DICTIONARY OF PENTECOSTAL AND CHARISMATIC MOVEMENTS

Stanley M. Burgess and Gary B. McGee
Editors
Patrick H. Alexander
Associate Editor

Regency
Reference Library
Zondervan Publishing House
Grand Rapids, Michigan

DICTIONARY OF PENTECOSTAL AND CHARISMATIC MOVEMENTS

REGENCY REFERENCE LIBRARY is an imprint of Zondervan Publishing House
1415 Lake Drive, S.E., Grand Rapids, Michigan 49506

Library of Congress Cataloging in Publication Data

Dictionary of Pentecostal and Charismatic movements / Stanley M. Burgess and Gary B. McGee, editors : Patrick H. Alexander, associate editor.
    p. cm.
    Bibliography: P.
    ISBN 0-310-44100-5
    1. Pentecostalism—Dictionaries. 2. Pentecostal churches—Dictionaries. I. Burgess, Stanley M.,
1937– . II. McGee, Gary B., 1945– . III. Alexander, Patrick H.
BR1644.D53 1988   88-28341
270.8'2–dc 19   CIP

Printed in the United States of America

89   90   91   92   93 / DH / 10   9   8   7   6   5   4   3   2

Contents

Editorial Preface vii

Editors and Contributors ix

Abbreviations xiii

The Pentecostal and Charismatic Movements 1

Dictionary Articles 7

Editorial Preface

The *Dictionary of Pentecostal and Charismatic Movements* is intended not only to increase the self-understanding of those inside the Pentecostal and charismatic movements, but also to introduce to the broader religious community the inner life and thought of a twentieth-century religious phenomenon that has had a significant impact on Christianity worldwide. The editors have sought to avoid apologetic and polemical approaches, and they have made every effort to present a balanced overview of the many perspectives that have grown out of a genuinely diverse set of traditions. Included among the contributors, therefore, are classical Pentecostals, charismatics representing a wide variety of denominational affiliations, and those who are not participants. Opinions expressed in this volume are intended to represent the diversity within the movements but are not necessarily those of the editors or of the publisher.

The work includes topical as well as biographical entries. Articles on books of the Bible focus on areas that are of special importance to Pentecostals and charismatics, especially the person and work of the Holy Spirit and his fruits and gifts. Articles on denominations or groups have as a rule been restricted to those with at least two thousand members.

The *Dictionary* is not a comprehensive treatment of Pentecostalism in its many forms worldwide. The vastness of these movements precludes complete coverage in a single volume. It could be argued that much of our focus should have been on Latin America, Africa, and Asia, where at the present time the majority of Pentecostals and charismatics are found. The editors felt, however, that in order to come to any understanding of the macrocosm, it is necessary first to concentrate on North America and Europe, where classical Pentecostalism and the charismatic movement originated.

Editors and Contributors

Editors

STANLEY M. BURGESS
Ph.D., University of Missouri—Columbia. Professor of Religious Studies, Southwest Missouri State University, Springfield, Missouri.

GARY B. McGEE
Ph.D., Saint Louis University. Associate Professor of Church History, Assemblies of God Theological Seminary, Springfield, Missouri.

Associate Editor

PATRICK H. ALEXANDER
M.A., Gordon-Conwell Theological Seminary. Academic Editor, Hendrickson Publishers, Peabody, Massachusetts.

Contributors

BEN C. AKER
Ph.D., Saint Louis University. Associate Professor of New Testament and Acting Vice President for Academic Affairs, California Theological Seminary, Fresno, California.

PATRICK H. ALEXANDER
M.A., Gordon-Conwell Theological Seminary. Academic Editor, Hendrickson Publishers, Peabody, Massachusetts.

DELTON L. ALFORD
Ph.D., Florida State University. Director of Music, Pathway Press, Cleveland, Tennessee.

FRENCH L. ARRINGTON
Ph.D., Saint Louis University. Professor of New Testament Greek and Exegesis, Church of God School of Theology, Cleveland, Tennessee.

J. MARTIN BALDREE
Ed.D., Southern Baptist Theological Seminary. Professor of Christian Education, Lee College, Cleveland, Tennessee.

DAVID B. BARRETT
Ph.D., Cambridge University. Research Consultant, Foreign Missions Board, Southern Baptist Convention, Richmond, Virginia; Research Secretary, Charismatic Renewal in the Mainline Churches; Vatican Consultant on world evangelization.

FRANCES BIXLER
Ph.D., University of Arkansas—Fayetteville. Assistant Professor of English, Southwest Missouri State University, Springfield, Missouri.

EDITH L. BLUMHOFER
Ph.D., Harvard University. Project Director, Institute for the Study of American Evangelicals, Wheaton, Illinois.

DAVID D. BUNDY
Lic., Catholic University of Louvain. Associate Professor of Christian Origins, and Collection Development Librarian, Asbury Theological Seminary, Wilmore, Kentucky.

STANLEY M. BURGESS
Ph.D., University of Missouri—Columbia. Professor of Religious Studies, Southwest Missouri State University, Springfield, Missouri.

DESMOND W. CARTWRIGHT.
Diploma in Ministerial Course, Elim Bible College. Official Historian, Elim Pentecostal Church, and Minister, Elim Pentecostal Church, Greenock, Renfrewshire, Scotland.

PAUL G. CHAPPELL
Ph.D., Drew University. Academic Dean and Professor of American Church History, School of Theology and Missions, Oral Roberts University, Tulsa, Oklahoma.

LARRY CHRISTENSON
B.Th., Luther Theological Seminary. Director, International Lutheran Renewal Center, St. Paul, Minnesota.

ITHIEL C. CLEMMONS
M.Div., Union Theological Seminary. Bishop for the Armed Forces and Institutional Chaplaincy, Church of God in Christ; Pastor, Wells Memorial Church of God in Christ, Greensboro, North Carolina, and Co-pastor, First Church of God in Christ, Brooklyn, New York.

JOSEPH COLLETTI
M.A., Fuller Theological Seminary. Birmingham, England.

CHARLES W. CONN
Litt.D., Lee College. Author and church historian, Cleveland, Tennessee.

GORDON D. FEE
Ph.D., University of Southern California. Professor of New Testament, Regent College, Vancouver, British Columbia.

JOSEPHINE MASSYNGBAERDE FORD
Ph.D., University of Nottingham. Professor of Theology, University of Notre Dame, South Bend, Indiana.

JAMES R. GOFF, JR.
Ph.D., University of Arkansas—Fayetteville. Lecturer in History, Appalachian State University, Boone, North Carolina.

GLENN W. GOHR
M.Div., Assemblies of God Theological Seminary. Archival Assistant, Assemblies of God Archives, Springfield, Missouri.

J. L. HALL
M.A., Emporia State University. Editor-in-Chief of Publications, United Pentecostal Church International, Hazelwood, Missouri.

JAMES ALLEN HEWETT
Ph.D., University of Manchester. Author and educator, Tulsa, Oklahoma.

PETER D. HOCKEN
Ph.D., University of Birmingham. Historian and theologian, Mother of God Community, Gaithersburg, Maryland.

STANLEY M. HORTON
Th.D., Central Baptist Theological Seminary. Distinguished Professor of Bible and Theology, Assemblies of God Theological Seminary, Springfield, Missouri.

RAY H. HUGHES
Ed.D., University of Tennessee—Knoxville. First Assistant General Overseer, Church of God (Cleveland, Tenn.), Cleveland, Tennessee.

HAROLD D. HUNTER
Ph.D., Fuller Theological Seminary. Executive Director, Sunday School Department, Church of God of Prophecy, Cleveland, Tennessee.

LARRY W. HURTADO
Ph.D., Case Western Reserve University. Associate Professor of Religion, University of Manitoba, Winnipeg, Manitoba.

CHARLES M. IRISH
B.D., Bexley Hall Divinity School. National Coordinator, Episcopal Renewal Ministries, Fairfax, Virginia.

DONALD A. JOHNS
Ph.D., Saint Louis University. Associate Professor of Bible and Theology, Assemblies of God Theological Seminary, Springfield, Missouri.

CHARLES EDWIN JONES
Ph.D., University of Wisconsin. Historian and bibliographer, Oklahoma City, Oklahoma.

DANIEL C. JUSTER
M.Div., McCormick Theological Seminary. General Secretary, The Union of Messianic Jewish Congregations, Gaithersburg, Maryland.

KLAUDE KENDRICK
Ph.D., University of Texas—Austin. Author and church historian, Rogers, Arkansas.

PETER KUZMIČ
Dr.Theol., Catholic Faculty of Theology, University of Zagreb. Director, Biblijsko-Teološki Institut, Osijek, Yugoslavia.

RONALD A. N. KYDD
Ph.D., University of St. Andrews. Pastor, Kanata Pentecostal Church, Kanata, Canada.

LEONARD LOVETT
Ph.D., Emory University. Pastor, Church at the Crossroads (Peniel Church of God in Christ), Los Angeles, California.

R. FRANCIS MARTIN
S.S.D., Pontifical Biblical Institute. New Testament scholar and theologian, Mother of God Community, Gaithersburg, Maryland, and Professor of New Testament, Dominican House of Studies, Washington, D.C.

L. GRANT McCLUNG, JR.
D.Miss., Fuller Theological Seminary. Assistant Professor of Missions and Church Growth, Church of God School of Theology, Cleveland, Tennessee.

WILLIAM G. MacDONALD
Th.D., Southern Baptist Theological Seminary. Author and educator. Front Royal, Virginia.

GARY B. McGEE
Ph.D., Saint Louis University. Associate Professor of Church History, Assemblies of God Theological Seminary, Springfield, Missouri.

J. RAMSEY MICHAELS
Th.D., Harvard University. Professor of Religious Studies, Southwest Missouri State University, Springfield, Missouri.

CHARLES NIENKIRCHEN
Ph.D., University of Waterloo. Associate Professor of Church History and Director of Spiritual Formation, Canadian Theological Seminary, Regina, Saskatchewan.

TIMOTHY POWELL
Ph.D., Fuller Theological Seminary. Associate Professor of Old Testament, California Theological Seminary, Fresno, California.

JOHN REA
Th.D., Grace Theological Seminary. Professor of Old Testament, CBN University, Virginia Beach, Virginia.

DAVID A. REED
Ph.D., Boston University. Assistant Professor of Pastoral Theology and Director of Field Education, Wycliffe College, Toronto, Canada.

FRANK M. REYNOLDS
B.S., Cornell University. Executive Director, Teen Challenge Training Center, Rehrersburg, Pennsylvania.

RICHARD M. RISS
M.C.S., Regent College. Author and church historian, Plano, Texas.

CECIL M. ROBECK, JR.
Ph.D., Fuller Theological Seminary. Associate Professor of Church History and Assistant Dean of Academic Programs, Fuller Theological Seminary, Pasadena, California.

ELIZABETH B. ROBINSON
Ph.D., Ohio State University. Associate Professor of Sociology, Southwest Missouri State University, Springfield, Missouri.

JERRY L. SANDIDGE
Ph.D., Catholic University of Leuven. Senior Pastor, Evangel Temple Christian Center, Springfield, Missouri.

SCOTT SHEMETH
M.A., Assemblies of God Theological Seminary. Springfield, Missouri.

JERRY W. SHEPPERD
Ph.D., University of Texas—Austin. Instructor in Sociology, Austin Community College, Austin, Texas.

RUSSELL P. SPITTLER
Ph.D., Harvard University. Professor of New Testament and Director of the David J. du Plessis Center for Christian Spirituality, Fuller Theological Seminary, Pasadena, California.

B. MAURICE STOUT
Th.M., Harvard University. Pastor, First Assembly of God, Jefferson City, Missouri.

STEPHEN STRANG
B.S., University of Florida. President, Strang Communications Company, Altamonte Springs, Florida.

FRANCIS A. SULLIVAN, S.J.
S.T.D., Pontifical Gregorian University. Professor of Theology, Pontifical Gregorian University, Rome, Italy.

H. VINSON SYNAN
Ph.D., University of Georgia. Chairman, North American Renewal Service Committee, Oklahoma City, Oklahoma.

JAMES S. TINNEY†
Ph.D., Howard University. Associate Professor of Journalism, Howard University, Washington, D.C.

HAROLD DEAN TRULEAR
Ph.D., Drew University. Associate Professor of Church and Society, Eastern Baptist Theological Seminary, and Pastor, Mt. Zion Baptist Church of Germantown, Philadelphia, Pennsylvania.

GRANT WACKER
Ph.D., Harvard University. Associate Professor of Religious Studies, University of North Carolina, Chapel Hill, North Carolina.

C. PETER WAGNER
Ph.D., University of Southern California. Donald A. McGavran Professor of Church Growth, Fuller Theological Seminary, Pasadena, California.

WAYNE E. WARNER
Diploma in Ministerial Course, Eugene Bible College. Director, Assemblies of God Archives, Springfield, Missouri.

J. RODMAN WILLIAMS
Ph.D., Columbia University. Professor of Theology, CBN University, Virginia Beach, Virginia.

DWIGHT J. WILSON
Ph.D., University of California—Santa Cruz. Professor of History, Bethany Bible College, Santa Cruz, California.

EVERETT A. WILSON
Ph.D., Stanford University. Academic Dean and Professor of History, Bethany Bible College, Santa Cruz, California.

LEWIS F. WILSON
Ph.D., University of California—Berkeley. Academic Dean and Professor of History, Southern California College, Costa Mesa, California.

JAMES R. ZEIGLER
M.A., Gordon-Conwell Theological Seminary. Librarian, Rhema Bible Training Center, Broken Arrow, Oklahoma.

Abbreviations

AB	Anchor Bible
AF	The Apostolic Faith
AG Heritage	Assemblies of God Heritage
ANET	Ancient Near Eastern Texts
ANF	The Ante-Nicene Fathers
Antiq.	Josephus, Antiquities
BAGD	Bauer, Arndt, Gingrich, and Danker, Greek-English Lexicon of the New Testament
BDB	Brown, Driver, and Briggs, Hebrew and English Lexicon of the Old Testament
BETS	Bulletin of the Evangelical Theological Society
Bib	Biblica
CA Herald	Christ's Ambassador Herald
CBQ	Catholic Biblical Quarterly
CBQMS	Catholic Biblical Quarterly Monograph Series
CCL	Classics of Christian Literature
CGE	Church of God Evangel
CT	Christianity Today
DThC	Dictionaire de Théologie Catholique
EBC	Expositors' Bible Commentary
EDT	Evangelical Dictionary of Theology
EPTA Bulletin	European Pentecostal Theological Association Bulletin
EQ	Evangelical Quarterly
ET	Evangelische Theologie
ExpT	Expository Times
FGMH	Full Gospel Missionary Herald
HMM	History of Methodist Missions
HNTC	Harper's New Testament Commentary
HTKNT	Herder's Theologischer Kommentar zum Neuen Testament
IB	The Interpreter's Bible
ICC	International Critical Commentary
IDB	The Interpreter's Dictionary of the Bible
ISBE	The International Standard Bible Encyclopedia
JBL	Journal of Biblical Literature
JETS	Journal of the Evangelical Theological Society
JNES	Journal of Near Eastern Studies
JRT	Journal of Religious Thought
JSPS	Pneuma—Journal of the Society for Pentecostal Studies
JSSR	Journal for the Scientific Study of Religion
JTS	Journal of Theological Studies

LRE	Latter Rain Evangel
LSJ	Liddel, Scott, and Jones, Greek-English Lexicon
LThK	Lexicon für Theologie und Kirche
LXX	Septuagint
MM	Moulton and Milligan, The Vocabulary of the Greek New Testament
MMD	Miracles and Missions Digest
MRW	Missionary Review of the World
NBD	The New Bible Dictionary
NCBC	New Century Bible Commentary
NIC	New International Commentary
NICNT	New International Commentary on the New Testament
NIDCC	New International Dictionary of the Christian Church
NIDNNT	New International Dictionary of New Testament Theology
NIGTC	New International Greek Testament Commentary
NSHERK	New Schaff-Herzog Encyclopedia of Religious Knowledge
NTS	New Testament Studies
NovT	Novum Testamentum
ODCC	Oxford Dictionary of the Christian Church
PE	Pentecostal Evangel
PG	Patrologia Graeca
PL	Patrologia Latina
RGG	Die Religion in Geschichte und Gegenwart
SBK	Strack and Billerbeck, Kommentar zum Neuen Testament aus Talmud und Midrash
SBL	Society of Biblical Literature
SJT	Scottish Journal of Theology
TDNT	Theological Dictionary of the New Testament
TF	Triumphs of Faith
TR	Theological Renewal
TS	Theological Studies
VetTest	Vetus Testamentum
WBC	Wycliffe Bible Commentary
WE	World Evangelism
WTJ	Westminster Theological Journal
ZAW	Zeitschrift für die alttestamentliche Wissenschaft
ZNW	Zeitschrift für die neutestamentliche Wissenschaft
ZPEB	Zondervan Pictorial Encyclopedia of the Bible

The Pentecostal and Charismatic Movements

Introduction

Since the beginning of this century, Christianity has witnessed the emergence of two great renewal movements of the Spirit: the Pentecostal movement, beginning in 1901, and the charismatic movement that developed several decades later. Whether through Pentecostal preachers Charles H. Mason, Aimee Semple McPherson, David Wilkerson, and Ray H. Hughes, or charismatics like Episcopalian Dennis Bennett, faith healer Oral Roberts, Roman Catholic Léon-Joseph Cardinal Suenens, and television personality M. G. ("Pat") Robertson, these movements and their participants (both men and women, clergy and laity) have proclaimed that the spiritual power of the first-century church can be the norm for Christians today. The impact of these movements has changed the face of Christianity around the world and ushered in a new era of Christian spirituality. In view of this, these movements merit careful investigation.

The terms "Pentecostal" and "charismatic" are often used interchangeably. Indeed, they do have many features in common, and even for the expert it is frequently difficult to draw a dividing line. When points of delineation are decided upon and connected, the resulting line is invariably crooked, perhaps broken, and sometimes split into various branches. For one venturing into the field of Pentecostal and charismatic studies for the first time, some kind of tour guide for distinguishing between the two is indispensable.

There are two approaches to differentiating between "Pentecostal" and "charismatic." One is theological, the other ecclesiastical. A theological differentiation might be along doctrinal lines, in particular Spirit baptism (also called the baptism in or of the Holy Spirit). It is oversimplified, but perhaps useful, to say that "Pentecostals" subscribe to a work of grace subsequent to conversion in which Spirit baptism is evidenced by glossolalia (i.e., speaking in tongues); for some, this baptism must also follow another act of grace, sanctification. "Charismatics," however, do not always advocate either the necessity of a second work of grace or the evidence of glossolalia as an affirmation of Spirit baptism. Yet both emphasize the present work of the Spirit through gifts in the life of the individual and the church.

An ecclesiastical differentiation especially concerns denominational affiliation. Thus "Pentecostal" describes those participating in classical Pentecostal denominations such as the Assemblies of God, the Church of God (Cleveland, Tenn.), the Church of God in Christ, and the International Church of the Foursquare Gospel. "Charismatics" would characterize persons outside these classical Pentecostal denominations, whether they are within mainline denominations or are part of an independent group.

Obviously, neither differentiation is entirely adequate. The theological approach overlooks the natural denominational lines drawn by history, while the strictly ecclesiastical tack ignores the tremendous theological diversity among and within denominational groups. For example, Roman Catholic charismatics express their understanding of Spirit baptism in a wide variety of ways, ranging from an almost Pentecostal "second stage" understanding to a perspective that rejects any notion of a second work of grace. Likewise, some within classical Pentecostalism are uncomfortable with denominational insistence that Spirit baptism is both subsequent to salvation and must be accompanied by the "initial physical evidence" of speaking in tongues.

For the purposes of this dictionary the theological ambiguity of the terminology has been left somewhat intact; each writer is working within his or her own set of understandings. Moreover, the theological and ecclesiastical differentiation predominating in this dictionary also functions in other scholarly discussions of the subject.

Historical Roots

Both twentieth-century Pentecostals and charismatics have an identifiable heritage throughout Christian history. In the West the emphasis on a life in the Spirit with an exercise of spiritual gifts has long been the portion of those who lived Christian lives beyond the expectations of the institutionalized church and thereafter were honored as saints. The stress on the work of the Holy Spirit has frequently also been found among fringe and heretical groups such as radical dualists and millenarians. But the modern Pentecostal belief that *all* believers can and should live in the Spirit, empowered and enlivened by his gifts, has not been the teaching of mainline Western Christendom since the third century A.D.

In contrast, Eastern Christianity has never ceased to place great emphasis on pneumatology and the interior life of the Spirit in the believer. Although there has been an ebb and flow in the practice of this ongoing theology of the Spirit, Eastern churches have always had a charismatic character and expectation. Sadly, this is a tradition long forgotten in the West, so that contemporary Pentecostals and charismatics view their movements as unique since the first century.

The advancement of modern Pentecostalism can be traced to at least five distinct theological developments in the last two hundred years. The first relates to two works of grace—justification and sanctification. It stems from the Wesleyan notion of conversion followed by a definable second work of grace—sanctification—in which the "stranglehold of sin is decisively broken" and Christian perfection can be realized. A second and closely related doctrinal development can be traced to Charles G. Finney and other "higher-life" teachers who emphasized the importance of a second experience following conversion which endued the believer with power for witness and service. Both the Wesleyan and higher-life advocates of the last century referred to this additional experience as the baptism in the Holy Spirit, although their definitions of the significance of that experience differed.

The third influence came from the emergence of premillennialism in the nineteenth century, particularly the dispensational brand originating from the Plymouth Brethren and the teachings of John Nelson Darby and Reuben A. Torrey. At the same time, the rise of the evangelical faith healing movement, with such leaders as Charles C. Cullis, A. J. Gordon, A. B. Simpson, John Alexander Dowie, and Maria B. Woodworth-Etter, generated a fourth impact. Many were attracted by their emphasis on the miraculous for physical well-being, which stemmed from the belief that the effects of the atonement of Christ extended beyond one's soul to the body.

The final and probably most significant development was the restorationist longing for the vitality and miracles of New Testament Christianity. The "early rain" poured out on the early church was thought by Pentecostals to be replicated in the "latter rain" at the end of history. These early Pentecostals were experiential primitivists in the sense that they consciously hailed back to the dynamic, Spirit-filled, Spirit-led first-century church—especially that of the Day of Pentecost and the church at Corinth.

Twentieth-Century Developments: The Pentecostal Movement

Historians often trace the origins of Pentecostalism in the American context to a revival that began on January 1, 1901, at Charles F. Parham's Bethel Bible School in

Topeka, Kansas. With the identification of speaking in tongues as the evidence of the baptism in the Holy Spirit, Parham and his students made a vital theological connection that has remained essential to much of classical Pentecostalism. While the immediate impact of this event was limited, Parham's ministry gained more acceptance several years later in a revival conducted outside Houston, Texas. From there William J. Seymour, a black Holiness preacher who had become convinced of the truth of Parham's teachings on Spirit baptism, traveled to Los Angeles, California, to preach the new message. The ensuing revival at the Azusa Street Mission (1906–09) represented an anomaly on the American religious scene. Blacks, whites, and Hispanics worshiped together. Men and women shared leadership responsibilities. The barrier between clergy and laity vanished, since participants believed that the endowment of spiritual power for ministry was intended for all to receive. The gifts of the Holy Spirit (1 Cor. 12), understood by most denominations as having ceased at the end of the first century, had been restored.

From Los Angeles, news of the "outpouring" of the Holy Spirit spread across the nation and around the world by word of mouth and the printed page. Before long, Pentecostal revivals could be found in Canada, England, Scandinavia, Germany, India, China, Africa, and South America. Some revivals overseas occurred without knowledge of the happenings at Azusa Street.

Theological issues soon began to divide the movement, however. Questions concerning the nature of sanctification, the gift of tongues, and the Trinity generated tensions that have remained. The racial harmony of Azusa Street waned within a few months, and as a result Pentecostalism remains racially divided with very limited progress toward reconciliation. While in the early years women enjoyed considerable freedom in ministry, often surpassing that of the established Protestant denominations, their prominence has declined with but few exceptions. However, an ecumenical ideal among Spirit-baptized believers has continued to be in evidence from the early decades despite their isolation from one another, particularly on the American scene.

Although several Holiness denominations in the southeastern part of the United States accepted Pentecostal theology, many participants in the new movement were rejected by their parent groups and were therefore skeptical of ecclesiastical organizations. Even with these reservations, however, Pentecostal mission agencies, "fellowships," and denominations began to evolve shortly thereafter. By mid-century they were outstripping most other Christian bodies in the rate of growth.

Twentieth-Century Developments: The Charismatic Movement

While early Pentecostalism was often associated with the lower socioeconomic classes and relegated to the fringe of evangelical Christianity, the desire for spiritual renewal in the historic and affluent mainline churches unexpectedly resulted in an increased interest in spiritual gifts, including glossolalia and physical healing. News of this renewal in the United States began to surface on the national level in 1960 with the publicity accorded to remarkable happenings in the ministry of Dennis Bennett, an Episcopal rector in Van Nuys, California. As the movement grew, it spread to other Protestant churches, the Roman Catholic Church, and finally to the Orthodox churches. Part of the groundwork for charismatic renewal, reflecting its deep roots in the Pentecostal movement, had been laid by the ministries of Oral Roberts, David J. du Plessis, and Demos Shakarian and the Full Gospel Business Men's Fellowship International. It quickly became apparent that this renewal, which also sought for the dynamic power of the Spirit, flowed out of what many believed to be a vacuum in American religious life as well as a longing to return to the essence of New Testament Christianity within one's particular church tradition.

The renewal in the Roman Catholic Church, which can in part be traced to the monumental changes ushered in by the Second Vatican Council, spread around the world and was experienced by both prelates and laity. To Roman Catholic theologian Peter D. Hocken, "the charismatic movement is a grace of God touching every aspect of the Christian life and is found across all the Christian churches. . . . The reappearance of the spiritual gifts thus represents something dramatically new in church history. Once you admit they are authentic and are the work of the Holy Spirit, you have to recognize that something of possibly unparalleled importance is happening" (1987, 46, 48).

The charismatic renewal, therefore, represents a transdenominational movement of Christians (both independent and denominational) who emphasize a "life in the Spirit" and the importance of exercising extraordinary gifts of the Spirit, including but not limited to glossolalia, in private prayer and in public worship.

While initially charismatics adopted the distinctives of classical Pentecostalism, in recent years they have explored their newfound experiences within their own traditions. Without roots in some of the extremes of the Holiness movement, they have typically been more overtly supernaturalistic and culture-affirming in their perspective on the Christian life than classical Pentecostals. As time passed, most of the renewal movements found a degree of recognition and approval within parent denominational structures.

With the outbreak of the charismatic renewal in the early 1960s, it became apparent to the church world that Pentecostalism in its various forms would have to be taken seriously not only because of its growth but also because of its successful penetration into virtually every corner of the Christian community and the world. Pentecostal-charismatic successes in evangelism may well constitute the most dramatic increase of believers in the history of the Christian church. Clearly what was initially a small, fledgling, and poorly regarded group of the sometimes disinherited was in 1958 labeled by Henry Pitney Van Dusen (then president of Union Theological Seminary in New York) as part of Christendom's "Third Force" alongside conventional Protestantism and Catholicism. In 1975 University of Chicago historian Martin Marty reported that some observers had identified the Pentecostal/charismatic movement as the "first force" in the Christian world, "while the more staid counterparts foundered or remained static" (quoted in Synan, 1975, 199).

Rapid growth in the Pentecostal and charismatic movements, however, also brought a considerable variety of worship patterns, cultural attitudes, ecclesiastical structures, and methods of evangelism. Wide differences in spirituality and theology become even more apparent when indigenous Third World groups are examined.

Pentecostal-Charismatic Tensions

From a separation that fed on rejection and its own early tendency toward isolation and intolerant exclusiveness, Pentecostalism has, since World War II, become interactive with Protestant Evangelicalism, and in certain cases even with the broader ecumenical Christian community. The result has been a relatively higher level of acceptance and respectability, which Pentecostals now share with nonseparatist charismatics who never suffered as high a level of rejection. Because many Pentecostals, fearing compromise of basic tenets that might lead to a loss of distinctiveness, are not yet entirely comfortable with this entrance into the mainstream of American Christianity, the movement tends to be divided between those who identify with the past and those who relish their newfound identification with the larger church world.

Growth pains became evident with the emergence of the charismatic movement. Pentecostals, who by mid-century were identifying closely with mainstream Evangelicals, initially applauded the movement. But when many charismatics remained in their own churches rather than shifting to classical Pentecostalism, some Pentecostals became frustrated with them. Dually aligned to their own church traditions and to the historic people of the Spirit, the charismatics have tended to recognize the ebb and flow of fervent spirituality in Christian history and have found their identity as part of the latest wave of renewal. Nevertheless, by the 1980s most Pentecostals recognized that the Holy Spirit was accomplishing a new work and sensed an affinity with it. The charismatic renewal brought pressures on the Pentecostals to broaden their identification within the universal church to groups previously considered apostate. In this regard, the untiring efforts of the late David J. du Plessis (1905–1987), one-time secretary of the Pentecostal World Conference, proved to be particularly instrumental in building bridges between Pentecostals and charismatics. Through such efforts, the earlier ideal of ecumenism among the Spirit baptized has extended beyond the Pentecostal World Conference, primarily made up of classical Pentecostals, to the recent North American Congresses on the Holy Spirit and World Evangelization (1986, 1987), which have encompassed all stripes of classical Pentecostals, together with charismatic Baptists, Episcopalians, Lutherans, Mennonites, Messianic Jews, Methodists, Presbyterians, Reformed, Greek Orthodox, and Roman Catholics. These events rank among the most important gatherings of Christians in the twentieth century, because of both their size and their theological significance.

Conclusion

The Pentecostals and charismatics have come to be identified with exuberant worship; an emphasis on subjective religious experience and spiritual gifts; claims of supernatural miracles, signs, and wonders—including a language of experiential spirituality, rather than of theology; and a mystical "life in the Spirit" by which they daily live out the will of God. The Holy Spirit fills and indwells their spirits, and because they anticipate the imminent return of Christ, this spiritual life is not merely to be enjoyed but also to serve as empowering to win others to Christ.

Undeniably, this development has spurred the various branches of Christendom to review their theological perspectives on the work of the Holy Spirit. Meanwhile, Pentecostals and charismatics continue to explore the meaning and implications of their unique perspectives on the Holy Spirit for their spirituality, theology, methods, expectations in evangelism, relationships with other Christians, and ultimately their place in the history of Christianity. The present generation of Pentecostal and charismatic scholars, while concerned about correct doctrine, tends to focus on these issues and exhibits a certain detachment from some of the dogmatic concerns that have divided Evangelicals and Fundamentalists in the last one hundred years.

As the writer of Ecclesiastes once suggested (1:9), there is nothing new under the sun. This certainly is true of these movements. Each of the characteristics mentioned above has appeared before in the rich and colorful tapestry of Christian spirituality through the ages. But the combination is new, and it has appeared all the more unique in the context of the traditional Christianity in which it was spawned. Regardless of one's position concerning the work of the Holy Spirit in the modern world, Pentecostalism, in all its forms, has nevertheless sparked an almost unprecedented expansion of the Christian faith, has brought renewal to branches of mainstream Christianity, and has challenged Christians everywhere to address the issues that have been raised.

Bibliography: R. M. Anderson, *Vision of the Disinherited* (1979); S. M. Burgess, *The Holy Spirit: Eastern Christian Traditions* (1989); idem, *The Spirit and the Church: Antiquity* (1984); C. Farah, "America's Pentecostals: What They Believe," *Christianity Today* (October 16, 1987), 22, 24–26; idem, "Differences Within the Family," *Christianity Today* (October 16, 1987), 25; J. L. Gresham, Jr., *Charles G. Finney's Doctrine of the Baptism of the Holy Spirit* (1987); M. P. Hamilton, ed., *The Charismatic Movement* (1975); P. D. Hocken, *One Lord One Spirit One Body* (1987); W. J. Hollenweger, *The Pentecostals* (1972); R. T. Hughes, "Christian Primitivism as Perfectionism: From Anabaptists to Pentecostals," in S. M. Burgess, ed., *Reaching Beyond* (1986); S. Lawson, "The Big Charismatic Get-Together," *Charisma* (September 1987), 56–58; H. I. Lederle, *Treasures Old and New* (1988); G. B. McGee, "The Azusa Street Revival and 20th Century Missions," *International Bulletin of Missionary Research* 12 (April 1988): 58–61; M. E. Marty, "Pentecostalism in the Context of

American Piety and Practice," in V. Synan, ed., *Aspects of Pentecostal-Charismatic Origins* (1975); J. T. Nichol, *The Pentecostals* (1966); R. Quebedeaux, *The New Charismatics II* (1983); H. B. Smith, "America's Pentecostals: Where They Are Going," *Christianity Today* (October 16, 1987), 27–30; V. Synan, *The Holiness-Pentecostal Movement in the United States* (1971); G. Wacker, "America's Pentecostals: Who They Are," *Christianity Today* (October 16, 1987), 16–21.

The Editors

A

ABRAMS, MINNIE F. (1859–1912). Missionary to India. Abrams first traveled (from Minneapolis, Minn.) as a missionary with the Woman's Foreign Missionary Society of the Methodist Episcopal Church to Bombay, India, in 1887. Working with Sarah M. DeLine, she helped establish and supervise a Christian girls' school. An orphanage and boarding school were added later. In 1898 she became affiliated with Pandita Ramabai's home for Indian widows (the Mukti Mission) at Kedgaon, reporting that God had spoken to her about this new course of ministry.

An American missionary to India in 1887, Minnie F. Abrams worked with children in schools and orphanages. She was baptized in the Spirit in 1905 and became instrumental in leading others into the movement.

When a Pentecostal revival occurred at the mission in 1905, Abrams received the baptism in the Holy Spirit. She described the revival and discussed its theological underpinnings in *The Baptism of the Holy Ghost and Fire* (1906). Sending a copy of it to May L. Hoover (Mrs. Willis C. Hoover) in Valparaiso, Chile, with whom she had attended the Chicago Training School for Home and Foreign Missions (Methodist-related), Abrams significantly influenced the beginnings of the Pentecostal movement in that country.

Later travels took Abrams to Oakland, California, where she visited Carrie Judd Montgomery in 1909 and Elmer K. Fisher's Upper Room Mission in Los Angeles the following year. While in the U.S. Abrams determined to return to India and preach the gospel to unreached peoples. Departing in October 1910, she led a party of seven single women missionaries, including Edith Baugh from Zion City, Illinois, to evangelize in the United Provinces, Fyzabad, and Bahraich. She later died from malaria.

Bibliography: M. F. Abrams, *The Baptism in the Holy Ghost and Fire*, 2d ed. (1906); Abrams, "A Note of Praise," *LRE* (October 1910), 11; W. C. Barclay, *Widening Horizons, 1845–1895*, HMM (1957); J. T. Copplestone, *Twentieth-Century Perspectives, 1896–1939*, HMM (1973); "Entered into Rest," *LRE* (January 1913), 14–15; W. C. Hoover, "The Wonderful Works of God in Chile," *LRE* (April 1911), 19–20; "Minnie F. Abrams, of India," *MRW* (February 1913), 156; R. Nalder, "Miracles of Salvation, Healing, Provision and Protection," *LRE* (November 1908), 7–12.

G. B. McGee

ALL-UNION COUNCIL OF EVANGELI-CAL CHRISTIANS—BAPTISTS See EURO-PEAN PENTECOSTALISM.

ALLELUIA (AUGUSTA, GA.) See CHARIS-MATIC COMMUNITIES.

ALLEN, ASA ALONSO (1911–70). Healing evangelist. A. A. Allen, born in Sulphur Rock, Arkansas, grew up in poverty with an alcoholic father and an unfaithful mother. By age twenty-one Allen also had become an alcoholic. A turnaround came in 1934 when he was converted to Christ. His wife, Lexie, had a strong influence on his spiritual life and ministry.

Licensed by the Assemblies of God (AG) in 1936, Allen's reputation as an evangelist grew slowly and even included a two-year pastorate because of financial hard times. The *Voice of Healing* magazine reported Allen's success as an evangelist in 1950, however. The next year he bought a tent and soon established headquarters in Dallas. He began broadcasting "The Allen Revival Hour," a radio program in 1953. His periodical, *Miracle Magazine*, began in 1954 (1969 circulation was 340,000).

"After Jack Coe died, he (Allen) had no rival as the boldest of the bold" (Harrell, 1975, 68). Where others avoided the hard cases, Allen thrived on them. Of all the evangelists during his time, Harrell credits Allen as being "the leading specialist at driving out demons" (Harrell, 1975, 88). His services drew all types of people, but he identified especially with the poor and blacks.

Allen ran into trouble with the AG in the mid

A. A. Allen was one of the better-known salvation-healing evangelists following World War II. He established his headquarters and a Bible school at Miracle Valley, Arizona.

1950s due to his extravagant claims. Many of the miracles were considered questionable or at least exaggerated. However, the claimed miracles, along with his preaching, continued to stir people.

A strong shadow was cast over Allen's ministry due to his arrest for drunken driving during a Knoxville, Tennessee, revival in 1955. In response to pressure, he resigned from the Voice of Healing organization. Also as a result of this incident, the AG suggested that Allen withdraw from public ministry until the matter was settled. Fearful that it would ruin his ministry, Allen claimed innocence but surrendered his credentials. Thereafter the arrest and the surrendered credentials made it difficult for Allen to work within AG churches.

In 1956 Allen started the Miracle Revival Fellowship (1956–70) while still headquartered in Dallas. Its Articles of Incorporation state that its purpose

shall be to encourage the establishing and the maintenance of independent local sovereign, indigenous, autonomous churches, home and foreign missionary activities; to establish schools . . . to engage in other related ministries . . . by means of sermons, radio, television, publication, and any means whatsoever. To work in cooperation with all believers . . . to minimize nonessential doctrinal differences which divide the flock of God (*Miracle Magazine,* October 1956, 2).

To become a member, one had to be a "sincere born again Christian" and uphold biblical standards of holiness. The articles provided for the licensing and ordaining of ministers. It claimed five hundred affiliated churches and approximately 10,000 members in 1983.

In a January 1958 revival in Phoenix, Arizona, Allen expressed a dream to establish a training center for preachers. A man came to the platform and presented Allen with a gift of approximately 1,200 acres in the San Pedro Valley in southeastern Arizona. Allen claimed that four years earlier God had inspired the donor to give this gift. With additional gifts, Allen purchased another 1,200 acres. In February 1958 Allen began readying his new headquarters in a community he would name Miracle Valley. Miracle Revival Training Center opened that October, and Allen began his stay there with a "Miracle Week" in January 1959. Allen viewed Miracle Valley as a "totally spiritual community" consisting of 2,500 acres, a 4,000-seat church, private homes, a training school, headquarters, and a radio and television outreach.

Allen survived the pressures of media, isolation, and declining interest in the healing revival. His fund-raising ability, innovation, and daring contributed to his success. He was one of the first to appeal for support by using the theme of financial blessing for the giver. He introduced gospel rock music into his services and employed skilled entertainers.

Allen authored several books, including *The Curse of Madness* (n.d.), *God's Guarantee to Heal You* (1950), *Receive Ye the Holy Ghost* (1950), *Power to Get Wealth* (1963), *The Burning Demon of Lust* (1963), and *God's Guarantee to Bless and Prosper You Financially* (1968).

The commitment to old-time faith healing campaigns was retained by Allen even though they were dying in the late 1950s and throughout the 1960s. As late as 1970 he announced his plans to conduct his services in the world's largest tent.

Allen's divorce from his wife Lexie in 1967 caused unrest in his organization. He died three years later in San Francisco from sclerosis of the liver while his team conducted a revival in West Virginia. The ministry fell to Don Stewart, Allen's associate since 1958, who renamed it the Don Stewart Evangelistic Association.

Bibliography: A. A. Allen, *My Cross* (1957); A. A. Allen and W. Wagner, *Born to Lose, Bound to Win* (1970); D. E. Harrell, *All Things Are Possible* (1975); C. E. Jones, *A Guide to the Study of the Pentecostal Movement* (1983); J. Randi, *Faith Healers* (1987); *Miracle Magazine,* "About Revival Fellowship" (October 1956), 2, 21; idem, "Miracle Week at Miracle Valley" (March 1959), 6, 10; idem, "The San Pedro Valley Is Canaan" (September 1958), 8–9, 15, 20.

S. Shemeth

AMERICAN BAPTIST CHARISMATIC FELLOWSHIP See BAPTIST CHARISMATICS.

AMERICAN EVANGELISTIC ASSOCIATION The purpose of the American Evangelistic Association (AEA) is to set professional standards and to license and ordain clergy and to coordinate independent missionary, educational, and charitable efforts in foreign countries. Established in

1954 by John Elwood Douglas, Sr., former Methodist and convert of A. A. Allen, and seventeen other independent ministers, the AEA grew rapidly. The Baltimore headquarters reported 2,057 members in 1968. It then claimed a combined membership of more than 100,000 in self-governing congregations served by member clergy. In 1979 its overseas arm, the Dallas-based World Missionary Evangelism, reported work in twelve countries. At that time it was sponsoring more than 30,000 children overseas.

Bibliography: D. E. Harrell, *All Things Are Possible* (1975); C. E. Jones, *Guide to the Study of the Pentecostal Movement* (1982); *Mission Handbook* (1979); A. C. Piepkorn, *Profiles in Belief*, vol. 3 (1979).

C. E. Jones

ANACONDIA, CARLOS See CHARISMATIC MOVEMENT.

ANCHOR BAY EVANGELISTIC ASSOCIATION (ABEA). The ABEA is the extension of the ministry of Roy John Turner (1880–1945) and the independent congregation he founded in New Baltimore, Michigan. In 1918 Turner, a Congregationalist physician trained at the University of Michigan, and his wife, Blanche, who two years before had become Pentecostal, brought the noted evangelist Maria B. Woodworth-Etter (1844–1924) to their town on Lake Sinclair northeast of Detroit. Afterward converts from this campaign, destined to provide the founding cadre for Bethel Temple and for the ABEA, met in the Turner home. Although from 1938 to 1940 Turner served the International Church of the Foursquare Gospel as an executive of Angelus Temple in Los Angeles, the New Baltimore congregation remained independent. Upon Dr. Turner's return, Bethel Temple became the cornerstone both of the ABEA and the Anchor Bay Bible Institute, essential to the success of both. At home Anchor Bay workers concentrate on ministry to orphans, prisoners, and the poor. Overseas their aim is to establish churches and educational projects on an indigenous, self-supporting basis. In 1979 the association had twenty North American workers in five fields. That year it spent $440,000 overseas. It holds membership in the Pentecostal Fellowship of North America.

Bibliography: C. E. Jones, *Guide to the Study of the Pentecostal Movement* (1982); *Mission Handbook* (1979); A. C. Piepkorn, *Profiles in Belief*, vol. 3 (1979).

C. E. Jones

ANDERSON, ROBERT MAPES (1929–). Social historian with specialist interest in American Pentecostalism. Anderson's interest was stimulated in his youth by acquaintance with a neighborhood storefront church in New York City, and this led to his Ph.D. dissertation on American Pentecostal origins at Columbia University (1969). Published in 1979 under the title *Vision of the Disinherited*, Anderson's study was rapidly acclaimed as authoritative. Despite his evident unbelief, Anderson has an unusual empathy for the world of early Pentecostalism, enabling him as a social historian to paint a fuller picture of the life situations from which the Pentecostal pioneers came. Skilled at distinguishing fact from legend and subsequent interpreta-

Robert Mapes Anderson, author of the acclaimed study of Pentecostals *Vision of the Disinherited*.

tion, Anderson sees the millennial expectation that "Jesus is coming soon" as primary among initial Pentecostal convictions. He is currently professor of history at Wagner College, Staten Island, New York.

P. D. Hocken

ANGELICA, MOTHER (1923–). Catholic television personality. Born Rita Francis, Mother Angelica entered a Franciscan convent in 1944, becoming in 1962 the foundress of Our Lady of Angels monastery, Birmingham, Alabama. She experienced a spiritual renewal in the early 1970s. Mother Angelica initiated a book apostolate reaching many nations from 1973 on. However, she only became nationally known when in 1981 she boldly launched the Eternal Word Television Network (EWTN), the first Catholic satellite cable network. EWTN's rapid success, far exceeding the television promotions of the official U.S. Catholic Conference, is attributed to the straightforward presentation of the gospel, backed by constant intercessory prayer of all the sisters in Mother Angelica's convent. Mother Angelica's ministry is much supported by people in the charismatic renewal. As of July 1986, EWTN had 317 affiliates in thirty-seven states.

Bibliography: D. O'Neill, *Mother Angelica — Her Life Story* (1986).

P. D. Hocken

ANGELUS TEMPLE Located at 1100 Glendale Boulevard in Los Angeles, California, the temple formed the headquarters congregation of the International Church of the Foursquare Gospel. On January 1, 1923, it was dedicated by Aimee Semple McPherson, who served as its pastor until her untimely death in 1944. As she traversed the continent, holding meetings of up to 16,000 people in cities like Denver; St. Louis; Dayton; Washington, D.C.; and Montreal, she shared the vision of the completed temple project,

Angelus Temple, Los Angeles, the church Aimee Semple McPherson built in 1923. (Photo c. 1937.)

much of which she designed herself. When it was opened, it was debt free, and people from a wide number of historical denominations had helped to make it so.

Constructed largely of steel-reinforced concrete, the temple, semi-circular in shape, seated 5,300 people. Its cornerstone proclaimed its dedication to the cause of interdenominational and worldwide evangelization. At that time it boasted the largest unsupported dome in the U.S. Situated at the intersection of major streetcar lines, the temple was easily accessible to commuters. Nationally renowned artist George W. Haskins was commissioned to design and construct eight stained-glass windows in the sanctuary at the cost of $15,000. A prayer tower, originally called the "Watch Tower," went into operation February 1923, with volunteers praying around the clock in two-hour shifts. Services were carried on the temple's own radio station, KFSG (Kall Four Square Gospel) beginning February 6, 1924.

From 1923 to 1926 "Sister" preached each evening and three times each Sunday. She drew standing-room-only crowds—some 25,000 worshipers weekly, who came to hear her vividly illustrated sermons, fully costumed operas, and cantatas. There was a hundred-voice choir, a large Kimball organ, and a "Silver Band." While Sundays featured a Communion service, as well as inspirational and revivalistic services, each Monday the emphasis was on deeper life; Tuesday the focus was on evangelism; Wednesday was dedicated to prayer and Bible Study; Thursday evening was reserved for baptismal services; Friday was set apart for the young people; and Tuesday afternoon and Saturday evening were given over to divine healing services.

The temple was active in both civic and social ministry in the community as well. "Sister" was a member of the Los Angeles Chamber of Commerce. She campaigned actively for high pay for Los Angeles police and fire departments. The temple entered floats in the famed Tournament of Roses Parade in Pasadena each year from 1923 through 1926, winning the coveted Sweepstakes trophy in 1925. When an earthquake occurred in Santa Barbara in 1925, she used the radio station to make a plea for food, clothing, and other supplies, and trucks to carry them. The caravan arrived in the town before governmental agencies were on the scene. In the late 1920s and early 1930s, the temple's commissary ran at full speed. Taking care of indigents and the unemployed, some of whom were referred by Los Angeles County, was a major concern. From August 1927 to May 1936, 99,520 families and 355,158 persons were fed while 257,686 articles of clothing and over 3,000 quilts were distributed. By July 1942 the commissary was said to have fed and clothed over a million persons. The temple's employment agency was also at work. In the nine months from September 1, 1935, to June 1, 1936, for instance, it supplied 4,850 jobs, 75 percent of which were permanent positions. An outgrowth of the temple's ministry also included the establishment of L.I.F.E. (Lighthouse of International Foursquare Evangelism) Bible College in March 1923. A bookstore was opened in 1927.

The temple is little changed from its beginning. Some internal remodeling has set the current seating capacity at 3,300. The congregation averages 2,000 and is divided into three smaller churches: the Anglo community is approximately 900; the Hispanic, 1,300; and the Korean, 30—

50. The college, bookstore, prayer tower, and radio station (KFSG-FM Stereo 96.3) continue to run as they were originally envisioned.

See also INTERNATIONAL CHURCH OF THE FOURSQUARE GOSPEL; MCPHERSON, AIMEE SEMPLE.

Bibliography: A. S. McPherson, *In the Service of the King* (1927); idem, *The Story of My Life* (1951); "The Opening of the Angelus Temple," *Triumphs of Faith* 43 (January 1, 1923): 20–21.   C. M. Robeck, Jr.

ANGLEY, ERNEST W. (1921–). Pastor and televangelist. Angley grew up in North Carolina as the son of a Baptist deacon and attended Lee College (Church of God, Cleveland, Tenn., 1941–43). He received the baptism in the Spirit in his teens and was called to preach when he was eighteen. He began his healing ministry when he was age twenty-three, after being healed of ulcers. Angley's faith healing services, which have been the benchmark of his ministry at Grace Cathedral (Independent) in Akron, Ohio, as well as his evangelistic crusades on four continents, are from four and one-half to five and one-half hours long. He also televises "The Ernest Angley Hour" into at least six countries. Angley Ministries has known controversy due to the methods employed during the healing services. While in Munich, Germany (1984), Angley was indicted for practicing medicine without a license.

Bibliography: E. W. Angley, *Miracles Are Real—I Got One!* (1975); idem, *Raptured* (1950); idem, *Untying God's Hands* (1977); G. Martin, "The Importance of Being Ernest," *Saturday Night* 99 (1984): 44–55; J. Randi, *The Faith Healers* (1987).   E. B. Robinson

ANGLICAN RENEWAL MINISTRIES (ARM). An organization founded in 1981 to establish an Anglican charismatic service committee in the U.K. Its primary inspiration came from the Canterbury Conference of 1978. Spurred by the closure of Fountain Trust, an ecumenical renewal organization, seventy clergy meeting at Scargill voted unanimously to begin the organization. The Reverend Lawrence Hoyle became its first coordinator. Other primary leaders were Thomas R. Hare and John Gunstone.

Among its activities ARM published a newsletter, *Anglicans for Renewal*, conducted annual national renewal conferences for clergy and leaders, led regional conferences about personal and parish renewal, and distributed teaching and resource material to help clergy and leaders in the same. ARM (U.K.) was joined by similar organizations in Scotland, Ireland, Canada, Australia, New Zealand, and many other places in the Anglican Communion.   C. M. Irish

ANOINTING WITH OIL Anointing with oil is used predominately in the modern church in conjunction with prayer for physical healing. For centuries the Roman Catholic church practiced the sacrament of extreme unction, known since Vatican II as the anointing of the sick. During the Middle Ages, kings and bishops began to be anointed with holy oil. From the third century a postbaptismal anointing and laying on of hands was practiced by the church to confer the gifts of the Holy Spirit.

Anointing with oil was used from early times throughout the East for cosmetic, preservative, and medicinal purposes. The OT regularly employs the roots *sûk* and *tûah* for this process (Ruth 3:3; 2 Chron. 28:15), words rendered in the LXX predominately by *aleiphō*. *Aleiphō* appears eight times in the NT, exclusively of the physical act of anointing people for personal hygiene (Matt. 6:17), as a sign of honor (Mark 16:1; Luke 7:38, 46), or for healing (Mark 6:13; James 5:14). Mark 6:13 and James 5:14 suggest medicinal properties for the oil, but the practice of exorcism may also serve as background, the casting out of demons being symbolized in the anointing with oil.

Anointing with oil also carried sacred or symbolic significance, indicated in the OT by the term *mašah*. Objects were anointed and consecrated to divine service (Exod. 30:26–29). Anointed persons received an infusion of divine presence and power, actualized for the Israelite by an endowment of the Spirit of Yahweh (1 Sam. 16:13). Kings were inducted into office by the pouring of oil over the head (1 Sam. 10:1). "Yahweh's Anointed" is a synonym for Israel's king (1 Sam. 12:3). Priests were set apart and ordained into office by anointing (Exod. 28:41). Elijah was commissioned to anoint Elisha as his successor in the prophetic office (1 Kings 19:16). "To anoint" is used metaphorically for the bestowal of divine favor in such passages as Psalm 23:5; 92:10.

The LXX regularly renders *mašah* by *chriō*, a verb used five times in the NT. Three occurrences of the related noun *chrisma* appear in 1 John. Both terms are used only in a figurative sense. Anointing is a metaphor for the bestowal of the Holy Spirit, special favor, or divine commission. At his baptism, Jesus was confirmed in his royal and priestly roles by the anointing of the Holy Spirit, an anointing that confirmed him as *Christos*, the "Messiah" (a direct transliteration of the Hebrew word "anointed"). Hebrews 1:9 connects anointing with Christ's elevation and enthronement as eschatological ruler and high priest. In 1 John *chrisma* involves the reception of the Holy Spirit (2:18, 27–28), the believer's Teacher and Guide, the one who enables the Christian to discern spirits (1 John 4:1–7). The reception of the Holy Spirit allows the believer to share in the messianic anointing of Jesus. The designation "Christian" connotes a member of the community of the "Anointed One."

Bibliography: D. Engelhard, "Anoint; Anointing," *ISBE*, rev. ed (1979), 1:129; W. Grundmann et al., "Chrio ktl.," *TDNT* (1974), 9:493–580; D. Muller, "Anoint," *NIDNTT* (1975), 1:119–24; H. Schlier, "Aleiphō," *TDNT* (1964), 1:229–32; S. Szikazai, "Anoint," *IDB* (1962), 1:138–39.   T. Powell

ANTIPENTECOSTALISM See BERLIN DECLARATION; HOSTILITY/PERSECUTION; FUNDAMENTALISM.

APOCALYPSE, BOOK OF THE The recent renewal of interest in the Apocalypse or Book of Revelation is reflected in the number of scientific studies and commentaries that have appeared on the subject of the Apocalypse. (For more extended information on these, the reader is referred to the bibliography, especially Collins, 1986, and Beasley-Murray, 1978.) After a few introductory remarks, I will treat two aspects of Revelation that are most particularly related to the scope of this volume: the role of the Holy Spirit and the question of Christ's thousand-year reign.

I. Introductory Remarks. The designation of the Book of Revelation as Apocalypse derives from its first word: "The revelation [*apocalypsis*] of Jesus Christ, which God gave to him, to show to his servants what must soon take place; he made this known by sending his angel to his servant John" (Rev. 1:1). After giving his name as John, the author goes on to describe himself as sharing with his audience the "tribulation, the kingdom, and the patient endurance that are ours in Jesus," adding that he is writing from exile on the isle of Patmos "because of the word of God and testimony of Jesus" (v. 9).

The author's name and a certain similarity of outlook between the Fourth Gospel and Revelation gave rise to the prevalent view in the early church that both works were by John, the Son of Zebedee. This view was challenged as early as the third century by the perceptive and moderate Dionysius, bishop of Alexandria, who nevertheless did not reject Revelation as noncanonical. Modern critical studies tend to confirm Dionysius' basic intuition while ascribing a more complex origin to all the works that form the Johannine block in the NT (Beasley-Murray, 1978, 32–38). These same studies also agree with the estimate of Irenaeus of Lyons that Revelation was composed "at the end of the reign of Domitian" (*Haer.* 5, 30, 3; Domitian's reign was 81–96 A.D.).

The uniqueness of Revelation does not result from its being a prophetic word addressed in letter form by a Christian leader to a group of communities in order to strengthen, enlighten, and correct them. We find these characteristics in 1 Peter, 2 Peter, 1 John, and, in fact, in most of the epistolary compositions of the NT. The particular uniqueness of Revelation results from its being a prophetic message that, after the initial addresses to the seven churches (Rev. 2–3), finds expression in a series of complex images and symbols deriving from the OT and the thought world familiar to western Asia Minor. The message is consistent: despite the suffering, injustice, and humiliation experienced by those who believe in Jesus Christ, all of history is subject to him and not to the human and demonic forces that seem to hold sway; what is being experienced now must be interpreted in the light of God's ultimate plan for human existence.

By authoritative use and modification of the symbols of the OT, particularly of Daniel and Ezekiel, and those of the mythic themes common to the time, the author orchestrates this same theme repetitively, thus enabling his readers to interpret their experience in the light of the reality and majesty of Jesus Christ. Revelation is neither a cryptically coded prediction of all future history nor an imaginative flight from the harsh realities being faced by those to whom it was addressed. It is rather a symbolic interpretation of history deriving from the experience of the author's time

and laying down the ultimate principles of Christian existence for all time as these came to the author by the "revelation of Jesus Christ."

II. The Pneumatology of Revelation.

A. The Role of the Holy Spirit in the Act of Revelation. The phrase "in the Spirit" (*en pneumati*) occurs four times in Revelation (1:10; 4:2; 17:3; 21:10). The first of these occurrences introduces the letters to the seven churches; the second introduces the remaining part of the work. The third and fourth occurrences refer to a visionary experience of being transported and allude to Ezekiel 37:1 and 40:2, respectively (see Bauckham, 1980, 71). John is using terminology here that would have been intelligible to his audience. He is not claiming that he was caught up out of his body, but that the source of what he is saying is the Holy Spirit. He is claiming prophetic authority.

That which he writes is "what the Spirit says to the churches" (Rev. 2:7, 11, 29; 3:6, 13, 22). By prefacing this with the address, "He who has an ear, let him hear," the author expressly alludes to the same remark recorded of Jesus (Matt. 11:15; 13:9 par.; 13:43; Mark 4:23; et al.), thus illustrating that "the Spirit will take from what is mine and make it known to you" (John 16:15). In asserting this activity of the Holy Spirit in Revelation, John is making his work a particular instance of that fulfilled prophecy in Joel 3:1–5 to which the early community appeals in explaining how its present life is a foretaste of the eschatological promise made available in the death and resurrection of Christ.

B. The Spirit of Prophecy. We read in Revelation 19:10 the solemn statement, "The witness of Jesus is the Spirit of prophecy." Given the frequency with which the early rabbinic tradition designated the Spirit of God as the "Spirit of prophecy," it is clear that Revelation is asserting two things: (1) the role of the Holy Spirit is linked to the witness of Jesus, and (2) this witness is prophecy. We must understand "the witness of Jesus" to be both the witness that Jesus bore (he is the faithful witness [Rev. 1:5; 3:14]) and that borne to him by believers (Rev. 12:17). This latter witness is explicitly linked to "the word of God" (1:2, 9; 20:4; also 6:9) and to the prophetic role (11:3), and includes giving one's life as a testimony (2:13; 11:7; 17:6). Indeed, it is by the blood of the Lamb and the word of their testimony that the witnesses who did not "shrink from death" overcame the "accuser of our brethren" (see Rev. 12:10–11).

In the Fourth Gospel, Jesus proclaims that the reason he was born and came into the world was "that I might bear witness to the truth" (John 18:37). The witness of Jesus, together with the witness borne to him, is prophecy because by it the Spirit interprets actual events in the light of the witness that Jesus bore "under Pontius Pilate" (1 Tim. 6:13), that is, by his death on the cross. "The Lord, the God of the spirits of the prophets, sent his angel to show his servants the things that must soon take place" (Rev. 22:6).

When the author of Revelation calls his own work a "prophecy" (1:3; 22:7, 10, 18, 19), he is asserting that it was accorded to him by revelation "in the Spirit." He is also claiming that it shares in the witness of and to Jesus which testifies to the ultimate meaning and goal of human history.

C. The Spirit and the Church. According to 1 John 5:7, the Spirit is "the one who bears witness" (*to martyron*) to the reality and power of the ministry and blood of Christ. He is a witness to Jesus, as in Revelation, which adds that the Spirit is the one who confirms for us the heavenly voice (14:13). He also prays within and with the Bride saying, "Come!" (22:17; see Rom. 8:26–27). By this Spirit the churches receive the testimony of Jesus (Rev. 22:16, 20).

The Spirit is the "Spirit of life" who, as in the vision of Ezekiel 37:5–10, brings the dead people of God (symbolized by the two witnesses) back to life to be honored by God (Rev. 11:11; see also 20:4–6). The manifold nature of the Spirit is denoted by the expression, "the seven spirits" (Rev. 1:3; 3:1), whose relation to the church is accented by being linked to the "seven horns" (power) and the "seven eyes" (presence/knowledge) of the Lamb (Rev. 5:6). In brief, the Spirit is the one who establishes the church in its unique identity as the Bride and witness of Jesus.

III. The Millennium. The interpretation of Revelation 20:1–10 serves to classify commentators. The three basic views of the text are that it is a depiction of historical events in the future (pre- and post-millennialists), an allegory (Origen and others), or a symbolic reference to the mystery of Christ (Augustine, followed variously both in ancient and modern times). The ten verses contain three narrative moments. First, Satan is bound for a thousand years (20:1–3). Second, those who were killed because of their witness come to life and reign with Christ for this same period of a thousand years: this is called the first resurrection (vv. 4–6). Third, at the completion of the thousand years, Satan is released, gathers Gog and Magog, wages war on the beloved city, is defeated, and is thrown into the lake of burning sulfur (vv. 7–10).

The characteristics of the whole book are present here as well. This is prophetic teaching on the ultimate meaning of what John's audience was suffering. The teaching is mediated through the symbolic use of OT motifs and contemporaneous religious and cosmic images (Gelin, 1957). The notion of a present world, an interim period, and a final period was common in the pagan world of the first century (Martin, 1967, 362). Some Jewish circles had already adapted this notion to a rhythm: this age, the age of the Messiah, and a final age ushered in by the judgment. Sometimes the age of the Messiah was considered to last for a thousand years, having been preceded by six thousand years of the present age (*Letter of Barnabas* 5:4–9; b. Sanh. 97b). The author of Revelation, working with symbols known to his audience, uses them in his own way to proclaim the word of the Lord.

Those who have insisted that the text must refer to realities in this world are correct: this is a word of prophecy for the disinherited. Those who see the application of this and other teaching of Revelation to their own time are also correct, and

there have been people who have so understood the text in nearly every century. At times, those people spoke as if the thousand-year reign here on earth were about to start or be terminated, depending upon their particular view. In this, as history has borne out, they were mistaken.

The profound teaching of this revelation is consistent with the message of the book as a whole. The forces of Satan in John's day, who were obstructing the witness of Jesus, found expression in the culture and government of the Roman Empire. The teaching was that these forces will be bound, Rome will fall, and those who have been killed will continue to reign with Christ until the end (see Boismard, 1959, 81). These forces may experience a resurgence, but their end has already been decreed. It is up to Christians of every generation to recognize the embodiment of these forces in the world around them and interpret their own suffering accordingly.

Those generations who identify the Spirit of prophecy with the spirit of their own age, no matter how "religious" it seems to be, have failed to understand the prophetic judgment of John's message. One may neither relegate the words of this prophecy exclusively to a distant future nor interpret them as a code by which one can chart the course of contemporary history. These words are prophetic teaching by which we may measure our own situation with an eschatological perspective.

See also ESCHATOLOGY, PENTECOSTAL PERSPECTIVES ON.

Bibliography: (entries marked "Bib." can provide the reader with more ample bibliographical material): R. M. Anderson, *Vision of the Disinherited. The Making of American Pentecostalism* (1979); R. Bauckham, "The Role of the Spirit in the Apocalypse," *EQ* 52 (1980):66–83; G. R. Beasley-Murray, *Revelation, NCBC* (1978) (Bib.); M. E. Boismard, *L'Apocalypse* (La Sainte Bible de Jérusalem) (1959); A. Gelin, "Millénarisme," *Dictionnaire de La Bible Supplément*, vol. 4 (1957), 1289–94 (Bib.); F. Martin, "Cosmic Conflagration," *NCE*, vol. 4 (1967), 362 (Bib.); W. Stringfellow, *An Ethic for Christians and Other Aliens in a Strange Land* (1973). R.F. Martin

APOSTLE

I. Apostle: The Gospels and Acts. Jesus chose from his disciples twelve "whom he also named 'apostles'" (Luke 6:13; cf. Acts 1:2, 13). Mark 3:14 (see Metzger, 1971, 80, on the textual support of the reading "whom also he named apostles") and Matthew 10:2 (no other Matthean references to "apostle" occur) have the same witness. "The Twelve" or "the twelve disciples" are also "the apostles." ("A disciple" may not be "an apostle," but "the disciples" or "the twelve disciples" are "the apostles"; cf. Rev. 21:14.)

Jesus gave to this innermost company "power and authority over all the demons and to heal sicknesses and he sent them away to preach the kingdom of God and to heal" (Luke 9:1–2; cf. Matt. 10:1; Mark 3:14–15; note the "sent" motif in John 13:16b ["neither is an apostle greater than the one who sent him"]). Though sent away bearing the authority of the sender, the apostles were expected to return (Mark 6:30; Luke 9:10).

Jesus did not establish them as agents of the kingdom of God apart from their disciple relationship to himself (Matt. 16:24–25 = Mark 8:34–35 = Luke 9:23–24). One may deduce five aspects to being a member of the first apostolic group: call, authorization, dispatch, going and acting in obedience, and return.

Although the apostles had intimate contact with Jesus and personal, private teaching from him, they did not adequately comprehend either his person (contrast Luke 9:20 and 45) or their role as his apostles (Luke 9:46–48). Their faith was lacking both before and after the resurrection of Jesus (Luke 17:5; 24:11). They did not have unalloyed commitment to him (cf. Luke 22:54–62 and parallels; Mark 14:50). Even Jesus' betrayer, Judas, was one of "the apostles" who ate Jesus' last meal with him (Luke 22:2–3, 14, 21).

Two considerations in particular suggest that Jesus did not establish an exclusive apostolate. (1) Jesus allowed nonfollowers to cast out demons "in Jesus' name" and rebuked John for having thought otherwise (Mark 9:38–41; Luke 9:49–50). (2) The twelve designated as "apostles" (Luke 9:1–2, 10) and the Seventy—who were not so designated—(Luke 10:1–12) had the same authority, abilities, and commission given to them. Jesus' intention was that selected persons—whether called "apostles" or not—were to be empowered and sent forth to preach the nearness and/or presence of the kingdom of God. Healing the sick and casting out demons were integral to that sent-forth-one's activity.

In the postresurrection community the apostolic tasks changed even as the relationship to Jesus did. Their tasks were preaching the word of God (cf. Acts 2:14, 37; 4:1–2, 33; 6:2; 10:36–43), accompanied by signs and wonders (e.g., 3:6–7; 4:29–31); teaching (2:42; 2 Peter 3:2; Jude 17); praying (6:4); and fairly distributing goods so that all the company of believers might be without need (4:34–5:11).

Central to the content of the apostles' preaching was that they be witnesses to Jesus' resurrection (Acts 1:22). Hence, at the outset, there were two criteria for Judas' replacement: (1) the man must have been a traveling companion in all the active historical ministry of Jesus so that he could witness with them to the resurrection of Jesus in the light of those historical experiences (vv. 21–22). (2) The heart of the man had to be acceptable before the Lord, who was to make the final choice (v. 24). The selection process involved the apostles' submission to the Lord even as in the pre-Passion context. Through prayer (v. 24) and the casting of lots (v. 26), they sought divine designation of the one whom the Lord himself had chosen (1:24b, 26).

No one person was designated as leader of the apostolic band, though in the early chapters of Acts Peter is quite clearly the vocal and forthright one. As one of the apostles, he became a dynamic, bold, tenacious witness for the risen Lord, but he worked under an authority from God that was confirmed by the Jerusalem apostles (8:14, 25; 15:7). In his dialogues with them he demonstrated an accountability toward them that was balanced with his own authority to challenge and silence the group (11:2–18; 15:7–11).

Until the dispersion of the saints into other areas (8:1), the apostles were the reconstituted Twelve, centered in Jerusalem, and an exclusive, nontraveling band. After the scattering, a change in the constituency of the apostles may be detected. In Acts 8:14 one reads, "Now when the in-Jerusalem apostles heard . . ." (author's translation). Luke just said the apostles remained in Jerusalem (v. 1). Now by his word order he draws attention to which apostles—those in Jerusalem. Acts 16:4 ("the apostles and elders, the ones in Jerusalem") is another example of such emphasis, strongly intimating that "apostle" per se has come to mean more than the original twelve or the eleven plus Matthias. Had there been only the apostles in Jerusalem, Luke's added "in Jerusalem" and "the ones in Jerusalem" would be superfluous. Acts 14:4, 14 confirm the existence of apostles other than those in Jerusalem with the naming of "apostles Barnabas and Paul."

In the course of time the Jerusalem apostolic *group* became less significant. Peter and John went to Samaria at their behest to confirm Philip's preaching (8:4–24). The Jerusalem apostles and, in particular, the "circumcision party" objected to Peter's mission "here and there" in Lydda, Sharon, Joppa, and among Gentiles of Caesarea (9:32–11:18). They had to yield, however, recognizing that God made the choice that Peter evangelize among the Gentiles (cf. 15:7). The Spirit had told him to go (11:12), and Peter had chosen not to withstand God (11:17–18). The authority of the group had to be subordinated to the will of God, Jesus, or his Spirit.

When Greeks in Antioch received the word of the Lord through converts from Cyprus and Cyrene (11:20–21; NB, not from the apostles at Jerusalem), "the church in Jerusalem"—not "the apostles"—sent Barnabas, who was not one of the original apostolic group, as their envoy (v. 22).

When the apostles of Jerusalem and the elders and prophets together with the whole church (15:6, 22, 32) determined to convene and declare a position concerning the issue of Gentile conversions and Mosaic law keeping, they sent no command to Antioch (15:23–29). Instead, they gave an exhortation as to how "you will do well" (v. 29).

Furthermore, this last recorded Lucan reference to the apostles in Jerusalem depicts neither Peter (15:7–11) nor James (vv. 13–21) nor any other individual as in control of the group. Both Peter and James spoke. Each made suggestions. But the letter to Antioch was from "the apostles and the elders" (vv. 22, 23; 16:4); the final position was that which "seemed good to the Holy Spirit and to us" (v. 28). Control of the group did not rest with any one person or clique. Equality, collegiality, and mutual submission under the leadership of the Holy Spirit appear to have ruled among the brethren during their deliberations and hearing of the report by Barnabas and Paul concerning "what signs and wonders God had done through them among the Gentiles" (15:12b). After these deliberations at Jerusalem, Luke does not again mention the apostles, their work or persons.

II. Apostle: A Transition Period. Philip was one of the seven chosen to handle the daily distribution (Acts 6:5) to the widows. He was a man full of the Spirit and wisdom. When next met, he is not serving tables; instead, he is in Samaria preaching Christ, casting out unclean spirits, and healing many paralyzed and lame persons (8:5–13)—all activities of the apostles.

When Saul of Tarsus was blinded, the Lord called a disciple of Damascus, Ananias, and sent him to Saul so that the latter might regain his sight and be filled with the Holy Spirit (9:17)—an appropriate activity for an apostle.

Prophets and teachers of the church in Antioch, under instructions from the Holy Spirit (13:1, 4), set apart Barnabas and Saul for evangelistic work. Their ministry was a proclamation of the "word of the Lord," accompanied by signs and wonders (13:7–12, 16–49; 14:3, 11) and persecutions from certain Jews and Gentiles of the region (13:50–52; 14:5; cf. 2 Tim. 1:11–12)—all activities and circumstances common to apostles. There are here three new elements: (1) Barnabas and Saul are chosen and sent "by the Holy Spirit." *The Holy Spirit, not the Lord Jesus, is now the one who calls, commissions, and certifies the activities of God's agents.* (2) The apostles of Jerusalem are now joined by others—the prophets and teachers of the church at Antioch—whom God uses as agents of commissioning and sending forth. (3) These sent-forth ones function in essentially the same capacity with like results and under the same circumstances of persecution as the original post-resurrection apostles, though for a while without the title "apostle."

III. Apostle: The Pauline Perspective.

A. Paul's personal apostleship. In his earliest letter Paul unhesitatingly introduces himself as "apostle, not from men neither through a man, but through Jesus Christ and God the Father" (Gal. 1:1; cf. 2 Tim. 1:1, 11). Consistent with the witness of Acts, Paul insists that he is an apostle because of a direct, *divine* calling, rather than any human selection process (Gal. 1:17–19). Later he also rejects the notion of being an apostle because of any personal qualifications (1 Cor. 15:9; 2 Cor. 12:5–11).

Undergirding Paul's apostleship is the fact that, like the original apostles of Jerusalem, he had seen Jesus the Lord (1 Cor. 9:1; 15:5–9; Gal. 1:16). Seeing the Lord, however, whether in the flesh or as the Risen One, does not thereby automatically qualify any person as an apostle. Neither is such an encounter introduced as a necessity for someone to be an apostle. In 1 Corinthians 15:6 there is no suggestion that the five hundred brethren are apostles. In Paul's case his vision of the Lord is coupled with the fact that he was "called [to be] an apostle" (1 Cor. 1:1), set apart and called before he was ever born (Gal. 1:15). To this should be added that the indicators of an apostle—namely, (1) effective proclamation of the gospel and (2) signs, wonders, and mighty works—accompanied Paul's ministry, thereby verifying his apostolic service (1 Cor. 9:2; 2 Cor. 12:11b–12; cf. Rom. 15:18–19).

Still, more must be said. Signs, wonders, and mighty works may verify an apostolic ministry, but they do not guarantee that a ministry is apostolic. Paul struggled against false apostles who were disguised as apostles of Christ and servants of righteousness but who in actuality were agents of Satan who disguises himself as an angel of light (2 Cor. 11:12–15; cf. Matt. 7:22–23).

After Matthias was chosen (Acts 1:23–26) there is no indication that personal vision of the earthly Jesus or the risen Lord is a requisite for other persons being an apostle. The initial insistence by the twelve apostles was that the only person who could be enrolled as an apostle was someone who had seen the risen Lord and had been a personal companion of Jesus during his earthly ministry (Acts 1:21–22). This precludes Paul himself, regardless of his Damascus Road experience. Having seen and accompanied the Lord was required prior to Pentecost and the outpouring of the Spirit because it was only as one related to Jesus that one was "in the Kingdom." After the outpouring of the Spirit at Pentecost one could know—by the Spirit—both the reality of the resurrection and the power of the risen Lord in one's life whether or not one had seen Jesus in flesh and blood (consider Paul's entire Gentile mission).

Being an apostle in the post-Pentecost church of God in Christ Jesus depends on *the calling of the Lord* and on *his enabling grace for apostleship.* In 1 Corinthians 12:27–31 Paul affirms that God established apostles in the church—not just the local congregation of Corinth, but "body of Christ" (v. 27). God himself graciously gave functional gifts to those called to be his one body (Eph. 4:1–6): whether apostles or prophets or evangelists or pastors-teachers.

Neither 1 Corinthians 12 nor Ephesians 4 is expressed as a temporal matter. Paul simply says that in the church or in "'one body' God has placed or given . . ." (Note well that God has given these gifts "in," not "over" the church.) It follows that these gifts are available wherever persons are open to receive the proffered gifts for their intended purpose: that we, the body of Christ, "grow up with regard to everything into him who is the head [of the body], Christ" (Eph. 4:15).

B. Nondominical Apostles. Epaphroditus (Phil. 2:25) exemplifies an apostle as a congregation's commissioned representative rather than God's. Persons whom Paul sent to Corinth are apostles (2 Cor. 8:23); that is, persons who are sent to assist Paul in the collection from the Gentiles for the poor in Jerusalem. When Paul described these, he called them "glory of Christ," just as he, speaking of his own ministry, said he conducted a work "for the glory of the Lord" (v. 19). Whereas these apostles are sent with authority to act, they are not free, independent agents. Apostles have externally assigned responsibilities and people to whom they must render accountability—whether to the churches or Philippi or Jerusalem or the Lord Christ.

See also GIFTS OF THE SPIRIT.

Bibliography: J. B. Lightfoot, *Galatians* (1866), 92–101; B. M. Metzger, *A Textual Commentary on the Greek New Testament* (1971); R. E. Nixon, "Apostle," *ZPBE* (1975), 1:216–20; K. H. Rengstorf, *"Apostolos,"* *TDNT* (1964), 1:398–445; W. C. Robinson, "Apostle," *ISBE* (1979), 1:192–95; M. H. Shepherd, Jr., "Apostle," *IDB* (1962), 1:170–72.   J. A. Hewett

APOSTOLIC CHURCH (AC). The smallest of the mainline Pentecostal groups in Britain. Established in 1916, the founders were brothers Daniel Powell Williams (1882–1947) and William Jones Williams (1891–1945). Both were converted in the Welsh revival 1904–05. Early association was with the Apostolic Faith Church founded by W. O. Hutchinson (1864–1928) in Bournemouth in 1908. D. P. Williams entered the full-time ministry in 1911 and was called to be an apostle in 1913. Following disagreement with the Bournemouth parent body, the majority of the Welsh assemblies broke away at the end of 1915 to form the nucleus of the Apostolic Church.

In 1918 the Apostolic Church was joined by the Burning Bush Assembly of Andrew Turnbull (1872–1937) of Glasgow, who brought in a number of other churches in Scotland. In 1922 Frank Hodges of Hereford brought in his assembly, and two years later a group of churches lead by H. V. Chanter of Bradford were added. Administrative headquarters were established at Penygroes, Carmarthen, Wales, with Dan Williams as chief apostle and his brother W. J. as prophet. Missionary headquarters were in Bradford and financial control at Glasgow. An annual convention is held at Penygroes in August, where a memorial hall was erected in 1922 with enlargements since with accommodation for three thousand. A Bible school was opened in 1936 and a more detailed constitution accepted in 1937.

The tenets of the AC proclaim church government by apostles and prophets. In addition they include the possibility of falling from grace and the obligatory nature of tithes and offerings. During the early 1930s they experienced a period of rapid growth in the number of churches, but this caused some friction with other groups. On the local level their churches tend to keep apart from others, although their leaders have always worked with the British Pentecostal Fellowship and other bodies. AC appears to be the only mainline group in Britain that is declining. It has a large missionary work in Nigeria and also in France, Italy, Denmark, and New Zealand.

Bibliography: T. N. Turnbull, *Brother in Arms* (1963); idem, *What God Hath Wrought* (1959).
D. W. Cartwright

APOSTOLIC CHURCH OF GOD IN RUMANIA See EUROPEAN PENTECOSTALISM.

APOSTOLIC CHURCH OF JESUS CHRIST See UNITED PENTECOSTAL CHURCH, INTERNATIONAL; PENTECOSTAL ASSEMBLIES OF THE WORLD.

APOSTOLIC CHURCH OF PENTECOST OF CANADA In 1921 Franklin Small (1873–1961) and ten others affiliated with the infant Pentecostal Assemblies of Canada withdrew in protest against the reception that year of congregations in the four western provinces previously affiliated with the U.S.-based General Council of the Assemblies of God. At issue was the Small faction's belief in the oneness of the Godhead. On October 25, 1921, they obtained a Dominion charter as the Apostolic Church of Pentecost of Canada, with oneness as the central tenet. Union in 1953 with the Evangelical Churches of Pentecost, which included many who held to the triunity of the Godhead, resulted in tolerance of both points of view. Baptism in the name of Jesus and the eternal security of the believer then became principal emphases.

The home constituency is concentrated in the prairie provinces. By 1979 the church was sponsoring outreach in fourteen countries. That year the Saskatoon headquarters received more than $250,000 for work overseas and had sixty North American workers in foreign areas.

Bibliography: C. E. Jones, *Guide to the Study of the Pentecostal Movement* (1982); R. A. Larder, *Our Apostolic Heritage* (1971); *Mission Handbook* (1979); A. C. Piepkorn, *Profiles in Belief*, vol. 3 (1979).   C. E. Jones

APOSTOLIC FAITH (BAXTER SPRINGS, KANS.) The Apostolic Faith (AF) became the earliest organized Pentecostal sect when Charles F. Parham initiated a loose program for his followers in the spring of 1906. Proclaiming himself "projector," Parham established three state directors over the areas most affected by his new doctrine—Texas, Kansas, and Missouri—and ordained local elders to serve individual assemblies of AF workers. The local assemblies met weekly for a period of prayer and devotion. Late in 1906, however, Parham's attempt at organization and personal leadership met an abrupt end. He was personally rejected by the Azusa Street AF Mission in Los Angeles (unrelated to Parham's AF), and, amidst rumors questioning his personal morality, much of his Midwestern alliance defected under the leadership of W. Faye Carothers and Howard Goss. Parham succeeded, however, in retaining several thousand followers and in 1909 established Baxter Springs, Kansas, as his home and informal headquarters of his small wing of the Pentecostal movement.

Parham never formulated another plan for organized fellowship. During the last two decades of his life, he led the collection of AF churches through the force of his own charismatic personality and the influence of his journal, the *Apostolic Faith*. Parham retained a small national constituency for his ministry and held campaigns throughout the country. Still, the bulk of his followers lived in the Midwestern states of Kansas, Missouri, Texas, Arkansas, and Oklahoma. At his death in 1929, Parham's journal registered fourteen hundred subscribers, and he had a regular following of four to five thousand.

After 1929 Sarah Parham assumed her husband's editorial work, and Robert Parham took the bulk of his father's preaching schedule. Upon Sarah Parham's death in 1937, Robert hoped gradually to reorganize the fledgling band of churches into a tighter organizational unit and to bring the sect into closer fellowship with other

A group of Christian workers with Charles F. Parham (seated in center) at Bryan Hall, Houston, Texas, 1905.

This is the ordination certificate of Howard A. Goss with the Apostolic Faith (Baxter Springs, Kan.), dated Aug. 26, 1906. It is signed by W. F. Carothers, field director, and Charles F. Parham, projector.

Pentecostal denominations. He died prematurely in 1944, however, and the AF was left without a leader who could control the diverse assortment of locally run churches.

In 1951 the AF alliance, linked only by the *Apostolic Faith* and an annual Bible school held in Baxter Springs, split in half. Progressive-minded ministers considered it essential to form some cooperative organization to take advantage of state and federal tax laws and to provide more efficient support of foreign missionaries. They also advocated increased contact with other Pentecostal sects and allowed greater emotional displays in their worship services. Other ministers,

The headquarters building of the Apostolic Faith Mission, Portland, Oregon, was occupied in 1980. Florence L. Crawford founded the organization in 1907.

conditioned by Pentecostalism's rejection of Charles F. Parham decades earlier, feared the trappings of organization and considered much of the emotional display a "counterfeit" spawned by the popularity of Pentecostal faith healers. In Spearman, Texas, in 1951 the progressive faction withdrew from the fellowship and established the Full Gospel Evangelistic Association (FGEA). This group created its own monthly periodical, *Full Gospel News,* and in 1960 organized Midwest Bible Institute in Webb City, Missouri. In 1971 the Bible school was relocated to a campus in Houston, Texas, and in 1976 permanent headquarters were also established there. Today FGEA claims 134 ministers, thirty-one active churches and mission stations, and approximately four thousand church members.

The older AF fellowship remains a loose band of churches centered around the monthly periodical—now the *Apostolic Faith Report*—and the Bible college in Baxter Springs. Recently totals listed 109 ministers and forty-seven churches. Church membership is estimated at slightly less than four thousand. Unlike the FGEA, the AF affiliation promotes Parham's unique theological stand on "conditional immortality" and "destruction of the wicked."

See also APOSTOLIC FAITH MOVEMENT, ORIGINS.

Bibliography: J. Goff, *Fields White Unto Harvest* (1988); A. Nehrbass, *This Is Full Gospel Evangelistic Association* (1980).   J. R. Goff, Jr.

APOSTOLIC FAITH MISSION (PORTLAND, ORE.)

The Apostolic Faith Mission emerged directly out of the Apostolic Faith (AF) movement supervised by William J. Seymour in Los Angeles. Its founder, Florence Louise Crawford, was a Holiness worker who embraced Pentecostal views at Azusa Street. Late in 1906 she left southern California for Oregon. Arriving in Portland on Christmas Day in 1906, she immediately began conducting mission services, out of which her organization developed.

During 1907 Crawford traveled to Seattle, Minneapolis, and Winnipeg, trying to determine where she should locate permanently. She decided to settle in Portland. In 1908 she acquired downtown property and began a faith publishing venture. Like Seymour (whose mailing list she took from Azusa Street), she called her paper *The Apostolic Faith.*

Crawford was critical of many aspects of Pentecostal practice. An ardent restorationist, she also subscribed wholeheartedly to Holiness teaching, divine healing, premillennialism, and faith living. She deplored centralized organization and minced no words in denouncing advocates of the finished work, those whose separation from worldliness she deemed inadequate, and the organization of Pentecostal denominations. Over the years, Crawford kept her group out of associations with other Pentecostals and Evangelicals.

Crawford's Portland mission soon spawned related efforts, most of which were on the West Coast. Together these constituted her AF movement. Although membership never reached much over five thousand, the movement's publishing efforts have been extensive. Those who affiliated with her were required to take "an uncompromising stand" for official doctrines and to espouse strictly enforced moral codes.

Crawford's movement espoused a three-stage Pentecostalism: first, justification by faith; then, entire sanctification; and finally, the baptism of the Holy Spirit. She demanded that her missions accept a "faith" stance: ministers could neither solicit funds nor receive regular offerings. An offering box near the church entrance sufficed. Her members not only relinquished dancing, card playing, theater attendance, smoking, and drinking, they also distanced themselves from those who practiced such activities. Proscribing all makeup and short hair for women, Crawford enjoined modest apparel and insisted that slacks, shorts, and short sleeves were inappropriate for women.

Unlike many Pentecostal groups, the Portland-based AF movement sponsors no Bible training school. The headquarters makes available various Bible studies as well as Crawford's sermons. It encourages the use of the KJV.

Florence Crawford died on June 20, 1936. Her son, Raymond Robert Crawford, who had served as assistant overseer under his mother, assumed leadership and served until his death on June 8, 1965. Loyce Carver succeeded him. See also APOSTOLIC FAITH MOVEMENT (ORIGINS).

Bibliography: *The Apostolic Faith* (1965).
E. L. Blumhofer

APOSTOLIC FAITH MOVEMENT, ORIGINS

The Apostolic Faith movement grew out of the restorationist dreams of a young Kansas evangelist, Charles F. Parham (1873–1929). Influenced during his childhood in Cheney, Kansas, especially by Methodism and the Winebrenner Church of God, Parham dedicated his life to the ministry. From his teens, he demonstrated a proclivity for intense spiritual experiences as well as impatience with structure and authority. Parham briefly attended the academy and normal school associated with Southwestern Kansas College, a Methodist institution. In mid 1893 he accepted an assignment as a lay preacher in the Methodist Episcopal Church in Eudora, Kansas. He served there until 1895. By then he had determined to preach what he understood to be NT Christianity. Essentially self-taught, Parham read the Bible to find its meaning for himself. This approach to Scripture had already led him to some nontraditional conclusions. He espoused conditional immortality, taught an experience of Spirit-baptism that "sealed" Christ's bride for the rapture, enthusiastically supported Zionism, and preached divine healing. He also lived "by faith." He traveled within Kansas, preaching in homes, school houses, and churches as invited, living wherever he was offered shelter, proclaiming his message.

By 1898 Parham (now married and the father of a growing family) established a base of operations in Topeka, where he opened a faith home, a mission, and a small publishing enterprise. Probably the central practice of his outreach was prayer for the sick. While in Topeka, he began to call his message of "living Christianity" the "apostolic faith." He began to issue a biweekly magazine, *The Apostolic Faith,* and to recognize his identity with a larger restorationist millenarian subculture.

Committed to recapturing fully the essence of primitive Christianity, Parham visited ministries that shared his hopes. His most important trip took him to Shiloh, Maine, in mid-1900. There the efforts of Frank Sandford deeply influenced him. Returning to Topeka in the late summer, Parham determined to open a Bible school patterned on Sandford's Holy Ghost and Us Bible School in Shiloh. Other evangelists had already taken over most of his congregation and his facilities, so he was free to embark on a venture to promulgate and further develop his views. In October 1900 he opened Bethel Bible School with some forty people (including dependents).

Bethel Bible School was unusual in several ways. It had one text, the Bible, and one teacher, the Holy Spirit—who presumably channeled his message through Parham. Students studied biblical passages together and endeavored to "pray in" the lessons of each passage. Long hours of prayer,

services of indefinite duration, and hours of visitation and evangelism filled each day. Parham stressed the NT views that he considered had constituted the apostolic faith. Toward the end of the year he turned the students' attention to a NT experience as yet unrealized among them—tongues speech. Basing his assertion primarily on Acts 2, he affirmed that speaking in tongues was the biblical evidence for an experience of Spirit baptism. Many of his contemporaries shared his emphasis on the baptism with the Holy Spirit; none, however, had posited a uniform biblical evidence for the experience.

As a result, in January 1901 Parham's students and other followers began to speak in tongues. The school disbanded in the wake of enthusiasm to spread the message that yet another dimension of the apostolic faith had been restored. Enthusiasm waned rapidly in the face of considerable ridicule and opposition, however. For two years Parham struggled to establish a setting in which he could preach and practice his variety of the NT faith.

The tide turned in 1903 when Parham, frustrated in his efforts to convince people of the validity of tongues speech as the evidence of Spirit baptism, focused again on healing. He distributed tracts at a popular southwestern Missouri health resort, El Dorado Springs, and conducted meetings in his rented rooms. The healing of Mary Arthur, a chronically ill resident of nearby Galena, Kansas, resulted in an invitation for Parham to visit Galena. There his efforts immediately evoked response. Daily services continued for months, with converts numbering near a thousand and nearly as many healings. Parham recruited dedicated young helpers in Galena who proved willing to share his itinerant "faith" life. He located his family in Baxter Springs, Kansas, and conducted services under the banner of the Apostolic Faith movement in surrounding towns.

The movement spread rapidly in the contiguous area of Kansas, Missouri, and Oklahoma. By 1905 Parham was in southern Texas, where he was to have some of his most dramatic success. He associated in the Houston area with a capable young lawyer who was also a licensed Methodist preacher, Warren Fay Carothers. Late in 1905 the two opened a faith Bible school in which several who later became prominent Pentecostals participated. Probably Parham's best known Houston protégé was William Seymour, who responded (against Parham's wishes) to an invitation to carry the movement's message to Los Angeles. He took not only Parham's message but also the name of the movement and called his message and his paper the Apostolic Faith.

The Apostolic Faith movement, according to Parham, had a twofold purpose: the restoration of "the faith once delivered to the saints" (Parham yearned for "the old-time religion"), and the promotion of Christian unity. In addition to evidential tongues (which Parham believed should be authentic human languages), the movement affirmed the necessity of crisis sanctification, proclaimed divine healing, espoused premillennialism, urged "faith" living for Christian workers, and valued the manifestation of spiritual gifts.

Once Seymour reached Azusa Street, leadership eluded Parham, except in the southern Midwest. Apostolic Faith missions sprang up in many places as people who embraced Parham's essential message carried it elsewhere. Usually leaders of such missions shared Parham's distaste for organization and did not acknowledge his authority.

Parham's influence remained strong in Texas through mid-1907, even after he was arrested on a charge of sodomy. Some of his followers regrouped, keeping the name Apostolic Faith movement but disassociating from Parham. Parham, meanwhile, retained a loyal following and also used the name, claiming that his efforts alone represented the true vision of his original Apostolic Faith. Gradually, adherents of Apostolic Faith missions in the Midwest that had disassociated from Parham replaced the designation "Apostolic Faith" with the less troublesome term "Pentecostal." Seymour's efforts in Los Angeles retained the name. Florence Crawford, who left Azusa Street for Portland, Oregon, introduced her efforts under the name "Apostolic Faith." The group she founded continues to use the name today, as does the remnant of Parham's followers in Baxter Springs, Kansas.

In one sense, then, the Apostolic Faith movement can be regarded as an early synonym for Pentecostal. It quickly came to have a more specific usage, however, describing participants in several Pentecostal ministries that operated independently of one another.

See also APOSTOLIC FAITH (BAXTER SPRINGS, KANS); APOSTOLIC FAITH MISSION (PORTLAND, ORE.).

Bibliography: R. M. Anderson, *Vision of the Disinherited* (1979); J. Goff, "Fields White Unto Harvest: Charles F. Parham and the Missionary Origins of the Pentecostal Movement," Ph.D. diss., University of Arkansas (1987).   E. L. Blumhofer

APOSTOLIC OVERCOMING HOLY CHURCH OF GOD

A black Oneness Pentecostal organization founded in Mobile, Alabama, in 1917 by William T. Phillips (1893–1974). A Holiness minister since 1913 and evangelist in 1916, Phillips embraced the Oneness doctrine as a Pentecostal. His own congregation, the Greater Adams Holiness Church, was incorporated in 1920 as the Ethiopian Overcoming Holy Church of God, with "Ethiopian" being changed to "Apostolic" in 1927. Due to Phillips's influence, the organization is the only Oneness body to hold the Holiness doctrine of sanctification. Wine is required in Communion, and footwashing is an ordinance. The episcopally governed body ordains women. The Apostolic Overcoming Holy Church of God Publishing House distributes literature and its periodical, *The People's Mouthpiece*. Headquarters are in Birmingham, Alabama, which in 1987 recorded its membership as 13,000 in 197 churches. The church has foreign works in Haiti and West Africa.

Bibliography: C. E. Jones, *Guide to the Study of the Pentecostal Movement*, vol. 1 (1983); W. T. Phillips, *Excerpts from the Life of Rt. Rev. W. T. Phillips and Fundamentals of the Apostolic Overcoming Holy Church of God, Inc.* (1967); A. C. Piepkorn, *Profiles in Belief*, vol. 3 (1979).   D. A. Reed

ARCHIVAL RESOURCES Until recent years researchers interested in the Pentecostal and charismatic movements generally had to discover a private collection, interview eyewitnesses to the revivals, or confer with a denominational official for archival resources. This is still true for certain resources, but since the late 1970s several denominations have organized repositories, and other non-Pentecostal libraries and archives have added Pentecostal and charismatic resources to their holdings.

Documenting the early years of the Pentecostal movement is difficult for at least two reasons. First, the movement was unorganized and few Pentecostals showed interest in organizing, wishing rather to remain independent. Second, across the movement it was believed that Christ's coming was imminent. With this belief firmly settled in their minds, there was little reason to keep records for historians to ponder.

Fortunately, as the movement developed, some early Pentecostals began to preserve diaries, periodicals, correspondence, photographs, and other documents. The items that have survived help tell the story of the movement's early years.

Likewise, documenting the charismatic movement has its difficulties, for it too has had little formal organization. Many who were baptized in the Spirit remained in their denominations while others formed independent congregations. However, more documentation is available for the recent charismatic movement than for the early Pentecostal movement simply because there has been more interest in documenting religious history in the latter half of the twentieth century than there was in the first.

I. Resource Centers. Several archival repositories that have developed in recent years are open to researchers. Each center has established certain collecting and research policies that they follow. Persons interested in researching a given repository are advised to check in advance with the center regarding the type of materials available and the hours the center is open. Often archival personnel can direct a researcher to other archives if their own does not have the desired documents.

• The Arch (Pentecostal Holiness Church), 7300 Northwest Expressway, Bethany, OK 73008: Denominational records that include taped interviews, missionary records, conference records, photographs, videos, memoirs, books, periodicals, newspaper and magazine clippings, and individual church histories.

• Archives of the Billy Graham Center, Wheaton College, Wheaton, IL 60187: An archives for nondenominational Protestant missions and evangelism. Collections include resources of groups and individuals having connections with the Pentecostal and charismatic movements, such as the National Religious Broadcasters and National Association of Evangelicals. Also included in the collections are papers and recordings of William Branham, Kathryn Kuhlman, Aimee Semple McPherson, and Corrie ten Boom.

• Archives of the David J. du Plessis Center for Christian Spirituality, Fuller Theological Seminary, 135 North Oakland, Pasadena, CA 91182: Collects documentation on the Pentecostal, char-

The importance of Pentecostal-charismatic archival research has become more evidenced in recent years. Here Fr. Peter Hocken, a Roman Catholic scholar, researches in the Assemblies of God Archives, Springfield, Missouri.

Some early records of the Church of God (Cleveland, Tenn.) stored in the Hal Bernard Dixon, Jr., Pentecostal Research Center in Cleveland, Tennessee.

ismatic, and ecumenical movements. Includes papers of David J. du Plessis and his collection of Pentecostal and charismatic ephemera. Other papers include the history of early Pentecostalism and its ethnic origins.

• Assemblies of God Archives, 1445 Boonville, Springfield, MO 65802: Collects materials pertaining to the denomination, the early Pentecostal movement, charismatic movement, Pentecostal Fellowship of North America, Pentecostal World Conference, and individual records; also has audio and video interviews and radio and television programs from the salvation-healing movement of the 1950s.

• Hal Bernard Dixon, Jr., Pentecostal Research Center (Church of God), P.O. Box 3448, Cleveland, TN 37311: This center's goal is to collect materials on the Pentecostal-charismatic movements worldwide. On their own denomination they have records, journals, correspondence, periodicals, minutes, early books, tapes of radio programs and church services, and other materials.

• Holy Spirit Research Center, Oral Roberts University, 7777 South Lewis, Tulsa, OK 74171: A collection of materials pertaining to the Pentecostal-charismatic movement with emphasis on groups and individuals after 1950. Collection includes books, periodicals, sermon tapes, recorded interviews, and other materials. The Oral Roberts Evangelistic Association also maintains an archives for the association and the university.

• Pentecostal Historical Center (United Pentecostal Church), 8855 Dunn Road, Hazelwood, MO 63042 (St. Louis area): This center is a part of the denomination's church division. The church division maintains denominational records. The center has several early periodicals published by Oneness groups that merged to form the United Pentecostal church: diaries, photographs, recordings, radio programs, various artifacts on display.

II. Other Sources. In addition to the above repositories, researchers will find resources in Pentecostal denominational headquarters that do not have organized archives. Resources on non-Pentecostal groups, such as the Holiness movement, are cataloged in denominational and college libraries and archives. The latter includes the Nazarene Archives, Kansas City, Missouri; Church of God Archives, Anderson, Indiana; B. L. Fisher Library, Asbury Theological Seminary, Wilmore, Kentucky; and the A. B. Simpson Historical Library, Nyack, New York. The library at CBN University, Virginia Beach, Virginia, also has Pentecostal-charismatic resources.

Local and state historical societies, local libraries, university libraries, newspaper files, court records, and other sources often turn up information on Pentecostal-charismatic research projects.

Bibliography: C. Jacquet, *Yearbook of American and Canadian Churches* (annual); C. Jones, *A Guide to the Study of the Pentecostal Movement* (1983).
                                                              W. E. Warner

ARGENTINIAN CHARISMATICS See CHARISMATIC MOVEMENT.

ARGUE, ANDREW HARVEY (1868–1959). Pastor and evangelist. A pioneering figure in the Pentecostal Assemblies of Canada (PAOC), A. H. Argue founded Calvary Temple, Winnipeg, for decades one of Canada's largest Pentecostal churches. Upon hearing of the Pentecostal outpouring in 1906, he traveled to Chicago, where he experienced the baptism in the Holy Spirit himself. Leaving a profitable business and his Winnipeg pastorate, he traveled extensively in the U.S. and Canada, for a time in the 1920s in campaigns with his daughter Zelma and son Watson. His meetings brought him into association with Maria B. Woodworth-Etter and Charles S. Price, and led to the establishment of several churches, including Evangel Temple, Toronto, in 1927.

Bibliography: Z. Argue, *Contending for the Faith* (1923); C. Brumback, *Suddenly . . . From Heaven* (1961); G. Kulbeck, *What God Hath Wrought* (1958); W. E. McAlister, "A. H. Argue With the Lord," *Pentecostal Testimony* 40 (3, 1959): 7, 15–16.
                                                              E. A. Wilson

ARGUE, WATSON (1904–85). Pastor and evangelist. Son of A. H. Argue, Watson Argue distinguished himself as a competitive swimmer, speaker, and gospel musician by age twenty. He held meetings in the United Kingdom in 1923 and in Angelus Temple upon the disappearance of Aimee Semple McPherson in 1926. He pastored Calvary Temple, Winnipeg (1937–48), and Calvary Temple, Seattle (1948–56). He was noted for his effective invitations at the close of an evangelistic message. His later ministry was devoted largely to overseas evangelistic crusades.

Bibliography: Z. Argue, *Contending for the Faith* (1923); C. Brumback, *Suddenly . . . From Heaven* (1961); G. G. Kulbeck, *What God Hath Wrought* (1958); W. Menzies, *Anointed to Serve* (1971).
                                                              E. A. Wilson

ARGUE, ZELMA (1900–1980). Well-known Pentecostal evangelist and teacher. Born in Winnipeg, Canada, the eldest daughter of A. H. and Eva Argue, Zelma was brought up in a strong Pentecostal home, becoming a zealous witness for Christ. She was ordained as an evangelist in the Assemblies of God in March 1920. She regularly accompanied her father, ministering with him on his evangelistic travels in the 1920s and 1930s. She realized the power of the printed word and became a prolific writer, contributing more than two hundred articles to the *Pentecostal Evangel*. Her books were: *What Meaneth This?* (1923), reprinted as *Contending for the Faith* (1928); *Garments of Strength* (1935); *Practical Christian Living* (1937); and one on her mother entitled *The Vision and Vow of a Canadian Maiden* (1940). With a reputation of being other-worldly, she was known as a powerful intercessor. She pastored in Los Angeles in the 1950s and spent her last years in California.
                                                              P. D. Hocken

ASCETICISM See FASTING.

ASHCROFT, JAMES ROBERT (1911–). College educator. An ordained minister of the Assemblies of God (AG), J. Robert Ashcroft has spent his life in Christian education: as a teacher at Central Bible College, as the national secretary of education (AG, 1955–59), as president of Central Bible College and Evangel College (1958–63), as president of Evangel College (1958–74), as president of Valley Forge Christian College (1982–84), and as president of Berean College (1984–). He is recognized internationally as a devotional speaker and writer (*The Sequence of the Supernatural and Other Essays on the Spirit-Filled Life* [1972]; *When You Pray* [1977]). As well, he is respected as a Bible expositor (*Ways of Understanding God's Word* [1960]). A staff member describes him as a "servant administrator" (Hedman, 1987, 69).

Bibliography: J. Hedman, "J. Robert Ashcroft," *Springfield Magazine* (September 1987), 40–41, 69.
F. Bixler

ASSEMBLEA CRISTIANA (The Christian Assembly). One of the more prominent ethnic churches that became part of the Pentecostal movement. The first Italian-Pentecostal Church in the U.S., the Assemblea Cristiana was established in Chicago in 1907. Its beginning is a story of the struggles of a group of Italian emigrants from Tuscany who entered into the life of one of the Italian ghettos located on the city's near north side. During the latter part of 1907, many of its initial members became Pentecostals after attending the meetings conducted by William H. Durham at the North Avenue Mission. Shortly afterward, these people established their own

J. Robert Ashcroft is an Assemblies of God college educator, having filled teaching and administrative positions for most of his adult life. His son John was elected governor of Missouri in 1984.

church at 256 W. Grand Avenue under the leadership of Peter Ottolini and Luigi Francescon. A few years later, church members elected their first pastor, Peter Menconi. Menconi remained as pastor until his accidental death in 1936. Shortly after its inception, members of the Assemblea Cristiana traveled for the next thirty years to other Italian communities, particularly in the U.S., Italy, and South America, and established hundreds of Italian-Pentecostal churches and converted thousands of Italians to Pentecostalism. Presently, many of the churches in the U.S. are organized under the Christian Church of North America.

Bibliography: R. Bracco, *Il Risveglio Pentecostale in Italia* (n.d.); L. DeCaro, *Our Heritage: The Christian Church of North America* (1977); *Fiftieth Anniversary: Christian Church of North America* (1977).
J. Colletti

ASSEMBLIES OF GOD The largest, strongest, and most affluent white Pentecostal denomination, the Assemblies of God (AG) was formed in 1914 to give coherence to broadly based Pentecostal efforts. It organized in Hot Springs, Arkansas, as a fellowship of Pentecostal ministers who believed that cooperative action would enable them to fulfill their shared objectives expeditiously. In spite of the preponderance of southerners among its early members, the AG emerged specifically to meet the needs of a nationwide constituency. As opposed to other Pentecostal organizations (most of which had existed prior to their embracing Pentecostalism), the AG was

A member of the well-known Argue family, Zelma Argue traveled with her father, A. H. Argue, during the 1920s and 1930s.

The AG has established churches of many foreign language groups in the U. S. This Chinese church is an example of that concern.

neither locally defined nor organized around a Wesleyan view of holiness.

Those whose efforts shaped the AG had encountered Pentecostal teaching—with its stress on restorationist goals—in various places. Many had roots in Charles Parham's Texas-based Apostolic Faith (AF) movement; others had been influenced by the Rochester, New York, ministries known as Elim; some brought experience and convictions molded by association with the Christian and Missionary Alliance (CMA); many had ties, direct or indirect, to John Alexander Dowie's Zion City or to other Chicago-area independent missions. These centers especially influenced those who led the denomination in its formative years.

The formation of the AG was the result of efforts initiated in 1913 by Eudorus N. Bell, Howard Goss, Daniel C. O. Opperman, Archibald P. Collins, and Mack M. Pinson. These men sought both to accomplish specific objectives and to repudiate unacceptable doctrines and practices. They issued a call to a general council through the *Word and Witness*, a periodical edited by Bell in Malvern, Arkansas. The announcement was publicized in other periodicals as well.

The announcement elicited varied response. Pentecostals tended to distrust organization, claiming that the NT offered no precedent for anything beyond local church order. Most Pente-

costals had distanced themselves from the denominations before embracing Pentecostal teaching; some had been forced to break denominational ties when they had begun espousing tongues speech and divine healing. Most were convinced that organization stifled the Holy Spirit.

Such hesitations resulted in the formation at Hot Springs of a loosely conceived agency that adopted neither a constitution nor a doctrinal statement. The denomination established its headquarters at a small Bible school in Findlay, Ohio. In 1915 it moved its base of operations to St. Louis.

Even as the organization took shape, however, some of its promoters accepted divergent views about the Trinity and began espousing more radically restorationist sentiments than most Pentecostals accepted. In 1915 the third general council endeavored to promote harmony. A showdown in the 1916 general council in St. Louis, however, resulted in the expulsion of advocates of the "New Issue" and assured the Trinitarian orthodoxy of the AG. The same general council adopted a Statement of Fundamental Truths, identifying acceptable doctrines. The original statement was not conceived as a full theological affirmation (e.g., it contained no reference to the Virgin Birth). Rather, it sought to help participants understand their Pentecostal emphasis. Further clarification came later.

Before the AG had organized, another disagreement had agitated independent Pentecostals. Early Pentecostals had tended to regard sanctification as a second, instantaneous, spiritual crisis. A Chicago mission leader, William Durham, had challenged that view after 1908 and had advocated, rather, "the finished work of Calvary." Responding to the extreme teachings some contemporary Holiness advocates urged, Durham insisted that penitent sinners received both Christ's pardon and cleansing at conversion. Their further responsibility was not to pursue crisis cleansing but to live an "overcoming" life.

Durham's views circulated widely through his periodical, *The Pentecostal Testimony,* and through his travels. E. N. Bell, a Southern Baptist pastor who became the first chairman of the AG, had embraced Pentecostalism in Durham's Chicago mission. Bell most likely encouraged his associates in the AF movement in Texas and Arkansas to accept Durham's views. Durham attended their camp meeting and convinced the majority of the leaders.

Durham's teaching coincided with the predilections of those who embraced Pentecostalism within the CMA and of those with roots in Zion, Illinois. They sparked intense controversy, especially with Charles F. Parham and Florence L. Crawford.

Since the AG did not seek to enforce doctrinal unity, it embraced people who held various views on sanctification. Participants at the first general council heard Mack M. Pinson advocate Durham's position. Early versions of the Statement of Fundamental Truths attempted to satisfy those with Holiness sympathies while identifying with Durham's essential approach. As time passed, it became increasingly evident that the AG supported Durham's understanding. The denomination's early leaders, accused by Holiness advocates of minimizing holiness, found it necessary to assert frequently that they believed in sanctification.

A third doctrinal issue that helped mold the AG emerged in 1918 when a popular evangelist, pastor, and former executive presbyter, F. F. Bosworth, resigned from the denomination in a disagreement about evidential tongues speech. Bosworth published his critique of the movement's espousal of tongues as uniform initial evidence of Spirit baptism in a pamphlet entitled "Do All Speak With Tongues?" His actions promoted thorough discussion of evidential tongues and marked the culmination in the AG of an evolution toward rigid promotion of evidential tongues. Early Pentecostals had not all accepted evidential tongues without qualification, but increasingly the movement had tended to do so. It became evident in 1918 how strongly the leadership of the AG was committed to that position. The denomination was saved a showdown by the force of Bosworth's magnanimous spirit. Only he and his brother resigned over the issue.

Under the leadership of its first chairman, Eudorus N. Bell, the AG issued a weekly paper which, in 1918, took the name *The Pentecostal Evangel.* Its current circulation exceeds 275,000, making it one of the larger Protestant denominational weeklies in the U.S. During the first several years, much of the actual editorial work was done by J. Roswell Flower, who had initially conceived the idea of a weekly publication. After several changes in editorial staff, an Englishman, Stanley H. Frodsham, became editor of the *Evangel* as well as editor-in-chief of publications for the growing AG publishing effort known as Gospel Publishing House. Frodsham served until 1949, when his long-time associate, Robert Cunningham, accepted editorial responsibility. On Cunningham's retirement in 1984, his assistant, Richard Champion, became editor.

Bell resigned from the chairmanship late in 1914 and was replaced by a fellow Texan and former Southern Baptist, Archibald P. Collins. In the Oneness turmoil in the fall of 1915, John W. Welch assumed the chairmanship, a post he held until Bell was returned to office in 1920. On Bell's unexpected death in 1923, Welch resumed office. W. T. Gaston succeeded Welch in 1925 and served until 1929. During his tenure, the AG adopted its constitution and bylaws. Under the new constitution, the chairman became the general superintendent. In 1929 Ernest Swing Williams was elected the first general superintendent, a post he held until his retirement in 1949.

Among the several purposes for establishing the AG was the support of foreign missions. J. R. Flower, the denomination's first missionary secretary, began the process of systematizing a missions program. The process was expedited when the 1927 general council ratified the selection of Noel Perkin as missionary secretary. Perkin, an Englishman by birth and a former independent Pentecostal missionary to Argentina, supervised an expanding missionary program until his retirement in 1959.

Another troublesome concern early in AG history was the provision of training for ministry. Pentecostals regarded Spirit baptism as "endurement with power for service," and, at least in the first several decades, the experience seemed to compel many to dedicate their lives to preaching and teaching ministries at home and abroad. The profusion of committed but untrained workers caused considerable difficulty in some places. Lacking both finances and inclination to commit the new denomination to a single institution, the early leaders endorsed various existing "full gospel" schools. These tended to be short-term. D. C. O. Opperman conducted numerous such training institutes in various places. Several small schools—such as Bethel Bible Training School in Newark, New Jersey—established themselves more permanently.

In 1920 the executives decided to cooperate with several AG districts in organizing a permanent school in Auburn, Nebraska. S. A. Jamieson, a former Presbyterian pastor, served as principal of this effort, known as Midwest Bible School. In spite of its dedicated staff, however, the school could not overcome financial and social problems. It closed in the spring of 1921.

That fall, AG leaders tried again, this time in Springfield, Missouri (where the denomination's headquarters had moved in 1918). Central Bible Institute began under the direction of Daniel W. Kerr, an elderly pastor who had spent most of his

An inner city church founded by Bill Wilson in Brooklyn, Metro Assembly of God ministers to hundreds of children in a high crime area.

ministry in the CMA. Kerr had already assisted in the formation of the two West Coast Bible colleges. During the 1920s, various men who would make lasting contributions to Central Bible Institute joined its faculty: Frank M. Boyd, Myer Pearlman, William I. Evans, and Ralph M. Riggs. As the only general council school, Central Bible Institute set the standard against which other locally sponsored AG institutions were evaluated.

The establishment of a council-sponsored school did not indicate unanimity about education, however. Strong sentiment against school-based training persisted for many years. Some were convinced that education hindered the Spirit; others, true to their restorationist origins, insisted that the NT offered no precedent for training beyond a form of apprenticeship with an experienced worker. The conviction of the imminence of the end also assured the persistence of the view that would-be workers had no time for specialized training.

During these years, the AG addressed questions relating to the place of women in the ministry. The first general council limited voting to males. It noted that women were to be subject to male leaders but acknowledged their right to be evangelists and missionaries. The key issue was authority: males refused to admit women to positions that granted them authority over men. They dismissed Galatians 3:28 ("There is neither male nor female: for ye are all one in Christ Jesus," KJV) as a basis for equality, alleging that the text meant only that "in the matter of salvation the lines of sex [were] blotted out."

Membership in the general council was limited to ministers. Numerous Pentecostal women had engaged in ministries before they had embraced Pentecostalism. Some had been ordained (though usually in nontraditional and highly irregular settings). Although their ordination was recognized by the AG such women could not vote at general councils until 1920. Full ordination of women by the AG was not granted until 1935. Even then the proviso "when such acts are necessary," was appended to women's permission to administer the ordinances.

Meanwhile, however, the *Pentecostal Evangel* had repeatedly informed women of their actual restrictions. In particular, E. N. Bell strongly opposed women pastors. He grudgingly accorded them temporary rights but urged the propriety of "pushing men" as soon as potential male leadership emerged in a female-led congregation. He considered that women ministers were God's second best—useful for instances in which men "failed God." He fully concurred with widespread early Pentecostal restrictions on their appropriate roles. Ernest S. Williams shared Bell's views. "God," he noted (even as women gained ordination during his administration), had "placed headship" in the males. According to Williams, even the much-cited daughters of Philip (Acts 21:8) had prophesied under the authority of their father. Males, then, properly controlled the environments in which women ministered. With such assumptions prevalent, it is hardly surprising that relatively few women sought ordination. None ever achieved national office. The masculine language of the constitution and by-laws continues to make mockery of claims that the denomination as a whole fully supports ministering women.

J. Roswell Flower was appointed as the first Assemblies of God missionary secretary-treasurer in 1919. He later served for many years as the denomination's general secretary.

Through the 1930s the AG developed in relative isolation from other religious groups. Awareness of circumstances in other Pentecostal denominations was fostered by occasional visits by Europeans and others, but no formal channels existed to express shared concerns. In 1942, however, this changed when Pentecostal participation in an evangelical gathering in St. Louis was solicited. Ernest S. Williams, J. Roswell Flower, and Noel Perkin represented the AG at the meeting, out of which the National Association of Evangelicals (NAE) emerged. Although some AG pastors expressed serious reservations about cooperation with Evangelicals who privately opposed Pentecostal teaching, most favored identifying their movement with the NAE. Closely related to the NAE was the National Religious Broadcasters Association, with which the AG has been deeply involved from the beginning.

Two other cooperative agencies emerged in the 1940s to foster Pentecostals' awareness of their participation in a broader movement. In 1947 the Pentecostal World Conference was formed in Zurich. The gathering was similar to some that had convened before World War II, except that North American participation was added. Despite the fears of some that regular meetings would result in international organization, the confer-

ences have continued with substantial support from AG leaders.

The Pentecostal Fellowship of North America (PFNA) emerged in 1948 to provide regular opportunities for contact among North American Pentecostal denominations. While this agency has never won support from major segments of the movement (Oneness Pentecostals are excluded by its doctrinal statement; black Pentecostals have chosen not to affiliate), the AG has played a significant leadership role.

Late in the 1940s, AG leaders began responding to the emergence of "Latter Rain" teaching in independent Pentecostalism. The rhetoric of Latter Rain advocates closely resembled that of early Pentecostals: they coveted a restoration of apostolic Christianity. They considered Pentecostalism a step in the direction of restoration but indicted the movement for organizing and "quenching the Spirit." To effect a restoration, they promoted an emphasis on prophecy, spiritual gifts, the restoration of the offices of NT Christianity and biblical organization. Emanating from Saskatchewan, they soon found response in some AG congregations.

While the teaching did not result in denominational division, it did prompt several resignations from the general council. More importantly, it was related to two other emerging issues that demanded assessment—healing revivalism and charismatic renewal.

Healing had historically been central to Pentecostalism. Adherents believed that miraculous results would follow fervent prayer. Wherever Pentecostal teaching spread, healing evangelism followed. Late in the 1940s, as Latter Rain advocates called Pentecostal denominations to task for betraying their heritage in numerous ways, healing became the central focus of several emerging ministries. William Branham, Oral Roberts, A. A. Allen, and Jack Coe were among the best known of hundreds of tent-toting prophets of the miraculous. Their efforts, coordinated for a time by AG minister Gordon Lindsay through an organization he called the Voice of Healing, gave the teaching more visibility than it had ever achieved.

The trouble was that some of the major revivalists—especially Allen and Coe—found it impossible to advocate healing without criticizing those who objected to their style. The AG became a principal target as it urged adherents to consider carefully the spiritual and financial issues raised by forceful independent leaders. For some, the promise of miracles seemed far more attractive than advice to read the Bible, pray, and support the local congregation. During the 1950s, most healing evangelists opted for independence, even from the guidelines Lindsay had advocated. As their claims became increasingly radical, and as some fell into disrepute, their direct influence within the AG dissipated. They touched sensitive chords, however, and left a permanent legacy.

Early in the 1950s, AG pastor David J. du Plessis had visited the office of the National Council of Churches of Christ in America to share his Pentecostal testimony. To his surprise, the leaders welcomed him and solicited his involve-

The Assemblies of God Headquarters complex in Springfield, Missouri, includes a four-story administration building, printing plant, publications distribution center, and the Assemblies of God Theological Seminary.

ment in a growing network of gatherings. Du Plessis ultimately gained acceptance among Protestants and Catholics who differed sharply with the fundamentalist assumptions of most AG adherents. His relationship with the AG became increasingly uneasy. Du Plessis found himself unable to adhere to restrictions advised by denominational leaders and, under pressure, submitted his resignation as an AG minister in 1962. His influence in the broadening charismatic movement continued to expand.

The charismatic movement posed numerous problems for Pentecostals who had long assumed that their theological persuasions were absolutely requisite to valid Spirit baptism. AG leaders offered no firm response, simply saying that their intention was to be identified with what "God was doing in the world." Many AG churches were influenced by the charismatic worship style and attempted to recover some of their own heritage by identifying with its exuberance and simplicity. Changing grassroots attitudes became apparent in a tendency to welcome du Plessis in AG churches. In 1980 du Plessis again became a credentialed AG minister.

After the long, stable administration of Ernest S. Williams, a succession of men served as general superintendents in the 1950s. Wesley L. Steelberg, Gayle F. Lewis, and Ralph M. Riggs supervised the creation of new departments, a growing radio outreach, and the formation of Evangel College, a liberal arts institution that was created—in spite of lingering doubts about its mission—in 1955. Berean School of the Bible, a correspondence institute that had been created in 1947, serviced a growing lay constituency. In 1985 it became Berean College of the AG. After it made a fourth and fifth year of work available in 1947, Central Bible Institute gained accreditation through the Accrediting Association of Bible Colleges.

The general council meeting in San Antonio in 1959 marked an important leadership transition. J. R. Flower and Noel Perkin, men whose careers had shaped the AG, resigned. J. Philip Hogan assumed direction of the growing missionary program. General superintendent Ralph Riggs was replaced by Thomas F. Zimmerman.

Zimmerman's administration began during an era of disappointingly slow growth. A strong leader, Zimmerman sought the reasons for this, developed programs to foster growth and determined to exploit AG participation in the NAE to bolster adherents' identity as Evangelicals. Over the years, Zimmerman became a familiar figure on the boards of various evangelical agencies. By 1982 his emphasis on church growth had won the denomination recognition as one of America's fastest growing denominations. Subtle changes were at work, however: a denomination that had once savored rejection by "the world" basked in growing popularity. Adherents accommodated increasingly to a middle-American lifestyle.

The year 1985 marked the end of another era. The general council, meeting again in San Antonio, turned from Zimmerman to G. Raymond Carlson for leadership. By then growth had slowed again: at best, it was unevenly concentrated in Spanish and newly formed Korean districts. By any standard, however, the emergence and development of the AG is an impressive story. From humble beginnings, the denomination has grown until its membership exceeds that of numerous long-established denominations. America's largest church buildings and several of its prominent televangelists have ties to the AG. Per capita giving to foreign missions exceeds that of any mainline denomination.

Bibliography: E. L. Blumhofer, *The Assemblies of God*, 2 vols. (1988); W. W. Menzies, *Anointed to Serve* (1971). E. L. Blumhofer

ASSEMBLIES OF GOD OF GREAT BRITAIN AND IRELAND (AGGBI). Founded in 1924 from a number of independent Pentecostal assemblies. On his first furlough in 1922, W. F. P. Burton attempted to bring together many of the scattered assemblies. This gave rise to the Sheffield Conference and the setting up of a Provisional Council. In 1923 Archibald Cooper of South Africa, with the support of John Nelson Parr of Manchester, went a step further, with the latter sending out a circular letter in November 1923 stating the reasons for an association: (1) To preserve the testimony to the full Gospel, including the baptism of the Spirit and to save the work from false teaching; (2) to strengthen bonds and create a

fuller degree of cooperation; (3) to cooperate in evangelistic and missionary work; (4) to present a united witness to outsiders; (5) to exercise discipline over the disorderly; (6) to save the assemblies from falling into unscriptural organizations. According to Parr, another major reason was to articulate their attitude toward war and thus obtain exemption from military service for their ministers (*Autobiography*, 1972, 26–27).

A meeting was arranged at Aston, Birmingham, in February 1924 to which many leaders were invited. A number were unable to be present owing to a railway strike, including Lewi Pethrus, who was visiting Britain at the time. The resolutions that were accepted contained the following:

. . . we do not intend identifying ourselves as, or establishing ourselves as a sect, that is a human organisation, with centralised legislative power . . . and usurps authority over Assemblies and has unscriptural jurisdiction over its members. . . . We . . . recognise the need . . . of scriptural methods and order of worship, unity and fellowship and business for God . . . disapproving all unscriptural methods, doctrines, and conduct.

The Fundamental Truths declared that speaking in tongues was the initial evidence of the baptism of the Holy Spirit, the return of Christ is premillennial, and those whose names are not in the Book of Life are to be everlastingly punished. Baptism should be by total immersion and deliverance from sickness is provided for in the Atonement.

A second meeting was held in Highbury, London, in May 1924 with eighty people present. A letter was received from the Elim leaders (who had been excluded from the invitation). When they arrived on the second day, E. J. Phillips suggested that they should work together, with Elim providing the evangelistic arm of the work. It was too bold for the time, but the proposal was to be put to the Elim workers in December. Among the leaders at this London meeting were Donald Gee (who joined later but had to consult his Leith Assembly), John Carter, Alfred H. Carter, and J. N. Parr. Thirty-seven assemblies in England and one in Belfast joined; thirty-eight from Wales and Monmouth joined in August. The Elim workers continued on their own, and the AGGBI became established.

At the end of 1925 several senior members of the Pentecostal Missionary Union (PMU) resigned. The remaining members representing the AGGBI took responsibility for their work, and the two bodies merged. A. H. Carter (1891–1971) had been in charge of the PMU Bible School at Hampstead, London, since February 1921. He was joined there by his brother John in March and in April 1923 by C. L. Parker (Fellow of University College, Oxford), T. J. Jones, and Harold Horton. Though the college maintained its independence, it became the Bible school for the assemblies. When it was destroyed in 1940–41, another building was used for a time until they moved to Kenley, Surrey, and amalgamating with the Bristol Bible College in 1951. Donald

Gee became the first principal in September 1951. They later moved to Mattersey, Doncaster, Yorkshire, in 1973. The offices were in Lewisham, London, until 1940, when they transferred to Luton, Bedfordshire, before returning to London in 1953. Eighteen years later they moved to Nottingham, where they remain.

The number of assemblies increased from 140 in 1927 to 200 in 1929. By 1933 there were 250; by 1939, 350. In 1946 there were 403 assemblies, and in 1957 there were 506. Today the figure is almost 600. The greatest impact was made in the period of 1926–28 as a result of the ministry of Stephen Jeffreys. Alfred Missen writes: ". . . his campaigns altered the whole character of the Movement. Small meetings gave place to crowded campaign services . . . to the select companies of mature Christians were added many hundreds of new converts."

Others, like Fred Squire (1933–36), John Carter (1927–34), and W. T. H. Richards (1917–74) pioneered churches on their own.

The strength of the fellowship lies in the local assemblies and in the twenty-four districts. The Midlands District, based in Nottingham (thirteen assemblies), is the largest, with fifty-four assemblies, followed by South Wales with fifty-two. The Annual Conference at Minehead now attracts 5,500, with nearly 500 delegates at the business sessions. The present constituency is 40,000.

See also EUROPEAN PENTECOSTALISM.

Bibliography: D. Gee, *Wind and Flame* (1967); A. Missen, *Sound of a Going* (1973).

D. W. Cartwright

ASSEMBLIES OF THE CHURCH OF JESUS CHRIST See ASSEMBLIES OF THE LORD JESUS CHRIST.

ASSEMBLIES OF THE LORD JESUS CHRIST

A Oneness Pentecostal organization founded in 1952 as a merger of the Assemblies of Jesus Christ, the Church of the Lord Jesus Christ, and the Jesus Only Apostolic Church of God. The racially integrated body is congregational in polity and calls its leader the general chairman.

Doctrinally it allows the use of either grape juice or wine in Communion, practices footwashing, teaches that women should not cut their hair, and disapproves of divorce and remarriage.

Headquarters, publishing house, and offices of its periodical, *Apostolic Witness*, are in Memphis, Tennessee. Its two Bible schools are in Memphis and Parkersburg, West Virginia. In 1987 numerical strength was approximately 20,000 members and four hundred ministers in three hundred churches throughout twenty-two states, with work in six foreign countries.

Bibliography: C. E. Jones, *A Guide to the Study of the Pentecostal Movement*, vol. 1 (1983); A. Piepkorn, *Profiles in Belief: The Religious Bodies of the United States and Canada*, vol. 3 (1979). D. A. Reed

ASSEMBLY OF CHRISTIAN CHURCHES

(est. 1938). A Pentecostal group with churches in New York and Puerto Rico. The Assembly of Christian Churches (ACC) was organized from the Puerto Rican congregations that had come into being under the influence of Francisco

Olazábal, the leading Hispanic evangelist during the 1920s and 1930s. Upon his death, the Atlantic coast churches were left with tenuous ties with the predominantly Mexican branch of Olazábal's Latin American Council of Christian Churches with headquarters in Texas. The first elected president of the newly formed ACC was Carlos Supúlveda Medina, a former Presbyterian minister who had studied at the University of Puerto Rico and the Evangelical Seminary. The ACC has 250 churches with a membership of 14,000, more than half of whom are in Puerto Rico.

Bibliography: D. Barratt, *World Christian Encyclopedia* (1982); R. Domínguez, *Pioneros de Pentecostés* (1971), 1:15–51, 167–73; F. Whitam, "New York's Spanish Protestants," *Christian Century* 79 (1962): 162–64; idem, "A Report on the Protestant Spanish Community in New York City," in C. Cortés, ed., *Protestantism and Latinos in the United States* (1980).
E. A. Wilson

ASSOCIATED BROTHERHOOD OF CHRISTIANS
The Associated Brotherhood of Christians (ABC) came out of the Oneness segment of the Pentecostal movement. Originally organized in 1933 as the Associated Ministers of Jesus Christ, it incorporated as the Associated Brotherhood of Christians during World War II to obtain exemption for its members from military service. In 1977 it numbered forty churches, two thousand members, and a hundred ministers in six states. The headquarters office is located in Hot Springs, Arkansas.

The primary motive for organization among the members was their view that a literal observance of the Lord's Supper is not essential for salvation. In matters of church polity, the pastor has dominant oversight of the local church. He may also differ with the *Articles of Faith* but not oppose them. *Our Herald* is the official publication of ABC and is printed in Wilmington, California.

Bibliography: E. L. Moore, *Handbook of Pentecostal Denominations in the United States* (1954); A. C. Piepkorn, *Profiles in Belief*, vol. 3 (1979).
S. Shemeth

ASSOCIATION OF FAITH CHURCHES AND MINISTRIES
(AFCM). Founded by Jim Kaseman in 1981 as the Upper Midwest Faith Churches and Ministries, Inc. Beginning with a small group of about 25 to 30 people, in 1988 the association has grown to about one hundred churches and more than four hundred ministers. The association issues ministerial credentials and provides teaching on current issues to its members. The main purpose, however, is to provide fellowship to those who are ministering in the "faith movement." In order to fulfill this goal, AFCM holds regular meetings and annual conventions.

Bibliography: Purpose statement from AFCM.
J. R. Zeigler

ASSOCIATION OF INTERNATIONAL MISSION SERVICES
(AIMS). A transdenominational organization that promotes the work of foreign missions among independent Pentecostal and charismatic churches, founded on March 21, 1985, in Dallas, Texas. Its primary aim is "to challenge and mobilize the church for World Missions and to expand its capabilities and opportunities to fulfill the Great Commission. AIMS will provide a framework for unity and fellowship among churches, mission agencies and training institutions in cooperative efforts for world evangelization." (AIMS, 1987, 2).

Since the charismatic renewal had not yet produced a structure for fostering unity between individual churches and mission agencies to further promote overseas evangelism, AIMS was formed with the following objectives: (1) to develop a consortium of participating churches and agencies; (2) to provide services to local churches for missions mobilization; (3) to provide services to mission agencies; (4) to provide services to training institutions involved in preparing missionaries; (5) to appoint regional coordinators and area representatives for promoting AIMS activities; (6) to foster relationships with other evangelical organizations in the U.S. and abroad; and (7) to determine overseas needs and develop sister organizations abroad. Since AIMS does not send or train missionaries under its own auspices, it focuses on improving the capabilities of those organizations that do.

By 1987 the agency claimed a membership of more than 140 churches, mission agencies, and training institutions. The main office is in Virginia Beach, Virginia. Howard Foltz, a professor at CBN University and former missionary who directed Eurasia Teen Challenge, serves as the president. Six full-time regional coordinators serve across the nation. The first North American Conference for AIMS was held in Denver, Colorado, from September 29, to October 1, 1987. The agency publishes *The AIMS Report* to promote its activities.

See also MISSIONS, OVERSEAS.

Bibliography: Association of International Mission Services, "Background Paper" (February 1987); *The AIMS Report* (1986–).
G. B. McGee

ASSOCIATION OF PENTECOSTAL ASSEMBLIES
See INTERNATIONAL PENTECOSTAL CHURCH OF CHRIST.

ATKINSON, MARIA W.
(1879–1963). Pioneer of the Church of God (CG, Cleveland, Tenn.) in northern Mexico. Born in Sonora, Mexico, Maria was a deeply religious young woman. In 1905 she and her husband moved to Douglas, Arizona, where he died soon afterward. In 1920 she married an American, M. W. Atkinson. She was healed of cancer and baptized in the Holy Spirit in 1924. Immediately she began to preach and pray for the sick in Arizona and Mexico.

In August 1931 Atkinson met J. H. Ingram and joined the CG. Her missions in Obregon and Hermosillo became the foundation of the CG in Mexico. The work has enjoyed great growth throughout northwest Mexico, where Atkinson became known as "La Madre de Mexico." She continued her ministry in Mexico until her death at age eighty-four in 1963.

Bibliography: C. W. Conn, *Where the Saints Have Trod* (1959); P. Humphrey, *Maria Atkinson—La Madre de Mexico* (1967).
C. W. Conn

ATTER, FRANCIS GORDON (1905–). Pastor, author, and district official for the Pentecostal Assemblies of Canada (PAOC). Francis Atter was born in Hamilton, Ontario, to a Methodist family which joined the Pentecostal movement when he was one year old. He was raised in a revivalistic atmosphere, his parents carrying the Pentecostal message to China in 1908 and then becoming pioneer Pentecostal preachers in Canada for thirty years. Atter preached his first message at age seventeen and pastored his first church at nineteen. His career includes pastoring, evangelism, Bible teaching, and serving in an executive capacity in many of the districts of Canada as well as on the general executive committee of the PAOC.

Atter is considered an authority on the history of the Pentecostal movement. He served on the faculty of Eastern Pentecostal Bible College in Peterborough, Ontario. His most noteworthy book is *The Third Force* (1962).

Bibliography: G. Kulbeck, *What God Hath Wrought* (1958).   S. Shemeth

AUSTRIAN PENTECOSTALS See Europe-an Pentecostalism.

AZUSA STREET REVIVAL The term given to events that ran from 1906 to 1913 in and around the Apostolic Faith Mission (AFM) located at 312 Azusa Street in Los Angeles, California. The mission, an outgrowth of cottage prayer meetings held at the Richard and Ruth Asberry home at 214 N. Bonnie Brae Street in the winter and early spring of that year, was established April 14, 1906, under the leadership of Elder William J. Seymour. While it is more or less possible to date the beginning of this revival to the founding of the mission, the end of the revival is more elusive. The culmination of the second international camp meeting sponsored by the AFM in the Arroyo Seco between Los Angeles and Pasadena in April–May 1913, however, seems to provide an adequate terminus.

The significance of what occurred in the former Stevens African Methodist Episcopal Church building that housed the mission on Azusa Street must be seen within a larger context. Several theological threads emerged in American religious life during the nineteenth century that eventually were woven into the tapestry of Azusa. Restorationism, for one, spawned several new religious movements that viewed the church as returning to her NT glory. In some cases it brought an expectation of a "latter rain" outpouring of the Holy Spirit with an accompanying revival. Appeal was also made to the "apostolic faith," "once for all delivered to the saints" (Jude 3) to demonstrate the relationship between the contemporary faith and that of the first apostles. Frontier revivalism contributed anxious benches, brush arbor and protracted meetings, tarrying sessions and altar calls for personal salvation, and holiness of life from evangelists such as Charles G. Finney. F. B. Meyer helped popularize the "overcoming life" taught at Keswick, which became very influential in many American churches. Personal holiness and sanctification as a "Pentecostal" experience of the "Full Gospel" were given a

theological framework in Asa Mahan's work on *The Baptism of the Holy Ghost* (1870). The Holiness movement also brought an understanding of the atonement of Christ as providing a "double cure for a double curse" that ultimately led to an emphasis on divine healing. Finally, concern for the Second Coming and prophetic events originating in Britain with J. N. Darby and the Plymouth Brethren came to the American context through a host of Bible prophecy conferences and the widespread usage of the *Scofield Reference Bible,* which provided annotated notes on Darby's scheme. By 1900 these threads were all present in the religious life of the Los Angeles area.

In 1904–05 reports came to Los Angeles of a substantial revival that was taking place in Wales, largely associated with the work of the young evangelist, Evan Roberts. In Chicago Holiness publisher S. B. Shaw wrote *The Great Revival in Wales* (1905), which was widely read in the Los Angeles area in 1905 and 1906. People who read the book began to establish cottage prayer meetings where they sought God for a similar revival among the churches of Los Angeles.

Prayer for revival was frequently offered in the Free Methodist colony at Herman, California, a suburb lying northeast of the downtown area. It was heard in the Holiness Church of Southern California, the Peniel Mission, the Holiness group known as the Burning Bush, and in a local tent meeting of the Household of God led by W. F. Manley as well. But it was a preeminent concern of Joseph Smale, pastor of First Baptist Church in Los Angeles.

So taken by reports of the Welsh revival was Smale, an immigrant from England, that in 1905 he made a trip home to meet with Evan Roberts and to observe firsthand the factors that made revival possible. Upon his return to Los Angeles, he began to preach a message that encouraged people to be open to the work of the Holy Spirit to convict of sin and to restore some of the more spectacular charisms. He organized his church into smaller home prayer groups and began a series of meetings that lasted for fifteen weeks.

Not everyone at First Baptist Church was satisfied with this approach. The board confronted Smale with the fact that they thought he had become too fanatical. He resisted them but soon resigned his pastorate, taking with him those who believed in what he was doing. With this core of followers, he founded the First New Testament Church. Because Smale had been the pastor of a prominent church in Los Angeles, the local press featured the novelty of his new congregation more than once. Yet Smale continued his search for revival.

In the spring of 1905 Second Baptist Church in Los Angeles was struck by division when several of its members embraced the "second work" teaching of the Holiness movement and attempted to teach it there. Julia W. Hutchins and several families were expelled from membership, and for a time they met with W. F. Manley's Household of God tent meeting at First and Bonnie Brae Streets. Soon they ventured to establish a small store-front mission at Ninth and

This old building at 312 Azusa Street, Los Angeles, became world famous as the Azusa Street Mission beginning in 1906. The pastor of the church, William J. Seymour, is standing on the porch.

Santa Fe Avenues, where they could teach their holiness doctrine freely. Their quest for a pastor led them to summon from Houston, Texas, a Holiness preacher with a Pentecostal message, Elder W. J. Seymour, who had been recommended to them by one of their members, Neely Terry.

Seymour arrived in Los Angeles on February 22, 1906, and began to hold meetings at the mission on Santa Fe two days later. Seymour's recent training had come from Charles Parham, founder of the Apostolic Faith Movement (Baxter Springs, Kans.), a group that claimed as many as 13,000 members in the south-central region of the U.S. A distinctive of the AFM involved speaking in tongues (unlearned foreign languages), which was thought to have an evidential relationship to baptism in the Spirit. When Seymour broached the subject of speaking in tongues to his new congregation, Hutchins, who disagreed with him, locked him out. He was forced to hold meetings, first in the home of Edward S. Lee with whom he was staying, then for several weeks at the home of the Asberrys on Bonnie Brae.

The Asberry home was small, but a number of people from Hutchins's mission, others from First New Testament Church, and still others from a variety of Holiness churches moved in and out of the prayer meeting and Bible study led by Seymour. Blacks and whites mingled freely, and high on their agenda was prayer for revival and an expectation that God was about to move in their midst.

On Monday, April 9, 1906, before Seymour left Edward Lee to go to the Asberry home for the evening meeting, Lee told him of a vision that he had had in which the apostles showed him how to speak in tongues. The two men prayed together, and in moments Lee was speaking in tongues. Seymour carried the news to his meeting on Bonnie Brae where Jennie Evans Moore and several others also broke into tongues. News spread rapidly, and people came to Bonnie Brae to see and hear for themselves. Within a week the group had rented 312 Azusa Street, and the mission had begun.

That this was a revival, however, was something that was not immediately apparent. By year's end critics still proclaimed that what was happening at Azusa was "of small moment." Even such a sympathetic observer as Carrie Judd Montgomery, whose husband George had visited Azusa in December of 1906 and had come away with glowing reports of what God was doing there, wrote the following month, "There is no real revival as a whole in Los Angeles, but only here and there a little company who are trusting God fully and receiving a rich experience of His grace."

For the most part these reports were accurate. Yet the opening of the Azusa Street Mission was something that did not escape the eyes of many, including members of the secular press. The Los Angeles Times sent a reporter to an evening meeting during the first week of its existence. The ensuing article served as free publicity in spite of its patently derogatory tone. Jennie Evans Moore, who was a member of First New Testament Church, spoke in tongues at the conclusion of the

Five early Pentecostal leaders pictured at the Azusa Street Mission. In the front are the mission pastor, William J. Seymour, and John G. Lake; standing are a Brother Adams, F. F. Bosworth, and Tom Hezmalhalch.

Easter morning (April 15) service at that church, causing quite a stir. She moved quickly to attach herself to Azusa Street on a permanent basis, and others soon followed.

At Azusa, services were long, and on the whole they were spontaneous. In its early days music was a cappella, although one or two instruments were included at times. There were songs, testimonies given by visitors or read from those who wrote in, prayer, altar calls for salvation or sanctification or for baptism in the Holy Spirit. And there was preaching. Sermons were generally not prepared in advance but were typically spontaneous. W. J. Seymour was clearly in charge, but much freedom was given to visiting preachers. There was also prayer for the sick. Many shouted. Others were "slain in the Spirit" or "fell under the power." There were periods of extended silence and of singing in tongues. No offerings were collected, but there was a receptacle near the door for gifts.

The upstairs at Azusa doubled as an office for the mission and as a rooming house for several residents, including Seymour and later his wife, but it was also sufficiently large to handle the overflow at the altar or to accommodate those who were tarrying for one or another experience with God. High on the agenda of most of those who tarried was a Pentecostal baptism in the Spirit and the ability to speak in tongues.

Arthur Osterberg, who later reminisced about the first service at Azusa, claimed that some one hundred people were present. The Los Angeles *Times* reported a "crowd" that included a majority of blacks with "a sprinkling of whites" when a reporter visited the mission on April 17. Frank Bartleman, who attended first on Thursday, April 19, said that it was somewhat smaller—"about a dozen saints," some black, some white. Weekend crowds were larger than those on week days.

Growth was quick and substantial. Most sources indicate the presence of about 300–350 worshipers inside the forty-by-sixty-foot white-washed, wood-frame structure, with others mingling outside before the end of summer, including seekers, hecklers, and children. At times it may have been double that. W. F. Manley reported in September 1906 that there were 25 blacks and 300 whites at the meetings he attended. But what had occurred at Azusa began to spread quickly to other churches.

Smale opened the doors of First New Testament Church, if somewhat cautiously, to those who had received the Pentecostal experience, offering room for the free expression of their newly discovered gifts of the Spirit, including tongues. A. H. Post, a Baptist pastor who had joined forces with Manley's Household of God, attempted to establish a Pentecostal work in Pasadena in July, but he met stiff resistance from some local residents. Frank Bartleman established a congregation at the corner of Eighth and Maple in Los Angeles in August. Seymour, the Lemons, and others from the mission held meetings in Whittier in August, September, and October of that year. Another group held Pentecostal meetings in the Holiness Church at Monrovia. Edward McCauley went to Long Beach, while Thomas Junk, Ophelia Wiley, and others went north to Oakland, Salem, Spokane, and Seattle. Still others like Abundio and Rosa de Lopez moved southward to San Diego.

Seymour believed greatly in what was happening at the mission. He knew that it was something important and new, but he sought first to acknowledge its relationship with the work of Charles Parham. In July 1906 he wrote to W. F. Carothers, field secretary to the AFM, asking for promised ministerial credentials from Parham. Carothers sent the note on to Parham, remarking that he had filled the request.

In September 1906 Seymour published a letter in Azusa's newspaper, *The Apostolic Faith*, in which Charles Parham told of his plans to visit the mission. The following month Seymour acknowledged that the message of Pentecost had been preached ever since Agnes Ozman's experiences in Parham's Topeka, Kansas, Bible school in 1901. Now, however, it had "burst out in great power" and was being carried worldwide from the Pacific Coast.

When Parham visited Azusa in October 1906 he did not approve of what he found but rather repudiated it. Theological, racial, and power issues all entered into his assessment and the resulting rupture. Seymour and the mission were left to an independent existence. This did not dampen the movement in Los Angeles but served to provide it with greater independence and freedom as it became the center of the Pacific Apostolic Faith movement. Parham's reputation was irreparably damaged among Pentecostals in 1907, when he was arrested on charges of committing "an unnatural offense" in San Antonio, Texas. Seymour and his mission, however, gained increasing respect as well as notoriety, spread in part through firsthand testimonies and also through *The Apostolic Faith*, which was published between September 1906 and May 1908 by members of the mission staff.

It appears that the core of the mission's membership ran no more than fifty or sixty people. The official membership was racially integrated, although predominantly black, but a disproportionate number of whites served in leadership positions. Seymour, the pastor, was black, as were trustees Richard Asberry and James Alexander. But whites Louis Osterberg (trustee), George E. Berg (secretary), Glenn Cook (business manager) and R. J. Scott (camp meeting organizer), also held responsible positions. Highly gifted black women such as Jennie Evans Moore, Lucy Farrow, and Ophelia Wiley were joined by white women Clara E. Lum and Florence Crawford in public leadership roles. They led in singing, read written testimonies, aided in the publication of the mission's newspaper and in visitation and outreach evangelism, and sometimes they "exhorted" the congregation. Indeed, Seymour served as pastor of an anomalous congregation in Los Angeles, a fully integrated work with leadership drawn from blacks and whites, with Hispanics and other ethnic minorities comfortably present in most of its services.

There appear to have been two periods in which the number of people worshiping at Azusa was much larger than the core membership. In each case, several hundred people were involved. The initial surge was in 1906–08, and the second one was in 1911. Attendance peaked at these times, with a major attendance dip between 1909 and 1911. Only days before the second big surge, it was reported that there were as few as a dozen blacks and no whites in attendance. While the second rise was short-lived, it was sufficient to cause Bartleman to describe it as "the second shower of the Latter Rain." In 1912 Anglican pastor and publisher of *Confidence,* A. A. Boddy, came from England and found a "good-sized" crowd though greatly reduced from that of the previous year.

In spite of the fact that Azusa was often described as a "colored" mission, the large crowds it attracted proved to be dominated by whites who were both volatile and extremely mobile. Evangelists such as Gaston B. Cashwell, Frank Bartleman, and "Mother" Elizabeth Wheaton came. Pastors Elmer Fisher, William Pendleton, William H. Durham, and Joseph Smale attended. Publishers such as Carrie Judd Montgomery (*Triumphs of Faith*), M. L. Ryan (*Apostolic Light*), and A. S. Worrell (*Gospel Witness*) passed through and quickly spread the news. Veteran missionaries such as Samuel and Ardelle Mead, and Mae F. Mayo were there, while church executives such as Charles H. Mason, from the Church of God in Christ, and Christian and Missionary Alliance District Superintendent George Eldridge attended. Some of them came for extended periods of time.

Most, but not all, seem to have come out of curiosity, though many came with the hope that they would receive something that they could take elsewhere—a new teaching, a renewed commitment, a new experience, or added power to their already existing ministries. Many who came were spiritually hungry, but there were also those who sought to establish a name for themselves, would-be preachers, and those who would occupy the fringe of the movement because of their fanatical antics. Charges of fanaticism, of "whipping up the saints," and of "wild-fire" were reported on occasion, and even Seymour wrote of his frustration with the whites who imported certain excesses into the mission. On the whole, though, Seymour provided the necessary leadership to ensure the success of the revival.

In terms of its local revival impact, by 1912 Azusa Street could directly be credited with contributing to the establishment of such congregations as Elmer Fisher's Upper Room Mission, Bartleman and Pendleton's Eighth and Maple Mission, William Durham's Seventh Street Mission, W. L. Sargent's Florence Avenue Pentecostal Mission, A. G. Osterberg's Full Gospel Assembly, John Perron's Italian Pentecostal Mission,

Frank Bartleman's *How "Pentecost" Came to Los Angeles*, published in 1925, was reprinted as *Azusa Street* in 1980.

James Alexander's (one of Seymour's original trustees) Apostolic Faith Mission on 51st Street as well as one other Apostolic Faith Mission at 7th and Sentous, W. F. Manley's Pentecostal Assembly, G. Valenzuella's Spanish Apostolic Faith Mission, William Saxby's Carr Street Pentecostal Mission, and an Apostolic Faith Rescue Mission on 1st Street.

Azusa's effect on the local religious establishment provoked the conservative churches of Los Angeles to work with the police commissioner so that they could hold "approved" street meetings. They added "prayer meetings" to their lists of services and bound their participants to agree that they would engage in substantial acts of "secret prayer, at certain intervals." All of this was to move toward a culmination in March 1907, in which these churches would sponsor a city-wide evangelistic campaign with special speakers from around the country.

The revival spread nationally with the establishment of new congregations and the transformation of existing ones. William Hamner Piper's Stone Church in Chicago joined the Full Gospel Assembly, or North Avenue Mission, begun initially by William Durham as a new and significant Pentecostal voice, complete with a major periodical (*The Latter Rain Evangel*) and a publishing house (Evangel Press). In New York City the Glad Tidings Tabernacle pastored by Marie Burgess Brown and her husband Robert Brown joined the Pentecostal ranks. Throughout the

South and Midwest many missions and churches were planted.

Internationally the message spread rapidly as people who believed themselves to have been freshly touched by the Spirit and, in many cases, to have been given a gift of languages (tongues) for purposes of missionary work, went abroad. Lucy Leatherman made a trip around the world, while Frank Bartleman circled the globe once and made a second two-year evangelistic tour to Europe. Thomas Junk as well as Bernt and Magna Bernsten went from Azusa to China. M. L. Ryan led a number of young people to missions in the Philippines, Japan, and Hong Kong. The George E. Bergs and the A. G. Garrs went to India, while Tom Hezmalhalch and John G. Lake went to South Africa. Pastor A. H. Post became a long-term missionary to Egypt, and a host of people, mostly black, including Edward and Mollie McCauley, G. W. and Daisy Batman, and Julia W. Hutchins took the Pentecostal message to Liberia. In Toronto the Hebden Mission was established.

Sometimes existing denominations were split, while others were totally transformed into Pentecostal vehicles. Among these were the Church of God in Christ, the Church of God (Cleveland, Tenn.), and the Pentecostal Holiness Church. A portion of the Free Will Baptist Church also fell into this category, becoming the Pentecostal Free Will Baptists. But new groups were formed as well. The Apostolic Faith (Portland, Oreg.), the Pentecostal Assemblies of the World (Los Angeles), and in 1914 the Assemblies of God, fell into this category. Indeed, nearly every Pentecostal denomination in the U.S. traces its roots in some way or other to the Apostolic Faith Mission at 312 Azusa Street. The Apostolic Faith Church of God (Franklin, Va.), whose founder, Charles W. Lowe, was appointed bishop of that group by William J. Seymour, is the most clearly identifiable denominational descendant of the Azusa Street Mission.

In order to assess the significance of the Azusa Street revival, one cannot look merely at what was initially perceived to be a ministry of W. J. Seymour to "the colored people of the City of Los Angeles." Its significance will be lost, too, if one concentrates on the growth in the number of people who attended Azusa Street in any ongoing way. By 1915 the congregation numbered but a handful, and the mission had been permanently lost to any further leadership role in a now burgeoning movement. W. J. Seymour died on September 28, 1922, and his wife continued to lead the congregation until her health broke. The building was demolished in 1931 and the land lost in foreclosure in 1938. Thus one must look at the impact of what took place outside the walls of the mission to grasp the full impact of the revival that was sparked there.

To look elsewhere for primary evidence of the revival's extent, however, should in no way detract from the fact that something very significant did take place at Azusa Street. It attracted many people—skeptics, seekers, and church leaders alike from around the world, people of all colors and from all stations in life. They came, and in many cases stayed there for an extended period of time. Unlike most churches of its day, Azusa was very much freely integrated in a day of racial segregation and jim-crow laws. It is not an insignificant fact that a black man, W. J. Seymour, provided its leadership and that everyone sensed a form of equality as sisters and brothers seeking God together.

Azusa was typically described by the press as a "colored" congregation that met in a "tumble-down shack" and made the night "hideous" through the "howlings of the worshipers," yet it was a church where whites, blacks, Hispanics, Asians, and others met together regularly and where from their own perspective the "color-line" was virtually nonexistent. Clearly, Seymour may be credited with providing the vision of a truly "color-blind" congregation. His was a radical experiment that ultimately failed because of the inability of whites to allow for a sustained role for black leadership.

The significance of the revival is equally related to its teaching about baptism in the Spirit and in the gift of tongues. Unlike later Pentecostals, and clearly in opposition to the Pentecostal message of the Upper Room Mission a few blocks away, Seymour moved away from a theology of tongues as the initial physical evidence of baptism in the Spirit. In point of fact, Seymour ultimately repudiated the "initial evidence" teaching as providing "an open door for witches and spiritualists and free loveism." From the beginning he taught that "baptism in the Holy Ghost and fire means to be flooded with the love of God and Power for Service." The gift of tongues, however, was viewed as a sign that would follow this baptism.

While tongues speaking played a significant role in the life of Azusa, it was the emphasis on power for ministry that most frequently sent people to the evangelistic or mission field. In some cases the gift of tongues was viewed as a form of supernatural endowment that equipped its recipients with the necessary ability to communicate the gospel to the lost of another culture. The experience of an immanent God in a day in which transcendence was the dominant theme set the mission apart from many churches, and the experiences of tongues, healings, and other "spectacular" gifts tended to underscore the immanence of God.

The significance of Azusa lies also in the testimonies of those whose lives were transformed by an experience of an immanent God, through the Holy Spirit. Many found their intellectual orientation transformed. Their own ministries suddenly gained new direction or power, their personal spiritualities were enriched, and their vision of the church's task immeasurably broad-ened. Thus the significance of Azusa was centrifugal as those who were touched by it took their experiences elsewhere and touched the lives of others. Coupled with the theological threads of personal salvation, holiness, divine healing, baptism in the Spirit with power for ministry, and an anticipation of the imminent return of Jesus Christ, ample motivation was provided to assure the revival a long-term impact. Today the site of the Azusa Street Mission is dominated by the Japanese-American Cultural and Community Center, unmarked except for the street sign. Yet the phenomenal worldwide growth of the Pentecostal movement and its sister, charismatic renewal in the historic churches, suggests that the Azusa Street revival continues to bear much fruit.

Bibliography: "Baba Bharati Says Not a Language," *Los Angeles Daily Times* (September 19, 1906), pt. 2, 1; F. Bartleman, *How Pentecost Came to Los Angeles* (1925, reprinted as *Azusa Street* [1980]); idem, "The Pentecostal Work," *Word and Work* 39 (1, January 1908); idem, "Praying Bands for Churches," *Los Angeles Express* (July 25, 1906), 6; idem, *Witness to Pentecost: The Life of Frank Bartleman* (1985); idem, "Work in Los Angeles," *Word and Work* 33 (6, June 1911): 180–81; F. Corum, *Like As of Fire* (1981); D. Dayton, *Theological Roots of Pentecostalism* (1987); S. H. Frodsham, *"With Signs Following"* (1926, 1941); H. A. Ironside, "Apostolic Faith Missions and the So-Called Second Pentecost" (pamphlet, n.d.); idem, "The Gift of Tongues," *Nazarene Messenger* 11 (24, December 13, 1906): 6; C. J. Montgomery, "The Work in Los Angeles," *Triumphs of Faith* 27 (2, January 1907): 14; D. J. Nelson, "For Such a Time as This," unpublished Ph.D. diss., University of Birmingham, England, 1981; A. M. Otis, "Apostolic Faith Movement," *Word and Work* 39 (2, February 1907): 51–53; "Queer 'Gift' Given Many," *Los Angeles Daily Times* (July 23, 1906), pt. 2, 7; C. M. Robeck, Jr., "The Earliest Pentecostal Missions in Los Angeles," *AG Heritage* 3 (3, Fall 1983): 3–4, 12; "Rolling on Floor in Smale's Church," *Los Angeles Daily Times* (July 13, 1906), 1; W. J. Seymour, *The Doctrines and Discipline of the Azusa Street Apostolic Faith Mission* (1915); J. H. Sparks, "Azusa Street Mission," *Word and Work* 33 (4, April 1911): 120; idem, "Convention in Los Angeles," *Word and Work,* 30 (5, May 1908), 150; George B. Studd, "My Convictions as to the Pentecostal Movement Irreverently Called 'The Tongues' " (pamphlet, n.d.); A. C. Valdez with James F. Scheer, *Fire on Azusa Street* (1980); "Weird Babel of Tongues," *Los Angeles Daily Times* (April 18, 1906), pt. 2, 1; "Weird Fanaticism Fools Young Girl," *Los Angeles Daily Times* (July 12, 1906), 1; A. S. Worrell, "At Los Angeles," *Confidence* 5 (10, October 1912): 232–34; idem, "Azusa's First Camp-Meeting," *Word and Work* 58 (1, January 1936): 1–2; idem, "Letter from Los Angeles," *Triumphs of Faith* 26 (12, December 1906): 247–52; idem, "A Meeting at the Azusa Street Mission, Los Angeles," *Confidence* 5 (11, November 1912): 144–245; idem, "The Movements in Los Angeles, California," *Triumphs of Faith* 26 (12, December 1906): 256–57.

C. M. Robeck, Jr.

B

BAKER, ELIZABETH V. (c. 1849–1915). Faith healer and educator. An important center of early Pentecostalism, established in Rochester, New York, was a result of the efforts of Elizabeth V. Baker, the eldest daughter of Methodist pastor James Duncan, and her sisters—Mary E. Work, Nellie A. Fell, Susan A. Duncan, and Harriet "Hattie" M. Duncan. From their ministry activities, spearheaded by Baker, came the Elim Faith Home, Elim Publishing House, Elim Tabernacle, and the Rochester Bible Training School.

Baker's early life indicates a great deal of personal grief. Her first marriage, entered into before she was twenty years old, ended in divorce due to an abusive husband. Some time after this she attended a lecture on the Ohio "Women's Crusade," a forerunner of the Woman's Christian Temperance Union. She felt little interest until the speaker referred to the women who in the power of Christ courageously entered saloons to protest the sale of alcoholic beverages and knelt in the sawdust on the sidewalks to pray. More than the temperance issue, Baker was confronted by the living Christ.

Several years later (c. 1881), a severe throat condition threatened her health. Her second husband, a medical doctor, called in specialists to treat her, but her condition worsened. Finally she was anointed and prayed for by C. W. Winchester, pastor of the local Asbury Methodist Episcopal Church, who had come to believe in faith healing. Immediately after his prayer she was able to swallow and her illness ended.

Baker and her husband eventually separated. This partially resulted from her embrace of the doctrine of faith healing and subsequent activities in that ministry.

By the time Baker and her sisters opened a mission and the Elim Faith Home in 1895, she had been influenced by the advocates of faith healing; the writings of George Müller, which depicted his life of faith; and the premillennial teachings of Adoniram J. Gordon. The faith home opened to meet the needs of those who sought physical healing and to provide a place "where tired missionaries and Christian workers could for a time find rest for soul and body" (Baker, 1926, 51).

Feeling directed by the Holy Spirit to visit India, Baker traveled there in 1898 and met the famous Pandita Ramabai, director of the Mukti Mission. This trip heightened the missionary vision of the sisters and their followers in Rochester. By 1915, $75,000 had been contributed to foreign missions—a considerable sum for that time.

Other activities followed. In 1902 the sisters began to publish *Trust,* a periodical edited by Susan A. Duncan and devoted to teaching the doctrines of salvation, faith healing, the Holy Spirit, premillennialism, and world evangelization. Several years later the Elim Tabernacle was constructed, and in 1906 the Rochester Bible Training School opened "for the training of those who felt His call to some special work, but lacked the educational fitness."

The news of the Welsh revival in 1904–05 had impressed Baker and her sisters of the need for a similar occurrence in Rochester. When word of the Azusa Street revival reached them, they pondered for a year the Pentecostal baptism accompanied by speaking in tongues. Through study and prayer, they concluded that it was valid. At their summer convention in 1907, the participants sought for this experience, and a Pentecostal revival followed.

The Duncan sisters were sensitive to the criticisms made by many about the legitimacy of women preachers. Baker justified her ministry because of a direct calling from the Holy Spirit. With the construction of the Elim Tabernacle, they prayed that God would send the right man as pastor. When no one suitable appeared, however, their leadership continued. Nevertheless, they refused ordination because they were women.

After Elizabeth V. Baker died at age sixty-six on January 18, 1915, her two sisters, Susan A. Duncan and Harriet "Hattie" M. Duncan, directed the ministries until they were too advanced in age to continue. The legacy of Baker and her sisters lived on through the students who attended their school. By 1916 seventeen of the students had traveled overseas as missionaries. Two of them, Beatrice Morrison and Karl Wittick, had died in Africa by this time. Other noteworthy Pentecostals attended, including Alfred Blakeney, John H. Burgess, Marguerite Flint, Ivan Q. Spencer, Ralph Riggs, Grace Walther, Charles W. H. Scott, and Anna Ziese.

Bibliography: E. V. Baker, et al., *Chronicles of a Faith Life,* 2d ed. (c. 1926); G. B. McGee, "Three Notable Women in Pentecostal Ministry," *AG Heritage* 1 (1986): 3–5, 12, 16.   G. B. McGee

BAKER, H. A. (1881–1971). Early Pentecostal missionary to Tibet, China, and Taiwan. At thirteen or fourteen years of age Baker was baptized in the Christian Church but professed that a real experience of conversion did not come until five years later. He entered Hiram College to prepare for ministry and while there served as president of the local chapter of the Student Volunteer Movement for Foreign Missions. After graduation in 1909 he married Josephine Witherstay and pastored in Buffalo, New York. In 1912 the couple went to Tibet as missionaries under the auspices of the Christian Church.

After five years of work on the Tibetan border,

the Bakers returned to the U.S. While on furlough they received the baptism in the Holy Spirit, having been influenced by Allan A. Swift, another missionary to China. They returned to China as independent Pentecostal missionaries to work in Yunnan Province, where they opened an orphanage for homeless children and eventually witnessed an outpouring of the Spirit among the tribal people. In his book *Visions Beyond the Veil* (c. 1938), Baker described the experiences these children had when they received visions of heaven and hell; this proved to be his most popular book and was eventually printed in thirteen languages. He also wrote *Through Tribulation* (n.d.) and *Tribulation to Glory* (c. 1951), in which he argued for a posttribulational rapture of the church, somewhat of a doctrinal novelty among American Pentecostal missionaries. His other publications included *God in Ka Do Land* (1937), *The Three Worlds* (1937), *Seeking and Saving* (1940), *Devils and Dupes* (n.d.), *Heaven and the Angels* (n.d.), *Plains of Glory and Gloom* (n.d.), and *The Adullam News* (booklets that described and promoted his ministry); his autobiography is entitled *Under His Wings* (n.d.).

H. A. Baker (pictured at 88 years of age) served as a pioneer missionary to China and authored many books.

Although Baker remained an independent missionary, he had strong links to the Assemblies of God. The Bakers remained in China until a year following the Communist takeover. Returning to the U.S., they ministered among the Navajo Indians in New Mexico. For the last sixteen years of Baker's life (his wife preceded him in death by several months) he ministered among the Hakka people of Taiwan until his death at the age of ninety. The Bakers' one son, James, and his wife, Marjorie, minister with Asian Outreach in Hong Kong.

Bibliography: H. A. Baker, "The Lord Opened the Way to China," *FGMH* (April 1924), 12–13; idem, *Under His Wings* (n.d.); "Pentecostal Pioneer Dies in Taiwan," *PE* (February 6, 1972), 14.   G. B. McGee

BAKKER, JAMES ORSEN ("JIM"), AND TAMMY FAYE (LA VALLEY) (1940–) and (1942–). Television evangelists and founders of the PTL Network. Jim Bakker was born to Raleigh and Ferne Bakker of Muskegon Heights, Michigan. In his autobiography, *Move that Mountain* (with R. P. Lamb, 1976), Bakker relates his modest origins, including his embarrassment over an unsightly house, his small and frail body, and his mediocre performance in school. He surrendered his life to God as the result of a crisis experience in which he ran over a child with his father's automobile. Following graduation from high school in 1959, Bakker attended North Central Bible College of the Assemblies of God (AG), where he met Tammy Faye La Valley.

According to Tammy's autobiography, *I Gotta Be Me* (with C. Dudley, 1978), she was the eldest of eight children born to the La Valley family of International Falls, Michigan. Raised by her mother and stepfather, Tammy suffered from convulsions. She was healed through the prayers of the local AG minister. In 1960 she chose to study at North Central Bible College (NCBC).

Several months after meeting, and in the middle of a school term, Jim and Tammy decided to marry (1961). This resulted in their expulsion from NCBC and marked the end of their formal education. For the next five years they lived as itinerant preachers, specializing in children's ministry, including the use of puppets. In 1964 Jim was ordained by the AG. In 1965 he was hired by Marion G. (Pat) Robertson (CBN) for a children's radio/TV show ("The Jim and Tammy Show") and as host of the new "700 Club." In 1973 Jim became cofounder of the California-based Trinity Broadcasting Network. The following year he inaugurated another Christian talk show—the "PTL Club" (originally meaning "Praise the Lord," later "People That Love") in Charlotte, North Carolina.

In this new venture, the Bakkers were phenomenally successful, as the "PTL Club" grew into the PTL Television Network with a worldwide outreach. By early 1987 they had developed a $172 million religious empire, including state-of-the-art TV production studios and Heritage Village (with the Grand Hotel, condominiums for those who wished to live in a Christian environment, a water amusement park, and a home for handicapped children). This Christian entertainment complex drew visitors at a rate third only to Disneyland and Disney World.

While it was quite apparent to the average viewer that the Bakkers had experienced difficulties in their marriage and crises in their ministry, the events of early 1987 came as a shock. Tammy was admitted into a California clinic,

Jim Bakker and his wife Tammy Faye hosted the PTL Club until 1987. The Bakkers founded Heritage USA near Charlotte, North Carolina.

suffering from drug dependency. Then on March 19, 1987, Jim Bakker announced that he had resigned as chairman of PTL ministries and from ministry in the AG. He claimed that a "hostile force" (later identified as fellow evangelist Jimmy Swaggart) was plotting to take over his religious empire, and that he was being blackmailed by former friends over a 1980 sexual encounter with church secretary Jessica Hahn. He explained that the tryst with Hahn had been an attempt to make his wife jealous at a time when their marriage was in trouble. Bakker then turned his empire over to another televangelist, the Reverend Jerry Falwell. Meanwhile, the public became aware that Richard Dortch, Bakker's assistant at PTL, had paid hush money to Jessica Hahn for "the sake of the ministry."

These revelations—called "Pearlygate" by the media—were followed by a "holy war" between televangelists Bakker, Falwell, and Swaggart. For several weeks, Bakker and his accusers dominated the news, including such TV shows as "Good Morning America" and "Nightline," with charges and countercharges. Swaggart declared that Bakker was a "cancer" that needed to be excised from the Body of Christ. Falwell contended that Bakker was the greatest scab and cancer on the face of Christianity in 2,000 years. John Ankerberg, a Baptist television personality, accused Bakker of bisexuality. Bakker countered by denying additional sins of the flesh and by demanding the return of his empire from Falwell, which he said the fundamental Baptist evangelist had promised. When Falwell refused, Bakker accused him of theft.

It soon became apparent that Bakker's early confessions only addressed the tip of a scandalous iceberg. Auditors discovered that the Bakker's

salary and bonuses for 1986–87 totaled $1.6 million (Bakker frequently had presented a "prosperity theology," arguing that God wanted his people to go first class). At the same time, it was revealed that the PTL ministry had piled up a $70 million debt. Shortly after the scandal broke, PTL lawyers petitioned for bankruptcy. An Internal Revenue Service investigation into the finances of PTL followed.

Tammy Faye and Jim Bakker meet with reporters in 1987 after appearing on television for the first time since leaving the PTL ministry.

The PTL enterprises survived the demise of the Bakkers until mid-1988. First Jerry Falwell and then David Clark guided the empire through the stormy period following the Bakker's exit.

In addition to the autobiographies mentioned above, Jim and Tammy Bakker have written several books. Jim's writings include *Eight Keys to Success* (1980), *Survival* (1981), and *You Can Make It* (1983). Tammy is the author of *Run to the Roar* (with C. Dudley, 1980). Together they have produced *How We Lost Weight and Kept It Off* (1979).

Bibliography: "Fresh Out of Miracles," *Newsweek* (May 11, 1987), 70–72; "Heaven Can Wait," *Newsweek* (June 8, 1987), 58–65. *Who's Who in America* (43d ed., 1984–85), 148.   S. M. Burgess

BALL, HENRY CLEOPHAS (1896–). Indigenous church pioneer and missionary. Henry Cleophas Ball was born in Brooklyn, Iowa, and was reared in Ricardo, Texas, by his widowed mother. Converted to Christ under the preaching of a Baptist minister, he nevertheless followed the lead of his mother and joined the Methodist church in Kingsville, Texas, in 1910. Inspired by the message of a missionary from Venezuela, Ball became burdened to minister to the Mexicans living in Ricardo.

His inability to speak Spanish did not deter his missionary impulse. Through inviting people to his services and relating his testimony in Spanish, Ball slowly began to master the language. Eventually he was able to preach in Spanish and give invitations at the end of the services for people to accept Christ. Such was the beginning of a lifelong ministry to Hispanics that would take him from Texas to Central and South America and the West Indies.

When Felix A. Hale, an Assemblies of God (AG) evangelist, preached in Kingsville, Ball was baptized in the Holy Spirit. This signaled an end to his Methodist affiliation. In 1915 Arch P. Collins, E. N. Richey, and Hale ordained him as a minister of the AG. His increasing activities in Hispanic evangelism led to his selection as the first superintendent of the Latin American Conference in 1918 (District 1925), a post which he occupied until 1939. Ball was deeply committed to establishing indigenous churches, partially reflecting the influence of his friend Alice E. Luce. He promoted annual conventions for the Mexican converts to provide fellowship and instruction. In 1916, while pastoring in Kingsville, he began the publication of the *Apostolic Light*. It later became the official publication of the Latin American District Council of the AG. This monthly magazine, designed as a tool for evangelism, made an enormous impact. Ball became a prolific writer, and his many publications gave positive direction to the growth of Hispanic Pentecostalism. He published a song book in Spanish called *Hymns of Glory*, which was printed without musical notation. Financed with money from his father's estate, Ball published a new edition with the music included in 1921. Both editions sold hundreds of thousands of copies. Other song books followed.

Another milestone passed with Ball's establishment of the Latin American Bible Institute in San Antonio, Texas, in 1926. The graduates of this institute preached the gospel in various parts of the U.S., Mexico, Spain, Nicaragua, Puerto Rico, and Cuba. Thus the impact of Ball's school in San Antonio reached beyond the borders of the U.S. to Latin America and Europe.

Faced with a lack of curricular materials, Ball wrote extensively to provide class notes for his students. These notes in turn were used in other Bible institutes in Latin America and are still highly valued.

Ball's activities eventually transcended educational, editorial, and district responsibilities to include a two-year period of missionary work in Chile from 1941 to 1943. In 1943 the AG Department of Foreign Missions appointed him to serve as the first overseas field secretary for Latin America and the West Indies. He continued in this capacity until 1953.

Ball's departure from this position afforded him the opportunity to devote his full attention to Spanish literature production. He had begun an agency for this purpose in 1946. It is currently known as Life Publishers International. His labors in evangelism, administration, Bible institute training, and Spanish literature production gained him widespread respect. In many areas he proved to be one of the most far-sighted and creative missionary strategists that the Pentecostal movement, and the AG in particular, has produced.

Bibliography: V. De Leon, *The Silent Pentecostals* (1979); G. B. McGee, "Pioneers of Pentecost: Alice E. Luce and H. C. Ball," *AG Heritage* 2 (1985): 5–6, 12–15; I. Spence, *Henry C. Ball: Man of Action* (n.d.).
                                                                        G. B. McGee

BAPTISM IN THE HOLY SPIRIT

    I. Introduction
   II. Baptism in the Holy Spirit and Other Terminology
  III. Baptism in the Holy Spirit and Salvation
   IV. Baptism in the Holy Spirit and Sanctification
    V. Baptism in the Holy Spirit and Speaking in Tongues
   VI. The Purpose of Baptism in the Holy Spirit
  VII. Baptism in the Holy Spirit and Water Baptism
 VIII. The Reception of the Holy Spirit

I. Introduction. In the Pentecostal and charismatic traditions the doctrine of baptism in (or with) the Holy Spirit occupies a place of critical importance. The Pentecostal Fellowship of North America (PFNA) affirms, "We believe that the full gospel includes holiness of heart and life, healing for the body, and baptism in the Holy Spirit with the evidence of speaking in other tongues as the Spirit gives the utterance." M. P. Hamilton's book on the charismatic movement offers the following prefatory statement: "The term *charismatic* applies to those who have experienced a 'baptism of the Holy Spirit' that involves receiving certain spiritual gifts" (Hamilton, 1975, 7). This article gives primary attention to Pentecostal understanding of baptism in the Spirit, although some reference to charismatic thinking also is made.

Baptism in the Holy Spirit is viewed as a distinctive Christian experience. For Pentecostals,

Spirit baptism refers to an experience whose basis is believed to be found in the Jerusalem event of Pentecost as recorded in Acts 2:1–4. At the beginning of Jesus' ministry John the Baptist preached "baptism of repentance for the forgiveness of sins" (Mark 1:4) so that many confessed their sins and were baptized in water. He also declared about Jesus, "I baptize you with water, but he will baptize you with the Holy Spirit" (Mark 1:8). Some three years later, shortly before Pentecost, Jesus talked with his apostles about a gift promised by the Father, and he then commanded: "Do not leave Jerusalem, but wait for the gift my Father promised, which you have heard me speak about. For John baptized with water, but in a few days you will be baptized with the Holy Spirit" (Acts 1:4–5). Hence the gift the Father promised would be the Holy Spirit; it would come from Jesus (as John the Baptist had said), and the reception of that gift would be baptism in the Holy Spirit. On the Day of Pentecost the promise was fulfilled—"all of them were filled with the Holy Spirit" (2:4). Thereafter the same gift was offered to the thousands who assembled: "Repent and be baptized, every one of you, in the name of Jesus Christ for the forgiveness of your sins. And you will receive the gift of the Holy Spirit. The promise is for you and your children and for all who are far off—for all whom the Lord our God will call" (vv. 38–39). Viewing this promise extended to all generations and peoples as the gift of the Holy Spirit, Pentecostals claim that they also have received this gift. They too have been baptized, or filled, with the Holy Spirit as a distinctive Christian experience.

II. Baptism in the Holy Spirit and Other Terminology. The expression "Baptism in [with] the Holy Spirit"—or, more precisely, "baptized in the Holy Spirit"—occurs twice in the Book of Acts. Its first use by Jesus has been noted; the other is found in Acts 11:16. Here Peter declared: "Then I remembered what the Lord had said: 'John baptized with water, but you will be baptized with the Holy Spirit.'" Peter was recalling the Caesareans—the Roman centurion Cornelius, his relatives, and close friends—who previously had been baptized in the Holy Spirit (10:44–46). Pentecostals view the Caesarean narrative as further evidence that Spirit baptism is not limited to the event of Pentecost but continues through the years.

Outside the Book of Acts there is one possible reference to Spirit baptism. According to Paul, "we were all baptized by one Spirit into one body" (1 Cor. 12:13). However, Pentecostals generally do not identify this baptism with baptism in the Spirit. Taking the usual reading of "*by* one Spirit" as the proper translation, they view the agent of baptism as the Holy Spirit: the Spirit baptizes us into the one body of Christ. On the other hand, when we are baptized in the Holy Spirit, Christ is the agent who baptizes us in the Holy Spirit. Hence, from the Pentecostal viewpoint, we must look to Acts for an adequate understanding of baptism in the Spirit.

Since the essential meaning of baptism is immersion, Pentecostals often emphasize that to be baptized in the Holy Spirit is to be immersed in the Holy Spirit. This signifies a total submergence within the reality of the Holy Spirit so that whoever is so baptized has a vivid sense of the Spirit's presence and power. According to one Pentecostal testimony: "Talking about a baptism, it was just like I was being plunged down into a great sea of water, only the water was God, the water was the Holy Spirit" (K. and D. Ranaghan, 1969, 16). Immersion, similar to that in water but in the reality of the Spirit, is a central emphasis in Pentecostalism.

Other terminology in Acts relevant to baptism in the Spirit is much used by Pentecostals. First, there is the language of *filling*. On the Day of Pentecost the text reads "All of them were filled with the Holy Spirit." Jesus had promised they would be baptized in the Spirit, but when the event actually occurred they were said to be filled. If the word "baptized" suggests a submergence within the Holy Spirit, "filling" points to an inner penetration or pervasion. Both are words expressing totality, without and within. In Acts 9:17 Saul (Paul) is ministered to by Ananias that he might be "filled with the Holy Spirit." Since "baptized" and "filled" in Acts 1 and 2 refer to the same event, Paul's resulting experience may also be viewed as a baptism in the Holy Spirit.

Pentecostals sometimes speak of this as the "infilling" of the Holy Spirit. Though the word "infilling" is not directly biblical, the reason for its usage is to differentiate this experience from the "indwelling" of the Spirit. Pentecostals generally acknowledge that all believers have the Spirit within them (Rom. 8:9–11; 1 Cor. 6:19); hence "filling" must refer to the full penetration of the indwelling Spirit. Some Pentecostals, especially charismatics, refer to this as the "release" of the Spirit: the Spirit within is released for a total inward occupancy.

Another term used in Acts is the "outpouring," or "pouring out," of the Holy Spirit. After the disciples on the Day of Pentecost were filled with the Holy Spirit, Peter declared that this was in fulfillment of the prophecy by Joel: "In the last days, God says, I will pour out my Spirit on all people. . . . Even on my servants, both men and women, I will pour out my Spirit in those days, and they will prophesy" (Acts 2:17–18, referring to Joel 2:28–29). Later Peter stated that this has happened through Jesus: "Exalted to the right hand of God, he has received from the Father the promised Holy Spirit and has poured out what you now see and hear" (Acts 2:33). The imagery of outpouring is also used many years thereafter to describe the Caesarean's experience: "The gift of the Holy Spirit has been poured out even [or "also," KJV] on the Gentiles" (10:45).

The language of "outpouring," like "baptizing" or "filling," suggests totality, but it also points to abundance. God does not give sparingly: "God gives the Spirit without limit" (John 3:34). It is not as if a person may have a partial measure of the Holy Spirit at one time and more later; the Spirit is given without measure. Pentecostals usually emphasize that such language as "outpouring" and "infilling" does not mean that one has more of the Spirit. Rather the Spirit who is totally present now totally claims the person. In popular Pentecostal language: "You may have the Spirit, but now the Spirit has you!" When the Spirit is poured out, there is abundance.

Another expression used in Acts is the "falling" of the Holy Spirit. In the account of the Samaritans, Peter and John come from Jerusalem to minister to them the Holy Spirit, for the Spirit "had not yet fallen upon any of them" (Acts 8:16 NASB). In Caesarea, just before reference is made to the Spirit being poured out, the text reads, "The Holy Spirit fell upon all those who were listening to the message" (10:44 NASB). The word "falling" suggests suddenness, forcefulness—as in the account at Pentecost when "suddenly a sound like the blowing of a violent wind came from heaven and filled the whole house" (2:2). The word "fall" has had much usage in Pentecostal circles where testimonies abound as to a certain occasion when the Holy Spirit fell. Agnes Ozman, whose experience is often viewed as the beginning of twentieth-century Pentecostalism, testified that "the Holy Spirit fell upon me and I began to speak in tongues, glorifying God" (Kendrick, 1961, 52).

One further term in Acts is "come on." In the earliest Acts account when Jesus spoke of the apostles' future baptism in the Spirit, he added the words, "you will receive power when the Holy Spirit comes on you" (Acts 1:8). Thus their later experience in Acts 2:4 of being filled was both a coming on and a baptism. Much later, when Paul ministered the Holy Spirit to the Ephesians, "the Holy Spirit came on them" (19:6). Hence the Ephesians likewise were baptized in the Holy Spirit. The language of "coming on," incidentally, may be related to another expression used in Luke 24:49, namely, "clothed with": "stay in the city until you are clothed with power from on high." Both terms, "coming on" and "clothed with," express an active, continuing endowment of the Spirit wherein there is both possession by investiture with the Holy Spirit.

For many Pentecostals the imagery of coming on, or upon, is particularly significant. "The Holy Spirit may be in you, but is he also on you?" This kind of question is more than semantical, because the latter is viewed as an additional operation of the Holy Spirit in relation to the believer. The Pentecostal "filling," accordingly, is not only an internal moving but also an external coming of the Holy Spirit. As a result, one is both Spirit-filled and Spirit-endowed.

All of this terminology—baptizing, filling, outpouring, falling, coming on—suggests a total experience of the presence of the Holy Spirit. In one sense it is an immersion, a submergence within (baptized); in still another it is an invasion from without (outpouring, falling upon, coming on). Such terminology is variously used by Pentecostals to describe their own experience.

Baptism in the Holy Spirit therefore is one of many expressions that relates to the gift of the Holy Spirit. However, both because it is language used by Jesus himself and also because it expresses a profound experience of the reality of God's presence, this phrase is used most often in the Pentecostal and charismatic traditions.

III. Baptism in the Holy Spirit and Salvation.

Pentecostals view baptism in the Holy Spirit as an experience that presupposes conversion. Preparatory to the event of Acts 2:1–4 Jesus had said to his apostles, "Do not leave Jerusalem, but wait for the gift my Father promised. For John baptized with water, but in a few days you will be baptized with the Holy Spirit" (Acts 1:4–5). Pentecostals hold that the apostles had already been converted. Many point to such Scriptures as Luke 10:20 ("Rejoice that your names are written in heaven"), John 15:3 ("You are already clean"), and John 17:14 ("They are not of the world") as signifying their conversion. Also attention is frequently called to the Resurrection Day scene in the Gospel of John where Jesus "breathed on them and said, 'Receive the Holy Spirit'" (20:22). This is often interpreted to refer to regeneration whereby the Holy Spirit comes to dwell within. Whether conversion/regeneration occurred during Jesus' ministry or on the day of his resurrection, the importance for Pentecostals is that it occurred prior to Pentecost. Hence it is assumed that the apostles and their company were already believers when they were baptized in the Holy Spirit. Salvation came first, then baptism in the Holy Spirit. Reinforcement for this view is pointed to in Acts 11:17, where Peter, speaking in relation to the gift of the Holy Spirit to the Caesareans, declares: "God gave them the same gift as he gave to us, who believed [or "after believing," NASB] in the Lord Jesus Christ." Peter and those with him at Pentecost accordingly were already believing when they were baptized in the Holy Spirit.

Sometimes an objection is raised against Pentecostals that the faith experience of this first apostolic group prior to Pentecost should not be used in relation to any event thereafter, since that was a unique situation. Against this objection Pentecostals point to other accounts in Acts in which they see a similar distinction between conversion and baptism in the Spirit. According to Acts 8, before Peter and John arrived to minister the Holy Spirit, the Samaritans had already come to faith and been water baptized: "They believed Philip . . . [and] were baptized, both men and women" (v. 12). Sometime later, through the ministry of the two apostles, the Samaritans "received the Holy Spirit" (v. 17). There can be little doubt that their conversion preceded their reception of the gift of the Holy Spirit. The occasion of Paul's being filled with the Spirit (9:17) occurred three days (v. 9) after his initial encounter with the risen Christ (vv. 4–6). Viewing this as Paul's conversion, Pentecostals see further biblical evidence of Spirit baptism as following conversion. In the narrative of Acts 19 the Holy Spirit comes upon the Ephesians after they have believed and been baptized. "On hearing this [the call to faith in Christ], they were baptized into the name of the Lord Jesus. When Paul placed his hands on them, the Holy Spirit came on them" (vv. 5–6). Based on these accounts, Pentecostals hold that there is good biblical evidence for baptism in the Holy Spirit subsequent to conversion.

Pentecostals often speak of baptism in the Spirit

as being both distinct from and subsequent to salvation. According to the Assemblies of God (AG), "This wonderful experience is distinct from and subsequent to the experience of the new birth." To Pentecostals this does not necessarily mean a chronologically separate experience, for they point out that in another account, namely that of the Caesareans (Acts 10), there is no reference to a later experience of receiving the gift of the Holy Spirit. After Peter calls for faith in Christ—"everyone who believes in him receives forgiveness of sins through his name" (v. 43), the next words are: "While Peter was still speaking these words, the Holy Spirit fell . . ." (10:44 NASB). Priority is still given to the Caesareans' believing before the falling of the Holy Spirit, even if the latter follows immediately upon the other. The important matter for the Pentecostal is not chronological but logical subsequence, viz., that even if salvation and baptism in the Spirit are at the same moment, salvation (conversion, regeneration) precedes Spirit baptism. Moreover, Pentecostals hold that there is nonidentity of the two, for the Caesareans' Spirit baptism is later attested to be a confirmation of their salvation. According to Acts 11, when Peter seeks to convince the church in Jerusalem that the Gentiles in Caesarea had come into salvation, he says to the apostles and brethren: "As I began to speak, the Holy Spirit fell upon them, just as He did upon us at the beginning" (11:15 NASB). This fact was unmistakable evidence to the church in Jerusalem of the Gentiles' salvation, for the Scripture later reads: "When they heard this, they had no further objections and praised God, saying, 'So then, God has granted even the Gentiles repentance unto life'" (11:18). The Caesareans' Spirit baptism, while not chronologically subsequent to their faith in Christ, was by no means identical with it. The falling of the Spirit was rather the certain sign of their conversion—their repentance unto life.

It is a Pentecostal distinctive, therefore, to affirm that salvation precedes baptism in the Spirit or, to put it a bit differently, that one may truly believe in Christ and not yet have received the gift of the Holy Spirit. In the account of the Ephesians in Acts 19, before Paul proceeds to water baptism and the laying on of hands, he asks them: "Did you receive the Holy Spirit when [or "after," NIV mg.] you believed?" (v. 2). The very question implies the possibility of believing in Christ without an accompanying reception of the Holy Spirit. The Ephesians had not yet come to a full faith in Christ, so Paul ministers Christian baptism and laying on of hands (vv. 3–6). Still the question itself remains with its clear implication. Whether the question is "when" or "after" (or "since," KJV) "you believed," baptism in the Spirit may not yet have followed upon faith in Christ. Hence, Pentecostals emphasize that one of the most pressing questions to be asked today of believers is that of Paul: "Did you receive the Holy Spirit when you believed?"

Pentecostals are quick to affirm that this question has nothing essentially to do with salvation. They do not mean to suggest that people may be only partially saved and that by Spirit baptism they may receive the rest. Rather, even as the

word about salvation relates to sinners, so the word about baptism in the Holy Spirit relates to saints. The former is the call to believe; the latter is the call to receive.

It should be added that in the charismatic movement there has been a wide range of views concerning salvation and Spirit baptism. While many have adopted the basic Pentecostal pattern as described, there are those who hold that there is no "second stage" beyond salvation. Larry Christenson, a Lutheran charismatic leader, speaks rather of an "organic view" of the Spirit's work that sees "the gift of the Holy Spirit . . . as being given to all Christians" (1976, 38). This means that the gift of the Holy Spirit (or being baptized in the Spirit) occurs with the experience of salvation. From this perspective, what Pentecostals really have been talking about is an experience of spiritual renewal, not a separate Spirit baptism. Brick Bradford, longtime general secretary of the Presbyterian Charismatic Communion (now known as Presbyterian and Reformed Renewal Ministries), writes that "we were 'baptized with the Holy Spirit' when we became Christians, but we find ourselves wanting to more fully experience the release of the power of the Holy Spirit in our lives in order to become more effectual Christians" (1983, 23). It seems to this writer that such views, while congenial to Lutheran and Reformed traditions, have difficulty with the record in the Book of Acts. The traditional Pentecostal viewpoint would appear to be a more adequate interpretation.

IV. Baptism in the Holy Spirit and Sanctification. Pentecostals in general affirm the importance of holiness in the Christian life. The PFNA (as earlier quoted) affirms "holiness of heart and life" as belonging to "the full gospel." Early Pentecostalism had its roots largely in the Wesleyan-Holiness tradition with its strong emphasis on sanctification. As a result, sanctification was held to be a "second work of grace" to be received prior to Spirit baptism. Sanctification was therein understood to be an instantaneous operation of heart purification following regeneration but preceding Spirit baptism. Many branches of Pentecostalism continue to affirm this viewpoint. The Church of God (CG, Cleveland, Tenn.) declares that "we believe . . . in sanctification subsequent to the new birth . . . and in the baptism of the Holy Ghost subsequent to a clean heart." This three-stage pattern is affirmed by other such major Pentecostal bodies as the Pentecostal Holiness Church and the Church of God in Christ.

Other Pentecostal churches, with non-Wesleyan origins, such as the AG, the Elim Pentecostal Church, and the International Church of the Foursquare Gospel, view sanctification as both given in salvation and progressive throughout the Christian life. Sanctification, therefore, is understood not to be a second work of grace prior to baptism in the Holy Spirit. Rather, from this perspective, the heart has been made essentially clean in regeneration; hence there is no need for heart purification before Spirit baptism may occur.

The charismatic tradition has generally held this

latter viewpoint. With its adherents largely in such non-Wesleyan denominations as Episcopal, Lutheran, and Presbyterian, there has been little, if any, recognition of an intervening stage between regeneration and the gift of the Holy Spirit. Sanctification is by no means denied, but such is not viewed as a second stage the believer must pass through before being eligible for baptism in the Holy Spirit.

It is difficult to deduce from the Book of Acts a second stage of sanctification between salvation and the gift of the Holy Spirit. There are two references to sanctification in Acts. In the first of these Paul, speaking to the Ephesian elders, says, "Now I commit you to God and to the word of his grace, which can build you up and give you an inheritance among all those who are sanctified" (20:32). In the other Paul quotes Jesus as saying to him that he was being sent to both Jews and Gentiles that "they may receive forgiveness of sins and a place among those who are sanctified by faith in me" (26:18). Sanctification in both cases would appear to be a given fact of the Christian life. In the latter instance, since forgiveness of sins and sanctification are juxtaposed, they would seem to refer to two aspects of the same experience.

V. Baptism in the Holy Spirit and Speaking in Tongues. The Pentecostal and charismatic traditions are often identified with speaking in tongues. Pentecostals have laid particular stress on speaking in tongues as "initial evidence" of baptism in the Spirit (as the PFNA statement attests). The word "initial" is emphasized since other evidence may be spoken of; however, the immediate evidence of Spirit baptism is viewed as speaking in tongues. Sometimes speaking in tongues (or glossolalia) is described as the "initial physical sign" (the Apostolic Faith movement) of baptism in the Holy Spirit. Whether evidence or sign, the point made is that the distinctive event of Spirit baptism is primarily exhibited through speaking in tongues.

Scriptural basis for the Pentecostal doctrine is again drawn from several Acts passages. In regard to the Day of Pentecost the first thing said about those who were filled with the Holy Spirit was that they "began to speak in other tongues as the Spirit enabled them" (Acts 2:4). At Caesarea the text reads that "the circumcised believers who had come with Peter were astonished that the gift of the Holy Spirit had been poured out even on the Gentiles. For they heard them speaking in tongues and praising God" (10:45–46). Speaking in tongues was unmistakable evidence to the Jewish believers that the Caesareans had experienced Spirit baptism. When Paul laid his hands on the Ephesians, "the Holy Spirit came on them, and they spoke in tongues and prophesied" (Acts 19:6). The coming of the Spirit is immediately followed by tongues and prophecy. However, the initial activity after the Ephesians' Spirit baptism is speaking in tongues.

Pentecostals further observed that in the account of the Samaritans' reception of the Spirit (Acts 8:17) speaking in tongues is implied. For "when Simon [the magician] saw" (8:18) that the Samaritans had received the Spirit through the laying on of hands, he offered money to the apostles, seeking to buy the power to bestow the same gift on others. What Simon saw, it may be assumed—and for which he was willing to pay—was the spectacle of the Samaritans' speaking in tongues. In regard to the account of Paul's being filled with the Holy Spirit (9:17), nothing is said about his speaking in tongues at that time. However, since Paul in one of his letters later attests to his own speaking in tongues—"I thank God that I speak in tongues more than all of you" (1 Cor. 14:18)—Pentecostals surmise that it could well have begun (as with the other apostles in Acts 2:4) when he was Spirit baptized.

On the basis of these five passages Pentecostals affirm that they have an adequate scriptural basis for their view of initial evidence. Further, they see in glossolalia an extraordinary sign of an extraordinary event—the gift of the Holy Spirit. Since the coming of the Spirit, however often repeated, is a supernatural happening, the supernatural occurrence of tongues is its peculiar immediate expression. For Pentecostals the dynamic connection seen between speaking in tongues and Spirit baptism again confirms their view that tongues occurred in all five of the narratives in Acts.

Further, when the nature of glossolalia is properly understood, Pentecostals claim, its connection with Spirit baptism is all the more apparent, for speaking in tongues is basically the language of praise. In the narrative of Pentecost the crowd, upon hearing the tongues, said in amazement, "We hear them declaring the wonders of God in our own tongues" (Acts 2:11). At Caesarea the close connection between tongues and praise is shown in the words, "They heard them speaking in tongues and praising God" (10:46). Accordingly, speaking in tongues may be understood as the way of praising God that goes beyond ordinary speech: it is transcendent praise. If such is the case, then the connection between Spirit baptism and glossolalia is readily seen: the dynamic experience of the presence of God in the Holy Spirit overflows in self-transcending speech glorifying God.

Pentecostals also frequently call attention to Paul's words in Ephesians 5:18–19: "Do not get drunk with wine . . . but be filled with the Spirit, speaking to one another in psalms and hymns and spiritual songs" (NASB). The intimate connection between being Spirit filled and manifold praise (including "spiritual songs," i.e., songs inspired by the Holy Spirit) is apparent. Fullness of the Spirit leads to fullness of praise. Thus do Spirit baptism, praise, and tongues fit naturally together.

In sum, from the Pentecostal perspective speaking in tongues as the speaking forth of praise is due to the dynamic presence of God in the Holy Spirit. It is hardly strange that the immediate response to such a holy presence may well be transcendent praise to God.

A word should be added about the charismatic movement and tongues. Though speaking in tongues is a common practice, there is less emphasis on tongues being *the* initial evidence. First, many charismatics do not find the evidence in Acts of glossolalia to be conclusive; second, because of the variety of gifts of the Holy Spirit (see esp. 1 Cor. 12:8–10), they often prefer to speak of spiritual gifts—any of which may signify the Spirit's coming. One Roman Catholic theologian, Edward O'Connor, reporting on the early movement among Catholics wrote: "Some people begin speaking in tongues at the moment of the [Spirit] baptism. Others do not begin until hours, days, or even weeks later, and some never do" (1971, 134). However, there are many charismatics that do affirm the close connection between the Spirit baptism and tongues. Dennis Bennett, early Episcopal charismatic leader, states about speaking in tongues: "It comes with the package! Speaking in tongues is not the baptism in the Holy Spirit, but it is what happens when and as you are baptized in the Spirit" (1971, 64). This statement seems better to accord with the evidence in Acts and more closely approximates the Pentecostal view.

VI. The Purpose of Baptism in the Holy Spirit. The primary purpose of Spirit baptism, according to the Book of Acts, is *power*. The biblical term is *dunamis*—power, strength, force—and represents an endowment of spiritual power. Jesus promised his disciples that upon being baptized in the Holy Spirit, "You will receive power when the Holy Spirit comes on you" (Acts 1:8). The command of Jesus in Luke 24:49 makes the same point: "Stay in the city until you have been clothed with power from on high." The power of God—transcendent power—is the purpose of the gift of the Holy Spirit.

At the beginning of Jesus' own ministry the Holy Spirit had already "descended on him" (Luke 3:22, also see other Gospel parallels). As a result Jesus was "full of the Holy Spirit" (Luke 4:1) and, after his temptations, "returned to Galilee in the power of the Spirit" (v. 14). Therefore Jesus intended that the same Spirit of power that rested upon him should rest upon his disciples. Further, since what Jesus received was power for ministry, it would be the same for his disciples. They would likewise be able to move in the power of the Spirit for the ministry that lay ahead. Hence, though the immediate response of the disciples to the gift of the Spirit will be the praise of God directed upward, the purpose of that gift will be the service of humanity and therefore directed outward.

Primarily, Spirit baptism will be a power for witness. Following Jesus' promise of power, he declared, "You will be my witnesses in Jerusalem, and in all Judea and Samaria, and to the ends of the earth" (Acts 1:8; cf. Luke 24:48—"You are witnesses of these things" prior to "stay in the city"). After the 120 spoke in tongues on the Day of Pentecost, Peter first explained the phenomenon and then bore witness to the gospel, saying, "Men of Israel, listen to this" (Acts 2:22). It was his powerful witness that brought about conviction of sin (v. 37), repentance, and forgiveness (v. 38), and thereby the salvation of some 3,000 persons (v. 41). That Spirit baptism is directly related to witness is also demonstrated in the account of Paul's being filled with the Spirit. Before Ananias laid hands on Paul he was told by the Lord, "Go! This man [Paul] is my chosen instrument to carry my name before the Gentiles and their kings and before the people of Israel" (9:15).

This power for witness in Acts is by no means limited to such apostles as Peter and Paul but also belongs to the whole community of Christians. On one occasion when the believers corporately prayed for greater boldness in witness, the result was that "they were all filled with the Holy Spirit and spoke the word of God boldly" (4:31). Hence, being Spirit-filled produces a powerful witness among believers in general.

Baptism in the Holy Spirit also enables the performance of *mighty works*. After Jesus returned in the power of the Spirit, he went throughout Galilee not only teaching and preaching but also "healing every disease and sickness among the people" (Matt. 4:23). According to Luke, "the power of the Lord was present for him to heal the sick" (5:17). Moreover, he cast out demons "by the Spirit of God" (Matt. 12:28) and wrought many miracles. Likewise, he said to his disciples: "I tell you the truth, anyone who has faith in me will do what I have been doing. He will do even greater things than these, because I am going to the Father" (John 14:12). After his ascension, Jesus would send believers the Holy Spirit to equip them to do these works. Thus shortly after the event of Pentecost, Jesus' apostles began to perform numerous mighty works: "Many wonders and miraculous signs were done by the apostles" (Acts 2:43). With Peter, so great was the anointing of the Spirit that his shadow alone was sufficient to bring healing (5:15). Handkerchiefs and aprons touched by Paul brought healing to the sick and deliverance from evil spirits (19:12).

However, it was not only apostles who did these works but deacons also. Stephen, "a man full of faith and of the Holy Spirit . . . did great wonders and miraculous signs among the people" (Acts 6:5, 8). Philip, also "full of the Spirit" (v. 5), did many "miraculous signs . . . evil spirits came out of many, and many paralytics and cripples were healed (8:6–7). Spirit-anointed men of God were performing mighty deeds.

Nowhere in the Scripture is there any suggestion that either the powerful witness or the mighty works would end with the NT period. According to Mark 16:17–18, "these signs will accompany those who believe," and among the signs listed are driving out demons, speaking in new tongues, and healing the sick. Jesus' mighty works will thereby be continued over the years through his people.

Pentecostals have no hesitation in affirming this continuity in the *dunamis* of the Holy Spirit down to the present day. They lay much emphasis on the power of the Spirit as essential for anointed witness and believe that mighty works such as miracles of healing and deliverance are vital components of a full-orbited ministry. On this latter point Pentecostals differ with many evangelical Christians who claim that miracles ceased with the apostolic times. Pentecostals view both a fully anointed witness and the working of miracles as inseparable: if the witness continues, so do miracles. Moreover, they maintain that both become truly effective through baptism in the Holy Spirit.

Here then is a critical point in the Pentecostal outlook. Pentecostals declare that what many Christians today need is precisely this baptism of power. In addition to being born of the Spirit wherein new life begins, there is also the need for being baptized, or filled, with the Spirit for the outflow of the life in ministry to others.

Pentecostals frequently draw a parallel between Jesus and believers by pointing out that he was first conceived by the Holy Spirit (Luke 1:31–35) and then thirty years later was filled with the Holy Spirit (3:21–22; 4:1). Though he was born as the Son of God, he still needed the empowering for ministry that occurred when the Holy Spirit came upon him. So it is with believers who have been reborn by the Spirit as sons of God. They need—surely far more than Jesus did—Spirit baptism to fulfill the ministry Christ gives them. It is the same Holy Spirit but in two distinct operations: one in birth (or rebirth) and the other in empowering for service. Pentecostals sometimes depict this by speaking of Jesus as fulfilling both the roles of Savior and Baptizer. According to the Fourth Gospel, John the Baptist on one occasion acclaimed Jesus as "the Lamb of God, who takes away the sin of the world" (John 1:29), hence the Savior. Shortly thereafter John spoke of the Spirit-anointed Jesus ("the man on whom you see the Spirit come down") as "he who will baptize with the Holy Spirit" (v. 33). There is need, accordingly, for Jesus as Savior to take away sins and as Baptizer to equip for participation in his ministry.

Returning to the matter of power as the purpose of Spirit baptism: Pentecostals emphasize that this is a special anointing of power. Whatever power there may be resident in a believer—and this is surely greatly due to the Holy Spirit within—Spirit baptism is an implication of that power. Pentecostals do not intend to say that the Spirit-baptized have experienced power, for the gospel itself "is the power of God unto salvation" (Rom. 1:16 KJV). However, they do urge that in addition—and for an entirely different reason than salvation—there is another action of the Holy Spirit that equips the believer for further service. This is not salvation but implementation; it is not transformation of a new creature but his commissioning for the sake of Christ and the gospel.

VII. Baptism in the Holy Spirit and Water Baptism. Pentecostals in general view water baptism as important but not essential to baptism in the Holy Spirit. With the Book of Acts again as basic guide, Pentecostals speak of water baptism as either preceding or following Spirit baptism but as having no necessary connection with it.

In the case of the Samaritans Philip preached the gospel, and many were baptized (Acts 8:12). However, it was only after Peter and John had come down from Jerusalem that the Samaritans were Spirit baptized. Prior to this "they had simply been baptized into the name of the Lord Jesus"; now when "Peter and John placed hands on them . . . they received the Holy Spirit" (vv. 16–17). The same thing was true with the

Ephesians. Paul baptized the Ephesians in the name of Christ and thereafter laid hands on them for the reception of the Spirit (19:5–6). Water baptism, in both instances, preceded baptism in the Spirit.

In two other cases water baptism followed Spirit baptism. While Peter was proclaiming the gospel to the Caesareans, the Holy Spirit fell upon his hearers (Acts 10:44). After this Peter said, "Can anyone keep these people from being baptized with water? They have received the Holy Spirit just as we have" (v. 47). Then the apostle proceeded with water baptism. In the other instance Paul first had hands laid on him by Ananias for Spirit baptism (9:17); then he was baptized in water (v. 18). Water baptism in both cases followed baptism in the Spirit.

It is also apparent from these accounts in Acts that water baptism was neither a precondition nor a channel for baptism in the Holy Spirit. On the matter of precondition, Peter's words on the Day of Pentecost might suggest such: "Repent and be baptized. . . . And you will receive the gift of the Holy Spirit" (Acts 2:38). However, since at Caesarea Peter baptized subsequent to the reception of the Spirit, there was clearly no precondition of water baptism. Moreover, in none of the Acts narrations is there any suggestion of water baptism conveying the gift of the Holy Spirit.

Pentecostals thus see no essential connection between water baptism and baptism in the Holy Spirit. This does not mean that for them water baptism is unimportant, but the importance lies at another point, namely, in relation to forgiveness and salvation. To complete Peter's words at Pentecost: "Repent and be baptized, every one of you, in the name of Jesus Christ for the forgiveness of your sins" (Acts 2:38). Water baptism is connected with forgiveness of sins not the gift of the Spirit that is thereupon promised. Pentecostals, however, do not view water baptism as essential to forgiveness (salvation), though water baptism is seen to be important as a sign or symbol of salvation.

With regard to the laying on of hands, Pentecostals view this to be more directly connected with baptism in the Spirit than is water baptism. Even as water baptism relates to salvation so does laying on of hands relate to the gifts of the Holy Spirit.

The relation of water baptism to baptism in the Holy Spirit is variously understood in the charismatic movement. For those whose traditions are less sacramental (e.g., Baptists, Methodists, Presbyterians), water baptism is not viewed as necessary for Spirit baptism. For charismatics whose traditions are more sacramental (e.g., Roman Catholics, Greek Orthodox, Lutherans), baptism in the Spirit is usually viewed as essentially connected with the sacrament of water baptism. From their perspective the Holy Spirit is often said to be given objectively in the sacrament of baptism. Accordingly, what these charismatics are really talking about in reference to Spirit baptism is an actualization or appropriation of what presumably they have already sacramentally received. Kilian McDonnell, a Roman Catholic theologian in the Catholic renewal, writes that

"Baptism, in its New Testament context, is always a baptism of the Spirit" (1975, 73). However, the occasion may come, McDonnell adds, when "the Spirit already present becomes a fact of conscious experience" (ibid., 82). This actualization or coming to consciousness may then be called Spirit baptism in a subjective and experiential sense. The problem with such a sacramental understanding is twofold: first, there is difficulty in harmonizing this view of the Spirit with the record in Acts (e.g., water baptism is in no place depicted as a rite in which the Holy Spirit is given); second, it reduces what charismatics have experienced to an actualization or appropriation of a prior sacramental action. It is apparent, however, both in Acts and today, that far more happens to people subjectively and experientially than the sacramental viewpoint can contain.

VIII. The Reception of the Holy Spirit.
Pentecostals hold that the basic requirement for receiving the Holy Spirit is faith. Even as salvation is received by faith, so is the Holy Spirit. Baptism in the Holy Spirit happens only to those who believe in Jesus Christ.

In all the Acts narratives the necessity of faith is apparent. Regarding the first Pentecostal reception of the Spirit, Peter later speaks of this as the "gift . . . he gave us, who believed in the Lord Jesus Christ" (Acts 11:17). So it was with the Samaritans who believed (8:12) and thereafter received (v. 17). Paul acknowledged Jesus as "Lord" (9:10) and later was "filled" (v. 17). The Caesareans heard Peter's proclamation, "Everyone who believes in him receives forgiveness of sins through his name" (10:43), and immediately the Holy Spirit fell upon them (v. 44). And the Ephesians were exhorted by Paul to believe in Christ (19:4) and shortly thereafter received the Holy Spirit (v. 6). The reception of the Holy Spirit was and is by faith.

Reference may be made also to two Pauline statements outside Acts. In Ephesians 1:13 Paul declares that "having believed, you were marked in him with a seal, the promised Holy Spirit" (cf. the "promise of the Spirit" in Acts 1 and 2). In Galatians 3:2 Paul asks, "Did you receive the Spirit by observing the law or by believing what you heard?" Faith is essential to the reception of the Spirit.

Pentecostals, while recognizing the necessity of faith, also hold that baptism in the Holy Spirit does not always occur at faith's inception. They point again to Acts, which shows the Spirit being received *after* faith has begun (e.g., the Samaritans and Paul, whose faith is presupposed). The Pentecostals particularly view Paul's question to the Ephesians, "Did you receive the Holy Spirit when ["after"—mg.] you believed?" (Acts 19:2) as undoubtedly implying a possible reception of the Spirit after the initiation of faith.

On the basis of a possible temporal separation between the beginning of faith and Spirit baptism, the Pentecostal tradition has commonly spoken of certain conditions. Whereas faith remains fundamental, additional factors are emphasized. Attention is often focused on such matters as prayer, obedience, and yielding.

In the matter of *prayer* Pentecostals call atten-tion to the company of disciples before Pentecost who "all joined together constantly in prayer" (Acts 1:14). Jesus had earlier said, "Tarry ye in the city of Jerusalem, until ye be endued with power from on high" (Luke 24:49 KJV). "Tarrying" meetings—often over long periods of time—were commonplace in early Pentecostal circles. Constancy in prayer, awaiting the coming of the Holy Spirit, continues to be emphasized. Pentecostals call attention not only to the Upper Room account of prayer prior to Pentecost but also to the preparatory nature of prayer in other accounts. In the Gospel of Luke Jesus himself is shown to be praying when the Holy Spirit first descended: "As he was praying, heaven was opened and the Holy Spirit descended on him" (3:21–22). Later he taught his disciples the importance of persistence in prayer—asking, seeking, knocking—and added: "Your Father in heaven [will] give the Holy Spirit to those who ask him" (11:13). In Acts several further accounts describe an atmosphere of prayer. Regarding the Samaritans, Peter and John "prayed for them that they might receive the Holy Spirit" (8:15); only after that did the apostles lay hands on others. Paul fasted and prayed for three days (9:9, 11) prior to his being filled with the Spirit (v. 17). The centurion at Caesarea was a "devout man who . . . feared God with all his household . . . and prayed constantly to God" (10:2 RSV). To these devout and prayerful people Peter preached, and upon them the Holy Spirit fell. Prayer was the background and context in which Spirit baptism occurred. Pentecostals, taking such things as their lead, emphasized the need for earnest prayer in preparing for the reception of the Holy Spirit.

Pentecostals also stress the importance of *obedience*. Peter on one occasion speaks of the Holy Spirit "whom God has given to those who obey him" (Acts 5:32). Obedience is usually understood in two ways. First, the believers in the Upper Room obeyed Christ's injunction to wait in prayer for the Holy Spirit to be given (1:14). Many people are unwilling to take the time to wait upon the Lord and thereby fail to receive his blessing. Second, obedience is also viewed in the larger context as obedience to Christ's commands. Jesus had earlier declared, "If you love me, you will keep my commandments. And I will pray the Father, and he will give you another Counselor . . . even the Spirit of truth" (John 14:15–17 RSV). The Holy Spirit will be given to those who obey Christ's commands. One who seeks to walk the way of righteousness is better prepared to receive Spirit baptism. The centurion of Caesarea and his family were already "devout and God-fearing" (Acts 10:2); they were among those who "do what is right" (10:34) even before they come to salvation. Their faith and obedience was honored by the outpouring of the Holy Spirit as Peter preached the gospel to them.

A third factor frequently mentioned by Pentecostals in relation to Spirit baptism is *yielding* or *surrender*. A parallel is often drawn between water baptism and Spirit baptism. In believer's baptism one must totally yield himself to immersion by another in water; likewise one must totally yield himself to be baptized by Christ in the Holy Spirit. Yieldedness in relation to speaking in tongues is particularly significant since the tongue is described as an "unruly evil" (James 3:8 KJV). It must also be surrendered to become ruled by the Holy Spirit and thereby speak a new language inspired by the Spirit. In any event, what is important is a total surrender to the lordship of Jesus Christ. Donald Gelpi, a Roman Catholic theologian, speaks of the need for "full docility to the Spirit of Christ" (1971, 183). Yielding, surrender, full docility—however expressed—is the attitude of one who is to receive the Holy Spirit.

The conditions just mentioned are best understood not as requirements in addition to faith but as expressions of faith. F. Dale Brunner in his book *A Theology of the Holy Spirit: The Pentecostal Experience and the New Testament Witness* (1970, 111) criticizes Pentecostalism for its various conditions as representing a call to "superhuman effort," hence going beyond "ordinary faith." Doubtless there is some merit in his criticism, for Pentecostals have at times so stressed conditions as to seem to leave faith behind. The basic concern of Pentecostals, however, is with active faith: praying in faith, the obedience of faith, faith as yielding. The Holy Spirit is still a gift of God's grace; there is no way of earning it or achieving it. God delights to give to those who are eager to receive.

See also GIFTS OF THE SPIRIT; GLOSSOLALIA; INITIAL EVIDENCE, A BIBLICAL PERSPECTIVE; INITIAL EVIDENCE, A HISTORICAL PERSPECTIVE.

Bibliography: D. and R. Bennett, *The Holy Spirit and You* (1971); B. Bradford, *Releasing the Power of the Holy Spirit* (1983); L. Christenson, *The Charismatic Renewal Among Lutherans* (1976); S. Clark, *Baptized in the Spirit and Spiritual Gifts* (1976); H. M. Ervin, *These Are Not Drunken, As Ye Suppose* (1976); R. M. Frost, *Set My Spirit Free* (1973); D. Gelpi, *Pentecostalism: A Theological Viewpoint* (1971); M. P. Hamilton, ed., *The Charismatic Movement* (1975); S. M. Horton, *What the Bible Has to Say About the Holy Spirit* (1976); H. D. Hunter, *Spirit-Baptism* (1983); K. Kendrick, *The Promise Fulfilled* (1961); K. McDonnell, *The Holy Spirit and Power: The Catholic Charismatic Renewal* (1975); E. O'Connor, *The Pentecostal Movement in the Catholic Church* (1971); K. and D. Ranaghan, *Catholic Pentecostals* (1969); R. M. Riggs, *The Spirit Himself* (1949); J. S. Schep, *Spirit Baptism and Tongue Speaking* (1970); J. R. Williams, *The Gift of the Holy Spirit Today* (1980).
J. R. Williams

BAPTISM IN WATER See ORDINANCES, PENTECOSTAL ; SACRAMENTS.

BAPTIST CHARISMATICS A. C. Piepkorn lists two Baptist Pentecostal denominations: the Pentecostal Free-Will Baptist Church, Inc. (PFWBC), and the Free-Will Baptist Church of the Pentecostal Faith (1979, 3:159–62).

According to Piepkorn, the

Pentecostal Free-Will Baptist Church traces its Baptist roots to the eighteenth-century Baptist preacher Benjamin Randall. It organized in Dunn, North Carolina in 1908 as a pentecostal church after G. B. Cashwell, who had himself experienced the Azusa Street revival, led many Free-Will Baptists into a pentecostal experi-

A praise and worship time at a Fulness Conference at Bethesda Community Church, Fort Worth, Texas.

ence. Today the PFWBC has some 13,000 members in 150 churches (1979, 3:159–60; cf. Synan, 1986, 54).

The Free-Will Baptist Church of the Pentecostal Faith is a group of South Carolina Baptists who share basically the same beliefs as the Pentecostal Free-Will Baptist Church. From 1943–58 the two were one church. Considering itself more conservative, the South Carolina group withdrew to form its own denomination in 1959 (Piepkorn, 1979, 3:161–62).

Within the mainline Baptist churches the charismatic renewal has met with mixed responses, from warm embrace to outright rejection and hostility. A support group for charismatics is the American Baptist Charismatic Fellowship in Pasadena, California. Annual summer conferences (since 1975) are held at the denomination's camp ground in Green Lake, Wisconsin. Rev. Howard Ervin, Th.D., an American Baptist minister and professor at Oral Roberts University, is one of their principal speakers and a leading advocate of Neo-Pentecostalism.

The Southern Baptist Convention (SBC), Protestantism's largest denomination in the U.S., has grown increasingly negative in its official public stance toward Baptist charismatics. In a January 7, 1988, letter, Don LeMaster, senior pastor of West Lauderdale Baptist Church in Fort Lauderdale, Florida, and a spokesman for many Southern Baptist charismatics, wrote:

In the light of all that is taking place in the convention it appears it is a matter of time for us [charismatics]. If the liberals gain control I am not sure we want to remain. If, however, it goes the other way, will they make room for us? . . . Another denomination would be just that "another denomination"—that we do not need. A fellowship of "Charismatic," "Fulness," "Full Gospel," or _____ (you fill in the blanks) is needed. In order for that to happen, we must form some kind of organization. Lord help us!

The struggle and uncertainty that mark his letter come in the wake of actions taken at the highest levels of the SBC. Among Baptists nationally, it is reckoned that fully 20 percent consider themselves Pentecostal or charismatic. That, however, is a minority, and the majority has unequivocally rejected charismatic practices, especially glossolalia. The SBC Home Mission Board, in July 1987, voted to forbid even the private practice of glossolalia among its missionaries. This is but a further intensification of the position set forth in "The Baptist Faith and Message" (1963), in which the SBC repudiated public glossolalia and public faith healing services where people are declared healed.

Prior to this 1987 decision many Southern Baptist pastors and lay persons had sought to maintain their affiliation with the SBC and their identification as a SBC church. LeMaster's letter includes a directory of "Fulness" pastors and churches (as the SBC charismatic community is sometimes named). These number more than a hundred. Some observers, including C. P. Wagner, professor of church growth at Fuller Theological Seminary, estimate the number to be between two and three hundred charismatic SBC congregations (Synan, 1987, 57).

Baptists who have personally participated in some aspect of the charismatic or Pentecostal experience have often not been welcome to remain within the SBC. C. H. Mason withdrew to found the Church of God in Christ. E. N. Bell was the first general superintendent of the Assemblies of God. William Branham and Tommy Hicks were Baptists who, after Pentecostal experiences, became leaders of the Pentecostal and healing revival of the late 1940s and 1950s. M. G. "Pat" Robertson, Jamie Buckingham, Ken Sumrall, Charles Simpson, John Osteen, Larry Lea, and James Robison represent but a few of the contemporary charismatic ministers or leaders who have come out of Baptist backgrounds. At the level of the laity "the Pentecostal churches have probably seen more adherents from among Baptists than from any other Protestant group in the United States" (Synan, 1986, 54).

Fulness magazine seeks to be an agency that fosters ministry without divisiveness among its SBC charismatic constituency, rather than highlighting any particular spiritual gift. The magazine, together with Fulness Ministries, seeks to foster "growth into the fulness of Christ." Fulness Conferences are held periodically throughout the nation.

See also CHARISMATIC MOVEMENT.

Bibliography: C. L. Howe, "The Charismatic Movement in Southern Baptist Life," *Baptist History and Heritage* 13 (3, 1978): 20–27, 65; Pentecostal Research Center, Oral Roberts University, Tulsa, Oklahoma, letter by D. LeMaster, including, "Directory of Fulness Pastors and Churches, January 1988"; J. Moody, "A Baptist Pastor Looks at the Charismatics," *Fulness* 10 (6, 1987): 26–29; A. C. Piepkorn, *Profiles in Belief,* 3 vols. (1979); "Southern Baptists Disagree Over Tongues," *Charisma and Christian Life* 13 (7, 1988): 22; V. Synan, "Baptists Ride the Third Wave," *Charisma and Christian Life* 12 (5, 1986): 52–57.   J. A. Hewett

"Mother" Mary Barnes began preaching the Pentecostal message early in the 20th century. She was associated with Mary Moise in rescue mission work in St. Louis.

BARNES, LEANORE O. ("MOTHER MARY") (1854–1939). An early Pentecostal evangelist in the Midwest. Although biographical data on her are sketchy, she apparently gained initial notoriety in a revival meeting she helped conduct in Thayer, Missouri, in 1909. Despite hoodlums threatening to kill the evangelists, a six-week meeting netted more than a hundred converts and at least fifty baptized in the Spirit. She was associated with the Pentecostal social worker "Mother" Mary Moise in St. Louis, beginning in about 1909. She became a charter member of the Assemblies of God in 1914 but later went into the Oneness movement. She taught at the Oneness Bible school in Eureka Springs, Arkansas, and was associated with a St. Louis church for many years. One of her daughters married an early Pentecostal preacher and writer, Bennett F. Lawrence.

Bibliography: " 'Mother' Barnes, Evangelist Here Many Years, Dies," *St. Louis Post-Dispatch* (May 9, 1939); W. Warner, "Mother Mary Moise of St. Louis," *AG Heritage* (Spring 1986), 6–7, 13–14.
                    W. E. Warner

BARNETT, TOMMY J. (1937–). Assemblies of God (AG) evangelist and megachurch pastor. Tommy Barnett is the son of H. W. Barnett of Kansas City, Kansas. He began his career at age sixteen with a series of revival meetings held for Ted Vassar, AG pastor in Seminole, Texas. Gifted with great personal charisma, Barnett soon became one of the most successful Pentecostal evangelists, drawing large crowds to hear his music and his simple yet powerful sermons.

In 1971 Barnett accepted the pastorate of Westside Assembly in Davenport, Iowa. It grew from an average of 76 to 4,400. In 1979 he moved to Phoenix, Arizona, as pastor of Phoenix First Assembly. Again, there was spectacular growth under his ministry. First Assembly's attendance increased from an average of 250 to more than 9,000 in nine years.

Church growth under Barnett's ministry can be attributed to several factors. In addition to his own drawing power, Barnett has relied heavily on a bus ministry. This outreach has been to children of all classes, and to the orthopedically handicapped. He also has outreach ministries to the elderly, to college groups, and to minorities. Barnett has a flair for the spectacular, including Easter, Independence Day, Thanksgiving, and Christmas productions, which have drawn as many as 130,000 to a week-long event. His success in church growth has led to training programs for ministers and church leaders (3,000 attended the early 1988 conference).

Barnett is married and has three children.

Bibliography: Vita and press releases provided by Tommy Barnett (February 1988).   S. M. Burgess

Thomas B. Barratt, a well-known Methodist minister in Oslo, Norway, came to the United States on a fund-raising project and was baptized in the Spirit.

BARRATT, THOMAS BALL (1862–1940). Norwegian Pentecostal leader. Thomas Ball Barratt was born in Albaston, Cornwall, England. Barratt's father, a miner, immigrated to Norway in 1867. Barratt attended school in England (ages eleven–sixteen) and, in Norway, studied art with O. Dahl and music with E. Grieg. At age seventeen he began preaching. He was ordained deacon (1889) and elder (1891) in the Methodist Episcopal Church of Norway and pastored several churches. In 1902 he founded the Oslo City Mission and in 1904 became editor of its paper, *Byposten*. During a visit to the U.S. (1906) he came into contact with the Pentecostal movement and returned to Norway an ardent proponent, becoming the founder of the Norwegian movement and a key figure in the establishment of indigenous Pentecostal churches throughout Europe and the Third World. His periodical, *Korsets Seier*, was published in Swedish, Finnish, German, Russian, and Spanish as well as Norwegian. From 1907 to 1916 Barratt was a freelance revivalist and prolific author. In 1916 he left the Methodist Church to found the Filadelfia Church in Oslo, where he was pastor until his death.

See also EUROPEAN PENTECOSTALISM.

Bibliography: Selected Works: T. B. Barratt, *Aimee Semple McPherson: liv, virke og praedikener* (1927); idem, *Erindringer* (1941); idem, *The Gift of Prophecy* (1909, reprint 1974); idem, *In the Days of the Latter Rain* (1909, rev. ed. 1928); idem, *Kvinnens stilling i menigheten* (1933); idem, *To Seekers After "The Promise of the Father"* (1911); idem, *Skrifter i utvalg, minneutgave* (1949); idem, *When the Fire Fell, and an Outline of My Life* (1929). **Selected Secondary Literature:** N. Bloch-Hoell, *Pinsebevegelsen, en undersøkelse av pinsebevegelsens tilblivelse . . .* (1956; partial English trans., *The Pentecostal Movement* [1964]); T. E. Dahl and John-Willy Rudolph, *Fra seier til Nederlag, Pinsebevegelsen i Norge* (1978); W. J. Hollenweger, *Handbuch der Pfingstbewegung* (1966), 05.21.007; S. Lange, *T. B. Barratt et Herrens Sendebud* (1962); M. Ski, *T. B. Barratt — Dopt i and og ild* (1979); E. Strand, E. Strom, and M. Ski, *Fram til ur-kristendommen, Pinsevekkelsen gjnnom 50 aår* (1956–59).   D. D. Bundy

BARTLEMAN, FRANK (1871–1936). Early Pentecostal evangelist, critic, and the primary chronicler of Pentecostal origins in Los Angeles. The third of five sons, he was born on a farm near Carversville, Pennsylvania, to Frank Bartleman, a stern Roman Catholic who immigrated to the U.S. from Württemberg, Germany, and Margaret (Hellyer) Bartleman, an American-born Quaker of English and Welsh descent. A relatively sickly youngster, he attended school and worked on his father's farm until he left home at age seventeen.

Moving to Philadelphia, the younger Bartleman worked a number of odd jobs and attended Grace Baptist Church, pastored by Russell H. Conwell. On October 15, 1893, he was converted. The following summer he received his call into full-time ministry and began formal preparation by attending Temple College. He also studied briefly at Moody Bible Institute. In succeeding years Bartleman ministered with the Salvation Army, the Wesleyan Methodists, Pillar of Fire, and the Peniel Missions, while working at a number of tent-making jobs.

On May 2, 1900, Bartleman married Anna Ladd, a Bulgarian-born woman who had been adopted and reared by American Methodist missionaries to Bulgaria. The Bartlemans had four children; the first, Esther, was born April 30, 1901, and died shortly after the family's arrival in

Los Angeles in December 1904. This tragedy affected Frank profoundly, and he reiterated his commitment to the ministry as a result.

From 1906 to 1908 Bartleman attended a few prayer meetings led by W. J. Seymour prior to the Azusa Street revival. For a time he supported Joseph Smale in the First New Testament Church, attended the Azusa Street Mission, and established another mission at 8th and Maple Streets in Los Angeles, then turned it over to W. H. Pendleton. But he seldom remained at one address or in one church for very long.

Bartleman preached as an itinerant evangelist for forty-three years. He crisscrossed the U.S. on several occasions, preached his way around the world (1910–11) while leaving his family in Los Angeles, and made a second extended evangelistic tour through Europe (1912–14), this time with his family.

Bartleman's most obvious contribution came in more than 550 articles, 100 tracts, and 6 books he authored during his ministry. His writings appear in popular religious journals of both the Holiness and Pentecostal movements in the U.S. and England. He was a frequent contributor to the *Way of Faith* (Columbia, S.C.), *Word and Work* (Framingham, Mass.), and *Confidence* (Sunderland, Eng.). His first book, *My Story: "The Latter Rain,"* published in 1909 by J. M. Pike, was superseded by Bartleman's own publication *From Plow to Pulpit* (1924), which described his life from his birth through 1904. *How Pentecost Came to Los Angeles* (1925) chronicled events in which he participated in Los Angeles from 1905 through 1911. These works were followed by *Around the World by Faith* (1925) and *Two Years Mission Work in Europe Just Before the World War: 1912–1914* (1924).

Theologically, Bartleman was always looking for the latest work of God. He wished for more unity among Pentecostals, and he wrote a book on *The Deity of Christ* (1926), arguing for liberty of conscience in the "Jesus Name" baptismal formula controversy. Always his own person, Bartleman was quick to write and speak his opinion on a wide range of topics. He criticized church leadership and denominational organization, and he argued strongly for separation in church-state relations, condemning the presence of national flags in church buildings. He harangued on the economic evils of communism and capitalism, the pitfalls of political involvement by Christians, and the nature of the controlled "free" press. He vehemently opposed all forms of militarism, including the purchase of War Bonds and the existence of Boy Scouts, and he argued passionately for a neutral pacifism in World War I.

Frank Bartleman died on the afternoon of August 23, 1936. He is buried at Valhalla Memorial Park in Burbank, California.

Bibliography: C. M. Robeck, Jr., "The Writings and Thought of Frank Bartleman," *Witness to Pentecost: The Life of Frank Bartleman* (1985), vii–xxviii; *Witness* is a reprint of four of Bartleman's autobiographical works; V. Synan, "Frank Bartleman and Azusa Street," in *Frank Bartleman, Azusa Street* (1908), ix–xxv.
                                                    C. M. Robeck, Jr.

One of the important figures in the early years of the Pentecostal movement, Frank Bartleman was involved in the Azusa Street Mission meetings. He also wrote articles and books about the revival and other themes.

BASHAM, DON WILSON (1926–). Bible teacher, editor, and author. Born in Wichita Falls, Texas, Basham was educated at Midwestern State University and Phillips University (B.A. and B.D.). He was reared in a Baptist home but joined the Christian Church while in college. It was there that he met his wife, Alice. Shortly after their marriage, the couple experienced a dramatic spiritual rebirth following the miraculous healing of a close friend. This resulted in a desire for Christian service. Basham and his wife were baptized in the Holy Spirit in 1952. He was ordained as a Disciples of Christ minister in 1955 and pastored churches in Washington, D.C.; Toronto, Canada; and Sharon, Pennsylvania. He left the pastorate in 1967, after the publication of his first book, to begin a freelance writing and teaching ministry, traveling extensively both in the U.S. and abroad. His teaching emphasis is on the Holy Spirit, faith, family relationships, spiritual authority, and deliverance. His book on deliverance, *Deliver Us From Evil* (c. 1972), has become well known. He has written fifteen other books.

Basham joined with Bob Mumford, Derek Prince, and Charles Simpson in Fort Lauderdale, Florida, under the name Christian Growth Ministries (CGM). Basham served as editor of CGM's monthly publication, *New Wine Magazine* from 1975 to 1981 and as chief editorial consultant until 1986. He moved to Mobile, Alabama, in 1978, when the magazine moved there.

Basham was among the first in the charismatic renewal to teach on deliverance. He and others became involved in the "ministry of deliverance." Although church leaders debated whether Christians could be influenced by demons, some staunch church members were freed of problems that had plagued them for years after going through deliverance. The debate about the practice raged for a time but has quieted. Most who practice deliverance say they agree a Christian cannot be "possessed" by a demon, although one can be "oppressed."

When *New Wine Magazine* ceased publication in 1986, Basham moved to Elyria, Ohio, where he now publishes a monthly newsletter, *Don Basham's Insights,* and continues his freelance writing and teaching ministry.

Bibliography: J. Buckingham, "New Wine Ceases Publication," *Ministries Today* (November–December 1986), 24; S. Strang, "The Discipleship Controversy Three Years Later," *Charisma* (September 1978), 14–24.   S. Strang

BAXTER, WILLIAM JOHN ERNEST ("ERN") (1914–). Pastor, Bible teacher, and author. Baxter was born in Saskatoon, Saskatchewan, Canada, to W. E. and Annie May Baxter, members of the Presbyterian Church. When influenced by the ministry of an itinerant evangelist, the Baxters became Pentecostals. The young Baxter rebelled against the faith of his parents but eventually discovered the grace of God. Later he traveled with a friend in conducting evangelistic meetings and received the baptism in the Holy Spirit at a camp meeting in 1932.

For a short time Baxter pastored a Pentecostal church, but doctrinal differences with the denomination forced his departure. Eventually he pastored an independent congregation in Vancouver, British Columbia. In 1947 Baxter came into contact with the ministry of William Branham. The latter, claiming to have been instructed by an angel to invite Baxter to be his traveling companion in evangelistic work, asked him to join his ministry. During this time, Baxter was also influenced by positive aspects of the Latter Rain movement that he observed. Although recognizing God's supernatural activity in these ministries, his concerns over "uncorrected sin, corruption, and unsound doctrine" caused him to separate himself from them and return to his church in Vancouver.

Influenced by the testimony of Dennis Bennett, Baxter became involved in the charismatic renewal. His concerns for Bible teaching and Christian nurture led him to develop a series of teachings on growth and development, both personal and corporate; as a consequence, he began to publish a monthly magazine called *New Covenant Times*. In 1974 Baxter was one of the speakers at a conference in Montreat, North Carolina. While at this conference he became involved with Christian Growth Ministries and *New Wine* magazine because of his interest in the shepherding teaching. He worked with this group, which had its headquarters in Mobile,

Alabama, until 1984 when he moved to El Cajon, California.

Bibliography: E. Baxter, *The Chief Shepherd of His Sheep* (1987); J. Buckingham, "New Wine Ceases Publication," *Ministries Today* (November/December 1986), 24; S. Strang, "The Discipleship Controversy Three Years Later," *Charisma* (September 1978), 14–24.   S. Strang

BEALL, JAMES LEE (1925–). Prominent figure of the charismatic renewal and pastor of Bethesda Missionary Temple in Detroit, Michigan. Son of Myrtle D. Beall, he was ordained in the late 1940s and became senior pastor of his mother's church of more than three thousand members in the late 1970s. Known for his nationwide radio broadcast, "America to Your Knees," Beall has contributed frequently to *Logos Journal* and to many other charismatic periodicals and has been in continual demand at charismatic conferences and workshops.

Bibliography: "James Beall—An Interview," *Pathfinders* 1 (March–April 1983): 26–28.   R. M. Riss

Myrtle D. Beall, pastor of the Bethesda Missionary Temple, Detroit, became a leader in the New Order of the Latter Rain Movement in 1948.

BEALL, MYRTLE D. (1896–1979). Founder and pastor of Bethesda Missionary Temple in Detroit, Michigan. Born in Hubbell, Michigan, as Myrtle Monville, she was reared in a devout Roman Catholic home. After success in preaching among Methodists, she felt a call to preach independently in the early 1930s, at which time she began a Sunday school for children. As more people became interested in her ministry, a church developed, which eventually became associated with the Assemblies of God. In 1947 she began construction of a three-thousand seat "armory." It was dedicated in 1949. Her church became a center for the 1948 Latter Rain movement, resulting in her withdrawal from the Assemblies of God in 1949. It attracted thousands of visitors seeking a fresh anointing from God. Churches in many parts of North America look to Bethesda for guidance and direction, many of them using for catechetical instruction *Understanding God* (1962) by Patricia D. Gruits, Mrs. Beall's daughter.

Bibliography: M. D. Beall, "A Hand On My Shoulder" (serial article), *LRE* (Detroit) (July 1951).
R. M. Riss

BELGIAN CHARISMATICS   See CHARISMATIC MOVEMENT.

BELGIAN PENTECOSTALS   See EUROPEAN PENTECOSTALISM.

BELL, EUDORUS N. (1866–1923). Former Baptist pastor and first general chairman (title later changed to general superintendent) of the General Council of the Assemblies of God (AG) (1914; 1920–23). Bell was one of the better-educated Pentecostals during the period.

Bell was a twin (his brother was Endorus) and was born at Lake Butler, Florida. Their father died when the boys were only two years old. E. N., as he preferred over Eudorus, was converted at an early age and felt a call into the ministry.

Bell received higher education at Stetson University in the 1890s, Southern Baptist Theological Seminary (1900–1902), and the University of Chicago (B.A., 1903). He pastored Baptist churches for seventeen years.

After hearing about the Pentecostal outpouring in William Durham's North Avenue Mission, Chicago, in 1907, Bell took a leave of absence from his church in north Fort Worth. For eleven months he sought the Pentecostal experience and then received it on July 18, 1908. He returned to Texas and offered his resignation, but the church asked him to stay, which he did for another year.

Bell's first Pentecostal pastorate was in Malvern, Arkansas, where he published a monthly paper, the *Word and Witness*. In December 1913 this paper published the "call" to Hot Springs that resulted in the organization of the AG. Characteristic of his generosity, he gave the *Word and Witness* to the newly formed AG. As editor and general chairman, he helped move the publishing interests to Findlay, Ohio, and then pastored again for two years. From 1917 to 1919 he edited the *Pentecostal Evangel* (also known as *Christian Evangel* and *Weekly Evangel*) and then was elected secretary of the AG in 1919, a position he filled until 1920 when he was once again named general chairman.

J. Roswell Flower, another early leader of the AG described Bell, whom he met in 1912, as the "sweetest, safest and sanest" man he had met in the Pentecostal movement.

Bell's influence in the Pentecostal movement

A Southern Baptist pastor who was baptized in the Spirit, E. N. Bell later became the first chairman of the Assemblies of God.

was far-reaching. When he was rebaptized during the early years of the Oneness controversy, it both shocked and pleased Pentecostals who were divided over the issue. Trinitarians, however, were relieved when he returned to their camp.

Selections from the answer column in the *Pentecostal Evangel* were compiled for a book, *Questions and Answers* (1923), which Gospel Publishing House published after Bell's death. He supported the creation of a Bible school in Springfield, Missouri, and hoped to teach there after completing his duties as general chairman, but he never lived to fulfill that wish, for he died in office in June 1923.

Bibliography: C. Brumback, *Suddenly . . . From Heaven* (1961); S. Frodsham, biographical sketch in E. Bell's *Questions and Answers* (1923); R. Lewis, "E. N. Bell, An Early Pentecostal Spokesman" (unpublished paper, 1985); W. Menzies, *Anointed to Serve* (1971).
W. E. Warner

BENNETT, DENNIS JOSEPH (1917–) **AND RITA** (1934–). Dennis Bennett is an Episcopal clergyman prominently identified with the charismatic renewal from the beginning. The movement is usually dated from the Sunday morning in 1959 when Bennett announced to his congregation in Van Nuys, California, that he had been baptized with the Holy Spirit and had spoken in tongues.

Bennett was born in England, the son of a Congregational minister. The family moved to the U.S. in 1927. He was ordained into the ministry of the Congregational Church in 1949 and served congregations in San Diego, California, from 1949 to 1950.

In 1951 Bennett was appointed lay vicar of St. Paul's Episcopal Church in Lancaster, California. He was ordained a deacon in the Episcopal Church in February of 1952 and a priest in October of 1952. He was called to be rector of St. Mark's Episcopal Church in Van Nuys, California, in 1953.

In 1959, along with many members of his congregation, Bennett received the baptism with the Holy Spirit. A small opposition group in the congregation challenged him to cease and desist from what later came to be called charismatic experiences. He voluntarily resigned his pastorate, feeling that he did not have adequate understanding to defend his position.

Bennett conferred with the presiding bishop of the Episcopal Church and with the other bishops on the West Coast. He was offered churches both in Oregon and Washington. In 1960 he accepted an invitation to become vicar of St. Luke's Episcopal Church in Seattle, Washington. St. Luke's was ready to be closed for the third time.

Within six years the little mission church had become a strong parish; in twelve years one of the strongest churches in the Northwest. For a decade it was the major center from which word of baptism with the Holy Spirit would spread worldwide, especially in the mainline denominations. Thousands of people experienced the baptism with the Holy Spirit as a result of hearing Bennett's testimony. He ministered throughout the U.S. and in many foreign countries; he lectured in major universities and theological schools worldwide; and he was one of the founders of the Episcopal Charismatic Fellowship, later called Episcopal Renewal Ministries. In 1981 he was designated a canon of honor of the Diocese of Olympia by Bishop Robert H. Cochrane, in recognition of his work in the charismatic renewal.

Bennett's first wife, Elberta, died in 1963. He married Rita Marie Reed of Tampa, Florida, in 1966. In 1981 he resigned as rector of St. Luke's to pursue a ministry of writing, traveling and speaking, and conducting seminars and conferences with his wife.

Bennett has authored several books, some with his wife, Rita, that set forth the significance of charismatic experience both for the individual and for the church as a whole. Together with her husband, Dennis, Rita Bennett has been a leading spokesperson of charismatic renewal, particularly in the Anglican Communion. She was born in Michigan, but her family moved to Florida in 1936, where she grew up and received her formal education.

Rita worked in the Florida State Department of Education in child welfare. She placed children in foster care, worked with juvenile court cases and adoption studies. She assisted her brother, Dr. William Standish Reed, in forming the Christian Medical Foundation. In 1963–64 she served as assistant editor of *Trinity* magazine, an influential

publication in the early years of the charismatic movement.

Dennis and Rita Bennett are two of the best-known Episcopalians in the charismatic renewal. They conduct charismatic seminars and have authored several books.

Two years after their marriage Rita and Dennis Bennett formed Christian Renewal Association to minister worldwide and transdenominationally in evangelization, healing, and church renewal. Rita made her mark as a writer with the best seller *The Holy Spirit and You* (1971), which she coauthored with her husband. By 1987 she had authored seven books, three with her husband.

Rita Bennett was in frequent demand as a speaker and Bible study leader for retreats, seminars, and churches in many denominations both in the U.S. and overseas.

See also CHARISMATIC MOVEMENT; EPISCOPAL RENEWAL MINISTRIES.

Bibliography: D. Bennett, *Nine O'Clock in the Morning* (1970); idem, *The Trinity of Man* (1979); D. and R. Bennett, *The Holy Spirit and You* (1971); idem, *The Holy Spirit and You Study Supplement* (1973); idem, *How to Pray for the Release of the Holy Spirit* (1985); idem, *Moving Right Along in the Spirit* (1983); R. Bennett, *Emotionally Free* (1982); idem, *How to Pray for Inner Healing for Yourself and Others* (1984); idem, *I'm Glad You Asked That* (1980); idem, *Making Peace With Your Inner Child* (1987).   L. Christenson

BERG, DANIEL (1884–1963). Swedish Pentecostal missionary. Daniel Berg was born on April 19, 1884, in the city of Vargon, Sweden. His parents were members of the Swedish Baptist movement, and through their influence Berg converted to the movement and was water baptized in 1899. Because of an economic depression, he left Sweden during March 1902 and arrived in Boston three weeks later. Once in the U.S., Berg shared a common history with Adolf

Gunnar Vingren for the next twenty years. Berg was introduced to the Pentecostal movement through a friend while visiting Sweden in 1909. Upon his return to America, he met Vingren during a Pentecostal conference sponsored by the First Swedish Baptist Church in Chicago and later attended several independent Pentecostal churches in the Chicago area, including William H. Durham's North Avenue Mission and the Svenska Pingst Forsamlingen. When Vingren accepted the pastorate of a Swedish Baptist church in South Bend, Indiana, Berg remained in Chicago and worked in a fruit shop. A year later he joined Vingren in South Bend and received the same prophecy from Adolf Uldine to go as a missionary to Para, Brazil. Together these two men returned to Chicago and attended the North Avenue Mission, where they were both dedicated as Pentecostal missionaries by William H. Durham. Shortly afterward they left America and arrived in Brazil on November 19, 1910. During the rest of the decade both men dedicated themselves to establishing the country's first Pentecostal church. As they struggled to organize a church, Berg began working for a shipping company and used part of his income to pay for Vingren's Portuguese lessons. On June 11, 1918, they officially registered their congregation as a church under the name "Assembly of God." From this church grew Brazil's largest Protestant body, the Assemblies of God (AG). After Vingren died in 1932 Berg continued to support Pentecostalism in Brazil. Just two years before his death Berg attended the fifteenth anniversary celebration of the Brazilian AG.

Bibliography: W. J. Hollenweger, *The Pentecostals* (1972); I. Vingren, *Pionjarens dagbok dagboksanteckingar* (1968).   J. Colletti

BERLIN DECLARATION (*Die Berliner Erklärung*). A statement strongly opposing the new Pentecostal movement issued in September 1909 by fifty-six leaders in the Gnadau Alliance, a body representing the Pietist-Holiness current in German Evangelical Protestantism (*Gemeinschaftsbewegung*). The declaration began with a statement, frequently quoted, that the Pentecostal movement was "nicht von oben, sondern von unten" (not from on high, but from below), stating that evil spirits from Satan were at work through cunning and deception to lead souls astray. Reasons given for this rejection included a list of disturbing manifestations alleged to characterize the movement, the practice of prophecy replacing obedience to the Word of God by enslavement to "messages," and the rejection of "the clean heart" doctrine associated with J. Paul, who was accused of teaching the possibility of a condition of *Sundlosigheit* (sinlessness).

The German Pentecostals responded with the Mülheim Declaration the following month, but this never acquired the publicity of the Berlin original. German Evangelicals became divided into a smaller party of "neutrals," who, while not accepting the Pentecostal movement, were open to dialogue and fellowship, and a larger party of *Gegner* (opponents), who refused all association with Pentecostals and stuck by the original declaration. The opposition to Pentecostalism was both fiercer and more theologically sustained than in any other country, and the shadow of the Berlin Declaration still hovered over German Evangelicalism when the charismatic movement arrived in the 1960s.

See also EUROPEAN PENTECOSTALISM.

Bibliography: E. Edel, *Der Kampf um die Pfingstbewegung* (1949); L. Eisenlöffel, . . . *bis alle eins werden* (1979); P. Fleisch, *Die Pfingstbewegung in Deutschland* (1957); E. Giese, *Und flicken die Netze* (1976).
                                                   P. D. Hocken

John Bertolucci, a Catholic priest, was baptized in the Spirit in 1969 and became a popular evangelist in the Catholic renewal through radio and television and other means.

BERTOLUCCI, JOHN (1937–). Catholic charismatic evangelist-preacher. Ordained priest for the diocese of Albany, New York, in 1965, Bertolucci spent much of his first six years as a priest teaching in Catholic schools. In February 1969 he was baptized in the Spirit at a nearby charismatic prayer meeting. From 1971 to 1976 Bertolucci served as vice-chancellor of the Albany diocese, then becoming pastor in Little Falls, New York (1976–80). During the early 1970s Bertolucci's gift for popular evangelism became evident and was recognized by his bishop. By 1980 he sensed the need for a Sabbath year and moved to Steubenville, Ohio, joining the faculty of the University of Steubenville as an assistant professor of theology. In 1981 Bertolucci established the St. Francis Association for Catholic Evangelism (F.A.C.E.), which supports his preaching and his radio and television ministry. His weekly television series, "The Glory of God," begun in 1981, was aired by many networks, cable systems, and television stations in the U.S., Canada, and the Caribbean. Bertolucci began a daily radio ministry in 1984 as host of the program "Let Me Sow Love." His media ministry was terminated in 1987 due to financial and personal stresses.

In 1983 Bertolucci became part of the F.I.R.E. team (see SCANLAN, MICHAEL). His personal story is told in *On Fire with the Spirit* (1984), and his other books include *The Disciplines of a Disciple* (1985), *Straight from the Heart* (1986), and *Healing: God's Work Among Us* (1987).

Bibliography: F. Lilly, "At the Heart of the Renewal," *Charisma* 12 (8, 1987): 16–21.   P. D. Hocken

BETHANY FELLOWSHIP   An organization founded in 1945 to train and support missionaries. Believing in the practice of the early church (Acts 2:45), members sold their possessions, pooled their resources, and purchased a headquarters to carry out their goal. The organization still operates in the same manner. Members live on the Bethany campus, a fifty-seven-acre tract in Bloomington, Minnesota, and work full-time in the various programs sponsored by the Fellowship. Students training for mission fields are involved in vocational as well as theological training.

I. Bethany Fellowship Missions. In the early years Bethany missionary graduates were sent by other missionary societies. In 1963 Bethany formed Bethany Fellowship Missions, a society that has ministry in Brazil, the Caribbean, Mexico, France, Indonesia, the Philippines, Pakistan, and Japan. In addition, Bethany graduates serve with several other missions in different countries, both as short-term and regular-term missionaries. Still other graduates are in full-time Christian service in the U.S.

Brazil was Bethany's first mission field and remains the largest. More than eighty foreign and national staff members are associated with the Brazilian field, which includes three Bible institutes, forty congregations, publishing and bookstore ministries, and various evangelistic outreaches.

II. School and Missions. Approximately two hundred young people are involved in various stages of missionary preparation at the fellowship headquarters. There are three specific areas of preparation: (1) *Academic*. Morning classes prepare students much like other Bible institutes. (2) *Evangelistic*. Each student is assigned to evangelistic activities. (3) *Vocational*. Afternoons are designed to train students in various vocational skills for missionary service, such as printing, construction, maintenance, cooking, cleaning, secretarial work, and manufacturing.

Students select either a theological missions course or a vocational missions course. The training also includes a one-year voluntary internship program. Students earn either a two- or three-year diploma.

III. Printing and Publishing. Thousands of pieces of literature are distributed each year through the printing and publishing divisions. Bethany House Publishers is a book publisher that has published hundreds of originals and reprints. In addition, cassette teaching tapes, tracts, and booklets are distributed. Bethany also publishes a bimonthly magazine, *Message of the Cross*, and has a commercial printing business.

IV. Bethany Missionary Church. This local church is closely related to Bethany Fellowship but is a separate organization. Born out of home Bible studies, the church sponsors many missionaries around the world.

V. Doctrinal Statement. Accepting the generally promoted evangelical view of Scripture, Bethany is a member of the National Association of Evangelicals. It also accepts the Pentecostal teaching on the gifts of the Spirit, believing that they are "still available for the edification of God's people and for the purpose of making them effective witnesses in today's world." Speaking in tongues is viewed as a gift for the church today but not as the evidence of the baptism in the Holy Spirit.

Bibliography: "Bethany School of Missions," packet (1986); *Message of the Cross* magazine.   W. E. Warner

BETHANY FELLOWSHIP (SUSSEX, ENGLAND)   See CHARISMATIC COMMUNITIES.

BETHESDA MISSIONARY TEMPLE   See MYRTLE D. BEALL.

BETTEX, PAUL   (1864–1916). Missionary. Bettex was born in Switzerland to Huguenot parents. His father, Jean Frederic Bettex, was a distinguished Christian apologist whose books were later published in English by Moody Bible Institute. The younger Bettex studied at the University of Geneva, various Italian schools, and the Sorbonne, with the intention of entering the French diplomatic corps.

Bettex was converted to Christ through the ministry of the Salvation Army in Paris. In 1886 he traveled to Ireland and then to Santiago, Chile, in 1889 to teach at an American Presbyterian mission. On the advice of a colleague, he enrolled at Princeton Theological Seminary in 1890. One biographer, Stanley H. Frodsham, claims that Bettex received the baptism in the Holy Spirit and spoke in tongues during a revival on campus. After pastoring rural churches near Detroit and Pittsburgh, Bettex traveled to Uruguay, Argentina, and Brazil for missionary service. Stories about his dedication and the hardships that he faced circulated back to the U.S., and he became a missionary hero in some circles.

Returning to the U.S. in 1903, Bettex taught at Central Holiness University in Oskaloosa, Iowa, during the winter of 1906. The trustees of the institution later dismissed him for what they considered to be fanatical behavior. He eventually attended the meetings at the Azusa Street revival in Los Angeles, California, and quickly joined the ranks of the Pentecostal movement. A burden for evangelism in China prompted him to travel there in 1910. While there he met and married Nellie Clark, a missionary with the London Missionary Society.

Although the circumstances surrounding the death of Nellie Clark Bettex in 1912 are contradictory, her passing aided in convincing some independent Pentecostals that the problem of missionary support needed to be addressed. Paul Bettex was murdered in China in 1916, and the events surrounding his death remain uncertain. He was buried in Canton, where a memorial chapel was erected. Although his methods were often unorthodox, his concern for world evangelization inspired others for the cause of foreign missions.

Bibliography: S. H. Frodsham, *Wholly for God* (n.d.); E. Gordon, *A Book of Protestant Saints* (1940); G. B. McGee, *This Gospel Shall Be Preached* (1986).

G. B. McGee

BHENGU, NICHOLAS BHEKINKOSI HEPWORTH (1909–86). Church leader and evangelist known throughout Africa as "the black Billy Graham." Nicholas Bhengu was born in Zululand, the grandson of a Zulu chief. His father was an evangelist at the Norwegian Lutheran mission church at Eshowe, Zululand, where Nicholas attended school. Later he enrolled at the Roman Catholic Institute there for his secondary education. As a youth he was attracted to Marxism but returned to Christianity by the time he was twenty. He later studied at the South Africa General Mission Bible Training School in Dumisa, Natal, Republic of South Africa. After graduating in 1937 he began work as a court interpreter because of his proficiency in several languages. Feeling called to the ministry, he resigned to enter full-time evangelism in 1938. He began to conduct "Back to God Crusades," having been inspired by a dream in which he heard the words, "Africa must get back to God." Eventually he became affiliated with the South African Assemblies of God (AG).

Bhengu traveled extensively in evangelistic work and financed his Africa crusades with funds he raised on preaching tours in the U.S. (1954, 1958), Canada, England, Scotland, and Norway. By 1959 he had established, directly or indirectly, more than 50 churches, with an approximate membership of 15,000. At the time of his death, there were 1,700 assemblies, 450 ministers, and 250,000 members.

Bhengu's preaching had a profound effect on the spiritual and moral values of South Africans. In some areas where he ministered, the crime rate dropped by as much as one-third. It was not unusual for people to respond to his messages by leaving their weapons (knives, blackjacks, brass knuckles) and stolen goods in piles at his feet. At one time, Bhengu set as his goal the reduction of crime in Johannesburg by 25 percent.

The South African AG eventually came to be closely governed by "apostles" who also spearheaded evangelism and church planting; Bhengu was considered one of the apostles and strongly defended this system of church government.

In 1974 Bhengu served as a Fellow at Selly Oak Colleges in England, teaching in the field of evangelism. Eleven years later he became ill with cancer. His memorial service was held in the Methodist Central Hall in Durban. Crowds upward of 20,000 attended the interment at Piet Marithberg.

Several weeks before Bhengu's death he wrote:

Build the Church of God. The names of our Churches are our own inventions and not God's! Let the Christians come together as God's children. Build the nation where you are remembering that you are part of that nation

and you are in it for a specific purpose for God. Pray for all leaders in Africa, support leaders of your nation and present Christ to them by all means. The Church is the light of the world. The Church is the salt of the earth and the Church should lead the nation to peace, unity and prosperity (Bhengu, 1986, 16).

Bibliography: N. B. H. Bhengu, *Revival Fire in South Africa* (1949); "The Black Billy Graham," *Time* (November 23, 1959), 69–70; W. J. Hollenweger, *The Pentecostals* (1972); Bhengu, "Farewell Message to the Church," *World Pentecost* (July 1986), 16; idem, "The Soul of South Africa," *Decision* (October 1974), 4, and (November 1974), 10; "The Growth and Expansion of Brother Bhengu's Work from 1945–To Date," "Homecall of 'The Black Apostle,'" "Nicholas Bhengu Was a Man With a Mission," *World Pentecost* (July 1986), 16ff.

G. B. McGee

BIBLE COLLEGES See BIBLE INSTITUTES, COLLEGES, UNIVERSITIES.

BIBLE INSTITUTES, COLLEGES, UNIVERSITIES
    I. Philosophy
    II. History
    III. Present

I. Philosophy. Pentecostals have generally been ambivalent about higher education, with many regarding it with open suspicion. Although from the beginning some groups recognized the need to provide at least basic theological training for their ministers, it was generally agreed that the historic denominations had lost their spirituality in direct relationship to their emphasis on education. In fact, higher education was thought to be so threatening in one's spiritual welfare that for decades few Pentecostals chose to enroll in any but Pentecostal schools.

Even though Pentecostals claimed it was not education that they opposed but an education that destroyed faith or reduced dependence on the Holy Spirit, the lack of Pentecostal liberal arts colleges, universities, and seminaries effectively limited most adherents to a modest Bible school education. As late as 1949 the General Council of the Assemblies of God (AG), the Pentecostal denomination with the largest number of schools, both refused to authorize the creation of a liberal arts college and took action to ensure that an academic degree could never be required for ministerial ordination. The Pentecostal experience rather than formal education had become the essential requirement for Pentecostal ministry. A residual belief that spirituality and higher education are basically incompatible has limited the support of Pentecostals for higher education throughout their movement's history.

The development of Pentecostal schools has also been affected by the movement's deep commitment to the doctrine of the imminent return of Christ. Because the Pentecostal revival was regarded as the fulfillment of Joel's prophecy of a latter rain that would prepare for the Second Coming (Joel 2:23), it followed that the limited time before that climactic event should be used for matters more urgent than building or even attending schools. This sense of urgency prompted more than one early Pentecostal to leave college to begin preaching, and it partially explains the great evangelistic and missionary emphasis of the movement. It also explains why Pentecostals have generously supported foreign missions and overseas Bible schools but, paradoxically, have been reluctant to adequately support the domestic colleges that prepare their missionaries.

Support for strong Pentecostal colleges and universities has also been compromised by the belief that, whatever its value, formal education is unnecessary. From the earliest days, Pentecostal ministers and laypersons alike seemed to do quite well without formal education. Many felt that as Christ had used untutored fishermen to begin his church, he could use "unlearned men" to complete it (Acts 4:13 KJV). Although of the twenty-seven early Pentecostal leaders identified in one study, 78 percent had received some postadolescent education, well above the national average for the time (Anderson, 1979, 102), many Pentecostal pioneers lacked any formal theological training, and a few were barely literate. One of the most admired of the early Pentecostals, Smith Wigglesworth, had been a semiliterate plumber before his Pentecostal experience propelled him into worldwide evangelism. His proud boast was that he had never read a book other than the Bible (Frodsham, 1951, 109). Almost any Pentecostal who wished to could find a place to preach without benefit of formal education, and as late as the mid 1950s, a significant number of Pentecostal ministers lacked formal theological training (Hollenweger, 1977, 40).

Few in the lower-middle-class constituency that comprised the membership of most of the classical Pentecostal churches in their formative decades had attended college. Not surprisingly, disciplined, hard-working Pentecostals who had succeeded as businessmen or farmers with little or no formal education tended to discount its value. Their bias was reinforced by the subtle or even overt criticism of higher education often heard in their churches. Some smaller Pentecostal groups have opposed all formal training for their ministers, adopting a policy of providing any needed preparation through the local church. Pentecostal ministers with limited educational credentials have continued to enjoy places of prominence, which seemingly proves that formal education is unnecessary or even harmful.

Even if Pentecostals had been more sympathetic to higher education, the practical problems of building and supporting colleges would have limited the enterprise. The early fragmentation of the Pentecostal movement into struggling and even competitive denominations worked against the establishing of large schools, and the limited financial resources of most modest Pentecostal congregations made it difficult to obtain the fiscal support required to create quality schools. The struggle to maintain even modest Bible institutes made the development of more comprehensive and expensive accredited colleges seem virtually impossible.

But in spite of this resistance to higher education, Pentecostals have always recognized that schools afford an effective means to train workers, perpetuate their distinctive doctrines and experiences, and deepen the devotion and commitment of their youth. Consequently, in their nearly ninety-year history, Pentecostals have established more than a hundred Bible institutes and colleges in the U.S. and well over three hundred in the rest of the world. The major Pentecostal denominations, strong local churches, and prominent Pentecostal personalities from Aimee Semple McPherson to Jimmy Swaggart have founded schools to share and perpetuate their visions. Over the decades, probably a majority of the Pentecostal clergy have attended some type of Bible institute or college. Most recognize the important role played by such institutions, remain loyal to their own schools, and give at least moral support to Pentecostal higher education.

Growth and prosperity among classical Pentecostals and the impact of the charismatic movement have brought some changes. More Pentecostal youth attend college, and a growing number of Pentecostal colleges have been accredited. Graduate programs and even charismatic universities have been established; however, the colleges have yet to earn academic distinction, and the universities, though promising, remain better known for their founders than their scholarship. In striking contrast to their achievements in church building, foreign missions, Sunday schools, and the electronic media, Pentecostals have been content with small, modestly funded, minimally staffed, and often unaccredited Bible institutes and colleges.

II. History. In the first two decades of their movement, the Pentecostals who wished formal study utilized two types of schools. Short-term Bible schools, such as Charles F. Parham's Bethel Bible School in Topeka, Kansas, where the twentieth-century Pentecostal movement may have begun, provided one option. Bethel opened in 1900 in a rented three-story residence, with Parham as the only teacher. Though he had attended college briefly, he lacked a degree and teaching and administrative experience. Students were attracted to the school by announcements in his bimonthly paper, *The Apostolic Faith*. No charge was made for tuition or living expenses. Students contributed whatever they could, including a cow, which was pastured in the back yard. Approximately thirty-five students enrolled, twelve of whom already held ministerial credentials with the Methodists, Friends, Holiness, or other groups. The Bible was the only textbook. A subject such as repentance, conversion, or healing was selected. References on the subject were located and Bible passages memorized for presentation to the class. Parham also gave lectures and ended the unit with an examination. Bethel was not intended to be a permanent school, and, in fact, lasted less than a year (Parham, 1930, 51–67).

Dozens of similar schools were conducted in the midwestern and southern states in the next two decades, including another that Parham opened in Houston, Texas, in 1905. Lacking textbooks, developed curricula, and permanent facilities, the schools had little more to offer than the skills and zeal of their teachers, which, in some cases at least, were substantial. D. W. Myland,

An important early center of Pentecostal ministry in the eastern part of the United States was Bethel Pentecostal Assembly on the right, and Bethel Bible Training School, left, in Newark, New Jersey.

who directed a short-term school at Plainfield, Indiana, was described by a knowledgeable student as "a prince among Bible teachers" (Brumback, 1961, 227). D. C. O. Opperman, who had headed John Alexander Dowie's educational system in Zion, Illinois, conducted scores of six-week Bible schools in midwestern states before becoming a highly respected leader in the AG.

Although the limitations of such schools were obvious, they did provide basic training in Pentecostal beliefs and experience. The stated purpose of Opperman's schools was to learn "How to pray, how to study the word, how to know God and walk with Him" (*Word and Witness*, December 20, 1913). Classes were sometimes interrupted by spontaneous prayer, praise, and the exercise of spiritual gifts. Some of the distinctive aspects of Pentecostal worship apparently developed in these classes. Certainly some of the future Pentecostal pastors and leaders received their training at such schools. Opperman alone is credited with the training of hundreds of Pentecostal ministers. The mobility of these schools allowed them to take their teaching to the people who could not attend a conventional school. However, none of them had more than a few dozen students, and thus their effectiveness and contribution were limited.

The early Pentecostal movement was also served by more permanent faith Bible or mission-ary training schools, such as Rochester Bible Training School in Rochester, New York. Elizabeth V. Baker and her four sisters founded the school in 1906 in conjunction with their Elim Missionary Home and Tabernacle just prior to their acceptance of the Pentecostal experience. Housed in a three-story brick building adjacent to the tabernacle, the school opened with twenty students and five teachers. The two-year course was described as "strictly Biblical having the Bible as our chief text-book" (Baker, 1984, 132). In addition to book-by-book surveys of the Bible, courses in theology, evangelism, homiletics, exegesis, dispensational truth, tabernacle studies, and missionary work were offered. The school operated on faith, and students who could contribute little or nothing were encouraged to learn to trust God by praying in their fees. A strong missionary emphasis led many of the students to leave for the mission field immediately after graduation. When the school closed after eighteen years of operation, it had trained four hundred graduates, including fifty foreign missionaries.

When a small group of southern Holiness churches accepted the Pentecostal experience in 1907, they continued to be served by Holmes Theological Seminary, a small but established Bible school in Greenville, South Carolina, that had been founded in 1898. The Gospel School in Finley, Ohio, which opened in 1908 and operated

Beginning with a graduate school of communications in 1977, Pat Robertson founded CBN University in Virginia Beach, Virginia.

for a decade before moving to Chicago; Beulah Heights Bible and Missionary Training School (1912), which operated in Dergen, New Jersey, for thirty years; and Bethel Bible Training Institute in Newark (1916) also provided a modest education for early Pentecostals.

These institutions rarely had more than forty students and emphasized practical training and personal piety more than academic excellence. They did provide a two-year course, a more extensive curriculum, and better facilities than the short-term schools. These modest institutions turned out an impressive number of pastors and future Pentecostal leaders who would shape and direct their infant churches. Several of their teachers were to have long and illustrious careers in Pentecostal education, thereby influencing the more permanent Pentecostal schools that were to follow.

By 1920 it was apparent that the Pentecostals had been isolated from the established churches, and in spite of their opposition to man-made organizations, had in effect established new Pentecostal denominations that required more permanent and structured schools for their workers. By that time the Bible institute, pioneered by A. B. Simpson, D. L. Moody, and A. J. Gordon in the 1880s, had been widely adopted as the appropriate means of training fundamentalist-evangelical youth. Many Pentecostals, including D. W. Myland and each of the principals at Bethel in Newark, had attended such schools and recognized them to be particularly applicable to the needs of the Pentecostal movement.

Bible schools required neither a college degree nor even a high school diploma for admission. Academic standards were of less importance than spiritual commitment. Low tuition allowed many to attend who would not have been able to attend a conventional college. At a time when few seminaries accepted women, Bible institutes were open to both sexes. Courses were designed to encourage faith in the power of the Bible as opposed to its critical analysis. Terms were short, and the entire course of study was rarely more than two years. The brief time in school was sufficient to inspire students with a vision for service while pushing them into ministry before the vision was lost. Every effort was made to maintain a spiritually charged environment that would encourage personal piety and prepare gospel workers while not using the limited time in theological speculation or unnecessarily subjecting students to controversial issues. Consequently a greater emphasis was placed on indoctrination than intellectual development, to avoid compromise and assure the propagation of the full gospel. And so the Bible institute became the Pentecostal answer to the challenge of providing ministerial training while protecting students from the perceived threats of higher education.

But even a simple Bible institute required greater resources than the embryonic Pentecostal denominations could muster, and the early Pentecostal schools proved to be only modest versions of the established and better-known Bible institutes. Although the Church of God (CG) at Cleveland, Tennessee, recognized the need for a school and formed a committee in 1911 to find a location and erect buildings, its first Bible institute did not open until 1918, when twelve students and one teacher met in a room over the denominational print shop (Conn, 148). It took the AG six years to open its first school, the Midwest Bible School in Auburn, Nebraska, and it lasted only nine months because of lack of support (Moore, 1954, 105).

Eventually, denominational schools were established. In addition to the school begun by the CG in 1918, the Pentecostal Holiness church, though served by Holmes Theological Seminary, opened a second school in Franklin Springs, Georgia, in

1919; the AG began Central Bible Institute in Springfield, Missouri, in 1922; Aimee Semple McPherson began the Lighthouse of International Foursquare Evangelism in 1923; and Bible Standard organization established its school in Eugene, Oregon, early in 1925. Over the next two decades forty other Pentecostal Bible institutes were established across the nation. Many were founded, owned, and operated by individuals or strong local churches though they sought to serve the wider Pentecostal community. After a slow start, the Oneness Pentecostals began their first school in St. Paul, Minnesota, in 1937, followed by nine other endorsed schools in America. Black Pentecostals were unsuccessful in their early attempt to start a Bible institute in Dallas, Texas, but did begin one in Goldsboro, North Carolina, in 1944.

Though each of these schools was unique, they shared certain characteristics. They were small. Until the late 1940s their enrollments ranged from fewer than 50 to more than 500 students, but few exceeded 200. Over a twenty-year period, one of the stronger schools averaged 17 in its graduating classes. Although this allowed a personal concern and intimacy that a larger school could not match, it also resulted in a high mortality rate. At least fifteen Bible institutes in the AG alone closed by 1941 (Menzies, 1971, 355). Those that survived into the 1950s tended to be stronger and larger, with some student bodies exceeding 500. However, in 1970 the seven remaining Oneness Pentecostal schools averaged 144 students.

These schools were located in a variety of facilities, from converted mansions to a former night club. They often met in or adjacent to a sponsoring church. On occasion new facilities were constructed. An imposing six-story reinforced concrete building to house students and classrooms was erected in San Francisco for Glad Tidings Bible Institute (GTBI) in 1924. Although that metropolitan school lacked a campus, Central Bible Institute (CBI) in Springfield, Missouri, was housed in a new brick building on what would become a fifty-acre site. Elim Bible Institute near Rochester, New York, founded in 1924, eventually moved to a historic eighty-five-acre campus that had housed colleges for 140 years.

A study of the English Bible was the heart of the curriculum, but classes in such subjects as English, biblical languages, music, and applied classes in soul winning, missions, and apologetics were gradually added. What passed as a library was usually little more than a few hundred largely donated volumes on religious subjects, shelved in a small room. An emphasis was placed on the mastering of doctrinal positions and the memorization of Scripture rather than critical thought or scholarly research. Study time was limited for students who were working their way through school and spending considerable time in applied ministry.

Teachers were not required to have degrees, and few did. As late as 1943 their average post-high-school education was less than four years (Menzies, 1977, 355). Graduate degrees were

even more rare. Experience, teaching gifts, or willingness to serve were the primary qualifications. Although some of the teachers were well trained and their classes became legendary, they were the exception. At times the wives of teachers were also given classes for which they had few apparent qualifications. No accreditation body existed to recognize or evaluate these schools, and transfer credit by accredited colleges was rarely expected or granted. Admission was opened to virtually anyone who professed conversion and a desire to study the Bible. Few academic records were maintained, and graduation was achieved by remaining in the school for the full course. Although the early Bible institutes initially offered only two years of study, a third was eventually added by most.

Particularly in their early days, the Bible institutes tended to be dominated by a strong leader. GTBI, which had opened in San Francisco in 1919, was led and controlled by its founders, Robert and Mary Craig. Craig, a former Methodist minister, became a veritable spiritual father, shaping the lives and ministries of his students through his daily early morning chapel sessions. The Craigs' influence was enormous, extending even to such personal matters as the choice of a marriage partner. Students who failed to fulfill the ministry expected of them were reluctant to return and meet the Craigs' disapproval, while the more successful were proud to report any achievements. Ivan Q. Spencer at Elim in Rochester; P. C. Nelson at Southwestern Bible School in Enid, Oklahoma; and W. I. Evans at CBI in Springfield, Missouri, were only a few of the other strong personalities who dominated their respective schools.

This education was designed to prepare students for the Pentecostal ministry, and, consequently, formal classes were only a part of the program. Spiritual development and applied ministry were of major importance. Students were expected to participate in such activities as mission services, street meetings, and jail ministry. The schools that were related to churches also required choir, orchestra, and prayer participation in regular services, in some cases on a nightly basis. Although a majority of the graduates at least attempted to enter full-time ministry as pastors, evangelists, or missionaries, the attrition rates for these ministries was high. As a result, the majority of students were educated for work they failed to pursue.

For this education students paid a tuition of only a few dollars a month when it was collected. In some cases, none was charged, and the schools operated by faith. This was made possible, in part, by employing teachers and staff who were willing to work for little more than a subsistence wage. The schools lacked endowment but depended on the gifts of friends. One founder's $80,000 inheritance made possible a new building (Brumback, 1961, 234). Because Pentecostals made little provision for the support of their schools, the normal procedure was for them to appeal to their constituencies for emergency offerings to keep the doors open in the frequent times of financial exigency.

This early Bible training school directed by D. C. O. Opperman operated in Eureka Springs, Arkansas, beginning in 1916. It became probably the first Oneness Pentecostal school.

Little social activity was provided and fewer recreational facilities. With rare exception, there were no organized intramural or intercollegiate athletic programs. Through the 1940s most schools required their women students to wear uniforms and men to wear ties and jackets. Strict regulations attempted to prevent romantic contact between the sexes, and marriage during the school year was a cause for immediate dismissal. In spite of this, many couples who were inspired with the same ministry ideals married soon after graduation.

Whatever their strengths or limitations, these schools shaped the Pentecostal churches. Their graduates became the pioneers of the majority of Pentecostal churches in the U.S. and the missionaries responsible for planting them around the world. The doctrines and practices they had learned provided the accepted norms for church administration, doctrine, and personal piety. Equipped with but two or three years of training, graduates often began ministry in their early twenties. Their modest education had given them few illusions about their professional standing, and because little or no financial support was available from their developing denominations, the Bible institute graduates were ready to make sacrifices, live modestly, and even work with their hands to support their families and build churches.

There were, however, less happy consequences. The meager quality of their education hardly prepared these committed souls for certain aspects of the ministry. Poorly trained ministers often remained at a given charge for only months before moving on, leaving an infant congregation behind. As a direct consequence of these rapid changes by eager but inexperienced pastors, Pentecostal churches in many communities failed to grow for many decades.

Those who did identify with the Pentecostals were more often from the working class, with limited education themselves. Educated professionals who were already biased against the supernatural and emotional aspects of Pentecostalism found little in these poorly trained ministers to attract them. The result was the creation of churches virtually without professionals such as doctors, lawyers, and teachers and without the financial and leadership resources they could provide. With limited contact to the intellectual community, Pentecostals became increasingly anti-intellectual, glorying in being the Lord's despised few. One result of this alienation was the development of something of a Pentecostal subculture. In spite of the impressive numerical gains of the Pentecostals, the movement appeared limited to a lower-middle-class constituency.

By the outbreak of World War II, there were signs that this trend was changing. Experience had demonstrated that Bible institute education had not prepared for the marketplace those students who had not entered, or at least remained, in the ministry. Recognizing this, several schools added business courses. Key Pentecostal denominations had considered the need for liberal arts colleges as early as 1935, though no apparent progress had been made in implementation. Progress in the development of junior colleges came first. Black Pentecostals began a small junior college in Lexington, Michigan, in 1918. The Bible Training School (later Lee College), operated by the Church of God, added a junior college division in 1941. Southwestern Bible Institute (AG) followed with a similar program in 1944.

In 1939, believing that a broader education was required to meet the needs of the fast-growing Pentecostal movement, Southern California Bible College (SCBC) in Pasadena added a fourth year and was recognized by the state as a degree-granting institution. During the war this allowed SCBC to train military chaplains, a fact not unnoticed by other Pentecostal schools. After the war thousands of Pentecostal servicemen returned ready for further education at government expense. To qualify to train these veterans, schools were required to meet certain standards. Nonetheless, mature servicemen recognized some of the deficiencies in the quality of the Pentecostal schools that were available to them and, in some cases, worked for their improvement.

The war had also brought new affluence to many first- and second-generation Pentecostal parents who wanted better educations for their offspring than they had enjoyed. A new educational discrimination became apparent as some parents began sending their Pentecostal children to better-developed evangelical or even secular colleges and universities. The fact that those who went off to non-Pentecostal schools were often lost to the movement contributed to a growing sentiment for better Pentecostal schools.

In 1947 the new National Association of Evangelicals was instrumental in forming the first Bible institute accrediting association, which would become the American Association of Bible Colleges (AABC). Pentecostals sat on its founding board, and a number of Pentecostal Bible institutes and colleges immediately applied for accreditation. To gain recognition with the new body, Bible schools were forced to meet higher library, record-keeping, and faculty educational standards. Eventually, more than twenty schools affiliated with five Pentecostal denominations became members of this body, substantially improving their educational offerings. After rejecting outside accreditation for many years, L.I.F.E. Bible College, the larger Foursquare school in Los Angeles, was accredited by the AABC in 1980.

Once begun, the movement toward accreditation proved hard to resist. Following the lead of many evangelical Bible institutes that had determined that the needs of their youth could be better served through regionally accredited liberal arts colleges, some Pentecostal educators began promoting and working for regionally accredited liberal arts colleges that would provide the education required for most graduate programs, teacher certification, and entrance into virtually all professions.

In 1962 SCBC, which in 1950 had moved from Pasadena to Costa Mesa, dropped Bible from its name, withdrew from the AABC, and two years later was accredited by the Western Association of Schools and Colleges as a four-year liberal arts college. It did so at the cost of at least temporarily alienating much of its constituency, who feared the school was following the path of the many church-related colleges that had lost their evangelical fervor and even their Christian commitment. In 1955 the AG opened Evangel College on fifty-nine acres in Springfield, Missouri, as a denominationally sponsored liberal arts college (Menzies, 1971, 362–63). Lee College of the CG, which had added a four-star liberal arts curriculum, received regional accreditation in 1969.

Accreditation required higher salaries, a more complex curriculum, science laboratories, a more extensive library, and other requirements that made liberal arts schools much more expensive than Bible colleges. And because Pentecostals had never learned to support higher education and their middle-class young people could not pay high tuition, maintaining the liberal arts colleges proved difficult. The alumni funds that assisted many schools were unavailable because many graduates served as low paid ministers or missionaries. A qualified faculty presented another problem. By its failure to emphasize higher education, the Pentecostal movement lacked the required supply of accredited doctorates in many academic disciplines.

Nonetheless, one by one Bible colleges saw the need and advantages of regional accreditation. To avoid alienating conservative supporters, the name "Bible" was retained and a substantial Bible requirement placed on all students. In a number of cases, the U.S. government contributed to the move toward accredited education by providing financial assistance through student loans, veterans' benefits, and state scholarships. Government programs to encourage the expansion of colleges in the postwar era even made possible the building of new buildings. Several major grants of surplus property assisted in the development of new college campuses (Nelson, 1987, 417–46). Though many Pentecostal schools have remained Bible colleges, at least ten regionally accredited Pentecostal colleges now exist.

Nationally known evangelist Oral Roberts had experienced the frustration of seeking an education within Pentecostal ranks, and he, believing that thousands of young people were being lost to the full gospel movement for want of a quality Pentecostal university, determined to provide a university to serve classical Pentecostals as well as the growing number of charismatics. Oral Roberts University opened in 1964 on 180 acres in Tulsa, Oklahoma. Its futuristic architecture and educational innovation won it immediate recognition, and in an unusually short six years it was granted accreditation by the North Central Association of Colleges and Schools. By recruiting outstanding athletic talent, ORU was soon competing with the nation's best-known universities and earning national recognition. The fund-raising ability of its founder allowed the continued development of the $60 million campus, including a $2 million aerobic center, a 10,000-seat special events center, and a 200-foot-high prayer tower. Subsidized tuition further assisted the rapid growth of the university so that by 1986 it had a student body of nearly five thousand, over twice the size of any other Pentecostal college. Professional schools were added in dentistry, law, medicine, nursing, social work, theology, and music. Accreditation for these programs led to prolonged, bitter, but eventually successful fights with the American Bar Association and the medical community (Harrell, 1985, 223).

Unlike the earlier Pentecostals, the new charismatics expected their youth to be educated, and many flocked to the beautiful new charismatic campus. By 1975 only half of the student body was associated with classical Pentecostal denominations even though its Pentecostal commitment remained strong.

In 1975 Pat Robertson, founder of the Christian Broadcasting Network (CBN), believed he was directed to buy two hundred acres of land in Virginia Beach, Virginia, to house a new headquarters and university. Over the next three years the vision developed so that in 1978 CBN University opened its doors with seventy-nine graduate students in communication. It was determined that the university would offer only graduate education and soon was drawing students from scores of secular and religious schools. Within six years it had won regional accreditation and had begun offering degrees in education, business administration, biblical studies, public policy, and journalism. In 1986 the law school that had been located at ORU was transferred to CBN. Enrollment exceeded nine hundred students coming from all fifty states and many foreign countries. Though the leadership of CBN is charismatic, only one-third of the students

indicating a church membership came from classical Pentecostal churches.

In the early 1980s, Youth With a Mission, a charismatic missionary-evangelistic ministry operating in many countries, founded Pacific and Asia Christian University in Hawaii. A nontraditional school, it alternates terms of study with extended periods of ministry in an attempt to join the theoretical with the practical. Its lack of a paid faculty, meager library, and limited curriculum indicate that regional accreditation may be difficult to obtain.

Southern California College also joined the move toward graduate education in 1984. With the collapse of Melodyland School of Theology in Anaheim, California, the college recognized that no regionally accredited programs existed in the western U.S. and began an M.A. program in biblical studies and church administration.

III. Present. This movement toward accredited education produced a reaction among many Pentecostals who believed the early unaccredited Bible institutes had better served the needs of Pentecostals. Some of the existing schools refused to move toward accreditation and continued to offer a traditional Bible college education. Gordon Lindsay, who had been a leader in the healing movement of the 1950s, founded Christ for the Nations in Dallas, Texas, in 1972 shortly before his death. Though its seventy-five-acre campus was modern and impressive, its curriculum and emphasis were a return to the earlier Bible and missionary training schools. It grew rapidly to over one thousand students who could earn an Associate of Practical Theology degree in two years. It has never sought accreditation.

In the 1970s and '80s numerous Bible institutes were founded across the nation that were designed to promote personal spiritual growth and service with no expectation of accreditation. Genesis, which began in Santa Rosa, California, and Rhema Bible Training Center in Tulsa, Oklahoma, were two of the earlier such institutions. Many of them were sponsored by local churches with classes offered exclusively at night. Housed in local churches without extensive libraries and expensive faculties, these schools were able to operate economically at a time when accredited Bible colleges were raising their tuition beyond the means of many.

In 1982, while the existing Pentecostal schools were struggling for finances and students, Evangelist Jimmy Swaggart announced the founding of a new Bible college in Baton Rouge, Louisiana. His name and resources as a leading television evangelist allowed him to construct within five years a handsome campus with an enrollment of 1,500 students. It has been announced that Jimmy Swaggart Bible College will seek accreditation with AABC. But the future of the college now is uncertain in the wake of Swaggart's confession of a liaison with a prostitute.

Currently Pentecostal higher education is offered in a wide range of options from modest local Bible institutes to accredited universities. Although this variety makes Pentecostal education widely available, it has also fragmented resources. If stronger colleges and universities that might better serve the Pentecostal movement are to develop, Pentecostals will have to recognize the need for such schools and make a commitment to support them.

Bibliography: R. Anderson, *Vision of the Disinherited* (1979); E. Baker, *Chronicles of a Faith Life* (1984); V. Brereton, *Protestant Fundamentalist Bible Schools 1882–1940*, Ph.D. thesis, Columbia University (1981); C. Brumback, *Suddenly . . . From Heaven* (1961); R. Chandler, "Melodyland School: The Spirit's Time," *Christianity Today* 17 (July 20, 1973): 42; C. Conn, *Like a Mighty Army* (1955); A. Flower, *Grace for Grace* (privately printed, n.d.), 1961); S. Frodsham, *Smith Wigglesworth, Apostle of Faith* (1951); D. Harrell, Jr., *Oral Roberts* (1985); W. Hollenweger, *The Pentecostals* (1977); C. Jones, *A Guide to the Study of the Pentecostal Movement*, 2 vols. (1983); R. Mitchell, *Heritage and Horizons: The History of Open Bible Standard Churches* (1982); W. Menzies, *Anointed to Serve* (1971); E. Moore, "Handbook of Pentecostal Denominations in the United States," M.A. thesis, Pasadena College (1954); L. Nelson, "The Demise of O'Reilly Hospital and the Beginning of Evangel College," *Missouri Historical Review* (1987), 117–46; J. Nichol, *Pentecostalism* (1966); S. Parham, *The Life of Charles F. Parham* (privately printed, 1930); *Word and Witness* 9 (December 20, 1913): 1.
L. F. Wilson

BIBLE STANDARD CONFERENCE See OPEN BIBLE STANDARD CHURCHES, INC.

BIBLE WAY CHURCHES OF OUR LORD JESUS CHRIST WORLDWIDE Charges of misgovernment in the Church of Our Lord Jesus Christ of the Apostolic Faith led to the calling of the 1957 ministers' conference in Washington, D.C., which established the Bible Way Church of Our Lord Jesus Christ World Wide. Approximately seventy congregations followed Elders Smallwood E. Williams (b. 1907), John S. Beane, McKinley Williams (b. 1901), Winfield Showall, and Joseph Moore into the new church. The Oneness teachings of the new body are identical to those of the parent. Members are required to tithe, to be present each time the Holy Communion is observed, and to attend all business meetings. Bible Way churches forbid the use of tobacco and alcohol and the remarriage of divorced persons as long as their original partners live. They label as fanatical those who preach against the straightening and shampooing of hair and the wearing of neckties or shoes without toes or heels. The denomination is centered in Bishop Smallwood Williams's church in Washington. By 1975 it claimed 350 congregations and 30,000 members in the U.S. and 16 congregations and 1,000 members in the U.K. It sponsors missions in Jamaica, Trinidad and Tobago, Liberia, and Nigeria.

Bibliography: C. E. Jones, *Black Holiness* (1987); A. C. Piepkorn, *Profiles in Belief*, vol. 3 (1979).
C. E. Jones

BIBLIOGRAPHY AND HISTORIOGRAPHY OF PENTECOSTALISM (U.S.)

I. Bibliography
II. Historiography
   A. The Governance of History
   B. The Direction of History
   C. Supernatural Versus Natural Causation in History
   D. The Definition of the Movement
   E. Geographical and Social Origins of Pentecostalism
   F. The Movement's Place in History

I. Bibliography. After years of benign neglect, scholarly resources for the study of American Pentecostalism are beginning to tumble off the presses at an astonishing rate. The literature on the subject has become so extensive that bibliographic guides are virtually indispensable. For serious researchers, Charles Edwin Jones, *A Guide to the Study of the Pentecostal Movement* (2 vols., 1983), looms as the most comprehensive listing of primary and secondary materials available in English. Most of its seven thousand entries refer to primary texts. The majority are doctrinal or devotional in nature, yet scores of dissertations and hundreds of historical and social scientific items are noted. Perhaps the most delectable treat for the hungry researcher is the large number of entries for tunebooks, pamphlets, and tracts, as well as articles in obscure or long-extinct popular magazines. The focus is on North American English-language materials, but the growth of Pentecostalism in other parts of the world is not ignored.

Additional bibliographies of varying comprehensiveness and emphasis are worth noting. Watson E. Mills, *Charismatic Religion in Modern Research: A Bibliography* (1985), contains 2,100 entries, primarily limited to more scholarly books and articles. Another helpful resource is the copious notes of Arthur Carl Piepkorn, *Profiles in Belief*, vol. 3, *Holiness and Pentecostal* (1979). David W. Faupel, *The American Pentecostal Movement* (1972), offers a much slimmer survey of the literature than the ones noted above, but for routine reference needs it is adequate and handily organized. Still more compact, but more up to date and broad ranging, are Cecil M. Robeck, Jr., "The Pentecostal Movements in the U.S.: Recent Historical Bibliography," in *Evangelical Studies Bulletin* 3 (March 1986): 7–9, and Russell P. Spittler, "Suggested Areas for Further Research in Pentecostal Studies," *Pneuma: Journal of the Society for Pentecostal Studies* (hereafter *Pneuma*) 5 (1983): 40–43. The semiannual *Newsletter* of the Society for Pentecostal Studies, which lists recent dissertations and publications, registers bibliographic trends in the field.

The most serviceable one-volume survey of the history and theology of Pentecostalism around the world is Walter J. Hollenweger, *The Pentecostals: The Charismatic Movement in the Churches* (1972, reprint 1988; German original, 1969). Although this work is marred by numerous factual errors and lacks a coherent interpretive thesis, it remains the most detailed general guide to the global expansion of Pentecostalism, especially in Europe, Africa, and South America. For the casual reader, *In the Latter Days: The Outpouring of the Holy Spirit in the Twentieth Century* (1984), by Vinson Synan, offers a brief and sprightly overview of worldwide trends, emphasizing recent developments in Third World countries. Synan sculpts a clear and therefore valuable typology of the various forms of Pentecostal piety in North America and elsewhere in "Pentecostalism: Varieties and Contributions," *Pneuma* 9 (1987): 31–49.

The most authoritative study of Pentecostal origins in the U.S. is Robert Mapes Anderson, *Vision of the Disinherited: The Making of American Pentecostalism* (1979). Anderson approaches the subject from a forthrightly naturalistic perspective, but his research is exhaustive, accurate, and methodologically sophisticated. Another useful survey, although less critical (in both senses of the term), is Vinson Synan, *The Holiness–Pentecostal Movement in the United States* (1971). In this volume he argues—a bit too insistently, perhaps—that the Wesleyan Holiness tradition served as the theological wellspring of the movement as a whole. Grant Wacker's article on "Pentecostalism," in Charles H. Lippy and Peter W. Williams, eds., *Encyclopedia of the American Religious Experience* (vol. 2, 1987), offers a chapter-length summary of the history of the movement, with particular attention to the early years.

In the mid-1950s many of the ideas and practices of old-line Pentecostalism started to erupt in the Roman Catholic church and in some of the mainline Protestant bodies. The literature on this phenomenon, which is commonly known as the Neo-Pentecostal or charismatic movement, already is extensive. Charles Edwin Jones, *Guide to the Study of the Charismatic Movement* (forthcoming, 1988), promises to serve as the standard bibliographic resource. The spread of Pentecostal piety among traditionally non-Pentecostal groups is traced in Richard Quebedeaux, *The New Charismatics* (1976, reissued in 1983 as *The New Charismatics II*), and in Vinson Synan, *The Twentieth-Century Pentecostal Explosion: The Exciting Growth of Pentecostal Churches and Charismatic Renewal Movements* (1987). The latter is especially useful, for it traces the growth of Pentecostal stirrings within particular—and seemingly unlikely—denominational families such as Lutherans, Mennonites, and Orthodox Catholics. For scholarly assessments of these trends, one should see James C. Connelly, C.S.C., "Neo-Pentecostalism: The Charismatic Renewal in the Mainline Protestant and Roman Catholic Churches of the United States, 1960–1971," Ph.D. dissertation, University of Chicago, 1977, and Meredith B. McGuire, *Pentecostal Catholics: Power, Charisma, and Order in a Religious Movement* (1982). Important primary sources bearing upon the charismatic movement and its relation to other Christian groups are collected in Kilian McDonnell, ed., *Presence, Power, Praise: Documents on the Charismatic Renewal* (3 vols., 1980). Statistical and poll data on the beliefs and practices of both old-line Pentecostals and the newer charismatics can be found in Kenneth S. Kantzer, "The Charismatics Among Us," *Christianity Today* (February 22, 1980), and in David Barrett, *World Christian Encyclopedia* (1982).

All of the major and several of the minor old-line Pentecostal denominations have been examined in book-length monographs. Not surprisingly, the Assemblies of God (AG), largest and strongest of such groups, has been treated most extensively and with most sophistication. By far

the best is Edith L. Blumhofer, *The Assemblies of God to 1941: A Chapter in the Story of American Pentecostalism* (forthcoming, 1989). Blumhofer meticulously explores the turn-of-the-century social and cultural context in which that denomination was born and breaks new ground by demonstrating how strongly restorationist impulses influenced the thinking of first-generation leaders. Margaret M. Poloma, *Charisma, Prophets, and Institutional Dilemmas: A Sociological Account of the Assemblies of God* (forthcoming, 1988), is a sympathetic study of that group's structure and ethos, with emphasis on the determinative role that the clergy has played in shaping the spiritual lives of its adherents. Particular aspects of that body's development are explored in various dissertations and monographs. Among the most valuable of these are Howard N. Kenyon, "A Social History of the Assemblies of God: Race Relations, Women and Ministry, and Attitudes Toward War," Ph.D. dissertation, Baylor University (forthcoming, 1988); and Gary B. McGee, *This Gospel Shall Be Preached: A History and Theology of Assemblies of God Foreign Missions to 1959* (1986), both of which deal with curiously neglected features of the Pentecostal story. The latter work, like Blumhofer's, is projected as the first of a two-volume set.

The growth of the Pentecostal Holiness Church, the Church of God (CG, Cleveland, Tenn.), and the Church of God of Prophecy, have been surveyed in, respectively, Vinson Synan, *The Old-Time Power: A History of the Pentecostal Holiness Church* (1973); Charles W. Conn, *Like a Mighty Army: A History of the Church of God* (1955, rev. 1977); and James Stone, *The Church of God of Prophecy: History and Polity* (1977). The story of the largest Oneness denomination, the United Pentecostal Church, is outlined in Arthur L. Clanton, *United We Stand* (1970). Joseph H. Howell, "The People of the Name: Oneness Pentecostalism in the United States," Ph.D. dissertation, Florida State University, 1985, offers an astute analysis of the religious and cultural dynamics that have animated the Oneness tradition since its inception.

The literature of black Pentecostalism is described in Charles Edwin Jones, *Black Holiness: A Guide to the Study of Black Participants in Wesleyan Perfectionist and Glossolalic Pentecostal Movements* (1987). No comprehensive treatment of black Pentecostalism in the U.S. exists, although the Synan (1971), Anderson, and Howell works noted above contain useful chapters, and several Ph.D. dissertations and published monographs have probed aspects of the black Pentecostal experience. These include Leonard Lovett, "Black Origins of the Pentecostal Movement," in Vinson Synan, ed., *Aspects of Pentecostal/Charismatic Origins* (1975); Morris E. Golder, *History of the Pentecostal Assemblies of the World* (1973); James C. Richardson, *With Water and Spirit: A History of Black Apostolic Denominations in the U.S.* (1980); and Lucille J. Cornelius et al., *The Pioneer: History of the Church of God in Christ* (1975). Cornelius is particularly attentive to the much-neglected role of women in black Pentecostalism. For anthropological and sociological case studies one should consult Melvin D. Williams, *Community in a Black Pentecostal Church* (1974), and Arthur E. Paris, *Black Pentecostalism: Southern Religion in an Urban World* (1982). The latter, an examination of three "storefront" black congregations, seeks to normalize that form of Pentecostal expression by showing how it serves enduring social, cultural, and religious needs.

Scholarly resources for the study of socially or culturally marginal Pentecostals are sparse for some groups, ample for others. Although non-English-speaking bodies generally have been overlooked, a beginning has been made by Louis De Caro, who surveys the Italian-American Christian Church of North America in *Our Heritage* (1977), and by Victor de Leon, who sketches the Latin American Assemblies of God in *The Silent Pentecostals* (1979). Snake-handling believers in the Southern Appalachians, on the other hand, have been, if anything, overstudied. The best known of such works is Weston LaBarre, *They Shall Take Up Serpents: Psychology of the Southern Snake-Handling Cult* (1962, rev. 1969). A classic and widely viewed one-hour documentary film, *Holy Ghost People,* graphically depicts the ritual practices of the snake-handling sects. The relation between chronic poverty and Pentecostal religion in that region is sensitively explored in Troy D. Abell, *Better Felt Than Said: The Holiness-Pentecostal Experience in Southern Appalachia* (1982).

A number of Pentecostal leaders have attracted the attention of professional historians. Oral Roberts is the subject of a magnificent and scrupulously objective biography by David Edwin Harrell, Jr., titled *Oral Roberts: An American Life* (1985). Aimee Semple McPherson's importance rivals Roberts's, but she has not fared as well in the scholarly literature. Lately Thomas, *Storming Heaven: The Lives and Turmoils of Minnie Kennedy and Aimee Semple McPherson* (1970), covers the first half of her career in a study that is lively, painfully funny, yet hardly objective. For a competent yet too-brief survey of McPherson's career, one should see William G. McLoughlin's essay in *Notable American Women* (vol. 2, 1971). Maria B. Woodworth-Etter never attracted wide recognition outside of Pentecostal circles, but her influence within them actually may have been greater than Roberts's or McPherson's ever was. Her ministry is traced in an exhaustively researched study by Wayne E. Warner called *The Woman Evangelist: The Life and Times of Charismatic Evangelist Maria B. Woodworth-Etter* (1986).

Virtually all historians of American Pentecostalism agree that Charles Fox Parham and William J. Seymour rank among the most important of the first-generation leaders. Parham is the subject of a forthcoming study by James R. Goff, Jr., *Fields White Unto Harvest* (1988), based on his University of Arkansas Ph.D. dissertation. Goff published a preview of his work in "Charles F. Parham and His Role in the Development of the Pentecostal Movement: A Reevaluation," *Kansas History* 7 (1984): 226–37. Blumhofer's history of the AG (noted above) also contains a revealing chapter on Parham and the early history of Parham's Apostolic Faith Movement. For Seymour, the best resource is Douglas J. Nelson, "For Such a Time as This: The Story of Bishop William J. Seymour and the Azusa Street Revival: A Search for Pentecostal/Charismatic Roots," Ph.D. dissertation, University of Birmingham, 1981. Nelson's work is flawed by a polemical attitude and tendentious use of data. Even so, he has unearthed a remarkable amount of evidence about Seymour as well as the Azusa Street revival. Curiously, no one has yet published a critical study of A. J. Tomlinson, who loomed as one of the most influential and, by any reasonable measure of such things, colorful figures in early Pentecostal history.

The theological origins of Pentecostalism in the sprawling evangelical subculture of Great Britain and the U.S. in the late nineteenth century are traced in Donald W. Dayton, *Theological Roots of Pentecostalism* (1987). Although Dayton stresses the Wesleyan contribution more than most historians, his work stands as the most learned and careful treatment of the theological tributaries to the Pentecostalism stream. Another study, which focuses almost exclusively on Reformed and Keswick (as opposed to Wesleyan) influences, is Edith L. Waldvogel (Blumhofer), "The 'Overcoming Life': A Study in the Reformed Evangelical Origins of Pentecostalism," Ph.D. dissertation, Harvard University, 1977. The theological heritage of the large minority of Pentecostals who adhere to the Oneness position is explored in David A. Reed, "Origins and Development of the Theology of Oneness Pentecostalism in the United States," Ph.D. dissertation, Boston University, 1978.

Particular aspects of the Pentecostal tradition— beyond those that have been noted already— have been studied closely and are worth mentioning here. Roger Robin's 1984 Harvard Divinity School thesis, "Worship and Structure in Early Pentecostalism," ranks as an exceptionally perceptive study not only of that topic but also of the ethos of the tradition as a whole. Factors that sustained the movement when the glow of the revival began to dim are suggested in Grant Wacker, "The Functions of Faith in Primitive Pentecostalism," *Harvard Theological Review* 77 (1984): 353–75. Richard M. Riss, *Latter Rain* (1987), describes a significant yet curiously understudied rigorist movement that rocked many Pentecostal churches in the middle decades of the century. The tradition's distinctive approach to biblical scholarship is analyzed in Russell P. Spittler, "Scripture and the Theological Enterprise," in Robert K. Johnston, ed., *The Use of the Bible in Theology: Evangelical Options* (1985). Attitudes toward ecumenism are probed in Cecil M. Robeck, Jr., "Pentecostals and the Apostolic Faith: Implications for Ecumenism," *Pneuma* 9 (1987): 61–84. Dwight Wilson, *Armageddon Now! The Premillenarian Response to Russia and Israel Since 1917* (1977), describes their eschatological views in general and their enduring fascination with Israel in particular. The movement's adeptness in using mass media and its recent affinity for right-wing politics are highlighted in David Edwin Harrell, Jr., *Pat Robertson: A Personal, Political and Religious Portrait* (1987). This work should be read in conjunction with Everett A. Wilson, "Sanguine Saints: Pentecostalism in El Salvador," *Church History* 52 (1983): 186–98; and Jay Beaman, "Pentecostal Pacifism: The Origin, Development, and Rejection of Pacific Belief Among Pentecostals," M. Div. thesis, North American Baptist Seminary, 1982. The latter two show that social and political conservatism are not as uniform in the Pentecostal tradition as the contemporary North American scene might lead one to suppose.

Although there is no comprehensive treatment of the Pentecostal view of healing, its origins are sketched in Dayton (noted above), and in Raymond J. Cunningham, "From Holiness to Healing," *Church History* 43 (1974): 499–513. Pentecostal attitudes toward human well-being in general and the post-World War II surge of interest in physical health and financial prosperity in particular, are discussed in Grant Wacker, "The Pentecostal Tradition," in Ronald L. Numbers and Darrel W. Amundsen, eds., *Caring and Curing: Health and Medicine in the Western Religious Traditions* (1986). The rise and partial demise of independent deliverance ministries in the mid twentieth century are traced in David Edwin Harrell, Jr., *All Things Are Possible: The Healing and Charismatic Revivals in Modern America* (1975). Two of the virtues of this exceptionally interesting book are its photographs and its extensive bibliographic essay on hard-to-find primary materials. Gordon Lindsay, *John Alexander Dowie: A Life Story of Trials, Tragedies and Triumphs* (1980), stands out as a wide-eyed yet informative biography of the father of modern healing evangelism. C. Douglas Weaver, *The Healer-Prophet: William Marrion Branham: A Study of the Prophetic in American Pentecostalism* (1987), considers the career of this uncannily gifted figure who nearly displaced Oral Roberts as the leader of deliverance evangelism in the 1950s and 1960s.

Predictably, Pentecostalism has sparked the interest of countless social scientists. Much of this literature is described in Kilian McDonnell, *Charismatic Renewal and the Churches* (1976). For a thought-provoking and surprisingly sympathetic study of the social and cultural fabric of the movement, one should see Luther P. Gerlach and Virginia H. Hine, *People, Power, Change: Movements of Social Transformation* (1970). Linguistic analyses of glossolalia and related behavior are summarized in William J. Samarin, *Tongues of Men and Angels: The Religious Language of Pentecostalism* (1972), and in H. Newton Malony and A. Adams Lovekin, *Glossolalia: Behavioral Science Perspectives on Speaking in Tongues* (1985). Several anthologies, which bring together scholarly assessments by historians, theologians, and social scientists, have been published in the past decade. The better ones include Vinson Synan, ed., *Aspects of Pentecostal/Charismatic Origins* (1975); Russell P. Spittler, ed., *Perspectives on the New Pentecostalism* (1976); and Watson E. Mills, ed., *Speaking in Tongues: A Guide to Research on Glossolalia* (1986).

Until recently, primary sources, especially from the crucially important pre-World War I years,

have been quite hard to come by. But growing historical consciousness, especially within the major denominations, has prompted a systematic effort to identify and collect textual and, to a lesser extent, material artifacts of Pentecostal culture. A one-volume anthology of documentary materials representing the various periods and aspects of the movement's history does not yet exist, but an awesome forty-eight-volume set does. The latter has been edited by Donald W. Dayton et al. as *"The Higher Christian Life": Sources for the Study of the Holiness, Pentecostal and Keswick Movements* (1984–85). This series contains photographic reproductions of works by early leaders such as Elizabeth V. Baker, Frank Bartleman, Andrew Urshan, G. T. Haywood, Frank Ewart, D. Wesley Myland, G. F. Taylor, B. F. Lawrence, Agnes [Ozman] LaBerge, Aimee Semple McPherson, Carrie Judd Montgomery, Charles Fox Parham, and A. J. Tomlinson. Most are taken from original or very early editions. All are relatively rare, some extremely so.

Other primary resources also have become available in recent years. The first thirteen issues of the Azusa Mission's newspaper, which ran from September 1906 through May 1908, have been photographically reproduced by Fred T. Corum under the title *Like as of Fire: A Reprint of the Azusa Street Documents* (1981). Wayne E. Warner, ed., *Touched by the Fire: Patriarchs of Pentecost* (1978; reissued as *Revival! Touched by Pentecostal Fire* [1982]), offers a somewhat sanitized yet revealing set of first-generation autobiographical accounts. Frank Bartleman's eyewitness account of the Azusa Street revival, published in 1925 as *How "Pentecost" Came to Los Angeles— How It Was in the Beginning*, may well be the most important primary document of all. This volume was edited by Vinson Synan and reissued in unabridged form in 1980 as *Azusa Street*. Bartleman's career is surveyed in C. M. Robeck, Jr., "The Writings and Thought of Frank Bartleman," Introduction to Donald W. Dayton et al., eds., *Witness to Pentecost: The Life of Frank Bartleman* (n.d., reprint 1985). Primary works that defended the distinctive features of Pentecostal theology and enjoyed wide support at one time or another include George Floyd Taylor, *The Spirit and the Bride* (1907); D. Wesley Myland, *The Latter Rain Pentecost* (1910); Lilian B. Yeomans, M.D., *Healing from Heaven* (1926); Ralph M. Riggs, *The Spirit Himself* (1949); Charles W. Conn, *Pillars of Pentecost* (1956); and Stanley M. Horton, *What the Bible Says About the Holy Spirit* (1976). From the 1920s to the 1960s no Pentecostal theologian exercised greater influence in the U.S. than the Englishman Donald Gee. Among his many books, *Concerning Spiritual Gifts* (1928, rev. 1937) remains the most influential.

Many of the founding figures wrote autobiographies or left autobiographical reminiscences in one form or another. More often than not they provide a rare glimpse into the inner world of early Pentecostalism. In this respect the life histories of Charles Fox Parham and A. J. Tomlinson are indispensable. The former was compiled by Sarah E. Parham under the title *The Life of Charles F. Parham, Founder of the Apostolic Faith*

Movement (1930). The latter was edited by Homer A. Tomlinson as *Diary of A. J. Tomlinson* (3 vols., 1949–55). Other autobiographical works, both early and recent, that are particularly worth noting include Elizabeth V. Baker, *Chronicles of a Faith Life* (n.d., reprint 1984); Maria B. Woodworth-Etter, *Signs and Wonders* (1916, reprint 1980); Thomas Ball Barratt, *When the Fire Fell and An Outline of My Life* (1927, reprint 1985); Aimee Semple McPherson, *This Is That: Personal Experiences, Sermons and Writings* (1919, rev. 1921, 1923, reprint 1985); Andrew Urshan, *The Life Story of Andrew bar David Urshan* (1967); J. H. and Blanche L. King, *Yet Speaketh: Memoirs of the Late Bishop Joseph H. King* (1949); Oral Roberts, *The Call: Oral Roberts' Autobiography* (1971); and Pat Robertson, *Shout It from the Housetops* (1972).

Finally, it should be noted that since 1979 the Society for Pentecostal Studies has published *Pneuma*, a quarterly that deals with a variety of historical, biblical, theological, and, occasionally, sociological subjects. The same is true of the papers given and made available in bound form each November at the annual meeting of the society. Both strive, not always successfully, to transcend the sectarian defensiveness that still limits the scholarly usefulness of most Pentecostal publications. And both offer a continual river of data, insights, and bibliographic tips for serious students of the subject.

I. Historiography. History and historiography are similar but not identical concepts—more like kissing cousins than like twins. The former is the study of past events. In practice this distinction is difficult to maintain, for it is virtually impossible to know the history of anything except as it has been mediated through the perceptions of earlier historians. Nonetheless, in principle, the difference is clear. History deals with the past, taken by itself, while historiography deals with scholarship about the past and especially the way that successive generations of historians presuppose and build upon each other's insights.

The historiography of modern Western religious movements—which is to say, movements that emerged within Euroamerican Christianity during the nineteenth or twentieth centuries—follows a predictable pattern. The first stage of that pattern is widespread lack of interest. This is true of both outsiders and insiders. For the former, if a new movement is small, they are bemused; if it is large, they are frightened. Either way, outsiders have better things to do than to worry about why it came into existence. Insiders too are slow to tell the story. Preoccupied with the task of proclaiming their message, they rarely take time to think, much less write, about their origins. And when they do, they instinctively assume that their beginnings were supernatural, directly launched by God outside the channels of ordinary human history. In time, however, movement leaders begin to grow self-conscious about who they are and where they fit on the religious landscape. At that point they also become curious about their roots. First one, then another, and then another sets down his or her recollections about the way it "really was" in the beginning.

Eventually, someone with a measure of formal education gathers these firsthand accounts into a coherent narrative that identifies the "relevant" influences, establishes the "proper" sequence of events, and orders the "true" hierarchy of importance among leaders.

The books that partisans initially write about themselves almost always come across as self-serving and triumphalist, more like parodies than serious works of history. Even so, they usually merit careful attention. Their musty pages bend under the weight of factual details not available anywhere else, and to the discerning eye, such details illumine the moods and motivations that sustained the revival during its formative years. Further, the first histories of a movement inevitably cast a long shadow over all subsequent efforts to tell the story. The former set the terms of the discussion, not only because of the things that they do say, but also, and perhaps more importantly, because of the things that they do not say. Every effort to include the factors that are deemed relevant to a movement's beginnings is at the same time an effort to exclude the factors that are deemed irrelevant. Later historians may tell the story and construe its significance in radically different ways, but they cannot ignore the interpretations set forth by the pioneer writers.

This article deals only with the earliest historians of the movement. To a remarkable extent, their work fits the pattern sketched above. It was fiercely apologetic, but it was packed with information gleaned from firsthand observations, and it offered priceless insights into the social structure and cultural texture of the early days. Later scholars necessarily built upon the primitive authors' labor, presupposing their research and borrowing their ideas more often than they realized. For this reason alone it is important to know who the original writers were and what the corpus of their work looks like.

The initial historians of the Pentecostal movement can be divided into two broad groups. The first consisted of authors who explicitly understood themselves to be writing a comprehensive account of the revival's beginnings. Significantly, no one attempted a work of this sort for more than fifteen years, but in 1916 B. F. Lawrence published *The Apostolic Faith Restored*. Although this slender volume purported to serve as a general survey of Pentecostal origins, it focused almost entirely on events in the lower Midwest, especially in Texas. About a third of it consisted of Lawrence's personal recollections, while the remainder consisted of extracts from periodicals and letters from various leaders. More a compilation than a composition, the book was, nonetheless, singularly valuable, for it was the first sustained effort by a Pentecostal writer to survey the movement's beginnings. (As things turned out, the book also proved valuable because it preserved meaty quotations from documents that later were lost.) In 1925 Frank Bartleman published *How "Pentecost" Came to Los Angeles—How It Was in the Beginning*. Bartleman structured this work as an autobiography, but it was much more than that, since he happened to be one of the leading actors in the unfolding drama in California as well as in other parts of the country. Like all the early writers, Bartleman was a relatively uneducated man. Yet he possessed shrewd historical instincts, a fine eye for significant details, and a colorful writing style filled with memorable one-liners (when Pentecost came to town, he deadpanned, an opposition group called the Pillar of Fire went "up in smoke"). The following year Stanley H. Frodsham published *"With Signs Following": The Story of the Latter-Day Pentecostal Revival* (rev. 1928, rev. and enlarged 1946). Perhaps four-fifths of this work consisted of extracts from periodicals and letters from converts in all parts of the world. Although Frodsham also was principally a compiler, he was the first to fully grasp the international dimensions of the revival. Precisely for this reason, perhaps, he drew upon a much wider range of sources, both in type and in geographical provenance, than either Lawrence or Bartleman.

Two additional attempts to forge a comprehensive account of Pentecostal origins did not come out until after World War II, but they should be mentioned here because they were based on notes taken during the initial flowering of the revival. One was the *Phenomenon of Pentecost: (a history of "The Latter Rain")*, published by Frank J. Ewart in 1947. Ewart was on hand nearly from the beginning (taking over William H. Durham's mission in Los Angeles in 1912), and he seems to have relied on his own carefully recorded diary entries. Ewart's work highlighted developments on the West Coast and in the Orient. In 1958 Ethel E. Goss, the second wife of Howard A. Goss, released *The Winds of God: The Story of the Early Pentecostal Days (1901–1914) in the Life of Howard A. Goss, as Told by Ethel E. Goss.* This volume purported to be a slightly edited version of her husband's personal diary, but since the latter is not publicly available, it is difficult to know exactly how much the published version differs from the original. However that may be, H. A. Goss loomed as a key figure in the growth of the movement in the lower Midwest, and he played a pivotal role in the organization of the AG. Thus his autobiography, like Bartleman's, bears a wider significance than the title suggests.

Besides these systematic, book-length efforts by Lawrence, Bartleman, Frodsham, Ewart, and Goss to describe the origins of the movement, there was another broad category of retrospective writings that might be called "incidental" observations. The latter included essays by authors like Henry G. Tuthill, Minnie F. Abrams, and Mother Emma Cotton, who tried to tell the story in a self-consciously historical fashion but devoted only a brief article or two to the task, usually in primitive periodicals such as *Faithful Standard, Word and Work,* or *Message of the "Apostolic Faith."* This category also included theological and polemical expositions by well-known figures such as Charles Fox Parham, William J. Seymour, and A. J. Tomlinson, and by some not-so-well-known figures such as Elizabeth V. Baker, A. A. Boddy, and J. G. Campbell. Such expositions were relevant to the growth of Pentecostal historiography when they contained, as they often did, recollections about the sequence of events or state of affairs in the early years. Still another source appropriately included under this rubric were observations by outsiders. Some, such as Alma White's five-volume autobiography, *The Story of My Life and Pillar of Fire* (1935), remained unremittingly hostile. Others, such as Charles W. Shumway's University of Southern California A. B. thesis, "A Study of the 'Gift of Tongues'" (1914), made no pretense of impartiality but did maintain a measure of objectivity. Documents of this sort were useful because they showed how Pentecostals were perceived by others or because they contained data preserved nowhere else or because they told a seamy side of the story that insiders understandably chose to overlook.

There were, of course, additional authors and perhaps other types of historical writings that might be considered, but this is enough to indicate at least the broad contours of the historiographic landscape. The task now is to describe the continuities of outlook and interpretation that bound these men and women together. This is not pure guesswork, yet it is a matter of inference, since the original writers simply did their work without taking time to talk about, much less analyze, the principles that informed their thinking. In order to understand these authors, in other words, we need to ask questions of them that they did not ask of themselves, at least not explicitly.

Our queries can be divided into two sets. The first set is: (1) How, in their minds, was history governed? (2) Where was it headed? And (3) How did supernatural causation interact with the natural causation? The second set is: (4) How was Pentecostalism to be defined? (5) How did it get started? And (6) Where did the revival fit in the overall pattern of human history? It should be evident that the first three questions, which are very general in scope, deal with the early writers' overarching philosophy of history, while the next three, which are quite specific, probe their understanding of the origins and historical significance of the Pentecostal movement itself. It is only by combining these two perspectives, the general and the specific, that we can gain an adequately nuanced perspective on the assumptions and arguments that the primitive historians brought to their work.

A. The Governance of History. Let us begin, then, with the first question. How did the primitive historians conceive the governance of history? Simply stated, who, in their minds, was in charge of human affairs—God or human beings? For most of the early writers the answer was more complicated than we might suppose.

To begin with, Pentecostals, like most Christians, assumed that history was providential, which meant that it moved by supernatural guidance from Creation to Final Judgment, whether humans cooperated or not. But unlike most Christians or at least most modern Christians, Pentecostals also believed that God's governance of history was intimately tied up with human responses. Simply stated, God was both sovereign and subject, both changeless and changeable. This state of affairs posed a logical contradiction, of course, but Pentecostals did not worry about it very much. They were content simply to assert that God stood wholly above and outside of history but at the same time also to assert that human repentance and obedience—or the lack of them—powerfully affected the timing and the placement of God's actions in history. To take a case in point, Pentecostals were certain that God himself had determined to bring about a worldwide revival to prepare men and women for the Lord's coming. Yet they were equally certain that the exact time and place of the revival largely depended on human responses. The terrible San Francisco earthquake of 1906 illustrated the paradox. Frank Bartleman argued that God had sent that calamity to that city to alert it to its spiritual peril, but he also insisted that God had been dissuaded by the prayers of the saints in Los Angeles from sending a similar disaster to the southern California area. No one knew why the prayers rising from Los Angeles had been more effective than the ones rising from San Francisco. All that they knew was that God had acted according to his own calculus, yet—and it was a big yet—humans had been permitted to stipulate the numbers.

Another way to describe the Pentecostal view of history is to say that in their minds it resembled a great black line stricken across a page, running from a divinely determined starting point at one end to a divinely determined ending point at the other. Although from a distance the line appeared to be a straight one, close up one could see that it harbored internal striations running in all directions. The overall pattern was fixed, but the details were not, for to a remarkable extent humans were free to obey or disobey God's law as they wished. And God, in turn, was free to stray from his own predetermined line of behavior as freely or as often as he wished. The whole scheme was a systematic theologian's nightmare, but the early historians instinctively sensed that the logic of religious experience usually is.

B. The Direction of History. If the governance of history was simultaneously divine and human, so too the direction of history was simultaneously linear and cyclical. This is to say that history was linear insofar as God exercised control; cyclical insofar as God permitted humans to use and misuse their freedom. Human freedom took a disturbingly repetitive form. Over time vibrant churches would become respectable churches, and respectable churches would become, almost by definition, spiritually cold and lifeless. Sooner or later a small body of saints, humble and repentant, would break away to set up their own fellowship. God would bless them, and for a while they too would prosper, but prosperity would lead to pride and pride would lead once again to spiritual death. Throughout the history of Christianity that pattern has been repeated countless times.

Pentecostals were certain, of course, that their own revival constituted the final cycle of renewal within the time line of history. Bartleman and perhaps one or two others feared that they too might backslide into apostasy and that another cycle might replace them, but most early writers seem never to have considered that possibility, much less worried about it. Their smugness

stemmed from two assumptions. One was that they expected the Lord's return momentarily, and thus they could not imagine that there would be time for a relapse. The other and more important assumption was that the historical time line was, in a sense, curving back to the beginning. The present revival promised to replicate both the form and the power of the apostolic revivals that had inaugurated the Christian era. Thus the current revival constituted not merely another round of decay and renewal, but also, and more fundamentally, it embodied the final cycle that would bring history full circle. When this process was complete, when the present had become a mirror of the beginning, history itself would come to an end.

First-generation Pentecostals sometimes talked about these matters in the terms we have been using—cycles of renewal, the full circle of history, and so forth—but ordinarily they expressed themselves in a quite different vocabulary. They called it the promise of the Latter Rain. To unravel the intricacies of Latter Rain theology would require a major essay in itself. Here it is sufficient to say that in their minds the signs and wonders of the apostolic age—including, most notably, speaking in tongues—were destined to reappear at the end of history. When the miracles of the NT church came back after centuries of apostasy and disuse, Christians would know that the Lord's return was at hand and that history itself was finally drawing to a close.

The early writers' conviction that their revival uniquely replicated the beliefs and practices of the apostolic church partly accounts for their studied *dis*interest (as opposed to simple lack of interest) in the centuries of Christian tradition stretching from the second to the twentieth centuries. The older denominations, B. F. Lawrence judged, had existed long enough to "establish precedent, create habit, formulate custom." But the Pentecostal movement possessed no such history. Rather it leaped the intervening years crying, " 'BACK TO PENTECOST!' " Admittedly, this deliberate disinterest in the Christian tradition sometimes was more apparent than real. From time to time Pentecostal historians compared their leaders with Martin Luther, George Fox, and John Wesley, or portrayed their revival as the direct successor to the Irvingite and Holiness revivals of the previous century. Their reasons for doing this are easy to see. Fear of being depicted as schismatics or heretics prompted them to claim at least some measure of continuity with the main body of Christians. Nonetheless, the movement's fundamental impulse was to deny its rootedness in Christian tradition and to insist, as noted above, that it represented the final renewal that would complete history by bringing it full circle.

C. Supernatural Versus Natural Causation in History. A third prominent feature of the early Pentecostal writers' general philosophy of history was their eagerness to use supernaturalistic principles of explanation whenever they wished to account for their own beginnings and successes. The opposite side of this trait—and another way of describing it—is to say that they resisted contextualist assumptions. The latter might be defined as the supposition, which was virtually universal among professional historians even then, that all social and cultural patterns are products of, and therefore explainable in terms of, antecedent social and cultural patterns. Admittedly, Pentecostals used contextualist principles adroitly enough whenever they wanted to explain (or more precisely, explain away) the motivations of the opponents. But when they considered their own origins, they instinctively dropped contextualist principles in favor of supernaturalistic ones. Examples are countless. Frank Bartleman was certain, for example, that the devil had tried to keep him from attending a revival service by electrocuting the motorman on the streetcar Bartleman was riding. When Charles F. Parham got into a fight with William H. Durham, another early leader, over the timing of sanctification, Parham publicly prayed that God would smite dead whoever was wrong—and crowed about the results when Durham died six months later.

This habit of mixing supernatural and natural principles of explanation helps explain the early writers' repeated assertions that God himself had directly produced the movement, with little or no involvement of secondary causes or agencies. The idea that the revival had dropped from heaven like a sacred meteor showed up in at least two ways. One was that the movement had burst into existence without human leadership. William J. Seymour, a founder of the Azusa Mission, made that point with memorable simplicity when he declared that "the source is from the skies." The denial or at best severe minimalization of human agency helps account for the movement's lack of curiosity about its beginnings. If the source was from the skies, and if human instruments were irrelevant, there really was not much to write about. It is significant that the first major effort by a Pentecostal historian to reconstruct the story of the AG was Carl Brumback's *Suddenly . . . From Heaven* (1961). Although this work reflected careful research in primary materials, its title hardly could have been more nonhistorical, if not antihistorical, in implication, if not in intent.

The sacred meteor theme took another form as well. This was the assertion that the Pentecostal fire had fallen more or less simultaneously in all parts of the world. This meant that the revivals on the various continents had been ignited not by sparks of influence from other revivals but by God himself. One historian typically insisted that the Pentecostal stirring had flared up in mission schools in India long before news from the U.S. could have reached them, and from there it swept around the world, "even though no one had brought the message. It was the Lord's doing." Granted, the early authors occasionally sketched the lines of communication that seemed to have linked one leader or group with another. Almost everyone noted, for example, that the North Carolina evangelist G. B. Cashwell had been instrumental in carrying the Pentecostal message from Azusa back to the camp meetings of the Southeast. Yet they traced those connections haphazardly rather than systematically, and primarily to indicate that there had been "giants in the land" worth emulating today, not to show

that each eruption could be accounted for in contextual terms. Figuring out who had talked to whom or who had converted whom served as interesting sidelights to the story perhaps, but only sidelights, for everyone knew that such connections had little to do with the real reasons the movement had emerged.

D. The Definition of the Movement. These broad assumptions about the governance, direction, and causal mechanisms that turned the wheels of history informed the early historians' interpretation of how the movement actually began. Before they could tackle the latter problem, however, they first had to decide what Pentecostalism was. Differently stated, it was necessary to settle the definitional question—who belonged and who did not—before they could determine where it had started and what kind of folk the Lord had used to get it going.

Modern Pentecostals tend to think that the practice of speaking in tongues, coupled with the doctrine that tongues is the sole initial physical evidence of the baptism of the Holy Spirit, is and always has been the definitional hallmark of the movement. There can be little doubt that this norm became the litmus test of orthodoxy among Pentecostals or at least among white ones after World War I, but throughout the first ten or fifteen years of the movement's life there was considerable debate about the essence of the Pentecostal message. Although it would be an overstatement to say that everything was up for grabs, grassroots evidence such as letters to the editor in the early periodicals leaves little doubt that the boundary lines were extremely porous. Today one might plausibly argue that John Alexander Dowie, A. B. Simpson, or even F. F. Bosworth, did not qualify as true-blue Pentecostals because they did not espouse the right views about speaking in tongues, but discriminations of that sort were not self-evident in the early 1900s.

The theological fluidity of first-generation Pentecostalism shows up in the work of the initial historians. To be sure, all of them assumed that the "foursquare" gospel of salvation, divine healing, speaking in tongues, and expectation of the Lord's return constituted the indispensable core of the movement. But the interpretation and priority they ascribed to one or another of these notions, and the array of doctrines, rituals, and social practices they tacked on to them, varied according to time and place. Howard Goss, for example, highlighted "fast music" as the distinguishing feature of the movement. J. G. Campbell, editor of the *Apostolic Faith* in Goose Creek, Texas, believed that the most notable aspect of Parham's Bible school in Topeka (both before and after 1901) was that all property was held in common and that no one held outside jobs. At one point Parham himself declared that conditional immortality (that is, the annihilation of the wicked) stood as the "most important doctrine in the world today," and he insisted that believers might possess the gift of tongues without ever experiencing the sign of tongues. An unnamed CG historian writing in the *Faithful Standard* ranked baptism by immersion with tongues and divine healing as cardinal doctrines of the movement. Indeed, Elizabeth V. Baker, a prominent evangelist and a founder of the Rochester Bible Training School, debunked the idea that tongues was the only valid evidence of baptism in the Holy Spirit. To say that stalwarts like Huss and Wesley did not have the baptism, she urged, was the "same as to say that one can live the most Christ-like life, bringing forth all the fruits of the Spirit, *without the Holy Spirit.*"

We must be careful not to overstate the case. For the early historians the outer boundaries of the movement may have been fuzzy, but the inner core was not. Frank S. Sandford's Shiloh Bible School near Brunswick, Maine, is a case in point. That institution was almost never mentioned in the early historical literature. Why? Throughout the 1890s and 1900s all of the characteristic beliefs and practices of Pentecostalism, including resurrections from the dead, took place at Shiloh. All, that is, except speaking in tongues. Although first-generation Pentecostals wrangled endlessly about the theological significance of tongues, none doubted that it was a highly coveted part of Christian experience. As a result, the absence of tongues at Shiloh precluded it from serious consideration as one of the fountains of the Pentecostal revival.

E. Geographical and Social Origins of Pentecostalism. Keeping these qualifications in mind, then, it is fair to say that the early historians' uncertainty—albeit limited uncertainty—about the precise boundaries of the revival naturally led to disagreement about where it had started. Some writers, manifestly trying to be as generous as possible, suggested that the movement did not have a single historical origin but grew from several sources. Thus Lawrence and Goss traced the movement's beginnings in about equal measure to the Houston and Los Angeles stirrings of 1905 and 1906, while Frodsham tossed in the Zion City revival of 1904 as another equally important wellspring.

Often, however, the question of origins provoked hot dispute. Tuthill, a CG historian, not surprisingly insisted that the first sprinkle of the Latter Rain had fallen not in Houston, Los Angeles, or Zion City, but in Cherokee County, North Carolina, way back in the 1890s. Bartleman blew up when Pentecostal newspapers in the Midwest asserted that the California revival had sprung from tributaries in other parts of the country. "We . . . prayed down our own revival," he shot back. "The revival in California was unique and separate as to origin." Seymour, too, traced the beginning of the "worldwide revival" to the Azusa Mission, barely acknowledging its connection, much less its provenance, in other streams. Parham was even more adamant about getting the story straight. Seymour, he charged, grown "drunken with power and flattery," was using all his abilities to prove that "Azuza [*sic*] was the original 'crib' of this Movement." But the plain truth was that the apostolic faith had started in Topeka, Kansas, January 1, 1901, and "all who now accept . . . the wildfire, fanatical, wind-sucking, chattering, jabbering, trance, bodyshaking originating in Azuza [*sic*]. . . will fall." In the end, however, Tomlinson took the prize for

historical ingenuity by insisting that his group, the CG had simply uncovered or made explicit the one true tradition that had been continuously present since the days of the apostles. Thus the revival had no American beginning at all; it had been passed down directly from the hands of Christ himself.

Just as there was measured disagreement about what the Pentecostal movement was and where it had begun, so too there was measured disagreement about who the first Pentecostals were. The early historians sometimes debated whether the Wesleyan or the Reformed traditions had fathered the movement, and sometimes they argued about which denominations and sects the initial converts came from, but in general none of them seems to have been deeply interested in either of these questions. From time to time the racial and ethnic make-up of the movement was discussed, yet by and large the early writers do not seem to have been strongly interested in the racial question either.

What all of the first-generation authors were interested in, however, was the movement's social composition. Two tendencies prevailed. One was to stress its lower-class character. Seymour proudly pointed out that the revival had started among poor people. If God had waited for (middle-class) people in the established churches to open their hearts to the Spirit, he wrote, it never would have happened. Seymour's outlook predominated, but there was another—and seemingly opposite—tendency among the early writers to stress the movement's middle- or even upper-middle-class origins. Goss, for example, boasted that some of the "best people" in Texas attended his services. A. W. Orwig remembered that the Azusa Mission attracted all types of people, "not a few of them educated and refined." Pentecostals rarely missed a chance to excoriate secular entertainment, but they also gloated about converts from that world. "One of the results of the revival [in Copenhagen]," Frodsham wrote, "was the salvation of a great Danish actress, Anna Larssen . . . Another Danish actress, Anna Lewini, was also saved and filled." Such remarks probably reveal more about the status hunger of the writers than the actual social position of the converts, but they do suggest that the movement was not, in its own historical perception at least, uniformly drawn from the most destitute ranks of society.

F. The Movement's Place in History. If the early writers evinced healthy disagreement about the theological, geographical, and social provenance of the movement, they displayed remarkable unanimity when they assessed its significance in the history of Christianity. Simply stated, they all believed, without exception, that the eyes of the world were fixed squarely upon them. Nine months after the Azusa Mission opened, Seymour headlined a brief survey of its development with the words: "Beginning of World Wide Revival." Eleven months later Bartleman exuberantly claimed that the California work was "spreading worldwide." Parham insisted that the events taking place in southeastern Kansas served as the pivot of a global revival, while Tomlinson, not surprisingly, suggested that the meetings in western North Carolina constituted its center. By 1922 the *Faithful Standard* was prepared to assure its readers that this was, quite simply, the "greatest revival the world has ever known." However stunningly parochial these spokesmen may have been, yet they also, paradoxically, reflected a global consciousness that was grandly imperial in scope.

The image, here, of a revival focal point radiating outward around the globe effectively contradicted the other image, which Pentecostals also cherished, of causally unconnected stirrings simultaneously springing up all around the world. But that did not bother anyone, because the issue was not causation but consummation; not "Where did it all come from?" but rather "What did it all mean?" In their minds the Pentecostal revival loomed as the very fulfillment of history, the end toward which everything was moving. As noted before, the early historians were certain that the present revival signaled the beginning of the Latter Rain, the apocalyptic events of the last days. Differently stated, the "signs and wonders" of the present revival were regarded as dispensational occurrences, designed, as evangelist Elizabeth V. Baker put it, to "ripen the grain before the Husbandman gathers it." In Tomlinson's words, the purpose of the outpouring was to bring about the "evangelization of the world, [the] gathering of Israel, [and the] new order of things at the close of the Gentile age." No one captured the universal and radically primitivist sweep of their vision better than Ewart: "By one great revolutionary wrench," he exclaimed, God "is lifting His church back over the head of every sect, every creed, every organized system of theology, and [putting] it back where it was in power, doctrine and glory, on and after the Day of Pentecost."

Recently the non-Pentecostal historian Robert Mapes Anderson has argued that "fratricidal warfare" stood out as one of the most pervasive features of early Pentecostal life. He is right, yet it is important to see that most of these brawls were not personal controversies but ideological disputes about one's spot in history. Jostling for pride of place provoked endless arguments over which branch of the movement was going to win in the long run. Ewart, for example, who stood on the Reformed side of the tradition, wrote off his Wesleyan rivals as "inconsequential . . . diehards." Parham dismissed those who were attempting to organize the AG as a "bunch of imitating, chattering, wind-sucking, holy-roller preachers." On and on it went. The one thing they all could agree on was that the Holiness churches, who had rejected the Pentecostal message, were all but washed up; the tide of history had passed them by. Most Holiness people, charged the *Faithful Standard*, were now back into "formal churches, or out all together . . . It is difficult to find a little group of Holiness people anywhere." Pentecostals were convinced beyond question that they, and they alone, were riding the crest of history. When Frodsham drew an analogy between the apostle John's effort to write a narrative of the "things which Jesus did," and his own effort to describe "how the Holy Spirit

fell in . . . this twentieth century," he may have revealed more about his assumptions than he intended.

This survey of the early historians' general philosophy of history; their variegated view of the theological, geographical, and social origins of the movement; and their unanimous conviction of its pivotal place in world history, brings us finally to the question of reliability. Is their work trustworthy? Are the golden oldies of Pentecostal historiography still worth playing?

The initial answer is no, not if we expect their books and articles to serve as reliable representations of what "really happened." All historical words are of course interpretive. None offers a God's-eye view of anything. But some come closer than others. And by the standards of modern, professional scholarship, the writings of self-ascribed historians such as Bartleman and Frodsham, not to mention the historical recollections of popular leaders like Parham and Tomlinson, were far from reliable. At this point we need to be as precise as possible. While simple factual errors of name, date, place, and sequence marred the works of all of the early writers, such mistakes probably were no more numerous than in a good newspaper such as the *New York Times*. The real problems, rather, were defensiveness and the absence of critical standards.

Defensiveness showed up as a determination to omit any aspect of the story that might reflect poorly upon the Pentecostal message. A few writers, such as Bartleman, let the chips fall where they might, but most steered clear of controversy. The long-standing eclipse of Parham offers a case in point. In the summer of 1907 Parham was arrested in Houston and charged with committing a homosexual act. He claimed that he had been framed by a rival, and there is some evidence to support his claim. No matter. From that point forward Pentecostal historians went out of their way to minimize his contribution. Some, such as Lawrence, mentioned his name two or three times but no more than absolutely necessary in order to tell the story. Others, such as Frodsham, simply pretended that Parham had never existed. (As far as that goes, by phrasing everything in the passive tense, Frodsham managed to write two entire chapters about Parham's schools and revivals in Kansas and Texas without once mentioning his name!) Unfortunately Frodsham set the tone for the next half-century. Not until 1961, when Klaude Kendrick published his University of Texas Ph.D. dissertation as *The Promised Fulfilled: A History of the Modern Pentecostal Movement*, was Parham's crucial role in the articulation and propagation of the Pentecostal message finally brought to light.

Frodsham's defensiveness was typical of the first-generation writers. If they had their way, the contribution of any leader who did not fully toe the line would have been forever buried in the mists of the passive tense. The sentiment was laudable, but the result was not, for in their zeal to protect the movement they omitted many deserving figures whom they disliked or considered theologically unsound. Besides being unfair, such edginess proved counterproductive. Sanitizing the story rendered it less than believable and thus guaranteed that unsympathetic outsiders would step in to fill the lacuna with exaggerated tales of sexual and financial misconduct.

A more serious deficiency in the work of the early historians was their lack of critical standards. By this I mean that they were unable or unwilling to see that sound historical writing consisted of the presentation of publicly available facts and the interpretation of those facts in terms of publicly available theories of human motivation and social change. More simply stated, they failed to recognize that history was not theology. Figuring out what God had or had not done in human history should have been the business of the theologian, not of the historian. But Pentecostal writers almost never understood this. They rarely realized that when they deliberately and openly made God the central actor in their stories, they rendered their works unpersuasive to outsiders. And the reason was not because outsiders were necessarily irreligious, or even unsympathetic, but because theological assertions smuggled in as historical "facts" violated the rules by which the game was supposed to be played.

That is not the end of the matter, however. If the golden oldies were unreliable as conventional historical works, they were, nonetheless, useful as "ritualizations" of Pentecostal history. This is to say that they presented a version of the past that was congruent with the theological and institutional needs of the movement at the time that they were written. Hence the data were filtered and the interpretations of the data were simplified and dramatized in order to make them serve the larger purposes of the movement. Davis Bitton's assessment of early Mormon history writing is relevant to early Pentecostals'. Ritualized history, he has pointed out, "was not invention." Rather it was history cast in the form of a morality play.

> Seized upon as a useful symbol of the struggle of darkness against light, of the triumph of the latter, and of God's providential care over his Saints, the incident was simplified, dramatized and commemorated. . . . New converts, as part of their assimilation into the body of the faithful, could easily master the simplified history and accept it as their own ("The Ritualization of Mormon History," *Utah Historical Quarterly* 43 [1975]: 83).

Examples of the ritualization of Pentecostal history abound. One of the more egregious was white racial bias. The problem here was not that the presence of blacks was denied but that the influence of secular black culture on white Pentecostalism (such as jazz and folk healing arts) was ignored. A more serious distortion was male bias. The primary evidence contained tantalizing indications that Lucy Farrow may have been as instrumental as William J. Seymour in bringing about the Azusa Street revival—but both black and white male historians overlooked that data. In retrospect it is increasingly clear that the pivotal role of women pastors and evangelists such as Aimee Semple McPherson, Maria B. Woodworth-Etter, Carrie Judd Montgomery, Elizabeth

V. Baker, and Susan Duncan was systematically eclipsed in the historical literature.

The most persistent form of distortion was, however, theological. Time and again the early historians allowed their theological desires to shape, if not create, their facts, rather than the reverse. One especially clear example of this tendency was the way that the events that took place in Parham's Bible school in Topeka, Kansas, in the fall and winter of 1900 was reported. As the conventional story went, the students in the school *first* read the account of the Day of Pentecost in the Book of Acts, *then* sought the baptism of the Holy Spirit with the evidence of speaking in tongues. There is, however, substantial evidence—which was simply ignored until non-Pentecostal historians such as Robert Anderson started to examine the record in the 1970s—that the events in the Topeka Bible School followed the reverse sequence. After sustained prayer and fasting, the students first started to speak in tongues, and then, in a frantic effort to figure out what it might mean, they started to search the NT for similar occurrences in apostolic times.

Why did the early, and for that matter, all subsequent Pentecostal historians until the 1970s, insist on telling the story the other way around? The answer is easy to discern: the "ritualized" version suggests that the normativeness of speaking in tongues was, or at least ought to have been, self-evident to anyone who read Acts 2 with an open mind and honest heart. As J. Roswell Flower put it in 1950 in a typescript history of the AG, "these students had deduced from God's Word that in apostolic times, the speaking in tongues was considered to be the initial physical evidence of a person's having received the baptism in the Holy Spirit. . . . It was this decision which has made the Pentecostal Movement of the Twentieth Century." Flower's last sentence is particularly revealing. From the beginning, the traditional Pentecostal denominations have distinguished themselves from other Evangelicals and especially from their Holiness rivals by their insistence on the necessity of tongues. Yet that doctrine has been perennially disputed, not only by outsiders, but also by a vocal minority within the movement. Thus institutional needs have determined that a particular version—a ritualization—of the events that took place in Topeka in 1901 would prevail.

In sum, the works of the primitive historians are not satisfactory for all purposes. By definition, they are simplified, designed to celebrate that which can be celebrated. "Those who probe more deeply," Bitton has written, "are bound to discover that men of the past were not one dimensional and, more essentially, that the past was not that simple. Historians have a duty to criticize and correct inaccurate, inadequate, or oversimplified versions of the past" (D. Bitton, "Ritualization of Mormon History," *Utah Historical Quarterly* 43 [Winter 1975]: 83). Yet it is equally important to remember that arguments about one's true history are usually struggles between forms of legitimacy, not between legitimacy and illegitimacy. Students of Pentecostal history need to learn, in short, how

to take the early histories in stride, use them for what they are worth, respect them for what they stand for, and remember that we all see through a glass darkly.
G. Wacker

BIOLLEY, HÉLÈNE (c. 1854–c. 1947). An important background figure in the origins of French Pentecostalism. Born in Switzerland, Biolley came to Le Havre, France, in 1896, opening a temperance hotel and restaurant, the Ruban Bleu, together with a gospel outreach and prayer meetings. Following a visit by Alexander Boddy in 1909, she regularly invited Pentecostal evangelists to visit and speak, e.g., Smith Wigglesworth (1920, 1921) and Douglas Scott (1927, 1930). Biolley's greatest contributions to French Pentecostalism were, however, her persuading Scott, who became the nation's foremost Pentecostal evangelist, to spend time in France before going to Africa, and her formative influence on three young men—Felix Gallice (France), Cristo Domoutchief (Romania), and Ove Falg (Denmark)—who became major figures in the French movement. Biolley translated into French Maria B. Woodworth-Etter's *Signs and Wonders* (1919), which ran to at least five editions.

Bibliography: G. R. Stotts, *Le Pentecôtisme au pays de Voltaire* (1981).
P. D. Hocken

BIRMINGHAM (ENGLAND) "ACTS 1986"
See CHARISMATIC MOVEMENT.

BITTLINGER, ARNOLD (1928–). European charismatic leader and scholar. Bittlinger, then evangelism director in the Protestant state church (*Landeskirche*) in Germany, first encountered charismatic renewal (CR) in the U.S. in late 1962. He arranged a German conference with L. Christenson the following summer. Bittlinger then became the main Lutheran leader of West German CR, which he promoted ecumenically, helping to establish an ecumenical center at Schloss Craheim in 1968. With J. Rodman Williams, he initiated the European Charismatic Leaders Conference in 1972. A biblical scholar, Bittlinger was one of the earliest charismatic exegetes to use the methods of biblical criticism. Of his many works, only *Gifts and Graces* (1967), *Gifts and Ministries* (1973), and *Letter of Joy* (1975) are available in English.

During a year's residence as Fellow of the Institute for Ecumenical and Cultural Research at Collegeville, Minnesota, Bittlinger coauthored with K. McDonnell *The Baptism in the Holy Spirit as an Ecumenical Problem* (1972). As a charismatic scholar, he participated in the first five years of the dialogue between the Catholics and the classical Pentecostals (1972–76). His doctoral dissertation on the dialogue was published under the title *Papst und Pfingstler* (1978).

Bittlinger was chairman of the committee that produced in 1976 theological guidelines for the charismatic parish renewal in the West German Evangelical Church. He resigned this position in 1978 when he became part-time consultant to the World Council of Churches (WCC) on CR and part-time pastor in Oberhallau, Switzerland. Helped by his linguistic abilities, he convened the WCC consultation on charismatic movements held at Bossey in March 1980 and edited its paper, *The Church Is Charismatic* (1981). At the WCC, Bittlinger took particular interest in the Third World, helping to arrange a further consultation in Zaire at the end of 1981. Later his WCC work was channeled into a study project for the Commission on World Mission and Evangelism. He has also become director of the Ecumenical Academy at Nidelbad and has opened an Ecumenical Information Office on Worldwide CR in Zurich.

Bibliography: U. Birnstein, *Neuer Geist in älter Kirche?* (1987).
P. D. Hocken

BJORNER, ANNA LARSSEN (1875–1955). Pioneer figure in the Pentecostal movement in Denmark. A well-known actress in Copenhagen, Anna Larssen was converted through the preaching of H. J. Mygind. She was baptized in the Spirit during a visit of T. B. Barratt in December 1908. She held Pentecostal meetings in her large house, attracting many colleagues from the stage, though she gave up her acting career in 1909. In 1912 she married Sigurd Bjorner, then general secretary of the Danish YMCA.

The Bjorners held Pentecostal meetings all over Denmark. In 1919 they were both baptized in water in Sweden, an act that finally excluded them from the Danish state church. Following a visit to Wales in 1923, the Bjorners' fellowship joined the Apostolic Church. This relationship was broken in 1936, when their assembly objected to other national Apostolic churches being under the British. Anna Bjorner died in 1955, two years after her husband.

Bibliography: N. Bloch-Hoell, *The Pentecostal Movement* (1964); T. N. Turnbull, *What God Hath Wrought* (1959).
P. D. Hocken

BLACK HOLINESS-PENTECOSTALISM
I. Introduction
    A. Movement of Several Denominations
    B. Belief in Baptism of the Holy Spirit
II. Beginnings
    A. Slaves' Religious Beliefs
    B. Holy Spirit Controversy
III. Growth
    A. Rise of Black Independent Churches
        1. Segregation
        2. Holiness Message
    B. Baptism in the Holy Spirit
        1. Azusa Street Revival Confirmation
        2. Churches Emerged
    C. Persecution
        1. Gave New Insight of the Holy Spirit
        2. Reasons
    D. Issues
        1. Finished Work
        2. Jesus Only
        3. Oneness
    E. 1920s and 1930s
        1. Rifts in Black Holiness-Pentecostal Churches
        2. Women's Participation
    F. 1940s and 1950s
        1. Spread Throughout the World
        2. Education
    G. 1960s and 1970s

       1. Further Institutionalization
       2. Polity rifts
  IV. Conclusion
      A. Contributions
      B. Active Discipleship to be Witnesses

I. Introduction.

A. Movement of Several Denominations.
Black Holiness Pentecostalism is not a denomination but rather a movement encompassing several denominations professing belief in Spirit baptism accompanied by various signs including speaking in tongues, with historic roots embracing, but not always restricted to, both a Wesleyan–Arminian and finished work of Calvary orientation. Participants believe that the baptism in the Holy Spirit is a normative postconversion experience available to all Christians for the purpose of becoming more effective witnesses in carrying out the Great Commission (Matt. 28:19).

B. Belief in the Baptism of the Holy Spirit.
Perhaps more than any other twentieth-century religious movement in the West, Black Holiness Pentecostalism is regarded by many as a highly significant catalyst and spawning ground for scores of denominations including the charismatic renewal, all emphasizing the centrality of the Holy Spirit. So little attention had been given to Black Holiness-Pentecostalism by historians that Dietrich Bonhoeffer, while visiting the U.S. from Germany, referred to its participants as the "stepchildren of modern church history." The early Black Holiness-Pentecostal pioneers, while often sequestered from the view of even major American church historians, have nevertheless spoken to our times and deserve their rightful place in history.

II. Beginnings. Black Holiness-Pentecostalism was born amidst the fleeting shadows of slavery in America. The movement encompasses those black religious groups whose leadership for the most part developed primarily from established mainline black Protestant denominations between 1885 and 1916. The genesis of Black Holiness-Pentecostalism occurred approximately twenty-five years after the signing of the Emancipation Proclamation, some fifteen years before the formation of the National Association for the Advancement of Colored People, and parallel to the ascendency of the illustrious Booker T. Washington, noted black educator.

A. Slaves' Religious Beliefs. While the importance and significance of African survivals within black religion in the New World have been the subject of much debate among anthropologists, sociologists, and historians, it appears from the evidence that Black Holiness Pentecostalism shares the legacy of black slave religion, whose historic roots are anchored deep in African and Afro-Caribbean religion. It was not coincidental that Philip the Evangelist in the NT baptized the high-born African treasurer to the Queen of Ethiopia, a ceremony that was symbolic of African involvement in the further spread of the Christian faith.

It should be stated at the outset that it is primarily in worship form, religious expression, and lifestyle rather than a codified belief system that Black Holiness-Pentecostalism shares in the rich tradition and legacy of black slave religion. Since most of the first slaves to be brought to the American colonies came from the Antillean subregion, it is quite possible that some of them had already made a partial transition from their native religions to Christianity prior to any systematic evangelization on the mainland. It was from slave religion that a "black style" of worship developed in an unstructured way as black slaves encountered the almighty God of their fathers.

The degree to which these Christianizing influences modified slave religion is a matter still under debate and requires a far more detailed treatment. While slaves were not educated in terms of Western standards and cultural ethos, their ancestral religions and the religious consciousness engendered were highly complex. Specific religious beliefs salvaged from Africa often came under vigorous assault by Protestant missionaries. It was the slave's adaptation to Christianity without being completely divested of his native religious worship style that later proved to be significant in its impact on black religious lifestyle.

Carter E. Woodson, a prominent black historian, reminded us several decades ago of the affinity of African religion with the Hebraic background of Christianity pointing to the fact that the African stories of creation and belief in the unity of God paralleled Christian theology. He contended that there was so much affinity between the two traditions that about the only changes that the black slave made was to label as Christian what he practiced in Africa. The resolution of the issue with regard to the survival of African cultured ethos is decisive for black Pentecostalism.

The issue of the survival of African influence was debated by E. Franklin Frazier, a prominent black sociologist who contended for a sharp break with the African past. He argued that due to the emasculating process of chattel slavery, blacks brought to America were completely stripped of all vestiges of the African past. Frazier focused on two basic institutions of the black community: the family and the church. He observed that "of the habits and customs as well as the hopes and fears that characterized the life of their forebears in Africa, nothing remains." However, once the black family was destroyed, it was the Christian faith rather than any vestiges of African culture or religious experience that provided a new basis of social cohesion for slaves.

A counter response to Frazier's view was presented by Melville J. Herskovits, the renowned cultural anthropologist who argued a case for the slaves' continuity with the African past. In his study of human behavior among large segments of persons undergoing acculturative change, it was difficult to distinguish between form and meaning. He observed that as persons moved from one culture to a new one, there was a tendency to adopt new forms more readily than new meanings. However, under acculturation, form changes more readily than meaning. Herskovits concluded that during this process, persons characteristically assign old meanings to new forms, thereby maintaining their preexisting systems of values and making the break with established custom minimal as far as their cognitive responses are concerned. On the emotional level persons tend to retain the satisfaction derived from earlier ways while adopting new forms that seem advantageous to them. Both viewpoints have their own value, and both serve to enrich each other and to foster the continuing discussion relative to the issue of African survival in the New World.

It is generally known that the Cavaliers and Huguenots controlled the southern colonies at the points where slaves were traded and were said to be far more tolerant with regard to their religious views than the Puritans in the Northeast. Their high degree of tolerance proved to be the proper setting for black slaves under acculturation who could very easily assign old meanings to new forms and in the very process maintain their preexisting system of religious values. At the emotional level they could readily cling to those values that had substance as they adopted new forms that symbolized survival. Under the influence of the Cavaliers and Huguenots, black slaves throughout the South revised where necessary and reinterpreted their religious practices. While the slaves were physically "in" enough to "feel" the spirit of their slave master's religion, their African cultural background to a large extent, kept them intellectually "out."

Only as black slaves were able to co-opt the outward observable acts of their masters and interpret them in terms of their African culture did they discover genuine spiritual meaning and religious vitality. During the long trek of slavery, the freedom to worship provided slaves with the best avenue of articulation and meaningful expression when other ways were closed. Under such conditions slaves developed a strong, simple faith permeated with ample superstition from their African past. Such conditions also provided fertile soil for the birth, growth, and development of a much later phenomenon known as Black Holiness sects.

It has been cogently argued that where European practices were relatively weak, the opportunities for the maintenance of African practices were correspondingly strengthened. The South was a natural habitat for the birth and development of Black Holiness-Pentecostalism. By 1836 several thousand slaves were taken into Texas annually. Bay Island in the Gulf of Mexico was a depot where at times as many as 16,000 Africans were on hand to be shipped to Florida, Texas, Louisiana, Mississippi, and other markets. Such cities as Vicksburg, Mississippi, and Memphis, Tennessee, received large contingents of imported slaves during this period. The presence of hostile white power and the early closing of the slave trade did much to crush the specific African religious memory but did not annihilate it.

B. Holy Spirit Controversy. Long before the Pentecostal revival at Azusa Street, Charles G. Finney in his "Letters to Ministers of the Gospel" had acknowledged that his instructions to converts had in former times "been very defective, for he had not clearly seen that the baptism of the Holy Ghost is a thing universally promised to

Christians under this dispensation and that blessing is to be sought and received after conversion." Finney's revival methodology had a pronounced influence on the Methodism of his day and proved to be decisive in its impact on the Holiness movement as it attempted to embrace primitive Wesleyanism, with its emphasis on sanctification. American revivalism planted the seeds for the much later Pentecostal movement.

The literature published in connection with the gradual development of the Holiness movement proved to be invaluable as well as decisive as a formative influence. William E. Boardman's *The Higher Christian Life* (1859) was said to have been the single most influential book in the literature of the Holiness movement. John P. Brook's *The Divine Church* (1891) became the bible for radical fringe groups labeled by older denominations as "come-outers." Also considered were Asa Mahan's *The Baptism of the Holy Ghost* (1870) and Finney's *Memoirs*, (1876) in which he relates his Spirit baptism. Finally, R. A. Torrey's important work *Baptism with the Holy Spirit* (1895) found its way into the hearts of many Holiness leaders who later became prominent within the development of the Pentecostal movement.

With a new interest in the Holy Spirit came controversy over Wesley's doctrine of sanctification, which resulted in a division within the Methodist church between 1880 and 1900. This was generated by Holiness advocates who stressed complete perfection characterized by "perfect love" or better yet, entire sanctification, while those of Pentecostal persuasion stressed baptism in the Holy Spirit as an experience subsequent to, and distinct from, conversion.

III. Growth.

A. The Rise of Black Independent Churches. The spirit of religious individualism soon found its true expression in the emergence and development of black independent Protestant churches. This trend had begun in the eighteenth century with such notable ecclesiastical leaders as Richard Allen, James Varick, Peter Williams, George Collins, and Christopher Rush. The precedent was set in the case of Richard Allen in the formation of the African Methodist Episcopal church (AME) in 1816, and Absalom Jones in founding the St. Thomas Protestant Episcopal church in 1794, in protest against white racism and discrimination in the body of Christ.

1. Segregation. The first few decades of the nineteenth century experienced a great deal of spiritual upheaval. New black churches were formed as black leaders sought to exercise their powers of leadership and to control their own affairs and destiny. By 1800 Peter Williams, James Varick, George Collins, and Christopher Rush had constituted a church they called "Lion" as a direct consequence of racial segregation. The Reverend Thomas Paul founded the first African Baptist Church in Boston by 1805 and later assisted in organizing a congregation in New York that became the Abyssinian Baptist Church. The First African Baptist Church in Philadelphia was founded in 1809 as a direct result of thirteen blacks who had been dismissed from a white

Baptist church. The Lombard Street Presbyterian Church in Philadelphia was also founded as a direct result of racial separation. The Dixwell Avenue Congregational Church was founded by blacks in New Haven, Connecticut, by 1829.

These native and original black churches emerged for several reasons. Some were initiated because blacks were encouraged to form separate congregations, often under white supervision, due to the vast size of the mixed congregations. Several congregations were founded as a direct result of missionary activity. Frequent cases of blatant discrimination and the desire of black Christians for equal privileges within mixed congregations also became the basis for separation. The disapproval by whites of black worship and lifestyle played a major role in the separation of blacks from mixed fellowships and in the founding of independent black churches.

2. *Holiness Message.* It was into this historical context that those persons were born who were destined to give leadership to what was to become the Black Holiness-Pentecostal movement. William Edward Fuller, born January 29, 1875, in Mountville, South Carolina, was destined to lead the Fire-Baptized Holiness Church of God of the Americas. Charles Harrison Mason was born September 8, 1866, on a plantation known as the Prior Farm near Memphis, Tennessee, to Jerry and Eliza Mason, who had been converted to the Christian faith; he later founded the Church of God in Christ (CGIC). Charles Price Jones, who later established the Church of Christ Holiness U.S.A., was born December 9, 1865, near Rome, Georgia, and grew up in the brokenness of post– Civil War black existence. These Black Holiness-Pentecostal leaders were the sons of devoutly religious slaves whose African roots were deep within the black religious tradition where freedom of worship and varied lifestyle were dominant motifs.

In 1892 Elijah Lowney, a former Methodist minister from Cleveland, Ohio, held a revival at Wilmington, North Carolina, where he preached the message of Holiness. Among the persons from various races and denominations gathered to hear this black scholarly Holiness advocate preach with unusual power and unction was Henry Lee Fisher, who was instrumental in the formation of the United Holy church in 1894 at Durham, North Carolina.

The emergence of Black Holiness-Pentecostalism from established black independent churches became more pronounced as in the case of Robert H. White, who had been a local preacher in the St. Stephens AME Church. When some accepted the Holiness message, he volunteered to provide leadership to the new converts who needed a place to worship and express their new-found experience. W. H. Fulford, a former member of the AME Zion church, had earlier embraced Holiness, having preached to integrated audiences; he later organized a congregation under the name New Covenant Church.

As a Holiness body the United Holy Church of America traces its genesis to a revival meeting held at Method, North Carolina, in 1885–86 parallel to that which started the Church of God

(Cleveland, Tenn.). Several personalities are associated with its beginnings: Isaac Cheshier, L. M. Mason, G. A. Mials, H. C. Snipes, W. H. Fulford, and H. L. Fisher, who later became president of the movement. The United Holy church originated as a typical Holiness group and later was among the first Holiness bodies on record to become Pentecostal. The first convocation convened at Durham, North Carolina, in 1894, resulting in the establishment of its headquarters in that city.

A division occurred during the early developmental period of the United Holy church over the belief in the necessity of the Lord's Supper for salvation, but this schism was resolved in 1907. When the Holiness message began to rapidly spread to other cities, some groups severed denominational ties while others retained them. Two organizations were formed, the United Holiness Convention and the Big Kahara Holiness Association. Those groups retaining denominational ties became known as the "in church people" and joined the Big Kahara Holiness Association. Those who severed their ties were known as the "come-outers" and later became members of the United Holiness Convention. Severe criticism of the "in-church people" by their denomination gradually forced the two groups into a merger. In 1900 both groups merged and consented to use the name Holy Church of North Carolina. "Virginia" was later added as the movement spread northward, and in 1916 at Oxford, North Carolina, the name was changed to the United Holy Church of America.

The example of the United Holy Church of America significantly illustrates that the same trend that occurred among advocates of white Holiness bodies in their genesis also occurred within black fellowships. Unlike the United Holy church, the Pentecostal Assemblies of the World and the Fire-Baptized Holiness Church of God of the Americas grew out of white Holiness-Pentecostal bodies.

The genesis of the Church of Christ Holiness, U.S.A. occurred between 1894–96 under the leadership of Charles Price Jones (1865–1949), a black missionary Baptist preacher in Jackson, Mississippi. While pastor of Tabernacle Baptist Church, Selma, Alabama, Jones became dissatisfied with his personal religious experience. After acceptance of the Holiness principle of entire sanctification, Jones attempted to remain pastor of the Mt. Helm Baptist Church in Jackson, Mississippi. He held a series of annual Holiness convocations and met objections by his Baptist brethren, later resulting in his expulsion. In 1900 Jones formed the Christ's Association of Mississippi of Baptized Believers and developed an antidenominational stance.

Jones, Mason, and other prominent Black Holiness-Pentecostal leaders participated in what was known as "the movement," which primarily consisted of persons who embraced the "new doctrine of entire sanctification." From "the movement" emerged a federation of loosely organized congregations bearing such titles as "churches of God" and "churches of Christ." They held dual membership in their own denominations and in the emerging new federations stressing sanctification. This emphasis could be traced to the leadership efforts of Phoebe Palmer, who used the National Association for the Promotion of Holiness as a vehicle to promulgate its message of Wesleyan perfectionism to the South.

B. Baptism in the Holy Spirit.

1. Azusa Street Revival Confirmation. These perfectionist teachings were heard by other prominent leaders such as Amanda Berry Smith, a convert of John S. Inskip, John and William Christian, and John Jeter, a companion to C. P. Jones. It was Jones who sent Mason, D. J. Young, and J. A. Jeter to Los Angeles in 1906 to scrutinize the revival being held at Azusa Street under the leadership of William J. Seymour. When Mason returned, laying claim to a third crisis experience, the baptism in the Holy Spirit, he was disfellowshiped by Jones and Jeter. There is now historical evidence to suggest that the Azusa Street revival was no more than confirmation of a phenomenon that had already begun among Black Holiness-Pentecostals. (One year prior to Mason's claim to sanctification in Preston, Arkansas, a black woman, Lucy Smith, testified to having received Spirit baptism in August of 1892.)

2. Churches Emerged. After his expulsion Mason reorganized the loosely federated band of churches in 1907 into the Church of God in Christ, the name divinely revealed to him according to Scripture (1 Thess. 2:14; 2 Thess. 1:1; Gal. 1:22) as he walked along a street in Little Rock, Arkansas, in 1897. Perhaps the greatest impetus in the founding of the Church of God in Christ was a successful revival in 1896 at Jackson, Mississippi, conducted jointly by Mason, Jones, Jeter, and W. S. Pleasant. The response was so overwhelming that opponents came from every direction and many persons were dramatically and miraculously healed by the power of faith. By 1897 the revival had made its way to Lexington, Mississippi, which was sixty miles north of Jackson. The late Elder John Lee gave Mason permission to use his living room, which was of no value within hours because of the throngs of persons. A Mr. Watson generously donated an abandoned gin house located on the bank of a little creek and gave Mason permission to use it for revival. Opposition increased to the point that gunshots were fired into the services, but none were fatal. The emerging movement chose C. P. Jones as general overseer and appointed Mason over Tennessee and Jeter over Arkansas. While a general assembly was in session at Jackson, Mississippi, in 1907, voting to sever the fellowship with Mason and his followers, a similar meeting was being held by Mason in Memphis. It was the latter meeting convened by Elder C. H. Mason that constituted the first general assembly of the CGIC. During this meeting he was unanimously chosen as chief apostle, a position held until his death on November 17, 1961.

Between 1890 and 1898 a small group originally formed as an "association" after separating from the Pentecostal Fire-Baptized Holiness Church with roots in Georgia. Under the leadership of its founder, Benjamin Hardin Irwin, the first general council of the Fire-Baptized Holiness Church convened at Anderson, South Carolina, on August 1, 1898. W. E. Fuller was the only black among the 140 founding members. By 1911 the problem of a biracial constituency proved too difficult for the times. One-third of the constituency was released by the Pentecostal Holiness church, the parent body, to follow W. E. Fuller. From 1910 to 1922 the group was known as the Colored Fire-Baptized Holiness Church of God, with "of the Americas" added four years later. The headquarters are currently in Atlanta, Georgia.

The Pentecostal Assemblies of the World emerged as a Oneness Pentecostal body between 1906 and 1914. Its first general assembly was held March 12, 1912, in Los Angeles, California, where J. J. Frazee of Portland, Oregon, was selected as its first general/superintendent. This group merged with the all-white general assembly of Apostolic Assemblies at St. Louis in 1918. With Garfield T. Haywood as one of its first bishops the body moved to Indianapolis, Indiana, where it began to thrive. It originally began as an interracial body, and by 1924 whites had formed the Pentecostal Church, Inc., a constituent body of the United Pentecostal church that was formed largely by merger in 1945. The Pentecostal Assemblies of the World is parent to the black Oneness fellowships that trace their spiritual genesis to G. T. Haywood.

C. Persecution. In a letter to the *Apostolic Faith* just two years after the beginning of the Azusa Street revival, C. H. Mason wrote: "The fight has been great. I was put out, because I believed that God did baptize me with the Holy Ghost among you all. Well, He did it and it just suits me. . . . His banner over me is love." Religious and civil persecution began to plague Black Holiness-Pentecostal adherents. It was in the providence of God that William Joseph Seymour, a Baptist preacher with Holiness affiliation, born in Louisiana around 1855, would be used as a catalyst to usher in twentieth-century Pentecostalism. The converted livery stable in the ghetto of Los Angeles, a former AME church, became in God's providence a beckoning beacon light to the world as well as a spawning ground from which virtually all Pentecostals trace their lineage; at least twenty-six church bodies trace their Pentecostal doctrine to Azusa Street. No revival prior to this outpouring bore such interracial and ecumenical fruits. Not only did persons of various races in America participate, but adherents from thirty-five nations responded to the mighty call of the Holy Spirit.

1. Gave New Insight of the Holy Spirit. However, a few years past this three-year revival, Black Holiness-Pentecostals found themselves facing suffering from within and without their celebrated enclaves. It was not long before they found themselves in a condition of triple jeopardy — black, poor, and Pentecostal. The harsh invectives imposed on these pioneers caused them to develop a world view much closer to the reality of the world than that of the privileged few. Unearned suffering imposed on Black Holiness-Pentecostal adherents gave them special insight into the working of the Spirit in the world. Their suffering forced them to reject the abstract god of the philosophers for a more concrete God who could be encountered and known at a deeply personal level.

2. *Reasons.* Lynchings and Klan activity were not the only plagues on the South and other parts of the nation at the turn of the century; another problem was paranoia among governmental officials that eventually brought pressure to bear on anyone who was openly opposed to warfare. C. H. Mason directed W. B. Holt (a white) and E. R. Driver, the CGIC West Coast representative, who had a legal background, to draft a statement reflecting the church's stance on war. The statement "We are opposed to war in all its various forms and believe the shedding of blood and the taking of human life to be contrary to the teachings of our Lord Jesus Christ," remains to this day the CGIC stance. The drafted document affirmed loyalty to the president, the constitution, civil laws, the flag, magistrates, and all God-given institutions; but on the other hand, it forbid members to bear arms or shed blood.

The CGIC conscientious objector stance set the stage for other newly formed Holiness-Pentecostal groups to follow. The strains of the First World War brought greater pressure on churches that openly encouraged others to disobey the draft law. The *Memphis Commercial Appeal* carried an article (April 1918) about Elder Jessie Payne, a CGIC pastor in Blythville, Arkansas, who was tarred and feathered as a result of "seditious remarks concerning the president, the war, and a white man's war." Mason had presented a clear message on "The Kaiser in the Light of the Scriptures" in which he condemned German militarism, but he was misinterpreted when under the power of the Spirit he admonished listeners

> not to trust in the power of the U.S., England, France, or Germany, but trust in God. The enemy [the devil] tried to hinder me from preaching the unadulterated word of God. He plotted against me and had the white people to arrest me and put me in jail for several days. I thank my God for the persecution. "For all that live godly must suffer persecution" (2 Tim. 2:12).

The impact of Mason's stance was so great on persons entering the military that the government tried in vain to build its own case against Mason for fraud and conspiracy. With other followers, he was subjected to a thorough and ongoing investigation by the Federal Bureau of Investigation, but all to no avail. When agents confiscated Mason's briefcase for what they knew would be incriminating evidence, they found only a bottle of anointing oil and a handkerchief with his Bible. The United States District Court in Jackson, Mississippi, failed to render a federal grand jury indictment against Mason and his followers. The "kangaroo court" in Paris, Texas, in 1918, dropped its case when the presiding judge looked at Mason, laid down his books, and said, "You all

may try him; I will not have anything to do with him."

No courtroom, no government, no amount of persecution or prosecution could withstand the powerful witness of those pioneers whose lips had been touched by divine fire. Throughout the deep South and throughout the U.S., the message of Pentecostalism spread. It was C. H. Mason who responded to the call of E. N. Bell and H. A. Goss, who convened a general council of "all the churches of God in Christ" and "Pentecostal or Apostolic Faith Assemblies" to meet at Hot Springs, Arkansas, in April 1914, where the Assemblies of God (AG) came into being. Significantly, many white ministers from the AG had been ordained by Mason for purely practical reasons because his organization had been officially chartered by the state of Tennessee.

D. Issues.

1. *Finished Work.* Between 1909 and 1915 the "finished work" controversy raised objections about sanctification as a definite second work of grace; opponents proposed a progressive view of sanctification. The challenge was raised by W. H. Durham, pastor of the North Avenue Mission in Chicago, Illinois. This issue wrought havoc among several Pentecostal denominations that were organized after 1911 but did not affect Black Holiness-Pentecostal denominations.

2. *Jesus Only.* The most notable controversy to affect all Pentecostal denominations after 1914 was the "New Issue" (Jesus Only) controversy espoused initially by R. E. McAlister and Frank J. Ewart. Ewart converted Glenn A. Cook, who later traveled to the Midwest and influenced G. T. Haywood. E. N. Bell, the general chairman of the AG, initially opposed this new doctrine but later accepted it.

3. *Oneness.* Between 1916 and 1922 several Oneness Pentecostal denominations were formed. W. T. Phillips, a former black Methodist preacher, founded the Apostolic Overcoming Holy Church of God at Mobile, Alabama. Robert Clarence Lawson founded in 1919 the Refuge Churches of Our Lord in Columbus, Ohio, and moved the headquarters to Harlem in New York City. The unity continued until 1930 when Sherrod C. Johnson, a native of Edgecombe County, North Carolina, withdrew and established the Church of the Lord Jesus Christ of the Apostolic Faith. Johnson, who succumbed in 1961, remained highly controversial until his death. His successor S. McDowell Shelton presides currently from the Philadelphia headquarters. The second division of Lawson's church came in 1957 when Smallwood E. Williams of Washington, D.C., founded the Bible Way Church of our Lord Jesus Christ World Wide due largely to the rigid authoritarianism of K. C. Lawson.

E. 1920s and 1930s.

1. *Rifts in Black Holiness-Pentecostal Churches.* In 1917 Lightfoot Solomon Michaux became licensed in the Church of Christ Holiness at Newport News, Virginia. The "Happy Am I" evangelist refused to leave his independently established Everybody's Mission to accept reassignment by his bishop and incorporated his work

as the Gospel Spreading Association. Known for his flamboyance, Michaux attracted widespread attention by sensational stunts, all preceded by a build-up in the mass media. With his death in 1968, the Church of God (Gospel Spreading) declined.

King Hezekiah Burruss also left the Church of Christ Holiness U.S.A. and formed the Church of God Holiness in 1920. Burruss and C. P. Jones had a personality clash rather than doctrinal differences. The church remained small until Burruss' death in 1963. The rigid authoritarian leadership was passed on to Burruss' son, Titus Paul Burruss, with its headquarters in Atlanta, Georgia.

William Christian, an associate of C. H. Mason, founded the Church of the Living God, Christian Fellowship Workers, initially, and changed the latter part of the name to Christian Workers for Friendship. Christian's movement contended that many biblical personalities were black and consequently affirmed its own racial pride. Finally, three groups formed from Christian's church. They are the Church of the Living God, General Assembly, founded by Charles W. Harris; the Church of the Living God, the Pillar and Ground of the Truth, incorporated initially under the leadership of Arthur Joseph Hawthorne in 1918; and a related movement affirming black people as the true Israel, founded by Frank S. Cherry around 1920: the Original Church of the Living God, the Pillar and Ground of the Truth.

Many Black Holiness-Pentecostal churches came into existence during the 1920s and 1930s over issues ranging from baptism to dressing attire. The exception was Elias Dempsey Smith, who claimed that God revealed to him through special revelation in 1897 (the same year C. H. Mason received the name CGIC at Little Rock, Arkansas) the name Triumph the Church and Kingdom of God in Christ at Issaquena County, Mississippi. Smith led his new church for approximately twenty years and left for Ethiopia, never to return again. This organization taught a highly controversial doctrine relative to the finality of life. It taught that sickness and death were signs that believers had lost the faith. It was this that C. H. Mason had in mind when he wrote a brief apologetic treatise addressing what he called the "no dying" issue. As a result, the issue was forthrightly opposed and did not create the expected rift in existing Black Holiness Pentecostal churches. The Triumph church remained relatively small and thrived mainly in a few southern states.

Rifts within newly established Black Holiness-Pentecostal churches resulted in the formation of several new organizations that later achieved denominational status. Such was the case of Bromfield Johnson in 1929, who formed the United Holy Church of America, accompanied by some two hundred followers. Johnson founded the Mount Calvary Holy Church of America, establishing its headquarters in Boston, Massachusetts. Some eighty churches in thirteen states represented the fruits of Johnson's labors at the time of his demise in 1972.

2. Women's Participation. Throughout the genesis and historical development of Black Holiness-Pentecostalism, women often have participated but usually in minor supportive roles. One has to recall the arduous evangelistic efforts of M. L. Esther Tate as the exception. Known affectionately among her followers as "Saint Mary Magdalene Tate," she, with her sons, F. E. Lewis and W. C. Lewis founded the Church of the Living God, the Pillar and Ground of the Truth in 1903. After its first general assembly, which convened at Greenville, Alabama, the organization splintered with dissension and schism upon the founder's demise in 1930.

A young deeply spiritual visionary, Ida Robinson, became disenchanted with the United Holy Church of America after a series of dreams and a ten-day fast. In 1924 after envisioning herself as a spiritual advisor to persons from many directions (a calling Ida attributed to the leading of the Holy Spirit), she founded the Mt. Sinai Holy Church of America. Not only did her group adopt a strict code of personal ethics, but it also gave women prominent roles in its hierarchy.

F. 1940s and 1950s.

1. Spread Throughout the World. The period between the 1940s and 1950s witnessed the spread and development of Black Holiness Pentecostalism throughout the U.S. and the world. Mass migration of blacks from the rural South to the midwestern and northern states during and after the war years proved to be a major social factor that impacted the movement's growth and expansion. The impact of cultural shock on these newly arrived settlers from the South often brought them face to face with the search for primary contacts and relationships that were often missing at the gatherings of established mainline black churches in the cities. This period sparked the heyday of several sociocultural messiahs, where the masses flocked. M. J. Divine, known as "Father Divine" established his earthly kingdom in Philadelphia, while "Daddy Grace" reigned in Detroit, Michigan. Gone were the embers and fires of Azusa with its dream of restoring Pentecostal spirituality to Western Christianity by way of the "Black face of church renewal."

However, this was the time when Riley F. Williams, an eminent CGIC preacher, without peer, would capture audiences with his preaching throughout the U.S. In 1933 he became one of the first five CGIC bishops appointed by Bishop Mason. Williams was instrumental in the planning, designing, and building of the Mason Temple in Memphis, Tennessee, the CGIC headquarters.

2. Education. With growth came the need for education—the foundation for institutionalization within denominations. Black Holiness Pentecostalism had indeed returned to the very same set of values that brought it into existence, the indictment of C. P. Jones that "denominationalism is slavery." The return to denominationalism found Black Holiness-Pentecostals with a different agenda, namely, how they could most effectively impact the larger society and at the same time overcome the stereotypes that had been imposed upon them since their inception.

Contrary to the common notion held by the larger society regarding education, Black Holiness-Pentecostal leadership maintained from the movement's early stages of development a vital concern about education in the lives of their constituents. As early as 1897 the Church of Christ Holiness U.S.A., under the visionary leadership of C. P. Jones had founded the Christ Missionary and Industrial College in Jackson, Mississippi.

Likewise, Bishop C. H. Mason, who had earlier heard God admonishing him that "salvation was not to be found in schools," utilized Miss Pinkie Duncan to establish Saints Industrial and Literary School at Lexington, Mississippi, in 1918. Mason further stated that the Lord spoke to him in special revelation and said, "If you will leave Arkansas Baptist College, I will give you a mouth of wisdom that your enemies cannot resist or gainsay." Even though Mason left that institution in 1926, he sent the youthful Arenia Cornelia Mallory, a protégé of Madame Mary McCleod Bethune, to develop the work initiated by professor James Courts, who died one month after she arrived on campus. She became the foremost educator in the CGIC.

In 1912 the Fire-Baptized Holiness Church of God of the Americas established the Fuller Normal and Industrial Institute, named in honor of its founder. The United Holy Church of America founded as a Bible training institute the United Christian College in 1944. The Bible Way Training School, established in 1945, served the (Oneness) Bible Way Church of Our Lord Jesus Christ World-Wide, led by Bishop Smallwood Williams at Washington, D.C. The Aenon Bible College, established in 1941, met the educational needs of the constituents of the Pentecostal Assemblies of the World.

So enamored by educational opportunities afforded to Black Holiness Pentecostals, the CGIC paved the way for Pentecostals of all races with its establishment of the first fully accredited Pentecostal seminary in North America. In 1970 Bishop J. O. Patterson, presiding prelate of the denomination, sent Leonard Lovett, who at that time was a young Pennsylvania preacher engaged in ministry at his first pastorate, to pioneer the C. H. Mason Theological Seminary and its system of Extension Schools in Atlanta, Georgia. Students from several Black Holiness-Pentecostal constituencies have received graduate theological education at this institution.

G. 1960s and 1970s.

1. Further Institutionalization. The period between the 1960s and 1970s attested to further institutionalization among Black Holiness Pentecostal churches in various ways. Major organizations, such as the CGIC and United Holy Church of America, witnessed ecclesiastical rifts within its leadership hierarchy that threatened the future existence and unity of both denominations to some degree. The thrust for civil rights, which set the stage for social ferment throughout the larger society, also spilled over into Black Holiness-Pentecostal churches.

2. Polity Rifts. As far back as 1932, Elder Justus Bowe, a pioneering comrade of Bishop C. H.

Mason left the CGIC over a dispute concerning its polity. He argued that the structure of the church was congregational, not episcopal. He founded the Church of God in Christ Congregational but later returned to the denomination in 1945. Upon the demise of Bishop Mason in 1961, the issue of leadership succession erupted into a major debate. At the annual convocation held in November 1962, Bishop Ozro Thurston Jones, Sr., was elected successor by acclamation, an action that was later disregarded and repudiated by the church, and led to several years of litigations. The extended dispute led to the departure in 1969 of fourteen bishops who met in Kansas City, Missouri, to form the Church of God in Christ International, which proved to be short lived. The year 1968 witnessed the formation of a new leadership structure for the CGIC, a twelve-man presidium, which recognizes one person as the presiding bishop, an honor accorded to James Oglethorpe Patterson, son-in-law and successor to the founder.

As recently as June 29, 1977, some within the United Holy Church of America organized at Raleigh, North Carolina, to form the Original United Holy Church International. The rift developed around a dispute over polity between Bishop W. N. Strobhar, denominational president, and Bishop J. A. Forbes, president of the Southern District Convocation.

IV. Conclusion.

A. Contributions. Throughout our history Black Holiness Pentecostal spiritual contributions have arisen from serious allegiance to God in Jesus Christ, through the power of the Holy Spirit, disregarding the divisive allegiances of the gods of this world. Allegiance to God's dominion called Black Holiness-Pentecostal leadership to a double discernment. In their early history they discovered how to say no to loyalties that divide and yes to the moving Spirit that heals and restores persons and institutions torn asunder by idolatrous loyalties.

B. Active Discipleship to be Witnesses. Throughout their brief history on the continent of North America Black Holiness-Pentecostals have rejected the abstract god of the philosophers and creeds and have opted for a more concrete god who could be encountered at a deeply personal level of existence. Black Holiness-Pentecostals perceive the baptism in the Holy Spirit to be an empowering symbol of active discipleship to be witnesses and servants of Christ, whose kingdom knows no caste or divisions.

The history of Black Holiness-Pentecostalism is exciting as well as embarrassing, full of triumphs as well as tragedies, full of promise and riddled with failures. It is the saga of people who heard the beckoning call of the Liberator, Jesus Christ, and took his urgent call to freedom seriously. Through them the "first love" of the kingdom broke through the boundaries of creeds, denominations, race, and class to demonstrate that God has once again, in his "saving moment" "chosen the foolish things of this world to confound the wise; . . . the things which are despised, to bring to nought things that are, that no flesh should glory in his presence."

See also BLACK THEOLOGY; CHURCH OF GOD IN CHRIST; PENTECOSTAL ASSEMBLIES OF THE WORLD.

Bibliography: R. Bastide, *African Civilization in the New World* (1971); B. Brawley, *A Social History of the American Negro* (1921); O. B. Cobbins, *History of Church of Christ Holiness U.S.A.* (1966); H. Courlander, *Negro Folk Music U.S.A.* (n.d.); W. E. B. Dubois, *The Negro Church* (1903); P. D. Dugas, ed., *The Life and Writings of Elder G. T. Haywood* (1968); J. H. Franklin, *From Slavery to Freedom* (1947); E. F. Frazier, *The Negro Church in America* (1963); E. D. Genovese, *Roll Jordan Roll: The World the Slaves Made* (1972); M. E. Golder, *History of the Pentecostal Assemblies of the World* (1973); idem, *The Principles of Our Doctrines* (n.d.); M. J. Herskovits, *Cultural Relativism* (1972); idem, *The Myth of the Negro Past* (1941); idem, *New World Negro* (1966); W. J. Hollenweger, *The Pentecostals* (1972); C. E. Jones, *Black Holiness: A Guide to the Study of Black Participation in Wesleyan Perfectionist and Glossalalic Pentecostal Movements* (1987); idem, *Perfectionist Persuasion: A Guide to the Study of the Holiness Movement* (1974); W. G. McLoughlin, *Modern Revivalism* (1959); H. Mitchell, *Black Preaching* (1970); D. Nelson, *The Black Face of Church Renewal* (1984); J. T. Nichols, *Pentecostalism* (1966); G. Ross, *History and Formative Years of the Church of God in Christ* (1969); L. B. Scherer, *Slavery and the Churches in Early America 1619–1819* (1975); W. J. Seymour, *Doctrine and Discipline of the Azusa Street Apostolic Faith Mission of Los Angeles* (1915); T. Smith, *Called Unto Holiness* (1962); idem, "Freedom Through the Sanctifying Spirit: A Forgotten Chapter in America's Theological History" (unpublished draft, August 1977); idem, *Revivalism and Social Reform in Mid-Nineteenth Century America* (1957); V. Synan, ed., *Aspects of Pentecostal-Charismatic Origins* (1975); idem, *The Holiness-Pentecostal Movement in the U.S.* (1971); D. M. Tucker, *Black Pastors and Leaders, 1919–1972* (1975); L. Turner, *Africanisms in the Gullah Dialect* (1949); W. C. Turner, "The United Holy Church of America: A Study in Black Holiness-Pentecostalism," Ph.D. diss., Duke University (1984); G. S. Wilmore, *Black Religion and Black Radicalism* (1972).   L. Lovett

BLACK THEOLOGY   There is consensus among most black American theologians and religious specialists that black theology is critical reflection about God through the prism of oppression and African cultural adaptation in North America. Black theology's roots are traceable to the eighteenth century within the corpus of the first black American "Independent churches." In the words of its contemporary seminal thinker, James Cone, black theology is said to be "Black God Talk" and is situational and contextual. In unequivocal terms, black theology insists on biblical grounds that the liberation of the poor and oppressed is at the very core of the Christian faith.

Black theology in its contemporary expression, developed as a response to the continuing debate among black religionists on the issue of racial integration or separation within the vortex of American society. Such racial dualism was represented by majority voices within the black churches and the Civil Rights movement. The late Dr. Martin Luther King, Jr., supported integration, while nationalists—from Bishop McNeal Turner of the African Methodist Episcopal (AME) Church to Malcom X—advocated separation. The first half of the 1960s was virtually dominated by the integrationist posture of King with a positive stress on love and nonviolence within the black religious community. After the assassination of Malcom X in 1965, Stokely Carmichael, a black nationalist, came to the fore espousing the notion of "Black Power." After the tragic demise of King in 1968, Black Power became more attractive even among black churchmen, with its emphasis on self-determination and political liberation by "any means necessary," as a possible viable alternative in deference to nonviolence. The attempt to resolve the continuing dilemma of how to reconcile Christian faith and Black Power became pronounced when an ad hoc committee of black churchmen published a position statement in the New York *Times*, in July 1966. In the ensuing debate, National Council of Black Churchmen (NCBC) clergymen endorsed the positive features of Black Power, and in the process a view of the Christian faith emerged that was radically different than traditional Western Christian theology. It was in such a context that black theology in its contemporary expression was born. From their interpretation of the gospel emerged a view of theology that embraced justice, hope, suffering, and liberation in terms of strong political implications, thereby maintaining solidarity with their suffering brothers and sisters in the urban ghettos of America. Just two years before the NCBC statement, a young articulate black interpreter of the black religious experience, J. Washington, published a book entitled *Black Religion* (1964), taking to task the exponents of the traditional view of black religion and stressing its unique relationship to its African heritage. Washington came under severe attacks by other black religionists, thus triggering a string of writings in black theology and lifting up racism as being heretical to the cause of the gospel. In 1968 Albert Cleage wrote *The Black Messiah*, while serving as pastor of the Shrine of the Black Madonna, Detroit, Michigan. Later, in his work entitled *Black Christian Nationalism*, Cleage pleaded with the masses to abandon whiteness totally and to reinstate blackness, beginning with the belief that Jesus, the Black Messiah, was a revolutionary leader sent by God to rebuild the black nation Israel and to liberate black people from the oppressive brutality and exploitation of the white Gentile world. Espousing a black nationalist posture, he contended that Jesus Christ was literally black and attempted to carve a theological position known as "Black Christian Nationalism." In 1969, a young scholar, James H. Cone, wrote the first book on black theology, *Black Theology and Black Power*. This work was preceded by an article entitled "Christianity and Black Power," Cone's first published essay serving as the basis for his first book. Cone argued that Black Power was not peripheral to Christian faith but is an authentic embodiment of the Christian faith in our time. The point of departure for black theology is the liberation of the oppressed. In this seminal work, the task of black theology is to analyze "black people's condition in the light of God's revelation in Jesus Christ with the purpose of creating a new understanding of black dignity among black people and providing the necessary soul in that people to destroy white racism." For Cone, self-determination, self-identity, emancipation from white oppression "by whatever means necessary," all of which are goals of the Black Power movement, are synonymous with his view of what God is doing in history in his task of liberation.

That black theology developed out of the corpus of the black experience can be seen in the social tensions of the times in which it emerged. The black insurrection in Watts, Detroit, Newark, and other parts of America impacted James H. Cone to search for a new way of viewing theology that would emerge out of the dialectic of black history and culture. Cone's quest led him to the Scriptures as the primary source for the new approach. He determined to find out what the biblical message had to do with the black power revolution. His first response came in his first book, *Black Theology and Black Power* (1969). The same problem emerged in a second work, *A Black Theology of Liberation*, and was probed in the light of the classical structures of theology. Those primary works left Cone dissatisfied, particularly after his earlier insistence that black theology has to emerge out of an oppressed community. The result was the publication of *The Spirituals and the Blues*, which was an inquiry about the theological significance of the black experience as reflected in such sources as sermons, sayings, songs, and stories. Cone had laid the foundations for further inquiry by insisting that Christianity, as espoused biblically, is essentially a movement of liberation and that the starting point for theology must be the liberation of the oppressed. Consequently, several subsequent debates among black theologians occurred around three categories of issues set forth initially by Cone: (1) black theology and black suffering; (2) black religion and black theology; and (3) liberation, reconciliation, and violence.

One of the first serious counter responses to Cone came from J. Deotis Roberts, who readily established himself as a major interpreter of black theological thought for this era. In contrast to Cone, Roberts proceeded to argue that we must not only lead the oppressed to liberation, but we are obligated by the demands of the gospel to reconcile the oppressor. It was that argument that sparked the title of his primary work, *Liberation and Reconciliation: A Black Theology*. Roberts proposed a theology that sought to retain a universal vision. By struggling between the tensions of the particular and universal categories, Roberts presents us with a universal Christ who will embrace the entire community of faith and at the same time participate in the task of liberation. In his less controversial and more balanced theological program, Roberts sought to bridge the gap between blacks and whites. He contended that intercommunication was a necessary task of black theology if reconciliation was to be achieved. For Roberts, liberation is personal and social, particular and universal. He refused to accept the view of many colleagues that black liberation versus white oppression was indeed an adequate formula to overcome the human condition of estrangement. He was not hesitant to suggest liberation between blacks and blacks as well as between blacks and whites in anticipation of the possibility that the oppressed would become the liberated. But what would happen to our theology? In reaction to Stokely Carmichael's Pan-Africanism, Roberts insisted that we must find a way to interracial togetherness in this country. This concern came to fruition in Roberts's second discussion, *A Black Political Theology*, in which he insisted that the only Christian way in race relations is a liberation experience of reconciliation for the white oppressor as well as for the black oppressed. Roberts attempts to resolve the theological tension in his system by insisting that reconciliation includes cross-bearing for whites as well as for blacks. Whites who are aware of the widespread and all-embracing effects of white racism have the responsibility to awaken and activate other whites to the end that racism may be overcome, root and branch. He was primarily concerned about the relationship of church and family in the black tradition as a basis for theological construction. Jones contributed to the dialogue in his *Black Awareness, A Theology of Hope*, under the influence of Jürgen Moltmann, Ernest Bloch, Wolfhart Pannenberg, and others; he insisted that a new direction for black theology was needed. The new direction was identified as the infusion of a Christian theology of hope into the black awareness movement while at the same time moving toward the goal of a radically new community beyond racism. The issue of the legitimacy of black theology and its relationship to black religion came to the fore of black theological debate. William R. Jones in his principal work, *Is God a White Racist?* influenced by Camus and Sartre, structures his theology upon the question of racism in light of the historic suffering of black people in their horizontal relationship with white people. For Jones theodicy is the point of departure for black theology. He radically questions Cone and challenges him to prove the assertion that God is the God of oppressed blacks, liberating them from bondage in the absence of an exaltation-liberation event. In *God of the Oppressed* not only does Cone identify primary sources for doing black theology, such as songs, sermons, testimonies, and slave narratives of the black religious tradition, he lifts up the Christ-event as the exaltation-liberation event to which Christians turn in order to resolve the theodicy issue posed by Jones. Charles Long, a renowned black scholar in the field of history of religion, in two key articles, "Perspectives for a Study of Afro-American Religion in the United States," and "Structural Similarities and Dissimilarities in Black and African Theologies," first raised the issue about the legitimacy of black theology to new levels of concern. Long's theoretical analysis questions the legitimacy of black theology during its infancy because of its reliance on Western theological constructs that have viewed the whole of religious reality through the bifocals of Immanuel Kant. As a provocative debater, Long persuades us to examine what he views as "a characteristic mode of orienting and perceiving reality"—an African rather than a European mode. Long identifies the process as the "historical and present experience of opacity, the meaning of which is not altogether clear, but definitely related to the otherness of Blackness."

Cecil Cone, the brother of James Cone, in his *The Identity Crisis in Black Theology,* and Gayraud Wilmore, in his *Black Religion and Black Radicalism,* set forth analyses of religion similar to Long, but neither rejects theology. Cecil Cone argues that the lack of a correct point of departure for black theology, namely black religion, and the tools derived from white seminaries are inadequate and that both are responsible for producing an identity crisis in black theology. Cone relies heavily on the vertical encounter with God in black slave religion as a viable option for empowering persons to transcend and transform negative oppressive situations into an oasis of hope. Wilmore sought to make black theology palatable to non-Christian blacks by lifting up its sources— the traditional religions of Africa; black folk religion; and the writings, sermons, and addresses of black preachers and public men of the past. C. Eric Lincoln, a distinguished black interpreter of religion, has cogently argued on behalf of the sustaining power of black religion and its peculiar genius for having made oppression less onerous for lives of black people.

Currently James Cone and several black theologians have shifted their focus to ecclesiology. Cone engages in what may be labeled an internal critique of the black church in his recent work, *My Soul Looks Back.* Cone critically assesses the past and present development of black theology as a servant to and for the black church. He helps us to understand that the identities of our theologies, whether they be black, African, Hispanic-American, Asian, Red, Latin American, Minjung, black feminist, or whatever, are determined by the human and divine dimensions of reality to which we are attempting to bear witness. In a most recent work, *Speaking the Truth,* Cone not only engages the issue of ecumenism, but links our struggle to the South African struggle and urges us to bear witness now to God's coming liberation by refusing to obey the agents of death. A similar concern comes to the fore in J. Deotis Roberts's most recent work, *Black Theology in Dialogue.* In utilizing the contextual approach, he proposes a theology concerned with specific and concrete situations while retaining a universal vision that relates black theology to African, feminist, Asian, Euroamerican, and liberation theologies. Roberts's contextual approach takes seriously the unique contribution of black church theology to the doctrine of the Holy Spirit in a chapter on the Holy Spirit and liberation. He uses the internal critique of Bennie Goodwin, James Tinney, James Forbes, and Leonard Lovett, to call into question the manifestation of racism within Pentecostal ranks. He concludes by reminding us that in the black church tradition, the Spirit is not merely a dove but wind and fire also. The Comforter is also the Strengthener. Justice in the social order for the black church, no less than joy and peace in the hearts of believers, is evidence of the Spirit's presence and power. Authentic Pentecostal encounter cannot occur unless liberation becomes the consequence.

See also BLACK HOLINESS–PENTECOSTALISM.

Bibliography: A. Cleage, *Black Messiah* (1969); idem, *Black Christian Nationalism* (1972); C. Cone, *The Identity Crisis in Black Theology* (1975); J. Cone, *Black Theology and Black Power* (1969); idem, *A Black Theology of Liberation* (1970); idem, "Christianity and Black Power," in *Is Anybody Listening to Black America?* ed. C. E. Lincoln (1968), 3–9; idem, "The Content and Method of Black Theology," *JRT* 33 (Fall–Winter 1975): 90–103; idem, *For My People* (1984); idem, *God of the Oppressed* (1975); idem, *My Soul Looks Back* (1982); idem, "Sanctification, Liberation and Black Worship," *Theology Today* (July 1978); idem, *Speaking the Truth* (1986); idem, *The Spirituals and the Blues* (1972); M. Jones, *Black Awareness* (1971); idem, *Christian Ethics for Black Theology* (1974); W. Jones, "Theodicy: The Controlling Category for Black Theology," *JRT* 30 (1, 1973): 28–38; idem, *Is God a White Racist?* (1973); M. L. King, Jr., *Where Do We Go From Here: Chaos or Community?* (1967); C. E. Lincoln, *The Black Church Since Frazier* (1974); C. E. Lincoln, ed., *The Black Experience in Religion* (1974); idem, *Race Religion and the Continuing American Dilemma* (1984); C. Long, "Perspectives for a Study of Afro-American Religion in the U.S.," *History of Religions* 2 (August 1971): 54–66; "Structural Similarities and Dissimilarities in Black and African Theologies," *JRT* 33 (Fall–Winter 1975): 9–24; L. Lovett, "Conditional Liberation: An Emergent Pentecostal Perspective," *Spirit* 1 (2, 1977): 24–30; J. D. Roberts, *A Black Political Theology* (1974); idem, "Black Theology and the Theological Revolution," *JRT* 28 (1, 1971): 5–20; idem, *Black Theology in Dialogue* (1987); idem, "Black Theology in the Making," *Review and Expositor* 70 (Summer 1973): 321–30; idem, *Liberation and Reconciliation: A Black Theology* (1971); idem, *Roots of a Black Future* (1980); H. Thurman, *Jesus and the Disinherited* (1949); J. Washington, *Black Religion* (1964); idem, *Black Sects and Cults* (1972); idem, "The Roots and Fruits of Black Theology," *Theology Today* 30 (July 1973): 121–29; C. West, *Prophesy Deliverance* (1982); G. Wilmore, "Black Messiah; Revising the Color Symbolism of Western Christology," *Journal of the Interdenominational Theological Center* 2 (Fall 1974): 8–18; idem, *Black Religion and Black Radicalism* (1973); idem, *Last Things First* (1982).
L. Lovett

BLACK, WARREN (1927–). Wesleyan charismatic leader. Warren Black is vice-chairman of the Wesleyan Holiness Charismatic Fellowship. Reared in a Nazarene community (Bethany, Okla.), he was a third-generation member of the Church of the Nazarene (thirty-two years) and a member of the official board of his church for fourteen years. He graduated from the University of Oklahoma (1949).

Black was controller for Nazarene Publishing House for nearly twenty years and sang in the Showers of Blessing radio choir and quartet for the Nazarene worldwide radio programs.

He was chairman for organizing business prayer groups in the Billy Graham Crusade, Kansas City; Midwest regional director of Christian Broadcasting Network and the 700 Club; nationwide speaker in Full Gospel Business Men's Fellowship International chapters; guest on "Good News" and "700 Club" TV programs, and Missouri coordinator of "Washington for Jesus '88."

For more than thirty years Black stammered so badly that he could not speak in public. He suffered from a debilitating lung condition and an enlarged hernia. God has healed him from all these and given him a ministry of healing and counseling. He continues to reside in Kansas City, Missouri.

Bibliography: Resume supplied to this author.
                                                    J. A. Hewett

BLAIR, CHARLES ELDON (1920–). Pastor. Blair was born into a poor family in Hiawatha, Kansas. As a youth he was converted in a Pentecostal church in Enid, Oklahoma, and he attended a small Bible school in that city.

Ordained at age twenty-three, Blair was elected the Nebraska District youth president for the Assemblies of God. After four years as an evangelist, he received a call to pastor Central Assembly of God in Denver, Colorado.

Beginning in a theater building, Blair's ministry in Denver started small but grew rapidly. The congregation built a 2,300-seat sanctuary, renamed the church Calvary Temple, and continued to grow with multiple services and an extensive missionary outreach.

Despite his wife's misgivings, Blair decided that it was God's will to build a geriatric center. He sold bonds for phase two of the project without an up-to-date prospectus. He believed everything would work out even though phase one ran into problems. When things did not work out, his failure to inform investors amounted to fraud under the law. Blair and an associate were convicted in 1976, and the "Life Center" declared bankruptcy. Blair and his church are sponsoring Second Mile, a program to repay investors.

Bibliography: C. Blair, *The Man Who Could Do No Wrong* (1981); S. Strang, "Fading Footprints," *Charisma* (March 1988), 6.
                                                    S. Strang

BLASPHEMY AGAINST THE HOLY SPIRIT Blasphemy against the Holy Spirit is the sin for which there is no forgiveness, the "unpardonable sin." It particularly denotes a saying of Jesus in three texts—Matthew 12:32; Mark 3:29; Luke 12:10—and while some may wish to interpret the "sin unto death" in 1 John 5:16 as equal to the "unpardonable sin," there is no justification for such an equation except in the broadest of terms, because, as it will be shown, even "blasphemy against the Spirit" is not understood in any monolithic sense in Scripture. Similarly, Hebrews 10:29, a reference to "insulting [*enybrisas*] the Spirit of grace," may have the same general implications, but it is not parallel to the Jesus saying in the strict sense. A text variant at 1 Peter 4:14 also contains a reference to blasphemy of the Spirit, which is an act attributed to those who revile believers. Some commentators think this text is original (Michaels, 1988).

"To blaspheme" (Gk. *blasphēmeō;* cf. the noun, *blasphēmia,* and the adjective, *blasphēmos*) is an especially strong word conveying insult, derision, abusive speech, or ridicule (Beyer, *TDNT,* 1:621). It particularly denotes religious profanation in the Scriptures, although this is not ordinarily the case in secular literature (LSJ, s.v.).

The word family is relatively rare in the Septuagint (LXX), with the verb appearing eight times; the noun "blasphemy," six; and the adjective/substantive "blasphemous"/"blasphemous one," six times. Of these twenty times, all refer to

religious blasphemy of God. Usually blasphemy is a verbal act (e.g., 2 Kings 19:4, 6, 22; Isa. 52:5; Ezek. 35:12; 2 Macc. 10:34), but it can denote an action directed against God (e.g., 1 Macc. 2:6; 2 Macc. 8:4; Sir. 3:16). Israel's enemies are typically "blasphemers" (e.g., Isa. 52:5; 1 Macc. 8:4; 10:34–36).

Blasphēmeō surprisingly occurs thirty-four times in the NT, appearing in fifteen books by eleven writers. The cognates *blasphēmia* and *blasphēmos* occur eighteen and four times respectively. Like the LXX, the NT conception of blasphemy is almost exclusively regarded as directed against God (Acts 6:11; Rev. 13:6), his name (Rom. 2:24; cf. Isa. 52:5), his word (Tim. 2:5), or indirectly against him (e.g., of "the way of truth," 2 Peter 2:2; but cf. Acts 13:45; 18:6; Paul is the object of Jewish "insults").

Blasphemy is also a charge frequently leveled against Jesus by his Gospel antagonists (e.g., Matt. 9:3; 25:65; cf. Mark 2:7; John 10:36). At the crux of the Jewish charge of blasphemy against Jesus lies the assumption that Jesus claimed equality with God (John 10:33–36; cf. Mark 2:7 with parallels). As a result of asserting his messiahship (Mark 14:61–62) Jesus is condemned to death for committing blasphemy (Mark 14:64). Ironically—and probably reflecting consummate literary design—his opponents "blaspheme" him (Matt. 27:39; Mark 15:29; Luke 22:65; 23:39).

It is within such literary settings that one must interpret what each Gospel writer has to say concerning blaspheming the Spirit. The issue of religious blasphemy is not unique to NT theology; the Jewish experts in the law were "thoroughly familiar with this concept under the rubric 'the profanation of the Name'" (Lane, 1974, 145). "The Holy One, blessed be he, pardons everything else, but on profanation of the Name [i.e., takes vengeance immediately" (Lane, ibid., citing Sifré on Deut. 32:38). Profanation of the Name (*hillul ha-Shem*), however, "includes every act or word of a Jew which disgraces his religion and so reflects dishonor upon God" (Moore, 1932, 2:108). Thus in Jewish casuistry there were several "unpardonable sins," including "murder, unchastity, apostasy, contempt for the Law, etc." (Jeremias, 1971, 149–50).

The saying about blaspheming the Holy Spirit occurs in three locations in the NT: Mark 3:28–30; Matthew 12:31–32; and Luke 12:10. (The Gospel of Thomas [logion 44] also records an interesting Trinitarian version in which the Father and Son cannot be blasphemed—only the Holy Spirit.) Apparently the saying circulated in two forms; one form occurs in the double-tradition material (Q), while Mark has the other, more original (e.g., Bultmann, 1963, 131; Manson, 1957, 110; but cf. Boring, 1976, who argues that the Q form was older). Dunn's assertion that both forms were probably derived from an Aramaic original seems logical, especially if one accepts this as an authentic saying of Jesus (Dunn, 1988; cf. Boring, who is reluctant to originate the saying with Jesus). Matthew's version reflects a union between Q and Mark, while Luke probably reflects the Q version.

Both Matthew and Mark associate the saying with the Beelzebub controversy (cf. Luke 11:14–16), while Luke makes no such connection, preferring instead to link it to a confession/denial lesson (Luke 12:8–11). Each evangelist shapes the saying's import, but Luke's repositioning of the text affects it most radically. Therefore, any blanket interpretation of what constitutes "blasphemy against the Spirit" ignores how each evangelist uses the saying. The context of each appearance will be analyzed below to determine differences, emphases, and similarities. Following that the implications of the Gospel teachings will be offered.

Mark 3:28–30. Jesus' mission in the Gospel of Mark is carried out under the power of the Spirit received at his baptism by John. Empowered by the Spirit, Jesus is portrayed in the earliest chapters of Mark as an exorcist par excellence (Mark 1:23, 27, 32, 34; 3:11), and the passage in which the saying about blaspheming the Spirit occurs is precisely such an exorcism story (Dunn suggests that "Mark or the pre-Markan tradition was right to link [the blasphemy saying] into the exorcism context" [1988]).

The Markan understanding of blasphemy against the Spirit is revealed in Mark 3:30, where the narrator interrupts the story with an explanation for why Jesus uttered this warning: "for [*hoti*] they were saying he had an unclean spirit [*pneuma akatharton*]." Of the evangelists, only Mark reads this. It is important both for Mark's perspective of who Jesus is and for what Mark's community is experiencing. While Mansfield's main thesis is perhaps exaggerated, he rightly sees Mark's editorializing here as one of the key signs that the Spirit continues to guide the Markan church in its understanding of "Gospel" (Mansfield, 1987, 5–7, 17–19, 61, 65–70). Those in the community who would wrongly appeal to Satan as the source for power wielded by either Jesus or his disciples—who are authenticated in terms of cross-bearing and self-denial and who have been granted "authority" (*exousia*) to drive out demons (3:15)—are in danger of blasphemy. The question is not *if* Jesus and his disciples drive out demons, but *how* they do it. The answer is—as the reader knows—Jesus does this by the power of the Spirit, not by Satan, who resists Jesus at every turn.

Mark underscores this both with the intercalated parable of the strong man and with his portrayal of Jesus' family and the scribes. The *"they"* of "they were saying" (v. 30) need not be limited to the scribes alone. For the observant reader notes that Jesus' family, who first appear in verse 21, reappear in verse 31, thereby bracketing the parable of the strong man and the saying against blasphemy. Their attitude parallels that of the teachers of the law from Jerusalem. His family thinks he is "mad" (*exestē,* i.e., "crazy," or possibly "in a state of ecstasy," v. 21), while the scribes say he is "possessed" (lit., "he has Beelzebub"; *Beelzeboul echei,* v. 22). Not insignificantly, it is his family who "stands outside" (*exō stekontes,* 3:31–32) and who is among those "on the outside [*exō*] to whom everything is given in parables" (4:11). Jesus' rejection in his own hometown of Nazareth further implies his family's rejection of him (Mark 6:1–6). Similarly, the scribes risk blasphemy by asserting that Jesus' power comes from Satan rather than from God. Ironically, it is they who are under the control of Satan, not Jesus or his disciples.

The Markan saying on blasphemy thus points up a problem in the Markan community. It is not necessary to go to the extent that Mansfield (following T. Weeden) does in trying to link the actions of Jesus' family as in some way representative of "pneumatic prophets who misunderstood and opposed (unknowingly?) the true Gospel of Jesus" (Mansfield, 1987, 65; cf. Alexander, 1985). If anything, Jesus' family represents the anticharismatic, more institutionally oriented element in Mark's community. Mark endeavors to salvage the charismatic ministry of the church; at the same time he wishes to safeguard against imitation. The genuine "charismatic" disciple not only does the "works" of Jesus, he or she lives the life of Jesus as well. The disciple denies self and takes up the cross, following the footsteps of the Lord.

A coinciding relationship between blasphemy and charismatic manifestations is also related in the *Didache,* an early Christian document. There it is blasphemous to "test" (*peirazō*) or "judge" (*diakrinō*) a prophet speaking by (*en*) the Spirit (Did. 11:7).

Matthew 12:31–32. Matthew's interpretation of the saying concerning blaspheming the Spirit is intelligible only in light of its immediate context. While Matthew apparently knows Mark (and Q), his application of the saying is quite different from Mark's. He does not incorporate Mark's explanatory comment in 3:30 that "He [Jesus] said this because they [the Pharisees] were saying, 'He has an evil spirit.'" Instead, Matthew reads the controversy as a question over the source of Jesus' power to drive out demons (Matt. 12:28). He further subordinates that issue to a larger one: the issue of Jesus' messiahship.

O. L. Cope has shown on the basis of the Targumic translation of the opening verse of Isaiah 42 (servant = "servant Messiah") as well as on the basis of redactional elements (the inclusion of *agapētos,* which is not in the LXX but points back to Jesus' baptism in Matt. 3:17) that Isaiah 42:1–4 is understood by Matthew to be a messianic text (Cope, 1976, 36). Further evidence pointing to this is implicit in the response of the crowd to Jesus' healing the demon-possessed man who was blind and mute. They exclaim, "Could this be the Son of David?" i.e., the Messiah? Only Matthew has this comment from the crowd. To counter the conclusions of the crowd, the Pharisees argue that Jesus exorcises demons by the power of Beelzebub. Jesus retorts with the parable of the strong man and with his own question, "And if I drive out demons by Beelzebub, by whom do your people drive them out?"

Jesus clarifies himself further by asserting that he casts out demons by "the Spirit of God." This forms a crucial link to the messianic interpretation of Isaiah 42:1–4, which confirms that God's servant will have God's Spirit upon him (cf. Isa. 42:1 with Matt. 13:18). The saying against blasphemy, accordingly, is affixed in this messianic frame. The question is not whether Jesus was exorcising demons—even the Pharisees had their "exorcists" (Matt. 12:27; cf. on this as a Jewish practice, Acts 19:13–16; Josephus, *Antiq.* 8.44–49); rather, the question is whether Jesus is doing this as God's Messiah, as the crowd believes. "To blaspheme" is to speak against the power by which God's servant the Messiah announces the arrival of the kingdom, since Jesus is indeed casting out demons "by the Spirit of God" (cf. 12:18, 28). For Matthew, "to blaspheme the Spirit" is to reject God and his purpose in Jesus as Messiah.

Luke 12:10. Unlike Matthew, Luke departs totally from the Markan sequence and wording. As a result, his understanding of blaspheming the Spirit is utterly different. The saying does not occur in the Beelzebub controversy as it does in Mark and Matthew (cf. Luke 11:14–28); instead, it surfaces in conjunction with an admonition about remaining faithful during trials the disciple of Jesus will inevitably face. The context is that of confession (*homologeō;* Luke 12:8) and denial (*arneomai;* Luke 12:9). Luke 12:11 envisions conditions of persecution and trial for the believer: "When you are brought before synagogues, rulers and authorities." Under such circumstances the Holy Spirit will instruct the disciple in what to say (cf. John 16:8–11).

It is not surprising that Luke should have Jesus provide such a postresurrectional glimpse of the fate of the disciples. Clearly this relates to Luke's own readers, who are enduring hardship for the sake of the gospel and who have been promised "power" (*dynamis*) specifically to bear witness (e.g., Luke 24:48–49; Acts 1:8). Thus, for Luke, to reject the Spirit's help at this critical juncture—and as a consequence to deny Jesus—is tantamount to blaspheming the Holy Spirit.

Implications. The teaching from Scripture concerning blaspheming the Spirit depends on whose version one reads, yet each evangelist can speak to the church today. A central scriptural lesson can be blended from this saying of Jesus in its various contexts. First, contrary to some thinking, God's grace is not irresistible; it can be spurned, rejected, and ignored; moreover, persistent denial of God's revealing himself in Jesus through the power of the Spirit can have eternal consequences. God's revelation of himself is not limited to, but certainly includes, manifesting his grace through the gifts of the Spirit. Any refusal of grace (i.e., salvation) is in a sense "unforgivable," because grace that is "given" must be "received." Second, blaspheming the Spirit concerns a willful rejection of God's grace and power. This especially includes attributing God's working through the power of the Spirit—whether in Jesus or his disciples—to Satan. To blaspheme the Spirit is also to reject both the offer of grace and the power to remain faithful to God. Thus the one blaspheming the Spirit rejects the very power through which grace is manifest and made available. Have those who have denounced Pentecostalism and the charismatic movements been guilty in any sense of

blaspheming the Spirit because they deny the validity of such manifestations? Certainly not, if they have accepted the greater gift of salvation through Jesus Christ, the ultimate manifestation of God's power and grace.

As Jeremias astutely points out, appreciating the uniqueness of blaspheming the Spirit lies in understanding that for Jesus' hearers the Spirit's activity had largely ceased. Jesus, though, knows the Spirit is active through his ministry and is himself revealing that presence. "In other words, Mark 3:28 speaks of sin against the God who is still hidden, v. 29 of sin against the God who is revealing himself. The former can be forgiven, the latter is unforgivable" (Jeremias, 1971, 150). Thus he rightly continues, "the unforgivable sin is not a particular moral transgression, as it is in the sphere of Rabbinic casuistry . . . ; rather, it is the sin that arises in connection with revelation" (ibid.).

Bibliography: P. H. Alexander; "A Critique of Theodore Weeden's *Traditions in Conflict,*" unpublished paper read before the Central States Regional Society of Biblical Literature, 1985; idem, "The Literary Function of Mark 6:6b–13 and Its Message to Mark's Church," *Debarim* (1982–83): 24–34; H. W. Beyer in *TDNT* (1964), 621–25; M. E. Boring, "The Unforgivable Sin Logion Mark III 28–29 Matt XII 28–32/Luke XII 10: Formal Analysis and History of the Tradition," *NovT* 18 (1976): 258–75; R. Bultmann, *History of the Synoptic Tradition* (1963); O. L. Cope, *Matthew. A Scribe Trained for the Kingdom, CBQMS* 5 (1976); F. Danker, *Jesus and the New Age* (1972); J. D. G. Dunn, *Jesus and the Spirit* (1975); J. A. Fitzmyer, *The Gospel According to Luke,* 2 vols., *AB* 28, 28A (1983, 1985); H. Gloer, ed., *Eschatology: Essays in Honor of George Raymond Beasley-Murray* (1988); J. Jeremias, *New Testament Theology. The Proclamation of Jesus* (1971); W. L. Lane, *The Gospel of Mark, NIC* (1974); *LSJ* (1968); M. R. Mansfield, *Spirit and Gospel in Mark* (1987); T. W. Manson, *The Sayings of Jesus* (1957); I. H. Marshall, *The Gospel of Luke, NIGTC* (1978); G. F. Moore, *Judaism in the First Centuries of the Christian Era. The Age of the Tannaim,* 2 vols. (1932).   P. H. Alexander

BLESSED TRINITY SOCIETY An organization founded in 1960 to publicize and support charismatic renewal in mainline Protestant churches. The founder, Jean Stone Willans, was active in St. Mark's Episcopal Church in Van Nuys, California, when Rector Dennis Bennett received the baptism in the Holy Spirit. After her own Pentecost experience Mrs. Willans began the society, which later claimed about seven thousand members.

The society first distributed booklets and tracts and supplied speakers to groups who wished to learn more about spiritual gifts. In 1961 the society's chief publication, *Trinity* magazine, began appearing quarterly. It was the first non-Pentecostal publication dedicated to promoting the Pentecostal experience. As interest grew they sponsored meetings in various cities to teach about and lead people to experience the spiritual gifts. When dissent among congregations occasionally led to division and resignations, the society provided assistance for some ministers until they could find new posts.

Debate and controversy chiefly centered around speaking in tongues. In 1963 the society's board

Pavel Bochian, president of the Apostolic Church of God in Romania, baptizing converts in Bucharest, Romania in 1972.

of directors stated its position. This included the belief that tongues should primarily be used for private devotions; that in public, tongues should always be interpreted; and that when a Christian receives the baptism in the Holy Spirit promised by Jesus (Acts 1:5, 8), the consequence is the ability to speak in tongues.

See also CHARISMATIC MOVEMENT; EPISCOPAL RENEWAL MINISTRIES.

C. M. Irish

BLOCH-HOELL, NILS EGEDE (1915–). Historian. The Norwegian historian Nils Bloch-Hoell, a Lutheran, was the first scholarly commentator to address the Anglo-American Pentecostal audience from a Scandinavian standpoint and from outside the movement's subjective confines. Sometime lecturer at the University of Oslo and the Teologiske Menighetafakutet and editor of *Tidsskrift for Teologi og Kirke,* Bloch-Hoell has produced two versions of his book: *Pinsebevelgelsen* (1956), revised and translated into English as the *Pentecostal Movement* (1964). In content, the principal difference between the Norwegian and English language versions was the reduction of pages devoted to Norway from 150 to 12 and expanded coverage of the American and British movements. In the process the bulk was reduced from 466 to 256 pages. Although, as is proper, giving close attention to North American origins, Bloch-Hoell highlights European developments, giving special attention to Norway and the other Scandinavian countries. The stress on Norway in the original book was in fact its unique feature. To Pentecostal readers unused at the time of publication to objective and critical scrutiny, the sociological and phenomenological analysis of their institutions, beliefs, and worship was at first unsettling. Taken together with the later work of W. J. Hollenweger, Bloch-Hoell's work proved to be a useful corrective to the earlier narrow-gauge,

apologetic works of American and British insiders.

Bibliography: N. Bloch-Hoell, *The Pentecostal Movement* (1964); R. Quebedeaux, *The New Charismatics II* (1983).   C. E. Jones

BOCHIAN, PAVEL (twentieth century). President of the Apostolic Church of God in Romania. The first Pentecostal church in Romania was established in 1922. As Pentecostalism grew, its adherents experienced considerable persecution from ecclesiastical (Romanian Orthodox) and governmental officials. Bochian, as a young Pentecostal minister, experienced many difficulties, particularly in the 1930s and 1940s. Full government recognition of the Pentecostal churches came in 1950. Over the years he has worked in important leadership posts, serving as president of the Apostolic Church of God (the official organization of Pentecostal churches) since 1962.

During his years in office the church has experienced intense pressures, witnessed remarkable growth, established a theological seminary (1976), and established fraternal links to the Church of God (Cleveland, Tenn.) in 1980.

Bochian attended the Ninth Pentecostal World Conference in Dallas, Texas, in 1970.

Bibliography: P. Bochian, "The Pentecostal Church in Rumania," *World Pentecost* (1, 1972), 26–27; Church of God (Cleveland, Tenn.), press release, September 8, 1980.   G. B. McGee

BODDY, ALEXANDER ALFRED (1854–1930). Early Pentecostal leader in Great Britain. Son of an Anglican rector, Boddy was heavily influenced by Keswick. He studied theology at Durham. He was ordained by Bishop J. B. Lightfoot and began ministry at Elwick before being appointed to Sunderland (1884–1922) and Piddington (1922–30). Boddy traveled widely, exploring western Canada, Egypt, North Africa, Palestine, and Russia. Books describing these trips won him membership in the Royal Geographical Society (England) and the Imperial Geographical Society (Russia). Concerned about the spiritual life of his parish, he investigated the Welsh Revival and in 1907 went to Oslo to study the Pentecostal revival. T. B. Barratt visited Sunderland (September 1907), and under his leadership several experienced the baptism of the Holy Spirit. Boddy became active in the Pentecostal revival in England. He hosted the Annual Whitsuntide (Pentecost) Pentecostal Conventions at Sunderland (1908–14). Participants included G. Polman from the Netherlands and J. Paul from Germany. Boddy also edited and published the Pentecostal periodical *Confidence* (1908–26).

Mary Boddy ministered along with her husband in his All Saints Church, Sunderland, England. It was she who laid her hands on Smith Wigglesworth when he was baptized in the Spirit in 1907.

An Anglican rector in Sunderland, England, A. A. Boddy was baptized in the Spirit in 1907. He edited the influential Pentecostal periodical *Confidence*.

See also EUROPEAN PENTECOSTALISM.

Bibliography: Works: A. A. Boddy, *By Ocean, Prairie, and Peak* (1896); *Christ in His Holy Land, A Life of Our Lord* (1897); *Days in Galilee and Scenes in Judea* (1900); *From the Egyptian Ramleh* (1900); *The Laying on of Hands, A Bible Ordinance* (1895); *To Kairwan the Holy* (1884); *With Russian Pilgrims* (1893); **Secondary Works:** J. V. Boddy (Mother Joanna Mary), "Alexander Alfred Boddy, 1854–1930" (unpublished typescript, c. 1970); E. Blumhofer, "Alexander Boddy and the Rise of Pentecostalism in Britain," *Pneuma* 8 (1986): 31–40; D. Gee, *Wind and Flame* (1967); idem, *These Men I Knew* (1980); W. K. Kay, "Alexander Boddy and the Outpouring of the Holy Spirit in Sunderland," *EPTA Bulletin* 5 (1986): 44–56; A. Missen, *Sound of a Going* (1973).   D. D. Bundy

BODDY, MARY (d. 1928). Wife of the Reverend Alexander A. Boddy, vicar of All Saints', Monkwearmouth, Sunderland, England. Daughter of an Anglican minister, she assisted Boddy during revival services in 1890. They were married in 1891. Mary was healed of asthma in 1899 and exercised a healing ministry before and after her Pentecostal experience, which occurred on September 11, 1907. Their two daughters, Mary and Jane, also spoke in tongues. Mrs. Boddy possessed musical ability and teaching skills, which were coupled with her healing ministry. She also had a special gift for helping seekers into the experience of the baptism of the Spirit. Among the number who received the baptism when she laid hands upon them were the Bradford plumber, Smith Wigglesworth, and G. R. Polman from Holland. For the last sixteen years of her life she was an invalid, but she still ministered healing to others, both in Sunderland and at Pittington, Durham, where the Boddys retired in 1922.

Bibliography: Mary Boddy, *"Pentecost" at Sunderland, The Testimony of a Vicar's Wife* (n.d.).
D. W. Cartwright

BODY OF CHRIST (B'NAI SHALOM), THE Following the death of William Sowders (1878–1952), the Gospel of the Kingdom movement divided into several factions. The body of Christ led by Elder Reynolds Edward Dawkins (d. 1965), "apostle and builder of the body of Christ," was among the most populous of these. Denying that it is a denomination, it refuses to capitalize "body" in its name. Adherents say that the "apostolic order" schema by which it is

The Pentecostal revival in Los Angeles began in this house on North Bonnie Brae Street in 1906. Because of the crowds, the meetings were moved to what became known as the Azusa Street Mission. The above house is still standing.

governed was given to Dawkins by divine revelation. The body of Christ, which is the "new Jerusalem" or "natural Israel," derives its authority from the twelve apostles and is the means whereby the love of God is transmitted to the rest of humankind. The Gospel of Peace Camp Ground and Peace Publishers and Company are both in Phoenix, Arizona. By 1975 the body of Christ had eight churches and about a thousand members in the U.S., with affiliates in Jamaica, the Netherlands, Nigeria (eleven churches), Israel, India, and Hong Kong.

Bibliography: C. E. Jones, *Guide to the Study of the Pentecostal Movement* (1983); A. C. Piepkorn, *Profiles in Belief,* vol. 3 (1979).   C. E. Jones

BONNIE BRAE STREET COTTAGE During the winter-spring months of 1906 a group of black Los Angeles Christians gathered at 214 (now 216) North Bonnie Brae Street, the home of a janitor and his wife, Richard D. and Ruth Asberry, for prayer and Bible study. Included among them was Mrs. Julia W. Hutchins, who, with eight other families, had been expelled from the Second Baptist Church in Los Angeles for embracing "Holiness" teaching. When the group proved to be too large for the Asberry home, Hutchins opened a storefront mission on Santa Fe Street.

William J. Seymour was called to serve as the pastor of this new congregation. He arrived by train on February 22, 1906, and commenced his ministry on February 24. At first all went well, but when Seymour argued that the ability to speak in tongues was a sign that would follow the baptism in the Holy Spirit, Hutchins had him locked out of the church.

Seymour had been staying in the home of Mr. and Mrs. Edward S. Lee on South Union Avenue, near First Street. They opened their small home so that those from the church who were interested could pursue their Bible study with Seymour. When the group grew to the size when it could no longer meet at the Lee's home, they moved back to the Asberry home.

At 6:00 on the evening of April 9, 1906, Edward Lee called Seymour and asked for prayer that he would at that time be given the gift of tongues. Seymour prayed, and Lee spoke in tongues. Seymour went immediately to the Asberry home for the 7:30 P.M. meeting. Following the singing of a song, a time of prayer, and a few testimonies, Seymour began to speak on Acts 2:4, sharing the news of Edward Lee's experience less than two hours ago. He never finished his study. Someone began to speak in tongues. That person was joined by others, among them Jennie Moore, who improvised a melody on the piano to accompany her gift of tongues. The meeting concluded about 10 P.M., and word traveled fast within the black community and into the white community. For the next several nights crowds gathered at the Bonnie Brae home so that the services moved to the ready-made pulpit of the front porch and the street below. On April 12, 1906, the front porch collapsed from the weight of the worshipers. Meetings were moved to 312 Azusa Street after a lease was negotiated with the Stevens African Methodist Episcopal Church, where several of the crowd had formerly been members.

The cottage remained in the Asberry family until 1985 when it was purchased by Pentecostal Heritage, Inc., a nonprofit entity under the leadership of Arthur E. Glass. The corporation intends to restore the house, to seek historical landmark status, and to open it to the public as a museum showplace.

See also AZUSA STREET REVIVAL.

Bibliography A. M. Cotton, "Inside Story of the Outpouring of the Holy Spirit, Azusa Street, April 1906," *Message of the "Apostolic Faith"* 1 (1, 1939): 1–3; R. L. Fidler, "Historical Review of the Pentecostal Outpouring," *International Outlook* (January–March 1963); C. W. Shumway, "A Study of 'The Gift of Tongues,'" A.B. thesis, University of Southern California, 1914.   C. M. Robeck, Jr.

BONNKE, REINHARD WILLI GOTT-FRIED (1940–). International evangelist. Reinhard Willi Gottfried Bonnke was born in Koenigsberg, Germany, on April 19, 1940, the son of a Pentecostal pastor belonging to the Federation of Free Pentecostal Churches (Bund Freier Pfingstmeinden [BFP]). Educated in Wales, he met George Jeffreys (1889–1962) as a youth. From his earliest days he felt called to be a missionary to Africa. His marriage to Anna Sulzle in 1964 produced three children: Kai-uwe (1966), Gabriele (1967), and Susanne (1969). After several years as a pastor and evangelist in Germany, he arrived in Africa in May 1967.

From 1967 to 1974, Bonnke labored with meager results as a traditional missionary for the BFP in Lesotho, Africa. In the latter year he received a call to minister "to the whole of Africa" with the assurance that "Africa shall be saved." His first mass healing crusade took place in Gaberones, Botswana, in April 1975, which began with only 100 persons in attendance and ended in a packed stadium with over 10,000 present.

In 1977 he purchased a 10,000-seat tent, which often was inadequate when as many as 40,000 attempted to enter. A blond-haired, blue-eyed German, Bonnke was at a loss to explain his popularity among the blacks with whom he identified. Everywhere he ministered, even in South Africa, Bonnke refused to practice racial segregation in his services.

A major attraction in Bonnke's meetings were the signs and wonders that accompanied his preaching, with thousands testifying to miracles of physical healing and exorcisms in his crusades. Also featured in many meetings were bonfires that were set as converts burned their magic amulets and charms associated with witchcraft. Everywhere Bonnke encouraged his converts to receive the baptism in the Holy Spirit with the evidence of speaking in tongues. Also, at times, thousands would be "slain in the Spirit" as he preached.

During the early 1980s Bonnke's crusades attracted some of the largest crowds in the history of mass evangelism. One crusade in Nigeria in 1986 attracted as many as 250,000 to one service. His crusades in Soweto attracted thousands of blacks and whites despite the official government policy of apartheid.

In 1983 Bonnke purchased the largest gospel tent ever built, one that would hold some 34,000 persons. Although it was torn apart in a severe storm in Capetown in 1984, it was rebuilt and put back into use by 1986. In the latter year, Bonnke's team reported 1,500,000 responses to the call for salvation, many thousands of whom were Muslims.

By the mid-1980s Bonnke also began conducting leadership conferences in Africa and Europe. His "Fire Conference" in Zimbabwe in 1986 drew thousands of African pastors and evangelists, while his "Eurofire" conferences in Frankfurt in 1987 and Birmingham in 1988 brought his ministry to the attention of Europeans. His ministry in the U.S. increased after speaking in the New Orleans Superdome in 1987 to the Congress on the Holy Spirit and World Evangelization.

In 1987 Bonnke moved his family from Johannesburg, where he had lived for many years, to Frankfurt, West Germany, where he set up headquarters for his organization which, since its legal beginning in 1972, has been known as Christ for All Nations (CFAN).

Bibliography: R. Steele, *Plundering Hell to Populate Heaven* (1987).   H. V. Synan

BOONE, CHARLES EUGENE ("PAT") (1934–). Singer, actor. With roots in the Church of Christ and currently an elder at the Church on the Way (Foursquare), Pat Boone has been active for many years as an evangelical witness for Christ. In 1955 his first record, "Two Hearts," became a best seller, helping to make him a teenage idol and a favorite of teenagers' parents. Boone went on to star in the movie *Bernadine*, while attempting to finish his college education. In June 1958 he graduated from Columbia University. Since these early successes, Boone has engaged in many other business ventures, singing appearances, and acting roles, all the while consistently encouraging young people to dedicate themselves to Christ. His book *'Twixt Twelve and Twenty* (1958) makes practical suggestions to teenagers for living.

Early in 1969 Pat Boone received the baptism in the Holy Spirit, singing in unknown languages in the Spirit. He had been influenced in charismatic directions by David Wilkerson when he was asked to act in the film *The Cross and the Switchblade* and by his wife, Shirley, who received a baptism in the Spirit late in 1968. In response to his new life in the Holy Spirit, Boone wrote his biography, *A New Song* (1970), describing the positive changes in his life that grew out of his dependence on the divine Spirit. Convinced of the importance of the supernatural in Christian living, Boone authored *A Miracle a Day Keeps the Devil Away* (1974). He has been actively involved in the Church on the Way.

Bibliography: B. C. Spicer, "Pat Boone Talks to Teen-Agers," *Ladies Home Journal* (August 1959), 76, 142–43. F. Bixler

BOSWORTH, FRED FRANCIS (1877–1958). Early Pentecostal pioneer, pastor, and healing evangelist. When Bosworth was young, his family moved to Chicago to be a part of John Alexander Dowie's church. He later became director of Dowie's Zion City, Illinois, band. When Charles F. Parham brought the Pentecostal message to Zion City in September 1906, Bosworth and Marie Burgess were baptized in the Holy Spirit on the same evening.

Persecuted for his Pentecostal beliefs, Bosworth went to Dallas, where in 1910 he pioneered a church that rose to prominence as a center of great revival. In 1912 Maria B. Woodworth-Etter held tent meetings at his church every night for several months. Many were healed of serious medical problems, and this attracted people from all parts of the U.S. (Woodworth-Etter, 1916, 159–60, 172–75). While pastor of this church, Bosworth suffered a great deal of persecution for befriending blacks and for holding racially integrated meetings.

Bosworth was a delegate to the First General Council of the Assemblies of God (AG) at Hot Springs, Arkansas, in 1914, and later became one of the sixteen members of its executive presbytery. However, Bosworth began to express his belief that the gift of tongues was only one of many possible indications that a person was baptized in the Holy Spirit. As a result of the ensuing "initial evidence" controversy, he resigned from the AG in 1918. He was permitted to attend a meeting of the General Council later that year, which, after a period of discussion, reaffirmed its commitment to the gift of tongues as the only initial sign of baptism in the Spirit.

As members of the Christian and Missionary Alliance, F. F. Bosworth, his brother B. B. Bosworth, and their wives, held healing campaigns in many major cities. At meetings in Pittsburgh in 1919, there were 4,800 reported conversions (Niklaus, 1986, 151). There were many dramatic healings; at a January 1921 meeting in Detroit, a woman was healed of blindness (Bosworth, 1948, 229–31). In 1922 and 1923 the Bosworth team held meetings in Toronto with Oswald J. Smith, Paul Rader, and the "Cleveland Coloured Gospel Quintette" (Sawin, 1986, 152; Bosworth, 1948, 215–20). Campaigns were held in many other cities, including Chicago, Ottawa (where more than 12,000 people attended nightly), and Washington, D.C. During these years, Bosworth became a pioneer in radio evangelism and established the National Radio Revival Missionary Crusaders, broadcasting over WJJD in Chicago.

During 1948–50, soon after William Branham began his healing ministry, Bosworth came out of semiretirement to join him in campaigns in Pensacola, Seattle, Miami, Zion, and Houston. Bosworth was an important influence on the healing evangelists of the post-World War II revival. T. L. Osborn wrote, "Old F. F. Bosworth used to share a lot of secrets with us" (Harrell,

F. F. Bosworth was an early Pentecostal who had roots in John Alexander Dowie's Zion City, Illinois.

1975, 15). Bosworth, in turn, had been influenced by E. W. Kenyon (Bosworth, 1948, 156). He gave the last six years of his life to the work of missions in Africa.

Bibliography: F. F. Bosworth, *Christ the Healer* (1924, 1948); C. Brumback, *Suddenly . . . From Heaven* (1961); D. E. Harrell, Jr., *All Things Are Possible* (1975); E. M. Perkins, *Fred Francis Bosworth: His Life Story* (1927); "Rev. and Mrs. F. F. Bosworth Work With Branham Party," *Voice of Healing* (May 1948), 1, 5; R. L. Niklaus, J. S. Sawin, and S. J. Stoesz, *All for Jesus* (1986); M. B. Woodworth-Etter, *Signs and Wonders* (1916). R. M. Riss

BOYD, FRANK MATTHEWS (1883–1984). Author and educator. A pioneer Assemblies of God (AG) educator, Boyd graduated from the Missionary Training Institute at Nyack, New York, in 1911 and served as the principal of Bethel Bible Training School, Newark, New Jersey, and then in the same capacity at Central Bible Institute. He was the dean of Bethany Bible College and later worked at Southern California College. He returned to Central Bible Institute as an instructor for sixteen years (1947–63). He simultaneously served as the director for correspondence education in the AG for ten years (1947–57). He wrote several books, including *Ages and Dispensations* (1955), *The Book of the Prophet Ezekiel* (1951), and *The Kenosis of the*

Lord Jesus Christ (1947). His major theological contribution was to adapt Scofield's pattern of dispensationalism to fit the Pentecostal experience. Boyd accomplished this by transforming the age of the church into the age of the Spirit. He also wrote numerous articles for the denominational magazine, the *Pentecostal Evangel*.

Bibliography: "With Christ," *PE* (February 26, 1984), 80.   B. M. Stout

Brick Bradford is the general secretary of the Presbyterian and Reformed Renewal Ministries.

BRADFORD, GEORGE CRAIN ("BRICK")

(1923–). Pastor and Presbyterian charismatic leader. Brick Bradford was born in Mercedes, Texas. He attended the University of Texas at Austin and earned a B.B.A. (1949) and J.D. (1952). In 1955 Brick married Marjorie Jane Lloyd. They have four children. Receiving a diploma from Austin Presbyterian Theological Seminary in 1957, he was ordained into the ministry of the present-day Presbyterian Church in the U.S.A.

Bradford pastored Faith Presbyterian Church at Pasadena, Texas (1957–62), and First Presbyterian Church at El Reno, Oklahoma (1962–68). He became the executive director of Christian Renewal Ministry in Oklahoma City in 1968. Bradford is also general secretary and editor for the Presbyterian Charismatic Communion with offices in Oklahoma City (1972–), a trustee for Literacy and Evangelism, Inc. (1973–), and was a regent for Melodyland School of Theology.

Bibliography: *Who's Who in Religion*, 2d ed. (1977).
                                                  G. W. Gohr

BRANDING, HARRY W.

(1891–1969). Pastor and church official. Born near Granite City, Illinois, Branding received the baptism in the Holy Ghost in 1929 through the ministry of Benjamin H. Hite. Shortly after, he began pastor-

ing and for thirty-four years he served the Apostolic Pentecostal Church in St. Louis, Missouri. Under his ministry it became one of the largest congregations in the United Pentecostal Church, International (UPC).

Denominational responsibilities for Branding included serving as general secretary of the Pentecostal Church, Incorporated; district superintendent of the Missouri District (1948–1969); and member of the following boards of the UPC: Foreign Missionary, Christian Education, Publication, and Tupelo Children's Mansion. He also served as chairman of the board of directors of Gateway College of Evangelism in St. Louis, which he helped found in 1968.

Bibliography: A. L. Clanton, *United We Stand* (1970).   G. B. McGee

BRANHAM, WILLIAM MARRION

(1909–65). Initiator of the post-World War II healing revival. Born in a dirt-floor log cabin in the hills of Kentucky, Branham carried his prophetic message of healing and deliverance to the far corners of the earth. A mystic from his youth, he reported divine visitations at ages three and seven. After a personal healing, he felt called to preach and became an independent Baptist. In 1933 he preached to three thousand people in a tent revival in Jeffersonville, Indiana, and later built Branham Tabernacle there. He attributed the death of his wife and baby in 1937 to his failure to heed the call to conduct revivals in Oneness Pentecostal churches.

Branham reported that throughout his life he was guided by an angel who first appeared to him in a secret cave in 1946. He was given the power to discern people's illnesses and thoughts. David Harrell reports of his popularity: "The power of a Branham service . . . remains a legend unparalleled in the history of the charismatic movement" (Harrell, 1975, 162). Branham's accuracy is attested by Walter J. Hollenweger, who interpreted for him in Zurich and "is not aware of any case in which he was mistaken in the often detailed statements he made" (Hollenweger, 1977, 354). But he further reports that although many healings were well attested, there were not as many as were claimed. Branham filled the world's largest auditoriums and stadiums. In contrast to the caricature of the image-minded evangelist, he lived moderately, dressed modestly, and boasted of his youthful poverty. This endeared him to the throngs who idealized him. He was self-conscious about his lack of education, but the simplicity of his messages had worldwide appeal.

By emphasizing healing and prosperity and neglecting his Oneness theology Branham was able to minister in Trinitarian Pentecostal circles as well. In 1947 he acquired as his manager Gordon Lindsay, who edited the *Voice of Healing* magazine, which served as an advertising vehicle for the rapidly multiplying healing evangelists. He was also highly touted by the Full Gospel Business Men's Fellowship International, but support declined as he became more controversial in the 1960s.

Branham's insistence that believers baptized by a Trinitarian formula must be rebaptized in the

Perhaps the most famous picture of the post-war salvation-healing movement is this 1950 photograph of William Branham in Houston. His followers described the light as "the pillar of fire."

name of "Jesus only" was a view shared by a number of Pentecostals. But other teachings placed him on the fringes of orthodoxy. His doctrine of the "serpent's seed" taught that Eve's sin involved sexual relations with the serpent. Some humans are descended from the serpent's seed and are destined for hell, which is not eternal, however. The seed of God, i.e., those who receive Branham's teaching, are predestined to become the Bride of Christ. There are still others who possess free will and who may be saved out of the denominational churches, but they must suffer through the Great Tribulation. He considered denominationalism a mark of the Beast (Rev. 13:17).

Branham proclaimed himself the angel of Revelation 3:14 and 10:7 and prophesied that by 1977 all denominations would be consumed by the World Council of Churches under the control of the Roman Catholics, that the Rapture would take place, and that the world would be destroyed. He died in 1965, but many of his followers expected him to be resurrected, some believing him to be God, others believing him to be virgin-born.

Branham's influence has continued in many churches where his prophecies are considered to be divinely inspired. His teaching on the power of the spoken word has been a characteristic of later revivalists. Kenneth Hagin identifies Branham as a prophet.

Bibliography: W. M. Branham, *Footprints on the Sands of Time* (1975); C. Dyck, *William Branham: The Man and His Message* (1984); D. E. Harrell, Jr., *All*

A William Branham healing campaign, Kansas City, April 1948. Branham is at the pulpit, and two influential editors can be seen on the extreme left and right: Gordon Lindsay on the left and Stanley H. Frodsham on the right.

Things are Possible: The Healing and Charismatic Revivals in Modern America (1975); W. J. Hollenweger, *The Pentecostals* (1977); G. Lindsay, *William Branham: A Man Sent from God* (1950).   D. J. Wilson

BRAXTON, S. LEE (1905–82). The first vice-president of Full Gospel Business Men's Fellowship International and a staunch worker with Demos Shakarian in its development. Braxton was a successful businessman and civic leader in North Carolina: mayor of Whiteville; organizer and, for thirteen years, chairman of the board of First National Bank of Whiteville; president of Braxton Enterprises; member of the local Rotary; president, vice-president, chairman, or director of numerous auto-related companies and civic groups; national director of Oral Roberts' "Coast-to-Coast" radio broadcast; director of Whiteville Merchants Association and Chamber of Commerce; and director of North Carolina Merchants Association.

In 1949 Braxton, who was by that time a millionaire considering retirement, began providing business counsel to Oral Roberts. For sixteen years he was chairman of the board of regents of Oral Roberts University and personal consultant to Roberts.

Bibliography: L. Braxton, "A Dream Come True," *Full Gospel Business Men's Voice* 1 (1, 1953): 12; idem, "A Better Way," *Full Gospel Business Men's Voice* 20 (4, 1972): 4–7, 28–30; O. Roberts, "One of the Greatest Laymen of This Century," *Abundant Life* 37 (2, 1983): 28–30.   J. A. Hewett

BRAZILIAN CHARISMATICS See CHARISMATIC MOVEMENT.

BREDESEN, HARALD (1918–). Pastor and conference speaker and an important figure in origins of the charismatic movement. Ordained a Lutheran minister in 1944, Bredesen was baptized in the Spirit at a Pentecostal summer camp in 1946. His proffered resignation was refused by the Lutheran authorities, which Bredesen took as a sign to remain within his church. Holding various nonpastoral church appointments, Bredesen witnessed to the baptism in the Spirit, being encouraged during these "years in the wilderness" by D. du Plessis and later by the Full Gospel Business Men's Fellowship International (FGBMFI). In 1957 he became pastor of Mount Vernon Dutch Reformed Church in New York City and soon began a charismatic prayer meeting. Bredesen had a remarkable flair for showing up in unexpected places, and many prominent figures speak of his role in their Spirit baptism, e.g., P. Boone, J. Sherrill, B. Slosser, and M. G. (Pat) Robertson, who was his student assistant (1958–59).

When Jean Stone (see J. S. Willans) formed the Blessed Trinity Society (BTS) in 1960, Bredesen became chairman of the board. Together with

Stone, he spoke at numerous "Christian Advances" sponsored by BTS. In 1963 Bredesen's mission on the Yale campus attracted national publicity. He and Stone coined the designation "charismatic renewal" in 1963, in contrast to "Neo-Pentecostalism" used in an *Eternity* editorial. In these years, Bredesen was featured in all the major media presentations of the movement, including Walter Cronkite's mini-documentary on "World News Tonight" (1963). Bredesen has traveled widely, often financed by the FGBMFI. After the beginnings of Catholic charismatic renewal, he played a part in its early stages in Colombia and Yugoslavia. Bredesen's ministry has also been marked by an ability to reach political leaders, including various heads of state.

Bredesen resigned from Mount Vernon in 1970, and after a break, he pastored Trinity Christian Center in Victoria, B.C., from 1971 to 1980, when he retired to Escondido, California, where he carries on his distinctive charismatic ministry. His earlier story is told in *Yes, Lord* (1972).

Bibliography: J. T. Connelly, "Neo-Pentecostalism: The Charismatic Revival in the Mainline Protestant and Roman Catholic Churches of the United States, 1960–1971," Ph.D. diss., University of Chicago (1977); J. Sherrill, *They Speak With Other Tongues* (1964); V. Synan, *The Twentieth-Century Pentecostal Explosion* (1987).   P. D. Hocken

A prominent Elim minister in Wales, Percy S. Brewster was an active participant in the Pentecostal World Conference.

BREWSTER, PERCY STANLEY (1908–80). British Pentecostal leader, pastor, and evangelist. Born in London, he was converted under the ministry of George Jeffreys. He was made youth leader at East Ham and was asked to assist in the follow-up after George Jeffreys's most successful crusade in Birmingham in 1930. He spent a short time at the Elim Bible College, London, before being sent to a joint charge.

Developing gifts found expression in evangelistic outreach. Following a vision in which he saw a hall packed with people, he lead a crusade in Neath, Wales. The hall they booked was the one seen in the vision. It was a great success, the first of more than forty that established new churches. This was a time when Elim's founder (George Jeffreys) was at the close of his major success. In 1939 Brewster became minister of Cardiff City Temple. He remained as minister until 1974. During this period he went forth from Cardiff twice a year conducting crusades and establishing churches all over Britain. At the close of the war he took a leading part in the new evangelistic thrust in Elim beginning in Wigan, Lancashire. He was superintendent in Wales, where in spite of his other duties he continued to pioneer new churches.

A man of vision and bounding energy, a gifted evangelist with a particular skill for gathering in converts, he combined this with a caring pastoral ministry. He was elected to the executive council of the Elim Foursquare Gospel Alliance in 1952 and served as president twice, becoming secretary-general in 1974–77. From 1964 he served on the advisory committee of the Pentecostal World Conference (secretary, 1970) and editor of *World Pentecost*. Known affectionately as "P.S." by his friends, "Mr. Brewster," by his younger ministers, he was "Pastor Brewster" to his loving congregation. He also traveled extensively in the interests of the worldwide Pentecostal movement, visiting New Zealand, Europe, the U.S., and Korea. He died in London in July 1980 following a brain tumor. He was buried in Cardiff, Wales, the land of his adoption.   D. W. Cartwright

BRITISH CHARISMATICS See CHARISMATIC MOVEMENT; UNITED METHODIST CHARISMATICS.

BRITISH PENTECOSTALS See APOSTOLIC CHURCH; ASSEMBLIES OF GOD IN GREAT BRITAIN AND IRELAND; ELIM PENTECOSTAL CHURCH; EUROPEAN PENTECOSTALISM.

BRITTON, BILL (1918–85). Founder and pastor of the House of Prayer in Springfield, Missouri, and proponent of the "sonship" message. He was highly regarded by many in the charismatic movement as an individual who moved in the realm of prophetic ministry. At the 1949 annual Sunday school convention of the Assemblies of God in Springfield, he heard about the Latter Rain revival and became involved in it. He became a prolific writer of books and pamphlets on some of the "deeper truths" of the Christian faith, which he mailed free of charge upon request. While his major emphasis was on growth to Christian maturity, some of his teachings became controversial, especially as others took some of his teachings and pushed them to extremes. As a result of the demand for his preaching, he traveled frequently and had an extensive influence both in the U.S. and in many foreign countries.

Bibliography: B. Britton, *Prophet on Wheels* (1979).
R. M. Riss

BRITTON, FRANCIS MARION (1870–1937). A Pioneer evangelist and leader of the Fire-Baptized Holiness Church (FBHC) in North Carolina. Britton was converted in 1888 at age eighteen and joined the Union Methodist Church. Early in 1907 he received the Holy Spirit baptism and immediately commenced a vigorous Pentecostal ministry. He introduced Pentecost to the South Florida Holiness camp meeting in 1907 and in 1908 established a FBHC in Florida. Also in 1908 he introduced Pentecost to the Beulah Holiness Bible School in Oklahoma.

As assistant general overseer of the FBHC, Britton helped to form its merger with the Pentecostal Holiness Church in 1911. He died in 1937, leaving one published book, *Pentecostal Truth* (1919).

Bibliography: F. M. Britton, *Pentecostal Truth* (1919); *The Pentecostal Holiness Advocate* (February 14, 1970).
C. W. Conn

One of the early Presbyterian leaders in the charismatic renewal, James H. Brown turned his Parkesburg, Pennsylvania, church into a popular charismatic center.

BROWN, JAMES H. (1912–87). Presbyterian charismatic leader. Brown was born in Pittsburgh, Pennsylvania, on March 27, 1912. He graduated from Grove City College, Pennsylvania, in 1935, and Princeton Theological Seminary in 1939. From 1939 to 1977 Brown pastored the Upper Octorara Presbyterian Church, Parkesburg, Pennsylvania. During his pastorate he served for twelve years (1946–58) as assistant professor of theology and ethics at Lincoln Theological Seminary.

In the early 1950s Brown had a decisive conversion experience through the witness of a Pentecostal meeting and Bible study. Toward the end of the 1950s he was baptized in the Holy Spirit. Soon thereafter the Upper Octorara Church became famed for its charismatic life, and people came literally from around the world especially to attend the Saturday night prayer and praise service.

Brown served as an early president of the Presbyterian Charismatic Communion (now Presbyterian and Reformed Renewal Ministries). His ministry carried him to many denominations across America, also to Europe, the Middle East, and Far East.
J. R. Williams

BROWN, ROBERT AND MARIE (1872–1948) (1880–1971). Founders and pastors of Glad Tidings Tabernacle in New York City. Robert was born in Enniskillen, Northern Ireland, the seventh of the twelve children of Christopher and Alice Reed Brown. After brief service on London's police force, Robert was converted under Methodist influences and dedicated his life to the Wesleyan Methodist ministry. He migrated to New York in 1898, where he found daytime employment to support his evening and weekend evangelistic efforts. In 1907 he met Marie Burgess, who conducted a Pentecostal storefront mission in midtown Manhattan. Burgess had been sent to New York by Charles F. Parham as a pioneer Pentecostal evangelist. Reared an Episcopalian in Eau Claire, Wisconsin, Burgess and her family had moved to healing evangelist John A. Dowie's religious community,

Robert and Marie Brown pastored Glad Tidings Tabernacle in New York, which for years was the leader in foreign missions giving among churches in the Assemblies of God.

Zion City, Illinois, after embracing divine healing teaching. In Zion in 1906 she encountered the ministry of Pentecostal pioneer Charles F. Parham, whose message she promptly accepted. In January 1907 she followed Parham's advice and embarked on full-time ministry.

In January 1908 Robert accepted Pentecostalism. On October 14, 1909, he and Marie Burgess were married in her parents' home in Zion City by prominent Pentecostal pastor William H. Piper. Their midwestern contacts led them into association with the loosely structured white Churches of God in Christ in 1912 and 1913. By 1916 they had affiliated with the Assemblies of God (AG).

Robert and Marie Brown's combined efforts in New York were fruitful: the congregation moved to larger quarters; extended them; then in 1921 purchased a large former Baptist church, which they named Glad Tidings Tabernacle. At least until World War II, Glad Tidings was a hub for northeastern Pentecostals. It supported a weekly radio broadcast, was the site of huge evangelistic rallies, and sent its young people to missions efforts around the world. From the 1920s through the 1940s, it typically led AG congregations in missionary giving. Robert served the AG as a general presbyter (1918–25) and played a prominent role in the 1918 General Council debate on the Pentecostal distinctive of evidential tongues. After her husband's death Marie continued to serve the congregation as pastor until her death in 1971.

Bibliography: "A Man Greatly Beloved," *Glad Tidings Herald* (May 1948), 1–11; E. L. Blumhofer, "Marie Burgess Brown," *Paraclete* (Summer 1987), 5–9.   E. L. Blumhofer

BRUMBACK, CARL (1917–87). Pastor and historian of the Pentecostal movement. Brumback was converted and received the baptism of the Holy Spirit at age fourteen in Washington, D.C. He attended Central Bible Institute, Springfield, Missouri, and served pastorates in Sperryville, Virginia; Tampa, Florida; Bedford, Ohio; and Silverspring, Maryland. In 1942 to 1944 a series of twelve radio sermons in Florida were expanded into his significant defense of Pentecostalism, "What Meaneth This?" (1947).

Brumback's *God in Three Persons* (1959) was a major contribution to the Trinitarian debate with the Oneness movement. He wrote the first official history of the Assemblies of God, *Suddenly . . . From Heaven* (1961). His writings brought him into full-time demand on the lecture and evangelistic circuit.

Bibliography: C. Brumback, *God in Three Persons* (1959); idem, *Suddenly . . . From Heaven* (1961); idem, *"What Meaneth This?": A Pentecostal Answer to a Pentecostal Question* (1947).   D. J. Wilson

BRUNER, FREDERICK DALE (1932–). Missionary, NT scholar, and author. Currently professor of religion at Whitworth College in Spokane, Washington, F. Dale Bruner studied at Princeton Theological Seminary and completed a Th.D. in 1963 at the University of Hamburg, Germany. His dissertation was revised for publi-

cation as *A Theology of the Holy Spirit: The Pentecostal Experience and the New Testament Witness* (1970), an important resource in Pentecostal studies. A Presbyterian, Bruner was influenced as a young man by Henrietta Mears of First Presbyterian Church of Hollywood, California (Bruner, 1970, 8). As a theological student, he came to a deep appreciation of Martin Luther in a quest for answers to questions raised by Pentecostalism (Bruner, 1970, 344). Although not a Pentecostal himself, he has done extensive research on Pentecostal doctrine and history. While he upholds the importance of new infillings of the Holy Spirit (for him, equivalent to new drafts of faith in Christ), he disagrees with the idea of a second crisis encounter with God as necessary for the fullness of the Spirit (Bruner and Hordern, 1984, 8). He argues that the Scriptures teach that the baptism with the Holy Spirit and water baptism belong together to form the "one baptism" of the church (Bruner, 1970, 193–94).

Bibliography: F. D. Bruner, *The Christbook* (1987); idem, *The Churchbook* (1988); idem, *A Theology of the Holy Spirit* (1970); F. D. Bruner and W. Hordern, *The Holy Spirit: Shy Member of the Trinity* (1984); J. D. G. Dunn, *Baptism in the Holy Spirit* (1970); H. M. Ervin, *Conversion-Initiation and the Baptism in the Holy Spirit* (1984); H. D. Hunter, *Spirit-Baptism: A Pentecostal Alternative* (1983); R. Stronstad, *The Charismatic Theology of St. Luke* (1984).   R. M. Riss

BRYANT, JOHN (1948–). Pastor, evangelist. Born in Baltimore, Maryland, son of an African Methodist Episcopal (AME) bishop, John Bryant returned there in 1975 as pastor of Bethel African Methodist Episcopal Church, one of the oldest (c. 1785) black congregations in the country. While serving in Africa with the Peace Corps, Bryant (D.Min., Colgate–Rochester) became "aware of a realm of the spirit" that he "could not explain away." Returning to the States, he experienced the power of the Holy Spirit, and his ministry took on new directions. Membership at Bethel is currently more than seven thousand, placing it among the largest charismatic congregations among mainline black denominations. Bryant locates Bethel's ministry squarely within the "full gospel" tradition of the black church, teaching baptism of the Holy Ghost (with the fruit of the Spirit as evidence, though glossolalia and other gifts are present in the church). There is also an emphasis on a social outreach program that meets needs for food, shelter, employment, and education. Notable among these programs is Bethel Bible Institute, offering an accredited associate of arts degree. Bryant also conducts an evangelistic ministry featuring crusades and radio and television programs.

Bibliography: J. Bryant, "Worship in the A.M.E. Context," in L. Campion, ed., *A Pastor's Manual for the A.M.E. Church* (1985); L. Creque, "St. Paul's A.M.E. Church," *Black Church* 2 (4, 1974): 24–25; "Shepherds in the Pulpit," *The Black Church Magazine* (May 1987), 8–17; "Silent the Giants Have Grown," *The Black Church Magazine* (May 1987), 15–16; G. Singleton, *The Romance of African Methodism* (1952).
H. D. Trulear

BUCKINGHAM, JAMES WILLIAM II ("JAMIE") (1932–). Pastor, columnist, and author. Buckingham was born in Vero Beach, Florida, and educated at Mercer University (A.B.) and Southwestern Baptist Theological Seminary (B.D. and M.R.E.). He was pastor of South Main Street Baptist Church for eight years and then pastored Harbor City Baptist Church, Melbourne, Florida, for fifteen months. Buckingham says, "After being fired from two churches because of my emptiness and pride and penchant to sexual immorality, I attended a Full Gospel Business Men's convention in Washington, D.C., while researching my first book, *Run, Baby, Run.* While there I responded to an invitation and was filled with the Holy Spirit."

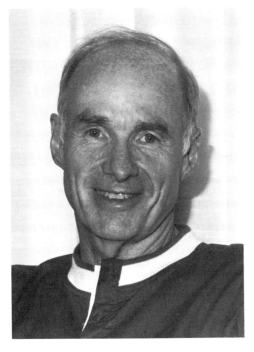

A Baptist charismatic, Jamie Buckingham developed into one of the most prolific writers of the charismatic movement.

In 1967 Buckingham formed Tabernacle Church (now nondenominational) in Melbourne, Florida, and has since served as pastor (now senior minister). The church grew from a small group to a present membership of four thousand.

Buckingham writes an award-winning column for *Charisma* and the Buckingham Report for *Ministries Today.* He has written thirty-eight books, including *Power for Living* (n.d.), which has been read by 30 million people.

Bibliography: J. Buckingham, *Where Eagles Soar* (1980).   S. Strang

BUFFUM, HERBERT (1879–1939). A Holiness-Pentecostal evangelist and prolific song writer with some 10,000 songs to his credit. Although a talented musician, he received no musical training. Most of his songs were sold for five dollars or less.

Herbert Buffum had no musical training, but a thousand of his gospel songs were published, including "Lift Me Up Above the Shadows," "I'm Going Thro', Jesus," "I'm Going Higher," and "The Old-fashioned Meeting."

Born in Illinois, Buffum later moved to California with his family. There he felt a call to the ministry after his conversion at age eighteen. He held credentials with the Church of the Nazarene. He also began to write songs, many of which were inspired by personal experiences. Some of these were, "My Sheep Know My Voice," "I'm Going Through," "The Old Fashioned Meeting," "I'm Going Higher Some Day," "When I Take My Vacation in Heaven," and "In the City Where the Lamb Is the Light."

When he died in 1939 the *Los Angeles Times* called him "The King of Gospel Song Writers."

Bibliography: W. Warner, "Herbert Buffum," *AG Heritage* 6 (Fall 1986): 11–14, 16.   W. E. Warner

BULGARIAN PENTECOSTALS See EUROPEAN PENTECOSTALISM.

BUNTAIN, DANIEL MARK (1923–). Missionary to India. Mark Buntain, born in Winnipeg, Manitoba, is the son of a Pentecostal minister. He left his work as a successful radio broadcaster and, after marrying Hulda Monroe in 1944, began pastoring churches in Saskatchewan. Before going to India as a missionary, he ministered as an evangelist in Canada, the U.S.,

Taiwan, the Philippines, Sri Lanka, Hong Kong, and Japan.

As a missionary to India, Mark Buntain saw the desperate needs of the sick and hungry. He was instrumental in building a hospital in Calcutta.

Buntain went to India in 1953 with a reluctant wife and a four-month-old baby. They started the Calcutta Mission of Mercy as a response to the cry he heard as he preached: "Don't try to give us food for our souls until you give us food for our stomachs."

Today the Buntains are pastors of the Assembly of God (AG) in Calcutta, which has more than 1,500 people in Sunday school each week and 4,000 parishioners representing six languages. He is the assistant superintendent of the AG in North India and airs a radio broadcast three times a week to a potential audience of 145 million listeners. The mission feeds 22,000 people each day. It is run by nearly 1,000 Indian nationals, and the operation contains a hospital, a school of nursing, six village clinics, a hostel for destitute youth, a drug prevention program, and twelve schools that provide instruction for 6,000 children. Since Buntain has been in India, more than 250,000 have been saved from hunger, more than 100,000 have had the chance to go to school, and tens of thousands have been treated at the hospital.

Bibliography: M. Buntain, "God Broke My Heart for India," *Mountain Movers* (April 1979), 3–6; R. Hembree, *Mark* (1979); Screen Communications, Inc., "Miracles of Love for Calcutta Mission of Mercy" (n.d.); D. Wead, *The Compassionate Touch* (1977).   S. Shemeth

BUNTAIN, DANIEL NEWTON   (1888–1955). Canadian churchman and executive. Beginning ministry among the Methodists, Buntain was ordained in Saskatchewan in 1918. The following year he moved to Winnipeg, Manitoba, to pastor a Methodist church and to attend Wesley College.

Buntain had come into contact with Pentecostalism in 1916, and in 1925 his interest deepened as a result of the ministry of Charles Price. This same year the Methodist Conference, in response, gave him the option of being left without a charge or being assigned to a rural parish. Buntain chose the former. Shortly thereafter he was baptized in the Holy Spirit, and three days later he became the pastor of Wesley Church, the largest Pentecostal Assemblies of Canada (PAOC) congregation.

Buntain quickly moved into leadership among the Pentecostals, becoming the first superintendent of the Manitoba District of the PAOC in 1928, a position he held until 1936 when he rose to national leadership through being elected general superintendent. He served in that office until 1944. The remainder of his life was spent in Edmonton, Alberta, where he was pastor of Central Pentecostal Tabernacle and president of Northwest Bible College, which he founded in 1947.

Buntain had a very significant impact on the PAOC. A man of intense spirituality, he was driven by a burden for missions, evangelism, revival, and prayer. At the same time, he was convinced that the church had to be organized in order to function efficiently. It was in this area that he made his most unique contribution. Under his leadership the PAOC endorsed the implementation of indigenous church principles on its mission fields, began to receive annual reports from its superintendent, and created national Sunday school and women's departments. Buntain also led the PAOC into the Canadian Association of Evangelicals, demonstrating the increasing self-confidence and self-awareness the denomination felt.

Bibliography: D. M. Buntain, *Why He Is a Pentecostal Preacher* (1944); D. N. Buntain, "He Leadeth Me!" *The Pentecostal Testimony* 17 (13, 1937): 8–9; G. G. Kulbeck, *What God Hath Wrought: A History of the Pentecostal Assemblies of Canada* (1958); R. A. N. Kydd, "The Contribution of Denominationally Trained Clergymen to the Emerging Pentecostal Movement in Canada," *Pneuma* 5 (1983): 30–32.   R. A. N. Kydd

BURGESS, JOHN HARRY   (1903–). Missionary, educator, and pastor. John H. Burgess was born in Muskegon, Michigan, to Harry and Winnie (Bakker) Burgess. He attended Rochester (N.Y.) Bible Training School (1924–25) and Bethel Bible Training School, Newark, New Jersey (1925–26). He later earned degrees in history (B.A., 1958; M.A., 1963) at the University of Michigan.

While a student at Rochester, Burgess met Bernice Frances Andrews (1901–) who was a student at Beulah Heights Bible and Missionary Training School in North Bergen, New Jersey. They were married in India in 1927; one son was born to their union, Stanley Milton Burgess (1937–).

In 1925, Burgess became pastor of the Assemblies of God (AG) church in White Plains, New York. Ordained in 1926, he left for India in the same year. He ministered for the next 25 years in the state of Travancore (now Kerala) on the Malabar coast, in such towns as Chenganur, Quilon, Mavelikara, and Punalur. Aware that missionaries alone were unable to convert the Indian masses to Christ, Burgess founded the Bethel Bible School (later College) at Mavelikara in 1927. The school was relocated to Punalur in 1949. Outside the United States, Bethel Bible College is the oldest AG institution for ministerial training in the world.

Burgess served as superintendent of the South India District Council of the AG and chairman of the South Indian Missionary Fellowship for many years. One of his primary objectives was to develop native leadership in the Indian church. This dream was realized since the church in Kerala now functions without missionaries, governed exclusively by Indian leaders.

In 1950 the Burgess returned to the United States because of Bernice Burgess' poor health. They pastored Trinity AG in Flint, Michigan from 1951–1965, when John Burgess joined the faculty of Central Bible College in Springfield, Missouri. He retired in 1972.

Bibliography: John Burgess, *Opportunities in South India and Ceylon* (c. 1934); interview with John Burgess, June 1987.   G. B. McGee

BURNETT, BILL (1917–). Prominent Anglican charismatic leader. Born in South Africa, Burnett was captured at Tobruk, Libya, in 1942, later escaping from a prisoner of war camp to be on the run in the Italian mountains for a year. Married to his wife Sheila in 1945, he was ordained an Anglican priest in 1947, becoming bishop of Bloemfontein in 1957. Burnett was general secretary of the South African Council of Churches (1967–70) when the council produced *The Message to the People of South Africa*, a theological refutation of apartheid. In 1970 he became bishop of Grahamstown, and in 1972 he was baptized in the Spirit. In 1974 Burnett was elected archbishop of Cape Town and metropolitan of the Anglican province of South Africa, the first native-born South African to hold these positions.

Burnett's ministry as bishop and archbishop was deeply changed through his baptism in the Spirit. The difference made to his opposition to racial injustice in South Africa is described in "The Spirit and Social Action," *Bishops' Move*, ed. M. Harper (1978). He exercised a strong influence for renewal in South Africa that resulted in several Anglican bishops there being baptized in the Spirit. He became a regular speaker at charismatic conferences throughout the world and participated in the World Council of Churches Consultation on Charismatic Movements at Bossey, Switzerland in 1980.

Since his retirement in 1981, Burnett has continued his teaching ministry with much international travel. His teaching has been characterized by an emphasis on the cross of Jesus triumphing over the forces of evil and leading to holiness of life and the transformation of society. Since its foundation in 1981, Burnett has been active in SOMA, the Anglican international renewal organization, becoming chairman of its international council. In 1982 he was led to concentrate on ministry in South Africa, forming support ministries to promote this work, which is described in *Ixthus*, its regular newsletter.

P. D. Hocken

BURNETT, CORDAS CHRIS (1927–75). Educator. A leader in Assemblies of God (AG) education, he served as the first executive vice-president of the denomination's seminary for nearly two years. In the initial structure of the seminary his position involved the oversight of the operation of the school under the aegis of the general superintendent. Prior to leading the seminary, Burnett was president of Bethany Bible College in Santa Cruz, California, for thirteen years. He also served as an instructor at Central Bible College, vice-president of Central Bible College, and secretary of education for the AG.

Burnett was known for his ecumenical spirit. He was involved in such organizations as NAE and Youth for Christ. His blend of formal education (B.A., DePaul; graduate study at Washington University; honorary D.D. from Southeastern Bible College) and a rich background in pastoral ministry in Indiana, Illinois, and Ohio qualified Burnett in the minds of denominational leadership as someone with academic credentials who was thoroughly Pentecostal in style as well as in substance.

Bibliography: "Goes to Be With Christ," *PE* (October 12, 1975). 27.   B. M. Stout

BURTON, WILLIAM FREDERICK PADWICK (1886–1971). British pioneer missionary and author. Born in Liverpool, son of a sea captain, he was trained as an engineer. Converted in 1905, he attended the Pentecostal Missionary Union (PMU) Bible School at Preston and pastored Henry Mogridge's Elim Mission, Lytham, Lancashire. (1911–14). He was to have sailed for Africa with James McNiell but came into conflict with the leaders of the PMU and sought an opening with other societies without success.

Burton left Britain in May 1914 to be joined in June 1915 by James Salter. With one other missionary, they arrived in Mwanza, Congo, in September. They joined the Pentecostal Mission in South and Central Africa, Burton being their legal representative. In 1917 he visited Dan Crawford's work in Luanza, and the lessons he learned there were put into practice at Mwanza. Because he was serving in an area where there were 250,000 people within a radius of forty miles, he had to go to South Africa to recruit new workers. He returned with four, including Hettie Trollip, whom he married in May 1918. Other workers came from the U.S., but the burden fell on Burton. He possessed great gifts as an artist, builder, engineer, and teacher. The impetuous youth became a wise counselor to officials and missionaries. He wrote twenty-eight books, in-

William F. P. Burton, along with James Salter, founded the Zaire Evangelistic Mission.

cluding a standard work on the Lubu religion. Honors were given to him, but he was content to be known as "the tramp preacher." He was named "Kapamu," the "rusher-forth." He became field director of the Congo Evangelistic Mission (later called the Zaire Evangelistic Mission) on its foundation in 1919 and served until 1954. When he left the Congo in 1960 there were sixty-five European missionaries out of a staff of eighty in thirteen stations. He died in South Africa in June 1971.

Bibliography: M. W. Moorhead, *Missionary Pioneering in the Congo Forests* (1922), C. C. Whittaker, *Seven Pentecostal Pioneers* (1983); H. Womersley, *Wm. F. P. Burton* (1973). D. W. Cartwright

BYRD, VERNON (1931–). Bishop (105th) of the African Methodist Episcopal Church. Born in Clinton, South Carolina, he began preaching at age thirteen and was ordained at age seventeen. Educated at Richard Allen and Boston Universities, he later served churches in South Carolina, Delaware, New Jersey, Pennsylvania, and Bermuda. He was elected to the episcopate in 1984 and assigned to West Africa. While in the pastorate he received the baptism of the Holy Spirit at a service sponsored by Kathryn Kuhlman. He returned to his church with a new "inner security" and "sense of fulfillment" in the ministry.

Drawing on the resources of black folk theology concerning the Holy Spirit, he began a crusade ministry that has taken him across the U.S. and abroad, emphasizing conversion, healing, and the laying on of hands for power. He has been one of the leading figures in the charismatic revival among black mainline denominations.

Bibliography: V. Byrd, *Book of Discipline of the A.M.E. Church* (1984). H. D. Trulear

C

CALIFORNIA EVANGELISTIC ASSOCIATION In 1933 Oscar C. Harms, a former Advent Christian pastor who had received an "infilling of the Holy Spirit," founded an independent church, the Colonial Tabernacle, in Long Beach, California. During the next six years, a small network of like-minded autonomous satellite churches sprang up, which in 1939 constituted themselves the California Evangelistic Association, with the mother church in Long Beach at its hub. Except for its amillennial stand, the association is in essential doctrinal agreement with the General Council of the Assemblies of God. In 1975 there were sixty-two churches and approximately 4,700 members in California, Oregon, and Washington.

Bibliography: C. E. Jones, *Guide to the Study of the Pentecostal Movement* (1983); A. C. Piepkorn, *Profiles in Belief,* vol. 3 (1979). C. E. Jones

CALL TO MINISTRY A significant aspect of the Pentecostal doctrine of the church is that the work of the ministry belongs to all believers (1 Peter 2:5; Rev. 1:6). All members of Christ's body have received a general call to ministry. Closely associated with that call is an endowment with spiritual gifts (Rom. 12:3–8; Eph. 4:11–12). The entire church is Pentecostal and charismatic; the whole people of God are prophets and priests. Therefore, believers have the obligation as well as the right to spread the gospel.

Besides the general calling, many Pentecostals believe that there is a specific call to the ministry of leadership and that appropriate spiritual gifts are given for such a ministry—especially the gifts that involve leadership responsibilities. This special call, which encompasses the activities of witness, pastoral care, and leadership in the church, is not from the community of believers, but from God himself. It is a call to participate in the continuing ministry of Christ to the world and to carry out a Christlike ministry. Personal integrity, purity, and holiness are seen by Pentecostals as being vital to the fulfillment of the work of the ministry.

The call to a leadership ministry comes from God but is confirmed by the church. The church recognizes the divine call and thus serves as a regulating community for ministry. The Holy Spirit works through the church, vivifying ministers and consecrating them for specific responsibilities (Acts 31:2–3). Consequently, authority for ministry is derived from God and the church. Though the church is empowered to test a person's call, Pentecostal expositors believe that the ultimate authority for ministry is derived from the Spirit and the Word. Therefore, the ultimate direction of ministry is from the One who calls.

Ministry rests on the call of God and on the power of the Holy Spirit, but God calls ministers in a variety of ways. Many Pentecostals testify that they have received their call through a crisis experience in their lives. Some tell of receiving their call through visions, dreams, an audible voice of God, or by some other miraculous manifestation. Other Pentecostals tell of providential circumstances, such as the pressures of life or a series of definite experiences, that brought them to devote their lives to the ministry. Regardless of the way they received their call, a result of their experience was a consuming desire to win the unsaved. With their call came a profound sense of obligation to proclaim the good news: "Woe to me if I do not preach the gospel!" (1 Cor. 9:16).

Bibliography: R. E. Fisher, ed., *In the Challenge of the Ministry* (1977); M. Harper, *Let My People Grow!* (1977); L. Melton, "Surrendering to God's Call: A Reassessment," *Church Administration* (July 1982), 24–35; F. E. Montgomery, "Calling Collect: From Damascus to Rome," *Church Administration* (October 1981), 3, 7–9; H. R. Niebuhr, ed., *The Ministry in Historical Perspectives* (1983); D. Watson, *I Believe in the Church* (1978). F. L. Arrington

CALVARY CHAPEL A congregation in Costa Mesa, California, that reached national prominence as a primary place of outreach during the "Jesus People" revival of the early 1970s. Originally a struggling congregation of twenty-five members, Chuck Smith was called to lead it, first as an associate pastor in 1965, then as its pastor. It began to grow as a result of Chuck's openness to a variety of young people in the counterculture of Southern California.

Through a series of Bible studies, disciplined prayer, and a genuine concern for "hippies," drug addicts, and societal "dropouts," the congregation soon became a vibrant center for worship and caring for culture and counterculture alike. It included Christian rock concerts with Maranatha Singers, Love Song, and Children of the Day. More staid congregations labeled it as "unorthodox" and "faddish" and accused it of soft-pedaling the gospel. To be sure, it was unconventional, but it managed to grab the attention of thousands of young people who had written off other forms of gospel proclamation.

In 1971, following a series of moves, Calvary Chapel purchased a ten-acre campus, where it is presently located. The auditorium was fitted with 2,500 seats and equipped with moveable furnishings designed for flexible use. Closed-circuit televisions are used in the fellowship hall and another auditorium that act as overflow areas.

Early in its ministry to "hippies" and former addicts it demonstrated the strength of community living for the new convert. By the mid 1970s, the church registered nine hundred conversions a month with eight thousand baptisms performed in a two-year period. It established a series of Christian communes, first in Costa Mesa, then in the San Bernardino/Riverside area, then at a number of other sites in the western U.S.

New converts were encouraged to share their experience with others. At the same time they were put into relationship with more mature Christians and were led through a range of Bible studies. As these converts matured they were encouraged to launch out in ministry. The result is that Calvary Chapel has grown to 35,000 members, making it the eighteenth largest congregation in the world. Since its facilities cannot handle its total membership adequately, multiple services are held, and twice each month Calvary Chapel meets for back-to-back services in the Anaheim Convention Center, enabling the majority of the members to enjoy fellowship with many who typically attend other services. Calvary Chapel has also spawned more than three hundred other Calvary Chapels throughout the U.S., and it has become the home of Calvary Chapel Ministries, which include an extensive tape ministry, some publications, and a weekly radio broadcast, "Word for Today," featuring Pastor Chuck Smith.

About 1983, a small group of Calvary Chapels that had come under the influence of John Wimber, then pastor of the Calvary Chapel in Yorba Linda, left Calvary Chapel ministries and gathered with a half-dozen Vineyards started by Ken Gullichson. Wimber's "Calvary Chapel" was renamed a "Vineyard," and Wimber was soon asked to head the new fellowship of congregations. Under the leadership of Wimber the Vineyard Christian Fellowship has grown to more than two hundred congregations. While Smith and Wimber have worked hard at maintaining a cordial relationship, their reasons for the separation involved the fact that both men were very strong leaders and that they took different positions with respect to their emphasis on the use of certain spiritual gifts. Chuck Smith's concerns have been expressed in his book *Charisma vs. Charismania* (1983), while Wimber's views have been popularized in *Power Evangelism* (1986) and *Power Healing* (1987).

In keeping with Smith's low profile approach to the "charismatic," Calvary Chapel is supportive of a range of more standard evangelical organizations. Until it developed its own Bible study program it enrolled its new converts in the respected Navigators program. It supports Wycliffe Bible Translators, whose headquarters are nearby, Campus Crusade for Christ, Missionary Aviation Fellowship, and a variety of mission endeavors in Latin America.

Bibliography: R. Enroth et al., *The Jesus People* (1972); C. Smith with T. Brooke, *Harvest* (1987); C. Smith with H. Steven, *The Reproducers: New Life for Thousands* (1972); J. Vaughan, *The World's Twenty Largest Churches* (1984).   C. M. Robeck, Jr.

CALVARY PENTECOSTAL CHURCH In

1931 a group of former Assemblies of God ministers, intent on achieving cooperative action without unnecessary interference from church

officials, organized the Calvary Pentecostal Church. Based in Olympia, Washington, the new fellowship experienced notable early growth. In 1944 it reported thirty-five churches and 20,000 members. Beginning in the mid 1950s, however, a contest of wills between key pastors and the executive board resulted in the eventual withdrawal of all but four member churches and the loss of flourishing affiliates in Brazil and India. The 1,500 remaining members support work in the Philippines.

Bibliography: C. E. Jones, *Guide to the Study of the Pentecostal Movement* (1983); A. C. Piepkorn, *Profiles in Belief,* vol. 3 (1979).   C. E. Jones

Ivey Campbell, while visiting Los Angeles in 1906, was baptized in the Spirit at the Azusa Street Mission. Reportedly, she was the first person to take the Pentecostal message to her home state of Ohio.

CAMPBELL, IVEY GLENSHAW (1874–

1918). Early Pentecostal evangelist. Campbell was born in Service (Beaver County), Pennsylvania, and reared in East Liverpool, Ohio, by United Presbyterian parents who practiced strict religious discipline in their home. Ivey (nicknamed "Iva") had two sisters: Sarah Agnes Campbell (1867–1948) and Alice Mary Campbell Kennedy (1872–1955). Ivey Campbell was a seamstress by profession. Although she faithfully supported her Presbyterian church, she later claimed to receive an experience of sanctification (c. 1901) during services held by a visiting evangelist; this prompted her pastor to condemn Holiness theology. Subsequently she joined a group of local men and women who opened the Broadway Mission (c. 1902) in East Liverpool. She became a prominent leader in this ministry and remained in it for four years.

In 1906 Campbell traveled to Los Angeles to

visit relatives. While there she attended services at the Azusa Street Mission and received the baptism in the Holy Spirit. Having written to Claude A. McKinney, pastor of the Union Gospel Mission in Akron, to share the news of revival with him, she returned to Ohio and, after visiting her home, began holding services at his church on December 5, 1906. Early Pentecostal leaders reported that she was the first person to bring the Pentecostal message from Azusa Street to Ohio. Other revivals took her to Cleveland, Ohio, as well as to Pittsburgh and Springboro, Pennsylvania. In June 1907 Campbell collaborated with McKinney and Levi R. Lupton to lead the Pentecostal camp meeting in Alliance, Ohio, that had a major impact on the spread of Pentecostalism in the northeastern U.S.

Campbell's later activities are currently obscure. Nevertheless, A. A. Boddy, reporting on his visit to Los Angeles in 1912, indicated that he had met her but observed that she was in poor health. Her last years were spent in California, where she died.

Bibliography: A. A. Boddy, "Some Los Angeles Friends," *Confidence* (November 1912), 246–47; P. Bowen, "Akron Visited With Pentecost," *AF* (January 1907), 1; I. Campbell, "Report from Ohio and Pennsylvania," *AF* (February–March 1907), 5; "Converts Claim Strange Powers," *The Evening Review* (East Liverpool, Ohio) (January 7, 1907), 1.   G. B. McGee

CANTEL, MARGARET (1878–1926). Early British Pentecostal. Born in America, Margaret L. Fielden was the daughter of one of J. A. Dowie's elders at Zion City, Illinois. She married Harry Eugene Cantel in 1907, who was overseer of Dowie's work in Britain from 1900. After their marriage she returned with her husband to London, where they introduced the Pentecostal message to their assembly in Islington. Renting a shop in Upper Street, Islington, they turned it into an assembly hall with Pentecostal gospel meetings four days a week. In 1909 the Cantels published a magazine, *The Overcoming Life* (February 1909–August 1910). Harry Cantel was a very successful evangelist with a healing ministry, but he died of peritonitis in August 1910. The Cantels had opened a guest house in Highbury called Maranatha. This was moved to 73 Highbury New Park and opened in October 1912 as a missionary guest house. Mrs. Cantel managed this home, and many Pentecostal missionaries stayed there. The guest list is a veritable "Who's Who." Donald Gee experienced Spirit baptism there. Mrs. Cantel died in March 1926.

Bibliography: G. Gardiner, "Out of Zion . . . Into All the World," *Bread of Life* 31 (July 2, 1982): 7ff.; D. Gee, *These Men I Knew* (1980).   D. W. Cartwright

CANTELON, WILLARD T. (1916–). Canadian-born international evangelist. Raised in a Pentecostal home, Willard Cantelon received the Holy Spirit as a youth in 1930 and immediately became an evangelist.

In 1941 Cantelon was invited by the Assemblies of God to evangelize in the U.S., where he was associated with Lorne F. Fox for five years. In 1951 he turned exclusively to foreign work, pioneering churches in Europe, Africa, and Asia. In 1958 he helped found Missions Televised, Inc.,

which started Christian television in the U.S. and expanded worldwide.

His writings focus on a conspiracy that will cause the fall of the world monetary systems and will necessitate a world dictator to restore order.

Bibliography: W. Cantelon, *The Day the Dollar Dies* (1973); idem, *Money Master of the World* (1976); idem, *New Money Or None?* (1979).   D. J. Wilson

CAPPS, CHARLES EMMITT (1934–). Leader in the Faith and Word movement (Positive Confession movement). Born in Brummett, Arkansas, to a family of farmers who joined the Assemblies of God (AG) in his youth. His marriage to Peggy Walls in 1951 produced two children: Annette (b. 1954) and Beverly (b. 1957). Converted at age thirteen, Capps became a lay minister in 1962. After hearing the faith message as taught by Kenneth Hagin in 1969, he began in 1973 an itinerant ministry emphasizing the power of the spoken word for victorious Christian living.

A leader in the Faith and Word church movement, Capps teaches that God's words "are the most powerful things in the universe," which, when spoken in faith, become "the creative power that releases God's ability within you." These teachings were promoted in his first and most important book, *The Tongue, a Creative Force,* published in 1976, and in his popular booklet entitled *God's Creative Power.* These books had sold more than 1.5 million copies by 1988.

In 1977 Capps began a national radio broadcast titled "Concepts of Faith." By 1979 he had forsaken farming to carry the faith message nationwide. In 1980 Capps was ordained by Kenneth Copeland and became a minister in the International Convention of Faith Churches.

Bibliography: C. Capps, *The Tongue, a Creative Force* (1976).   H. V. Synan

CARLSON, GUY RAYMOND (1918–). Author, college president, and denominational executive. Carlson was born in Crosby, North Dakota, and was converted to Christ under the ministry of Evangelist Blanche Britton in 1925. From 1934 to 1935 he attended Western Bible College. In 1938 he married Mae Steffler; they have three children.

Carlson's pastoral ministry began in Thief River Falls, Minnesota, and ordination with the Assemblies of God (AG) followed in 1941. In 1944 he was elected as a district presbyter of the North Central District of the AG and also served as its Sunday school superintendent. Four years later he became the district superintendent and remained there until he became president of North Central Bible College in 1961. When he left that office in 1969, the college conferred an honorary doctor of divinity degree on him for services rendered to the institution, the district, and the AG.

Carlson was elected as one of five assistant general superintendents of the AG in 1969. With the reorganization of the AG in 1971, he became the sole assistant superintendent. Carlson later succeeded Thomas F. Zimmerman as the general superintendent of the denomination in 1985. During his years in national leadership, he has been involved in various projects and has served

G. Raymond Carlson became general superintendent of the Assemblies of God in 1985.

on the boards of directors of the Ministers Benefit Association, Central Bible College, Evangel College, the Assemblies of God Theological Seminary, and the Executive Committee of the National Association of Evangelicals (NAE). He currently serves as chairman of the Pentecostal Fellowship of North America. His preaching ministry has taken him across the U.S., Canada, and to many foreign countries.

Carlson has written extensively for church publications. His books include *Preparing to Teach God's Word* (1975), *Spiritual Dynamics* (1976), *Our Faith and Fellowship* (1977), *The Acts Story* (1978), *Prayer and the Christian's Devotional Life* (1980), and *The Assemblies of God in Mission* (1970) with D. V. Hurst and Cyril E. Homer.

During his tenure as general superintendent, Carlson was faced by the fall-out from the PTL and Jimmy Swaggart scandals. His personal integrity and his call for spiritual renewal and biblical holiness brought comfort and assurance to the AG constituency during that stormy period.

Bibliography: AG Office of Information, media release (n.d.); W. W. Menzies, *Anointed to Serve* (1971).
G. B. McGee

CAROLINA EVANGELISTIC ASSOCIATION Established in 1930, the Carolina Evangelistic Association is the vehicle through which the Garr Memorial Church, an independent congregation in Charlotte, North Carolina, conducts its evangelistic and missionary outreach. Alfred Goodrich Garr (1874–1944), Azusa Street convert and pioneer missionary to Hong Kong, launched both the Charlotte church and the association following a landmark revival campaign he and his son directed there that year. At the end of thirty-five years the thousand-member congregation had sent more than a hundred ministers and other full-time workers into the field. It was airing a daily radio broadcast and supporting missionaries in nine fields. Two-thirds of the $25,000 annual missions budget was then being sent overseas. Following his death, Garr's widow, Hannah Erickson Garr, and son assumed oversight of the work. See also GARR MEMORIAL CHURCH.

Bibliography: Encyclopedia of Modern Christian Missions (1967), 298; C. E. Jones, *Guide to the Study of the Pentecostal Movement* (1983); A. C. Piepkorn, *Profiles in Belief,* vol. 3 (1979).
C. E. Jones

CAROTHERS, MERLIN R. (twentieth century). Chaplain and author. Army chaplain whose work *Prison to Praise* (1970) received tremendous attention in charismatic circles in the 1970s.

Carothers served in the 82nd Airborne Division as a demolition expert during World War II. After attending Marion College and Asbury Seminary, he served as a Methodist pastor in Claypool, Indiana, for three years. He reentered the Army in 1953 and served as a chaplain in several countries, including Vietnam.

His works focus on pragmatic reasons for praising God for all circumstances. It is his contention that praise not only alters the attitude of the person involved but transforms the actual situation. Carothers writes in an anecdotal style supported by loose proof texting of Scripture. He was the first person to write on the subject of praise during the cresting of interest in the subject in charismatic circles. He also wrote *Bringing Heaven into Hell* (1976), and *Praise Works* (1973).
B. M. Stout

CAROTHERS, WARREN FAY (1872–1953). Attorney, judge, pastor, denominational executive, ecumenist. Carothers was born in Lee County, Texas. He married and had one daughter. In April 1894, after reading law in Giddings and Beeville, Texas, law offices, Carothers was admitted to the bar. In 1923 he formed a law partnership with J. E. Niday and, upon the death of Niday, with R. S. Bowers. His offices in 1923 were located in Houston. In 1933 he received an appointment as a U.S. commissioner judge.

Carothers's interests also included real estate. In 1908 he managed the Houston Abstract Company, which he converted into a title company. While serving there, he also helped to found the Houston Real Estate Board.

Always a religious man, Carothers entered the ministry in 1896, and in 1899 he was licensed as a "local preacher" by the Methodists. While serving as pastor of Texas Holiness Church in Brunner, Texas, in 1905, Carothers and his congregation came into contact with C. F. Parham's ministry and entered the Pentecostal movement. Carothers perceived himself to be a teacher, but in 1906 he was appointed to serve as Parham's field director in the Apostolic Faith (AF) movement. He trained pastors and evangelists, selected other directors, oversaw the annual AF conventions, awarded William J. Seymour his credentials, and authorized his move to Los Angeles. During this period he authored *The Baptism with the Holy*

Ghost (1906–07) and *Church Government* (1909) for AF use.

By early 1912 Carothers and Parham had parted company. Carothers informed the readers of *Word and Witness,* "the withdrawal of the Parhamites left a unity that God can consistently bless. . . ." That the separation was a difficult one is clear from Parham's later references to Carothers. The issue appears to have been one that focused on Christian unity and the form of organization the AF movement was taking. In spite of the break, Carothers appears to have continued to hold AF in high regard.

Carothers entered the newly formed Assemblies of God (AG) in 1914, and for a time he served as a pastor and executive presbyter. In 1921 he acknowledged the General Council of the Assemblies of God as the "authorized Council of our day." His hand is apparent in the resolution of "World-wide Cooperation" passed by the general council in 1921. It lamented the divisions prevalent among Pentecostals in the U.S. and established a committee, of which he was one member, with a view to calling for the formation of an "Ecumenical Union of Pentecostal Believers."

Apparently this action bore little fruit that would satisfy Carothers. The following year he formed a committee with H. A. Goss and C. B. Fockler to promote visible Christian unity. For the sake of consistency, on April 10, 1923, he wrote to E. N. Bell and withdrew from the AG to establish an independent church in Houston, where he expected to carry forth his message on unity. His one criticism was that he did not believe that the AG was "*the* church." His suspicion that AG leadership at the time held this position was quickly denied by E. N. Bell.

Carothers held unity conferences in St. Louis, Missouri (October 24, 1922); Chicago, Illinois (November 11, 1923); and Owensboro, Kentucky (July 11–14, 1924). He published *The Herald of the Church* to draw others into dialogue, arguing that the church was universal and that ultimately a universal council would coordinate local manifestations of the church with appeal to Scripture *and* prophetic gifts. By May 1934 the movement had foundered and disappeared. Carothers continued in the legal profession until his death in February 1953.

Bibliography: W. F. Carothers, *The Baptism With the Holy Ghost* (1906); idem, *Church Government* (1909); idem, "The Gift of Interpretation," *LRE* 3 (1, 1910): 7–10 (reprinted in *Confidence* 3 [11, November 1910]: 255–57); idem, *The Herald of the Church* 1 (3, 1925); idem, "Two Ways," *AF* (Fort Worth) 7 (1, 1911): 2–3; Letters: Seymour to Carothers, November 12, 1906; Carothers to Bell, April 10, 1923; Bell to Carothers, April 14, 1923; "W. F. Carothers, Realty Board Founder Dies," *Houston Chronicle* February 12, 1953; C. F. Parham, "A Glimpse Into the Heart of God," *LRE* 4 (11, 1912): 19–22; idem, "Houston Heights, Tex.," *Word and Witness* 8 (8, 1912): 2; idem, "Leadership," *AF* (Baxter Springs) 1 (4, 1912): 7; idem, "My Debt to the Movement," *Word and Witness* 9 (6, 1913): 4; idem, "The Work Still Progressing in Houston," *The Weekly Evangel* 129 (March 4, 1916): 5.   C. M. Robeck, Jr.

CARROLL, R. LEONARD (1920–72). Twelfth general overseer of the Church of God (CG, Cleveland, Tenn.). Born in Franklin County, Georgia, Carroll received academic degrees from Furman University (B.A., 1947) and the University of Tennessee (M.S., 1955; Ed.D., 1958). He was president of Lee College for five years (1952–57) and executive director of general education for two (1968–70). He also served as chairman of the commission on education for the Pentecostal Fellowship of North America and the National Association of Evangelicals.

Carroll was general overseer of the CG less than two years (1970–72) and died of a heart attack while serving in that office. A frequent writer, his final and most popular published work was *Stewardship: Total Life Commitment* (1967).

Bibliography: Archives of the Church of God (Cleveland, Tenn.).   C. W. Conn

CARTER, ALFRED HOWARD (1891–1971). British Pentecostal leader and educator. After several visits to Sunderland, England, Carter became a Pentecostal (1915). He pastored briefly at Saltley, Birmingham, but was imprisoned as a conscientious objector during World War I. From 1921 to 1948 he was principal of Hampstead Bible School (London). He also developed a program of correspondence study. A founding member of the Assemblies of God in Great Britain and Ireland, he served as vice-chairman (1929–34) and chairman (1934–45). Carter traveled widely as a preacher and conference speaker.

Bibliography: A. H. Carter, *Cyril J. Duxbury As I Knew Him* (n.d.); idem, *The Gifts of the Holy Spirit* (1946); idem, *Questions and Answers on the Gifts of the Spirit* (1946); idem, *Questions and Answers on Spiritual Gifts* (1946); idem, *Spiritual Gifts and Their Operation; Anecdotal Lectures* (1968); idem, *When the Time Flew By* (1957); J. Carter, *Howard Carter, Man of the Spirit* (1971); D. Gee, *Wind and Flame* (1967); L. F. Sumrall, *Adventuring with Christ* (1939).   D. D. Bundy

CARTER, JOHN H. (1891–1981). British Assemblies of God leader. Carter was born in Birmingham and saved in the Churches of Christ. He was introduced to the Pentecostal movement and attended the Sunderland Convention in 1913. After engaging in pastoral ministry in Birmingham, he joined the Elim Evangelistic Band in Belfast in 1919. He left in 1921, joining his brother Howard to pastor the Lee Assembly, London. As Tutor at Hampstead (1923–28), he engaged in evangelistic ministry (1928–34). A founding member of the Assemblies of God in Great Britain and Ireland (AGGBI) in 1924, he served as general secretary (1936–63); editor of *Redemption Tidings* (1934–49); tutor at Kenley Bible College (1955–63); and principal at Kenley (1966–70). Carter also served as a member of the advisory committee of the Pentecostal World Conference (1955–61) and chairman of AGGBI conferences in 1952 and 1964. Gracious, efficient, and hard working, he died at Mattersey, Doncaster, in April 1981.

Bibliography: J. H. Carter, *A Full Life* (1979); A. Missen, *The Sound of a Going* (1973). D. W. Cartwright

CASHWELL, GASTON BARNABAS (1862–1916). The apostle of Pentecost in the South. Gaston Barnabas Cashwell was born in Sampson County, North Carolina, near the city of

Dunn. As a young man he became a minister in the North Carolina Conference of the Methodist Episcopal Church, South. In 1903, under the influence of A. B. Crumpler (1862–1952), he left the Methodist Church to join the newly formed Pentecostal Holiness Church (PHC), then known as the Holiness Church of North Carolina (HCNC).

Cashwell made a name in the Holiness movement as an evangelist, ministering to both blacks and whites in tent meetings and local Holiness churches. Although his relationship with Crumpler and the leadership of the church was often stormy, Cashwell became a leading minister in the church.

Upon hearing of the Azusa Street meeting in California, Cashwell was overcome with a desire to receive the baptism in the Holy Spirit with the evidence of speaking in tongues as taught by William J. Seymour (1870–1922), the pastor of the Azusa Mission. His knowledge of the California Pentecost came from reports by Frank Bartleman in the *Way of Faith* magazine published by J. M. Pike in Columbia, South Carolina.

In November 1906 Cashwell borrowed money to travel by rail to Los Angeles. His letter to the annual conference in Lumberton, North Carolina, explained his absence and asked forgiveness for wrongs done to anyone he had offended. In his first service at Azusa Street he was taken back by some practices that to him seemed "fanatical," but overall he felt that "God was in it." On first seeking for the baptism in the Holy Spirit, he was antagonized by his aversion to being prayed for by blacks. He went to his hotel room where he "suffered a crucifixion" and "died to many things," including his racial prejudice. He went the next night requesting that Seymour and other blacks lay hands on him. He promptly received the Pentecostal experience, and according to his own account spoke in "English, German, and French."

After an offering in which the Azusa Street congregation bought him a new suit and a train ticket back home, Cashwell returned to Dunn, North Carolina, where he brought the Pentecostal message to the local Holiness church on December 31, 1906. Invitations were sent to the ministers of the Holiness churches of the region to attend Pentecostal services in January in Dunn. Due to the intense interest in the meeting, Cashwell rented a three-story tobacco warehouse by the railroad tracks to hold the crowds.

The Dunn meetings lasted through the month of January 1907 and became an East Coast counterpart to the Azusa Street meetings. Most of the ministers of the Holiness churches in the area came to Dunn and received the tongues experience, including G. F. Taylor, H. H. Goff, and F. M. Britton. Through the Dunn meetings, the PHC, the Fire-Baptized Holiness Church (FBHC), and the Pentecostal Free-Will Baptist Church entered the Pentecostal movement.

In February 1907 Cashwell visited J. H. King (1869–1946), general overseer of the FBHC in Toccoa, Georgia, where King received the Pentecostal experience. Also through a whirlwind series of tent meetings in South Carolina, N. J. Holmes

and the Holmes Bible and Missionary Institute in Greenville, South Carolina, was swept into the Pentecostal movement. In the summer of 1907 Cashwell visited Birmingham, Alabama, where O. N. Todd, Sr., and future founders of the Assemblies of God, M. M. Pinson and H. G. Rodgers were baptized in the Holy Spirit.

In January 1908 Cashwell was invited by A. J. Tomlinson to speak in Cleveland, Tennessee, to leaders of the Church of God (CG). While Cashwell was preaching, Tomlinson fell to the floor speaking in tongues. Thereafter, the CG with its subsequent branches became part of the Pentecostal movement.

In order to promote Pentecostalism in the South, Cashwell began publication in 1907 of the *Bridegroom's Messenger,* a paper that carried news of the spreading Pentecostal revival. In the space of six months he had established himself as the apostle of Pentecost in the South.

The major obstacle to the sweep of Cashwell's ministry was the leader of his own church, A. B. Crumpler, who began a campaign to stop the spread of Pentecostalism in his HCNC. While Cashwell and G. F. Taylor led the Pentecostal faction, Crumpler attacked the initial evidence theory in the church periodical the *Holiness Advocate.* In the Annual Conference of 1908 the issue was settled in favor of the Pentecostals, after which Crumpler left the church forever. Cashwell and the victorious Pentecostal party then redrafted the Articles of Faith to include the initial evidence theory.

By 1909 Cashwell himself left the PHC, evidently over disappointment at not being elected to head the church after successfully leading the Pentecostal revolution. Until his death in 1916 he conducted revivals in independent churches in the South, but his reputation as a Pentecostal pioneer was firmly established by his barnstorming ministry in 1907 which forever altered the religious landscape of the South.

Bibliography: V. Synan, *The Old-Time Power* (1973).   H. V. Synan

CASTING OUT DEMONS See EXORCISM.

CATHOLIC APOSTOLIC CHURCH See EDWARD IRVING.

CATHOLIC CHARISMATIC RENEWAL
   I. History
      A. Context: The Post-Vatican II Catholic Church
      B. Beginnings of the Catholic Charismatic Renewal (CCR) in the U.S.
      C. Progress of the CCR in the U.S.
      D. International Outreach
   II. "Pentecostal Movement in the Catholic Church"
      A. Historical Links With Pentecostalism
      B. Sharing a Common Experience
      C. Ecumenical Outreach of the CCR
   III. Distinctive Aspects of the CCR
      A. Doctrine
         1. Respect for Tradition
         2. Catholic Sacramental Theology
         3. Consequences for Catholic Interpretations of Baptism in the Spirit

4. Consequences for the Catholic Understanding of Charisms
B. Distinctive Catholic Practices
   1. Celebration of the Eucharist
   2. Expression of Devotion to the Blessed Virgin Mary
   3. Retreats and Seminars
C. Organization
   1. Within the Prayer Group
   2. Among Prayer Groups
      a. Diocesan and Regional
      b. National Organization
      c. International Organization
   3. Organization of Covenant Communities
      a. Within Communities
      b. Among Communities
D. Relationship With Church Authority
   1. With Local Authority: Parish Priest and Bishop
   2. With Episcopal Conference
   3. The Role of Cardinal Suenens
   4. With Roman Authorities

I. History.

A. Context: The Post-Vatican II Catholic Church. While some individual Catholics had been touched by the Pentecostal movement and had been baptized in the Spirit prior to 1967, the formation of a prayer group among faculty members and students at Duquesne University, Pittsburgh, in February 1967 is generally looked upon as the beginning of the charismatic renewal in the Catholic church. There are several reasons for seeing it as providential that this beginning took place after the Second Vatican Council, which concluded its final session on December 1, 1965. Indeed, it seems unlikely that any form of Pentecostalism among Catholics would have been accepted by the bishops and the pope if it had not been for some important decisions that they themselves had made at the council.

The first of these decisions was that the Catholic church should become a full and active participant in the ecumenical movement. This involved the recognition

> that whatever is wrought by the grace of the Holy Spirit in the hearts of our separated brethren can contribute to our own edification. Whatever is truly Christian can never conflict with the genuine interests of the faith; indeed, it can always result in a more ample realization of the very mystery of Christ and the Church (Decree on Ecumenism, 4; Abbott, 1966, 349).

Given the previously negative attitude of the Catholic church toward what other churches might have to offer, this positive assessment of the Christian values to be found among the "separate brethren" surely was an important factor in the acceptance of the idea that Pentecostalism might have something to contribute to the spiritual renewal of the Catholic church.

Another decision of Vatican II that opened the way to the acceptance of a charismatic renewal in the Catholic church was the recognition of the vital importance of charismatic gifts in the life of the church. Such recognition had been strongly contested by some council members, but Cardinal Suenens led a successful effort to have the statement on the charisms of the faithful retained and approved by an overwhelming majority. A key sentence of this text declares:

> These charismatic gifts, whether they be the most outstanding or the more simple and widely diffused, are to be received with thanksgiving and consolation, for they are exceedingly suitable and useful for the needs of the church (Dogmatic Constitution on the Church, 12, Abbott, 1966, 30).

While the bishops making this statement in 1964 could hardly have anticipated that within a few years many of their Catholic faithful would be manifesting such gifts as tongues and prophecy, their subsequent acceptance of those gifts as an integral part of the charismatic renewal surely owes a great deal to the intervention of Cardinal Suenens at the council, who of course at that time could have had no inkling of the role he was to play in the renewal.

A third element in the teaching of Vatican II that contributed to the acceptance of the charismatic renewal in the Catholic church was its insistence that the call to holiness and to active sharing in the building up of the body of Christ is universal, embracing all of the lay faithful as well as clergy and those with religious vows. In its chapter on the laity in the Constitution on the Church, the council declared:

> If everyone in the church does not proceed by the same path, nevertheless all are called to sanctity and have received an equal privilege of faith through the justice of God (cf. 2 Peter 1:1). And if by the will of Christ some are made teachers, dispensers of mysteries, and shepherds on behalf of others, yet all share a true equality with regard to the dignity and to the activity common to all the faithful for the building up of the Body of Christ (Abbott, 1966, 58).

If it had not been for this new emphasis given by the council to the role of the laity in the life of the church, it is doubtful that the priests and bishops would have been so open to a movement of spiritual renewal whose origin, growth, and leadership owe so much more to the initiative of lay Catholics than to that of the clergy.

B. Beginnings of the Catholic Charismatic Renewal (CCR) in the U.S. Ralph Keifer and Patrick Bourgeois were young lay instructors in the department of theology at Duquesne University, a Catholic institution under the direction of the Holy Ghost Fathers. Their interest in the Pentecostal movement was stimulated by the reading of two books: David Wilkerson's *The Cross and the Switchblade* (c. 1963), and John Sherrill's *They Speak With Other Tongues* (1964). Desirous to experience for themselves the spiritual awakening that Wilkerson and Sherrill described as the effect of being baptized in the Spirit, and having learned of the existence of a Pentecostal-type prayer group in the Pittsburgh area, they sought and received an invitation to attend the meetings of this group, which were held in the home of a Presbyterian laywoman. It is significant that it was such a prayer group, made up of people from the mainline Protestant churches, that provided the bridge between Catholics and Pentecostals, as it would undoubtedly not have occurred to Keifer and his friends to attend services in a Pentecostal church. At the second meeting in which they took part, they asked for prayer that they might receive the baptism in the Spirit; they had the typical Pentecostal experience, including the gift of tongues. In the following weeks they shared their discovery with close friends and prayed with them for the baptism in the Spirit. In mid February 1967 they, together with a group of about thirty of their students who had also read *The Cross and the Switchblade*, decided to spend a weekend in prayer, reflecting on the first four chapters of Acts and seeking the will of God for their lives. In the course of the weekend, at various times and in different ways, each of these young people experienced a new outpouring of the Spirit. The first Catholic charismatic prayer group manifesting the gifts and fruit of the Spirit that are characteristic of the Pentecostal movement thus came into existence.

Having begun on the campus of a university, the movement soon found adherents at two other universities: Notre Dame and Michigan State. A visitor from Duquesne brought the movement to Notre Dame in early March. At about the same time, two recent graduates of Notre Dame, Ralph Martin and Stephen Clark, having heard of the events at Duquesne, went there themselves, were baptized in the Spirit, and started a prayer group when they returned to Michigan State. During the weekend of April 7–9, 1967, about a hundred students and several faculty members from these universities gathered on the Notre Dame campus for a weekend of prayer and reflection on the new experiences they shared after their baptism in the Spirit. What was particularly noteworthy about this meeting was that it attracted the attention of the press: first of student publications, and then of two widely read Catholic weeklies, *The National Catholic Reporter* (April 19, 1967) and *Our Sunday Visitor* (May 14, 1967). In this way the existence of a "Catholic Pentecostalism" came to be known to the general public. It was likewise spread by word of mouth when the students scattered to various parts of the country during their summer vacation. At the end of this summer a second meeting at Notre Dame brought together a number of people who had been touched by the movement. In September of that same year Ralph Martin and Stephen Clark accepted an invitation from the Catholic chaplain at the University of Michigan in Ann Arbor to assist him in campus ministry, and shortly thereafter they initiated a prayer group which has subsequently had a major impact on the development of the CCR. Since that time, South Bend, Indiana, and Ann Arbor, Michigan, have been the most influential centers of the renewal among Catholics in the U.S. They have also played an important role in the worldwide expansion of this movement.

C. Progress of the CCR in the U.S. Among the outstanding events in the history of the CCR in the U.S. have been the annual conferences that have been held on the University of Notre Dame campus. At the second of these conferences, in March 1968, there were about 150 participants, most of them from the Midwest. One who attended as an observer and subsequently played an important role in obtaining the approval of this movement by the National Conference of Catholic Bishops, was Fr. Kilian McDonnell, a Benedictine monk from St. John's University in Collegeville, Minnesota. Fr. McDonnell had previously collaborated in a study of the Pentecostal movement prior to its inception among Catholics and so was well qualified to reach a well-informed judgment on the Catholic Pentecostal movement. He was a member of a committee that prepared a report concerning this movement to present to the Catholic bishops at their annual meeting in November 1969. This positive report gave new impetus to the spread of the renewal, especially among Catholic clergy and religious sisters, a great many of whom came into the renewal when they attended summer sessions at the Catholic universities where prayer groups had already been formed.

An index of the growth of the charismatic renewal among American Catholics is provided by the number of adherents who have taken part in the annual conferences at Notre Dame. The third such conference, held in April 1969, attracted more than 450 people from most of the states and from several provinces of Canada. The fourth conference, in June 1970, drew more than 1,300 people from all parts of the U.S. and Canada. The fifth, by now justly named an international conference, was attended by nearly 5,000 people, including representatives of ten foreign countries, some as far away as Korea and Australia. The 1972 conference was attended by more than 11,000 people from sixteen countries. In 1973 more than 20,000 took part, so that the general assemblies had to be held in the football stadium. About five hundred priests concelebrated the final Eucharist, at which a Canadian archbishop, James Hayes, presided, and a Belgian cardinal, Leon Joseph Suenens, gave the homily. After 1976, when the number attending the Notre Dame conference reached 30,000, the decision was taken to promote regional conferences and to limit the registration at Notre Dame to about 12,000, so that the plenary sessions could be held indoors. Since then the number attending the annual Notre Dame conferences has dropped to about 8,000, while the total number taking part in all the regional conferences has become far greater. One such regional conference, held at Atlantic City in 1977, attracted more than 37,000 participants.

The principal form that the renewal has taken in the U.S. has been the prayer group. In 1986 the total number of such groups was estimated at more than six thousand. At the present time there is a tendency to reduce the overall number of groups, by encouraging several small groups to coalesce into one large group, wherever this can be done. Experience has shown that small groups often suffer for lack of a sufficient number of people with gifts for leadership, teaching, and the like, and that this problem can be solved by having them pool their resources in one larger group.

D. International Outreach. The events are recent enough and memory fresh enough so that it would be possible to gather firsthand accounts of how the charismatic renewal arrived in each of the more than a hundred countries where it is now thriving. However, such is not the scope of this article. Some few indications will have to suffice of approximately when and how the renewal reached out to various parts of the world.

The first extension over the border of the U.S. seems to have been to Canada, where it was introduced to the Madonna House community in Combermere, Ontario, in August 1968. After first spreading among English-speaking Canadians, a year or so later it began to take hold in the province of Quebec as well. Not long after its expanse to the north, it was also carried south, into Latin America, in many cases by North American missionaries working there who came to know the renewal on a visit home, and in other cases by those already involved in the renewal who were invited south to give conferences or retreats. Such was the origin of the renewal in Bolivia (1969), in Mexico and Peru (1970), and in Puerto Rico (1971). In 1973 a meeting took place in Bogota, Colombia, that brought together leaders of the renewal in eight Latin American countries. At that meeting a decision was taken to establish a communication center, Encuentro Carismatico Catolico Latino-Americano (ECC-LA). The renewal has since expanded to all of the countries of Latin America, and some of them are still among the most thriving regions of the CCR in the world.

Attendance at the Notre Dame conferences shows that by 1971 the renewal had reached at least ten foreign countries, including Korea and Australia. The same year saw the beginnings of the Catholic movement at two of the most important Catholic universities in Europe: in Belgium at the American College at the University of Louvain, and in Rome, where some Americans and a Canadian began an English-speaking prayer group that has had an important impact on the worldwide expansion of the renewal. The very fact that it became known quite early that there was a charismatic prayer group holding its meetings in Rome at the Pontifical Gregorian University did much to assure Catholic clergy around the world that this was a legitimate Catholic movement. And secondly, this Roman group was largely made up of priests and sisters from all parts of the world who, after their studies or other assignments in Rome, would carry the renewal to wherever they returned or were sent on mission.

The year 1972 saw the spread of the renewal in Ireland, France, Germany, Japan, India, and New Guinea, among other places. An index of the rapid spread of the renewal at this time is the fact that by the end of 1972, *New Covenant* magazine was being sent to subscribers in approximately ninety countries. Toward the end of this same

year, the leaders of the movement in the U.S. established an International Communications Office (ICO) in Ann Arbor, with Ralph Martin as its director. After the 1973 Notre Dame conference, a special meeting was held with 200 leaders who had come from twenty-five different countries, and the decision was made to hold an international leaders' conference in December of that year. This meeting was held in Grottaferrata, a town in the vicinity of Rome, with the participation of Cardinal Suenens and 120 leaders of the renewal from 34 countries. At the request of Cardinal Suenens, a special audience was granted to a dozen of these leaders, who were warmly received by Pope Paul VI. Encouraged by this reception at Rome and by the rapid growth of the renewal throughout the world in the following year, the ICO made the bold decision to hold an international congress in Rome during 1975, which Pope Paul had declared a holy year, a year of special pilgrimages to Rome. Just prior to the opening of this congress, a second international leaders' conference was held, with 220 participants from 50 countries. Then the congress itself took place, with 10,000 in attendance; at its close on Pentecost Monday, its participants had the joy of being received in St. Peter's Basilica by Pope Paul VI and hearing his encouraging message to the CCR.

Musicians sing and play at the 1973 Catholic Charismatic Renewal Conference at the University of Notre Dame.

By the end of 1975 *New Covenant* magazine reported that it had close to 60,000 subscribers in more than a hundred countries. In 1976 the ICO was moved to Brussels to be in closer contact with Cardinal Suenens, to whom Pope Paul VI had given a special mandate of oversight with regard to the worldwide Catholic renewal. In 1978 a third international leaders' conference was held, with participants from 60 countries, followed by an international congress in Dublin, attended by 20,000. Since 1981, when the ICO moved from Brussels to Rome and changed its name to International Catholic Charismatic Renewal Office (ICCRO), the international leaders' conferences have been held in Rome: the fourth, in 1981, with 94 countries represented, and the fifth, in 1984, with leaders from 108 countries present. Both of these were addressed in encouraging fashion by Pope John Paul II, who also confirmed the mandate given Cardinal Suenens. The sixth international leaders' conference was held in Rome in May 1987.

Given the worldwide extent of this movement in the Catholic church and the great variety of situations in which it finds itself, it is evident that the state of the renewal will vary from region to region. In some areas it is still enjoying vigorous growth; in others there has been a leveling off or a drop in the number of groups and participants. However, the overall impression one gets from the reports given at the international leaders' conferences is that the CCR is solidly rooted in the life of the Catholic church and that it is not likely to fade away.

II. "Pentecostal Movement in the Catholic Church." Kevin Ranaghan and his wife Dorothy, who were among the first group at Notre Dame to be baptized in the Spirit, have the distinction of being coauthors of the first book to be published about this new movement in the Catholic church. They entitled their book *Catholic Pentecostals* (1969). Two years later Fr. Edward D. O'Connor, a professor of theology at Notre Dame, who was also among the early participants in the renewal there, published his account of it, under the title *The Pentecostal Movement in the Catholic Church*. The titles that the Ranaghans and O'Connor gave to their books shows that they recognized what was happening to be a Catholic manifestation of the larger Pentecostal movement. For a few years following the publication of these books, the terms "Catholic Pentecostalism" and "Catholic Pentecostal" were commonly used to describe this movement and its participants. However, to avoid confusion with members of the various Pentecostal churches, the suggestion was made quite early on, and has been generally adopted, to use the term "Catholic Charismatic Renewal" (even though this has given rise to the unhappy practice of referring to participants in the renewal as "the charismatics," as though they claimed a monopoly on such gifts).

It is important to note that the dropping of the term "Catholic Pentecostals" does not signify any intention to deny the Pentecostal roots of this movement. The purpose of this section of the article is to point out a number of reasons that justify understanding the CCR as just what Fr. O'Connor called it: the Pentecostal movement in the Catholic church.

A. Historical Links With Pentecostalism. As we have seen, it was not from "classical" Pentecostals but from a charismatic group composed mainly of Episcopalians and Presbyterians that the men at Duquesne learned how to pray for the baptism in the Spirit. The existence of a Pentecostal movement in such "respectable" churches certainly facilitated its entry into the Catholic church. Previous relationships between Catholics and Pentecostals had generally been anything but cordial. Many Catholics knew of the Pentecostals only by their reputation as "holy rollers," and many Pentecostals were convinced that the Holy Spirit had long since abandoned the Catholic church. Hence it was easier for Catholics in the first years of their experiences of the Pentecostal movement to find sympathetic advisers among the many Protestants who had already been involved in charismatic prayer groups in the decade or so since Dennis Bennett had introduced prayer for the baptism in the Spirit into the Episcopal Church.

However, Edward O'Connor's account of the beginnings of the renewal at Notre Dame shows that the Catholics involved there received encouragement and friendly counsel from members of the Pentecostal churches in South Bend. The first of these was Ray Bullard, at that time president of the South Bend chapter of the Full Gospel Business Men's Fellowship International (FGBMFI) and a deacon at a local Assemblies of God. O'Connor describes him as "a kind of spiritual godfather for the charismatic community that was beginning to form at Notre Dame" (1971, 46). Bullard was typical of the many Pentecostals, active members of the FGBMFI, who, having for some years had the experience of seeing the Pentecostal movement accepted by Protestants, were now open to the idea that Catholics too could receive the baptism in the Spirit and the charismatic gifts without having to leave their own church. However, it was not only members of this fellowship, but other ministers and lay people from Assemblies of God churches in the South Bend area, who gave support and encouragement to the Catholic charismatic group at Notre Dame.

In his detailed account of the early years of the Catholic renewal, "The Charismatic Movement: 1967–1970," in the book edited by the Ranaghans, *As the Spirit Leads Us* (1971, 211–32), Fr. James Connelly, of the University of Notre Dame, mentions a number of Pentecostals and charismatic Protestants who had an influence on the leaders of the Catholic renewal during those early years. Among others, he names Ray Bringham, of Inter-Church Team Ministry, an interdenominational group of ministers who had been spreading the Pentecostal movement among Protestants, and who now likewise encouraged the Catholic version of it. Other pastors of this group addressed the conference held at Notre Dame in the summer of 1967, as did Lloyd Weber, a United Church of Christ pastor and leader of a charismatic community in a Chicago suburb. Others instrumental in bringing Catholics into the baptism in the Spirit in those early years were

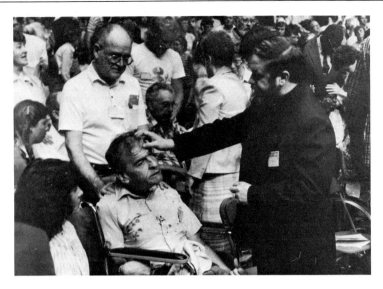

The practice of laying on of hands for the sick during a Catholic charismatic conference.

Agnes Sanford, Tommy Tyson, Derek Prince, and Harald Bredesen.

Among "classical" Pentecostals who had an important influence on the CCR, special mention must be made of David du Plessis, who in his address to the conference at Notre Dame in April 1969, urged the participants to be Pentecostal within their Catholic tradition and not to try to imitate everything they saw the older Pentecostals doing. The CCR owes a great deal to the wise counsel that David du Plessis shared with it on that and on many subsequent occasions.

The number of Pentecostals and Protestants involved in the Pentecostal movement who have been invited to address the conferences at Notre Dame and other important meetings of the Catholic renewal is further proof of the recognition by the leaders of this renewal that they are sharing in a common movement and that they have much to learn from those who have had a longer experience of it.

B. Sharing a Common Experience. Besides the historical links between the CCR and the older Pentecostal movement, an even more decisive reason for recognizing this renewal as "Catholic Pentecostalism," is to be found in the basic identity of the experiences that Catholics have come to share with others in this movement, namely the baptism in the Spirit and the charisms that typically follow. The fact that Catholics may prefer a theological interpretation of baptism in the Spirit that differs from the Pentecostal interpretation does not negate the identity of the experience as such. What all participants in the Pentecostal movement have come to know is that in the course of Christian life one can begin to experience the power of the Spirit in a radically new way. Catholics have learned from Pentecostals to be open to such a new outpouring of the Spirit, to seek it, to dispose oneself as well as one can to receive it, and to pray for it, especially with

the help of others who have already received it. All know that it is not something that one can achieve by human effort, no matter how intense; it is essentially a free gift, but one that is often given in answer to sincere prayer. Accompanying the transforming gift, or subsequent to it, Catholics, like Pentecostals, expect to experience some new gift of the Spirit, most often that of praying in tongues. It is true that generally Catholics will not insist, as most Pentecostals do, that every authentic baptism in the Spirit will be marked by the recipient's speaking in tongues. But there can be no doubt about the important role that the gift of tongues plays in the identification of a Catholic prayer group as "charismatic." It may well be that in most cases the manifestation of this gift will be in the form of a wordless but sometimes quite harmonious "singing in the Spirit" that wells up in the group, especially in a time of praise. But a distinguishing mark of any Pentecostal prayer group, Catholic or Protestant, will be the reception of prayer in tongues as a normal and expected manifestation of the Spirit.

Similarly, a positive attitude toward the appearance of the gift of prophecy, even in otherwise ordinary and simple people, is as common to Catholics as it is to other participants in the Pentecostal movement. Likewise, Catholics have learned to pray for physical and spiritual healing with faith in the power of the Lord to cure all ills and have had tangible proof that the Lord does act powerfully in answer to such prayers of faith.

Given all these elements shared in common, there is a sound basis for judging that the CCR is a genuine manifestation of the Pentecostal movement.

C. Ecumenical Outreach of the CCR. It has already been suggested that the participation of Catholics in the Pentecostal movement could hardly have been approved by the bishops if it had not been for the positive attitude that they had expressed at Vatican II toward the Christian values present in other churches. But if Catholic ecumenism was a prior condition for the acceptance of Catholic Pentecostalism, the latter has had consequences for the cause of ecumenism that hardly anyone could have foreseen at the time of the council. For at that time, if anyone had listed the other churches in the order of their closeness to, or distance from, the Catholic church, the Pentecostal churches would surely have been named among the most distant. While it would be overly optimistic to claim that relations have everywhere become ideal, still there is no denying the key role that Catholic Pentecostalism has had in breaking down what had seemed to be insurmountable barriers between Catholics and Pentecostals.

In the previous section we have already mentioned the help that Catholics received from other Christians already participating in the Pentecostal movement, especially in the early years when they had so much to learn. While at first it was mostly a question of other Pentecostals being invited to speak at Catholic meetings, it was not long before leaders in the Catholic renewal were being invited to address Protestant Pentecostal gatherings as well. Mutual understanding and respect have led to the building of cordial relationships and often of warm friendships between representatives of churches whose previous relationships had been cold or even hostile.

An important factor here has been the formation of interdenominational prayer groups and communities and the acceptance by the authorities of the several churches of the participation of their members in such groups. As a result of coming together regularly for praise and worship and experiencing the same gifts of the Spirit, participants of such mixed groups have come to appreciate how much they share in common with other Christians and to recognize the evident work of the Spirit in them and in their churches. The existence of a large number of such ecumenical prayer groups, and even in some cases of ecumenical communities, is surely an important factor in what is often termed "grassroots ecumenism."

It is unfortunately true that in some cases the potential for ecumenism has been lost when such mixed prayer groups have settled for mere nondenominationalism, drawing their members away from adherence to their own churches. The maintenance of a truly ecumenical approach, seeking to achieve reconciliation and full communion among Christian churches while preserving and strengthening the sound elements found in each of them, calls for leaders who are understanding of and deeply committed to genuine ecumenism. While this has not always been the case, there is reason to judge that, on the whole, the Pentecostal movement, in bringing so many Catholics together with other Christians for prayer and fellowship, has made a positive contribution to the cause of ecumenism, which is all the more important in that it comes from an area where it would have been least expected.

Mention should be made here of the official Pentecostal-Catholic dialogue, which in 1985 began the third of its five-year mandates. Key figures in the history of this dialogue have been the late David du Plessis and Fr. Kilian McDonnell. The Vatican Secretariat for Christian Unity has sponsored this dialogue from the beginning, while it is only gradually that official sponsorship has come from the leadership of the Pentecostal churches. During the first five-year period, many of the non-Catholic participants were leaders of the charismatic renewal within Protestant, Anglican, and Orthodox churches. However, in subsequent sessions there has been more active participation in the dialogue on the part of some Pentecostal churches that have authorized their representatives to take part in it.

The participation of prominent leaders of the Pentecostal movement in other churches has been a regular feature of all the major conferences of the CCR. Similarly, Catholics have regularly participated in interdenominational meetings and conferences sponsored by other communities. Perhaps the most striking manifestation of the ecumenical nature of the charismatic renewal thus far was the Conference on Charismatic Renewal in the Church that took place in Kansas City in July 1977. This conference was prepared by a committee composed of leaders in the renewal from a large number of churches, under the chairmanship of Kevin Ranaghan. About 45,000 persons gathered in the local football stadium for each of the evening sessions. During the mornings there were meetings of ten distinct conferences, of which the largest was the Catholic one, with about half the total number of those present at the plenary sessions. Other conferences were for members of Baptist, Episcopal, Lutheran, Mennonite, Methodist, Pentecostal, and Presbyterian churches. During the afternoons the participants could choose among the workshops offered by the various conferences for anyone who wished to come. In his address to the Catholic conference, Cardinal Suenens hailed this congress as an example of what authentic ecumenism means: coming together with other Christians without losing one's identity.

Europe also has witnessed a remarkable proof of the ecumenical outreach of the CCR in the conference held at Strasbourg in May 1982, organized by a committee of leaders representing Catholic, Anglican, Lutheran, Reformed, and Evangelical churches. The number of participants from all these and other churches grew from about 10,000 at the opening session to nearly 20,000 at the close. The organization of this conference was facilitated by the fact that ecumenical European leaders' conferences had been held annually during the decade preceding it in which Catholics had regularly taken part.

More recently, in North America leaders of the Pentecostal movement from all the major denominations have formed the North American Renewal Service Committee, which sponsored the Leaders' Conference on the Holy Spirit and World Evangelization that brought together 7,500 leaders of the renewal from forty different churches and ministry fellowships at New Orleans in October 1986. Here, as at Kansas City in 1977, the largest single group was the Catholics.

The same committee prepared the general Congress on the Holy Spirit and World Evangelization for July 1987, which drew approximately 35,000 participants from all the major churches. While Kevin Ranaghan was not the chairman of this committee, he and other leaders of the CCR played an important role in preparing this congress, and a very large number of Catholics took part in it.

III. Distinctive Aspects of the CCR. Having considered the many common elements that justify speaking of the CCR as the "Pentecostal movement in the Catholic church," we must now turn our attention to those aspects of Catholic Pentecostalism that are distinctively Catholic. The four aspects that we will consider have to do with doctrine, practice, organization, and relationship to church authority.

A. Doctrine. Obviously it is not a question here of treating all the aspects in which Catholic doctrine would be different from that of Protestants in general or Pentecostals in particular. What we are concerned about are the factors that have led Catholics to propose theological interpretations of their Pentecostal experiences that differ from the interpretations that would more likely be given by Pentecostals or by evangelical Protestants.

There is every reason to believe that the experiences as such are substantially the same. But it is in the nature of theology to seek a deeper understanding of one's faith experience. And it is appropriate that if it is a question of a new faith experience, one will look for an understanding of it that is consistent with all that one already believes. Of course it is possible that a new faith experience might be so radically at variance with one's previous beliefs that one would either have to reject the validity of the new experience or modify one's beliefs in the light of it. No doubt there have been some Catholics who have thought that their Pentecostal experience was incompatible with their previous beliefs and have embraced the faith of the group or church in which they discovered the Pentecostal gifts. But the overwhelming majority of Catholics who have had the experience of baptism in the Spirit during the past twenty years have seen in this nothing that is inconsistent with their Catholic faith. Indeed, the acceptance of a "Pentecostal movement" by the authorities of their church would have been out of the question if there had been any contradiction between its basic experience and Catholic doctrine. What this means, of course, is that the Pentecostal experience has been recognized as susceptible of an interpretation that is consistent with Catholic faith.

Such an interpretation will most probably be different, at least in some respects, from one offered by Christians of a different theological tradition. For it is to be expected that people who are thoroughly convinced of the truth of their faith will seek an interpretation of a new spiritual experience in the light of what they already believe. First, then, we shall describe some elements of a distinctively Catholic understanding of the Christian faith and then show how these have influenced the Catholic interpretation of the spiritual experiences that are typical of the Pentecostal movement.

1. Respect for Tradition. One of the distinctive elements of Catholic faith is the role that it assigns to tradition as a bearer and interpreter of divine revelation. Catholics, of course, revere the sacred Scriptures as the inspired Word of God. But they are also convinced that as the books of the NT are the written record of the faith of the apostolic church, so these books must continue to be read and understood in the light of that same faith as it has been handed down from the beginning in the beliefs, practices, and worship of the Christian church.

The consequences of this is that when Catholics are confronted with a new spiritual experience, they will seek to interpret it not only in the light of Scripture but also in the light of tradition. They will proceed on the assumption that while some aspects of this experience may be new, it will not involve a radical break with the church's traditional faith or spirituality. They will look for the basic elements of continuity between this new experience and what history tells us about spiritual experience of the past. Catholics will instinctively reject the idea that for most of its history the church had lacked something as essential as the experience of the power of the Holy Spirit and that it regained this only at the beginning of the twentieth century with the onset of the Pentecostal movement. This does not involve a denial or rejection of what is new in Pentecostalism, but it does involve the presumption that there will be a basic continuity between whatever is essential to Christian life here and traditional Christian experience. It also involves the conviction that both Scripture and Catholic tradition must be taken into account when seeking a theological interpretation of baptism in the Spirit or any other distinctive feature of Pentecostalism.

2. Catholic Sacramental Theology. A basic element of Catholic faith is the belief that there are seven acts of public worship given to the church by Christ that are uniquely efficacious signs of his power to confer the grace of the Holy Spirit on his people. In each case there is a human minister of the sacrament, and for most of the sacraments it is required that the minister be duly ordained. The effectiveness of the sacrament, however, does not depend on the faith or holiness of the minister, since Christ himself is understood to be the one who confers grace through these acts of worship. At the same time, the effectiveness of the sacraments to confer the gifts of the Spirit does depend on the faith of the recipients and their being properly disposed to receive such grace. Lack of faith or refusal to renounce grave sins would prevent a sacrament from having its intended effects. However, in the case of the baptism of infants, Catholics, relying here on Christian tradition, hold that the faith of the church and the intention of the parents to bring up the child as a Christian justify the belief that the infant receives the saving grace of Christ at baptism without being able to make an act of personal faith at that time. Of course he or she must make such an act of faith when capable of it, and the special occasions for this confession of faith will be at the reception of confirmation and the Eucharist, which complete that person's Christian initiation.

There are several aspects of Catholic belief about the sacraments that give rise to some differences between a Catholic interpretation of baptism in the Spirit and one that is more typical of Pentecostals or evangelical Protestants. Since Catholics believe that the saving grace of Christ is given in baptism, even to infants, they insist neither on its necessity for salvation nor on an adult crisis experience of conversion to Christ. Of course they do insist that one baptized as an infant must subsequently make an act of personal faith in Christ, but they are not accustomed to seeing this as a crisis experience. They do recognize that a Catholic's life of faith may possibly involve such a crisis experience, but they are more accustomed to associating the major advances in the life of grace with the reception of the sacraments, such as confirmation, Eucharist, matrimony, and holy orders. They will generally expect the course of Christian life to be a matter of gradual growth rather than a series of crisis experiences.

3. *Consequences for Catholic Interpretations of Baptism in the Spirit.* The word "interpretations" is plural here, because Catholics have proposed more than one way of understanding what happens when a person is baptized in the Spirit. Here two such interpretations will be explained: one stresses the sacramental element in Catholic theology, and another relies on a traditional Catholic understanding of the "missions" or "sendings" of the Holy Spirit.

When Catholics began to share the Pentecostal experience, they realized that they had to make it clear that this in no way conflicted with Catholic belief that the Holy Spirit was already given in the sacraments of Christian initiation: baptism and confirmation. Above all they wished to avoid giving the impression that they now looked on the first of these as a mere "baptism in water," as though it were only through a Pentecostal experience that a person really received the Holy Spirit.

In the light of this preoccupation, the interpretation of baptism in the Spirit that was most commonly given in the literature of the CCR was based on the assumption that one could speak of the Spirit as actually being given or imparted only through one of the sacraments. Catholics were reluctant to speak of a new imparting of the Spirit except through the reception of a sacrament, as though this would be incompatible with Catholic theology. Furthermore, it was seen as crucial to insist that the sacrament of baptism was a true "baptism in the Spirit," since it was a matter of Catholic faith that every valid and fruitful baptism conferred the gift of sanctifying grace, which involved the indwelling presence of the Holy Spirit in the person so graced.

The solution proposed was to distinguish between the sacramental baptism in the Spirit, whereby the gift of the Holy Spirit was actually conferred or imparted, and the Pentecostal baptism in the Spirit, which was interpreted as a "release" of the power and gifts of the Spirit, hitherto present in the soul but not previously

Catholic charismatics during a celebration at Notre Dame in 1986.

experienced. Some even spoke of the sacrament of baptism as conferring a "total gift of the Spirit" with all the gifts and graces that a person might subsequently become aware that he or she possessed. In this case the function of the Pentecostal baptism in the Spirit was to initiate the awareness and exercise of the gifts that were already there.

The interpretation proposed in the first of the Malines Documents was to distinguish between a "theological sense" of baptism in the Spirit and an "experiential sense." Baptism in the Spirit in the "theological sense" would involve the actual giving or imparting of the Holy Spirit. In the supposition that the Holy Spirit could be given only through the reception of a sacrament, only sacrament baptism would qualify as baptism in the Spirit in the theological sense. Baptism in the Spirit in the experiential sense would be the coming into conscious experience of the gifts of the Spirit already received in the sacraments, and this of course would apply to the Pentecostal kind of baptism in the Spirit (see O'Connor, 1974, 30–31).

As already mentioned, another interpretation of what happens when people are baptized in the Spirit in the charismatic renewal is based on a traditional Catholic understanding of the missions or sendings of the Holy Spirit. Proponents of this view do not accept the idea that it would be incompatible with Catholic doctrine to speak of an actual imparting of the gift of the Spirit except through the reception of a sacrament. They do not see how one can fully explain the "coming into conscious experience of the power and gifts of the Spirit" that happens through Pentecostal baptism in the Spirit, as merely a change in one's subjective consciousness. They argue that if a person becomes conscious of the power of the Spirit in a radically new way, it must be because the Spirit begins to work new effects of grace in him or her, and that involves the Spirit's being present in a new way. But if the Spirit begins to be present in a new way, that means that there must have been a new sending of the Spirit, because the Spirit is present in us precisely as sent by the Father and the Son.

It was a common teaching of medieval Catholic theologians that one could attribute every real increase in grace or virtue to a new imparting of the Holy Spirit. The greatest of these theologians, St. Thomas Aquinas, did not reject this opinion outright but made it clear that he preferred to speak of such a new sending of the Spirit only when it was a case of a genuine "innovation" produced in the spiritual life of the person, such that one could say that the person had been moved into some new act or new state of grace. His teaching on this matter is found in the passage of his *Summa Theologiae* where he is addressing the question of whether there can be a new sending of the Divine Person to someone in whom the Holy Spirit is already indwelling by grace. His answer is as follows:

There is an invisible sending also with respect to an advance in virtue or an increase of grace. . . . Such an invisible sending is especially to be seen in that kind of increase of grace whereby a person is moved forward into some new act or some new state of grace: as, for instance, when a person is moved forward into the grace of working miracles, or of prophecy, or out of the burning love of God offers his life as a martyr, or renounces all his possessions, or undertakes some other such arduous thing (*Summa Theologiae* I, q.43, a.6, ad 2um).

There is nothing in the text or its context that would suggest that St. Thomas thought that a new sending of the Spirit with effects such as these could be had only through the reception of a sacrament. If we recall that in biblical language "sending the Spirit," "pouring out the Spirit," and "baptizing in the Spirit" are simply different ways of saying the same thing, the conclusion follows that it is quite in accord with traditional Catholic theology for baptized and confirmed Catholics to ask the Lord to "baptize them in the Spirit." What they are asking for, in the language of St. Thomas, is a new sending of the Holy Spirit, which would begin a decisively new work of grace in their lives. The examples given by St. Thomas show that he would not have been surprised if such a new work of grace involved a charismatic gift.

Believing in the holiness of the church, Catholics believe that there have been genuinely holy people in every period of Christian history, and from reading the lives of the saints, they know that the lives of a great many of them have been marked by such spiritual "innovations" as have decisively changed their lives and moved them into new states of grace. If we agree with St. Thomas that such innovations must involve a new presence of the Spirit in that person, then it follows that the experience at the heart of the Pentecostal movement is really not something altogether new. It has been happening to people ever since the Spirit was poured out at Pentecost. What is new, however, besides the use of the biblical term "baptism in the Spirit" to describe it, is the fact that so many people have discovered how much it helps to pray explicitly and perseveringly for such an outpouring of the Spirit, to ask others to pray with them, and to direct such prayer to the Lord Jesus Christ, with the desire that he become the Lord of one's life in a new way through the working of the Holy Spirit.

4. Consequences for the Catholic Understanding of Charisms. The consequences here follow not from sacramental theology but from the Catholic emphasis on the importance of tradition. The first is the agreement between Catholics and Pentecostals in rejecting the "dispensationalist" idea that charisms such as tongues, prophecy, and healing were restricted to the apostolic age. While these have certainly not always been as common as they are today, Catholics accept the sovereign freedom of the Spirit to distribute his gifts when and to whom he chooses, in any age. Furthermore, their historians of spirituality and biographers of saints assure them that no age of the church has lacked its truly charismatic people. At the same time, familiarity with the lives of the saints will make them aware that there is a great variety of charisms and that the Spirit has adapted his gifts to the needs of the church in every age. Hence they will not rigidly limit the spectrum of charisms to those mentioned by St. Paul in 1 Corinthians 12:8–10, or claim that to be charismatic one must necessarily have one or more of those nine gifts.

In particular, Catholics will hardly accept the claim that every authentic baptism in the Spirit must be marked by the person's speaking in tongues. On the one hand, this would mean that hardly anyone had received such a transforming and empowering gift of the Spirit during all the centuries when the known cases of people manifesting this gift are quite rare.

On the other hand, Catholics have discovered in Christian tradition some practices that do resemble the modern gift of tongues: in particular the practice of "singing in tongues." St. Augustine, in his commentary on the Psalms, frequently explains and encourages the practice of what he termed "singing in jubilation," which he describes as a kind of a joyful singing by which one can still praise God even when one has gone beyond the bounds of real words. Such "singing in jubilation" was actually a common practice for centuries in the Christian churches during the Easter season, when, after singing the threefold "Alleluia," the whole congregation would be called upon to continue singing, without set words or melody, until they had satisfied their desire to express Easter joy. Such "jubilation," as it was termed, was also practiced by some saints in their private prayer.

Another charism that Catholics know has never been absent from the life of the church is that of healing in answer to prayer. It is true that for many centuries Catholics did not expect such charisms to be found except in the lives of exceptionally holy people. In fact it is the practice of the Catholic church to require that miraculous healings have taken place through prayers of a holy person before he or she can be declared certainly among the blessed in heaven. Nonetheless, it has always been part of Catholic practices to pray for the healing of the sick, and the lives of many saints have been marked by outstanding gifts of healing. Hence it was not so great a surprise for Catholics as it might have been for Christians of another tradition to discover that gifts of healing might become as abundant as they are in the charismatic renewal.

B. Distinctive Catholic Practices. If one compares a typical prayer meeting of a Catholic charismatic group with meetings of other Christians involved in the movement, the similarities will far outweigh any details that would distinguish a Catholic group from all the others. However, there are some practices that are distinctive of Catholic groups, and we shall mention them here.

1. *Celebration of the Eucharist.* For Catholics, participation in a weekly prayer meeting is quite distinct from their weekly participation in the official worship of their church. However, many Catholic groups do arrange to have a celebration of the Mass either before or after their prayer meeting if the place where they meet is appropriate for that. The celebration of the Eucharist is regularly a feature of special days of renewal, weekend retreats, and conferences of the Catholic renewal. Such celebrations are typically marked by great joyfulness and enthusiasm and provide special occasions for the exercise of spiritual gifts. At the large conferences and congresses, the Eucharist is particularly impressive, with hundreds of priests and several bishops concelebrating with the presiding prelate. Perhaps the most memorable of such celebrations was the one at which Cardinal Suenens presided in St. Peter's Basilica on Pentecost Monday, 1975, with the 10,000 people gathered in Rome for the international conference participating.

2. *Expressions of Devotion to the Blessed Virgin Mary.* On the one hand, one who is at all familiar with the CCR will question the statement that meetings that are typical of this renewal are solidly focused on God: Father, Son, and Holy Spirit, and in a very special way on Jesus as Lord. I have never attended a Catholic charismatic prayer meeting that was especially focused on Mary. On the other hand, it is distinctive of Catholic groups (along with those of Orthodox Christians) that from time to time a hymn may be sung in honor of Our Lady, or a prayer will be said, requesting her intercession. Sometimes, when such a prayer is said, reference will be made to her role at the wedding at Cana, when she presented the needs of the people there to her Son. Catholics believe that the doctrine of the communion of saints justifies their trust that the saints do intercede for them, and they have special confidence in the intercession of the Blessed Virgin Mary. In a certain sense, participation in the charismatic renewal confirms their trust in the effectiveness of intercessory prayer, because they

so often experience the fruits of the prayers that other members of the group offer for them. Since it proves beneficial to request the prayers of their companions here on earth, they find it all the more appropriate to request the prayer of those who are close to the Lord in heaven. And this applies in a unique way to Mary, his mother.

3. *Retreats and Seminars.* It will be recalled that a weekend retreat was the occasion of the first outbreak of the Catholic renewal at Duquesne. Several of the earliest and most influential leaders of the renewal were previously active in weekend retreats, such as those of the Cursillo movement, and those called "Antioch weekends." It is not surprising that the practice of conducting such weekend retreats has been a common feature of Catholic prayer groups. Such retreats will usually include one or two typical prayer meetings, some longer teachings, periods of private prayer and meditation, the sharing of Scripture, perhaps a penance service with the opportunity for the sacrament of reconciliation, and regularly the celebration of the Eucharist. In many places there will be a monthly "day of renewal" for members of all the prayer groups in the area, involving some of the elements of a weekend retreat.

A practice that originated in the Word of God community in Ann Arbor and has since become typical of the CCR is the conducting of Life in the Spirit seminars for those seeking the baptism in the Spirit. Not long after they began praying with newcomers for the baptism in the Spirit, the leaders of this group came to the conclusion that more serious preparation was needed, at least in most cases, before people would be properly disposed to receive the gifts that the Lord had in mind for them. To meet this need, they began to require that those who wished the group to pray with them for the baptism should first participate in what they called Life in the Spirit seminars. These are a series of spiritual exercises, usually lasting seven weeks, intended to help people to reach the best possible dispositions with which to pray for the gift of the Spirit. The thrust of the seminars is evangelization rather than catechesis: the intention is to help people to face the challenge of the gospel and to respond to it in a new way, renouncing whatever in their life has been incompatible with it and making a new, adult commitment to Jesus as their Lord. For Christians who were baptized in infancy and confirmed in early adolescence, this can well be the first time that they have ever made such a personal adult ratification of what was done for them at their Christian initiation.

After some experience in conducting such seminars, Stephen Clark and other members of the Word of God community composed a manual for the use of those leading the seminars and a booklet for participants suggesting Scripture passages for daily prayer during the seven weeks of the seminars. Both of these have been very widely and fruitfully used, and the conducting of these or similar "seminars" has become a typical practice of Catholic charismatic prayer groups throughout the world.

C. Organization. In this section we shall describe the forms of internal organization that

Catholic charismatics celebrating the Eucharist.

have developed within the CCR. In the following section we shall consider the relationships between the renewal and the various levels of authority in the Catholic church.

1. Within the Prayer Group. The most common form of organization within a prayer group is to have a team of members who share leadership responsibility for the group. This is often described as the "pastoral team." One member of the team will usually be designated as the coordinator, but decisions are made in collegial fashion. The manner in which members of the prayer group are chosen for the pastoral team normally involves a process of prayerful discernment by the actual team rather than election by the whole group. The team itself will also generally choose one of its members as the coordinator. Each member of the pastoral team may have special responsibility for some particular ministry in the group, such as caring for newcomers, conducting Life in the Spirit seminars, leading and teaching at the prayer meetings, leading music, etc. Other people in the group will be part of each of these ministry teams, and all those involved in any kind of ministry, along with the pastoral team, may make up a "core group" within the larger group.

2. Among the Prayer Groups.

a. Diocesan and Regional. In the U.S., within the past five years there has been a very significant trend toward the establishment of diocesan renewal centers, with a view to the more effective communication and collaboration among all the prayer groups within each diocese. There are such diocesan centers now in about fifty dioceses in the U.S. They do not claim or exercise authority over the prayer groups in the diocese but rather seek to provide services for them, such as helping to organize diocesan conferences and days of renewal, helping to provide the teaching and training needed by those called to leadership in the groups, and being a center of communication among the groups and with others who seek information about the renewal, especially the local

bishop. The diocesan centers are staffed by local participants in the renewal and are financially supported by the prayer groups in the diocese.

As has been mentioned earlier, since 1976 there has been a strong development of regional conferences in the U.S. The preparation and conducting of such conferences has usually required the setting up of a regional committee, some of which have then developed into permanent regional service committees. One such regional organization is the Southern California Renewal Communities, which coordinates the many activities of the renewal in that area and conducts a large annual conference.

b. National Organization. Since the national organization in the U.S. was the first to be established and has set a pattern that has been substantially followed in most other countries, under this heading it will suffice to explain how the renewal is nationally organized in the U.S.

In April 1969, after the Notre Dame conference, a group of leaders from around the country approved the suggestion of the Notre Dame community that a communication center be set up at Notre Dame to serve the renewal, which was already becoming nationwide. After the 1970 conference, a committee was formed, called the Catholic Charismatic Renewal Service Committee, made up very largely of the leaders of the Notre Dame and Ann Arbor communities, which had already provided the national services such as the Notre Dame conferences, the communication center, and *New Covenant* magazine. Within that year a much larger advisory committee was also formed, made up of leaders from all the regions of the country where the renewal was already flourishing. The initial statement of the Service Committee concerning its function is worth quoting here:

The Service Committee does not exist to plan a renewal, but it exists to be of service to a renewal that God is bringing about. It is attempting to discern what the Lord is doing, and to make specific contributions to it; contributions which it feels it is equipped to make. . . . The Service Committee does not claim any authority over groups or individuals involved in the charismatic renewal of the Church. Its only authority is over the services which it provides, and within those services it exercises the normal supervision. . . . Because the charismatic renewal is a renewal (an unorganized movement) there can be no authority that comes from services well performed. . . . In order to provide a regular opportunity to have its work reviewed by a representative group of mature leaders, the Advisory Committee has been established (*New Covenant* [July 1971], 7).

From its inception until 1984, the National Service Committee (NSC) continued to be very closely associated with the Notre Dame and Ann Arbor communities, People of Praise and Word of God, with participants of these two communities constituting the majority of its membership. Relying very heavily on the services provided by these two large communities, the NSC continued to sponsor the annual conferences at Notre Dame, annual leaders' conferences, and many regional conferences, as well as to publish *New Covenant* magazine. Along with a number of other services to the renewal in the U.S., it also contributed the major share of financial support to the international office of the renewal.

In 1984 it was decided that while these two covenant communities should continue to provide those services with which each one had been primarily involved (e.g., People of Praise with the Notre Dame conferences and the national book and tape ministry; Word of God with *New Covenant* and Servant Publications), the NSC should no longer be so closely identified with these communities. At the meeting in January 1984 four members of the NSC (two from People of Praise and two from Word of God) resigned in order to make room on the committee for greater representation of the renewal at the regional and diocesan levels. This change reflected the recognition of the importance of the development of strong regional and diocesan centers for the promotion of the renewal in local prayer groups. The NSC now sees the fostering and strengthening of such regional and diocesan renewal centers as one of its primary functions. The national advisory committee has also been enlarged to about sixty members, with one or two from each of the ecclesiastical provinces of the U.S., nine "at large" members, and six representatives of the renewal among Spanish-speaking people in the U.S.

As has already been noted, the pattern of national organization established in the U.S. has been substantially followed in most other countries, so that there are now more than one hundred such national service committees around the world.

c. *International Organization.* In describing the worldwide expansion of the Catholic renewal, we have already had occasion to mention the estab- lishment in 1972 at Ann Arbor of the International Communications Office (ICO), with Ralph Martin as its director. While still located at Ann Arbor, this office prepared and conducted the international conferences at Grottaferrata in 1973 and Rome in 1975. In 1976, at the suggestion of Cardinal Suenens, Ralph Martin and his staff moved the ICO to Brussels, where it organized the international conferences held at Dublin in 1978. In that same year an international council was formed, composed of two prominent leaders of the renewal from each continent, with the function of overseeing the work of the office. At that time Ralph Martin was named chairman of the council, and Fr. Tom Forrest became director of the office.

In 1981 the name was changed to International Catholic Charismatic Renewal Office (ICCRO), and it was moved to Rome, with Tom Forrest as chairman of the council and Fr. Fio Mascarenhas as director of the office. Since that time the International Leaders' Conferences (1981 and 1984) have been held in Rome, and another is in preparation for 1987.

The functions of ICCRO and the International Council are best described in the statement that they presented to Pope John Paul II in 1979:

The International Catholic Charismatic Renewal Office, known as ICCRO, is a service offered to the worldwide Renewal. It makes no claims of authority for directly supervising the Renewal, and understands clearly that in every area of the world where the Catholic Charismatic Renewal exists, it is always subject to the authority of the local ordinary. At the same time, the Office attempts to assure the pastoral and theological soundness of renewal groups everywhere. Its basic goals could be expressed in the following way: To be a center for information regarding the history, development and activities of the Renewal, to organize activities of a worldwide nature and to serve as a center of unity for the Renewal within the Church, and with all elements of the Renewal throughout the world.

The International Office is under the direct supervision of the International Council of the Catholic Charismatic Renewal. This Council, made up of a limited group of leaders of the Renewal, representing all areas of the world, has direct responsibility for the office, with authority to make final decisions regarding its functions and directions. It also has the right to supervise financial matters regarding the office, including its yearly budget. Membership on the International Council does not convey authority or leadership over any local or regional area of the Renewal.

General purposes:

(a) Serve as the international center for unity for the worldwide Renewal, thus avoiding regional fragmentation into autonomous parts in no way identified with each other. "Unity" here means oneness in diversity, rather than some type of imposed uniformity.

The Mother of God community choir singing at Eastern General Conference of the Catholic Charismatic Renewal, Atlantic City, in 1978.

(b) To be of service to the leaders of the Renewal around the world whenever possible. This includes making useful material available, paying visits, attending the more important conferences, giving encouragement, developing ways to share positive and fruitful experiences of the Renewal, suggesting the best directions to take, helping to develop prudent positions regarding more difficult and delicate pastoral practices, etc.

(c) Work to deepen the identification of the Renewal with the Universal Church. This would include being active as liaison between the Renewal on the international level and bishops and theologians of the Church. The desire here is to clearly place the Renewal at the heart of the Church: within rather than at the fringe of Church life.

(d) Do everything possible to serve and stimulate world evangelization. This would include supporting the beginnings of Charismatic Renewal in areas of the world where it has not yet appeared.

(e) Serve as an information center both for the Renewal internally, and for those who wish to become acquainted with it.

(f) Without becoming in itself a structural organization such as some movements, and without seeing itself as the first doer of the work of the Renewal, ICCRO should have a flexibility in responding to opportunities that present themselves for serving the Renewal of the Church and the work of evangelization.

(g) Help to direct the strength of the Renewal from those areas where it is more developed and economically stronger, towards less developed and poorer areas. In other words, ICCRO is to have a missionary focus. (Unpublished document, quoted with permission of the chair of the International Council of ICCRO, Fio Mascarenhas, S.J.)

One of the important activities of ICCRO is to promote the holding of regional international conferences and to take an active part in them whenever this is possible. Some such conferences during the year 1985 were the thirteenth annual conference organized by ECCLA, bringing together leaders from all the countries of Latin America; the third Asian leaders' conference, held in Bangalore, India, which drew seventy-two delegates from fourteen countries of Asia; the third Scandinavian conference, with fifty delegates from Sweden, Norway, Denmark, and Finland; and the conference of the leaders of the renewal in the nine French-speaking countries of Africa, held in Kinshasa, Zaire.

3. *Organization of Covenant Communities.*

a. *Within Communities.* While being far less numerous than the prayer groups, the covenant communities, of which there are about sixty in the worldwide renewal, have played a vital role in the leadership of this movement. Such communities have usually developed out of prayer groups, when people who had formed close bonds through praying together felt ready to make a deeper commitment to one another. Such a commitment, expressed in a "covenant," usually involves sharing at least some degree of financial resources, praying, and taking meals together at regular intervals, accepting mutual correction, and submitting to the appointed leaders of the community. The larger communities, consisting in some cases of more than a thousand persons, are subdivided into "households" made up of people who live in the same house or close enough to one another to share prayer and meals more frequently. People of all walks of life and in most cases of several different Christian churches are members of such covenant communities. Most households are centered around one or two families, but there are also households made up of single men or women, and there are also some of single persons who have committed themselves to a life of celibacy.

Each household recognizes one of its members as its "head," who will normally be the father of the family the household is structured around. If it is a household of singles, one member will be appointed as its head; in most communities a woman can be the head only of a household of women. A group of households, consisting of up to a hundred people, will be under the pastoral care of one of the "coordinators" of the community; all the coordinators, and thus the whole community, will be under the pastoral care of two or three "over-all coordinators."

b. Among Communities. The oldest and largest of the covenant communities, such as Word of God and People of Praise, have from early years shared the fruit of their experience with other groups wishing to develop into covenant communities or with younger communities needing help in solving their problems. In this way each of these older communities has established bonds with a group of others that tend to share their distinctive style of community life. In recent years these informal relationships have become more structured, with the formation of associations or federations of such communities. The best-known of these is the international federation of communities called The Sword of the Spirit, which recognizes the leadership of the Word of God community in Ann Arbor. There are now several such federations of covenant communities in the CCR, but there are also communities that have remained independent of them.

D. Relationship With Church Authority.

1. With Local Authority: Parish Priest and Bishop. A survey of Catholic prayer groups in the U.S. taken in 1981 showed that about two-thirds described themselves as "parish-centered." Such a designation could mean that the group consisted totally or almost totally of members of one parish, that it was officially recognized as the "parish prayer group," that it had its meetings in the church or church hall, and that it had its meetings announced in the weekly parish bulletin. Such a group would obviously be in close association with the parish priest, and either he or one of his assistants might attend the prayer meetings, in some cases as an active participant in the renewal. Other Catholic prayer groups might still describe themselves as "parish-centered," even though their association with a parish or its priests were not as close as described above. However, any group that describes itself as parish-centered would no doubt enjoy the approval of the local Catholic pastor and would respect his authority over the group in any question concerning Catholic faith or practice. Normally, however, the parish priest would not interfere in the leadership of the group unless there were some problem that called for his pastoral intervention.

Well over five hundred Catholic prayer groups that responded to the 1981 survey did not describe themselves as parish-centered. Such groups would draw their members from a number of different parishes and not see themselves as especially centered on any of them. This is more likely to be the case where the meetings take place in premises that do not belong to any parish church, such as a convent, a monastery, a retreat house, or school run by a religious order, etc. In such cases, where the group is not in close association with any particular parish priest, it will see itself as directly subject to the pastoral authority of the bishop of the diocese.

In most diocese in the U.S., the bishop has appointed a "liaison person" (in most cases a priest, and often one personally involved in the renewal) for maintaining contact with the renewal groups in his diocese and for providing pastoral care when there is need for it. Since 1978 these "liaisons" have formed a national association with an elected steering committee, and they gather together annually for the discussion of questions of common interest. They have also sponsored a number of theological symposia on questions relating to the renewal. The growing influence of these liaisons in the CCR in the U.S. is an aspect of the current trend to center the renewal more firmly in the diocese, with the establishment or strength of diocesan renewal centers. Another indication of this growing influence may be seen in the fact that Fr. Ken Metz, after his term as chairman of the liaisons' steering committee, was chosen in 1984 to be chairman of the NSC.

2. With Episcopal Conferences. One of the decisions of the Second Vatican Council was that the bishops of each country should form an episcopal conference in order to be able to exercise their pastoral care in a collegial manner in matters that concerned the whole nation. One function of such conferences has been to prepare a common response to various issues that present themselves to the bishops and to publish pastoral statements on such issues. In the past twenty years many of these national conferences have issued pastoral statements concerning the renewal in their country. The texts of all those issued prior to 1980 have been published with introduction and commentary by Kilian McDonnell in his three-volume collection of statements by various church authorities: *Presence, Power, Praise* (1980). The conference of bishops of the U.S. has published three statements concerning the charismatic renewal. The first of these was a report that the Bishops' Committee on Doctrine presented to the conference at its annual meeting in 1969. The chairman of the committee, Bishop Alexander Zaleski, had enlisted the help of Fr. Kilian McDonnell in the preparation of this report, which expressed a positive judgment on this movement, while noting its need of careful pastoral guidance.

In order to keep the conference well informed about the renewal and to provide such pastoral care as the bishops might be called upon to give, the episcopal conference established an ad hoc committee in 1973 to foster closer ties between the bishops and the leaders of the renewal in the U.S. One member of this committee, Bishop Joseph McKinney, was already an active participant in the renewal and was serving as episcopal adviser to the NSC. In 1975 this Bishops'

Committee issued a second statement about the renewal, entitled "Guidelines for the Catholic Charismatic Renewal." While still fairly positive, this statement put the major emphasis on the areas in which careful pastoral guidance was needed to prevent excesses and misdirections. Ten years later (1984) the Bishops' Committee, with the help of Kilian McDonnell, prepared a third document that was published by the conference with the title "A Pastoral Statement on the Catholic Charismatic Renewal." This statement, while offering sound pastoral advice, gave much generous approval and encouragement to the renewal than the previous statement had done. Shortly after this statement was issued Bishop McKinney was named chairman of the Bishops' Committee, which was given a new title: Bishops' Liaison Committee with the Catholic Charismatic Renewal. In recent years this committee has worked closely with the national association of diocesan liaisons and with the NSC to foster the development of diocesan renewal centers for the better formation of leaders and to encourage the involvement of priests in the pastoral care of those involved in the renewal.

3. *The Role of Cardinal Suenens.* Leon Joseph Cardinal Suenens, archbishop of the see of Malines-Brussels in Belgium, played a key role at the Second Vatican Council as one of the four presidents named by Pope Paul VI. As has already been noted, when the question of the charismatic element in the church was being discussed at the council, he made a decisive speech in favor of the positive statement which the council eventually made on this issue. An indication of his openness to the work of the Spirit may be seen in his choice of the motto: "In the Holy Spirit," which he had chosen much earlier when first ordained as a bishop. When news of the charismatic renewal reached him, he determined to see for himself what was going on, and in the spring of 1973 he visited several of the charismatic communities in the U.S. As a result of the favorable impression he received there, he attended the Notre Dame conference in June 1973; and in December of that year he took an active part in the first international leaders' conference at Grottaferrata, during which he arranged to have a group of the leaders received in private audience by Pope Paul VI. From this time Cardinal Suenens made no secret of his personal participation in the renewal. He was one of the main speakers at the Notre Dame conference in 1974 and that same year published his book *A New Pentecost?* which introduced the renewal to a large public. He played a key role in facilitating the holding of the international congress of the renewal in Rome in 1975. On that occasion Pope Paul VI gave him a special mandate to exercise pastoral supervision over the worldwide renewal in the Catholic church. In order to exercise this role more effectively, he invited Ralph Martin to move the International Communications Office from Ann Arbor to Brussels, where it remained until the move to Rome in 1978, when the new pope, John Paul II confirmed his mandate of oversight for the renewal. Even after his retirement as archbishop of Malines-Brussels, Cardinal Suenens continued to serve as episcopal adviser to ICCRO, a charge he relinquished only in 1982, at the age of seventy-eight. During the years of his papal mandate he played a very active role in the guidance of the renewal, attending and speaking at the major conferences and providing his advice and encouragement both in person and in the series of Malines Documents of which he was a principal author. He also actively encouraged the ecumenical potential of the renewal, both by his Malines Document on the issue, *Ecumenism and the Charismatic Renewal* (1978), and by taking an active part in such ecumenical conferences as the one held at Kansas City in 1977.

4. *With Roman Authorities.* We have already mentioned the favorable reception that Pope Paul VI gave to the leaders whom Cardinal Suenens presented to him at the first International Leaders' Conference in 1973. During the international congress held in Rome in 1975, one of the many signs of papal approval was the permission granted to Cardinal Suenens to celebrate Mass for the participants in St. Peter's Basilica, at the close of which, Pope Paul VI received the whole congress in special audience and delivered a warm and encouraging address.

Pope John Paul II has likewise received those gathered in Rome in 1981 and 1984 for the international leaders' conferences, and on both occasions has expressed his appreciation of the renewal. In his 1981 address he especially encouraged priests to fulfill their pastoral role with regard to it, observing that "the priest, for his part, cannot exercise his service on behalf of the renewal unless and until he adopts a welcoming attitude toward it" (*New Covenant* 11 [2, 1981]: 9).

Since the 1982 resignation of Cardinal Suenens from his role as episcopal adviser to ICCRO, his mandate with regard to the worldwide renewal has been entrusted by Pope John Paul II to the head of the Pontifical Council on the Laity, Bishop Paul Cordes. He has accepted invitations to address several important conferences of the renewal and in various ways has shown his appreciation of it as a movement making a valuable contribution to the spiritual life of the Catholic church, especially of its laity. Another proof of his positive attitude toward the renewal was his personal intervention that resulted in the obtaining of office space for ICCRO in the Palazzo della Cancelleria in Rome. The very location of the International Office of the CCR in the heart of Rome, in a building belonging to the Vatican, is a tangible sign of the fact that the charismatic renewal, in the short span of twenty years, has achieved recognition as a movement which, while conscious of its debt to Pentecostalism, deserved to be welcomed with open arms into the Roman Catholic Church.

See also CHARISMATIC MOVEMENT; CURSILLO MOVEMENT; DIALOGUE, ROMAN CATHOLIC AND CLASSICAL PENTECOSTAL; LIFE IN THE SPIRIT SEMINARS; MARY AND THE HOLY SPIRIT; MEDJUGORJE; VATICAN II.

Bibliography: N. A. Abbott, ed., *The Documents of Vatican II* (1966); J. Fichter, *The Catholic Cult of the Paraclete* (1975); R. Laurentin, *Catholic Pentecostalism*

Morris Cerullo has been involved in the salvation-healing movement since the 1950s, both in the U. S. and overseas.

(1977); K. McDonnell, *Charismatic Renewal in the Churches* (1976); idem, *Presence, Power, and Praise* (1980); G. T. Montague, *Riding the Wind* (1974); E. D. O'Connor, *The Pentecostal Movement in the Catholic Church* (1971); idem, *Theological and Pastoral Orientations on the Catholic Charismatic Renewal* (1974); K. and D. Ranaghan, *Catholic Pentecostals* (1969); idem, *As the Spirit Leads Us* (1971); L. J. Suenens, *A New Renewal* (1978); F. A. Sullivan, *Charisms and the Charismatic Renewal* (1982).   F. A. Sullivan

CATHOLIC PENTECOSTALS See CATHOLIC CHARISMATIC RENEWAL.

CATTA, HERVÉ-MARIE Leader in the Catholic Charismatic Renewal (CCR) in France. By the early 1970s Catta was a practicing lawyer in Paris with brilliant career prospects. Brought to a profound conversion and baptized in the Spirit through the witness of the Emmanuel community in Paris, Catta joined Emmanuel and began a life characterized by eucharistic adoration and street evangelism. He married Martine Laffitte, a medical doctor and a founding member of Emmanuel, and became part of the community leadership. He then studied theology, obtaining a license and then a master's degree in ecumenical theology from the Institut Catholique in Paris.

In 1979 Catta became a member of the Council of the International Catholic Charismatic Renewal Office (ICCRO), assuming responsibility for contact with French-speaking regions of the world, serving on ICCRO until 1987. He has been closely involved in Emmanuel's outreach in Africa and has constantly emphasized the urgency of public evangelism.   P. D. Hocken

CENTRAL AMERICAN CHARISMATICS
See CHARISMATIC MOVEMENT.

CERULLO, MORRIS (1931–). Missionary evangelist and faith healer. Morris Cerullo was raised in an Orthodox Jewish orphanage in New Jersey. A Christian woman who worked at the orphanage talked to the young man and gave him a NT. This action lead to her dismissal. At the age of fourteen Cerullo left the orphanage and was supernaturally led to the woman who had befriended him and who now took him into her home. Morris Cerullo began attending a Full Gospel church and soon received the Baptism of the Holy Spirit and a call to preach the gospel. Cerullo was ordained by the Assemblies of God in the early 1950s, and in 1956 he began a healing ministry. He was active with the Voice of Healing organization in his early ministry and has been quite closely associated with the Full Gospel Business Men's Fellowship International. Cerullo's own organization is called World Evangelism and is based in San Diego, where an annual school for the training of ministers is held.

Bibliography: M. Cerullo, "From Jewish Orphanage to the Christian Pulpit," *World-Wide Revival* (September 1968), n.p.; D. E. Harrell, Jr., *All Things Are Possible* (1975).   J. R. Zeigler

CHAMBERS, GEORGE AUGUSTUS (1879–1957). Prominent Canadian Pentecostal leader. A native of Ontario, Chambers studied in Cincinnati, Ohio, becoming a pastor with the New Mennonite Brethren. His first contact with the Pentecostal movement was with the Hebden mission in Toronto. Influenced by A. G. Ward, he began preaching the baptism in the Spirit and opened a Pentecostal mission, though he only received the baptism himself later at Elkland, Pennsylvania.

On the organization of the Pentecostal Assemblies of Canada (PAOC) in 1919, Chambers was elected general superintendent, a post he held until 1934. An indefatigable traveler, he played a major part in the steady expansion of PAOC. He served pastorates in Vineland, Ottawa, Arnprior, Peterborough, and Kitchener. Near the end of his life he wrote an autobiography, *Fifty Years in the Service of the King: 1907–1957* (1960).

Bibliography: G. G. Kulbeck, *What God Hath Wrought* (1959).   P. D. Hocken

CHAMBERS, NORA I. (c. 1883–1953). An early Church of God (CG, Cleveland, Tenn.) evangelist, scholar, and teacher. Chambers united with the CG in 1910 and was licensed to preach the same year. In the early years she and her husband preached in North Carolina and Georgia amidst harsh deprivation and persecution. Because of her ability and education (Holmes Bible School), she was soon called into other service.

When the Church of God Publishing House opened in 1917, Chambers was a proofreader. On January 1, 1918, when the CG instituted a Bible training school (now Lee College), she was appointed its first teacher. For six years she taught many who would become leaders in the CG.

Mrs. Chambers also served as a matron of the home for children in Cleveland, Tennessee, and taught two years in her alma mater, Holmes Bible School, in Altamont, South Carolina.

Bibliography: C. W. Conn, *Like a Mighty Army* (rev. 1977).　　　　　　　　　　　　　C. W. Conn

CHAMBERS, STANLEY WARREN

(1915–). General superintendent of the United Pentecostal Church (UPC; 1968–78). Born and reared in Ohio, Chambers was converted in a Pentecostal church in 1927 and received the Holy Spirit in 1930. In 1943 he was ordained and became pastor of a church in Hazelton, Pennsylvania. Chambers became the first general secretary of the UPC in 1945, a position he held until he was elected general superintendent. He now serves as the superintendent of the Missouri District of the UPC and as president of Gateway College of Evangelism in St. Louis, Missouri.

J. L. Hall

A long-time editor for Assemblies of God publications, Richard G. Champion was named editor of the *Pentecostal Evangel* on the retirement of Robert C. Cunningham in 1984.

CHAMPION, RICHARD GORDON

(1931–). Editor and author. Born in Elkhart, Indiana, and raised in Muskegon, Michigan, Champion graduated from Central Bible College in 1953 with a B.A. in Bible. He then became associate pastor of First Assembly of God, Macomb, Illinois, and was ordained in 1955. He married Norma Jean Black in 1953. She is currently a professor of communications at Evangel College. The Champions have two children.

From 1955 to 1957 Champion was advertising and circulation manager for the *Pentecostal Evangel*. Champion supervised publications for the national youth department of the Assemblies of God (AG) and was editor of the *C.A. Herald* and *C.A. Guide* from 1958 to 1964. He then served as managing editor for the *Pentecostal Evangel* from 1964 to 1984, becoming editor upon the retirement of Robert C. Cunningham.

Champion has written numerous magazine articles, curriculum publications, and youth materials. He has taught journalism at Central Bible College since 1961 and is in demand as a speaker for writing seminars across the nation.

Bibliography: *PE* (June 10, 1984), 24.　　G. W. Gohr

CHARISM See GIFTS OF THE SPIRIT.

CHARISMA IN MISSIONS A Catholic charismatic agency for missionary evangelization founded by Marilynn Kramar in December 1972 that seeks to evangelize and bring renewal among Spanish-speaking people in particular. The organization has its headquarters in Los Angeles, California, and sponsors various ministries: the annual International Latin Encounter for Renewal and Evangelization, Latin Encounter for Youth, Annual Married Couples Evangelization Convention, Catholic Campaign of Faith, Missions of Evangelization, the one-day faith rally "Presence" connected with the work of the Archdiocese of Los Angeles, as well as various courses, seminars, and retreats. These efforts assist in the training of Catholic lay evangelizers—one of the major goals of the organization.

Charisma in Missions was approved as an official international apostolate in the Archdiocese of Los Angeles by Cardinal Timothy Manning.

Bibliography: *Charisma in Missions* (n.d.).　　G. B. McGee

CHARISMATA See GIFTS OF THE SPIRIT; GLOSSOLALIA; PROPHECY; BAPTISM IN THE HOLY SPIRIT.

CHARISMATIC BIBLE MINISTRIES A fraternal fellowship of charismatic organizations. Sponsored by Oral Roberts and founded on January 21, 1986, the fellowship's stated purpose is to create an organization "far bigger than any denomination" (*Abundant Life*, 10). Designed for charismatic organizations, not individuals, Charismatic Bible Ministries (CBM) held its first major conference on June 23–25, 1986, in Tulsa, where the benefits of membership were described. Such benefits would include a pension plan; health-care at the City of Faith Health-Care Center; group plans for purchasing equipment, goods, and services; and seminars on subjects such as church insurance needs, long-range financial planning, and legal counseling. Oral Roberts was elected as chairman, Kenneth Copeland as secretary, and Paul Yonggi Cho as honorary international chairman.

Bibliography: "Charismatic Bible Ministries," *Abundant Life* (March–April 1986), 10–13.　　F. Bixler

CHARISMATIC COMMUNION OF PRESBYTERIAN MINISTERS See PRESBYTERIAN AND REFORMED CHARISMATICS.

CHARISMATIC COMMUNITIES From its earliest days, the charismatic movement sparked an interest in Christian community. Whereas the first Pentecostals had seen "Pentecost" primarily in eschatological terms, charismatics rooted in historical church traditions have not generally anticipated an imminent Parousia but have seen the restored charismata as divine equipment for renewing the body of Christ. While many local church congregations touched by the Holy Spirit in charismatic renewal have experienced renewal in their corporate life and ministry, the term "charismatic communities" is here used to refer to intentional communities with explicit forms of commitment over and above regular patterns of church initiation. Many are better known as "covenant communities," being constituted by a form of covenant agreement made corporately by committed members before the Lord.

Charismatic communities are bodies of Christians seeking through a common commitment to the Lord and to each other to translate the grace of baptism in the Spirit into a shared lifestyle. They typically see this new life and power of the Holy Spirit forming a faith-filled community as a sign to both church and world of the truth and efficacy of the gospel. Though some charismatic communities have not yet had members make an official life commitment, fully committed membership ordinarily presumes some intention of permanence.

The basic unit in the life of most communities is the "household." A household is a group of community members living under the same roof and committed to a corporate lifestyle. It may consist of one family with or without other community members living with them, or of a group of young singles. Often those single people committed to a life of celibacy live together and collectively may be known as the "Brotherhood" or "Sisterhood." Some communities use the language of "nonresidential household" to refer to small groups of people who do not live under the same roof but who meet frequently for shared meals, worship, and personal exchange. Community covenants customarily express the obligations and vision accepted by the members, including commitment to a discipline of personal prayer, participation in community meetings, and acceptance of the authority of pastoral leaders. Ordinarily all members belong to small fellowship groups within the larger community, with the leaders of such groups normally having immediate pastoral care of their members.

Almost all the charismatic communities of this type have a membership drawn preponderantly from the historic church traditions, frequently with a large or total Roman Catholic participation. They ordinarily encourage their members to continue their existing denominational commitment, and the communities of ecumenical composition generally see themselves as contributing to the reunion of divided Christendom.

Most charismatic Christians from backgrounds with a Congregationalist ecclesiology (e.g., Baptist, Mennonite, many Pentecostals) drawn toward communal life in the Spirit have been led into "nondenominational" assemblies seeking to be fuller corporate expressions of the body of Christ. Many of these assemblies are now known as "covenant churches," often having origins in some way related to the discipleship movement in the U.S. or to the House Church movement in

Great Britain. These assemblies can be seen as a form of Free Church charismatic community, but they do not ordinarily see themselves in ecumenical terms, nor do they expect lifelong commitment to one community.

I. History. The first impulse toward charismatic community with widespread repercussions was in the Episcopalian parish of Holy Redeemer, Houston, Texas. From 1965, under the leadership of W. Graham Pulkingham, a core of committed members lived for some years in households and developed a powerful corporate ministry. Houston's long-term importance may lie primarily in its influence on other places, particularly through Michael Harper's book *A New Way of Living* (1973), which was translated into several languages.

However, the first of the major charismatic communities to survive and exercise a major influence was the Word of God community (WG) in Ann Arbor, Michigan, founded in 1967 by Ralph Martin, Stephen Clark, and others soon after their baptism in the Spirit. Though the founding leaders were all Catholics, WG soon had an ecumenical composition and identity. Two covenant communities were formed at South Bend, Indiana: first, True House, which encountered difficulties and did not survive, and later, the People of Praise (PP), led by Kevin Ranaghan and Paul DeCelles. PP has always had some Protestant members, though fewer than WG.

Word of God from its earliest days served as a model and a beacon for charismatic prayer groups, particularly for those in the Catholic Charismatic Renewal (CCR), who felt drawn to a deeper life of mutual commitment. WG leaders were the first organizers of leadership training in CCR, and visitors came to Ann Arbor from many parts of the world. The writings of WG leaders, especially Clark, provided much guidance for aspiring communities. In addition, WG and PP collaborated to serve CCR nationally and beyond through publishing *New Covenant* magazine, begun in 1971, through Charismatic Renewal Services and through their strong influence within the National Service Committee. WG services the Pastoral Renewal Center, and its monthly magazine, *Pastoral Renewal*, has its own publishing house, Servant Publications, and has played a major role in founding *Allies for Faith and Renewal*, an ecumenical coalition. PP has serviced annual CCR conferences at Notre Dame, Indiana, and the major charismatic renewal congresses at Kansas City (1977) and New Orleans (1987).

Another major community of American origin is Mother of God (MG), Gaithersburg, Maryland. Developing from the 1966 relationship of two newly Spirit-baptized housewives, Edith Difato and Judith Tydings, MG has grown into a strong community noted for its emphasis on depth of spiritual formation and for its scholarly strength. While predominantly Roman Catholic in membership, it has acquired an appreciation for the spiritual authors of many Christian traditions, both Roman Catholic and evangelical, with a focus on the blood and the cross of Christ. MG's monthly, *The Word Among Us*, begun in 1981, with Japanese and Spanish editions from 1987, is primarily a biblical aid to daily prayer and Christian living. MG has about a thousand members, including children, plus outreach in England, Ireland, and Canada. Since 1981 it has also helped to launch Christian businesses operated on Christian principles by community members.

A rather different American charismatic community developed at Orleans, Massachusetts, on Cape Cod. Its origins preceded the public manifestation of charismatic renewal when one foundress, Judy Sorensen, was instrumental in the healing of the other, Cay Andersen. From their joint association in healing ministry came the Rock Harbor Fellowship, which, following the leaders' baptism in the Spirit, became in 1970 the Community of Jesus (CJ). CJ is interdenominational, with strong Anglican associations and several resident clergy, mostly Presbyterian, and has three hundred members at Cape Cod, including children, and a nonresident membership of six hundred.

In Europe the strongest flowering of charismatic communities has been in France. The major communities are Emmanuel, founded in Paris in 1972, pioneers in street evangelism and by far the largest of the European communities, with more than three thousand members; Théophanie, a more monastic foundation begun in Montpellier in 1972, but evolving in a direction away from identification with CCR; Chemin Neuf, founded in Lyon in 1973, the only large French community of ecumenical composition; and Lion de Juda, another monastic-type community, larger than Théophanie, founded at Cordes in 1974. The network of community-forming organizations founded at Poitiers in 1974 as the Communauté Chrétienne de Formation, is now known as La Fondation. La Sainte-Croix, begun in Grenoble in 1974, was dissolved in 1984. The development of the French charismatic communities has been thoroughly documented and researched through the works of Monique Hébrard. The French communities have a notably different ethos from the American, with more attention paid to theological formation and more rapid acquisition of official church status. All have multiplied developing foundations in several places, within France and beyond, and have earned the respect of the French Catholic bishops, who have entrusted them with pastoral tasks. They have been more influenced by traditional religious life than the American communities, and thus members typically make their personal commitments in groups rather than all members renewing the community covenant together, the prevailing pattern in North America.

Other European countries have seen the formation of charismatic communities, of which only Maranatha Community in Brussels, Belgium, and some communities related to WG in the Sword of the Spirit (SS, see below) exceed a hundred members. However, in Austria, Great Britain, Holland, Ireland, Italy, Spain, Switzerland, and West Germany, there are developing communities of a small size. Outside North America and Europe, the charismatic community with the largest influence has been Emmanuel in Brisbane,

Australia, formed in 1975 and led by Brian Smith, with an extensive outreach in Oceania and Southeast Asia.

II. Classification. While each community or family of communities has its own distinctive identity and ethos, there is a similarity of vision and purpose among the major urban communities, which, combining families and celibates, ordained and unordained, are microcosms of the church as the body of Christ. They seek to be strong bodies of believers, focusing on personal renewal and evangelism more than on specialist ministries. In a society ravaged by individualism and self-gratification, such communities testify to the reconciling power of the gospel and are effective instruments for deep renewal of family life.

Other communities are more monastic, such as Lion de Juda, Théophanie, and Kreuz Bruderscheft (Melchtal, Switzerland), having a more contemplative thrust while exercising a strong formative influence in their countries. CCR has also given rise to charismatic monasteries and convents, both with older orders (e.g., the Pecos Benedictines in New Mexico) and with the formation of new congregations (e.g., the Disciples of the Lord Jesus Christ in Channing, Tex.).

Another category is the ministry-oriented community, formed primarily for more effective service to the church. These are more common in Europe, often acquiring large properties to run as charismatic conference centers. Found equally among Catholics and Protestants, these communities generally have a less permanent membership.

Some charismatic communities do not readily fit into these categories, like the influential Reba Place Fellowship in Evanston, Illinois (with a strong Mennonite component and a call to inner-city ministry), and the Bethany Fellowship in Sussex, England, led by Colin Urquhart (with a strong ministry orientation and some similarities to "house church" restorationist assemblies).

III. Networks of Communities. In 1975 "an association of communities" was formed by WG and PP, assisted by Servants of the Light, Minneapolis, Minnesota; the Work of Christ, East Lansing, Michigan; the Lamb of God, Baltimore, Maryland; and Emmanuel, Brisbane, Australia. This association ended after four years, since the emphases and visions of the founding communities were too disparate. One larger community, Alleluia, Augusta, Georgia, which has substantial Episcopalian as well as Roman Catholic membership, has remained unattached since the dissolution of the association.

Word of God then formed a new network, the Sword of the Spirit, to embody its ecumenical and prophetic convictions. SS has been established as one international community with member communities becoming branches of SS. In spring 1987 SS had twelve branches, twenty-five affiliated groups, and six associated communities. Among the larger branches besides WG are the Joy of the Lord, Manila, Philippines; the City of God, Managua, Nicaragua; the Lamb of God, Baltimore; and the Community of the King, Belfast, Northern Ireland. As of spring 1987, SS had 7,600 committed adult members of whom 1,505 were in WG (two-thirds Catholic).

People of Praise, less structured than SS, then integrated affiliated communities into its branches, including the greater part of the Minneapolis community, and organized the Fellowship of Communities, a loose coalition of kindred bodies. As of early 1987, PP consisted of some 3,000 people, including children, living in eighteen locations.

In 1983 Emmanuel (Brisbane, Australia) and the Community of God's Delight (Dallas, Tex.) launched a new association known as International Brotherhood of Communities (IBOC) as a consultative fellowship body, including communities from Malaysia (the Light of Jesus Christ, Kota Kinabalu, Sabah; the Servants of Yahweh, Kuala Lumour); Australia (Heohzibah, Canberra; Bethel, Perth) and New Zealand (Lamb of God, Christchurch).

Bibliography: S. Clark, *Building Christian Community* (1972); S. Clark, ed., *Patterns of Christian Community* (1984); M. Hébrard, *Les Nouveaux Disciples* (1979); idem, *Les Nouveaux Disciples Dix Ans Après* (1987); P. Hocken "The Significance of Charismatic Communities," *Charismatic Renewal in the Churches*, ed. P. Elbert (forthcoming); D. and N. Jackson, *Living Together in a World Falling Apart* (1974); R. Quebedeaux, *The New Charismatics II* (1983).   P. D. Hocken

CHARISMATIC MISSIONS   See MISSIONS, OVERSEAS.

CHARISMATIC MOVEMENT   The term *charismatic movement* is here understood in its most common usage to designate what Donald Gee in the late 1950s called "the new Pentecost," namely the occurrence of distinctively Pentecostal blessings and phenomena, baptism in the Holy Spirit (BHS) with the spiritual gifts of 1 Corinthians 12:8–10, outside a denominational and/or confessional Pentecostal framework. Although this designation sometimes refers specifically to this work of the Spirit within the historic church traditions, it is here used in a wider sense to include "nondenominational" patterns of charismatic Christianity. That is to say, "charismatic movement" here refers to all manifestations of Pentecostal-type Christianity that in some way differ from classical Pentecostalism in affiliation and/or doctrine.

The subject is here treated as follows:

I. Its Development in North America
   A. Earliest Stirrings (Pre-1960)
   B. The Emergence of the Movement (1960–67)
   C. The Movement Takes Shape (1967–77)
   D. Consolidation (1977–87)
II. Its Development in Europe
   A. Origins
   B. Development and Expansion
     1. The British Isles
     2. West-Central Europe
     3. Eastern Europe
     4. Scandinavia
     5. The Latin Countries
     6. Overview
   C. Developments at Continental Level
III. Its Development in Latin America
   A. Protestant Beginnings
   B. The Ecumenical Period
   C. Separate Development
IV. Analysis
   A. The Essential Elements in Charismatic Renewal
     1. Focus on Jesus
     2. Praise
     3. Love of the Bible
     4. God Speaks Today
     5. Evangelism
     6. Awareness of Evil
     7. Spiritual Gifts
     8. Eschatological Expectation
     9. Spiritual Power
   B. A Comparison With the Pentecostal Movement
   C. The Significance of the Movement

I. Its Development in North America.

A. Earliest Stirrings (Pre-1960). The roots of the charismatic movement in North America go back more than a decade before the 1960 event commonly seen as the birth of the movement, namely Dennis Bennett's public announcement to his Episcopal congregation at St. Mark's, Van Nuys, California, that he spoke in other tongues. Already in the late 1940s, healing evangelists, such as William Branham, Oral Roberts, Gordon Lindsay, and T. L. Osborn, were instrumental in spreading "Spirit-baptized" Christianity beyond explicitly Pentecostal milieux. Although these evangelists were virtually all Pentecostal in doctrine and some in church membership or close association, their independent ministries were not under denominational control. While in the popular view these men were "healers," most saw themselves as evangelists, saving souls for Jesus through healing signs and wonders. Their ministries produced a following of Spirit-baptized believers who could not all be classified as Pentecostal. These believers did not constitute a readily identifiable category because of the itinerant and varied character of these healing ministries. In this way, many people belonging to mainline Protestant denominations received BHS in the 1940s and 1950s.

This Pentecostal outreach beyond explicit Pentecostal boundaries received its first organized expression in the Full Gospel Business Men's Fellowship International (FGBMFI), formed by Demos Shakarian, a California millionaire dairy-farmer of Armenian background. From the start, FGBMFI was closely associated with the leading healing evangelists, and its first meeting at Los Angeles in October 1951 had Oral Roberts as the guest speaker. FGBMFI, which had its first national convention in 1953, was conceived as an organization of Spirit-filled businessmen to evangelize and witness to non-Pentecostals. Its ministry was mainly accomplished through prayer breakfasts and larger conventions, regional and national, supplemented from 1953 by its monthly magazine *Voice*, edited by Thomas R. Nickel. Not only did FGBMFI extend beyond Pentecostal circles with its outreach, its local chapters provided a forum for regular "charismatic" fellowship for non-Pentecostal Christians. Most of the first printed witnesses to BHS by mainline Protestant Christians are to be found in the early issues of *Voice*. FGBMFI was able to be successful in reaching many mainline Protestants with the Pentecostal message because it did not attempt to make its "converts" become denominational Pentecostals. As an early article in *Voice* stated, "God never intended that the Full Gospel or Pentecostal groups should have a religious monopoly on the Baptism of the Holy Spirit" (Hoekstra, 1956, 23).

While the healing evangelists and FGBMFI helped to create and influence a clientele of Spirit-filled Christians outside Pentecostal boundaries, both saw the filling with the Spirit as an individual work of spiritual blessing and empowerment. They did not have any vision of the Holy Spirit renewing the historic churches. This element, central to much of the charismatic movement as it later developed, first entered North American thinking through the vision and witness of David du Plessis.

Although du Plessis' distinctive ministry of Pentecostal truth to those within the historic church traditions did not fully emerge until the early 1960s, the call and the preparation went back to a prophecy of Smith Wigglesworth in South Africa in 1936. This prophecy spoke of a coming Pentecostal revival in the churches, of which du Plessis would be a part. The first steps toward its fulfillment came in 1949, when du Plessis felt called to visit the New York City office of the WCC. Throughout the 1950s, du Plessis' contacts with historic church leaders increased, a work that helped prepare the way for later church acceptance of charismatic renewal (CR). During these years, his Pentecostal exclusiveness was being broken and replaced by a vision of the Holy Spirit renewing the churches through BHS. By the mid-1950s, du Plessis was regularly reporting the thrilling news that God was pouring out his Spirit on Christians of the "denominational churches" in many lands.

Throughout the history of the Pentecostal movement, ministers from the historic churches had occasionally received BHS, but they generally joined a Pentecostal church or became independent. The first significant case of an American minister remaining within a historic church framework after BHS was Harald Bredesen, then a young Lutheran minister, who received BHS in 1946. Another was Tommy Tyson, then pastor of a United Methodist church in North Carolina, who was baptized in the Spirit in 1951. Without any knowledge of spiritual gifts, Tyson was touched by the Lord following a congregational study of Acts 2.

A major influence in the spread of the Pentecostal experience within the historic church traditions was Agnes Sanford. With several years' experience in healing ministry, she experienced the strong inner working of the Spirit around 1953–54, when two friends laid hands on her to receive the Holy Spirit and shortly afterward she received the gift of tongues. From this time, Sanford often spoke privately of BHS to those to whom she was ministering. The scope for such ministry expanded in 1955 when Sanford and her husband started the "Schools of Pastoral Care," week-long conferences for those involved in healing (ministers, doctors, and nurses). In these conferences they spoke of "the power of the Holy Spirit working in men and women to the healing of their physical, mental and social ills."

Sanford was also active in the Order of St. Luke (OSL), founded by Reverend John Gayner Banks and Ethel Tulloch Banks in 1947. Although it was interdenominational, OSL had a strong Episcopalian membership. It sought to promote the restoration of "the Apostolic practice of Healing as taught and demonstrated by Jesus Christ." Although OSL's official declarations did not speak of healing as one of the spiritual gifts of 1 Corinthians 12:8–10, it was not surprising that when some OSL members rediscovered the power of the Lord in healing, they were led to experience other spiritual gifts, including tongues, even though the OSL leadership was unsympathetic and in 1963 came out openly against any practice of glossolalia under its auspices. One of the first priest-members of OSL to receive BHS was Richard Winkler, rector of Trinity Episcopal Church, Wheaton, Illinois. Winkler, who received BHS in April 1956 at a meeting of an AG evangelist, was already holding healing meetings in his home but began a public prayer meeting after a healing mission by Sanford in the fall of 1956. Following the public meeting in church, there was a smaller meeting in a lounge with exercise of the spiritual gifts and charismatic ministry. This was the first Pentecostal-type prayer meeting among Episcopalians.

Around 1956, a Presbyterian minister, James Brown, was baptized in the Spirit and began a prayer meeting with the exercise of the spiritual gifts in his church, Upper Octorara Presbyterian Church in Parkesburg, Pennsylvania. The Parkesburg services had a wide influence, aided by Brown's reputation and high standing among local Presbyterians. In 1957 Bredesen accepted the pastorate of Mount Vernon Dutch Reformed Church in New York, and this church soon became another center with Pentecostal prayer meetings. It also became a point of referral for interested persons.

Another milieu in which many "mainline" Christians first heard of BHS was Camps Farthest Out (CFO), founded by Glenn Clark in 1930 to aid Christians to become "athletes of the Spirit." CFO conferences, like those of OSL, proved to be an environment receptive to the Pentecostal message, even though the organizers eventually came out against any identification with the charismatic movement. CFO gatherings, usually a week in length, gave much scope to the camp leaders—who over the years included Sanford, Tyson, Bredesen, Brown, Derek Prince, and many others who had been baptized in the Spirit. As a result many people received BHS at CFOs, one of them being Don Basham in the early 1950s.

A major instrument for alerting the evangelical public to the power of the Holy Spirit in BHS was the monthly *Christian Life*. Its editor, Robert Walker, was baptized in the Spirit around 1952. Without using explicitly Pentecostal terminology, he soon began to publish items dealing with a fuller life in the Spirit. Myrrdin Lewis's 1953 article "Are We Missing Something?" elicited unusual interest. Beginning in 1959, *Christian Life* regularly published articles on congregations that had experienced awakening through a Pentecostal-type outpouring of the Spirit.

By the end of the 1950s, there was a considerable Pentecostal stirring reaching beyond the Pentecostal churches. Much of it was not congregationally based or congregationally organized, though there were the beginnings of Pentecostal groups in mainline church traditions at Parkesburg, Pennsylvania; Mount Vernon, New York; and the Lutheran Bethany Fellowship in Minneapolis, Minneapolis, as well as less openly at Wheaton, Illinois. As the only organ for this expansion was *Voice* magazine, the overall perspective was one of Pentecostal expansion beyond Pentecostal boundaries, with little sense of unity and cohesion among those in the historic churches who had been baptized in the Holy Spirit.

B. The Emergence of the Movement (1960–67). The events that brought the nascent movement into public view and consciousness occurred among Episcopalians in California. In the spring of 1959, a young couple, John and Joan Baker from Holy Spirit Parish at Monterey Park, received BHS with the sign of tongues following contact with some Pentecostals. Soon a small group of ten parishioners had experienced BHS and met for worship. The vicar, Frank Maguire, was troubled and sought counsel from a neighboring pastor, Dennis Bennett of St. Mark's, Van Nuys. In November 1959, both Bennett and Maguire received BHS. Bennett was soon sending over interested people from St. Mark's and by spring 1960, some seventy people from St. Mark's—including the leaders of most of the key parish organizations—had received BHS and were meeting for prayer. Unknown to the people in Monterey Park and Van Nuys, a small group of Episcopalians in St. Luke's, in Monrovia, another Los Angeles suburb, experienced tongues, interpretation, and prophecy in the fall of 1959.

After several months of widening Pentecostal blessing and increasing rumors at Van Nuys, Bennett felt obliged to share his experience publicly in his parish. This he decided to do on Passion Sunday, April 3, 1960. At all three morning services Bennett explained in a quiet, unemotional way how he had been led to receive the power and the fullness of the Holy Spirit, and how this had included "the Gift of Unknown Tongues." After the second service, an associate priest resigned, and a church officer called for Bennett's resignation. Bennett announced his resignation at the third service. The bishop of Los Angeles then wrote a pastoral letter to the people of St. Mark's, temporarily forbidding any group to meet under parish auspices if "speaking in tongues is encouraged or actually engaged in." In fact, the Pentecostal Episcopalians in the parish formed two different groups, one simply a private prayer group, the other with a more evangelistic vision, led by Jean Stone.

These events would have had little effect beyond the Los Angeles area had Stone not been determined to make them known. She contacted *Newsweek* and *Time*, which respectively ran stories under the headlines "Rector and a Rumpus" (July 4) and "Speaking in Tongues" (August 15). Only with these reports did the Van Nuys story, with a focus on glossolalia, reach the church press. It was this publicity that first generated the sense of a new movement of the Spirit, with the newness being seen in the combination of Pentecostal blessing and historic church attachment.

These developments in southern California and the ensuing publicity gave rise to two main thrusts in the charismatic movement. The first was in the life and ministry of Dennis Bennett. By the time of the national publicity, Bennett had received a welcome from the bishop of Olympia (western Washington state) and was being installed as vicar of St. Luke's in Seattle, Washington, a mission the bishop had thought of closing. Within a year, church attendance had quadrupled from seventy-five to three hundred. Two events that year triggered this expansion: one, a joint clergy conference of the Episcopal dioceses of Olympia and Oregon, at which many priests asked Bennett to share his experience; the other, a visit to St. Luke's from Richard Winkler, when Winkler brought the issue right out into the open by asking the parishioners, "Does anyone here want to receive the baptism in the Holy Spirit?" It was somewhat paradoxical that Winkler, whose Pentecostal experience had been kept quiet for several years, should so prod Bennett, whose similar experience had reached the national media. From this point, St. Luke's, Seattle, developed as a parish whose committed members were baptized in the Spirit and where seekers from elsewhere regularly came for this blessing. After his arrival in Seattle, Bennett received invitations to speak to Christian groups of many traditions. Part of the importance of his witness was his clarity on the compatibility of this Pentecostal BHS and his Episcopal churchmanship.

The second thrust that developed from the Van Nuys events centered on the group led by Jean Stone. In 1961 this group became the Blessed Trinity Society (BTS), which produced a number of pamphlets and a quarterly magazine, *Trinity*, the first issue, dated "Trinitytide 1961," appearing in the fall of that year. Stone mailed copies of this first issue to every Episcopal priest in the country, just as she had done with the issue of *Voice* that featured Bennett's witness. The members of Trinity's board of directors were all Episcopalians except for du Plessis and Bredesen. Bredesen became for a time a close associate of Stone; together they traveled across the western states, presenting the Pentecostal message at gatherings known as Christian Advances.

For the next five years *Trinity* and *Voice* were the two publications promoting this movement of the Spirit. Both magazines advocated BHS and spiritual gifts, both gave prominence to personal testimonies, both had lay editors, and both were run from California. However, while *Voice* included both Pentecostal and Neo-Pentecostal items, *Trinity* was more oriented to the mainline churches and did not ordinarily mention merely Pentecostal news. Thus, though *Voice* had a vastly

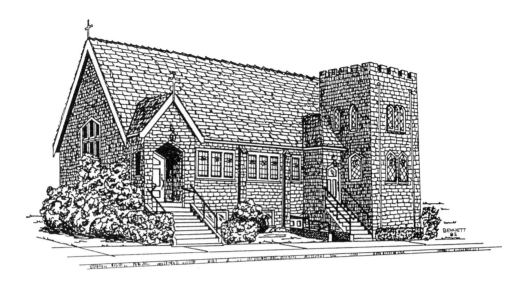

Dennis Bennett, following his baptism in the Holy Spirit, transferred to this church, St. Luke's Episcopal, Seattle. It became one of the leading charismatic churches in the U.S.

larger circulation, *Trinity* played a definite role in the growing consciousness of a new movement that was characterized by the appearance of the Pentecostal blessing in the historic Protestant traditions.

The beginnings of charismatic renewal (CR) in Canada, at least in attracting attention, occurred in a remote area of British Columbia—in Prince Rupert, were a young Anglican priest returned from a visit to California in September 1961 with news of the Pentecostal outbreak among Episcopalians. Soon the dean of the Anglican cathedral, George Pattison, and some clergy of the town were baptized in the Spirit. Controversy broke out; the bishop forbade glossolalia in public, and the clergy involved felt constrained to leave the area. CR that had greater longevity began in Ontario in 1962 under the leadership of Ron and June Armstrong, who both received BHS without contact with charismatics. Ron, an Anglican priest, soon began praise meetings in his parish, St. Elizabeth's, in Etobicoke. Some other Anglicans received BHS following contacts made at the international Anglican Congress at Toronto in 1963.

By the early 1960s people in virtually every major Protestant tradition were receiving BHS (Baptists, Lutherans, Mennonites, Methodists, and Presbyterians). By 1963 these developments had come to the attention of most Protestant leaders and editors, a larger number of church journals publishing items on glossolalia in that year. Among these was the evangelical monthly *Eternity*, whose editor, Russell Hitt, wrote an article entitled "The New Pentecostalism," which affected the nomenclature of the movement. Hitt's article elicited a response in *Trinity* from Bredesen and Stone; they objected to the "Neo-Pentecostal" label, preferring "charismatic renewal," the first time this designation was used in a definitive manner. The term *Neo-Pentecostal*, however, came into common usage in scientific studies of the movement by outside observers.

One of the first denominational groups to come together on this issue was the American Baptists. The charismatic pastors attending the 1963 denominational convention in Detroit, Michigan, heard a presentation, "The Ministry of the Charismatic Church," by Harold Jackson of Arcata, California. From that time on, American Baptist charismatics came together at each convention for a dinner and late-night worship.

The largest penetration was among the Episcopalians. It was influenced by Bennett, Sanford, and Stone and encouraged by a positive statement of the Episcopal bishops in 1962—"New Movements in the Church." Among other denominations, the early history of CR is less well-documented, save in the few cases where the first recipients later became major charismatic leaders.

One of these pioneer leaders was an American Lutheran pastor, Larry Christenson of San Pedro, California. Christenson, who was baptized in the Spirit in August 1961, had been active in OSL for some years but actually received the baptism of the Spirit following contact with a Pentecostal. Christenson made his experience public at Pentecost 1962. This caused some dissension, which he narrowly survived. Christenson's role as Lutheran leader was actually enhanced because, in a more theological tradition, he consciously sought to relate the Pentecostal experience to Lutheran tradition. His pamphlet "Speaking in Tongues . . . a Gift for the Body of Christ," had a wide influence and was translated into German. Christenson's visit to Germany in 1963 is noted under Section II, "Its Development in Europe."

Christenson's denomination, the American Lutheran Church (ALC), was the first church to address the issue of the charismatic revival. (Earlier Episcopalian studies and statements had been conducted by individual diocesan bishops, not the Protestant Episcopal Church as a whole.) The ALC concern began in 1962 following complaints that an ALC evangelist, Herbert Mjorud, had been emphasizing glossolalia in his ministry. Mjorud had been baptized in the Spirit following a visit to Bennett's parish in Seattle. A Committee on Spiritual Gifts was established to study and make recommendations concerning both glossolalia and "extra-medical" healing. The report of this committee in 1963 was followed in 1964 by an official ALC statement against any promotion of glossolalia and restricting its usage to private devotions.

A more aggressive opposition to CR grounded in doctrinal objections came from the Lutheran Church–Missouri Synod (LC-MS). The initial confrontation concerned Donald Pfotenhauer, a pastor in Minneapolis, Minnesota, who was baptized in the Spirit at the end of 1964. In March 1965, Pfotenhauer was suspended by his district president, beginning five years of church litigation that ended to Pfotenhauer's disadvantage in 1970. During the church trials, the main objection was not to glossolalia, but to prophecy, which was seen as derogating from the uniqueness of God's word in Scripture. Despite these discouragements, other LC-MS pastors continued to receive BHS (including Rodney Lensch, Delbert Rossin, Don Matzat, and theologian Theodore Jungkuntz).

Another church in which Pentecostal experience became a contentious issue was the Presbyterian Church. Although J. Brown of Parkesburg, Pennsylvania, never encountered difficulties with his Presbyterian authorities, others were not so fortunate. Robert Whitaker, a United Presbyterian pastor in Chandler, Arizona, baptized in the Spirit in the fall of 1962, was removed from office in 1967 after several years of dispute. In 1966, the difficulties of Whitaker and other Presbyterian ministers in the movement led Brown and others to form the Charismatic Communion of Presbyterian Ministers, the first denominational charismatic body to be formed. Its full-time secretary was George C. ("Brick") Bradford, a former attorney who had also been expelled from the ministry and who then helped Whitaker win his appeal against expulsion. Of major importance was a retreat Bradford organized in Austin, Texas, in 1967. At this retreat the speakers were two theologians—J. Rodman Williams, who was to make a valuable theological contribution from within CR, and John A. Mackay, a former president of Princeton and a respected international church leader. Mackay's advice and influence helped to end the harassment of charismatic Presbyterian pastors and contributed to the movement's being taken more seriously by the United Presbyterian Church, whose 1970 report, "The Work of the Holy Spirit," remains one of the most comprehensive church studies of the charismatic movement.

It is almost impossible to gauge the precise influence of particular leaders and publications in CR's accelerating spread. However, specific mention should be made of two men whose contributions may easily be undervalued, David du Plessis and Harald Bredesen. Du Plessis commenced his unique globe-trotting ecumenical witness in this period. His distinctive contribution was to emphasize that what the charismatics were receiving was indeed BHS, the same blessing that had characterized the Pentecostal movement. Through his talks, his book *The Spirit Bade Me Go* (1961), and his quarterly personal newsletter, du Plessis disseminated a vision as he recounted the worldwide scope of CR. He was also responsible for the first meeting of leaders from many traditions held near Columbus, Ohio, in October 1962.

Harald Bredesen was in some way instrumental in almost all CR impacts on the mass media. He was featured in nationwide presentations on CBS's "The World Tonight" and on Walter Cronkite's "World News Tonight." He also had a gift for reaching key people and telling them of BHS. Bredesen had an indirect hand in both of the books that had the greatest influence in the spread of CR in the 1960s, for he introduced John Sherrill to David Wilkerson. Wilkerson's book *The Cross and the Switchblade* (1963) vividly describes the impact of the Holy Spirit on young drug addicts in New York City, while Sherrill's *They Speak With Other Tongues* (1964) is a journalist's personal investigation into glossolalia, which led to his own BHS.

C. The Movement Takes Shape (1967–77). More than any other development, the spread of CR to the Roman Catholic church affected decisively the shape of the wider movement. While individual Catholics had been baptized in the Spirit before 1967 (e.g., Barbara Shlemon, as also some visitors to Bennett's parish in Seattle), the development of Catholic charismatic renewal (CCR) was determined by the events at Duquesne University, Pittsburgh, Pennsylvania, and South Bend, Indiana, in February 1967 and their immediate aftermath. These events differed in significant ways from the origins among Protestants: (1) They occurred in a university setting; thus the first Catholic charismatics were well-educated, a factor ensuring that CCR would not begin with an anti-intellectual bias. (2) These pioneers, from whose ranks CCR leadership is drawn, were young lay Catholics; the first priest participants, such as Fr. Edward O'Connor, acted more as theological and spiritual advisers, an important but complementary role. (3) These lay leaders had almost all worked and worshiped together in Notre Dame campus activities over the preceding three to four years; this helped from its inception to give CCR a cohesion the movement had not achieved in other churches. (4) These Catholics had been strongly influenced by the debates, ethos, and decrees of the Second Vatican Council, recently ended. They were "renewal-minded" and already desired to realize the renewal that the council envisioned for the Catholic church. As a result, they interpreted this outpouring of the Spirit in relation to Vatican II. They saw it as God's answer to Pope John's prayer that the Council might be a new Pentecost for the church and immediately recognized that this outpouring must be for the sake of the whole church. Thus from its inception, CCR had a sense of mission to the Catholic church.

Decisive in the development of CCR was the coming together of Stephen Clark, Ralph Martin, Gerry Rauch, and Jim Cavnar to form the basis of the Word of God community in Ann Arbor, Michigan. Clark and Martin were working as staff members of the Cursillo movement, for which Clark had done much strategic thinking and training. These men were convinced that for the renewal to affect the whole church, it was essential to train leaders and give them a thorough formation. So from its early days, CCR was characterized by conferences with an emphasis on teaching and by the production of literature for wider diffusion. From 1967, Days of Renewal were held in Williamston, Michigan, as occasions for initiation and teaching, gathering people interested in this move of the Spirit together with members of the growing number of charismatic prayer groups. These became a model widely followed by CCR in many countries. Each year from 1969, CCR leaders were invited to a conference at Ann Arbor, at which Clark and others shared their vision and strategy for church renewal through CCR and BHS. Life in the Spirit Seminars were developed within the Word of God community to prepare people for BHS, and these were soon made available for wider use. This prominence of the Word of God community ensured that covenant community became a dominant model and an attractive option for many Catholic charismatic groups.

While Clark was the strategist behind these formative initiatives, close links remained between the Ann Arbor leaders and those in South Bend, Indiana, where each spring an annual CCR conference was held. In 1969 a Center for Service and Communication was formed to serve CCR. Out of this center grew Charismatic Renewal Services as an agency to service CCR with literature, tapes, and prayer group directories. In 1970 a National Service Committee (NSC) for CCR was formed with nine members, all from the southern Michigan–northern Indiana area, combining the administrative experience of the South Bend leaders and the teaching gifts at Ann Arbor. Such structures, unthinkable in early Pentecostalism, can be seen as a fusion of Pentecostal elements with Catholic expertise in organized Christian formation. As a result, CCR acquired within four years a sense of identity with a coordinated leadership and the channels of communication needed for rapid expansion.

These Catholic patterns were soon to have a major impact on CR in other churches. The greater publicity given to this unexpected latecomer "Catholic Pentecostalism" with its rapid expansion challenged the charismatics in other churches. They were stimulated to relate their charismatic experience more actively to their tradition and encouraged to have a vision for church renewal through the Holy Spirit. As a result, charismatics in other traditions began to hold their own conferences and organize their own fellowships. Some were denominational (such as the Episcopalian), though more of them represented confessional families (such as the Lutheran, the Mennonite, and the Presbyterian). Although the Presbyterian Charismatic Communion was formed before CCR began, it was then limited to ministers, commencing its promotional role only following the Catholic lead. The chart on the next page illustrates the sequence of these developments in the wake of the organization and expansion of CCR.

Among these confessional or denominational groupings, the Episcopalians and the Lutherans were the strongest. This may reflect a greater sense of confessional identity in liturgical and sacramental traditions, though it also reflects factors intrinsic to the renewal movement. Among Episcopalians, the influence of Dennis Bennett and St. Luke's, Seattle, was further enhanced by his best-selling book *Nine O'Clock in the Morning* (1970). By the mid-1970s more than 150 pastors from the Seattle area had been baptized in the Spirit through the ministry of Bennett's church, and a pastors' fellowship that sponsored several teaching conferences was formed. Another major Episcopalian influence antedating CCR was the developments at Holy Redeemer Parish, Houston, Texas, under the able leadership of W. Graham Pulkingham. Although the Holy Spirit's work of renewal began there in 1965, it was in the early 1970s that it received wide publicity and became a model not only for the integration of the denominational and the charismatic elements but also for the formation of church community and its potential for social transformation. Another characteristic of Episcopalian renewal favoring denominational integration was the connection with the movement in Britain, with Michael Harper and a strong Anglican presence in the Fountain Trust.

The emergence of a strong current of CR among Lutherans was fostered both by the emergence of Larry Christenson as foremost leader and by the geographical concentration of American Lutherans in the Upper Midwest. The annual Lutheran renewal conference in Minneapolis, Minnesota, attracted an attendance second only to the Catholic conferences. Lutheran charismatics were also drawn together to defend their orthodoxy against the accusation that they fell under Luther's condemnation of sixteenth-century Spirit enthusiasts as *schwarmerei* (swarmers). In fact, a major impetus for Lutheran renewal came from S. Clark and the leaders of the Word of God community, who with their Lutheran members helped to host two national leaders conferences for Lutherans in 1974 and 1975.

The early to mid-1970s saw a steady stream of official church reactions to CR in North America. Only a minority of denominations clearly opposed the movement: the Church of the Nazarene (1970) declared the incompatibility of glossolalia with their formularies, while the LC-MS came out with lengthy though consistently negative statements, whose regularity (church documents of 1972 and 1977 and a seminary statement of 1975) itself pointed to the extent of charismatic activity within LC-MS. LC-MS regarded CR as both unscriptural and un-Lutheran (1975),

Church Tradition	First National Conference	Service Agency	Year Formed	Newsletter First Issued
Catholic	1970 (1968)	National Service Council	1970	*Pastoral Newsletter* *New Covenant* (1971)
Episcopalian	1973	Episcopal Charismatic Fellowship renamed Episcopal Renewal Ministries	1973 1980	*Acts 29* (1973)
Lutheran	1972	Lutheran Charismatic Renewal Services	1974	*LCRS Newsletter* (1975)
Mennonite	1972	Mennonite Renewal Services	1975	*MRS Newsletter* (1976) *Empowered* (1983)
Methodist	1974	United Methodist Renewal Services Fellowship	1977	*Manna* (1977)
Orthodox	1973	Service Committee for Orthodox Spiritual Renewal	1977	*Logos* (1968) *Theosis* (1978)
Presbyterian	1972	Presbyterian Charismatic Communion renamed Presbyterian and Reformed Renewal Ministries International	1966 1973 1984	*PCC Newsletter* (1966) later *Renewal News* (1980)

though it did not deny authenticity to every aspect of charismatic experience. Although the denomination did not call for the expulsion of charismatics and called for charismatic pastors to be "allowed time to wrestle with their consciences" (1977), their seminary in Springfield, Illinois (later in Fort Wayne, Ind.) established procedures to exclude professed charismatics from ordination (1975).

The majority of denominations adopted positions of cautious openness, neither welcoming CR with enthusiasm nor rejecting it as inauthentic. They generally accepted in principle the validity of Pentecostal experience and the availability of the charismata but rejected the Pentecostal theology of a second baptism subsequent to conversion and the necessity of glossolalia. Most, however, make a genuine effort to recognize the positive elements of new life brought by CR to the churches. This is in general the position of the United Presbyterian Church (1970); the Presbyterian Church in the U.S. (1971); ALC (1973); the Lutheran Church in America (1974); the Presbyterian Church in Canada (1974, 1975, 1976); the Reformed Church in America (1975); the Roman Catholic Church in the U.S. (1975); the Roman Catholic Church in Canada (1975); the United Methodist Church (1976); and the Mennonite Church (1977). The statements of the Lutheran and Reformed churches tend to be the most theological, while the thrust of the Catholic statements is predominantly pastoral.

CR frequently encountered strong resistance in the largest white Protestant denomination in the U.S., the Southern Baptist Convention (SBC), though no denominational statement was made at the national level. Some charismatic Baptist congregations were expelled by their state associations, like the large Beverly Hills Baptist Church in Dallas, Texas, pastored by Howard Conatser; this church, however, continued its membership in the national SBC until Conatser's death in 1978. Others simply withdrew in face of the opposition and suggestions that charismatics had no place in SBC. Many others continued as charismatic congregations within SBC, keeping a low profile by not advertising their charismatic involvement.

Among the American (Northern) Baptists CR encountered much less resistance, a fact demonstrated by the holding of regular and popular workshops on CR within the American Baptist denominational conventions. Throughout the 1970s, effective leadership for American Baptist charismatics came from the First Baptist Church, Chula Vista, California, led by Ken Pagard. Their local church newsletter, *Our Life Together*, was expanded around 1972 to serve the denomination more widely. Pagard's church emphasized community life and developed an extensive system of residential households, rather similar to Holy Redeemer fellowship in Houston among Episcopalians. An important teaching role was played among American Baptist charismatics by Howard Ervin, professor of OT at Oral Roberts University in Tulsa.

These years of denominational organization in CR did not prevent or inhibit constant cross-fertilization and interaction across all boundaries of church and nation. While leaders in particular church traditions began to exercise greater influence within their own territories, the charismatic rank and file were generally eager to accept the teachings and inspiration of any Spirit-filled preacher. The early 1970s saw a torrent of charismatic literature, some from new Pentecostal-charismatic publishing houses like Logos International, Plainfield, New Jersey, begun by Dan Malachuk in 1971, others from existing publishers, such as Fleming H. Revell and the Paulist Press, who saw the potential in the charismatic market. Several charismatic books became bestsellers, by both mainline-church authors such as Kevin and Dorothy Ranaghan (*Catholic Pentecostals* [1969]) and Dennis Bennett (*Nine O'Clock in the Morning* [1970]) as well as independent writers like Merlin Carothers (*Prison to Praise* [1970]), Pat Boone (*A New Song* [1970]), and Don Basham (*Deliver Us From Evil* [1972]). Toward the mid-1970s, there began a wave of new books on healing, from authors such as Francis MacNutt, Dennis and Matthew Linn, Michael Scanlan, Barbara Shlemon, and Ruth Carter Stapleton. All these books achieved sales crossing denominational boundaries and contributed to the wider spread of the movement.

The period that saw the organization and mushrooming of CR in the historic churches was also the time of the dramatic rise and growth of "nondenominational" Spirit-filled assemblies and networks and the first signs of major charismatic use of the mass media. These years saw the rise of Melodyland Christian Center in Anaheim, California (under Ralph Wilkerson), the expansion into the media of the teaching ministry of Kenneth Hagin in Tulsa, the founding by Pat Robertson of the Christian Broadcasting Network (CBN) in Virginia Beach, Virginia, and the spread across Canada of *Crossroads*, led by David Mainse in Ontario, as well as the proliferation of many other ministries, such as those of Charles and Frances Hunter, Kenneth and Gloria Copeland, John Osteen, Roxanne Brant, Gerald Derstine, and Bob Weiner. With many of these independent ministries, the labels of "charismatic" and "Pentecostal" are sometimes used interchangeably. Even if independents whose ethos and doctrine are indistinguishable from those of classical Pentecostal preachers are termed "independent Pentecostals," and those whose patterns and teaching are influenced by non-Pentecostal sources are called "charismatic," the independent Pentecostals would still need mention in any history of CR. For the clientele of the independent Pentecostals has been primarily outside the Pentecostal churches, with vast numbers of hearers and viewers coming from mainline church membership.

Among the independent developments having a major impact on the American scene was the rise of Christian Growth Ministries (CGM) and the *New Wine* magazine in Fort Lauderdale, Florida. CGM was originally known as the Holy Spirit Teaching Mission (HSTM); it was begun by a committee of forty who were mostly denominational charismatics in search of solid teaching. HSTM organized teaching conferences, the teachers including four men who later became the basic CGM team: Derek Prince, a classics scholar with some years in Pentecostal missions in Kenya; Don Basham, a pastor originally from the Disciples of Christ; Charles Simpson, a Southern Baptist pastor from Mobile, Alabama; and Bob Mumford, a former Pentecostal who had then trained at Reformed Episcopal Seminary. In 1969 HSTM began the monthly magazine *New Wine* to promote solid teaching to help the vast members of new charismatics to mature in their faith. In 1970 Basham, Mumford, Prince, and Simpson were asked to become more involved in HSTM when a moral problem and financial difficulties threatened its future. These four men soon sensed a call to submit their lives to one another for mutual protection and direction. All four maintained their existing personal ministries, while submitting to each other the basic pattern of their lives and ministries.

The initial thrust of CGM was to bring Spirit-baptized Christians to maturity and to teach church-building. In 1972 they terminated the regular teaching conferences at Fort Lauderdale, sensing a need to spread these across the nation. Even though the issues for which the CGM team became known in the mid-1970s, discipling and pastoring, were consciously pursued only from 1972 to 1973, the leaders had already practiced discipling for a few years, preparing young men for ministry through the sharing of life on the model of Jesus' training of the Twelve. As they began to reflect more systematically on the patterns of biblical pastoral authority, they taught explicitly on such topics as authority, submission, discipleship (training of Christians for ministry), and pastoring-shepherding (pastoral care of practicing ministers). As a result, large numbers of charismatic pastors began to be shepherded by the CGM leaders, a development that went uncharted but not unnoticed. It was uncharted because these relationships were personal and not institutional, so there were never any published lists of pastors and congregations being shepherded by CGM leaders, who were joined in 1974 by Ern Baxter. It did not pass unnoticed because involvement with CGM changed local patterns of ministerial cooperation, and problem cases caused growing friction between the CGM teachers and other charismatic leaders, particularly heads of other independent ministries. In 1975 these difficulties erupted in public controversy. While many respected leaders were opposed to the CGM discipleship teaching (e.g., D. Bennett, D. du Plessis), matters came to a head when Kathryn Kuhlman refused to speak at the Holy Spirit Conference in Jerusalem if Mumford was on the platform, Pat Robertson banned CGM speakers from CBN programs, and Demos Shakarian likewise excluded them from FGBMFI gatherings.

The key concepts in contention were authority, submission, shepherding, and discipleship. The CGM team saw these as scriptural principles, much needed to combat Protestant individualism and charismatic free-lancing. In this, they found

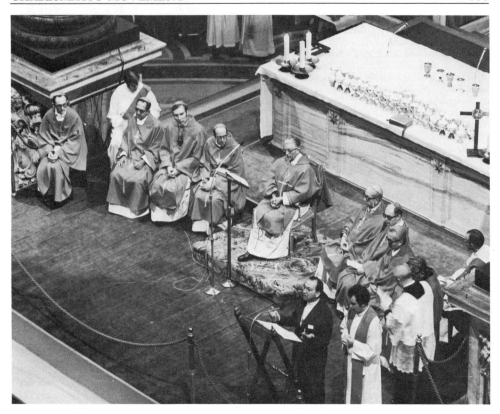

Léon-Joseph Cardinal Suenens presides at concelebrated mass at the main altar of St. Peter's Basilica during a Rome conference in 1975.

support from the Catholic leaders of the ecumenical Word of God community, Ann Arbor, Michigan, particularly S. Clark and R. Martin, with whom they had collaborated in holding Shepherds Conferences at Montreat, North Carolina (1974), and Kansas City (1975). Their positions also found support in the book *Disciple* by the Argentinian Juan Carlos Ortiz, published in 1975. The opponents of CGM saw themselves as the defenders of the Reformation heritage of the priesthood of all believers threatened by new sources of authority and teaching over and above the Word of God. A series of meetings were held between the summer of 1975 and the spring of 1976 involving CGM teachers, some of their principal critics, and other respected CR leaders. These led to "a statement of concern and regret" by the CGM leaders, in which they affirmed the essential soundness of their teachings but asked forgiveness for the pastoral mistakes that they had made. The discipleship debate received extensive coverage in charismatic journals, especially *Logos*, *New Wine*, and *New Covenant*.

Despite such headlines as "Deepening Rift in the Charismatic Movement" (*Christianity Today*, Oct. 10, 1975), this controversy probably contributed to the overall maturing of the movement. It led to a meeting of most of the disputants for prayer and discussion, with a common recognition of the need for reconciliation. This somewhat

uncommon occurrence in ecclesiastical disputes made both sides face up more squarely to what all recognized to be important issues. Concretely, as a result, an annual meeting of charismatic leaders became more formally constituted as the "Charismatic Concerns Committee," which has subsequently met each year at Glencoe, Missouri. Further, the more formal organization made possible the participation of persons from both sides of the dispute in the Kansas City conference of July 1977.

This 1977 Conference on CR in the Christian Churches at Kansas City concluded this formative period of American CR. In many ways Kansas City summed up the achievements and advances of the previous decade. It brought together in one demonstration more than 50,000 charismatic faith leaders and people from virtually all strands of the movement: denominational CR leaders, independent teachers, both discipling and antidiscipling, Messianic Jews, and a few Pentecostal leaders. Its format recognized both the distinctiveness of each grouping (the morning sessions were arranged according to church membership) and the overall unity of this work of the Spirit (all met together for plenary sessions each evening in the Arrowhead stadium). The conference reflected the confident forward surge of CR and provided many memorable vignettes of God's power to transcend human expectations—of Cardinal

Suenens of Belgium seated alongside Thomas F. Zimmerman of the AG; of the first major impact on CR of the Messianic Jews with their chant and the footwashing at their symposium; of the joint witness to reconciliation by Bill Burnett, white archbishop from South Africa, and James Forbes, a black Pentecostal preacher.

Participants in Kansas City (July 1977) experienced the conference as an outstanding ecumenical event. It strongly reinforced people's sense of CR as a remarkable work of God intentionally spanning all the churches and with an evident power to transcend inherited patterns of division. It gave signs of a new maturity and depth, as in the prophecies that summoned Christians, particularly church leaders and pastors, to repentance for attachment to their own priorities, and to "mourn . . . weep . . . for the broken body of my Son."

The conference by its organization and structure underlined the importance of the denominational renewal fellowships, and indeed helped to ensure their formation in some church traditions previously without any charismatic service agency, such as the United Methodists and the United Church of Christ. The decade from 1967 to 1977 thus ended with denominational CR firmly established with its own structures, yet with a recognition of CR's ecumenical character, plus a plethora of independent ministries of evangelism, healing, and teaching.

D. Consolidation (1977–87). This most recent phase is not surprisingly the most difficult to describe and evaluate. The heading "Consolidation" indicates agreement with the subtitle of Richard Quebedeaux's *New Charismatics II,* "How a Christian Renewal Movement became part of the American Religious Mainstream." However, what has been happening to CR besides more widespread recognition can be variously interpreted. Some speak of the movement in America peaking in the early 1980s; the majority, however, see CR as still spreading, but having moved into a new and less sensational pattern of growth. Certainly, CR in the historic churches was no longer a novelty and attracted less attention than in the previous decade. Moreover, most would agree that the élan and promise of the Kansas City conference did not last.

Some of the Kansas City ecumenical enthusiasm was manifest in the Jesus rallies held on Pentecost Sunday for a number of years. The first rally, "Jesus '78," in Meadowlands, New Jersey, was the brainchild of Dan Malachuk, a Pentecostal who was strongly supported by Catholic Fr. Jim Ferry. This rally drew 55,000 people. In the following years, Jesus rallies were held in many U.S. cities, reaching more than one hundred in 1980. They were intended to be manifestations of Christian unity in praise and witness, animated by, but not restricted to, charismatic Christians. In many places, the Jesus rallies were the largest and most representative Christian gatherings ever held, and they did much to impart a sense of the grass-roots ecumenical thrust of CR. Their momentum, however, did not continue long into the 1980s.

That things were never quite the same after

Kansas City was more quickly evident in CCR. The era of the big conferences ended, partly because the leaders of some major covenant communities believed they had served their purpose and that the future thrust should be the formation of strong and lasting communities. Thus no subsequent annual CCR conference at Notre Dame ever reached the numbers that attended prior to 1977. The year 1978 saw the last of the large East Coast CCR conventions at Atlantic City, New Jersey, which did not survive a change of venue to New York City. Business at Charismatic Renewal Services and other agencies in CCR began to level out and then decline.

The impression of decline or peaking seems to have been a predominantly Catholic perception, though with lesser echoes elsewhere, as among the Presbyterians. This undoubtedly reflects the different patterns in CCR from CR in other churches. CCR is largely made up of charismatic prayer groups, only loosely associated with official church structures; such informal groups do not have a high survival rate in an eclectic and highly mobile society. The strength and continuity in CCR has been most marked in the covenant communities (see CHARISMATIC COMMUNITIES). While in the mid-1970s the alternative to communities was sought in parish prayer groups, in the 1980s the thrust of CCR outside the covenant communities has been much more associated with the diocesan liaisons. Since the mid-1970s, Catholic bishops in the U.S. had been appointing individuals (generally priests but occasionally religious sisters and lay people) as liaisons between the bishop and CCR in the diocese. By the late 1970s, the liaisons were organizing themselves nationally, with a national newsletter and annual conferences (from 1978) augmented by an annual theological symposium (from 1979). By the mid-1980s, most liaisons had become full-time diocesan coordinators for CR. The number of diocesan pastoral centers for CR, or for spiritual renewal but staffed by CR people, has soared (over fifty in 1986, over eighty in 1987), and these have provided new focal points for the movement locally. CCR conferences have become regional, sometimes diocesan, organized by local service committees. Among the most successful was Southern California Renewal Communities (known as SCRC), led by Fr. Ralph Tichenor until his death in 1983.

The rapid diffusion of CR among Catholics has stimulated much greater Catholic interest in Bible reading and Bible study. This need has been met principally by two monthly magazines—*God's Word Today* and *The Word Among Us. God's Word Today,* begun in 1979 and edited by George Martin, is a daily guide to reading Scripture, with a focus on particular books of the Bible, whereas *The Word Among Us,* begun in 1981, is more an aid to daily prayer based on the Scriptures and is written by members of the Mother of God community, Gaithersburg, Maryland, to share more widely the anointing on their life.

In most of the historic Protestant denominations CR has grown steadily during this decade, particularly in churches with denominational or confessional renewal fellowships. Their conferences, with the exception of the Lutherans, who are more geographically concentrated in the upper Midwest, were relatively small in numbers and attracted less attention. However, the number of denominational renewal conferences has multiplied during the 1980s, as have the staff of the denominational fellowships and the size and circulation of their newsletters (the Episcopalian *Acts 29* had increased circulation from 20,000 to 40,000 between 1985 and 1987, and the Methodist *Manna* printing has increased steadily to 15,000). CR among American Baptists had been flagging in the late 1970s, in part because the community model and style of the Chula Vista, California, church had become a contentious issue, but it took on new momentum in 1982. Gary Clark, formerly of Salem, New Hampshire, took over the leadership of the American Baptist Charismatic Fellowship, changing it from an informal body into a legal organization and forming a national service committee in 1983.

In the Protestant churches in Canada CR was much slower to develop national structures than in the U.S., as both geography and economics favored north-south communications (to/from the U.S.) rather than east-west. A Renewal Fellowship was established in the United Church as an association of evangelical Christians as early as 1965. Over the years more of its chapters have become charismatic in some sense, currently reaching 80 percent. Its magazine, *The Small Voice*, was changed to a larger format in 1986. In the Anglican Church of Canada, there are many parishes with small charismatic groups, but as yet few in which rectors have been leading whole congregations into renewal. Anglican Renewal Ministries is run from Nepean, Ontario, while *Tongues of Fire,* a quarterly, has been published from Calgary, Alberta, since 1986. In general, Protestant opposition to CR in Canada, unlike in the U.S., comes more from traditionalist circles than from the more liberal.

CR in the Protestant churches has concentrated more on congregational renewal, in contrast to CCR, where many parish prayer groups have been formed, but few charismatically renewed parishes have resulted. The main thrust of Protestant denominational renewal fellowships has been to foster and encourage the emergence of strong renewed congregations. This concern led in 1981 to the establishment of the interdenominational Parish Renewal Council. The council did not lead to the results hoped for, and the organization did not long survive the first reassessment of its goals.

Whereas the strength of CCR is in the covenant communities, the role models in Protestant CR are the renewed parishes, in which there has been an integration of denominational and charismatic elements over many years. Local churches that have been recognized in their denominations and sometimes beyond as pioneering models of renewed congregational life include the following:

American Baptist: First Baptist, Salem, N.H. (under Gary Clark, then Clement Sutton); First Baptist, Chula Vista, Calif. (under Kan Pagard, then Richard Hensgen); Bethlehem Baptist, Lake Oswego, Ore. (under Jack Matthews); Redeemer Baptist, Monroe, Mich. (under F. Joseph Atkinson).

Episcopal: St. Luke's Episcopal, Seattle, Wa. (under Dennis Bennett, then Trevor Dearing, and later Kevin Martin); St. Paul's Episcopal, Darien, Conn. (under Terry Fullam); Truro Episcopal, Fairfax, Va. (under John Howe); St. Jude's Episcopal, Burbank, Calif. (under Michael Flynn); St. Luke's Episcopal, Bath, Ohio (under Charles Irish and then Roger Ames).

Lutheran: North Heights Lutheran, St. Paul, Minn. (under Morris Vaagenes); Faith Lutheran, Geneva, Ill. (LC-MS, under Delbert Rossin); Our Savior's Lutheran, Albany, N.Y. (LC-MS under Walter Litke, then James Roberson); Resurrection Lutheran, Charlotte, N.C. (LC-MS, under Herbert Mirly, then William Gittner); Trinity Lutheran, San Pedro, Calif. (ALC, under Larry Christenson, then Paul Anderson); Christ the King Lutheran, North Olmsted, Ohio (Independent Lutheran, under Ward Potts).

Mennonite: Trinity Mennonite, Morton, Ill. (under Mahlon Miller); Hopewell Mennonite Elverson, Pa. (under Merle Stoltzfus); English Lake, North Judson, Ind. (under Art Good); Communion Fellowship, Goshen, Ind. (under Doug Fike).

Methodist: First United Methodist, Tulsa, Okla. (under L. D. Thomas and then James Buskirk); Trinity United Methodist, Savannah, Ga., the mother church of Georgian Methodism (under Sanford Brown); Bay Shore United Methodist, Tampa, Fla. (under Frank Seghers); First United Methodist, Bedford, Tex. (under Lee Bedford); Aldersgate United Methodist, College Station, Tex. (under Terry Teykle).

Presbyterian Reformed: Our Lord's Community (Reformed Church in America), Oklahoma City, Okla. (under Robert Wise); St. Giles Presbyterian, Richmond, Va. (under Earl Morey); New Covenant Presbyterian, Pompano Beach, Fla. (under George Callahan); Kempsville Presbyterian, Virginia Beach, Va. (under David Anderson); St. Giles Presbyterian, Charlotte, N.C. (under Percy Burns); College Hill Presbyterian, Cincinnati, Ohio (under Jerry Kirk and Ron Rand, assisted by Gary Sweeten); Silver Lake Presbyterian, Los Angeles, Calif. (under Robert Whitaker).

Southern Baptist: First Baptist, Coral Springs, Fla. (under Jimmy Brookins); West Lauderdale Baptist, Fort Lauderdale, Fla. (under Don Le Master).

United Church of Canada: Alderwood United, Toronto, Ont. (under Harold Moddle); Victoria Avenue United, Chatham, Ont. (under John Neal); Echo Place United, Brantford, Ont. (under John Tweedie); Pilgrim United, Victoria, B.C. (under Tom Ridewood); Lawrencetown United, Porter's Lake, N.S. (under Michael Kaye).

The decade since 1977 has seen an increased emphasis on teaching among mainline Protestant charismatics. The only Protestant church grouping using the Word of God community Life in the Spirit seminars to any appreciable extent is the Episcopal, though Episcopalian charismatics also use the *Saints Alive* program from Britain. The Presbyterians have developed their own initiation-teaching program known as *Spirit Alive Missions.* This is a three-year series, with the first year focusing on the lordship of Jesus Christ, the second on the healing ministry of the church, and the third on discovering and ministering one's gifts. There are several initiation programs among the Methodists, while among the Lutherans individual congregations have formulated their own patterns of teaching.

Opposition to CR has been fiercest and most sustained among the leaders of the Orthodox church, whose bishops and theologians view the movement as intrinsically Protestant. A small group led by Fr. Boris Zabrodsky continues to produce *Theosis,* but almost all the Orthodox priests renewed in the Spirit over the past twenty years have withdrawn under pressure. Fr. Eusebius Stephanou, formerly of Fort Wayne, Indiana, was canonically suspended for a number of years, and Fr. Athanasios Emmert, faced with a choice between CR and Orthodoxy, became a Melkite Catholic at the end of 1987.

While the opposition to charismatics had been declining in many other denominations, opposition continued in LC-MS and SBC. However, CR continued to spread among Southern Baptists. Many Southern Baptists baptized in the Spirit use the term *fulness* rather than *charismatic* to describe Spirit-filled Christian life, avoiding explicitly Pentecostal terminology and doctrine (e.g., tongues as initial evidence) and other emphases seen as extreme or narrow. It is estimated that there are some four hundred Fulness churches in SBC. Since 1978, the bi-monthly *Fulness,* published in Forth Worth, Texas, by a Southern Baptist layman, Ras Robinson, has sought to build bridges between Fulness people and traditional Southern Baptists. The ministry of James Robison, a Southern Baptist pastor in Euless, Texas, has increasingly had a charismatic dimension, with prayer for the sick and the exorcism of evil spirits. His bi-monthly *Restoration* testifies to "God's move to return His Church to the power, purity and majesty He intended it to have in preparation for the coming of Christ in glory."

This decade also saw a multiplication in the number of healing ministries. New developments included the emergence of Catholic healing ministries concentrated in parishes and dioceses, such as those of Ralph DiOrio of Worcester, Massachusetts, and Edward McDonough of Boston, Massachusetts. Ministries focusing on inner healing saw major expansion: among Protestants, with John Sanford, an Episcopal priest and son of Agnes Sanford, and with Leanne Payne; and among Catholics, the continued growth of the ministry of Briege McKenna, the Linn brothers, Barbara Shlemon, and others. Some noticeable differences have emerged among those ministries that have a stronger psychological base, often Jungian, and those with a greater spiritual empha-

sis on repentance for sin. While these healing ministries have been charismatic in experience and expression, though not all in origin, the people they have reached have been the sick, whether they were interested in CR or not. As with the healing evangelists of the 1950s and 1960s, these divine healers of the 1980s are contributing to the spread of charismatic experience but not by the formation of explicitly charismatic groups.

This period is particularly characterized by an explosion of nondenominational charismatic assemblies, among whom a complete classification is virtually impossible. However, the majority of these assemblies tend to acquire affiliation or connections with some network or association of charismatic assemblies and/or pastors. These cover a spectrum ranging from explicit acceptance of the transcongregational authority of a charismatic leader to occasional participation in leaders' fellowships that in no way restrict congregational autonomy.

The largest association representing a particular bloc of convictions is the National Leadership Conference (NLC), formed in 1979 largely because of the initiative of Ken Sumrall. NLC brought together leaders whose ministries already served networks of charismatic assemblies, in particular Sumrall of Liberty Church, Pensacola, Florida. (now with some 350 to 400 local churches); Gerald Derstine of Bradenton, Florida. (who followed Sumrall as president); Bill Ligon of Brunswick, Georgia; Russ Williamson of Hopewell Junction, New York; Ernest Gruen of Kansas City; Bob Heil of Hillsboro, Missouri, and Bob Wright of Davidsonville, Maryland. The director of the NLC is Jim Jackson, of Montreat, North Carolina. As this list indicates, the NLC constituency is almost entirely east of the Mississippi. NLC is clear that it is not a new denomination, but a fellowship of charismatic leaders with common convictions and a similarity of vision. NLC churches are often named "Community Church" or "Covenant Church," reflecting a conviction that they are bound together by regeneration in the one new covenant of Jesus Christ. This "covenant" usage is thus different from that of the "covenant communities" constituted by an explicit covenant commitment. It reflects rather a desire for unity in the body of Christ and a willingness to fellowship with all in whom they recognize the work of the Spirit. NLC churches practice believers' baptism and regard BHS as part of normal Christian life. They expect to see the fivefold ministry of Ephesians 4:11 operative in their churches without entitling leaders with particular ministries. The NLC committee is made up of leaders recognized to have an apostolic dimension to their ministry. Thus groupings within NLC represent more organized networks under an apostolic leader, but NLC itself is a nondirective fellowship of likeminded leaders.

A similar pattern of "nondenominational" charismatic Christianity is found in the network associated with Larry Tomczak and C. J. Mahaney. They founded a church in Wheaton, Maryland, in 1977 and now lead the 1,200-member Covenant Life Church in Gaithersburg, Maryland. In 1982 they founded People of Destiny International to provide pastoral care for other local churches and the training of leaders. By 1987 there were sixteen churches in this network. These assemblies are similar in many ways to the churches linked to NLC, both in their style of worship and in their presbyterian patterns of church government. Their main distinction is a stronger emphasis on God's restoration of the NT church in the end-times, a point on which Tomczak and Mahaney have been influenced by the Bradford (Harvestime) network of the House Church movement in Britain. Their bi-monthly magazine, *People of Destiny*, is similar to the Bradford bi-monthly, *Restoration*. This group also has close links with the Maranatha Christian churches arising from the campus and youth ministry of Bob Weiner, based in Gainesville, Florida.

Another stream is the Fellowship of Covenant Ministers and Conferences (FCMC) formed by Charles Simpson in 1987. FCMC, with approximately 350 members, represents the sector of the discipling-shepherding ministry of CGM that survived the final dissolution of the old CGM team in 1985. The FCMC theology of covenant is similar to that of NLC, except that a functional commitment (not regarded as a covenant) is made between the pastoring pastor and the pastored pastor. Simpson's ministry and Covenant Church of Mobile, Alabama, now produces *Christian Conquest* from the office that previously published *New Wine*, but this is not an organ of FCMC.

Alongside these independent charismatic assemblies is the controversial phenomenon of the "electronic church," the world of the television evangelists. Some of these are Pentecostal in ministerial affiliation, as were Jim Bakker (until 1987) and Jimmy Swaggart (until 1988), whereas others are independent, like Kenneth Copeland and Kenneth Hagin. Pat Robertson had Southern Baptist credentials until he resigned in 1987 in view of his presidential candidacy. These and other TV ministries have become multimillion dollar industries, with enormous followings. Studies show that members of historic denominations form a large part of their clientele, including many Catholics. Concern about aspects of these ministries, such as their lack of accountability, found clearer expression following the scandals uncovered in the Bakkers' PTL ministry at Charlotte, North Carolina, in 1987. There can be no doubt that many have heard gospel truths through these programs, though a question mark may remain over the permanence of their impact and the depth of life imparted.

In Canada, where access to media time is more regulated, a rather different pattern emerged in charismatic media ministry. In 1977 David Mainse began daily Christian TV, known by the address of his Toronto studios: 100 Huntley Street. Mainse, a minister of PAOC, accepted denominational regulations regarding accountability with PAOC representatives on his board. At the same time, Mainse made 100 Huntley Street a vehicle for all Spirit-filled Christianity, inviting charismatic participation by having two priests on his staff, Al Reimers (Anglican) and Bob MacDougall (Roman Catholic). In many ways, "100 Huntley Street" has provided a distinctive Canadian charismatic focal point in a country where national organization has been slow to develop. In 1984, with support from Mainse, MacDougall started a separate Catholic charismatic ministry, *Food for Life*.

Besides the associations of "nondenominational" assemblies already mentioned, one grouping that is Pentecostal in origin and confession has evolved to become more like the NLC assemblies than the old-line Pentecostal denominations. This is the International Communion of Charismatic Churches, led in the U.S. by Bishops John Meares of Evangel Temple, Washington, D.C., and Earl Paulk of Chapel Hill Harvester Church, Decatur, Georgia. Prior to any influence from CR this grouping of Pentecostals was led to a ministry more focused on worship, teaching, and church building than on dramatic preaching and healings. Other large city churches that followed the same path were those pastored by Charles Green in New Orleans, Louisiana (Green has formed his own Network of Christian Ministries), and James Beall of Detroit, Michigan. In addition, a number of Pentecostal churches have been renewed through their contact with CR, one being the Calvary Assembly of God, Orlando, Florida, out of which came the initiative for the monthly *Charisma*, edited by Stephen Strang, which perhaps uniquely spans the Pentecostal and charismatic public.

The International Convention of Faith Ministries (ICFM), headquartered in Tulsa, Oklahoma, was formed in 1979 as an "organization without denomination." ICFM holds regular conventions at many levels and has a particular emphasis on leadership training. Its current president is Happy Caldwell, and its secretary is Terry Mize. A looser fraternal fellowship entitled Charismatic Bible Ministries (CBM) was established by Oral Roberts in 1986 "for the advancement of the Unity of the Body of Christ through Love and Mighty Signs and Wonders." CBM brings together for mutual support both Pentecostal and nondenominational ministers and currently has 1,200 members across the U.S., many of whom are involved in closer forms of fellowship and association already noted. CBM has a Statement of Beliefs, which mentions the spiritual gifts, including tongues as "the prayer language of the Spirit," but without any mention of BHS.

Besides the nondenominational assemblies forming part of wider associations, there are independent charismatic churches without any such links. Many of these are former Southern Baptist churches, whose convictions about congregational autonomy discouraged them from participation in any national networks. There remain some independent teachers, such as Judson Cornwall, who are unaffiliated and have opposed discipleship teaching.

One of the most dramatic new developments of the 1980s has been the rise of the "Signs and Wonders" praxis and teaching associated with John Wimber and his Vineyard Fellowship, based in Yorba Linda, California. While the origins of the Vineyard go back to 1978, Wimber's distinc-

Catholic charismatics in a joyous worship service during a 1978 conference in Dublin, Ireland.

tive ministry came to prominence in 1983 through publicity given to the "Signs and Wonders" course offered at Fuller Theological Seminary in Pasadena by C. Peter Wagner, assisted by Wimber. Wagner was responsible for labeling the resulting movement "The Third Wave"; he saw the "Signs and Wonders" teaching as a third phase in some continuity with, but distinct from, the Pentecostal and charismatic movements. The proliferation of Vineyard Fellowships across the American continent (two hundred churches in 1987) has given rise to another grouping of nondenominational charismatic assemblies.

The "Third Wave" terminology was introduced because Wimber's teaching was welcomed in many evangelical circles previously closed to CR. Wimber's wider acceptability partly resulted from his emphasis on signs and wonders as a normal element in evangelism and church growth rather than any second-blessing experience. Ministers were reassured by his openness to evangelical scholarship, shown in his links with Fuller, and by his down-home style and lack of self-promotion in contrast to some more flamboyant ministries. Wimber's ministry undoubtedly gave CR a boost in the mid-1980s, as shown by the increased attendance at the events in which he participated. His "Signs and Wonders" teaching has been accepted in many charismatic milieux, as, for example, among the Episcopalians where Bishop David Pytches of England has formulated this emphasis in an Anglican framework.

The "third wave" terminology is still too new to be definitive. As initially used in close connection with Wimber's message and ministry, it is too narrow to be compared with the first two waves (Pentecostal and charismatic). It has however come to be used (e.g., by David Barrett) of the widespread occurrence of Pentecostal phenomena among Christians, especially evangelical Protestants who refuse the "charismatic" label and often do not practice glossolalia while manifesting other spiritual gifts. While it appears certain that a widespread diffusion of spiritual gifts and associated power is occurring throughout the world, this extension beyond the acknowledged ranks of CR may be too disparate and diverse to be given any one distinctive label.

The ecumenical dimension of CR received a new fillip from the New Orleans conference of October 1986 (leaders) and July 1987 (general public) organized by the North American Renewal Service Committee, with Vinson Synan as chairman. The committee established for the purpose represented a wider range of denominations and charismatic networks than that for Kansas City ten years previously. The newcomers included Pentecostal denominations such as PHC, CG, CGP, and ICFG, as well as groupings like Youth With a Mission (YWAM) and Maranatha Christian Churches. Both conferences linked the outpouring of the Spirit with world evangelization and were planned as part of a process leading to a world congress in 1990 followed by a decade of evangelism to win at least half the world for Christ by the year 2000.

Neither New Orleans conference drew the crowd the organizers hoped for and initially predicted. The numbers at the general conference in July 1987 reached 35,000 and may have been reduced by the Bakker scandal and associated publicity. As at Kansas City, the Catholics constituted 50 percent of the attendance. New Orleans 1987 lacked something of the prophetic thrust and élan of Kansas City 1977, but any gathering of this size that associates such a wide variety of participants in extended worship must have incalculable effects. The dynamic of the New Orleans congresses may prove to reverse the loss in CR's ecumenical cohesion.

The number of Americans claimed to be involved in CR varies according to sources and methods of computation. A *Christianity Today* poll in 1980 found that between 18 and 21 percent of adult American Baptists, Catholics, Lutherans, and Methodists considered themselves charismatic. However, the same poll discovered that only a small fraction of the professed charismatics have ever spoken in tongues (17 percent of all Pentecostals and charismatics, higher among Pentecostals and lower among charismatics). There is no reason to doubt the accuracy of the poll statistics; however, they tabulate how American Christians understand their own experience and do not provide evidence for active participation in charismatic groups. The statistics, however, do suggest that church people in general view CR positively and accept it as part of the religious mainstream. CR leaders in the Lutheran and Presbyterian churches have estimated that at least 10 percent of their ordained ministers are charismatic, a higher percentage than among the laity. American Catholics active in CR are calculated in the mid-1980s as 250,000 in some 6,000 groups.

Continued ascent or commencing decline? The overall evidence suggests that the number of Spirit-baptized Christians in North America has continued to increase throughout the 1970s and 1980s. But the increase is not equal in every sector. A Presbyterian leader has estimated that 50 percent of Presbyterian charismatics leave to join independent charismatic or Pentecostal churches. It seems likely that this percentage is similar to that in other mainline church traditions. The membership of major Pentecostal denominations, such as AG, has soared during the years of CR, and their leaders agree in attributing their extraordinary growth rate to the accession of many charismatics who are unable to accommodate their new spiritual fervor within their previous church. The fastest growth, however, has been among "nondenominational" charismatics, with perhaps the most significant expansion being among those like the NLC grouping, which practice a corporate leadership. In other words, the overall Pentecostal-charismatic movement in North America continues to grow as fast as ever, but the slowest growth is in some sectors of CR within the historic churches. One implication is that the challenge of CR has not been addressed within the historic American churches as much as either denominational CR leaders or church officials would like to think.

II. Its Development in Europe.

A. Origins. In Europe more than in America CR shows some elements of continuity with the ecumenical origins of the Pentecostal movement prior to its denominationalization. Seen in this light, European CR had its precursors in those Pentecostal pioneers who never left their churches of origin: in England, Alexander Boddy and Cecil Polhill; in Germany, Jonathan Paul, Karl Ecke, and C. O. Voget; in Norway, Morten Larsen; in Sweden, J. Ongman and the Orebro Baptists; in Switzerland, C. E. D. DeLabilliere, and later Jean and Fritz de Rougemont; in Belgium, Henri de Worm. However, the only direct link between these "old church" Pentecostals and the later charismatics appears to be through Louis Dallière, with whom de Worm worked closely in the 1930s, and the Union de Prière (UP) in France.

Although the charismatic movement in Europe did not acquire a clear-cut identity or develop recognizable structures until the 1960s, there were, besides the Ardeche revival and UP, a number of other anticipatory strands of Pentecostal blessing outside the Pentecostal churches by the 1950s. In Germany from 1945 there were manifestations of spiritual gifts with Basilea Schlink and the Mary Sisters in Darmstadt. In Britain various strands are traceable back into the 1950s: the largely ex-Brethren independent groups associated with David Lillie and Arthur Wallis; the incidence of glossolalia among those involved in healing ministries, such as the London Healing Mission and the Evangelical Divine Healing Fellowship; the Methodist lay preacher Edgar Trout; and the Pentecostal search of men active in prayer fellowships for revival, such as W. B. Grant and Eric Houfe. In Holland, the "New Pentecost" goes back to student milieux in the early 1950s, within which Wim Verhoef started the *Vuur* (Fire) group. In these preparatory strands, virtually none owed their beginnings to American contacts, though several (Lillie; the London Healing Mission; Trout, Grant, Houfe; *Vuur*) stemmed from links with European Pentecostals.

The emergence of a conscious movement of CR in the early 1960s was primarily the consequence of news from America of the outbreak among Episcopalians at Van Nuys, California, under Dennis Bennett, publicized in *Newsweek* and *Time*. Of particular importance for British awareness was Philip E. Hughes's description of a visit to California in *The Churchman* of September 1962. Some 39,000 copies of Hughes's editorial were circulated in leaflet form. Of great importance too were the visits of David du Plessis, spreading the news of "Pentecost outside Pentecost." He visited England, Holland, and Switzerland in the fall of 1963, while 1964 saw him in Britain for a month, in France (Alsace), Holland, and Switzerland.

The deliberate correlating of the Pentecostal life with a received church tradition began in Holland with Verhoef's separation from the nondenominational Karel Hoekendijk and the launching in 1957 of *Vuur* magazine, the first charismatic journal in the world in the sense of affirming Pentecostal experience with traditional denominational commitment. *Vuur* was described as an ecumenical monthly by 1961, with the editorial board composed of members of both Reformed churches and the Remonstrants, extending to a Baptist and a Catholic by 1964. The explicit combining of Pentecostal and denominational convictions was especially the work of Michael Harper in England and Arnold Bittlinger in West Germany. The English movement developed rather more quickly for several reasons: the wider number of preparatory strands, the ready availability of American literature, and Harper's resignation from parish work and his establishment of the Fountain Trust (FT) in 1964 as a service agency for CR. The West German origins followed Bittlinger's American visit in late 1962 which led to Larry Christenson's addressing the Enkenback conference in August 1963. In East Germany, the first charismatic manifestations occurred in the early 1960s in church centers associated with evangelism and revival helped by links with some West German Protestant religious communities.

B. Development and Expansion. The later origins in other European countries and the development of CR throughout the continent will be described country by country according to geographical blocs.

1. *The British Isles.* The growth of CR in Britain was slow but steady during the years 1964–70. The main thrust of expansion came from the work of Michael Harper at FT. The FT residential conferences begun in January 1965 featured the best-known teachers in the British movement (Cecil Cousen, Campbell McAlpine, Edgar Trout, Arthur Wallis) and its bimonthly magazine *Renewal* served CR nationally from January 1966. In the first years there was some influence by Pentecostal preachers, but this declined after the mid-1960s, as the two movements settled for largely friendly coexistence rather than close cooperation. The American literature, especially David Wilkerson's *Cross and the Switchblade* (1963) and John Sherrill's *They Speak With Other Tongues* (1964), accelerated the spread of the movement, as did regular tours by David du Plessis and visits by Jean Stone (1964) and Dennis Bennett (1965, 1968).

The initial impact of the movement in Britain was strongest among evangelical Anglicans. At the time of his BHS, Harper was an assistant priest at the prominent Central London evangelical parish of All Souls', Langham Place, then under the leadership of John Stott. The first Anglican parish to become a focal point for CR (from 1963) was St. Mark's, Gillingham, Kent, under John Collins, a former assistant at All Souls. Collins' two assistants, David Watson and David MacInnes, soon became major figures in the movement. Other parishes in which CR had a definite impact by the mid-1960s were St. Andrew's, Chorleywood (under John Perry), and then St. Cuthbert's, York (under David Watson). Stott's opposition to the movement from early 1964 was supported by other evangelical leaders, creating an evangelical-charismatic tension that was only overcome with the joint statement "Gospel and Spirit" in 1977.

Some Anglo-Catholic and more "high church" clergy were involved from quite an early stage (of whom John Gunstone was to become a valued teacher), but the main impact in these circles came in the late 1970s. After the Anglicans, the Baptists were the most affected in the early years, with the main leadership coming from David Pawson, Douglas McBain, Barney Coombs, Harold Owen, Edmund Heddle, and Jim Graham. Headway was slower among the Methodists, though the first denominational initiative in British CR was Charles Clarke's *Newsletter for Methodists Interested in Charismatic Renewal,* begun in 1968.

The first impetus to "restorationist" thinking in Britain among those baptized in the Spirit came from the Devon conferences convened by Lillie and Wallis between 1958 and 1962. Its subsequent development is treated under House Church Movement (HCM). A boost to charismatic revival among Free Church and independent circles was given by the Capel (Surrey) Bible week, held annually from 1970 to 1976. This was initiated by Fred Pride, ex–Plymouth Brethren, who had organized the evangelical Abinger Convention for many years and now saw in the Capel Bible week its charismatic successor. Capel brought together a wide spectrum of non-Anglican charismatics: later Restoration leaders like Bryn Jones, Wallis Coates, and Gerald Coates; independent Baptists like Owen and Michael Pusey; teachers like Cousen and McAlpine, who were acceptable in all circles.

The high point of FT's contribution to CR in Britain was from 1971 to 1976, the era of the major conferences: Guildford (1971), Nottingham (1973), and Westminster (1975). These conferences, though small by American standards, were nonetheless national gatherings, giving the movement a higher profile and a stronger sense of identity. They also drew wider European participation, which was significant for later international fellowship. During this period, Harper was first assisted and then succeeded by Thomas Smail, whose arrival strengthened theological reflection on the movement, particularly through the journal *Theological Renewal.*

This same period saw the rise of CCR in Britain. Its beginnings were less influenced by contacts with mainline Protestant charismatics than by circles associated with the young Dominican Simon Tugwell and by their contacts with British Pentecostals, by some priests' contacts with American Catholics, and by the work of an American layman, Bob Balkam, whose work in Britain began with an ecumenical society concentrating on CR. The first Catholic prayer groups developed days of renewal in London around 1970 and a National Service Committee (NSC) in 1973. NSC worked closely with FT with the latter's closure in 1980.

While CCR gave rise to many prayer groups, most of them with fewer than fifty members, CR among Anglicans and Baptists during the 1970s caused some parishes to acquire a reputation as centers of renewal. Besides Watson's work in York (since 1973 at St. Michael-le-Belfrey) and St. Andrew's, Chorleywood, Hereford (now under Bishop David Pytches), CR made a major impact on St. Hugh's, Luton, Bedfordshire (first under Colin Urquhart and later under David Gillett); in St. Philip and St. James, Bristol (under Malcolm Widdecombe); in St. John's, Harborne, Birmingham (under Tom Walker); and (from the late 1970s) at Hawkwell, Essex (under Tony

Higton). St. Aldate's, Oxford, welcomed a charismatic dimension under Michael Green, a development confirmed by the appointment of David MacInnes as Green's successor in 1987. Centers such as Lamplugh House, Yorkshire (under Lawrence Hoyle), and Whatcombe House, Dorset (for a long time led by Reg East), had consistent influence. Some prominent Baptist charismatic churches became independent: Woking (Owen), Basingstoke (Coombs), and Farnborough (Pusey) in effect becoming new restorationist networks alongside the various strands of HCM. Other Baptist churches such as Streatham, London (under McBain), and Gold Hill, Bucks (under Graham), continued within the Baptist Union.

With the voluntary closure of FT at the end of 1980, when its trustees were convinced it had completed its task, the thrust of the movement within the churches shifted to denominational groupings. CR among Anglicans received a boost from an international conference held at Canterbury in July 1978 immediately before the bishops' Lambeth conference. This led the more Anglo-Catholic London Committee for Renewal to launch in 1979 the newsletter *Anglicans for Renewal.* In 1981 the General Synod of the Church of England published their favorable report, *The Charismatic Renewal in the Church of England,* and in the same year Anglican Renewal Ministries was established as a service agency, taking over *Anglicans for Renewal,* retitled *ARM-Link* in 1988. Many Anglican parishes are using a nine-week course called *Saints Alive!* by John Finney and Felicity Lawson to prepare church members for BHS. An Anglican survey conducted in 1984 reported between 1 and 33 percent of parishes per diocese experiencing renewal through CR, with a national average of 7 percent.

The Methodists had produced their own charismatic magazine, *Dunamis,* since 1972, edited for some years by William Davies, Ross Peart, and Charles Clarke. With the growing denominationalization of the movement, the *Dunamis* editors took the initiative in forming the Dunamis Renewal Fellowship in 1983. Both the United Reformed GEAR (Group for Evangelism and Renewal), dating from 1974, and the Baptist for Life and Growth, begun in 1978, are church renewal groups wider than CR, but both have had significant charismatic membership and influence. The movement among Catholics lost impetus in the late 1970s and early 1980s after the initial excitement but in the mid-1980s has acquired new dynamism with the rise of new charismatic communities and the accession of Charles Whitehead as chairman of the NSC. This new lease on life is also shown by the doubling in size of the NSC's bi-monthly *Goodnews.*

The 1980s saw increasing friction between CR in the mainline church traditions and some sections of HCM, particularly those centered on Bradford in Yorkshire and the bi-monthly *Restoration.* The point of contention included *Restoration's* antidenominationalism and accusations of "sheep-stealing" and proselytism. Many charismatics from mainline denominations and several local churches (among them some Pentecostal assemblies) joined HCM networks, partly through frustration at the apparent slowness of CR in the older churches, partly by being persuaded that HCM networks offered a more fully biblical pattern of church life. However, not all HCM leaders distanced themselves from CR in the historic churches, and John Noble of Romford has played a major role in the All Saints Celebrations in London, bringing together Spirit-filled believers from many traditions.

The movement's growth in Scotland and Northern Ireland was somewhat slower. After an initial flurry of charismatic life in the Motherwell area in Scotland (1962–64), conferences on the movement were held at Crieff (1966) and Dunblane (1967), but the death in 1974 of D. P. Thomson, the founder of St. Ninian's Lay Training Centre at Crieff, deprived the movement of a respected leader. Various ministers in the Church of Scotland and the Free churches were baptized in the Spirit, but the Scottish movement lacked a focus for many years. The Fountain Trust's activities in Scotland increased in the mid-1970s with more regular teaching conferences, while in 1974 their link-man, David Black, a Baptist minister, launched Scottish Churches Renewal, which he directed, editing its bulletin, until 1980. CCR in Scotland was slower developing, with a National Service Committee being formed in 1977, but the participation of Bishop Maurice Taylor of Galloway and their magazine, *The Vine,* produced by the Risen Christ community in Glasgow, has provided a more solid base for the movement. The Scottish Episcopal Renewal Fellowship was formed in 1982 under the leadership of Duncan Sladden.

In Ireland, CR among Protestants was found at least by 1963, when a Presbyterian missionary in India, David McKee, was baptized in the Spirit while on furlough in Belfast. Some Elim Pentecostal pastors helped other ministers to receive BHS. Around 1968 CR became more visible among Northern Irish Protestants, with the arrival of Tom Smail from Scotland as minister at Whiteabbey Presbyterian Church in Belfast. The Hollywood Fellowship (Pentecostal) under Keith Gerner had much involvement with the new charismatics.

CCR in Ireland began in Dublin in early 1972 at a meeting addressed by Smail and an Irish Catholic priest, then working in England, Fr. Joe McGeady. Several other Irish Catholics received BHS around this time through American contacts. In its origins, Irish CR was notably ecumenical, and in 1974 a national committee of four Catholics and two Protestants was formed; no other such committee existed anywhere in the world. In the strife-torn north of Ireland, CR aroused great hope in being the first grassroots movement to touch both sides of the religious divide. The CR New Year conference in Belfast remains the only major ecumenical event in the province with popular participation. The ecumenical dimension has been strongly supported by the Christian Renewal Centre at Rostrevor, County Down, founded by Cecil Kerr in 1974, with an emphasis on reconciliation.

However, the rapid growth of CR among Catholics in the south led to the organization of

The ACTS '86 Conference filled this auditorium in Birmingham, England.

national conferences in Dublin beginning in 1974. Although Protestant speakers were invited, these conferences were not organized by the national committee but by Catholics only, and in Eire the earlier ecumenical dimension became largely lost. The Light of Christ community in Dublin, initially led by Fr. Martin Tierney and Tom Flynn, helped to host the larger internation-al CCR conference in Dublin in 1978 and to produce the CCR monthly *New Creation*. In a strongly Catholic country with a less secularized media, the Dublin conference attracted more attention than such events in other places. CCR in Ireland has declined somewhat in the mid-1980s, though some small covenant communities have developed and show signs of increasing impact.

2. *West-Central Europe*. Initial trends toward Holy Spirit revival in the German churches were particularly associated with new communities, such as the Mary Sisters in Darmstadt (see Schlink, Basilea), the Jesus Brüderschaft, and the Julius Schniewindhaus near Magdeburg. Some openness to the spiritual gifts occurred among those groups who were aware of the nineteenth-century healing ministry of J. C. Blumhardt. The influence of these renewal centers and the impact of the movement have been stronger in East Germany (GDR) than in the West (FRG). For GDR see below under Eastern Europe.

CR in FRG has been marked from the start by a strongly theological interest. The first major gatherings began in 1965; these were the ecumen-ical Königstein conferences near Frankfurt on the theme "Church and Charisma." These conferences were as much theological explorations as pastoral or evangelistic expositions. In 1968 a residential community for Christian Unity was formed at Schloss Craheim by the leaders mainly responsible for the Königstein conferences—namely Arnold Bittlinger and R. F. Edel (Lutheran), Wilhard Becker and Siegfried Grossman (Baptist), and Eugen Mederlet (Catholic). For virtually the next decade Schloss Craheim was the focal point for CR in FRG, with Bittlinger as main author and Edel as publisher.

CCR in FRG came from two main sources: (1) a visit of Fr. Herb Schneider of Manila, Philip-pines, to Innsbruck, Austria, in 1971 and (2) the meeting of Fr. Hubertus Tommek of West Berlin with some American charismatics in Lyon, France, and receiving BHS in Grenoble at Pente-cost 1972. Since the mid-1970s, there have been two contrasting strands of the renewal movement among Catholics in FRG. The larger strand has been marked by the well-known Paderborn theo-logian, Heribert Mühlen, originally influenced by his participation in the Catholic-Pentecostal dia-logue. Mühlen has promoted *Charismatische Gem-einde Erneuerung* (CGE), parish renewal led by the clergy and based on the renewal of the sacraments, expounded in the magazine *Erneuer-ung in Kirche und Gesellschaft*. Mühlen distin-guishes CGE from CCR, which he sees as theologically "Neo-Pentecostal." The lesser strand—led by Tommek, Otto Knoch, and Nor-bert Baumert—identifies with worldwide CCR and publishes *Rundbrief für Charismatische Er-neuerung in der Katholischen Kirche*. By the mid-1980s, however, the contrast between CGE and CCR was less marked, a welcome change that was due in part to the rise of new leaders in CGE and to the work of the theological commission for CGE established by the West German bishops.

CR among Protestants in the state churches of FRG, notably stronger in Bavaria than in the northern provinces, has been influenced by the CGE model, with a leadership role being taken by Wolfram Kopfermann, whose church (St. Peter's, Hamburg) has been a center of renewal since 1978. Other centers of parish renewal in the West German Evangelical Church are Bendorf am Rhein (under Peter Gleiss) and Herschweiler-Pettersheim (under Günter Moll). The CGE pattern has also been followed by many Catholics and Protestants in Austria and Switzerland. In German-speaking Switzerland, the *Albanarbeit*, a charismatic parish in the Reformed Church, under Johannes Cswalina, exercises a strong influence. Other Reformed CR centers are Calvin House in Biel (under Markus Jakob) and the Basileia Group in the Johanneskirche in Bern under Marcel Dietler. Dietler was often the Swiss representative at European CR meetings. In Austria, the main CGE leader has been Msgr. Johann Koller, pastor of a major parish in Vienna.

Independent centers exercising an important influence in FRG have been Jesus-Haus in Düsseldorf, led by Gerhard Bially, which produces the magazine *Charisma*, and the organization Projektion J, founded by Günter Oppermann. Projektion J introduced John Wimber and his "Signs and Wonders" message into Germany.

In France, a charismatic movement within the French Reformed Church arose in the early 1930s in the Ardèche revival. It was associated with the preaching of the Pentecostal missionary Douglas Scott and the leadership of Louis Dallière. Although Dallière became disillusioned with Pentecostal sectarianism, his ecumenical charismatic vision found its expression in the Union de Prière, formed after World War II; however, the beginnings of CR proper in France did not stem from this source. Beginning in 1968 several Protestant pastors received BHS through contact with Pentecostals, particularly Clément le Cossec and the evangelical center at Carhaix in Brittany. In 1971 a significant meeting was held at Charleville in northeast France with Protestant pastors from France and Belgium. At this meeting the American Presbyterian J. Rodman Williams presided. Links between UP and the new wave of CR were established especially through Thomas Roberts, Arnold Bremond, and Jean-Daniel Fischer. In 1971 in the Protestant center "La Porte Ouverte" near Châlon-sur-Saône, Roberts was instrumental in beginning an annual charismatic conference, which within a few years became one of the more important ecumenical teaching gatherings in Western Europe.

The beginnings of CR among French Catholics occurred through a visit to France of Jean-Paul Régimbal of Quebec and through individual French visitors to the U.S. Xavier le Pichon, a layman from Brest, and Albert de Monléon, a young Dominican theologian, both encountered CCR during visits to America. French CCR particularly dates from a meeting near Paris in February 1972. The meeting was attended by Pierre Goursat and Martine Lafitte, who became the founders of the Emmanuel community. CCR's rapid spread in the years 1972–75 was aided by the translation of American literature, especially the Ranaghans' book, *Catholic Pentecostals*. The French movement in those years was notably ecumenical, with two important meetings in 1973, a theological consultation at Montpelier, and a conference for leaders at Viviers; organized by UP; presided over by Roberts; and addressed by du Plessis, Harper, Bittlinger, and the Catholic Val Gaudet. At this Viviers conference, the UP conviction about the centrality of Israel in God's purposes was manifest, and this emphasis has since influenced much of French CR.

The movement among Protestants has been strongest in Alsace, aided by the influence of J. D. Fischer of Mulhouse (d. 1983) and the current leadership of Kurt Maeder in Strasbourg. Besides the Porte Ouverte conventions, an important center for CR among French Protestants is the largely Baptist group called the Pierre Vivante community in Lille, led by David Berly. This community is well known for its television work. Although charismatics have not been welcomed enthusiastically by the major French Protestant denominations, a consultation organized in 1984 by the Protestant Federation of France on the place of CR in church life has led to some reconciliation and more positive attitudes.

CCR has had more impact in France than in other European countries, with some 500,000 participants. Many communities have arisen (see CHARISMATIC COMMUNITIES), and the urban communities have exercised a strong leadership in the national movement. The shrine at Paray-le-Monial in central France, long associated with devotion to the Sacred Heart of Jesus, has been rejuvenated through becoming a center for CCR, with a succession of teaching conferences each summer. Another pilgrimage center at Ars has also had an increasing charismatic presence. The magazines *Il est Vivant!* (published by Emmanuel in Paris from 1975), *Tychique* (more scholarly, though not technical, published by Chemin Neuf from 1977), and *Feu et Lumière* (published by the Lion de Juda community since 1983) are of an impressive quality. The movement has been taken more seriously by more Catholic theologians in France than elsewhere, these theologians being both sympathetic observers (such as Yves Congar) and participants (such as René Laurentin, Jean-Claude Sagne, Albert de Monleon, and Juan-Miguel Garrigues). A positive report on CR was made to the Catholic bishops in 1982 by Msgr. Marcus, bishop of Nantes, and many French bishops have entrusted significant pastoral responsibilities to CR groups, particularly in the major communities. This greater church acceptance has been accompanied by some loss in ecumenical expression, with some disappointment among Protestant charismatics earlier excited by the ecumenical beginnings. The major ecumenical thrust in French CCR comes from the Chemin Neuf community centered in Lyon, though the intercessory emphases of the Lion de Juda community are almost identical with the aims of UP (conversion of souls, the restoration of Israel, unity of Christians, Parousia).

The charismatic movement in Holland was associated from an early date with the magazine *Vuur*, edited by Wim Verhoef and described as an "ecumenical monthly for revival." The 1958 Dutch campaign of the healing evangelist T. L. Osborn gave a further impetus to CCR. Important for reaching ministers in the historic churches were the visits of du Plessis, who as a native Afrikaans-speaker was able to preach without an interpreter. It was at a du Plessis meeting in Utrecht in 1965 that Fr. Jos Biesbrouck, later prominent in CCR in the Low Countries, was baptized in the Spirit.

In 1972, following the European leaders' meeting at Schloss Craheim, three organizations (*Vuur*, Oase, and the Near East Mission) joined forces to form the "Charismatische Werkgemeenschap Nederland" (CWN; Dutch Charismatic Working Fellowship). The Near East Mission soon left but was replaced by the Dutch CCR. The central role of CWN has resulted in the Dutch movement being more strongly ecumenical than in many other countries, though in the 1980s there has been greater ecumenical reticence on the part of some Catholic charismatics.

In recent years, CR has made the most impact on the Re-reformed churches, the most Calvinist groupings, and their national organization has established a committee for official relationships with CWN. Besides Verhoef, the most prominent leader in CR among Protestants is Willem (Wim) van Dam of Geldorp. The parachurch movement Youth With a Mission (YWAM) has also had considerable impact in Holland, especially through the ministry of Floyd McClung.

The movement in Holland was always rather theological (Verhoef being theologically qualified) and attracted the attention of a few theologians—e.g., Hendrik Berkhof (Reformed), J. Veenhof (Re-reformed), and Piet Schoonenberg (Catholic). Since 1978, the CWN theological commission has produced the quarterly *Bulletin voor Charismatische Theologie*.

CR in French-speaking Belgium was primarily influenced from France. Belgian CCR has been marked with the involvement and influence of Cardinal Léon-Joseph Suenens, Catholic Primate of Belgium (1961–79). Suenens, whose episcopal motto was *"In Spiritu sancto"* (In the Holy Spirit), first encountered CCR in the U.S. in 1972. For several years he sent Belgian priests to the U.S. to learn more about the movement and appointed Fr. Paul Lebeau his theological assistant for CCR. At Suenens's invitation, the International Catholic Charismatic Renewal Office (IC-CRO) was established in Brussels, and a community was formed in Brussels under Ralph Martin and Stephen Clark from the Word of God community, Ann Arbor, Michigan. This association did not last, with transatlantic differences proving too strong. CCR in Belgium has received the strong backing of Suenens's successor, Cardinal Godfried Danneels.

3. *Eastern Europe*. CR in Eastern Europe exists in widely varied conditions of harassment and persecution. Relatively greater freedom exists in GDR, Poland, Hungary, and Yugoslavia, though state regulations prohibit all unofficial church gatherings. More information is available about these countries than for the other Communist lands of Eastern Europe, in which all church life is tightly restricted and often forcibly suppressed. Especially for the latter it is more difficult to speak of a movement, for Christians baptized in the Spirit have little opportunity for fellowship and are often forced to live their faith in isolation.

Around 1962–63, instances of CR occurred in the GDR in two parishes that were also retreat centers: Grosshartmannsdorf (under Christoph Richter) and Bräunsdorf (under Gerhard Küttner). These centers, together with the Julius Schniewindhaus at Schönebeck (under Bernhard Jansa) and the parish center at Slate (under Erwin Pähl), became the focal points for CR in GDR. It is now estimated that four hundred Protestant pastors are participants, about 10 percent of the clergy of the Protestant (Lutheran) churches.

The movement in the GDR, which follows the CGE pattern of parish renewal, has given rise to more thorough theological analysis and reflection than in any other country, especially through the work of Gottfried Rebner and Paul Toaspern. A series of theological studies on the movement in the GDR was issued in the late 1970s (part of one document is in McDonnell).

The CGE model of renewed parish congregations without separate charismatic structures has found acceptance in the GDR, Poland, and Yugoslavia. In GDR there are many hundreds of prayer and Bible groups in private houses as steps to renewed parishes. Since 1976 many renewed Christians meet at the annual Interconfessional Conference on Spiritual Renewal of the Church (*Interkonfessionelle Konferenz für geistliche Gemeindeerneuerung*) in East Berlin, attended by eight hundred participants in 1987. There are also annual pastors' conferences in several locations. International contacts and imported literature are much valued, due to state restrictions in GDR, where only one book on CR has been published (by the theological department of the Evangelical churches).

In Poland the way was prepared by a visit of the American music group *The Living Sound*, who were welcomed by the then archbishop of Krakow, Cardinal Wojtyla. The first charismatic groups among Catholics date from 1975 (Poznan) and 1976 (Warsaw), springing from people who had encountered the movement in America or Western Europe.

CCR's spread in Poland has been much aided by the Oasis renewal movement, known since 1976 as Light-Life. In 1977 the Catholic University of Lublin held its annual theological week on CR, the first occasion on which the future Pope John Paul II met active participants in CCR from the West. This visit was the occasion for the founder of Light-Life, Fr. Franciszek Blanchnicki, who was already in touch with Campus Crusade and YWAM, to enlist help from CCR. As a result many Light-Life members took part in Life in the Spirit seminars and received BHS. From this point, CCR in Poland spread more rapidly as a result of its permeation of the Light-Life movement, which has 50,000 committed members and has influenced even more Polish people.

In Hungary, CR among Reformed Christians had begun by the early 1970s, and in the mid-1970s among Catholics. In both cases, Hungarian charismatics encountered opposition. Among Protestants there was initial conflict between "revival" Evangelicals and charismatics and a hostile reception from church leaders. Now the Reformed Church does not promote CR but tolerates it. CR leaders meet monthly. Among Catholics, CR found the greatest welcome among the Basic Communities led by Fr. Bulanyi; these communities encountered difficulties with the hierarchy on other grounds—e.g., pacifism.

In Czechoslovakia, repression of church life has been persistently strong. CR has been strongest in Prague; however, there are more and more prayer groups all over the country among Lutherans, Reformed, and Catholics. There are increasing contacts between CR in FRG, Hungary, and Czechoslovakia. Among Catholics, there has been some influence from Poland.

In Soviet Russia, charismatic faith is mostly represented by various types of Pentecostal Christianity. There are known to be some Lutheran charismatics in Latvia and Estonia, mostly influenced from Scandinavia. In the central Soviet republics, there is evidence of CR arising in some Protestant groups—e.g., Baptists—but any corporate expression of charismatic fellowship tends to lead to expulsion and the formation of independent churches.

4. *Scandinavia.* CR in the Scandinavian countries has arisen and developed in ways particular to each country. In general, it was later arriving than in Western Central Europe, and the movement burgeoned in the 1970s rather than in the 1960s. Pentecostal influence on the movement has been somewhat stronger than in the rest of Europe.

In Denmark, CR began when Michael Harry, an English doctor working in Denmark, was baptized in the Spirit after attending the FGBMFI international convention in London in 1965. In the late 1960s and early 1970s Harry organized visits to Denmark by Harper and Cousen, and this helped to spread the movement. The first surge was in western areas of the country, but the movement lacked integration in the state church because of the absence of Lutheran pastors, and some leaders were rebaptized in Pentecostal churches. From the early 1970s, some Lutheran pastors became involved, and by the late 1970s some forty to fifty were active in the movement. For some years CR in the Copenhagen area was more ecumenical, but in 1981 charismatic leaders in Copenhagen and the rest of Zealand formed the Spirit and Light group to focus CR in the state church.

Finland was one of the last European countries to be reached by CR. The beginnings go back to a 1971 conference with Harper and Harry, but the movement did not became fully established in Finland until 1977 when Pentecostal preacher Niilo Yli-Vainio drew many Lutherans to his meetings and did not seek to undermine their church affiliation. In 1978 a coordination committee for the "Spiritual Renewal of the Church" was formed. Since then, CR has grown faster and more evenly in Finland than in the rest of Scandinavia, with 173 state-church parishes reporting its presence by 1983. A prominent Lutheran leader has been Olli Valtonen, a pastor who became well-known in Finnish television and edits *Sana,* an evangelistic magazine that has penetrated the secular market. The movement in the state church is seen in continuity with the distinctively Finnish revival movements, Lutheran and Pietist, and has cooperated closely with evangelical and Neo-Pietistic organizations. It has not been at ease with the terminology of BHS, and like OASE in Norway (see below) the movement has spoken of the filling of the Spirit as a continuation and renewal of God's work in water baptism. Glossolalia has been less prominent than healing, with indications that perhaps one-tenth of Lutheran participants in Finland speak in tongues.

In Norway the emergence of CR is generally dated to the large FGBMFI convention held in Oslo in October 1970. At this convention a well-known Lutheran pastor, Hans-Jakob Frøen, testified to his charismatic experience. However, the way had been prepared in previous years, on the one hand by the ministry of the independent Pentecostal evangelist Aril Edvardsen, who had already been reaching many people within the majority state church, and on the other hand by the writings of an early twentieth-century theologian and revival preacher, Ole Hallesby, who taught the need for a postbaptismal "filling with the Spirit." Following the FGBMFI convention, Frøen formed an organization, *Agape,* in 1971 to promote charismatic revival in Norway. The *Agape* society was somewhat influenced by the FT model in Britain, though Frøen was not as committed to all aspects of Lutheranism as Harper was to the Church of England. For some years, the main thrust of CR for Norwegian adults was provided by Frøen through *Agape* and by Edvardsen through his center at Kvinesdal. However, in 1971–72 groups influenced by the Jesus movement were formed, reaching many young people: the Peace of God community in Oslo, YWAM, and Young Vision; however, none of these currents really penetrated the Lutheran state church, which itself has a tradition of revival outside the parish structures.

Moves toward a more integrated Lutheran renewal began among students at the Free Faculty of Theology at Oslo as they were influenced by Hallesby's theology of the Spirit. A conference convened by H. C. Lier and Jens-Petter Jorgensen in February 1977 was a turning point, leading the one hundred people who were present through a "Holy Spirit seminar." The success of the seminar led to further conferences and in 1980 to the formation of the OASE Foundation with Jorgensen as chairman; the purpose of the Foundation was renewal in the Lutheran churches. OASE conferences have been held in southern Norway each summer, with from five to seven thousand participants. The OASE teaching does not use baptismal language of the initial charismatic experience, neither does it link this with glossolalia. It is estimated that there are about 50,000 charismatics in the Lutheran churches.

In Sweden, CR in the state church owes much to the indigenous Pentecostal groupings, such as the Baptist Orebro Mission with its annual conferences and to impulses from outside Sweden, such as that of the English evangelist Harry Greenwood. These early influences were aided later by the translation of many books from English originals. The movement nationally received a major boost from the ecumenical conference at Stockholm in October 1972 under the leadership of David du Plessis, Harper, the Catholic George di Prizio, and the Pentecostal pioneer Lewi Pethrus. CR in Sweden has had particular impact in the southwest of the country, where the bishop of Gothenburg, Bertil Gartner, has encouraged the movement led by Pastor Carl Gustaf Stenback, with many pastors being affected. From the late 1970s the retired bishop, Helge Fosseus, working from a significant conference center, has given further focus for CR in the state church.

In Iceland, a particular impact has been made in the Lutheran parish. The movement here was led by Halldor Grondal with help from YWAM.

5. The Latin Countries. In Italy the beginnings of CCR occurred in late 1970, through American students in Rome and a Canadian priest, Val Gaudet, who had received BHS after a meeting with the Dutch Fr. Biesbrouck. During 1971 regular prayer meetings began at the Jesuit Gregorian University, led from 1971 to 1973 by the American Francis Martin. Meeting in Rome, this English-language prayer group with its international membership rapidly became an instrument for diffusing CCR throughout the world. The American Jesuit theologian Francis Sullivan attended the meetings almost from the beginning, having been initially invited by church authorities who were concerned about the movement. Although the first Italian Catholic charismatic prayer group in Rome began in early 1972, CCR in Italy did not gather momentum until the late 1970s following the International Conference in Rome on Pentecost Day in 1975 and the participation of respected priest-theologians, such as Robert Faricy and Domenico Grasso (who, like Sullivan, were professors at the Gregorian University) and the patristic scholar Raniero Cantalamessa of Milan, who soon after was appointed special preacher at the Vatican.

The bi-monthly *Alleluja* began publication in 1976 and prompted the formation of the Italian National Service Committee for CCR and the annual conferences held in Rimini since 1978. The Service Committee has organized Italian CCR with regional councils and numerous delegates for specific tasks. Since 1985 it has produced its own monthly *Rinnovamento nello Spirito Santo*. *Alleluja* still continues as an independent venture; so does another magazine, *Risuscito*, produced since 1977 by Comunita Maria, a group founded by Alfredo and Jacqueline Ancellotti. *Risuscito* has from the beginning maintained its own independence from *Alleluja* and later official CCR publications. Pope John Paul II has twice spoken in encouraging terms to large gatherings of Italian Catholic charismatics in St. Peter's, Rome (1980, 1986). CCR in Italy numbered about eight hundred prayer groups, totaling some 70,000 to 80,000 participants. In Italy there has been virtually no ecumenical dimension to CR, with Italian Pentecostals mostly rejecting any possibility of authentic Pentecostal life within the Roman church.

CCR in Spain appeared around 1973–74 when several prayer groups began to meet in Salamanca and Madrid. The first steps toward national coordination occurred in 1976, with a leaders' conference in Salamanca, the formation of a national service committee (led by Fr. Manuel Casanova, baptized in the Spirit in India in 1972) and the beginning of the bi-monthly *Koinonia* (initially edited by Fr. Luis Martin of Barcelona). CCR in Spain has grown steadily since that time, with the beginnings of small communities in Madrid, Granollers (Barcelona), and Saragossa. In 1987 there were 275 CCR prayer groups in Spain, with some 20,000 participants.

The first CCR prayer meeting was held in Portugal in late 1974. As in Spain, national organization began in 1976 with the formation of a service committee and the launching of a bi-monthly periodical, *Pneuma*, edited by Fr. José da Lapa of Lisbon.

6. Overview. From the brief national summaries it can be seen that the 1970s saw the blossoming of CR in non-Communist Europe, from the early 1970s in the north to the mid-to-late 1970s in the south. As in America, the spread of CR to the Roman Catholic church provided an added impetus for the whole movement. This added impetus came first from the fascination of the very idea of "Catholic Pentecostals" and was strongly supported by the Catholic tendency to organize the movement, with the emerging patterns of national conferences in many countries.

In the 1980s there has been a definite concern to relate CR to the historic traditions. This is evident not only in CCR but also among Anglicans in Britain and Lutherans in Germany and Scandinavia. This has led to an acceleration of renewal in Protestant churches where CR is mainly parish-based, though much depends on the quality of national leadership and often on the rise of renewed congregations which can serve as models for the wider church. Among Catholics, for whom CR is mostly organized in prayer groups, not all of them parish-based, fuller integration with church structures has not always resulted in greater penetration. In countries with established charismatic communities, the main thrust of CCR has come from their midst, as such communities have the resources to provide the leadership, the personnel, and the continuity needed for expansion.

C. Developments at Continental Level. The idea of gathering European leaders in CR seems to have come first to J. Rodman Williams and took shape during the sabbatical year he spent at St. John's, Collegeville, Minnesota, with Larry Christenson and Arnold Bittlinger in 1971–72. As a result, the first European Charismatic Leaders' Conference was held at Schloss Craheim, West Germany, in 1972, with sixteen countries represented. These conferences have been held regularly ever since, generally at intervals of two years. At the third meeting in 1975, three theses were adopted on the theme "Charismatic Renewal and the Unity of the Church" (printed in *Presence, Power, Praise,* ed. Kilian McDonnell, II, 14). Between 1976 and 1984, the meetings were organized and chaired jointly by Smail and Lebeau. The British churches, together with those from the Low Countries, France, West Germany, and Switzerland, have generally been well represented, Scandinavia intermittently and the Mediterranean countries rather poorly.

The vision of a European-wide gathering to celebrate jointly the work and power of the Holy Spirit was given to Thomas Roberts in 1978. Pursued at the leaders' meeting in Strasbourg in 1980, this vision became reality in 1982, when twenty thousand Christians from many different backgrounds, mostly charismatic, came together at Strasbourg to celebrate "Pentecost over Europe." This conference seems to have had an effect in Europe similar to that of the 1977 Kansas City conference in the U.S., deepening the sense of the ecumenical grace of CR and leading to a call for a common humbling before the Lord in repentance and mutual reconciliation.

A large ecumenical European charismatic conference called "Acts 1986" was held at Birmingham, England, in July 1986, following an initiative by Michael Harper and the formation of a European committee. Whereas Strasbourg 1982 was primarily made up of French and German speakers, Birmingham 1986 had a participation that was mostly English-speaking, though significant groups came from Scandinavia, especially Finland, and from Hungary.

In 1988 a larger European Charismatic Leaders Conference was held in Berlin, Germany, bringing together the leaders from the older meetings begun in Schloss Craheim and the members of the Acts 1986 committee.

III. Its Development in Latin America. CR has been less researched and analyzed in Latin America than in North America and Europe. It is easier to obtain information about CCR than about CR among Protestants as CCR has developed national and continental structures that interact with the International Catholic Charismatic Renewal (ICCRO) in Rome. The distinction between CR among Protestants and in the Pentecostal movement is more difficult to make in Latin America than elsewhere for reasons that will emerge in the following short survey.

A. Protestant Beginnings. Brazil was the first Latin American country to experience widespread outbreaks of Pentecostal phenomena within historic church traditions (aside from the patterns at the beginning of the Pentecostal movement, as in Chile). There were stirrings in Brazil in the mid-1950s, just as there were in America and Europe at that time, with small groups of praying Christians seeking a deeper spiritual life. Many found help and encouragement from a Southern Baptist missionary, Rosalee Appleby, who was increasingly burdened for world revival. Public preaching of BHS began in some Baptist circles in 1958, particularly in Belo Horizonte, under José de Nascimento, and as a result Baptist pastors and people were being baptized in the Spirit. By the

mid-1960s Pentecostal outbreaks were also being reported among the Methodists, the Presbyterians, the Congregationalists, and the Seventh-day Adventists. All these experiences of renewal (the designation preferred by these Christians) attracted opposition within their denominations. The first to be expelled from the parent body were the charismatic Baptists, who formed themselves into the Igreja do Renovacao (Church of Renewal). Subsequent conflicts led to other new denominations—the Igreja Metodista Wesleyana (Wesleyan Methodist Church), the Igreja Crista Presbiteriana do Brasil (Presbyterian Christian Church of Brazil), and the Igreja Adventista da Promessa (Adventist Church of the Promise). These denominations tend to prefer the language of renewal or of restoration rather than being labeled Pentecostal. Together they probably now account for 140,000 or more committed Christians.

In Colombia, a spontaneous movement began around 1960 in the north Colombian forest under the leadership of Victor Landero, with manifestation of spiritual gifts following intense spiritual seeking and reading of the Book of Acts. Like many other such groups in Latin America, the assemblies linked with Landero call themselves *renovacion,* reject the label "Pentecostal," and are affiliated with the Association of Evangelical Churches of the Caribbean, a non-Pentecostal body.

In Argentina, CR began among the Hermanos Libros (the Open Brethren segment of the Plymouth Brethren) in a prayer meeting in the Buenos Aires home of business executive Alberto Darling in February 1967, helped by the ministry of Keith Bentson. Soon after, a missionary with Pentecostal experience, Orville Swindoll, conducted a mission in an independent church in Villa Soldati, pastored by Jorge Himitian. The success of this mission led to fusion of the Darling and Himitian meetings, which became a focus for Pentecostal renewal. In the ensuing expansion, important teaching and guidance roles were played by Swindoll, Bentson, Ed Miller of the Peniel Bible Institute in La Plata, and Juan Carlos Ortiz, pastor of Central Assembly of God Church in Buenos Aires. Swindoll's influence was increased by his magazine, *Vision Celestial.* The Baptists and the Mennonites soon saw pastors and congregations being affected by this movement that was being called *Renovacion* (Renewal). The charismatic Brethren, who numbered five thousand within three years, were forced out of their fellowship, and the movement was denounced as "spiritistic." Among the Brethren who received BHS was Daniel Somoza, who had edited the main Brethren magazine for many years. Opposition also arose among the Baptists, who expelled some pastors. One former Baptist prominent in CR was Alberto Motessi. As a result of this opposition, the development of CR among Argentinian Protestants was to be primarily in the independent sector, with the discipleship teaching of Ortiz playing an important part in the growth of many assemblies.

An Anglican missionary to Chile with the South American Missionary Society, Kath Clarke, was baptized in the Spirit while on furlough in England in the mid-1960s, and on her return she was the instrument of charismatic blessing in the seminary where she taught. Asked to desist from Pentecostal practices by the church authorities, Clarke complied, but the Spirit of Pentecost was already spreading and soon touched David Pytches, first assistant bishop and then bishop of the Anglican diocese of Chile, Bolivia, and Peru. Also in Chile during this period, CR began among Methodists around the city of Tome.

B. The Ecumenical Period. The beginnings of CCR in Latin America flowed from a visit paid to Colombia by Harald Bredesen and an ecumenical team of charismatics from North America. During this visit F. Rafael Garcia-Herreros, who was well-known in Colombia for his TV program, *El Minuto de Dios*, was baptized in the Spirit. In the early 1960s, Fr. Garcia had launched the construction of a new estate to rehouse the homeless in an area then on the edge of Bogota. Fr. Garcia communicated his new-found enthusiasm for the Lord to a young priest, Diego Jaramillo, who in 1970 rejoined him to work in the housing development that became known as *El Minuto de Dios*. Jaramillo later became a prominent leader in Latin American CCR and its main international spokesman.

One of the first centers of CR in Central America was the Templo Biblico of the Evangelical Association of Bible Churches in San Jose, Costa Rica. The Christians here experienced Pentecostal blessing through the invited ministries of the Argentinian pastors Alberto Motessi and Juan Carlos Ortiz and the unexpected visits of the U.S. Catholics Francis MacNutt and Barbara Shlemon. In Guatemala, Timothy Rovenstine was instrumental in bringing Catholics and Protestants together in the beginnings of CR, aided by visiting members of FGBMFI and of the Word of God community, Ann Arbor, Michigan, as well as MacNutt.

In the early to mid 1970s this ecumenical character marked CR in the Latin American countries, especially in Central America. A pattern repeated in many places was the success of teams of charismatic Protestants and charismatic Catholics working together. Of particular importance was the teaming up of the Catholic Francis MacNutt with a Methodist, Joe Petree. In 1970 they visited Costa Rica, Peru, and Bolivia, along with another Methodist, Tommy Tyson. This unprecedented combination opened many doors and attracted great interest, MacNutt being invited to speak in an evangelical seminary and at Templo Biblico in San Jose, Costa Rica. Ecumenical teams with some of these same men visited Ecuador, Peru, and Bolivia in early 1971 and Costa Rica later the same year. Another ecumenical team, with Catholic priests Jim Burke and George di Prizio, plus Petree and a Protestant businessman from North Carolina, conducted a retreat in Puerto Rico in November 1971. At this retreat Fr. Tom Forrest, then working in Aguas Buenas, was baptized in the Spirit, an event that let loose a flood of charismatic blessing on the island. CCR also began with explosive power in the Dominican Republic, where the French Canadian missionary Fr. Emilian Tardif returned from sick leave in 1974, healed and baptized in the Spirit.

The First Latin American Renewal Congress was held in Buenos Aires in 1972, bringing together eighty leaders, mostly Protestant, at a Catholic retreat center; but within a year the second congress at Porto Alegre, Brazil, drew two thousand participants. The first international CCR meeting occurred early in 1973 when twenty-three leaders representing eight Latin American countries—priests, sisters and one Baptist—met in Bogota, Colombia, and laid the foundations for ECCLA (Encuentro Carismatico Catolico Latino-Americano), a body that has since developed its own structures and holds regular congresses.

Latin American CR is characterized by a populist enthusiasm that has gathered huge crowds to football stadia and other public places. Such gatherings tended to attract the masses of every religious background and those with none, whatever the denomination of the visiting speaker. Many TV evangelists from the U.S., such as Rex Humbard and Jimmy Swaggart, have held such campaigns. One remarkable instance of this populist character was the ministry of a young Catholic, Julio Cesar Ruibal, who was initially converted at a Kathryn Kuhlman meeting in California. Returning to Latin America, he began preaching and praying for the sick, with remarkable results that attracted vast crowds. Between December 1972 and February 1973, over 200,000 people were touched by God during Ruibal's virtually unplanned three-day campaigns in La Paz, Santa Cruz, and Cochabamba, Bolivia. In Colombia he appeared on the Catholic TV program *El Minuto de Dios,* and when he spoke in Medellin, the soccer stadium was filled. Ruibal's ministry belongs to the ecumenical beginnings, for his campaigns initially received support from Catholics, especially those already in CCR, while inspiring Protestants by his gospel preaching.

Ruibal is but one more dramatic example of a leader in a process that has occurred throughout CCR—namely, that in this grassroots movement of the Holy Spirit, those first finding themselves in positions of ministry and leadership were not all priests but included many lay people with little or no theological and spiritual formation. These lay leaders often found ecumenical contacts with Spirit-filled Christians in other churches much easier to make than did the priests and religious with their traditional Catholic formation. Filled with a desire to know the Scriptures following their BHS, many of these lay leaders welcomed the help that many evangelical Protestants were keen to give them, particularly in Central America. In this situation were sown the seeds of future developments.

C. Separate Development. While Pentecostal-charismatic Christianity has continued to spread in Latin America, both among Catholics and Protestants, it has not preserved the ecumenical openness and hope of its beginnings. The reasons for this are less to be sought in deliberate suppression by unsympathetic church authorities than in the situation of interchurch relations when

Anglican clergymen participating in worship at the charismatic Conference for Spiritual Renewal, Canterbury Cathedral, July 1978.

CR appeared. Unlike North America and Europe, where there had been growing patterns of ecumenical relationship over recent decades, accentuated by Vatican II, in Latin America Catholics and Protestants lacked such frameworks and still viewed each other with suspicion if not outright hostility. Catholics tended to view evangelical Protestants as proselytizing interlopers, luring away their faithful with a simplistic creed, whereas evangelical Protestants would regard Catholics as little better than pagans lost in a morass of superstition.

Faced with this unexpected grassroots ecumenical eruption, the Catholic hierarchy was concerned about the influence of Protestant teachers on lay Catholic leaders, a concern that saw its justification in the generally unecumenical stance of the Evangelicals concerned and their evident antipathy toward the Catholic faith. On the other hand, many Latin American Catholic bishops, particularly in Colombia, Venezuela, and Mexico, were sympathetic to CCR, sensing its potential for spiritual rejuvenation of the Latin American church. The result was a more explicit promotion of CCR, with priests appointed to lead and teach. Especially from the late 1970s, the structuring of CCR throughout the continent proceeded at all levels with regular ECCLA meetings for leaders from all nations, with national and diocesan directors, conferences, and guidelines. Of particu-

lar importance has been the leadership in Colombia, with Bishop Uribe Jaramillo of Sonson Rio Negro and Fr. Diego Jaramillo, then of Bogota. Since 1977 annual charismatic retreats for priests from all Latin America have been held at La Ceja in Bishop Jaramillo's diocese, which has also seen more recently a conference for Latin American bishops on CCR.

The Rome office of ICCRO estimates that in 1987 there were two million Catholic charismatics in twenty-one Latin American countries. The ECCLA VII meeting in Belo Horizonte, Brazil, in 1982 authorized the establishment of a CCR Latin American office in Bogota, Colombia, and decided to initiate meetings of theologians and CCR leaders to study such problem topics as healing and deliverance, as well as the relationship of CCR and social action. Father Diego Jaramillo, who in 1987 was appointed director of ICCRO in Rome, stated at an earlier ICCRO meeting: "The distinguishing characteristic of the Renewal in Latin America is the special effort to incorporate the Renewal into Church structures, and to enter into serious dialogue with priests and bishops." (ICCRO *International Newsletter* 8 [6, November–December 1982]: 1).

In this process of Catholic structuring, many of the pioneer lay leaders were unhappy with the clerical authority provided for them. As a result, numerous charismatic groups formed in the first wave of CCR have not continued within the Roman Catholic church, becoming independent charismatic assemblies under their former lay leaders. Sometimes such groups exist in uneasy tension between their Catholic past and the evangelical Christian world with its suspicions of that background. In Bolivia, the Eklesia Mission stemming from Ruibal's campaigns became independent and is now under a new leader.

One ecumenical bridge in the late 1970s and early 1980s was the John 17:21 Fellowship associated with David du Plessis. The John 17:21 Fellowship was established in Guatemala City after the major earthquake there in 1976. A Latin American branch of John 17:21 coordinated by Robert Thomas of Los Altos, California, worked closely with Fr. Alfonso Navarro and the Catholic Missionaries of the Holy Spirit to form UC-ELAM, the Christian Union for Evangelizing Latin America, with annual conferences in Mexico City. UCELAM teams whose leaders included Bill Finke and Juan Carlos Ortiz spoke in several Latin American countries in the early 1980s.

Among Latin American Protestants it has been estimated that by 1987, 80 to 85 percent were Pentecostal or charismatic. Of those who are not in Pentecostal denominations, only a small percentage are in the historic Protestant denominations (Anglican, Baptist, Lutheran, Methodist, Reformed-Presbyterian, Mennonite). In most of these bodies, charismatic outbreaks have occurred, but where these have led to any coherent charismatic groupings, they have often encountered resistance from church authorities. In many cases the results have been either expulsion or voluntary withdrawal under heavy pressure. Most of these groups formed new denominations, as in Brazil in the 1960s, while far more new indigenous churches of a Pentecostal type grew from scratch. In Latin America, these denominations and assemblies are regarded as Pentecostal, except for a minority of more middle-class bodies that have refused that designation, preferring the language of *Renovacion* or *Renovacao*.

Thus charismatic Protestant Christianity in Latin America outside the major Pentecostal churches is overwhelmingly in the independent sector, unaffiliated with any of the major confessional families. A small percentage is found within the historic churches, particularly the Anglican Communion, in which some bishops endorse, some tolerate, and some oppose CR. In Ecuador the Anglican diocese, which in 1971 had only three congregations catering to expatriates and had grown to over a hundred congregations, saw a remarkable expansion from 1986 following the visits of SOMA teams invited by bishop Adrian Caceres. A majority of the priests in the Ecuador diocese have received BHS, and the influx of converts includes many youth, with a resulting indigenous church of 220 congregations and 16,000 members by 1987.

In Brazil, CR has developed since the late 1970s among a group of independent Lutheran churches in the area of Porto Alegre sparked by the leadership of a former LC-MS pastor, Aloisio Hoffmann. In addition, the Brazilian Lutheran church of German background (Igreja Evangelica da Confissao Luterana no Brasil) has seen since the early 1970s an extensive renewal movement known as *Encontrao*, characterized by evangelism, praise, and healing, though without the CR emphasis on the word-gifts and glossolalia. These movements, like the new Renovacao denominations, are found in more middle-class Brazilian society than the Pentecostal churches.

Among the many independent churches of a charismatic type that have sprung up are the Templo Biblico in San Jose, Costa Rica, and that in Caracas, Venezuela, pastored by Sam Olsen. The church in Caracas is the largest Protestant church in the country. Some independent churches have become charismatic since their original establishment, such as the Union Church in San Jose, Costa Rica. In Argentina the fastest-growing currents outside the Pentecostal churches are flowing from the independent charismatic ministries of evangelist Carlos Anaconida, of Omar Cabrera, and of Pastor Gimenez. While these assemblies and currents are not called charismatic, they are the Latin American equivalent of North American nondenominational CR. That is to say, their differences from denominational Pentecostals lie in their foreign contacts (independents rather than Pentecostals) and in the espousal in many cases of teachings as on discipleship generally suspect among the Pentecostals.

These developments in Latin American CR suggest that the growth of a Catholic movement with little ecumenical contact and of Protestant Pentecostal-charismatic faith mostly outside the mainline denominations is at least partly the result of the absence of prior ecumenical relationships. When CR arrived, neither side had sufficient recognition of the Lord's presence and activity through the others. In this situation, although the charismatic explosion has multiplied basic Christian evangelism, the challenge presented by the Holy Spirit's transcendence of inherited patterns seems to have been more than either side could handle.

IV. Analysis. This analysis is based on the evidence presented by CR in the sense described above. It does not take into account Christian movements with charismatic characteristics and phenomena that arose prior to CR (e.g., various indigenous movements in Africa) and that did not exert any detectable influences on its origins.

A. The Essential Elements in Charismatic Renewal While there are some continental and national differences in CR as to origins, development, emphases, and style, the distinguishing characteristics of the movement are everywhere the same. These common characteristics are evidently the essential elements in CR, not only because they are present wherever CR is found and are there recognized as essentials but also because of their intrinsic importance in the Christian life.

1. Focus on Jesus. CR is everywhere marked by a focus on Jesus Christ. Witnesses to baptism in the Spirit (BHS) constantly refer to an encounter with Jesus, a deeper yielding to Jesus, and a fuller acceptance of Jesus as Lord. This focus on Jesus is expressed in the common conviction that Jesus is the baptizer in the Holy Spirit. The proclamation "Jesus is Lord" has been the most characteristic banner and slogan in CR. All the distinctive elements of the movement subsequently listed are in fact manifestations of the exercise of Jesus' lordship. Thus Jesus is known as the living Lord at the heart of Christian worship, the Lord who speaks in the present, who speaks through the Word, who delivers from evil, who heals now, etc.

2. *Praise.* CR is universally recognized as evoking the praise of God and of his Son Jesus Christ. The first result of the coming of the Holy Spirit in BHS is a flow of praise from within the believer, a verification of John 7:38. As a result, the believer has a new capacity to give glory to God, evident in the spontaneity of charismatic praise and symbolized in the gift of tongues. Together with this flow of praise has come a great explosion of new songs of praise, possibly unparalleled in Christian history.

3. *Love of the Bible.* Despite some Evangelical fears that the charismatic emphasis on experience and on spiritual gifts devalues the Scriptures, CR has been consistently marked by a great love and thirst for the Scriptures. Charismatics are typically Bible-carriers. The widespread accusation that CR is fundamentalist, less true in mainline church renewal than the accusers generally think, itself bears witness to the importance of the Scriptures within CR.

4. *God Speaks Today.* CR is everywhere characterized by the conviction that God speaks to his people, corporately and personally, as directly and as regularly as in the first Christian century. People baptized in the Spirit hear the Lord. They experience a directness of communication and guidance from the Lord in a way that shocks or puzzles, attracts or repels other Christians. This experience of God speaking is experienced as intrinsic to knowing God as a loving Father who converses with his children and opens up his inheritance to them. Although personal messages from the Lord to believers often attract attention, experience in CR in general confirms John 16:13–15, that what God most wants to reveal through the Holy Spirit is his Son and his saving plan for creation centered in Jesus.

5. *Evangelism.* The coming of the Spirit in BHS regularly leads to evangelism. For some, this is an evangelism with a new effectiveness; for others, an inner impulse to evangelize for the first time. Just as Christians baptized in the Spirit have a new capacity to speak freely to God in praise, so they have a new capacity and freedom to speak to others about the Lord.

6. *Awareness of Evil.* The advent of CR in the experience of BHS is typically followed by a new awareness of the reality of Satan and the powers of evil. Charismatics see this as following the pattern of Jesus' own experience, in which the temptations in the wilderness quickly followed his baptism in the Jordan. This awareness has caused deliverance and exorcism to acquire new relevance and usage in CR.

7. *Spiritual Gifts.* The features most readily identifiable as characteristic of CR are the spiritual gifts listed in 1 Corinthians 12:8–10. While this Pauline list specifies nine charismata, the gifts that are most prominent and most discussed in CR are glossolalia, prophecy, and healing. What is new within the mainline churches with the advent of CR is not the occurrence of any of these gifts, but the expectation that they are currently available and the conviction that the gifts as a whole form an intrinsic part of God's equipment of each local church for its mission.

8. *Eschatological Expectation.* CR is generally accompanied by an increased expectancy and longing for the Parousia. While many charismatics think the end of the world will occur in the near future, the more widespread conviction is of the imminence of Christ's return in the sense of history's moving toward its climax, with Christians ardently longing for the completion of all things as they pray, "Come, Lord Jesus."

9. *Spiritual Power.* Power, which is a recognized aspect of charismatic Christianity, has been listed last, as it is in fact a dimension in almost every aspect of CR. The spiritual power that accompanies BHS is manifest in the capacity to praise, in the capacity to evangelize, in all ministries of deliverance and the overcoming of evil, and in the exercise of the spiritual gifts. This power of the Spirit is experienced as a gift of the risen Lord Jesus, flowing from obedience to God's Word and manifested in every form of Christian ministry and service, in Word and in sacrament, in ministries within the body of Christ, and in service to those outside.

While these characteristics are seen as the essential elements of CR, they are universally seen by charismatics as the consequences of the core-experience, most commonly termed the baptism in the Holy Spirit. Thus, while outside observers commonly pay most attention to the visible characteristics, especially the more phenomenally unusual, participants focus on BHS as the most basic characteristic of CR. This is why charismatic testimonies regularly focus on the event of BHS, while other features vary from one testimony to another.

B. A Comparison With the Pentecostal Movement. A comparison of CR with the Pentecostal movement will indicate that these nine elements characterize both movements. The differences concern the framework, both ecclesiastical and theological, in which they occur, the social milieu being most penetrated. It is undeniable that CR, at least in the First World, has made most progress in the white middle-class sectors of society, whereas the Pentecostal movement in its beginnings was largely a proletarian phenomenon among poor people of all colors. However, CR has from the late 1970s made great progress among the churches of the Third World, most dramatically perhaps in Asia, where it is clearly not the preserve of the middle classes. The probable conclusion is that the milieux penetrated by CR are those where the historic churches have their strongest membership.

A comparison of the origins of CR and of the Pentecostal movement shows that the charismatic origins were more diverse than the Pentecostal. There has never been any charismatic equivalent of Azusa Street. In the origins of CR there were many paths by which believers were led to BHS: direct contact with Pentecostals or charismatics already baptized in the Spirit, growing experience of spiritual gifts following rediscovery of the power of God in divine healing, outbreaks of glossolalia in circles praying for revival (more in Europe than in America), Bible studies (especially on the Book of Acts), and sovereign interventions of God among people who knew nothing of Pentecostal blessing. While there are instances of these latter sources in Pentecostal beginnings, they seem to have been more widespread and decisive in the origins of CR.

CR in the mainline denominations did not immediately unleash the missionary drive that characterized Azusa Street and the beginnings of Pentecostalism. In the early stages of CR, the main evangelistic thrust was toward fellow church members to bring them to BHS, rather than toward the pagan and the unchurched. The strongest consistent missionary thrust among charismatics has come from restorationist "nondenominational" circles and from parachurch groups with a strong charismatic membership, such as Operation Mobilization and the Pentecostal-originated YWAM, though in the 1980s some covenant communities with a sizable Catholic membership have developed a strong missionary outreach.

Holiness of life was a much more dominant concern among first-generation Pentecostals than among first-generation charismatics. This aspect reflects the Holiness background of many pioneer Pentecostals, whereas the charismatics have come from a wide variety of church and confessional backgrounds. This difference helps to explain a constant source of Pentecostal suspicion about charismatic authenticity, namely depth of conversion and moral transformation. This concern also reflects a difference between the original Pentecostal pattern of "tarrying for the baptism" with much soul-searching and intensity and the widespread charismatic practice of immediate "praying over" people for BHS. Many charismatics, particularly Catholics, have dealt with this problem by preparing candidates for BHS by teaching and formation courses, often known as Life in the Spirit seminars.

CR has had more sense of the corporate work of the Holy Spirit than has classical Pentecostalism. The widespread conviction that CR is for the renewal of the church recognizes that the coming of the Holy Spirit creates *koinonia* in the body of Christ. This conviction appears to have been strongest among charismatics in the sacramental-liturgical traditions, among the independents of restorationist tendencies who have rediscovered covenant relationships, and among groups like the Mennonites, who have always had a more corporate sense than mainline Evangelicalism has had. CR in these groupings has a stronger sense of the close link manifested in the Pauline Epistles between the spiritual gifts and the corporate life of the body of Christ.

The power to form *koinonia* across confessional boundaries has been more evident in CR than in the Pentecostal movement. Thus CR abounds in examples of spiritual fellowship and bonds arising between Christians traditionally seen as most incompatible. The rise of ecumenical covenant communities is itself a proof of the power of the Spirit to overcome historic barriers. Nonetheless, CR, like the Pentecostal movement, also has a history of division, with doctrinal disputes on discipleship and on modes of baptism, with unresolved conflicts among leaders, with unseemly rivalry and competition. The evidence suggests that the immediate fruit of BHS is reconciliation but that its maintenance is a harder task, requiring the crucifixion of fleshly desires (Gal. 5:24). Where this depth is achieved, the fruit is impressive; where it is not, the promise can give way to scandal.

Both movements have had their share of scandals, magnified in recent times, particularly in America, by enormous budgets and media publicity. The most vulnerable seems to be independent entrepreneurs, because of their independence of church tradition and pastoral supervision. The stronger sense of *koinonia* in some sectors of CR is an important protection against the dangers of moral and doctrinal aberration to which independent and successful Christian ministries are more subject.

Some sectors of CR have seen a close link between the contemporary outpouring of the Holy Spirit and the fulfillment of God's purposes for Israel, a development significantly different from the origins of the Pentecostal movement. This concern was linked with charismatic experience in the French pastor Louis Dallière and UP that he founded, whence it has influenced other French Christians, Catholic (as the Lion de Juda community) and Protestant (especially Thomas Roberts). This burden for Israel has also marked the Evangelical Sisterhood of Mary in Darmstadt, West Germany. A similar concern has arisen among some Protestant charismatics in the Anglo-Saxon world, such as David Pawson in Britain and the American groups associated with the International Christian Embassy in Jerusalem, but it has evoked few echoes among English-speaking Catholics. This development has been connected in the last twenty years with the growth of Messianic Judaism, leading to the formation of synagogues of Jews who have accepted Jesus as the Messiah.

Both the Pentecostal movement and CR have seen the rise of restorationist currents, emphasizing not simply the restoration of the spiritual gifts of 1 Corinthians 12:8–10 but also the fivefold ministries of Ephesians 4:11. However, the restorationist currents have always been minority currents among classical Pentecostals, and the major Pentecostal denominations have tended to view their emphases as dangerous and deviant. While CR in the historic denominations has adopted a similar caution, many nondenominational segments of the movement have welcomed the restorationist message. Thus the restorationist current arising within CR has become much stronger in the 1970s and 1980s than it ever was in the Pentecostal movement.

Charismatics in the mainline churches have not generally accepted the dispensationalist premillenarianism common to most Pentecostals and evangelical fundamentalist groups. However, they do manifest a heightened "end-times" consciousness, a feature that has also accompanied previous outbreaks of the spiritual gifts on a lesser scale.

Healing has become as prominent a ministry among charismatics as among Pentecostals, although the patterns of healing ministry show obvious contrasts. Whereas physical healing with demonstrative styles of ministry has been more emphasized among Pentecostals, inner healing with a focus on the healing of emotions has characterized many charismatic ministries. This contrast reflects differences in social background and theology. Awareness of mental states is more characteristic of middle-class milieu than of working-class people, and the theology of many charismatics is more sympathetic to psychology than that of many Pentecostals.

The area of theology manifests another obvious contrast between Pentecostals and charismatics, especially those from Christian traditions with a rich theological inheritance, whether Catholic, Orthodox, Lutheran, Reformed, or Puritan. Charismatics from these traditions, especially priests and ministers, attach more importance to a coherent theological basis for the Pentecostal experience than do Pentecostals and independent charismatics. The spread of CR to the Roman Catholic church led to a rapid rise in theological output on topics of BHS and charismata, and the NSC sponsored a theological symposium in Chicago in 1976 (papers published in *Theological Reflections on the Charismatic Renewal*, ed. John D. Haughey, 1978). But the second decade of CCR has probably produced less charismatic theology of quality than the first decade, and the provision of a truly charismatic theology of God, Christ, the church, and Christian initiation (including BHS) remains as much a need as an accomplishment. The theological task imposed by CR has been perhaps most recognized by Lutheran leaders, as shown in the book *Welcome, Holy Spirit*, edited by Larry Christenson (1987), produced by an international team of Lutheran scholars and pastors.

Most charismatics have continued to use the Pentecostal terminology of BHS. Like the Pentecostals, they commonly associate this spiritual event with the gift of tongues, though few charismatics would accept the AG and majority Pentecostal position of "No tongues, no baptism." Many charismatic teachers in liturgical-sacramental traditions have had reservations about the term BHS, on the grounds that it makes BHS appear to be another sacrament and because there is only "one baptism" (Eph. 4:5). Although these reservations have led many continental European Catholics, for example, to use alternative terminology, as *Effusion de l'Esprit, Tauferneuerung* and *Geisterfahrung*, in the English-speaking world BHS has remained the common designation, even within Catholic circles. There is a widespread sense that the baptismal language is important, even if it poses some theological questions that are not easily resolved.

The grounds of opposition to the Pentecostal movement and to CR have varied very little, thus confirming the basic spiritual unity and identity of the two currents. Many Evangelicals objected to the belief in one post-conversion reception of the Spirit and to an alleged devaluation of the Word by belief in contemporary revelation in the Spirit. In both movements, groups of dispensationalist Christians opposed the contemporary availability of spiritual gifts on a priori grounds. In both cases, the focus of opponents was initially on glossolalia, which was perceived as irrational and possibly pathological. However, CR has helped to promote greater scholarly investigation, demonstrating the psychological normalcy of glossolalics, as in Kilian McDonnell's *Charismatic Renewal and the Churches* (1976).

C. The Significance of the Movement. The significance of CR can be seen by considering the list of its essential elements. All are clearly central to Christian life and the mission of the church. They concern every aspect of the church's life: personal relationship with God in Jesus, worship, community formation, evangelism, and mission. The evidence thus confirms the common charismatic conviction that CR is not simply a prayer movement or an evangelistic movement, but a grace for the renewal of the church in all its dimensions.

A comparison with other Christian movements also underlines the importance of CR. Its genesis indicates that it had no one human founder, that its arrival was unexpected and unplanned, that it did not come as a set of coherent ideas or with any strategic methodology, and that it was not in its origins the product of any one Christian tradition more than others. People were first baptized in the Spirit, and then they faced the question of its meaning and what to do with it.

These characteristics clearly differentiate CR from all movements with identifiable human founders, whether movements of Catholic origin (such as Cursillo, Focolari, Marriage Encounter, Comunione e Liberazione in Italy, and Light-Life in Poland), of Orthodox origin (such as the Lord's Army in Rumania), or of Protestant origin (like the Haugean revival in Norway and such parachurch organizations as the Student Christian Movement, YWAM, Operation Mobilization, and Campus Crusade). All such movements have a self-understanding that comes from the life and thinking of the founder. They reflect the founder's theology and church background, and they have clear-cut forms of membership, enrollment, and participation.

If this analysis is correct, the argument follows that an unplanned and unexpected movement, without any one human founder or place of origin, and whose essential characteristics are the fruit only the Holy Spirit of God can produce (knowledge of Jesus, heartfelt praise of God, love of the Scriptures, greater sensitivity to powers of evil), must represent a sovereign intervention of the Lord.

As such a sovereign divine intervention (in origin an unexpected happening rather than a planned organization), CR is similar to previous unplanned divine visitations such as the Great American Awakening of the early 1800s, the Welsh revival of 1904–06, the East African revival that began in the 1930s, and the Indonesian revival from the 1960s. The significance of particular sovereign interventions will then be manifested by their distinctiveness.

In terms of extent of occurrence, CR has a claim to major significance. First, it is found in all continents of the world. Second, it is found in virtually all Christian traditions, being the first sovereign grassroots movement touching equally both Catholic and Protestant churches. There has been minimal penetration of Eastern Orthodoxy, on which see Andrew Walker, "The Orthodox Church and the Charismatic Movement," in *Strange Gifts?* edited by David Martin and Peter Mullen (1984). Walker states, "In no sense . . . should the renewal be seen as a purely western phenomena [sic] (as some Orthodox erroneously think)" (163–64).

CR shows one other interesting and potentially highly significant difference from other sovereign divine interventions of recent centuries, namely the restoration of elements of Christian life largely unknown since the early days of Christianity: the spiritual gifts of 1 Corinthians 12:8–10 and the reappearance of an authentically Jewish Christianity.

All these factors taken together suggest that CR is not simply a sovereign divine intervention for this age but a grace that is healing and repairing the wounds and the weaknesses of many centuries. Although in local settings CR has rarely had the dramatic impact made by some more local awakenings, it has already had more impact on worldwide Christian life than has been generally recognized.

The transconfessional composition of CR underlines its essentially ecumenical character. Not coming out of any one tradition, even the Pentecostal, and touching people from every church, denomination, and tradition, CR is one work of the Holy Spirit in all the churches for their renewal and their unity. Thus it is falsifying the nature of this grace when Catholic charismatic renewal, Lutheran charismatic renewal, or any other denominational renewal is regarded as a distinct movement, rather than as a part of one worldwide transdenominational outpouring of the Spirit of God.

The data cumulatively suggest that the grace of BHS confers on the recipient tangible evidence of the basic Christian reality, centered on a relationship to the Father through his Son, Jesus Christ, in the communion of the Holy Spirit. In their experience of this fundamental reality, Christians of all traditions can recognize the heart of their faith tradition. The history of interchurch dialogue suggests that such a realized spiritual unity, however inchoate, would have been impossible without such a divine intervention. In other words, progress beyond comparative Christian experience and theology to an experienced unity in the Spirit required a "new" grace beyond what was currently known by either Catholic or Protestant.

To assert the extraordinary significance of CR for world Christianity and all the churches is not to ignore its weaknesses and its areas of immaturity. But the weaknesses and immaturity flow from its nature as an unplanned spontaneous eruption, and from its being a movement where people are participants as a result of their experience, not as a consequence of specific training. These weaknesses point, not to any reduced significance of CR as such, but to the fragility of this work of God and the dangers of its full goals not being realized. Recent scandals in independent ministries highlight the need for fellowship and mutual accountability. In other words, the negative aspects of CR are not reasons for dismissal but incentives to ensure that this extraordinary grace of God is not wasted.

Because CR is an unexpected and unplanned grace of God for the churches, its significance has to be sought out in humble prayer and reflection on all the data. Unlike the movements with human founders, the meaning of CR is not given with the experience of BHS. Reflection on what happens in BHS and its effects in the life of the Christian and of the church is a task and responsibility given with that grace. That task is incomplete.

In seeking what is most characteristic of the movement, insufficient attention has been paid to the directness of personal communication with the Lord that is involved in and flows from BHS. There seems to be something distinctive in relation to divine revelation in the Spirit that CR shares with the Pentecostal movement—something that has been lacking in inherited patterns of Christian life. Evidently there have always been holy and dedicated Christians in every church tradition who have known and heard the Lord. But BHS opens up a directness of communication with the Lord Jesus as part of ordinary Christian discipleship. With BHS it is an intrinsic element in Christian initiation and is no longer a sign of advanced holiness of life. With this expectation shared with other members of the body of Christ comes the possibility of corporate Christian life being supernaturally directed by the Spirit of God.

This directness of relationship seems to have made possible the identity of the "charismatic experience" among Christians of diverse traditions, as this directness has in some way got beyond the apparatus of theological formulation and ritual performance. In other words, the significance of CR appears to be closely related to the element identified as "God Speaks Today"—namely, that CR restores to "normal Christianity" the experience of revelation in the Spirit. It would then be this element of inner revelation from God that grounds the immediacy of charismatic praise to the Lord and the life-giving power that transforms people.

If initiating inner revelation in the Spirit is central to BHS, then what is so revealed is the fullness of God and his plan centered on his Son. That is to say, CR is intrinsically concerned with the restoration both of the Spirit's means of communication to God's people and of the fullness of its content. However, openness to divine revelation in the Spirit is inseparable from vulnerability to deception and makes imperative constant discernment of spirits. In this light, a test of the maturity of CR is the extent to which revelation in the Spirit focuses on the central truths of Christianity. Are charismatics being led to a deeper grasp of the glory of the triune God, of the devastation caused by sin, of the cross of Jesus as death to sin, as the manifestation of God's righteousness and the divine conquest of Satan, of the resurrection as the inauguration of the new creation under the headship of Jesus, of the church as the Spirit-filled body of Christ, "the fulness of him who fills all in all" (Eph. 1:23)?

Revelation in the Spirit restores to the Christian people a more consistently divine view of reality. It thus deals a major blow to the anthropomorphism that evaluates everything from a merely human perspective. This divine vision is not an instant possession, however, but an ongoing gift that presupposes increasing death to the flesh in union with the cross of Christ.

This vision of CR again indicates the essential character of its ecumenical composition. As the separated churches allow the Holy Spirit to reveal their need for those elements of divine revelation more fully conserved in other traditions, they will be opened to a greater fullness of divine revelation and so be brought into closer union with each other.

These considerations point to the immediacy of the Spirit's work in CR being concerned with fullness: the fullness of divine revelation, the full equipment of the church for its mission. That is to say, the Lord's purpose is the full gospel being preached by a Spirit-filled "whole" church to the whole world. Thus will "we all attain to the unity of the faith and of the knowledge of the Son of God, to mature manhood, to the measure of the stature of the fulness of Christ" (Eph. 4:13) so that to God the Father may be all "glory in the church and in Christ Jesus to all generations, for ever and ever. Amen" (3:21).

See also BAPTIST CHARISMATICS; CATHOLIC CHARISMATIC RENEWAL; CHARISMATIC RENEWAL SERVICES; EPISCOPAL RENEWAL MINISTRIES; HOUSE CHURCH MOVEMENT; LUTHERAN CHARISMATICS; MENNONITE CHARISMATICS; NONDENOMINATIONAL PENTECOSTAL AND CHARISMATIC CHURCHES; STEPHANOU, EUSEBIUS A.; PENTECOSTAL AND CHARISMATIC MOVEMENTS (INTRODUCTORY ESSAY); PRESBYTERIAN AND REFORMED CHARISMATICS ; STATISTICS, GLOBAL; UNION OF MESSIANIC JEWISH CONGREGATIONS; UNITED CHURCH OF CHRIST, FELLOWSHIP OF CHARISMATIC CHRISTIANS IN THE; UNITED METHODIST CHARISMATICS; WESLEYAN CHARISMATICS.

Bibliography: J. Bax, *The Good Wine* (1986); A. Bittlinger, ed., *The Church Is Charismatic* (1981); L. Christenson, ed., *Welcome, Holy Spirit* (1987); P. Elbert, ed., *Charismatic Renewal and the Churches* (forthcoming); M. Harper, *None Can Guess* (1971); D. E. Horrell, *All Things Are Possible* (1975); M. Hérard, *Les Nouveaux Disciples Dix et Aprés* (1987); P. Hocken, *One Lord One Spirit One Body* (1987); idem, *Streams of Renewal* (1986); R. G. Hoekstra, "God Is Breaking Through All Barriers!" *Voice* 4 (1,1956): 23; W. J. Hollenweger, ed., *Pentecostal Research in Europe* (1988); C. Hummel, *Fire in the Fireplace* (1978); K. McDonnell, ed., *Presence, Power, Praise*, 3 vols. (1980); R. Quebedeaux, *The New Charismatics II* (1983); D. A. Rausch, *Messianic Judaism* (1982); A. Reimers, *God's Country* (1979); J. Sherrill, *They Speak with Other Tongues*

(1964); V. Synan, *The Twentieth-Century Pentecostal Explosion* (1987); C. P. van der Laan, *Pinksteren in Beweging* (1982); J. Williams, *The Gift of the Holy Spirit Today* (1980); See also bibliography for CATHOLIC CHARISMATIC RENEWAL.　　　　　　P. D. Hocken

CHARISMATIC RENEWAL SERVICES

Service agency for Catholic Charismatic Renewal (CCR) in the U.S. Charismatic Renewal Services (CRS) was formally incorporated in South Bend, Indiana, in 1971 by the newly formed Catholic Charismatic Renewal Service Committee, later known as the National Service Committee for CCR (NSC), to develop and continue services begun by the Communications Center at Notre Dame. These services included the organization of the annual CCR conferences at Notre Dame, the compilation of a national prayer group directory, the publication of the CCR monthly, *New Covenant*, the retailing of charismatic literature and cassettes, together with the publication of a few books. In 1975, due to accelerating expansion, CRS was made organizationally distinct from the NSC and became in effect a distribution center for all CCR materials in the U.S. Until 1979 CRS was serviced jointly by the People of Praise Community in South Bend and the Word of God community in Ann Arbor, Michigan, but the Ann Arbor operations, including *New Covenant*, were then withdrawn from CRS and incorporated as Servant Publications.　　　　　　P. D. Hocken

CHAWNER, C. AUSTIN (1903–64).

Missionary to Africa, author, composer, publisher, and linguist. Chawner, Canadian born, moved to South Africa when he was six years old (1909) with his father, Charles Chawner, who was the first Pentecostal Assemblies of Canada (PAOC) missionary to South Africa. He graduated from Bethel Bible Training School in Newark, New Jersey, where he received the baptism in the Spirit in 1923. Upon being ordained in London, Ontario, in 1925 and returning to South Africa as a PAOC missionary in the same year, Chawner took the gospel message to many areas where it had never been heard. Chawner and Ingrid Lokken, who was affiliated with the Norwegian Pentecostal Assemblies and later became his wife (c. 1935), were the first PAOC missionaries in Mozambique (c. 1929) and Rhodesia (c. 1942).

Chawner's evangelistic methodology emphasized education and publishing. He started the first Pentecostal Bible schools in South Africa (1930) and Mozambique (c. 1935) in order to train national leaders for an indigenous church. Chawner wrote, composed, translated, and published gospel tracts, Bibles, hymn books, free correspondence Bible courses, and gospel literature on the Emmanuel Press in forty-four different languages. More than 24.5 million pieces of literature were distributed by this press in 1959 alone. When the Mozambique government prohibited further Protestant missionary work (c. 1950), the two hundred churches that Chawner had established in the country were ready to survive under the leadership of national ministers with the support of literature produced by the Emmanuel Press in Nelspruit, South Africa, near the border of Mozambique.

Part of Chawner's success in establishing churches was due to his achievements in six languages. He helped to develop written Tsonga and wrote a Tsonga grammar book (1938), Bible studies, and hymns. Chawner held many important positions: managing director of Emmanuel Press, member of the Orthography Committee of the Tsonga language, member of the Translation Committee of the British and Foreign Bible Society, field secretary for the PAOC in Africa, and general secretary of the South African Assemblies of God.

Bibliography: F. Burke, "Austin Chawner–South Africa," a typed report (1979); C. A. Chawner, *Step by Step in Thonga* (1938); idem, "Trip Through N. E. Transvaal," *PE* (November 12, 1927), 20–21; W. J. Hollenweger, *The Pentecostals* (1972); G. G. Kulbeck, *What God Hath Wrought* (1958); E. A. Peters, *The Contribution to Education by the Pentecostal Assemblies of Canada* (1970).   E. B. Robinson

CHEMIN NEUF (LYONS, FRANCE) See CHARISMATIC COMMUNITIES.

CHEROKEE COUNTY (N.C.) REVIVAL

One of the earliest known outpourings of the Holy Spirit in America. The Cherokee County revival occurred in 1896 in the Unicoi Mountains along the North Carolina and Tennessee border. Ten years before the outpouring, R. G. Spurling and his Baptist followers organized a Christian Union (which is now the Church of God) on the Tennessee side of the mountain region. In 1892 a kindred fellowship was organized by W. F. Bryant on the North Carolina side. The two congregations were effectually the same, with only the state line between them. In the summer of 1896 three lay evangelists conducted revival services in the Shearer schoolhouse that served as a meeting place for the area. William Martin, a Methodist, and Joe M. Tipton and Milton McNabb, both Baptists, were the evangelists. The Wesleyan emphasis on sanctification was their insistent theme. It was a time of spiritual renewal and religious fervor, with numerous conversions of sinners.

The meetings closed at the schoolhouse and were continued in the Bryant home, where a new thing happened. Numerous men, women, and children began to speak in tongues and otherwise manifest the presence of the Holy Spirit. At first the people were puzzled by these occurrences, but a search of the Scriptures revealed that they were experiencing an outpouring of the Holy Ghost such as that in Acts 2:4; 10:46; and 19:6. The revival continued all summer (1896) and about 130 were filled with the Spirit and spoke in tongues. Other hundreds were converted and numerous sick persons were healed.

The people did not immediately become evangelistic about their experience and formulated no doctrine about it. They simply thanked God for "the blessing" and wished that all people had it. That universal outpouring would begin ten years later, 1906, in far away California.

See also CHURCH OF GOD (CLEVELAND, TENN.).

Bibliography: C. W. Conn, *Like a Mighty Army* (rev. ed., 1977); H. Hunter, "Spirit-Baptism and the 1896 Revival in Cherokee County, North Carolina," *Pneuma* 5 (2, 1983): 1–17.   C. W. Conn

CHESSER, H. L. (1898–). Sixth general overseer of the Church of God (CG, Cleveland, Tenn.), whose tenure was from 1948–52. After attending Bible training school (1923–26) he served as pastor in Florida in the 1930s and 1940s. Chesser was an effective counselor and state overseer; in 1948 he was elected general overseer, a post he filled for four years. Also in 1948 he was a member of the Pentecostal Fellowship of North America constitution committee and the National Association of Evangelicals executive committee. During his tenure as general overseer he led the CG in its amalgamation with the Full Gospel Church of South Africa (1951). In 1954 Chesser returned to a local ministry in his native Florida.

Bibliography: Archives of the Church of God (Cleveland, Tenn.); C. W. Conn, *Like a Mighty Army* (rev. 1977).   C. W. Conn

CHI ALPHA Assemblies of God (AG) national campus ministry program. Founded by the AG in the fall of 1953, Chi Alpha is the national society for Christian witness on non-Christian campuses in recognition of the fact that the university has always been the center of changing ideas and religious awakenings. The first chapter was formed in Springfield, Missouri, by J. Calvin Holsinger on the campus of Southwest Missouri State College. Its purpose was to minister to students in secular colleges with a four-pronged program—worship, Bible study, social life, and community outreach. Other chapters were established on college and university campuses in the U.S., providing a Pentecostal ministry. The Greek letters stand for *Christou—Apostoloi*, Christ's Sent Ones or Ambassadors.

Bibliography: J. C. Holsinger, "Epiphany Day 1984," Assemblies of God Archives, Springfield, Missouri.   F. Bixler

CHILD EVANGELISTS See GORTNER, HUGH MARJOE ROSS; WALKER, DAVID DAVILLO "LITTLE DAVID"; EVANGELISTS.

CHILDREN OF GOD See FAMILY OF LOVE.

CHILEAN CHARISMATICS See CHARISMATIC MOVEMENT.

CHO, PAUL YONGGI (1936–). Positive-thinking Korean prophet who is pastor of the world's largest congregation. Raised as a Buddhist, Paul rejected his religion as he was dying of tuberculosis and aspired to become a medical doctor, but Jesus later appeared to him in the middle of the night dressed as a fireman, called him to preach, and filled him with the Holy Spirit.

After graduation from an Assemblies of God (AG) Bible school, he started a tent church in Seoul in 1958. By 1962 he was able to build a 1,500-seat downtown "revival center," soon changing the name to Full Gospel Central Church. Divine healings at the dedication stimulated growth to a membership of 2,000 by 1964. Cho suffered a nervous breakdown but was divinely guided to delegate responsibility. In

1966 he became general superintendent of the Korean AG. He found time to complete a degree in law at the National College of Korea in 1968 and was awarded an honorary doctor of divinity degree from Bethany Bible College, Santa Cruz, California, the same year.

A 10,000-seat auditorium was dedicated in 1973 by Billy Graham. By 1974 there were 23,000 members; by the end of 1979 100,000; and by 1987, over half a million. The church has hundreds of assistant pastors and thousands of home cell group leaders, the majority of both groups being women—a breakthrough in Korean culture.

Former Buddhist Paul Yonggi Cho is pastor of the Yoido Full Gospel Church in Seoul, Korea, which has the world's largest congregation.

Pastor Cho's success formula is a combination of positive thinking and positive confession: "Think it. See it. Speak it—in *boldness*." (Kennedy, 1980, 202). He teaches that through the power of the spoken word the Spirit-led believer can "create and release the presence of Jesus Christ" (Cho, 1979, 81). He emphasizes being specific in prayer; one must visualize and specify exactly what is needed. This implies financial prosperity, but it is not an instant cure-all. Answers to prayer may take weeks or months.

Coming out of the Oriental tradition, Cho has emphasized the mystical, including the power of satanic forces; but at the same time he has elevated the believer even more—to the "class of gods" as children of God who have power over the angelic class (including Satan). This is the language of the mystic, not the lawyer-theologian, and must be interpreted as such. He has been criticized for mind-power statements such as: "Through visualizing and dreaming you can incubate your future and hatch the results." But these must be interpreted in their context: "The subconscious has certain influence, but it is quite limited, and cannot create like our Almighty God can" (Cho, 1979, 42, 44). He teaches that only the Holy Spirit can bring the true understanding of Scripture. Such traditional subjectivism among Pentecostals has always had the potential for abuse.

See also CHURCH GROWTH.

Bibliography: J. Buckingham, "The World's Largest Pastorate," *Charisma* (June 1982), 20–23; P. Y. Cho, *The Fourth Dimension* (1979); N. L. Kennedy, *Dream Your Way to Success* (1980).   D. J. Wilson

CHRIST FOR THE NATIONS INSTITUTE

(CFNI), Dallas, Texas. This two-year educational institution serving the charismatic and Pentecostal traditions was founded in 1970 by Gordon and Freda Lindsay, longtime leaders of the healing movement. This was not the Lindsays' first involvement in education. In 1959 the Lindsays had established the World Correspondence Course, which by the late 1960s had over 11,000 students enrolled. The library established to provide research resources for writing the courses provided the core of the CFNI library.

To supplement the educational background of regional evangelists and teachers, a series of seminars dealing with theological, ministry, and missiological concerns was conducted at the Dallas Christian Center where Lindsay was pastor and director of the center's various publishing, mission, and educational efforts. This proved popular, and the Lindsays were encouraged to develop a Bible school to train pastors, evangelists, and lay workers.

CFNI opened in 1970 with one full-time teacher in addition to Lindsay, 45 students, and few resources. Gordon Lindsay was president. By the time of Gordon Lindsay's death (1973), the school had grown to about 250 students. Freda Lindsay was elected president, a position that she held from 1973 to 1985. Her son, Dennis Lindsay, succeeded her as president. Freda Lindsay remained chairperson of the board of trustees and chief executive officer.

Enrollment peaked during the mid 1980s at 1,500 and has declined to about 900 (in 1988) because of a daring educational experiment. Concerned that many foreign students, as well as students from areas lacking strong charismatic churches were being taken from their environment never to return, CFNI has been instrumental in establishing Bible schools in Bad Gandersheim (West Germany), Montego Bay (Jamaica), and New York City (Long Island). CFNI alumni have established schools modeled after CFNI in Argentina, Finland, Mexico, Malaysia, Spain, and Thailand. These events and the life of CFNI have been reported in *Christ for the Nations* (1967, formerly the *Voice of Healing*). A yearbook (variously titled) published by the student association reports annual events and records the student population.

See also VOICE OF HEALING.

Bibliography: F. Lindsay, *Freda* (1987), idem, *My Diary's Secrets* (1976); G. Lindsay, *The House the Lord Built* (1972).   D. D. Bundy

One of the early leaders in the Lutheran Charismatic movement, Larry Christenson wrote *The Charismatic Renewal Among Lutherans* and edited *Welcome, Holy Spirit.*

CHRISTENSON, LAURENCE DONALD ("LARRY")

(1928–). Lutheran charismatic and author. Christenson was born in Northfield, Minnesota, to a Norwegian Lutheran family. His father served at the time as the football coach at St. Olaf College in Northfield. Christenson was married to Nordis Evenson in 1951, who bore their four children.

During World War II, Christenson served as a parachutist in the Army Air Corps. Before graduating from St. Olaf in 1952 he entertained hopes of being a playwright but decided to enter the ministry in 1955. Graduating from Luther Theological Seminary in St. Paul in 1959, he was called to serve as pastor of Trinity Lutheran Church (ALC) in San Pedro, California, in 1960.

Through reading the works of Agnes Sanford, Christenson became interested in Pentecostalism. In 1961 he was baptized in the Holy Spirit and spoke in tongues in a Foursquare Gospel church. Leading his church into a Pentecostal revival, he immediately became a national leader in the Lutheran charismatic renewal movement.

Author of *The Christian Family* (1970) and *The Renewed Mind* (1974), Christenson soon gained influence as an ecumenical leader in the interna-

tional charismatic movement. In 1974 he was instrumental in organizing a renewal organization known as Lutheran Charismatic Renewal Services. After retiring from the pastorate in San Pedro in 1983, he became director of the International Lutheran Renewal Center in St. Paul.

See also LUTHERAN CHARISMATICS.

Bibliography: L. D. Christenson, *The Charismatic Renewal Among Lutherans* (1976).   H. V. Synan

CHRISTIAN AND MISSIONARY ALLIANCE

(CMA). Incorporated in 1897, was the product of an amalgamation of two organizations, the Christian Alliance and the Evangelical Missionary Alliance (later renamed the International Missionary Alliance), founded in 1887 at Old Orchard, Maine, by the Canadian-born Albert Benjamin Simpson. Since its inception, the CMA has evolved into a missionary denomination composed of churches in fifty-one nations with over two million adherents. Its international headquarters are located in Nyack, New York.

Reflecting its roots in the American Holiness movement of the later nineteenth century, the Alliance has historically highlighted the doctrines of the Spirit-filled life and healing in the Atonement. Articles 7 and 8 of the Alliance Statement of Faith (1965) read as follows:

7. It is the will of God that each believer should be filled with the Holy Spirit and be sanctified wholly, being separated from sin and the world and fully dedicated to the will of God, thereby receiving power for holy living and effective service. This is both a crisis and a progressive experience wrought in the life of the believer subsequent to conversion.

8. Provision is made in the redemptive work of the Lord Jesus Christ for the healing of the mortal body. Prayer for the sick and anointing with oil are taught in the Scriptures and are privileges for the church in this present age.

Various pioneers of the Pentecostal movement acknowledged their connection with A. B. Simpson and the CMA. In 1900 Charles Parham visited "Dr. Simpson's work in Nyack," where spiritual truths were being "restored." Agnes Ozman warmly recalled the time she spent at the Missionary Training Institute at Nyack, New York, where she was exposed to the teachings of A. B. Simpson and his colleagues. Thomas Barratt recounted his seeking of the baptism of the Holy Spirit in 1906 while staying in the Alliance guest house in New York City. Alexander Dowie derived inspiration from Simpson's healing ministry and once invited the Alliance founder to accompany him across the U.S. on a healing tour. Other prominent Pentecostal personalities who were influenced by the CMA include Alice Belle Garrigus, founder of the Pentecostal Assemblies of Newfoundland, and D. Wesley Myland, founder of the Gibeah Bible School near Indianapolis.

Out of Simpson's Missionary Training Institute came Pentecostal pastors, administrators, and missionaries. William I. Evans and Frank M.

An early leader of the Christian and Missionary Alliance in Canada, John Salmon was baptized in the Spirit but remained in the Alliance.

Boyd became deans of Bethel Bible Training School in Newark, New Jersey, and Central Bible Institute in Springfield, Missouri. On the Canadian scene, R. E. Sternall, the first pastor of the influential Pentecostal assembly in Kitchener, Ontario, received the Pentecostal baptism at Nyack in 1911. The three-year Bible institute model perfected by A. B. Simpson and D. L. Moody, in which the atmosphere of the school was geared more to spiritual development than the academic performance, became the dominant strategy for the preparation of Pentecostal leadership.

According to Assemblies of God (AG) historian Carl Brumback, the Pentecostal movement owes the CMA a sevenfold debt: (1) doctrines borrowed from the Alliance; (2) the hymns of Simpson; (3) the books of Simpson, Pardington, Tozer, and others; (4) the terminology "Gospel Tabernacle," which, when supplemented with "Full," became a popular name for churches among Pentecostals; (5) the polity of the early Alliance Society, after which the AG was styled; (6) a worldwide missionary vision; and (7) numerous leaders converted and trained in Alliance circles (*A Sound From Heaven*, 1977, 92). Aimee Semple McPherson's "Foursquare Gospel," which she claimed was given directly to her by divine revelation, was noticeably similar to A. B. Simpson's "Fourfold Gospel." The emblem of the Foursquare movement, a cross, a laver (representing healing), a dove, and a crown, bore a marked resemblance to the already existent Alliance symbol, which included a cross, laver (representing sanctification), a pitcher of oil, and a crown.

The incursion of Pentecostalism into the ranks of the CMA during the first two decades of the twentieth century constituted the most severe crisis faced by the Alliance during its entire history. The years 1908–12 were particularly stressful as attitudes toward Pentecostalism within the Alliance polarized. Many of those Alliance persons who had received the Pentecostal baptism felt constrained to leave and identify themselves with the burgeoning Pentecostal movement in which they quickly emerged as leaders. Significantly, there were notable persons such as Robert Jaffray and John Salmon, who received the gift of tongues and chose to remain within the Alliance. Losses to the Alliance were substantial among branch members, official workers, and missionaries. In 1912, in order to protect itself, the Alliance adopted as part of its new constitution, the controversial "reversion clause," which ensured that the property of local branches, schools, and undenominational churches would "revert to and become the property of the CMA as incorporated under the laws of the State of New York."

Throughout the Pentecostal controversy, A. B. Simpson affirmed the orderly expression of supernatural gifts within the Alliance. During the post-Simpson period, however, the Alliance has increasingly distanced itself from the Pentecostal and charismatic movements. In 1963, responding to the spread of Neo-Pentecostalism within established Protestant churches, the Alliance board of managers issued an official statement regarding the charismatic movement that reiterated Simpson's earlier assessment of Pentecostalism made in 1908. The statement asserted:

Certainly some persons of impeccable Christian character are associated with the present charismatic movement. But the gift of tongues belongs in the category of things earlier imitated and by the very nature of it is capable of abuse and wild excesses. . . .

. . . We do not believe that there is any scriptural evidence for the teaching that speaking in tongues is the sign of having been filled with the Holy Spirit, nor do we believe that it is the plan of God that all Christians should possess the gift of tongues.

Under the influence of A. W. Tozer, the board of managers proposed the phrase, "Seek not, forbid not," as embodying the "wisdom for this hour" regarding the gift of tongues. The widespread notion that this expression originated with A. B. Simpson is erroneous.

An unofficial report entitled "Dealing with the Charismatic in Today's Church" was distributed to all North American Alliance workers in 1977 with the recommendation that it be received as "scriptural and consistent with the Alliance position." While insisting that the Alliance had never endorsed a cessationist view of the gifts of the Holy Spirit, the study nonetheless proscribed Neo-Pentecostalism as "the most devastating and dangerous of all the other charismatic movements

This photograph taken at the 1906 Old Orchard Convention in Maine reflects the early link between the CMA and the emergence of Pentecostalism. (1) Henry Wilson, who investigated Pentecostalism within the Alliance; (2) Mrs. A. B. Simpson; (3) A. B. Simpson; (4) W. C. Stevens, principal of the Missionary Training Institute; and (5) Minnie T. Draper, prominent Alliance official and speaker who later helped in the founding of the Bethel Pentecostal Assembly, Newark, New Jersey, and the Pentecostal Mission in South and Central Africa.

in the twentieth century." It further advised that tongues speaking, though legitimate, nevertheless should be prohibited in "certain services of the church."

As a result of its unpleasant encounter with the Pentecostal movement during the early years of the twentieth century, the CMA has tended to diminish its working relationships with groups of Holiness, Pentecostal, or charismatic persuasion. It has sought instead to maintain fidelity to its traditional emphasis on the "deeper life" while aligning itself more closely with non-Pentecostal, evangelical Protestant bodies.

Bibliography: R. Niklaus, J. Sawin, S. Stoesz, *All for Jesus* (1986); S. Stoesz, *Understanding My Church* (1983); idem, *Footprints* (1981); A. E. Thompson, *A. B. Simpson* (1960). C. Nienkirchen

CHRISTIAN ASSEMBLY See CRISTIANA ASSEMBLEA.

CHRISTIAN BROADCASTING NETWORK See ROBERTSON, MARION GORDON "PAT."

CHRISTIAN CHURCH OF NORTH AMERICA
A cooperative Pentecostal fellowship that has a congregational form of government governed by overseers and presbyters. Their doctrine and emphasis on missions is very similar to the Assemblies of God (AG). Christian Church of North America (CCNA) is affiliated with Assembles di Dio d'Italia (ADI), Iglesia Cristiana Pentecostal De Argentina, and the Italian Christian Churches of North Europe. It has close affinity with the Association of Italian Pentecostal Churches in Canada and has membership in the Pentecostal Fellowship of North America and the National Association of Evangelicals. CCNA is headquartered in Transfer, Pennsylvania, and has two official organs, *Il Faro* and *Vista*.

The religious heritage of CCNA includes: (1) the Pentecostal revival that started in Topeka, Kansas (1901), and (2) a group of Italian Evangelicals living in a Chicago (near the north side) Italian community. W. H. Durham received the baptism in the Spirit at Azusa Street (1907) and carried the Pentecostal message back to Chicago. Luigi Francescon and Pietro Ottolini, mosaic artisans, who had already left the Italian Presbyterian Church in Chicago, heard Durham preach at the North Avenue Mission and received the baptism in the Spirit (1907). On September 15, 1907 (the Sunday after Ottolini received the baptism in the Spirit), the power of God was manifested at Grand Avenue Mission, Assemblea Cristiana, and many people in Ottolini's Italian evangelical group received the baptism in the Spirit. This marked the beginning of the Pentecostal movement among Italian-Americans. The power of the Spirit continued to be manifested at the mission, with healings and additional baptisms in the Spirit. The membership expanded, and some became missionaries to other Italian populations in the U.S. and around the world. Their efforts produced churches in thirteen states and in several foreign lands. This growth was without the benefit of organization; however,

dissension in 1927 indicated that structure was needed.

Structure for the movement developed as a result of three needs: (1) to resolve dissension, (2) to facilitate foreign missions, and (3) to balance foreign missions with evangelization of the U.S. The first need, to resolve dissension over the interpretation of Acts 15:13–29—Should Christians drain all blood from meat before they eat it or not?—resulted in Luigi Francescon, Maximilian Tosetto, and Joseph Petrelli combining their efforts to solve the problem during the first general convention of the movement at Niagara Falls, New York. Francescon was a charismatic leader and disliked formal organization. In contrast, Tosetto was an organizer. Petrelli, however, disapproved of formal organization and provided written expression of the early theology. The result of this convention was: (1) adoption of twelve articles of faith, (2) publication of a hymnal, (3) formation of the general council, (4) adoption of the name Unorganized Italian Christian Churches of the United States, (5) the call for an annual conference, and (6) the historical beginning of CCNA (1927).

The need to facilitate missions was accomplished by: (1) forming a missions fund (1929), (2) electing a missions committee to administer the fund (1929), (3) creating the office of missionary secretary/treasurer (1943), (4) incorporating as the Missionary Society of the CCNA (June, 1948), and (5) making the director of missions the first permanently, fully supported office of CCNA (1953). This emphasis led to established major works in Brazil and Italy but to the neglect of the growth of CCNA at home.

Subsequently, CCNA drew up an eight-point program to correct the imbalance in growth; restructured their organization; incorporated as a legal religious denomination under the name General Council of the CCNA (1963); expanded the home missions organization; regionalized their world mission fields; and made the general overseer's office a permanent, fully supported position (1965). This structure has enabled the directors of missions (Richard L. Corsini [1943–69], Guy BonGiovanni [1969–81], Richard Tedesco [1981–85], and John DelTurco [1985–]) and the general overseers (Carmelo Paglia [1952–54], Frank P. Fortunato [1954–75], Carmine Saginario [1975–84], and Guy BonGiovanni [1984–]) to develop missions in seventeen nations and the church at home. Currently CCNA has a national executive board consisting of overseers and directors utilizing management by objective; five U.S. districts being governed by district presbyteries, 125 churches in twelve U.S. states; and five hundred credentialed workers. One annual goal is to establish two new churches in each district.

Initially CCNA defined their purpose as evangelizing all Italian people; however, now it considers its mission as being multiethnic. During World War II the organization dropped the Italian identity from the denominational name in order to express loyalty to the American government. In 1961 CCNA began to expand its home missionary outreach beyond ethnic Italians. Today approximately 20 to 50 percent of the U.S. ministers and 75 to 85 percent of the U.S. members are non-Italian as a result of CCNA members being assimilated into the American culture and making an effort to evangelize Korean, Hispanic, Black, Vietnamese, Haitian, and Portuguese Americans.

The Italian-American Pentecostals felt the consequences of not being incorporated in Italy and the U.S. During the early years, the movement splintered into many independent, unincorporated groups, including CCNA, Evangelical Christian Pentecostal Churches (ECPC), Ottolini's group, and Petrelli's group. An attempt was made to merge these groups in Chicago (1945); however, the attempt failed. This was followed by the merger of ECPC into the AG as the Italian Branch of the AG (January 1948), today called the Italian District of AG (IDAG). IDAG tried to merge CCNA into their district (1959). The merger attempt failed; however, approximately 25 percent of CCNA did join IDAG. Today most of the churches have merged into CCNA or IDAG; some members attend the conventions for both groups. A few independent Italian-American churches exist in the US.

These Pentecostal groups established many churches in Italy starting with the work of layman Giacomo Lombardi in 1908. As a result of persecution before, during, and after World War II, the American AG offered to help them at the first Pentecostal World Conference in 1947. Later that year many of these churches took the name Assembles di Dio in Italia (ADI), and an agreement of association was signed between ADI and the American AG (December 1947). CCNA continued to form churches in Italy. However, the Italian government stated CCNA churches in Italy should affiliate with a legal church in the U.S. if they wanted religious freedom (1953). CCNA combined its work in Italy with ADI (1953). ADI became incorporated in Italy six years later. CCNA and ADI eventually signed an agreement of association in 1977. ADI, which has received substantial support from both the American AG and the CCNA, had in 1987: 107,000 members; 838 churches and outstations; 421 ministers; and one Bible school, the Italian Bible Institute.

Bibliography: G. BonGiovanni, *CCNA 60th Anniversary Ricordo* (1987); idem, "The Christian Church of North America," a pamphlet (1987); idem, *The Ministry of Reconciliation in the Christian Church of North America* (1983); J. Colletti, "A Sociological Study of Italian Pentecostals in Chicago: 1900–1930," unpublished paper presented at Society for Pentecostal Studies, 1986; A. F. Dalton, "Field Focus: Italy," AG Foreign Missions Report (1988); L. DeCaro, *Our Heritage: The Christian Church of North America* (1977); A. Erutti, *The Life and Early Ministry of Leonard Erutti* (c. 1982); S. Galvano, ed., *The Fiftieth Anniversary of the Christian Church of North America, 1927–1977* (1977); C. E. Jones, *A Guide to the Study of the Pentecostal Movement,* (1983); R. T. McGlasson, "Observations on the Work of the Assemblies of God in Italy," unpublished, March 10, 1952; P. Ottolini, *The Life and Mission of Peter Ottolini* (c. 1962); A. Palma, *The Articles of Faith* (1987); N. Perkin, "Persecution Continues in Italy," *PE* (March 22, 1953), 6; A. Piraino, "Minutes of Convention of Italian Brethren Held in Grace Tabernacle Syracuse, N.Y. on January 15, 16, 17, 1948 for the Purpose of Forming, if Feasible and Expedient, an Italian Branch of the Assemblies of God" (1948); R. Tedesco, ed., *General Council of Christian Church of North America Annual Report Book—1977* (1977); E. S. Williams, J. R. Flower, N. Perkin, U. N. Gorietti, R. Bracco, and P. A. di Domentio, "Agreement for Association Between the General Council of the Assemblies of God With Headquarters in Springfield, Missouri, U.S.A. and the Assemblies of God of Italy With Headquarters in Rome, Italy," unpublished, 1947.

E. B. Robinson

CHRISTIAN CHURCHES, CONFERENCE ON CHARISMATIC RENEWAL IN THE See KANSAS CITY CONFERENCE.

CHRISTIAN DAY SCHOOLS As society has become more secular, public schools have increasingly become non-Christian. In American colonial times, according to evangelical Christian educators, education was Christian in purpose, curriculum, and practice, and was usually private, provided by church or parents. Particularly in the Middle Colonies and New England, the purpose of education was to teach reading so that the pupils could read the Bible for themselves. The curriculum frequently reflected evangelical theology and ethics and Christian conduct was a goal as expressed in *McGuffey's Readers*, which were almost universally used for over a century. As the population of the U.S. became increasingly diverse ethically and religiously during the nineteenth century, public schools began to take a neutral stance toward Christianity. By the middle of the twentieth century, most large public school systems in the U.S. had become completely secular if not anti-Christian, in the opinion held by many Christians.

Parochial schools are usually thought of as those sponsored by Roman Catholics, Lutherans, Seventh-day Adventists, etc. Christian day schools generally refer to those schools that are sponsored by evangelical churches and stress Christian commitment in lifestyle and curriculum. These independent church-sponsored educational programs give strong emphasis to biblical principles and are considered a vital ministry of outreach and evangelism. The day school is often included as a part of the Christian education program along with Sunday school, youth ministry, weekday clubs, etc. Some independent schools are sponsored by parents or are under an independent school board that may represent several churches.

The Christian day school is a protest school that has chosen to break step with the philosophy of life that predominates in public schools. Christian schools argue that any education that leaves out God does not give students an accurate picture of the "real world" because God is the center of life for Christians. Relativistic, secular humanism presents students in public schools with a "religious" education based on faith that humankind can solve all its problems without divine assistance. The foundation, then, for Christian day school philosophy is not just human reason, but is in the Bible, God's revelation to humanity. Since this revelation is true, the philosophy of education must be based on this true revelation.

The major Pentecostal denominations belong

to the National Association of Evangelicals (NAE). Theological statements of NAE would thus be common ground for building a philosophy of education. Many charismatic churches also build on the same theological foundation. One distinctive of Pentecostal philosophy that goes beyond the NAE formulations is the emphasis on the Person and work of the Holy Spirit. Pentecostals and charismatics believe that the Person of the Holy Spirit has a relationship with believers and that he is not merely a power given to help believers do Christian service.

The purpose of Christian day schools is to complement the home and the church in providing students an excellent academic program from a definite Christian viewpoint. Some Christian schools have sought to meet state standards of education to show their strength or to demonstrate excellence. Most schools reject state supervision or regulations as being incapable of evaluating Christian schooling. The arrest and conviction of pastors who have refused to observe state regulations have led some state legislatures to write better and fairer laws for governing private education.

Since 1925 when the U.S. Supreme Court struck down an Oregon law requiring public school attendance of pupils between the ages of eight and sixteen, U.S. courts have recognized parental rights to send their children to nonpublic schools. Parents are responsible for the education of their children. For the Christian this means an education that includes not only the truths found in God's world but the truth revealed in his Word ("All truth is God's truth," to quote Frank E. Gaebelein).

As in any educational endeavor, the teacher is a key factor in the success or failure of the school. Some schools require only that teachers be born again. However, the majority of schools prefer teachers who are Pentecostal in belief and practice. The *Assemblies of God Educator* (28:5) states it well: "Personnel in Assemblies of God schools should also be Spirit-filled, have formal Bible training, adhere to the Assemblies of God Statement of Fundamental Truths, become an active member of the sponsoring assembly, and desire to advance professionally."

As the Christian day school movement becomes stronger and the number of pupils increase, the demand for better and more professionally trained teachers and administrators will also increase. Pentecostal colleges have begun programs for training Christian teachers. West Coast Christian College, Fresno, California, Church of God (CG), and Southeastern Assemblies of God College, Lakeland, Florida, are two examples. The Association of Christian Schools International (ACSI) has developed a certification program that Christian colleges can adopt in preparing teachers for Christian day schools. ACSI also has a certification program for administrators. Oral Roberts University offers an M.A. in Christian day school administration.

Adequate curriculum development has been one of the most difficult areas for Pentecostal and charismatic Christian day schools. Many schools have chosen to use state-approved textbooks for most subjects and have used teacher-developed materials for Bible study. This was necessary because the Bible courses available were strongly Baptistic and often anti-Pentecostal. The Assemblies of God (AG) have developed the first Pentecostal Bible textbook series, *Radiant Bible Curriculum*. Editor Lorraine Mastrorio says, "Our philosophy was to produce a curriculum in which the Bible is taught without compromise to the Person and work of the Holy Spirit. Whenever a passage deals with the Spirit our material deals with Him." All Bible lessons in this curriculum are centered around biblical truths, not situational ethics. The curriculum encourages students to seek salvation and the baptism of the Holy Spirit. *Radiant Bible Curriculum* is available for kindergarten through eighth grade. High school materials are being prepared for publication before 1990. Pentecostal and charismatic schools not only want to develop the mind but to influence the spiritual lives of students.

Curriculum development in Christian day schools has been affected by the type of school organization adopted by the church—individualized versus traditional. The traditional school with conventional grading is considered the better of the two. It provides traditional grades with trained teachers in each room. Christian textbooks published by A Beka Book Publications are often used. The individualized approach in curriculum permits students to study on the level of their ability in each subject according to entrance examinations. Two well known publishers of individualized programs are Alpha Omega Publications and Accelerated Christian Education (ACE).

In individualized programs students are usually assigned study carrels where they learn according to their ability and level of motivation. Emphasis is placed on self-motivation rather than competition with others. Because schools buy curricular materials needed by each student on his or her individual level, large initial expenditure for curriculum is avoided. A majority of Pentecostal and charismatic day schools use individualized programs. One of the advantages of Alpha Omega or ACE is that a small church can begin a Christian school with only a few students scattered from kindergarten through twelfth grade. There is also an economic advantage, because the school can use church facilities with some adaptation.

A number of Pentecostal day schools have enrollments of over five hundred. Some have excellent facilities and could compete with any private or public school. An example is Mount Paran Christian School (CG) in Atlanta, Georgia. It begins with three-year preschool and goes through twelfth grade. A program of art, music, and sports is offered in a "country day school" setting. The school employs media specialists and bus drivers and offers hot lunches. Special counseling and a program for the gifted are included. First Assembly Christian School, Memphis, Tennessee, is another strong school whose football team ranked in the top ten in the state Class A in 1983. Evangel Tabernacle (AG) in Louisville, Kentucky, has a large and extensive program from preschool through college. A well known charismatic school is Victory Christian School in Tulsa, Oklahoma. Many of the larger Pentecostal and charismatic schools are located in California, Florida, and the north-central U.S. Larger schools usually have their own buildings apart from church Christian education facilities.

Many of the problems faced by Pentecostal and charismatic schools also are common with most day schools: financial instability, inadequate buildings, insufficient equipment, curricular offerings limited to basics, unwillingness to seek accreditation, rapid turn-over of staff because of low salaries, and lack of enrollment of minority students. Few, if any, Christian schools are racially segregated by design. All of the Christian-school and denominational associations have rules that prevent member schools from practicing racial segregation.

Inadequate finances for the typical small Christian school is a major problem that also exacerbates most of the other problems. This has led some churches to decide not to have schools. They support public schools by emphasizing the Christians' responsibility to teach and otherwise participate in public schools and seek to improve conditions. Others have emphasized parental responsibility for Christian training and that parents are not to expect public schools to teach Christian values. Lack of financial stability contributes to Christian school closings each year. The number of new schools opened each year is reported by various publications, but not the number that are closed.

Although many Christian day school students score higher on national tests in basic academics, the majority of schools do not offer much in their curricula beyond the basics. This is a disadvantage for students gifted in music, athletics, and writing. This also presents problems for students who may return to public school.

Lack of accreditation of many Christian day schools has been by design. A reason often given is that schools do not want their curricula or objectives to be dictated by secular evaluators. Accreditation by regional agencies, however, does not change the purpose or curriculum of schools but evaluates whether a school is satisfactorily meeting its self-determined goals. Each year the number of accredited Christian schools increases. Because of small enrollments in many schools, lack of accreditation will remain a perennial problem.

Admission of Christian day school graduates to state universities has also been a problem. However, most Christian colleges will accept these students.

Several years ago the CG began a national Christian school association which in 1987 reported almost two hundred schools. The CG is moving toward establishing accreditation for its schools. The AG recently established the National Association of Assemblies of God Christian Schools, patterned after the successful Florida League of Assemblies of God Schools (FLAGS). The AG reports more than 1,200 schools, including preschools and day care centers. Both of these denominational agencies plan annual conferences, publish information for and about member

schools, and serve as clearinghouses for employment services and other resources.

The Oral Roberts University Education Fellowship (ORUEF) was organized in 1983 to provide information, workshops, athletic events, and guidance for Christian day schools, Bible schools, and colleges that are charismatic, full gospel, or Pentecostal in persuasion. ORUEF also hopes to serve those who are teaching their children at home. "The ORUEF," according to a 1987 brochure,

> is composed of schools whose curricula are built on the complete and uncompromised Word of God, and whose staffs, faculties, students and administrators have agreed to be led by the Holy Spirit. These Fellowship Schools, under the guidance of Oral Roberts University, agree to provide support to one another in seeking continuous spiritual development, academic credibility, and financial stability in the context of educating the whole person . . . body, mind, and spirit . . . under God's authority.

The future of Christian day schools seems bright. Increasingly, parents and churches see the need for Christian schools for their children as our society moves more toward a secularized, pagan world view. Christian schools are not adjunct to the church, but are a vital ministry where order, authority, and Christian standards combine "reading and writing" with "right and wrong."

Bibliography: H. W. Byrne, *A Christian Approach to Education* (1977); F. E. Gaebelein, *The Pattern of God's Truth* (1973); P. A. Kienel, *The Philosophy of Christian School Education* (1980); idem, *The Christian School: Why It Is Right for Your Child,* (1974); R. W. Lowrie, Jr., *Christian School Administration* (1966); idem, *Guidelines for the Establishment of Church of God Christian Day Schools* (n.d.).   J. M. Baldree

CHRISTIAN EDUCATION   See CHRISTIAN DAY SCHOOLS; SUNDAY SCHOOLS.

CHRISTIAN GROWTH MINISTRIES   See HOLY SPIRIT TEACHING MISSION; INTEGRITY COMMUNITCATIONS.

CHRISTIAN MINISTERS' ASSOCIATION A Canadian ministers' association. Previously called Evangelical Churches of Pentecost, the Christian Ministers' Association had earlier roots in the Full Gospel Missions (1927–46) and was formed in 1976. It has a statement of faith but offers latitude in interpretation. This group teaches a triunity of the Godhead but baptizes in the name of Jesus. The association awarded credentials to 225 ministers in 1987. Offices are in Surrey, British Columbia.

Bibliography: "Constitution and By-Laws of the Christian Ministers' Association"; C. Jones, *A Guide to the Study of the Pentecostal Movement* (1983).
                                                            W. E. Warner

CHRISTIAN PERFECTION (A PENTE-COSTAL PERSPECTIVE) A Holiness/ Pentecostal belief that moral perfection is taught by the Scriptures as an attainable goal and ideal state for the followers of Christ. Belief in Christian perfection played a great part in the development of the Pentecostal movement even though it did not originate with, and was not universally held by, Pentecostals. It is noteworthy that even those fellowships that have not declared perfectionism as a doctrine have nonetheless given evidence of such belief in their practices and codes of conduct.

Our consideration of the subject will therefore follow a scriptural-historical pattern:

I. Introduction
   A. A Definition of Terms
   B. Background
II. The Old Testament
   A. God's Call to Holiness
   B. Individual Examples
     1. Enoch
     2. Noah
     3. Job
   C. Between the Testaments
     1. The Essenes
     2. "The Pious People" (Pharisees)
III. The Perfect Christ
IV. The Life of Holiness
   A. Imparted Grace
   B. The Human Factor
     1. Deliverance and Overcoming
     2. Personal Examination
     3. Personal Cleansing
     4. Personal Walk
V. The Divine Nature
VI. Particulars of Perfection
   A. Progressive Likeness
   B. Distinctions of Perfection
   C. Hindrances to Holiness
     1. Hindrance by Indifference
     2. Hindrance by Carnal Behavior
       a. Temptation and Sin
       b. Carnal Thoughts
       c. Worldliness
       d. Specifics of Worldliness
VII. Summary

I. Introduction.

A. Definition of Terms. "Christian perfection" is but one of several terms that refer to the same experience or state of grace, others being "holiness," "sanctification," and "perfect love." These refer to a spiritual experience that follows regeneration and can be attained only by those who are already redeemed by Christ. Beyond the conversion experience there is a further, deeper plane of total commitment to Christ and his purpose.

The term "Christian perfection" became popular with John Wesley in the 1700s and was given wide attention by the early Methodist clergy. They preached much about a state of holy living attainable through the grace of Christ and the devotion of the believer. This experience, which was seen as an instantaneous work of grace, has ever since been spoken of as "sanctification," "holiness," or "Christian perfection." The terms are often used interchangeably, but there are different scriptural or theological shades of meaning between them.

The word *sanctification* denotes consecration and purification—a setting apart for sacred service in the OT, and spiritual purification in the NT. The word *perfection* speaks of completeness, or wholeness, of Christian character, including free-

dom from sin. Christian perfection is the possession of all the graces of the Spirit of Christ.

The word *holiness,* which is most widely used today refers to wholeness and perfection of soul. Holiness originates in conversion and covers the whole span of the Christian experience in constant growth and cleansing. It is a state of separation and purity wherein souls move toward the perfect likeness of Christ.

Both "perfection" and "holiness" are supported by scriptural references with such phrases as these in the KJV:

"We speak wisdom among them that are perfect" (1 Cor. 2:6).

"Let us go on unto perfection" (Heb. 6:1).

". . . make you perfect in every good work" (Heb. 13:21).

". . . make you perfect, stablish, strengthen, settle you" (1 Peter 5:10).

". . . for the perfecting of the saints" (Eph. 4:12).

". . . perfecting holiness in the fear of God" (2 Cor. 7:1).

". . . holiness, without which no man shall see the Lord" (Heb. 12:14).

"Sanctify" and "sanctification" are common scriptural terms that have a dual meaning. In the OT, the word *sanctify* meant a separation for divine service and referred to objects as well as persons (Exod. 29:43; 30:29; Lev. 20:7). In the NT, the word has the meaning of moral purification and refers almost entirely to persons. It is the purifying process by which holiness is possible. Jesus prayed for his disciples, "Sanctify them through thy truth: thy word is truth. . . . And for their sakes I sanctify myself, that they also might be sanctified through the truth" (John 17:17, 19).

B. Background. The quest for the perfect spiritual life can be said to predate Christianity itself. Even though the OT laid the foundation for the doctrine of perfectionism, it was in the teachings of Christ that it found its greatest expression and expectation. Through the centuries, many followers of Christ have laid claim to the promise and sought such an ideal state of grace. No people emphasized perfectionism more boldly or sought it more earnestly than those of the great Evangelical Revival of the 1700s. The movement fostered such capable spokesmen as William Law, Henry Martyn, George Whitefield, and John Wesley, whose writings still stand as effective statements of the doctrine.

In the late 1800s and early 1900s there was a growing impression by some Holiness believers that the direct spiritual heirs of Wesley had betrayed their trust. These Holiness people then took up the standard with great vigor, spawning numerous Christian bodies that were faithful to the Holiness tradition. Among them were several bodies that later became primary parts of the Pentecostal revival. Among the more prominent perfectionist Pentecostal bodies were the Church of God (Cleveland, Tenn.), the Fire-Baptized Holiness Church, the Pentecostal Holiness Church, the Church of God in Christ, the Congregational Holiness Church, and the Mountain Assembly Church of God.

The beliefs of these groups were almost identical to the time-honored beliefs of Wesley and the early Methodist Church concerning holiness of doctrine and life. Thus the teaching of Christian perfection was a vital part of the early Pentecostal message. Not all of the Pentecostal bodies came out of the Holiness tradition, but the earliest bodies did, and the most prominent views of the nineteenth-century Holiness movement became part and parcel of the twentieth-century Pentecostal movement.

An examination of humanity's quest for Christian perfection and the reasons for man's hope must center in the Holy Scriptures.

II. The Old Testament

A. *God's Call to Holiness.* God created man with a longing to be like his Creator. When God said, "Let us make man in our image, after our likeness" (Gen. 1:26 KJV), the prospect of godliness was implied. Man's likeness to God was to be spiritual rather than physical, a truth that became clear when God later said to the Israelites, "I am the LORD who brought you up out of Egypt to be your God; therefore be holy, because I am holy" (Lev. 11:45) and used similar language in several places in the Torah—Leviticus 11:44; 19:2; 20:26; Deuteronomy 7:6; 14:2.

In all of these instances, God called on his people to be separated from all things that were profane and unclean. This made God's holiness a pattern for man to follow, an entirely appropriate way in which man can be Godlike.

Holiness is an attribute that God shares with man and even expects of man. In no place does the Bible state or imply that God shares with man such attributes as omnipotence, omniscience, or omnipresence. Such sovereign attributes belong to God alone, and any pretense of man's sharing them is false. Before the creation of man, Lucifer made the presumptuous boast that he would be like God in power and sovereignty (Isa. 14:12–14), but he showed no desire to be like him in holiness. That unholy aspiration formed the seedbed of all heresy. Adam and Eve were induced to seek Godlikeness (Gen. 3:5) but not the holiness that is characteristic of him. These perverse notions of being like God in sovereignty serve mainly to underscore the fact that God will share with man only that likeness that exalts man's character, morals, and ethics. Grievous error always results from human effort to emulate God's attributes of power.

But God calls on man to reach for his pattern of purity and separateness. "Make every effort to live in peace with all men and to be holy; without holiness no one will see the Lord" (Heb. 12:14).

B. *Individual Examples.* Several persons in the OT were noted for their high degree of holy living. They lived between the fall of Adam, whereby a sinful nature was imputed to all people, and the advent of grace, wherein people can attain through Christ a state of holiness patterned after him. Through the sin of Adam the nature of man was fatally injured (Rom. 5:12–17) and man lived under a sentence of death. Nevertheless, even before the advent of Christ, there arose a few noble persons who reached upward toward that perfection for which man was created.

1. *Enoch.* The first person mentioned in Scripture for his singular devotion to God was Enoch, who "walked with God; and he was not, for God took him" (Gen. 5:24). In the NT, the translation of Enoch is mentioned as a reward for his faith: "By faith Enoch was taken from this life, so that he did not experience death; he could not be found because God had taken him away. For before he was taken, he was commended as one who pleased God" (Heb. 11:5).

Jude called Enoch a prophet and quoted his prophecy: "See, the Lord is coming with thousands upon thousands of his holy ones" (Jude 14). Enoch is pictured as one looking toward a time when holiness will fill people's hearts and control their lives.

2. *Noah.* The piety of Noah is seen against the backdrop of a sinful world following the Fall. When God wearied of the corruption of mankind (Gen. 6:11–12) and determined to punish the world with a flood, only Noah was deemed worthy to survive. "Noah was a righteous man, blameless among the people of his time, and he walked with God " (v. 9). The KJV translates this verse as "Noah was a just man and perfect in his generations." The words "blameless" and especially "perfect" have caused problems for some extreme views of Christian perfection, because Noah did not always exemplify the holiness called for in Scripture. When the Flood ended, he was recorded as being both drunken and uncovered (Gen. 9:21), hardly the condition for a blameless or perfect man. But this flawed state of holiness is understood by the words "in his generations." The generations of Noah were before the grace of Christ provided for the purification of the human heart; when people offered sacrifices that brought forgiveness but not the eradication of sin. By sacrifices people could be forgiven but not sanctified in heart, and so the sacrifices had to be made anew year after year (Heb. 10:3–4, 11).

The OT call for sanctification, and holiness was a call for physical separation from the profane and unclean things of life. Yet in them there was the anticipation of Christ and his perfection, by which the heart of man could be perfected (Heb. 5:9).

3. *Job.* A more Christlike figure than Noah was Job, who in many ways reflected a Christian purity of heart. Twice the Lord spoke of him as being unlike any other man: "He is blameless and upright, a man who fears God and shuns evil" (Job 1:8; 2:3). Once again, the KJV uses the word "perfect" for "blameless." No higher commendation is possible than for God to deem a person blameless, which is precisely what Peter called upon Christians to be: "You ought to live holy and godly lives . . . make every effort to be found spotless, blameless and at peace with him" (2 Peter 3:11, 14). This can be called the ideal statement of Christian perfection.

In his generation Job gave evidence of those pure qualities that are expected of modern-day Christians. He was patient, kind, faithful, generous, and Godward in his life. Some modern-day individuals who are embarrassed by Job's suffering because it contradicts their beliefs about prosperity and health have tried to demean his spiritual character, but it was God who pronounced him blameless. And yet, as Christlike as he was, there were imperfections in Job's perfection. While a detailing of those deficiencies is not necessary for this study, a recognition of them does underscore the unique nature of Christian perfection.

C. Between the Testaments. The patriarchs and prophets were noted for a singular piety as each endeavored to abide by the commandment "Be holy, for I am holy." There were also occasional sects of the Jews who endeavored to follow the commandment, the most notable of which flourished in the intertestamental period. At times when Israel experienced defeat and humiliation at the hands of such heathen nations as Assyria, Babylonia, Greece, and Rome, the need of spiritual renewal and devotion became apparent to many. The place of holiness was recognized by the prophet Isaiah, who envisioned the holiness of God and the profanity of the people (Isa. 6:2–5ff.). Ezekiel also wrote powerfully that the nation's troubles were due to its departure from God's requirement of holiness (Ezek. 22:26).

1. The Essenes. One of the several sects that arose for the preservation of the Law and piety was the Essenes. This brotherhood of seekers for truth and holiness was formed two centuries before Christ and survived until after the Roman destruction of Palestine. The Essenes lived in the area of the Dead Sea and apparently influenced John the Baptist. Although their emphasis on being holy made considerable impact on the Jewish people, the monastic brotherhood is best remembered because it hid copies of the Scriptures in caves near its Dead Sea community and thereby preserved ancient texts of the sacred Word. These became known as the Dead Sea Scrolls.

2. "The Pious People." Of considerably greater influence on the early Christian era was a well-known brotherhood known as the *Hasidim*—The Pious Ones. This major sect set out nearly four hundred years before Christ to establish a perfect body of the faithful. Later known as the Pharisees, they are portrayed for the most part as the chief antagonists of Christ; and yet it should still be remembered how devoutly they undertook to preserve the law of Moses, maintain the integrity of the nation, and perfect the holiness of the Lord.

The Scriptures reveal many noble qualities of the Pharisees, a once-admirable group who held an orthodox theology and a pious pattern of life. For a great period of their existence they did preserve the Scriptures and keep faith alive. They are given credit in the NT for their zeal and beliefs. They held rigidly to the inspiration of the Scriptures (John 5:39), the resurrection of the dead (Acts 23:6), the efficacy of prayer (John 9:31), the forgiveness of sins (Luke 5:21), the reality of the spirit world (Acts 23:8), eternal life (John 5:39), obedience of the Sabbath law (Matt. 12:2), fasting as religious regimen (Luke 18:12), tithing (Matt. 23:23), a strong missionary effort (v. 15) and other emphasis on pious practices.

In fact, the Pharisees' intent upon perfection makes what they became by the time of Christ all the more tragic. It also accounts for much of what he said to his followers about them, such as "Be on your guard against the yeast of the Pharisees, which is hypocrisy" (Luke 12:1) and "The teachers of the law and the Pharisees sit in Moses' seat. So you must obey them and do everything they tell you. But do not do what they do, for they do not practice what they preach" (Matt. 23:2–3).

So, two of the three great religio-philosophic bodies leading up to the time of Christ had high ideals regarding righteousness, but their performance was dangerously below what they preached. The Lord warned the people, "Unless your righteousness surpasses that of the Pharisees and the teachers of the law, you will certainly not enter the kingdom of heaven" (Matt. 5:20).

III. The Perfect Christ. It is basic to an understanding of Christian perfection to bear in mind that the law could not provide for the high expectations contained in the law. Those expectations pointed to Christ, who was the perfection of all contained in the law. The law pointed to Christ and all who kept the law lived in spiritual anticipation of him. "For what the law was powerless to do in that it was weakened by the sinful nature, God did by sending his own son in the likeness of sinful man to be a sin offering. And so he condemned sin in sinful man, in order that the righteous requirements of the law might be fully met in us, who do not live according to the sinful nature but according to the Spirit" (Rom. 8:3–4).

Jesus was perfection incarnate. It was his life on earth that set an example of holiness, and it was his sacrifice on the Cross that made holiness possible. Paul wrote to the Corinthians that "God made him who had no sin to be sin for us, so that in him we might become the righteousness of God" (2 Cor. 5:21). In him man can experience redemption from sin and reconciliation to God, so that the mandate "Be holy, because I am holy" becomes both a possibility and an expectation. Through the propitiation of Christ, "who is holy, blameless, pure, set apart from sinners, exalted above the heavens" and "who has been made perfect forever," we have access to all grace whereby the righteous can be made perfect (Heb. 7:26–28).

John Wesley, the foremost preacher of Christian perfection in the 1700s, preached that the life of Christ, culminating in the Cross, is a way we must imitate. This way is a possibility only for those who are justified by faith in Christ and have received him as Savior and follow him as Lord. The possibility of this perfection begins with Christ the Reconciler and continues with Christ the Pattern. The term "imitation of Christ" has often been used in reference to the demands laid on Christians to pattern their lives after Christ. "Be imitators of God, therefore, as dearly loved children and live a life of love, just as Christ loved us" (Eph. 5:1–2). The admonition to follow the pattern of Christ is explicit throughout the NT, a requirement that begins with our entering a state of grace. It is understood in the Scriptures that those who are encouraged toward spiritual perfection, perfect love, sanctification (or any of the other terms used to identify the deeper spiritual experience) have already accepted Christ as Savior. It would be futile and a kind of mockery to encourage unregenerate men and women to a position of Christian perfection. In the teaching of Scripture the spiritual life is seen as a progressive maturity of the soul. That was clearly the import of Paul's words to the immature Corinthians, "I could not address you as spiritual but as worldly—mere infants in Christ" (1 Cor. 3:1); and of Peter's forceful direction, "Like newborn babies, crave pure spiritual milk, so that by it you can grow up in your salvation, now that you have tasted that the Lord is good" (1 Peter 2:2).

The simile used by Peter and Paul is consistent throughout the NT, beginning with Jesus' statement that we must be born again (John 3:3). As allowance is made for babies to grow up through childhood to adulthood, so allowance is made for Christians to mature in the same manner. The grace of Christ covers all stages of development. A babe in Christ is not cut off just because he is not yet a perfect man or woman of God—for he is still a perfect child; and in each child there is the promise of adulthood. We can be perfect Christians without being perfect men and women. The apostles were not such perfect men that they did not seek personal advantage or sometimes feel jealousy or vindictiveness. Yet they were perfect in obedience and teachableness. In the grace of Christ we are accepted and loved at whatever stage of development we are. As C. S. Lewis wrote, if we have a will to walk, God is pleased even when we stumble. The pathway to perfection is paved with human desire and divine grace. Christ's call to perfection is clear and undeniable—with the understanding that it presupposes our position in him. He said to the rich young man, "If you want to be perfect, go, sell your possessions and give to the poor, and you will have treasure in heaven. Then come, follow me" (Matt. 19:21). In John 17:23 he prayed that his disciples might be made perfect in unity (KJV), and in Matthew 5:48 he said most tellingly, "Be perfect, therefore, as your heavenly Father is perfect."

Equally emphatic are the further calls to perfection in the epistles. Paul pointed out that the purpose of teaching is the perfecting of the saints. See Ephesians 4:11–12 (KJV); Colossians 1:28; 2 Timothy 3:16, 17 (KJV). In these verses we see the progression into perfection by those who are already converted to Christ; we see the state of their mature and complete devotion to Christ. The Holiness revival of the eighteenth century identified it as sanctification, an experience effected by grace for our continued purification unto perfection. The life of holiness is made possible by the continuing work of Christ within us.

IV. The Life of Holiness. An analysis of the words "holy" and "holiness" leads us along an interesting and beautiful path. In the OT, where the Hebrew word *qadesh* is used in connection with God himself, it refers to his divine nature, his transcendence, his separation from all that is earthly and human (Exod. 15:11; Ps. 47:8; Isa. 6:3). It speaks first of ceremonial purity, but in a narrower sense, to the purity of God's character. Thus in its most frequent OT usage holiness of persons referred to a ceremonial separation for divine purposes, yet the higher sense of moral purity was always present. Moral implications are assuredly in much of the law, such as "I am the LORD your God; consecrate yourselves and be holy, because I am holy. Do not make yourselves unclean by any creature that moves about on the ground" (Lev. 11:44).

In the NT the preponderant use of the word "holiness" (*hagiotes*) has reference to purity, with the sense of separation always present. Separation and purity are entwined in the sense that holiness is separation from sin and separation to God. So God "disciplines us for our good, that we may share in his holiness" (Heb. 12:10). When we go further into the meaning of the word, we find that it is related to the words *whole, hale, healthy,* and so on.

In the life of the Christian, holiness, or Christian perfection, is purity of heart and mind and freedom from defilement and contamination. Positively it is separation unto God and negatively, a separation from sin. It is perfect health of soul, that is, the healthy development of the divine nature of God within us. Having been born of God, we have the beginning of a life wherein lies the possibility of perfect likeness to him. "But now that you have been set free from sin and have become slaves to God, the benefit you reap leads to holiness, and the result is eternal life" (Rom. 6:22); "Put on the new self, created to be like God in true righteousness and holiness" (Eph. 4:24).

A. Imparted Grace. Human holiness is predicated on God's holiness. He is holy, and we are called to be like him in holiness. "But just as he who called you is holy, so be holy in all you do" (1 Peter 1:15). With these words Peter repeated the command of the law and put a Christian emphasis on it. God expects us to share in his holiness and disciplines us that we may do so (Heb. 12:10). God's crowning attribute is holiness; it is the fountainhead of all his moral attributes: his love, his mercy, his justice, his faithfulness, his love of goodness and hatred of evil in man. Holiness is also God's communicable attribute, which means that he imparts to us the essence of his own holy nature. If we are to be perfect even as he is perfect—and that remains his commandment to us—we must be partakers of his nature, his holiness.

God does not impute holiness—he imparts it. By sanctification through the blood of Christ he imparts to man purity of heart, mind and soul. This impartation is a positional holiness not attained by man's own efforts. In his 1880 study of *Perfect Love*, J. A. Wood said: "Holiness in man, wrought by grace and power of Christ, is precisely the same as the holiness of God. The same in 'kind'—the one is 'original,' and the other is derived and inwrought by the Holy Ghost. 'Be ye holy, for I am holy.' God is both the model and the source of all holiness" (53).

Another writer of the past century, Mark Guy Pearse, wrote in *Thoughts on Holiness* (1884): "We think and talk of holiness as if it were getting into the King's garden, climbing over a wall by tremendous effort, or getting in as a great favor. . . . No: holiness is ours only when we open the door of our heart unto the King, that He himself may come in and make this barren place the garden of the Lord, a very paradise wherein he may walk and talk with his child" (163).

It is clear that God's holiness becomes essentially our holiness and his perfection makes our perfection possible—he the perfect Father and Lord, and we the perfect child and follower. We must have this impartation in order to keep such commandments as this: "Love the Lord your God with all your heart and with all your soul and with all your mind and with all your strength" (Mark 12:30). Such a commandment is impossible if we have nothing more than natural or human resources. To love him with all our heart we must conform our will to his will; to love him with all our soul we must feel as he feels about all things and worship him as sovereign in all things; to love him with all our mind we must think as he thinks and let him rule our thoughts; to love him with all our strength we must endeavor to do his work in all the situations of life. This kind of obedience comes only by his holiness within us. There is no other way.

B. The Human Factor. Although Christian holiness is inwrought by the grace of Christ, much is left for Christians to do in the progression and refinement of their experience. The degree of spiritual watchcare that is left to this human factor is quite remarkable. Every person who will be perfect in Christ is responsible for the maintenance of his holiness. Through sanctification we are not only purified but also empowered to overcome sin. We have an important part in safeguarding our holiness experience.

1. *Deliverance and Overcoming.* It is notable that in Scripture we read equally of deliverance and overcoming. The word "overcome" suggests conflict and victory. While there is no question that God is able to deliver the Christian from every occasion of trouble, he does not always do so. He frequently chooses for us to overcome evil by a united effort of the soul and the power of his grace (2 Cor. 12:7–10). His grace is always sufficient to deliver the believer from trouble or temptation, but it is often more beneficial for the believer to gain the victory by overcoming the difficulty. For this reason there is a special blessing in God's Word for those who overcome (e.g., 1 John 4:4; 5:4; Rom. 12:21; Rev. 21:7). The only way one can overcome weakness or evil is to be allowed to come to grips with it, and for this reason God does not deliver people from every presence of temptation or evil. He expects them by his grace to overcome their deficiencies and carnal inclinations. It must be understood, however, that within themselves people are not able to overcome evil and achieve a holy life. They must overcome by the power of his grace and thereby become the spiritually strong persons God calls them to be.

2. *Personal Examination.* It is the responsibility of each person to keep his life under constant and honest surveillance lest there enter his heart any desire or motive that is contrary to the Spirit of God. Paul encouraged self-examination as a means of appraising one's spiritual well-being: "Examine yourselves to see whether you are in the faith; test yourselves. Do you not realize that Christ is in you—unless, of course, you fail the test?" (2 Cor. 13:5). The basis of this watchfulness should be the Word of God, for it is obedience to his Word that perfects God's love in the Christian heart (1 John 2:5).

Jesus frequently reminded the disciples to "watch" or "beware" lest temptation or covetousness or absorption with the world overcome them. The writer to the Hebrews affirmed that counsel in this way: "Make every effort to live in peace with all men and to be holy; without holiness no one will see the Lord. See to it that no one misses the grace of God and that no bitter root grows up to cause trouble and defile many" (Heb. 12:14–15). It is only by Scripture reading and meditation, coupled with prayers that personal safeguards can be established.

3. *Personal Cleansing.* Holiness is perfected by those who purify themselves from everything that contaminates body and spirit (2 Cor. 7:1). The Bible speaks here of an ongoing process of purging out all unchristian habits or attitudes that flaw the Christian character. John, repeating the strong admonition of Paul, wrote, "Everyone who has this hope in him purifies himself, just as he is pure" (1 John 3:1–3).

If, as in Paul's admonition, a Christian must purify himself from things that contaminate body and spirit; and, in John's words, he must purify himself as Christ is pure, then the Christian's situation becomes quite clear. God's grace and love and hope provide the strength whereby he can purify himself continually from things that are unlike the Lord.

These instructions would not have been written if they were beyond the reach of man. The procedure of obedience is simple—what Christ would not do if he were on earth should be purged from the Christian's personal life. If Christ would not engage in a physical habit or indulgence, or would not allow the poison of bitterness or envy or hate to enter his spirit, then it must be purged from the believer's spirit. He requires those who are his to purify themselves from all that is contrary to him.

4. *Personal Walk.* A further way Christians are to follow the pattern of Christ is mentioned by both Peter and John as following in his steps. Peter wrote, Christ "suffered for you, leaving you an example, that you should follow in his steps" (1 Peter 2:21); and John wrote, "Whoever claims to live in him must walk as Jesus did" (1 John 2:6). Peter clearly was speaking of how believers should bear up under persecution: "For it is commendable if a man bears up under the pain of unjust suffering because he is conscious of God" (1 Peter 2:19), while John was more general in his teaching, which emphasized the necessity of Christian love: If the believer is obedient to Christ's commands even in the face of suffering, then love is perfected in him.

It is clear from the teachings of the NT that Christ begins the work of perfection in the believer, and yet he expects the believer to grow in him and become increasingly like him. This can be done only by prayer and devotion and taking his Word into one's life. It also requires resolve and fortitude. Christian perfection, the life of perfect holiness, must result from divine grace and human devotion united in the believer's life.

V. The Divine Nature. Man alone cannot live a Christian life, no matter how noble his efforts and intentions may be. He must have a change of nature so profound that it is referred to as being born again (John 3:5–6; 1 Peter 1:23); a new creation (2 Cor. 5:17; Gal. 6:15); a new man (Eph. 2:15); and a new self (Eph. 4:24; Col. 3:10). The one who comes to Christ receives a divine power so sufficient that he is a new person. Second Peter 1:3–4 assures us that God's "divine power has given us everything we need for life and godliness through our knowledge of him who called us by his own power and goodness. Through these he has given us his very great and precious promises, so that through them you may participate in the divine nature and escape the corruption in the world caused by evil desires."

The ineffable glory of participating in the divine nature is beyond any human right or merit, as well as beyond any imagination or expectation. It is a benefit that Christ gives to his believers, a boon by which they are able to experience a growth of soul that is ever expanding with his likeness. This participation in the divine nature enables the believer to escape the world's corruption and attraction and to attain the perfection of spirit unknown to the worldly minded.

On his last evening with his disciples, as he faced the horrors of the Cross, Jesus shared a remarkable intimacy with his friends. He spoke of a unique relationship that surpassed other relationships he had already revealed to them. Earlier, he had referred to himself as the Shepherd and to the disciples as the sheep, and to himself as the Gate of the sheepfold (John 10:7, 11, 14); he had spoken of himself as Master and to them as brethren (Matt. 23:8); and, earlier on this final evening he referred to himself as Teacher and Lord and to them as his servants and messengers (John 13:13–14, 16). But none of these were as revealing and profound as what he said toward the end of his long discourse to them. John records these words of Jesus:

> I am the true vine and my Father is the gardener. He cuts off every branch in me that bears no fruit, while every branch that does bear fruit he prunes so that it will be even more fruitful. You are already clean because of the word I have spoken to you. Remain in me, and I will remain in you. No branch can bear fruit of itself; it must remain in the vine. Neither can you bear fruit unless you remain in me. I am the vine; you are the branches. If a man remains in me and I in him, he will bear much fruit. . . .

> This is to my Father's glory, that you bear much fruit, showing yourselves to be my disciples (John 15:1–5, 8).

This entire section must be studied in order to see the openness with which Christ disclosed the continuing relationship he wishes to have with his followers. It is a relationship as valid in modern times as it was on the fateful evening when he first revealed it.

In this portion of Christ's word we see the divine nature as it operates between the Lord and his people, and we see the oneness that exists in the ideal spiritual life. The vine and the branches are essentially one, for they cannot be different. A grape vine does not produce fig branches, for the branches must be the same as the vine that produces them. The vine and its branches live in a threefold relationship, which was emphasized in the Lord's discourse: (1) they are joined together; (2) they are of the same nature; (3) they serve the same purpose.

The branches are dependent upon the vine for life; any branch that loses its union with the vine "is thrown away and withers." It is essential to understand that people become Christians only by being "in Christ," a term used 6 times in the quoted verses. Paul spoke 164 times of himself as being a man "in Christ." It is not enough to accept Christ only as a teacher or only to read his words or only to follow his ethical example or do any of the things that may make a good Buddhist or Hindu or Muslim. To be a true Christian, we must have a spiritual union with him; we must be in him and he in us.

This union commences at conversion but deepens and strengthens as we remain in him and his words remain in us. His purpose is more fully revealed in us as we progress in devotion to him.

The vine and the branch must be of the same essence, the same nature, the same spirit. Just as it is biologically impossible for a branch to be different from the tree on which it grows, so it is impossible for a true Christian to be of a nature that is contrary to the nature of Christ. What he is in holiness and love, we must become. It is more than patterning our lives after him through self-effort. This means in particular that it is important but not sufficient that we abstain from things he abstained from. In Christian perfection it is necessary to perfect those qualities of holiness that were present in Christ: He was loving, so we must love; he was forgiving, so we must forgive; he was kind, so we must be kind. That was the true intent of his discourse about the vine and the branches (John 15:9–10, 12–13, 17). Christian perfection is not to be viewed as the sum of our restrictions and taboos. It is important that we refrain from unholy practices, but it is more important that we abstain because we have no inclination or disposition for them. Christian self-denial should come from the Spirit of Christ flowing freely in us.

It is significant that the only time Jesus ever spoke of sanctification was when he prayed in the course of his final evening with his disciples: "Sanctify them by the truth; your word is truth. . . . For them I sanctify myself, that they too may be truly sanctified" (John 17:17, 19). Note carefully that Christ specified the means by which sanctification should be achieved—"by the truth," the Word of God.

Paul wrote to the Ephesians that "Christ loved the church and gave himself up for her to make her holy, cleansing her by the washing with water through the word" (5:25–26). The Word of God must take root in our lives so that we by our very nature are guided by it, reproved by it, comforted by it, pruned by it until we manifest the very nature of Christ. "If you remain in me and my words remain in you, ask whatever you wish, and it will be given you" (John 15:7). When the spirit, the essence, the nature, the word of Christ dwell in you, you will not "ask with wrong motives that you may spend what you get on your pleasures" (James 4:3), but you will ask only in accordance with the purposes of Christ the Vine.

Christian perfection does not consist only of chaste and godly behavior. There is also a responsibility for service. The third truth of Christ's discourse on the vine and the branches is this: the purpose of the branches is to bear the fruit of the vine. It is not enough for the fig branches to have the nature of the fig tree—they must bear figs. The Lord gave a graphic lesson in this when he cursed the barren fig tree because it bore leaves without bearing fruit. He did not spare the tree because of the multiplicity of bad fruit it did not bear, but he cursed it because it did not produce the good fruit its leaves proclaimed was there. The branches must bear fruit, for "he cuts off every branch . . . that bears no fruit" (Mark 11:12–14).

In some earlier emphases on Christian perfection less has been said about service than about emotions and behavior, but the twentieth-century Pentecostal has emphasized that the healthy branch is a fruitful branch. (John 14:12) Christian perfection is being a healthy, holy, productive branch of Christ the Vine. It consists of doing what is right in equal measure with not doing what is wrong. Jesus' repeated reference to love in the discourse makes it clear that love is a primary fruit of holiness. But love is more than a passive emotion—it is a force that serves and blesses other persons. First Corinthians 13 gives a list of what love does: it makes people patient and kind; it causes them to rejoice in the truth, to protect, trust, hope, and persevere. This chapter also lists what love restrains people from doing: they will not be envious, boastful, proud, rude, self-seeking, or easily angered; they will not keep a record of wrongs or take delight in evil.

So it is with all the fruit of holiness—it is not only being good but also doing good. This active goodness can be accomplished only by the power of the Holy Spirit, who has been sent in Christ's stead for this dispensation. He empowers the branches to bear the fruit of the vine, that is, to do in their generation what Christ would do if he were on earth today (Luke 4:18–19).

VI. Particulars of Perfection. The work of perfection in the Christian life is not always easy to understand. There are practical aspects that result from the spiritual experience, and these do not always correspond to human expectations or imperfect preferences. We are called to be perfect even as our heavenly Father is perfect, and yet we seem never to attain that state. No one who knows his weaknesses and frailties, his shortcomings and imperfections, can seriously consider

himself to be perfect. Nor should he, for perfection is essentially a process of becoming.

A. Progressive Likeness. The biblical call to perfection is a call to be like Christ, who was the incarnate Word of God, called both Son of God and Son of Man. Jesus, in order to assume the likeness of man, found it necessary to experience growth and development while he lived on earth. Luke's account of Christ's life reveals an aspect of his perfection that is easily overlooked—at least in its significance to what perfection is: "And the child grew and became strong in spirit" (1:80); "and Jesus grew in wisdom and stature, and in favor with God and men" (2:52). In both Zechariah's prophecy and the historical record we see Christ growing and gaining in strength and wisdom. Yet he was perfect from the beginning— and final perfection cannot be improved.

Nature shows that a perfect infant is not a perfect man or woman, nor is a perfect child or a perfect youth yet a perfect man or woman. The perfection is in each stage of the person's development and growth. Perfection does not mean completion, for then nothing of growth would remain. The glory of perfection is that it is perfect at each appropriate stage. Christian perfection is a purging from the principles of sin so that the nature of Christ can course without obstruction in the heart of the believer. In so doing the likeness of Christ is more and more evident in the believer's life. The spirit of love and devotion, made perfect in nature through sanctification, will grow and expand, encompassing more and more of life and its relationships.

B. Distinctions of Perfection. This requires an understanding of what is meant by the term *perfection.* With the sin principle destroyed by sanctification, does it become impossible to sin? That is never the assurance of Scripture, as is seen in such statements as that of John: "My dear children, I write this to you so that you will not sin. But if anybody does sin, we have one who speaks to the Father in our defense—Jesus Christ, the Righteous One" (1 John 2:1).

A distinction must be made between Christian perfection and absolute or sinless perfection. John Wesley, despite the accusations of George Whitefield to the contrary, denied believing in or preaching sinless perfection. But, Wesley elaborated, that position must be understood in the light of willful sin and involuntary sin. Strictly speaking, sin is any disobedience of the commands of God, and the likelihood of never breaking one is remote indeed. Sinless perfection is a goal that can hardly be attained in this life, but Christian perfection can be attained. A Christian may sin because he is still human, and there is no human perfection; but being a perfect Christian, he will respond to his circumstance according to the perfection of Christ's life within him. In this manner even the apostle Paul could correct his errors (Acts 23:3–5; 2 Cor. 12:13). There are numerous terms in the Bible that disprove sinless human perfection, among which are "error," "wrong," "fault," "deceived," and "stumble," for, as James said most tellingly, "We all stumble in many ways. If anyone is never at fault in what he says, he is a perfect man, able to keep his whole body in check" (3:2).

Charles Wesley, who took issue with his brother John's extreme view of perfection, wrote to John: "One word more, concerning setting perfection too high. That perfection [in] which I believe, I can boldly preach because I think I can see five hundred witnesses of it. [But] that perfection which you preach, you do not even think you see any witnesses at all." Charles continued in his letter, "Where are the perfect ones? I verily believe there are none upon earth, none dwelling in the body. . . . Therefore I still think to set perfection [too] high is effectually to renounce it" (*Letters*, vol. 20).

John admitted to the impossibility of sinless perfection when it meant the involuntary transgression of a known law.

I believe there is no such perfection in this life as excludes these involuntary transgressions which I apprehend to be naturally consequent on the ignorance and mistakes inseparable from mortality. Therefore, *sinless perfection* is a phrase I never use, lest I should seem to contradict myself. I believe a person filled with the love of God is still liable to these involuntary transgressions. Such transgressions you may call sins, if you please; I do not . . . ("A Plain Account of Christian Perfection," *Works of Wesley* 1:396).

From the time of the Holiness revival to the present the issue has been whether the scriptural statements about perfection refer to absolute sinlessness in the voluntary sense or whether the statements refer to the human attachment to a sinless Christ. Christians must constantly strive for the likeness of Christ, even when it means trusting in his perfect love when our perfection is imperfect. One may sin because he is an imperfect person, but if he is a perfect Christian he will repair the wrong and cling all the closer to the perfect Christ.

The Greek word *teleios*, which with its derivatives is translated "perfect" in the KJV (Matt. 5:48; Gal. 3:3; Eph. 4:13; Phil. 3:15; Col. 1:28; 4:12; James 1:4), means complete or full-grown, as being mature in moral character. The word indicates the achievement of a desired purpose, as when Christ, who knew no sin, was made "perfect through suffering" (Heb. 2:10). A study of the cited Scriptures reveals that our own perfection is manifested by various spiritual achievements such as faithfulness in times of trial (James 1:4), dependence on the Holy Spirit (Gal. 3:3), and sensitivity to the will of God (Col. 4:12). These qualities of spiritual maturity make people like Christ, a state of perfection that reaches its fulfillment only when we enter eternal life with him (John 3:2).

C. Hindrances to Holiness. There are many forces that hinder the holy life, some of which are of the world and some of which are of the flesh. There are inner forces that war against the soul, not outward antagonisms that overwhelm it. There is an inescapable tension between the world and those who profess a life of holiness, which by

its very nature is antiworldly. Jesus prayed for his believers, who would be subjected in all ages to the fierce antagonisms of the world: "My prayer is not that you take them out of the world but that you protect them from the evil one. They are not of the world, even as I am not of it" (John 17:15–16).

The history of the Christian faith shows that it has been unhindered by persecution. That has been equally true of the Holiness movement of later years and the Holiness Pentecostal revival of this present era. (See HOSTILITY/PERSECUTION.)

1. Hindrance by Indifference. Realization of the sanctified life is hindered by the attitudes and behavior of the individual believers. The promises of grace, including that of perfect love, are for those who ardently seek them. "Blessed are those who hunger and thirst for righteousness, for they will be filled" (Matt. 5:6).

Philip Doddridge said in his spiritual autobiography, *The Rise and Progress of Religion in the Soul:* "To allow yourself deliberately to sit down satisfied with any *imperfect* attainments in religion, and to look upon a more confirmed and improved state of it as what you do not desire, say, *as what you secretly resolve that you will not pursue,* is one of the most fatal signs we can well imagine that you are an entire stranger to the first principles of it." (In Wood, *Perfect Love,* 219; Doddridge was a famous nonconformist minister and educator in Northampton, England, who encouraged, and was encouraged by, John Wesley and the Methodist pioneers.)

M. G. Pearse wrote that holiness is "perfect health of soul. And what is perfect health anywhere, in anything? It cannot be other than this—perfect distribution of all that life depends upon. . . . This is holiness. This reception checked, then at once the life is a sickly one. This reception stopped, then the sickness is unto death" (*Thoughts on Holiness,* 24). Just as hunger and thirst are necessary for the development of a healthy body, so spiritual hunger and thirst are necessary for health of soul and for our likeness of God. Indifference and lukewarmness in the life of Christ cannot produce the divine nature that is necessary to be like him, for health of soul is both the source and the product of an endless hunger and thirst for more of Christ. There is an insatiable longing for more and more of Christ in those who are fully committed to him, which is to say that those who do not have these longings are deficient in their commitment to him. When a person loses his physical ability to be hungry, he is sick, in need of healing, a circumstance no less true in the spiritual life; one who lacks appropriate spiritual hunger is in need of healing.

Jesus made the deficiencies of indifference even more graphic in his remonstrance to the church of Laodicea: "I know your deeds, that you are neither cold nor hot. I wish you were either one or the other! So, because you are lukewarm—neither hot nor cold—I am about to spit you out of my mouth" (Rev. 3:15–16). Those Christians who wish not to be lukewarm and ineffective witnesses for Christ must go on to perfection. There is no middle ground—they will either go forward or they will ultimately fall back and bring reproach to the cause of Christ. The apostle Paul disclaimed that he had "already been made perfect, but I press on to take hold of that for which Christ Jesus took hold of me. Brothers, I do not consider myself yet to have taken hold of it. But one thing I do: Forgetting what is behind and striving toward what is ahead, I press on toward the goal to win the prize for which God has called me heavenward in Christ Jesus" (Phil. 3:12–14). There is no time or place in the holy walk to stop pressing, stop growing, stop hungering, for however deep in Christ we go, there is still more, much more, ahead.

2. *Hindrance by Carnal Behavior.* This precious grace of sanctification has been given so that we may be free from the corruption of the world (2 Peter 2:20). It is therefore damaging to the spiritual life when carnal attitudes intrude unchecked into the Christian's heart and mind.

a. *Temptation and Sin.* Carnal temptations will inevitably come into the sanctified life, and saints have often doubted their perfection because of such dark whisperings in the mind. But a firm distinction must be made between temptation and sin. When Christ was tempted, it was through the words that Satan spoke to him. Although there was never a moment when Christ came near to yielding to the suggestions, they were clear enough in his mind to be recorded in the Holy Scriptures (Matt. 4:3, 5, 7).

Perfect love cleanses a person from sin but does not remove him from the possibility of sinning. Proof of this lies in the fact that one can be tempted, which would be impossible if sin were impossible. But many who seek a life of holiness have difficulty in knowing when temptation becomes sin. This problem arises from the fact that temptation comes in the form of thoughts, and Jesus said, "Out of the heart come evil thoughts" (Matt. 15:19). He certainly did not mean that tempting thoughts are evil thoughts, for he was tempted in every way, just as we are and yet was without sin (Heb. 4:15). Almost all, if not all, temptation comes to us through the process of thought, as evil speaks and we hear it. But because Jesus suffered the onslaughts of temptation, he is able to help those who are tempted (Heb. 2:18). J. A. Wood gave a thoughtful solution to the following question:

The object of temptation must exist intellectually or there could be no temptation. The temptation may exist to this extent without sin, and hence evil suggestions that are presented to our minds but have no effect on our desires or will are only temptations. No temptation or evil suggestion to the mind becomes sin till it is cherished or tolerated. Sin consists of yielding to temptation. So long as the soul maintains its integrity so that temptation finds no sympathy within, no sin is committed and the soul remains unharmed, no matter how protracted or severe the fiery trial may prove (*Perfect Love*, 62, 63).

Temptation becomes sin when it is acted upon, or finds concurrence in the will. When wrong thoughts become yearning or take residence in the mind, there is sin, for then the evil thoughts proceed from the mind. The mind should be a fortress for the soul, a bulwark that repels evil before it takes root in the heart. That is one intent of the word: "Do not conform any longer to the pattern of this world, but be transformed by the renewing of your mind" (Rom. 12:2).

b. *Carnal Thoughts.* The possibility of carnal thoughts must still be regarded as a primary hindrance to holy living. The numerous references to the mind's role in spiritual integrity attest to its importance and vulnerability in the spiritual process (Isa. 26:3; 2 Cor. 3:14; Phil. 4:7; Titus 1:15; Heb. 10:16). When the gateway of the mind is broken down, all manner of sin can invade the soul. "Those who live according to the sinful nature have their mind set on what that nature desires; but those who live in accordance with the Spirit have their minds set on what the Spirit desires. The mind of sinful man is death, but the mind controlled by the Spirit is life and peace; the sinful mind is hostile to God" (Rom. 8:5–7). As he did to the Romans here, Paul constantly articulated the importance of a pure and strong mind in spiritual warfare (Eph. 4:22–23).

Jesus named many sins that are lodged in the carnal mind, none of which can be seen with the eye, but all of which bring death to the spiritual man. In the life of holiness one must be constantly vigilant against the intrusion of attitudes that are a normal part of the natural life. Among the deadly occupations of the mind are hate, pride, envy, jealousy, covetousness, greed, lust, bitterness, unbelief, anger, arrogance, and hidden desires—all of which are named in Scripture as poisons of the soul.

Hate is a mental attitude of wishing ill toward a fellow person. If unchecked before it takes root in the mind, it will transform itself into malicious actions, a fact strongly affirmed by John's blunt warning: "Anyone who hates his brother is a murderer, and you know that no murderer has eternal life in him" (1 John 3:15). Note that hate, although it seems to be a passive sin of the mind, is revealed in an active sin against both God and the hated person.

The same is true of *lust,* which is mentioned by James as being frequently related to aggression and violence: "What causes fights and quarrels among you? Don't they come from your desires ["lusts," KJV] that battle within you?" (James 4:1ff.). Jesus was equally emphatic in making the connection between lust and active sin: "You have heard it was said, 'Do not commit adultery.' But I tell you that anyone who looks at a woman lustfully has already committed adultery with her in his heart" (Matt. 5:27).

While evil thoughts cannot be observed with the eye in the same way that sin is seen, they are evil nonetheless and originate in the carnal heart (Mark 7:21). Just as hate leads to violence and lust to immorality, so all evil thinking corrupts the soul of man. The list of carnal thoughts that beset us is vast, and these thoughts are too powerful to be controlled without the restraining power of holiness in the heart. Only the sanctifying work of Christ can expel hate, lust, pride, arrogance, malice, anger, covetousness, greed, unbelief, envy, jealous, bitterness, selfish ambition, and the like from the believer before they take root and corrupt him. If such thoughts are allowed to occupy the mind, they will destroy the spiritual life.

Christ's warnings against these sins were made to his disciples, those who were already cleansed by his word (John 15:3). They needed more than forgiveness of prior sins; they needed also a continuing state of purification. Paul was writing "to the saints in Ephesus, the faithful in Christ Jesus" when he admonished them, "Put off your old self, which is being corrupted by its deceitful desires . . . be made new in the attitude of your minds . . . put on the new self, created to be like God in true righteousness and holiness" (Eph. 4:22–24). The Ephesian believers were further warned not to give the devil a foothold (v. 27) and not to let any unwholesome talk come out of their mouths (v. 29). They were told, "Get rid of all bitterness, rage and anger, brawling and slander, along with every form of malice. Be kind and compassionate to one another, forgiving each other, just as in Christ God forgave you" (Eph. 4:31–32).

The key to this manner of life was for the Ephesians to "be imitators of God . . . and live a life of love" (Eph. 5:1–2). That was the ideal set before the early Christians, and it remains the ideal for Christians today. By patterning their lives after Christ, and by that alone, can believers attain the state of perfection required of them.

c. Worldliness. The world is a constant obstacle to holy living, yet the Christian must live in the world and exemplify the life of perfect love (John 17:13–19). The enmity between the worldly life and the spiritual life is relentless and dangerous, as can be seen from the numerous warnings against the world. "Do not love the world or anything in the world. If anyone loves the world, the love of the Father is not in him" (1 John 2:15).

There is a world system of opposition to Christ in both the secular and spiritual realms. It manifests itself in many forms of physical and spiritual hostility to the cause of Christ and his people. The opposition comes constantly from without and frequently from within the Christian body, which makes the threat of the world all the more acute. Satan is called the god of this world (2 Cor. 4:4); Paul testified to being crucified to the world (2 Tim 4:10); James said that anyone who is a friend of the world becomes the enemy of God (James 4:4); and Peter warned Christians to escape the corruption in the world caused by evil desires (2 Peter 1:4).

The "world" is a spirit or attitude that ties a person to this world, to the neglect or disrepair of spiritual values. It is living as if this world is the only one that he will ever know. He therefore seeks to enjoy in this life all the possessions, pleasure, status, power—or whatever else appeals to him—that he will ever have. A worldly person is one who becomes so absorbed with the affairs or trappings of this world that he loses sight of his spiritual self. Unlike Moses, who "chose to be mistreated along with the people of God rather than to enjoy the pleasures of sin for a short time" and who "regarded disgrace for the sake of Christ as of greater value than the treasures of Egypt, because he was looking ahead to his reward" (Heb. 11:25–26), a worldly man chooses the benefits of the present world over the promise of a world to come.

It has become common to focus on the effects of worldliness more than on its cause. That is especially true among many who feel that holiness consists of the multiplicity of things they do not do. But one is not worldly because he does worldly things—he does worldly things because he is worldly in his heart. The world attaches itself to his thoughts and desires and attitudes, and so his deeds reflect the condition of the inner man. John made that point clear when he said, "Do not love the world or the things in the world. If any one loves the world, love for the Father is not in him. For all that is in the world, the lust of the flesh and the lust of the eyes and the pride of life, is not of the Father but is of the world" (1 John 2:15–16 RSV). Note the emphasis on lust and pride—both of which are carnal thoughts that produce worldly behavior—and it is clear why Paul said, "Do not conform any longer to the pattern of this world, but be transformed by the renewing of your mind" (Rom. 12:2). This transforming of the mind is essential to Christian perfection.

From the earliest days of Christianity people have agreed on compacts and regulations aimed at either creating or preserving perfection. But without the transformed mind, the pure heart, the new creation, and the changed nature, no set of regulations can either create or preserve holiness.

The perfection of Christ's life in us will be seen in our behavior, a certainty that does not change from generation to generation. The sanctified person will by nature and impulse do the things that glorify Christ, and he will abstain from things that are unlike him. "Whoever claims to live in him must walk as Jesus did" (1 John 2:6). "No one who lives in him keeps on sinning. No one who continues to sin has either seen him or known him" (1 John 3:6). "No one who is born of God will continue to sin, because God's seed remains in him" (1 John 3:9).

These truths translate into practical issues pertinent to every generation. Greed is sin in the present time just as much as it was in earlier days. The manifestations of it may vary with time, but the sin is the same. Lust is lust, whether it was in the brothels and dark corners of ancient times or in the cinema or television of modern times. Ancient pride in houses and dress was no different from pride in cars and finery of dress in our time. The dress and possessions changed, but the pride has remained the same. Pomp and power among the ancients was the same pride of life that infects those who are status-conscious and power-hungry today. Conditions and circumstances are individual to each generation, but the sin does not change. Nor does the Lord's expectation of his people change. Worldliness is anything that comes between the believer and Christ, anything that obscures the clear vision of him, anything that lessens devotion to him or interferes with the pure worship of him. Worldliness is any spirit or desire or pleasure or pursuit that omits him as Lord and companion.

d. Specifics of Worldliness. The world is a relentless, pervasive enemy of Christ and Christians, at constant war against godliness and the life of holiness. It has been a danger to Christian devotion since the time of Christ, a threat of many faces and attractions. Worldliness is a spirit that comes against the holy life in forms suitable to the vogue of every generation. Because worldliness is a frame of mind or attitude of the heart, its specific devices and appeals are in constant flux. That is why it is difficult to pinpoint specific manifestations from one generation to another. Even Paul wrote that Demas had deserted him "because he loved this world," though Paul did not specify the form of that love (2 Tim. 4:10). That is why the Bible deals with the world principle but leaves finer specificity to the requirements of each generation (see 1 John 2:12–17).

Accordingly, those who claim or seek Christian perfection have almost always identified and proscribed the worldly intrusions of their time. Warnings and guidance have often ended up becoming church law rather than scriptural guidelines to encourage Christians in sanctity. The Shakers of England and America in the eighteenth century had literally hundreds of regulations in their codes of conduct.

Despite the changing times, there are some principles and standards that do not change. Such spiritually (and physically) harmful practices as drinking alcoholic beverages, the abuse of drugs, the use of tobacco, gambling, dancing, and participation in frivolous and vulgar amusements have almost always been discouraged or forbidden by those who emphasize holiness or Christian perfection. Methodist J. A. Wood wrote, "The Lord has made ample provision for the healthful happiness of his children, in the gift of the Holy Ghost, the Comforter, and therefore they do not need amusements, such as dancing, games, theaters, and the like, which worldly people seek" (*Perfect Love,* 303). In earlier years of the present holiness revival, medicine shows, fairs, festivals, concerts, the reading of novels, undue attention to fashionable dress and most forms of entertainment were regarded as worldly and therefore a hindrance to Christian perfection.

In all periods, any practice or interest that supplants the hunger for righteousness or diverts a Christian's attention from Christ or mars the image of Christ in him is of the world and should be avoided at all costs. Any love or desire, overt or covert, that diminishes the love and desire for Christ is of the world and should be expelled from the heart. Perfection is secured by the pursuit of Christ and abstinence from all that is unlike him.

VII. Summary. Perfection is the ideal of God's relationship with his people. Christians are to be his perfect children, not because they can of themselves be so, but because his seed in them makes them so. There may never be a time when anyone can regard himself as a finished product, for even the most fruitful life must be pruned in order to be even more fruitful. Perfection by its very nature is a state of becoming as is true of all living things. That which ceases to increase begins to decrease, and that which stops growing begins to decay. To be spotless, Christians must faithfully purge out spots that appear; and to be without wrinkle, they must forever endure the heat of the iron that presses the wrinkles out. Only by possessing the virtues and qualities of Christ in increasing measure can the perfect Christian be effective and productive in knowledge and service to the Lord Jesus Christ.

Bibliography: C. W. Conn, *Why Men Go Back: Studies in Defection and Devotion* (1966); S. C. Henry, *George Whitefield: Wayfaring Witness* (1957); F. J. McConnell, *John Wesley* (1939); M. G. Pearse, *Thoughts on Holiness* (1884); W. M. Smith, *The Word of God and the Life of Holiness* (1957); J. Wesley, *A Plain Account of Christian Perfection* (reprint 1977); A. S. Wood, *The Burning Heart* (1967); J. A. Wood, *Perfect Love—Or, Plain Things for Those Who Need Them Concerning the Doctrine, Experience, Profession and Practice of Christian Holiness* (1880).   C. W. Conn

CHRISTIAN WORKERS' UNION In 1935 the majority of its members having affiliated with the General Council of the Assemblies of God, the Christian Workers' Union disbanded. Its Framingham (Montwait), Massachusetts, based organ, *Word and Work,* continued for a few issues as a district council paper, then suspended publication. First issued in Springfield, Massachusetts, the paper was then in its fifty-seventh year. Its readership was practically synonymous with the constituency of the union, whose activities it promoted. Representative of such was the camp meeting on Oak Street in Wellesley, which in 1929 it sponsored jointly with the Russian and Eastern European Mission. After they became Pentecostal, the paper and the union joined in bringing evangelists such as Stanley H. Frodsham (1882–1969) and Aimee Semple McPherson (1890–1944) to the attention of New England. The Harvard-trained attorney Fred Corum (1900–1982), a nephew of the Azusa Street convert Rachel Sizelove (1864–1941), was the last editor of *Word and Work* under union auspices.

Bibliography: C. E. Jones, *A Guide to the Study of the Pentecostal Movement* (1983).   C. E. Jones

CHURCH GROWTH
    I. Overview
       A. The Largest Family of Protestants
       B. The Chief Categories
       C. African Independents
       D. Chinese Believers
       E. Global Totals
          Graph: Worldwide Pentecostal-charismatics
       F. What About the Future?
    II. The Third Wave
    III. Signs, Wonders and Church Growth
       A. Church Growth Without Signs and Wonders
       B. Signs and Wonders Without Church Growth
       C. Church Growth With Signs and Wonders
         1. Assemblies of God
           Graph: Assemblies of God
         2. Rates of Pentecostal Growth
           Graph: Korea

          Australia
          Singapore
          New Zealand
     3. Super Churches
  IV. Spot Checking the World
     A. Europe
     B. Latin America
     C. Africa
     D. Asia
   V. Coming Home to America
     A. Early Growth
        Graph: Decadal Growth Rates
     B. Classifying the Groups
     C. The Problem of the Church of God
        in Christ
     D. Current Growth
        Graphs of Pentecostal Growth
        Graphs Comparing Denominational
        Decadal Growth Rates
        Graph: Charismatic Renewal Move-
        ment
     E. Adding It Up
  VI. Church Growth Principles
     A. International Institutional Factors
       1. Biblical Triumphalism
       2. Targeting the Poor and Oppressed
       3. Multiple Tracks to Ordination
       4. High Local-Church Autonomy
       5. The Apostolic Model of Church
         Planting
       6. Schism
     B. Local Institutional Factors
     C. Some Possible Dangers
       1. The Dark Side of Respectability
       2. St. John's Syndrome
       3. Ministerial Elitism
  VII. Selected References

I. Overview. One of the most amazing phenomena related to the world religious scene in the latter part of the twentieth century has been the unprecedented growth of evangelical Christianity. Patrick Johnstone says, "The harvest of people into the Kingdom of God in recent years has been unprecedented. Never in history has such a high percentage of the world's population been exposed to the gospel, nor the increase of evangelical Christians been so encouraging" (*Operation World* 1986, 35). While many factors have combined to produce this growth, among the most significant, according to many observers, has been the explosive increase of the Pentecostal and charismatic movements.

A. The Largest Family of Protestants. Drawing on the findings of the *World Christian Encyclopedia* (Oxford University Press, 1982), Pentecostal historian Vinson Synan lists the number of adherents of the major Protestant families of the world in 1980 as follows (*In the Latter Days,* 1984, 17):

Pentecostals	51,167,000
Anglicans	49,804,000
Baptists	47,550,000
Lutherans	43,360,000
Presbyterians	40,209,000
Methodists	29,782,000
Charismatics (not in other	
denominations)	11,000,000

Synan comments, "Probably the most unexpected finding in the table is that the Pentecostals now comprise the largest family of Protestants in the world" (1984, 16). A similar observation was made by *Time* editor Richard N. Ostling: "The biggest distinct category of Protestants today does not consist of traditional Reformation groups, such as Lutherans, but the Pentecostalists—at 51 million strong, a leading strain of the worldwide Evangelical movement" (*Time,* May 3, 1982, 67).

The numbers are all the more remarkable given the fact that the appearance of Pentecostal-charismatic Christians is a twentieth-century phenomenon. Whether providentially or coincidentally, the distinctive beginning of the Pentecostal movement occurred at Bethel Bible School in Topeka, Kansas, on January 1, 1901, precisely the first day of the twentieth century. While Pentecostal churches experienced good growth rates during the first half of the century, the total impact on world Christianity was minimal. It was mainly a period for building momentum, which would mushroom after World War II. The greatest growth for Pentecostals, joined by charismatics in 1960, has come in the latter half of the century.

B. The Chief Categories. Scholars have not yet agreed on a standard classification of the ecclesiastical traditions we are discussing. There is broad consensus, however, that lines of demarcation can be seen between classical Pentecostals, charismatic renewal groups in traditional denominations, independent charismatic churches, and indigenous Pentecostal-charismatic churches.

Classical Pentecostals trace their origins to the Topeka, Kansas, event of 1901 or to the Azusa Street revival in Los Angeles in 1906–1909. These movements have mostly taken on formalized denominational structures that self-consciously identify themselves as Pentecostals, such as the Assemblies of God (AG), International Church of the Foursquare Gospel, Church of God in Christ, Pentecostal Holiness Church, Church of God (Cleveland, Tennessee), and scores of others (see C. E. Jones, *A Guide to the Study of the Pentecostal Movement,* 1983).

Charismatic renewal groups are informal gatherings of believers who minister with spiritual gifts of healing, deliverance, tongues, prophecy, and others, most of whom regard themselves as "Spirit filled," testifying to having received a "baptism in the Holy Spirit" subsequent to conversion, but who choose to remain within their traditional, non-Pentecostal churches and denominations. Strong charismatic renewal groups can be found in Catholic, and Orthodox churches as well as among most varieties of Protestants. Nearly all major denominational families in the U.S. recognize officially approved charismatic organizations.

Independent charismatic churches strongly resemble Pentecostal churches to outsiders, but they are perceived by themselves and by Pentecostals as having a discrete identity. There are certain key differences in doctrine, in lifestyle, and in liturgy that are dealt with in other parts of this volume. In several countries of the world, including the U.S. and Great Britain, the independent charismatic churches are the fastest growing segment of Christianity.

Indigenous Pentecostal-charismatic churches are those that originate within a particular nation or people group with little or no influence from outside ecclesiastical agencies. They are sometimes referred to as nativistic movements. The two largest groupings of these churches are the African Independent churches and the house church movement in mainland China.

In order to develop a global picture of the growth of Pentecostal-charismatic movements, all four of these categories need to be included. As those involved in church growth research will testify, it is not a simple matter to come up with figures acceptable to all involved. Some nations ask religious questions in their national census, others, such as the U.S., do not. Some denominations keep accurate statistics on a yearly basis, others do not. Even prestigious publications such as C. H. Jacquet's *Yearbook of American and Canadian Churches* lack data for such important categories as independent charismatics. Counting only what is reported in such sources as hard data is not an adequate methodology, since it does not reflect the true state of affairs. A considerable amount of educated interpolation is thereby called for, and this admittedly involves some subjectivism. A case in point is the difficulty in obtaining reasonably accurate figures for the U.S. Churches of God in Christ described in another section of this article. Serious efforts are being made by such researchers as Patrick Johnstone (*Operation World*, 1986), Vinson Synan (*The Twentieth-Century Pentecostal Explosion*, 1987), and especially David Barrett, whose detailed statistical table appears in this volume (see STATISTICS, GLOBAL).

C. *African Independents.* What to do with the African Independent churches in a study like this is a subject of considerable discussion. Some 30 million African persons belong to newer denominations with unusual names such as First Miracle Healing Church, Sacred Cherubim and Seraphim Church of God, Emissaries of Divine Light, Church of the Lord (Aladura), Zion Apostolic in Jerusalem Church, or the Divine Healing Church of Israel. In recent times new African denominations have been forming at the rate of one per day.

Professor Walter J. Hollenweger of the University of Birmingham, England, argues that most of the African Independent churches should be regarded as part of Pentecostalism. He points out that historical links can be found to early Pentecostal missionaries in many cases. And in the others, "the phenomenological pattern of spirituality, worship and theology is so strikingly similar to early Pentecostalism that one can speak with justification of one movement, even if there is no organizational link between the different churches" ("After Twenty Years' Research on Pentecostalism," *International Review of Mission*, 75 [297, 1986]: 9–10).

Professor Dean S. Gilliland of Fuller Seminary in Pasadena, California, is more cautious. He sees the African Independent churches on a spectrum from primary Evangelical-Pentecostal to secondary Evangelical-Pentecostal to revelational indigenous to indigenous eclectic. He would regard only the first two categories and part of the third as Christian. The indigenous eclectic group has incorporated so much African traditional religion that it would not be proper to characterize those churches even as Christian, much less Pentecostal-charismatic, according to Gilliland. (See "How 'Christian' Are African Independent Churches?" *Missiology: An International Review*, 14 [3, 1986]:259–72.) Phenomenologically some of the African churches may look Pentecostal, but theologically they exclude themselves.

D. *Chinese Believers.* The other recently emerging challenge is to ask: How Pentecostal are the house churches of China? The growth of Christianity in China, particularly since 1976, has been a phenomenon unmatched in Christian history. When the missionaries were driven out of China in 1949–50, they left about one million Protestant believers. By the 1970s many believed that the Christian community there had been wiped out by Chairman Mao, the Red Guard, the Cultural Revolution, and the Gang of Four. Instead, Christians multiplied until by the mid-1980s the number was conservatively estimated at 50 million, with some suggesting twice that number. This means that the Christians in China have increased from less than 2 percent of the population to perhaps between 5 and 10 percent in less than twenty years. This has caused Howard A. Snyder to identify this growth as one of the top ten major world trends that will dramatically affect the future of Christians and the church: "From Communist China to Christian China" (*Foresight*, 1986).

There has been no religious census of China nor any recent survey resembling a Gallup poll. However, two expert China watchers have come to virtually identical conclusions as to the percentage of Pentecostal-charismatics in China. Denominationalism as we know it is for all practical purposes nonexistent in China. Distinctions are made between Three Self (government approved) churches, the Roman Catholic church, and house churches. A few other groups, such as the Little Flock, still maintain an identity. But none of these is helpful in counting Pentecostal-charismatics.

Both Paul Kauffman, president of Asian Outreach, and Jonathan Chao, director of the China Church Research Center head up Hong Kong-based organizations that actively engage in research on the churches in mainland China. These men, both born and raised in China, visit the mainland frequently, as do key members of their staffs. They regularly interview Christians who travel to Hong Kong from the mainland. Each organization has a network of representatives in China, especially throughout the house church movement. Kauffmann is a Pentecostal and Chao is not, which helps balance their mutual perspective. My estimates of the situation in China lean heavily on the findings of these two researchers.

Of the 50 million believers in China, some 20 to 25 percent (10 to 12 million) are probably tongues speakers. If speaking in tongues is regarded as the crucial Pentecostal distinctive, this would give us our figure for China. However, a considerably larger number of Chinese believers would be perceived by most observers as phenomenologically Pentecostal-charismatic. Their normal ministry is characterized by prophecies, healings, signs and wonders, miracles, deliverances, upraised hands, and the like. Both Kauffmann and Chao estimate that 85 percent of Chinese believers would be phenomenological Pentecostal-charismatics, giving us a figure of 42.5 million. Some have argued that the figure should be larger because there actually are more than 50 million Christians in China. Others have argued that the 85 percent Pentecostal-charismatics is too high. In my judgment, the 42.5 million is a moderate and reasonable figure.

The modern growth of the Chinese churches began in earnest after 1970 and increased dramatically after 1976. Some researchers estimate that there were 15 million believers in 1980. If so, this would mean that Pentecostal-charismatics in China grew from some 12.8 million in 1980 to 42.5 million in 1985, an increase—mostly by adult conversions from non-Christian backgrounds—of some 30 million persons. As a point of comparison, this itself is a higher figure than the total population of Kenya or Canada or Peru or Afghanistan or Australia or scores of other nations of the world.

E. Global Totals. No one has devoted more research time to estimating the current number of Pentecostal-charismatics than David Barrett. His figures are being published here for the first time (see STATISTICS, GLOBAL), so they have not as yet come under the scrutiny of other researchers. But I am of the opinion that, if the explanatory footnotes are taken at face value, Barrett's estimates are the most complete and the most accurate presently available.

The following graph incorporates Barrett's figures for 1975 and 1985 (totaling what he refers to as First Wave and Second Wave). Then by extrapolating backwards, I have made the estimates for the previous decades.

Worldwide Pentecostal-Charismatics
(in millions)

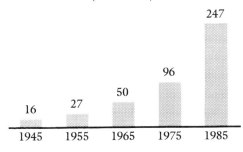

Barrett's 1985 breakdown is as follows:

First Wave: Pentecostalism	149.7 ml.
Second Wave: Charismatic Movement	97.5 ml.
Total	247.2 ml.

Notice that these figures include "post-Pentecostals" (2 million), "postcharismatics" (64 mil-

lion), and "radio/television charismatics (2.9 million). Post-Pentecostals and postcharismatics are individuals who were at one point identified with a Pentecostal denomination or charismatic renewal group but who no longer are. However, they are not denied the validity of their Pentecostal-charismatic experience. Some may raise questions concerning the appropriateness of including these categories, but I agree with Barrett that, if we want an accurate picture of the whole movement, including them is better than excluding them.

Also note that Barrett's figures include baptized members, their children and infants, catechumens, inquirers, and attenders, but exclude interested non-Christian attenders, casual attenders, visitors, etc. This in itself will account for discrepancies with some other compilations of data that count members only.

The 1975–85 decadal growth rate (DGR) from the above graph figures out to 157 percent. If accurate, it represents what would undoubtedly prove to be one of the highest if not *the* highest recorded rate of growth of a nonpolitical, nonmilitaristic human movement across history.

Much of this comes as a surprise to many non-Pentecostal Christian leaders, however, since the magnitude of Pentecostal-charismatic church growth has been all but ignored by prominent evangelical researchers. For example, a high-quality document entitled "Christianity in the World: An Overview" (1986) was prepared by World Vision for the seven thousand participants in the Billy Graham-sponsored Amsterdam 1986 conference for itinerant evangelists. In over six thousand words, the wide-ranging survey makes no specific mention of the phenomenon described above. Similarly, Patrick Johnstone's influential *Operation World* (1986) opens with a fifty-page survey of world Christianity containing only a three-line mention of Pentecostalism's growth "tempered by sadness" due to "the divisiveness that, in many lands, has afflicted Pentecostal churches" (65).

The January 1987 issue of *Missiology: An International Review* carries seven articles in 107 pages on the theme "The Future of the Christian World Mission" and makes no explicit reference to the Pentecostal-charismatic phenomenon. Nor do the twenty-one articles over 116 pages in the January 1987 issue of *International Review of Mission* on "The Future of Mission."

The figures take on more meaning when seen in comparison to the growth rates of other branches of the Christian movement worldwide. David Barrett charts the growth rates of all world religions over the fifteen-year period 1970–85 (*World Christian Encyclopedia,* 1982, 6). Of eighty-eight categories and subcategories, only five grew more than an annual rate of 12 percent, and four of those five were Pentecostal-charismatic groups:

Catholic Pentecostals	22.71% per year
Orthodox Pentecostals	19.42%
Anglican Pentecostals	18.86%
Protestant neo-pentecostals	16.39%
Black Muslims	12.00%

In contrast, for example, Christians in general grew 1.64 percent, Hindus 2.30 percent, Buddhists 1.67 percent, and Muslims 2.75 percent.

F. What About the Future? To put the current Protestant-charismatic decadal growth rate of 157 percent into perspective, the following comparative scale has been found helpful in analyzing the growth rates of local congregations, judicatories, or denominations:

25 %	per decade	marginal growth
50 %	per decade	fair growth
100 %	per decade	good growth
200 %	per decade	excellent growth
300 %	per decade	outstanding growth

Please note that the most frequent scale for measuring growth rates used in this essay is decadal growth rate or DGR. The meaning of this is obvious for figures ten years apart such as 1975–85. But the DGR is also used for measuring growth over periods longer or shorter than ten years. The DGR is used to indicate the percentage of growth the church would have experienced if the rate for the shorter or longer period had been sustained over a ten-year period. This provides a standardized measuring tool that can be used to compare all growth situations. The methods used for calculating DGR are explained in *The Church Growth Survey Handbook* by Bob Waymire and C. Peter Wagner (Overseas Crusades, 1984), 16–17.

It must be recognized that the larger and older a church or movement becomes, the more difficult it is to sustain a high rate of growth. For example, as we will see again later, the growth of third- and fourth-generation classical Pentecostals in the U.S. is currently 52 percent DGR, lower than the growth rate of independent charismatic churches, which are still in their first generation. Whether a 157 percent worldwide DGR will be sustained throughout the remainder of the twentieth century is unknown, but somewhat doubtful. David Barrett projects 562 million Pentecostal-charismatics by the year 2000. Time will tell.

II. The Third Wave. An important phenomenon, closely related to the growth of the Pentecostal-charismatic movements is the recent appearance of what is being identified as the "Third Wave." Characteristics of the Third Wave are explained elsewhere in this volume (see THIRD WAVE). While the Third Wave is chiefly a phenomenon of the 1980s in which members of traditional evangelical churches and denominations have begun to minister in healings, deliverances, signs and wonders, prophecies, and the like, much on the order of Pentecostal-charismatics, Barrett also discerns a number of "crypto-charismatics" dating back to about 1970. His 1985 total of mainstream third-wavers and crypto-charismatics is 20.7 million, with a projected 65 million in A.D. 2000.

Combining all three waves (149.7 million First Wave plus 97.5 million Second Wave plus 20.7 million Third Wave), the 1985 total is 267.9 million or 19 percent of the world's church-member Christians. By the end of the century, the projection is 562.5 million or 29 percent of Christians.

III. Signs, Wonders and Church Growth. What some refer to as the "signs and wonders movement," sparked in the late 1970s and early 1980s by John Wimber of the Vineyard Christian Fellowship and others, has stimulated an increasing amount of research focusing on "power evangelism" (see J. Wimber, *Power Evangelism,* 1985). One of the major questions deals with the relationship of supernatural signs and wonders to the growth and multiplication of Christian churches. At this stage, three generalizations can be made from the research:

1. There is vigorous church growth in some parts of the world with no discernible emphasis on signs and wonders or other characteristics of the Pentecostal or charismatic movements.

2. There are places in the world where dramatic manifestations of signs and wonders have been experienced, but which have resulted in little or no church growth.

3. Across the board, however, the growth and multiplication of churches in which healings, deliverances, prophecies, and other miraculous works of the Holy Spirit are normative components of ministry is substantially greater than in the churches in which they are not.

A. Church Growth Without Signs and Wonders. It would be a mistake to emphasize the third generalization without the first two. For example, the Evangelical Churches of West Africa (ECWA) is reportedly the largest national denomination in Nigeria with 650,000 adult members (P. Johnstone, *Operation World,* 1986, 323). This was pioneered by the Sudan Interior Mission, a member of the U.S. Interdenominational Foreign Mission Association, which specifically excludes charismatics from membership. While some changes have been taking place under African leadership in recent years, most of the church growth has occurred during the period in which speaking in tongues, miraculous healings, receiving words of knowledge, and the like were at best frowned upon and at worst forbidden. Not only has ECWA planted over seventeen hundred churches in Nigeria, but they have also taken the leadership among all Third World denominations in recruiting, supporting, and sending out cross-cultural missionaries. Their Evangelical Missionary Society, led by Panya Baba, now supports over six hundred Nigerian missionaries. Similar examples of church growth without an emphasis on signs and wonders can be found on all six continents.

B. Signs and Wonders Without Church Growth. One of the developments of the Pentecostal and charismatic movements has been an affinity for large-scale evangelistic and miracle crusades. Some of the largest crowds of human beings ever seen are currently gathering under the anointed ministry of Pentecostal evangelists. For example, in the mid-1980s the world's leading evangelist, if measured by the size of crusade meetings, was probably German missionary Reinhard Bonnke. Starting his ministry in South Africa, Bonnke had to exchange an evangelistic tent that accommodated 10,000 for another that accommodates 34,000. Even that is often inadequate. In 1986, for example, Bonnke held a crusade in Blantyre, Malawi, in the open air. The opening meeting drew a crowd of 25,000. But as word spread of the lame walking, the blind seeing, and the deaf hearing, the crowds swelled to an estimated 150,000 per night before the sixteen days of meetings were over.

Few questions would be raised as to the purity of the gospel preached or as to the authenticity of the signs and wonders. Conversions are genuine. Healings are verified. People are marvelously blessed. Some of the converts certainly end up in Christian churches. But questions have been raised as to the net result of this type of meeting on the subsequent growth of the participating churches. What percentage of those who register a "decision for Christ" are brought into congregations of believers? How many of those who commit themselves to Christ also commit themselves to the body of Christ? Research to answer these questions is rarely either sponsored or encouraged, much less reported, by those who hold the crusades. Some observers interpret what little evidence is available to indicate that the total effect on church growth may be about the same in a Reinhard Bonnke crusade with signs and wonders following as in a Billy Graham crusade without them. Signs and wonders *by themselves* may not be the secret of closing the follow-up gap.

A similar phenomenon may be observed on the local church level. Consider, for example, a hypothetical district of the AG in the U.S. Virtually every pastor in the district will profess a belief in divine healing and affirm that healing is a normative part of the pastoral ministry of the congregation. Yet, while some of those churches will be growing, a significant number will be on a plateau or declining at the same time. This confirms that church growth is always an intricate interweaving of institutional and contextual factors under the sovereignty of God. It is not always accurate to reduce the reasons for growth or nongrowth to any single cause including presence or absence of Pentecostal-charismatic distinctives.

C. Church Growth With Signs and Wonders. Having said this, I must add that the major purpose of this article is to highlight examples from around the world that reflect a wedding of signs and wonders with church growth such as we see in the Book of Acts. Many today are perpetuating the ministry of the apostle Paul who summed up years of spreading the gospel in these words: "I will not venture to speak of anything except what Christ has accomplished through me in leading the Gentiles to obey God by what I have said and done—by the power of signs and miracles, through the power of the Spirit" (Rom. 15:18–19). Generally speaking, where this is happening churches are growing and multiplying more rapidly than where it is not.

1. Assemblies of God. The largest classical Pentecostal denomination in the world is the Assemblies of God (AG). Their worldwide expansion through 1,396 missionaries sent out by their Division of Foreign Missions and over 90,000 national ministers serving around the world has

been dramatic, particularly over the last twenty years. The number of churches has multiplied from just over 16,000 in 1965 to 107,415 in 1985. Growth of members and adherents is reported as follows:

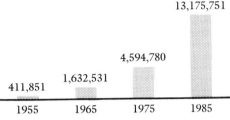

**Assemblies of God
Worldwide Members & Adherents**

1955	1965	1975	1985
411,851	1,632,531	4,594,780	13,175,751

Note that these numbers reflect only reports actually received from the field. They do not attempt to interpolate figures from local churches, districts, or national groups that for any number of reasons have not reported. According to G. Edward Nelson, secretary of foreign missions relations of the Division of Foreign Missions of the U.S. AG, approximately two-thirds of the national church bodies do not submit reports. In other instances they attempt to use conservative figures when possible. For example, the Brazilian AG is the largest of the national fellowships with 7,500,000 members and adherents in 1985. Alternate reports of up to 12 million have not been used by U.S. AG leadership, which desires to maintain the highest degree of integrity.

Also note that, according to Barrett (see STATISTICS, GLOBAL), if AG teenagers and children are counted, the 1985 figure rises to 22 million instead of 13 million.

A remarkable feature of AG growth has been sustaining a high decadal growth rate even though the movement has become very large. The rates over the past three decades have been as follows:

1955–65	296%
1965–75	181%
1975–85	187%

Despite the fact that most of the numerical increase has come over the past ten or twenty years, the AG has already become the largest or second largest national Protestant denomination in American Samoa, Argentina, Benin, Bolivia, Brazil, Burkina Faso, Burma, Cuba, Dominican Republic, Egypt, El Salvador, French Guiana, Guatemala, Honduras, Iran, Italy, Mauritius, Nicaragua, Panama, Peru, Portugal, Puerto Rico, Reunion, São Tome & Principe, Senegal, Togo, Uganda, Uruguay, Venezuela, and Zimbabwe. At the current rate of growth, this list of thirty nations will undoubtedly be considerably longer before the end of the century.

In one city alone, São Paulo, Brazil, the Assemblies of God report no fewer than 2,400 congregations. These are more churches than entire U.S. denominations such as Baptist General Conference, Christian and Missionary Alliance,

Korea

Decadal Membership Growth Rates 1969–82
(Jae Bum Lee, *Pentecostal Type Distinctives and Korean Protestant Church Growth*, Ph.D. dissertation, Fuller Seminary, 1986, p. 234)

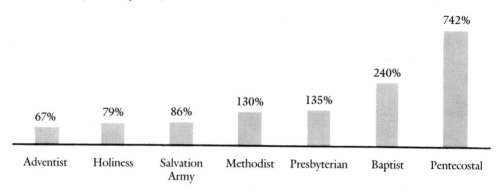

| 67% | 79% | 86% | 130% | 135% | 240% | 742% |
| Adventist | Holiness | Salvation Army | Methodist | Presbyterian | Baptist | Pentecostal |

Australia

Decadal Growth Rates 1976–81
(Barry Chant, *Heart of Fire*, Australia: House of Tabor, 1984, p. 224)

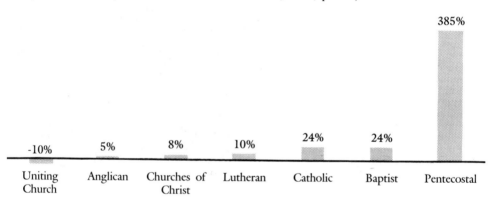

| -10% | 5% | 8% | 10% | 24% | 24% | 385% |
| Uniting Church | Anglican | Churches of Christ | Lutheran | Catholic | Baptist | Pentecostal |

Reformed Church in America, Mennonite Church, or Salvation Army report.

2. *Rates of Pentecostal Growth.* Although hard data to confirm these are not yet available, many researchers suspect that when rates of church growth over the past decade or so are examined in countries that now have a significant Christian presence, Pentecostal-charismatic churches will be found to be the fastest-growing group of churches in at least 80 percent of the nations. Examples of this phenomenon in four nations are shown on the accompanying chart.

3. *Super Churches.* An informative study of the world's super churches has recently been published by Professor John N. Vaughan of Southwest Baptist University in Bolivar, Missouri, (*The World's 20 Largest Churches*, Baker, 1984). In it he reports that eight out of the first ten churches in worship attendance in 1981–82 were Pentecostal-charismatic. These include Yoido Full Gospel Church (Seoul, Korea), Evangelical Cathedral of Jotabeche (Methodist Pentecostal, Santiago,

Chile), Calvary Chapel (Santa Ana, Calif.), Deus e Amor (São Paulo, Brazil), Miracle Center (Benin City, Nigeria), Melodyland Christian Center (Anaheim, Calif.), Brazil for Christ (São Paulo, Brazil) and Sung Rak Baptist Church (Seoul, Korea) (1984, 287).

While John Vaughan's list includes two Brazilian churches, they are so difficult to calculate that more of them may deserve to be there. For example, eight AG churches in Brazil report members and adherents ranging from 20,000 to 110,000 (1984, 260), but none of them is on the list. Several other churches have risen to metachurch proportions since Vaughan's research. Among those are the Vision of the Future of Argentina (145,000 members in 1986) and Deeper Life Church of Lagos, Nigeria (42,000 members in 1986), both Pentecostal-charismatic type churches. These, and several others, would probably qualify for an updated list.

Given current world trends, it would not be a high risk to suppose that by the end of the century

Singapore

Decadal Membership Growth Rates early 1970s to early 1980s
(Keith Hinton, *Growing Churches Singapore Style*. Singapore: OMF (1985), 116)

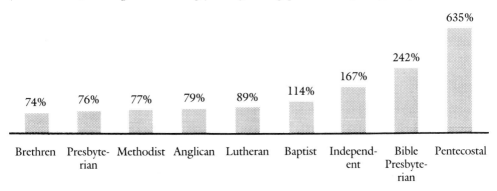

New Zealand

Decadal Growth Rates 1971–81
(National Census Data, 1981)

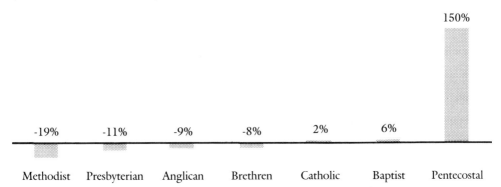

virtually all the world's largest churches may be Pentecostal-charismatic. For example, as of 1987, Thailand, traditionally a nation of very small churches, had seen four large churches of five hundred to fifteen hundred members emerge in the 1980s. All four emphasize a ministry accompanied by signs and wonders. The largest and fastest-growing church in Sweden is the Word of Life Community in Uppsala. Pastor Ulf Ekman has constructed a sanctuary seating four thousand, said to be the largest Protestant church building in Europe.

Carl F. George, director of the Charles E. Fuller Institute for Evangelism and Church Growth, is currently doing the cutting-edge research on the dynamics of the transition from the megachurch (several thousands of members) to the metachurch (several tens of thousands of members). He is finding that the phenomenon, with few notable exceptions, is occurring mostly among Pentecostal-charismatics.

IV. Spot Checking the World. Data are not currently available for a country-by-country analy-

sis of Pentecostal-charismatic church growth worldwide. Lacking that, I will simply report some relevant church growth information from selected areas of Europe, Latin America, Africa, and Asia.

A. Europe. Pentecostalism was taken to Europe in the early years of this century by such pioneers as Norwegian Thomas Ball Barratt, Italian Luis Francescon, and Swede Lewi Pethrus. Although there was some growth in Norway, Finland, and Sweden, where the well-known Filadelfia Church in Stockholm grew to seven thousand members, not much impact was made either in England or in the German-speaking countries. The cultural entrenchment of Anglicanism and Lutheranism, together with the anti-Pentecostal "Berlin Declaration" of 1909, combined to create a very negative climate for Pentecostal growth. In southern Europe, slow growth was also experienced in Spain, Portugal, and France, but Italy emerged as the most receptive nation.

In Italy the AG, pioneered by Francescon, had grown to 250 churches and 5,000 members by the time the Fascist regime closed the country down to the spread of the gospel in 1934. After World War II, despite the ten-year setback, the Assemblies of God entered a vigorous growth period, increasing to 166,736 members in 1980. With a healthy 44 percent decadal growth rate, the number was up to 200,000 by 1985. Adding adherents to members, the total rises to approximately 400,000. This now represents more than 80 percent of all the Protestants in Italy.

Other than Italy, and with the possible exceptions of Portugal, Bulgaria, Romania, Finland, and Russia, Pentecostal growth is slow in Europe. However, over the past twenty-five years charismatic renewal growth in many countries has been vigorous, particularly in the traditional churches in Italy, France, Sweden, Norway, Germany, and England from 1980 to 1985. In Norway 20 percent of practicing Christians are charismatic (rising to 35 percent among those who are college educated). In England an estimated 10 percent of Church of England clergy are charismatic.

In England the independent charismatic churches are known variously as the "house church movement" (although only 2 percent actually meet in houses) or the "restoration movement" or simply the "renewal movement." According to researcher Peter Brierley, independent charismatic churches increased from 190 in 1980 to 650 in 1985. By far the most rapidly growing segment of British Christianity, the house churches, had an estimated membership of some 75,000 with an attendance of 94,000 in 1985 (P. Brierley, ed., *U.K. Christian Handbook 1987/88,* 139). While there was much transfer growth in the 1970s, only about 15 percent of the growth in the 1980s can be attributed to transfer. The conversion rate is currently very high. All this is producing a new spiritual climate that is helping increase the growth rates of other denominations, particularly the Elim Pentecostal churches and the AG.

B. Latin America. The evangelical movement has experienced rapid growth in Latin America throughout the twentieth century. An estimate of 50,000 Evangelicals in 1900 has increased to over 50 million in the mid-1980s and is projected at 137 million by the end of the century. Since the middle of the century, most of that growth has been among Pentecostals and independent charismatic churches.

The charismatic renewal movement within the Roman Catholic church is not included in the above figures. The growth rates of the Catholic charismatic movement, at least in the three countries reported by Brinkerhoff and Bibby ("Circulation of the Saints in South America: A Comparative Study," *Journal for the Scientific Study of Religion* 24 [1985]: 39–55), compare with the rates shown for the European charismatic movements:

Latin American Catholic Charismatics 1970–84

	1970	1984	DGR
Bolivia	1,000	9,000	380%
Brazil	5,000	500,000	2583%
Peru	1,000	40,000	1294%
Totals	7,000	549,000	2155%

In thirteen of the twenty major Latin American republics, a Pentecostal denomination was the largest of the Protestant groups reported in 1985. In four other countries (Costa Rica, Venezuela, Colombia, and Dominican Republic) they were exceeded only by the Seventh-day Adventists. In only three republics (Ecuador, Paraguay, and Haiti) Pentecostal-charismatics have not as yet risen to leadership in church-growth statistics.

Two of the three largest churches in the world are in Latin America. While neither surpasses the 500,000 plus of the Yoido Full Gospel Church of Seoul, Korea, they are enormous. The Vision of the Future Church in Argentina, pastored by Omar Cabrera and his wife, Marfa, counted 145,000 members in 1986. There are some difficulties in recording it as a single church, as meetings are held on forty-five different locations throughout the central belt of Argentina. However, it is not a central church with satellites as are many of the Brazilian super churches. It is one body of believers under one senior pastor who travels some seven thousand miles per month, mostly by automobile, to care for the flock. In my opinion it is properly thought of as a church, rather than a denomination. A central meeting point with a sanctuary to accommodate 17,000 is under construction near the city of Cordoba. Cabrera is known for a very effective ministry of breaking the power of territorial demons through spiritual warfare.

The world's second largest church is the Evangelical Cathedral of Jotabeche (Methodist Pentecostal), pastored by Javier Vasquez and located in Santiago, Chile. Estimates of membership at Jotabeche vary, but the official church report for 1986 registered 312,843 baptized members (including children, since they baptize infants). They claim a "total membership" of 478,605. Members are assigned one Sunday per month when they are allowed to attend the central cathedral, which seats 16,000. The other three Sundays find them in one of the 324 neighborhood *templos* (seating over 600 each) or 60 *locales* (seating under 600) scattered around the city of Santiago in a ten-mile radius of the cathedral (Vaughan, 1984, 211).

With Pentecostals leading the way, some of the most rapid church growth on national levels has been seen in Central America. As recently as 1979 Nicaragua was estimated at 3 percent evangelical. Despite the reign of the Marxist Sandinistas, the percentage rose to 12 percent in 1983 and was estimated by researcher Clifton Holland to be 20 percent in 1986. Guatemala was the first Latin American nation with an evangelical president, charismatic Efrain Rios Montt. Evangelicals comprise more than 25 percent of the population with an expectation of 30 percent by 1990, by far the highest on the continent.

Although the Vision of the Future Church in Argentina is one of them, independent charismatic churches are a relatively new feature in Latin American evangelicalism. However, they may well constitute an increasingly significant element of church growth in the near future throughout the continent. Paul E. Pretiz of the Latin America Mission says, "In some Latin American countries, these are now the largest churches—a growing stream that leaves many of the others in the backwaters." He points out that their appearance fulfills what foreign missions had long dreamed of: "The gospel taking root in native soil and springing up in new plant forms that carry no foreign interference and are fully expressive of a people who live out their Christian faith in their own cultural style" ("God Forms a People in Bogota," *Latin America Evangelist* [October–December 1986], 8). As an example, Pretiz describes the Christian Crusade Church of Santa Isabel, pastored by Marcos Antonio Diaz, which at 2,600 members has become one of the largest churches in Bogota, Colombia.

C. Africa. In Africa the Christian movement south of the Sahara is increasing from 10 million at the beginning of our century to a projected 400 million by the end. This will raise the proportion of Christians from 8 to 50 percent.

I have previously described the growth of the African Independent Movement, with more than 12,000 denominations, according to Prof. G. C. Oosthuizen of the University of Durban, and 30 million members and adherents. One of these denominations, the Zion Christian Church of South Africa, conducts what could be the largest regular gathering of human beings in history. Their annual Easter conference held near the city of Pietersburg reportedly attracts a crowd of 1 to 2 million persons to celebrate their faith in the resurrection of Christ. A bank in Pietersburg is said to close for the week after Easter, just to count the money deposited from the offering. In 1987 the traffic was backed up for an estimated 200 miles on the main roads as the conferees returned home.

The most rapidly growing Lutheran church in the world is the Mekane Yesus church in Ethiopia. It has grown from approximately 140,000 in 1970 to 750,000 in 1986 despite Marxist persecution. In the early 1970s the Mekane Yesus church commissioned a Norwegian scholar to make a major survey of the congregations—their economy, structure, and growth. It was discovered that in those congregations that showed the highest growth rate a major factor of growth was supernatural signs and wonders. In these congregations a full 60 to 80 percent of the members interviewed quoted these signs as the major reason for the growth of the church. The signs included expulsions of evil spirits, healings, and power encounters. Here is an example of a sizeable church that is not counted among the Pentecostals or charismatics, even though from the point of power evangelism they would have much in common.

Classical Pentecostal denominations do not play as much of a part proportionally in church growth in Africa as they do in Latin America. They are the largest Protestant denomination in only eight of the forty-six African nations south of the Sahara Desert: Angola, Benin, Burkina Faso, Burundi, Mauritius, Reunion, São Tome & Principe, and Zimbabwe. Undoubtedly the rise of the African Independent churches has satisfied the spiritual needs of many African people who otherwise might have been drawn to Pentecostal churches.

The extent of the independent charismatic church movement, so far as it can be distinguished from the African Independent churches, is not known on a continental scale. However, in the urban areas of South Africa, for example, the fastest growing nonblack churches since 1980 have been the independent charismatics. Nonblack means that they are mostly under white leadership but open to all races. Some three hundred of them are affiliated with the International Fellowship of Charismatic Churches. In Pretoria the Hatfield Christian Centre has built a sanctuary for 4,000. In Johannesburg the Rhema Church has more than 10,000 members and meets in a sanctuary for 5,000, which contains fifteen kilometers of seating and is said to be the largest unsupported steel roof in the Southern Hemisphere.

The Miracle Center in Benin City, Nigeria, pastored by Benson Idahosa, is of the independent charismatic type, with ties to Kenneth Hagin, Kenneth Copeland, Earl Paulk, T. L. Osborne, and others. They have constructed a sanctuary seating 20,000—one of the largest in the world. Among other things, Idahosa reports seeing seven people raised from the dead.

D. Asia. Evangelical church growth in Asia had been relatively slow until recent years. Centers of current rapid growth have been Korea, the Philippines, Indonesia, Singapore, Northeast India, Burma, and, of course, China. However, in none of the twenty-five Asian nations has a classical Pentecostal denomination risen to the top of the Protestant membership list.

Growth rates give a different picture. When the Pentecostal-charismatic movement is taken as a whole, it will be found that its rate of growth will surpass that of other similar groups in many countries. For example, three large churches currently emerging in countries traditionally known for small churches and slow growth are the Hope of Bangkok Church in Thailand; the Full Gospel Church in Tokyo; and Calvary Church of Kuala Lumpur, Malaysia. The first two were started since 1980. In Bangkok, Pastor Kriengsak Chareonwongsak reported 2,300 members in 1987, the first Christian church of its size in 160 years of missionary activity. Miraculous healings are a normal part of church life there. In Tokyo the Full Gospel Church, a daughter of Paul Yonggi Cho's Yoido Full Gospel Church in Korea, also numbered 300 in 1987, the largest Protestant congregation in Japan. The largest church in Malaysia is the Calvary Church (AG) pastored by Prince Guneratnam. More than 2,000 were attending in 1987, and a sanctuary for 5,000 is planned.

We have already seen graphs of the rates of growth for Singapore and Korea. In Singapore, Pentecostals are growing at 635 percent decadal growth rate (DGR), while the second-place Bible Presbyterians are showing a 242 percent DGR. The largest church in Singapore is the English-speaking Calvary Charismatic Center, which reportedly has over 4,500 members and gives $1.2 million per year to missions.

In Korea, Pentecostals have a 742 percent DGR compared to Baptists, who are second with 240 percent. But this does not tell all. The largest Baptist church in Korea is the Sung Rak Baptist Church in Seoul, pastored by Ki Dong Kim. With over 40,000 adult members, it is the largest of any church related to the ministry of the U.S. Southern Baptists. A sanctuary seating 20,000 is on the drawing board. Although Pastor Kim is not included on any Pentecostal or charismatic roster, he himself reports being used to raise ten people from the dead, casting out thousands of demons, and praying for fifty-nine totally crippled people who are now walking. Similarly, the Central Evangelical Holiness Church in Seoul, pastored by Mahn Shin Lee, is the largest specifically Holiness church in the world, with 6,000 members. Divine healing is a prominent element in Lee's philosophy of ministry.

The three largest Methodist churches in the world are in Korea, with memberships between 20,000 and 30,000 each. The pastors of the two largest ones, Ho Moon Lee from Incheon and Hong Do Kim from Seoul, are both disciples of Paul Yonggi Cho, and their ministry has much in common with Pentecostals.

This might well be a pattern in many parts of Asia and one of the reasons why self-identified Pentecostal-charismatics may be as visible as in other parts of the world. Many of them would fall into the recently identified Third Wave category. Baptist growth in Northeast India is another example. Unlike most Baptists in the U.S. or in Latin America, those in Northeast India have frequently ministered with power encounters and supernatural healings simply because they have assumed it was the biblical way to minister. If they were in the U.S., many would be regarded as charismatics.

One does not usually associate Campus Crusade for Christ with the Pentecostal-charismatic movements. Nevertheless, the Jesus film they have produced has given similar results. This high-quality film on the life of Jesus uses only the Gospel of Luke as narrative, with vernacular languages dubbed in. Nontechnological village dwellers take its message literally and believe that Jesus heals the sick and casts out demons today. New converts begin healing ministries almost as soon as they are saved. Campus Crusade's Paul Eschleman tells story after story of the signs and wonders that follow the Jesus film in the Third World (*I Just Saw Jesus,* Here's Life Publishers, 1985). Currently an estimated 500,000 people see the Jesus film every day, and around 50,000 make decisions for Christ. Many of them are brought into home fellowship groups that minister in a charismatic style, even though they are not counted as Pentecostal-charismatics, but as Third Wavers.

The Jesus film, signs and wonders, and home fellowship groups have been important factors in the vigorous growth of the churches in Nepal, particularly since 1980. Open evangelism is forbidden, but the message spreads through word of mouth. In 1976 there were only 500 baptized believers, but by 1986 the number had swelled to 60,000. Some whole villages have become Christian. Most churches are affiliated with the Nepal Christian Fellowship, not known as a Pentecostal-charismatic denomination, but ministering in much the same way.

The growth of the churches in China to a conservative estimate of 50 million believers mostly in the last ten years has been reported above. It should be reiterated, however, that, while classifications of Pentecostal or independent charismatic have little meaning to most Chinese believers, the Spirit of God is ministering in some 85 percent of the churches in what we would regard as Pentecostal-charismatic ways. Because of the dramatic church growth there, five books have recently been written on the church in China: Paul E. Kauffman, *China, the Emerging Challenge* (1982), Carl Lawrence, *The Church in China* (1985), Leslie Lyall, *God Reigns in China* (1985), David H. Adeney, *China: The Church's Long March,* (1985), and Arthur Wallis, *China Miracle* (1986). Every one of these authors stresses the important role that supernatural signs and wonders have played in the spread of the gospel. One of Wallis' chapters, for example, is titled, "Where Supernatural Is Natural."

V. Coming Home to America. Since historians trace the roots of the Pentecostal-charismatic movements back to Topeka, Kansas, in 1901 and Los Angeles, California, in 1906–1909, the U.S. can generally be considered the home of the movements. It is important, therefore, to take a fairly close look at church growth patterns in the U.S.

For years, Elmer L. Towns, one of America's leading church growth researchers, published a list of America's fastest-growing Sunday schools. In 1980 Pentecostals were leading in fifteen of the fifty states. By 1985 Towns had changed his list to the fastest-growing *churches.* While some have raised questions about whether Baptists are sufficiently represented, his findings indicate that no fewer than forty of the fifty states are led by Pentecostal-charismatic churches. Twenty-nine of them (58 percent) have "Assemblies of God" in their names (*Ministries Today* [September–October, 1986], 58).

A. Early Growth. Growth did not come easily for Pentecostal churches in the first part of the century. Considered by theologians as a false cult, scorned as "holy rollers," socially and physically persecuted in many places, and ridiculed as adhering to a "hillbilly religion," the early Pentecostal churches found the going rough. Both theologically and socially the countercultural features of Pentecostalism could have been seen as restrictions to growth. Nevertheless, as is the case with many sect-type movements, substantial growth did occur over a sixty-year period as the following charts show:

Membership 1926–86

	1926	1970	1986
Assemblies of God	47,950	626,660	2,036,453

Church of God (Cleveland)	23,247	243,532	505,775
Pentecostal Holiness	8,096	66,790	113,000
Totals	79,293	937,162	2,655,228

Decadal Growth Rates

1926–70   75% DGR

1970–86   92% DGR

Decadal growth rates of 75 and 92 percent for a movement of this size are considerable. If the three denominations selected above can be considered representative of the whole, we may surmise that some growth-restricting factors of the early years were somewhat alleviated more recently. One of these can easily be identified as when, after World War II, Pentecostal denominations were admitted into the National Association of Evangelicals; the period of ridicule began changing into a period of respectability. As we will see later, however, respectability for religious movements can at times turn out to be a mixed blessing.

B. Classifying the Groups. While classical Pentecostal denominations such as those listed above represented virtually the entire movement to 1960, the picture has now become more complex. For the purpose of studying growth rates, the following classification of Pentecostal-charismatic groups is being used:

1. Classical Pentecostals
   a. Wesleyan (Holiness)
   b. Baptistic (finished work)
   c. Oneness
2. Charismatics
   a. Independent charismatic churches
   b. Charismatic renewal movement
     (1) Protestant charismatics
     (2) Catholic charismatics

C. The Problem of the Church of God in Christ. Before displaying the statistics for American Pentecostal-charismatic growth, the matter of the membership figures of the Church of God in Christ (CGIC) should be discussed. This is the largest of a number of statistical inconsistencies that must be dealt with in calculating the size and growth rates of different churches. Who is actually counted in statistical reporting will vary from denomination to denomination. Are only adults counted, or are children included as well? If only adults, is eighteen years of age the cutoff period? Or fifteen? Or twelve? Are regular attenders included with members? Are nominal members included with active members? Is it required that members have experienced baptism in the Holy Spirit and have then spoken in tongues in order to be counted? Is water baptism necessary? Answers to these questions are so varied that the most reasonable procedure is to accept whatever number is reported by the denominational office.

This is what has been done in this study with the exception of the CGIC, a black Wesleyan-type Pentecostal denomination, which is one of the largest and probably the fastest-growing of all the classical Pentecostal groups. How large it is and how fast it is growing, however, are difficult to determine because accurate record keeping has never been a high priority for its leaders. The *Yearbook of American and Canadian Churches 1986* reports 3,709,661 members as of 1984, with 9,962 churches. This would mean that the average church has 372 members, a figure suspiciously high in view of two other considerations. First, the 1974 *Yearbook* report lists 425,000 members in 4,500 churches, or 94 per church. Second, a spot check of four Southern California jurisdictions of the CGIC reveals an average of 79 per church. Furthermore, five other black Pentecostal denominations show an average of 50 per church. This is not to deny that there are some large churches, such as Bishop Charles Blake's West Angeles CGIC of Los Angeles with more than 3,000 members.

Leonard Lovett, pastor of the Church of the Crossroads Peniel CGIC of Los Angeles and a contributor to this volume, confirms that the number 3,709,611 is probably an inflated figure and that a more realistic number is 1.5 or 2 million. Admitting that this may be the best figure for the CGIC, I nevertheless need to exercise my editorial responsibility of making a subjective decision. In my calculations of black Pentecostal churches I have chosen to use 76 members per church across the board. This is important because it seems that several black Pentecostal denominations keep a fairly accurate record of the number of congregations but not of members. I frankly acknowledge that at this point there is considerable room for statistical variation.

D. Current Growth. In the following set of graphs, the category under examination will be listed with the total numbers of members in 1984 revealed by a fairly thorough study of American Pentecostal-charismatic groups. Decadal growth rates (DGR) will be indicated on a bar graph with the rate for the decade 1974–84 first and under it the DGR for the five-year period of 1979–84. This will allow one to see at a glance whether the rate of growth of each category is increasing or decreasing.

1. All Pentecostals and Charismatics (8,972,863)

1974–84   175% DGR

1979–84   173% DGR

2. All Classical Pentecostals (4,004,798)

1974–84   55% DGR

1979–84   52% DGR

  a. Wesleyan (Holiness) (1,800,198)

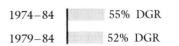

1974–84   62% DGR

1979–84   48% DGR

  b. Baptistic (finished work) (1,597,012)

Decadal Growth Rates 1980–84

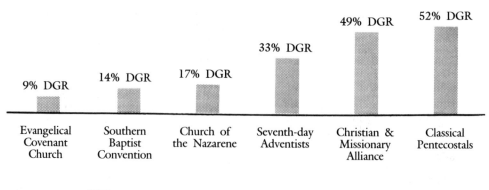

9% DGR	14% DGR	17% DGR	33% DGR	49% DGR	52% DGR
Evangelical Covenant Church	Southern Baptist Convention	Church of the Nazarene	Seventh-day Adventists	Christian & Missionary Alliance	Classical Pentecostals

1974–84   50% DGR

1979–84   56% DGR

c. Oneness (607,588)

1974–84   50% DGR

1979–84   48% DGR

The one category of classical Pentecostals that is increasing the growth rate is the Baptistic type. This includes, among others, the rapidly growing Assemblies of God, which alone comprises 30 percent of all American classical Pentecostals, if the conservative full membership figure of 1,189,143 is used (as here). If the inclusive membership of 2,036,453 for the Assemblies of God were used (assuming that some of the others might use this instead of full membership), the figure rises to 42 percent.

Before we move on to look at the growth rates of charismatics, it would be well to see how the current 52 percent DGR of classical Pentecostals compares to some of the other denominations in America. Some groups such as the Evangelical Lutheran Church in America, the Episcopal Church, the United Methodist Church, the United Church of Christ, the Presbyterian Church (U.S.A.), the Reformed Church in America, the Mennonite Church, the Christian Church (Disciples of Christ), and others are actually losing members. Some of the growing denominations are shown here by way of comparison:

3. All Charismatics (4,968,065)

1974–84   804% DGR

1979–84   457% DGR

a. Independent Charismatic Churches (750,000)

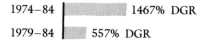

1974–84   1467% DGR

1979–84   557% DGR

The drop in growth rate of the independent charismatic churches from 1,467 to 557 percent is not a cause for alarm. Most of the growth of the independent charismatics has come since 1980, meaning that there was a relatively small number of them in 1974, and this tends to distort the rates. The 557 percent DGR is extraordinarily high; even half of that percentage of growth would be remarkable. As such, so far as American church growth is concerned, the independent charismatic churches are currently the most rapidly growing segment of American religion. The charismatic renewal movements that follow are also growing rapidly, but since they are contained within existing churches and denominations, they do not figure in the overall church-growth picture.

Our research on independent charismatics was difficult because no overall reporting or accountability system is in place. The growth rates above are based on eighteen groups, which reported 1,090 churches and 235,524 members. Those that did not report included major groups such as Rhema Ministerial Association (Kenneth Hagin), with 525 churches; International Ministers Forum (Louise Copeland), with 500 churches; and many others. It also excludes the new Charismatic Bible Ministries (Oral Roberts). The Full Gospel Chaplaincy, led by Jim Ammerman, claims 1.5 million independent charismatics affiliated with their agency. Some leaders are estimating that there are as many as 80,000 independent charismatic churches which, if our documented membership per church is assumed, would total a rather unbelievable 17 million members in 1985. To stay on the conservative side, however, I am using the 750,000 figure in the totals, although I am tempted to say that 1.5 million may be more realistic.

b. Charismatic Renewal Movement (4,218,065)

1974–84   782% DGR

1979–84   463% DGR

i. Protestant Charismatics (2,779,565)

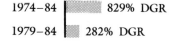

1974–84   829% DGR

1979–84   282% DGR

ii. Catholic Charismatics (1,439,000)

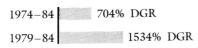

1974–84 ▨ 704% DGR

1979–84 ▨ 1534% DGR

A breakdown of the estimated percentage and number of charismatics reported by leaders in some of the traditional U.S. denominations in 1984 is shown in the following list:

Roman Catholics (3%)	1,439,000
Southern Baptists (3%)	400,000
United Methodists (4%)	400,000
Episcopalians (11%)	300,000
Presbyterian & Reformed (8%)	250,000
American Baptist (5%)	76,000
Mennonite (13%)	12,000

E. Adding It Up. How many Pentecostal-charismatics do we currently find in the U.S.?

The survey outlined here identified about 9 million. Undoubtedly there were some who were not counted, especially independent charismatics. So the number must be considered conservative.

Some confusion entered the picture in 1980 when *Christianity Today* (February 22, 1980) published the results of a Gallup survey that claimed that 19 percent of American adults identified themselves as Pentecostal-charismatic. This calculated to 29 million adults. However, only 4 percent of American adults, or 5 million, had spoken in tongues. All of this was hard to understand, and at the time several leaders were groping to provide some explanation for these findings.

However, another Gallup poll, sponsored by CBN (the 700 Club), was taken in 1984. Americans were asked, "Are you involved with or do you participate in the charismatic movement?" Three percent said they did, which would total 5.8 million adults. The same number said they had spoken in tongues. If we assume that some classical Pentecostals would not identify themselves with the charismatic movement, these figures are nearer to our findings.

Given this information, a reasonable estimate of the number of Pentecostal-charismatics in the U.S. in 1985 would be 9 to 10 million active weekly adult attenders. At the current rate of increase, we could expect there to be some 15 million Pentecostal-charismatics by 1990 and 41 million by the turn of the century. (Note that Barrett's figures are higher because he is counting children of believers as well as postcharismatics.)

VI. Church Growth Principles. On both a national and a worldwide scale, Pentecostal-charismatics are front and center in terms of rates of church growth. Why is it that these movements are growing more rapidly than other segments of Christianity at the present time? The question will be addressed by first examining some international institutional factors, then examining some local institutional factors, and in conclusion indicating some danger areas that could slow the growth in the days to come.

A.   International   Institutional   Factors. Church growth analysis usually addresses national institutional factors, but we are here dealing with the Pentecostal-charismatic movements on an international scale. It must be recognized that the major overriding growth factor for Pentecostal-charismatic churches is the same as for Baptist, Presbyterian, Episcopal, or any other churches, namely the sovereign power of God. Church growth is not like growth of an industry or a political party or a trade union. Jesus said, "I will build my church" (Matt. 16:18), and he alone does it through the power of his Holy Spirit and for his glory. However, there are certain attitudes and methodologies that Jesus seems to bless at certain times and places. The six factors listed below are not absent from all non-Pentecostal churches, but they should be recognized as key factors that have contributed specifically to Pentecostal-charismatic church growth.

1. Biblical Triumphalism. It has become stylish among theologians to disparage so-called triumphalism. This mood of pessimism, however, does not impress many Pentecostal-charismatic leaders who more readily identify with the apostle Paul who says, "Thanks be to God, who always leads us to triumphal procession with Christ and through us spreads everywhere the fragrance of the knowledge of him" (2 Cor. 2:14). Pentecostals, while not downplaying the Cross and its implications, have a large capacity to believe that God is doing, and will continue to do, great things through them.

2. Targeting the Poor and Oppressed. The Bible teaches that, while God loves all people, he has a special bias for the poor and oppressed. While there are some notable exceptions, the rule is that Pentecostal churches worldwide are churches of the poor. And church-growth research has shown that, not coincidentally, those at the lower end of the socio-economic scale are more receptive to the gospel than the rich and powerful, just as they were in Corinth (see 1 Cor. 1:26).

3. Multiple Tracks to Ordination. The constitution and by-laws of the AG in the U.S. specifically state that no educational requirements will ever be made for ordination. This is one of the most significant growth advantages that Pentecostal-charismatics have over any number of other Christian groups. Academic training does not disqualify men and women from ordination, but neither is it regarded as a substitute for spiritual gifts, divine calling, Holy Spirit anointing, and confirmation of the call through apprenticeship training. (See C. P. Wagner, "Seminaries in the Streets," in *Spiritual Power and Church Growth,* 1986.)

4. High Local-Church Autonomy. With few exceptions, Pentecostal-charismatic groups give a large degree of freedom to local congregations for developing and implementing a philosophy of ministry. This helps avoid the creation of top-heavy bureaucratic structures that tend to draw extraordinary amounts of finances, energy, and creativity from local churches.

5. The Apostolic Model of Church Planting. Operating under the assumption that the gift of apostleship, like the other NT spiritual gifts, is in operation today, many of the Pentecostal-charismatics (but not all) expect that church planting will be done according to the pattern of the apostle Paul. This permits the exercise of strong spiritual (as over against legal) authority on the part of leaders recognized by themselves and their colleagues as having the apostolic gift. Ed Roebert of Pretoria, South Africa, is a typical contemporary apostle. Working from a base of the Hatfield Christian Center, itself with over five thousand members and some five hundred home fellowship groups, in 1987 he was planting an additional new church every four days. At this writing, no fewer than 161 other churches have voluntarily submitted to his apostolic authority in the NT style.

6. *Schism.* It may seem strange to include schism on this list of positive growth factors, but research has shown that in many parts of the world it has been a strong factor underlying Pentecostal-charismatic church growth. While schism is usually unplanned and unprayed-for, it has frequently resulted in two growing churches or denominations instead of one. Just as the apostle Paul seemed to be able to weather the storm of schism in his mission (see Acts 15:36–41), likewise many Pentecostal-charismatic leaders seem to be able to experience schism and perceive the hand of God to be working through it all.

B. Local Institutional Factors. Recent studies have been made of new large churches in the U.S. that have been established in the 1980s and have grown to at least one thousand within two years. Almost all of these are Pentecostal-charismatic churches. If they can be taken as typical, the following common growth factors can be seen as important for Pentecostal-charismatic local church growth:

1. Conservative evangelical theology is unquestioned. There is no debate on biblical authority or the priority need of saving lost souls from hell.

2. Strong pastoral leadership is encouraged. The pastors exercise extraordinary authority, they have unbounded optimism and vision, and they model radical obedience to the lordship of Jesus Christ.

3. Prayer is a significant, explicit, up-front component of the church's philosophy of ministry. Instead of affirming prayer simply in theory, particularly the new independent charismatic churches have discovered how to organize the congregation's prayer life, enlist believers' participation, and experience and share exciting, tangible answers to prayer. Some even hire a staff member as pastor of intercession.

4. Openness to the person and work of the Holy Spirit is maintained at all times. Heightened spirituality through the baptism of the Holy Spirit and the release of all spiritual gifts—but especially those of healings, tongues, deliverance, and prophecy—draws believers close to God as he manifests his power in their midst.

5. Abundant financial support of the work is forthcoming. Money is rarely a problem, since the believers are excited about what their church means to them and others and are highly motivated to give to it. Tithing is the norm, even among the poor.

6. Worship is a central feature of church life. Contrasted to performance-oriented worship characteristic of many traditional churches, Pentecostal-charismatic worship is participant-oriented, with freedom for the use of body language such as uplifted hands or dancing. Hymnology is based more on praise and worship choruses composed since 1980 than on traditional hymns. Contemporary instruments such as synthesizers and guitars have supplemented or replaced the pipe organ and piano.

7. Participation in lay ministry is expected of all church members. Many churches have developed high-caliber in-house training programs designed to equip lay persons for effective ministry. An increasing number of gifted laypeople are being recruited for paid staff positions.

8. Extensive Bible-teaching ministry is focused on the felt needs of church members such as physical health, material prosperity, social relationships, emotional stability, and lay-ministry challenges more than on the historical-grammatical exegesis of the content of scriptural passages. The teaching is communicated not only from the pulpit but also through voluminous sales of audio tapes distributed through well-stocked bookstores, which do most of their business before and after Sunday services.

C. Some Possible Dangers. How long will the vigorous rate of growth of the Pentecostal and charismatic movements be sustained? Pentecostal leaders are fond of poking fun at their early detractors by reminding them that they predicted the movement would soon blow over. "They were right," is the reply. "It has now blown over the whole world!" At the present moment there are no signs that a slowdown is around the corner. But the lifecycle of similar human movements has been analyzed sociologically, and certain pitfalls can be identified in order that they may be avoided in the future. If, as many Pentecostal-charismatic preachers affirm, we are witnessing the fulfillment of the end-time part of the prophecy of Joel, nothing will be able to stop the movement. But if lessons can be learned from some of the Pentecostal movements that have stagnated, the earlier Holiness movement, and numerous other churches that started with obvious manifestations of the Spirit of God, it might be well also to recognize at least three areas of possible danger.

1. *The Dark Side of Respectability.* It was earlier mentioned that the latter half of the twentieth century saw Pentecostalism moving from the era of ridicule to the era of respectability. This has been a positive growth factor, but it can all too easily lead to what church-growth theory calls "halting due to redemption and lift." Whereas the Pentecostal movement began as a church of the poor, many of the first- and second-generation leaders who were born into poverty have experienced the blessing of the Lord and have been lifted out of it. Many of their children, now entering positions of leadership, have never known poverty firsthand. Their tendency may be to gear their ministry toward the middle class, neglecting the poor from whose lot they are thankful to have been delivered.

Linked to this is the desire for wider ecclesiastical respectability. Particularly among some Pentecostals who have sensed the call of God toward intellectual pursuits and who presumably will be the shapers of future Pentecostal theology, the drive to erase the stigma of "hillbilly religion" has at times led to a reluctance to defend Pentecostal doctrinal distinctives with any degree of conviction so as not to alienate newly found academic colleagues. Some have even left the denomination of their parents. Some of those who have remained may be more interested in impressing non-Pentecostal leaders than in giving outspoken theological leadership to their own movement.

2. *St. John's Syndrome.* Church-growth pathology has identified St. John's Syndrome as a potential growth-obstructing disease (see C. Peter Wagner, *Your Church Can Be Healthy,* 1979). It is the disease the apostle John diagnosed when he wrote to some of the churches in Asia Minor in Revelation 2 and 3. After forty years those fervent, Spirit-filled churches were becoming lukewarm and losing their first love. The all too frequent story of second-generation churches is that nominalism sets in and the level of commitment goes down. This apparently has been one of the problems encountered in some of the older European Pentecostal churches.

So far, St. John's Syndrome has been avoided in the U.S. chiefly because Pentecostalism has been able to maintain a high level of evangelistic fervor. As long as a steady stream of first-generation adult converts continues to feed in, nominality can be prevented and growth can be sustained.

3. *Ministerial Elitism.* The establishment of accredited theological seminaries may bring blessings to the Pentecostal-charismatic movements, but the potential dangers must also be recognized. The Pentecostal churches of Chile wisely avoided any formalized system of ministerial training for over fifty years chiefly because they perceived that it could slow their growth. North American Pentecostals feel that if seminaries supplement rather than replace nonformal ministerial training routes, they will not be harmful. This may turn out to be the case.

But another scenario is possible, particularly if steps are not consciously taken to avoid it. In the first generation, seminary-trained pastors find themselves receiving calls to the larger, wealthier, more prestigious congregations. They are then promoted to denominational positions. Because like begets like, they advocate seminaries as the superior route to ordination. A layer of first-class seminary-trained pastors develops over against another layer of second-class nonseminary-trained pastors. By the third generation motions are made in the general assembly to change the rules in order to "upgrade the ministry." By this time, predictably, stagnation of a denomination may be setting in.

The danger may seem unreal at this moment of explosive Pentecostal-charismatic growth. While this may not cripple the entire movement, it could well affect the growth momentum of some prominent segments of it.

See also STATISTICS, GLOBAL; HISPANIC PENTECOSTALISM.

Bibliography: D. B. Barrett, ed., *World Christian Encyclopedia* (1982); C. H. Jacquet, Jr., ed., *Yearbook of American and Canadian Churches,* published annually; P. Johnstone, *Operation World* (1986); C. E. Jones, *A Guide to the Study of the Pentecostal Movement* (1983); L. G. McClung, Jr., ed., *Azusa Street and Beyond: Pentecostal Missions and Church Growth in the Twentieth Century* (1986); P. A. Pomerville, *The Third Force in Missions* (1985); V. Synan, *In the Latter Days: The Outpouring of the Holy Spirit in the Twentieth Century* (1984); idem, *Twentieth-Century Pentecostal Explosion* (1987); J. N. Vaughan, *The World's 20 Largest Churches* (1984); C. P. Wagner, *On the Crest of the Wave* (1983); idem, *Spiritual Power and Church Growth* (1986).
C. P. Wagner

CHURCH LEADERSHIP

I. Introduction. Pentecostals and charismatics place a distinctive emphasis on the Holy Spirit's involvement in all aspects of leadership within the body of Christ. This emphasis does not denigrate human abilities such as vision, courage, integrity, and boldness. It encompasses all things human and recognizes the Spirit's role both in the granting of gifts that make for leadership and in the directing of human instruments toward effective implementation of the will of Christ on earth.

II. Leadership and the Holy Spirit. Since the Day of Pentecost the administration of the affairs of the church has been the role of the Holy Spirit. From that time forward the Spirit's presence in the church was to be perpetual (John 14:12), and his continuing office was to be that of Administrator (1 Cor. 12:5–11). Everything in the church is to be subject to his will. The presidency of the Spirit was exhibited in the church so that undergirding the apostle Peter, the apparent leader, was the Spirit who stood as the real Administrator of affairs (Acts 5).

The Holy Spirit is thus seen as the Leader controlling all subordinate offices so that they shall be occupied only by certain types of men full of the Spirit (Acts 6:3–5). The Holy Spirit chose, separated, and sent forth the first two missionaries of the church yet not without the church also being involved (Acts 13:1–3). Later the Spirit is seen not only in his lofty sovereignty but condescending as a fellow Counselor. Such should be the true character of all church councils (Acts 15:28).

Even a cursory glimpse of the NT reveals that the Holy Spirit played a major role in leadership among early Christians. Luke recognizes this when he opens his treatise by writing, "He was taken up to heaven, after giving instructions *through the Holy Spirit* to the apostles he had chosen" (Acts 1:2, italics mine).

Not only did Paul depend on the Holy Spirit for strength and guidance, but he stated this principle of leadership specifically when he wrote to his fellow Christians: "It seemed good to the Holy Spirit and to us not to burden you with anything beyond the following requirements" (Acts 15:28). This is the announcement of the conclusions and decisions of the church council at Jerusalem. The Holy Spirit unites with them in a joint conclusion. He sat with them as chief Counselor in their deliberations and sealed their conclusions with his approval.

III. The Gift of Leaders. Though he preached to the multitudes, Jesus Christ spent most of his time teaching and instructing key men, his disciples. He was concerned that these give leadership to the church after he returned to the Father. Many passages support the idea that leaders are themselves chosen of God and presented as gifts to the body of Christ.

Paul referred to himself as one "called to be an apostle of Christ Jesus by the will of God" (1 Cor. 1:1). He saw himself divinely ordained to minister. Speaking to the elders at Ephesus, Paul said, "The Holy Spirit has made you overseers" (Acts 20:28). The Ascension gift of Christ was the baptism of the Holy Spirit (*dōrea*). He also gave gifts, and the apostle gives us a list of these office bearers who were given to the church: "some to be apostles, some to be prophets, some to be evangelists, and some to be pastors and teachers" (Eph. 4:11).

Paul wrote to the Corinthians: "Now you are the body of Christ, and each one of you is a part of it. And in the church God has appointed first of all apostles, second prophets, third teachers, then workers of miracles, also those having gifts of healing, those able to help others, those with gifts of administration, and those speaking in different kinds of tongues" (1 Cor. 12:27–28).

Clearly, what Paul means is that each individual has been saved by God's grace. Each is in turn presented as a unique member of the body of Christ for ministry to others. This ministry will be both confirmed and affirmed in life-practice as the individual lives out his/her ministry on this earth.

IV. Spiritual Gifts. God endows believers with spiritual gifts that are distinct from natural talent, or natural gifts, that come at birth or that are developed by experience. Paul's most familiar listing of spiritual gifts, and the one traditionally emphasized by Pentecostals, is found in 1 Corinthians: (1) the message of wisdom, (2) the message of knowledge, (3) faith, (4) gifts of healing, (5) miraculous powers, (6) prophecy, (7) the ability to distinguish between spirits, (8) the ability to speak in different kinds of tongues, and (9) the interpretation of tongues (12:8–10). Paul gives us a slightly different listing of gifts in Romans: "If a man's gift is prophesying, let him use it in proportion to his faith. If it is serving, let him serve; if it is teaching, let him teach; if it is encouraging, let him encourage; if it is contributing to the needs of others, let him give generously; if it is leadership, let him govern diligently; if it is showing mercy, let him do it cheerfully. Love must be sincere" (12:6–9). The image drawn here is clearly that of servanthood. We are to serve one another in the Spirit of Christ.

V. Pentecostal Role Models. Peter overcame his Jewish prejudice through direct ministry of the Holy Spirit (Acts 10:9–23). Later he defended his actions before the brethren in Jerusalem (Acts 15–18). James modeled Pentecostal leadership when he opened his Epistle with the words, "James, a servant of God and the Lord Jesus Christ" (James 1:1). Paul established his concept of leadership by referring to Christ, who "did not please himself" (Rom. 15:3). He wrote to the Corinthians, "I will very gladly spend for you everything I have and expend myself as well" (2 Cor. 12:15); and he often altered his plans and projections as a missionary in response to the bidding of the Holy Spirit (Acts 16:9).

Pentecostals view this as the only proper attitude for church leaders. The Holy Spirit is always in charge, and we are servants ready to do his will.

VI. Self-Perception Among Pentecostal Leaders. NT examples mandate that true leaders of the church perceive themselves as "shepherds of God's flock" (1 Peter 5:2), not as masters who command but as servants who give of themselves in the Spirit of Jesus Christ (Matt. 20:27). This forbids carnality, the exalting of human personality, and the erecting of cultic bureaucratic organizations that perform under the guise of the church.

Leaders must always recognize and acknowledge that they are ambassadors of Christ (2 Cor. 5:20), messengers sent forth by him, charged to speak and to act only in his name (John 14:13; 15:16).

To properly grasp the nature and scope of leadership as interpreted here, one must see the philosophical and theological background from which Pentecostals perceive themselves as human instruments playing a subservient role to the Holy Spirit.

VII. Conclusion. For the Pentecostal, therefore, leadership is first of all a calling, that which is and shall always remain under the sovereignty of God. Leadership is diverse and individually distinct, consisting of all those varied natural human talents with which God providentially endows men and women, and worked out through the same providence in terms of circumstances and daily happenings. Yet it is more.

Pentecostal leadership is predicated on human submissiveness to the Holy Spirit, a man or woman's willingness to listen and to be obedient to the promptings of the Spirit within. Leaders who thus yield themselves in obedience to the Holy Spirit are further aided by special gifts of the Spirit, gifts that supernaturally counteract the devices of Satan and open doors and bring spiritual victories beyond mere human efforts. Herein the church *can* and *does* always triumph, remaining under the lordship of Christ and being submissive to his Spirit.

See also PASTOR, ROLE OF.

Bibliography: H. T. Armerding, *Leadership* (1978); T. W. Engstrom, *The Making of a Christian Leader* (1976); K. K. Kilinski and J. C. Wofford, *Organization and Leadership in the Local Church* (1973); M. Wilson, *How to Mobilize Church Volunteers* (1983).
R. H. Hughes

CHURCH MEMBERSHIP Membership in the local Pentecostal church today differs little from other evangelical groups. Most churches do not equate the body of Christ only with those baptized in the Spirit, therefore a Pentecostal experience is not required of members. Church discipline of members tends to reflect the Holiness traditions and manifests the same taboos.

I. Historical Developments. Early Pentecostals did not attach great significance to the formal matter of church membership. They equated the mainline church with apostate Babylon or Antichrist and emphasized that church membership did not equate with salvation as a part of the true body of Christ. Participation in fellowship and worship was the bonding element rather than the institutional legalism of membership. As a result, open rather than closed Communion is the general practice. Some had been ejected from their former church denominations and were so suspicious of ecclesiastical structures that they even rejected the whole idea of a membership list. They were one in the unity of the Spirit.

With the development of church polity, however, institutional structures became standard. Particularly important was the power of a voting membership in a congregational decision such as who the pastor would be. Membership, though, does not bestow power in all groups; only male members of the Church of God (Cleveland, Tenn.) have votes in the local conference.

In some of the modern charismatic fellowships, membership is not exclusive. Members may hold dual memberships, in the local fellowship as well as in a historical Catholic, Orthodox, Anglican, or Protestant church.

II. Requirement for Membership. All Pentecostal churches require testimony of a conversion experience for admission to membership. Most do not emphasize water baptism as a prerequisite to joining, but it is an expected compliance in all. It is required in some Assemblies of God churches and in all United Pentecostal churches. In Pentecostal Holiness churches parents may follow the Wesleyan pattern and have their infants baptized or merely dedicated if they prefer. Of particular interest is the fact that only in a few instances, such as in the United Pentecostal Church, is the uniquely Pentecostal experience of the baptism in the Spirit required for membership. Many second-generation Pentecostals either have not been baptized in the Spirit or do not continue the practice of speaking in tongues after a childhood or adolescent experience. Those who do not claim Spirit baptism may, however, become somewhat second-class saints as they are barred from positions of church leadership or kept from advancing to the clergy.

Financial support of the church may be either an explicit or implicit obligation. Tithing may be required, as in the Pentecostal Church of God, or a commitment to support may be demanded, as in the Foursquare Church, but enforcement may not be consistent. Members who do not attend worship for extended periods of time, from one to six months, may be dropped to an inactive status on the rolls. This is not so much a disciplinary matter as it is a means of keeping rosters current to be able to meet legal quorum requirements when conducting church business.

Loyalty and cooperation are required by all groups, but toleration of dissent may vary widely. In many independent charismatic fellowships that developed in the 1960s membership meant submission to authority figures in the details of life that most Christians consider private.

III. Standards of Conduct. Church members represent the body to the public and, therefore,

standards of ethical conduct are imposed. The early Pentecostals emphasized the Bible as the authoritative rule of *faith* and *practice*, but the deemphasis on creeds left the *practices* as the focus of tensions. The issues were the taboos of the holiness and revivalistic traditions. Urbanization and affluence have eroded these standards over the years, but they still remain points of contention in many fellowships. Alcohol, tobacco, and dancing are still generally not permitted, but television has eroded the opposition to theater attendance. A few groups do not even allow television, and some do not permit women to cut their hair or wear makeup. The modern charismatic movement, however, has not been characterized by these traditional Holiness taboos.

See also CHURCH, THEOLOGY OF THE; ECCLESIASTICAL POLITY.

Bibliography: W. J. Hollenweger, *The Pentecostals* (1972); J. T. Nichol, *Pentecostalism* (1966); R. Quebedeaux, *The New Charismatics: The Origins, Development, and Significance of Neo-Pentecostalism* (1976); K. M. Ranaghan, "Conversion and Baptism: Personal Experience and Ritual Celebration in Pentecostal Churches," *Studia Liturgica* 10 (1974): 65–76.   D. J. Wilson

CHURCH OF CHRIST IN THE ANTILLES See IGLESIA DE CRISTO EN LAS ANTILLAS.

CHURCH OF GOD (1957 REFORMATION) See CHURCH OF GOD, JERUSALEM ACRES.

CHURCH OF GOD (ANDERSON, IND.) CHARISMATICS See WESLEYAN CHARISMATICS.

CHURCH OF GOD (CLEVELAND, TENN.) (CG). The Church of God, with headquarters in Cleveland, Tennessee, is one of the oldest and largest Pentecostal bodies in America and very likely in the world. It has local congregations in all 50 states, and mission outposts in 107 countries. In 1986 the 1,650,000-member denomination celebrated its centennial under the theme "A Century of Pentecostal Witness," which signified that its earliest years of searching and preaching resulted in a Pentecostal outpouring and that its subsequent ministry has been a multifaceted witness of Pentecostal truth and experience.

I. History. The CG was instituted under the name Christian Union on August 19, 1886, in Monroe County, Tennessee. R. G. Spurling, a Missionary Baptist preacher who led in the organization, was joined by only eight others, one of whom was his son, Richard G. Spurling, Jr., also a Missionary Baptist preacher. The original compact of this small group was "to take the New Testament, or law of Christ, for your own rule of faith and practice, giving each other equal rights and privilege to read and interpret for yourselves as your conscience may dictate, and . . . sit together as the Church of God to transact business as the same. . . ." Their stated intention was "to restore primitive Christianity and bring about the union of all denominations." They chose the name Christian Union because it

Two of the first leaders of the Church of God, R. G. Spurling and W. F. Bryant, at the first General Assembly in Cherokee County, North Carolina, January 1906.

expressed the simple agreement that bound the original members together.

A. Beginnings. The elder Spurling died soon afterward, and the younger Spurling carried on alone. In 1892 a second fellowship was formed twelve miles away in Cherokee County, North Carolina, in the home of W. F. Bryant, a Baptist lay preacher. Spurling and Bryant ministered in the isolated Unicoi Mountain region for four years before there was any significant response to their efforts. Then in the summer of 1896 a revival was conducted in the Shearer Schoolhouse in Cherokee County that resulted in a strange and wonderful occurrence—men and women became enraptured by the Holy Spirit and spoke in unknown tongues. During the outpouring about 130 persons received the experience, which was identified in the Scriptures as the baptism of the Holy Ghost. It was also recorded that numerous afflicted persons were healed. Such things had never been seen or even heard of in the mountains. Few knew what to make of it, so much opposition followed. The opposition turned hateful, and a period of violent persecution swept across the mountains and tested the faith and courage of the believers. Churches and homes were burned; the people were flogged, shot at, stoned, and otherwise tormented for almost a decade. They were opposed in more subtle ways for many years thereafter.

On May 15, 1902, the church added guidelines and regulations to its policy and changed its name to the Holiness Church. On June 13, 1903, a new minister, A. J. Tomlinson, who had recently come to the mountains from Indiana, joined the church and was chosen as pastor. Soon thereafter another preacher and newcomer to the mountains, M. S. Lemons, joined the growing body.

By 1905 there were four congregations in three contiguous states: Tennessee, North Carolina, and Georgia. On January 26–27, 1906, these four came together for a "general assembly" in Cherokee County, North Carolina. Thereafter, an annual or biennial general assembly would be a prominent feature of the CG.

As early as 1904 the center of activities began to shift westward from the mountains to the town of Cleveland, Tennessee. By 1907 the move was complete and permanent. On January 11, 1907, the church officially adopted the name Church of God, the name that had been used in the original compact in 1886.

From 1906 onward the CG became more aggressive in preaching the baptism of the Holy Spirit. Although many of the members had received the experience as early as 1896, they seem to have thought of it as a phenomenon that had happened only to them; they testified to the experience and wished that others would share "the blessing," but they did not aggressively preach it to others. From 1906, when their experience was reaffirmed with news of similar outpourings in other places, particularly California, the people of the CG became more evangelistic in proclaiming the Holy Spirit baptism as a doctrine and spiritual experience for all believers.

B. Early Expansion. In 1909 the CG created its first administrative office, that of general

A general assembly of the Church of God. The denomination in 1986 had a worldwide membership of 1,652,000 with congregations and missions in 107 countries.

overseer, for full-time supervision of the affairs of the church. A. J. Tomlinson was elected to the post and proved effective in pressing the Pentecostal message across the southeastern U.S. Congregations were established in Tennessee, North Carolina, Georgia, Alabama, Florida, Kentucky, and Virginia. This led the church to the most creative year of its early history, 1910. In January of that year the first CG missionaries went to a foreign country, the Bahama Islands; in March 1910 the church began publication of a denominational journal, the *Church of God Evangel*; in August 1910 the teachings of the CG were formally codified for the first time; and the evangelists were so effective that the church almost doubled in size during the year, from 1,005 to 1,885 members. With the surge of growth, overseers were appointed in 1911 to supervise the work and lead the evangelistic effort in the separate states.

From these early days the CG endeavored to use scriptural designations and terms for its operation. This was seen in its use of names, such as "Church of God," "Evangel," and "overseers." This practice was particularly evident in the adoption of the tithing plan of finances. The plan had been encouraged from the formative days, but it was officially adopted and developed from 1914 to 1917. In 1917 the CG agreed that each congregation would retain 80 percent of the tithes paid by its members and send 10 percent each to the state headquarters and general headquarters. The result was a dramatic increase of funds for such purposes as evangelism, missions, publishing, and general expansion. The individual states and the CG in general were soon able to expand their ministries into new fields and services.

The Assembly of 1916 created the most powerful body of the CG—a council of twelve men to care for the affairs of the church between its general assemblies. Following the pattern of Scripture, it was called "Council of Twelve" or "Elders Council." This influential body has provided the CG with leadership, balance, and strength through the years. It presently meets with the full-time executive committee as an executive council. (In 1986 the body was made international and enlarged by six seats to a "Council of Eighteen.")

With growing resources and leadership, the CG moved ahead boldly into new areas of ministry. It began its own publishing plant in 1917 for printing its expanding Sunday school literature and church journals. This plant grew well and is today a productive arm of the church (see PATHWAY PRESS).

In 1917 the CG instituted a Bible Training School, a dream that had occupied the church since 1911. The first class began on January 1, 1918, in the midst of World War I and the influenza epidemic of 1918. Despite the difficulties, the school survived and grew under the leadership of such teachers as Nora Chambers, Flavius J. Lee, and J. B. Ellis. Today it is Lee College, a four-year, fully accredited liberal arts college of 1,400 students.

Another long-cherished dream of the CG, an orphanage or home for children, was realized in 1920 when a home was opened in Cleveland, Tennessee. Lillian Kinsey was the first matron. Almost immediately new homes were built to accommodate the critical need.

1. Transition. The CG suffered a painful disappointment in 1923 when A. J. Tomlinson, upon being replaced as general overseer, withdrew from the denomination and organized a separate group. The break occurred when leaders of the CG, especially members of the Council of Twelve, became unhappy with Tomlinson's autocratic style of leadership and sought a change of administration. Tomlinson took the position that the council could not remove him, for he had been elected "for life" in 1914. The impasse was not resolved, and the unfortunate break occurred in June 1923.

Flavius J. Lee, a singularly pious man and effective teacher was elected to replace Tomlinson. Under Lee's leadership the CG regained its unity and sense of direction. This was due in large part to the high character and spiritual depth of the new leader. The CG enjoyed considerable growth and expansion and by 1926 had 25,000 members in thirty-one states. It maintained foreign missions in the Bahama Islands and Jamaica.

When Lee died in 1928, S. W. Latimer succeeded him as general overseer. The Great Depression shortly thereafter had an adverse effect on the CG in some ways, particularly in the area of finances, but it did not dampen the spiritual ardor or evangelistic zeal of the church. In many respects the Depression period can be called "a golden era." Camp meetings, which had been a part of each state's annual calendar since 1909, became even more important times of fellowship, evangelism, and devotion. Outstanding preachers arose in most parts of the CG, and numerous new programs were begun. In 1929 a few local youth organizations resulted in a national organization called Young People's Endeavor (YPE). The YPE fueled such enthusiasm among the youth that they became a dynamic new force in the CG. A national youth magazine, *The Lighted Pathway,* was begun in 1929 by Alda B. Harrison at her own expense. After a year the denomination assumed responsibility for the journal and made it its official youth magazine.

2. *Missions Outreach.* The decade of the 1930s saw the opening of new missions in several lands in the Western Hemisphere: Mexico (1932), Turks Island (1932), Haiti (1933), Guatemala (1934), Costa Rica (1935), and Panama (1935). The principal missionary force of the period was J. H. Ingram, who became a factor in world outreach for more than three decades.

When the CG emerged from the Depression in 1936, it was fifty years old and had 64,000 members. Behind the vigorous leadership of J. H. Walker, general overseer, and J. H. Ingram, missions field representative, the membership was in an expansive mood. The CG utilized its fiftieth anniversary to quicken an awareness of the world's need of the gospel. During a "Golden Jubilee World Tour" in 1936, Ingram brought the South India mission work of R. F. Cook into the fellowship of the CG and opened missions in several other lands. Also in 1936 Herman Lauster returned to his native Germany and began a vigorous work in the face of Nazi tyranny. Within the North American continent, congregations were established in virtually every state and in Saskatchewan, Canada.

a. *The Modern Era.* In 1942–43 the CG was one of the founding organizations of the National Association of Evangelicals (NAE). It was a significant move for Pentecostal churches to develop such strong bonds with some of the very churches that they had withdrawn from only a few years earlier. It was a remarkable move, and a wise one. The fellowship was genuine, and the results were good for everyone. This was followed in 1947 by the formation of the Pentecostal World Conference (PWC) and in 1948 by the Pentecostal Fellowship of North America (PFNA). These moves indicated that the CG, along with the entire Pentecostal movement, had come of age.

The CG set limits in 1946 on the time its leaders could serve in executive offices. This plan of limited tenures proved to be popular with the ministers, and the church has been treated to a notable succession of administrators at both general and state levels.

b. *Amalgamations.* Twice in the modern era the CG has formed an amalgamation with a kindred body outside America. The first was in 1951, when the church formed a union with the Full Gospel Church of South Africa. The 30,000-member South African church altered its name to Full Gospel Church of God. The immediate result was a remarkable growth in South Africa and increased opportunities for evangelism on the African continent.

The second amalgamation was formed in 1967 between the CG and the 70,000-member Bethel Full Gospel Church of Indonesia. The Indonesian leader, Ho L. Senduk, was a member of the CG, but his work was not a part of the denomination's missionary program. The union of the Gereja Bethel Indonesia and the CG resulted in an international Bethel Church of God, with congregations in all of the twenty-seven provinces of Indonesia and in Holland.

II. Ministries. The modern ministry of the CG consists of a full range of Christian activities and endeavors. These include such departments as (1) evangelism and home missions, (2) world missions, (3) publications, (4) higher education, (5) youth and Christian education, (6) benevolences, (7) radio and television, (8) women's ministries, (9) lay ministries, (10) stewardship, and other special ministries.

A. The Church of God and Race Relations. Since 1909 the CG has had a considerable number of black ministers and congregations. Despite the fact that its roots were in the South, where racial discrimination was strong, the denomination made no official distinction between black and white churches or ministers until well after 1920.

Edmond S. Barr, a Bahamian, was licensed in 1909 and ordained on June 3, 1912. The first official register of ministers in January 1913 included eleven black ministers (three with full ordination) without any reference to race or color. Five others were added to the ranks before the end of 1913. Most of the black constituency of that period was in Florida, although there were black congregations in Tennessee. There is no record of the number of black members in predominantly white congregations, although there were many.

There was a dubious separation of the black and white congregations in 1926. Even though it came at the request of the black ministers, the unfortunate division was probably a consequence of prevailing social attitudes of the period. For forty years the separation existed but with close harmony and fellowship between the two entities. The CG struck down all official barriers in 1966 and returned to the racial idealism that prevailed in the earliest years of the church.

The international headquarters of the Church of God was built in 1968. It is located in Cleveland, Tennessee, along with the publishing house, Lee College, the School of Theology, and the Pentecostal Resource Center.

In 1986 there were about eight hundred CG ministers and four hundred congregations in the U.S. that were totally or predominately black. Yet there are no official barriers to whites or blacks in their choices of local congregations, congregational or denominational schools, or any other church participation. It was mandated in 1986 that the Council of Eighteen always have black membership. Much earlier, 1932–38, a black minister, J. H. Curry, served on that important body, and several others later served as ex officio members.

B. The Missions Cause. In 1909 the earliest CG missionaries went beyond the U.S. when R. M. Evans and his wife, of Florida, went to the Bahama Islands. The couple arrived in Nassau on January 4, 1910, and worked with Bahamians Edmond S. and Rebecca Barr. At the same time Lillian Trasher, a young woman of North Carolina associated with the Dahlonega, Georgia, church went to Assiout, Egypt, and established a mission and orphanage. Both Evans and Trasher went at their own expense, there being in 1910 no missions fund to support Pentecostal missionaries. The *Church of God Evangel* constantly appealed to its readers to support the missionaries. The support was so inadequate that R. M. Evans had to return home, and Lillian Trasher ultimately found other sponsorship for her Egyptian mission.

Although the CG continued its Bahamian work without a break, it was not until 1918 that another successful missionary ministry was begun in Jamaica. A missions board was appointed in 1926 to promote the missions cause, examine applicants, and raise funds for missions. After this rather tardy step, the missions cause took on new vigor. From its beginning the CG had a vision of reaching the world but no clear understanding of how it was to be done, a circumstance true in most other denominational efforts in world ministry. It is therefore understandable that many of the most vigorous foreign undertakings were independent or nondenominational.

In the 1930s the CG missionary program finally came into its own, with consistent financial support from the homeland but with the use of native converts as ministers wherever that was possible. Each new field was opened with the aim of making it indigenous as soon as possible. This was effected as schools were established in the various countries for the purpose of training workers. In 1966 the foreign membership of the CG surpassed that in the U.S., a trend that has continued for the past twenty years. The U.S. and Canadian membership was 547,000, of a worldwide membership of 1,652,000. Local congregations and missions have been established in 107 countries and territories on every continent. These are grouped in six general territories: (1) Atlantic and the Caribbean, (2) Central America, (3) South America, (4) Europe and the Middle East, (5) Far East and Oceania, and (6) Africa. American missionaries presently serve in many, but not all, of the 107 countries. Non-American missionaries, especially from European and Latin American countries, also go from their homelands to other parts of the world.

Several programs of internationalization were begun by the CG in 1973. This has included bilingual general assemblies (plus interpreters for many languages); international congresses in Mexico (1973) and Puerto Rico (1977; 1985), and in 1986, the requirement that no less than two members of the Council of Eighteen come from outside the U.S. In 1986 members were elected to the council from Mexico, Bermuda, and Korea.

C. Education. After establishing Lee College in 1918, the CG established numerous other colleges and schools, mostly Bible colleges. In 1935 Northwest Bible College was established first at Lemmon, South Dakota, and later at Minot, North Dakota; in 1936 International Bible College was established in Saskatchewan,

Canada; in 1949 West Coast Christian College was instituted in Fresno, California; and in 1976 East Coast Bible College was established in Charlotte, North Carolina.

The Church of God School of Theology was instituted in Cleveland, Tennessee, in 1975, and like Lee College, it is fully accredited by the Southern Association of Colleges and Schools. The seminary campus adjoins that of Lee College; the two institutions share a Pentecostal Resource Center, which houses a library of 116,000 volumes and a modern media resource center. The resource complex features the Pentecostal Research Center, a comprehensive collection of Pentecostal literature, materials, and memorabilia from the worldwide Pentecostal movement.

Other college-level educational institutions are operated by the CG in South Africa (two colleges), Indonesia, Korea, Puerto Rico, Germany, Panama, Mexico, Argentina, and the Philippines. Schools of institute level also are operated in fifty-two countries.

III. Special Ministries. In addition to its traditional ministries, the CG also operates several nontraditional agencies that serve contemporary societal needs. These are specialized ministries that have been introduced to meet the needs and crises that torment modern society.

A. Ministries to the Military. Following World War II the CG responded to the needs of its servicemen with a worldwide program of servicemen's centers and fellowships. Begun in Germany and Japan in 1961, the ministry now maintains sixty-one centers in all parts of the world and conducts a regular program of servicemen's retreats that minister to military personnel of all denominations. There are also twenty-three CG chaplains in the U.S. Armed Forces.

B. Ministries of Restoration. The CG has long operated a wide range of special ministries (e.g., prison evangelism, ethnic ministries, and home for children) to which have now been added new ministries that are restorative in purpose. These are in response to contemporary societal problems, such as child abuse, drug abuse, and unwed motherhood. It sponsors the Peniel Ministry (for drug rehabilitation) in Harrisburg, Pennsylvania; Jireh House (for unmarried mothers) in Portland, Oregon; and the Raymond E. Crowley Center (for abused children) in Sevierville, Tennessee. These and other CG ministries to the ills of humankind reflect a consciousness of the diverse responsibilities that come with age and experience.

C. Beyond the Walls. The CG launched its second century in August 1986 with growing emphasis on reaching beyond its walls to help those who are not a part of the denomination. This reflects the 1886 compact of the church, when it was called Christian Union, and reveals a continuing awareness that Christians should "by love serve one another" (Gal. 5:13). Several ministries of the CG are designed to help those in need for the simple reason that they are in need, when there can be no reasonable expectation of returns to the denomination. Most obvious among those extramural efforts are those restorative ministries already mentioned. This maturity is

deemed to be natural—a coming to that place God intends his people to reach. In addition to its present outreach to servicemen, to the unfortunate, the disenfranchised, and the abused of the world, the CG has involved itself in ministries that strengthen the whole brotherhood of Christ rather than only the CG itself. Thus the leaven of holiness can influence the whole body of believers, and thus the branch can truly bear the fruit of the vine (John 15:1–5).

Bibliography: Archives of the Pentecostal Research Center (Cleveland, Tenn.); C. W. Conn, *Like A Mighty Army* (rev. ed., 1977); L. H. Jullerat, ed., *Book of Minutes* (1922); E. L. Simmons, *History of the Church of God* (1938).   C. W. Conn

CHURCH OF GOD (CLEVELAND, TENN.) IN CANADA

The Church of God (CG), with headquarters in Cleveland, Tennessee, was organized in Canada in 1920. The small congregation in the rural town of Scotland Farm, Manitoba, was at first regarded as part of the foreign missions work, and offerings were given for its support. With the earnest evangelization of Saskatchewan and Ontario in the 1930s, however, the Canadian work was regarded as one with the U.S. In 1936 a Bible school was established in Consul, Saskatchewan, which continues today as International Bible College in Moose Jaw.

From 1939 to 1962 the Canadian work was administered mainly from the U.S., with most of its activities correlated with the U.S. churches. Now it is under the direction of a superintendent of Canada. The Canadian churches have provided the CG with many of its most effective ministers, missionaries, and teachers.

Bibliography: C. W. Conn, *Like A Mighty Army* (1977).   C. W. Conn

CHURCH OF GOD (HUNTSVILLE, ALA.)

Born December 9, 1943, this quasi-denomination's first twenty-five years centered around the life of Homer A. Tomlinson. Exact figures of the membership, then and through the years, have been wanting. The numbers (like 30 million) released by Homer were inclusive of his projected spiritual domain and do not relate to any actual denominational allegiance. It seems that actual membership through all the years would, at best, be in the hundreds. Initially, most of the constituency came from the Church of God of Prophecy (CGP), and perhaps the whole of the North American Church of God of Prophecy has sometimes been included in the figures released.

Under the leadership of Homer Tomlinson, the church built on the twenty-nine prominent teachings of the CGP. The Church of God (Huntsville, Ala.) continues to use the CGP flag, slightly altered, and Homer repeatedly used this flag when before the media, thereby leading many to the mistaken view that he was the leader of the CGP. Homer was highly esteemed by his church ministers and enjoyed virtually unquestioned authority. A primary manifestation of this is the thirtieth teaching ("kingdom of God on Earth") adopted by the group and the work the small group generated in assisting Homer in his political campaigns. The self-perception of the average church member has been, simply put, that they are obedient Christians. In the main, they were supporters of traditional Holiness/classical Pentecostal thought.

At Homer's death in 1968, his designated successor, Voy M. Bullen, assumed the leadership of the piecemeal denomination. Bishop Bullen moved the working headquarters from the Queens residence to his home in Huntsville, Alabama. Bullen's literary abilities are limited, but the church periodical continues to be released, and at times Homer and/or A. J. Tomlinson are featured on the front page. In his annual address for what is counted as the seventy-ninth general assembly (1984), Bullen said that he was still carrying out the doctrines of Homer. The church paper, titled simply *The Church of God*, gives ongoing attention to politics along with local church news and apocalyptic sermons. The political agenda spans usual items about Israel and identifying Pat Robertson as prefigured in Homer. The printed program of the 1986 general assembly included auxiliary programs and state marches known from the CGP along with a report from the "Theocratic party for better government."

Bibliography: *The Church of God Book of Doctrines: 1903 to 1970* (1970); Interview with Voy Bullen in Huntsville, Alabama, February 26, 1981. Also subsequent correspondence.   H. D. Hunter

CHURCH OF GOD (ORIGINAL)   In 1919
J. L. Scott withdrew from the Church of God (Cleveland, Tenn.) and founded the (Original) Church of God (OCG) in Chattanooga, Tennessee. He opposed the Church of God's emphasis on tithing and A. J. Tomlinson's autocratic leadership.

Scott and his followers claimed to follow the "teachings of the Church of God as originally set up in 1886." The OCG followed the structure and doctrine of the Church of God, with an annual general assembly and general overseer. There are about fifty congregations and 2,500 members in six states other than Tennessee. The OCG operates a publishing house in Chattanooga and works with the Church of God of the Mountain Assembly, though the two are not related.

Bibliography: *Manual of Discipline of the (Original) Church of God* (1966).   C. W. Conn

CHURCH OF GOD (QUEENS, N.Y.)   See
CHURCH OF GOD (HUNTSVILLE, ALA.).

CHURCH OF GOD BY FAITH   (CGF).
Founded in 1919 and chartered in 1923, the Church of God by Faith has its headquarters in Jacksonville, Florida. Elder John Bright was its founder and first moderator. Its doctrine and teachings are centered in the principles of holiness and Pentecost, with strong emphasis on "sanctification and clean living."

The predominantly black church reports five thousand members and one hundred churches, mostly in Florida, Georgia, Alabama, and South Carolina. There are a few churches in other states, plus foreign mission works in Nigeria.

The CGF is led by a bishop, an executive secretary, and three ruling elders. Its official journal is *Spiritual Guide*.

Bibliography: Church of God by Faith, *Handbook for the Laymen*, (n.d.); idem, *Ritual of the Church of God by Faith, Inc.* (1984).   C. W. Conn

CHURCH OF GOD, HOUSE OF PRAYER
(CGHP). Organized by H. W. Poteat in 1939, this Pennsylvania-based organization was started with dissident congregations of the Church of God (CG, Cleveland, Tenn.). Poteat served as state overseer for the Church of God in Pennsylvania (1922–34) and Maine (1924–36). When he was assigned to Montana in 1936, Poteat objected and returned to Pennsylvania and set up the new organization with churches supportive of him. Poteat organized the Church of God, House of Prayer in 1939 and openly tried to induce CG congregations to join with him. In 1942 the CG legally blocked further raids, whereupon some churches that originally joined Poteat became independent congregations. The CGHP has thirty churches and 1,500 members, with headquarters in Markleysburg, Pennsylvania.

Bibliography: E. L. Simmons, *History of the Church of God* (1937); P. H. Walker, *Paths of a Pioneer* (1970).   C. W. Conn

CHURCH OF GOD IN CHRIST (WHITE)
An association of Pentecostal ministers operating primarily in the South and Southwest, between 1910 and 1914. Howard A. Goss, who had been associated with Charles F. Parham since 1903, received permission from Charles H. Mason, bishop of the black Church of God in Christ, to use his organization's name to ordain some white ministers. The new group issued credentials and was able to obtain clergy railroad discounts under the borrowed name. Since there are apparently no minutes extant of meetings conducted by this group, there is a certain amount of confusion as to when they actually started, where they met, who they ordained, and other details. Existing ministerial credentials give the organization's name as "The Church of God in Christ and in unity with the Apostolic Faith Movement." This only adds to the confusion, because several founding ministers of the group left what was known as the Apostolic Faith movement, directed by Charles F. Parham.

Another ministerial association, one of the many groups to use the name Church of God, apparently merged with the Church of God in Christ (white) in 1913. This Church of God was formed as a loose fellowship of Pentecostal ministers at Dothan, Alabama, in 1909. Four of the leaders were H. G. Rodgers, M. M. Pinson, D. J. Dubose, and J. W. Ledbetter.

By the end of 1913 a published list of ministers of merged groups numbered 352. Five of the men on the list—M. M. Pinson, A. P. Collins, H. A. Goss, D. C. O. Opperman, and E. N. Bell—prepared and published "The Call" to what became the organizational meeting of the Assemblies of God (AG). Apparently, with the forming of the AG, the Church of God in Christ (white) ceased to exist. Its importance was to bring Pentecostal ministers together in an association and prepare the way for the formation of the AG.

A communion service during a National Convocation of the Church of God in Christ.

Bibliography: C. Brumback, *Suddenly . . . From Heaven* (1961); J. Flower, *History of the Assemblies of God* (1949); W. Menzies, *Anointed to Serve* (1971); V. Synan, *The Holiness-Pentecostal Movement in the United States* (1971).   W. E. Warner

CHURCH OF GOD IN CHRIST, INTER-NATIONAL In 1969 dissatisfaction over governmental changes following the death of Bishop C. H. Mason, the founder, caused fourteen bishops to leave the Church of God in Christ (CGIC). Doctrinally the new body they formed at Kansas City, Kansas, that year, differed in no way from the parent. Memory of the original conflict soon began to fade with a corresponding return to the CGIC, a course made graphic in membership trends. The Church of God in Christ, International (CGICI) reported only 200,000 members in 1982 as contrasted with more than one-half million eleven years earlier. As its membership continues to plummet, it seems possible that the CGICI may in time be entirely reabsorbed into the parent body.

Bibliography: C. E. Jones, *Black Holiness* (1987); A. C. Piepkorn, *Profiles in Belief*, vol. 3 (1979).
                        C. E. Jones

CHURCH OF GOD IN CHRIST (CGIC). The largest black North American Pentecostal body, the Church of God in Christ, is the extension of a network of black congregations led for over a half-century by Charles H. Mason (1866–1961). In 1893 Mason claimed entire sanctification. Two years later he withdrew from the Missionary Baptist church and organized an independent congregation in a cotton gin shed in Lexington, Mississippi. His intention, Mason said, was to establish a church that would stress entire sanctification and outpourings of the Holy Spirit. Two years later, at Jackson, Mississippi, C. P. Jones (1865–1949) instituted a series of annual Holiness convocations that Mason, J. A. Jeter (1854–1945), and other former Missionary Baptists attended. Out of these meetings came a nondenominational fellowship, Christ's Association of Mississippi of Baptized Believers, from which in a few years emerged the Churches of God in Christ. (Local affiliates used a variety of names.)

Although Mason had made spiritual progress, he feared that his inability to heal the sick and cast out demons was an indication that he had not yet received the fullness of the Spirit. So in 1906, hearing of a great revival in Los Angeles, he with J. A. Jeter and D. J. Young went to check out the meeting at Azusa Street. Elder Mason returned, claiming the baptism of the Holy Ghost with tongues as the initial evidence. Upon arrival, he discovered that Glenn A. Cook, another Azusa convert, had visited Memphis while he had been away and convinced many in his congregation of

Presiding Bishop J. O. Patterson, Sr. of the Church of God in Christ is the pastor of this Pentecostal Institutional Temple in Memphis.

the validity of the new teaching. Elders Jones and Jeter were not won over, however, and at the 1907 convocation the group split. A majority supported elders Jones and Jeter in disfellowshiping Mason. By 1911 they had reorganized, taking a new name: the Churches of Christ (Holiness) U.S.A.

The fourteen congregations in Tennessee, Mississippi, Arkansas, and Oklahoma that sided with Mason reorganized in August 1907 as the Church of God in Christ, with Mason as general overseer and chief apostle (bishop) and D. J. Young as editor of the official organ. The founder said that the name, which is based on 1 Thessalonians 2:14, 2 Thessalonians 1:1, and Galatians 1:22 had been revealed to him ten years earlier while walking along a Little Rock, Arkansas, street. At first the church was held together by Mason's charisma, an annual convocation in Memphis, and a periodical (the *Whole Truth*). By 1934 the CGIC claimed 345 churches in twenty-one states and the District of Columbia. Membership totaled more than 25,000. Five bishops (I. S. Stafford of Detroit, E. M. Page of Dallas, W. M. Roberts of Chicago, O. T. Jones of Philadelphia, and R. F. Williams of Cleveland) whom Mason had consecrated a year previous to this, were with him and ten other state overseers put in charge. Under this plan, growth was phenomenal. Membership increased tenfold during the next three decades. In 1962 (a year after the founder's death), it totaled at 382,679.

Doctrinally, the CGIC under Mason stood in the Wesleyan camp, holding that entire sanctification (subsequent to justification) would be evidenced by holiness of life and that the full blessing of Pentecost (the baptism of the Holy Spirit) would be witnessed to by speaking in tongues. (Because of this, the wide belief that the CGIC is the black counterpart of the General Council of the Assemblies of God, cannot be sustained.) Observing the Lord's Supper, baptism by immersion, and washing of the saints' feet as ordinances, the CGIC held to strict standards of dress and personal conduct. The founder designated O. T. Jones (1890–1972), one of the first bishops, as his successor. After Mason's death this appointment resulted not only in a prolonged constitutional crisis and the seating of Mason's son-in-law, J. O. Patterson (b. 1912), rather than Jones as presiding bishop, but in the blurring of doctrinal and disciplinary distinctives as well. Although in 1969 a major split rent the body, dynamic leadership and quiet rapprochement resulted in spectacular growth. With a reported 3,709,661 members in 1982, the CGIC was nearly ten times as large as it had been twenty years earlier. Part of the increase may be attributed to the friendship its leaders have extended to the charismatic movement, a stance unique among black denominations.

See also BLACK HOLINESS–PENTECOSTALISM; MASON, CHARLES HARRISON.

Bibliography: "Church Celebrates 50th Anniversary," *Ebony* 13 (March 1958): 54–56, 58–60; H. N. Kenyon, "An Analysis of Racial Separation Within the Early Pentecostal Movement," unpublished M.A. thesis, Baylor University, 1978; L. Lovett, "Aspects of the Spiritual Legacy of the Church of God in Christ," *Mid-Stream* 24 (October 1985): 389–97; J. O. Patterson, *History and Formative Years of the Church of God in Christ* (1969); V. Synan, *The Twentieth-Century Pentecostal Explosion* (1987).   C. E. Jones

CHURCH OF GOD, JERUSALEM ACRES

The Church of God, Jerusalem Acres (Cleveland, Tenn.), reckons itself to be the NT church. Its version of church history traces the true early church up to the Council of Nicea in A.D. 325. After that it is swallowed up, not to reemerge until June 13, 1903, when the church was rediscovered. It is said that A. J. Tomlinson provided the true lineage through the 1922–23 controversy (see TOMLINSON, A. J.) as did Grady R. Kent facing similar circumstances in 1957.

Grady R. Kent, born in 1909 in Rosebud, Georgia, was converted at age twenty-one in a Congregational Holiness church. His Spirit baptism soon followed in the Church of God (Cleveland, Tenn.). Church officials insisted that because of Kent's speech impediment and literary crudeness, he attend Bible school if he wanted a ministerial license. By 1931 he had joined the Church of God of Prophecy (CGP), and he received a ministerial license in 1932. From 1934 to 1936 he served as state overseer of Minnesota and then spent the next two years in the same capacity in Nebraska. In 1938 he went to Egan, Georgia, as pastor. He received considerable attention in the following year as a result of his part in a highly publicized trial of members of the Ku Klux Klan who had severely beaten him. The governor of Georgia, Gene Talmadge, attended the court proceedings as did A. J. Tomlinson, who after remaining through the completion of the trial, brought Kent to Cleveland to pastor the local church that met in the Tabernacle House of Blessings. On September 1, 1940, Kent's sermon focused on Micah 4:1 and Psalm 132:4–6. He and Tomlinson had previously discussed biblical prophecy, and as a result of their conversation that afternoon, Tomlinson purchased a place he named Fields of the Wood and started a new auxiliary, Church of Prophecy Marker Association, over which Kent was placed as world supervisor in 1943. Kent was a stirring speaker, although rude in speech, who could hold audiences for two to three hours. His continued influence was evident in various projects like the "white angel fleet" (i.e., airplanes), which he called Ezekiel's cherubim.

Confronting a problem previously centered in the likes of the Zwickau prophets, Hoffman (1530s), Spiritual Franciscans, Jansenists, Seekers, John Alexander Dowie, and Frank Sandford, the 1956 general assembly of the CGP passed the following resolution: "The Church does not endorse attempts by its ministers to identify themselves or other ministers as the Two Witnesses mentioned in Rev. 11. Neither does it approve of anyone indicating that he is John the Revelator." This action was clearly directed at Kent, later called St. John II. The following January he printed and began to circulate his view that he was in the spirit and power of John the Revelator. M. A. Tomlinson, general overseer, called on Kent to recant or resign, and he did the latter on February 13, 1957.

Kent saw the above as the next great reformation of the Bible church, because in his view, M. A. Tomlinson had, in 1948, wrongly given the general assembly priority over the general overseer, thus failing true theocracy. On February 17, 1957, counted as the second reformation of the last days Church of God or Zechariah's third part, Kent formed his group of three hundred as the Church of God of All Nations. Kent declared himself the chief bishop, formed seven auxiliaries, restored the offices of twelve apostles (with names changed to Apostle Emerald, Apostle Chrysopraus, etc.), seven Spirits of God (or Seven Men of Wisdom), female prophets (ministers), and the Seventy (this group, also known as the elders, was never full). He grew a beard as a constant reminder of the revolution, and many male members did likewise. The official publication, The Vision Speaks, was first issued in April, and the next year a church flag, modified from that belonging to the Church of God of Prophecy, was released. On August 1, 1958, he bought a seven-acre tract of land in Cleveland to be called Jerusalem Acres, that intended to be a more complete fulfillment of John's Revelation than Fields of the Wood. On August 20, 1958, the name "The Church of God" was adopted.

By 1962 Kent was preoccupied with the Jewish people. The resultant approach was called NT Judaism. Some evidences of this were: forbidding of certain meats, worshiping on Saturday rather than Sunday, using the Jewish calendar, surnaming, using staffs, observing various Jewish festivals (their general assembly is also the Feast of Pentecost). Kent retained his position for seven years, until his death on March 31, 1964. Attention was drawn to the concurrent Passover celebration and the great earthquake in Alaska. Various steps, including an open grave, were taken to comply with the belief that soon Kent was to rise from the dead. In the meantime, although two of his sons, along with David Williams, thought themselves his successor, the council chose Marion W. Hall, apostle to the Gentiles, as the chief bishop. Hall retained this position until 1972, when he was replaced by Robert S. Somerville, who served until 1980.

The church has increasingly come on hard times financially, since the membership base was never very large and has declined in recent years.

Bibliography: J. D. Garr, *The Lost Legacy* (1981); G. R. Kent, *Basic Bible Teachings* (n.d.); idem, *Manual of Apostles' Doctrine and Business Procedure* (n.d.); idem, *Sixty Lashes At Midnight* (1942, reprint 1962); idem, *Treatise of the 1957 Reformation STAND* (n.d.); idem, *The Vision Speaks* 18 (12, 1976). H. D. Hunter

CHURCH OF GOD OF PROPHECY, THE

(CGP). The Church of God of Prophecy (the name since 1952) historically shares some of the early years of the Church of God (CG, Cleveland, Tenn.). A. J. Tomlinson, a dynamic Pentecostal pioneer, was the church's most prominent figure of the first half of this century (see TOMLINSON, AMBROSE JESSUP). In this limited amount of space we cannot adequately treat the multiplex of events that resulted in Tomlinson's becoming the head of the CGP as a distinct organization in 1923. Suffice it to say that numerous sociological, theological, historical, and personal factors plus different views of church government and financial dilemmas were involved. Failure was not limited to any one category or group.

Relations between the two groups were tense for some time. The legal consequences included the small group being designated the "Tomlinson Church of God" by the chancery court of Cleveland, Tennessee. By 1952 the court's judgment allowed the group to use the name "Church of God of Prophecy" in its "secular affairs." During that time and to this day the church refers to itself as the "Church of God" (with A. J. Tomlinson and then M. A. Tomlinson as general overseer). The strained relationship between the CG and the CGP has become more relaxed through the years, and since the late 1960s there have been various regional, national, and educational concerns jointly addressed by the two churches.

The CGP has laid considerable emphasis on many events prior to 1923. One of the most tangible evidences of this line of thought is realized in that it counts among its binding polities those decisions of the general assemblies from 1906 onward, unless later clarified or reversed by the CGP. Also, the home that hosted the first general assembly of 1906 is owned by the CGP. An annual service is held by the church in

This headquarters building for the Church of God of Prophecy is located in Cleveland, Tennessee.

the house to commemorate the first assembly and to honor the participants, activities, and resolutions.

The theme most often sounded about these early years is related to June 13, 1903. This was the date that A. J. Tomlinson joined the Holiness Church at Camp Creek. A total of five joined that day, bringing the number to twenty. A. J. Tomlinson was made pastor of the congregation and later general overseer of the fledgling church that grew to a membership of 21,076 by 1922. The local body had been formed in May 1902 and included persons from the now defunct Christian Union (1886) and the 1896 revival in Cherokee County, North Carolina, that included speaking in tongues. A. J. Tomlinson had previous contact with some of these people and had joined other groups, but when he joined them that day he meant for it to be a final decision. The CGP also owns the property that includes the site of the meeting place for the Camp Creek church. The site is now called Fields of the Wood, situated near Murphy, North Carolina (see FIELDS OF THE WOOD). Following Tomlinson's death in 1943, his youngest son, Milton, was chosen his successor by the assembled state and national overseers, whose decision was determined by an interpreted message in tongues. This verdict was accepted and confirmed by the 1944 general assembly. M. A. Tomlinson continues (1988) to serve as the general overseer, making him third, after Charles H. Mason and J. H. King, in his longevity as an international Pentecostal church head.

A central focus of the CGP has been that worship services are considered an essential part of the Christian pilgrimage. Thus members have often been engaged in at least four services a week and some specialized meetings that have lasted for several weeks. Some of these services have lasted for several hours, including some late into the night. Further, members have been generally engaged in prayer meetings, various forms of evangelism, and special times of fellowship.

Revival campaigns traditionally included serv-

ices every night for at least a week, and one went for ten weeks. The 1980s still record some revivals of eight-week duration. Often these services last for hours and center on invigorating music, stirring preaching, intense prayer for spiritual experiences, healings, and for reaching the unconverted in the U.S. and abroad. The preaching at these meetings has often been issue-oriented. Evangelists have been particularly concerned to confront the individual's relationship with God. The manner in which they have done this is of such a nature that it might be labeled the "divine drama." Ministers would often engage in various forms of physical agitation when it was believed that this aided the cosmic battle between good and evil.

The time spent at the altar, a bench built to accommodate seekers of spiritual experiences, has always been a centerpiece to any worship service and especially to revival meetings. This was the place that one surrendered all to God, sought God, and received blessings ranging from salvation to physical healing and to specific directives ("calls") from the Lord. Prayers of many kinds have been encouraged as central to the believer's walk. Some have regularly prayed one hour a day and some have engaged in twelve-hour prayer sessions along with short- or long-term fasting. In a public service, most members of the congregation kneel and pray while different ones pray for the seekers gathered at the altar. Some are "slain in the Spirit" on the floor and others "shout" (i.e., physically demonstrate) their praises to God. It is not unusual for the flow of the service to be interrupted by those who want to pray for whatever need is at hand. These and like things, along with charismatic outbreaks such as a "message in tongues" could result in the scheduled sermon being replaced by an extended prayer session. This kind of activity is not understood as minimizing the importance of Scripture but rather as undergirding it by obedience to the pertinent directives.

Church of God of Prophecy members have

shared a distinct ethos with the majority of early Pentecostals. Among the characteristics are the following: intensity of faith, sincerity, devoutness, commitment, praxis, and humility. This translated into criteria like "the anointing" and/or "the calling" as basic to judging the usefulness of members and especially ministers. The local church, in addition to state, national, and international leadership, has been routinely involved in implementing the guidelines. Pentecostals in general and the CGP in particular are not rightly understood by those outside the movement if doctrinal formulas and behavioral studies are alone given priority. Any comprehensive analysis must reckon with matters of ethos. Not surprisingly, the last generation has seen a gradual deterioration of emphasis on ethos and a simultaneous preoccupation with various propositions.

In terms of officially determined doctrinal propositions, at the center stands an Arminian version of the *ordo salutis* that includes a special emphasis on sanctification. It culminates with a doctrine of Spirit baptism that regards tongues speech as the initial evidence. Other prominent teachings from the well-publicized list of twenty-nine include an imminence-oriented eschatology that involves a premillennial return of the risen Jesus; a call for the sanctity of the nuclear family, which includes denial of a multiple marriage of an adulterous person—fornication as related to a person who can remarry is defined as a single person marrying a person who has a living married companion; practice of water baptism by immersion and rebaptism after "reconversion"; the Lord's Supper (with grape juice) and the washing of the saints' feet; total abstinence from intoxicating beverages and tobacco; a concern for modesty in all dimensions of life; and an emphasis on nine Holy Spirit charisms with special attention given to divine healing. For the most part the result of the formulas has been to stabilize many of the adherents, but also there have been some aberrant results. Included in the failure column has been the refusal to purchase life insurance, opposition to formal education, antimedicine to the extent that pain and death were accepted rather than formal medical treatment, and dissolution of existing marriages.

One of the results of the restorationist impulse of the CGP is the exclusive body ecclesiology. The restorationist impulse produced a view of history that said Jesus founded the church on Mount Hattin (Mark 3:13ff.). This survived until A.D. 325, at which time it ceased to exist as before because it was layered over with much foreign matter. But layers began to be removed by Luther, then Wesley, etc., until the complete revelation was unveiled on June 13, 1903. This is the ancestry that the CGP has claimed as its own. Although this ecclesiology was not originated by A. J. Tomlinson, he became its most forceful advocate, and it has been reinforced by M. A. Tomlinson. One result has been the ongoing, repeated exaltation of "the Church." Those outside the organization often view this as self-indulgence, while those inside have thought they were glorying in Jesus Christ. A typical service can include someone lifting up "the Church" with the rejoinder that members are unworthy of such a thing and prove their humility by their various failures to fulfill Christian obligations. A person joins the church by publicly covenanting his or her allegiance to the Scriptures as the final authority. Further, although the doctrine of salvation is predicated on a rugged individualism, this ecclesiology insists that no person seek celebrity recognition but be immersed in the group identity.

Some of the other noteworthy results of this teaching is that the CGP has not joined the National Association of Evangelicals (NAE) or the Pentecostal Fellowship of North America (PFNA). An interesting by-product of this and like prohibitions is that the church has not undergone "evangelicalization" or "charismatization" and has retained more of the original Pentecostal agenda than other similar Pentecostals, with the exception of Oneness Pentecostals. Thus, although the CGP does not ordain women, they have one of the highest percentages of female ministers who serve as pastors and state, national, and international leaders. The following ranks of ministry are presently observed: authorized teachers, lay ministers, evangelists, deacons (a distinction is made between those who preach and those who do not), and bishops. The current practice is that female ministers receive no license higher than that of an evangelist, and they cannot lead marriage ceremonies or administer sacraments. This shows the strength of oral tradition, because there is no general assembly ruling on record that limits women in this regard. Also, the church may be the most racially integrated Pentecostal church in the world, judged by the number of racially mixed congregations and the integrated state, national, and international leadership. The CGP may have been the first church to defy Jim Crow laws in their worship services, and they have long opposed the Ku Klux Klan. The church has also been generally unencumbered by the conservative battle plan with regard to a specific view of biblical inspiration and science versus Scripture. While the church has not participated in formalized ecumenical efforts, it continues to call for a oneness in Christ that transcends human expectations and is truly organic.

The term "theocracy" has been used throughout church history from the likes of John Calvin in Geneva to John Alexander Dowie in Zion. The CGP has long used this term to describe its government. The premise is that things of polity and doctrine are ultimately, and sometimes quite directly, determined by God. Thus the annual general assembly is the highest tribunal for the organization, and no resolution is accepted without a unanimous decision of the attending male members. Women are excluded from the decision-making process, but no distinction of clergy and laity or nationality, etc., exists among the males. The impact of oral tradition is well illustrated by the fact that the practice of unanimous decision did not become an official assembly ruling until September 4, 1986. A "unanimous decision" often means that some who disagree simply have to defer to the prevailing view, but should they persist in supporting their view, that particular item fails to pass at that time. A form of episcopacy is utilized by the church as the general overseer (since 1911) appoints state and national overseers, who in turn appoint their staff and pastors, who in turn determine the local leaders. This practice has not been uniformly observed through its history, because into the 1950s the churches "called" pastors.

In the 1980s the 10,000-seat auditorium in Cleveland, Tennessee, annually draws 20,000 registered attendees to a meeting that is principally a time of celebration and fellowship with church members from around the world. Various projects are promoted by the international departments, and there is much fervent preaching (some delivered in Spanish and everything translated into Spanish and French) and praying, while the doctrinal and business concerns are held to a minimum. The greatest attendance at each assembly is during the annual address by the general overseer, M. A. Tomlinson. Much time is devoted to state and national marches (started in 1925), which are swept along by the Bahama Brass Band. Many of these things characterize the state and national annual conventions.

The governmental system that evolved to insure the success of prioritized concerns centers on five departments. Each of these departments has a comprehensive network of international, state or national, district, and local directors. These are still commonly referred to as "auxiliaries," which in order of appearance are: Sunday School—1906; Assembly Band Movement (ABM)—1916, 1928; Women's Missionary Band (WMB)—1928; Victory Leaders' Band (VLB)—1928; and Church of Prophecy Marker Association (CPMA)—1941. Sunday schools exist as part of almost every congregation in the world and engage students of all ages in the study of Scripture.

A. J. Tomlinson opened an orphanage in Cleveland, Tennessee, in 1919 and another one in 1928. There are a variety of like homes and schools around the world maintained today by the church. In 1932 the Emergency Fund was begun to assist members during financial crises. The general assembly of 1933 adopted a distinctive church flag. The colors and symbols were carefully chosen to represent important biblical themes like truth, purity, and the blood of Jesus. Some zealous adherents have at times made an icon of the church flag, but this has been despite the official pronouncements of the assemblies. In 1939 a white field secretary was added to assist the general overseer. In 1941 a black field secretary joined the staff, and a Hispanic field secretary completed the group in 1953. This missions orientation of the church evidenced itself by not only insisting that members tithe their income and give in regular offerings but also give sacrificially to missions. A general secretary was appointed to head this work in 1938, followed in 1940 by a foreign language department. A department focusing on the needs of retired and disabled ministers was established in 1941 along with a short-term school known as Bible Training Camp (BTC). BTC is now called Bible Training Institute in its fifty-plus sessions held around the world. In 1951 a radio and recording ministry was firmly established, and it led (1953) to the weekly program "Voice of Salvation" (now in four languages). This was followed by a limited television ministry initiated in 1971 and revived in 1987 (the 1952 and 1957 assemblies ruled against members owning television receivers). In 1964 a public relations department was established, and a full-time music department followed the next year. The year 1966 saw the birth of Tomlinson College, a two-year liberal arts accredited college that has produced more than a thousand graduates. The servicemen's department was founded in 1967 and the evangelism department in 1970.

The influence of the Holiness movement is quite apparent in several ways. One product of this influence is a list entitled "Advice to Members." This first appeared in the assembly minutes of 1919 and was last revised in 1968. The document opens with exhortations to an obedient church life shown in things like manifesting fellowship, being courteous, and being cautious in conversation. Subsequent revisions focused on clothes and recreation. Specifically prohibited were wearing such things as shorts in public, rings and lipstick, and going to movie theaters and public swimming areas. Compliance with some of the latter has increasingly related to matters of socioeconomic and cultural concerns. The power of oral tradition is again evidenced in that, despite the lack of an assembly ruling, a person is not accepted for membership if he or she is wearing any jewelry, including a wedding band.

The official mouthpiece is the biweekly periodical *White Wing Messenger*. The magazine is run in eight languages and has 20,204 subscribers. The CGP reported in November 1987, a membership of 74,588 in the U.S. with 2,085 churches, while eighty-nine countries outside the U.S. had an aggregate membership of 172,153 with 3,048 churches. In the earlier decades the membership was almost exclusively from a low socioeconomic stratum. Yet the "working poor" have been increasingly replaced by the middle class in the industrialized West. Accompanying the social upward mobility of the membership has been a moderation of many of the sectarian idiosyncrasies and a concomitant lack of membership gains in the U.S. The organization at large continues its anti-intellectual tradition, while the official doctrinal formulas increasingly fade in significance for the middle-class constituency.

See also FIELDS OF THE WOOD.

Bibliography: *Book of Minutes: General Assemblies of the Churches of God* (1922). The brief history was taken from A. J. Tomlinson's *Last Great Conflict;* Cyclopedia *Index of Assembly Minutes of the Church of God of Prophecy: 1906 to 1974* (1975); C. T. Davidson, *Upon This Rock,* 3 vols. (1973–76); *Evangels, Faithful Standards, White Wing Messengers,* tracts, brochures, assembly minutes, court proceedings, etc.; B. M. Johnson, *Written in Heaven* (1972); J. Stone, *Church of God of Prophecy: History and Polity* (1977); A. J. Tomlinson, *Last Great Conflict* (1913, reprint 1984); idem, *Historical Annual Addresses,* 3 vols. (1970–72); H. A. Tomlinson, *The Great Vision of the Church of God* (1939).

　　　　　　　　　　　　　　　　　　　　　H. D. Hunter

CHURCH OF GOD OF PROPHECY IN CANADA

The Church of God of Prophecy in Canada (CGPC) traces its heritage to a group of believers who met for prayer and Bible study in Cherokee County, North Carolina, on August 19, 1886. From this gathering came the Church of God (Cleveland, Tenn.), with Ambrose Jessup Tomlinson as general overseer (1909–23). When a "disruption" affected the ranks in 1923, the Tomlinson loyalists formed the Church of God (Tomlinson) in 1923, considered by its membership to be the true successor of the original organization. The name was later changed to Church of God of Prophecy. The denomination has churches in all fifty states of the U.S.

In 1937 the first CGPC congregation was organized in Swan River, Manitoba. Fifty years later there were eighty-eight ordained clergy and thirty-eight congregations found in British Columbia, Manitoba, Alberta, Saskatchewan, Ontario, and Quebec, with a total membership of 2,091. Sunday or Sabbath schools numbered forty-three, with an enrollment of 2,871. The national headquarters is located in Brampton, Ontario. National and provincial meetings are held annually. The two national overseers are Bishops Richard E. Davis (Canada East) and John Doroshuk (Canada West). The latter also serves as president of the board of directors. The CGPC publishes two periodicals: *Canadian Trumpeter* and *Maple Leaf Communique*.

Bibliography: C. H. Jacquet, Jr., *Yearbook of American and Canadian Churches* (1987).   G. B. McGee

CHURCH OF GOD OF THE APOSTOLIC FAITH

(CGAF). The Church of God of the Apostolic Faith, with headquarters in Tulsa, Oklahoma, has its roots in the revivals of Charles F. Parham. Organized near Ozark, Arkansas, in 1914, it has churches in Oklahoma, Kansas, Arkansas, and Missouri. It is led by a general superintendent and twelve elders, who are elected in an annual general conference.

Congregational in polity, local churches of the CGAF elect their pastors and arrange for their support. Each church determines whether or not it will keep a membership roster. The National office publishes the *Church of God Herald* and *Christian Youth*. The denomination, which consists of twenty-seven congregations and 1,500 members in the U.S., sponsors a missionary work in northern Mexico called Iglesia Cristiana Evangelica Mexicana.

Bibliography: E. Buckles, *A Brief History of the Church of God of the Apostolic Faith* (1935). C. W. Conn

CHURCH OF GOD OF THE MOUNTAIN ASSEMBLY

(CGMA). With headquarters in Jellico, Tennessee, the Church of God of the Mountain Assembly has an extensive outreach in the mountains of Kentucky and Tennessee. It also has extended its ministry into the Midwest, the Southwest, and as far as California. In 1986 it reported a world membership of 6,911.

Like many of the churches that arose around the turn of the century, CGMA came about because of dissatisfaction with the existing churches in its region. In 1903 several ministers were turned out of the United Baptist Church of the South Union Association for preaching "a closer communion with God and the danger of apostasy." More specifically, they preached that it is possible for a person to be lost after regeneration. Five congregations withdrew from the Baptist fold to protest the harsh stand taken by the association.

On August 24, 1906, ministers S. N. Bryant, J. H. Parks, Newt Parks, and Andrew Silcox and five congregations met in council at Jellico Creek, Whitley County, Kentucky, and formed a new organization. (They first called themselves the Church of God, but in 1911 they learned of the Cleveland, Tennessee, group with that name and added "Mountain Assembly" to their name.) Andrew Silcox was chosen as general moderator of the new church. The following year, 1907, S. N. Bryant succeeded Silcox and served as the denomination's leader until 1938.

Because the CGMA was strongly Pentecostal and Holiness in its doctrine and practices, it was subject to fierce persecution in its formative years. It grew, however, to a membership of 966 in 1912, and 1,612 in 1914. This was remarkable in the face of the hostility that confronted the church all across the mountains.

In 1919 the church adopted the tithe plan as its financial base, which enabled it to do more evangelistic work following World War I. Also in 1919 the church instituted a board of twelve elders, who were responsible "to plan the program for the future course of the church." With the improved organization and financial system in place, the church grew to more than two thousand members in 1922 and erected a new tabernacle for its permanent headquarters in Jellico, Tennessee.

The CGMA experienced both advances and setbacks in the decades that followed. A new system of government was adopted in 1944, following a long static period, and a general overseer, A. J. Long, became the chief executive of the church. The present administrative structure consists of a general overseer, two assistants, and a general secretary-treasurer.

In 1968 the CGMA began a missions outreach in Brazil and in 1986 reported missionary works in Jamaica, Haiti, and India. Missions in Liberia, Nigeria, Malawi, and Zambia also were taken into the fellowship of the church in 1986.

Bibliography: L. Gibson, *History of the Church of God of the Mountain Assembly* (1954); *Minutes of the Assemblies of the CGMA* (1907, 1986).   C. W. Conn

CHURCH OF GOD OF THE UNION ASSEMBLY

(CGUA). A predominantly southeastern U.S. denomination founded in 1921. With headquarters in Dalton, Georgia, it added "Union Assembly" to its name to distinguish it from other groups with similar names. It is not related to any other group. The CGUA was formed by C. T. Pratt, who was general overseer until his death in 1967; his son Jesse F. Pratt succeeded him. Jesse F. Pratt, Jr., is the present general overseer. The *Covenant* of the church emphasizes holiness, the "perfecting of the saints," the baptism of the Holy Ghost, and divine healing.

The principal CGUA congregations are in

Georgia and Tennessee, although congregations have been organized in about seventeen states. No records are available, but the church claims to have more than five thousand members.

Bibliography: The *Charter* and *Covenant* of the Church of God of the Union Assembly. C. W. Conn

CHURCH OF JESUS CHRIST Established in 1927 by Bishop M. K. Lawson (d. 1962), the Church of Jesus Christ holds as essential doctrines repentance for sins, baptism in the name of Jesus Christ, and the infilling of the Holy Spirit. It is a Oneness body and opposes the taking of oaths, participation in secret societies and the military, and marriage outside the church. The organization's principal function appears to be the licensing and ordaining of ministers. Candidates pay for credentials. Registered with the headquarters, which in 1975 moved from Kingsport to Cleveland, Tennessee, are five hundred clergy serving congregations with a combined membership of approximately 37,500. In some cases, local churches modify the name. The congregation at Stanton, Delaware, for instance, is called Full Gospel Church of Jesus Christ.

See also ONENESS PENTECOSTALISM.

Bibliography: D. B. R. Jackson, "The Full Gospel Church of Jesus Christ: A Description and Analysis," unpublished B.A. thesis, University of Delaware, 1973; A. C. Piepkorn, *Profiles in Belief,* vol. 3 (1979); R. W. Sapp, *Upon This Rock I Will Build My Church: The Church of Jesus Christ* (1976). C. E. Jones

CHURCH OF JESUS CHRIST MINISTE-RIAL ALLIANCE In 1962 disagreement in the Church of Jesus Christ over ministerial courtesy at the death of its founder, Bishop M. K. Lawson, resulted in formation of the Church of Jesus Christ Ministerial Alliance. Doctrine was not an issue. In 1975 the new organization took the first steps toward reunion. At that time it claimed three hundred ministers, eighty-five churches, and approximately six thousand members. Bishop J. Richard Lee of Portage, Indiana, was chairman.

Bibliography: A. C. Piepkorn, *Profiles in Belief,* vol. 3 (1979). C. E. Jones

CHURCH OF THE LIVING GOD, CHRIS-TIAN WORKERS FOR FELLOWSHIP Organized at Wrightsville, Arkansas, in 1889, the Church of the Living God, Christian Workers for Fellowship (CLGCWFF) resembles the Church of God in Christ in several ways. The founder, William Christian (1856–1928), a former Baptist minister, was in fact an early associate of C. H. Mason (1866–1961). The CLGCWFF differs, however, in permitting tongues speech in recognizable languages only, and it rejects the initial-evidence theory. It recognizes three biblical sacraments: baptism by immersion, the Lord's Supper (using unleavened bread and water), and the washing of the saints' feet. Each ordinance is administered only once. It holds that the Lord's Prayer is the only prayer "to be prayed by all Christians." It upholds the racial pride of its members by asserting that many biblical saints were black. Following its founder, who was a mason, it approves the essentials of freemasonry. Churches are called temples and are numbered consecutively by dates of organization. In 1964 the CLGCWFF reported 276 churches and 45,320 members. Headquarters moved from St. Louis to Cincinnati in 1984.

Bibliography: *Glorious Heritage: The Golden Book* (1967); C. E. Jones, *Black Holiness* (1987); A. C. Piepkorn, *Profiles in Belief,* vol. 4 (1979). C. E. Jones

CHURCH OF THE LORD JESUS CHRIST OF THE APOSTOLIC FAITH A multiracial Oneness Pentecostal organization founded in Philadelphia by Bishop Sherrod C. Johnson (1897–1961). The organization grew from a local church established in 1919, primarily by means of an effective radio ministry begun by Johnson in 1935. The predominantly black body teaches the multiracial nature of the church. Other distinctive teachings by Johnson include a variant Oneness view that the Sonship of Jesus ceased with his death, the use of wine in Communion, the practice of footwashing, and the rejection of all military service. Condemned are celebration of Christmas and Easter, remarriage after divorce, and ordination of women. Women are to cover their heads when praying or prophesying, shun cosmetics, and wear plain, long dresses. With one schism in 1961, Bishop Johnson's successor, S. McDowell Shelton, continues as "apostle and general overseer" of a membership of approximately seven thousand in ninety-two churches throughout thirty states, with work in the West Indies, West Africa, Belize, and England. The periodical *The Whole Truth* has a circulation of 2,300.

See also ONENESS PENTECOSTALISM.

Bibliography: C. Jones, *A Guide to the Study of the Pentecostal Movement,* vol. 1 (1983); L. McCoy, *A True History of the True Church* (rev. ed., 1977); A. Piepkorn, *Profiles in Belief,* vol. 3 (1979). D. A. Reed

CHURCH, THEOLOGY OF THE
 I. Pentecostal. Pentecostals commonly believe that the one church of Christ is composed of all who are regenerate in Jesus through repentance and faith. This conviction is explicitly stated in some denominational declarations of faith (Assemblies of God [AG]; AG of Spain; Elim Pentecostal Church of Great Britain and Ireland; International Church of the Foursquare Gospel [ICFG]; Apostolic Faith [AF] of Baxter Springs, Kansas; Pentecostal Apostolic Church of God of Romania), but its absence from other denominational statements reflects its lack of centrality in Pentecostal faith rather than a different ecclesiology. Denominations with no mention of church in their statements of faith include AF of Portland, Oregon; Church of God (CG, Cleveland, Tenn.); AG of France; and AG of Italy. The United Pentecostal Church (UPC) has one tangential reference. Some Pentecostal declarations only mention the church in relation to patterns of church government (Apostolic Church and AG of Great Britain and Ireland) and another only in relation to the spiritual gifts (Church of God of Prophecy [CGP]).

Almost all Pentecostal denominations are pre-tribulational and premillennial, believing that this invisible church of all the saints will be raptured by Christ prior to the Great Tribulation, after which Christ will reign on earth with the saints for a thousand years. These convictions concerning the Rapture and the Millennium feature in the majority of denominational declarations of faith, whether or not the term *church* is used.

While Pentecostals have nearly always affirmed the invisibility of the universal church, they have regularly used the term *assembly* of the visible local congregation. However, with some restorationist exceptions (see below), they do not correlate entire denominations with the theological concept of the church, typically seeing the church in spiritual rather than institutional terms. Thus Pentecostals often say that the church is an organism, not an organization, an emphasis reflected in the Pentecostal Assemblies of Canada's (PAOC) expressed faith in "Christ's Lordship over the Church."

Though the Pentecostal movement is characterized by belief in a postconversion baptism in the Holy Spirit, this is virtually never regarded as necessary for salvation and but rarely as constituting membership of the church. However, for many Pentecostals of earlier generations only those baptized in the Spirit had the Holy Spirit, an attitude framed in times of expulsion and exclusion. Thus for a time some Pentecostals did not readily accept the Christian character of non-Pentecostal denominations.

The concept of the church has not generally been central to Pentecostal faith, though it has been more prominent among those churches formed and living in situations of hardship and oppression. Thus the black Pentecostal churches generally manifest a greater social consciousness as church, though their self-understanding as God's people together delivered from bondage is more distinctively black than Pentecostal. The most articulate theological reflection among Pentecostals has probably come from the Pentecostal Apostolic Church of God of Romania, where conditions of persecution have deepened the bonds of church fellowship. In the movement at large, however, there are signs in recent decades of increasing attention to ecclesiology. Past and present Pentecostal understanding of church can be illustrated from a summary of developing attitudes and convictions.

A. Initial Presuppositions. The first-generation Pentecostals brought with them the understanding of church commonly found among revival-conscious evangelical Protestants. The exciting message of Azusa Street that "Pentecost has come," was understood as individual blessing on a large scale. However, this personal focus did not totally exclude church consciousness. Their understanding of church reflected two distinct thrusts found in some tension in early Pentecostalism, the apocalyptic and the restorationist.

The apocalyptic thrust, very vocal and emphasized in the study of Robert Mapes Anderson, focused on the imminence of the Parousia, seeing the outpouring of the Spirit in the "baptism" as empowerment for effective evangelism of the entire world before the end came. In this perspective the dominant image of the church was the bride awaiting the coming of the bridegroom and her consequent rapture. Charles F. Parham's view

distinguishing the bride from the church (1986) was a minority view.

The restorationist strand, owing something to Disciples inspiration, saw the outpouring of the Spirit for the restoration of authentic NT Christianity. The Pentecostal outpouring was heralded as the culmination of divine interventions to restore authentic Spirit-filled Christianity: first, the restoration of the gospel of justification by faith at the Reformation; then the restoration of the Spirit's work of sanctification in the Wesleyan movement; and last, in the Pentecostal movement the restoration of divine power with the baptism in the Holy Spirit and the full range of spiritual gifts. Although the term "restoration" later came to have negative connotations for many mainline Pentecostals (being associated with groups seen as deviant), this reading of church history is restorationist. While rarely focusing on the concept of church, it clearly had ecclesiological implications.

These two strands in early Pentecostalism came together in the Latter Rain concept. The ecclesiology of the first Pentecostals is then best characterized as an implicit and largely unformulated Latter Rain theology. The Latter Rain idea, based on Joel 2:23 and James 5:7, contained both an apocalyptic "end-times" message (this rain is the final downpour immediately preceding the end) and a restorationist emphasis (it restores NT intensity blessing). Virtually all first-generation Pentecostals saw their movement in terms of "the Full Gospel" and not simply as the most powerful demonstration of the Spirit since the first century; however, for most Pentecostal groups the church was not really part of the "Full Gospel" but was commissioned to proclaim it with the church growing from its proclamation.

The restoration of the "Full Gospel" was seen in a few circles as restoring the church according to the mind of God in the Scriptures. This restorationist strand was more explicit in the CG. First R. G. Spurling and then A. J. Tomlinson saw the church in theocratic terms with a focus on the government of God's people. The structures given to the people of Israel in the wilderness received as much attention as passages in the NT. As late as 1916 Tomlinson was saying, "We are diligently searching for the original system of Church government" (*Book of Minutes*, 1922, 216). However, this restorationist vision has faded in the CG, though it survives somewhat more in the CGP.

A different form of church restorationism is found in the Apostolic Church (AC) in Great Britain. The restoration of the fivefold ministries of Ephesians 4:11 was central in the formation of the AC, with the church constitution of 1937 providing for the ordination of apostles, prophets, etc., and for the regulation of these ministries. D. P. Williams, one of the founding brothers, wrote, "We believe that the Apostolic Church, as at present working, gives the freest expression to the New Testament form of Church government, ministry, and relationships" (Williams, n.d., xxiv). This restorationist emphasis on the fivefold ministries of Ephesians 4:11 was to reappear in the late 1940s in the Latter Rain movement that broke out in Saskatchewan, Canada, and subsequently influenced centers such as Elim Bible Institute in Lima, New York, and Bethesda Missionary Temple in Detroit, Michigan.

Another Pentecostal milieu with a modified restorationism giving increased attention to the church issue is the fellowship of the International Communion of Charismatic Churches under the leadership in the U.S. of Bishops John Meares and Earl Paulk. Paulk's "Kingdom Now" teaching has aroused controversy, particularly on eschatological grounds, but it touches sensitive Protestant nerves because of its emphasis on authority within the church. Paulk represents a Pentecostal theology in which the church concept is more central and in which the invisible has to be made visible and the visible is called to be one.

B. Factors Promoting Attention to Church.

1. Concern for Unity of Movement. The Azusa Street revival in Los Angeles from 1906 to 1909, which triggered off the worldwide Pentecostal explosion, was a powerfully unifying event. Its astonishing interracial character and its unusual interdenominational make-up demonstrated that "Pentecost" was the outpouring of the Holy Spirit upon "all flesh." Thus there was an awareness of a God-given spiritual unity among the Spirit-baptized. This unity occasioned frequent comment in the first years, as, e.g., a statement in *Apostolic Faith* (Azusa Street): "This Pentecostal movement is too large to be confined in any denomination or sect. It works outside, drawing all together in one bond of love, one church, one body of Christ."

That this experience of Christian unity did not generate an explicit ecumenical vision was partly due to the movement's populist and largely proletarian character. Moreover, the subsequent racial segregation and the doctrinal divisions in the movement obscured the unifying power of the Spirit of Pentecost. Those leaders who saw the unity of the movement as a sign of its heavenly origin were deeply disturbed by emerging rivalries and divisions and became ardent advocates of Pentecostal unity. These figures included Thomas Ball Barratt, Alexander Boddy, W. F. Carothers, William Hamner Piper, Gerrit Polman, and William J. Seymour. Piper had preached a sermon, "The Prayer of Jesus Must Be Answered: His Body Must Be United: The Gifts and Offices of the Early Church Must Be Restored," as early as August 1908 (*LRE*, October 1908). In 1911 Barratt's *Confidence* article, "An Urgent Plea for Charity and Unity," argued: "We have to do with facts: that people, honestly professing to having received the Holy Ghost, do not agree in everything on doctrinal points. . . . What is there to be done? We must either find some form of union, or stand as separate bodies, and aim at some form of alliance between these" (February 1911, 31). Boddy emphasized Pentecostal unity during his American tour of 1912, getting leaders to agree not to engage in mutual condemnation in relation to the "Finished Work" (*Confidence*, November 1912, 246). In the mid 1920s Carothers held several "unity conferences," spreading his message through his magazine, *The Herald of the Church*. While none of these authors systematically stud-

ied the relationship between fellowship in the Spirit and understanding of the church, their concern for unity necessarily had an ecclesiological component.

The most common Pentecostal position has seen the unity of the Spirit-baptized as a sovereign work of God, based on the working of the Holy Spirit within each believer. "Within the Pentecostal Revival itself a profound, and indeed unique, unity of the Spirit has been given to us by Christ Jesus: it leaves nothing for us to 'make,' but much that we must zealously endeavor to 'keep' " (Gee, 1947, 2). This spiritual unity was thus seen as personal rather than as institutional.

2. The Denominationalization of the Movement. Greater attention to the concept of church was thrust on Pentecostals by the formation of new Pentecostal denominations from the 1910s in America and the 1920s in Europe. In these years the local Pentecostal congregations came to be known more as "assemblies" and less as "missions," the original terminology. Somewhat paradoxically, the formation of new denominations initially hindered rather than promoted reflection on the nature of the church, diminishing the sense of the unity of the movement, at least until the launching of the Pentecostal World Conferences in 1947. The church issue was largely restricted to patterns of church government.

Apart from those lesser Pentecostal denominations, which were like family businesses, and those that regarded themselves as the restored NT church, the new denominations were formed for pastoral and pragmatic rather than doctrinal reasons: the need to have ministerial credentials for protection against unknown itinerant preachers; the need for accreditation of missionaries and some central organization for disbursement of mission funds; the need for some basic statements of Pentecostal belief.

In fact, Pentecostal churches have adopted virtually every form of church government known to Christians. There are denominations with episcopal government (the Pentecostal Methodist Church of Chile; the International Evangelical Church); denominations with congregational patterns of church government (the Scandinavian churches; most of the Russian Pentecostals); churches with a mixture of presbyterian and congregational polity (AG); churches with a centralized national organization (Elim Pentecostal Church); churches with a form of monarchial government by one charismatic leader (many smaller denominations, especially in their first generation). The process of denominationalization did not therefore produce any distinctively Pentecostal view of the church, except for those bodies seeking to restore the fivefold ministry of Ephesians 4:11.

The formation of Pentecostal denominations inevitably hastened the tendency toward a full-time ordained ministry trained in Pentecostal colleges. A full-time pastorate tends to raise interest in church questions, and the development of ministerial training produces more schematic studies that can hardly avoid the issue of church.

3. Church Growth Theory. The church growth movement pioneered by Donald McGavran in the

Fuller Seminary School of World Mission in Pasadena, California, since the mid 1960s has contributed indirectly to greater Pentecostal attention to the church. Because Pentecostal churches have been among the fastest-growing in the world, McGavran's scientific study of what causes churches to grow has attracted the attention of Pentecostals, particularly in North and Central America. This current has reinforced the trend fostered by Melvin Hodges (see below), leading Pentecostals to think more precisely about the formation of churches and not just about the multiplication of converts.

4. *The Catholic-Pentecostal Dialogue.* Although only a minority of classical Pentecostals have supported this dialogue, its third series begun in 1984 has necessitated more Pentecostal attention to church. In 1985 Miroslav Volf and Peter Kuzmič of Yugoslavia presented a paper entitled "Communio Sanctorum: Toward a Theology of the Church As a Fellowship of Persons," and in 1987 the charismatic Baptist Howard Ervin made the presentation "Koinonia, Church and Sacraments," implying that Pentecostalism should strengthen the vision of the church as corporate human participation in the inner life of the Trinity.

C. Pentecostal Presentations of the Church. Explicit treatments of the theology of the church have not been common among Pentecostal authors and publications. It is noticeable that Ernest S. Williams's three-volume *Systematic Theology* (1953) has no treatment of the church. W. A. C. Rowe's *One Lord, One Faith* treats the church only in subsections under "Governmental," while the volume *Pentecostal Doctrine* (1976), edited by Percy S. Brewster, has one item by Ramon Hunston, "The Church—the Body of Christ." Russell P. Spittler's small book, *The Church* (1977), is written for a more popular readership.

An interesting book on the church from a restorationist background by Hugh Dawson of the AC has the rather daunting title *Through Analogy to Reality* (1968). A characteristic Pentecostal view of church history from a CGP perspective is provided by Daniel D. Preston in *The Church Triumphant* (1969). The work of an early Pentecostal, Eugen Edel of Germany, was reprinted in 1971 under the title *Das Symbol der Stiftshutte und die Kirche Jesu Christi.* Possibly the most creative Pentecostal work on the church is by the Romanian leader Pavel Bochian, who presents an ecclesiology grounded in the faith life and worship of the community with an eschatological orientation (see review by D. Bundy in *EPTA Bulletin* 4 [2, 1985]: 56–58).

The most recent textbook, *Foundations of Pentecostal Theology* (1983), by Guy P. Duffield and Nathaniel M. Van Cleave (from ICFG) gives increased attention to church with one out of ten chapters. Duffield and Van Cleave illustrate a Pentecostal tendency to treat the local church as a visible body of Christ but remain reluctant to speak of any visible embodiments of the universal church. This partly reflects a historic Protestant mistrust of church institutions and partly a concern not to make exclusive claims for one's own denomination. However, they make one interesting statement concerning NT understanding: "Every local church was considered to be the physical manifestation of the Universal Church in that community" (422).

An important address giving greater centrality to the church was G. Raymond Carlson's keynote address, "Committed to the Church," at the AG forty-second general council in Oklahoma City in 1987. Carlson spoke of the church as a "divine institution" that is "a shining light in the darkness of a crooked and perverse generation," a position that sees a visibility of the church beyond the local assembly.

D. Distinctive Pentecostal Contributions. The most distinctive Pentecostal contribution to ecclesiology might be made in the understanding of the local church. Here there are two distinct but complementary thrusts. The first sees the spiritual gifts as an intrinsic element in the life and equipment of the local church. Rather as Orthodox and Catholics see baptism and Eucharist as constitutive of church, so some Pentecostals see these charismatic endowments of the Holy Spirit not just as evangelistic equipment but as forming and shaping the church. Thus a Pentecostal view of the church expects the full range of the spiritual gifts to be manifested in each local assembly, even though this is not actually verified in most American and European churches. However, in such well-known works as those of Donald Gee and Harold Horton on the spiritual gifts, this position is more implicit than spelled out. W. G. Hathaway (1933) is more explicit: "While the gifts rest in individuals they are only given *through* individuals to *the Church*" (Hathaway, 1963, 20–21). Unusually, Hathaway argues that every gift belongs to the whole church, not just to the local church assembly.

A Pentecostal vision of the local church rooted in the power of the indwelling Spirit has been presented more recently by the Elim pastor John Lancaster in *The Spirit-filled Church* (1973, rev. 1987) and the Dutch pastor Willem J. Lentink in *De Bijbelse Gemeente* (1980). These works are typical in being not theological treatises but pastoral teachings on congregational life ordered under the lordship of Jesus in the power of the Holy Spirit. They characteristically emphasize both worship and ministry. This vision has also been prominent in the vision communicated by Lewi Pethrus and the movement in Scandinavia.

The second thrust has come from reflection on Pentecostal missionary experience. While many Pentecostal assemblies initially experienced rapid growth through the Holy Spirit's endowment of all members, some missionary labors led to numerical expansion but not to the equipment of all believers. This led some missionaries to reflect on the missionary purpose, producing a greater focus on the nature of the church. The pioneer missiologist was Melvin Hodges of the AG, whose book *The Indigenous Church* (1953) broke new ground. Hodges saw that initial conversion to Christ had to be followed by conscious building of church. He argued that each NT church was self-propagating, self-governing, and self-supporting. While Hodges's book and his later *Build My Church* (1957) were important correctives to colonial patterns of American Pentecostal missions, his treatment seeks practical rather than theological principles from the Scriptures. He ends pragmatically advocating an AG-type church polity, combining an independence of local congregations with some national structures and leadership.

A study of the Pentecostal contribution to ecclesiology ought to take into account the writings of Donald Gee. Gee's editorials in *Pentecost* from 1947 to 1966 constitute the most penetrating and honest reflection of Pentecostal life and convictions to date. Though such reflection is an essential element in ecclesiology, Gee's writings did not directly encourage the emergence of a distinctively Pentecostal theology of the church. This was because he saw the Pentecostal movement as a Holy Spirit revival weakened by denominationalization and because he consistently argued that it was but a part, though the most vital part, of the worldwide body of Christ. Nonetheless, Gee pointed the way to a more constructive Pentecostal theology by his defense of intelligence enlightened by supernatural faith and by his lack of fear in relating to the non-Pentecostal Christian world.

II. Charismatic. Within the many streams constituting the worldwide charismatic renewal movement (CR), there are three contrasting attitudes to church: (1) the position of charismatics committed to the historic church traditions, both Catholic and Protestant; (2) the restorationist position of those intentionally rejecting all forms of denominationalism; and (3) the attitudes of independent charismatics who pay little attention to the church.

A. Charismatics Committed to Historic Church Traditions. The emergence of CR as a distinct movement of the Holy Spirit or as a clearly new phase in an existing movement of the Spirit occurred when leaders and teachers became committed both to the Pentecostal experience of baptism in the Holy Spirit and to their own historic church traditions. Unlike the Pentecostals, these charismatic Christians immediately saw this outbreak of the *charismata pneumatika* in relation to the church and its renewal. In 1964 Michael Harper wrote: "It is the renewal of the Church that God is principly [*sic*] concerned about—not that of the gifts. The gifts are for the building up of the Church—in order that it may become once more a powerful and influential force in the world. It is the recovery of New Testament Church life which is our greatest need today" (Harper, 1964, 5).

This view became common among charismatics, but since charismatic teachers were pastors and not theologians, the initial presentations of CR and the gifts of the Spirit being for the renewal of the church are mostly in popular periodicals or more descriptive works like Harper's book, *A New Way of Living* (1973), describing Holy Redeemer Episcopal Church in Houston, Texas.

More theological reflection on CR and church began in Europe, first in Holland in the circles associated with the monthly *Vuur*, edited by W. W. Verhoef, who combined a dedication to

serious theology and regular association with Pentecostals. More scholarly biblical studies came from Arnold Bittlinger in West Germany in 1967–68, later translated into English. Bittlinger brought to his exegesis a more systematic theological mind than was then found among the more pragmatic Pentecostals. He writes of Jesus as being himself the internal order of his body. "Just as in him all the charismata are united, so he is also the prototype of all church ministries" (Bittlinger, 1973, 98).

Among Protestant charismatic theologians, Thomas A. Smail, at one time director of the Fountain Trust in Britain, has written on the church, particularly in *Theological Renewal* (*TR*). Smail's theological reflections on CR are strongly ecclesial, with the constant emphasis that church life reflects the patterns of the Trinity. (See, e.g., "Towards the Trinitarian Renewal of the Church," *TR* 25 [November 1983]: 15–22.)

The Protestant charismatics interacting most seriously with their own theological and liturgical traditions have been the Lutherans, who brought a strong sense of their confessional identity to their reflections, without, however, much explicit attention to the church. Theodore R. Jungkuntz of the Lutheran Church—Missouri Synod has explicitly repudiated the accusation that Lutheran charismatics made baptism in the Spirit the basis for church fellowship instead of Word and sacrament. More recently, a group of Lutheran leaders and theologians under the leadership of Larry Christenson has produced a study of CR entitled *Welcome, Holy Spirit* (1987), of which a substantial portion is devoted to the church.

With the spread of CR to the Roman Catholic church, there was a sharp increase in charismatic reflection on ecclesiological themes. Several Catholic theologians baptized in the Spirit were already specialists in ecclesiology (Heribert Mühlen, Paul Lebeau, Francis Sullivan). Mühlen was in fact the author of one of the most original contributions to Catholic ecclesiology since the era of John XXIII and one that centered on the role of the Holy Spirit. In his book *Una mystica persona: Die Kirche als das Mysterium der Identität des Heiligen Geistes in Christus und den Christen* (1964), Mühlen presented the nature of the church as "one Person in many persons," that is to say, the person of the Holy Spirit in Christ and in Christians. A glimpse of Mühlen's position can be seen from his contributions to *The Holy Spirit and Power*, ed. Kilian McDonnell (1975). Rejecting as ambiguous the widespread Catholic view of the church as the continuation of the Incarnation, Mühlen saw the continuity in the mission of the Holy Spirit. Although Mühlen has continued a considerable theological output, he has not attempted a major work on the church since his own spiritual renewal in the early 1970s.

Another Catholic theologian whose writings unconsciously prepared the way for the integration of CR into the Catholic church was Karl Rahner (1904–84), who emphasized that the unpredictable charismatic work of the Holy Spirit belongs to the nature of the church, which cannot be reduced to merely institutional factors. Rahner's essay "The Charismatic Element in the

Church," is published in *The Dynamic Element in the Church* (1964) and *The Spirit in the Church* (1979). A similar study can be found in *Theological Investigations* (12:81–97).

Catholic reflections on CR all insist on seeing this grace of the Spirit in relation to church. This innate Catholic tendency had been strengthened by the inclusion in Vatican Council II's constitution on the church of a passage on charismata as both universal and contemporary (para. 12). This passage owed much to a speech by Cardinal Suenens of Belgium, who a decade later was to encourage Catholic theological reflection on CR. While Catholic writers on CR gave most attention to baptism in the Spirit, spiritual gifts, and believers' relationships with the persons of the Trinity, these topics were all addressed in relation to the body of Christ.

More explicit reflection on ecclesiological issues focused on the following points:

1. *The church as constituted by the distinct divine missions of the Son and the Spirit* (J. H. Nicolas; A. de Monleon; E. O'Connor). Thus the renewal of ecclesiology is dependent on a balance between christology and pneumatology, a point recurring in the writings of Yves Congar, the major contemporary Catholic theologian to devote attention to CR.

2. *The first point grounds the second, the complementary nature of the institutional and the charismatic; both are integral to healthy church life* (J. Haughey; E. O'Connor). Charism and church office mutually belong like the Spirit and the Son in the Trinity (N. Baumert). Institutional ministries can themselves be seen as charisms (P. Lebeau). The charisms are ways the Spirit structures the church from within (R. Laurentin).

3. *The work of the Spirit in conversion and baptism in the Spirit has an inner dynamic toward the formation of community and integration into ecclesial life* (D. Gelpi; F. Martin; K. McDonnell).

4. *Study of interchurch dynamics in CR has led to some reflection on essentials and inessentials in each tradition.* Kilian McDonnell has urged attention to be given to "theological ecclesial cultures," referring to the coherence in each tradition of belief, worship, piety, church government and law, theology and ethos.

5. *Received traditional patterns of theology and church life have influenced Pentecostal and charismatic understanding of CR and baptism in the Holy Spirit* (F. Sullivan).

Heribert Mühlen has insisted that CR is "the church in movement, not a movement in the church." Peter Hocken has maintained that CR's movement character is inherent in its ecumenical nature as a work of God across all the churches. At issue here are different models of what is meant by the integration of CR into the life of the churches, a goal endorsed by all committed to the historic church traditions.

B. Restorationists Intentionally Rejecting All Denominationalism. A different kind of restorationist thinking appeared in CR's earliest days in Great Britain. While restorationist groups have gained many recruits from charismatics disenchanted with CR in the historic churches, the existence of this current cannot be attributed

to such a reaction. The father of restorationist thinking about the church within CR is David Lillie of Exeter, England. Lillie brought with him from his Plymouth Brethren background clear convictions about the centrality of the church in God's plan, the unscriptural character of the historic denominations, the governmental independence of each local church, and the organic rather than organizational bonds between authentic local churches. Lillie, suspended by the Brethren for his Pentecostal interests, was baptized in the Spirit in 1941; and helped by G. H. Lang, he came to see the baptism in the Spirit and the spiritual gifts as poured out for the sake of the restoration of the NT church.

Lillie's scope to spread this "Pentecostal-Brethren" vision of the church expanded in the late 1950s through fellowship with Arthur Wallis and the conferences to which they invited sympathetic pastors and preachers. Some men later prominent in the House Church movement first met at these conferences (Bryn Jones, Graham Perrins, Barney Coombs). Lillie was the main teacher on the church, his audience including other former Plymouth Brethren already well-disposed to this ecclesiology. Notwithstanding the role of Cecil Cousen in these conferences, restorationist thinking in British CR did not arise from previous Pentecostal restorationist currents (AC or the Latter Rain movement).

The characteristics of this Brethren ecclesiology were the priesthood of all believers, to which was added the charismatic equipment of church members with the gifts of the Spirit, and the rejection of "special ministry" (professional pastors and the one-man pastorate) and "special membership" (i.e., denominational exclusivity by which membership in one denomination excludes membership in another). Each local church is a full manifestation of church, called to be self-sufficient, self-governing, self-supporting, and self-edifying. Communion between local churches is not a matter for external authority.

However, by the early 1970s as the British House Church movement was gathering momentum, the majority of leaders departed from Lillie's strict congregationalism by espousing the fivefold ministries of Ephesians 4:11 (apostles, prophets, evangelists, pastors, teachers) with apostles having authority across a range of local churches. This vision was particularly embodied in the Harvestime network centered in Bradford, Yorkshire, in which Bryn Jones was seen as a leading apostle, and in a somewhat lower key in the networks led by Terry Virgo of Hove, Sussex, and Tony Morton of Southampton, Hampshire. Their convictions are expressed in numerous publications, such as the bimonthly *Restoration;* David Matthew's history, *Church Adrift;* and Virgo's *Restoration in the Church.* Since the early 1970s, these British restorationists have been perceived as advocating a "Come Out" policy toward charismatics in the historic churches, provoking controversy over their goals and methods. Michael Harper's book *That We May Be One* (1983) addressed this troubled situation.

Meanwhile there were parallel developments in the U.S., though the American approach was generally more pragmatic and less dogmatic than the British. In the early 1960s, a magazine, *A Voice in the Wilderness,* edited by John Myers of Northridge, California, presented restorationist views with positive reports on CR. In the early 1970s the leaders of Christian Growth Ministries in Fort Lauderdale, Florida, focused on church formation through the tools of discipling and shepherding. However, they never favored the "Come Outism" often stimulated by a restorationist view of the NT church.

Much American charismatic restorationism has been fueled by a growing sense of the covenantal nature of relationships in the body of Christ. This stronger sense of the corporate character of Christian ministry is perhaps most widely represented among the churches associated with the National Leadership Conference, as well as the Covenant churches associated with Charles Simpson of Mobile, Alabama. The churches associated with Larry Tomczak and C. J. Mahaney of Gaithersburg, Maryland, are nearer to the British style of restorationism, with their magazine *People of Destiny* resembling the British *Restoration.*

C. Independent Charismatics With Little Concern About Church. Since the beginnings of CR, some people baptized in the Spirit have had an individualistic view of salvation and the Christian life. Teachers and leaders with such an outlook have not seen the need to relate to any church tradition nor to seek to build a corporate expression of life in Christ. Many of these charismatics have come from an Evangelical background and are probably more numerous in North America where people have fewer ties to the Christian past.

III. Overview. Such a survey of Pentecostal and charismatic understandings of the church suggests that this overall movement of the Spirit has not yet done justice to the ecclesiological implications of Pentecost. For different reasons, the Pentecostals and the charismatics (whether mainline or restorationist) have not elaborated a theology of the church that captures the distinctive thrust of this outpouring of the Spirit and that manifests the scope of its challenge to received ecclesiologies. The Pentecostals have not done so, partly because their forte has been action, not reflective theology, partly perhaps through a Protestant fear that focus on church diminishes focus on Christ. The mainline charismatics, especially the Catholics, have given more attention to ecclesiological issues, but no theologian has attempted a major study on the church from a distinctively charismatic perspective. The restorationists are the people who have focused most on the nature of the church and its significance in God's plan, but their interest has been practical rather than academic, and their works lack the theological weight of the best Brethren writers of the last century.

That a truly Pentecostal-charismatic theology of church is yet to be elaborated can be seen from the failure of later generations to capitalize on the seminal study of Lesslie Newbigin, *The Household of God* (1953). Newbigin sensed the originality of the Pentecostal eruption of the twentieth century, seeing that the Pentecostals represented a third type of Christianity distinct from the Catholic and the Protestant. In contrast to the Catholic, which stressed the continuation of Christ's saving mission, and the Protestant, which emphasized the gospel message as the content of the apostolic witness, the Pentecostal sees the church as where the Holy Spirit is recognizably present with power. Newbigin's typology points to a certain disharmony between the received evangelical view of the invisibility of the church and the Pentecostal insistence on the visibility of evidence for Spirit-baptism.

The distinctiveness of Pentecostal-charismatic understanding of the church is indicated by considering the inherited patterns of Christian worship. Whereas the preecumenical Catholic pattern presented a hierarchically ordained priest acting *in persona Christi* offering the eucharistic sacrifice at the altar for the people, and the Protestant pattern presented an educated preacher expounding the Word of God from the pulpit, the Pentecostal pattern is of the Upper Room, an entire congregation filled with the Holy Spirit, giving praise to Almighty God. J. Gordon Davies has illustrated this point in his contribution on church architecture to *Pentecostal Research in Europe* (ed. Walter J. Hollenweger).

While Word and sacrament should have a major place in Pentecostal-charismatic church life, this movement poses a radical challenge to the inherited clericalism of both Catholic altar and Protestant pulpit. A Pentecostal-charismatic theology of church will then unpack the fuller implications for all aspects of ecclesiology (ordained ministry, Word and sacrament, differentiation of ministries, pastoral authority, marriage and family, evangelism, and nurture) on the basis of all members being indwelt, moved, and filled with the Holy Spirit. Pentecostalism thus takes up a concept dear to the Reformation heritage, the priesthood of all believers, but invests it with more existential content in terms of active deputation to worship and service in ministry.

As Nigel Wright has written: "If it should seem right to expect the restoration to the church of New Testament gifts, why should we not also expect the restoration of New Testament ministries?" (*The Radical Kingdom,* 1986, 76). If this is correct, the restorationist resurrection of the Ephesians 4:11 ministries may be in line with the movement's basic impulse rather than a deviation. This would be the case where the fivefold pattern is presented as a distribution of ministries that in fact belong to the whole body, and where they are not a restriction of apostolic, prophetic, evangelistic, etc. activities to church leaders. It would seem that the mainline Pentecostal rejection of such restorationism owes more to negative pastoral experience than to theology or exegesis and to the fear that contemporary apostles could easily become absolute monarchs. These reflections point to the restorationist currents, apparently the fastest-growing sector of the movement, being more important than has so far been recognized by Pentecostals and other charismatics.

Study, prayer, and dialogue are then needed about the relationship between historic patterns of Christian ministry and the patterns emerging in

The City of Faith is part of the Oral Roberts University complex in Tulsa, Oklahoma. In the center is the 60-story clinic; the 30-story building on the right is the 277-bed hospital; and on the left is a 30-story research tower. The complex was opened in 1981.

restorationist circles. Theologians in the sacramental-liturgical traditions will argue that the historic pattern of bishop-priest-deacon reflects a participatory understanding of Christian ministry as deputation to act *in persona Christi,* a role that none can take to themselves. The revival of other ministries, most explicitly in the restorationist currents but less officially throughout CR, questions the adequacy of "one pastor" ministries (whether more sacramental or more evangelical or even Pentecostal) and raises the relationship between ordination as empowerment-deputation and ordination as recognition of graces already bestowed by the Lord. It poses the difficult question as to whether a higher synthesis is possible between traditional patterns of "one person" ministry, especially the historic threefold pattern, and patterns of complementary ministries forming teams within the body of Christ.

See also CHURCH LEADERSHIP; CHURCH MEMBERSHIP; ORDINANCES, PENTECOSTAL; SACRAMENTS.

Bibliography: R. M. Anderson, *Vision of the Disinherited* (1979); A. Bittlinger, *Gifts and Ministries* (1973); *Book of Minutes* of the Church of God, Cleveland, Tennessee (1922); L. Christenson, ed., *Welcome, Holy Spirit* (1987); H. Dawson, *Through Analogy to Reality* (1968); G. P. Duffield and N. M. Van Cleave, *Foundations of Pentecostal Theology* (1983); D. Gee, "Editorial," *Pentecost* (1, 1947), 2; M. Harper, *Prophecy* (1964); idem, *That We May Be One* (1983); W. G. Hathaway, *The Gifts of the Spirit in the Church* (1963); W. J. Hollenweger, *The Pentecostals* (1972); M. L. Hodges, *Build My Church* (1957); idem, *The Indigenous Church* (1953, rev. 1976); J. Lancaster, *The Spirit-Filled Church* (1987); D. Lillie, *Beyond Charisma* (1981); K. McDonnell, ed., *The Holy Spirit and Power* (1975); L. Newbigin, *The Household of God* (1953); C. F. Parham, *A Voice Crying in the Wilderness* (1944); A. C. Piepkorn, ed., *Profiles in Belief,* vol. 3 (1979); R. Prenter, *Le Saint-Esprit et le Renouveau de l'Eglise* (1949); K. Rahner, *The Spirit in the Church* (1979); R. P. Spittler, *The Church* (1977); D. Watson, *I Believe in the Church* (1978); D. P. Williams, *Apostolic Church: Its Principles and Practices* (n.d.); N. Wright, *The Radical Kingdom* (1986).   P. D. Hocken

CITY OF FAITH An impressive ultramodern medical and research center established debt-free in 1981 by Oral Roberts. It occupies eighty acres adjacent to Oral Roberts University (ORU), Tulsa, Oklahoma. It is the primary teaching facility for the ORU School of Medicine and the Anna Vaughn School of Nursing.

Although initially opposed by other medical facilities in Tulsa, a certificate of need was granted by the Oklahoma Health Planning Commission (1978) and upheld by the Oklahoma Supreme Court (1981). The clinic was opened in June 1981, and the hospital opened later that year. The commission denied Roberts's original request for a 777-bed hospital, granting instead a total of 294 beds. After five years of operation, the inpatient daily average was 125. The hospital is accredited by the Joint Commission of Accreditation for Hospitals.

The City of Faith is composed of a sixty-story clinic tower, a thirty-story hospital, and a twenty-story research tower. The three towers and four-story base total two million square feet of floor space.

Roberts drew criticism not only from the other hospitals in Tulsa but also from Pentecostals and others who felt he was compromising his belief in faith or divine healing by building a hospital. He paid little attention to the critics, preferring rather to listen to what he believed was the voice of God. Several financial crises in the first few years of operation threatened to close both the City of Faith and ORU. During one especially trying time Roberts told his partners that he saw a vision in which a nine-hundred-foot Jesus stood over the City of Faith.

The City of Faith bills itself as the first hospital to combine medicine and prayer. "For the first time in history," promotional material claims, "these two sources of healing [spiritual and emotional along with physical] are combined under one roof." Other church-related hospitals, however, argue that the combining of prayer and medicine originated long before the City of Faith was built.

See also HEALING MOVEMENTS.

Bibliography: R. Brown, "Oral Roberts and the 900-Foot Jesus," *Christian Century* (April 22, 1981), 450–52; issues of *Abundant Life* (1978–); promotional materials, Office of Creative Development, ORU.
W. E. Warner

CLANTON, ARTHUR LEE (1915–76). Pentecostal preacher, author, songwriter, and editor-in-chief of United Pentecostal Church (UPC) publications. Born in Texas in a Southern Baptist family, Clanton received the Holy Ghost in 1930 and accepted his call to the ministry in 1932. He held pastorates in Texas and Louisiana before accepting the position of editor-in-chief with the UPC in 1955, the position he held at the time of his death. He served on the general board, executive board, and board of publication of the UPC. Clanton is the author of *United We Stand* (1970), a history of the UPC. He also wrote fifty-two hymns.
J. L. Hall

CLARK, STEPHEN B. (1940–). Prominent teacher in Catholic charismatic renewal and pro-

moter of Christian communities. Educated at Yale, Freiburg (West Germany), and Notre Dame, Clark worked for the Cursillo movement, authoring *The Work of the Cursillos and the Work of Renewal* (1967). With his friend and colleague Ralph Martin he was baptized in the Spirit in the spring of 1967 and became a cofounder of the Word of God community in Ann Arbor, Michigan.

In the charismatic renewal among Catholics, Clark became a valued teacher, a gift illustrated in his books *Baptized in the Spirit* (1969), *Spiritual Gifts* (1970), *Growing in Faith* (1972), and *Knowing God's Will* (1974). He was also the strategist, applying the concepts he had developed in Cursillo to the ecumenical situation opened up in charismatic renewal. A member of the national service committee (1970–78), he sought ways to structure the renewal so as to promote lasting fruit within the churches. Clark was primarily responsible for the Life in the Spirit Seminars, first developed within the Word of God community and then published for wider use. His strategic thinking was developed in *Building Christian Communities* (1972) and *Where Are We Headed?* (1973).

Within the Word of God community, Clark was overall coordinator (1972–82) and has led "the brotherhood" of men called to be "single for the Lord" as well as serving younger communities throughout the world. With the formation of the Sword of the Spirit international community in 1982, of which he is assembly president, Clark has reduced general charismatic ministry to concentrate on building strong Christian communities as instruments for the shaping of a Christian culture. He authored the major studies *Unordained Elders and Renewal Communities* (1976) and *Man and Woman in Christ* (1980), and he edited *Patterns of Christian Community* (1984).
P. D. Hocken

CLARKE, CHARLES J. (1903–84). Pioneer figure among Methodist charismatics in Britain. As a young minister, Clark was much influenced by Samuel Chadwick's *The Way to Pentecost*. A prolonged inner search, intensified by the death of his wife, culminated in his being baptized in the Spirit in early 1963. Clarke, a minister in the English Midlands, developed his quarterly, *The Quest*, begun in 1961, into a vehicle for charismatic renewal. Long interested in revival, Clarke saw the new move as the start of a new outpouring. After his retirement (1967) Clark, assisted by his second wife, Mary, concentrated on calling Christians to holiness and depth of prayer by making known the great Christians of the past, as in *Pioneers of Revival* (1971). A member of the Fountain Trust's advisory council, Clark merged *The Quest* into *Renewal* in 1966. Clarke's *Newsletter for Methodists Interested in Charismatic Renewal* (1968–72) was superseded by *Dunamis*, of which he became coeditor.

Bibliography: P. D. Hocken, *Streams of Renewal* (1986).
P. D. Hocken

CLASSICAL PENTECOSTALISM The classical Pentecostal churches, which had their origins in the U.S. at the beginning of this century, have

The *Los Angeles Times* described this building as "a tumble-down shack," but it became widely known as the Azusa Street Mission (or Apostolic Faith Gospel Mission), scene of a Pentecostal revival beginning in April 1906.

since grown to be the largest family of Protestant Christians in the world. Known at first simply as "Pentecostal" churches, they were given the added designation "classical" about 1970 to distinguish them from the "Neo-" Pentecostals in the mainline churches and the "charismatic" Pentecostals in the Roman Catholic church.

The roots of modern Pentecostalism lie in the nineteenth-century Holiness and Higher Life (Keswick) movements in England and America that stressed "second blessing" sanctification and the baptism in the Holy Spirit as an enduement of power for service. From these earlier movements the Pentecostals emphasized a postconversion experience known as "the baptism in the Holy Spirit." The unique teaching of the Pentecostals, however, was that gifts of the Spirit (or charismata) should normally accompany this baptism experience and continue to be manifested in the life of the believer and in the church thereafter. The gifts most often singled out by Pentecostals were speaking in tongues and divine healing.

Most histories date the beginning of the movement to January 1, 1901, when Agnes Ozman spoke in tongues in the Bethel Bible School in Topeka, Kansas, operated by former Methodist preacher Charles F. Parham. It was Parham who subsequently formulated the "initial evidence" teaching that is central to the theology of most of the classical Pentecostal churches of the world. This teaching holds that speaking in tongues (glossolalia) unknown to the speaker is the necessary first sign that one has received the Pentecostal experience. This teaching was based on the fact

that tongues appeared as the Spirit was poured out in the primitive church in Acts 2, 10, and 19, and were implicit in Acts 8 and 9.

The effect of this doctrine was to deny the "cessation of the charismata" teaching that had been the standard understanding of the Western churches since the days of Saint Augustine. The cessation view held that the charismata had been withdrawn from the church at the end of the apostolic age. Classical Pentecostalism thus forced the church to reexamine this position in the light of the many claims it made for current manifestations of the gifts. Along with the manifestation of tongues as evidence of the baptism in the Holy Spirit, the Pentecostals also emphasized divine healing "as in the Atonement" for modern believers.

Pentecostals also taught that all the other gifts of the Spirit had likewise been restored to the church. From the beginning the restoration of the charismata was seen as a sign of the imminent second coming of Christ. This "latter rain" outpouring of the Holy Spirit, the movement taught, was clear proof that the end of the age was near.

The new Pentecostal movement received its greatest impetus from the Azusa Street revival of 1906–09 led by William J. Seymour, a black Holiness preacher from Texas. This revival launched Pentecostalism into a worldwide movement. Located at 312 Azusa Street in Los Angeles, the Azusa Street Mission became the international mecca for those seeking the Pentecostal experience. From Azusa Street, the movement spread throughout the world through the mission's newspaper, *The Apostolic Faith,* and by pilgrims who flocked to Los Angeles to experience tongues.

The first persons to receive the experience were poor and disinherited people from the mainline churches, primarily those from the Methodistic and Holiness movements that flourished in the late nineteenth century. The first avowedly Pentecostal churches were the Pentecostal Holiness Church, led by Joseph H. King, the Church of God (CG, Cleveland, Tenn.) led by A. S. Tomlinson, and the Church of God in Christ (CGIC), led by C. H. Mason. These churches were formed as Holiness denominations before the advent of the Pentecostal movement.

The Pentecostal movement soon spread far beyond the Holiness movement to practically every Protestant denomination in America. In time, Pentecostal converts without roots in the Holiness movement formed newer churches. Led by E. N. Bell, the Assemblies of God (AG) was formed in 1914 to serve those from a "Baptistic" background. Other churches of this type were the Pentecostal Church of God, founded in 1919 by John Sinclair, the International Church of the Foursquare Gospel founded by Aimee Semple McPherson in 1927, and the Open Bible Standard churches formed by an amalgamation of two smaller organizations in 1935. Doctrinal divisions concerning the "second work" and "finished work" views of sanctification continue to this day.

In 1916 the infant AG organization was torn by a division concerning the Godhead known at the time as the "New Issue." Adherents of the "Jesus' Name" Pentecostal movement taught a modalistic view of the Godhead that denied the Trinity while ascribing to Jesus Christ the deity of the Father, the Son, and the Holy Spirit. Those who left formed "Oneness" denominations known today as the United Pentecostal Church and the Pentecostal Assemblies of the World, among others.

Because of their teachings and their noisy and expressive worship, all the early Pentecostal groups were criticized and persecuted by the mainline churches. Ironically, the most bitter criticism came from the older Holiness and Fundamentalist churches that were nearest to the Pentecostals in theology and practice.

With little public acceptance, the growth of the movement in America was slow between 1901 and World War II. Yet seeds of future massive growth were planted around the world through the development of aggressive missionary programs, especially by the AG. By 1920 the movement was firmly planted in Europe, Latin America, Africa, and Asia.

Pentecostalism began to experience unprecedented growth in America and around the world immediately after World War II. Under the impetus of the divine healing and deliverance crusades of Oral Roberts, Tommy Hicks, and Jack Coe, masses of people flocked to Pentecostal churches. By 1953 Pentecostalism entered the living rooms of the nation through the pioneering television ministry of Roberts.

Countless others were led into the Pentecostal experience by the Full Gospel Business Men's Fellowship International, which was founded by Los Angeles dairyman Demos Shakarian in 1952. The mass healing crusades of T. L. Osborn in Europe, Africa, Latin America, and East Asia led to burgeoning growth in the developing nations of the Third World.

The postwar period also saw the beginnings of Pentecostal ecumenism. Although Pentecostals had been disfellowshiped by organized Fundamentalism in 1928, relations improved with the more moderate Evangelicals, who began to distance themselves from the Fundamentalists during World War II. By 1942 the Pentecostals were admitted as charter members of the National Association of Evangelicals (NAE). This was done despite the strong objections of Carl McIntire and his fundamentalistic American Council of Christian Churches.

Relationships with mainstream Evangelicals continued to improve in the decades after World War II. The most positive sign of this new atmosphere was the election of T. F. Zimmerman, general superintendent of the AG, to serve as president of the NAE in 1960. Another sign was the positive reception of Pentecostal evangelist Oral Roberts at the 1966 Berlin World Congress on Evangelism sponsored by the Billy Graham organization.

In 1948, due to contacts made in the NAE, the American Pentecostals formed the "Pentecostal Fellowship of North America" (PFNA), a fraternal body that included most of the major North American Pentecostal denominations. Although blacks did not join and Oneness Pentecostals were excluded, the PFNA represented the mainstream of classical Pentecostalism in the U.S.

Most of these American groups also cooperated with the Pentecostal World Conferences, which first convened in Zurich, Switzerland, in 1947. After the outbreak of the Neo-Pentecostal movement in the mainline Protestant churches in 1960 and the Catholic charismatic movement in 1967, the most important voice calling for fellowship and cooperation was David J. du Plessis, a South African Pentecostal minister who immigrated to the U.S. after the war.

By 1980 the classical Pentecostals had grown to be the largest and fastest-growing family of Protestant Christians in the world. They also led the world in church growth, with the largest Protestant congregations in the world counted in the Pentecostal camp. In 1987 David Barrett estimated the world constituency of the classical Pentecostal churches at 146,906,360.

See also ASSEMBLIES OF GOD; AZUSA STREET REVIVAL; BLACK HOLINESS–PENTECOSTALISM; CHURCH OF GOD (CLEVELAND, TENN.); CHURCH OF GOD IN CHRIST; CHURCH OF GOD OF PROPHECY; HISPANIC PENTECOSTALISM; HOLINESS MOVEMENT; INITIAL EVIDENCE, A HISTORICAL PERSPECTIVE; INTERNATIONAL CHURCH OF THE FOURSQUARE GOSPEL; INTERNATIONAL PENTECOSTAL HOLINESS CHURCH; KESWICK HIGHER LIFE MOVEMENT; HOLY SPIRIT, DOCTRINE OF THE; ONENESS PENTECOSTALISM; OPEN BIBLE STANDARD CHURCHES; PENTECOSTAL ASSEMBLIES OF CANADA; PENTECOSTAL FELLOWSHIP OF NORTH AMERICA;

PENTECOSTAL WORLD CONFERENCE; UNITED PENTECOSTAL CHURCH, INTERNATIONAL.

Bibliography: D. Barrett, ed., *World Christian Encyclopedia* (1982); W. J. Hollenweger, *The Pentecostals* (1972); V. Synan, *The Holiness-Pentecostal Movement in the United States* (1971).   H. V. Synan

CLEMMONS, ITHIEL CONRAD (1921–).

Pastor, bishop, and denominational executive. He was born in Washington, North Carolina, to Frank and Pauline (Williams) Clemmons. His mother had been reared as a Baptist, and his father had been in an independent Holiness church since 1908. By the time of his birth they had joined the Church of God in Christ (CGIC). The third of seven children and the eldest to survive those early years, he lived in North Carolina until 1926, when the family moved to Brooklyn, New York, where his father became the pastor of the earliest CGIC there. Clemmons received a B.A. from Long Island University (1948), M.A. from College of the City of New York (1951), and M.Div. from Union Theological Seminary (1956). In the mid 1960s he studied at the Urban Ministries Institute in Chicago and was one of the first Pentecostals to participate in the College of Preachers at Washington Cathedral in Washington, D.C. He is currently a Ph.D. candidate in church history in a joint Union and New York Theological Seminary program in American church history.

Reared in a pastor's home, Clemmons came to faith at a young age and entered the ministry. In 1955 he pastored Gethsemane Church of God in Christ in Clairton, Pennsylvania. Twelve years later he moved to New York, where he copastored First Church of God in Christ in Brooklyn with his father. Since 1975 he has served as copastor of Well's Memorial Church of God in Christ in Greensboro, North Carolina.

Clemmons played a significant role in helping to map strategy for the civil rights work of Dr. Martin Luther King, Jr., in New York in 1963. In 1964–65 he was heavily involved in Robert Kennedy's Bedford-Stuyvesent restoration project. He was also the founding president of the Foundation for Urban Ministries from 1967 to 1977, and he worked with Leon Sullivan to establish Opportunities Industrialization Centers in 1968–69.

In April 1977 Clemmons was consecrated to the CGIC board of bishops and was also named commissioner for the Armed Forces and Institutional Chaplaincies, a position he continues to hold. During that same year he served on the planning committee of the large and very significant Charismatic Conferences held in Kansas City, Missouri. A member of the Society for Pentecostal Studies since 1972, he was elected to serve as its president in 1981. His challenging presidential address was later published in *Pneuma*. He has written numerous articles on prayer and the devotional life in a variety of magazines and journals.

Clemmons is married to the former Clara Agnes Cantrell. They have three daughters, (Mrs.) Pamela Rosborough, Constance, and Debra.

Bibliography: D. Manuel, *Like a Mighty River* (1977); "True Koinonia: Pentecostal Hopes and Historical Realities," *Pneuma* 4 (1, 1982): 46–56.
                                              C. M. Robeck, Jr.

Flamboyant salvation-healing evangelist Jack Coe is shown here holding his daughter in a Miami courtroom where he was tried for practicing medicine without a license.

COE, JACK (1918–56).

Healing evangelist. Born in Oklahoma City, Coe was abandoned by his parents and reared in an orphanage. He left the orphanage at age seventeen and became a heavy drinker. While in the army during World War II, he received a miraculous healing and decided to become a minister. He began conducting revival meetings while still in the service and was ordained by the Assemblies of God in 1944.

Coe had a dynamic personality and quickly won the allegiance of thousands as he conducted healing revivals all across the U.S. In 1950 he began to publish the *Herald of Healing* magazine, which eventually had a circulation of 300,000. That same year he opened a children's home in Waxahachie, Texas (near Dallas). Coe established a ministry in Dallas known as the Dallas Revival Center in 1952. He was expelled from the AG in 1953 when church leaders became increasingly frustrated and embarrassed by some of his methods and teachings. Coe's church became one of the largest churches in Dallas, and in 1954 he began a television series, but it was short-lived.

In February 1956 at a healing crusade in Miami, Florida, Coe was charged with practicing medicine without a license. A trial ensued, but eventually the judge dismissed the case. Then in December of that year, Coe became critically ill and was diagnosed with bulbar polio. He died within a matter of weeks.

After Coe's death, his widow Juanita continued to hold healing campaigns for a while, but she soon began to direct her energies to the support of foreign missions and to the children's home at Waxahachie. Mrs. Coe, along with her second husband, Dan Hope, continued to pastor the Dallas Revival Center until the early 1970s.

Bibliography: D. E. Harrell, *All Things Are Possible* (1975).   G. W. Gohr

COLLEGES See BIBLE INSTITUTES, COLLEGES, UNIVERSITIES.

COLUMBIAN CHARISMATICS See CHARISMATIC MOVEMENT.

COMMUNITY GOSPEL FELLOWSHIP
(CGF). A small U.S. denomination organized by homosexuals for evangelism in the gay community. In 1982 a former minister of the United Pentecostal Church (UPC), Alvis Strickland, founded Community Gospel Center in Houston, Texas. In 1983 a branch church was opened in Dallas.

Strickland's successor, Ronnie D. Pigg, spearheaded the formation of CGF in 1987. More than twenty-two congregations in seven states (mostly midwestern) are affiliated. Some had earlier ties to the Universal Fellowship of Metropolitan Community Churches (UFMCC).

Community Gospel Fellowship embraces Trinitarians, although UPC influence is reflected in the ambiguity of articles of faith concerning the Godhead and order of salvation. Polity resembles UFMCC with an annual general conference and board of elders. Clerk is Samuel Kader of Dayton, Ohio.

Bibliography: *Community Gospel Fellowship Bylaws* (1987).   J. S. Tinney

COMMUNITY OF JESUS (ORLEANS, MASS.) See CHARISMATIC COMMUNITIES.

CONFERENCE ON CHARISMATIC RENEWAL IN THE CHRISTIAN CHURCHES See KANSAS CITY CONFERENCE.

CONATSER, HOWARD (1926–78). Pastor and Baptist charismatic leader. A graduate of Southwestern Baptist Theological Seminary in Fort Worth, Texas, Conatser was pastor, until his death, of the Beverly Hills Southern Baptist Church, Dallas. At that time Beverly Hills Church was the denomination's most renowned charismatic congregation. Though W. A. Criswell, pastor of the First Baptist Church of Dallas, vigorously opposed Conatser and his charismatic ministry, the church grew to more than five thousand members by the mid 1970s. Conatser was a leader and speaker in the first National Southern Baptist Charismatic Conference, July 21–23, 1976.

Bibliography: "Excluding the Charismatics," *Christianity Today* (November 7, 1975), 65–67; V. Synan, "Baptists Ride the Third Wave," *Charisma* 5 (12, 1986): 54.   J. A. Hewett

CONCILIO LATINO-AMERICANO DE IGLESIAS CRISTIANAS Formed in 1923, the Concilio Latino de Iglesias Cristianas (CLAIC) owes its existence to Francisco Olazábal (1886–1937), a Mexican national who six years earlier had received the baptism of the Holy Spirit under the ministry of George and Carrie (Judd) Montgomery in California. Until that time a minister of the Methodist Episcopal Church, South, Olazábal at first worked with the Assemblies of God (AG) but withdrew with his followers because of the attitude of the leader the AG placed over the Spanish-speaking churches. A proposed union of the CLAIC and the (Tomlinson) Church of God failed to be consummated because of the founder's death in an automobile accident near Alice, Texas, in 1937. Miguel Guillén of Brownsville, Texas, who then assumed leadership, became president for life in 1956. Under his leadership the CLAIC Seminary opened in Los Angeles. By the mid 1970s CLAIC claimed 105 churches and 4,200 members in nine states of the U.S., and 55 churches and 2,200 members in five states of Mexico. Half of the U.S. membership was in Texas.

Bibliography: M. Guillén, *La Historia del Concilio Latino-Americano de Iglesias Cristianas* (1982); A. C. Piepkorn, *Profiles in Belief,* vol. 3 (1979).   C. E. Jones

CONCILIO LATINO-AMERICANO DE LA IGLESIA DE DIOS PENTECOSTAL DE NEW YORK In 1956 work begun in the New York area five years earlier by the Iglesia de Dios Pentecostal de Puerto Rico became autonomous. Taking the name Concilio Latino-Americano de la Iglesia de Dios Pentecostal de New York, Incorporado, it established "affiliation" with the parent body and continued contributing to its support. By the mid 1970s the Manhattan-based Concilio Latino-Americano had about seventy-five churches and eight thousand members in the metropolitan area. It was sponsoring missionary work in the Netherlands Antilles and Central America. At that time Abelardo Berrios was president.

Bibliography: A. C. Piepkorn, *Profiles in Belief,* vol. 3 (1979).   C. E. Jones

CONGO EVANGELISTIC MISSION See ZAIRE EVANGELISTIC MISSION.

CONGREGATIONAL HOLINESS CHURCH The Congregational Holiness Church (CHC), with headquarters in Griffin, Georgia, resulted from a split in the Pentecostal Holiness Church (PHC) in 1920. Watson Sorrow, a minister of the Georgia Conference of the PHC, had sharp doctrinal disagreements with his denomination, particularly on the subject of divine healing. In the vein of those early days, some influential PHC leaders took the position that it was sinful to resort to medicine or physicians in times of sickness. According to his view, healing was provided for in the Atonement, and any reliance upon human remedies was wrong.

Watson Sorrow and a few others disagreed with this teaching and with some aspects of denominational polity. F. M. Britton and G. F.

Taylor held to the episcopal form of government practiced by most Holiness groups, while Sorrow and Hugh Bowling believed in a congregational form of government.

The conflict ended in Sorrow's and Bowling's expulsion from the PHC in 1920. On January 29, 1921, Sorrow led a large part of the Georgia Conference in organizing the CHC. The name of the new group reflected its views on local church autonomy. The 1921 preface to the *Discipline of the Congregational Holiness Church* states:

> . . . Our purpose is to follow the teachings of the Bible. So, in form of government we believe in a Congregational Government, while no actions taken by the few or many will glorify God unless we let the love of God rule in our hearts and lives. But we observe how both State and Church have suffered when a few held the reins of government. . . .

The CHC was chartered in 1925 and began publication of *The Gospel Messenger* to carry regular news of the young church. Under the leadership of Joe Sorrow, the first general moderator and brother of Watson, the CHC showed considerable vitality. Joe Sorrow was followed as moderator by such men as Watson Sorrow, B. L. Cox, Terry Crews, Cullen L. Hicks, and James Martin. The CHC has strength and influence far beyond its numerical size.

In 1986 there were eight thousand members and 175 churches in the U.S., mostly in Georgia and other southeastern states. There are a few congregations in Illinois and Texas. It is estimated that there are more members in other countries than in the U.S. The denomination has 126 congregations in Mexico and operates missions in Honduras, Guatemala, Costa Rica, Nicaragua, Brazil, and India.

Bibliography: *Discipline of the Congregational Holiness Church* (1980); W. Sorrow, *Some of My Experiences* (1954). C. W. Conn

CONN, CHARLES WILLIAM (1920–). Author, editor, educator, and former general overseer of the Church of God (CG, Cleveland, Tenn.). Born in Atlanta, Georgia, Conn married Edna Louise Minor in 1941 and was ordained by the CG in 1946. The Conns had twelve children. Conn was involved in pastoral work before serving as director of Sunday school and youth literature for the CG in 1948. That same year he became editor of *The Lighted Pathway*. Later he worked as editor-in-chief of publications and editor of the *Church of God Evangel* (1952–62). After serving as assistant general overseer (1962–66), Conn served as general overseer (1966–70) and president of Lee College (1970–82). Since 1977 Conn has served as the official historian of the denomination.

Conn is well-known in evangelical and Pentecostal circles. He has been a member of the Society for Pentecostal Studies and served on the executive committee for the Pentecostal Fellowship of North America (1962–70) and on the board of directors for the National Association of Evangelicals (1966–70).

A prolific writer, Conn has written for numer-

Charles W. Conn is an educator and historian with the Church of God (Cleveland, Tenn.). He is the author of *Like a Mighty Army*, the history of his denomination.

ous publications and has contributed to several encyclopedias and reference works. He is the author of the following books: *Like a Mighty Army* (1955, rev. ed. 1977); *Pillars of Pentecost* (1956); *The Evangel Reader* (1958); *Where the Saints Have Trod* (1959); *The Rudder and the Rock* (1960); *The Bible: Book of Books* (1961); *A Guide to the Pentateuch* (1963); *Christ and the Gospels* (1964); *A Certain Journey* (1965); *Acts of the Apostles* (1965); *Why Men Go Back* (1966); *A Survey of the Epistles* (1969); *The Pointed Pen* (1973); *Highlights of Hebrew History* (1975); *A Balanced Church* (1975); *Candle of Pentecost* (1981); *Poets and Prophets of Israel* (1981); *The Anatomy of Evil* (1981); *Our First 100 Years, 1886–1986: A Retrospective* (1986); and *Images of a People* (1986).

The Promise and the Power (1980), edited by Donald N. Bowdle, was published as a Festschrift dedicated to Charles Conn.

Bibliography: C. Conn to G. W. Gohr, April 20, 1988; *Contemporary Authors* (1983); *Who's Who in Religion*, 2d ed. (1977). G. W. Gohr

COOK, GLENN A. (1867–1948). Early Pentecostal evangelist and advocate of the Oneness doctrine. Originally a Baptist from Indianapolis, he worked for a daily newspaper in Los Angeles. At the onset of the Pentecostal revival in 1906, he resigned his position to work with W. J. Seymour. During this time, Cook handled the finances and correspondence at the Azusa Street

Mission and began assisting in the publication of *The Apostolic Faith*. During early 1907, he brought the message of Pentecost to Indianapolis, which quickly became a center for the new movement, as well as to the Church of God in Christ. C. H. Mason, its coleader, who had just been baptized in the Spirit while at Azusa Street, returned to Memphis, Tennessee, to find that many people in his organization had already received this experience through Cook's ministry. Cook also held highly successful campaigns in Oklahoma, Arkansas, and Missouri.

Glenn A. Cook took the Pentecostal message from the Azusa Street Mission to Indianapolis in 1907. He later united with the Oneness movement.

Beginning in 1914, Cook traveled throughout the Midwest and the South proclaiming the "Jesus Only" message, after he and Frank J. Ewart had baptized one another in the name of Jesus in Belvedere, near Los Angeles. Others rebaptized by Cook included G. T. Haywood, who later became general secretary of the Pentecostal Assemblies of the World, a Oneness organization, and L. V. Roberts, who later rebaptized E. N. Bell and H. G. Rodgers, although these three men later repudiated Oneness teachings. Cook later worked for many years with Ewart in the Los Angeles vicinity.

Bibliography: G. A. Cook, *The Azusa Street Meeting* (n.d.); G. A. Cook, "The Truth About E. N. Bell," *Herald of Trust* (August 1947), 3; F. J. Ewart, *The Phenomenon of Pentecost* (rev. ed., 1975); V. Synan, *The Holiness-Pentecostal Movement in the United States* (1971).   R. M. Riss

COOK, RALPH G. (1899–1981). Pastor and denominational official. Cook was born in Boston, Massachusetts, and reared in a Methodist church. He later attended services in several

Holiness churches but did not profess conversion until age sixteen in a Pentecostal church in Chelsea, Massachusetts. In 1917 he adopted Oneness Pentecostal theology. He was ordained to the ministry by N. Alexander in Boston, and he traveled to Indianapolis in 1919 to attend Garfield T. Haywood's church. From there he pastored various churches: Bloomington, Indiana; Carrollton, Illinois; a congregation in Louisiana; Hot Springs and Little Rock, Arkansas; Foxboro, Massachusetts; and Lancaster, Ohio.

Cook served in various administrative capacities: district elder of the Pentecostal Assemblies of the World; member of the General Board of the Pentecostal Assemblies of Jesus Christ (1938–1945); district superintendent of the Ohio District of the United Pentecostal Church, International (1945–1954); and member of the UPC Foreign Missionary Board. He was elected as assistant general superintendent of the UPC in 1963 and served in this capacity until 1971. A biography of his life, *He Stands Tall* (1980), was written by Mary H. Wallace.

In 1917 Cook married Hattie Lowell, who died a year later during the influenza epidemic. Three years later he married Nellie Reppond, a young evangelist.

Bibliography: A. L. Clanton, *United We Stand* (1970).   G. B. McGee

COOLEY, ROBERT EARL (1930–). Archaeologist, educator, and seminary president. Born in Kalamazoo, Michigan, Cooley received his academic training at Central Bible College (three-year diploma, 1952), Wheaton College (B.A., 1955), Wheaton College Graduate School (M.A., 1957), and New York University (Ph.D., 1968). In 1952 he married Eileen H. Carlson; they have two sons. The Michigan District of the Assemblies of God ordained him in 1958.

Since 1960, Cooley has been involved with supervising archaeological expeditions in Israel (Dothan, Ai) and Egypt (Tell Retaba). He has also been involved in archaeological excavations in New York (Oyster Bay) and Missouri (James River Basin and Smith Cabin site). Guest lectureships have taken him to Belgium, Brazil, Israel, Korea, and Portugal. He was appointed annual professor at the W. F. Albright Institute for Archaeological Research in Israel for the spring term of 1980. Since 1959 he has conducted fifty study trips to Europe, Mediterranean countries, and the Middle East.

Cooley's extensive teaching and administrative experience has included service at the following institutions: Central Bible College, New York University, Wheaton College, Dropsie University, Evangel College, and Southwest Missouri State University. At the latter he directed the Center for Archaeological Research from 1973 to 1981. A member of numerous professional societies, he served as president of the Evangelical Theological Society in 1970, the only Pentecostal to be elected to that office. His published works include "Learning Through Travel in Israel," *The Journal of Educational Sociology* (April 1963); with Joseph Callaway, "A Salvage Excavation at Raddana, in Bireh," *Bulletin of the American*

Schools of Oriental Research 201 (February 1971); "Four Seasons of Excavation at Khirbet Raddana," The Bulletin of the Near East Archaeological Society 5 (1975); "Gathered to His People: A Study of a Dothan Family Tomb" in The Living and Active Word of God: Studies in Honor of Samuel J. Schultz, ed. Morris Inch and Ronald Youngblood (1980). He also served as the principal investigator for the Cultural Resource Management Studies (106 monographs published by the Center for Archaeological Research at Southwest Missouri State University).

In 1981 Cooley was appointed president and professor of biblical studies and archaeology at Gordon-Conwell Theological Seminary in South Hamilton, Massachusetts. Fuller Seminary professor Russell P. Spittler observed that Cooley's appointment to that office "completed the evangelicalization of the Assemblies of God."

Bibliography: Personal resume supplied to this author (1987); R. P. Spittler, "The Cooley Inauguration: A Celebration of Sovereignty," Agora 5 (Summer 1981): 13–14.
G. B. McGee

COPELAND, KENNETH (1937–). Televangelist, author, and leading proponent of the "Word of Faith" message. Copeland consecrated his life to God in 1962. Five years later he enrolled in Oral Roberts University (ORU), where he became a copilot on Oral Roberts's cross-country crusade flights.

While at ORU Copeland attended Kenneth Hagin's Tulsa seminars. Unable to pay for Hagin's tapes, he offered the title to his car for them. Hagin's manager, Buddy Harrison, took one look at the car and said, "Just go ahead and take the tapes. Bring the money in when you can" (Hagin, 1985, 67).

In 1968 Copeland and his wife, Gloria, returned to Fort Worth, Texas, where they founded an evangelistic association. Their meetings began as Bible studies in local homes but grew rapidly. In 1973 the Copelands began publishing the Believer's Voice of Victory. Two years later, after an extended time of prayer, Copeland reported that the Lord had commanded him to "preach the Gospel on every available voice" (Copeland, 1981, 6). The following year the Copelands began radio broadcasts that quickly spread throughout North America. In 1979 they launched an equally successful television ministry that soon became international in scope. Copeland began to use special satellite communications in 1981, initiating a global religious broadcast the following year.

Copeland's ministry has been accompanied with many reports of healings, even for victims of cancer (Copeland, 1981, 8) and of AIDS (Charisma, January 1988, 61). Jerry Savelle (1982, 31–32) reported that at one meeting Copeland jumped off the platform, pointed to a man paralyzed from the neck down, grabbed him by the hand, and ran around the church with him.

Heavily influenced by E. W. Kenyon, Copeland emphasizes that for those who do not love their own lives but submit themselves totally to God's purposes, there is great prosperity: a flourishing of spirit, soul, and body (G. Copeland, 1985, 6–7).

Bibliography: G. Copeland, "Love Not Your Life," Believer's Voice of Victory 13 (April 1985): 6–7; K. Copeland, "And God Said," Believer's Voice of Victory 9 (September 1981): 2–10; "Copeland Reaches Out to AIDS Victims," Charisma & Christian Life (January 1988), 61; K. Hagin, Jr., "Trend Toward Faith Movement," Charisma (August 1985), 67–70; J. Savelle, If Satan Can't Steal Your Joy (1982).
R. M. Riss

COPLEY, ALBERT SIDNEY (1860–1945). Pastor, teacher, songwriter, and editor, with most of his ministry in Kansas City, Missouri. Copley taught the unconditional eternal security of believers and rejected any type of church organization (helping instead to form "grace" assemblies). Converted in the Evangelical Church near West Salem, Ohio, Copley graduated from the denomination's college at Naperville, Illinois. He was ordained and ministered in Illinois, Canada, Oregon, and Ohio. For a short period of time he was associated with the Christian and Missionary Alliance. He received the Pentecostal experience at Levi Lupton's 1907 camp meeting in Alliance, Ohio. He established the Christian Assembly in Kansas City and became the publisher of the Grace and Glory magazine (formerly J. Roswell Flower's The Pentecost), which is still published at Mountain Grove, Missouri.

Bibliography: W. Franklin, A. S. Copley (1983).
W. E. Warner

CORNWALL, ESPIE JUDSON (1924–). Itinerant teacher and writer. Born in San Jose, California, Cornwall was educated at Southern California Bible College (B.A.) and Fountain Gate Bible College (M.A. and Th.D.). He reports to have been called into the ministry at age five and to have begun preaching at age six. An Assemblies of God pastor for twenty-nine years, Cornwall served five churches in Washington, Oregon, and California. Since then he has spent fifteen years in conference ministry with an emphasis on praise and worship, traveling some 100,000 miles each year. For several years he appeared regularly on the television program "Manna." He has written seventeen books, including Meeting God (n.d.) and Eat What You Serve (n.d.).

Bibliography: J. Cornwall, "How to Receive a Traveling Ministry," Ministries (Fall 1984), 44–47.
S. Strang

CORRELL, NORMAN L. (1926–). Missionary and administrator. Born in Bridgeport, Nebraska, Correll attended North Central Bible College at Minneapolis, Minnesota, and was ordained by the Assemblies of God in 1951. He married Norma Jane Shoff in 1946. They have two children.

After several years of pastoral and evangelistic work, Correll served as a missionary to Tanzania, East Africa, from 1958 to 1966. He became the national Mobilization and Placement Service (MAPS) representative in 1966 and was named national Christ's Ambassadors secretary in 1968. From 1975 to 1979 Correll was dean of evangelism and Christian education at the International Correspondence Institute in Brussels, Belgium.

Having served as secretary of missions support for the Division of Foreign Missions from 1979 to 1982, he now is administrative assistant to J. Philip Hogan, the executive director of the Division of Foreign Missions.

Bibliography: Personal data sheet, AG Office of Information (1980). G. W. Gohr

CORVIN, RAYMOND OTHEL (1915–1981).

Pastor, church leader, and educator. Corvin was born on a farm near Ada, Oklahoma. A childhood friend was Oral Roberts, who was born in the same region. Converted in a rural congregation of the Pentecostal Holiness Church (PHC) in 1932, Corvin immediately enrolled in Holmes Bible College in Greenville, South Carolina. In 1939 he married Eula Kathleen Staton, a union that produced two daughters.

Ordained in the Upper South Carolina Conference of the PHC in 1935, Corvin served churches in South Carolina and Oklahoma before being elected general secretary of the denomination in 1945. He held this position until 1969 when he was elected vice-chairman of the PHC.

During these years, Corvin earned two doctoral degrees and founded Southwestern Bible College in Oklahoma City. In 1962 he served as founding chancellor of Oral Roberts University (ORU) in Tulsa. He also served as the first dean of the ORU Graduate School of Theology. In his later years he pioneered in developing modular education programs for home ministerial training.

Bibliography: D. Harrell, Jr., *Oral Roberts—An American Life* (1985); V. Synan, *The Old-Time Power* (1973). H. V. Synan

COTTON, EMMA L. (1877–1952).

Evangelist, church planter, pastor, and editor. Born in Louisiana of Creole descent, Emma Cotton first appeared at the Azusa Street revival in 1906. She was attracted by word of "the great awakening of the Spirit." At Azusa she was healed of "weak lungs and cancer," the latter disease having attacked her nose. Emma was married to Henry C. Cotton (1879–1959), who worked as a cook on a railway run between Los Angeles and San Antonio, Texas. Henry's frequent trips left "Mother" Cotton free to engage in evangelistic work throughout California. In 1916, for instance, she held divine healing services at the Pentecostal Assembly in San Jose. By 1933 she had founded independent Pentecostal churches in Bakersfield, Fresno, and Oakland. She was described as courageous, hard working, and dedicated by those who knew her.

During the early 1930s Mother Cotton enjoyed a friendship with Aimee Semple McPherson, who encouraged her to establish a church in Los Angeles. Known as "Azusa Temple," it was located at 27th and Paloma. Together, Emma and Henry, who held credentials with the Church of God in Christ (CGIC), copastored this independent congregation. The church remained independent during Mother Cotton's lifetime since the CGIC did not ordain women, and Mother Cotton did the bulk of the preaching. Today the church is known as Crouch Memorial Church and is an important congregation affiliated with the CGIC.

In April 1939 Mother Cotton edited and published a four-page paper called the *Message of the "Apostolic Faith,"* intended to be the first volume of a regular series. She included her eyewitness account of events surrounding the 1906 outpouring of the Holy Spirit in Los Angeles in that volume. No other issues are known to exist. About 1950, after a reprieve of nearly half a century, her cancer reappeared. Mother Cotton died on December 27, 1952. Emma and Henry Cotton are buried in Lincoln Memorial Park in Compton, California.

Bibliography: S. H. Frodsham, *With Signs Following* (1941); *Los Angeles City Directory* (1910, 1920); *Message of the "Apostolic Faith"* 1 (1, 1939); T. R. Nickel, *Azusa Street Outpouring* (1979, 1986); *Triumphs of Faith* 36 (6, 1916): 127. C. M. Robeck, Jr.

Howard P. Courtney served the Foursquare Church as general supervisor from 1944 to 1974. He was also active in the National Association of Evangelicals and the Pentecostal World Conference.

COURTNEY, HOWARD PERRY (1911–).

Pastor, teacher, author, denominational executive, and churchman. Howard Courtney was born in Frederick, Oklahoma, to Christopher Columbus and Dotty Lee (Whelchel) Courtney. Educated in public schools, Howard Courtney was reared in Santa Monica. He attended L.I.F.E. Bible College, receiving his diploma in 1932. On March 21, 1932, he married Vaneda Harper and entered the ministry. His first pastorate (1932–34) was in Racine, Wisconsin. While serving in Racine, he was ordained in 1933 by the International Church of the Foursquare Gospel (ICFG). His ordination was followed by a short term in Terre Haute, Indiana (1934). In 1935 Howard Courtney moved to Portland, Oregon, where he served as an assistant pastor, but entered for the first time, denominational administration. From 1935 to 1936, while he was in Portland, he served as the assistant supervisor of the Northwest District of the ICFG. The Courtneys moved to Riverside, California, in 1936, where Howard served as pastor until 1939 while teaching adjunctively at L.I.F.E. Bible College. Following another short pastorate in Urbana, Illinois (1939), Howard Courtney was named district supervisor of the Great Lakes District in 1940, a position he held until 1944.

Before the death of Aimee Semple McPherson in September 1944, leadership of the ICFG was already shifting to Rolf McPherson. Howard Courtney was called to serve with him in national office and was one of the last appointments made by Aimee McPherson. He was named general supervisor and director of foreign missions for the denomination and was awarded an honorary doctor of divinity degree from L.I.F.E. In 1950 he was named general supervisor and vice-president of the ICFG, and for the next four years (1950–1953) he also served as copastor of Angelus Temple.

During his years in national office with the ICFG (1944–1974), Courtney regularly offered classes on church administration on a part-time basis at L.I.F.E. Bible College. He authored several booklets, including "The Vocal Gifts of the Spirit" (1956) and "The Baptism in the Holy Spirit" (1963). He was instrumental in helping the ICFG move into the larger Pentecostal world when he chaired the constitutional drafting committee for the Pentecostal Fellowship of North America (PFNA), and in 1948 he was elected vice-chairman of the PFNA. He served as the chair of the PFNA in 1953, 1954, and again in 1965–66. Courtney also chaired the advisory committee to the 1958–61 triennium of the Pentecostal World Conference, chairing the 1961 conference in Jerusalem. Once the ICFG joined the National Association of Evangelicals (NAE) in 1952, Courtney was an active member of the board of that organization. In 1966 he preached a plenary address, "Christ and Modern Man," at its annual convention.

Since 1974, when Courtney resigned as general supervisor of the ICFG, he has participated in a variety of ministries. Notable among them was his participation in the planning committee of the 1977 Conference on the Charismatic Renewal in the Christian Churches held in Kansas City, Missouri. From 1977 to 1981 he served as pastor of Angelus Temple. He currently resides with his wife in Glendale, California, and continues to serve on the board of directors, the missionary cabinet, and the executive council of the ICFG.

Bibliography: D. Manvel, *Like a Mighty River* (1977); W. Menzies, *Anointed to Serve* (1971); *United Evangelical Action* 25 (1, March 1966): 6; *Who's Who in America* (1976–77); *Who's Who in Religion* (1977).
C. M. Robeck, Jr.

COUSEN, CECIL (1913–). British pastor and teacher. Son of a founding member of the Apostolic Church who had been an associate of Smith Wigglesworth at the Bowland Street Mission in Bradford, England, Cousen was baptized

in the Spirit at the age of ten, becoming one of the first Pentecostals to go to university (Cambridge). In family business for some years (1934–48), he became a pastor and was sent to Hamilton, Ontario (1949–51). Receiving new depth of active faith through the Latter Rain movement, Cousen took some practices back to Britain, including imposition of hands for the baptism of the Holy Spirit. Expelled by the Apostolics in 1953, Cousen formed the Dean House Christian Fellowship in Bradford, which he pastored until 1968. A gifted Bible teacher, Cousen taught at many British conferences from the mid-1950s and later in Denmark. He edited *A Voice of Faith* (1957–77). As the charismatic movement developed, Cousen became one of its most valued teachers, being closely associated with the Fountain Trust and a member of its advisory council from 1969. He authored *The Gifts of the Spirit* (1986).

Bibliography: P. D. Hocken, *Streams of Renewal* (1986).
P. D. Hocken

COVENANTED COMMUNITIES See CHARISMATIC COMMUNITIES.

COX, RAYMOND LESTER (1924–). Foursquare pastor, author, and denominational leader. Raymond Cox pastored churches in the Northwest and Canada beginning in 1946. A prolific writer, he has had more than 2,600 articles published in more than a hundred periodicals worldwide. Since 1975 he has written a monthly column for the *Foursquare World Advance*, "Current Events and Comments." He is the author of four books: *The Verdict Is In* (the alleged kidnapping of Aimee Semple McPherson, 1984); *The God-Shaped Vacuum* (1967); *The Foursquare Gospel* (1970); *Aimee Semple McPherson, The Story of My Life,* (1973, reprinted as *Aimee,* 1979).

In addition to being involved in activities in his denomination, Cox has held offices in the National Association of Evangelicals (Oregon president 1986–) and other interdenominational groups. He is also a photographer and musician and a Fellow of Royal Geographical Society, London.

Bibliography: *Who's Who in Religion* (1977).
W. E. Warner

CRAIG, ROBERT J. (1872–1941). Pastor and educator. A Methodist minister at the time of the 1906 San Francisco earthquake, Craig later received the baptism in the Holy Spirit and a vision for reaching 100,000 souls. His mission on O'Farrell Street grew into a strong church with new facilities completed in the Fillmore District in 1925. Craig became the first superintendent of the northern California and Nevada districts of the Assemblies of God in 1919. Frequent extended meetings with prominent evangelists made Glad Tidings Temple and Bible Institute a center of Pentecostal activity on the West Coast.

Bibliography: C. Brumback, *Suddenly . . . From Heaven* (1961); R. J. Craig, "A San Francisco Church," *Glad Tidings* 16 (10, 1941): 4; idem, "How I Received the Baptism in the Holy Ghost," *PE* (February 14,

1931): 4; W. W. Menzies, *Anointed to Serve* (1971).
E. A. Wilson

CRAWFORD, FLORENCE LOUISE

(1872–1936). Founder of the Apostolic Faith evangelistic organization in Portland, Oregon, in 1907. The mother of two, Florence Crawford was active in social work and women's organizations in spite of a childhood injury and spinal meningitis. Her parents were atheists, but she had had a conversion experience before attending the Azusa Street Mission in 1906. After the experiences of sanctification and Spirit baptism, she was healed. She assumed an active role in the mission. She was soon parted from her building contractor husband of sixteen years, Frank Mortimer Crawford, who did not accept her faith until after her death. A series of evangelistic trips to the Northwest and Canada returned Crawford to her native Oregon. For the next thirty years "Mother" used her position as general overseer of the Apostolic Faith Church to maintain a strict Holiness standard of doctrine and practice. Crawford's relationship with W. J. Seymour was strained for two reasons: Seymour's 1908 marriage, of which Crawford disapproved, and Crawford's transfer of the *Apostolic Faith* paper and its mailing lists from Azusa Street to Portland despite Seymour's objections. Though the Apostolic Faith organization had fewer than three thousand members at Craw-

Florence Crawford became one of the first Pentecostals at the Azusa Street Mission in Los Angeles in 1906. She later founded the Apostolic Faith organization, Portland, Oregon.

ford's death, branch churches extended its influence around the world.

Bibliography: *A Historical Account of the Apostolic Faith* (1965); *The Light of Life Brought Triumph* (1936); D. J. Nelson, "For Such a Time As This: The Story of Bishop William J. Seymour and the Azusa Street Revival," Ph.D. diss., University of Birmingham, 1981.
L. F. Wilson

CRAWFORD, RAYMOND ROBERT

(1891–1965). General overseer of the Apostolic Faith Church in Portland, Oregon, from 1936 to 1965. As a teenager Crawford joined his mother, Florence Crawford, the founder of the church, in Portland, where he was converted, received the experiences of sanctification and Spirit baptism, and began to preach. He attended a local business college and was an accomplished musician. In 1919 he was licensed to fly and purchased a plane for evangelistic efforts. He also captained a series of boats used in missionary endeavors along the Northwest Coast. Through evangelistic trips he assisted branch churches, and on his mother's death he succeeded her as general overseer. During his tenure, the church grew to nearly five thousand members in forty-three congregations while maintaining a commitment to its distinctive doctrines and standards of conduct.

Bibliography: *A Historical Account of the Apostolic Faith* (1965); Thelma L. Miles, comp., *Saved to Serve* (1967).
L. F. Wilson

Robert J. Craig founded Glad Tidings Temple, San Francisco, California, in 1913. Glad Tidings Bible Institute (now Bethany Bible College, Santa Cruz) was added in 1919.

CROSS, JAMES ADAM (1911–). The ninth general overseer of the Church of God (CG, Cleveland, Tenn.). A second generation Pentecostal preacher, the son of W. H. Cross of Florida, James A. Cross was ordained in 1936. He served as a CG evangelist, pastor, and administrator in numerous states of the Southeast and Northwest. He was elected to the office of general overseer of the CG in 1958 and served for four years. He then served as president of Lee College (1966–70).

Beyond the CG, Cross served as chairman of the Pentecostal Fellowship of North America (1962–64) and was prominent in the National Association of Evangelicals and the Pentecostal World Conference for many years. His published books include *The Glorious Gospel* (1956), *Healing in the Church* (1962), and *A Treasury of Pentecostal Classics* (1986).

Bibliography: Archives of the Church of God (Cleveland, Tenn.); C. W. Conn, *Our First 100 Years* (1986).
C. W. Conn

Bibliography: *Billboard* (March 22, 1986); *Cashbox* (October 12, 1985).
L. F. Wilson

Television personality Paul F. Crouch is founder and president of Trinity Broadcasting Network, which originated in 1973.

Andraé Crouch became a popular gospel singer and composer during the 1970s.

CROUCH, ANDRAÉ (1940–). Contemporary gospel singer, composer, and producer. The son of a Los Angeles street preacher, he became a Christian at age nine and two years later determined to use his musical gifts for the glory of God. He directed a Teen Challenge choir and performed with local groups before signing a record contract in 1971. His thirteen albums to date present the gospel songs he learned as a child in a contemporary form. He has performed in the most prestigious concert halls in over forty countries and has appeared on popular secular and Christian television programs. His songs have won six Grammy and three Dove Awards and have been recorded by secular and religious artists. He received an Oscar nomination for his music in the film "The Color Purple."

CROUCH, PAUL FRANKLIN (1934–). Founder and president of the Trinity Broadcasting Network (TBN), which owns and operates a growing number of Christian television stations across the U.S. After graduating from Central Bible College in Springfield, Missouri, Crouch worked in radio and television for several years before moving to California in 1961 to direct film and TV production for the Assemblies of God. In 1973 he and his wife Jan, together with Jim and Tammy Bakker, established TBN's flagship station in Santa Ana. Under Crouch's leadership the station prospered, and in the process, he became known by millions. Within four years TBN acquired a station in Phoenix, Arizona, and the following year the network was licensed to broadcast across the nation by satellite. Additional full-powered, low-powered, and cable stations have extended the ministry of TBN and the influence of its president across the nation and to many other countries.

Bibliography: M. K. Evans, "Where Miracles Are a Way of Life," *Christian Life* (May 1983), 28–32.
L. F. Wilson

CROWLEY, RAYMOND ELSON (1922–). General overseer of the Church of God (CG, Cleveland, Tenn.) since 1986. A native of Chincoteague, on the eastern shore of Virginia, Crowley received the baptism in the Holy Spirit at age fourteen and began preaching a year later (1937).

As a teenage preacher, he pastored churches in Michigan (1939–40) and Pennsylvania (1941–43). His later pastorates were in Maryland (1945–60) and for ten years in Canton, Ohio (1960–70).

Crowley's distinguished service as a pastor and evangelist led to administrative assignments: the National Radio–TV Board (1968–74) and as overseer of northern Ohio (1970–74). In 1974 he was elected assistant director of evangelism and home missions. Elevated to the directorship in 1978, he served with the department until 1982, when he was elected to the executive committee as assistant general overseer.

As assistant, Crowley was executive director of the CG Ministry to the Military. This work carried him into many parts of the world as evangelist and administrator. When the CG celebrated its centennial at the 1986 general assembly, Crowley was selected as the general overseer to lead the denomination into its second century of witness for Christ.

Bibliography: Archives and official records of the Church of God (Cleveland, Tenn.).   C. W. Conn

CRUMPLER, AMBROSE BLACKMAN
(1863–1952). Holiness evangelist, pastor, and church leader. Ambrose Blackman Crumpler was born near Clinton, North Carolina, at the height of the Civil War. In the late 1880s he moved to Missouri, where he was converted and licensed as a local preacher in the Methodist Episcopal church. In 1890, under the preaching of Beverly Carradine, he received an experience of entire sanctification as taught by the Holiness Association movement.

In 1896 Crumpler returned to North Carolina determined to establish the Holiness message in his native state. Holding meetings in both Methodist churches and in gospel tents, he ignited Holiness revivals across eastern North Carolina. Everywhere he went, people shouted, danced before the Lord, and "fell under the power" when they received the second blessing. He was more noted, however, for his claim that he had not sinned since his sanctification experience in 1890. This claim led to much discussion and controversy wherever he preached.

In time Crumpler's ministry attracted enough Methodist support to form a regional component of the National Holiness Association movement for the state of North Carolina. Accordingly, on May 15, 1897, in the town of Magnolia, the North Carolina Holiness Association was formed with Crumpler as president. From this organizational base, he conducted further meetings throughout the state.

His attacks on religious coldness and worldliness soon included his own Methodist denomination, which since 1894 was moving to curtail the Holiness movement within its ranks. In the general conference of 1898, southern Methodism passed a resolution known as "Rule 301," which forbade evangelists to hold meetings in a local Methodist charge without permission of the pastor.

In the summer of 1898 Crumpler tested the rule by holding a tent meeting in Elizabeth City,

North Carolina, without the prior approval of the pastor. When he was criticized for this infraction, he left the Methodist Church in November of 1908 to form a new group in Goldsboro, North Carolina, which he called the Pentecostal Holiness Church (PHC). This became the first continuing congregation of the new denomination to bear the PHC name.

The next year, Crumpler rejoined the Methodist Church determined to overturn Rule 301. After holding a meeting near Stedman, North Carolina, without pastoral approval, he was tried by an ecclesiastical court in October 1899 for the "immorality" of violating Rule 301. Although acquitted in the trial, Crumpler once again left Methodism to lead in the formation of the new church.

In 1900 G. B. Cashwell conducted a convention in Fayetteville that resulted in the formation of the PHC as an ecclesiastical body modeled on the Methodist Church. A "Discipline" was adopted as well as a periodical edited by Crumpler known as the *Holiness Advocate*. Of the dozen or so churches associated with the movement, the one in Goldsboro grew to be the largest. By 1902, under Crumpler's pastoral leadership, it had grown to more than a thousand members and for a time was one of the largest Holiness congregations in America. In 1903 the group adopted the name Holiness Church of North Carolina.

In 1906 Crumpler's infant denomination was wracked by controversy engendered by the introduction of Pentecostalism by a minister in the church, G. B. Cashwell of Dunn, North Carolina. In a historic meeting in Dunn in 1907, practically the entire ministerium of the church received the baptism in the Holy Spirit evidenced by speaking in tongues. At first Crumpler cooperated with the new movement and published positive reports of Cashwell's meetings in the *Holiness Advocate*. But by 1908 Crumpler began to oppose those in the church who insisted on tongues as the only initial evidence of the baptism.

The controversy came to a head in the convention of the church that convened in Dunn, in November 1908. The Pentecostal faction led by Cashwell and G. F. Taylor easily defeated Crumpler and the few anti-Pentecostal delegates who were present. Despite his opposition to the Pentecostal majority, Crumpler was reelected to head the church. The next day, however, he left the convention and the church he had founded. Thereafter, he returned to the Methodist Church, where he remained for the rest of his life.

In his later years, Crumpler accepted location (laicization) from the itinerant Methodist ministry and practiced law in Clinton. His occasional ministry in Methodist churches until his death in 1952 mainly involved his interest in the prohibition movement.

Bibliography: J. Campbell, *The Pentecostal Holiness Church, 1898–1948* (1951); V. Synan, *The Old-Time Power* (1973).   H. V. Synan

CRUZ, NICKY (1938–). Youth evangelist.
Nicky Cruz was born in Puerto Rico in 1938. He came to New York City at age fifteen and shortly

thereafter became involved with the Mau Mau street gang.

Former New York gang leader Nicky Cruz was converted under the ministry of David Wilkerson's Teen Challenge. ©Stegner Portraits.

The story of Cruz's conversion has been detailed in *The Cross and the Switchblade* (1963) by David Wilkerson and *Run, Baby, Run* (1968) by Nicky Cruz. Since his conversion and training at Latin American Bible Institute, La Puente, California (1958–61), he has been active in ministry with Teen Challenge and city-wide crusades.

Cruz has traveled to many Latin American countries by invitation of the churches and governments. In 1985 he was in Hungary for crusades. As a result of those meetings, the government granted permission for a Teen Challenge center in Budapest.

The conversion of Nicky Cruz was one of the keys to the break up of the gangs of the 1950s in New York City. It also inspired many other ministries to youth on the streets in other metropolitan areas in the U.S. and overseas.

Bibliography: N. Cruz, *Run, Baby, Run* (1968); D. Wilkerson, *The Cross and the Switchblade* (1963).
F. M. Reynolds

CULPEPPER, RICHARD WESTON
(1921–). Evangelist. R. W. Culpepper was converted while stationed in Havana, Cuba, during World War II as a staff sergeant in the U.S. Army. When Normandy was invaded, he was serving in England. He was baptized in the Holy Spirit while he was fellowshiping within a hollowed-out haystack with a group of Pentecostal soldiers. After he quite reluctantly taught this group one night, God audibly told Culpepper, "I

want you to preach the gospel" (Culpepper, 1960, 8–9).

For about two years after the war Culpepper traveled in the U.S. as an evangelist. Settling in the Los Angeles area, he held two pastorates until 1957, when he was called into foreign evangelism. Many articles in *The Voice of Healing*, of which he was chairman of conventions from 1959–61, featured his international, evangelistic, healing ministry: around the world.

Culpepper, David Nunn, Morris Cerullo, and W. V. Grant in 1958 formed the World Convention of Deliverance Evangelists. Culpepper was an active leader until the group ceased meetings in 1965.

Culpepper's own organization was a "missionary church" supporting missionaries "in East, West, and South Africa, India, the Philippine Islands and Jamaica and orphan children in India" (*World-Wide Revival Reports* 2 [12, 1963]: 2). In 1968 Culpepper supported "more than 90 missionaries and native evangelists around the world" (*World-Wide Revival Reports* 6 [4, 1968]: 4).

In 1970 Culpepper joined A. C. Valdez, Sr., as copastor of the Milwaukee Evangelistic Temple.

Bibliography: R. W. Culpepper, "God Works in Mysterious Ways His Wonders to Perform," *Voice of Healing* 13 (2, 1960): 8–9; R. W. Culpepper, ed., *World-Wide Revival Reports* (1961–70); *Full Gospel Business Men's Voice*, 1 (1, 1953): 14; D. E. Harrell, Jr., *All Things Are Possible* (1975); G. Lindsay, ed., *Voice of Healing* 11 (4, 5, 9); 12 (7); 13 (2, 3, 5, 6); 14 (3, 4, 6, 7).
J. A. Hewett

CUMMINGS, ROBERT WALLACE (1892–
1972). Missionary, educator, and mystic. Robert Cummings, an American citizen born in India, was the son of United Presbyterian (UP) missionaries and attended UP schools. While studying the Bible as a UP missionary (he was a third-generation missionary to India), he became convinced that he needed to receive the baptism in the Spirit in order to be effective. After two years of seeking, he received this experience in 1925. Cummings went to India seven times (twenty-one years total) as a missionary. The last two times he went as an Assemblies of God (AG) missionary, with whom he affiliated in 1944. He served as AG field secretary for Southern Asia (India and Ceylon) from 1946 to 1948. Cummings earned four degrees: B.A., Westminster College; B.Th. and M.Th., Pittsburgh-Xenia Theological Seminary; and M.A., Kennedy School of Missions. He also served as a Central Bible College teacher in Springfield, Missouri. Cummings's gifted life was marred by two episodes of mental illness. He is remembered for his missionary work, his worship of God, and the idea that Christ can help each individual to be victorious over his own Gethsemane, which he wrote about in *Gethsemane* (1944).

Bibliography: M. Craig, *Prepared by God: Robert Cummings* (1962); R. W. Cummings, *Gethsemane* (1944); idem, "*Unto You Is the Promise*" (c. 1940).
E. B. Robinson

CUNNINGHAM, LOREN (1935–). Founder of Youth With a Mission. The son of Assemblies of God pastors, Loren Cunningham attended Central Bible Institute in Springfield, Missouri.

Cunningham's vision for interdenominational youth missionary work led to his separation from the AG in 1964 after eight weeks of successful ministry in the Bahamas. Youth With a Mission (YWAM) has a twofold vision of loving God and loving neighbor. Each young person going with YWAM is responsible for raising his or her support for short-term trips to foreign fields. YWAM grew until more than 15,000 young people were going out on missions trips in 1983. One of the notable successes of YWAM was its effective ministry following the tragedy at Munich during the 1972 Olympics. YWAM established a school of ministry in Hawaii in 1977 and outfitted a mercy ship that has been used in relief work around the world.

Bibliography: L. Cunningham, *Is That Really You, God?* (1984).   J. R. Zeigler

After Canadian Robert C. Cunningham completed his studies at Central Bible College in 1937, he went to work at the Gospel Publishing House as an editor. He later became editor of the *Pentecostal Evangel*, a position he kept for 35 years.

CUNNINGHAM, ROBERT CYRIL

(1914–). Magazine editor. Cunningham was born and educated at Peterborough, Ontario, and came to the U.S. in 1935. He graduated with a B.A. from Central Bible College and later received an M.A. from the Assemblies of God Theological Seminary. He married Helen Marian Platte in 1941. They have four children.

In 1937 Cunningham became a member of the editorial staff at the Gospel Publishing House. He also served as a supply pastor for various churches

near Springfield, being ordained by the Assemblies of God (AG) in 1945.

Cunningham became editor of the *Christ's Ambassadors Herald* in 1939 and associate editor of the *Pentecostal Evangel* in 1943.

When Stanley Frodsham resigned in 1949, Cunningham became the editor of the *Pentecostal Evangel*. He helped organize the International Pentecostal Press Association in 1970. After thirty-five years as editor, Cunningham retired in 1984 and was succeeded by Richard G. Champion.

Bibliography: *Who's Who in America,* 43d ed. (1984–85).   G. W. Gohr

CURSILLO MOVEMENT A renewal movement within the Roman Catholic Church (RCC). The techniques of Cursillo have been adapted by other denominations, including the United Methodists (Emmaus Walk) and Episcopal Church (Episcopal Cursillo). Cursillo is crucial for understanding the Catholic Charismatic Renewal (CCR).

Cursillo, Spanish for "little course" (officially, Movimiento de Cursillos de Cristiandad) began in Spain in the 1940s as an effort by a Mallorca layman, Eduardo Bonnin, to make Catholic Action Retreats to Santiago de Compostella more meaningful. This was supported by Bishop Juan Hervas, and a priest, Juan Capo Bosch. The bishop was disciplined by the church for his involvement and was transferred to Cuidad Royale, where he continued to defend the movement as a means of pastoral planning and priestly direction. The origins of Cursillo are debated within the movement as official church documents indicate Hervas as founder or cofounder. Cursillo thus became an issue in the discussion of the role of laypersons within the RCC. Eventually, Cursillo was accepted as a legitimate renewalist movement. A national secretariat was organized in Spain (1962–73), and the movement soon spread to most Spanish-speaking countries. It was first introduced to the U.S. in 1957 by Spanish pilots being trained in Texas.

It was not until 1966 that Pope Paul VI gave approbation to the efforts in his address published by Cursillo, *Christ, the Church, the Pope Are Counting on You* (1966). Since that time there have been a number of international leadership meetings; the proceedings of several have been published: *Corrientes nuevas en los Cursillos de Cristiandad* (1972); *Los Cursillos se Renuevan* (1973); *El M.C.C. Agente de Evangelizacion* (1976); and *Los Cursillos y Puebla* (1982).

An extensive literature has been produced by Cursillo, but little effort has been made to examine it beyond the brief bibliographic essay of Stephen Clark, *The Evolution of the Cursillo Literature* (1971), and the only history of the movement, Ivan Rohloff, *The Origins and Development of Cursillo* (1976). The basic perspectives of North American Cursillo are expounded by Stephen Clark, *Developing Christian Communities* (1972), and in a volume produced by the World Encounter, translated and revised as *Fundamental Ideas of the Cursillo Movement* (1974).

Cursillo endeavors to produce vital Christians

who as a committed community will lead in the development of parish spirituality. The rationale of the method is described in E. Bonnin, *The How and the Why* (1966) and F. Forteza, *Ideario* (rev. ed., 1971). The basic formula of the Cursillo program has changed little since its inception in Spain. There are four elements to the structure: Pre-Cursillo, Cursillo, Closing, and Ultreya. Pre-Cursillo involves both recruitment of potential participants and establishing relationships between a sponsor and prospective participants. Cursillo is a three-day retreat with a carefully constructed set of activities and homilies. The closing is the point at which the individual is encouraged to testify to the personal significance of the retreat before friends and family. Ultreya, or post-Cursillo, are regular meetings designed to encourage living as a renewed Christian. Detailed descriptions of the Cursillo program are available in W. Alcuin et al., *Cursillo Spiritual Director's Manual* (1976), *The Cursillo Movement's Leader's Manual* (1981), and *Our Fourth Day* (1985). *A General Commentary on the Lay Talks of the Cursillo Weekend* (1984) seeks to provide for continuity within the programs. Participatory observations of the life of a Cursillo community are found in M. Marcoux, *Cursillo, Anatomy of a Movement* (1982).

Several of the early leaders of the CCR were involved in the leadership of Cursillo in the U.S.

but separated from the movement over the issue of "spiritual gifts," especially glossolalia. Stephen Clark and Ralph Martin brought to the CCR the ambiguous attitudes toward episcopal authority and a pattern for renewal that has been adapted into the *Life in the Spirit Seminars* (n.d.) and a number of support publications.

See also CATHOLIC CHARISMATIC RENEWAL; LIFE IN THE SPIRIT SEMINARS.

Bibliography: A. Augustinovich, *Lineas biblicas del movimiento de cursillos* (1970); E. Bonnin, *The Cursillo Movement: Explanation and Purpose* (n.d.); idem, *The Cursillo Movement: The Precursillo* (n.d.); idem, *Structure of Ideas* (1965); J. Capmany, *Presencia del cristiano en el mundo* (n.d.); J. Capo Bosch, *The Basic Concepts of the Cursillo Movement in the Light of Vatican II* (n.d.); idem, *The Cursillo, Yesterday and Today* (1974); idem, *The Group Reunion: Theory and Practice* (1969); idem, *Lower Your Nets* (n.d.); H. Castano, *New Men* (1967); S. Clark, *The Work of the Cursillos and the Work of Renewal* (1967); J. M. Fernandez, *Los cursillos y el cambio del hombre* (1977); C. Gil, *Los cursillos y la evangelizacion* (1976); J. Hervas, *Cursillo's in Christianity* (1965); idem, *The Priest and the Cursillos* (n.d.); idem, *Questions and Problems Concerning Cursillos in Christianity* (1966); G. Hughes, *The Postcursillo, Group Reunion and Ultreya* (n.d.); D. Knight, *Cursillo Spiritual Direction Program* (1984). D. D. Bundy

CZECHOSLOVAKIAN CHARISMATICS
See CHARISMATIC MOVEMENT.

D

Finis Dake was a Bible teacher and author whose most famous and influential work is the *Dake's Annotated Reference Bible*.

DAKE, FINIS JENNINGS (1902–87). Author of the famous *Dake's Annotated Bible* (1961, 1963), teacher, and pastor. The twenty-four-year-old Dake resided with his wife in Amarillo, Texas, at the time of his ordination to the New Mexico–Texas district of the Assemblies of God (AG) in 1927, following two years of pastoral ministry there. In the mid 1920s Dake attended Central Bible Institute. He pastored in the Dallas area for approximately nine months before becoming an evangelist. During his stint as an evangelist (1928–31) he lived in Tulsa and Enid, Oklahoma.

Dake accepted the pastorate of the Christian Assembly in Zion, Illinois, in October 1932. Shortly after arriving in Zion, Dake spoke with his church board about purchasing the home and carriage house of John Alexander Dowie for the purpose of establishing "Shilo Bible Institute," which would later be renamed "Great Lakes Bible Institute" (Knight, 1972, 147) and would eventually merge with Central Bible Institute.

Dake's stay in Zion was not without controversy. On February 9, 1937, Dake received a six-month jail sentence in the Milwaukee County jail after pleading guilty to a charge of violating the federal Mann Act by transporting sixteen-year-old Emma Barcelli from Kenosha, Wisconsin, to East St. Louis, Illinois (with hotel stops in Waukegan, Bloomington, and East St. Louis under the name Mr. and Mrs. C. Anderson). Although pleading guilty, Dake insisted that he did not harm the girl. Despite the fervent loyalty of his wife and parishioners at Christian Assembly, as a consequence of this "unfortunate mistake," as Dake's lawyer called it, Dake's relationship with the AG ended in 1937. He later joined the Church of God (Cleveland, Tenn.) and finally became an independent. He remained Pentecostal nonetheless and did not allow this unfortunate event to ruin his life.

Dake was the author of numerous books, tracts, and pamphlets (e.g., *Revelation Expounded*, 2d ed. [1950]; *God's Plan for Man; Contained in Fifty-two Lessons, One for Each Week of the Year* [1949]; *Foundation Studies of Scripture; or, Dispensational Truth* [1946]). Sales of these and other books crested 180,000 by 1988 (Love and Owen, 1988, 40).

Dake is best known, however, for the notes in the strongly dispensationally oriented *Dake's Annotated Reference Bible*, published by the family-operated Dake Bible Sales, Incorporated, of Lawrenceville, Georgia. In 1961 the NT was published together with Psalms, Proverbs, and Daniel. Based strictly on the KJV, the Old and New Testaments were published jointly in 1963. This Bible contained a "Complete Concordance and Cyclopedia Index" as well as maps of the Holy Land, charts of the "Ages and Dispensations," and Dake's prized marginal "Notes." Until the appearance of Dake's decidedly Pentecostal brand of dispensationalism, *Scofield's Reference Bible* held sway. But the Pentecostal ingredients of "Dake's" (as it was popularly known) soon made it a favorite among Pentecostals. His impact upon conservative Pentecostalism cannot be overstated. His "notes" became the "bread and butter" of many prominent preachers and the "staple" of Pentecostal congregations. Thus Jimmy Swaggart, in a tribute to Dake, could say, "I owe my Bible education to this man" (1987, 44). Indeed, a recent article in *Charisma* on *Dake's Annotated Reference Bible* was titled "The Pentecostal Study Bible" (Love and Owen, 1988, 39).

Finis J. Dake died in 1987. Dake Bible Sales, Incorporated, continues under the leadership of his son, Finis J. Dake, Jr. Since 1961, 372,000 volumes have rolled off the presses of Dake Bible Sales. Each year 28,000 to 30,000 copies of *Dake's* in its various forms (paperback, large-print, leather-bound) are sold, according to Finis J. Dake, Jr. (Love and Owen, 1988, 40).

Bibliography: AG Archives, "Finis J. Dake"; *Dake's Annotated Reference Bible* (1961, 1963); C. E. Jones, *A Guide to the Study of the Pentecostal Movement*, 2 vols. (1983); H. V. Knight, *Ministry Aflame* (1972); R. Love and J. B. Owen, "The Pentecostal Study Bible," *Charisma* (January 1988), 39–40; "Petting Parson Sent to Jail," *Chicago Tribune*, February 10, 1937, p. 1; J. Swaggart, "In Memory. Finis Jennings Dake 1902–1987," *Evangelist* 9 (1987): 44.　　P. H. Alexander

DAKE'S REFERENCE BIBLE See DAKE, FINIS JENNINGS.

DALLIÈRE, LOUIS (1897–1976). Precursor of charismatic renewal in the French Reformed Church and founder of the Union de Prière. Ordained as pastor of Charmes-sur-Rhône in 1925, Dallière initially combined his pastorate with creative theological and philosophical writing. Convicted by the preaching of D. Scott, Dallière sought the Lord, receiving a fullness of the Spirit in 1930 and the gift of tongues two years later. In 1932 he wrote *Daplomb sur la Parole de Dieu*, a monograph on the Pentecostal revival. From 1932 until 1939 he collaborated with H. T. de Worm of Belgium on a monthly *Esprit et Vie* to promote the revival. Increasingly distressed by Pentecostal sectarianism, Dallière withdrew to his pastorate, still nourishing his ecumenical vision of a charismatic revival within the churches, which found expression in the charter of the Union de Prière, formed in 1946. He urged and practiced baptismal immersion in view of the Lord's return, which he saw neither as "rebaptism" nor as denying previous water baptism.

Bibliography: A. and E. Brémond, *Sur le Chemin du Renouveau* (1976); D. D. Bundy, "Pentecostalism in Belgium," *Pneuma* 8 (1, 1986): 41–56.
　　P. D. Hocken

DAMASCUS CHRISTIAN CHURCH (Concilio de las Iglesias Cristianas Damasco) A Hispanic church organization formed in 1939 by Francisco and Leoncia Rosado. The church teaches a Wesleyan form of Pentecostalism. Intended as an outreach to Spanish-speaking people in New York City, the group now ministers in New York, New Jersey, Florida, Ecuador, Mexico, the Dominican Republic, the Virgin Islands, and Puerto Rico—with a total of fifty-six churches in 1987. The group operates five Bible institutes and an outreach to drug addicts and conducts street evangelism. Since 1981 the organization has also included English-speaking churches.

The church is governed by an executive board of seven members. Engrique Melendez has been president since 1964. Angel M. Rios, converted and delivered from drug addiction and alcoholism through the efforts of the church, is secretary. Headquarters for the church is in Queens, New York (formerly in the Bronx).

Bibliography: "Constitution and Articles of Faith of the Council of the Damascus Christian Church and Missions" (1984); *Damascus Christian Church Directory* (1986–87).　　W. E. Warner

DANCING IN THE SPIRIT Physical movement akin to dancing presumably done while under the influence and control of the Holy Spirit. According to T. Burton Pierce, "Most older Pentecostal believers who have participated in spiritual revivals over a period of years have witnessed what is known as 'dancing in the spirit'" (1986, 9). Pierce lists humility, gracefulness, and beauty as characteristics of a person engaged in this form of worship. He also suggests that these persons are usually "shy, ungainly," and not normally given to attracting attention to themselves.

Pentecostal believers in the revival occurring during the early twentieth century eschewed dancing as a social activity in their zeal to become more Christlike. Thus, it is a bit surprising that "dancing in the Spirit" became an acceptable mode of worship. However, another characteristic of early Pentecostal movements was their flexibility in accepting new spiritual phenomena. Pierce's description matches oral reports by older Pentecostals who have observed this phenomenon, though some are hesitant to fully endorse it. Many reservations grow out of the fear that encouraging people to "dance in the Spirit" opens the door to excesses ranging from the need to be noticed to the breaking of necessary decorum in the church service. Other reservations stem from a certain caution regarding the credibility of the act itself. Thus, while many older Pentecostals refuse to eliminate "dancing in the Spirit" as a form of worship, many of them also express strong doubts that it is "Spirit-filled."

E. Louis Backman, a professor of pharmacology at the Royal University of Uppsala, writes of the "ritual significance" of dance to all religions:

> The types of dance varied even in the earliest Church. Frequently there seems to have been a question of round dances, usually with stamping and hopping, but always with clapping of hands and a certain rhythm. Sometimes the dance was a solo dance and in such cases it appears to have been a typical pirouette (1952, 329).

Backman asserts that a close relationship between the urge to dance and the need for healing is nearly always apparent in church dances. The Dance of the Angels, practiced for centuries in the church, was often described as an attempt to mirror the ecstasy of the Resurrection. Church dancing did degenerate into what Backman calls "dance epidemics" (1952, 331). People tried to find relief from pain or sickness through dancing. Backman now believes that the cramping and twitching experienced by the dancers can be traced to poor nutrition and ergot poisoning of grain and bread. Some of the dance epidemics took on characteristics of demon possession and were treated by the church as such. Especially during the Middle Ages, choreomaniacs presented a special problem for the church because of their irrational behavior (1952, 333).

In the 1980s similar dance epidemics have occurred in some Pentecostal and charismatic churches. These epidemics cannot be linked to malnutrition but may more closely coincide with a strong need on the part of a congregation for physical evidence of the presence of the Holy Spirit. Contrary to the spontaneous movement of earlier times, these dances appear structured, even loosely choreographed, giving rise to some doubt that the dancers are moving under the control of the Holy Spirit.

See also Worship.

Bibliography: E. L. Backman, *Religious Dances in the Christian Church and Popular Medicine* (1952). T. B. Pierce, "The Dance and Corporate Worship," *PE* (November 2, 1986), 8–10.   F. Bixler

DANIEL, BOOK OF

Due to the general acceptance of premillennialism and an emphasis on the immanence of Christ's return, most Pentecostals have shown a great interest in the Book of Daniel. It has been considered a key to the study of prophecy and to the pretribulational Rapture taught by many.

Invariably, Pentecostal writers, being supernaturalists, accept the entire book as coming from Daniel's time. The second-century date suggested by antisupernatural higher critics is usually not even mentioned; or if it is, it is dismissed as the product of unbelief. Professors in Pentecostal Bible colleges and seminaries, however, do defend the traditional dating of the book. Thus, both popular writers and Pentecostal scholars take the sequence of empires in chapter 2 to be Babylon, Medo-Persia, Greece, and Rome. Most see the same sequence in chapter 7, with Antiochus Epiphanes taken to be a type of the Antichrist. Daniel's seventieth week in chapter 9 is also generally understood to be a yet future period of tribulation at the end of the church age.

The Book of Daniel does not give any specific attention to the Holy Spirit. It does record how the Babylonians spoke of "the spirit of the holy gods" in Daniel (5:11). This was their way of recognizing that there was something supernatural about Daniel's knowledge, wisdom, and prophetic gifts. The NT, however, clearly recognizes Daniel's inspiration, with Jesus seeing future fulfillment (Matt. 24:15).

Bibliography: G. L. Archer, *A Survey of Old Testament Introduction* (1974); J. G. Hall, *Prophecy Marches On*, vol. 1, "Daniel" (1962); S. M. Horton, *Welcome Back, Jesus* (1967); idem, *What the Bible Says About the Holy Spirit* (1976); R. Riggs, *The Story of the Future* (1968); C. M. Ward, *What You Should Know About Prophecy* (c. 1975).   S. M. Horton

DANISH CHARISMATICS

See Charismatic Movement.

DANISH PENTECOSTALS

See European Pentecostalism.

DAOUD, MOUNIR AZIZ

(twentieth century). Missionary evangelist. M. A. Daoud's work in faith healing and evangelism during the 1950s and 1960s is chronicled in *Miracles and Missions Digest* (*MMD*). With his wife, Jane Collins Daoud—a faith healer and missionary even prior to her marriage—he circled the globe, consistently sending back to the U.S. testimonies of healing and salvation. The secular presses, government and police officials, and those involved

reported healings of the blind, deaf, and lame. Lepers, cancer victims, and those afflicted with numerous other sicknesses were cured (*MMD* 6 [3, March 1961]: 4–5, excerpt from *Uganda Egozera* newspaper, February 8, 1961, Kampala, Uganda).

The Daouds' Voice of Miracles and Missions, Inc., has sought to reach those where no other churches or evangelists have gone. It is

> a Full Gospel non-denominational organization . . . for . . . spreading the gospel of the Lord Jesus Christ around the world. Through [sic] preaching the Gospel with signs following and printing Christian literature. Sending [sic] forth American Missionaries to the ends of the earth, training and supporting native preachers in different fields of the world (*MMD* 4 [7, July 1959]: 13).

In 1970 the Daouds opened the "Old Fashioned Holiness Bible School" in Dallas, Texas. The International Bible Association was formed in 1972 to spread among missionaries and native populations "the PURE WORD OF GOD"— the King James Version of the Bible (Newsletter, November 21, 1972 [their capitals]). In the years that followed, the Daouds' efforts have largely been directed to Bible and literature distribution. *MMD* (1987–88) reports that hundreds of thousands of Bibles, New Testaments, and Bible portions have been distributed in English, Spanish, and various African and Indian languages.

Bibliography: J. C. Daoud, *Miracles and Missions and World-Wide Evangelism* (1953); M. A. Daoud, *Bringing Back the King* (1956); M. A. Daoud and J. C. Daoud, eds., *MMD* 4 (7, 1959): 13; 5 (6, 1960): 6; 6 (3, 1961): 4–5; 31 (1, 1988).   J. A. Hewett

DAVID J. DU PLESSIS CENTER FOR CHRISTIAN SPIRITUALITY

Established in 1985 as an organizational unit of Fuller Theological Seminary, Pasadena, California. As he neared his ninth decade, Pentecostal ambassador-at-large David du Plessis naturally gave thought to the future of his personal papers and library—an extensive collection acquired over nearly sixty years of ministry. Around 1983, du Plessis shared a conference platform with David Allan Hubbard, President of Fuller Seminary. Their conversation planted an idea in the mind of du Plessis: perhaps he could move to Pasadena, reducing the arduous travel that so long had characterized his itinerant ministry and giving himself to writing and consulting. With the advice and support of a close circle of friends on making such a change, Anna and David du Plessis sold their home of twenty years in Oakland, California, and moved to Pasadena. On February 7, 1985, Du Plessis' 80th birthday, a formal academic convocation at Fuller Seminary marked the establishment of the Du Plessis Center.

Du Plessis was particularly attracted to Fuller by the commitment of the seminary to ecumenical breadth coupled with its friendly openness to the Pentecostal and charismatic sectors of the church. From then until his death on February 2, 1987, Du Plessis served as Resident Consultant for

Ecumenical Affairs at the seminary, located a block from his new home.

The Du Plessis Center aims to facilitate the study and practice of Christian spirituality over a broad range of ecumenical diversity. It encourages research in the literature, practice, institutions, and movements of spirituality within the Christian church. By late 1987 the first major phase of the work of the Du Plessis Center was concluded—the completion in the seminary library of an archive for the Du Plessis papers and correspondence. The Du Plessis papers, which bear dates as early as the 1930s (a number of which are in his native language, Afrikaans) form an important resource for the development of three movements through the middle quarters of the twentieth century: the Pentecostal movement, the ecumenical movement, and the charismatic movement. Preserved records contain valued correspondence with such Pentecostal leaders as Stanley Frodsham, Donald Gee, Kathryn Kuhlman, Joseph Mattsson-Boze, Lewi Pethrus, and Carlton Spencer. They include correspondence with ecumenical leaders such as Visser 't Hooft, John Mackay, and Henry P. van Dusen, as well as with Roman Catholic churchmen such as Augustin Cardinal Bea and Jan Cardinal Willebrands. The archive also holds letters exchanged with charismatic leaders including Dennis Bennett, Larry Christenson, and Harald Bredesen. Among the resources in the Du Plessis archive are his personal collection of correspondence, published addresses and sermons, minutes, and conference papers related to the first fifteen years of the Pentecostal World Conference (1947-1962). Since 1986, the National Council of Churches has designated the Du Plessis Center as the west coast depository of its printed materials.

Gathered personal effects of Du Plessis include momentos of his personal friendship with three popes and numerous awards presented over his lengthy and distinguished ecumenical career. To the papers of Du Plessis, which by late 1987 had been sorted and positioned in permanent containers for access by scholars and researchers, have been added the papers of other Pentecostal leaders. Notable among these are the extensive correspondence of Joseph Mattsson-Boze (who was born the same day as Du Plessis, February 7, 1905), papers related to early twentieth-century ethnic immigrant Pentecostalism (especially Italian and Swedish), and the effects of several minor Pentecostal figures.

The Du Plessis archive participates in an informal network of evangelical, Pentecostal, and fundamentalist archival efforts. Joseph Colletti serves as the first archival assistant, and he largely has been responsible for the refinement of the collection. The formation of the Du Plessis archive has had the able guidance of consultant Nicholas Olsberg, head archivist of the famed Getty Museum of Santa Monica, California. Fuller faculty member and Pentecostal minister Russel P. Spittler served as the founding director of the Du Plessis Center.

As it grows, the Du Plessis Center projects sponsorship of seminars, conferences, and courses that will enhance and communicate the spiritual and ecumenical values characteristic of David du Plessis. In 1986, the Center sponsored the only session (of thirteen through 1987) of the International Roman Catholic–Pentecostal Dialog ever to have been held outside the European continent. This venue was arranged particularly to honor Dr. du Plessis.

During 1986, the Du Plessis Center sponsored the presence of visiting research scholars especially interested in religious ecstasy in antiquity. In 1987, it hosted an invitational conference of evangelical social activists and charismatics involved in socially ameliorative ministries.

It is an aim of the Du Plessis Center to deepen trust among diverse sectors of leadership in the church. With the Pentecostal and charasmatic movements combined now numbering in excess of twenty percent of the world's known Christians of any persuasion, the need and opportunity for a Center combining ecumenical and Pentecostal interests is clear and apparent.

Bibliography: Cecil M. Robeck, Jr., "David J. du Plessis Center Established," *Glad Tidings* (May 1985), 3; Chris Woehr and Steve Lawson, "Doors Open at Du Plessis Center," *Charisma* (January 1987), 68.

R.P. Spittler

DAYTON, DONALD WILBER (1942–). Educator, author, and specialist in the Holiness movement as an antecedent to Pentecostalism. As a student in the 1960s, Dayton left an evangelical college to become a civil rights advocate. He soon discovered, however, that the nineteenth-century Evangelicals who founded such institutions had been social activists. This prompted him to study the American Holiness movement, for which he wrote an extensive bibliography in 1971. As a Ph.D. student at the University of Chicago, he wrote an award-winning paper tracing the origin and development of the term "baptism of the Holy Ghost" within the Holiness movement (Synan, 1975, 39).

Dayton has done a great deal to preserve works valuable for the study of the milieu from which Pentecostalism arose, and to remind us of the emphasis of these works upon social justice. He is editor of the forty-eight-volume series, "The Higher Christian Life" (1985), a collection of facsimile reprints of original sources for the study of the Holiness, Pentecostal, and Keswick movements. He is also coediting a collection of secondary works on these topics, "Studies in Evangelicalism" (1980–), published by Scarecrow Press.

Bibliography: D. W. Dayton, *Discovering an Evangelical Heritage* (1976); idem, "From 'Christian Perfection' to the 'Baptism of the Holy Ghost,' " in V. Synan, *Aspects of Pentecostal-Charismatic Origins* (1975), 39–54; idem, "The Rise of The Evangelical Healing Movement in Nineteenth Century America," *Pneuma* 4 (Spring 1982): 1–18; idem, *Theological Roots of Pentecostalism* (1987).

R. M. Riss

DE LEON, VICTOR, JR. (1927–82). Author, editor, and district official for the Assemblies of God (AG). Born in Cottle County, Texas, De Leon married Sofia Calzada in 1947. They had nine children. Ordained in 1959, De Leon pastored churches in California until becoming assistant superintendent of the Pacific Latin American

District in 1971. During these times he also worked as the AG sectional presbyter in Riverside and San Bernardino, California (1958–59); youth president of the Latin American District (1960–64); and district executive presbyter (1960–76).

De Leon received the following degrees: B.A., Southern California College; M.A., Azusa Pacific University; M.Div., Melodyland School of Theology; and Ph.D., Union University Graduate School. He also served as a professor and member of the board of the Latin American Bible Institute and Seminary in La Puenta, California. His book *The Silent Pentecostals* (1979) is noteworthy for its contribution to understanding the history of the Hispanic Pentecostal movement in the twentieth century.

Bibliography: *Who's Who in Religion* (1977).
S. Shemeth

DELIVERANCE MINISTRY See Exorcism.

DEMON POSSESSION See Exorcism.

DEMONS See Exorcism.

DENNY, RICHARD ("DICK") (1923–). Lay leader in the Lutheran charismatic movement. Together with his wife, Betty, Denny served as manager and coordinator of a variety of activities and ministries among Lutheran charismatics. He was one of the original sponsors of the International Lutheran Conference on the Holy Spirit (1972), which became the chief annual gathering of Lutheran charismatics.

He and his wife experienced marked conversions and the baptism with the Holy Spirit shortly after their oldest son was killed in Vietnam in 1968. As a result, Denny sold a successful business and became a business manager for Lutheran Youth Encounter, a Minneapolis-based youth organization that ministered on college campuses and in local Lutheran congregations.

Later Denny served as lay assistant at North Heights Lutheran Church, St. Paul, Minnesota. In 1975 he became executive secretary for Lutheran Charismatic Renewal Services, which subsequently became a part of a merger of Lutheran charismatic leadership to form the International Lutheran Renewal Center (ILRC) (1983). Denny became ILRC's coordinator of national ministries. He traveled widely, teaching and counseling congregations in regard to charismatic renewal. He and his wife became officially accredited lay ministers in the American Lutheran Church.

Bibliography: L. Christenson, ed., *Welcome, Holy Spirit* (1987).
L. Christenson

DERSTINE, GERALD (1928–). Evangelist and church leader. Born and reared a Pennsylvania Mennonite, Derstine was converted in a T. L. Osborne crusade (1949). Shortly thereafter Derstine was healed of chronic stuttering.

With his Mennonite wife, Beulah Hackman, Derstine established a mission and then a church among the Chippewa Indians of northern Minnesota (1953). After being ordained as pastor of the Strawberry Lake Mennonite Church, Ogema, Minnesota, he was asked to leave (1955) when he

and members of his church experienced a week of Pentecostal experiences like those of the first-century believers.

Gerald Derstine was one of the first Mennonite ministers to be baptized in the Spirit in the 1950s.

Derstine's subsequent evangelistic, healing revival efforts were first sponsored by Henry Brunk, a Mennonite and Florida building contractor who had earlier established "Gospel Crusade" (1953, a nondenominational missions organization).

Derstine is founder and director of Christian Retreat Conference Center in Bradenton, Florida (1968), which he has developed as a center for lay education and renewal, including an "Institute of Ministry" (1975) and a "Pastoral Training School" (1982). Additional Centers include Christian Retreat Campgrounds, Ogema, Minnesota, and Christian Retreat Campgrounds, Russel, New York.

Derstine is vice-president of Gospel Crusade Ministerial Fellowship, a body that ordains and licenses men and women to active Christian ministry; president of Gospel Crusade, Inc.; and vice-president on the board of the National Pastor Leadership Conference Committee. He is also on the committee of the Charismatic Bible Ministries Fellowship, Tulsa, Oklahoma.

Gospel Crusade, Inc., supports ministries in Haiti, Honduras, Philippines, the Middle East, Jamaica, Mexico, and thirty-eight other nations.

Bibliography: G. Derstine, *Following the Fire* (1980); idem, *Three Decades of World-wide Ministry* (1983); G. Derstine, ed., *Harvest Time* 1 (1, 1958ff.).   J. A. Hewett

DeWEESE, ROBERT F. (1910–). An associate evangelist to Oral Roberts beginning in

1951. DeWeese was converted in a meeting conducted by Charles S. Price in 1928 and then went on to graduate from L.I.F.E Bible College. He pioneered and pastored churches in the International Church of the Foursquare Gospel and Open Bible Standard Churches and served as an elected official. He became well known as the campaign manager and afternoon speaker for the Oral Roberts campaigns. He and his wife Charlotte have written articles about their healings from a heart attack and acute leukemia.

DeWeese is a trustee of the Oral Roberts Evangelistic Association and chairman of the board of regents for Oral Roberts University.

Bibliography: R. Mitchell, *Heritage and Horizons* (1982). W. E. Warner

DIALOGUE, ROMAN CATHOLIC AND CLASSICAL PENTECOSTAL

Approximately sixty years after the formation of the first Pentecostal denominations the international dialogue between the Vatican Secretariat for Promoting Christian Unity and some members of the Pentecostal churches began. Significant things happened on both sides that made it possible for some form of theological discussion to take place.

I. Historical Background. Initial contact between Roman Catholics and classical Pentecostals came about through the ecumenical ministry of David J. du Plessis. In 1961 du Plessis visited Rome and was received by Augustin Cardinal Bea, president of the Secretariat for Promoting Christian Unity (SPCU). As a result of this meeting, Cardinal Bea invited du Plessis as an observer to the third session of the Vatican Council (1964). Then, at the Fourth Assembly of the World Council of Churches (WCC) in Uppsala, Sweden (1968), du Plessis became acquainted with Fr. Kilian McDonnell, OSB, a Benedictine theologian whose specialty was Protestant theology. It is out of the friendship between du Plessis and McDonnell that a dialogue eventually became a reality.

In 1969 the Reverend Ray Bringham, a charismatic Church of God (Anderson, Ind.) minister and personal friend of du Plessis, visited Rome while on a trip to Europe. He met John Cardinal Willebrands, president of the SPCU and Father (now Bishop) Basil Meeking. They discussed the possibility of a dialogue between the SPCU and representatives of the Pentecostal and charismatic movements. Bringham informed du Plessis of these discussions, which they had talked about prior to Bringham's trip.

In November 1969 Cardinal Willebrands spoke at the annual plenary meeting of the Secretariat in Rome (his speech was later published in *Information Service*), declaring:

> The problem of establishing an ecumenical contact with the Christians who do not belong to any of the Churches and ecclesial communities created by the Reformation of the sixteenth century remains an open one. I am thinking of those who are sometimes called "conservative Evangelicals," for example Pentecostals, the Seventh Day Adventists and others. As a result of their fanaticism and their refusal of any form

of institution they are often considered as sects. They represent a large and growing group of Christians. In Latin America they constitute between 80 and 90% of the non-Catholic Christians. Even after the integration of the International Missionary Council into the World Council of Churches the latter still does not include more than about one third of all Protestant missionary activities, largely because of the missions of these independent groups. (*Information Service*, no. 9 [1970]: 7).

David du Plessis read this article and, remembering the visits of Ray Bringham in Rome a few months before, wrote Cardinal Willebrands in June 1970 requesting that a dialogue be established. Willebrands responded favorably, suggesting that there be a "small, informal and private meeting in September to explore whether it is possible to have such a dialogue, and if so, what the method might be." The first preliminary discussion was held in September 1970. After two days of meeting, it was decided to meet again to discuss the possibilities further.

A second preliminary meeting was held in June 1971 where several important decisions were made: (1) unanimous desire to enter into dialogue was expressed; (2) there should be six to eight persons on each side in the sessions; (3) there would be five meetings over the next three years; and (4) a steering committee was chosen to select topics for discussion and to administrate the deliberations.

A third and final preliminary meeting was held in Rome in October 1971 by the steering committee. Details of the dialogue were finalized. There would be cochairpersons to moderate the dialogue. On the Roman Catholic side it would be Kilian McDonnell and on the Pentecostal side, David du Plessis. There would be five meetings in as many years (a quinquennium). Pentecostal participants would include classical Pentecostals and charismatics (Neo-Pentecostals) from the historic Protestant churches. Theologians on each side would be asked to present papers on topics to be selected by the steering committee. Each side would bring nine persons to the dialogue table. At the end of each dialogue week there would be an "agreed account" and a press release prepared, summarizing the discussions.

The steering committee also outlined the reasons for such a dialogue being established. Their seven-page report said in part:

> In an age of spiritual crisis a dialogue on spirituality seems much in place, especially since such a dialogue is concerned with the centrality of prayer. . . . It is therefore not inappropriate that prayer, spirituality and theological reflection be shared concerns at the international level in the form of a dialogue between the Secretariat for Promoting Christian Unity and Pentecostal Churches and participants in the charismatic movement within the Protestant and Anglican Churches.

The steering committee report goes on to explain that the dialogue "will give special attention to the meaning for the Church to fullness of life in the Holy Spirit." The desire is to "share in the reality of the mystery of Christ and the Church, to build a united Christian testimony, to indicate in what manner the sharing of truth makes it possible for us Roman Catholics and Pentecostals to grow together." A significant objective was for the dialogue to serve as an exchange of information "rather than action." The dialogue was not to "concern itself with the problems of imminent structural union but with unity in prayer and common witness" (*New Covenant* [1972], 6–7).

II. First Quinquennium (1972–76). The first series of discussions has been well documented in Arnold Bittlinger's *Papst und Pfingstler* (1978). The "agreed accounts" and Final Report can be found in *Presence, Power, Praise,* 3:373–95. Most of the theological papers were published in *One in Christ,* a Roman Catholic ecumenical journal, between the years 1973 and 1976.

The deliberations for the five years touched the concerns of the charismatic renewal. In this first series the dialogue "covered the scriptural basis for fullness of life in the Spirit, the relation of baptism in the Holy Spirit to Christian initiation, the role of the gifts in the mystical tradition, the charismatic dimensions and structures of sacramental and of ecclesial life, psychological and sociological dimensions, prayer and worship, common witness, and evangelism" (McDonnell, 1980, 3:373).

At the end of the quinquennium several topics were suggested for further discussion, most of which were presented in the second five-year series. The Final Report made it clear that the conclusions reached did not necessarily reflect the official teaching of the Roman Catholic church or the classical Pentecostal churches. The report did not bind either side to the theological positions expressed. "Rather, the reports are the result of serious study by responsible persons who submit the reports to the churches 'for suitable use and reaction'" (McDonnell, 1980, 376).

III. Second Quinquennium (1977–82). John Cardinal Willebrands authorized a second series of discussions in August 1976. The *first* series was composed of persons involved in the Pentecostal movement and those in the charismatic renewal in the historic churches — Anglican, Baptist, Lutheran, Orthodox, Presbyterian, and others. It was decided that for the *second* quinquennium only classical Pentecostals would be invited. There were at least three reasons for this change: (1) Roman Catholics wanted to get closer to the world-wide Pentecostal movement; (2) there were national or international dialogues already going on between Roman Catholics and the various non-Roman churches represented by the charismatic renewal; and (3) the Pentecostals desired to involve more of the Pentecostal denominations in the dialogue process.

During this series David du Plessis introduced the idea of "observers" to the dialogue. His desire to get word of the dialogue more widely spread among Pentecostals could be facilitated by inviting a larger number (twelve to fifteen persons) of Pentecostals to attend. In order not to dominate the discussions (since there were only nine Roman Catholics), observers were limited in their participation and were mostly "absorbing" the dialogue process.

The dialogue for 1978 was canceled because of the death of Pope John Paul I. He died on September 28, 1978, and the dialogue was scheduled for October 16–20. Karol Cardinal Wojtyla was elected Pope John Paul II on October 16, the same day the dialogue was to begin. This, along with the other factors, caused the 1977 session to lose continuity with the remaining four years of the second quin- quennium.

In 1979 Kilian McDonnell introduced the concept of "hard questions" into the process. This was an attempt to get the difficult theological issues more readily on the table and reestablish continuity. This procedure did much to move the dialogue sessions more quickly and effectively into the substantive issues discussed in the theological papers.

A total of sixteen theological papers were presented, covering such topics as speaking in tongues, faith and experience, hermeneutics, healing, tradition, the church as communion, Mary, and ministry. (Six of these papers have been published in *One in Christ* between 1983 and 1985.) The Final Report for the second series ended with optimism:

> The members of the dialogue have experienced mutual respect and acceptance, hoping that the major points of difference will provide an occasion for continuing dialogue to our mutual enrichment. It is the consensus of the participants that the dialogue should continue in this same spirit. Every effort will be made to encourage opportunities for similar bilateral theological conversation at the local level. The dialogue was to be affirmed as an ongoing instrument of communication. (*Information Service,* no. 55 (1984).

IV. Third Quinquennium (1985–89). At the close of the last series, it was decided by the steering committee to take a brief break for a time of "assimilation and reflection" over the effectiveness of the dialogue. It would also allow time to publish the theological papers and the "Final Report" and persons on both sides could familiarize themselves with these documents.

Kilian McDonnell and David J. du Plessis had served as the chairpersons for the dialogue from its inception in 1972 through the 1982 session. At a steering committee meeting in Rome (1983), each resigned as cochairperson but remained on the steering committee as "chairperson emeritus." The new chairperson for the Pentecostal side became Justus T. du Plessis, the Ecumenical Liaison of the Apostolic Faith Mission (AFM) of South Africa. He had been in the dialogue since 1974 and served on the steering committee. As a younger brother of David, he would carry on the ministry of the dialogue in the same spirit but with his own gift of leadership. After careful review, the Roman Catholic side asked Kilian McDonnell to remain as chairperson of their side. At a second steering committee meeting held in

The Roman Catholic/Pentecostal Dialogue participants at their 1981 meeting in Vienna.

1. Fr. Robert J. Wister
2. Fr. Pierre Duprey, WF
3. Fr. Jerome Vereb, CP
4. Fr. William J. Dalton, SJ
5. Rev. James H. Carmichael
6. Fr. Kilian McDonnell, OSB
7. Rev. William L. Carmichael

8. Fr. Laurence R. Bronkiewicz
9. Rev. Jerry L. Sandidge
10. Rev. David J. du Plessis
11. Rev. Howard M. Ervin
12. Rev. Ronald McConnell
13. Miss Marigloria Iani
    (secretary)

14. Rev. Martin Robinson
15. Rev. John L. Meares
16. Rev. Justus T. du Plessis
17. The Very Rev. Liam G.
    Walsh, OP
18. Rev. H. David Edwards

Rome (1984) it was decided to begin a new five-year series in May 1985, following the basic theme for the entire five years of "The Communion of Saints." Topics for this quinquennium included; "Communion of Saints" (1985), "The Holy Spirit and the New Testament Vision of Koinonia" (1986), "Koinonia, Church and Sacrament" (1987), and "Koinonia and Baptism" (1988). The 1989 session will be used to prepare the Final Report for the quinquennium and to discuss future plans.

The Pentecostal side of the steering committee decided that for the third series of dialogues every effort would be made to create a better "mix" in the Pentecostal delegation by inviting theologians, pastors, and denominational leaders. Various Pentecostal denominations with representation from several countries would be invited to send delegates. This has been accomplished with some success in that official representatives have attended the third quinquennium of dialogue from the Apostolic Church of the Faith in Jesus Christ (Mexico), Apostolic Faith Mission of South Africa, Church of God (Cleveland, Tenn.), Church of God of Prophecy, Independent Assemblies of God International, International Church of the Foursquare Gospel, and International Evangelical Church, all of the U.S. Some leaders have attended with the approval of their church—though not necessarily in an official capacity—from the British Isles, the Netherlands, and Sweden.

V. Ecumenical Significance. The cochairman of the dialogue, Kilian McDonnell, has spoken to the question of the ecumenical importance of this dialogue: "One of the more obvious results of this kind of formal dialogue is the death of mythologies." Ignorance on each side about the other is removed and a broader understanding of each other is attained. A further effect of the dialogue will be for Roman Catholics to reevaluate "the personal dimensions of faith." Pentecostals, on the other hand, must see their need to "reevaluate the social dimensions" of the Gospel. Both sides need to "examine typologies of sanctification other than their own." Finally, it is possible that formal dialogue will help both Roman Catholics and classical Pentecostals to rethink their "ecumenical presuppositions." Rome must not think or speak of unity merely in terms of "return." Pentecostals should not be so suspicious of organizations within an ecumenical context (K. McDonnell in Spittler [1976], 246–68).

Not only is the dialogue relevant to Roman Catholics and Pentecostals themselves, but also for the WCC. A first contact of the World Council with participants of the dialogue took place on Pentecost Sunday (1975) in Rome. Seventeen men, of whom thirteen (both Roman Catholic and Pentecostal-charismatic) were members of the dialogue team, met to discuss "steps which might be taken to hold a conference of theologians on the Holy Spirit and also to see how wider relations might be opened up between member churches of the WCC, members of Charismatic Renewal movements and the Pentecostal Churches." The meeting, sponsored by the Commission on Faith and Order's subunit on Renewal and Congregational Life, was led by the Reverend Rex Davis from the WCC. Two recommendations surfaced from this meeting: (1) that the WCC be asked to convene a theological consultation on the experience of the Holy Spirit, including participants from the charismatic renewal, member churches of the WCC, Pentecostal churches, and the Roman Catholic church, and (2) "that as soon as convenient an Ecumenical Congress of the Charismatic Renewal be held to celebrate and experience the theological, pastoral, and community significance of the work of the Holy Spirit in renewal of the church and in our time" ("Memorandum," 1975). Planning meetings were held at Stony Point, New York (Sept. 1978), and at Schloss Schwanberg, Bavaria, West Germany (Dec. 1978), and a "Consultation on the Significance of the Charismatic Renewal for the Churches" in Bossey, Switzerland (March 1980). Results of these meetings have been published by the WCC in A. Bittlinger, editor, *The Church Is Charismatic* (1981).

There were national dialogues that grew out of these sessions. This dialogue directly influenced the start of a Pentecostal dialogue with charismatic renewal in West Germany. In New Zealand a Pentecostal participant was able to initiate an Apostolic Church/Presbyterian dialogue, as well as an Apostolic/Baptist dialogue. In Belgium there have been several meetings between representatives of the Flemish Pentecostal churches and leaders in the Roman Catholic Charismatic Renewal. In South Africa the AFM initiated bilateral dialogue with each of the three branches of the Dutch Reformed Church. The executive council of the AFM voted in August 1981 to create a new position in their church, that of "Ecumenical Liaison." Justus T. du Plessis, the retiring general secretary, was asked in April 1982 to fill this position.

Members of the Pentecostal steering committee for the dialogue have been invited as ecumenical guests to the last three International Leaders' Conferences of the Roman Catholic Charismatic Renewal in Rome (held in 1981, 1984, and 1987).

VI. Evaluation. By 1989 there will have been fifteen sessions of the Roman Catholic/Pentecostal dialogue. Several important lessons have been learned in the process. For example, Roman Catholics are trained in the historical-critical method of biblical exegesis, and the Pentecostals are generally skeptical of this approach. Sometimes the two sides have not understood each other very well when discussing biblical themes, and this has resulted in a diminishing of the exchange. The fact that there is very little doctrinal unity among Pentecostals often complicated the process for Roman Catholics. Second, Roman Catholics came to the dialogue far more experienced at the technique of theological dialogue. For Pentecostals, this is an experience that only a few have learned with skill. Also, it is essential that Pentecostals approach dialogue with Roman Catholics with a thorough acquaintance of the documents of Vatican II. Roman Catholicism must not be interpreted based solely on its pre-Vatican II posture.

Third, Pentecostals often approach theological issues from a personal witness or pastoral dimension. Testimony, oral theology, and narrative approaches are an essential part of Pentecostalism. Roman Catholics, on the other hand, are more gifted in precise theological formulations and are less comfortable with testimony and the sharing of personal thoughts and feelings. This difference in method often led to a lack of clear understanding of the other partner in dialogue. Fourth, Pentecostals generally emphasize spiritual experience, crisis moments of faith, and the *power* of the Holy Spirit. Roman Catholics spoke more of the role of the sacraments, the life of the church, and the Trinitarian dimension of the Holy Spirit. The *crisis* paradigm of sanctification is followed largely by Pentecostals, whereas the *growth* paradigm is the approach of Roman Catholics. Fifth, this dialogue is between a movement (Pentecostals) and a church (Roman Catholicism). It is extremely difficult for Roman Catholics to dialogue with a movement as opposed to a church. For Pentecostals, it is a challenge to integrate the centuries of church history, church councils, and traditions of the Roman Catholic church into a composite whole.

The fruit of this dialogue must not be expected immediately in terms of the unity of the church. If necessary, there must be a commitment to decades of discussion rather than a few years. Great patience is needed. Each side is growing in acceptance, understanding, and respect for the other. Amid all the known differences there have been many surprises of agreement and harmony. One thing is sure: these ecumenical encounters have been lessons in spiritual growth for participants on both sides.

See also CATHOLIC CHARISMATIC RENEWAL; CHARISMATIC MOVEMENT; VATICAN II.

Bibliography: A. Bittlinger, *Papst und Pfingstler: Der römisch katholisch-pfingstliche Dialog und seine ökumenische Relevance* (1978); P. Duprey, "L'Eglise catholique et le dialogue oecumenique," *Episkepsis*, 10, 212 (15 June 1979): 6–16; N. Ehrenstrom and G. Gassman, *Confessions in Dialogue* (1975); M. Harper, *Three Sisters* (1979); *Information Service*, No. 9 (1, 1970): 7; No. 32 (3, 1976): 32–37; No. 55 (2–3, 1984): 72–80; K. McDonnell, "Classical Pentecostal/Roman Catholic Dialogue: Hopes and Possibilities," in R. P. Spittler, ed., *Perspectives on the New Pentecostalism* (1976), 246–68; idem, ed. *Presence, Power, Praise: Documents on the Charismatic Renewal*, 3 vols. (1980); idem, "The Experiential and the Social: New Models From the Pentecostal/Roman Catholic Dialogue," *One in Christ* 9 (1973): 43–58; H. Meyer and L. Vischer, eds., *Growth in Agreement* (1984); *One in Christ*, various issues between 1973–1977, 1983ff; D. du Plessis and B. Slosser, *A Man Called Mr. Pentecost* (1977); J. F. Puglisi and S. J. Voicu, *A Bibliography of Interchurch and Interconfessional Theological Dialogues* (1984); J. L. Sandidge, *Roman Catholic/Pentecostal Dialogue (1977–1982): A Study in Developing Ecumenism* (1987); idem, "Roman Catholic/Pentecostal Dialogue: A Contribution to Christian Unity," *Pnuema* 7 (Spring 1985): 41–60. *Documentation Catholique* (1972–83); *Irenikon* (1972–81); *Service d'information* (1972–81); and *Unité de Chrétiens* (1978–83); "Vatican Enters Dialogue on Pentecostalism," *New Covenant* 7 (1, 1972): 6, 7; "Memorandum of a Meeting Held at the Centro Pro Unione, 30 via St. Maria dell'Anima, Rome, Italy, Tuesday, May 20, 1975" recorded by Rex Davis.
J. L. Sandidge

DIFATO, EDITH (1924–). Cofoundress of the Mother of God community, Gaithersburg, Maryland. Difato, from an Italian-American background in Philadelphia, and the mother of five children, had a sovereign experience of the Lord Jesus in 1966. She soon came to know J. Tydings, who had an almost identical experience around the same time. Difato and Tydings sensed that the Lord was calling them to a mutual commitment, on which he would build a corporate work. After hearing of the outpouring of the Holy Spirit on Catholics at Duquesne and South Bend in 1967, they started in 1968 the first Catholic charismatic prayer meeting on the U.S. East Coast. As this group grew and some Protestants also joined, it developed into the Mother of God community, which now has an international outreach. Difato has combined her life of prayer with extensive prayerful reading of Christian classics, Catholic and Protestant, finding confirmation and wisdom in such writers as Catherine of Siena, Ignatius Loyola, George Müller, Henri Lacordaire, Andrew Murray, Jessie Penn-Lewis, T. Austin-Sparks, and D. M. Lloyd-Jones. She has emphasized that inner revelation is central to baptism in the Spirit and that the object of all revelation is to glorify the incarnate Son of God. In all this Difato has been convinced that community life is essential for a deep appropriation of the gospel and that dedicated communities are for the service of the wider church. She has been a major influence in the monthly *The Word Among Us* and has helped to rework the Life in the Spirit seminars in the Mother of God community to stress the role of the blood of Jesus in the cleansing from all sin and the work of the Cross in putting to death every movement of the flesh within the Christian.
P. D. Hocken

DiORIO, RALPH A. (1930–). Catholic priest with full-time healing ministry. A second-generation Italian-American, DiOrio was ordained priest for the Scalabrini Fathers, a religious order of Italian origin. In 1968 he transferred to the diocese of Worcester, Massachusetts. DiOrio's first contacts with charismatic renewal were in 1976 when he attended healing services led by Fr. Edward McDonough. There he experienced God's power flowing through him for healing, a ministry that developed during two years in St. John's parish, Worcester. In 1979 DiOrio was authorized by his bishop to move his Apostolate of Prayer for Healing Evangelism to Leicester, Massachusetts. DiOrio's main ministry outside his home base is in officially sponsored healing services, both diocesan rallies and parish missions. His story is told in *The Man Beneath the Gift* (1980); his other works include *Called to Heal* (1984), *A Miracle to Proclaim* (1984), and *The Healing Power of Affirmation* (1985).
P. D. Hocken

DISCERNMENT OF SPIRITS, GIFT OF
The expression "discernment of spirits" (*diakriseis pneumatōn*) occurs in the Scriptures only in 1 Corinthians 12:10. Understanding the expres-

sion will be achieved, however, only if viewed in the context of discernment as a whole. This article will discuss, first, general biblical teaching regarding discernment; second, the gift of discernment of spirits; and third, the ways in which this gift has been considered throughout the centuries to today.

I. General considerations.

A. The Old Testament.

1. The Requirements of Faith. Discernment is required, basically, because God calls humankind to a goal beyond itself. The response to this call is faith, a trusting and obedient commitment of oneself to God based on his solemn word of promise. It is imperative that each person, and God's people as a whole, be able to discern God's voice directing him or her to this goal and to distinguish his voice from Satan's or from the illusory desires of the human heart.

2. Discerning Prophecy. A prophet is someone called by God and entrusted with a message for God's people. Since this word reveals God's thoughts concerning his people (Amos 3:7), it is extremely important to be able to distinguish true from false prophecy. The criteria for this discernment were developed particularly in the Deuteronomic tradition and in Jeremiah (Guillet, 1957, 3:1225–26). (1) A prophet who prophesies woe may be believed, but one who prophesies peace must await the fulfillment of his prophecy (Deut. 18:21–22; Jer. 28:8–9). This criterion is modified in the new covenant because of the presence of the fulfillment of all God's promises (see Mark 1:14–15). (2) A true prophet works signs as part of his credentials (Jer. 28:16–17), but this must be accompanied by true doctrine (Deut. 13:1–3), an upright life (Jer. 23:13–15), and a pure intention to proclaim God's word (Mic. 3:5–7). (3) Finally, the criterion to which the prophets themselves make appeal is their personal experience of being called by God (Isa. 6; Jer. 1; Ezek. 1–3; Hos. 1–3; Amos 7:14–15).

3. Discerning the Human Heart. Jeremiah declared the heart "deceitful above all things," "beyond cure" and known only to the Lord (Jer. 17:9–10). The Wisdom tradition applied itself to the work of discerning the ways of the heart and of teaching men how to walk in the light of the "secret purposes of God" (Wis. 2:22). Qumran, despite its dualistic tendency, perpetuated this practical approach in the light of prophetic teaching and was a factor in the Jewish matrix of Christianity which rendered the early Christians sensitive to the need to discern the movements of the heart in order to make a judgment. The *Manual of Discipline* (3:13–14) says that the leader must learn and teach others "the nature of all the children of men according to the kind of spirit they possess, the signs identifying their works," and the ultimate end of their actions. Not only at Qumran, but also elsewhere, we have indications that the Jewish people had been rendered sensitive to the need to look into the human heart to discern its dominant influence.

B. The New Testament.

1. The Synoptic Gospels and Acts. We frequently read of Jesus' discernment in the synoptic Gospels. The better reading of Matthew 9:4 speaks of his "*seeing* the thoughts" of his adversaries, and several texts speak of his knowing their thoughts and interior debates (Mark 2:8/Luke 4:22; Matt. 22:18/Mark 10:21/Luke 20:23; et al.). He not only confronts evil spirits and drives them out, he is able to see behind their strategy of openly acknowledging him to be Son of God in order to discredit him (Mark 1:25/Luke 4:35; Mark 1:34/Luke 4:41).

On another level the very presence of Jesus and his activity of preaching and healing compel his contemporaries to discern: "If by the Spirit/finger of God I cast out demons, then the kingdom of God has come upon you" (Matt. 12:28/Luke 11:20).

Luke portrays the disciples as continuing the above two aspects of Jesus' ministry. Both Peter and Paul are endowed with the capacity to discern what is in the heart: Acts 5:3 (Ananias); 8:23 (Simon); 13:6 (Elymas); 16:16–18 (the girl at Philippi).

The witness of the preaching and of the miracles of the disciples also forces people to discernment: "Know this, you and everyone else in Israel: 'It is by the name of Jesus Christ of Nazareth whom you crucified but whom God raised from the dead, that this man stands before you completely healed'" (Acts 4:10).

2. The Pauline Writings. Paul uses two different verbs to designate what we call "discern"; *dokimazein* (put to the test, evaluate), and *diakrinein* (in the sense which we are considering here, corresponds to our English "differentiate" or "judge as to worth"). Continuing the OT notion of the need for a pure faith in order to discern the call of God, Paul speaks of "evaluating" what God's will is, what is more pleasing to him (Rom. 12:2; Phil. 1:10 et al.). Believers should also evaluate themselves (1 Cor. 11:28), their works (Gal. 4:6), and their faith (2 Cor. 13:5), just as God evaluates them (1 Thess. 2:4; 1 Cor. 3:13; et al.; see also 1 Peter 1:7).

In 1 Corinthians 11:29 Paul speaks of those who eat and drink judgment on themselves, "not discerning [*diakrinōn*] the body of the Lord," and he goes on to say in verse 31 that if we were to judge ourselves as to our worth (*diekrinomen*), we would not be judged (*ekrinometha*). (For the enigmatic Rom. 14:1, one may consult the commentaries.)

3. The Johannine Writings. Except for 1 John 4:1, which we will consider shortly, neither of the two terms characteristic of Paul occurs in the body of writings associated with the name of John. On the other hand, no other NT writings so accent the fact that the presence of Jesus forces people to discern and decide: "For judgment I have come into this world, so that the blind will see and those who see will become blind" (John 9:39). In addition, criteria are offered by which the world will be able to discern the disciples of Jesus: "*By this* will all know that you are my disciples" (John 13:35). In 1 John the disciples themselves are given the signs by which they may know that they have eternal life (1 John 5:13).

4. Summary. The presence and activity of the risen Jesus make the need for faith discernment all the more urgent, and thus the Spirit must help us know what God has given us (see 1 Cor. 2:12). This work of the Spirit will confess Jesus (1 Cor. 12:3; Rev. 19:10), will build up the community (1 Cor. 12:7, 26; 14:4), will produce genuine signs along with the peace, patience, and humility of a true disciple (2 Cor. 12:12; 1 Thess. 1:4–5; Rom. 14:17–18), and by the constant exercise of their faculties under the influence of his gifts, he will enable the mature to discern "good and evil" (Heb. 5:14).

II. The Discernment of Spirits.

A. The Terminology. There are three NT texts speaking of evaluating or discerning in the specific case of prophecy, and the word "spirit" (*pneuma*) occurs in each case. In 1 Thessalonians 5:19–21 Paul says, "Do not extinguish the Spirit; do not despise prophecies; evaluate [*dokimazete*] everything; hold fast to what is good; keep away from every form of evil." Paul is enunciating general norms though he has prophecy in mind in a special way throughout this passage (Bruce, 1982, 125–27). In telling the Thessalonians to "evaluate" everything, he is implying that there is something of great worth in genuine prophecy.

The same two key words occur in 1 John 4:1–3. The writer tells his people not to put faith in "every spirit" but rather to "evaluate the spirits" (*dokimazete ta pneumata*), giving as his reason "because many false prophets have gone out into the world." This same use of "spirit" (*pneuma*) to designate prophecy is found in 2 Thessalonians 2:2. In such cases the presupposition is that the source of what is proclaimed is spiritual but that not everything spiritual is of God. Both the source and the fruits of this spiritual impulse must be tested/evaluated: "Every spirit that confesses that Jesus Christ has come in the flesh is of God" (1 John 4:3). This is the criterion by which true and false prophetic spirits may be distinguished.

The verbal and conceptual constellation in the two previously considered texts throws light on the use of the phrase "discernments of spirits" found in the list of "manifestations" of the Spirit in 1 Corinthians 12:8–10. Many authors have pointed to a certain logic in this list: first, the "words" of wisdom and knowledge; then "faith" and its outworking in healings and miracles; then prophecy and its control, "discernments of spirits"; then tongues and its control, interpretation. Primarily, then, the gift of discernment of spirits is the Spirit-conferred capacity to judge the origin and content of prophecy.

While Paul's immediate concern in this passage is with prophecy, it is legitimate to apply his terminology to the gift of discerning the origin and content of any spiritual manifestation. Under this aspect, any of the gifts can be called a "spirit," which Paul himself does in 1 Corinthians 14:12. The use of *diakrisis* here rather than words related to *dok* was probably dictated by two reasons. First, the capacity Paul emphasizes is distinguishment and judgment rather than testing and evaluating. He retains this terminology in 1 Corinthians 14:29: "Let the others discern [*diakrine-tōsan*]." Second, nouns such as *dokimasia* or *dokimē* refer more to the test itself or its result rather than to the ability to evaluate. The use of

the plural here ("discernments") alludes to the multiple exercise of the gift not only by one person on many occasions but also by the many persons on specific occasions.

B. The Subject and Object of Discernment.

1. The Subject of Discernment. Discernment of spirits as a gift of the Holy Spirit resides in an individual person, yet its exercise is presumed to be collaborative as well. Thus the instructions in 1 Thessalonians 5:21 and 1 John 4:1 are addressed to the whole community, and 1 Corinthians 14:29 speaks of "the others" discerning what the prophets say. The local church, living by the Spirit, is able to recognize his gifts in their midst, including that of discerning spirits. Individuals who possessed this gift in varying degrees would have been expected to make a corporate judgment regarding the source and doctrinal authenticity of prophecy and other gifts. This is the most probable meaning of the enigmatic statement in 1 Corinthians 14:32 that the *pneumata* (spiritual activities) of the prophets are subject to the prophets (who discern).

2. The Object of Discernment. The answer to the question of what is discerned may be brief. As in the OT, the two primary areas of discernment are the origin of prophecy (and other spiritual manifestations), and the movements of the human heart. Discernment differs from prudence in that, although the criteria of love, service, peace, order, etc. are important corroborations of discernment, its essence lies in being able to make out the *source* of spiritual activity (Martin, 1971, 18:58). Each person must accordingly judge him/herself (1 Cor. 11:28, 31), and those who have the gift and spiritual authority must also discern those spiritual manifestations that affect the life of the community.

III. Discernment of Spirits in the History of the Church.

While not ignoring the role of discerning spiritual manifestations in others, most early Christian teaching on discernment of spirits dealt with identifying the source of movements within the individual heart. The possible sources are four: God, an angel, oneself, or an evil spirit. Basing themselves on the list of "thoughts" (*dialogismoi*) in Mark 7:21–22, the Christians of the first four centuries developed a very refined spiritual anthropology that has formed the basis of personal discernment to our own day (Bardy et al., 1957, 3:1247–81).

The age of enlightenment with its "closed system" of thinking tended even in religious circles to reduce discernment to prudence or character evaluation. With the abundant reappearance of spiritual manifestations, the true role of discernment has become once again apparent. Because the Spirit of God moves in the human heart, bestowing his gifts, especially that of prophecy, and because these can be counterfeited by Satan and by the human spirit, we see the need once again to pray for the gift of the discernment of spirits so that we may know "those things given to us by God" (1 Cor. 2:12).

See also GIFTS OF THE SPIRIT; PAULINE LITERATURE.

Bibliography: G. Bardy, F. Vandenbroucke, and J. Pegon, "Discernement des Ésprits," *Dictionnaire de Spiri-*

tualité (1957), 3:1247–81; A. Bittlinger, *Gifts and Graces. A Commentary on 1 Corinthians 12–14* (1967); F. F. Bruce, *1 & 2 Thessalonians* (1982); J. D. G. Dunn, *Jesus and the Spirit* (1975); G. D. Fee, *The First Epistle to the Corinthians* (1987); J. Guillet, "Discernment des Esprits. Dans l'Ecriture," *Dictionnaire de Spiritualité* (1957), 3:1222–47; A. Linford, *A Course of Study on Spiritual Gifts*, 2d ed. (n.d.). F. Martin, "Le discernment communautaire," *Animation spirituelle de la communauté, Collection "Donum Dei," Cahiers de la CRC* (1971), 18:45–63.   R. F. Martin

DISCIPLESHIP MOVEMENT   See SHE-
PHERDING MOVEMENT.

DISPENSATIONALISM   Dispensationalism
has not been part of the major theological traditions of Reformed and Wesleyan Christianity, though many of its advocates get their general orientation from one of these traditions. Nevertheless, the dispensational system has had a strong influence in the church and is widespread. It was popularized by John Nelson Darby's commentaries and has entered into millions of homes by the *Scofield Reference Bible* (1909). The system has been advocated by such prominent educational institutions as Moody Bible Institute and Dallas Theological Seminary. Lewis Sperry Chafer, the founder of Dallas Theological Seminary, claims that his eight-volume *Systematic Theology* (1948) has the distinction of being unabridged, premillennial, and dispensational. The grafting of dispensationalism to the traditional body of Christian doctrine does make Chafer's work a different kind of theological system.

The interpretation of dispensationalism varies, but its basic assumption is that God deals with the human race in successive dispensations. According to the *Scofield Reference Bible*, "A dispensation is a period of time during which man is tested in respect to his obedience to some specific revelation of the will of God" (p. 5). Each dispensation has its point of beginning, its test, and its termination in judgment due to humanity's continual failure. Some interpreters identify as many as seven—namely, the dispensations of innocence, conscience, civil government, promise, law, grace, and the kingdom.

Dispensationalism has influenced Pentecostal theology, but the earliest Pentecostal teachings were not tied directly to dispensationalism. From its inception the modern Pentecostal movement gave prominence to eschatology. Gerald T. Sheppard makes this point in his observation: "Pentecostals commonly thought of the twentieth century outpouring of the Spirit as evidence of the 'latter rain' or at least as a sign of a 'last days' restoration of the Apostolic church prior to the return of Christ" (1984, 7). A strong eschatological perspective permeated the revival in 1901 in Topeka, Kansas, and in 1906–09 at Azusa Street, Los Angeles. O. W. Orwig, who attended some of the Azusa Street meetings, recalled a decade later the principal themes of Pentecostal preaching at the revival as:

the teaching that the baptism in the Spirit was upon the sanctified, evidenced by speaking in tongues, however brief, as on the day of Pentecost. . . . The subject or doctrine, of divine healing received special attention. . . . Likewise was the doctrine of the premillennial coming of Christ ardently promulgated" (*The Weekly Evangel* [March 18, 1986], 4).

Charles F. Parham, the leader of the Pentecostal revival at Topeka, affirms also that the prevailing mood of premillennialism was at the very heart of early Pentecostalism (1985, 47–61).

Dispensationalism began to flourish with the rise of the Pentecostal movement. Since Pentecostals as a whole shared the premillennial vision of the future, dispensationalism with its intense emphasis on futuristic eschatology had a strong appeal to them. The statements of faith of Pentecostal denominations such as the Church of God (Cleveland, Tenn.), the Pentecostal Holiness Church, and the Assemblies of God commit them to premillennialism but not necessarily to dispensationalism. It has, however, been an easy exercise for many Pentecostals to adopt essential aspects of the Scofieldian dispensational system because it provides a convenient method of organizing biblical history and teaches that it is possible to fit the full range of prophetic Scripture into something like a complicated puzzle.

Nevertheless, the marriage of the Pentecostal emphasis to dispensationalism was strange in light of the dispensational assertion that the gifts of the Spirit, especially what has been called "the sensational gifts" or "sign gifts" (healing, faith, working of miracles, and tongues), were confined to the apostolic age. The dispensational teaching of the Scofieldian type that denies the possibility of a modern Pentecostal experience has been glossed over with minor Pentecostal adaptations, to allow for the continuation of all the spiritual gifts in the church today. Such accommodations have been made by Pentecostals who saw the dispensational system as a helpful aid to emphasizing the premillennial second coming of Christ, the rapture of the church, the seven years of Great Tribulation, the Millennium, and the cataclysmic judgment of the present order.

Scofieldian dispensationalism maintains that the gifts of the Spirit, such as speaking in tongues and working of miracles, are not for the postapostolic age and that they should be forbidden because God no longer bestows such gifts. Pentecostals have taken exception to the dispensational teaching that "sign gifts" or "sensational gifts" granted to the apostolic church were temporary; nevertheless the dispensational understanding of the church as well as eschatology has influenced Pentecostal theology. Dispensationalism teaches that the people of God in the OT are completely unrelated to the church in the NT. The OT prophets, however, did see a relationship.

For a number of years a standard textbook in a number of Pentecostal Bible institutes and colleges was Myer Pearlman's *Knowing the Doctrines of the Bible* (1937). Pearlman's exposition of eschatology fits the dispensational vision of the future, but he does not make a sharp separation between Israel and the church. Contrary to dispensationalism, he sees real continuity between the congregation of Israel and the Christian church (pp. 348–49). Like Pearlman, other

Pentecostal writers, such as George L. Britt, Ralph M. Riggs, E. S. Williams, A. A. Ledford, and Ray H. Hughes, depend on a dispensational posture in both eschatology and ecclesiology (*Ages and Dispensations* [1949]). In agreement with the dispensational hermeneutic, Pearlman interprets some sections of the Bible as dealing with the nation of Israel and some others as being concerned with only the church. On the assumption that the church began at Pentecost he argues against calling Israel the "church" and never describes the church as "spiritual Israel" or "new Israel."

In recent years there has been less dependency among Pentecostal scholars on the dispensational system. Excellent examples of this are two books on eschatology: Stanley Horton, *The Promise of His Coming* (1967) and R. Hollis Gause, *Revelation: God's Stamp of Sovereignty on History* (1983). Both of these scholars are premillennial, but neither is dispensational. The term "dispensation" does not appear in Horton's book, and Gause affirms progressive revelation that does not make the dispensational divisions of biblical history. Neither does Gause distinguish between the church and Israel, but he sees the character of God and the character of salvation as progressively revealed.

See also DAKE, FINIS JENNINGS; ESCHATOLOGY, PENTECOSTAL PERSPECTIVES ON; HERMENEUTICS, HISTORICAL PERSPECTIVES ON PENTECOSTAL AND CHARISMATIC; SCOFIELD REFERENCE BIBLE.

Bibliography: C. W. Buxton, *What About Tomorrow?* (1974); L. S. Chafer, *Systematic Theology* (1948); D. P. Fuller, *Gospel and Law: Contrast or Continuum?* (1980); W. C. Meloon, *We've Been Robbed* (1971); C. C. Ryrie, *Dispensationalism Today* (1965); G. T. Sheppard, "Pentecostals and the Hermeneutics of Dispensationalism: The Anatomy of an Uneasy Relationship," *Pneuma* (Fall 1984), 5–31; G. F. Taylor, *The Second Coming of Jesus* (1950).   F. L. Arrington

DIVINE HEALING See HEALING MOVEMENTS;HEALING, GIFT OF.

DOOR OF FAITH CHURCHES OF HAWAII A small Pentecostal denomination resulting from the missionary work of Mildred Johnson (later Brostek), who was sent to the Hawaiian Islands by the Pentecostal Holiness Church (PHC) in 1936. After Johnson married an army officer, she left the PHC and established the Door of Faith in 1940 as an independent ministry. In 1987, with the seventy-six-year-old Brostek still leading the organization, the ministry in Hawaii reported forty churches, three thousand members, and a Bible School. In addition, there are ordained ministers serving in Canada, Singapore, Japan, the Philippines, New Zealand, Indonesia, Okinawa, and Mexico. Brostek was in Honolulu when Pearl Harbor was bombed and remained during the war.

Bibliography: R. Donavan, *Her Door of Faith, The Lifestory of Mildred Johnson Brostek* (1971); C. Jones, *Guide to the Pentecostal Movement* (1983).
                    W. E. Warner

DOUGLAS, JOHN ELWOOD Missions executive. John E. Douglas, Sr., is director of World Missionary Evangelism, Inc. (WME), an organization that was founded in 1958 and is dedicated to supporting "thousands of children in Children's Homes, Food for Hunger Centers, schools and day care centers, besides mission farms and vocational training for children." Activities and programs are in progress in Mexico, Nicaragua, Guatemala, Haiti, Philippines, Indonesia, Korea, Nepal, Bangladesh, India, Kenya, Nigeria, Ethiopia, Costa Rica, and Uganda (*WE*, 1988, 15).

WME activities are organized around a "12 Point Program of Love": orphan homes—over two hundred are in operation; Christian schools—operating in every country where WME is active; special homes—serving handicapped children; Save-a-Child Club—providing food, clothing, and free education for children in very poor families; medical clinics; emergency relief; national ministers; tools for evangelism—e.g., bicycles and public address systems; churches—over two thousand have been built and water wells; preaching conventions; literature; and radio ministry.

Douglas's ministry began after his conversion under A. A. Allen's preaching. For several years he worked with Allen, and then in 1958 he worked with Juanita Coe.

Bibliography: J. E. Douglas, Sr., ed., *WE* 29 (6, 1987): 3, 8–9; 30 (1, 1988): 15; D. E. Harrell, Jr., *All Things Are Possible* (1975).   J. A. Hewett

John Alexander Dowie became a strong proponent of divine healing at the turn of the 20th century and established Zion City, Illinois, as a religious community.

DOWIE, JOHN ALEXANDER (1847–1907). Faith healer, founder of Zion City, Illinois, and the Christian Catholic Church. Dowie—who became a prominent advocate of heal-

The white building is Dowie's Shiloh Tabernacle which seated nearly 8,000. The smaller building on the right is the Zion radio station WCBD which went on the air in 1923.

ing—was a sickly child. When he was thirteen his family migrated to Australia, where he began to earn his living. At the age of twenty he decided to enter the ministry and began to prepare for the university. In 1848 he left Australia for Edinburgh University, where he studied at the Free Church School. After three years, Dowie returned to Australia. On April 1, 1872, he accepted a call to the Congregational Church in Alma. The next year he took a church in Manly Beach. In 1875 he moved again, this time to a church in the Sydney suburb of Newton. There, he later claimed, he became convinced of the practical message of divine healing.

On May 26, 1876, Dowie married his cousin, Jean. In 1878 he left the Congregational Church and launched an independent ministry, first in Sydney and later in Melbourne. After an unsuccessful try for a seat in the Australian parliament, Dowie gained notoriety for his stubborn opposition to the liquor traffic. During the 1880s he also renewed his focus on healing.

Dowie and his wife and their two children (William Gladstone and Esther) migrated to the U.S. in 1888. After two years of itinerant healing evangelism, which took him to many parts of the country, Dowie established a base of operations in Evanston, Illinois, in 1890. During the 1893 Chicago World's Fair, he conducted meetings across the street from popular attractions, and his ministry began to grow as people testified to healings. He started a publication, *Leaves of Healing,* and opened a divine healing home in Chicago. Local controversy only increased his audiences. Soon several homes and an enlarged publishing effort took shape, and Dowie began conducting services in his spacious Zion Tabernacle. In 1895 Dowie organized his followers into the Christian Catholic Church.

Intensely evangelistic, Dowie stressed consecration and holiness and welcomed participation from blacks and women. The primary focus of his work, however, was healing. Dowie insisted that those who sought his prayers relinquish all medicine and, instead, exercise faith. He also demanded that his followers abstain from use of all pork products. Stubborn and aggressive, Dowie

seemed to welcome conflict: over the years, his sharp criticism alienated virtually every other significant American exponent of divine healing.

In 1900 Dowie unveiled plans for a religious community that would be molded by his own views of what a holy society should be. The community—known as Zion City and located north of Chicago on Lake Michigan—grew to approximately six thousand persons during the next few years. Dowie, meanwhile, became increasingly eccentric. He reasserted his restorationist hopes and announced in 1901 that he was the prophesied Elijah, the Restorer. In 1904 he told his followers to anticipate the full restoration of apostolic Christianity and revealed that he had been divinely commissioned the first apostle of a renewed end-times church.

In September 1905, as Dowie prepared to announce plans for the planting of Zions in other areas, he suffered a stroke. This followed several major confrontations with critics, first in New York during a much heralded visitation in 1903, then in Australia, where his attacks on the vices of the reigning British monarch gained international press attention. While traveling in the interests of both his health and his Zion in 1906, he lost control of his community. Individuals there had suffered severely as a result of financial mismanagement. He died in 1907, disgraced and ignored by most of the thousands who had acclaimed him.

Dowie's end-time expectations, his message of divine healing, and his restorationist vision made him an important forerunner of Pentecostalism. Many of his followers accepted Pentecostal views; some became prominent leaders in a movement that regarded itself as an end-time restoration. Most Pentecostal leaders with roots in Zion affiliated with the Assemblies of God. Some, however, more committed to a thoroughgoing restorationism, moved on into Oneness Pentecostalism.

See also HEALING MOVEMENTS.

Bibliography: G. Lindsay, *John Alexander Dowie* (reprinted 1980); G. Wacker, "Marching to Zion," *Church History* 54 (December 1985): 496–511.
                                                                E. L. Blumhofer

DRAPER, MINNIE TINGLEY (1858–

1921). Faith healer and missions executive. Although born in Waquit, Massachusetts, Minnie T. Draper grew up in Ossining, New York. She never married and for a time supported herself and her mother through teaching. A Presbyterian, she faithfully attended a local church.

The strain of overwork broke Draper's health, and for four years she lived as an invalid. Physicians were consulted but could not relieve her suffering. Hearing about the doctrine of faith healing, she was anointed with oil and prayed for at A. B. Simpson's Gospel Tabernacle in New York City. Miraculous healing followed, and at the same time, the Lord also "definitely sanctified and anointed her with the Holy Ghost and power" (Lucas, 1921, 3). Convinced, as a result, that Christ is the Healer for every believer, she never again went to a physician or took any form of medicine.

Successful evangelistic work followed Draper's healing, and for many years she served as an associate of A. B. Simpson, assisting him in conventions that were held at Rock Springs, Pennsylvania; New York City; and Old Orchard, Maine.

Prayer for the sick is what Draper is best remembered for. However, she also chaired various committees and served for several years as a member of the executive board of the Christian and Missionary Alliance (CMA) until it was reorganized in 1912.

When news of Pentecostal happenings reached Draper in 1906, she was initially cautious. At the same time, however, she earnestly desired a deeper work of the Spirit in her own life. One night in her room the Lord appeared to her and "hours elapsed wherein she saw unutterable things and when she finally came to herself she heard her tongue talking fluently in a language she had never learned" (Lucas, 1921, 3).

Draper identified with Pentecostal believers and participated in the development of several important ministry enterprises. She assisted in the organization of at least two churches: the Bethel Pentecostal Assembly, Newark, New Jersey (c. 1907), and the Ossining Gospel Assembly, Ossining, New York (1913). She remained in the CMA until 1913.

Draper's greatest achievements in Pentecostalism resulted from her involvement with the Bethel Pentecostal Assembly of Newark. In 1910 the executive council of the Bethel Pentecostal Assembly, Inc., organized "to maintain and conduct a general evangelistic work in the State of New Jersey, in all other states of the United States and any and all foreign countries" (McGee, 1986, 4). People often referred to the council as the "Bethel Board." Draper served as president of the board until her death in 1921, even though she was a member of the Ossining church.

Most of the institutions founded by the board, the Pentecostal Mission in South and Central Africa (1910), and the Bethel Bible Training School (1916), remained independent due to a restriction in the constitution and bylaws. The Newark congregation joined the Assemblies of God in 1953.

Bibliography: C. J. Lucas, "In Memoriam," *FGMH* (April 1921), 3; G. B. McGee, "Three Notable Women in Pentecostal Ministry," *AG Heritage* 1 (1986): 3–5, 12, 16.
                                                                       G. B. McGee

DU PLESSIS, DAVID JOHANNES (1905–

87). South African born (but naturalized American) ecumenical and international Pentecostal spokesman. The oldest of nine sons of David J. and Anna C. du Plessis, he was born on February 7, 1905, in a town called Twenty-four Rivers that is near Cape Town at the far southwestern tip of Africa. Of Huguenot stock, his parents were religious people who became Pentecostals under the influence of John G. Lake and Thomas Hezmalhalch. These were turn-of-the-century missionaries from John Alexander Dowie's mission in Zion City, Illinois. They also had connections with the Azusa Street Mission. David's father was a carpenter and a sometime lay preacher. In 1916 the senior du Plessis family moved to Basutoland (since 1966 known as Lesotho), an enclave for tribal blacks. There, until the family moved to Ladybrand in 1917, the carpenter assisted missionaries in the construction of a mission compound. While there, du Plessis in his twelfth year was deeply impressed with the joyfulness of the blacks all about the mission compound. His conversion, as he tells it in *A Man Called Mr. Pentecost* (1977), came in 1916 during a sudden severe storm en route back to the compound from a mail run to a distant town. Water baptism came the next year, under the auspices of the Apostolic Faith Mission (AFM), the South African church of his parents in which he was to serve until 1947. In 1918, at about thirteen years of age, he was baptized in the Holy Spirit at meetings held by an English evangelist, Charles Heatley, in a coffin warehouse.

While du Plessis remembers his mother as a compassionate peacemaker, he recalls his father as a stern disciplinarian. Following early Pentecostal practice not limited to South Africa, the elder du Plessis forbade the use of medicine and consultation of physicians in his family, not even for plagued cattle, whose needless deaths led to a brief imprisonment (that ended when a friend paid the fine). When David du Plessis went off to Grey University in Bloemfontein for a few years of college training, his father—disturbed over the son's involvement with education—voluntarily surrendered his lay preacher's license, overwhelmed by a sense of paternal failure. In addition, because of the prohibitive distance and because he thought his son—at age twenty-two—too young to marry, the father did not attend David's wedding and refused to welcome his bride until after the birth of their first child, when a reconciliation occurred.

In an oft-told story, when a visiting missionary asked for donkeys to use in mission work, the senior du Plessis brought young David by the ear to the platform and presented the embryonic ecumenist as "David the Donkey," lacking a suitable animal. Characteristically, du Plessis in later years spoke of the "D. D." given him by his father in that episode—which was in fact a sincere act of devotion on the part of his father.

Known affectionately as "Mr. Pentecost," David J. du Plessis was reared in South Africa but later moved to the U.S. and joined the Assemblies of God. His work with ecumenical groups brought both acclaim and criticism. ©

As a young pastor, du Plessis was asked to speak with a woman named Anna Cornelia Jacobs, who had absented herself from church meetings over a minor misunderstanding. She was restored, but what is more, they married on August 13, 1927, and their marriage lasted just short of sixty years. Seven children were born to this marriage: Anna Cornelia (1928–), Eunice Elizabeth (March–December 1932), David Johannes, Jr. (1933–1985), Philip Richelieu (1940–), Peter Louis le Roux (1944–), Matthew Kriel (1947–), and Basel Somerset (1949–). (du Plessis' mother, wife, and only surviving daughter were all named Anna Cornelia.) Both David and his wife became naturalized citizens of the U.S. in 1968.

The earliest ministry in the AFM found du Plessis a teenage street preacher. At age fifteen, he undertook an apprenticeship in the denominational printery, a move that took him out of the family home in Ladybrand to Johannesburg. His stay there was short-lived, and du Plessis returned home to undertake college study first at Ladybrand and later at Bloemfontein. In the middle 1920s, seeking fulfillment of his call to full-time ministry, du Plessis variously served part-time and full-time pastoral roles (including a period of employment at the railway) in the cities of Benoni, DeAar, and Pretoria. He was ordained April 11, 1930, at the age of twenty-five.

By age thirty du Plessis played a leading role in

the AFM, the strongest Pentecostal church in South Africa. He edited *Comforter/Trooster,* the bilingual house organ of the denomination. Placing second in the election for general secretary of the AFM in 1932, he won that spot in 1936 and kept it until he resigned in 1947 for the first steps in what was to become a global ministry.

Apart from brief trips abroad, du Plessis remained in South Africa through the Depression years and World War II until 1947. During these years he operated the denominational bookroom and edited the denominational periodical *Comforter,* which had fallen into bad times. Du Plessis was active in an effort in 1935 to merge the AFM with a group known as the "Full Gospel Church" (in which his wife had grown up). The merger effort was abortive, and the Full Gospel group fell into a relationship with the American Church of God (Cleveland, Tenn.)—a denominational fellowship with which du Plessis was to spend his earliest years in America. Drawing on personal experience during a 1937 visit to America, du Plessis introduced the camp meeting to his church. By 1940–41, he was involved in Bible school work. Among his administrative accomplishments were the creation of a retirement system for ministers through the use of a mandated tithe from all ministers; he also was responsible for the purchase of a campground, the establishment of an orphanage, and the construction of denominational offices. Through the later war years, du Plessis led in the reorganization of the AFM constitution. The revision was published in the March 1946 issue of the *Comforter.*

It was during this South African period, actually at the annual AFM conference at Johannesburg on December 13–20, 1936, that from an illiterate English evangelist—he could not read road signs—du Plessis heard a prophecy that was to guide him over the next fifty years. Smith Wigglesworth had been commended by British Pentecostal leader Donald Gee to du Plessis, following the evangelist's successful meetings in Australia and New Zealand. Du Plessis was his interpreter for Afrikaans congregations. The prophecy itself grew over the years, and it was reinterpreted (details: Robinson, 85–91). An account of it was not published until 1964, though a privately printed tract by du Plessis in 1951 referred to the prophecy. But the gist of the inspired words abruptly announced to du Plessis by Wigglesworth was that the South African would find himself giving witness in the remote parts of the world—provided only that du Plessis would remain obedient and faithful to the Lord. Du Plessis often recalled that the evangelist at the time specifically prayed for the continued health of the budding ecumenist.

The war's end brought travel opportunity. Already at the 1937 General Council of the Assemblies of God (AG) in Memphis, Tennessee, du Plessis (who with others, including Donald Gee, had been invited by general secretary J. Rosewell Flower), had discussed possible worldwide joint efforts of Pentecostals. Du Plessis knew many Pentecostals through the publications he exchanged for his own in an effort to keep up with global Pentecostalism. Scandinavian Pentecostals, perennial foes of any formal organization outside the local church, hosted a European conference in Stockholm in 1939 to thwart the unitive tendencies they feared.

The first Pentecostal World Conference (PWC) was held in Zurich during May 1947. Du Plessis obtained a leave of absence from his AFM secretarial post and arrived a week ahead of time. Swiss Pentecostal pastor Leonard Steiner was the organizing secretary. When AFM leaders refused Steiner's request to extend du Plessis' leave of absence, du Plessis took the bold and prophetic step of resigning as their general secretary—an office he had formally held a dozen years (1935–47). In 1947 he sent a cable to Anna with the direction to sell all and come to Basel, where du Plessis would provide leadership in the forthcoming PWCs.

Du Plessis served as organizing secretary for the PWC for nearly a decade, from its 1949 meeting in Paris to its 1958 gathering in Toronto. He resigned after the 1952 London meeting but was requested again to serve following the 1955 Stockholm conference.

A fully supported office in Switzerland to serve the worldwide Pentecostal movement did not materialize, owing to the diversity and regional interests that marked global Pentecostalism. By August 1948 du Plessis left for America. There he worked to facilitate the formation of the Pentecostal Fellowship of North America—an event that occurred in October 1948 as du Plessis lay critically injured in a Beckley, West Virginia, hospital—the result of a severe auto-train accident while traveling with Church of God pastor Paul Walker.

Between 1949 and 1951, du Plessis taught at Lee College, the Church of God school in Cleveland, Tennessee. During 1952–54, du Plessis worked with the Far East Broadcasting Company. By 1952 he had moved his family to Stamford, Connecticut, where for a year he served as interim pastor at the Stamford Gospel Tabernacle (AG) in that city. For that reason, he affiliated in 1955 with the American AG as one of its ordained ministers (though he never relinquished his ordination with the South African AFM). Between 1956 and 1959 he lived in Dallas, where he was the organizing secretary for Gordon Lindsay's Voice of Healing Fellowship.

For du Plessis, the 1950s opened with efforts at uniting world Pentecostals. As that decade closed, increasingly he became involved in the ecumenical movement. While in Stamford, he was moved to visit WCC offices, uninvited and unannounced, in New York City. Hearing some hard words for Latin American Pentecostals from John Mackay, president of Princeton Seminary, du Plessis wrote to Mackay, and the two became friends. Mackay was du Plessis' gate into organized ecumenism. As president of the International Missionary Council, Mackay brought du Plessis to the 1952 meeting at Willigen, West Germany, and had him address the 210 delegates. Probably because of du Plessis' interviews with more than half of the global ecclesiastical representatives, most of whom had never seen a rational Pentecostal, he there earned the title "Mr. Pentecost."

At Willingen, W. A. Visser t' Hooft invited du Plessis to the 1954 World Council Assembly at Evanston, Illinois. By 1959 du Plessis was giving lectures at major theological centers—Princeton, Yale, Union, Colgate, Bossey, and others. He was received by three Roman Catholic pontiffs—John XXIII, Paul VI, and John Paul II.

Although around 1960 du Plessis' favor rose in the ecumenical world, his ministry increasingly drew the ire of the Pentecostal denominational establishment. By 1960 a changed situation in Pentecostal history aggravated the uneasiness of his peers. In May of that year, Dennis Bennett, an Episcopal priest serving in Van Nuys, California, at a Sunday morning service declared that he had received the baptism in the Holy Spirit and had spoken in tongues. The charismatic movement was born. Du Plessis blessed it; establishment Pentecostals were in turn bewildered, angered, and hostile.

Meanwhile, the North American Pentecostal establishment luxuriated in its postwar acceptance among Evangelicals. In 1961 Thomas F. Zimmerman, who in 1959 had become general superintendent of the AG, was returned for a second year to the post of elected president of the National Association of Evangelicals.

It was an era that completed the evangelicalization of Pentecostalism. In 1961, the only change (other than the rearrangement of the original seventeen into sixteen points) ever made to the Statement of Fundamental Truths of the AG was accomplished under Zimmerman's leadership. The added elements were evangelical accents: the virgin birth, deity, and sinlessness of Jesus—items too widely assumed to have been expressed when the 1916 Statement was crafted.

An editorial in the *United Evangelical Action* (June 1961, 28ff.), house organ of the NAE, protested du Plessis' coziness with the World Council of Churches (WCC), particularly objecting to his reputation in ecumenical circles as a spokesperson for the Pentecostal movement—while in fact he had no official authority. Clearly embarrassing was the circulation of a minister of the AG, widely noted in the religious press, within World Council and National Council circles when the chief executive officer of the Assemblies of God was the elected president of the rival NAE. Out of this environment emerged a demand for du Plessis to cease and desist from such ecumenical ministry. Du Plessis sought counsel from a hundred friends, asking advice on whether to quit the ecumenical circle. He interpreted their response to mean he should by no means forsake this emerging acceptance among ecumenists. Declining a request to withdraw, he was—in 1962—asked to surrender his credentials as an ordained minister of the AG. He retained membership, however, in the First Assembly of God, Oakland, California, where he and his family had moved in 1954. From 1962 until 1980, when he was reinstated as an ordained minister, du Plessis served as an uncredentialed and unofficial Pentecostal ambassador-at-large.

This period saw du Plessis' increasing participation in ecumenical events. While both du Plessis and Donald Gee were invited to the WCC Third

Assembly at New Delhi, Gee declined in deference to the concerns of Pentecostal brethren. But du Plessis went, revealing their contrasting styles. By invitation of Augustin Cardinal Bea, he was an invited guest at the third session of Vatican II (1963–65). He attended all six assemblies of the WCC, from Amsterdam (1948) to Vancouver (1983), that were convened during his lifetime.

The crown of his ecumenical achievements lay in the development of the Roman Catholic–Pentecostal Dialogue, one of a wide series of discussions with "separated brethren" begun as a result of Vatican II. Efforts to enter formal dialogue with the North American establishment churches of Pentecostalism were unsuccessful, largely because frontier Pentecostal missionary enterprises, especially in Latin America, reflected conflict between Pentecostal missionaries and local Roman Catholic clerics. The churches could not politically afford to engage in friendly discussion with those who, according to distressing field reports, so strongly opposed their missionaries.

With official dialogue thus impossible, coupled with du Plessis' rising role as "Mr. Pentecost," a proposal emerged to draw together a surrogate group of representative Pentecostal leaders who would speak *as* Pentecostals when it was not feasible to engage those who would speak *for* the Pentecostal movement. (Initial explorations for what became the International Roman Catholic–Pentecostal Dialogue were made actually by the Reverend Ray Bringham, a charismatic leader earlier associated with the Church of God [Anderson, Ind.].) Benedictine monk Fr. Kilian McDonnell, an authority on Protestant theology and a consultant to the Vatican's Secretariat for Promoting Christian Unity, solicited the aid of David du Plessis in constructing such a dialogue. McDonnell and du Plessis served as cochairpersons of the first ten sessions (1972–82), after which Justus du Plessis succeeded his older brother as cochair for the Pentecostal team.

At the invitation of the joint faculties of Fuller Theological Seminary in Pasadena, California, du Plessis formally donated to the seminary his papers and personal library. An archive was established. For the final two years of his life, du Plessis served the seminary as Resident Consultant for Ecumenical Affairs and supervised the sorting of his papers and library. During routine gall bladder surgery in August 1986, inoperable abdominal cancer was discovered. He died in 1987 at Pasadena, a week short of his eighty-second birthday, and is buried (and with him the cremains of David, Jr.) at Mountain View Cemetery in the adjacent city of Altadena, California.

For all his editorial and organizing work in South Africa and with the PWC, du Plessis—true to his Pentecostal tradition—left no tightly argued theological writings. Two of his three published volumes (*Mr. Pentecost* [1977] and *Simple and Profound* [1986]) were actually written by others following extensive interviews. *The Spirit Bade Me Go* (1961, 1970) is a collection of miscellaneous writings, whose periodic revision clearly reflected historical currents in his ministry.

Du Plessis preferred to consider "speaking in tongues" a consequence—rather than "the evidence"—of the coming of the Spirit. Asked if one *had* to speak in tongues as a sign of the Holy Spirit's baptism, he would reply: "You *must* not; but you *will*." Gifts of healing, he taught, were given to the sick and not to the evangelists who prayed for them. The gift of interpretation, in his view, could be identified with thoughts that came after a glossolalic address. And he was never content with the jargon "message in tongues," which he repeatedly exposed as unbiblical terminology. Speaking in tongues was always addressed to God, not to humans. And more often than not, he said, it was prophecy and not "interpretation" that followed glossolalic outbursts in Pentecostal assemblies. In his practical wisdom, he counseled scores of newly Spirit-baptized charismatics to stay in their churches—to the unending consternation of establishment Pentecostals. He stood firm for "the ecumenicity of the Holy Spirit." He exemplified in his own life the virtues and values of forgiveness, and his simple lifestyle was in stunning contrast to the opulence of certain highly visible Pentecostal televangelists.

No stranger to controversy, du Plessis never outgrew the conviction formed in the 1920s to the 1940s that South African apartheid was a workable scheme, given social realities. Nor was he thanked by many of his Pentecostal peers for favorable comment on the apparitions of Mary reported at Medjugorje in Yugoslavia—which he personally visited. Clearly his confrontational behavior often proved irksome to ecclesiastics, as does that of prophets of any age.

Even apart from his leadership in the Roman Catholic–Pentecostal Dialogue, the PWC, the charismatic movement as a whole, du Plessis' catalytic role affected a wide range of Pentecostal institutions: the Full Gospel Business Men's Fellowship International, Women's Aglow, the Pentecostal Fellowship of North America, and the Society for Pentecostal Studies. Predictably, all of these were multidenominational in character.

No one in the twentieth century so effectively linked three of the major movements of the time—the Pentecostal movement, the ecumenical movement, and the charismatic movement. *Time* magazine (September 9, 1974, 66) reported the choice of seven editors of religious publications for the leading "shapers and shakers" of Christianity. Du Plessis was among them, along with people like Billy Graham, Hans Küng, Jürgen Moltmann, and Rosemary Ruether (the editors had eliminated Cesar Chavez, Harvey Cox, Norman Vincent Peale, and Oral Roberts). Kilian McDonnell spoke of du Plessis as "a national treasure." In 1976 St. John's University in Collegeville, Minnesota, presented to him the prized Pax Christi award, clear evidence of his high repute in Roman Catholic circles. He was the first non–Roman Catholic ever to have received (in 1983) the distinguished Benemerenti award, presented on the pope's behalf by Jan Cardinal Willebrands. In 1978 du Plessis received an honorary doctorate from Bethany Bible College (Santa Cruz, Calif.). His example, his wry and rabbinic teaching style—if not his consistent logic—inspired hundreds of younger Pentecostal leaders and subtly molded the emerging theology of a major force in Christendom. For the twentieth century at least, he was indeed "Mr. Pentecost."

Bibliography: Though no definitive biography exists, many details are given in Martin Robinson's Ph.D. thesis "To the Ends of the Earth: The Pilgrimage of an Ecumenical Pentecostal, David J. du Plessis (1905–1987)," University of Birmingham, 1987. Selected facts appear in the autobiography ("as told to Bob Slosser") *A Man Called Mr. Pentecost: David du Plessis* (1977) as well as within du Plessis' two other published works, *The Spirit Bade Me Go* (rev. and enlarged, 1970) and *Simple and Profound* (1986). Du Plessis' role in the Roman Catholic–Pentecostal dialogue emerges in J. L. Sandidge, "Roman Catholic-Pentecostal Dialog: A Contribution to Christian Unity," *Pneuma* 7(1985): 41–61. Details of the first five years: A. Bittlinger, *Papst und Pfingstler: Der römisch katholisch-pfingstliche Dialog und seine ökumenische Relevanz* (1978). The second five years: J. L. Sandidge, *Roman Catholic/Pentecostal Dialog [1977–1982]: A Study in Developing Ecumenism* (1987). The personal papers of David du Plessis are housed in an archive at Fuller Theological Seminary in Pasadena, California.   R. P. Spittler

DU PLESSIS, JUSTUS TELO (1917–).
Pastor and honorary secretary for Ecumenical Affairs for the Apostolic Faith Mission (AFM) of South Africa; cochairman of the Roman Catholic/Classical Pentecostal Dialogue (1982–). A descendant from the French Huguenots who settled South Africa in 1688, Justus Telo du Plessis was born in the Lesotho territory of South Africa to godly parents who became believers under the ministry of Andrew Murray. Justus du Plessis was saved at age seventeen under the ministry of his eldest brother, David, who would later become known as "Mr. Pentecost."

During more than fifty years of ministry, du Plessis served as a missionary, pastor, district chairman, and member of the executive council of the Apostolic Faith Mission, the oldest and largest Pentecostal church in South Africa, with a membership of approximately a half million. In 1970 du Plessis was elected general secretary of the AFM, a position he held until his retirement in 1982. Progressive steps taken under his leadership include the establishment of a fund for higher education and the creation of the AFM pastor's pension fund. One of his most significant contributions to the church was his key role in working for a better understanding and greater acceptance of Pentecostalism in South Africa. In the area of higher education, du Plessis' role as liaison with the South African government allowed him to negotiate changes in educational curriculum that met the needs of churches that did not subscribe to the Calvinistic doctrines taught in state-supported schools.

Like his brother David, Justus became active in the charismatic renewal movement worldwide. Since 1974 he has participated in the Roman Catholic/Classical Pentecostal Dialogue, and in 1982 he succeeded his brother David as cochairman of the Dialogue.   P. H. Alexander

DUFFIELD, GUY PAYSON (1909–).
Foursquare pastor, educator, and author. Duffield was born in Hingham, Massachusetts, to evangelical Christian parents who, shortly after the birth of their son, moved to Toronto, Ontario. While there, the younger Duffield was converted to Christ as a child and, at age ten, consecrated his life to Christian ministry during a missionary rally conducted by evangelist Paul Rader. He later entered L.I.F.E. Bible College in Los Angeles and graduated in 1928.

Early ministry took Duffield to Vancouver, British Columbia, where he served for a year at Canadian L.I.F.E. Bible College. After this his pastorates included Senlac and Evesham, Saskatchewan, and Victoria, British Columbia. During this time, he met and married Orpha Audrey Strong (1907–) of Rocanville, Saskatchewan. They have one daughter, Darlene Starr, who is married to Harold Sala, president of "Guidelines for Living," a worldwide radio and television ministry. Together the Duffields traveled in evangelistic work and pastored in Hillsboro, Oregon; Bellingham, Washington; Pomona, California (1940–56); and Vancouver, British Columbia (pastor of Kingsway Foursquare Church and dean of Canadian L.I.F.E. Bible College, 1956–58). He then received the call to pastor Angelus Temple in Los Angeles (1958–74) and to join the faculty of the adjacent L.I.F.E. Bible College (1958–85). In recognition of his service to the International Church of the Foursquare Gospel, L.I.F.E. Bible College conferred two honorary degrees on him (S.T.D., 1959; D.D., 1968).

Duffield's literary contributions include *Pentecostal Preaching* (1957), *Handbook of Bible Lands* (1969), and (with Nathaniel M. Van Cleave) *Foundations of Pentecostal Theology* (1983). He currently lives with his wife in Laguna Hills, California, and continues to minister in churches.

Bibliography: Personal correspondence, G. P. Duffield to G. B. McGee, December 29, 1987, and January 9, 1988.   G. B. McGee

DUNCAN, SUSAN A. (1854–1935).
Important early Pentecostal teacher and cofounder of Elim Tabernacle in Rochester, New York. With her sisters, Hattie M. Duncan, Nellie Fell, and M. E. Work, she founded Gospel Mission in 1887. Their eldest sister, E. V. Baker, joined them in 1894, and they founded Elim Faith Home the following year. In 1901 they established a publishing house and began publishing *Trust*, which Susan Duncan edited for more than thirty years. Elim Tabernacle was established a few years later. In 1906 they founded Rochester Bible Training School, where they taught many early Pentecostal leaders, including the great teacher John Wright Follette, who later joined the faculty.

Susan Duncan had charge of the work during E. V. Baker's visit to India in 1898–99 and after her sister's death in 1915. In 1924 Elim Memorial Church was founded, and by 1935 they had sent out more than sixty missionaries and had spent more than $100,000 in support of foreign missions without any solicitation of funds.

Bibliography: S. A. Duncan, "Incidents Connected With My Call," in E. V. Baker, *Chronicles of a Faith Life* (n.d.); idem, *Talks About Faith* (n.d.); "Elim Church Founder Dies," *Democrat and Chronicle* (Rochester) (October 2, 1935), 13.   R. M. Riss

DUNN, JAMES DOUGLAS GRANT

DUNN, JAMES DOUGLAS GRANT
(1939–). Author, professor, and minister. Dunn
studied economics and statistics at the University
of Glasgow, graduating from that institution in
1961. He received a B.D. in 1964 and in that
same year was ordained by the Church of Scotland. Presently Dunn is professor of divinity at
the University of Durham, England. He is recognized worldwide as a NT scholar and author. He
has authored countless articles and many books,
including *Jesus and the Spirit* (1975), *Unity and
Diversity in New Testament Theology* (1977),
Christology in the Making (1980), and *The Evidence for Jesus* (1985).

Dunn's most important book for Pentecostalism came out of his doctoral work at Clare
College, Cambridge, under C. F. D. Moule. His
dissertation, *Baptism in the Holy Spirit: A Re-
examination of the New Testament Teaching on the
Gift of the Spirit in Relation to Pentecostalism
Today*, was revised and reprinted as a monograph
in the Studies in Biblical Theology series (2d ser.,
no. 15 [London: SCM], 1970). This study,
which was designed "to introduce scholars, students and ministers to the most distinctive aspect
of Pentecostal theology—baptism in the Holy
Spirit," while quite irenic in tone, challenged the
Pentecostal doctrine that Spirit baptism is an
experience subsequent to salvation (e.g., Dunn,
1970, 136–38). He also contested the sacramen-
talist understanding that water baptism is synonymous with Spirit baptism.

Dunn argued that Spirit baptism was essentially
the same as—or was part of the "process" of—
becoming a Christian ("conversion-initiation" in
Dunn's parlance). The effect of Dunn's work was
twofold. First, by implicitly inviting Pentecostals
to engage in theological dialogue he really opened
the scholarly door to their opinions. Second, this
also made Pentecostals take a delayed but hard
look at their own theology in light of his exegesis
of the NT text. Harold Hunter—some thirteen
years after Dunn's *Baptism in the Holy Spirit*—
offered a response with his dissertation *Spirit-
Baptism: A Pentecostal Alternative*. A year later
(1984) Howard M. Ervin responded with a
frontal attack on Dunn with a work entitled
*Conversion-Initiation and the Baptism in the Holy
Spirit: A Critique of James D. G. Dunn's Baptism
in the Holy Spirit*. More subtle protests to Dunn's
hermeneutic are taken up in such works as Roger
Stronstad's *The Charismatic Theology of St. Luke*
(1984). Thus, almost twenty years later, scholarly
Pentecostal works cannot ignore Dunn's *Baptism
in the Holy Spirit*.

Dunn's impact upon Pentecostal and charismatic studies has continued with his own peripheral involvement with the Society for Pentecostal
Studies. At the 1982 meeting of that organization
Dunn read a paper on "Ministry and the Ministry:
The Charismatic Renewal's Challenge to Traditional Ecclesiology," which would later be included in a book of essays coming out of that
conference (C. M. Robeck, Jr., ed., *Charismatic
Experiences in History*, 1985). In that same year
he contributed to *Essays on Apostolic Themes*
(1984), a Festschrift for Southern Baptist charismatic Howard Ervin.

Bibliography: J. D. G. Dunn, *Baptism in the Holy
Spirit* (1970).   P. H. Alexander

DUQUESNE WEEKEND See CATHOLIC
CHARISMATIC RENEWAL.

DURASOFF, STEVE (1922–). Missionary,
educator. Steve Durasoff pastored for eleven years
in the Assemblies of God (AG), earned a Ph.D. in
religious education at New York University
(1968), worked for the Oral Roberts Evangelistic
Association for five years, and taught at Oral
Roberts University in the Department of Theology for fifteen years. He has also traveled extensively in eastern Europe and the Soviet Union as a
missionary evangelist. Among his publications
are: *The Russian Protestants: Evangelicals in the
Soviet Union, 1944–1964* (1969); *Pentecost Behind the Iron Curtain* (1972); *Bright Wind of the
Spirit: Pentecostalism Today* (1972); and "Communist World at Our Seaport," *PE* (July 5,
1981), 8–9. Currently Durasoff serves as president of Continental Bible College in Brussels,
Belgium (AG).

Bibliography: S. Durasoff, *Bright Wind of the Spirit:
Pentecostalism Today* (1972).   F. Bixler

DURHAM, WILLIAM H. (1873–1912).
Dynamic leader of the early Pentecostal movement and proponent of the doctrine of Christ's
"finished work." Originally from Kentucky, Durham joined the Baptist Church in 1891 but was
not converted to Christ until seven years later
while in Minnesota, where he experienced a vision
of the crucified Christ. He immediately devoted
himself to full-time ministry and became pastor of
Chicago's North Avenue Mission in 1901. When
the gifts of the Spirit became evident there in
1906, Durham visited the Azusa Street Mission in
Los Angeles, where he received the baptism of the
Holy Spirit and spoke in tongues on March 2,
1907, at which time W. J. Seymour prophesied
that wherever Durham preached, the Holy Spirit
would fall upon the people.

When Durham returned to his church in
Chicago, the Pentecostal revival spread quickly
through his ministry. His overcrowded meetings
lasted far into the night and sometimes until
morning. Durham reported in his periodical, *The
Pentecostal Testimony*, that "it was nothing to
hear people at all hours of the night speaking in
tongues and singing in the Spirit" (Brumback,
1961, 69). A "thick haze . . . like blue smoke"
often rested upon the mission. When this was
present, those entering the building would fall
down in the aisles (Miller, 1986, 123).

Frank Ewart (1975, 99) wrote that "thousands
came to hear Durham preach, and all went away
with the conviction that he was a pulpit prodigy."
At one point there were as many as twenty-five
ministers from out of town at his meetings
seeking the baptism of the Holy Spirit.

Many people who later became prominent
pioneers of the Pentecostal movement attended
Durham's meetings, including A. H. Argue; E. N.
Bell; Howard Goss; Daniel Berg, founder of the
Assemblies of God in Brazil; and Luigi Frances-
con, a pioneer of the Pentecostal movement in
Italy. Aimee Semple, before her marriage to

Harold McPherson, was instantaneously healed of a broken ankle through Durham's ministry in January 1910.

William Durham pastored Pentecostal churches in Chicago and Los Angeles but is best known for his teaching on the "finished work of Calvary."

Durham's church soon became a leading center for the Pentecostal movement worldwide. The *Assemblea Cristiana* of Chicago, which had received the Pentecostal message as a result of Durham's friendship with Luigi Francescon, became the mother church of other Italian assemblies in the U.S., Italy, and South America. F. A. Sandgren, a Norwegian elder in Durham's mission, published a Scandinavian periodical, *Folke Vennen,* resulting in several Swedish, Norwegian, and Danish Pentecostal missions in Chicago. A group of Persians under the leadership of Andrew Urshan also received encouragement from Durham.

Durham became well known for his repudiation of the Holiness doctrine of sanctification as a "second work of grace," arguing that the "finished work" of Christ on Calvary becomes available to the believer at the time of justification. The benefits of Calvary are therefore appropriated for sanctification over the entire period of the Christian's life, rather than at a single subsequent moment, as was believed by most Pentecostals in Durham's day.

Durham went to Los Angeles with this message, and upon his return to Chicago, contracted a head cold. Returning to Los Angeles, he died of pneumonia during the summer of 1912.

See also FINISHED WORK CONTROVERSY.

Bibliography: R. M. Anderson, *Vision of the Disinherited* (1979); F. Bartleman, *How Pentecost Came to Los Angeles,* 2d ed. (1925); C. Brumback, *Suddenly From Heaven* (1961); J. Colletti, "Sociological Study of Italian Pentecostals in Chicago, 1900–1930," in *Papers of the Sixteenth Annual Meeting of the Society for Pentecostal Studies* (1986); F. Ewart, *The Phenomenon of Pentecost* (rev. ed., 1975); S. Frodsham, *With Signs Following* (1946); D. Hayes, *The Gift of Tongues* (1913); W. J. Hollenweger, *The Pentecostals* (1972); A. S. McPherson, *This Is That* (1919); T. W. Miller, "The Significance of A. H. Argue for Pentecostal Historiography," *Pneuma* 8 (Fall 1986): 120–58. R. M. Riss

DUTCH CHARISMATICS See CHARISMATIC MOVEMENT.

DUTCH PENTECOSTALS See EUROPEAN PENTECOSTALISM.

E

EASTERN EUROPEAN MISSION   See
RUSSIAN AND EASTERN EUROPEAN MISSION.

EASTERN EUROPEAN PENTECOSTALS
See EUROPEAN PENTECOSTALISM.

EASTERN ORTHODOX CHARISMATICS
See HOLY SPIRIT, DOCTRINE OF: THE ANCIENT
FATHERS; HOLY SPIRIT, DOCTRINE OF: THE
MEDIEVAL CHURCHES; STEPHANOU, EUSEBIUS A.

ECCLESIASTICAL POLITY   The organization, governance, and discipline of the older
Pentecostal denominations reflect the wide spectrum of traditional church structures of Episcopalian, Presbyterian, or congregational organizations. In contrast, the charismatic movement,
which originated in the 1960s, has tended to
retain an informal or extrachurch structure under
the leadership of dominant personalities, paralleling the early twentieth-century Pentecostal movement.

I. The Local Church. The early participants in
the Pentecostal movement were not welcome in
mainline denominational churches because of the
enthusiastic style of revivalistic worship and particularly because of the phenomenon of speaking
in tongues. The antipathy was mutual, however,
as a sense of spiritual elitism led Pentecostals to
condemn the "dead" denominational churches.
Local units were formed in makeshift upper
rooms or barnlike tabernacles under the charismatic leadership of itinerant evangelists heralding
the "Full Gospel" of Pentecostalism.

These believers perceived their churches as the
restoration of NT faith and practice based solely
on the Bible. They were consistently suspicious of
ecclesiastical systems, some even to the extent of
refusing to organize and have a name or even a
membership list. Leadership was based on charisma, both in the biblical sense and in the sociological usage of Max Weber. Many of the leaders
defined themselves by the biblical terms of "apostles" or "prophets." At first nearly all the churches
were staunchly independent, refusing any external
guidance or discipline, believing themselves to be
Spirit-led. Some still retain their autonomy and
have refused to follow the general trend into
regional and national associations. One earlier
leader, Charles Fox Parham, advocated local
congregationalism under the guidance of elders,
to the extent that he refused the invitation of
William J. Seymour to assist in bringing discipline
to the extreme manifestations at Seymour's Azusa
Street Mission in Los Angeles.

The same issues that drove the Pentecostals out
of the mainline churches haunted them as independents. Spirit baptism produced a split-level
hierarchy of superior and inferior saints; those
who could not show evidence of Spirit baptism

usually were not allowed leadership roles in the
local organization. Ardor versus order remained a
tension as moderate pastors attempted to restrain
the ecstatic extremes.

These tensions burst into open conflict in the
late 1940s in the "Latter Rain" movement.
Bethesda Tabernacle, Detroit, and the Wings of
Healing Temple, Portland, Oregon, became centers that radiated the teaching of extreme congregationalism and a restoration of the apostolic
ministry of laying on of hands. This apostolic
succession produced a class of gifted Christians
claiming superiority to the old-line Pentecostals.
Prophetic guidance in the hands of the laity and
the deliverance derived from the confession of sin
to fellow believers tended to undermine the
traditional authoritarian role of the Pentecostal
pastor.

Local groups evolving out of the 1960s charismatic movement were also frequently beset by
issues from what are known as the "shepherding"
or "discipleship" movement. Churches were organized into authoritarian hierarchies for purposes of guidance and spiritual discipline, with
strong emphasis on the interests of the local
community. This phenomenon paralleled the
communalism of the "hippie" era.

The Civil Rights movement and Women's
Liberation movement of the late twentieth century made the Pentecostal churches, like others,
self-conscious about the roles of minorities and
women in the local church as well as in the
denominations. Most churches continue to be
divided along ethnic and racial lines, although no
denomination has any formal ethnic or racial
limitations. Those churches that include significant minority elements usually set them apart,
such as the Latin American districts of the
Assemblies of God or the work among racial
minorities of the Church of God (CG, Cleveland,
Tenn.). Minorities are infrequently selected for
leadership in integrated local churches and even
less frequently raised to ministerial status. Although some Pentecostal churches have always
ordained women, the role of women as active,
head pastors has declined; and with the notable
exception of Aimee Semple McPherson, they have
not traditionally been elevated to denominational
leadership positions. On the other hand, the CG
is an example of the other extreme that does not
even allow women to be voting members of the
local church and limits their ministerial status to
"exhorters," which does not permit administration of the sacraments. A similar pattern is
reflected in one of the major institutions of the
recent charismatic movement; Melodyland Christian Center, Anaheim, California, will not ordain
women or allow them to be elected to the
governing board.

II. National Denominations. Most Pentecostal groups just after the turn of the twentieth century had no polity structure outside the local church and did not require a higher authority for ministerial ordination. Fellowship among these groups was characterized by conventions, camp meetings, and six-week Bible schools. Denominationalism and ecclesiasticism were feared as the Babylon that might seduce the new movement away from its spiritual dynamism. Nevertheless, informal social structures centered on such charismatic figures as Charles F. Parham and Florence L. Crawford. Gradually regional associations were found to be beneficial. The necessity of controlling fanatical and unethical itinerant preachers required structures for credentialing a qualified clergy. Traditional ecclesiastical structures were particularly tempting because of the practice of the railroad companies of granting free passes to clergy, who were required to verify their status within a recognized religious body. Some congregations, however, favored a worldwide body of unorganized believers, led only by the Spirit, while others claimed the biblical pattern of Acts 6 and 8 to justify overseers and voting processes. These tensions caused further splintering in the fledgling groups.

The call for a national, as opposed to a regional, organization was issued in 1914 and resulted in the formation of the General Council of the Assemblies of God. This call was based on the desirability of doctrinal unity; the legal advantages of chartered churches; and the efficiency of a unified missionary, publishing, and educational endeavor. Although the original Preamble and Resolution on Constitution recognized the inclusion of foreign countries, in practice the organization has followed the culturally and pragmatically established pattern of nationalism and colonialism in its polity without attempting any scriptural justification for the denomination's correspondence to these human institutions. The organization responded to the antiestablishment sensibilities by carefully guaranteeing the autonomy of the local churches. In terms of traditional polity, the structure is a centralized Presbyterian form that retains the autonomy of the local congregation. Ordination is by the presbytery, not the local body. This general pattern has also been adopted by many other Pentecostal groups, such as the Pentecostal Church of God of America.

The earlier regional organizations, such as the CG and the Pentecostal Holiness Church (PHC), gradually expanded also into national organizations with more centralized polity based on the episcopal backgrounds of their Holiness and Wesleyan traditions. This strongly centralized pattern is also reflected in the largest black Pentecostal group in the U.S., the Church of God in Christ. The structure reflects the strong personal leadership of the founder, Charles H. Mason. Similarly, the centralized structure of the International Church of the Foursquare Gospel results from the dominant personality of founder Aimee Semple McPherson.

A congregational type of polity was manifested in a 1921 revolt against the episcopal centralization of the PHC, resulting in the formation of the Congregational Holiness Church. This form has also been a staunch characteristic of the Scandinavian Pentecostal churches as well, their background reflecting the free church's resentment of the hierarchical domination of the state church.

III. Suprachurch and Extrachurch. Fear of an apostate, liberal ecumenism has generally prevented the Pentecostals from joining the World Council of Churches. Two Chilean groups, however, Mision Iglesia Pentecostal and Iglesia Pentecostal de Chile, joined that body in 1961. Some Pentecostals in the U.S. have been part of the moderate National Association of Evangelicals since its inception in 1942. The fear of ecclesiastical hierarchies sidetracked attempts to form an international Pentecostal fellowship at Amsterdam in 1921 and at Stockholm in 1939, but at Zurich in 1947 the Pentecostal World Conference was formed. This in turn spawned regional and national organizations such as the Pentecostal Fellowship of North America (1948) and the British Pentecostal Fellowship (1948).

The Full Gospel Business Men's Fellowship International (1951) and the Fountain Trust (1964) are leading examples of charismatic organizations that are ecumenical in spirit but exist apart from the denominational structures of the churches themselves.

See also CHURCH, THEOLOGY OF THE; CHURCH LEADERSHIP; CHURCH MEMBERSHIP.

Bibliography: R. H. Gause, *Church of God Polity* (1958); W. J. Hollenweger, *The Pentecostals* (1972); K. Kendrick, *The Promised Fulfilled: A History of the Modern Pentecostal Movement* (1961); J. T. Nichol, *Pentecostalism* (1966); R. Quebedeaux, *The New Charismatics: The Origins, Development, and Significance of Neo-Pentecostalism* (1976). D. J. Wilson

ECHO PARK EVANGELISTIC ASSOCIATION See INTERNATIONAL CHURCH OF THE FOURSQUARE GOSPEL.

ECUMENISM See CHARISMATIC MOVEMENT; DIALOGUE, ROMAN CATHOLIC AND CLASSICAL PENTECOSTAL; INTERNATIONAL COMMUNION OF CHARISMATIC CHURCHES; KANSAS CITY CONFERENCE; NATIONAL ASSOCIATION OF EVANGELICALS; NORTH AMERICAN CONGRESSES ON THE HOLY SPIRIT AND WORLD EVANGELIZATION; PENTECOSTAL FELLOWSHIP OF NORTH AMERICA; PENTECOSTAL WORLD CONFERENCE; WORLD COUNCIL OF CHURCHES.

EDUCATION See BIBLE INSTITUTES, COLLEGES, UNIVERSITIES; CHRISTIAN DAY SCHOOLS; SEMINARIES AND GRADUATE SCHOOLS; SUNDAY SCHOOLS.

EDVARDSEN, ARIL (1938–). Norwegian evangelist with world-wide Pentecostal ministry. Born and brought up in Kvinesdal in southwestern Norway, Edvardsen was converted in 1956, soon after marrying his wife, Kari. Baptized in the Spirit in 1958, Edvardsen soon began an evangelistic ministry, starting in 1961 *Troens Bevis* (*Evidence of Faith*), a magazine now having 50,000 readers in Scandinavia. Giving priority to the unreached and unchurched, his evangelism supports national missionaries and national churches. Edvardsen's home valley has become the center of this missionary enterprise, with camping facilities for major conferences and studios for gospel radio and television. His ministry has become increasingly ecumenical since the Kvinesdal conferences of 1970 and 1971, which contributed significantly to the rise of charismatic renewal in Norway. Edvardsen has held campaigns in many countries, including the Soviet Union. He opened an American office in Fort Lauderdale, Florida, in 1983 under the title "International World Ministries." Edvardsen's life and ministry is described in *Dreaming and Achieving the Impossible* (1984).   P. D. Hocken

ELDRIDGE, GEORGE N. (1847–1930).
Pastor and district leader of the Assemblies of God (AG). The poverty of George Eldridge's widowed mother forced him to leave school, but he was able to return to seminary and become a Methodist pastor in Maine. His wife's health resulted in a move to Wyoming, where he accepted the doctrines of divine healing and the premillennial return of Christ. After a meeting with A. B. Simpson, he joined the Christian and Missionary Alliance and was made a superintendent for four central states. On a visit to California, he came into contact with the Azusa Street Revival and received the Pentecostal experience. Leaving the Alliance, he established Bethel Temple in Los Angeles and assisted in the founding of the Southern California District of the AG in 1919. Ill health caused him to retire from ministry in 1927.

Bibliography: G. N. Eldridge, *Personal Reminiscences* (1920); S. H. Frodsham, "Dr. G. N. Eldridge With the Lord," *PE* (February 22, 1930), 12.
L. F. Wilson

ELIM EVANGELISTIC BAND   See ELIM PENTECOSTAL CHURCH.

ELIM FELLOWSHIP
An international ecumenical and Pentecostal organization serving pastors, churches, missionaries, and other Christian workers, with headquarters in Lima, New York. It began in 1933 as an informal fellowship of churches, ministers, and missionaries, originating from a nucleus of people who had been trained at the Elim Bible Institute.

The school was founded in 1924 by Ivan Q. Spencer, who had attended the "Old Elim," Rochester Bible Training School operated by the Duncan sisters. Before founding Elim Fellowship, Spencer had been a member of the Assemblies of God (1919–24).

By 1987 the group numbered forty-one affiliated churches and 461 credentialed ministers and Christian workers. A high percentage of its credential holders serve on foreign mission fields.

Spencer's original simple, interdenominational concept, rather than another denomination, is still the guiding force at Elim. He envisioned that his ecumenical body of believers would "provide a vehicle for fellowship without imposing all of the strict controls and regulations that most denominations have developed." Service to others is stressed, and frequently missionaries go out to assist previously established national movements rather than to start new Elim ministries.

Although basically adopting the classical Pentecostal statement of faith—the entire statement has fewer than 250 words—the organization is perhaps more tolerant of other beliefs and practices than most Pentecostal groups. It is a charter member of the Pentecostal Fellowship of North America and National Association of Evangelicals.

Always listening for what he believed to be God's voice for guidance, Spencer began the Bible school with very little money but a lot of faith. Emphasizing missions, Spencer saw 10 percent of the students go into foreign service during the first decade of the school's existence.

Never content with the status quo in Pentecostal experience, Spencer looked for perpetual revival and was disappointed when it was not sustained. Spencer was often criticized by outsiders when he accepted questionable prophecies and impulses that he felt came from God. Critics looked at Elim as a group that permitted and even encouraged fanaticism. Another complaint was that Spencer and others embraced the teaching of a "selective rapture" of believers; some, it was taught, would be left when Christ returned for his church. Still another belief was that of the "Manchild Company," which meant believers could have victory over death—both for the soul and the body.

Perhaps the greatest break between Elim and other Pentecostals came in 1948 when Spencer introduced the New Order of the Latter Rain to the fellowship. After visiting Myrtle Beall's Bethesda Temple in Detroit, Spencer was certain that the Latter Rain was the revival movement that would restore unity to the body of Christ. Spencer and other leaders later saw, however, that excesses in the movement caused deep divisions within and criticism outside the fellowship. He and the fellowship tried to become a moderating force and called for believers to avoid extremes.

The fellowship publishes the *Elim Pentecostal Herald*, which Spencer founded in 1930. Most of the churches and members are concentrated in New York and Pennsylvania. Spencer's son Carlton followed his father as the fellowship's leader.

Beginning as the Elim Ministerial Fellowship (1933–47), the fellowship became Elim Missionary Assemblies in 1947 and Elim Fellowship in 1972.

Bibliography: "People Serving People, A Closer Look at Elim Fellowship" (n.d.); M. Meloon, *Ivan Spencer, Willow in the Wind* (1974).
W. E. Warner

ELIM FOURSQUARE GOSPEL ALLIANCE   See ELIM PENTECOSTAL CHURCH.

ELIM MINISTERIAL FELLOWSHIP
See ELIM FELLOWSHIP.

ELIM MISSIONARY ASSEMBLIES
See ELIM FELLOWSHIP.

ELIM PENTECOSTAL ALLIANCE
See ELIM PENTECOSTAL CHURCH.

ELIM PENTECOSTAL CHURCH
Founded by Welsh evangelist George Jeffreys. The Elim Evangelistic Band was formed in Monoghan,

Ireland, in January 1915. The first church in 1916 was a former laundry in Hunter Street, Belfast. George Jeffreys drew up a statement of faith that formed the basis of the later Fundamentals. The name Elim was chosen following the Welsh custom of giving churches names and also after the Elim Mission, Lythan, Lancashire. In 1919 the Elim Pentecostal Alliance was created as a property-holding body on the advice of John Leech. An advisory council was set up with Leech as president and William Henderson as secretary. By the end of 1920 there were fifteen assemblies and twenty-one workers in Ireland. George Jeffreys preached all over Britain but did not establish his first church until 1921 at Leigh on Sea, Essex. Their headquarters were in Belfast, but in 1922 Jeffreys shifted his attention to England, joining his brother Stephen at Grimsby. An aggressive evangelistic policy was adopted, and George moved to Clapham, London, from 1922 to 1924. The brothers spent five months in Canada and the U.S. in 1924 shortly after the formation of the Assemblies of God of Great Britain and Ireland. They returned to Barking, London, where large crowds were attracted and many outstanding miracles of healing were witnessed. Stephen separated from his brother, who continued in Ilford and East Ham. But P. S. Brewster, Douglas Scott, and D. B. Gray, leader of the London Crusader Choir, joined Elim. Brewster was saved and Scott healed. A Bible school was commenced at Clapham in 1925, and in January 1926 the former Redemptorist Convent in Clarence Road, Clapham, was opened as the Elim Bible College.

The Elim Evangelistic Band was a closely knit company with only basic rules. These were replaced by a constitution in 1922, which was revised twice before 1929 when the Elim Foursquare Gospel Alliance (EFGA) was created. The name highlighted the distinctive tenets: Jesus Christ as Savior, Healer, Baptiser, and Coming King. In 1928 there were 70 churches; another 108 were added by 1934. In 1924 E. J. Phillips (1893–1973), pastor of Armagh, editor of *Elim Evangel* and former Preston student, was asked to take over the administration at Clapham. The structure was modeled on the Salvation Army (E. C. Boulton and others had been Salvationists). In 1934 administrative control was transferred to an executive council of nine men, with Principal George Jeffreys having appointed three. E. J. Phillips was secretary-general. The supreme governing body was the annual ministerial conference of the EFGA. This followed the pattern of Methodism, and a deed poll was drawn up in April 1934.

After 1934 George Jeffreys was less successful in Britain. He achieved spectacular results in Europe, particularly in Switzerland, where he had 12,000 converts in 1935, with a further 2,000 in two weeks in 1936. He continued his vain search for the ideal form of church government, devoting his efforts to established or affiliated churches rather than pioneering new ones. The constant changes and agitation lead to conflict with the majority of the executive and the ministerial conference. Substantial concessions were made,

but Jeffreys resigned from the Alliance in December 1939. A small group of ministers joined him and formed the Bible Pattern Church Fellowship at Nottingham in November 1940. Coming so soon after the outbreak of the war in Europe, it was a severe blow. It was a barren time, as the consequent restrictions, evacuation, and bombing as well as the internal problems reduced the number of churches. It left many disheartened.

In 1944 an evangelistic committee was formed, and P. S. Brewster began with a pioneer crusade in Wigan, Lancashire. This was the first of several successful efforts. The number of churches rose to 250 in 1953, reaching 300 in 1962. A group of ten Full Gospel Testimony churches founded by Fred Squire (1904–62) joined the Alliance in 1954. In 1964 a group of 21 churches in the eastern counties joined the Alliance. A proposal in 1957 to seek affiliation with the Church of God (Cleveland, Tenn.) failed by only seven votes to achieve the required 75 percent majority.

E. J. Phillips retired as secretary general in 1957. In 1965 the four-acre site in Clapham was acquired by the local authority, and offices were built in Cheltenham and opened in 1968. The Bible college moved to a thirty-acre site in Capal, Surrey, where it remained until its removal to Nantwich, Cheshire, in 1987. The constitution has been adapted over the years to meet changing conditions. A much greater emphasis is now given to shared leadership and team ministries. A number of churches have adapted their buildings to provide accommodation in multipurpose developments, particularly in city areas. The rate of opening new churches has slowed, but there has been growth within many local churches, and the Elim Pentecostal Church is larger now than at any time in its history. There are 380 churches in Britain, with a constituency of 38,000.

The first missionaries went to Africa in 1920 to work with W. F. P. Burton. The Elim Missionary Council was formed in 1929 (later named Elim Missionary Society; now Elim International Missions). It works in sixteen countries, with an annual budget of £400,000. In 1978 nine missionaries and four children were killed in Rhodesia.

Bibliography: E. C. Boulton, *George Jeffreys—A Ministry of the Miraculous* (1928); D. W. Cartwright, *The Great Evangelists* (1986); W. J. Hollenweger, *The Pentecostals* (1972); B. R. Wilson, *Sects and Society* (1962). D. W. Cartwright

ELLIS, VESPHEW BENTON (1917–88).

Pastor and gospel songwriter. V. B. "Vep" Ellis was pastor for the past sixteen years of the Harvest Temple Church of God (Cleveland, Tenn.) in Largo, Florida. During this pastorate he also conducted weekly television and daily radio programs.

Ellis, a minister in the Church of God (Cleveland, Tenn.) for forty-nine years, also served for six years as music director and soloist for Oral Roberts tent crusades. He was one of the founding regents for Oral Roberts University.

Ellis was a prolific gospel songwriter, publishing more than five hundred of his songs and recording five albums plus numerous singles. For

A minister, singer, and composer, V. P. "Vep" Ellis is perhaps best remembered for his gospel songs, "Do You Know My Jesus?" "Let Me Touch Him," and "My God Can Do Anything."

seven years he was music director of the Tennessee Music and Printing Company.

Bibliography: "Funeral Rites Scheduled for Rev. Vesphew Ellis," *Tulsa World* (May 3, 1988), B–11, 12.
J. A. Hewett

EMMANUEL (BRISBANE, AUSTRALIA)
See CHARISMATIC COMMUNITIES.

EMMANUEL (PARIS, FRANCE) See CHARISMATIC COMMUNITIES.

EMMANUEL HOLINESS CHURCH One of the most recent of Pentecostal churches, the Emmanuel Holiness Church (EHC) was organized in Whiteville, North Carolina, on March 19, 1953. Its founding members withdrew from the Fire-Baptized Holiness Church (FBHC) because of a feeling that the parent church had become lax in its Holiness standards. The newly formed group was opposed to such things as the wearing of neckties, racial integration, ordination of "double married" persons, and its members' participation in armed conflict. In its doctrines, however, the EHC remains in essential agreement with the parent FBHC.

The EHC reports fifty congregations and two thousand members, mostly in the southeastern U.S. Its official publication is the *Emmanuel Holiness Messenger*.

Bibliography: V. Synan, *The Holiness-Pentecostal Movement* (1971).
C. W. Conn

EMMANUEL'S CHURCH OF JESUS CHRIST See UNITED PENTECOSTAL CHURCH, INTERNATIONAL.

ENCUENTRO CARISMATICO CATOLICO LATINO–AMERICANO See CHARISMATIC MOVEMENT.

END TIMES See ESCHATOLOGY, PENTECOSTAL PERSPECTIVES ON.

EPISCOPAL CHARISMATIC FELLOWSHIP See EPISCOPAL RENEWAL MINISTRIES.

EPISCOPAL CHARISMATICS. See BLESSED TRINITY SOCIETY; CHARISMATIC MOVEMENT; EPISCOPAL RENEWAL MINISTRIES.

EPISCOPAL RENEWAL MINISTRIES
Episcopal Renewal Ministries grew out of what was once known as the Episcopal Charismatic Fellowship (ECF). That organization began in early 1973, when approximately three hundred Episcopal clergymen interested in charismatic renewal, gathered at St. Matthew's Cathedral in Dallas, Texas. The meeting, a brainchild of the Reverend Dennis J. Bennett and the Reverend Wesley (Ted) Nelson, enabled the participants to share the excitement generated by their common experience of the baptism with the Holy Spirit. Until that conference the extent of the outpouring of the Holy Spirit in the Episcopal Church was unknown.

Speakers at the Dallas meeting included the Right Reverend William C. Frey, the Reverend Robert B. Hall, and the Reverend George W. Stockhowe, Jr. The conference statement reflected the joy the participants expressed after discovering that the outpouring of the Holy Spirit had touched many lives: "We were drawn together by a shared awareness . . . and the power and love of the Risen Christ . . . and the renewing presence of the Holy Spirit." It was during this conference that ECF was established, with Ted Nelson as the president of the board and the Reverend Robert H. Hawn, Sr., as its executive secretary.

ECF was headquartered for three years in Denver, Colorado; then for two years in Winter Park, Florida. During this time it launched a series of charismatic conferences around the country and became a sponsor for the large ecumenical conference held in Kansas City in 1977. Hundreds of laity and clergy who participated in the various conferences came into the experience of the baptism with the Holy Spirit. These conferences were mainly concerned with conversion to Jesus Christ, the baptism with the Holy Spirit, gifts of the Spirit, and life in the Spirit.

Early in its existence, ECF began to publish a newsletter called "ACTS 29." It was the basic communications device for those who identified themselves as charismatics and members of ECF. During this time, a work was started to regionalize ECF's activity, but it languished for lack of clergy involvement.

In 1974 the Reverend Tod W. Ewald was elected president of the executive board. It was during this time that ECF changed its thrust from one of leadership to one of servanthood. The decision was based on a belief that ECF should

Episcopalians gathered at the first meeting of the Episcopal Renewal Ministries, St. Matthew's Episcopal Cathedral, Dallas, in 1973.

not direct but rather assist the Episcopal Church in renewal. This, they believed, would prevent them from being perceived as an elitest organization. During its formative years, however, a commonly accepted vision for the organization never emerged.

A new direction, however, did emerge in 1977. At this time the ECF executive board ratified the vision that they should be dedicated to fostering parish renewal. The executive board did this, believing that if charismatic renewal was ever to be useful to the church it should be the catalyst for the renewal of parishes. This move from personal renewal to corporate renewal bore fruit in subsequent years. Thus the role began to shift toward a more proactive leadership in the process of renewal. In 1977 the Reverend Everett L. (Terry) Fullam was elected president of the executive board.

In 1978 two other changes occurred. The first was the changing of ECF's name to Episcopal Renewal Ministries (ERM). This was done to reflect the actual ministry in which it was engaged and to avoid the misunderstandings that existed over the word "charismatic." The second came when Hawn resigned to become part of a religious community. The ERM executive board then appointed the Reverend Charles M. Irish to become its national coordinator. Irish assumed

this work while continuing to serve as rector of St. Luke's Episcopal Church in Bath, Ohio.

ERM's vision was broadened with the conviction that charismatic renewal should be normative to church life. To aid in this expression every bishop and priest of the Episcopal Church was added to the mailing list of "ACTS 29." Then, in 1979 fourteen conferences on parish renewal were conducted throughout the U.S. Scores of similar conferences were conducted in subsequent years, which not only launched ERM into the parish renewal ministry but became patterns for parish renewal conferences conducted by other denominational renewal organizations.

As part of its emerging role, ERM changed from serving a constituency of like-minded people to that of serving the entire Church. Its motto became: "Dedicated to the renewal of people and parishes through Apostolic teaching, biblical preaching, historic worship and charismatic experience."

With ERM's new thrust and the addition of clergy to its list, the "ACTS 29" mailing list increased dramatically and by 1988 numbered over 42,000. The purpose of the newsletter was to provide renewal information and inspiration for the entire church. "ACTS 29" continues to be published as a result of voluntary contributions and the prayers of the people.

By 1977 only a handful of Episcopal parishes were fully affected by charismatic renewal, so as to be "lighthouse" churches. Many Episcopalians, converted and filled with the Holy Spirit, found that they were unwelcome in their own churches and thus found homes in Pentecostal and charismatic churches. The efforts of ERM toward parish renewal helped change this situation, and by 1988 more than 400 parishes of the 7,800 in the Episcopal Church were fully involved in renewal. In addition, another 800 were beginning to be changed. The laity involved in renewal is estimated at over 300,000.

In 1986 Irish resigned from St. Luke's Church to become the first full-time National Coordinator for ERM. It was at this time, and through the encouragement of Truro Episcopal Church, that ERM moved its offices to Fairfax, Virginia. By this time ERM's work expanded to include clergy placement, conference planning, networking of clergy, parish renewal, and distribution of books and tapes. ERM also helped sponsor the Congress on the Holy Spirit and World Evangelization held in New Orleans in 1987.

In 1988 the Reverend Carl E. Buffington, Jr., was added to the staff to take leadership in ERM's regional development and to promote its new work called "Christian Formation Series."

See also BLESSED TRINITY SOCIETY; CHARISMATIC MOVEMENT.

Bibliography: "ACTS 29;" executive board minutes.
C. M. Irish

ERICKSON, CLIFTON O. (1915–). Healing evangelist. Born to emigrants from Norway, Clifton O. Erickson was dedicated by his mother to the Lord with hope of his becoming a minister. At age five Erickson felt that call. He grew up in Wenatchee, Washington, where he was converted in a revival campaign. Shortly thereafter he became a youth leader and teacher and traveled with his uncle (who was a pastor) as a song leader.

Four years after his conversion, Erickson received the baptism in the Holy Spirit. Erickson claimed that by revelation the Lord informed him that after three days of fasting and praying, God would baptize him at 10:00 P.M. At the designated time, the power of God came to him and he was Spirit-baptized.

Erickson testifies of how God gave him three revelations of his future ministry. It was to be a healing ministry, a ministry of the miraculous, and international in scope. Licensed with the AG in 1945, Erickson was ordained in 1948. He attended the First Convention of Healing Revivalists in Dallas, Texas, in 1949.

Although Erickson had persistent problems with a sick child, both he and his wife, Vivian, experienced healings. Through severe trials, the work went on. A turning point came when Oral Roberts laid hands on him (at Erickson's request). He reported, "I felt the power immediately . . . henceforth He was going to manifest through me the ministry of healing" (Erickson, 1962, 22). Gordon Lindsay described the miraculous power of God through Erickson's ministry in Chile in 1952. A Chilean newspaper reported that thirty-nine evangelical leaders in Chile praised Erickson as a man of faith. The peak crowd in his crusade there reached 75,000.

In collaboration with Lester Sumrall in Manila in 1954, a church was built with a Sunday morning attendance of 7,000. This became the site of another spectacular revival.

Erickson authored *Supernatural Deliverance* (1950) and collaborated with Lester Sumrall in an account of the Manila revival entitled *Modern Manila Miracles* (1954). In 1962, Erickson, along with Lester Sumrall, started a new publication, *World Harvest*. He later retired in Florida.

Bibliography: C. O. Erickson, *My Testimony* (1962); International Evangelistic Association, *Deliverance* 3 (January 1959); *The End Time* (1957).   S. Shemeth

ERICKSON, ERIC C. (1898–1982). Swedish-American evangelist. As a young boy, Erickson attended the Sister Bay Church, a Swedish Baptist church in northeastern Wisconsin, with his family. As a result of their conversion to Pentecostalism in 1911, Erickson, his family, and a few church members left the church and began to conduct Pentecostal meetings in their homes. Deeply influenced by the local church polity that the Sister Bay Church practiced, he remained convinced that local church autonomy was the correct biblical pattern for each local church. Erickson, who was ordained as a minister with the Assemblies of God (AG) in 1918, staunchly believed that the independent Scandinavian Pentecostal churches in the area should not join the North Central District of the AG when it organized in 1922. He believed that these churches should remain autonomous and free from any denominational affiliation. Erickson organized a meeting in 1922 in St. Paul, Minnesota, during which several Scandinavian Pentecostal churches agreed to remain independent from the AG and to fellowship with one another under the name Independent Assemblies of God. Today these churches are under the name Fellowship of Christian Assemblies. For the rest of his life Erickson pastored the Duluth Gospel Tabernacle, which became one of the most influential Scandinavian Pentecostal churches in the U.S. during his pastorate. For several years he was editor of the *Herald of Faith,* which for years was the leading Scandinavian-Pentecostal periodical in the U.S.

Bibliography: J.R. Coletti, "Lewi Pethrus: His Influence Upon Scandinavian-American Pentecostalism," *Pneuma* 5 (2, 1983): 18–29.   J. Colletti

ERVIN, HOWARD MATTHEW (1915–). Biblical scholar, author, educator, and presently professor of OT at Oral Roberts University, where he has taught for more than twenty-one years. A Baptist by profession since his conversion more than forty years ago, Howard Ervin is one of the earliest academically trained voices in the modern charismatic movement. He holds an A.B. and Th.B. from Eastern Baptist Theological Seminary in Philadelphia, an M.A. in Near Eastern Studies from the Asia Institute in New York, and a B.D. from New Brunswick Theological Seminary (N.J.). His Th.D. in OT was awarded by Princeton Theological Seminary, and he took postdoctoral studies at the Institute of Holy Land

A Baptist Charismatic, Howard M. Ervin is a professor of Old Testament at Oral Roberts University.

Studies in Jerusalem and Dropsie College for Hebrew and Cognate Learning in Philadelphia.

As a pastor, lecturer, and teacher, Ervin is recognized both in the U.S. and abroad. His participation in the International Roman Catholic/Pentecostal Dialogue since 1979 has done much to open ecumenical channels between these two groups, and he continues to have a burden for spiritual renewal of the whole church.

Ervin is perhaps equally well known for his writing career, which has spanned more than twenty years. His *These Are Not Drunken, As Ye Suppose* (revised in 1987 as *Spirit Baptism: A Biblical Investigation*) remains a classic exegetical defense of the Pentecostal and charismatic experience of Spirit baptism. He has also penned a series of essays on the practical implications of Spirit baptism (*This Which Ye See and Hear*, 1972) and numerous articles on charismatic renewal. Another important work, *Conversion-Initiation and the Baptism in the Holy Spirit* is a refutation of James D. G. Dunn's classic, *Baptism in the Holy Spirit* (1970). Dr. Ervin and his wife, Marta, who have three daughters and five grandchildren, reside in Tulsa, Oklahoma.

Bibliography: Autobiographical statement supplied to this writer; C. Farah, Jr., and S. Durasoff, "Biographical Sketch" in P. Elbert, ed., *Essays on Apostolic Themes* (1985).   P. H. Alexander

ESCHATOLOGY, PENTECOSTAL PERSPECTIVES ON

For most Christians the present determines the future; they believe they will reap what they sow. But for most Pentecostals the future determines the present; their view of eschatology governs their view of current events. Their interpretation of prophecy has had a very significant effect on their perception of world historical events and on their political and social response to those events. On a smaller scale their eschatological views have affected their own history by stimulating evangelistic and missionary endeavors.

I. Theological Background. The Pentecostal views of eschatology are not uniquely Pentecostal but are widely shared with the fundamentalist churches. The Pentecostals, however, are unique in viewing the outpouring of the Spirit as itself a fulfillment of end-time prophecy. Some anti-Pentecostal others have seen it likewise but as satanic in origin.

A. Premillennialism. In general, Pentecostal eschatology may be characterized as premillennial, expecting the second advent of Christ prior to the establishment of the thousand-year kingdom of Revelation 20. This may be contrasted with the dominant nineteenth-century view of postmillennialism that foresaw the church gradually bringing about a Christian millennium, after which Christ would return as King. The medieval view tended to be amillennial, viewing the Millennium merely as a symbol of the church age.

B. Dispensationalism. Premillennialists may be further divided into historicist and futurist persuasions. The Pentecostals are overwhelmingly futurists, expecting the major fulfillment of biblical prophecies to lie in the future, and nearly all expect those fulfillments to be imminent. In contrast, the historicists see the fulfillment of prophecies within the historical church age. Historicist premillennialists were discredited in the midnineteenth century by the Millerites, but the futurist position, known as dispensationalism, was later developed by English-born John Nelson Darby (1800–1882). It was popularized in the U.S. by James H. Brookes. *The Scofield Reference Bible* (1909) became the source of dispensationalism that has dominated Pentecostalism.

C. Pretribulationism. Futurists may be further divided into pretribulationists and posttribulationists. Most Pentecostals have followed the prevailing view of the late-nineteenth-century prophetic conference movement, expecting the rapture, or removal, of the church prior to a time of tribulation. Some, however, continue to expect the church to remain through the Great Tribulation until the return of Christ to set up an earthly kingdom. A smaller segment envisions a rapture in the middle of the Great Tribulation, the midtribulationist view. The doctrine of pretribulation rapture has allowed Pentecostals on the one hand to pessimistically preach impending doom with "wars and rumors of wars" as a sign of the end, while on the other hand optimistically offering "the blessed hope" of the rapture of the church.

D. Antinomianism. Most Pentecostals' view of the moral issues surrounding the fulfillment of latter-day prophecies may be characterized as antinomian. Since fulfillment of the prophecies are predestined by the determined will of God, they are welcomed, therefore, as a sign of the end, and in their view are justified—not subject to ordinary measurements of God's moral laws. The end justifies the means. They have applauded the restoration of Israel, no matter what the means employed, whereas they have deplored rising crime rates and have consequently wished to reverse the trends. Yet they viewed both of these phenomena as fulfillment of prophecy. The application of the principle has not been consistent. This moral problem was not new, for Jesus had dealt with it regarding his own betrayal: "The Son of Man will go as it has been decreed, but woe to that man who betrays him" (Luke 22:22).

II. Israel. The Pentecostals' perception of history has been most influenced by their premillennialist belief that the restoration of Israel to Palestine is a sure sign of the soon return of Christ. Belief in the restoration of Israel had been an important part of Puritan theology as well as of the prophetic conference movement, but the Pentecostals associated the development of modern Zionism with the era of the outpouring of the Spirit, thus producing a sense of kindredness.

Pentecostals were thrilled during World War I by the announcement by the British Foreign Secretary, Arthur Balfour, that Britain favored the establishment in Palestine of a home for the Jews. Just over a month later, the Turks abandoned Jerusalem to the British. The event was heralded as the end of the times of the Gentiles. The eventual establishment of the state of Israel in 1948 and the capture of the old city of Jerusalem by the Israelis in 1967 would likewise be interpreted as the end of the times of the Gentiles. The whole purpose of World War I, according to some, was the freeing of the Holy Land from the Turks.

After the war Britain was given control of Palestine under a mandate from the newly established League of Nations. British leaders attempted to limit Jewish migration to Palestine, for they had also promised in the Balfour Declaration to look out for the civil rights of non-Jews in Palestine. These limitations were severely criticized as violating the divine plan. In 1937, in the face of irreconcilable differences between the Arabs and the Jews, the British recommended the partitioning of the land into two separate states. This plan was criticized at first but was later reevaluated as a direct fulfillment of prophecy. Over the long haul, though, interpreters expected and cheered the prospect of the entire Holy Land being restored to Jewish autonomy in spite of the Arabic dominance in the region for centuries.

Between the world wars rumors were rampant that the Jerusalem temple was about to be rebuilt and that the Jews were preparing for the restoration of Mosaic sacrifices. These stories would also flourish after the 1967 war, and they continue to crop up.

The Jewish-Arab rioting culminated in the British withdrawal from Palestine in 1948, and the Jews won the ensuing battles and established an independent state of Israel. The United Nations had attempted a partition of the land, but this was rejected by both parties, and the victorious Jews refused to be bound by the suggested borders. Pentecostal preachers exhorted everyone to rejoice over the failure of the partition plan, give thanks for the glorious sign of the end times, and prepare for the Rapture that was, of course, even more imminent than the establishment of the earthly kingdom in Jerusalem.

It is interesting to note that prior to 1948 one major interpretation of the prophecies, following the scheme of the *Scofield Bible,* called for the Jews to be converted *prior* to the restoration to the land. Even after 1948 some voices continued to separate the coming religious restoration from the existing political restoration, but the overwhelming majority simply reinterpreted the prophecies after the fact when faced with the awesome reality of what they called the greatest event of the century. Even though many had been wrong in the specifics of their interpretation, the establishment of Israel greatly enhanced the credibility of the premillennialists in general.

Some moderate voices decried the Jews' treatment of the Arab refugees, lamenting that the methods were not of God even though the fulfillment of prophecy was of God. At the same time, however, they pointed out that the Jews would have been justified in taking all of the land including that across the Jordan River—which they had not been able to do.

In 1956, in response to Arab pressures and to the Egyptian nationalization of the Suez Canal, the Israelis, in conjunction with the French and British, attacked Egypt. Under pressure from both Russia and the U.S., the Israelis were forced to withdraw. Pentecostal response was that the attack had been brash, but that, nevertheless, it was likely in the divine plan because it would probably hasten the coming Russian attack at the Battle of Armageddon, which would occur during the Great Tribulation.

Israel's 1967 June War brought a more critical attitude among the wider Christian community toward Israeli expansionism. But the annexation of all of Jerusalem was enthusiastically received by the Pentecostals. Former general superintendent of the Assemblies of God (AG), Ralph M. Riggs, asserted that the 1967 war confirmed that God gave Palestine to the Jews. Israeli officials developed the policy of cultivating the support of the premillennialists in order to influence public opinion in their favor. Particularly useful were highly visible figures such as Oral Roberts, who was invited to the Holy Land and given red carpet treatment.

Support for Israel has continued through the Yom Kippur War of 1973, the attack on Iraq in 1981, and the invasion of Lebanon in 1982. Pentecostals are admonished that it is their duty to stand behind Israel and are reassured that Israel will never be destroyed by the Arabs. This is usually accompanied by an appeal to self-interest: that the Jews are God's chosen people and that he will bless those who bless Israel. In the 1980s that support has followed the direction of right-wing Fundamentalism and has become more political in nature. The appeal has gone to Pentecostal congregations to sign petitions and send money for lobbyists to get the U.S. government to move its embassy to Jerusalem and thus recognize

Israel's claims to territory conquered in war—which is strictly prohibited under international law. Laypersons influenced by Pentecostal dispensationalism have become influential in Christian lobbies such as the American Christian Trust headed by Mrs. Bobi Hromas. This group maintains a continuous prayer vigil across the street from the Israeli embassy in Washington, D.C., and sends money to Israel to support Jewish settlements in the occupied West Bank.

III. Anti-Semitism. While Pentecostals have been staunch backers of Zionism, they have at the same time ironically been tolerant of anti-Semitism. Persecution of the Jews has been treated matter of factly as God's means of driving the Jews out of the lands of their dispersion back into their God-given homeland of Palestine. This was not antinomianism, however, for the perpetrators of crimes against God's chosen people would be punished, and those who blessed Israel, "the apple of his eye," would be rewarded. The victory of tiny Japan over giant Russia in 1905 was seen as a punishment for Russian persecution of the Jews. The execution of Czar Nicolas I by the Bolsheviks was God's retribution for his treatment of the Jews. In 1931, as the U.S. began its slide into the Depression, it was depicted, nevertheless, as a prosperous nation being blessed by God for its kindly treatment of the Jews.

The Pentecostals shared in the anti-Semitism that pervaded American culture. In the 1920s a forged document entitled the *Protocols of the Elders of Zion,* which was purportedly written by Jewish conspirators who were bent on taking over the world, was circulated. These were widely distributed by Henry Ford and were accepted as legitimate by Pentecostals as well as by other premillennialists. This tended to reinforce the endemic American anti-Semitism and thus perpetuated the apathy of the church community toward the forthcoming Jewish Holocaust. When the Germans and Russians joined forces in the 1937 Nazi-Soviet pact, the binding force was simplistically viewed as anti-Semitism. It was not until World War II was over and six million Jews had been exterminated that the AG passed a resolution opposing anti-Semitism.

IV. The Arabs. Like most Americans, the Pentecostals found little in common with the Islamic peoples, whereas the Jews shared with Western civilization the Judeo-Christian traditions. Premillennialists identified with people who at least worshiped the same God, even if they did reject his Son. But even beyond this, the Pentecostals were indifferent to the existence of the native Palestinians, both Moslems and Christians alike. Their cavalier treatment of the likely destruction of the Moslem shrines in Jerusalem is particularly revealing of an underlying aggressiveness. At the time of the fall of Jerusalem in World War I, they were delighted by the prospect that British planes might bomb the Dome of the Rock and make way for the Jewish temple to be rebuilt. Reports of plots to destroy the shrines are usually editorialized with the observation that if the Jews do not tear them down, then God will do so with an earthquake.

As conflicts between Jews and Arabs developed in the Holy Land, the Pentecostals consistently sided with the Jews. At the time of the 1936–37 disturbances the Jews were identified as peacemakers who were trying to explain to the Arabs their ultimate intentions. When the British in 1939 attempted to restrict immigration, the Pentecostal analysts observed that it did not make any difference anyway, for the whole land was eventually to belong to the Jews. In 1948 some admitted that the Jews had no rights in the land at all, but they would return anyway, for it had been prophesied. There was criticism of the Jews' treatment of the Arabs, but that too was interpreted prophetically: the Jews were building up an antipathy that would in turn bring the Great Tribulation upon them. In 1956 the Suez crisis was justified because the Arabs were, after all, trespassing on the Jews' God-given land. In 1982 the invasion of Lebanon was given similar justification.

V. Russia. Since 1917 Christianity has shared an antipathy toward communist Russia because of the militant atheism of the revolutionaries. In addition, the Pentecostals have inherited an earlier premillennialist anti-Russian attitude that stems from two sources: (1) the Russian anti-Semitism and (2) the identification of Russia as "Gog" and "Magog" in Ezekiel 38–39 and as a participant in the Battle of Armageddon in Revelation 16:16. More than anticommunism, and even more than anti-Russian imperialism, the Pentecostals' attitude is sheer anti-Russianism. Since World War I they have persistently identified world events as always leading to an imminent Armageddon—to be preceded, of course, by their own escape from it all in the Rapture.

This system predetermines that Russia will eventually attack, and therefore all peace overtures or disarmament schemes are ultimately doomed to fail. In a curious contrast to the antinomian welcome of Israel's inevitable expansion and fulfillment of her destiny, they have generally supported resistance to Russia's expansion in fulfillment of her prophetic role. No one is ever exhorted to rejoice that the Russians are coming.

Even peripheral events may take on apocalyptic significance. The 1924 Japanese exclusion act precluding Japanese immigration to America was interpreted as God's means of driving Japan into an alliance with Russia at Armageddon. Japan's invasion of China in 1931 and again in 1937 identified Japan as the "kings of the east" (Rev. 16:12), which would also be gathered to Armageddon. After World War II this label was given to India or China as they took the headlines.

Between the world wars the Russian army was identified as preparing for Armageddon. And the Far East, the Near East, or Europe were all designated as places where the battle might break out. The start of World War II was depicted as leading to Armageddon, and some lamented America's unholy alliance with Russia, while others perceived the chief result of the war would be the rise of Russia to dominance.

As the Cold War developed between Russia and the U.S. after World War II, the arms race was seen as a harbinger of Armageddon. Prophetic voices were euphoric in 1948 as Russian aggression brought the Berlin Blockade and the overthrow of Czechoslovakia in the same year that Israel became a state. This was the peak of prophetic interest, not to be surpassed even by the occupation of Jerusalem in 1967.

The expected Armageddon became even more ominous as the Russians joined America as a nuclear power. As the nuclear arms race produced enough bombs to destroy the earth many times over, the premillennialists drew the conclusion that the Armageddon battle would be a nuclear one. But they had a unique twist to their fatalism: humanity would not be destroyed; for according to their prophetic model, many events were to transpire after Armageddon—Christ would eventually set up an earthly kingdom—so there was no need to fear the holocaust. War was certain, but so was survival. While other Christian groups attempted to be peacemakers and advocated nuclear disarmament, the Pentecostals were resigned to divinely ordained war and were militantly anti-Russian and anticommunist. These were demonic forces that must be resisted in spite of their fulfillment of prophecy.

Interest somewhat waned in the era of detente, but in the 1980s it was further stimulated by Russian intervention in Afghanistan as she moved south toward Israel. Public opinion became more widely influenced by this eschatology as millions followed the teachings of popular television evangelists; almost all were premillennialists and Pentecostal. Television personality Pat Robertson guaranteed the fulfillment of Ezekiel concerning Russia by the fall of 1982. Pentecostals claimed that President Ronald Reagan was premillennialist, as he had come under the influence of Pentecostal laymen and clergymen as governor of California and then as president. These included Herb Ellingwood, George Otis, Harald Bredesen, and Secretary of Interior James Watt. Critics were uneasy about having a president who believed that nuclear war was inevitable yet did not fear his own destruction. The whole idea of a nuclear deterrent to war seemed to be breaking down.

VI. Europe. The interpretation of events in Europe has been pervaded by the expectation of a latter-day revival of the Roman Empire in some form or another to be presided over by the Antichrist. There is a variety of scenarios, a leading one identifying "Gomer" in Ezekiel 38:6 as Germany, who will form a northern confederacy with Russia. England has been identified with Ezekiel 38:13; her former colonies, including the U.S., being the "young lions."

Following World War I, the first candidate to be the revived Roman Empire was the League of Nations, a sign of the soon-coming Armageddon. Predicted for the league was the role of defending the Jews against the Russians, Russia not being a member of the group. Mussolini's self-conscious revival of the empire, however, soon gained precedent. Italy's intervention in the Spanish Civil War in 1937 was depicted as a model for Mussolini's possible intervention in the Middle East that would naturally lead to Armageddon. Some authors asserted that Mussolini was the Antichrist. It was more usual, though, to identify such world figures tentatively as probabilities or

possibilities, the list including Hitler, Stalin, and Franklin D. Roosevelt. After World War II Hitler would be identified with the "hunters and fishers" of Jeremiah 16:16, whose function was to drive the Jews back to Palestine.

Prior to the Nazi-Soviet pact of 1939 there was much predicting that such an alliance would take place. When it did happen, the premillennialists virtually gloated in their accuracy. Then in 1942 when Hitler junked the treaty and attacked Russia, there was sheepish silence on the subject.

A flurry of apocalyptic interest accompanied World War II. In the first three months of 1941 thirty-one out of the ninety major articles in the AG *Pentecostal Evangel* were about prophecy and the war in Europe. After the war there was great excitement about the United Nations. Just as the case with its predecessor, the League of Nations, it was depicted as a forerunner of a one-world government that would be set up by the Antichrist. Students of prophecy were deeply suspicious of such associations, especially when the goal was world peace, which the Pentecostals considered to be a wild fantasy anyway.

The 1949 North Atlantic Treaty Organization (NATO), which included the U.S., was identified as a revival of the Roman Empire. Many teachers believed that the U.S. would be one of the nations destroyed at the Battle of Armageddon. Even though the church would escape all this in the Rapture, this was not a teaching popular with patriotic Americans and was not stressed. The European Common Market in 1958 was also depicted as the revived Roman Empire, and its eastern counterpart, the 1955 Warsaw Treaty Organization's Council for Mutual Economic Assistance, chartered in 1959, was now seen as the great northern confederacy. Similar themes continued to be stressed among Pentecostals in the 1970s and '80s. David Wilkerson has promised America that it will be destroyed by a hydrogen holocaust, and television evangelist Jimmy Swaggart has advocated U.S. withdrawal from the United Nations and increased armaments.

VII. The Pentecostal Movement. The outpouring of the Holy Spirit is seen by Pentecostals as an important sign of the end. A sense of urgency has been an important motivation for missionary endeavor and evangelism, making the Pentecostals the fastest-growing segment of Christianity, which they attribute to the work of the Spirit. The terror of impending doom and the imminent Blessed Hope have been the heart of their evangelistic appeal. Many also believe that Christ will not return until the gospel has been preached to the ends of the earth. They have a duty, therefore, to facilitate his return by spreading the Good News. Since the end is near, they are indifferent to social change and have rejected the reformist methods of the optimistic postmillennialists and have concentrated on "snatching brands from the fire" and letting social reforms result from humankind being born again.

While the Pentecostals have interpreted the ecumenical movement as the great apostate church symbolized by Babylon, some Seventh-Day Adventists have depicted the modern charismatic-Pentecostal revival as the very means of unification for that ecumenical apostasy. Evaluations may vary, but the growth is undeniable. Whether that growth is because of the Pentecostals' identification of nearly every current event as a sign of the end, or in spite of it, remains to be seen.

See also DAKE, FINIS JENNINGS; DISPENSATIONALISM; SCOFIELD REFERENCE BIBLE.

Bibliography: G. Halsell, *Prophecy and Politics: Militant Evangelists on the Road to Nuclear War* (1986); W. M. Menzies, *Anointed to Serve: The Story of the Assemblies of God* (1971); E. R. Sandeen, *The Roots of Fundamentalism: British and American Millenarianism 1800–1930* (1970); G. T. Sheppard, "Pentecostalism and the Hermeneutics of Dispensationalism: Anatomy of an Uneasy Relationship," *Pneuma* 6 (2, 1984): 5–33; T. P. Weber, *Living in the Shadow of the Second Coming: American Premillennialism 1875–1925* (1979); D. Wilson, *Armageddon Now! The Premillenarian Response to Russia and Israel Since 1917* (1977).   D. J. Wilson

EUCHARIST See ORDINANCES, PENTECOSTAL; SACRAMENTS.

EUROPEAN PENTECOSTAL FELLOWSHIP See EUROPEAN PENTECOSTALISM.

EUROPEAN PENTECOSTAL THEOLOGICAL ASSOCIATION (EPTA). Following discussions at the Pentecostal European Conference at Hague, Holland, in 1978, EPTA was formed on March 16, 1979, in Vienna, Austria. Its stated purpose was "the promotion of Pentecostal learning, ministerial training and theological literature, and the fostering of exchange and cooperation between member institutions." Membership is either institutional (Pentecostal Bible schools and theological colleges) or individual. EPTA holds annual conferences, and the presiding officers hold office for two periods.

EPTA differs from the North American Society for Pentecostal Studies (SPS) in several respects. It is strictly for Pentecostals and does not include charismatics. It is more institution-oriented, addressing the concerns of Pentecostal education and training colleges. Thus papers at EPTA conferences treat pastoral and administrative issues facing these institutions as well as strictly academic questions. EPTA also has an international and intercultural role, seeing the diversity of languages and cultures between Finland and Portugal, Ireland and Yugoslavia.

One of the most valuable services of EPTA is the *EPTA Bulletin,* published quarterly since 1981. D. Bundy, the first editor, has been followed by J. Karsten (Zeist, Holland) and D. Smeeton (Brussels, Belgium). Most space was initially given to book reviews (including books by charismatics and others of interest to Pentecostals), but since 1985 issues also regularly contain quality historical or theological surveys on Pentecostal topics.   P. D. Hocken

EUROPEAN PENTECOSTALISM

   I. Background
   II. Origins
   III. Regional and National Expansion
      A. The British Isles
      B. Scandinavia
      C. West-Central Europe
      D. Eastern Europe
      E. Southern Europe
   IV. European Dimensions

I. Background. As in America, the main background to the Pentecostal movement in Europe is to be found in the Holiness movements of the late nineteenth century. The European Holiness currents, already evident in the writings of the Irish Methodist William Arthur, were intensified by the visits to Britain and Germany of Robert Pearsall Smith, aided by the British campaign of D. L. Moody, which all led to the annual Keswick conventions held in northwestern England each July from 1875. The same period saw the revitalization of Pietist cells (*Gemeinschaft*) in the state churches of Germany. A European tour by R. A. Torrey in 1903 spread the concept of a post-conversion baptism in the Spirit as an empowerment for ministry and service.

There were, however, significant differences between the European and American Holiness groups: (1) while the Keswick conventions did teach and encourage the expectation of an experiential coming of the Holy Spirit to give the Christian a breakthrough in the struggle against temptation, they gave greater emphasis to the ongoing faith proclamation of Jesus' victory; (2) Keswick and German circles rejected the view, widespread in the U.S., of Christian perfection as the eradication of the flesh by nature, and proclaimed instead an ongoing victory over temptation, with slogans such as "the victorious life" and "the overcomer." Of the American Holiness teachers, European Holiness leaders felt most at home with the circles associated with A. B. Simpson and D. L. Moody; (3) there was less Wesleyan-Methodist influence on the European than on the American Holiness movements. Holiness teaching in Europe was mostly Calvinistic (among many Anglican Evangelicals at Keswick and among Welsh Calvinistic Methodists) or Lutheran (as in much of the *Gemeinschaftsbewegung,* the Holiness movement within the Protestant state churches in Germany).

Holiness currents were equally present in European Pentecostal origins as in America, though in general less visibly. The advent of glossolalia was more immediately divisive in America, where it disrupted newly formed Holiness denominations, than in Europe, except for Germany with its rejection by the *Gemeinschaftsbewegung* in the Berlin Declaration. Early Pentecostal teachings in Europe are suffused with Holiness teaching on the victorious, overcoming life, e.g., with Mary Boddy and Jonathan Paul. The influence of the Welsh revival (1904–06) was more marked in Europe, with some Pentecostal pioneers visiting Wales during the period of intense revival.

II. Origins. The Pentecostal movement in Europe developed from the ministry of Thomas Ball Barratt, a naturalized Norwegian of English birth, who was baptized in the Spirit in New York in November 1906. On his return to Oslo (then Christiania) the following month, Barratt held meetings in a large gymnasium to preach the Pentecostal message. These meetings received extensive publicity so that many flocked to hear

SPEAKERS, ETC., AT SUNDERLAND CONVENTION.
Read from left to right. Back Row: Mr. Cecil Polhill and Mr. W. H. Sandwith (Treas., P.M.U.)
Middle Row: Mr. John Leech, K.C., Bro. Techner, Pastor J. H. King, Bro. Stanley Frodsham, Bro. T. Moggs.
Front Row: Bro. Smith Wigglesworth, Rev. T. Hackett, M.A., Pastor Polman, Pastor Paul, Pastor Barratt, Prediger
Humburg, Prediger Schilling, "Pastor" Boddy. (Photo., Taylor, High Street, Sunderland.)

P.M.U. Annual Balance Sheet—continued.)	£ s. d.	List of Contributions received during
Brought over	781 0 3	May, 1912.

This group attending a Sunderland, England, Convention in 1912, includes the leading European Pentecostals of the time. Front row, left to right, Smith Wigglesworth, T. Hacket, Gerrit Polman, Jonathan Paul, Thomas B. Barratt, Emil Humburg, a Mr. Schilling, and A. A. Boddy. Center, John Leech, a Mr. Techner, J. H. King, Stanley Frodsham, and T. Moggs. Back row, Cecil Polhill and W.H. Sandwith.

Barratt, including Alexander Boddy from England (March 1907) and Jonathan Paul from Germany (April 1907).

All the countries in Western Europe in which the Pentecostal movement became established before World War I received the message from Norway, except Holland and Italy; that is, Sweden: early 1907 (a Barratt visit expanded the small beginnings sparked by Andrew G. Johnson, a Swedish-American baptized in the Spirit at Azusa Street); Great Britain: March 1907 (Boddy's return, boosted by Barratt's Sunderland mission in September 1907); Germany: Spring 1907 (two Norwegian visitors from Oslo); Denmark: early 1907 (Barratt's first visit); Switzerland: summer 1907 (visit of the same young Norwegian women, followed by a Barratt visit in 1908); Finland: fall 1911 (visit by Barratt).

Although there were small pockets of Pentecostal believers before World War I in Belgium, France, the Baltic states, and Russia, these assemblies did not form a nucleus for the movement, which grew later from new roots. In Holland, the Polmans in Amsterdam heard of Azusa Street through receiving *Apostolic Faith* magazine. Wilhelmina Polman was baptized in the Spirit in Holland in 1907, some months before her husband Gerrit received the baptism in England. In Italy, the movement's beginnings in 1908 came through Italian-American missionaries bringing the message from the U.S. to their homeland.

The factors contributing most to the expansion of the Pentecostal movement in Northern Europe before World War I were, in probable order of importance:

1. *Personal witness.* From the beginning, the movement was strongly evangelistic, with Pentecostal people proclaiming their experience to all who would listen. While newcomers were frequently baptized in the Spirit at Pentecostal meetings, the witness of Pentecostal believers was often the initial attraction.

2. *Literature.* In five countries (Britain, Norway, Germany, Holland, and Switzerland) leaders were producing Pentecostal monthlies within two years of the movement's arrival (by 1908–1909). All reported the worldwide spread of the movement and were augmented by an array of pamphlets, joined before long by magazines and bulletins issuing from other Pentecostal sources.

3. *Annual conferences.* Annual conferences were held in such Pentecostal centers as Sunder-

Scandinavian Pentecostal leaders discussing Bible doctrines. From the left, Lewi Pethrus, (Sweden), Mrs. Barratt and T. B. Barratt (Norway), Anna Larssen Bjorner and her husband Sigurd (Denmark).

land, England; Mülheim, Germany; and Orebro, Sweden. Other major conferences were held in Hamburg (1908) and Oslo (1911). Sunderland in particular attracted speakers and participants from other lands, emphasizing the international character of the Pentecostal movement.

4. *Press coverage.* In some places the Pentecostal outbreak drew comment in the secular press, usually skeptical and sometimes derisive. Though the Pentecostals were presented as credulous fanatics, such publicity—e.g., in Norway and Britain—often produced more interested enquirers. Hostile comment in Christian journals tended to be more damaging to the movement, as in Germany with the controversy surrounding the negative Berlin Declaration of 1909.

5. *Travels by major figures.* The early Pentecostal leaders, such as Barratt, Boddy, Polman, and Paul, all visited each other, with closer links between Britain, Holland, and Germany than between these and Norway. These leaders undertook regular preaching tours, though Paul traveled less than the other three.

6. *Visitors from the U.S.* Many American Pentecostal pioneers made trips around the world, often visiting Europe on their way home. These included Frank Bartleman, Joseph Hillery King, Daniel Awrey, A. H. Post, and Elizabeth Sisson. They do not, however, seem to have contributed significantly to the European beginnings.

P. D. Hocken

III. Regional and National Expansion. This survey is organized according to blocs of European countries. The blocs are identified primarily on the basis of common cultural, linguistic, political, and religious factors.

A. The British Isles. Pentecostalism in Britain has never attained the prominence that it has achieved in Sweden or parts of South America. It

has not produced the massive churches that have been features in other countries. What it has done is to provide the worldwide church with outstanding leaders, both teachers and evangelists. It has also given training to many leaders of Pentecostal churches throughout the world and has sent out an army of missionaries.

Reports of the Azusa Street revival in Los Angeles and T. B. Barratt's work in Norway began to attract attention in the Christian press. Anglican minister Alexander A. Boddy of Sunderland spent three days in Norway in March 1907 and urged Barratt to visit Britain. Barratt arrived on August 31 and stayed until October 18. Meetings were held in the vicarage and in the church hall. During that time seventeen persons were baptized in the Spirit and spoke in tongues. These included Alexander's wife, Mary; their daughters Jane and Mary; his brother-in-law, the Reverend James Pollock (who soon retracted); and a black preacher from London, T. Brem Wilson. The meetings did not attract much attention at first, but after a month a report in the *Sunderland Echo* was picked up by the London *Daily Chronicle.* Within days the vicarage was besieged by reporters, and Boddy found himself the object of considerable curiosity.

The first person to speak in tongues in Britain in connection with the Pentecostal movement was Mrs. Catherine Price of Brixton. This was in London in January 1907. By December, fifty had spoken in tongues at Sunderland, including Smith Wigglesworth. In May 1908, when A. A. Boddy began publishing his magazine, *Confidence* (1908–26), he stated that up to five hundred had spoken in tongues in Britain. Some, like Smith Wigglesworth, were able to return to their small missions or their more fashionable churches. Most of them were asked to leave.

The first building to be erected and opened as a Pentecostal church in Britain was Emmanuel Mission, Winton, Bournemouth. It was opened in November 1908 by Cecil Polhill for William Oliver Hutchinson (1864–1928), founder of the Apostolic Faith Church (AFC). Among those who joined at Bournemouth were Baptist minister James Brooke (1883–1960) and Salvation Army officer E. C. W. Boulton (1884–1959). In Wales, Dan P. Williams (1882–1947) also joined. In 1916 most of the Welsh assemblies left the AFC to form the Apostolic Church, with Williams as leader and prophet.

After preaching in the Sunderland Convention in 1913, George Jeffreys was invited to northern Ireland, where he founded the Elim Evangelistic Band in 1915. This later became the Elim Pentecostal Church.

In 1924 some seventy independent assemblies came together to form the Assemblies of God of Great Britain and Ireland (AGGBI). The essential difference between Elim and the AGGBI was that the former was centrally governed while the latter are congregational with local autonomy (subject to district approval). The AGGBI insists that speaking in tongues is the initial evidence of the baptism of the Holy Spirit, but the Elim Church declares it to be "with signs following."

There has been a number of smaller groups. Fred Squire (1904–62) established a number of churches for the AGGBI (1933–36), founding the Full Gospel Testimony in 1936. These were absorbed into Elim and AGGBI in 1954. Squire concentrated his work at his International Bible Training Institute at Burgess Hill, Sussex. Previously he had been at Leamington Spa (where Walter Hollenweger was a student).

After leaving the Elim Church in 1940, George Jeffreys founded the Bible-Pattern Church Fellowship (BPCF) in Nottingham. At one time there were some fifty-five churches in this group. Many of the surviving churches have joined the Elim Church Incorporated, as have most of their ministers. BPCF allows the teaching of British Israelism, though few of their ministers have ever held this view.

A number of groups having links with parent bodies in the U.S. are also represented. The largest of these is the New Testament Church of God with some ninety churches. It began in 1953 among West Indian immigrants in Wolverhampton and Birmingham by O. A. Lyseight, and they established sixty-five churches by 1965. National headquarters were in Birmingham (1962–76). A former school building was purchased at Overstone, Northampton, in 1980 to become a Bible school and headquarters.

The Pentecostal Holiness Church has a handful of churches, and a few belonging to the Foursquare Gospel Church have been established, mainly to cater to American servicemen.

There are a good number of independent churches that are not linked to any of the mainline groups or with the house churches. Some, like Kilsyth, Scotland (from 1908), are of long standing; others have been founded by new leaders, some of whom have left their denominations but have not joined with any other established group.

The growth in the number of the mainline Pentecostal churches has slowed down in recent years, but the total number continues to rise and it has been within the existing churches that the largest growth has been witnessed. There is a greater degree of freedom, and many churches have several ministers and full-time staff members who are committed to a total program of social involvement to the community.

This former Jewish synagogue was bought and renovated by the Pentecostal Church in Osijek, Yugoslavia, where Dr. Peter Kuzmič is the pastor. The church is the fastest growing and numerically the largest Pentecostal and evangelical congregation in Yugoslavia.

See ASSEMBLIES OF GOD OF GREAT BRITAIN AND IRELAND; APOSTOLIC CHURCH; ELIM PENTECOSTAL CHURCH.

Great Britain. Leading Figures: A. A. Boddy, P. S. Brewster, W. F. P. Burton, Howard Carter, John Carter, Donald Gee, Harold Horton (1881–1969), George Jeffreys, Stephen Jeffreys, J. N. Parr, Cecil Polhill, E. J. Phillips (1893–1973), James Salter, Smith Wigglesworth, D. P. Williams.

Pentecostal Groupings [churches/ministers (constituents)]: AGGBI: 596/693 (40,000). Elim: 379/565 (38,000). Apostolic: 144/80 (5,298). NTCG: 92/90 (7,000). Elim and AGGBI issue a Year Book, and these contain lists of churches and names of ministers. The Annual Conference in May accepts new churches.

Bible Schools: Pentecostal Missionary Union (1909), AGGBI: Hampstead, Bristol, Kenley, Mattersey (109 students). Elim: Clapham, Capel, Nantwich (113 students). International Bible Training Institute, Leamington Spa, Burgess Hill (40 students). Apostolic: Penygroes, Carmarthen (currently used by Teen Challenge). NTCG: Overstone, Northampton (19 students).

Karl Erik Heinerborg and Lewi Pethrus, in center, play host to two American Pentecostal leaders in this 1972 meeting in Stockholm. On the left is David J. du Plessis and on the right is Joseph Mattsson-Boze.

Publications: *Confidence* (1908–26), ed. A. A. Boddy, Sunderland); *Elim Evangel* (1919, weekly); AGGBI: *Redemption Tidings* (1924–85, weekly); *Redemption* (1985, monthly); Apostolic: *Riches of Grace* (monthly).

Missions: AGGBI work in 24 countries but chiefly in South Africa, Kenya, Zaire. Income: £190,000. Elim work in 23 countries. Income: £360,000. Main areas: Belgium (11 churches), Ghana (2,200 churches, 160,000 members), New Zealand (37 churches, 44 ministers), Eire (4 churches), Tanzania, Transvaal, Zimbabwe. Apostolic: Main areas: Nigeria (320,000 members), Denmark, Italy, Canada, Switzerland, New Zealand.

Bibliography: I. V. Brooks, *Where Do We Go From Here?* (1982); D. W. Cartwright, *The Great Evangelists* (1986); D. Gee, *Wind and Flame* (1967); T. N. Turnbull, *What God Hath Wrought* (1959); K. White, *The Word of God Coming Again* (1919).
D. W. Cartwright

B. Scandinavia. Of the five blocs, the Scandinavian countries represent the most homogeneous pattern in terms of Pentecostal life and thought. This homogeneity results from features common to the movement in the Nordic lands:

1. Although, as elsewhere, the beginnings of Scandinavian Pentecostalism were marked by Holiness concerns, it was seen in continuity with the tradition of indigenous Scandinavian revival movements (e.g., the Haugean movement in Norway and the Laestadtian movement in Finland). This perspective has influenced the nomenclature of the major Pentecostal groupings in each country, which in English would be termed "the ——— Pentecostal Revival Movement."

2. The movement in the Scandinavian countries is marked by a strongly congregationalist ecclesiology. Scandinavian Pentecostals have typically resisted all forms of supracongregational organization, seeing such structures as unbiblical. The major secessionist movements in Finland, Norway, and Sweden all upheld this strict congrega-

tionalism. This emphasis came from an early influx of Baptists into the Swedish movement, beginning with Lewi Pethrus's Baptist church in Stockholm becoming Pentecostal in 1913. This congregational polity then gained the weighty support of the Pentecostal "patriarch," Thomas Barratt of Norway, around the time of World War I. The annual conferences at Nyhem have been important for the unity of the movement in Sweden.

3. The distinctive character of Scandinavian Pentecostalism reflects the unparalleled influence and prestige of Lewi Pethrus. Among European Pentecostal leaders, only Donald Gee of Britain has had a comparable standing. Whereas Gee's influence was more extended across the world, Pethrus's was more intensive in and close to his native Sweden. Though there were two crises in the Swedish movement in which schisms followed challenges to Pethrus's standing and authority (by A. P. Franklin in 1929 and by Sven Lidman in 1947), his reputation as leader, teacher, and statesman of the movement held firm. The characteristic features of Scandinavian Pentecostalism were in fact the distinctive emphases of Pethrus, though he disavowed all authority over other assemblies. Even the recent mitigation of absolute congregationalism in Sweden is primarily due to the influence of the national ventures started by Pethrus after his retirement in 1958.

4. In all the Scandinavian countries except Denmark and Iceland, Pentecostalism has emerged as the largest Christian movement outside the Lutheran state churches. This growth was initially helped by major Pentecostal recruitment from the Scandinavian free churches, particularly from the Methodists in Norway and the Baptists in Sweden. It was later aided by the movement's revival character in contrast to the more doctrinal emphases of other Protestant bodies. As a result, the Pentecostal movement in Norway, Sweden, and Finland has an air of confident progress and

relative prosperity that contrasts with much continental European Pentecostalism, which retains more of its earlier "back-street mission hall" character.

5. Pentecostal strength among non-Lutheran Christians has contributed to Scandinavian Pentecostalism's greater public presence and outreach, especially in Sweden and Finland. The Swedish movement has taken up a distinctively Swedish institution, the "Folk High School," offering adult courses from one month to three years on Christian and other topics. Swedish Pentecostals have produced more quality literature than elsewhere and have the only Pentecostal daily journal, *Dagen*, begun in 1945. Swedish Pentecostals have had more influence on public life than Pentecostals elsewhere, e.g., through the Christian Democratic Party founded by Pethrus, which has influenced local more than national politics. The Stockholm assembly under Pethrus was responsible for launching IBRA (International Broadcasting Association), which reaches into Europe, Africa, Asia, and Latin America. The Swedish Pentecostals now have their own TV studio, selling programs to the state TV company. This greater self-confidence of Scandinavian Pentecostals has led in Finland to an official dialogue between the Pentecostals and the state Lutheran church.

Pentecostals form approximately one-half of all Scandinavian missionaries, with main concentrations in Africa and Brazil. Missionary organizations were formed in both Norway and Sweden, but they were accused of usurping the authority of local congregations. The coordination and supervision of missionary work has thus been a delicate topic, raising substantive theological issues for Scandinavian Pentecostals.

In the statistics given, the first figure given for each denomination represents the number of worship centers (unless stated to be churches that have their own pastors) and the second is of committed adult membership, with an occasional third figure in parentheses representing the total attendance-participation. In all countries, there are very small denominations not listed.

Denmark. Leading Figure: Anna Larssen Bjorner.

Pentecostal Groupings: Pentecostal Revival Movement of Denmark (*Pinsebevaegelsen*): 38/4,400. AC: 37 churches/2,500 (10,000). Elim 33/3,400 (10,000).

Publications: *Korsets Evangelium* (semiweekly). Missionaries: 24 in 11 countries.

Finland. Leading Figures: G. Olsen-Smidt, Norwegian, ex-Salvation Army, pioneer pastor in Helsinki (1912–25); Eino Manninen (1896–1967), pastor in Helsinki (from 1925) and host pastor for seventh PWC (1964); Niilo Yli-Vainio (1920–81), best-known Finnish Pentecostal and powerful revival preacher.

Pentecostal Groupings: Pentecostal Revival Movement of Finland (*Helluntal-Ystavat*): 190 Finnish and 35 Swedish/40,000 and 3,000. Pentecostal Friends: 25/3,600. Free Pentecostal Revival of Finland: ?/2,000. Maranatha Revival: ?/2,000.

Publications: *Ristin Voitto* (monthly).

Nicholas and Martha Nikoloff were early Pentecostal missionaries to Eastern Europe.

Missionaries: 327 in 26 countries.

Iceland. Movement founded in 1920. Pentecostal movement in Iceland: 50/600.

Norway. Leading Figures: Thomas Ball Barratt, G. F. Tollefsen (–1966), missionary pioneer and organizer.

Pentecostal Groupings: Norwegian Pentecostal Assemblies (*Pinsebevegelsen*): 770/36,105 (70,000). Free Pentecostal Friends: ?/1,000. Apostolic Faith Church: 7/200. Maranatha Revival: ?/200. AC: 2/50.

Publications: *Korsets Seier* (weekly). Missionaries: 300 plus in 30 countries.

Sweden. Leading Figures: Lewi Pethrus; Sven Lidman (1882–1960), poet, author, missions promoter; Samuel Nystrom (1891–1961), missionary to Brazil, then missionary secretary in Sweden, active in PWCs; Allan Tornberg (1907–56), missions executive, song writer, pastor.

Pentecostal Groupings: Pentecostal Revival Movement (*Pinqstväckelsen*): 540 churches/100,674 (230,000). Orebro Mission Society: 350/19,650 (44,650). Maranatha Revival: ?/10,000 (late 1970s, but declining).

Publications: *Evangelii Harold* (weekly, Stockholm); *Hemmets Van* (weekly, Orebro). Missionaries: 838 in 48 countries.

C. West-Central Europe. The least homogeneous European region in terms of Pentecostal

Rumanian Pentecostal church leaders meeting in Bucharest in 1967. In front row are A. Vamvu; D. Matache; Andre Nicholle, visiting French Pentecostal leader; Pavel Bochian, president of the Apostolic Church of God; and Trandafir Sandru, director of the Pentecostal Theological Seminary.

patterns and presence is west-central Europe, covering three language groupings (German, French, and Dutch-Flemish). The Pentecostal movement has been present uninterruptedly since the beginning in Germany and Holland (1907), present in Switzerland since the beginning though less steadily (1907), with a weak presence in France from 1909, Le Havre providing the only continuity with the later French movement (1930), and only present from a later date in Austria (1923).

German Pentecostalism has been heavily marked by opposition from German evangelical Pietists, expressed in the Berlin Declaration. The Mülheim Association, the oldest branch of the German movement, is unique in representing a framework combining Pentecostal experience and convictions with the possibility of remaining within older denominational structures. It has continued the Holiness teaching of the *Gemeinschaftsbewegung,* which other Pentecostals at the 1921 Amsterdam conference found too oppressive. The Mülheim Association does not teach tongues as "initial evidence."

The Free Church Pentecostal Assemblies in Germany sprang up after World War II, largely from the influx of refugees from Eastern Europe, where German communities had experienced revival. Due to evangelical opposition, the German Pentecostals have been more isolated than in many other countries, and it is only in the last decade that there has been regular fellowship among different Pentecostal bodies.

The movement in the Netherlands is characterized by a plethora of Pentecostal bodies, none numerically dominant. The clearest denomina-

tional structure belongs to the Brotherhood of Pentecostal Assemblies, formed in 1952 but having this title only since 1959. Several Pentecostal groupings have resulted from revival movements led by dynamic preachers such as Karel Hoekendijk, J. E. van den Brink, and Johan Maasbach. In addition, there are three groupings of Indonesian Pentecostals. Some Dutch Pentecostals were open to the charismatic movement, which began earlier in Holland than in most European countries, and in 1962 the Brotherhood produced a statement "*De Pinkstergemeente en de Kerk*" (The Pentecostal Assemblies and the Church) in reply to a statement of the Dutch Reformed Church.

French Pentecostalism is less marked by the Holiness movement. The major shaping influence was a foreign evangelist, Douglas Scott from England, who communicated his Elim evangelistic vision to the French assemblies, so that French Pentecostals see the movement primarily in terms of evangelistic effectiveness. The French movement had its roots in Le Havre and Rouen (the scene of the labors of Pierre Nicolle), with Normandy continuing to be a center for Pentecostal revival. Particularly notable in the history of French Pentecostalism has been the gypsy revival under the ministry of Clément le Cossec since 1952. This gypsy movement separated from the Assemblies of God in France in 1968 by amicable arrangement and now numbers in excess of 100,000 people with their own pastoral structures.

Austria. Pentecostal Groupings [churches/ministers (constituents)]: Free Christian Assemblies (*Freie Christengemeinden*): 18/800 (2,000).

Rumanian Pentecostals gather for an Easter service in 1970.

Publications: *Lebens Botschaft* (monthly).

Belgium. Leading Figures: Henri Théophile de Worm (1893–1964), Reformed pastor at Paturages, a center for Pentecostal revival from 1932 to 1939; Johannes Rietdijk (1901–85), scholarly author and pioneer pastor in Kiel, near Antwerp; Johannes Benjamin van Kesteren (1905–81), pioneer church builder who bridged the French-Flemish linguistic divide.

Pentecostal Groupings: AG in Belgium (French language): 40/3,750. Flemish Pentecostal Assemblies (*Broederschap van Vlaamse Pinkstergemeenten*) 40/2,000. Pentecostal Churches (French language; Scandinavian background): 10/475.

France. Leading Figures: Hélène Biolley; Douglas Scott; Pierre Nicolle (1882–1972), ex-Baptist pastor who became founding pastor of Rouen assembly, which became a focal point for the French AG; Félix Gallice (1887–1960), pioneer pastor in Le Havre; Clément le Cossec (1921–), founder of international Pentecostal mission to gypsies.

Pentecostal Groupings: French AG (*Assemblées de Dieu en France*): 324/50,000 (65,000). Gypsy Mission (*Mission Evangélique des Tziganes*): 500 preachers/40,000 (100,000). AC: 40/1,000. *Fédération des Associations de Réveil:* 18/3,000.

Publications: *Viens et Vois* (1923–73, monthly); *Pentecôte* (1974– , monthly).

Missionaries: AG: 48 in 15 countries.

Germany (undivided until 1945, West Germany since 1945). Leading Figures: Jonathan Paul; Emil Humburg; C. O. Voget (1879–1936), Reformed pastor in Friesland, who became a leading teacher in the Mülheim Association; Erwin Lorenz (1906–85), pioneer founder and leader among the "free church" Pentecostals; Christian H. Krust (1896–1973), successor to Humburg and theologian of the Mülheim Association.

Pentecostal Groupings: Mülheim Association: ?/11,000. Federation of Free Church Pentecostal Assemblies (*Bund Freikirchlicher Pfingstegemeinden in Deutschland,* BFP): 150/16,000. People's Mission of Committed Christians (*Bolksmission Entschiedener Christen*): 80/2,500 (5,500). CG (*Gemeinde Gottes*): 52/1,637. AC: 7/500.

Publications: *Heilszeugnisse* (monthly, Mülheim Association); *Wort und Geist* (monthly, BFP).

Missionaries: CG: 6 in 2 countries.

The Netherlands. Leading Figures: Gerrit R. Polman; Wilhelmina Polman; Nicolaas Vetter (1899–1945), missionary in Venezuela, who returned to pastor church in Rotterdam; Piet Klaver (1890–1970), missionary in China and Java, who returned to lead church in Amsterdam; Pieter van der Woude (1895–1978), pastor in Rotterdam and key leader in generation after Polman; Karel Hoekendijk (1904–87), major figure in origins of *Stromen van Kracht* (Streams of Power) revival; J. E. van den Brink (1909–), pioneer of *Kracht van Omhoog* (Power From on High) movement; Johannes Maasbach (1918–), healing evangelist and founder of Full Gospel World Mission.

Pentecostal Groupings: Brotherhood of Pentecostal Assemblies (*Broederschap van Pinkstergemeenten*): 38/5,500. Full Gospel Assemblies (*Volle Evangelie Gemeenten Nederland):* 45/5,500. *Kracht van Omhoog* 25/4,000. Bethel Assemblies, Indonesian Dutch (*Bethel Pinksterkerk Nederland*): ?/3,085. Bethel Full Gospel, Indonesian Dutch (*Volle Evangelie Bethel Kerk):* ?/2,500. Johan Maasbach World Mission: 10/2,150. Independent Pentecostal Churches: ?/20,000.

Publications: *Parakleet* (quarterly) and *Gouden Schoven* (monthly) from Brotherhood; *Herstel* (quarterly) and *Kracht van Omhoog* (monthly) from Kracht; *Nieuw Leven* (monthly, Maasbach); *Opwekking* (monthly, B. Hoekendijk).

Missionaries: 163.

Switzerland. Leading Figures: Anton B. Reuss (1872–1934), British founder of Bern assembly in 1920; Heinrich Steiner (1876–1945), founder of St. Gallen assembly; Leonhard Steiner, son of Heinrich Steiner; Jakob Zopfi (1932–   ), currently president of the Swiss Pentecostal Mission, editor of *World Pentecost*, first president of newly formed Pentecostal European Fellowship, and secretary to advisory committee of the Pentecostal World Conference.

Pentecostal Groupings: Swiss Pentecostal Mission (*Schweizerische Pfingstmission*, SPM): 60 churches/5,000 (6,500). Apostolic Church (*Gemeinde für Urchristentum*): 75/2,600. Free Swiss Assemblies (*Freie Christengemeinden der Schweiz*): 21/1,400. Eglise Evangélique du Réveil: 17/1,700.

Publication: *Die Verheissung des Vaters*, later absorbed into *Wort und Geist* (monthly, SPM).

Missionaries: SPM: 25 in 4 countries.

D. Eastern Europe. Eastern Europe encompasses the European nations with Communist governments. The Pentecostal movement reached Eastern Europe in a variety of ways. Small Pentecostal groups were reported to be in Estonia as early as 1907, probably stemming from Scandinavian influence, which continued in the Tallinn and St. Petersburg areas. One branch of Russian Pentecostals, the Smorodintsy, are "Oneness" in their theology, their founder N. P. Smorodin having received the Pentecostal message from A. D. Urshan in Finland around 1911. Eleanor Patrick and Edwin Dennis from Frankfurt, Germany, did Pentecostal work among German-speaking Christians in the Baltic countries for some years from 1909. Pastor Fetler exercised a Pentecostal ministry in imperial Russia for some years before the 1917 revolution.

Most accounts of Russian Pentecostalism attribute the main thrust of the movement to the missionary labors of Ivan E. Voronaev, though his work may be best-known because of his contacts in the West. A Russian Baptist pastor forced to emigrate, Voronaev was baptized in the Spirit and formed the first Russian Pentecostal Church in New York City in 1919. Hearing a divine command to return to Russia, Voronaev traveled to Bulgaria in 1920, laying the foundations of Pentecostal work there before going on to Odessa and Leningrad. The 1920s were optimum years for Pentecostal mission, when the Soviet authorities hoped that freedom for Russian Protestants would help undermine the Orthodox church. Voronaev established some 350 congregations in the Soviet Union, many in the Ukraine, before his arrest and imprisonment in the late 1920s. Initial headway was commonly made in Baptist assemblies.

Other missions in Eastern Europe were spearheaded by emigrés to America who later returned to their native lands with the Pentecostal message. Notable among these were Gustave Herbert Schmidt (1891–1958) and Nicholas Nikoloff (1900–1964), who from 1927 worked in the Russian and Eastern Europe Mission (REEM),

which had close links with the AG in the U.S. Schmidt founded a Bible school in Danzig, and the Pentecostal work in Poland stemmed from his labors. Nikoloff worked in Bulgaria from 1926, but later succeeded Schmidt in Danzig. The Pentecostal assemblies in Rumania arose from American Pentecostal literature reaching Gheorghe Bradin (1895–1962) in 1922. Assemblies were formed, and despite persecution, the association of Pentecostal assemblies was formed in 1929 into the Apostolic Church of God.

The Communist takeover in Eastern Europe following World War II intensified the difficulties of Pentecostal Christians already facing unsympathetic state churches and governments. In almost all Eastern European lands, the Pentecostals have been faced with the dilemma of either registering with the state authorities and suffering close state supervision of all church life, or refusing to register and risking harsh penalties for illegal association.

In the Soviet Union, registered Pentecostals were constrained by the state in 1945 to join the All-Union Council of Evangelical Christians-Baptists (AUCECB), in which the Pentecostals are one of four distinct church streams. This "union," which appeared on paper to be an acceptance of Pentecostal assemblies into a wider denomination, was often an absorption of Pentecostal believers into Baptist congregations. Since glossolalia was explicitly excluded from AUCECB worship, the majority of Pentecostals refused to join, and some that did soon left. The war years, and the period between Stalin's death and the Khrushchev persecution (1953–58) were years of rapid growth, and the release of many from labor camps in remote areas of the U.S.S.R. led to the founding of Pentecostal assemblies in those parts.

Since the early 1970s, some Pentecostal assemblies outside AUCECB have been allowed to register, thirty having done so by 1977. It is estimated that there are 25,000 Pentecostals within AUCECB, a few thousand in other registered churches, and at least 100,000 in unregistered assemblies. Russian Pentecostals almost all attribute great importance to foot-washing. Persecution has hit them as hard as any Soviet Christians, glossolalia often being presented by state persecutors as harmful to health, and opposition sometimes intensified by Pentecostal objection to military service.

In Poland the Pentecostals were the largest of five groups in the Evangelical United Church of the Gospel, with almost 200 congregations. A reorganization occurred in 1987 with the establishment of the Pentecostal Church in Poland, numbering 86 local churches and about 10,000 members. One area with many Polish Pentecostals was absorbed into the Soviet Union in 1945, strengthening the movement in Belorussia (White Russia). In Czechoslovakia, the Pentecostals are part of a Union of Free Congregational Churches, and in East Germany they are in the Association of Evangelical Free Church Congregations.

The Pentecostals in Bulgaria, Hungary, and Rumania have been allowed to form their own denominations without forcible association with other Protestant groups. Much the largest is the

The Biblical Theological Institute, Osijek, Yugoslavia, with 40 resident students representing nine nationalities. The school has about 200 extension students and is the largest evangelical training school in eastern Europe.

Apostolic Church of God in Rumania, with a membership of over 100,000, though it is estimated that there are more than 200,000 Pentecostal believers in Rumania. The registered Bulgarian Pentecostals have about 100 congregations with more than 10,000 members, while the unregistered Church of God is thought to have more than 4,000 members. The main Pentecostal denomination in Hungary, formed in 1935, is the Primitive Christian Brethren (the Apostolic Church) with about 3,000 members. In Yugoslavia, the Kristova Pentekostna Crkva had its origin among German-speaking people and has about 3,000 members, with its main strength in Croatia and Slovenia.

There are signs of significant Pentecostal theology developing in Eastern Europe, notably with Trandafir Sandru (Rumania, 1924–   ) and Peter Kuzmič (Yugoslavia, 1946–   ). This surprising development may be helped by their life situation, in which Pentecostals are less likely to be involved in exegetical encounter with other Christians than in the confrontation between eternal issues and social tensions.

In this section, available approximate statistics have been given in the text. No classifications are given by nations due to the difficulty of obtaining reliable information.

E. Southern Europe. The most notable characteristic of Mediterranean Pentecostalism is its opposition to the dominant Roman Catholicism (Italy, Portugal, Spain) and Eastern Orthodoxy (Greece). In these lands, where historic church-state connections are still operative, Pentecostals have encountered persecution and hostility, perhaps most markedly in areas of evangelistic success, though with some diminution in Catholic countries since Vatican II. In 1987, a historic agreement was reached between the Italian AG and the government that gave the Pentecostals full liberty to develop and evangelize. In these countries there is implacable opposition to all forms of ecumenical dialogue, and virtually no collaboration or fellowship with Catholic charismatics. The perceived moral laxity of the prevailing culture has produced in Pentecostals a strongly negative attitude toward some pastimes and amusements.

In Italy and Portugal the Pentecostal movement represents the most numerous and fastest-growing segment of evangelical Protestantism. In the Mediterranean lands, Pentecostal impact has been greatest among the poor, especially the peasant class. Latest AG statistics show Pentecostal growth as fastest in the south, especially in Sicily. Some observers have noted that the strongest opposition to Pentecostalism comes in areas where the local oligarchy sees Pentecostal faith as withdrawing the poor from their control.

Italian Pentecostalism, the strongest in the Mediterranean region, is unique in resulting wholly from evangelistic campaigns led by returning emigrés from the U.S. This occurred at a very early stage in the movement, with Giacomo Lombardi returning to Italy in 1908, the year after the first Italian-Americans were baptized in the Spirit in Chicago. However, Portuguese Pentecostalism, now numbering between 20,000 and 30,000 adherents, also came from the New World, through J. Placido da Costa of Brazil (1913) and Daniel Berg, the founder of the Brazilian AG (1921). In Spain the largest Pentecostal group is the Iglesia Filadelfia, the church of the gypsies. This work began around 1964 as an expansion of the French mission of Clément le Cossec and is strongest in the northern provinces. It now has some 1,500 preachers and has outgrown the gypsy mission in France.

Greece. Movement began about 1924.
Pentecostal Groupings (churches/ministers [constituents]): AG: 16/2000.

Italy. Leading Figures: Giacomo Lombardi (1864–1934), pioneer evangelist; Roberto Bracco (1915–83), pastor and author; Francisco Toppi, general superintendent of the AG in Italy.
Pentecostal Groupings: AG in Italy: 935/104,000 (200,000). International Evangelical Church: 16/5,000. AC in Italy: 74/2,400 (5,000). CG: 10/350 (1,000)
Publication: *Risveglio Pentecostale* (monthly from AG).

Portugal. Leading Figures: Jose de Matos (1888–1958), pioneer evangelist and founder; Paulo Branco (1959–), historian of movement and now pastor in Cadiz, Spain.

Pentecostal Groupings: AG: 470/25,000 adult (33,000).

Publication: *Novas de Alegria* (monthly).

Spain. Pentecostal Groupings: *Iglesia Filadelfia:* 1,500 preachers/100,000 (200,000). AG: 70/3,000 (5,000) CG: 15/2,000.

Publication: *Fiel* (monthly).

IV. European Dimensions. In the first decade of the movement, contacts between Pentecostal leaders in different European countries were closer than in subsequent years. The major leaders regularly attended and spoke at each other's conventions and kept up frequent correspondence. These bonds were formalized in the International Pentecostal Council, formed in 1912, which, while welcoming some leaders from America, was in effect a European council.

These bonds of fellowship were disrupted by World War I, which restricted travel and communications. After the war the degree of closeness was never recovered despite the international conference held at Amsterdam in 1921. The 1920s were years of denominationalization, a process that inevitably introduced rivalries and led to the term "movement"—preferred by Pentecostals to church terminology—becoming applied to particular denominations. Nonetheless, the common experience of baptism in the Holy Spirit with signs following was distinctive enough for the whole Pentecostal movement in Europe to retain a sense of its particular identity even amid diminished international contacts. This sense was enhanced in the 1920s and 1930s by the evangelistic campaigns of Smith Wigglesworth, who was not aligned with any one Pentecostal denomination, and the developing teaching ministry of Donald Gee, which was valued in all strands of the movement.

Gee was the prime mover in an attempt to gather Pentecostals from all European groups into one conference, and this was finally held at Stockholm in June 1939. This conference was the only occasion in Pentecostal history when doctrinal and theological issues have been openly debated between delegates from a variety of allegiances. Here was manifest a problem that bedeviled subsequent attempts at Pentecostal unity: the clash between those espousing a strict congregationalism (notably the Scandinavian Pentecostals, but also the French AG) and those with an element of denominational centralization. The former were deeply suspicious of all attempts to form any Pentecostal organization, whether at national, continental, or worldwide level.

Collaboration across national boundaries was reinforced after World War II by the inauguration of Pentecostal World Conferences, of which the first was held at Zurich, Switzerland, in 1947. It was at the Paris PWC in 1949 that the organizational issue caused another confrontation. The desire to form some kind of Pentecostal world organization was vehemently opposed by the Scandinavians. It was agreed simply to hold the PWC together with five advisers, with the secretary's responsibility limited to contacts in view of the next PWC. Rumblings among the Scandinavians continued for several years, as they were fearful of the secretary (then David du Plessis) being seen as a spokesman for the whole movement. Gee did much to assuage fears and keep international communications open.

There were no specifically European Pentecostal groupings until the 1960s. In 1966, the European Pentecostal Fellowship (EPF) was formed in Rome, bringing together Pentecostal denominations with national organizations. Initially comprising mostly AG-type denominations, EPF was later joined by the Church of God (Germany) and Elim (Britain). Congregational-type Pentecostals began in 1969 to hold Pentecostal European Conferences (PEC), initially on a small scale in Sweden, but from 1972 every three years in various European centers. In 1987 the European fellowship sought for so long became a reality when EPF and PEC amalgamated to form the Pentecostal European Fellowship (PEF). From discussions at the PEC at The Hague, Holland, in 1978, the European Pentecostal Theological Association was formed.

Less-frequent academic conferences on "Pentecostal and Charismatic Research in Europe" have been held since 1980, when first convened by David Bundy and Jerry Sandidge in Leuven, Belgium. These conferences (Leuven, 1980 and 1981; Birmingham, England, 1984; and Gwatt, Switzerland, 1987) are open to all scholars interested in Pentecostalism and charismatic renewal, and they have been strongly supported by Professor Walter Hollenweger and his doctoral students' tackling Pentecostal topics.

Bibliography: N. Bloch-Hoell, *The Pentecostal Movement* (1964); P. Branco, *Pentecostes un Desafio al Mundo* (1984); D. D. Bundy, "Charismatic Renewal in Belgium: A Bibliographical Essay," *EPTA Bulletin* 5 (1986): 76–95; idem, "Early European Scholarly Perspectives on Pentecostalism," *EPTA Bulletin* 5 (1986): 4–23; idem, "Historical Perspectives on the Development of The European Pentecostal Association," *Pneuma* 2 (1980): 15–25; idem, ed., *Papers Presented at the Second Meeting of the European Pentecostal Theological Association* (1980); idem, "Pentecostalism in Belgium," *Pneuma* 8 (1986): 41–56; idem, "The Roumanian Pentecostal Church in Recent Literature," *Pneuma* 7 (1985): 19–40; B. Carlsson, *Organizations and Decision Procedures Within the Swedish Pentecostal Movement* (n.d.); S. Durasoff, *Pentecost Behind the Iron Curtain* (1972); P. Fleisch, *Die Pfingstbewegung in Deutschland* (1957); W. C. Fletcher, *Soviet Charismatics* (1985); D. Gee, *Upon All Flesh* (1947); idem, *Wind and Flame* (1967); W. J. Hollenweger, *The Pentecostals* (1972); idem, ed., *Die Pfingstkirchen* (1971); C. H. Krust, *50 Jahre Deutsche Pfingstbewegung* (1958); idem, *Was wir glauben, lehren und bekennen* (1963); I. Lundgren, "Lewi Pethrus and the Swedish Pentecostal Movement," in *Essays on Apostolic Themes*, ed. P. Elbert (1985); L. Pethrus, *A Spiritual Memoir* (1973); C. E. Sahlberg, *The Pentecostal Movement* (1985); W. Sawatsky, *Soviet Evangelicals Since World War II* (1981); R. P. Spittler, ed., *Perspectives on the New Pentecostalism* (1976); L. Steiner, *Mit Folgenden Zeichen* (1954); G. R. Stotts, *Le Pentecôtisme au pays de Voltaire* (1981); E. Strand et al., *Fram til urkristendommen,* 3 vols. (1956–59); A. Sundstedt, *Pingstväckelsen,* 5 vols (1969–73); C. and P. van der Laan, *Pinksteren in beweging* (1982); J. Zopfi . . .*auf alles Fleisch* (1985).   P. D. Hocken

EUROPEAN PIETIST ROOTS OF PENTE-COSTALISM Pietism has been influential in the development of Pentecostalism both in Europe and the U.S. From those two centers various emphases and concerns of Pietism have been transferred to Pentecostal and charismatic movements throughout the world. To describe the influence of various expressions of Pietism within the Pentecostal traditions, it is first necessary to look at the heritage of Pietism, its adaptation in the eighteenth-century Wesleyan revivals, and developments in late-nineteenth- and early-twentieth-century European Pietism, as well as the role of American revivalism, both Wesleyan-Holiness and Keswick articulations.

What is Pietism? It has never been a monolithic movement. Pietism is ideologically and socially diverse; however, its main identifying characteristics are (1) affirmation of the possibility of a personal experience of God, beginning with a "new birth" by the Holy Spirit; (2) insistence that the experience of God has direct implications for the manner in which a Christian person may live (sanctification); (3) requirement of Christian community, a community that often understands itself to have a reformist stance over against the larger social context; (4) chronologically, designation of the particular confluence of these concerns after the development of confessional orthodoxy and before the Enlightenment, as well as groups and ideas tracing their heritage to this period; and (5) its near-exclusive use for Protestant groups although similar ideas and emphases are found among Roman Catholic and Orthodox Christians.

I. Heritage of Pietism. The major impetus for Pietism within the Lutheran tradition came from the work of Johann Arndt (1555–1621). Arndt edited writings of Thomas Aquinas and John Tauler, thereby making Catholic mysticism available to Lutheran believers. He contributed essays on "True Christianity" in which he insisted on the mystical union with God (new birth) and argued that Christian commitment is to result in a life of active piety, congruent to the model provided by Christ.

These emphases were picked up by many Lutheran theologians who articulated them primarily in tractates designed to edify the literate layperson and to exhort the clergy. However, it was only with Philipp Jakob Spener (1635–1705) that Pietism became a movement with defined goals. A scholarly pastor, he was well acquainted with the writings of the Reformers and counter-reformers. He concluded that it was not enough to provide doctrinal purity. The inner life of the individual was to be transformed. Spener suggested a method in *Pia Desideria* (1675) and introduced eschatological expectations as a motivational device. The method was to (1) develop Bible study sessions at which laypersons would be involved in the interpretation of Scripture, (2) implement the "priesthood of believers," (3) give the practice of Christian truth priority over Christian dogma, and (4) develop the interior life of the Christian. Each aspect of this proposal received criticism from the more traditional Lutheran theologians.

Perhaps the most effective supporter of Spener was August Hermann Francke (1663–1727), pastor and theologian at Hamburg and then Halle. Francke's description of his conversion, emphasizing the role of the conscience, both in its unease and assurance, became paradigmatic for conversion within the Pietist movement. He argued that the soul senses the emptiness of love for the world, that it responds to the call of God with repentance that leads to conversion. This results in joy and assurance, both of which are reinforced by resisting the persecutions and temptations of the world. This understanding of conversion became central to Wesley's experience and was adapted by revivalist movements throughout Europe and North America. Francke also undertook serious and extensive efforts at social and economic reform.

One of Francke's students was Count Nikolaus Ludwig von Zinzendorf (1700–1760). Zinzendorf contributed to the survival of the movement by developing communitarian structures (Herrnhut) and critically interacting with and adapting to the Enlightenment in Germany. His critique of the Enlightenment influenced Goethe, Schleiermacher, and other German intellectuals. Zinzendorf was also more ecumenical in his understanding of the church, and this contributed to the spread of Pietist ideals beyond the confines of German Lutheranism.

Pietist biblicism developed in southern Germany. Johann Albrecht Bengel (1687–1752) was the most important early Pietist contributor to developing biblical studies, especially in textual criticism. His magisterial commentary on the NT, *Gnomen Novi Testament* (1742), later served as the basis for John Wesley's *Explanatory Notes Upon the New Testament* (1755). It also contributed directly to Pentecostal hermeneutics in Western Europe and North America.

Another Pietist emphasis, primitivism, developed gradually within Germany and was directly related to the issue of whether or not the group should remain in the Lutheran church. Some of the radical pietists opted for separatism. It was Gottfried Arnold (1660–1714) who most definitively articulated the primitivist vision in *Die erste Liebe der gemeinden Jesu Christi, das ist Wahre Abbildung der ersten Christenen nach ihrem lebendigen Glauben und heiligen Leben* (1696). Versions of this text are kept in print by Pentecostal publishing houses in Europe. It argues that the true church is not defined by its doctrinal stance as judged by the confessional decisions but by its fidelity to the new birth by the Holy Spirit. He provided the framework for what would eventually become the standard Pentecostal historiography, the "history of heresies" tradition. Primitivists have argued that the NT tradition is to be paradigmatic, and they have reevaluated many groups judged heretical by the established churches, reinterpreting them as reform or renewalist movements seeking to reestablish the NT model.

II. Pietism in the Wesleyan Revivals. Pietism influenced various aspects of English church life before 1800, including the Society of Friends (Quakers), Puritans, and Anglican theologians of the Carolingian period. Each of these has influenced Pentecostalism. However, the most significant channel by which Pietist concerns flowed into the Pentecostal theological synthesis is that of Methodism in its various forms and derivative movements. The primary leader of the Methodist revivals was John Wesley (1703–1791), who received his early theological formation from his mother, who had personal roots in the Puritan tradition, and from his father, who had studied the Carolingian theologians. Wesley drew from both traditions and became attracted to German Pietism when he met a spiritually confident Moravian on board ship during a severe storm. A visit to Herrnhut brought him into direct contact with that center. He also adapted the insights of Spanish and French Roman Catholic mystics to articulate his vision for Christian spirituality, adding to the Pietist understanding, concepts of human divinization found in fourth-century Christian writers.

Wesley's chosen theologian, John Fletcher (1729–85), was the first to use the term "baptism of the Holy Spirit" to describe the process of sanctification and the accompanying assurance of spiritual well-being. True to his Pietist heritage, he emphasized the internal spiritual changes of "new birth" and lifestyle as well as Christian responsibility for relief work and social reform. Fletcher became the Methodist theologian of choice in North America. His works were published in more editions than those of Wesley!

The Wesleyan-Fletcher theological synthesis was shaped by Pietist concerns. It developed in three overlapping primary arenas within North America: (1) the Methodist Church, (2) the perfectionistic revivalist movements, and (3) in other denominations—a phenomenon that has been described as the "arminianizing of America" or the "Methodist century." The central concerns were those of the seventeenth-century German pietists described above. Prominent evangelists and theologians included Charles G. Finney, Asa Mahan, Phoebe Palmer, James Caughey, Orange Scott, and Thomas Upham. The 1858 revival gave impetus to the Pietist concerns. D. L. Moody, William E. Boardman, Charles Cullis, Hannah Whitall Smith, Robert Pearsall Smith, George Müller, William Arthur, A. B. Simpson, S. D. Gordon, Andrew Murray, and R. A. Torrey became important exponents of the "higher Christian Life." Hannah Whitall Smith's *Christian's Secret of a Happy Life* (1875) became the standard interpretation of the spiritual life advocated by the revivalist movement.

Smiths and Boardman were instrumental in establishing the series of meetings that became known as the Keswick movement. Because of the personal moral problems of Robert Pearsall Smith and the different cultural conditions in which Keswick initially functioned, American perfectionist expectations were separated from the doctrine of sanctification as was Pietist social concern. Keswickian perspectives significantly influenced the Reformed wing of the American Holiness movement. As Juhuni Kuosmanen, *Herätyksen Historia* (1979); Daniel Brandt-Bessire, *Aux sources de la spiritualité pentecôtiste*

(1986); and especially Donald Dayton, *The Theological Roots of Pentecostalism* (1987) have demonstrated, both Keswickian and Wesleyan perfectionist elements of the Holiness movement provided theological paradigms and leadership to the nascent American Pentecostal movement.

III. Nineteenth-Century European Pietism and Pentecostalism. The traditions of classical Pietism that have influenced Pentecostalism are diverse and regionally specific. Also the extent of direct influence is problematic, as relationships and reading patterns of early adherents are difficult to define. Examination of several early European Pentecostal periodicals indicates that American and British Holiness-Keswick authors are cited more frequently than all other traditions combined. The most frequently cited authors are W. Boardman, H. W. Smith, C. Finney, D. L. Moody, A. J. Gordon, S. D. Gordon, W. Arthur, A. B. Simpson, R. A. Torrey, J. A. Dowie, E. Irving, and A. Murray. They are used as definitive authorities on spiritual life, theology, mission, and evangelism. Melvin Dieter, *The Holiness Revival of the Nineteenth Century* (1980), discusses the transference of American Wesleyan-Holiness spirituality to Britain and the Continent as well as its transformation in that context.

However, there were important parallel or complementary traditions in Europe. In Germany, the efforts of Robert Pearsall Smith, later reinforced by R. A. Torrey, were institutionalized and indigenized in the *Heiligungsbewegung* or *Gemeinschaftsbewegung*. Leaders included T. Christlieb, E. Schrenk, C. H. Rappard, E. Modersohn, and J. Vetter. Theodor Jellinghaus (1841–1913), author of *Das völlige gegenwartige Heil durch Christum* (1880, 5th ed. 1903) and Jonathan A. B. Paul were the most important theologians. The movement later split, as chronicled in Dieter Lange, *Eine Bewegung Bricht sich Bahn* (1979), over the issue of Pentecostalism; however, the popular theological and spirituality books of *Gemeinschaftsbewegung* writers have continued to circulate in Pentecostal churches.

In Scandinavia there were other Pietist traditions. While there was significant interchange across changing political boundaries, Hans Nielsen Hauge (1771–1824) was particularly influential in Norway, while Lars Levi Laestadius (1880–61) and Peter Waldenström (1838–1917) were especially influential in Sweden and Finland. Methodist, Baptist, and Darbyist thought was significant throughout Europe, as was the example of the Salvation Army.

Other European Pietist figures became paradigmatic of how the Pentecostal theological synthesis should be lived in Europe. Andrew Murray provided a model for theological writing, Otto Stockmeyer and A. Monod were known for preaching and pastoral skills, and J. F. Oberlin was exemplary of Pietist social analysis and social ministry. Johann Christoph Blumhardt's experiences with healing at Möttlingen provided a counterbalance to Anglo-Saxon traditions; the Bad Boll healing ministry continued by his son, Christoph Blumhardt, suggested institutional forms, as did the ministries of Friedrich and Friedrich von Bodelschwingh (father and son).

IV. Conclusion. Through these and other sources, Pentecostals in North America and Europe were influenced by classical Pietist concerns. Pentecostals on both continents have continued to articulate the central foci of Pietist thought. The differences in theology and praxis are in significant measure due to the divergent expressions of Pietism encountered at crucial stages in the development of national movements.

See also HOLINESS MOVEMENT.

Bibliography: K. Aland, *Pietismus und Bibel* (1970); idem, *Spener Studien* (1943); idem, *Frömmigkeit und Theologie. Gesammelte Aufsätze zum Pietismus und zur Erwekungsbewegung* (1980); idem, *Geschichte des Pietismus* (1978); idem, *Studien zur Theologie Zinzendorfs* (1962); E. Bayreuther, *Der junge Zinzendorf* (1957–1961); D. Blaufuss, *Spener Arbeiten* (1980); N. Bloch-Hoell, *Pinsebevegelsen* (1956); D. Dayton, D. Faupel, and D. Bundy, *The Higher Christian Life* (1985); J. D. Douglas, ed., *The New International Dictionary of the Christian Church* (1974); idem, *Evangelisches Gemeindelexikon* (1978); P. Fleisch, *Die moderne Gemeinschaftsbewegung in Deutschland* (1912); idem, *Die Pfingstbewegung in Deutschland* (1957); E. Geise, *Und flicken die Netze: Dokumente zur Erwekungsgeschichte des 20. Jahrhunderts* (1976); M. Gerhardt and A. Adam, *Friedrich von Bodelschwingh*, 3 vols. (1955–1958); P. Grunberg, *Philipp Jakob Spener* (1893–1906); N. Holm, *Pingstströrelsen* (1978); W. Koepp, *Johann Arndt und sein Wahres Christentum* (1959); G. Kramer, *August Hermann Francke* (1880–1882); G. Malzer, *Bengel und Zinzendorf* (1968); idem, *J. A. Bengel. Leben und Werk* (1970); J. Müller-Bohn, *Entschiedende Jahrhundertwende. Geistlichgeschichtliche Beurteilung der Jahre 1895–1945. Originaldokumentation der Erwekungszeit 1895–1945* (1972); J. Ohlemacher, *Die Gemeinschaftsbewegung in Deutschland: Quellen zu ihrer Geschichte 1887–1914* (1977); A. Outler, *John Wesley* (1972); E. Peschke, *Bekehrung und Reform. Ansatz und Wurtzeln der Theologie A. H. Franckes* (1977); idem, *Studien zur Theologie A. H. Franckes* (1964–66); H. Renkewitz, *Im Gesprach mit Zinzendorfs Theologie* (1980); A. Ritschl, *Geschichte des Pietismus* (1880–86, reprint 1961); J. Sauter, *Die Theologie des Reiches Gottes beim alteren und jungeren Blumhardts* (1962); M. Scharfe, *Die Religion des Volkes* (1980); M. Schmidt, *Der Pietismus als theologische Erscheinung* (1984); idem, *Pietismus* (1972); idem, *Wiedergeburt und neuer Mensch. Gesammelte Studien zur Geschichte des Pietismus* (1969); F. E. Stoeffler, *German Pietism During the Eighteenth Century* (1973); idem, *The Rise of Evangelical Pietism* (1965); Patrick Streiff, *Jean de la Flechère . . . ein Beitrag zur Geschichte des Methodismus* (1984); Henryk Ryszerd Tomaszewski, "Grupy Chrzescijańskie Typu Evangeliczno-Baptystycznego na Terenie Polski od 1858–1939," diss. Warsaw, 1978; C. P. van Andel, *Gerhard Tersteegen. Leben und Werk* (1973); J. Wallmann, *P. J. Spener und die Anfange des Pietismus* (1970).

D. D. Bundy

EVANGELICAL CHURCHES OF PENTECOST See CHRISTIAN MINISTERS' ASSOCIATION.

EVANGELICALISM
The NT Greek word *euangelion* has been called the richest word in the Christian vocabulary. Its biblical usage, "good news" refers to the central core of the Christian message of salvation, its primary meaning to this day. Since the Protestant Reformation, however, the word *evangelical* has taken on various specialized doctrinal and denominational meanings used to define several Christian traditions.

The Reformation use of the word and its derivatives is seen in the names of several Lutheran denominations and institutions such as The Evangelical Lutheran Church in the United States, the Evangelical and Reformed Church, and the National Association of Evangelicals (NAE). The first person to employ the word *evangelical* to denote a specific doctrinal tradition was Martin Luther, who used it to define those Christians who stressed justification "by faith alone" and who used the Bible as the final authority in contrast to the Roman Catholic ecclesiastical system, which allowed a place for tradition and good works along with faith.

In addition to the foregoing basic assumptions, Luther added the universal priesthood of believers in contrast to Roman claims for an exclusive priesthood of the ordained clergy. Therefore, Roman Catholic theologians such as Erasmus, Thomas More, and Johannes Eck labeled the Reformers "Evangelicals," a term not accepted by Luther, for he saw the evangel as the essential core of Christian truth and not restricted to any sectarian meaning.

Nonetheless, the Treaty of Westphalia in 1648, and the *Corpus Evangelicorum* of 1653 recognized the Reformers as "Evangelicals." This usage was further entrenched in 1817 when the union of Lutheran and Reformed churches in Germany referred to both groups as "evangelical."

From that time forward, the word was freely applied to all Protestants in general, with no understanding that it defined any particular tradition within Protestantism. Thus, to this day in most predominantly Catholic countries the term *evangelical* is the popular word used to identify all Protestant Christians, regardless of any particular theological tradition within the various churches.

It was in the foregoing sense that Calvin and his followers in the Reformed tradition were also called "Evangelicals." Calvin's *Institutes,* while promoting the predestination theory for which he became famous, agreed with Luther's basic contentions concerning justification by faith, the primacy of Scripture, and the priesthood of all believers. Added to these principles was the necessity of a conscious conversion experience to settle the question of election for the individual.

This understanding brought the action words *evangelize* and *evangelization* into the Protestant lexicon as methods of bringing persons to an understanding and acceptance of their election to eternal salvation. Nowhere was this more evident than among the Puritan Reformers in England and America.

The necessity of an evangelical conversion experience was an article of faith among the American Puritan settlers of New England. They were the first major group of evangelical settlers in North America. They created many of America's first colleges, including Harvard and Yale, as ministerial training centers for preparing evangelical pastors and leaders.

After the early Puritan communities evolved into the third and fourth generations, church leaders were vexed by the large number of church members born in the church who never had undergone a conversion experience. By means of the Halfway Covenant of 1657, those citizens of Massachusetts who had never undergone a conversion experience were nonetheless allowed to be members of the churches, although without voting or ministerial rights.

This emphasis on a conversion experience became part of the American religious folklore and an essential element in the various awakenings and revivals that have swept over the nation through its history. Vivid and often emotional conversion experiences were seen as necessary to salvation, despite the various understandings of the churches regarding water baptism and the other sacraments and ordinances of the churches.

The extraordinary revivals of Jonathan Edwards in Northampton, Massachusetts, in the 1730s and the mass evangelism of George Whitefield a few decades later had as their goal the conversion of many who were already church members. The story of John Wesley before and after his Aldersgate experience in 1738 clearly demonstrated the difference between the sacramental approach he followed before Aldersgate and the evangelical approach he followed for the rest of his life.

Most historians speak of the eighteenth-century Wesleyan movement in England as the "evangelical revival." Wesley clearly identified himself as an Evangelical although he never severed his relationship with the Anglican Church. Since Wesley, Anglicans have been classified as high church Anglo-Catholics or low church Evangelicals in the tradition of Wesley and the Puritan Reformers. In Britain, therefore, the term *evangelical* took on a new meaning, i.e., that of a particular party within an existing church tradition.

The term also became synonymous with any Protestant who refused to countenance the liberalizing influences that continually arose within Protestant churches. Thus the New England Unitarian movement led by William Ellery Channing, Ralph Waldo Emerson, and Theodore Parker was opposed by such Evangelicals as Timothy Dwight and Nathaniel Taylor. In a similar vein, when Horace Bushnell promoted a new "halfway covenant" theology with his 1857 book *Christian Nurture,* it was the opposing Evangelicals who held firmly for the necessity of a conversion experience.

In Europe during the same century, there were forces and events that further helped to define the meaning of the word *evangelical* as it applied to Protestants. In the light of a perceived new threat from Roman Catholicism and the gradual loss of a clear evangelical witness in the major Protestant bodies, a call was issued for Evangelicals to meet in London in 1846. This meeting, which was led by Thomas Chalmers (Scotland), Merle D'Aubigne (Switzerland), S. S. Schmucker (U.S.), and F. Tholuck (Germany), formed the Evangelical Alliance, which was to carry the evangelical cause into the twentieth century.

The Evangelical Alliance formulated a doctrinal statement whose nine affirmations placed the evangelical movement squarely in the mainstream of traditional Protestant orthodoxy. These statements affirmed: (1) the inspiration of the Bible, (2) the Trinity, (3) the depravity of man, (4) the mediation of Christ, (5) justification by faith, (6) conversion and sanctification by the Holy Spirit, (7) the return of Christ and the Final Judgment, (8) the ministry of the Word, and (9) the sacraments of baptism and the Lord's Supper.

Because the foregoing statements made more liberal members uncomfortable, the Alliance was unable to exercise a major influence in the mainline Protestant churches beyond 1900. Thereafter, the liberals went their separate way, creating their own agenda; this ultimately led to the founding of the Federal Council of Churches and the World Council of Churches. On the other hand, the conservative Evangelicals moved in the direction of Fundamentalism.

The nineteenth century also saw tremendous growth among Methodists and Baptists in England and America. This growth greatly strengthened the evangelical cause. The Methodists, who spread rapidly across the American frontier, went beyond the conversion experience common to all Evangelicals, to emphasize a postconversion crisis that Wesley and his followers called variously "entire sanctification," "perfect love," the "second blessing," or "Christian perfection." Along with this emphasis on inner spirituality, the Wesleyans also stressed social responsibility and reform, typified by Wesley's famous opposition to slavery.

The Methodists came to America in 1766 and were organized as a distinct denomination in 1784. After the extraordinary camp meeting at Cane Ridge, Kentucky, in 1800, the Methodists practically preempted the camp meeting as a tool of evangelism. Throughout the century various Methodists also attempted to renew and perpetuate the teaching of second blessing sanctification in the church. These included Timothy Merritt and Phoebe Palmer after 1830, and John Inskip with his colleagues in the National Holiness Association (NHA), formed in 1867 at the close of the Civil War.

The revivalist movement unleashed by Charles G. Finney in the middle of the century also carried the evangelical message to the cities and towns of America. Finney, America's first "professional evangelist" preached a modified Perfectionism, which demonstrated the ecumenical appeal of the Holiness emphasis so dear to the heart of the Methodists. The Oberlin Theology promoted by Finney and Asa Mahan became central to the message of mainstream Evangelicalism in America. This emphasis greatly moderated the hard-line Calvinism that had characterized much of American Protestant theology since the days of Jonathan Edwards.

A stream distinct from the Perfectionism promoted by the Methodists and other revivalists was the fundamentalist movement that arose in the latter years of the nineteenth century. Arising in reaction to the liberalism in the mainline churches, the Fundamentalists felt threatened by the scientific challenges of Darwinism and other emerging sciences that seemed to constitute a threat to the biblical accounts of creation. In the latter decades of the century a theological movement known as "higher criticism" arose in Germany, which attempted to make an accommodation with these developments.

After the turn of the century, those who favored this type of accommodation began to call themselves "Modernists." Conservatives who opposed this movement were first called "Fundamentalists" in 1920, using the term made famous with the 1910 publication of *The Fundamentals*, a set of twelve booklets explaining the five essential and nonnegotiable fundamentals of the faith. They included: the deity of Christ, the Virgin Birth, the substitutionary Atonement, the inerrancy of Scripture, and the visible return of Christ. Edited by A. C. Dixon and R. A. Torrey, they were financed by California oil millionaires Lyman and Milton Stewart.

By 1919 an umbrella organization for like-minded defenders of the orthodox faith was formed under the leadership of William Bell Riley, an aggressive Baptist pastor from Minneapolis. Called the World's Christian Fundamentals Association (WCFA), the new organization brought some focus to the movement.

The struggles that ensued between Modernists and Fundamentalists were especially severe among Baptists and Presbyterians, eventually resulting in splits producing the fundamentalist "Bible" and "Regular" Baptist churches, and the Presbyterian Church in America (later the Orthodox Presbyterian Church) founded by J. Gresham Machen.

The nadir of the fundamentalist cause was the famous "Monkey Trial" of 1925 held in Dayton, Tennessee, where a local high school teacher, John T. Scopes, was convicted of teaching evolutionary theory in the public schools in violation of a newly passed Tennessee law. Although no less a person than William Jennings Bryan led the prosecution, the defense of Clarence Darrow succeeded in painting all Fundamentalists as anti-intellectuals who opposed the march of scientific and academic progress.

Thereafter, the Fundamentalists withdrew themselves from public debate, entering into a separatistic world of bitter censure against all who compromised the faith. This movement toward separation included the founding of many independent Bible schools and splinter denominations. By the 1930s it seemed as if Modernism had won the day in the mainline American Protestant denominations.

In the meantime, a powerful new evangelical movement was forming out of the remnants of the separatistic Holiness movement that had left Methodism after 1894. This was the Pentecostal movement that was born in 1901 in Topeka, Kansas, under the leadership of former Methodist Charles Fox Parham. This movement, which shared most of the basic presuppositions of Fundamentalism, went beyond second-blessing holiness and the five points of Fundamentalism to stress the present-day exercise of the gifts of the Spirit, especially those of divine healing and speaking in tongues.

The Pentecostal movement was given worldwide impetus through the Azusa Street Mission in Los Angeles pastored by the black Holiness preacher, William J. Seymour. From 1906 to 1909 thousands of Azusa Street pilgrims were baptized in the Holy Spirit and spread the Pentecostal message around the world. By 1920 the movement had crystallized into three streams:

(1) the Holiness Pentecostals, who continued to stress a second-blessing sanctification experience; (2) the Baptistic Pentecostals, who taught a finished work theology that denied the necessity of a second blessing; and (3) the Oneness Pentecostals, who denied the doctrine of the Trinity while emphasizing a Unitarianism of the Son, Jesus Christ.

It soon became apparent that the Pentecostals were something different from the Fundamentalists, who thereafter reasserted the ancient cessation of the charismata theory. This theory denied the possibility of supernatural gifts in modern times. Warfield's 1918 anticharismatic book, *Counterfeit Miracles,* established the fundamental opposition to the rising Pentecostal movement. The dispensational scheme accepted by most Fundamentalists left no place for a Pentecostal "Latter Rain" teaching that called for a last day restoration of signs and wonders before the end of the age and the second coming of Christ. In 1928 the WCFA rejected the Pentecostals as "fanatical" and "unscriptural."

Until World War II the conservative Evangelicals in America consisted of a dwindling and defeated minority in the mainline denominations, the splinter groups that had separated from the mainline churches, the Holiness and Pentecostal churches, and the generally disorganized independent fundamentalist groups centering around such leaders as Bob Jones and Carl McIntire. The public image of Fundamentalism was that of negative, censorious legalists who were more interested in attacking their enemies than in proclaiming a positive gospel.

In 1941 Carl McIntire attempted to bring all Fundamentalists together in a new coalition that he called the American Council of Christian Churches (ACCC). He regarded this as a counter movement to the liberal Federal Council of Churches (FCC). By this time, however, there were many conservative Evangelicals prepared to shed the image of the fighting Fundamentalist and return to the classical Evangelicalism exemplified by the Evangelical Alliance, which predated the fundamentalist controversy. Leaders in this movement were Harold J. Ockenga of Boston's Park Street Church, and Carl F. H. Henry.

These men led in the creation of a new evangelical coalition that stressed the basic affirmations of Fundamentalism but with a new name and image that distanced it from the unfortunate associations of the past. Against the wishes of McIntire, the new National Association of Evangelicals (NAE) was formed in 1942. To the further chagrin of the Fundamentalists, the NAE accepted the Pentecostals and refused to join forces with the ACCC. The NAE thereafter became the home of a "new Evangelicalism" and provided a base for the phenomenal growth of evangelical Christianity after World War II.

Giving intellectual leadership to the movement was Carl F. H. Henry, whose 1948 book, *The Uneasy Conscience of Modern Fundamentalism,* became the textbook for the new movement. By 1948 Billy Graham began crusades that soon made him the outstanding evangelist of his generation. Always working closely with the

NAE, Graham helped Henry establish the central organ of the movement in 1956, the fortnightly magazine *Christianity Today*. This periodical soon became the intellectual counterweight to the liberal *Christian Century* magazine.

By the 1960s, with the Fundamentalists now on the sidelines, the struggle for leadership in the churches was between the new Evangelicals and the liberal establishment that still dominated the ecclesiastical machinery of most major Protestant denominations. Largely ignored were the Fundamentalists, who were not taken seriously again until the rise of Jerry Falwell with his new brand of activist Fundamentalism in the 1980s.

During this period, the campaigns of Graham and the growth of the Pentecostal churches were contrasted with the drastic membership declines in the mainline liberal churches. Another sign of rising evangelical strength was the growth of the evangelical Southern Baptist Convention, which by 1970 surpassed the more liberal United Methodist Church to become the largest Protestant denomination in the U.S.

Evangelicalism was brought to the attention of the nation and the world with the election of Jimmy Carter—a Southern Baptist—as president of the United States in 1976. A committed evangelical, Carter popularized the term "born again" to a nation that had largely forgotten its evangelical heritage.

"Born again" religion also received a boost with the rise of the charismatic movement in the mainline churches. This movement represented the incursion of Pentecostalism into the older traditional churches after decades of rejection. The first Neo-Pentecostal to make headlines was Dennis Bennett, pastor of Saint Mark's Episcopal Church in Van Nuys, California, whose 1960 experience of speaking in tongues shocked the religious establishment. Soon thousands of ministers and laypersons in all the mainline churches were speaking in tongues and attempting to stay in their churches. Encouraging them was the traveling Pentecostal ecumenist David J. du Plessis, who advised them to "bloom where you are planted."

By 1967 the Pentecostal movement had entered the Roman Catholic church, bringing Evangelicalism into previously unthinkable territory. By 1979 a Gallup poll conducted on behalf of *Christianity Today* found that 19 percent of the American population (44 million adults and children) considered themselves to be "Pentecostal or Charismatic Christians." Part of the explanation of this phenomenon was the advent of the electronic church, which saw the rise of Pat Robertson's Christian Broadcasting Network (CBN) to prominence as an alternative to secular television. Following Robertson's lead were such evangelical television entrepreneurs as Jim Bakker (PTL [Praise the Lord or People That Love] Network) and Paul Crouch (Trinity Broadcasting Network [TBN]).

These television ministries followed the pioneering work of Billy Graham and Oral Roberts, who also helped found the National Religious Broadcasters (NRB). This coalition of evangelical broadcasters arose after World War II when the Federal Council of Churches attempted to gain a monopoly on religious broadcasting in America, which would have kept the Evangelicals off the air.

The election of Ronald Reagan in 1980 marked a symbolic national political triumph for the new Evangelicals. Some claimed that the born again Americans had put him in the White House. Whether true or not, it was obvious that Reagan's positions on abortion and prayer in public schools were items on the evangelical agenda. The religious right instead of the liberal religious establishment became the spiritual advisors to the president.

David Barrett's *World Christian Encyclopedia* estimated that in the U.S. in 1976 some 69 million Christians described themselves as Evangelicals. The world figure in 1985 stood at 174,202,200 persons. This represented a remarkable comeback for the evangelical cause from the dark days of the 1920s. By this time the Evangelicals had apparently not only survived their struggles with liberalism but were thriving in a world where the liberal churches were in a state of decline.

See also CHURCH GROWTH; EVANGELISM; MISSIOLOGY; MISSIONS, OVERSEAS.

Bibliography: G. Marsden, *Fundamentalism and American Culture* (1980); R. Quebedeaux, *The Young Evangelicals* (1974); D. Wells and J. Woodbridge, *The Evangelicals* (1977).   H. V. Synan

EVANGELISM

I. Introduction. Evangelism has been a priority among Pentecostals throughout their history. The historical self-image of the major Pentecostal church bodies is that they were raised up to be an instrument of evangelism in the world. Traditionally, therefore, it has been felt that to be a Pentecostal is to be an evangelistic witness. Pentecostals see aggressive evangelism in the pages of the NT, and due to their high regard for the Bible and their literal interpretation of Scripture, they interpret the Pentecostal experience as a mandate for evangelism in its various forms and methods.

II. Definition and Nature of Evangelism. There is a multitude of explanations and definitions for the term "evangelism." The Madras Conference of the International Missionary Council came up with some thirty-one definitions. The word's history from the NT reveals a twofold usage—as a noun and as a verb. The noun is *euangelion*—"good news," and occurs seventy-five times. The verb is *euangelizomai* and means "to publish good news." It appears twenty-four times. The gospel is the evangel, the Good News. Evangelism is the act of proclaiming the good news of Jesus Christ in the power and anointing of the Holy Spirit with the intention that men and women will come to put their trust in Christ for salvation and serve him in the fellowship of his church.

For Pentecostals evangelism involves much more than simply proclaiming the gospel. Evangelistic proclamation is not an end in itself but a means to an end—the persuasion of sinners to accept Christ as Lord and to follow him as responsible, reproducing members of a local church. Pentecostal evangelism would reject the liberal tenets of universalism that say the work of evangelism is simply to inform people that they are *already* saved. Neither do Pentecostals believe that proclaiming only for the sake of giving objective information is sufficient. Pentecostal evangelism involves the good news of deliverance over against the bad news that humanity is dead and bound in the oppression of sin. Pentecostal evangelism therefore calls for a confrontation; it is the conveyance of truth-as-encounter. The Pentecostal witness preaches for a verdict and expects results.

This is the sense in which Jesus announces his mission of evangelism under the anointing of the Holy Spirit:

> The Spirit of the Lord is on me, because he has anointed me to preach good news to the poor. He has sent me to proclaim freedom for the prisoners and recovery of sight for the blind, to release the oppressed, to proclaim the year of the Lord's favor (Luke 4:18–19).

There is, therefore, a persuasiveness and aggressiveness in Pentecostal evangelism characterized by the preaching of the apostle Paul as he seeks to persuade King Agrippa to become a believer. Paul indicates that he has been rescued in order to rescue others through evangelism. God's commission to him is central to his evangelistic testimony:

> I will rescue you from your own people and from the Gentiles. I am sending you to them to open their eyes and turn them from darkness to light, and from the power of Satan to God, so that they may receive forgiveness of sins and a place among those who are sanctified by faith in me (Acts 26:17–18).

III. Biblical/Theological Foundations for Evangelism.

Pentecostals have seen their evangelistic outreach as more than the mere extension of a religious movement or recruitment to a particular ideology or experience. From the outset of the modern Pentecostal movement there was a sense of "divine destiny," the participation with God in a new work for the last days. The theological mood and atmosphere set by premillennialism and the actualization of the experiences and promises of Scripture (particularly the "outpouring" passages such as Joel 2:28–32 and Acts 2:16–21) caused Pentecostals to view evangelism as an extension of the purposes of God for the world.

Pentecostals have seen redemption as the central purpose of God in Scripture and evangelism as the comprehensive method for fulfilling that purpose. Their literal biblicism has caused them to be aggressively obedient to the Great Commission passages in the Gospels. Acts 1:8 could be claimed as the golden text for their style of evangelism: "But you will receive power when the Holy Spirit comes on you; and you will be my witnesses in Jerusalem, and in all Judea and Samaria, and to the ends of the earth."

For Pentecostals, the connection of the "power" in Acts 1:8 to the evangelistic task is quite clear: only the coming of the power of the Holy Spirit to those who are witnesses for Christ makes the work of evangelism possible. In this light the "power" passages of Acts 1:8 and 2:1–4 and the "enduement" passage of Luke 24:48 have been central to Pentecostal preaching and teaching on evangelism.

Therefore, evangelism, not other spiritual gifts or manifestations, should be seen as the primary result of the baptism of the Holy Spirit and the operation of spiritual gifts. Evangelism occupies the central place in the growth of Pentecostal churches. Other supernatural manifestations revolve around it. Donald Gee contended that evangelism was a natural expression of the spiritual gifts of 1 Corinthians 12. In his writings he argued for a combination and balance between the manifestations of spiritual gifts and evangelistic proclamation to unbelievers. He believed that if spiritual gifts could not flourish in the arena of public witness, there was something wrong with their usage (see Gee, 1932 and 1963).

Theologically, evangelism cannot be limited to the work of the Holy Spirit alone. "Evangelism," says Harold John Ockenga, "must be Trinitarian if it is to be biblical." The Great Commission itself incorporates the desire and activity of the triune God in that we are to go, to teach, and to baptize all nations in the name of "the Father, and of the Son, and of the Holy Ghost" (Matt. 28:19). The Bible honors each member of the Trinity, says Ockenga, in that "the New Testament makes it clear that the Father elects, which is predestination; that the Son redeems, which is atonement; and that the Holy Spirit regenerates, which is salvation (Henry, 1967, 2:96).

IV. Motivation for Evangelism.

A sense of participation in what is central to the nature and heart of God motivates Pentecostals toward evangelism. Emerging from this central desire of God for evangelism come additional facets of the Pentecostals' motivation for reaching the unconverted.

First, Pentecostals have understood an obedience to evangelize as one of the primary steps of obedience in Christian discipleship. Therefore, evangelism is not an end within itself once a person has been reached and led to personal belief in Christ. Immediately this new convert is urged to testify to others and to begin preaching. He is "saved to serve."

In early Pentecostalism in particular, one finds many accounts of people who stood up to preach within a few days of their conversion. C. Peter Wagner's study of the dynamic growth in Latin American Pentecostalism indicates that personal witnessing and street evangelism by the newly converted were some of the central marks of their outstanding expansion (Wagner, 1986).

Second, it has been crystal clear in the theology of Pentecostal evangelism that humankind is lost and is under the judgment of eternal punishment unless reached with the good news of the gospel (Ezek. 18:4; Luke 13:3–5; Rom. 2:12; 3:23; 5:12; 6:23; 2 Thess. 1:7–8; James 1:15; 2 Peter 3:9). The doctrinal confessions of all major Pentecostal organizations reflect their belief in

Oral Roberts pleading to the unconverted to step forward to receive Christ as Savior in a 1959 crusade. These respondents were later ushered into a smaller tent for prayer and counseling.

"eternal life for the righteous and eternal punishment for the wicked," with no liberation from annihilation (in terms of "second chance" salvation).

This is related to a third motivation for evangelism: the imminent return of Christ and the end of all things. There is an "eschatological urgency" inherent in evangelistic theology and practice of Pentecostals. Thomas F. Zimmerman, former general superintendent of the Assemblies of God (AG), has stated the surety of impending doom

and judgment that hangs over the world in a coming retribution that will be both universal and final. Out of this reality he says, "Men must be told!" (Henry, 1967, 2:65–66).

V. Supernatural Evangelism. The "telling" in Pentecostal evangelism, however, has involved more than verbal proclamation. Pentecostals have understood miraculous signs and wonders to be demonstrations of "the Lord working with them, and confirming the words with signs following" (Mark 16:20). This was clearly the proclamation strategy of early Christians (Rom. 15:19; 1 Cor. 2:1–5).

This makes Pentecostal evangelism distinctive since it proceeds from a world view of power leading to what Ray H. Hughes, first assistant general overseer of the Church of God (CG, Cleveland, Tenn.), calls "supernatural evangelism" (Hughes, 1968, 63). Divine healing, for example, has been an evangelistic door-opener that leads to verbal proclamation (Acts 3). For Pentecostals, every healing and miracle and every spiritual manifestation or "power encounter" in exorcism becomes an "earnest" of the kingdom of God and the means whereby the message and dominion of this kingdom are actualized in the lives of people who are delivered. Pentecostal evangelists and missionaries would identify with the report of one missionary from England to Le Havre in 1930: "Every new work is opened on the ministry of Divine Healing; for without the supernatural it would be impossible to get any interest created in the gospel message . . ." (Frodsham, 1946, 91–92).

This conviction of "God among us and working with us" is one of the key factors in the persuasive attraction of Pentecostal–charismatic worship. That Pentecostal worship is a key evangelistic factor has been agreed upon by both inside interpreters and outside observers of Pentecostal church growth. Central to Pentecostal worship is the unique style of preaching in Pentecostal evangelism. It is "a Spirit-endowed preaching which is pungent and penetrating," says Hughes, who claims that there is a "miracle element" present in Pentecostal preaching, making it a powerful evangelistic force (1981, 149; see also McClung, 1986, 73).

Supernatural evangelism has also been called "power evangelism," a concept first articulated in the Fuller Theological Seminary School of World Mission and popularized by John Wimber, a contemporary proponent of its Church Growth school of thought:

> By power evangelism I mean a presentation of the gospel that is rational but that also transcends the rational. The explanation of the gospel comes with a demonstration of God's power through signs and wonders. Power evangelism is a spontaneous, Spirit-inspired, empowered presentation of the gospel. Power evangelism is evangelism that is preceded and undergirded by supernatural demonstrations of God's presence (1986, 35).

VI. Evangelism and the Media. Being aggressively intent upon evangelizing every available person, Pentecostals have made extensive use of radio and television for the propagation of the gospel. Pentecostal radio preachers began blanketing the U.S. with gospel broadcasts in the 1920s and 1930s. Leading denominations established departments of radio and television as the church moved into the electronic age.

One of the earliest television pioneers was Rex Humbard, who constructed the Cathedral of Tomorrow in Akron, Ohio, to televise a local worship service into America's living rooms. Oral Roberts moved from the tent to the tube and expertly used the medium of television to telecast his healing campaigns and television specials. By 1985 he commanded an audience of 2.5 million households.

Later the pioneers of televangelism were joined by a new breed of television evangelists. Pat Robertson founded the Christian Broadcasting Network (CBN) and its popular "700 Club," which eventually drew 4.4 million viewers daily. Jim Bakker began his broadcast career under Robertson's tutelage and later founded the PTL Network ("Praise the Lord"). Jimmy Swaggart began with the radio broadcast "The Campmeeting Hour" and eventually moved to television. By mid-1987, Swaggart was viewed by 3.6 million viewers per day and received 40,000 letters weekly at his headquarters in Baton Rouge, Louisiana.

Robertson's ministry pioneered televangelism as a two-way medium with the establishment of phone-in prayer lines. Annually, CBN and the PTL Network were recording hundreds of thousands of conversions and miraculous healings. This was also the pattern established in the televangelism ministry of Paul and Jan Crouch through the Trinity Broadcasting Network in Southern California.

Contrary to the critics of televised Pentecostal preaching, there was an established effort among televangelists to bring new converts into established local churches—Pentecostal, charismatic, and evangelical. In many instances, televangelism was combined with mass crusades in overseas missionary preaching and new church planting.

Eventually, televangelism was to make a wider contribution to humanitarian ministries and higher Christian education. Oral Roberts established Oral Roberts University and the City of Faith Medical Center. Swaggart funneled some $12 million dollars annually into the foreign missions enterprises of the AG and funded an international child care program to feed, clothe, educate, and heal some 250,000 children in Third World countries. In addition, he founded a Bible college for the training of evangelists, pastors, and missionaries. Robertson funded "Operation Blessing," providing food and medical attention to needy people in the U.S. and abroad. Bakker's PTL ministry opened a home for handicapped children and another for unwed mothers. Pentecostals have effectively and positively used the media as a channel to preach the gospel of salvation.

VII. The Future of Evangelism. As Pentecostals and charismatics move into the 1990s there does not appear to be any departure from their aggressive stance on the need to evangelize. There is continued commitment toward training and deploying evangelists. There have been congresses and consultations held on the strategy of evangelism, particularly in the great urban centers of the world. Two statements, A Declaration at St. Louis (1968) by the AG and A Covenant on World Evangelism (1983) by the CG, reveal strong sentiments of self-identity as agencies for evangelism.

Bibliography: "America's Pentecostals," *Christianity Today* (October 16, 1987), 16–28; A. A. Biddle, "The Holy Spirit Prompting Evangelism," *Pentecostal Doctrine* (1976); D. J. Bosch, *Witness To The World* (1980); R. Champion, E. S. Caldwell, G. Leggett, eds., *Our Mission in Today's World* (1968); S. H. Frodsham, *With Signs Following* (1946); D. Gee, *Pentecost* (1932); idem, *Spiritual Gifts in the Work of the Ministry Today* (1963); C. F. H. Henry and W. S. Mooneyham, eds., *One Race, One Gospel, One Task*, vol. 2 (1967); R. H. Hughes, *Church of God Distinctives* (1968); idem, *Pentecostal Preaching* (1981); A. P. Johnston, *The Battle For World Evangelism* (1978); L. J. Lord, "An Unholy War in The TV Pulpits," *U.S. News & World Report* (April 6, 1987), 58–65; L. G. McClung, Jr., ed., *Azusa Street and Beyond: Pentecostal Missions and Church Growth in The Twentieth Century* (1987); C. P. Wagner, *Spiritual Power and Church Growth* (1986); idem, *Strategies for Church Growth* (1987); J. R. Williams, *The Pentecostal Reality* (1972); J. Wimber, *Power Evangelism* (1986).
L. G. McClung, Jr.

EVANGELISTS

I. Introduction. The term "evangelist," though briefly mentioned in the Bible, is not specifically defined. The term originates from the Greek word *euangelistēs*, "one who proclaims good news." A Pentecostal evangelist has traditionally been one who devotes himself or herself entirely to a full-time itinerant ministry of preaching the gospel, especially the message of salvation and deliverance. In this regard, an evangelist is one with a specialized ministry that involves more than being a witness for Christ—a duty expected of all believers in the Pentecostal-charismatic heritage.

II. Biblical Descriptions and Models. The word "evangelist" is used only three times in the NT (Acts 21:8; Eph. 4:11; 2 Tim. 4:5). Although Philip is the only person specifically called an evangelist (Acts 21:8), other workers may have functioned in the same role: Timothy (2 Tim. 4:5), Luke (2 Cor. 8:18), Clement (Phil. 4:3), and Epaphras (Col. 1:7; 4:12). Evangelists are seen as a gift to the church by the ascended Christ (Eph. 4:11) and have traditionally been classed with apostles and prophets as itinerant workers in contrast to pastors and teachers who are attached to local assemblies (though this may be an imposition from church history more than an interpretation of the Scripture itself). Many Pentecostal pastors, in the spirit of the young pastor Timothy, have seen themselves in a dual role of pastor-evangelist (2 Tim. 4:5). Indeed, in the history of Pentecostal tradition an itinerant evangelist often established a local congregation, continued to pastor it as founding pastor, and conducted occasional revival/evangelistic crusades away from the local church base.

The composite picture of a Pentecostal evangelist would identify with the lessons emerging from Philip, a NT evangelist (Acts 8).

A. He (or she) is one from among the people, chosen as a deacon but gifted with a preaching ministry (Acts 6:5; 8:5). The roots of most early Pentecostal evangelists were from the common people of the poorer class. Most were lay preachers later ordained to the clergy.

B. Miracles typically follow the evangelist's preaching (8:6). Divine healing and miracles of deliverance have been emphasized in the preaching of Pentecostal evangelists as inclusive in the salvation message.

C. The evangelist crosses cultural, racial, and economic barriers to preach Christ (8:5). The crowds attending the crusades of itinerant evangelists have typically been racially integrated.

D. The evangelist baptizes converts (8:12, 38). Evangelists have not always left this to the work of local pastors (a source of tension). Itinerant evangelists have established a "following," initially through informal literature and later through the use of the electronic media.

E. The evangelist is flexible, preaching from city to city, ready to follow the leading of the Holy Spirit to another place or person (8:26, 29, 40). The leading of the Holy Spirit, even to another country, has been a hallmark of traveling evangelists. Many would not limit themselves to a calendar of specific dates for a crusade but would leave the conclusion of evangelistic crusades openended, depending on the work of the Holy Spirit and the response of the crowds.

III. The Evangelist in Christian Tradition. Stephen Neill has traced three main types of evangelists in the expansion of Christianity: (1) A person raised up by God to perform evangelistic ministry in a specified geographic area among a designated group of people; (2) a paid agent representing a missions society in itinerant evangelism to areas where the church or missions society has not yet been firmly established; (3) a lay preacher or pastor entrusted with the care and oversight of an existing congregation (Neill, 1971, 200).

IV. Evangelists in the Pentecostal Tradition. Pentecostal evangelists would fit into all three of Neill's classifications but would not necessarily be bound by them, particularly those among the independent "healing" evangelists with ministries of larger or more visible proportions. Menzies indicates that the Pentecostal evangelists of the 1920s and 1930s had ministries that were farreaching in their influence (1971, 170–71). Harrell traces the self-sustaining and extensive ministries of evangelists in what he calls "the healing revival (1947–1958)," and "the charismatic revival (1958–1974)" in his *All Things Are Possible* (1975). His bibliographic essay is a valuable resource for researchers on Pentecostal evangelists (1975, 240–54).

A complete listing of all names in the history of Pentecostal evangelists would not be possible in this overview. No one evangelist could be said to be the prototype of all modern Pentecostal evangelists. Nevertheless, a survey of the literature of Pentecostalism suggests that many outstanding figures had ministries of impact during various eras. Gordon Atter had "Biographical Sketches of Pentecostal Pioneers" as a separate chapter in his review of Pentecostal history. He includes persons such as Frank Bartleman, W. T. Gaston, Howard A. Goss, C. H. Mason, Claude A. McKinney, Charles F. Parham, W. W. Simpson, A. H. Argue, Charles E. Baker, Marion Keller, Alexander Boddy, Stephen and George Jeffreys, and Lewi Pethrus in his review of some forty-five Pentecostal pioneers from the U.S., Canada, and

Great Britain (1962, 57–85). Others of note are Aimee Semple McPherson, Charles S. Price, Smith Wigglesworth (Menzies, 1971, 170–71); William F. P. Burton, Teddy Hodgson (Whittaker, 1983, 146–98); J. W. Buckalew, A. J. Tomlinson, J. F. Rowlands (Conn, 1977); Edith Mae Pennington (Warner, 1987, 6); Mary C. Moise, and Maria B. Woodworth-Etter (Blumhofer, 1985, 11). Harrell's study highlights the more recent figures of William M. Branham, Oral Roberts, Gordon Lindsay, Jack Coe, T. L. Osborn, A. A. Allen, W. V. Grant, Don Stewart, and Morris Cerullo (1975; see also Harrell, 1985).

Typical methodologies of Pentecostal evangelists have been the use of mass crusades incorporating music, testimonies, prayer for the sick, and the extensive use of publishing (tracts, magazines, and paperback pamphlets and books). Many of the early evangelists combined an itinerant preaching schedule with the planting of new churches, often "preaching them out" and turning them over to associates or an organized denomination (Menzies, 1971, 170). Many began as children, and the phenomenon of the child evangelist (or "boy preacher") was popularized in Pentecostalism. "Little David" Walker and Marjoe Gortner are notable examples (Harrell, 1975, 81, 166, 233).

The message of Pentecostal evangelists has been typically centered on salvation and deliverance, with a popular highlighting of divine healing. Prayer lines for the sick have been common as well as confrontations with spiritual oppression resulting in exorcisms. In addition, evangelists have prayed for seekers to be baptized in the Holy Spirit. Eventually, the North American healing evangelists saw their calling to extend beyond their border to the international arena (Harrell, 1975, 94; Quebedeaux, 1976, 42–47).

Many evangelists have remained independent, not allowing themselves to be "tamed" or controlled by any denomination. This has traditionally been a source of tension and has caused contempt for the ministry of the evangelist in church circles. On the other hand, nonaffiliated evangelists have often seen their work as interdependent with the missions outreaches of established church departments of home and foreign missions. Harrell notes that there has been isolation and fragmentation among the healing evangelists themselves although some efforts have been made to form networks and associations (1975, 144). Many early independent evangelists, however, were incorporated into the polity and structure of newly formed denominations (Conn, 1977, 74).

V. Pentecostal Evangelists and the Future.
Pentecostal-charismatic trends indicate that the ministry of the itinerant evangelist will continue into the twenty-first century with more attention being given to integrity and accountability.

Major Pentecostal denominations encourage the ministry of evangelists, holding conferences for mutual exchange and providing training for evangelistic ministry (Champion, 1968). Pentecostals have participated in interdenominational conferences designed for itinerant evangelists, such as the gathering of four thousand evangelists at the International Conference for Itinerant

Evangelists in Amsterdam, Netherlands, in July 1983 (Douglas, 1984). In addition, there continues to be an emphasis upon the development of lay evangelists in the charismatic movement and new Pentecostal-charismatic evangelists are becoming prominent in the non-Western world.

See also EVANGELISM; GIFTS OF THE SPIRIT; MISSIONS, OVERSEAS; PREACHING, A PENTECOSTAL PERSPECTIVE.

Bibliography: G. F. Atter, *The Third Force* (1962); E. Blumhofer, "The Role of Women in Pentecostal Ministry," *AG Heritage* (Spring 1985), 11, 14; R. Champion, E. S. Caldwell, and G. Leggett, eds., *Our Mission in Today's World* (1968); C. W. Conn, *Like A Mighty Army* (1977); J. D. Douglas, *The Work of an Evangelist*, (1984); G. P. Duffield and N. M. Van Cleave, eds., *Foundations of Pentecostal Theology* (1983); D. Gee, *The Pentecostal Movement* (1949); D. E. Harrell, Jr., *All Things Are Possible: The Healing and Charismatic Revivals in Modern America* (1975); idem, *Oral Roberts: An American Life* (1985); W. W. Menzies, *Anointed to Serve* (1971); S. Neill, G. H. Anderson, and J. Goodwin, eds., *Concise Dictionary of the Christian World Mission* (1971); R. Quebedeaux, *The New Charismatics* (1976); W. Warner, "From the Footlights to the Light of the Cross," *AG Heritage* (Winter 1987), 6–9, 20; C. Whittaker, *Seven Pentecostal Pioneers* (1983).

L. G. McClung, Jr.

EVANGELIZATION SOCIETY, THE
(TES) A missions agency connected with the Pittsburgh Bible Institute and founded by Charles Hamilton Pridgeon on August 18, 1920, following prayer and the voluntary commitment of several hundred people to support its work. The first board of directors (self-perpetuating) included Pridgeon as general director, Louise Shepard Pridgeon, Edgar L. Clementson, William H. Hammon, and Grace D. Dorchester. Following its inception, several couples traveled overseas as missionaries.

The purpose of the society is "the propagation of Christianity and the doing of Christian and charitable work at home and abroad in association with and supplementary to the work of the Pittsburgh Bible Institute" (*Charter of the Evangelization Society,* n.d., 2). With the decline of the Pittsburgh Bible Institute and the growth of TES, the latter has more recently focused on forming "branches and centers to promote prayer and the study of the word among those who will cooperate in the spread of the Gospel at home and abroad and help as He enables in its many forms of Christian activity" (Vogel to McGee, 1988).

While the earlier work of TES has come to an end in China, it currently has mission outreaches in the U.S., consisting of five churches; Zaire, with two hundred churches and 55,000 members; and ministries in India and Taiwan. The work is supported by unsolicited donations, reflecting the concept of faith held by the British Christian philanthropist George Müller. The agency also ordains qualified applicants for Christian ministry. TES is evangelical and Pentecostal in doctrine and has discarded Pridgeon's doctrine of universalism called the "restitution" or "reconciliation" of all things.

The headquarters office for TES is located in Gibsonia, Pennsylvania. David W. Vogel currently serves as the general director.

Bibliography: H. P. Beach and C. H. Fahs, *World Missionary Atlas* (1925); Charter of The Evangelization Society (n.d.); E. L. Clementson, *Louise Shepard Pridgeon* (1955); G. D. Clementson, *Charles Hamilton Pridgeon* (1963); *The Encyclopedia of Christian Missions: The Agencies* (1967); D. W. Vogel to G. B. McGee, January 29, 1988.   G. B. McGee

EVANS, R. M. (c. 1847–1924). The first Church of God (CG, Cleveland, Tenn.) missionary. Evans was a retired Methodist minister when the Pentecostal message reached his home in Florida. He and his wife, Ida, joined the CG in May 1909, then sold their possessions and used the proceeds to go as missionaries to the Bahama Islands. Their friends, Edmond and Rebecca Barr, native Bahamians, preceded them there, and the four worked together after the Evanses arrived in Nassau on January 4, 1910. With no missions fund to support them, the personal funds of the Evanses were soon used up. The work prospered, however, and a strong missions ministry resulted in the Bahamas. After two years Evans and his wife returned to Florida sick and destitute. He died in 1924 and was buried in Live Oak, Florida.

Bibliography: C. W. Conn, *Where the Saints Have Trod* (1959); J. Cossey, *R. M. Evans, The First of His Kind* (1985).   C. W. Conn

EVANS, WILLIAM IRVIN (1887–1954). Assemblies of God (AG) educator and executive presbyter. Raised by Methodist parents, William Evans received the baptism in the Holy Spirit at the Missionary Training Institute in Nyack, New York. He served as pastor in Richmond, Virginia; Ossining, New York; and Butler, New Jersey. In 1917 he joined the faculty of the year-old Bethel Bible Training School in Newark, New Jersey, under the principalship of W. W. Simpson and then Frank M. Boyd.

When Boyd left in 1923 to head the recently formed Central Bible Institute (CBI) in Springfield, Missouri, Evans became principal at Bethel. In 1929 Evans, in turn, became principal at CBI when the two schools merged. He remained in dynamic leadership there a quarter century, the institution reflecting the image of the man.

Bibliography: W. I. Evans, *This River Must Flow! Selections From the Writings and Sermons of W. I. Evans* (1954).   D. J. Wilson

EWART, FRANK J. (1876–1947). Pentecostal preacher and author. Born in Australia, Ewart began his ministry in the Baptist Church as a bush missionary. In 1903 he immigrated to Canada and served as pastor of a Baptist church. After he received the baptism in the Holy Spirit in 1908 he was dismissed by the Baptist organization. In 1911 he became the assistant pastor to William H. Durham in Los Angeles, and when Durham died in 1912 Ewart became the pastor. In 1913 he heard R. E. McAlister preach at the Arroyo Seco camp meeting on water baptism in the name of Jesus Christ, and the following year he openly began preaching the shorter formula and rebaptizing Pentecostals. Ewart was one of the first Pentecostals to teach the Oneness of God rather than the doctrine of the Trinity. He spread the Oneness message throughout the Pentecostal

One of the most influential spokesmen for the Oneness movement in its early years, Frank J. Ewart was the author of *The Phenomenon of Pentecost.*

movement in his periodical *Meat in Due Season.* In 1919 he founded a successful church in Belvedere, California, and he continued to pastor this church until his death. He is the author of at least eight books: *Jesus, the Man and Mystery* (1941), *The Name and the Book* (1936), *The New Testament Characters X-Rayed* (1945), *The Modern Rip Van Winkle* (n.d.), *The Revelation of Jesus Christ* (n.d.), and *The Phenomenon of Pentecost* (1947). He was an ordained minister of the United Pentecostal Church.   J. L. Hall

EXORCISM Though the *New International Dictionary of the Christian Church* describes exorcism as "the practice of expelling evil spirits by means of prayer, divination, or magic" (Toon, 1974, 365), Pentecostal/charismatic theology would not understand the means of exorcism in any other source than the power of God. Instead, exorcism would be "the act of expelling evil spirits or demons by adjuration in the name of Jesus Christ and through His power" (Richardson, 1974, 5).

A review of the literature, history, and oral "stories" of Pentecostalism reveals the centrality of the practice of exorcism in the expansion of the Pentecostal and charismatic movements. While there is some general agreement in theology and practice, there remains a broad diversity in specific beliefs and ministries surrounding exorcism.

No clarified doctrinal statement on demonology and exorcism exists among major Pentecostal bodies. There are Pentecostal expositions such as Duffield and Van Cleave's *Foundations of Pentecostal Theology* (1983). Much of these discussions, however, are the reworking of earlier evangelical commentaries on the subject. Like many themes in Pentecostal/charismatic belief and practice, exorcism has been practiced but not formally theologized.

I. Scriptural Data. Since the Gospels are replete with the accounts of the power of Jesus over demons, Pentecostals have seen the ministry of Jesus as the biblical paradigm for the practice of exorcism. This would also be true of the work of the apostolic church in the Book of Acts. Almost every Pentecostal/charismatic writing on the subject will include a case study from the story of the Gerasene demoniac (Matt. 8:28–34; Mark 5:1–20; Luke 8:26–39).

In addition to the many general statements in the Gospels regarding the work of Jesus in the lives of demonized persons (see, e.g., Matt. 4:24; 8:16; Mark 1:32–34, 39; 3:11; 6:13; Luke 4:41; 6:18; 7:21), Michael Green has noted seven specific accounts of his work with individuals:

1. The man with the unclean spirit in the synagogue (Mark 1:21–28; Luke 4:31–37).

2. The blind and mute demoniac (Matt. 12:22–29; Mark 3:22–27; Luke 11:14–22).

3. The Gerasene demoniac (Matt. 8:28–34; Mark 5:1–20; Luke 8:26–39).

4. The Syrophoenician woman's daughter (Matt. 15:21–28; Mark 7:24–30).

5. The epileptic boy (Matt. 17:14–21; Mark 9:14–29; Luke 9:37–43).

6. The woman with a spirit of infirmity (Luke 13:10–17).

7. The mute demoniac (Matt. 9:32).

Along with this list, Green includes "with probability" the healing of Simon's mother-in-law (Luke 4:39), whose fever Jesus "rebuked." He notes that three incidents were deemed important enough to appear in all three Synoptics—the Beelzebub controversy, the Gerasene demoniac, and the epileptic boy (Green, 1981, 127–30).

One is impressed with the clear authority with which Jesus cast out demons. In terms of his own self-understanding of his authority and mission, Jesus most certainly believed that he was liberating the demonized completely (in other words, it was not psychological transference or unfulfilled hope). This fact was also immediately visible by observers and witnesses. Jesus gave proof of his divinity and authenticity through his actions. His language of exorcism exhibits expressions consistent with his divine authority: "He *commanded* the unclean spirit"; "Jesus *rebuked* the devil"; "He *cast out* many devils"; "He *suffered not* devils to speak" (italics mine; see Duffield and Van Cleave, 1983, 486; Conn, 1981, 104).

The deliverance ministry of exorcism continued in the early church as normative and expected. In fact, the disciples understood it as inclusive in the Great Commission of the Lord Jesus (Mark 16:15–17). Apostolic practices and subsequent correspondence to the newly established churches evidenced exorcism as an ongoing practice (Acts 8:6–7; 16:16–18; 19:11–12; 26:18; Eph. 2:2; Col. 1:13; 2 Tim. 2:25–26; 1 John 5:18). A complete listing of Scripture references to Satan and evil spirits is found in Michael Scanlan and Randall J. Cirner's *Deliverance From Evil Spirits* (1980).

II. Exorcism in the Christian Tradition. There is evidence for the practice of exorcism in the Christian tradition from the time of the apostles to the present day. Harper reviews the special clerical position of "exorcist" in the historic churches and includes samples of older forms and rituals of exorcism used in church liturgy (1970, 125–27).

Mainline Pentecostals and Protestant charismatics would not separate the duties of clergy and laity in the performance of exorcism. All believers equally share in the power of exorcism according to the biblical teaching of the priesthood of all believers (Mark 16:15–17; 1 Peter 2:9). Philip the deacon (Acts 6:5) was instrumental in the exorcism of demons (Acts 8:4–8). Typically, however, exorcism in Pentecostal ranks has been exhibited through missionaries, pastors, and evangelists, especially those seen to have a special "deliverance" ministry.

There has been a general skepticism in classical Pentecostalism toward those claiming to have a specialized ministry in this area. British Pentecostal George Canty expresses this attitude:

> In this connection, nobody was ever given a special gift for "exorcism," only for discernment, as part of the protection of the Church, chiefly against false teachers with lying and deceitful doctrines of demons. Nobody manifested a ministry exclusively for dealing with demons. This would draw attention more to Satan than to Christ (1976, 255).

Though some orders have been established in the historic churches for a special class of persons called "exorcists," this model was not incorporated into the classical Pentecostal awakening or the charismatic revival.

The influence of Pentecostals upon evangelical thought is especially seen in the marketplace of mission and the extension of the church. Missiologists have been among the first to recognize the Pentecostal contribution to world evangelization through a serious confrontation with Satan's power. This is the conclusion of Arthur F. Glasser, a respected Presbyterian missionary dean:

> Besides this, the Pentecostals were willing to tackle the "dark side of the soul" and challenge the growing phenomenon of occultism, Satan worship and demon possession. Whereas IFMA [Interdenominational Foreign Missions Association] people and other noncharismatic evangelicals (particularly the Baptists!) had found it relatively easy to expose the extravagance of the occasional charlatan, they were silenced in the presence of the Pentecostals' serious confrontation of the hard realities of the spirit world. Here was a spirituality which could not be ignored (1983, 119–20).

III. Special Issues.
A. Exorcism and Healing. The diversity of opinion regarding the source of disease (whether

from demons or natural causes) and the connection (or separation) of exorcism to healing is as broad as the number of authors one wishes to consult. There is no monolithic agreement in doctrine and practice.

For example, "There seems little doubt that every accident, misfortune, quarrel, sickness, disease, and unhappiness is the direct result of the individual work of one or more wicked spirits," says one Pentecostal writer (Whyte, 1969, 27). Others, particularly from a North American middle-class perspective, would argue a distinction between sickness from natural causes and demon-related disorders (based on an understanding of such references as Matthew 4:23–24; 8:16; Mark 1:32; Luke 7:21). Thus, as Longley believes, "We do not exorcise sickness itself, only demons who cause sickness. Prayer for the sick within various Christian ministries is totally different from casting out demons" (n.d., 93).

Many Pentecostal writers are careful to point out that Jesus healed diseases *and* cast out devils, citing such examples as Matthew 8:16 and Luke 13:32. In addition, mention is made of examples of healing without the notation of any presence of demons as in John 11:3–4; Philippians 2:25–27; 1 Timothy 5:23; and 2 Timothy 4:20 (Duffield and Van Cleave, 1983, 487; Conn, 1981, 105; Canty, 1976, 250). Canty concludes:

Even in Mark 16, where healing and deliverance from demons are mentioned together, they are not confused as if they were both the same thing. The language is that some would be sick and need healing, and that some would be possessed and need spirits to be cast out. Sheer lack of Scriptural suggestion about demon possession and sickness being one and the same thing obliges us to reject such a doctrine, while recognizing that the one or two cases recorded make it possible that violent possession will also (as we might expect) have effects on the body (1976, 251).

The practice of some, therefore, ". . . who in ministering to the sick always try to cast out a demon, is not biblical procedure" (Duffield and Van Cleave, 1983, 487). This would be Green's conclusion, who points out that in his mission charge to the Twelve, Jesus empowered them

. . . in two respects, not one: to have authority over demons and to heal diseases (Luke 9:1–2). Demons are expelled: diseases are healed. In other words, the Gospel writers seem to indicate that illness may be caused by direct demonic invasion though it certainly need not be. They are abundantly clear that there is a difference between healing and exorcism (1981, 127).

While John Wimber understands this view of an "either/or" distinction as built upon Western dichotomization, he argues for a more holistic approach in dealing with sickness: "Jesus frequently spoke the same way to fevers as he did to demons, because he saw the connection between sickness and Satan" (Wimber, 1986, 100). Because of Western secularization, Wimber argues,

modern Christians find it easier to compartmentalize faith and science away from each other.

Often, of course, there are psychological or physical explanations for illness. But more frequently than many Christians realize, the cause is demonic (1986, 98).

B. Classifications and Terminology. Classical Pentecostal writings have traditionally made a distinction between demon possession and demon influence. While allowing for demonic affliction, Pentecostal commentators have been adamant against any possibility of demon possession among believers (Duffield and Van Cleave, 1983, 487, 494–96; Conn, 1981, 105, 132; Longley, n.d., 86–90; the reader is also referred to the official statement of the general presbytery of the Assemblies of God, "Can Born-Again Believers Be Demon Possessed?" May 1972).

To differentiate types of demonic activity, Pentecostal/charismatic writers have used a trilogy of "states of demonic control": oppression, obsession, and possession (Whyte, 1974, 29; Lindsay, 1977, 26–32; Bubeck, 1975, 83–85). Lindsay sees them in a progression and adds a fourth in the series: "oppression, depression, obsession, and possession." He views demonic activity in a number of ways and uses the terms, "attacking, harassing, and actually dominating." He includes "professing Christians" as objects of demonic offensives (1972b, 23).

Regarding Christians, Bubeck understands "oppression" as attacks from the outside in terms of spiritual warfare. "Obsession," he says, has traditionally meant the subject's "uncontrollable preoccupation" with demonic forces or phenomena.

It is something less than total commitment or ownership, but is a step in that direction. A Christian who has of his own will developed overt curiosity about the occult, or in other ways has habitually given ground to Satan, may find himself demonically obsessed as traditionally defined (1975, 84).

Possession, says Bubeck, is total control by the evil spirit as exhibited by the command of a person's will and by ownership of the person. He claims that the word "possession," though an English expression, is not a word of the original language and agrees with classical Pentecostals that

no believer can be possessed by an evil spirit in the same sense that an unbeliever can. In fact, I reject this term altogether when talking about a believer's problem with the powers of darkness. A believer may be afflicted or even controlled in certain areas of his being, but he can never be owned or totally controlled as an unbeliever can (1975, 85, 87–88).

In terms of classifications and terminology, says Green, Jesus made no distinction between oppression or possession:

The Greek word is *daimonizomai*, "to be demonized" or sometimes *echein deimonion*, "to have a demon." The modern distinction between oppression and possession has no basis in the Greek New Testament (1981, 131).

Wimber also prefers the broader term, "demonization" (1986, 187). In discussing "How Evil Spirits Affect Mankind" (ch. 3), Scanlan and Cirner prefer the threefold classifications of "temptation, opposition, and bondage" and make no mention of "oppression, obsession, and possession" (1980, 27–36).

C. Types and Orders of Demons. Pentecostal literature, especially from the ranks of evangelists, has asserted that all demons are *not* alike. Pentecostals have said that the Bible speaks of many kinds of evil spirits, discerned by their manifestations or effects they have in those they afflict. Richardson says the Bible refers to spirits of fear, unclean spirits, foul spirits, spirits of error, perverse spirits, lying spirits, deceiving spirits, spirits of emulation, spirits of jealousy, spirits of whoredom, spirits of infirmity, and familiar spirits (1974, 39).

Others would add the spirit of bondage; deaf and mute spirits; and spirits of heaviness, whoredoms, and haughtiness (Lowery, n.d., 33ff.; Garrison, 1976, 1). Lindsay devotes a chapter to this discussion (titled "Different Orders of Demons") and claims that certain demons are specifically adapted to afflict the bodies of people. He refers to "demons of the sense organs" (deaf and blind spirits, infirm spirits) and lying spirits that cause oppression in the brain (1972c, 14–21).

IV. Methodology and Practices.

A. Discernment. Citing biblical support for supernatural insight (1 Cor. 12:10; 1 John 4:1), Pentecostal/charismatic writers have stressed the need for discernment. "We do not have to rely on a sensation or a hunch," says Green (1981, 134), and it would be dangerous to do so (Richardson, 1974, 20). Lindsay devotes a special chapter to discernment, along with a fourfold test for discernment. He, along with most others, would assert that the discernment gift, "is particularly designed to detect the presence of demons" (1972b, 30–38).

Authors also suggest various signs of demonization. Green, for example, lists such things as an irrational and violent reaction against the name of Jesus, unnatural bondage to sexual perversion, strange behavior or moodiness, and sudden changes of voice or emotions (1981, 134–35).

B. Preparation. In some instances confrontation with a demon-possessed person is immediate and there is no time for prolonged preparation. In these instances, the long-term maturity and preparedness in the Christian readies him or her for the confrontation. In cases where there is time for preparation, fasting and praying has been held up as the primary way to ready oneself (Richardson, 1974, 21; Green, 1981, 138; Lindsay, 1972a, 19).

Green provides a checklist of preparatory steps, including giving time to confession and prayer, claiming the victory of Christ, studying the Bible, gathering the support of a team, etc. (1981, 137–39). Harper stresses the importance of personal holiness:

We should never go lightly into this ministry. First we should seek personal cleansing, in the same way as a surgeon will wash before an operation. We should repent of any sin, and relinquish any trust or confidence in ourselves. We must confess, if necessary, any unbelief in the power of our Lord and the authority of His word (1970, 111).

C. Action. To cast out demons "in the name of Jesus" would indicate that it is being done under his authority and by his power. In his commission, Jesus said that his followers would cast out devils in his name (Mark 16:17; Acts 16:18). This is not to be taken as a magic formula or special ritual. Richardson notes, "Enunciating the name 'Jesus' or even claiming the protection of Christ's blood is meaningful only if the person has a genuine relationship with Jesus and exercises his position of authority that is in Christ" (1974, 25).

This should not mean, however, that we must constantly quote or repeat the name of Jesus with every act we do in his name. Duffield and Van Cleave point out that demons left people when the name of Jesus was not uttered (Acts 5:15–16; 19:11–12). The casting out of demons, they insist,

> does not require a barrage of words with voluminous repetitions of the word "Jesus" or "Christ." We have authority, and can use it, as "ambassadors" (2 Co 5:20), but we must avoid treating it as a magic incantation, like a piece of abracadabra or spell. When we utter "Lord Jesus Christ" it indicates that he is the Lord of the one who speaks, otherwise we are like the sons of Sceva, unknown to the spirits (1983, 490).

There are varieties of methodologies recorded in Pentecostal/charismatic sources. In the NT even aprons and handkerchiefs from the hand of Paul were instrumental in exorcism (Acts 19:11–12). Some may lay hands on the demonized; others may not. There is no actual record in the Scriptures of deliverance from demons by the laying on of hands. Neither is there any data on coughing up or spitting out demons (though this is reported in some contemporary deliverances). In addition, the Scripture does not give us any encouragement to hold conversations with demons (Duffield and Van Cleave, 1983, 490–91).

Harper (and others) state that the name or nature of the demon may be revealed and, in that case, we name the spirit when we command it to leave the person. However, the practice followed by some,

> of asking the demons for their names has no scriptural warrant. There is no instance of Jesus doing it; in Mark 5 he asked the *man* what his name was, and it is the man who answers, "my name is legion," although the demons would seem to have added the words "for we are many" (Mark 5:9). As for carrying on a conversation with them, this is extremely dangerous and scripturally unwarranted (1970, 117).

Harper also emphasizes the need for "after-care" in the life of the delivered person. He speaks of filling (baptism of the Holy Spirit), healing (emotional), self-discipline, faith, and praise (1970, 119–22). Green also points out the need for encouragement and pastoral care after one has been delivered (1981, 145).

V. Exorcism and the Mission of the Church. Green sees exorcism as a natural part of the growth and extension of the church into new areas of darkness. He refers to the commission of Jesus to the Seventy (Luke 10:19) and says that demonic opposition is to be expected when the kingdom of God is being advanced (1981, 146–47). Paul Pomerville says that the power encounter involved in exorcism has been an intentional church growth strategy among Pentecostals (1985, 109).

Church growth proponents have noted that seriously dealing with demonic opposition has been one of the distinctive marks of Pentecostal growth. McGavran cited exorcism as a part of the answer to his question, "What makes Pentecostal churches grow?" Pentecostals, he said,

> accept the fact that most men and women today believe that demons and evil spirits (varying forms of Satan and dark thoughts) do invade them, bind them, and rule over them. Pentecostals believe that the mighty name of Jesus drives out evil spirits and heals all manner of sickness (1977, 98).

Wagner concluded that exorcism was a key factor in the exploding growth among Latin American Pentecostals (1986, 126–29), and De Wet believes that is the only way to successfully deal with the world view of Animists and the unseen spiritual resistance in the Muslim world (1986, 163–64).

Bibliography: M. I. Bubeck, *The Adversary* (1975); G. Canty, "Demons and Casting Out Demons," *Pentecostal Doctrine* (1976); C. W. Conn, *The Anatomy of Evil* (1981); C. De Wet, "The Challenge of Signs and Wonders in World Missions for the Twentieth Century," *Azusa Street and Beyond,* ed. L. G. McClung, Jr. (1986); G. P. Duffield and N. M. Van Cleave, *Foundations of Pentecostal Theology* (1983); M. Garrison, *How to Try a Spirit* (1976); A. F. Glasser and D. A. McGavran, *Contemporary Theologies of Missions* (1983); S. D. Glazier, *Perspectives on Pentecostalism: Case Studies From the Caribbean and Latin America* (1980); M. Green, *I Believe in Satan's Downfall* (1981); M. Harper, *Spiritual Warfare* (1970); M. L. Hodges, *A Theology of the Church and Its Mission* (1977); W. J. Hollenweger, *The Pentecostals* (1972); G. Lindsay, *Demon Manifestations and Delusion,* vol. 3 (1972b); idem, *Fallen Angels and Demons,* vol. 2 (1972a); idem, *The Ministry of Casting Out Demons* (1977); idem, *The Origin of Demons and Their Orders* (1972c); D. M. Lloyd-Jones, *The Christian Warfare* (1976); idem, *The Christian Soldier* (1977); A. Longley, *Christ Made Satan Useless* (n.d.); T. L. Lowery, *Demon Possession* (n.d.); S. E. McClelland, "Demon, Demon Possession," *Evangelical Dictionary of Theology* (1984); D. A. McGavran, "What Makes Pentecostal Churches Grow?" *Church Growth Bulletin* (1977); J. T. Nichol, *Pentecostalism* (1966); J. Penn-Lewis, *War on the Saints* (1977); J. D. Pentecost, *Your Adversary the Devil* (1969); R. Peterson, *Are Demons for Real?* (1972); P. A. Pomerville, *The Third Force in Missions* (1985); C. Richardson, *Exorcism: New Testament Style* (1974); M. Scanlan and R. J. Cirner, *Deliverance From Evil Spirits* (1980); L. J. Suenens, *Renewal and the Powers of Darkness* (1983); P. Toon, "Exorcism," *NIDCC* (1974); M. F. Unger, *Demons in the World Today* (1971); C. P. Wagner, *Spiritual Power and Church Growth* (1986); H. A. M. Whyte, *Dominion Over Demons* (1974); J. Wilson, *Principles of War* (1964); J. Wimber, *Power Evangelism* (1986).   L. G. McClung, Jr.

EZEKIEL, BOOK OF

I. Introduction to Ezekiel. The Book of Ezekiel bears its name not only because Ezekiel is its main character, but also because the book claims him as its author. Ezekiel was a priest who was deported by Nebuchadnezzar of Babylon in 597 B.C. along with Jehoiachin, king of Judah (see 2 Kings 24:10–17; 2 Chron. 36:9–10). At that time Nebuchadnezzar deported the upper economic classes, including the nobility, craftsmen, and the elite troops of the king. Evidently Ezekiel's priestly family qualified as being in the upper classes, for he was deported.

The book itself can be divided according to the visions and oracles that Ezekiel reports. They are too numerous to catalog here, but they run in length from a few verses to several chapters.

The time of several of the oracles and visions can be dated with some precision. Most of the dates are relative to the deportation of King Jehoiachin (1:1–2; 8:1; 20:1; 26:1; 29:1, 17; 30:20; 31:1; 32:1, 17; 33:21 [relative to "our exile"]; 40:1 [relative to "our exile" and to the fall of Jerusalem]), and others give a time period separating oracles or actions of Ezekiel (3:16; 12:8; 24:18; 33:21–22). Zimmerli (1979, 11), for example, thus assigns the call of Ezekiel to July 31, 593 B.C., and the latest dated oracle (29:17) to April 26, 571 B.C. There is one date given for the fifth, sixth, seventh, tenth, twelfth, twenty-fifth, and twenty-seventh years; five dates are given for the eleventh year. Since the dates in chapter 29 are out of chronological sequence, it may be that other undated oracles are not entirely in sequence, either. One date, "in the thirtieth year" (1:1), remains enigmatic, though some have suggested that it refers to Ezekiel's age at the time of his prophetic call and would translate it "in *my* thirtieth year" (e.g., NIV margin).

Ezekiel is known for extensive use of symbolic actions. For example, God commanded Ezekiel to use a brick to prophesy the siege of Jerusalem and to shave his head and beard and to use the hair to portray the fate of the inhabitants of Jerusalem (see Ezek. 4–5). Ezekiel also used a large number of speech forms to communicate the divine message. Students of Ezekiel have concluded that many of the texts in the book were never delivered orally but were originally composed in written form.

II. Terminology. The term "spirit," *rûah* in Hebrew, often refers to such things as wind, breath, life or principles of life, heart in the sense of the core of personality, and anger. It can also refer to the Spirit of God. In view of the range of meanings, it is best to consider *rûah* to point directly to the Spirit of God only when one or more of the following factors suggest it: (1) phraseology, e.g., "*rûah* of God," "his [God's] *rûah*"; (2) statements within the context that move the thought away from a physical meaning (wind, breath) toward "Spirit"; or (3) a clear reference to God's Spirit in the context.

In Ezekiel the phrase "the hand of the LORD" is used closely with the "Spirit of the LORD" so that at times "the hand of the LORD" seems to mean "the Spirit of the LORD." Texts where "the hand of the LORD" is used this way are Ezekiel 1:3; 3:14, 22; 8:1; 33:22; 37:1; and 40:1. The clearest text is 8:1–4. The hand of the Lord came upon Ezekiel, and he entered a vision in which he saw the glory of the Lord in a rather anthropomorphic way, described in much the same terms as in 1:26–28. The hand of this glorious figure reached out and grabbed Ezekiel by the hair, apparently preparatory to lifting him up by his hair, but then the Spirit actually lifted him up and took him in visions of God to Jerusalem. The transition from the hand of the Lord to the hand of this glorious figure to the Spirit indicates that the hand of the Lord can be used almost interchangeably with the Spirit in certain contexts.

This conclusion can be validated by examining several of the other texts in the list above. The initiation of the vision in 37:1 is similar: the hand of the Lord is upon Ezekiel, and the Lord brings him out by means of the Spirit of the Lord into the valley. In 1:3 it is the hand of the Lord that induces the vision, as it is in 40:1–2. In 3:22 the hand of the Lord is upon Ezekiel, and then the Lord speaks to him, which is similar to 3:24 and 33:22. Wilson (1980, 261) would concur, stating that the phrase "the hand of the LORD was upon" is a clear indication of Spirit-possession.

III. Visions of God. In several texts the Spirit lifts Ezekiel up and transports him in a vision to another location. The texts are as follows: Ezekiel 3:12, 14; 8:3; 11:1, 24; 40:1–2; 43:5.

The account of the first vision of Ezekiel runs from 1:1 to 3:15. The opening description makes it clear that a vision is intended. Ezekiel was among the exiles at the river Kebar when the hand of the Lord fell upon him and he entered an altered state of consciousness and received the vision. At the end of the vision, when the Spirit returned him to the exiles beside the river, it was as if he were physically transported to his original location (which, of course, he never actually left): "the Spirit then lifted me up and took me away" (3:14; cf. v. 12).

Another complete vision is described in Ezekiel 8–11. Again the hand of the Lord was upon Ezekiel. In 8:1–4 the Spirit lifted him up into the air and took him "in visions of God" to Jerusalem to the north gate of the inner court of the temple. Later in the vision (11:1) the Spirit again lifted him up and took him to the east gate of the temple. Finally, when the vision was complete (11:24), the Spirit lifted him up and took him in the vision to the exiles in Babylonia, i.e., returned him to his normal state of consciousness.

Ezekiel 37:1 likewise involves transportation in a vision, this time to a valley full of dried bones. The status of this text as a vision is confirmed when the Lord explains the metaphoric symbolism of the vision in verse 11: "These bones are the whole house of Israel." The valley is real only in the vision; it is not a physical place. Ezekiel does not describe the return from the valley, and the reader knows that the vision is over when Ezekiel abruptly begins a new section with an introductory formula in verse 15, "The word of the LORD came to me."

The final two texts are in Ezekiel's vision of the temple, 40:1–2 and 43:5. In the first, the hand of the Lord came upon Ezekiel, and the Lord transported him in visions of God "there," i.e., presumably to Jerusalem, although this was a vision of what would be, not what was. In the vision Ezekiel was escorted around the temple, but at one point, narrated in 43:2–4, the glory of the Lord arrived and entered the temple. Then the Spirit lifted Ezekiel up and brought him into the inner court.

In several of these texts, then, the Spirit is responsible for initiating a prophetic vision. These visions are of various types: a vision of the glory of God, involving a prophetic commissioning; a vision of an actual state of affairs in Jerusalem; a symbolic vision where dried bones stand for Israel; and a vision that is of Jerusalem and the temple, yet not as they then existed. (Whether this temple will be physically constructed and whether its significance is symbolic or spiritual are questions that are debated, but their resolution is not of great relevance to this study.) The initiation of each vision is described in terms of transportation to another location (except for 1:3–4), as is the return to normal consciousness, when it is reported. It is evident that during these visions Ezekiel's whole perception came from the vision and that he was totally unaware of his physical surroundings.

During two of these visions the Lord commanded Ezekiel to speak, and Ezekiel did speak, i.e., prophesy. In 11:13 the result was the death of one of the elders of Israel; in 37:7–10 the result was that the dry bones came to life. Since the latter is symbolic, it may also be that the former is not meant to be taken literally, either, though it is much more specific regarding the person and location.

Contrasts may be made on two points: first, in Ezekiel 3:22–24 when the Lord wanted Ezekiel to move from one physical location to another, he told Ezekiel to get up and go; he did not physically transport Ezekiel. Second, Ezekiel's experiences contrast with the reputation of Elijah for being picked up and carried by the Lord from one location to another (1 Kings 18:12; 2 Kings 2:16).

IV. The Lord Speaks. In several texts the presence of the Spirit of the Lord is connected with the Lord speaking to Ezekiel. The connection is the closest in 11:5, where the RSV reads, "The Spirit of the LORD fell upon me, and he [the LORD] said to me." In this case, the primary, or perhaps only, reason for the Spirit coming upon Ezekiel is to communicate the word of the Lord to him. In 3:22, under the term "the hand of the LORD," a similar link appears: "the hand of the LORD was upon me there, and he [the LORD] said to me. . . ." In both texts there is a switch in the gender of the verb from feminine to masculine, indicating a change in subject from the feminine nouns "spirit" and "hand" to "the LORD," a masculine noun. Thus the LORD himself is the speaker, not the Spirit, yet the presence of the Spirit is an important element in the prophetic experience of the divine word.

Similarities are present in the opening lines of the book as well, where in 1:3 "the word of the LORD came to Ezekiel. . . . There the hand of the LORD was upon him." In this text the lines of distinction between the word of the Lord and visions of God seem somewhat blurred. Other texts involve a looser connection between the presence of the Spirit and the Lord speaking to Ezekiel. In 33:22–23 the hand of the Lord was upon Ezekiel during the evening, and the Lord opened his mouth: Ezekiel should have suspected that a message from God would be forthcoming. (The reader must remember 3:24–27, where God took from Ezekiel the ability to speak, except when God had a message for him to deliver to the people of Israel.) The final two texts involve the Spirit initiating a vision in which the Lord speaks to Ezekiel. In 8:1–5 the Spirit took Ezekiel in a vision to Jerusalem, where he saw the glory of God, then God spoke to him. Finally, in 37:1–3, the hand of the Lord was upon Ezekiel, the Lord brought him out by the Spirit of the Lord in a vision, and then the Lord spoke to him.

It is possible to conclude from these texts that the presence of the Spirit was an important factor in Ezekiel's experience of the word of the Lord. We have already seen that such was the case in the visionary strand of his prophetic experience; now it should be evident that the two strands, the visionary and the auditory, are intertwined. All of Ezekiel's visions included God speaking to him; on the other hand, God did not always use a vision to speak to him. In these cases, Ezekiel used the expression "the word of the LORD came to me" (e.g., 3:16). In other cases, Ezekiel could use the terminology of the hand of the Lord or the Spirit (e.g., 3:22–24, which is not described as a vision, though it may have been one; and 33:22) being upon him, then the Lord speaking to him.

V. The Spirit Revives. When Ezekiel saw his first vision of the glory of the Lord, he fell down on his face. He retained consciousness but apparently could not move. God told him to get up, and as God spoke, the Spirit entered Ezekiel and raised him to his feet (Ezek. 1:28–2:2). In 3:23–24, Ezekiel again saw a vision of the glory of the Lord and again fell facedown. As by the Kebar River, the Spirit came into him and raised him to his feet.

These two texts may be unconnected with the other Spirit material in Ezekiel, but it seems probable that they are related to those texts in the "New Spirit" category. Ezekiel is known for the symbolic actions that he performed—perhaps this draining and then granting of strength was intended as a symbolic lesson to him near the beginning of his prophetic vocation, for these events were not repeated again after the second time.

VI. A New Spirit. It is not until Ezekiel 36:26–27 that the reader receives the clue needed to put together this theme in Ezekiel. In the first part of verse 26 the Lord states that he will give Israel, i.e., each Israelite, a new heart and a new spirit. In itself, this statement is strongly reminiscent of 11:19, where the reader would be justified in taking "spirit" as nearly equivalent to "heart." "One heart" of the Hebrew text is well rendered by the NIV "undivided heart": no longer will Israel be torn by the rivalry between idolatry and the Lord, because Israel will be faithful to him. The structure of Ezekiel 36:26–27, however, leads the reader to question the easy equation of "heart" and "spirit." The second half of verse 26 (like 11:19) explains the "new heart" imagery: the Israelites have hearts of stone that God will remove and replace with hearts of flesh. Deadness and hardness will be replaced by life and responsiveness. The next verse functions in a similar way, i.e., to explain what the Lord means by a "new spirit." The "new spirit" that God will give the Israelites is *his own Spirit;* the result again parallels 11:20: the Israelites will follow God's decrees and be careful to keep his laws.

It is therefore probable that the other "new spirit" texts in Ezekiel should be interpreted in the light of 36:26–27. One of these is 18:31, where God chides Israel for not repenting and so getting themselves a new heart and spirit. The longest passage is 37:1–14, in Ezekiel's vision of the valley of dry bones. In this vision there is an interplay of three meanings of *rûaḥ*: "spirit," "breath," and "wind." The first use of *rûaḥ* in verse 1 sets the overtones for the passage: God's Spirit brought Ezekiel out in the vision into the valley. The next two occurrences, verses 5 and 6, parallel the giving of *rûaḥ* with the giving of life. The NIV rightly translates *rûaḥ* as "breath," but there are strong overtones of the *rûaḥ* from God giving life. The *rûaḥ* in verse 8 is again "breath" in the sense of "life": Ezekiel has prophesied as the Lord told him to do, and though the bones came together and flesh covered them, "there was no breath in them." God then tells Ezekiel to prophesy to the *rûaḥ*: "Come from the four winds [plural of *rûaḥ*], O breath [*rûaḥ*], and breathe into these slain, that they may live" (v. 9). Verse 10 relates that breath (*rûaḥ*) entered them, and they stood up.

The Lord then interprets the vision to Ezekiel. The bones are Israel, scattered among the nations, feeling that their bones are dried up and their hope is all gone. The Lord, however, promises that he will gather the Israelites back into their own land; it will be as though their graves would be opened and they would be brought back from the dead. In order to give them life, he will put his Spirit in them. At this point the reader can make the connection with the Spirit and the vision. The *rûaḥ* of the vision that enters the bodies is the *rûaḥ* of the Lord that will be given that Israel may live. This giving of the Spirit implies a restoration of the hope that was lost and is also connected with the return to the land (for the latter, cf. 11:16–20 and 36:24–28).

In 39:29 God promises (in a mild contrast with putting his Spirit *within* the Israelites) to pour out his Spirit *on* the Israelites. In the paragraph (NIV) that begins with verse 25, the return of Israel to its own land is prominent. God will no longer hide his face from Israel, for he will pour out his

Spirit upon its people, and they will be faithful to him.

VII. Summary and Conclusions. Ezekiel is an outstanding example of a prophet possessed by the Spirit. During these times of possession, Ezekiel retains consciousness, but it is a consciousness that receives all seemingly sensory data (taste, vision, and hearing) from a nonsensory source (the Spirit). Some of the mental experiences thus created by the Spirit involve transportation in a vision to places that also exist in the real world; other places do not exist except in the vision.

The presence of the Spirit is also linked in Ezekiel with his receipt of the word of the Lord. Ezekiel did not perceive the Spirit as speaking— that would have to wait for the prophetic experience in NT times (see, e.g., Acts 13:2; 1 Tim. 4:1; and Rev. 14:13). Rather, the presence of the Spirit is presented as a factor preparatory to receiving the divine word.

"The hand of the LORD" terminology creates an image of organic connection of the Spirit with the Lord. Perhaps the effect is to depict the Spirit as an extension of the Lord's power in operation, since there are uses of the hand of God terminology in Ezekiel that do not involve the Spirit. On the other hand, the wind imagery in Ezekiel 37 presents a picture of the Spirit as more distinct, since the *rûaḥ* comes from the four winds.

Finally, God promises to pour out his Spirit upon Israel as part of their return to their own land. Israel would repent of their idolatry. In response to their repentance, God would transform their hearts from cold, dead, unresponsive stone to warm, living flesh; God would give them a new spirit—his own. The Spirit would produce hope and life and faithfulness to the demands of God for righteousness.

Bibliography: R. Wilson, *Prophecy and Society in Ancient Israel* (1980); W. Zimmerli, *Ezekiel 1* (1979).
D. A. Johns

F

FAITH HEALING See HEALING MOVEMENTS.

FAITH HOMES Hospices for healing, especially prevalent from about 1882 until the first decade of the twentieth century. One of the expressions of the Holiness movement of the late nineteenth century had been the parallel healing movement, which eventually gave rise to rest homes operated on a faith basis for the sick and terminally ill. Faith homes were often closely tied to Holiness missions and/or Bible schools operated by the same personnel and therefore became important outlets for teaching, preaching, and evangelism.

Faith homes were an important component of the Holiness milieu out of which the Pentecostal movement arose. The Pentecostal revival was spread by Holiness pastors and lay people as they testified at other Holiness missions about the baptism of the Holy Spirit, the gift of unknown tongues, and the outpouring of the Holy Spirit at the Holiness mission at Azusa Street, Los Angeles, in 1906. Because some of these missions were associated with faith homes, it is not surprising that healing became an important aspect of the Pentecostal message.

Most faith healing homes were financed without any solicitation of funds. This method had its origins in the work of George Müller, who in 1835 began an orphanage in Bristol, England, which he financed by prayer. Every year Müller published an annual report on the income he had received and on what had been accomplished during that year, but he and his staff did not appeal for assistance even under very difficult financial conditions, believing that they were to trust God for all of the needs of the work. This method became very popular in America, not only for faith homes, but for many Holiness missions and Bible schools.

Although some of the first faith homes were for very sick patients who had nowhere else to go, many became open to others seeking healing, rest, or spiritual or material help, or to missionaries on furlough. Mrs. Elizabeth V. Baker wrote of Elim Faith Home in Rochester, New York:

We take all guests alike whether rich or poor, for a limited time, longer or shorter as the Spirit directs. All sit down at the same table, and share equally in the comforts and advantages of the Home both temporal and spiritual. Immediately after breakfast, . . . all come together where an hour is taken up over the Word of God in exposition and prayer. God has especially honored this morning study of His Word, and often the Spirit has fallen upon us in a remarkable way, sometimes holding us till dinner time. Special prayer and instruction is given each guest privately as the case requires. Hundreds have been healed in answer to prayer alone . . . (Baker, n.d., 63–64).

The idea for faith homes may have arisen from the establishment of a faith home by Johann Christoph Blumhardt at Bad Boll, Germany, in 1852. Blumhardt had been a Lutheran minister in nearby Möttlingen, and in 1842 one of his parishioners, a young girl named Gottlieben Dittus, was diagnosed by doctors as "demon-possessed." Blumhardt and others prayed for two years for this girl, who not only suffered from a strange nervous disorder, but in whose home numerous psychic phenomena had been observed. One day, as Blumhardt was praying with Gottlieben's sister, she heard the voice of a girl that said, "Jesus is victor." From this time onward, there was renewal on an unusual scale, and people began converging upon Möttlingen from all parts of Europe seeking healing. To accommodate them, Blumhardt opened the church manse as a faith home, where he conducted Bible studies and provided guidance and prayer at regular intervals for each patient. After Lutheran ecclesiastical authorities ordered Blumhardt to release those in the manse into the care of physicians, he resigned his church and purchased and renovated Bad Boll, a bankrupt gambling and health spa. This facility became the center of Blumhardt's ministry, which was continued for many years after his death in 1880 by his two sons and by Gottlieben Dittus.

Another important influence upon the American healing movement was Dorothea Trudel of Männedorf, Switzerland, who prayed successfully for many victims of an epidemic there in 1851. People from many parts of Europe traveled to Männedorf seeking healing, where she eventually opened her own home in order to minister to them. She then began acquiring additional homes as more and more people sought her help.

The first home in America was established by Charles Cullis, a physician who purchased a home in Boston for the terminally ill in 1864. He financed it on the same basis that George Müller had run his orphanages in Bristol, expanding it to include a local church, an evening school, an orphanage, and a publishing house. Within a few years Cullis became familiar with the ministry of Dorothea Trudel and began in 1870 to pray for the healing of the sick people under his care. The first person healed under Cullis was Lucy Drake, who had had an inoperable brain tumor until Cullis prayed with her. After three months there was no longer any sign of a tumor.

In 1882 other faith homes began to appear in America and England. One of the first was Bethshan Institute of Healing, opened by Mrs. Elizabeth Baxter in London, where the great South African preacher Andrew Murray was healed of a throat disorder that had threatened to end his public ministry. During the same year, Miss Carrie F. Judd founded Faith Rest Cottage in Buffalo, New York, which soon became widely recognized as a center for divine healing, prayer, and spiritual renewal. She used this facility for her extensive teaching, writing, and publishing ministries. She later married George Montgomery and moved to California, where she established the Home of Peace at Beulah Heights, near Oakland, in 1893.

A. B. Simpson, inspired by these developments, opened The Home for Faith and Physical Healing in 1883 in New York City, a precursor of Berachah Home, which he established the following year with generous donations from E. G. Selchow, a businessman who had been healed at Simpson's first healing center.

By 1887 more than thirty faith homes had already been established in the U.S., but many had become targets of intense criticism. In 1885, for example, a faith cure home in St. Louis was under investigation as a result of the death of a child under its care. Until this time newspapers had given favorable publicity to the faith cure establishments, helping to spread positive public awareness of the healing movement, but later publicity became much less favorable. Healing centers were sometimes accused of refusing medical aid for their patients and of viewing the use of physicians and medicines as demonstrations of lack of faith. In response to such criticisms, A. B. Simpson wrote in 1890:

We do believe that God heals His sick and suffering children when they can fully trust Him. At the same time we believe that no one should act precipitately or presumptuously in this matter, or abandon natural remedies unless they have an intelligent, Scriptural and unquestioning trust in Him alone and really know Him well enough to touch Him in living contact as their Healer (Niklaus, Sawin, and Stoez, 1986, 88).

In 1894 John Alexander Dowie opened "Divine Healing Home Number One" in downtown Chicago. The Chicago Commissioner of Health responded by passing an ordinance requiring such homes to be attended by a licensed physician. Dowie, however, rejected the use of medical science and was arrested several times for the violation of this ordinance, but charges were eventually dropped and the ordinance declared invalid. These events generated a great deal of publicity for Dowie, who then opened two additional homes to accommodate the multitudes who flocked to Chicago for his prayers. All of these facilities were consolidated into the splendid seven-story former Imperial Hotel of Chicago, which Dowie acquired in 1896, naming it the Zion Divine Healing Home.

In 1898 Charles Parham opened Bethel Healing Home in Topeka, Kansas, "to provide home-like comforts for those who were seeking healing, while we prayed for their spiritual needs as well as their bodies. We also found Christian homes for orphan children, and work for the unemployed"

(Parham, 1930, 39). Parham used this home as the center for his ministry, publishing *The Apostolic Faith* twice a month and holding services. Two years later Parham left this home in charge of two Holiness preachers in order to visit other homes, including Dowie's in Chicago; the Eye-Opener in the same city; Malone's work in Cleveland; A. B. Simpson's work, which had moved to Nyack, New York; and Frank W. Sandford's Holy Ghost and Us society at Shiloh, in Durham, Maine. When Parham returned he found that "the ministers I left in charge of my work had not only taken my building but most of my congregation" (Parham, 1930, 48). Parham then opened a Bible School at a mansion known as "Stone's Folly," where the Pentecostal movement was born in the beginning of 1901.

Other faith homes in operation during this era included the Fourfold Gospel Mission at Troy, New York, established by Sara M. C. Musgrove; Arthur and Kittie Sloan's faith home in Stratford, Connecticut; Miss Fannie Curtis's home in the same city; Mrs. Lucy Drake Osborn's Home for Incurables in Brooklyn; Miss M. F. Barker and Miss H. M. Anderson's home in Ilion, New York; J. D. Asbough's Faith Cure Home in St. Louis; the Louisville Home in Kentucky founded by J. T. Burghard; J. R. Newton's home in New York City; the Pink Cottage in Stanford, Kentucky, founded by George O. Barnes; Mother Moise's Home in St. Louis; Beulah Rescue Home in Chicago; the Missionary Home in Alliance, Ohio; Mrs. S. G. Beck's Kemuel House in Germantown, Pennsylvania; Miss M. H. Mossman's Faith College in Ocean Grove, New Jersey; Mrs. J. P. Kellogg's Home in Utica, New York; and Mrs. Dora Dudley's home in Grand Rapids, Michigan (Anderson, 1979, 50, 73; Cunningham, 1974, 504–5; Chappell, 1983, 99–100, 166–68).

Faith homes also became an important part of the Pentecostal movement in the years following the outpouring of the Holy Spirit in 1906, especially since many of them accepted the message of Pentecost during the first few years of the revival. The experience at Elim Faith Home in Rochester, New York, may have been typical: "Later we heard about the work in Los Angeles accompanied with speaking in tongues . . . but not till our convention season was there any manifest outpouring. . . . While the meeting was going on in the church a few had gathered in Elim Home for further waiting, and it was there the power fell" (Baker, n.d., 134–35).

See also HEALING MOVEMENTS.

Bibliography: D. Albrecht, "Carrie Judd Montgomery: Pioneering Contributor to Three Religious Movements," *Pneuma* 8 (Fall 1986): 101–19; R. Anderson, *Vision of the Disinherited* (1979); E. Baker, *Chronicles of a Faith Life* (n.d.); E. Blumhofer, "The Christian Catholic Apostolic Church and the Apostolic Faith: A Study in the 1906 Pentecostal Revival," in C. Robeck, Jr., *Charismatic Experiences in History* (1985): 126–46; A. Brooks, *Answers to Prayer from George Müller's Narratives* (n.d.); P. Chappell, "The Divine Healing Movement in America," Ph.D. diss., Drew University, 1983; R. Cunningham, "From Holiness to Healing: The Faith Cure in America 1872–1892," *Church History* 43 (December 1974): 499–513; D. Dayton "The Rise of the Evangelical Healing Movement in Nineteenth Century America," *Pneuma* 4 (Spring 1982): 1–8; R. Niklaus, J. Sawin, and S. Stoesz, *All for Jesus* (1986); S. Parham, *The Life of Charles F. Parham* (1930); E. Prange, *The Gift Is Already Yours* (1980).

R. M. Riss

FAITH MOVEMENT See POSITIVE CONFESSION THEOLOGY.

FAITH, GIFT OF After the two "word" gifts mentioned in 1 Corinthians 12:8, Paul lists "faith" *(pistis)* as another "manifestation of the Spirit," and follows this with "charisms of healings" and "workings of [deeds] of power." Since Paul lists "faith" here as a special gift, he is describing something different from that faith by which a person is justified. This article will first study instances in which this special aspect of faith is narrated or described in the NT, discuss briefly the significance of the term in 1 Corinthians, and then proceed to consider how the charismatic gift of faith has been viewed in the history of Christianity.

I. The Charismatic Gift of Faith in the New Testament

A. In the New Testament Outside 1 Corinthians 12:9. Generally, the NT uses the word *pistis* (faith) to describe that act by which people accept God's witness concerning what he has done for the human race in the life, death, and resurrection of Jesus Christ, and come to confess Jesus as Lord and to receive the effect of God's saving action in their own selves. This faith is "the work of God" (John 6:29) to which the one believing agrees. As Thomas Aquinas expressed it, "Not that righteousness is merited through faith, but rather the very act of believing is itself the first act of righteousness that God works in someone. From the fact that he believes in God who makes righteous, he submits himself to God's righteousness and thus receives its effect" *(Commentary on Romans,* 4:5).

It is significant, however, that this same word "faith" is used to describe a very particular actualization of that same acceptance, trust, and knowledge in connection with mighty works of God. The Synoptic Gospels, sensitive to the general NT teaching regarding saving faith, exploit the ambiguity of the Greek *sōzein* (heal/save) to make some of the healing miracles a symbolic teaching regarding this faith. In the story of the woman with the flow of blood, the actual healing is used to symbolize the salvation of the Gentiles healed as Jesus makes his way to the daughter of the synagogue's ruler. The Synoptics record Jesus' words as: "Your faith has healed/saved you" (Matt. 9:22/Mark 5:34/Luke 18:42; cf. Matt. 9:29); and they are taken up by Luke in regard to the healed and grateful leper (Luke 17:19), and to the forgiven and grateful woman (7:50). A similar notion, exploiting the same ambiguity, underlies Luke's report that as Paul looked intently at the cripple in Lystra, he saw that he had "faith to be healed/saved" (Acts 14:9; see also 3:16; cf. Acts 16:31; Rom. 1:16–17, etc.). In all the above instances, *pistis* describes an inner attitude of trust, abandonment, and belief that results in the

believers' healing, a symbolic expression of their salvation.

There is another series of Synoptic texts that present Jesus' teaching regarding the relation of *pistis* to the performance of works outside the believer. Much of this is linked to Jesus' saying about faith moving mountains, which we find in four places: Matthew 21:21 and Mark 11:22ff. as Jesus' reply to the disciples' astonishment at the withered fig tree; in Matthew 17:20 in his reply to their question concerning their inability to cast out a demon (cf. Mark 9:29, and see the whole discussion of faith in the Marcan account); and in Luke 17:6 in response to their request for an increase in faith (Luke changes "mountain" to "sycamore tree"). The general context of this last Lucan use of the saying is forgiveness and unity among the believers, and this is reflected in the further Marcan teaching which transposes Jesus' saying about forgiveness (see Matt. 6:14–15) and adds it to the powerful saying, "Therefore I say to you: all that you pray and ask for, believe that you have received it, and it will be done for you." (Mark 11:24/Matt. 21:22; see John 11:40.) The same notions of unity, forgiveness, and the "prayer of faith" are combined in James 5:15–16.

The kind of faith described in Mark 11:24 is illustrated in the variant reading of Acts 6:8, which describes Stephen performing great wonders and signs "full of God's *faith* [text, 'grace'] and power." We can find it as well in Paul, who, after receiving a word from the Lord, told all his companions about to face shipwreck that they would not be harmed: "So keep up your courage, men, for I have faith in God that it will happen just as he told me" (Acts 27:25).

B. Pistis in 1 Corinthians 12:9. Paul is aware of the general NT tradition concerning Jesus' teaching on faith. This is evident from his allusion in 1 Corinthians 13:1–3 to the saying of Jesus during his comparison of the gifts he has just mentioned in chapter 12 with love. We read there, ". . . if I have all faith so as to move mountains, but I do not have love, I am nothing" (13:2).

The *pistis,* then, to which Paul refers in 1 Corinthians 12:9 is that faith which renders someone apt to be an instrument of the Holy Spirit in performing "healing" and "works of power" *(dynameis),* and generally in praying efficaciously (see 1 John 5:14). The fact that it is listed among the other "manifestations" of the Spirit sheds an important light on Paul's concept of these manifestations or "spiritual things" *(pneumatika)* or "gifts" *(charismata).* The charismatic gift of faith is a particular intensification of that basic attitude toward God in Jesus Christ by which we accept his saving act, his authority, and his complete trustworthiness, and base our lives on his Word. It is possible to have the right relationship to God and be thus justified by the blood of Christ through faith without having the particular gift called faith: "to *another* faith in the same Spirit" (1 Cor. 12:9). On the other hand, it is possible to have a minimal faith, even without a great love of God (1 Cor. 13:2) and be able to move mountains. The ideal, however, is that the basic faith relationship to God be elevated so that a person goes beyond the usual boundaries of human existence and, in the power of God, lays hold of and gives human existence to God's desire to perform a particularly wonderful work that can lead to salvation. Johannes Bengel describes this gift of faith as "a most ardent and realistic [*praesentissima*] laying hold of God, most especially in regard to his will" (cited by Robertson and Plummer, 1914, 266). F. Prat (1945, 1:426) describes it thus: "an invincible confidence, founded on theological faith and assured by a supernatural instinct that God, in a given case, will manifest his power, his justice, or his mercy."

II. The Gift of Faith in the Life of the Church. From earliest times, commentators were aware of the relation between this gift and the performing of signs and wonders. John Chrysostom says that the faith to which Paul refers in 1 Corinthians 12:9 is not that regarding the articles of faith (*dogmatōn*) but miracles (*sēmeiōn*), and that such faith is the "mother of miracles" (*PG* 61, 245). Cyril of Jerusalem first notes that the faith of others can bring about a healing. He appeals to the fact that Jesus "saw the faith" of those who brought the paralyzed man to him (Matt. 9:2/Mark 2:5/Luke 5:20), and he also cites John 11:40. He remarks in regard to the "second kind" of faith that it is not only doctrinal but also effects things beyond human power. He includes among these things the ability to contemplate God and to grasp the mystery of the universe and the history of the world. He urges his hearers, "Regard highly therefore, that faith which comes from yourself and is directed to him, that you may also receive from him that faith which effects things beyond man's power." (*Catechesis* 5, 10–11, *PG* 33, 517–20.)

The gift of assured and efficacious prayer is part of the charismatic gift of faith. We see this in men like George Müller of Bristol who was able to care for thousands of English orphans through his prayer to God for what they needed. Another common instance of this gift is to be found in those with an authentic healing ministry. It seems that the faith of the minister of healing can be imparted to the one to be healed and enable him to reach out and "lay hold" of the will of God. J. Brosch describes it this way: "Faith as a gift is essentially a tremendous assurance, received only by divine grace; an assurance which draws the supernatural into the natural world. An immovable faith such as this is particularly suited to win the weak and establish them" (cited by Bittlinger, 1967, 33). By insisting on the fact that this gift is a divine work, we can lift from the shoulders of the sick the unjust burden imposed by those who tell them that they are not healed because they "do not have enough faith." On the other hand, we should all pray as the disciples did, "Lord, increase our faith" (Luke 17:5).

Bibliography: A. Bittlinger, *Gifts and Graces. A Commentary on 1 Corinthians 12–14* (1967); J.D.G. Dunn, *Jesus and the Spirit* (1975); G.D. Fee, *The First Epistle to the Corinthians* (1987); F. Prat, *The Theology of St. Paul* (1945); A. Robertson and A. Plummer, *A Critical and Exegetical Commentary on the First Epistle of St. Paul to the Corinthians* (1914).   R. F. Martin

FALLING UNDER THE POWER See SLAIN IN THE SPIRIT.

FAMILY OF LOVE An American cult with charismatic-like tendencies. Known until 1983 as the Children of God, the Family of Love consists of followers of David Berg (b. 1919), self-named Moses David. In 1967 the founder, former Christian and Missionary Alliance minister and public relations person for Fred Jordan's American Soul Clinic, became head of the Teen Challenge branch in Huntington Beach, California. Soon renamed the Light Club, this center became the rallying point of Jesus People ready to take Berg seriously when in 1969 he revealed that an earthquake was imminent in California and that the Children of God should leave. Berg and his followers started out on an eight-month trek throughout the Southwest that ended at the Soul Clinic mission in Los Angeles, where Fred Jordan volunteered ranches he owned at New Thurber, Texas, and Coachella, California, for their use. Within a year conflict had developed between the Children of God and Jordan, and he evicted them. Coincident with this, parents of members in San Diego organized the Parents Committee to Free Our Children from the Children of God and retained Ted Patrick to capture, if necessary, and to deprogram them of its teachings.

After 1971 the Children of God dispersed into several dozen small communities in the U.S., with a majority—including the renamed leader, Moses—going overseas. The group supported itself from assets individual members surrendered at the time they joined and from the sale of publications. The dispersed community was held together, and uniformity of belief and outreach was fostered by the periodic issuance of circular communiques, the "Mo Letters," Mo being the sobriquet for Moses David (i.e., David Berg). The "Mo Letters," which eventually numbered into the hundreds, were addressed to members only and covered every aspect of their common life, especially recruitment of new members. Widespread rumors founded on certain "Mo Letters" that came under scrutiny by outsiders were that female Children of God members were expected even to use sex, if necessary, to attract new members. In the late 1970s publicity of defections gained by the deprogrammers and of the "flirty fishing" strategem for making converts drove the leaders and a large portion of the members into hiding. At its height the movement had approximately eight hundred colonies in eighty countries. At one time there were approximately three thousand adherents in the U.S. and one thousand in the U.K.

Bibliography: D. Davis, *The Children of God: The Inside Story* (1984); R. Davis, "The Organization and Functioning of the Children of God," *Sociological Analysis* 37 (1976): 321–39; J. G. Melton, ed., *Encyclopedia of American Religions*, vol. 2 (1978); T. Moore, "Where Have All the Children of God Gone?" *New Times* 3 (October 4, 1974): 32–41; New York Charity Frauds Bureau, *Final Report on the Activities of the Children of God* (1974); T. Patrick, *Let Our Children Go!* (1976); W. D. Pritchett, *The Children of God/Family of Love: An Annotated Bibliography* (1985).   C. E. Jones

A theology professor at Oral Roberts University graduate school, Charles Farah, Jr., is author of *From the Pinnacle of the Temple.*

FARAH, CHARLES, JR. (1926–). Pastor, author, professor of theology. Farah was born in Akron, Ohio, and educated at Wheaton College (B.A. and M.A.), Fuller Theological Seminary (B.D.), Edinburgh University (Ph.D.), and Hebrew University, Jerusalem (postgraduate studies).

In 1952 Farah was ordained to the Presbyterian ministry, attended Presbyterian College in Montreal, and while there pastored a parish of three churches in northern New York.

When serving as an area director for the Navigators and having listened to a tape by Dennis Bennett, Farah received the baptism in the Holy Spirit.

In 1967 Farah became associate professor of historical studies at Oral Roberts University. He is now professor of theology at the Oral Roberts University graduate school and ministers as an elder at Tulsa Christian Fellowship.

Farah is also the author of *From the Pinnacle of the Temple* (1979), which addresses the problem of presumption in faith healing.   S. Strang

FARICY, ROBERT (1926–). American Jesuit theologian and leader in Catholic Charismatic Renewal (CCR). Ordained in 1962, Faricy has been professor of spirituality at the Gregorian University, Rome, since 1971. Involved in a charismatic prayer group at the Gregorian University from 1975, Faricy became a member of the Italian national service committee in 1976.

Besides the CCR, Faricy has specialized in the theology of prayer, Christian involvement in the world, and the future of religious life. Coeditor with Sr. Lucy Rooney of *Renewal in the Spirit,* a newsletter for the renewal of religious life (eighteen issues, 1979–85), Faricy has sought to encourage spiritual renewal among Catholic religious men and women through the renewal of their charisms of poverty, chastity, obedience, and the specific charisms of their founder or foundress.

Bibliography: R. Faricy, *The End of the Religious Life* (1983); idem, *Medjugorje Up Close* (1986); idem, *Seeking Jesus in Contemplation and Discernment* (1983); R. Faricy and S. Blackborow, *Healing the Religious Life* (1986); R. Faricy and L. Rooney, *The Contemplative Way of Prayer* (1986).   P. D. Hocken

FARROW, LUCY F. (twentieth century). Pastor, evangelist, and missionary. Noted to be a woman of prayer who laid hands on many who received their Pentecost during the early days of the Azusa Street revival. Lucy Farrow was born in slavery in Norfolk, Virginia. A niece of the famous abolitionist-journalist Frederick Douglass, Farrow showed outstanding leadership qualities. She entered the Pentecostal picture through contact with Charles F. Parham. In 1905 she was serving as a pastor of a small Holiness church in Houston when she was engaged by Parham to work as a governess for his family that summer. William J. Seymour filled the pulpit in her absence. When she returned to Houston later that year, she had experienced speaking in tongues. While in Houston, she served as the cook for Parham's Bible school and persuaded Parham to enroll Seymour as a student.

In February 1906 Seymour went to Los Angeles to serve as a pastor of a small Holiness church. Recognizing the capabilities of Lucy Farrow and a man, J. A. Warren, he sent money to cover their fare to Los Angeles. Lucy Farrow was described as an "anointed handmaid" who not only brought the full gospel to Los Angeles but whose ministry included the laying on of hands through which "many received the Pentecost and the gift of tongues."

In August 1906 Farrow made a trip to Norfolk, Virginia, via Houston and New Orleans. En route, she preached in Houston, sharing with the state encampment of Parham's Apostolic Faith Movement. There she laid hands on at least 25 people and many spoke in tongues. She also prayed for the sick along the way and shared her testimony. Arriving in Virginia, Farrow held a series of meetings in Portsmouth. The meetings lasted several weeks, and ultimately it was reported that 150 had received "the baptism of the Holy Ghost." About 200 were reported saved as a result of her Portsmouth campaign.

By December 1906 Farrow had determined that she had a call to go as a missionary to Monrovia, Liberia, a city governed by expatriated American slaves. She sent word to Azusa, asking for replacement personnel to continue the work in Portsmouth, then she proceeded to New York. There she was joined by the G. W. Batmans; Julia W. Hutchins; Mr. and Mrs. Samuel J. Mead; and the Shidelers, who were on their way from Azusa to Liberia; and Mr. F. M. Cook, who received his Pentecost when they laid hands on him. While in New York, this band of missionaries held two weeks of meetings. The Meads and Shidelers went to Bengilela, Liberia, while the others proceeded to Monrovia via Liverpool, England. They arrived in Liberia in late December.

Farrow settled in Johnsonville, Liberia, about twenty-five miles from Monrovia, where she preached and ministered until August 1907. During that time she reportedly brought many into the faith. Many were sanctified and healed, and twenty received their Pentecost.

Farrow's missionary ministry was a faith venture, financed largely by supporters from Azusa. Receiving direction from the Lord, as well as the necessary funds, Lucy Farrow returned to Azusa in the latter half of 1907 again by way of Virginia and the South. She held meetings in Littleton, North Carolina, in November for an Apostolic mission there.

Upon her return to Azusa, Lucy Farrow continued to minister from a small "faith cottage back of the mission." Those who came to her there were reported to have been healed, baptized in the Spirit, or to have received "a greater filling."

Bibliography: *AF* 1 (1, 1906): 1; *AF* 1 (4, 1906): 3; *AF* 1 (6, 1907): 8; *AF* 1 (12, 1908): 4; *AF* 2 (13 [*sic*], 1908): 2; "Latest Report From Our Missionaries to Africa," *AF* 1 (5, 1907): 3; B. F. Lawrence, *The Apostolic Faith Restored* (1916); D. J. Nelson, "For Such a Time as This: The Story of Bishop William J. Seymour and the Azusa Street Revival," Ph.D. diss., University of Birmingham, 1981; "Pentecost in Portsmouth," *AF* 1 (4, 1906): 1; "The Work in Virginia," *AF* 1 (2, 1906): 3.   C. M. Robeck, Jr.

FASTING   Fasting, the voluntary abstaining from physical nourishment for spiritual purposes, has been practiced by modern Pentecostals from the outset of the movement. Fasting is a long-standing practice in Christianity, and clearly people fasted for church revival and personal needs well before the outpouring of the Holy Spirit in Los Angeles. In some regions of the world fasting was undoubtedly a part of the spiritual condition that led to the Spirit's infilling.

I. The Background of Fasting. The Pentecostal regimen of fasting is only the latest in a long history of the practice. Perceived as a form of sacrifice to God, fasting has been a constant feature of humanity's search for, and communion with, God. For a fast to be beneficial it must be made in a spirit of reverence toward God, in which the one who fasts acknowledges his dependence on God and worships him as Creator and Lord. Fasting is basically a quest for spiritual mastery over the sensory appetites, an elevation of thoughts to God and his will. Because fasting is a normal inclination of those who are eager to express love for God and manifest dependence on him, the Pentecostal believer comes easily to accept it as a spiritual, beneficial practice.

A. The Old Testament. Fasting has an abundant record and validity in both the OT and the NT. The religious fast for specific purposes was frequently mentioned in the OT. In its strictest sense it meant going without both food and drink for a designated period of time, as mentioned by Esther to Mordecai: "Hold a fast on my behalf, and neither eat nor drink for three days, night or day. I and my maids will also fast as you do" (Esth. 4:16 RSV).

Annual fasts by the entire congregation were prominent in Hebrew religious practice. Fasting on the Day of Atonement was spoken of as a time for afflicting oneself (Lev. 16:29, 31; 23:27–32; Neh. 9:1). This indicates the earliest reason for fasting: the affliction of one's flesh so that one might be more susceptible to things of the spirit.

Zechariah 8:19 mentions four annual fasts that were observed in the fourth, fifth, seventh, and tenth months of the Jewish year. These were spoken of as commemorative fasts, to be observed with joy and gladness. Esther 9:31 refers to the origin of still another annual fast, known as Purim, which commemorated the Jews' survival in Persia.

Israel had special times of prayer, sometimes prompted by national need or calamity (Judg. 20:26; Joel 1:14). These occasions emphasize the spiritual impulse to humble oneself in times of personal distress.

Frequently OT fasting is mentioned in connection with repentance, both national and personal. "They drew water and poured it out before the LORD. On that day they fasted and there they confessed, 'We have sinned against the LORD'" (1 Sam. 7:6; see also Deut. 9:3–4; 1 Kings 21:27; Neh. 9:1–2). In this regard fasting might be predominantly an expression of self-punishment. While all fasting has the underlying purpose of subjugating the flesh, it is not in all instances punitive in nature.

There was fasting as a means of expressing grief: "They mourned and wept and fasted until evening for Saul and for his son Jonathan, and for the army of the LORD and the house of Israel, because they had fallen by the sword" (2 Sam. 1:12). Fasting for divine guidance was also prevalent in OT times. Moses said, "When I went up the mountain to receive the tables of stone, the tables of the covenant which the LORD made with you, I remained on the mountain forty days and forty nights; I neither ate bread nor drank water" (Deut. 9:9 RSV; see Exod. 8:21–23; 2 Sam. 12:16–23; 2 Chron. 20:3–4).

B. The New Testament. In the NT fasting is more sharply focused than in the OT. Of the annual fasts mentioned in the OT, only the Day of Atonement is mentioned in the NT (Acts 27:9). While fasting in the OT was only occasionally personal and specific, in the NT it is almost altogether so. The Pharisees, who regarded fasting as one of the three most important works of righteousness, were said to have had a set schedule of fasting (Luke 18:12). Anna was said to have fasted often (Luke 2:37).

Jesus had much to say about fasting and assumed that his hearers fasted frequently: "When you fast, do not look somber as the hypocrites do, for they disfigure their faces to show men they are fasting. . . . But when you fast, put oil on your head and wash your face, so that it will not be obvious to men that you are fasting . . . and your

Father, who sees what is done in secret, will reward you" (Matt. 6:16–18).

The only recorded occasion of Jesus' fasting was during his forty days in the wilderness (Matt. 4:1–4), and that occasion seems to have been less formal in nature than a matter of immediacy. He was apparently so intent upon his confrontation with Satan that he did not eat. Also, the fact that Satan tempted him to turn stones to bread suggests that there was no food available in the wilderness.

Jesus emphasized the personal nature of fasting on an occasion when the disciples of John the Baptist asked him, "How is it that we and the Pharisees fast, but your disciples do not fast?" (Matt. 9:14). Jesus replied that his disciples had no need to fast while he was with them but that they would fast when he was taken from them (v. 15). This reveals that formal fasting was not encouraged or expected by him but that urgent spiritual need would later bring it about.

There was much fasting by the disciples after Jesus was taken away. At times the apostles did without food because there was none available, as is strongly implied in the case of Peter (Acts 10:9–10) and Paul (2 Cor. 6:5; 11:27). Although some fasting came about because food was unavailable, it is also clear that voluntary fasting for spiritual reasons was regarded as a worthy and pious practice. This was particularly so with regard to the selection of ministers. Jesus' extended fast in the wilderness of Judea preceded his calling of the twelve apostles. The church at Antioch fasted before the selection of Barnabas and Paul to go out as missionaries (Acts 13:2–3). Paul and Barnabas then "appointed elders for them in each church and, with prayer and fasting, committed them to the Lord" (14:23).

II. The Modern Practice. With its strong reliance on Scripture patterns and spiritual resources, the Pentecostal movement has always emphasized the appropriateness of fasting.

A. Spiritual Aspects. There are important points to be observed in the readiness of Pentecostals to accept and practice physical deprivation for spiritual benefit. To begin with, fasting is so thoroughly scriptural that sincere Christians cannot neglect it. The example of Jesus and the early church was clear for those who daily endeavored to be like him. Furthermore, fasting was viewed as being linked with self-control ("temperance" in the KJV), which is a fruit of the Spirit (Gal. 5:23). Just as self-control is an essential part of the spiritual life, gluttony is a hindrance to it. Fasting therefore benefits spiritual well-being as a conditioning for Christian growth and an encouragement of faith and meekness. The body is the "temple of the Holy Spirit" (1 Cor. 6:19), and it must bring honor to God. Fasting rather than gluttony encourages the spiritual nature of the human temple.

Fasting is spoken of in the Scriptures as a source of spiritual power. It is contrary to natural reasoning to deplete oneself of physical energy at a time when it is needed most. But the diminished bodily strength is replaced by a spiritual energy necessary for spiritual needs.

When Jesus healed the epileptic youth after his disciples had failed to do so, they wondered at their failure. Jesus replied, "But this kind does not go out except by prayer and fasting" (Matt. 17:21). The joining of prayer with fasting is mentioned in numerous places and must be regarded as a necessary part of any fast (See 2 Sam. 12:16; Acts 13:3; 14:23; 1 Cor. 7:5).

B. Practical Aspects. The Pentecostal emphasis on fasting is a necessary accompaniment to the equally strong emphasis on the gifts of the Spirit, particularly the gifts of healing. Although every type of revival has been accompanied by periods of private and congregational fasting, the occurrences of healing and miracles have been especially attended by such devotion.

As in earlier Christian times, fasting among Pentecostal churches has been largely voluntary, with each person free to determine whether or not he shall fast—and to what degree. Scheduled fasting has at times been practiced, especially in times of congregational need; e.g., the selection of pastors and other personnel, financial needs, effectiveness of ministries, and other group concerns. The practice has never been mandated, for it is viewed as a private and voluntary matter between the believer and God.

There are errors and dangers to be avoided in the practice of fasting. In particular, fasting can become a source of self-righteousness, as it was with the Pharisee who prayed, "God, I thank you that I am not like other men—robbers, evildoers, adulterers—or even like this tax collector. I fast twice a week and give a tenth of all I get" (Luke 18:11–12).

Then there are people who fast for self-serving purposes, such as the achieving of particular political ends or social reforms. While these may be admirable in intent, they are not the kind of fasts referred to in Scripture. (Neither is the fast [or "hunger strike"] intended to force one's will upon another.) The true fast is a sacrifice made as an act of worship to God and is certainly not an effort to obligate God to the one fasting. Fasting should not be done in order to demonstrate the faster's spirituality or piety. It is not for the purpose of favorably impressing either God or man. That is why Jesus called it erroneous to make any show of fasting: "When you fast, put oil on your head and wash your face, so that it will not be obvious to men that you are fasting, but only to your Father, who is unseen; and your Father, who sees what is done in secret, will reward you" (Matt. 6:17–18).

See also SPIRITUALITY, PENTECOSTAL AND CHARISMATIC.

Bibliography: H. A. G. Belben, "Fasting," *NBD* (1962); C. W. Conn, *A Balanced Church* (1975), 93–94; W. W. Kelly, "Fast, Fasting," *Baker's Dictionary of Theology* (1960).   C. W. Conn

FAUSS, OLIVER F. (1898–1980). General superintendent of the United Pentecostal Church (UPC) and author. During his early childhood in Oklahoma, Fauss attended a Methodist church. After moving to Texas, he received the baptism in the Holy Spirit in 1911 and began evangelizing in 1915. In the same year he accepted water baptism in the name of Jesus Christ. He was ordained in

1917. Fauss served as the chairman of the Apostolic Church of Jesus Christ from 1928 to 1930 and as the chairman of the South Central Council of the Pentecostal Assemblies of Jesus Christ from 1930 to 1935. He became the assistant general superintendent of the UPC in 1947 and served in this position until 1972. After the death of General Superintendent A. T. Morgan in 1967, Fauss served the remainder of the term. Fauss is the author of *Baptism in God's Plan* (1955), *Buy the Truth and Sell It Not* (1965), and *What God Hath Wrought* (1945). These three books were combined in one volume in 1985 under the last title.

Bibliography: A. L. Clanton, *United We Stand* (1970).   J. L. Hall

FEAST OF PENTECOST   See PENTECOST, FEAST OF.

Gordon Fee is a NT scholar, author, and educator. He is also an ordained Assemblies of God minister.

FEE, GORDON DONALD   (1934–). NT scholar, author, and educator. The son of Assemblies of God (AG) minister, Donald Fee, Gordon Fee is himself an ordained AG minister (since 1959), having pastored the Des Moines, Washington, Assembly of God from 1958 to 1962 and having served as interim pastor for the Magnolia Congregational Church in Magnolia, Massachusetts, during the first quarter of 1975. Fee was conferred the Ph.D. degree in NT studies by the University of Southern California in 1966.

During a teaching career that spans more than two decades, Fee has taught at Southern California College (AG, 1966–69) in Costa Mesa; Wheaton College (1969–74), Wheaton, Illinois; and Gordon-Conwell Theological Seminary (1974–86), South Hamilton, Massachusetts. Since 1986 he has been professor of NT at

Regent College in Vancouver, British Columbia. His arrangement with Regent is such that six months out of each year Fee and his wife of thirty-one years, Maudine (Lofdahl), teach overseas in Bible colleges and seminaries. They have taught at the Far East Advanced School of Theology (AG) in the Philippines and at the East Africa School of Theology, Nairobi, and they expect to be in Europe during 1988. The Fee's joint overseas tours of duty reflect their deep commitment to missions.

As a teacher, Fee is known for his contagious enthusiasm and passionate love for Scripture. He also has a reputation for insisting on conscientious and careful scholarship. A demanding teacher, he attracts students from a variety of traditions. He has convinced many that excellence in scholarship can be coupled with a deep devotion to God.

Fee is internationally known and respected for his work as a NT text critic, and in addition to countless articles in his field of specialization, he has written several books on NT studies, including *New Testament Exegesis: A Handbook for Students and Pastors* (1983), *1 and 2 Timothy and Titus: A Good News Commentary* (1984), and *How to Read the Bible for All Its Worth* (with D. Stuart, 1982). His *Commentary on the First Epistle to the Corinthians* (1987) appears in the prestigious New International Commentary series.

Within Pentecostal circles Fee is both admired and denounced. To some, Fee epitomizes the heretofore oxymoron, "a Pentecostal scholar." His careful regard for "the text" and his skills as a NT exegete render him a voice to be reckoned with; moreover, his zeal behind the pulpit and his passion for the Pentecostal message of the Spirit's presence in this age authenticate him as one deeply committed to the Pentecostal experience. Yet, to others, Fee's hermeneutic challenges the traditional Pentecostal hermeneutic (which Fee labels "pragmatic," 1976, 121–22) and is regarded as an implicit threat to the Pentecostal doctrine that tongues are the "initial physical evidence" of Spirit baptism (e.g., see Fee's *How to Read the Bible for All Its Worth*, ch. 6, "Acts and Historical Precedent"; and Fee, 1985, 87–99). Despite often finding himself at the center of controversy, Fee's reputation as both a thoroughgoing Pentecostal and a dedicated biblical scholar remains intact.

Bibliography: G. D. Fee, "Baptism in the Holy Spirit: The Issue of Separability and Subsequence," *Pneuma* 7 (2, 1985): 87–99; idem, "Hermeneutics and Historical Precedent," in *Perspectives on the New Pentecostalism*, ed. R. P. Spittler (1976); personal curriculum vitae supplied to this writer (1987).   P. H. Alexander

FELLOWSHIP OF CHARISMATIC NAZARENES   See WESLEYAN CHARISMATICS.

FELLOWSHIP OF CHRISTIAN ASSEMBLIES   This organization originated during the spring of 1922 when approximately twenty-five Scandinavian ministers agreed to meet in St. Paul, Minnesota, to discuss the possibility of creating an informal fellowship of autonomous local churches. About half of these ministers were pastors of independent local assemblies within the upper Midwest region. The other half were pastors within the same region that had previously incorporated as a body of local independent churches in 1918 under the name of Scandinavian Independent Assemblies of God. During their first year of existence, they published their own periodical called the *Sanningens Vittne*, which later became the primary periodical for all the Scandinavian assemblies in the U.S. The gathered ministers decided to merge together as a fellowship of churches under the name the Independent Assemblies of God. The basis of their unity was founded on their belief that each local church was free to manage and direct its own affairs without being responsible to any denominational organization. The "New Order of the Latter Rain" controversy divided the fellowship in 1951. Those ministers supporting the new revival separated from the fellowship and organized under the name Independent Assemblies of God, International. The other group continued under the original name until 1973, when they changed their title to the Fellowship of Christian Assemblies. Presently this fellowship has more than three hundred ministers in churches in the Midwest, East Coast, West Coast, and in the four Canadian provinces of Alberta, British Columbia, Ontario, and Saskatchewan.

See also INDEPENDENT ASSEMBLIES OF GOD, INTERNATIONAL.

Bibliography: *The Fellowship of Christian Assemblies: An Experience in Inter-church Fellowship* (1978); A. C. Piepkorn, *Profiles in Belief,* vol. 3 (1979), 154; J.R. Coletti, "Lewi Petrus: His Influence Upon Scandinavian-American Pentecostalism," *Pneuma* 5 (2, 1983): 22–24.   J. Colletti

FELLOWSHIP OF COVENANT MINISTERS AND CONFERENCES   See CHARISMATIC MOVEMENT.

FIELDS OF THE WOOD   A 216-acre biblical theme park located in Cherokee County, North Carolina, maintained and operated by the Church of God of Prophecy (CGP). The original acreage was purchased in 1939–40 as a result of A. J. Tomlinson's desire to preserve the site that housed the events of June 13, 1903—the "rediscovery" of the NT church. The first temporary marker was erected on November 15, 1940, on the site of the W. F. Bryant home. Three days later the purchased acreage was officially named Fields of the Wood by A. J. Tomlinson. This grew out of his understanding of Psalm 132:6, which was introduced to him by Grady R. Kent. Starting in 1941, a series of services memorializing like events was initiated. The annual meetings of this nature, which have survived to this day, are the following: June 13, 1903, the service prior to each general assembly, reenactment of the first Thanksgiving Day, and an Easter pageant. Also several tent revivals and special youth activities have been held there. Including the revival participants and youth groups, approximately 200,000 people come to Fields of the Wood each year.

The designs of Fields of the Wood were first influenced by the Church of Prophecy Marker Association (CPMA), General Secretary Grady R. Kent, and Auxiliary Designer L. S. Rhodes. Commensurate with Kent's preoccupation with apocalyptic literature, the Fields of the Wood has four gates (Rev. 21). Prominent also is an airplane marked "Wings of Prophecy" from the White Angel Fleet, which at its peak included a hundred airplanes. Growing out of A. J. Tomlinson's 1939 interpretation of Isaiah 60:1, 8, (which started with Grady Kent), a connection was made with the Wright brother's first successful flight, which occurred in the same state and in the same year that A. J. Tomlinson joined the fledgling Church of God. One large structure, now changed to include a summary history, included a list of churches honored as related to a Holiness doctrine of perfection. One mountain slope has an enlarged version of the Ten Commandments (letters 4 feet by 6 feet) topped by a huge Bible (34 feet by 24 feet) opened to Matthew 22:37–40. This design, created by Rhodes, illustrates how the Law and Prophets find fulfillment in the love of God in Christ. Smaller markers around record the Beatitudes, the Twenty-third Psalm, and the Lord's Prayer. Individual marble markers describe each of the twenty-nine teachings and the five departments known as auxiliaries. Several markers testify to June 13, 1903, and its implications. Some came to see this multimillion dollar project as a fulfillment of texts like Habakkuk 2:2–3 (while the September 7, 1941, erection of the church flag in a tree was said to have been predicted in Isa. 13:2). Also included are a pavilion from which indoor services are moderated and a baptismal pool.

Among the early markers is the replica of the tomb of Joseph of Arimathea, the Bethlehem star, and a large cross on one of the mountain tops that sometimes displays flags from all nations that have a CGP congregation. This theme, which moves away from the earlier cultish influence of Kent, was enhanced in 1986 with the introduction by Wade Phillips, then general CPMA secretary, of a reduplication of the place called Golgotha.

See also CHURCH OF GOD OF PROPHECY.

Bibliography: C. T. Davidson, *America's Unusual Spot* (1954); P. Gillum, *These Stones Speak* (1985); interviews with Wade Phillips, 1986–87.
H. D. Hunter

FILLED WITH THE SPIRIT   See BAPTISM IN THE HOLY SPIRIT.

FINISHED WORK CONTROVERSY   A major controversy of the early Pentecostal movement over whether sanctification is a second definite work of grace. Except for the Keswick movement in England and the Christian and Missionary Alliance (CMA), in the U.S., the Holiness movement of the nineteenth century had held the view of sanctification taught by John Wesley in his *Plain Account of Christian Perfection,* according to which there is an instantaneous experience of "entire sanctification" or "Christian perfection" distinct from the conversion experience. As former members of the Holiness movement, Charles F. Parham, William J. Seymour, and the other early pioneers of Pentecostalism retained the Wesleyan view, modifying it by

The Fields of the Wood, shown here in an artist's conception, is a Bible theme park in Cherokee County, North Carolina, operated by the Church of God of Prophecy.

regarding the baptism of the Holy Spirit with tongues not as a third work of grace but as a gift of power upon the sanctified life. Beginning in the late nineteenth century, most people within the Holiness movement had come to consider "entire sanctification" to be synonymous with "the baptism in the Holy Spirit," although they did not believe that the gift of tongues was the initial evidence of this experience. The early

Pentecostal leaders, however, believed that entire sanctification and Holy Spirit baptism were two separate experiences and that the latter experience was always accompanied by the gift of tongues. There were, therefore, three stages of Christian experience: conversion (or justification), entire sanctification, and the baptism of the Holy Spirit.

The finished-work controversy began in 1910 when William H. Durham, the renowned pastor of North Avenue Mission in Chicago, who had received the Pentecostal experience at Azusa Street in 1907, began criticizing the Wesleyan idea of entire sanctification. He believed that the finished work of Christ on Calvary provided not only for the forgiveness of sins but for the sanctification of the believer. Thus for sanctification the believer need only appropriate the benefits of the finished work of Calvary that were already received at the time of regeneration. Sanctification for Durham was a gradual process of appropriating the benefits of the finished work of Christ, not a second instantaneous work of grace subsequent to conversion. Durham therefore did not restrict the time of sanctification either to the moment of regeneration or to any other particular subsequent moment in the Christian experience. He objected to the doctrine of entire sanctification because he felt it circumvented the need for an ongoing sanctification process in the life of the Christian.

When Durham first publicly aired his views on this matter at a 1910 Pentecostal convention held in Chicago, it caused considerable controversy. However, during the same year, Howard Goss invited Durham to a camp meeting in Malvern, Arkansas, where Durham was able to convince Goss and many of Parham's former followers in the southern Midwest of his views.

The following February, Durham went to Los Angeles with his message. He was refused a hearing at Elmer K. Fisher's Upper Room Mission, which had become a major center for the Pentecostal movement. However, he went to Azusa Street Mission, and in William J. Seymour's absence, began preaching. Here "the fire began to fall at old Azusa as at the beginning" (Bartleman, 1925, 145), and these meetings soon became known as the "Second Azusa outpouring" (Valdez, 1980, 26). When Seymour returned, however, he locked Durham out of the Azusa Street Mission.

Undaunted, Durham began holding meetings at a large building on the corner of Seventh and Los Angeles Streets in Los Angeles, where over a thousand people attended the Sunday meetings, several hundred attending on week nights. Some of the people who assisted Durham in ministry at this time were Harry Van Loon and Frank J. Ewart. Ewart wrote that he found it easy to accept Durham's message, since he had believed it while still in the Baptist church (1975, 102).

After several months Durham returned to Chicago, where G. Smidt, one of the founders of the Pentecostal movement in Finland, visited Durham's church and became convinced of the finished work view. Smidt returned to Finland, where considerable controversy erupted, especially since T. B. Barratt, the Norwegian pioneer of Pentecostalism who had considerable influence in Finland, steadfastly resisted Durham's opinions on this issue.

Durham wrote some strongly polemical articles on the finished work of Christ in the periodical that he published, *The Pentecostal Testimony*, and his adversaries were just as adamant in their opposition to his views. Parham believed Durham's view to be "diabolical," as did Florence Crawford, who had become a leader of the Apostolic Faith movement in the Pacific Northwest. Other Pentecostal leaders who did not accept Durham's viewpoint included G. B. Cashwell, C. H. Mason, and A. J. Tomlinson. These people held to the three-stage understanding of Christian experience, since they had had an experience of entire sanctification prior to being baptized in the Holy Spirit and speaking in tongues and were wary of anyone who could receive the baptism of the Spirit "on an unsanctified life" (Hollenweger, 1972, 25). These views were usually held by those who came into the Pentecostal movement as Methodists, Wesleyans, Free-Will Baptists, or as members of most Holiness groups. The various Apostolic Faith groups, the Church of God (CG, Cleveland, Tenn.), the Pentecostal Holiness Church (PHC), and other Pentecostal denominations that had formerly been part of the Holiness movement therefore did not accept the teachings of Durham on sanctification.

On the other hand, Pentecostals who had formerly been part of the CMA generally accepted the finished work view, because the CMA did not hold to a belief in a second work of grace after conversion. This was also true of those who had been Baptists or Presbyterians.

Although Durham died in 1912, the finished work controversy continued to rage. When A. A. Boddy of Sunderland, England, visited California later that year, he found that "the Pentecostal people in Los Angeles were just about tired of shaking fists at one another" over this question. Here and at other important Pentecostal centers he introduced a nonpartisan resolution that those involved "refrain from condemning one another on the matter" (Boddy, 1912, 6).

Nevertheless, the issues that Durham had raised continued to be a source of controversy within the early Pentecostal movement. At the 1914 convention held in Hot Springs, Arkansas, where the AG denomination was established, the opening address, delivered by M. M. Pinson, was entitled "The Finished Work of Calvary." Although the "Basis of Union" adopted at these meetings had no statement of faith, this keynote address set the stage for an organization that held to the finished work doctrine. From this time onward this understanding of sanctification spread rapidly, becoming the majority view among Pentecostals by the end of the next decade. One of the reasons for the success of Durham's viewpoint was that many people seemed to be receiving the baptism of the Holy Spirit without first having experienced entire sanctification, despite the belief by second work of grace advocates that entire sanctification was a necessary prerequisite.

The Pentecostal movement remained split into two opposing camps for about thirty-five years over the issue of sanctification, and both sides often adopted extreme positions on the question. Those who believed in sanctification as a second work of grace began to refer to the experience of entire sanctification as an eradication of one's sinful nature, not merely a complete surrender to God. Finished work advocates, on the other hand, often minimized the need for experiential sanctification in the life of the believer, resting in the knowledge that provision for this had already been made by the death of Christ. With the closer cooperation that arose among the Pentecostal groups after the Second World War, which resulted in the formation of such bodies as the Pentecostal Fellowship of North America, extremes of this kind became modified.

Bibliography: R. M. Anderson, *Vision of the Disinherited* (1979); G. Atter, *The Third Force,* 3d ed., (1970); F. Bartleman, *How Pentecost Came to Los Angeles,* 2d ed. (1925); E. Blumhofer, *The Assemblies of God: A Popular History* (1985); A. A. Boddy, "They Two Went On," *LRE* (October 1912), 1–7; C. Brumback, *Suddenly . . . From Heaven* (1961); F. Ewart, *The Phenomenon of Pentecost,* rev. ed. (1975); W. J. Hollenweger, *The Pentecostals* (1972); R. A. Larden, *Our Apostolic Heritage* (1971); W. W. Menzies, *Anointed to Serve* (1971); idem, "The Non-Wesleyan Origins of the Pentecostal Movement," in V. Synan, ed., *Aspects of Pentecostal-Charismatic Origins* (1975), 81–98; A. C. Valdez, Sr., *Fire on Azusa Street* (1980).   R. M. Riss

FINNISH CHARISMATICS See Charismatic Movement.

FINNISH PENTECOSTALS See European Pentecostalism.

FIRE-BAPTIZED HOLINESS CHURCH (FBHC). Founded by Benjamin Hardin Irwin of Lincoln, Nebraska, in 1895. Beginning as a radical offshoot of the Iowa Holiness Association, the FBHC embraced Irwin's teaching of a "third blessing" beyond justification and sanctification. This "baptism of fire" was accompanied by varied shouting manifestations familiar to the frontier American camp meeting. Those receiving "the fire" also at times would see balls of fire or feel fire burning in their bodies.

The classical Holiness movement soon disowned Irwin and what they called "third blessingism," thus forcing the Fire-Baptized movement to follow an independent path. Irwin organized a national body in Anderson, South Carolina, in August 1898 that was called the Fire-Baptized Holiness Association (FBHA). The new church body represented regional associations in ten American states and two Canadian provinces. The headquarters of the movement was located in Olmitz, Iowa, where Irwin published a paper known as *Live Coals of Fire.*

Irwin spread the Fire-Baptized movement through tent campaigns in the South and Midwest. Thousands attended his crusades, which also featured divine healing for the sick. In time, Irwin added more "baptisms" in addition to the third blessing, which he named the baptisms of dynamite, lyddite, and oxidite. He also formulated a strict lifestyle for his followers that went beyond the usual Holiness dress codes of the day. Added to plain dress for women was a code which forbade Fire-Baptized men to wear neckties.

Added to these strictures were dietary prohibitions from the OT forbidding the eating of pork and other "unclean" meats. Fire-Baptized members thus gained the pejorative name, "The no-necktie, no hogmeat people."

Despite these teachings, the movement continued to grow under the charismatic leadership of its founder, who had himself appointed "general overseer" for life. This growth came to an abrupt end in 1900 when Irwin confessed to "open and gross sin" and left the movement in confusion. In many areas the church disappeared.

Remnants of the movement were held together, however, by Irwin's young assistant, Joseph H. King, who moved the headquarters of the church to Royston, Georgia, in 1902. Under King's leadership the church abandoned the baptisms of dynamite, lyddite, and oxidite but continued to hold to a separate baptism in the Holy Ghost "and fire."

The church was radically changed in 1907 when King and most of the ministers of the church received the baptism in the Holy Spirit evidenced by speaking in tongues, as taught by G. B. Cashwell, who had been to Azusa Street in 1906. In April 1908 the church amended its doctrine to include the Pentecostal view on tongues, thus becoming the first official Pentecostal denomination in the U.S.

Because of similarities in doctrine and practice, the FBHC merged with the Pentecostal Holiness Church (PHC) in Falcon, North Carolina, in 1911. Although the FBHC was larger, the new church adopted the name of the smaller PHC.

Three branches of the FBHC remain to this day. The black branch of the church requested autonomy in 1908 and was granted a friendly separation by the parent body. This group was led by Bishop William E. Fuller, who built his denomination into a national body, which today has more than three hundred congregations. It is now known as the Pentecostal Fire-Baptized Holiness Church of God of the Americas.

A white splinter group also withdrew from the PHC in 1916 in an effort to reconstitute the original movement. A third group in Kansas never entered the Pentecostal movement and is now known as the Fire-Baptized Holiness Church (Wesleyan).

Bibliography: J. Campbell, *The Pentecostal Holiness Church, 1898–1948* (1951); J. and B. King, *Yet Speaketh, The Memoirs of the Late Bishop Joseph H. King* (1949).   H. V. Synan

FIRE-BAPTIZED HOLINESS CHURCH OF GOD OF THE AMERICAS The Fire-Baptized Holiness Church of the Americas is a predominantly black Pentecostal denomination with roots in the Fire-Baptized Holiness Church (FBHC) founded by B. H. Irwin in Anderson, South Carolina, in 1898. The founder of the church, William E. Fuller (1875–1958), from Mountville, South Carolina, was a convert from Methodism. From 1898 to 1908, the FBHC was interracial, with Fuller serving on the executive council. In this capacity, he founded many black FBHC congregations in the South.

In 1908 the blacks under Fuller's leadership requested the right to separate and form their own church. An amicable agreement of separation from the parent body resulted in the organization of the "Colored FBHC" in Anderson, South Carolina, that same year. The doctrines of the new church were the same as the parent body, i.e., justification by faith, sanctification as a second work of grace, baptism in the Holy Spirit evidenced by speaking in tongues, divine healing, and the imminent second coming of Christ.

The church conferred the title of bishop on Fuller in 1922 and renamed the church the "Fire-Baptized Holiness Church of God" (FBHCOG). The words "of the Americas" were added in 1926. In 1912 the church founded the Fuller Normal and Industrial School in Atlanta. It was moved to Greenville, South Carolina, in 1923.

By 1978 the church claimed 15,450 members in 775 churches and missions. Since 1958 the church has been headquartered in Atlanta under the leadership of Bishop W. E. Fuller, Jr.

Bibliography: C. Jones, *Black Holiness* (1987); H. V. Synan, *The Old-Time Power* (1973). H. V. Synan

FIRST CHURCH OF JESUS CHRIST
(FCJC). A Oneness group established by H. E. Honea in 1965, with headquarters in Tullahoma, Tennessee. Bishop Honea reported in 1986 that the group had thirty-five churches, 225 ministers, and about 15,000 members. The churches are located in ten southern and midwestern states. Honea had formerly ministered in the Church of Jesus Christ. The FCJC will license ministers at age sixteen and ordain at eighteen; women can receive a license to preach, but the church does not ordain women. The FCJC's articles of faith include the generally accepted Pentecostal doctrines. However, the FCJC believes that the baptism in the Holy Spirit, with speaking in tongues, is necessary to become a part of the kingdom of God; and it considers footwashing to be as "much a divine command as any other New Testament ordinance." The FCJC has national churches in Haiti, Jamaica, Africa, and the Philippines. The official periodical is *Banner of Love*.

Bibliography: "Articles of Faith and By-Laws for FCJC" (1985). W. E. Warner

FISHER, ELMER KIRK (1866–1919). Early
Pentecostal pastor. Born in Wintersville, Ohio, to Methodist parents William R. Fisher and Lydia Jane (Kirk) Fisher. Fisher graduated from Moody Bible Institute and in 1894 married Clara Daisy Sanford, the daughter of Heman Howes Sanford, a professor of classical languages at Syracuse University. Early in his ministry Fisher evangelized for the Christian (Congregational) church and then for the Northern Baptists. He pastored a Baptist church in Camarillo, California (1903–05); from there he went to the First Baptist Church of Glendale, California (1905–06). In 1906 he received the Pentecostal baptism in the Spirit at the New Testament Church in Los Angeles, pastored by Joseph Smale. Afterward he went to Azusa Street and worked with William J. Seymour. He was left in charge there for four months while Seymour evangelized in the South. He then started the Upper Room Mission at 327½ South Spring Street with three hundred in attendance. From there he went to Mercantile Place, then Kohler Street, then Los Angeles Street. After turning the church over to his son-in-law, Harry S. Horton, he pastored a large group of Armenians in Boyle Heights for a time. Then he evangelized in Seattle, in Canada, and

opened a mission in Denver. Later he returned to Los Angeles, where he died in the influenza epidemic on January 19, 1919, and was buried from the Church of the Open Door. Frank Bartleman criticized Fisher because he believed in order and did not allow everyone to speak who thought they were moved by the Spirit. Fisher's grandsons include Dr. Stanley M. Horton and Rev. Wesley P. Steelberg of the Assemblies of God, and Dr. Robert E. Fisher of the Church of God (Cleveland, Tenn.).

Bibliography: Interview with Harold Fisher, November 13, 1986; Upper Room Mission, *The Upper Room* (1909–11). S. M. Horton

The son of missionary parents, George M. Flattery founded the International Correspondence Institute (ICI) under the auspices of the Assemblies of God Division of Foreign Missions.

FLATTERY, GEORGE MANFORD
(1936–). Missionary, educator, and president of the International Correspondence Institute (ICI). Born in Three Sands, Oklahoma, to George W. and Stella Flattery, Assemblies of God missionaries to Burkina Faso, West Africa. He received a B.A. at Central Bible College (1956); M.R.E., Southwestern Baptist Theological Seminary (1958); B.A., Southern Methodist University (1959); and Ed.D., Southwestern Baptist Theological Seminary (1966). In 1955 he married Esther Scheuerman; two sons were born to their union: George Warren (1956) and Mark Douglas (1960).

Flattery began his ministry as minister of education at Oak Cliff Assembly of God, Dallas, Texas (1960–62), and later founded Calvary

Chapel, Richardson, Texas (1962-66). On December 26, 1967, he received appointment with the Assemblies of God Division of Foreign Missions as president of the International Correspondence Institute (ICI), a bold new venture in theological education by extension. Flattery, having served as an educational consultant to the Division, was a major driving force in the establishment of the new program. With headquarters in Brussels, Belgium, ICI's goals are to evangelize, instruct, and train people by means of extension education. It offers a college degree program for ministerial training, as well as programs in Christian service, Christian ministry, and evangelism. In addition to other responsibilities, George and Esther Flattery host "World Alive," a television program for the American audience. Through his leadership, ICI has become one of the foremost programs in theological education by extension. Central Bible College named him Alumnus of the Year in 1977.

Bibliography: Assemblies of God Office of Information press release, December 26, 1967; Central Bible College Alumni Association, "Citation for George Flattery, 1977 Alumnus of the Year."   G. B. McGee

FLOWER, JOSEPH JAMES ROSWELL
(1888–1970) **AND ALICE REYNOLDS** (1890–). Pioneer leaders in the Assemblies of God (AG). J. Roswell Flower (he later dropped the name "James") was born in Belleville, Canada, to George Lorenzo and Bethia Rice Flower, both members of the Methodist Church. While still a young man, Flower's parents and grandparents came into contact with followers of John Alexander Dowie. In 1902 the family moved to Dowie's community of Zion City, Illinois. Disillusionment, however, prompted the family to move to Indianapolis, where they soon identified with the Christian and Missionary Alliance (CMA). The younger Flower accepted a position with the Indiana Seed Company and began to "read law" with a local attorney in preparation for a career in law.

Alice Reynolds was born to Charles Ernest and Mary Alice Reynolds in Indianapolis. Her father had been reared as a Quaker and her mother as a Methodist. After the latter received a physical healing, the spiritual tone of the family was deepened. Eventually the family became part of the local branch of the CMA, the "Gospel Tabernacle," in Indianapolis, pastored by George N. Eldridge.

When the Pentecostal message came to Indianapolis in January 1907 through the ministry of Glenn A. Cook, it strongly impacted the congregation of the Gospel Tabernacle. As the revival continued, Flower surrendered his life to Christ (April 14) and shortly after became active in ministry. When Thomas Hezmalhalch arrived, having attended the Azusa Street revival in Los Angeles, Alice Reynolds received the baptism in the Holy Spirit on Easter Sunday (March 31). In June, Flower attended the Pentecostal Camp Meeting in Alliance, Ohio, sponsored by Levi R. Lupton, C. A. McKinney, and Ivey G. Campbell. This gave him broad exposure to other early Pentecostal leaders.

On his way to assist a church in Kansas City in 1908, Flower stopped at the faith home operated by "Mother" Mary Moise and "Mother" Leonore Barnes. While there he sought for the baptism in the Holy Spirit, reporting: "I spent a whole month there and found this period of seeking to be hard work at first. It appeared to be a battle of faith. So I went at it in that spirit." After realizing that he had to exercise faith to receive the Pentecostal baptism, and following a lengthy time of prayer one day, he experienced the power of the Holy Spirit and said, "It seemed as though a great light shone around me and I was filled with holy joy and laughter" (Skoog, 1957, 2). After several months "the delayed evidence" of glossolalia came to him (ibid.).

While in Kansas City, Flower assisted (along with Fred Vogler, a later leader in the AG) A. S. Copley until 1910. During this time he and Copley issued a monthly magazine that Flower had begun publishing in Indianapolis with C. T. Quinn entitled *The Pentecost* (1908–10; later changed to *Grace and Glory*). Flower served initially as foreign editor and later as associate editor. His contributions clearly demonstrate his familiarity with many personalities and facets of the emerging Pentecostal movement.

J. Roswell Flower and Alice Reynolds were married in 1911. During the following year they traveled and preached in northern Indiana. Later they joined D. W. Myland, a long-time friend and former leader in the CMA, and his wife in conducting services in Ohio. With the leadership of the Mylands, the Flowers assisted in the establishment of the Gibeah Bible School in Plainfield, Indiana. While there, several important events in 1913 occurred: (1) J. Roswell began his first pastorate in neighboring Indianapolis; (2) he received ordination from the World's Faith Missionary Association; (3) the couple began publishing the *Christian Evangel* (later the *Weekly Evangel* and since 1919 the *Pentecostal Evangel*); and (4) Myland and Flower organized the Association of Christian Assemblies for interested Pentecostal churches in Indiana and the surrounding states; this was a precursor to the General Council of the Assemblies of God, founded a year later.

With the organization of the AG at Hot Springs, Arkansas, April 2–12, 1914, the group selected E. N. Bell as general chairman and Flower as secretary-treasurer. Following the council, the Flowers moved to Findlay, Ohio, to continue publishing the *Evangel*, now listed as an official periodical of the AG. With the development of the "New Issue" (Oneness Pentecostalism) in the AG, Flower strongly argued for the orthodox view of the Trinity and played a particularly vital role in helping the organization to retain that doctrinal posture.

When the AG relocated its executive offices and the printing plant to St. Louis in 1915, the Flowers moved there as well. Eventually the family moved to Stanton, Missouri, and Flower began an itinerant ministry, conducting "Bible conventions" in churches. Nevertheless, he maintained close contact with the AG leadership and assisted in the search for affordable property to expand the work of Gospel Publishing House.

J. Roswell and Alice Reynolds Flower served as leaders in the Assemblies of God from its beginning. They founded the *Pentecostal Evangel* (then *Christian Evangel*) in 1913.

Flower supported Bell's recommendation of purchasing property in Springfield, Missouri, which has been the site of the organization's headquarters since 1918.

With the growth of the AG missions enterprise, Flower was selected to serve as the first missionary secretary-treasurer in 1919, although he had never served as a missionary. In that year, the family moved to Springfield, where he assumed his new responsibilities. Flower worked with distinction, and during his tenure in 1921 the AG adopted a significant statement defining the goals of its foreign missions effort. The office, however, was divided in 1923, and Flower received the second position of missionary treasurer. He had struggled with the financial turmoil of the missionary department during these years, and his outspoken recommendations for changes may have been responsible for the general council choosing an older man (also with no missionary experience) to become missionary secretary in 1923. He continued as treasurer until 1925 when he was voted out of office due to his (and John W. Welch's) recommendation at the council meeting that the AG adopt a constitution (ironically, it adopted one at the next gathering in 1927).

With this turn of events, the Flowers accepted a pastorate in Scranton, Pennsylvania, in 1926. While pastoring, Flower was elected as the Eastern District secretary and served in this additional capacity until 1929 when he became superintendent of the Eastern District (New York, New Jersey, Pennsylvania, and Delaware). As a result, the Flowers moved to Lititz, a suburb of Lancaster, Pennsylvania. As superintendent he selected Green Lane, Pennsylvania, to be the site of the annual district-sponsored camp meetings; the property that was purchased became known as

"Maranatha Park." A summer Bible school at the camp site started in 1932 and became a permanent institution in 1938. It has been known through the years as Eastern Bible Institute, Northeast Bible Institute, and currently as Valley Forge Christian College located in Phoenixville, Pennsylvania.

In 1931 Flower was elected to serve as the nonresident assistant general superintendent and held that position until 1935 when he was selected to serve as general secretary-treasurer (he continued as assistant superintendent until 1937); he subsequently moved with his family to Springfield, Missouri. When the AG established the position of general treasurer in 1947 Flower continued as general secretary until retirement in 1959. During these years he played key roles in the development of the denomination as well as in its entry into the National Association of Evangelicals (NAE) and participation in the Pentecostal Fellowship of North America and the Pentecostal World Conference. While serving on the NAE's executive board in its early years, Flower became acquainted with Bob Jones, Sr., well-known fundamentalist evangelist and educator. The latter, impressed by Flower's administrative work in the AG, arranged for Bob Jones College (later, University) to confer on him an honorary doctor of laws degree in 1946, a surprising event considering the normally hostile attitude of Fundamentalists toward Pentecostals. Flower was also a supporter of AG higher education and strongly urged the adding of a fourth year of specialized missions studies at Central Bible Institute (CBI) in 1943. An active community leader, he served on the Springfield city council from 1953 to 1961.

For many years the name J. Roswell Flower was synonymous with AG. The significance of his multiple contributions to the denomination cannot be underestimated. In addition, his typewritten lecture notes at Central Bible Institute in 1949 entitled "History of the Assemblies of God," have proven to be a valuable source of information on the development of the organization.

Alice Reynolds Flower has also made important contributions to the AG, particularly through her speaking, writing, and teaching. Her work has been widely published, and she has contributed to the *Pentecostal Evangel*. Furthermore, she has reared six children, five of whom were ordained in the AG and have had important ministries: Joseph R. Flower (former superintendent of the New York District and elected in 1975 as general secretary), Adele Flower Dalton (missionary and writer), George E. Flower (d. 1966; sometime superintendent of the Southern New England District), Suzanne F. Earle (homemaker and pastor's wife), Roswell S. Flower (died in 1941 while a student at Central Bible Institute preparing for missionary service), and David W. Flower (former superintendent of the Southern New England District and pastor).

Alice Flower's devotional writings have made a major contribution to the literature of Pentecostal spirituality. They include *Love's Overflowing* (1928); *From Under the Threshold* (1936); *A Barley Loaf* (1938); *Straws Tell* (1941); *The Set of*

Your Sails & Other Twilight Chats (1942); *Open Windows* (1948); *Threads of Gold* (1949); *Building Her House Well* (1949); *The Home, A Divine Sanctuary* (1955); *Grace for Grace* (1961); *The Child at Church* (1962); *Springs of Refreshing* (1975, I. M. Isensee, comp.); *Along a Gently Flowing Stream* (1987); *The Altogether Lovely One* (n.d.); *Blossoms From the King's Garden* (n.d.); *The Business of Coat-Making* (n.d.); *The Out-poured Life* (n.d.); and *What Mean Ye By These Stones?* (n.d.).

Bibliography: M. T. Boucher, "J. Roswell Flower" (unpublished, 1983); S. F. Earle, "Her Children Shall Call Her Blessed," *Christ's Ambassadors Herald* (May 1958): 4–7; A. Flower (Dalton), "This Is My Dad," *TEAM* (July–September 1957): 3–8; A. R. Flower, *Grace for Grace* (1961); J. R. Flower, "Publishing the Pentecostal Message," *AG Heritage* 2 (Fall 1982), 1, 8; J. R. Flower, interview by W. W. Menzies, June 26, 1967, AG Archives; "J. R. Flower With Christ," *PE* (August 16, 1970), 4; J. Henderson, "J. Roswell Flower: An Essay on Practical Spirituality" (unpublished); J. Kleeman (Newburn), "Mother Flower," *Springfield! Magazine* (May 1984), 48–49; G. B. McGee, *This Gospel Shall Be Preached* (1986); W. W. Menzies, *Anointed to Serve* (1971); S. Overstreet, "Mother Flower Remembers," *The News-Leader* (Springfield, Mo.) (December 1, 1984), 4B; D. Skoog, "Soldier of Faith," *Live* (June 2, 1957), 2–3.   G. B. McGee

FLOWER, JOSEPH REYNOLDS (1913–). Pastor and denominational executive. Joseph Reynolds Flower was born in Indianapolis, Indiana, to J. Roswell and Alice Reynolds Flower. Reared in a devout Christian home, the younger Flower received the baptism in the Holy Spirit in 1926 during a revival conducted by William Booth-Clibburn. He later enrolled at Franklin and Marshall College in Lancaster, Pennsylvania. Impacted by the ministry of Charles S. Price at the Ebenezer Camp near Buffalo, New York, he transferred to Central Bible Institute (College after 1965) and graduated from there in 1934. He began his ministry that year by pastoring in Bethlehem, Pennsylvania; ordination followed in 1943. Flower pastored and pioneered other Assemblies of God (AG) churches in Stroudsburg and Pottstown, Pennsylvania; Dansville, Buffalo, and Syracuse, New York; Dover-Foxcroft, Maine; and Melrose, Massachusetts. Between pastorates on two occasions he engaged in evangelistic work.

After moving to Syracuse, Flower was elected as the assistant superintendent and presbyter of the then New York–New Jersey District and as a sectional secretary in the same district. From 1954 until 1975 he served as superintendent of the New York District. For ten of those years (1965–75) he represented the northeastern area of the U.S. on the denomination's executive presbytery. Elected as general secretary in 1975, he has held that position since then. His gentle demeanor, personal integrity, and fervent spirituality have had a significant influence on ministers within the denomination.

Flower has authored numerous articles for AG publications, including the *Pentecostal Evangel*. One of his most important contributions came with the writing of "Does God Deny Spiritual Manifestations and Ministry Gifts to Women?" (mimeographed, 1979). In 1940 he married Mary

Jane Carpenter. They have three children: Joseph Reynolds, Jr.; Mary Alice; and Paul William.

Bibliography: A. R. Flower, *Grace for Grace* (1961); W. W. Menzies, *Anointed to Serve* (1971).   G. B. McGee

John Wright Follette was a Bible college teacher and evangelist. He also authored the popular book, *Broken Bread*.

FOLLETTE, JOHN WRIGHT (1883–1966). Pentecostal teacher, poet, and artist. Follette was a descendant of Huguenots who first settled in the Catskill Mountains in the early 1660s. His fifth great-grandfather, Hugo Frere, was among the twelve who established the community of New Paltz. He received his college and ministerial training at the New York Normal School in New Paltz, Taylor University, and Drew Theological Seminary.

Follette was raised a Methodist. In 1911, however, after receiving the baptism of the Holy Spirit, he was ordained by a council of Pentecostal ministers at Elim Tabernacle, Rochester, New York. He affiliated with the Assemblies of God (AG) in 1935. He soon became a favorite speaker at church conferences, summer Bible camps, and retreats for missionaries around the world. He also taught at Elim Bible Institute in Rochester and at Southern California Bible College (AG).

Possessing a sensitive, artistic temperament, Follette expressed himself in prose, painting, musical compositions, and especially in his poetry. Being a lover of nature he had an awareness and a keen insight into its mystical language. He once remarked, "Who can always catch and interpret the subtle and ever-changing rays of light sifting through nature or flashing from the human heart?" Spiritual truth shines through his poetry and ministers to needs at various levels, whether taken literally or allegorically.

Follette's writings include *Arrows of Truth* (1969), *The Bethany Household* (n.d.), *Broken Bread* (1957), *A Christmas Wreath: A Collection of Christmas Poems, Written One Each Year Between 1919 and 1965* (1968), *Fruit of the Land* (n.d.), *Old Corn* (1940), *Psalms, Hymns and Spiritual Songs* (a hymnal of original compositions, 1968), *Smoking Flax and Other Poems* (1936), *This Wonderful Venture Called Christian Living* (1974), and inspirational booklets in the *Poured Out Wine* series.

Follette died at New Paltz in 1966, following a stroke. Characteristically, he chose to make his own funeral a moment for teaching by earlier recording the sermon that was played at that time.

Bibliography: Documents provided by AG Archives; interview with John H. Burgess, January 21, 1988; Clara Schwager and Shirley Scribner, "A Word About the Author," in John Wright Follette, *A Christmas Wreath: A Collection of Christmas Poems, Written One Each Year Between 1919 and 1965* (1968), v–viii.
                                                        S. M. Burgess

FOOTWASHING See ORDINANCES, PENTE-COSTAL.

FORBES, JAMES ALEXANDER (1935–). Joe R. Engle Professor of Preaching at Union Theological Seminary in New York and a leading preacher and homiletician in the black Pentecostal tradition.

Married, and with one son, Forbes is a graduate of Howard University, Union Theological Seminary, and Colgate-Rochester Divinity School. He pastored in North Carolina and Virginia before serving as the associate director of Inter/Met Seminary for three years (1973–76). This was an experimental school designed to train students for ministry through local congregations.

In 1976 Forbes was invited to Union, where he still teaches. He is an ordained minister in the Original United Holy Church International.

Forbes combines electric delivery with exegesis, employing the historical-critical method. The simple messages he proclaims are based on enjoyable yet complex images. His style is inspirational and exegetical, motivational and theological.

Bibliography: J. A. Forbes, "A Pentecostal Approach to Empowerment for Black Liberation," D.Min. diss., Colgate-Rochester Divinity School, (1975); idem, "Ministry of Hope to a Double Minority," *Theological Education* 9 (Summer Supplement): 305–16. D. F. Williams, "James Alexander Forbes: A Biographical Sketch," unpublished ms (1987).   B. M. Stout

FORD, JOSEPHINE MASSYNGBAERDE (1928–). Catholic Scripture scholar. Born in Nottingham, England, Ford qualified as a nurse; then, as an Anglican she studied theology, obtaining her Ph.D. from the University of Nottingham (1965). Becoming a Catholic, she taught in Uganda. She moved in 1965 to the University of Notre Dame, South Bend, Indiana, where she was in turn assistant professor, associate professor, and (from 1980) professor of biblical studies. She authored the Anchor Bible volume on Revelation (1975).

Ford became involved early in Catholic Charis-matic Renewal, writing numerous articles and booklets, including *The Pentecostal Experience* (1970) and *Baptism in the Spirit* (1971). Soon disputing the movement's main direction, especially concerning the role of women and its relationship to Catholic sacramental life, she produced more critical writings, including *Which Way for Catholic Pentecostals?* (1976). Her most detailed Pentecostal article, "Toward a Theology of 'Speaking in Tongues,' " is reprinted in *Speaking in Tongues: A Guide to Research on Glossolalia,* edited by W. E. Mills (1986).

Bibliography: R. Quebedeaux, *The New Charismatics II* (1983).   P. D. Hocken

FOREIGN MISSIONS See MISSIONS, OVERSEAS.

FORREST, TOM (1927–). International Catholic charismatic leader and promoter of evangelism. Born in Brooklyn, New York, Forrest was ordained priest in the Redemptorist order in 1954, working in the Dominican Republic and then in Puerto Rico. He was baptized in the Spirit in 1971, soon becoming pastor of Aguas Buenas, which then became a center for charis-matic renewal in the Caribbean and parts of Latin America. From 1978 to 1984 he was director of the International Catholic Charismatic Renewal Office and chairman of the associated international Council for Catholic Charismatic Renewal, first in Brussels and then in Rome.

Forrest, a dynamic preacher, returned to the U.S. after coordinating the Worldwide Retreat for Priests in the Vatican (October 1984). More recently he has returned to Rome to coordinate the planning for his vision of a decade of evangelism from 1990 to 2000.   P. D. Hocken

FOUNTAIN TRUST (FT). The primary service agency for charismatic renewal in Great Britain from its formation in July 1964 until its voluntary dissolution in 1980. The Fountain Trust was formed by Michael Harper. He was assisted by his wife and some professional friends, who became the trustees. Devised as a service agency to promote renewal in the Holy Spirit, FT had neither members nor branches but utilized conferences, meetings for praise and teaching, tapes, and (initially) books to spread its work. Its magazine, *Renewal,* first published in January 1966, has continued under independent auspices since the trust's closure. From its inception FT sought to service renewal in all the British churches by forming an advisory council representative of all strands in the movement. Though its thrust was more toward renewal in the historic churches, it included leaders such as A. Wallis with "nondenominational" convictions; tensions later developed between FT and the House Church movement. The International Conference at Guildford in 1971 was described as the charismatic movement's "coming of age" in Britain but attracted some criticism for including a Roman Catholic speaker. However, FT did not waver in welcoming Catholic charismatics, collaborating closely with the Catholic National Service Committee from its formation in 1973. FT had earlier engaged in periodic talks with British Pentecostal leaders. In 1972 Harper was joined at FT by Thomas Smail, who took over as director in 1975. Smail's theological gifts complemented Harper's talent for popular presentation, and he initiated first a theological workshop on renewal and then the thrice-yearly magazine, *Theological Renewal* (1975–83). In 1978 Smail was followed by an Anglican priest, Michael Barling. The FT model of an agency serving renewal across the churches influenced other Commonwealth countries, and similar agencies were set up in Australia and New Zealand.

See also CHARISMATIC MOVEMENT.

Bibliography: E. England, *The Spirit of Renewal* (1982); P. Hocken, *Streams of Renewal* (1986).
P. D. Hocken

FOURSQUARE GOSPEL CHURCH OF CANADA
The Foursquare Gospel churches of Eastern and Western Canada were originally affiliated respectively with the Eastern and Northwest districts of the International Church of the Foursquare Gospel (ICFG), the parent organization with headquarters in Los Angeles, California. A district for Western Canada was formed in 1964 with Roy H. Hicks, Sr., as supervisor. In 1976 the Church of the Foursquare Gospel of Western Canada was chartered as a provincial society. Incorporation of the Foursquare Gospel Church of Canada as a federal corporation came about in 1981, including all Canadian Foursquare Gospel churches. The current president and general supervisor is Victor F. Gardner. The church's headquarters and L.I.F.E. Bible College of Canada, a ministerial training school, are located in Burnaby, B.C.

The organization includes thirty-nine churches, an inclusive membership of 2,433, Sunday school enrollment of 1,554, and ninety-three ordained clergy. A national convention meets annually for inspiration and to address the needs of the organization. It publishes two periodicals: *The Canadian Challenge* and *News & Views*.

Bibliography: C. H. Jacquet, Jr., *Yearbook of American and Canadian Churches* (1987).
G. B. McGee

FOURSQUARE GOSPEL
See INTERNATIONAL CHURCH OF THE FOURSQUARE GOSPEL; MCPHERSON, AIMEE SEMPLE; ANGELUS TEMPLE.

FOX, LORNE FRANKLIN
(1911–). Assemblies of God (AG) missionary evangelist. Having been healed under the ministry of Charles S. Price in 1923 of severe heart disease and St. Vitus's Dance, Lorne Fox began his own evangelistic ministry soon after. His message was one of hope in the good news of the gospel and in God's healing power—a message that eventually took him all over the world. As a young man, Willard Cantelon became a member of the Fox party and traveled extensively with them. Fox also encouraged faith through a number of publications: *Africa Safari* (1967); "Is Physical Healing in the Atonement?" *PE* (October 8, 1950), 4–6; "One Hour Inside the Pearly Gates," *PE* (February 11, 1951), 3, 12–13; "Sickness and Demon Possession," *PE* (April 15, 1950), 2–3; and *This Is My Story*, (n.d.); *With Signs Following* (n.d.). Fox's

early career has been documented by E. Fox, *Bless the Lord, O My Soul* (1973).
F. Bixler

FRANCESCON, LUIGI
(1866–1964). Italian-American evangelist. Born in Cavasso Nuova, a province of Udine, Italy, Francescon immigrated to the U.S. and arrived in Chicago, Illinois, on March 3, 1890, where he began to work as a mosaic artisan. In December 1891 Francescon attended a service conducted by a small group of Italian Waldensians in Chicago's Railroad YMCA Hall and converted from Catholicism to Presbyterianism. Shortly afterward he became a member of the First Italian Presbyterian Church. On August 25, 1907, Francescon attended a Pentecostal meeting conducted by William H. Durham at the North Avenue Mission and experienced the baptism in the Holy Spirit with the evidence of speaking in tongues. Durham later prophesied that Francescon was divinely called to preach the Pentecostal message of Spirit baptism to the Italian people. In 1907 Francescon helped establish the first Italian-American Pentecostal church, the Assemblea Cristiana. In the following year, Francescon traveled to other cities in the U.S. such as Los Angeles, Philadelphia, and St. Louis and helped establish Pentecostal churches within the Italian communities. In 1909 he went to Argentina and helped establish the Italian Pentecostal movement in that country, which is presently incorporated as the *Iglesia Cristiana Pentecostal De Argentina*. Francescon's greatest evangelistic success began in 1910 in Sao Paulo, Brazil. Out of his evangelistic efforts grew one of the largest Pentecostal churches in Brazil, the *Congregacioni Christiani*.

Bibliography: The autobiography of Louis Francescon, untitled (privately published, June 1951); G. Bongiovanni, *Pioneers of the Faith* (1971); W. Hollenweger, *The Pentecostals* (1972); P. Ottolini, *Storia dell' Opera Italiana* (1945).
J. Colletti

FREE GOSPEL CHURCH
(FGC). A Pentecostal organization that two brothers, Frank and William Casley, founded in 1916. The Casleys were associated with the Christian and Missionary Alliance in about 1907 when they received the Pentecostal experience. A few churches they had organized became Pentecostal as well. The Free Gospel Church was known as the United Free Gospel and Missionary Society until 1958 when the name was shortened. The group operates the Free Gospel Bible Institute, which was organized in 1958, in Export, Pennsylvania. In 1987 there were more than 150 students enrolled. FGC supports thirteen foreign missionaries in Indonesia, the Philippines, Sierra Leone, and India, with an annual budget of $130,000. Total membership attending the twelve FGC churches is about one thousand, and twenty-four ministers belong to the group. In addition, about fifty other churches cooperate in FGC's foreign missions program. Offices are in Export, Pennsylvania. FGC is a member of the Pentecostal Fellowship of North America.

Bibliography: "Free Gospel Church" (pamphlet, rev. 1976); C. Jones, *Guide to the Pentecostal Movement* (1983).
W. E. Warner

FREE METHODIST CHARISMATICS See WESLEYAN CHARISMATICS.

FREE WILL BAPTIST CHURCH OF THE PENTECOSTAL FAITH In 1923 Free Will Baptists in South Carolina who had accepted Pentecostalism formed a statewide conference. Twenty years later this body joined three like-minded conferences in North Carolina—Cape Fear, Wilmington, and New River—in a general conference. Cooperative effort, which at first was limited to production of educational materials, led to overtures by the North Carolina conferences for organic union. South Carolina responded by withdrawing from the general conference. And in 1959, while their brethren to the north were forming the Pentecostal Free-Will Baptist Church, the South Carolina conference incorporated as the Free-Will Baptist Church of the Pentecostal Faith. In 1961 it issued a discipline, and two years later it ratified a new constitution. Nontheological issues, such as clergy pensions, have impeded merger negotiations with the Pentecostal Free-Will Baptist and Pentecostal Holiness churches. In the mid 1970s the Elgin, South Carolina, headquarters reported thirty-eight congregations (including one in Georgia and two in North Carolina) and 1,300 members.

Bibliography: A. C. Piepkorn, *Profiles in Belief,* vol. 3 (1979).   C. E. Jones

FREEMAN, HOBART E. (1920–84). Pastor and faith healer. Born in Ewing, Kentucky, Freeman suffered polio as a child. While he claimed to have been healed (one leg was shorter than the other), he was forced to wear special shoes. His education included study at Bryant and Stratton Business College and culminated at Grace Theological Seminary with a Th.D. in OT. Freeman taught at Grace Theological Seminary from 1961 until 1963 when doctrinal differences forced his departure. Moody Press published his *An Introduction to the Old Testament Prophets* in 1969.

Formerly a Baptist, Freeman started a small church in his home in Winona Lake, Indiana, in 1963. The congregation went through several names and locations before moving to the hamlet of Wilmot, Indiana, in 1978. Six years later 2,000 people worshiped at the church, which by that time was known as Faith Assembly.

Freeman was once in the mainstream of the charismatic renewal and faith-healing movement. He eventually adopted a sectarian position that isolated him from other leaders. He came to the attention of the national media in 1978 following the deaths of children in his congregation who had been denied medical assistance because of his teachings.

A former colleague, John Davis, president of Grace Theological Seminary, stated that "Freeman believed that all doctors and medicine have their roots in witchcraft . . . and that such witchcraft is demonically inspired. He believed that if you expose yourself to doctors and medical care, you are exposing yourself to demonic activity." The church had a type of midwife to assist in births, which were to take place at home, not in a hospital. Church members claimed hundreds of miraculous healings. However, Davis says as many as a dozen people in the congregation, including children, died of medically treatable ailments.

Church members David and Kathleen Bergmann were sentenced to ten years in prison as a result of being convicted of charges that they allowed their child to die without receiving medical assistance. At the time of his death Freeman was under indictment on the charge of aiding and inducing reckless homicide of a fifteen-year-old girl. The girl's parents, James and Ione Menne, were also indicted and later convicted, receiving suspended sentences.

Freeman conducted closed worship at Faith Assembly, which meant that no nonmembers were permitted to attend. He taught against education and television and forbade his congregation to receive religious teachings from anyone outside their church.

Freeman succumbed to broncho-pneumonia and what medical examiner Dr. Patricia Newhouse defined as "heart failure" complicated by an "ulcerated leg." He had not received medical treatment for these problems.

Bibliography: S. Lawson, "Faith Preacher Hobart Freeman Dies," *Charisma* (February 1985), 110; C. Lutes, "Leader's Death Gives Rise to Speculation About the Future of His Faith-healing Sect," *Christianity Today* 29 (January 18, 1985): 48.   S. Strang

FREEMAN, WILLIAM W. (twentieth century). Pastor and evangelist. Born in Stone County, Missouri, of intensely devout parents, Freeman experienced visitations from God even as a boy. Through the Great Depression and the 1930s he labored as a poor Pentecostal pastor and evangelist in the Midwest.

In 1946 Freeman was ministering in Salem, Oregon, when his wife had a nervous breakdown. Not long thereafter, he himself collapsed with heart trouble. Considering his ministry over, he resigned his pastorate. When a cancerous growth formed on his leg he sought divine healing all the more—which he received. In early 1947 he went forth as an itinerant evangelist, strengthened by a divine vision of the Lord standing upon a cloud and himself preaching before a vast congregation.

Teaming with Gordon Lindsay, who featured Freeman in the *Voice of Healing* (1948–52), he held "union meetings" throughout the Midwest and on the West Coast. Both the *Voice of Healing* and Freeman's own journal, *The Healing Messenger* (1949–56), contain numerous accounts of healings and the conversion of thousands.

Freeman was noted for being a powerful preacher, using "the straight Word of God" without "carnal programs, entertainers, side line attractions, etc" (Harrell, 1975, 77). In 1952 his services were broadcast on three radio stations; by 1956 he was on sixteen.

Freeman retired in 1956, settling in Chicago after ceasing the publication of his journal and canceling a projected 1957 overseas revival campaign.

Bibliography: W. Freeman, "My Life Story," *The Healing Messenger* (March 1949), 3; D. E. Gossett, "The Life and Ministry of William W. Freeman," *The Healing Messenger* (March 1954), 6; D. E. Harrell, Jr.,

All Things Are Possible (1975), 75–77; G. Lindsay, "The Story of the Great Restoration Revival: Part III," *Voice of Healing* 11 (2, May 1958): 4; H. A. Rogers, "William W. Freeman, Evangelist," *The Healing Messenger* (February 1950), 8.   J. A. Hewett

FRENCH CHARISMATICS See CHARISMATIC MOVEMENT.

FRENCH PENTECOSTALS See EUROPEAN PENTECOSTALISM.

FRODSHAM, ARTHUR W. (1869–1939). First generation Pentecostal pastor and evangelist. The eldest brother of Stanley H. Frodsham, Arthur heard early in 1909 of Stanley's baptism in the Spirit in England. Receiving this news in Winnipeg, Manitoba, Arthur immediately sought the baptism for himself, receiving that and healing for a long-standing stomach disorder in February 1909. He did evangelistic work based in Fort William, Ontario, for a few years, though during visits to Britain he helped with *Victory*, the journal started by his brother in Bournemouth.

After pastoring a church at Fergus, Ontario, Frodsham applied in 1916 for accreditation as an Assemblies of God (AG) pastor, moving in 1918 to Fredonia, New York. In 1923, he moved to California, where he pioneered and built AG churches at Glendale (1923–30) and Manhattan Beach (1932–39), with two intervening years at Burbank. He was for some years secretary of the Southern California and Arizona District Council.
                                P. D. Hocken

FRODSHAM, STANLEY HOWARD (1882–1969). Writer, editor, and teacher who ministered in the Pentecostal movement beginning in 1908. Wanting to become a writer, Frodsham studied hard to learn proper grammar, history, and literature at a private school in his native England.

After Frodsham's conversion in the London Young Men's Christian Association (YMCA), he spent a year in Johannesburg as the secretary for the newly formed YMCA. Then he traveled to Canada. All this time he sought for a deeper spiritual experience. Back in England in 1908 he found what he was searching for at All Saints Church in Sunderland when he received the baptism in the Holy Spirit.

Frodsham began his publishing ministry in 1909 when he introduced *Victory*, a monthly paper that reported on the Pentecostal revivals in various parts of the world.

Following his marriage to Alice Rowlands, Frodsham took his wife to America in 1910. In 1916 he began his ministry with the General Council of the Assemblies of God (AG). That year he was elected the general secretary; the next year he became the missionary treasurer; and in 1921 he was elected as editor of all AG publications, which included the weekly *Pentecostal Evangel*. In addition to his writing and editing of the *Evangel*, he wrote for Sunday school papers and quarterlies. His first book, *The Boomerang Boy and Other Stories*, was published in 1925. Of the fifteen books that Frodsham wrote, the best known is *Apostle of Faith* (1948), a biogra-

Stanley H. Frodsham edited the *Pentecostal Evangel* for nearly 30 years and wrote 15 books. In his later years he identified with the New Order of the Latter Rain.

phy on his friend Smith Wigglesworth. Another popular book is *With Signs Following* (1926, 1946). He edited another book for Wigglesworth, *Ever Increasing Faith* (1924), which also became very successful.

He left the AG employment two times to take editorial positions with other organizations: The Russian Missionary Society (1920–21) and the Christian Workers' Union (1928–29). He returned each time to edit the *Evangel*.

In 1949 Frodsham retired as editor of all AG publications and gave up his credentials. For the next several years he ministered in Latter Rain circles, teaching for a time at Elim Bible Institute.

Bibliography: F. Campbell, *Stanley Frodsham, Prophet With a Pen* (1974).   W. E. Warner

FROEN, HANS-JACOB (1912–). Norwegian charismatic pioneer. A pastor in the Lutheran state church, Froen had an experience of the Holy Spirit in 1938, later recognized as the "baptism," receiving a prophecy about his future ministry. Serving thirty-one years in the Mission to Seamen in Oslo, he was for ten years chairman of the Evangelical Alliance of Norway. Hearing of charismatic revival in America, Froen prayed for its outbreak in Norway. Froen became the recognized leader of the movement in Norway in 1970, when he attended A. Edvardsen's summer camp and then spoke publicly of his experience at a Full Gospel Business Men's Fellowship International convention in Oslo. From 1971 to 1981 he directed Agape, a service agency for charismatic renewal, editing its magazine *Dypere Liv (Deeper Life)*. Froen won friends by his personal warmth and evangelistic zeal, but his growing dissatisfaction with confessional Lutheran theology reduced Agape's impact on the state church.

Bibliography: T. Engelsviken, "Charismatic Renewal in the Lutheran Church of Norway," in *Charismatic Renewal in the Churches*, ed. P. Elbert (forthcoming).
P. D. Hocken

FROST, ROBERT C. (1926–). Author and teacher. Robert Frost was trained as a biologist (B.A., M.A., Ph.D.) but has developed a ministry as a teacher of the Spirit-filled life. He taught biology at several colleges before his baptism in the Holy Spirit in 1955. Since this experience Frost has written several books about life in the Spirit: *Aglow With the Spirit, Set My Spirit Free, Life's Greatest Discovery*, and *Overflowing Life*. Active in the charismatic circles of Oral Roberts University and the Full Gospel Business Men's Fellowship International, Frost has taught at Evangel College (Springfield, Mo.), Oral Roberts University (Tulsa, Okla.), and, most recently, at Melodyland School of Theology (Anaheim, Calif.).

Bibliography: R. C. Frost, *Overflowing Life* (1973).
J. R. Zeigler

FRUIT OF THE SPIRIT The expression "the fruit of the Spirit" appears only once in the Bible, in Galatians 5:22–23, and is there defined as consisting in nine behavioral qualities: "love, joy, peace, patience, kindness, goodness, faithfulness, gentleness, and self-control." The immediate context of the phrase is Galatians 5:13–6:10, in which Paul turns from a more doctrinal discussion concerning the importance of Christ and the question of the efficacy of circumcision for his converts, and exhorts them to embrace certain ethical commitments. The nature of this hortatory section is vital for a precise appreciation of what "the fruit of the Spirit" represents here. This context shows that the phrase refers specifically to behavioral qualities to be manifested in the Christian treatment of others, especially other Christians. Although the appeal must be responded to by individuals and although personal attitudes are obviously involved, the "fruit of the Spirit" is exhibited primarily in Christian interpersonal relationships and corporate life in the congregation.

I. Context. In Galatians 5:1 Paul reminds his readers that they have been set free "for freedom," and he urges them not to allow themselves to be entrapped anew in a "yoke of slavery," the latter phrase referring to the commitment to circumcision and Torah (law of Moses) observance promoted by Paul's opponents in Galatia. In the next several verses (5:2–12), Paul makes plain the stark alternatives for his Gentile readers: either trust in Christ as sufficient basis for standing before God, or turn from him to the futile attempt to obtain justification by observance of "the whole law."

Then, in 5:13, Paul returns to the term "freedom" (*eleutheria*) mentioned in 5:1 in order to warn the Galatians not to abuse their freedom from Torah, and to make the point that Christian freedom entails very clear obligations. These obligations Paul summarizes in two ways. First, in a clever but profound turn of phrase, Paul states that Christians have been freed in order to "serve (*douleuete*) one another in love." Then, with the Galatian preoccupation with the Torah in mind, Paul declares that "the entire law is summarized in a single command: 'love your neighbor as yourself'" (v. 14). These initial statements of the ethical section of the letter show that Paul's major concern here is to urge a practical and yet radical commitment to one another. The next comment, "[But] if you keep on biting and devouring each other, watch out or you will be destroyed by each other" (v. 15), suggests that Paul's teaching here is not simply general exhortation but is apparently fired by actual problems of conflict within the Galatian churches.

Beginning in 5:16 Paul employs the Spirit/flesh contrast he uses elsewhere (cf. 3:3; 4:29; Rom. 8:1–17) to distinguish two types of life. (English translations render "flesh" [*sarx*] in a variety of ways, in Gal. 5:16–6:10, passim, e.g., the NIV consistently translates the term by "sinful nature.") Using a variety of figures, Paul refers to the Spirit as the dynamic of the life he advocates. He exhorts the readers to "walk [*peripateite*] by the Spirit" (5:16), to be "led [*agesthe*] by the Spirit" (5:18), to "keep in step [*stoicheō*]" with the Spirit (v. 25), and to "sow to [*speirō eis*] the Spirit" (6:8). The contrast is to gratify the "desire of the flesh" (5:16), which is directly contrary to the Spirit (5:17). Those who belong to Christ have crucified the flesh with its passions and desires (5:24). Whoever "sows to the flesh" (6:8) will reap destruction. In the context of this running contrast between the flesh and the Spirit, the reference to the "fruit of the Spirit" is one of several figurative expressions used by Paul to connect the behavior he advocates here with the Holy Spirit.

II. The Spirit and Christian Life in Paul. Indeed, Paul characteristically links Christian life with the Spirit and makes the Spirit the source of the power for Christian ethical obedience. Earlier in this letter Paul has reminded the Galatian Christians that their initiation into Christian life was by the power of the Spirit (3:3) and that God gives them the Spirit freely (3:5; and cf. 4:6, "God sent the Spirit of his Son into our hearts"). Likewise, in 1 Corinthians 12:13, Christians are those who have been "baptized by one Spirit into one body" and have all been "given the one Spirit to drink." In Romans 8:9–11 Paul says that the presence of the Spirit is the assurance of all Christians (cf. 5:5), and in 8:13–14 he calls for Christians to draw upon the Spirit to "put to death" the misdeeds arising from selfish desires. Therefore, although the image of "fruit of the Spirit" is unique to Galatians 5:22, the underlying idea of the Spirit as the empowering source of Christian endeavor is an amply attested Pauline theme. Especially interesting in comparison with this passage is Romans 14:17, where, in another passage dealing with strife in the Christian community, Paul describes the kingdom of God as involving "righteousness, peace, and joy in the

Holy Spirit," qualities that are substantially paralleled in Galatians 5:22–23.

III. The "Fruit" Image. Before turning to a more detailed consideration of Galatians 5:22–23, we should note that early Christian sources show a widespread reference to "fruit" as an image for human behavior. For example, in Philippians 1:11, Paul's prayer for the readers includes the desire that they be filled with the "fruit of righteousness." The same figure appears in James 3:18, a similar expression in Hebrews 12:11. Note also Ephesians 5:9, where we read of the "fruit of light" that consists in "all goodness, righteousness and truth."

The metaphor of deeds as "fruit" is reflected also in other places in the NT, such as 2 Peter 1:8, which warns against being "unfruitful [*akarpos*, NIV "unproductive"] in your knowledge of our Lord Jesus Christ"; Ephesians 5:11, which refers to "fruitless deeds of darkness"; and Jude 12, where false teachers are described as being "without fruit." In Romans 7:4–5 Paul contrasts his readers' preconversion way of life with their new responsibility as Christians by employing the images of bearing fruit (*karpophoreō*) formerly "for death," but now "to God." The same verb appears in Colossians 1:6, where the gospel message is described as "producing fruit" everywhere it has gone, and in 1:10, where Paul prays that his readers will live a proper Christian life, "bearing fruit in every good work."

In fact, of course, the use of "fruit" as a metaphor for human actions is commonplace in the ancient background of the early Christians. Several OT passages reflect this imagery (e.g., Prov. 1:31; 13:2; Jer. 17:10; 21:14; Hos. 10:12–13; Amos 6:12). This is indicated also in several passages in the Gospels, such as Matthew 3:8, where the Baptist demands of his hearers "fruit in keeping with repentance," and Matthew 7:15–20, where Jesus states of false prophets, "By their fruit you will recognize them." Certainly among the most well-known uses of the imagery is John 15:1–8, where Jesus' followers are described as "branches" who are to "bear fruit." (Although some sermonic treatments of this passage have taken the fruit to be converts made through the efforts of Christians, the image much more likely refers to the full range of Christian obedience.)

As these passages show, the "fruit" of human actions may be either good or bad and thus reveals the nature and purposes of the human actor. In the NT passages where the image is used as an ethical metaphor, the emphasis is on the moral quality of the actions (e.g., "fruit of *righteousness*"). In several of the passages, God is implored to enable or assist Christians to "bear fruit," indicating that the writers understand the righteous behavior referred to as at least to some degree the result of divine activity and not purely a matter of human striving. By the phrase "fruit of the Spirit," Paul certainly underscores this note, making the behavioral qualities in view in Galatians 5:22–23 emphatically the ethical manifestation of the Holy Spirit.

As indicated already, the contextual contrast in Galatians 5:13–6:10 between the "flesh" and the divine Spirit no doubt supplies the immediate reason for the appearance of the phrase in this passage. That is, the phrase "fruit of the Spirit" arises out of the ethical dualism reflected in the context. This ethical dualism removes ambiguity from the realm of human actions and makes all behavior a result either of self-oriented human desires or of the impulse supplied by the Spirit of God. However, by calling the behavior listed in 5:22–23 the "fruit of the Spirit," Paul did not mean to portray Christians as automata manipulated by the Spirit. Rather, his intention was to portray the sort of behavior that could properly be taken as evidence of God's Spirit and that could be approved and promoted in the Christian fellowship.

IV. The Nature of the Fruit of the Spirit. Certain contextual factors in Galatians 5:13–6:10 have already been mentioned that indicate that "fruit of the Spirit" has to do here with the way Christians treat fellow believers. A more detailed analysis of the two contrasting lists that constitute respectively the "works of the flesh" and the Spirit's "fruit" will further confirm and clarify this conclusion.

The items listed as springing from the "flesh" form one of several so-called vice lists in the NT. These lists overlap somewhat, but each seems fitted to its context. None of them was intended to give anything more than a representative list of evil works. For example, in 1 Corinthians 6:9–11 Paul lists ten vices characterizing the "wicked." A still longer list appears in Romans 1:28–32 in a more global discussion of the results of human moral darkness. Comparison of the evils in Galatians 5:19–21 with these other vice lists indicates that this list tends to emphasize sins that manifest chaotic selfishness and that tear at the fabric of Christian fellowship. Note that in addition to commonly condemned vices such as "sexual immorality" (*porneia*) and associated sins ("impurity and debauchery," *akatharsia, aselgeia*) and other evils of Greco-Roman society such as idolatry (*eidōlolatria*), "witchcraft" (or "sorceries," *pharmakeia*), drunkenness, and "orgies" (*kōmoi*), eight of the fifteen items in the list refer to attitudes and actions that violate relationships with others: "hatred, discord, jealousy, fits of rage, selfish ambition, dissensions, factions, and envy."

The Spirit desires "what is contrary to the sinful nature [flesh]" (v. 17), and the description of the Spirit's "fruit" makes this explicit, consisting in a ninefold list of interpersonal attitudes and actions that enhance Christian fellowship (cf. other lists of virtues in, e.g., Rom. 5:3–5; 2 Peter 1:5–7). The nine terms are not simply to be seen as inner attitudes or personality attributes that one seeks so as to claim a certain personal spiritual attainment or to make one in Stoic-like fashion personally immune to circumstances in life. Rather, these terms describe personal behavior essential to corporate Christian life and reflect an attitude that has others in view rather than one's own private religious aims. That is, the primary context for the "fruit of the Spirit" is life together in Christ, and the Spirit's fruit does not consist in passive qualities that operate within the inner world of the individual but represent very active qualities of behavior directed outwardly toward those who have been made one's "brothers." Thus, although there is a limited similarity of a few of the terms, such as "self-control" (*enkrateia*), with the ideals of some of the Greco-Roman philosophical traditions, the intent and tenor of the list here is substantially different.

There have been attempts to find some sort of inner organization or structure in the list of nine qualities given in Galatians 5:22–23, but all such efforts convey a strong impression of weakly founded speculation. H. D. Betz, for example, offers an elaborate scheme involving three triads of concepts that descend from divine to human action (1979, 286–88). It is true that nine can yield three groups of three, but there is no hint here of anywhere else in early Christian literature that Betz's triads were recognized as fixed groups. Paul does seem to have been drawn to the use of triads, such as (with variations) the triad of "faith, hope, and love" (e.g., 1 Cor. 13:13; cf. 1 Thess. 1:3; 5:8), but the triads that Betz finds within the nine terms in Galatians 5 do not appear as such elsewhere. Paul's nine terms may well be the product of a rhetorical style that tended to speak of Christian virtues in ad hoc groupings of threes, here producing a group of terms that collectively is a threefold list of threes, but there is little indication that the list has the more fixed and detailed inner structure that Betz pictures.

It is certainly no accident that this list is headed by "love" (*agapē*), the chief virtue in early Christian ethical instruction and already twice emphasized by Paul in this passage (Gal. 5:13–14) as the essence of Christian ethical responsibility. In the NT *agapē* most commonly refers to love for other Christians and involves much more than affectionate feelings. In view of modern romanticized associations of the term, which tend to focus on the subjective, emotional experience of love, it has to be emphasized that the NT demand for Christian love always expects fulfillment in practical and tangible *actions*. That is, to love someone is to demonstrate active concern for that person's welfare, even in preference to one's own desires (cf., e.g., Phil. 2:1–4).

"Joy" and "peace" are elsewhere associated in Paul (Rom. 14:17; 15:13), and in numerous other references Paul says that joy is an important aspect of Christian existence. It is worth noting that these other Pauline references to joy tend to connect it with Christian fellowship in various ways. For example, Paul takes joy in his converts (Rom. 15:32; 2 Cor. 7:4; Phil. 1:4–5; 1 Thess. 2:19–20; 3:9; Philem. 7); he expects his converts to share in his joy over their fellow converts (2 Cor. 2:3; Phil. 1:25–26); he praises Macedonian Christians whose joy was manifested in generosity for the Jerusalem believers (2 Cor. 8:1–4); and he makes his joy dependent on good relations among his converts (Phil. 2:2). The "joy" referred to here in Galatians 5:22 accordingly fits the context where interpersonal Christian relations are the focus and therefore equals joy arising from and directed toward the Christian fellowship.

"Peace" in Paul carries overtones of his Semitic background where *shalom* involves total well-being, as indicated in the "grace and peace" salutations with which Paul opens his letters (e.g., Gal. 1:3). However, Paul also ties peace directly to Christian fellowship with God (Rom. 5:1) and with other Christians (Rom. 14:19; 1 Cor. 7:15; 14:33; 16:11). The present context suggests that the personal peace given by God's Spirit is to be manifested in the Galatians' relations with one another.

"Patience" (or "longsuffering," *makrothymia*), "kindness" (*chrēstotēs*, a pun on *christos*, "Christ"?), and "gentleness" (or "humility, courtesy," *praütēs*) are all easily recognized as qualities expressed almost entirely in personal relations, but the remaining terms are also to be seen in this setting. "Goodness" (*agathōsunē*) is here probably to be taken as "generosity," doing good practically to others (cf. 6:10, where the Galatians are to "do good [*to agathon*] to all people, especially to those who belong to the family of believers"). "Faithfulness" (*pistis*) here has to do with a steadfastness toward others that grows out of confidence in God.

The last term, "self-control" (*enkrateia*) is rarely used in the NT (elsewhere only in Acts 24:25; 2 Peter 1:6; and cf. the verb form in 1 Cor. 7:9; 9:25, and the adjective in Titus 1:8) but appears more frequently in the noncanonical literature of early Greek-speaking Christianity (e.g., 1 Clement 35:2; 62:2; Barnabas 2:2; Polycarp, to the Philippians 4:2). It is also a frequent term both in Greco-Roman philosophy in the writings of Greek-speaking Jews of the day (e.g., 4 Macc. 5:34; Jos. *Wars* 2:120, 138; *Antiq.* 8:235). Particularly in the Jewish and noncanonical Christian writings, the term is often, though not always, associated with control of one's sexual appetite. Here, however, the term probably carries a more general connotation, such as we find in its other NT uses, referring to control of one's passions, which issues in behavior that is orderly and pleasing to God.

Betz (1979, 288) suggests that the final position of "self-control" in the list gives it a certain intended prominence and that the term implies that Christian ethics is presented here as fulfilling "the central demand of Greek ethics." However, we are dealing with something different from the Stoic idea of control of one's inward responses to circumstances. In the present list, "self-control" represents a treatment of others that subordinates one's own selfish desires to the higher aim advocated in 5:13–14 to "serve one another in love." No doubt Paul's first readers would have caught the verbal echoes of Greek philosophical ideals pointed out by Betz, but careful consideration of the context indicates that here Paul gives to the term a characteristically Christian nuance that emphasizes one's behavior toward others.

V. The Fruit of the Spirit and Christ. As R. B. Hays has cogently shown, the entirety of the ethical section of Galatians (5:13–6:10) is governed by Paul's christology. Paul's exhortations to the Galatians, epitomized in 5:13b ("serve one another in love"), call for behavior that conforms to the paradigm given in Christ, whom Paul elsewhere refers to as the Son of God "who loved me and gave himself for me" (2:20). The fruit of the Spirit is to be the way of life of "those who belong to Christ Jesus" (5:24). Those who so live by the Spirit "fulfil the law of Christ" (6:2). That is, the "fruit of the Spirit" listed in 5:22–23 is both the product of the operation of the Holy Spirit in believers and also the manifestation of participation in Christ. Paul has already referred to the Holy Spirit as "the Spirit of his [God's] Son" (4:6). It is therefore quite fitting that the "fruit" of this Spirit should be behavior that reflects the "crucifixion" of selfish desires of the "flesh" (5:24), Paul's language alluding, of course, to Christ's own sacrificial death.

The fact that Christ is the foundation for and paradigm of the behavior called "the fruit of the Spirit" makes the connection apparent between Galatians 5:13–26 and other Pauline passages such as Romans 13:8–14. There, as in the Galatians passage, after emphasizing that mutual love is the central Christian obligation (13:8–10), Paul proceeds to contrast a list of similar vices to be rejected (vv. 12–13) with an opposite and wholly new type of behavior there described in simple but powerful imagery: "Rather, clothe yourselves with the Lord Jesus Christ" (v. 14). The Galatians metaphor, "fruit of the Spirit," focuses on the agency enabling Christians to conform their lives to Christ, and the ninefold definition of the spiritual fruit makes more specific than the Romans passage what Christian love for one another involves.

VI. Conclusion. Paul's reference to the "fruit of the Spirit," unique to the Galatian letter, forms part of an important section of ethical instruction often overlooked in the historical concentration on the doctrinal issues in this fiery writing and supplies Christian tradition with a memorable and evocative metaphor for understanding Christian ethics. Three things may be emphasized about this "fruit": (1) It refers to active attitudes and behavior directed toward others in the Christian fellowship and aimed at enhancing and preserving that fellowship. (2) It is not the result of mere ethical striving or of one's own spiritual exercises but is manifestation of the gift of God's Spirit allowed sway in one's life. (3) It rises from and is conformed to the sacrificial paradigm of Christ's own self-sacrifice.

See also HOLY SPIRIT, DOCTRINE OF THE.

Bibliography: H. D. Betz, *Galatians* (1979); F. Hauck, *TDNT*, 3:614–16; R. B. Hays, "Christology and Ethics in Galatians: The Law of Christ," *CBQ* 49 (1987): 268–90; R. Hensel, *NIDNTT* 1:721–23.

L. W. Hurtado

FULL GOSPEL BUSINESS MEN'S FEL-LOWSHIP INTERNATIONAL (FGBMFI)

Interdenominational organization of charismatic lay people. Demos Shakarian, a lay leader in the southern California area felt God leading him to start an organization of businessmen who could come together from all different denominations to share their faith in Christ. In 1951 he founded the first chapter of the FGBMFI. The speaker for the first meeting was Oral Roberts, who had just completed a healing campaign in Los Angeles. Roberts encouraged Shakarian in his efforts and prayed at that first meeting that God would raise up a thousand chapters throughout the world and that the gospel would go forth through this organization.

The FGBMFI began with breakfast meetings held on Saturday mornings at Clifton's Cafeteria in downtown Los Angeles. However, the idea just did not seem to be working, and after the first year Shakarian was very discouraged. One Friday night he told his wife and his house guest, evangelist Tommy Hicks, that he felt he must pray that God would give him an answer regarding the future of FGBMFI. While in prayer, God took Shakarian around the world in a vision and showed him humankind as dead and lifeless and then as alive and full of joy as the Spirit of God was poured out. As he saw this vision his wife, Rose, spoke through tongues and interpretation to describe what he was seeing. The next morning at the FGBMFI meeting he received a check for $1,000, and Thomas R. Nickel offered the services of his press to print a magazine for the group. Nickel was appointed editor of the magazine called *The Full Gospel Business Men's Voice*.

During the next year eight more chapters of the FGBMFI began around the country, and the first annual convention was held in Los Angeles. The attendance at the initial meeting was about three thousand. The speakers included almost all the noted independent ministers who were associated with the healing revival: Oral Roberts, Jack Coe, Gordon Lindsay, Raymond T. Richey, O. L. Jaggers, and Tommy Hicks.

The FGBMFI continued to grow at a startling rate. By the mid-'60s it had more than three hundred chapters, with a total membership of 100,000. Growth did not stop, and in 1972 there was a membership of 300,000. By 1988 the fellowship had more than 3,000 local chapters and had spread to 87 countries.

The original vision of the FGBMFI was of a nonsectarian fellowship of laity who could come together to share what God had done in their lives without any apology—even if that testimony included healing or tongues or deliverance from demonic forces. The impact of the FGBMFI on the Pentecostal and charismatic movements has been considerable and not without controversy. The typical meeting usually held in a hotel ballroom or a restaurant was often a marked departure from the traditional Pentecostal meetings of the past. The FGBMFI took the message of the power of the gospel to heal and deliver and of the baptism of the Holy Spirit from the tents to the hotels and convention centers of America. Often speakers were laymen who told of God's remarkable and miraculous intervention in their lives and businesses. They offered prayer for the sick and many were saved, healed, and filled with the Holy Spirit in these services. This was certainly not the traditional revivalist meeting of the past, nor was it like any of the usual interdenominational testimony meetings. Many of the traditional ministers from Pentecostal denominations could not adjust to this new approach; and although the stress was that the FGBMFI was *not* a replacement for the local church, many pastors felt threatened by this open ecumenical fellowship.

This modern office building is the headquarters for the Full Gospel Business Men's Fellowship, International, in Costa Mesa, California.

The FGBMFI was in large part responsible for the rise of the teaching ministries of many of the prominent "faith teachers." The members were usually from churches that had not stressed nor taught on faith or healing or the ministry of the Holy Spirit and so teachers like Kenneth E. Hagin, Sr., Kenneth Copeland, and others were much in demand to teach at the regional and annual conventions.

The FGBMFI started a television program called "Good News" in the 1970s that at one time was seen in 150 cities. This half-hour program was hosted by Demos Shakarian and, like many local meetings, consisted of ordinary businessmen telling extraordinary stories about their faith in Christ.

The leader of the FGBMFI since its beginning has been Demos Shakarian. Shakarian suffered a stroke in 1984 that resulted in his taking a less active role in the day-to-day operations of the fellowship. In March 1988 the board of directors voted to remove Shakarian as president but to retain him as spiritual director. This move may well reflect the need for change felt by the younger members of the organization who are looking for new ways to fulfill the vision of God's people coming together to share the good news of the Gospel.

See also CHARISMATIC MOVEMENT.

Bibliography: B. Bird, "FGBMFI: Facing Frustrations and the Future," Charisma (June 1986), 25, 26, 28; D. E. Harrell, Jr., All Things are Possible (1975); D. Shakarian, The Happiest People on the Earth (1975); idem, "FGBMFI Struggles Toward the Future," Charisma (March 1988), 24.   J. R. Zeigler

FULL GOSPEL CHURCH ASSOCIATION

(FGCA). A small church organization founded by Dennis W. Thorn in 1952. Thorn, formerly with the Assemblies of God, sought to organize independent Pentecostal churches and ministers in a cooperative fellowship primarily in the southern and western sections of the U.S. Except for minor stipulations (KJV to be used, every church to have an altar), FGCA's statement of faith is similar to other Pentecostal "finished work" groups.

Thorn died in 1984, and the leadership was assumed by his widow. In 1986 FGCA was composed of about fifty churches and two thousand church members. Most of the ministers associated with the group are evangelists. Offices are in Amarillo, Texas. FGCA sponsor's foreign missions in Mexico and the Philippines.

Bibliography: C. Jones, *Guide to the Pentecostal Movement* (1983); D. Thorn (comp.), "FGCA Constitution, Faith & Teaching" (1958).   W. E. Warner

FULL GOSPEL EVANGELISTIC ASSOCIATION (FGEA).

Originally comprised of ministers who were a part of the Apostolic Faith (AF, Baxter Springs, Kans.) and who were interested in forming a foreign missions outreach. The group formed the Ministerial and Missionary Alliance of the Original Trinity Apostolic Faith in 1951, but they were disfellowshiped by the AF. The next year the group organized as the Full Gospel Evangelistic Association. Thus a more progressive element within Charles Parham's AF was on its own. Parham's daughter-in-law, Pauline Parham, became active in the new organization and served as the first superintendent of Midwest Bible Institute, which is sponsored by FGEA.

FGEA ordains ministers, supports foreign missions, and has an affiliation with local churches. By 1987 there were 175 ministers, thirty member churches and institutions, plus mission stations and cooperating churches.

Midwest Bible Institute was established in 1959 and began operating at Webb City, Missouri, the next year. The best-known instructor at the school in its formative years was the English Pentecostal Charles H. E. Duncombe. The school moved to Houston in 1971. FGEA has its office on the campus.

Taking a classical Pentecostal position, FGEA is Trinitarian, accepts sanctification as a "definite work of grace," believes in divine healing and health, is premillennial, and practices footwashing.

The missionary emphasis has been on Latin America, with missionaries serving in Mexico, Guatemala, and Peru. Other missionaries have been sent to Taiwan.

FGEA publishes *Full Gospel News* as its official periodical. The affiliated churches use Sunday school literature published by Pentecostal publishers.

See also APOSTOLIC FAITH (BAXTER SPRINGS, KANS.).

Bibliography: "By-laws, FGEA" (n.d.); C. Jones, *Guide to the Pentecostal Movement* (1985); "This is Full Gospel Evangelistic Association" (1980).   W. E. Warner

FULL GOSPEL FELLOWSHIP OF CHURCHES AND MINISTERS INTERNATIONAL (FGFCMI).

Serving as a credential-granting agency for independent ministers and a fellowship for independent congregations, the Full Gospel Fellowship of Churches and Ministers International was founded in 1962 at a convention in Dallas, Texas. Gordon Lindsay and W. A. Raiford were instrumental in organizing this loosely structured association; J. C. Hibbard and John Meares were also incorporating officers. In addition to serving independent ministers and churches, David Edwin Harrell, Jr., sees another reason for the formation of FGFCMI: "They hoped [FGFCMI] could bridle the stampeding charismatic movement. The effort was unsuccessful because the Neo-Pentecostal phenomenon was much too nebulous to take very much organization, and what fellowship was needed was already provided by the Full Gospel Business Men's Fellowship International" (1975, 167).

FGFCMI's constitution is clear from the opening paragraphs that the organization "shall never have any ecclesiastical or hierarchical authority over its members." Each church affiliated with FGFCMI is free to conduct its own business and ministry at home and abroad and to ordain ministers if it chooses. FGFCMI regards itself as a fellowship of the body of Christ rather than as "a closed communion."

Underscoring the liberty of its members, the Tenets of Faith provide few positions for debate and much doctrinal latitude. Its basis of faith is the doctrine of Christ as given in 2 John 9–11 and the seven principles of Christ in Hebrews 6:1–2. Citing differences of opinion in the Apostolic Church, FGFCMI's constitution maintains that each church and minister is to function with "Apostolic liberty of conscience," but it disapproves of those who would "use that liberty to divide brethren." A sample copy of suggested articles of faith—which has the appearance of an abbreviated Assemblies of God statement—is provided for local churches but with a qualifying note that articles can be revised in any way to suit each church.

In its twenty-fifth year, FGFCMI listed (worldwide) 450 affiliated churches, 850 ministers, and church membership of about 125,000. Other nonaffiliated churches that are pastored by FGFCMI ministers could increase church membership by as many as 60,000 people, according to a church spokesperson. General offices are in Dallas.

Bibliography: "FGFCMI Constitution and By Laws (1980); D. Harrell, Jr., *All Things Are Possible* (1975); C. Jones, *Guide to the Pentecostal Movement* (1983).   W. E. Warner

FULLAM, EVERETT L. ("TERRY")

(1930–). Episcopal priest, teacher, and conference leader. Ordained as a priest in 1967, Fullam taught philosophy at the University of Rhode Island and biblical studies at Barrington College. In 1972 he became rector of St. Paul's Episcopal Church in Darien, Connecticut. Under his leadership the parish became one of the most active Episcopal churches in the U.S., increasing Sunday attendance from 250 to 1,200 in five years.

A number of the innovations Fullam instituted at St. Paul's are now widely practiced by congregations active in spiritual renewal. Among these are the policy of moving under the headship of Jesus Christ and making decisions in unity of the Spirit; using liturgy as an outline for worship; tithing resulting from walking in a covenant with Christ; pastoral care through smaller and more intimate "shepherd" or "home" groups; and the audio and video taping and distribution of sermons and lectures.

Fullam's teaching ministry in parish renewal extended to both clergy and laity in all denominations worldwide. He was also the president of the executive board of Episcopal Renewal Ministries.

Everett (Terry) Fullam is one of the leaders in the Episcopal Renewal Ministries, serving at St. Paul's Church, Darien, Connecticut.

Fullam's publications include: *Living the Lord's Prayer* (1981); *Facets of the Faith* (1982); *Your Body, God's Temple* (1984); *Riding the Wind* (1986); *How To Walk With God* (1987).

Bibliography: B. Slosser, *Miracle in Darien* (1979).
C. M. Irish

FULLER, WILLIAM E. (1875–1958). Church planter and executive. William Edward Fuller was born in Mountville, South Carolina, the son of sharecroppers. Raised as a Methodist, he was attracted to the Holiness movement through the ministry of B. H. Irwin and the Fire-Baptized Holiness Association, which he joined in 1897. An interracial group in its beginnings, the Fire-Baptized Holiness Church (FBHC) elected Fuller as a member of the executive board at its national organizational meeting in Anderson, South Carolina, in 1898. By 1900 he had organized more than fifty black FBHC congregations in South Carolina and Georgia.

In 1908 Fuller and his black colleagues petitioned the church for permission to form a separate black version of the denomination. This was granted in an amicable separation with properties deeded over to the new church, which from 1908 to 1922 was known as the Colored Fire-Baptized Holiness Church.

In time, Fuller moved the headquarters of the church to Atlanta, Georgia. Before his death in 1958 the church had changed its name to the Fire-Baptized Holiness Church of God of the

Americas and had given Fuller the title of presiding bishop.

Bibliography: V. Synan, *The Old-Time Power* (1973).   H. V. Synan

FULNESS MINISTRIES See BAPTIST CHARISMATICS.

FULNESS PASTORS AND CHURCHES See BAPTIST CHARISMATICS.

FUNDAMENTALISM Fundamentalism refers to a movement among theologically conservative Protestant churches that reached its height in America during the 1920s and survives in resurgent post-World War II fundamentalist and evangelical churches and movements. With roots in nineteenth-century millenarianism, Fundamentalism arose as a reaction to the liberal teachings of the nineteenth-century higher critics and the subsequent movement known as "Modernism." Fundamentalists saw themselves as defenders of orthodox Christianity against those in the churches who were attempting to accommodate the faith to the realities of the modern world.

Although an elaborate system of particular doctrines emerged from the movement, all Fundamentalists stressed the verbal and inerrant inspiration of the Bible, which was seen as the final and complete authority for faith and practice. Fundamentalism also preached a rigorous lifestyle that often precluded the use of alcohol, tobacco, drugs, and attendance at places of "worldly amusement," such as the stage and later the movie theaters.

After its zenith in the 1920s, Fundamentalism and the modernist movement against which it struggled, suffered drastic declines. Fundamentalism gained its greatest attention in the famous "Monkey Trial" of 1925, during which John T. Scopes was tried for teaching the theory of evolution in the public schools of Dayton, Tennessee. As a result of publicity surrounding this trial, Fundamentalists were regarded as anti-intellectuals who stood in the way of social and academic progress.

Despite this perception, Fundamentalism, in its more respectable form known as "Evangelicalism," has not only survived the negative image of the 1920s, but has flourished in the latter half of the century.

I. The Roots of the Movement. Modern Fundamentalism had its origins in the Evangelical and millenarian movements of nineteenth-century England and America. The movement toward Fundamentalism began in England in the wake of the French Revolution. When Pope Pius VI was exiled in 1798 and a new regime installed in revolutionary France with a new calendar and the seeming overthrow of the established order, some Christians believed that they were living in the last days before the end of the age. English Evangelicals thus began to seek answers for these events in biblical prophecies relating to the end times. Leaders in this pursuit were Lewis Way, an Anglican; Edward Irving, a Presbyterian; and John Nelson Darby, founder of the Plymouth Brethren.

In their studies, these men saw in Scripture the

teaching of the imminent rapture of the church at the second coming of Christ, which would occur before the Millennium (the thousand years of peace predicted in the Apocalypse). They saw biblical prophecies concerning the return of the Jews to the Holy Land and a new outpouring of the Holy Spirit "on all flesh," with the restoration of the charismata, as signs of the last days. They expected these signs to take place in their time. Indeed, when prophecy and glossolalia broke out in Irving's London Presbyterian congregation in 1830, he was sure that the end was near. But his Presbyterian elders felt otherwise. After being tried and expelled from the presbytery for teaching heresy concerning the person of Christ, Irving founded the Catholic Apostolic Church, which, along with the term *Irvingism,* became a byword among the enemies of the movement.

Darby, however, continued to popularize the teachings of the movement among his own English followers and among large groups of Americans during his several preaching tours of the U.S. One avid teacher of the new millenarian doctrines in America was William Miller of New York. He boldly predicted that the second advent of Christ would take place on or before the year 1843. His growing group of followers, which swelled to some 100,000 believers, were disappointed and scattered after the expected event failed to occur. This experience also gave Adventism a bad name, and "Millerism" became as unpopular in America as "Irvingism" was in Britain.

Despite the negative results of the Irving and Miller episodes, interest in the premillennial second coming of Christ continued to increase throughout the century and gained powerful allies in America before 1900. In 1872 the Niagara Bible Conferences in Ontario, Canada, stirred new support. Led by Baptists James Ingles and Adoniram J. Gordon, Presbyterian James H. Brookes, and Episcopalian William R. Nicholson, the prophetic movement began to flourish in America centering around Bible conferences devoted to biblical prophecy.

In addition to millenarianism, these teachers added to their set of doctrines a vigorous defense of the literal, or verbal, inspiration of the Scriptures. In time, belief in the "inerrant" original autographs of Scripture became a bedrock teaching of the movement. The absolute authority of Scripture gave at one and the same time a defense against the twin evils of Modernism and Roman Catholicism, of which Roman Catholicism was fast becoming the largest denomination in the U.S.

The major enemies of these teachers, however, were not the Roman Catholics but the higher critics who more and more called themselves Modernists. When the modernist movement began to gain strength under the influence of such leaders as Shailer Matthews, Charles Briggs, and A. C. McGiffert, Sr., prophetic leaders saw themselves as the defenders of the faith against the German "higher critics" and their modernist American followers. By the late 1890s the millenarians had won no less a personage than Dwight L. Moody to their cause. Their greatest prizes,

however, were the Princeton Seminary professors Charles Hodge and Benjamin Warfield, who were destined to give important biblical and intellectual support to the movement. Although not supportive of the millenarian aspects of Fundamentalism, Hodge and Warfield stressed the inerrant authority and inspiration of the Scriptures. Their distinctive work was known as the Princeton Theology.

II. Institutionalization. The fundamentalist movement began to crystallize after the turn of the century with the organization of the American Bible League in 1902 and the World's Christian Fundamentals Association in 1919. The latter organization came into being under the influence of the publication of a series of twelve pamphlets entitled *The Fundamentals* between 1910 and 1915. Financed and sent free to 250,000 ministers and laymen by California oil millionaires Lyman and Milton Stewart, these booklets contained an exposition of the five points of the movement. They were (1) the verbal inerrancy of the Scriptures, (2) the deity and virgin birth of Christ, (3) the substitutionary atonement, (4) the physical resurrection of Christ, and (5) Christ's bodily return to earth. Edited by A. C. Dixon and R. A. Torrey, they gave the movement its popular name and distilled its distinctive theology.

In addition to these teachings, a dispensational eschatological schema called "dispensationalism" was popularized before the turn of the century. This interpretation of history and prophecy divided spiritual history into seven periods or "dispensations" according to the differing methods of God's dealing with humankind. These periods were those of (1) innocence, (2) conscience, (3) human government, (4) promise, (5) law, (6) grace, and (7) kingdom. Darby, the originator and promoter of this teaching, also popularized it in the U.S. between 1866 and 1877. In Darby's system the church age, or "age of grace," began with the birthday of the church and was destined to end with the rapture of the church at the second coming of Christ. Then the seventh dispensation, the millennial reign of Christ, or the "kingdom" age would begin.

Although Fundamentalists and dispensationalists strongly supported the miracles of the Bible as one of the bedrock fundamentals of the faith, they denied the presence of miracles in modern times. Thus they added to the dispensation of the church age a subdispensation in which the charismata ceased after the canon of Scripture was completed. The fundamentalist belief in miracles was limited to the historical fact that they had occurred in biblical times.

Buttressing this claim was the book by Warfield titled *Counterfeit Miracles* (1918), which held that not one single documented miracle had occurred since the death of the last apostle. Much of this view was based on a refusal to accept the miraculous claims of the Roman Catholic church. This view also predisposed the Fundamentalists to oppose the Pentecostal movement, which had appeared at the beginning of the century.

Major dispensational leaders were A. C. Gaebelein and C. I. Scofield. The dispensational scheme was most widely publicized through the notes of the *Scofield Bible* (1909), which continued to enjoy heavy sales among Evangelicals throughout the rest of the century. Despite its antimiraculous teachings, many Pentecostals joined the dispensationalist camp and taught the scheme in their Bible colleges with appropriate modifications to accommodate glossolalia and divine healing.

III. The Fundamentalist Controversy With the Modernists.

While liberalism was small and ineffectual before World War I, it grew greatly in influence after the war. Although some denominations feared and opposed the new views, more and more theologians and seminaries joined the modernist ranks. Although some large Protestant denominations, such as the Southern Baptists and Missouri Synod Lutherans were largely unaffected, others, such as the Methodist and Episcopal communions found increasing numbers of Modernists in their ranks.

The outstanding liberal voice in the land was that of Harry Emerson Fosdick, pastor of New York's First Presbyterian Church (although he was a Baptist) and professor of homiletics at Union Theological Seminary. Fundamentalists found Fosdick a popular target. After preaching a controversial sermon in 1922 titled "Shall the Fundamentalists Win?" he was removed from his Presbyterian pulpit, whereupon he founded the influential Riverside Church in New York City with help from John D. Rockefeller.

Another target of the Fundamentalists was the Federal Council of Churches, which by 1920 was largely under the control of the Modernists. Formed in 1908, it was seen by Fundamentalists to be under the control of evolutionists and higher critics. A first line of attack was to root the Modernists out of the mainline Protestant denominations. In the 1920s skirmishes broke out in several churches where Fundamentalists attempted to oust leading Modernists and gain control of the denominational machinery. The ensuing battles resulted in the defeat of the Fundamentalists, however. In their attempts to drive Modernists from the northern Presbyterian and Baptist churches, the Fundamentalists were themselves rejected.

The climax of the conflict between Fundamentalists and Modernists came in 1925 in the famous Scopes trial in Dayton, Tennessee. Charged with teaching evolution contrary to a recently passed Tennessee law, high school teacher John T. Scopes was defended by the most famous trial lawyer in America, Clarence Darrow. Coming to aid the prosecution was the most famous Fundamentalist in the land, thrice-defeated Democratic presidential candidate William Jennings Bryan, a committed Presbyterian Fundamentalist.

Although Scopes lost the trial and was fined a hundred dollars, the Fundamentalists lost in the court of public opinion. Because of the trial, Fundamentalists were seen as anti-intellectual and were derided by the press and especially by the universities. Despite this drastic setback, Fundamentalists refused to die. The strength of the movement was seen in the fact that it not only survived the Scopes trial but that it continued in a more moderate form as Evangelicalism in future years.

After 1925 the Fundamentalists largely abandoned the seminaries and universities to the Modernists and concentrated on building Bible institutes where their faith would be safe from the glare of the liberal media and the intellectuals who, like H. L. Mencken, found Fundamentalists to be easy targets to lampoon. Such schools as Moody Bible Institute in Chicago and the Bible Institute of Los Angeles became havens of Fundamentalist theology. Some Fundamentalists left their denominations to found new ones, such as the Presbyterian Church of America (later the Orthodox Presbyterian Church) founded by J. Gresham Machen in 1936 and the General Association of Regular Baptist Churches founded by breakaways from the Northern Baptist Convention. Others joined smaller groups, such as the Christian and Missionary Alliance and the Evangelical Free Church.

IV. Controversy With Pentecostals.

An important area of influence for Fundamentalism was the rising Pentecostal denominations that appeared after 1906. Although disagreeing with the cessation teaching of the dispensationalists, most Pentecostals during the 1920s and 1930s thought of themselves as Fundamentalists "with a difference." Especially influential to Pentecostals was the premillennial rapture of the church teaching. The reappearance of the charismata had been closely tied to the rapture of the church from the times of Edward Irving. Pentecostals saw in the renewal of healing and tongues a sure sign of the end of the age and of the rapture of the church. The prominence given to the rapture of the church in Pentecostal preaching and teaching led historian Robert Mapes Anderson to the conclusion that early Pentecostalism was more a Second Coming movement than a tongues movement.

The disagreement with Pentecostals over miracles eventually led to a break between Fundamentalists and Pentecostals. Although no Pentecostal groups had formally joined the World's Christian Fundamentals Association after 1919, they were formally rejected by the organization in 1928. The resolution that disfellowshipped the Pentecostals stated:

> Whereas the present wave of Modern Pentecostalism, often referred to as the "tongues movement," and the present wave of fanatical and unscriptural healing which is sweeping over the country today, has become a menace in many churches and a real injury to sane testimony of Fundamental Christians,
>
> Be it resolved, that this convention go on record as unreservedly opposed to Modern Pentecostalism, including the speaking in unknown tongues, and the fanatical healing known as general healing in the atonement, and the perpetuation of the miraculous sign-healing of Jesus and His apostles, wherein they claim the only reason the church cannot perform these miracles is because of unbelief.

From this point on, it was impossible to classify the Pentecostals as Fundamentalists, although the general public then and to this day is unaware of the differences. Indeed, in many minds the Pentecostals were and continue to be falsely thought of as the hyperfundamentalists.

V. From Fundamentalism to Evangelicalism. When it became clear that the Fundamentalists had lost the battle for the minds of mainstream American Protestant Christianity, they withdrew more and more into a social and theological shell. Eventually a spirit of censoriousness and condemnation took over the rhetoric of the movement with leaders such as Bob Jones and Carl McIntire denouncing those who had fallen from the straight and narrow way. These and others began to build institutional bastions for future warfare in defense of the faith. In 1927 Bob Jones created his university in Cleveland, Tennessee, not far from Dayton, where the famous trial had taken place.

In 1941 Carl McIntire founded his American Council of Christian Churches (ACCC) to counteract the influence of the Federal Council and later of the National Council of Churches. The creation of the ACCC came at a point when more moderate voices were being heard. In the emergency of World War II many conservative Christians began to fellowship together in unprecedented ways. Leaders among these men were theologian Carl F. H. Henry and Harold J. Ockenga, pastor of Boston's historic Park Street Church. A group of moderate Fundamentalists meeting in Chicago in 1943 were invited to join McIntire's group, but they were repelled by his belligerent spirit. When discussions of merger began, the presence of Pentecostals in the moderate group became the bone of contention that ended all hopes of union.

McIntire regarded the Pentecostals as apostates with whom he could have no fellowship. He refused to accept them or other Evangelicals who fellowshipped with them in his new ACCC. In a historic moment the moderates rejected the Fundamentalists, accepted the Pentecostals, and adopted the name National Association of Evangelicals. This was the final break with the discredited militance characterized by the older Fundamentalists. It marked the beginning of a new era where evangelists such as Billy Graham would preach under the banner of Evangelicalism rather than of Fundamentalism. It also marked the first time in Christian history that a charismatic move-

ment was accepted into the mainstream of the church.

Since that time Pentecostals have grown to be the majority force in the NAE, with Pentecostals such as Thomas F. Zimmerman (Assemblies of God) and Ray H. Hughes (Church of God, Cleveland, Tenn.) serving as presidents of the organization. The crusades of Billy Graham after 1948 were strongly supported by Pentecostals around the world, often making up the majority of his audiences in Third World countries. For this and other reasons, Graham was denounced by Bob Jones and other Fundamentalists for compromising the purity of the gospel.

VI. Fundamentalism Today. The most prominent Fundamentalist of the last quarter of the century has been Jerry Falwell, whose "Old Time Gospel Hour" has taken him into the living rooms of the people of America. His brand of conservative political activism harked back to the heady days before 1925 when Fundamentalism was a force to be reckoned with in American life. His "Moral Majority" is believed to have played a key role in the election of Ronald Reagan in the 1980 presidential election.

But the prime religious forces in America after World War II were Evangelicalism and Pentecostalism, both of which played leading roles in the religious revival of the 1950s. Paralleling the evangelistic crusades of Billy Graham were those of Oral Roberts, who introduced Pentecostalism to the American public with his televised healing services under the big tent.

The growth of the Pentecostal churches and the outbreak of the charismatic movement in the mainline churches left the Fundamentalists far behind the attention of the American public. In the opinion of this writer, the breaks with Fundamentalism in 1928 and 1943 turned out to be a blessing that freed the rising Pentecostals from the dead cultural and theological baggage of a discredited movement and opened up the way for unparalleled influence and growth in the last half of the twentieth century.

See also EVANGELICALISM.

Bibliography: G. Marsden, *Fundamentalism and American Culture* (1980); W. Menzies, *Anointed to Serve* (1971); E. Sandeen, *The Roots of Fundamentalism* (1970).   H. V. Synan

G

An early missionary to Liberia, Henry B. Garlock later became the first field secretary for the Assemblies of God in Africa.

GARDNER, VELMER JAMES (1913–). Healing evangelist. In 1965 Velmer Gardner, one of the healing evangelists gathered around the Dallas-based evangelist and editor Gordon Lindsay (1906–73), was himself forced to leave the field because of ill health. The son of a Mansfield, Washington, alcoholic, Gardner was converted as a teenager following his father's conversion and accidental death. Called to the ministry, Gardner entered Northwest Bible Institute in Seattle, graduating in 1938. Shortly thereafter he married Wilma Estelle Burns and launched into itinerant evangelism and several brief pastorates. He was ordained by the Assemblies of God (AG) in 1942. The next year he entered the evangelistic field to stay. Inspired by Oral Roberts, Gardner stressed healing. By 1958 he was questioning the conservative stance taken by church officials toward the healing revival. Three years later he left the AG because of it.

Bibliography: V. J. Gardner, *My Life Story* (1954); D. Gossett, *Courageous Christians* (1968); D. E. Harrell, Jr., *All Things Are Possible* (1975); G. Lindsay, *Men Who Heard From Heaven* (1953).   C. E. Jones

GARLOCK, HENRY BRUCE (1897–1985). Missionary, administrator, and pastor. The eldest child of Edmund and Jessie Garlock, Henry Garlock attended Beulah Heights Bible Training School, North Bergen, New Jersey (1918–20). He first preached in the Pentecostal Holiness Association (F. S. Perkins), which supported him as a missionary to Liberia (1920–23), where he married Ruth E. Trotter (b. August 18, 1897) on June 28, 1921. Ordained in the Assemblies of God (AG) (1924), he served as missionary to Ghana (1932–36) and Malawi (1953–57) and as the first African field director (1943–53) for the AG. Garlock pastored in Atlantic City, New Jersey (1923–26), Colorado Springs, Colorado (1926–29), Wichita (1929–32), and Kansas City, Kansas (1936–43).

Bibliography: H. B. Garlock, *Before We Kill and Eat You* (1979); G. Lindsay, *Maria Woodworth-Etter, Her Life and Ministry* (1981); J. L. Sherrill, "Cannibal Talk," *God Ventures: True Accounts of God in the Lives of Men,* ed. I. B. Harrell (1970), 13–17; *Assemblies of God Ghana 1931–1981* (n.d.); Obituary, *PE* 3716 (July 28, 1985).   D. D. Bundy

GARR, ALFRED GOODRICH, SR. (1874–1944). Early Pentecostal missionary, evangelist, and pastor. Alfred Goodrich Garr was born in Danville, Kentucky, to Oliver and Josephine Garr. At eight years of age during a Baptist revival meeting, "A. G." Garr was baptized and joined the church. Intense spiritual questions remained until he found peace with God at age fifteen. Called to the ministry, he began preaching in the hills of Kentucky. Realizing the need for academic preparation, he enrolled at Center College, Danville, Kentucky, and later transferred to Asbury College in Wilmore, Kentucky. While there he met and married Lillian Anderson, the daughter of a Methodist bishop. Following their studies, the Garrs traveled to California to pastor the Burning Bush Mission in Los Angeles.

Hearing of the revival at the Azusa Street Mission, Garr attended and received the baptism in the Holy Spirit with speaking in tongues on June 16, 1906, thus becoming the first white pastor of any denomination to claim this experience there. His wife received the baptism shortly afterward. However, when his church board refused to accept his new experience and teaching, Garr resigned. A week later he felt called to India as a missionary. Announcing his intention to the Azusa participants, they immediately gave hundreds of dollars, enough to send a party of five. Garr and his family traveled to Chicago in July to meet with the Burning Bush leaders and then to Danville, Virginia, to prepare for passage to India.

Like other Azusa Street participants, the Garrs believed that tongues-speaking had equipped them to minister in (previously unlearned) languages abroad. In the words of historian Vinson Synan, "this was the outstanding attempt at carrying out Parham's teaching concerning the missionary use of tongues and it ended in failure" (1971, 111). Unlike some early Pentecostal missionaries, however, who returned home because of disillusionment with their inability to preach in foreign languages and the living conditions abroad, the Garrs persevered in their overseas ministry.

One of the first to be baptized in the Spirit at the Azusa Street Mission, A. G. Garr served as a Pentecostal missionary in India and Hong Kong, beginning in 1907.

Arriving in Calcutta in 1907, Garr preached at a convention of missionaries where many received the baptism in the Holy Spirit. He later ministered at Pandita Ramabai's Mukti Mission (near Poona), and also held services in Bombay and Colombo, Ceylon (Sri Lanka). Following an invitation to Hong Kong, the Garrs arrived there on October 9, 1907, and began conducting services in the Congregational Board Mission. While their ministry was quite effective, the Garrs suffered personal tragedy with the death of two daughters and an associate, Maria Gardener; they also faced other difficult circumstances. Ministry in Japan followed, but they resumed their work in Hong Kong on October 4, 1909. Several months later they took a year's furlough in the U.S. and returned to China on April 9, 1911. After a short stay, they departed for America in December 1911.

Following their return to the U.S., the Garrs traveled in evangelistic work and A. G. became well-known in Pentecostal circles for his faith-

healing ministry. Three years after the death of his wife in 1916 (a son, Alfred, Jr., was born to them in China), he married Hanna Erickson (1919).

Garr's ministry of itinerant evangelism continued until he conducted a revival in Charlotte, North Carolina, in 1930. Because of the tremendous response to his preaching, Garr settled there and established a church that was eventually housed in the old city auditorium; as a result, it became known as the Garr Auditorium. For many years this congregation was one of the best-known Pentecostal churches in the southeastern U.S. On January 12, 1940, the Garr School of Theology opened with Dr. Charles William Walkem as the dean; it closed in 1943, however, when many of its students entered the war effort. Following the death of Garr, his wife and son pastored the church.

Bibliography: R. P. Downing, "God Works in Mysterious Ways His Wonders to Perform" (n.d., typewritten); H. and A. Fritsch, eds., "Letters from Cora" (1987). B. Gann, ed., The Trailblazer—The History of Dr. A. G. Garr and the Garr Auditorium (n.d.); "Good News from Danville, Va.," AF (September 1906), 4; "In Calcutta, India," AF (April 1907), 1; E. M. Law, Pentecostal Mission Work in South China (c. 1916); "Pentecost in Danville, Va.," AF (October 1906), 2; V. Synan, The Holiness-Pentecostal Movement in the United States (1971);   G. B. McGee

GARR MEMORIAL CHURCH A prominent urban Pentecostal church in Charlotte, North Carolina. A. G. Garr, founder of the church, had a fruitful ministry before going to Charlotte in 1930. He was pastor of a Holiness mission in Los Angeles in 1906 and was one of the first persons to receive the baptism of the Holy Spirit at the Azusa Street Mission.

Garr went in 1907 to India, expecting God to enable him to speak the language of the people, which was an early belief of how God would exercise the gift of tongues. The venture failed, however, and Garr made use of an interpreter. In 1908 he and his wife went as missionaries to Hong Kong, where they studied the Chinese language and established a strong mission station. Many missionaries who passed through Hong Kong and visited the Garr's mission continued to spread the Pentecostal message throughout the Orient.

In the spring and summer of 1930 A. G. Garr and his wife, Hanna, conducted a tent revival in Charlotte, North Carolina, that attracted city-wide attention. Garr remained in the city and in 1931 established an independent church. The church purchased and rebuilt the city auditorium as its sanctuary. It was first named Garr Auditorium and is now the Garr Memorial Church.

Garr, his wife, and son, Alfred, were partners in the ministry from the beginning. Hanna Garr began a daily radio broadcast, "Morning Thought," in 1937 and continued it for forty-eight years. When Garr died in 1944, she became pastor of the church, a post she held for twenty-nine years. Alfred Garr, Jr., succeeded his mother as pastor in 1973 and led the church for fourteen years. He then became pastor emeritus and executive director of the church's Camp Lurecrest near Charlotte. He was succeeded as pastor by Karl D. Coke, Ph.D.

See also CAROLINA EVANGELISTIC ASSOCIATION.

Bibliography: Files of the Garr Memorial Church, Charlotte, North Carolina; "Garr Memorial Church Jubilee" (phonograph record of the church's music, with a historical review), 1980.   C. W. Conn

In 1910, at the age of 52, Alice Garrigus founded what became the Pentecostal Assemblies of Newfoundland.

GARRIGUS, ALICE BELLE (1858–1949). The founding mother of the Pentecostal Assemblies of Newfoundland. Garrigus went from the U.S. to St. Johns, Newfoundland, as a mature woman of fifty-two with a clear purpose: "to preach the full gospel—Jesus as Savior, Sanctifier, Baptizer, Healer and Coming King" (Janes, 1983, 2:137). Her full-gospel message always emphasized the subjective element of the faith but never at the expense of personal decorum or religious fanaticism. Garrigus was a leader strong enough to control any fanatics yet sufficiently pliable to yield to the Spirit's work.

Garrigus began her labors in a simple, unpretentious setting, Bethesda Mission, which grew under her leadership to become a denomination, Bethesda Pentecostal Assemblies, later known as the Pentecostal Assemblies of Newfoundland. The church serves in both Newfoundland and Labrador, as well as in numerous mission stations around the world.

Bibliography: B. K. Janes, *The Lady Who Came,* 2 vols. (1982–83).   J. A. Hewett

GAUSE, RUFUS HOLLIS (1925–). A contemporary theologian and scholar, and a professor at the Church of God (CG, Cleveland, Tenn.) School of Theology. Gause attended Emmanuel College (1944), Presbyterian College (B.A., 1945), and Columbia Theological Seminary (M.Div., 1949). He later earned a Ph.D. at Emory University (1975).

In 1947 Gause began his teaching career at Lee College, where he served in the religion department until 1972. From Lee he became the first dean and director of the CG School of Theology in 1975.

Gause was president of the Society for Pentecostal Studies (1971–72) and a member of the board. His published works include *Church of God Polity* (1973), *Living in the Spirit* (1980), *Revelation* (1984), and *The Preaching of Paul* (1985).

Bibliography: Archives of the Church of God (Cleveland, Tenn.).   C. W. Conn

GAY PENTECOSTALS See PENTECOSTAL COALITION FOR HUMAN RIGHTS; COMMUNITY GOSPEL FELLOWSHIP.

GEE, DONALD (1891–1966). Pastor, author, educator, conference speaker, editor, and ecumenist. Gee, son of a London sign painter (d. 1900), was converted (1905) in Finsbury Park Congregational Church (London) through the preaching of Seth Joshua, a Methodist influenced by the Welsh revival. With his mother, Gee joined a Baptist congregation (1912) and became a Pentecostal believer in March 1913. He continued his sign painter's occupation until forced to find alternative service on a farm to avoid imprisonment because of his conscientious objection to military service in World War I. In the countryside he led a small Pentecostal fellowship and after the war accepted appointment (1920–30) to a small chapel in Leigh, a suburb of Edinburgh. Congregational growth resulted in the building of Bonnington Toll Chapel. The events of this decade are narrated in *Bonnington Toll—and After: The Story of a First Pastorate* (1943, 1960). Gee's first involvement with the larger Pentecostal movement occurred during this period as he attended the International Pentecostal Conference in Amsterdam in 1921.

A competent musician, Gee was often invited to serve as pianist or organist for large gatherings, and he produced the first *Redemption Tidings Hymn Book* (1924). He began contributing articles to Pentecostal periodicals in 1924.

In 1928 Gee accepted an invitation to serve as a Bible teacher in Australia and New Zealand, where he spent seven months. On the way he wrote his first book, *Concerning Spiritual Gifts* (1928). Until World War II restricted his freedom to travel, Gee lectured all over the world. He taught in the Danzig Bible School and Filadelfia Bible School (Stockholm) as well as in North American camp meetings. His travel on five continents provided data for his history of Pentecostalism, *Upon All Flesh* (1935), in which he argued that the Pentecostal revival is a diverse world-wide movement transcending national interest and united by a shared experience. As a teacher he was renowned for his judicious counsel and the thoughtful care with which he avoided extreme positions on issues of contention within the Pentecostal movement. This tendency led to his being known as the "Apostle of Balance," a reputation that resulted in his being elected vice-chairman of the British Assemblies of God (AG) (1934–44) and chairman (1945–48).

A leader in the Pentecostal movement, Donald Gee preached in many countries throughout the world and wrote several books on the baptism in the Spirit and spiritual gifts.

Gee's experiences throughout the world led him to think in terms of Pentecostal ecumenism and resulted in the European Pentecostal Conference at Stockholm (1939). The next conference was organized by Gee and David du Plessis in Zurich (1947). At this conference Gee was appointed editor of *Pentecost* (1947–66), in which he would publish some of his most important and provocative essays. Some of these were in response to harsh criticism by Pentecostals for his cooperation with the 1954 Billy Graham Evangelistic Campaign in London and of his attending the meeting of the World Council of Churches' Faith and Order Commission in St. Andrews, Scotland (1960). Gee was invited to be an observer at the New Dehli Assembly of the World Council of Churches (1961), but because of pressure organized by American AG general superintendent Thomas Zimmerman at the Jerusalem Pentecostal World Conference, Gee was forced to decline the invitation. However, despite growing concern in his own church and in the American AG, he established and maintained contact with the leaders of the early charismatic renewal in Europe and North America.

In 1951, at age sixty, Gee embarked on a career as principal of the newly reorganized Bible school of the British AG at Kenley, Surrey, near London. It was a formidable task. Funds were scarce, and critics of Bible school training within the AG were vocal. This context, while restricting Gee's freedom to travel, allowed him time for his editorial responsibilities, for extensive reading and reflection as well as productive years of writing.

In 1964 Gee was relieved of his position as principal. His last two years were spent with editorial work, teaching at International Bible Training Institute, and occasional lecturing. He died of heart failure on July 20, 1966, in London.

A self-educated man, Gee became a prolific author, writing more than thirty books. The number of periodical articles is formidable. From 1924 he contributed more than five hundred articles to *Redemption Tidings* alone (sometimes under the pen name "Circumspectus"). His articles appeared in nearly every Pentecostal periodical around the world. Books and articles, many of which were revised and republished by Gee himself, have been translated into many languages and continue to be reprinted. His complete bibliography has not been established.

Bibliography: J. Carter, *Donald Gee: Pentecostal Statesman* (1975); D. Gee, *After Pentecost* (1945); idem, *All With One Accord* (1961, reprinted as *Toward Pentecostal Unity* [n.d.]); idem, *Concerning Shepherds and Sheepfolds, A Series of Studies Dealing With Pastors and Assemblies* (1930, reprint 1952); idem, *Concerning Spiritual Gifts* (1928, reprint 1937, rev. ed. 1972); idem, *The Fruit of the Spirit, A Pentecostal Study* (n.d.); idem, *Fruitful or Barren?* (1961); idem, *The Glory of the Assemblies of God* (n.d.); idem, *God's Grace and Power for Today, The Practical Experience of Being Filled with the Holy Ghost* (1936, reprint 1972); idem, *God's Great Gift, Seven Talks Together About the Holy Spirit* (n.d., reprint 1972); idem, *Keeping in Touch, Studies in Walking in the Spirit* (1951); idem, *Messages Preached at the Fifth Triennial Pentecostal World Conference . . . ,* ed. D. Gee (n.d.); idem, *The Ministry Gifts of Christ* (n.d.); idem, *The Missionary Who Stayed at Home* (n.d.); idem, *Pentecost* (1932); idem, *The Pentecostal Movement, A Short History and an Interpretation for British Readers* (1941); idem, *The Pentecostal Movement, Including the Story of the War Years (1940–1947)* (1949); idem, *Proverbs for Pentecost* (1936); idem, *Spiritual Gifts in the Work of the Ministry Today* (1963); idem, *Studies in Guidance* (1936, rev. ed. 1941); idem, *Temptations of the Spirit-Filled Christ* (1966); idem, *These Men I Knew, Personal Memories of Our Pioneers* (1980); idem, *"This is the Will of God . . . ," The Bible and Sexual Problems* (1940); idem, *"To the Uttermost Part," The Missionary Results of the Pentecostal Movement in the British Isles* (1932); idem, *Trophimus I Left Sick: Our Problems of Divine Healing* (1952); idem, *Why Pentecost?* (1944); idem, *Wind and Flame, Incorporating the Former Book, The Pentecostal Movement, With Additional Chapters* (1967); idem, *World Pentecostal Conference, 1952 . . . ,* comp. and ed. H. W. Greenway, D. Gee, I. MacPherson (1952); W. J. Hollenweger, "The Pentecostal Movement and the World Council of Churches," *Ecumenical Review* 18 (1966): 310–20; idem, *Enthusiastisches Christentum. Die Pfingstbewegung in Geschichte und Gegenwart* (1969), 191–200; English. ed., *The Pentecostals* (1972), 206–17; Spanish ed., *El Pentecostalismo, Historia y Doctrinas* (1976), 207–17; J. L. McNamee, "The Role of the Spirit in Pentecostalism: A Comparative Study," diss., Tübingen, 1974; A. Missen, *The Sound of a Going: The Story of the Assemblies of God* (1973); R. M. Ross, "Donald Gee: In Search of a

Church, A Sectarian in Transition," Th.D. thesis, Knox College, Toronto (1974); idem, "Donald Gee, Sectarian in Search of a Church," *Evangelical Quarterly* 50 (1978): 94–103.   D. D. Bundy

GELPI, DONALD L. (1934–). Catholic charismatic theologian. Gelpi became a Jesuit as a young man and was ordained as a priest in 1964, early specializing in theology. Spiritual concerns were prominent in his first publications, e.g., *Functional Asceticism: A Guideline for American Religious* (1966) and *Discerning the Spirit: Foundations and Futures of Religious Life* (1970). Baptized in the Spirit in 1969, Gelpi directed his mind to God's work in Pentecostal blessing, writing *Pentecostalism: A Theological Viewpoint* (1971), the first systematic study of charismatic renewal by a Catholic theologian, and *Pentecostal Piety* (1972). Gelpi's later writings manifest a concern to develop a more indigenous American theology with a sound philosophical basis rooted in American experience and culture. Works reflecting his charismatic experience as well as these concerns include *Charism Sacrament: A Theology of Christian Conversion* (1976); *Experiencing God: A Theology of Human Emergence* (1978); *The Divine Mother: A Trinitarian Theology of the Holy Spirit* (1984). Gelpi is currently professor of historical and systematic theology at the Jesuit School of Theology, Berkeley, California.   P. D. Hocken

GENERAL ASSEMBLY OF THE APOSTOLIC ASSEMBLIES See UNITED PENTECOSTAL CHURCH, INTERNATIONAL.

GERMAN CHARISMATICS See CHARISMATIC MOVEMENT.

GERMAN PENTECOSTALS See EUROPEAN PENTECOSTALISM.

GIBSON, CHRISTINE AMELIA (1879–1955). Educator and pastor. A champion of the faith principle, Christine A. Gibson headed the Zion Bible Institute, East Providence, Rhode Island, during the first thirty-one years of its existence. Born in British Guiana, she was orphaned as a small child and converted at age twenty-one. In 1905 a series of circumstances brought her to the U.S. and to a Holiness faith home in East Providence. Soon after she became pastor of the church connected with the home, she received the Pentecostal baptism while on a visit to Rochester, New York. In 1910 she married Rueben A. Gibson (d. 1924), who afterward joined her in the work in East Providence. The faith principle, the keystone in the operation of both church and home, was enshrined also in the administration of the worker training school Gibson opened the year after her husband's death. Although she died in 1955, the school continued for decades to rely on prayer rather than on advance pledges or fees. In other ways, such as the requirement that female students wear uniforms, Zion continued traditions set by its founder and other Pentecostal pioneers.

Bibliography: Zion Bible Institute, *Zionian* (1974), 29–30, 36–87.   C. E. Jones

GIFT OF DISCERNMENT OF SPIRITS See DISCERNMENT OF SPIRITS, GIFT OF.

GIFT OF FAITH See FAITH, GIFT OF.

GIFT OF HEALING See HEALING, GIFT OF.

GIFT OF INTERPRETATION See INTERPRETATION, GIFT OF.

GIFT OF KNOWLEDGE See KNOWLEDGE, WORD OF.

GIFT OF MIRACLES See MIRACLES, GIFT OF.

GIFT OF PROPHECY See PROPHECY, GIFT OF.

GIFT OF TONGUES See GLOSSOLALIA.

GIFT OF WISDOM See WISDOM, WORD OF.

GIFTS OF THE SPIRIT The Holy Spirit is called a "gift" three times in the Book of Acts (2:38, 10:45, 11:17), and once specifically "the gift of God" (Acts 8:20; cf. also John 4:10). Yet this terminology (Greek: *dōrea, dōron, doma, dōrema*) is *not* used in the NT to refer to the varied powers and activities of those who have received the Spirit. "Gifts" in the NT are normally either sacrifices (Matt. 5:23–24; 8:4; 15:5; 23:18–19; Luke 21:1, 4; Heb. 5:1; 8:3–4; 9:9; 11:4) or material gifts of some kind (e.g., Matt. 2:11; 7:11; Mark 7:11; Luke 11:13; Phil. 4:17; Rev. 11:10), while the singular "gift" in a more profound sense refers to salvation, righteousness, or eternal life, or even to Jesus Christ himself (see, e.g., Rom. 5:15–17; 2 Cor. 9:15; Eph. 2:8; 3:7; 4:7; Heb. 6:4; James 1:17). Only in Ephesians 4:8 are "gifts" (Greek: *domata*) viewed in relation to the ministries of the church, and even here the choice of words is not Paul's own, for he is quoting from Psalm 68:18. The reference is not to a divinely given power to perform these ministries, but to the persons who perform them: apostles, prophets, evangelists, and teachers.

The more characteristic NT expressions for what Christians today call "gifts of the Spirit" are "spiritual things" (Greek: *pneumatika*), "graces" or "favors" (*charismata*), and "showings" or "manifestations" (*phanerōseis*). Two other terms used for similar phenomena are "workings" (*energēmata*), and "ministries" (*diakoniai*). All of these are ways of getting at what could be called the plurality of the Holy Spirit. The Spirit of God is one according to both Jews and Christians, just as God is one, yet because the Spirit's activity in the ancient church was seen as often in relation to individuals as to groups, the diversity or plurality of the Spirit's power and presence was constantly in evidence. Already in the Hebrew Scriptures the Spirit of God could be viewed as plural when an author wanted to dramatize a number of different virtues, as in relation to the expected Messiah: "And the Spirit of the Lord shall rest upon him— the spirit of wisdom and understanding, the spirit of counsel and might, the spirit of knowledge and the fear of the LORD " (Isa. 11:2; cf. 1 Peter 4:14).

Even the word "spirit" itself was occasionally used in the plural, not only of evil spirits (as in the Gospels or in 1 Peter 3:19), but also of the varied activities of the Holy Spirit of God. John, for example, sent greetings to the seven churches of Asia from God and "from the seven spirits who are before his throne" (Rev. 1:4; cf. 5:6). The author of 1 John warns his readers not to

> believe every spirit, but test the spirits whether they are of God; for many false prophets have gone out into the world. By this you know the Spirit of God: every spirit which confesses that Jesus Christ has come in the flesh is of God, and every spirit which does not confess that Jesus Christ has come in the flesh is not of God. This is the spirit of the antichrist (1 John 4:1–3).

According to this writer, both the "spirit of truth" and the "spirit of error" (4:6) can be viewed as either singular or plural.

The best known statement of the Apostle Paul on the subject of "spiritual gifts" (1 Cor. 12:1–11) centers on this issue of unity versus plurality. "There are different gifts *[charismata],* Paul writes, "but the same Spirit; and there are different ministries *[diakoniai]* but the same Lord; and there are different workings *[energēmata],* but the same God who works them all in everyone" (1 Cor. 12:5–6). The plurality or diversity in the Corinthian congregation is clear for anyone to see. What Paul wants to do is affirm unity in the face of this diversity. From a list of specific examples (vv. 7–11) he concludes, "All these are the work of one and the same Spirit who distributes to each differently as God decides." The varied "workings" of the Spirit of God to which Paul appeals here are "a word of wisdom," "a word of knowledge" (v. 8), "faith," "gifts of healings" (v. 9), "workings of miracles," "prophecy," "discernment of spirits," "various tongues," and "interpretation of tongues" (v. 10). There is no evidence that the list is intended to be systematic or exhaustive. Some items fall into pairs, such as "tongues" and "interpretation of tongues," "prophecy" and "discernment of spirits," "word of wisdom" and "word of knowledge," and (possibly) "gifts of healing" and "workings of miracles." Yet a "prophecy" and a "word of wisdom" or "word of knowledge" seem to overlap, while "faith" shows no particular relationship to any other item in the list. Most of the gifts are gifts of *speech,* yet at least two (healings and miracles) are gifts of *action* (cf. 1 Peter 4:11: "If anyone speaks, let it be as words coming from God; if anyone ministers, let it be out of the strength God provides"). If this is Paul's organizing principle, it is again difficult to know how "faith" is to be classified. Is it a gift of speech or a gift of action?

Paul introduces the metaphor of the human body in 1 Corinthians 12:12. He crowns his emphasis on unity with the conclusion that "by *one* Spirit we were all baptized into one body—whether Jews or Greeks, whether slaves or free—and we were all given *one* Spirit to drink" (v. 13). Far from being in tension, unity and diversity reinforce each other in Paul's argument. Only the recognition of the Spirit's unity can legitimize for him the Spirit's diverse expressions. Paul

introduces a kind of fable in verses 14–26, in which he imagines different parts of the human body each talking about its relationship to other parts or to the body as a whole (e.g., "Because I am not a hand, I do not belong to the body," v. 15; "I have no need of you," v. 21). The application comes in verses 27–30, where Paul again speaks explicitly of *charismata,* or "gifts": "first apostles, second prophets, third teachers, then miracles, then gifts of healings, doing helpful deeds, carrying out responsibilities, various kinds of tongues" (v. 28). He then asks rhetorically, "Are all apostles? Are all prophets? Are all teachers? Do all [work] miracles? Do all have gifts of healing? Do all speak in tongues? Do all interpret?" (vv. 29–30). The rhetorical questions repeat in part the immediately preceding list in verse 28, which in turn invites comparison with Paul's earlier list in verses 7–11.

The most conspicuous difference between the lists of spiritual gifts in 1 Corinthians 12:7–11 and in 12:28–30 is that the latter begins with three items that refer not to powers or activities but to persons of status in the ancient church: apostles, prophets, and teachers (cf. Eph. 4:11; also 2:20; 3:5). These are set off from what follows by being numbered from one to three, giving the impression that Paul has deliberately combined two types of lists, one applicable to the Christian church generally and one adapted specifically to a local congregation (in this instance Corinth). Of the six remaining items in verses 28–30, four coincide with the list in verses 7–11: "miracles" and "gifts of healings," "tongues" and the "interpretation of tongues." The only new items introduced are references to "doing helpful deeds" (Gk: *antilēmpseis)* and "carrying out responsibilities" *(kybernēseis).* These are also the only two items from verse 28 that are not picked up in verses 29–30. Paul asks, "Are all apostles? Are all prophets? Are all teachers? Do all work miracles? Do all have gifts of healings? Do all speak in tongues? Do all interpret?" The questions he does *not* ask are, "Do all do helpful deeds?" and "Do all carry out their responsibilities?"

The reason for the omission is not hard to find. The doing of helpful deeds and the carrying out of routine responsibilities in the congregation were not the sort of "gifts" that made others in the congregation envious. They are clearly the least "charismatic" of all the gifts in 1 Corinthians 12 (with the possible exception of "faith" in v. 9), and may not have even been counted among the "spiritual gifts" by anyone other than Paul. Those who contributed to the work of the congregation by "doing helpful deeds" and "carrying out responsibilities" were probably the ones most tempted to say, "Because I am not a hand [or an eye], I do not belong to the body" (i.e., because I do not prophesy or work miracles or speak in tongues, I do not really count in the life of the congregation).

Paul's purpose in 1 Corinthians 12 is not to list all the varied gifts of the Spirit, much less rank them, but to attribute them all to the same Holy Spirit, and to make sure that simple and humble acts of service were not overlooked in the congregation's zeal for miracles and inspired speech.

This is probably the point of his rather obscure reference in verses 22–24 to the "less honorable" or "unpresentable" parts of the human body which are "indispensable," and which are consequently treated with "special honor" or "special modesty." To introduce a modern analogy, the "helpers" and "servers" in the congregation were like the coaching staff of a talented basketball team. Though they lack the ability to run, jump, or dunk the ball like their players, their team can hardly survive without them. Paul appears to be making a case for the apparently "ungifted" helpers and even leaders in the congregation, that their gifts too might be recognized and appreciated as the work of the Spirit. Near the end of 1 Corinthians, Paul refers explicitly to "the household of Stephanas . . . the first converts in Achaia" as those who "devoted themselves to the service of the saints. I urge you, brothers and sisters, to submit to such as these, and to everyone who joins in the work and keeps at it" (1 Cor. 16:15–16; cf. 1 Thess. 5:12–13). It is likely that he has in mind people of this sort already in chapter 12 and wants it clearly understood that their labors too are gifts of the Spirit. This emphasis also sets the stage for Paul's celebration of love in chapter 13. If love is the motivation of those who help and those who serve in the congregation without attracting attention to themselves, it must govern as well the exercise of all the spiritual gifts. Then, without jealousy or arrogance, the gifts of the Spirit will be used to unify and build up the congregation, not to divide or destroy it.

At the same time, Paul urges his readers to "eagerly desire the greater gifts" (12:31). He has carefully avoided specifying what the "greater gifts" are, yet in chapter 14 he pointedly ranks two of them: "Pursue love, and eagerly desire the spiritual gifts, but especially that you may prophesy" (14:1). Prophecy is "greater" than speaking in tongues because it communicates meaning and therefore has the possibility of "building up" the congregation. Tongues speaking also has this possibility, but only if it is accompanied by interpretation; otherwise it divides the hearer from the speaker. Paul can say, "I thank God that I speak in tongues more than all of you," yet add almost in the same breath, "But in the congregation I would rather speak five intelligible words to instruct others than ten thousand words in a tongue" (14:18–19).

Clearly, Paul was a "charismatic," yet the thrust of his argument in 1 Corinthians is to channel the charismatic experiences of his readers in such a way as to make them better servants to each other in the body of Christ. In Romans 12 he accents the gifts of helping and serving even more than in 1 Corinthians, and makes no mention of tongues speaking, healing, or miracles:

We have gifts [charismata] that differ according to the grace given us: if it is prophecy, let it be in proportion to our faith; if it is service, let it be in serving; for the teacher, let it be in teaching; for the preacher, in preaching; let the one who contributes money do so generously; let the one who gives leadership do so faithful-

ly; let the one who shows mercy do so cheerfully (Rom. 12:6–8).

Then he adds, in the spirit of 1 Corinthians 13,

Let love be genuine; hate what is evil; cling to what is good. Show each other warm brotherly affection. Honor one another above yourselves. Don't waver in your zeal, be fervent in the Spirit, serve the Lord. Be joyful in your hope, patient in affliction, constant in prayer. Contribute to the needs of the saints. Practice hospitality. (Rom. 12:9–13.)

If there is one conclusion that emerges from this survey, it is that "spiritual gifts" are defined very broadly in the NT, encompassing both the "natural" and the "supernatural," both the visible miraculous signs that gave evidence of the Spirit's presence at Pentecost and the deeds of love, kindness, and service that were part of the believer's obligation already in the OT and Judaism. The Holy Spirit was indeed plural as well as singular to the earliest Christians, and the wisest among them resisted all efforts to limit the Spirit's gifts to one kind of activity or one set of phenomena. Though the Pentecostal and charismatic movements have strongly emphasized the gifts of tongues and prophecy in particular, they have also called the attention of the Christian church to the crucial importance of "gifts of the Spirit" generally, and in so doing have served as an agent of renewal in the last half century.

See also DISCERNMENT OF SPIRITS, GIFT OF; FAITH, GIFT OF; GLOSSALALIA; HEALING, GIFT OF; INTERPRETATION, GIFT OF; KNOWLEDGE, WORD OF; MIRACLES, GIFT OF; PROPHECY, GIFT OF; WISDOM, WORD OF; PAULINE LITERATURE.

Bibliography: C. K. Barrett, *A Commentary on the First Epistle to the Corinthians* (reprint, 1988); D. Bennett, "The Gifts of the Holy Spirit," in *The Charismatic Movement*, ed. M. Hamilton (1975); A. Bittlinger, *Gifts and Graces* (1967); D. Bridge and D. Phypers, *Spiritual Gifts and the Church* (1973); F. D. Bruner, *A Theology of the Holy Spirit* (1970); H. Conzelmann, *1 Corinthians* (1975); J. D. G. Dunn, *Baptism in the Holy Spirit* (1970); idem, *Jesus and the Spirit* (1975); E. E. Ellis, *Prophecy and Hermeneutic in Early Christianity* (1978); G. D. Fee, *The First Epistle to the Corinthians* (1987); idem, "Tongues—Least of the Gifts? Some Exegetical Observations on 1 Corinthians 12–14," *Pneuma* 2 (1980): 3–14; R. Y. K. Fung, "Ministry, Community and Spiritual Gifts (in Pauline Theology)," *EQ* 56 (January 1984): 3–20; J. Koenig, *Charismata: God's Gift for God's People* (178); R. P. Martin, *The Spirit and the Congregation: Studies in 1 Corinthians 12–15* (1978); P. D. Opsahl, ed., *The Holy Spirit in the Life of the Church* (1978); S. Smalley, "Spiritual Gifts and 1 Corinthians 12–16," *JBL* 88 (1968): 427–33.

J. R. Michaels

GIMENEZ, JOHN AND ANNE (NETHERY) (1931–) (1932–).

Pastor and copastor of Rock Church, Virginia Beach, Virginia. Born in New York City, John dropped out of school after the eighth grade and was in and out of reform school and prison from age eleven until age thirty-one when he was converted. He traveled in ministry with converted drug addicts.

Anne was born in Houston, Texas, and at age fourteen moved with her parents to Corpus Christi, Texas. She was converted in a T. L.

Pastors of the Rock Church, Virginia Beach, Virginia, John and Anne Gimenez.

Osborn tent crusade in 1949. At age thirty she went into full-time evangelistic ministry.

John and Anne were married in 1967 and a year later established Rock Church. Attendance reached nearly five thousand by 1987. The couple founded Rock Christian Network and produce "Rock Alive," a daily television ministry. John was the national chairman of Washington for Jesus rallies in 1980 and 1987 and founder of the National Organization for the Advancement of Hispanics. Anne founded International Women in Leadership and is the author of *Emerging Women* (n.d.).

Bibliography: E. C. Martin, "Anne Gimenez: Co-Pastoring Beside Her Beloved," *Ministries* (Winter 1985–86), 59–62.   S. Strang

GLAD TIDINGS MISSIONARY SOCIETY
A Latter Rain organization growing out of Glad Tidings Temple, Vancouver, British Columbia. At one time six churches in Canada and Washington State were associated with the Vancouver congregation, with approximately four thousand in membership. This organization was an early participant in the New Order of the Latter Rain and was formed in 1950. Early teachings of the group can be found in the *Pastor's Pen*, by Reg Layzell and compiled by B. M. Gaglardi, dealing with the Latter Rain and God's plan and method—restoration, the laying on of hands, and an eyewitness account of the Latter Rain meetings in North Battleford, Saskatchewan, in 1948.

Bibliography: C. Jones, *Guide to the Pentecostal Movement* (1983); R. Layzell, *Pastor's Pen* (1965).
W. E. Warner

GLAD TIDINGS TABERNACLE Glad Tidings Tabernacle was for many years one of the leading Pentecostal congregations in the Northeast. Affiliated with the Assemblies of God (AG), the congregation was established in 1907 by Marie Burgess, a Christian worker with varied home missions experience who accepted Pentecostalism in Zion City, Illinois, in October 1906. Two months later she complied with Parham's wish that she bring the Pentecostal message to New York.

Burgess began services in midtown Manhattan in January and met with immediate response, especially from participants in the Christian and Missionary Alliance. These men and women provided a strong nucleus for the growing congregation, which dated its origins to the opening of Burgess's mission on May 5, 1907. In 1909 Burgess married Robert Brown, an Irish immigrant who was a dedicated Wesleyan Methodist lay preacher before he embraced Pentecostal views at Burgess's mission.

The growing congregation moved to bigger facilities, enlarged those, and finally purchased a commodious church building on 33rd Street in Manhattan. The Browns shared a strong missionary vision, and through the World War II era their congregation usually led all AG congregations in missionary giving. The congregation commissioned many workers from its own numbers. A weekly radio broadcast carried the Sunday afternoon services across the metropolitan area. Through the 1940s Glad Tidings Tabernacle functioned as a center for New York area Pentecostals.

Robert Brown exerted considerable influence as a denominational presbyter and district leader. Stubborn and opinionated, he was nonetheless revered and loved. After his death in 1948 his wife continued to give leadership to the congregation, assisted by her nephew, R. Stanley Berg. By that time changing urban conditions had influenced the size and character of the congregation. When Marie Brown died in 1970, she had served the church for sixty-three years.

Bibliography: G. P. Gardiner and M. E. Brown, *The Origin of Glad Tidings Tabernacle* (1955).
E. L. Blumhofer

TONGUES, GIFT OF See GLOSSOLALIA.

TONGUES, SPEAKING IN See GLOSSOLALIA.

GLOSSOLALIA Usually, but not exclusively, the religious phenomenon of making sounds that constitute, or resemble, a language not known to the speaker. It is often accompanied by an excited religious psychological state, and in the Pentecostal and charismatic movements it is widely and distinctively (but not universally) viewed as the certifying consequence of the baptism in the Holy Spirit.
    I. Terminology
    II. Non-Christian Varieties
    III. Biblical Data
    IV. Theological Nuances
    V. Historical Survey
    VI. Varied Explanations

VII. Evaluation

I. Terminology. Not used in English before 1879, the technical term *glossolalia* derives from *glōssais lalein*, a Greek phrase used in the NT meaning literally "to speak in [or "with" or "by"] tongues." Its inclusion in the list of spiritual gifts (*charismata*) given in 1 Corinthians 12:8–10 accounts for the popular equivalent expression "the gift of tongues," though that precise phrase nowhere occurs in Scripture. A French scholar coined the term *xenoglossia* (or *xenoglossy:* French *xenoglossia*) in 1905 to describe a spiritualist medium who, in trance, wrote in modern Greek though she had no acquaintance with that language. *Xenographia*, it was later argued, would be more accurate. *Xenolalia*, a more frequent synonym of *xenoglossia*, describes glossolalia when the language spoken is identifiable as one among the over three thousand known to occur on the globe. Two other terms describe *xenoglossia*: the longer *xenoglossolalia* and *heteroglossolalia* ("speaking in other languages"). *Glossographia* refers to automatic writing that is inspired from a higher power but results in no known language. In recent times, scholars have coined still other words for related phenomena: *propheteialalia*, the inspired vernacular speech of the prophet; *akolalia* (perhaps better *akuolalia*), the perceived hearing of another language even when one is not spoken; *ermeneglossia*, a technical term for interpretation of tongues; *echolalia*, the agitated repetition of the words of another; *idiolect*, a glossolalic dialect peculiar to an individual. "Prayer language" as a synonym for glossolalic prayer (cf. 1 Cor. 14:14) appears to be of recent origin, made popular by Pentecostal and charismatic televangelists and talk-show hosts. Fortunately a term used late in the second century by Tatian, an early Christian apologist, never got picked up in the modern European languages; he used *glossomania* to refer to the insane speech of the Greek philosophers against whom he wrote (*Oration, 3*). Although the OT contains records of ecstatic religious speech, there is no Hebrew equivalent for the term *glossolalia* nor any use of the expression *glōssais lalein* in the Septuagint (the Greek translation of the OT in common use during NT times). The singular *glōssa lalein* does appear in the Septuagint, but not in reference to glossolalia.

II. Non-Christian varieties. Whatever its origin, glossolalia is a human phenomenon, not limited to Christianity nor even to religious behavior among humankind. *Dramatic glossolalia* occurs in television situation comedies when actors spontaneously initiate a language, then put the punch line in the vernacular. No external source for such speech, neither divine nor devilish, need be imagined beyond the stage talents of the speakers. *Spiritualistic glossolalia* and related phenomena among spiritual mediums were among the first studied by psychologists near the beginning of the twentieth century. Pentecostals have attributed a satanic origin to such cases, even though proof lies outside scientific methods of sociopsychological inquiry. *Pathological glossolalia* is known to medicine and psychiatry, the result of such causes as organic neurological damage, effects of drugs, or psychotic disorders. Schizo-phrenic disorders have furnished examples of glossolalia. Research conducted by social scientists (Malony/Lovekin, 1985) over the past two decades have corrected earlier views that all glossolalia, even and especially its Christian varieties, arose from mental illness or social and economic deprivation.

More relevant to Christian glossolalia are clearly reported cases of *pagan glossolalia*, both ancient and modern. These have varied in the degree of religiousness involved—some more or less culturally routine, others evincing marks of singular prophetic distinctiveness.

Among ancient parallels, the Delphic Oracle (Parke, 1956) is best known. Located at the city of Delphi less than fifty air miles across the Corinthian Gulf to the northwest of Corinth, the Delphic Oracle flourished in the high classical period of Greek culture (the fifth century B.C., Nehemiah's time in Israel), but its popularity had declined by NT times. Private citizens or public officials consulted the oracle in order to acquire, as they believed, divine guidance regarding particular issues like marriage decisions, business ventures, and battle strategies. An inquirer would first undergo purification rites and present sacrificial offerings. Then the inquirer would be brought into the presence of a young woman, a priestess of Apollo said to possess a "pythonic spirit" (named for the serpent said to have been slain by Apollo: such a priestess is mentioned in Acts 16:16). A male prophet of the temple received the question of the inquirer. The young priestess fell into a state of frenzied ecstasy and spoke out words that were unrecognizable. The attending priest supposedly translated these into understandable Greek of the period and presented the oracular response to the seeker of the will of the gods. The result, though often ambiguous, was taken to strengthen the intent or preference of the inquirer who was thus led to believe the action taken reflected the divine will.

Scholars do not agree regarding what produced the ecstatic state. Researchers have variously proposed a narcotic effect from chewing leaves of a nearby tree or use of a sacred drink. Now discounted is an earlier theory of intoxicating gases that escaped from a cleft in the earth at that vicinity. Some suggest a demonic spirit. Whatever the cause, the Delphic ecstatic speech formed, not only a parallel to, but also a precedent for, the glossolalia at Corinth. It may be that the popularity of speaking in tongues at Corinth in part was fueled by a misguided Christian effort to match the speech of surrounding pagan deities.

An important study by anthropologist L. Carlyle May (1956) that predates the rise of the charismatic movement shows the widespread occurrence of *contemporary pagan, or non-Christian, glossolalia* among twentieth-century cultures. Using a taxonomy of glossolalia that ranges from mumbles and grunts through esoteric priestly languages and imitations of animal speech to widely related instances of xenolalia, May shows that cases outside Christian influence have been reported in Malaysia, Indonesia, Siberia, Arctic regions, China, Japan, Korea, Arabia, and Burma, among other places. He found that it was used sparingly among American Indians but was widespread in African tribal religions. He concludes that glossolalia on the whole occurs infrequently and has not been reported to appear in whole tribal groups except where affected by Christianity. More often it produces religious leaders rather than followers, but it is by no means a necessary feature even of ecstatic religious leaders.

Reports of such cultural, pathological, and dramatic cases of glossolalia are descriptive: it does not lie within the methods of social science or historical research to conclude that any given instance of glossolalia, Christian or non-Christian, may have a divine (or devilish) origin. What exists—phenomena that appear—can be described by all observers. The observer, from his or her own world view, determines what he or she believes is the spirit—or Spirit—that impels the glossolalist.

III. Biblical Data. If sheer quantity of text is the measure, more is said in Scripture about glossolalia than about the Virgin Birth or the ordination of women. Roy Harrisville (1974) counts thirty-five references to the phenomenon in Mark, Acts, and 1 Corinthians—twenty-eight of them in 1 Corinthians, twenty-three of which are in chapter 14. These texts chronologically locate glossolalia from just prior to the ascension of Jesus and the first Christian Pentecost around A.D. 30, through the middle 50s at Corinth in Greece, to Paul's mission in Ephesus in Asia Minor around A.D. 60. The phenomenon therefore, as reported in NT records, spanned three decades, flourished in both Jewish (Jerusalem) and Gentile (Corinth) centers, and appeared in widely separated parts of the Mediterranean—Corinth is nearly 1,500 air miles from Jerusalem—in places that marked the eastern and western limits of Paul's missionary enterprise. If glossolalia appears with surprising infrequency over the centuries in the life of the church, that does not rise from a lack of biblical accounts of its origin.

The most frequent phrase, which appears in Mark, Acts, and 1 Corinthians puts "tongues" in the plural glōssais lalein. "In tongues" (or "with tongues") is the appropriate translation whether or not the preposition en appears. The singular, "to speak in a tongue," occasionally occurs, but only in 1 Corinthians 14:2, 4, 13, 27 (where, in the KJV, "unknown" is italicized to show there is no comparable Greek word underlying the English adjective). There are "new" tongues (Mark 16:17), "tongues of men and of angels" (1 Cor. 13:1), and "other tongues" (Acts 2:4). Besides speaking in tongues, one may also "pray" in tongues (1 Cor. 14:14). The parallel structure of 1 Corinthians 14:14–16 suggests that to "sing in the Spirit" and to "bless in the Spirit" also are glossolalic acts. One may even "have" (1 Cor. 14:26) a tongue. There are "kinds [species, varieties] of tongues" (1 Cor. 12:10, 28).

A large consensus among biblical scholars concludes that Mark's Gospel ended at Mark 16:8. Among several alternative endings that appear in copies of NT manuscripts, Mark 16:9–20 seems to have been added to the original Gospel in the late second century. The textual

history is complicated and conclusive proof is impossible. Accepted theories of the origins of the canonical Gospels make it clear that sayings of Jesus and stories about him circulated orally for decades before they were ever gathered into written Gospels (cf. Luke 1:1). An example appears in Acts 20:35: "Remembering the words of the Lord Jesus, how he said, 'It is more blessed to give than to receive' "—a saying not found in any of the four Gospels. What is striking about the "Markan Appendix," as Mark 16:9–20 is called, is this: of all the sayings and stories of Jesus that were still circulating in the second century, the one that got attached to a canonical Gospel distinctly reflected charismatic interests, including speaking "in new tongues." This suggests that interest in glossolalia clearly persisted into the second century.

Three clear occurrences of glossolalia, besides at least two other strong allusions, appear in the Book of Acts. Acts 2 describes the descent of the Holy Spirit on the first Christian Day of Pentecost, a late spring Jewish holiday that earlier celebrated the agricultural harvest but later observed the harvest of Sinai, the giving of the law through Moses. On this day "they were all filled with the Holy Spirit and began to speak in other tongues as the Spirit gave them utterance" (Acts 2:4). Said the listeners, "We hear them telling in our own tongues the mighty works of God" (2:11). This was in Jerusalem, among Jews, on a Jewish holiday. Later, yet in Palestine, but in a Gentile household, the address of Jewish leader Peter was interrupted when the Spirit fell on the foreign group. Peter's fellow Jews who had made the trip to Caesarea with him "were amazed, because the gift of the Holy Spirit had been poured out even on the Gentiles. For they heard them speaking in tongues and extolling God" (10:45–46). Still later, in Ephesus, a leading city in western Asia Minor, Paul met a group of people who knew only of John's baptism. After Paul laid hands on them, "the Holy Spirit came on them, and they spoke with tongues and prophesied" (19:6).

Luke's interest in the Book of Acts seems to include a sort of theological geography. In his Gospel, Luke took Jesus from rural Galilee to the Jewish capital of Jerusalem; likewise, in Acts he takes Paul from the Jewish center to the imperial capital of Rome. In doing so, Luke seems to mark the movement of the gospel westward by gradual stages—each characterized by the descent of the Holy Spirit—Jerusalem (Jews alone), Caesarea (Gentiles on Jewish soil), Ephesus (Gentiles in Greek territory). At each step, the Holy Spirit falls, and glossolalia is an accompanying feature.

"Samaria" (Acts 8:14–24)—a nation of half-Jews—could be inserted between "Jerusalem" and "Caesarea" above, but glossolalia is not mentioned. Many commentators conclude its presence, however, since there was some aspect of the episode that led the magician Simon to offer money to acquire the trick of giving the Spirit by the laying on of hands. Connections flourished in those days between magic, nonsense syllables, and popular piety.

The other place where glossolalia originally

may have appeared in the text of Acts describes the effects of prayer following the safe release of Peter and John: "After they prayed, the place . . . was shaken. And they were all filled with the Holy Spirit and spoke the word of God boldly" (Acts 4:31). Many NT scholars, Rudolf Bultmann among them, believe the original text may have read ". . . filled with the Holy Spirit and spoke in tongues." No surviving manuscript, however, preserves such a reading.

It is Paul's first letter to the Corinthians that most speaks of glossolalia. The setting of the letter is crucial to its interpretation. First Corinthians is not a zero-based treatise on spiritual gifts. Rather, it is a forceful pastoral letter sent to correct rumored wrongs in a church founded a half-dozen years earlier by the apostle Paul in Corinth, the capital city of southern Greece. Paul's unnamed successor(s) warped teachings he had left. The congregation, at least an influential and troublesome part of it, developed a distorted doctrine of Christianized human nature such that it overemphasized the spiritual side of the Christian life to the neglect even of basic morality (e.g., incest was arrogantly tolerated [1 Cor. 5:1–13]). With that mindset, using glossolalia would attest a supposed higher spirituality.

Paul's response to the Corinthian superspirituality lay in his appeal, not to end the use of glossolalia, but to govern its use by three guidelines: (1) recognition of the diversity of charismata graciously given by the triune God (1 Cor. 12); (2) the supremacy of love, without which no charisma counts (1 Cor. 13); and (3) the priority of congregational edification over personal benefit (1 Cor. 14).

Is glossolalia at Corinth the same phenomenon that appeared in Jerusalem a quarter century earlier? Acts describes xenolalia on the Day of Pentecost (2:14). The hearing of identified languages is not mentioned in the other two instances where glossolalia is mentioned in Acts (10:46; 19:6)—though the vocal consequence consisting in "extolling God" (10:46, cf. 2:11) may imply that the content of the glossolalic speech was understood. In any case, Acts is theological history—a work composed by its author freely at will. First Corinthians, by contrast, is a pastoral response in the form of a straightforward but longer-than-average letter that addresses specific problems in a particular congregation.

Glossolalia in Acts is heard as "our own languages" (2:11). Corinthian glossolalia is addressed to God, "no one understands him," and "he speaks not to men but to God" (1 Cor. 14:2). Glossolalia in Acts is an outcome of the Spirit's arrival. In Corinth it is a charisma, one among others. (Luke does not use the term *charisma* in Acts or in the Gospel: it is, except for 1 Peter 4:10, a Pauline word.) Corinthian glossolalia occurred in a settled congregation and required the companion gift of interpretation to extend its usefulness beyond the speaker. Paul, not Luke, speaks of "interpretation": there is no uninterpreted glossolalia in Acts. In Acts 2 at least, the tongues are immediately perceived as various native languages. The glossolalia of Acts seems

once-for-all, at least initiatory: that at Corinth habitually recurred. Phenomenologically, the glossolalia of Acts and 1 Corinthians may be the same. But Luke in Acts makes a theologically symbolic use of glossolalia entirely appropriate to the genre of Acts, while in 1 Corinthians the phenomenon crops up as a pastoral problem rising from overzealous charismatic piety.

A clear precedent for NT glossolalia appears in the tradition of ecstatic prophetism in the OT. Israel's prophets were given to dreams, visions, and a variety of abnormal behaviors that included broken speech. Samuel directed Saul to Gibeah and said, "You will meet a band of prophets coming down from the high place with harp, tambourine, flute, and lyre before them, prophesying, then the Spirit of the LORD will come mightily upon you, and you shall prophesy with them and be turned into another man" (1 Sam. 10:5–6). Earlier, when Moses gathered seventy elders to the meeting tent, "then the LORD came down in the cloud and spoke to him, and took some of the spirit that was upon him and put it upon the seventy elders; and when the spirit rested upon them, they prophesied. But they did so no more" (Num. 11:25). Contagious ecstatic prophetism is an acknowledged part of Israel's past and an unavoidable topic in OT theology. What is striking is the nearly universal voice effects coupled with emotive experience.

In nonbiblical Jewish literature roughly contemporary with NT times, the Testament of Job 48–50 furnishes the nearest parallel to Paul's reference to "tongues of angels" (1 Cor. 13:1). Facing his impending death, Job distributed his goods among his children, saving the best—a triple stranded charismatic sash—for the three daughters. As each daughter tied one of the strands about herself, her "heart was changed" (cf. 1 Sam. 10:5–6) and she "no longer cared for earthly matters." The first daughter then spoke "ecstatically in the angelic dialect, sending up a hymn to God." The mouth of the second daughter "took on the dialect of the archons and she praised God." The third daughter "spoke ecstatically in the dialect of those on high . . . in the dialect of the cherubim." No evidence exists that Paul knew of the Testament of Job.

IV. Theological Nuances. Nearly all classical Pentecostal groups adhere to the doctrine that speaking in tongues certifies the personal experience of the baptism in the Holy Spirit. Representative is the doctrinal formulation of the American Assemblies of God:

The baptism of believers in the Holy Ghost is witnessed by the initial physical sign of speaking with other tongues as the Spirit of God gives them utterance (Acts 2:4). The speaking of tongues in this instance is the same in essence as the gift of tongues (1 Cor. 12:4–10, 28), but different in purpose and use.

Nineteenth-century Holiness groups sought to recover Wesley's emphasis on personal holiness. Donald W. Dayton (1987) shows that over the decades of that century, Wesley's language of "pure love" and "entire sanctification" was gradually replaced by the phrase "baptism in the Holy Spirit"—commonplace among Holiness people and revivalists as the end of the nineteenth century drew near. A simultaneous development, it can be argued, was the shift from Wesley's "assurance" to the notion of "evidence." This exchange was doubtlessly facilitated by the rise of a popular scientism after the Civil War. Darwin published *Origin of the Species* in 1859 and *Descent of Man* in 1871. Holiness seekers, who also resisted imported German higher criticism, opposed the "evidence" argued by the new biological and biblical sciences. Adamantly opposed to the conclusions, they may well have been captured by the method: one gets at truth by "citing evidence." This pop intellectualism accounts for the way the question was put at century's end, when Charles F. Parham's Bible School students gathered in Topeka in 1900. As he left for ministry elsewhere, Parham, founder of the Apostolic Faith Movement, charged his students to search the Scriptures and to discover the Bible evidence for the baptism in the Holy Spirit. The answer identified by the students gave birth to the Pentecostal movement: speaking in tongues is the initial physical evidence of the baptism in the Holy Spirit.

Classical Pentecostals account for the difference between Acts and 1 Corinthians by maintaining a distinction between speaking in tongues as the *evidence* of the baptism in the Holy Spirit (as the frequent outcome of the Spirit's descent in Acts) from the *gift (charisma)* of tongues mentioned in 1 Corinthians. Most Pentecostals admit the difficulty of supporting the doctrine of initial evidence from 1 Corinthians. In truth, the doctrine finds its sole support from the historical precedent of the cases of the Spirit's descent in Acts 2, 10, and 19.

Not all classical Pentecostals teach initial evidence. Exceptions include organized classical Pentecostal churches in Scandinavia, Germany, the United Kingdom, and Latin America. Admittedly, the case for initial evidence is not as strong as that for major doctrines such as the sinfulness of humankind or the efficacy of the Atonement. Yet historical precedent as a basis for belief should not be belittled. Jesus himself appealed to precedent: did not the Pharisees, chagrined that Jesus' disciples picked and ate grain on the Sabbath, recall that David "unlawfully" entered the sanctuary and ate consecrated bread? (Mark 2:23–28).

V. Historical Survey. What counts for glossolalia in Christian history depends on how the term is defined. The technical term *glōssais lalein* (in the plural) is limited to the NT itself, until the phrase is picked up by patristic commentators citing the NT. But if ecstatic speech and nonsense-written syllables are counted, then glossolalia can be sporadically located over the whole history of the church until its exponential spread in the twentieth-century Pentecostal and charismatic movements.

The first full generation of glossolalia is recounted in Acts: thirty years elapsed between the Jerusalem Pentecost (Acts 2, around A.D. 30) and the Ephesian descent of the Spirit (Acts 19:1–6, about A.D. 60). Over the next hundred years, little is recorded. By the third generation of the second century, however, the magical use of esoteric nonsense syllables occurs in Christian Gnosticism, and a prophet named Montanus (who flourished in Phrygia in central Asia Minor) announced that he had become the Paraclete. Doing combat with heretics, both Irenaeus (c. A.D. 180) and Tertullian (A.D. 207 or later: he had himself become a Montanist) offered as apologetic defense the existence in their communities of the apostolic charismata.

But for Origen in the third century and Augustine in the late fourth and early fifth, it is clear that charismatic phenomena, including glossolalia, were valued as marks of the birth of the church centuries earlier. Augustine made a metaphor: the church, by his day spread over the then-known world, collectively spoke in virtually all the languages of the inhabited globe. It was Augustine who established the belief, deeply held by many to the present day, that the charismata ended with the days of the apostles.

Saints through the Middle Ages are often credited with the capacity to speak in tongues, though careful historical research has to be applied to determine where such attributed endowments are little more than stylized encomium.

Neither Luther (1483–1546) nor Calvin (1509–64) reflected firsthand encounters with glossolalia. For Luther and his foes, "speaking in tongues" had to do with the Roman Mass offered in Latin: Luther said the vernacular is needed. Calvin saw the tongues of the Jerusalem Pentecostal as symbolic of the inclusion in the church of non-Jews.

Persecution from Louis XIV against seventeenth-century French Protestants produced the French prophets of the Cevennes mountain region in southeastern France. Records describe extraordinary phenomena—trances, faints, shakings, and glossolalic sounds. Some of the Camisards, as they were known, escaped to England, where they later forced John Wesley's attention to glossolalia. Wesley (1703–91) theoretically defended the contemporary relevance of the charismata and thought kindly of the Montanists. Reactions to his own preaching included some who were "constrained to roar." While he supported deep personal experience of the sanctifying Spirit, it seems to be too much to claim Wesley was himself a glossolalic.

The nineteenth century opened with the Shakers well situated in upstate New York. It closed with the birth of the Pentecostal movement. In the 1820s and 1830s, both among the Shakers and the followers of Edward Irving, a popular London Presbyterian pastor, glossolalia occurred repeatedly. In the 1840s, glossolalia emerged with the rise of Mormons: both Joseph Smith and Brigham Young spoke in tongues. Latter-Day Saint doctrinal formulations to this day include the practice.

Throughout the nineteenth century, the Holiness movement grew. Its pursuit of restored holiness and the "perfect love" engendered by Wesley the century before traced a shift, as Donald W. Dayton (1987) shows, in terminology from terms like "entire sanctification" and "Christian perfection" toward a rising preference for "baptism in the Holy Spirit." In the 1890s, four renowned Bible teachers who did not have Wesleyan roots—A. J. Gordon, Reuben A. Torrey, A. B. Simpson, and C. I. Scofield—wrote books that, though their preferred terminology varied, urged the fullness of the Spirit upon every believer.

The stage was thus set for the birth of the Pentecostal movement. It took only the linkage of speaking in tongues with the evidence of the baptism in the Holy Spirit to bring about the Pentecostal movement. That happened in the closing days of 1900 among Charles Parham's Topeka Bible School students: when glossolalia was pronounced to be the initial physical evidence of the baptism in the Holy Spirit, the classical Pentecostal movement was born. The rest is history (Synan, 1971; details in this section have been drawn largely from Williams/Waldvogel, 1975).

VI. Varied Explanations. How does glossolalia occur? What are its effects and significance? Responses to these and similar queries turn on the world view of the inquirer and the methodology adopted. Even Third World illiterate Pentecostals are entitled to their uncomplicated view that God has filled them with himself and they speak in tongues under the direct drive of the Holy Spirit.

Research conducted by social scientists (Malony and Lovekin, 1985) has been the kind of inquiry most productive of theories. The earliest psychological investigations viewed glossolalia as the by-product of an unhealthy mind or a disordered personality. It has been attributed to hysteria or hypnosis, suggestion or regression. Some researchers view it as an altered state of consciousness, others as learned behavior or narcissistic self-preoccupation.

Buddhist doctrine explains xenolalia as a linguistic survivor from a prior existence. Jungian theory views glossolalia as an individual breakthrough from the collective unconscious. It has been described as the consequence of stimulation of Broca's Area in the left cerebral hemisphere and as a form of right-brain speech. It can be styled as the suspension of the rational or as a mix of a cry (anticipating death) and a laugh (celebrating birth: Hutch, 1980) or as a kind of mysticism—although glossolalia played no major role in the classical Christian mystical tradition.

Pentecostals are gratified to learn that they have been, in more recent research, accorded healthy normal personalities—if, as a whole, a bit more anxious than others. In fact history, psychological analysis, and personal testimony converge to suggest occasional coincidence of personal or social stress and the use of glossolalia. Ongoing research will add to the common understanding of the phenomenon, but research cannot exhaust the meaning of the experience to the individual believer.

VII. Evaluation. A few summarizing and interpretive conclusions can be offered.

1. Glossolalia is a human phenomenon, not limited to Christianity nor even to religious behavior. Speaking in tongues "embraces every ecstatic oral-auditory phenomenon from speaking a language not generally known . . . to speaking in forceful declamations, incantations, and other verbal effusions that are more likely to be psychological-spiritual projections of inner speech than some authentic language itself" (Williams/Waldvogel, 1975, 61).

2. The impulse for glossolalia, not readily accessible to scientific determination, may rise from the speakers themselves, from a demonic spirit, or from the Holy Spirit. Even if glossolalia occurs in a balanced Pentecostal environment, any one of the three sources may apply. The discernment of the community is essential. On the other hand, glossolalia of simply human origin is probably more frequent than recognized. That explains, for example, the humanities scholar who "taught himself" to speak in tongues and can do so at will.

3. It is equally wrong to conclude (1) that glossolalia did not occur between the first and the twentieth centuries or (2) that it is a regular and predictable outcome of revivalistic religious fervor. Despite emotional excesses at the Kentucky Cane Ridge revival in the early 1800s—surely the most emotional of American awakenings, where appeared such phenomena as shaking, barking, falling, and fainting—no clear cases of glossolalia are reported. Nor do any come from the lay-led prayer revival of the 1850s. The charismatic renewal after the 1960s, on the other hand, is replete with reports of glossolalia among many quiet and controlled mainline Christians.

4. If the doctrine of speaking in tongues as the initial physical evidence of the baptism of the Holy Spirit can be labeled the distinctive teaching of the Pentecostal churches, the belief that *distinguishes* the movement can only wrongly be thought of as describing the *essence* of Pentecostalism. The Pentecostal family of Christians are, on the whole, balanced evangelical believers with a high view of Scripture, a penchant for deeply personal (but not mystical) religious experience, and a conspicuous passion for global evangelization.

5. Even deaf people speak in tongues. But this has been little studied among social scientists and, for that matter, rarely observed among Pentecostals.

6. "That a phenomenon has a psychological explanation does not exclude it from being a gift of the Spirit" (McDonnell, 1976, 154). That an experience is human cannot mean it is not Christian, as the Incarnation itself discloses. Given the theology of the Book of Hebrews, one may conclude that Christians in fact have a better chance of becoming truly human than non-Christians.

7. Xenolalia is at the same time the most difficult variety of glossolalia to document, yet the most widely reported among global cultures.

8. Most instances of glossolalia seem not to consist in the extraordinary use of some identifiable language. The significance of glossolalia for the individual speaker may lie in its capacity to vent the inexpressible—hence the observed connection with stress. But in congregational life the good of the group exceeds that of the individual and the companion charisma "interpretation" is

required. Such interpretation need not be considered literal translation of the speech given in tongues but rather an explanation of the meaning of that glossolalic utterance for the gathered Christians. Eccentricities arise when interpretations are preserved and assigned a value above Scripture and the tradition of the local church or the Christian family of which it is a part.

9. After all self-induced and demonically originated glossolalia has been accounted for, there remains a variety—one could say a level—of encounter with the Holy Spirit, the consequence of which is speaking in tongues. The capacity for speech distinguishes human nature among living beings; it likewise differentiates—in OT theology—God from the many other gods. It is not to be wondered at that one of the finest varieties of religious experience links divine and human speech. Nor is it surprising that the result of that mix transcends rational thought.

10. Genuine Christian glossolalia is temporary, a feature of the present age between the first Christian Pentecost and the second coming of Christ. "Tongues . . . will cease" (1 Cor. 13:8); there will be no speaking in tongues in heaven. Glossolalia is therefore supremely eschatological, a broken speech for the broken body of Christ till perfection arrives.

See also BAPTISM IN THE HOLY SPIRIT; HOLY SPIRIT, DOCTRINE OF THE; INITIAL EVIDENCE, A BIBLICAL PERSPECTIVE; INITIAL EVIDENCE, A HISTORICAL PERSPECTIVE; INTERPRETATION, GIFT OF; LUKE-ACTS; PAULINE LITERATURE.

Bibliography: L. Barnett, and J. P. McGregor, *Speaking in Tongues: A Scholarly Defense* (1986: independent Pentecostal, voluminous but sophomoric); D. A. Carson, *Showing the Spirit* (1987: evangelical, noncharismatic); D. Christie-Murray, *Voices from the Gods* (1978: anthropological); S. D. Currie, " 'Speaking in Tongues': Early Evidence Outside the New Testament Bearing on 'Glōssais Lalein,' " *Interpretation* 19 (1965): 274–94; G. B. Cutten, *Speaking With Tongues* (1927); D. W. Dayton *Theological Roots of Pentecostalism* (1987); F. D. Goodman, *Speaking in Tongues: A Cross-Cultural Study* (1972: involves an altered state of consciousness); H. Gunkel, *The Influence of the Holy Spirit* (1888, reprint 1979); R. H. Gundry, " 'Ecstatic Utterance' (NEB)?" *JTS* 17 (1966): 299–307 (actual human languages); R. W. Harris, *Spoken by the Spirit* (1973: classical Pentecostal collection of seventy-five anecdotal reports); R. Harrisville, "Speaking in Tongues: A Lexicographical Study," *CBQ* 38 (1976): 35–48; W. H. Horton, *The Glossolalia Phenomenon* (1966: classical Pentecostal); A. L. Hoy, "Public and Private Uses of the Gift of Tongues," *Paraclete* 2 (1968): 10–14 (classical Pentecostal); H. D. Hunter, *Spirit-Baptism* (1983); R. A. Hutch, "The Personal Ritual of Glossolalia," *JSSR* 19 (1980): 255–66; C. O. Ishel, "Glossolalia and Propheteialalia: A Study of I Corinthians 14," *WTJ* 10 (1975): 15–22; M. T. Kelsey, *Tongue Speaking* (1964: Jungian); J. P. Kildahl, *The Psychology of Speaking in Tongues* (1972: not known languages, yet religiously useful); E. Lombard, *De la glossolalie* (1910); W. G. MacDonald, *Glossolalia in the New Testament* (n.d.: classical Pentecostal); A. Mackie, *The Gift of Tongues* (1921: pathological); H. Malony and A. Lovekin, *Glossolalia: Behavioral Science Perspectives* (1985: reviews a century of social science research); I. J. Martin, *Glossolalia in the Apostolic Church* (1960); L. C. May, "A Survey of Glossolalia and Related Phenomena in Non-Christian Religions," *American Anthropologist* 58 (1956): 75–96; K. McDonnell, *Charismatic Renewal and the Churches* (1976: misleadingly titled, best summary of psychological research on glossolalia to 1975); P. C. Miller, "In Praise of Nonsense," in A. H. Armstrong, ed., *Classical Mediterranean Spirituality* (1986: on the use of nonrational syllables in ancient magic and gnosticism); W. E. Mills, *Glossolalia: A Bibliography* (1985: over 1,150 entries and a useful, sometimes flawed, bibliographic essay); idem, ed., *Speaking in Tongues: A Guide to Research on Glossolalia* (1986: mainly reprinted technical articles, exegetical, historical, psychological in perspective); E. Mossiman, *Das Zungenreden* (1911); H. W. Parke and E. Wormell, *History of the Delphic Oracle* (1956); C. Richet, "Xenoglossia: L'écriture automatique en langues étrangères," *Proceedings of the Society for Psychical Research* 19 (1905–07): 162–94; J. L. Sherrill, *They Speak With Other Tongues* (1964: popular); F. Stagg et al., *Glossolalia* (1967: noncharismatic Southern Baptist assessment); C. G. Williams, *Tongues of the Spirit* (1981).

R. P. Spittler

GORTNER, JOHN NARVER (1874–1961). Pastor, teacher, poet, and leader in the Assemblies of God (AG). Son of a Methodist pastor-missionary, Gortner was educated at Garrett Biblical Institute and pastored Methodist churches in the Midwest before moving to California in 1909. Five years later he was baptized in the Holy Spirit at a Pentecostal camp. After another five years as a Methodist pastor, he joined the AG and accepted a pastorate in Cleveland, Ohio. Returning to California in 1924, he pastored in Los Angeles and built a large church in Oakland before beginning a ten-year ministry as teacher and administrator at Glad Tidings Bible Institute in San Francisco. Ill health forced him to retire from active ministry in 1946. He was a regular contributor to Christian periodicals. His books included a nationally recognized volume of poems, *Dust from Chariot Wheels,* and two on prophecy, *Studies in Daniel* (c. 1948) and *Studies in Revelation* (c. 1948).

Bibliography: C. Brumback, *Suddenly . . . From Heaven* (1961); W. E. Warner, "J. Narver Gortner" (Part 1) *AG Heritage* 8 (Spring 1988): 13–16; (Part 2) (Summer 1988): 12–14.

L. F. Wilson

GORTNER, HUGH MARJOE ROSS (1944–). Evangelist and actor. Gortner traveled across the U.S. from 1949 to 1957 as "the world's youngest ordained preacher," playing several musical instruments and preaching memorized sermons. The son of Pentecostal preachers and grandson of J. Narver Gortner, the precocious boy was carefully prepared for public ministry from his earliest days. By his fifth birthday he had been ordained, and he received national publicity for performing a California wedding. Within three years his musical and dramatic talents had attracted large audiences, but the novelty could not be sustained. His parents separated, and the aging and disillusioned boy preacher retired at thirteen. For eleven years he experimented with jobs, lifestyles, and marriage before returning to itinerant evangelism. After three years he sought to expose evangelists as exploiting entertainers in a book and film before entering the film industry as an actor.

Bibliography: S. Gaines, *Marjoe* (1973); D. E. Harrell, Jr., *All Things Are Possible* (1975).

L. F. Wilson

The Gospel Publishing House, and the Assemblies of God office, occupied this St. Louis building from 1915-18. Here are the employees in c. 1916. Longtime Assemblies of God leader J. Roswell Flower is in the center.

GOSPEL ASSEMBLY (JOLLY) In 1965 Tom M. Jolly, pastor of the Gospel Assembly in St. Louis, led his congregation and twelve others in disassociating themselves from the movement founded by William Sowders (1878–1952). At that time Jolly had been a pastor in the parent movement for thirty-one years. In 1970 about thirty "autonomous, independent; unorganized, unaffiliated" assemblies were in fellowship with Jolly. The combined members numbered approximately four thousand. At that time, Kansas City, Missouri, represented the westernmost extent of the movement.

Bibliography: A. C. Piepkorn, *Profiles in Belief*, vol. 3 (1979).   C. E. Jones

GOSPEL ASSEMBLY (SOWDERS) In 1927 William Sowders (1878–1952) established the Gospel Tabernacle in Louisville, Kentucky, the mother church of the Gospel Assembly movement. Here Sowders promulgated what he called the Gospel of the Kingdom in a long service each Sunday afternoon called the School of the Prophets. This elaborate dispensational schema includes distinctive teachings concerning the Godhead and the restoration of the Jewish nation. At its height Sowders's following consisted of an estimated 75,000 believers in three hundred congregations in thirty-one states. Following the founder's death, however, factionalism splintered the movement. In 1970 approximately 10,000 adherents in ninety-two assemblies in twenty-two states remained in the original fellowship. Nearly three-fourths of these had "Gospel Assembly" in their names.

Bibliography: A. C. Piepkorn, *Profiles in Belief*, vol. 3 (1979).   C. E. Jones

GOSPEL PUBLISHING HOUSE (GPH). The publishing division of the General Council of the Assemblies of God (AG). After the AG was formed at Hot Springs, Arkansas, in April 1914, T. K. Leonard offered his printing facilities in Findlay, Ohio, as a temporary headquarters and printing plant. The name Gospel Publishing House was adopted (this name was used by an earlier company in New York). AG had assumed ownership of two periodicals: the *Christian Evangel* (later called the *Weekly Evangel*, 1915–18; *Christian Evangel*, 1918–19; and the *Pentecostal Evangel*, 1919–), and the *Word and Witness* (discontinued in 1915). The council moved to St. Louis in 1915 and then to Springfield, Missouri, in 1918. By this time Sunday school curriculum and books were being published along with the *Evangel*. The present plant was occupied in 1949, and other buildings were added to the complex, including a four-story administration building in 1961.

GPH, with more than three hundred employees, operates a complete modern printing plant, producing twenty-two tons of books, music, periodicals, and Sunday school literature every working day. The Sunday school literature, "Radiant Life" curriculum, is used not only by Assemblies of God but also by other denominations. In the fall of 1987 GPH began publishing "Vida Radiante," a Spanish curriculum. Earnings from GPH sales are channeled into various AG ministries.

Bibliography: M. Hoover, "Origin and Structural Development of the Assemblies of God," M.A. thesis, Southwest Missouri State University, 1968; W. Menzies, *Anointed to Serve* (1971); "PCPA Welcomes Three New Members," *The Round Table* (November–December 1986), 2–3. W. E. Warner

GOSS, HOWARD ARCHIBALD (1883–1964). First general superintendent of the United Pentecostal Church (UPC). Converted in 1903 under the ministry of Charles F. Parham, Goss attended Parham's short-term Bible school in Houston, Texas, in 1905. While riding a train with other Pentecostals in 1906, he received the baptism of the Holy Ghost. In the same year Parham appointed him to be field supervisor of the Apostolic Faith movement in Texas. After moral charges were brought against Parham in 1907, Goss separated from Parham and evangelized in Texas, Arkansas, Kansas, Iowa, Illinois, and Missouri, establishing several Pentecostal churches. Goss and E. N. Bell were chiefly responsible for organizing the Assemblies of God (AG) in 1914, and Goss was elected to serve on the first executive presbytery and as the person

Special Gospel
SERVICES
You are invited to attend The Special Gospel Services CONDUCTED BY

MR. and MRS. GOSS
of Hot Springs, Ark. at
The Pentecostal Tabernacle
228 ALBERT STREET
Sunday 10.30 a. m., 2.30 and 7.30 p.m.
Meetings every night except Saturday

This gospel service advertisement is for meetings in Ottawa in 1919. Howard and Ethel Goss were leaders in the Oneness movement.

issuing credentials to ministers in the South and West. E. N. Bell rebaptized Goss in the name of Jesus Christ in 1915. After the division of the Oneness ministers from the AG in 1916, Goss served on the credentials committee of the General Assembly of the Apostolic Assemblies. In 1919 he moved to Canada and established a church in Toronto, serving as its pastor until 1937. In the U.S. Goss was a member of the organizing board of presbyters for the Pentecostal Ministerial Alliance and served as the first chairman of this organization from 1925 to 1932. In 1939 he became the general superintendent of the Pentecostal Church, Incorporated. At the merger that formed the UPC in 1945, Goss became the first general superintendent of the new organization and served until 1951. With his wife, Ethel, Goss wrote *The Winds of God* (1958), a history of the early years of the Pentecostal revival.

Bibliography: A. L. Clanton, *United We Stand* (1970). J. L. Hall

GRADUATE SCHOOLS See SEMINARIES AND GRADUATE SCHOOLS.

GRANT, WALTER VINSON (1913–). Author, healing evangelist. W. V. Grant, born in Arkansas, was a successful businessman before becoming an Assemblies of God (AG) minister in 1945. Rising as an early leader in the faith healing revival of the late 1940s and 1950s, he launched his first campaign in 1949. Poor health stopped him in 1956. Staying involved in the movement, he became vice-president of the Voice of Healing organization and a consultant to many healing evangelists. Grant admits that he did not attract theologians but common people.

Writing was one of Grant's strengths. He started the *Voice of Deliverance* in 1962, and eleven years later the circulation reached two million. In addition, he authored scores of books. Harrell notes that after Lindsay, Grant was "the most prolific and important writer in the revival" (Harrell, 1975, 80). Grant authored such books as *Raising the Dead* (n.d.), *Must I Pray for a Miracle?* (n.d.), and *Power to Detect Demons* (n.d.). His son, W. V. Grant, Jr., has continued to sell his father's books and engages in his own faith healing ministry.

Bibliography: W. V. Grant, *The Grace of God in My Life* (1952); D. E. Harrell, Jr., *All Things Are Possible* (1975). S. Shemeth

GRAVES, FREDERICK A. (1856–1927). Songwriter. Ordained at age sixty-two, F. A. Graves is remembered chiefly as a gospel songwriter. Born in Williamstown, Massachusetts, "Freddie" was orphaned at nine and discovered to have epilepsy at fourteen. He was converted in childhood and joined the Congregational Church. At age twenty-one, still struggling to overcome periodic seizures, Graves moved to Nobles County in southwestern Minnesota. Soon afterward, believing that he had been healed, he served briefly as an organizer and evangelist for the American Sunday School Union. Short courses in Bible and music followed in Chicago and Northfield, Massachusetts. Upon return,

Graves went to hear healing evangelist John Alexander Dowie (1847–1907) in Minneapolis. There, despite a relapse, he experienced permanent healing, a pivotal event in his spiritual journey, and the backdrop for two long-lasting songs: "Honey in the Rock" (1895) and "He'll Never Forget to Keep Me" (1899).

Before Dowie's downfall, Graves moved his family to Zion City, Illinois, where he was to remain the rest of his life. Acceptance of Pentecostalism enhanced his popularity, and his family's contributions to the Pentecostal cause magnified his ministry. He was ordained to the ministry of the General Council of the Assemblies of God in 1918. All of his children attended Central Bible Institute, Springfield, Missouri. Arthur Graves (1902–73) became a prominent pastor and president of Southeastern Bible College, Lakeland, Florida; Carl, a missionary in Ceylon and pastor in Michigan; and Irene, wife of Myer Pearlman (1893–1943), a convert from Judaism noted as a teacher at Central Bible Institute and a writer on doctrine. (Pearlman recalled that in the first Pentecostal mission service he attended in San Francisco, they had sung "Honey in the Rock.") F. A. Graves died in Zion City (population five thousand) in January 1927. Nearly a thousand attended his funeral.

Bibliography: C. Brumback, *Suddenly . . . From Heaven* (1961); F. A. Graves, *So He Made It Again* (1924); I. P. Pearlman, *Myer Pearlman and His Friends* (1953).   C. E. Jones

GREAT COMMISSION, INTERNATIONAL An interdenominational organization with headquarters in Hanford, California, and whose primary function is to publish an inspirational quarterly, *Testimony*, and books on Pentecostal and prophetical themes. Great Commission was founded in 1962 by Thomas R. and Ruth D. Nickel. Thomas R. Nickel (1900–) was the founding editor of *Voice*, the magazine published by the Full Gospel Business Men's Fellowship International. Nickel believes that God wants him and the Great Commission—with help from other believers—to open Tibet to the gospel so that Christ can return. The organization has promoted trips to Israel, Jewish messianic congregations, Azusa Street revival anniversaries, and other interdenominational activities. Nickel is arranging an Azusa anniversary in 1991 and "every five years until Jesus returns."

Bibliography: "Jesus People Are Drawn From All Walks of Populace," *Sentinel* (Hanford, Calif.) (September 25, 1971); *Testimony* (1962–).   W. E. Warner

GREEK PENTECOSTALS See EUROPEAN PENTECOSTALISM.

John Gunstone is one of the leaders in the Anglican charismatic movement in England.

GUNSTONE, JOHN (1927–). One of the main teacher-leaders in the charismatic movement in the Catholic wing of the Church of England and a popular author of books on pastoral liturgy. As a vicar near London (1964) Gunstone was one of the first Anglo-Catholics baptized in the Spirit, and his numerous writings reflect a strong churchmanship, wide scholarship, and ecumenical commitment. His books include *Greater Things Than These* (1974), a personal account of the renewal; *The Beginnings at Whatcombe* (1976), the story of four years spent in the Barnabas Fellowship, a small community-based team ministry; *A People for His Praise* (1978), on renewal and congregational life; *Pentecostal Anglicans* (1982); *Live by the Spirit* (1984); and *The Lord Is Our Healer* (1986). Since 1975 Gunstone has been secretary of the Greater Manchester County Ecumenical Council and has been active in Anglican Renewal Ministries since its formation in 1981.

P. D. Hocken

H

HAGIN, KENNETH E. (1917–). Teacher, prolific author, and advocate of the "Word of Faith" message. Born prematurely with a deformed heart, he was not expected to survive, yet he managed to function fifteen years before becoming an invalid. He reported that the following year, during a ten-minute period, his vital signs failed three times. On each occasion he witnessed the horrors of hell. This experience resulted in his conversion on April 22, 1933. The following year he was healed, and he soon began a ministry as a lay preacher for a small multidenominational country church in Texas, attended predominately by Southern Baptists. His baptism in the Holy Spirit in 1937 led him into ministry as a Pentecostal in the same state, where he pastored six churches successively.

Hagin began an itinerant ministry as a Bible teacher and evangelist in 1949. During the following fourteen years he had a series of eight visions of Jesus Christ, who in the third vision granted him the gift of discerning of spirits, enabling him to pray more effectively for the healing of the sick. As a result of his final vision in 1963, he set up his own office at his home in Garland, Texas, for the distribution of his tapes and books. Three years later he moved to Tulsa, Oklahoma, where he has remained for more than twenty years.

Hagin founded Rhema Bible Training Center in 1974. By 1988 more than 10,000 students had graduated, and his daily radio program, "Faith Seminar of the Air," was being broadcast on more than 180 stations in thirty-nine states, with a short-wave audience in about eighty other nations. By this time more than three million of his eighty-five books and almost a half million cassette tapes of his sermons were being distributed annually.

With respect to his prophetic ministry, Hagin (1972, 109) has written, "When the word of knowledge began to operate in my life after I was filled with the Holy Ghost, I would know things supernaturally about people, places, and things. Sometimes I would know through a vision. Sometimes while I was preaching, a cloud would appear and my eyes would be opened so that I would see a vision concerning someone in the congregation."

Kenneth Hagin emphasizes the message of uncompromising faith in God's desire to bless in every area of life all who do not doubt him. Although he has been criticized as the leader of the "Word of Faith" and "Positive Confession" movements (Hunt, 1987, 56; McConnell, passim), his message emphasizes the need to pray only according to God's principles as found in the Judeo-Christian Scriptures. At one point he wrote, "I do not understand how some people can

go around spouting off things, endeavoring to believe, and calling it faith, when it is only presumption and folly" (Hagin, 1979, 25). In other cases (Hagin, 1978, 112–13), he has provided examples of negative "prophecies" that did not come to pass.

Kenneth Hagin, Sr., is a leader in the "faith" movement. He is founder of Rhema Bible Training Center, Broken Arrow, Oklahoma.

Bibliography: K. E. Hagin, *How You Can Be Led by the Spirit of God* (1978); idem, *I Believe in Visions* (1972); idem, *I Went to Hell* (1982); idem, *What to Do When Faith Seems Weak and Victory Lost* (1979); D. Hunt, *Beyond Seduction* (1987); D.R. McConnell, *A Different Gospel* (1988).   R. M. Riss

HALL, FRANKLIN (twentieth century). Teacher, healing evangelist. Raised in poverty, Franklin Hall became a devout Christian and traveled in his early ministry as an independent evangelist. His book *Atomic Power With God Through Prayer and Fasting* (1946) brought a measure of recognition to his ministry.

Hall carried on a ministry of teaching throughout the 1960s and 1970s. He began publishing *Miracle Word* magazine in 1965, which eventually reached a peak circulation of 24,000.

Unlike some faith healers, Hall emphasized

teaching. His extremist views in the area of fasting and healing were considered unacceptable to many evangelists. He attributes the tapering down of the revival of the 1950s to the lack of fasting and to spiritual coasting by the leaders. Extreme in the area of healing, he held to a "body-felt salvation." Accordingly, the fire of the Holy Spirit, if fully applied to a person (which would take about thirty days), would eliminate the potential for sickness, tiredness, and even body odor. These extremes and the discipline they entailed severely limited his following. In 1956 Hall founded his Deliverance Foundation, and in 1970 it reported thirty-two affiliated churches and two thousand members.

Hall wrote several books, including *Glorified Fasting* (1961), *The Fasting Prayer* (1947), *The Body-Felt Salvation* (1968), *Formula for Raising the Dead* (1960), and *Our Divine Healing Obligation* (n.d.).

Bibliography: D. E. Harrell, Jr., *All Things Are Possible* (1975); C. E. Jones, *A Guide to the Study of the Pentecostal Movement*, 2 vols. (1983).   S. Shemeth

HALL, HOMER RICHARD (twentieth century). Healing evangelist. H. Richard Hall was born in poverty. With the influence of a Pentecostal mother, he started preaching at age fourteen and received ordination with the Church of God of Prophecy (CGP) at age twenty-four. Hall reported that in 1952 God audibly told him to preach deliverance. Immediately resigning as CGP state overseer of Colorado, he left to pursue his new ministry outside denominational walls.

Hall was a small-town evangelist throughout the 1950s and for the most part remained such throughout his career. By 1972, his magazine, *The Shield of Faith* (started in 1956 as *The Healing Broadcast*, then *The Healing Digest*), had a circulation of 100,000.

The United Christian Ministerial Association was established by Hall in 1956 as an organization of independent clergy and churches. In 1972 he had ordained more than two thousand ministers. Hall worked in cooperation with Pentecostal denominations but never won their support. He emphasized healing and, like William Branham, whom he admired, frequently exercised the gift of knowledge.

Hall identified with social outcasts and with those outside the churches, especially the youth of the rebellion of the 1960s and 1970s, by campaigning with college-age talent and attempting to relate to youth. He felt that the rebellion expressed a hunger for food.

Bibliography: D. E. Harrell, Jr., *All Things Are Possible* (1975); C. E. Jones, *A Guide to the Study of the Pentecostal Movement*, (1983).   S. Shemeth

HAMMOND, HATTIE PHILLETTA (1907–). Evangelist. Born and raised in Williamsport, Maryland, Hammond grew up in the Brethren church with headquarters in Ashland, Ohio. At age seventeen she attended a Pentecostal camp meeting in 1924 conducted by evangelist John J. Ashcroft, father of J. Robert Ashcroft. Hattie was saved and baptized in the Holy Spirit at that meeting and began witnessing to her teachers and classmates.

Feeling a definite call to preach, Hammond began traveling on the evangelistic field and was asked by George Bowie to speak in Cleveland, Ohio; by J. Narver Gortner in Oakland, California; by Robert and Marie Brown in New York City; and by E. S. Williams in Philadelphia.

Hammond was ordained by the Assemblies of God in 1927. She has ministered all over America in colleges, conventions, Bible schools, churches of all denominations, and in more than twenty-seven countries.

Bibliography: Interview by Wayne E. Warner (August 16, 1982).   G. W. Gohr

An Anglican minister in England, Michael C. Harper has been an important figure in the Charismatic renewal since 1962.

HARPER, MICHAEL CLAUDE (1931–). Pioneer figure in charismatic renewal in Britain, leader in worldwide renewal in the Anglican Communion, and prolific author. Converted as an undergraduate at Cambridge, Harper was ordained as a priest in 1956. From 1958 to 1964 he served at one of London's major evangelical churches, All Souls, Langham Place, under John Stott. In the fall of 1962 he had an enlivening and empowering experience of the Holy Spirit, receiving the gift of tongues in August 1963. Harper sponsored talks by F. Maguire, L. Christenson, and D. du Plessis in 1963, and organized residential conferences at Stoke Poges in February and June 1964. Publishing Christenson's booklet on tongues and his own on *Prophecy* by the summer of 1964, he resigned from All Souls and became the first full-time general secretary of the Fountain Trust. The Trust embodied Harper's goals and ideals, focusing on new life in the Spirit for Christians of all churches in the context of the renewal of the body of Christ. His organizational, teaching, and writing work now multiplied, with a first trip to the U.S. in 1965 and to Australia and New Zealand in 1967. Editing the Fountain Trust's magazine, *Renewal,* from its inception in January 1966, Harper changed to director in 1972, but in 1975 he resigned as director and editor to concentrate on international teaching ministry from a parish near Heathrow airport. Instrumental in convening a charismatic conference for Anglicans immediately prior to the Lambeth Conference in July 1978, he began to concentrate on renewal within the Anglican Communion. The Canterbury initiative led in 1981 to the formation of SOMA (Sharing of Ministries Abroad), of which he was appointed full-time international director in 1984. Moving to Haywards Heath, Sussex, in 1981, Harper became a canon of Chichester Cathedral in 1984. He was a principal organizer of the Acts 1986 European charismatic conference in Birmingham. Throughout his ministry Harper has been supported by his wife, Jeanne, herself musically gifted and active in the Lydia Fellowship for women. Harper's gifts are illustrated in his steady literary output. His practical spiritual teaching is seen in *Power for the Body of Christ* (1964), *Walk in the Spirit* (1968), and *Spiritual Warfare* (1970). His narrative skills shine in *As at the Beginning* (1965), an account of Pentecostal origins and the first blossoming of charismatic renewal; *None Can Guess* (1971), his own personal story; and *A New Way of Living* (1973), on the Church of the Redeemer in Houston, Texas. His ability to clarify contemporary issues in the light of the gospel is seen in *Let My People Grow* (1977), *Three Sisters* (or *This Is the Day,* 1979), and *The Love Affair* (1982).

Bibliography: B. England, *The Spirit of Renewal* (n.d.); P. D. Hocken, *Streams of Renewal* (1986); M. Robinson, *Two Winds Blowing* (n.d.).

P. D. Hocken

HARRELL, DAVID EDWIN, JR. (1930–). Church historian, university professor, and writer. David Harrell is a prolific writer on religious themes, but he is best known in Pentecostal and charismatic circles for his highly acclaimed *All Things Are Possible* (1975) and *Oral Roberts: An American Life* (1985), both published by Indiana University Press. He was reared in the Church of Christ but later regarded himself as nondenominational. Harrell's Vanderbilt University Ph.D. dissertation was "A Social History of the Disciples of Christ, 1800–1866," published in 1973. He also wrote *White Sects and Black Men in the Recent South* (1971). In addition, he has contributed major articles to numerous journals. He was the senior Fulbright lecturer at the University of Allahabad, India (1976–77). In 1985 Harrell was named university scholar in history and chairman of the department at the University of Alabama at Birmingham.

Bibliography: *Who's Who in America,* 41st ed. (1980–81).

W. E. Warner

HARRIS, RALPH WILLIAM (1912–). Religious journalist. As editor-in-chief for church

school literature (Assemblies of God [AG]) from 1954 to 1976, Ralph Harris shaped Sunday school curricula and developed new pedagogical techniques. He is the founder of Speed-the-Light (AG), a program designed to gather funds for missionary equipment; author of *Now What?* (1964), a booklet for new converts; executive editor of the *Complete Biblical Library,* vols. 1 and 2 (1986, 1987; fourteen vols., forthcoming); author of *Spoken by the Spirit* (1973), an account of incidents of glossolalia in a known language; and author of "It's a Great Life" (*PE* [August 30, 1987], 10–11).

F. Bixler

HARRIS, THORO (1874–1955). Black composer and publisher. A child prodigy whose compositions in the Methodist Holiness style found appreciation among Pentecostals, Harris published the first of his several hymnals about 1900. His wide range of musical interests reflected his classical training and acquaintance with the church music tradition. As owner of Windsor Music Company in Chicago, he associated with well-known figures in gospel music, including Peter Bilhorn, James Rowe, and Henry Date. He is remembered for "More Abundantly" (1914), "Jesus Loves the Little Children" (1921), "All That Thrills My Soul Is Jesus" (1931), and "He's Coming Soon" (1944). He composed "Pentecost in My Soul" in 1948.

Bibliography: C. Brumback, *Suddenly . . . From Heaven* (1961); P. Kerr, *Music In Evangelism* (1962);

David Edwin Harrell, Jr., has published acclaimed works on the salvation-healing movement.

F. J. Metcalf, *American Writers and Composers of Sacred Music* (1925). E. A. Wilson

HARRISON, ALDA B. (1875–1959). Pioneer leader in the Church of God (CG, Cleveland, Tenn.). The wife of a Presbyterian minister, Harrison was filled with the Holy Spirit in 1908 at the Pleasant Grove, Florida, camp meeting. She became zealous in the Pentecostal cause but remained faithful to her responsibilities in the Presbyterian Church. She joined the CG in 1911 and began a ministry to its young people.

When Harrison's husband moved to Cleveland, Tennessee, she became active in youth efforts under the name of Bertie Harrison and in 1929 was instrumental in the organization of the Young Peoples Endeavor. That same year, at age fifty-four, she began publication of a youth magazine, *The Lighted Pathway,* and personally financed the project. Until her death in 1959 Mrs. Harrison remained the inspiration of the youth movement and editor emeritus of *The Lighted Pathway.*

Bibliography: A. Harrison, *Mountain Peaks of Experience* (n.d.). C. W. Conn

HARVEY, ESTHER BRAGG (1891–1986). Missionary to India. Born at Port Huron, Michigan, Esther Bragg was converted in a Methodist revival as a teenager and later healed of an incurable illness when some Pentecostal friends prayed with her. In 1911 she attended a small Bible school in Norwalk, Ohio, and received the baptism of the Holy Spirit. Being ordained by the school in 1913, she went with a group of missionaries to Nawabganj, India, to help James Harvey.

After a short courtship, James and Esther were married in November 1914 at a Methodist church in Lucknow. Ordained by the Assemblies of God in 1917, the Harveys established Sharannagar Mission as a home for widows and orphans and a training school for boys. After James Harvey died in 1922, Esther continued to maintain the mission and school until 1961, when she returned to the U.S. after forty-eight years of service in India.

Bibliography: E. B. Harvey, *The Faithfulness of God* (1945). G. W. Gohr

HAWN, ROBERT HAROLD (1928–). Episcopal priest and administrator. A U.S. Army officer who won numerous decorations, he returned to divinity school and became ordained in 1961. After serving a decade as an army chaplain, he retired and took a variety of teaching and parish positions.

Hawn became the first national coordinator of the Episcopal Charismatic Fellowship (ECF; now known as Episcopal Renewal Ministries) in 1973. Under his administration the ECF expanded into a nationwide organization, and a system of diocesan representation became necessary; so local, regional, and national conferences were organized. Publications he initiated included a booklet about charismatic renewal entitled *Acts 29* and a newsletter of the same name. He also served on the planning committee for the 1977 ecumenical charismatic conference, Jesus Is Lord, held in Kansas City.

Robert Hawn became an Episcopal priest after being decorated as a U.S. Army officer. He served as the first national coordinator of the Episcopal Charismatic Fellowship.

Hawn left the ECF in 1978 to speak and teach. From 1983 to 1986 he was rector of a parish in Cuernavaca, Mexico. He later moved to California. C. M. Irish

HAWTIN, GEORGE R. (1909–). Prominent early leader in the 1948 Latter Rain revival. In 1935, as a pastor of the Pentecostal Assemblies of Canada (PAOC), he pioneered Bethel Bible Institute in Star City, Saskatchewan, which moved to Saskatoon in 1937. Disputes between Hawtin and PAOC officials led to his resignation under pressure in 1947. Joining Herrick Holt of the North Battleford, Saskatchewan, Church of the Foursquare Gospel in an independent work that Holt had established, Sharon Orphanage and Schools, Hawtin became president of Sharon's Global Missions. The following February, revival broke out at the Bible school at Sharon, catapulting him, with his brother, Ern Hawtin, into prominence during the resulting Latter Rain movement. Within a year or two the Hawtin brothers became less prominent as others began to take on leadership roles in the movement. George Hawtin later began an independent work in nearby Battleford, publishing a periodical, *The Page.*

Bibliography: G. R. Hawtin, *Mystery Babylon* (n.d.); R. M. Riss, *Latter Rain* (1987). R. M. Riss

HAYES, NORVEL L. (1927–). Businessman and traveling teacher, born in Benton, Texas. Hayes's mother died when he was nine years old, and his grandmother subsequently reared him. During his teen years he dropped out of high school and worked in a food store. Hayes later became a successful business executive and for a time resided in Indianapolis, Indiana.

Moving to Cleveland, Tennessee, Hayes met Rev. M. E. Littlefield, a Pentecostal minister, and worked with him for seven years in a ministry of compassion to the poor; they also worked together in a local church. Hayes started to develop his own ministry to high school and college students and became involved in tract distribution; a ministry of deliverance, healing, and teaching also followed. He was greatly influenced by Kenneth Hagin, Sr., and Lester Sumrall and has worked closely with them for more than twenty years. The author of thirty books, he has also produced more than twenty audio tape teaching series.

In addition to his business corporation, Hayes is founder and president of New Life Bible College in Cleveland, Tennessee, established in 1977. His other ventures have included homes for unwed mothers and abused children, and the restoration of backslidden ministers.

Bibliography: "Runners Up," *Charisma* (August 1985), 132–33; P. Wagner, "Norvel Hayes," *So Great A Cloud of Witnesses* (n.d.).   S. Strang

Jack Hayford, popular Charismatic speaker, composer, and pastor of the Church on the Way, Van Nuys, California.

HAYFORD, JACK WILLIAMS, JR.

(1934–). Influential pastor, author, musician, and educator. Though Jack Hayford's family attended a variety of churches, they early identified with the International Church of the Foursquare Gospel (ICFG). He attended L.I.F.E. Bible College in Los Angeles and affiliated with the ICFG. After a pastorate in Indiana, he served terms as national youth director, dean of students,

teacher, and eventually president of L.I.F.E. In 1969 he accepted the pastorate of the First Foursquare Church of Van Nuys, which in time became the Church On the Way, growing from eighteen to more than six thousand members including many celebrities from the entertainment industry. He has written more than 350 songs, including "Majesty" and the award-winning "We Lift Our Voices Rejoicing." He hosts a daily radio program and is a popular conference speaker.

Bibliography: J. Hayford, *Church on the Way* (1982); S. Lawson, "Pastor on the Way," *Charisma* (June 1985), 20–26.   L. F. Wilson

As a pastor, denominational leader, composer, and editor, the gifted G. T. Haywood was one of the most influential early leaders in the Pentecostal movement.

HAYWOOD, GARFIELD THOMAS

(1880–1931). Pastor, church executive, and songwriter. Haywood was born to Benjamin and Penny Haywood of Greencastle, Indiana. The third of nine children, he was reared in a Christian home, attending both Baptist and Methodist churches. When he was three his parents moved to Indianapolis, where Haywood spent the remainder of his life.

Educated in the public school system in Haughville, Haywood attended through his sophomore year. During his high school years he discovered artistic talents, later selling his abilities as a cartoonist to two black weekly papers, *The Freedman* and *The Recorder*. On February 11, 1902, he married Ida Howard of Owensboro, Kentucky. They had one daughter, Fannie Ann.

News of the Pentecostal revival taking place at the Azusa Street Mission arrived in Indianapolis in late 1906. It was largely through the efforts of another black man, Elder Henry Prentiss (from

Azusa Street he went to Whittier, California, where he held open air meetings) that the scattered "Pentecostals" in Indianapolis found a pastor. Henry Prentiss led Haywood into the Pentecostal experience and the latter wrote to *The Apostolic Faith* newspaper to share his testimony (July–August 1908, 1).

By the end of 1908 Henry Prentiss had turned the Indianapolis work over to Haywood, who continued on as its pastor. Under his leadership the congregation grew rapidly. Haywood obtained credentials with a small organization in 1911 called the Pentecostal Assemblies of the World (PAW). Yet his world was much wider, for he ministered in churches and camp meetings and joined in some of the early general councils of the Assemblies of God (AG), which formed in 1914. The fact that he was given the floor in an early council of the Assemblies has led some to speculate that he was a minister with that movement, an assumption that he heartily denied. Yet it does demonstrate how highly his leadership was regarded by that nearly totally white group.

January 1915 was pivotal in Haywood's career in that it was during this time that Glenn A. Cook took the message known as the "New Issue," including baptism in Jesus' name, to Indianapolis. At first Haywood was reticent to accept it, but finally he received the message. Warned too late by the AG leader J. Roswell Flower, Haywood was rebaptized in Jesus' name, and his congregation swiftly followed him in his action. He never faltered from that position. Between 1918 and his death on April 12, 1931, G. T. Haywood served as a pastor; field superintendent; and then with the reorganization of the PAW in 1919, which he helped to incorporate, as general secretary. In 1922 he became executive vice-chairman and in 1923, secretary. In 1925 he was named presiding bishop when the PAW moved to an episcopal polity.

Haywood's leadership has been described as balanced, visionary, and progressive. He was a prolific writer who often illustrated his works, e.g., *The Finest of the Wheat* (n.d.), *The Victim of the Flaming Sword* (n.d.), or *Before the Foundation of the World* (1923). He was famous for his charts and paintings, which depicted his theological understanding. Perhaps his most widely acknowledged contribution to Pentecostalism was his music, which is still sung in most Pentecostal congregations, including those outside the Oneness movement. His spirituality is evident in such songs as "I see A Crimson Stream of Blood" and "Jesus the Son of God."

Bibliography: P. D. Dugas, compiler, *The Life and Writings of Elder G. T. Haywood* (1968); M. E. Golden, *The Life and Works of Bishop Garfield Thomas Haywood (1880–1931)* (1977); idem, *History of the Pentecostal Assemblies of the World* (1973).   C. M. Robeck, Jr.

HEALING, GIFT OF At both the beginning and the end of his discussion of "manifestations" of the Spirit in 1 Corinthians 12, Paul mentions "gifts of healings" (*charimata iamatōn*: 1 Corinthians 12:9, 28, 30). These are the only explicit designations of this reality in the NT, but the fact of healing is frequently narrated and described in the Gospels and elsewhere. This article will deal first with a biblical view of healing in general. Then, after a brief consideration of the role of healing in Jesus' ministry and the disciples' ministries, it will proceed to a specific treatment of what is designated by the Pauline phrase "gifts of healings."

I. An Old Testament View of Healing. Health and sickness are viewed according to the implicit or expressed anthropology of a given culture. (See Martin, 1978, and bibliography given there.) God's successive revelation to the Jews created a prophetic interpretation of reality which, while refracted through the culture, also acted in turn upon the culture, making of it the vehicle for a revealed understanding of the human condition. The interpretation of health and sickness that we find in the OT is just such a prophetic interpretation of these realities.

A. The Experience of Health and Sickness. It is significant that there is no one word in Hebrew that means "healthy." The state of being healthy is expressed in terms that indicate vigor, life, even "being fat" (*br'*), or simply by *shalom*, which we usually translate as "peace" but which really means the presence in a person, or a relationship, of all that ought to be there. Sickness, on the other hand, is most commonly described in words derived from the root *hlh*, which connotes "weakness," "exhaustion," "lacking vitality," etc. The most common way of expressing the recovery of health is through the root *hyh*, meaning "life." To be sick is to approach that state of absolute weakness and diminution which is death, while to recover health is to receive life once again. The most awful aspect of sickness is that a human being risks coming to that state where there is no praise of God. For people of the Old Covenant, that was death: "The grave cannot praise you, death cannot sing your praise. . . . The living, the living—they praise you, as I am doing today" (Isa. 38:18).

From this point of view it is easy to understand how the "death" threatened to Adam and eventually set loose in the world was linked in the Hebrew mind with sickness. Any loss of vitality indicates a certain separation from God, who is life, just as any recuperation implies a renewal of the divine presence.

In the deeply intuitive and symbolic anthropology of the OT, an experience of sickness is an experience of sin. Thus, prayers for deliverance from sickness always include an avowal of sin (Pss. 38:2–6; 39:9–12, et al.), while praise of God for such deliverance mentions forgiveness (Pss. 30:2–5; 32:1–11; 103:3, et al.). The linking of sickness/death and sin is expressed in the oldest stratum of the Yahwistic tradition now found in Genesis 2 and 3. The placing of this text at the beginning of the Torah by the inspired redactor is one more instance of the theological judgment that proposed a prophetic interpretation of all human suffering. It is not that the OT taught that every sickness was related to a personal sin; it is rather that every sick person was a physical expression of the weakness of the people who were alienated from God. Only God knows the degree of personal culpability. On the same principle, the prophets looked forward to the presence in Zion of a restored and purified people: "No one living there will say, 'I am sick;' for the people who dwell there will have their sins forgiven" (Isa. 33:24).

Healing, the restoration to life, is always the work of Yahweh. Asa is condemned because, when he is sick, "he did not seek Yhwh, but healers [by implication, magicians]" (2 Chron. 16:12). It was not forbidden, however, to have recourse to those who were skillful in binding up wounds or broken bones as prophetic allusions to these actions indicate (Isa. 1:6; Ezek. 30:21, et al.). The use of herbs and other means of healing were certainly practiced (2 Kings 20:7; Isa. 38:21), and considered part of wisdom (1 Kings 5:9–14 [Heb.]; Wisd. Sol. 7:20). In the biblical tradition, Sirach (38:1–15) praises the doctor, stating that his wisdom comes from God, that the doctor must also pray to God, and that God has provided healing herbs to be used wisely. The last line of this passage once again links sickness and sin, though the exact tenor of the expression is difficult to interpret.

Throughout the whole history of Israel, including intertestamental times, are instances as well of charismatic healers who have a power from God to restore to life. Even in the pagan world, people instinctively turned to God, as they understood him, for healing and restoration. (For examples of biblical and extra-biblical narratives of such healings, see Martin, 1988.)

B. The Symbolic Understanding of Sickness and Healing. Very early, the OT tradition began to speak of the wholeness of the people when they were faithful to God and the debilitated state that resulted from their sins in terms of health and sickness. This type of predication was facilitated by the symbolic anthropology characteristic of a culture that expressed psychological and spiritual states in terms of the body, especially the eyes, heart, limbs, etc. (see Wolff, 1974; Lack, 1973).

The Lord's act of rescuing his people from bondage is termed a "healing" in Exodus 15:27 and Hosea 11:3. However, the people's further infidelities resulted in sickness and wounds that only God can heal (Hos. 5:13; 7:1; Isa. 1:5–7; 6:10). He promises to heal their apostasy (Hos. 14:5; Jer. 3:22). The sickness of an individual may be directly related to this illness of the people as in Jeremiah 17:14, or the link may be more remote as in Psalms 30:3; 32:1–5. The symbolic use of terms relating to health and sickness is continued in the later tradition of Judaism, both in regard to the nation and to the individual (e.g., 1QH 2:8; CD 12:4; 13:9–10; b. Sanh. 101a; b. Ber. 5a; Mek. Besh. 5; Tg. Jer. 33:6; Tg. Isa. 35:1–6; 61:1–3). We may cite as one example a targumic tosephta found in connection with Genesis 22: ". . . our sins do not allow us to find healing . . . upon repentance depends our healing" (Grelot, 1957, 24). This mentality throws light on sayings of Jesus, such as, "Those who are healthy do not need a doctor, but rather those who are sick. I did not come to call the just, but sinners" (Mark 2:17/Luke 5:31–32; cf. Matt. 9:12–13).

II. Healing in the New Testament.

A. The Ministry of Jesus. Jesus responded to the emissaries from the Baptist by appealing to their own experience that promises such as Isaiah 35:5–6; and 61:1 were being fulfilled (Matt. 11:4–6/Luke 7:22–23.) This same view is reflected in texts such as Acts 10:38. Again, in nearly all the statements in the synoptic Gospels that summarize the activity of Jesus, healing is mentioned. Matthew frames his account of the Sermon on the Mount and the first ten wonders wrought by Jesus with the notice that "He went about in all Galilee teaching in their synagogues and preaching the good news among the kingdom, and healing every disease and every sickness among the people" (Matt. 4:23; see 9:35.) This same type of statement is repeated frequently. Some examples are Matthew 4:24–5:2; 8:16–17; 12:15–16; 15:29–31; Mark 1:32–34; 3:7–13; Luke 4:40–41; 6:17–19, et al.

Jesus, by his preaching, by his manner of life in associating with marginalized people (Matt. 9:12–13 par.; Luke 15:1–2), and by his healings and exorcisms manifested the fact that "The kingdom of God has come!" (Mark 1:14 par.). The word of the Lord had described a servant, anointed by Yahweh, who would preach the good news to the poor, bind up the brokenhearted, open the eyes of those who had no vision and comfort those who mourn (Isa. 61:1–2). In applying this promise to himself, Jesus was announcing that in his person the kingdom of God was breaking in (Luke 4:17–21). By healing from disease and casting out demons, Jesus inaugurated the kingdom and embodied it (Matt. 12:28; Luke 11:20).

The importance of this ministry can be seen in the light of the symbolic anthropology described above. Through healing, Jesus was evidencing the power and compassion of God to free human beings from all aspects of the power of evil. He himself made this explicit at times (Luke 13:16), and this is intensified by the fact that the Gospels may describe someone "demon-possessed" as "healed" by the word of Jesus (see Matt. 15:22–28; compare Mark 7:25–30; see also Luke 9:42). In addition, the healings worked by Jesus embody and symbolize that healing work by which he will heal the people of their sins and infidelity (Matt. 8:17).

B. The Healing Ministry of the Church. The healing ministry of the church is based on the apostolic commission given to the disciples during Jesus' lifetime: "He called his twelve disciples to him and gave them authority to drive out unclean spirits and to cure every disease and every sickness. . . . As you go, preach, saying: 'The kingdom of heaven has come.' Heal the sick, raise the dead, cleanse lepers, cast out demons . . ." (Matt. 10:1, 7–8; Mark 6:7–12; Luke 9:1–6). It is obvious, then, that healing and deliverance from demonic power are integral parts of evangelization.

We see this principle at work, not only in the summary of the signs that "accompany those who believe" (Mark 16:17) and in such texts that describe the characteristics of an apostle ("signs, wonders, and miracles . . . great patience" [2 Cor. 12:12]), but also in the Book of Acts where Luke is careful to narrate many instances of healing done by the servants of the Lord. Such actions witness to the resurrection of the Lord Jesus (4:33), and, in the symbolic nature of all Christian healing, witness as well that "Salvation/healing (sōtēria) is found in no one else, for there is no other name under heaven given to men by which we must be saved/healed (sōthēnai)" (4:12).

As in the life of Jesus, healing and teaching are considered aspects of one activity, namely, preaching the gospel. In the Gospels are three instances where Matthew records that Jesus healed while, in parallel places, Mark speaks of teaching. Luke, in one of these, mentions both activities (Matt. 14:14/Mark 6:34/Luke 9:11; Matt. 19:2/Mark 10:1; Matt. 21:14/Mark 1:17). In the same way, after Paul had struck Elymas blind, the proconsul who saw what happened "believed, for he was amazed at the teaching of the Lord." (Acts 13:12).

The witness to the Resurrection made through healing can take place in the midst of believers, as in the case of Dorcas (Acts 9:36–43) and Eutychus (Acts 20:9–12). However, the primary purpose of healing is to demonstrate tangibly God's intention and ability to lead people to the ultimate salvation which is eternal life—i.e., the fruit of healing is conversion. This is demonstrated frequently in Acts, as can be seen in Luke's notice concerning belief recorded after a healing or a deliverance. Some examples are Acts 4:4, 31; 5:14–15; 9:35–42.

III. The Gift of Healing.

A. In the Early Community. The only explicit mention of the gift of healing, as has been noted, is found in the discussion in 1 Corinthians 12:9, 28, 30 where both terms (gift, healing) are in the plural. This, along with the related expression, "workings of powerful deeds" (energēmata dynameōn, 1 Cor. 12:9; see v. 29) is probably meant to evoke the sense of abundance and variety in the gifts that spring from faith. The gifts of healing and of miracles are distinguished because of the particular symbolic power of healing to evidence God's action freeing humankind at every level from bondage to evil and the effects of sin.

Since the charismatic gift of faith is itself a specific intensification of the basic attitude toward God by which we are brought to salvation (see FAITH, GIFT OF), "gifts of healings" refers to a particular specification of the general power to preach the gospel conferred upon the whole body of believers and realized in different ways within the body.

James 5:13–16 describes an established function in the community whereby someone who is ill or weak (asthenei) is to call in the elders, a specific group, who are to anoint him in the name of the Lord. The prayer of faith (cf. 1 Cor. 12:9) will heal/save (sōsei) the ill or enervated (kamnonta) person, and the Lord will raise him up (egerei, undoubted resurrection overtones); and if the person has committed sin (see above, I.A.), it will be forgiven him/her. This passage does not speak of a charisma of healing but of a power in the community of faith expressed through its leaders. On the other hand, 1 Corinthians 11:30 speaks of the weakness, sickness, and death that occur when the community does not discern the body of the Lord. This notion of individual health and sickness on every level of human existence being an embodied symbol of the whole community is a matter of experience that finds expression and confirmation in the theological anthropology already begun in the OT.

While it is easy to distinguish the charisma of healing from those healings effected by the Lord through the community's prayer of faith, the same cannot be said for the function of healing that is part of the apostolic commission to preach the gospel. In the first place, the NT restricts its accounts of healing on the part of the disciples to instances involving the well-known preachers of the gospel. We must bear in mind as well that the gifts of healing and of miracles are of their nature manifestations of God's existence and power, and they witness to Jesus. Thus, though Paul seems to have the internal life of the Corinthian community in mind (1 Cor. 12–14), he lauds even prophecy for its capacity to convict and change the unbeliever (1 Cor. 14:24).

In light of the NT presentation of healing, we may draw four conclusions. First, the preaching of the word is itself sufficient to bring about healings; this is confirmed in modern experience. Second, those who are sent to preach the gospel are often endowed with the gift of healing as part of their empowerment to bring people to salvation. Third, God works healings through the ministry of the elders and the prayer of faith. Finally, there is a specific gift, possessed by some but not by others, which provides for healing both within and outside of the community and, in both instances, witnesses to the power of the Resurrection to offset the moral and physical consequences of individual and communal sin. The writings of the early ecclesiastical Fathers bear abundant witness to the presence of this gift in their communities (see Kydd, 1984).

B. Healing in the Modern Church. God heals in answer to prayer. This is sometimes in the context of the ministry of the elders within a community of faith. God also heals in order to provide an "audio-visual aid" when the gospel is being preached. Finally, God brings about healing through special charismata, and it is to this last manner of healing that we will address a few concluding remarks.

All life, vigor, and strength come to us from our Lord Jesus Christ who, as he now lives "to God," applies the restoring power of his cross to our lives. Healing is a symbolic foreshadowing of the full life to which humankind is called, "our adoptive sonship, the redemption of our bodies." (Rom. 8:23). As healing takes place within the body of believers, we are given on the level of our existence in this world an unmistakable demonstration of that power "for us who believe," which the Father "exerted in Christ when he raised him from the dead" (see Eph. 1:19–20).

When unbelievers experience healing at the hands of Christians, they are being given a presentation of the Good News, "not simply with words, but also with power, with the Holy Spirit, and with deep conviction" (1 Thess. 1:5 NIV).

Charismatic gifts of healing are qualities given to certain members of the body in and through which God demonstrates his saving power so that the response of faith will rest "not on men's wisdom, but on God's power" (1 Cor. 1:5 NIV).

In every century, the Spirit has unceasingly given the gifts needed to build and protect the body of Christ. The challenge particular to the gift of healing is that it can easily be imitated or co-opted by evil powers so that what was once a demonstration of God's Good News can become a source of pride and vainglory, leading both the minister and those to whom he ministers into a state of distraction or even ruin. The possession of this gift, with which certain persons are obviously more highly and permanently endowed than others, is a concretization of God's call to a life of love, humility, and that form of ministry by which one becomes and remains the "servant of all."

There is a great need for "gifts of healings" in our age. As we become sensitive to the unity of the human person and of the human race, we see how physical healing does more than rectify disorders of the body; it makes God present to the one healed and to all those joined to that person. As our modern understanding of the psychology of health and sickness expands, we grow to appreciate more profoundly the wisdom of the inspired theological anthropology of the Scriptures, which sees these states as symbolic embodiments of individual and societal alienation from God.

To heal a poor person of the effects of malnutrition is to reverse a process created by the structures of sin of which the person may be an innocent victim. To heal a person of AIDS is to claim the victory of the Cross of Christ not only over physical disorder, but also over the very forces of death that lead to eternal ruin. To heal an angry or anxious person of heart disease or cancer is to initiate a process of reconciliation and restoration that derives from the power of the Cross. To free someone from Satan's domination, gained through a life exposed to alienation and violence, is to liberate a human memory from the power of evil so that it can generate thoughts and attitudes that correspond to the truth of the gospel and become a temple in which the Father is adored in spirit and truth. In brief, healing is an essential part of preaching the gospel and of bearing witness to the reality and majesty of Jesus Christ.

See also GIFTS OF THE SPIRIT; PAULINE LITERATURE; HEALING MOVEMENTS

Bibliography: P. Gelot, "Une tosephta targoumique sur Genèse xxii dans un manuscrit liturgique dans la Geniza du Caire," *RÉJuivHJud* 16 (1957):5–26; R. Kydd, *Charismatic Gifts in the Early Church* (1984); R. Lack, *La Symbolique du Livre d'Isaïe* (1973); F. MacNutt, *Healing* (1974); F. Martin, *Narrative Parallels to the New Testament* (Resources for Biblical Study) (1988); idem, "The Charismatic Renewal and Biblical Hermeneutics," in *Theological Reflections on the Charismatic Renewal*, ed. J. Haughey (1978), 1–38; H. W. Wolff, *Anthropology of the Old Testament* (1974).

R. F. Martin

HEALING MOVEMENTS One of the notably significant, yet controversial, phenomena to develop in the modern history and theology of the American church is the doctrine and ministry of divine healing. Few practices within Christianity have had a more legitimate ancestry than praying for the healing of the sick. The tradition of divine healing within the church has been long and well-documented. Christians in all ages have believed in the miraculous intervention of God to heal. At times the practice has been normative in the life of the church, but at other periods it has existed only on the church's periphery. In America the seventeenth and eighteenth centuries witnessed scattered demonstrations of healing within various religious communities. Since the latter half of the nineteenth century, however, a discernible interest in the divine healing movement has existed in America, a movement fully endowed with its own doctrine, leaders, and popular following. This movement, whose doctrine and practices have been adopted by others through the years, has been variously referred to as the faith healing, faith cure, divine healing, or healing movement. It refers to that group of people who maintain the belief that physical disease or illness is cured by the supernatural intervention of God in response to the prayer of faith. The significance of the movement lies in its uniqueness to popularize in America a concept of salvation that includes health and healing as an integral part. Since the inception in America of the Pentecostal movement and the later charismatic movement, divine healing has been an integral and universal part of their *Gestalt* of doctrines.

I. Historical Antecedents. In the early years of the nation, several religious groups included the belief and practice of healing within their ranks. Divine healing was never the dominating motif within any of these groups, but each advocated the doctrine, and manifestations of supernatural healing were recorded. One of the earliest to advocate healing was the Society of Friends. Members of the Friends had migrated to America from England as early as the mid-seventeenth century. George Fox, the founder of the Quakers, had a significant healing ministry, and his reputation of praying for the sick preceded his evangelistic travels to America. As he itinerated in America in 1672, he reported the physical healing of many for whom he prayed. When he prayed for the sick, he practiced the laying on of hands and insisted that their healing was under the divine sovereignty of God. Thus, if healing did not immediately follow the prayer of faith, the person was not chastised for lack of faith. Under Fox's ministry most healings occurred instantaneously, but gradual healings were also acknowledged. His journal contains the records of many who were physically healed, and after his death a "Book of Miracles" was discovered which documented in detail 150 of the healings under his ministry. Fox and the Quakers acknowledged the miraculous power of the Holy Spirit working among the people to heal sickness just as in the NT era. At the same time they demonstrated their confidence in both medicine and medical doctors. For the Quakers, instances of divine healing did not serve as proofs of their ministry but were seen as simply one part

Giant circus tents and salvation-healing meetings were a common sight in major cities during the 1950s. R. W. Schambach, a former associate of A. A. Allen, continued using tents into the 1980s. Here he prays for the sick in a tent crusade.

of their total ministry. The practice continued by American Friends into the nineteenth century.

Another early group advocating divine healing was the Brethren or "Dunker Church" founded by Alexander Mack, Sr. These persecuted German Pietists resettled in America in the Pennsylvania region during the early 1700s. One of the basic Brethren tenets and practices was the anointing of the sick with oil as prescribed in James 5:14–15. The Pietist scholar John Albert Bengel, in his *Gnomon of the New Testament,* insisted that the purpose of this anointing was to produce miraculous healing and that God intended this practice to remain in the church always. The literature of the movement records many testimonies of miraculous cures. Eventually the Brethren split into four denominations, but each maintained the emphasis upon healing.

In the century before 1850 many of the manifestations of divine healing occurred in religious movements that were related to the religious fervor of revivalism as propagated in the "burned-over" district of western New York. Many of the more sectarian and sometimes colorful groups such as the Shakers, Mormons, Noyesites, and Adventists either originated in or were influenced by this region. The Shakers, for example, regularly reported healings through the prayer of faith and the laying on of hands by either their founder, Mother Ann Lee, or their elders. This group believed the power to heal the sick had been transmitted by Christ to his disciples and was established as one of the signs of a true Christian church. Many of those healed attested to their healing by affidavits as a witness against skeptics. The early Shakers were radicals in their belief regarding healing by prayer to the exclusion of physicians or medicine. Gradually, as time separated them from their founder, they began emphasizing personal hygiene and other preventive health measures as well as the use of herbal medicines. By the 1830s the Shakers had elevated the use of herbal medicines to a plane of respectability and were marketing medical formulas to drug firms nationwide. These developments led the society to alter their doctrine on healing and to maintain that miraculous gifts were used solely to usher in new dispensations of God's grace.

Two of the cults that developed during this period and advocated and prayed for healing were the Mormons and Noyesites. As early as 1835 Joseph Smith, founder of the Mormons, was reporting numerous cases of divine healing. When he was unable to pray personally for the sick, he would anoint handkerchiefs and send them to those who were suffering. Recognizing that not all persons possessed the faith to be healed, Smith encouraged people to use medical means since God had prepared the medicinal qualities of plants and roots for the purpose of removing the causes of disease. Another sectarian group that advocated divine healing was John Humphrey Noyes' Oneida Community. This community openly expected miraculous and supernatural demonstrations to be exhibited just as they had been in the apostolic church. Noyes advocated a novel theology regarding disease. He maintained that the immediate cause of disease was the committed sins of each individual (not original sin) and the power of evil spirits. He believed that if the world could be freed of all diabolical powers there would be no disease.

The Adventist movement under Ellen Gould White arose in the late 1840s with miraculous healings in answer to the prayer of faith as a normative expectation. As White traveled throughout western New York and New England, demonstrations of the healing power of prayer in her ministry were manifested. Following the example of James 5 she anointed the sick with oil and laid hands upon them. In her early years she taught that the use of medical assistance was a denial of faith in God to heal. As with the Shakers, White gradually shifted her focus from divine healing to an emphasis upon health and healthful living. So convinced did she become that diet, medicine, and faith should be combined in the treatment of disease that she opened a sanitarium in 1866 in West Battle Creek, Michigan, where such a combination of treatment could be practiced. The clinic was staffed only by Christian physicians. To train them White founded a medical school at Loma Linda University in 1910. Today Adventists operate more than three hundred medical facilities around the world. Gradually the miraculous was displaced in White's ministry and the principles of preventive health care and temperance became predominant.

II. European Influences. In the early nineteenth century, Edward Irving, minister of the National Scottish Church in Regent Square, London, began calling for a new expectation on the part of the church for supernatural manifestations of God through physical healings. Irving believed that the contemporary church was not experiencing the miraculous interventions of God in physical healing because pastors were not teaching believers to expect God to heal. By 1830 Irving's congregation began to experience supernatural healings as well as "the speaking in other tongues." Irving believed all healing was from God and thus encouraged the joining of the prayer of faith with medical assistance. His influence and ministry were propagated in Britain through the Catholic Apostolic Church, which was founded in 1830. He later influenced the American church through the ministry of John Alexander Dowie who considered Irving the most influential person in his life.

The immediate European influences on the American healing movement centered on the ministries of Johann Christoph Blumhardt, Dorothea Trudel, and Otto Stockmayer. Their ministries were to be both inspirational and exemplary for the leaders of the American movement and were to be widely imitated. The healing ministry of Johann Blumhardt, a Lutheran pastor, began in 1843 in the small village of Mottlinger in the heart of Germany's Black Forest. In praying for a dying young girl, Katarina Dittus, he discovered that the testamentary words of Christ, "They shall lay hands on the sick and they shall recover," were not outdated. The supernatural healing of the girl at his hands created a marked sensation. Revival broke out in the local parish. Reminiscent of the earlier religious awakenings in both Europe and America, people with tears and lamentations flocked to the churches to confess their sins and seek deliverance from the wrath of God.

As newspapers spread reports of these events across Europe, multitudes of the sick from throughout the continent migrated toward Mottlinger seeking the healing prayers of Blumhardt. The Lutheran ecclesiastical authorities ordered Blumhardt to cease praying for the sick and to advise only patience and submission in sickness. In 1852 he withdrew from the denomination and established a faith home at the famous Bad Boll, a former gambling and health spa that accommodated more than 150 invalids at a time. Here the sick were instructed in the biblical message of healing within a faith-building atmosphere to enable them to obtain spiritual power over their sickness. So successful was the faith home concept that R. Kelso Carter reported in 1887 that more than thirty such healing centers operated in America.

Regarding the cause of sickness, Blumhardt firmly supported the views of Origen, Augustine, Cyprian, and other church fathers who believed that sickness was the result of sin and emanated from the devil. Therefore, Blumhardt argued that the forgiveness of sins and healing are related. Reflecting upon this view, Karl Barth was later to assert that Blumhardt's emphasis upon sickness as the result of the human struggle with the devil contributed to a better understanding of healing in the NT than that which was proposed by the older orthodox, pietistic, and rationalistic Protestant groups, including the Reformers. To Barth, Blumhardt made it plain that sickness is the manifestation of an ungodly and inhuman reality to which the Christian's attitude must be one of indignation and conflict. The Christian must cooperate with God by exercising faith in him and praying to him for the elimination of this evil.

Having accepted this theological position, Blumhardt insisted there could be no cure unless there was believing contact of the person's spirit with God. Thus, Blumhardt always charged seekers to search their hearts and to confess their secret sins before God. He urged seekers to acknowledge their faults to those whom they had wronged and to make restitution as far as possible. Furthermore, he believed God cured without the aid of medicines or physicians since he believed that healing was provided for in Christ's atonement. But he never urged people to give up either one. Blumhardt carefully cautioned that healing was not effected by the mere laying on of hands or any physical exertion, but by simple prayer alone. In fact, he never intimated that his presence was necessary and frequently prayed for people by means of letters or telegrams.

A second notable healing ministry in Europe that inspired the American scene was that of a young florist, Dorothea Trudel. In 1851 several of her coworkers in the Swiss village of Mannedorf on Lake Zurich fell ill and steadily grew worse as their sicknesses resisted all medical treatment. Acting upon the promise of James 5:14–15, Dorothea anointed them with oil and prayed for them. Instantaneously they were healed; thus began her healing ministry. This event propelled Trudel into the forefront of the public and brought people from throughout Europe to seek her prayers. In order to accommodate these masses Trudel opened several faith homes. Her assistant and successor in this enterprise was Samuel Zeller.

In 1856, because of her praying for the sick, Trudel was charged with "practicing the healing art without a license." This is the first recorded instance of such a formal charge being leveled against a faith healing practitioner in modern history. In her trial before the Zurich tribunal of justice she was acquitted of all charges. The massive publicity from the trial, however, attracted such large multitudes to her faith homes that most had to be turned away. To reach the multitudes, Trudel began the practice of including prayers in her correspondence with the sick. This means became normative in America, and by it faith healing practitioners were able to extend their ministries far beyond their local environs.

If Blumhardt and Trudel were inspirational examples and patterns to be imitated in regard to their faith homes and methodology, Otto Stockmayer was to provide the most systematic presentation of the theology undergirding the movement. His introduction to faith healing came on Easter 1867 when Samuel Zeller laid hands upon him and prayed for his healing. Several years later he opened his own faith home in Switzerland, where he employed the same methodology as that used in Mannedorf. Stockmayer's book, *Sickness and the Gospel* (n.d.) and his frequent participation in the early Keswick conventions made his ministry familiar to both British and American audiences. A. J. Gordon, one of the leading American advocates of divine healing, referred to Stockmayer as the "theologian of the doctrine of healing by faith." The basic presupposition of divine healing, that deliverance from sickness could not be separated from the whole work of redemption, was articulated by Stockmayer in his thesis. He found justification for this view in what

he considered the important connection between Matthew 8:16–17 and Isaiah 53:4. Using the Matthean Scripture to interpret Isaiah 53:4, he concluded that Christ had borne humankind's physical as well as spiritual sufferings on the cross. The connection between these two Scriptures, according to Stockmayer, shows that it cannot be God's final will for people to suffer physical infirmities and diseases since Christ had borne them on the cross for all humankind.

William Branham initiated the post-war healing movement in 1947. He later proclaimed himself the angel of Revelation 3:14 and 10:7.

Stockmayer insisted, along with Blumhardt, that the promises of God are not self-fulfilling, but their realization depends upon people. Thus, in order for them to be delivered from sickness, they must do so by faith just as they experience freedom from sin. In addition, Stockmayer emphasized that sick believers were not to be directed to those with gifts of healing or working of miracles because these gifts are deposited with the church. From the beginning Christ gave the power to heal the sick in connection with the work of evangelism, i.e., the work of extending the kingdom of God. This power was first given to the apostles, who in turn appointed elders who received the same power. According to Stockmayer, James 5:16 made healing no longer dependent upon the prayer of the elders, but rested it with the effectual and fervent prayer of any righteous person. Thus the circle widened and all the children of God were exhorted to pray for one another in the case of sickness. This development revealed the acute need for persons to be cleansed of sin (sanctified), since it is the prayer of a righteous person that is answered.

III. American Holiness Influence. The most significant theological influence upon the divine healing movement came from the nineteenth-century American Holiness movement. With its emphasis upon purification from sin and the power of the Holy Spirit in individual lives, the Holiness movement provided the theological environment for faith healing in America. In teaching the doctrine of Christian perfection, Holiness advocates emphasized certain characteristics that were important for the divine healing movement. First, most Holiness advocates insisted that the experience of perfection or entire sanctification was a second and separate work of grace that was realized instantaneously by the supernatural intervention of God. Wesley regarded this as a definite experience, but he taught it as a point in a process of growth and gradualism. In the 1830s, however, under the teachings of Charles G. Finney and Phoebe Palmer, the instantaneous emphasis virtually eclipsed the gradual aspect of the experience. Part of the divine healing movement reflected this position by declaring that healing always occurred instantaneously, and if it did not, it was owing to a lack of faith or existing sin on the part of the sick person. On the other hand, the Keswickian branch of the Holiness movement allowed for the progressive aspect of the experience by teaching a practical deliverance from continuance in known sin by an instant abandonment of sin and of every known weight that hinders progress. Practitioners of divine healing who reflected the Keswickian view of sanctification believed that when God is petitioned in faith for healing, he immediately confers it although the actual manifestation of healing may occur gradually.

In addition to entire sanctification being an instantaneous experience, the Holiness movement emphasized that the experience is "immediate salvation." Palmer insisted that believers must "venture now" to receive the experience of perfection, for God stands waiting to bestow it. When asked how soon a person could expect to experience this state of perfection, she replied in her book *Faith and Its Effects* (1854) that "just so soon as you come believingly . . . come complying with the conditions and claim it . . . it is already yours. If you do not now receive it, the delay will not be on the part of God, but wholly with yourself." The entire faith healing movement echoed these views by emphasizing that a person could receive his healing now, immediately.

Finally, in the 1850s Palmer began to refer to Christian perfection variously as "the baptism with the Holy Ghost and with fire," "an endue-ment with power," "the baptism of fire," and as a "Pentecostal baptism." She was one of the first to adopt and popularize the "baptism of the Holy Spirit" terminology. Feeling that the Holiness movement was in the midst of the dispensation of the Holy Spirit, she concluded that now, as in the earliest days of the Spirit's dispensation, Pentecostal blessing brings Pentecostal power. Asa Mahan also supported the use of the terminology "baptism of the Holy Ghost" to identify the perfectionist experience. He noted that power was one of the most striking characteristics of this baptismal experience and that it was clearly the privilege of all believers to receive and exercise this power.

He based this assumption on Acts 1:8, "Ye shall receive power, after that the Holy Ghost is come upon you." Included within this common heritage of every believer were the gifts of the Spirit, such as prophecy and divine healing.

By propagating the doctrine of Christian perfection or the baptism of the Holy Spirit as purification from sin, the enduement with power, and the living of a consecrated life of holiness, the nineteenth-century Holiness movement provided the basic theological milieu in which the supernatural gifts of God, and in particular divine healing, would flourish. After acknowledging that the Pentecostal power of Acts was still available today for all believers, it was a logical step to allow for the accompanying supernatural signs. When one accepts the basic presupposition of the faith healing movement that all sickness is ultimately related to sin and Satan, and the presupposition of the Holiness movement that the believer is endued with the Pentecostal power of Acts, then the sanctified believer, who through God has power over sin and Satan, also has power over sickness. This thesis provided the fundamental basis for the intimate connection between perfectionism and divine healing. As the Holiness scholar Melvin Dieter has observed, with this renewed activity of the Holy Spirit working in the believer's life, many Holiness adherents experienced increased occurrences of miraculous physical healings as demonstrations of the new dispensation of the Spirit. The belief in and the witness to divine healings attended the Holiness movement at every turn.

The pioneers of divine healing in America clearly demonstrate the interwoven connection between the Holiness and divine healing movements, and between the European and American healing movements. These pioneers were among the foremost proponents of Christian perfection. In fact, the man commonly referred to by his contemporaries as the father of the divine healing movement in America, Ethan O. Allen, in 1846 became the first member of the American healing movement to associate officially the doctrine of Christian perfection with divine healing. Like the founder of Methodism, Allen believed that Christ's atonement provided not only for justification but also for purification of the human nature from sin. Agreeing with Stockmayer that sickness was caused by sin, Allen maintained that the purification of human nature from sin by the experience of sanctification would eliminate illness.

While in his late twenties, Allen had been healed of tuberculosis by the prayer of faith at a meeting of Methodist class leaders in 1846. He immediately began to pray for the sick, becoming the first American to make the faith healing ministry his full-time vocation. The beginning of his work was contemporaneous with that of Dorothea Trudel, although at the time he had no knowledge of the supernatural events that were occurring under her ministry. Without any instruction in the methods or techniques of praying for the sick except for the examples of the NT, Allen ventured ahead with his new ministry. Unlike his European counterparts who established their ministries at one location, Allen itinerated. His ministry was basically, but not exclusively, limited to the disinherited of society. His itineration to individual homes, poorhouses, the developing faith homes, camp meetings, and churches enabled him to spread his message widely. But his shyness and especially his unschooled ways prevented him from obtaining a larger audience. For fifty years he traveled throughout the eastern half of the U.S., praying for the sick and teaching divine healing.

Over the years Allen was instrumental in bringing a number of persons into the faith healing ministry. The most important of these was Mrs. Elizabeth Mix, a black woman from Wolcottville, Connecticut, who had been healed of tuberculosis under Allen's ministry. She was well-educated, articulate, and persuasive. Under Allen's tutelage she became the first black healing evangelist in the nation. Her healing ministry was so well received that even the most outspoken opponents of divine healing, such as James Buckley, editor of the *Christian Advocate*, respected her and her accomplishments. Interestingly, even physicians sent their patients to her for prayer.

It is significant to note Mrs. Mix's articulation of an important and universal principle of the divine healing movement. She instructed patients to pray in faith and then to act upon their faith. She emphasized that it is not necessary to feel some particular emotion, but it is essential for patients to act as though they believe what they profess to believe. That is, petitioners must act out their faith by making physical exertions to demonstrate their professed belief that God is actually healing.

Allen and his disciples provided the first systematic beginning of the divine healing movement in America. However, Charles Cullis, a medical doctor in Boston, did more than any other person to propagate faith healing and to draw the attention of the American Church to the doctrine. He was the single most important figure in the development of the divine healing movement in America. Cullis functioned as a vital link between the Holiness and divine healing movements, and his significance in linking these two movements is demonstrated by his success in convincing prominent Holiness leaders that full salvation included not only salvation or healing of the spirit but also the healing of the physical body. Included among these leaders were John Inskip, first president of the National Camp Meeting Association for the Promotion of Holiness (1867–84); William McDonald, second president of the National Camp Meeting Association (1884–92); William E. Osborn, founder of the Ocean Grove Camp Meeting; Daniel Steele, professor of NT at Boston University; William E. Boardman, author of *The Higher Christian Life* (1859); A. J. Gordon, founder of Gordon College in Massachusetts; A. B. Simpson, founder of the Christian and Missionary Alliance (CMA); and two Friends, Hannah Whitall Smith of Philadelphia, and David B. Updegraff, a leader in the Ohio Yearly Meeting.

In addition, Cullis's endeavors to spread the messages of perfection and divine healing led to his founding of a publishing firm, the Willard Tract Repository, which was the first press in the nation to begin regular publication of divine healing materials, including the works of Blumhardt, Trudel, and Stockmayer from Europe. Cullis also founded a faith healing home, conducted weekly faith healing services in his local church, and held faith healing conventions across the nation. By the time of his death in 1892, the doctrine of divine healing was firmly established in the American religious community.

In the midst of a personal crisis in 1861–62, Cullis underwent an intense and profound spiritual experience in which he professed salvation and vowed to serve God with his talents. Following his attendance at Phoebe Palmer's Tuesday Meeting for the Promotion of Holiness in New York City, he received the experience of sanctification and vowed to take the gospel of love and care to the poor, the hopeless, and especially the terminally sick and neglected. Knowing that indigent consumptives had nowhere to seek relief, since both hospitals and poorhouses denied them admittance owing to their incurable status, he determined to pioneer a home where such victims could have proper care during their dying days. His first consumptive home was opened in 1864, and the sick were able to receive free the comforts of a warm home and complete medical care. During the decade of the 1880s Cullis's faith work grew until it became a constellation of charities. It eventually included not only homes for consumptives, a school of nursing, a publishing house that produced three monthly magazines, five churches, various urban missions, a high school, and a Bible college; but also two orphanages, a home for those with cancer, a home for people with spinal problems and another for paralytics, a faith-cure home, a home for "fallen women," a home for the insane, a mission to American Jews, a college and orphanage for black freshmen in the South (Boydton Institute), a mission to the Chinese in America, a school at Renick's Valley in West Virginia, an evangelistic outreach to the blacks in Oxford, North Carolina, and several missions in California. His work became international in scope when he sent missionaries to India and South Africa.

This extensive benevolent ministry was keynoted by Cullis's ministry of faith healing. It was the reading of the *Life of Dorothea Trudel* in 1869 that convinced Cullis that healing in answer to the prayer of faith was a permanent privilege for the people of God. In 1870 he demonstrated his new belief when Lucy Drake was healed of a brain tumor that had completely immobilized her for five months. This healing was the turning point of Cullis's ministry. He immediately began converting the Holiness leadership to his new discovery regarding physical healing by faith. Following a four-month trip to Europe in 1873, where he visited the faith works of Blumhardt, Trudel, and George Müller, he began conducting annual faith conventions at Framingham, Massachusetts, and later at Old Orchard Beach, Maine. These conventions constituted typical nineteenth-century Holiness camp meetings with an emphasis upon Christian perfection, but included the added

The best known evangelist in the salvation-healing movement, Oral Roberts, prays for a woman in his Portland, Oregon, crusade, c. 1953.

dimension of divine healing. The meetings quickly became internationally known. In the words of critic James Buckley, Cullis was credited with having given Old Orchard Beach the same "reputation among his followers as the grotto of Lourdes among the Roman Catholics."

Cullis's faith conventions did more to focus attention on the message of divine healing throughout America than any single event. The outpouring of articles from both secular and religious presses across the country on the faith conventions and on divine healing in general was extraordinary, considering that the topic had seldom appeared in the news media before this date. *Christian Advocate* reported that the "remarkable scenes" witnessed at Cullis's faith conventions brought the subject of divine healing into prominence. Regardless of the stance taken on the issue of faith healing by different editors and reporters, massive publicity during the years 1881–85 effectively spread interest in the doctrine across the land. One needs only to consider the large number of articles on the subject by local, regional, and national papers during this period to understand that the nation was becoming aware that a new movement was being born.

R. Kelso Carter, one of the leading apologists for the movement, called this period of widespread publicity and attention the "wonder" stage of the modern development of divine healing. This "wonder" stage is illustrated by an editorial in the *Christian Advocate* in 1882, which concluded that at the present time divine healing "should neither be pushed aside as unworthy of notice, nor received with unquestioning credulity." Writing in *Century Magazine* Carter insisted that "the mass of evidence offered, the multitude of witnesses arising, and the words of Scripture on the subject, demand at least a respectful hearing, and invite the closest scrutiny into the . . . practice of Divine Healing." By 1887 he would observe that "True or False, there is no belief rising more swiftly before the churches everywhere than that of Divine Healing."

With this new surge of interest created in divine healing as a result of the widespread publicity the doctrine received in the early 1880s, Cullis decided to carry his faith conventions beyond the confines of Old Orchard Beach. He began staging faith conventions in the major cities throughout the country, including Philadelphia, Baltimore, New York, Chicago, Boston, Pittsburgh, and Detroit. The climax of these faith conventions came when William Boardman convened the International Conference on Divine Healing and True Holiness in the great Agricultural Hall of London, England, in which more than two thousand persons gathered in 1885. This was the first such international gathering of its kind. It also was the first gathering of the major advocates of the movement. The conference was followed immediately by a series of small faith conventions throughout the U.K.

The interest in divine healing that Cullis's faith conventions helped to generate was increased by the proliferation of publications concerning the topic. The decade of the 1880s saw an outpouring of popular testimonial works such as Cullis, *More Faith Cures; or Answers to Prayer in the Healing of the Sick* (1881); Carrie Judd, *The Prayer of Faith* (1880); R. Kelso Carter, *Miracles of Healings; and* Theodore Monod, *The Gift of God*. More importantly, however, this was the decade of the first doctrinal and theological treatises on the subject. Most of these first apologetics were published by the Willard Tract Repository, since they were written at the personal request and encouragement of Charles Cullis. One of Cullis's biographers, the Reverend William Daniels, identified the repository as one of the key instruments in making Cullis's faith work the center of the American divine healing movement. Next to the faith conventions, Daniels declared the repository to be the "chief visible" cause for advancing the doctrine of divine healing into one of the most prominent questions before the Christian world in the nineteenth century.

The first of these doctrinal treatises was produced by a leader of the Keswick Holiness movement, William Boardman, and was entitled, *"The Lord that Healeth Thee" (Jehovah Rophi)* (1881). This volume, which launched Boardman into a career as one of the leading authorities and practitioners of faith healing in the nineteenth century, was written with the same care and thoroughness as his 1859 defense of the doctrine of sanctification, *The Higher Christian Life* (1859). Another significant volume was A. J. Gordon's *The Ministry of Healing: Miracles of Cure in All Ages* published in 1882. This was a lengthy historical and doctrinal study on faith healing from the early church fathers progressing through the post-Reformation period. Gordon's theological and scriptural defense of divine healing was considered by the doctrine's most hostile critic, B. B. Warfield, to be an "ingenious" apologia and a "very persuasive" argument.

A year later (1883) R. L. Stanton's volume *Gospel Parallelisms: Illustrated in the Healing of the Body and Soul* appeared. Stanton, a former president of Miami University in Ohio and a moderator of the general assembly of the Presbyterian Church, set out to demonstrate that Christ's atonement had laid a foundation for deliverance from both sin and disease. He insisted that it was vital to include both in any true conception of what the gospel offers to humankind. However, the volume that quickly became the leading apologia for the doctrine was R. Kelso Carter's *The Atonement of Sin and Sickness; or A Full Salvation for Soul and Body* (1884). Carter's thesis was that the Atonement provided for the body the same total healing which it provided for the soul. Carter's rootage in the American Holiness movement was obvious in his maintenance that the Atonement was instantaneous in its applica-

tion to unrighteousness or inward depravity. This doctrine of Atonement embraced cleansing from all traces of inherited depravity and considered sickness a trace of humankind's inherited depravity and thus as being from the devil. The vicarious atonement of Christ is explicitly for all depravity, including sickness. *Century Magazine* proclaimed this work "the leading authority" on the subject of faith healing, and the Chicago periodical *Inter-Ocean* identified the publication as the "best writing upon this subject." So popular was this volume that four years later John B. Alden revised and enlarged the work under the new title *Divine Healing or The Atonement*. An additional important apologia published in the late 1880s was R. L. Marsh's *"Faith Healing": A Defense, or The Lord Thy Healer* (1889). This volume was originally presented as a bachelor of divinity thesis at Yale Divinity School.

These theological and historical treatises published in defense of divine healing tended to legitimatize the movement by providing a systematic approach to the doctrine theologically, and by demonstrating a solid rootage of the church historically through the tracing of the practice of divine healing throughout the centuries. Since faith homes and faith conventions such as those operated by Cullis focused upon the experiential aspect of healing, these scholarly apologetics provided a needed balance to the movement. Even critics of the doctrine acknowledged the respect and stability these works brought.

IV. The Expanding Movement. Through the aggressive outreach of Cullis's ministry, the doctrine and practice of divine healing was brought to the forefront of the American Christian community and made a permanent feature. During his lifetime his name had become synonymous with the faith healing movement. R. Kelso Carter was correct in his observation that to Cullis belonged the distinction of having done more than any other person to bring healing by faith to the attention of the church in the nineteenth century. Perhaps, however, his most significant contribution was the conversion of other individuals who were to provide theological and practical leadership to the movement. Among the most important of these was William E. Boardman, already cited as one of the leaders in the American Holiness movement. As a Holiness advocate, Boardman's most significant publication, referred to above, was *The Higher Christian Life*, a doctrinal and historical defense of Christian perfection that sold over 100,000 copies. In 1875 he published the volume *In The Power of the Spirit*, in which he delineated the differences between the gift of the Spirit for conversion and that for sanctification. He concluded that the baptism of the Spirit is not a gift of miraculous powers conferred upon a few, but is the normative gift of the Holy Spirit himself provided for all the children of God who will receive him.

As one of Cullis's earliest converts to the doctrine of divine healing, Boardman traveled with him in 1873 to Europe to visit healing ministries. Following Cullis's return to America, Boardman teamed up with Robert Pearsall Smith to establish the Higher Life movement in Europe.

In this 1948 Kansas City meeting, two of the biggest names in the salvation-healing movement—William Branham and Oral Roberts—are together. From the left, Young Brown, Jack Moore, Branham, Roberts, and Gordon Lindsay.

The climax of this effort to advance the cause of Holiness came in a series of camp meetings at the Broadlands, Oxford, and Brighton. Following these successful campaigns Boardman returned to America and campaigned extensively with Cullis. In 1875 he returned to England, making it his permanent home. After consulting extensively with Otto Stockmayer in Switzerland, Boardman published the book *The Lord That Healeth Thee* (1881), which thrust him forth as an international teacher of healing. In this volume Boardman presented Christ as the sin-bearing and pardoning Savior, as the Deliverer from present sin and its power, as the Sanctifier of the human heart, and as the Deliverer of all the consequences of sin, including disease. He emphasized that healing by faith, like initial salvation and sanctification, was to be a continuous work of the church. Since James 5:14–15 placed it within the permanent provisions of the gospel, it was not to be relegated to the category of special signs and wonders from previous periods in the history of the church.

By 1882 Boardman, along with Charlotte C. Murray and Mrs. Michael Baxter, opened a faith home in London to accommodate those seeking healing under his ministry and named it "Bethshan," Hebrew for "House of Rest." The chapel of the home seated 600 persons, and healing services were conducted several times a week while matrons instructed the sick daily in the doctrine of divine healing. Unlike Cullis's faith homes, medicine and medical treatment were not dispensed.

Mrs. Baxter, cofounder of Bethshan, was the wife of the editor of the *Christian Herald* in London and of the New York *Christian Magazine*. She was deeply involved in evangelistic work, was an enthusiastic advocate of both holiness and divine healing, and used the family's publications to support and propagate these messages. Following the death of her husband, she initiated another periodical entitled *Thy Healer*, which featured testimonies and doctrinal studies on healing. Her popularity was such that she frequently toured America on speaking engagements and was a regular participant in Cullis's faith conventions.

It should be noted that Bethshan was not the only center for healing in London. Before Boardman or Bethshan, a significant healing ministry was conducted at Metropolitan Tabernacle, pastored by Charles H. Spurgeon. Most of Spurgeon's healing ministry took place through his pastoral visitation, although he both spoke on the topic and regularly prayed for the sick from his pulpit. Russell H. Conwell, Spurgeon's biographer, reports that it was common for parishioners to request the prayers of the church for healing and that thousands of cases of healings could be documented.

One of the most prominent and significant individuals to receive physical healing at Bethshan was the Reverend Andrew Murray, a native of South Africa, and one of the leading international Evangelicals of the late nineteenth and early twentieth centuries. Murray had been convinced of the truth of the divine healing message in 1882 by both William Boardman and Otto Stockmayer. His acceptance of this doctrine, however, was initially inspired by the study of Charles Cullis's faith work and the multitude of healing testimonies flowing from it. In his homeland, Murray pastored one of the most prestigious and influential churches in the country. He was considered the "chief and most honored teacher of the Dutch Reformed Church," served as moderator of the South African Dutch Reformed Church for six terms, and fathered the Keswick movement in his country. In addition, he published over 240 books and tracts which were issued in as many as fifteen languages, and he traveled worldwide to proclaim the messages of holiness and divine healing. The influence of this man upon the church continues today through the increasing number of his works that are being reprinted and via such recent influential giants in the modern international charismatic movement as David du Plessis, who claimed him as his spiritual father.

In 1879 Murray faced the most profound crisis of his life when his physician ordered him to stop preaching due to a throat problem. This forced upon him the imposition of almost total silence for two years. Having exhausted the best medical efforts, he went to London in 1882. Pastor Stockmayer convinced him that according to James 5:13–14 sickness was healed by the prayer of faith. Having read Boardman's *The Lord That Healeth Thee*, he submitted himself to Bethshan and within three weeks was completely healed. Within two years he published the volume *Divine Healing*, which systematized the biblical basis for divine healing and presented a set of practical rules by which one could obtain healing. In these guidelines he emphasized that sickness is a chastisement for sin, but that God promises that it is his will to heal. By an act of faith, however, a believer must accept Jesus as healer and physician. He must also exercise his faith and his will and begin to act as one healed or beginning to be healed even if the manifestation is not visible. Murray's simple but straightforward rules were well received by the public and were to be a pattern for other practitioners to use in instructing the sick in faith healing. Although Murray visited America only once, his acceptance by Moody, Torrey, and the Northfield Convention constituency gave him a strong influence with a wide audience.

Another articulate spokesman for the divine healing movement and an ardent supporter of Cullis's ministry, was Dr. Adoniram J. Gordon. Recognized by his contemporaries as an almost unmatched example of the union, in one man, of deepest spirituality with broadest intellectual powers, Gordon became a significant figure in the divine healing and Keswick Holiness movements. Gordon was the pastor of the prestigious Clarendon Street Church in Boston for the last quarter of the nineteenth century.

Gradually, Gordon succeeded in convincing his congregation that the church was a hospital whose proper mission was to serve as a "cure" for souls. He and his church participated in the founding of the Boston Industrial Temporary Home for treating drunkards; they were in the forefront of the Prohibition Party, the women's rights movement, relief for the unemployed, protection of Chinese immigrants, and the defense of secular, state-controlled schools against ultramontanism. Gordon's church also initiated evangelistic outreach to such ethnic groups as the Jews and the Chinese. In 1889 the church founded the Boston Missionary Training School (later renamed Gordon College), which before the end of the century was sending missionaries around the world including such places as Africa, China, India, and even to the Indian reservations of Oklahoma.

Beginning in the early 1870s Gordon became a leading supporter of the multi-faith ministries of his Boston neighbor, Charles Cullis, and served for years as a trustee of Cullis's Faith Work. Gordon was impressed with Cullis's courage and efforts to reach out to the poor, the needy, the destitute, and the rejected of society. He applauded Cullis's multiple efforts at health care, education, social services, and spiritual nurture.

As early as 1873 Gordon was exposed to the concept of divine healing through his close association with Cullis. During that year Cullis had announced to his supporters, for the first time, the healings that had occurred through his ministry and had openly begun to speak of his experiences with others. At this time, Gordon expressed interest and appreciation but no personal involvement in this belief. It was during Moody's 1877 meetings in Boston when Gordon observed an opium addict and a missionary's cancerous jaw healed instantaneously through the prayers of concerned believers that he seriously began a study of Scripture concerning this topic. By 1882 Gordon had become one of the leading advocates and apologists for the faith healing movement. In that year he published his famed book, *The Ministry of Healing*, with the strong support and encouragement of Cullis. This work, as previously mentioned, was respected even by the critics of the faith healing movement and remains a significant statement of the topic today. Gordon argued in his various writings that Christ's earthly ministry was twofold; he healed the sick and forgave the sinner. He frequently referred to what he called the Hebrew parallelism of Psalm 103:3: "Who forgiveth all thine iniquities, who healeth all thy diseases." Recovery for the soul and restoration for the body were the parallel expressions of the life of God being communicated to humankind. In addition, Matthew 8:17 seemed to suggest, according to Gordon, that physical healing was provided for in the atonement of Christ. Thus Christ was both the sickness-bearer and the sin-bearer of his people. To support further his thesis, Gordon emphasized the promise in the great commission that "They shall lay hands on the sick and they shall recover." The commission, he observed, was constantly exercised in the Acts of the Apostles. The ministry of the apostles was "the exact facsimile of Christ's." The promise of recovery is explicit and unconditional, for the Bible says, "The prayer of faith shall save the sick and the Lord shall raise him up."

Gordon questioned how this twofold cord of the church's ministry had been unraveled into a single strand. He believed it incongruous for the modern church to assign one part of this cord (divine healing) to the exclusive use of the apostolic period, while maintaining the other as the foundation of one's Christian hope. Gordon confessed he suspected that the modern church had framed the excuse that the age of miracles was past simply to camouflage its own impotence. If the age of miracles was past, it was due to the church's lack of faith.

One of the most influential voices in the spreading of the doctrine of divine healing was A. B. Simpson, founder of the CMA and one of the great spiritual leaders of the last century. According to Kenneth MacKenzie, one of his closest ministerial associates, divine healing was the most influential aspect of his ministry. His famous Friday healing service became a shrine to thousands in New York City. Simpson's conversion to the doctrine and experience of divine healing came under the ministry of Charles Cullis in 1881. Although Simpson became the pastor of the fashionable and prestigious Thirteenth Street Presbyterian Church in New York City in 1879, within two years he was plagued by physical infirmities. Having had a fragile constitution since his youth, by 1881 the doctors had given him only a few months to live. In an effort to regain his health he retired to Old Orchard Beach, Maine, for rest. Here he encountered Charles Cullis's famous annual faith convention and was healed.

As a result he returned to New York City, resigned his church, and began a new independent work with the goal of reaching the unchurched masses. By 1889 his new church had become an association; the mother church, the Gospel Tabernacle, was located in a new six-story building one block from Times Square. During this time he had started branch churches to different ethnic groups in New York, established a half-dozen rescue missions, a home for the rehabilitation of prostitutes, several temperance homes, a free dispensary, social services for the destitute and suffering, a prison reform ministry, a large orphanage, a strong missionary program, and a coeducational Missionary Training College (the school exists today as Nyack College). During 1887 Simpson formed the Christian Alliance, which was a fraternal alliance uniting Evangelicals who believed in Christ as Savior, Sanctifier, Healer, and Coming Lord. This fourfold gospel was the cornerstone of his personal ministry and of the Alliance organization. The idea for the Alliance came while he was participating in the 1885 International Conference on Divine Healing and True Holiness convened by Boardman.

Praying for the sick was a central part of Simpson's ministry. His official biographer acknowledged healing to be the most influential aspect of his work and noted that his healing meetings in New York City created a marked sensation. His magazine *Word, Work, and World* carried many articles on the topic. Healing was a frequent focus of his books: *A Cloud of Witnesses* (2d ed., 1900), *The Discovery of Divine Healing* (1903), *The Four-Fold Gospel* (1925), *Friday Meeting Talks* (3 vols., 1894, 1899, 1900), *The Gospel of Healing* (1896), and *Inquiries and Answers Concerning Divine Healing* (1887). Following the example of Cullis he established ten-day conventions at Old Orchard Beach for meetings focusing on holiness and healing. Among the speakers at these conventions were R. A. Torrey, A. T. Pierson, A. J. Gordon, Otto Stockmayer, Andrew Murray, and Carrie Judd. Simpson also established Berachah Home, a faith healing home patterned after the work of Cullis.

Kathryn Kuhlman filled auditoriums across America in her "miracle" services. Here she stands with a crippled boy who had received prayer.

Divine healing was clearly an integral and vital part of the four-fold gospel which Simpson propagated. Whenever he presented his theological position on the doctrine of divine healing, he always asserted his basic presupposition that divine healing is part of the completeness of the redemption of Jesus Christ. He agreed with the normative view of the divine healing movement that sickness is the result of the Fall, thus his insistence that the fundamental principle of divine healing rests on the atoning sacrifice, since the atonement of Christ reaches as "far as the curse is found." As a result, healing, according to Simpson, became a redemption right which we simply claim as our purchased inheritance through the blood of his Cross. Believers must commit their bodies to Christ and simply claim their promise of healing by faith. Carrie Judd's influence is obvious in Simpson's insistence that the believer "act" faith, claiming and believing that Christ has begun the healing. He, more than most propagators of divine healing, emphasized that believers ought not to be looking for immediate removal of the symptoms. He cautioned believers to ignore them and press forward, claiming the reality of their healing.

It should be noted that Simpson was a radical in the divine healing movement, for he allowed only limited use of physicians and medicine. He firmly maintained that once a person believed and claimed the promise of healing he must count it as "forever settled, and step out solemnly, definitely, irrevocably . . . on God's promise." This meant that the person must abandon at once all remedies and medical treatment, since any human attempt at helping would imply a doubt of the reality of the healing.

For thirty-seven years, A. B. Simpson stood as one of the most effective and popular exponents of the divine healing message in America. His conventions, Friday meetings, healing homes, and prolific publications on the topic made him one of the most significant figures of the movement. Although his theological views and defenses of the doctrine of divine healing were generally the normative ones within the movement, his organizational abilities and persuasiveness were superior. Unlike most of the early leaders of the movement, Simpson left behind an extensive permanent structure (the CMA with its hundreds of ordained ministers) to perpetuate the message of divine healing worldwide. No single individual in the movement who was influenced by Charles Cullis touched so many lives with the message of healing as Simpson or persuaded so many individuals to enter full-time ministry with faith healing as a vital aspect of that ministry.

The only significant figure to participate in the formative years of the divine healing movement in the 1880s and to live until the beginning of the healing revival in the post-World War II era was Carrie Judd Montgomery. Her ministry also demonstrated the close relationship between the Holiness and divine healing movements as illustrated by the subtitle of her *Triumphs of Faith: A Monthly Journal Devoted to Faith-Healing and to the Promotion of Christian Holiness.* Her teachings on divine healing are reminiscent of Phoebe Palmer's "altar theology." She also represented an organic link between the divine healing and Pentecostal movements when she became a participant in the latter movement in 1908. She was responsible for the establishment of the first faith healing home on the West Coast and was the first woman to itinerate from coast to coast as a healing evangelist. Judd attributed her entrance into full-time faith healing ministry to the inspiration of Charles Cullis.

In 1879, Judd, an Episcopalian from Buffalo, New York, was healed of a severe disability under the ministry of Elizabeth Mix. The local newspaper carried the story of her miraculous healing, and newspapers as far away as England reprinted it. The next year she published her testimony in a volume entitled *The Prayer of Faith* (1880), which was distributed internationally and launched her into notoriety as a divine healing proponent of some magnitude. Following the example of Cullis, she established the "Faith Rest Cottage," a faith healing home, as the center of her ministry. She soon became associated with A. B. Simpson and the CMA and served as the organization's first recording secretary and later as vice president.

In her many writings, she emphasized that physical healing was provided through the atonement of Christ. To receive healing, she insisted according to Psalm 107:20 that we must simply believe we are healed by the Word of God. When by faith we accept the Bible literally, then our bodies will be freed from sickness. Acceptance of belief in God's Word in spite of feelings or circumstances was considered an essential principle if divine healing was to be received. Judd emphasized that the argument of James 2:4–26 teaches that those who profess to have faith in God show by their works whether or not that faith is more than a mere profession. Therefore, she stressed that the showing forth of works was the natural and inevitable result of faith. Faith for the obtaining of God's promised blessings, Judd maintained, is not a "feeling faith" but an "acting faith." It is unnecessary for us to feel some particular emotion in order to receive God's promised healing; all we need to do is to act as though we believe what we profess to believe. Judd insisted that if we continue to praise God, our feelings will naturally align themselves with God's truth. Having the assurance from the Bible that our petitions are granted before they are physically manifested, we must act upon faith's reckonings and take a course which will justify our professed belief.

In 1890 Judd married George Montgomery and moved to California. In San Francisco they founded a rescue and healing mission, established a temperance town five miles from Oakland, and there built a spacious faith home, the Home of Peace. She also established a Bible training college, an orphanage, a home for orphaned babies, the Cayadero Worldwide Camp Meeting, a foreign missions operation, and a Monday afternoon faith healing service in downtown Oakland which she conducted for twenty-five years. In 1906 Mr. Montgomery visited William J. Seymour's services on Azusa Street and received the Pentecostal experience being taught there. It would be two years before Judd would receive the "fullness of the Holy Spirit" and speak in tongues. She would later become a charter member of the Assemblies of God. As a member of the new Pentecostal movement, she took part in the first World Pentecostal Conference in London sponsored by Alexander A. Boddy. On her trip home she visited her friend and colleague A. B. Simpson in Nyack and told him of her new Pentecostal experience. Simpson was sufficiently impressed so that he arranged for her to speak of this new experience at his Old Orchard Beach camp meeting. Interestingly, Simpson, who never endorsed the Pentecostal doctrine of the baptism of the Holy Spirit being evidenced by tongues, was specifically to request Judd to relate her experience to his congregation on her future trips to Nyack.

Judd's support of the healing and Pentecostal movements continued through the operation of the Home of Peace and *Triumphs of Faith* even after her death in 1946. She was the product of the first generation of faith healing propagators in America and the only West Coast faith healing advocate to be personally familiar with and molded by those pioneers. Her popular work on the West Coast was eventually supplemented and surpassed by the works of another generation of faith healing advocates which included such persons as Florence L. Crawford, Phinias Yoakum, John G. Lake, Aimee Semple McPherson, and Charles S. Price.

A contemporary of Carrie Judd but one not directly influenced by the work of Charles Cullis and his colleagues was Maria B. Woodworth-

Etter. As the wife of a local pastor and with little formal education to guide her, Etter began extended revivalistic tours in 1882 with remarkable success. She was to crisscross the country for more than forty years conducting union meetings with crowds reaching, at the height of her popularity, 25,000 in a single service. So powerful were her meetings that newspapers everywhere gave them thorough coverage. It was not uncommon for journals such as *Fremont Evening Tribune* to run front-page headlines like "Cripples Walking After Prayers of the Divine Healer . . . Blind See, Deaf Hear." Described as a revivalist with remarkable power, she began her ministry as a part of the United Brethren Church but left it in 1884 to join the Churches of God in Indiana.

Etter's meetings were characterized by signs and wonders and many physical phenomena such as those that occurred in America's Second Awakening. There were always multitudes healed, prophecies given, singing in the Spirit, and people slain under the power of the Spirit. Others spoke in tongues, danced in the Spirit, or went into trances. Detailed accounts of these events are given in her testimonial volume *Acts of the Holy Ghost* (1922), which was to be revised and updated under several titles. Across the country newspapers gave first-hand reports of the limbs of hopeless cripples straightened, of hearing restored to the deaf, of sight restored to the blind, and of a multitude of healings which defied the work of medicine and science. Etter strongly advocated that the power given the apostles had never been taken from the church, but that the churches had sunk to the level of the world and were without the unlimited power that effects healing. Her success in ministry also brought persecution and condemnation. She was frequently denounced as an impostor, a pharisee, or a hypocrite, and on various occasions was arrested for "practicing medicine without a license."

By 1890 Etter was itinerating with the largest tent in the country, one seating 8,000. In her 1889 Oakland, California, revival she met Carrie Judd and formed a life-long friendship. Judd was impressed with the manifestations of Holy Spirit power in Etter's meetings. Another young female healing evangelist to be influenced by Etter was Aimee Semple McPherson, who occasionally preached for her at the Woodworth-Etter Tabernacle in Indianapolis. By 1912 Etter was taking a prominent role in the Pentecostal movement. In that year she conducted a five-month campaign for F. F. Bosworth in Dallas where miracles of healing seemed almost common and the list of influential Pentecostals who flocked to Dallas was like a "Who's Who" of early Pentecostalism. This revival became a key Pentecostal rendezvous. The following year she was the featured preacher at the Los Angeles World-Wide Camp Meeting, which was one of the high-water marks in the early Pentecostal movement. Etter became a strong link between the divine healing movement and the Pentecostal movement.

As described earlier, the Holiness movement provided the foundation and ethos for the development of the divine healing movement in the latter half of the nineteenth century. It also played a significant role in the spread of the doctrine through the various Holiness associations and denominations that were formed during this period. As the doctrine of entire sanctification swept across the land so did the doctrine of divine healing. As early as 1862 the founder of the Free Methodist Church and editor of the *Earnest Christian and Golden Rule*, B. T. Roberts, shared with his reading audience the reality that Christ was still the healer in the present day. Because the leadership of the Holiness movement actively supported the doctrine of divine healing, by the end of the century the practice and doctrine were common features of the movement. However, debate did continue within Holiness circles whether provision for healing was in the Atonement to the same degree as salvation. Many did not accept healing theologically as a provision in the Atonement equal to that of salvation. But some supported it as a ministry of the church as advanced in James 5:14–16. Almost all members of the movement were to agree with Daniel Steele, NT professor at Boston University and a leading advocate of Holiness, that the ministry of healing had been in the church in all ages and was a normative part of the church's ministry. By 1895 W. B. Godbey, Holiness leader and author of a popular multivolume commentary on the NT, acknowledged that in the last twenty-five years divine healing had become commonplace in the movement and was no longer a matter of controversy. Charles J. Fowler, third president of the National Holiness Association, in his book *Thoughts on Prayer*, quotes Methodist Bishop W. F. Warren as proclaiming divine healing as a prominent doctrine of Scripture and a common practice of great Christian leaders. In his 1897 volume *The Ideal Pentecostal Church*, Seth Cook Rees also emphasized that divine healing was an integral part of the church's ministry. By the turn of the century most Holiness groups had adopted a positive position toward the doctrine and practice of divine healing. Significantly, the General Holiness Assembly meeting in Chicago in 1901 declared in article five of their six-point statement of faith that the sick are healed through the prayer of faith. They emphasized that divine healings would be more numerous if Christians would measure up to the NT standards of holy living.

During the period of 1893 to 1907 thousands of local independent Holiness congregations and dozens of Holiness sects and associations were formed especially in the South, Southwest, and Midwest. Most of these new Holiness churches and groups emphasized the ministry of healing. Several of them even radicalized the doctrine and maintained that any use of doctors or medicine demonstrated a lack of faith in the healing Christ. Various prominent Holiness leaders spoke out against such unwarranted extremes and fanaticism and cautioned that these extremes should not cause people to neglect the healing gospel.

The two largest Holiness denominations eventually to be formed following this sect formation period were the Church of the Nazarene and the Pilgrim Holiness Church. Both embraced healing, as did the sects they were formed from, and

Evangelists who emphasized divine healing usually published their own monthly magazines. The magazines above were published by Jacob Filbert (*The Herald of Deliverance*), F. F. Bosworth (*Exploits of Faith*), Jack Coe (*International Healing Magazine*), Gordon Lindsay (*The Voice of Healing*), and A. A. Allen (*Miracle Magazine*).

incorporated the belief into their statements of faith. The Church of the Nazarene was created in 1914 as a merger of the People's Evangelical Church (1887), the Pentecostal Churches in America (1894), the New Testament Church of Christ (1894), the Church of the Nazarene (1895), the Pentecostal Mission (1898), and the Independent Holiness Church (1900). The Pilgrim Holiness Church began in 1897 in Cincinnati under the leadership of the famed Holiness leader, Martin Wells Knapp. It was a merger of the International Apostolic Holiness Union, the Holiness Christian Church, the Pentecostal Rescue Mission, and the Pilgrim Church.

A number of Holiness groups that arose during this period were to become part of the later Pentecostal movement. One of the most radical of these which propagated healing was Benjamin Hardin Irvin's Fire-Baptized Holiness Church, which began in 1895 in Iowa. This group was an outgrowth of the Iowa Holiness Association, the largest regional Holiness association in the nation. The group held to the radical belief that it was wrong to use doctors or medicines and insisted on the prohibition of various foods such as hog meat, catfish, oysters, or anything forbidden by the dietary laws of the OT. The group merged with the Pentecostal Holiness Church in 1911 and took the name of the latter group.

Also born of the Holiness movement was a large group of churches, each of which identified itself as the Church of God (CG). Almost all of these groups embraced divine healing. Generally those formed before 1894 remained in the Holiness movement after Azusa Street and those formed after 1894 were to become part of the Pentecostal movement. The pre-1894 groups tended to be less radical in their views regarding divine healing. For the post-1894 churches, healing was placed almost on the same level as salvation. Medicines were viewed as poisons dispensed by doctors to the faithless, and Christians consulting doctors were considered weak or even lost. Whether a part of the Holiness or Pentecostal movements, the CG denominations have grown to include a constituency of millions.

V. John Alexander Dowie. In popularity and outreach, John Alexander Dowie was to the divine healing movement at the turn of the twentieth century what Oral Roberts has been to the movement since the Second World War. A. B. Simpson's lifelong associate Kenneth Mackenzie identified Dowie as "unquestionably the apostle of healing of his day." At the peak of his ministry from 1894 to 1905 he was known by more people throughout America than any other propagator of the message of divine healing in the nation's history. His periodical, *Leaves of Healing,* enjoyed the largest worldwide circulation of any publication of the movement. Through his Divine Healing Association (the first such organization in American history) and later his Christian Catholic Church, Dowie set up a worldwide network of followers. He established the largest divine healing home in the world; founded a Christian utopian community, the city of Zion, Illinois; and built a tabernacle seating eight thousand, which he filled every Sunday.

Among the leaders of the American divine healing movement, Dowie was the most vocal and radical. He was a flamboyant and persuasive healing evangelist who focused his ministry almost exclusively upon the practice of healing during his first decade of ministry in America. Dowie's radicalism was shown by his insistence that supernatural healing always occurred instantaneously and by his vigorous opposition to the use of physicians and medicines. The title of his popular sermon, "Doctors, Drugs and Devils; or the Foes of Christ the Healer," succinctly stated his viewpoint. Also, unlike other members of the early healing movement, Dowie frequently and publicly condemned other propagators of the doctrine such as A. J. Gordon, Marie Woodworth-Etter, R. A. Torrey, and A. B. Simpson whenever he ascertained practical or theological disagreements between himself and them.

Dowie emphasized that his healing ministry was simply an imitation of that of Christ's, who, according to Matthew 4:23 and 9:35 "went about all the cities and villages, teaching . . . and preaching . . . and healing every sickness and every disease among the people." Matthew 8:16–17 clearly stated that Christ "healed all that were sick," for "Himself took our infirmities, and bare our sicknesses." Healing, Dowie insisted, occurred "through faith in Jesus, by the power of God," and Scripture states that Jesus "forgiveth all thine iniquities . . . healeth all thy diseases" (Ps. 103:2–3). There were two basic presuppositions to his ministry of healing. First, Christ "is the same yesterday, today and forever, and being so, He is unchanged in power and in will." Second, "Disease, like sin, is God's enemy, and the devil's work, and can never be God's will." These presuppositions led to Dowie's projections of "The Two Chains" of life. There exists in life the Chain of Good, which begins with Christ and brings salvation, healing, life, and ultimately heaven. On the other hand, there is the Chain of Evil, which was originated by Satan and results in sin, disease, death, and hell. Since Christ has delivered humankind from "the power of the enemy" (the Chain of Evil), there is redemption for both spirit and body (Rom. 8:11, 23; 2 Cor. 4:11). Dowie refused to pray for the healing of the unregenerate. He insisted that first there must be salvation and then the active pursuit of holiness. Regarding healing, he simply maintained, "Sin is a cause, of which Disease, Death and Hell are the inevitable effects and consequences . . . Holiness is a cause, of which Health, Eternal Life and Heaven are the glorious effects and consequences."

In 1888 Dowie arrived in America from Australia establishing his headquarters in San Francisco. For two years he itinerated on the West Coast and established branches of his healing association. By 1890 when the "First General Convention of the Branches of the American Divine Healing Association" convened, he had more than five thousand members. During the same year he moved his headquarters to the Chicago area. In 1894 when Sadie Cody, the niece of Colonel W. F. Cody (the famed "Buffalo Bill"), and Amanda M. Hicks, cousin of Abraham Lincoln, were healed at his hands, Dowie instantly became a national figure. As a result, thousands of people flocked to his meetings, leaving behind them their crutches, braces, canes, cots, and surgical appliances as they were healed. People traveled from across the nation to have Dowie pray for them, and he received more than three thousand letters per week asking for prayer. To accommodate those pouring into Chicago, he obtained the seven-story Imperial Hotel and converted it into a Faith Healing Home. The *Chicago Daily Chronicle* reported that he preached to the largest crowds ever gathered in Chicago for a religious service. His national popularity was indicated by the personal audiences which were granted him with two presidents of the U.S., McKinley and Roosevelt.

In 1896 Dowie decided to institutionalize his teachings on salvation, healing, and holy living into a new denomination, the Christian Catholic Church. With this action he began reaching out, as Charles Cullis had years earlier, to the disinherited of society to offer healing to those with physical, spiritual, economic, and social hurts. His church members canvassed the poorer tenements of Chicago to care for the poor and elderly, distributing food, clothing, and fuel; cooking meals; scrubbing floors; finding employment, etc. As a social reformer he campaigned for a free national system of education, and fought discrimination, racism, anti-semitism, pornography, birth control measures, gambling, drugs, tobacco, breweries, saloons, and secret organizations. On December 31, 1899, Dowie announced that he had purchased 6,500 acres of land north of Chicago for the purpose of building the City of Zion, a self-supporting utopian community which was to be a working model of a godly society. Before Dowie was stricken with a paralyzing stroke in 1905, his utopian community had grown to 10,000 residents. As a result of the stroke and charges of financial mismanagement, Dowie never resumed leadership of Zion or of his church. His achievements had been phenomenal, however. No individual within the healing movement had ever reached so many people worldwide with the message of divine healing as John Dowie. Importantly, the worldwide following which he had developed produced an army of imitators who were to play a significant role in the healing and Pentecostal movements of the twentieth century. Dowie became the paradigm of the twentieth-century healing evangelists. Interestingly, even the use of radio and television as future vehicles for spreading the message of healing was prophesied by Dowie before 1904.

VI. Pentecostal Movement.

Into the splintered and disunited City of Zion came Charles Parham, the father of the twentieth-century Pentecostal movement, in September 1906. It had been a year since Dowie had been stricken with his stroke, a year in which a people accustomed to the miraculous workings of God in their midst had experienced a famine of his visible presence.

Parham had achieved notoriety in 1901 at his Bethel Bible College in Topeka, Kansas, when he became the first person to insist that speaking in other tongues is an inseparable part of the baptism of the Holy Spirit and was the only Bible evidence for this experience. For the next several years Parham was unable to find wide acceptance for his new doctrine. However, in 1903 when he began to renew his earlier emphasis upon divine healing, the new Pentecostal message was readily accepted. Parham's healing ministry had begun in 1897 when he was healed of a major heart problem and several months later started his public ministry of preaching divine healing and praying for the sick in Ottawa, Kansas. His healing ministry was so well received that he moved to Topeka in 1898 and established a divine healing home to which people came from all parts of the nation to receive healing, and "mighty miracles" took place. Desiring to learn through other healing ministries, he traveled to Chicago in 1899 to visit Dowie's healing home; to Nyack, New York, to visit Simpson's Berachah Home; and to A. J. Gordon's work in Boston.

In 1903 Parham was invited to conduct a healing revival at El Dorado Springs, Missouri, and many were healed. Concluding this campaign he was invited to Galena, Kansas, where he conducted a three-month revival that brought national attention to his ministry. As a result of these meetings, he began to acquire the title "The Divine Healer." Significantly, Parham discovered that in an atmosphere where divine healing was emphasized and experienced, he encountered little opposition to his doctrine of speaking in tongues as the evidence of the baptism of the Holy Spirit.

During the winter of 1905 Parham opened a Bible school in Houston, Texas, and among those attending was a black Holiness minister, William J. Seymour. It was Seymour whom Parham sent to Los Angeles in response to a request from a black woman for Parham to share his Pentecostal message with her local church. Seymour's meetings in Los Angeles quickly became known nationally as the Azusa Street revival and attracted people nationwide. Seymour reported that large numbers of people were baptized with the Holy Spirit and healed of all manner of sicknesses. From the Azusa Street revival the Pentecostal message was spread worldwide, and from 1906 until 1932 Pentecostal denominations were formed across the country. By the summer of 1906 Seymour was requesting Parham to assist him at Azusa Street, but at about the same time Parham received an urgent request to minister in Zion City to a fragmented people. Parham decided to visit Zion on his way to Los Angeles. His meetings there were successful. Once again the people of Zion began to see God demonstrate his presence through divine healing, and for the first time many began to experience the baptism of the Holy Spirit as evidenced by speaking in tongues. The effect of Parham's ministry in Zion was to establish the city as the second most significant center in the world for the spreading of the new Pentecostal message. As mentioned above, Parham's personal experience had taught him that where people readily received the message of divine healing, the acceptance of the baptism of the Holy Spirit evidenced by speaking in tongues was also strong. Parham traveled to different branches of the Christian Catholic Church throughout America and Canada and was successful in converting most to the Pentecostal doctrine. Some of Parham's Zion followers were responsible for planting the Pentecostal message in different countries such as South Africa, Australia, Holland, Switzerland, Jamaica, and India. In addition, due to Parham's success in combining divine healing and the Pentecostal message of the baptism in the Holy Spirit, there went out from Zion a number of famous independent healing Pentecostal evangelists who would achieve national and international prominence.

Among this group and perhaps the most successful was Fred F. Bosworth whose healing campaigns in the 1920s packed the largest auditoriums in the U.S. and Canada and attracted as many as 20,000 to a single meeting. Bosworth eventually established a large independent church in Dallas, Texas, and became a pioneer of radio evangelism when he established the National Radio Revival Missionary Crusaders and began broadcasting regularly over WJJD in Chicago. In just a few years his radio ministry processed over a quarter of a million letters. His international influence continued to be felt into the 1940s and 1950s through the ministry of William Branham, with whom Bosworth worked for a number of years. In the post-World War II healing revival Bosworth became a great resource to that generation of revivalists concerning revival techniques and healing ministry. His 1924 book, *Christ the Healer,* which is a compilation of healing messages, continues to be printed by Revell as a significant statement on healing. John G. Lake of Zion also established a worldwide evangelistic healing ministry which seemed particularly fruitful in South Africa where he helped to found one of the largest organized Pentecostal works in the country, the Apostolic Faith Mission. In 1914, Lake settled in Spokane, Washington, and established a large church with multiple branches up and down the West Coast. Through his and Parham's ministries, Gordon Lindsay, who was born in Zion, came into the healing Pentecostal ministry and later became famous as the editor of the *Voice of Healing* magazine. Through the auspices of this magazine, Lindsay developed a ministerial fellowship for dozens of America's most popular healing evangelists during the 1950s. Today, Lindsay's ministry is carried on through the Christ for the Nations Institute and ministry organizations in Dallas, Texas. Included among other significant independent healing Pentecostal evangelists whose ministries arose from Parham's work in Zion were L. C. Hall, E. N.

This 1936 issue of the *Pentecostal Evangel,* the official voice of the Assemblies of God, emphasizes divine healing.

Richey (the mayor of Zion City), and Raymond T. Richey.

Parham influenced many Zion people. Among the most significant of those who later founded independent churches were Cyrus B. Fockler, William Hamner Piper, and Mrs. Martha Robinson. Fockler established the famous Milwaukee Gospel Tabernacle and was responsible for training a large number of workers who went throughout the nation founding churches within the healing Pentecostal tradition. Of later significance for the movement, Fockler made a profoundly positive impression upon young David J. du Plessis during a two year preaching/healing campaign he conducted in South Africa during the second decade of the century (du Plessis was to become internationally know as "Mr. Pentecost"). It is also important to note that through the

influence of Fockler's ministry the Ridgewood Pentecostal Church in Brooklyn, New York, was founded, and eventually its national publication, *Bread of Life,* and a significant collection of Pentecostal churches organized into the Ridgewood Pentecostal Fellowship.

William Hamner Piper founded the prestigious Stone Church of Chicago and edited the important Pentecostal magazine, *The Latter Rain Evangel.* Stone Church and *Evangel* became a crossroads for the early independent healing Pentecostal leaders. The disciples of Cullis, Boardman, Judd, Dowie, and Parham were all familiar with this ministry and frequently ministered there and wrote articles for the magazine. *Evangel* became an unofficial organ for many itinerant healing evangelists and a means of keeping in touch with the broader movement. Also coming out of Zion as a Parham convert was elder David A. Reed, who became the operator of Piper's faith healing home, Bethesda. Reed was later to work extensively with the famous Aimee Semple McPherson, founder of the Foursquare Gospel denomination. Another convert was Mrs. Maria Wing Robinson, who founded the Faith Homes and the Zion Bible School in Zion City. Out of these Faith Homes and the Bible school came hundreds of missionaries, ministers, and Christian workers trained to propagate the healing/Pentecostal message around the globe. In addition, Marie Burgess became an itinerant evangelist and later founded the important Pentecostal work in New York City, the Glad Tidings Tabernacle.

Parham's ministry in Zion City not only helped to establish the healing/Pentecostal message through dozens of independent evangelistic/healing ministries, independent churches, and healing homes, but also by its direct influence upon what was to become the largest Pentecostal denomination in the nation, the Assemblies of God (AG). Dozens of Parham's Zion converts became a part of this organization. Undoubtedly, the most important of these individuals was J. Roswell Flower, one of the founders of the denomination and a part of the church's leadership from its inception until his retirement in 1959. He was also the founding editor of *Christian Evangel* which was the first Pentecostal weekly periodical in existence. This magazine became *Pentecostal Evangel*, the official organ of the AG. Of note, Flower was also one of the organizers of the National Association of Evangelicals in 1942 and of the Pentecostal Fellowship of North America in 1948.

Among Parham's other Zion City converts who became important leaders in the AG were Fred Vogler, assistant general superintendent of the denomination for more than fourteen years; Daniel C. O. Opperman, who was one of the initial five conveners to call for a "General Convention of Pentecostal Saints" and the first assistant general superintendent; also E. N. Richey and Cyrus Fockler, who were participants at the founding meeting of the church at Hot Springs, Arkansas. Interestingly, three out of the original eight persons to serve as executive presbyters of the first general council in 1914 were Zion men—Flower, Fockler, and Opperman. Obviously, the Zion City Pentecostals had a significant role in the formation and governance of the AG.

Charles Parham and his multitude of Zion converts to the Pentecostal message played a vital role in the institutionalizing of the doctrine of divine healing as a permanent part of the twentieth-century Pentecostal movement. Through the ministry of Parham, of his disciple W. J. Seymour at Azusa Street, and of his converts at Zion City, the two doctrines of divine healing and the baptism of the Holy Spirit evidenced by speaking in tongues became permanently associated in the *gestalt* of beliefs for the twentieth-century Pentecostal movement. The influence of the Azusa Street revival tended to be focused upon bringing existing Holiness churches into the new Pentecostal movement, whereas the Zion City revival

focused upon founding new independent ministries and independent churches, although it did bring a large portion of Dowie's worldwide following into the new movement.

The influence of Dowie and Parham upon the divine healing movement was profound. Although Dowie personally rejected the doctrine of the baptism of the Holy Spirit evidenced by speaking in tongues, his worldwide healing ministry with its emphasis upon the supernatural provided a springboard for a large constituency to accept the Pentecostal message. Charles Parham served as the instrument that enabled Dowie's disciples to make the transition into the Pentecostal movement. Thus, from the birth of the movement, divine healing has been an integral and distinctive part. Through the movement and its grandchild, the charismatic movement, divine healing has become a normative emphasis for a large and significant portion of Christendom.

The formative years of development for the classical Pentecostal churches were from 1907 to 1932. As the movement aggressively grew and spread, so the doctrine and practice of divine healing was extended since it was one of the movement's cardinal doctrines. Pentecostalism did suffer setbacks, such as a rebuke by a meeting of the World's Christian Fundamentals Association in 1928. The association condemned the movement as a threat to the Christian church. The Fundamentalists also condemned the "fanatical" doctrine that healing was provided for in the atonement. The healing movement, however, continued to expand during this period. By the end of World War I, a number of healing evangelists began building independent revival ministries and their crusades attracted national attention. Many of these evangelists came out of Dowie's ministry. There were also several British evangelists who toured the U.S. and became popular for their healing ministries, the most important of whom was Smith Wigglesworth. The two most significant healing evangelists of this period were Aimee Semple McPherson and Charles S. Price.

McPherson was the most widely known healing evangelist of the 1920s and 1930s. A Canadian, she was reared in the home of a Salvation Army captain and married an evangelist/missionary. After her husband died in China, she returned to the states and eventually began to evangelize. Between 1918 and 1923 McPherson made eight transcontinental preaching tours across the United States. She preached in tents, churches, theaters, and auditoriums, always packing them to capacity as people sought to hear this anointed preacher and to receive healing. In 1922 she became the first woman to preach on radio and later purchased her own station. Deciding to make her headquarters in Los Angeles, she built one of the largest church structures in America, the 5,300 seat Angelus Templ, which was dedicated in 1923. To accommodate the multitudes who sought her ministry and healing, she personally conducted an average of twenty-one services each week. To communicate with her large national following she published *Crusader*, a weekly magazine, and *Bridal Call*, a monthly

JESUS HEALS!

MRS. M. B. WOODWORTH-ETTER

Camp Meeting

OTTUMWA

JULY 8 TO 30

WEST PARK AVE.

COURT HILL CAR TO PARK AVE., THEN
GO FOUR BLOCKS WEST FROM
OTTUMWA CEMETERY.

Salvation For Soul
Healing For Body

THREE MEETINGS DAILY

Good Song Service at Each Meeting

Mrs. Woodworth-Etter has had a marvelously successful minstry of over forty years
throughout the U. S. Her work has been
blessed in the salvation of multitudes. Many
thousands have been healed of all manner of
diseases by the prayer of faith and through
the laying on of hands. (Mark 16: 17, 18
James 5: 13, 14.)

Come bring the sick and afflicted to be healed

without money and without price through the name of JESUS.

Those desiring to rent tents, cots, mattresses , or comforts please give 3 days notice.. Bring
toilet articles, sheets and pillows.. Meals may be secured on the camp ground.

Address communications to JOSEPH A. DARNER, 131 W. 2ND .ST. OTTUMWA,

After Reading, Please Hand to Some One Sick or Afflicted, or Tack Up to be Read

Maria B. Woodworth-Etter began praying for the sick in her 1880s meetings.
This poster advertises her 1922 meeting in Ottumwa, Iowa.

magazine. In 1944 these were combined and renamed *Foursquare Magazine*. To assist her growing ministry she founded L.I.F.E. Bible College to train ministers, and organized the International Church of the Foursquare Gospel. The latter name indicated the fourfold ministry of Christ as the Savior of the world, the Baptizer with the Holy Ghost, the Great Physician and Healer of our bodies, and the coming King of kings. Upon her death in 1944 the denomination had over 400 churches, 200 mission stations abroad, and 3,000 ordained ministers.

One of McPherson's converts to the Pentecostal experience was the Methodist pastor, Dr. Charles S. Price. Price, who was born in England and earned a law degree from Oxford, had entered the ministry through a series of spiritual crises. Following acceptance of the Pentecostal message, he became a full-time evangelist. His ministry was immediately successful and because of his background, he was able to reach non-Pentecostal

Christians effectively. In 1925 he began publishing his monthly magazine *Golden Grain*, which highlighted the successes of his popular healing ministry and helped extend his teachings on healing to an expanding audience. Price was also one of the outspoken critics of the divisiveness of Pentecostal groups over their doctrinal issues. Their controversies were making union crusades almost impossible in the 1930s. Just before his death in February 1947 he recognized that a cooperative spirit was growing among Pentecostals, and began to anticipate that God was going to move in a special way with his miraculous power in that divinely appointed hour. The great post-war healing revival was about to begin.

VII. Post-War Healing Revival. Following the spiritual drought of World War II, two major national revivals burst upon the American scene: the evangelical revival represented by Billy Graham and the healing revival symbolized by William Branham and Oral Roberts. The healing revival was "a signs-gifts-healing, salvation-deliverance, Holy Ghost miracle revival." Between 1947 and 1958 dozens of healing evangelists crisscrossed America praying for the sick. Their stories are best followed in the pages of Gordon Lindsay's *Voice of Healing* magazine or in David Harrell's volume *All Things are Possible* (1975). Significantly, the revival was responsible for the unexpected growth of Pentecostalism in modern America. By reaching across denominational lines and socio-economic levels, the healing revival gave birth to the modern charismatic movement in the late 1950s and early 1960s. The person universally acknowledged as the revival's "father" and "pacesetter" was William Branham. The sudden appearance of his miraculous healing campaigns in 1946 set off a spiritual explosion in the Pentecostal movement which was to move to Main Street, U.S.A., by the 1950s and give birth to the broader charismatic movement in the 1960s, which currently affects almost every denomination in the country.

Branham was an ordained independent Baptist minister who had been reared in poverty and had received only a marginal education. He began his ministry in 1933, pastoring the church he founded in Jeffersonville, Indiana, the Branham Tabernacle. The pivotal point of his career came in May 1946 when he experienced an angelic visitation in which he was promised the gift of healing and opportunities to preach before thousands. Following this visitation, Pastor Robert Daugherty summoned him to St. Louis to pray for Daugherty's dying daughter. He complied and the girl was healed. In the revival that followed, praying for the sick was highlighted. His reputation quickly spread. Following St. Louis, Branham conducted a healing revival in the Bible Hour Tabernacle in Jonesboro, Arkansas, pastored by Rex Humbard's father. Over 25,000 people from 28 states attended the meetings. Branham had struck into the heartland of fervent Pentecostalism, one which was starved for the message of old-time miracle power. With these meetings, the post–World War II American healing revival was born.

As testimonies of incredible healings increased, Branham's fame and ministry grew. Within months he had assembled an able management team of Jack Moore, Gordon Lindsay, and W. J. Ern Baxter. Lindsay initiated *Voice of Healing* magazine to publicize Branham's ministry, although within several years it became the voice of dozens of healing evangelists. In May 1948 Branham discontinued his crusades for five months due to physical exhaustion, but when he resumed the campaigns, he added the famed Pentecostal evangelist, Fred F. Bosworth, to his team. Bosworth added enormous prestige to the ministry.

In the dramatic and important campaign held in Houston, Texas, in 1950 Bosworth debated the Rev. W. E. Best, pastor of Houston Tabernacle Baptist Church, on the doctrine of divine healing and the debate received national press coverage. In the same year Branham's team made the first campaign tour of Europe by a major healing revivalist. Branham's success in Scandinavia was startling and brought international publicity to the emerging phenomenon of healing revivals. Internationally renowned church historian W. J. Hollenweger reported that "Branham filled the largest stadiums and meeting halls in the world." The European campaign also won Branham the endorsement of the internationally respected Pentecostal leader Donald Gee, editor of *Pentecost,* the voice of international Pentecostalism.

The most famous healing in the history of the revival was effected by Branham on William Upshaw, a U.S. Congressman from California who had been crippled from birth. This healing in 1951 made Branham's healing power a worldwide legend. Branham's ministry continued to grow until the mid-1950s when it encountered severe financial difficulties. When the healing revival was transformed into the broader charismatic revival in the late 1950s, Branham could not readily adapt. Although he continued to engage in healing campaigns, the thrust of his ministry shifted from healing to doctrinal teaching.

The great healing crusades that Branham initiated in 1946 revitalized the American Pentecostal movement and popularized the doctrine of divine healing in America as never before. When the healing revival attracted hundreds of thousands of Americans from all denominational and cultural backgrounds, the charismatic movement was born. As the pacesetter of the healing revival, Branham was the primary source of inspiration in the development of other healing ministries. He inspired hundreds of ministers to enter the healing ministry and a multitude of evangelists paid tribute to him for the impact he had upon their work. As early as 1950, over 1,000 healing evangelists gathered at a *Voice of Healing* convention to acknowledge the profound influence of Branham on the healing movement.

The second giant of the post-war healing revival was Oral Roberts. Roberts has been identified by historian David Harrell as "one of the most influential religious leaders in the world in the twentieth century." Harrell contends that Roberts has influenced the course of modern Christianity as profoundly as any American religious leader. In this century no other name has been so inextricably identified with divine healing. Healed of tuberculosis as a youth, Roberts became an evangelist and pastor in the Pentecostal Holiness Church. In 1947, one year after Branham began the post-war healing revival, Roberts launched his ecumenical healing ministry. In the course of the next thirty years, he conducted over 300 major healing crusades and personally prayed for over one million people. He traveled across America with the largest portable tent ever used to promote the gospel. His most significant impact came in 1955 when he initiated a national weekly television program which took his healing crusades inside the homes of millions who had never been exposed to the healing message. Through this program, which was the number one syndicated religious program on television for almost thirty years, the message of divine healing was extended to its widest audience in history. In addition, his radio program was heard on over

500 stations. In 1969 he undertook the most ambitious television outreach of any healing evangelist in history, the production of prime-time religious variety shows. His success was remarkable, reaching as many as 64 million viewers. Programs were intentionally entertaining to reach nonbelievers, but each ended with an eleven-minute sermon and a prayer for the healing of the sick. By 1980 he was receiving more than five million letters annually from supporters requesting the prayer of faith.

Indicative of his wide ecumenical appeal, Roberts transferred his denominational affiliation to the United Methodist Church in 1968. Just three years earlier he had opened regionally accredited Oral Roberts University which by 1978 was to include seven graduate schools—medicine, dentistry, nursing, law, business, education, and theology. The $250 million university with its ultra-modern campus is considered the premier charismatic university in the world. The ministry of healing and signs and wonders is at the heartbeat of the institution. It is the only major university in the world forged on the anvil of healing evangelism. In 1981 Roberts opened City of Faith Medical and Research Center with the goal of merging prayer and medicine, the supernatural and the natural, in the treatment of the whole person. Over a hundred years after Charles Cullis, a practitioner of divine healing was still combining the supernatural power of God to heal with God's natural means of healing.

VIII. Charismatic Movement. The post-war healing revival with its ecumenical appeal to mainline church believers gave birth to the charismatic movement in the 1960s. Illustrative of this, Oral Roberts had noted by 1965 that over half of his audiences were composed of non-Pentecostals seeking the miraculous power of God to heal.

One of the most prominent advocates of divine healing associated with the charismatic movement was Kathryn Kuhlman. Although her healing ministry had begun in 1946, her focused constituency were those within mainline churches. In 1950 she was invited to lead a special service at Carnegie Hall in Pittsburgh, Pennsylvania. The response was so tremendous that she made it her headquarters for the next twenty years. By 1965 her strongest appeal was to those within the emerging charismatic movement. In that year she began conducting weekly healing meetings in Shriner Auditorium in Los Angeles, with a capacity crowd of 7,000 each week. Oral Roberts called her "the greatest evangelist of the ministry of God's miracle power in my lifetime." *Time* magazine referred to her as a "one-woman shrine of Lourdes." Kuhlman attracted large numbers of mainline church believers into the charismatic movement.

David Barrett, author of *World Christian Encyclopedia,* reports that by 1988 the charismatic movement had grown to over 359 million followers worldwide and that its growth rate of 21% made it the fastest growing religious movement in America and the world. The movement has tripled in size during the past ten years. It encompasses various theological traditions, but is unified by the common belief that the supernatu-

ral gifts of the NT are operative today. The charismatic movement is composed of several major groupings. Among these is the Charismatic Renewal, which is made up of those persons who accept the operation of the *charismata* as normative today and who have remained within traditional denominations. This group accepts the doctrine and practice of divine healing as openly as any Pentecostals. Because of their own church traditions, they are more open to sacramental healing, especially through the sacrament of the Lord's Supper. This is especially true of the Episcopalians and Roman Catholics. Actually, Anglicans have had a Rite of Healing in *The Book of Common Prayer* since the sixteenth century. Throughout the Roman Catholic church there is a significant rediscovery of the power of prayers for the sick. Following the recommendation of Vatican II, the church officially redefined the "Rite of Anointing," or extreme unction, from preparation of the soul for death to the more ancient rite of anointing for healing, a return to the church's pre-Medieval position. Several individuals personify this strong renewal of healing within the Roman Catholic church. Father John Bertolucci who conducts healing meetings throughout the country took the healing ministry to the television airwaves. Most influential has been Francis MacNutt (Ph.D. from Harvard and former priest) whose ministry and books on healing have had a significant impact on the ministry of healing in America. No longer is the emphasis placed only upon the instantaneous, but rather upon the process of healing. MacNutt has popularized the concept of "soaking" prayer and degrees of improvement, whereas the healing evangelists basically taught believers to expect the instantaneous. MacNutt has also done much to popularize deliverance ministry and exorcism among grassroots believers. His books *Healing* (1974) and *The Power to Heal* (1977) provide a comprehensive approach to the ministry of healing. MacNutt's ministry was significantly influenced by the healing ministries of Agnes Sanford (author of *The Healing Light*) and the Reverend Alfred Price (one of the Episcopalian founders of the healing ministry, The Order of St. Luke the Physician).

A second grouping within the charismatic movement is commonly referred to as the Faith Movement or the Word Movement. This movement began as a grassroots, parachurch activity consisting of a mixture of evangelistic revivalism, fundamentalist literalism, and Pentecostal experientialism. The acknowledged father of this movement is Kenneth Hagin. The national religious press has acclaimed him "the granddaddy of the Faith teachers." Undoubtedly, every major Faith ministry in America has been influenced by his teachings. Most prominent among these are Kenneth Copeland, Fred Price, Jerry Savelle, Charles Capps, Norvel Hayes, Robert Tilton, etc. Hagin's syndicated radio program is on approximately 180 stations, his *Word of Faith* monthly magazine has a circulation of almost 200,000, and his $20 million Rhema Bible Training Center has over 2,000 students. His ministry is one of the largest in the nation. Hagin's theology is a unique blend of evangelical orthodoxy, biblical fundamentalism, charismatic theology, and metaphysical thought. He differs from most advocates of divine healing in his use of positive confession, sensory denial (particularly as it relates to physical symptoms of illness), and implicit rejection of medical science. Criticism of these latter aspects of his teachings on healing has come from within the charismatic movement because of their origin in the metaphysical teachings of New Thought/Christian Science as presented by E. W. Kenyon. Hagin has been significantly influenced by Kenyon in these areas. However, his emphasis that divine healing is in the Atonement and that believers have authority to bind demonic powers in the name of Jesus echoes the teachings of the American healing movement for the past century.

A third grouping within the charismatic movement is what Peter Wagner calls the "Third Wave Revival." He refers to these as mainstream conservative Evangelicals who are experiencing the same miraculous power of the Holy Spirit as the Pentecostals, but who prefer not to be identified as such. The emphasis of this group is not so much upon the *charismata* as it is upon the power and ministry of the Holy Spirit to heal. As a church growth specialist, Wagner focuses upon the importance of "signs and wonders" and healing in the growth of the church. Recently three professors at conservative Dallas Theological Seminary became participants in "Third Wave" charismatic ministry and were forced to resign or be fired. Wagner predicts phenomenal growth in this grouping in the next decade.

The fourth grouping within the charismatic movement is the Charismatic Independent, which is the fastest-growing segment of the movement. This grouping is composed of thousands of independent churches across the country. Many of them are among the largest and fastest growing churches in the nation. All of them are characterized by an emphasis upon praise and worship, divine healing, and the operation of the charismata. Some of these churches are now beginning to form cooperative fellowships. Among these are the Vineyard Fellowships associated with John Wimber, the Church of the Rock of North America associated with Larry Lea, and Victory Ministry Fellowship under Billy Joe Daugherty's leadership. Among this growing group, John Wimber has one of the most extensive international healing ministries. Wimber has developed and teaches what he refers to as an "integrated model of healing" which is being adapted worldwide with tremendous success.

In the mid-1850s Horace Bushnell, one of America's leading theologians, predicted that the most widely attested dispensation of miracles and supernatural demonstrations to occur in centuries was about to commence. The growth of healing ministries in the twentieth century affirms his prediction, for as never before, healing is a dominant part of the life of the Christian church.

Bibliography: K. Bailey, *Divine Healing* (1977); N. Bloch-Hoell, *The Pentecostal Movement* (1964); W. Boardman, *Faith Work Under Dr. Cullis* (1874); idem, *"The Lord That Healeth Thee"* (1881); F. Bosworth, *Christ the Healer* (1924); R. K. Carter, *The Atonement for Sin and Sickness* (1884); idem, *"Faith Healing" Reviewed* (1897); P. Chappell, "The Divine Healing Movement in America," Ph.D. diss., Drew University (1983); A. J. Gordon, *The Ministry of Healing* (1882); D. E. Harrell, Jr., *All Things Are Possible* (1975); idem, *Oral Roberts: An American Life* (1985); W. J. Hollenweger, *The Pentecostals* (1972); C. Judd, *The Prayer of Faith* (1880); M. Kelsey, *Healing and Christianity* (1973); F. MacNutt, *Healing* (1974); idem, *The Power to Heal* (1977); W. McDonald, *Modern Faith Healing* (1892); A. Murray, *Divine Healing* (1900); A. B. Simpson, *The Gospel of Healing* (1915); V. Synan, *Aspects of Pentecostal-Charismatic Origins* (1975); idem, *The Holiness-Pentecostal Movement in the U.S.* (1971); E. Waldvogel, "The Overcoming Life: A Study in the Reformed Evangelical Origins of Pentecostalism," Ph.D. diss., Harvard University (1977); J. Wimber, *Power Healing* (1987); M. Woodworth-Etter, *Acts of the Holy Ghost* (1922). P. G. Chappell

HEBDEN, JAMES (d. c.1919) **AND ELLEN K.** Pentecostal pioneers in Toronto, Ontario. The Hebdens were involved in Christian work in Yorkshire, England, where James Hebden was a building contractor. After an abortive missionary visit to Jamaica, they arrived in Toronto in late 1904. An experience of healing raised their faith expectations, and without knowing any Pentecostals, Mrs. Hebden was baptized in the Spirit in November 1906, and her husband received the baptism in December. The Hebden mission on Queen Street, East, was the first Pentecostal assembly in Canada. Many there received the baptism. Several missionaries went out from this mission (the Chawners, Atters, Slagers, and Semples). The Hebdens' absolute opposition to any Pentecostal organization contributed to the decline of the Queen Street Mission, and in 1910 they left Toronto as missionaries to Algiers, North Africa. James Hebden died c. 1919, but his wife survived him for many years.

Bibliography: T. H. Miller, "The Canadian 'Azusa': The Hebden Mission in Toronto," *Pneuma* 8 (1, 1986): 5–29. P. D. Hocken

HEBREWS, EPISTLE TO THE

I. Introduction. The Epistle to the Hebrews is an anonymous work, and although many Bibles still give the title of this book as the Epistle of Paul to the Hebrews, there is very little evidence to suggest that Paul wrote it. No other major figure of the early church fits well as the author though many possibilities have been suggested.

The letter was probably written to a congregation at Rome (see 13:24) that was predominantly Jewish Christian but included some Gentiles. Its main pastoral concern is for these Jewish Christians who were in some danger of returning to the old covenant. Much of the letter is directed toward showing how the new covenant is vastly superior to the old.

Hebrews presents a modified dualism contrasting the world above, the unseen, and the world below, that which is seen; it also contrasts the present time with the age to come. The new covenant deals with the unseen and heavenly realities, while the old dealt with visible, inferior images of the heavenly spiritual realities.

The decade of the 60s best fits the evidence for the date of writing. There are serious questions as to whether or not Hebrews is actually a real letter.

It lacks the opening that was standard for letters of the time (sender, addressee, greetings). Perhaps it could be described as an exposition or homily partially in the form of a letter.

II. Holy Spirit As Speaker of Old Testament Scriptures. One of the major concerns of the author was to relate the old revelation to the new revelation in Christ. This concern shows up in the first few lines of the book: the old was spoken by God, but it was spoken through prophets and was fragmentary. The new spokesman, however, is of a higher order and status: he is God's Son. Thus, although the covenantal ceremony and regulations no longer retain their force because of the new covenant that the Son established, the prophetic message (broadly defined) retains its validity as revelation.

The Spirit is an important factor in allowing the prophetic message to retain its validity. The author of Hebrews, in 9:8–9, views the Holy Spirit as the author of the Pentateuchal material regarding the construction of the tabernacle. The Spirit, he states, meant that the very existence of the tabernacle here on earth was to indicate that the way to the (true, heavenly) Holy Place was not yet known or open. Were it open, there would have been no need for an earthly tabernacle. Thus the author finds a significance in the Holy Spirit as originator of Scripture for the original recipients. He is more interested, though, in the significance of the Spirit's meaning for the present, which becomes explicit in verses 9–10. The new covenant has come, and in Scripture God speaks to the present, testifying that the old was imperfect and temporary.

The case is much the same in 10:15–17. Having already quoted Jeremiah 31:31–34 in 8:8–12, the author now wants to focus on two parts of this longer passage that bear on sacrifice: a new law and an obliteration of God's memory of sins. These two factors, the author reasons, require an ultimate, truly atoning sacrifice after which no more atonement is necessary or even possible. Introducing the fuller quotation in 8:8, God is identified as the historical speaker. Here the Spirit is designated as the speaker, but his role is not historical; it is present: "The Holy Spirit also testifies to us about this" (10:15).

The same significance may be seen in 3:7, the introduction of a quotation of Psalm 95: "So, as the Holy Spirit says. . . ." The quotation itself begins with "Today, if you hear his voice, do not harden your hearts." The Spirit is speaking through the text, and he is speaking "today." Yet the text is not without historical significance to the author (3:16–18). The psalm that he quotes refers to the forefathers who rebelled in the desert, and he acknowledges the historical reference. The psalm itself refers "you" both to those who rebelled and to those to whom it appeals. The author does not pick up this note of solidarity but reserves "they" and "them" for the desert rebels and does not think of the psalmist's contemporaries at all. The "you" of the text are his readers, and the one who speaks is the Spirit.

Thus there is a tension in the author's presentation of Scripture. He tends to minimize the human development, placing more emphasis on the divine as the origin. On the other hand, he also speaks of the Pentateuchal Law as spoken by angels (2:2), probably reflecting an old rabbinic tradition. The angels are God's messengers and do not speak independently; but given his attitude toward the angelic, it is a statement that downgrades the significance of that revelation when compared to Jesus. Further, when he does speak of the human agents of revelation, they, too, are compared to Jesus and found inferior (1:1; 3:3–6).

Still, since the Spirit is the one who speaks (present tense) in Scripture, Scripture does retain authority as revelation and as the voice of God.

III. The Spirit in the Life of the Believer.

A. As the Agent in the Offering of the Sacrifice of Christ. One of the themes of Hebrews is that the sacrifice offered by Christ is far superior to the sacrifices of the OT. The sacrifices of the old covenant involved merely external defilement and cleansing; they could not effect an inner change in the heart of the worshiper. Christ's sacrifice is better because it does offer an inner cleansing. Part of the reason that Christ's sacrifice can offer this cleansing lies in its nature: it was himself (e.g., 9:26; 10:10). Another factor, however, is that the offering was made through the Spirit (9:14). Much of the author's doctrine of atonement is based analogically on the OT ritual; the role of the Spirit in the atonement by Christ finds little parallel in this ritual, so it is hard to determine the author's precise meaning. The analogy shows that just as the decisive act of sacrifice was not the slaying of the animal but rather the offering of its blood (representing the life of the animal given up in death [Lev. 17:11]) to God, so the decisive action that constituted the death of Christ a sacrifice was not his death itself but rather the offering of his life given up in death (spoken of here as the "blood of Christ") to God. Under the old covenant, the act of presenting the blood involved the priest catching the blood of the victim and then sprinkling it against the sides of the altar (see, e.g., Lev.1:5). The offering made by Christ as priest was in the heavenly sanctuary but did not involve physical blood. Since this offering involved not physical substance but spiritual realities, including Jesus' life itself, it is only natural that the Spirit be the means or agent of presenting it to God. It is also probable that the participation of the Spirit in the act of offering is a factor in making the sacrifice applicable for everyone for all time, since he is designated as the "eternal Spirit" in this text.

B. Communication of the Benefits of Atonement. Another reason that the sacrifice of Jesus offers inner cleansing is that the benefits of the sacrifice are applied to the individual believer by the Spirit. This principle can be seen in 10:29, where the Spirit, viewed as the agent of grace, is linked with the cleansing of the individual by the sacrifice of Christ. This text describes a person who had been a member of the new covenant, i.e., who had been a Christian, but who now has rejected the covenant. The rejection is described in three ways: trampling the Son of God under foot, treating the blood of the covenant as unholy, and insulting the Spirit of grace (probably a more detailed description of the "fall away" in 6:6). The first either was figurative or involved a symbolic action. The last two are related to each other and should be read in light of 9:14, where the author previously mentioned the blood, cleansing, and the Spirit together. By rejecting the covenant based on the sacrifice of Christ, a (former) believer thereby insults the Spirit by whom the sacrifice was offered and who communicated its benefits to him.

C. *Sharing the Holy Spirit.* Not only is the Spirit active at the beginning of the Christian experience; he is also integrated into the life of the believer. This theme is evident in the author's discussion concerning those who have been Christians but have fallen away. He states that it is impossible to make them repent. Discussions of this text (6:1–6) often focus on the prior status of the person as a "Christian": Was the person really in a saving relationship with God or not? Those who hold to some form of eternal security will say that the person only appeared to be a Christian. Those who reject this doctrine will still face theological problems with Christians who fall into sin and who subsequently repent: Was their apostasy only apparent? One interpretation that attempts to resolve these problems is to note that the text does not say that it is impossible for that person to repent, only that it is impossible to cause that person to repent. The other facet of the text that moves toward a resolution, and the item that is of interest to this study, is that these people had shared in the Holy Spirit. The term "shared" is used two other places in Hebrews to indicate an actual experience in common with others (3:1; 12:8), once to indicate personal relationship (1:9) and once that could be read either way (3:14). Both meanings, however, point to the same conclusion: This person had previously had a personal relationship with God in common with the other members of the believing community. Further, the parallel term "tasted" points strongly to actual experience (cf. 2:9).

Thus the author sees an experience of the Spirit as constitutive of the Christian experience of God's salvation. It is not entirely clear whether he views this experience as a union of the divine and human spirits in the Pauline-Johannine mold or as a personal relationship as in 1:9. In either case, we should note the conjunction of this experience with the other items in the list: (1) enlightenment (although this term could relate to baptism); (2) experience of the word of God, which for our author may be equivalent to God himself at work within (cf. 4:12–13, where this equation seems to be made) or which may relate to an experience along the lines of an OT prophet; and (3) experience of the power of God that will characterize the age to come. In addition, we must again observe that this relationship with the Spirit follows the work of the Spirit in cleansing the believer by applying the Atonement to him or her.

D. *The Charismatic Spirit.* Finally, Hebrews also mentions, in 2:4, the charismatic experience of the Spirit. As the message of salvation is preached, God himself attests to its veracity. His testimony consists of the miraculous described in several terms, one of which is "gifts of the Holy Spirit." The term is a different one than those used in 1 Corinthians 12, where Paul enumerates a list of gifts. Here the term is *merismos,* a distribution or apportionment (BAGD) of the Spirit, i.e., the Spirit manifesting himself in a miraculous way through those who were preaching the gospel (cf. 1 Cor. 12:7 for the charismata as manifestations of the Spirit and Heb. 6:5 for experiencing the powers of the age to come parallel with experiencing the Spirit).

IV. Summary and Conclusions. In general, the teaching of the Letter to the Hebrews on the Holy Spirit can be divided into two broad themes: the Spirit in relationship to Scripture and in relationship to the believer. In the former, while showing that the old revelation has been superseded and the regulations of the old covenant are no longer binding, the author still views Scripture as the voice of the Spirit to the present. In the latter theme, the Spirit is active in several phases of the Christian's relationship with God: the provision of atonement, its application to the individual believer in cleansing, dwelling in the individual and community, manifesting himself in the miraculous, and attesting to the truth of the gospel as it is proclaimed.

Bibliography: F. F. Bruce, *The Epistle to the Hebrews* (1964); G. W. Buchanan, *To the Hebrews* (1972); G. Hughes, *Hebrews and Hermeneutics* (1972); R. Jewett, *Letter to Pilgrims* (1981); E. Kasemann, *The Wandering People of God* (1984); H. Montefiore, *Commentary on the Epistle to the Hebrews* (1964); G. Milligan, *Theology of the Epistle to the Hebrews* (1899).
D. A. Johns

HERITAGE VILLAGE, U.S.A See Bakker, James Orsen ("Jim") and Tammy Faye.

HERMENEUTICS, HISTORICAL PERSPECTIVES ON PENTECOSTAL AND CHARISMATIC The frame of reference and theological orientation out of which the Bible is studied influence one's interpretation of Scripture. Pentecostals have understood that the Scriptures can be interpreted properly only through the agency of the Holy Spirit (cf. John 14:26; 16:13). Convinced of the importance of the Holy Spirit to the interpretive process, they bear a distinctive witness to an experience and life in the Spirit, out of which Pentecostal hermeneutics and theology have emerged. A review of Pentecostal hermeneutics from a historical perspective discloses some of the key aspects of the Pentecostal reality of life in the Spirit and their implications for the Pentecostal approach to the Scriptures.

I. Definitions
    A. Hermeneutics
    B. Pentecostal/Charismatic
II. Foundations for Interpretation
    A. Historical Background
        1. Wesley
        2. Holiness Movement
    B. Theological Presuppositions
        1. Classical Pentecostals—Three Periods
        2. Oneness Pentecostals—Hermeneutical Difficulties

      3. Neo-Pentecostals—Harmonization
  C. View of Scripture
      1. Inspiration
      2. Authority
      3. Infallibility
III. Method of Interpretation
  A. Pneumatic
      1. Basis in Inspiration
      2. Pentecostal Epistemology
      3. Harmony in Interpretation
      4. Recognition of a Danger
  B. Experiential
      1. Experience Drawn From Interpretation of Scripture
      2. Experience Informing Interpretation
      3. Dialogical Relationship of Experience and Interpretation
  C. Historical Narrative
      1. Challenge of Dispensationalism
      2. A More Recent Challenge
      3. Pentecostal Response
IV. Direction for Interpretation in the Future
  A. Hermeneutical Tools
  B. A Pentecostal Model
  C. A Broad Perspective

I. Definitions.

A. Hermeneutics. This term can be generally defined as the principles, rules, and methods of the interpretation of literary texts. Interpretation refers here to a specific twofold process that is initiated with a methodical search for the original meaning of a text (exegesis) and is concluded with a determination of the meaning of this same text for the modern reader. Throughout this process the interpreter must deal with any linguistic, cultural, geographical, or temporal barriers that hinder his or her understanding of the text.

While the general definition previously offered encompasses the interpretation of all literary texts, the immediate concern is the interpretation of the biblical text alone. The interpreter must immediately recognize that the Bible presents a unique set of hermeneutical problems that demand attention.

First, while the Bible presents itself as a single book in terms of revelation, it is not a single book in terms of language (Hebrew, Aramaic, and Greek), authorship (Moses the ruler, Ezra the scribe, Matthew the publican, Luke the Gentile physician, etc.), time (from pre-Hebrew history to the first-century church), literary genre (historical narrative, legal code, poetry, wisdom literature, apocalyptic, gospel, epistle, etc.), or theological perspective (e.g., prophecy/fulfillment, national preservation/international evangelism, etc.). Second, the Bible is considered an "inspired" document and as such represents not only a witness to God but God's voice itself speaking directly to the heart of the reader. Third, the Bible is self-interpreting; the product of this self-interpretation offers insight and often presents new problems to the modern interpreter. Fourth, there are problems of harmonization between biblical texts, i.e., synoptic problems (cf. the synoptic Gospels, the three Acts accounts of Paul's conversion, Kings/Chronicles narratives, etc.) that the

interpreter must address. The Bible as a literary work thus presents the interpreter with all of the typical problems associated with the interpretation of literary texts, and as the inscripturated word of God it presents the interpreter with a new set of difficulties not encountered in other literary texts.

B. Pentecostal/Charismatic. The view that there exists a distinctive Pentecostal/charismatic hermeneutic presents yet more problems to an understanding of the interpretative process. First, the term *Pentecostal* itself must be defined; however, upon investigation, it quickly becomes evident that those who call themselves "Pentecostal" do not comprise a homogeneous group. Some are classical Pentecostals whose theological roots lie in the Wesleyan and Keswick Holiness movements of the eighteenth and nineteenth centuries. They teach that conversion to Christ is followed by an experience known as the baptism or infilling with the Spirit and that at the moment of this experience all speak in tongues as the initial evidence of the baptism with the Spirit. Others are Jesus Only or Oneness Pentecostals characterized by their Unitarian theology. Finally, some others are Neo-Pentecostals who are generally identified with the charismatic movement. This movement is transdenominational and spans the entire spectrum of Christianity including Roman Catholic, Eastern Orthodox, Lutheran, and Reformed traditions. Richard Quebedeaux expresses the broad ecumenical impact of the charismatic movement in positing that "close doctrinal agreement is not a prerequisite for unity or fellowship" (1946, 123). Furthermore, classical Pentecostal Hollis Gause observes that the perception of a unity of faith simply on the basis of a common experience of the phenomenon of glossolalia potentially hides differences of commitment (Spittler, 1976, 113). The wide-ranging theological perspectives of the groups called "Pentecostal" bring to the hermeneutical process different interpretational presuppositions. Therefore, it is imperative that an initial admission be made that the Pentecostal interpretational scheme brings to the hermeneutical task various currents of theological thought.

Naturally the theological currents present in the Pentecostal movement have had a decisive influence on the hermeneutics of Pentecostals. Our approach to the issue of Pentecostal hermeneutics is to begin with an examination of the foundational aspects. From that point the focus will move to a discussion of the methodology of Pentecostal hermeneutics. Finally, a suggested agenda is offered for the future direction of the Pentecostal hermeneutic.

II. Foundations for Interpretation. The initial area of concern is the foundation of the Pentecostal hermeneutic. At this stage the inquiry focuses on the predispositions and presuppositions that the Pentecostal interpreter brings to the hermeneutical task. The interpreter can by no means divorce himself/herself from the accumulated history when engaging the biblical text. Therefore, in order to appreciate more fully the dynamics of Pentecostal interpretation, it is advantageous to recognize and understand these factors.

A. Historical Background. The first place to look for such predispositions is the history from which the movement emerged. The cradle from which classical Pentecostalism emerged was primarily the Wesleyan and Holiness movements.

1. Wesley. The hermeneutical tendencies of eighteenth-century preacher and theologian John Wesley bear tremendous implications for the study of Pentecostal hermeneutics. Wayne McCown recognizes four dominating hermeneutical principles emerging from Wesley's work. First, "Wesley approached the Scriptures most often with a view to reading longer (chapter-length) passages. . . . Wesley himself became a 'living' Bible. Its language and thoughts were spontaneously interwoven into his mode of self-expression." This embracing of Scripture demonstrated the passion of the man for the text, a passion so consuming that it transformed his very patterns of speech. This is not mere Scripture quoting or proof texting but an integration of the biblical text into the fabric of his own thought. Second, Wesley regarded Bible study not only as an academic exercise but as a devotional experience tempered by heartfelt prayer. Third, Wesley regarded the Bible as the primary authoritative source for doctrine that would feed into his writing and preaching. Finally, Wesley saw application of the biblical message as a necessary conclusion to the hermeneutical task (McCown and Massey, eds., 1982, 2:3–6). The purpose of Scripture study was, for Wesley, to discover the will of God and then to act on that discovery. Wesley's strong affirmation of biblical authority for doctrinal formulation and practical response provided a strong foundation upon which Pentecostal thought could later grow.

2. Holiness Movement. The Holiness movement also has had a decisive influence on Pentecostal hermeneutics and theology. Building upon Wesley's thought, a distinctive Holiness theology emerged in the nineteenth century that established the thought patterns and theological agenda that would later be elaborated upon by Pentecostals. R. C. Dalton recognizes this progression:

> The rediscovery by these men of the truth of a Spirit baptism subsequent to regeneration contributed more than is generally recognized to the acceptance of Pentecostal teaching by the early Pentecostalists at the beginning of the 20th century. Dwight L. Moody, R. A. Torrey, A. J. Gordon, Andrew Murray, James Elder Cumming, and C. R. Vaughan, all writing before 1900, distinctly take a doctrinal position on a spiritual experience known as the baptism in the Holy Spirit subsequent to regeneration. . . . All stress the experience as climactic, and all agree that its purpose is to give power in Christian service (1973, 3).

These men saw that the opportunity had been afforded every believer to partake of a special spiritual experience subsequent to regeneration. While two of these Holiness preachers, Torrey

and Murray, later wrote that speaking in tongues is not the initial physical evidence of this subsequent experience (Dalton, 1973, 3–4), it yet remains that their teaching provided the propositional groundwork upon which the Pentecostal theology of subsequence of Spirit baptism to conversion could be erected and upon which Pentecostal interpretation could be practiced.

B. Theological Presuppositions. In addition to the principles established by its predecessors, the Pentecostal movement's own theological presuppositions also impact the movement's interpretative principles. Because doctrine is necessarily an outgrowth of biblical interpretation, it seems at first a case of circular reasoning to speak of Pentecostal theology as a foundational aspect of Pentecostal hermeneutics. While there is admittedly an element of truth in this assessment, it must then be remembered that no one interprets in a theological vacuum. Interpretation, indeed, the very approach to the task of interpretation, is shaped by the theological presuppositions that the interpreter brings to the process.

1. Classical Pentecostals—Three Periods. For the classical Pentecostal, these theological presuppositions have passed through three phases. Historically, the first Pentecostals emerged from the Keswick and Wesleyan Holiness movements. The Wesleyan Holiness Pentecostals maintain a three-fold *ordo salutis* of the Christian experience that includes conversion, entire sanctification, and the baptism in the Holy Spirit. These are considered three distinct works of grace that must be experienced in serial order. The Pentecostals with Keswick antecedents see instead two definite works of grace. They dispense with a second definite work of sanctification by emphasizing instead the sanctifying work inherent in the conversion experience and a process of gradual sanctification that ensues conversion. And indeed, the interpretational concerns of classical Pentecostals largely paralleled those of their predecessors. It became a time to enunciate their own theological distinctives in relation to the theological definitions developed by the Holiness movements from which they came. For example, in the earliest Pentecostal literature, there is great effort taken to distinguish between "the anointing of the Holy Spirit" and "the baptism in the Holy Spirit."

Charles F. Parham, whose ministry was associated with the initiation of the modern Pentecostal movement, explains the difference between the anointing and Spirit baptism:

> This . . . is the anointing: To illuminate the Word, to give revelation of truth, and is an in-filling of the Holy Spirit. This is the phase of the Holy Spirit's power received by all truly sanctified persons, which they mistake for and call the Baptism of Pentecost. . . . While there is an attendant blessing as sweet as honey-dew, yet Pentecost is given to us for power to witness and to enable us to give out to others what the anointing has been filling us with. The anointing is within you a well of water (artesian); the baptism lends the pressure or power to compel that well to flow from your inward

parts in "streams of living water" to your fellowmen (Parham, 1911, 70).

This distinction between the anointing and the Spirit baptism is clearly an effort to speak to the equation of these two experiences by Holiness preachers. While this is more precisely a discussion of early Pentecostal theology rather than of hermeneutics, it nevertheless reveals the concern for defining Pentecostal thought that influenced the early Pentecostals' interpretational labors. This was then a period of *definition* for the early Pentecostals. This need for definition was precipitated by the dramatic, unexpected outpouring of the Holy Spirit upon these people. They sought to explain (as much for themselves as for outsiders) the relationship of this twentieth-century renewal to the historical precedent they saw for their experience in the biblical record.

Soon thereafter, the definitions derived by the early Pentecostals had come to be presuppositions in their own right. Primary among these Pentecostal distinctives are the two interrelated doctrines: (1) that the Spirit baptism is a work of grace distinct from and subsequent to the initial experience of salvation, and (2) that speaking in tongues is the initial physical evidence of baptism in the Spirit. These distinctive doctrines of subsequence and initial evidence were affixed to the holiness doctrines as the primary Pentecostal theological presuppositions. While much Pentecostal doctrine retained a Holiness emphasis, there was no longer any need to engage in such arguments as the distinction between the anointing of the Holy Spirit and the baptism in the Holy Spirit. Instead, this becomes a time for *defense*. Pentecostal theology had been defined and published by the pioneers of the movement, and this had drawn fire from outside detractors. Thus the most penetrating Pentecostal study of Scripture was approached with a view to defend the doctrines espoused by the earliest Pentecostals.

Recently, classical Pentecostal theology has drawn critiques from more theologically sophisticated quarters. Representative of these critical works is *Baptism in the Holy Spirit* (1970) by James D. G. Dunn, who is sympathetic toward the Pentecostal movement but has strong reservations regarding its hermeneutic and theology. Therefore, these latest criticisms have attacked not only the distinctives of Pentecostal theology but the basis for these distinctives, the Pentecostal hermeneutic, as well. Such astute criticism has caused much reflection upon and reconsideration of the biblical basis for the theology of classical Pentecostals. The result is a new wave of Pentecostal scholarship that continues to affirm the prevailing Pentecostal doctrines but that provides a sounder hermeneutical footing for these doctrines. This third era is then best characterized as one of *reflection*. In this latest period much effort has been expended to reevaluate the interpretive foundation of Pentecostal theology. This introspection has resulted in some questioning of the theological distinctives by Pentecostals themselves but has primarily concluded with a strong endorsement of the well-established Pentecostal theology upon a sounder hermeneutical footing. The particulars of this recent Pentecostal work are discussed later.

2. Oneness Pentecostals—Hermeneutical Difficulties. Generally Pentecostals have embraced the Trinitarian view of the Godhead, but as a variation, Oneness Pentecostalism has proclaimed an "evangelical Unitarianism" of the Second Person of the Godhead. The effort of this Pentecostal branch has been to harmonize the Trinitarian formula of Matthew 28:19 with what this group perceives as a non-Trinitarian pattern in the Book of Acts. They observe that in Acts baptism is administered in the name of the "Lord Jesus" or "Jesus Christ." To resolve the interpretive problem they affirm the pattern of Acts 2:38, insisting that Jesus is the full manifestation of the Godhead in this dispensation. Hermeneutically, this position creates various difficulties with which the mainline Pentecostal movement must contend. Representative of these difficulties are the dispensational understanding of the Trinitarian involvement of God in history and the relationship of the work of Christ and the work of the Holy Spirit as described in the NT. These theological presuppositions have relevance for understanding the Oneness view of the Godhead, but they express nothing that is universally characteristic of the Pentecostal hermeneutics and theology (Dayton, 1985, 9–10).

3. Neo-Pentecostals—Harmonization. Neo-Pentecostals come from a wide variety of theological backgrounds and have been able to remain within their respective movements. Because they do not represent a clearly defined group, it is difficult to offer a comprehensive treatment of their theological and hermeneutical presuppositions. Nevertheless, they represent a mindset that endorses traditional hermeneutics as a basis for sound theology. It should be noted that those involved in each of the various Charismatic groups have attempted to reconcile the Pentecostal dimensions of their religious experience with the theological deposit of their respective traditions. Gause maintains that, in fact, they "want an experience that does not interfere with doctrinal and traditional commitments already made" (Spittler, 1976, 114). Therefore, the Pentecostal experience is integrated within the existing theological framework. Representative of this integration is the typical charismatic perspective that the baptism in the Holy Spirit is not a subsequent work of grace but an actualization of the latent spiritual potential made available in Christian conversion/initiation. It is just such doctrinal maneuvering that renders the thrust of Neo-Pentecostal interpretation as an effort of *harmonization*.

C. View of Scripture. A third hermeneutical foundation is the view of Scripture held by Pentecostals. For Pentecostals divine truth may come in song, in testimony, in sermon, or through spiritual gifts; but all such means lead back to the Scriptures. Classical Pentecostals embrace the principle of the Protestant Reformation that the Scriptures are the only rule for faith and practice. This principle is foundational to Pentecostal hermeneutics.

1. Inspiration. The Pentecostal movement insists that the basis for inspiration lies in the very nature of God. It is God's nature to communicate. He took the initiative to share himself with others by sending his Son into the world, and by providing the gift of his Spirit. God's desire to communicate or to reveal himself finds expression in the inscripturation of the Bible as well. As the Incarnation and the gift of the Holy Spirit reveal God to humankind, so does the biblical text. The implication is that the Bible is no longer seen as a secondary witness to God but as the voice of God himself speaking across the ages through the hands of human authors. It is a primary witness to God because it is the speech of God recorded in the biblical text through the inspiration of the Holy Spirit; and as a primary witness, the Bible is a "saving witness." This view of the Bible rests on the fact that an encounter with the Holy Scriptures is in fact an encounter with the living God.

The problem for Pentecostals has been to understand the role of the human authors in the process of inspiration. It is recognized that the biblical writers all enjoyed a particular experience with the Holy Spirit and that the fruit of that experience is the biblical text. The problem is in comprehending the coalescence of the human and the divine in the production of the text. It is a problem that bears profound similarity to the discussion of the human and the divine natures in the incarnate Christ and the cooperation of the divine and human wills in election.

Early Pentecostal responses to this problem saw the biblical writers as passive instruments in the hands of God, as mere channels through which the word of God was spoken. The result was an understanding of inspiration as dictation. This early Pentecostal comprehension is demonstrated by the fact that Pentecostal interpretation placed little or no significance upon the historical context in which the texts were inscribed. Biblical statements were understood at face value with no appreciation for the ancient context in which they were delivered.

In time, this understanding of inspiration was found to be unsatisfactory. Instead, there is seen a full cooperation of the human and divine in the writing of the Bible. The result is a Bible that is equally the word of God and the words of man. To be more precise, the Scriptures are fully divine and fully human. Just as Christ, from the time of his incarnation, is fully man and fully God and just as his divine and human natures are indivisible, so in a similar manner, the Bible is both fully human and fully divine. Yet the mechanics of this cooperative process of the divine and human in the writing of the Scriptures, as George Florovsky keenly observes, remain a profound mystery:

The Scriptures are "inspired," they are the Word of God. What is the inspiration can never be properly defined—there is a mystery therein. It is a mystery of the divine-human encounter. We cannot fully understand in what manner "God's Holy men" heard the Word of their Lord and how they could articulate it in the words of their own dialect. Yet, even in their human transmission, it was the voice of God (Florovsky, 1972, 27).

To proclaim the Bible a human document in no way lessens the reality or the scope of its inspiration. "All" Scripture is inspired by God; "all" Scripture is written by man. The Bible is entirely the word of God, and it is at the same time entirely the words of men. The two elements cannot be separated, for they each pervade the whole of Scripture; to attempt to separate these two elements would only serve to destroy the Bible. The divine element present in the Bible cannot be separated from the human, for God has chosen to act in human history. Human history is the vehicle through which God chooses to reveal himself; therefore, it is in vain that one attempts to discover God's word in the Scriptures apart from the human element that is present in them.

2. Authority. It is appreciation for the inspiration of the Bible that has led the classical Pentecostal to defend ardently the inherent authority of Scripture. From its inception, Pentecostalism, although caricatured as a movement of emotionalists who were most concerned with their unique "experience," has held an extremely high view of scriptural authority. F. D. Bruner, whose work is sharply critical of Pentecostal theology, recognizes that "Pentecostalism quite openly declares that unless it can support its case biblically it has no finally compelling reason to exist" (Bruner, 1972, 63). This concern to accede to biblical authority is in fact extended to every facet of Pentecostal faith and religious practice. Demonstration of this fact is seen in the following excerpt from the minutes of the 1912 General Assembly of the Church of God (CG):

Each year has brought perplexing questions, and every question has been discussed with a view to settle it in perfect harmony with the Scripture. . . . On the part of all there has been that honest, earnest and sincere desire for truth, light and Scriptural systems. It has never been our custom to try to bend the Scriptures to suit our conveniences and accommodations, but have always proposed to yield our own views and harmonize everything to suit the Scriptures, which we are obligated to defend ("Annual Address of the General Overseer of the Churches of God," as published in the *Minutes of the Seventh Annual Assembly of the Churches of God,* 1912, 4).

The context of this great concern for "harmony with the Scripture" is simply the discussion of the scheduling of future assemblies; these early Pentecostals indeed saw far-reaching implications for the authority of Scripture within the body of Christ. The Assemblies of God (AG) affirms this conviction in positing that "the Bible is our all-sufficient rule for faith and practice" ("Constitution of the General Council of the Assemblies of God Revised to August 23, 1977," Article V. Statement of Fundamental Truths, as published in the *Minutes of the Thirty-Sixth Session of the General Council of the Assemblies of God,* 1977, 113). But the reign of biblical authority extends beyond the church to the personal life of the believer apart from the gathered body. The Bible is affirmed as the norm against which every word and experience of our lives is to be measured. While this sense of overarching authority is not an innovation of Pentecostalism (this view of Scripture finds its roots in the Reformation that called for biblical authority alone against tradition), it bears noting that this Pentecostal insistence on the authority of Scripture contradicts the popular assessment of Pentecostalism as a movement that is directed only through its own ecstatic experiences.

In early Pentecostalism this insistence on biblical authority found expression in a devout anti-creedalism. Early Pentecostal literature was filled with attacks on "man-made traditions." These polemical statements in many respects parallel the literature of the early Reformation period, which lifts Scripture to a preeminent position above the ecclesiastical traditions of Roman Catholicism. The following citations from early Pentecostal publications demonstrate these strong convictions:

> If I should say no more than this—"Lay aside all man-made teachings, or traditions, and take the whole truth of God," I would have said enough. We reject the authority of tradition in sacred things and rely only on the written Word of God (Payne, 1915, 1).
>
> It is impossible to set up a creed for a man to preach and the Holy Ghost guide into all truth. . . . Whether they be truth or error it differs not. If every article were as pure as gold, it would break God's law as Moses broke the table of God's law (Spurling, 1920, 25–26).

In the growth of Pentecostalism, this harsh anticreedalism has moderated. It was recognized that "creeds are not Scripture, but neither are they the memorabilia of a dead past" (Ervin, in Elbert, 1985, 33). Pentecostals discovered for themselves the value of codifying their fundamental beliefs for deterring heretical excesses. However, they continued to maintain their strong conviction that creedal statements, "traditions," only have derived authority, an authority reliant on the inherent authority of the Bible.

While charismatics insist that they share this same appreciation for biblical authority and that they embrace the Reformation principle of *sola scriptura*, the perception of some charismatics of the ongoing work of the Holy Spirit (particularly in Christian prophecy and glossolalia interpretation) tends to undermine this insistence. As Mark McLean perceives, there is a "tendency of charismatic groups to abandon the canon for 'fresh and authoritative revelations' of the Holy Spirit" (McLean, 1984, 35). While scriptural authority is explicitly defended, it is implicitly circumvented by the emphasis on this "living word" of charismatic Christian prophecy, this so-called *rhema* word. The remarks of Richard Quebedeaux provide ample evidence of this excessive exaltation of charismatic prophecy: "In Neo-Pentecostalism, then, spiritual authority rests ultimately in the present activity and teaching of the Holy Spirit at least as much in the Bible itself, whose essential

truth is made known to individuals only by the power of the Spirit" (1976, 113).Though classical Pentecostals and charismatics believe that God speaks today as he spoke to the biblical authors, Quebedeaux's remarks unfortunately distort the historical significance of the Pentecostal/charismatic movement. Pentecostalism does not claim to espouse a new revelation (as does Mormonism, for example); it instead perceives itself as a revival movement that calls the church to relive the apostolic experiences that are related in the NT.

Cecil M. Robeck, Jr., offers three insights with which Pentecostals readily identify and which help to delineate the distinctions between the authority of Scripture and Christian prophecy. First, while God's revelation in Scripture is normative for all matters of our Christian faith and practice, those other means by which he leads his people (including the gift of prophecy) are subject to testing against this scriptural norm to ensure their validity. Second, while Scripture proclaims for itself an inherent and therefore independent authority, the authority of charismatic prophecy is determined by its consistency with the Bible. Finally, while "Scripture is a universal authority with universal applications," charismatic prophecy speaks "to specific people at specific times in specific situations" (Robeck, 1979, 28–30). The emphasis of charismatic prophecy is therefore on its immediate hortatory value to its hearers. The ongoing revelatory work of the Holy Spirit is seen not as a challenge to biblical authority but as a specific application of the biblical message that is limited both in its subjection to Scripture and in its applicability.

3. Infallibility. Another by-product of the Pentecostal insistence on an inspired canon as foundational to the hermeneutical process is the recognition of the infallibility of Scripture. Like their fellow Evangelicals, Pentecostals have struggled with the definitions of infallibility and inerrancy as they apply to the biblical text. In regard to this issue, Pentecostals have sought to avoid each of two opposing excesses. First, Pentecostals have denied the liberal appraisal that sees the Bible as a human document replete with human error that merely contains the word of God. Pentecostals saw that such a position undermines biblical authority because it leaves the interpreter the task of separating fact from fiction, truth from error. This process puts the interpreter in authority over the text instead of the text exercising authority over the interpreter. As a result, scientific biblical criticism has been met with suspicion among Pentecostals. The sanctity of a Spirit-inspired canon is typically seen by the Pentecostal as standing above human faculties, and thus Scripture becomes the standard against which our own critical efforts are evaluated. Instead of scientific criticism evaluating the truth of Scripture, the Pentecostal sees the truth of Scripture determining the validity and relevance of criticism.

On the other hand, Pentecostals stop short of the extreme Fundamentalist view of Scripture as a static deposit of truth that the interpreter approaches through his/her rational faculties alone. Therefore, Pentecostals are freer to examine the difficulties of Scripture without recourse to the defensive posture assumed by many Fundamentalists. Certainly Pentecostals affirm the infallibility of the Bible; but while biblical infallibility is an assumption on which Pentecostals build their hermeneutic, they recognize that they have neither the ability nor the responsibility to demonstrate this infallibility. Because the Bible is inspired by an infallible God, it is infallible. No further demonstration of its infallibility is either necessary or possible.

III. Method of Interpretation. The discussion now turns to the manner in which Pentecostals engage the biblical text, the methodology of Pentecostal interpretation. Because Pentecostals possess a unique perception of the nature and function of the Holy Scriptures, they use equally unique approaches to the interpretation of the biblical text.

A. Pneumatic. The Pentecostal method of interpretation is essentially *pneumatic,* or *charismatic.* This is to say that the interpreter relies on illumination by the Holy Spirit in order to come to the fullest comprehension of the significance of the text.

1. Basis in Inspiration. This pneumatic mode of interpretation finds its basis in the inspiration of Scripture. Because the human author has been guided and assisted at every juncture of the inscripturating process, the human interpreter is believed to require this same guidance and assistance. Such a view recognizes a spiritual kinship between the ancient authors of the text and the modern reader. When the modern reader's experience of the Holy Spirit reenacts the apostolic experience of the Spirit, the Spirit serves as the common context in which reader and author can meet to bridge the historical and cultural gulf between them. The Bible is then a book for the believer. The commonality of the experiences of the modern reader and the ancient author lies in their shared faith in Jesus Christ and their walk with the Paraclete whom he promised them. It is within the context of faith that the Bible was inspired; therefore, it is within the context of faith that the Bible must be interpreted.

The question arises, then, whether the unbeliever can comprehend the Scriptures. In one respect, the answer to this question is in the affirmative. The tools of scientific exegesis are certainly at the disposal of the nonbeliever. There are scholars who deny the deity of Christ and who are yet exegetes of Scripture. And so, in a certain sense, the Scriptures are open to all. To argue otherwise is to claim that the Bible is on the surface incoherent, thereby asserting a gnostic view of the text in which the secrets of its meaning are only discernible to the initiated members of the community of faith. The result is a purely allegorical approach to the Bible that denigrates the literal meaning of the text. The Pentecostal takes no such approach but nonetheless contends that there is a deeper significance to the biblical text that can only be perceived through the eyes of faith. As Howard Ervin posits, "It is not possible to penetrate to the heart of its message apart from the Holy Spirit" (Ervin, 1985, 29). The apostle Paul attests the fundamental importance of the pneumatic dimension to sound hermeneutics: " 'No eye has seen, no ear has heard, no mind has conceived what God has prepared for those who love him'—but God has revealed it to us by his Spirit" (1 Cor. 2:9–10a).

2. Pentecostal Epistemology. Deeper insight into Scripture afforded the believer is a function of the Pentecostal or pneumatic epistemology. Pentecostals see knowledge not as a cognitive recognition of a set of precepts but as a relationship with the One who has established the precepts by which we live. The teachings of Scripture remain ambiguous until the Holy Spirit, who searches even the deep things of God (1 Cor. 2:10), illuminates human understanding to the mysteries of the gospel, but such a pneumatic epistemology finds its roots in the Scripture itself. Thus the believer knows God as Adam knew Eve, and he comes to know God through his Christian walk in fellowship with the Spirit. His belief then is not merely an intellectual acceptance of precepts but is a lived response to his lived relationship with the Spirit of God. As a result, the believer comes to understand the Word of God only in his relationship with its ultimate author, the Spirit of God.

3. Harmony in Interpretation. Early Pentecostals, in their search for theological definition, were keenly aware of the need for pneumatic leading in the hermeneutical process. Their main concern was to achieve harmony in interpretation. As there is one God and this one God is the embodiment of all truth, then the conclusion of the early Pentecostal was that there was one truth and therefore one correct interpretation of Scripture. The following excerpt from a 1914 *Church of God Evangel* serves to demonstrate this point:

> Since there is only one Bible . . . it becomes a mystery how so many different doctrines have been originated since the Reformation by Martin Luther. Every different sect claims they are right and that their creed and articles of faith are based on the Scriptures and yet all are different. This leads us to exclaim, There is a wrong somewhere (1914, 1).

These early Pentecostals knew well that they were but a minute sect within the church universal and that many of the conclusions that they were drawing from Scripture were contradictory to popular interpretations. So they sought affirmation of their doctrines, and this affirmation would be found in biblical unity, a unity not achieved by human means but only through the Spirit. The leader of the Topeka Bethel Bible College revival, Charles F. Parham, contended that "unity cannot be accomplished by . . . the minorities yielding to the majority in the interpretation of Scripture, thus crushing out all personal views" (Parham, n.d., 10). The apologetic tone of this statement should not be missed, for Parham here defends the perceptive interpretations of the tiny Pentecostal minority from the intimidating fact that most of Christendom was opposed to their interpretations.

Their insightful interpretations were worthy of this adamant defense. Despite their limited exegetical skills, these early Pentecostals derived many profound interpretations from the Bible text that have weathered well the storm of stringent academic criticism in the intervening years. It seems that the Spirit of Truth was indeed guiding their hermeneutic.

4. *Recognition of a Danger.* There is, however, an imminent danger in relying solely on this pneumatic guidance in the hermeneutical process. This danger lies in the potential that the interpreter confuses his or her own (or some other) spirit with the Spirit of God. Because the interpreter has claimed divine guidance, the resulting interpretation is assumed to be above questioning and thus implicity demands an authority on par with Scripture itself. This unchallenged status ostensibly renders the interpretation itself as inspired, infallible, and inherently authoritative. I. Howard Marshall takes specific exception to this practice:

> There are people who have claimed to be led by the Spirit who have promulgated shocking heresies. . . . Such people depended purely on what they conceived to be the Spirit's help and so landed themselves in a subjective approach. They failed to compare Scripture with Scripture and . . . they failed to listen to the voice of the Spirit as He spoke to other interpreters of Scripture within the fellowship of the Christian church over the centuries. In scriptural interpretation, as in any other area, it is essential that we "test the Spirits" (1 John 4:1) (n.d., 7).

This hermeneutical excess is not a necessary outcome of pneumatic interpretation. In fact, the correction to the problem lies in the realization that this pneumatic dimension to the Pentecostal hermeneutic rightfully places the task of interpretation "within the pneumatic continuity of the faith community" (Ervin, 1985, 33). It does not give the interpreter free rein to interpret the Scriptures privately without any form of accountability. Instead, pneumatic interpretation, properly exercised, does just the opposite; it forces the interpreter to address the illumination of the text that the Spirit has afforded other believers of all ages and to be informed by their responses to the text. Ervin trenchantly summarizes the responsibility that rests on the pneumatic interpreter: "This must not be construed as a plea for a spiritualizing (allegorical) interpretation. Rather, it is a truly existential and phenomenological response to the Holy Spirit's initiative in historical continuity with the life of the Spirit in the Church" (Ervin, 1985, 23–24).

B. Experiential. The experiential dimension of the Pentecostal hermeneutic is another facet of the method of interpretation. Here there are two distinct yet interrelated issues. First, concern is centered on the way in which the interpretations drawn from Scripture impact Pentecostal experience. Second, concern is centered on the manner in which personal and corporate experience inform the Pentecostal hermeneutical process.

1. *Experience Drawn From the Interpretation of Scripture.* Donald Dayton has called the Pentecostal hermeneutic a "subjectivizing" hermeneutic (Dayton, 1985, 17). By this, Dayton means that the Pentecostal draws from the scriptural description of apostolic life the rightful pattern for one's own life. The Bible, therefore, is not studied in a detached, objective manner; instead, the Pentecostal believer enters into an existential continuity with apostolic believers and thereby subjectively shares in their experiences. The vehicle for this subjective experience is the fresh outpouring of the Holy Spirit on the twentieth-century Pentecostal church; this "latter rain" of the Spirit provides the twentieth-century believer experiential continuity with the NT church.

Because the Pentecostal feels this close affinity to the apostolic believers, there has been some tendency among Pentecostals to ignore the church of the intervening centuries. The truth remains, however, that a subjectivizing hermeneutic predates Pentecostalism. The Pietists and the nineteenth-century "Higher Life" groups applied scriptural patterns to their own subjective experience in a normative manner (Dayton, 1985, 17–18). Therefore, believers of other eras have shared in this subjective experiencing of apostolic life.

2. *Experience Informing Interpretation of Scripture.* Early Pentecostals were acutely sensitive to the provision given them in the Holy Spirit to live out the experience of the apostles. The common testimony of Pentecostal believers was that they had received "their Pentecost." The experiences of Acts 2 had been appropriated into their own lives. The following testimony of Pentecostal pioneer Smith Wigglesworth is demonstrative of this enthusiasm for reliving the Upper Room outpouring:

> I found myself speaking in other tongues. The joy was so great that when I came to utter it my tongue failed, and I began to worship God in other tongues as the Spirit gave me utterance. . . . I had received the Bible evidence. This Bible evidence is wonderful to me. I knew I had received the very evidence that the Apostles received on the Day of Pentecost. . . . I knew I had the biblical baptism in the Spirit. It had the backing of Scriptures (1924, 113).

For the Pentecostal, Scripture is not merely the historical record of God's working among the ancients; the Bible is the primary source book for living the Pentecostal life. Because the NT believers shared in this Pentecostal experience with the Holy Spirit, they demonstrated the experiences available to the Latter Rain Pentecostal.

The assumption is not that glossolalia is the only phenomenological parallel between the NT church and twentieth-century Pentecostalism. All the miraculous works of the Holy Spirit are understood to occur today as they did in the apostolic church. Thus the Pentecostal expects all the supernatural manifestations that are ascribed to the Holy Spirit in the NT to be realized during the present era. This includes not only tongues but exorcisms, divine healing, miracles, dreams, visions, audible voices, and all of the various charismatic gifts described in the NT. Consequently, the Pentecostal expects the mode of God's presence to be the same today as in biblical times. This expectation is maintained by charismatic groups as well. Quebedeaux claims that among charismatics "biblical doctrine becomes almost existential" (1976, 123). This criticism is justified if the perceived existential significance is no longer grounded in the historical significance of the text. Thus the empirical approach of Friedrich Schleiermacher, which attaches no significance to the historical context of the Scripture but imposes meaning on the text through a purely subjective rationalistic approach, has no place in a sound Pentecostal hermeneutic. The Pentecostal preserves the historical significance of the text because it is precisely this ancient history that has been recreated. The Pentecostal perceives an undeniable historical continuity between the apostolic age and the twentieth century.

While Pentecostals readily endorse a hermeneutic that draws upon the text to inform personal experience, they often resist placing experience on the front end of the hermeneutical process. Assemblies of God scholar William W. Menzies voices the following reservation toward such an approach: "It would be manifestly out of order if priority were given to personal experience as a basis for theology. . . . However, it should not be thought improper to include personal experience and historical accounts at some point in the process of doing theology" (1979, 20). Menzies denies the propriety of placing experience before interpretation; he demonstrates that the Pentecostal doctrines have not been derived by such a hermeneutic. He notes that "the inductive study of the Bible" led to the initial outpouring at the turn of the century in Topeka, Kansas (ibid.). His reckoning is validated by the personal testimony of Agnes N. Ozman, the first to receive the baptism in the Holy Spirit at Bethel Bible College in Topeka.

On the other hand, attempts have been made within the Pentecostal movement to question the validity of its hermeneutic. Gordon Fee argues that Pentecostal experience has indeed preceded the hermeneutical process. He argues that "the Pentecostal tends to exegete his experience" (Spittler, 1976, 122). Fee further contends that the Pentecostal doctrine of subsequence "did not flow naturally out of his [the Pentecostal's] reading of Scripture" but was derived from his own experiences (ibid.). Neither Fee nor Menzies wants to deny that personal experience plays some rightful part in the hermeneutical process. They are both apparently contending that if a doctrine is determined through a process of informed biblical interpretation, then it is only natural to expect personal experience either to validate or to deny the conclusions drawn by that interpretation.

3. *Dialogical Relationship of Experience and Interpretation.* Experience can and does impact the hermeneutical task. Mark McLean, a Pentecostal scholar, offers the following paradigm for the integration of personal experience (and other forms of "extrabiblical evidences") into the interpretative process:

The question is how do we know when the extrabiblical evidence requires a modification of our understanding of the biblical revelation. . . . There are three possibilities. . . . First, one's interpretation of the biblical evidence is correct and the understanding of the extrabiblical evidence is faulty. The second possibility is that one's interpretation of the extrabiblical evidence is correct . . . and one's understanding of the biblical evidence is faulty. Finally, both one's understanding of biblical evidence on any given issue and of the extrabiblical evidence are wrong (1984, 42–43).

Fee and Menzies agree that when experience becomes the starting point for interpretation, it tends to usurp biblical authority. They perceive that the inescapable result is interpretation that is only directed to the end of justifying the personal experience. Thus the perceived meaning of Scripture becomes easily susceptible to distortion by the presuppositions of the interpreter.

The warning of Fee and Menzies must be taken seriously, but wholesale concession to their argument is unwarranted. The failure of their argument lies in a linear view of the hermeneutical task with respect to personal experience. Instead, the relationship of personal experience and Scripture interpretation is dialogical. At every point, experience informs the process of interpretation, and the fruit of interpretation informs experience. It is certainly true that God communicates revelation through personal experience as well as Scripture, and it may be justifiable to recognize further that such experiential revelation can unlock previously undiscovered scriptural truths. The problem is not necessarily that personal experience "precedes" the hermeneutical task; the problem is that personal experience can displace Scripture as the "norm" against which all proposed revelation is to be tested. But until scholars of the Pentecostal movement confront this issue and establish a clearer definition of the appropriate relationship of experience and Scripture, they risk the unsound interpretation against which Fee and Menzies warn. In confronting this issue, Pentecostals must first determine the present relationship of their personal experience to their hermeneutic. Second, they must demonstrate that this relationship is justifiable. Third, they must determine how best to limit the undeniable potential for misinterpretation that arises in this dialogue between experience and Scripture. Such an approach will enable Pentecostal interpreters to avoid the pitfall of manipulating the Scriptures in order to substantiate a predetermined theological position.

C. Historical Narrative. Pentecostal theology reflects a heavy dependence on historical narrative, specifically the historical narrative of Acts. The appropriate interpretation of historical narrative texts emphasizes the accurate discernment of the author's intent. For Pentecostal hermeneutics, the specific concern is that the interpreter does not distort the message of Acts either through the imposition of foreign meanings upon Luke's text or through the omission of intended meanings from it.

It is because the Acts narratives serve as the foundation for the two primary Pentecostal doctrines of subsequence and initial evidence that this is such a crucial hermeneutical issue. Five Acts pericopae in particular form this foundation. They are the Pentecost narrative (Acts 2), the Samaritan Pentecost (Acts 8), the conversion and calling of Saul (Acts 9), the Gentile Pentecost (Acts 10), and the Ephesian Pentecost (Acts 19). Each of these accounts records the experience of the baptism in the Holy Spirit in the apostolic church. Pentecostals claim that there is evidence for the doctrine of subsequence in each of these five pericopae. They further note that tongues are explicitly mentioned in three instances and are implicit in two of the accounts. While tongues are not mentioned in Samaria (Acts 8), Pentecostals note that some charismatic manifestation must have precipitated the reaction of Simon Magus (Acts 8:18–19). This manifestation, they argue, was most probably glossolalia. Tongues are also not mentioned when Ananias laid hands on Saul so that he would be filled with the Spirit (Acts 9:17). But Pentecostals argue that Paul's remark to the Corinthians, "I speak in tongues more than all of you" (1 Cor. 14:18), implies that he did indeed speak in tongues at the laying on of Ananias's hands. Thus the Pentecostal claims biblical substantiation for the doctrines of subsequence and initial evidence.

1. Challenge of Dispensationalism. The early attacks on the Pentecostal understanding of Acts denied the validity of the tongues experience in the twentieth-century church. Arguing from the vantage point of Fundamentalist dispensationalism, critics claimed that tongues were restricted to the apostolic age and that the Pentecostal's "Latter Rain" experience was aberrational.

Contrary to what might be expected, many Pentecostals adopted a dispensational view of Scripture. According to Gerald T. Sheppard, the Pentecostal's motivation for adopting dispensationalism was "to find acceptance and legitimation from the dispensationalist-fundamentalist movement" (1984, 5). But the cause seems more immediate. It stems from the Pentecostal self-identity. Pentecostals have seen themselves as an eschatological community; they insist that these are the last days as proclaimed by Peter in Acts 2:19; they see this Latter Rain of the Holy Spirit as a harbinger of the Parousia and their baptism in the Holy Spirit as an empowering for missionary labors to reap the final harvest before the *Eschaton*. For this reason, Pentecostals have a keen interest in eschatology, and dispensationalism provided a comprehensible, systematic approach to eschatology.

It is this clarification of mysterious eschatological issues that has primarily attracted Pentecostals to dispensationalism. But dispensationalism is not simply a theological construct. It is a system that proposes a hermeneutical model and a system with specific interpretive presuppositions that aid in theological definition. Foremost is the presupposition that revelation is confined to each age and that the revelation given in any age has no significance for either prior or antecedent ages.

The result is that dispensationalism bears profound ecclesiological implications in addition to its eschatological implications. The immediate relevance for the Pentecostal lies in the dispensationalist insistence that the prophecy of Joel that Peter recalls in Acts 2 cannot be applied to the church. Thus the charismatic experiences of the apostles belong not to the church age but to an interdispensational period. Glossolalia, divine healing, and other divine manifestations are limited to the apostolic period. The twentieth-century outpouring of the Spirit is then rendered illegitimate; and until the Rapture inaugurates the Great Tribulation, God's activity is limited to the illumination of Scripture through the agency of the Holy Spirit and through the proclamation of the gospel.

The ongoing problem for the dispensationalist Pentecostal has been to divorce the eschatological implications of the system from its ecclesiological ramifications. The necessary inconsistency of these endeavors, as the Pentecostal is forced alternately to defend and then decry the dispensational system, has been problematic. Thus Pentecostals have reacted in two ways. Some have more firmly embraced the tenets of dispensationalism: "In several cases, a more consistent dispensational eschatology has led later Pentecostals to a more consistently dispensational ecclesiology, one that could challenge even the most basic doctrines common among Pentecostals" (Sheppard, 1984, 26). Other Pentecostals have clearly discerned the problem of the wedding of Pentecostalism to dispensationalism and have reacted to the inconsistency by denying the dispensational hermeneutic. They have opted to forsake the eschatological schemes offered by dispensationalism in order to be more faithful to Pentecostal ecclesiology. Thus some Pentecostals have reevaluated their eschatology, especially dispensationalism's strict separation of national Israel from the church.

2. A More Recent Challenge. The Pentecostal reliance on the Acts narratives has met a more recent and more serious challenge. The critique of Clark Pinnock and Grant Osborne made an early contribution to the discussion of the Pentecostal use of Acts. Because Acts is descriptive of life in the church, they rejected the dispensational assessment and determined that it is reasonable to assume glossolalia is to be expected in the church today (1971, 8). On the other hand, they denied that Luke had any theological intent in writing Acts beyond the preservation of the historical record of the exploits of the leading apostles. Therefore, they found it unreasonable to turn to the Acts narratives as the sole basis for establishing a normative Christian experience. It was unsound, they reasoned, to establish Christian doctrine on a text that itself has no theological emphasis. It was an attack on Pentecostal doctrine that cut to the heart of the Pentecostal hermeneutic. The following excerpt summarizes their position: "Didactic portions of Scripture must have precedence over historical passages in establishing doctrine. We ought to move here from the teaching of First Corinthians to the narrative of Acts rather than the reverse. When one follows this proper methodology, one notes that there is no manifestation of tongues that is normative" (Pinnock and Osborne, 1971, 8). The issue that Pinnock and Osborne address is the doctrine of initial evidence. The significant word in their argument is *normative*. They do not deny the validity of tongues in the Christian experience. They do deny that tongues is a normative evidence of the baptism in the Holy Spirit. There is, in the estimation of these two scholars, no reason to insist that Spirit baptism is contingent upon the evidence of glossolalia (Pinnock now concedes that Pentecostal theology is more intellectually convincing; see the foreword to Roger Stronstad's *The Charismatic Theology of Luke* [1984]).

The argument of Pinnock and Osborne did not go unfelt in Pentecostal circles. In fact, their contention has been affirmed by some in the Pentecostal movement. Gordon Fee, for example, speaks from this same perspective. Fee posits that biblical precedent—in this case the Acts narrative—does not serve to reveal "repeatable patterns" for Christian experience. Therefore he rejects the Pentecostal position that biblical precedent can establish normative experience (Fee in Spittler, 1976, 128–29). In so arguing, Fee seeks to undermine the Pentecostal doctrines of the baptism in the Spirit as subsequent to conversion and tongues as initial evidence of that experience. His position is based on the redactional issue of Luke's theological intent in writing Acts. Fee contends:

> The major task of the interpreter is to discover the author's intent. . . . It is one thing for the historian to include an event because it serves the greater purpose of his work, and yet another thing for the interpreter to take that incident as having didactic value apart from the historian's larger intent. . . . Historical precedent, to have normative value, must be related to intent. That is, if it can be shown that the purpose of a given narrative is to establish precedent, then such precedent should be regarded as normative (Fee in Spittler, 1976, 125–26).

The challenge then offered to Pentecostals who would defend the doctrines of subsequence and initial evidence is twofold. First, the Pentecostal is invited to demonstrate that Luke did indeed have a theological purpose. If this theological intention can be shown, the Pentecostal is then challenged to show that Luke's intent was indeed to establish baptism in the Spirit as distinct and subsequent to the experience of salvation and tongues as the initial evidence of Spirit baptism. Intentionality is then the key to establishing normativity.

3. *Pentecostal Response.* Initial Pentecostal responses to this challenge worked within the hermeneutical paradigm proposed by Pinnock and Osborne. Pentecostal scholars offered a more sophisticated articulation of the Pentecostal approach to Acts; however, Roger Stronstad observes that they conceded "the legitimacy of the sharp and rigid distinction between history and *didaché* in the New Testament literature" (Stronstad, 1984, 6). Stronstad proposes Ronald Kydd's pamphlet "I'm Still There" as an example.

But Stronstad, enlisting the capable support of I. Howard Marshall and Martin Hengel, argues convincingly that this is a false distinction. He points out that this distinction is contrary to the NT assessment of historical writing. For example,

Paul maintains that the wilderness experiences of Israel "happened to them as an example, and they were written for our instruction" (1 Cor. 10:11). He used all of the OT to set forth his doctrine, not just the didactic passages. In fact, he makes no distinction between Scripture that serves the purpose of doctrine and Scripture that is simple history. In Galatians 4 he appeals to the historical narrative of Hagar and Sarah to develop the contrast between slavish obedience to the law and the liberating power of the gospel. In Romans 15:4 he explains his approach to the Scriptures: "For everything that was written in the past was written to teach us, so that through endurance and the encouragement of the Scriptures we might have hope." From the same broad approach he writes in 2 Timothy 3:16–17, "All Scripture is God-breathed and is useful for . . . training in righteousness, so that the man of God may be thoroughly equipped for every good work." There is no doubt that Paul has in mind the OT, but his hermeneutical methodology is equally valid in reference to the NT. In the NT there can be found no rigid distinction between historiography and teaching that some Evangelicals have used to reject the didactic content of Acts.

Given these facts, Stronstad makes this observation: "If for Paul the historical narratives of the Old Testament had didactic lessons for New Testament Christians, then it would be most surprising if Luke, who modeled his historiography after the historiography of the Old Testament, did not invest his own history of the origin and spread of Christianity with a didactic significance" (1984, 7). Luke, then, is a theologian in his own right. Unlike Paul, Luke constructs his theology through the selection and arrangement of historical events into the narrative framework of Acts. It is, as Stronstad astutely observes, a charismatic theology, a theology communicated in the charismatic working of the Holy Spirit upon and through the apostles of the NT church. Thus the Pentecostal practice of theologizing from a Lukan perspective is perfectly legitimate. On the other hand, the dichotomization of history and *didaché* proposed earlier illegitimately forces the interpreter to view the Lukan text through Pauline eyes. At this point the Pentecostal hermeneutic stands vindicated.

But the issue of the interpretation of Lukan narratives deserves further consideration. It is not sufficient simply to demonstrate that Luke had a theological purpose in his text. It must be shown that Pentecostal interpretation of Acts coincides with that theological purpose. Again, the emphasis turns to the intentionality of the author.

The problem before the Pentecostal interpreter who insists that Luke intends to communicate theological instruction in Acts is to interpret Luke on his own terms. They must avoid the imposition of Pauline theology upon the Lukan text that others have forced into the process. They must also avoid pressing the Scripture's analogy of faith beyond its intended sphere by taking a promise-box view of Scripture. James D. G. Dunn states the problem in the following manner: "The common error . . . is to treat the New Testament (and even the Bible) as a homogeneous whole, from any part of which texts can be drawn on a chosen subject and fitted into a framework and system which is often basically extrabiblical" (1970, 39). To avoid this error, which Dunn rightly notes, the interpreter must make an effort to search out the particular theological concerns of the individual writer. For the Pentecostal, it will not suffice to recite repeatedly the five Spirit baptism pericopae in Acts in order to substantiate Pentecostal doctrines. It is in recognition of the Lukan sermons that significance of these events is best understood; thus, the Pentecostal interpreter must take a systematic approach to interpreting these Lukan narratives. An inductive approach to Scripture study is best suited to fulfill this need. To glean the full import of these favorite passages and thereby offer irrefutable support for Pentecostal doctrine, the interpreter must address this need.

If the interpreter realizes first that Luke expresses a theology in the Acts and second that comprehension of this theological intent is crucial to the hermeneutical task, it becomes imperative that this Lukan theology not be misconstrued. This has been the failure of Fundamentalist dispensationalism, which imposed its own ecclesiological presuppositions upon Lukan theology. This is also the failure of James Dunn's landmark work. It is his artificial imposition of a Conzelmannian "threefold scheme of salvation history" upon the Lukan narrative that distorts his conclusions (Dunn, 1970, 41). Dunn follows in a long line of scholarship that denies the "theological homogeneity of Luke–Acts" in spite of its overt literary unity (Stronstad, 1984, 3). He adopts an interpretative scheme that "has an almost homiletical symmetry, but like all too many sermons, it subordinates substance to rhetorical form" (Ervin, 1984, 18).

Stronstad offers instead a Lukan theology that attempts to remain faithful to the text of Luke–Acts and at the same time endorses Pentecostal doctrine. He sees throughout Luke–Acts an emphasis on the charismatic gift of the Holy Spirit, a gift that is by nature prophetic, empowering, and experiential (1984, 75–76). Thus Stronstad derives a theological framework from the whole of the Lukan corpus and offers that framework to the interpreter as a template with which to interpret the historical narrative of Luke–Acts. Such an approach to historical narrative offers the greatest hope for the Pentecostal hermeneutic.

IV. Direction for Interpretation in the Future. The directions available for Pentecostal and charismatic interpretation are innumerable. The Pentecostal must therefore choose carefully the path that is most faithful to his/her high view of Scripture but that also best serves to elucidate the text. In order to achieve that balance, the Pentecostal interpreter must be willing to preserve the hermeneutical tensions directing his/her efforts.

A. Hermeneutical Tools. The Pentecostal must give proper recognition to both the divine and human elements that coexist in the Scriptures. Appreciation of these two facets of the nature of Scripture must be held in constant tension in order to avoid hermeneutical excesses. The interpreter must approach biblical interpretation with reverential awe for the Bible's divine origin and with a ready dependence on illumination of the Holy Spirit. Yet, at the same time, critical tools must be used to evaluate Scripture. Grammatico-historical-contextual exegesis, redaction criticism, form criticism, and narrative theology provide valuable assistance to the interpreter and should not be neglected by Pentecostals. If they will but keep their awareness of the divine and human elements of Scripture in tension, Pentecostals can effectively use such tools without denigrating the text and sacrificing the historicity of Scripture. Pentecostals will be best served by an inductive approach to interpretation in order to address the challenges with which they are confronted. Such an approach begins with the data of Scripture; and when properly exercised, it gives proper recognition to the diversity of Scripture. Yet it can at the same time address the analogy of faith inherent in Scripture, the result of the single, unchangeable source in which it finds its ultimate authorship.

B. A Pentecostal Model. At the Jerusalem Council the believers gathered around the Word of God in the power of the Spirit to address the theological question of what is required for salvation—the works of the law as circumcision or faith alone. In 1906 the same commitment to the Word and the Spirit motivated early Pentecostals to come together for the first general assembly of the Church of God (CG). They gathered around the Word in the Spirit, with an explicit appeal to the Jerusalem Council of Acts 15:

> It seemeth good to the Holy Ghost and us; being assembled together with one accord, with the Spirit of Christ in the midst and after much prayer, discussion, searching the Scriptures and counsel, to recommend these necessary things and that they be ratified and observed by all the local churches (*Minutes of Annual Assembly of the Churches of East Tennessee, North Georgia and Western North Carolina*, held January 26 and 27, 1906, at Camp Creek, N.C., p. 18).

As well as a guide to early Pentecostals, Acts 15 may provide a framework for the further development of a Pentecostal hermeneutic. The chapter describes a truly Pentecostal meeting in that the decision of the council was a corporate response to the Holy Spirit. As a result, James was able to declare, "It seems good to the Holy Spirit and us" (v. 28). The believers in Jerusalem were convinced of the guidance and the authority of the Holy Spirit. The activity of the Holy Spirit at the Jerusalem Council, as well as other instances of the Spirit's guidance in the NT, underscore the centrality of the Holy Spirit to the hermeneutical task and to the whole life of the church.

Furthermore, at the council appeals were made to the Scriptures, experience, tradition, and reason. James asserted that Scripture fully concurred with Peter's argument and that all of the prophets, particularly Amos, agreed that God's eternal purpose was to include Gentiles in his family (vv. 14–18; cf. Amos 9:11–12). Paul and

Barnabas told of their missionary experience in preaching the gospel to the Gentiles (v. 12). Peter reminded the council of his personal call to preach to the Gentiles and of the experience of Cornelius and his friends (vv. 7–11). Tradition rooted in Scripture was appealed to by James as ground for asking the Gentiles to observe the four prohibitions (vv. 20–21; cf. Lev. 17:8, 10–12, 13; 18:6–23). On the basis of the purification of the Gentiles by faith and the outpouring of the Spirit on them Peter reasoned that uncircumcised Gentiles should be accepted into the church (vv. 8–11). Likewise James reasoned on the basis of Scripture and tradition that circumcision was not to be required of Gentile believers (vv. 13–21). Consequently, under the guidance of the Holy Spirit the council reached a common position.

The interplay of Scripture, experience, Pentecostal tradition, and reason under the direction of the Spirit have strong implications for a Pentecostal approach to hermeneutics. Out of the Pentecostal reality and dimension of life in the Spirit emerges a uniquely Pentecostal hermeneutic. The Holy Spirit addresses us through the gifts of the Spirit (1 Cor. 12, 14; Rom. 12; Eph. 4) and in more subtle ways (Rom. 8:1–27). Speaking to this point, Rick D. Moore (1987, 4) observes:

There is a vital place for emotion as well as reason, for imagination as well as logic, for mystery as well as certainty, and for that which is narrative and dramatic as well as that which is propositional and systematic. Consequently, we appreciate Scripture not just as an object which we interpret but as a living Word which interprets us and through which the Spirit flows in ways that we cannot dictate, calculate or program.

By some the Pentecostal faith has been caricatured as an experience-based faith. Yet "Pentecostals do see an inseparable interplay between knowledge and lived-experience, where knowing about God and directly experiencing God perpetually inform and depend on one another" (Moore, 1987, 4). In contrast to the common secular understanding of knowledge, this view is biblical and "points beyond the conceptualization of an object to the actualization of a relationship" (ibid.; cf. Jer. 1:5; 22:16; 31:34; 1 John 4:8). Therefore, Pentecostal preaching or Bible study involves not only the recognition of the truth but also an overt response to the transforming call of God's Word. This approach has been and must continue to be fundamental to Pentecostal hermeneutics.

The Spirit calls every believer to be a witness to the gospel (Acts 1:8). At the very roots of Pentecostal heritage have been the priesthood (1 Peter 2:5, 9) and prophethood (Num. 11:27–29; Joel 2:28–32; Acts 2:16–20) of all believers. Among Pentecostals the conviction that the whole people of God should be priests and prophets has a distinct reality in the experience of the Spirit being "poured upon all flesh" (Acts 2:17). Active participation in the Pentecostal community of faith is vital to Pentecostals, especially for personal edification and evangelizing the

lost. In fact, Pentecostal faith has its beginnings in the gathering together of believers (Acts 2:1–4) and continues to be nurtured and sustained by the same communion of saints (Acts 4:42–47). The Spirit speaks and manifests his gifts as nowhere else. Therefore, the fellowship of believers, where members of Christ's body are bound together with bonds of mutual love, interdependence, and accountability, provides the context for the practice of a distinctly Pentecostal approach to Scripture and for deeper understanding of God's presence among his people that will "not put out the Spirit's fire" (1 Thess. 5:19).

C. A Broad Perspective. To be on sound footing a Pentecostal hermeneutic must be pneumatic and must rest on Scripture as the infallible rule for faith and conduct. However, to facilitate the development of a distinctive and viable "Pentecostal hermeneutic," Pentecostal scholars must begin to realize the broad ramifications of Pentecostal theology for the church at large. Interpretation needs to be faithful to the movement's theological distinctives, but there is also a need for developing a systematic approach to discover its rightful role within the broad scope of evangelical theology. Pentecostalism deserves a holistic hermeneutic, one that seeks to provide a sound footing for the current deposit of Pentecostal theologizing. In this manner, Pentecostal interpretation can both address forthcoming issues and still remain faithful to its heritage.

See also DISPENSATIONALISM.

Bibliography: D. Bruner, *A Theology of the Holy Spirit* (1972); R. C. Dalton, "Pentecostal Doctrine Before Nineteen Hundred," *Paraclete* 7 (3, 1973): 3–9; D. W. Dayton, "Toward a Theological Analysis of Pentecostalism," a paper presented to the Society for Pentecostal Studies (1985); J. D. G. Dunn, *Baptism in the Holy Spirit* (1970); P. Elbert, ed., *Essays on Apostolic Themes* (1985); H. M. Ervin, *Conversion-Initiation and the Baptism in the Holy Spirit* (1984); idem, "Hermeneutics: A Pentecostal Option," *Pneuma* 3 (2, 1981): 11–25; G. D. Fee, *New Testament Exegesis: A Handbook for Students and Pastors* (1983); G. Florovsky, *Bible, Church, Tradition: An Eastern Orthodox View* (1972); M. Hengel, *Acts and the History of Earliest Christianity* (1980); R. H. Hughes, ed., *Understanding the Holy Spirit* (1982); R. K. Johnston, ed., *The Use of the Bible in Theology: Evangelical Options* (1985); H. Küng and J. Moltmann, eds., *Conflicts About the Holy Spirit* (1979); I. H. Marshall, *Luke: Historian and Theologian* (1970); F. Martin, "Spirit and Flesh in the Doing of Theology," a paper presented to the Society for Pentecostal Studies (1985); W. McCown and J. Massey, eds., *God's Word for Today: Wesleyan Theological Perspectives*, vol. 2 (1982); M. D. McLean, "Toward a Pentecostal Hermeneutic," *Pneuma* 6 (2, 1984): 35–56; A. S. McPherson, *The Four Square Gospel* (1969); W. W. Menzies, "Synoptic Theology: An Essay on Pentecostal Hermeneutics," *Paraclete* 13 (1, 1979): 14–21; R. Moore, "Pentecostal Approach to Scripture," *The Seminary Viewpoint* 8 (1, 1987): 1–2; C. F. Parham, *The Sermons of Charles Parham* (1911); T. S. Payne, "Traditions and How to Get Rid of Them," *CGE* 6 (3, 1915): 1ff.; "Pentecost Has Come," *AF* (September 1906; reprinted in *Azusa Street and Beyond*, ed. L. G. McClung, Jr., [1986]); C. H. Pinnock, *The Scripture Principle* (1984); C. H. Pinnock and R. Osborne, "A Truce Proposal for the Tongues Controversy," *Christianity Today* 16 (1, 1971): 6–9; R. Quebedeaux, *The New Charismatics* (1976); C. M. Robeck, Jr., "The Gift of Prophecy and the All-Sufficiency of Scripture," *Paraclete* 13 (1, 1979): 27–

31; G. T. Sheppard, "Pentecostals and the Hermeneutics of Dispensationalism: The Anatomy of an Uneasy Relationship," *Pneuma* 6 (2, 1984): 5–34; R. P. Spittler, ed., *Perspectives on the New Pentecostalism* (1976); R. G. Spurling, *The Lost Link* (1920); R. Stronstad, *The Charismatic Theology of St. Luke* (1984); "There Is a Wrong Somewhere." *CGE* 5 (18, 1914): 1–2; S. Wigglesworth, *Ever Increasing Faith* (1924).

F. L. Arrington

HETEROGLOSSOLALIA   See GLOSSOLALIA.

Thomas Hezmalhalch, better known as "Brother Tom," took the Pentecostal message to South Africa with John G. Lake and others in 1908.

HEZMALHALCH, THOMAS (1848–1934).
Early Pentecostal evangelist and missionary. Known widely as "Brother Tom," Hezmalhalch was one of the many Pentecostals who went out from the Azusa Street Mission. An Englishman who came to the U.S. in the 1880s, he was a Holiness preacher before he was baptized in the Spirit. His name is associated with Pentecostal revivals in U.S. cities, including Zion, Illinois; Pueblo, Colorado; and Indianapolis, Indiana.

He is perhaps best known for his ministry with John G. Lake in South Africa beginning in 1908. The Apostolic Faith Mission was formed there as a result of the Pentecostal outpouring in that country. Several Pentecostal periodicals, including *Pentecost, The Upper Room,* and the *Latter Rain Evangel*—kept their readers abreast of that early movement of the Spirit. Brother Tom's ministry in South Africa began after he had reached sixty years of age.

Although he was not considered a great preacher by some contemporaries, Hezmalhalch's name is legendary in both the U.S. and South Africa as a man who walked in the Spirit and who

had great influence in the early Pentecostal movement. He even tells of picking up a poisonous viper in California to convince a taunting atheist that there is a God. This bizarre incident, however, seems to be an exception in his ministry.

In his later years Hezmalhalch stayed in the home of friends in southern California and taught an adult class at Bethany Church, Alhambra.

Bibliography: A. Flower, "The Ministry of 'Brother Tom,'" W. Warner, ed., *Touched by the Fire* (1978); *AF* (Los Angeles) (1906–07); "Gone Home," *Trooster Comforter* (May 1934), 5.   W. E. Warner

Marilyn Hickey founded her own ministry in 1976, which includes programs on radio and television and a publishing ministry.

HICKEY, MARILYN SWEITZER (1931–).
Bible teacher. Born in Dalhart, Texas, Hickey moved to Denver, where she attended high school. She earned a B.A. at the University of Northern Colorado. After serving as a high school teacher, she entered the ministry with her husband, Wallace. He currently is pastor of the Happy Church (AG) in Denver.

The Lord called Hickey in 1976 to "cover the earth with the Word." A Bible study class in her home paid for her first radio teaching broadcasts. Now Marilyn Hickey Ministries has expanded to 120 radio stations and some 35 television outreaches. Her magazine is read in about 200,000 homes.

In 1983 Hickey heard the Lord say, "Go to Ethiopia." She raised money to purchase Bibles and food for the hungry in Haiti, the Philippines, Bangladesh, and Honduras, as well as distributing Bibles in Iron Curtain countries.

Bibliography: D. M. Hazard, "Marilyn and Wally Hickey: They Make a Great Team," *Charisma* (October 1985), 26–34.   S. Strang

Roy H. Hicks, a well-known minister in the International Church of the Foursquare Gospel.

HICKS, ROY H. (1920–). Foursquare executive and preacher. In the years that followed his graduation from L.I.F.E. Bible College in 1943, Roy Hicks, a native of Big Sandy, Tennessee, became a leader in the International Church of the Foursquare Gospel (ICFG). In 1982 he was named general supervisor of the denomination's one thousand congregations, a position he held until 1986. He considers his ministry as that of a prophet and teacher. He frequently speaks in charismatic circles such as Rhema Bible Training Center, Christ for the Nations Institute, and in meetings conducted by the Full Gospel Business Men's Fellowship International. This close association with charismatic groups sets him apart from most classical Pentecostal officials.

Hicks is the author of nine books, including *Praying Beyond God's Abilities* (1977), *Another Look at the Rapture* (1982), *Keys of the Kingdom* (1984), *Healing Your Insecurities* (1982), and *Faith, Use It or Lose It: The Word of Faith* (1976). L.I.F.E. Bible College awarded Hicks an honorary doctor of divinity degree in 1975.

Bibliography: ICFG Public Relations, press release.
W. E. Warner

HICKS, TOMMY (1909–73). Missionary evangelist, faith healer. Tommy Hicks is noted for his work as an overseas evangelist. Successful on several continents in the mid 1950s, his work in Argentina in 1954 was the most outstanding of all. Because of the crowds, the revival had to be moved to the Huracane Football Stadium (seating capacity, 110,000), which overflowed. It lasted two months; 3 million are reported to have attended, with 300,000 decision cards filled out, many healings manifested, and 50,000 New

Evangelist Tommy Hicks conducted huge meetings in Argentina in the early 1950s. Here he is pictured with President Juan Perón during a meeting Hicks held in Buenos Aires.

Testaments and Bibles distributed. Hicks was well accepted in the country, the vice-president being among the reported converts. The success overseas gained Hicks sustained support from the Full Gospel Business Men's Fellowship International.

Hicks wrote *Capturing the Nations in the Name of the Lord* (1956), *Millions Found Christ* (1956), *Manifest Deliverance for You Now!* (1952), and *It's Closing Time* (1958).

Bibliography: D. E. Harrell, Jr., *All Things Are Possible* (1975); G. G. Kulbeck, *What God Hath Wrought* (1958); L. Stokes, *The Great Revival in Buenos Aires* (1954). S. Shemeth

HISPANIC PENTECOSTALISM
    I. "The Fastest Growing Church in the
       Hemisphere"
       A. The Hispanic Peoples

B. Implications of Hispanic Pentecostal Growth
C. Hispanic Pentecostal Denominations
D. Hispanics and Non-Pentecostal Protestantism
E. Characteristics of Hispanic Pentecostals
II. Beginnings of Hispanic Pentecostal Churches in the U.S. and Puerto Rico
A. Hispanics and the Early Pentecostals
B. Hispanic Pentecostal Beginnings in Texas
C. Hispanic Pentecostal Beginnings in California
D. Hispanic Pentecostal Beginnings in Puerto Rico and on the East Coast
E. Francisco Olazábal and the Latin American Council of Christian Churches
F. Institutionalization of the Early Revival
III. Development of the Movement Since World War II
A. Hispanic Pentecostals on the Atlantic Coast and in Puerto Rico
B. The Asamblea Apostólica de la Fe en Cristo Jesus
C. The Latin American Churches of the Church of God
D. The Latin American Districts of the Assemblies of God
IV. Assessments of Hispanic Pentecostal Churches

I. "The Fastest Growing Church in the Hemisphere." The rapid growth that Pentecostalism has registered in Latin America has occurred also among Hispanics in North America, beginning early in the century and accelerating since World War II. As early as 1962 *Time* magazine referred to these vigorous, grassroots movements as "the fastest growing church in the hemisphere." The combined membership of the various organizations in the U.S. and Puerto Rico is now approaching a half million adults.

A. The Hispanic Peoples. "Hispanic" is the currently preferred term to describe the ethnically diverse peoples whose common heritage, in addition to ascribed cultural and psychological traits, includes the Spanish language and the Roman Catholic religion. These peoples include past and recent immigrants and their descendants from the Spanish-speaking countries of the Caribbean and Central and South America, as well as Spaniards and their descendants, some of whom have resided in the Southwest since before the American Revolution.

Hispanic culture has been perpetuated by the various people who have merged in Latin America since the sixteenth-century Spanish conquest of the New World, including the several million Africans brought in colonial times, the native peoples, and successive waves of European and Asian immigrants. While many American Hispanics remain close to their cultural traditions, others, like actor Anthony Quinn, son of Mexican immigrants and briefly associated with Pentecostals in his youth, have identified completely with North American values and lifestyles.

The 20 million Hispanics in the U.S. who constitute the nation's second largest ethnic minority have increased by 30 percent since 1980. Besides a birth rate exceeding that of the general population, growth has resulted from the Central American conflict, which has brought a million refugees to the U.S. in the past decade, and the pressure of Mexico's faltering economy, which has driven several millions more north across the border. America's Cuban population, centered in Florida but widely dispersed and easily assimilated, now numbers a million persons. The 3.5 million Puerto Ricans, U.S. citizens who since 1952 have been a self-governing commonwealth, enjoy unrestricted access to the mainland. There are 2 million persons of Puerto Rican origin in the U.S.

Table 1. Percentage of Hispanics by Country of Origin	
Mexico	63%
Puerto Rico	12%
Central and South America	11%
Cuba	5%
Other	9%

Source: Bureau of the Census (*U.S. News and World Report* [September 21, 1987]).

Although numerous differences distinguish the subcultures within the Hispanic population, as a whole Hispanics are younger, poorer, and less educated than the general population. Hispanics are overwhelmingly urban (88 percent), with half of all Hispanics found in metropolitan inner cities. Despite heavy continued immigration, more than half of all Hispanics are at least third-generation Americans, yet the Spanish language, a unifying force, persists as the preferred or second language of 10 million people in the U.S. Cultural conservatism and social disadvantage, it has been suggested, have contributed to the spread of Pentecostalism among Hispanics.

Hispanics are expected to increase from 6.4 percent of the national population in 1980 to 9 percent in A.D. 2020, making them also the fastest growing ethnic minority. Along with heightened cultural consciousness that has come with political and social recognition in recent years, continued immigration makes Hispanics an increasingly important element in American religious life.

B. Implications of Hispanic Pentecostal Growth. The emergence of the Hispanic Pentecostal movement has implications for both the future of American Pentecostalism and the assimilation of Hispanic Catholics into American Protestantism. Opinion polls report that while 52 percent of Americans and 54 percent of American Catholics consider religion to be "very important" to them personally, the response from Hispanics was 64 percent. The growth of Hispanic Pentecostalism, as well as indicating some Hispanic predisposition to this form of Protestantism, may affect the future course of American Pentecostalism.

The spread of Pentecostalism has drawn com-

Mexican believers worshiping in Faith, Hope, and Love Center, Mexico City.

ment from Roman Catholic spokesmen who lament the resulting loss of tradition and community solidarity. The nation's Hispanics make up more than a third of all American Catholics and are expected to account for half of all the nation's Catholics within a generation. In California and the Southwest the proportions already exceed 50 percent. While an estimated 90 percent of American Hispanics are baptized Catholics, 60 percent consider themselves to be "practicing Catholics," and according to some estimates, as few as 12 percent regularly attend Mass. Meanwhile, from 10 to 15 percent are believed to have affiliated with some other religious group, especially the Jehovah's Witnesses and Pentecostals, both noted for their aggressive proselytism (San Jose *Mercury News* [August 1, 1987], 14C; [November 3, 1981], 8A).

In recent years, however, disproportionate growth in the primarily white Assemblies of God (AG) and Church of God (CG, Cleveland, Tenn.) has come from the denominations' ethnic branches, especially from their Hispanic churches. While AG members increased by 18.2 percent between 1980 and 1987, the Hispanic membership grew by 18.9 percent. With 108,000 members in the group's seven Hispanic districts and at least half that number attending Anglo churches, the AG is considered 15 percent Hispanic. The CG has also had rapid Hispanic growth. Nationally the denomination reports 271 Hispanic congregations, with an additional 185 in Puerto Rico. With only 30 such churches in California in the mid 1970s, there are now 75. The CG held its first national Hispanic convention in 1985 with 500 delegates from five ethnic districts. Both denominations have recently created districts in the Southeast to provide for the growth among Florida's Cuban and Central American population. Such sustained increases may arrest the

tendency of these denominations to become increasingly white middle-class churches.

C. Hispanic Pentecostal Denominations. Current estimates of Hispanic Pentecostal adherents in the U.S. reach 240,000, while those of Puerto Rico are reported as 150,000. In addition to the several predominately Anglo Pentecostal churches that have organized Spanish-language branches, there are exclusively ethnic denominations like the Iglesia Apostólica de la Fe en Cristo Jesus (Apostolic Church of the Faith in Jesus Christ) in the Southwest and the Spanish Christian Churches of the East Coast that contribute importantly to Hispanic Pentecostalism. Tables 2 and 3 indicate that about a third of the membership of the Hispanic Pentecostals in the U.S. belongs to these exclusively ethnic organizations. These groups, sometimes referred to as indigenous churches, account for four-fifths of Puerto Rican Pentecostals. The origins of several of these groups in the AG and the tendency for Pentecostals to fragment organizationally are important considerations in their emergence.

In addition to these denominations, large numbers of independent congregations are found among Hispanics, especially in Puerto Rico and among East Coast Puerto Rican communities. A study of New York Hispanic churches in 1960 identified 240 Pentecostal congregations, half of which (117) were not denominationally affiliated. Meanwhile, David Barratt reported 20,000 unspecified "indigenous" Protestants, largely Pentecostals and including the 5,000-member Mita group, a marginally Christian movement, in Puerto Rico. Elsewhere the appearance of various revival centers and social outreach ministries like Teen Challenge and Victory Outreach have found a response among Hispanic youth, sometimes former gang members and addicts who find in

Column A: Congregations
Column B: Communicants

Table 2. Hispanic Pentecostal Denominations in the United States

	A	B
Asamblea Apostólica de la Fe en Cristo Jesus	195	24,000
Asamblea de Iglesias Christianas	100	4,000
Damascus Christian Church	12	925
Latin American Council of Christian Churches	105	4,200
Spanish Christian Churches	240	18,500
Total	652	51,625

Source: D. Barratt, *World Christian Encyclopedia* (1982). Some current estimates are substantially higher.

Table 3. Pentecostal Denominations With Hispanic Branches

	A	B
Assemblies of God (Hispanic Districts)	1,100	93,000
Church of God, Cleveland (Hispanic Districts)	271	30,000
Church of God of Prophecy	40	2,000
International Church of the Foursquare Gospel	96	8,500
Total	1,507	133,500

Source: Published or verbal reports issued by the denominational offices.

Table 4. Puerto Rican Pentecostal Churches

		A	B
Asamblea de Iglesias Cristianas	(58)	150	8,000
Asambleas de Dios (included in Table 3)	(35)	179	19,000
Iglesia de Cristo Misionera	(56)	125	7,000
Iglesia Defensores de la Fe	(60)	125	8,000
Iglesia de Dios (Mission Board)	(100)	185	17,000
Iglesia de Dios de la Profecía	(25)	24	900
Iglesia de Dios Pentecostal	(207)	450	70,000
Iglesia del Evangelio Cuadrangular	(9)	12	400
Iglesia Pentecostal de Jesucristo	(45)	50	1,200
Iglesia Universal de Jesucristo*	(31)	50	3,000
Total	(626)	1,350	132,500

Source: An average of estimates provided by several Puerto Rican Pentecostal leaders. Figures confirmed for Asamblea de Dios, Iglesia de Dios (Mission Board), Iglesia de Dios de la Profecía, and the Iglesia del Evangelio Cuadrangular from groups' respective U.S. denominational offices. Figures in parentheses are from Barratt, *World Christian Encyclopedia* (1982).

Pentecostalism a resolute, emotionally satisfying form of Christianity.

Hispanic membership reports may omit large numbers of children, relatives, and sympathizers who take part in the activities of the church community without having advanced to communicant status. Rigid demands on personal conduct and commitment to the work of the congregation, including tithing and acceptance of the group's authority, appear to trim membership to a dedicated nucleus. Missiologists sometimes multiply the number of communicants by a factor of two or more in order to determine the total number of participants. If the membership figures included in this study for Hispanic Pentecostals were doubled, the Hispanic Pentecostal commu-

nity in North America would approach a million persons.

Pentecostal statistics must also take into consideration the difficulty of identifying and following membership recruited from a population that in the past was often deeply prejudiced against Protestants and largely excluded from the benefits of American life. Hispanic congregations have often contended with unemployment and shifting jobs, limited resources and inadequate facilities, unsupportive and even hostile neighborhoods and, too frequently, the indifference of Anglo-Pentecostals. Congregations are often youthful, comprised disproportionately of women and children, and lack recognition within the Hispanic community. Yet the descriptions of these organizations suggest vitality and institutional strength, as well as substantial numerical growth. A comparison of Pentecostal growth with that of other Protestant denominations is instructive.

D. Hispanics and Non-Pentecostal Protestantism. If adverse conditions, authoritarian traditions, and expressiveness and spontaneity in religion make Pentecostalism especially suited to Hispanics, as has sometimes been asserted, relatively few American Hispanics (no more than 5 percent) have turned to the movement for relief or satisfaction. Catholic observers readily point out that the American Catholic church has not easily accommodated the needs of Hispanic Catholics, and the large proportion of Hispanics who are not practicing their faith are hardly inclined to Protestantism. A major study of Mexican-Americans concludes simply that "Protestantism is not important in the Mexican-American population" (Grebler et al., 487). A half-century of effort by the mainline denominations appears to have demonstrated the point.

As early as 1912 the Interdenominational Council on Evangelical Work Among the Spanish-Speaking attempted to establish missions to Hispanics. By 1923 the Methodists in Southern California had twenty-six preaching circuits reaching fifty-four points, of which the largest had a congregation of 179 persons. Baptists, Presbyterians, and Adventists all had begun work by 1930. As the Hispanic population burgeoned, reaching 1,400,000 born in Mexico or whose parents were Mexican by birth, the Home Missions Council reported in 1930 that the number of Spanish-language churches was 453, representing fourteen denominations with a combined membership of 28,000. The study found that no more than 2 percent of the Hispanic population was Protestant; and the largest grouping, the Methodists, had 10,000 members. Baptists claimed 6,500 and Presbyterians 6,700. Other major religious bodies had fewer than ten congregations and 800 adherents each. The report, submitted by Thomas F. Coakely, concluded that the Mexican-American "is not adequately cared for either religiously or socially. The whole area [of Hispanic evangelism] is practically untouched."

E. Characteristics of Hispanic Pentecostals. A popular account of the rise of Pentecostalism identifies features that appeal both to the masses of Latin America as well as to the Hispanic populations of the U.S. "Most adherents are poor, few of them well educated," the article revealed.

Their minister is likely to be a factory worker himself, secure in the Pentecostal belief that "a man of God with a Bible in his hand has had training enough." Many Pentecostals attend church every night for a two-hour service. Loud Bible readings and spontaneous testimonials are part of every service, punctuated by shouts of "Aleluyah" and "Gracias a Dios." The hymns well over a rhythmic clapping, generally accompanied by a guitar, drums, tambourines, a bass fiddle, piano or small combo. Part of Pentecostals' appeal—particularly to immigrants—is their total, emotional participation.

The writer quoted a Chicago Presbyterian pastor who commented, "When you walk into a Pentecostal service, you are likely to be asked, no matter who you are, your name, where you are from, and 'Brother, do you have a word to say for us?' "

Few Hispanic Pentecostal churches are static and secure. Most involve rapidly changing communities of migrant laborers or marginally employed industrial and servile workers. Although congregations are generally comprised of families, most of them first-generation Protestants, members are often alienated from their extended families. Many churches are in effect family-operated missions or congregations dominated by two or three extended families linked by intermarriage. As the more successful and established members of the church find employment and housing outside the barrio, association with the church is likely to become complicated by social mobility and changing values. Where mobility and generational differences—often in the form of loss of Spanish fluency among the younger people—are overcome, the church may lose its appeal for recent, unacculturated newcomers. In fact, leading Hispanic churches throughout the U.S. have acquired the sleek look of affluence and success, with comfortable buildings, well-dressed parishioners, and social acceptance.

II. Beginnings of Hispanic Pentecostal Churches in the United States and Puerto Rico.

A. Hispanics and the Early Pentecostals. At the Azusa Street Mission in Los Angeles, focus of the 1906 West Coast revival, ethnic diversity was notable. The meetings were noticeably "free of all nationalist feeling," according to an early account. "If a Mexican or a German cannot speak English he gets up and speaks in his own native tongue and feels quite at home, for the Spirit interprets through his face and the people say 'Amen.' No instrument that God can use is rejected on account of color or dress or lack of education. That is why God has so built up the work." But the successors of the short-lived Azusa Street Mission soon split along ethnic as well as doctrinal and regional lines in ways that are still reflected in the extreme diversity among Hispanic Pentecostals.

"Mexicans were present at Azusa Street at an early date," writes historian Robert Mapes Anderson, "and soon initiated missions of their own. Within a decade," he continues, "Pentecostal preachers of Spanish extraction had firmly planted Pentecost among the 'floating population' of migrant Mexicans in many cities and towns from San Jose to Los Angeles to San Diego and throughout the outlying farm areas." Along the Texas border with Mexico, Oscar Nelson responded to rejection by the white community by writing, "The Lord told us, 'The white people have rejected the gospel and I will turn to the Mexicans' " (Anderson, 1979, 126). Reports of the AG in Texas in 1926 indicate that two-fifths of the membership was Mexican, even after a dozen or more churches had been lost in a defection. Although these congregations developed alongside Anglo churches, they largely assumed responsibility for their own work from the beginning.

The "Oneness" controversy that divided Pentecostals after 1916 also affected Hispanic churches. Early preachers Juan Navarro, Francisco F. Llorente and Marcial De La Cruz accepted the Oneness position and established churches as early as 1914, a year after the doctrine was propounded at the Arroyo Seco camp meeting. The work was taken up in 1917 by Antonio Nava, a recent Mexican immigrant, who established a congregation in Yuma, Arizona, in 1919 and pastored in Calexico from 1920 to 1928. By 1925, with twenty-three churches scattered along the border from California to New Mexico, the group's pastors gathered in San Bernardino to organize. Only seven of the congregations had buildings, but an official name was adopted and an effort was made to establish criteria for ministerial credentials. Although the fledgling denomination suffered serious reverses in the following years, it survived to reorganize as the Asamblea Apostólica de la Fe en Cristo Jesus (Apostolic Assembly of the Faith in Jesus Christ) at the group's sixth general convention in San Bernardino in 1930. During the interim the Apostolics in Mexico continued to grow and emerge after World War II as a major source of further growth and leadership in the U.S. Although the church was separated from other Pentecostals by its authoritarian rigidity, as well as by its theology, it nevertheless remained effective in the postwar years. A leading study of Mexican Americans published in 1970 considered it to be "the predominant Mexican-American sect."

B. Hispanic Pentecostal Beginnings in Texas. Of the nearly 400,000 members of Hispanic Pentecostal denominations reported currently, at least two-thirds trace their origins to the work that began with Henry C. Ball and his associates working in Texas, elsewhere in the Southwest, and California. The Pentecostals of Puerto Rico, including the work of the Church of God, can be traced to the efforts of Juan L. Lugo, Francisco Olazábal, and other ministers who were influenced also by Ball and the work he helped structure. It is thus possible by tracing the development of the early AG to indicate the origins of most of the present Hispanic Pentecostal organizations.

Henry C. Ball, reared by his mother near the Mexican border, exhibited remarkable spiritual sensitivity and an affinity for Hispanic peoples while he was still a teenager. He started a Methodist church in a school in Ricardo, Texas, before coming under the influence of a Pentecostal preacher and affiliating with the recently organized AG in 1914. As his parish grew, Ball moved to nearby Kingsville, where his congregation shared facilities with the Anglo AG congregation. The challenge of providing instruction for new converts and guidance to new congregations brought into being by his members whose work took them to other locations defined Ball's ministry for years to come. Within a short time a fellowship of Mexican pastors met to organize and provide suitable training for workers. By 1922 there were fifty Mexican churches in towns along the border.

During this formative period Ball was assisted by Alice E. Luce, a former Anglican missionary to India who had experienced the revival that erupted in the girls' home operated by Pandita Ramabai. Luce had come from Canada seeking entry to Mexico and had met Ball en route. She accompanied Sunshine Marshall, a young woman who also aspired to missionary work, in a short-lived venture in Monterrey, Nuevo Leon, from which they soon withdrew because of the hazards of the Mexican revolution then in progress. Returning to Texas, Marshall married Henry C. Ball, and Luce continued to Los Angeles to open the Pentecostal work there.

C. Hispanic Pentecostal Beginnings in California. Alice E. Luce has been credited with being the catalyst that encouraged other workers to initiate ministry among the Hispanic peoples of California. Capable, well-educated, and committed to the task, she prepared much of the printed materials used for instruction among the early Hispanic Pentecostals and encouraged formal preparation of pastors and evangelists. The school she founded in San Diego in 1926, later named the Latin American Bible Institute and located in La Puente, produced several generations of Hispanic leaders, including Robert Fierro, a distinguished evangelist whose ministry became well known throughout the AG in both the U.S. and Latin America. While Luce was laying these educational foundations, the work progressed throughout the state.

Accounts of the earliest AG churches in Los Angeles revolve around several key families whose influence and resources gave the nascent work stability. Several of these leaders had previous backgrounds in other denominations and shared with Luce concern for establishing the work on a sound theological basis. From the origins of a mission at what is now Olvera Street, Los Angeles, churches were begun in Watts, Huntington Park, Santa Paula, and Irwindale. Two young Welsh brothers, Richard and Ralph D. Williams, whom Luce had recruited previously for Hispanic ministry, opened churches in San Diego and took the Pentecostal message to the San Joaquin Valley.

Meanwhile, the work in northern California was emerging among the mixed communities of Mexicans, Puerto Ricans, and Portuguese in San Francisco, San Jose, and the East Bay. After a beginning in Danville, the work spread to Niles and Hayward, as Domingo Cruz, a fiery, illiterate, one-legged preacher became a legend for his persuasive preaching and his remarkable effectiveness in overcoming his handicaps. In addition to establishing strong churches and producing effective leadership, Pentecostalism in northern California gave rise to two of the most important figures among the early Hispanic Pentecostals, Francisco Olazábal, the movement's leading evangelist, and Juan L. Lugo, who initiated the work in Puerto Rico.

D. Hispanic Pentecostal Beginnings in Puerto Rico and on the Atlantic Coast. Juan L. Lugo is recognized as the pioneering missionary

A Spanish congregation in Los Angeles visiting after a service.

to Puerto Rico. Converted in Hawaii as a youth, Lugo accompanied his pastor to the mainland, where he was ordained with the AG and began his long, productive ministry. In 1917 Lugo received the promise of financial support from Bethel Church, Los Angeles, an Anglo congregation, to enable him to fulfill his vision of taking the Pentecostal message to his homeland. Lugo conferred with J. Roswell Flower at the AG headquarters in St. Louis, Missouri, en route to the East Coast, and was joined soon after his arrival in Puerto Rico by a colleague from California, Salomón Feliciano. After attempting to start a work in Santurce, where he succeeded in reaching immigrants from St. Thomas, Lugo proceeded to Ponce, his family's home. There the missionaries gathered a sufficient following to produce an open rupture with the other evangelical pastors and to establish the judicial basis for their religious work. Within two years eight congregations had been formed, and Lugo returned to the mainland to attend the 1919 General Council in Chicago. Accompanied by his bride, the daughter of a Puerto Rican physician, Lugo continued on to the Pacific Coast to visit his family, returning to Puerto Rico via Texas, where he conferred with Henry C. Ball and met a recent addition to the Pentecostal ranks, Francisco Olazábal.

By 1921 the eleven churches and six hundred members of the thriving work were brought under the AG. The majority adopted the name Iglesia de Dios Pentecostal (Pentecostal Church of God) in order to include the term church (*iglesia*) for clear identification in legal matters, although the group remained an integral part of the AG. A small defection occurred at the time, as some leaders chose to retain the name Asambleas de Dios for their churches. Subsequent growth

under Lugo's leadership was accelerated with the addition of other missionaries, including Frank O. Finkenbinder, who arrived with his bride in 1921. Before his family's health forced him to leave Puerto Rico fifteen years later, Finkenbinder had assisted the work to grow from a dozen churches, none of which had its own facilities, to forty churches, most of which had permanent buildings.

This Pentecostal growth in Puerto Rico led in time to the opening of churches among the Puerto Ricans of New York. By 1929, with twenty-five churches in Puerto Rico, Juan L. Lugo left to pastor a church in the Greenpoint district of Brooklyn. The acquisition of a former synagogue gave the congregation an identity and adequate facilities for the large church that emerged under Lugo's leadership. Within a decade more than thirty Puerto Rican Pentecostal churches had come into being, as works were begun in the various Hispanic districts of metropolitan New York, and Francisco Olazábal directed much of his energies to establishing churches on the East Coast.

E. Francisco Olazábal and the Latin American Council of Christian Churches.

Francisco Olazábal stands out as the dominant figure among the early Hispanic Pentecostals. A convert influenced by George and Carrie Judd Montgomery in California at the turn of the century, Olazábal returned to Mexico in preparation for the Methodist ministry. He later pastored briefly in El Paso and attended Moody Bible Institute, where he became acquainted with Reuben A. Torrey. As an effective Methodist evangelist and overseer of the denomination's work in northern California, Olazábal once again was influenced by the Montgomerys in San Francisco to seek the Pentecostal experience. In 1917 he accepted credentials with the AG and joined Henry C. Ball in Texas as pastor of the church in El Paso. By 1920 his congregation had grown to four hundred members. Ball sent his own associate, Demetrio Bazán, from San Antonio to assist Olazábal.

In 1922 Mexican ministers of the Texas–New Mexico District requested the formation of a Latin American District within the AG to give them greater voice in the administration of their churches. Ball, who had received prior notification that the proposal had been denied, responded at the 1922 meeting of the Mexican ministers in Victoria, Texas, with what was taken by some ministers as an insensitive rejection of their wishes. Reportedly, about twenty pastors met in Houston the following March to secede from the general council and to form the Latin American Council of Christian Churches (LACCC), with Francisco Olazábal as their leader.

The extraordinary work of Olazábal, and the significance of the organizational split for the future of the movement can hardly be overestimated. Considered the most effective Hispanic Pentecostal minister to that time—and perhaps since—he was referred to as the "great Aztec" by a contemporary biographer. Imposing and forthright, his superior preparation, his articulate, persuasive presentation, and his close identification with the Hispanic people and their aspirations all contributed to his remarkable influence.

Olazábal established the headquarters of the LACCC in Texas and began a ministry that soon radiated throughout the country. He traveled widely, conducting healing meetings in rented halls and establishing churches with unusual effectiveness for the next fourteen years. His work in New York and Chicago led to the establishment of dozens of new churches, as did his campaigns in Los Angeles and Puerto Rico. His emphasis on evangelism and healing were combined with concern for the social needs of the Hispanic communities. By the late 1930s his organization had fifty churches and an estimated adherence of 50,000 persons. Olazábal was apparently at the height of his career when he was killed in an automobile accident in Texas in 1937.

F. Institutionalization of the Early Revival. The many unanswered questions regarding Olazábal's work have left much room for conjecture about what might have been had he survived or had he remained with the AG. Victor De Leon concluded that "the probability will always exist that had Francisco Olazábal remained with the General Council, he would have been the first Latin American superintendent of the [Hispanic] convention, and much earlier than 1939"—the date when leadership devolved to a Hispanic (1979, 30). In fact, Henry C. Ball remained prominent in the formation of the Hispanic work for the next sixteen years, opening the Latin American Bible Institute in San Antonio in 1926, concurrently with the San Diego school founded by Luce; cultivating the work in Mexico and Central America in the formative stages; publishing his paper, the *Luz Apostólica*; and preparing

hymnals, one of which (*Himnos de Gloria*) came into general use throughout the Spanish-speaking world. Not only did Ball provide stabilizing leadership at a time when Pentecostals often belittled formal preparation, but his personal influence was important in the development of a number of qualified leaders, including Rubén J. Arévalo and Juan Consejo Orozco, both of whom served as superintendents of the AG of Mexico, and Josué Cruz and Horacio Menchaca, notable in establishing the church in the U.S.

Not the least of Ball's contributions was his success in recovering some of the losses sustained by the AG with the secession of 1923 and his recruitment of able men who succeeded him in the denomination's leadership. In 1929 the Mexican convention in the AG, which had operated under the Texas–New Mexico District, was converted to the Latin American District Council, with Ball serving as superintendent. At the same time the churches in Mexico were placed entirely under national control, with two of Ball's former students as superintendent for extended periods of time. In the meantime Ball's former assistant, Demetrio Bazán, had led the move to rejoin the AG the year after the defection and accepted Ball's former pastorate in Kingsville. He successively pastored in Laredo, Houston, and San Antonio before accepting the invitation to the church in Denver in 1932. In turn Bazán recruited able leadership in the Rocky Mountain States, including Augustín López, pastor of an independent congregation in Denver, and José Girón, a Presbyterian who was to succeed him as superintendent of the Latin American District in the post-World War II era. By 1937, with the approaching retirement of Henry C. Ball, Demetrio Bazán had emerged as the dominant figure in the Hispanic ministry in the U.S. His election as superintendent of the Latin American District Council of the AG in 1939 introduced a new era in the development of the Hispanic Pentecostal work.

III. Development of the Movement Since World War II.

A. Hispanic Pentecostals on the East Coast and in Puerto Rico. World War II marked the beginning of a new era for Hispanic Pentecostalism in several respects. The rising tide of Puerto Rican nationalism under Governor Luis Muñoz Marín brought religious pluralism and tacit support for Protestantism. In the ensuing economic development program and the recognition of commonwealth status for the island, the Pentecostal churches benefited from the assertiveness of the popular groups in demanding a larger place in Puerto Rican society. With the flood of Puerto Ricans who arrived in New York and other eastern cities, a community of 500,000 immigrants ready to adapt to American life provided a receptive field for the already established Hispanic Pentecostal groups and soon engendered additional organizations.

Moreover, the influence of Olazábal both in Puerto Rico and New York had helped establish the work in the 1930s. With his death in 1937 the churches he had opened tended to fragment, creating new organizations and unleashing new leadership within the ranks of the Pentecostals.

When the Puerto Rican churches in the East broke with the Texas-based, Mexican-dominated LACCC the following year, a primary beneficiary was the Asamblea de Iglesias Cristianas (Assembly of Christian Churches), whose work was introduced into Puerto Rico in 1940.

Olazábal's impact on Puerto Rican Pentecostalism had been notable even earlier in the formation of the Defensores de la Fe (Defenders of the Faith), that dated from his association with a former Christian and Missionary Alliance minister, Juan Francisco Rodríguez Rivera, in 1934. Rodríguez, who was influenced by the Fundamentalist evangelist Gerald B. Winrod about the same time, formed a group that has been considered at least marginally Pentecostal. The Defensores began work in New York in 1944 and reported twenty-six churches in Puerto Rico by 1948.

A third group traced to Olazábal's ministry is the Iglesia de Cristo en las Antillas (Church of Christ in the Antilles), whose emergence is not attributed to any single founder. When the ministers of this association changed its name to the Iglesia de Cristo Misionera (Missionary Church of Christ) in 1938, the original congregation separated, retaining the former name and giving rise to a new denomination. By 1980 the two churches, of approximately equal size, reported a combined total of 250 congregations and 15,000 members in Puerto Rico. Subsequently the Iglesia de Cristo en las Antillas changed its name to the Iglesia de Cristo Universal (Universal Church of Christ).

The Iglesia Pentecostal de Jesucristo (Pentecostal Church of Christ), a group formed by a former pastor of the Iglesia de Dios Pentecostal in 1938, and the Iglesia de Dios (Church of God), organized by a group of nine pastors in 1940, further contributed to the proliferation of Pentecostal organizations in Puerto Rico. The former church reported forty-five churches and the latter seventy-five by 1980. A similar Pentecostal organization, the Samaria Iglesia Evangelica (Samaria Evangelical Church) was founded by a former Catholic whose conversion in a Baptist church followed an intense spiritual struggle. Given to fasting, prayer, and the exercise of the gifts of healing and exorcism, Julio Guzman Silva, a blacksmith, formed his own church in 1941 and was the leader of an association of twenty-five churches by 1980.

These demonstrations of local initiative were matched by the introduction of several denominational missions in the postwar period. The Foursquare Church (Iglesia Cuadrangular) arrived in 1930, the Church of God of Prophecy (Iglesia de Dios de la Profecía) in 1938, and the Church of God (CG, Cleveland, Tenn.), in 1944, the Open Bible Standard Churches in 1958, and the United Pentecostal Church in 1962. Of these, the CG was by far the most successful, benefiting from the denomination's association with Antonio Collazo, Juan L. Lugo's son-in-law, in the years just after World War II. Collazo had separated from the Iglesia de Dios Pentecostal previously and emerged as the main influence in the new organization. Next to the Iglesia de Dios

Pentecostal, this group has become the largest Pentecostal group in Puerto Rico in recent years, using the name Mission Board to distinguish it from a small, previously organized indigenous Iglesia de Dios.

The Iglesia de Dios Pentecostal, affiliated with the General Council of the AG beginning in 1921, has continued to grow rapidly since 1945. By 1950 it registered a larger membership than any other Protestant group in Puerto Rico, with 12,000 members in the late 1940s and 70,000 according to recent estimates. In 1956 the group separated from the AG, forming an entirely autonomous organization and opening the way for a new Asambleas de Dios affiliated with the mainland denomination. The growth of the new organization, an integral district of the general council, has resulted in 179 churches and 19,000 communicant members to the present.

The Hispanic Pentecostal churches on the East Coast showed the same tendency to fragment in the postwar era. While it was reported that there were about 25 such groups in 1937, a comprehensive study identified 240 in 1960. In addition to the denominations whose work began as missions, the AG, the CG, and the Church of God of Prophecy, the Hispanic groups in the metropolitan East include the Asamblea de Iglesias Cristianas and autonomous groups fraternally linked to the Puerto Rican churches, such as the Defenders of the Faith. The congregations formerly associated with the Puerto Rican Iglesia de Dios Pentecostal are now independent of the Puerto Rican organization and are designated the Spanish Christian churches. A much smaller organization, the Damascus Christian church, and a larger number of independents, many with names similar to the affiliated churches, make up the balance of the East Coast Hispanic Pentecostal churches. There is relatively little difference operationally and doctrinally between all the local churches of these groups, although those with wider associations presumably benefit from the exchange of a larger pool of leadership and resources. These churches have moved out from their initial locations in New York City and the immediate environs. The Spanish Eastern District of the AG, for instance, reports churches in Massachusetts, Connecticut, and Rhode Island, as well as in Pennsylvania, Delaware, and Ohio, although the preponderance remain in New York and New Jersey.

B. The Asamblea Apostólica de la Fe en Cristo Jesus. The growth of the Asamblea Apostólica in the U.S. has been a major development of Hispanic Pentecostalism in the postwar years. After the 1930s, when the Mexican population in the U.S. experienced little net increase and agricultural laborers were repatriated, the churches demonstrated increased awareness of the larger society and encouraged better internal organization. The Apostolic Bible Training School was organized in Hayward, California, in 1949. Between 1950 and 1962 forty-two new churches were occupied, and evangelists started works in Washington, Oregon, Pennsylvania, and Florida. The group also attempted to send foreign missionaries to Central America and Italy. By 1970 the group had better defined its relationship with the Mexican Apostolics and had organized the North American churches into thirteen districts, each administered by a bishop. Clearly the group represents the most conservative position of any of the Pentecostal groups, retaining an episcopal hierarchy and centralized control; authoritarian pastors in the local churches; and rigid demands on tithing, dress, and conduct considered worldly. Many of the pastors support themselves with secular employment, full or part-time. Holland notes that the strength of the Apostolic movement is found in the rural labor camps and in small southwestern towns that to some extent replicate the social conditions of rural Mexico (1974, 370).

C. *The Latin American Churches of the Church of God.* Although the CG only organized its Hispanic work formally after World War II, the group's Central American work flourished in the 1930s. When, under the aegis of Dr. Vessie Hargrave, the work was organized in 1946 under the supervision of Josué Rubio, the Hispanic work grew rapidly. Rubio promoted the church in several parts of the country, working on the West Coast, the Atlantic Coast, and in Texas. Table 5 indicates the national distribution of the denomination's Hispanic churches. Church of God congregations function autonomously, although they work under the same organizational structure as the Anglo churches. Contributions are directed exclusively for use within the administrative territory of the Hispanic churches. The CG's rapid growth makes it the second largest Hispanic Pentecostal group in the U.S.

Table 5. Church of God (Cleveland, Tenn.) Hispanic Churches by Region

	Churches	Year Territory Organized
South Central Territory	51	1946
Western Territory	74	1962
Northeastern Territory	90	1968
Southeastern Territory	26	1978
North Central Territory	40	1979

D. *The Latin American Districts of the Assemblies of God.* The AG entered a new phase in its Hispanic work with the accession of leadership by Demetrio Bazán. Faced with the problems of cultural difference and distance, Bazán promoted the separation of the Spanish Eastern District from the Latin American District. In 1956 this entity was made a separate administrative unit, although the two districts continued to work under the supervision of the denomination's Home Missions Department until 1973, when they were given status equal to the church's geographical districts. At that time the Puerto Rican church was given similar status. In 1981 a seventh district was created for the largely Cuban population in the southeastern states that in the

next five years grew to include sixty churches and a membership of 6,000. In the 1980s the number of AG Hispanic ministers has increased 20 percent to 2,732.

Table 6. AG Hispanic District Churches/Members

	Churches	Members
Puerto Rico	179	18,991
Spanish Eastern	209	24,221
Southeastern Spanish	74	5,046
Midwest Latin American	52	3,312
Gulf Latin American	295	29,323
Central Latin American	110	6,640
Pacific Latin American	270	24,840

Source: *Pentecostal Evangel,* July 19, 1987, p.14.

IV. Assessments of Hispanic Pentecostal Churches. Several observations may be made about the future of Hispanic Pentecostalism, based on the experience of past immigrant groups, the findings of students of these ethnic churches, and the concerns of the Catholic church. In the latter case, it has been frequently pointed out that the church has until recently neglected its Hispanic communicants. Hispanic representation within the local parish, especially, has proved troublesome and less easily remedied than the elevation of Hispanic bishops. While there were no Hispanic bishops in 1970, there are now thirteen; but while Hispanics in the Southwest make up as many as 80 percent of the parishioners, they account for only 4 percent of the priests. Nationwide fewer than 2 percent of the 58,000 priests are Hispanic, and of these less than 1 percent are American born. In a San Antonio parish, Aldolfo Valdivia found that a minority of the Hispanic families considered themselves to be Catholic, and thousands were indifferent to religion. Valdivia found "other groups"—Baptists, Pentecostals, and Jehovah's Witnesses—thriving. The atmosphere in these churches, he reported, was "upbeat and inviting." On Mexican Independence Day, September 15, 1987, the Los Angeles *Times* ran a full-page ad announcing, "Welcome Back! Perhaps you are among those baptized Catholics who no longer practice your religion. To you, we issue a special invitation. Much has happened in the Catholic Church in recent years. There is a new surge of involvement and commitment and understanding going on within our Catholic community. To make our family complete, we need and want you back with us. We think you may be pleasantly surprised."

Other observers see the growth of Protestant groups in the Hispanic community in terms of the Hispanics' cultural assimilation. According to Margaret Sumner,

Accepting a form of Protestantism reflects a tentative identification with America's predominantly Protestant culture. Experience in a Protestant church might be expected to lead gradually to a complete acceptance of what might be called the "American" world view with its emphasis upon activity in this world, control over the self and nature, a hopeful view of the future, and stress on personal responsibility (1970, 225–33).

Sumner points out that identification with Protestants often involves a high cost within the Hispanic community, where the "social tone" is that of Roman Catholic society. And other writers doubt that assimilation is accelerated by affiliation with Hispanic Protestant churches that tend to isolate their members.

A major study of Mexican-American culture sees the main reason for Pentecostal growth as the groups' "familistic" quality.

> The atmosphere is one of total acceptance: personal and family troubles are made public for congregational help through prayer; embraces between pew neighbors at the close of a service enhance the sense of warmth and all-encompassing community. Pentecostal groups tend more than the classic denominations to reach the hard-to-reach in a meaningful fashion (Grebler et al. 1970, 505).

The authors go on to point out that in comparison with paternalistic groups like the mainline Protestant denominations and the Evangelicals who vacillate between paternalism and self-determination, the Pentecostals provide equality of status through ethnic exclusiveness and sectarian autonomy.

Implicit in these discussions are the suggestions that Hispanic Pentecostals are either essentially traditionalists who adhere to fundamentalistic Christian faith as a means of retaining values threatened by the prevailing culture and the dissolution of the family, the community, and religion, or, in contrast, progressives who have abandoned custom to embrace a more individualistic and liberating form of Christianity. Despite authoritarianism and marginality, these groups provide opportunities for community recognition and independence from restrictive traditions. Members are assured of a supportive, intimate circle of friends, reinforcement of values like respect for elders and marital fidelity, and legitimation of their quest for social and material security.

Possibly the ambivalence of Pentecostal practices is itself vital to its appeal for Hispanics, many of whom are seeking a bridge between the traditional and the modern. Whatever importance Pentecostals attribute to the uniqueness of their doctrines and experiences, they have obviously found an effective formula for institutional survival and growth. Hispanic Pentecostalism, in particular, has demonstrated its suitability for peoples in transition.

Bibliography: R. Andersen, *Vision of the Disinherited* (1979); H. Ball, "Forty-three Years of Progress in the Latin American District," *PE* (January 25, 1959), 14; T. Coakley, "Protestant Home Missions Among Catholic Immigrants," *The Commonweal* 28 (16, 1933): 386; V. De Leon, *The Silent Pentecostals* (1979); R. Domin-

guez, *Pioneros de Pentecostes* (1971); "The Fastest Growing Church in the Hemisphere," *Time* (November 2, 1962), 56; L. Grebler, Moore, and Guzman, "Protestants and Mexicans," *The Mexican-American People* (1973), 487; K. Haselden, *Death of a Myth* (1964); "Hispanics in the Assemblies of God Outpace General U.S. Spanish Population in Rapid Growth," *PE* (July 19, 1987), 14–15; C. Holland, *The Religious Dimension in Hispanic Los Angeles* (1974); La Ruffa, "Pentecostalism in Puerto Rican Society," in S. Glazier, ed., *Perspectives on Pentecostalism* (1980), 49–65; J. Lugo, *Pentecostes en Puerto Rico* (1951); G. McGee, "Pioneers of Pentecost: Alice E. Luce and Henry C. Ball," *AG Heritage* 5 (2, 1985): 5–6, 12–15; D. Moore, *Puerto Rico Para Cristo* (1972); S. Stern, "Catholicism Losing Its Grip on Hispanics," *Tribune* (Oakland) (September 15, 1987), B-1; M. Sumner, "Mexican-Americans in the United States" (1970), 225–33; F. Whitam, "New York's Spanish Protestants," *Christian Century* 79 (1962): 162–64.

E. A. Wilson

HISTORICAL BOOKS

I. Joshua. It is evident that the Book of Joshua contains much eyewitness material. John Rea in *The Wycliffe Bible Commentary* (1962, 205), suggests that the book is a unity and was written during the judgeship of Othniel. (For a discussion of various other views see Woudstra, 1981.)

When God told Moses his time had come to die, Moses' first concern was for the people. He asked God to appoint a new leader so that they would not be "like sheep without a shepherd" (Num. 27:17). God had already prepared Joshua for this place of leadership. He had been Moses' assistant for many years (Exod. 17:9–14). But, more importantly, God declared him to be "a man in whom is the Spirit" (Num. 27:18). The same Spirit that was on Moses (Num. 11:17) would be the source of power and guidance for Joshua. Deuteronomy 34:9 does seem to indicate that Joshua was filled with the Spirit because Moses had laid his hands on him, but this surely cannot be the case. God had already told Moses that Joshua was a man "in whom is the Spirit." The word *because* (Heb., *ki*, Deut. 34:9) can also mean "so that." Thus, the laying on of hands by Moses, like NT ordination, was simply the recognition of ministry that God had already given.

Though the Book of Joshua does not mention the Holy Spirit, Joshua's leadership shows that he was indeed filled with the Spirit's wisdom and power. We can see the Spirit's quiet presence in his life. On two occasions Joshua did trust his own judgment (Josh. 7:2–4; 9:14), but these were not characteristic of his leadership.

II. Judges. Internal evidence shows that the Book of Judges was probably written during the reign of King Saul, possibly by Samuel or one of his contemporaries. The judges were more than judges in the modern sense. They were leaders raised up by God and empowered by the Holy Spirit to deliver Israel from its enemies. Then they proceeded to rule the people under the guidance of God.

Again and again we read that the people did not drive out the Canaanites, nor did they conquer all their cities (Josh. 15:63; 16:10; Judg. 1:21, 27–31, 33). The result was spiritual decline. "Another generation grew up, who knew neither the LORD nor what he had done for

Israel" (Judg. 2:10). That is, they had heard about the Lord and the miracles of deliverance he had given, but they did not know the Lord in their own experience nor had they seen any miracles themselves.

This new generation was attracted to the culture of the Canaanites and to the prestige of their ancient temples and high places. Soon God used those very Canaanites to bring judgment on them. Then the people cried out to the Lord. God sent judges to deliver them, and they served the Lord as long as the judge lived. After that they fell back under the influence of Canaanite religion and immorality. This cycle was repeated over and over.

Five judges get special attention: Othniel, Deborah, Gideon, Jephthah, and Samson. Othniel had already accepted Caleb's challenge to conquer Kirjath-Sepher (Judg. 1:11–13). Thus he was already a man of faith when the Spirit "was [Heb. *tehi*, "proceeded to be"] on him" (Judg. 3:10).

Because Deborah was a prophetess, she was already "carried along [Gk. *pheromenoi*, "led along"] by the Holy Spirit" (2 Peter 1:21). Thus, unlike the other judges, the people accepted her as a judge before there was a victory. They came to her because the Spirit gave her the wisdom to settle their disputes, answer their questions, solve their problems, and comfort them in their sorrows.

Instead of encouraging others, Gideon himself had to be encouraged again and again. It took an angel, fire from a rock, fleeces, and the assurance of Israel's victory given in a Midianite's dream before he dared to step out in faith and obedience. "Then the Spirit of God came upon Gideon" (Judg. 6:34). The Hebrew word here for "came upon" (*labeshah*) is an unusual one and means "clothed himself with." This can only mean that the Spirit filled Gideon and was inside doing the work; Gideon was just the clothes.

Jephthah first tried to negotiate with the Ammonites. When they refused, he moved against them with the Spirit of the Lord coming upon him. In the heat of the battle, however, he forgot to depend on the Spirit and tried to bargain with the Lord with a foolish vow. Yet the Lord still gave him the victory.

The angel of the Lord commanded Samson's mother to drink no alcoholic beverages and to eat nothing unclean, for Samson was to be a Nazirite for life (Judg. 13:7, 14; see Num. 6:1–21). As Samson grew, the Lord blessed him and the Spirit began to stir him to action (Judg. 13:25). On three occasions the Spirit literally rushed in (Heb. *titslah*) on him with a great burst of mighty power (14:6, 19; 15:14). Samson, of course, was still in control of his faculties, but he acted in faith with expectation that the Spirit would supply the strength he needed. Even after the outward sign of his Nazirite consecration was broken by the cutting of his hair, he still thought, "I'll go out as before and shake myself free" (16:20). But this time the Spirit's power and strength was not there, for "the LORD had left him" (v. 20).

When Samson's hair grew, his strength did not automatically return. But he prayed for God to strengthen him once more. Then he pushed with all his (God's) might (Judg. 16:28–30). Thus, by another manifestation of the Spirit's might and power Samson won a final victory.

III. Ruth. The Book of Ruth gives us a picture of another side of the period of the judges. It also gives us a genealogy that leads to David and was probably written during his reign. Though the Spirit is not specifically mentioned in the book, the influence of Spirit-filled judges was still evident in Bethlehem. Naomi's influence on Ruth, Ruth's decision to serve Naomi's God, and the quiet faith and faithfulness of Boaz all point to this.

IV. First and Second Samuel. First and Second Samuel were originally one book. Internal evidence indicates that it must have been written after the death of Solomon. The attention focuses on three key characters: Samuel, Saul, and David. Samuel brought revival and united the twelve tribes for the first time since Joshua. Saul organized the kingdom but failed to establish it. David established the kingdom and brought it to a point that prepared for Solomon's prosperity.

Though the Philistines stole the ark and destroyed Shiloh and its temple (Jer. 7:12; 26:6, 9), Samuel brought the people to a renewed faith in God. Soon there were groups of prophets who went through the country with musical instruments such as a psaltery (a small triangular harp), tabret (tambourine), pipe (flute), and harp (guitarlike lyre). They prophesied, speaking for God in song, and thus encouraged the people to worship the Lord.

The Bible, however, draws special attention to Samuel as the anointer of kings and as a powerful intercessor for Israel. He anointed both Saul and David with special anointing oil that set them apart and consecrated them for the service of God and his people. This oil, made of olive oil compounded with four spices (Exod. 30:23–24), was symbolic of the anointing of the Spirit. We can see a contrast, however, between the way Saul responded to the Spirit and the way David responded. Saul apparently did not know the Lord in a personal way before Samuel anointed him. Not until after the anointing did God change his heart (1 Sam. 10:9). Then, as Samuel had predicted, "a procession of prophets met him; the Spirit of God came upon him (Heb. *titslah*) in [a mighty rush of] power, and he joined in their prophesying" (10:10). That is, he joined these prophets in singing for God as he was moved by the Spirit. But his experience with the Spirit, like that of Samson, was temporary and intermittent.

David, on the other hand, already knew the Lord in a personal way. As a boy he recognized the Lord as his Shepherd (Ps. 23:1) and cried out that the heavens declare the glory of God (19:1). Thus when Samuel anointed him the symbolism became real, for "from that day on the Spirit of the LORD came upon David in power" (1 Sam. 16:13). The Hebrew indicates a further difference between David's experience and Saul's. The Spirit came or rushed *upon* (Heb. *al*) Samson and Saul. But the Spirit came *to* (Heb. *el*) or, better, *into* David, from that day *upward* (Heb. *ma'elah*).

David's experience with the Spirit was a continuing, growing one.

Saul, by acts of disobedience, lost his rights to the throne. The Spirit of the Lord departed from him, "and an evil spirit from the LORD tormented [and terrified] him" (1 Sam. 16:14). This "evil" spirit even caused Saul to prophesy (1 Sam. 16:16, 23; 18:10; 19:9). However, the word "evil" (Heb. *ra'ah*) used here is often used of the judgments of God. In such cases the NIV usually translates it "disaster" (1 Kings 21:20; Isa. 45:7; Jer. 4:6; 6:19). In Isaiah 45:7 it is the opposite of prosperity (Heb. *shalom*, "peace"; but including prosperity, blessing, health, and well-being). Thus the "evil" spirit was a spirit of judgment that our Holy God sends upon rebellious sinners. Only David's Spirit-anointed playing on the harp counteracted to a degree the effects of this judgment on Saul. (Note that on occasion Saul hurled his spear at David.)

On only one other occasion did the Spirit of the Lord come upon Saul. During Saul's pursuit of David he sent messengers three times to arrest him. Each time the Spirit of the Lord came upon them when they reached Samuel and his company of prophets. Each time God's blessing made them turn back without accomplishing their mission. Saul then went to Samuel himself to demand David's arrest. Before Saul arrived at Samuel's headquarters in Ramah the Spirit of the Lord came upon him and he proceeded to prophesy. Then, in Ramah, he stripped off his royal robes and prophesied all that day and night (1 Sam. 19:19–24).

Notice the contrast between this occasion and the first time the Spirit came upon Saul. The first time the Spirit rushed upon him with power, preparing him to reign as king, and he prophesied among the prophets. This time he stripped off his royal robes and lay on the ground. This time, instead of being open to the Spirit and to the will of God, he was rebelling, and God used this to give David an opportunity to escape.

The Holy Spirit never left David. Even when David sinned he was aware of God's presence in the Spirit's convicting power. When he was faced with his sin he repented and cried out for God to create in him a pure heart and asked God not to take his Holy Spirit from him. David knew he needed the Spirit's help to keep him from falling again and to help him to teach sinners God's ways and turn them back to the Lord (Ps. 51:10–13). Thus the Lord restored David, and before he died he was still able to say, "The Spirit of the LORD spoke through me; his word was on my tongue." He was still God's Spirit-anointed singer of songs for Israel (2 Sam. 23:1–2).

V. Kings and Chronicles. The Books of Kings were originally one book, as were the Books of Chronicles. Kings concludes the historical sequence that began with the Book of Joshua. In it the kings form the framework of the history, and each king is introduced with a cut and dried formula. The accounts of the work of the prophets is injected into this framework. After the account of Solomon's reign, the prophets become the real heroes of the book, and they lay the foundation for the future. The book carries us down past the capture of Jerusalem in 586 B.C. and lets the exiles know that idolatry was the reason they were carried away to Babylon.

Chronicles was written after the return from Babylon to help the people make a connection with the good things in their past, especially with the worship. It goes back to the beginning and reviews the history from Adam on, adding spiritual and moral reasons and reflections to the material found in Samuel and Kings. Archaeology has confirmed much of the additional material found in it.

When Amasai, "chief of the thirty," joined David, the Spirit "put him on as clothes" just as the Spirit did Gideon (1 Chron. 12:18; Judg. 6:34). By the Spirit he proclaimed the loyalty of his men to David and promised success to David and his men. The rest of Kings and Chronicles mention the Spirit only in connection with the ministry of the prophets.

Solomon, of course, knew the Spirit's gift of wisdom. But after Solomon's death the kingdom was divided. The kings of the northern ten tribes all worshiped the golden calves set up in Bethel and Dan. In the southern kingdom of Judah were good kings, like Asa, Jehoshaphat, Hezekiah, and Josiah who saw revival. But the majority of the kings in both kingdoms practiced idolatry and were not true servants of the Lord. Thus God in his faithfulness raised up prophets who warned the people, called for repentance, and challenged them with the assurance that God would keep his promises and bring restoration to a remnant of both Israel and the nations.

Among the early prophets in Judah who were moved by the Spirit were Azariah, who encouraged King Asa (2 Chron. 15:1–8), and Jahaziel, who helped King Jehoshaphat to let God give the nation a victory (2 Chron. 20:14–17). Then in northern Israel God raised up Elijah and sent fire from heaven to bring the people to a decision (1 Kings 18:36–39). The Spirit was so evident in his life and ministry that when Elisha knew Elijah was to be taken from him, he asked for a double portion of his spirit (2 Kings 2:9). The double portion was the portion of the chief heir. Thus Elisha was asking for the same Spirit of God to come on him that gave Elijah leadership among the prophets of that day.

Not only did other prophets recognize that the Spirit of Elijah was upon Elisha, so did kings and the people (2 Kings 2:15; 4:9). Even Naaman, the general of the Assyrian army recognized him as a holy man of God (2 Kings 5:14–15). Yet at times Elisha was surrounded with unbelief. Once the unbelief was so strong that he asked for a harpist to come. While the harpist played worshipfully, Elisha looked to the Lord and created his own atmosphere of faith around him. Then "the hand of the LORD came upon Elisha" (2 Kings 3:15)—that is, the power of the Lord came upon him through a mighty move of God's Spirit.

Earlier God used the prophet Micaiah to let King Ahab know that a lying spirit was causing other prophets to promise victory. One of the prophets, Zedekiah, slapped Micaiah and asked, "Which way did the spirit of the LORD go when he went from me to speak to you?" (1 Kings 22:24). Though Zedekiah was wrong about his own inspiration, at least he recognized that true prophecy was inspired by the Spirit of God.

The Spirit "clothed himself" (Heb. *labeshah*) with another prophet in this period. Thus the Spirit spoke through Zechariah (not the author of the Book of Zechariah) to rebuke the apostasy of King Joash. Instead of repenting, Joash had him stoned to death. He was not the only Spirit-filled prophet who was martyred for speaking God's Word, but he was the last one mentioned in Chronicles (2 Chron. 24:20; Matt. 23:35; Luke 11:51).

VI. Ezra and Nehemiah. Nehemiah 8:2 indicates that Ezra was Nehemiah's contemporary. This means Ezra's return was in 457 B.C., the seventh year of Artaxerxes I (Ezra 7:8). Nehemiah returned in 444 B.C. The first part of Ezra records the building of the temple in 520–516 B.C., though 4:6–23 is a parenthesis continuing the story of Samaritan opposition into Ezra's own day.

Both Ezra and Nehemiah gave more attention to the reading and teaching of God's Word that was already given (Ezra 7:10; Neh. 8:1, 8–9). The great prayer of Nehemiah 9 expresses how God gave his "good Spirit to instruct" the Israelites in the desert (9:19–20). God, also by his Spirit, "admonished them" through his prophets (v. 30). The prayer recognizes that it was important for later generations to give attention to these things and learn from them.

VII. Esther. Esther takes place in the reign of Xerxes and gives the background for the Jewish feast of Purim. E. J. Young and G. L. Archer suggest that it was written in the latter half of the fifth century B.C. by someone who was familiar with the facts and who still remembered the palace of Xerxes (which was destroyed within thirty years of Esther's time). Though the Holy Spirit is not mentioned, the name of God is not mentioned either. Yet the providence of God and God's ability to overrule the laws of chance are clearly evident.

Bibliography: G. L. Archer, *A Survey of the Old Testament* (1974); P. Cassel, *Judges and Ruth* (reprint 1965); G. A. Cooke, *The Book of Judges* (1918); A. B. Davidson, *The Theology of the Old Testament* (1904, reprint 1955); W. Eichrodt, *Theology of the Old Testament* (1961); S. M. Horton, "The Holy Spirit in the Book of Judges," *Paraclete* 2 (1969); idem, *What the Bible Says About the Holy Spirit* (1976); C. F. Keil, *Bible Commentary on the Old Testament* (n.d.); A. F. Kirkpatrick, *The First Book of Samuel* (1888); J. M. Myers, *I Chronicles* (n.d.); G. F. Oehler *Theology of the Old Testament* (reprint 1883); J. Rea, "Joshua," *Wycliffe Bible Commentary* (1962); S. J. Schultz, *The Old Testament Speaks* (1960); M. H. Woudstra, *The Book of Joshua* (1961); E. J. Young, *Introduction to the Old Testament* (1949). S. M. Horton

HISTORIOGRAPHY See BIBLIOGRAPHY AND HISTORIOGRAPHY OF PENTECOSTALISM (U.S.).

HITE, BENJAMIN HARRISON (1888–1948). Pentecostal preacher and leader. Born in Kentucky, Hite received the baptism in the Holy Spirit in 1912 in Nashville, Tennessee. He evangelized in Tennessee, Arkansas, Oklahoma, Illi-

nois, and Missouri, establishing many missions that grew into churches. In 1921 he founded the First Pentecostal Church in St. Louis, Missouri, and remained pastor there until his death. He was the first chairman of the Pentecostal Church, Incorporated, serving from 1934 to 1939. He was then elected to serve as the superintendent of the Central District in the Pentecostal Church, Incorporated, from 1939 to 1945, and later as the superintendent of the Missouri District of the United Pentecostal Church. He was known for his unusual ministry of healing.

Bibliography: A. L. Clanton, *United We Stand* (1970). J. L. Hall

HOCKEN, PETER DUDLEY (1932–). Roman Catholic historian and theologian. Born in Brighton, Sussex, England, and reared as an Anglican, Peter Hocken converted to Roman Catholicism in 1954. Subsequently he studied at Oscott College, Birmingham (1958–64), and was ordained to the priesthood February 23, 1964, serving the Diocese of Northampton in pastoral work until 1968. From 1968 to 1976 he taught moral theology at Oscott College, interrupted only by his pursuit (1964–71) of the S.T.L. from the Accademia Alfonsiana in Rome. Since 1976 he has served the Mother of God community in Gaithersburg, Maryland.

Through the years Hocken has maintained a strong ecumenical interest and has been actively involved in such interests since 1965, including membership on the Bishops' Ecumenical Commission for England and Wales (1973–76). Since 1972 he has served on the editorial board of *One in Christ*, a Roman Catholic ecumenical journal. In 1971 he became involved in the charismatic movement. This experience contributed to his Ph.D. studies undertaken at the University of Birmingham. He has authored numerous articles in both scholarly and popular journals and has been a contributor to *New Heaven? New Earth?* (1977) and *The Church Is Charismatic* (1981). His most recent publications included *Streams of Renewal* (1986) on the origins of the charismatic movement in Britain, and *One Lord One Spirit One Body* (1987) on the ecumenical grace of the charismatic movement. He served as the president of the Society for Pentecostal Studies in 1986. C. M. Robeck, Jr.

HODGES, MELVIN LYLE (1909–88). Author and missionary to Latin America. Melvin Hodges was born in Lynden, Washington, to parents who had left the Methodist church because of their new-found Pentecostal experiences. At age ten he was baptized in the Holy Spirit and called to the ministry. Two years later his family moved to Colorado. His father, a minister, taught him Greek at home; at age fifteen young Hodges pursued additional study in the language at Colorado College. In 1928 he married Lois M. Crews; they had three children. He began his ministry as an evangelist in Colorado and received ordination from the Assemblies of God (AG) in 1929. While pastoring there, he was chosen to serve as district youth director (1931–33). After moving to Wyoming, he became the first presbyter from that state to serve the Rocky Mountain District (1933–35).

Melvin Hodges' name was synonymous with indigenous church principles through his books and teaching. He served as a missionary and field director for the Assemblies of God in Latin America.

Hodges received appointment from the AG in 1935 as a missionary to Central America. Arriving in El Salvador in 1936, he assisted missionary Ralph D. Williams in Bible institute teaching. Moving to Nicaragua, he was elected as the general superintendent of the Pentecostal churches and founded the Nicaraguan Bible School at Matagalpa. While there he began to redirect the church polity from a paternalistic structure, dependent upon American financial assistance, to one based on indigenous church principles.

In 1945 Hodges returned to the U.S. for a brief time to edit the *Missionary Challenge*, a promotional magazine for the AG Division of Foreign Missions. During his last term in Central America (1950–53), he served as the chairman of the AG missionary fellowship for the region, superintended the work in El Salvador, and continued his Bible institute administration and teaching.

His missiological insights were strongly molded by the writings of Roland Allen. Asked by Noel Perkin to give a series of lectures at a missionary conference in 1950, he later expanded them for publication by Gospel Publishing House in 1953 under the title *The Indigenous Church*. Moody Press reprinted it the following year. This was the first book on missiology published by a Pentecostal and reflects the principles of Allen, Hodges's expertise in building indigenous churches in Central America, and his Pentecostal pneumatology. Since forces within Pentecostalism

were currently at work to return overseas missions to a paternalistic approach, the timing of Hodges's book proved to be of crucial importance.

Hodges later took office as field director for Latin America and the West Indies for the AG Division of Foreign Missions in 1954. During these years his efforts to build strong evangelistic national churches contributed significantly to the spectacular church growth among Pentecostals in Latin America.

After retiring from his field director's position in 1973, Hodges received appointment as professor of missions at the Assemblies of God Theological Seminary, Noel Perkin Professor of World Missions in 1980, and professor emeritus in 1986. Northwest College of the AG conferred an honorary D.D. degree on him in 1974. A prolific writer, his books include: *The Indigenous Church* (1953), *Build My Church* (1957), *Growth in Your Christian Ministry* (1960), *Spiritual Gifts* (1964), *When the Spirit Came* (1972), *A Guide to Church Planting* (1973), *A Theology of the Church and Its Mission: A Pentecostal Perspective* (1977), and *The Indigenous Church and the Missionary* (1978).

Bibliography: J. P. Hogan, "Breaks New Ground," *PE* (August 12, 1973), 16–17; J. Hurst, "Melvin L. Hodges—Pentecostal Missions Leader of the Twentieth Century" (1985, unpublished ms.); G. B. McGee, *This Gospel Shall Be Preached* (1986); *Who's Who in Religion, 1975–1976*.   G. B. McGee

HODGSON, EDMUND ("TEDDY") (1898–1960). British missionary and martyr. Born in Preston, Lancashire, he was called up in 1916 and served as a gunnery instructor. After being wounded he returned to Preston, where he became a master cabinetmaker. He sailed with James Salter to the Belgian Congo in 1920, where his practical skills resulted in boat building and church construction. Barely surviving blackwater fever, he returned to England in 1923. On recovering health he returned to the Congo in 1924 and in 1930 carried out extensive deputation work for the Congo Evangelistic Mission (CEM).

An unspoiled man, Hodgson was greatly loved. In 1932 he married Linda Robson, but she died in 1933. In 1938 he married nurse Mollie Walshaw of Halifax; she died in 1952 at age forty.

Hodgson became field director of the CEM (later the Zaire Evangelistic Mission) in 1954 in succession to W. F. P. Burton; his last furlough was in 1958–59. Following independence from Belgian rule in June 1960 and a period of unrest, most of the CEM workers were withdrawn to Kamania for safety. When New Zealander Elton Knauf sought to return to his station at Lulungu, Hodgson accompanied him. They were both murdered on November 23, 1960.

Bibliography: E. Hodgson, *Fishing for Congo Fisher Folk* (1934); idem, *Out of Darkness* (1946); C. Whittaker, *Seven Pentecostal Pioneers* (1983).   D. W. Cartwright

HOGAN, JAMES PHILIP (1915–). Missionary and Pentecostal missions executive. Born on a ranch near Olathe, Colorado, to Mr. and Mrs. James E. Hogan and converted as a child during a revival meeting conducted by two women evangelists, J. Philip Hogan received the baptism in the Holy Spirit a year later in 1923. Hogan later attended Central Bible Institute (CBI; College after 1965) and graduated in 1936. He married (Mary) Virginia Lewis, daughter of Gayle F. Lewis (at the time superintendent of the Central District and later an Assemblies of God [AG] denominational executive), following her graduation from CBI in 1937. They have had two children: James Richard (d. 1956) and Phyllis Lynne (Hilton).

After serving as a missionary in China and Taiwan and as a staff member of the Division of Foreign Missions of the Assemblies of God, J. Philip Hogan became executive director in 1959.

After graduation Hogan began his ministry as an evangelist. Later pastoral ministry included churches in Springfield, Missouri; Painesville, Ohio; and Detroit, Michigan. While in Detroit, Hogan invited Leonard Bolton, a missionary to China (L. Bolton, *China Call* [1984]), to conduct a missions convention in his church. He and his wife subsequently responded to Bolton's call for committed Christians to serve abroad as missionaries.

The AG approved the Hogans as missionaries in 1945, and they went to the University of California at Berkeley to study Chinese language and culture. Appointed to North China on January 15, 1946, they sailed in February 1947. Traveling to Ningpo, they ministered at the Bethel Mission founded by Nettie D. Nichols. There Hogan taught in the Bible school, led evangelistic teams, and learned the local dialect. They remained there for eighteen difficult months with the threat of a Communist takeover making their situation ever more perilous. Leaving Ningpo, they went to Shanghai, where they conferred with AG missionaries Howard and Edith Osgood and the Garland Benintendises. Eventually the

Hogans and Benintendises traveled to Formosa for ministry. With the imminent threat of a Communist invasion of Formosa, the Benintendises, Virginia Hogan, and their children returned to the U.S. J. Philip Hogan stayed in Formosa, training a national minister and baptizing about fifteen converts. After six months, conditions forced him to return home (1950). A brief pastorate followed in Florence, South Carolina.

In 1952 Noel Perkin, director of AG foreign missions, invited Hogan to become a field representative for the promotions division of the agency. He accepted this assignment and moved his family to Springfield. Two years later he received appointment as secretary of promotions and traveled widely among AG churches and conventions promoting foreign missions. During his years in this office (1954–59) new and more effective programs were implemented to advance the cause of missions.

With the retirement of Perkin in 1959, the general council selected Hogan to become the executive director of the Division of Foreign Missions, based on the confidence he had gained among the council's ministers through his missionary experience, preaching ministry, editorials in the *Pentecostal Evangel*, and other promotional work. With his encouragement, important and creative international ministries have developed during his administration: Brazilian Extension School of Theology (BEST), Christian Training Network (CTN), International Correspondence Institute (ICI), International Media Ministries (IMM), and Center for Ministry to Muslims (CMM). His commitment to indigenous church principles fostered the already growing number of overseas theological institutions (Bible institutes, Bible colleges, and advanced schools of theology) that have been established for the training of national ministers and lay workers.

In addition to his administrative and promotional work, Hogan has also served as a key strategist for the missions program. Whether with the Global Conquest initiative in 1959 or the forthcoming Decade of Harvest program for the 1990s (a fraternal effort of the AG in the U.S. with national AG church organizations overseas to evangelize the world before the turn of the century), Hogan's imprint can be seen on the development of the missions enterprise.

Hogan's stature among evangelical and Pentecostal missions executives has led to his serving three terms as president of the Evangelical Foreign Missions Association (EFMA; 1968–70, 1976–78; 1983–85; the missionary branch of the National Association of Evangelicals [NAE]). He is also a member of the World Relief Corporation board of directors, also related to the NAE. In addition he is a member of five AG boards of directors: the executive presbytery, foreign missions board (chairperson), Berean College, Evangel College, and the Assemblies of God Theological Seminary, all located in Springfield, Missouri. In recognition of his service to AG missions, two colleges have conferred honorary doctorates of divinity on him: Southern Asia Bible College, Bangalore, India (1970); and

North Central Bible College, Minneapolis, Minnesota (1975).

During Hogan's tenure, the number of AG missionaries has grown from 753 (1959) to 1,464 (1987); the budget from $6,734,780 to $76,679,376; the number of overseas churches from 13,975 to 110,608; and the overseas constituents of national AG church organizations from 627,443 to 14,241,714. During the years of his leadership, and for many reasons, the AG missions effort has seen its most spectacular growth.

Bibliography: AG Division of Foreign Missions press release; G. B. McGee, *This Gospel Shall Be Preached* (1986, 1989); W. W. Menzies, *Anointed to Serve* (1971).

G. B. McGee

HOLINESS CHURCH OF GOD A denomination of about twenty-eight congregations centered in North Carolina and adjacent states. The church began with a 1917 revival in Madison, North Carolina, led by Elder James A. Foust. The revival continued for three years and brought much attention to the Holiness doctrine and the gifts of the Spirit. Several older Holiness congregations of the Winston-Salem area were drawn to the Pentecostal faith.

In 1920 the Holiness Church of God was organized, and in 1928 it was legally incorporated in Winston-Salem. The denomination has only a few thousand members, mostly in North Carolina, but there are several congregations in Virginia, West Virginia, and New York.

Bibliography: Files of the Holiness Church of God, Winston-Salem, North Carolina.   C. W. Conn

HOLINESS MOVEMENT The Pentecostal movement owes its inspiration and formation to the Wesleyan Holiness revival of the nineteenth century. It was born in the midst of Holiness retreat from attempts to reshape Methodist institutions to conform to the practices of camp-meeting evangelists and at the outset of the adaptation of these practices to work among rural newcomers in the cities. The retreat, so clear in hindsight, was to many contemporaries neither inevitable nor desirable. Nor was it uniform, representing as it did the growing rift between the Eastern Methodists, who in 1867 had founded the National Camp Meeting Association for the Promotion of Holiness, and their converts, who as years progressed increasingly dominated the affiliated state associations. The latter predominated in the independent churches and missions that appeared after 1880. And it was from this group, concerned as it was with healing, eschatology, and ecclesiology (issues outlawed for discussion by the national leaders), that most early Pentecostals were drawn. Considered radicals among radicals, future glossolalists were absent from leadership in the insurgent independent group. Not one future Pentecostal leader, for instance, is listed as attending or endorsing the General Holiness Assembly of 1901 in Chicago, the last and most impressive move toward the creation of a comprehensive national Holiness denomination. It is not as a cohesive group within the Holiness ranks, however, that they were shut out. Rather, it is their espousal of issues deemed either controversial or heretical that placed many future Pentecostals on the fringes of Christian perfectionism.

The issues that gave rise both to Holiness independency and to Pentecostalism can be attributed to the aims of the original promoters of the nineteenth-century revival, who traced the church's malady to lack of the marks of sanctification. Other issues were secondary at best. National Holiness leaders, all of whom in the first decades were Methodists, insisted that those affiliated with it and its auxiliaries be members in good standing in some Christian body. They also required that meetings conducted by National Association workers be conducted in accordance with association regulations concerning doctrine and decorum. Agitation concerning church politics or emphasis on doctrines or experiences other than entire sanctification had no place, they said, in National Holiness meetings. An entirely sanctified membership would result in blameless conduct and peace in the church.

The die of Holiness conflict over independent churches was cast in the decade following 1880 with the birth of three bodies later known as the Church of God (Anderson, Ind.), the Church of God (Holiness), and the Holiness Church of California. Although ecclesiology rather than doctrine was at issue, the emergence of these groups witnessed to the vitality of issues other than Holiness teaching in the movement and to the powerlessness of the Methodist Holiness evangelists to guide and control converts, especially in the Midwest, West, and South. All three churches conformed to strict Holiness orthodoxy. By their very existence, however, they opened the way to experimentation that both associations and independent church bodies were ill-fitted to cope with. Pentecostalism became one of the chief end-products.

The Holiness independents envisioned churches of saints meeting together for worship, edification, and watch-care. Daniel Sidney Warner (1842–95) and John P. Brooks (1826–1915), theoreticians of the two Church of God groups, believed that the NT provided a specific plan for church government and that local congregations should be set in order according to that plan. In each place, the Church of God consisted of the wholly sanctified living out the divine command under the Scripture-mandated name. No membership roll had to be kept, for true saints recognized one another. As a human body, the local church was subject to mistakes in administration. As to its true members, however, it could never be in error. Since the Lord himself admitted those who were being saved, he alone determined who were true members. George M. Teel, theologian of the Holiness Church of California, described a church also composed solely of the entirely sanctified. Unlike the Church of God, however, the Holiness Church kept a membership roll, a feature of Brooks' "church of sect" adopted at organization by later Holiness and Pentecostal bodies, which never came into the light of the truth of the one NT church of God. Differences aside, reliance on the guidance of the Holy Spirit occupied a prominent place in the thinking of Holiness independents and so opened the avenue to experience-centeredness and Spirit-guidance so often revealed in later Pentecostal thought. Future Pentecostals in the Holiness ranks started in this direction intellectually very soon thereafter.

Administrative difficulties attendant on the reliance of Holiness independents on Scripture and Spirit soon surfaced in the form of the so-called anti-ordinance heresy. Originating among the infant Church of God ranks in north Missouri, the revolt against baptism and the Lord's Supper rapidly spread over the central and southern plains area. Based on the idea that the true believer depends on the guidance of the Holy Spirit alone, extremists came to discount even the Scripture, the church, and common sense as standards of authority. Stories abounded of marriages contracted for and broken up on spiritual impulse. Faced with charismatic leaders among the new insurgents, conservative Holiness independents stood defenseless. In the years following 1881, this mode of thinking nearly destroyed the infant Texas Conference of the Free Methodist Church. Although within a decade or two the anti-ordinance movement died of its own excesses, its existence demonstrated the potential explosiveness of reliance on charisma, emotion, and Spirit-guidance, factors inherent in the rise of Pentecostalism a few years later.

Close on the heels of the anti-ordinance agitation arose another doctrinal novelty that appealed to a similar clientele and sprang from similar impulses. Invented by Benjamin Hardin Irwin (b. 1854), an independent evangelist who operated on the fringes of the National Association, the Fire-Baptized teaching distinguished between entire sanctification and the baptism with the Holy Spirit and posited the latter as a third experience of grace. Like John Fletcher (1729–85), Wesley's colleague, Irwin regarded the sanctified Christian as the potential recipient of multiple infusions of power, the baptism of the Holy Spirit and fire being but the first. Later blessings he characterized by various explosives: dynamite, lyddite, oxidite. Beginning in 1895 with Iowa, Irwin organized state and provincial Fire-Baptized associations wherever he preached, and these in turn became units of the Fire-Baptized Holiness Association of America, formed at Anderson, South Carolina, three years later. The life tenure granted the founder as general overseer and the baptism-of-fire doctrine both ended with exposure of Irwin's moral failings in 1890. The group's acceptance of third-work Pentecostalism under his successor, Joseph Hillery King (1869–1946), seven years later can be attributed partially to their earlier belief in the postsanctification experience of the baptism of the Holy Spirit and fire. Similarly, adoption of a three-work schema by the Cleveland, Tennessee-based Church of God about the same time may be attributed to the influence of this teaching. Emphasis on Spirit-guidance, faith healing, and premillennialism, which pervaded these Holiness groups, remained intact after they entered the Pentecostal group. The phenomenology of the experience of fire also remained. George Floyd

Taylor (1881–1934), theologian and educator in the Pentecostal Holiness Church with which the Fire-Baptized group merged in 1911, recalled testimonies of Irwin's followers concerning physical sensations of warmth and burning coincident with the spiritual experience. Likewise Charles Fox Parham (1873–1929), father of the doctrine of tongues as the initial physical evidence of the baptism of the Holy Spirit, had attended B. H. Irwin's meetings and, although not favorably impressed, observed the shouting and ecstatic demonstrations that accompanied the experience. At the height of the Azusa Street revival, Irwin reappeared as a Pentecostal worker in Oakland and San Francisco. Apparently there was a tie between those attracted to experiences witnessed by fire and tongues.

Pentecostalism sprang not only from tensions between the established Methodist leaders of the National Holiness Association and their radical, independent Holiness brethren, but also from the commitment to Wesleyan perfectionism, which united them. Perfect love, both groups taught, was both a Methodist doctrine and a Bible doctrine. Resulting in heart purity, the experience of entire sanctification was essential not only to Methodists but to all true Christians. The Tuesday Meetings of Phoebe Palmer (1807–74) and the National Holiness camp meetings, therefore, welcomed comers from all evangelical denominations. Congregationalists, Baptists, Presbyterians, Episcopalians, Quakers, and Mennonites were accepted. Profession of a holiness experience by non-Methodists resulted in unpredictable changes both in doctrine and in the non-Wesleyan churches to which new Holiness believers returned. As the movement expanded, Holiness believers from Methodist backgrounds increasingly taught that purity of intention and eradication of unholy desire was the essential fruit of entire sanctification, a theory taken to its extreme by the eccentric, scholarly evangelist W. B. Godbey (1833–1920). Non-Wesleyans, on the other hand, rallied around the teaching of the Keswick Convention for the Promotion of Practical Holiness (from 1875 on held annually in the Lake District of northwest England) that power for Christian service was the principal fruit of sanctification and that suppression of sinful desire, not eradication of it, was the best the higher Christian life had to offer. Claiming less of a transformation than Wesleyan perfectionists, the Keswick Holiness advocates were also more tolerant of discussion of healing and eschatology. For potential Pentecostalists it was a short step from the baptism of the Holy Spirit as a means of spiritual power to the acceptance of tongues as the initial witness of such a baptism. Anglican Pentecostal pioneer A. A. Boddy (1854–1930) early sensed the connection. He circulated his published Pentecostal testimony at Keswick in 1908. In America the center most sympathetic to the Keswick teaching was Moody Bible Institute in Chicago. This city—contributor of William H. Durham (1873–1912), E. N. Bell (1866–1923), and Andrew Urshan (1884–1967) to Pentecostal leadership—was the early center of the so-called Finished Work of Calvary teaching, which among

Pentecostal theologies bears the closest resemblance to Keswick. A. B. Simpson (1843–1919), Presbyterian founder of the Christian and Missionary Alliance, from which many early Pentecostals were drawn, tried to bridge the Wesleyan-Keswick chasm by saying that he taught neither eradication nor suppression, but habitation. To say the least, the situation on the edges of the National Holiness movement at the turn of the century was a fluid one, susceptible to a multitude of interpretations and methodologies beyond the scrutiny of ecclesiastical or academic critics. Anglicans like Boddy, George B. Studd (1861–1946), Cecil H. Polhill (1860–1938), Robert Phair (1837–1931), and J. Eustace Purdie (b. 1880); Presbyterians like N. J. Holmes (1847–1919); Quakers like Levi Lupton (1860–1929) and A. J. Tomlinson (1865–1943); and Mennonite Brethren in Christ like George A. Chambers (1879–1957) all were ready to accommodate the niceties of received doctrine and tradition to new spiritual experiences.

By the turn of the century, worship patterns and mission strategies developed in Holiness cottage, camp, and band meetings, and in independent churches and missions these patterns were ripe for adoption and adaptation by the infant glossolalia-centered movement. The system of self-support that Bishop William Taylor (1821–1902), a National Holiness member, developed to utilize European and American businessmen in his quasi-independent foreign missionary enterprise had evolved by the 1890s into so-called faith work, in which unsalaried young people went to the field without formal backing or advanced pledges, depending solely on faith and prayer for support. Future Pentecostal strongholds in India, Chile, and West Africa grew out of the pioneer Holiness efforts of Taylor workers, Willis C. Hoover (1856–1936) in Chile being the outstanding example. A corollary of this method was a trial period spent in slum or rural work at home using the faith principle as a test of the suitability of candidates for foreign service. Workers who proved themselves in this way would be given transportation to the field but no guarantee of support after arriving. A large number of independent city missions sprang up in the U.S. and Europe under this plan, which was at the height of its popularity at the time of the Topeka, Houston, and Los Angeles revivals.

Not only had the plan of organization and support been established but the content and manner of conducting worship as well. Beginning with the "Cleansing Wave" of Phoebe Palmer, a new genre of Holiness-experience songs emerged in which the whole congregation testified, shouted, and at times gave expositions of Scripture and doctrine. Destined to provide the core repertoire of the hymnodies of both Holiness and Pentecostal movements for well over a half century, these songs abounded with images drawn from the Bible and John Bunyan (1628–88): the Exodus, the Promised Land, and heaven in analogies derived from the camp meeting ground, the railroad, and debt and hard times. These songs drew worshipers into sympathy one to another at the same time they were reinforcing teaching

from the pulpit and creating a common doctrinal and behavioral standard.

In the 1890s both Wesleyan and Keswick Holiness advocates increasingly identified the second crisis with Pentecost, and references to the Upper Room event began to appear in church names and song texts. Use of the Pentecostal designation was thematic rather than dogmatic, however. Holiness people in both camps sang hymns such as "The Comforter Has Come" by Frank Bottome (1823–94) for more than a decade before it gained permanent standing in the Pentecostal repertoire by repeated use at Azusa Street. Between 1891 and 1911 Hope Publishing Company of Chicago issued six volumes of *Pentecostal Hymns* compiled by Henry Date. Other Holiness contributions were song books issued by the Pepper Publishing Company of Philadelphia, the Christian Witness Company of Chicago, the Christian Alliance Publishing Company of New York, the Pickett Publishing Company of Louisville, and the Pentecostal Mission Publishing Company of Nashville. Notable individual contributions as composer or compiler were made by A. B. Simpson, F. A. Graves (1856–1927), R. Kelso Carter (1849–1926), L. L. Pickett (1859–1928), Charlie Tillman (1861–1943), D. Wesley Myland (1858–1943), and Herbert Buffum (1879–1939), all of whom were white; and C. P. Jones (1865–1949) and Thoro Harris (1874–1955), blacks.

Due to their roots and the roots of their followers in the Holiness movement, Charles Fox Parham and William J. Seymour (1870–1922) acted at Topeka, Houston, and Los Angeles in an already familiar arena. Parham, who tacitly encouraged female followers to challenge the ascetic Holiness dress code, had intimate knowledge of the independent and National Holiness movements in the plains area. Seymour, a black, had ties with the Revivalist people of Cincinnati and the Evening Light Saints (Church of God [Anderson, Ind.]) in Indiana and Louisiana. Both were familiar with Holiness inner-city missions and with Holiness communalism. Parham's Bethel Healing Home and his Bethel Bible School in Topeka were markedly similar to the World's Faith Missionary Association home in Shenandoah, Iowa, where Clara Lum (d. 1942), an Azusa Mission worker, trained; the God's Bible School and Missionary Training Home, which Seymour visited in Cincinnati; N. J. Holmes' Altamont Bible and Missionary Institute in Greenville, South Carolina; and the healing home in East Providence, Rhode Island, which Christine Gibson (1879–1955) was to transform into Zion Bible Institute, a faith school. In the last decades of the nineteenth century a Holiness language of several dialects had been formulated; it encompassed a like number of doctrinal, racial, ecclesiastical, and social constituencies. For several months in 1906, 1907, and 1908, a number of these dialects merged into a unified one in a multiracial slum mission on Azusa Street in Los Angeles. Although they were destined to separate, those Holiness people were so marked by this experience that they were permanently redirected. To the movement launched at Azusa, however, the new Pentecostals brought a richly diverse inheritance of Holiness doctrine, ecclesiology, worship, and institutionalism—all of which were henceforth both to unite and divide them.

See also BLACK HOLINESS–PENTECOSTALISM; KESWICK HIGHER LIFE MOVEMENT; INITIAL EVIDENCE, A HISTORICAL PERSPECTIVE.

Bibliography: R. M. Anderson, *Vision of the Disinherited* (1979); J. P. Brooks, *The Divine Church* (1891); C. Brumback, *Suddenly From Heaven* (1961); J. E. Campbell, *The Pentecostal Holiness Church, 1898–1948* (1951); C. W. Conn, *Like a Mighty Army* (1977); C. E. Cowen, *A History of the Church of God (Holiness)* (1948); D. W. Dayton, *Theological Roots of Pentecostalism* (1987); M. E. Dieter, *The Holiness Revival of the Nineteenth Century* (1980); idem, "Wesleyan-Holiness Aspects of Pentecostal Origins: as Mediated through the Nineteenth Century Holiness Revival," in V. Synan, ed., *Aspects of Pentecostal-Charismatic Origins* (1975), 55–80; C. C. Fankhauser, "The Heritage of Faith: an Historical Evaluation of the Holiness Movement in America" (M.A. thesis, Pittsburgh State University [Kansas], 1983); S. H. Frodsham, *With Signs Following* (1946); J. R. Goff, "Charles F. Parham and His Role in the Development of the Pentecostal Movement: a Reevaluation," *Kansas History* 7 (Autumn 1984): 226–37; idem, "Fields White unto Harvest: Charles F. Parham and the Missionary Origins of Pentecostalism," Ph.D. thesis, University of Arkansas, 1987; C. E. Jones, *Perfectionist Persuasion: the Holiness Movement and American Methodism, 1867–1936* (1974); A. M. Kiergan, *Historical Sketches of the Revival of True Holiness and Local Church Polity from 1865–1916* (1972); L. Lovett, "Black Origins of the Pentecostal Movement," in V. Synan, ed., *Aspects of Pentecostal-Charismatic Origins* (1975), 123–41; W. W. Menzies, *Anointed to Serve* (1971); D. J. Nelson, "For Such a Time as This: The Story of Bishop William J. Seymour and the Azusa Street Revival, a Search for Pentecostal/Charismatic Roots," Ph.D. thesis, Birmingham University, 1981; R. L. Niklaus, J. S. Sawin, and S. J. Stoesz, *All for Jesus* (1986); S. E. Parham, *The Life of Charles F. Parham, Founder of the Apostolic Faith Movement* (1930); D. R. Rose, *Vital Holiness: a Theology of Christian Experience* (1975); M. H. Schrag, "Benjamin Hardin Irwin and the Brethren in Christ," *Brethren in Christ History and Life* (Dec. 4, 1981): 89–125; idem, "The Spiritual Pilgrimage of the Reverend Benjamin Hardin Irwin," *Brethren in Christ History and Life* 4 (June 1981): 3–29; J. W. V. Smith, *The Quest for Holiness and Unity* (1980); T. L. Smith, *Called Unto Holiness* (1962); V. Synan, *The Holiness-Pentecostal Movement in the United States* (1971); idem, *The Old-Time Power* (1973); G. M. Teel, *The New Testament Church* (1901); E. L. Waldvogel [Blumhofer], "The 'Overcoming Life': A Study in the Reformed Evangelical Origins of Pentecostalism," Ph.D. thesis, Harvard University, 1977; D. S. Warner, *The Church of God; or, What Is the Church and What Is Not* (1902); G. H. Williams and E. Waldvogel [Blumhofer], "A History of Speaking in Tongues and Related Gifts," in M. P. Hamilton, ed., *The Charismatic Movement* (1975). C. E. Jones

HOLLENWEGER, WALTER JACOB

(1927–). Swiss theologian and professor of mission, University of Birmingham (U.K.). Born in Antwerp, Belgium, Hollenweger became a youth leader and pastor in the Schweizerische Pfingstmission and attended the International Bible Training Institute, Burgess Hill, U.K. He studied at the University of Zurich, where he produced the *Handbuch der Pfingstbewegung*, 10 vols. (inaugural dissertation, Zurich, 1966), portions of which were revised and published as

Enthusiastisches Christentum. Die Pfingstbewegung in Geschichte und Gegenwart (1969; rev. English trans., *The Pentecostals* [1972], rev. Spanish trans., *El Pentecostalismo, Historia y Doctrinas* [1976]). He also served as the secretary for evangelism of the World Council of Churches. Hollenweger is now a clergyman in the Swiss Reformed Church and is a prolific author.

Walter J. Hollenweger is professor of mission, University of Birmingham, England. He is author of *The Pentecostals*.

Hollenweger has argued that Western theologians need to develop an awareness of the intercultural dimensions of the Christian traditions, especially of those movements that offer alternatives to and variations on the traditional European and North American churches. Theologians able to relativize their own culture conditioning have the potential to create bridges from the barriers between people, offering possibilities of communication and understanding. This, Hollenweger contends, is how the Pentecostal movement functioned in the early period when it understood its goal to be the renewal of the church. It soon came to believe that its reason for being was the perpetuation of its own organization and structures. There was a corresponding decline in influence and an isolation from the rest of society. He has characterized the charismatic movement as a "new chance" for the churches.

Hollenweger suggests that in Third World indigenous Pentecostal (and related) churches, priorities of the early movement have been maintained for liturgical structures and architecture, and theological thought and praxis have not been confined to Graeco-Roman thought forms and Western "respectable" traditions.

Bibliography: W. J. Hollenweger, *Erfahrungen der Leibhaftigkeit* (1979); idem, *Evangelism Today: Good News or Bone of Contention?* (1976); idem, *Pentecost Between Black and White* (1974); idem, *Umgang mit Mythen* (1982); idem, *Wie aus Grenzen Brücken werden;* idem, *Ein theologisches Lesebuch* (1980).

D. D. Bundy

HOLMES, NICKELS JOHN (1847–1919). Pastor, educator, and church leader. Born in Spartanburg, South Carolina, and trained in law at Edinburgh University. Holmes decided to enter the Presbyterian ministry and was ordained by the Enoree Presbytery in South Carolina in 1888. He served as pastor of the Second Presbyterian Church of Greenville, South Carolina, from 1892 to 1895.

In July 1896 he received an experience of sanctification after a visit to hear D. L. Moody in Northfield, Massachusetts. After this he organized the "Tabernacle Presbyterian Church," a small Holiness denomination in South Carolina. Prior to this, he had begun to hold classes for young ministers on Parris Mountain near Greenville, South Carolina. By 1898 these classes became the "Holmes Bible and Missionary Institute." The school operated then as it does now as a "faith" school, not charging students for educational costs.

In 1907 Holmes and his entire Bible institute accepted the Pentecostal message from G. B. Cashwell, an Azusa Street pilgrim. After speaking in tongues, Holmes and the institute continued to teach a Wesleyan theology, staunchly defending the sanctification experience as a second blessing while promoting glossolalia as "initial evidence" of the baptism in the Holy Spirit.

In 1915 the Tabernacle churches merged with the Pentecostal Holiness Church (PHC) in Canon, Georgia. Holmes and the institute did not join in the merger although the school was later related to the PHC. His institution, now known as the Holmes College of the Bible, is the oldest Pentecostal educational institution in the world.

Bibliography: N. Holmes, *Life Sketches and Sermons* (1920).

H. V. Synan

HOLY LAUGHTER See SPIRITUALITY, PENTECOSTAL AND CHARISMATIC

HOLY SPIRIT, DOCTRINE OF THE

I. A Distinct Divine Person
II. The Spirit's Work of Inspiring Scripture
III. The Spirit's Work in Creation
IV. The Spirit's Work in the Old Testament
V. The Spirit in the Life and Ministry of Jesus
VI. The Holy Spirit in the New Testament Church

Throughout the Bible we read of people who were touched by the Spirit of God. In the NT especially, we see the Holy Spirit given a prominent place. Yet over the major part of the history of the church, the Holy Spirit has been the neglected member of the Trinity. Too many treated him as if he were a mere influence of little real importance. Most of the books dealing with systematic theology had very little to say about him, his work, and his gift.

Thomas Goodwin, a Puritan writer of 1660, admitted, for example, that the Christians of his day did not give the Holy Spirit the glory due him. George Smeaton said in 1882, "We may safely affirm that the doctrine of the Spirit is almost entirely ignored" (Smeaton, 1882, 1). W. G. T. Shedd in his *Dogmatic Theology* of 1888 has only brief mentions of the Holy Spirit here and there. A. H. Strong in 1906 wrote, "We still wait for a complete discussion of the doctrine of the Holy Spirit, and believe that widespread revivals will follow the recognition of the omnipotent Agent in revivals" (Strong, 1907, 340). His *Systematic Theology* has no special section on the Holy Spirit and deals with him only briefly in connection with other doctrines. Even in 1939, L. Berkhof has only a few pages that deal with the Spirit and has no discussion of the Spirit's gifts.

At the beginning of the twentieth century the Pentecostal revival began to bring a change. Since the middle of the century, further growth of Pentecostal churches and the rise of the charismatic movement have brought more and more attention to the Holy Spirit. Many books by Pentecostal authors are being circulated widely, and more and more Christians are recognizing that the Bible does teach the Pentecostal experience. Stanley Horton's *What the Bible Says About the Holy Spirit* (1976) has been translated into a number of languages and is being used as a textbook in almost every part of the world where the Pentecostal message has gone. In addition to books from every continent, journals such as *Paraclete* (Springfield, Mo.: Gospel Publishing House), *JSPS* (Pasadena, Calif.: Society for Pentecostal Studies), and *EPTA Bulletin* (Brussels: European Pentecostal Theological Association) are specifically devoted to the doctrine of the Holy Spirit. Obviously, more people are recognizing that the Holy Spirit is a real person who still works in our hearts and lives today.

I. A Distinct Divine Person. Throughout the Bible we see the Holy Spirit as a real person, doing things that only a person can do. We see him with a mind, intelligence, and knowledge (Rom. 8:27; 1 Cor. 2:11). He has a will (1 Cor. 12:11). He shows love and affection (Rom. 15:30). He spoke to Philip (Acts 8:29). He commanded Peter (Acts 11:12). He told the church to separate Paul and Barnabas for the ministry to which he had called them (Acts 13:2, 4). On one occasion he forbade Paul to preach in the province of Asia (Acts 16:6–7). He spoke to the churches (Rev. 2:7, 11, 17, 29). He joins with the church to invite others to come (Rev. 22:17).

We see also that the Spirit can be vexed or grieved (Isa. 63:10; Eph. 4:30), blasphemed or insulted or outraged (Matt. 12:31; Heb. 10:29), lied to (Acts 5:3), and tempted or tested (Acts 5:9). No impersonal force such as lightning or electricity shows either grief or love. People in the Bible could respond to him or resist him, but they treated him as the Spirit of God (Gen. 6:3; Exod. 31:3; Judg. 6:34; Isa. 61:1; Rom. 8:9; 2 Cor. 3:3). He is the Spirit of the Father (Matt.

10:20) and the Spirit of his Son (Gal. 4:6). He is truly God, just the Father is God and the Son is God, and, like them, he has divine attributes. He is omnipresent (Ps. 139:7–8). He is omniscient (Isa. 40:13; 1 Cor. 2:10–11). He is omnipotent (Zech. 4:6). He is eternal (Heb. 9:14). He is also good in the same way that God is good (Neh. 9:20; Ps. 143:10).

The fact that he is a distinct person is seen also in such passages as Isaiah 48:16, "And now the Sovereign LORD has sent me with his Spirit." Jesus recognized the Spirit as a distinct person when he quoted Isaiah 61:1, "The Spirit of the Sovereign LORD is on me, because the LORD has anointed me." Then Hebrews 9:14 declares that Christ "through the eternal Spirit offered himself unblemished to God" (see Bickersteth, 1959, 58–59). Jesus further referred to the Holy Spirit as "another Counselor" (John 14:16). The Greek, *allon parakleton*, indicates that he would be another of the same kind: a helper, friend, and teacher to them, just as Jesus had been. Though in perfect unity and working in perfect cooperation with the Father and the Son, he has his own distinct person and work (John 14:26; 15:26; 16:7).

Many other passages show that perfect unity and cooperation. First Corinthians 12:4–6 shows that the Spirit, the Lord Jesus, and God the Father are parallel. Ephesians 4:4–6 reveals them as perfectly coordinate. They all dwell in the temple as God (1 Cor. 3:16; 6:19; Col. 1:27). These teachings were often contradicted during the early centuries of the church. Some Gnostics considered the Holy Spirit a mere emanation or radiance. In the third century A.D., Origen put the Spirit in a subordinate status. The Macedonian cult treated the Spirit as an uncreated being, yet did not call him God. In the fourth century Arians, who thought of Jesus as a created being, did not accept the deity of the Spirit. It is not hard for those who follow in their train to consider the Spirit a mere impersonal power or influence.

Others, like Sabellius in the third century, denied the Trinity in a different way. He taught that the one divine person manifested himself in different ways, modes, or capacities. Most Pentecostals see that the Bible teaches a triunity with three distinct persons whose distinctness does not infringe on the unity of the being of God.

They would agree, for example, with the so-called Athanasian Creed, which explicitly states: "We worship one God in Trinity, and Trinity in Unity, neither confounding the Persons, nor dividing the substance. For there is one Person of the Father, another of the Son, and another of the Holy Spirit; but the Godhead of the Father, of the Son, and of the Holy Spirit is all one, the glory equal, and the majesty eternal." Later creeds sometimes subordinated the Holy Spirit in some way. But most Pentecostals, like the early Methodists in their statement of 1789, have avoided such controversies. Pentecostals usually accept the person of the Holy Spirit and give more attention to what the Bible says about his work.

II. The Spirit's Work of Inspiring Scripture. The Bible shows that God is good and that he loves us. The greatest evidence of his love is the gift of his Son to die in our behalf and in our place. But that did not come about apart from God's work carried on down through many centuries to prepare for the coming of Christ. For the good news of God's salvation to be spread, the written record of both the Old and New Testaments is needed.

The Bible makes strong claims for its inspiration by the Spirit. Sometimes the Spirit inspired the writers in a direct way, giving them the words to say. Sometimes they heard the words of the Lord directly. Sometimes the Spirit used a variety of ways to reveal God's message (Num. 17:8–10; 2 Sam. 23:2; Acts 9:5; Rev. 1:10–11).

Again and again the prophets proclaim that the word of the Lord came to them, or they called on the people to hear the word of the Lord (e.g., Hos. 1:1; 4:1; Joel 1:1; Amos 1:3, 6, 9). God called the prophets, prepared them, took them through experiences that would help them, and led them along by his Spirit until they were ready to receive the message the Spirit wanted them to give in the way he wanted them to give it. To guide them, he sometimes gave them dreams, visions, and other manifestations of his presence and of the Spirit (2 Tim. 3:16–17; 2 Peter 1:20–21).

God is the true author of Scripture, for it is God's Word. This was God's claim in Hosea 8:12: "I wrote for them [Israel] the many things [the myriad things, the ten thousand things] of my law [my instruction, the written Scriptures up to that time]." Thus, though God used Moses and other prophets to write and the Spirit inspired them, God was the real author.

No biblical writer ever sat down and on his own decided what would be nice to write. Because God had prepared them, however, the Spirit was able to use their own vocabularies, styles, and experiences to proclaim the truth. Thus their writings were not mere dictation. Neither were they just the product of elevated human inspiration. They were divinely inspired, fully inspired, God-breathed words.

For most Pentecostals the fact that Jesus called the Holy Spirit the Spirit of truth (John 16:12) is sufficient grounds for believing in the dependability and reliability of all that the Bible says. The "Statement of Fundamental Truths" of the Assemblies of God, for example, makes this its first point: "The Scriptures, both the Old and New Testament, are verbally inspired of God and are the revelation of God to man, the infallible, authoritative rule of faith and conduct (1 Thess. 2:13; 2 Tim. 3:15–17; 2 Peter 1:21)." The Holy Spirit makes the Bible a new book to Pentecostals, and it is common for them to say that they believe the Bible from cover to cover.

This means also that the Spirit who inspired the Word uses it. The Word is the Spirit's only sword, the Spirit's only tool for accomplishing the work and will of God (Eph. 6:17). With the Word in our hearts, minds, and hands, we become the Spirit's agents, and he makes us ambassadors for Christ, fellow workers with the Lord.

III. The Spirit's Work in Creation. The Bible first introduces us to the work of the Spirit as he was "hovering over the waters" of the primeval earth in preparation for the six creation days. Since the Hebrew word for spirit (*ruach*) can also mean wind or breath, some interpret Genesis 1:2 as a description of a mighty wind that swept over the waters. But in this chapter God is doing the action all the way through. Furthermore, "hovering" (Heb. *merahepheth*) is a word used elsewhere of a mother bird hovering over the birds in her nest (Deut. 32:11). Clearly the Holy Spirit cooperated with the Father and the Son in creation. (See also John 1:3.)

From this we can see that though the Bible does not mention the Spirit in the creation of Adam and Eve, the Spirit must have been just as active in Genesis 1:26–28 as he was in Genesis 1:2. As Ephesians 3:16; 4:24 indicates, the image and likeness of God in humanity involved the capabilities for true righteousness and holiness.

Some interpret Genesis 2:7 (KJV) to mean that God breathed the Holy Spirit into Adam so that he became a living soul (Heb. *nephesh hayah*) and that therefore the soul is made up of the body plus the Holy Spirit. Others take it to mean that after God created the physical body the Holy Spirit had to give it life before it became a soul. Still others say that the soul is made up of the body plus the human spirit. Actually, the word *soul* (Heb. *nephesh*) is used in the Bible to mean being, person, or individual. In Genesis 1:20–21, 24 the same Hebrew phrase (*nephesh hayah*) is used of birds, fish, and animals, for they are also living beings, given life by God. Humankind alone, however, bears the image of God and is capable of fellowship with him and capable of responding to the Spirit of God.

Genesis 9:6 shows further that though the image of God in human beings was marred by the Fall, it was not destroyed altogether. God, for example, was able to anoint and use Cyrus by the Holy Spirit even though Cyrus did not know God (Isa. 45:1–4).

On the other hand, because the results of the Fall led to increasing corruption and violence, and because sinful people took God off the throne in their lives and put self on the throne, God gave them up, so that the effects of their sin would bring part of their judgment on them (Rom. 1:24–26). Yet God did not cease loving the world, nor did he give up his plan of redemption. His purpose was still to make a way to give us a new birth, a new creation, a salvation by grace through faith—all made real in our lives by the Spirit who gives life.

IV. The Spirit's Work in the Old Testament. In the days before the Flood, the Spirit continued to work. Noah was a preacher of righteousness (2 Peter 2:5). As such he must be considered a prophet, with the Spirit of Christ in him (1 Peter 1:11). Yet we see that God set a limit on the length of time the Spirit would continue to "contend with" people "to restrain them from their evil ways" (Leupold, 1950, 1:255–56) or "judge among" (Heb. *yadon* from the root *din,* "judge, govern") humanity before the Flood would bring judgment (Gen. 6:3).

History has been dominated by Spirit-filled men and women (Barclay, 1960, 11). Abraham

was a prophet, a spokesman for God (Gen. 20:7). So were Isaac, Jacob, and Joseph (Ps. 105:15). Even Pharaoh recognized Joseph as a Spirit-filled person (Gen. 41:38). Moses was also Spirit-filled (Num. 11:17; 12:6–8). God filled Bezalel and Aholiab with the Spirit to do beautiful work and to teach others (Exod. 31:2–3; 35:30–31). He also took the same Spirit who was on Moses and put him on seventy elders so they could help him with the spiritual leadership of the people (Num. 11:17). This led Moses to express the wish that all God's people would be prophets and that he would put his Spirit upon them (Num. 11:29). That wish was never fulfilled in OT times, but by expressing it, Moses recognized that being filled with the Spirit should be the normal experience of all. Joshua also saw this, and by the time he was chosen to replace Moses, God recognized him as a man in whom the Spirit was continually resident (Num. 27:18).

The judges who followed Joshua were men and women aroused, moved, and filled by the Spirit. "They turned the hearts of the people to God, led them to victory, and inspired them to serve the Lord" (Horton, 1976, 35). Deborah was a prophetess. Gideon was literally the clothes for the Spirit, with the Spirit doing the work in and through him (Cook, 1918, 80). In spite of their weaknesses, even Jephthah and Samson were moved and empowered by the Spirit to win victories for the people.

Samuel, as a prophet and spokesman for God anointed Saul and David with a special oil symbolic of the anointing of the Spirit now available to every believer (1 John 2:20). For Saul the experience became a reality when he joined in with a group of prophets who were singing and playing musical instruments for God under the inspiration of the Spirit (1 Sam. 10:9). David, however, experienced a filling of the Spirit as soon as he was anointed, and the Spirit continued with him and in him "from that day forward" (Heb. *ma'elah,* "upward," for it was a growing, continuing experience; 1 Sam. 16:13 KJV). Saul, because he continued in self-will, lost that anointing of the Spirit. David sinned also, but because of his genuine repentance, God responded to his cry (Ps. 51:10–13) and did not take away his Holy Spirit from him as he did from Saul. At the end of David's life, the Spirit still spoke by him and inspired the psalms he wrote (2 Sam. 23:2).

The Spirit's activity in the rest of the OT is seen in the way he inspired and worked through the prophets. Elijah, for example, was so characterized by the Spirit that when Elisha knew Elijah was to be taken from him, he asked for a double portion (the portion of the heir) of the same divine Spirit. Micah declared that the reason he was full of power was that he was full of the Spirit (Mic. 3:8). Ezekiel was moved again and again by the Spirit (Ezek. 2:2; 3:12, 14, 24; 8:3; 11:1, 5, 24; 37:1; 43:5). Thus, all the true prophets were inspired, moved, and led along (Gk. *pheromenoi*) by the Spirit (2 Peter 1:21).

The prophets also looked ahead and saw the Spirit resting on the Messiah (Isa. 11:1–5; 61:1–4). The sevenfold Spirit of Isaiah 11:2

shows how the Spirit would manifest himself through the Messiah as well as what he will do for us. He is above all the Spirit of the Lord who makes God's redemption effective in us and gives us purpose for living. As the Spirit of wisdom, he gives insight, applies truth to life, and helps us to make right choices. As the Spirit of understanding, he gives comprehension and helps us to recognize good and evil. As the Spirit of counsel, he gives divine direction and helps us to come to right conclusions. As the Spirit of knowledge he reveals God and truth to us. As the Spirit of the fear of the Lord, he inspires reverence and helps us to worship and to submit to the lordship of Christ.

The prophets also saw future outpourings of the Spirit on God's people (Isa. 32:16–18; 44:3; Ezek. 11:19–20; 18:31–32; 36:26–27; 37:14; 39:29; Joel 2:28). In the latter passage the Hebrew (eshpok) indicates what is normally progressive or repeated action, thus making the outpouring of the Spirit available continually from that point on (Laetsch, 1965, 128).

From all the Spirit's work in the OT we can see why God declared that his work must always be done, not by human might or power, but by his Spirit (Zech. 4:6). We see also that teaching was an important ministry of the Spirit in the OT and that he inspired the prophets when God commanded them to write. He is still the teacher Spirit, and every fresh move of the Spirit always involves illumination of the same written Word he inspired.

V. The Spirit in the Life and Ministry of Jesus. During the four hundred years between Malachi and Christ's birth, the Spirit was not entirely neglected. Apocryphal and pseudepigraphal writings, as well as Philo and Josephus, mention him, though the latter do not use the term "Holy Spirit." The opening chapters of Luke also show that the Holy Spirit was active in the events surrounding the birth of Christ, filling John the Baptist and his mother and father, moving Simeon, and inspiring Anna the prophetess.

Jesus himself was born of the Spirit, identified by the Spirit to John the Baptist, proclaimed as the baptizer in the Spirit and as the baptizer in fire by John the Baptist, and was driven by the Spirit into the wilderness to be tempted by the devil. He was led by the Spirit and rejoiced in the Spirit, and in all his ministry of teaching and healing he did his Father's work in the power of the Spirit.

Twice Matthew emphasizes that Jesus was born of or by the Holy Spirit (Matt. 1:18, 20). Luke tells how the angel Gabriel told Mary that the Holy Spirit would come upon her, and the power of the Most High, that is, of God, would overshadow her like a cloud so that the holy child would be called the Son of God (Luke 1:35). Luke does not suggest, however, that the Holy Spirit contributed anything of himself. Rather, the creative act that made possible the Virgin Birth was God's act (Alford, 1883, 1:447–48). Later, the Bible emphasizes that God sent his own Son, born of a woman, in the likeness of sinful humanity (Rom. 8:3; Gal. 4:4).

The direct agency of the Holy Spirit in the birth of Jesus probably indicates that he was indwelt by the Spirit from the time of his birth. Then at his baptism in the Jordan River by John he had a further distinct experience with the Holy Spirit that identified him as the baptizer in the Holy Spirit. He would not only pour out the Spirit but would also cause us to be immersed in him and saturated with him, so that life would never need to be drab, inadequate, futile, or earthbound (Barclay, 1960, 24–25).

The "baptism in fire" prophesied by John the Baptist is taken by some to mean an experience of purification or sanctification. Others take the fire to mean zeal or enthusiasm expressed in the ministries and gifts of the Spirit (Carr, 1886, 100). Others relate it to the tongues as of fire on the Day of Pentecost (Montefiore, 1968, 2:388). However, since those tongues of fire preceded the outpouring of the Spirit, they can hardly have been part of it.

Actually, every time Jesus spoke of fire he meant the fire of judgment. John the Baptist also spoke of fire in reference to judgment (Matt. 3:10, 12). Thus, though John did not see the time difference between them, he was speaking of two alternatives. Jesus was to baptize in the Spirit; then, as Paul shows, he will come back in blazing fire to punish those who do not know God (2 Thess. 1:7–8).

After John baptized Jesus in the Jordan River, Jesus came up out of the water (Matt. 3:16; Mark 1:10) and was on the bank praying (Luke 3:21–22) when the Holy Spirit descended in the form of a dove and remained on him. Pentecostals see here that Jesus' baptism in water and the descent of the Spirit were two distinct and separate events. We note a parallel here to the fact that prayer and praise often preceded the believers' baptism in the Holy Spirit (Luke 24:53; Acts 1:14; 4:24; 8:15; 10:30). Jesus' experience was unique, of course, for God gave him the Spirit without limit (John 3:34). Yet the Holy Spirit does come on us to stay, and he comes on us from the Father (vv. 16, 26).

By being baptized in the Jordan, Jesus identified with humanity. Then, when the Spirit came on him, he continued to submit to the Spirit's leading, first by being led (Mark says, "driven out"; Gk. ekballei) into the desert to be tempted by the devil, then by going in the power of the Spirit into Galilee for ministry (Luke 4:14). At Nazareth he made it clear that his ministry was fulfilling the prophecy of Isaiah 61:1–2. Later Matthew recognized that his healings fulfilled the ministry of the Spirit-anointed servant of Isaiah 42:1–4 (Matt. 12:15–21). Luke records also how Jesus was "full of joy through the Holy Spirit" when he saw how his disciples were responding to the truth (Luke 10:21).

Even the enemies of Jesus recognized that he had supernatural power, but they refused to believe his power was divine. Instead, they deliberately tried to discredit Jesus by attributing his power to the devil. Jesus met their challenge first by pointing out that a disunited kingdom is laid waste and a disunited city or house will not stand. If Satan's kingdom is disunited, with Satan casting out Satan, how can his kingdom stand?

But if Jesus was casting out demons by the Spirit of God, then the kingdom or rule of God was actually in operation in the people's behalf. Luke used the expression "the finger of God" in referring to the Spirit of God. The OT often used the hand of God for the power or the Spirit of God. Jesus, no doubt, used both expressions for the power of the Spirit. Then he gave a warning about blasphemy against the Holy Spirit.

The warning is serious, but most people still have a great many questions about it. W. E. Biederwolf summarized some of the interpretations (1903, 111–26). He pointed out that some identify it with the apostasy of Hebrews 6:4–6; 10:29 and say that only the regenerate can commit it.

Others say that only the unregenerate who attribute Jesus' miracles to Satan can commit this sin. John Wesley held this view. Jerome and Chrysostom went further and said that only those who did this while Jesus was on earth could be guilty. John Broadus said only those who see miracles done by the Holy Spirit and attribute them to Satan can be guilty. Because he believed the day of miracles was past, he thought no one today could be guilty.

Some people doubt that the Pharisees in Jesus' day committed this sin, since Jesus prayed on the cross, "Father, forgive them." It is hard to be sure also whether a single expression of blasphemy or a person's whole attitude is what makes him guilty. Some say it involves only the final state of the soul after continuing blasphemies. Franz Delitzsch said, "It is not the individual word of blasphemy itself, or the individual deed of blasphemous opposition, but these taken in connection with the disposition of mind which is manifested in them, that constituted the unpardonable sin" (cited in Biederwolf, 1903, 121).

It should be kept in mind also that the apostle Paul before his conversion could well have attributed the work of the Spirit through the believers to the devil. He certainly knew about Jesus (Acts 26:26), and he heard Stephen's defense. But he did these things in ignorance and was forgiven (1 Tim. 1:13).

Some Pentecostals suppose that those who say that all speaking in tongues today is of the devil have committed the unpardonable sin. But most of those who say that simply lack correct teaching. Many today still have a zeal for the Lord but say such things in ignorance (Rom. 10:2–3; 11:25). It is dangerous for us to judge their motives. Nevertheless, it is known that the devil has imitated this gift in some instances.

Jesus did more than warn, however. He gave much teaching, especially to his disciples, about the Holy Spirit. He emphasized that the Spirit is God's gift, and the Spirit brings all the good things God has for his children (Matt. 7:7–11; Luke 11:9–13). He assured them that the Spirit would be with them to anoint their ministry in every circumstance and would help them even when they would be arrested and brought to trial (Matt. 10:16–20; Mark 13:9–11; Luke 12:11–12; 21:12–15). Finally, he commissioned them to baptize believers in the name of (that is, into the worship and service of) the Father, Son, and Holy Spirit (Matt. 28:19); but they had to stay (Gk. *kathisate*, "sit") in Jerusalem until they were "clothed with power from on high" (Luke 24:49). Only then could they be his witnesses in the way and to the extent he wanted them to be (Acts 1:8).

Most of the teaching of Jesus about the Holy Spirit is recorded in John's Gospel. On three occasions he used water as a symbol of the Spirit. "Born again" (Gk. *gennēthē anōthen*) or, as the phrase also means, "born from above" is equated with "born of water" (John 3:3–8). Sacramentalists generally take the water to refer to water baptism (Hunter, 1957, 134). Others take the water to refer to physical birth. But this does not fit with the strong contrast made between natural and spiritual birth in John 1:12–13. Thus others take the water to mean the Word (John 15:3; Eph. 5:26; James 1:18; 1 Peter 1:23, 25). Yet in John's Gospel water is usually symbolic of the Spirit himself as the giver of life (John 4:10, 14; 7:37–39). Since the Greek word *kai*, "and," can also mean "even," we may take John 3:5 to mean "born of water, even the Spirit" (Horton, 1976, 116).

Jesus promised further that the Spirit whom they would later receive would be "streams of living water" flowing from within them (John 7:38–39). This looked ahead to the Day of Pentecost when the age of the Spirit began.

Jesus' final instructions before his death included much about the Holy Spirit, the Comforter (KJV) or Counselor (NIV) or Helper (NAS), whom he identified as the "Spirit of truth" (John 14:16–17, 26; 15:26; 16:13). "Helper" is probably the most common meaning of the Greek *paraklētos* (Horton, 1967, 5–8). It was most often used of a friend who became a mediator, intercessor, adviser, or helper (BAGD, 1979, 618).

Jesus himself was the first Paraclete of his disciples, for he called the Holy Spirit "another Counselor," meaning another of the same kind (John 14:16). Thus the Holy Spirit is the kind of helper for us that Jesus was for his disciples (see Mark 13:11; Rom. 8:24–26). "He is the same kind of personal friend to us on earth that Jesus now is to us in heaven" (Horton, 1976, 8). Acts 9:31 illustrates this, and the context shows that the Holy Spirit brought about the growth of the church by being the kind of teacher and helper who made the truth of Christ real in their lives and gave them the power, boldness, and encouragement that made their witness effective.

John 16:8–11 then points out that in dealing with humanity in general the Spirit would convict people of guilt with regard to sin, righteousness, and judgment. The world ignores or denies these things, showing that the essence of sin is unbelief, the true nature of righteousness is seen in Christ, and Christ's victory on Calvary's cross means that Satan and all those who follow him will surely be judged (cf. Matt. 25:41; Acts 17:31; Rom. 2:16).

After his resurrection Jesus breathed on his disciples and said, "Receive the Holy Spirit" (John 20:22). Some critics call this the Johannine Pentecost, postulating that it comes from a different tradition than Acts 2. Others suppose this was just the breath of God, symbolizing power (Johnston, 1970, 11). Still others take the breathing as prophetic of what would happen on the Day of Pentecost and believe that nothing happened at the time when Jesus gave the command (Simpson, 1895, 2:22; Richardson, 1872, 90–93; Ladd, 1974, 288–89; Cumming, 1965, 90). The language, however, is parallel to that of Genesis 2:7 and fits an actual impartation (Biederwolf, 1903, 56).

Christ's death on the cross put the new covenant into effect (Heb. 9:15–17), making the disciples a new covenant body; they were already the church, already in right relationship with the Lord. Up to this time, however, the Spirit had been *with* them, but not *in* them (John 14:17). But now they received the same measure of the Spirit that all believers still receive in regeneration.

VI. The Holy Spirit in the New Testament Church. Pentecostals emphasize the fact that Jesus intended the work of the church to be done in the power of the Holy Spirit (Acts 1:8). This power comes to individuals through the baptism in the Holy Spirit (Acts 2:4) and through the gifts the Spirit distributes to each one "just as he determines" (1 Cor. 12:11).

What we know about the baptism in the Spirit comes primarily from the Book of Acts. Some people object to the use of a historical book like Acts to establish doctrinal teaching about the Spirit. But, though Acts is indeed history, it is more than history. All through the Bible we see God coming down into the stream of human life and history to bring truth into the world's darkness. We see also that when Paul wanted to establish doctrinal teaching he did not hesitate to go back to historical passages in the OT. Thus the Book of Acts was written, not to satisfy our curiosity about the history of the early church, but to teach us the truths the church learned as believers were filled, led, and used by the Spirit.

Pentecostals use the term "baptism in the Spirit" to refer to the initial filling of the believer with the Spirit and take it to be the same empowering experience that was accompanied by the speaking in tongues on the Day of Pentecost (Acts 2:4). That experience was a pouring out of the Spirit on them (2:17, 33), a pouring out of the gift (10:45), an active taking of the gift (2:38), a falling on them (8:16; 10:44; 11:15), and a coming on them (Acts 19:6). Then in Acts 11:15–17 Peter pointed out that the experience of the Gentiles in the house of Cornelius was identical (Gk. *isēn*) to the experience of the 120 on the Day of Pentecost. He also saw it as a further fulfillment of the promise of Jesus that they would be baptized in the Spirit. Thus there were other baptisms in the Spirit after the Day of Pentecost. There is a variety of terms, but the experience was and is the same.

It is clear also that the Holy Spirit gave fresh, new fillings after the Day of Pentecost. When Peter was before the Sanhedrin, he was filled (Gk. *plēstheis*, aorist tense, indicating here a new, fresh filling) with the Spirit to meet that challenge (Acts 4:8). The same Greek word (*plēstheis*) is used in Acts 13:9, where Paul faced the challenge

of Elymas the sorcerer. Another aorist tense (*eplēsthēsan*) in Acts 4:31 indicates that the whole group of believers received a new filling to meet the challenge of the Sanhedrin's warnings.

In Acts, three of the five instances of initial reception of the Spirit mention speaking in tongues (languages different from the speaker's own), and in the other cases tongues were undoubtedly present. From this and especially from the fact that a convincing evidence was needed at the house of Cornelius and tongues was the evidence given (Acts 10:46), Pentecostals regard tongues as the initial outward evidence of the baptism in the Holy Spirit.

Some non-Pentecostals are willing to admit that from the Book of Acts it seems that speaking in tongues is the initial evidence (e.g., Ryrie, 1959, 113). But they use the question "Do all speak with tongues?" (1 Cor. 12:30) for an argument against this. "Speak" (Gk. *lalousin*), however, is a present tense that is normally continuous. Paul was simply pointing out that not all have a ministry of tongues in the assembly.

Other evidences of the baptism in the Holy Spirit will follow the experience. These include "a deeper reverence for God (Acts 2:43; Heb. 12:28); a more intense dedication and consecration to God and his Word (Acts 2:42); and an ever-increasing and more active love for Christ, for the Bible, and for the lost (Mark 16:20)" (Horton, 1976, 261).

Pentecostals emphasize that the baptism in the Spirit is an empowering experience (Acts 1:8) that is distinct from conversion as well as from water baptism. Acts 19:1–7 shows that the disciples at Ephesus were not filled with the Spirit and did not speak in tongues until after they believed and were baptized in water. Dunn (1970, 86) argues against this, saying that those who argue that the aorist participle "having believed" (Gk. *pisteusantes*) indicates action prior to the receiving of the Spirit have an inadequate grasp of the Greek grammar. However, Pentecostal and charismatic scholars have pointed out that Dunn's examples are unconvincing, and numerous passages—such as Matthew 22:25; Acts 5:10; 13:51; 16:6; and 16:24—show that the action of the aorist participle normally precedes the action of the main verb (Horton, 1976, 159–62; Ervin, 1984).

A similar distinction is seen in Ephesians 1:13, where the Greek also uses an aorist participle. It is literally "by whom [i.e., by Christ] also having believed [Gk. *pisteusantes*] by the Holy Spirit of promise. . . ." Thus the believing precedes the sealing. The sealing here indicates a present outward acknowledgement that we are the Lord's. The seal is a sign of ownership and brings the impress of Christ with the intent that Christ be formed in us (Gal. 4:19). The sealing therefore represents the baptism in the Holy Spirit and is connected with the earnest or first installment of the Spirit. That is, through the baptism in the Holy Spirit we begin to enjoy our inheritance, an inheritance that will be ours in its fullness when Jesus comes again. Those who object to this interpretation forget that the baptism in the Holy

Spirit was the normal experience of all believers in NT times.

Another controversial passage is 1 Corinthians 12:13. Some non-Pentecostals wish to translate it, "For in one Spirit also we all were baptized so as to form one body." Pentecostals point out that the Greek word *en* is used four times to mean "by" in verses 3 and 9 of the same chapter. The entire passage shows that the unity of the body is seen when the gifts are given by the one Holy Spirit. Thus the Holy Spirit baptizes the believer into the body of Christ. Then, in a distinct experience, Jesus baptizes us into the Holy Spirit.

As Pentecostal scholar Anthony D. Palma points out, "This distinction between being baptized *by* the Holy Spirit and being baptized *in* the Holy Spirit is not the result of a Pentecostal hermeneutical bias. A comparison of the translation of the preposition *en* in the major versions indicates a decided preference even by non-Pentecostals for the translation *by*" (Palma, 1980, 16; Horton, 1976, 215). This Pentecostal position has been further explained by many Pentecostal writers, including former AG general superintendents E. S. Williams and R. M. Riggs, as well as Bible teachers such as P. C. Nelson, Myer Pearlman, Donald Gee, and L. Thomas Holdcroft. Holdcroft also shows how a rejection of the Pentecostal position often leads to neglecting the Spirit's work in the life of the believer. He adds that "quite apart from the issue of tongues, it is clearly of manifest spiritual importance to enjoy a meaningful, personal baptism with the Spirit" (1967).

Paul also calls for a lifestyle in which we are filled with the Spirit (Eph. 5:18, where the Gk., present, *plērousthe*, probably indicates the repeated filling seen in the Book of Acts). It is clear also that the Spirit continues to indwell the believer whether there are special manifestations of his guidance and gifts or not. Actually, the first-century believers were marked more by faithful, everyday Christian living than by spectacular interventions. "Yet, this was no drab existence. The gifts of the Spirit and the presence of Christ were daily their portion in both work and worship. It was a life of growth in grace and in the fruit of the Spirit as well" (Horton, 1976, 256–57).

We must recognize that our new life in the Spirit puts a responsibility on us to keep putting to death our old nature and winning victories by the Spirit. "The whole work of sanctification is the work of the Spirit which receives by far the greatest attention in the NT. It takes precedence over witnessing, evangelism, giving, and every other form of Christian service" (Horton, 1976, 258; see also Dieter, 1987).

The power for service, however, comes by means of the gifts of the Spirit. These are given freely and generously. Some early Pentecostals treated the baptism in the Holy Spirit as a climactic experience, but the majority of their leaders have always recognized that it is only the beginning of a new life of service and worship. Most recognize the importance of teaching on the gifts of the Spirit.

Some insist that all gifts must fit within the classes named in 1 Corinthians 12:8–10 (Horton, 1975, 80). However, by examining the other lists (in Rom. 12:6–8; 1 Cor. 12:28–30; and Eph. 4:11) many see twenty or more gifts, all supernatural, all given by the Spirit.

The gifts have been classified in various ways. For convenience I have listed them in three groups. First, there are the gifts of Christ for establishing the church and bringing believers to maturity. These include the apostles, prophets, evangelists, and pastor-teachers of Ephesians 4:11–16. Second, there are the nine gifts of 1 Corinthians 12:8–10: the word of wisdom, the word of knowledge, faith, gifts of healing, the workings of miracles, prophecy, the discerning of spirits, kinds (families) of tongues (languages), and the interpretation of tongues. These are for the edification of the local assembly and are distributed as the Holy Spirit wills. Third are gifts of administration, ruling, ministry, giving helps, mercy, and exhortation. These contribute to service and outreach.

All the gifts are received by grace through faith. As *charismata*, they are bestowed by the grace or unmerited favor and goodness of God. "This rules out the slightest thought of any credit being due us for them or for their use, since the faith to exercise them is also from God" (Horton, 1976, 192).

In dealing with the gifts, the apostle Paul found that the believers in Corinth needed more teaching and also some correction. But before he gave specific correction he pointed them to love (Gk. *agapē*) as the governing principle for the exercise of all the gifts. There was, however, no intention in 1 Corinthians 13 to substitute love for the gifts. Love is a fruit of the Spirit. Both love and the gifts are necessary for the life and ministry of the church. The contrast is not between love and the gifts but between gifts without love and gifts with love. Love will want the assembly to be edified by the gifts. Love will want tongues to be interpreted. Love will want to see a variety of expression in order to meet a variety of needs. Love will avoid confusion and bring peace and blessing.

It is clear also that Paul did not want to stop the manifestation of the gift of tongues. Several times in 1 Corinthians 14 he indicates that the gift of tongues continues to have a place in the worship of the church as well as in the private worship of the believer. The purpose of his limitations on tongues was to give opportunity for other gifts in the public meeting, and he warned against forbidding to speak in tongues (1 Cor. 14:15, 39). Those who speak in tongues edify themselves (build themselves up spiritually) and thus are better prepared to edify others. But a variety of gifts is needed if the whole body is to be edified.

Instead of depending on human resources, Pentecostals proclaim (and should practice) a dependence on the power and gifts of the Holy Spirit. Where believers have done this, they have accomplished and are still accomplishing the impossible.

See also JESUS AND THE SPIRIT; JESUS CHRIST; SPIRIT IN SCRIPTURE.

Bibliography H. Alford, *The Greek New Testament* (1883); W. Barclay, *The Promise of the Spirit* (1960); L. Berkhof, *Systematic Theology* (1939); E. H. Bickersteth, *A Help to the Study of the Holy Spirit* (1974 reprint from 1903); A. Bittlinger, *Gifts and Graces* (1967); A. Carr, *St. Matthew* (1886); H. Carter, *Spiritual Gifts and Their Operation* (1968); G. A. Cooke, *The Book of Judges* (1918); J. E. Cumming, *Through the Eternal Spirit* (1965); M. E. Dieter, *Five Views on Sanctification* (1987); J. D. G. Dunn, *Baptism in the Holy Spirit* (1970); H. M. Ervin, *Conversion-Initiation and the Baptism in the Holy Spirit* (1986); idem, *These Are Not Drunken As Ye Suppose* (1968); D. Gee, *A New Discovery* (1932); idem, *Concerning Spiritual Gifts* (n.d.); idem, *Now That You've Been Baptized in the Spirit* (1972); R. W. Harris, *Spoken by the Spirit* (1973); L. T. Holdcroft, "Spirit Baptism: Its Nature and Chronology," *Paraclete* (Fall, 1967), 27–30; H. Horton, *The Gifts of the Spirit* (1975); S. M. Horton, "Paraclete—What Does It Mean?" *Paraclete* 1 (1967): 5–8; idem, *What the Bible Says About the Holy Spirit* (1976); A. M. Hunter, *Introducing New Testament Theology* (1957); G. Johnston, *The Spirit-Paraclete in the Gospel of John* (1970); G. E. Ladd, *A Theology of the New Testament* (1974); T. Laetsch, *The Minor Prophets* (1965); H. C. Leupold, *Exposition of Genesis*, 2 vols. (1950); A. D. Millard, "The Holy Spirit and Us," *Paraclete* 2 (1968): 20; C. C. Montefiore, *The Synoptic Gospels* (1968); A. Palma, "Baptism *by* the Spirit," *Advance* (June 1980), 16; R. Richardson, *Scriptural View of the Office of the Holy Spirit* (1872); R. Strong, *Systematic Theology* (1907); H. B. Swete, *The Holy Spirit in the New Testament* (1910); R. A. Torrey, *Person and Work of the Holy Spirit* (1974).   S. M. Horton

THE HOLY SPIRIT, DOCTRINE OF: THE ANCIENT FATHERS

I. Before the Council of Nicea
  A. The Apostolic Fathers
  B. The Early Apologists
  C. The Impact of Early Heresies on Christian Pneumatology
    1. Gnostic Religions
    2. Montanism
    3. Marcionism
    4. Dynamic and Modalistic Monarchianism
  D. The Response of Later Apologists and Polemicists
    1. Irenaeus
    2. Tertullian
    3. Two Early Christian Martyrs
    4. Clement of Alexandria
    5. Origen
    6. Novatian
    7. Hippolytus
    8. Cyprian
II. The Nicene and Post-Nicene Period (to the End of the Sixth Century)
  A. Theological Controversies and Creedal Formulae
  B. Eastern Christianity From the Fourth Through the Sixth Centuries
    1. Eusebius of Caesarea
    2. Cyril of Jerusalem
    3. Didymus the Blind
    4. Athanasius
    5. John Chrysostom
    6. Basil of Caesarea
    7. Gregory of Nyssa
    8. Gregory of Nazianzen
    9. Ephrem of Syria
    10. Narsai
    11. Pseudo-Macarius
    12. Pseudo-Dionysius the Areopagite
  C. Western Christianity From the Fourth Through the Sixth Centuries
    1. Hilary of Poitiers
    2. Ambrose
    3. Augustine of Hippo

I. Before the Council of Nicea (A.D. 325). Theological understanding of the person and work of the Holy Spirit grew slowly during the first three hundred years of the Christian era. In part, this resulted from the need to address significant christological questions. But it also can be attributed to the fact that during this period Christians suffered persecution, which made it all but impossible for leaders of the church to gather in a general council to resolve theological issues.

In addition, much of the apostolic awareness of the work of the Spirit seemingly was lost, partially because of a diminishing in both prophetic ministry and ecclesiastical emphasis on the gifts of the divine Spirit. It resulted from the inability of prophets and priests to find common goals for the church, from prophetic excess and abuse, and from an institutionalization process in which Spirit *charismata* came to be localized in the office of the bishop. It also was reserved for certain truly exceptional Christians, such as those who were to be martyred, those who became confessors (suffered persecution but were not martyred), and, by the late third and early fourth centuries, the ascetics. By default, after the late second century the most prominent exercise of the charismata was to be in heretical and fringe groups, such as the Gnostics and the Montanists.

Admittedly, during the first three Christian centuries, significant strides were taken in conceptualization of Spirit doctrine and in pneumatological definition. For example, in the writings of Tertullian, a late second-/early third-century North African father, expression is given to the distinctive personhood and work of the Spirit and to a Trinitarian understanding of God as "three in one," a concept that would eventually be adopted by the larger church in the Nicene formula. There was further definition of the salvific role of the Holy Spirit in the waters of baptism, and of his reception, first thought to occur in baptism, and later understood to be in *chrismation* (in the East) and in the laying on of hands (*baptisma Spiritus*) or confirmation (in the West). Certain of these Fathers also added significantly to the Christian conceptualization of the nature of the Godhead by more clearly defining terminology such as "Trinity" and divine "persons."

A. The Apostolic Fathers. The earliest church fathers—sometimes called "apostolic fathers" because they were thought to have known the apostles—wrote occasional pieces that responded to local contemporary needs, rather than systematic theological treatises. Their references to the Spirit do very little to define the person and office of the divine Spirit beyond that of canonical writings. Two of them (Pseudo-Clement and the writer of the *Shepherd of Hermas*) even confuse the Holy Spirit with the Son or Word of God. Others, such as Clement of Rome and Ignatius of

Antioch, speak of the Father, Son, and Spirit with a much clearer understanding of the separateness and the divine status of the Spirit.

Because prophetic ministry was still prominent in the church (according to Pseudo-Barnabas it would seem that it was even normative), the apostolic fathers were concerned to distinguish between the true and the false prophets. The *Didache* identifies false prophets as those who ask for money, stay longer than two days, and do not have "the ways of the Lord." The author of the *Shepherd of Hermas* also warns against those who use "prophecy" to collect money for themselves, give empty answers, have an earthly spirit, and attempt to gain a prominent place. The latter writer also suggests that the Holy Spirit and an evil spirit can possess a person at the same time.

Like canonical writers, Clement of Rome and Ignatius of Antioch, both bishops, claimed to be inspired by the divine Spirit to write to the churches. Both recognize the operation of spiritual gifts among average Christians, although this is tempered by their stress on the importance of obedience to the bishop. Ignatius writes to yet another bishop, Polycarp of Smyrna, encouraging him to pray that he would be deficient in nothing and might abound in all gifts. The *Martyrdom of Polycarp* is the first noncanonical work to recognize the support given by the Spirit to martyrs. It also includes the first doxology outside of Scripture in which the Holy Spirit is exalted with the Father and the Son.

B. The Early Apologists.

Struggling to defend the church against pagan Roman attacks, the apologists made the first attempt to conceptualize and interpret Christian theology with the tools of classical philosophy. They were so concerned with christology—especially Logos theology—that they gave little place to the Holy Spirit. Perhaps because of inadequate vocabulary, but certainly because of undeveloped Trinitarian concepts, they, like certain of the apostolic fathers, used the term *spirit* to express the preexistent nature both of Christ and of the divine Third Person. They occasionally used the term to denote all three Persons.

In fairness, however, it should be pointed out that the apologists were actually experimenting with vocabulary, an effort that was eventually to result in the more adequate expression of emerging orthodox theology. For example, Theophilus is the first Christian to apply the word *Trinity* to the Godhead. Athenagoras presents the first clearcut definition of the relationship of the Holy Spirit to the rest of the Trinity, in language that anticipates the great creedal statements of the next several centuries. (Although he labels the three as "God, Word, and Wisdom," Theophilus also refers to the Holy Spirit as "Wisdom.")

One of the tendencies of classically trained Christian apologists was to follow Platonic metaphysical systems, especially the concept of emanation, in explaining the nature of the Trinity and its interrelationships. By emanation is meant the notion that all creatures issue from the One, and eventually return to that One. In expressing the nature of the Godhead in Platonic terms, therefore, it was understandable that certain apologists, such as Justin Martyr, would introduce subordinationism—placing the Son below the Father, and the Spirit below both of the other divine persons. Another apologist of the second century, Tatian, argues against the integration of Neoplatonism into Christian thought, although he too seems to imply subordination, at least in the function of the divine persons. The same subordinationist tendency appears again in third-century Alexandria, especially in the writings of Origen, but eventually it was struck down as heresy at the councils of Nicea (325) and Constantinople (381) in the struggle against the Arians and Macedonians.

It is apparent from the early apologists that the charismata were in evidence in the second-century Christian community. Justin Martyr explains that the prophetic gifts exercised by OT figures had been transferred to Christian believers. Theophilus goes a step further, arguing that the ancient Greeks had been given similar gifts.

C. The Impact of Early Heresies on Christian Pneumatology.

Orthodoxy can exist and be so defined only in the presence of heresy—the teaching of the losing side in struggles with orthodoxy. In addition, there certainly is more reason for the mainstream church to formulate theological positions when it is threatened by opposition that it considers to be in error. So it was in the early church. Challenges from competing groups led mainstream polemicists to a clarification and systematization of basic doctrine.

1. Gnostic Religions. Perhaps the most serious challenge came from gnostic religions, which flourished from the first through the third centuries A.D., some continuing well into the Middle Ages. The Gnostics agreed on several significant tenets, including a whole system of radical dualism. They understood the spirit of each human to be unalterably divine, and the body to be evil, imprisoning the spirit that had not received special revelation. Salvation to the "Christian Gnostic" was not through the sacrificial death of Christ but rather through a gift of higher knowledge through the Holy Spirit—quite different from a gospel view of redemption in which the Spirit works on the moral nature of man, rather than by merely enlightening his mind. Those individuals who recognize the presence of the divine Spirit within them were called pneumatics or the elect, whereas others less fortunate were identified with matter.

Individuals who received special knowledge were given gifts of the Spirit; but these were not to be shared with the common "ignorant" people, who lacked *gnosis*. Apparently these gifts included glossolalia, of which we have several written examples (although these may be merely barbarizations of language). It seems that gnostic prophets abounded, and opponents were quick to point out charlatans (e.g., Irenaeus in his account of Marcus, a follower of Valentinus).

Gnostic theologies are highly complex and allegorically expressed, although little attempt is made to articulate the nature of God who is understood to be incomprehensible. Both the Son and the Spirit are viewed as emanations, which by definition subordinates them to the Father. Several times in gnostic texts, the Holy Spirit is referred to as the divine mother. Again, Christ is said to have been born of a virgin—the Holy Spirit. Whoever becomes a gnostic Christian is said to have gained both a father (God the Father) and a mother—the Spirit of God.

Several sacraments are present in Christian Gnosticism, including baptism, Eucharist, unction, sealing, and bridal chamber. The unction of the Holy Spirit is of a higher order than traditional sacraments, and anointing by the Spirit is valued above baptism.

It can be assumed that antagonism to the Gnostics led the mainline church to fear anyone who claimed a "special knowledge" or "revelation." Thus the place of the prophet was diminished, with more authority placed into the hands of the priest.

2. *Montanism*. If Gnosticism was damaging to the influence of those who claimed prophetic gifts within the broader church, a derivative of Gnosticism in Asia Minor, Montanism, proved to be fatal. About A.D. 155, Montanus, a former priest of Cybele who had converted to Christianity, began to prophesy in his new context. His prophecies gained immediate attention, in part because of his manner of delivery—he was said to have lost control of himself, fallen into a sort of frenzy and ecstasy, and raved, babbled, and uttered strange things (certain Pentecostal historians take this to be glossolalia), and prophesied in a manner contrary to established custom. He was joined by two prophetesses, Maximilla and Priscilla (or Prisca), who deserted their husbands with Montanus' sanction, and claimed the same prophetic gifts their founder enjoyed. (Apparently Montanist women continued to exercise a prophetic gift after the death of these three, for Tertullian, himself a convert to Montanism, tells of an early third-century woman who fell into ecstasy during services but did not deliver her prophetic message until the congregation had departed.)

All three of these early Montanist leaders believed that their prophecies would be God's final word to man. Montanus identified a new holy place—Pepuza in Phrygia—where Christ would return, and gathered his followers to await that event. The Montanists believed that the Old and New Testaments were superseded by the new prophecies, which were put into written form (all of these writings soon disappeared, probably as the result of the persecution meted out on the Montanists). The authority of the mainline Catholic church as well as its avenues for imparting grace were rejected, to be replaced by the authority of the new prophets and a new and more demanding discipline. They practiced a perfectionist lifestyle with a new extreme of intolerant exclusiveness. The product was a legalistic requirement of additional fasting, rejection of second marriages, and promotion of other forms of self-denial and unreserved preparation for martyrdom.

Intolerance was answered by intolerance. But the mainline church was impotent to wipe out the new prophecy until it was itself legitimatized by the state. From the beginning of the fourth century, however, the Montanists suffered acute persecution by the orthodox faithful, until at last they were exterminated in the sixth century under Justinian.

Paul Tillich recognizes four effects of the victory of Christianity over Montanism: the canon was victorious against the possibility of new revelations, the traditional hierarchy was confirmed against the prophetic spirit, eschatology became less significant, and with the loss of the strict Montanist discipline, a growing laxity infected the church (Tillich, 1968, 41).

3. *Marcionism*. Marcion, a wealthy shipowner from Asia Minor who moved to Rome shortly before A.D. 140, was excommunicated from the orthodox community for his radical teachings. He proceeded to form a rival religious community. His church flourished in the late second century to the extent that the final victor in his controversy with the mainline church was in doubt.

Marcionist teachings, like those of gnostic religions, centered on radical dualism. Unlike the Gnostics, however, Marcion never claimed special gnosis and did not argue that salvation comes by knowledge as opposed to faith. He distinguished between a god of the Old Testament—the creator of matter (which was evil), and the God of love—the true God of the New Testament. As a docetist, Marcion would not allow for an Incarnation, because the very notion of a divine Redeemer participating in materiality was repugnant to him.

Rejecting the Old Testament and much of the New, Marcion was devoted to the writings of the apostle Paul, in large measure because of Paul's distinction between law and grace. Notwithstanding, Marcion seemingly found no place for the Holy Spirit, and this seems strange for someone so devoted to the apostle. He seems to have identified the Spirit of God with Christ, the giver of supernatural life.

Because of his success in winning converts, Marcion became the target of the leading Trinitarian writers in the early-second- and early-third-century church. Origen argues that Marcion could not really have been a Paulinist, because of his rejection of the Paraclete. It is impossible to experience the blessings of the gospel while at the same time rejecting the gospel. Tertullian agrees, adding that Marcion quenched the Spirit by denying ecstatic prophecy. He challenged Marcion to show that there are gifts of the Spirit functioning in his church, adding that they are fully in operation within his own true Christian community.

Marcion's rejection of the Holy Spirit prompted the ablest contemporary defenders of the faith—Irenaeus, Tertullian, and Origen—to rise in support of the church's belief in the divine third Person. In so doing, they amplified and further developed the church's doctrine of the Spirit. But they also chose to address the ongoing charismatization of the church in the late second century, a witness to the continued functioning of the Spirit through his gifts—a witness that might not otherwise be available.

4. *Dynamic and Modalistic Monarchianism*. Certain early Christians reacted against what they

considered "tritheism" in Trinitarian teachings. They stressed the "one man rule" or "monarchy" of the Father, rather than that of the Logos, whom they saw as a second god, or of a third, the Holy Spirit. These unitarians came to be known as monarchians.

Such dynamic monarchians (or adoptionists) as Theodotus of Byzantium in the West and Paul of Samosata in the East taught that Jesus was merely a man on whom the divine Spirit descended at his baptism in the Jordan River, giving him power for his messianic mission. The man Jesus was adopted and filled with the divine Logos or Spirit (qualities of God, not persons in the Godhead). But Jesus was not God.

Modalistic monarchians, such as Noetus of Smyrna, taught that God appears in different modes, in different ways. Praxeas, against whom Tertullian wrote, taught that God the Father was born through the Virgin Mary and that he, the only God, suffered and died. The leading Modalistic Monarchian was Sabellius of Libya; he believed that God changes masks throughout history, as an actor would on the stage. He appears as the Father in his functions of creating and lawgiving; he takes on the countenance of the Son in his work of redemption; and he assumes the guise of the Spirit in his work of sanctification. The one God only appears to be a Trinity.

As with the threat of Marcionism, the Monarchian challenge impelled leading Trinitarians such as Tertullian, Hippolytus, and Novatian to reflect further on the nature of the Godhead and to develop new terminology to better express these concepts. Certainly the challenge of heresy within the church led ultimately to a more adequate understanding of the divine "three in one."

D. The Response of Later Apologists and Polemicists. With the writings of the apologists who defended the church against Roman persecution and of the polemicists who guarded against false teachings, the doctrine of the Holy Spirit matured significantly during the second and third centuries. Trinitarian concepts and vocabulary developed further, and the role of the Spirit in salvation was clarified. This also was the period in which the Spirit and authority were united formally. This fusion of prophetic and priestly functions was completed under Cyprian. In turn, the institutional church allowed the charismata (1 Cor. 12) to die, rendering them powerless in the hands of others. The result was that the prophetic spirit came to center in sectarian movements. These, of course, were immediately in conflict with the institutional church.

1. Irenaeus (c. A.D. 130–202). A disciple of Polycarp of Smyrna who became bishop of Lyons in Gaul, Irenaeus was the most influential of all early church fathers. Recognizing the gnostic threat, he chose to defend the young church by giving the first systematic exposition of its beliefs. In the process, he said much about the Holy Spirit.

Reacting against the gnostic teaching of emanation, Irenaeus speaks of the Son and the Spirit as inherent in the very life of God, rather than as proceeding from the Father. His anti-Gnosticism

also led him to stress the role of the Son and the Spirit (the "Word" and the "Wisdom") in creation. Furthermore, he reacted against Marcion's depreciation of the OT by emphasizing the Spirit's inspiration of christological prophecy in the OT. Gnostic teachings that Jesus merely seemed to take on human flesh prompted Irenaeus to emphasize the Incarnation and the act of the Spirit that united the Word of God with the flesh of Jesus in the womb of Mary. This stress on the Incarnation also is in reaction to the Adoptionists, who argued that Jesus was merely a man until the Spirit descended on him at his baptism in the Jordan.

Irenaeus insists that mankind is redeemed by Christ through the regenerating power of the Holy Spirit, but not as the result of having received a special knowledge (gnosis) from God. Furthermore, the redemptive act is for all those who have faith in Christ as Savior and is not reserved for those who claim to be spiritually elite.

The bishop of Lyons recognizes the ongoing operation of the Spirit in the life of the church—a recognition far beyond other writers of the second century, with the possible exception of Tertullian. Where the church is, there is the Spirit of God; and where the Spirit of God functions, there is the church. The Christian life is an ascent to God, and the Spirit serves as the ladder.

Irenaeus also recognizes the continued operation of charismatic gifts, including prophecy, among the brethren in his own church. He warns, however, against certain false Gnostics (especially one named Marcus) who fabricated spiritual gifts to win the favor of others, especially rich women in the congregation. The only real answer to such gnostic novelty is for the truly spiritual person to hold to the apostolic tradition as handed down by the succession of Catholic bishops. Irenaeus' advice was to be followed by the Catholic church, with the result that spiritual gifts soon were located in the office of the bishop and were institutionalized in the sacraments. Although the Mass became the central Spirit experience, it usually was not known as such. When the act lost its name, the breadth of its significance was gone.

2. Tertullian (b. c. A.D. 150). Born in Carthage, Tertullian was trained as a lawyer. In mid-life he moved to Rome, where he was converted to Christianity. Later he returned to Carthage, where he began writing in support of his new faith. Attracted by the extreme asceticism of the Montanists, he broke with the Catholics in Carthage in about 207 and joined with the "New Prophecy."

The first important "pentecostal" theologian, Tertullian adds measurably to the church's understanding of the person and work of the Holy Spirit. He gives to Christianity its language of "Trinity" and of "Persons" in the Trinity. Certainly in part from his Montanist experience of the Spirit, he is able to distinguish the operation of the divine Third Person from that of the Father and the Son. They are separate in function, yet one in essence. The uniqueness of the Spirit's role is demonstrated in his salvific work. Regenerated in waters of baptism, which the Spirit sanctifies, the Christian then is anointed with the Spirit by God the Father ("blessed unction" or "chrismation"). Indeed, argues Tertullian, it is these very distinctions of personhood and function in the Godhead that separate Christianity from Judaism.

In his writings, Tertullian introduces a form of dispensationalism that argues that although the Spirit was poured out on the first-century church, it was the Montanist "New Prophets" who would be instruments in revealing the full provision of the Spirit. Spiritual insights gained through visions received by the prophets in dreams and in states of ecstasy, and the prophetic utterances that followed, become norms for his own hyperascetic teachings. He assumed that the functioning of Spirit gifts is clear evidence of the true spirituality of the Montanist movement, and he challenged the heretic Marcion to show similar evidence of the charismata.

Tertullian always felt that he was true to traditions handed down from the primitive church. As the result, he reacted against the tendency he perceived in the mainline church to live beneath the extraordinary ascetic requirements of the New Prophecy and to squelch or to institutionalize prophetic ministry. But admittedly the very force of his apologetics on behalf of the message of his prophets undoubtedly accelerated the institutionalization process he wished to abort.

3. Two Early Christian Martyrs. In A.D. 202, during the persecution by Septimius Severus, five Christians gave their lives for their faith in the arena at Carthage. These included Vivia Perpetua and her maid-servant Felicitas. Their martyrdom is recorded by an anonymous author with unmistakable Montanist leanings (perhaps Tertullian). Not only does the text suggest the importance of end-time events in the history of the church—a clear reference to the New Prophecy—but it also includes a passage describing the final moments of the two women, who face death with triumphant ecstasy (reminiscent of Polycarp of Smyrna).

The significance of this martyrology for our study is that the women's most unexpected reaction of triumphant joy is attributed to the presence of the Holy Spirit, who is understood to provide strength and comfort for those summoned to martyrdom. Here we have a recognition of the legitimate exercise of spiritual gifts by a class of believers who lived beyond the expectation of the rest of the church. This principle later would be applied to monks and virgins as well. Of course, this also implied that the charismata should not be expected to function as readily in the lives of more ordinary Christians.

4. Clement of Alexandria. With the decline of Athens, Alexandria became the intellectual capital of the late Roman Empire. Here blends of philosophy and religious belief were common. It is understandable that certain Christian writers trained in Neoplatonic thought would bring their philosophic understanding to bear on Christian theology. Clement of Alexandria (d. before A.D. 216) argued that philosophy was given by God to the Greeks for the same purpose as law had been given to the Hebrews, namely, to bring them to Christ.

When referring to God, Clement depends on Neoplatonic doctrine, which makes heavy use of negative theology (i.e., that nothing can be said directly about God, for he cannot be defined). But Neoplatonic concepts of emanation and hierarchy *are* applied to the Christian Trinity. The result is more than a hint of subordination of the Son to the Father, and of the Spirit to the other two divine Persons.

The Spirit's work is most important, however. Clement states that the believer is combined with regal gold, the Holy Spirit, in contrast with the Jews, who are silver, and the Greeks, who are a third element. The more the Christian becomes a true Gnostic, the closer (s)he will be to the light of the Spirit. All true knowledge comes from the Spirit of God. In addition, all spiritual gifts also flow from the Spirit. The perfect man or Gnostic can be distinguished by the reception of the charismata (here Clement refers to the 1 Cor. 12 list of gifts).

5. Origen. One of the greatest scholars of the ancient church, Origen was born about A.D. 185, probably in Alexandria. He became a student of Clement in the catechetical school there and eventually succeeded his mentor as head. He viewed philosophy as the prelude to an understanding of Christianity, with the Christian Scriptures as the highest object of scholarly activity.

Neoplatonism recognized God as the One, the unspeakable being from whom all other beings emanate, including intermediate beings between the One and the creatures of earth. This hierarchical concept, when applied to Christian theology, led to the subordination of the Son and the Spirit in Origen's early writings. In time, however, he seems to have become somewhat uncomfortable with this concept and more inclined by the time he wrote his great treatise, *On First Principles,* to a recognition of the equality of members in the Godhead.

Origen struggled over whether the Spirit is to be described as "generate," like the Son, or "ingenerate," like the Father. As a consequence of these speculations, he seems to be moving toward the concept of the procession of the Spirit in his later writings, but he is lacking in those terms and definitions necessary for adequate expression of these concepts. The Spirit is associated in honor and dignity with the Father and the Son, yet his work also is distinct. The chief function of the Holy Spirit is to promote holiness among believers in Christ. He *is* their holiness. He turns the human mind to the things of God and assists the faithful in apprehending spiritual truth and in promoting holiness among believers in Christ. He turns the human mind to the things of God and assists the faithful in apprehending spiritual truth and in avoiding falsehood. He leads toward spiritual maturity or perfection, although this is not gained in a moment of time, but is progressive.

Origen sought to refute claims of the pagan philosopher, Celsus, who had attempted to discredit the charisma exercised by individuals in the church. Spiritual gifts given to the apostles still were operating in Origen's day, though not to the same extent. Origen reports that evil spirits were expelled, healings did occur, and the future was foretold in his own church. He places considerable emphasis on the validating force of signs and wonders. These are to be exercised by those who are led by the Spirit, but not by all Christians.

6. *Novatian.* The third-century church had numerous "holiness" factions, including the Novatians, who vigorously denied the right of a priest or bishop to be reinstated in the event that he had apostatized (or recanted the faith) in the face of persecution. The leader, Novatian, led the group out of the Catholic church, arguing that it was contaminated by those who had given restitution.

Novatian was the first Latin writer of the Roman church. In his *Treatise Concerning the Trinity,* penned before his separation from the mother church, we find a description of the offices of the Spirit in the Old Testament and the early church—a description that is as rich as the writing of any ante-Nicene father. The church is perfected and completed by the gifts of the Spirit. While Novatian demanded a higher standard of perfection among Christians in his own day, he also recognized that such holiness is the product of the operation of the Spirit through his gifts. Where the Spirit is, the church is perfect and complete.

7. *Hippolytus.* Hippolytus of Rome (d. A.D. 136), a disciple of Irenaeus, was openly hostile to fringe and heretical groups. He struggled against the Gnostics, Marcionists, Montanists, and Monarchians. His purpose was to maintain tradition established in the first and second centuries. His primary work, the *Apostolic Tradition,* is our most detailed picture of the Roman church at the beginning of the third century. It also is a window into the exercise of spiritual gifts within the established structure of the church, though Hippolytus does not limit the operation of the Spirit to the ecclesiastical hierarchy, as Cyprian later did.

The election of the bishop was to be by Spirit-led laity and clergy alike. Hands were laid on the ordinant, and prayer was offered for the descent of the Spirit. The Holy Spirit also was poured out on the presbyter at the time of his ordination, when the bishop laid on hands and prayed. Similarly, the ordination of the deacon involved a petition for the granting of the Spirit. There was no need to lay hands on the confessor, who already had emerged triumphantly from the trials of persecution. Again, the Spirit was seen as descending on those who suffer for Christ.

If any claimed to have the gift of healing, hands did not have to be laid on them, for it would soon be apparent whether the Spirit functioned within them when they prayed for the sick. Here is clear evidence that the third-century church at Rome was acquainted with the gift of healing. Another important gift, according to Hippolytus, is that of teaching. The Spirit-led teacher's words would be profitable to the hearers, as the healer's would be to the sick. Hippolytus placed considerable emphasis on the Spirit's instruction through the Word at weekday morning gatherings. So the Spirit is functioning through the hierarchy, through gifted laity, and in the assemblies of believers. This is the last generation in the West in which it would be said that the Spirit does indeed deal directly in and through the entire church.

8. *Cyprian.* Cyprian, bishop of Carthage from A.D. 248 to 258, taught that the church is the indispensable ark of salvation. He also contended that the church exists only wherever the bishop is. But Cyprian also was strongly charismatic. Therefore, he contended that spiritual gifts are vested in the bishop, who has the sole claim to exercise the charismata.

With Cyprian the process of institutionalization of the prophetic element was completed. Office and charismata were now one. The sacraments had become the sole vehicle for the expression of spiritual gifts. And when gifts were no longer emphasized and the priesthood only rarely exercised the prophetic function outside the sacraments, the charismata fell into disuse. Only those who attempted to reach beyond their fellow Christians—monks, virgins, and radical fringe groups—kept the prophetic tradition alive.

II. The Nicene and Post-Nicene Period (to the End of the Sixth Century)

A. Theological Controversies and Creedal Formulae. The church's dark night of Roman persecution ended early in the fourth century (A.D. 303 in the West and 324 in the East). Constantine created a religious pluralism in which Christianity became one of the legitimate religions of the Empire. In 381 came the final stage in the evolution of the church from persecution to dominance when Theodosius declared the empire to be solely a Christian state.

Constantine's hopes that the church would be a uniting factor in the empire soon were dashed, because Christendom itself was deeply divided. Divisive issues became even more apparent after Christians were freed from their struggle for survival. Chief among these was the conflict over the relationship of persons in the Trinity. Neoplatonic theories of subordination led to the Arian teaching that the Son was inferior to the Father, and it eventually led to the heresy of the Macedonians—that the Holy Spirit was inferior to both Father and Son.

Arius, an Alexandrian presbyter, declared that the Son had a separate existence from the Father. He was not consubstantial (of the same essence) or coeternal with the Father. Arius did not take this reasoning to its inevitable conclusion, however. Nowhere did he declare that the Spirit was not equal to the Son.

Athanasius, a deacon and secretary to the bishop of Alexandria, vigorously opposed Arius. His case was based on the soteriological principle that no half-god could accomplish the redemption of mankind. But Athanasius still did not raise the companion question of the relationship of the Holy Spirit in the Godhead.

Emperor Constantine called the First Ecumenical Council at Nicea in 325, to deal with the Arian threat. After considerable debate the council issued a creedal statement that declared that the Son is coeternal and equal in substance with the Father. Nothing is said like that about the Spirit, however. Creedal writers were content to include the statement "And [we believe] in the Holy Ghost." Unfortunately, ecclesiastics throughout history have tended to react to present challenges to the truth rather than to anticipate areas of potential heretical growth and church division.

While Arianism officially was expelled from the empire, it reemerged in a different form in Egypt. Here a group of Arians who had come to admit the Nicene position regarding the Son, refused to recognize the Spirit in the Godhead, declaring him to be the greatest of creatures. They came to be known as "trope-mongers" (tropes are metaphors) or "Tropici," because they dismissed the Scripture that went against their position as being merely figures of speech. Their most prominent leader was the Arian bishop of Constantinople, Macedonius. So they later came to be called Macedonians. Athanasius also spoke of them as "enemies of the Spirit," or "Pneumatomachi."

Although several synods attempted to deal with the Macedonians, final action was not taken until the Second Ecumenical Council was summoned by Theodosius to meet at Constantinople in 381. The Macedonians were condemned, and a passage was added to the third article of the Nicene Creed "And [we believe] in the Holy Ghost"; namely, the terminology, "the Lord and Giver-of-Life, who proceedeth from the Father, who with the Father and the Son together is worshipped and glorified, who spake by the prophets." Thus, while the Constantinople addition to the Nicene Creed does not explicitly declare the deity of the Holy Spirit, it does so implicitly by requiring for him divine dignity and worship.

In declaring that the Spirit proceeds from the Father, the council rejected the Arian position. Unfortunately, this did not entirely settle the relation of the third Person to the Trinity. There still remained the question of his relation to the Son. By the fourth century the Greek church already was teaching a procession from the Father *through the Son,* while the Western Latin church was soon to follow Augustine's position that the procession was from the Father *and the Son (filioque).* Since the early Middle Ages, this has proven to be the most irreconcilable issue between Eastern and Western Christendom.

Still another theological controversy emerged in the East—the dispute over the natures of Christ and the relationship that the Holy Spirit bears to the incarnate Word. The central figure in this dispute was Nestorius, a monk at Antioch, who became patriarch of Constantinople in 428. He rejected the popular term used to describe the Virgin, *theotokos,* or "bearer of God," in favor of the expression *Christotokos,* or "Christbearer," or even *theodochos,* or "God-receiving." By his reasoning, the Spirit did not conceive the Logos but formed within the Virgin's womb the man who was assumed by the Word. Afterward the Spirit came down on him at baptism, glorifying him and giving him power to do miraculous works. The Spirit also gave him authority over unclean spirits and ultimately gave him the power to ascend to heaven.

Nestorius's opponents, led by Cyril of Alexandria, found in his teachings that the Logos did not truly become man and that the incarnate Son received the Spirit of God as by a superior power. In short, they accused Nestorius of radical dy-

ophisism (two natures in Christ that were not hypostatically united). Emperor Theodosius II called the Third Ecumenical Council at Ephesus in 431 to deal with Nestorianism. Nestorius was excommunicated and deposed from his see, his teachings were condemned, and the term *theotokos* was reaffirmed. The first permanent split in the history of the church resulted.

Decisions of the Council of Ephesus proved to be of critical importance, not only to an understanding of the natures of Christ but also in its treatment of the Virgin Mary and of the Holy Spirit. Paul Tillich has observed that from the very time that the Spirit was declared to be divine (at the Council of Constantinople in 381), the divine third Person was gradually replaced in popular piety by the Virgin Mary (Tillich, 1968, 78). Perhaps this can be explained in part by the institutionalization of the Spirit's gifts (third century) and by the greater emphasis on his transcendence than his immanence after the Council of Constantinople (381).

But the reaffirmation of the term *theotokos* certainly played a part in the ever-increasing veneration of the Virgin in both East and West. Remember, however, that by the post-Nicene period the Virgin had become the model in how the Holy Spirit operated in human life. So Mary was now being portrayed as the earthly locus of the Spirit (later she became known as the "spouse of the Holy Spirit").

In Eastern churches, the Spirit remained, and continues to be, an object of Christian piety. However, in the West, with but a few exceptions, the divine Spirit was never again to be as important for piety for the vast majority of Christians.

B. Eastern Christianity From the Fourth Through the Sixth Centuries.
The earliest centers of theology in the Greek East were Alexandria and Antioch. Eusebius of Caesarea, Didymus the Blind, Athanasius, and the three Cappadocians: Basil of Caesarea, Gregory of Nyssa, and Gregory of Nazianzen were leading figures in the Alexandrian school. Theodore of Mopsuestia and John Chrysostom belonged to the school of Antioch. Alexandrians tended to be Platonists and emphasized the allegorical-mystical interpretation popularized in the third century by Origen. They also emphasized the transcendence of God in which Word and Wisdom (Son and Holy Spirit) were viewed as intermediate beings between God and the world. Those in Antioch preferred Aristotle and were inclined toward a grammatical-historical explanation of Scripture.

1. Eusebius of Caesarea. The court theologian of Emperor Constantine, Eusebius (c. 260–339), was the first important Christian historian. That he was a follower of Origen is evident from his doctrine of the Trinity, in which the Son is subordinated to the Father. At the Council of Nicea he served as a mediating agent and agreed to sign the Nicene Creed, which declared the Son to be of "the same substance as the Father." Although Eusebius never became an Athanasian, he never again defended Arianism.

As a historian, Eusebius provides information on individuals who enjoyed unusual richness of life in the Spirit. One of these was a man named Quadratus, who, along with the daughters of Philip, was renowned for prophetic gifts and through whom wonderful works were accomplished by the power of the Spirit. Eusebius also tells of a Melito, bishop of Sardis, who probably lived during the reign of Marcus Aurelius (161–180). Melito was known as a prophet, as a "eunuch who lived altogether in the Holy Spirit" (*Ch. Hst.* 4.26.1; 5.24.5).

Eusebius was not so kindly disposed toward the self-styled "New Prophets" or Montanists, however. He writes of Christ's distinction between true and false prophets. The Montanists were inspired by the devil, not by the Holy Spirit, he concludes (*Ch. Hst.* 5.16.4ff.). Against the Montanists, Eusebius also gathered the witness of other writers: Asterius Urbanus, Miltiades, Apollinus, and Serapion. (*Ch. Hst.* 5.16.17–19.4)

Above all, Eusebius stands for unity in the body of Christ. Those who claim to be Spirit-directed and do not work toward this unity are anathema.

2. Cyril of Jerusalem (d. 386). The early church had developed a long and arduous process for preparing adult converts for baptism. They were enrolled as "catechumens" under the care and instruction of a teacher. By the fourth century, the forty days before Easter (i.e., Lent) had been designated for the preparation of catechumens to be baptized on Easter. The twenty-four catechetical lectures of Cyril, bishop of Jerusalem, were pastoral teachings aimed at these baptizands.

Because baptism is a sacrament of the Spirit, Cyril refers frequently to the divine third Person, although he attempts to confine himself to what is said of the Spirit in Holy Writ. Anything additional is vain, even dangerous, speculation. Such was the error of the Gnostics, Montanists, and Marcionists.

Again and again Cyril refers to the grace of the Spirit as water. By water all things exist and are renewed. Cyril draws the Eastern Christian connection between the waters of creation, the waters of deliverance (Red Sea), and the waters of recreation (the womb of Mary and the waters of baptism). In each case the Holy Spirit is the active agent.

In baptism, the Spirit is present to remit sins and to seal the believer. But he is also present to grant supernatural power, the gift of prophecy, his own presence and protection, fruits as listed in Galatians 5:22–23, and gifts of all varieties. It is interesting to note that Cyril adds the gifts of chastity, virginity, voluntary poverty, and preparation for martyrdom to scriptural lists. All spiritual gifts are antidotes for the defilement of the believer.

When the newly baptized Christian came up from the water, he was anointed with scented oil while receiving the laying on of hands. This was the sacrament of "chrismation," of which the "unction" or anointing was the most important part (in the Latin West the term *confirmation* developed later). The anointing balm introduces the presence of the Spirit in sanctifying power, and a life in the Spirit, which for Cyril was indescribably rich.

3. Didymus the Blind. Born early in the fourth century, Didymus of Alexandria lost his sight when he was only four years of age. He prayed for and received inner light, which to him more than compensated for his physical handicap. His writings on the Holy Spirit include three books on the Trinity and a separate protest against Macedonianism.

He depicts the Spirit as one with the Father and the Son—the same in honor, in operation, in divine nature, and in essence. The Three also share in function, though the Spirit has a unique operation. Through his unction the soul is strengthened so as to share in the life of God and is permitted to drink at the everlasting fountain. Baptism is the sacrament of the Spirit. Those who are martyred before baptism, having been washed with their own blood, are given divine redemption by the Spirit.

Among all Eastern fathers, Didymus appears closest to the Western doctrine of the *filioque* clause. According to his formula, the Spirit goes forth from the Father, is sent by the Son, but still is indivisibly one with the Person who sent him. The Spirit has no substance except that which is given him by the Son.

4. Athanasius (c. 296–373). The great champion of Trinitarianism, Athanasius vigorously fought Arianism—which challenged the equality of the Son to the Father—and its companion heresy, Macedonianism—which challenged the equality of the Holy Spirit to the rest of the Godhead. Present and victorious at the Council of Nicea in 325, he did not live to attend the Second Ecumenical Council at Constantinople in 381. His influence *was* present, however, through his writings and the work of his disciples.

Athanasius' arguments for the full deity and Godhead of the Spirit are based primarily on the Spirit's divine activity within the Trinity. He is what he does. He performs and exhibits characteristics that could be ascribed only to God. He is the effective principle in the Trinity who apportions to us what the Father accomplishes through the Son. The Spirit is the instrument of the Son in both creation and sanctification. The Spirit receives his mission from the Son, but he proceeds from the Father. There is no statement of double procession in Athanasius' writings.

Athanasius shows that any rejection of the full divinity of the Spirit would ruin Christianity. To deny the Spirit is to deny the very agent of grace who has been provided by the Father through the Son to sinful mankind.

5. John Chrysostom (347–407). The greatest teacher and preacher of the ancient Greek church, John Chrysostom lived as a hermit monk for six years, rose to the office of presbyter in the church at Antioch, and in 397 was chosen patriarch of Constantinople. Because of his impassioned sermons, however, Chrysostom later was banished. He died in exile.

Chrysostom's sermons emphasize the influence of the Holy Spirit on human ethical behavior. The Spirit gives life, knowledge, and Christlikeness—which is a sign to unbelievers of the validity of the gospel. The Spirit searches the heart, helps with human infirmities, and makes intercession for the saints. It is absolutely essential that the Christian listen to the voice of the Spirit.

Obviously, Chrysostom calls for character (the fruit of the Spirit), rather than for the charismata (the extraordinary gifts). Indeed, he insists that while spiritual gifts played a vital role in the beginning of the church, they have ceased. Specifically, Chrysostom declares that tongues no longer were necessary after the church was established. In this, his reasoning is similar to that of Augustine of Hippo, a Western contemporary.

6. *Basil of Caesarea* (in Cappadocia). Cappadocia, in what is now central Turkey, produced in one generation three of the greatest fathers of Eastern Christendom. These were Basil of Caesarea; his brother Gregory of Nyssa; and their associate, Gregory of Nazianzen. With the Cappadocians the doctrine of the Holy Spirit was brought to a new pitch of development. From Athanasius came their desire to define the Spirit's *homoousios*—that he is of one and the same nature with the Father and the Son. From Origen came their concern to strengthen the doctrine of the three hypostases. By restricting the term *ousia* to define the Godhead as one (essence), and *hypostasis* to that wherein the Godhead is three, the Cappadocians introduced much needed clarification into Trinitarian terminology. They also added the insight that each hypostasis indwells and reciprocates with the other two. From their synthesis came the "three in one" concept that has remained the basis of orthodoxy from the time of the Council of Constantinople (381).

Basil was born c. 330 in Caesarea of Cappadocia and was trained in Greek literature, philosophy, and oratory. He was drawn to a life of Christian asceticism and founded the monastic system in Pontus. He is best known for the Basilian rule, which remains standard for Eastern ascetics even today. His monks were encouraged to be actively involved in providing relief to Christians, pagans, and Jews alike. On the outskirts of Caesarea he built a complex of buildings to house travelers, the sick, and the poor. This later was called the Basilead.

Basil came to be known as a champion of the Spirit (and eventually, "Doctor of the Holy Spirit") from his rejection of any suggestion that the divine third Person was a created Being, and his insights into the relationship of the Spirit and the church in his writings. He endeavored to mediate differences between East and West, and even to win back semi-Arians to the Catholic fold. Therefore, he avoided dogmatic statements concerning the deity of the Spirit, concentrating instead on subtle indicators of that divinity. For example, he declares that the Spirit is not a creature, that he is no stranger to the divine nature, that he is intrinsically holy, one with the blessed divine nature and inseparable from the Father and the Son. The same glory, honor, and adoration must be given to all three Persons in the Godhead.

On the matter of procession, Basil is more direct. The Spirit proceeds out of God, not by generation like the Son, but as the breath of his mouth. Here then, is one of the classic Eastern Christian statements on procession.

But Basil's grasp of the full range of the Holy Spirit's work in the life of the believer is perhaps the most exceptional in the ancient world. As the Spirit is the conductor of the symphony of creation, so too he is the creator of the church (again a symphony operating in the harmony of the Spirit), which sanctifies all of creation through the work of the Spirit. The church is a body composed of individual members, each of whom is assigned a particular charisma by the Spirit. Edification or life in the Spirit occurs when there is mutual cooperation of its members in the exercise and participation of the individual charismata.

The charismata are not ends in themselves but instruments of virtue. No one can possess all of the charismata. But when those gifted by God live together, they reap the fruits of sharing in the gifts of the Spirit. Ministry is a charisma of the Spirit, to be exercised for the benefit of others.

Basil places earthly goods and services alongside gifts delineated by Paul under the rubric of charismata. Teachers are quickened by divine grace to provide spiritual nourishment for the hungry. Office, however, is less important to Basil than the functioning of spiritual gifts. A simple monk may spiritually lead those in high ecclesiastical position. Basil allowed one named Musonius, his junior, to preside over episcopal assemblies because of his many charismata. To become a pneumatophor—an active receptacle, carrier, and distributor of the Holy Spirit and his gifts—it is necessary first to become detached from this life. Life in the Spirit involves spiritual freedom that is worked out in a life of self-denial, discipline, and obedience. All Christians, however, are recipients of the charisma of life, the highest of all the charismata bestowed by the Spirit.

7. *Gregory of Nyssa* (b. c. 335/336). The younger brother of Basil the Great, Gregory of Nyssa was highly studious, but weak in health and shy in disposition. Against his will, he was named bishop of Nyssa by his brother. In 381 he attended the Council at Constantinople, influencing its decisions greatly and writing the additions to the Nicene Creed (including the most significant statement concerning the Holy Spirit), which were sanctioned by the council.

Gregory of Nyssa is one of the great mystics of the church. He recognized that humans are at a disadvantage in exploring the depths of the divine mystery. Notwithstanding human limitations, however, he does delve into the nature of God and particularly into the Spirit's transformation of humans into the image of God.

In defending Christianity against charges of tritheism, Gregory of Nyssa argues that when we speak of God the Father, God the Son, and God the Holy Spirit, we are not naming three Gods, for the Three share a common divine essence. We are naming three Persons in the Godhead. While the Son is the Word of God, the divine Spirit is the "Breath of God." Each Person has his individual work but does not operate separately from the other two.

Each member of the Trinity must be distinguished by origin. The One is the cause; the other two are caused. The Son is directly from the

Father, while the Spirit is from the Father through the Son—clearly the Eastern formula of procession.

Perhaps the most instructive of Gregory's teachings involve the sanctifying role of the Spirit, in transforming humankind back to the image of God. This process can be compared to an aim of ancient teachers known as *paideia*, the training of the physical and mental faculties to produce a broad enlightened and mature outlook harmoniously combined with maximum cultural development (Jaeger, 1961). This is accomplished through the sacraments or "mysteries" of the church, by participation in which the Christian grows from glory to glory in the process of "deification" (sharing in the characteristics, though not in the essence of God).

The Spirit of God transforms common or material elements—whether water, bread, wine, or oil—through his sanctifying power, so as to transform the participant in spiritual rebirth. Water becomes the agent of re-creation; bread and wine are transformed into the body and blood of Christ; and the Spirit is bestowed by anointing with the oil of chrism.

After a person has been cleansed, the Holy Spirit comes to set that soul on fire, giving the grace of his fruit. Gregory uses the symbol of a "fertile dove" for the Spirit, and his gifts are the offspring of that dove. Grace given by the Spirit increases as a person is nurtured and grows to perfect maturity. Eventually, those who hold communion with the Spirit have the assurance that he will also quicken them for life everlasting.

Gregory of Nyssa describes such a person of the Spirit, his own saintly sister, Macrina, who lived a contemplative and rigorously ascetic existence. At the end of her life she suffered intensely, but her conversation and demeanor served to lift those around her to "heavenly sanctuaries." Even through death, her advance in perfection continued on from glory to glory in the infinite and eternal realm.

8. *Gregory of Nazianzen.* A lifelong friend of Basil the Great, Gregory of Nazianzen studied in Palestine, Alexandria, and Athens before returning to his native Cappadocia. He was strongly attracted to a life of solitude but chose to live in the world under a strict ascetic rule. Basil eventually named him bishop of Sasima, and later he became archbishop of Constantinople.

Gregory's orations and homilies refer frequently to the Holy Spirit. The most important of these are his oration *On the Holy Spirit* and his sermon on Pentecost. He struggled against those who, like the Sadducees, denied the existence of the Holy Spirit and those who admitted to his existence but denied his full deity. Gregory argues that the Spirit is not contingent; that he is neither a creature nor a servant; that he is not generate or generated, but proceeds; that he is not just a second Son of God. The Spirit reveals the Son, who in turn takes us to the Father. He is the divine Person in whom we worship and through whom we pray.

Figures of speech and imagery borrowed from the world of nature are not adequate to depict relationship within the Trinity or to describe members in the Godhead. Time and again he resolves to depend on "few words" to describe the nature and work of the Spirit. He couples this economy of words with a strong distaste for irreverent inquiry, especially the tendency to become "frenzy-stricken for prying into the mystery of God" (*On the Holy Spirit* 8).

In *The Oration on Pentecost* Gregory presents a masterly account of the supernatural work of the Spirit leading up to the climax of Pentecost. He reminds the reader of the Spirit's ongoing creativity in bringing individuals in the Old and New Testaments to their ultimate potential in God. The Spirit turns the shepherd into a psalmist, fishermen into proclaimers of the gospel, and Saul into the apostle Paul. But such Spirit-activity is not simply in the past—he was equally active in Gregory own's day. Gregory also points out that, while the divine third Person *is* active in an ecclesiatical context, he is not limited to established avenues provided in the church. He works within the believer as he wills, not as humans command.

Although John baptized with water, Jesus baptizes with the Holy Spirit—and this is the perfect baptism. The Spirit moves upon the waters of baptism, thereby "deifying" the believer in baptism. And the Spirit indwells those whom he has regenerated. In *The Oration on Pentecost* Gregory presents a magnificent picture of the *koinonia* of the Spirit, especially as operating in his own life and those around him. Gregory could function fully as priest only as he lived in the Spirit. In obedience to the Spirit's beckoning he moved, he spoke, or he was silent.

He also related instances of divine healing in his time, including that of his own father and mother. He even reported that his parents had visions of his own danger during a storm at sea and prayed for his deliverance. Indeed, he confidently declared, the Holy Spirit had chosen presently to provide a wide diversity of gifts to many, bringing them together in a unity of the Spirit.

Gregory even offered a theory to explain the late development of the teaching about the Holy Spirit. He reasoned that in the Old Testament the Father is revealed and the Son hinted at. In the New Testament the Son is fully revealed, the Spirit adumbrated. The era of the church has brought the doctrine of the Spirit to full development.

9. *Ephrem of Syria* (c. 306–373). Ephrem, called "the Harp of the Spirit" by his fellow Syrians, has the distinction of being the only Syrian writer to be publicly recognized by the Western church. Although he was born to a Christian mother, his pagan father expelled him from his home in Nisibis when he found friends in the church. Tradition reports that Ephrem later founded a school at Edessa where he met with numerous disciples. But he is best remembered for his prolific writings, which include biblical commentaries, homilies, hymns, and odes.

Ephrem remained aloof from Greek modes of thought, never searching for precise definitions nor being preoccupied with areas that lie beyond the experience and capability of the human intellect. He believed that the nature of the

Godhead, the mystery of the Incarnation, the immanence of the holy in this world through the sacraments and the office of the divine Spirit, and sacred or liturgical time are beyond human probing. These subjects can be approached only by means of the languages of metaphor or symbolism and in the context of prayer and wonder. Poetry thus becomes the most appropriate tools for the practitioner of symbolic theology.

Beginning with Paul's first-Adam/second-Adam typology, Ephrem found connections between everything. What is hidden in the Old Testament is revealed in the New, and what is revealed in this world through the sacraments points to what is for us the hiddenness of God. But symbols are more than mere pointers. They are within themselves the actual presence of what they symbolize. This is possible only in the realm of sacred or liturgical time (eternity), wherein all moments in ordinary linear time converge to a single point. The participant enters sacred time through the working of the Holy Spirit, who effects the conjunction of the two times. Therefore, baptism is seen as humanity's entry into paradise, the kingdom of heaven. Participation in the Eucharist actually is involvement with the hosts of heaven (including the saints of all ages) in the marriage supper of the Lamb. By the Spirit, the "not yet" is made into the "already." For Ephrem, the Christian life is allowing the Holy Spirit to effect this entry into sacred time at every moment of life. The Spirit also removes scales from the eyes so that the Christian can recognize the world as transfigured and the kingdom of God as existing within. The Spirit is central in this blending of earth and heaven, of time with the timeless, of known with the unknown.

The nature of the Trinity and of the interrelationships of the three Persons are ineffable. Human knowledge is merely feeble twilight to that of the angels, which in turn is but a little twinkling to the knowledge of the Spirit. Ephrem argues that the Father, the Son, and the Spirit are comprehended by their names only. On the question of how one God can be three Persons, Ephrem introduces a number of symbolic triads, the most frequently used being that of flame (Father), heat (Son), and light (Spirit). Here is a one that is three and a three that is one. Similarly, wheat is composed of the root, the stalk, and the ear; each complete in itself, yet parts of the same plant.

Ephrem also articulates the doctrine of *perichoresis* or circumincession—the reciprocal being of the three Persons of the Trinity in one another. The three are blended, though not confounded; distinct, though not divided. The Spirit is not merely the love by which the Father and the Son love each other—a doctrine common in the medieval Western church. Rather, the love of one Person is common to all three. This reciprocity exists both at the transcendent level and in divine immanence. Every act of members in the Godhead is the work of the whole Trinity. For example, the Son is present in the Eucharist by the will of the Father and by the intervention of the Holy Spirit.

Spirit activity is apparent throughout the entire panorama of salvation, reaching in ordinary linear time from creation to the end of time. Yet it is seen in sacred or liturgical time as a single act. Thus the Spirit's work at creation, in which he brooded or moved on the waters, is part of the same act wherein the Spirit parted the Red Sea for the children of Israel, effected the Incarnation of the Son in the water-filled womb of Mary, and brings re-creation through waters of baptism to the Christian.

One of the most beautiful images that Ephrem employs is that of the pearl, which is used to give meaning to the Incarnation. According to ancient mythology, the pearl is created when lightning strikes the mussel in the sea. The Spirit is the fire that enters the mussel, giving birth to Christ the Great Pearl. He who dives for the pearl goes through the same process as the one who is baptized: first he strips, then is covered with oil (anointed), and finally dives into the water to find the pearl. Again at the Eucharist, Christ gives pearls beyond price—his body and blood—to the participant. The fire of the Spirit also descends to give the pearl at the *epiklēsis* (the invocation of the Holy Spirit to come to bless the bread and wine).

Early Syrian writers conceived of the Holy Spirit as feminine. This concept began to decline during the fourth century as devotion to the person of Mary grew. Ephrem is a key transition figure because he placed equally strong emphasis on both the Mother-Spirit and on Mary. There also seems to be a similar trend among most Syrian writers to move away from seeing the dove as a symbol of the Holy Spirit, transferring this imagery also to Mary. Ephrem appears to be moving in this direction, for he relates Noah's dove to Mary.

In all Syrian baptismal services the holy oil or myron is poured onto the waters shortly after the *epiklēsis* (or invocation) to the Holy Spirit. With the oil the Spirit imprints his marks on his followers. Oil depicts the image of Christ, the restoration of the "image of God" that Adam had spoiled. This is the mark of being separated out by God—a "hidden circumcision" and a symbol of the newly born Christian's holiness.

By the work of the Holy Spirit, the eucharistic participant is allowed to enter sacred time, though still living in historical time. The Spirit effects the transformation of the elements into the body and blood of Christ. For Ephrem, this is symbolic of the Spirit's work in the formation of Christ's body in Mary's womb, and of the miracle at Cana, when water was turned to wine. The fire of the Spirit is imparted through the eucharistic mystery; his divine warmth provides clothing for the otherwise naked. The Spirit crushes the icy bond of sin and the devil, bringing springtime to the church.

The Spirit's salvific provision is a continual source of amazement to Ephrem. But he also understands the created world as sacrament. Even everyday provisions, including food, cause him to wonder. To a person born of the Spirit and guided by his hand, it is possible to live in a continuous attitude of awe and praise as all things are rendered holy.

Ephrem recognizes that the Spirit's work is not limited to the sacramental mysteries as narrowly defined. He carefully guards against putting God in a box, recognizing that the Spirit's activities are beyond defining and spill over all boundaries of human expectation. To illustrate this, he shares several of his own experiences, which he had while reading the Bible. He reports that while reading the Genesis paradise narrative, he was filled with joy and was lifted up and transported into paradise itself. Here he learned unspeakable truths, even beyond those recorded by the writers of Scripture.

It was clear to Ephrem that one who heeds the Holy Spirit's prompting to seek divine riches rather than the transitory things of the earth will become a harp of the Spirit and a treasurer of his riches, speaking as a fountain of divine words and inwardly singing God's good will.

10. *Narsai* (413–c. 503). Narsai was the most profound and original thinker of the great church of the East (Assyrian, or the more familiar but less satisfactory name, Nestorian). He taught at and eventually headed the famed School of Edessa, which supplanted the School at Antioch as the center of radical dyophysitism (distinguishing sharply between the two natures of Christ). Like Ephrem of Syria, Narsai's Assyrian supporters styled him "the Harp of the Holy Spirit," though his enemies labeled him "the leper."

According to Narsai's homilies, the Holy Spirit is an eternal being, equal to the Father and the Son in essence and in the Godhead. The three Persons are three hypostases of fatherhood, generation, and procession in one God—a mystery hidden from all. The Spirit proceeds from the Father in a manner that is beyond searching and gives life—or re-creation—to those he has created.

Narsai teaches that at his baptism in the Jordan River the man Jesus received the Spirit and was anointed with hidden power so that by the Spirit he was able to banish demons and heal the sick. When Jesus died on the Cross, the Word did not share in his sufferings. The mortal vessel of flesh, built by the Spirit, fell, and the Spirit rent the sanctuary veil. But the second Adam arose and gave life to Adam and to his offspring.

The victorious King of Heaven then promised that he would open the treasury of the all-enriching Spirit. His disciples would be clad with the armor of the all-prevailing Spirit to engage in a contest against the Evil One. Consistent with his dyophysite christology, however, Narsai differentiates between the essence and the power of the Spirit (a distinction that Gregory Palamas later popularized in the Byzantine church). Narsai teaches that the Spirit who descended at Pentecost did not come in his essence or nature, but rather in his power.

At Pentecost the treasure of the Spirit was delivered into the hands of a new priesthood to dispense. By the laying on of hands, the priest receives the power of the Spirit, so that he is enabled to perform the divine mysteries. By administering the "drug of the Spirit" in the Eucharist, the priest can purge iniquity from the mind. He nourishes the faithful with this "food of the Spirit," prepared as a living sacrifice at the table of life. He summons the divine third Person to come down on the assembled congregation so that it might be worthy to receive the body and the blood. The Spirit causes the power of the Godhead to dwell in the bread and the wine, completing the mystery of the Lord's resurrection from the dead.

The priest also consecrates the bosom of the waters of baptism, and the Spirit bestows the adoption of sons and daughters on those who are baptized. Narsai likens the baptismal vat of water to a furnace in which the Spirit heats the weak clay that is the person. Then, instead of clay, the baptized emerges from the water recast as spiritual gold, with the hue of heavenly beings. The priest is a painter of the Spirit, without hands. The "drug of the Spirit" is in the water as in a furnace, to purify the image of men from uncleanness.

After baptism it behooves those who have sickness in their souls and iniquity in their thoughts to run to the priest continuously so as to receive this drug of the Spirit. The priest causes spiritual babes to grow with the Spirit's nourishment (the food of the bread and the drink of the wine). He calls for the Spirit to come down to give power to the elements, changing them into the body and blood of Christ.

Like so many other Eastern Christian mystics, Narsai placed great emphasis on the sense of awe and fear that must accompany the Spirit's work in the mysteries. This is the riches of the Spirit, the promise of the King that cannot be broken.

11. *Pseudo-Macarius* (late fourth century?).

St. Macarius of Egypt was the spiritual hero of the Egyptian monastic community in the desert of Scete. He was famed for his virtue and life of prayer (he was said to have been in a state of continual ecstasy). By the age of forty, Macarius was exercising gifts of healing and of forecasting the future. Some of his contemporaries believed that he raised a dead man for the purpose of persuading a heretic who did not acknowledge bodily resurrection.

The fifty-seven homilies, twenty dialogues, and other writings ascribed to Macarius have had a wide and lasting influence, not only on Eastern Christendom but also on the Western churches even to our day. Modern scholarship, however, has seriously questioned whether these works were in fact authored by Macarius. The issue may never be settled. What is certain is that the spirituality of the writings attributed to him is consistent with the picture of Macarius as drawn by his early biographers. They present a daily anticipation of the miraculous, a dependence on divine gifts of grace to overcome demonic forces, a deep awareness of the effects of sin, a resulting life of prayer, and an ascetic lifestyle that reaches toward an extremely high ideal of perfection.

The writings of Pseudo-Macarius represent an experiential tradition of spirituality. After experiencing evil, the penitent sinner must seek an experience of grace in which there is the gradual cessation of evil. With grace abounding in a Christian's life, the virtue and the fruit of the Spirit become as perceptible to that person as sin is. The goal of the ascetic life, then, is progress in grace, and it is the Spirit of God who is the essential maker of that progress.

Pseudo-Macarius recognized the incomprehensibleness of the transcendent God. But the greatest mystery is that the Almighty chose to reveal himself immanent to man. The Holy Spirit's power and effectual working, which is the kingdom of God on earth, was inaugurated with the advent of the Savior. Because of Christ's propitiatory sacrifice, humans can attain the heavenly kingdom. By putting off sin and putting on "the soul of the Holy Spirit" the Christian is delivered from sin and begins to grow in the Spirit's image. The Christian begins a new life in the habitation or heavenly house of the divine Spirit, and puts on Christ, the Pearl of Heaven, who cannot be worn by one who has not been begotten by the Spirit.

In his treatment of the operations of the Holy Spirit, Macarius is full of awe and exaltation. God's wealth *is* the working of the Spirit. But the Spirit's activity is not only provision. It is also metacognition or awareness of the divine process in oneself. As a royal treasury his gifts are beyond measure. He provides nourishment, repose, consolation, joy, delight, animation, and a spiritual investiture of untold beauty. These provisions will result in a Spirit-given inebriation that is ineffable.

Pseudo-Macarius, like so many other Eastern spirituals, describes the Spirit as unspeakable light. This was the brightness that shone in the face of Moses, and the brightness that became a guiding pillar of light and cloud. This light is the life of the soul. The Christian's mind is always in heavenly flame because of the indwelling light of the Spirit. All true knowledge is revealed by the Spirit, who leaves secret and unutterable impressions in the human mind. Those who are truly led by the light of the Spirit, Pseudo-Macarius said, cannot learn from another person, but in their mind should pass, by the operation of the Spirit into another age—that of the heavenly kingdom.

Gifts of the Spirit ("royal gifts") are given to those who ask. They are not to be sought after as ends in themselves, but rather they are dispensed by Christ to those who seek a life in him. Each person is adorned uniquely, each retaining his or her own personality and nature, though filled with the same Spirit. Such gifts are given so that the Christian can have power and can fly over all wickedness into the very air of the Godhead.

Pseudo-Macarius lays great stress on experiencing the indwelling Spirit of God. He is not satisfied with mere head knowledge and correct notions. Those who are children of God and born of the Spirit should anticipate a wide variety of experiences as part of their Spirit-led lives. There are times when they will be, as it were, entertained at a royal banquet, rejoicing with joy and inexpressible gladness. On other occasions, they will be like a bride reposing in communion with her bridegroom. At still other times, they become like angels without bodies, light and unencumbered in body. Sometimes they are like those inebriated with strong drink, being exhilarated and intoxicated with the Spirit, experiencing his divine and spiritual mysteries. On occasions they are in weeping and lamentation for the human race, being consumed by the love of the Spirit for humanity. Frequently they are fired by the Spirit with such love that, if it were possible, they would take every person—good or bad—into their own hearts. Sometimes they are humbled by the Spirit, or live in unspeakable joy, or in great quietness, with no sense of anything but spiritual pleasure. Occasionally, they are like a mighty champion who comes upon the enemy, defeating him with the heavenly weapons of the Spirit. But there are also times when the soul is instructed by grace in a kind of unspeakable understanding and wisdom, in things that are impossible to utter with tongue and speech. Having been considered worthy of such gifts, it is possible for one to advance toward perfection, being translated from glory to glory, and from joy to perfect joy.

Perhaps more than any other desert father, Pseudo-Macarius speaks to modern Christians because of his emphasis on personally experiencing the divine Spirit and on the growth toward perfection that results. His desert life also reminds the busy, modern church that true communion with God is possible only as an individual takes time to enter a quiet place for solitary prayer.

12. Pseudo-Dionysius the Areopagite. Pseudo-Dionysius was an anonymous author who attributed his writings to Dionysius the Areopagite, a first-century A.D. convert baptized by the apostle Paul after delivering his sermon at Mars Hill in Rome (Acts 17:34). Actually Pseudo-Dionysius was a disciple of Proclus (d. 485), whom he quotes almost word-for-word in one of his writings. He was himself first quoted by Severus at Constantinople in 533. His writings were composed, therefore, between 480 and 530. He obviously was Eastern—perhaps a monk with strong Neoplatonic training. But it is otherwise impossible to identify the author, who managed to dissociate himself from historical events, even from the christological controversies raging during his lifetime.

Elusive as his identity has been, Pseudo-Dionysius remained perhaps the most influential intellectual father and spiritual master of Christian contemplatives in both East and West for a thousand years.

Pseudo-Dionysius introduces the question of whether it is possible to know God. From there he develops his negative theology, declaring that the essence of God is beyond description and human understanding. What we do not know about things divine is what we know. We can affirm many of God's attributes, but this knowledge cannot reach to the essence of God, which transcends all of these qualities and is indescribable in its dynamic reality. Names applied to God in the Scriptures identify his attributes, but even these do not give us any understanding of his essence, which transcends all of these qualities and is indescribable in its dynamic reality.

To acquire the boundless meaning of God's nature, which is the end to which mystical contemplation leads, demands that the soul pass beyond sense experience and the operations of the intellect into "the darkness of unknowing." Here the impressions of the sense and all preconceived ideas are set aside and all the faculties are quieted. In this darkness the soul is elevated to a vision of God as light more luminous than all the stars of the universe combined. This is a transcendent level of truth achieved through the mystical life. The realization of God's inner light, this intimate union with him in a near identification with his eternal way of existence, is what Dionysius means by "deification" (sharing in his attributes, although not in his essence). This is the end of negative theology, and of the mystical steps of purgation, illumination, and perfection.

Pseudo-Dionysius' neo-Platonic system of thought is not marked by the specifically Christian revelation of God as Father, Son, and Holy Spirit. The Godhead is attributed a Trinitarian nature only as a natural expression of its supernatural fruitfulness. Because it was untenable by the fifth and sixth centuries for a Christian to deny that a difference exists within the Trinity, Pseudo-Dionysius declared that distinctions within the Godhead are essentially whatever theologians say are differences. But it is not possible either to speak or to think of what these are, because the power of human intellect is limited.

For our purposes, Dionysius is important because of his notion of a transcendentally ineffable God who can be approached experientially beyond the bounds of sense perception and reason. Because there is no place for an immanent God in Pseudo-Dionysius' celestial world, however, his writings necessarily were reinterpreted by his spiritual descendants, beginning with Maximus Confessor. Maximus makes provision for distinctions between three divine Persons who deal in human affairs, especially in the redemptive process—a God who has chosen to be revealed in the Son by the Spirit.

C. Western Christianity From the Fourth Through the Sixth Centuries. Western Christianity was saved from much of the devastation experienced in the East, devastation that resulted from its struggles against Arianism. This was due in part to the long-established Trinitarian tradition in the West (especially the formulae of Tertullian), together with the Latin emphasis on practical, nonspeculative theology and the influence of Stoicism with its stress on divine immanence—in contrast to Eastern Neoplatonic concern with divine transcendence. To be sure, all Western theologians of this period were dependent in varying degrees on Eastern writings. But when the Arian threat in the form of Germanic invaders did come to the West, it developed its own expression of Trinitarian doctrine. Augustine of Hippo accomplished for the Latin West what Athanasius and the Cappadocians gave to the Greek East: a unique synthesis of Trinitarian doctrine.

1. *Hilary of Poitiers.* Hilary, Bishop of Poitiers in Gaul, was exiled to Phrygia in Asia Minor by the Arian Emperor Constantius II. While in exile he came into contact with Eastern Christian thought, which he subsequently brought back to the West. He argued in defense of Nicene orthodoxy and Athanasius, and in so doing summarized for the West the issues at stake in the Arian controversy.

Like Athanasius, Hilary championed the deity of the Spirit. The divine third Person is at the same time the Spirit of God and the Spirit of Christ. He has the same nature as the Father and the Son. They are equal in perfection and dignity as well. The Spirit, however, remains distinct from the Father and the Son. He is a real Person within the Trinity. Yet he is beyond defining, for he is incomprehensible. It is best not to speak where Scripture is silent. Here Hilary betrays his Eastern inclinations.

On the subject of procession Hilary approached what became, with Augustine of Hippo, the Western doctrine of the *filioque*. While the Spirit proceeds from the Father *through* the Son, Hilary discounts any difference between receiving from the Son and proceeding from the Father. Therefore, his views are consistent with the *filioque* doctrine.

Hilary had a well-developed understanding of what Pentecostals and charismatics call "life in the Spirit." The Spirit sanctifies and enlightens the believer. The Holy Spirit is God's great gift to his church. In turn, various Spirit-gifts are given for edification. But in order to make full use of the great gift of the Spirit, it is essential to exercise his charismata. From Hilary's writings it is quite apparent that these were functioning in the church of his day. Hilary writes that the grace of the Spirit was revealed in a contemporary, St. Honoratus, through his prayers, his fruit, and his charismatic gifts. It is the heretics and unbelievers who lack the Spirit and consequently are led into error.

2. *Ambrose.* Ambrose, bishop of Milan, was raised in Gaul and moved to Rome, where he studied law. His success as a lawyer led to his appointment in 370 as governor of Liguria and Aemila. Four years later, with the death of the intended Arian bishop of Milan, he was elected by acclamation to the bishopric, though he was still but a catechumen. Eight days after his baptism he was consecrated bishop. Recognizing the weight of his responsibilities and his lack of theological training, Ambrose began to read heavily in the Eastern fathers—especially Athanasius, Basil, and Didymus. Like Hilary of Poitiers, therefore, he served as a carrier of the rich Eastern Christian tradition to the emerging West, laying the groundwork for his great follower, Augustine of Hippo.

Holy Scripture was for Ambrose an immense sea that does not readily reveal its secrets to the superficial observer. In order to gain a higher knowledge of God and his purpose, it is necessary to discern various layers of meaning that lie in each verse. The Holy Spirit reveals these hidden but higher truths. To a literal interpretation of Scripture, Ambrose added the allegorical, which he understood to be of a higher significance. Even the Spirit must be understood as a mystery.

Ambrose accepts the Eastern belief that water blessed by the Spirit is salvific—whether in creation, deliverance (Re[e]d Sea), the Incarnation (watery womb of Mary), or baptism. The Spirit is the stream flowing from the living fount of God, which Joel promised (2:28). In turn, from the one river of the Spirit flow many streams, representing various Spirit-gifts. He is the great Dispenser of God's blessing to the human race.

Together with the Father and the Son, the Spirit possesses certain divine properties, including power, creativity, life, and light. Members of the Godhead are one in substance and in operation and one cannot be conceived of without the others. Notwithstanding, each of the three constitutes a separate Person. The Spirit has personal characteristics that indicate his personality. For example, he is said to be grieved and tempted. He also has unique functions—he reveals, he is the Author of the Incarnation, he descends with complete power, he gives birth to the church, he is the primary link binding Christ to his church, and he infuses his gifts to individual souls.

For Ambrose, life in the Spirit begins with the sacraments. In baptism the water, the blood, and the Spirit play essential roles. The water washes, the blood redeems, and the Spirit renews and resurrects. Baptism is closely associated with the Incarnation as a watery work of re-creation.

In the Eucharist, the Spirit actualizes the mystery of salvation. Again, the Incarnation, a work of the Spirit, is actualized through the Eucharist. At the same time, the Eucharist anticipates the Resurrection, which also is a work of the Spirit.

In the sacrament of confirmation the Spirit seals the soul and provides his sevenfold gift. In ordination the Spirit provides power to the priest to forgive sins. Indeed, the very office of the priesthood is considered a gift of the Spirit.

Life itself is dependent on the Spirit of God. Where the Spirit is, there is life; where life is, there is the Holy Spirit. Through him the Christian can enjoy a more abundant life of holiness, purity, creativity, and conformity to the image of God.

3. *Augustine of Hippo.* Certainly the greatest theologian and thinker of the ancient Western church was Augustine, bishop of Hippo. Although reared in a strong Christian home by his mother, Monica, he sowed wild oats as a youth. His indiscretions resulted in a strong consciousness of the sinful nature of mankind. With his relatively negative anthropology Augustine, more than any other theologian, shaped Christian soteriology in the West. Augustine taught that all humans are cursed by original sin and are fallen to the extent that their wills are impaired. No one has more than a very limited capability of positively effecting his or her own salvation. Therefore Augustine placed great emphasis on Christ's propitiatory sacrifice on the cross. The primary salvific role of the Holy Spirit is to reprove of sins and then to forgive the penitent. Outside the church there is no Holy Spirit and no such forgiveness.

Unlike Eastern fathers who begin with the three divine hypostases and then proceed to the unity of God, Augustine begins with the unity of God and proceeds to the Persons. In part, Augustine's emphasis of unity over diversity in the Godhead is a reaction against his predecessor

in the West, Marius Victorinus, who spoke of God as "a triple being." For Augustine, the unity of the Godhead is inseparable, and there is equality in deity. The Spirit is consubstantial and coeternal with the Father and the Son. He is the Spirit of both the Father and of the Son. Augustine concludes that the Holy Spirit is the communion of divine love between the other two divine Persons—a concept that remained central to Western Catholic pneumatology from that time onward.

Because the third divine Person is the Spirit of both the Father and the Son, it follows that he proceeds from both. In this proposition, Augustine gives definitive shape to the Western church's position, which stands in contrast with the Eastern Christian concept of single procession. After 1500 years, this remains as the primary theological difference separating Western Christians from their counterparts in the East.

In an attempt to explain distinction of operation within the Trinity, Augustine likens God's Trinitarian being to the memory, intellect, and will in the human psyche. The Holy Spirit is likened to the faculty of the human will. Therefore, the Spirit of God is the energizer who renews the human moral faculty so that humankind can obey God's law, and the heavenly teacher leading humanity into all truth as Christ was the great teacher while on earth. The Spirit gives to believers a love for God which aids in the pursuit of righteousness. The very presence of the Holy Spirit is God's law written in human hearts. He is the "finger of God" reaching out to touch mankind.

The church was born of the Spirit on the Day of Pentecost. When God's great gift, the Holy Spirit, was poured out on the faithful, a new law was written on human hearts—a law of love, and not of fear. Since that time, the Spirit is received only in the church and with the imposition of hands. But whenever a person secedes from the church, the Spirit also withdraws.

The Spirit's operations in the church are many. The charismata are like stars in the sky, on which the babe in Christ must be contented to stare until able to look at the sun. But these gifts must be tested carefully, as one examines a pot to see whether it is cracked. If the gift or gifts give off a dull sound, they are not genuine. But if they ring full and clear, they are of God.

On several occasions Augustine explicitly states that the gift of tongues was only for the first-century church. Glossolalia served as a sign to the first-century unbeliever, but it was not to be expected in his own generation. Far more important than tongues is love, a gift of the Spirit that transcends time and circumstance.

Despite his rejection of tongues as an ongoing gift of the Spirit, Augustine quite readily admitted to numerous contemporary miracles. He directly related certain wonders occurring in his own church at Hippo to the "gifts of healing" mentioned by Paul in 1 Corinthians 12:9. While no one person seemed to possess a gift of healing, these miraculous recoveries involved divine intervention in response to the prayers of the Hippo congregation and those healed.

Augustine's impact on the medieval Catholic church and on evangelical Protestantism can hardly be overstated. His formulation of Western Trinitarian dogma, his conception of the Spirit as the love between the Father and the Son, and especially his articulation of the double procession of the Holy Spirit mark him as one of the most important pneumatological thinkers in Christian history.

Bibliography: J.L. Ash, "The Decline of Ecstatic Prophecy in the Early Church," *Theological Studies* 35 (June 1976): 227–52; L. Bouyer, "Charismatic Movements in History within the Church," *One in Christ* 10 (2, 1974): 148–61; B. L. Bresson, *Studies in Ecstasy* (1966); S. M. Burgess, *Reaching Beyond: Studies in the History of Perfectionism* (1986); idem, *The Holy Spirit: Eastern Christian Traditions* (1988); idem, *The Spirit and the Church: Antiquity* (1984); J. P. Burns and G. M. Fagin, *The Holy Spirit* (1984); B. de Margerie, *The Christian Trinity in History* (1982); G. S. Hendry, *The Holy Spirit in Christian Theology* (1956); A. I. C. Heron, *The Holy Spirit* (1983); W. Jaeger, *Early Christianity and Greek Poideia* (1961); B. Krivocheine, "The Holy Trinity in Greek Patristic Mystical Theology," *Sobornost* 21 (3, 1957): 462–69; W. Lewis, *Witnesses to the Holy Spirit: An Anthology* (1978); P. D. Opsahl, ed., *The Holy Spirit in the Life of the Church: From Biblical Times to the Present* (1978); F. Stagg, E. G. Hinson, and W. E. Oates, *Glossalalia: Tongue Speaking in Biblical, Historical, and Psychological Perspective* (1967); H. B. Swete, *The Holy Spirit in the Ancient Church* (1912); P. Tillich, *A History of Christian Thought* (1968); C. Williams, *The Descent of the Dove: A Short History of the Holy Spirit in the Church* (1939); G. Williams and Edith Waldvogel (Blumhofer), "A History of Speaking in Tongues and Related Gifts," in M. P. Hamilton, ed., *The Charismatic Movement* (1975).   S. M. Burgess

THE HOLY SPIRIT, DOCTRINE OF: THE MEDIEVAL CHURCHES

I. Medieval Eastern Christianity
  A. Assyrian and Non-Chalcedonian
    1. 'Abdīsho' Hazzāya
    2. Isaac of Nineveh
    3. Gregory of Narek
  B. Byzantine (Chalcedonian)
    1. Maximus the Confessor
    2. Photius
    3. Symeon the New Theologian
    4. Gregory Palamas
II. The Medieval Roman Catholic West
  A. The Eleventh Council of Toledo in 675
  B. Controversy Over the *Filioque*
  C. The Scholastics
    1. Anselm of Canterbury
    2. Peter Abelard
    3. Richard of St. Victor
    4. Peter Lombard
    5. Joachim of Fiore
    6. Thomas Aquinas
    7. Bonaventure
  D. Popular Piety in the Medieval Roman Catholic West
III. Radical Dualism
  A. Messalians
  B. Paulicians
  C. Bogomils
  D. Cathars

I. Medieval Eastern Christianity. Pneumatology has always been at the very heart of Eastern

Christian theology, certainly occupying a place much more central than in the christologically inclined West. In part this has resulted from the fact that Eastern churches from the time of the three Cappadocian fathers (Basil the Great, Gregory of Nyssa, and Gregory Nazianzen) have emphasized the uniqueness of function of the three divine hypostases, while the West, following Augustine, has tended to stress the unity of the divine nature or essence. The East, however, has balanced this concept of individuality in the Godhead by recognizing the reciprocal being (*perichoresis* or circumincession) of these hypostases in each other. No member of the triune God functions without the involvement of the other two.

Eastern pneumatology differs in emphasis as well. Because Eastern Christians have a more positive view of humanity than is found in the West, they emphasize the role of the Spirit in perfecting believers, restoring in them the image of God that was tarnished in the Fall. God the Creator re-creates humankind and all of nature. He intends for the ultimate end of humanity to be *theosis*, or "deification"—meaning that through the work of the Holy Spirit humanity becomes Godlike, sharing in divine characteristics (though not in divine essence). In contrast, the West, influenced by Tertullian and Augustine's conception of humanity's cataclysmic fall (or original sin), places greater emphasis on the sacrificial death of the Savior, with the Spirit serving as prime agent in regeneration.

Eastern and Western Christianity were divided in the early Middle Ages over the mystery of the origin or procession of the divine Spirit, and this remains the chief stumbling block in the path of their unity today. Eastern Christians almost universally declare that the Holy Spirit proceeds from the Father through the Son, while the West—at least since the ninth century—has argued that the third Person issues from the Father *and the Son* (hence the *filioque* controversy).

Numerous mystics in both Oriental and Occidental Christendom have insisted that God can be personally experienced. Eastern Christians, however, have placed a greater emphasis on sensorial perception than have their counterparts in the West. By the Spirit, spiritual eyes are enlightened, and other senses—such as those of smell, taste, and touch—are quickened. Certain Eastern mystics even contend that the Spirit is higher than all the images and representations in our creation that we experience through our senses. To these mystics God must be experienced at a level higher than natural powers can reach and human language can describe.

The East always has been inclined toward an understanding of God as transcendent. As such he is essentially unknowable and indescribable. Eastern spiritual writers, therefore, have approached these subjects by means of the language of metaphor—the use of symbolism. The symbol becomes the language of mystery, a vehicle to represent that which is other than human—of the hidden which calls out for description. Symbolic language, then, attempts to express the inexpressible as the communicator seeks to know the unknowable. It can be postulated that one of the reasons why pneumatology has remained so central a doctrine in the East is that oriental Christianity early developed a symbolic vocabulary to express both the nature and work of the Holy Spirit.

Through the centuries, Eastern Christians have also placed a greater emphasis on the gifts of the Holy Spirit—yet another means for the unknowable, infinite and undefinable God to become known to humanity. Pre-twentieth-century Western Christians traditionally have understood the gifts functioning in the church as being confined to the Isaiah 11:2 list (wisdom, understanding, counsel, might, knowledge, and fear of the Lord). Eastern Christians also have tended to incorporate the Pauline lists in 1 Corinthians 12 (word of wisdom, word of knowledge, faith, gifts of healing, prophecy, discerning of spirits, tongues, and interpretation of tongues), Romans 5 (peace, faith, hope, glory in tribulation, patience, experience, and love), Romans 12 (prophecy, ministry, teaching, exhorting, giving, ruling, and showing mercy), Ephesians 4 (apostles, prophets, evangelists, pastors, and teachers), and 2 Timothy 1 (power, love, and a sound mind).

Not only has Eastern Christianity operated from the expectation of a wider range of spiritual gifts, but also it never has ceased to be actively charismatic. Perhaps this has resulted from the fact that Eastern monasticism has always remained contemplative, and never became active, as in the Roman church. But it also seems to have stemmed from the fact that the East never was beset with the level of clericalism found in the West. Lay people until recent times assumed teaching and preaching ministries. Simple and unordained Eastern monks became recognized and venerated as Spirit-filled spiritual fathers and counselors. But above all, there simply has been a greater expectation of functioning charismata in the East.

The individuals described below are representative of Eastern Christianity during the Middle Ages (seventh through fifteenth centuries). It must be remembered that after the early eighth century, Islam quickly conquered most of their homelands. Therefore, with the exception of the Byzantine Empire, which finally succumbed to the Turks in 1453, and part of the Assyrian church, which was too far east for Islam to reach, Eastern Christians fell under the dominion of the followers of Muhammad. The most creative Christian theological writings tended to cluster in the period immediately before and just after the Islamic conquest.

A. Assyrian and Non-Chalcedonian.

1. ʿAbdīshoʿ Hazzāya. We know little about the life of ʿAbdīshoʿ Hazzāya, the great seventh-century East Syrian mystic. He wrote extensively on the nature of monastic life, on certain of the writings of Pseudo-Dionysius and Evagrius Ponticus, and about the visions of Ezekiel and of St. Gregory. In all of these works, the Holy Spirit is given a prominent place.

ʿAbdīshoʿ is most concerned with the work of the Spirit in the soul of the Christian who reaches beyond toward perfection. The divine third Person is the "treasure of life" whose power is received at baptism. Having become an heir of God, the Christian is stamped with the seal of the Spirit and is set over the treasures of the heavenly Father. Chief among these spiritual treasures is the Spirit-led rise toward perfection. The move upward from the corporeal state to purity is accomplished as the Spirit frees those in whom he dwells from human passions, entering the soul as a fiery impulse. As divine heat expands in the soul, exhaling sweet odors of a perfume that cannot be described, the person moves from darkness into light, from doubt to certainty, from the vision of corporeal things to that of intelligible things and the consciousness of the next world. Here is the kingdom of heaven, with security, peace, and joy in the Holy Spirit.

In this vision of fiery impulse or holy light, the mental faculties become intoxicated as with strong wine, and they are enraptured. The mind moves beyond thought. Mysteries and revelations that the human mind can receive spiritually only from the divine Mind are manifested. This is a sphere of incomparable light, accompanied by ecstasy and tears of joy, which flow uncontrollably. The soul is imbued with love for all of humanity, and the Spirit allows it to hear "a fine sound of glorification" that cannot be explained by human tongue.

The highest state in the rise to perfection is achieved when self is viewed not as a material body, but only as the fire in which it is clad. The human mind that reaches this sphere of perfection has no image or likeness of itself. Instead it is swallowed up in the hidden glory of the Trinity so that it is impossible to distinguish its nature from that of holy light. The soul feeds on the Holy Spirit, and there is no need of natural food. But even at this most lofty height, ʿAbdīshoʿ reminds the reader, no one can know God's essence, which resembles neither fire nor the light of the sun.

ʿAbdīshoʿ suggests that it is possible to distinguish the work of the Holy Spirit from that of a demon. The first sign of the Spirit's operation is that the love of God burns in the human heart like fire, leading to complete renunciation of the world and a love of asceticism. The second sign is the growth of true humility of the soul. The third sign is true kindness to all people—demonstrated by a gift of tears, whenever one's thoughts are extended to others. The fourth sign is true love with an ineffable vision of God as pure light. The final sign of the working of the Spirit is the illuminated vision of the mind that receives the light of the Trinity. At this stage the firmament of the heart is turned to a sapphire sky. The individual is elevated to an unutterable ecstasy from which flow spiritual speech and the gift of knowledge. Here one has a consciousness of the mysteries of future things, together with a holy smell and taste. Here one is transported into sacred or eternal time.

ʿAbdīshoʿ also identifies characteristics of being led by a demon. The demon of fornication begins by heating the body, causing the mind to be perturbed and numb. These attacks of the Evil One are to be countered by vigil and prostrations before the Cross, walking, recitation of the Psalms, and reading.

Ultimately, one must rely on a kind of spiritual intuition as an indicator of whether a given vision is from God or the enemy. If the soul contracts and the heart is afflicted, it is caused by demons. But if peace and quietness reign over the thoughts, it is certain that God's grace is working within through his Spirit.

2. *Isaac of Nineveh.* Isaac, bishop of Nineveh, in the late seventh century, is representative of the mysticism that flourished in the East Syrian church during the early centuries of Islamic domination. He was strongly influenced by the heretical Syrian dualists known as Messalians, from whom he gained an appreciation of the spirituality of experience and of a life in the Spirit. Because of his Spirit-emphasis, Isaac was something of an ecumenist, appealing to Greek Chalcedonians and Syrian non-Chalcedonians as well.

Isaac assumes that God is too hard for the intellect to grasp and scrutinize. God can be known only through spiritual knowledge, which begins with a childlike spirit that Isaac sees as part of dying to the world. Asceticism is the mother of saintliness and the beginning of spiritual knowledge. By the Spirit one lives a virtuous life, successfully struggling with passions because senses and mind are made one by the Spirit. Spiritual eyes now see the divine treasure that is hidden from the sight of the sons of flesh.

Detachment from the world results in flashes of intuition in which the soul is raised to God, enters a state of ecstasy or spiritual drunkenness, and receives the gift of tears. It is at such times that divine gifts are bestowed. Spiritual intoxication, or ecstasy, and the gift of tears are available to all who seek them, as are nightly visions, freedom from the pangs of torture, unusual warming of the body during prayer, great joy in the Holy Spirit, and wisdom and humility from the Spirit.

When a person receives the gift of the Comforter and is secretly taught by the Spirit, there is no need of material things. God's Word becomes a bottomless source of incomprehensible ecstasy and joy in God. All of God's provisions become available to the person who lives in the Spirit.

3. *Gregory of Narek.* Perhaps the most outstanding figure in Armenian literature, Gregory of Narek (Grigor Narekatsi) was born in the tenth century. After losing his mother in infancy, he entered a monastery where he was educated. He was ordained a priest and lived the rest of his life in the cloister. Gregory's fame stems not only from his writings but also from the many miracles attributed to his ministry.

Gregory stresses the three-in-one relationship of the Godhead. The Trinity is inscrutable and bathed in ineffable light, inaccessible to the highest soaring of the human intellect and beyond all limits and comparisons in quality and quantity.

While sharing in the same power and substance as the Father and the Son, the Spirit also is active by himself, with unique functions. He created the law, inspired prophets, glorified the Son, and prompted the writings of the apostles.

But the Holy Spirit continues to be active in the hearts of those who hunger after God. The eyes of the redeemed become like doves as one grows in perfection. The Spirit digs up the hardened field that is the human heart of flesh and plants spiritual seed to make it productive. Then he provides "spiritual springtime." Gregory cried out for forgiveness, so that he might be refashioned in the image of the Holy Spirit.

Gregory interjects numerous personal notes which suggest his heavy dependence on the Holy Spirit. He writes at the Spirit's direction and with his strength. He prays that the Spirit will be present with him when he speaks, so that the church will be edified. He has come to recognize that the Spirit is the true craftsman for effectiveness of ministry and for life itself.

B. Byzantine (Chalcedonian).

1. *Maximus the Confessor.* A citizen of the Byzantine Empire in the seventh century, Maximus became a champion of Orthodoxy against a wide variety of nascent heresies. Eventually he fell out of favor with the emperor and was brought to trial for his efforts. He was flogged, his tongue was plucked out, and his right hand was cut off. He died shortly thereafter (662), broken in body but not in spirit.

A prolific writer, Maximus restated and reinterpreted Pseudo-Dionysius' system, which purported to be Christian but lacked a Christocentric emphasis. Strongly influenced also by the Cappadocian fathers, he proceeded to turn apophatic or negative theology around. For him the Trinity was not simply a Christian name for the superessential Monad but the revelation of the transcendent, dynamic, and personal reality of the Godhead. The same God is both Unity and Trinity.

God creates by his consubstantial Word and Spirit out of the infinite goodness of his essence. As created, humanity enjoyed a natural disposition toward God. The fall of Adam, however, led to ignorance about God, with accompanying self-love and disorder of the soul. The human soul was disharmonized from the body, and the unity of the entire earth with its creator was undermined.

But even human beings' sins against God did not alter the fact that they were created in the divine image and likeness. It remained God's purpose that humankind be re-created and united with him. Maximus calls this "deification"—the ultimate fulfilling of humanity's capacity for God, in which it is possible to share in his characteristics, though not in his essence. The agent of re-creation is the Holy Spirit, who cooperates with the life of asceticism. Life in the Spirit is the kingdom of God, in which the human mind receives clear impressions of God and is seized by divine light and love. Human deification on earth, however, is but a momentary experience—just a glimpse of the everlasting deification, which is eternal union with the Triune God.

Maximus the Confessor served as a carrier to the Medieval East of the ideas of Origen, Evagrius, the Cappadocians, Cyril of Alexandria, and Pseudo-Dionysius. In so doing, he synthesized these various strands into mature Byzantine theology, preserving the unique Eastern understanding of the nature and office of the Holy Spirit. This he did with unusual eloquence, combining as successfully as any Christian writer the language of spirituality and the language of theology.

2. *Photius*. Best known as the great Eastern Christian champion of single procession, Photius was born early in the ninth century and passed away near its end.

At a time when relations between Byzantium and Rome were badly strained, especially over the clashes of rival missionaries in the Balkans, Photius was called on to defend the Eastern position of the single procession of the Holy Spirit. He argued this on three grounds. First, he stated that Jesus himself declared the same in John 15:26, for he clearly indicated that the Spirit would receive "from that which is mine," meaning from the Father. Secondly, the decrees of Holy Synods overwhelmingly support single procession. Finally, he based his argument on the weight of support found in the church fathers. Only a few—including Augustine, Ambrose, and Jerome—had opposed this position.

Photius argued that the Spirit would have gained nothing by proceeding from the Son that he did not already possess through his procession from the Father. Double procession actually results in the heretical doctrine of subordination, which the Macedonians taught. Again, the very immutability of the hypostatic properties necessarily founders if the Spirit proceeds from the Son. Admitting to two causes in the Trinity diminishes the majesty of the monarchy. Logically, double procession results in the Spirit's being relegated to the position of grandson.

Photius's determination to have the "truth," as he understood it, won out, and the intransigence of both sides in the controversy resulted soon after his death in a final schism between East and West (1054). The tragedy is that the controversy he engaged in is still the primary theological barrier between Orthodoxy and the West, and eleven centuries later the arguments on both sides remain much the same.

3. *Symeon the New Theologian*. Symeon (949–1022) was born in Paphlagonia in Byzantine Asia Minor and was brought by his uncle to Constantinople to finish his studies. Instead, he began a life of piety, eventually becoming a monk at the age of twenty-seven.

When he was about twenty, Symeon received his first vision of God as light. He reported that as he prayed, he was blessed with abundant tears, and everywhere experienced divine light. These visions were repeated throughout his life, including the time when he served as abbot. Because of the richness of his spiritual experiences, Symeon attempted to lead other monks to a similar ongoing and direct experience of God. Many of his fellow monks revolted against his leadership, and Stephen, archbishop of Nicomedia—the chief theologian at the emperor's court—reacted strongly against his enthusiasm or charismatic approach. Eventually Stephen and other enemies succeeded in having Symeon exiled, and, although he was later exonerated by the patriarch and the emperor, he remained in exile until his death.

Symeon was one of the most personal writers in Eastern Christian spirituality. He revealed as few others did his own interior experiences of the indwelling Trinity. He exposed both the ecstatic heights of spiritual life and the ascetical struggle that are essential features of Eastern Christian spirituality. Above all, he highlighted the cooperation in the Christian life of the Holy Spirit. For this he became famous both in his own day (when he was known as the one who possessed the true science of the Spirit) and in subsequent centuries, because he felt a call by the Spirit not only to preach but also to write.

According to Symeon, the Godhead—especially the quality of being both three and one—is ineffable. He often refers to the Trinity as light, and the Spirit as inhabiting light. Because God is luminous, he is able to make persons light as well. Because of this, it is possible to participate in the life of God in this present existence.

Symeon argued that the most dangerous heresy is to suggest that it is impossible to possess the same fullness of mystical graces as did the early church. It is possible, indeed absolutely essential, that a person have a direct personal mystical experience of God by seeing him, feeling him, and knowing the transcendent and ineffable one in an intimate relationship. This is the work of the Holy Spirit. Without him, humanity is dead now and eternally. With him, all of the treasure of the Trinity is made available, together with a full consciousness of the abiding and vivifying Spirit in the interior life. This life in the Spirit begins when a person is baptized in the Holy Spirit.

Water baptism is separate from baptism in the Holy Spirit. While the first confers the grace of the indwelling Trinity, the latter is a gateway to a greater conscious awareness that one lives in the presence of God through the illumination of the Holy Spirit. Baptism in the Spirit results in a greatly intensified experience (or sensation, knowledge, awareness, power) of the indwelling Trinity. It is not enough that Christians rationalize their faith; they must be consciously aware of divine life within, just as a pregnant woman is aware that new life stirs within her. They must feel the well of living water spring up in their souls. They must be aware that they possess divine light and be aware of its effects on them. Only a cadaver would not recognize the Spirit's presence within it.

Symeon's argument that it is necessary to consciously experience the Holy Spirit is based on the grounds that a person who is "deified" must experience this union with God just as God the Logos was conscious of becoming man. In addition this awareness is like that which the Father and the Son have in their union. And so Symeon encourages others to pursue a life in the Spirit. He also continuously pleads with God for the Holy Spirit in his own life.

There must be preparation for a baptism of the Holy Spirit. First the heart must be purified, for the Spirit cannot fill an unclean vessel. Then the Spirit begins a growth of meekness and humility, of compunction (awareness of one's guilt before God), and of penitence. Finally, there is the purification of many tears. No one ever receives the Spirit without constant tears. Tears shed in repentance flow into tears that issue in response to divine radiance.

Although Symeon's references to a "baptism of the Holy Spirit" and to "seeking the Spirit" remind the reader of modern Pentecostal and charismatic terminology, there are significant differences. Unlike Pentecostals, Symeon had no expectation that a miraculous gift of tongues would accompany the infilling of the Spirit (although he claimed to exercise tongues-speech). Rather, the Spirit's reception is accompanied by the gift of tears, an intensified sense of compunction, and an intensified conscious awareness of the divine Trinity as light dwelling within. Symeon also anticipated that the fruit of the Spirit (mentioned in Gal. 5) and other ascetical virtues would accompany the presence of the Holy Spirit, *for these also are his gifts.*

After a person receives the baptism of the Spirit, the Spirit's vivifying presence in the interior life opens the door to all divine graces (1 Cor. 2:9), which Symeon associated with *theosis* or deification of the Christian. These graces include reception of life through the sacraments. The Holy Spirit transforms the waters of baptism, as well as the bread and wine of the mystery, into life. The Spirit then gives new eyes to see the invisible world and works of God, and new ears to hear the divine voice whenever it speaks through a human voice. As a person comes to experience the Triune God as light, he or she is overcome by great spiritual joy and perception.

Symeon also prays for additional gifts of the Spirit: words of wisdom, words of knowledge, divine intelligence, direct language, strength, and power to speak. His biographer, Nicetas, tells us that he did indeed exercise these various charismata—especially gifts of knowledge, healing, and victory over demons.

Perhaps with greater fervor than any other voice in the Middle Ages, Symeon called on Christians to return to a radical living of the gospel, to the charismatic and prophetic life of the primitive church. The emphasis that he draws from Scripture on the necessity of a second baptism—that of the Spirit—is especially unique for his time. He clearly enlarged the horizons of Oriental Christian spirituality and has challenged and inspired Christians in both East and West for almost a millennium.

4. *Gregory Palamas.* Raised in a noble family close to the court of the Byzantine emperor, Gregory Palamas (1296–1359) entered monastic life at the age of twenty. He is remembered for his prolonged debate with a Greek Italian "philosopher," Barlaam the Calabrian, over the issue of whether humans could directly experience God.

Barlaam rejected the claims of the Hesychasts to spiritual knowledge of God. He insisted that only a secular education providing for the acquisition of wisdom could lead to a true knowledge of God. The hesychastic practice of continually reciting the Jesus Prayer was particularly offensive to the rationalistic Barlaam.

Gregory Palamas recognized the seeming inconsistency between a belief in the absolute transcendance of God, and Hesychasm, which was confident that an immanent God would indeed be known, experienced and in which a person could participate. To him it was imperative that he find a middle ground reconciling these seeming opposites.

Palamas' solution to this dilemma was that God cannot be known, communicated with, or participated in as he is in his essence; but he can be known, communicated with, and participated in as he is in his energies. In a sense, then, God exists in two modes and is equally present in both. Mankind can participate in the divine energies by grace and thereby share the life of God and be "deified" by participation in that life. Through his energies—the uncreated light that took on flesh in Christ Jesus, and the deifying gift of the Holy Spirit—God reveals himself positively to the spiritual senses, without losing anything of his transcendence.

Humanity was created by the energy of the whole Trinity. The first human received a created body and the divine Spirit, who is an ineffable uncreated divine energy. The Fall resulted in mankind's loss of the Spirit of God, and therefore the likeness of God also was lost. But the image remained untouched, though the loss of likeness resulted in a dimming and distorting of that image. So it was that in the Old Testament period mankind could participate in divine grace only incidentally and apocalyptically, but not permanently. Since the Incarnation, however, grace has operated permanently and has become available for participation by humanity, if the divine Spirit is received anew.

The deifying gift of the Holy Spirit is a mysterious light, which transforms into light (or transfigures) those who receive its richness, so that they shine like the sun. The human mind that is overshadowed by the energy of the Holy Spirit is driven upward by the Spirit of wisdom and becomes itself entirely radiant. The saints, as a consequence, become instruments of the Holy Spirit, having received the same energy as he has. As proof of this, Palamas cited such graces as the gifts of healing, miracles, foreknowledge, irrefutable wisdom, diverse tongues, interpretation of tongues, and the word of instruction as operating at times of intense mental prayer, and even on occasion without prayer. Palamas lays particular emphasis on the practice of "Paul's laying on of hands" for receiving such gifts.

Through the concentration of the intellect during prayer, a person may also experience ecstasy—a condition in which human powers are elevated above their natural state, so that the individual receives a vision of divine light and is received into that light. All mental activity ceases, and union with God *(theosis)* occurs.

With Gregory Palamas the Eastern Christian tradition of experiencing the absolutely transcendent God received its most accepted theoretical explanation. Palamas more than any other Oriental writer unfolded the mystery of how the incomprehensible uncreated light chose to make himself known to created humanity through his Spirit, even to the extent of transfiguring and "deifying" those created in his image and accepting his grace.

II. Medieval Roman Catholic West. Augustine's theological synthesis—which reasoned that humanity through original sin in the Garden had fallen cataclysmically so as to be wholly dependent on divine grace for salvation—resulted in a highly christological emphasis in Western medieval theology. As a result, the Holy Spirit came to be understood in Roman Catholic thought as the mutual love existing between the Father and the Son and/or as the agent of Christ in redemption. The Occident, therefore, did not place as much emphasis in general on pneumatology, especially on the unique offices of the divine Spirit, as did the Christian Orient. The Holy Spirit became "the dark side of the moon" in Western theology.

A. The Eleventh Council of Toledo in 675.
Augustine's doctrine of the double procession of the Holy Spirit was added to the Nicene-Constantinople Creed at the Eleventh Council of Toledo in 675. It spoke of the Spirit as the third Person of the Trinity, who was God coequal and consubstantial with the Father and Son, not begotten or created, but proceeding from *both* the Father *and the Son (filioque)*. The three Persons are inseparable in existence and operation but distinct in personal properties. The Father has eternality without birth, the Son eternality with birth, and the Holy Spirit eternality without birth but with procession.

Of particular signficance to our study is the statement of double procession and the declaration that the Spirit is not distinct from the Father and the Son in operation. Both clauses are markedly different from the teachings of the Christian East.

It was thought in the West that the insertion of the *filioque* clause was decisive against Arianism. There is no reason to believe that Catholic Christians had any awareness that their doctrine of double procession was an advance on earlier teaching. Little did they realize that the issue of *filioque* would remain the primary theological issue dividing East and West for the next thirteen hundred years.

The refusal to admit unique functions for the Spirit was also crucial—though few have recognized its importance. This was a natural outgrowth of the Western inclination to begin with the unity of the Godhead and then to move to the Persons, as opposed to the East, which begins with the unique qualities of the three divine Members and only then turns to qualities of unity. While the East places equal weight on each member of the Trinity, the Western position tends to relegate the Spirit to a position of lesser importance than the Son.

B. Controversy Over the Filioque.
Controversy between East and West over the procession of the Holy Spirit erupted in the early ninth century when Charlemagne attempted to have the *filioque* inserted in the Nicene Creed. Open conflict broke out between individuals of the two persuasions, who competed as missionaries in the Balkans. Soon Photius was on the offensive, declaring that the divine Spirit proceeds from the Father alone.

Writing at the request of Pope Nicholas I, Ratramnus (d. 868) maintained that the *filioque* stemmed from the very teachings of Christ and was handed down from the apostles to the Fathers. He cited Augustine in the West, and

Eastern fathers such as Athanasius, Gregory of Nazianzus, and Didymus.

In contrast, John Scotus Erigena (c. 813–891), the greatest theologian of the Carolingian Renaissance, did not champion the *filioque*. Thoroughly Neoplatonic in orientation, Scotus taught the essential oneness of philosophy and religion. He agreed with fellow Carolingians on the unity and eternity of God. The Trinity is a threefold light, a threefold goodness, three substances in one Essence—Father, Son, and Holy Spirit—one God. However, he maintained that the Spirit proceeds from *(ex)* the Father through *(per)* the begotten Son. Furthermore, because he was a Neoplatonist, it is not surprising that he broke with fellow Carolingians like Alcuin over the existence of evil. There is little room in Scotus's theology for the regenerative operation of the Holy Spirit.

There was no important Western theologian on the Holy Spirit in the tenth century. In 1054, however, the final schism between Eastern and Western Christendom occurred. Once again Western writers come to the defense of the *filioque* clause. Among these was Peter Damian (d. 1072), who argued that the Father, Son, and Holy Spirit are one in essence, but differ from one another by their originational properties. He insisted that the *filioque* must be accepted because it is taught by Scripture and the Fathers. Quoting the creed of the Eleventh Council of Toledo, Damian stated that the Spirit proceeds from both Father and Son, but he then added that this is for the sanctification of creatures.

C. The Scholastics.
1. Anselm of Canterbury. From the eleventh century to the end of the Middle Ages, the scholastics dominated Western theology. Scholasticism was not a philosophy per se, but rather an approach to all intellectual inquiry through the use of Aristotelian logic. In the area of pneumatology, scholastics attempted to defend the double procession and to work toward a solution to the very difficult question of the precise difference between the origin of the Son and the origin of the Spirit.

Anselm (1033–1109) is the first scholastic theologian of real significance. His theology of the Holy Spirit is to be found in his *Monologion*, written c. 1070 when he was abbot of Bec, and in a treatise *De Processione Spiritus Sancti*, composed at Canterbury where he became archbishop. A rationalist by approach, Anselm on the one hand takes from Augustine of Hippo his analysis of the Spirit's activities—understanding and love. On the other hand he considers of secondary importance his great spiritual ancestor's mystical concept of the Spirit as the mutual love between the Father and the Son.

For Anselm the Holy Spirit was first and foremost the love of himself proceeding from his memory and thought. This concept results from his reasoning that the supreme Spirit is capable of an act of understanding, of remembering himself, and necessarily also loving himself. This is seen as the basis for the existence of the divine third Person. In this supreme Spirit, memory is the Father, and understanding is the Son. It is therefore evident to Anselm that the Holy Spirit proceeds from both.

Notwithstanding, having found rationale for his position on double procession, Anselm concluded that the Trinity actually is a mystery beyond the human intellect. From this basis it can be argued that he actually ascribed to reason far more competence than can be justified, projecting his theological speculations much too far into the realm of the unknowable.

2. Peter Abelard. One of the greatest and certainly the most controversial of the early scholastics, Abelard (1079–1142) dealt with the Trinity as his primary subject. He began with the premise that the church's creed must be tested by reason. In reacting against his first master, Roscellin, who had tritheistic tendencies, Abelard perhaps went too far to the other extreme—that of overemphasizing the unity of the Godhead. As a result he was soon confronted with the charge of modalism—i.e., of making Persons in the Trinity into mere modes of the divine Being. This attack was characteristic of the period (and similar to many of the attacks Abelard inflicted on his opponents). But in this case it was not really fair, for he also insisted on the fullness of the personality of each divine Person.

Having emphasized the personal distinctions in the oneness of the Godhead, Abelard dwelt on the procession of the divine Spirit. It is the nature or distinctive character (*proprium*) of the Spirit to proceed from both Father and Son. Here Abelard drew special importance from Jesus' breathing of the Spirit upon the disciples, and the witness of the church fathers. Further, he reasoned that if the Spirit is eternal, his procession from the Father and the Son also must be eternal. Therefore, he must equally be the Spirit of the Son as of the Father.

Abelard became embroiled in a theological controversy with Bernard of Clairvaux (d. 1153), who insisted that Abelard the rationalist did not give sufficient place to the cross and the atonement of Christ. At the Council of Sens (1141) Abelard was condemned for heresy and put to silence. Charges against him included allegations that he rejected the omnipotence of the Son and the Holy Spirit, that he denied the consubstantiality of the Spirit with the Father, that he denied the coequality of the Spirit with the Father and the Son, and that he denied the Father's equality with the Son and Spirit in wisdom. He died the following year. Whether or not the charges against him were justified, Abelard left a heritage that has significantly influenced Western thought in medieval and modern times.

3. Richard of St. Victor. During the last half of the twelfth century, the abbey of St. Victor in Paris was a center for intense theological discussion in a climate that combined deep spirituality and a trust in the power of reason. Richard of St. Victor (d. 1172) wrote a treatise on the Trinity in which he attempted to demonstrate by means of reason the existence of the triune Godhead, including that of the second and third Persons. The perfect deity has everything, including perfect love. To be charity, love must tend to another, for charity cannot exist as private love of self. Such love implies that there is one who is personally over and against that perfect presence and who is the Son. The love that is simply given is the Father. The love that gives is the Son. But there is also a third Person: the love that receives is the Holy Spirit.

On the issue of procession, Richard argues that the third Person proceeds both from the one who was born and from the one who cannot be born. Beginning with the one who cannot be born, there is an immediate procession, that of the Love-Son, and one that is simultaneously immediate (from the Father) and mediate (from the Son), that is the Holy Spirit.

No other being or person proceeds from the Spirit, but it is through the Spirit that God as love is given to the believer and takes root in him. The Spirit, then, is best described as the divine "gift."

Interestingly, Richard suggests that his ideas are based not merely on rational deduction, but also on spiritual experience—known in part to humanity through human experiences of love. But this does not mean that Richard presents a well-rounded and full pneumatology. He offers only a definition of the triune Godhead that probably was more convincing to his own generation than to Christians today.

4. Peter Lombard. Having studied under Abelard at Paris and having been closely related to the theologians at St. Victor, Peter Lombard (d. 1160), bishop of Paris, created a systematic and traditional summary of the Christian faith that became a standard throughout the Middle Ages—the *Book of Sentences.* His reasoning on behalf of a Godhead that is united in essence and plural in Persons is based on an analogy to the human mind. Love naturally proceeds from pure intellect and its conception or idea. The Spirit then proceeds essentially from the Father and the Son. The Holy Spirit is the Spirit of both by virtue of proceeding from both.

The Holy Spirit loves by himself without the medium of any virtue; however, the divine Spirit also is the love by which people love God and their neighbors. In human existence the Spirit prompts acts of faith and love through the medium of virtues of faith and hope.

Peter Lombard became the great authority for medieval theological students in the West. This was not without challenge, however. Joachim of Fiore charged him with heresy, arguing that he actually had taught a Quaternity in God. Lombard eventually was cleared of the charge by the Fourth Lateran Council (1215), fifty years after his death.

5. Joachim of Fiore. Perhaps the most important prophetic figure of the Middle Ages, Joachim of Fiore (c. 1130–1202), had a series of visions that he believed helped him to understand the mysteries of Scripture and from which he developed a dispensational system that he applied to human history. He tried to show the historical concordance between the unfolding of history in the Old and New Testaments and in the process to understand the future.

Joachim taught that human history could be divided into three overlapping time periods: the age of the Father (from creation to Christ), the age of the Son (reaching from the ninth or seventh centuries B.C. to A.D. 1260), and the age of the Spirit (from c. A.D. 500 to the end of the world). The three ages represented ongoing spiritual progress. During the age of the Spirit, humankind and the church will be perfected, and the world will be evangelized. All humans will be brought by the Holy Spirit into religious life in which they will be inspired by the love of God to despise this world and worldly things. The purified church will be under monastic leadership. The Holy Spirit will complete the teachings of Christ and impart to each one knowledge and grace to achieve perfection and to persevere in it, walking in light and truth up to the end. The age of the Spirit, then, is to be a time of utopian perfection structured on the principles of monasticism in which the various members of Christ's mystical body will achieve great spirituality and harmony of purpose. The process of individual perfection will be completed.

A new form of free and spiritual religion will replace the obsolete ecclesiastical order, which struggles over the letter of the gospel. The spiritual person of the third age will know the truth without veil and will receive directly from the Holy Spirit all the charismatic gifts necessary for perfection.

As the institutional church will be transformed into the true spiritual church, so the kingdoms of this world will yield to the kingdom of God. This globe will then become "spiritualized" and heaven will descend upon earth.

At a certain point, however, Joachim's description of the future utopia of the Spirit seems less than clear or complete. As with most visionaries, Joachim thought he was viewing the promised land, but was not being permitted to enter it himself.

Joachim's dreams of a third age of the Spirit are reminiscent of Montanus' dreams of a new era in which the Spirit would reveal all things. They both anticipated that the future utopia would be led by ascetics, although details are radically different. Both Montanist and Joachimite prophecies failed to materialize, and followers of both Montanus and Joachim of Fiore were harshly persecuted by the mainstream church as heretics.

6. *Thomas Aquinas.* Aquinas (1224–1274) was the greatest philosopher and theologian of the medieval Western church and the "Prince of the Scholastics." He developed a synthesis of Aristotelian philosophy and Christian thought. As a rationalist, Aquinas believed that reason played an important role in understanding God and his relationship to humankind. But in delving into the nature of the Godhead and interrelationships between divine Persons, reason was limited. It was possible to reveal the unity of the divine essence through reason. But it was impossible to know rationally the distinctions of Persons in the Godhead.

Aquinas agrees with Augustine and Anselm that the Holy Spirit is the bond of love between the Father and the Son; however, he readily admits that this did not provide a sufficiently intellectual force to form a basis for organizing his treatise on the Trinity. He prefers to argue the origins of the Son and the Spirit from analogy. He begins with the premise that there are two origins in the Trinity: that of generation and that of procession. This he does by relating the intellectual acts of understanding and willing. Generation of the Son is essentially a likeness-producing act. But the Spirit proceeds by will, which is not a likeness-producing act, but instead an impulse-producing act. In sum, the Son is generated by intellect, and the Spirit proceeds by will.

On the issue of double procession, Aquinas argues that if the Spirit did not proceed from the Son, he would not be distinguished from him. As always, he deals with this question in a dialectic and highly rationalized way. The Greeks are wrong in assuming that Jesus' statement "All that the Father has is mine; therefore I said that he will take what is mine" (John 16:15) refers to his humanity. The words can be applied only to his divinity.

Although Thomas accepts the *per Filium* (double procession), he is careful to exclude any inequality in the Godhead. He also is much more concerned to affirm the unity of the hypostases than to stress their order and source of origin.

Aquinas teaches that the gift of sanctification belongs to the Holy Spirit. While the Son is the author of holiness, the divine Spirit is its sign. The Spirit makes one holy. The church is holy because the Spirit of God is present within it.

Virtues of the Christian life are strengthened by the Spirit's deep and lasting gifts (Thomas understands the Isaian list to be the permanent charismata). By spiritual gifts the believer is able to function beyond natural human means, for the mind is moved by a higher than human principle. The gifts are dispositions that make the Christian ready to grasp and follow the inspirations or promptings of the Spirit.

This is a position far removed from a purely rational moral attitude. For Aquinas morality is based on the saving and perfecting divine will, according to norms that go far beyond human reason. Gifts of the Spirit are at the service of moral and theological virtues that unite mankind to God himself ("All who are led by the Spirit are sons of God" [Rom. 8:14]).

In attempting to determine precisely how the gifts influence the practice of moral and theological virtues, Aquinas ties one gift of the Spirit and one of the beatitudes to each of the virtues. To each of these combinations he then attempts to join one of the elements of the fruit of the Spirit as listed in Galatians 5:22–23. For example, Thomas states that happiness is a great virtue—the final end of human life. Children are said to be happy because they are full of hope. The apostle Paul says that Christians are saved by hope. The Beatitudes pronounce benedictions on those who are childlike or poor in spirit. The poor in spirit are those who dwell with humility.

Aquinas distinguishes between gifts and charisms. As we have seen, gifts (Isa. 11:2–3) are permanent and are received by all Christians from the Holy Spirit, enabling them to be receptive to God. Charisms (1 Cor. 12:8–10) are temporary actions of God. For example, he distinguishes between the gift of wisdom, which is common to all individuals in a state of grace, and the charismatic gift, *sermo sapientiae*, which is extraordinary. Thomas identifies several charisms, each of which he places in a distinct category. These include revelatory or prophetic charisms—illumination, revelation, utterance under divine empowerment, and performance of miraculous signs. Speech charisms comprise tongues (preaching in other languages), interpretation of speeches (not just tongues), utterance of wisdom, and knowledge. Miracles and healings are action charisms. The highest charism is prophecy, and the highest form of prophecy is illumination.

Thomas was a supernaturalist, both theologically and experientially. In centering his discussion around the manifestation of 1 Corinthians 12:8–10 rather than on verses that speak of ministries and offices, he is in agreement with both modern Pentecostals and most early Christian thought. Unlike Pentecostals, however, Thomas believes charismata may be given by God as blessings to believers and unbelievers alike. In addition, he argues that charisms are given, not primarily to supply ecstatic experiences, as some modern Pentecostals would claim, but rather to provide divine revelatory knowledge.

We have ample evidence that Thomas personally experienced the presence of God. On one occasion he reported experiencing a transport of heavenly grace while celebrating the Mass. Again, near the end of his life, he was reported to have been in a ecstatic state for almost three days.

Unfortunately, in his own time and in the centuries that followed, Thomas Aquinas has been thought of simply as a great rationalist. As a result of this unbalanced overgeneralization, his sensitive discussion of mystical themes—such as the distinction between ordinary gifts and charisms—and his experiences in the Spirit usually have been overlooked. Certainly Aquinas did provide the great medieval Western theological synthesis, and it still speaks to modern Christians who attempt to find a balance between reason and revelation, tradition and experience.

7. Bonaventure. While Thomas Aquinas supplied a theological synthesis for Western Christendom, Bonaventure (c. 1217–74) provided a spiritual synthesis. Bonaventure was born at the time that the young Franciscan movement was beginning to gain considerable popularity. He reported being healed from a serious illness through the prayers of Francis of Assisi. This event clearly established a close bond between Bonaventure and Francis. In 1226 Francis died.

About 1234 Bonaventure went to study at the University of Paris, and in 1243 he entered the Franciscan Order. He taught for many years in Paris, eventually becoming minister general of the Order. Bonaventure proved to be a moderate leader, facing various challenges to the Franciscans.

Bonaventure's spirituality combined the mysticism and negative theology of Pseudo-Dionysius with the Franciscan devotion to the humanity and passion of Christ. His overriding purpose was to portray the journey of the inner person inward and upward into the mystery of the Triune God.

For him, the soul's journey was a growth in the Spirit—and expansion of the heart in love and the other great virtues through the three stages of purgation, illumination, and perfection.

His doctrine of the Trinity is based on the Pseudo-Dionysian principle of the self-diffusion of God. The Father is the fountain-source of divine fecundity. Out of his boundless fecundity, the Father generates his Son, expressing himself in his perfect image, his eternal Word. This fecundity issues further in the procession of the Spirit from the Father and the Son as their mutual love and the Gift in whom all other spiritual gifts are given. In turn, all creatures emanate out of God and return to God. This doctrine of emanation is the basis of Bonaventure's understanding of rational creatures as vestiges and images of divine in the soul's journey to God.

The crucified Christ was the center of Bonaventure's spiritual synthesis. Through the Cross the charity of the Holy Spirit is nourished in devout hearts and the sevenfold grace is poured out. Then the Spirit brings devotion to the crucified Christ.

Bonaventure personally wrestled with the Spirit and received that spiritual and mystical ecstasy that gives rest to the intellect and through which natural affections pass over entirely to God. In this state the very marrow of a person is inflamed by the fire of the Holy Spirit. Aware of the importance of this mystical wisdom, Bonaventure insisted that emphasis should be on unction rather than inquiry, on inner joy rather than on the tongue, on God's gift to humanity—the Holy Spirit, rather than on words and on writing.

Bonaventure had a great reverence for Francis of Assisi and the workings of the Spirit in and through him. In his biography of Francis, the saint is portrayed as a man of the Spirit. The joy of the Spirit came over him, and he was assured that all his sins had been completely forgiven. He was rapt in ecstasy and totally absorbed in a wonderful light. In this state his heart was expanded, and he saw clearly what would transpire for him and his followers in the future.

Francis learned in prayer that the presence of the Spirit for whom he longed was granted more intimately to those who invoke him and withdraw from the noise of worldly affairs. Francis was frequently lifted up by the Spirit into ecstasy beyond human understanding (also described as being "drunk in the Spirit"). On these occasions he was unaware of time and of the place and people that he passed. But these ecstasies always brought greater devotion to the crucified Christ. For Francis, to know Christ and him crucified was a gift of the Spirit.

The Spirit led Francis in establishing the Franciscan rule. Wherever Francis went, the Spirit of the Lord was with him, giving him words of sound teaching and miracles of great power. Francis directed his efforts chiefly to the exercise of those virtues that by the inspiration of the Holy Spirit he knew most pleased God. He exercised the gifts of wisdom and knowledge, bringing hidden things to light. The spirit of prophecy also was apparent in him, for he foresaw the future and had insight into the secrets of the hearts of those around him. Whatever was hidden by man was revealed to him by the Spirit. In short, he was so often moved upon by God that he seemed to live among others more like an angel than a human being.

Having been called by their leader to penance and gospel perfection, a large number of Francis' followers experienced the work of the same Spirit. One such disciple had been an abusive husband who opposed his wife's Christian commitment. Francis heard about this and assured her that her husband soon would be a comfort to her. She returned home to discover that the Holy Spirit had come upon her spouse, making him a new man. Thereafter, they both took the vow of celibacy, becoming followers of Francis.

Bonaventure reports that Francis lived so completely in the presence of the crucified Christ that late in life he miraculously also received the stigmata (the wounds of Christ). These remained with him to his death.

Bonaventure's formulating of the dynamics of growth in the Spirit has become one of the classical expressions of Western spirituality. In the fifteenth century he was given the title of Seraphic Doctor or *Doctor Devotus* (Devout Teacher) because of the extent·to which he displayed the Spirit's unction in his life and writings.

D. Popular Piety in the Medieval Roman Catholic West. Charismata, or gifts of the Spirit as described by Paul in 1 Corinthians 12, were exercised widely in the Catholic West during the Middle Ages. But most Catholic theologians taught that it was not to be expected that they would function in all believers. These were extraordinary gifts reserved for the ministries of the most pious, and so they marked the lives of the saints. For example, certain of the saints spoke in earthly languages not their own: Dominic in German, Colette in Latin and German; Clare of Monte Falcone in French; Angelus Clarenus in Greek; Stephen in Greek, Turkish, and Armenian; and Jean of the Cross in Arabic. Hildegarde is said to have written numerous books on music, the lives of saints, medicine, and devotional subjects—all in Latin, a language completely unknown to her.

Sometimes the miracle was in the hearing of the listeners: Vincent Ferrer was understood by Greeks, Germans, Sardinians, and Hungarians as he preached in Spanish. The Spanish of Louis Bertrand was comprehended by Indian natives in the Western Hemisphere. Francis Xavier's Portuguese was understood by both Japanese and Chinese.

Known cases of ecstatic utterance in an unknown tongue are far rarer. Hildegarde is said to have sung in unknown tongues to the extent that her biographer refers to these occasions as "concerts." It is reported that Francis Xavier was heard to speak the language of angels. Clare of Monte Falcone engaged in holy conversation, speaking heavenly words about heavenly things.

In at least three bulls of canonization the gift of tongues was listed among the evidences of piety that were used in support of the elevation of these individuals to the status of saints. These men were Vincent Ferrer, Francis Xavier, and Louis Bert-

rand. On the other hand, it is most curious that in the eleventh-century *Rituale Romanorum*, speaking in and interpreting unknown languages, was considered a sign of demon possession. It would seem that the orthodoxy of the individuals involved in tongues-speaking determined whether the phenomenon was viewed as a sign of sainthood or of demon possession.

Numerous other charismatic gifts were apparent in the lives of the saints. For example, St. Colette enjoyed the gift of knowledge and the gift of discernment, along with a reputation for ministering healing to lepers and raising the dead. Vincent Ferrer was famous for his prophetic gift and many miracles of healing. It was reported that Francis Xavier had a ministry of healing—ranging from deliverance from barrenness to relief from pain in childbirth. Louis Bertrand laid hands on the sick in a hospital, with the results that people regained their sanity and the dead were raised to life.

In his *Sounds of Wonder: A Popular History of Speaking in Tongues in the Catholic Tradition*, Eddie Ensley argues that, from the ninth through the sixteenth centuries, spontaneity of worship, improvised songs of jubilation, clapping of hands, and even dance movements were apparent in the lives not only of saints and mystics, but also of many ordinary believers. The word *jubilation* means spiritual inebriation. By the language of jubilation Ensley means going beyond ordinary speech into a transcendent language of praise—which he views as the equivalent of speaking in tongues.

Ensley also points to a high level of devotion to the Holy Spirit in the medieval Catholic West. This was a time when hymns to the Spirit such as "Veni, Creator" ("Come, Creator Spirit") and "Veni, Sancte Spiritus" ("Come, O Holy Spirit") were popular. Congar adds that churches were dedicated to the Holy Spirit in this period. The town of Saint-Saturnin was renamed Pont-Saint-Esprit. In the early twelfth century, confraternities of the Holy Spirit, which cared for the poor and for deserted children, appeared in the Auvergne. A brotherhood of the Holy Spirit was founded in 1177 at Benevento. Hospitals and hospices under the patronage of the Spirit appeared in numerous places, especially along pilgrimage routes.

Ensley suggests that popular devotion often took the form of spontaneity in praise and the giving of self to God and in a greater docility toward the inspirations of the Spirit. Among the faithful, there was a nearly childlike credulity about things religious, including a widespread belief in miracles. Wandering preachers were amazingly similar in preaching style to modern Pentecostals. Healing services were frequent. In a spirit of renewal, nobles and commoners often worked together as volunteers to build great cathedrals and other church structures. During such times miracles abounded, and it was common to hear group singing in the Spirit, as practiced in the present-day charismatic renewal.

III. Radical Dualism. From well before the beginning of the Christian era, perhaps even as far back as the Persian prophet Zoroaster, radical dualism has reared its deterministic head. Dualism assumes the existence of two cosmic forces—one of light or good, the other of darkness or evil—which to a greater or lesser extent control each individual. Radical dualism teaches that such control is virtually complete, leaving very little, if any, free will or individual responsibility. In Christian terms, this usually has been described as the struggle within humanity between the devil and his evil spirits and God through his Holy Spirit.

Historically, radical dualism appears in Gnosticism and its offspring: Manichaeism, Messalianism, Paulicianism, Bogomilism, and Catharism. Each of these appeared sequentially in movement from East to West. Each was considered a significant threat to the established and orthodox Christian community. In part this was a threat because radical dualism reinterpreted Christian anthropology, calling attention to the divine element within the human spirit, while depreciating the physical body as a prison for the spirit. This led as well to a reinterpretation of soteriology. Certain chosen individuals (a kind of "elect") claimed to receive special divine knowledge from the Holy Spirit for salvation. Others less "gifted" either acquiesced or were condemned by the intolerantly exclusive dualists. In all cases, radical dualists purported to exercise spiritual gifts, but because of their rejection of commonly accepted theology—especially established means of grace such as the sacraments—they were branded as heretics and often persecuted by the mainstream church.

While it would not be fair to label the majority of modern Pentecostals and charismatics as radical dualists, there *are* striking similarities. In most cases they do teach a cosmic struggle between the forces of good and evil. They stress the importance of a baptism in or with the Holy Spirit and of the exercise of supernatural gifts in order to be "victorious" in this conflict and to understand divine purposes, though they believe that these charismata are for all believers, not simply for an elect few. They often reject or minimize established order. These connections have not escaped certain Pentecostal historians, such as B. L. Bresson, who openly identifies with historic dualists.

A. Messalians. A sect probably originating in Edessa and in surrounding parts of Mesopotamia c. A.D. 360, the Messalians survived in the East until the ninth century. They also were known as Euchites, or "praying people," from the Greek translation of their oriental name (Aramaic *mezalin,* participle of *zela,* to pray), because they placed such an emphasis on individual prayer.

Christian Messalians were radical dualists, believing that every person is possessed from birth by a personal demon. Even the body of Christ had to be purified from devils by the Logos, though through glorification Christ became like the Father. They even taught that Satan and the Holy Spirit dwelt together in the individual—probably after baptism, although this is not certain.

Water baptism, the church's traditional answer to demonic forces, did not satisfy the Messalians. The individual demon must be driven out through unceasing fervent prayer and other ascetic exercises and the reception of the Holy Spirit.

The demon's departure is perceived in visual fashion by images such as smoke, black serpents, or a sow with her litter. The subsequent indwelling of the Spirit of God is perceived through sensory experiences. Sometimes the Spirit was seen to enter the soul with the appearance of an innocuous fire, and at other times the Spirit's coming is likened to sexual intercourse (Spirit-baptism as intimate communion with the heavenly Bridegroom). Experiential evidence was necessary so that it was certain that the Spirit had indeed been received. The Messalians also practiced the laying on of hands for the reception of the Spirit.

The Messalians claimed prophetic gifts by which they even knew the states of departed souls and by which they could read the hearts of individuals. It was said that when they had visions of demons, some of the people danced in order to trample the evil forces that appeared to them.

As with most dualists, the Messalians had a contempt for churches. After all, had they not personally received the Holy Spirit? Were they not especially blessed, having been freed of all sins and made perfect and superior? Their orthodox enemies reported that they lived far from perfect lives, living promiscuously, dissolving legitimate marriages, and even allowing their women a high place in their communities!

Because of their religious and social counterculturalism, the Messalians were persecuted mercilessly. The movement ceased to exist in the Eastern Mediterranean world by the ninth century. It reappeared in the Balkans, however, under the name Bogomil.

B. Paulicians. The Paulicians were radical dualists who during the early Middle Ages spread throughout Asia Minor and Armenia and finally into the Balkans. It appears that they were quite diverse in theological emphasis.

Like the Messalians, the Paulicians condemned the Christian establishment and its hierarchy, questioned a large part of its sacramentally based soteriology, rejected its Mariology, refused to venerate its saints and images, and interpreted the New Testament in an individualistic way. However, they placed a heavier emphasis on the authority of Scriptures than did the more experientially oriented Messalians.

Byzantine Paulicians appeared more Marcionist than their Armenian brothers, distinguishing between the good God of the NT and an evil God of the OT who created the world. Because they rejected as evil all of creation, especially flesh, they taught against the Incarnation and were decidedly docetic. In contrast, the Armenian Paulicians were adoptionist—stressing the humanity of Jesus.

According to *The Key of Truth,* which numerous scholars think is a handbook of Armenian Paulicians, Christ's faithful followers, who, like their Master, acquit themselves nobly, will receive the same grace of the Spirit as he. They take on themselves the same prophecy and ministry as Jesus, they preach and suffer, they yield in like manner to the Spirit as Jesus did after his baptism.

The Key also teaches that the Holy Spirit enters the catechumen immediately after the third handful of water is poured over his head in the Spirit's honor. The Spirit enters to exclude evil spirits. This is not a separate and distinct baptism of the Spirit, as the Messalians taught, however.

Like the Messalians, the Paulicians developed a two-class system. The spiritually adopted are set apart from common unbelievers or misbelievers who are dependent on the ineffectual infant baptism offered by the mainline church as the vehicle for elimination of original sin.

A well-known Paulician leader, Sergius Tychicus, who reformed the movement, had great evangelistic abilities and successes. Married people abandoned their spouses, and monks and nuns broke their monastic vows. But his opponents also claim that he exalted himself, even to the point of identifying himself with the Holy Spirit and offering himself to be worshiped. These charges are remarkably similar to those leveled against Mani, as well as against Paul of Samosata, who is thought by some scholars to have been the founder of the Paulician movement.

Byzantine Paulicians remained strong and militant in their resistance to Orthodoxy until the tenth century, when they were decimated and dispersed. Some of them amalgamated with the dualistic Bogomils of the Balkan Peninsula. In Armenia, Paulicianism seems to have lasted at least another century, eventually to be swamped by the rising tide of Islam.

C. Bogomils. The Bogomils were members of a medieval Balkan sect that originated in Bulgaria, but whose roots probably go back to Manichaeism via Paulicianism. Their name appears to mean "beloved of God."

The Bogomils taught that the devil or Satanael was the elder of the two sons of God; he fell from his lofty position and created the visible world, including mankind. In order to escape his domination, all contact with matter and especially flesh must be avoided. The Bogomils, therefore, were especially known for their extreme asceticism; they rejected lawful marriage and maintained that reproduction of the human species was a law of the demon. They also forbad the eating of meat and the drinking of wine, and the sacraments in general. They had an aversion to baptized children. The cross was called an enemy of God, churches were material creations and therefore abodes of the devil, and icons and relics were rejected. They spurned the order of priesthood, the apostolic succession, and the Orthodox hierarchy.

The Bogomils were intolerantly exclusive. True Christianity could be found only in their own communities. Hence they claimed for themselves the sole right to the name of Christians. They alone lived "according to the Spirit."

In creation when Satanael made Adam's body, he begged his Father to send down his Holy Spirit on Adam. Satanael agreed that mankind would belong to both of them. God agreed, and Adam came to life, with a corrupt body and a divine soul.

In Bogomilism, it seems that the Son and the Spirit were not distinct hypostases but different names and emanations of the Father—two rays proceeding from the lobe of his brain. In this teaching, the Bogomils seem to resemble early Sabellianism or modalistic monarchianism.

They taught that each person was inhabited by a demon. Even Christ or the Holy Spirit could not withstand their potential to harm, since the Father had not yet deprived them of their power. In this, the Bogomils differed from the Messalians, who taught that the Holy Spirit could completely fill and dominate a person.

The Bogomils, like other dualists, believed in a distinction between the "perfect" or "chosen" on one hand and the "believer" or "hearer" on the other. An elect person was considered a receptacle of the divine Spirit, and was consequently called *theotokos* or God-bearer, a name usually reserved for the Virgin Mary in the Orthodox Christian world. Having denied the incarnation of Jesus, it was Bogomil teaching that each of them as *theotokos* "gave birth to the Word" by teaching. They claimed to experience the Trinity personally and therefore no longer to be subject to the law, having been made incapable of sin.

Apparently the Bogomils had a rite of initiation called the Baptism of Christ through the Spirit, which they distinguished from water baptism. In this rite the Spirit was invoked and the Lord's Prayer sung, while the Gospel of John was placed on the head of the initiate.

Bogomilism spread rapidly in the Balkans and even in Asia Minor in the eleventh century. During the time it also passed into Italy and France, where its adherents were called Patrines or Cathari. During the thirteenth and fourteenth centuries, Bogomilism actually became the national religion of Bosnia. In the fifteenth century persecution forced many into Herzegovina, which became the final bastion of Bogomilism. The movement in the Balkans eventually was wiped out or merged into Islam.

D. Cathars. Catharism (known in France as Albigensianism) was the most powerful heresy in the medieval West. This movement seems to have grown out of Balkan Bogomilism, appearing in the West in the twelfth century and growing to such threatening proportions in the thirteenth century that it was considered the prime object of the Inquisition. It lasted until the fourteenth century when it finally succumbed to intense persecution.

As with earlier dualists, the Cathars believed that the God of the Old Testament was one of love and that he created the human soul. Therefore, humanity was in a most difficult position: the soul was spiritual and good, but the flesh was evil. So it was necessary to liberate the soul from the flesh as effectively as possible. According to the Cathars, one could escape the flesh by participating in the rite of *consolamentum* (which may have been the equivalent of the Bogomil *baptisma*) and by observing their system of radical asceticism, which they believed led to perfection.

The Cathars taught that water baptism was not profitable for salvation. Instead they believed that to enter the company of their elite, the *perfecti*, it was necessary to take the *consolamentum* or initiatory sacrament. This was a baptism with fire and the Holy Ghost, performed by the imposition of hands. Through this rite they believed that mortal sins were forgiven and the Holy Spirit was received.

Enemies of the Cathars reasoned that the consolamentum was called a baptism with fire because the participants were surrounded by a circle of lanterns, the fire of which was to dispel the darkness of their secret meeting place.

The preliminaries to attaining the status of perfecti were extremely arduous. The candidates had to be approved by the other perfect ones, and had to show fitness to undertake their life by a year's probation, in which they fulfilled their fasts on every Monday, Wednesday, and Friday as well as during three penitential seasons—all on bread and water. At no time could the Catharist eat what they defined as a product of coition: meat, milk, eggs, and cheese. Fish was allowed because it was thought to be a product of the water itself, not of coition. Because sexuality formed part of Satan's creation, sexual contact in any form was strictly forbidden. If married, a candidate had to abandon his or her partner.

The Cathars who had received the consolamentum faced a lifetime of rigid observance of the group's precepts. They encouraged each other in their tense battle for perfection. Any breach involved the sinner once again in Satan's world and resulted in a loss of the consolamentum.

The Cathars rejected the Trinity in favor of a subordination of two Persons to the Father. They could not admit that Christ was God, nor could they agree to his humanity. Like most other Gnostics, they rejected the Incarnation, the atoning death, and the resurrection of Jesus Christ. They believed that Jesus' mission was to convey to human prisoners of the flesh instructions for effecting an escape from the body.

Bibliography: N. Arseniev, Mysticism and the Eastern Church (1979); P. B. T. Bilaniuk, Theology and Economy of the Holy Spirit: An Eastern Approach (1980); B. L. Bresson, Studies in Ecstasy (1966); S. M. Burgess, "Medieval Examples of Charismatic Piety in the Roman Catholic Church," in R. Spittler, ed., Perspectives on the New Pentecostalism (1966); idem, ed., Reaching Beyond: Chapters in the History of Perfectionism (1986); idem, The Holy Spirit: Eastern Christian Traditions (1989); Y. M. J. Congar, I Believe in the Holy Spirit (1983; French 1979–80); G. B. Cutten, Speaking in Tongues (1927); I. H. Dalmais, "The Spirit of Truth and of Life. Greek Pneumatology and Latin Pneumatology: Are They Conflicting or Complementary?" Lumen Vitae 28 (1, 1973): 41–53; J. Dupuis, "Western Christocentrism and Eastern Pneumatology," Clergy Monthly 35 (1971): 190–98; E. Egert, The Holy Spirit in German Literature until the End of the Twelfth Century (1973); E. Ensley, Sounds of Wonder: A Popular History of Speaking in Tongues in the Catholic Church (1977); M. A. Fahey and J. Meyendorff, Trinitarian Theology East and West (1977); L. Gillet ("A Monk of the Eastern Church"), Orthodox Spirituality: An Outline of the Orthodox Ascetical and Mystical Tradition (1978); G. S. Hendry, The Holy Spirit in Christian Theology (1956); R. Knox, Enthusiasm: A Chapter in the History of Religion (1962); H. Küng and J. Moltmann, Conflicts About the Holy Spirit (1979); W. Lewis, Witnesses to the Holy Spirit: An Anthology (1978); V. Lossky, The Mystical Theology of the Eastern Church (1976); idem, The Vision of God (1963); J. Meyendorff, Byzantine Theology: Historical Trends and Doctrinal Themes (1974); R. Murray, Symbols of Church Kingdom: A Study in Early Syriac Traditions (1975); P. O'Leary, "The Holy Spirit in the Church in Orthodox Theology," Irish Theological Quarterly 46 (3, 1979): 177–84; P. D. Opsahl, ed., The Holy Spirit in the Life of the Church: From Biblical Times to the Present (1978); R. Payne, The Holy Fire: The Story of the Fathers of Eastern Church (1980); H. M. B. Reid, The Holy Spirit and the Mystics (1925); S. Runciman, The Medieval Manichee: A Study of the Christian Dualistic Heresy (1947); D. Staniloae, "The Holy Spirit in the Theology and Life of the Orthodox Church," Sobornost 1 (7, 1975): 4–21; E. Timiades, "The Centrality of the Holy Spirit in Orthodox Worship," Ekklesiastikos Pharos 60 (1–2, 1978): 317–57; C. N. Tsirpanlis, "Pneumatology in the Eastern Church," Diakonia 13 (1, 1978): 17–26; H. Watkin-Jones, The Holy Spirit in the Medieval Church (1922); G. Williams and Edith Waldvogel (Blumhofer), "A History of Speaking in Tongues and Related Gifts," in M. P. Hamilton, ed., The Charismatic Movement (1975).   S. M. Burgess

HOLY SPIRIT, DOCTRINE OF: MODERN PERSPECTIVES

See QUAKERS; EUROPEAN PIETIST ROOTS OF PENTECOSTALISM; SHAKERS; EDWARD IRVING; HOLINESS MOVEMENT.

HOLY SPIRIT TEACHING MISSION

(HSTM). An interdenominational charismatic agency based in Fort Lauderdale, Florida. The Holy Spirit Teaching Mission (HSTM) grew out of a charismatic Bible study in Fort Lauderdale, which around 1966 became a weekly prayer fellowship in the home of Eldon Purvis. This interdenominational meeting was one of the first charismatic groups in south Florida. A committee of some fifteen men was formed, known as the Committee of Forty, coordinated by Purvis to promote and sponsor charismatic teaching events. Later in 1966 the HSTM was incorporated with the Committee of Forty as the board of directors.

HSTM organized annual teaching conferences in Fort Lauderdale, which drew charismatics from all over the U.S. Among the teachers were Don Basham, Derek Prince, Harry Greenwood (from South Chard, England), Joseph Mattsson-Boze, Bob Mumford, and Charles Simpson. By 1969 the HSTM was sponsoring seminars in California, Georgia, and Ohio, besides several cities in Florida, and was beginning four-week leadership courses four times a year in Montego Bay, Jamaica. In addition, HSTM sponsored several witnessing and teaching tours and cruises.

HSTM began a monthly magazine, New Wine, in June 1969. In 1970, when serious problems arose in the leadership, Basham, Mumford, Prince, and Simpson, already members of the editorial board, were asked to become the main leaders. From this point, the HSTM is the first phase in the story of Christian Growth Ministries (CGM), to which its name was changed in 1972.

The HSTM conferences were an important influence within the American charismatic movement, providing teaching and formation for many future leaders. The teaching emphasized personal formation leading to spiritual maturity. The discipleship teachings of CGM developed after the change of name. Worship was also important at the HSTM conferences, with a significant contribution being made by the visitors from Chard, England.   P. D. Hocken

HOMOSEXUALITY See COMMUNITY GOSPEL FELLOWSHIP; PENTECOSTAL COALITION FOR HUMAN RIGHTS; PERRY, TROY DEROY.

An American Methodist missionary to Chile, Willis C. Hoover founded a Pentecostal organization in 1909.

HOOVER, WILLIS COLLINS (1856–1936). Father of Pentecostalism in Chile. The patriarch of Chilean Pentecostalism, W. C. Hoover is unique among foreign missionaries in having become leader of a major indigenous movement. He was born on July 20, 1856, in Freeport, Illinois, to Methodist parents. In youth, while gaining professional credentials in medicine (M.D., 1884) and architecture, he received an inner impression repeatedly in the words: "South America, South America, South America." So urgent was the call, in fact, that he made willingness to accompany him to the field a condition in his proposal to his future wife, Mary Anne Hilton. Although devoid of formal training in theology, Hoover gained appointment in 1889 as rector of the Colegio Inglés de Iquique (Iquique English School) in northern Chile under the quasi-independent mission of Methodist bishop, William Taylor (1821–1902).

Soon thereafter he began his studies for ordination. In 1893 when the Taylor work was absorbed into the new South American Conference of the Methodist Episcopal Church, Hoover was received from the Cincinnati Conference as a probationer in the second year. At that time he was serving a Spanish-language congregation in Iquique, which he had established two years earlier. A pioneer in the Spanish (as distinct from English) work, he was elevated to superintendent of the Iquique District when Chile was divided into three administrative areas in 1897, and appointed pastor in Valparaiso, the largest church in the conference, in 1902. There he expanded the already extensive evangelistic thrust which included branch chapels, class meetings, house-to-house visitation, and cottage meetings, devices destined to widespread use in his later ministry as a Pentecostal. A *caudillo*-type leader, Hoover deployed the evangelistic energies of converts drawn from peasant newcomers to Valparaiso in ways similar to those used earlier by Methodist circuit riders on the American frontier.

He monitored the activities of other evangelists, such as Evan Roberts (1878–1947) in Wales and A. B. Simpson (1843–1919) in the U.S., learning of the Pentecostal outpouring in India through an eighty-page book of Minnie F. Abrams, a former classmate of Mrs. Hoover in the Methodist-related Chicago Training School for Home and Foreign Missions. Entitled *The Baptism of the Holy Ghost and Fire* and received by the Hoovers in 1907, the book told of a spectacular revival two years earlier among widows and orphans in a school and home operated by Pandita Ramabai, a high-caste Indian, where Miss Abrams was then working. Upon reading it, Hoover made inquiries in North America and other places about the phenomena, which, with the exception of tongues, seemed to differ little from the emotional expression of pioneer Methodism. As superintendent of the Central District and pastor of the main church in Valparaiso, he sought the new experience and encouraged others to do so as well. Although Pentecostal phenomena during the 1909 Chile Conference session at Temuco brought no reaction from Bishop Frank M. Bristol (1851–1932), Hoover's continued activity and that of Nellie Laidlaw, a new convert and prophetess he had endorsed, cost him the superintendency, but not his pulpit, at the 1910 conference session in Valparaiso. Effective May 1, that year, however, Hoover resigned from the ministry and membership of the Methodist Episcopal Church, taking most of his own and two other congregations with him. Reorganized as the Iglesia Methodista Nacional, the Hoover-led body experienced phenomenal growth and soon outstripped its U.S.-sponsored parent. When nationalist sentiment and other issues split this movement in 1932, the founder established still another, the Iglesia Evangelica Pentecostal de Chile, which he headed until his death four years later. Under Chilean leadership, the two churches he fathered have prospered greatly, ranking as the first and second largest Protestant denominations in the country. In 1975 they reported a combined adult full communicant membership of 350,000, as compared with 7,676 in the non-Pentecostal parent body. Both regard 1909 as their birth date.

Bibliography: J. T. Copplestone, *Twentieth-Century Perspectives: The Methodist Episcopal Church, 1896–1939* (1973); C. Lalive d'Epinay, *Haven of the Masses* (1969).
C. E. Jones

A former minister with the Apostolic Faith, Portland, Oregon, Fred Hornshuh helped found the Bible Standard Church which later amalgamated with the Open Bible Evangelistic Assn. to form the Open Bible Standard Churches, Inc.

HORNSHUH, FRED (1884–1982). A Pentecostal pioneer in the Northwest, Hornshuh evangelized and founded numerous churches for the Apostolic Faith (AF, Portland) and later Bible Standard. He was the youngest of eight children and lived on a farm in Oregon until he was sixteen. His parents sent him to John Alexander Dowie's Zion College for two years. In 1908 he received a degree from Willamette University.

Hornshuh was baptized in the Spirit in an AF meeting in Portland in 1909 and preached for this group for several years. Because of disagreements with the AF leadership, Hornshuh and others left to form what they called the Bible Standard Mission. In 1935 this group became a part of the Open Bible Evangelistic Association, which was later changed to Open Bible Standard Churches. He founded a magazine in 1919, *Bible Standard*, which was later called *The Overcomer*.

Today Hornshuh is best known for founding the Lighthouse Temple, Eugene, Oregon (1919), and other churches in the Northwest and what is now Eugene Bible College (1925).

Bibliography: R. Mitchell, *Heritage and Horizons* (1982).
W. E. Warner

HORTON, HAROLD LAWRENCE CUTHBERT (1880–1968). British Pentecostal educator and author. Horton was trained as a Methodist minister but was converted to the Pentecostal tradition early in the revivals. He became a prolific author and contributed to most English language Pentecostal periodicals. Horton was very influential in the development and defense of the "initial evidence" doctrine within the British Assemblies of God in Great Britain and Ireland (AGGBI) as well as in the U.S. AG, where many of his essays are kept in print. He taught for most of his life at the AGGBI Bible School at Hampstead, London.

Bibliography: H. L. C. Horton, *Arrows of Deliverance* (n.d.); idem, *The Baptism of the Holy Spirit* (1961); idem, *Chords From Solomon's Song* (1937); idem, *The Gifts of the Spirit* (1934, 2d ed. 1946); idem, *Preaching and Homiletics* (1946, 2d ed. 1949); idem, *Receiving Without "Tarrying"* (n.d.); idem, *The Sons of Jeshurun, Illustrating Spiritual Types and Characteristics* (1944); idem, *Talks on Occupying the Land, A Challenge and a Call to Fuller Inheritance* (n.d., reprint 1944); idem, *What Is the Good of Speaking With Tongues?* (1946).
D. D. Bundy

HORTON, STANLEY MONROE (1916–). Author, educator, and premier theologian of the Assemblies of God (AG). Stanley M. Horton was born to Harry and Myrle Horton. His father was an evangelist from Owen Sound, Ontario, and his mother was the daughter of Elmer K. Fisher, pastor of the Upper Room Mission in Los Angeles. The younger Horton was converted and baptized in water in 1922. He received the baptism in the Holy Spirit in 1936 and felt called to a teaching ministry four years later. He was ordained through the New York–New Jersey district of the AG in 1946 (since 1948 he has

An Assemblies of God educator and writer, Stanley M. Horton is a third-generation Pentecostal. His grandfather, Elmer K. Fisher, pastored the Upper Room Mission in Los Angeles.

been a member of the Southern Missouri District). In 1945 he married Evelyn G. Parsons of Boston, Massachusetts. They have three children: Stanley, Jr.; Edward; and Faith.

Horton received his educational training at the following schools: A.A., Los Angeles City College (1935); B.S., University of California at Berkeley (1937); M.Div., Gordon-Conwell Theological Seminary (1944); S.T.M., Harvard University (1945); and Th.D., Central Baptist Theological Seminary (1959). Additional studies were completed at the Biblical Seminary of New York (now New York Theological Seminary).

Horton's employment began with the California Packing Corporation Land Research Department (1938), followed by four years at the Bureau of Chemistry of the California Department of Agriculture (1938–42). After graduation from Harvard, he began teaching at Metropolitan Bible Institute, North Bergen, New Jersey (1945–48), which was followed by a lengthy term of service at Central Bible College, Springfield, Missouri (1948–78). Since 1978 Horton has taught at the Assemblies of God Theological Seminary in the same city. The seminary's board of directors awarded him the title of "Distinguished Professor of Bible and Theology" in 1987 in recognition of his scholarship and long-term service to the denomination. In 1979–80 he served as president of the Society for Pentecostal Studies. In his extensive travel abroad Horton served as guest professor (1962) at the Near East School of Archaeology in Jerusalem, as well as teaching classes at AG colleges and seminaries in India, Belgium, Germany, Taiwan, the Philippines, and Singapore.

Horton has made notable contributions to the Pentecostal movement and to the AG in particular through his prolific writing. For more than twenty-five years he authored the *Adult Teacher's Quarterly* as well as books and manuals for Gospel Publishing House, the publishing arm of the AG. His books include *Into All Truth* (1955), *The Promise of His Coming* (1967, later published as *Welcome Back, Jesus*), *Desire Spiritual Gifts . . . Earnestly* (1972), *It's Getting Late* (1975), *What the Bible Says About the Holy Spirit* (1976), *The Holy Spirit* (1979, Study Guide for International Correspondence Institute), and *The Book of Acts* (1981). He has also contributed the following chapters: "The Assemblies of God View" in *Encounters with Eternity* edited by C. J. Johnson and M. G. McGee (1986), and "The Pentecostal View" in *Five Views of Sanctification* (1987). In addition to these works, he has written more than two hundred articles and book reviews.

Stanley M. Horton became an influential writer in the AG at a time when only a few were professionally trained at the graduate level in theology and the biblical languages. Theologically, his firm commitment to the entire trustworthiness of Scripture, concern for evangelism, Pentecostal pneumatology, and nondispensational premillennialism have had a profound influence on the course of AG theology in the last four decades. His warm personal blend of Pentecostal spirituality and academic expertise has also provided an important model for many of his

students who have pursued advanced degrees in theological studies. To honor his achievements, a collection of scholarly essays entitled *Faces of Renewal* (ed. Paul Elbert), was presented to him in 1988.

Bibliography: "A/G Editors Honor Stanley Horton for 25 Years of Writing Ministry," *PE* (April 27, 1975), 26; S. M. Horton, "I Believe . . . the Bible," *PE* (December 29, 1986), 5–6; *Who's Who in Religion,* 2d ed., 1977; resume supplied to this author.
G. B. McGee

HORTON, WADE HENRY (1908–). Twice general overseer of the Church of God (CG, Cleveland, Tenn.). Horton began his ministry in 1933 and pastored churches in South Carolina, North Carolina, and Washington, D.C. He is noted for his vigorous preaching on the practical aspects of Christianity.

After six years of service in world missions (1952–58) and two as state overseer of Mississippi (1960–62), Horton was called upon in 1962 to lead the denomination as its tenth general overseer. During his tenure (1962–66) the CG experienced such progress that he was returned to the office for a second tenure (1974–76). He was the first man to serve two separate tenures. Horton also served on the CG executive council for a total of thirty years.

Among his published works are *Pentecost: Yesterday and Today* (1964); four books of sermons; and a compiled study of tongues speaking, *The Glossolalia Phenomenon* (1966).

Bibliography: Archives of the Church of God (Cleveland, Tenn.).   C. W. Conn

HOSTILITY/PERSECUTION Malicious and destructive acts against a people because of their religious beliefs and practices. Jesus spoke of an innate hatred that exists in the world toward spiritual men: "If the world hates you, keep in mind that it hated me first. If you belonged to the world, it would love you as its own. As it is, you do not belong to the world, but I have chosen you out of the world. That is why the world hates you" (John 15:18–19). This hostility is rooted in the contrast between the world and Christ. Because it hated him it follows that it will also hate those who are like him. It is inescapable that a tension exists between Christ-likeness and world-likeness, a tension that results in hostility toward those who have renounced the world for Christ.

I. The Apostolic Church. Paul, speaking of the hostility he endured, made this observation: "Everyone who wants to live a godly life in Christ Jesus will be persecuted" (2 Tim. 3:11–12). Paul could understand this inevitable hostility because of his own early hatred of Christians. At least six times in his writings he recounted or alluded to his persecution of the church. The most extensive account was to King Agrippa: "On the authority of the chief priests I put many of the saints in prison, and when they were put to death, I cast my vote against them. Many a time I went from one synagogue to another to have them punished, and I tried to force them to blaspheme. In my obsession against them, I even went to foreign cities to persecute them" (Acts 26:9–11).

Persecution was often the lot of early Pentecostals, and one of the common forms was tarring and feathering the victims.

Paul recognized persecution to be a senseless, obsessive, violent reaction to something one does not understand or accept. This violence can be transposed into a belief that it is the right and proper reaction to its object: "I too was convinced that I ought to . . . oppose the name of Jesus of Nazareth" (Acts 26:9). Jesus said, "They will put you out of the synagogue; in fact, a time is coming when anyone who kills you will think he is offering a service to God" (John 16:2). Such delusion explains why a man's enemies can be even the members of his own household (Matt. 10:36). It was in such light that the early Christians understood the hostility of the world. Because they were different from the world, the world was suspicious of them and did them great harm.

II. The Plain People. In the same way the followers of Christ have suffered through the centuries, sometimes at the hands of ungodly men and sometimes at the hands of those who thought of themselves as servants of God. The greatest outbreaks of persecution have been directed toward those whose religious beliefs are in sharpest contrast to their time. The greater the contrast between the church and the world, whether in belief, appearance, or practice, the greater the antagonism. This was the unmistakable case with such groups as the Amish in Switzerland, the Waldenses in Italy, and the Shakers in England. These plain-dressed, nonpolitical, gentle folk were so harassed in their homelands that they took refuge in America.

III. Persecution of Pentecostals. As the Pentecostal movement arose at the turn of this century and spread around the world, it encountered opposition and hostility everywhere. The Pentecostal people were distinct from the world in several ways: they were gentle in nature, nonpolitical in interests, plain of dress, and assertive in their faith. So the world was hostile toward them. The persecution of Pentecostals in America in the early years was particularly spiteful and virulent, equaled or surpassed only by the violence that drove the Mormons from Illinois to Utah in 1844.

A. America. When the early Holiness people of North Carolina and Tennessee received the Holy Ghost baptism in 1896, what was at first only ridicule and scorn among their detractors burst into physical violence. The Holiness people were expelled from the churches of their birth and barred from the schoolhouse where they first worshiped. When the people built churches of their own, these were torched and dynamited; their homes became targets of vandalism and destruction by fire, gunshot, and stoning.

The people themselves were physically abused. The men were beaten with clubs and stones, flogged with horsewhips, and sometimes even ambushed and shot. The women suffered less, but the water springs and wells were polluted and poisoned, regional tradespeople refused them provisions, and the children were subjected to verbal abuse from teachers and physical abuse by fellow students. It was an extended period of relentless persecution, with the persecutors vowing to stamp out the belief in sanctification and the Holy Ghost baptism.

In the forefront of the atrocities was a branch of the Ku Klux Klan called the "Night Raiders," a hooded mob that spread violence and mayhem across the countryside. The Ku Klux Klan was a vigilante group that arose during the Reconstruction Days following the Civil War, setting themselves against everything unlike themselves in race, religion, politics, or moral values. The Pentecostal people became prime targets of their prejudice and punishment. The hooded assailants would descend upon a victim's home, drag him far away into the woods, tie his upstretched arms to a limb of a tree, and flog him into unconsciousness. Then they cut the thongs and let him fall to the ground. When the victim regained consciousness he made his way back home as best he could.

Similar hostility was encountered as the Pentecostal revival spread from town to town and state to state. As late as the 1930s there were incidents of flogging, not always in the rural mountains, but often in sophisticated and metropolitan areas. The lash seems to have been a favorite later weapon of the enemies of Christ, surpassed only by the earlier stones and clubs and guns.

Fire, too, has been widely used to hinder or discourage the spread of the gospel. The Pentecostal journals of the 1910s and 1920s constantly printed reports of burned churches, homes, and gospel tents. Typical is a *Church of God Evangel* account in 1910 of how three evangelists were falsely arrested in Alabama: "They marched us out from our tent and up the street to the stone jail. . . . Immediately they left the jail and returned to the tent, cut it down, and set fire to it. While the flames were ascending we were in the iron cells praising God that we were counted worthy to suffer shame for His sake."

That seems to have been the positive spirit with which the people faced all opposition and violence. They regarded the early apostles as their examples of how to meet persecution. The apostles were flogged and ordered not to speak in the name of Jesus, yet they rejoiced "because they were counted worthy of suffering disgrace for the Name. Day after day, in the temple courts and from house to house, they never stopped teaching and proclaiming the good news that Jesus is the Christ" (Acts 5:41–42).

It was commonplace in some areas for the Pentecostal people to be waylaid on their way to or from worship, or their churches to be vandalized, or the ministers to be arrested as disturbers of the peace or on other trumped-up charges. The most widespread abuse was slander or calumny, such as reports that the Pentecostal people caused fits by the use of powders, or that their worship was orgiastic or even orgasmic in nature or effect. A favorite way of slurring the Pentecostals was to call them "holy roller," a tired old epithet that has long been used to insult people who are emotional in their worship.

B. Worldwide. Hostility toward the Pentecostal revival has taken various forms during the past seventy-five years, but usually at a personal or community level rather than as a state or national policy. Pentecost in America has never faced the official opposition or prohibition that earlier Christians suffered. In other lands, especially in non-Christian or even non-Protestant lands, there have been, and still are, times of well-organized persecution of Pentecostals. The opposition in most communist countries has been relentless and widespread. There were sizable Pentecostal missions in China before World War II that have now disappeared. In Russia the Pentecostal Christians have demonstrated a remarkable durability in the face of danger. The plight of some Pentecostals in Russia was dramatized in 1978 when seven members took refuge in the American embassy in Moscow, fleeing from state-sponsored persecution. The group of seven remained in the embassy for four years, during which time other believers tried without success to join them. When their endeavors to immigrate to America failed, the people were left with an uncertain future in their homeland. Even in the 1980s reports frequently come to American and European denominations of pastors who have been arrested and imprisoned in Eastern-bloc countries for preaching without a license. The churches are closed, and the people carry on alone or underground.

The evidence suggests that believers in such places have resorted to the age-old practice of worshiping undercover. They believe that that is the caution advised by Jesus when he said, "I am sending you out like sheep among wolves. Therefore be as shrewd as snakes and as innocent as doves" (Matt. 10:16). An example was in Nazi Germany, especially from 1936 to 1945, when the Pentecostal churches worshiped mainly in homes and out of the sight of the Gestapo. In Spain before 1967 the Pentecostal believers were in constant danger of exposure and punishment. Some of the ministers moved from town to town in order to escape official hostility and punishment. In 1967 there was a change in national policy that recognized evangelical churches in Spain and permitted them to operate openly.

C. Violence in Christian Countries. Even in countries where there is no state or religious policy that discriminates against particular beliefs, there have been incidents of persecution that seemed to be sanctioned by official authority. For instance, in 1933 and 1934 missionary Maria Atkinson of Mexico was slandered and maligned as "a dope peddler passing as an American missionary, a witch, as a hypnotist using her glasses to make people do odd things, an immoral devil-possessed old woman fostering a spirit of fornication." Bending to such accusations from newspapers and antagonistic pulpits, the governor of Sonora ordered the Pentecostal churches closed. The people worshiped in secret until the closure was rescinded.

A worse outrage occurred in Veracruz in 1944, when a mob destroyed the church property, including several homes, of the La Gloria congregation. With some police reportedly encouraging the mayhem, the mob raped, flogged, and stabbed the people. Some of the church members fled to the hills and woods, where they hid in caves and underbrush and ate roots and wild fruit. Nine persons were killed or died during the persecution. The Mexican government struck hard against the crime and punished its perpetrators. Wide publicity was given to the incident, and the victims were restored to their community with full religious liberty.

D. Contemporary. The persecution of Pentecostals has not resulted in death as frequently as it did for some earlier Christians. Yet it has happened often enough to remind us of the hatred that is possible toward those who are different from the world. In revolutionary lands, such as certain Latin American countries during the past decade, entire congregations have been abducted and killed. While no statistics are available, it is known that in the 1980s hundreds of believers are held hostage or have been killed. Church buildings have been confiscated as political meeting places or burned to the ground. Because they are of the common people, without political or material strength, the Pentecostals are at constant risk in volatile situations.

In June 1978 a brutal mob set upon a mission compound of the Elim Pentecostal Church in Ruangwa, Rhodesia, and killed thirteen men, women, and children. The victims were all European missionary teachers. In mourning its dead, the Elim Church called upon its people to "seek as never before to promote the gospel of Jesus Christ in our land and beyond our land across the world."

This was the spirit of Paul, who was "convinced that neither life nor death, neither angels nor demons, neither the present nor the future, nor any powers, neither height nor depth, nor anything else in all creation, will be able to separate us from the love of God that is in Christ Jesus our Lord" (Rom. 8:38–39).

Bibliography: C. Brumback, *Suddenly . . . From Heaven* (1961); C. W. Conn, *The Evangel Reader* (1958); idem, *Where the Saints Have Trod* (1959); periodical files of the Pentecostal Research Center (Cleveland, Tenn.).   C. W. Conn

HOUSE CHURCH MOVEMENT (HCM). The designation of the networks of nondenominational charismatic assemblies in Great Britain. The name has stuck in popular parlance, even though almost all groups have outgrown the house fellowships of their origins. Among their own memberships, the term "restoration" is most widely used to describe the goals and character of the movement.

HCM's main thrust has become the restoration of the NT church, with the fivefold ministries of Ephesians 4:11, many streams emphasizing the ministry of apostles. Apostles are seen as church planters and generally act as heads of apostolic teams. While HCM has avoided particular millenarian positions, church restoration is typically seen as preparation for the Lord's return. Christian life is presented as a radical discipleship, kingdom living, with members accepting leaders' authority, which in most streams includes the discernment of all areas of life: family, finance, career, work, possessions. HCM assemblies are mostly subdivided into housegroup cells for pastoral formation and deepening of mutual relationships.

HCM roots lie in a series of conferences convened by D. Lillie and A. Wallis in the late 1950s and early 1960s. At this stage, the emerging cluster of convictions that later characterized HCM combined a vision for the restoration of the NT church, without at the time any mention of apostles, and the Pentecostal experience of baptism in the Spirit and the spiritual gifts. Many HCM leaders are former Plymouth Brethren members, expelled for their Pentecostal testimony; their vision of church restoration in many ways equals "Brethren teaching plus Pentecost."

When the term HCM was first coined, it referred among other things to two networks now of lessening importance: (1) the groups associated with South Chard, Somerset, begun by S. Purse (ex-Brethren) around 1951; (2) the groups relating to a charismatic Holiness teacher, G. W. North, with centers particularly in the Wirral (Merseyside) and Exeter, Devon. At Chard, Purse has been supported by V. Dunning, I. Andrews, and H. Greenwood.

During the 1960s, independent charismatic fellowships in Britain increased in number, helped by the ministries of men such as D. Clark, C. McAlpine, E. Trout, and A. Wallis. Some assemblies were independent on doctrinal grounds that excluded any transcongregational *episcope* (as that of D. Lillie) and others more pragmatically. A conference, entitled "Our Generation," of about fifty invited leaders in Paignton, Devon, in 1970, was the first meeting together of almost all the men who later became leaders of HCM networks. Around the same time, a group of independent charismatic leaders in the London area, including G. Coates, D. Mansell, J. Noble, and M. Smith, began regular meetings. From this circle came *Fulness* magazine, published from 1970 to 1982.

Early in 1972 Wallis convened a meeting of leaders to share God's vision for the end times. Six attended (A. Wallis, B. Jones, P. Lyne, D. Mansell, G. Perrins, and H. Thompson), and from this group (to which J. Noble was added) came unforeseen a covenant of mutual commitment. This group of seven was soon expanded to fourteen, a step that many later saw as a mistake. From 1972 to 1974 there was a growing interest, first in London, then in Bradford, Yorkshire, in teachings on apostleship, eldership, and discipling. One forum for such teaching was the annual Capel Bible Week in Surrey, at which E. Baxter from Fort Lauderdale, Florida, spoke in 1974. This American connection led to an increase in emphasis on discipleship and submission.

In 1976 the group of fourteen divided, with two main blocs emerging. An attempt of Baxter to mediate failed, ending any Fort Lauderdale influence. This split marked a clear contrast between the two groups. One group, termed R1 by Walker, was more authoritative, organized, and exclusive. It was influenced especially by Jones and Wallis, most strongly represented in Bradford, and had its expression in *Restoration* magazine, begun in 1975. The other group, termed R2, was more relaxed, in some areas more permissive, and less organized. It was associated with G. Coates and J. Noble and was mostly found in the London area. Its periodical was *Fulness*. In 1980 Jones encouraged T. Virgo of Hove, Sussex, to develop an apostolic team, now known as "New Frontiers," in the South of England; and in 1981 another team known as "Cornerstone," was formed under T. Morton of Southhampton, Hampshire, soon joined by Wallis. Key events in HCM growth have been the annual Bible weeks, first the Lakes and then the Dales Bible weeks in the North, organized from Bradford (1975–86) and later the Downs Bible weeks in the South, organized from Hove since 1979.

While the R1–R2 distinction has a definite foundation, it does not easily accommodate the growing importance of Virgo's network, probably now the largest in HCM. Nor does it take account of the networks, originating from charismatic Baptist churches that became independent and adopted plural leadership, notably Basingstoke, Hampshire (B. Coombs and V. Gledhill); Woking, Surrey (H. Owen); and Aldershot, Hampshire (D. Brown and M. Pusey). All these have clusters of local assemblies under their leadership.

Some London leaders, especially Noble, have sought in the 1980s to build bridges to the wider charismatic movement, in contrast to the strident antidenominationalism of *Restoration*. The other major HCM figures have largely adopted an intermediate position, with fewer links to denominational charismatic renewal than Noble, but unlike Jones, taking an active part in the Evangelical Alliance.

Despite the divisions and not uncommon changes of individual allegiance, HCM has some sense of shared vision and concerns, and there are no networks in which all communications with other leaders have been broken off.

See also CHARISMATIC MOVEMENT.

Bibliography: *Restoration* (May–June 1987); J. V. Thurman, *New Wineskins* (1982); T. Virgo, *Restoration in the Church* (1985); A. Walker, *Restoring the Kingdom* (1985); A. Wallis, *The Radical Christian* (1981).
P. D. Hocken

HUGHES, RAY HARRISON (1924–). A Church of God (CG, Cleveland, Tenn.) minister and prominent Pentecostal preacher and administrator. Twice Hughes was general overseer of the CG (1972–74; 1978–82), and twice he was president of Lee College (1960–66; 1982–84). He received academic degrees from Tennessee Wesleyan College (B.A., 1963) and the University of Tennessee (M.S., 1964; Ed.D., 1966).

The son of Pastor J. H. Hughes, Ray H. Hughes began his ministry in 1941 as an evangelist of notable effectiveness. Evangelism has always been his foremost ministry, although he has been successful as pastor, state overseer, and denominational executive. He came upon the national scene in 1946 as speaker at a mass rally of Pentecostal youth in the Hollywood Bowl in Los Angeles. He has frequently been the featured speaker for the British Pentecostal churches at Royal Albert Hall

in London and for numerous other international and interdenominational meetings. He has spoken at six Pentecostal World Conferences, numerous Pentecostal Fellowship of North America (PFNA) conventions, and the National Association of Evangelicals (NAE) conferences. Hughes has served as chairman of the PFNA and president of the NAE.

A prominent minister in the Church of God, Ray H. Hughes has also been active in interdenominational efforts such as the Pentecostal World Conference, the National Association of Evangelicals, and the Pentecostal Fellowship of North America.

Hughes' administrative ministry in the CG has included several positions; e.g., he was concurrently director of the CG radio ministry "Forward in Faith" (1960–63) and president of Lee College (1960–66).

Among Hughes' published works are *Religion on Fire* (1956), *What Is Pentecost?* (1963), *Church of God Distinctives* (1968), *The Outpouring of the Spirit* (1980), and *Pentecostal Preaching* (1981). His most popular album of recorded sermons is "The Anointing Makes the Difference."

Bibliography: Archives of the Church of God (Cleveland, Tenn.); C. W. Conn, *Our First 100 Years* (1986).
C. W. Conn

HUMBARD, ALPHA REX EMMANUEL (1919–) **AND MAUDE AIMEE** (1921–). Traveling evangelists, gospel singers, pastor and television pioneers.

Born in Little Rock, Arkansas, the son of a minister, Rex Humbard grew up in gospel work. His family traveled throughout the country pioneering churches and conducting revival crusades. When his family moved their musical ministry to Dallas, Humbard met Maude Aimee Jones. Rex and Maude Aimee married in 1942 and set out together on the road with Rex's family. In 1952 after a successful meeting in Akron, Ohio, he decided to leave his family's ministry and remain in Akron to build a church. One of the notable successes in establishing the work was the series of meetings held with Kathryn Kuhlman. Humbard had a vision for the role of television in gospel ministry and built the Cathedral of Tomorrow to accommodate his weekly telecasts. A large network of television stations carried his Sunday morning services in the late '60s and early '70s. In 1973 Humbard became involved in controversy because of questionable investments. The aura of scandal hung over his ministry for several years.

Although Rex Humbard came from a Pentecostal background, he did not emphasize the baptism of the Holy Spirit in his ministry. The following statement was made by the director of public relations for his church: "The Cathedral of Tomorrow is not Pentecostal; neither is the pastor or any of the staff. Neither are we affiliated with any Pentecostal organization, and the magazine is not slanted at the Pentecostal message at any time. We are an interdenominational evangelistic church" (Harrell, 1975, 192). The above statement should not be interpreted to mean that the church was anticharismatic, but rather that it was determined to avoid controversy. Prayer for the sick and anointing with oil were a regular part of the service, but the stress was always on the message of salvation. It was a formula that worked with a great deal of success.

Maude Aimee began singing at the age of nine and has had a long career as a successful gospel singer. She was a featured soloist on the Humbards' weekly telecast. In addition she accepted the responsibility of raising a family and occasionally preaching. The Humbards have been considered pioneers in the field of Christian television, and have served as role models for many of the ministry couples now seen on television.

In 1986 Rex Humbard served for a brief time on the new board of directors chosen by Jerry Falwell to head the PTL ministry. Humbard resigned from this board after a short time but is still involved in television ministry, working with Robert Tilton on a project in South America and appearing on the Trinity Broadcasting Network from time to time.

Bibliography: D. E. Harrell, Jr., *All Things Are Possible* (1975); R. Humbard, *Miracles in My Life* (1971).

J. R. Zeigler

HUMBURG, EMIL (1874–1965). German Pentecostal leader. After two years' ministry in the newly established *Gemeinschaft* (holiness society) in Mülheim-Ruhr, Humburg became leader on the death of its pastor in 1907. Welcoming the Pentecostal message, he attended conferences at Hamburg (December 1908) and Sunderland, England (June 1909), receiving the baptism in the Spirit with many others at Mülheim in the summer of 1909. As pastor of the largest Pente-

costal assembly in Germany, Humburg was with J. Paul and others in the forefront of defense against the Berlin Declaration, becoming one of the main writers and the publisher of the German movement. In 1911 he became president of the *Hauptbrudertag* (senior pastors' conference), a position he held until 1957. Humburg carried a major burden in the difficulties facing the German assemblies after the two world wars and made an unsuccessful attempt in 1934 to get the Berlin Declaration withdrawn.

Bibliography: C. H. Krust, *50 Jahre Deutsche Pfingstbewegung* (1958). P. D. Hocken

HUNGARIAN CHARISMATICS See CHARISMATIC MOVEMENT.

HUNTER, CHARLES EDWARD AND FRANCES (FULLER) (1920–) (1916–). Healing team. Charles was born in Palo Pinto, Texas. He earned an associate of business administration degree and served as a captain in the Air Force and as president of a certified public accounting firm. He experienced a spiritual life-change at age forty-eight.

Frances was born in Saratoga, Illinois. Frances says that God visited her in the hospital following eye surgery when she was forty-nine. She accepted Jesus as Savior and Lord nine months later and became in her words an "instant fanatic."

Although the couple was from the non-Pentecostal Church of God, Anderson, Indiana, they were baptized in the Holy Spirit through listening to a tape left with them by George Otis.

The "Happy Hunters" have coauthored thirty-two books and have conducted "healing explosions" across the U.S. and in other countries. They teach Christians how to administer healing to the sick to "fulfill the Great Commission."

Bibliography: S. Strang, "The Happy Hunters," *Charisma* (September 1977), 12–15. S. Strang

HURST, WESLEY ROBINSON (1922–87). Pastor and missionary. Hurst was born in Mineral, Illinois, to Rev. and Mrs. Wesley R. Hurst, Sr., pastors in the Christian Advent church who later joined the Assemblies of God (AG). Reared in Minnesota and Nebraska, Hurst later attended North Central Bible College and graduated with a diploma in 1943 (B.A. in 1978). In the same year he married June Van Dover. He held pastorates in Bruce and in Britton, South Dakota; Tulsa, Oklahoma; and Kalispell, Montana. He also spent three and a half years in itinerant evangelism. Feeling called to overseas missions work in the late 1940s, the Hursts received appointment with the AG and traveled to Tanganyika (later Tanzania) in 1953. Organizing the Pentecostal believers that he found there, Hurst opened a Bible institute at Mbeya and contributed to the founding of the Tanzanian AG.

After seven years (1960) the Hurst family returned to the U.S., and Wesley became the secretary of promotions for the AG Division of Foreign Missions. Ten years later he succeeded Maynard L. Ketcham as field director for the Far East. In this capacity Hurst focused on training national church leaders, providing advanced ministerial education through the Far East Advanced

School of Theology (FEAST), using advanced media technology in spreading the gospel, and promoting the development of the Assemblies of God Asian Mission Association (AGAMA), a network of Asian AG national church organizations working together to evangelize the region. For his contributions to missions, Northwest College of the AG conferred an honorary doctor of divinity degree on him in 1981. He died in 1987, shortly after dedicating the new facilities for FEAST in Baguio City, Philippines. He is survived by his wife and three children: Judy Mitchell, Wesley Randall Hurst, and Jhan Hurst.

Bibliography: "He Dared to Dream," *Mountain Movers* (April 1987), 6–7; "Wesley R. Hurst With Christ," *PE* (March 1, 1987), 9.   G. B. McGee

HYMNOLOGY See MUSIC, PENTECOSTAL AND CHARISMATIC.

I

IGLESIA DE CRISTO EN LAS ANTILLAS
In 1934, following the Puerto Rican campaign of Evangelist Francisco Olazábal (1886–1937), an independent church was organized in the barrio La Dolores of Rio Grande. Soon twelve additional congregations were established in the area. The next year these churches and the one at La Dolores met in general council and formed the Iglesia de Cristo en las Antillas (ICA). In the 1938 assembly a majority of the churches voted to change the name to Iglesia de Cristo Misionera. The mother church at La Dolores of Rio Grande, however, refused to accept the decision. It withdrew and, continuing under the original name, developed another network of satellite churches. In 1970 ICA reported thirty-one congregations and 2,100 members in Puerto Rico and a mission in New York.
See also MISSIONARY CHURCH OF CHRIST.

Bibliography: C. E. Jones, *Guide to the Study of the Pentecostal Movement* (1983); A. C. Piepkorn, *Profiles in Belief,* vol. 3 (1979).   C. E. Jones

IGLESIA DE DIOS PENTECOSTAL DE PUERTO RICO In 1912 American Pentecostal missionaries en route to the Orient stopped in Hawaii long enough to make several converts among Puerto Ricans living at the government experimental station near Honolulu. As a result, a congregation was organized with Francisco D. Ortiz, Sr., as pastor. In 1916 Juan L. Lugo, one of the members who had gone to California to work, felt called to return to Puerto Rico as a missionary. He was soon joined by other homeward-bound members of the Hawaiian congregation, including the pastor. The work grew rapidly. A street meeting in Ponce provided a nucleus for the first congregation. After four years there were eight churches; after five years, thirteen. In 1921 a convention met in Arecibo and formed the Iglesia de Dios Pentecostal de Puerto Rico (IDPPR), which incorporated the next year.

En route from California to Puerto Rico, Lugo stopped over in St. Louis, where he met the secretary of the newly formed General Council of the Assemblies of God (AG). Consequently, until 1947, when it was refused the status of a domestic district, the Puerto Rican group considered itself part of the AG fellowship. The years of uncertain relations that followed coincided with the migration of many islanders to the continental U.S., particularly to New York. Organization of stateside churches followed. In 1955 the American AG proposed the union it had refused eight years earlier, only to be rejected this time by the Puerto Rican brethren. The next year the IDPPR formally announced its independence and granted practical autonomy to its New York area churches under the name Concilio Latino-Americano de la Iglesia de Dios Pentecostal de New York. It, however, retained jurisdiction over other mainland work. In 1970 it reported 207 churches and 30,000 members in Puerto Rico.

Bibliography: A. C. Piepkorn, *Profiles in Belief,* vol. 3 (1979).   C. E. Jones

INDEPENDENT ASSEMBLIES OF GOD
See FELLOWSHIP OF CHRISTIAN ASSEMBLIES; INDEPENDENT ASSEMBLIES OF GOD, INTERNATIONAL.

INDEPENDENT ASSEMBLIES OF GOD INTERNATIONAL The Independent Assemblies of God International shared a common history with the Fellowship of Christian Assemblies until 1951. Prior to this time the two groups were united under the name Independent Assemblies of God. The "New Order of the Latter Rain" controversy that began in 1947 divided the two groups. In October 1949 ministers of the Independent Assemblies of God met at the Philadelphia Church in Chicago for their annual meeting. The two groups were already divided. The larger group argued that the New Order movement supported unscriptural teachings and practices, such as the casual way in which spiritual gifts and prophecies were given by the laying on of hands and the belief in the restoration of apostles and prophets. The smaller group led by Andrew W. Rasmussen supported these teachings and practices. By the time the annual meeting of 1951 convened, a permanent rift had grown between the two groups. The pro-New Order group decided to separate from the other body and organize themselves under their present name. Their headquarters currently are located in San Diego, California, under the administration of Rasmussen. Its official publication is entitled *Mantle.* Presently there are more than 1,800 ministers listed in its 1986 ministerial handbook.
See also FELLOWSHIP OF CHRISTIAN ASSEMBLIES.

Bibliography: J. Colletti, *Pneuma,* "Lewi Pethrus: His Influence Upon Scandinavian–American Pentecostalism" 5 (2, Fall 1983): 18–29; A. C. Piepkorn, *Profiles in Belief: The Religious Bodies of the United States and Canada,* vol. 3 (1979), 152–54.   J. Colletti

INGRAM, JAMES HENRY (1893–1981). A missionary leader of the Church of God (CG, Cleveland, Tenn.) for fifty years. Ingram served as a missionary ambassador and traveled to many countries rather than serving in only one. His earliest missions work was in Bermuda in 1921. Following several assignments to the British colony and later missions work in the U.S., Ingram began the CG missions endeavor in Mexico, where he served from 1932 to 1943. In the course of his Mexican ministry, he also opened works in Panama, El Salvador, Costa Rica, and Argentina.

Ingram's most notable work was his Golden Jubilee World Tour in 1936 to celebrate the fiftieth anniversary of the CG, during which he brought numerous independent congregations into the denomination. The missions in China and India proved to be fruitful fields for the Pentecostal message. His efforts led to the establishment of strong Pentecostal works in more than a dozen other countries. A prolific writer, Ingram aroused the awareness of the CG to its missionary responsibility and emphasized the needs of the world. A compilation of his missionary writings, *Around the World With the Gospel Light,* was published in 1937.

Long after most men decline in activity, Ingram continued his worldwide ministry. Even past age eighty he traveled widely and nurtured those fields he had opened to the message of Pentecost. He died in California in 1981 at the age of eighty-eight.

Bibliography: C. W. Conn, *Where the Saints Have Trod* (1959); P. Humphrey, *J. H. Ingram—Missionary Dean* (1966); J. H. Ingram, *Around the World With the Gospel Light* (1937).　　　　　　　C. W. Conn

INITIAL EVIDENCE, A BIBLICAL PERSPECTIVE Traditional Pentecostalism distinguishes between the work of the Spirit in regeneration and his work in empowering believers for ministry. When one has received this empowering, it is referred to as the baptism of the Spirit. The person knows that she/he has received this baptism if, at that time, she/he spoke in tongues. Speaking in tongues is called "the initial evidence." This initial speaking in tongues is distinct from the gift of tongues spoken about in 1 Corinthians 12–14. Though it is of the same essence, it is distinguished in part by noting that the initial evidence of tongues is immediate, the gift of tongues is permanent (Duffield and Van Cleave, 1983, 320). This initial evidence is emphasized around the world (cf. Hollenweger, 1972, 32–33, 330–47; see especially the footnotes for international representation, 513–22); however, in these same places, there is much controversy regarding it.

I. The Need for Clarification.

A. Terminology. What does this initial evidence of speaking in tongues mean? The exact wording of this doctrine varies from place to place. For example, in the literature of the Assemblies of God, "initial evidence" is not adequate. Its statement of doctrine reads, "initial physical evidence." But this has not always been the case. In Pearlman's early edition of *Knowing the Doctrines of the Bible,* only "initial evidence" occurs (1937, 313). As has been noted above in Duffield and Van Cleave, the Foursquare movement has only "initial evidence." And the Church of God (Cleveland, Tenn.) literature reflects some ambiguity regarding the wording of this doctrine. In two of its publications "initial physical evidence" is found (Conn, 1966, 26; Hughes, 1963, 30), while another one has only "initial evidence" (Slay, 1963, 88). What is meant in each case, however, is that there is some accompanying,

visible witness/evidence along with the baptism of the Spirit (a work that the Spirit does in the personality) and that such a work cannot be doubted, either by one experiencing this baptism or by observers.

B. Logical Relationship With Other Charismata. Another difficulty surfaces in understanding the relationship between the initial evidence of tongues and other gifts/manifestations of the Spirit. Wiebe has raised questions about the logic that Pentecostals use regarding the sequencing of initial evidence and these other manifestations (1984, 465–72) and finds some inconsistency and a lack of clarity in how Pentecostals understand this sequencing.

II. The Challenge of the Biblical Evidence.

A. Traditional Interpretations. Support traditionally has come from the Book of Acts, where some sort of precedent theology based upon specific, repeated events evidence miraculous phenomena, some of them clearly expressing tongues and/or prophecy (cf. also in Luke's Gospel where the Spirit's coming results in prophecy: e.g., 1:41ff., 67ff.).

For example, in Acts 2:1–4 the Holy Spirit filled the "house," and "all of them were filled with the Holy Spirit and began to speak in other tongues as the Spirit enabled them." In the account of Cornelius in 10:44ff. the Spirit came upon the ones who were listening to Peter's message. The circumcised believers who had accompanied Peter were astonished, "for they heard them speaking in tongues and praising God." Later tongues are mentioned in 19:1ff., when Paul came to Ephesus and immediately questioned the disciples there as to whether or not they had received the Spirit. They replied that they had not. Paul then placed his hands on them, the Spirit came on them, and they spoke in tongues.

Classical Pentecostals include Acts 8:4–24, the so-called Samaritan Pentecost, among these other texts in Acts as a basis for this doctrine. Traditionalists argue that tongues are the sign of the coming of the Spirit here, even though tongues are not explicitly mentioned with this coming. They say that these Samaritans already believed (vv. 12–13), had seen signs and miracles, but had not yet received the Spirit's baptism (vv. 14–16). Apparently Peter and John had been sent there to oversee Philip's work. When they arrived they placed their hands on these believers, who then received the Spirit (v. 17). Traditionalists note that (1) the Samaritans believed prior to the coming of the apostles; (2) the people had seen signs and miracles; and (3) something unique, other than signs and miracles, captured their attention. Therefore, this something unique must have been tongues.

B. Hermeneutical Challenges.

1. Paul Versus Luke? The paucity of biblical references makes understanding and supporting the classical doctrine of initial evidence difficult. Pentecostals argue mainly from Acts, where such evidence is found. In contrast, non-Pentecostals argue from a Pauline perspective and interpret Acts in light of Paul; accordingly, they believe that these texts in Acts refer to conversion. That is, they see no distinct experience between regeneration and the "empowering" (cf. from England, Dunn, 1970, and an American response from Ervin, 1984). Among others, Stronstad, a Canadian Pentecostal, has shown that it is poor hermeneutics to impose the meaning of one biblical author onto that of another (1984). It is essential to note that Paul does not stress the empowering of the Spirit in his works but that Luke does.

2. *Genre and Theological Precedent.* Another challenge arises over the question of genre. Acts, according to some, simply gives a historical account of what happened, not a theology of what ought to happen. Tongues are valid and *normally* happen, but it cannot be said that they ought to be *normative*, based on Acts as history (cf. Fee and Stuart, 1982, ch. 6, "Acts—The Problem of Historical Precedent," 87–102; Fee's argument is found in a number of other places and has been known for some time, especially among American Pentecostals like Fee himself). This argument attempts to guard against a pseudoexperience in which those who do not really receive the gift of the Spirit but, nonetheless, because of pressure, speak in some sort of gibberish of their own doing.

C. A New Response From Biblical Evidence.
1. *Expanding Theological Precedent.* The way traditional Pentecostals use theological precedent in Acts is weak in itself, but it can be substantially strengthened by extending the scope of research and following a better hermeneutic. While the lives of the early believers in Acts do not establish precedent, certainly precedents can be discovered in the life of Jesus. Therefore, what must be considered is Jesus' anointing in Luke 3:21–22; this event sets the precedent for what follows in the lives of the apostles in Acts. In Luke 3:21–22 John's name and Jesus' water baptism are distanced from Jesus' baptism in the Spirit so as to make this an empowerment for ministry. Jesus is a model for the apostles (cf. Aker, 1988). (But this only raises the difficult question for traditionalists, why did Jesus not speak in tongues at his anointing?)

2. *Genre.* According to some, Acts is history. What is repeated there is not necessarily to be considered a theological datum. But the genre of Acts as merely history is being challenged. It is shown that Luke's purpose and methods are the same in both his Gospel and Acts. Luke and Acts are in fact one work by the same author. It is therefore not valid to separate these two in terms of genre and hermeneutics (cf. Aker, 1988). Luke must be interpreted in light of his own practical and theological interests and not in light of Paul. And different hermeneutical principles should not be used: one for Luke as Gospel and one for Acts as "history." The major difficulty in this is that we do not have other accounts of the story of this period with which to compare Acts. In contrast we can fruitfully compare Luke with the four Gospel accounts. But we can gain much by comparing Luke with other Gospels. It is important to realize that Luke's own theological interests can be ascertained. In addition, the comparison of Luke with other Gospels proves to be beneficial. Then we can read Acts in light of Luke and note similar concerns and interests. In other words, one should employ both synchronic (examine other Gospels) and dischronic/linear (examine Luke and Acts) methods.

3. *Old Testament Evidence.* We can also expand the biblical evidence for this initial evidence doctrine. Speaking in tongues as initial evidence is attached to prophecy, which is, in turn, the sign that one has experienced the benefits (especially power in Luke) of the eschatological community. This can be seen from several NT sources and from the OT material they draw upon. The OT serves as the source of Luke's theology of the baptism in the Spirit (cf. Stronstad, 1984), as can be seen from a number of texts centering on Israel's early history, including its deliverance out of Egypt and its becoming a new nation.

a. *Numbers 11.* Numbers 11 tells of an episode when the people of Israel were complaining about Moses. In response, God tells Moses to gather seventy of the elders of Israel at the tent of meeting, where he will take of the Spirit that is upon Moses and place it upon them (vv. 16–17), thus preparing them to take care of the complaining people. It is not the organization of the elders that, in the mind of the writer, prepares these elders for this service—it is the Spirit. Moses had already chosen the elders in Exodus 16:24–26, and they had begun to function in administrative roles. Embedded in this text in Numbers, then, is a concern for charismatic ability. Something is lacking in these elders that only the Spirit can supply. Later, in Numbers 11:24–25, they gather at the tent, and the Spirit that was upon Moses comes upon them and they prophesy.

It is significant to notice several things. First, the purpose for which these elders received the Spirit was not prophetic—it was administrative. But the evidence for the Spirit's presence was prophecy. There was a community understanding that linked the Spirit with prophecy. To shatter that view and suggest something different, such as the Spirit's empowerment in the caring for Israel's needy, was challenging. Second, this text suggests this understanding by mentioning the accompanying prophecy, although an ambiguous statement ends verse 25. The difficulty involves what it means and how some manuscripts have tried to overcome the difficult reading by substituting other words. Should it indicate that they prophesied no more after that time, or should it mean that they continued to prophesy? Whichever choice one opts for makes no difference regarding the point of the argument. Prophecy uniquely indicates the presence of the Spirit, and after receiving it, the elders function in a role different from that of the prophets. Prophecy acts as an initial sign that the Spirit had come and was at work.

b. *1 Chronicles 16:19–22; Psalm 105:12–15.* The charismatic tradition manifested in Numbers 11 is also found in other places in the OT. There was a tradition that regarded the first group of Israelites, referred to as patriarchs, to be prophets. For instance, 1 Chronicles 16:19–22, paralleled in Psalm 105:12–15, speaks about this small band of sojourners wandering from place to place, the victims of persecution. The relevant verses (the Hebrew is identical in 16:22 and 105:15) read in synonymous and chiastic (inversely parallel) fashion:

> "Do not touch my anointed ones;
> do my prophets no harm."

These texts refer to more than just the two or three patriarchs; all of their families are included. It also extends to future generations. The theme of wandering is important in biblical history regarding the concept of the people of Israel being prophets. This explains well the pervasive theme attached to the prophetic tradition that all prophets have a sense of alienation and uprootedness. This is in fact part of their call—to challenge the world's *Weltanschauung* (world view), which is foreign to Yahweh's. True prophets, consequently, risk being persecuted and killed.

c. Joel 2:28–32. The future anticipation of salvation in terms of the coming of the Spirit and of all being prophets also occurs in another OT text, Joel 2:28–32. This text speaks about the future restoration of God's people in terms that do not distinguish between salvation and baptism in the Spirit and that are loaded with controversy in the twentieth century. In Joel, which reflects ancient Near Eastern anthropology, no distinction existed among various elements of salvation. That the future community would be prophetic is signified in the structure and content of Joel 2:28–29.

A "I will pour out my Spirit on all people.
B Your sons and your daughters will prophesy,
C your old men will dream dreams,
C' your young men will see visions.
B' Even on my servants, both men and women,
A' I will pour out my Spirit in those days" (v. 29).

The first and last lines express the comprehensive extent of the pouring out of the Spirit; the inner lines give specific information about who is included in this outpouring. The meaning is clear—all of God's people will receive the Spirit. Furthermore, the nature of this eschatological community is given. Prophecy is explicitly mentioned, but another phenomenon associated with prophecy is listed synonymously alongside prophecy: dreams/visions.

4. New Testament Evidence.

a. Luke–Acts. All of the OT texts we have noted provide examples and models for Luke. For instance, the episode in Numbers 11 (and Exod. 16:24–26) finds some parallelism in Acts 1. Luke goes to some pains to show that it is important that the leadership of the church (the eleven apostles, plus the newly elected one and the one hundred or so others) is set in place, much like the seventy elders of early Israel. The function of these leaders in Acts takes on a purposeful role and bears upon the raison d'être for the work. The baptism in the Spirit could be confused with the practice of magic so prevalent during those times

and evidenced especially in the account of Simon the magician in Acts 8. Luke goes out of his way to show that what the Spirit does is different from magic. One of the reasons that Luke's community needed the moving of the Spirit was because, out of fear of confusing magic with the working of the Spirit, the believers withdrew from such spiritual manifestations. Luke avoids the formula used by Hellenistic magicians and emphasizes the openness of doing miracles and "empirical evidence" (cf. the Lukan "bodily form" in Luke 3:22 and "tongues like fire" in Acts 2:3). He also emphasizes proper modes of behavior in connection with miracle, and often the OT prophetic call for rectitude is present (cf. Hull, 1974).

Another reason for Luke's call in his double work for the outpouring of the Spirit was theological. One particular group, the disciples of John the Baptist, did not believe in Spirit baptism. The amount of attention devoted to this group in Luke–Acts and how Luke handles it suggests that this group influenced his church considerably (cf. Aker, 1988).

Throughout the Acts narrative, leadership provides proper direction and oversight. Everywhere that new churches start, leadership, through all the apostles—but especially Peter and Paul—is there to ensure experiential and theological standards. This is the case regarding the baptism of the Spirit, especially when it does not occur at the outset. This baptism is normal, and tongues and/or prophecy accompanies the Spirit when he fills people. Note, for example, 8:4–25, the Samaritan episode, and 19:1–7, the "Ephesian Pentecost."

Persecution and alienation are also themes in Luke–Acts as they are in many prophetic contexts of the OT. (Certainly this is prominent in other NT books, and often in eschatological contexts at that, such as in Matthew, Mark, John, 1 Peter, and Revelation.) In Luke, Christ is the prophet par excellence—he is persecuted and killed. In like manner, his disciples walk the same path. Luke 13:29, in contrast to the other Gospels, includes "all the prophets" with the names of the three patriarchs, thus suggesting that Luke identifies this ancient community with the eschatological one.

Peter's speech in Acts 2 quotes, with slight revision, Joel 2:28–32. And its place there is significant. First, this speech explains the tongues phenomenon as a sign that Joel's prophecy is fulfilled. Nowhere is it more acutely disclosed that the eschatological community manifests what is alien and radically different from the traditional expectations of the present age than in Acts 2. As in the twentieth century, so in this first instance, people, even religious ones, were confused by God's breaking in.

Second, Luke (or Peter) has modified Joel's prophecy by disrupting the parallelism and has indicated something about this community. He adds to the Septuagint of Joel *kai prophēteusousin* at the end of verse 18 to interpret and thus to emphasize clearly what sons and daughters (v. 17) are to do. They are to prophesy! Others have noted this fact about Luke as well. E. Schweizer notes that for Luke prophecy is central to the work of the Spirit and that the eschatological community is prophetic (1968, 6:408). K. Lake and H. J. Cadbury similarly claim that "few things are more necessary for an understanding of early Christianity than a perception of the fact that it was essentially a prophetic movement" (1979, 130). Both Judaism and Christianity perceived the people in the age to come to be a community of prophets. All people, according to Judaism, will receive the Spirit. Finkel notes, for example, that the background for Luke resides in both the Essene movement and the rabbis and their expectations in messianic times. In Luke's version of the Lord's Prayer in chapter 11, the Aramaic words for "father," "your name," "holiness," "for tomorrow," "our sins," and "trial" spell out acrostically the word for "I will baptize them with grace [i.e., the Spirit]" ('*eSHaQem Hen*). (For the significance of the Lord's Prayer in Luke's theology of the Spirit, see Aker, 1988). In Luke a reference to this request for the coming of the Spirit occurs also in 24:49 and Acts 1:5. But the promise of Joel 2:28 is described in Acts 2. In Judaism, this request for the Spirit was tied to Joel, Zechariah 12:10, and the benediction in Numbers 6:25. The Essenes and rabbis took this promise to refer to the coming of the Spirit or illumination (Finkel, 1981, 153–54).

Furthermore, in Acts 2, the word for "enabled" (NIV) in verse 4 is the same for Peter's "addressed" (NIV; *apophtheggesthai*) in verse 14. The Greek word means "to speak under inspiration." Luke thus connects this tongues phenomenon with the prophecy of Joel. When he does this, he places tongues (the 120) and prophecy (Joel's prediction and Peter's prophetic "sermon") on the same level.

What about other supernatural phenomena? Are they also not a sign that the Spirit is at work? The response to this important question is also found in the NT. Schweizer has observed that in Luke the Spirit is no longer God's power manifested in healings and exorcisms. These phenomena are connected with the person, power, or name of Jesus; or with prayer; or with bodily contact with the disciples or with other objects (1968, 6:407). There is a reason for this. In Luke–Acts prophecy focuses on Jesus. In fact, *martys* in Acts 1:8 is associated with the Spirit and prophecy, whose content is Jesus. And here is where tongues contrasts with other signs as evidence of the Spirit. Other signs can be duplicated by demonic power (cf. Rev. 13), and tongues and prophecy can be falsified. Also significant is that Judaism expected a prophet to prove his identity by miraculous signs (Brown, 1975, 2:629; Strack-Billerbeck, 1924–61, 1:127, 726ff.; 2:480; 4:316–17).

Acts 2 connects the coming of the Spirit and the speaking in languages with Jesus in Peter's speech in verses 22ff. In 2:33 it is Jesus who is exalted at God's right hand, who has received from the Father the promise of the Spirit, and who has poured out the Spirit.

b. Johannine Literature. In Luke the Spirit gives special revelation, and this is prophetic and rooted in Spirit baptism. But in John the ability to know spiritual things (i.e., special revelation) is based on regeneration. John 3:34 reads, *hon gar apesteilen ho theos ta rhēmata tou theou lalei, ou gar ek metrou didosin to pneuma* ("for he whom God sent speaks the words of God, for he gives the Spirit not by measure"). The subject of "speaks the words of God" (i.e., Christ) is the same subject of "gives the Spirit not by measure" (i.e., Christ). The second "for" in "gives the Spirit not by measure" explains "he who speaks the words of God" (de la Potterie, 1972, 448). This giving of the Spirit directly refers to 7:37–39 and approximates that in Acts 2:33, where Jesus pours out the Spirit, but its meaning is quite different. In Acts it does not refer to regeneration but to the baptism of the Spirit. In John it clearly relates to regeneration. In other places (4:10; 6:63; 7:38–39; 14:17; 15:16; 16:13; 1 John 4:6) John connects Jesus and his word (Jesus is the one who brings revelation from God to humanity) with Spirit, life, and truth (cf. JOHANNINE EPISTLES and JOHN, GOSPEL OF).

In noting the use of signs in John's Gospel, there are two differing viewpoints. To those who followed Jesus for the wrong reasons, signs as the basis of faith were inadequate (cf. John 2:11, 22–24). On the other hand, signs (and Jesus' word, cf. 2:22) were useful to solicit faith (cf. 20:30–31). Other NT references respond negatively toward signs, especially when they portray the Jews as seeking signs (e.g., Matt. 16; 1 Cor. 1:22).

The Book of Revelation also signifies that the eschatological community is a prophetic one, although tongues are not mentioned. Luke is unique among NT writers in this regard. But the important element, the prophetic nature of the Christian, can be demonstrated by briefly examining Revelation 22:8–9 (cf. 19:10), where specifically a Christian is called a prophet. Verse 9 states, "I am a fellow servant with you and with your brothers the prophets and of all who keep the words of this book." "Prophets," a noun, and the participle, "those who keep," are parallel. The *kai* ("and") that connects them is epexegetical and is translated "even." Both "prophets" and "those who keep" modify "brothers." This is signified because of two "yous" (*sou*) that modify "fellow slave" and "brothers." In other words, everyone who keeps the words of Jesus (i.e., Christians) is a prophet.

c. 1 Corinthians. Paul's view of understanding spiritual knowledge (i.e., revelation) is similar to John's, surprisingly so in light of 1 Corinthians 12–14. Paul's anthropology of the spiritual person (i.e., the one who has been regenerated) in 1 Corinthians 2:6–16 is the basis for knowing the things of God, even for the gift of discernment found later in 12:10 ("discernment" occurs in both contexts). It is even possible to assume that all of the congregation is to discern the prophetic utterance. For instance, the "others" of 12:29 can just as easily refer to all rather than just to the two or three prophets. At any rate, Paul places no more importance on the prophet than on other Christians. All have the same access to God through Christ. For these reasons it is appropriate to note that Paul and John emphasize the inner dynamic of the Spirit, as in regeneration and sanctification, while Luke emphasizes the outer, an empowerment for ministry.

III. Conclusion. Classical Pentecostals believe in an experience subsequent to salvation called "Spirit baptism." When one first receives this baptism, he/she will speak in another language. This first speaking is known as the "initial evidence of speaking in tongues." Initial evidence for these Pentecostals is an important doctrine, for they argue that this experience is necessary for maintaining a high visibility of the supernatural working of God, something that has been missing from many churches. The lack of a specific sign, such as this "initial evidence," dilutes the experience, ultimately causing Spirit baptism to cease.

However, there are problems with this doctrine. First, there is the terminology itself. What does it refer to? Second, does one support this doctrine and use traditional hermeneutical methods? Acts is usually interpreted so as to establish precedent theology based on repeated occurrences of speaking in tongues. Is Acts history or theology? And the paucity of texts speaking directly to these issues does not help. There is, however, biblical evidence for the doctrine. By applying the same interpretive method to both Luke and Acts, precedents for the doctrine of initial evidence can be seen in the life of Jesus.

Although the evidence of tongues is not foundational to Christian life, the NT writers make it clear that regeneration is. What is paramount in Luke–Acts is that the evidence of tongues is an experience of the eschatological community—not a doctrine to divide those who are regenerate.

See also BAPTISM IN THE HOLY SPIRIT; GLOSSOLALIA; HOLY SPIRIT, DOCTRINE OF THE; INITIAL EVIDENCE, a HISTORICAL PERSPECTIVE; LUKE–ACTS.

Bibliography: C. Brown, *NIDNTT* (1975); C. W. Conn, "Glossolalia and the Scriptures," in *The Glossolalia Phenomena*, ed. W. H. Horton (1966); G. P. Duffield and N. M. Van Cleave, *Foundations of Pentecostal Theology* (1983); J. D. G. Dunn, *Baptism in the Holy Spirit* (1970); P. Elbert, ed., *Faces of Renewal* (1987); H. M. Ervin , *Conversion—Initiation and the Baptism in the Holy Spirit. An Engaging Critique of James D. G. Dunn's Baptism in the Holy Spirit* (1984); idem, *Spirit Baptism: A Biblical Investigation* (1987); G. D. Fee and D. Stuart, *How to Read the Bible for All Its Worth* (1982); A. Finkel, "The Prayer of Jesus in Matthew," *Standing Before God: Studies on Prayer in Scriptures and Tradition with Essays, in Honor of John M. Oesterreicher*, ed. A. Finkel and L. Frissell (1981); W. J. Hollenweger, *The Pentecostals: The Charismatic Movement in the Churches* (1972); R. H. Hughes, *What Is Pentecost?* (1963); J. M. Hull, *Hellenistic Magic and the Synoptic Tradition* (1974); K. Lake and H. J. Cadbury, "The Acts of the Apostles" in *The Beginnings of Christianity*, ed. F. J. Foakes Jackson and K. Lake (1979), vol. 4; W. G. MacDonald, *Glossolalia in the New Testament* (n.d.; originally published in *BETS* (1964). M. Pearlman, *Knowing the Doctrines of the Bible*; I. de la Potterie, "Studiorum Novi Testamenti Societas: L'esprit saint dans l'evangile de Jean," *NTS* 18 (1972): 448–51; E. Schweizer, "*Pneuma, Pneumatikos*," in *TDNT* (1968), 6:389–451; J. L. Slay *This We Believe* (1963); R. Stronstad, *The Charismatic Theology of St. Luke* (1984); C. H. Talbert, *Reading Luke: A Literary and Theological Commentary on the Third Gospel* (1986); P. H. Wiebe, "The Pentecostal Initial Evidence Doctrine," *JETS* 27 (1984): 465–72.   B. C. Aker

INITIAL EVIDENCE, A HISTORICAL PERSPECTIVE The twentieth-century Pentecostal movement introduced into Western Christendom an element that would give rise to considerable controversy. That element was glossolalia, or speaking in other tongues. The Pentecostals maintained that a Holy Spirit baptism, validated and evidenced by "speaking in tongues," was a normative postsalvation religious experience that was available to all Christians. The early twentieth-century classical Pentecostals further complicated the confusion by insisting that the gift of tongues, one of the nine gifts discussed in 1 Corinthians 12, was divinely intended to be endowed by the Holy Spirit to certain Spirit-baptized believers. Thus there was a universal tongues experience, given as a sign or evidence of the baptism in the Holy Spirit, and a gift of tongues, given only to those believers who received this communicating vehicle from the Holy Spirit. The reaction and response of Christendom to this innovative doctrine were varied and complex.

Prior to the charismatic renewal, mainline denominations insisted that glossolalia was only for the establishment of the church on the Day of Pentecost (Acts 2:4). They thus deemed tongues inappropriate and unnecessary in the Christian experience. Dispensationalist segments alleged that tongues were intended only for the period of the early church, a position thought to be supported by the scarcity of references to the phenomenon in church history after that time. This position also facilitated the explanation of the presence of glossolalia in the Book of Acts and 1 Corinthians.

There were several reactions to the Pentecostal baptism with the evidence of tongues among Holiness bodies and Keswick adherents that had developed in the last quarter of the nineteenth century. Both of these groups believed in a second spiritual experience, generally called the baptism in the Holy Spirit. The Holiness groups held that this experience was synonymous with sanctification and that it provided grace to achieve personal purity and was often accompanied by ecstatic joy. Those with Keswick leanings, on the other hand, held that the baptism in the Holy Spirit resulted in a deeper spiritual experience that empowered the believer for service. D. L. Moody, R. A. Torrey, A. J. Gordon, A. B. Simpson, and J. Wilbur Chapman were outstanding names connected to this latter group.

Several Holiness bodies (the Church of God, Cleveland, Tenn.; the Pentecostal Holiness Church; and the Church of God in Christ, to name some of the more prominent ones) resolved the problem by quickly embracing the Pentecostal posture on the baptism in the Holy Spirit with the evidence of tongues, adding this as a third spiritual experience to those of salvation and sanctification; thus reflecting the influence of Benjamin Hardin Irwin's perspectives on the baptism in the Spirit. These bodies fused into the Pentecostal movement and have played a significant role in its development.

Most of the Holiness bodies, however, adamantly rejected the Pentecostal tongues baptism, referring to it as an unscriptural doctrine. The response of the Church of the Nazarene is somewhat characteristic of the resistance of these groups to the Pentecostal movement. This body had been organized as the result of a merging of several small Holiness groups as the Pentecostal Church of the Nazarene. Because of its anti-Pentecostal stance, the term "Pentecostal" in its title became a source of embarrassment. Consequently, in 1919 the name was changed to the Church of the Nazarene, thus precluding it being associated with the Pentecostal movement. These bodies continued to support two spiritual experiences, salvation and the "second blessing" of sanctification.

There was no broad acceptance of the tongues evidence of the baptism in the Holy Spirit within the Keswick groups. Though many in this cluster of bodies continued to embrace a second "deeper spiritual" experience, the Pentecostal evidence was strongly opposed. An enduement of power for Christian service continued to be the primary purpose for the experience. The opposition to the practice of tongues was eventually based by many on the conversion-initiation or dispensational positions on tongues.

A. B. Simpson and the church he headed, the Christian and Missionary Alliance (CMA), reflected yet another reaction to the Pentecostal baptism in the Holy Spirit. In 1907 Simpson was forced to appraise seriously his relationship with the Pentecostals. By that time many of the CMA churches had embraced the Pentecostal baptism, and in that year manifestations of tongues were noted in the Alliance's annual convention, in its Nyack Missionary Training Institute, and in several of its large camp meetings. After agonizing over these happenings Simpson issued a manifesto that denied the Pentecostal teaching that the baptism of the Holy Spirit is always evidenced by speaking in tongues and urged his leaders and members to "neither seek to speak in tongues, nor to forbid it." In practice he said that tongues could be one of several evidences of the baptism in the Holy Spirit when it was being exercised as the gift of tongues, one of the nine gifts of the Spirit listed in 1 Corinthians 12. Though this response was made in a magnanimous and conciliatory manner, many of his constituents who were now committed to the Pentecostal theology left the CMA and greatly influenced the ongoing development of the Pentecostal movement. It is a matter of interest that the Pentecostal posture holding glossolalia as the biblical initial evidence of the baptism in the Holy Spirit has repeatedly been challenged within the Pentecostal movement, most notably in the Assemblies of God (AG) in 1918. To prevent the erosion of this tenet, the AG, the largest Pentecostal body, in recent years has required its ministers to attest to their continuing support of this position. There have especially been conflicting positions espoused in the later charismatic movement. A substantial number of these constituents hold that tongues is only one of several evidences of the baptism in the Holy Spirit.

After World War II relationships between the Pentecostal bodies and the communions that have roots in Holiness and Keswick traditions have become much more conciliatory, though no doctrinal accommodations have been made by either camp. This has come about through participation in the National Association of Evangelicals.

See also HOLINESS MOVEMENT; INITIAL EVIDENCE, A BIBLICAL PERSPECTIVE.

Bibliography: C. Brumback, *What Meaneth This?* (1947); J. D. G. Dunn, *Baptism in the Holy Spirit* (1970); H. M. Ervin, *Conversion-Initiation and the Baptism in the Holy Spirit* (1970); K. Kendrick, *The Promise Fulfilled* (1961); W. W. Menzies, *Anointed to Serve* (1971); J. T. Nichol, *The Pentecostals* (1966); V. Synan, ed., *Aspects of Pentecostal-Charismatic Origins* (1975); idem, *The Holiness-Pentecostal Movement in the United States* (1971); R. A. Torrey, *The Person and Work of the Holy Spirit* (1974). K. Kendrick

INTEGRITY COMMUNICATIONS The fountainhead of the discipling/shepherding doctrine. Integrity Communications is probably better known by either of its previous names: Holy Spirit Teaching Mission and Christian Growth Ministries. It adopted its present title in 1982 when it shifted its base of operations from Fort Lauderdale, Florida, to Mobile, Alabama. Founded in 1969, Integrity Communications is the creation of five Neo-Pentecostal preachers: Don Basham (Disciples of Christ), Ern Baxter (Pentecostal), Derek Prince (Pentecostal), Bob Mumford (Pentecostal), and Charles Simpson (Southern Baptist), with Mumford and Simpson as its present most frequently quoted spokesmen. They declared the church radically independent of ecclesiastical structures. Instead they substituted a vision of the church as the body of Christ. As described in *New Wine* magazine, the true body of Christ is composed of believers who submit to one another, giving obedience and paying tithes to shepherds whom the Lord places over them. As a whole, the body of Christ is a pyramid of spiritual authority and responsibility. Hundreds of unconventional churches sprang up in the U.S., Canada, and Great Britain using this model, and conflict with denominational charismatics followed. A confrontation in 1975 between representatives of each brought subtle reforms and an uneasy truce between Simpson and Mumford and other charismatics.

Bibliography: J. Maust, "Charismatic Leaders Seeking Faith for Their Own Healing (1980) [and] The Secret Summit Reconstructed (1975)," *Christianity Today* 24 (April 4, 1980): 44–46; K. Philpott and R. L. Hymers, *Why We Reject Simpsonism-Mumfordism* (1978). C. E. Jones

INTERNATIONAL BROTHERHOOD OF COMMUNITIES See CHARISMATIC COMMUNITIES.

INTERNATIONAL CATHOLIC CHARISMATIC RENEWAL OFFICE (ICCRO). Originally called the "International Communication Office" (ICO), this organization serving worldwide Catholic charismatic renewal (CCR) was set up by the U.S. National Service Committee in October 1972. With R. Martin as director in Ann Arbor, Michigan, ICO began as a service from North America, with greater numbers,

The five principal leaders in Integrity Communications: from the left are Ern Baxter, Derek Prince, Charles Simpson, Don Basham, and Bob Mumford.

resources, and experience to CCR elsewhere. The process from ICO in Ann Arbor to ICCRO in Rome, Italy, with an international staff drawing on worldwide resources passed through several stages: the removal of the ICO office and staff to Brussels, Belgium, in 1976 at the invitation of Cardinal Suenens; the formation of an international council for ICO in 1978 with nine members representing all continents; the replacement of R. Martin by T. Forrest as director at the end of 1978 and his regular visitation of all parts of the world; and the removal of the ICO office from Brussels to Rome in 1981, followed immediately by the change of name to ICCRO.

The contribution of ICCRO to international CCR has been primarily: (1) through the work and travels of the full-time staff (F. Mascarenhas from India served as director from 1981 to 1987, followed by K. Metz, U.S.); (2) through the organization of international conferences—e.g., general conferences in Rome and in Dublin, Ireland (1975, 1978), leaders' conferences (1973 and triennially since 1975), and an international retreat for priests in the Vatican (1984); (3) through a newsletter, originally *ICO Newsletter* (first issued July 1975, monthly) and since 1978 *International Newsletter Serving the Charismatic Renewal in the Catholic Church* (bimonthly); (4) through channeling aid from the wealthier countries to CCR in the Third World; (5) through emphasizing evangelism. Links between ICCRO and the Catholic hierarchy were first assured through Cardinal Suenens at the request of Paul VI, and since Suenens' retirement more formally through Paul Cordes of the Council for the Laity, the Vatican department assigned responsibility for CCR.

See also CATHOLIC CHARISMATIC RENEWAL.

P. D. Hocken

INTERNATIONAL CHURCH OF THE FOURSQUARE GOSPEL

(ICFG). Founded January 1, 1923, with the opening of Angelus Temple, by the gifted evangelist Aimee Semple McPherson. Incorporated December 30, 1927, in California.

"Sister," as the founder was affectionately called, entered the ministry with her husband, Robert Semple, as a relatively young convert. Ordained together by William H. Durham on January 2, 1909, the Semples pastored, worked in the Full Gospel Assembly in Chicago, and aided Durham in evangelistic meetings during 1909–10. In mid-1910 the couple began a term as missionaries in China. Robert Semple's untimely death in August 1910 brought that dream to an end. Aimee Semple returned to the U.S. with the couple's newly born infant daughter, Roberta. Aimee remarried in late 1911, to Harold Stewart McPherson. Following the birth of their son, Rolf, the couple embarked on an evangelistic ministry.

Beginning in 1915, "Sister" ministered in Ontario, Canada, then in 1916–18 conducted a series of tent revivals along the Eastern Seaboard from Maine to Florida. She purchased a "gospel auto" on which she painted slogans such as "Jesus is coming soon—get ready." Her sermons were enthusiastically received, her message clear and simple; her method was broadly appealing, and, as a result, her reputation increased and her crowds grew.

In June 1917 she began to publish *The Bridal Call* (since 1964, *The Foursquare Advance*), a monthly magazine with articles that she authored.

This magazine, as well as Mrs. McPherson's participation as an editor with the New England Pentecostal monthly *Word and Work* helped to broaden her appeal and solidify a supportive constituency. By 1918 she had begun a series of transcontinental evangelistic campaigns in a number of major U.S. cities. She also embarked on a successful international campaign to Australia (1922), where she held meetings in Melbourne, Sidney, and Adelaide.

The name "Foursquare" was derived from an experience Sister McPherson had in her July 1922 Oakland, California, crusade. There in a moment of "divine inspiration," while preaching on Ezekiel's vision (Ezek 1:4–10) of the four cherubim with four faces which she understood to typify the fourfold ministry of Christ, she declared it to stand for "The Foursquare Gospel." The four cardinal doctrines of "Foursquare" were all descriptive of Jesus Christ. He was identified as "Savior," "Baptizer with the Holy Spirit," "Physician and Healer," and "Coming King." These four emphases were already present in the nineteenth-century Holiness movement, especially in the work of A. B. Simpson, who in 1890 had authored a book on *The Four-fold Gospel.* Simpson had identified Christ as Savior, *Sanctifier, Healer,* and Coming King, but these themes were uniquely appropriated, "pentecostalized," and popularized by "Sister." She formed the Echo Park Evangelistic Association and solicited the signatures of hundreds, regardless of denomination, who would preach these points.

McPherson's transcontinental trips led to broad-based support in many denominations. Along the way these people contributed thousands of dollars, making possible the building of the denomination's parent organization, Angelus Temple. Originally intended as a building where "Sister" would hold evangelistic meetings while she was in town, but whose pulpit would be shared with other evangelists when she was away, her adherents in Los Angeles soon encouraged her to settle there. Under the auspices of the Echo Park Evangelistic Association the temple was constructed, and the evangelistic association became responsible for the buildings and grounds.

To the temple were added the Prayer Tower (February 1923); the radio station KFSG (Kall Four Square Gospel, February 1924); a five-story building housing the Lighthouse of International Foursquare Evangelism (L.I.F.E.) Bible College (January 1926), founded in March 1923 to train pastors, evangelists, and missionaries; a denominational bookstore, "Ye Foursquare Book Shoppe" (1927); and the Angelus Temple Commissary (September 1927). Students who graduated from L.I.F.E. formed branch churches referred to as Foursquare Gospel Lighthouses. By 1927 it was clear that a new corporation was needed, and in December it was formally incorporated as the Church of the Foursquare Gospel.

Aimee Semple McPherson served as founder and president of the organization until her death on September 27, 1944. During her lifetime, Angelus Temple continued to function as the centerpiece of the denomination while it gained nationwide prominence. From its pulpit the gospel was proclaimed as many as twenty-one times weekly by McPherson. She was also actively involved in local community causes, and during the Depression more than 1.5 million needy individuals were helped through the Temple Commissary. The constant draw upon the financial resources of Angelus Temple to meet the needs of the ministry, especially of the commissary, led to a severe financial crisis in the mid-1930s. The help of Giles N. Knight was solicited, and by the end of the 30s, the movement was financially sound and fully prepared to face the future.

During the 1920s and 1930s, the organization of the fellowship was carefully established. Sister McPherson was designated president for life, and a board of directors was brought into existence. It included John Goben, Mae Waldron Emmel, Harriet A. Jordan, Herman Reitz, T. A. Overgard, and James Abbott. A general supervisor and various supervisors were appointed to manage regional or district affairs. The board, the district supervisors, and five other individuals were elected by the convention body at its annual meeting from a missionary cabinet to serve in an advisory capacity to the president and board.

The doctrinal position of the ICFG is found in its declaration of faith, penned by its founder. It is Trinitarian with respect to the Godhead, and progressive in its view of sanctification, exhorting the Foursquare faithful to "live and walk in the Spirit moment by moment, under the precious blood of the Lamb." The Declaration of Faith teaches on the baptism of the Holy Spirit that "the believer may have every reason to expect His [the Spirit's] incoming to be after the same manner as that in . . . Bible days," and supports that position with references to John 14:16, 17; Acts 1:5, 8; 2:4; 8:17; 10:44–47; 19:6; and 1 Corinthians 3:16. Little separates the doctrinal position of the ICFG from that of the Assemblies of God, except for minor nuances.

At the time of Sister McPherson's death in 1944, Rolf McPherson, her son, who for several years had carried administrative responsibilities alongside his mother, became president of the organization for life "unless or until he should desire to resign or retire." Aimee had left a legacy of more than 400 churches in North America; 200 mission stations; 22,000 church members, more than 3,000 of whom had graduated from L.I.F.E. and received ministerial credentials. The presidency of "Doctor" McPherson, as Rolf is most often referred to, is one that has brought accelerated growth to the ICFG around the world. According to figures released in January 1988, Foursquare had grown by the end of 1986 to include 1,250 churches in the U.S. and a total of 15,051 worldwide. It ministers in 59 countries, supporting 141 missionaries, and gives over 4.1 million dollars to missions annually. It claimed 383,774 new converts in 1986 bringing its total membership in the U.S. to 188,757, with a worldwide total membership of 1.1 million. Denominational assets rose to nearly $479 million, a tribute to the acute business sense of "Doctor" McPherson.

Rolf McPherson's leadership has also been

typified by action in which the ICFG has reached beyond itself and interacted with other Pentecostals and the larger evangelical world in a positive way. During the decade of the 40s, Rolf McPherson brought the ICFG into membership in the Pentecostal Fellowship of North America and enrolled the denomination in the Pentecostal World Conference. Howard P. Courtney played significant roles in both groups. Due to concerns that some Evangelicals had regarding Foursquare, the ICFG was not among the first Pentecostal groups to join the National Association of Evangelicals. Yet in 1952 McPherson successfully led the fellowship into that association, where it has played an important role, especially through Commission representation. Since joining the NAE, the ICFG has also taken membership in the National Religious Broadcasters.

The year 1987 was an important one for ICFG history. Rather than remaining in office for life, President McPherson announced his retirement. In a series of meetings that followed, John R. Holland was nominated and ratified as president-elect of the fellowship. In February 1988 he moved into ICFG headquarters to work alongside McPherson until "Doctor" officially retired at 2 P.M. on May 31, 1988. Thus, Holland became president at that time, elected to a four-year term. For the first time since its founding, the ICFG is being led by someone outside the McPherson family. Holland has been a minister and/or supervisor in the ICFG both in the U.S. and Canada since 1953.

The future of the ICFG is a bright one, thanks to those who have led it to its present position. The movement shows particular vigor in California, Oregon, Washington, and the Great Lakes region, especially Illinois. It has proven itself to be innovative on the mission field and, like most Pentecostal denominations in 1988, it is among the fastest-growing denominations in the world, especially in Brazil, the Philippines, Colombia, and Nigeria. The ICFG supports nearly sixty Bible schools, and in North America L.I.F.E. Bible College has been joined by L.I.F.E. of Canada and L.I.F.E. Bible College East, Christiansburg, Virginia.

Foursquare continues with its long-held vision for helping the poor. Work in the commissary goes on unabated. The ICFG has also participated in disaster-relief programs all over the world, supported in large part by its women's organization, United Foursquare Women. It continues to recognize a significant role for women in ministry with over 40 percent of its ministerial rolls consisting of women. It is also producing a number of vital churches. Among its best-known congregations is the Church on the Way in Van Nuys, California, served by Jack Hayford.

Bibliography: Articles of Incorporation and Bylaws of the International Church of the Foursquare Gospel (1985); P. Damboriena, *Tongues as of Fire* (1969); "International Church of the Foursquare Gospel—A History of Spiritual Achievement," *Congressional Record-House* (February 5, 1973), H 712; C. Duarte, "Historical Resume of the International Church of the Foursquare Gospel" (1979); "80 Facts You Should Know Concerning the Decade of Destiny in the 1980s"

(n.d.); "Foursquare Gospel Church Joins N.A.E.," *United Evangelical Action* 11 (1952); J. W. Hayford, *The Church on the Way* (1982); idem, "Why Do We Call Ourselves 'Foursquare'?" *Foursquare World Advance* (1976); "International Church of the Foursquare Gospel" (1983); A. S. McPherson, *Aimee* (1979); idem, *The Story of My Life* (1973); idem, *This is That* (1919, 1921, 1923); "Meet the Hollands," *Foursquare World Advance* 24 (1988); "'Doctor'—A Doer that Worketh," *Foursquare World Advance* 24 (1988); J. Montgomery, *Fire in the Philippines* (1975 rev. ed.); V. Synan, *The Twentieth-Century Pentecostal Explosion* (1987); R. Williams, "The Selection of a President," *Foursquare World Advance* (1987). C. M. Robeck, Jr.

INTERNATIONAL COMMUNICATIONS OFFICE See INTERNATIONAL CATHOLIC CHARISMATIC RENEWAL OFFICE.

INTERNATIONAL COMMUNION OF CHARISMATIC CHURCHES (ICCC). A communion of some Pentecostal churches with episcopal government closely related to the International Evangelical Church (IEC). ICCC was formed in 1982 by Bishop John Meares of Evangel Temple, Washington, D.C., and Bishop Robert McAlister of Igreja Pentecostal da Nova Vida in Rio de Janeiro, Brazil. Meares and McAlister saw the need for an international forum to share ideas, ministry resources, and spiritual direction among those Pentecostal leaders sharing their concern for the Kingdom message.

By 1983 five bishops composed the college of bishops for ICCC. Besides Meares and McAlister were Benson Idahosa of Miracle Centre, Benin City, Nigeria; Earl Paulk of Chapel Hill Harvester Church, Atlanta, Georgia; and Herro Blair of Deliverance Center, Kingston, Jamaica. All except Blair are also part of the IEC.

While IEC is primarily a legal entity to serve civil and ecclesiastical purposes, ICCC is a framework for pastoral and spiritual fellowship and collaboration. ICCC brings together the bishop-leaders of clusters of Pentecostal churches: McAlister's Igreja Pentecostal da Nova Vida in Brazil, Paulk's network of Harvester Churches; Idahosa's Nigerian churches listed under Church of God Missions; Blair's churches known as Deliverance Centers, together with the churches coming under Meares's supervision.

Besides their adoption of episcopal government, ICCC churches are characterized by their Kingdom message (the designation "Kingdom Now" especially applied to Paulk's teaching is that of critics). Systematic teaching aims at the formation of Christians whose lifestyles will reclaim whole sectors of living for the kingdom of God. Thus churches in ICCC are often characterized by programs whereby converted Christians can help change the social and economic environment. Their U.S. churches have large black memberships. The ICCC is committed to "the maturity, unity and preparation of the Body of Christ for the manifestation of Christ's Kingdom on earth as it is in heaven." The Eucharist is more important than in most Pentecostal churches.

ICCC's episcopal college meets for several days each year, and the bishops regard their college relationship as providing their "spiritual covering" in major ministry decisions. Expansion has been by invitation following growing pastoral relationships. Bishop Meares currently presides at college meetings.   P. D. Hocken

INTERNATIONAL CONVENTION OF FAITH CHURCHES AND MINISTERS

Established in 1979, the Tulsa-based International Convention of Faith Churches and Ministers consists of more than eight hundred pastors and congregations committed to the word of faith (so-called "name it, claim it") teaching of its most prominent founding members: Doyle Harrison; Kenneth Hagin, Sr.; Kenneth Copeland; Frederick K. C. Price; Norvel Hayes; Charles Capps; Jerry J. Savelle; and John H. Osteen. Dependent on ideas first promulgated by E. W. Kenyon (1867–1948), they head large churches in Tulsa; Fort Worth; Houston; Los Angeles; and Cleveland, Tennessee. All teach that the faithful can rightfully possess things from God after having publicly confessed them. Television ministries and publishing are principal means of spreading the message, dissemination of which has brought strong reactions from other charismatic leaders. The official organ is the *International Faith Report*. Papers issued by individual members, such as Hagin's *Word of Faith* (Tulsa); Price's *Ever Increasing Faith Messenger* (Los Angeles); and Copeland's *Believer's Voice of Victory* (Fort Worth); and the Tulsa-based Harrison House, a book publishing firm founded in 1975, also serve the International Convention constituency. Schools serving the movement are the Rhema Bible Training Center, Tulsa, and the Crenshaw Christian Center School of Ministry, Los Angeles.

Bibliography: C. Farah, *From the Pinnacle of the Temple* (1979); J. G. Melton, *Encyclopedia of American Religions* (1987); V. Synan, "Faith Formula Fuels Charismatic Controversy," *Christianity Today* 24 (December 12, 1980): 65–66.   C. E. Jones

The headquarters for the International Correspondence Institute is in Brussels, Belgium. Here a crowd gathers to dedicate the facility in 1975.

INTERNATIONAL CORRESPONDENCE INSTITUTE

George M. Flattery, founder and president of the International Correspondence Institute, laid the foundation of this worldwide correspondence school and, with the enthusiastic support of J. Philip Hogan, executive director of Assemblies of God (AG) foreign missions, recommended its implementation to the Division of

Foreign Missions of the AG in 1967. The International Correspondence Institute (ICI) was developed to supplement the training of national ministers and lay workers overseas and to coordinate the many different correspondence programs being developed by AG missionaries around the world. By 1971 a curriculum committee of missionary educators had chosen five levels of study for ICI: Evangelism, Christian Life, Christian Service, Christian Ministry, and College.

After five years of operating from a two-room office on the campus of Central Bible College in Springfield, Missouri, ICI transferred its operation to Brussels, Belgium, in 1972. After three years the rented facilities became inadequate, and a new modern five-story building was completed in 1975.

ICI received full accreditation by the National Home Study Council in Washington, D.C., in 1977. The school offers various associate of arts and bachelor of arts degrees. ICI also produces courses on audio tape and videocassettes; and it conducts radio and television ministries in the U.S. and in many foreign countries.

In addition to the international ICI office in Brussels, Belgium (with national offices in more than 110 countries), a stateside office has operated from Fort Worth, Texas, since 1982.

Bibliography: *Until the Day Dawns: The Story of International Correspondence Institute* (1987).
                      G. W. Gohr

INTERNATIONAL EVANGELICAL CHURCH

Originally known as the International Evangelical Church and Missionary Association, the International Evangelical church (IEC) was incorporated in the U.S. in March 1964 to provide a legal basis under an Italo–U.S. pact for the independent Pentecostal work begun in Italy in 1959 by John McTernan. McTernan was president of IEC until his death in 1974, when this responsibility passed to the vice-president, John L. Meares.

Besides the U.S. churches under Bishop Meares of Washington, D.C., the IEC includes in its framework a network of Brazilian churches under Bishop Robert McAlister of Rio de Janeiro, a large number of churches in Nigeria led by Bishop Benson Idahosa of Benin City, and some Italian churches whose senior pastor is Silvano Lilli of Rome.

In 1982 Meares and McAlister joined with other Pentecostal leaders of similar convictions to form the International Communion of Charismatic Churches (ICCC), which sees itself not as a denomination but as a communion of kindred churches. While ICCC is a little wider in scope than IEC, it represents much the same Pentecostal constituency, with IEC serving the official, legal, and organizational needs and ICCC filling the spiritual and fellowship roles. Thus IEC, besides being an entity recognized in civil law, has become a member of the World Council of Churches (WCC) (1972), sending two delegates, one being David du Plessis, to the Vancouver assembly in 1983. It was also the first Pentecostal denomination to participate officially in the Catholic-Pentecostal dialogue.

In 1985 there were approximately 450 IEC churches worldwide. There are 20 in the U.S., with a membership of around 13,500. The U.S. also has three Bible schools, with approximately 1,300 students. Latin America has 45 IEC churches, with a membership of around 60,000. Italy has 22 churches, with a membership of 3,000, while Jamaica has only 1, with a membership of around 350. The largest contingency of IEC churches is in Africa, where there are 400 churches, with membership of around 150,000. Africa also has two Bible schools, with a total enrollment of nearly 2,700.   P. D. Hocken

INTERNATIONAL EVANGELISM CRUSADES A fellowship that grants ministerial credentials, charters churches, and operates International Theological Seminary (ITS) in Van Nuys, California. Frank E. Stranges, who attended North Central Bible College (Assemblies of God), founded International Evangelism Crusades (IEC) in 1959 and ITS in 1976. He is president of both and serves as pastor of a local church in Van Nuys, the IEC Christian Center. In 1967 Stranges founded the National Investigations Committee on Unidentified Flying Objects (NICUFO) and has published books on the subject. IEC's statement of faith is similar to that of other Pentecostal groups. In 1986 IEC claimed 12,000 members and 1,200 credentialed ministers worldwide. In the U.S. the fellowship claims 2,400 members and sixty chartered churches. ITS operates with four academic sessions each year and has attracted twenty-five to thirty Korean students for each session.

Bibliography: IEC, ITS Catalogue (1985); IEC Newsletter (1986).   W. E Warner

INTERNATIONAL LUTHERAN RENEWAL CENTER See LUTHERAN CHARISMATICS.

INTERNATIONAL MINISTERIAL ASSOCIATION (IMA). A Oneness ministerial and church fellowship organized in 1954 by W. E. Kidson and other ministers who withdrew from the United Pentecostal Church and other Oneness bodies. In 1987 the association had 105 affiliated churches in the U.S. and 1,140 ministers worldwide. Glen Yeazel, Arvada, Colorado, serves as chairman. A. D. Van Hoose, Evansville, Indiana, a former chairman, is editor of the association's magazine, *Herald of Truth*. The headquarters for the group is located in St. Louis. IMA is also affiliated with the Apostolic World Christian Fellowship, South Bend, Indiana.

Bibliography: IMA Constitution (1987).   W. E. Warner

INTERNATIONAL PENTECOSTAL ASSEMBLIES See INTERNATIONAL PENTECOSTAL CHURCH OF CHRIST.

INTERNATIONAL PENTECOSTAL CHURCH See INTERNATIONAL PENTECOSTAL CHURCH OF CHRIST.

INTERNATIONAL PENTECOSTAL CHURCH OF CHRIST (IPCC). A Wesleyan Pentecostal organization that is the result of a 1976 amalgamation between the International

Pentecostal Assemblies and the Pentecostal Church of Christ. The two groups trace their history to the early outpouring of the Holy Spirit in this century. The IPCC has its headquarters in London, Ohio.

I. International Pentecostal Assemblies. Holiness preacher G. B. Cashwell went to Los Angeles in 1906 because he had heard about the Azusa Street Mission revival. He returned to his North Carolina home baptized in the Spirit and eager to spread the message throughout the South. Many believed and also received the experience, including a group in Atlanta. A new Pentecostal church was established there in the fall of 1907, and Cashwell founded a Pentecostal paper that he called the *Bridegroom's Messenger*. Later the *Pentecostal Holiness Advocate* stated that Cashwell intended the paper "to take care of the Pentecostal work of the South" (Synan, 1971, 127). Mrs. E. A. Sexton became Cashwell's associate editor and later the editor.

In 1919 Paul and Hattie Barth, who were pastors of the church in Atlanta, founded Beulah Heights Bible School. The Atlanta church and a few Pentecostal churches in the Southeast founded the Association of Pentecostal Assemblies (APA) in 1921. An amalgamation took place in 1936 when the APA and the International Pentecostal Church joined forces, calling the new group the International Pentecostal Assemblies (IPA). The IPA continued publishing the *Bridegroom's Messenger* and operating Beulah Heights. The first chairman of IPA was John W. Pitcher of Baltimore.

II. Pentecostal Church of Christ. John Stroup, who was an elder of the Methodist Church in South Solon, Ohio, received the baptism in the Holy Spirit in 1908. He ministered in the Ohio Valley between 1913 and 1917, and in May 1917 he invited ministers and church representatives to meet at Advance (now Flatwoods), Kentucky. There they organized the Pentecostal Church of Christ (PCC) with Stroup as the bishop.

For six years, beginning in 1928, two other groups were associated with the PCC. They were the United Pentecostal Association of Conneaut, Ohio, and the Full Gospel Pentecostal Church of Maryland. Both groups had withdrawn by 1934.

Beginning in 1923, the *Pentecostal Witness* was the official publication for the PCC. It consolidated with the *Bridegroom's Messenger* in 1974 when the trial merger began.

III. The Merger—IPA and PCC. At a general conference at London, Ohio, August 10, 1976, the two groups voted to merge and become the IPCC. Chester I. Miller, who served as PCC's general overseer, became the leader of the new organization.

IPCC operates a home for the elderly in Harpers Ferry, West Virginia, and Beulah Heights College in Atlanta. In 1985 IPCC reported ninety-nine churches in the U.S., 188 ministers, and 4,500 members. Missionaries serve in several countries.

IV. Statement of Faith. IPCC's statement of faith is similar to that of other Wesleyan Pentecostal groups that belong to the Pentecostal Fellowship of North America. They regard footwashing as an ordinance, but its practice in local assemblies is optional. The group is pacifistic regarding war.

Bibliography: The *Bridegroom's Messenger* and the *Pentecostal Witness;* Minutes of the IPCC (1984, 1985 supplement); Statement of Faith of IPCC (n.d.); V. Synan, *The Holiness-Pentecostal Movement in the United States* (1971). W. E. Warner

INTERNATIONAL PENTECOSTAL COUNCIL

A consultative body of Pentecostal leaders, mostly European, that met four times during its short existence (1912–14). The council was formed during the Sunderland, England, convention at the end of May 1912. It has no formal membership, but the main European leaders who took the initiative in its formation invited visiting American leaders to participate (J. H. King was a signatory to the May 1912 statement).

The council was formed "to protect this [Pentecostal] work from wrong teaching, or false teachers." This concern found expression in its rejection of teachers claiming direct divine inspiration in a way that denied any need for discernment by fellow Christians (1912), in warning against itinerant teachers without credentials from other assemblies as well as repudiating a teaching on the "eunuch life" (1913), and in denouncing the placing of inspired divine messages on the same level as Holy Scripture (1914).

Probably more important than the warnings against deviations were two positive statements made by the council, one on the "Baptism of the Holy Ghost and Fire" (May 1912) and "Declaration" (December 1912). (A third declaration mostly sought to refute the anti-Pentecostal allegations in *War on the Saints* by J. Penn-Lewis and E. Roberts [May 1913]). The first statement was brief, manifesting a clear concern to issue a statement on the baptism of the Holy Ghost that all leaders could sign: this speaks of the baptism in terms of the Holy Spirit indwelling the believer in His fullness "and is always borne witness to by the fruit of the Spirit and the outward manifestation, so that we may receive the same gift as the disciples on the Day of Pentecost." The concern for unity in the movement, especially championed by Boddy and Barratt is clear in the Amsterdam Declaration of December 1912: the "present outpouring . . . we consider to have been granted . . . in these last days . . . for the edifying and perfecting of the Body of Christ, and its preparation for the 'rapture.'" It also reflects the strong concern for holiness of life, emphasized by J. Paul, stating that there often has to be a progressive entering into the fullness of blessing implied in this baptism. All true deepening is a work of the Holy Spirit and cannot be effected by "merely human or self-originated efforts."

The International Pentecostal Council witnesses to the unusually close fellowship and warm friendship existing among the first major European Pentecostal leaders, especially Boddy, Barratt, Paul, and Polman. It is one of the tragedies of Pentecostal history that this international communion was interrupted by the outbreak of World War I in August 1914 and never fully recovered.

Bibliography: *Confidence* (June and December 1912; July 1913; June 1914); C. van der Laan, "The Proceedings of the Leaders' Meetings (1908–1911) and of the International Pentecostal Council (1912–1914)," *EPTA Bulletin* 6 (3, 1987): 76–96. P. D. Hocken

INTERNATIONAL PENTECOSTAL HOLINESS CHURCH

The International Pentecostal Holiness Church (IPHC) is one of the oldest and largest Pentecostal denominations in the U.S. With roots in the nineteenth-century Holiness movement, it was formed before the advent of the Pentecostal movement. Directly influenced by the Azusa Street revival, it was one of the first organized denominations to adopt a Pentecostal statement of faith.

The roots of the church lie in the National Holiness Association movement with beginnings in Vineland, New Jersey, in 1867. The western part of the church had its origins in the Iowa Holiness Association, which began in 1879, while the eastern part began its existence in 1896 as the North Carolina Holiness Association. The original impulse of these movements was the attempt to revive the Wesleyan experience of entire sanctification.

The present church represents the merger of three groups: the Fire-Baptized Holiness Church (FBHC), the Holiness Church of North Carolina (HCNC), and the Tabernacle Pentecostal Church (TPC). All three of these were Wesleyan groups that accepted the Pentecostal revival after 1906.

I. The Fire-Baptized Holiness Church. The oldest of the three groups was the Fire-Baptized Holiness Church (FBHC), which was founded by Benjamin Hardin Irwin as the Iowa Fire-Baptized Holiness Association in Olmitz, Iowa, in 1895. Before entering the Baptist ministry, Irwin had practiced law in Lincoln, Nebraska. After his conversion in 1879 he came under the ministry of preachers in the Iowa Holiness Association, becoming in his words, a "John Wesley Methodist." He soon joined the Wesleyan Methodist Church and began a ministry of tent evangelism featuring divine healing. After a study of Wesley and Wesley's colleague, John Fletcher, Irwin sought for and received an experience that Fletcher referred to as a "baptism of burning love." It then became Irwin's contention that after the "second blessing" of entire sanctification, there was a "third blessing" for all the sanctified called the "baptism of fire."

This teaching set Irwin and his followers apart from the mainline Holiness leaders, who denounced it as the "third blessing heresy." In addition to the "fire" experience, Irwin required his people to follow OT dietary rules against eating pork and insisted on a strict dress code which, in addition to the usual holiness code for women's dress, forbade men to wear neckties. To detractors, Irwin's followers were called the "no ties, no hog-meat" people. Worship in fire-baptized meetings was characterized by shouting and dancing before the Lord.

By 1898 the Fire-Baptized movement had spread to eight states and two Canadian provinces. In August of that year, a national organization was effected in Anderson, South Carolina, with Irwin designated as general overseer for life.

He also began the publication of a periodical called *Live Coals of Fire*. The church grew rapidly under the dynamic preaching of its founder until 1890 when Irwin resigned from the church after confessing to "open and gross sin." His young assistant, Joseph H. King of Georgia, took over the church and attempted to hold it together after Irwin's fall.

II. The Holiness Church of North Carolina. The HCNC had its beginning in the same period under the leadership of Ambrose Blackman Crumpler, a North Carolina Methodist preacher who was sanctified under the ministry of Beverly Carradine in 1890 while living in Missouri. In 1896 he moved back to North Carolina, determined to bring the Holiness movement to his native state. After organizing the North Carolina Holiness Association in Magnolia, North Carolina, in 1897, he began a ministry of tent evangelism featuring sanctification and divine healing.

By 1898 Crumpler began to organize independent congregations to shepherd his converts, although he was still an ordained Methodist minister. The first church to bear the Pentecostal Holiness name was organized in Goldsboro, North Carolina, on November 4, 1898. He also began publication of a periodical for the Association known as *The Holiness Advocate*. His fiery preaching and disregard for church polity caused controversy among North Carolina Methodists.

In 1899 near Elizabeth City, North Carolina, Crumpler was tried under charges for violating Rule 301 of the Methodist *Discipline,* which forbade evangelists to preach in a local parish without an invitation of the local pastor. Although he was acquitted, Crumpler decided to organize a separate denomination, which he called the Pentecostal Holiness Church of North Carolina (PHCNC). This transpired in Fayetteville in 1900. The PHCNC adopted a "discipline" based on the Holiness Church of Donelsonville, Georgia. Crumpler's new church was identical in doctrine and government to the Church of the Nazarene, which was forming at the same time.

In 1901 the church voted to drop the word "Pentecostal" from its name. This was done because many members identified themselves as Pentecostal rather than bearing the "reproach" of the word "Holiness." In this period the word "Pentecostal" did not denote tongues speaking but was a widely used synonym for the Holiness experience.

III. The Tabernacle Pentecostal Church. The third group that ultimately merged to form the church was the TPC, which began in South Carolina in 1898 under the leadership of Nickles John Holmes. A Presbyterian pastor trained at the University of Edinburgh, Holmes had practiced law before entering the ministry. In 1896, while pastor of the Second Presbyterian Church of Greenville, South Carolina, he journeyed to Northfield, Massachusetts, where he accepted the second blessing teaching of D. L. Moody.

Due to pressure from the Enoree presbytery concerning his teachings on sanctification, Holmes left the Presbyterian Church in 1898 to found an independent congregation in Greenville as well as a Bible college on Parris Mountain outside the city. Other churches following his lead formed the Brewerton Presbyterian churches, mostly in South Carolina. These congregations later changed their name to TPC.

All three of these small Holiness groups joined the ranks of the Pentecostal movement after 1906 under the ministry of Gaston Barnabas Cashwell, a minister in Crumpler's North Carolina church. Traveling to Azusa Street in 1906, Cashwell returned to Dunn, North Carolina, to open a Pentecostal revival in December. By 1908 all three churches had accepted the Pentecostal "initial evidence" teaching that glossolalia was the necessary first sign of the baptism in the Holy Spirit.

By the end of 1907 practically all the ministers of the three tiny denominations had not only received the tongues-attested baptism but had led their congregations to accept the new experience and teaching. King and Holmes quickly experienced glossolalia, but Crumpler refused to countenance the new movement. In January 1908, when it became apparent that his church had become Pentecostal, Crumpler left the convention of the denomination he had founded and returned to the Methodist Church. In January 1908, under Cashwell's leadership, the HCNC adopted a Pentecostal article of faith requiring all ministers and members to accept the doctrine. In 1909 it changed its name to Pentecostal Holiness Church (PHC).

The FBHC also adopted a similar article in April 1908 with the understanding that tongues was the reality that the church had been seeking under Irwin's "Fire-baptism" teaching. Holmes and the school and churches under his influence also accepted the new teaching.

IV. Mergers. Now with similar doctrines and experiences, the leaders of the FBHC and PHC began negotiations in 1909 to merge the two churches. Sentiment soon arose in favor of a merger since both churches operated in the same territory and had shared fellowship for many years. On January 31, 1911, the merger took place in the camp meeting village of Falcon, North Carolina. At the time of merger, the FBHC was the larger of the two groups. Altogether the membership of the united churches was about two thousand persons.

In 1915, in the village of Canon, Georgia, the TPC merged with the PHC. Although the Holmes Bible and Missionary Institute did not join in the merger, the school became the major center for training pastors and missionaries for the church. By the 1940s Holmes Bible College became directly related to the church.

The theology of the church was typical of the Holiness Pentecostal groups that represented the first wave of American Pentecostalism. The church's teachings were distilled in its five "cardinal doctrines," i.e., justification by faith; sanctification as a second definite work of grace; the baptism in the Holy Spirit evidenced by speaking in tongues; divine healing as in the Atonement; and the imminent, premillennial second coming of Christ.

The government of the church reflected its Methodistic roots. The highest government body was the general conference, which met quadrennially, while the licensing, ordination, and assigning of pastors was the province of the regional annual conferences. In 1937 the general superintendent was given the honorary title of bishop. Beginning in the 1960s, the church moved toward a modified congregational polity in contrast to the centralized episcopacy that characterized the early years. In 1975 it changed its name to International Pentecostal Holiness Church.

V. Growth and Development. In the years following the mergers the church developed several institutions, mainly under the leadership of George Floyd Taylor, who served as general superintendent from 1913 to 1917. In the latter year, Taylor inaugurated the official organ of the church, known as the *Pentecostal Holiness Advocate,* and in 1919 he became the founder and first president of the Franklin Springs Institute located near Athens, Georgia. This in time developed into Emmanuel College, the first liberal arts college owned by the denomination. Also, in 1919 Taylor sold his privately owned Sunday school literature business to the church, which ultimately became known as Advocate Press.

The foreign missions program of the church began in 1909 when the first missionary was sent to Hong Kong, China. A second field was opened in India in 1910, while the first missionary to South Africa went out in 1913. Other fields were opened in South America by the 1930s.

The church suffered its only schism in 1920, when Watson Sorrow and Hugh Bowling, leaders in the Georgia Conference, objected to the general teaching in the church that the use of medicine or doctors was an admission of a lack of faith in divine healing. Those following Bowling and Sorrow left the denomination in 1921 to found the Congregational Holiness Church, which accepted medicine as well as prayer. In time this church planted congregations in the southeastern U.S.

The IPHC grew slowly during the 1920s and 1930s under the long-time leadership of Joseph H. King, who served as head of the church from 1917 until his death in 1946 (with the exception of the years 1941–45 when Dan T. Muse served as chairman of the general board).

The church moved outward in the years following World War II. One influence in bringing Pentecostals together was the healing-deliverance crusades of the era led by IPHC evangelist Oral Roberts. For the first time, pastors of the various Pentecostal bodies cooperated in these crusades, becoming better acquainted with each other. Also, the exigencies of World War II had demonstrated the need for closer cooperation between the churches.

In 1943 the IPHC, along with several other sister Pentecostal bodies, joined the National Association of Evangelicals (NAE) as charter members. Building upon relationships created in the lobbies of the NAE, the IPHC became one of the founders of the Pentecostal Fellowship of North America (PFNA) when it was formed in Des Moines, Iowa, in 1948. After the Pentecostal World Conference (PWC) was formed in Zurich, Switzerland, in 1947, the church also played an active part in the triennial Pentecostal World Conferences that followed. A leader in building these relationships was Bishop J. A. Synan who headed the church from 1950 to 1969.

This spirit of Pentecostal ecumenism also led the church to form affiliations with the Iglesia Metodista Pentecostal de Chile (MPC) in 1967 and the Igreja Metodista Wesleyana do Brasil in 1984. In the U.S., affiliations were also formed with the predominantly black Original United Holy Church in 1977 as well as with the Congregational Holiness and Pentecostal Freewill Baptist Churches in 1980.

The post–World War II era was also a period of tension within the church over the ministry of Oral Roberts, a member of the East Oklahoma Conference who gained national prominence for his healing crusades after 1948. Roberts' opponents in the church included Paul F. Beacham, longtime president of Holmes Bible College, and H. T. Spence, editor of *The Advocate.* Roberts' friends were able to win acceptance for his ministry in the 1953 general conference when his friend Oscar Moore was elected bishop. Roberts also gained new respect and acceptance within the church after his positive reception at the Berlin Congress of 1966. The new Oral Roberts University, which he opened in 1965, was staffed largely by IPHC people. Many of his friends in the church were puzzled when he left the denomination in 1969 to become a United Methodist.

Like most American classical Pentecostal bodies, the church experienced mixed feelings about the charismatic movement in the traditional Christian churches after 1960. A leading voice encouraging fellowship with the charismatics was Vinson Synan (son of Bishop J. A. Synan), who led the New Orleans Charismatic Congresses in 1986 and 1987.

The growth of the IPHC over the years was steady but not spectacular. The size of the church in the U.S. by decade was as follows: 1920: 6,000; 1930: 12,000; 1940: 22,000; 1950: 40,000; 1960: 53,000; 1970: 70,000; 1980: 110,000. With the accession of the Chilean and Brazilian churches, the worldwide statistics of the church soared in the 1960s and 1980s. By 1985 the world constituency of the church stood at 1.5 million members (including affiliates). By the end of the 1980s, the church had missions work in thirty-two nations and had plans to expand into other areas of the world.

Bibliography: A. Beacham, Jr., *A Brief History of the Pentecostal Holiness Church* (1983); J. Campbell, *The Pentecostal Holiness Church, 1898–1948* (1951); V. Synan, *The Old-Time Power, A History of the Pentecostal Holiness Church* (1973). H. V. Synan

INTERNATIONAL PENTECOSTAL PRESS ASSOCIATION

(IPPA). Founded in 1970 by Pentecostal journalists in cooperation with the Pentecostal World Conference (PWC). Member periodicals are not required to belong to the PWC but to remain in sympathy with that organization's goals and statement of faith. International Pentecostal Press Association has no members from the Oneness or Catholic charismatic traditions. Purposes include: to meet and encourage cooperation among members, to gather and disseminate information of the Pentecostal movement, and to promote excellence in the journalistic profession. A general meeting of IPPA is conducted in association with the triennial meeting of the PWC. Continental chapters meet annually. IPPA publishes a quarterly newsletter and the *World Directory of Pentecostal Periodicals*. Scholarships are awarded to deserving students, with some preference given to Third World applicants.

Bibliography: IPPA Constitution and By-laws (rev. 1976); *Pentecost: International Report* (quarterly).
W. E. Warner

INTERPRETATION OF TONGUES, GIFT OF

The spiritual gift *(charisma)* by which one so endowed makes clear to the congregation the unintelligible utterance of one who has spoken in tongues. This gift, and not speaking in tongues as often stated, appears at the end of three lists of charismata (1 Cor. 12:10, 30; 14:26), not because it is least valued, but because of its necessarily close relation to glossolalia—which it follows immediately in all these places.

Interpretation *(hermēneia)* itself is a charismatic gift, no less extraordinary than any other charisma. The overall corrective pastoral advice given by Paul in 1 Corinthians 12–14 calls for the elimination of uninterpreted glossolalia in the congregation (14:5). For this reason, those who speak in tongues should pray for the ability to interpret (v. 13). But a different person may interpret (v. 27). Since it can be determined if an interpreter is present (v. 28), this charisma may habitually reside with certain persons known for such ability. Not all are interpreters (12:30). Speakers in tongues should not exercise their gift but speak to themselves if no interpreter is present (14:28). Interpretation shares with prophecy the end result of an uplifting message that bears meaning for the whole congregation. Coupled with speaking in tongues, the double event gains a sign value when unbelievers are present (v. 22).

According to Acts 2:6–8, 11, the speaking in tongues that occurred on the first Christian Day of Pentecost was heard by the gathered Jewish pilgrims in their own native dialects. No interpretation was necessary, nor is any interpretation of tongues reported in Acts 10:46 or 19:6. Acts knows of no gift of interpretation. Both "interpretation" (in the sense of a charismatic gift) and "charisma" are Paul's words, not Luke's. Luke does use the *hermēneia* cluster of words in a noncharismatic sense, to indicate translation from one language to another: for example, "Tabitha, which *means* Dorcas" (Acts 9:36).

In the patristic and Reformation eras, interpretation was understood narrowly as "translation," because the Fathers and the Reformers generally understood speaking in tongues to mean using foreign languages, after the model of Acts 2. In the early Pentecostal movement, newly Spirit-baptized believers undertook overseas missionary ventures, convinced that speaking in tongues would be God's way of equipping them for that task without language study. Early Pentecostal leader Charles F. Parham never relinquished that view of the purpose of glossolalia. W. F. Carothers by 1910 found it necessary to write an article cautioning his Pentecostal peers against construing interpretation as a means of personal or group guidance. Classical Pentecostal teachers over most of the twentieth century have viewed interpretation as a rendering of the essence of the glossolalic utterance in the vernacular. Particular Pentecostal teachers developed nuances: (1) expecting the interpretation to match in length or patterns of intonation the glossolalic utterance it translates; or (2) insisting that the interpretation must, like speaking in tongues, be addressed "to God" (1 Cor. 14:2) and therefore be a prayer (these might also teach that any interpretation that began, "Thus saith the Lord . . ." was thereby out of order). But these views seem needlessly restrictive. Among the new charismatics, especially in Roman Catholic charismatic groups organized as communities, prophecy rather than "tongues and interpretation" prevails—with Pauline warrant.

Both social scientists and theologians have focused on glossolalia, surely the most studied charisma, to the neglect of interpretation. In the rare instances where speaking in tongues issued in the use of an identifiable language, interpretation expectedly would be translation. But the idea of *hermēneia* is broader, ranging from "speech" that expresses what is unclear, through "translation" that exchanges from one language to another, to "commentary" that explains or interprets" (Robinson, 1964). In all uses of the word the movement from obscurity or unintelligibility to clarity of expression prevails. Thiselton (1979), considering the way the word cluster "interpretation" is used by Philo and Josephus (near-contemporaries of Paul), concludes that the gift of interpretation means "to put into words, to say it articulately." He assumes that glossolalia is ecstatic speech. Behm (1964, 1:665) says that the gift of the interpretation of tongues consists in "the conversion of what is unintelligible into what is intelligible and therefore an explanation of the spiritual movement which fills the ecstatic."

It is not necessary to look for one-to-one correspondences between a glossolalic speech and its interpretation. It is enough to acknowledge that for the uplift of the gathered church the Holy Spirit who moves one to broken speech moves another (or the same one) to clarify what the Spirit says to the church at that time.

Bibliography: D. Basham, *A Handbook on Tongues, Interpretations and Prophecy* (1971); J. Behm, *"hermēneia,* etc." *TDNT* 2:661–66 (New Testament word cluster for "interpretation"); E. Best, "The Interpretation of Tongues," *SJT* 28 (1975): 45–62 (wordplay title: treats what to make out of glossolalia for today); W. F. Carothers, "The Gift of Interpretation: Is It Intended to Be a Means of Guidance?" *LRE* (Chicago) (October 1910): 7–10; D. G. Dunn, "The Responsible Congregation (1 Cor. 14:26–40)," in L. de Lorenzi, ed., *Charisma und Agape* (1983); D. Gee, *Concerning Spiritual Gifts* (1949, reprint 1980); W. Grudem, "A Response to G. Dautzenberg on 1 Cor. 12:10," *Biblische Zeitschrift* 22 (1978): 253–70 (rejects Dunn's proposal that "discernment of spirits" should rather be translated "interpreting the revelations of the Spirit"); A. L. Hoy, "The Gift of Interpretation," *Paraclete* 3 (1969):

Celebrating the Eucharist at the 1983 Episcopal Renewal Ministries National Priests' Conference is Charles M. Irish, national coordinator of ERM.

28–31 (classical Pentecostal view); W. Peremans, "Les hermeneis dans l'Egypte greco-romaine," in G. Grimm, ed., *Das römisch-byzantinische Agypten: Akten des internationalen Symposiums 26.–60. Sept. 1978 in Trier* (1983); J. Robinson and H. B. Cobb, eds., *The New Hermeneutic* (1964); A. C. Thiselton, "The 'Interpretation' of Tongues: A New Suggestion in the Light of Greek Usage in Philo Josephus," *JTS* 30 (1979): 15–36; H. Weder, "Die Gabe der hermēneia (1 Cor. 12 und 14)," in H. F. Geisser and W. Mostert, eds., *Wirkungen hermeneutischer Theologie* (1983).

R. P. Spittler

IRISH CHARISMATICS See CHARISMATIC MOVEMENT.

IRISH, CHARLES MANNING (1929–). A leader in the charismatic movement within the Episcopal Church and national coordinator of the Episcopal Renewal Ministries. A veteran of the Korean War, Irish was in business for ten years prior to entering the ministry. He graduated from Bexley Hall Seminary to become vicar of St. Luke's Mission in Bath, Ohio, in 1969. Following a charismatic experience in 1970 he led St. Luke's into becoming a nationally known charismatic parish. He attended the first Episcopal charismatic clergy conference in 1973 and two years later was a member of the national board of the Episcopal Charismatic Fellowship. In 1978 he was elected its national coordinator and editor of *Acts 29.* Under the new name, Episcopal Renewal Ministries, headquarters were moved in 1986 to Fairfax, Virginia, where he directs the work full time. Theologically he teaches the baptism in the Holy Spirit as a definite second work of grace. He is committed to spiritual renewal in the historic churches. His teaching and conferences model practicality, with emphasis on parish renewal and ministry of the laity.

D. A. Reed

IRVING, EDWARD (1792–1834). Scottish-Presbyterian pastor, theologian, considered a founder of the Catholic Apostolic Church, also known as Irvingites. Irving studied mathematics at the University of Edinburgh (ages thirteen–

seventeen). He taught briefly at Haddington and later at Kirkcaldy. Interest in theology persisted, and by following lectures at the university, Irving passed his theological examinations in 1815 and was licensed to preach by the presbytery of Kirkcaldy. In 1818, after difficulties in the parish, he returned to the university to study science and linguistics in anticipation of missionary service in Persia. However, he became the assistant to Dr. Thomas Chalmers at St. John's Glasgow (1819). After three difficult years, he was ordained in Annam presbytery (1822) and became minister to a small congregation in London. In London he quickly achieved recognition and published a series of sermons, *For the Oracles of God, Four Orations. For Judgement to Come, an Argument in Nine Parts* (1823). The church became too small to accommodate the crowds, and a new church was built in Regent Square.

Influenced by the ideas of Samuel Taylor Coleridge and Thomas Carlyle, Irving became convinced that he was to function as a prophet and priest. His study of the biblical accounts of the early church persuaded him that since the fivefold offices of apostles, prophets, evangelists, pastors, and teachers had been abandoned, the Holy Spirit had, as a result, left the church to its own devices. This conviction was reinforced and provided with an interpretative key by the millenarian and apocalyptic views espoused by Henry Drummond (1786–1860), a wealthy banker with whom Irving became closely associated after 1825. A group for the study of spiritual concerns sponsored by Drummond at Albury, his estate in Surrey, had a significant influence on Irving; he, in turn, became its leader. In 1825 Irving preached on "Babylon," developing these ideas and predicting the end of the world in 1868. These sermons were published as *Babylon and Infidelity Foredoomed by God* (1826). He also published, with an extensive introduction, an apocalyptic treatise written by a Spanish Jesuit, M. Lacunza, *The Coming of the Messiah in Glory and Majesty* (1827), and a three-volume set of *Sermons, Lectures, and Occasional Discourses* (1828).

In the latter, along with his apocalyptic views, Irving began to publish his ideas on the liturgy and christology. His apocalyptic dualism resulted in a view of the Incarnation quite out of keeping with Presbyterian theology. At this time, prayer groups were established to seek a new outpouring of the Holy Spirit, and many were led, by Irving's assistant, Alexander Scott, to seek the "charismata" described in the NT as part of early Christian spirituality. Anticipation was increased during Irving's preaching tours to Scotland in 1828, 1829, and 1830. In early 1830 parishioners near Glasgow began to experience charismata, especially glossolalia, and understood these in light of Irving's analysis. A delegation from Albury was sent to investigate and concluded that the manifestations were indeed of divine origin.

The general presbytery of the London area called Irving to account for his christological views expressed in *The Orthodox and Catholic Doctrine of Christ's Human Nature* (1830). Meanwhile, the Albury groups began to experience glossolalia and prophetic utterances. By early 1831 many in Irving's church and other churches throughout Britain had begun to prophesy and speak in tongues. In October 1831 the practice of these charismata had become part of the worship in Irving's church. He considered them to be of divine origin and revelatory. Irving was censured by the London Presbytery in 1832 for violating liturgical regulations by allowing women and men not properly ordained to speak in the services. He was expelled from his pulpit on April 26, 1832, and led about eight hundred members from the Regent Street Church to form the first congregation of what would become the Catholic Apostolic Church. Irving's status as a clergyman in the Church of Scotland was removed by the presbytery of Annam on March 13, 1833. On returning to London, he found himself relegated to a minor role in his congregation because he himself had received no charismata.

As the form of the new church took shape, Irving was recognized as an "angel," while Drummond, Cardale, and Taplin were declared "apostles." It was a conscious decision to remove Irving from his position of leadership within the movement. The members in London were divided into seven churches. Finally, in an effort to further remove him from the center of power, Irving was sent (1834) to Glasgow by the "apostles," where he died and was buried in the cathedral.

After Irving's death the development of the organization continued. In 1835 the collegium of apostles was brought to twelve. Reshaping of the liturgy according to J. B. Cardale's understanding of early Christian practice resulted in the gradual assimilation of Roman Catholic and Orthodox liturgical elements and architecture. Prophecy became less functional, and after the publication of Cardale's *Prophesying and the Ministry of the Prophet in the Christian Church* (1868), it virtually ceased in British churches. The tradition remained "enthusiastic" longer in Germany and the Netherlands where, under the leadership of T. Carlyle

and other dissidents, continental apostles were chosen and the movement became indigenized as the *Neu-Apostolische Gemeinde.*

Irving and his church became important features of Pentecostal historiography as historical precedents were sought for revivals with emphasis on the charismata, especially glossolalia. It is evident from early periodical articles that the Irving phenomenon became an interpretative grid by which Pentecostal theologians came to understand and evaluate their own experience. This historiography has been continued by writers such as J. Nichol, *The Pentecostals* (1966); D. Gee, *Wind and Flame* (1967); V. Synan, *The Holiness-Pentecostal Movement* (1971); and J. Kuosmanen, *Heratyksen Historia* (1979). The best analysis of the significance of Irving for Pentecostals is by D. Brandt-Bessire, *Aux sources de la spiritualité pentecôtiste* (1986).

Bibliography: (1) On Irving: (a) Works: E. Irving, *Collected Works,* 5 vols., ed. G. Carlyle (1864–65). (b) Dictionaries: A. Algermissen, "Irving," *LThK* 5 (1960): 771; *Dictionary of National Biography* (1891–92), 10:489–93; J. D. Douglas, "Irving, Edward," *NIDCC* (1974), 517; T. Kolde, "Irving, Edward," *NSHERK* (1910), 7:33–34; *New Catholic Encyclopedia* (1967), 7: 660; *ODCC* (1957), 702. (c) **Studies:** T. Carlyle, *Reminiscences* (1932); A. Dallimore, *Forerunner of the Charismatic Movement, the Life of Edward Irving* (1983); A. L. Drummond, *Edward Irving and His Circle* (1937); W. Jones, *Biographical Sketch of Rev. Edward Irving* (1835); D. Ker, *Observations on Mrs. Oliphant's Life of Edward Irving* (1863); T. Kolde, *Edward Irving* (1901); O. W. Oliphant, *The Life of Edward Irving, Illustrated by His Journals and Correspondence* (1862, 2d. ed. 1865); J. C. Root, *Edward Irving, Man, Preacher, Poet* (1912); P. E. Shaw, *The Catholic Apostolic Church* (1946); G. Strachan, *The Pentecostal Theology of Edward Irving* (1973). H. C. Whitley, *Blinded Eagle* (1955). (2) **On the Catholic Apostolic Church: (a) Dictionaries:** K. Algermissen, "Katholisch-Apostolische Gemeinden," *LThK* 6 (1961): 73–74; A. Humbert, "Irvingiens," *DThC* 7(2, 1923): 2566–70; T. Kolde, "Catholic Apostolic Church," *NSHERK* (1908) 2:457–59; W. Lohff, "Irvingianismus," *LThK* 5 (1950): 771–72; *ODCC* (1957), 251; J. G. Simpson, "Irving and the Catholic Apostolic Church," *Encyclopedia of Religion and Ethics* (1914), 422–28; T. C. F. Stunt, "Catholic Apostolic Church," *NIDCC* (1974), 203–4. (b) **Studies:** S. J. Andrews, *God's Revelation of Himself to Men* (1886); R. A. Davenport, *Albury Apostles* (1970); O. Eggenberger, *Die neuapostolische Gemeinde* (1953); K. Kandtmann, *Die Neu-Irvingianer* (1907); E. Miller, *The History and Doctrines of Irvingism* (1878); H. M. Prior, *My Experience of the Catholic Apostolic Church* (1880); J. Robert, *Catholiques-apostoliques et neo-apostoliques* (1960); A. Weber, *Die Katholisch-apostolischen Gemeinden* (1978).   D. D. Bundy

IRVINGITES   See EDWARD IRVING.

IRWIN, BENJAMIN HARDIN   (b. 1854). Holiness preacher and church executive. Born near Mercer, Missouri. In 1863 the Irwin family moved to Tecumseh, Nebraska, where Benjamin early acquired an interest in law. After becoming a lawyer, Irwin practiced law in Tecumseh until 1879 when he was converted in a Baptist church. He soon became a preacher and pastor in his local church.

By 1891 Irwin received a sanctification experience through the ministry of preachers in the Iowa Holiness Association. He then immersed himself in the writings of Wesley, Fletcher, and other Methodist leaders. Though he described himself as a "John Wesley Methodist," Irwin was especially impressed with John Fletcher's idea of a "baptism of burning love," which he felt came after the experience of entire sanctification.

From 1892 to 1895 Irwin served as a traveling evangelist in the Wesleyan Methodist church, holding meetings in Kansas, Nebraska, and Iowa. Many of his meetings were in Brethren in Christ congregations. His ministry was radically changed in 1895 when he experienced a "baptism of fire" in Enid, Oklahoma. In short order he began teaching a "third blessing" called "the fire" and began organizing Fire-Baptized Holiness Associations (FBHA) where he went. The first one was organized in Iowa in 1895.

By 1896 Irwin was preaching tent revivals in Georgia, South Carolina, and Canada, organizing associations as he went. In August 1898 he organized an international FBHA in Anderson, South Carolina, with regional associations in eight states and two Canadian provinces. He also began publication of a periodical titled *Live Coals of Fire*.

The teachings of the new church included a strict external holiness code as well as adherence to the dietary laws of the OT. Furthermore, he also began to encourage his followers to seek further experiences that he called the baptisms of dynamite, lyddite, and oxidite. The mainstream of the Holiness movement, however, rejected his teachings as the "third blessing heresy."

In 1900 Irwin fell from the leadership of the church after confessing to "open and gross sin," after which leadership passed on to his young assistant, Joseph H. King. In 1907–8, the church accepted Pentecostalism and became one of the first denominations to teach officially the "initial evidence" theory of the baptism in the Holy Spirit.

In 1911 the major stream of the movement merged with the Pentecostal Holiness Church (PHC) in Falcon, North Carolina, to form the present PHC. The black members of the movement separated in 1908 under the leadership of William E. Fuller and continue to this day as the Fire-Baptized Holiness Church of God of the Americas.

Irwin's career after 1900 is largely unknown, although there is some evidence that he became a Pentecostal after 1906. See also HOLINESS MOVEMENT.

Bibliography: J. Campbell, *Pentecostal Holiness Church, 1898–1948* (1950); M. Schrag, "The Spiritual Pilgrimage of the Reverend Benjamin Hardin Irwin," *Brethren in Christ History and Life* 4 (June 1, 1981): 3–29; V. Synan, *Old-Time Power* (1973).   H. V. Synan

ISAIAH, BOOK OF

I. Introduction. The quotations and allusions to this book in the NT cause many to call it "The Gospel According to Isaiah." It contains, along with Joel and Ezekiel, some of the most important prophecies about the Holy Spirit. Moses told Joshua, "I wish that all the LORD's people were prophets and that the LORD would put his Spirit on them!" (Num. 11:29). All the OT sees

prophecy as an important activity of the Holy Spirit. Isaiah is one of the prophets who saw that Moses' desire would indeed be fulfilled.

From the Dead Sea Scrolls it is clear that in the second century and probably the third century B.C. all sixty-six chapters of Isaiah were included in the one book and accepted as written by Isaiah. Not until the time of J. C. Doederlein (1775) did literary critics begin to spread the idea that Isaiah 40–66 was written by a second, or "Deutero," Isaiah. This proposed great unknown was presumed to live in about 540 B.C. when Cyrus was already on the scene making his way toward Babylon. These critics have continued their disintegration of the book until some form critics, like Gressman and Gunkel, reduced it to a mass of disordered fragments.

Those who denied that Isaiah wrote the entire book based their claims initially on three grounds. First, they said that Babylon was off the horizon in Isaiah's day so that an eighth-century prophet would not have known or cared about it. Second, they claimed that the basic standpoint of Isaiah 40–66 and the passages in the first part of the book that mention Babylon are that of the late Babylonian exile (540 B.C. or later). Third, they tried to reinforce their conclusion by pointing to differences in style and theology between the two parts of the book.

It is true that Assyria was the dominant empire in Isaiah's day. Isaiah 10:5–7 recognized that even though Assyria did not realize it, God was using Assyria to bring his judgment on Israel and Judah. Yet archaeological records show that the central focus of Assyria's attention in Isaiah's day was on Babylon. The Assyrian kings, Sargon and Sennacherib, spent a great deal of time consolidating their control of Babylon. Babylon was important to them, for it was the cultural, religious, and commercial center of the whole Mesopotamian basin.

When Sennacherib came to the throne in 705 B.C. Merodach Baladan tried to take over Babylon. Sennacherib took care of that and, according/to his records, moved 208,000 captives out of Babylonia. Then he felt free to move toward Egypt, taking control of other nations along the way. In 701 he threatened Jerusalem and, according to his records, took over 200,000 captives from the forty-eight walled cities of Judah that he destroyed. He probably took them to Babylon, for in 700 he was back in Babylon, where he again drove off Merodach Baladan. It is probable also that he replaced the 208,000 he took from Babylonia earlier with the 200,000 he took from Judah.

Then for more than ten years he was kept busy trying to settle things in Babylon. In 691 Babylonian priests hired Elamites to fight against him, and he suffered his first major defeat. Two years later, in 689, Sennacherib swept down, leveled Babylon to the ground, made a swamp out of it, carried off the great images of Bel and Nebo (Isa. 46:1–2), and, because he was angry with the priests, encouraged his soldiers to destroy the rest of the images of Babylon (Isa. 37:19).

The whole world of that day was shocked by this destruction of Babylon. These events were in the center of world attention. It would have been very strange if Isaiah had not said something about Babylon. Certainly it was not off his horizon as some critics say. In fact, what his book does say about Babylon fits Isaiah's day, not the later Babylon of 540 B.C. From this it is evident that the standpoint of the passages about Babylon is not 540, but Isaiah's own day. An examination of chapters 40–66 shows also that the picture is that of the trees, valleys, and hills of Palestine, not the flat plains of Babylon.

The differences in style are minor and can easily be explained by the difference in audience and subject matter. In Isaiah 36:21 the people took a stand of faith and listened to Hezekiah because of Hezekiah's trust in God. Then the deliverance of Jerusalem in fulfillment of Isaiah's prophecy discredited the war party. God also gave Hezekiah fifteen added years of peace. Thus Isaiah no longer had to use any war terminology or references to those who trusted in Egypt, for Egypt also had been defeated. God gave Isaiah new prophecies that looked to the future and to the suffering and victory of the Messiah, God's anointed Servant. With Manasseh's taking the throne, however, idolatry was again a problem, and the later prophecies of Isaiah reflect an idolatry that fits that time, not the time after 540 B.C. All through the book the Lord is the Holy One of Israel, and there is no good reason to postulate a supposed second Isaiah.

II. The Holy Spirit Dealing with Sin. Isaiah sees the Spirit active in dealing with sin. He looks ahead and sees that: "those who are left in Zion, who remain in Jerusalem, will be called holy [dedicated to God, consecrated to God], all who are recorded among the living in Jerusalem. The Lord will wash away the filth [excrement] of the women [daughters; that is, inhabitants, both men and women] of Zion; he will cleanse the blood-stains [caused by murders] from Jerusalem by a spirit of judgment [or the Spirit of justice] and a spirit [or the Spirit] of fire" (4:3–4). This will prepare the messianic glory to come. C. von Orelli (1895, 32) took the Spirit here to be a burning, cleansing wind. However, the work is God's work done by his Spirit bringing the fire of his wrath and the fire of his cleansing.

III. The Holy Spirit and the Messiah. The Book of Isaiah presents an unfolding picture of the Messiah. An important part of that picture is the way the Spirit of God rests on him. The description of the virgin-born Son who will reign and who will make David's throne eternal finds its climax in 11:1–5, with the Spirit of the Lord resting continually upon him. The description of the Suffering Servant who triumphs through death and resurrection is tied to the prophecies of his reign by the promise of the Spirit upon him in Isaiah 61:1–4.

Isaiah 11:1 shows that when the virgin-born Son appears, the kingdom of David could be compared to a stump of a tree that had been cut down; all its outward glory would be gone. The members of the Davidic line would be reduced to poverty, but God would bring a new shoot from that stump, a branch that would draw new life from its roots. (Many believe it is significant that the word "branch" here is the Hebrew *netser* or *nezer*, from the same root word as Nazareth and Nazarene.)

As Franz Delitzsch (1949, 1:282–83) pointed out, the Spirit of the Lord in 11:2 may be compared to the central shaft of a sevenfold lampstand. The three groups of manifestations of the Spirit could then be like the three pairs of branches of such a lampstand. Delitzsch classified the first pair as dealing with the mind or intellect, the second pair with the practical life, and the third pair with the relationship to God.

This writer (Horton, 1976, 61–62) believes that each aspect of this sevenfold Spirit is significant. The Spirit of the Lord is also the Spirit of prophecy, the Spirit working in redemption. Wisdom includes ability to see what is in a person, as Jesus did when he saw Nathaniel (John 1:47) and when he refused to trust himself to the crowds who had a superficial belief because they saw his miracles (John 2:24–25). Understanding includes the ability to see beyond external appearances and distinguish between good and evil. Counsel includes the ability to see what the facts are and give correct guidance. Might (Heb. *gevurah*) includes not only strength but the courage to do what God asks. Knowledge is more than knowledge about God and spiritual things. It includes personal relationships with him and personal knowledge of his love and grace. The fear of the Lord is not a cowardly fear, but a reverence that gives God his proper place and that becomes the beginning of all wisdom (Job 28:28; Ps. 11:10; Prov. 1:7; 9:10).

When the Spirit of the Lord descended on Jesus after his baptism, all this would be brought to the minds of those who knew the OT Scriptures. John, in Revelation 5:6 undoubtedly had all this in mind also when he saw the sevenfold Spirit as seven horns of power and seven eyes of wisdom in the Lamb who still bore the marks of having been slain. This fullness of power and wisdom John saw going out into all the earth, showing that the Spirit ministers the power and wisdom of Christ to us in its sevenfold fullness during this age.

Isaiah 11:3–5 goes on to show that because the Spirit continues to rest on the messianic King, he will be the kind of judge the world needs. "He will not judge by what he sees with his eyes, or decide by what he hears with his ears; but with righteousness he will judge the needy, with justice he will give decisions for the poor of the earth." The judges and juries in our courts today have to make their decisions by what they hear and see. They do the best they can, but they do make mistakes, especially when some of the facts are not available to them. But the decision of the virgin-born, Spirit-anointed Judge and King will always be right.

Isaiah 11:6–9 goes to show that the Spirit's work through the messianic King will be effective in the age to come and will bring about the ideal conditions that will mark the Millennium. Even more important, the teaching ministry of the Messiah through the Spirit will cause the earth to be "full of the knowledge of the LORD as the waters cover the sea."

Isaiah 28:5–6 adds, "In that day the LORD Almighty will be a glorious crown, a beautiful wreath for the remnant of his people. He will be a spirit of justice to him that sits in judgment, a source of strength to those who turn back the battle at the gate." "Strength" (Heb. *gevurah*) is the same courageous strength mentioned in Isaiah 11:2. Clearly, God wants to give the same sevenfold Spirit to his people as well.

Isaiah 42:1–4 develops the same thought of bringing justice through the Spirit-Anointed One. Here Isaiah sees that he is doing this as the servant of the Lord. In Isaiah 41:8 God called Israel his servant because he had a work for Israel to do. But Israel as a nation could not do the work of redemption that God wanted. So Isaiah prophesies another Servant who would be able to accomplish the work of God, the work of salvation. God calls him "my chosen one in whom I delight" and says, "I will put my Spirit upon him and he will bring justice to the nations." Justice (Heb. *mishpat*) includes all God's decisions, decisions intended to help us worship and serve him as well as giving guidance for practical everyday living. This Servant will himself "be a [new] covenant for the people and a light for the Gentiles, to open eyes that are blind, to free captives from prison, and to release from the dungeon those who sit in darkness" (Isa. 42:6–7).

Though Isaiah 61:1–3 does not call the speaker the servant of the Lord, it is clear that Isaiah 42 and Isaiah 61 are parallel and that they are talking about the same person. He is also the same person God sends with his Spirit in Isaiah 48:16 (where the Heb. is better translated, "God has sent me and has sent his Spirit").

Jesus at Nazareth (Luke 4:16–21) claimed that Isaiah 61 found its fulfillment in him. He indeed preached good news to the meek, the poor, and the humble. He proclaimed freedom for the prisoners who were taken captive by sin and Satan in a spiritual warfare that is still going on. He brought recovery of sight not only to those who were physically blind, but to those who were blind to the truth of the gospel. He released the oppressed and brought them deliverance and salvation. He also proclaimed the year of the Lord's favor, which was shown by his blessings.

Though the passage does go on to speak of the future judgment, the climax of the passage is really the year of the Lord's favor, which is the place where Jesus stopped. Many take this to refer to a new and better "Year of Jubilee." The Year of Jubilee was a time when people gained back lost inheritances (Lev. 25:10–13). Through Jesus both Jews and Gentiles enter into an inheritance that belongs to the family of God and that is ours through faith in Christ not just for one year but for always.

IV. The Holy Spirit and the Future. One of the characteristics of the Book of Isaiah is the way he contrasts his own day and its failures with the promised future day of restoration and blessing.

In 30:1 Isaiah pronounces woe from the Lord on obstinate children who form an alliance with Egypt, "but not by my Spirit." In verse 18 he adds, "Yet the LORD longs to be gracious to you."

Chapter 32 talks about the destruction that will come upon the land "till the Spirit is poured upon us from on high, and the desert becomes a fertile field" (32:15), thus transforming both the people and the land. In fact, the rest of the world will enjoy its effects.

Isaiah 40:3 recognizes the sovereignty and supreme wisdom of the Spirit in contrast to the smallness of the nations of the world. Yet 44:3, like 32:15, speaks of God outpouring his Spirit and his blessing. This is compared with water being poured out in abundant streams on a dry ground. God is concerned both with outward restoration and with salvation and spiritual renewal.

Isaiah 59:18–21 brings another contrast between the Spirit's work in judgment and his work in restoration. Verse 19 is best translated: "And they shall fear the name of the LORD from the west and his glory from the rising of the sun, for he [God] shall come like the river [the Euphrates] narrowed, the Spirit of the Lord driving it on." Just as the Euphrates River speeds up where high banks narrow it down, and sweeps everything before it, so the Holy Spirit will sweep God's enemies away. On the other hand, when the Kinsman-Redeemer (Heb. *goel*, the one who restores the inheritance that was lost) comes to Jews who repent of their rebellion, God will give a covenant that the Spirit (which came upon them when they were restored to God, as in Ezek. 36:27; 37:14) will not depart, neither will God's words, which the Spirit puts in their mouths, depart.

V. A Lesson Not Learned. Isaiah's last specific references to the Spirit are in a passage that looks back to God's mercy and compassion in Israel's past history. Beginning with 63:7 Isaiah gives praise to God for all the good things he had done for Israel and how "in his love and mercy he redeemed them; he lifted them up and carried them all the days of old" (63:9). In contrast to this and in spite of this, "they rebelled and grieved his Holy Spirit. So he turned and became their enemy and he himself fought against them" (v. 10).

This caused the people to remember the days of Moses and ask, "Where is he who brought them through the sea. . . . Where is he who set his Holy Spirit among them, who sent his glorious arm of power to be at Moses' right hand?" (63:11–12).

We see that the Holy Spirit can be grieved and is thus treated as a person here. Yet God's Holy Spirit is also parallel to his glorious arm of power. That does not mean, however, that his power is an impersonal force.

"Setting his Holy Spirit among" them can also be translated "setting his Holy Spirit within him"—that is within Moses. Numbers 11:17 lets us know that the Spirit of the Lord was upon Moses. Numbers 27:18 calls Joshua "a man in whom is the Spirit." Miriam was a prophetess and therefore a woman of the Spirit. So it is true that the Spirit was among them. However, the emphasis in verse 12 is on Moses, so the KJV seems preferable.

Then Isaiah compares the Spirit's leading of

Israel into the rest of Canaan to a good shepherd leading a flock into green grass and beside still waters. Thus Isaiah praises God for the Spirit-filled leaders of the past. At the same time he recognizes that the Spirit of the Lord was the One who was really guiding them.

Bibliography: J. M. Adams, *Ancient Records and the Bible* (1946); W. F. Albright, *Recent Discoveries in Bible Lands* (1955); J. A. Alexander, *Commentary on the Prophecies of Isaiah* (2 vols. in 1, 1846–47, reprint 1953); O. T. Allis, *The Unity of Isaiah* (1972); G. L. Archer, *A Survey of Old Testament Introduction* (1964); J. A. Bewer, *The Prophets* (1955); C. Boutflower, *The Book of Isaiah (Chapters I–XXXIX)* (1930); J. M. Cook, *The Persian Empire* (1983); F. Delitzsch, *Bible Commentary on the Prophecy of Isaiah*, 2 vols. (1881, reprint 1949); C. H. Gordon, *The Ancient Near East* (1965); idem, *Introduction to Old Testament Times* (1953); L. L. Honor, *Sennacherib's Invasion of Palestine* (1926); S. M. Horton, "A Defense on Historical Grounds of the Isaian Authorship of the Passages in Isaiah Referring to Babylon," Th.D. diss., Central Baptist Theological Seminary, 1959); idem, *What the Bible Says About the Holy Spirit* (1976); A. Kaminka, *Le Prophet Isaie* (1925); D. D. Luckenbill, *Ancient Records of Assyria and Babylonia,* 2 vols. (1926–27); idem, *The Annals of Sennacherib* (1924); G. C. C. Maspero, *The Passing of the Empires* (1900); A. T. Olmstead, *The Book of Isaiah* (1948); I. M. Price, *The Monuments and the Old Testament* (1946); G. L. Robinson, *The Bearing of Archaeology on the Old Testament* (1941); idem, *The Book of Isaiah* (rev. ed., 1954); S. J. Schultz, *The Old Testament Speaks* (1980); J. W. Thirtle, *Old Testament Problems* (1916); D. H. Van Zeller, *Isaias: Man of Ideas* (1938); C. von Orelli, *The Prophecies of Isaiah* (1895); Th. C. Vriezen, *An Outline of Old Testament Theology* (2d ed., rev. 1970); H. Winckler, *Geschichte Babyloniens und Assyrians* (1892); E. J. Young, *An Introduction to the Old Testament* (1954); idem, *Studies in Isaiah* (1954).
S. M. Horton

ITALIAN CHARISMATICS See CHARISMATIC MOVEMENT.

ITALIAN PENTECOSTAL CHURCH OF CANADA Ministering to Italians in Canada, this small group originated in 1912 when several members of an Italian Presbyterian Church in Hamilton, Ontario, formed a mission, Chiesa Cristiana Italiana Independente. The next year the mission became Pentecostal after several members received the baptism in the Holy Spirit. Other Italian congregations sprang up in other cities as a result of the mission's evangelistic efforts. Early leaders of the Italian Pentecostal Church of Canada (IPCC) included Luigi Ippolito, Ferdinand Zaffato, and Giuseppe DiStaulo. Although the group had operated for more than forty years, it did not apply for a provincial charter until 1958; it was granted the next year.

IPCC is closely associated with the Pentecostal Assemblies of Canada, with identical beliefs, but has retained its identity to minister to Italians. The group is also associated with the Christian Church of North America and the Assemblies of God of Italy and is a member of the Pentecostal Fellowship of North America. Headquarters are in Montreal. *Evangel Voice* is published bimonthly in Italian and English.

Bibliography: D. Ippolito, "Origin and History of the IPCC" (1986).   W. E. Warner

ITALIAN PENTECOSTALS See EUROPEAN PENTECOSTALISM.

J

JAGGERS, ORVAL L. (1917–). Founder and head of the World Church in Los Angeles. The son of an Assemblies of God pastor, he began preaching with that denomination in 1941, rising to prominence in the healing movement of the late 1940s. In 1952 he began his ministry in Los Angeles, using radio, TV, and newspaper advertising to assemble a following. His orthodox Pentecostal doctrines gave way to extraordinary teachings and practices that isolated him from his former colleagues and other churches. With his second wife, Velma, he continues to direct a colorful church complete with a transubstantiation altar and illustrated sermons featuring cages lowered from a forty-foot ceiling. He unsuccessfully sought to found a sectarian city near Camarillo, California, blaming his problems on a communist conspiracy.

Bibliography: D. E. Harrell, Jr., *All Things Are Possible* (1975), 78–79; P. Martin, "Faith and Fear for $1.07," *Christian Herald* (July 1967), 13–49.

L. F. Wilson

JAMES, BOOK OF The so-called Letter of James, first of the Catholic Epistles, lacks virtually all of the earmarks of a true letter. While it has been called, among other things, paranesis, sermon, and at one time wisdom literature, it is probably best understood as modeled after a "diaspora letter" (cf. 2 Macc. 1:1–10a; 1:10b–2:18; 2 Bar. 78–87; or Acts 15:23 [from James!]; cf. also Jer. 29:4; 1 Peter). The "diaspora letter" was a type of formal communication from Jerusalem (cf. 1 Peter) that circulated among Jewish communities scattered in the Diaspora.

If James the brother of Jesus is accepted as the author, then a date c. A.D. 62 (the conjectured martyrdom of James) is the terminus ad quem for its production. Conversely, those who hold that James could not have been written by Jesus' brother or by his contemporaries posit a date of composition c. A.D. 80+.

James is marked by its hortatory style and contains proverbs, admonitions, commands, and instruction; however, James is not a disjointed collection of aphorisms and platitudes. Many of the sayings are reminiscent of words of Jesus, especially the Sermon on the Mount (James 1:2/Matt. 5:12; James 1:5/Matt. 7:7; James 1:22; 2:14/Matt. 7:26; James 4:11/Matt. 7:1). James also shares concepts found in Hellenistic writings (cf. James 1:19/Sir. 5:11; James 4:14/Wisd. 2:4). He is influenced by and familiar with the OT(e.g., James 2:8/Lev. 19:18; James 2:11/Exod. 20:13–14; Deut. 5:17–18; James 2:23/Gen. 15:6; James 4:6/Prov. 3:34 [LXX]). The author further reflects great affinity with Judaism (cf. James 2:8–13 [keeping the law]; 2:20–26 [Abraham's righteousness]; James 3:9 [humankind created in God's image]; James 4:4 [the image of adulterous people]; James 5:10 [prophets of old]; 5:17–18 [Elijah's example]).

Several "themes" are recognizable within James. First, the writing seems directed at those undergoing trial or persecution originating from *within* the community (e.g., 1:2–4, 12; 5:7–11, 13). Second, the recipients are under some threat of being deceived, either by insiders, outsiders, or both (1:13–16, 22; 3:1–2[?]; 4:1, 8; 5:19). A third theme may actually reflect the specifics of the first two: The rich are exploiting the poor (2:6; 5:1–6), who, "being deceived," are not only allowing them to do this, but they have been tempted and have fallen in league with them (1:13–14; cf. 1:27; 2:14–17; 4:2–4; cf. 4:7; 4:13–17). This brings us back full circle to the admonitions to "endure," "be patient." These are now best understood as directed to those who have not succumbed to the pressures of the rich and powerful. They continue to suffer at the hands of the rich. They are also encouraged to "save" (*sōzō*) a brother who has wandered from the truth onto the path of deception, which leads to death (5:20). A true faith/righteousness expresses itself in action both on behalf of those in need (1:26–27; 2:14–17) and against those who oppress the poor (1:12–16; 4:4–10).

The Holy Spirit. The Holy Spirit (*hagios pneuma*) is not mentioned in James, although "spirit" (*pneuma*) occurs twice. James 2:26 reads: "As the body without the spirit [*pneuma*] is dead, so faith without works is dead." Every translation consulted rendered this anarthrous *pneuma* as "spirit" rather than "Spirit" (e.g., NIV, RSV, NASB, PHILLIPS, TEV), although the lack of the article does not disallow *pneuma*'s being a reference to "Spirit" (e.g., Matt. 1:20; 12:28; 22:43; Mark 1:8; Luke 1:15, 67; 11:13; John 1:33; 7:39). On the basis of James 1:15, "Sin, when it is full-grown, gives birth to death," and James 5:20, "Whoever turns a sinner from the error of his way will save him from death"—both references to the death brought by sin—one might argue that the "body without [the] Spirit [i.e., the unsaved] is dead [spiritually]." The evidence is too slim, however, to be conclusive; and the sense of the saying would not be radically changed except for those who discern Hellenistic dualism in James 1:15. Its interpretation might impact how one reads James 4:5.

James 4:5. James 4:5 is more problematic: "Or do you not think Scripture says without reason that the spirit he caused to live in us envies intensely?" Notorious for being thorny, James 4:5 offers the interpreter several problems. First, if a Scripture is being cited, which one? Despite a plethora of suggested renditions or hypothetical, unknown translations, no one has satisfactorily answered that question. Second, how should the verse be translated? A comparison of just a few versions demonstrates the difficulty: "The spirit he caused to live in us envies intensely" (NIV), "the spirit God placed in us is filled with fierce desires" (TEV), "He [God] yearns jealously over the spirit which he has made to dwell in us" (RSV), "the Holy Spirit, whom God has placed within us, watches over us with tender jealously" (LB). Other versions only continue to reflect the same interpretive apoplexy (e.g., KJV, NASB, NEB) created by the difficult syntax and unusual vocabulary of the verse. (Davids offers a good summary of the entire discussion and should be consulted [1982, 162–64]).

Wisdom. Some Pentecostal groups—and by default many charismatics—contend that the "wisdom" mentioned in James 1:5; 3:13; and 3:17 equals the "word of wisdom" referred to in 1 Corinthians 12:8 (e.g., Pearlman, 1937, 321–22). The "word of wisdom" in 1 Corinthians is normally associated with a supernatural "utterance" or with divine "insight." Furthermore, it is not regarded as the product of human effort. Granted, it is clear that the source of wisdom in James is God—the giver of all graces; this is not to say, however, that the "wisdom" spoken of in James 1 and 3 is synonymous with the traditional Pentecostal understanding of wisdom as a gift of the Spirit.

Within the context of James, "wisdom" almost certainly refers to the wisdom God gives for living a godly life, especially in the face of oppression and persecution. Wisdom loves peace, is considerate, compassionate, impartial, and sincere (James 3:17). It stands in contrast to "earthly" wisdom (i.e., the "rich" in James), which is boastful, envious, denies the truth, and is disruptive (v. 15). The "foolish person" (anthrōpē kenē) does not equate faith with lifestyle (2:20). True wisdom—from above—expresses itself in lifestyle (3:13). Such an understanding places James 1:5, "If any of you lacks wisdom," in a new light. The issue is not that God will answer any petition as long as we do not waver in our belief that he will perform it. Rather, the issue is whether the believer will meet the demands of the gospel and live justly in an unjust world (i.e., to exhibit faith) or whether he or she will succumb to the temptation of the world, which invites the foolish to avoid the trials of life—in other words, to succumb to doubt (cf. 1:12).

James 5:14–16. Although belief in divine healing waned during the Reformation, a resurgence in interest in "anointing the sick with oil" naturally developed during the great American healing revival of the nineteenth century under the leadership of such persons as Charles Cullis, Carrie Judd Montgomery, A. J. Gordon, and A. B. Simpson and greatly impacted Pentecostalism (see Dayton, 1988, 115–17). Indeed, Dayton can comment that "the crucial biblical text for Cullis had been James 5:14–15." This practice greatly influenced Pentecostalism, which adopted many of the tenets and techniques of the healing movement.

James 5:14, "Is any one of you sick? He should call the elders of the church to pray over him and anoint him with oil in the name of the Lord," has long been used as justification for anointing the sick or dying with oil. One could say that today, almost without exception, scholarship reads James 5:14–15 as a reference to supernatural physical healing (e.g., Dibelius, 1976, 253–55; Davids, 1982, 192; Ropes, 1916, 303–9; Mussner, 1967, 218–25; Laws, 1980, 232). But where does this reading originate?

Judaism knows of no rite of anointing the sick with oil in ritual fashion or otherwise, although oil plays a significant role in the rituals of Israel (e.g., bKerithoth 5a–6a; bHorayoth 11b; bShebu'oth 14b). In the OT pseudepigraph Life of Adam and Eve there is an interesting account of oil that flows from the tree of life. Adam asks Seth to go to Paradise to obtain the oil of life from God so that he might be anointed to "rest from his pains." When Seth reaches Paradise he is told that the oil of mercy is reserved for the last days (42). The gnostics pick up on this story and apply it to Christ (Christ's Descent into Hell, 3), who they regard as having descended into Hades to anoint those who have already died. There is also much baptismal imagery involved here. In any case, healing of physical sickness seems only secondary to the point that the time in which this oil is to be made available has indeed arrived in Christ.

Although the rite of anointing with oil has a longstanding tradition in Western Christendom and has been practiced in the Greek Orthodox Church for centuries, it was usually practiced in conjunction with baptism. The ritual on behalf of the sick apparently did not become a part of church practice until after the third century (unless one assumes that Mark 6:13 is speaking of the same thing). Eastern churches like the Ethiopians and Nestorians had the rite but have allowed it to discontinue (Douglas, 1978, 994). The rite is never mentioned in the apostolic fathers or Ante-Nicene fathers; and in one relatively early (4th–5th cent.) anonymous work, "Two Epistles Concerning Virginity" (ANF, 7:59–60), which does outline some rules for assisting the sick, no mention is made of anointing with oil or the prayer of faith. It is certain, though, that the author knew James (cf. the Shepherd of Hermas and the Epistles of Cyprian, 75 [ANF, 5:397–98] speaks of an anointing at Eucharist as well). In one of his "epistles" Cyprian (d. A.D. 258) fails to refer to anointing when speaking of the practice of baptizing the sick, although he does seem to see some physical healing possible through baptism (ANF, 5:402). Hippolytus of Rome (d. c. 236), Apostolic Tradition, 5, contains references to the oil of baptism and confirmation (the latter being the sealing of the believer by the Spirit; Quasten, 1950, 2:191, 192), as do the Apostolic Constitutions, 29 (c. A.D. 381). In the latter the oil and the water of baptismal chrismation are seen to have healing properties (ANF, 7:494). No association with James 5:14 is made, however.

That James 5:14–15 need not refer to physical healing finds further support from the larger context of James. The poor and afflicted are not promised recovery in this life; rather, they must depend on God in their affliction and wait for the judgment of the eschaton (5:7). Their examples in the face of suffering are "the prophets who spoke in the name of the Lord." Those who persevere, like Job, are blessed (5:11).

The "weary" (asthenei) therefore are those who are faltering in the face of persecution and affliction. If they have sinned against the community by yielding to the pressures of the rich, they will be forgiven if they confess their sins and "turn from the error of [their] way" (v. 20). Elijah's example of prayer stems from verse 16, "the prayer of a righteous man is powerful and effective." The lesson of Elijah's prayer is applied in verses 19–20: "If one of you should wander from the truth and someone should bring him back, remember this: Whoever turns a sinner from the error of his way will save him from death and cover over a multitude of sins."

On the one hand, James 5:14–16 is not to be read solely as a formula for administering physical healing in the name of the Lord. On the other hand, the weight of tradition and the teaching of the church certainly make anointing with oil a viable symbolic gesture, and indeed God still heals those in physical need.

Bibliography: P. H. Alexander, "James 5:14–16. Magic, Medicine, Miracle, or Metaphor?" unpublished paper read before the Central States SBL, April 1988; *Ante-Nicene Fathers*, 10 vols., ed. A. Roberts and J. Donaldson (reprint 1982); J. Bonsirven, *Textes Rabbinique des Deux Primiers Siècles Chrétiens* (1955); P. Davids, *Commentary on James*, NIGTC (1982); D. Dayton, *Theological Roots of Pentecostalism* (1987); M. Dibelius and H. Greeven, *James*, Hermeneia (*ET*, 1976); J. D. Douglas, ed., *NIDCC*, s.v."Unction" (1978); F. Exler, *The Form of the Ancient Greek Letter* (1923); A. S. Geyser, "The Letter of James and the Social Condition of His Addresses," in *Neotestamentica 9* (1975): 25–33; A. J. Gordon, *Ministry of Healing* (n.d.); S. Laws, *The Epistle of James*, HNTC (1980); B. Metzger, *The New Testament, Its Background, Growth, and Content* (1965); F. Mussner, *Der Jakobusbrief*, HTKNT (1967); *Oxford Dictionary of the Christian Church*, s.v. "Unction" (1974); M. Pearlman, *Knowing the Doctrines of the Bible* (1937); J. H. Ropes, *James*, ICC (1915, reprint 1973); J. Quasten, *Patrology*, 4 vols. (1950); A. B. Simpson, *The Gospel of Healing* (1915); J. L. White, *Light From Ancient Letters* (1986).

P. H. Alexander

JEFFREYS, GEORGE (1889–1962). Founder and leader of the Elim Foursquare Gospel Alliance (Elim Pentecostal church). George Jeffreys was the sixth of eight sons of miner Thomas Jeffreys and his wife Kezia, born in Nantyffylon, Maesteg, Wales, February 28, 1889. The family belonged to the Welsh Independent (Congregational) church. Together with older brother Stephen, George was converted November 20, 1904, at Siloh Chapel, under the preaching of the minister Glassnant Jones. George was working at the Co-Operative Stores, and his brother Stephen was a coal miner. A sister, four brothers, and their father had all died. George was frail in health and suffered from a speech impediment and showed the beginnings of facial paralysis.

When Pentecostalism was introduced to Wales early in 1908 George and Stephen were opposed to the movement. However, Stephen's son, Edward, was baptized in the Spirit and spoke in tongues while on holiday, and uncle and father sought the experience. George was baptized by immersion in the Llynfi River in April 1911. He was baptized in the Spirit and healed. Joining a small group of Pentecostals, he began preaching. In September 1912 he applied to the Pentecostal Missionary Union and was sent to Preston to train under Thomas Myerscough. He was "set apart for the ministry by the Independent Apostolic Church known as Emmanuel Christ Church . . . Maesteg, 13 November 1912."

In January 1913 Stephen requested George's help in a mission he was conducting near Swansea. Following this success the brothers went on to mid Wales and then to London before George was requested to return to Preston to complete his training. In May he was invited by A. A. Boddy to speak at the Sunderland Convention. He stayed on to hold special meetings for the vicar. A visitor from Ireland who heard George preach invited him for meetings and enclosed the fare. Meetings were advertised in Monaghan, but when it was learned that Jeffreys was Pentecostal, the owners of the hall canceled the booking. In January 1915 George met a group of men in Monaghan, and they formed the Elim Evangelistic Band. George was left a sum of money in a will and was advised to register his group, which took the name Elim Pentecostal Alliance. He traveled extensively in Britain after establishing his first church in Belfast in 1916. Confining his church building work to Ireland, he established his first English work in 1921. Joined by Stephen, he went to Grimsby and Hull before moving to London in 1922. In 1924 they spent five months in Canada and the U.S. On their return they were together for a time in London before Stephen went on his own. George then embarked on a sustained period of evangelistic activity lasting ten years (1925–34). Everywhere there were huge crowds, dozens of healings, thousands of converts. From Plymouth to Dundee, from Swansea to Rochester, churches were established. The most successful crusade in Birmingham recorded 10,000 converts. Without support from other churches, usually with only a handful at the start, he went from place to place and within a short time established flourishing new churches.

George was not satisfied that he had found the right method of church government (though the rules were all made by him). He began to bring in one change after another. Setting up an annual ministerial conference in 1933, he constantly agitated for change. Finally, in 1939, after granting major concessions, the ministerial conference rejected his demands and he resigned. He was asked to stay but finally totally resigned in November 1940 and founded the Bible-Pattern Church Fellowship in Nottingham. This was a congregational group, and for a time there was considerable antagonism between the two groups. George himself was a sick man, and though he continued to hold campaign meetings he was never again to achieve the success of former years.

Not only in Britain but in mainland Europe Jeffreys was a great success. In Switzerland he had

Considered England's greatest evangelists since Wesley and Whitefield, George (left) and Steven Jeffreys founded the Elim Pentecostal Church.

14,000 converts (1934–36). He visited Sweden several times and was the chief preacher in the great European Pentecostal Conference in Stockholm in June 1939. From Holland in 1922 to France in 1950, his ministry was widely accepted. Though the later years left Jeffreys increasingly isolated, he was for ten years the greatest evangelist produced in Britain since Whitefield or John Wesley. He died quietly among friends in his Clapham home on January 26, 1962.

Bibliography: E. C. W. Boulton, *George Jeffreys — A Ministry of the Miraculous* (1928); D. W. Cartwright, *The Great Evangelists* (1986); A. W. Edsor, *George Jeffreys: Man of God* (1964); W. J. Hollenweger, *The Pentecostals* (1972); R. Landau, *God Is My Adventure* (1935); Bryan J. Wilson, *Sects and Society* (1961).
D. W. Cartwright

JEFFREYS, STEPHEN (1876–1943). British Pentecostal evangelist. Third of eight sons of miner Thomas Jeffreys and his wife Kezia. He spent twenty-four years as a coal miner (1889–1912). A member of Siloh Independent Chapel, Maesteg, where he played in the flute band, he was converted there on November 20, 1904, during the height of the Welsh revival.

In 1898 Jeffreys married Elizabeth Lewis, daughter of Joseph Lewis, deacon at Siloh and miner. They had three daughters and one son, Edward (1899–1974), founder of Bethel Evangelistic Society, who eventually became an Anglican minister. Stephen was a simple, lovable man

who delighted in preaching. Without theological training and having only a few sermons, he was thrust into evangelistic work through the recommendation of his brother, George, who asked him to preach at Cwmtwrch near Swansea in October 1912. A further visit in December extended to a seven-week mission in which there were 130 converts in the small village. He had to telegraph his brother at the Preston Bible School to assist him. With very favorable coverage in *The Life of Faith*, Stephen left the mine. In response to many requests, the brothers went on to mid Wales and thence to London for meetings. Later in 1913 Stephen preached in a Llanelly Baptist church and stayed on, accepting the pastorate of Island Place Mission. In July 1914 a vision occurred while Jeffreys was preaching. The face of a lamb appeared on the wall of the Mission and then changed to the face of the Man of Sorrows. This vision was witnessed by hundreds. It was widely reported by the local press and created considerable interest. Stephen was frequently away preaching though remaining pastor there to 1920. Meetings in Dowlais were so successful that a building was rented and then purchased, and Stephen became pastor. Joining his brother George's Elim Evangelistic Band he still continued to preach wherever he could.

In 1924 Stephen went with George and three others on a five-month tour of Canada and the U.S. On their return he left Dowlais (November

1924) and was engaged as a full-time evangelist in London. These arrangements were short lived, and early in 1926 he went off independently. The newly formed Assemblies of God of Britain and Ireland (AGGBI) invited him to hold meetings, and for the next three years he traveled extensively in pioneering churches.

In Bedford, Bishop Auckland, Bury, Chesterfield, Doncaster, Dover, Manchester, Sunderland, and many other places Jeffreys established or strengthened assemblies. Outstanding miracles were witnessed. People sometimes stood in line all night to obtain seats. At Sunderland mounted police were needed to control the crowds. Jeffreys's work dramatically changed the character of the AGGBI and the rate of growth. He established many churches and also inspired others to do the same. By the middle of 1928 he became the object of a totally unjustified attack by a hostile section of the press, though he ignored this and went on preaching. After meetings in Newcastle he left for the U.S., where he drew large crowds at Springfield, Missouri, and Los Angeles. From there he went on to New Zealand, where he remained until going on to Australia for a few meetings before visiting South Africa.

On Jeffreys's return his health began to deteriorate, and he became increasingly incapacitated. His wife died in 1941, and he went to live with his daughter May in Porthcawl, Wales. He lived his last eight years in quiet seclusion. He preached his last sermon a few weeks before his death on November 17, 1943. He was indeed a beloved evangelist. In Bishop Auckland four brothers who were converted became ministers in the AGGBI. In Manchester, J. N. Parr left business to become a full-time pastor of his greatly enlarged congregation following Jeffreys's mission. Jeffreys was happy to move on to the next place and could not turn down any offer to preach.

Bibliography: A. Adams, *Stephen Jeffreys* (1928); W. J. Adams, *Miracles of Today* (1927); D. W. Cartwright, *The Great Evangelist* (1986); E. Jeffreys, *Stephen Jeffreys—Beloved Evangelist* (1946); C. Whittaker, *Seven Pentecostal Pioneers* (1983).   D. W. Cartwright

JENKINS, LEROY (1935–). Tent evangelist and faith healer. Jenkins's ministry began with the spectacular healing of his almost completely severed arm in an A. A. Allen tent meeting in Atlanta, Georgia, in May 1960. Jenkins recounts in his autobiography, *I Met the Master,* that he had run from a divine call his entire life and considered the accident that injured his arm to be divine judgment. Immediately following his healing Jenkins began to preach and pray for the sick with what was considered to be great success. With the help of the business manager of the deceased Jack Coe, he was able to obtain Coe's 10,000-seat tent and hold meetings with great success all over the country throughout the 1960s.

Although for a short period of time he attended a Presbyterian church, Jenkins was raised by his mother in a Pentecostal atmosphere and declared himself to be "thoroughly Pentecostal in belief and doctrine." Jenkins's ministry was known for his "fantastic miracles," but they were not enough

to keep him from trouble. Jenkins was divorced from his wife and was arrested several times in cases involving drugs and alcohol. Jenkins began a new phase by founding "The Church of the What's Happening Now" in Columbus, Ohio, in the early 1970s. Jenkins had moved completely away from his early Pentecostal roots, but he still found a following for his unique brand of religion.   J. R. Zeigler

JERICHO MARCH See SPIRITUALITY, PENTECOSTAL AND CHARISMATIC.

JERNIGAN, JOHN C. (1900–1980). The fifth general overseer of the Church of God (CG, Cleveland, Tenn.). A Tennessee native, Jernigan was converted in 1921, entered the CG Bible Training School, and began preaching before the year ended. He pastored churches in Tennessee, Texas, and Illinois before he was assigned to a state overseership in 1926. An effective administrator, he was elected general overseer in 1944, a position that he held for four years. As general overseer he not only served his denomination but also helped organize the Pentecostal Fellowship of North America (PFNA) in 1948. He was chairman of the constitution committee in 1948 and the first president of the PFNA, 1948–50.

Jernigan published numerous sermon outlines and other books; among them are his autobiography, *From the Gambling Den to the Pulpit* (1927) and *Advice to Ministers* (1948).

Bibliography: Archives of the Church of God (Cleveland, Tenn.); C. W. Conn, *Like a Mighty Army* (rev. 1977).   C. W. Conn

JESUS CHRIST The two foci of the Christian gospel resolve into two interdependent questions: (1) Who is Jesus? (2) What was the meaning or accomplishment of his life? How any religious group thinks about Jesus of Nazareth and responds to the evangelical (i.e., "gospel"-bearing) questions about his identity and significance tell us as much about the group as it does about Jesus.

The "holy Scriptures" provide us the last word on "Jesus, who is called Christ." Theologies, on the other hand, are calibrated from their emphases as derived from the *biblical records,* but also from *tradition,* and from our *experience* of relating with God—whether we admit it or not. When Jesus leads his twentieth-century Pentecostals to their Caesarea Philippi examination and asks, "How do you understand my identity and mission?" how have they characteristically responded?

I. Difficulties of Literary Accessibility. At the outset it must be noted that one must distill Pentecostal christology primarily from *oral tradition,* because for the first half-century and more, Pentecostals, untrained in formal theology as most were, did not write christologies or even lives of Jesus. Their message communicated Christ regularly by preaching and in a lesser way by ephemeral literature. And when that message was written down, whether in tract form, evangelistic booklets of sermons, or tabloid articles, it was almost always—except for denominational statements of faith—meant to be appropriated and acted on as by altar-like responses, just as if it were heard live.

The earliest Pentecostals of this century descended in their spiritual heritage from some established form of the Christian faith. A vast majority of them had been discipled in a habitat where *vital experience* with God was highly valued—either in the Methodist Holiness movement or in Reformed revivalism. Traditional creeds promulgated by the orthodoxy of the fourth and fifth centuries correspondingly were considered to be part of the baggage of Christianity. But in no way were the creeds deemed as having an authority commensurate with the Bible itself. The Bible introduced Jesus as someone a humble person could love and relate to. Philosophical constructs (e.g., "begotten, not made"; "one substance") had an unfamiliar ring to the pure biblicist, and did nothing to endear Jesus to the one encountering them in the creeds—if, indeed, he or she ever had such an encounter.

Pentecostals delighted in taking their views of Jesus straight from the Bible. The creeds, associated with nominal Christianity for fifteen hundred years, generally were not thought to be needed for interpreting Jesus in the Bible, since true believers had the Spirit to reveal him (John 14:25–26; 15:26; 16:12–15), not only through the holy words of Scripture, but in a parallel fashion in one's experience (John 14:16–24; 2 Cor. 3:18).

II. The Centrality of Jesus in Pentecostal Faith. The exhortation in Hebrews 12:2, "Looking to Jesus the author and finisher of our faith" (KJV) had the power of a proverbial slogan to conserve that faith Jesus initiated and consummates in history, doctrine, and experience. He is the concrete object of trust, the subject of teaching, and the ethos of everlasting life. The exhortation to focus faith on Jesus was often coupled with that other standard summation of the Pentecostal faith found in Hebrews 13:8, "Jesus Christ [is] the same yesterday and today and forever." The composite exhortation to look to the living Jesus, who has not changed from what he was and did in Bible days provided them a glorious world-and-life view (in lieu of a philosophy), and a centerpiece for theology (in lieu of a "system").

In a movement that highly valued and proclaimed the activities of the Spirit of God, the place of Jesus as God's "Christ," i.e., "Anointed," and Spirit dispenser, nevertheless, has been central. As with the gifted teachers of the movement, it has never been a simplistic choice based on the either-or fallacy—either pneumatology or christology. The principle has been reiterated time and time again: The more of the Spirit pervading one's total experience, the more one will have a preoccupation with Jesus as the object of adoration, the focus of doctrine as "the Word of God" (John 1:1; Rev. 19:13), the model of spirituality, and the paragon for ethical integrity and fruitfulness. This, of course, presupposes his oneness with God (John 10:30; 17:11, 21) and his bearing the unmeasured fullness of the Spirit of God (John 3:34).

The doctrine of the Spirit's being a constant promoter of Christ has instant authenticity with Pentecostals, not because of the grandeur of the teacher(s) stating it, but because it essentially quotes and interprets the words of Jesus: "But when he, the Spirit of truth, comes, he will guide you into all truth. He will not speak on his own; he will speak only what he hears . . . He will bring glory to me by taking from what is mine and making it known to you. All that belongs to the Father is mine. That is why I said the Spirit will take from what is mine and make it known to you" (John 16:13–15).

Not the institutional church, not the creeds, and not the seminaries—but the Bible itself, read, not in the Hebrew and Greek texts in which it originated, but in the KJV—was the authoritative source in early Pentecostalism for knowing and proclaiming Jesus. The reception of the Spirit in fullness was intended to empower one specifically as a *witness of Christ* (Acts 1:8).

To "preach the word" (2 Tim. 4:2) meant to "preach Christ" (Acts 8:5; 1 Cor. 1:23; Col. 1:28). And that process meant transformation. The Christ of the Bible had to be experienced before he could really be understood. Direct holy experience with him is cherished above all extra-biblical formal configurations of the knowledge of him. Neither the high-church congregational chanting of the Apostles' Creed (with its late addition of the "descended into hell" clause in the fifth century), nor of any of the other creeds—the Nicene Creed (A.D. 325), the Niceno-Constantinopolitan Creed (A.D. 381), the Chalcedonian Formula (A.D. 451), the so-called Athanasian Creed (c. A.D. 475–500)—but *present experience of the same Jesus* who traversed Galilee doing such wonderful things and rising from the dead, provides that transforming intimate knowledge of the Lord.

III. The Centrality of the Bible for Formulating Biblical Christology. Neither having nor desiring great theologians of their own, and not being enamored of the theologians of other eras and traditions, the early Pentecostals were left pretty well unobstructed in their concentration on the Bible, considered to be an open book to all conscientious believers. Read constantly, memorized extensively, and quoted or paraphrased rather than "interpreted" more often than not, in the process of evangelism and in-house edification, the Bible, especially as its message culminates in the NT, produced a facile Christocentricity.

The personal name "Jesus," occurring some 919 times in the NT (almost all of which refer to him), was revered continually in prayer and worship, and cherished like that of a family member and close friend. His title, "Christ," denoting his Jordan bankside experience of the Spirit, and occurring more than 500 times in the NT, meant that Jesus, too, was Pentecostal, the charismatic par excellence, as well as the one who poured forth from heaven, as the second stage of his glorification, all that was seen and heard at Pentecost (Acts 2:33).

The NT literature is structured around Jesus. In the Gospels, the compassionate and dying Lord can be seen in action on the earth, conveying the very words of God and making the atonement. In the Acts the living Lord who ascended to heaven can be seen relating to his people, and reaching by his Spirit across all barriers to draw all peoples to himself. In the Epistles Christ can be seen as the focus of life: "Christ, who is your life" (Col. 3:4); and he would be seen as the unifying factor in the church, his body: "Christ is all, and is in all" (Col. 3:11). In the Revelation he can be seen as the evaluator of the church and the one whose kingdom will displace all the kingdoms of the world with his righteous one.

The biblical Christ is both awesome and winsome. The Christ generated as the product of fourth-and-fifth-century creedal formulations seemed to be as devoid of vitality as a dissected biological specimen lying on the laboratory table. The biblical Christ is always alive and whole as "the way, the truth, and the life"—not as an abstraction, but as the "wonderful counselor" . . . "the prince of peace" . . . "the savior" . . . the one who is "faithful and true."

IV. The Centrality of Christ for All Biblical Theology. Theology over the Christian ages has typically looked to philosophy to provide an absolute to become its organizing center (e.g., Absolute Will disguised as Sovereignty; Nature; Reason). Pentecostals were interested not in abstracting absolutes to impress the philosophers of this world, but in following the Good Shepherd and co-seeking for the lost. Consequently, they would not develop *a philosophy of Christ* to gain status on the world's theological charts.

Their outlook was simple, sure, and positive: Having eyes for Jesus, they would follow him in whatever he was saying and doing. He had provided the answer to humankind's greatest conundrum, death. Because he rose from the dead and by his Spirit was present in the worshiping community, they did not need to go for a conceptual center beyond him, or to place a theological framework over him. He is alive and interactive among his people. The Christian faith is spelled out from A to Z in him. He is "the First and the Last" (Rev. 1:17).

A. Borrowing From Barth's Christocentric Theology. On the surface it may appear that Pentecostal christocentricity has strong affinities with the concomitant rise in the twentieth century of Karl Barth's theology, dubbed by his critics as Christomonism. Avowing to move away from every philosophical base, Barth was determined to build on Christ as the full Revelation of God. The final verdict on Barth may not yet be in, but it is clear from his writings that Karl Barth's "Christ" evolved in certain ways to resemble a philosophical construct. Barth's God who at first was "Wholly Other" became instead, as his theology matured (*The Humanity of God*), a God who eternally was partly human. This meant that Barth would assert not only the preexistence of Jesus' deity, but also the preexistence of his humanity, making the human Jesus antedate Adam, the first man. But one of the most human characteristics of each person is that he or she had a temporal beginning; consequently, one must deal for decades sometimes with the question of self-identity.

Whereas Barth "eternalized" the humanity of Jesus, making his humanity to that degree different in kind from ours, Pentecostals have taken the "yesterday" of Hebrews 13:8 as referring to time,

especially his time on the earth. With the evangelical mainstream, they have confessed his *true* and *full* humanity, as well as his *true* and *full* deity. In harmony with 1 John 4:2–3, "This is how you can recognize the Spirit of God," Pentecostals have held that the Incarnation, that is, the concrete humanity of Jesus as historically revealed, occurred in space and time as God's self-revelation.

Philosophy is always inclined to keep divine things in the celestial safety zone of the Platonic ideals above space and time. But the Spirit of God calls attention to the fact that Jesus came in the human zone of "water and blood" (1 John 5:6–8). The flesh of God's human Son was drenched in the waters of the Jordan and in the blood of the cross. That coming by water and blood is what we know for sure, and with that Karl Barth would agree, but when one would hypothesize preexisting *eternal* flesh, it necessitates a philosophical way of thinking alien to the Bible.

In summary, both Barth and the Pentecostals featured "Christ" or "Jesus" in their biblical theology. But he is not the same in the one as in the other; and there is no evidence that Pentecostals, immersed as they were in Fundamentalism, were in any way influenced by Barthian christology, a species of neo-orthodoxy.

B. Christ in the Old Testament. One of the more formidable questions raised by biblical theology, however, asks how—or whether—Christ is present in the OT. The prima facie response made according to a straight-forward biblicism uses the words of Jesus: "the Scriptures . . . testify about me" (John 5:39). He is found there in the testimony of prophecy (Rev. 19:10). He is found there also in oneness with God: "Before Abraham was born, I am!" (John 8:58). He is found there moreover in type (John 1:29, 36, 51 [Bethel]; 2:19; 3:14; 6:32, 35; 7:37–38; 1 Cor. 10:4). But when one goes further and inquires whether Jesus was physically appearing there in at least eighteen incidents, one already has presumed something about his humanity—a presumption that will have a shaping effect on the answer.

The Pentecostals as Fundamentalists were heirs of the conservative theology of the nineteenth century. As such their heritage included E. W. Hengstenberg's three volume *Christology of the Old Testament*. This influential 1836 work championed the appearance of Jesus in the flesh whenever "an/the angel of the Lord" appeared and even in cases where only the word angel occurs. Put in its starkest terms the question becomes: Did Jesus have veal and yogurt with Abraham, visit Ishmael but not Isaac, provide fire protection for the three Hebrews in the king's furnace, wrestle with Jacob, and become the executioner of firstborn sons and animals all over Egypt?

To the degree that these queries were answered in the affirmative by Pentecostal Bible proclaimers, to that degree—by predicating pretemporal flesh—did they lean toward Barth, the only difference being that the human substance of his Christ was eternal, and theirs, though not necessarily eternal, existed about 2,000 years before

Mary's conception in Nazareth when the Lord's angel came to her.

The point is this: Not wanting to miss Jesus anywhere in the Bible, for the most part, they would score points for him in the supposed Old Testament "Christophanies," even if those points would later have to be subtracted from the uniqueness of the Incarnation. In so doing they, perhaps unconsciously, broke with the position of Stephen (Acts 7:30, 38, 53) and Paul (Gal. 3:19) that the old covenant was mediated by angels and the new covenant by Christ, to follow Reformed teaching that makes Christ the mediator of both covenants. Suffice it to say that not by any means have all Pentecostals contended that for Christ to be the center of all biblical theology he must be the physically present star of the Old Covenant as well as the New.

C. Doctrinal Analysis. The centrality of Christ for all *biblical* theology—and Pentecostal doctrine is nothing if not Bible-based—is expressed in the following thesis: *Every biblical doctrine has Christ as its focal point and radiates his light.* The following analysis examines the great doctrines of Scripture:

Holy Scripture: Christ is the cohesive theme of the Bible (Luke 24:25–27, 44–45; John 5:39b; Acts 17:2–3), the focus of its vision, the unifying factor in its prophecies and its doctrines, the key to interpreting its historical progression, the quintessence of its wisdom and spirit, and the ultimate model of its message.

Revelation: Since no one can see God, and since only the Son understands the Father (and those with whom he shares that understanding), all the revelation of God received by human beings can be divulged by Christ only through his Spirit (Luke 10:22; John 1:18; Col. 2:2–3).

God: Christ is the visible image of the invisible God (Col. 1:15), fully depicting God (Col. 1:19; 2:9). *God's Word* is fully expressed in him (John 1:1; Rev. 19:13), and *God's Spirit* is fully presented in him (2 Cor. 3:17–18), and thus God's glory is fully resplendent in him (Heb. 1:3), and he is fully authorized to bear *God's Name* (Matt. 1:23; 21:9; 23:39; John 5:43; 10:25; 12:13; 17:11–12; Phil. 2:9–10).

Creation: Everything that exists was "created by Christ and for him" (Col. 1:16; John 1:3). Therefore, he is the owner of all creation, old and new (2 Cor. 5:17).

Preservation: Christ sustains everything from the microcosm to the macrocosm, from quarks to quasars (Col. 1:17), including his people (2 Tim. 1:12).

Humankind: Christ is the model of a perfect human being, one in whom the image of God is resplendent (Rom. 8:29; Eph. 4:13; Phil. 2:15; Heb. 12:2).

Law: The law, serving to reveal one's need of God, was designed "to lead us to Christ" (Gal. 3:24).

Gospel: The "Good News" preached by the apostles (Rom. 15:19) was "the gospel of the glory of Christ" (2 Cor. 4:4).

Christology: The various aspects of the doctrine of Christ—his deity, humanity, work of redemption—are the heart of theology.

Pneumatology: The "one Spirit" (1 Cor. 12:13) that is God's is "the Spirit of Christ" (Rom. 8:9). The Spirit (John 20:22) is Christ's presence in the church (John 14:16–18; 2 Cor. 3:17–18), and the Spirit's gifts are Christ's presents to his church (Acts 2:33; Eph. 4:7–13).

Soteriology: Christ's work of atonement at the cross provides the only hope and the all-sufficient means for the salvation of sinners (Eph. 1:7; Acts 4:12; 10:39–43).

Grace: God's giving us himself in Christ (John 3:16) and Christ's giving us himself in the Spirit (John 14:16–20; Heb. 10:29) specify the "gift" nature of grace.

Resurrection: The resurrection of Jesus is the cornerstone for the whole doctrine of the new creation (Acts 10:39–41; Rom. 4:25; 10:9–10; 1 Cor. 15:3–5, 14, 17; 1 Peter 3:21; Rev. 1:5).

Justification: Subsequent to his resurrection (Rom. 4:25), all justification must be "in the name of the Lord Jesus Christ and by the Spirit of our God" (1 Cor. 6:11).

Regeneration: Jesus said: "Because I live, you also will live" (John 14:19). So he "breathed on them and said, 'Receive the Holy Spirit'" (John 20:22; cf. Gen. 2:7; Titus 3:4–5).

Sanctification: "You are in Christ Jesus, who has become for us . . . holiness" (1 Cor. 1:30). "Clothe yourselves with the Lord Jesus Christ, and do not . . . gratify the desires of your sinful nature" (Rom. 13:14). We were baptized into his death, co-crucified with him, and co-raised with him (Rom. 6:3–7). "In the same way [that Christ died "to sin" once for all but now lives "to God"], count yourselves dead to sin but alive to God in Christ Jesus (Rom. 6:11).

Maturation: We must go on to maturity (Heb. 6:1–3) until "in all things [we] grow up into . . . Christ" (Eph. 4:15).

Election/Predestination: The church was chosen corporately "in Christ" (Eph. 1:3, 4, 5, 6, 7, 9, 11, 13)—not on one's own, but "in the one he loves," before the creation of the world.

Incorporation: Individuals from all backgrounds are integrated with the body of Christ upon the occasion of their regeneration, becoming a part of him in his church (1 Cor. 12:12–13).

Glorification: Seeing Christ when he appears will mean transformation to share in his glory and to be patterned after his glorious body (Phil. 3:21; 1 John 3:2).

Ecclesiology: Christ is the supreme head of his body, his "fullness," the church he purchased with his blood and endowed with his Spirit and gifts (John 20; Acts 2:4, 33; 20:28; Eph. 1:22; 4:7–11).

The Blessed Hope: The Christian hope hinges upon the bodily return of Christ to this world to receive his living church into glory (Acts 1:9–11; Titus 2:13–14; Rev. 1:7).

Final Judgment: God has committed to Christ the judgment of all people during the Day of the Lord "because he is the Son of Man" (John 5:25–27; Acts 10:42; 17:31; 2 Cor. 5:10).

Consummation: "Then the end will come, when [Christ] hands over the kingdom to God the Father after he has destroyed all dominion, authority and power. For he must reign until he has put all his enemies under his feet" (1 Cor. 15:24–25).

V. The Centrality of Jesus in "Oneness" Pentecostal Doctrine. Separating from Trinitarian Pentecostalism in the teens of the twentieth century, Unitarian Pentecostalism rejected the classical catholic contention for the threeness of God, while keeping the distinctively Pentecostal doctrines. It must be noted that only once in the KJV is the numeral "three" applied to God (1 John 5:7); and that text is a very late gloss (thirteenth-century Latin and sixteenth-century Greek [1520]), omitted responsibly by modern translators, since it is inauthentic.

Like the rest of the early Pentecostals, these believers in "one God" were strong biblicists. They found that the NT stated categorically and repeatedly that "God is one" (Mark 12:29; Rom. 3:30; Gal. 3:20; 1 Cor. 8:4, 6; Eph. 4:6; 1 Tim. 2:5; James 2:19). Not finding in any authentic text of the Bible *any* of the twenty or more terms used as building blocks to construct a triplex view of God (viz., three, person, *treis hypostaseis, tres personae, circumincession, perichoresis,* ingenerateness, generation, procession, *una substantia, mia ousia,* Second Person, Third Person, spiration, subsistence ["the mode by which substance becomes individualized"]/subsistential, triune, *ad intra/ad extra,* efflux, *diairesis* ["division"], one principle, trinity), they gravitated to what Scripture had to say about the unity of God, using "One God" and "Jesus' Name" as their concrete way of understanding that teaching.

The heart of the matter is well stated by one of their teachers: *"There is no possibility of separating God and Jesus, and there is no God visible outside of Jesus"* (D.K. Bernard, 1983, 29). This statement is insightful in two important respects: (1) It confesses an evangelical unitarianism in contradiction to the antichrist unitarianism (1 John 2:22–23) that was influential throughout the nineteenth century and until the middle of the twentieth century. (2) It provides the real operational criterion for their analysis of the biblical doctrine of God.

It is the second of these that elicits our attention here. Instead of accepting the teaching of the so-called Athanasian Creed, worked out by the theological heirs of Augustine who codified his doctrine, the unitarian Pentecostals took a Hebraic approach, completely antithetical to philosophy and aligned to visual orientation. They found nothing biblically that says God is a trio of persons subsisting from one essence and originating "as by one principle." What they did find was this: The key to understanding God, his Word, and his Spirit, and the statements in Scripture about the Father and Son was to be found in the Bible's own emphasis on the *visible* God (John 1:14—"We have seen his glory") and the *invisible* God (John 1:18—"No man has ever seen God") who is "spirit" (John 4:24), and who became fully *visible* in Jesus, his perfect "image" (John 1:18; Col. 1:15).

In their view of God they contend for his inseparability. Augustine, on the other hand, denied the inseparability of God by saying that

though the Incarnation was accomplished by "the whole Trinity" only "the person of the Son" was "brought forth" from Mary (*Enchiridion,* 38). Yet Jesus would reiterate in a lengthy explanation that the Father was truly visible in himself if one wanted to see God the way one sees the world (John 14:7–11; cf. 12:44–45; 14:17). To deny that the Father and Spirit (John 14:17) are incarnately visible in Jesus is tantamount to the Colossian heresy, though coming at it from a different direction (Col. 1:19; 2:9).

The key term for understanding unitarian Christology is "the Son of God." The term refers to his *human* nature that fully depicts the nature of God. According to Psalm 2:7 and Hebrews 1:5–6 the Son was begotten on a special day, and according to Galatians 4:4 that Day of the Son's arrival was in the fullness of time during the tenure of the Law. Since the Bible never uses the term "God the Son," we have to recognize the term the Bible does use, that is, "Son of God," which became the biblical designation for God incarnate as Mary's baby (Luke 1:35)—not for the eternally existing God who is spirit, or eternal Spirit prior to the incarnation. When "the Son of God" died on the cross, the human being died, but we cannot say that *God the Son died.* The immortal God does not die. It can be said as does Scripture that the Son died, but it cannot be said correctly that the Father died. This is because "Father" refers to deity alone, while "Son of God" refers to the historical one who reflected the glory of God in his humanity, who as Luke wrote *"will* be called the Son of God." Thus the Father is not the Son (D.K. Bernard, 1983, 127) (and the eternal Spirit is not the Son) but the Father is *in* the Son (John 14:10).

It remains to speak of the *name* of the one covered by the Hebraically descriptive title as "the Son of God." The incarnate one received the name "Jesus." Many texts teach that Jesus was fully human and at the same time "the mighty God, the everlasting Father" (Isa. 9:6), the one in whom divine fullness dwelt. Thus it can be recognized that Jesus was not only the Son in his humanity but also the Father in his deity as long as one regards the Father biblically as being "invisible" and "spirit"/Spirit. The name "Jesus" is Yahweh's identity/"the only name" (Zech. 14:9), and as such can be used to refer to his divine or human nature or both as the Lord. The Great Commission passages (Matt. 28:19; Mark 16:17; and Luke 24:47) unitedly speak of the name of the Lord—*not* names. So the church baptized believers in the name of Jesus Christ (Acts 2:38; 8:16; 10:48; 19:5; 1 Cor. 1:13).

VI. The Five Great Works of Jesus in "the Fourfold Gospel." Pentecostals have championed in their proclamation of the Good News five activities Jesus was noted for—activities not generally recognized, experienced, or hoped for in the traditional church at large. With all those who proclaimed that Jesus forgives the *guilt* of sin by his atonement at the cross, they said the "amen" of confirmation. But they insisted it is stopping short of the "full gospel" to end the message there. Jesus is also sanctifier, healer, baptizer in the Holy Spirit, and returning king.

A notable number of leaders came from the Christian and Missionary Alliance into the Pentecostal movement. They brought with them their heritage of a fourfold gospel as framed by A. B. Simpson: "Christ our Savior, Christ our Sanctifier, Christ our Healer, and Christ our Coming King." Into this quartet they had to insert a new voice, "Christ our Baptizer in the Holy Spirit" without eliminating any of the other features of his work. It could not be a mere substitution of the Baptizer in power for the Sanctifier in holiness. Two doctrinal courses of action presented themselves: (1) Keep all five emphases distinct; (2) Merge the Sanctifier with the Savior and keep the gospel foursquare like the points of the compass. One group that did this enshrined the fourfoldness of Christ's post-resurrection activity in the name of their denomination: "International Church of the Foursquare Gospel."

A. Savior-Sanctifier. If the Roman Catholics stressed salvation from hell at the end of life, and the evangelical Protestant church emphasized salvation from the guilt of sin that can ruin a personality, the Pentecostals, while not failing to touch these bases, brought with them virtually all of the precepts inculcated by the Holiness movement in which so many had been spiritually conditioned. This meant that they would emphasize that Jesus delivers people here and now from the *power* of sins to control believers any longer. He would free believers from the clutches of the devil so sin would no longer be able to tyrannize them with its attendant fear and death.

The traditional church at large had taught for far too long that the Lord's atonement had no salvific effect on one's immediate life; it could only "save" one from the punishment due sinners. However, had God's plan been to save people *in their sins* (Ps. 130:3; 143:2) as was normative during the Old Covenant (Rom. 6:14; 8:3; Heb.7:19; 10:1), it is inconceivable Jesus would have expended so much grief in the pouring out of his life until it was all expended in death, if the result would accomplish nothing more than a continuation of the Old Covenant with its associated slavery to sin (Rom. 6:6, 14, 17, 20). The cycles of sin and restoration had to be broken to make it possible for one to live above sin the way Jesus did.

In the old eras, both before and under the law, there was justification but no sanctification—except the ceremonial sanctification depicted in the rituals of the law. "*In Christ*" there is not only the objective sanctification accomplished by his crucial work "for us," but there is also subjective sanctification, accomplished by his holy presence "in us," freeing us from the slavery of sinning (Rom. 6:14), and making us slaves "to righteousness" and "to God" (Rom. 6:18, 19, 22).

Sanctification is not to be had mystically as in sacramentalism by the application of "a holy thing" (sacrament) to an individual by a priest. But it is to be had spiritually in personal relationship with the victorious power of Jesus to conquer sin in one's life (John 8:36). The full visual model of the believer's being buried with Jesus in baptism and raised with him from death to live again is provided to keep his faith and experience riveted on Jesus. He identified himself with mankind's sin when he submitted himself to baptism at the hands of John the Baptist. He drank the cup of God's judgment on sin in the Garden of Gethsemane and then he became the scapegoat to carry away our sins outside the city at the cross.

To make the cycle of victory complete, we identify with him in his death and resurrection and in so doing we participate in his conquest of sin. In other words we receive not only the "forgiveness of sins" in his name (Luke 24:47); we also are freed from the law that brings out the sin in the person living under it (Rom. 7:8), and just as importantly we are freed from the inveterate sin that would relentlessly control us (Rom. 7:17–24). The deliverance from sin comes "through Jesus Christ our Lord" (Rom. 7:25), and "No one who lives in him keeps on sinning. No one who continues to sin has either seen him or known him (1 John 3:6).

B. Healer. The Pentecostals brought with them from the spiritual bounty of the nineteenth century the great truth that the risen Jesus still heals the sick. A number of works had been influential, including the following: A.B. Simpson, *The Gospel of Healing* (1885); A. J. Gordon, *The Ministry of Healing* (1882); Charles Cullis, *Faith Cures* (1879); R. Kelso Carter, *The Atonement for Sin and Sickness* (1884). In the twentieth century the premier book because of its closely reasoned logic supporting an unmodified positive position was F. F. Bosworth, *Christ the Healer* (1927).

There were two great Pentecostal pillars that supported the healing side of the foursquare temple. One was exegetical, and one was implicational. The Matthean interpretation (8:16–17) of Jesus' healing ministry as the fulfillment of Isaiah's prophecy (53:3–12) that the Messiah would suffer vicariously so we might be healed, made healing a benefit of his atonement. Jesus' healings prior to his cross do not in themselves disconnect those healings from his cross, for he had already been symbolically baptized, necessitating his cross by his voluntary identification with the fallen race. Some of those who question today the grounds for healing in the Matthew 8:16–17 passage have said that the Isaiah 53:4 quotation used in Matthew 8:17 means that Jesus only *took away* sicknesses from individuals on a case by case basis, not that he *received* them and *carried* them in his own person to the cross. Such reasoning, if sustainable, would effectively sever healing by Christ and his atonement. But the actual Greek words used in Matthew's rendering do not use the readily available terms that mean "remove" and decisively use the verbs "take/receive" and "bear/carry."

Now the implicational pillar is just as sturdy as the exegetical one, though that theoretically would seem impossible. This pillar is not freestanding but actually is based on Hebrews 13:8, applying it in light of what one reads throughout the four Gospels and Acts. That rationale goes like this: Physical healing is prevalent in the ministry of Jesus as recorded in the NT. If he is alive and active in the world today as he was during the days of his ministry, there should be evidences of his healing power in operation, because his character and power are the same "today" as "yesterday." Thus the "full gospel" includes the good news about Jesus being the healer of "all my diseases" just as he forgives "all my sins" (Ps. 103:3).

C. Baptizer in the Holy Spirit. The most pronounced and most frequently recorded prophecy of John the Baptist concerning Jesus was that he would immerse the faithful in fiery holy Spirit (Matt. 3:11; Mark 1:7–8 "in holy Spirit"; Luke 3:16; John 1:26–33 "in holy Spirit"; Acts 11:16 "in holy Spirit"). Pentecostals construe this great Jordanian prophecy by John as saying that Jesus' ministry would contrast remarkably with John's. One was an immerser in water—a natural element. The other was an immerser, too,—but in Spirit, symbolized by fire. The Spirit-immersion was to be a supernatural event. And even if understood analogically in terms of the natural elements—water and fire—the contrast could hardly have been greater.

Therefore, if one's theology of Spirit-experience under the Christian faith needs only the great Baptist as model, something incoherent is thereby introduced in John the Baptist's often recorded declaration about Jesus. If baptism in water for the forgiveness of sins explains John's statement about Jesus at all—let alone exhausts its meaning—then why should we desire to move on from John to Jesus? Why not stay with the original baptizer?

Yet Jesus' immersion of believers in his riverine fullness of the Spirit (John 7:37–39) had to do with a fullness of God that went beyond the clearing up of our negative past in "the forgiveness of sins." At the very least, under a parallel metaphor to immersing in the Spirit, it meant that Jesus would clothe those who believed in his resurrection with heavenly power (Luke 24:49; Acts 1:8) such as that which had been upon him (Acts 10:38). Thus the "full gospel" deals with something more than justification; it claims the Spirit's power fully to represent Christ through his followers in an antichrist world (Acts 1:8b). It remains to be underscored that the work of Spirit-baptism is that of Jesus alone. Neither a sacramental institution, nor a how-to-do-it spiritual self-improvement formula, nor zealous co-pray-ers and spiritual giants, nor anyone but Jesus can immerse a believer in the depths of the Spirit.

Because one must yield oneself completely to Jesus, even to the depth of one's speech faculty, the effect of a genuine immersion by the Lord in the Spirit is not only the promised power and boldness, but a heightened sense of the glory and wonder of Jesus and a holy familiarity with him that affects everything thereafter in mutual relationship with him. One becomes sensitized to his lordship, since the one so baptized has yielded to him all there is of oneself to surrender. There will remain plenty of room to grow in the Spirit's fruits over a period of time in the process of becoming more and more like Jesus. But his baptizing work can take place in a moment of full yieldedness and faith.

D. Returning King. Believers will not go on forever meeting the Lord in death. For to one privileged generation living on the edge of history he will return to terminate the world systems with the kingdom of God. He will raise the dead, transform the believing living, and judge all humanity past and present.

Under the "faith" (or was it delusion?) that the church could by its power and influence bring in the kingdom of God on earth, the church, sometimes for centuries at a stretch, had either forgotten or forsaken the doctrine and "blessed hope" of Christ's return. The adventist (i.e., second coming) hope was revived in part of the church during the nineteenth century and was passed on and picked up by the "full gospel" Pentecostals in the twentieth century. The prospect of Jesus returning is one more factor that keeps the Christian faith from being a philosophy of Christ. He will appear again. "His own," this time around, will receive him with open arms. That glorious encounter with the glorified Christ will result in those who have kept the faith being glorified with his glory and receiving a spiritual body like his glorious body (Phil. 3:20–21; 1 John 3:2).

VII. Jesus as the Model for Spiritual Experience. Encompassing the Christian faith as its pioneer and perfecter (Heb. 12:2), and being the one who identified himself as "the way" (John 14:6), Jesus was destined to become in himself an *example* for believers (John 13:15; 1 Peter 2:21), and he taught that "everyone who is fully trained will be like his teacher" (Luke 6:40). Paul also taught the same great truth that Jesus, the Son of God, is the model we are being conformed to so that "he might be the firstborn among many brothers" (Rom. 8:29). Another author harmonizes that "he had to be made like his brothers in every way" (Heb. 2:17). Moreover, Jesus taught "As the Father has sent me, I am sending you" (John 20:21).

Pentecostals have found in Jesus a role model not only for "Christian" [in the most literal sense] character but also for Christian experience—specifically, spiritual experiences analogous to the great ones preserved in the record about him. A holy human being entempling the Holy Spirit, he became the prototype for those recreated in his image.

A. Jesus' Human Birth by the Spirit. When Jesus was born, his birth was brought about by the agency of the Spirit of God. And he was "holy" from the very first moment of life onward (Luke 1:35, NIV, note). Consequently, his physical birth *by the Spirit* has a likeness to our new birth *by the Spirit* in the sense that we are born again by the Spirit just as he was born of the Spirit, never needing to be born again beyond that original *spiritual* birth. So all of his natural life he modeled for us what the Christian spiritual life should be, including all the fruit of the Spirit in full abundance.

B. Jesus' Anointing With the Spirit. Jesus had two distinct experiences in succession—one in the Jordan River and one on the bank of the Jordan. He was baptized in water by John the Baptist. Then "he went up out of the water"

Three Stages in Jesus' Glorification and Their "Spiritual" Results.

Event	Biblical Scene	Effect for Believers
1. Resurrection	Post-Easter Night (John 20:19–23)	Regeneration (Spiritual life and breath: John 14:19; 20:22)
2. Ascension and Session	Pentecost	Clothing with Power to Serve/Anointing/Baptism in the Holy Spirit (Luke 24:49; Acts 1:8)
3. Return to Earth in Glory	*Parousia* (1 Cor. 15:23, 52)	Glorification (A *Spiritual* body: 1 Cor. 15:44)

(Matt. 3:16; Mark 1:10) and during a season of prayer (Luke 3:21) his Father anointed him (Luke 4:18; Acts 4:27; 10:38) with the power of the Holy Spirit. His water baptism identified him with the fallen race. His anointing with the Spirit identified him as the holy One marked and equipped by the Spirit to fill his role as the servant of the Lord.

The easiest way to misunderstand his Jordan experiences is to assume that they represent only one monolithic experience for him, indistinctly foreshadowing the conversion experience of believers. But note the contrasts in the two experiences:

Jesus' Baptism		Jesus' Anointing
by the prophet	—agent—	by God
in the Jordan	—place—	beside the Jordan
river water	—symbol—	dove
cleansing	—action—	inauguration of a peaceful king
man down under water	—movement—	Spirit down from heaven
one following many	—number—	only one

In the experience of baptism he shows his submission to God by following sinners into the water where all their sins had been washed off symbolically. It was his human spirit yielding to water baptism and all the consequences it would have for him that is featured. In his prayer before the anointing his human spirit remains submitted, but the Spirit of God is featured as descending emblematically upon him. In summary:

His birth prepared him for life in the Spirit.

His baptism prepared him for the Cross by his facing it symbolically.

His anointing prepared him for his ministry.

C. **Jesus' Relationship With the Spirit.** Throughout his life Jesus was the model of a person submitted perfectly to the Spirit and benefiting from the Spirit.

1. He was conceived by the Spirit in a miraculous birth (Luke 1:35).

2. He bore the fruit of the Spirit all through his life from childhood on (Luke 2:51–52).

3. He was anointed with the Spirit to become prophet, priest, and king (Luke 4:18–19).

4. He was led by the Spirit to go out and to return from temptation (Luke 4:1–14).

5. He had his ministry in Israel by the power of the Spirit (Acts 10:38) and exorcised demons (Matt. 12:28).

6. He was enabled to go through with the cross by the Spirit (Heb. 9:14).

7. He was raised from the dead by the Spirit (Rom. 1:4).

In his resurrection Jesus was glorified (cf. John 7:39) and thereafter the Spirit was given by him in three impartations, each of which was commensurate with a stage in his glorification. His resurrection, then, is the pivotal point. It is the last event in his serene submission to the Spirit's control of his life and ministry and the first event in his glorification, from which time on the Spirit is disbursed by him.

Each stage of Jesus' glorification brings successive gifts to his church, which are respectively:

(1) a share of his own holy *vitality* in spiritual presence and peace

(2) a share of his own holy *power* in ministries and spiritual gifts

(3) a share of his own holy *glory* in a resurrection body

So although all NT spiritual disbursements from the Lord come after his resurrection, they have a "spiritual" model in the experiences of Jesus as one submitted fully to God.

Jesus the Paragon of Spiritual Experience

Events in Jesus' life	Experiences That Parallel Jesus' Life in the Spirit
1. Birth by the Spirit (Luke 1:35)	1. Regeneration: New Birth
2. Anointing by the Spirit (Acts 10:38)	2. Baptism in the Holy Spirit: New Power
3. Resurrection by the Spirit (Rom. 1:4; 8:11)	3. Glorification: New Body

The one spiritual gift not explicitly modeled in Jesus was the Spirit's speaking through believers in other languages when they are baptized in the power of the Spirit. Pentecostals have held that the international languages at Pentecost were symbolic of God's interest in all nations. Jesus, the "wonderful counselor" that he was, continually was speaking words that were "spirit and life" but in the language of the Hebrews. Tongues are a lesser gift than his superior gift of holy speech appropriate to the prophets of the Old Testament epoch *in which he lived out his life*. That does not mean he was against tongues or aloof to speaking in tongues, for we are told that he was the one responsible for what was seen and heard on the day of Pentecost (Acts 2:33).

D. Jesus as the Life-Giving Spirit. The Apostle Paul contrasted the "first Adam"—"a living being"—with the "last Adam"—"a life-giving spirit" (1 Cor. 15:45). One man lived. The other man gives life. At the literary climax of John's Gospel (20:19–23), we see the last, final, ultimate man revealing the glory of his life-giving self. Having come to his fearful followers for their first group meeting after his resurrection he pronounced two blessings of peace upon them. The first restored their old relationship with him and made them eyewitnesses of his resurrection. The second created the new life in them that would characterize new covenant relations with him. He breathed upon them and offered them the breath of eternal life—his own intimate spiritual life. By this afflation of his holy breath they would understand what it means to have "Christ in you, the hope of glory"—"the mystery that has been kept hidden for ages and generations, but is now disclosed to the saints" (Col. 1:26–27).

Jesus' resurrection opened to the world the Age of the Spirit. By the Spirit he reigns in his church and gives gifts to those who worship and obey him. He is the Alpha and Omega of the Christian faith, the head of his church, and the bright morning star signifying the coming of a new day that never ends.

See also JESUS CHRIST AND THE SPIRIT; MATTHEW, GOSPEL OF; MARK, GOSPEL OF; LUKE–ACTS; JOHN, GOSPEL OF; PAULINE LITERATURE.

Bibliography: D. K. Bernard, *The Oneness of God* (1983); D. W. Dayton, *Theological Roots of Pentecostalism* (1987); W. G. MacDonald, "Christology and 'The Angel of the Lord,' " *Current Issues in Biblical and Patristic Interpretation*, ed., G. F. Hawthorne (1975); Aimee Semple McPherson, *The Foursquare Gospel*, compiled by R. L. Cox (1969).   W. G. MacDonald

JESUS CHRIST AND THE SPIRIT The relationship between Jesus and the Holy Spirit is as complex as the Trinity itself; moreover, Scripture does not speak monolithically or extensively about this alliance. With some justification one can speak of the Spirit and Jesus or the Spirit and the Risen Christ. Generally speaking, while the earthly Jesus' connection with the Spirit is expressed in terms of power, authority, and divine approbation, the relationship between the Risen Christ and the Spirit is conveyed in terms of the power which raised Jesus (thereby showing divine approval) and who now dwells within believers, both authenticating their status as children of God and empowering them to live as disciples. The focus below will concentrate on the relationship between the "historical" Jesus of the Gospels and the Spirit rather than the Risen Christ, although ultimately it must be admitted that the portraits of Jesus in the Gospels are shaped by that apostolic view. Three areas of the Spirit's activity of particular concern to Pentecostals and charismatics will be examined: (1) The Incarnation/Birth and Childhood of Jesus; (2) Jesus' ministry in the power of the Spirit; and (3) Jesus, the Spirit, and discipleship. Finally, a general summary concerning the relationship between Jesus, the Spirit, and disciples will be offered.

I. Incarnation/Birth/Childhood of Jesus. The Gospels are not univocal in their coverage of the birth of Jesus. Mark makes no immediate mention of Jesus' origins (cf. Mark 6), choosing instead to open his Gospel with the appearance of John the Baptist and the start of Jesus' ministry. John's Gospel, likewise, has no birth narrative, but celebrates the eternal nature of the Logos. Of the synoptic Gospels only Matthew and Luke contain an account of Jesus' birth, and both of them independently report the activity of the Spirit surrounding the events.

According to Matthew's Gospel, Mary is "found to be with child 'through the Holy Spirit' " (Matt. 1:18), and the angel tells Joseph that "what is conceived in her is from the Holy Spirit" (Matt. 1:20). Brown is certainly warranted in cautioning the interpreter against reading the activity of the Spirit as the "male element in union with Mary" (Brown, 1979, 124). The conception of Jesus is not a result of physical union of any kind, such as one might find in mythology, but is instead the consequence of divine action. Although "the Holy Spirit" might just as easily read "a holy spirit" in Matthew 1:18, there is no question that it is God who is at work in Mary. Apart from the two references to the involvement of God's Spirit in Mary's pregnancy, "Spirit" plays no other role in the Matthean birth narrative.

Matthew's emphasis is upon the divine source of Mary's pregnancy, and the presence of the Spirit does not directly concern the child Jesus as it does, for instance, in Luke's account. According to Luke's Gospel, the angel Gabriel announces to Mary that "the Holy Spirit will come upon you, and the power of the Most High will overshadow you" (Luke 1:35). The parallelism between the "Holy Spirit" and the "power of the Most High" is self-evident. The outcome of this "overshadowing" pertains not so much to Mary as to the child she will bear. It is also consistent with Luke's emphasis elsewhere that the Spirit is virtually synonymous with power (cf. Acts 1:8, which even uses the same language for "come upon"; Acts 8:10; 10:38; cf. Luke 4:14). The future "will come upon you" in Luke 1:35 is noteworthy, for there is no explicit fulfillment of this prediction. Indeed, the angel leaves with Mary's wish that what the angel said come true. The mention of Elizabeth (v. 36) immediately after the announcement that the child will be holy and the Son of God, in all likelihood alerts the reader that she will play a role in the scene of the fulfillment of this promise. Accordingly, the next frame pictures Mary visiting Elizabeth, who at the sound of Mary's greeting is filled with the Holy Spirit and prophesies. In turn, Mary speaks, or perhaps more correctly, Mary prophesies too (e.g., Ellis, 1966, 74–75; Shelton, 1988, 82–83; cf. Danker, 1972, 15, who regards the speaker of the Magnificat as Elizabeth). This is almost certainly the realization of the promise of the angel in verse 35 that the Spirit would come upon Mary. At the moment of Jesus' conception, Mary breaks out in a prophetic song that is decidedly christological in emphasis. The "Mighty One has done great things" (cf. v. 35) to Mary, and through the son she will bear, God is extending mercy to all. The role of the Holy Spirit in Luke's birth narrative, therefore, is to verify that Mary's child is an accomplishment of the power of the Most High God (1:35).

When the Spirit moves again in conjunction with Jesus' birth, he moves in the temple upon Simeon. Simeon had been assured by the Holy Spirit that he would not die before he saw the Lord's Messiah (Luke 2:26). When Mary and Joseph take Jesus to the temple to be circumcised, Simeon, upon seeing the child, prophesies a christological affirmation that Jesus is the Savior of all people. In the same temple scene the prophetess Anna, though she is not explicitly said to be filled with the Spirit, recognizes Jesus as the "redemption of Israel" in much the same way as Simeon saw Jesus as the promised Messiah. In each instance of the prophetic activity of the Spirit in the Lukan birth narrative, Luke draws attention to the identity of the child Mary will bear— he is the Son of God who will save all peoples from their sin.

Matthew makes no mention of Jesus' childhood and does not refer to the Spirit in relation to Jesus until his baptism in the Jordan River. Although Luke does give us some glimpses into Jesus' childhood, the Spirit is not alluded to in this connection. At the same time, it is probably not without significance that the childhood scene that Luke does relate takes place in the temple (*ieron*), which in the passage immediately preceding has been the locus of the Spirit's activity (Luke 2:1– 40). In any case, Luke highlights for the reader the unique relationship Jesus has to the temple by having Jesus refer to it as his "Father's house" (*en tois tou patrou mou;* see Marshall, 1978, 129). Whether this scene is historical or not, it is plain that Luke regards Jesus as the Son of God from the moment of the Holy Spirit's conception of Jesus in Mary's tomb (cf., Luke 1:32). He does not become Son via the baptism in the Jordan with the accompanying descent of the Spirit (contra Dunn 1975, 65ff.).

Neither does Luke recognize his role as Son only at the moment of baptism. In keeping with the Spirit's activity throughout the birth narratives and the passage concerning Jesus' childhood, it is, on the one hand, unimaginable that Jesus— the one conceived by the Spirit—should not be conscious of who he is. On the other hand, Michaels is certainly right when he advises that Jesus' baptism is not simply a case of "a divine Being, conscious of his own perfection deciding to stand beside others in a ritual for which he felt

no personal need, simply to identify with them or to put his endorsement on John's ministry" (Michaels, 1981, 26). From the perspective of the evangelists—who were not really focusing on the divine self-consciousness of Jesus at this juncture—Jesus' baptism by John is a unique moment in the dynamic between Jesus, the Father, and the Spirit. If Jesus was motivated by personal need to experience baptism by John, God responded by sending the Spirit to affirm Jesus as the sinless one who is God's salvation. It is a key role of the Spirit, not only in the birth narratives, but in the baptism of Jesus, to confirm that Jesus is God's Son and Messiah.

II. Jesus' Ministry in the Power of the Spirit. If the baptism of Jesus with the accompanying manifestation of the Spirit is an "affirmation rather than a conferral" of Jesus' sonship (Autry, 1983, 31), it is also the moment of his being empowered for ministry (e.g., Luke 3:23; 4:1, 14). Despite the seeming paradox that the one who has always been the Son should "need" the power of the Spirit, it is unquestionable (according to canonical tradition, cf., e.g., the Infancy Story of Thomas) that Jesus did not perform miracles, heal the sick, or begin his mission as God's agent prior to the Spirit's descent upon him in the Jordan. While Mark's associating the descent of the Spirit with the empowerment of Jesus for ministry is less discernible, it is nonetheless apparent that the Spirit does become the source of Jesus' authority and power (cf., Mark 3:28–29; Mansfield, 1987 offers an elaborate discussion of this relationship).

We note especially in passages like Luke 4:18ff: "The Spirit of the Lord is on me, because he has anointed me to preach good news to the poor" (cf. Isa. 61:1), and Matt. 12:18: "I will put my Spirit on him and he will proclaim justice to the nations" (cf. Isa. 42:1) that the Spirit's anointing sets Jesus apart for his messianic task. In addition, for Luke particularly, "sonship" is virtually synonymous with "messiahship" (cf. Luke 1:32–35; 2:26, 38; Aker, 1988, 110–11).

Even the Fourth Gospel, which does not strictly recount Jesus' baptism by John, begins Jesus' ministry only after an encounter between Jesus and John the Baptist in which John testified that he saw the Spirit descend and "abide" (*menō*) on Jesus. Thus, for the Fourth Gospel, which stresses the eternality of uncreated Logos, the Spirit's anointing signals the beginning of Jesus' ministry and affirms Jesus' status as God's Son and Messiah. And although John's Gospel does not explain Jesus' ability to perform miracles in terms of the Spirit's presence, the author says that Jesus "speaks God's words because God gives Jesus the Spirit without measure" (John 3:34; Autry, 1983, 40), and he characterizes Jesus' words as "Spirit and life" (John 6:63). John also portrays the Baptist as interpreting the Spirit's descent as a messianic sign as well; for instance, in John 1:37–42 Jesus' first disciples are convinced he is Messiah on the basis of John's testimony. Significantly, whereas messianic expectation during the time of Jesus was varied, there may have been, as Johnston calls it, one "common article of faith," namely, that *"God would qualify his chosen agent by empowering him with spirit*" (Johnston, 1970, 54).

That the Spirit empowers Jesus merits further discussion. The Spirit is explicitly associated with Jesus' ministry on limited but strategic occasions (e.g., Mark 3:29; Luke 4:1, 14, 18; Matt. 12:18, 28; cf., Luke 11:20). However, the Spirit's role is implicit at every turn, often couched in terms like "authority" (*exousia*) or "power" (*dynamis*), whose meanings are closely aligned with the Spirit in the OT (Schweizer, *TDNT* 1968, 6:403). Matthew forcefully bonds the coming of the kingdom with the presence of the Spirit through his shaping of a double tradition saying, "But if I drive out demons by the Spirit of God, then the kingdom of God has come upon you" (Matt. 12:28; cf. Luke 11:20; most scholars agree that Luke preserves the original). Most likely Matthew read "Spirit of God" where the source read "finger of God." The change is inconsequential in terms of meaning, but significant in underscoring for the reader that Jesus accomplished his exorcisms via the power of the Spirit. In the alteration of his source Matthew also resonates with Isaiah 42, which he has just cited (Matt. 12:18), and confirms once more Jesus' messiahship by virtue of the Spirit's work in him. Matthew also expands his Marcan source (Mark 2:1–12) slightly (see below) and reiterates that it is Jesus' authority to forgive sins that dumbfounds the onlookers.

There is a solid link between Jesus' power and authority in his charismatic ministry in the early chapters of Mark. Jesus' teaching "with authority" (Mark 1:27) encompasses his power to cast out demons (1:23–27, 32–33, 39, 40–42), an ability attributed to the power of the Holy Spirit in Mark 3:28 (cf. 3:22). Furthermore, Jesus' power includes the authority to forgive sins, a prerogative reserved for God alone (Mark 2:6–12; cf. Mansfield, 1987, passim).

Luke portrays the Spirit-filled Jesus as empowered to heal the sick and cast out demons as well as preach the Good News. Luke reports that "full of the Holy Spirit" Jesus is led into the desert to be tempted. Following the temptation, Jesus returned "in the 'power of the Spirit' into Galilee, and news about him spread through the whole countryside." What prompted the news about Jesus would have included the miraculous (healings, exorcisms) as well as his authoritative teaching (cf. Mark 1:22, 27; Luke 4:36–37). The reference to the Spirit's power in Luke 4:14 (*dynamis*) does not point back to power by which Jesus overcame temptation (cf. 4:1?); rather, the second half of the verse indicates that it was the "power of the Spirit" working in Jesus which caused the news to spread. Thus, while Luke 4:18–19 (cf. Isa. 61:1–2) are programmatic for Luke's narrative, Jesus' ministry by the power of the Spirit began earlier (as Luke 4:23 confirms).

Jesus expects his divine commission to preach the good news of God's kingdom (4:18, 43) to be carried out by the power of the Spirit. God has anointed him specifically for this task (Luke 4:18; cf. Isa. 61:1–2), and he regards the effects of the Spirit's power to be evidence for the people that he is carrying out his assignment as God's anointed one (Luke 11:20; cf. Matt. 12:28).

The communion between Jesus and the Father in the context of Jesus' mission is maintained through the abiding presence of the Spirit, as Jesus' baptism in the Jordan makes plain. Outside the baptismal scene, however, glimpses of this dynamic are rare. One instance is notable, though. Luke 10:21 (not paralleled in Matt. 11:25) makes the fascinating comment that when the disciples' return from a charismatic mission, "Jesus, full of joy through the Holy Spirit, said, 'I praise you, Father, Lord of heaven and earth.'" This unique portrayal of Jesus as "inspired" (cf. Shelton, 1988; Stronstad, 1984) recalls the prophetic outbursts of praise found in the infancy narratives. Once more, we discover that a chief role of the Spirit concerns the relationship between the Father and Son. Less striking and perhaps debatable with respect to whether they refer to the Spirit or spirit in Jesus are texts that describe Jesus as "being troubled in S/spirit" (cf., John 11:33; 13:21) or "knowing in his S/spirit" (Mark 2:8). In these latter cases it would probably be unwise to press the Gospel writers for subtleties not made elsewhere.

III. Jesus, the Spirit, and Discipleship. Not only is Jesus anointed with the Holy Spirit, he himself will baptize others in the Holy Spirit (and with fire, Matt./Luke). This promise is recorded in various forms in all four Gospels (Matt. 3:11; Mark 1:8; Luke 3:16; John 1:33) and Acts (1:5; 11:16), although it is difficult to establish a corresponding fulfillment of this promise in each Gospel. To say that Pentecost is that fulfillment only holds true for Luke's story. Mark and Matthew never elaborate on how they see this baptism. Luke–Acts contains several allusions to the promised baptism that use language other than "baptize in the Spirit" (e.g., Luke 24:49; Acts 1:8, 2:4, 18, 33; 10:45; see Stronstad, 1984).

John even goes so far as to describe Jesus as "the one who baptizes in the Spirit" (present tense), yet he does little to show the reader how this transpires in his Gospel (Windisch, 1968, 30–31, 33). John does refer to the sending of the Paraclete, but this is apparently not the same event as the baptism in the Spirit. The Paraclete bears witness to Jesus and is Jesus' representative in the community (John 14:15–19; 16:25–26). There is no evidence that enthusiastic experiences took place in the Johannine community; instead, love appears to be "proof" that Jesus is present in the Spirit (John 14:21–24; 15:9–11, 17). The Spirit teaches and instructs in Jesus' stead; he is the Spirit of truth (e.g., John 16:13; Schnackenburg, 1982, 138–54). As Paraclete the Spirit encourages believers to stand fast and to bear witness to the truth (John 15:18–27). Moreover, just as Jesus was sent to bear witness to the truth, now disciples are sent to do the same (John 17:16–19).

In actuality, the comment of John the Baptist in John's Gospel that Jesus was the one who baptizes in the Spirit cannot be realized until after Jesus' glorification, according to John 7:39; however, there is nothing in John to indicate that the author had the Pentecost event in mind as the time after Jesus' "glorification." John 20:22 can only forcibly be equated with conversion (e.g., in 20:17 Jesus refers to "my Father and yours" and calls the disciples "brothers"). The case for its being a reference to Pentecost is historically indefensible; nonetheless, there does appear to be some sense in which Jesus confers authority (or power?) upon the disciples to forgive sin (John 20:23), and Jesus does "send" the disciples on a mission after the fashion of the mission he was sent on by his Father (e.g., John 17:18). If we are looking for John to provide missing pieces to a theological construct, we discover the pieces belong to a different puzzle.

IV. Summary. What can be said generally about Jesus and the Spirit? The Spirit is the active power behind the ministry of Jesus, including his working of miracles, casting out of demons, and healing the sick. The Spirit of the Lord anoints Jesus to proclaim the Good News of the kingdom and is evidence of its in-breaking. Just as the Father sends Jesus on a mission equipped with the Spirit, so Jesus sends his disciples equipped with the power of the Holy Spirit to bear witness to the truth of his death, resurrection, and exaltation. Jesus "pours out the Spirit" (Acts 2:33) to initiate the beginning of the last days. With the coming of the Spirit, the New Age breaks through and the Old Age begins to pass away. As the eschatological power of the last days, the Spirit continues to work through believers. The Spirit is given to the church to equip the saints; this "equipping" includes both the miraculous manifestations of the Spirit as recorded in 1 Corinthians 12–14 and the not-so-spectacular gifts of service, teaching, administration, and showing mercy. In the sense that the Spirit working in Jesus empowered him to carry out his divine mission, so disciples of every age are empowered by the Holy Spirit to live as people of God.

See also JESUS CHRIST; LUKE–ACTS; PAULINE LITERATURE.

Bibliography: B. C. Aker, "New Directions in Lucan Theology: Reflections on Luke 3:21–22 and Some Implications," *Faces of Renewal*, P. Elbert, ed. (1988); A. C. Autry, "Christ and the Spirit in the NT and in Christian Thought of the Second Century." Unpublished diss., Baylor University (1983); R. E. Brown, *Birth of the Messiah* (1979); F. W. Danker, *Jesus and the New Age* (1972); J. D. G. Dunn, *Baptism in the Holy Spirit* (1970); idem, *Jesus and the Spirit* (1975); E. E. Ellis, *The Gospel of Luke* (1966); P. D. Hocken, "Jesus Christ and the Gifts of the Spirit," *Pneuma* 5 (1, 1983): 1–16; M. R. Mansfield, *Spirit & Gospel in Mark* (1987); I. H. Marshall, *Commentary on Luke* (1978); J. R. Michaels, *Servant and Son* (1981); P. D. Opsahl, ed., *The Holy Spirit in the Life of the Church* (1978); R. T. Schnackenburg, *The Gospel According to John*, 3 vols. (1982–87); E. Schweizer, *TDNT* (1968) 6:389–455; J. B. Shelton, " 'Filled with the Holy Spirit' and 'Full of the Holy Spirit': Lucan Redactional Phrases," P. Elbert, ed., *Faces of Renewal* (1988); R. Stronstad, *Charismatic Theology of St. Luke* (1984); H. Windisch, *The Spirit-Paraclete in the Fourth Gospel* (1968).

P. H. Alexander

JESUS CHURCH, THE See YAHVAH TEMPLE.

JESUS' NAME DOCTRINE See ONENESS PENTECOSTALISM; UNITED PENTECOSTAL CHURCH INTERNATIONAL; PENTECOSTAL ASSEMBLIES OF THE WORLD.

JESUS ONLY DOCTRINE See ONENESS PENTECOSTALISM; UNITED PENTECOSTAL CHURCH INTERNATIONAL; PENTECOSTAL ASSEMBLIES OF THE WORLD.

JESUS PEOPLE A sobriquet for young converts to Pentecostal and Baptist beliefs from the street culture of the late 1960s and early 1970s. An umbrella for a many-faceted and much-fragmented movement, the term suddenly gained currency with the inauguration of a spate of free newspapers designed to appeal to West Coast street people: *Hollywood Free Paper, Right On!* (Berkeley) and *Agape* (Seattle) in 1969, and *Maranatha* (Vancouver) and *Truth* (Spokane) the next year. A massive assault on the sexual promiscuity, drug addiction, and lure of Oriental religions, the Jesus movement stripped the gospel message to bare essentials, the chief tenet being that Jesus is the "one way" to God. Pragmatism characterized evangelistic efforts. Street preaching, introduced as early as 1966 by Tony and Susan Alamo in Los Angeles, became commonplace there and in San Francisco and other Pacific coast cities. Under its college minister, Don Williams (b. 1937), even the wealthy Hollywood Presbyterian Church developed a program for street people. A Seattle coffee house called the Catacombs, started by Linda Meissner, was replicated in hundreds of storefronts and church basements as the movement spread eastward like a prairie fire. Along the way it joined hands with Teen Challenge, by then a national and even international evangelistic "cold-turkey" drug rehabilitation program that had been established in Brooklyn in 1958 by David Wilkerson (b. 1931), an Assemblies of God minister. Much-publicized mass baptisms in the Pacific Ocean and the emergence of superchurches such as Melodyland Christian Center in Anaheim, the Vineyard Christian Fellowship in Yorba Linda, and Calvary Chapel in Costa Mesa, which attracted many formerly disaffected young people, gave the movement widespread notoriety. Hippies carried many customs developed in the street into their new life, unconventional dress and long hair being the most conspicuous. They developed a new genre of sacred song with a secular beat and guitar accompaniment. The informality of their worship made assimilation in existing churches difficult, and the desire of converts for like-minded companions with similar tastes led to establishment of dozens of independent churches and communes with the Bible, not sex or drugs, as their focus. Leader-centered, these included the Lighthouse Christian Fellowship, the Children of God (renamed Family of Love in 1983), and the Tony and Susan Alamo Christian Foundation. Many Jews converted to Christianity, giving rise to Jews for Jesus, Bob Weiner's Maranatha Christian churches, and the like. Such conversions reinforced the image of the movement as one that manipulated disaffected youths into revolt against parents and family traditions. Actions of Tony Alamo (a convert from Judaism), David (Moses) Berg (b. 1919), and some other more radical

New converts of the Jesus Movement are being baptized in an ocean-side service as hundreds watch along the shore. At one service conducted at Corona del Mar, California, Chuck Smith and his Calvary Chapel staff, Costa Mesa, baptized 700 people.

leaders seemed to lend credence to parental fears of brainwashing. To counteract the power of communal leaders, some families resorted to deception, even kidnapping, in attempts to win their young adults and children back. Some retained deprogrammers (the best known being the California black Ted Patrick) to argue their offspring back to reason.

The overwhelming majority of Jesus youth, however, were simply conservative, unconventional Evangelicals, little akin to those being deprogrammed. Some of the earliest Roman Catholic charismatics were among them. A minority joined established fellowships such as the Assemblies of God, a group willing to allow local affiliates to use names such as Christian Center or Faith Chapel. Some congregations allied with loosely constructed networks such as the Chicago-based Jesus People U.S.A. Most, however, remained unattached, their members becoming more and more indistinguishable from independent Pentecostals and Baptists, so that by 1985 the now middle-aged Jesus People had practically disappeared from sight.

Bibliography: G. Adler, *Die Jesus-Bewegung* (1972); N. Albin, *Die Jesus-Revolution* (1971); R. F. Berkey, "Jesus and the Jesus People," *Christian Century* 89 (March 22, 1972): 336–38; N. E. Bloch-Hoell, "Den Hellige and i Pinsebevegelsen, den Charismatiske Bevegelse og i Jesus-Vekkelsen," *Norsk Teologisk Tidsskrift* 77 (2, 1976): 75–86; L. Boisset, *Movement de Jesus et renouveau dans l'Esprit* (1975); J. Duchesne, "*Jesus Revolution*" *Made in U.S.A.* (1972); R. S. Ellwood, *One Way: The Jesus Movement and Its Meaning in the Age of Aquarius* (1972); D. Frielinghaus, *Sie wissen, was sie tun* (1973); W. Kroll, *Jesus kommt! Report der Jesus-Revolution unter Hippies und Studenten in USA und anderswo* (1971); M. McFadden, *The Jesus Revolution* (1972); J. G. Melton, *Encyclopedia of American Religions*, vol. 2 (1978); D. Pederson, *Jesus People* (1971); E. E. Plowman, *The Underground Church* (1971); D. Williams, *Call to the Streets* (1972).   C. E. Jones

JOEL, BOOK OF   The second book of the twelve Minor Prophets (known collectively as the Book of the Twelve in the Hebrew canon).

Joel's writing contains the passage (2:28–32) to which the apostle Peter referred in explaining the supernatural events of the outpouring at Pentecost (Acts 2:16–21). Therefore the prophecy of Joel is one of the most significant books of the OT for modern Pentecostal and charismatic readers. Peter's quotation from Joel ranks as one of the longest OT portions to be found in the NT (107 words in Greek; 54 words in the original Hebrew).

I. Author and Date. The author, Joel, son of Pethuel, cannot be identified with any of the other dozen individuals bearing this name in the OT. He is not mentioned outside of Joel 1:1 and Acts 2:16. Most certainly he lived in the land of Judah. If not a resident of Jerusalem, he was deeply concerned for its citizens (1:2, 3, 19) and was well acquainted with the liturgical practices of the priests (e.g., 1:13–14; 2:12–17). This familiarity has led some scholars to conclude that Joel was a cultic prophet attached to the temple (Kapelrud, Williamson). By contrast, others think he stood in tension with the Jerusalem priesthood (Ahlström, Wolff, Redditt). In either case, the interpretation of his book is not dependent on a correct assessment of Joel's relationship to the temple.

The date of the book is an unsettled issue. The main views that modern scholars have held are:

A. Early Preexilic. The position of Joel as second in the Book of the Twelve is claimed to point to an early date. The absence of the name of a Jewish ruler fits the minority of King Jehoash (Joash) c. 835–820 B.C., when the godly high priest Jehoiada governed Judah in fact (2 Kings 11:21–12:2) and Assyria was not yet threatening Jerusalem. The Book of Joel, however, does not allude to any problem with idolatry, whereas Jehoash and Jehoida did not rid the land of high places (2 Kings 12:3).

B. Mid Preexilic. Patterson (1985, 7:231–33) argues strongly for an early eighth-century date during the reign of King Uzziah when Judah was prosperous and before the campaigns of Tiglath-pileser III in 743 and 732 B.C. But Uzziah's name is not listed in Joel 1:1 (contrast Hos. 1:1; Amos 1:1).

C. Late Preexilic. The Book of Joel has strong affinities in its pronouncements about the Day of the Lord with Zephaniah's writings and with the religious outlook of Jeremiah. Thus it is claimed that they were contemporaries.

D. Early Postexilic. The majority of OT scholars now prefer a postexilic dating. Meyers, Ahlström, and Allen place Joel during or soon after the rebuilding of the second temple (c. 520–500 B.C.). The great powers go unmentioned as enemies of Judah, because the book was written *after* the fall of Babylon in 539 B.C. The rulers of Persia had treated the Jews kindly and so were not considered foes. The historical allusions in 3:2–6 most nearly fit the destruction of Jerusalem in 586 and the ensuing exile. Furthermore, Joel (2:32) undoubtedly is quoting from Obadiah (v. 17): "For on Mount Zion . . . there will be deliverance, as the LORD has said." Obadiah's prophecy is God's oracle against Edom for her conduct in 586 against Jerusalem. The absence of a king, the positive attitude toward priestly leadership and ritual, and the possibility of summoning the entire community to the temple reflect conditions in the early decades after Zerubbabel's return from Babylon. The reference to Sabeans (3:8) suggests no later than 500 B.C., after which they lost control of the Arabian caravan routes.

E. Late Postexilic. A time around 400 B.C., after the rebuilding of Jerusalem's defenses by Nehemiah in 444, is suggested by reference to the city wall in Joel 2:7, 9. But if 2:1–11 is an eschatological prediction, mention of the wall would have no bearing on the date of writing.

In view of strong Jewish tradition that Malachi (fifth century B.C.) was the last of the prophets, it is best to date Joel about 500 B.C. Therefore it is Joel who seems to have borrowed numerous phrases from the writings of Jonah, Amos, Micah, Isaiah, Nahum, Zephaniah, Jeremiah, Obadiah, and Ezekiel and not vice versa.

II. General Message. The message of Joel is a cry for repentance in view of the imminent Day of the Lord (the *yôm Yahweh*) with the hope of restoration to follow. The people of Judah had

Part A. 1:2–2:17

1. 1:2–14	parallel with	2. 1:15–2:17
2–3	announcement	1:15; 2:1–2
4–7	army	2:3–11
8–12	drought	1:16–20
13–14	repentance	2:12–17

Part B. 2:18–3:21

1. 2:18–27	parallel with	4. 3:17–21
18–19a	historical note	
19b, 26	no shame	
20, 25	invasions	17b, 20–21a
21–22, 24	productivity	18a, 19
23	water	18b
27	God in Zion	17a, 21b

2. 2:28–32	parallel with	3. 3:1–16
28a	preface	1
28b–29	Spirit/judgment	2–14
30–31	signs in heaven	15
32	survivors	16

been instructed frequently by earlier prophets that the Day of Yahweh was a time of chastisement and subsequent blessing for Israel and judgment for the nations. The destruction of Jerusalem in 586 B.C. had been *a* day of Yahweh for that generation (Ezek. 7:7–19). Yet God's word to Joel is that *the* Day of Yahweh will strike again on Israel with far greater intensity if the people do not repent and humble themselves before God. God's preparation of his people to survive the apocalyptic Day of Yahweh will be the outpouring of his Spirit on them (Joel 2:28–32). In that day Yahweh will decide the fate of the threatening nations (3:1–2, 12–16). Then Jerusalem will be holy, Judah will know bountiful harvests, and Yahweh will dwell in Zion among his people (3:17–21)—his ultimate goal in redemption (Ezek. 37:25–28; 48:35; Rev. 7:15–17; 21:3).

III. Composition and Structure. A majority of recent commentators accept unity of authorship for the Book of Joel. The question remains, did the author intend the main division to come after 2:17 or 2:27? If the latter analysis is followed, then 1:2–2:27 most logically is concerned with near-at-hand visitations of God on Palestine in the realm of nature (locusts, drought) and his reversal of judgment in the prophet's lifetime; and only 2:28–3:21 foretells eschatological blessings for Judah and judgment for the nations. If the former analysis is correct, the summons to repent may more readily be taken as valid for every age, because the Day of Yahweh is understood as always imminent. Wolff, Allen, and Williamson argue for the second division to begin at 2:18 and thus are able to compare the description of the present and future disasters and the cries to repent of the first part with the divine assurances of economic and spiritual renewal of the second. The exegete can detect numerous parallels between the two divisions as well as balancing ideas within each division. Chiastic

structures also are evident in several passages, especially 2:19b–26 and 3:17–21. The parallels may be aligned in tabular form:

IV. Outline.

I. The Prophet's Urgent Call to Repentance (1:2–2:17)
    A. Lament and Summons Because of Present Economic Distress (1:2–14)
    B. Alarm Concerning the Imminent Day of Yahweh and Summons to Repent (1:15–2:17)

II. Yahweh's Response: Promised Restoration and the Day of Yahweh (2:18–3:21)
    A. Economic Renewal of Yahweh's Land, Present and Future, to Reverse the Judgments of 1:2–2:17 (2:18–27)
    B. Spiritual Renewal Before the Day of Yahweh and Deliverance for All of His People (2:28–32)
    C. Final Judgment of the Nations in the "Valley of Jehoshaphat" (3:1–16)
    D. Ultimate Spiritual and Economic Prosperity of Judah and Jerusalem (3:17–21)

V. Interpretation. In Joel's time a double calamity had recently struck the land of Judah: first, a terrible locust plague and then a searing drought (1:2–12). These were harbingers of an always imminent Day of Yahweh (v. 15). Every natural catastrophe should be construed as a visitation of God and as a foreshadowing of the ultimate fulfillment of the Day of Yahweh—clear reason to repent (vv. 13–14).

In 2:1–11 the prophet warned of the invasion of an army that appears to be more than mere locusts; instead they may be apocalyptic creatures, perhaps the demon-possessed horsemen and horses who go forth following the sounding of the sixth trumpet (Rev. 9:13–21). God had already used first Assyria and then Babylonia as his divine war club to execute judgment on Judah and other nations (Isa. 10:5–6; Jer. 51:20–23; Hab. 1:6). Likewise, he will send "his army"—far more terrifying—in conjunction with cosmic phenomena in that great and dreadful day (Joel 2:10; cf. 2:31). Even in 500 B.C. such a fearful judgment was imminent. On that basis the prophet again urged his countrymen to return to Yahweh their God (2:12–17).

Then Joel announced that the consequences of their genuine repentance (that evidently followed his prophetic exhortation) was the beginning of restoration. The four verbs of 2:18–19a (preceding "I am sending") should be translated in the past tense, as in the ASV, RSV, NEB, and the marginal readings of the NASB and NIV. But the Lord's promises of the return of agricultural productivity and national honor (2:19b–27) extend far beyond any fulfillment in Judah in biblical times or for the Jewish people who have suffered the Holocaust in modern times. The promise in 2:20 of the removal of the northern army (literally, "the northerner") seems to be eschatological, evidently the same invading army already described in 2:2–11. The stench of their unburied corpses will be unbearable (cf. Isa. 34:3; 66:24; Ezek. 39:11–16). Conversely, the mention of "my great army" of locusts in Joel 2:25 is a deliberate reference to the locust plague of 1:4–6. Yahweh's presence among his people will be characteristic of the ultimate Day of Yahweh (cf. 3:17, 21).

Amidst the section foretelling Yahweh's renewal of his land to benefit his people (2:18–27) is a cryptic statement regarding the rains: "for he has given you the autumn rains (hammôreh) in righteousness. He sends you abundant showers, both autumn (môreh) and spring rains, as before" (2:23). The verse stands within Joel's call to praise (2:21–24), answering in detail his laments regarding the recent drought (1:10–12, 16–20). Therefore the primary reference must be to the seasonal rains of Palestine (cf. Ezek. 34:26). However, the word môreh usually means "teacher" (Job 36:22; Prov. 5:13; Isa. 30:20; Hab. 2:18 NASB), whereas yôreh is the usual spelling for the early (October) rain (Deut. 11:14; Jer. 5:24). The only other occurrence where môreh is translated "autumn rain" is Psalm 84:6[7]; but this verse too may by word play refer to the heavenly Teacher; interestingly, the LXX translated môreh in 84:6 as nomothetôn, "lawgiver." Isaiah makes a strong connection between teacher and rain (30:20, 23). The close association between the concepts of rain and righteousness may be seen in Isaiah 45:8 and especially in Hosea 10:12, "until he comes to rain righteousness on you" (NASB)—or, "comes and teaches righteousness to you" (literal). As Bewer explains, ṣᵉḏāqâ is used in the OT only in a moral or religious sense (1911, 120). Wolff claims that contrary to much recent scholarly opinion neither Joel 2:23 nor Hosea 10:12 provides the origin of the title "Teacher of Righteousness" found in the Dead Sea Scrolls; the extant Qumran texts never

relate that title to either of these verses (1977, 63–64).

Buechler (1979, 11–13), on the other hand, believes Joel is making a veiled reference to the outpoured Spirit in 2:23 in the expression hammôreh liṣᵉḏsāqâ. Translating it as "the teacher for righteousness" (NIV mg.) clarifies that possibility. Jesus promised that the Holy Spirit would come as the Spirit of truth, teaching us all things, convicting the world of guilt in regard to sin and righteousness and judgment, and guiding us into all truth (John 14:26; 16:8, 13; cf. 1 John 2:20, 27). Nowhere else does Joel's prophecy refer to the Messiah. It is more in keeping, therefore, with 2:28–29 to expect an allusion to God's gift of his Spirit than of his Son. God's Spirit is "the one giving instruction in righteousness" in Joel 2:23 (on this participial use of hammôreh see Patterson, 1985, 7:254).

Joel 2:28–3:21 changes the subject to describe the Day of Yahweh particularly with regard to the spiritual blessing of the people of Zion and Jerusalem. The text of 2:28 literally says: "And it will come about afterward ('aḥᵃrê kēn)." It does not mean "after this" (NASB), as something following chronologically after 2:18–27 but is a more general term for the future, for eschatological times in general, as found also in Jeremiah 49:6; Isaiah 1:26 (NIV); and Ezekiel 20:39 (NIV). Peter interpreted it to mean "in the last days" (Acts 2:17), altering the LXX of Joel 2:28. Peter's phrase suggests the entire period between the first and second advents of Christ.

The outpouring of the Spirit is to occur "in those days" (2:29), not merely on one day. From the study of this and other OT passages (Isa. 44:3–5; Ezek. 39:29 with 37:14–27; Zech. 12:8–10) as well as the NT, we may conclude that there was an initial fulfillment of Joel's prophecy of the outpouring at Pentecost, a continuing fulfillment during the church age, and an ultimate fulfillment at the Second Advent. Then the outpouring will be a veritable fountain of life flowing out from the Lord's house to water and heal the desert lands (Joel 3:18; Ezek. 47:1–12; Rev. 22:1–2). God promises that he will pour out (Heb. š-p-k) his Spirit as freely as water in far more abundant measure than the promised rain (2:23). Just as he pours out his wrath in judgment (Isa. 42:25; Ezek. 7:8; Hos. 5:10— šāpak in each of these verses), so he will pour out his Spirit in prophetic power. Different but synonymous verbs for "pouring out" the Spirit are used in Isaiah 32:15 ('ārâ) and 44:3 (yāṣaq). "Dreams" and "visions" are traditional forms of prophetic revelation (Num. 12:6). Joel's prophecy indicates that in the messianic age everyone would be his own prophet. Moses' wish would be fulfilled (Num. 11:29). Instead of only on a few, the Spirit would be poured out on believers of all races and categories. The term kāl bāśār, "all flesh" (KJV), bears the meaning of "all mankind" (NASB) or "all people" (NIV); the expression seldom if ever is restricted to "all Israel."

The purpose of the supernatural outpouring in Joel 2:28–32 is to prepare God's people for the coming of the great and dreadful Day of Yahweh. Spirit-empowering will enable them to survive, to be among "those who escape" (v. 32 NASB). The gifts or manifestations of the Spirit are already enabling those persecuted around the world to endure. In that day those who are delivered will then participate in the era of peace and prosperity that Zion will enjoy (3:17–21; Isa. 4:2–6).

Bibliography: Commentaries and monographs: G. W. Ahlström, *Joel and the Temple Cult of Jerusalem* (1971); L. C. Allen, *The Books of Joel, Obadiah, Jonah and Micah* (1976); J. A. Bewer, *Commentary on Joel* (1911); C. H. Bullock, *Introduction to the OT Prophetic Books* (1968); A. S. Kapelrud, *Joel Studies* (1948); C. F. Keil, *The Minor Prophets* (1875); R. D. Patterson, "Joel," *EBC* (1985), 7:226–29; W. K. Price, *The Prophet Joel and the Day of the Lord* (1976); J. A. Thompson, "The Book of Joel," *IB,* vol. 6 (1956); H. W. Wolff, *Joel and Amos* (1977).

Articles: P. D. Beuchler, "Studies in the Book of Joel," unpublished ms, Melodyland School of Theology (1979); H. Hosch, "The Concept of Prophetic Time in the Book of Joel," *JETS* 15 (1972): 31–38; W. C. Kaiser, Jr., "Participating in and Expecting the Day of the Lord—Joel 2:28–32," *The Uses of the Old Testament in the New* (1985), 89–100; J. M. Myers, "Some Considerations Bearing on the Date of Joel," *ZAW* 74 (1962): 177–95; P. L. Redditt, "The Book of Joel and Peripheral Prophecy," *CBQ* 48 (1986): 225–40; C. Roth, "The Teacher of Righteousness and the Prophecy of Joel," *VetTest* 13 (1963): 91–95; J. A. Thompson, "Joel's Locusts in the Light of Near Eastern Parallels," *JNES* 14 (1955): 52–55; H. G. M. Williamson, "Joel," *ISBE,* rev. ed., 3 vols. (1982).   J. Rea

JOHN, LETTERS OF In keeping with the scope of this dictionary, this article will concentrate on the pneumatology of the letters of John. More thorough discussion of the letters will be found in the works listed in the bibliography.

I. Introductory Remarks. Today a consensus exists that the three letters of John were written subsequent to the Fourth Gospel and were, in different ways, occasioned by it. Since a date near A.D. 90 is usually assigned to the Fourth Gospel, the letters were most probably written between 90 and 100. All the letters seem to have the same author and were probably written in the order in which tradition has preserved them. It is quite certain, however, that the author of the letters is not the same as the author(s) of the Fourth Gospel, though all these works are rooted in the community which owes its existence to the teaching and apostolic activity of John, the son of Zebedee.

The second and third letters are basically short communications, able to fit on one piece of parchment, addressed to various small communities or house churches in the vicinity of the main community, which was probably located at Ephesus. Despite their brevity, they are theologically profound (Marshall, 1978). What is called the First Letter of John is, on the other hand, a "'paper' which sets out to expound Johannine teaching and ideas" (Smalley, 1984, xxvii). It must have been sent out as a circular letter to all those under the influence of "the elder" (2 John 1; 3 John 1).

The author of the first letter states that his purpose in writing is "that you might know that you have eternal life, you the believers in the name of the Son of God" (1 John 5:13). He sets out to show that the proper faith relationship to

Jesus recognizes him as the Christ, the Son of God, come in the flesh. This faith produces a transformed life that is recognizable in its effects, particularly in a living knowledge of God expressed in obedience to him and love of the brethren. He proposes a set of criteria by which it can be demonstrated that those who hold this faith are in communion with God. This is what distinguishes them from the world and the schismatic teachers who have gone over to the world. The criteria are usually introduced by the formula, "by this we [will] know . . . " (see de la Potterie, 1971, 110). Some of the criteria are moral: the absence of sin (3:6), walking in the light (1:7), keeping the commandments (2:3–5; 3:24; 5:2), practicing justice (2:29; 3:10), practicing love (4:7). Some of the criteria are doctrinal: believing and confessing that Jesus is the Christ come in the flesh (2:23; 4:2; 5:2–10), remaining in the teaching received (2:23), listening to those who so teach (4:6). Finally, there is the criterion: "He has given us of his Spirit" (3:24; 4:13).

The error that prompted the elder's concern had to do with the relationship between Jesus and the Christ/Messiah. It seems as though the opponents, basing themselves on the teaching of the Fourth Gospel, maintained that there was such a reality as the Christ, an eternal figure, who is the Son of God; but they denied that *Jesus* was this person. It is likely that John 20:31 already addresses itself to this issue (Carson, 1987). They seemed to consider the lowly "flesh" state of the earthly Jesus as unworthy of such an exalted personage either because of their suspicion of matter (Gnostics) or, as is more probable, their inability to conceive of divine reality in such proximity to humanity (former Jews). It is difficult to be more precise concerning these adversaries, though indications in the writings of Ignatius and Irenaeus give us some idea of views circulating a few decades later than the letters of John (see Marshall, 1978, 14–22). Brown (1982, 51) notes a series of dogmatic assertions in 1 John as well as denunciations leveled against the tenets of those who "went out from us, but did not really belong to us" (1 John 2:19). The assertions include: Jesus is the Christ (1 John 5:1); Jesus is the Christ come in the flesh (1 John 4:2; 2 John 7); Jesus is the Son (1 John 2:23; 3:23; 5:11–12); Jesus is the Son of God (1 John 1:3, 7; 3:8, 23; 4:9–10, 15; 5:9, 10, 11, 12, 13, 20); Jesus Christ is the one who came by water and blood (1 John 5:6). On the other hand, the denunciations are directed against those who deny that Jesus is the Christ/Messiah (1 John 2:22); the Son (1 John 2:23); Jesus Christ as coming in the flesh (2 John 7; 1 John 4:2–3).

Their erroneous views about Jesus are the source, according to the elder, of the adversaries' moral aberrations. They claim to have fellowship with God (1 John 1:6, 8, 10), to know God (1 John 2:4), and to be without sin (1 John 1:8), yet they do not manifest the most fundamental criterion for these claims, already laid down in the gospel: obedience to the commandments of God and Jesus (1 John 2:3; 3:23b; see John 14:15, 21; 15:10–14, et al.). The gospel command insisted upon repeatedly in the Johannine correspondence by which the true disciples are to be discerned (John 13:35) is, of course, love for one another (1 John 2:9–11; 3:10–18, 23b; 4:7–12, 19–21). This love is itself obedience to the commandments of God (1 John 5:2; 2 John 6), and includes righteousness (1 John 3:10) and imitation of Jesus Christ (1 John 2:6; 3:16). In brief, the Johannine letters reflect the biblical teaching that knowledge of God is best described by our English term "recognition," which can apply to both perception and acknowledgment. Authentic knowledge of God includes experience of God and practical acknowledgment of his authority (see Martin, 1974).

In seeking to understand the letters of John, particularly 1 John, by identifying the position of the "false prophets" (1 John 4:1), we must bear in mind that although the situation of conflict may explain some of the terminology and even accent of the treatise, it does not explain the *content* of what is being taught. Historical information provides valuable understanding of the context of an utterance, but it does not give knowledge of its referent. It is vitally important, for instance, to understand the social and political realities of the U.S. in the 1960s if one wishes to grasp the context of the speeches of Dr. Martin Luther King, but this knowledge does not give one an understanding of the realities about which he spoke: brotherhood and mutual love in obedience to Christ, freedom for all people, a "faith dream" for all humanity. This illustrates the fact that historical study may help in understanding what a text *says*, but another form of knowledge is needed to grasp what it is *talking about*. Applied to our topic, we may say that the pneumatology of the Johannine letters is part of the prophetic and pastoral teaching of the elder on the true source and fruit of communion with God. This teaching was occasioned by erroneous interpretations of the Fourth Gospel concerning the identity of Jesus, the Christ.

After having considered the occasion of the correspondence, we may now, in the light of our understanding of its context, proceed to consider what it teaches about the action of the Spirit of God in the life of the believer and the believing community.

II. The Role of the Holy Spirit According to First John. Since the word *pneuma* (S/spirit) occurs only in 1 John, we may concentrate our attention on this letter, making references to the other two letters as need arises. The pneumatology of 1 John is found in five passages. In order to understand their significance, we will locate each passage in the overall structure of the treatise. (For a discussion of structure of 1 John, see Marshall, 1978, 22–27; Brown, 1982, 116–29.)

A. 1 John 2:18–28. This section has been aptly entitled "Faith as the eschatological criterion distinguishing believers from heretics" (Malatesta, 1978, 192). The elder can appeal to a tradition well known to his audience ("you heard") to establish the fact that this is the ultimate (*eschatē*) hour. The proof is the presence of the antichrists, that is, those who oppose God's plan by falsifying the identity of the Christ, who is Jesus. Echoes of this notion are found elsewhere in the NT (Matt.

24:23–24/Mark 13:21–22; 2 Thess. 2:3–4; Rev. 19:20; 20:10).

By contrast, John tells his communities, "You have the oil of anointing (*chrisma*) from the Holy One, and you all have knowledge. I did not write to you because you do not know the truth but because you know it, and that every lie is not of the truth" (1 John 2:20–21). The liar is then defined as "the one who denies that Jesus is the Christ" (2:22). Such a person is cut off from communion with the Father and the Son, while those who allow that which they heard from the beginning to remain in them "will abide in the Son and in the Father" (2:24). After mentioning the promise of eternal life and warning them once again concerning those who are deceiving them, the author reiterates, "The oil of anointing which you received from him abides in you, and you have no need for anyone to teach you. Rather as his oil of anointing teaches you about all things, and is true and is not a lie, and as it taught you, abide in him" (2:27).

The *charisma*, or oil of anointing, gives the faithful believer the possession of knowledge (alluding to Jer. 31:31–34), knowledge of the truth; it teaches about all things and teaches the person to abide in Christ. In fact, the *charisma* itself abides within the believer and can be referred to as "that which you heard from the beginning" (2:24).

Drawing from the teaching of the Fourth Gospel concerning the true disciples who abide in the word of Christ (John 8:31–32), or who have his words abide in them (John 15:7), the author coins a new term, *chrisma*, to denote this teaching of and about Jesus which he links to the role of the Holy Spirit who teaches "all things" (John 14:26; 1 John 2:27). The oil of anointing, then, is the teaching about Jesus rendered capable of mediating a knowledge of his reality by that action of the Holy Spirit which brings one into living communion with the risen Christ. Because of this action, believers can know the truth, that is, they "possess the intimate conviction that Jesus is the Christ, and the Son of God; they know that he abides in them and they in him" (de la Potterie, 1977, 587). In one way or another, the teaching of the Johannine letters is consistent concerning this role of the Spirit which brings us into that truth "which abides in us and will be with us forever" (2 John 2).

B. 1 John 3:19–24. These verses occur at the end of a consideration of love (3:11–24). Verse 19 of chapter 3 has in common with 2:5 and 4:6 the fact that the criterion to which it refers is found in what immediately precedes it: "Little children, let us not love with word and tongue, but in deed and truth. *In this* we will know that we are of the truth. . . . " Such a statement points to a fundamental Johannine principle, namely, that exterior actions manifest their source and in this manner can establish the truth or falsity of the claim to "know God."

After adducing obedience to the commandments as the reason for having confidence in regard to God (obedience itself being an exterior manifestation of a deeper source of action), the author goes on to specify that the commandment is twofold: believing in the name of his Son Jesus Christ (the first explicit mention of faith in the letter), and loving one another as he (probably the Father through Jesus) gave us command (3:23). Then, for the first time in 1 John, we encounter the word *pneuma*: "The one keeping his commandments abides in him, and he in that person; and in this we know that he abides in us, from the Spirit he has given us" (3:24). This statement combines the promise of the other Paraclete, the indwelling Spirit of truth in John 14:15, with the promise of the manifestation of Jesus and the indwelling of the Father and the Son in John 14:21–23. All three of these texts mention the keeping of the word/commandments of Christ. What is new here is the fact that the presence of the indwelling Spirit is adduced along with the keeping of the commandments as a criterion by which one may be certain of the mutual indwelling between the Father and the believer. Keeping the commandments is related to the evidence provided by the Spirit as fruit relates to the tree. "It is doubtless more nearly correct to say that 'keeping the commandments' (like 'fellowship with one another,' 1:7) is not the condition but rather the characteristic of the knowledge of God" (Bultmann, 1973, 25); that is, just as the Spirit reveals himself by providing "intimate conviction" concerning the true reality of Jesus Christ, he also manifests himself as the source of life by which we keep the commandments.

C. 1 John 4:1–6. The mention of the Spirit in 1 John 3:24 serves as a "hinge," concluding one section and opening another in which the word S/spirit occurs seven times. The present section is a consideration of faith, and it corresponds to the preceding consideration of love. Since all discernment is a determination of the source of an action (see DISCERNMENT OF SPIRITS, GIFT OF), the author points to two different sources that give rise to two different actions. The confession of the false prophets derives from the spirit of the antichrist and is discernible because it does not confess Jesus as the Christ come in the flesh. The criterion for discerning the Spirit of God is clear: "In this we know the Spirit of God: every spirit [spiritual source of action] which confesses Jesus [to be] the Christ come in the flesh is of God" (4:2). The elder goes on, asserting prophetic authority for himself, to render this principle more precisely: "We are of God [and not of the world]. The one who knows God listens to us [those who preach the truth, see John 18:37]; he who is not of God does not listen to us: in this we know the Spirit of truth and the spirit of error" (4:6).

Once again, it is clear that an exterior action reveals its interior source: "That is to say, the possession of the Spirit of God—the Spirit that confesses Jesus as the Christ (4:2)—is the objective and infallible sign that God is abiding in us" (Law, 1914, 263). John is here developing the teaching in the Fourth Gospel (John 15:26) which, in turn, is a development of the Synoptic teaching (Mark 13:11/Matt. 10:20/Luke 12:12) concerning the witness of the Spirit and the

disciples to the transcendent and glorious position of Jesus Christ.

D. 1 John 4:7–16. In keeping with the alternating style of the letter and as a further confirmation of the twofold commandment in 1 John 3:23, the consideration of faith in 4:1–6 is followed by a discussion of love (1 John 4:7–21) in which, however, the notion of confessing faith is still present.

In the small section constituted by 1 John 4:11–16, there is a repetition of the themes of 4:7–10, but under a different aspect. Both begin by an address to the "Beloved" and an exhortation to love, speaking of God's love as the foundation of our own (4:7–8; 11–12). In 4:9–10, the love of God is described "objectively": "In this the love of God is made manifest in us: God sent his only begotten Son into the world that we might live by him. . . . [He] loved us and sent his Son, the propitiation for our sins." In 4:14–16, this same reality is proclaimed from the viewpoint of its recipients: "we have seen and bear witness that the Father sent the Son, the Savior of the world . . . and we have come to know and have believed the love which God has in us."

After the further introduction in 4:11–12, we find as a link joining the "objective" and "subjective" dimensions of the revelation of God's love the phrase: "In this we know that we abide in him and he in us: he has given us of his Spirit." This line is found between two statements concerned with divine indwelling. In 4:12, we read ". . . if we love one another God abides in us and his love is made perfect in us." Then in 4:15 the author states, "Whoever confesses that Jesus is the Son of God, God abides in him and he in God." The conclusion is clear: the action of the Spirit interiorizes the historical events by which humankind was saved so that they become the inner source of confessing belief in Jesus, the Son of God, and of that mutual love that is the infallible sign of true disciples (John 13:35). The Spirit reveals his presence through that act of faith and love by which the believer is able to be present to God who abides with him. As Augustine put it, "Love your neighbor, and look within yourself to the source of that love: there you will see, as you are able, God" (*On the Gospel of John*, 17:8; CCL 36, 174).

E. 1 John 5:6–8. These difficult verses are found at the center of the last dogmatic section of the Letter (1 John 5:1–12), which is dedicated to a final consideration of faith. This time, the author places the accent on the interior attitude of faith rather than on its external confession: the verb *pisteuein* (to believe) occurs five times in this passage along with the only occurrence of the noun "faith" in either the Gospel or the Letters, while the verb *homologein* (to confess) does not occur at all.

The faith of which John speaks "overcomes the world" (5:4). In the following verse, it is stated once again that the one who believes that Jesus is the Son of God overcomes that world which the author already described as the native environment of those who do not believe and who are moved by the spirit of the antichrist (1 John 4:3–5).

Once again, the author insists on the total human dimension of God's act of redemption in Jesus: "This is he who has come through water and blood: Jesus Christ. Not in water only but in water and blood; and the Spirit is the one who bears witness, because the Spirit is the truth. For there are three who bear witness, the Spirit, the water and the blood; and these three are of one accord" (1 John 5:6–8).

In this passage, the roles of Jesus and the Spirit are defined respectively as "he who has come" (*ho elthōn*) and "he who bears witness" (*ho martyroun*). The reference to Jesus as "having come" utilizes common NT parlance when speaking of his being sent by the Father and accomplishing the work of redemption (Schneider, 1964, 668–75). In saying that he came in/through (*dia*) both water and blood, the author is most probably denying an opinion that minimized the saving power of Jesus' death (Smalley, 1984, 278–80). It may have been similar to a view attributed to Cerinthus and others, according to which the Logos or the Christ entered Jesus at his baptism, thus enabling him to be a revealer of divine truth, but left him at his Passion. The elder insists that the "coming" of Jesus, by which the work of the devil was destroyed (1 John 3:8), included the whole of his earthly life, summed up in the moment of his commitment to be the servant of God at his baptism, and was completed by the pouring out of his life-blood on the cross. The Spirit bears witness to these realities *now* because the Spirit "is the truth," that is, he confers knowledge of the truth concerning the Father revealed by Jesus through his life, death, and resurrection: "For this was I born, for this I came into the world: to bear witness to the truth" (John 18:37).

The text goes on to speak of the three witnesses—the Spirit, the water, and the blood—and describes their testimony as convergent (*eis to en*). The action of the Spirit is of a different order than the other two. The "water" refers to the baptism of Jesus and all that it implies: his whole life, his teaching and miracles. The "blood" is his sacrificial death (*hilasmos* in 2:2; 4:10), which still purifies us from sin (1:7). These events, which transpired within the limits of human history, have an interior dimension which relates to and reveals God. The witness of the Spirit is that action by which the faith of the believer assimilates these events in their interiority so that they become an actual source of revelation and, therefore, life for him/her personally.

John has taken the teaching of the Fourth Gospel on the blood and water that flowed from the pierced side of Christ, and to which the beholder bears solemn witness, and explains it by modifying it. The water is not only the Spirit as in John 19:34 (see John 7:37–39, etc.); it is also the whole life of Jesus upon whom the Spirit came to rest at his baptism (John 1:33). The blood is the outpoured life by which the sin of the world was borne away (John 1:29). In our present text, the role of the Spirit who brings to faith is mentioned first and, explicitly, no longer under the symbol of water. He is the one who bears witness, now in the heart of the church and of each believer, so

that we may gaze on the One who was pierced (John 19:37) and receive life from him who was raised aloft for this very purpose (John 3:14–15; 8:28; 12:32). It is by this action of the Spirit that we "put our faith in the name of the Son of God" (5:13).

Conclusion. This brief consideration of the principal passages in the Johannine correspondence allows us to conclude by describing the pneumatology contained there.

The Spirit dwells within us, bearing witness to the reality and majesty of Jesus, the Christ of God and the Son of God. His witness consists in producing in us that faith by which we accept God's witness and confess boldly and publicly who Jesus really is. This faith, in turn, is the source of loving "in truth" by obeying the commands of God (5:2) and by laying down our lives for fellow believers (3:16). These actions both cause and manifest the reciprocal indwelling between the Trinity and ourselves. Only the Spirit can manifest this reality to the human conscience.

Bibliography: M. E. Boismard, "La Connaissance dans l'Alliance nouvelle d'après la Première Lettre de saint Jean," *Revue Biblique* 56 (1949): 364–91; R. E. Brown, *The Epistles of John*, AB, (1982), 30; R. Bultmann, *The Johannine Epistles*, Hermeneia (1983); G. Burge, *The Anointed Community: The Holy Spirit in the Johannine Tradition* (1987). D. A. Carson, "The Purpose of the Fourth Gospel: John 20:31 Reconsidered," *JBL* 106 (1987): 639–51; I. de la Potterie, "Anointing of the Christian by Faith," in *The Christian Lives by the Spirit* (1971); idem, *La Vérité dans Saint Jean*, Analecta Biblica, 73/74 (1977); R. Law, *The Tests of Life* (1914, reprint 1968); E. Malatesta, *Interiority and Covenant*, Analecta Biblica, 69 (1978); I. H. Marshall, *The Epistles of John*, NICNT (1978); F. Martin, "The Humanity of Christian Mysticism," *Cross Currents* 24 (1974): 233–47; J. Schneider, "*Erchomai* (etc.)" *TDNT* (1964), 2:666–84; S. S. Smalley, *1,2,3 John*, WBC (1984). R. F. Martin

JOHN 17:21 FELLOWSHIP See CHARISMATIC MOVEMENT.

JOHN, GOSPEL OF

I. Introduction
  A. Theories About the Background
    1. A Literary-Fragmentary Theory
    2. A Sociological Theory
    3. The Historical Theory
  B. The Spirit in John
    1. A Review of Theories on the Spirit
    2. Observations on the Term *Spirit* in John
  C. Signs
  D. Presuppositions: Themes in John
II. Interpreting the Gospel of John
  A. The Proem (1:1–18)
  B. The Manifestation of Jesus to the World (1:19–12:50)
    1. Introduction (1:19–51)
    2. Two Signs (2:1–4:54)
    3. The Healing at the Pool (ch. 5)
    4. The Bread of Life (ch. 6)
    5. The Feast of Booths to Hanukkah (chs. 7–10)
    6. The Raising of Lazarus and the Anointing of Jesus (chs. 11–12)

C. The Manifestation of Jesus to the
Disciples (chs. 13–21)
1. Discourses for the Disciples
(chs. 13–17)
2. The Crucifixion and Resurrection
(chs. 18–21)
III. Conclusion

I. Introduction.   The Gospel of John is
frequently called the Fourth Gospel, not merely
because it is fourth in the canonical order but
because it is different in a number of aspects from
Matthew, Mark, and Luke—which are called the
Synoptic Gospels. John provides a different chronology of events, the most famous inconsistency
being the early cleansing of the temple (in ch. 2).
In the other Gospels the cleansing comes in the
Passion narrative. John has no parables as in the
Synoptics, either—the word "parable" is not even
found there. The style and vocabulary, too, are
dissimilar. In fact, it is difficult to discern the
differences between Jesus' speech and John's
narration. And John's Gospel has long discourses
that differ from the Synoptic narratives.

Differences such as these have brought into
question the historicity of this Gospel. Two
conclusions can be noted here: (1) Scholars now
think that the writer of this Gospel used oral
tradition that is common to both the Synoptics
and the Fourth Gospel. This explains both the
similarities and the differences. (2) The Fourth
Gospel is the most theological. The life and
teaching of Jesus are so much a part of John that
it comes through in John's experience. Jesus is
truly internalized in John's person so as to make
an impact on his world view. But history and
theology have been understood differently. Some,
like Martyn, have seen a convergence of the
historical Jesus on the one hand (i.e., Jesus'
teaching) and disputes with the synagogue in
John's day on the other. By reading between the
lines of Jesus' dialogue with the Jews in the
Gospel, one can discern the disputes with John
and his opponents at a later time.

A. Theories About the Background.
1. A Literary-Fragmentary Theory. In regard to
the historicity of the Fourth Gospel, there are
several schools of thought. One school, which
follows in the path of the great German scholar
Rudolf Bultmann, thinks that the Gospel went
through several stages of compilation by different
redactors, each using diverse sources, none of
which comes from the apostle John and perhaps
one being Palestinian or at least Jewish. One of
the main sources according to this school of
thought is a so-called signs source, which forms a
basic document of the first twelve chapters or so.
This school is well known for its fragment
approach, seeing aporia (literary seams) everywhere. It also believes the final stages of redaction
to be quite late. Discoveries of manuscript fragments of the Gospel, however, have forced
scholars to find an earlier time for its writing.
2. A Sociological Theory. Another theory can be
classified as sociological because it considers the
Gospel to have been produced by a "community
of the beloved disciple/Johannine school." Among
others, two prominent scholars adhere to this
view: R. E. Brown, an American, and Stephen

Smalley, from Britain. Brown's view is the most
complex in that he opts for five stages of redaction. Smalley commits himself to only three
stages. Both, however, believe that later disciples
reshaped a basic Johannine apostolic tradition,
Palestinian in origin. This school opts for a late-
first-century date at the earliest for the last
redaction.

Studies on sociological factors other than on
"community" have been forthcoming. One of
these factors is in regard to an issue Bultmann
raised. He noted that one of the sources for the
Gospel was Jewish. Some, such as C. H. Dodd,
R. E. Brown, C. K. Barrett, and R. Schnackenburg, consider John's Gospel to be more Jewish
than just this one source Bultmann mentioned.
Brown, for instance, contends that there were
several Jewish groups: John the Baptist and some
Jewish people that followed Jesus for a while. But
Brown and others hold that John's Gospel is no
longer concerned with Jewish issues. The writer/
redactor is now facing questions from the larger
Hellenistic world.

In light of the predominance of the fragmentary theory among scholars several decades ago,
when R. E. Brown began work on his commentary on John, he was considered to be quite
conservative because he regarded the Gospel
tradition to come from the apostle and to be
transmitted through his disciples.

3. The Historical Theory. A third, conservative
theory considers that John the apostle actually
wrote the Gospel and used the facts of Jesus' life
as they were. This school generally thinks that the
Gospel was written earlier than most others
believe it was written, usually sometime in the
mid-eighties.

B. The Spirit in John. The approach in this
article will be to analyze the book section-by-
section. But attention will be devoted to Pentecostal-charismatic issues as they surface within
this analysis. Yet here it will be helpful to discuss
in an introductory way one of these issues—that
of the term *Spirit.*

1. A Review of Theories on the Spirit. The Spirit
in John's Gospel was the topic of *Studorum Novi
Testamenti Societas,* a seminar in Holland that was
reported in "L'esprit saint dans l'evangile de
Jean," *NTS* 18 (1972): 448–51. First, I will offer
a brief overview of the main theories; next I will
examine current theories about the Spirit in John.

The congress addressed three themes of the
Spirit in John. The first theme focused on "the
word and the Spirit." Three of the four points of
this theme come from 3:34; 6:63; and 9:10 and
elaborate on the connection between Jesus' word,
the Spirit, and life. The fourth deals with the title
"the Spirit of truth" and notes that this identifies
the function of the Spirit, which is to communicate to the believer the truth of Jesus.

The second theme concentrated on the difficult
title *Paraclete.* First, H. Riesenfeld presented
different views regarding the status of research.
He cited R. E. Brown, an influential scholar
regarding the research of this title (1970, 1136–
37), who notes that (1) the term has a passive
sense according to the etymology of *parakalein;*
(2) the same verb had an active sense, which

included the idea of intercessor; (3) according to another meaning of *parakalein*, it meant consoler; and (4), more in line with the form *paraklēsis*, it meant exhortation.

Riesenfeld then gave the various theories regarding the background for the title: pre-Mandean Gnosticism (Bauer, Windsch) and Judaism (Mowinckel, Johannson, O. Betz), based on a number of intermediaries such as Moses and Elijah. Riesenfeld then argued for a background in the wisdom tradition. He noted that the LXX a number of times (Prov. 8:4–11; Eccl. 4:11; Ecclus. 17:15ff.; Wisd. of Sol. 1:1–10) applied the verb *parakalein* to the sages and that the function in these places is very similar to that which is attributed to the Paraclete in John 14–16.

Later, discussion expanded to include other possible contacts between the wisdom tradition and Paraclete in John. And finally, C. H. Giblin criticized recent interpretations that associate the Johannine Paraclete with Jewish angelology.

The third theme focused on the connection between the mission of Jesus and that of the Spirit in John 20:22–23. One point examined the context of John 20 and noted the significance of the Spirit's communication to the disciples in 20:17 after Jesus' resurrection and before he returned to the Father and the significance of the day (20:19) on which Jesus spoke to them. This first day of the week was also the first of the fifty days of Pentecost. This was the so-called Johannine Pentecost.

The problem of sources for the John 20 passage was also discussed, mainly in light of G. Hartman (*ZNW* 55 [1964]: 197–220), who thought that 20:21–22 came from John's *Vorlage* (source). A. Jaubert examined the relationship between John 20 and Luke 24, noting a number of similarities: peace, joy, the work of the Spirit and the understanding of Scripture, repentance and the remission of sins, mission, and the presence of the Spirit. On the other hand, a number of differences were noted, such as Jesus' breathing on the disciples; Jesus' presentation of his hands and his side, which provoked their joy; and the motive of their mission.

Discussion added information to this theme. Riesenfeld brought out the similarity between John 20 and Revelation 5 in reference to the crucified Lamb. In addition, de la Potterie said that the pneumatology in John 20 added significantly to the Johannine theology of the Spirit in that, by drawing attention to Calvary and the day of Passover and to Jesus' breathing the Spirit upon the disciples, it provided continuity between Jesus and the Spirit.

Scholars from the Evangelical and Pentecostal traditions interpret Spirit texts in John in light of their respective theological concerns. Evangelicals, in contrast to Pentecostals, generally do not believe in an experience subsequent to regeneration called "Spirit baptism."

Interpretation of references to the Spirit in John 3 and 4 follow these two lines. One is a clear reference to being "born again" (regeneration). This is particularly the meaning of 3:5. Thus G. M. Burge, a charismatic, believes that this text emphasizes the Spirit's activity in giving the believer life from above, though, in a somewhat sacramental way, baptism is referred to and is important in this experience (1987, 159–69).

According to the Pentecostal interpretation, being "born from above" is not an end in itself. It is only the first step toward living in the Spirit (Horton, 1976, 115). Burge also suggests this for the significance of the Spirit in 3:34. There it is Jesus who is anointed with the Spirit without measure (1987, 81–84). This is commensurate with his interpretation of Jesus' baptism in 1:29–34; John's account is about Jesus' anointing by the Spirit (50–62).

The reference to the Spirit in 4:23–24 (e.g., "God is Spirit") usually is interpreted to mean a special worship condition the Christian is to be in (cf. Horton, 1976, 117). Pentecostals, on the one hand, believe that this condition is assisted by having the Spirit baptism. Burge, on the other hand, notes that the medium between heaven and earth is the Spirit. To possess the Spirit one must be born from above through Jesus. This brings about a new worship situation (1987, 190–97).

Another text, John 7:37–39 (the Spirit flows like a river from the side of Jesus), implies both Spirit baptism and regeneration, according to S. M. Horton (1976, 130–31). L. Morris (1971, 427) relates this text to both the Cross and the work of the Spirit, a position similar to Horton's (but see Morris, 1986, 268). Whose side it is, is not immediately clear in the text of Scripture.

Pentecostals argue for a distinction between regeneration and empowerment on the basis of John 14–16, which includes, among other material, the promise of the coming of the Paraclete. Particularly, they note a difference between the clauses *par' humin menei* ("he will abide with you") and *en humin estin* ("he is in you") in 14:17. "He [the Spirit] will be with you" substantiates Spirit baptism, while "he is in you" speaks about regeneration.

John 20:19–23 is much discussed by scholars from these two traditions. Some consider this passage to refer to a symbolic gesture by Jesus. Others, like Morris (1971, 846) and J. D. G. Dunn (1979, 177), believe that it refers to another giving of the Spirit (as in Acts 2) for empowerment and life. M. C. Tenney believes that it was "the initial announcement of which Pentecost was the historic fulfillment" (1981, 193). Some Pentecostals take this breathing to refer to a real experience of regeneration and believe that Acts 2 refers to an empowerment only (Horton, 1976, 128–29; Aker, 1983, 13–16; Ervin, 1987, 31).

2. *Observations on the Term* Spirit *in John.* The term *Spirit* occurs rather frequently in John but in different ways, especially in comparison to Luke–Acts. Luke's favorite term is "Holy Spirit," while John's is simply "Spirit." John often speaks of the Spirit in apologetic circumstances. According to John, the true people of God are marked by the presence of the Spirit. Thus the Spirit comes on Jesus first (1:29–34); Jesus is the temple of God, the true dwelling place of the Spirit, in the same way that the people of God are. It is the Spirit's presence on Jesus, and consequently among his

believers, that characterizes the eschatological community—a community that is struggling with disciples of John the Baptist and resurging Judaism.

Furthermore, in John's Gospel (and his Epistles) the Spirit is the means of rebirth, of imparting eternal life, of making spiritual people. In this respect, rebirth is the way one is able to receive revelation from God. Each one thus born of the Spirit is a prophet who believes and follows Jesus. This view of "prophet" is also articulated in 1 John and Revelation. In Revelation the Spirit bears witness through the true prophet to Jesus. In contrast, seducing spirits (false prophets) lead the whole world astray—they especially entice those who follow Jesus.

"Paraclete" in John 14–16 is a special name used in reference to the Spirit. John seems to use this term for the Spirit specially to connote the Spirit's activity in reassuring the believer that he or she is a member of God's community. This is necessary because opponents are placing pressure on the community—believers are wavering in commitment to Jesus, God's Son, the head of this community. The Paraclete's function is to provide the same kind of assurance that Jesus provided while he was on earth.

C. Signs. Another issue in John relevant for Pentecostals and charismatics is the use of signs. A brief word about them is in order. In John, faith is a prerequisite for a proper understanding of signs. Signs can be negative. If people do not follow Jesus for the right reasons, signs lead away from rather than to "belief."

Signs in John function mediatorially. That is, they point beyond themselves to something else, a deeper level of faith. They point to Jesus and the Father, never to themselves. Signs do not primarily authenticate one's person or ministry—they reveal God at work in Jesus.

D. Presuppositions: Themes in John. The frequent references to Jewish feasts and holy sites, in addition to the dialogues of controversy (Streitgesprache) between Jesus and the Jews, are important features in the Gospel of John. One of the better explanations for the presence of these features is that they reveal a resurgence of Judaism in the late first century in the Ephesus area.

It is especially in the controversial dialogues, beginning in chapter 2 and concluding in chapter 12, that disagreement in four theological areas occurs: pneumatology, christology, soteriology, and ecclesiology. What is taught in these first chapters, however, is consummated in the Passion narrative of the Gospel. In fact, all four of these issues are related and bear on the theology of the Spirit in Johannine material. The Sitze im Leben (settings in life) for the Epistles and Revelation, however, differ. Still, especially in Revelation, Jewish themes and material appear—many of them linked to the Fourth Gospel.

It is also important to note that a John the Baptist sect was probably influencing the Johannine church as well. Support from this comes from the large amount of material about John the Baptist. At several points John is contrasted with Jesus, who is always the superior one. Also in this regard, in John's Gospel John the Baptist does not baptize Jesus with water; rather, he only witnesses that the Spirit came upon Jesus and that Jesus is the Lamb of God. In this respect Matthew and Mark record that Jesus was baptized with water. But John comes close to Luke in that both present this event as Jesus' anointing.

II. Interpreting the Gospel of John.

A. The Proem (1:1–18). Revelation is the main concern in the proem, and it is given a christological orientation. In verse 4 the statement "that life was the light of men" signifies this orientation. This is determined by noting the relationship between "of men" and "light." "Of men" is an objective genitive expressing the object of light. The life (Jesus) was in the world to bring revelation to "men" from God. The last verse (18) of the proem supports this interpretation. There it is said that no one has ever seen God, but the Son, who is in God's bosom, has explained (exēgēsato) him. But the proem also notes that humankind was incapable of receiving this light (v. 5) without some sort of transformation. The purpose, then, of Jesus' coming (i.e., the Incarnation, v. 14) was to redeem humanity from its sin and to give birth from above by the Spirit (vv. 12–13). This new birth was the means by which people could now receive this revelation of the Father. So, revelation here has a distinctly christological focus—Jesus is content, form, and means by which the objects are enabled to receive him).

The function of this proem is to summarize the contents of the Gospel. Consequently, the proem was added later, after the document was completed. It is no surprise, then, to find that the entire book "breathes" with these proem themes.

B. The Manifestation of Jesus to the World (1:19–12:50).

1. Introduction (1:19–51). In 1:19–51, which could well be called the "Introduction," significant themes of the Gospel are presented: (1) Jesus' opponents, portrayed by the leaders of Judaism; (2) John the Baptist; (3) John's disciples; (4) the presentation of the ideal Israelite; (5) the true meaning of Jesus' function as Messiah; and (6) the Spirit as the way to recognize the people of God. These themes are summarized in the thee major issues of christology, soteriology, and ecclesiology.

The major opponents of John's church are the leaders of Judaism, and they are often presented as Pharisees (it is important to note that Sadducees are not mentioned in John). In this section their representatives asked John the Baptist about his ministry, and he replied that he was not the Messiah, an answer to a major question that the Baptist sect and some in his church were asking.

This question regarding the Messiah is important, for Judaism and Christianity disagreed over it, and the Fourth Gospel underscores this. These leaders considered their messiah in typical Judaistic terms, certainly terms that would exclude a deified Messiah with a new and different way of salvation.

Nathanael's confession (v. 49), then, is significant. It culminates the introduction in which Jesus is presented as the Lamb of God. This eschatological Lamb, which will take the place of the Jewish Passover lamb, transcends the Jewish

Passover as the way of salvation (the Jewish Passover did not initiate salvation; it maintained salvation. To understand Jesus as the new Passover Lamb, then, is quite distinct, for it emphasizes here the point of entry, although this is not to say that the Eucharist, the Christian Passover in John, does not maintain salvation in some sense). John announced this Lamb twice: verses 29 and 36. The first time he announced that the Lamb would take away the sin of the world. "Sin," which is singular and has the definite article, denotes a particular sin, the sin that separated God and humankind. This can be understood as objective sin. It is not discussed in plain terms, but it is evident that the sin of the first man is in view here and that it has passed on to all people (cf. 1:9ff.; 8:39–47; the "amen, amen" saying in 8:34 is like a creed on sinful nature). All people, then, need a new beginning, and this is what this Gospel emphasizes.

It has been noted that the new creation motif is prevalent in John, especially in the phrases "on the next day" (vv. 29, 35, and 43) and "on the third day" (2:1). These approximate the six creation days of Genesis. Also, John intentionally began his Gospel in a style similar to that of Genesis: "in the beginning." Jesus is thus the Son of God, Israel's King (i.e., Messiah) who must die as the Lamb of God and create a new people of God.

The term *Israel* in John is reserved for the "true" people of God—those who, like Nathanael, look for and believe in Jesus as the Messiah who had to die and provide a new way to God. In a similar manner, John's disciples, Peter and Andrew, followed Jesus. They, too, acted like true Israelites.

But the portrayal of John the Baptist suggests that his followers were also part of the problem to or in John's church. In the Fourth Gospel references to John the Baptist occur numerous times in such ways as to place him in an inferior position to Jesus and to have him—along with Abraham, signs, the Father, the Scripture and the Spirit—assume a witnessing role. This portrayal is similar to that in Luke–Acts. There, too, John is simply John (not the Baptist). John's main function was to witness, not to baptize Jesus. In both Gospels, the emphasis is on the Spirit's anointing of Jesus. (This suggests a similar provenance for Luke–Acts and John.)

The Spirit plays an important role in the anointing scene as well. Because of the presence of the Spirit, John knew that Jesus was the Lamb of God, the one who would baptize with the Spirit. In parallel statements in verses 31–33, John says that he would not have recognized Jesus as God's Son except by the Spirit's coming and remaining on him. The presence of the Spirit, then, signifies who the true Son of God is, the one who possesses the Spirit. The Spirit here has a larger role than in Luke–Acts where he empowers people to prophesy and perform miracles. The Spirit in John ushers one into the kingdom of God by giving eternal life. This is what "baptism" in 1:33b means. Jesus is the one who gives the Spirit, as in 20:22. "Remaining" in 1:32–33 is important in Johannine literature. "Remain" (Gk. *menō*) is a Johannine word for sanctification and

perseverance, which are tests for the true believer, i.e., one who has the Spirit.

2. Two Signs (2:1–4:54). There is good reason to consider these verses to belong to the same section, even though A. Feuillet gives cogent reasoning not to do so (1965, 39–51). John enumerates these two signs but not the others: "first" (2:11, *archēn*) and "second" (4:54, *deuteron*). Furthermore, the only times he mentions Cana is with these two signs (2:1 and 4:46) The same themes run through these verses: (1) new creation, (2) eternal life, (3) being born from above, (4) opposition, and (5) revelation. These two signs can function like brackets and hold this material together.

The first sign is significant in that it sets forth from the start what Jesus is to do. Admittedly, this first sign of the changing of the water into wine fits in a different manner with the wedding at Cana. However, it can be explained in the following way:

First, we note that these two accounts in John 1 are held together by brackets, which are clues for the reader. In verses 12 and 19 the ordinal ("third") and numeral ("three") are used. It is on the third day that the wedding occurred and on the third day when Jesus (the new temple) was to be raised. Second, the new wine in the wedding signifies that Judaism was bankrupt (i.e., empty water pots; the water usually stored in them was used for ablutions, v. 6) and that Jesus' new creation, the church, would supersede Judaism (the new wine tastes great!).

What adds further significance to this view is the cleansing of the temple. John placed this account in a different order from its place in the Synoptics, but this placement is what gives us clues to the importance of this first sign. It tells us about the new people of God, presenting a view that is similar to that of the church in Ephesians. Jesus in John 2 spoke about his body as the temple of God. Note the play on words: Jesus' literal body is equated with the spiritual body of the church. His resurrection will raise others to be part of his body.

But the church is identified in soteriological terms. First, this *cleansing* occurs during the "passover of the Jews" (v. 13). Second, the OT quote (*darash*) in verse 17 signifies a substitutionary sacrifice. Finally, "destroy" in verse 19 refers to his death on the cross, while verse 22 mentions Jesus' resurrection.

Thus these two accounts state that what Jesus was to bring by his death and resurrection transcends what Judaism offers. He was to create his church and to raise his body after three days. People can experience this new creation by believing the Scriptures and his word (v. 22). The Scriptures (OT) and Jesus' word, placed on an equal par here, refer specifically to the Psalm 69:9 quote in verse 19 and to the words of Jesus in the paragraph. "The disciples' remembering" in verses 17 and 22 emphasizes this connection. Furthermore, the OT and Jesus' word serve as the basis of faith and discipleship. In contrast, the belief of the many in Jerusalem, which follows in 2:23–25, was based on signs for something rather than on Jesus' word or the Scripture, which leads to discipleship. Jesus consequently did not commit himself to them.

Chapters 3 and 4 contain dialogues with two individuals: Nicodemus (a "leader," v. 1), probably a rabbi, and a Samaritan woman. Nicodemus was the man who came to Jesus at night. It was typical for rabbis to work during the day and study Torah (law) in the evening. Rabbis were lay ministers. Chapter 3 contains irony. Nicodemus was not bright in regard to spiritual matters. He was a teacher of Israel (v. 10) and did not know about spiritual birth? Indeed, this is what the irony demonstrates: he was not born by the Spirit, so he could not know spiritual things.

The point of the Nicodemus dialogue is regeneration. This dialogue functions as a narrative to interpret the sign in chapter 2. What Judaism (here Nicodemus) could not do (i.e., through water ablutions take away sin and make people part of God's community), Jesus does (i.e., takes away sin and gives the Spirit to create people anew). This rebirth gives ability to understand spiritual things—thus regeneration is prophetic and revelatory.

Nicodemus is "bigger than life" here. He stands for Judaism or at least for unbelieving people who question Jesus about salvation. Note that a shift in number occurs at verse 11. The number is singular up until then. Then in the "amen, amen" saying the "I" becomes "we" and singular "you" becomes plural (in Greek). "We know what we speak and what we have seen we bear witness to, and our witness you [plural] do not receive." Likewise in verse 12: "I speak to you [plural] and you [plural] do not believe." This is evidence of a dialogue between John's church and those outside.

And then there is the matter about the "amen, amen" sayings in verses 3 and 5. By noting the structure, we can make some observations:

Verse 3

A Jesus answered and said to him,
  B Amen, amen, I tell you,
    C Except one is born from above,
      D he is not able to see the
        kingdom of God.

Verse 5

A′ Jesus answered,
  B′ Amen, amen, I tell you,
    C′ Except one be born of water and
      spirit,
      D′ he is not able to go into the
        kingdom of God.

Several comments are in order. The "amen, amen" saying became formulated into a creedlike theological statement of the church concerning the necessity of being born again. This statement arose out of a controversy with Judaism over the identity of the true people of God.

Further, this amen, amen saying in the sign narrative comments on the sign in chapter 2. And this is how we are to understand the second such saying in verse 5. There, the oft-discussed "by water and spirit" is to be taken as a hendiadys and translated "by spiritual water" as opposed to the

water in baptism, i.e., Jewish baptism in the water pots in chapter 2. In other words, one enters the kingdom (v. 5), sees the kingdom (v. 3) by being born of the Spirit, and this is what "spiritual water" means. John's meaning of being in the kingdom has to do with being regenerated by the Spirit. And while he does not deny other NT views of the kingdom, e.g., Luke's emphasis on and meaning of the kingdom, because of his situation he emphasizes the kingdom in terms of regeneration—something that comes from above by the Spirit. This interpretation does away with a sacramental view of this passage. Consistently in John, the symbol for the Spirit is water. And a similar use of the symbol exists in Judaism. John's emphasis on being born from above extends into 1 John as well.

This interpretation of "spiritual water" is supported by the parallel saying in verse 3. The parallel member is "born from above," which refers to the Spirit. And this rendering has further support. If verse 5 refers to regeneration of the Spirit, then we can note a similar reference to the activity of the Spirit at the end of the chapter. The "Spirit" then acts as a bracket to all of the chapter. Note further, however, in verse 34, that "he gives the Spirit not by measure." "Measure" (*metrou*) here is unique in the NT, and scholars have had a difficult time trying to interpret it satisfactorily. With this interpretation of Spirit in 3:5, however, and the connection of the Spirit and "without measure" in 3:34, we can compare chapter 3 with chapter 2 and discover what "measure" means and how it is used in 3:34. If the Christian experience of regeneration by the Spirit (ch. 3) is contrasted with Jewish ablution (ch. 2), and the water pots are mentioned with specific measurements (2:6; note there the same root *metr* for "measure"), then we know that "without measure" refers to regeneration by the Spirit. In contrast to the water pots that hold a finite amount, the Spirit who has no limits gives birth—and he comes from above.

The paragraph of 3:16–21 explains why sinners do not follow Jesus. They are already under judgment for their sins, for they reject God's Son. They do not want their evil deeds exposed by coming to the light. This paragraph further explains the spiritual ignorance of "Israel," depicted by Nicodemus. This paragraph is connected with the former, 3:1–15, by one of Rabbi Hillel's interpretive rules. The rule says that whatever can be said of one, a similar thing can be said of another. Thus, as Moses lifted up the serpent in the wilderness (and people lived), so Jesus must be exalted in order for people to live (i.e., have eternal life). The "so" in verse 16 does not speak of the extent (greatness) of God's love; it speaks rather of the *manner* of God's love. God loved people infinitely more by giving his Son to be lifted up on the cross.

The paragraph on John the Baptist (vv. 22–30) further underscores the superiority of Jesus, not only over Judaism but also over "Christian" sectarianism such as this John the Baptist sect. Here John says that he must decrease but that Jesus must increase.

Chapter 4 presents a dialogue with another

individual, a Samaritan woman. The point in this chapter is also regeneration. This material has caused a few scholars to believe that the destination of John was somewhere in Samaria. This view is rejected by most, however. The point remains, though, that we must give some sort of explanation for the inclusion of the material. The theme of chapter 3 is eternal life, and here water is mentioned again—this time from Jacob's well.

In John 4 an important Jewish tradition, though Samaritans are associated with it, is contravened. This Jewish tradition is related to a holy site, Jacob's well, located south of the ancient city of Samaria. In part, what John wants to do is to show that Jesus brings the true water of life, as opposed to this well, and that Jesus brings a new worship situation. This new worship differs from both the religion of Judaism and the religion of the Samaritans and results from the eternal life that comes from Jesus: "Indeed, the water I give him will become in him a spring of water welling up to eternal life" (4:14). This is the meaning of 4:24: "God is spirit, and his worshipers must worship in spirit and in truth." The worshiper must partake of God's nature through the birth that is from above. This is the situation that allows one to communicate with, or worship, God. This new worship situation suggests a new temple as well, a theme noted already in chapter 2. The ubiquitous Spirit, the line of communication between the believer and heaven, renders geography unimportant for the believer. And Jacob, one of the patriarchs of Israel, is no longer to be considered the source of blessing for Israel. The patriarchs, two of whom are mentioned in John (Abraham and Jacob), in the Judaism of John's day were continual sources of the promises of God (i.e., salvation) to their sons. And John overturns the value of both of them for salvation purposes.

In contrast to the Jews, the Samaritans received Jesus well. Their contact with him was through a prostitute who came out to draw water at an unusual time of day. Like other Samaritans, she was expecting a messiah (*Taheb*). Jesus filled all of their expectations for this messiah—and they received him as such (this contrasts with the view that this woman attempted to divert Jesus with her questions so as to avoid making a decision to be saved, an interpretation used by people teaching lessons on personal evangelism from this text).

3. *The Healing at the Pool (ch 5).* The sign in this chapter, like the signs in chapters 2 and 4, emphasizes eternal life, but in new ways. The man at the pool (aside from the textual difficulties in this passage) receives wholeness from Jesus. This wholeness is interpreted to mean eternal life. This point comes out in the chiastic section in verses 19–30.

A (19) The Son does nothing on his own
B (20–23) The Father and the Son do
   the same works
  C (24–25) Amen, amen: the dead live
B' (26–29) The Father and the Son do
   the same works
A' (30) The Son does nothing on his own

Two "amen, amen" sayings serve as the focal point of the chiastic verse and give the point of the entire chapter: he who hears Jesus' word and believes on the Father who sent him will have eternal life, now given in terms of passing from death to life. Furthermore in lines B and B', the Father and Jesus have unoriginated life (aseity) in themselves.

This is the first place we read of intense opposition from the Jews, and it is in the context of the conflict between Christian and Jewish traditions. Jesus healed the lame man on the Sabbath, an act that in itself does not break the Sabbath. But Jesus' command to the man to carry his pallet is what aggravated the religiosity and provoked their charge of Sabbath violation. The Jews then brought another charge against Jesus—blasphemy—for Jesus made himself equal with God.

This chapter offers four witnesses, more than enough to meet the legal requirement: John the Baptist (vv. 31–35), Jesus' works (v. 36), the Father (v. 37), and Moses (vv. 45–46; the OT).

4. *The Bread of Life (ch. 6).* This long chapter contains three major accounts: the feeding of the five thousand, walking on the water, and Jesus' discourse on the Bread of Life. The first two are really signs/miracle stories, and the third interprets the first two.

Scholars have debated long about the nature of this chapter. Some deny that it is eucharistic in nature, while others see evidence of the Eucharist in it (and consequently consider it sacramental). P. Borgen (1965) says that 6:31–58, comprised of Haggadic words of manna and the gift of Torah at Sinai, were interwoven with Gospel fragments from the institution of the Eucharist. He believes that especially the manna argued against a docetic christology (cf. esp. pp. 2–3). That is, docetists believed that Christ was not fully human. To counteract that position, John emphasized the flesh of Jesus (cf. "eats my flesh," v. 53). Indeed, many of the synoptic words of institution occur in John 6. But we do not need to see Gnosticism here.

A solution can be explained in the following way. The position taken here is that it is eucharistic but not sacramental. I will elaborate on this point later, but it must be said here that John's Gospel does not have the synoptic material about Jesus' eating the Passover with his disciples in the Passion narrative. There are reasons for John's omission. For one thing, because of problems with Jewish pressure, he did not want to connect the Lord's Supper with the Jewish Passover, as the Synoptics had done. In the Synoptics, Jesus ate the Passover, but in John, Jesus was the Passover lamb; so he could not eat it. John simply avoided the word *Passover* and called it a dinner. But John connected the Passover with the Lord's Supper in a different sense. He linked it with the Passover in chapter 5 and with messianic expectations in Judaism, namely, the miracles of feeding the five thousand and the walking on water. Jesus is shown to be as Yahweh who feeds the people in the wilderness and who controls "natural" forces. Thus, we have the manna (in the Exodus) tradition, which is connected with the Bread of Life material.

This chapter continues the theme of Jesus' provision of eternal life—a theme that, in the dialogue between Jesus and the crowd in 6:31–33, is the heart of this account. Here Jesus says to them that the Father has given them the true Bread from heaven (Jesus in contrast to Moses), who will give life to the world. This is connected to the feeding of the five thousand in an "amen, amen" saying at 6:26. Later, in 6:34–40, this theme of the Bread of Life is expanded.

Opposition and Jewish rejection also occur with the theme of eternal life and demonstrate that regeneration and community identity were big factors in John's context. The Jews rejected the new way of salvation, Jesus. In turn, John argued that the new people of God had life from above, given by Jesus, received by faith, and created by the Spirit. This is how one knew that he was a member of the true community of God. This supports my thesis—the main emphasis given to the Spirit's role in regeneration.

5. *The Feast of Booths (Tabernacles) to Hanukkah (chs. 7–10)*. These chapters are considered together here because two feasts, one in the fall and the other in the winter, serve as the skeleton for John's message. The first was Succoth (Booths), an important celebration for both Judaism and Jewish Christianity during the first century or so. The second was Hanukkah (10:22). In Judaism, beginning with the new year, the fall festivals featured atonement for Israel's sins and anticipated the new year. Even Hanukkah, the winter feast, was considered part of this fall configuration. This is why it is not unusual for the themes of chapters 7–8 to run into chapters 9–10. Nevertheless, it must be said that 7–8 has literary features that make it distinctive: inclusions at the beginning and end (e.g., "in secret," 7:4; "went out secretly," 8:59) and the Feast of Succoth material itself.

But the literary and textual difficulties in chapters 7–8 are well known, the most famous of which is the pericope of the woman taken in adultery. By all accounts, this story, though it may well be authentic, does not belong within 7 and 8.

Jewish opposition reached new levels. The two themes that occurred earlier reappeared: Sabbath breaking and blasphemy. The opposition became more diversified in terms of the numerous groups mentioned, especially in 7 and 8. What makes it difficult to identify these groups with any certainty is that some of them became "believers" but in a short while wanted to kill Jesus (cf. esp. 8:30–47).

A question arises again about the identity of Jesus. The crowds did not know who he was. But in this context Jesus emerged in a new light: he was a Messiah different from any messianic conception the Jews had had. And he was greater than Abraham because he was before Abraham (a high christology; i.e., Jesus is deity). Abraham was important for salvation during this feast. In the liturgy Jews could call on him and receive mercy from God (through imputation). In contrast, John relegates Abraham to a lesser role, that of a witness, and places Jesus as the one who saves all who believe in him. In short, John presents Jesus as the eschatological Messiah who brings a new way of salvation and who creates a new people of God. Jesus is divine to John, but to the Jews he was a demon-possessed blasphemer.

The three "amen, amen" sayings in 8:34, 51, and 58 address these issues. The last speaks about the divinity of Jesus, the one in verse 51 about this new creation (i.e., "will never see death"), and verse 34 voices a creed about the sinfulness of humankind. The creed is important in this debate between Jesus and the Jews in regard to the identity of Jesus and the true people of God. For instance, because the Jews did the works of their father the devil, they were not free from sin, and they were not able to "see." They rejected Jesus' words. They were blind; i.e., they could not understand revelation, a vital theme in John and the key to understanding prophecy in this literature. Thus the healing of the blind man in chapter 9 comes into play. This man was born blind so that the works of God could be done. That is, mankind has original sin and is in need of the Spirit to create life (e.g., 9:39). This gives further evidence about John's emphasis on the Spirit and the context out of which the theology of the new birth develops.

Jesus fulfills the expectations of the Feast of Succoth, the context for a significant reference to the Spirit. One of these expectations concerned a water-pouring ceremony and was connected with the coming of the Spirit. Based on such texts as Ezekiel 37 and Zechariah 14:8, the water ablution on the altar in the temple symbolized what God would do in the future when the Messiah came— he would bring deliverance and restore by means of the Spirit. This gushing stream of water from the altar toward the Dead Sea, invigorating everything in its way, symbolized the activity of the Spirit in this restoration.

In light of the water-pouring ceremony, then, 7:37–39 is meaningful. Verse 39 is often debated. Out of whose side does the water flow— Jesus' or the Christian's? It can be argued that it is from Jesus', both on the basis of the background of this water ceremony and on the basis of the text itself.

First, in regard to the background of this ceremony, note that the water flows from underneath the altar. Furthermore, the altar is the place where God and the worshiper meet. Moreover, in John, new "temple theology" is already present. Jesus is the temple (stone) where heaven and earth meet, the place of revelation (cf. 1:51). In the temple he replaces the altar (i.e., the new foundation stone; this stone altar was considered the foundation of the world in Judaism). In 16:7 Jesus said that he would send the Spirit; in 19:34 water (symbolical of Spirit) and blood flowed out of Jesus' side. Furthermore, Revelation 22:1–2 describes a river of living water coming from the throne of God and the Lamb. The setting of Revelation 22 also is the Feast of Succoth. Revelation 22 is a Christian interpretation and adaptation of this feast.

Second, the text can also support this interpretation. Of course, several different ways of punctuating these words of John appear in various texts and translations. In contrast to the UBS text and the NIV, for example, I punctuate it as follows: "If anyone thirsts, let him who believes in me come and drink. Just as Scripture says: 'Living water will flow out of his [Jesus'] belly.' This spoke he about the Spirit which they who would believe were to receive." I place the first part of verse 38, "he who believes in me," not with "as the Scripture has said" (NIV), but with the pronoun "him" of the former sentence. This allows the *darash* (the OT commentary), "as the scripture said . . . ," to remain free from the intrusion "he who believes on me," and to refer to Jesus. Furthermore, verse 39 speaks about the believer receiving the Spirit (i.e., from Jesus)— not the Spirit flowing out of him. And the coming of the Spirit is associated with Jesus' glorification in that verse also.

Another expectation of the feast concerns the lighting of the lampstand. Zechariah 14:6–7, a text behind the first-century observation of the feast, mentions the coming of Yahweh, the day when he conquers his enemies, a day character- ized as light. In John 8:12, Jesus fulfills this expectation when he says that he is the light of the world. And light is connected with life. The Spirit is the one who gives life and the one who brings light.

The theology of the Spirit in the Feast of Succoth is significant. Jesus ushered in the new age by bringing salvation, gaining victory over God's enemies by providing atonement. This new age, ushered in by the glorification of Jesus, meant that the Spirit had come. One thing the Spirit did was to regenerate sinners who placed their faith in Jesus. This coming of the Spirit also included the work of the Spirit in miraculous power, noted as signs in John.

This theology of the Spirit has implications for Evangelicals and Pentecostal-charismatics. Many Evangelicals fall short in both theology and experience, especially in experience. They mainly relegate the Spirit's work to regeneration and subsume the Pentecostal-charismatic dimension under the category of regeneration, making no distinction between them—often denying even the power aspect of the Spirit. However, some Pentecostals lean in the other direction and all but isolate regeneration from Spirit baptism. In this way they associate sanctification with Spirit bap- tism and virtually deny a relationship between sanctification and regeneration. A better option is to see the Spirit at work in manifold ways. It is appropriate, though, like John, to emphasize one and then, like Luke-Acts, to emphasize the other as congregational needs arise.

In contrast to the Pentecostal position regard- ing sanctification noted above, John says that sanctification comes from regeneration (similarly in Paul in Galatians 5:16–17, 22–23; these Galatians texts are often erroneously taken by Pentecostals to refer to the baptism of the Spirit). In 1 John 3:4–10 it is said that Jesus came to destroy the works of the devil, usually interpreted by Pentecostals to refer to exorcism. This refers, instead, to being born again. Of course, this does not take away the cooperation of the person in the process of sanctification (cf. 1 John 2:1–2).

Moreover, "to remain in the words of Jesus" is a Johannine way of encouraging Christians to stay in the community. John's opponents were causing some to leave. This "remaining" also refers to sanctification and pertains to a perfectionistic position in 1 John 3:4–10. Although this text appears to support a perfectionistic position, it does not. First John 3:4–10 is to be understood in the light of John's view of regeneration and of his definition of the new community of God— they possess the Spirit. (Some erroneously think that this perfectionism comes from a different source, usually gnostic.)

6. The Raising of Lazarus and the Anointing of Jesus (chs. 11–12). Chapters 11 and 12 prepare for the final major section, which contains the exaltation and death of Jesus. These chapters continue the themes of life, light, and the rejec- tion of Jesus.

The raising of Lazarus in a sense becomes the ultimate sign pointing to what Jesus would do by his death and resurrection. Jesus would forgive sins and give the Spirit. As Lazarus was raised to life, so they who are dead in sin (i.e., unable to understand or receive revelation) are resurrected to new life by believing Jesus, being justified, and receiving the same Spirit that raised Jesus.

Chapter 12 begins at the house of Lazarus. This reference to Lazarus connects chapter 12 to chapter 11 theologically. That is, the significance of the raising of Lazarus is ultimately found in what occurs next. Here Jesus is shown to be a different messianic King than the one the Jews were expecting. This difference comes out in the process of Jesus' exaltation and enthronement, which begin here. Three steps in this process are the giving of a festival meal, his anointing, and a solemn procession. This meal took place on an ordinary day (i.e., six days before the Passover, 12:1) outside Jerusalem (i.e., Bethany, 12:1). At that meal Jesus was anointed with a special kind of oil (cf. 12:3). The difference between rabbinic expectations and this account in John is that the rabbis expected the head to be anointed, not the feet, as in the case of Jesus' anointing. Further- more, in Judaism the feet of the dead were anointed. That this tradition is behind this epi- sode is brought out in the following verses where Jesus says, "Leave her alone . . . she should save this perfume for the day of my burial." But this is the point: the cross was to be his throne—he would suffer and die. Jesus' reign will bring about atonement for sins. Preparing for burial was a most important act of mercy in Judaism, just as it is in John. In this case, Jesus relates a correspond- ing act of mercy—"you will always have the poor among you" (12:8). Then there follows the solemn procession in 12:12–15, based on Psalm 118, the procession psalm chosen in the OT and Judaism for the ascension of the king.

The disciples found it hard to understand this. With irony, the disciples are depicted as not receiving the point that Jesus made about Laza- rus' situation. The disciples did not understand because they did not have light (11:4–12; Mar- tha in 11:39b–40). (Light did not come until Jesus gave the Spirit in 20:22.) Again, having spiritual perception (revelation) is a concomitant of having life.

In 11:45–54 the Jews plotted to kill Jesus. They recognized that he did miraculous signs, but they did not believe in him. Because of this plot, Jesus no longer moved about publicly among the Jews. In 12:37–41 they continued in their unbelief, though they had seen Jesus' miracles. This unbelief fulfills the word of Isaiah concerning the blinded eyes of these people. Blindness, as in chapter 9, characterizes the unregenerate, who cannot understand spiritual things (revelation)—i.e., the words that Jesus spoke.

C. The Manifestation of Jesus to the Disciples (chs. 13–21). Chapters 13–18 contain lengthy discourses without parallel in the Synoptics. These discourses contain unique personal instructions on discipleship in terms of the ethical dimensions of brotherly love and humility. In them John also gives a new interpretation of "community" and provides instructions on the Spirit. The apostle connects chapters 14–18 with 7–8 by way of the Feast of Succoth. And certainly, what John says covertly in chapter 13 is important: he does not call the Lord's Supper a Passover meal.

1. Discourses for the Disciples (chs. 13–17). The ethical dimensions given in these chapters suggest that the Johannine community was sectarian in nature and that this community was threatened by outsiders, causing some to leave and others to feel disenfranchised. The exhortation to love the brothers and not the world speaks of a threatened and isolated community that made walls around itself and closed the gates tightly. In this situation, theology becomes more important and religious demands (and indoctrination) increase. Judaism, feeling threatened, also made demands; those who could not meet these demands were expelled from the synagogue (from about A.D. 85 on). Furthermore, previously the Jews could "follow" a messiah, such as Jesus, as long as he was not considered divine. More than likely, no distinction between Jesus the divine Christ or Jesus the human messiah was made before this time—no one emphasized the theological points that were inherent all along. The Johannine community could not go along with any other perception of Jesus than that he was fully divine.

But these demands in John are of a love nature, though they are turned inward toward the members of the community. The command to love one another is a new *halaka* (a "legal" guideline given by the leader of the community, similar to what the rabbis did in Judaism) given by Jesus to his disciples in such a threatened situation. Sectarianism in this instance can be positive—it can, in others, be counterproductive.

In chapter 15 John gives the analogy of the vine, a familiar metaphor in the OT and in Judaism to represent the people of God. By observing what he has done with the vine imagery, we can see that John establishes new foundational roles for this community. In other places of the NT the patriarchs are important as founding fathers, indeed as they are in Judaism. For example, Matthew (the genealogy) and Paul (Rom. 4, 9–11) maintain the importance of Abraham. He is the foundation, or the trunk, at least. But now in John, church and synagogue confront each other over who are the true people of God. And John removes this role for Abraham. As we have seen, Abraham is simply one who witnesses about Jesus (8:31–59). In John 15 Jesus is the trunk, and the father is the vineyard tender. All branches, then, relate to Jesus and bear the fruit of love. If anyone does not remain in Jesus, he is cut off—he ceases to be part of the community.

The word *monai* ("dwelling places") in 14:2 bears out that John has reinterpreted the community of believers in the manner described above. "Dwelling places" in apocalyptic literature describes the kingdom of heaven and the eternal dwelling place of the patriarchs. For instance, in 1 Enoch 41:1–2, the kingdom *in* heaven was a place where the righteous lived and from which the ungodly were expelled. And in Testament of Abraham the patriarchs are said to live in eternal bliss in "mansions" (*monai*). In John the church and the kingdom are synonymous (cf. 8:35, where "household" is equivalent to this use of *monai*, as in 15:2). (The verb *menō* ["to dwell"], a Johannine word, is from the same root as *monai*.)

But more seems to be suggested with Jesus' words "I am going there to prepare a place for you" (14:2). One explanation of this saying is to explore how it may have been understood in the Jewish culture of its day. In Judaism there was an anticipation that in the age to come it would be Yahweh himself who would build the huts for the Feast of Succoth. His people would dwell in them forever. If this interpretation is correct, then one of Hillel's interpretive principles comes into play. This principle says, in Christian terms, "Whatever is said of Yahweh can equally be said of Jesus." Yahweh builds these booths—Jesus builds these booths. The use of this principle ascribes divinity to Jesus. (Note also that both the Father and Jesus send the Spirit.) Jesus' crucifixion, resurrection, and ascension together are his "going" to prepare these places.

John's reinterpretation of church, then, is important for ecclesiology, especially Pentecostal-charismatic theology. Pentecostals, under the influence of dispensationalism, often state that the church began on the Day of Pentecost (Acts 2). The theology of this statement places the church's foundation as the coming of the Spirit, something foreign to Luke and John. In contrast, Jesus is the foundation of the church.

It is in the context of this sectarianism, then, that we are to understand the teaching on the Paraclete in John's Gospel. Several themes connect this section (especially chs. 14–16) with 7:1–8:59. We have already noted that John connects the eschatological fulfillment of the Feast of Booths with the coming of Jesus in these chapters. Other features related to this feast are also found in chapters 14–16: the Spirit and justification/atonement.

It is in response to religious pressure, for instance, that chapter 14 encourages the believer. It is the work of the Paraclete as consoler to reassure believers that they have not been abandoned by God. When the Messiah comes, he consoles believers in their trials (one of the names for messiah in Judaism was *menahem* [consoler]— i.e., the consolation of Israel). The time of the Messiah is a time of salvation (*shalôm*), and one of its traits is the presence of joy among the community's members (cf. 16:20–24). This joy is directly related to the presence of the Spirit in the community.

Atonement also is referred to in 14:27–31. In 27–31 Jesus offers peace to those who follow him. This peace also is the result of the coming of *shalôm,* salvation. The most significant meaning of Paraclete in this section, then, has to do with peace and joy. Paraclete means advocate here— i.e., one who stands in court to argue someone's case. The context of this word is legal-judicial. For instance, it was believed that during the Feast of Succoth arguments between Satan and God occurred. Satan would accuse worshipers; others, especially Abraham, would present arguments in favor of the accused. In the process, God extended salvation to his people. Now, in similar fashion (except that Jesus has replaced the patriarch) John argues that when Jesus would go away, the Spirit—as "the Spirit of Jesus"—would assure (i.e., argue the case for) the believers that they are the true people of God and that their sins have been forgiven. This is the witness of the Spirit. The Spirit is to be the messianic Spirit (the Paraclete), always with the believer (cf. the "Spirit of Christ"—i.e., the messianic spirit in Romans 8:9, also a justification context).

Jesus, then, fulfills what the Feast of Succoth anticipates: the Messiah comes, provides atonement, and gives the Spirit. But this community experiences persecution and a sense of alienation. Not knowing where they belong, the believers are set adrift. It is the work of the Spirit to teach them the truth about Jesus, the true Savior and Messiah (cf. 14:15–31; 15:26–27). They have the ability to receive revelation because they have life (14:6, 19). On the other hand, those who do not have life (i.e., the Spirit) do not recognize Jesus as Messiah and Savior. It is the work of the Spirit to reveal to them their guilt (16:8–11). Unbelievers hate the believer as they did Jesus (15:18–25).

A note about John's presentation of the Lord's Supper is in order. The way he reinterprets this meal in this section also indicates that his community was sectarian in nature and that he was defending or defining more explicitly an important rite in his church. For instance, at the beginning of John 13, the writer clearly states that preparation was made for this dinner before the Passover Feast. It should go without saying, but it needs to be said, nonetheless, that he intends to separate the Passover from the Lord's Supper. Another thing he does is to call the dinner by another name, in comparison to what the Synoptics call the meal. John calls it simply a "dinner" (*deipnon*, v. 2); the Synoptics, "Passover." Since John presents Jesus as the eschatological Passover Lamb, and since the lamb is eaten at Passover, Jesus then cannot eat the meal. However, by making this distinction, John places the modern interpreter in a dilemma concerning how to reconcile this with the Synoptic version of the Last Supper. One way to explain this apparent

incongruency is to say that John uses a Jewish calendar for the Passover. This particular calendar allowed an extra day for those in the Diaspora to observe the feast. John simply took advantage of this extra day.

Jesus' prayer in chapter 17 also suggests a sectarian milieu. In this prayer Johannine themes, which we have noted, emerge. For instance, it is Jesus alone who gives life. The authority to give this life comes from the Father, and the purpose of life is to "know" (by revelation) the Son and the Father (cf. 17:1–4). Jesus prayed to the Father to keep the disciples who were not of the world, though they were in it (17:15–16). Furthermore, as the Father had sent Jesus into the world, so Jesus sent the disciples (17:18). In this way, the transference of authority is accomplished as they engage in their mission (authority is signified by the word *sent*).

2. *The Crucifixion and Resurrection (chs. 18– 21).* We can understand why Jewish people had difficulty with those in John's community, especially in light of the Passion narrative. It is here that John's christology and soteriology converge. In several places Jesus is presented as being equal with Yahweh. He also becomes the King, the Messiah and eschatological Lamb, who creates a new community of people by atoning for their sins and giving them the Spirit. He then sends the apostles on a mission into the whole world.

In seven scenes (cf. Brown, 1966–70, 2:859) from 18:28 through 19:16, although Jesus is on trial, he is, nevertheless, presented as King. Through the questionings of Jesus by the religious and political officials (18:33, 36, 37–38, 19:12, 14–15) and through the clothing worn by Jesus (19:1–2, 5), this theme becomes clear. Furthermore, the innocence of Jesus in his trial also emerges. Innocence is crucial to John's presentation of Jesus as the eschatological Lamb, a theme connected with that of King. The theme of King also occurs in the scenes of Jesus' crucifixion (19:19–24) and in the paragraph on his burial (19:38–41).

It is clearly in chapter 19, concerning Jesus' resurrection, that the theology of the eschatological Lamb occurs. There are several ways this theology is expressed. To begin with, John states three times (in 19:14, 31, 42) that it is the preparation for the Passover. This was the time for all leaven to be removed from the household and all preparations to be made for the offering of the lamb. Explicitly, John says that the death of Jesus occurred before the time the Jews ate the Passover meal later in the evening and during the time of the offering of the lambs in the temple.

Verse 14 particularly notes, "It was the day of Preparation of Passover Week, about the sixth hour. 'Here is your king,' Pilate said to the Jews." Several observations are in order. First, "king" is tied to the Passover lamb. Second, this exclamation occurred on the Day of Preparation, about the time when other lambs were being prepared for offering (i.e., the "sixth hour"). Third, while Pilate cried out to the Jews, "Here is your king," the high priest in the temple would be crying out in a similar way as he lifted the official Passover lamb: "Behold the lamb of our salvation."

This theology of the Lamb is expressed in another way. Jesus hung on the cross from about noon to 2:30, the approximate time for the Passover lamb to be offered in the temple. There is a difference—only Jewish males could look on the lamb in the temple. In contrast, Jesus was crucified outside for all the world to view. This Lamb was for the whole world.

And finally, John expressed his theology of the Lamb by noting particularly that the bones of Jesus were not broken (19:32–37). This fulfilled the Passover requirements in Exodus 12:46.

There are several places where the Spirit plays a significant role. However, one that is open to question is 19:34, where it is said that a soldier pierced Jesus' side, and blood and water gushed out. It is highly possible that this verse refers to 7:38–39, especially when we recall that John's theology places Jesus as the new temple foundation, the new temple rock from which, symbolically, the water (Spirit) pours out. Atonement and Spirit—thus blood and water—are connected in John.

Another significant paragraph is 20:19–23. The context of this paragraph seems to be the Lord's Supper. Remember that John has reinterpreted the Lord's Supper to give it new origins and meaning. In this case, John's account is close to Luke's in wording. Furthermore, late on the first day of the week (John 20:1 [early on Sunday], 19: it is the Jewish equivalent of Sunday), the disciples had gathered when Jesus appeared. Jesus' words ("peace," two times, vv. 19, 21; "giving the Spirit"), and his breathing suggest a first-century Sunday observance in which the Supper would be eaten. The theology of the Supper connotes the forgiveness of sins (the meaning of peace) and the reception of the Spirit (regeneration). That Jesus forgives sins and gives the Spirit is noteworthy. John uses one of Hillel's rules in which Jesus is seen to be equal with Yahweh of the OT. He (Jesus) creates the new community and forgives sins. God's act of breathing and creating (also connected with Spirit) is embedded in the OT and in Jewish tradition. It is appropriate to call this a Supper now, the Lord's Supper. For John it is not connected to the Passover—it has superseded that festival. This is also the significance of the "first day of the week." It denotes a new beginning—a new creation—and establishes the Christian (Johannine) custom of worshiping on Sunday. In this case, it is also appropriate to call it the eschatological meal. The function of verses 19–23 is partially etiological (i.e., it describes where, when, and under what circumstances the Supper originated; in no wise, according to John, did it originate in a Jewish context).

This passage, 20:19–23, is much debated by Pentecostals and Evangelicals. But even those who disagree over its interpretation quite often agree that the church began in Acts 2, when the Spirit came. But the similarity of John 20:19–23 with Luke 24:36–49 may mean that John was well aware of Luke's account of Pentecost (Acts 2). (It is hard to believe that John would not know about such a significant event as that recorded in Acts 2—though, admittedly, other

NT evidence to that event is not clear.) Because of John's own need, he made sure that his church knew that they were founded on Jesus, not on the Spirit. The church began, then, on this resurrection day.

In the ending of his Gospel John has a different commission from that of the Synoptics (e.g., Matthew). Jesus commissioned the apostles when he breathed on them and said, "If you forgive anyone his sins, they are forgiven; if you do not forgive them, they are not forgiven" (20:22–23). The reference to the Spirit occurs with this commission; however, it is in the context of regeneration—the Lord's Supper. Furthermore, it is the Passover season (despite John's anti-Judaistic stance) and not the Feast of Weeks as in Acts 2. That more is meant in this commission than Evangelicals and Pentecostals see is signified in John's context. It is by the transmission, even the transferal, of the Spirit that the disciples are given their authority. It is in the same line of transferal/sending of that between the Father and Jesus. It is the Spirit that effects this relationship of power and authority between the Father and Son, the Son and the disciples. The Spirit and Jesus are closely related in the earthly mission.

This commission is not related to the binding and loosing of Matthew 18:18–20. There, binding and loosing probably refers to community authority to permit or forbid certain action, to make new *halakah* (religious laws). Though this commission may appear to be similar to Matthew's, it is not. It is simply John's "great commission," and it comes from Jesus himself (as it does in Matthew).

This brings us to chapter 21. Here Jesus met his disciples at the Sea of Galilee in an unusual way. They had returned to fishing, but on this occasion they had caught nothing. After following Jesus' directions, as he stood on the bank, they caught a great number of fish, 153 to be precise. The key to understanding this chapter lies in this number. The best way to understand this unusual number is to take it as having some sort of symbolic meaning. One tradition in Judaism says that in the world 153 species of fish existed. If this is behind John's use of this number, it becomes significant for a missions enterprise of the Johannine community. This approximates the Great Commission in Matthew 28:19–20 in which Jesus told the apostles to go into all the world to make disciples. This view fits well with Jesus' commission in 20:22–23 and witnesses that John was attempting to arise above the sectarian weakness of closing the doors to world evangelization. In trying to preserve the saints, he intimates, one should never forget the sinners.

III. Conclusion. John was having difficulty with Jews who were being stirred up by a resurgent Judaism. A major problem focused on the identity of the people of God—both Christianity and Judaism confessed to be just that. John argued that the presence of the Spirit was the way to determine this, and the way to tell if people had the Spirit was to see if they believed the words of Jesus. Jesus himself taught a new way of salvation. Many witnesses supported his claim: the Father, signs, the OT, John the Baptist, and the Spirit.

This new way was portrayed in Jewish terms and feasts, especially as the eschatological Lamb of God. Furthermore, Jesus was not only the Messiah, the King; he was divine—he had the right to convey life and the Spirit. If anyone did not receive (believe) this teaching, he was not born again—he did not have the Spirit. This new birth was the means by which people could receive revelation from the Father. Thus, in John, there is a new emphasis on the Spirit, prophecy, and revelation. Rather than being rooted in a "charismatology" as in Pentecostal-charismatic emphases, the Spirit was rooted in a new anthropology—just like Paul's. John's doctrine of the Spirit, then, must be seen in this context. John's problem was regeneration—not Spirit baptism. If John's opponents could not understand such things as this new way of salvation and Jesus' deity, how could they understand other spiritual things—such as Spirit baptism?

See also JESUS CHRIST; JOHN, LETTERS OF; APOCALYPSE, BOOK OF THE.

Bibliography: S. Aalen, " 'Reign' and 'House' in the Kingdom of God in the Gospels," *NTS* 8 (January 1962): 215–40; B. C. Aker, " 'Breathed': A Study on the Biblical Distinction Between Regeneration and Spirit-Baptism," *Paraclete* 17 (Summer 1983): 13–16; C. K. Barrett, *The Gospel According to St. John*, 2d ed. (1978); T. Barrosse, "The Seven Days of the New Creation in St. John's Gospel," *CBQ* 21 (October 1959): 507–16; J. H. Bernard, *A Critical and Exegetical Commentary on the Gospel According to St. John*, 2 vols. (1928); O. Betz, *Der Paraklet*, (1963); P. Borgen, *Bread from Heaven: An Exegetical Study of the Concept of Manna in the Gospel of John and the Writings of Philo* (1965); R. E. Brown, *The Community of the Beloved Disciple* (1979); idem, *The Gospel According to John*, 2 vols. (1966–70); R. Bultmann, *The Gospel of John: A Commentary* (1975); G. M. Burge, *The Anointed Community* (1987); K. L. Carroll, "The Fourth Gospel and the Exclusion of Christians from the Synagogue," *BJRL* 40 (1957): 19–32; R. A. Culpepper, *Anatomy of the Fourth Gospel: A Study in Literary Design* (1983); J. Daniélou, "Les quartre-temps de Septembre et la Fête des Tabernacles," *La Maison–Dieu* 46 (1956): 114–36; W. D. Davies, *The Gospel and the Land* (1974); I. de la Potterie, "S.N.T.S. Reports on Noordwijkerhout Seminars: L'esprit saint dans l'evangile de Jean," *NTS* 18 (July 1972): 448–51; D. D. Duke, *Irony in the Fourth Gospel* (1985); P. Ellis, *The Genius of John. A Compositional-Critical Commentary on the Fourth Gospel* (1984); H. M. Ervin, *Spirit Baptism: A Biblical Investigation* (1987); A. Feuillet, *Johannine Studies* (1964); R. T. Fortna, *The Gospel of Signs: A Reconstruction of the Narrative Source Underlying the Fourth Gospel* (1970); E. Grässer, "Die Antijüdische Polemik im Johannesevangelium," *NTS* 11 (October 1964): 74–90; A. Guilding, *The Fourth Gospel and Jewish Worship. A Study of the Relationship of St. John's Gospel to the Ancient Jewish Lectionary System* (1960); S. M. Horton, *What the Bible Says About the Holy Spirit* (1976); E. C. Hoskyns, *The Fourth Gospel* (1947); R. H. Lightfoot, *St. John's Gospel* (1960); B. Lindars, *The Gospel of John* (1972); W. F. Lofthouse, "The Holy Spirit in the Acts and the Fourth Gospel," *ET* 52 (1940–41): 334–36; A. Loisy, *Le quatrième Évangile* (1921); J. L. Martyn, *History and Theology in the Gospel of John* (1979); L. Morris, *The Gospel According to John* (1971); idem, *The New Testament and the Jewish Lectionaries* (1964); idem, *New Testament Theology* (1986); B. N. Newman and E. A. Nida, *A Translator's Handbook on the Gospel of John* (1980); H. Odeberg, *The Fourth Gospel* (1968); R. Schnackenburg, *The Gospel According to St. John*, 3 vols. (1968–

82). S. Smalley, *John: Evangelist and Interpreter* (1976); A. Wilkenhauser, *Das Evangelium nach Johannes* (1961).

B. C. Aker

JOHNSON, BERNHARD (1931–). Missionary to Brazil and evangelist. Johnson was born in California and taken to Brazil (1940) by his parents, Assemblies of God (AG) missionaries. The younger Johnson obtained his training at Central Bible College in Springfield, Missouri. He was ordained in 1954 by the AG and returned to Brazil in 1957 as a missionary.

Johnson is known for his Good News Crusades. Each crusade, lasting up to eight days, has daily attendance of 3,000 to 175,000 (representing as much as 30 percent of a city's population), with as many as 1,050 to 13,500 people accepting Christ during the crusade. Furthermore, 12 to 67 percent of those who accept Christ are established in churches a year later. Johnson and his team of twenty-five Brazilians have been conducting approximately eight crusades a year since 1967. The crusades emphasize the salvation message and are frequently accompanied by signs, wonders, miraculous healings, and people being baptized in the Spirit. Like his parents, Johnson has had his life threatened due to testifying for Christ; a gunshot whizzed past his head during one crusade.

Johnson has held many responsible positions: director of Good News Crusades in Brazil; area representative of Brazil for the International Correspondence Institute (ICI); executive officer of the Brazilian Bible Society; executive officer of the Brazilian AG; chairman of AG Field Fellowship in Brazil; president of Children of Brazil Outreach; president of Brazil Extension School of Theology, headquartered at Campinas, Brazil; and president of Bernhard Johnson Ministries, with headquarters in San Jose, California. This organization has: (1) utilized the ministries of AG Light for the Lost, ICI, and Teen Challenge; (2) developed weekly national radio and TV evangelism ("Words of Life," "Good News," and "Bernhard Johnson Presents"); and (3) extended the crusades into Portuguese-speaking areas of Europe, Africa, and the Far East.

Bibliography: B. Braithwaite, "Over 12,000 Saved in Bernhard Johnson Crusade in Rio," *PE* (October 7, 1984), 8–9; J. D. Douglas, *The Work of an Evangelist* (1984); T. Gibbs, "Bernhard Johnson Presents," *PE* (October 26, 1980), 19; B. Johnson, "Good News Crusades and the Brazilian Revival," *Advance* 18 (March 1982): 4–5; idem, " 'Reverend Johnson . . . What's Your Gimmick?' " *PE* (April 14, 1974), 16–17; idem, "The Stretcher Was Empty!" *Mountain Movers* 23 (1981): 13; idem, "What Jesus Said Before He Left," *PE* (May 18, 1975), 16–17; S. Montgomery, "Missionary-Evangelist Reports 1,050 Accept Christ in Brazil," *PE* (October 25, 1987), 30; L. Triplett, "The 'Best' Bible School Training in Latin America," *PE* (September 17, 1978), 16–17.

E. B. Robinson

JONES, BRYN (1940–). Dynamic leader in the "Restoration" or "House Church" movement in Great Britain. Born near Swansea, Wales, son of a miner, Jones was converted in 1957 and baptized in the Spirit one year later at a Pentecostal church. He studied at the Bible College of Wales (1958–61) and then pioneered several churches in Guyana (1963–66). In 1968 Jones began to pastor an independent church in Bradford, England. Receiving a vision for God's corporate work of restoring the NT church, he was one of a group of independent leaders who covenanted together in 1972. Pastoring a church in St. Louis, Missouri (1978–83), Jones has become a leading apostle in the Harvestime network of churches based in Bradford and a major influence in establishing their many forms of outreach. Convinced that charismatic renewal was only a phase prior to emergence of restorationist movement, Jones has stated, "The charismatic awakening that does not deal with the root of independence, individualism, sectarianism, and denominationalism will be deficient."

Bibliography: J. Thurman, *New Wineskins* (c. 1982); A. Walker, *Restoring the Kingdom* (1985).

P. D. Hocken

JONES, CHARLES EDWIN (1932–). Librarian, archivist, bibliographer, and historian. Born in Kansas City, Missouri, Jones received his education at the Bethany-Peniel College (Oklahoma) and the Universities of Michigan (M.A.L.S., 1955) and Wisconsin (M.S., 1960; Ph.D., 1968). He has worked as librarian and archivist (Nazarene Theological Seminary, Park College, University of Michigan, and Brown University) and as professor of history (Houghton College).

Jones's dissertation, *Perfectionist Persuasion: A Social Profile of the National Holiness Movement within American Methodism, 1867–1936,* (published in 1974 with the subtitle *The Holiness Movement and American Methodism, 1867–1936*), provides a backdrop for understanding the sociological and ecclesiological bases for the rise of the Pentecostal movement. His bibliographical publications—*A Guide to the Study of the Holiness Movement* (1974), *A Guide to the Study of the Pentecostal Movement* (1983), and *Black Holiness: A Guide to the Study of Black Participation in Wesleyan Perfectionist and Glossolalic Pentecostal Movements* (1987)—have made significant contributions to the study of those movements.

Bibliography: C. E. Jones, *Perfectionist Persuasion: The Holiness Movement and American Methodism (1867–1936)* (1974); *Contemporary Authors*; *Library and Information Professionals* (1988).

D. D. Bundy

JONES, OZRO THURSTON, JR. (1922–). Pastor, editor, missionary, author, general board member (Church of God in Christ [CGIC]), bishop of Pennsylvania. Jones confessed salvation and the call to ministry at age twelve. Upon graduation from college and seminary he served as a missionary to West Africa. He distinguished himself as the second youth leader in CGIC, having succeeded his father as editor of the Young People Willing Worker literature series. Under his leadership the youth conferences grew into one of the largest mass meetings held by the denomination. He was further distinguished as being one of the first in the denomination to receive an earned doctorate in sacred theology (Temple University), having written as his dissertation, "The Meaning of the Moment in the Existential Encounter According to Kierkegaard" (1962). He is married to Regina Shaw, who bore twin sons, now in training to become astronauts. His preaching and influence has been significant.

L. Lovett

JONES, OZRO THURSTON, SR. (1891–1972). Pastor, evangelist, youth educator, bishop of Pennsylvania, and successor to Bishop C. H. Mason as senior bishop of the Church of God in Christ. He confessed salvation under the ministry of the late Elder Justus Bowe in 1912. In 1914 he was appointed as the first leader of the National Youth Department of the denomination. Through his profound preaching ministry he established several congregations in the Midwest and South, having conducted integrated revivals in Coffeeville, Kansas, as early as 1917. He held the distinction of being one of the five original bishops consecrated in 1933 by Bishop Mason and was the last to succumb. He is best remembered as a peerless and profound gospel preacher (he addressed the Pentecostal World Conference, Toronto, 1958), a pioneering educator of youth, a family-oriented Christian with a godly character. He was married to Neanza Williams of St. Louis, Missouri, who bore six children. He was a shepherding leader to the whole people of God.

L. Lovett

JONES, THEA F. (1920–). Healing evangelist. The faith healing ministry of T. F. Jones was incorporated as Thea Jones Evangelistic Association in Cleveland, Tennessee, in 1949. In 1954 Jones bought the Philadelphia Metropolitan Opera House and started a church. By the mid 1970s the church claimed membership of 6,000 with an inclusive membership of more than 22,000.

Jones's books include *Miracles, Signs and Wonders: Compiled from the Ecclesiastical History of Eusebius* (n.d.); *Mistakes of Satan* (n.d.); *What's in the Manger?* (n.d.); *Miracles in My Life* (n.d.); and *Mr. Jones Goes to Town* (n.d.).

Bibliography: C. E. Jones, *A Guide to the Study of the Pentecostal Movement,* 2 vols. (1983).

S. Shemeth

JUDE, EPISTLE OF Last of the so-called Catholic Epistles; purported to be written by "Jude the brother of James." This "James" has been regarded as the brother of Jesus, thus implying that Jude also was a brother of Jesus (e.g., Mark 6:3). Factors such as language, rhetorical skill, and concerns that appear to reflect a later situation, favor those who argue that the work was not written by Jude, the brother of Jesus. A good case has been made, however, that "brother" here refers to a coworker, perhaps the prophet Jude of Acts 15, who collaborates in the drafting of the Jerusalem letter and indeed is one of the bearers of the letter (Ellis, 1978, 228–30).

It was probably Jude's use of Jewish apocryphal works (e.g., 1 Enoch, Assumption of Moses) that resulted in the work being classed among Eusebius's "disputed" writings (*Eccl. Hist.* 2.23.24–25), so arguments against authenticity on the basis of its being "disputed" are weak. Regarding the complex literary relationship between Jude and 2 Peter, many see Jude as the source of 2 Peter (e.g. Kümmel, Bauckham).

Dating the document largely depends on how one views its authorship and its purpose. For those who regard the letter as combating some form of Gnosticism, a second-century date is demanded. Others, who regard the letter as belonging to the "milieu of apocalyptic Jewish Christianity and [combating] teachers of antinomian libertinism" date the letter sometime within the latter half of the first century. Jude's extensive use of Jewish material does not rule out Jewish gnostics as the opponents, but it does suggest a date prior to Christianity's separation from Judaism.

Scholars are also divided over whether Jude was a "catholic" treatise devoted to combating heresy in general (so Wisse, 1972) or whether it was addressed to "a specific situation in which a specific group of false teachers were troubling a specific church or group of churches" (Bauckham, 1983, 3). Some take a mediating position in which the author is writing a "circular letter to a considerable number of communities, nevertheless to specific communities that are facing a common problem from the same dangerous persons" (Ellis, 1978, 230).

Jude refers explicitly to the Holy Spirit only twice (vv. 19, 20), although the letter clearly has a "charismatic" world view. This is most apparent in his polemic against the false teachers. Jude uses a *pesher* style ("this is that"; cf. e.g., Acts 2) of interpretation in which he sees the fulfillment of OT prophecy and apostolic prophecy in his present situation. Thus in verse 4 he explains that the condemnation of certain men was "written about long ago" (i.e., in the OT). Furthermore, he asserts that the "apostles foretold" that in the last times there would be "scoffers who would follow their own ungodly desires" (vv. 17–18; see Ellis's comments for why this need not reflect a postapostolic situation, 1978, 228f.). The prophecy of Enoch in verse 14 is also a *pesher* type of prophecy.

The entire controversy of Jude may in fact be an issue similar to Paul's problem with radical pneumatics in 1 Corinthians. The opponents in Jude, on the basis of "prophetic revelation" (*enypniazomenoi*, Baucknam, 1987, 55; Ellis, 1978, 231), invoke the freedom of the Spirit as license for lawlessness and the rejection of authority (v. 8; cf. vv. 12, 16). Actually they are *pseuchikoi* ("unspiritual"), not having the Spirit (v. 19), although they regard themselves as *pneumatikoi* (see Dunn, 1975, 246).

Jude urges his readers to "pray in the Holy Spirit." Dunn is quite confident in asserting that "a reference to charismatic prayer, including glossolalic prayer, may therefore be presumed for Jude 20" (Dunn, 1975, 246). To pray "in the Holy Spirit" functions to "build up" the believers (1 Cor. 14:4). It is not necessary to impose a strictly Pauline understanding of praying in the Spirit, despite verbal similarities with Ephesians 6:18. The text merely reflects the pneumatic character of early Christian prayer (cf. Rom. 8:15–16, 26–27; Gal. 4:6; 1 Cor. 14:15; cf. John 4:23). For Jude the "building up" found in praying in the Spirit contrasts the destructive nature of the false teachers (v. 19). Praying in the Spirit promotes unity and allows the community as a whole to endure and thwart the threat of the false teachers. The strength gained in praying in

the Spirit manifests itself in love, patience, and mercy (20–23).

Bibliography: R. J. Bauckham, *Jude, 2 Peter* (1983); J. C. Beker, "Jude," *IDB*, 2:1009–11; J. D. G. Dunn, *Jesus and the Spirit* (1975); E. E. Ellis, *Prophecy and Hermeneutic in Early Christianity* (1978); W. G. Kümmel, *Introduction to the New Testament* (1973); F. Wisse, "The Epistle of Jude in the History of Heresiology," in M. Krause, ed., *Essays on the Nag Hammadi Texts in Honour of Alexander Böhlig* (1972).

P. H. Alexander

A leader in the Lutheran charismatic movement, Theodore Jungkuntz, has taught theology at Valparaiso University, authored several books, and pastors a Lutheran church in Michigan.

JUNGKUNTZ, THEODORE (1932–). Lutheran theologian and author. Jungkuntz is perhaps best known for giving strong theological direction to the Lutheran charismatic movement. He received a Th.D. from Erlangen University, once the leading center of confessional Lutheran theology in Germany. In 1968 he became involved in the charismatic movement while teaching theology at Valparaiso University, Valparaiso, Indiana.

Jungkuntz articulated a theology that demonstrated the consistency of charismatic renewal with the Lutheran confessions. He authored several books and numerous articles dealing with the two themes of the Lutheran confessions and charismatic theology. He was a major contributor to *Welcome, Holy Spirit* (1987), a pastoral and theological perspective on charismatic renewal prepared by an international Lutheran charismatic theological consultation.

In 1984 Jungkuntz became pastor of Cross and Resurrection Lutheran Church, a congregation associated with the Word of God, an ecumenical Christian community in Ann Arbor, Michigan.

Bibliography: L. Christenson, ed., *Welcome, Holy Spirit* (1987); T. Jungkuntz, *Confirmation and the Charismata* (1983); idem, *Formulators of the Formula of Concord: Four Architects of Lutheran Unity* (1977); idem, *A Lutheran Charismatic Catechism* (1979).

L. Christenson

JUNK, THOMAS Twentieth-century evangelist and missionary. Earliest records place Junk at the Azusa Street Mission early in the revival. A German American, Junk and his wife accompanied Florence Crawford and four others on an evangelistic tour of Oakland, California, in August 1906, moving north through Salem, Oregon, and into Seattle. There Junk reported moderate success in bringing the Pentecostal revival. He established and preached at a small racially integrated storefront Pentecostal mission on Seventh Avenue in Seattle. T. B. Barratt cites a testimony given by a young Jewish convert, Lewis Rudner, in *The Household of God*, that describes a service in which Thomas Junk and others recited a number of Scriptures and sang songs in Hebrew as a manifestation of the gift of tongues. As a result, the man was converted.

Toward the end of 1908 or the beginning of 1909 Mrs. Junk died. Thomas Junk went to Tsao-Hsien, Shantung, in northern China, where he served as a missionary for several years. His letters indicated that his ministry was focused on new convert evangelism, punctuated with healings, miracles, and exorcisms. North China was frought with famine during his time there. He collected a following of deserted children and provided them with food, clothing, and the gospel. The Stone Church of Chicago and the Upper Room Mission in Los Angeles supported Junk's ministry in China.

Bibliography: *AF* 1 (3, 1906): 1, 3, 4; 1 (4, 1906): 3; 1 (5, 1907): 3; T. B. Barratt, *In the Days of the Latter Rain* (rev. 1928, reprint 1985), 167–69; *LRE* 2 (7, 1910): 12; 2 (10, 1910): 14; 3 (6, 1911): 14; 3 (12, 1911): 12; "Slow to Arrive," *Daily Oregon Statesman* (Salem, Oreg.) (October 10, 1906), 2; *The Upper Room* 1 (6, 1910): 5; 1 (10, 1910): 6; 1 (11, 1910): 8; 2 (3, 1910): 6, 8; 2 (5, 1911): 5.   C. M. Robeck, Jr.

K

KANSAS CITY CONFERENCE The first general ecumenical gathering of Pentecostals and charismatics from the mainline denominations in North America took place July 20–24, 1977, in Kansas City, Missouri. Since most of the American denominational charismatic renewal groups conducted annual conferences, it was decided that all of them would meet together at the same time and place. The format called for a general conference that would safeguard the identity of the sponsoring groups while giving expression to a common unity of purpose in the plenary sessions. Denominational gatherings were held in the mornings in various locations around the city and common workshops were offered in the afternoons. In the evenings all the separate groups came together as one in the sessions in Arrowhead Stadium.

Kansas City was in reality a conference of conferences. The supporting groups included Catholic charismatics, Episcopalians, Baptists, Methodists, Presbyterians, Lutherans, Pentecostals, Mennonites, Messianic Jews, and persons from several nondenominational streams. Serving as chairman for the conference was Kevin Ranaghan, a leader of the Roman Catholic "People of Praise" Community in South Bend, Indiana. One-half of all registrants were Roman Catholics.

The conference theme was "Jesus Is Lord," a phrase that summarized the basic doctrinal ground for the unprecedented unity and cooperation displayed in the meeting. This theme was stressed by the keynote speakers, which included Bob Mumford, Larry Christenson, Kevin Ranaghan, and James Forbes.

The most memorable prophecy given to the conference followed the refrain "mourn and weep, for the Body of My Son is broken." Many messages called for the reconciliation of the churches. Major churchmen who participated in the conference were: Léon-Joseph Cardinal Suenens, primate of Belgium and papal liaison to the Catholic Charismatic Renewal; Bishop J. O. Patterson, presiding bishop of the Church of God in Christ; and Thomas F. Zimmerman, general superintendent of the Assemblies of God.

The conference followed the "three streams" approach put forth by Ralph Martin—i.e., that the major sources of the renewal consisted of (1) the classical Pentecostal churches, (2) the mainline Protestant charismatic movements, and (3) the Catholic charismatic movement. Thus the conference was organized around leadership representing these elements, with an executive committee made up of Ranaghan (Catholic), Christenson (Lutheran), and Vinson Synan (Pentecostal).

The larger planning committee was composed of leaders from the foregoing three streams. They were composed of: Ranaghan, Christenson, Synan, along with Nelson Litwiller (Mennonite), Carlton Spencer (Pentecostal), Brick Bradford (Presbyterian), Bob Hawn (Episcopalian), Roy Lamberth (Baptist), David Stern (Messianic Jewish), Howard Courtney (Pentecostal), Ken Pagard (Baptist), and Robert Frost (nondenominational).

The Kansas City Conference was the largest ecumenical conference in the history of the nation, with some 50,000 registered for the sessions. The next decade saw the greatest growth of charismatics and Pentecostals in North America and the world in the history of the movement. At the time of the Kansas City Conference there was an estimated 50 million Pentecostals and charismatics in the world. By the time of the next ecumenical conference in New Orleans in 1987 that number had surpassed the 200 million mark.

The Kansas City Conference was important in that it demonstrated a unity never before seen in the Pentecostal-charismatic movement. The songs and intense worship experienced in Kansas City spread rapidly to all sectors of the renewal around the world.

See also CHARISMATIC MOVEMENT.

Bibliography: D. Manual, *Like a Mighty River* (1977); V. Synan, *In the Latter Days* (1984).
H. V. Synan

KASEMAN, JIM (1943–). Pastor, evangelist and founder of the Association of Faith Churches and Ministries.

Although successful by human standards—a college graduate and officer in the Army National Guard, married, and the father of five children—it was not until after Jim Kaseman was "born again" at a small Bible study in 1972 that he was delivered from the torment of his alcoholism and his frequent thoughts of suicide. In 1975 Kaseman answered a small ad in a magazine and soon enrolled in the first class of Rhema Bible Training Center in Tulsa, Oklahoma. After graduating from Rhema, he moved to Willmar, Minnesota, where he pastored a small church. Eight months into his pastorate he felt the Lord leading him into a traveling ministry and by 1979 Kaseman had helped found twenty-seven churches in North and South Dakota and Minnesota. Then through a remarkable set of circumstances Kaseman found himself invited to Finland to spread the message of faith. In 1981 he founded the Association of Faith Churches and Ministries. In 1982 God spoke to him to translate twenty-seven books by Kenneth E. Hagin, Sr., into the Russian language. As of 1988 over one million books have been translated, printed, and smuggled into the Soviet Union for distribution.

Bibliography: J. Kaseman, *The Jim Kaseman Story* (1983).
J. R. Zeigler

KELLER, OTTO C. (1888—1942) **AND MARIAN (WITTIK)** (1889–1953). Missionaries to Kenya. A Canadian from Parry Sound, Ontario, Marian was raised in the Church of England. As a teenager she began to feel a call to missionary service. After attending some evangelistic meetings, she made a renewed commitment to God and was baptized by immersion. She later received the baptism of the Holy Spirit in 1909. Soon afterward Reverend Robert J. Craig recommended she attend Rochester (N.Y.) Bible Training School before going into missionary work. While attending the school, Marian met her first husband, Karl Wittick.

The Witticks left for Tanganyika in October 1913. After three months on the field, Karl died from poison in their water supply. Marian also was ill, but she recovered and remained on the field to supervise the building of a mission in Tanganyika.

In 1914 Marian was joined by several workers, including Otto C. Keller, an American Pentecostal missionary. Marian and Otto were married in 1918 and began a work together in Kenya, British East Africa. In 1924, to receive government recognition for their mission, the Kellers needed the backing of a chartered organization. They gained affiliation with the Pentecostal Assemblies of Canada (PAOC), and over the next two decades several missionaries from Canada joined them in their work. Their missionary society, with headquarters in Nairobi, Kenya, became known as the Pentecostal Assemblies of God (affiliated with the PAOC). Today there are hundreds of national pastors in Kenya.

Otto Keller passed away in 1942, and Marian carried on the work until other missionaries came to take over. She lived the last years of her life in Victoria, British Columbia.

Bibliography: M. Keller, *Twenty Years in Africa* (1933).   G. W. Gohr

KELSEY, MORTON TRIPPE (1917–). Episcopal priest, university professor, and author. Born in Depue, Illinois, and raised in Palmerton, Pennsylvania, Kelsey graduated with honors from Washington and Lee University. After graduate study at Princeton University, he received his B.D. from Episcopal Theological Seminary in Cambridge, Massachusetts. He pursued further study at Claremont College in California and under C. G. Jung at the Jung Institute in Zurich, Switzerland. After twenty years as rector of St. Luke's Episcopal Church, Monrovia, California, he taught for a number of years at the University of Notre Dame beginning in 1969.

Early in his career, Kelsey escaped from the dead end of philosophical agnosticism through studying the works of Baron Friedrick von Hügel and A. E. Taylor, later broadening this outlook through the understanding of the psychologist C. G. Jung, whose theories of the unconscious he employs as an interpretive model. Endorsing much in the charismatic movement he has written more than twenty-three books of considerable length and erudition on a variety of Christian and psychological topics, including books on healing in Christianity and tongues-speaking.

Bibliography: M. T. Kelsey, *Encounter With God* (1972); idem, *Tongue Speaking: The History and Meaning of Charismatic Experience* (1964).   R. M. Riss

KENDRICK, KLAUDE (1917–). AG minister, educator, educational administrator, and writer. Kendrick was born in Arizona and later graduated from Southwestern Assemblies of God College (at that time located in Enid, Okla.) in 1938. He completed the B.A. at Texas Wesleyan College in 1945, the M.A. at Texas Christian University in 1948, and the Ph.D. at the University of Texas in 1959. His graduate studies concentrated on history and college administration.

Kendrick served Southwestern Assemblies of God College as instructor, dean of men, business manager, and finally vice-president (1940–55). From 1955 to 1960 he served Evangel College, Springfield, Missouri, as academic dean and president. In 1960 he returned to Southwestern, where he was president until 1965. In 1965 he joined Texas Wesleyan College as chairman of the Division of Social Sciences, serving until 1977. From 1977 to 1979 he was academic dean of Southern California College.

Since Kendrick's formal retirement in 1977, he has accepted a number of challenging assignments at various churches and educational institutions. For two years he was responsible for upgrading the Far East Advanced School of Theology in Baguio, Philippines, to the graduate level. During that assignment he served as the school's president for more than a year.

Kendrick is married and has two children. He has written numerous articles and books, chief among which is *The Promise Fulfilled* (1961), a history of the modern Pentecostal movement.

Bibliography: Vita supplied by Klaude Kendrick (February 1988).   S. M. Burgess

KENNEDY, MILDRED ("MINNIE") (1862–1947). Mother of Aimee Semple McPherson. Orphaned at age twelve, "Minnie" was reared by Salvationists and became heavily involved in that movement. The second wife of a widower, James Morgan Kennedy (1836–1921), at first she did not accept Aimee's involvement in Pentecostalism, but she soon came to accept it. Following the death of Aimee's husband, Robert Semple, she spent the fall and winter months in New York City involved with the Salvation Army and providing moral support to her daughter. Moving back to Ingersoll, Ontario, she provided support to Aimee, who by this time had begun an active evangelistic ministry along the Eastern Seaboard and up into Canada.

When Aimee settled in Los Angeles, Minnie also moved there. Both mother and daughter were legally responsible for the Echo Park Evangelistic Association. "Mother" as she was called, showed remarkable skills in providing the primary financial and business leadership to the association in its early days. When Aimee disappeared in May 1926, Minnie dominated the business conducted at the temple, and upon initial reports of Aimee's apparent drowning, Minnie issued a telegram to George Jeffreys, inviting him to come immediately to conduct meetings. He could not come, and within days Aimee had reappeared.

After a decade as a widow, "Mother" Kennedy remarried on June 28, 1931, to Guy Edward Hudson. The courtship was short, the marriage unanticipated. Shortly after their wedding, charges of bigamy were filed against Hudson by another woman. The marriage to "Minnie" was annulled less than a month after it had been entered. Later that year the bigamy charges lapsed and Hudson obtained a "quickie" divorce in Las Vegas. Minnie met him there, and they were remarried. On July 4, 1932, she announced a separation; divorce followed in November 1932.

As with many mother-daughter relationships, it was not always easy for these two very strong women to see things alike. The newspapers reported a deep rift between them, with such spectacular headlines as "Police Guarding Aimee from 'Ma,'" and much was made of a broken nose, which "Mother" was quoted as having received in an altercation with Aimee. To what extent the rift was real is difficult to assess, but when Aimee's daughter, Roberta, disagreed with Aimee on certain elements of temple administration in 1937, Minnie sided with Roberta in the ensuing highly publicized court scene. The least that may be said following that incident is that mother and daughter continued to drift apart.

Following Aimee's death in 1944, Minnie declined into relative obscurity. She never fully recovered from the effects of an automobile accident in early 1947 and died on November 23, 1947, in Hermosa Beach, California.

Bibliography: D. Cartwright, *The Great Evangelists* (1986); "Police Guarding Aimee from 'Ma,'" *San Francisco Chronicle* (September 3, 1930), 1; L. Thomas, *Storming Heaven* (1970).   C. M. Robeck, Jr.

KENYON, ESSEK WILLIAM (1867–1948). Evangelist, pastor, educator, and author. Born in upstate New York, Kenyon preached his first sermon at a Methodist church in Amsterdam, New York, at age nineteen. After attending various schools and pastoring several churches in New England, he founded Dudley Bible Institute in Dudley, Massachusetts, a faith venture that he financed with proceeds from his evangelistic meetings in Canada, Chicago, and many parts of the Northeast, where there were thousands of reported conversions and healings. The school soon moved to Spencer, Massachusetts, and was renamed Bethel Bible Institute, where he continued as president for twenty-five years. The school later moved to Providence, Rhode Island, and became Providence Bible Institute.

In 1923 Kenyon founded Figueroa Independent Baptist Church in downtown Los Angeles, where he became a pioneer in radio evangelism with broadcasts from KNX every morning. After doing a few broadcasts from Tacoma, Washington, in 1931, he began a daily program from KJR in Seattle, "Kenyon's Church of the Air," which led to the founding of a church there of the same name, later known as New Covenant Baptist Church.

Kenyon later devoted himself more fully to itinerant ministry and writing. His sixteen books

A Bible teacher and author, E. W. Kenyon has had an important influence on the "word of faith" wing of the Pentecostal movement.

have enjoyed an extensive circulation and influence. Although he was not a Pentecostal, his work, *The Wonderful Name of Jesus* (1927) was widely read among Oneness Pentecostals (Reed, 1975, 160–62). His writings have had a broad acceptance in the Deeper Life and charismatic movements. Various aspects of his theology later became an important influence on such diverse people as W. J. "Ern" Baxter, F. F. Bosworth, David Nunn, T. L. Osborn, Jimmy Swaggart, and many others (Gossett and Kenyon, 1977, 3). Kenyon's writings also became seminal for the ministries of Kenneth Hagin, Kenneth Copeland, Don Gossett, Charles Capps, and others in the Word of Faith and Positive Confession movements.

Although Kenyon has been criticized for holding to a form of Gnosticism, the similarities between Kenyon's theology and the gnostic system are only superficial. Although Kenyon held that Jesus died both spiritually and physically (1964, 135–37), the ancient Christian gnostics held that Jesus did not die physically, some maintaining that Jesus himself was in need of redemption. For gnostics, redemption involved deliverance from the world and from the physical body, all matter being inherently evil. On the other hand, Kenyon (1964, 97–106) believed in the physical resurrection of Christ, the redemption of the physical bodies of believers, the centrality of the Incarnation, the necessity of the Virgin Birth, and the importance of the preexistence of Christ, all of which were antithetical to the central tenets of Gnosticism.

Bibliography: D. Gossett and E. W. Kenyon, *The Power of the Positive Confession of God's Word* (1977);

R. K. Housworth, letter to R. M. Riss (February 26, 1988); D. Hunt, *Beyond Seduction* (1987); E. W. Kenyon, *The Father and His Family* (1964); R. Kenyon [Housworth], "He Is At Rest," reprint from *Herald of Life* (April 1948); J. A. Matta, *The Born Again Jesus of the Word-Faith Teaching* (1987); D. R. McConnell, *A Different Gospel* (1988); D. Reed, "Aspects of the Origins of Oneness Pentecostalism," in V. Synan, ed., *Aspects of Pentecostal-Charismatic Origins* (1975).

R. M. Riss

KERR, DANIEL WARREN (1856–1927). Pioneer pastor and educator. Daniel W. Kerr is representative of a number of seasoned clergy drawn into the Pentecostal movement in its infancy. A native of Center County, Pennsylvania, he was founder of two Bible institutes—the Southern California Bible School (1920) and Central Bible Institute (1922)—and an early executive presbyter of the General Council of the Assemblies of God (AG). From 1911 to 1919 he was pastor of the large Pentecostal Church of Cleveland, Ohio. Previous to this Kerr had served in Illinois and Ohio under the Evangelical Association and the Christian and Missionary Alliance (CMA). In 1907, while pastor at Dayton, Kerr and his wife, Mattie, received the Pentecostal experience while attending the Beulah Park camp meeting east of Cleveland. Transferred four years later to the CMA church in Cleveland, they found a largely Pentecostal congregation ready to declare its independence. After eight years he resigned from this congregation to move to California. Venerated by the AG as a pastor and schoolman, Kerr died in 1927 at age seventy-one in Springfield, Missouri. He is buried in Cleveland.

Bibliography: C. Brumback, *Suddenly . . . From Heaven* (1961); *PE* (April 16, 1927), 4.   C. E. Jones

KESWICK HIGHER LIFE MOVEMENT
This renewalist tradition takes its name from an English village that has been the site of annual conventions devoted to the cultivation of the "higher Christian life" since 1875.

I. The History of Keswick. From the early decades of the nineteenth century, evangelists from the American Holiness movement became regular features of British church life. These men and women, as well as their publications, stirred interest in the Spirit-filled life. W. E. Boardman's *The Higher Christian Life* (1859) was especially influential. Robert Pearsall Smith contributed *Holiness Through Faith* (1870) and *Walk in the Light* (1873). His wife, Hannah Whitall Smith, wrote *The Christian's Secret of a Happy Life* (1875).

During 1873 the Smiths and Boardman were in England and became involved in a series of sessions of clergy and laity focusing on the "higher life." In 1874 W. Cowper-Temple hosted at his Broadlands estate a meeting of about a hundred persons, chaired by R. P. Smith, including Theodore Monod, George MacDonald, and Amanda Smith. August 1874 saw another meeting at Oxford. Speakers included the Smiths, Theodore Monod, Otto Stockmayer, Evan Hopkins, Asa Mahan, and W. E. Boardman. The Oxford Conference had significant influence on the Continent, and what became "Keswickian" in

England is known as the "Oxford movement" in the rest of Europe. The proceedings were published as *Account of the Union Meeting for the Promotion of Scriptural Holiness* (1875).

Brighton was the site of another meeting led by the Smiths (May 29–June 7, 1875) with speakers such as Mahan, Hopkins, and T. Monod. The proceedings of Brighton were published as *Record of the Convention for the Promotion of Scriptural Holiness* (1875). Smith also began a periodical, *The Christian's Pathway to Power* (1874–78), which became *The Life of Faith* (1878–), the official organ of the Keswick convention.

T. D. Harford-Battersby and Robert Wilson invited the Smiths to conduct a "Union Meeting for the Promotion of Practical Holiness" at Keswick (June 29–July 6, 1875). Smith withdrew from evangelistic work before the meeting, and its leadership fell to Battersby. The conventions at Keswick became annual events and served as the model for similar conferences through the world, many of which bear the name "Keswick."

II. The Development of a Theological Tradition. A product of the American Holiness movement, the Keswick Convention soon developed an indigenous tradition. Keswick theologians rejected the absolutizing by the parent movement (during the late nineteenth and early twentieth centuries) of sanctification, which was often expressed in terms of "sinless perfection" by radical American preachers. However, they retained the emphasis that a normative Christian life is characterized by "fullness of the Spirit." It is this, they argued, that gives power for living a consistent Christian life. Keswickians teach that reception of "fullness of the Spirit" is a definite act of faith distinct from but usually coincident with regeneration. The actualization of this power usually develops throughout Christian life. The experience provides for victory over temptation and sin, but did not result in the eradication of tendencies to sin. For times of special need, "fillings" of the Holy Spirit are available. "Fullness" and "fillings" are to be sought by all Christians following the biblical paradigms.

III. The Influence of Keswick. Jessie Penn-Lewis's *The Awakening in Wales* (1905), indicated that the Welsh revival had its roots in Keswick, a thesis accepted by most historians. The teaching of Keswick found its way to the Continent through the efforts of O. Stockmayer, T. Monod, R. A. Torrey, R. P. Smith, T. Jellinghaus, E. Modersohn, and others. On the Continent it achieved its most permanent form in the German Holiness movement. One of the influential authors and preachers of this group, J. Paul, became a founder of the German Pentecostal movement. A. Boddy, English Pentecostal leader, also attended Keswick, and through his influence and that of his periodical *Confidence*, a Keswickian understanding of "baptism of the Holy Spirit" (and therefore of the evidence for the reception of the Spirit) became normative for most Pentecostal movements.

A. B. Simpson, founder of the Christian and Missionary Alliance (CMA), influenced by A. J. Gordon and W. E. Boardman, adopted a Keswickian understanding of sanctification. Simpson's

Fulness of Jesus (1890) and the work by CMA theologian G. P. Pardington, *The Crisis of the Deeper Life* (1906), articulate this perspective. Simpson was attracted to the Pentecostal understanding of "baptism in the Holy Spirit," but apparently did not experience glossolalia. His theological treatise, *The Four-Fold Gospel* (1925), organized around the doctrine of Christ as Savior, Sanctifier, Healer, and Coming King, became a paradigm for early North American Pentecostal theological formulations. Other Keswick theologians such as H. A. Ironside and W. Graham Scroggie became opponents of Pentecostalism.

See also HOLINESS MOVEMENT.

Bibliography: S. Barabas, *So Great Salvation* (1952); D. Brandt-Bessire, *Aux sources de la spiritualité pentecôtiste* (1986); D. Bundy, *Keswick: A Bibliographic Introduction to the Higher Life Movements* (1975, reprint 1986); D. Dayton, *The Theological Roots of Pentecostalism* (1987); G. Marsden, *Fundamentalism and American Culture: The Shaping of Twentieth-Century Evangelism 1870–1925* (1980).   D. D. Bundy

KETCHAM, MAYNARD L. (1905–). Missionary to India. Maynard L. Ketcham lost his father when he was five months old. His godly mother raised him in the Methodist Church. When Ketcham was five years old, Fanny Simpson, a missionary to India, came to their church and laid hands on him and claimed him as a missionary to India.

Shortly after entering Massachusetts Institute of Technology (MIT) with a strong desire to become an engineer, he left to attend Beulah Heights Bible Training School in North Bergen, New Jersey, and later Taylor University. Following graduation, he taught at Beulah Heights, where he met his wife Gladys Koch. They were married in 1928 and have had three children— Jimmy, who died of polio; David; and Marjorie.

Ketcham left in 1926 to take over the mission station at Behar, India, that had been established by Simpson. He was ordained with the Assemblies of God (AG) in 1927 and established the Door of Hope Orphanage at Puruila and pioneered churches throughout Bangladesh and India.

At the beginning of his second term in India, Ketcham was elected superintendent of the AG of North India and also chairman of the North India Field Fellowship and later as general secretary of the All-India Pentecostal Fellowship. He held this position until he moved to Springfield, Missouri, to assume responsibilities as field secretary for southern Asia in 1951. Ketcham was eventually made field secretary for the Far East in 1955. In Korea he helped initiate training for national workers. Under his direction, the Evangelistic Center in Seoul, Korea, was organized and built. Today this church is the largest in the world and is pastored by Paul Y. Cho. The Ketcham's have been made honorary lifetime pastors of that church.

After retiring from his position as field secretary for the Far East in 1970, Ketcham became an instructor for the missions departments of Central Bible College and Evangel College in Springfield. Later Ketcham worked as an elder to PTL ministries and became an adviser for PTL prison

ministries. Most recently he has been involved with writing letters to prison inmates who correspond with the Prison Ministries program of the chaplaincy department of the AG. He received an honorary doctor of divinity degree from Bethany Bible College, Santa Cruz, California, in 1975 for his distinguished missionary service.

Bibliography: "Dear Uncle Maynard," *PE* (February 26, 1984), 10–11; M. L. Ketcham, *Pentecost in the Ganges Delta* (1945); idem, *Tigers That Talk* (1979); Maynard L. Ketcham, interview with D. Womack, March 3, 1970, Office of Promotions, AG Division of Foreign Missions.   S. Shemeth

Delivered from a bitter and hostile attitude, Ben Kinchlow ministered to runaways and addicts before joining "The 700 Club" as co-host in 1975.

KINCHLOW, HARVEY BEN (1936–). Minister and television cohost. Kinchlow was born in Uvalde, Texas. Following high school he joined the U.S. Air Force and served for thirteen years.

Kinchlow had much to overcome. Bitter and hostile, he followed the hate-fueled philosophies of Black Muslim leader Malcolm X. Ironically, John Corcoran, a white minister, penetrated the inner wall of hatred.

After his discharge from the Air Force, Kinchlow went to Southwest Texas Junior College (A.A.), where he met the Lord. During that time he opened His Place, a ministry to teenage runaways. Later he became the executive director for Christian Farms, a drug and alcohol rehabilitation ministry. While there he became an ordained minister in the African Methodist Episcopal Church. During that time he was interviewed by Pat Robertson on the "700 Club." He joined the Christian Broadcasting Network (CBN) as Director of Counseling for the Dallas, Texas, center. In

1975 he transferred to CBN headquarters in Virginia Beach, where he became cohost and in 1985 was promoted to executive vice-president. He resigned from CBN in 1988.

Kinchlow is author (with Bob Slosser) of *Plain Bread* (1985).

Bibliography: D. Hazard, "Ben Kinchlow: Off-Camera & Off-the-Cuff," *Charisma* (March 1986), 21–24.
                                                    S. Strang

KING, JOSEPH HILLERY (1869–1946). A founder and the first bishop of the Pentecostal Holiness Church (PHC). Born in Anderson County, South Carolina, to a family of poor sharecroppers, and one of eleven children, he moved with his family to Franklin County, Georgia, in 1882. In 1885, on his sixteenth birthday, King was converted in a Holiness-oriented Methodist camp meeting in Carnesville, Georgia. Later, on October 23, 1885, he received the "second blessing" of entire sanctification. Soon afterward he felt a call to preach and to assist in several local revivals. His first application for a Methodist exhorter's license was denied due to lack of education.

In 1890, after serving a short term in the U.S. Army, he married Willie Irene King. This marriage soon ended in divorce, however, since his new wife had no intention of being the wife of a Holiness minister. Because of his convictions against divorce and remarriage, King vowed to remain celibate as long as his first wife lived. In 1891 he was licensed to preach in the Georgia Conference of the Methodist Episcopal Church (the northern branch of Methodism) and was assigned as pastor of the Rock Spring-Walton circuit near his home. He also served several other charges at this time. He was assigned in 1895 to the Lookout Mountain circuit near Chattanooga. Because of his thirst for knowledge, he decided to attend the U.S. Grant University School of Theology. Despite his lack of earlier education, he graduated in 1897.

While in Chattanooga, King became disenchanted with the increasingly negative policy of the Methodist church toward the Holiness movement. He also came in contact with Benjamin Hardin Irwin's "Fire-Baptized Holiness Association" (FBHA), which promised a third experience after sanctification called "the fire." After receiving this experience and graduating from the university, he joined Irwin's group in 1897. When Irwin formed a national movement in Anderson, South Carolina, in 1898, King was one of the charter members.

After the Anderson convention, Irwin sent King to Toronto, Canada, where he pastored a local congregation and led in planting churches in eastern Canada. In 1900 Irwin called him to the church's headquarters in Iowa to assist him in editing the denominational journal, *Live Coals of Fire*. Soon after King's arrival, Irwin left the church in disgrace after confessing to "open and gross sin." The thirty-one-year-old King then became general overseer of the badly demoralized church. In prayer, he was assured that the FBHA would survive and that he would die as its leader. By 1902 King had not only succeeded in

holding remnants of the church together but had moved the headquarters to Royston, Georgia, near his family home. He then led the church in dropping the word "Association" from its name and adding the word "Church" (FBHC). For five years the growth of the church was slow, until the Pentecostal movement reached the church through the ministry of G. B. Cashwell, a preacher from the Holiness Church of North Carolina, who had been to Azusa Street in 1906 and experienced glossolalia. Most of King's preachers received the Pentecostal experience in Cashwell's historic meeting in Dunn, North Carolina, in January 1907. The next month, King invited Cashwell to preach the Pentecostal message in his FBHC congregation in Toccoa, Georgia. After some theological struggles, King accepted the experience and spoke in tongues himself in Cashwell's meeting.

King immediately led the church in adopting a Pentecostal statement of faith; this was done in January 1908. Thus the FBHC became the first denomination to embrace Pentecostalism officially. Thereupon, King and his followers agreed that the tongues-tested baptism was the reality they had been seeking in the earlier "baptism of fire" experience.

Pentecostalism injected such new life into the movement that King was kept busy developing new institutions for the now-growing denomination. In 1909 he moved his center of activities to Falcon, North Carolina, where he founded the monthly *Apostolic Evangel* and a new orphanage for the church.

In 1911 King took a two-year trip around the world in the interest of world missions. On this trip he preached for Thomas Ball Barrett in Oslo, Norway, and for Canon Harford-Battersby in Sunderland, England. While he was away on the world tour, the FBHC merged with the PHC (the smaller group) in Falcon, North Carolina, to form the present Pentecostal Holiness Church. Because he was away, King was not chosen to head the newly united church but was elected assistant general superintendent in charge of world missions. For four years he pastored the Memphis, Tennessee, church while heading the world missions department.

King was elected general superintendent of the church in 1917, a position he was to hold for the rest of his life with the exception of the years 1941–45 when Dan T. Muse was elected chairman. In 1920, after learning of the death of his first wife, he married Blanche Leon King, a teacher in the new Franklin Springs Institute near his home in Royston. They had four children, Easter Lily, Joseph, Jr., Virginia, and Mary Ann. In 1937 King was given the honorary title of bishop, the first man in the PHC to be so honored.

King's chief theological contribution was his 1911 book *From Passover to Pentecost*, which gave classic expression to the Holiness-Pentecostal teachings of the early Pentecostals. Over the years it became required reading for the ministers of the church.

When Bishop King died in Anderson, South Carolina, in 1946, he still held the chairman's position that he had inherited in 1900. At the time of his passing, the PHC had grown to include 26,000 members in seven hundred churches in the U.S., with hundreds of churches on the foreign mission fields.

Bibliography: J. Campbell, *The Pentecostal Holiness Church, 1898–1948* (1951); J. and B. King, *Yet Speaketh, The Memoirs of the Late Bishop Joseph H. King* (1949).   H. V. Synan

KINGDOM OF GOD It is unfortunate that the Hebrew *malkûth* and the Greek *basileia* are translated by the word "kingdom." In the Bible these are not geographical terms and do not speak of a territory governed by a king. They stand primarily for the sovereignty, the authority, and the power of God as king and refer to the *time* when he establishes his kingdom *rule*. The spiritual *realm* or *sphere* of this rule is implied. Better translations would be *reign, rule,* or *kingship*. It is primarily a soteriological concept that finds its main expression in the life and teaching of Jesus through whom the redemptive reign of God has become dynamically present in history. Since the Day of Pentecost the executive agent of God's redemptive activity and rule is the Holy Spirit. The return of Christ will bring the kingdom to its completion.

I. Historical Interpretations
II. Jewish Hopes and Expectations
III. The Central Theme of Jesus
IV. The Kingdom as Already Present
V. The Kingdom as a Future Event
VI. Pentecost and the Community of the Spirit
VII. The Apostolic Proclamation
VIII. Pentecostal-Charismatic Perspective

I. Historical Interpretations. In the first two centuries of the postapostolic Christian church, the kingdom of God was by and large conceived of as a hope belonging almost exclusively to the future triumphal reign of God. This was interpreted in millenarian terms. However, for the believers of the early church the kingdom was also an internalized spiritual reality that was to be experienced in an individual's reception and enjoyment of God's blessings. When the church was still a minority suffering external persecution and greatly concerned about its inner purity, it developed a tendency to withdraw from worldly affairs, awaiting the future coming of the kingdom to vindicate its cause.

The adoption of Christianity by Emperor Constantine (313) provided the religio-political context in which the church with its new and privileged status increasingly became a correlative term for the kingdom. The theologians of the Byzantine court developed the notion of the Christian imperium under the slogan "one God, one Logos, one Emperor, one Empire." The kingdom of God came to be seen as the *Corpus Christianum,* ruled by the *regnum* and *sacerdotum*. The church became a state church, the servant of the interests of the empire and at times ruling over it. Both the Eastern imperial theology and the Western episcopal theocracy actually reduced the understanding of the kingdom of God to the present earthly realities of caesaro-papal rule and power.

The medieval church followed Augustine, who in his influential *De Civitate Dei* (*The City of God*) identified the kingdom of God with the visible ecclesiastical system. This view has led to the sanction of the subsequent alliance of church and state with all of its tragic consequences, such as attempts to create by force a "pure" Holy Roman Empire and the "holy" crusades as replacements for the Christian mission.

The Reformers and their followers identified the kingdom of God with the invisible church. To them the kingdom was primarily a religious concept, a present spiritual reality of believers. Calvin went beyond that by developing a christocratic theology of the kingdom as exemplified by the experiment in Geneva where the church embodying the values of the kingdom of God was to have control over the secular affairs.

The debate about the kingdom of God over the last two centuries has been largely academic, with little relevance for the life and mission of the church. Albrecht Ritschl (1822–89) and his followers regarded the kingdom of God as a present reality at work within the evolutionary progress of human history moving toward higher levels of civilization and moral society. The eschatological expectations were totally discarded. This was the most prevalent view of liberal Protestantism in the latter part of the nineteenth century. It was an integral part of the religious ideology of humanism and corresponded well with the optimistic view of humanity and history characteristic of that period.

At the turn of the century, German NT scholarship, particularly reflected in the work of Johannes Weiss and Albert Schweitzer, reacted strongly against Ritschl's immanentistic conception in different ways and rediscovered the eschatological emphasis of Jesus' teaching. Their view became known as "consistent eschatology" or "thoroughgoing eschatology." It discounts the concept of an already-present kingdom in the life and ministry of Jesus, claiming that he expected an entirely future, apocalyptic reality that was to arrive through a world catastrophe in his own lifetime. This is also the view of Rudolf Bultmann and his followers, who deny the supernatural origin and mission of Jesus. They emphasize the primacy of those sayings of Jesus that point to that future apocalyptic coming of the kingdom and then reinterpret it in existential categories of present experience of humanity as it is continually faced with the challenges of decision for "authentic existence."

The opposing view, named "realized eschatology," was offered by Charles H. Dodd and other British scholars. They argued that the early church mistakenly interpreted the apocalyptic elements in the teaching of Jesus in a literal way. They are to be taken as merely symbolic for the kingdom of God as an already-present fact with the appearance and ministry of Jesus. In this view there is no room for God's final apocalyptic act at the end of history but only the historical outworking of God's redemptive action already undertaken.

The interpretations of both "thoroughgoing eschatology" and "realized eschatology" are one-sided and ignore the integrity of the teaching of

Jesus. Subsequent careful biblical studies (W. G. Kümmel; Oscar Cullmann; Joachim Jeremias; A. M. Hunter; Rudolf Schnackenburg; and, among Evangelicals, Herman Ridderbos and George E. Ladd) show convincingly that Jesus spoke of both the presence and the future coming of the kingdom, although in his sayings he did not always rigidly separate these two aspects. In his thorough and balanced study, Ladd (although very weak on the pneumatological aspect of the kingdom!) summarizes it succinctly: "For Jesus, the Kingdom of God was the dynamic rule of God which had invaded history in his own person and mission to bring men in the present age the blessings of the messianic age, and which would manifest itself yet again at the end of the age to bring this same messianic salvation to its consummation" (1964, 303).

II. Jewish Hopes and Expectations. In the OT the word "kingdom" is rarely used in relation to God. There is only one occurrence of the actual phrase "kingdom of God" in the form "kingdom of the LORD" (*malkûth Yahweh*) in 1 Chronicles 28:5. There are a few cases where the "kingdom," occasionally translated as "dominion," is ascribed to God (Pss. 22:28; 45:6; 103:19; 145:11–13; 1 Chron. 17:14; 29:11). The dynamic concept of God as King, ruling over all of his creation and especially over his people Israel is, however, implied or explicitly taught throughout the OT. God is recognized as king especially in the so-called enthronement psalms in the exclamation "Yahweh has become King" (Pss. 47:6–8; 93:1; 96:10; 97:1; 99:1) where the Hebrew "God reigns" is usually translated in English versions as "the Lord reigns." God's kingship is explicitly proclaimed by the prophets, especially Isaiah, Jeremiah (see e.g., his prophecies to the nations: Jer. 46:18; 48:15; 51:57), Ezekiel, and Daniel. The earliest use of the title King for Yahweh appears in the context of a vision Isaiah had when he saw "the King, the Lord Almighty" (Isa. 6:5). The eternal kingship of God is assumed in all the OT and Jewish thought.

In the OT prophetic visions there is also a strong eschatological element related to God's future kingship when his rule is to be universally acknowledged. This hope is combined with the messianic expectations (see Isa. 9:6–7; 11:1ff.) of the time when the future messianic successor of David will exercise royal authority over the redeemed people of God and his universal kingship will be recognized by all (Isa. 24:23; 45:23; Zech. 14:9; et al.). Daniel 4:34 speaks of God's rule as "an eternal dominion" and of "his kingdom [which] endures from generation to generation." More explicit is the prophecy of the time when "the God of heaven will set up a kingdom that will never be destroyed"; while it brings to an end all other kingdoms, "it will itself endure forever" (Dan. 2:44). The apocalyptic vision of the passing of all earthly empires as opposed by God's transcendent and eternal kingdom is climaxed in Daniel 7, where the heavenly "Son of Man" (royal title) is given "authority, glory and sovereign power" and is universally worshiped, and "his kingdom is one that will never be destroyed" (v. 14).

The Jews of the intertestamental period clung to the OT promises of the messianic deliverance. Their hope was further elaborated through apocalyptic imagery and intensified during the difficult times of suffering at the hands of foreign Gentile oppressors. They expected a Messiah who would soon bring about an apocalyptic reversal overthrowing the evil powers and restoring justice to the chosen people. They pictured a Davidic king (cf. 2 Sam. 7; Ps. 89:3–4, 29–37), a mighty conqueror over all the enemies of Israel, a heavenly supernatural Son of Man (as in the vision of Daniel). The promised kingdom of God that they were looking for (cf. Luke 2:25, 38; 23:51) and that fired their imaginations and inspired their political hopes of liberation explains why they "understood" and were ready without initial surprise to hear the message of John the Baptist: "Repent, for the kingdom of heaven is near" (Matt. 3:2).

The same message was adopted and further elaborated on by Jesus (Matt. 4:17) and, upon his special commission, proclaimed by the apostles (Matt. 10:7). God's appointed time had arrived, the kingdom had come in the very person of Jesus, who was the Son of Man of the vision of Daniel. It soon became clear, however, that the popular expectations of the Jews were not met by Jesus. He did proclaim justice, perform miracles, and draw large crowds. There were even moments such as the feeding of the five thousand when they were certain that he was the one whom they were eagerly expecting, and so in their zealous impatience they even tried to make him their king by force (John 6:15). Even his own disciples were not immune to these false hopes, both before and after the Resurrection (cf. Luke 24:21; Acts 1:6). He, however, did not come as a mighty king with glory and splendor, but rather as a Suffering Servant of Isaiah (part of the messianic prophecy, which they ignored), in humility, poverty, and weakness. His mission was totally different from their hopes and expectations. He was not to be their political liberator and earthly king, nor was he to fulfill their nationalistic dreams, take revenge on their enemies, and bring them material blessings.

Because of their special covenantal relationship with God, the Jews were to be the natural "sons of the kingdom" (Matt. 8:12; NIV inexactly translates *huioi* as "subjects"). Jesus was mindful of this, and the kingdom was at first offered "to the lost sheep of Israel" only (Matt. 10:5–7). But the Jews rejected the offer, and Jesus clearly told their religious leaders, "The kingdom of God will be taken away from you and given to a people who will produce its fruit" (Matt. 21:43). The promises and blessings, along with the special mission among the nations, which earlier belonged to Israel, were to be inherited by a new people of God, the church of Jesus Christ.

III. The Central Theme of Jesus. The idea of the kingdom of God occupies a place of supreme importance in the teaching and mission of Jesus. This "master-thought" of Jesus, as it has been called, is the central theme of his proclamation and the key to understanding his ministry. In the synoptic Gospels the term "kingdom" is used 121 times (not including parallels, over 60 times). The phrase "kingdom of the heavens" occurs 33 times and is limited to Matthew. Parallel passages make it clear that it is a linguistic variation of the same concept. It was a frequent Jewish practice to substitute an appropriate term for deity (cf. Matt. 21:25; Mark 14:61; Luke 15:21). For the identity of meaning see Matthew 19:23–24, where both expressions are used. Modern critical scholarship, despite various presuppositions and methodologies, agrees that the phrase "kingdom of God" expresses the focus of Jesus' proclamation and (in its Aramaic form) represents his authentic voice.

The ministry of Jesus begins with the announcement "The time has come. The kingdom of God is near. Repent and believe the good news" (Mark 1:15; cf. also Matt. 4:17). In these and other passages the Gospel writers consistently summarize the ministry of Jesus in terms of the kingdom of God. "Jesus went through all the towns and villages, teaching in their synagogues, *preaching the good news of the kingdom* and healing every disease and sickness" (Matt. 9:35; cf. also Luke 4:43; 8:1; 9:11). Jesus never defined the kingdom, although he convincingly demonstrated its power and illustrated it variously, especially through parables (e.g., Matt. 13; Mark 4). It was also the key message he instructed his disciples to proclaim when he sent them on missions (Matt. 10:7; Luke 9:2; 10:9, 11).

In the Gospels four basic meanings of the term "kingdom" can be discerned: (1) an abstract meaning of the reign or rule of God; (2) a future apocalyptic order into which the righteous will enter at the end of the age; (3) the presence of the kingdom already among people, the present challenge and the power already operative in the world; and (4) a present realm or sphere into which people are entering now (Ladd, 1964, 119).

It is clear from the teaching of Jesus that in terms of its realization the kingdom of God is both a present reality and a promise of a future fulfillment. It focuses on Jesus (the King) with whose arrival the new age of salvation has already begun. In the Incarnation, through the death and resurrection of Jesus (the unique and unrepeatable Christ-Event) God has definitely acted within human history in order to accomplish his redemptive purposes. Throughout the NT the concept of the "two ages" is presupposed. The followers of Christ live as "between the times," within the two-advent structure of salvation history. The present reign of Christ thus has two crucial points of reference. The first is a foundational one, the past accomplished act of redemption by the death and resurrection of Jesus, who inaugurated his rule in the believing community. The kingdom has already come in the person of Jesus. The second point of reference lies still in the future return of Christ, which will bring the drama of redemption to its completion. In his person and ministry the messianic salvation foretold by the prophets was already fulfilled, but there still remained a future eschatological consummation. What was *already* begun when Jesus inaugurated

the kingdom is *yet* to be fully realized when he comes in power and glory.

Such an understanding of salvation history is based on the teaching of Jesus himself and further elaborated in the rest of the NT, especially in the Pauline writings. The sayings of Jesus about the kingdom of God clearly though paradoxically imply both that the kingdom is already present in the person and acts of Jesus and that it will come in a final apocalyptic arrival and completion at the end of the age. The attempts to bring these two into one consistent pattern, as done by either "futurist" or "realized" eschatologists, are exegetically unacceptable. Both aspects of the teaching of Jesus have to be recognized and the tension between the two (the "already" and the "not yet") acknowledged also as the distinguishing mark of the present age.

IV. The Kingdom as Already Present. Jesus makes it very clear that in his own person the kingdom of God has already entered human history. To the question of the Pharisees as to "when the kingdom of God would come," he replied, "The kingdom of God is among you" (Luke 17:20–21). In another difficult saying Jesus indicated that the kingdom of God is present and forcefully at work in such a way that men are now seizing it or are being violently seized by it (Matt. 11:12–13; Luke 16:16). The overthrow of Satan's reign has already begun, the power of the future age is already operative in the present world, and the messianic blessings are available to those who respond. In the Beelzebub controversy Jesus clearly states that his power over the evil spirits is a sign of the arrival of the kingdom. "If I drive out demons by the Spirit [Luke: "finger"] of God, then the kingdom of God has come upon you" (Matt. 12:28; Luke 11:20). Jesus is the stronger man, now on the scene, who is able to bind the strong man (devil) and spoil his goods (Matt. 12:29; Mark 3:27).

In Jesus the presence of the kingdom is manifested primarily in two ways: in his preaching-teaching of the kingdom and in the miraculous demonstrations of the power of the kingdom. Jesus understood that the proclamation of the kingdom was his primary mission. His days of ministry are characterized as the time in which "the good news of the kingdom of God is being preached" (Luke 16:16). When shortly after his inaugural and programmatic sermon in Nazareth, the people of Capernaum, impressed by his miracles, tried to keep him from leaving them, he told them, "I must preach the good news of the kingdom of God to other towns also, because that is why I was sent" (Luke 4:43). Almost consistently, however, the verbal announcement of the nearness or arrival of the kingdom was accompanied by powerful demonstrations of victory over evil through miracles in general and the casting out of demons in particular.

In his "Nazareth Manifesto" Jesus quotes the messianic announcement of Isaiah 61: "The Spirit of the Lord is on me, because he has anointed me to preach good news to the poor. He has sent me to proclaim freedom for the prisoners and recovery of sight for the blind, to release the oppressed, to proclaim the year of the Lord's favor," and then Jesus explicitly identified himself with its fulfillment: "Today this scripture is fulfilled in your hearing" (Luke 4:18–21). In a similar way, pointing to his miracles and proclamation, he answered the question of John the Baptist as to his identity: "The blind receive sight, the lame walk, those who have leprosy are cured, the deaf hear, the dead are raised, and the good news is preached to the poor" (Matt. 11:5). The same pattern is evident in Jesus' sending out of his disciples with the twofold task of proclaiming the kingdom and performing the signs that characterize its arrival—healing the sick and casting out demons (Matt. 10:7–8; Luke 10:9, 11, 17). In summary, the preaching of the gospel and the miracles of healing and exorcism are signs of the presence of the kingdom of God.

To simply equate the arrival of the kingdom with the presence of the person of Jesus is, however, to ignore another significant biblical emphasis: the role of the Holy Spirit in the inauguration and ministry of the kingdom. Jesus knew that at his baptism he was uniquely "anointed with the Spirit" (Matt. 3:16; Mark 1:10; Luke 3:22). "Whatever else this meant, it meant equipment with divine power," for it is clear that "his conquest of disease and the devil are inspired by God's Spirit. His 'acts of power' reveal the energizing of God's Spirit through himself for the saving of sick and sinful men and women" (Hunter, 1950, 85).

The pneumatological aspect of the ministry of Jesus has until recently been widely neglected in the studies of the kingdom of God. It is, however, clear from the gospel accounts that the reception of the Spirit at his baptism was a turning point for the self-understanding of Jesus, launching him into his charismatic ministry. Thus it is of crucial importance for the understanding of our theme. "The decisive indication that the kingdom was present for Jesus was the presence of the Spirit working in and through him. The break between John and Jesus must therefore have been occasioned by Jesus' awareness of the Spirit: the eschatological Spirit was already upon him—therefore John's message and ministry was already superseded" (Dunn, 1975, 64).

V. The Kingdom as a Future Event. The kingdom of God, which in Jesus Christ became the present reality (the "already"), is at the same time a promise that is to be fulfilled in the future end of the age (the "not yet" aspect of the kingdom). While the kingdom of Satan has already been invaded by Jesus in the power of the Spirit, there yet remains a future eschatological consummation accompanied by the final destruction of Satan and the complete victory over all evil and its consequences. The Son of Man will come in power and glory (Matt. 24:30; 26:64; Mark 8:38; Luke 9:26). The final separation will take place when the wicked will be judged and the righteous will "inherit the kingdom" (Matt. 13:36–43; 25:31–46). The great reversal will be accompanied ("the first will be last and the last will be first"), the material order will be transformed, and eternal life will be given as an inheritance to the followers of Jesus (Matt. 19:28–30; Mark 10:29–31; Luke 18:29–30).

Several times Jesus pictures the time of the eschatological fulfillment of the kingdom in terms of a messianic banquet or marriage feast (Matt. 8:11; 22:1ff.; 26:29; Mark 14:25; Luke 14:15–24; 22:28–30). In various ways he describes this fullness of eschatological salvation as an *entrance* into eternal life (Mark 9:45; 10:17, 30; cf. also Matt. 25:46), into the age to come (Mark 10:30), and into the kingdom of God (Mark 9:47; 10:24). The return of the King will be a total surprise and requires watchfulness (Matt. 24:37–44; 25:1–13; Luke 12:35–48; 13:22–30). Jesus promised his disciples that in the age to come they would share his fellowship and his authority to rule (Matt. 26:29; Luke 22:29–30).

Jesus is not elaborating on the chronology of the consummation of the kingdom. His primary concern is "with its essential character, the demands it makes upon its members, the righteousness it requires, and its ultimate perfect consummation" (Ladd, 1952, 73). The Gospels focus on a single redemptive end-time event centering in the return of the Son of Man, to be accompanied by resurrection (Luke 20:35–36) and final judgment (Matt. 25:31ff.). Whether there are two future stages of the consummation as interpreted by premillennialists on the basis of Revelation 20 is a much-debated question.

VI. Pentecost and the Community of the Spirit. The resurrection of Jesus was the key redemptive event ushering the powers of the age to come into the present age by transforming the finality of the death of Jesus into a triumph over it. This significant event marked off the disciples of Jesus as the community who believed in the risen Lord. The risen One, has, however, announced another end-time event of determinative significance for their life and mission—"You will be baptized in the Holy Spirit" (Acts 1:5). This was to be a part of the fulfillment of the OT prophecy for the messianic age of the "last days" (Joel 2:28; Acts 2:17). However the "Johannine Pentecost" (John 20:22) is interpreted, it is clear that John emphasizes a theological continuum between the Cross, the Resurrection, the Ascension, and the outpouring of the Holy Spirit. The Spirit is to "replace" Jesus as the "other Paraclete" (John 14:16) and is given as a guarantee of the efficacious continuity of Christ's work in the community of his believers. The power of the kingdom was no longer to be limited to Jesus and the apostolic circle. The Pentecostal promise of God—"I will pour out my Spirit on all people"— was fulfilled. This means that in and through the church the Spirit is to continue and to universalize the kingdom ministry of Jesus himself.

The way the central concern of Jesus (the kingdom of God) is tied in with Pentecost and the apostolic church is indicated by Luke in the opening verses of Acts. In his postresurrection appearances Jesus "spoke about the kingdom of God" (1:3). It was in this context that he commanded his followers to "wait for the gift of my Father" to be "baptized with the Holy Spirit" (1:4–5). To their question about the timing of the restoration of the "not yet" kingdom, he responds pointing to the "already" pneumatological aspect of his reign—"But you will receive power when the Holy Spirit comes on you; and you will be my witness . . . to the ends of the earth" (1:6–8; cf. also Luke 24:49). From the Day of Pentecost on, "all that Jesus began to do and to teach" (Acts 1:1), as the One who was anointed by the Spirit to inaugurate the kingdom of God, was to be carried on by the new Spirit-filled community.

The fulfillment of the promise of Jesus was the Pentecostal experience of the mighty, visible, and audible manifestation of the divine power when "all of them were filled with the Holy Spirit and began to speak in tongues as the Spirit enabled them" (Acts 2:4). "The Pentecostal narrative is the story of the transfer of the charismatic spirit from Jesus to the disciples . . . having become the exclusive bearer of the Holy Spirit at His baptism, Jesus becomes the giver of the Spirit at Pentecost" (Stronstad, 1984, 49). The Pentecost event became crucial for the launching and the constitution of the Christian church, the new eschatological community bound together by their loyalty to the risen Lord and their common experience of the Spirit. The beginning of the age of the Spirit is thus coterminous and coextensive with the age of the church, the community of the Spirit. Baptized in the Spirit, the early Christian community tasted the powers of the age to come, and it is not impossible that the outpouring of the Spirit and the beginning of the church was at first understood by them as a fulfillment of Jesus' words about the coming of the kingdom of God. It is a possible interpretation that Jesus meant the Pentecost event when he said that some of his disciples "will not taste death until they see the kingdom of God come with power" (Mark 9:1; cf. Matt. 16:28; Luke 9:27; the context primarily points, however, to the miracle of the Transfiguration). Pentecost certainly represents the "already" aspect of the coming of the kingdom with power.

The coming of the Spirit, the kingdom power, at Pentecost, marks the transfer of Jesus' kingdom ministry to his followers. In ways similar to Jesus at his baptism, the empowerment from above results in public witness, the proclamation of the gospel of the kingdom, which is accompanied by signs and wonders. The Spirit-filled community becomes a witnessing, missionary-oriented movement, battling against the forces of Satan and extending God's rule among the nations. The Book of Acts portrays a church that is essentially a community of the Spirit, experiencing at its very inception an apocalyptic-like harvest and taking the gospel to the ends of the world. This mission of the church is not something that is carefully planned and executed according to a preconceived strategy of the apostolic leadership in Jerusalem. It is a spontaneous Spirit-driven and Spirit-controlled movement proceeding from the nature of the Spirit-filled community. "The initiative is with the Spirit; the Church follows" (Newbigin, 1980, 39).

VII. The Apostolic Proclamation. A frequent modern charge by liberal Christianity against the early church and especially against the apostle Paul was that it reduced the message of Jesus about the kingdom of God to a religion about Jesus. This is a misplaced accusation. Although it is true that the phrase "kingdom of God" is used less frequently than in the Synoptic Gospels, it is not totally absent from the apostolic proclamation (see, e.g., Acts 17:7; 19:8; 20:25; 28:23, 31; Rom. 14:17; 1 Cor. 4:20). The term *basileia* appears eight times in Acts and fourteen times in the Pauline Epistles and the contexts reveal that the concept of the kingdom is of major importance in the preaching of Paul and essentially synonymous with its use by Jesus.

On the other hand, Paul the missionary-theologian of the Gentiles, took the original messianic language of the kingdom of God as used by Jesus and translated it with a "dynamic equivalent," using the more familiar language of his new audience in the wider mission field. The evangelist John for similar contextualizing reasons more or less replaced the term "kingdom of God" with "(eternal) life," retaining the continuity of meaning (cf. John 3:3, 5 with 3:36 and further use of "life" in John). In the Book of Acts the term "kingdom" gives way to the term "gospel" or simply to "Jesus," but it is obvious that the message is the same. The person of Jesus and his accomplished work of redemption rightfully replaced the kingdom of Christian proclamation. The proclaimer of the kingdom became the proclaimed One. This is not a betrayal but an expression of faithfulness to the original message of Jesus in whom the kingdom was present. "If they had simply preached the kingdom of God there would have been no gospel. The *news* is that 'the kingdom of God' is no longer merely a theological phrase. There is now a name and a human face" (Newbigin, 1980, 32). The message of the kingdom is inseparable from the name of Jesus. "The apostle would have denied the central message of Jesus if he had not made that shift of language from 'kingdom' to 'Jesus' " (ibid., 33).

The synonymous uses of these terms in the apostolic kerygma are the best illustration of our point. Philip, the charismatic evangelist, "proclaimed the Christ" and "preached the good news of the *kingdom of God* and the *name of Jesus Christ*" (Acts 8:5, 12). The Acts account similarly ends with two summaries of Paul's final ministry in Rome. He "declared to them the *kingdom of God* and tried to convince them *about Jesus*" and in the final words, "preached the *kingdom of God* and taught about the *Lord Jesus Christ*" (Acts 28:31). The Pauline Epistles make it clear that in their use the *lordship of Christ* is the same as the *kingship of Jesus*. Paul finds the best expression in a term that was widely used in a number of convergent areas of the wide Mediterranean basin: the Septuagint (Greek OT), in which Yahweh is "LORD," Roman politics marked by Caesar's claim to be the sole *Lord*, the heathen temple and the slave market. The (baptismal) confession of faith that "Jesus [Christ] is Lord" (cf., e.g., Acts 16:31; Rom. 10:9; 1 Cor. 12:3; 2 Cor. 4:5; Phil. 2:11) becomes thus the equivalent of the acknowledgment of Jesus as King and the point of entrance into the realm of his kingdom. This aspect of proclamation of the early church is summarized by K. L. Schmidt:

We can see why the apostolic and the post-apostolic Church of the NT did not speak much of the *basileia tou theou* explicitly, but always emphasized it implicitly by its reference to the *kurios Iēsous Christos.* It is not true that it now substituted the Church (*ekklēsia*) for the Kingdom as preached by Jesus of Nazareth. On the contrary, faith in the Kingdom of God persists in the post-Easter experience of Christ (Schmidt, TDNT, 1964, 1:589).

Thus the apostolic "to know Christ" became an equivalent of the synoptic "entry into the kingdom." This further confirms that in the NT the kingdom of God is a dynamic and primarily a soteriological concept.

VIII. Pentecostal-Charismatic Perspective.

The biblical motif of the kingdom of God provides the essential theological framework for understanding the contemporary Pentecostal-charismatic phenomenon. The two basic characteristics that mark the age of the church—the witness of Jesus and the activity of the Holy Spirit—are hallmarks of Pentecostal-charismatic Christianity. They exemplify in a remarkable way that "the kingdom is known by the dynamic activity of Christ in the church as it proclaims His name in the power of the Holy Spirit" (Pomerville, 1985, 157).

Pentecostals and charismatics are convinced, with the apostle Paul, that "the kingdom of God is not a matter of talk but of power" (1 Cor. 4:20), and expect that the preaching of the Word of God be accompanied by mighty acts of the Holy Spirit. They model their ministry after Jesus who, "anointed with the Holy Spirit and power," not only preached the gospel of the kingdom, but also demonstrated its presence as "he went around doing good and healing all who were under the power of the devil" (Acts 10:38). In the model ministry of Jesus the miracles were "far from being an addendum to his gospel, they were an integral part of it; they were, in one phrase, the kingdom of God in action. Preaching and mighty acts were complementary parts in one great campaign against the dominion of evil" (Hunter, 1950, 56). Equally for the followers of Jesus who believe the "whole/full gospel," the commission to preach the good news of the kingdom of God is linked with the equipping power of the Holy Spirit to overcome the forces of evil. The gift of the Spirit was not just a historical sign of the coming of the new age but also the opening of the era of the Spirit in which the power of the kingdom is to be continuously and presently manifested. Wherever the presence of the kingdom is experienced through the mediation of the Spirit, preaching and healing along with deliverance are not regarded as disparate tasks. Pentecostals and charismatics believe that the same power and blessings that were evident in the ministry of Jesus and experienced by apostolic Christianity are also available to the modern-day followers of Jesus.

The Pentecostal and charismatic movements are marked by a revitalization of the eschatological orientation of the Christian faith. While they joyfully *participate* in the blessings of the kingdom as it is *already* manifested through the Holy Spirit, they also keep alive the eager *expectation* of the return of the Lord "in power and glory."

The classical Pentecostals interpret the Azusa Street revival and the subsequent phenomenal growth of their movement as an eschatological outpouring of the Holy Spirit. Joel's prophecy (2:28–30) was one of the most frequently cited texts by early Pentecostals as they perceived their experience of Spirit baptism as an indication that they were living in "the last days." Such an understanding of participation in the climax of salvation history gave a special urgency to the task of world *evangelization* for which they felt empowered by the Holy Spirit (Acts 1:8). The readiness to obey the Great Commission was linked with faith in "the signs following" (Mark 16:17) and their mission interpreted in the eschatological framework of Matthew 24:14—"this gospel of the kingdom will be preached in the whole world . . . and then the end will come." Pentecostal missiologists thus argue that "the view of the Pentecostal movement as a missionary phenomenon is, in a sense, a manifestation of the very present and powerful kingdom of God" (Pomerville, 1985, 60).

The manifestation of biblical charismata, the experience of "joy in the Holy Spirit" (Rom. 14:17), and the anointed ministry in which signs and wonders confirm the proclamation of the Word are the distinguishing marks of the kingdom of God at work. In the age of rationalism, theological liberalism, and religious pluralism, Pentecostals and charismatics believe that evidential supernatural activity of the Holy Spirit validates the Christian witness. As in the apostolic days, the Holy Spirit is the very life of the church and its mission, not replacing but always exalting Christ the Lord. This is the Spirit's primary mission and the way in which the kingdom of God is actualized in the believing community. Christ rules where the Spirit moves!

Bibliography. O. Cullman, *Christ and Time* (1950); J. D. G. Dunn, *Jesus and the Spirit* (1975); A. M. Hunter, *The Work and Words of Jesus* (1950); D. B. Kraybill, *The Upside-Down Kingdom* (1978); W. G. Kümmel, *Promise and Fulfillment* (1957); P. Kuzmič, "The Church and the Kingdom of God," in B. J. Nicholls, *The Church: God's Agent for Change* (1986), 49–81; G. E. Ladd, *Crucial Questions About the Kingdom of God* (1952); idem, *Jesus and the Kingdom* (1964), rev. ed. as *The Presence of the Future* (1974); G. T. Montague, *Holy Spirit: Growth of a Biblical Tradition* (1976); L. Newbigin, *Sign of the Kingdom* (1980); N. Perrin, *The Kingdom of God in the Teaching of Jesus* (1963); P. A. Pomerville, *The Third Force in Missions* (1985); H. Ridderbos, *The Coming of the Kingdom* (1962); P. Robertson, *The Secret Kingdom* (1982); K. L. Schmidt, "Basileia," TDNT (1964), 1:574–93; R. Schnackenburg, *God's Rule and Kingdom* (1963); H. A. Snyder, *The Community of the King* (1977); R. Stronstad, *The Charismatic Theology of St. Luke* (1984); W. Willis, ed., *The Kingdom of God in Twentieth-Century Interpretation* (1987); J. Wimber, *Power Evangelism* (1986).   P. Kuzmič

KNIGHT, CECIL BRIGHAM (1925–). The

fifteenth general overseer of the Church of God (CG, Cleveland, Tenn.). A native of Alabama, Cecil B. Knight began his ministry in 1944 and pastored churches in Mississippi, Alabama, and Florida before being assigned to youth and Christian education work in 1956. While he served in CG youth and Christian education, he also served as Pentecostal Fellowship of North America youth commission secretary. He earned degrees from the University of Southern Mississippi (B.S., 1948) and Butler University (M.A., 1968). His work in Christian education produced a book on *Keeping the Sunday School Alive* (1959).

Knight's two-year tenure as general overseer (1976–78) was followed by four years as president of the Church of God School of Theology (1978–82). He was the first full-time president of that institution. In 1982 he was reelected to his denomination's executive committee.

Bibliography: Archives of the Church of God (Cleveland, Tenn.).   C. W. Conn

KNIGHT, GILES N. (d. 1968). Minister, administrator, and personal manager for Aimee Semple McPherson, 1936–44. A faithful member of the Angelus Temple staff, Giles N. Knight, one of the first two persons awarded an honorary doctor of divinity degree from L.I.F.E. Bible College, worked his way up through the ranks of "Sister's" staff. During 1936 it became obvious that the Angelus Temple Commissary, while meeting thousands of needs in the area, was causing a substantial drain on the financial resources of the congregation. Threatened by foreclosure on certain temple properties, on July 10, 1936, Sister McPherson named Giles Knight to the post of assistant business manager. He was given the responsibility to place the temple on a "cash basis." Knight's appointment and subsequent hard-line fiscal policies led to some friction with Roberta Semple (who had previously held Knight's position); Harriet Jordan, dean of the college; and Rheba Crawford, associate pastor. Ultimately, "Sister" threw her support totally to Knight, who through hard work and extensive fund-raising activities was able to retire the temple's indebtedness by 1938. During these and subsequent years he managed Aimee's personal schedule as well. Knight held the position of vice-president and secretary-treasurer of Angelus Temple, L.I.F.E., and the Echo Park Evangelistic Association until he was succeeded by Rolf McPherson on February 1, 1944. Giles Knight died on July 13, 1968, in Santa Barbara, California.

Bibliography: A. Semple McPherson, *Aimee Semple McPherson: The Story of My Life* (1973); L. Thomas, *Storming Heaven* (1970).   C. M. Robeck, Jr.

KNOWLEDGE, WORD OF

Introduction. The actual phrase "word of knowledge" (*logos gnōseōs*) is found only once in the NT, as the second in the list of nine "manifestations of the Spirit" in 1 Corinthians 12:7–10. To grasp its significance, we will first consider the NT notion of knowledge in general, then the word of knowledge in particular and, finally, some ancient and modern applications of the term to aspects of church life.

I. Some General Considerations Regarding "Knowledge" in the New Testament. (For OT

and intertestamental background, see bibliography under Brown and Bultmann). The word *gnōsis* ("knowledge") occurs 29 times in the NT, 21 of which are in the recognized Pauline writings (16 in 1 and 2 Corinthians). The correlate *epignōsis* occurs 20 times, mostly in the Pauline literature but never in the Corinthian correspondence. The verb form *ginōskein* is found 221 times, mostly in the Johannine writings (82 times), while *epiginōskein* occurs 44 times (Acts, 13 times; Pauline writings, 12 times; never in Johannine literature). Most of the theologically significant occurrences of these words occur in John and Paul, with John using the verb form exclusively (as he does for *pisteuein* [except for 1 John 5:4]) and Paul making use of the substantive form as well as the verb.

A. Johannine Usage. While exploiting and transposing the rich OT notion of the "knowledge of God," John distinguishes that act by which one comes to know God or the things of God (*ginōskein*) from the fact of possessing knowledge (*eidenai*; see de la Potterie, 1959). Eternal life is coming to know God and growing in that knowledge of him as well as of Jesus Christ whom he has sent (John 7:3). In the better reading of John 14:7, Jesus tells Philip, "If you knew me, you will know my Father; and from now on you do know him and have seen him." Those who have really seen Jesus, that is, come to know him, have begun to see and know the Father. Such knowledge is the fruit of faith: "We have believed and come to know that you are the Holy One of God" (John 6:69).

B. Pauline Usage.

1. General. The Fourth Gospel and the Johannine writings in general are but an intensification of movements of thought begun much earlier in the Christian community. The overall Pauline use of words related to the root *gnō* is a good illustration of this, though the distinction between this root and the other root expressing knowledge (*id*) is not developed as in John.

Paul speaks of an "ignorance of God" (1 Cor. 15:34; see 1 Peter 2:15; also Acts 17:30; Eph. 4:18; 1 Peter 1:14) and of the Gentiles who "have no knowledge of God" (*eidotes*–Gal. 4:8; 1 Thess. 4:5; 2 Thess. 1:8; compare LXX Ps. 78:6). He asserts in the tradition of the OT that God can be known through his works (Rom. 1:19ff.; cf. Job 12:7–9; Wisd. Sol. 13:1–9); and that it is precious to know the will of God (Hos. 4:6; Mal. 2:7; Rom. 12:2; Phil. 1:9; Col. 1:9), to walk in the way that pleases him, and to come to know him (Col. 1:10; see Eph. 1:17). Important as it is to know God, however, it is more important to be known by him (Gal. 4:9; 1 Cor. 8:3; 13:12; esp. Rom. 8:29) and to be in awe of his wisdom and knowledge (Rom. 11:33).

For Paul, all that was promised in the old covenant is transcendently fulfilled in "knowing Christ" (Phil. 3:8, 10) in whom are hidden all the treasures of wisdom and knowledge (Col. 2:3; see Philem. 6), and on whose face shines the light of the new creation, giving knowledge of God's glory (2 Cor. 4:6). This consideration of Paul's teaching on knowledge is in keeping with the teaching of the Christian community at large.

This same teaching is retained but receives particular accent in what is termed his First Letter to the Corinthians.

2. *In the Corinthian Correspondence.* The density of the occurrence of the word *gnōsis* in the Corinthian correspondence noted above (ten times in 1 Corinthians alone) indicates that Paul is dealing with a problem whose particular shading and choice of vocabulary is due to the situation at Corinth. He begins by complimenting the Corinthians for being rich in "all word and all knowledge" (1 Cor. 1:5) but continues by finding fault with them because their community is riddled by "factions" (1:11). Realizing that their divisions arise from fleshly thinking about divine relatives, he proposes as a remedy the "word of the cross" (1:18) and goes on to speak of the nature of true wisdom, describing it as the result of God's revelatory action through the Spirit (2:10), expressed not in "words of human wisdom but in those taught by the Spirit" (2:13).

Paul returns to the theme of "knowledge" in his discussion of meat offered to idols (1 Cor. 8:1–13). His ironic use of the term allows us to see that one particular instance of fleshly thinking at Corinth was the Corinthians' pride in having "knowledge" regarding the spiritual forces in this world and the manner in which these find expression in idols. This knowledge makes them superior to pagans and weaker Christians but, as Paul points out, it only puffs them up since it does not lead to love and service (8:1).

II. The Word of Knowledge.

Finally, in chapter 12, Paul arrives at another source of pride and division among the Corinthians: their misunderstanding of charismatic gifts and their exaggerated esteem for the more dramatic of these gifts. Here, his response is, first, to point to the Trinitarian source of all Christian charisms, services, and forms of work and, then, to give a list of "manifestations" of the one and same Spirit. The first two are described this way: "To one, through the Spirit is given a word of wisdom, to another a word of knowledge according to the same Spirit" (12:8).

Two things must be noted here. First, the accent is on the notion of "word." This corresponds to the twofold compliment in chapter 1 as well as to the distinction between words of human wisdom and those taught by the Spirit in 1 Corinthians 2:13, and to the distinction between "word" and "knowledge" made in 2 Corinthians 11:6. The gift is the capacity to express verbally either wisdom or knowledge. Commentators as diverse as Chrysostom, *Homily 29 on 1 Corinthians PG* 61, 245; Aquinas, *In Primam ad Corinthios* 12, Lect. 2; Robertson and Plummer, 1914, 265; Allo, 1956, 325; and Fee, 1987, 592–93, have noted this.

Second, we may note that Paul is making a distinction in descending order. Wisdom is named first and is "through the Spirit," thus accenting the fact that both content and expression are the direct work of the Spirit through both revelation and *logos*, respectively. Knowledge is named second and is "according to the Spirit." Its content may or may not be the result of revelation and seems to do with "knowledge of

creatures as they reveal God's plan" (Aquinas) or "Christian insight into the realities of Christian existence here and now and its practical consequences" (Pearson, 1973, 42). Paul is talking about the charismatic capacity to communicate this insight and thus seems to be touching upon certain aspects of teaching. This has been frequently suggested.

In the other occurrences of the word *gnōsis* in his discussion of spiritual gifts, Paul does not restrict himself to a meaning for it that is distinct from wisdom. Thus in 13:2 he describes the result of prophecy as knowing "all mysteries [refer to 2:7, 10] and all knowledge." His long consideration of knowledge in 13:8–12 certainly uses the term generically, as does his mention of speaking "either by [*en*] revelation, or by knowledge, or by prophecy, or by teaching" (14:6). In another context (Rom. 15:14), Paul seems to divide the gifts into "knowledge" and "power" in much the same way as 1 Peter 4:11 divides them into "speaking" and "serving."

Given this diversity of reference and yet occasional distinction between wisdom and knowledge, we may say that when Paul draws a difference, wisdom refers to divinely conferred revelational understanding of God and his plan of salvation while knowledge refers to an understanding of the practical working out of that plan here and now. We may then define the gift of "word of knowledge" as being the charismatically endowed capacity to express some aspect of God's plan as it is at work in creation here and now, revealing something of God.

III. The Word of Knowledge in Tradition.

Tradition often reflects the fluid use of the term *gnōsis* that we have noted in Paul (Dupont, 1960), often extending this to include the phrase "word of knowledge." For instance, Origen linked both the word of wisdom and the word of knowledge to the understanding of Scripture (*On Principles* 1:8; *PG* 11:119), while Diadochus of Photike taught that *gnōsis* described experiential, transforming knowledge of God and *sophia* referred to the gift of being able to teach divine things (*One Hundred Chapters*, 9; *Sources Chrétiennes*, 5bis, 88ff.). Because of the gnostic heresy, this type of terminology became infrequent.

In our own day, a very special gift, that of knowing what God is doing at this moment in another's soul or body, or of knowing the secrets of another's heart (the ancients' *kardiagnōsis*), is often described as a "word of knowledge." This gift is particularly common among Pentecostals and those involved in the charismatic movement. The existence of the gift and its divine origin and fruit are unquestionable. (See bibliography under Madre and Linford.)

The word of knowledge serves a valuable purpose since by revealing to one person what God is doing in another person, God stirs up faith and allows someone to reach out more firmly for the gifts of healing, consolation, etc. that he is offering. In such contexts, the word of knowledge works in close harmony with the charismatic gift of faith (see FAITH, GIFT OF).

If the definition given above of the "word of

knowledge" is accepted, then this modern use has a certain basis in Scripture. In strictly Pauline terminology, the gift could perhaps better be classified as a type of revelation (1 Cor. 14:30) pertaining to prophecy (1 Cor. 14:24–25). It might also be termed a certain type of discernment.

See also GIFTS OF THE SPIRIT, PAULINE LITERATURE.

Bibliography: E. B. Allo, *Saint Paul. Première Epître aux Corinthiens* (1956); C. Brown, ed., *The New International Dictionary of New Testament Theology,* s.v. "Knowledge" (1971), 2:390–409; R. Bultmann, "Ginōskō," *TDNT* (1964), 1:689–718; I. de la Potterie, "Oida et ginōskō, les deux modes de la connaissance dans le quatrième Evangile" *Biblica* 40 (1959): 709–25; J. Dupont, *Gnosis. La Connaissance Religieuse dans les Epîtres de Saint Paul,* 2d ed. (1960); A. Linford, *A Course of Study on Spiritual Gifts* (n.d.); P. Madre, *Le Charisme de Connaissance,* 2nd ed. (1985); B. Pearson, *The Pneumatikos-Psychikos Terminology in 1 Corinthians,* SBL diss., 12 (1973); A. Robertson and A. Plummer, *A Critical and Exegetical Commentary on the First Epistle of St. Paul to the Corinthians, ICC,* 2d ed. (Clark, 1914).
R. F. Martin

KUHLMAN, KATHRYN (1907–76). The world's most widely known female evangelist. After completing the tenth grade—all that was offered—Kathryn Kuhlman began her ministry at age sixteen, assisting her sister and brother-in-law. She was soon on her own, itinerating in Idaho, Utah, and Colorado, finally settling down in Denver in 1933 in the Kuhlman Revival Tabernacle. By 1935 she had established the 2,000-seat Denver Revival Tabernacle. She effectively used the media and established an influential radio ministry. Her marriage to an evangelist, who divorced his wife to marry Kuhlman, destroyed her Denver ministry. They continued to evangelize, but apparently after about six years—she was silent on the subject—she left him and started over again on her own.

In 1946 in Franklin, Pennsylvania, a woman was suddenly healed of a tumor during one of Kuhlman's services. This was to develop as a characteristic phenomena of the "miracle services." Kuhlman would call out the specific disorder that was being cured in a certain area of the auditorium, and it would be received by the appropriate individual. She again developed a daily radio ministry. In 1948 she moved to Pittsburgh, which remained her headquarters as she held regular services in Carnegie Hall and the First Presbyterian Church. She was catapulted toward national fame by a seven-page laudatory article in *Redbook* magazine.

From California in 1965 came the insistent invitation of Ralph Wilkerson of Anaheim Christian Center (later Melodyland). She began services at the Pasadena Civic Auditorium, which seated 2,500, but later moved to the Los Angeles Shrine Auditorium, where she regularly filled the 7,000 seats for ten years. She also continued the Pittsburgh meetings while expanding into television, producing more than five hundred telecasts for the CBS network. In 1972 she received the first honorary doctorate awarded by Oral Roberts University.

It was not until the mid 1960s that Kuhlman

Kathryn Kuhlman became one of America's best-known evangelists during the 1960s and 1970s.

became particularly identified with the charismatic movement. The older Pentecostals out of the Holiness tradition found her twice suspect: she was a divorcee, and she did not satisfy them by giving testimony in her ministry to any personal experience of speaking in tongues. She did not permit tongues in the regular course of the miracle services.

Kuhlman objected to the appellation "faith healer" and gave the credit to the power of the Holy Spirit. Believing that gifts of healing were for the sick, the only gift she claimed, if any at all, was that of "faith" or "the word of knowledge" (1 Cor. 12:8–9). She had no explanation of why some were healed and some not, but she emphasized that the greater miracle was the regeneration of the new birth and always referred to herself as an evangelist.

Apart from the well-documented healings, the most sensational phenomena associated with Kuhlman was "going under the power" (sometimes referred to as "slain in the Spirit") as people fell when she prayed for them. This sometimes happened to dozens at a time and occasionally hundreds.

Kuhlman was an incessant worker and gave meticulous attention to every detail of her services; everything had to be first-class. Conducting them herself, she was on her feet from four to five hours at a time. She was very dramatic in gesture and consciously deliberate in speech. She was a strikingly tall redhead and dressed elegantly. Her friend and biographer Jamie Buckingham admits: "She loved her expensive clothes, precious jewels, luxury hotels, and first class travel" (1976, 247). She was a star, even until her death just short of her seventieth birthday.

Bibliography: J. Buckingham, *Daughter of Destiny: Kathryn Kuhlman . . . Her Story* (1976); H. K. Hosier, *Kathryn Kuhlman: The Life She Led, the Legacy She Left* (1976).   D. J. Wilson

KUZMIČ, PETER (1946–). Author, educator, pastor, and church planter. Born into a Pentecostal pastor's home in Nuskova (Slovenija), Yugoslavia. His theological studies were taken at a Pentecostal Bible school in Erzhausen, West Germany (1970); B.A., Southern California College (1971); M.A., Wheaton College (1972); Dr.Theol., Catholic Faculty of Theology, University of Zagreb (1981).

Kuzmič is secretary of the governing body of *Kristova Pentecostal Crkva*, the organization for Pentecostal churches in Yugoslavia; cofounder and director of Biblijsko Teološki Institut in Osijek, Yugoslavia; and also pastor of a Pentecostal church there. In 1987 he gained recognition from the Assemblies of God (AG) Division of Foreign Missions as an "Approved Minister Abroad," while remaining in his native country.

An authority on Christianity and Marxism, Kuzmič has participated in many theological conferences and seminars in Western and Eastern Europe, India, Burma, the Philippines, South and Central Africa, and the U.S. He serves as chairman of the theological commission of the World Evangelical Fellowship; member of the executive committee of the Fellowship of European Evangelical Theologians; member of the Lausanne Committee for World Evangelization; and adjunct professor at the Assemblies of God Theological Seminary, Springfield, Missouri, and Fuller Theological Seminary, Pasadena, California.

His broader ecumenical work has taken him to the Sixth Assembly of the World Council of Churches, Vancouver (1983), and the Roman Catholic–Pentecostal Dialogue (1985). In addition to numerous journal and magazine articles, he authored *The Gospel of John* (1974), a study guide for the International Correspondence Institute.

Bibliography: "The Church Within Socialism," (interview with Peter Kuzmič) *World Evangelization* (June 1987), 5–6; P. Kuzmič, "BTI: A School With a Purpose," *PE* (May 31, 1987), 20–21; idem, "Evangelical Witness in Eastern Europe," *Serving Our Generation* (1980).   J. L. Sandidge

L

LA FONDATION See CHARISMATIC COMMUNITIES.

LABERGE, AGNES N. OZMAN See OZMAN, AGNES N.

LAKE, JOHN GRAHAM (1870–1935). Faith healer, missionary, and pastor. John G. Lake was ordained to the Methodist ministry at the age of twenty-one but chose a career in business rather than the appointment that he was offered. Lake became a very successful businessman, founding a newspaper and then moving into real estate and finally into the insurance business. Although he was offered a $50,000 a year guarantee to be the manager of an insurance trust, Lake felt that God was dealing with him to devote all of his energy to preaching the gospel.

The breakthrough of God into Lake's life centered around several remarkable healings in his family, culminating in the instantaneous healing of his wife from tuberculosis under the ministry of John Alexander Dowie in 1898. After experiencing these healings, Lake became associated with Dowie's ministry and served as an elder in the Zion Catholic Apostolic Church. Later, after leaving Dowie, Lake became involved in ministry at night while continuing in his business activities in the daytime. Lake sought God for the baptism in the Holy Spirit, and after nine months of seeking, Lake felt the power of God come upon him in answer to his prayers.

Shortly after receiving the baptism in the Holy Spirit in 1907 Lake felt God directing him to Africa. He left his job and distributed his funds and set out for Africa in faith that God would supply his family's needs. Lake, his wife and their seven children, and four other adults arrived in South Africa in the spring of 1908. The party of missionaries found that God had gone before them and prepared the way. A lady met them at the boat and provided them with a house because the Lord had spoken to her to provide for his servants. Unfortunately these miraculous provisions did not continue. The people thought that the missionaries were rich Americans, and so while Lake and his party poured all of their resources into the work, they were often without sufficient food to feed themselves.

Mrs. Lake died in December of 1908 while Lake was away on a preaching trip. It has been suggested that she died of overwork and malnutrition. Her death was a severe blow to Lake, and although he continued to minister in Africa for four more years, he was often stricken with loneliness, which eventually caused his return to the U.S. After returning to the States, Lake married Florence Switzer in 1913 and settled in Spokane, Washington, a year later.

It is estimated that during the next five or six years thousands of healings occurred through Lake's ministry. He moved to Portland, Oregon, in May 1920 and started a work similar to his work in Spokane. Lake's health did not allow him to complete his vision of a chain of healing institutions throughout the country, and he died of a stroke in 1935.

Following missionary service in South Africa, where he helped establish the Apostolic Faith Mission, John G. Lake started churches and healing centers in the Northwest.

Bibliography: J. G. Lake, *The Astounding Diary of Dr. John G. Lake* (1987); idem, *Spiritual Hunger and Other Sermons* (1987); G. Lindsay, *John G. Lake— Apostle to Africa* (1981).   J. R. Zeigler

LAMBERTH, ROY Twentieth-century pastor and Baptist charismatic leader. As pastor of Fern Creek First Baptist Church, Louisville, Kentucky, Lamberth gained a majority vote of personal support in the face of opposition to his involvement in the charismatic movement. Nonetheless, he resigned to become pastor of Trinity Baptist Church of Fern Creek. He was a preacher for the first national Southern Baptist Charismatic Conference in 1976.

Bibliography: T. Nicholas, "Singing in the Spirit: A New Tune for an Old Movement," *Southern Baptist Home Missions Magazine* (July–August 1976), 37.
          J. A. Hewett

LASOURD, SARAH CATHERINE MARSHALL See MARSHALL, SARAH CATHERINE.

LATIN AMERICAN COUNCIL OF CHRISTIAN CHURCHES See CONCILIO LATINO-AMERICANO DE IGLESIAS CRISTIANAS.

LATIN AMERICAN COUNCIL OF THE PENTECOSTAL CHURCH OF GOD OF NEW YORK See CONCILIO LATINO-AMER-

ICANO DE LA IGLESIA DE DIOS PENTECOSTAL DE NEW YORK.

LATTER RAIN See JOEL, BOOK OF.

LATTER RAIN MOVEMENT A Pentecostal movement of the mid twentieth century that, along with the parallel healing movement of that era, became an important component of the post-World War II evangelical awakening. Although highly controversial, the "New Order of the Latter Rain," as it was called by its opponents, bore certain similarities to the early Pentecostal movement that originated at Azusa Street, Los Angeles, in 1906. While its impact was on a small scale, its effects were nevertheless felt worldwide, and it became one of several catalysts for the charismatic movement of the 1960s and 1970s.

The movement was characterized by many reports of healings and other miraculous phenomena, in contrast to the preceding decade, which was described by Pentecostals as a time of spiritual dryness and lack of God's presence. It stressed the imminence of the premillennial return of Jesus Christ, preceded by an outpouring of God's Spirit, which was expected in accordance with the "former rain" and the "latter rain" of Joel 2:28 (KJV). This was interpreted as a dual prophecy of the Day of Pentecost as described in Acts 2 and of the outpouring of the Holy Spirit that was to immediately precede the coming of the Lord. There was an emphasis on spiritual gifts, which were to be received by the laying on of hands, in contrast to the old Pentecostal practice of "tarrying" for the Holy Spirit that had become widespread during the years prior to the revival.

Some of the influence precipitating the Latter Rain includes (1) William Branham, who exercised the laying on of hands in his healing ministry; (2) healing evangelist Franklin Hall's emphasis on fasting and prayer; (3) the church government format in use by the Independent Assemblies of God, which stressed the autonomy of the local church; and (4) the emphasis on the "new thing" of Isaiah 43:19 (KJV), which had found its way into the movement years after it was stressed during the meetings of the early Pentecostal revival at the turn of the century.

The Latter Rain movement originated at Sharon Orphanage and Schools in North Battleford, Saskatchewan, Canada, as a spark igniting an explosion of revival among many Pentecostals. It spread quickly throughout North America and many places around the world.

The president of Sharon's "Global Missions" was George Hawtin, who had been a pastor of the Pentecostal Assemblies of Canada (PAOC) and had founded Bethel Bible Institute in Star City, Saskatchewan, in 1935. Two years later the Institute moved to Saskatoon, and it became PAOC property in 1945 in order to achieve full PAOC recognition. Disputes between Hawtin and PAOC officials led to Hawtin's resignation under pressure in 1947; another Bethel teacher, P. G. Hunt, resigned in sympathy.

In the fall of 1947, George Hawtin and P. G. Hunt joined Herrick Holt of the North Battleford, Saskatchewan, Church of the Foursquare

Gospel in an independent work that Holt had already established. Milford Kirkpatrick joined them as "Global Missions" secretary, while George Hawtin's brother, Ern, came as a member of the faculty. During this time, the students began to gather to study the Word of God, with fasting and praying. According to Ern Hawtin, on February 12, 1948, God moved into their midst in a

strange new manner. Some students were under the power of God on the floor, others were kneeling in adoration and worship before the Lord. The anointing deepened until the awe of God was upon everyone. The Lord spoke to one of the brethren. "Go and lay hands upon a certain student and pray for him." While he was in doubt and contemplation, one of the sisters who had been under the power of God, went to the brother saying the same words, and naming the identical student he was to pray for. He went in obedience and a revelation was given concerning the student's life and future ministry. After this a long prophecy was given with minute details concerning the great thing God was about to do. The pattern for the revival and many details concerning it were given (E. Hawtin, 1949, 3).

After they had spent a day searching the Scriptures, it seemed on February 14 "that all Heaven broke loose upon our souls and heaven above came down to greet us" (G. Hawtin, 1950, 2). Ern Hawtin wrote, "Soon a visible manifestation of gifts was received when candidates were prayed over, and many as a result began to be healed, as gifts of healing were received" (E. Hawtin, 1949, 3). As people became aware of these events, they flocked to North Battleford from all parts of North America and many parts of the world to the camp meeting conventions at Sharon publicized by *The Sharon Star*. Before long, the teachers from Sharon began receiving invitations to minister throughout North America.

At the invitation of Reg Layzell in Vancouver, British Columbia, George and Ern Hawtin held meetings at Glad Tidings Temple during November 14–18, 1948. Myrtle D. Beall, pastor of Bethesda Missionary Temple in Detroit, Michigan, traveled 2,500 miles by car to attend these meetings and returned to her church to spark revival there, attracting people from all parts of the country, including Ivan and Carlton Spencer (the founder of Elim Bible Institute and his son). They had been in attendance at the Zion Evangelistic Fellowship in Providence, Rhode Island, for a Pentecostal Prayer Fellowship gathering in December 1948 when a latecomer arrived and shared "what he had heard of a visitation in Detroit." Ivan Spencer and his wife went to Detroit within a few days and returned to ignite revival at Elim Bible Institute.

Mrs. Beall wrote a letter describing the revival at Bethesda to Stanley Frodsham, who had been a pioneer of the early Pentecostal movement, a leader of the Assemblies of God denomination in the U.S., and the editor of the *Pentecostal*

Evangel, its official periodical, for twenty-eight years. As a result of this letter, he went to Mrs. Beall's church in January 1949, where "he was moved deeply by scenes of people under great conviction of sin, making confession and finding peace" (Menzies, 1971, 232).

In February 1949 Dr. Thomas Wyatt of Portland, Oregon, invited the Hawtin party to his church, Wings of Healing Temple, where George Hawtin and Milford Kirkpatrick ministered to ninety preachers from almost every part of North America. One of the pastors attending was Dr. A. Earl Lee of Los Angeles, California, whose church became a center of revival soon after he returned.

By 1949 the North Battleford brethren were becoming less central to the movement, and leadership began to emerge in other circles, partly as a result of tendencies toward sectarianism among the former. This was one of the reasons that the Latter Rain soon became anathema among many denominational Pentecostals. However, such Pentecostal stalwarts as Lewi Pethrus of Sweden continued to endorse the movement. As leaders of the Apostolic Church, Elim Bible Institute in New York State, and Bethesda Missionary Temple in Detroit, Michigan, continued to move in the revival, the movement progressed with lasting effects.

One of the most important publications of the Latter Rain movement was *The Feast of Tabernacles* by George Warnock, which later came to be republished by Bill Britton of Springfield, Missouri, and was widely disseminated during the next several decades. The thesis of Warnock's book was that although the Feast of Passover was fulfilled in the death of Christ and although the Feast of Pentecost had had its fulfillment in the outpouring of the Holy Spirit on the Day of Pentecost, the third of Israel's great feasts, the Feast of Tabernacles, is yet to be fulfilled. Those involved in the Latter Rain revival felt that this and many other insights into the Word of God had been given by the Holy Spirit within the context of the 1948 revival by prophetic revelation. This "blaze of prophetic light" was not restricted to the penetration of mysteries within the Bible but included the "unveiling of peoples' lives and hearts through the agency of the Spirit of God" working through the laying on of the hands of "prophets and apostles of His choosing." While many people received renewed faith and hope with respect to their gifts and callings as a result of prophetic ministry of this type, there were a few people whose faith had become shipwrecked, perhaps after receiving the laying on of hands with prophecy from inexperienced people or from others who may have engaged in these practices with mixed motives. The controversy that raged as a result of these problems served to discredit the entire movement in the eyes of most of the major Pentecostal denominations, including PAOC, the AG in the U.S., the PHC, and the Apostolic Church. Many experienced pastors were dropped from the rolls of these and other bodies for their involvement in the Latter Rain movement. At the third annual convention of the Pentecostal Fellowship of North America (PFNA) in 1950, for example, Ivan Q. Spencer

resigned under pressure from membership in the PFNA board of administration. He discovered later that the Elim Missionary Assemblies had been dropped from the list of associates because Spencer and this group of churches, which he represented, were actively involved in the Latter Rain movement.

Stanley Frodsham was also active in the movement. In a letter to his daughter, Faith Campbell (May 7, 1949), he wrote that it was inappropriate to associate "this new revival which God is so graciously sending, where so many souls are being saved, where so many lives are being transformed, where God is so graciously restoring the gifts of the Spirit, with the fanatical movements of the past 40 years." In 1949, under pressure and eligible to retire, Frodsham resigned from the editorship of the *Pentecostal Evangel* and withdrew his name as an ordained minister of the AG.

While there was not a general acceptance of the doctrines and practices of the Latter Rain within the denominational churches, there was a significant extent to which they were received outside of the major Pentecostal denominations. Many hundreds of "revival churches" became visible, particularly in North America, during the Latter Rain revival, not a few of which had been in existence prior to the revival. Most of these churches were independent and autonomous, and many became mother churches to numerous others that were established or nurtured by members of the mother church.

There were many other similarities between the early Pentecostal movement and the 1948 Latter Rain revival, both of which were known as the "Latter Rain movement." Both arose during a time of spontaneous evangelical awakening, and both were characterized by a strong expectation of the imminent coming of Christ. Both employed the laying on of hands for the impartation of gifts of the Spirit, and both reported the supernatural occurrence of "heavenly singing" by "Spirit-filled" congregations, the sounds of which were likened to the sounds of a great pipe organ. Both recognized the existence of present-day apostles, prophets, evangelists, pastors, and teachers, and both were characterized by widespread repentance and "brokenness" before the Lord. Such people as Stanley Frodsham, who had been present at both revivals, often remarked that there was the same strong atmosphere of the presence of the Lord in both cases.

Both movements were also severely criticized by the denominations of which they were originally a part. Walter J. Hollenweger (1965–67, 02a.02.144, 758) has observed that the institutional Pentecostal denominations at this time began to experience anew what had come about at the inception of their own movement but this time from the opposite standpoint: that of the conservative denominations that they had criticized at the time of their own inception.

The churches either spawned or influenced by the Latter Rain were usually independent assemblies with little or no central organization, and for this reason the extent of the influence of the Latter Rain was not always fully evident. However, many of those involved in the Latter Rain carried on and developed principles that had arisen in the late 1940s, becoming a vital part of the charismatic renewal in the 1960s and 1970s. Marion Meloon wrote of a blind woman on the staff of Elim Bible Institute, Rita Kelligan, who, at a fall convention in 1949, developed a gift of setting psalms to music, "giving us the rich heritage that forms part of the charismatic renewal worship today" (1974, 160). Some of the other distinctive beliefs and practices of the Latter Rain that found their way into the charismatic renewal were the "foundational ministries" of Ephesians 4:11, tabernacle teaching, the Feast of Tabernacles, and the "foundational truths" of Hebrews 6:1–2.

The influence of the Latter Rain on the charismatic renewal of the 1960s and 1970s can also be seen in the continuity of many of the institutions of the Latter Rain with those of the charismatic movement. For example, *Logos Journal,* one of the most widely circulated magazines of the charismatic renewal, grew out of an earlier publication, *Herald of Faith/Harvest Time,* edited by Joseph Mattsson-Boze and Gerald Derstine. Mattsson-Boze played an important part in the 1948 Latter Rain revival, and Gerald Derstine was associated for several years with J. Preston Eby, who had been forced to resign from the PHC in 1956 due to his Latter Rain teaching and practice.

Other important components of the charismatic renewal also had roots in the 1948 Latter Rain revival, including John Poole's church in Philadelphia, which had been pastored by his father, Fred C. Poole, who had been very active in the Latter Rain movement until his death in 1963. The Elim Missionary Assemblies, a fellowship of churches closely associated with Elim Bible Institute, located first in Hornell, New York, and later in Lima, New York, also helped to carry on the beliefs and practices of the Latter Rain into the charismatic movement. The same was true of the Bethesda Missionary Temple in Detroit, where James Lee Beall succeeded his mother, Myrtle Beall, as pastor. The Independent Assemblies of God International, a loose fellowship of several hundred churches of Scandinavian origin, also served to carry on the principles of the Latter Rain after a serious split over this issue in 1949 with the Fellowship of Christian Assemblies, of which it had been a part.

J. Preston Eby succinctly stated a major emphasis of the Latter Rain when he made reference to preparation for the coming outpouring of the Holy Spirit

which shall finally bring the FULLNESS, a company of overcoming Sons of God who have come to the measure of the stature of the fullness of Christ to actually dethrone Satan, casting him out of the heavenlies, and finally binding him in the earthlies, bringing the hope of deliverance and life to all the families of the earth. This . . . great work of the Spirit shall usher a people into full redemption—free from the curse, sin, sickness, death and carnality (1976, 10).

Bibliography: G. F. Atter, *The Student's Handbook: Cults and Heresies* (1963); F. Campbell, *Stanley Frodsham: Prophet With a Pen* (1974); W. Cathcart, *To Glory from "Gloom"* (n.d.); J. P. Eby, "The Battle of Armageddon, Part IV" (1976); M. Gaglardi, *The Pastor's Pen, Early Revival Writings of Pastor Reg Layzell* (1965); E. Hawtin, "How This Revival Began," *The Sharon Star* (August 1, 1949), 3; G. Hawtin, "The Church—Which Is His Body," *The Sharon Star* (March 1, 1950), 2; T. Holdcroft, "The New Order of the Latter Rain," *Pneuma* 2 (Fall 1980): 46–60; W. J. Hollenweger, *Handbuch der Pfingstbewegung* (10 vols., 1965–67); M. E. Kirkpatrick, *The 1948 Revival & Now* (n.d.); M. Meloon, *Ivan Spencer: Willow in the Wind* (1974); W. W. Menzies, *Anointed to Serve: The Story of the Assemblies of God* (1971); A. W. Rasmussen, *The Last Chapter* (1973); R. M. Riss, *Latter Rain* (1987); idem, "The Latter Rain Movement of 1948," *Pneuma* 4 (Spring 1982): 32–45.   R. M. Riss

LATTER-DAY SAINTS See MORMONS.

LAURENTIN, RENÉ (1917–). Well-known Catholic scholar and church journalist. Born in Tours, France, Laurentin had his seminary studies interrupted by World War II, during which he spent five years as a prisoner of war in Germany, later being awarded the *Croix de Guerre* and the *Légion d'Honneur.* Ordained as a priest in 1946, he pursued his studies as a biblical exegete with a particular interest in Mary, the mother of Jesus. He obtained his Litt.D. from the Sorbonne (1952) and his doctorate in theology from the Institut Catholique, Paris (1953). Besides his exegetical study *Structure et Théologie de Luc I–II* (1956), Laurentin became the premier Catholic authority on Marian apparitions, editing seven volumes of documents on Lourdes, on which he also wrote a six-volume history.

Laurentin became a professor of theology at the Catholic University of Angers in 1952 and served as a consultant to the preparatory commission for Vatican II, later being appointed a theological expert at the council. During the council, his gifts for informed theological journalism found expression in a series of books on the council and on the episcopal synods that followed. In addition, Laurentin has written about the lives of several modern French saints.

Laurentin's ability to keep in touch with significant new developments in the Roman Catholic church brought him into contact with Catholic Charismatic Renewal (CCR) as early as 1967, though it was 1970 before he had firsthand experience during a visit to the U.S. His interest and personal experience of blessing led to his books *Catholic Pentecostalism* (1977) and *Miracles in El Paso* (1982). Since then Laurentin has spoken at major CCR conferences and is a respected voice supporting the movement. Since 1981 he has become the principal chronicler of the Marian apparitions at Medjugorje, Yugoslavia. His major exegetical study, *The Truth of Christmas, Beyond the Myth, The Gospels of the Infancy of Christ,* appeared in English translation in 1986.   P. D. Hocken

LAUSTER, HERMAN (1901–64). Founder of the Church of God (CG, Cleveland, Tenn.) in Germany. Born in Stuttgart, Germany, Lauster came from a staunch Lutheran family. In 1926 he and his bride, Lydia, emigrated from Germany to Grasonville, Maryland, where he became a merchant. He was converted in 1930 and filled with the Holy Spirit in 1934. He united with the CG and in 1936 went back to Germany as a Pentecostal missionary.

Nazi control of Germany made Lauster's efforts difficult, but three churches were secretly established in the Swabian region. In 1938 Lauster came to the unfavorable attention of the Nazis and was imprisoned in Welsheim Prison. Nevertheless, seven new churches were established during World War II. Lauster survived the war and its aftermath. He died in 1964 while preaching at a U.S. servicemen's retreat in Berchtesgaden, Bavaria.

Bibliography: B. Lauster, *Herman Lauster—One Man and God* (1967); C. W. Conn, *Like a Mighty Army* (rev. 1977).
C. W. Conn

LAWRENCE, BENNETT FREEMAN

(1890–). An early Pentecostal preacher in the Midwest. He was associated in evangelism efforts with his mother-in-law, "Mother" Mary Barnes, J. Roswell Flower, Fred Vogler, and others as early as 1908. He was a charter member of the Assemblies of God and was elected assistant secretary at the Second General Council in the fall of 1914. After he united with the Oneness movement in 1916, little more was heard of him. He is best known for the first history of the Pentecostal movement, *The Apostolic Faith Restored* (1916).

Bibliography: C. Brumback, *Suddenly . . . From Heaven* (1961); B. Lawrence, *The Apostolic Faith Restored* (1916).
W. E. Warner

LAYING ON OF HANDS

The laying on of hands in the Pentecostal and charismatic traditions includes three principal areas: the healing of the sick, the impartation of the Holy Spirit, and various practices of commissioning.

I. Healing. From the beginning of the Pentecostal movement there has been strong emphasis on divine healing. The "full gospel," according to Pentecostals, includes healing as one of its components. The doctrinal statement of the Pentecostal Fellowship of North America (PFNA) contains the affirmation: "We believe that the full gospel includes . . . healing of the body." In connection with healing the laying on of hands is commonly practiced.

Biblical basis for laying on of hands in relation to healing is drawn from numerous NT accounts. Jesus himself often laid hands on people for healing. In an early statement about his ministry we read: "The people brought to Jesus all who had various kinds of sickness, and laying his hands on each one, he healed them" (Luke 4:40). Particularly in the Gospel of Mark there are many references to Jesus' use of hands in healing, e.g., to take by the hand (Peter's feverish mother-in-law [1:31]; Jairus' dead daughter [5:41]; a demonized boy [9:27]), to touch (a leper [1:41]; a deaf mute [7:33]), as well as to lay hands on (various sick people [6:5]). Through manual contact there was a transference of spiritual physical vitality from Jesus to those needing healing. This continues in the Book of Acts. Peter

took a lame beggar by the hand, and he was healed (3:7). Tabitha was raised from the dead, and Peter, taking her by the hand, lifted her up (9:40–41). Even handkerchiefs and aprons that had touched Paul's body were used to heal the sick (19:12), and on the island of Malta Paul laid hands on Publius' father so that he was made well (28:7–8). In addition to these accounts about Jesus, Peter, and Paul there are the words of Mark 16 regarding believers: "these signs will accompany those who believe. In my name . . . they will place their hands on sick people, and they will get well" (vv. 17–18).

Pentecostals, accordingly, view the laying on of hands for healing to continue as a practice available in principle to all believers. They see no reason to assume that such a practice should be limited to the early church: it is to continue with "those who believe" through the ages. Further, healing will happen, as Jesus said, "in my name," not in the name or authority of the one who lays hands. So Pentecostals from the earliest days have made use of laying on of hands (manual contact of whatever kind) in the name of Jesus for the healing of the sick. The Pentecostal conviction about healing, however, is by no means limited to the laying on of hands. Jesus himself and the apostles often healed by simply a word spoken. Likewise, those today in the Pentecostal and charismatic movements in various ways may pronounce healing in Jesus' name without any physical touch. However, there is strong emphasis on the value of personal contact through hands.

II. The Impartation of the Holy Spirit. Pentecostals also recognize a close connection between laying on of hands and the gift of the Holy Spirit. For those who have come to faith, there is frequently the laying on of hands to receive the Holy Spirit.

Scriptural basis for this practice is drawn primarily from the Book of Acts. In the account of the Samaritans, after Philip had proclaimed the gospel and baptized them, Peter and John came down from Jerusalem and laid hands upon them to receive the Holy Spirit: "Peter and John placed their hands on them, and they received the Holy Spirit" (8:17). Some three days after Saul of Tarsus had recognized Jesus as Lord, Ananias went to Saul (Paul) and "placing his hands on Saul" declared both Paul's healing from temporary blindness and his being filled with the Holy Spirit (9:17). Paul himself many years later ministered to a number of disciples in Ephesus. They came to faith in Jesus, were baptized in his name, and thereafter "when Paul placed his hands on them, the Holy Spirit came on them" (19:6). In these accounts, receiving, being filled with, and coming on refer essentially to the same activity—the impartation of the Spirit. The laying on of hands was done in immediate conjunction with all three.

The experience of Agnes Ozman that initiated the Pentecostal movement occurred through the laying on of hands. She was a student at Charles Parham's Bethel Bible College in Topeka, Kansas. According to one account it happened thus:

Charismatic believers laying on hands and praying during North American Congress on the Holy Spirit and World Evangelization, New Orleans, 1987.

About 7:00 P.M. [January 1, 1901] when meditating in her devotions, Agnes Ozman was reminded that believers in the New Testament church were "baptized in the Spirit" on several occasions when hands were laid on them. Acting on an impulse when Parham had returned [from a brief mission], she asked Parham to lay hands upon her in biblical fashion. Refusing the request at first, he finally relented and said a short prayer as he laid hands on her. According to Miss Ozman's own testimony: "It was as his hands were laid upon my head that the Holy Spirit fell upon me and I began to speak in tongues glorifying God" (Kendrick, 1961, 52–53).

It is quite interesting that the first laying on of hands that began the Pentecostal revival was done reluctantly!

Pentecostals, however, also affirm that there is frequently the reception of the Holy Spirit without the laying on of hands. God sovereignly moves without making use of any human medium. Scriptural basis for this is seen in the accounts of the first coming of the Spirit in Jerusalem and the later outpouring in Caesarea. On the Day of Pentecost those who had been waiting in Jerusalem were "all. . .filled with the Holy Spirit" (2:4). Hands obviously could not have been laid, because these persons were the first to receive. At Caesarea some time later while Peter was still preaching the gospel to the centurion and his friends, the Holy Spirit suddenly "came on all who heard the message" (10:44).

There was neither need nor opportunity for the laying on of hands.

A Presbyterian minister and early charismatic, James H. Brown, speaks of how "there came a day and hour when the Spirit of God invaded our small Saturday evening prayer group, where we met to pray for the Sunday worship service. Literally, the Spirit fell! He electrified everyone in the room!" (Jensen, 1962, 6). In this testimony, typical of many in the movement of the Spirit, there is no reference whatever to laying on of hands: God simply "invaded"!

In the Catholic Charismatic Renewal (CCR) an important concern has been that of relating the laying on of hands in the sacrament of confirmation to baptism in the Holy Spirit. According to official Catholic teaching, when the bishop lays hands on one of the confirmed, the Holy Spirit is given for the person's inner strengthening and outward witness. Thus confirmation is sometimes called "the Pentecostal sacrament." How then does this sacrament, said to objectively give the Holy Spirit, relate to laying on of hands practiced by believers in general who pray for people to receive the Holy Spirit? Catholic charismatics have differentiated between sacramental laying on of hands and laying on of hands in the charismatic movement in various ways. Some view the latter as a prayer for the one confirmed that he will have "full docility" to the grace received in the sacrament (Gelpi, 1971, 179–83). In somewhat similar vein others have spoken of baptism in the Spirit as the release of the power of the Spirit already given in sacramental confirmation. Through this additional laying on of hands wherein Spirit baptism occurs one experiences "the effects of confirmation" (Clark, 1969, 15). Still another approach is that of placing less stress on the sacrament of confirmation as actually giving the Holy Spirit, and viewing it rather as "an offer" that needs to be personally accepted (Mühlen, 1978, 141, 203). In this last case, the emphasis has moved from sacramental laying on of hands as an objective medium of Spirit baptism to an offer of that which has yet to be received. Presumably, a later laying on of hands when a person is open in faith could be the occasion for the actual reception of the Holy Spirit.

There clearly is need in the church at large for a better understanding of the relationship between laying on of hands and the gift of the Holy Spirit. The Book of Hebrews speaks of the laying on of hands as an elementary doctrine that we should go beyond: "Let us leave the elementary teachings about Christ and go on to maturity, not laying again the foundation of repentance from acts that lead to death, and of faith in God, instruction about baptisms, the laying on of hands, the resurrection of the dead, and eternal judgment" (6:1–2). Since in these verses laying on of hands most likely refers to the impartation of the Holy Spirit, we can hardly "go on to maturity" without some basic reconsideration. If Catholics tend to overemphasize the sacramental, many Protestants have little or no comprehension of what is at stake. Pentecostals here have much to contribute by their closer approximation of laying on of hands to the NT practice.

III. Commissioning. Pentecostals, like many other bodies of Christians, practice laying on of hands for commissioning (ordaining, appointing). According to Acts 6:5–6, seven men were chosen by the Jerusalem believers to serve ("deacon") tables, and thereafter the apostles prayed and laid their hands on them. Some years later prophets and teachers in the Antioch church, after fasting and praying, laid hands on Paul and Barnabas and sent them off (Acts 13:1–3). During one of their missionary journeys Paul and Barnabas appointed (literally, "chose by stretching out the hand") elders in a number of churches (Acts 14:23). The Pentecostal practice of commissioning persons with the laying on of hands is in general accord with these NT examples. Pentecostals, however, do not view any such practice as sacramental, i.e., that imposition of hands in and of itself imparts some special grace for ministry.

In relation to ordination, many non-Pentecostal churches also make use of some statements of Paul to Timothy about hands laid on him. Paul refers first to this laying on of hands as being done by the body of elders: "Do not neglect your gift, which was given you through a prophetic message when the body of elders [or "presbytery" KJV] laid their hands on you" (1 Tim. 4:14). In his second letter Paul admonishes Timothy: "I remind you to fan into flame the gift of God, which is in you through the laying on of my hands (2 Tim. 1:6). Both of these declarations to Timothy are frequently utilized, especially in ordaining persons by the laying on of hands to the gospel ministry.

Pentecostals, while commonly following a similar practice, lay a larger stress on the prophetic side. Though hands are involved, the more important aspect is the gift (charisma—"Spiritual gift") bestowed by prophetic utterance. Paul not only speaks of this utterance in 1 Timothy 4:14 but also earlier refers to "the prophecies once made about you [Timothy], so that by following them you may fight the good fight" (1:18). In accordance with Paul's emphasis on prophecy, some Pentecostal bodies are primarily concerned about what is declared by the body of elders (or presbytery). Through such prophecy accompanied by the laying on of hands, the candidate to be commissioned is basically equipped for his further ministry in the body of Christ.

See also HEALING MOVEMENTS; HEALING, GIFT OF.

Bibliography: S. B. Clark, *Confirmation and the "Baptism of the Holy Spirit"* (1969); D. L. Gelpi, *Pentecostalism: A Theological Viewpoint* (1971); J. Jensen, ed., *Presbyterians and the Baptism of the Holy Spirit* (1962); K. Kendrick, *The Promise Fulfilled* (1961); E. Lohse, *TDNT*, 9:431–34; H. Mühlen, *A Charismatic Theology* (1978); E. D. O'Connor, *The Laying on of Hands* (1969); D. Prince, *Laying on of Hands* (n.d.); H. G. Schütz, *NIDNTT* 2:150–52; J. R. Williams, *The Gift of the Holy Spirit Today* (1980).   J. R. Williams

LEA, LARRY (1950–). Founder and pastor of Church on the Rock, Rockwall, Texas. The son of a wealthy Texas businessman, Lea was converted to Christ at age seventeen while in a psychiatric ward. After graduating from Dallas Baptist College in 1972, he became youth minister of Beverly Hills Baptist Church in Dallas and began attending Southwestern Baptist Theological Seminary in Fort Worth. After answering a call to faithful and extensive prayer, Lea established an independent charismatic work, Church on the Rock, in 1980. By 1987 the church had grown from 13 members to over 11,000. He became vice-president and dean of theological and spiritual affairs at Oral Roberts University in 1986, continuing with his pastoral responsibilities in Rockwall. Heavily influenced by Paul Yonggi Cho of South Korea, he has emphasized the need for prayer and obedience in the Christian life.

Bibliography: L. Lea, *Could You Not Tarry One Hour?* (1987).   R. M. Riss

LEBEAU, PAUL (1925–). Belgian Jesuit theologian. Lebeau studied in the U.S. from 1954 to 1958, when his interest in ecumenism was first enkindled. His active involvement in the charismatic renewal began early in 1974, and he was soon invited to become theological adviser to Cardinal Suenens in relation to the latter's responsibility for Catholic Charismatic Renewal. On the faculty at Lumen Vitae, Brussels, from 1974, Lebeau became in 1982 president of Institut d'Études Théologiques, also in Brussels. He was, with T. Smail, cochairman of the European Charismatic Leaders' Conferences in 1976, 1978, and 1980, playing a significant role with his linguistic ability and irenic manner. A specialist in ecclesiology and concerned about the social im-

Flavius J. Lee, who is described as "a singularly pious man and effective teacher" by Church of God historian Charles W. Conn, was elected general overseer following the dismissal of A. J. Tomlinson. Lee College is named for him.

pact of the renewal, Lebeau's writings are only available in article form, mostly in French (two English items are in *Theological Renewal*).

                                                    P. D. Hocken

LEE, FLAVIUS JOSEPHUS (1875–1928). The second general overseer of the Church of God (CG, Cleveland, Tenn.). Born in Cleveland, Tennessee, Lee was deeply religious even as a youth and was choir director of the local Baptist church. On August 28, 1908, he was filled with the Holy Spirit in a revival conducted by A. J. Tomlinson, pastor of the local CG. The experience changed Lee's life, and he soon became a minister of deep piety and great effectiveness.

In 1909 Tomlinson was elected to the newly created office of general overseer and Lee became his companion in labor. In 1911 Lee succeeded Tomlinson as pastor of the local church and in 1913 was appointed overseer of Tennessee. Soon he was second only to Tomlinson in influence in the CG. In 1922 he succeeded Tomlinson as superintendent of the recently established (1918) Bible Training School. That post also placed Lee on the newly created executive committee.

In 1923 a growing dissatisfaction with Tomlinson's autocratic leadership led to his removal from the office of general overseer. The CG, through its council of twelve, selected Lee to fill the vacated office. The five years of Lee's overseership were difficult, but there was steady growth and expansion. He led the CG away from the external fanaticism that threatened Pentecost in the southeastern U.S. at that time. Lee's ministry was cut short by death in 1928; on October 28 he died of cancer. Having consistently preached divine healing as scriptural truth, he declined medical treatment during his illness.

Lee's writings included *Demonology* (c. 1925), an unpublished diary, and a posthumously published book of sermons (1929). In 1947 the CG renamed its oldest college, Lee College, in his honor.

Bibliography: C. W. Conn, *Like a Mighty Army* (rev. 1977); F. J. Lee, unpublished diary; Mrs. F. J. Lee, *Life Sketch and Sermons of F. J. Lee* (1929).   C. W. Conn

LENSCH, RODNEY (1934–). Pioneer itinerant teacher in the Lutheran charismatic movement. Lensch graduated in 1959 from Concordia Seminary, Springfield, Illinois, a seminary of the Lutheran Church–Missouri Synod (LCMS). Seven years later, while serving in his second LCMS congregation, he experienced the baptism with the Holy Spirit. When called to testify before synod officials, he elected to resign from his call rather than cause divisions, though he had not been faulted theologically.

After leaving the congregation, Lensch took up a traveling ministry as a conference speaker and counselor to pastors and congregations, living first in St. Louis, Missouri, and later in St. Paul, Minnesota, where he helped initiate the annual International Lutheran Conference on the Holy Spirit.

He moved to Albany, New York, in 1983 to affiliate with Our Savior's Lutheran Church, the mother church for charismatic renewal in LCMS. He continued his traveling ministry in the U.S. and also in Australia and Brazil.

Bibliography: L. Christenson, ed., *Welcome, Holy Spirit* (1987); R. Lensch, *Fundamentals of the Spirit-Filled Life, Course I* (1974); idem, *My Personal Pentecost* (1968).   L. Christenson

LEONARD, THOMAS KING (1861–1946). Pastor and executive presbyter of the Assemblies of God (AG). Ordained by the Christian Church in 1901, he received the baptism of the Holy Spirit at a meeting conducted by C. A. McKinney in 1907. He then purchased an old saloon in Findlay, Ohio, which he converted into a church. Leonard also began a print shop and started a Bible school in the upstairs part of the building.

When the AG was founded in April 1914, Leonard was elected to the first executive presbytery. He also proposed that the church body call itself the "Assemblies of God" and establish its first headquarters at Findlay.

In 1917 Leonard's Gospel School in Findlay merged with Andrew Fraser's Mount Tabor Bible School in Chicago. Leonard, however, continued to pastor his church in Findlay, but from 1929 to 1938 he held credentials with the International Church of the Foursquare Gospel. He was later reinstated in the AG and retired from pastoring in 1941.

Bibliography: W. W. Menzies, *Anointed to Serve* (1971).   G. W. Gohr

LEWER, ALFRED (d. 1924). Pioneer British missionary to the Tibetan border of China. Born in London, he was a member of the Congregational Church and close friend of Donald Gee. Together they joined A. E. Saxby's (1873–1960) Baptist Church. Baptized in the Spirit in September 1913, he spent a short time in the Pentecostal

Missionary Union (PMU) Training Home, Hackney. In October 1915 he sailed with W. J. Boyd and David Lee to serve with the PMU. In spite of his limited education he became very proficient in the difficult Chinese language. He endeared himself to the people, sharing their food, sleeping out of doors, and settling their disputes.

Known affectionately as "Brother Alf," his labors were truly apostolic. In 1916 he married Mary Buckwalter of Philadelphia. By stages they moved to the borders of Tibet but later settled in Wei Hsi, an important town on the main route from southwest China. Forays into the surrounding areas met with considerable success among the Lisu people. Tragically, though a strong swimmer, he drowned crossing the swollen Mekong River in September 1924.

Bibliography: D. Gee, *Alfred G. Lewer* (1928); idem, *These Men I Knew* (1980).　　　　D. W. Cartwright

LEWIS, GAYLE F. (1898–1979). A pastor and administrator in the General Council of the Assemblies of God (AG). He became general superintendent at the death of Wesley R. Steelberg in 1952 but was returned to the position of assistant superintendent in 1953.

As a Methodist, Lewis received the Pentecostal experience and a call into the ministry. He attended Rochester (New York) Bible Training School and then pastored at Austinburg, Ohio, beginning in 1921. From 1930 to 1945 he was the superintendent of the old Central District of the AG. In 1945 he was elected as an assistant general superintendent. Among other duties at the national headquarters (1945–65), he directed the Gospel Publishing House and the home missions department. He was active in the Pentecostal Fellowship of North America, the National Association of Evangelicals, and the Pentecostal World Conference.

Bibliography: "Gayle F. Lewis, 1898–1979," *PE* (October 21, 1979), 7.　　　　W. E. Warner

LIFE IN THE SPIRIT SEMINARS A practical course of preparation for receiving the baptism in the Spirit.

I. Origins. Unlike the origins of the Pentecostal movement, in which those seeking "the baptism" customarily tarried in persistent prayer like the apostles in Jerusalem, the beginnings of the charismatic movement were characterized by seekers being "prayed over" by having hands imposed to receive the baptism of the Spirit. Life in the Spirit seminars as a means of preparing people for this "praying over" were first devised in the Word of God community in Ann Arbor, Michigan, some six months after the community's foundation in the fall of 1967. The Word of God seminars were first published in 1971, with a small booklet for participants and a larger book, the *Team Manual,* with detailed guidance for the team conducting the seminars. In the following eight years, 130,000 copies of the *Team Manual* were printed and circulated throughout the English-speaking world, predominantly among Roman Catholics.

What led these charismatic leaders to devise the Life in The Spirit seminars and why did they arise first among Catholic charismatics? Most basically,

the authors realized that baptism in the Spirit is not just an exciting experience nor a mere addendum to the Christian life but is the foundation for an ongoing life in the Spirit fully surrendered to the Lord. They were also aware that without previous biblical teaching leading to repentance for obvious sin, any "praying over" for baptism in the Spirit would only produce ambiguous and short-lived results. These objectives are spelled out in S. Clark's introduction to the 1971 and 1973 editions. Seminars were first produced by Catholics primarily because many of these young men (R. Martin, S. Clark, J. Cavnar, G. Rauch) had previously worked together in Catholic renewal organizations like the Cursillo movement, which had clear-cut training programs and encouraged a strategic approach to pastoral formation.

II. Content. The Ann Arbor seminars involve two introductory sessions for explanation and sign-up, and then seven seminars called God's Love, Salvation, The New Life, Receiving God's Gift, Praying for Baptism in the Holy Spirit, Growth, and Transformation in Christ. Two main lines of criticism of these seminars subsequently developed among Catholic charismatics: the first, that they were insufficiently Catholic, being unrelated to the sacraments; the second, that they are really more of a preparation for conversion, and that is too soon to teach people about charisms and baptism in the Spirit.

The first criticism led to a minor revision of the Ann Arbor seminars in 1979, with separate Catholic and ecumenical editions. However, they purposely avoided much sacramental explanation, clearly from the conviction that the seminars are a retreat type of situation in which doctrinal explanation can be a distraction from repentance for sin and turning to Jesus in faith. This sacramental and Catholic concern led two nuns, Srs. Burle and Plankenhorn of St. Louis, to produce alternative seminars: *You Will Receive Power* (1977). Most of the European versions follow this more doctrinal emphasis: P. Philippe *Afin que vous portiez beaucoup de fruits* (1977); H. Mühlen *A Charismatic Theology* (1978); D. Grasso *Vivere nello Spirito* (1980).

The second criticism has led the Mother of God community to introduce a twenty-week seminar on basic Christianity entitled "Growing in Faith Prior to Life in the Spirit," so that only clearly converted believers enter on the latter, which then focuses on death to the flesh, so that the power of the risen life of the Spirit may animate the Christian.

See also CATHOLIC CHARISMATIC RENEWAL.

Bibliography: P. Hocken, article in *Clergy Review* (November 1980), 404–8.　　　　P. D. Hocken

LINDSAY, GORDON (1906–73) **AND FREDA THERESA** (1916–). Leaders of the healing movement, publishers, editors, founders and directors of Christ for the Nations Institute. Gordon Lindsay's parents were members of J. A. Dowie's Zion City, Illinois, communitarian experiment when he was born. The bankruptcy of that city forced the family west, where they temporarily became participants in the communi-

Gordon and Freda Lindsay worked together as a team, first in pastoral ministry and then as leaders of the Voice of Healing and Christ for the Nations Institute. Following Gordon's death in 1973, Freda took the leadership of the school and its enterprises.

tarian experiment of Finis Yoakum at Pisgah Grande, California. When this community also failed because of leadership and financial problems, the family moved to Oregon. Lindsay attended high school in Portland, Oregon, where he was converted in a meeting at which Charles F. Parham preached. He came under the influence of John G. Lake, former resident of Zion City, missionary to South Africa, and founder of the Divine Healing missions in Spokane, Washington, and Portland, Oregon. Lindsay joined the healing and evangelistic campaigns of Lake, traveling throughout California and the southern states. Lindsay began his own ministry in California as pastor of small churches in Avenal and San Fernando.

Lindsay returned to Portland, where he and Freda Schimpf were married in the Foursquare Gospel Church. When World War II began, travel restrictions and financial concerns caused the Lindsays to accept a pastorate in Ashland, Oregon. In 1947 Lindsay resigned from the church to become manager of the William Branham campaigns. In an effort to report and publicize those campaigns, Lindsay published the first issue of the *Voice of Healing* in April 1948 (1948–67; *World-Wide Revival,* March 1958 to August 1959; *Christ for the Nations,* 1967–). Lindsay's decision to report on other revivalist healing campaigns caused Branham to break (1948) relations with his manager.

Thereafter, Lindsay used the periodical to facilitate healing movement efforts, report the results of meetings, and discuss the theological significance of the healing ministries of a large number of evangelists. Itineraries of individual evangelists were published, and in return individuals adhered to the loose set of guidelines established for the Voice of Healing organization. In addition to publishing activities, Lindsay organized conventions of healing evangelists. These were held in Dallas (1949) and Kansas City (1950). The intent was to coordinate the activities of the evangelists, prevent misunderstandings, and avoid conflict with the established Pentecostal churches. Eventually, many of the healing evangelists found it more lucrative to establish their own magazines and to avoid tacit endorsement of their competition. The number of healing evangelists participating in Voice of Healing activities decreased.

In 1956 Lindsay established Winning the Nations Crusade, which, on the model of the Osborne Native Church Crusades, sent "deliverance teams" on missions throughout the world. Later Lindsay would develop his own Native Church Crusade (1961) which has supplied resources to Third World church-controlled building programs. Remarkably this money has been provided with no requirements for allegiance or submission to the American organization.

Recognizing the need for literature articulating the theology and history of the healing and charismatic movements, Lindsay became a prolific author and historian of the healing movement. He wrote more than 250 books and pamphlets in addition to the continuous flow of articles for the *Voice of Healing.* Through the Native Literature Work, millions of volumes were published and circulated throughout the world. He also established a radio program and, together with W. A. Raiford, organized the Full Gospel Fellowship of Churches and Ministers International (September 1962; first convention, St. Louis, June 1963).

Their hope was that this organization could provide leadership and structure to the charismatic movement. The effort could not compete with the already established Full Gospel Business Men's Fellowship International. However, Gordon and Freda Lindsay have made major contributions to interdenominational and interconfessional understanding among Pentecostals and charismatics.

Prior to 1966 these ministries functioned under the aegis of the Dallas-based Voice of Healing, Inc. In 1966 the headquarters relocated to Dallas Christian Center. The various projects were reorganized and renamed (1967) Christ for the Nations, Inc. Seminars dealing with ministry and theological and missiological issues became popular. In 1970 Christ for the Nations Institute (CFNI) opened under the direction of Lindsay, who devoted the last three years of his life to establishing this center of theological and spiritual formation for the charismatic and Pentecostal movements. Lindsay died on April 1, 1973, while seated on the platform during the Sunday afternoon worship service at CFNI.

Freda Lindsay was elected president of CFNI, and the real growth of that institution came under her leadership. See also HEALING MOVEMENTS; VOICE OF HEALING.

Bibliography: D. E. Harrell, *All Things Are Possible. The Healing and Charismatic Movements in Modern America* (1975); F. Lindsay, *Freda* (1987); idem *My Diary's Secrets* (1976); G. Lindsay, *All About the Gifts of the Spirit* (1962); idem, *The Chaos of Psychics*, 4 vols. (1970); idem, *Crusade for World Fellowship* (n.d.); idem, *Gifts of the Spirit*, 4 vols. (n.d.); idem, *God's Master Key to Success and Prosperity* (1959); idem, *The House the Lord Built* (n.d.); idem, *John G. Lake—Apostle to Africa* (n.d.); idem, *The John G. Lake Sermons* (1949); idem, *The Life of John Alexander Dowie* (1951); idem, *Men Who Heard From Heaven* (1953); idem, *Miracles in the Bible*, 7 vols. (n.d.); idem, *Sorcery in America*, 3 vols. (1971); idem, *William Branham: A Man Sent From God* (1948); idem, *The World Today in Prophecy* (1953).
　　　　　　　　　　　　　　　　D. D. Bundy

LION OF JUDAH (LION DE JUDA, CORDES, FRANCE)　See CHARISMATIC COMMUNITIES.

LITWILLER, NELSON　(1898–1986). Mennonite missionary, bishop, and charismatic leader. Nelson Litwiller was born, reared, educated, lived, and died a Mennonite. He graduated with a B.A. from Goshen College and a B.D. from Bethany Biblical Seminary (1925).

In 1925 Litwiller was ordained by the College Mennonite Church, Goshen, Indiana. He served, with his wife, Ada Ramseyer (married 1919), from 1925 until 1956 under the Mennonite Board of Missions in Argentina. In 1947 he was appointed a bishop in the church. As a missionary to Uruguay from 1956 to 1967, Litwiller founded the "Montevideo Mennonite Seminary," which he served as president for ten years.

In June 1970 Litwiller attended several midweek prayer meetings led by Kevin Ranaghan at St. Joseph's high school in South Bend, Indiana. During a time of special prayer he was baptized in the Holy Spirit.

From that time until shortly before Bishop

Litwiller succumbed to cancer he was intensely active in efforts to bring reconciliation and unity first between traditional Mennonites and Mennonites who were embracing the Pentecostal experience, and then, among Protestants and Catholics, Evangelicals and Pentecostals. In 1975 he helped establish Mennonite Renewal Services. His zeal helped bring the 1977 Kansas City Conference on the Holy Spirit to realization. He envisioned the New Orleans Congresses on World Evangelization and the Holy Spirit of 1986 and 1987.

The Mennonite Renewal Services featured Nelson Litwiller in their winter 1987 issue. The cover photo was taken at the Festival of the Holy Spirit, Goshen, Indiana, 1972.

Bibliography: G. Derstine, "Nelson Litwiller (1898–1986)," *Charisma* 12 (January 6, 1987): 75; N. Litwiller, "Revitalized Retirement," *My Personal Pentecost*, ed. R. S. and M. Koch (1977), 106–17; "Litwiller Honored at New Orleans '86," *Empowered* 5 (1, 1987): 2; "Remembering the Bishop," *Chariscenter USA Newsletter* 12 (2, 1987): 2.　　　J. A. Hewett

LOGOS INTERNATIONAL FELLOWSHIP, INC.　A charismatic publisher founded in 1966 by Dan Malachuk that distributed an estimated 45 million books worldwide. By 1981, however, Logos International Fellowship (LIF) filed bankruptcy on indebtedness that exceeded five million dollars.

In 1965 Malachuk, president of a retail jewelry business in Plainfield, New Jersey, obtained U.S. publishing rights to a series of lectures written by former spiritualist medium Raphael Gasson of England. It was published as *The Challenging Counterfeit* (c. 1966). Malachuk then asked Jamie Buckingham to work with Nicky Cruz, a Teen Challenge convert, on a book entitled *Run, Baby, Run* (1968), which sold more than eight million copies. Then came other very successful titles, including books by Merlin Carothers (*Prison to*

in this issue:
Kathryn Kuhlman: My First Healing   The Jesus People Are Coming
A Man And A Movement—Demos Shakarian   Speaking In Tongues
Through The Ages   Divine Guidance—From Where?

September - October '71
50 cents

formerly HERALD OF FAITH
HARVEST TIME

ΛΟΓΟΣ **L**OGOS **J**OURNAL
an international *charismatic publication*

A CHAPTER FROM:

THE HOLY SPIRIT AND YOU

By DENNIS And RITA BENNETT

The leading charismatic periodical in the 1970s, the *Logos Journal*, was published by Dan Malachuk and his Logos, International, Plainfield, New Jersey.

Praise [1970], etc.) and Dennis Bennett's *Nine O'Clock in the Morning* (1970) and *The Holy Spirit and You* (with Rita Bennett, 1971). Other best sellers quickly followed. By the mid 1970s some fifty books a year were being published. The *Logos Journal* soon became popular among Pentecostals and charismatics and within three years boasted nearly 50,000 subscribers.

Logos later became LIF, a nonprofit organization, and listed several well-known personalities on its board of directors, including David du Plessis, Gen. Ralph Haines, Dennis Bennett, Jamie Buckingham, and others. LIF also sponsored conferences on the Holy Spirit.

Malachuk created a biweekly newspaper, the *National Courier*, but it became a financial burden and all but destroyed LIF. The staff was headed by Bob Slosser, formerly with the *New York Times*. Former staffer Jamie Buckingham later described it as "an incredibly exciting and expensive operation." The *Courier's* nearly 100,000 circulation was far below what it needed to break even. In an attempt to keep the paper operating,

Malachuk began borrowing money for LIF— about $5 million from several hundred individuals.

The *Courier* ceased publication in 1977, and its indebtedness became a heavy load for LIF to shoulder. Authors were told that the company would pay royalties later. By 1981 more cuts were made in an attempt to save LIF. The *Logos Journal* went the way of the *Courier*. The prosperity theme of many successful best-selling LIF titles seemed to have a hollow ring.

LIF finally filed for bankruptcy in 1981, thus leaving many creditors, investors, and authors without much hope of ever recovering their money. Part of the LIF operation was taken over by Bridge Publishing, whose president, Raymond Stanbury, hoped to make restitution for the LIF indebtedness.

Following LIF's closing, Malachuk moved to Peterborough, New Hampshire, and founded Inspirational Publishing Services, a subsidy publisher.

Bibliography: BP Newsletter (March 1982); J. Buckingham, "End of an Era: Final Chapter of the Logos Saga," *Charisma* (December 1981), 48–49, 51, 54–55; D. Malachuk, letter to Logos authors (December 13, 1979).   W. E. Warner

LOGOS MINISTRY FOR ORTHODOX RENEWAL See STEPHANOU, EUSEBIUS A.

LORD'S SUPPER See ORDINANCES, PENTECOSTAL; SACRAMENTS.

LUCE, ALICE EVELINE (1873–1955). Indigenous church pioneer and educator. With a French Protestant (Huguenot) ancestry, Alice Eveline Luce was born in Cheltenham, England. Her father, the Reverend J. J. Luce, served as vicar of St. Nicholas Church (Anglican) in Gloucester, England. She was converted to Christ at age ten and felt a strong inclination to the Christian ministry. Following high school she was educated at the Cheltenham Ladies' College and later studied nursing and theology.

Luce's intense desire for ministry led her to journey in 1896 to India as a missionary under appointment with the Church Missionary Society (CMS). She settled in Azimgarh, United Provinces, and worked in a school there and among women isolated in harems.

With the emergence of the Pentecostal movement early in this century, news of the baptism in the Holy Spirit finally reached Luce in India. Hearing of two women who had received this experience, she visited them to find out more about this baptism. Convinced that this was from God, she prayed until she received it (c. 1910).

Before long, Luce became ill from drinking

A missionary to India in 1896, Alice Luce became a Pentecostal about 1910 and devoted the rest of her life to missions, writing, and training others.

contaminated water. After a period of convalescence she returned home in 1912. In the following year the CMS loaned her to the Zenana Bible and Medical Mission (now known as the Bible and Medical Missionary Fellowship). Secretarial work with this agency required her to move to Vancouver, British Columbia, Canada. In 1914 she resigned from the CMS on medical grounds.

While serving in Canada Luce felt called of God to go to Mexico as a missionary. The Mexican Revolution, however, altered her plans and eventually she moved to Texas. It was there that she became acquainted with Henry C. Ball, Sunshine Marshall, Mack M. Pinson, and Lloyd Baker. This association with other Pentecostal believers led to her ordination in 1915 by Pinson into the newly organized General Council of the Assemblies of God (AG).

Two years later Luce and Sunshine Marshall traveled to Monterrey, Mexico, for missionary work. Because of the Revolution, however, they were forced to return to the U.S. Following this disappointment, Luce moved to Los Angeles to begin evangelistic work among the Hispanics living in that city.

Realizing that the best way to evangelize the Hispanic population was through training pastors and evangelists, she founded the Berean Bible Institute in 1926 in San Diego and served there until her death in 1955. The school is currently known as Latin American Bible Institute and is located in La Puente, California.

The significance of Alice E. Luce in the history of the AG and Hispanic evangelism is threefold. First, her efforts at Bible institute training prepared the way for many young people to minister effectively to their own people.

Luce's second area of influence resulted from her many publications. In the first twenty years of the Bible institute where she served, most of the curricular materials (books and notes) were prepared by her. Gospel Publishing House published three of her books: *The Messenger and His Message* (1925), *The Little Flock in the Last Days* (1927), and *Pictures of Pentecost* (n.d.). Other Latin American institutes also used her materials. Luce's literary output was enormous. She also regularly contributed to the *Apostolic Light* published by Henry C. Ball. Writing in English for Gospel Publishing House, she wrote lesson comments for intermediate and senior Sunday school teachers' quarterlies for many years.

The articulation of a missionary strategy for the AG constitutes Luce's third contribution and explains the direction of her ministry. Early in 1921, before the general council met, Luce contributed a series of three articles to *The Pentecostal Evangel* entitled "Paul's Missionary Methods." This represented the first exposition of indigenous church principles to ever appear in that publication, although brief references to them had been made before. Luce articulated principles aimed at the establishment of self-supporting, self-governing, and self-propagating New Testament churches, having been influenced by the publication of Roland Allen's *Missionary Methods: St. Paul's or Ours?* (1912). As a Pentecostal, however, Luce went beyond Allen in her view of NT evangelism. Luce believed that apostolic methods would be followed by the power and demonstration of the Holy Spirit.

A clear attitude of humility is apparent in these three significant articles. The picture of NT ministry is the servanthood of Jesus Christ. Luce noted that the unconverted can easily sense an attitude of cultural or racial superiority on the part of Pentecostal missionaries if such a feeling exists. While foreign leadership may be necessary for a time, this must be based on greater experience or spirituality, not on nationality. Luce believed that this attitude of humility and obedience to the Holy Spirit would serve as a model to the converts and young ministers. Consequently, when they follow in the same footsteps, their ministries will bear much fruit because they are following the NT pattern.

Bibliography: V. De Leon, *The Silent Pentecostals* (1979); A. E. Luce, "Paul's Missionary Methods," *PE* (January 8, 1921), 6–7; *PE* (January 22, 1921), 6, 11; *PE* (February 5, 1921), 6–7; G. B. McGee, "Pioneers of Pentecost: Alice E. Luce and Henry C. Ball," *AG Heritage* 2 (1985): 5–6, 12–15.   G. B. McGee

LUGO, JUAN L. (1890–1984). Pioneer Pentecostal missionary in Puerto Rico. A Puerto Rican living in Hawaii early in the century, Lugo was converted in 1913 and soon began ministry in California in company with his pastor, Frank Ortiz. Lugo was ordained by the Assemblies of God (AG) in San Jose, California, in 1916 and felt a call to evangelize his homeland. He received assistance from Bethel Church, Los Angeles, and left the same year for the Atlantic coast, conferring en route with J. Roswell Flower in St. Louis and Robert Brown in New York. After an initial effort in Santurce, Lugo continued to Ponce, his family home, where he was met by Salomón Feliciano, with whom he had worked in California. The several congregations that emerged from these efforts affiliated with the AG in 1921, with Lugo serving as executive head. After a profitable decade of expanding work, Lugo began ministry in New York City, establishing a church in a former synagogue. He returned to Puerto Rico to start a Bible institute in 1937 and resided permanently in New York after 1940. Lugo's wife, Isabel, from a socially established Catholic family, has been credited with having contributed much to the couple's ministerial success.

Bibliography: V. De Leon, *The Silent Pentecostals* (1979); R. Domínguez, *Pioneros de Pentecostés* (1971), 1: 55–122; J. Lugo, *Pentecostés en Puerto Rico* (1951); D. Moore, *Puerto Rico Para Cristo* (1969).
E. A. Wilson

LUKE–ACTS

I. The Unity of Luke–Acts
II. The Author: Historian or Theologian?
III. The Birth and Infancy Narratives
IV. John the Baptist
V. Jesus: The Inaugural Events
VI. Jesus: The Promise of the Father
VII. The Power of Pentecost
VIII. The Spirit in Jerusalem
IX. Samaria and the Gentiles
X. Paul and the Westward Mission
XI. Conclusions: Luke–Acts and the Pentecostal Tradition

I. The Unity of Luke–Acts. The canonical order of the books of the NT conceals the fact that the Gospel of Luke and the Book of Acts are two parts of a single work. In his brief introduction to the Book of Acts, the author looks back at his "former book," which told "all that Jesus began to do and to teach until the day he was taken up to heaven, after giving instructions through the Holy Spirit to the apostles he had chosen" (Acts 1:1–2). Such language makes it clear that Acts was preceded by a Gospel, and the explicit mention of "Theophilus" (1:1) leaves no room for doubt that Luke's Gospel is specifically in view (cf. Luke 1:3, "most excellent Theophilus").

Only Luke among the Gospel writers introduces his work formally in the manner of a Greek or Jewish historian (Luke 1:1–4; cf., e.g., Josephus, *Against Apion* 1.1–3). But is the preface at the beginning of Luke's Gospel intended to introduce the Gospel alone, or the entire two-part work? The author's reference to "many" predecessors refers most appropriately to Luke's Gospel; it is unlikely that "many" prior to this author had undertaken to write the story of the beginning of the Christian church. The things "handed down to us by those who from the first were eyewitnesses and servants of the word" (Luke 1:2) are probably the words and deeds of Jesus, as recorded by Mark and others from the testimony of Jesus' disciples. Yet the author's claim to have "investigated everything from the beginning," so that Theophilus might know "the certainty of the things [he had] been taught" (Luke 1:3–4) points to a more comprehensive goal. Moreover, the phrase "the things that have been fulfilled among us" (1:1) fits the events described in Acts just as well as the events of Luke's Gospel. Although the content of the Gospel of Luke is naturally first in the author's mind in composing the preface, the Book of Acts is also part of the plan from the start. The preface emphasizes careful investigation, promising an "orderly account," and "certainty," yet what distinguishes this work from all previous attempts to tell the Christian story is its sheer scope. The author has "investigated everything," and offers therefore a more complete account than ever before of the Christian beginnings. No other first-century Christian writer, not even Paul, attempted so much.

If the preface to Luke's Gospel has both the Gospel and the Book of Acts within its horizons, the briefer preface to Acts (1:1–2) is secondary in importance and depends on the Gospel preface for its meaning. "Most excellent Theophilus" is now just "Theophilus"; their "former book" (Luke) is summarized in half a sentence, and instead of explaining what he now proposes to do (as Josephus, for example, does in *Against Apion* 2.1–7), the author simply picks up the thread of the story. Probably the only reason Luke–Acts is not a single continuous work is that it would not fit on a single papyrus scroll (it is no accident that several NT books, Matthew, Luke, Acts, John, Revelation, nicely fill the maximum length of a papyrus scroll, and none exceed it). The "former book" is actually the "former scroll"; as the author begins a new scroll, a brief word to the reader is in order.

But who is the reader? More precisely, who is "Theophilus"? The most plausible answer is that Theophilus is the author's patron, like the "Epaphroditus" to whom Josephus addressed both his *Antiquities* (1; *Vita* 430) and his treatise *Against Apion* (1.1; 2.1, 296). This would mean that Theophilus was a man with a strong interest in the Christian movement and who had the financial resources to see that the work was copied and distributed. Consequently, the dedication was the author's way of getting the work published.

II. The Author: Historian or Theologian?

Unfortunately the author does not identify himself (or herself) as clearly as the work's patron is identified. Luke's Gospel, like the other NT Gospels, is anonymous. Tradition assigns the work to Luke, the "beloved physician" and companion of Paul mentioned in Colossians 4:14 (cf. 2 Tim. 4:11; Philem. 24), and there is evidence in the Book of Acts that parts of the narrative at least come from a person who traveled with Paul on some of his journeys (note the use of "we" in Acts 16:10–18; 20:5–15; 21:1–18; 27:1–28:16). Luke the physician is a plausible guess because he is not mentioned by name in the Acts narrative, but the identification is far from certain. For the sake of tradition and convenience, however, I will refer here to the author as "Luke."

More important than the author's identity is the purpose of Luke–Acts. Is the two-part work history or theology or both? The question is of particular importance in connection with the many references in Luke–Acts to the Holy Spirit and to such experiences as "receiving the Spirit," being "filled with the Spirit," and being "baptized in the Spirit." Is it possible to speak of a Lukan "theology of the Holy Spirit," or even (with Roger Stronstad) of a distinctly "charismatic theology" as Luke's contribution to the theology of the NT? Or is Luke primarily a historian? Does he provide information about these experiences of the Holy Spirit simply because they happened and because he does not want to leave anything out? Are these experiences—e.g., prophecy, tongues-speaking, visible tongues of fire—models for Christian experience in subsequent generations, or are they signs given once and for all to mark decisive milestones in the realization of the divine plan in history? Is Luke simply reporting events or using these events to teach Christian believers about the work of the Holy Spirit in their own lives and communities?

Christian theology has traditionally based itself more on the letters of Paul than on the Gospels because Paul is explicitly teaching his readers what to believe or how to behave, while the Gospel writers are merely telling a story. Within the Gospels, the sayings attributed to Jesus are often given priority over the accounts of his travels and miracles, not only because of who Jesus is but because the purpose of stories is supposed to be to inform and not to instruct. Even parables, the stories told by Jesus himself, have often taken second place to the specific commands and pronouncements attributed to him. And what is true of the Gospels is even more true of the Book of Acts, where few sayings of Jesus are cited. The same traditional theologians who have warned students for generations, "Never base a major doctrine on a parable," have also insisted repeatedly that the Book of Acts is "history rather than doctrine"—and therefore not a sure guide to Christian faith and practice.

Recent developments in biblical studies, however, have modified these conclusions. The discipline of redaction criticism has emphasized that the Gospel writers were not mere compilers of stories and traditions but conscious editors of the material they collected and indeed creative authors in their own right, with their own distinctive theological concerns and perspectives. This approach was applied to Luke's Gospel by Hans Conzelmann as early as 1954, in *The Theology of St. Luke,* and before that by Ned B. Stonehouse in *The Witness of Luke to Christ* (1951). More recently, the method has been applied to Luke–Acts as a unified work in numerous monographs (see the recent books by Stronstad, Tiede, Juel, Maddox, Jervell, and others in the bibliography). Narrative has come into its own alongside discourse or formal instruction as a legitimate vehicle of theology. Biblical scholarship has discovered not only that it is possible to "do theology" by telling stories, but that Jews and Christians (among others) have been doing exactly that for a very long time. To ask whether Luke was a historian or a theologian is not a proper question. Quite clearly he was both. He wanted Theophilus to know the "certainty" of what happened but also the implications of those events for understanding Christian experience in his own time. Because the "Spirit" or "Holy Spirit" is a reality spanning the whole of Luke–Acts, the work cannot be adequately interpreted without asking what the Spirit's "coming" meant and what the act of "receiving" the Spirit, whether individually or corporately, meant to the author and to those for whom he was writing.

III. The Birth and Infancy Narratives.

The first mention of the Holy Spirit in Luke–Acts is hardly typical of the work as a whole. Zechariah the priest was told by the angel Gabriel that the son to be born to him and his wife Elizabeth (i.e., John the Baptist) would be "filled with the Holy Spirit even from his mother's womb" (Luke 1:15 RSV). That this means "from conception" and not simply "from birth" (NIV) will be vividly demonstrated in 1:41, 44, where the unborn infant John is said to have leaped in Elizabeth's womb in joyful testimony to the coming birth of Jesus. On the one hand, the phrase "filled with the Holy Spirit" is probably linked to the notion that John was himself "holy" to the Lord from conception, like the Nazirites in Israel (Num. 6:3) or like Samson in particular (Judg. 13:7; 16:17), and that consequently he would never drink "wine or other fermented drink." On the other hand, it calls attention to his future role as a prophet of God, like Elijah (cf. Luke 1:17, "in the spirit and power of Elijah"; for John as a prophet, cf. also Luke 1:76; 3:1–2; 7:26).

Despite John the Baptist's uniqueness in

Luke–Acts, whether as a holy man or as a prophet, he is by no means the only person "filled with the Spirit" in the birth narratives. His mother Elizabeth is said to have been "filled with the Spirit" in Luke 1:41—at the prompting, to be sure, of the unborn prophet in her womb—and to have "exclaimed in a loud voice" a blessing on Mary ("Blessed are you among women, and blessed is the child you bear!"), with an acknowledgment of Mary as "the mother of my Lord." Though Elizabeth is not called a prophetess (like Anna in 2:36), there is little doubt she is prophesying, for she gives utterance to things she could not possibly have known by natural means. Luke is more explicit about Zachariah, who "was filled with the Holy Spirit and prophesied" (1:67) when he uttered the song of praise and salvation known as the Benedictus (1:68–79). Of Simeon, who saw the infant Jesus at the time of his presentation in the temple, Luke writes: "He was a righteous and godly man, waiting for the consolation of Israel, and *the Holy Spirit was on him*. It had been *revealed to him by the Holy Spirit* that he would not die until he had seen the Lord's Messiah. So he came *in the Spirit* to the temple" (Luke 2:25–27 [italics mine]). Although the phrase "filled with the Holy Spirit" is not used of Simeon, the triple reference to the Spirit's activity toward him leaves no doubt that it is implied. And although Luke does not call him a prophet in so many words, the content of his announcement—praise to God in verses 28–32 and a predictive oracle to Mary in verses 34–35—puts him unmistakably in that category. Anna is called a "prophetess" (2:36), and though her oracle is not recorded, Luke leaves the impression that it is similar in character to Simeon's (2:38) and spoken, like his, in the Spirit's power.

Luke's birth narratives give the impression that Jesus and John the Baptist were born into Jewish communities that were at once devout in their adherence to the law (e.g., Luke 1:6, 59; 2:22–25, 37), "messianic" in their eager anticipation of Israel's redemption (2:25, 38), and "charismatic" in their consistent accent on the Holy Spirit and prophecy. Although Mary is never said to have been "filled with the Spirit" or to have "prophesied," the birth of her son is described in an unparalleled way as the Holy Spirit's work: "The Holy Spirit will come upon you," the angel Gabriel told her, "and the power of the Most High will overshadow you. So that the holy one to be born will be called Son of God" (Luke 1:35). Jesus, like John the Baptist, was "holy" from his mother's womb, but his holiness was not that of a Nazirite (note the sharp contrast between John and Jesus as adults in Luke 7:31–35). Neither does Luke characterize Jesus as being "filled" with the Spirit or "moved" by the Spirit's power before baptism. At most, Luke is willing to say that Jesus as a child "grew and became strong; he was filled with wisdom, and the grace of God was on him" (2:40), and that he "grew in wisdom and stature, and in favor with God and the people" (2:52).

It is surprising that Jesus the Son of God was not "filled with the Spirit" in a setting where almost everyone else was! Even his mother Mary uttered a song with many of the same "charismatic" qualities evident in the other songs and hymns of the Lukan birth narratives (Luke 1:46–55, beginning with the words "My soul praises the Lord, and my spirit rejoices in God my Savior"). The only words attributed to Jesus in Luke 1–2 reinforce his identity as "Son of God" (2:49; cf. 1:35) but with none of the characteristics of prophecy or of speaking in the Spirit. Why is the Holy Spirit not linked to Jesus more directly and from the beginning of his life? The apparent reason is that the purpose of both the Spirit and prophecy in the first two chapters of Luke's Gospel is to bear testimony either to Jesus or to the coming of God's kingdom in Israel. Jesus was at that point the *object*, not the *subject*, of the Spirit's testimony. His own prophetic ministry was still to come.

The Holy Spirit in these opening chapters of Luke is best understood as "power," whether the power given to Mary to conceive a child (1:35: note the parallelism between "Holy Spirit" and "power"), the power to praise God as the angels do (1:46–55, 68–75; 2:28–32, 38; cf. the angelic praise of 2:13–14), or the power to serve God through the proclamation of God's word (1:15–17, 76–80). "Prophecy" for Luke seems to include both the second and third of these functions. Although the Spirit *announces* redemption, there is no indication in the birth or infancy narratives of Luke that the Spirit *is* redemption in the sense that those who have the Spirit or are "filled with the Spirit" are redeemed, while those who do not have the Spirit are unredeemed. Being "filled with the Spirit" is by no means to be equated with the Johannine experience of being "born of the Spirit," or "born again," as a metaphor for Christian salvation (cf. John 3:3–8). It refers for the most part to special utterances of praise and prophecy that have God as their source and God in Christ as their object. The other key expression, "baptized in the Holy Spirit," does not occur in the Lukan birth stories. Its meaning can be determined only in connection with the ministry of John the Baptist and the experience of the early Christians in the Book of Acts.

IV. John the Baptist.

The impression that John the Baptist was to be a prophet is confirmed in Luke 3:1–2, where he is introduced with the classic formula for describing a prophet's ministry: "In the fifteenth year of the reign of Tiberius Caesar . . . the word of God came to John the son of Zechariah in the desert" (cf., e.g., Jer. 1:1–2; Hos. 1:1; Joel 1:1; Jonah 1:1; Mic. 1:1; Zeph. 1:1; Hag. 1:1; Zech. 1:1). Even without mention of "the Spirit," the reference to "the word of God" in this formula makes it unmistakably clear that "John the son of Zechariah" was now a prophet. The promises made at his birth were about to be fulfilled (cf. 1:68, 76), for his time had come to be "manifested to Israel" (1:80). Like Israel's ancient prophets, John called the people to repentance (Luke 3:3, 8–9) and social justice (3:10–14).

John the Baptist's unique contribution to the Lukan understanding of the Spirit came not in his initial proclamation about repentance and its implications, but in his response to the questioning of the people "whether perhaps he mighty be the Messiah" (Luke 3:15). It is at this point that he introduced into Luke's narrative the expression "to baptize in [or with] the Holy Spirit" (3:16; cf. Acts 13:25, "as John was finishing his course"). That the phrase is metaphorical is clear from Luke 3:3, 7, and 12, where the verb "to baptize" refers to a bath in the Jordan River signifying repentance. "Baptize" properly goes with water (cf. Luke 11:38, where it means "wash"); only as a figure of speech can it go with a transcendent reality such as the Holy Spirit. John is here using his own practice of water baptism as a metaphor for the activity of a mightier One to come. John rejected the notion that he was the Messiah by introducing to his questioners the Messiah of his own expectation (vv. 16–17).

The matter is complicated by the fact that the future "baptism" of which John speaks is not just "in the Holy Spirit," but "in the Holy Spirit and fire" (Luke 3:16). "Fire," in fact, is its most conspicuous feature. John's Messiah is one whose "winnowing fork is in his hand to clear his threshing floor and to gather the wheat into his barn, but he will burn up the chaff with unquenchable fire" (3:17). Baptism in fire is here explained as destructive judgment, a judgment intimated already in 3:9, where John had said to the crowds coming for baptism: "Already the axe is laid to the root of the trees; every tree therefore that does not bear good fruit is to be cut down and thrown into the fire." If baptism in fire is explained by the burning of the chaff in the harvest of final judgment (v. 17b), baptism in the Holy Spirit appears to be explained by the promise that the mightier One will "gather the wheat into his barn" (v. 17a). John the Baptist was announcing final salvation and final judgment at the same time, though his emphasis was unmistakably on the latter. This is why he adopted "baptism" as his metaphor; water baptism and "baptism in the Holy Spirit and fire" have in common the twin aspects of salvation and judgment. John's message was that only by acknowledging one's sins and submitting to God's righteous judgment in water baptism could an individual hope to have a part in the coming salvation.

It is important to understand this emphasis in the ministry of John the Baptist because it helps explain why so many interpreters of Luke–Acts have understood "baptism in the Holy Spirit" as a conversion or initiation experience (see, e.g., James Dunn's influential *Baptism in the Spirit*). At the same time, it must be kept in mind that this interpretation rests more on one of Luke's sources than on the distinctive testimony of Luke–Acts itself. Both Luke 3:7–9 and 3:16–17 are closely paralleled in Matthew (for a pattern of almost verbal agreement, cf. Matt. 3:7–12). Most of this material in common is not found in Mark, suggesting that it comes from a sayings source (usually designated "Q") from which Matthew and Luke have drawn independently. Only Luke 3:16 has a parallel in Mark, where the wording is slightly different: "After me comes One who is mightier than I, the thongs of whose sandals I am

not worthy to untie. I have baptized you with water, but he will baptize you with the Holy Spirit" (Mark 1:7–8). At certain points Luke's wording agrees with Matthew's against that of Mark; e.g., "I baptize" rather than "I have baptized," and especially "He will baptize you in the Holy Spirit and fire" instead of Mark's shorter form, "He will baptize you with the Holy Spirit."

This is one of the rare instances in the Gospels where Matthew and Luke agree against Mark. It suggests that Mark and the "Q" source overlapped, in that "Q" as well as Mark had material about John the Baptist's announcement of the mightier One. Because they were following "Q" anyway in Luke 3:7–9/Matthew 3:7–10 (where Mark provides no information at all), it was natural for Matthew and Luke to continue following this source to the end rather than switching over to Mark for just one statement (they seem to have made the same choice in the Temptation narrative, preferring the dialogue between Jesus and the devil found in "Q" to Mark's very brief summary). So the interpretation of "baptizing in the Holy Spirit and fire" as salvation/judgment is an interpretation that rests on the "Q" material, not on anything distinctive to Luke. It is evidently a very old interpretation and may indeed represent John the Baptist's own understanding of what he proclaimed. That it may not be Mark's interpretation is suggested by Mark's omission of the words "and fire" in John the Baptist's pronouncement: the mightier One (whom Mark understands as Jesus) will simply "baptize with the Holy Spirit" (Mark 1:8). Mark includes nothing of the imagery of the harvest or of trees being cut down and thrown into the fire. Though Luke includes all of this, Luke's interpretation is shaped by the fact that he places it within a two-part work. This makes it necessary to ask how the promised baptism "in the Holy Spirit and fire" comes to realization in the Book of Acts.

John the Baptist passed from the scene long before Acts begins, yet Acts holds the key to Luke's understanding of John's ministry. Although the Pentecost experience in Acts 2 is never explicitly identified as the baptism in the Holy Spirit and fire, the language used to describe it evokes John's earlier prophecy. Luke mentions "a sound like the rush of a might wind," and "tongues as of fire" resting individually on Jesus' disciples as "they were all filled with the Holy Spirit and began speaking in other tongues as the Spirit gave them utterance" (Acts 2:2–4). Peter, interpreting what happened, referred not only to God's Spirit being poured out on all people (Acts 2:17–18), but to "wonders in the heaven above and signs on the earth below, blood and fire and billows of smoke" (Acts 2:19). More to the point, the Pentecost experience is linked to a prediction of Jesus that is linked in turn to the ministry and message of John the Baptist. The risen Jesus told his disciples not to leave Jerusalem but to "wait for my Father's promise which you heard from me, that John indeed baptized with water, but you will be baptized in the Holy Spirit in a few days" (Acts 1:4–5). Two things about this promise are noteworthy: First, it appears to be a quotation (by the risen Jesus) of something Jesus had said *before* his death and resurrection (for another example of a saying of Jesus not picked up in the Gospels but cited in the Book of Acts, cf. Acts 20:35); second, its structure identifies it as a saying of Jesus restating John the Baptist's pronouncement in Luke 3:16. John said, "I baptize you in water . . . but he will baptize you in the Holy Spirit and fire"; on Jesus' lips it becomes, "John baptized with water, but you will be baptized in the Holy Spirit." Peter cites the same saying of Jesus in Acts 11:16, whether from its resurrection setting in 1:5, or from an earlier occasion within Jesus' ministry. The saying of Jesus cited in Acts 1:5 and 11:16 serves as Luke's transition from John the Baptist's pronouncement about Holy Spirit and fire in Luke 3:16 to the coming of the Spirit at Pentecost. The concluding words, "in a few days," in Acts 1:5 make the connection unmistakable (in 11:16, where they are not necessary, they do not appear).

By means of this transition, Luke accents "Holy Spirit" and downplays "fire" in the prophecy of John the Baptist. Even though "fire" is part of the Pentecost experience as described in Acts 2, its place in the story is marginal. Tongues and prophecy continue to characterize the work of the Holy Spirit in the Book of Acts, but not visible "tongues of fire." More important, the transition from John the Baptist to Pentecost in Acts 1:5 gives Luke the opportunity to shift the significance of "baptism in the Holy Spirit" from the theme of salvation/judgment to that of prophetic testimony or proclamation. This he does with the accompanying promise of the risen Jesus: "You will receive power when the Holy Spirit comes on you; and you will be my witnesses in Jerusalem, and in all Judea and Samaria, and to the ends of the earth" (Acts 1:8; cf. Luke 24:49, "stay in the city until you are clothed with power from on high"). The purpose of baptism in the Holy Spirit in this passage is to confer, not salvation, but power for witness, a power coming to realization at Pentecost and afterward in praise, prophecy, tongues, and a worldwide mission. Luke has here adapted John the Baptist's "salvation/judgment" terminology to a quite different use, that of describing the "charismatic" life of Jesus' followers after his resurrection.

John the Baptist himself shows no awareness of this adaptation. From his perspective the time is too short for charismatic experiences to be of any great significance; from Luke's perspective John's time is limited in a quite different sense, cut short by imprisonment at the hands of Herod Antipas (3:19–20). John is in the narrative chiefly to bear testimony to Jesus (Luke 3:15–17; cf. 1:41, 44; Acts 13:25, 19:4). Luke downplays even John's role in the baptism of Jesus by taking him from the scene before the actual description of the Holy Spirit's descent on Jesus and the voice from heaven (Luke 3:20–21). Yet John is a proclaimer of the "gospel" or good news about Jesus, and Luke makes it clear that John said far more than what is recorded (Luke 3:18; cf. Luke's comment on Peter's Pentecost address in Acts 2:40). The sense that only a sampling of John the Baptist's words have been given is perhaps what legitimizes

for Luke the adaptation of John's message to his larger purposes in Luke–Acts as a whole.

V. Jesus: The Inaugural Events. The baptism and temptation of Jesus, his return to Galilee, and his reading of the Scripture in the synagogue at Nazareth are presented in Luke as one connected series of events inaugurating Jesus' ministry and linked together by the leading of the Holy Spirit. The importance of the baptismal story in Luke is that the Spirit's descent on Jesus at the time he was baptized (Luke 3:22) lays the basis for his announcement at Nazareth that "the Spirit of the Lord" was on him (4:18). Luke never refers to Jesus' baptism as a "baptism in the Holy Spirit," yet it was obviously a baptismal act in which the Holy Spirit was decisively involved. Significantly, perhaps, it is not an act of salvation, judgment, or initiation, but of authorization and empowerment for ministry, in keeping with Luke's understanding of baptism in the Holy Spirit in the Book of Acts.

In contrast to all previous Lukan examples of the Holy Spirit's activity, the Spirit comes on Jesus "in bodily form as a dove" (Luke 3:22); the closest parallel in Luke–Acts is perhaps the reference to visible "tongues of fire" resting on each of the apostles on the Day of Pentecost according to Acts 2:3. More than a mere "charismatic experience," the dove is for Luke a visible display of the Spirit's presence and power, laying a basis for the activity of the Spirit throughout Jesus' ministry even as the tongues of fire laid a basis for the Spirit's activity throughout the Book of Acts. For Luke it is not important who saw the Spirit so revealed, any more than it is important who saw the tongues of fire. What is crucial in each case is that the revelation is real and not a mere vision. The reality of these visible displays will be amply demonstrated by subsequent events recorded in Luke's Gospel and in the Book of Acts respectively.

The voice from heaven at Jesus' baptism was God's explicit recognition of a relationship already firmly established. Jesus did not become "Son of God" by his baptism, for Luke clearly indicated that he was God's Son already at birth (Luke 1:35) and in the temple at twelve years of age (2:49). Now at the age of thirty his sonship is confirmed (3:23). The genealogy (3:23–38) is a kind of postscript to the baptism story, reinforcing the voice from heaven by tracing Jesus' lineage back beyond Abraham, even beyond Adam, to God the Creator (3:38).

Jesus' temptation by the devil in the Judean desert begins an itinerary that brings him from the Jordan River to Jerusalem and thence to Galilee and Nazareth. The temptation story is framed by twin notices of the Holy Spirit's role in this inaugural journey:

Jesus, *full of the Holy Spirit*, returned from the Jordan and was *led by the Spirit* in the desert (Luke 4:1).

Jesus returned to Galilee *in the power of the Spirit*, and news about him spread through the entire countryside (Luke 4:14).

Between the two references to the leading of the Spirit, Jesus is said to have been "led" by the devil, first into the mountainous regions overlooking the Dead Sea and the Judean desert (Luke 4:5), and then farther up the mountains to Jerusalem and to "the highest point of the temple" (4:9). The temptation began in the desert but did not end there. Luke presents it not as a desert experience but as a journey to Jerusalem, anticipating the much longer and decisive journey to come (cf. Luke 9:51–19:44). At Jerusalem the issue raised by the devil is the risk of death: "If you are the Son of God, . . . throw yourself down from here" (4:9). For the moment Jesus rejected that option with the reminder from Scripture that to court death in this way would be to "put the Lord . . . God to the test" (4:12; cf. Deut. 6:16). Later, when the time was right, he returned to Jerusalem with the firm and specific intent of being "taken up" to God in death and resurrection (Luke 9:51; cf. 13:33), but he went there to fulfill his destiny on his own initiative, not that of the Enemy.

The itinerary continues with Jesus moving on to Galilee from Jerusalem (not from the desert) still "in the power of the Spirit" (Luke 4:14). The implication is that he had been under the Spirit's power and direction all along, even when the devil was doing the actual "leading" from the desert up to Jerusalem through the series of three exchanges that comprise the temptation experience. Luke implies that it was because Jesus was "full of the Holy Spirit" and "led by the Spirit" (4:1) that he was able to withstand the test and put the tempter to flight for the time being (4:13). When he came to the synagogue at Nazareth, therefore, and began to read from Isaiah, "The Spirit of the Lord is on me" (Luke 4:18; cf. Isa. 61:1), the reader understands why this passage of Scripture applies to Jesus himself. Jesus rolled up the scroll, sat down, and announced, "Today this scripture is fulfilled in your hearing" (4:21), for the Spirit of the Lord rested on Jesus by virtue of his baptism, and the same Spirit had led him all the way from the Jordan River through the desert to Jerusalem and on to Galilee. The Scripture read in the Nazareth synagogue in effect interprets for Luke the story of the baptism. What it means, Jesus said, is that God "has *anointed* me to proclaim good news to the poor. He has sent me to announce release to the captives and recovery of sight to the blind, to set at liberty the oppressed, to announce the acceptable year of the Lord" (Luke 4:18–19). By virtue of his baptism Jesus is the "anointed" one; though the actual title was not used, the implication is that he is "the Messiah" (Hebrew) or "the Christ" (Greek), for both words literally mean "the anointed."

The same point is made much later, in the Books of Acts, when Peter announced in the house of Cornelius "the good news of peace through Jesus Christ . . . beginning in Galilee after the baptism that John preached—about Jesus of Nazareth, and how God *anointed* him with the Holy Spirit and power, and how he went around doing good and healing all who were under the power of the devil, because God was

with him" (Acts 10:36–38). Although many people were "filled" with the Holy Spirit in Luke–Acts, only Jesus of Nazareth was "anointed" with the Spirit, for only he is "the Christ" (cf. Acts 4:26–27, where the phrase, "against his Christ" from Psalm 2:2 is interpreted by the phrase, "against your holy servant Jesus, whom you anointed"). Yet Jesus is not anointed in order to *be* something so much as to *do* something: in Acts 10:38, to travel around doing good and healing; and in Luke 4:18–19, to proclaim good news to the poor, freedom for the oppressed, and sight for the blind.

These activities interpret for Luke what "Christ" or "Messiah" means. Jesus' use of Isaiah 58:6 and 61:1–2 in the synagogue reading at Nazareth (Luke 4:18–19) suggests that he may have been identifying himself (as "anointed" or "Christ") with the servant figure mentioned repeatedly in Isaiah 40–66, and this is borne out by the phrase "your holy servant Jesus," attributed to the disciples in Acts 4:27. The allusion calls attention not to Jesus' death in particular (cf. Isa. 52:13–53:12), but to his entire ministry of proclamation and healing. His ministry in Luke's Gospel is a prophetic ministry; unique in his identity as "Son of God" and "Christ," Jesus of Nazareth was nevertheless a servant of God and prophet, even as John the Baptist had been a prophet, and as a prophet he spoke in the power of the Spirit. One contribution of Luke's Gospel to the christology of the NT, in fact, is its interpretation of the "Messiah" or "Christ" as a prophetic figure (cf. Luke 7:16, "A great prophet has appeared among us").

The impression that Jesus' words to the congregation at Nazareth, brief as they are, are words of the Holy Spirit, is confirmed by the initial reaction of his hearers: "They all spoke well of him and were amazed at the gracious words that came out of his mouth" (Luke 4:22). But their reaction changed abruptly when Jesus reminded them that a true prophet is not sent to his own people but to others. When he cited a proverb to the effect that "no prophet is acceptable in his home town" (4:24), the point is not that his home town was unwilling to accept him—the people of Nazareth had accepted Jesus gladly up to that point—but that a prophet is not "acceptable" *to God* if he stays home! A true prophet is an itinerant prophet, always on the move! In the accompanying biblical examples (4:25–27), Elijah and Elisha were not rejected by their fellow Israelites, but by virtue of their own prophetic calling moved beyond Israel to minister to needy foreigners. Jesus too was a prophet on the move, impelled by the Spirit of God. Later, after spending some time in the neighboring town of Capernaum, he said, "I must proclaim the good news of the kingdom of God to the other towns also, for that is why I was sent" (Luke 4:43). And much later, on his way to Jerusalem, he added, "I must keep going today and tomorrow and the next day, for a prophet cannot die anywhere but in Jerusalem" (Luke 13:33).

It was this compulsion in the Spirit to move on that offended the townspeople of Nazareth. They wanted their prophet all to themselves, and when they could not have him, they drove him from their town and threatened to throw him from the cliff on which the town was built (Luke 4:28–29). It is like a reenactment of the confrontation with the devil on the highest point of the temple in Jerusalem earlier in the chapter (cf. 4:9–12). Once again Jesus was face to face with death, and once again Luke makes it clear that the time for his death had not yet come (cf. John 7:30; 8:20, 59; 10:39). Jesus "passed through their midst and *went on his way"* (Luke 4:30). He resumed his itinerary, presumably still "in the power of the Spirit" (cf. 4:14). The incident at Nazareth is for Luke a kind of extension of the temptation story, except that instead of confronting the devil Jesus confronted the flesh-and-blood hostility of his own people, a hostility that surfaced again both in the Passion narrative of the Gospel and in the Book of Acts.

VI. Jesus: The Promise of the Father. It is a striking feature of Luke's Gospel that the Holy Spirit is never mentioned explicitly during Jesus' Galilean ministry after the confrontation at Nazareth (i.e., between 4:31 and 9:50). Once the Spirit had "launched" Jesus into his ministry, Luke is content simply to describe Jesus' words and actions without reminding the reader that his every move was at the Spirit's direction. Yet occasional references to Jesus as "prophet" (Luke 7:16; cf. 7:39; 9:8, 19) and as "the Christ" (Luke 4:41; 9:20) stand as evidence that the inaugural events involving the Holy Spirit had not been forgotten. On the contrary, they were the tacit presupposition of everything Jesus did.

Although his ministry was itinerant throughout, at Luke 9:51 it began to be pointed toward a specific goal, the city of Jerusalem. Here, with a notice that Jesus would be "taken up," Luke glimpses momentarily the end of the Gospel story and (implicitly at least) the beginning of the Book of Acts (cf. Acts 1:2, 22). From here to the end of Luke's Gospel there are only four explicit references to the Spirit (10:21; 11:13; 12:10, 12), and two of the four (Luke 12:10, 12) look beyond the immediacy of Jesus' ministry to the circumstances of his followers after his death and resurrection. Both the warning about those who "blaspheme against the Holy Spirit" (12:10) and the promise to Jesus' disciples "The Holy Spirit will teach you in that very hour what you must say" (12:12) are Lukan adaptations of sayings found in Mark (cf. Mark 13:11) or in the "Q" source (cf. Matt. 12:32). They were first preserved in settings where there was not a Book of Acts to follow, and they look prophetically toward a future time when Jesus' followers would be brought "before the synagogues and the rulers and the authorities" (Luke 12:11; cf. 21:12–15). Luke provides for these sayings a fulfillment in the Book of Acts, where the apostles faced just such situations and were given the courage and the words with which to respond (cf., e.g., Acts 4:1–12; 5:17–18, 27–32; 6:12–7:60; 24:10–21; 25:7–11).

In at least one instance Luke passes up an opportunity to mention the role of the Spirit in Jesus' ministry of healing: in Luke 11:20 Jesus says, "If I by the finger of God cast out demons, then the kingdom of God has come upon you"

(the parallel in Matthew 12:28 begins, "If I by the *Spirit* of God cast out demons . . . "). The only explicit reference to the Holy Spirit in connection with Jesus himself after the inaugural events of chapters 3–4 is found in Luke 10:21. That this is a decisive pronouncement and that it comes at a decisive moment in Jesus' ministry is clear from the verses that immediately precede it. The seventy disciples had just returned with joy from the mission on which Jesus had sent them, saying, "Even the demons are subject to us in your name" (10:17). Jesus' reply is striking: "I saw Satan fall like lightning from heaven. Look, I have given you authority to tread on serpents and scorpions, and on all the power of the Enemy. But do not rejoice that the spirits are subject to you; rejoice that your names are written in heaven" (Luke 10:18–20). Then "in that very hour" Jesus did exactly what he had just commanded his disciples to do: "He *rejoiced in the Holy Spirit* and said, 'I praise you, Father, Lord of heaven and earth, that you have hidden these things from the wise and understanding, and have revealed them to little children. Yes, Father, for this was your good pleasure!' "

Here if anywhere, Luke's Gospel portrays Jesus as a charismatic. His word of praise to the Father was clearly intended as an expression of his "joy in the Holy Spirit." There is every reason to believe that he continued to speak in the Spirit in the following verse, where no specific audience is in view: "All things have been committed to me by my Father. No one knows who the Son is except the Father, and no one knows who the Father is except the Son and anyone to whom the Son chooses to reveal him" (Luke 10:22). These pronouncements are recorded in Matthew as well (11:25–27) but without the notice that Jesus "rejoiced in the Holy Spirit." At this point in the Gospel narrative, Jesus' disciples participated fully in his itinerary by going out "two by two ahead of him to every town and place where he was about to go" (Luke 10:1). Now they were shown to be the objects of God the Father's "good pleasure" (cf. 2:14), as Jesus himself was in his baptism (cf. 3:22), and victorious over Satan, as Jesus was in his temptation. As those who belonged to the Father they had access to the Holy Spirit, yet the Spirit is not mentioned in connection with the mission on which Jesus had sent them, nor in connection with their recent victories over the powers of evil. For the time being the Spirit remained for them a promise rather than a present reality.

The promise becomes explicit in Luke 11:13, where Jesus asked rhetorically, after a series of illustrations, "How much more will the Father from heaven give the Holy Spirit to those who ask him?" It is likely that Luke has in mind here (just as in 12:10–12) the gift of the Spirit in the Book of Acts. The risen Jesus alludes to the Holy Spirit (without using the actual term) just once near the end of Luke's Gospel with this announcement: "I am sending upon you *the promise of my Father;* you, however, must stay in the city until you are clothed with *power from on high"* (Luke 24:49). The phrase "power from on high" clearly refers to the Holy Spirit (cf. "power" in Acts 1:8;

6:8), while the phrase, "promise of my Father" will be echoed significantly in Acts 1:4 ("wait for the promise of the Father") and in Acts 2:34 ("having received from the Father the promise of the Holy Spirit"). The notion of the coming of the Spirit as a fulfillment of the Father's promise looks back at the ministry of Jesus, but what specific promise is being cited? As we have already seen, Jesus referred in Acts 1:5 to his own earlier restatement of the words of John the Baptist: "John baptized with water, but you will be baptized in the Holy Spirit" (cf. also Acts 11:16). The future passive form of the verb ("you will be baptized") is a form often used in the NT to imply that God is the subject of the action. Thus, in contrast to John the Baptist, Jesus identified God rather than a coming Messiah as the one baptizing in the Spirit. Yet there is no mention of "the Father" in this saying. This makes it likely that Luke 11:13 is also in mind—at least in Luke's mind—in connection with the recurring notion of the Spirit as "the promise of the Father" in Luke 24 and Acts 1–2. The Spirit is not given or withheld arbitrarily or by some divine whim. Because God is Father, first to Jesus (Luke 1:35; 2:49; 3:22) and then to his disciples (Luke 10:21–22), he will give the Holy Spirit freely to his children. All they have to do is ask (cf. Luke 11:5–13).

Perhaps in recognition of this element in the teaching of Luke's Gospel, some later scribes substituted for the petition "Thy kingdom come" in the Lukan form of the Lord's Prayer a petition for the Holy Spirit: "Let thy Holy Spirit come upon us and cleanse us" (see Metzger, 1971, 154–56). Though not original, this petition undoubtedly captures something of Luke's understanding of the Spirit in relation to prayer both in Luke's Gospel and in the Book of Acts.

VII. The Power of Pentecost. Nothing in the first chapter of the Book of Acts suggests that the Holy Spirit was about to come among the people of God as a power and presence never known before. On the contrary, Luke begins his second volume with the information that Jesus, before he was "taken up" to heaven, had commanded his chosen apostles "through the Holy Spirit" (Acts 1:2; cf. Luke 24:45–49), while Peter later referred to "what the Holy Spirit said before through the mouth of David" concerning the fate of Judas Iscariot (Acts 1:16; cf. 4:25). Yet the risen Jesus makes it unmistakably clear to his disciples that the Spirit was about to come in a new and unprecedented way. The "promise of the Father" was soon to be fulfilled, not for one or two prophets or a few gifted individuals but for the entire group of disciples (120 in all, Acts 1:15) who had accompanied Jesus from Galilee to Jerusalem, and to whom Jesus appeared repeatedly over a forty-day period (cf. Acts 13:31). The content of the promise is that they would all be "baptized with the Holy Spirit" (1:5), and this phrase from the vocabulary of John the Baptist is then interpreted to mean, "You will receive power when the Holy Spirit has come upon you; and you will be my witnesses in Jerusalem and in all Judea and Samaria, and to the last part of the earth" (1:8). From Luke's perspective, this bap-

tism in the Spirit comes to realization at Pentecost not as conversion or salvation but as empowerment, specifically empowerment for witness or ministry, and above all for an itinerant ministry. Just as in the case of Jesus, the coming of the Holy Spirit in the Book of Acts confers on his recipients power and freedom in speech—whether praise or prophecy—and directs them on a sacred journey toward a divinely appointed goal. If Jesus' itinerary took him from the Jordan River to Jerusalem to Galilee and back to Jerusalem again, the itinerary of his followers was to take them from Jerusalem to Rome—and eventually beyond.

Two crucial questions about Pentecost for charismatics and Pentecostals are, What, if anything, is unique and unrepeatable about the Pentecost experience? and What, if anything, is repeatable about it, or even normative for all serious believers everywhere? The first question can be addressed by noticing what is unique about the Pentecost story within Luke–Acts itself. Both in its placement and in its significance, Pentecost in the Book of Acts can be appropriately compared to the baptism of Jesus in the Gospel of Luke. One unique feature of each of these narratives is that the Holy Spirit became visible, first in the "bodily form" of a dove (Luke 3:22), and then in "tongues of fire" (Acts 2:3). In each case, Luke is sensitive enough to Jewish ideas of God to avoid a literal identification: the visible dove is not actually the Spirit of God, but the Spirit appears "as" a dove; by the same token the visible tongues over the disciples are "as" fire. In each case too, the visible manifestation of the Holy Spirit comes "on," or "upon," someone: first on Jesus at his baptism, then on the disciples in Jerusalem after Jesus' resurrection. Never again in either Luke's Gospel or the Book of Acts does the Spirit become visible as in these two programmatic events.

The visible "tongues of fire" in Acts 2:3 serve as a signal to Luke's readers that the "baptism with the Holy Spirit and fire" predicted by John the Baptist was coming to realization not as judgment but as empowerment for ministry. The use of the word "tongues" in connection with the fire links the visible appearance to the spoken "tongues" that immediately follow: the disciples "were all filled with the Holy Spirit and began to speak in other tongues as the Spirit gave them utterance" (Acts 2:4). For the first time in Luke–Acts, the ability to speak in "other tongues" becomes the evidence that people were "filled with the Holy Spirit." If the visible "tongues of fire" were unique and unrepeatable, what about the audible "other tongues" in which the disciples spoke? The crowds were immediately aware that even though the speakers were all Galileans, they were hearing, each in his "own native dialect" (vv. 8), and that they were hearing them speaking in the people's "own tongues the mighty works of God" (v. 11). The reaction makes it clear that the "other tongues" being spoken were the very real human languages and dialects represented by the various ethnic groups listed in verses 9–11. No interpretation was necessary.

Although the precise term "other tongues"

does not occur again in the Book of Acts, speaking in tongues is mentioned twice more (Acts 10:46; 19:6). Of these, the phenomenon described in Acts 10:46 is explicitly said to match the Pentecost experience. While Peter was preaching in the house of Cornelius, "the Holy Spirit fell on those who heard the word" (10:44). Then the Jewish believers who had accompanied Peter were amazed because "they heard them speaking in tongues and magnifying God" (v. 46). Nothing is said here of a variety of specific languages, yet the reference to "magnifying God" makes it clear that the tongues speaking was understood (cf. "the mighty works of God" in 2:11). This is confirmed by Peter's remark that Cornelius and his companions had received the Holy Spirit just as the Jewish believers had" (10:47) and by his subsequent testimony: "When I began to speak, the Holy Spirit fell on them *just as on us at the beginning*" (11:15). This experience he identifies as the baptism in the Holy Spirit promised by John the Baptist (11:16).

The only remaining reference in Acts to speaking in tongues is less explicit. When Paul laid hands on some newly baptized believers in Ephesus, "the Holy Spirit came on them, and they spoke in tongues and prophesied" (Acts 19:6). Nothing is said of the content of their speech or of how it was heard, and no direct comparisons are drawn with what happened either at Pentecost or in the house of Cornelius. What is stated, however, is that tongues speaking was accompanied by prophecy, and it is fair to assume that the prophecy at least was understood by those who heard. The association of tongues with prophecy is characteristic of the Pentecost narrative as well.

If the facts of the Pentecost experience are sketched in Acts 2:1–4, the significance of those facts is set forth in Peter's speech in 2:14–36. Luke places both the event and its interpretation within the larger framework of action and response between the disciples of Jesus on the one hand and the crowds gathered in Jerusalem for the festival of Pentecost on the other. The chapter as a whole can be outlined as follows:

1–4 The Pentecost Experience
5–13 Reaction of the Crowd—"What does this mean?" (vv. 12–13).
14–36 Peter's Explanation of the Meaning
37 Reaction of the Crowd—"What shall we do?"
38–40 Peter's Call to Repentance
41–47 Response and Conclusions: A New Community

The heart of the exchange is Peter's long explanation in verses 14–36 of the remarkable display the crowd has just witnessed. Luke skillfully sets the stage for Peter's sermon with the crowd's introductory question, "What does this mean?" in verse 12, accompanied by a mocking suggestion that the disciples had had "too much wine" (v. 13). Even though everyone heard in their respective languages what the disciples were saying, they seem to have heard unintelligible sounds as well, so as to give the impression of drunkenness.

Peter began with a light touch (these people cannot be drunk because it is only nine o'clock in the morning!), but he quickly moves on to a serious explanation of the disciples' behavior. Just as the descent of the Holy Spirit on Jesus at his baptism was interpreted by the Scripture that he read later at the synagogue in Nazareth (Luke 4:18–19), so the descent of the Spirit on the disciples at Pentecost was interpreted by a passage of Scripture, in this case Joel 2:28–32 (or, in the Greek translation, 3:1–5), as cited in Acts 2:17–21. Just as Jesus simply read the text from Isaiah 61:1–2 and confined his interpretation to the announcement, "Today this scripture has been fulfilled in your hearing" (Luke 4:21), so Peter quotes his text in its entirety, prefaced by the simple declaration that *"this* [i.e., what they had just witnessed] is what was spoken by the prophet Joel" (Acts 2:16). The key word *this* was echoed later, in verse 33: "Being therefore exalted at the right hand of God, and having received from the Father the promise of the Holy Spirit, [Jesus] has poured out *this* which you see and hear."

The prophecy of Joel was that God would some day pour out his Spirit on everyone—male and female, young and old alike—and that therefore everyone would prophesy. Their prophecies would be accompanied by terrifying wonders in the sky and on the earth, signaling "the great and spectacular day of the Lord." Those who are saved at that time will be those who "call on the name of the Lord." Peter's sermon as Luke records it makes few modifications in the text of Joel: the indefinite "some day" or "after this" becomes "in the last days" (Acts 2:17), and the phrase, "they shall prophesy" is used not once but twice (i.e., "your sons and daughters shall prophesy," v. 17; "I will pour out my Spirit . . . and they shall prophesy," v. 18). To Peter, and apparently to Luke, the evidence that the Holy Spirit was poured out was that all the people of God now had the gift of prophetic utterance. Luke's assumption is that the remarkable phenomenon of speaking in other tongues is the "prophesying" to which Joel referred. Unlike Paul, Luke makes no distinction between tongues speaking and prophecy; tongues are simply one specific form of the more general gift of prophetic utterance.

Paul's distinction between tongues and prophecy is that "a person who speaks in a tongue speaks not to humans but to God; for no one understands him, but he utters mysteries in the Spirit. On the other hand, he who prophesies speaks to human beings for their upbuilding and encouragement and consolation. He who speaks in a tongue edifies himself, but he who prophesies edifies the congregation" (1 Cor. 14:2–4). Paul was saying that tongues speaking is a form of prayer or praise, while prophecy is more like preaching. But Paul was dealing with a type of tongues speaking that is unintelligible to the hearers without an interpreter (1 Cor. 14:10–13). As soon as the tongues are "translated," either by the speaker or by someone else in the congregation, they begin to function in much the same way as prophecy, and the congregation is encouraged and edified. The tongues speaking on the Day of Pentecost in Luke–Acts was very different in that no "translation" was needed. Luke is very clear that "each one heard them speaking in his own language" (Acts 2:6; cf. v. 11). This was the whole point of the Pentecost miracle.

Therefore, to make any kind of sharp distinction between speech addressed to God and speech addressed to human beings is to miss the point of Luke's account. Prophecy for Luke is simply speech in the power of the Holy Spirit, whether that speech is praise directed toward God or proclamation directed toward a human audience. When Luke says that the disciples at Pentecost were "telling the mighty works of God" (Acts 2:1), does he mean that they were telling the crowd how great God is, or that (in the hearing of the crowd) they were extolling God himself for his greatness and power? It is not altogether clear, nor (from Luke's perspective) does it matter. Those who were "filled with the Holy Spirit" or who spoke in the power of the Spirit in Luke's Gospel could be represented as speaking either to human beings (e.g., Luke 1:42–45, 67–79; 2:34–35) or to God (2:29–32; 10:21). The important thing was that in either case their words were the Spirit's words and in that sense genuine prophecy. The stunning news of Pentecost was that prophecy was no longer the prerogative of a few exceptional individuals but had now broken out in a whole community. The text from Joel was now beginning to be fulfilled. What would be next?

According to Joel, the universal gift of prophecy would be accompanied and confirmed by strange portents both in the sky and on earth. Peter in the Book of Acts modifies the oracle slightly to distinguish between "wonders" in the sky and "signs" on the earth; subsequently in Acts "wonders and signs" are used together for the miracles performed by the apostles in the course of their mission (Acts 2:43; 4:30; 5:12; 6:8; 14:3; 15:12; cf. also the reference to Jesus in Acts 2:22 and to Moses in 7:36). Joel also mentions "blood and fire and columns of smoke" and the phenomenon of the sun turning to darkness and the moon to blood. Peter could easily have ended his quotation before these words (just as Jesus ended his quotation of Isaiah 61:1–2 in Luke 4:18–19 before the words "the day of vengeance of our God"), but he did not. The fact that he did not raises the question of how Peter—or Luke—intended these words to be understood. In some sense, as we have seen, they are anticipated and dramatized by the visible tongues of fire over the heads of the apostles (Acts 2:2), but it is doubtful that Luke regards this phenomenon as the "fulfillment" of Joel's prediction in quite the same way as the tongues speaking fulfills the prediction of universal prophecy or the performance of miracles will begin to fulfill the prediction of "signs and wonders." Luke knows that these things are still in the future. The tongues of fire are at most a token of what is to come. Luke's presentation of Jesus' last discourse places the "signs in the sun and moon and stars" and the shaking of "the powers of the heavens" (21:25–26) at the end of the age, after Jerusalem's desolation and just before the coming of the Son of Man. The implication of Peter's speech at Pentecost in Acts is that all these things are very near; if the universal prophesying of young and old, and of male and female, has begun, the other and more spectacular signs of the end cannot be far behind. The sense of nearness lends urgency to the final words from the prophet Joel: "And it shall be that everyone who calls on the name of the Lord shall be saved" (Acts 2:21).

It is perhaps the reference at the end of the Joel quotation to being "saved" that has led to a significant difference between Pentecostals and non-Pentecostals over the meaning of the Pentecost account in Acts 2. Is it a matter of empowerment for service, or is it a matter of salvation? After proclaiming the resurrection of Jesus as a fulfillment of Scripture and linking the resurrection to the outpouring of the Spirit (Acts 2:22–36), Peter addressed the crowd directly on the issue of being "saved": "Repent and be baptized every one of you in the name of Jesus Christ for the forgiveness of your sins, and you shall receive the gift of the Holy Spirit. For the promise is to you and to your children and to all who are far off, as many as the Lord our God calls" (Acts 2:38–39). Luke comments that Peter spoke "many other words" on that occasion and gives one pointed example to conclude the whole speech: "Save yourselves from this crooked generation" (2:40). The end of Peter's sermon echoes in a number of ways the proclamation of John the Baptist—e.g., the call to repentance and baptism for the forgiveness of sins (v. 38; cf. Luke 3:3); the question of the crowd, "What shall we do?" (v. 37; cf. Luke 3:10, 12, 14); the reference to a "crooked generation" (v. 40b; cf. Luke 3:5, 7–9); and the indication that more was said than what is recorded (v. 40a; cf. Luke 3:18).

To what experience was Peter inviting this crowd of worshipers at Pentecost? Was it to the same experience of empowerment by the Spirit that they had just witnessed among Peter and his companions? Or was it to salvation and the forgiveness of their sins? Is a distinction necessary between "Pentecost" as an experience of the gathered disciples of Jesus (Acts 2:1–4) and as an experience of those who heard Peter's sermon? Luke says nothing about any tongues speaking in the latter instance, only that "those who received his message were baptized, and there were added that day about three thousand souls" (Acts 2:41). The description of the daily life of these new believers places little emphasis on prophecy or any other typically "charismatic" activities: "They devoted themselves to the apostles' teaching and fellowship, to the breaking of bread and the prayers" (v. 42). Although Luke mentions "wonders and signs," he indicates that these were done "through the apostles," not by all believers. The community had their possessions in common, attended the temple daily, and shared meals in their homes, but only a brief reference to "praising God and having favor with all the people" (v. 47) hints at anything close to the sort of charismatic speech described in the early part of the chapter (e.g., in v. 11, "telling . . . the mighty works of God").

Charismatics and Pentecostals have tended to look at Pentecost in terms of the experience of Jesus' disciples in Acts 2:1–13—consequently as empowerment for service by being "filled with the Holy Spirit," with prophetic utterance (specifically tongues) as the outward evidence. Noncharismatics (whether Baptists, Anglicans, Campbellites, or whatever) are drawn more to the experience of the three thousand who responded to Peter's message according to Acts 2:37–47. Theirs is a more "normal" experience by non-Pentecostal standards, or so it might seem: "receiving the word," "being baptized," "joining the church," and getting involved in prayer and praise meetings and in the Lord's Supper. Only the sharing of property seems strange and unfamiliar to most Christians, and this is the case no matter what views they may have on tongues and prophecy.

It is difficult to deny that Acts 2 is dealing *both* with empowerment for service *and* with salvation. Within Luke–Acts, the emphasis on empowerment for service goes back to the prophetic utterances of Luke 1–2, the baptism and temptation of Jesus, and his presentation of himself as prophet and Messiah in the synagogue at Nazareth. The emphasis on salvation goes back to John the Baptist, his call to repentance and baptism, his warning of divine judgment, and his promise of baptism "in the Holy Spirit and fire." Luke merges the two traditions in this chapter. The baptism "in the Holy Spirit and fire" came to realization for Jesus' disciples in the form of empowerment for ministry, dramatized by tongues of fire and demonstrated in the prophetic tongues speaking of 2:4. They were supernaturally empowered to preach, and one of them, Peter, did preach on behalf of the whole group. But the immediate object of his preaching was not that three thousand more should in turn be empowered to preach or prophesy or speak in tongues, but that three thousand should be "saved from this crooked generation" (Acts 2:40). Still playing on the text from Joel, Peter matched the phrase "everyone who calls on the name of the Lord" (Acts 2:21; Joel 2:32a) with a corresponding phrase that he had not quoted before: "as many as the Lord calls" (2:39; cf. Joel 2:32b). The promise of salvation extends beyond the present moment to "your descendants" and beyond Jerusalem and Palestine "to all who are far off" (v. 39).

Luke's justification for merging the notion of salvation with that of empowerment for service is that the same Holy Spirit who calls people into a right relationship to the God of Israel calls them as well to prophecy and praise (whether in their own languages or in "other tongues") and to an itinerant mission in the world. The very words "call" and "calling" encompass both aspects of the Spirit's work. It can well be assumed that many, perhaps all, of the three thousand new believers of Acts 2:41 at some point prophesied or announced in some way the "mighty works of God," as the disciples had done in their hearing (cf. v. 11), but Luke is not interested in the precise nature or circumstances of these continuing displays of divine power.

One more aspect of the Pentecost narrative in Acts remains to be explored, and it is without question the most important. The heart of Peter's explanation of the Pentecost phenomenon is his rehearsal of the work of God through Jesus Christ in Acts 2:22–36: first, Jesus' ministry of "miracles, wonders, and signs" (v. 22); anticipating both the ministry of the apostles (cf. v. 43) and the end of the age (cf. v. 19); then his death by crucifixion (v. 23); and finally, and at much greater length, his resurrection (vv. 24–32) and ascension to heaven (vv. 33–36). In connection with the last two, Peter introduced quotations from the Psalms to demonstrate that David spoke not of his own resurrection in Psalm 16 (vv. 25–31), nor of his own exaltation in Psalm 110 (vv. 34–35), but that, "being a prophet" (v. 30), he was pointing in each instance specifically to his descendant Jesus. Between the two biblical references, Peter summarized concisely the two stages of Jesus' vindication as Luke–Acts has portrayed them: his resurrection from the dead on Easter morning (v. 32) and his ascension to heaven forty days later (v. 33). The resurrection rests on the testimony of the apostles ("we are all witnesses," v. 32); the crowds may believe their report or not. The ascension is different, Peter said, in that the crowds could see with their own eyes and hear with their own ears its effects: "Being therefore exalted to the right hand of God, and having received from the Father the promise of the Holy Spirit, *he has poured out this which you see and hear*" (v. 33; cf. v. 16). The Spirit was the evidence of Jesus' ascension, and prophecy in "other tongues" was the evidence of the Spirit. If the function of the Holy Spirit in Luke's Gospel was to empower Jesus to testify to the kingdom of God, the Spirit's function in the Book of Acts is to testify to Jesus himself as risen and ascended Lord (v. 36, "Let the house of Israel . . . know assuredly that God has made him both Lord and Messiah, this Jesus whom you crucified"). Prophecy and tongues are therefore never an end in themselves but a means of glorifying Jesus and the God who exalted him.

VIII. The Spirit in Jerusalem. Even though the Holy Spirit is not explicitly mentioned in Luke's description of the daily life of the three thousand in Jerusalem who accepted Peter's message (Acts 2:42–47), the Spirit's presence soon became evident in a variety of ways. Peter healed a lame man at the temple gate called Beautiful (Acts 3:1–10); once again a "notable sign" (cf. 4:16) called for an interpretation, and once again Peter attempted to provide one in the form of a sermon (3:11–26). He and his companions were interrupted and arrested by the Sadducees and temple authorities, but when Peter was questioned the next day, he took up the message again (4:5–12). The thrust of his interrupted sermon on the healing of the lame man is that the miracle had been accomplished by the power and in the name of the risen Jesus (Acts 3:12, 16; 4:10) and that those who had seen it had to repent: "Repent . . . and turn again so that your sins may be blotted out, and times of refreshing may come from the presence of the Lord" (3:19). The phrase "times of refreshing" is another of Luke's variant expressions for the Holy Spirit, like "promise of my Father" and "power from on high" in Luke 24:49. Peter's invitation to the crowd in Acts 3:19 echoes his earlier invitation in 2:38, with the added promise that Jesus would return as Messiah to establish his kingdom (Acts 3:20–21; cf. 1:6). The response of the crowd was similar, for the number of those who believed increases from three thousand to five thousand (4:4). The next day, when Peter was given the opportunity to continue, Luke notes that he was "filled with the Spirit" (4:8) and that he again invited his hearers to be saved: "There is salvation in no one else, for no other name under heaven has been given to humanity; by this name we must be saved" (4:12). The pattern of Acts 2 thus repeats itself in chapters 3–4, as the apostles (Peter and John, but especially Peter) were given the Holy Spirit for empowerment, while the crowds were invited to receive the Spirit for salvation.

Later in Acts 4, after being warned by the authorities not to preach any more in the name of Jesus, Peter and John returned to the congregation of believers, who "lifted their voices together to God" in prayer (4:24–30). Woven into the prayer (vv. 25–28) is an exposition of Psalm 2, in much the same fashion in which Peter had expounded Psalms 16 and 110 in his Pentecost sermon. David is said to have spoken the words of Psalm 2:1–2 "by the Holy Spirit" (v. 25), and Luke's apparent assumption was that the explanation of the Psalm was given by the same Spirit. The "Gentiles" who "rage" are seen as personified in Pontius Pilate, while the "people" who "imagine vain things" are understood as the "people of Israel" represented by Herod Antipas. Both groups had "gathered together" against Jesus, the Anointed One of God to do what had been decreed (vv. 27–28; cf. Luke 23:12). The content of the prayer was, "Lord . . . enable your servants to speak your word with all boldness, as you stretch out your hand for healing, and as signs and wonders are done through the name of your holy servant Jesus" (vv. 29–30).

The prayer to "speak your word with all boldness" is essentially a prayer for the Holy Spirit (cf. Luke 11:13), and it was dramatically answered in verse 31: "When they had prayed, the place in which they were gathered together was shaken; and they were all filled with the Holy Spirit and spoke the word of God with boldness." The physical effect of shaking recalls the "mighty wind" of Acts 2:2, and though there is no mention of tongues speaking, the "boldness" given to the Jerusalem believers serves Luke equally well as evidence of the Spirit's power. The principle at work is that on each occasion the Holy Spirit provided exactly what was needed: in one instance miraculous communication with an audience representing many languages and cultures; in the other, courage to speak in the face of persecution, just as Jesus had promised (cf. Luke 12:11–12).

The presence of the Holy Spirit in Jerusalem was also vividly dramatized in the incident involving Ananias and Sapphira. Nothing was said earlier of any specific connection between the coming of the Spirit and the practice of the

Jerusalem community of having all their possessions in common (Acts 2:44–45), but in chapter 5 it becomes apparent that this too was part of the Spirit's unique ministry (the story of Ananias and Sapphira serves as a reminder that the Spirit's activity may be presupposed in the Book of Acts even in passages where it is not explicitly mentioned). Peter's first words to Ananias are, "Why has Satan filled your heart, that you have lied to the Holy Spirit and kept back part of the proceeds of the land? . . . You have not lied to humans but to God" (Acts 5:3–4). To Sapphira he says, "How is it that you have agreed together to tempt the Spirit of the Lord?" (v. 9). The "holy" Spirit is revealed to be indeed a Spirit of *holiness*, defining a holy community, with all the implications of purity and reverence that the word implies. The Spirit is also revealed once again as "power," this time with the message that power can destroy as well as save. Luke concludes the story with the comment that "great fear came over the whole congregation, and over everyone who heard of these things" (Acts 5:11).

Luke returns to the theme of the Holy Spirit as helper in persecution in Acts 5:29–31. Peter and the other apostles, after a miraculous release from prison, defied the high priest and the Sanhedrin with the announcement "We must obey God rather than men" (v. 29); another brief rehearsal of the death, resurrection, and exaltation of Jesus (vv. 30–31); and the claim "We are witnesses to these things, and so is the Holy Spirit whom God has given to those who obey him" (v. 32; notice the repetition of the word "obey," an emphasis all the more poignant against the background of the disobedience of Ananias and Sapphira).

A new source of persecution surfaces in chapter 6, after the appointment of seven additional leaders to assist the apostles. These seven were to be "full of the Spirit and of wisdom" (Acts 6:3; cf. the descriptions of Jesus in Luke 2:40, 52). When the seven are set apart by prayer and the laying on of hands (6:6), the point is not that by these procedures they received the Spirit, but that these procedures were followed because these leaders were already recognized as Spirit-filled individuals. Stephen in particular was singled out as "a man full of faith and of the Holy Spirit" (6:5), or "full of grace and power," so that he did "great wonders and signs among the people" (6:8). Stephen too was the one who becomes the focus of a new wave of opposition, this time from certain synagogues of the Jewish diaspora who "could not withstand the wisdom and the Spirit with which he spoke" (6:10). The implication is that Stephen was a prophet and that the long sermon attributed to him in Acts 7:2–53 was uttered in the Spirit's power. Stephen concluded his sermon before the high priest and the Sanhedrin with the charge "You always resist the Holy Spirit" (i.e., by persecuting the prophets and Christ and by disobeying their own law, vv. 51–53). As his hearers moved to put him to death, Stephen, "full of the Holy Spirit, gazed into heaven and saw the glory of God, and Jesus standing at the right hand of God, and said, 'Behold, I see the heavens opened, and the Son of Man standing at the right hand of God'" (vv.

55–57). For Stephen the fullness of the Spirit finally meant not only boldness of speech but clarity of vision (cf. Jesus' visions in Luke 10:18 and 22:43). Consequently, in his dying he was like Jesus in two ways: he commended his own spirit to God (cf. Luke 23:46) and he asked forgiveness for his tormentors (cf. Luke 23:34). The vision of a dying martyr and the actions that followed it are further evidence of the presence and power of the Holy Spirit as Luke understands it.

IX. Samaria and the Gentiles. After the stoning of Stephen, persecution forced many of the Christians out of Jerusalem, scattering them throughout Judea and Samaria (Acts 8:1). Luke focuses attention on Philip, another of the seven chosen by the apostles in chapter 6, and his ministry in Samaria (8:4–8). As a result of healings and exorcisms there, people "paid attention" to Philip's proclamation of the good news about Jesus Christ; there was joy in the city, and a number were baptized (vv. 6–8, 12). The distinctive feature of the Samaritan experience is that the Holy Spirit came only when Peter and John were sent from Jerusalem to pray for the new believers (cf. Luke 11:13) and lay hands on them (vv. 14–17). Previously the apostles had laid hands on certain individuals *because* they were filled with the Holy Spirit (cf. 6:3, 6); here the laying on of the apostles' hands *confers* the Spirit! The effects or evidences of the Spirit's coming are not stated in this account. Luke does not say whether or not there was prophecy or tongues among the Samaritan believers. He mentions "much joy" (v. 8), but this was *before* the ministry of Peter and John. Luke is more interested in the false prophet Simon (vv. 9–11) and his efforts to buy the power to confer the Spirit (vv. 18–24). Whatever the Spirit's effects, they were visible enough that Simon "*saw* that the Spirit was given through the laying on of the apostles' hands" (v. 18). The likely implication is that Simon witnessed prophecy and/or tongues speaking among the new believers and wanted to control this new source of power for his own purposes.

In any event, the Samaritan episode poses acutely the question of whether the coming of the Holy Spirit in the Book of Acts was for empowerment or for salvation. In the Pentecost narrative the accent was on the former in connection with the apostles and on the latter in connection with the crowds who heard Peter's message. It is fair to assume that in Samaria the crowds received salvation when they "believed Philip as he preached good news about the kingdom of God and the name of Jesus Christ" (Acts 8:12) and were "baptized in the name of the Lord Jesus" (8:16). Those who had "paid attention" to Simon the magician and his message about himself now "paid attention" to Philip. Luke mentions that "even Simon himself believed, and was baptized," and "followed Philip everywhere, astonished by the great signs and miracles he saw" (8:13).

Some have inferred from this example that there was something wrong or false about the faith of the Samaritans until they received the Spirit at the hands of the apostles from Jerusalem (see, e.g., J. Dunn, *Baptism in the Holy Spirit*,

64–65), but nothing in the text bears this out. Simon the magician is in no way typical of the Samaritans as a group. The implication of Luke's account is rather that many in Samaria had genuinely believed and had been baptized and that consequently "there was much joy in that city" (v. 8), presumably because their sins had been forgiven. Neither joy nor the forgiveness of sins seem to have hinged on receiving the Holy Spirit. When they did receive the Spirit from the Jerusalem apostles, therefore, it must have been for empowerment and not for salvation.

Whether all the Samaritan believers or only certain individuals among them received the Spirit must remain an open question. For example, did Simon the magician himself receive the Spirit? If not, did he think that he had? Luke's narrative of the ministry in Samaria leaves many issues of this kind unresolved. What it does make clear is that the apostles from Jerusalem were indeed Spirit-filled men. This is seen not only in the effectiveness of the laying on of their hands, but in the power of their prayers (v. 15) and in their clarity of vision. Like Stephen, Peter had a vision given presumably by the Spirit, and on the basis of that vision he pronounced judgment on Simon the magician: "I *see* [i.e., foresee] you in the gall of bitterness and the bond of iniquity" (v. 23). Simon's fate is left in limbo at the story's end, as Simon pleads, "Pray for me to the Lord, that nothing of what you have said may come upon me" (v. 24). The positive side of such a petition is that the Holy Spirit would come on Simon as on the others at Samaria, but Luke leaves Simon's fate unresolved. Instead he notes that the Jerusalem apostles completed Philip's mission to Samaria, "preaching the gospel to many villages of the Samaritans" as they returned to Jerusalem (v. 25). The implication is that the empowerment given by the laying on of the apostles' hands enabled the Samaritans who received the Spirit to carry on the mission for themselves among their own people. Luke, however, does not pursue either the subsequent history of the Samaritan communities or the subsequent machinations of Simon (for the latter, cf. Irenaeus in his late second-century treatise *Against Heresies* 1.23; also the *Acts of Peter* 6–18).

Peter was a visionary again in the story of Cornelius, the first Gentile convert, in Acts 10. The promise of Joel, "Your young men shall see visions and your old men shall dream dreams," (Acts 2:17) comes repeatedly to fulfillment as the Holy Spirit leads the Christian movement across ever-new cultural barriers. After the interrelated visions of Saul of Tarsus and of Ananias of Damascus in chapter 9 (see below), Luke uses again the technique of two separate visions in separate places to bring individuals together so that the Holy Spirit might be given. In this case, the centurion Cornelius at Caesarea "saw clearly in a vision an angel of God" (Acts 10:3), while Peter the next day at Joppa "fell into a trance and saw the heavens opened, and something descending, like a great sheet, let down by four corners on the earth" (10:11). Peter's vision, repeated twice (vv. 11–16), broke down for him the distinction between clean and unclean as he had always understood it, and impelled him to respond to the messengers from Cornelius: "And while Peter was pondering the vision, *the Spirit* said to him, 'Three men are looking for you. Rise and go down, and accompany them without hesitation; for *I have sent them'*" (vv. 19–20; cf. 11:12). The italicized words show the extent to which the Holy Spirit was orchestrating the whole process of Cornelius' conversion and the extension of the Christian message to the Gentile world. The Spirit is both the source and the interpreter of the decisive visions by which barriers are broken and boundaries crossed.

The role of the Spirit in what happened later in the house of Cornelius is well known. After Peter's sermon (Acts 10:34–43), Luke reports, "the Holy Spirit fell on all who heard the word. And the circumcised believers who came with Peter were amazed that the gift of the Holy Spirit had ben poured out even on the Gentiles" (vv. 44–45; cf. 11:15). The evidence here, as at Pentecost, was that "they heard them speaking in tongues and magnifying God" (cf. 2:11). There was no need for the laying on of hands, because it was evident to everyone present that the Holy Spirit was already one step ahead of Peter and his companions.

It is fair to assume that in the case of Cornelius no less than at Pentecost, the Spirit was given not for salvation but for empowerment. The only reference to the Spirit in Peter's sermon in verses 34–43 is that Jesus himself had been anointed "with the Holy Spirit and with power" (v. 38) and that by the Spirit's power he "went about doing good and healing all who were oppressed by the devil, for God was with him" (v. 39). But empowerment presupposed salvation. After the display of tongues speaking, Peter asked his Jewish Christian companions, "Can anyone forbid water for baptizing these people [i.e., Cornelius, his family, and his close friends, v. 24] who have received the Holy Spirit just as we have?" His rhetorical question was based on an argument from the greater to the lesser: if these Gentiles have already received the Holy Spirit for empowerment, there can surely be no doubt of their having been forgiven and having been saved. Even at the beginning of the chapter Cornelius was said to have been "a devout man who feared God with all his household, gave alms liberally to all the people, and prayed constantly to God" (v. 2). An angel told him, "Your prayers and your alms have ascended as a memorial before God" (v. 4).

A modern Christian reader is apt to object that at this point Cornelius, as a "God-fearer," was the equivalent of a "good Jew" but was not yet "saved" by becoming a Christian. Luke is not interested in distinctions of this kind; neither is he interested in pinpointing the time of Cornelius' "salvation" or of the forgiveness of his sins. What is important to the story is that the reception of the Spirit evidenced by the gift of tongues was proof that by that time Cornelius and those with him were already Christian believers and therefore appropriate candidates for water baptism. It is a little like the case of the "sinful woman" in Luke

7:36–50, whose behavior toward Jesus demonstrated that she had already been forgiven (v. 47).

In the story of Cornelius, just as in the story of Pentecost, the gift of repentance and the gift of the Spirit are closely related, yet not identical. Peter, in retelling the story, emphasized that the "Holy Spirit fell on them just as on us at the beginning" (Acts 11:15), and finally he asked, "If God gave the same gift to them as he gave us when we believed in the Lord Jesus Christ, who was I that I could withstand God?" (11:17). From the fact, evidenced by the gift of tongues, that God had given the Holy Spirit to the Gentiles for empowerment, Peter's Jewish companions "glorified God" and drew the only possible conclusion: "So then, God has granted even to the Gentiles repentance unto life" (11:18). As a result, Cornelius and his friends were baptized "after the fact" (Acts 10:48), somewhat belatedly by the standards of John the Baptist or of Peter in Acts 2:38–41, but on the ground of prior evidence that they were indeed genuine believers.

The second stage of the story is not told, but its implication is that Gentiles like Cornelius, now empowered by the Holy Spirit, began to spread the Christian message among their own people. Luke leaves the same implication in the case of the Ethiopian eunuch to whom Philip spoke after his mission in Samaria was taken over by the apostles from Jerusalem. An "angel of the Lord" told Philip to go south through the desert toward Gaza (Acts 8:26). When he encountered a chariot and an Ethiopian eunuch, "the Spirit" told him to join the chariot and speak with the eunuch (v. 29). Somehow the "angel of the Lord" and "the Spirit" fulfill much the same function. After the eunuch was baptized, "the Spirit of the Lord took Philip away, and the eunuch saw him no more" (v. 39). Philip later "was found" at Azotus, and continued his mission from there to Caesarea (v. 40). Once more the Holy Spirit directed the movements and journeys of those who had put themselves at the Spirit's disposal—in Philip's case by immediate supernatural intervention. Nothing is said of the eunuch's own experience of the Holy Spirit—e.g., whether he prophesied or spoke in tongues or saw visions—but the apparent purpose of the story is to suggest that he not only came to believe in Jesus but was empowered by the Spirit to spread the Christian message to his own country. This may be Luke's way of accounting for the existence of Christian communities, of which he had heard in Ethiopia.

X. Paul and the Westward Mission. Whatever may be implied by his story, the Ethiopian eunuch is forgotten in Luke's narrative after his encounter with Philip. The dominant geographical movement in the Book of Acts is westward, not southward, and the dominant figure in the latter two-thirds of the book is the apostle Paul. Paul was first introduced as "Saul" in connection with the martyrdom of Stephen (Acts 8:1) and was then seen ravaging the church in Jerusalem and Judea, hauling people off to interrogation and prison (8:3), and "breathing threats and murder against the disciples of the Lord" (9:1). On the way to Damascus to bring Jewish Christians back to Jerusalem for trial, Saul saw a vision of the risen Jesus that is reported three times in the Book of Acts, once by Luke acting as narrator (9:3–9) and twice in retrospect by Paul himself (22:6–11; 26:12–18). The immediate result of the vision was that Saul was struck blind: "They led him by the hand and brought him into Damascus; for three days he was without sight, and neither ate nor drank" (9:8–9). Simultaneous with Saul's vision (cf. the almost simultaneous visions of Cornelius and Peter in Acts 10) is a vision of the Lord given to a certain Ananias of Damascus (9:10–19; cf. 22:12–16). Ananias was told that Saul, now in the house of a certain Judas in Damascus praying, had "seen a man named Ananias come in and lay hands on him so that he might regain his sight" (9:11–12). Apparently he was also told of Saul's vision on the road, for when he arrived, he announced to Saul, "Jesus, the Lord who appeared to you on the road by which you came, has sent me so that you may regain your sight and be filled with the Holy Spirit" (9:17). This is exactly what happened as soon as Ananias laid his hands on Paul: "Immediately something like scales fell from his eyes and he regained his sight. Then he got up and was baptized, and took some food and was strengthened" (vv. 18–19; cf. 22:13, 16). Just as in the case of Cornelius in the next chapter, the evidence that Paul was "filled with the Spirit" serves also as evidence of his faith in Jesus and repentance of his earlier crimes against Jesus' disciples. According to Paul's later report of the incident, Ananias said to him, "And now why do you wait? Get up and be baptized, and wash away your sins as you call on his name" (22:16).

It should be noted that in Saul's case the initial evidence of being "filled with the Holy Spirit" was the regaining of his sight (cf. the case of Zechariah, who according to Luke 1:67 was "filled with the Holy Spirit" just after regaining his speech). Clarity of vision, not tongues or prophecy, was the sign that Saul had been touched and empowered by the Spirit of God. It was a vision that took away his sight to begin with, and it was on the basis of this vision of Jesus that he was called to become God's messenger to the Gentiles. As he retold the story later before the Jewish people in Jerusalem, Paul quoted Ananias as saying, "The God of our fathers appointed you to know his will, *to see the Righteous One* [i.e., Jesus] and to hear a voice from his mouth" (Acts 22:14). Then, he says, "When I had returned to Jerusalem and was praying in the temple, *I fell into a trance and saw him saying to me,* 'Quick! Leave Jerusalem at once, for they will not accept your testimony about me!'" (22:17–18). Still later Paul testified to King Agrippa, "I was not disobedient to *the heavenly vision,* but declared first to those at Damascus, then at Jerusalem and in the whole country of Judea, and to the Gentiles, that they should repent and turn to God, performing deeds worthy of their repentance" (Acts 26:19–20).

These examples not only demonstrate the importance of Paul's first vision of Jesus on the way to Damascus in the Book of Acts, but suggest the continuing importance of visions in his westward mission (e.g., the appearance to Paul of a "man of Macedonia" in Acts 16:9–10, and a vision of Jesus in Corinth in 18:9). Through such visions and through the testimony of prophets, the Holy Spirit directs and orchestrates the Christian mission throughout the Book of Acts. Barnabas, Paul's companion-to-be, is called "a good man, full of the Holy Spirit and of faith" (11:24; cf. 4:36–37; 9:27). He and Saul (not yet "Paul") were sent from Antioch to Jerusalem to deliver money for famine relief on the basis of an oracle of a prophet named Agabus, who "by the Spirit" had predicted a severe world-wide famine (11:28–30). Barnabas and Saul are also listed among five prophets and teachers in the church at Antioch (13:1). Luke reports that "while they were worshiping and fasting, *the Holy Spirit said,* 'Set apart for me Barnabas and Saul for the work to which I have called them.' So after fasting and prayer they laid their hands on them and sent them off" (vv. 2–3). This amounted to being *"sent on their way by the Holy Spirit"* (v. 4).

When Saul encountered Elymas the magician at Paphos on Cyprus in a way reminiscent of Peter's encounter with Simon in Samaria, he was again "filled with the Holy Spirit" (13:9), and Luke chooses this moment to shift to the name Paul in reporting his journeys. The Spirit in this instance gave Paul the power to inflict on Elymas divine judgment, the same judgment (temporary blindness) to which Paul himself had earlier been subject. The physical evidence of the Spirit's power and presence was what convinced the proconsul Sergius Paulus to believe Paul's message about Jesus (vv. 10–12). Although the impression is left that Saul of Tarsus was renamed after his first identifiable convert, "Paul" was probably his name as a Roman citizen all along. After his first major sermon, at Antioch of Pisidia (13:16–41), Paul encountered opposition from the synagogue so that he and Barnabas turned decisively to the Gentiles (v. 46), and shook the dust of that city from their feet (v. 51; cf. Luke 10:10–11). But Luke's parting word of hope about the ministry in Pisidian Antioch is a brief notice that "the disciples [i.e., the new converts of vv. 42–43] were filled with joy and with the Holy Spirit" (v. 52).

The centrality of the Spirit, whether in the Jerusalem church, the church at Antioch of Syria, or the new churches established by Paul and Barnabas on their journey, is dramatized by the language of the decree sent from Jerusalem to the Gentile churches according to Acts 15:23–29. The crucial expression in verse 28, "it seemed good to the Holy Spirit and to us" (virtually equivalent to "Be it resolved"), indicates the extent to which the deliberations and decisions of these early Christian communities were attributed to the Spirit's leading. Luke portrays them as charismatic communities in the strictest sense of that word. Paul, after helping to deliver the decree to Antioch of Syria, embarked on a return journey to churches he had established, only now with Silas as his companion—and possibly Luke himself (note the use of "we" beginning in 16:10). Whether Luke was part of the company or not, it is noteworthy that the Spirit's direction is made more explicit than at any other point in Luke–Acts (with the possible exception of the inaugural events in the ministry of Jesus in Luke 3–4). First, Paul and Silas are said to have crossed Phrygia and Galatia because they "had been forbidden by the Holy Spirit to speak the word in the province of Asia" (Acts 16:6); second, "when they came to the border of Mysia, they tried to enter Bithynia, but the Spirit of Jesus would not permit it. So they passed by Mysia and went down to Troas" (vv. 7–8); third, a night vision in which a Macedonian said to Paul, "Come over to Macedonia and help us," directed the party into Europe (vv. 9–10). The effect of all these experiences of the Spirit as Luke records them was to thrust the Christian movement ever westward, toward Greece and finally Rome. Although the Spirit is not mentioned in connection with Paul's stay in Corinth in Acts 18, Paul does have a vision of Jesus at night telling him, "Do not be afraid, but speak and do not be silent; for I am with you, and no one is going to attack or harm you; for I have many people in this city" (Acts 18:9). It is fair to assume that Luke could just as easily have said that the Holy Spirit told Paul these things.

Only once more in the Book of Acts (in addition to the Pentecost story, the mission to Samaria, and the Cornelius incident) does the reception of the Holy Spirit become in any sense a theological issue. This happens in connection with a unique community of disciples in Ephesus, a community that Paul himself had not established (Acts 19:1–7). Luke prepares for the story with a brief account of a Jewish believer from Alexandria named Apollos who came to Ephesus after Paul's first visit there (18:24; cf. vv. 19–23). Apollos is described as "an eloquent man, well versed in the Scriptures" who had been "instructed in the way of the Lord" and who, "being fervent in the spirit, spoke and taught accurately about Jesus, though he knew only the baptism of John" (vv. 24–25). Apparently in connection with this last statement, Luke mentions that Paul's friends Priscilla and Aquila instructed him "more accurately" in the way of God (v. 26). The implication is that they explained to him baptism "in the name of Jesus" (cf. 19:5), but whether or not he was then baptized, the account does not say. In any event, Apollos moved on to Corinth, where he "vigorously refuted the Jews in public debate, proving from the Scriptures that Jesus was the Messiah" (v. 28). It is difficult to know whether Apollos received the Holy Spirit as a result of the instruction he was given by Priscilla and Aquila, or whether he was already "filled with the Spirit" and only needed more information about the work of Jesus. The phrase "fervent in spirit," used of Apollos in 18:25, does not have to refer to the Holy Spirit, but neither does it prove that Apollos was without the Spirit. The question must therefore remain open. Luke's description of Apollos' ministry at Corinth in verses 27–28 strongly indicates, however, that by that time the power of the Holy Spirit was on him.

When Paul returned to Ephesus, he found "some disciples" (19:1) whose experience seems to have corresponded at least in one respect to that of Apollos—i.e., the only baptism they knew was the baptism of John. Luke's narrative does not specify whether they were "disciples" only of John the Baptist, or of Jesus as well. The use of the term "disciples" without qualification suggests that they were in some sense disciples of Jesus, yet the fact that Paul had to remind them of John's testimony to "the one coming after him, namely Jesus" (19:4; cf. 13:25) points to the likelihood that their knowledge about Jesus, especially about his death and resurrection, was incomplete. Moreover, they had no knowledge of the coming of the Holy Spirit, at Pentecost or anywhere else (v. 2). On the basis of Paul's message, Luke reports, "they were baptized in the name of the Lord Jesus"; then Paul laid hands on them, and "the Holy Spirit came on them, and they spoke in tongues and prophesied" (vv. 5–6). Once again some of the phenomena of Pentecost were repeated, though no one calls attention to the similarity as Peter did in the case of Cornelius (cf. 10:47; 11:17).

Luke concludes the brief account with the significant notice that "there were about twelve of them in all" (v. 7). The number, matching the twelve who had been with Jesus (cf. Luke 6:12–16, 22:30; Acts 1:15–26), can hardly be coincidental, and Luke must surely have been aware of strong irony in the fact that these "twelve" received the Holy Spirit by the laying on of the hands of the apostle Paul! The implication is not that these twelve were replacing the Jerusalem twelve, but Luke does want to emphasize that Ephesus would become the base for the last stage of the church's mission to Rome and the "end of the earth." The Ephesus twelve are presumably the "elders" to whom Paul addressed his farewell speech at nearby Miletus in Acts 20:17–35. The centrality of the Holy Spirit in their experience is echoed in Paul's reminder to them of the Spirit's role in his own mission ("I am going to Jerusalem bound in the Spirit," 20:22; cf. 19:21) as well as the Spirit's testimony through prophets of the dangers awaiting him (20:23). It is echoed even more pointedly in Paul's command to them: "Take heed to yourselves and to all the flock *over which the Holy Spirit has made you guardians*. Be shepherds to the church of God which he purchased with his own blood" (20:28). They were Paul's own "apostolic college," but with a reversal of roles: Paul was the one sent "bound in the Spirit," while their apostolate was to stay where they were and maintain Paul's testimony to Christ in Asia Minor.

Aside from prophetic warnings confirming the dangers awaiting Paul in his last visit to Jerusalem (Acts 21:4, 10–11), the Holy Spirit is mentioned only once in the last eight chapters of Acts, as Paul in Rome pronounced the Spirit's verdict on those who reject the message of Jesus and the kingdom of God: "The Holy Spirit spoke the truth to your fathers by saying through Isaiah the prophet, 'You shall indeed hear but never understand, and you shall indeed see but never perceive. For this people's heart has grown dull, and their ears hard of hearing, and they have closed their eyes" (Acts 28:25–27). Consequently, Paul announced (for the third time; cf. 13:46–47; 18:6), "This salvation of God has been sent to the

Gentiles; they will listen" (28:28). Despite the Spirit's word of judgment, the effect of the Spirit's ministry in Luke–Acts is not to close off anyone from salvation but to open its doors to those previously excluded. For two years in Rome prior to his trial, Paul "welcomed *all* who came to him, preaching the kingdom of God and teaching about the Lord Jesus Christ boldly and without hindrance" (Acts 28:30–31). If "boldness" is indeed a sign of the Spirit's power and presence (cf., e.g., Acts 4:13, 29, 31; 9:27–28; 13:46; 18:26), then the Holy Spirit is very much in the picture to the end of the Book of Acts, even where the actual term does not occur. Once Luke has made his point that the Holy Spirit directs the mission of the apostles, especially Paul, and guides the congregations that have been established, explicit references to the Spirit decrease in number. This phenomenon in Acts parallels the Gospel of Luke, where references to the Holy Spirit also became fewer after it had been firmly established that the Spirit was directing the movements of Jesus of Nazareth. Luke's apparent assumption is that when a movement or a community has been adequately defined as "charismatic," or "filled with the Spirit," it is unnecessary to refer constantly to the Spirit's presence or to charismatic phenomena. They are seen rather as an integral aspect of the movement's life and growth.

XI. Conclusions: Luke–Acts and the Pentecostal Tradition. The strength of the Pentecostal and charismatic tradition in the interpretation of Luke–Acts lies in the insistence that the Holy Spirit comes as a tangible, sometimes visible, reality with identifiable physical evidences. This insistence, whatever its justification in other NT writings (e.g., John's Gospel or the letters of Paul), is fully in keeping with Luke's intention both in his Gospel and in the Book of Acts. The Holy Spirit in Luke–Acts is not primarily a moral influence enabling believers to "keep the law" or to "lead more righteous lives," or even to "love one another." Luke is not interested in enumerating "fruits of the Spirit" in this sense. Rather, the Spirit in Luke–Acts is a power enabling believers see things they would otherwise not see, speak words they would otherwise be unable to speak, and perform mighty deeds that would otherwise lie beyond their abilities. These visions and words and deeds are the evidences of the Spirit's active presence, and most of Luke–Acts is devoted to the description of them and of their consequences.

The weakness in some expressions of the Pentecostal and charismatic understanding of Luke–Acts is the tendency to schematize, and so to limit, the physical evidences of the Holy Spirit—often in order to accent the centrality of tongues speaking. There is no doubt that speaking in tongues was one of the most conspicuous evidences of the Holy Spirit in the early church as Luke describes it, and certainly no doubt of its centrality in the Pentecost narrative. But in the larger framework of Luke–Acts, it appears that Luke regarded tongues speaking as one specific form of prophecy and that he understood prophecy very broadly, to include both inspired speech directed toward human beings (i.e., prophecy as it is commonly understood) and inspired speech directed toward God (i.e., Spirit-filled prayer, praise, thanksgiving, and rejoicing). Any of these forms of prophecy could be given in one's own language or in "other tongues," whether understood by the hearers or not. And any of them could serve as evidence (even initial evidence) of the Spirit's coming—at least so far as Luke is concerned.

The three other identifiable evidences of the Holy Spirit in Luke–Acts are clarity of vision, the sacred journey, and miracles. The promise of Joel was not only "Your sons and daughters shall prophesy," but also "Your young men shall see visions and your old men shall dream dreams" (2:17), and this promise, as we have seen, was amply fulfilled both in the experience of Jesus in Luke's Gospel and in the experience of his followers in the Book of Acts. Another common feature spanning Luke's Gospel and Acts is that of the journey. When the Spirit comes on Jesus at his baptism, the result is movement—first to the desert, then up to Jerusalem, then to Nazareth and Galilee, then back to Jerusalem. After Jesus' resurrection, the disciples waited in Jerusalem until the Spirit came on them; then (not immediately but eventually) they moved out through Judea and Samaria to Antioch, Asia Minor, Macedonia, Greece, and finally Rome. Though this is not usually thought of by Pentecostals or charismatics as one of the "physical evidences," the movement is surely both physical and geographical. One of the most important characteristics of the Holy Spirit in Luke–Acts is that the Spirit impels the servants of God to a world-wide mission. The miracles attributed both to Jesus and to the apostles, though not explicitly connected with the ministry of the Holy Spirit (note Luke's phrase "finger of God" in place of Matthew's "Spirit of God" in Luke 11:20), are seen as accompanying that mission. The prophet Joel had promised "wonders in the heaven above and signs in the earth below" (Acts 2:19); in the "signs and wonders" displayed in Jerusalem and continuing in the mission of Peter and Paul and others, Luke saw the Spirit at work bringing the ancient prophecy to fulfillment.

A lasting contribution of Pentecostal and charismatic hermeneutics to NT theology is the recognition that Luke deserves a place as a first-century theologian of the Christian movement, alongside Paul and John. Although this insight could be dismissed by some as arising out of denominational, even sectarian, interests, and though it has been misused by some in an overzealous search for a schematized formula for Christian experience, the insight stands. Critical scholarship has independently come to similar conclusions through "redaction history" and "narrative theology" (not without abuses of its own!). Criticism and a traditional faith have in this instance worked together to lay to rest the notion that Christian doctrine must be based solely on "didactic" works such as the letters of Paul and that Christian experience must conform to the guidelines that doctrine (so derived and so defined) lays down. It is not necessary to choose between Luke the historian and Luke the theologian, for Luke–Acts stands as an eloquent testimony to the fact that he was both.

See also BAPTISM IN THE HOLY SPIRIT; HOLY SPIRIT, DOCTRINE OF THE; GLOSSOLALIA; HERMENEUTICS, HISTORICAL PERSPECTIVES ON PENTECOSTAL AND CHARISMATIC; INITIAL EVIDENCE, A BIBLICAL PERSPECTIVE; JESUS CHRIST.

Bibliography: C. K. Barrett, *The Holy Spirit in the Gospel Tradition* (1966); F. D. Brunner, *A Theology of the Holy Spirit* (1970); H. Conzelmann, *The Theology of St. Luke* (1960); J. D. Dunn, *Baptism in the Holy Spirit* (1970); idem, *Jesus and the Spirit* (1975); M. Ervin, *Spirit Baptism: A Biblical Investigation* (1988); D. Ewert, *The Holy Spirit in the New Testament* (1983); M. Green, *I Believe in the Holy Spirit* (1975); L. T. Holdcroft, *The Holy Spirit: A Pentecostal Interpretation* (1979); S. M. Horton, *What the Bible Says About the Holy Spirit* (1976); J. H. E. Hull, *The Holy Spirit in the Acts of the Apostles* (1967); J. Jervell, *Luke and the People of God* (1972); D. Juel, *Luke–Acts: The Promise of History* (1983); R. Maddox, *The Purpose of Luke–Acts* (1982); B. M. Metzger, *A Textual Commentary on the New Testament* (1971); G. T. Montague, *The Holy Spirit: Growth of a Biblical Tradition* (1976); E. Schweizer, *The Holy Spirit* (1980); A. M. Stibbs and J. I. Packer, *The Spirit Within You: The Churches' Neglected Possession* (1967); N. B. Stonehouse, *The Witness of Luke to Christ* (1951); J. R. W. Stott, *Baptism and Fulness: The Work of the Holy Spirit Today* (1975); H. B. Swete, *The Holy Spirit in the New Testament* (1976); D. L. Tiede, *Prophecy and History in Luke–Acts* (1980).   J. R. Michaels

LUM, CLARA E. (d. 1946). Participant at the Azusa Street revival and editor. Lum played a significant role in widely publishing the events of the Azusa Street revival between 1906–08.

Formerly a white servant in the home of Charles F. Parham, Lum was "sanctified and anointed" about 1897. She arrived at Azusa Street in 1906 seeking the "baptism," and after receiving it, stayed to help in a secretarial capacity. Clara regularly exercised the gifts of tongues and interpretation of tongues and was featured in worship services at the mission, where she read testimonies from those who wrote in. She recorded in shorthand testimonies and "messages in tongues" given at Azusa then published them in *The Apostolic Faith.*

In an early scandal Lum was accused of taking "French leave" of the mission in 1908, purloining the newspaper and its mailing lists. She relocated in Portland, Oregon, where she continued to publish *The Apostolic Faith* for Florence Crawford's fledgling group. An explanation that may be understood as an apology for taking the paper with her was printed in *The Apostolic Faith* (21 [May–June 1909], 2).

Local records indicate that Clara Lum had relatives in the Portland area. A brother, William, lived in Portland, and a sister, Mrs. Mary Brooks, resided in Waldport, Oregon. Clara never married and lived in no fewer than fifteen Portland locations. Her primary stability seems to have been derived from her work with the Apostolic Faith. In 1909 she reported her occupation as a teacher at the Apostolic Faith school. Later she was listed as an editor (1911–13), as an editor of a children's paper (1916–17), and as a stenographer (1918–36) or typist (1938, 1941). Clara

apparently retired to Gresham, a suburb of Portland, in the mid-1940s. She died there on December 15, 1946.

Bibliography: *AF* 1 (4, 1906): 3; 1 (6, 1907): 8; *AF* (Portland) 21 (May–June, 1909): 2; *The Bridegroom's Messenger* 1 (3, 1907); F. T. Corum, *Like As of Fire* (1981), preface; *Oregon Journal* (December 18, 1946), 22; *The Oregonian* (December 18, 1946), 20; *Portland City Directory* (1909–44); C. W. Shumway, "A Study of the 'Gift of Tongues,'" unpublished A.B. thesis, University of Southern California, 1914.
                                             C. M. Robeck, Jr.

LUPTON, LEVI RAKESTRAW (1860–1929). Evangelist and missions advocate. Lupton was born in Smith Township, near Beloit, Ohio, to devout Quaker parents. Years later in a business venture, Lupton and his wife Laura and others moved westward and founded the village of Lupton, Michigan. In 1885 he professed to have been converted, sanctified, and called to the ministry. Returning to Ohio, Lupton was ordained by the East Goshen Monthly Meeting (a local church). In 1896 he reported a physical healing while attending the annual conference of the Ohio Yearly Meeting of Friends.

Evangelistic ministry followed, reflecting Lupton's Wesleyan-Holiness theology and belief in faith healing. In 1900 Lupton conducted revival services in Alliance, Ohio, that culminated in the organization of the First Friends Church. He later founded the World Evangelization Company (1904) with his associates to expedite his interest in foreign missions; a periodical called *The New Acts* (1904–10); and the Missionary Home (1905), which functioned as a Bible institute and camp meeting site. All were located near Alliance. These parachurch ministries, as well as Lupton's careless financial practices, generated tension within the Ohio Yearly Meeting.

When a Pentecostal revival under the leadership of Ivey Campbell occurred at C. A. McKinney's Union Gospel Mission in Akron, Ohio, Lupton and his supporters attended. Upon his return to Alliance, Lupton held services, hoping for such a revival there. He subsequently received the baptism in the Holy Spirit on December 30, 1906; his wife claimed that "a halo lit upon his brow." On February 9, 1907, the Damascus Quarterly Meeting (the local district) dismissed Lupton for disloyalty and refusal to abandon his independent ministries; the controversy over glossolalia was side-stepped.

With C. A. McKinney and Ivey Campbell, Lupton envisioned Alliance as "the headquarters for this gracious Pentecostal movement in this part of the country." As a result he sponsored a camp meeting in June 1907 that had a major impact on the development of Pentecostalism in Ohio and the Northeast. Speakers included Frank Bartleman, A. S. Copley, W. A. Cramer, and Joseph H. King. More than seven hundred people attended from twenty-one states and Canada; among those in attendance were George Fisher, J. Roswell Flower, and Alice C. Wood. Significantly, the camp meeting was interracial in composition. At the close, Lupton and several others organized the Apostolic Evangelization Company, with him as director, carrying the title "the Apostle Levi." However, little came of this effort.

At the 1908 camp meeting, the participants adopted a "missionary manifesto" urging the formation of a missionary agency; this was the first call among Pentecostals for such an enterprise. Realization of this goal came about the following year when the Pentecostal Missionary Union in the U.S. was established.

From 1907 to 1910 Lupton traveled widely as a popular speaker in Pentecostal circles, perhaps becoming the most articulate advocate of foreign missions in the movement. Unfortunately his ministry, the institutions he founded, and the Pentecostal Missionary Union in the U.S. collapsed in December 1910 after he confessed to adultery and his followers questioned the sincerity of his repentance. Because of this embarrassment, later Pentecostal writers, notably Bartleman, Flower, and King, referred to the 1907 camp meeting but refused to mention Lupton by name, thus effectively eliminating his memory and contributions for many years. Nevertheless, C. E. McPherson, a local newspaper reporter in Alliance, wrote his biography entitled *Life of Levi R. Lupton* (1911), possibly the first biography written about an early Pentecostal leader.

Bibliography: G. B. McGee, "Levi Lupton: A Forgotten Pioneer of Early Pentecostalism," *Faces of Renewal*, ed. P. Elbert (1988); C. E. McPherson, *Life of Levi R. Lupton* (1911); W. M. Smith, *Chapters from the New Acts* (n.d.). G. B. McGee

LUTHERAN CHARISMATICS In the summer and fall of 1961 small groups of Lutherans in scattered locations in the U.S. began to have what later came to be known as "charismatic experiences." These initial experiences were often sparked by ecumenical contacts, principally with Episcopalians. By mid-1962 Lutheran charismatics began to meet and correspond with one another.

I. The American Lutheran Church (ALC). Most of those affected at the outset were from the ALC, located principally in Minnesota, Montana, Southern California, Illinois, and North Dakota. Herbert Mjorud, an ALC evangelist, became a prominent exponent of charismatic renewal and was instrumental in the initial spread of the movement. Other early participants who remained visible in the leadership of the movement included Larry Christenson, Dick and Betty Denny, James Hanson, Morris Vaagenes, and George Voeks.

The initial response in the ALC was one of cautious interest. A study commission was appointed to look into the matter of speaking in tongues. A team consisting of psychiatrist Paul Qualben, clinical psychologist John Kildahl, and NT theologian Lowell Satre visited Zion Lutheran Church in Glendive, Montana, and Trinity Lutheran Church in San Pedro, California, where they interviewed and tested members who had experienced speaking in tongues. They found some convictions among those interviewed which they deemed un-Lutheran, such as equating "Spirit-filled" with speaking in tongues. On the other hand, they noted beneficial results in the personal lives and dedication of those who had entered into charismatic experience. The study commission published a report in 1963 that discouraged speaking in tongues in public gatherings but allowed it in one's private devotions. In 1972 Paul Qualben reported on their research in a seminar at Wartburg Seminary in Dubuque, Iowa. "We had two preconceptions when we went to these congregations," he said. "We expected to encounter people who were emotionally unstable, and we expected the phenomenon to be short-lived. We were wrong on both counts. The people we interviewed were a normal cross-section of a Lutheran congregation, and today, ten years later, the movement is still growing."

II. The Lutheran Church—Missouri Synod (LC–MS). In the mid 1960s some LC–MS pastors entered into similar experiences. These included Robert Heil, Theodore Jungkuntz, Rodney Lensch, Donald Matzat, Herbert Mirly, Donald Pfotenhauer, Erwin Prange, and Delbert Rossin.

The Commission on Theology and Church Relations produced two reports on the charismatic movement, one in 1972, another in 1977. The reports were generally cool toward the movement. They suggested that charismatic gifts were primarily for the apostolic age, though they did not disallow them.

Nevertheless, the movement continued to grow in LC–MS circles. LC–MS congregations, such as Faith Lutheran Church in Geneva, Illinois, and Resurrection Lutheran Church in Charlotte, North Carolina, became prominently associated with the renewal and exerted considerable influence both inside and beyond the LCMS.

III. The Lutheran Church in America (LCA). The LCA had fewer participants in the renewal than the ALC or LC–MS, but by the late 1960s prominent LCA pastors like Paul Swedberg in Minneapolis and Glen Pearson in York, Pennsylvania, together with their congregations, were openly identified with charismatic renewal.

In 1974 the LCA produced a pastoral perspective on charismatic renewal that was generally more positive toward the movement than any previous Lutheran statement.

IV. Growth. The growth of the Lutheran charismatic movement in the U.S. during the 1960s was more widespread than most people realized. Even those involved in the movement were surprised when, with little publicity or fanfare, the first International Lutheran Conference on the Holy Spirit drew more than nine thousand people to Minneapolis in 1972. This conference became an annual event and a focal point for renewal, with increasing attendance throughout the 1970s.

The movement grew significantly during the 1970s. By the middle of the decade it was conservatively estimated that about 10 percent of the Lutherans in the U.S., clergy as well as laity, identified with the charismatic movement. A relatively small number of Lutheran congregations—in 1975 fewer than twenty, by 1986 about eighty—could be described as "charismatic" in the sense of identifying visibly with this renewal and integrating the charismatic dimen-

Lutherans gather for a worship service in a charismatic conference.

sion into the total life of their church. A larger number of congregations, however, were significantly influenced by charismatic renewal. By the mid 1970s there was scarcely a Lutheran congregation in the country that did not have some members who were charismatic. Lutherans were the third largest group represented when an ecumenical charismatic congress was held in Kansas City in 1977, drawing more than 50,000 people.

The leadership of the renewal in the U.S. developed in clusters of regional leaders who met annually, and in the International Lutheran Renewal Center (ILRC) located in St. Paul, Minnesota. The ILRC sponsored conferences, publications, leaders' meetings, congregational and community renewal events, and theological research. Larry Christenson served as director of the center, with Dick Denny, W. Dennis Pederson, and Delbert Rossin coordinating various aspects of the center's ministry.

V. Theological Perspective. ILRC coordinated the work of a thirty-two-member international Lutheran theological consultation that produced *Welcome, Holy Spirit, a Study of Charismatic Renewal in the Church* (1987). It dealt with a broad range of issues and was the most comprehensive theological work to come out of the charismatic movement. On the sensitive issue of baptism with the Holy Spirit, they struck a mediating position. The biblical material is clear enough: John the Baptist prophesied that Jesus would baptize his followers with the Holy Spirit; Jesus confirmed it; believers in the early church experienced it. The term is used in reference to two events in Acts: Pentecost and the outpouring of the Spirit in the household of Cornelius.

However, theological explanations about the coming of the Spirit had come to sharp disagreement here. The Pentecostal view saw baptism with the Spirit as a "second blessing" by which someone who has already received salvation is empowered for service. The sacramental and evangelical views both took exception to this interpretation. They held that baptism with the Spirit was either identical with or invariably happened along with water baptism or salvation. Thus every believer has been baptized with the Spirit.

The Lutheran consultation recognized that the case is hard to resolve on purely exegetical grounds. Neither in the Gospels, where it is used prophetically, nor in Acts where it is used descriptively, is the term precisely defined; and its use in Acts is somewhat ambiguous. It is difficult to make Pentecost out to be a salvation event for the disciples. Jesus' words to them in Acts 1:4–8 speak not in terms of salvation but rather in terms of power for witness. Jesus' expression "you shall be baptized with the Holy Spirit" (Acts 1:5) is not a reference to baptism with water, since the disciples were not baptized at Pentecost when the promise was fulfilled. It was rather a metaphorical expression denoting the experience that the disciples would have of being filled with the Holy Spirit and manifesting it in a demonstrable way. That was exactly what happened to those who were gathered together on Pentecost: "And they were all filled with the Holy Spirit and began to speak in other tongues as the Spirit gave them utterance" (Acts 2:4). On the other hand, the primary interpretation that the apostles in Jerusalem put on that which happened in the household of Cornelius was that it was a salvation event (Acts 11:18).

"Baptized with the Holy Spirit," despite its presence in the NT, is terminology that was little used in the history of the church until the advent of the Holiness and Pentecostal movements. Even in the later writings of the NT it does not occur. Luke himself gives greater weight to the term "filled with the Spirit."

In the twentieth century, however, through the Pentecostal and charismatic movements, the term "baptism with the Holy Spirit" broke on the scene with dramatic results. The Lutheran consultation noted that to give disproportionate emphasis to a teaching or a term that has relatively little biblical or historical weight could lead to distortion.

The Lutheran consultation contended, however, that the term should not be abandoned or neglected. They noted that some mainline churches with venerable theological traditions tended to acknowledge the vitality and growth of Pentecostal Christianity while at the same time belittling its exegesis and theology generally, and its doctrine of baptism with the Spirit in particular. They allowed that it would be theoretically possible for the Spirit to enliven the life and worship and witness of Pentecostals, prosper their missionary endeavors in an unprecedented way, yet make little headway with them in regard to their understanding of Scripture and their theology. Authentic experience can be inaccurately assessed and explained. But they suggested that to make such a judgment in regard to a movement with the scope and significance and history of worldwide Pentecostalism would be audacious. They warranted that the Spirit might want to correct some aspects of Pentecostal teaching; a second wave of Pentecostalism in the twentieth century, the charismatic movement, could be the Spirit's occasion for addressing some new questions to Pentecostal theology. But they pointed out that it might equally be the Spirit's occasion for Catholics and Protestants to give more respectful consideration to the exegesis and theology of Pentecostals.

In considering the coming and the working of the Holy Spirit in the post-Pentecost Christian community, the Lutheran consultation found it instructive to study the NT, especially the historical sections, from a perspective of the Spirit's *strategy*. They observed that there are a number of basic factors or elements that Scripture links to the coming of the Spirit. The way that they occur, however, suggests a discriminating and varied use of the different factors—sovereign and often surprising *strategies* that the Holy Spirit employs to accomplish particular objectives. This approach suggested a fresh way of looking not only at the biblical material but also at some of the traditional systematic approaches to the topic.

The Lutheran consultation considered the three systematic approaches to the coming of the Spirit that are prominent in the church today: the *sacramental*, the *evangelical*, and the *Pentecostal*. Simply stated, the sacramental approach teaches that the Holy Spirit is given in water baptism. The evangelical approach links the gift of the Spirit to regeneration; you receive the Holy Spirit when you are born again. The Pentecostal approach says that one receives the Holy Spirit when you are baptized with the Holy Spirit, an event that happens subsequent to regeneration.

They proposed neither an alternative systematic nor a critique of systems already on the scene but simply a different way of looking at the reality of the Spirit's coming—a way that gives perhaps greater attention to the sovereign strategy of the Spirit in varying situations.

They found that a strategic approach to the coming of the Spirit answers to the realistic way in which the NT presents the kingdom of God and the kingdom of this world in conflict with one another. It helps identify fundamental truths in the scriptural revelation yet recognizes that the Spirit is sovereign in applying these truths to specific situations.

In considering baptism with the Spirit strategically, they saw that it answered to the need for a signal outpouring of the Spirit's power to initiate or renew witness and ministry. In Acts, both times the term occurs it describes a dramatic initial outpouring of the Spirit. The history of the Pentecostal and charismatic movements tended to echo this: a key factor in the spread of the movements was the widely shared personal experience of an outpouring of the Spirit. For many, perhaps most, this initiated a new sense of the Spirit's presence and power for life and ministry.

The experience was commonly accompanied by a manifest demonstration of the Spirit's presence through charismatic gifts, and this they found was also consistent with the scriptural witness. In the theology of Luke, the experience of being filled with the Holy Spirit consistently resulted in a manifest demonstration of the Spirit's presence, usually in the form of exalted speech—they spoke in tongues (Acts 2:4; 10:46; 19:6), prophesied (19:6), extolled God (10:46), spoke the word of God with boldness (4:31); or it was accompanied by a supernatural sign—a healing (9:17–18), a divine judgment (13:9–11), or a rapturous vision (7:55).

To state that such events, or such charisms, are "not necessary" in terms of systematic theology, the consultation said, would miss the point. They recognized that a specific outpouring of the Spirit with the manifestation of spiritual gifts is not "necessary" either for salvation or for fruitful ministry. One could argue the case both from Scripture and history—systematically. (One would have but to mention a handful of prominent and universally respected movements or believers outside the Pentecostal tradition to make the point.) But, they pointed out, that would be like saying, "It is not necessary that an airstrike precede an infantry engagement in order for a battle to be won." However, if the commander has planned things that way, then another kind of necessity comes into play: the necessity of paying heed to the commander's strategy.

Given the worldwide spread and witness of the Pentecostal and charismatic movements, given a history of more than eighty years, the Lutheran consultation contended that the church as a whole must consider questions not only of exegesis and systematic theology but also of the Spirit's strategy. They recognized that non-Pentecostals might not agree with some aspects of the Pentecostal way of explaining the coming of the Spirit. They allowed that Pentecostals and charismatics might have oversystematized their own perception and experience of the Holy Spirit. But they acknowledged that Pentecostals have accurately perceived the Spirit's strategy: he is calling believers to receive a personal outpouring of the Holy Spirit; he is calling them to be filled with the Holy Spirit in a way and to a degree that they have not done before.

The Lutheran consultation observed that one of the great misconceptions that circulates around discussions of the Holy Spirit is the notion that we *have* everything that we state in our doctrines. That, they said, is like claiming a victory on the battlefield because one has a textbook on military strategy. The strategy of the Spirit is calling the church to experience more of what the doctrines talk about—to go beyond an intellectual belief in the Third Person of the Trinity to a demonstration of the Spirit and power; to extend our expectation of the Spirit's working to the horizons of Scripture. They did not see this happening simply through reasserting traditional doctrines of the Holy Spirit. They saw it calling for an obedient response to the strategy of the Spirit: a personal encounter with Jesus, who fills followers with the Holy Spirit.

Whether one understands this as an appropriation of something already received (sacramental, evangelical) or a receiving of something promised (Pentecostal), the strategy of the Spirit, the consultation concluded, would be served: the Spirit would be poured out, believers would talk about the Holy Spirit with a new sense of reality, they would walk in a new dimension of his reality and power, and the Lord's people would register gains against the powers that oppose the gospel.

See also CHARISMATIC MOVEMENT.

Bibliography: L. Christenson, *The Charismatic Renewal Among Lutherans* (1985); idem, *Welcome, Holy Spirit* (1987); E. Jorstad, *Bold in the Spirit* (1974); D. Matzat, *Serving the Renewal* (1978); K. McDonnell, ed., *Presence, Power, Praise—Documents on the Charismatic Renewal*, vols. 1–3 (1980). P. Opsahl, ed., *The Holy Spirit in the Life of the Church* (1978); See following articles: "Anointing and Healing," LCA/USA, 1962; "A Report on Glossolalia," ALC/USA, 1963; "A Statement With Regard to Speaking in Tongues," ALC/USA, 1964; "Christian Faith and the Ministry of Healing" ALC/USA, 1965; "The Charismatic Movement and Lutheran Theology," LC–MS/USA, 1972; "Guidelines," ALC/USA, 1973; "The Charismatic Movement in the Lutheran Church in America: A Pastoral Perspective," LCA/USA, 1974; "Policy Statement Regarding the Neo-Pentecostal Movement," LC–MS/USA, 1975; "The Lutheran Church and the Charismatic Movement: Guidelines for Congregations and Pastors," LC–MS/USA, 1977; "The Lutheran Church of Australia and Lutheran Charismatic Renewal," February 1977; "Report of the Lutheran Council in the United States," Lutheran Council, USA, 1978.

L. Christenson

M

McALISTER, HARVEY (1892–1978). Pastor and evangelist. The brother of R. E. McAlister and a signer of the Pentecostal Assemblies of Canada charter in 1919, Harvey McAlister has been called the "delightful expositor of divine healing." McAlister taught school before his ordination in 1913. He pastored churches in Toronto, Winnipeg, and Calgary before embarking on a teaching ministry that eventually took him to fifty countries. He emphasized signs and wonders in his meetings, combining exposition with an evangelistic appeal. In a career that lasted almost seventy years, he preached a six-week meeting in Hong Kong at age seventy-five.

Bibliography: C. Brumback, *Suddenly . . . From Heaven* (1961); G. G. Kulbeck, *What God Hath Wrought* (1958); W. Menzies, *Anointed to Serve* (1961); "With the Lord" (editorial), *Pentecostal Testimony* 60 (1, 1979). E. A. Wilson

McALISTER, ROBERT EDWARD (1880–1953). Pastor and executive officer of the Pentecostal Assemblies of Canada. R. E. McAlister is considered to have made strategic administrative contributions during the denomination's formative years. Reared in a Presbyterian family, he briefly attended Bible school in Cincinnati before entering evangelistic work in western Canada. He was a participant in the Azusa Street meetings in Los Angeles in 1906, returning to Canada as an enthusiastic Pentecostal. He established churches in Westmeath, Ontario, and Ottawa. He pastored London Gospel Temple, London, Ontario, for almost twenty years (1920–39). In 1919 he joined with several other ministers to charter the Pentecostal Assemblies of Canada, with the intention of receiving government recognition and providing a fellowship where "everyone would speak the same thing." He served as secretary and treasurer of the new organization (1919–32), as well as editor of the *Pentecostal Testimony*. He is remembered for his competent, untiring efforts to advance the new movement. A persuasive debater and inspiring expositor, it was said that he was able to "frame resolutions in such clear-cut language as to end all debate."

Bibliography: C. Brumback, *Suddenly . . . From Heaven* (1961); S. Frodsham, *With Signs Following* (1941); G. G. Kulbeck, *What God Hath Wrought* (1958); W. E. McAlister, "Called Home," *Pentecostal Testimony* 34 (11, 1953): 3. E. A. Wilson

McCLAIN, SAMUEL C. (1889–1969). Pentecostal preacher, educator, author, and leader. Born in Georgia, McClain was converted in a Baptist church in Arkansas in 1903. After he received the Holy Spirit in 1912 he conducted prayer meetings. Ordination followed in 1914, and he accepted baptism in the name of Jesus Christ in 1916. He conducted revivals in Arkan-

sas, Kansas, Oklahoma, Texas, and New Mexico, establishing several churches. He pastored in Arkansas, Texas, New Mexico, Mississippi, and Idaho. McClain taught in the Bible school in Eureka Springs, Arkansas (1918–20), and in the Pentecostal Bible Institute in Tupelo, Mississippi (1947–50). From 1921 to 1925 he served as Arkansas state overseer in the Pentecostal Assemblies of the World and as a presbyter for the Texas District of the Pentecostal Church, Incorporated (1934–35). He edited *The Apostolic Herald*, the official periodical of the Pentecostal Church, Incorporated, from 1937 to 1940 and wrote *Student's Handbook of Facts in Church History* (1965).

Bibliography: A. L. Clanton, *United We Stand* (1970). J. L. Hall

Kilian McDonnell is one of the foremost scholars of the Catholic charismatic movement.

McDONNELL, KILIAN (1921–). Order of St. Benedict, Roman Catholic theologian. McDonnell was educated in public schools, graduating from high school in Velva, North Dakota, in 1940. McDonnell entered the Benedictine monastic life at St. John's Abbey in Collegeville in August 1945. Receiving his B.A. from the Benedictine St. John's University in Collegeville, Minnesota, in 1947, he undertook graduate work in liturgy at Notre Dame in 1948 and in library science at the Catholic University, Washington, D.C., in 1949. He was ordained to the Roman Catholic priesthood in 1951 and served in parish work in Hastings and Detroit Lakes, Minnesota, for four years.

McDonnell's pursuit of theological studies led to the licentiate in theology at the University of Ottawa in Ontario, Canada, in 1960. After receiving that degree he pursued research in several German, Swiss, French, and British universities and ecumenical institutes through 1964, when he obtained the S.T.D. from the Theology Faculty of Trier, Germany. Known early as a Calvin scholar, with his major work, *John Calvin, The Church and the Eucharist* (1967), McDonnell's sights broadened to include extensive work in ecumenical issues as well as Pentecostal and charismatic research. Currently he serves as professor of theology in the graduate school of St. John's University.

In 1967 McDonnell became the founder and executive director of the Institute for Ecumenical and Cultural Research. He has served as the president of its board since 1973, when a new director was named. Housed on the campus of St. John's, the center is designed to bring people together for dialogue and to conduct research on subjects with cross disciplinary and ecumenical implications. Among the early figures he invited to study at the institute were renewal leaders Arnold Bittlinger, Larry Christenson, and J. Rodman Williams.

McDonnell's commitment to issues bearing upon Christian unity have led him to serve on national consultations between Roman Catholics and Presbyterians, Lutherans, and Southern Baptists. On the international level he has engaged in meetings with the World Council of Churches and in consultation with the United Council (Presbyterians and Congregationalists), Disciples of Christ, and Methodists; and for nearly fifteen years he has cochaired the Roman Catholic–Pentecostal Dialogue beside David and, now, Justus du Plessis. In 1983 he received the *Pro Pontifice et Ecclesia,* a papal award for his work on ecumenism, and the following year St. John's University granted him the *Pax Christi* award for work done in the same field.

McDonnell's interest in the Pentecostal and charismatic renewal movements has led to a stream of literature on the subject from his hand. It was he who first coined the term "classical Pentecostalism" to refer to that which was present in the Pentecostal churches founded since 1900 and to distinguish it from charismatic renewal in the historic churches. At the suggestion of Cardinal Suenens in 1973 he was the principle author of the first attempt to explain the renewal in a document that had international significance, the "Statement of the Theological Basis of the Catholic Charismatic Renewal." The following year he was the principle author of the first "Malines Document" titled *Theological and Pastoral Orientations on the Catholic Charismatic Renewal.* These documents established him as a primary interpreter of the Roman Catholic Charismatic Renewal and as an informal liaison to the Vatican (1974–85), and formally for the National Service

Committee of Catholic Charismatic Renewal and American Catholic Bishops. In this latter capacity his hand may be seen in the formal statements issued by this committee.

McDonnell has combined pastoral concern with theological precision, enabling him to bring scholarship and the renewal into contact with each other. His own *Charismatic Renewal and the Churches* (1976) brought new levels of "responsibility" to tongues-speakers, with its assessment of all the pertinent psychological studies to date. In 1978 his book *The Charismatic Renewal and Ecumenism* (Paulist) attempted to outline an ecumenical theology with guidelines for implementation. His *Magnum opus* to date, however, is the massive three-volume edited work entitled *Presence, Power, Praise* (Liturgical Press, 1980), in which he collected, often translated, and contextualized over a hundred documents issued by Protestant and Roman Catholic churches between 1973 and 1980 on the charismatic renewal. His work continues, with a major study on the Holy Spirit anticipated in the near future.

C. M. Robeck, Jr.

McKENNA, BRIEGE (1946–). Catholic charismatic sister with healing ministry. Born and brought up in Northern Ireland, McKenna entered the Poor Clare nuns at age fifteen, following determined persistence. She soon developed a crippling rheumatoid arthritis, which led her superiors to send her in 1967 to their convent in Tampa, Florida. In December 1970 at a charismatic retreat, she was dramatically healed and baptized in the Spirit. Six months later at Pentecost 1970, McKenna heard an inner voice say, "You have my gift of healing. Go use it." Later in the year she heard a call to minister to and intercede for priests. McKenna's world-wide ministry is now largely devoted to priests, especially in giving diocesan clergy retreats. Her life and ministry is described in her book *Miracles Do Happen* (1987).

P. D. Hocken

McKINNEY, CLAUDE ADAMS (1873–1940). Pastor and evangelist. Born in Oil City, Pennsylvania, McKinney received his early education in Long Island, New York. Saved in a Methodist church, he became involved in church work and singing gospel songs. He also helped with Salvation Army street meetings, where he met Elizabeth Ream ("Libby") Sawyer. Claude and Libby attended A. B. Simpson's Bible institute in New York and served as missionaries to the Belgian Congo, where they were married in 1897.

In 1900 McKinney pioneered the Gospel Church at Akron, Ohio, and started the Union Gospel Mission to minister to the destitute of the city. He was ordained by the Christian and Missionary Alliance in 1902.

Soon after hearing about the Pentecostal outpouring at the Azusa Street Mission in Los Angeles, California, McKinney received the baptism of the Holy Spirit in late 1906. He withdrew from the Alliance in 1908 and organized the Pentecostal Church at Akron in 1914. He was ordained by the Assemblies of God in 1918.

Bibliography: N. Sparlin, *Our Heritage: First Assembly of God* (1965).　　　　　G. W. Gohr

MacKNIGHT, JAMES MONTGOMERY

(1930–). Pastor and administrator. MacKnight was born in Campbellton, New Brunswick. He graduated from Eastern Pentecostal Bible College in 1953 and was ordained in April 1955 by the Pentecostal Assemblies of Canada (PAOC). MacKnight pastored several churches in Ontario: Verona, Belleville, Oshawa (King Street), and Ottawa (Bethel). He has ministered extensively in Canada and the U.S. at conferences, camp meetings, conventions, and other types of special services. He served three years as senior evangelist of Canada for Christ Crusades. His most recent pastorate was at Central Pentecostal Tabernacle in Edmonton, Alberta, from 1978 to 1982.

MacKnight was elected general superintendent of the PAOC in 1982. He is presently giving leadership to a new forward thrust in church planting and church growth in Canada and in target cities around the world.

Bibliography: Biographical sketch (April 1986); *The Pentecostal Testimony* (January 1983), 2.　G. W. Gohr

McLELLAN, CYRIL A.

(1928–). Musician, arranger, and choir director. Born and reared in Vancouver, British Columbia, Cyril McLellan began violin lessons at age eight. He also received training through the London Royal School of Music (L.R.S.M.) and received a diploma from Vancouver Normal School. McLellan received music degrees from Central Bible College (1954) and Evangel College (1961) and received an advanced degree in performance (M.M.) from the University of Missouri at Kansas City. He received Assemblies of God ordination in 1958. Since 1952 he has been the "Revivaltime" radio choir director and a part-time instructor in music at Central Bible College. He is also a choir director and instructor at Evangel College and directs choral workshops and clinics. His publication credits include twenty books of choir arrangements. He has recorded a violin album, *Celebration Praise Strings;* has directed twenty-four record albums for the Revivaltime Choir; and has led the choir on more than a hundred tours. He has won numerous awards for his music and was named Central Bible College alumnus of the year in 1971.

Bibliography: *The Cup* yearbooks, Central Bible College (1952–).　　　W. E. Warner

MacNUTT, FRANCIS SCOTT

(1925–). Priest and faith healer. Born in St. Louis, Missouri, MacNutt received his B.A. at Harvard, M.F.A. at Catholic University of America, and Ph.D. at Aquinas Institute of Theology. Ordained to the Catholic priesthood in 1956, he was elected president of the Catholic Homiletic Society and later was founding editor of its magazine, *Preaching.* In 1967 he received the baptism in the Holy Spirit at a retreat in Tennessee and became active in reintroducing the message of Christ's healing power in the Roman Catholic church as well as among charismatic groups. He was a pioneer in the charismatic renewal in foreign lands, particu-

Francis MacNutt was one of the first Catholics involved in the charismatic renewal. He later withdrew from the priesthood.

larly in Latin America among priests and other church leaders.

In 1980 MacNutt married Judith Sewell, whom he had met five years earlier. This sent shock waves through the National Service Committee of the (Catholic) charismatic movement as well as through his own Dominican order, and it resulted in his excommunication (now lifted). He now leads Christian Healing Center in the Episcopal Diocese in Jacksonville, Florida. He has written *Healing* (1974), *Power to Heal* (1977), and *The Prayer that Heals* (1981).

Bibliography: J. Pugh, "Francis MacNutt: Catholic in Exile," *Charisma* (November 1983), 18–22.
　　　　　　　　　　　　　　　　　S. Strang

McPHERSON, AIMEE SEMPLE

(1890–1944). Gifted missionary, evangelist, editor, author, and founder of the International Church of the Foursquare Gospel (ICFG).

Born Aimee Elizabeth Kennedy on October 9, 1890, on a small farm near Ingersoll, Ontario, Canada, to James Morgan Kennedy (1836–1921) and his second wife, Mildred "Minnie" (Pearce) Kennedy (1862–1947), she was reared in a Christian home. Her father, a farmer and bridge builder, was a Methodist organist and choir director who taught his young daughter to play the piano and organ, while her mother, orphaned at age twelve, had been reared by Salvationists. Aimee was a good student, whose faith was shaken for a time by exposure in her local high school to teaching on the theory of evolution.

During the winter months of 1907–08, Robert James Semple, a Pentecostal evangelist, held storefront meetings in an attempt to establish a work in Ingersoll. It was there that Aimee made a firm commitment of faith. On August 12, 1908, Robert Semple and Aimee Kennedy were married in a simple Salvation Army ceremony performed in the apple orchard of Aimee's parents' home, "Kozy Kot."

Aimee Semple McPherson, founder of the International Church of the Foursquare Gospel and Angelus Temple, Los Angeles.

Following their honeymoon, the couple settled for a short time in Stratford, Ontario, then went to London, Ontario, where they pioneered a church. By January 1909 they had moved to Chicago. Robert and Aimee Semple were ordained by William H. Durham on January 2, 1909. For several months, the couple accompanied Durham on evangelistic tours in the northern U.S. and Canada.

From their courtship days, the couple was determined to serve as "faith" missionaries in China. Departing from Chicago in 1910, they left for China with a stop at Semple's home near Belfast, Ireland, and a visit in London; then they traveled on through the Suez Canal. They arrived in Hong Kong in June 1910 and were immediately immersed into language study and literature distribution. Within weeks of their arrival, Robert Semple contracted malaria and died on August 19, 1910, leaving Aimee a widow before her twentieth birthday. With few financial resources, Aimee stayed in Hong Kong until after the birth of the Semples' daughter, Roberta Star, on September 17, 1910.

Aimee returned to New York City that fall, where she was joined by her mother, Minnie. She worked with the Salvation Army, serving lunch in a Rescue Mission, then collecting money in Broadway Theater lobbies. While in the city, she met Harold Stewart McPherson (1890–1968).

After a brief courtship the couple went to Chicago with Roberta in tow. They were married on October 24, 1911, in a simple parsonage ceremony.

While living in Chicago, Aimee again became active in church work, but within a year the couple moved to Providence, Rhode Island, where their son Rolf Potter Kennedy McPherson was born on March 23, 1913. After a time Aimee returned to Canada with the children and became actively involved in ministry. Harold followed her, and for a time the two ministered together. Harold acted as the advance man, obtaining the necessary site permits and the tents needed to make possible the evangelistic meetings in which Aimee preached. In 1917 Aimee began to publish *The Bridal Call*, a monthly magazine in which she wrote many articles on the basic essence of her teachings. This move helped to solidify a constituency of followers especially along the Eastern Seaboard. But the evangelistic activity of the McPhersons was difficult, and it took its toll on both of them. Ultimately Harold McPherson left the evangelistic party, returning to Rhode Island. The couple was divorced in August 1921.

In 1919 Aimee received *ordination* with the Assemblies of God (AG) as an "evangelist." She held these credentials with the general council until January 5, 1922, when she returned her fellowship papers to Chairman E. N. Bell. While her recent divorce might have posed some problems, it was actually the issue of property ownership that sparked her resignation. E. N. Bell responded to her concerns by holding out the possibility that were she to acknowledge that the tabernacle then under construction, Angelus Temple, was not held in her name, the executive committee would look favorably on her continuation in the Assemblies. She chose not to do so and parted from the AG without prejudice.

Denominational loyalties were lightly held in those days, especially in Holiness and Pentecostal circles. It comes as no surprise, then, that while Aimee had credentials with the AG, because of her popularity she was granted credentials by others, even when she did not seek them herself. In December 1920, for instance, she received membership in the Philadelphia-based C. C. Hancock Memorial Church of the Methodist Episcopal Church. That same day she was *licensed* as an exhorter with the Methodist Episcopal Church. Her ministry continued through the Midwest, to St. Louis and Wichita, back to Denver, then on to California. There, on March 27, 1922, she was *ordained* by the First Baptist Church in San Jose, again at their encouragement. This ordination was a controversial one that was never ratified by the larger Baptist association. Her ability to appeal broadly across denominational lines was rare among early Pentecostals. Her meetings were always interdenominational or ecumenical. They were supported by many people and pastors within historic mainline churches. Her vision was interdenominational from the start, and the cornerstone of Angelus Temple was inscribed to read that the Temple was dedicated to "the cause of interdenominational and world-wide evangelism." In Los Angeles the evangelist looked for a suitable place to preach. She decided in 1921 to build her own and, purchasing the property near Echo Park, designed and built Angelus Temple. She crisscrossed the nation, raising funds and proclaiming the gospel. In 1922 she even held an evangelistic tour in Australia. By January 1, 1923, when the 5,300-seat temple was dedicated, it was clear that she needed to settle down and pastor her growing flock. The ICFG was born that day, although its formal incorporation did not come until December 1927.

The 1920s were important years for "Sister," as she came to be known. She continued to write and publish her own works. First came such works as *This Is That* (1919, 1921, 1923) her initial autobiography, then *Divine Healing Sermons* (n.d.) and *The Second Coming of Christ* (1921). The year 1922 brought her inspiration for "The Foursquare Gospel" in the midst of a sermon on Ezekiel 1:4–10, which she preached in Oakland, California. Jesus Christ was preached henceforth as Savior, Baptizer in the Holy Spirit, Healer, and Coming King. She preached her first radio sermon that same year, and in 1924 opened radio station KFSG in Los Angeles, which is still operated at the ICFG. She was the first woman to receive an FCC license to operate a radio station. Where she envisioned sending out other evangelists she saw the need for training and in 1923 established the Lighthouse for International Foursquare Evangelism (L.I.F.E.) Bible College. The early 1920s saw her investing in foreign missions as well, and in 1927 she opened the Angelus Temple Commissary.

McPherson captured the imagination of the lower classes while she captivated the hearts of many in the middle and upper classes. Her commissary met the physical needs of over 1.5 million people during the Depression, regardless of race, creed, or color. She fought for higher wages and greater benefits for police and fire fighters, and railed against organized crime. Her vision provided an expanded role for Pentecostal women to engage in ministry. Many Foursquare Gospel Lighthouses were pioneered and pastored by women for whom she became the role model. Black evangelist Emma Cotton was encouraged by McPherson to establish the church that would ultimately become the formidable Crouch Temple of the Church of God in Christ. McPherson also led the Temple to engage in disaster relief efforts when earthquakes hit Southern California.

But the later 1920s were difficult years. McPherson preached sometimes over twenty times weekly while she oversaw her burgeoning work. In May 1926 she had become a highly publicized international figure when she suddenly disappeared, apparently drowned off Venice Beach while swimming. A month later she was found in Mexico, with a story of her kidnapping by some people who feigned to need her help. Rumors spread and she was embroiled in controversy about an alleged affair in Carmel, California, with a former employee, Mr. Kenneth Ormiston. A grand jury investigated her, but while it was not in session the district attorney charged her with the obstruction of justice, and suborning perjury. Ordered to stand trial, she was ridiculed daily

from pulpit to press. Ultimately the charges were dropped for lack of evidence, and the district attorney became personally embroiled in his own legal dilemma. McPherson authored her account of things through *In the Service of the King* (1927); shortly thereafter an unauthorized biography, *Sister Aimee* (1931), was written by N. B. Manity. In some minds the issue was never settled, and books and TV reconstructions have left much to the imagination. But Aimee was much more resilient than is often acknowledged, and Angelus Temple and Foursquare people proved to be loyal to her during this critical time.

The 1930s brought their share of problems, too. McPherson suffered a nervous breakdown in 1930, and entered an ill-fated marriage to David L. Hutton on September 13, 1931. The vision of the commissary brought with it an increasing indebtedness and threatened the work of Foursquare to the brink of bankruptcy. But again she persevered, and the work continued to prosper through her hard choices and gifted capabilities.

During the 1930s, Aimee took advantage of opportunities to expand the ministry. In spite of some trouble with the loyalties of a few of her associates, she consolidated the work of the Temple with a few well-chosen appointments. Among them was Giles Knight, who helped put the organization on a solid financial footing. In 1934 she engaged in several widely publicized public debates, arguing with avowed atheist Charles Lee Smith about the existence of God, and in North Little Rock, Arkansas, she engaged in debate with Elder Ben M. Bogard on the subject of the continuation/cessation of miracles and divine healing in the *Bogard-McPherson Debate*. Issues such as the efforts of the higher critics, modernism, and evolution led her to pen "What's the Matter?" in 1928. These issues remained problematic in her portrayal of the larger church throughout the 1930s.

Always one who enjoyed music, as early as 1923 Aimee had published the *Tabernacle Revivalist*, including her own composition "Former and Latter Rain" and her own selection of responsive readings covering the four cardinal doctrines that she preached. In the 1930s came *Four-Square Melodies*, including more of her compositions. To this volume she appended the Apostles' Creed, the Ten Commandments, and additional readings from the Psalms. In 1937 she published her *Foursquare Hymnal* with a supplement featuring sixty-four of her own compositions as well as those of other Pentecostals, including Thoro Harris and C. W. Walkem. This work was revised in 1957. In all, she wrote some 180 songs, many of which have never been published. She composed, with the aid of arranger Walkem, seven full-length sacred operas, including "The Bells of Bethlehem," "Regem Adorate," and "The Crimson Road." Several of her works were also released as sheet music in arrangements for use by soloists and choirs.

A 1936 trip around the world resulted in her plea *Give Me My Own God* (1936), published in a revised format from London under the title *I View the World* (1937). Her travels reinforced her concerns about Hitler, Mussolini, and Stalin, and she spoke often of them and the danger they held for world peace. When war finally materialized, she actively participated in raising money for war bonds and drew many illustrations from the conflagration for her vividly illustrated, partially acted sermons. She also did much to popularize a restorationist view of church history with her vision the "Dispensation of the Holy Ghost" repeatedly shared in her very popular sermon "Lost and Restored." During the 1930s this was reinforced through an annual "Cavalcade of Christianity" and other similar productions on the Angelus Temple platform or in the Shrine Auditorium of Los Angeles.

During World War II Aimee paid special attention to military personnel who visited Angelus Temple, inviting them to the platform and giving them Bibles. She continued to hold evangelistic meetings around the U.S. and in Canada, though on a sharply reduced scale. She did much to demonstrate Foursquare loyalty to the war effort and sent her magazine the *Foursquare Crusader* to army camps. In 1943 she was able to take a vacation in Mexico, but while there she contracted a tropical fever that left her sometimes incapacitated for weeks.

In 1944, perhaps for the first time recognizing her own physical limitations, "Sister" named Rolf McPherson vice president of Foursquare. She also called Howard Courtney to serve alongside him in the national office as general supervisor and director of foreign missions. These were among the last appointments she made. During September 1944, she began a crusade in the Oakland, California, Civic Auditorium. She preached a sermon the evening of September 26. That night she went to bed and was found the following day, dead from what was described as "shock and respiratory failure" following an apparently accidental overdose of a medical prescription. She was buried in Forest Lawn Cemetery in Glendale, California, on October 9, 1944, in one of the largest funerals ever held in Los Angeles.

The impact of the life and ministry of Aimee Semple McPherson is a significant one by all accounts. She was a colorful, sometimes controversial, figure. But she was also an extremely gifted communicator and organizer; a competent musician; a prolific writer; in many ways a servant of the people, especially the poor; and an instiller of vision who challenged her followers to trust in Jesus Christ, "the same yesterday, today, and forever" (Heb. 13:8), a theme prominently displayed in many Foursquare churches today. She was undoubtedly the most prominent woman leader Pentecostalism has produced to date.

Bibliography: R. Bahr, *Least of All Saints: The Story of Aimee Semple McPherson* (1979); O. Coats, "The Ordination of Mrs. McPherson," *Moody Monthly* 22 (1922): 1026–27; R. L. Cox, *The Verdict Is In* (1983); idem, *Bogard-McPherson Debate* (n.d.); idem, *There Is a God Debate* (n.d.); R. L. Cox, comp., *The Four-Square Gospel* (1969); T. B. Cox, *Getting "It"* (1927); J. D. Goben, *'Aimee' the Gospel Gold Digger!* (1932); A. S. McPherson, *Aimee: Life Story of Aimee Semple McPherson* (1979); idem, *Aimee Semple McPherson: The Story of My Life* (1973); idem, *Give Me My Own God* (1936); idem, *In the Service of the King* (1927); idem, *I View the World* (1937); idem, *The Story of My Life* (1951); idem,

This Is That (1919, 1921, 1923); A. S. McPherson, sermons: *Divine Healing Sermons* (n.d.); idem, *Fire From on High* (1969); idem, *The Foursquare Gospel* (1946); idem, *The Holy Spirit* (1931); idem, *The Second Coming of Christ* (1921); idem, *When the Fig Tree Putteth Forth Her Leaves* (n.d.); correspondence: A. S. McPherson to E. N. Bell (January 5, 1922); E. N. Bell to A. S. McPherson (Feb. 2, 1922); A. S. McPherson to Bro. Welch and Bro. Bell (March 28, 1922); C. H. Magee, *Antics of Aimee: the Poetical Tale of a Kidnapped Female* (1926); N. B. Mavity, *Sister Aimee* (1931); R. P. Shuler, "McPhersonism" (n.d.); idem., "Miss X" (n.d.); L. Thomas, *The Vanishing Evangelist* (1959); idem, *Storming Heaven* (1970).

C. M. Robeck, Jr.

Assuming leadership of the International Church of the Foursquare Gospel at the death of his mother, Rolf McPherson held the position for 44 years.

McPHERSON, ROLF KENNEDY (1913–). Pastor, administrator, and denominational executive. McPherson was born Rolf Potter (Kennedy) McPherson on March 23, 1913, in Providence, Rhode Island, to Harold Stewart McPherson and Aimee Elizabeth (Kennedy) Semple McPherson. On July 21, 1931, he was married to Lorna De Smith. The couple had two daughters, Kay Sterling (b. 1932) and Marleen Beth (b. 1932, d. 1961).

In 1933 McPherson graduated from the Southern California Radio Institute. He has used his media experience to develop several Foursquare video productions. He attended L.I.F.E. Bible College in 1933–34. Ordained to the ministry in 1940, he served as editor of the *Foursquare Magazine* from 1940 to 1943. He was awarded the honorary Doctor of Divinity from L.I.F.E. Bible College in 1941.

Early in 1944 McPherson was named vice-president of the International Church of the Foursquare Gospel (ICFG) and aided his ailing mother, Aimee, in her last year of leadership.

Upon her death in September 1944, "Doctor," as he is fondly called, assumed the presidency of the ICFG. His administrative acumen and financial skills have helped to build the denomination from 492 churches in 1944 to one of 12,628 (September 1986), serving 1.1 million members and adherents worldwide. During his tenure as president, the denomination took membership in the National Association of Evangelicals and in the Pentecostal Fellowship of North America. McPherson has served on the administrative boards of both of these organizations. On May 31, 1988, McPherson retired from the presidency and was succeeded by John R. Holland. McPherson serves as president emeritus and remains a member of the board of directors of the organization.

Bibliography: *Who's Who in America* (1976–77); "Foursquare Gospel Church Joins NAE," *United Evangelical Action* (May 1, 1952), 21.　　C. M. Robeck, Jr.

A minister with the Pentecostal Assemblies of Canada, David Mainse began a television ministry in 1962 and continues to host *100 Huntley Street*, a television program produced in Toronto.

MAINSE, DAVID (1936–). Pastor and radio and television personality. Mainse was born in Campbells Bay, Quebec, the son of a missionary to Egypt. He was educated at Eastern Pentecostal Bible College and ordained in the Pentecostal Assemblies of Canada.

Mainse pastored churches in eastern Canada, and in 1962, while at Pembroke, he began a television ministry that grew into Crossroads Christian Communications. "Crossroads" came to be released on 150 master and satellite stations by 1976. He is host of the popular "100 Huntley Street" telecast, which includes programming in ten languages, has its headquarters in Toronto, and is said to reach three-fourths of the popula-

tion of Canada. The program is also released on PTL, TBN, and VPN networks and on twenty-six other U.S. stations.

Mainse is the author of three books: *100 Huntley Street* (1983), *God Keep Our Land* (n.d.), and *Past, Present, and Promise* (n.d.).

Bibliography: D. Mainse, *100 Huntley Street* (1983).
　　　　　　　　　　　　　　　　　　　　S. Strang

Founder of Logos, International, Daniel Malachuk was the publisher of millions of books and started the *Logos Journal* and the *National Courier*.

MALACHUK, DANIEL (1922–). Founder of charismatic religious publishing company Logos International (1966), which published books, the *Logos Journal*, and the *National Courier* newspaper. In his youth Malachuk was a member of the famous Glad Tidings Tabernacle in New York City.

Malachuk led Logos to become the world's largest charismatic book publisher before it went bankrupt in 1981. He was an international director of the Full Gospel Business Men's Fellowship and was a founding regent of Oral Roberts University. He was director of several overseas spiritual renewal conferences, including the World Conference on the Holy Spirit, Jerusalem (1974).

Malachuk founded a subsidy publishing company after Logos went bankrupt, and he is the author of *Stained Glass Religion—Who Needs It?* and coauthor of *Prophecy in Action*.

Bibliography: J. Buckingham, "End of an Era, Final Chapter of the Logos Saga," *Charisma* (December 1981), 48–49, 51–52, 55.　　W. E. Warner

MALINES DOCUMENTS See CATHOLIC CHARISMATIC RENEWAL.

MALLORY, ARENIA CORNELIA (1905–77). Educator, teacher, church parliamentarian, and college president in the Church of God in Christ (CGIC). In October 1926, at the request of Bishop Charles H. Mason, Mallory caught a jim-crow train to begin her assignment as the new head of Saints Industrial and Literary School at Lexington, Mississippi (CGIC). She established the first high school and band for Negroes in Holmes County. She attempted to integrate her school faculty long before the Supreme Court legalized integration, but she was repudiated by a mob. She organized a singing group called the Harmonizers who traveled the entire U.S. in recruitment and fund-raising efforts. During the Kennedy administration she served as manpower specialist and consultant for the U.S. Department of Labor. More than anyone in the church's history she was distinguished by the scores of leaders she influenced. She was protégé of Mary Mcleod Bethune and was the church's most distinguished educator.   L. Lovett

Author and speaker Betty Malz is best known for her book *My Glimpse of Eternity*, which describes her death experience.

MALZ, BETTY PERKINS (1929–). Author and speaker. Betty Perkins was born in Terre Haute, Indiana, to parents who pioneered nine Assemblies of God churches. Her first husband, John Upchurch, died during open heart surgery. They had two daughters. She is now married to former missionary Carl A. Malz, former executive vice-president of Trinity Bible College, Ellendale, North Dakota.

Malz wrote an article for *Guideposts* that resulted in an invitation from Catherine Marshall to write her first book, *My Glimpse of Eternity* (1977). It described her death experience (dead twenty-eight minutes; in a coma for forty-four days). It is now available in eighteen languages. She has written five books since: *Prayers That Are Answered* (1981), *Super Natural Living* (1982), *Angels Watching Over Me* (1984), and *Women in Tune* (n.d.).

Malz has been a guest on "The 700 Club," "PTL," "100 Huntley Street," and Gary Moore's "To Tell the Truth." She has been a featured speaker at prayer conferences in forty-six states.

Bibliography: B. P. Malz, *My Glimpse of Eternity* (1977).   S. Strang

MARANATHA CAMPUS MINISTRIES, INTERNATIONAL (MCMI). A collegiate campus ministry founded by Robert T. "Bob" Weiner and his wife Rose in 1972 in Paducah, Kentucky, following a successful evangelistic effort with high school students. The first campus church was started at Murray State University, Murray, Kentucky, later in the same year.

The goal of the organization focuses on reaching collegians around the world with the gospel. As they are won to Christ, MCMI disciples them through the establishment of churches on or near college and university campuses, known as Maranatha Christian churches. These churches develop full-fledged programs with children's ministries, Bible training classes, community involvement, etc., but retain their evangelistic outreach to the nearby campuses.

As a denomination MCMI conducts regional, national, and international conferences, the Maranatha Satellite Prayer Network (MSPN), the Maranatha Leadership Institute, *The Forerunner* (a newspaper), and other literature. To foster campus outreach, each church is encouraged to have the following full-time staff positions: campus evangelist, international student director, Champions for Christ director, and Society for Creation Science director.

The international office is located in Gainesville, Florida, and the staff works under the direction of an executive board. Weiner has served as president since 1972.

Although not without controversy in the past, MCMI is firmly evangelical and charismatic in theology, with membership in the National Association of Evangelicals. It has also worked to upgrade the quality of staff training in recent years. Currently the organization has thirty-eight churches in the U.S. with ministries to approximately two hundred college and university campuses; there are also twenty-five churches overseas in eighteen countries. MCMI is served worldwide by approximately five hundred full-time staff members.

Bibliography: B. Nolte to G. B. McGee, November 16, 1987; L. Warren to G. B. McGee, February 16, 1988; "A Team of Cult Watchers Challenge a Growing Campus Ministry," *Christianity Today* (August 10, 1984), 38–40, 43.   G. B. McGee

MARANATHA COMMUNITY (BRUSSELS, BELGIUM) See CHARISMATIC COMMUNITIES.

MARK, GOSPEL OF The Gospel of Mark is a quick-paced account of the ministry of Jesus beginning with Jesus' baptism in answer to the call of John the Baptist and continuing on through the ministry in Galilee and the final conflict in Jerusalem, which culminates in Jesus' execution and resurrection. The exact ending of Mark is a major textual problem and will be discussed later in this article.

I. Date and Origin
II. Basic Outline
III. Mark's Plot and Major Themes
    A. Jesus' True Identity
    B. Secrecy
    C. Discipleship and Mission
      1. Discipleship as Following Jesus
      2. Failures of the Twelve
    D. Miracles
      1. Miracles and Magic
      2. Miracles and Jesus' Identity
      3. Miracles and the Cross
IV. The Holy Spirit in Mark
V. The Ending of Mark

I. Date and Origin. Since the nineteenth century, the Gospel of Mark has commonly been recognized as the earliest of the canonical Gospels, indeed, as the writing that probably initiated the Gospel genre. In recent decades a vocal but small minority of NT scholars have attempted to overturn this view, usually arguing for the priority of Matthew; nevertheless, an overwhelming majority of specialists of all confessional positions remain persuaded by the hypothesis of Markan priority. The precise date of the writing remains somewhat conjectural, though opinions tend to place Mark at some point between A.D. 65 and 75.

A major question in the dating of Mark is whether it was written before, during, or after the great Jewish-Roman war of A.D. 66–72. The references to the destruction of the Jewish temple in Jerusalem in 13:1–2 and to great distress in Palestine in 13:14–19 are crucial. Some take these as prophetic words recorded before or at the outbreak of this war, while others see in them after-the-fact descriptions of the Jewish revolt. Given the OT precedents of prophetic condemnations of Israel and predictions of divinely sent catastrophes, such as Jeremiah's oracles concerning the Babylonian invasion and destruction of Jerusalem (e.g., Jer. 7:1–15), it is not unrealistic to think that Jesus and early Christians after him may have prophesied a similar judgment upon the city on account of its rejection of Jesus. Thus a date for Mark in the tense years leading up to the revolt is not impossible, though a majority of scholars tend to date Mark around A.D. 70.

The hypothesis of Markan priority carries with it the conviction that the writers of Matthew and Luke probably used Mark as the major narrative source in the writing of their own Gospels. Some 90 percent of Mark's material occurs also in Matthew, and approximately 60 percent of Mark reappears in Luke. Further, the general ordering of events in these other two synoptic Gospels follows the Markan order. Finally, where Mark and one or both of the others have the same material, the accounts in Matthew and/or Luke quite often show obvious stylistic divergencies in the direction of more polished and sophisticated Greek style. Thus, if there is some sort of direct literary relationship connecting Mark and the other Synoptics, it is more likely that the others

used (and altered) Mark than that the writer of Mark drew upon the others.

If the other Synoptic writers used Mark as their primary narrative source and guide, this means that this writing acquired an early and influential status in ancient Christian circles. (Matthew and Luke are commonly placed sometime between A.D. 70 and 85.) From Mark the other Synoptic writers drew both specific material and the general form of a Gospel writing. At the same time, Matthew and Luke show additional material and somewhat altered ideas of the overall plan of what they wanted to write. Therefore Mark may have been influential but was apparently regarded as insufficient for some church needs by these writers. It should be noted that the other Synoptics not only show stylistic changes and additional material, but also reflect differences in thematic emphases. Thus, although a sizable amount of Markan material can be found in the others, Mark's Gospel preserves distinctive and important theological emphases and should by no means be neglected. Later we shall mention some of these noteworthy Markan themes.

Ancient church tradition agrees in attributing the Gospel of Mark to a companion and interpreter of Peter, traditionally the John Mark of Acts 12:12; 15:36–39 (e.g., Irenaeus, *Adv. Haer.* 3.1.1; Eusebius, *HE* 3.39.15–16). The Gospel is said to reflect Peter's preaching, and its origin is sometimes placed in Rome after Peter's work there. Modern biblical scholarship has tended not to be bound by this tradition and in recent decades has concentrated more on trying to describe the intentions of the author and the characteristics of the Christian groups with which he was familiar, leaving the name of the author unspecified. However, Hengel has recently mounted a renewed defense of the traditional view of the authorship of Mark (1985, 30) and has at least shown that the case for the traditional authorship of Mark is stronger than many might have presumed.

In spite of its apparent influence on the writers of Matthew and Luke, and its prestige reflected in being included into the fourfold Gospel collection of the NT canon, the Gospel of Mark was not really the favorite among ancient Christians, who tended to prefer Matthew and John. Mark was often dismissed as a mere abbreviation of Matthew, and the modern conviction that Mark was the earliest Gospel was not widely shared in earlier centuries. However, the modern preoccupation with the NT writings as historical sources for reconstructing the ministry and message of Jesus and the life of the earliest churches, combined with the widely shared conviction that Mark was the earliest of the surviving Gospels, propelled this writing into the limelight of modern NT scholarship where it has remained for over a hundred years.

This intense investigation of Mark has produced a good deal of widely shared conclusions, but a number of issues remain unsettled. It is commonly recognized that Mark's Greek style is relatively unsophisticated, but it is increasingly clear to most scholars (in spite of some opinion to the contrary) that the writer has arranged his material with care and that he was capable of using such literary techniques as allusion to OT passages (e.g., the allusion to Isa. 35:1–7 in 7:31–37), repetition (e.g., the three Passion predictions in 8:31; 9:30–31; 10:32–34), irony (e.g., numerous features of the Crucifixion account in 15:16–39), and "bracketing" one story with another so as to make the reader see connections between the two stories (e.g., the interrogation of Jesus and the probing of Peter in 14:53–72). Indeed, only careful reading of Mark with sensitivity to his subtle shaping of his story can lead to a full appreciation of his abilities and the product he has left us.

II. Basic Outline. Scholars differ over the details of Mark's organization, but there is almost unanimous agreement on the basic units of material. The prologue, 1:1–13, summarizes the ministry of John the Baptist and describes Jesus' baptism at John's hands and the subsequent temptation in the wilderness. After the summary statement in 1:14–15, Mark describes Jesus' ministry of preaching, healing, and exorcizing demons, and his debating with religious opponents, mainly located in Galilee. This takes us as far as 8:26. This part of Mark is characterized by several editorial statements summarizing Jesus' ministry (1:39; 3:11; 4:33; 6:6).

From 8:27 through 10:52 there is much teaching material dealing with Jesus' own mission and the nature of discipleship set within a narrative that takes Jesus and the Twelve from Galilee to the outskirts of Jerusalem. The rest of the Gospel, from 11:1 on, is set in or near Jerusalem and within the last few days of Jesus' ministry. There is conflict set within the temple (11:1–12:44), culminating in Jesus' prediction of the temple's destruction and the woes for his followers during that period (13:1–36). Then, from 14:1 there follows the quick-paced narrative of Jesus' last supper, betrayal, arrest, interrogations, execution, and resurrection.

Although he frequently refers to Jesus as "teacher" and mentions teaching as an important part of Jesus' ministry several times, Mark does not contain as much teaching material as is found in Matthew's well-known five discourses of Jesus' teaching (e.g., the "Sermon on the Mount" in Matt. 5–7). However, there are blocks of teaching material in 4:1–34; 7:1–23; and 13:1–37, as well as numerous other smaller units of Jesus' teaching scattered about the narrative. Important among the latter units of material are the three cycles (chs. 8–10) where each prediction of Jesus' death is followed by an incident illustrating the disciples' failure to understand the significance of Jesus' words and more teaching by Jesus likening discipleship to his own path and destiny (8:31–38; 9:30–50; 10:32–45).

Other recognizable collections of material within the larger units mentioned above include the series of conflict stories in 2:1–3:6 and the similar series of debates in the temple in 11:27–12:44. It is quite clear, then, that Mark has not given us a haphazard collection of Jesus' tradition but has attempted to organize his material in a sensible fashion. It must be noted, however, that his arrangement does not appear to give us a firm

basis for drawing up a chronological description of Jesus' ministry, beyond very basic matters such as the fact that he carried on an itinerant ministry in Galilee before going to Jerusalem for the final conflict that led to his execution. The nineteenth-century quest to write a definitive biography of Jesus after the fashion of modern biographies foundered on the fundamental difficulty of drawing chronological and psychological conclusions about Jesus' ministry on the basis of the Gospels, which were not prepared for such purposes.

III. Mark's Plot and Major Themes. Besides arranging his material with some care, Mark has also built into the narrative certain themes that propel the story line along. These themes will be missed unless one reads Mark as a whole so as to see the way they connect the narrative and give it depth.

A. Jesus' True Identity. The opening words of Mark fix upon titles that refer to the higher significance of Jesus, "Christ" and "Son of God" (1:1). The careful reader soon realizes that these words ironically introduce a narrative in which the question of who Jesus of Nazareth really is recurs in such a way as to make the question dominating theme. Various human characters in the story ask in bewilderment about Jesus' significance (usually after some impressive display of authority or miraculous power, e.g., 1:27; 4:41; 6:2–3), or blindly regard him as a serious sinner possibly in league with evil (e.g., 2:6–7; 3:22; 14:63–64), or wrongly identify him by various honorific but inadequate labels (e.g., 6:14–16; 8:27–28), or misunderstand and underestimate the meaning of such proper labels as "Christ" (e.g., 8:29–33; 10:35–45). In powerful irony, Jesus' spiritual opponents, the demons, instantly recognize him for what he is, blurting out acclamations of him as "Holy One of God" (1:24) and "Son of God" (3:11; cf. 5:7). But Jesus silences these voices, refusing to allow them to speak of him publicly (1:25, 34; 3:12).

The theme of Jesus' true identity receives even greater emphasis when Jesus himself puts the question directly to his disciples in 8:27–30 and commands silence about their messianic answer. Likewise, Jesus commands silence about the Transfiguration experience (9:9), where he is revealed to some of his disciples in radiant glory.

These passages highlight the twin pressures in the narrative. On the one hand, the human characters in the story are driven by events in Jesus' ministry either to wonder if he is not of some higher than ordinary status or to label him as the opposite, a blasphemer or sorcerer. On the other hand, Jesus actively prevents demons and his disciples from openly acclaiming him with the very sort of titles that the reader knows are the appropriate ones to use.

The fact that the demonic acclamations are ironically correct as to Jesus' higher identity is confirmed by the most important voice in the whole Markan narrative—God's. In the all-important baptismal scene (1:9–11), while the Spirit descends on Jesus, God speaks from heaven, "Thou art my beloved Son" (KJV). And again in the Transfiguration episode, the divine voice declares to the disciples on the mount with Jesus, "This is my beloved Son" (9:7 KJV).

And, of course, Jesus himself uses this kind of self-descriptive language in the crucial parable of the vineyard in 12:1–12, which culminates with his mention of "a beloved son" who is the last envoy from the "owner" to the "tenants." Likewise, in 13:32 Jesus calls himself "the Son" in his answer about the date of the end of time. In light of these things, the reader is to understand that Jesus' riddle in 12:35–37 about how the Christ can be called "son of David" (the title by which Bartimaeus addresses Jesus in 10:46–52) is intended to point beyond traditional notions of the Messiah to divine sonship as the proper category for one whom David calls "my Lord." Most explicitly, in the climactic trial scene (14:61–62) Jesus affirms strongly that he is indeed "the Christ, the Son of the Blessed One."

Thus Mark presents Jesus of Nazareth as really both the Christ, the true King of Israel (as the ironic account of the Crucifixion makes clear in 15:1–32), the true Son of David (e.g., 10:46–52), and also, in some still higher sense, the Son of God. The latter category and title probably expressed for Mark more loftily and more precisely Jesus' ultimate significance, and with this title we approach the preferred Markan answer to the repeated characters and groups scattered across the Markan narrative.

B. Secrecy. From the first, the reader knows who this Jesus really is, but the human characters in the story seem unable to grasp the truth, and Jesus seems bent on hiding it. This secrecy motif is to modern scholars a well-known feature of Mark's narrative, having been isolated (but improperly understood) by W. Wrede in 1901 (*The Messianic Secret*, 1971).

But there is a deep theological dimension to Mark's emphasis on secrecy and the difficulty experienced in understanding Jesus' true status, even by his own disciples (who are even described as having "hardened" hearts in 6:52 and 8:17, like the unbelievers of 3:5). The disciples in the Transfiguration episode are told to say nothing of what they have seen "until the Son of Man had risen from the dead" (9:9). This points us to the key. The acclamation of Jesus as God's Son, the disclosure of his heavenly significance, cannot proceed without misunderstanding until Jesus fulfills his mission to suffer and die in the will of God on behalf of the "many" who are to be redeemed through him (10:45).

What the demons say is true: Jesus is the Son of God. Peter's conclusion in 8:29, "You are the Christ," is likewise technically correct. But Mark's story is intended to show that any acclamation of Jesus that does not take account of, and is not informed by, a proper understanding of the Crucifixion and resurrection of Jesus does not really disclose the full truth and can even be misleading. This is most powerfully illustrated by the fact that immediately after his confession of Jesus as the Christ, Peter must be rebuked in the strongest terms for his wrong-headed refusal to accept Jesus' teaching that as the Christ he must be rejected and be killed (8:31–33). The opening words of Mark's Gospel show us that the iden-

tification of Jesus as the Christ is not wrong. Peter's great mistake in this instance is that he fails to accept Jesus' predicted rejection and execution as the culminating portion of the earthly ministry of Jesus the Christ.

Indeed, the only human character in the story who seems to portend the proper confession of Jesus is the Roman centurion in charge of the crucifixion squad (15:39)—more of Mark's perfect irony!—who calls the *crucified* Jesus "Son of God." This Roman prefigures the reception of the Gospel by the Gentiles, but his acclamation also dramatizes Mark's point that true faith is that which recognizes the Crucifixion as the climactic revelation of Jesus as the Son of God.

C. Discipleship and Mission. There can be little question that Mark's main concern is to emphasize Jesus' true significance and that christology is therefore Mark's central theme. But closely tied in with this theme is an emphasis on what it means to be a true follower of Jesus. The discipleship theme emerges quite quickly in 1:16–20, where Jesus calls several men to join him in his mission. Thereafter, wherever Jesus goes, disciples accompany him, sometimes all twelve of the apostles and sometimes an inner circle of Peter, James, and John.

After the Last Supper (14:26–31) Jesus predicts that his disciples will all abandon him in the Gethsemane scene that is imminent and in the coming ordeal they seem unable to recognize. Jesus' prayer, apart even from the inner circle (14:35–42), is the first stage of a rapid isolation of Jesus from his followers that characterizes his trial and crucifixion. But Jesus also predicts a reunion with his disciples and their restoration to his fellowship beyond the ordeal of his death (14:28); the messenger in the empty tomb tells the women (and the readers) that this promise is to be fulfilled (16:7) now that Jesus is risen from death. Thus the final word of Mark's story is this reunification and restoration to discipleship, making the Twelve a continuing representation of following Jesus. Their failure is reckoned with and overcome by Jesus' gracious promise to restore them.

This overall narrative pattern of discipleship is fleshed out by numerous passages that amplify and clarify what following Jesus means for Mark. A full appreciation of these passages requires us to recognize Mark's intention to present the Twelve as instructive examples (sometimes good and sometimes bad) for the readers.

Three of the five conflict stories in 2:1–3:6 concern Jesus' disciples. He defends his welcome of such people as Levi the tax collector (2:13–17) and defends the behavior of his disciples in not observing ritual fasts (2:18–22) and in foraging on the Sabbath (2:23–28) in the course of their itinerant mission with him. These stories all concern disciples engaged in mission, and this is the characteristic way Mark portrays disciples of Jesus, as those called to join in Jesus' work. Thus, in 3:13–19 the Twelve are called to be with him, to be sent out to preach and to have authority to cast out demons—exactly the characteristic actions of Jesus in this part of the story. In 3:31–34 Jesus points to his disciples and calls them his true mother and brothers, for they do the will of God in endorsing and participating in his mission (v. 35).

1. Discipleship as Following Jesus. It is in the central section of Mark (8:27–10:52) that we have the most concentrated body of material on discipleship. And here following Jesus is shown to be taken quite literally. After telling of his coming crucifixion, Jesus warns followers that they must be prepared likewise to be executed (8:34–38). In the first-century church this statement can only have been taken as a real warning that discipleship might mean one's death, though later centuries have made taking up one's cross a spiritual metaphor for general stresses of Christian living. After the second Passion prediction in 9:30–32, Jesus uses a child to make the point that following him means committing oneself to obedient service like a child (9:35) and to the welfare of other disciples (9:36–50).

Preceded by teaching about marriage and children, 10:17–45 is a solid block of material on following Jesus. The rich man who cannot face the sacrifice Jesus requires of him (10:17–22) is contrasted with the twelve who have forsaken all for Jesus' mission (vv. 23–31). But the latter are warned in words of memorable irony that they have no continuing material reward in this life (vv. 29–31). Jesus tells his disciples that they will have a hundred houses and families—none of them really their own, of course—as they follow him in an itinerant ministry (and sometimes refugee status) that is dependent on the hospitality of others. (The concluding irony, "with persecutions," indicates the situation in which these many houses and "relatives" will be found!)

After the third Passion prediction (10:32–34), the request of the Zebedee brothers for preferred status in Jesus' kingdom requires Jesus to emphasize yet again that following him means being prepared to undergo his fate (Jesus' "cup" and "baptism," vv. 38–40) and to serve fellow disciples selflessly (vv. 42–45) after the pattern of his own self-giving (v. 45).

Another important passage dealing with discipleship and mission is the discourse on the future in 13:1–37. Two themes seem to dominate this passage, a concern to dampen misguided eschatological excitement that might lead to deception by false teachers (vv. 5–8, 21–23, 32–33) and an emphasis on faithfulness to the mission of proclaiming the gospel no matter what opposition arises (vv. 9–13, 34–37). Indeed, it is striking to note that the only genuine "sign" of the end Jesus gives here—the only eschatological condition that must be fulfilled for the end to come—is the proclamation of the gospel to "all nations" (v. 10)! And it bears noting that Mark, distinctively of the Evangelists, twice refers to disciples as those who sacrifice life (8:35) and other amenities (10:29) for the sake of Jesus "and for the gospel," probably meaning the work of mission associated with the gospel message.

2. Failures of the Twelve. In the light of the emphasis on discipleship and his presentation of the Twelve as the ones chosen to join Jesus in his ministry (3:13–19) and to participate in the spiritual force at work in that ministry (6:7–13),

it is striking that Mark also shows the Twelve in such an unfavorable light.

This underscoring of the failures and dullness of the Twelve is more emphatic in Mark than in the other Gospels. For example, Matthew's account of Jesus walking on the water (14:22–33) concludes with the disciples worshiping Jesus and saying, "Truly you are the Son of God" (14:33). But in Mark's version (6:45–52) the episode ends with a reference to the disciples' astonishment and their failure to understand the true dimension of Jesus' person, for "their hearts were hardened" (v. 52). And the curious discussion between Jesus and the Twelve about the meaning of the feeding miracles in 8:14–21 simply has no parallel in any of the other Gospels. If Matthew and Luke used Mark as their major source, they must have omitted this passage, perhaps because they found it too critical of the Twelve.

Another interesting comparison is in the Synoptic accounts of the confession of Peter at Caesarea Philippi (Mark 8:27–33; Matt. 16:13–23; Luke 9:18–22). In Mark, immediately after Peter's confession, Jesus predicts his own execution. This elicits Peter's rebuke of Jesus and Jesus' prompt counterrebuke of Peter as a "Satan" who is not on God's side. In Matthew, Peter's confession is immediately followed by the famous words of Jesus about Peter the rock, to whom (representative of the Twelve) is given the "keys of the kingdom of heaven" (16:17–19). Matthew then recounts the conflict between Jesus and Peter, but the preceding words of praise soften the negative picture of Peter considerably in comparison to Mark's account. In Luke the whole conflict between Jesus and Peter is simply not recounted at all!

Examples of Mark's somewhat severe picture of the Twelve could be multiplied, but these examples will suffice. Some scholars of a few decades ago argued that this critical view meant that Mark was against the Twelve as authority figures in the early church, but this view has justifiably failed to gain acceptance. Instead, nearly all NT scholars recognize that Mark's critical picture of the Twelve is meant to serve a more profound purpose than merely attacking them, and that, as indicated earlier, Mark's final word about the Twelve is that they have been reconciled to Jesus and called again to follow him (16:7).

The negative aspects of Mark's portrayal are meant to present the Twelve as more powerful hortatory examples for the readers. By observing the boasting and failure of Peter and the others, by noting that even those given special power to cast out spirits and participate in Jesus' mission failed the crucial test when the time came to be faithful to death at Jesus' arrest, the readers are warned against overconfidence in their own faithfulness under fire. The disciples' vain comparisons of themselves with one another (9:33–34) and the jockeying for positions of eminence by the Zebedee brothers (10:35–37) serve to rebuke any tendency among later followers of Jesus to see discipleship as an opportunity for personal advancement rather than as a call to service.

The only flawless model held up for the readers is Jesus himself. This is not because Mark wishes to attack the apostles, but rather because in Mark's theology there can be no other basis for and adequate model of discipleship than Jesus himself in his selfless service and obedience even to the point of death. That is, Mark's view of discipleship is deeply tied to his christology. Jesus is not only the Redeemer but also the pattern of service for the redeemed. Just as Mark emphasizes that a proper understanding of Jesus requires doing justice to his crucifixion as the culminating revelation of his mission and significance, so Mark insists that discipleship must be conformed to the pattern of Jesus' own ministry of obedience and sacrifice.

D. Miracles. No reader of Mark can fail to be impressed with the amount of space given to describing Jesus' authority and power exhibited in various miracles. Analyses of the material in the four Gospels show that Mark devotes proportionately more space to this emphasis than the other Evangelists do. Two obvious questions arise. First, what is the meaning of all these miracles in Mark? Second, how does this emphasis on Jesus' miracles fit with Mark's emphasis on Jesus as the obedient Son whose true nature is ironically most clearly revealed in his ignominious death on the cross?

The first thing to recognize is that in Mark (as in the other Synoptics) Jesus' ministry has to do primarily with the approach of the kingdom of God, the eschatological action of God in reasserting his lordship over this world. The initial summary of Jesus' message in 1:14–15 makes this theme prominent, and it is reasserted at various points later on in the narrative. For example, the disciples are those given "the secret of the kingdom of God" (4:11), and accepting Jesus' message is receiving the kingdom of God (10:13–15). This kingdom is the eschatological redemption that challenges and invalidates the old order with its rules and regulations, as indicated in the parables of wedding joy, new cloth, and new wine in 2:19–22 (cf. 7:1–23).

But God's kingdom is also the end of the regime of Satan and evil spirits that afflicts God's creation. This is made clear in the controversy in 3:22–30, where Jesus describes his exorcisms as indications of the overthrow of Satan's kingdom. Thus the prominence given to exorcism in Mark (see the summary statements in 1:39; 3:11; 6:7) and his tendency to describe other types of miracles as combat with evil forces (e.g., rebuking the wind in 4:39 and healing the epileptic boy in 9:17–29) form part of Mark's emphasis that the kingdom of God does not appear in a vacuum but establishes itself over against the opposing powers of darkness. Jesus, as the bearer of this kingdom of God, is not simply a teacher or prophet, but the divine Son engaged in conflict with these evil powers, and as such Jesus comes mighty both in word and in miraculous deed.

Jesus' miracles are not simply evidential signs but are themselves specific examples of the advance of the kingdom of God over against the powers of evil (cf. Acts 10:38). This is why Jesus, who works so many miracles in Mark, can also be shown rejecting the Pharisees' demand for a "sign from heaven" (8:11–13). Mark means to show that, on the one hand, eyes truly open to God's kingdom would have recognized God's hand upon Jesus in his deeds and words without needing some special stunt beyond the things recounted in Mark; and, on the other hand, Jesus can spare no time for submitting to the accreditation demands of these insensitive and self-appointed teachers of Israel. He performs no stunt to impress jaded eyes but throws his effort into dismantling the regime of Satan by means of the spiritual power given to him, including the power to work mighty works.

The Markan miracle stories are thus further vehicles for the christological emphasis on Jesus as the divinely authorized Son. But they also sometimes serve as opportunities to call for faith on the part of the disciples and the readers. In the "sandwiched" stories of the healings of Jairus' daughter and the woman with a flow of blood (5:21–43), Jesus commends the faith of the woman and calls for faith from Jairus (vv. 34, 36). Likewise, in the healing of the epileptic boy Jesus summons the father to have faith (9:23), and subsequently he congratulates Bartimaeus for his faith (10:52). In fact, after the miraculous withering of the fig tree, Jesus urges that faith in God makes any prayer request possible (11:24).

All this means that miracles form an integral and important part of Mark's picture of the ministry of Jesus. Though a few scholars have argued that Mark regarded the traditions about Jesus' miracles in a negative light, the prominent place given to recounting Jesus' mighty works renders this view implausible. Instead, Mark affirms strongly and clearly the picture of Jesus as a worker of miracles, and he seems to believe that followers of Jesus are called on to have faith for such mighty works in the continuing life of the church, as the exhortations about faith in God seem to imply. If, as some have argued, Mark sought to correct the christological views of some of his readers, any such correction did not involve denying or minimizing the tradition of Jesus' miracles.

1. Miracles and Magic. Mark does, however, seem concerned to distinguish Jesus' miracle working from the various types of wonder workers in the ancient Greco-Roman world. In Mark, Jesus speaks and acts with exceptional authority (1:27–28), and the crowds are astounded with the sweep of his healing power (7:37). There were others in the first century who claimed powers of exorcism and mighty works. Such figures characteristically are described as using various magical techniques like incantations, spells, and magical objects.

In several passages it appears that Mark is trying to distinguish between Jesus and these magical practitioners. For example, in a few places Mark shows Jesus speaking to the patient in an Aramaic phrase, which would have sounded foreign to his Greek-speaking readers. Indeed, such foreign phrases could be seen as similar to the use of incantations by ancient magicians and exorcists. These incantations often involved the use of strange, sometimes incoherent, and foreign words and phrases, as the ancient magical papyri reveal. But when Mark shows Jesus using an

Aramaic phrase, he *always* gives a translation, showing the Aramaic phrase to have been some unremarkable statement in itself, not something done in magical practices, for it would break the magical power of the phrase to do so. This practice of translating these Aramaic phrases may therefore have been intended to emphasize that Jesus did *not* work by means of mysterious incantations and spells, but rather spoke simple commands that were effective because of who he was.

To Jairus' daughter, Jesus speaks a phrase that Mark says means merely "Little girl, I say to you, arise" (5:41). To the deaf man with a speech impediment, Jesus commands simply, "Be opened" (7:33–34). This translating of Aramaic phrases accords with Mark's practice of translating in other situations in Jesus' ministry, as in the Gethsemane prayer ("Abba, Father," 14:36) and the famous cry on the cross (15:34). The translations of the phrases spoken in the miracle narratives remove the air of mystery from the Aramaic phrases and thereby implicitly place emphasis on the personal authority of Jesus.

The distinction between Jesus' miracle power and the common magical practices of the Greco-Roman period seems intended also in the stress on the demonic acclamation of Jesus and his power to silence the demons. The demonic cries of Jesus' secret identity as Son of God, etc., are to be seen in the context of the ancient magical notion that knowledge of the name of a person or a god could carry the power of incantation and control over the one named. The demonic cries are then probably attempts by the demons to prevent Jesus from expelling them by invoking against him knowledge of his transcendent identity. In 5:7 the demons adjure Jesus to leave them alone in a formula that looks very much like an attempt at a magical invocation.

The fact that Jesus can so consistently silence the demons with a simple command shows that the principles of magic have no effect on him. His exorcisms are thus more specifically examples of spiritual conflict between Jesus the Son of God and the powers of evil, which dramatize Jesus' decisive superiority over both the demons and the whole body of magical technique such as the demons attempt to use against him.

2. Miracles and Jesus' Identity. In addition, Mark seems concerned to show that the particular miracles of Jesus do more than serve as examples of mighty power; they reveal something about Jesus' nature and purpose. The exorcisms, which show the sacking of the reign of Satan (3:26–27), have already been mentioned. Other important examples include stilling the storm in 4:35–41, after which the disciples ask in wonder, "Who is this? Even the wind and the waves obey him!"

For readers familiar with the OT—the kind of audience Mark seems to expect—the miracle and the disciples' question would certainly allude to OT passages that celebrate power over the sea as one of God's major attributes (e.g., Pss. 65:7; 89:9; 106:9; 107:23–32). Though the disciples are unable to penetrate their own dullness, the readers are supposed to understand this sea

miracle as a veritable revelation of the transcendent status of Jesus.

Likewise, the healing accounts in Mark 7:24–37 contain terms perhaps in allusion to Isaiah 35. The concluding statement of the crowd in verse 37—"He even makes the deaf hear and the mute speak"—further underscores the association with the works of God promised in the Isaiah passage. In fact, Mark often presents Jesus as doing the sort of miracles that fulfill OT expectations and/or correspond to the sort of actions attributed to God in the OT. The intended effect can only have been to indicate that Jesus is not just a wonder worker but, more correctly, does the work of God and is himself so closely associated with these works of God that no category such as thaumaturge, prophet, Davidic messiah, or eschatological herald is adequate to describe him.

Nevertheless, for all Mark's emphasis on Jesus as a worker of miracles, it is clear that Mark does not regard these actions as giving a sufficiently clear picture in themselves of Jesus' mission and significance. It is worth noting that, in spite of the significance the readers are to see in Jesus' miracles (as already indicated), these mighty works are never said to produce faith and understanding for the characters in the story. The crowds are amazed (*thambeō*, 1:27; *existasthai*, 2:12) and astonished (*ekplēssō*, 6:2; 7:37), marvel (*thaumazō*, 5:20), and take offense at Jesus (*skandalizō*, 6:3). Critics see his wonders and accuse him of being a sorcerer (3:22). Even his disciples do not get beyond amazement (4:41), in spite of direct exposure to wondrous actions (6:52; 9:6).

We saw earlier that sometimes Jesus congratulates people for the faith that moved them to approach him for healing (5:34; 10:52) and urges stronger faith (5:36; 9:23). This makes it all the more striking that Mark never recounts a single case where a miracle *produces* faith. Thus the Markan enthusiasm for recounting Jesus' miracles cannot dispute a subtle but clear limitation set on their effectiveness in leading to true faith in and understanding of Jesus. However, this limitation in the effectiveness of Jesus' miracles in Mark did not arise from an antimiracle attitude or from any misgivings about the authenticity of the tradition that Jesus worked such wonders. Rather, Mark's point about the limited effect of Jesus' miracles has to do with a profound theological and christological point of view.

3. Miracles and the Cross. This brings us to the second of the two major questions raised earlier about the miracles of Jesus in Mark: the relationship of the emphasis on miracles to the Markan emphasis on the Crucifixion. Though Martin Kähler's description of the Gospels as Passion narratives with extended introductions (*The So-Called Historical Jesus and the Historic Biblical Christ*, 1964, 80) is a bit of an exaggeration of the facts, it is true that Mark shows in various ways a strong conviction about the theological importance of Jesus' crucifixion, as we have already noted. If, as is commonly agreed, Mark's Passion account begins with the entrance into Jerusalem (ch. 11), slightly more than one-third of the Gospel is devoted to this subject. But Jesus' threefold predictions of his death (chs. 8–10) and the mention of a plot to destroy Jesus (3:6) cast the shadow of the Cross over a much larger portion of the narrative. This emphasis on the redemptive and revelatory significance of Jesus' crucifixion explains Mark's subtle critique of the effect of Jesus' miracles.

By themselves, Jesus' miracles are powerful displays of his transcendent status as the Son of God and are dramatic indications that Jesus' ministry is the fulfillment of OT promises of divine redemption. But Mark's point with reference to the miracles is precisely that it is not enough simply to recognize these truths about Jesus in an abstract sense. To confess Jesus intelligently, to understand properly God's redemptive plan, to be "on the side of God" (8:33) and not be an unwitting opponent of God's purpose, one must confess the crucified and risen Jesus as God's Son. Therefore, no earthly character in the Markan story understands who Jesus really is or is allowed to use Mark's favored confessional titles, "Christ" and "Son of God," openly and intelligently until the crucial redemptive and revelatory events take place.

More systematically than the other Evangelists, Mark prevents his earthly characters from displaying the christological understanding of the church that was formed after the crucifixion and resurrection of Jesus. And this is not because Mark simply remembered more completely than the other Gospel writers that the Crucifixion and Resurrection did force Jesus' disciples to rethink all previous notions of God's redemptive plan and the meaning of messiahship. Besides his awareness of this historical fact, Mark seems also to have been concerned to make the important theological point we have noted above.

That is, in his narrative Mark sought not only to preserve tradition about Jesus and his disciples, but also to instruct his readers about proper Christian faith and understanding in the continuing life of the church of his own time. If Jesus' opponents rejected his miracles as satanic, this was an indication of their spiritual hardness and "leaven" of resistance to God's purposes (8:11–15). If the more neutrally presented crowds were unable to progress beyond bewilderment at his miracles, this could be seen as a result of a milder form of spiritual dullness, for they had not been given "the secret of the kingdom of God" (4:11–12). But even his disciples, who witnessed the miracles firsthand and were given a share in his miracle power (3:13–15; 6:7), failed to grasp and welcome the nature of God's purposes in Jesus. As the narrative unfolds, Mark makes it progressively clearer that their problem was precisely that they attempted to believe in Jesus and follow him without making his suffering central to their view of him and to their understanding of discipleship.

Christian readers of Mark have found in the Twelve the characters with whom they can identify themselves most easily. This was no doubt as true of the first readers as of those who have come after through the centuries. And from the first it is likely that Mark's Gospel was read both as sacred tradition and as sermonic instruction, that is, as a holy record of Jesus' ministry and as a lesson in following him. It is also likely that this was just as Mark intended his narrative to be used. That is, the distinctively Markan emphasis on the disciples' failure to grasp the nature of Jesus' mission—a failure that led to their abandonment of Jesus at his arrest—probably served to instruct and warn Mark's readers to learn from this failure and to develop their own theology and Christian discipleship accordingly.

Moreover, by giving such prominence to the miracles as genuine revelations of Jesus' transcendent status and yet at the same time showing how the miracles did not in themselves suffice to bring true faith and understanding, even among the Twelve, Mark makes the revelatory significance of the Cross and Resurrection all the more emphatic. Mark clearly believed that Jesus worked many miracles and seems to have expected that his followers would continue to see such manifestations of divine power in answer to their faith as a part of the ministry of the gospel. But just as clearly Mark subordinated miracles to the gospel of the crucified and risen Jesus.

This qualification on the revelatory efficacy of miracles in themselves is most evident in 13:21–23, where the readers are warned that false christs and false prophets will "perform signs and miracles to deceive the elect—if that were possible." So miracles by themselves cannot suffice to indicate the true Christ, and the readers are warned about uncritical preoccupation with such deeds.

IV. The Holy Spirit in Mark. At least to judge by frequency of mention, it cannot be said that the Holy Spirit is a major theme in Mark's Gospel. Mark's references to the Spirit are fewer than one finds, for example, in Luke. Yet the Spirit is mentioned in interesting ways in Mark, and here it is appropriate to address these references. We can observe some interesting distinctives of Mark's references to the Spirit by comparison with parallel passages in Matthew and Luke.

The first reference to the Spirit is in 1:8, where John the Baptist predicts one mightier than he, who is to come soon to "baptize you with the Holy Spirit." In John's prediction, baptism with the Spirit is the major work of the one mentioned. Moreover, in comparison with parallels in Matthew 3:11–12 and Luke 3:16–17 that refer to a baptism of the Spirit and a baptism of fire, the Markan form of John's saying seems to place more emphasis on the Spirit.

Mark almost certainly saw John's prophecy as pointing to Jesus, even though he nowhere else shows Jesus engaged in this Spirit baptism. Other passages, which demonstrate Mark's familiarity with the work of the Holy Spirit in the ministry of Jesus (1:12; 3:26–30) and the post-Easter church (13:11), tend to confirm implicitly the connection between Jesus and the Spirit established in John's statement. Mark does not elucidate what he understood the metaphor of Spirit baptism to represent, but it is a reasonable suggestion that he saw it as referring to the eschatological salvation that Jesus brought and that was exhibited in the experiences of the Spirit which were conferred in Jesus' name in early Christian communities.

Two more references to the Spirit follow in quick succession in the accounts of the baptism and the wilderness temptation of Jesus. Jesus' baptism (1:9–11) is marked by the opening of heaven, the descent of the Spirit upon him, and the voice from heaven addressing him as God's "beloved Son" (KJV) with whom God is "well pleased." If, as many commentators believe, the latter part of the heavenly statement alludes to Isaiah 42:1, where we read of God's servant "in whom I delight," the descent of the Spirit may be seen as fulfilling another statement there: "I will put my Spirit on him." In any case, other early Christian tradition makes it evident that Jesus was seen as specially "anointed" with the Spirit for his ministry (Acts 10:38), and the Markan baptismal scene dramatizes this empowerment.

Immediately after the baptism, the Spirit "drove" (ekballei, 1:12) Jesus into a wilderness where he was tempted by Satan for forty days. This verb is the same one Mark uses to describe Jesus' expulsion of demons (e.g., 1:34; 3:22). It is interesting that both Matthew and Luke prefer to describe Jesus as "led" by the Spirit (anēchthe, Matt. 4:1; ēgeto, Luke 4:1). The effect of Mark's choice of words is not necessarily to make Jesus resistant to the Spirit's direction (though Mark also seems to emphasize more than the other Synoptics Jesus' Gethsemane desire to avoid the Crucifixion, for 14:35 has no parallel), but the verb does seem to make emphatic the initiative of the divine Spirit.

The final Markan reference to the Spirit in connection with Jesus' ministry is in the account concerning the controversy over Jesus' exorcisms in 3:22–30. Mark has certain Jerusalem scribes attribute Jesus' power to possession by Beelzebub (3:22), and a bit later this is recounted as an accusation that Jesus "has an unclean spirit" (3:30). Jesus' parables (3:23–27) are intended both to make the accusation illogical and to claim that his exorcisms mark the end of Satan's tyranny. Then (3:28–29) comes the interesting warning about blasphemy against the Holy Spirit, "an eternal sin" for which there is no forgiveness.

In the Markan context, it is obvious that this blasphemy consists in writing off Jesus' ministry as a work of evil and that Jesus' power of exorcism is properly to be seen as a manifestation of the Holy Spirit. Mark's final comment in 3:30 directly contrasts the scribal accusation that Jesus is empowered by an unclean spirit with Jesus' implicit claim to be working in the power of God's Spirit. Once again we seem to be in touch here with the sort of tradition about Jesus' ministry that is encapsulated in Acts 10:38. This passage further confirms the suggestion that the descent of the Spirit at Jesus' baptism is to be seen as both a mark of divine favor and an enduement for his ministry.

The Gospel writers do not belabor the theme that Jesus worked in the Spirit's power, and Barrett (1970) has persuasively shown that the reason was probably christological. The Evangelists were apparently concerned to avoid giving the impression that Jesus was essentially another of the many "pneumatic" figures of popular legend. As Messiah and Son of God, Jesus was for the Evangelists the bearer of the Spirit par excellence. But what set Jesus apart in the faith of the early church was not his Spirit enduement; it was his own personal status and authority. In the early church, many were seen as endued with the Spirit and able to work wonders (see, e.g., the treatment of Peter, Stephen, Philip, and Paul in Acts). Therefore Mark neither downplays nor emphasizes greatly the claim that Jesus' ministry was done in the power of the Spirit. He presents the claim but is more concerned to draw attention to the person of Jesus himself.

Thus, in several passages Mark prefers to attribute the powerful nature of Jesus' ministry to Jesus' "authority" (exousia, e.g., 1:27; 2:10; 11:28–33). Likewise, when Mark mentions the disciples as empowered to partake of Jesus' ministry of exorcism, he refers to Jesus' giving them his "authority" over the demons (3:15; 6:7). All this has the effect of focusing attention primarily on Jesus rather than on the idea of his being endued with the Spirit.

Yet, in 13:9–13 Jesus warns his disciples of coming persecutions and trials before various tribunals, and he instructs them to be brave and to "say whatever is given you at that time, for it is not you speaking, but the Holy Spirit" (v. 11). This surely is evidence that Mark understood the mission of the church as empowered by the Holy Spirit, who could even supply those on trial for their faith with prophetlike inspiration to defend their faith with eloquence. So, although Mark did not choose to elaborate on the connection between Jesus' ministry and the Spirit's empowering of the Christian community for mission, he must have seen some such connection. Those on trial in 13:9–13, Jesus says, are persecuted "for my sake" (vv. 9, 13 KJV) and are involved in proclaiming the gospel (v. 10). The assistance of the Spirit, therefore, is specifically assistance in bearing witness to Jesus.

V. The Ending of Mark. The major text-critical problem in Mark is the question of how the Gospel originally ended. The ancient manuscripts show that four different endings circulated in early Christian circles:

1. The two oldest complete Greek manuscripts end Mark at 16:8, and other early witnesses show that the material in 16:9–20 was either not known or was regarded with some suspicion.

2. Several witnesses of the Byzantine period contain verses 9–20, but after verse 6 have (some with minor variations) the following statement: "But they reported briefly to Peter and those with him all that they had been told. After this Jesus himself sent out by means of them, from east to west, the sacred and imperishable proclamation of eternal salvation."

3. Jerome attests another expanded ending of Mark that involved verses 9–20 and other additional material. This ending is preserved in only one Greek manuscript, Codex Washingtonianus, in which we read after verse 14:

And they excused themselves, saying, "This age of lawlessness and unbelief is under Satan, who does not allow the truth and power of God to prevail over the unclean things of the spirits. Therefore reveal thy righteousness now"—thus they spoke to Christ. And Christ replied to them, "The term of years of Satan's power has been fulfilled, but other terrible things draw near. And for those who have sinned I was delivered over to death, that they may return to the truth and sin no more, in order that they may inherit the spiritual and incorruptible glory of righteousness which is in heaven" (translations of these endings are from B. Metzger, *A Textual Commentary on the Greek New Testament* [1971, 123–24]).

4. There is the traditional ending of Mark, verses 9–20, made familiar to English readers through the KJV.

Thorough study of the textual evidence enables us to dismiss endings 2 and 3 immediately. Their support is slight, and their Greek style and contents make them unlikely to have come from Mark's hand. The traditional ending (4) is attested quite early but is likewise in all probability an early attempt to supply a more satisfactory ending to Mark than what seems to be the earliest surviving ending at 16:8. Scholarly opinion is somewhat divided over the question of whether 16:8 is Mark's intended ending to the Gospel or whether the original ending was somehow lost quite early before many copies of Mark had been made.

The long ending (4) is attested in the great majority of witnesses to the text of Mark, and by the medieval period it had certainly become the standard ending. Moreover, this is the ending to Mark that was familiar to Christians throughout most of church history, and it has therefore functioned for many Christians as part of the canonical text. Especially in early Pentecostal circles of the modern period, this passage was part of a repertoire of NT texts used to defend the view that the proclamation of the gospel should continue to be accompanied by miraculous signs such as exorcisms, tongues speaking, and healing. Most other Christians have simply seen the text as referring to the signs that accompanied the initial apostolic proclamation of the gospel; but Pentecostals tended to emphasize that Jesus' promise is that signs shall follow "those who believe," not simply apostles or first-generation witnesses to the gospel, and that the signs are attached to the gospel, not to apostles (v. 20).

In the "snake handler" Pentecostal circles, regarded as intolerably extremist by all other Pentecostal Christians, this passage is the biblical basis offered for the ritual handling of poisonous snakes in the setting of a church service. The ability to pass around rattlesnakes without harm is regarded in these small and remote groups as outward proof of one's salvation. Outside these circles, however, this passage is usually understood as teaching that the signs of verses 9–20 are to accompany specifically the continued proclamation of the gospel and are not required as proof of the validity of individual Christian salvation.

Modern scholarly study of the passage has mainly been devoted to the text-critical question

of whether the passage was part of the original text of Mark and where and when it might have first appeared. Little time has been spent investigating in detail the contents of the passage. A careful reading shows that an important theme is the contrast between unbelief and belief. In verse 11, the resurrection report of Mary Magdalene is received with unbelief. Likewise, the resurrection appearance reported by the two unnamed disciples in verses 12–13 is not believed. Then, in verse 14, Jesus appears to the eleven apostles and scolds them for their unbelief (*apistia*) and hardness of heart (*sklērokardia*) because they had not believed the report of those who had seen the risen Lord. Finally, in his commission to the Eleven (vv. 15–18), Jesus promises salvation for those who believe and condemnation for those who do not believe (v. 16), and he assures those who believe that miraculous signs (*sēmeia*, v. 17) will "follow" them (meaning, no doubt, as they go forth in the evangelistic mission Jesus commands).

The unbelief illustrated in the passage is a repeated refusal to believe the reports of Jesus' resurrection, and it is interesting that it is "the Eleven" (the "Twelve" minus Judas) who are pictured as failing here. Yet Jesus himself takes the trouble to make his resurrection manifest to these same unbelieving disciples and gives to them the commission to preach his gospel to the whole world (v. 15).

The idea of "signs" accompanying the early proclamation of the gospel is found in other NT writings (e.g., Acts 2:43; 4:29–30; Heb. 2:3–4; Rom. 15:17–19), and the specific signs listed in verses 17–18 include some things attested elsewhere in early tradition, such as exorcisms (e.g., Acts 6:7), healings (e.g., Acts 3:6–10), tongues speaking (e.g., Acts 2:3–4), and surviving unhurt after being bitten by a snake (Acts 28:3–6). However, it is not entirely clear that to "pick up serpents" (v. 18) is quite the same thing as what happened to Paul on Malta, and we have no clear indication of what may be intended by the accompanying reference to drinking "any deadly thing."

It is probable, however, that whoever wrote this passage saw all these signs both as powerful corroborations of the truth of the gospel and as more specific indications that the message announced eschatological redemption from God. This is suggested by the reference to "*new* [*kainais*] tongues," an adjective often associated in early Christian usage with eschatological hope (e.g., 2 Cor. 3:6; 5:17). Also, the expulsion of demons in Jesus' name and the power over poisonous serpents may both have been intended to connote the eschatological triumph of God's purposes (cf. e.g., Rom. 16:20; Luke 10:19). Though the passage is brief, it is possible that careful investigation might be able to throw more light on the beliefs and purposes of its author.

See also JESUS CHRIST; JESUS CHRIST AND THE SPIRIT.

Bibliography: C. K. Barrett, *The Holy Spirit and the Gospel Tradition* (1970); E. Best, *Following Jesus: Discipleship in the Gospel of Mark* (1981); M. Hengel, *Studies in the Gospel of Mark* (1985); L. W. Hurtado, *Mark: A*

Good News Commentary (1983); J. D. Kingsbury, The Christology of Mark's Gospel (1983); W. L. Lane, The Gospel According to Mark (1974); P. Pokorný, "Das Markusevangelium. Literarische und theologische Einleitung mit Forschungsbericht," in H. Temporini, Aufstieg und Niedergang der Römischen Welt 2, 25/3:1970–2035; D. Rhoads and D. Michie, Mark as Story: An Introduction to the Narrative of a Gospel (1982); J. M. Robinson, The Problem of History in Mark (1968).

L. W. Hurtado

MARSHALL, SARAH CATHERINE

(1914–1983). American author. Born in Johnson City, Tennessee, Catherine Wood was the daughter of a Presbyterian minister. She married Peter Marshall, also a Presbyterian minister, in 1936.

From March 1943 to the summer of 1945 she was bedridden with tuberculosis. One night she had a vision of Jesus and trusted in God for healing. She soon recovered.

When her first husband died of a heart attack in January 1949, Catherine began her literary career by collecting his sermons in Mr. Jones, Meet the Master. She wrote his biography, the best-selling A Man Called Peter, in 1951 and Christy in 1967.

Catherine served as woman's editor for Christian Herald magazine from 1958 to 1960. She married Leonard Earl LeSourd, executive editor of Guideposts, in 1959 and became an editor of the magazine in 1961. In 1975 Marshall and LeSourd established Chosen Books, a publisher of inspirational literature. She died in Boynton Beach, Florida.

Bibliography: Contemporary Authors (1983).

G. W. Gohr

A Catholic charismatic New Testament scholar, Francis Martin was baptized in the Spirit in 1968 and has since that time been a leader in the renewal.

MARTIN, R. FRANCIS (1930–). Catholic Scripture scholar and leader in the Catholic

Charismatic Renewal (CCR). Born Robert Martin in New York City, he took the name Francis when entering the Cistercian abbey at Spencer, Massachusetts, in 1950. He was ordained priest in 1956 and was sent to study Scripture in Rome. Martin taught Scripture at Spencer (1961–65) and then at Madonna House Community, Combermere, Ontario (1965–71). He did further studies in Rome (1971–76), was a visiting professor at the Ecole Biblique in Jerusalem (1976–78), and gained his doctorate at the Pontifical Biblical Institute, Rome, in 1978.

Martin was baptized in the Spirit in 1968, following a visit to Combermere by two young men from Ann Arbor, Michigan. During his years in Rome and Jerusalem, he was active in CCR, acquiring a reputation as a dynamic teacher who combined the scholarly with the spiritual. Martin is a brilliant linguist and became known to CCR leaders in many countries through his translation work at the CCR International Conference in Rome in 1975. In those years he published three books that led to many conference talks: Touching God (1975), Footprints of God (1976), and The Songs of God's People (1978).

At the beginning of 1979 Martin moved from Madonna House to the Mother of God Community in Gaithersburg, Maryland, from a sense of the Lord calling him to "the heart of the renewal." He has been a regular contributor to The Word Among Us, a monthly magazine to help readers establish a daily prayer life based on the Scriptures, and has taught Scripture at the University of Steubenville, Ohio, and academic institutions in Washington, D.C. He has been a major speaker at the Conference for Priests and Deacons held at Steubenville since 1975. More recent works include Baptism in the Holy Spirit (1986) and Stories Comparable to New Testament Narratives (1988).

P. D. Hocken

MARTIN, RALPH (1942–). Prominent lay leader in the Catholic Charismatic Renewal (CCR). Having a conversion experience through a Cursillo just before graduating with a degree in philosophy from Notre Dame in 1964, Martin worked with Stephen Clark on the national secretariat of the Cursillo movement (1964–70). He was baptized in the Spirit in the spring of 1967 after hearing of the "Duquesne week-end."

In November 1967, Martin and three colleagues began the prayer meeting at Ann Arbor, Michigan, that grew into Word of God community. Closely associated with Word of God's outreach, he was the first editor of New Covenant (1971–75), directs Servant Ministries (1980–), and chairs the council for the Sword of the Spirit, an international community formed by Word of God and other communities in 1982.

Martin has been one of the most respected leaders in the charismatic renewal among Catholics. As well as serving on the national service committee (1970–75), he contributed to its international expansion, becoming the first director of the International Communications Office (1975–79), moving with the office to Brussels in 1976 to work more closely with Cardinal Suenens.

Ralph Martin is a prominent leader in the Catholic charismatic Word of God community, Ann Arbor, Michigan.

Martin's role has been important as both teacher and prophet. He has constantly stressed the call to repentance for sin, the demands of the holiness of God upon his people, and the importance of basic Christian orthodoxy, giving striking prophecies in St. Peter's, Rome, in 1975 and at the Kansas City conference in 1977. Since 1983 this message has been spread through F.I.R.E. (with John Bertolucci, Michael Scanlan, and Ann Shields), as well as through his weekly television program "The Choices We Face." His publications include: *Unless the Lord Build the House* (1971); *Hungry for God* (1974); *Fire on the Earth* (1975); *Husbands, Wives, Parents, Children* (1978); *A Crisis of Truth* (1982); and *The Return of the Lord* (1983).   P. D. Hocken

MARY AND THE HOLY SPIRIT In popular terms Mary, the Mother of Jesus, has been described as the "first Pentecostal." Commenting on Laurentin's treatment of Mary as the model charismatic, Carluer states: "In this portrait of Mary the author defines her essentially as the prototype of the charismatic. It is a portrait that in its broad outline is quite acceptable to an evangelical Christian" (Carluer, 1974, 74). The epithet "charismatic," or Spirit-filled, is rooted in the biblical tradition. The Gospels of Matthew (1:18–25) and Luke (1:26–38), both writing independently, know a tradition about Mary's virginal conception of Jesus through the Spirit. This "virginal conception" should be carefully distinguished from "virginal birth," which would indicate that Mary's hymen was not broken when she delivered her baby son: this mythological feature is found only in the Apocryphal NT. Luke portrays Mary conceiving Jesus through the "overshadowing" of the Holy Spirit. The verbs used are *eperchesthai* ("come upon") and *episkiazein*

("overshadow"). *Eperchesthai* is also used of the Spirit's coming on those assembled in the Upper Room on the Day of Pentecost (Acts 1:8), but Luke may also have in mind Isaiah 32:15: "until the Spirit from on high is poured on us." The verb *episkiazein* (cf. the transfiguration of Jesus [Matt. 17:5; Mark 9:7; Luke 9:34; and Acts 5:15]) means "to cover." It is used to describe God's presence under the symbol of the cloud over the tabernacle (Exod. 40:35 [29]) and of his powerful protection of the chosen people (Pss. 91:4 [90:4]; 140:7 [139:8]). The Spirit's power both implements a unique form of procreation through Mary and bestows on Mary's son a special character. From a literary point of view Luke's account is constructed according to the OT birth-announcement narrative, but the unique feature is found in the virginity of Mary. However, the Annunciation pericope itself is primarily christological, not mariological: It emphasizes Jesus' human origin as well as his divine nature. The subject of Mary's biological virginity was debated very little for sixteen hundred years (A.D. 200–1800) but has emerged as a matter of discussion in the Roman Catholic church since the Second Vatican Council. The position is, perhaps, best summarized in the *Dutch Catechism* (1967): "They (Matthew and Luke) proclaim that this birth does not depend on what men can do of themselves—infinitely less so than in other human births. That is the deepest meaning of the article of faith, 'born of the Virgin Mary'" (74–75).

Scholars have recognized that the NT makes no explicit connection between the divinity of Jesus and his virginal conception. However, Mary is addressed as the one "highly favored." In Pentecostal terms the blood of the Lamb finds its origin in Mary and, while she is informed that Jesus will be a successor of King David, she is also told that he will be called "great" (a title usually predicted of God) and "Son of the Highest." The Annunciation pericope itself bears some close affinity to the Palestinian Aramaic text from Qumran Cave 4 (4 Qps Dan Aa).

1. He will be great (cf. Luke 1:32).

2. He will be called Son of the Highest (cf. Luke 1:32).

3. He will be called Son of God (cf. Luke 1:35).

4. He will reign . . . forever (cf. Luke 1:33).

5. . . . will come upon you (cf. Luke 1:35) (see Fitzmyer, 1973–74).

Luke also presents Mary as the "handmaid of the Lord" (1:38 KJV), and he shows her as a true disciple, a member of the eschatological family of Jesus who hears the Word of God and believes (cf. 8:19–21). She is, therefore, the model who receives the Spirit's abundant blessing (cf. 1:45). She may also have been present with the other men and women disciples at the Last Supper.

This disciple aspect of Mary is also expressed in the Gospel of John in two pericopes. In the first (2:1–12) Mary requests Jesus to assist at the marriage feast at Cana where the wine had run out and where Jesus performs his first sign, namely, of changing water into wine: verse 12 shows Mary as a disciple following Jesus to Capernaum after the wedding feast. In the second (19:25–30) John presents Mary as standing at the foot of the cross (*para tō staurō*) in contrast to the women in the synoptic tradition who stand at a distance (*apo makrothen*). She stands there in the capacity of a disciple closely united to Jesus carrying his cross. Jesus commends her to the disciple John, and John to Mary. This Johannine scene contains profound symbolism. In the "hour" of Jesus, Mary in the person of John receives the commission (role) of maternal, spiritual care for the post-Resurrection community. Mary and John are seen as representatives of a small community of believing disciples who persevere in the hour of trial. Mary may also symbolize Israel, who gives birth to the Christian community. This emotive scene occurs just before Jesus bows his head and transmits the Spirit (v. 30; there is a Johannine play on the word *paradidomi*). Thus the Spirit begets Jesus' eschatological family at the foot of the cross. Mary seems to have been an important person for the Johannine community.

Mary is also closely associated with the Holy Spirit, for Luke specifically mentions that she and other women were present in the Upper Room with the apostles prior to the descent of the Holy Spirit on the Feast of Pentecost. Mary is the only person to be mentioned by name on this occasion except for the eleven apostles. Thus Luke, as well as John, presents Mary as a member of the believing Christian community after the Resurrection. The coming of the Spirit at the time of Jesus' conception was a foreshadowing of the coming of the Spirit upon the entire community on Pentecost. Thus Mary is regarded as one of the first to receive the "baptism in the Spirit" even prior to Pentecost.

Mary has been linked closely to the charismatic renewal within the Catholic church but more enthusiastically in France and Canada than in the U.S.

The Catholic Charismatic Renewal (CCR) focuses on "Mary's Spirit-animated presence in the communion of saints" and Mary as the model of the church in a way that is "truly biblical and ecumenical" (Laurentin, 1977, 194). Mary is also seen as the model of Christians who are baptized in the Spirit. Suenens (1974, 199) says, "Mary is the one who, beyond all others, has been sanctified, the daughter of Sion visited by the Spirit, who, moreover, in her response to the angel showed herself to be moved by the Spirit at a depth unique to herself." Mary is also the model of the charismatic life in that she exercised the charisma of prophecy when she recited the Magnificat (Luke 1:45–56); according to Catholic tradition, on account of her assumption into heaven like Elijah the prophet and Enoch; because she is a woman of prayer and reflection on the mysteries of God (Luke 2:19, 51); and as a teacher (the Orthodox Church calls her the "fiery chariot of the Word"). She also is associated with many miracles, healings, and private revelations. But she is regarded by some moderns as a "liberation theologian." Gutierrez asserts, "The Magnificat . . . is one of the New Testament texts which contains great implications both as regards liberation and the political sphere" (207, see also Ford, 1983).

Most importantly, however, Mary is seen by Roman Catholics to possess the epitome of the fruits of the Spirit (Gal. 5:23). This is really the implicit biblical background to the greatly misunderstood doctrine of the Immaculate Conception of Mary's soul (Ford, 1973). In the Catholic title *Mater Misericordiae* (Mother of Compassion) Mary is also venerated as the protector and intercessor for all the poor and troubled of the world. Thus she is associated with social consciousness. Montague (1974, 98) says: "The experience of Mary is one of the most precious gifts of the Spirit. She is a charism of the Spirit in person. From her we learn to believe more purely, to discern the Spirit more clearly, to listen to the Word more intently, and to wait more creatively the hour of the Lord's coming."

See also CATHOLIC CHARISMATIC RENEWAL; MEDJUGORJE.

Bibliography: R. E. Brown, "Luke's Description of the Virginal Conception," *TS* 35 (1974): 360–62; idem, *The Virginal Conception of the Bodily Resurrection* (1973), 21–28; idem, *Cahiers marial, "Croyons-vous au Saint-Esprit?"* 90 (November 15, 1973), special issue on Mary; R. E. Brown et al., eds., *Mary in the New Testament* (1978), 105–34; J. Y. Carluer, "Un livre courageuxi Pentecôte chez les catholiques!" *Experiences* 16 (8, 1974): 78; D. Daube, *The New Testament and Rabbinic Judaism* (1957); G. J. M. M. Farrell and G. W. Kosicki, CSB, *The Spirit and The Bride Say "Come!" Mary's Role in the New Pentecost* (1981); J. A. Fitzmyer, "The Virginal Conception of Jesus in the New Testament," *TS* 34 (1973): 541–75; idem, "The Contribution of Qumran Aramaic to the Study of the New Testament," *NTS* (1973–74), 382–407, esp. 391–94; J. Massyngbaerde Ford, *My Enemy Is My Guest: Luke and Violence* (1983); idem, "Our Lady and the Ministry of Women in the Church," *Marian Studies* 23 (1972): 79–112; G. Gutierrez, *Theology of Liberation: History, Politics and Salvation*, trans. and ed., Caridad Inda and John Eagleson (1973); R. Laurentin, *Catholic Pentecostalism, An In-depth Report on the Charismatic Renewal*, trans., M. J. O'Connell (1977); J. McHugh *The Mother of Jesus in the New Testament* (1975); G. T. Montague, *Riding the Wind: Learning the Ways of the Spirit* (1974); L. Pfaller and J. Alberts, *Mary Is Pentecost: A Fresh Look at Mary From a Charismatic Viewpoint* (1973); Cardinal L. Suenens, *A New Pentecost?* (1974). J. M. Ford

MASON, CHARLES HARRISON (1866–1961). Founder of the Church of God in Christ. One of the most significant figures in the rise and spread of the modern Pentecostal movement, Mason was born September 8, 1866, on Prior Farm just outside of Memphis in an area that is today the town of Bartlett, Tennessee. His parents, Jerry and Eliza Mason, former slaves, were members of the Missionary Baptist Church, a source of strength for them in the distressing times that followed the Civil War.

As a young boy, Mason was religious in bent. He often joined his mother and her neighbors in prayer. Mason said he prayed earnestly that God would give to him "above all things a religion like the one he had heard about from the old slaves and seen demonstrated in their lives" (Mason,

A Holiness minister and church leader, Charles H. Mason was baptized in the Spirit at the Azusa Street Mission in 1906.

1934, 6). It was this yearning for the God of his forebears that became the dynamic of his life.

When Charles was twelve years old, a yellow fever epidemic forced Jerry Mason and his family to leave the Memphis area for Plumersville, Arkansas, where they lived on John Watson's plantation as tenant farmers. The plague claimed his father's life in 1879. During those fearful and difficult days the younger Mason worked hard and had little chance for schooling.

In 1880, just before his fourteenth birthday, Mason fell ill with chills and fever. His mother despaired of his life. However, in an astounding turn of events on the first Sunday in September 1880, he was miraculously healed. He and his mother went to the Mt. Olive Baptist Church near Plumersville, where the pastor, Mason's half-brother, the Reverend I. S. Nelson, baptized him in an atmosphere of praise and thanksgiving. Mason went throughout the area of southern Arkansas as a lay preacher, giving his testimony and working with souls on the mourners' bench, especially during the summer camp meetings.

Mason was licensed and ordained in 1891 at Preston, Arkansas, but held back from full-time ministry to marry Alice Saxton, a beautiful daughter of his mother's closest friend. To his greatest disappointment and distress, she bitterly opposed his ministerial plans. She divorced him after two years and later remarried. Mason fell into such grief and despair that it is said that at times Satan even tempted him to take his own life (Lee, 1967, 5).

The year 1893 marked a crucial turning point in Mason's life. Following his heart-rending divorce, Mason was determined to get an education. That same year Meyer and Brothers of

Chicago published a significant and widely read volume: *An Autobiography: The Story of the Lord's Dealing With Mrs. Amanda Smith, The Coloured Evangelist.* That autobiography deeply impressed Mason as it did many blacks throughout the nation, especially in the South. Amanda Smith (1839–1915), a disciple of John Inskip, became one of the most influential, widely traveled, and respected black Holiness evangelists of the nineteenth century. Her life story swept many blacks into the Holiness movement, including Mason.

After reading her autobiography, Mason claimed the grace of divine sanctification and at Preston, Arkansas, preached his first sermon on the subject of Holiness. He chose as his text 2 Timothy 3:12–13, which begins, "Thou therefore endure hardness as a good soldier of Jesus Christ." This sermon stayed with him throughout his life.

On November 1, 1893, Mason entered Arkansas Baptist College, founded by Dr. E. C. Morris, pastor of Centennial Baptist Church at Helena, Arkansas, and president of the Arkansas Baptist State Convention. Mason was deeply disturbed by the new higher criticism that Dr. C. L. Fisher, a top graduate of Morgan Park Seminary (now the University of Chicago Divinity School) had brought to Arkansas Baptist College. He had both hermeneutical and cultural suspicions of the methods, philosophy, and curriculum at the college. He came to the personal conclusion that for him the school would be of no help in his task of preserving the vitality of slave religion. He left there in January 1894.

In 1895 Mason met Charles Price Jones, newly elected pastor of the Mt. Helms Baptist Church at Jackson, Mississippi. They became fast friends. Jones was a graduate of Arkansas Baptist College. Like Mason, Jones had come under the influence of the Holiness movement and in 1894 claimed the experience of sanctification while pastoring Tabernacle Baptist Church at Selma, Alabama. By preaching sanctification as a second definite work of grace subsequent to conversion, Mason and Jones caused no small stir among black Baptists. From 1896–99, the Holiness conventions, revivals, and periodicals of Mason and Jones split the Baptists and, in a few cases, the Methodist churches, causing the development of independent "sanctified" or "holiness" congregations and associations. Mason, Jones, and their colleagues were vehemently opposed and eventually expelled from the Baptist churches (the National Baptist Convention). After much praying and studying of Scripture in search of future direction for these independent "sanctified" congregations, Mason, while walking along a certain street in Little Rock, Arkansas, received the revelation of a name, the Church of God in Christ (CGIC) (1 Thess. 2:14; 2 Thess. 1:1). Thus in 1897 a major new black denomination was born. From the seventeenth century through the nineteenth century most blacks had encountered Christianity under aegis of Baptist or Methodist churches. Mason and Jones changed the religious landscape in the black community and broadened the black religious experience. Through the dynamic preaching of Mason and prolific writings and hymnology of

Jones, Sanctified or Holiness churches sprang up throughout the South and Southwest bearing the name Church of God in Christ.

As the new work progressed, Mason continued to seek a more complete consecration of his life. During the latter half of 1906, he received reports of the Pentecostal revival in Los Angeles. He traveled to California, and under the ministry of W. J. Seymour, Mason received the baptism of the Holy Spirit and spoke in tongues. After some five weeks in Los Angeles, Mason returned to Memphis and Jackson eager to share his additional experience of the Lord with his brethren. However, when he presented his Pentecostal message to the church, he and his message were rejected. After days and nights of intensive debate, Mason and Jones separated, and the church split. Those who agreed with Mason met in September 1907 to reorganize the CGIC. They elected C. H. Mason as general overseer and appointed D. J. Young—Mason's constant companion, as editor of the new periodical, The Whole Truth.

By ordaining ministers of all races, Mason performed an unusually important service to the early twentieth-century Pentecostal movement. He appears to have been the only early convert who came from a legally incorporated church body and who could thus ordain persons whose status as clergymen was recognized by civil authorities. This recognition allowed clergy to perform marriages and carry out other ministerial functions having legal consequences and entitled them to certain economic advantages such as the right to obtain reduced clergy rates on railroads. As a result, scores of white ministers sought ordination at the hand of Mason. Large numbers obtained credentials carrying the name CGIC. In the years 1909–14, there were as many white Churches of God in Christ as there were black, all carrying Mason's credentials and incorporation. Ironically, Mason, who viewed his lifelong task as one of simply preserving the "spiritual essence" and the "prayer tradition" of the black religious experience, found himself in a unique and pivotal historical position.

By 1913 it had become increasingly clear that as Pentecostals moved toward denominationalism, they would follow the segregating practices of American culture. The color line that had been washed away in the blood of Jesus at the Azusa Street revival reappeared.

On December 20, 1913, elders E. N. Bell and H. A. Goss issued a call to convene a general council of "all pentecostal saints and Churches of God in Christ," to meet the following April at Hot Springs. This invitation went only to the white saints. E. N. Bell's periodical, Word and Witness, was not distributed in the black religious community. On the first week in April 1914, Mason traveled to the Hot Springs convention to invoke God's blessings on the newly formed General Council of the Assemblies of God. He preached on Thursday night to more than four hundred white Pentecostal preachers (with one black—G. T. Hayward of Indianapolis, who would become the leader of a new body called the Pentecostal Assemblies of the World).

Despite this new racial separation, Mason maintained a warm fellowship with the white Pentecostals. He preached in their conventions, maintained a strong fellowship with A. J. Tomlinson of the Church of God (CG, Cleveland, Tenn.) and J. H. King of the Pentecostal Holiness Church (PHC, Franklin Springs, Georgia). In 1952 he was the elder statesman attending the Pentecostal World Conference at London, England.

The Federal Bureau of Investigation (FBI) developed a file on C. H. Mason because of his pacifism and interracialism. In 1918 some white followers of Mason in Los Angeles were identified as being of German extraction. Mason was jailed at Lexington, Mississippi, for allegedly preaching against the war, although he sold bonds to help the war efforts. William B. Holt, one of the white brethren targeted by the FBI as suspicious, was a lawyer and former Nazarene preacher. He traveled to Lexington and posted a two-thousand-dollar cash bond for Mason's release.

A reference from the 1918 FBI report is instructive. After quoting from one of Mason's tracts, it comments: "It is clear that Mason and his followers felt it to be of far reaching significance that one of the great religious movements of the twentieth century was founded by a member of the African race."

Later scholars have echoed the same conclusion as the FBI report. Dr. Gayraud Wilmore, a most careful and respected scholar, says, "This movement begun by C. H. Mason and W. J. Seymour at the turn of the century, has been one of the most powerful expressions of Black religion in the world" (Wilmore, 1972, 210–13). Wilmore's assessment is supported by Yale historian Sidney Ahlstrom, who observed that the lives of W. J. Seymour and C. H. Mason personify a process by which black piety exerted its greatest direct influence on American religious history (Ahlstrom, 1972, 1059–60).

Mason led the CGIC until his death in 1961. Under his leadership the church experienced phenomenal growth. Thousands of Mason's followers, migrating from south to north and southwest to far west, carried his teachings and evangelistic spirit to virtually every major city in America. At his death in 1961, the CGIC, which had begun in a gin house at Lexington, Mississippi, claimed some 5,500 congregations and 482,679 members. At least ten other church bodies owed their origins to Mason's church. Since his death the church has continued its rapid growth. Mason stamped his personality on his church far more emphatically than any other Holiness leader. He lived to see the CGIC become a major denomination and one of the largest Pentecostal bodies in the world, with a graduate seminary to its credit. Mason traces the church's phenomenal growth to a covenant-promise that the Lord gave to him. He died at age ninety-five in Harper's Hospital, Detroit, Michigan, on November 17, 1961. Martin Luther King, Jr., preached his last sermon from Mason's pulpit—Mason Temple, headquarters of the CGIC, Memphis Tennessee, where Mason's remains are entombed to this day.

See also BLACK HOLINESS–PENTECOSTALISM; CHURCH OF GOD IN CHRIST.

Bibliography: S. E. Ahlstrom, *A Religious History of the American People* (1972); I. Clemmons, ed., *Profile of a Churchman: The Life of Otha M. Kelly in the Church of God in Christ* (1976); O. B. Cobbins, *History of the Church of Christ (Holiness), U.S.A., 1895–1965* (1966); L. J. Cornelius, *The Pioneer History of the Church of God in Christ Compiled* (1975); C. T. Gilkes, "Cultural Constituencies in Conflict: Religion, Community, Reorganization and the Rise of the Saints, 1890–1925," *Association of Black Sociologists and the Society for the Study of Social Problems* (1983); C. E. Jones, *Black Holiness: A Guide to the Study of Black Participation in Wesleyan Perfectionist and Glossolalic Pentecostal Movements* (1987); E. Lee, *C. H. Mason, A Man Greatly Used of God* (1967); L. Lovett, "Aspects of the Spiritual Legacy of the Church of God in Christ: Ecumenical Implications," *Midstream* 24 (4, 1985): 389–97; M. E. Mason, *The History and Life Work of Elder C. H. Mason and His Co-Laborers* (1934); D. J. Nelson, *A Brief History of the Church of God in Christ* (1984); A. W. Peagues, *Our Baptist Ministers and Schools* (1892), 18–21; C. H. Pleas, *Fifty Years of Achievement, The Church of God in Christ* (1957); H. V. Synan, "The Quiet Rise of Black Pentecostals," *Charisma* 11 (June 1986): 45–48, 50–55; G. S. Wilmore, *Black Religion and Black Radicalism* (1972). I. C. Clemmons

MATTHEW, GOSPEL OF The first Gospel of the NT is among the three synoptic Gospels; Mark and Luke are the other two. The synoptic Gospels present, in general, common views of the life and ministry of Jesus. Most scholars think that Mark was the first one written and that Matthew and Luke used portions of Mark in their accounts. They also think that these Gospels were written to minister to distinct congregations with different needs. This is one way to explain the relationship between these "common" Gospels. The need for a satisfactory explanation of the relationship between them is known as the "synoptic problem."

Matthew, besides containing some material found otherwise only in Luke and generally known as Q (from the German *Quelle*, meaning "source"), contains verses that are unique to this Gospel. In these verses, especially, the writer's interests can be noted.

I. Background
  A. The Destination of the Gospel
  B. The Date of Writing
  C. Problems
  D. A Hermeneutical View
II. Matthew's Content
  A. Introduction
  B. The Use of the Term "Holy Spirit"
    1. The Neutral Use of the Term
    2. An Emphatic Use of the Term
    3. The Liturgical Use of the Term
    4. Summary
  C. Matthew's Use of a Special Formula for Citing the Old Testament
    1. Introduction
    2. Analysis of the Special Formula "It Is Fulfilled"
    3. Summary
  D. Healing and Other Miracles in Matthew
  E. Prophecy and Prophets
    1. The Role of Prophecy and Prophet
    2. False Prophets in Matthew
  F. Jesus and the Kingdom
    1. Introduction
    2. The Term "Kingdom" in Matthew
    3. Spirit and Kingdom
    4. John the Baptist, Jesus, and the Kingdom: Continuation and Consummation
    5. Entering the Kingdom: The View From Below
    6. Exclusion of the "Sons of the Kingdom"
  G. The Jewish Mission
  H. The Anthropology of Matthew's Community
    1. Introduction
    2. A Kinship Society With a New Identity
      a. Definition
      b. Societal Parameters
      c. "Church," Community, and Jesus
      d. Matthew and Paul
III. Conclusion

I. Background.

A. The Destination of the Gospel. In one of the passages containing material unique to Matthew, many scholars find hints about the destination of the Gospel. In 4:26 Syria is mentioned. From this mention it is concluded that Matthew wrote to a congregation or several congregations there or at least in an area somewhere between upper Galilee and Syria.

B. The Date of Writing. Theories about when Matthew was written depend, in part, on how one resolves the synoptic problem. If the author did use Mark and Q, then the time of writing would have been late enough to allow for Mark to become more widely known, especially if Mark's destination was Rome. The internal evidence suggests a time after the destruction of Jerusalem (A.D. 70). For instance, after the destruction of the "holy city" (mentioned only in Matt. 4:5 and 27:53) and the temple, messianism filled Palestine. Many were traveling around the country claiming to be the Messiah. These claims, of course, would confuse Christians, especially Jewish Christians who believed that Jesus was the true Messiah.

C. Problems. False messiahs were precisely one of the problems facing Matthew. Persecution was also a problem for his community, and the source of it may have been Judaism, for it particularly affected the community's evangelizing efforts aimed at the Jewish people. Another problem concerns the nature of the church. Matthew pays much attention to obeying the law; on the other hand, he urges people to go beyond the external manifestation of the law (legalism). Because of this emphasis, some think that Matthew's church consisted of both Jews and Gentiles. This theory cuts across religious and ethnic lines but does not utilize anthropological categories to analyze Matthew's community.

D. A Hermeneutical View. The perspectives of one modern school of interpretation, dispensationalism, concerning Matthew bear consideration. Dispensationalism generally breaks biblical history into seven eras. The sixth of these, the era of the church (between the two comings of Jesus), is a parenthesis. Specifically, this era interrupts the continuation of God's dealings with his people, who are considered to be national Israel. This school views the kingdom of God in nationalistic terms. National Israel, then, will be restored after the second coming of Jesus and during his thousand-year reign. The Gospel of Matthew, with its strong reflection of Jewish thinking (especially the Sermon on the Mount), belongs to the era of Israel. The emphasis on the law in the Sermon on the Mount outlines the way of salvation, the way Israelites were saved in the earlier dispensation of law (i.e., the Mosaic period; nondispensationalists interpret the sermon as setting grace over against law). Consequently, the Gospel pertains mostly to national Israel. Little of it relates to the church. Matthew is like the OT in that regard. Many Pentecostals are dispensationalists and are influenced by this approach to Matthew.

II. Matthew's Content.

A. Introduction. With this brief introductory information, which is quite relevant to our purpose, we can proceed to discuss the Gospel of Matthew. It is not the intention of this article to address all of the issues in this Gospel; rather it is to focus on issues that relate to the Pentecostal/charismatic traditions. We will begin by noting something about how the term "Spirit" is used in the First Gospel.

B. The Use of the Term "Holy Spirit."

1. The Neutral Use of the Term. The term "Spirit" or "Holy Spirit" is not a special Matthean concern. The significance of this observation will become obvious. In using this term, Matthew follows Mark in most instances. For example, all three Gospels refer to the Spirit in John the Baptist's preaching (Matt. 3:11–12; Mark 1:7–8; Luke 3:15–18), Jesus' baptism (Matt. 3:13–17; Mark 1:9–11; Luke 3:21–22), Jesus' temptation (Matt. 4:1–11; Mark 1:12–13; Luke 4:1–13), the blasphemy of the Spirit (Matt. 12:31–37; Mark 3:28–30; Luke 12:10), and the question about David's son (Matt. 22:41–46; Mark 12:35–37; Luke 20:41–44). Matthew's use of the Spirit (1:18, 20) in the birth narrative parallels Luke's (1:35).

Matthew's account of Jesus' prediction of the disciples' persecution, found also in the other Synoptics, reflects no special understanding of *pneuma.* Matthew 10:20 has the "Spirit of your Father," while Mark 13:11 and Luke 12:12 have "Holy Spirit." Matthew probably simply means "the father."

Matthew also does not elaborate on *pneuma* in the Beelzebub controversy, which occurs in all of the Synoptics. Only Matthew and Luke have references to Jesus' claim that his ability to cast out demons is a sign that the kingdom has arrived. Matthew 12:28 has "by the Spirit of God," while Luke 11:20 has "the finger of God."

2. An Emphatic Use of the Term. In another place common to all three Gospels (Matt. 22:41ff.; Mark 12:35ff.; Luke 20:41ff.), Matthew does give some emphasis to the term. But he does it in such a way as to stress Jesus as Messiah

(perhaps also in Matt. 1:18, 20). In this account a question about David's son and the Messiah arises. The answer is supported by a quote from Psalm 110:1 (LXX 109:1). Matthew and Mark include "Spirit" in their introductions of this quote. Matthew says that "David, speaking by *the Spirit,* calls him 'Lord'" (22:43), and Mark says, "David himself, speaking by *the Holy Spirit,* declared . . ." (12:36). Luke, on the other hand, says, "David himself declares in the Book of Psalms . . ." (20:42), replacing "by the Spirit" with "in the Book of Psalms." But what Matthew does in addition is significant. He adds that "David calls him [the Messiah] 'Lord'" (22:43 and 45). Mark and Luke place this information only after the quote. It is evident that "Lord" comes from the quote, but Matthew decisively employs it twice to emphasize Jesus as Messiah. Thus the Spirit is subjugated to enhance Jesus' messianic role. In a similar way, Matthew's OT quote in 12:18 emphasizes the Spirit's empowerment of the servant of God:

"Here is my servant whom I have chosen,
    the one I love, in whom I delight;
I will put my Spirit on him,
    and he will proclaim justice to the
        nations."

Verses 18–21 have no parallel in the other Gospels. With this observation, we are able to see that Matthew intentionally has a Christocentric view of pneumatology. He subordinates the Spirit to Jesus the Messiah, and christology is his primary concern.

3. The Liturgical Use of the Term. One final reference needs comment: the strictly Matthean Great Commission passage (28:19). The Spirit is named, along with the Father and Son, in the baptism formula. This Trinitarian formula emerges in a burgeoning Christian community that is distinguishing itself from Judaism.

4. Summary. Our survey of the term "Spirit" has revealed two elements. First, in one text (28:19) Matthew equates the Spirit with the Father and Son. Second, and by far the more pronounced, Matthew subordinates the Spirit to Jesus. In the relationship between Jesus and the Spirit, it is the Spirit who empowers Jesus; however, the accent falls on the person and authority of Jesus. For instance, the strictly Matthean quote of Isaiah 53, "He took up our infirmities and carried our diseases," in 8:17 illustrates this point. Jesus has authority because of who he is: he is the son of David, the heir to the throne. Immediately before this quote, Jesus casts out spirits with a word and heals. Only Matthew has "with a word" (in contrast to what a twentieth-century Pentecostal/charismatic response may be, "by the Spirit"), thus emphasizing Jesus' authority. Further, Matthew begins his introduction to this quote (the introduction and the quote are strictly Matthean) with a *hopos* ("in order that") clause, which correlates these deeds, and an OT quote from Isaiah. This linking of OT texts with Jesus is important for Matthew. By doing this, the accent falls on Jesus' person, his authority, and his redemptive work instead of on the Spirit.

These observations about Matthew's use of the Spirit can be further advanced by examining Matthew's special introductory formula for citing OT material.

C. Matthew's Use of a Special Formula for Citing the Old Testament.

1. *Introduction.* Matthew often introduces OT quotes with the clause, "It is fulfilled" (although one of these references contains an allusion without any specific OT text in mind). Though this clause introduces OT Scripture or allusions to it several times in John and Luke, Matthew's use is special (cf. Brown, 1977, 96–104; Gundry, 1982, 24, thinks that this formula reflects the tradition behind Luke 1:20, 70, and he also says that there are eleven of these that are Matthean). An analysis of Matthew's use of this formula uncovers information relevant to the Pentecostal/charismatic concerns of this article.

2. *Analysis of the Special Formula "It Is Fulfilled."*

a. Four instances of the formula "it is fulfilled," speak about the birth of Jesus.

(1) 1:22: This verse gives the details of his birth.

(2) 2:15 and 2:23: These verses speak about the family's flight to Egypt and return to Nazareth.

(3) 2:17: This reference is to the slaying of the infants.

b. One instance of the formula "it is fulfilled" involves John the Baptist (3:3), but the Lukan parallel (Luke 3:4) has, "As is written [*gegraptai*] in the book of the words of Isaiah the prophet." Later, in Matthew 11:10, John is connected to the OT by *gegraptai*. Mark (1:4) has no introduction to John the Baptist like this, unless 1:2 is so considered. Matthew, then, introduces the preparation of Jesus' ministry by noting that it fulfilled prophecy.

c. Many of these instances of "it is fulfilled" involve Jesus' ministry.

(1) 4:14: This passage inaugurates and gives the scope of Jesus' ministry—it will extend to the Gentiles. Jesus' ministry to Gentiles finds its consummation in the Great Commission in 28:19–20.

(2) 8:17: This text underscores Jesus' authority.

(3) 12:17: Jesus' salvific activity is given here.

(4) 13:14, 35: Jesus' opponents are spoken about here—that is, those who are not his true disciples and are, therefore, "hard of hearing." For this reason, God (Jesus) speaks in parables to them.

(5) 21:4: Jesus enters Jerusalem, the beginning of the end.

(6) 26:54, 56: These references refer to the events surrounding Jesus' arrest as being "fulfilled." Of the passages in Mark and Luke, only Mark 14:49b parallels Matthew 26:56—Mark does use *plēroō*, but Matthew inserts the additional reference to fulfillment in 26:54.

d. One reference prophesies about the fate of Judas: 27:9.

e. Specific prepositions are used with this formula. *Dia* ("through") occurs when the prophet as agent is intended; *hupo* ("by"), when

God is the source. The content focuses on Jesus. Only one reference has no preposition (13:14), but its subject is "prophecy."

f. One text in the Sermon on the Mount that has "fulfill" in it and that bears out Matthew's significance of connecting the OT (no specific reference to an OT text) to Jesus is Matthew 5:17: "Do not think that I have come to abolish the Law or the Prophets; I have not come to abolish them but to fulfill them." According to the material in this passage and the surrounding context, Matthew is struggling with opposing viewpoints. He employs this material in 5:17 to show that Jesus does not do away with the Scripture—it is eternal (cf. a differing view by Meir, 1976, 164ff.). Since this belief in the eternality of Scripture is also held by Judaism, and if his opponents come from the synagogue, why then does Matthew employ this material here? In light of the contrasting interpretations that follow (six times in ch. 5 [vv. 21, 27, 31, 33, 38, 43]) Jesus uses the rather highly stylized clause *ekousate hoti errethe* ("you have heard that it was said"), or some variable form of it, to refer to some ethical command, which usually has an OT text behind it. The repetition of this clause could simply be an appeal to the authority of Scripture, but both Matthew and his opponents could appeal to the OT. And these opponents could think that Matthew (Jesus) was setting aside Scripture in light of the interpretations that follow. If these opponents came from the synagogue, and the reference to the scribes and Pharisees in verse 20 suggests that they did, then the Jewish community would not necessarily be guilty of the social sins in this listing. The themes in the sermon are found in Jewish prayers, but the appearance of these themes in Jewish prayers does not necessarily indicate major difficulties in the synagogue.

What can be said then is this: Matthew's community was using a christological, hermeneutical principle embodying Jesus as the center. And the use of *plērōsai* ("to fulfill," v. 17) suggests that Matthew counteracted certain Jewish "prophets" who were Antinomian and interpreted the tradition with some amount of freedom. These interpretations gave them the support for such ethical behavior. Thus Jesus is the interpreter ("but I tell you"), whose decisions become *halakah* ("law"); ethical issues, issues that are similar to those in the synagogal tradition, are important. The emphasis falls upon Jesus as the center of prophecy (OT Scripture and its fulfillment) and certain behavioral responses. This emphasis appears throughout the Sermon on the Mount and in other places in the Gospel. Jesus, or his tradition, as the hermeneutical key is also important in the Gospel.

One pertinent text to mention in regard to our argument that Jesus' words are the hermeneutical key in Matthew's Gospel is 4:4b, a Matthean addition to the Temptation account: "but on every word that comes from the mouth of God." This reads literally, "every word which comes out through (*dia*) the mouth of God." In other places we note that "through" (with *plēroō*) indicates agency. It is somewhat strange, then, that Matthew uses "through" here. What he probably means is that everyone must live by the words that

Jesus (i.e., God) speaks. Already Matthew has said that Jesus is "God with us" (Gundry, 1982, 56).

g. This introductory formula, employing the verb "fulfill," stands in contrast to those introductions that use *gegraptai* ("it is written"), such as 2:5, where the chief priests and scribes say of the Messiah, "thus it *is written* through the prophet." *Gegraptai* does not occur often in Matthew, and when it does it comes from the synoptic tradition and introduces material containing dialogue between Jesus and his adversaries. For example, in the Temptation narrative (Matt. 4:1–11; Luke 4:1–13; the Temptation also occurs in Mark but in an abbreviated form that does not have "it is written") Satan is Jesus' opponent. In Matthew 11:7–19 (Mark 1:2; Luke 7:24–35) Jesus addresses the crowds about John the Baptist, for they seem to be seeking John inappropriately. And in 21:12–17 (Mark 11:15–17; Luke 19:45–46) Jesus speaks to the moneychangers. In 26:24 and 31 (the stories are found in Luke and Mark, but only Mark has *gegraptai*), Jesus does speak to the disciples, but they are placed in "opposition" roles. Judas (26:24) will betray him, and the other disciples will be "scandalized" and scattered (26:31).

On the surface, the way Matthew uses "it is written" and "it is fulfilled," reflects no difference in method. Note, e.g., 26:24. Here, without any specific reference in mind, "it is written" refers to the Son of Man's betrayal in the same way that "it is fulfilled" in 1:22 relates to a virgin giving birth to Immanuel. Whether one believes these to be a *darash* ("interpretation") or a *pesher* ("this is that" form of Jewish interpretation) in form makes no difference. There appears to be a typological/allegorical element (for a similar use of "it is said" [*sn'mr*] in rabbinic material, cf. Mekilta on Exodus 12:36; many examples of this exist in Mekilta). In the Temptation, Satan uses *gegraptai* in a fulfillment sense (4:6). On the other hand, Matthew does use *gegraptai* in a nonfulfillment way. He uses it in 4:4, 7, and 10 to support a statement that gives direction to any pious believer. The same use of "it is written" occurs in Paul (cf. Rom. 1:17 et al.; Paul also uses some of Hillel's rules, cf. Rom. 4:1ff.). But the main difference remains. Goppelt notes appropriately that Paul emphasizes "promise" while Matthew stresses "fulfillment" (1982, 2:56–57; Goppelt also notes a difference between Luke and Matthew in this regard, cf. 2:270–71; *TDNT*, 6:294ff.; Johnson, 1951, 238. Metzger, 1951, 306–37, has a different outlook: he says that these are eschatological and christological, contra Fitzmyer, 1974, 13–14; cf. Moule, 1967–68, 293–320. Kingsbury, 1975 31–32, 35, builds from such elements a particular Matthean history: OT time as prophetic and Jesus' time as fulfillment).

What is significant about Matthew's use of "it is fulfilled" is that it does not just involve prediction, a common element in prophecy. He sees that God was already at work in the future when he spoke through the OT prophets these things about Jesus. On the other hand, Matthew intends for his interpretation of the events of Jesus to explicate

the OT text. It is this point that makes Matthew different from Judaism.

h. These observations suggest that opposition to certain elements of the "historical" Jesus—his virgin birth, ministry, and death—exists.

i. This introductory formula is strictly Matthean.

3. *Summary.* But what is Matthew's purpose for using this introductory formula? One answer is that there is some sort of confrontation between church and synagogue. At the least we can say that it comes from people, more than likely Jewish, who consider themselves to be prophets and whose messages do not focus on the historical Jesus as Messiah but point to a different conception of Messiah, one that comes from Judaism. In doing this, they have followed subjective, "charismatic revelation," part of which has come from their tradition. According to Matthew, they need the "control" of the historical Jesus and the OT. But Matthew is not anticharismatic. For instance, he uses the prophetic phrase, "it is fulfilled." This term would have significant meaning among Matthew's charismatics. Matthew limits prophecy by submitting it to an "objective" criterion, focusing on Jesus, and by relegating the predictive element in the OT to its fulfillment in Jesus.

D. Healing and Other Miracles in Matthew. Miracles are of special interest to Pentecostals and charismatics. We have just noted that Matthew does not discard prophecy. Matthew is not opposed to miracles either. Jesus performs them not because he has the Spirit—though Matthew does not deny this—but because he is the Messiah and has the authority. In Matthew, Jesus' water baptism is where he identifies with sinful Israel so that he may redeem her. Jesus' anointing with the Spirit is secondary. In regard to healing miracles in Matthew, J. P. Heil notes that according to Matthew all healing power comes through Jesus and that though the disciples are expected to heal, Matthew emphasizes the salvific power of Jesus' messianic activity in the church through such miracles (1979, 274–87; cf. especially 286). In this case, healing is part of Jesus' salvation work, concluding in his work of atoning for the sins of Israel and for the rest of the nations of the world. But as such, healings are not "charismatic." Therefore, Matthew is a good model for contemporary noncharismatic congregations that practice healing.

There is a special case in Matthew 8:17, a text that uses the special Matthean introductory formula, that connects Jesus' ministry of healing with Isaiah 53:4. Matthew uses the word "took" (*elaben*) as opposed to the LXX "bore" (*pherei*). The Hebrew word is "bore" (*nasa'*). *Elaben* by itself in Matthew does not have soteriological significance; however, in the larger picture in Matthew and in his view of the kingdom of God, Jesus does offer salvation. And Jesus' death is a significant aspect of this. The sign of the kingdom's presence is healing and the casting out of demons (cf. 4:17; 4:23ff.). The individual's response to this offer is to do the will of the Father (cf. 7:21–23). Pentecostals generally interpret this verse in such a way so as to find support for the theological position of healing in the Atonement. This view certainly conveys Matthew's intention.

E. Prophecy and Prophets.

1. The Role of Prophecy and Prophet. In regard to prophecy, another Pentecostal/charismatic concern, Matthew emphasizes it more as an interpretive task in relating the historical Jesus to the OT. The "false prophets" disturbing Matthew's community, then, could not claim to be legitimate simply by "having the Spirit." According to Matthew, such revelations were viable only when coming from the Father and centering on the historical Jesus. Furthermore, this saying authenticates the apostles (especially Peter) because they bore witness to the historical Jesus, received revelation from the Father about Jesus' messiahship, and transmitted Jesus' tradition. It is also evident that the entire community discerned such revelations. A strong, charismatic, dictatorial figure is not supported by Matthew (Kingsbury, 1979, 67–83). What we see in Matthew, then, is a stage in history when prophetic religion was becoming more of a book religion. The prophet was more of an interpreter and transmitter of Jesus' experience than an orator (Cothenet [1978, 281–308] believes the prophet to be a preacher; cf. Matt. 23:34), predictor, and interpreter of events. The true prophet, therefore, discerns the teachings and lifestyles of those in the tradition according to Jesus' role in history and according to the Father's witness. The community, on the other hand, discerns all prophets in the same way.

2. False Prophets in Matthew. Matthew opposes false prophets and their messages, as he first indicates at the end of the Sermon on the Mount (7:21–23). According to this passage, no one can enter the kingdom by having prophesied, having cast out demons in Jesus' name, or having performed many miracles. The way to enter, Jesus says, is to do the will of the Father. The surprising element is that these "prophets" called upon Jesus and performed miracles. One might ask how they were allowed to do that. This passage gives us a clue to their identity: they were "insiders." (One view believes that they were itinerant.) The reference to future judgment and entrance to the kingdom tells us that Jesus granted them a time in which they could change. In contrast, the present verb "does" ("the will of [the] Father") in verse 21 implies an immediate situation. These "insiders" may well have been false prophets and deceivers.

The surrounding context applies to these "prophets," at least from verses 7–27. Themes relating to proper conduct, entering the kingdom, judgment, and prophets occur there. With this background in view, we can see more clearly what Matthew has done with a saying from Q in these verses. Verse 11 says, "If you, then, though you are evil, know how to give *good gifts* to your children, how much more will your Father in heaven give *good gifts* to those who ask him!" (italics mine; Luke [11:13] has "the Holy Spirit" instead of "good gifts"). Matthew avoids "Spirit" in this context because he is correcting these prophets' practice and behavior. They did not "need" the Spirit—they needed help to respond obediently to Jesus' tradition. In their request to

the Father, then, good gifts refer to the Father's help in this matter.

The false prophets in verses 15ff. (found only in Matthew) intimate that prophets may be on the inside, and Matthew exhorts the community to beware of them. They deceive—this is what sheep's clothing suggests. That is, they need to be discerned, and the criterion for this discernment is "good or evil fruit." Sheep's clothing also suggests that Matthew is concerned about external and internal modes of religiosity. These people may be quite religious on the outside, i.e., they keep the law scrupulously, but in the heart they are deficient. The Sermon on the Mount especially addresses this inner quality of religion in Jesus' tradition. A disregard for this is called "lawlessness" in 7:23.

Lawlessness is precisely the situation in chapter 23: the scribes and the Pharisees teach good things ("whatever they say," 23:3) but do not "do"/"keep" them. It is difficult to connect the scribes and Pharisees with these prophets otherwise, except to note that the denunciation of these scribes and Pharisees occurs in the same context as the eschatological discourse in which Jesus warns about false prophets.

Within the eschatological discourse at 24:11, it is said that many false "prophets" will come and lead many astray. Earlier, in verse 5, the community is warned that false "messiahs" will come and lead many astray. These ideas merge as a significant point of this discourse (24:23–28) and of Matthew: (1) false prophets who speak against the historical Jesus as if he were not the real one, since they spoke about other messiahs; and (2) a proper ethical response to Jesus.

The false prophets taught that one could tell by certain catastrophic events when the Messiah was coming: when society was in disarray, such as during times of war, and when great natural signs were happening, such as earthquakes and famine. These signs were called "birth pangs of the Messiah" in Christianity and in Judaism and are precisely what Jesus argued against in the context of 24:3. War, famine, and earthquake do not portend the coming of the Son of Man (the Messiah) (vv. 6–8). "The end is still to come" (v. 6) and "all these are the beginning of birth pains" (v. 8). Furthermore, events do not "make" the end come (23–28); it is God (24:36) alone who does—and no one knows when this will be, not even the Son of Man. The Christian responds by enduring (24:13) and discipling all nations. Only then will the end come (24:14; 28:19–20).

A relevant time for the activity of these prophets—and for the writing of Matthew (Palestine, northern Galilee, or Syria for the place)—is either before or after the Jewish War of A.D. 68, when Jewish messianic expectations filled the air and catastrophic events fed Jewish longings. In contrast, Matthew said that the coming of the Son of Man was not imminent. Jesus said that the time would be delayed (24:48; 25:5, 19) and that no one could know when it would happen (24:36, 42, 44, 50; 25:13). Several parables or parable-like sayings emphasize this point.

One such saying is the story recalling the days of Noah in 24:37–39, which is often interpreted in just the opposite way that Matthew intended it—to show how the things mentioned in it point to decay in society and consequently to the coming of Jesus. Matthew intended to show that "normal" events will be happening when Jesus comes. These events include wars, famines, and earthquakes. Since catastrophic events such as the Flood were not expected in Noah's day, so it will be when the Son of Man comes. Furthermore, there is nothing evil about marriage, giving in marriage, or eating and drinking. Matthew intended this to refer to a breakdown in the church rather than in society. Society remains evil. The warning given here relates only to the church. Outsiders would not understand—only insiders could decode this language. The only thing wrong with these activities is that in Matthew's case they show a church that has a warped value system with no true regard for the lordship of God, a church that is devoid of a reformed lifestyle that would prepare them for judgment and cause them to do what 25:31ff. implores—to help the afflicted, to visit those who have been imprisoned for preaching the gospel, and to feed the hungry and clothe the naked. As in Noah's time, so it was in Matthew's day: there was no regard for true prophetic teaching and living. They would thus be caught off guard.

The parable of the ten virgins (25:1–13) well illustrates how the people would be caught off guard. The kind of faith these "prophets" have and produce in others is a "fire escape" faith. They only serve God when signs, according to their prophecies, indicate the coming of the Son of Man and when they want to escape hard times. The parable in 24:45–51 points this out as well. There the wicked servant (his wickedness comes out in the delay of his master) is caught off guard. Note the three steps in which this servant's "true" faith surfaces. First, doubt arises in his heart, and he says to himself, "My master's coming is delayed." Second, he beats his fellow slaves, which means that he breaks fellowship, a severe thing to do in that culture (and group-oriented society). Third, he establishes a new circle of friends, one that includes the ungodly rich. In this parable leadership receives the brunt of Jesus' attack. They need to be discerned by the community, as we have noted.

F. Jesus and the Kingdom.

1. Introduction. Also important to our discussion is Matthew's presentation of Jesus and the kingdom. The presence of false prophets in his community explains why Matthew does not emphasize the Spirit and why he emphasizes Jesus instead. We can better understand this by looking briefly at Matthew's presentation of the kingdom of God and Jesus.

2. The Term "Kingdom" in Matthew. Matthew uses the term "kingdom" (e.g., God's; one should not make too much of his more popular "kingdom of heaven") about forty-nine times in his Gospel, more often than the other Gospel writers (Mark uses it about sixteen times; Luke, about forty-one; and John, five). This tells us something about Matthew's audience: the term would be more meaningful in a Jewish, Palestinian setting.

3. Spirit and Kingdom. Furthermore, in only one place does Matthew connect the Spirit with the term "kingdom." And there Matthew follows Q (12:28; Luke 11:20). He does not relate the Spirit with the kingdom as, e.g., Paul (see, e.g., Rom. 14:17), Luke, and John do. Several passages are worthy of observation and comment.

In Luke's version of the Lord's Prayer in 11:2–4 the believer is to pray for the coming of the kingdom. From the context, the object of praying is to receive the Spirit (v. 13). And the coming and manifestation of the Spirit is a coming of the kingdom.

On the other hand, "Spirit" does not occur in the context of Matthew's version (6:9–13). Matthew places in his context guidelines for such things as forgiveness and fasting, things integral to the kingdom, which, as we have noted, are his concerns in regard to false prophets.

4. John the Baptist, Jesus, and the Kingdom: Continuation and Consummation. Another Matthean distinction regarding the kingdom is to be noted in a pericope containing the presentation of John the Baptist (Matt. 3:1–6; Mark 1:2–6; Luke 3:1–6). Matthew records John announcing repentance and the kingdom of God (3:2), the same message Jesus preaches (4:17), while Mark (1:4) has John preaching only a baptism of repentance unto forgiveness of sins. It is not until Mark 1:14–15 that the kingdom is mentioned, and it is in the preaching of Jesus. Mark separates and distinguishes John and the coming of Jesus by an adverbial, infinitive clause. Matthew intends to connect the kingdom to Israel's past history (in a spiritual sense), as can be seen in the way he associates Jesus with OT texts and in the construction of Jesus' genealogy. At the same time, Matthew shows that Jesus ushered in a new era of the kingdom, the age of the Messiah (cf. Waetjen, 1976, 205–30). Matthew does state in one place that a distinction between John's era and that of Jesus does exist (11:11–19; Luke 16:16).

Matthew also notes in 25:34 that the kingdom was prepared from the foundation of the world. This is strikingly similar to the thinking in Judaism that a plan for humankind was conceived in the mind of God prior to creation. Abraham was one who was regarded to have a part in carrying out God's plan. But according to Matthew, God's promise to Abraham (Gen. 18:18) is fulfilled in Jesus. While Abraham is still an important figure in Matthew (cf. 8:11), his serving in the foundational role of the people of God, as it is in the OT and Judaism, is removed. Peter now partly serves that purpose (cf. 16:13ff.), and the special revelation that was given to Abraham as Israel's patriarch is now reserved for Peter. In regard to David, Jesus is his son and heir to the throne. He will rule forever. Matthew's christology is a royal messianism—Jesus fills and completes Israel's history.

This distinction between the past and present must include the fact that Matthew considered the Jewish people to be sinners in need of salvation (cf. 1:21: "You are to give him the name Jesus, because he will save his people from their sins"). So, while there is a continuation of the kingdom, there is also a radical shift in its manifestation.

There is an emphasis on its future aspect combined with what people must do to enter it. This combination implies that the perseverance of the Christian is essential, that the Christian may fail along the way and need to repent, and that the Judgment is the ultimate point of entry.

5. *Entering the Kingdom: The View From Below.* The Synoptics do speak about entering the kingdom (cf. Matt. 19:13–15 and parallels), but Matthew has additional texts that emphasize what one must do to enter the kingdom. One of them is found in 5:17–20. Verses 19–20 occur only in Matthew. Here Matthew emphasizes the importance of keeping the law to enter the kingdom: "For I tell you that unless your righteousness surpasses that of the Pharisees and the teachers of the law, you will certainly not enter the kingdom of heaven" (v. 20). Furthermore, one must keep the law to be called great in the kingdom.

A later text on greatness also states something about entering the kingdom. Matthew 18:1–5 parallels Mark 9:33–37 and Luke 9:46–48, but Matthew adds several significant items to his account. Only in Matthew is the kingdom mentioned. Later Mark and Luke (18:17) have this saying about becoming as children, but they write, "Anyone who will not receive the kingdom of God like a little child will never enter it" (Mark 10:15; Luke 18:17), while Matthew stresses the need for repentance by saying, "Unless you change and become like little children, you will never enter the kingdom of heaven" (18:3).

In 18:23–35 the kingdom of God is compared to what a king does to an unforgiving servant. The problem with the servant is his failure to repent. The application occurs in verse 35: this is what God does to those who do not forgive their brothers. This parable is only in Matthew and concludes a lengthy section on how to restore sinning brothers and how to discipline. This parable culminates with what was taught at the beginning of the chapter on entering the kingdom: one must repent and forgive.

Significant references to the kingdom exist in Matthew 19:14, 23–24. These bracket and hold together three incidents: (1) children as models for subjects of the kingdom (vv. 13–15); (2) a rich person's coming to Jesus, asking how he may enter the kingdom (vv. 16–22); and (3) Jesus' application of his conversation to his disciples (vv. 23–30). But this term is not the only one that is used as a bracket. Matthew uses several synonymous terms to assist. One of these is "eternal life" and occurs in verses 16 and 29 (cf. "life" at v. 17). In verse 29 "life" is inherited in the same way as the kingdom. Another term that is synonymous with life and kingdom is salvation (v. 25). This material, which is bracketed by these terms, emphasizes what people must do to enter the kingdom. They must do what the law fully intends; and the law emphasizes both internal principle and external manifestation.

The rich man in 19:16 asks Jesus what good thing he may do to get eternal life (later Matthew has "enter life," v. 17). "Good" is significant because Matthew has done something unique with it. (This material has parallels in Mark 10:17–22 and Luke 18:18–23.) While both Mark and Luke have the motif of "eternal life," "good" means something else. In them, "good" pertains to the nature of God. In Matthew, however, "good" is first connected to this rich person's works and his inheriting the kingdom. Therefore, Matthew has "good" with reference to God, at least by implication. Matthew also adds, "If you want to enter life, obey the commandments" (v. 17). Mark and Luke simply have, "You know the commandments" (Mark 10:19; Luke 18:20). "Life" in Jewish literature, especially rabbinic, is associated with keeping the law. Matthew is in line with that reasoning. In light of the specific commandments that he lists and that the man has "kept," we can see that Matthew emphasizes a religion of the heart, the attitude behind the external manifestation. This thinking is commensurate with the synagogue but not with the prophetic antagonists of Matthew's community.

But a different aspect of entering the kingdom comes into play in Matthew 19:23ff., where Jesus turns and addresses his apostles regarding what this means for them. The rich have difficulty in entering the kingdom because of their failure to adhere to one of its principles, in this case using one's wealth to bless those whom God specifically has great concern for: the poor. The disciples ask, "Who then can be saved?" And Jesus answers, "With man this is impossible, but with God all things are possible." The point is made for the disciples: they must not allow riches to get in the way; they must give up everything if they expect to inherit the kingdom—a stinging indictment for Matthew's charismatics who wish to accumulate wealth. The kingdom is not material[istic]—it is spiritual (cf. the Beatitudes, especially the first one in 5:3).

The things the disciples must give up have significance for the divorce pericope at the beginning of this paragraph (19:1ff.). Or better, one of the elements that is not in the list is also missing in Mark (10:28–31), but Luke has it (18:29): "wives." It is not enough to say that Matthew simply followed Mark. The explanation can be found by examining the context of Matthew's second divorce reference (19:12). The first one is in 5:27–32; both have the same exceptive clause. That there are two sayings about divorce and that both have these exceptive clauses make Matthew's case different from the other Synoptics. Especially in chapter 19, Matthew underscores the unity of the couple. Matthew's community, then, was experiencing a breakup of marriages, probably because married men were wanting to leave their wives for traveling ministries, such as the prophetic. In Matthew, Jesus reflects the position of the school of Shammai, where the only legitimate reason for divorce was adultery (cf. b *Gittin* 9:10; cf. also Fitzmyer, 1981, 79–111). Matthew adds the information about the three different eunuchs: one from birth, one by men, and one who is a eunuch for the kingdom of God. In other words, the kingdom requires everyone to place God first but requires only some to live in singleness if they have that gift, for some ministries require it. The Christian husband has obligations to his wife. In context, this, too, is a requirement of the kingdom. Apparently, some of those who were married wanted to divorce for "the sake of the kingdom." This is the reason Matthew does not include "wives" in his list— some men were already divorcing.

To heighten what Matthew does with these terms relating to the kingdom and the absence of the Spirit, it is helpful to examine a passage in John that strikingly contains this same terminology. "Entering the kingdom" also occurs in one significant place in John 3:1ff. There the Spirit plays a major role. The two parallel "amen, amen" sayings (vv. 3, 5) should be considered synonymous.

In contrast to Matthew, John speaks negatively of the law. In John 1:16–17 the law of Moses is contrasted with the true grace that came through Jesus. Jesus brings life—law does not.

These conclusions bring the discussion to a major point about the kingdom in Matthew: Who will inherit it?

6. *The Exclusion of the "Sons of the Kingdom."* Matthew gives considerable attention to this "Jewish-Christian" question regarding the kingdom. A clear reference to this occurs after his conclusion of the sermon in 8:5–13, where Jesus heals the centurion's servant. This story follows the cleansing of the leper. However, the order of events differs in Luke. There the cleansing of the leper is in 5:12–16 and the healing of the centurion's servant in 7:1–10. The exclusion of some people occurs in Luke 13:28–29. In Mark only the cleansing of the leper occurs. So Matthew has rearranged the order of Q to juxtapose his material in such a way as to bring out several points. First, Jesus makes unclean people clean (i.e., free from sin; in 1:21 Jesus came to deliver Israel from her sins). Second, this cleansing includes Gentiles (i.e., the centurion's servant). Thus, in these miracle stories salvation (the kingdom) arrives. But because the "sons of the kingdom" lack faith, they will be excluded: Jesus has not found in Israel such faith as in this centurion.

Several distinctions exist in Matthew. One is the Matthean phrase, "sons of the kingdom." Luke simply has "you." Matthew intends this to refer to those Jews who, like the Pharisees, will not enter the kingdom. (The future judgment is in view here, a point already made above.) He gives a certain definition to the kingdom: it is not to be understood in national or ethnic terms. It is spiritual in nature. The kingdom was intended especially but not exclusively for these Jews. And the requirement for entrance was the kind of faith expressed in this context.

Matthew differs from Luke in the list of those who are in the kingdom. Matthew has Abraham, Isaac, and Jacob; Luke has Abraham, Isaac, Jacob, and all the prophets. Matthew's omission is significant, then, for our understanding. On the other hand, Luke's mention of "prophets" is important for him because he perceives his community to be prophets. "Prophets" probably stood in Q because of the emphasis on prophecy in that community as well.

Matthew suggests that national Israel is excluded from the kingdom in the latter part of his

Gospel as well. In 19:16ff., as we have seen, the matter of the true intent of the law is brought into focus in the rich young man's failure to keep the law. This pericope concludes with the saying, "Many who are first will be last, and many who are last will be first" (v. 30). Within this story is a comment about the Son of Man, who will sit on his throne of glory while the twelve apostles sit on twelve thrones to judge the twelve tribes of Israel. Apparently, the spiritual, eschatological Israel is in view (cf. Jeremias, 1958). Only two or two and one-half tribes existed in the thinking of some Jewish authors at that time. According to Matthew, only those who follow Jesus will inherit the kingdom on that day. And Israel is in danger. This is brought out in the next chapter (ch. 20) in another parable of the kingdom.

This parable of the workers in the vineyard occurs only in Matthew. It speaks about workers who are hired at different times of the day to work in the vineyard. At the end of the day each is given the same wages, which causes the ones who worked longer to be disgruntled. (Such an attitude is also reflected in some of the Jewish literature when the authors react negatively toward Gentiles.) This suggests that some in Matthew's church had difficulty in allowing Gentiles into the kingdom. Clearly, Jesus does not manifest vengeance, which many Jews had toward Gentiles (cf. Jeremias, 1958). Moreover, Matthew goes beyond this. The kingdom is being given to others, although it will be understood in OT and Jewish terms. Furthermore, the same saying, with variations, concludes the story of the rich young man in 19:30 and the parable of chapter 20. Thus we are to understand this information together.

Between this material and the eschatological discourse in Matthew 24 are a number of stories and themes that distinguish between national and eschatological Israel. Chief among these themes is that Jesus must suffer and die by the hands of chief priests, teachers of the law, and the Gentiles (cf. 20:17–19; Matthew is not anti-Semitic; e.g, he presents Jewish people in a good light and Gentiles in a bad light in 20:24ff.). Anyone who sits with Jesus in his kingdom must follow the same path; he must be the servant of all (20:27). The difficulty in understanding this is compared to blind men (20:29–34) who have no sight to follow Jesus; when they do, they follow him. So it is with anyone; God needs to give this "spiritual" sight.

Another theme involves the idea of temple. It is significant that the cleansing of it occurs prior to the beginning of the eschatological discourse. The eschatological Israel will be the new temple; temple building in Jerusalem will be abandoned, destroyed (24:1–2). The chief cornerstone will be rejected (21:42; found in the triple tradition: Mark 12:1–12; Luke 20:9–19). Following this OT reference, Matthew includes material unique to him. He adds, "Therefore I tell you that the kingdom of God will be taken away from you and given to a people who will produce its fruit" (v. 43). This reference concludes a parable about tenants who killed the landowner's son who was sent to them to collect his part of the fruit. The landowner will come and "bring those wretches to a wretched end" and rent the vineyard to other tenants (v. 41).

The parable of the two sons (21:29–32), which precedes the parable just discussed, also brings out that the kingdom will be handed over to others. One son said he would not go and work in his father's vineyard but later changed his mind and went. The second son said he would and did not go. This illustration suggests that "the tax collectors and the prostitutes are entering the kingdom of God ahead of you [Jews]" (21:31).

In light of this information, one can understand what Matthew means with the story of the cursing of the fig tree in 21:18–22. The conclusion is that national Israel is not the kingdom. It was dead (bare tree). Consequently, it will remain dead.

But Matthew will implore that God has made attempts to call them to the kingdom. This is the meaning of the parable that follows in chapter 22. A king prepared a banquet for his son's marriage and sent out his servants to those who had been invited to the banquet to tell them to come, but they refused to come. Then he sent out other servants, yet the invited guests still paid no attention. At this, the king's servants went to the street corners and invited everyone: good and bad. Once inside, there was one who was not clothed with the wedding garment, and he was cast out. This parable says two things: (1) the "sons of the kingdom" did not respond to Jesus' invitation, and (2) some were living inappropriately (the one without the wedding garment who was cast out; this one fits Matthew's *Tendenz*, which we noted earlier—about his interest in the future of the kingdom and the concepts of repentance and perseverance). This understanding of national and eschatological Israel partially explains Matthew's community's mission to the Jewish people and the difficulty it faced.

G. The Jewish Mission. Evangelism and missions are important to Pentecostals and charismatics. This topic then is relevant to our discussion. The commission of the disciples to a strictly Jewish mission in Matthew 10 has long been a difficult passage to understand in light of Matthew's frequent assertion to evangelize the world (28:19). What, then, was happening in Matthew's community that caused him to emphasize Jewish missions (ch. 10)?

The following suggestions are offered. By and large the same material occurs in Mark (e.g., 3:13–19; 6:8–11; 13:9–13) and Luke (e.g., 6:12–16; 9:2–5; 12:11–12; 21:12–19), but Matthew has notable differences. He includes the instructions to the disciples (10:5–6) not to go the ways of the Gentiles (*ethnē*) or to the city of the Samaritans; rather, they were to focus on the villages and cities of the lost Jewish people of Palestine. Further, they were not to charge for their services but to "give freely" as indeed they had received from God (v. 8). They were to live on what people would give them; the workers were certainly worthy of these love offerings (v. 10). But they were also warned that they would receive great opposition. Some of the sayings about opposition and persecution occur in the eschatological discourses of Mark and Luke.

But Matthew has collected them and placed them here in the context of this strictly Jewish mission. Matthew says that these missionaries would be betrayed and brought before Jewish councils and other local governments (Gentiles). Indeed, families would be split. This can be understood in light of the particular group orientation of some Oriental peoples. When family members convert to Christianity, they are ostracized, and some are even killed. The rite of baptism is especially significant in these cultures. Baptism implies an ontological change. People who undergo baptism, then, are no longer considered family members. This is significant for missions. These stern measures would discourage evangelization, the very issue facing Matthew. Jewish members of his community were slack in their duty to convert their own people.

However, when they were brought before councils, they were not to worry about what they were to say (10:19–20). The Spirit of their Father would tell them that. In contrast, Luke has "Holy Spirit" (12:12). In light of our discussion Matthew simply means, "the Father will give you words to say."

H. The Anthropology of Matthew's Community.

1. Introduction. Pentecostal/charismatic groups tend to be dominated by strong "charismatic" leaders. A brief analysis of the nature of Matthew's community will be profitable.

Others have attempted to understand Matthew's community on a strictly ethnic or religious basis. However helpful these studies are, they are not broad enough. More comprehensive studies on Matthew are yet to appear. Some preliminary remarks of an anthropological nature can offer here some insight that will help to understand this community:

2. A Kinship Society With a New Identity.

a. Definition. An important question to ask of Matthew's community concentrates on the modality of human interrelations. Societies have two basic orientations in this regard. One is contractual (individualistic); the other is kinship (group). With the contractual society, one's identity comes largely from within, and the world view is oriented from this perspective.

b. Societal Parameters. "Sin" for kinship orientation comes by breaking an internal law. "Internal law," though it may come from the outside, is understood in the kinship frame of reference. Sin is a wrong involving the *individual*. Guilt is the felt consequence. Repentance takes on an individualistic meaning, then. People in this instance tend not to feel the need for restitution or for telling others that they have wronged them. The felt need is to experience an inner release of guilt.

On the other hand, people in kinship-oriented societies receive identities from their social unit. And sin is understood more in social terms—it threatens the group in terms of its identity and well-being. The consequence of sin, then, is manifested in personal shame ("personally" is different from "individually"). Repentance becomes community oriented.

c. "Church," Community, and Jesus. Matthew's community is a kinship society. Notice, for instance, that of all the Gospels, only Matthew has "church" (*ekklēsia*, 16:18; 18:17). His presentation of Jesus in the Infancy narratives and in the Temptation account signify this. In 2:13–15 Joseph, Mary, and Jesus flee to Egypt, from where, in typological fashion, God calls his Son (vv. 14–15). Typologically, as in the Exodus experience when God called his people out of Egypt, Jesus, God's Son [i.e., people], is called out of Egypt. In the OT, Israel is called God's son. Similarly, in his temptation, Jesus, like Israel in the Exodus, is tempted. In contrast, however, Jesus does not fail as Israel did. Furthermore, Jesus, as Israel's Messiah, is the one from whom the community receives its life and identity. And in this respect, the community will have no one over it who usurps this authority. Some scholars have noted that Matthew has no developed church structure. Usually this reflects an early situation or a charismatic orientation. In contrast the evidence suggests that Matthew's community was rather well developed and noncharismatic in nature. The social situation evidenced in this Gospel offers new conditions that current studies need to consider (cf. Kee's discussion on Max Weber and others, 1980, especially 54–73). Matthew certainly is different from sectarian Judaism (Qumran) and Pharisaism, for instance. And though his community is on the periphery of Palestinian society, the people (Matthew) feel quite acceptable in their differences. But they do feel threatened by certain Pharisees and prophets. Matthew reacts against the prophetic type of charismatic figure.

Part of this reaction stems from the social structure that these prophets desire to implement. They have the strong, authoritative, dictatorial, charismatic leader mentality. But Matthew is rejecting that—for it assumes the role, according to him, that is reserved for Jesus the Messiah. Of all the relevant statements against the scribes and Pharisees in chapter 23 that address our topic here, the comments in verses 8–12 are most appropriate:

"But you are not to be called 'Rabbi,' for you have only one Master and *you are all brothers.* And do not call anyone on earth 'father,' for you have one Father, and he is in heaven. Nor are you to be called 'teacher,' for you have one Teacher, the Christ. The greatest among you will be your servant. For whoever exalts himself will be humbled, and whoever humbles himself will be exalted" (italics mine).

Furthermore, the greatest in the community are the new Christians. This is what Matthew 18 signifies. There the "little child" is equated with Jesus—whoever rejects such a one also rejects Jesus, and to offend such a one has grave consequences. God's will is depicted in the good shepherd who goes after the straying sheep until it is found. Order is maintained in the community by repenting and securing forgiveness. If personal relationships are not restored, the offending party is excommunicated by the community that has the authority to do so (this is the meaning of binding and loosing in 18:18). Matthew's law-keeping

emphasis places responsibility on the older members of the community. In contrast to the Essenes, no limits are placed on new Christians for their acceptance into the community: no probationary period exists and no ablutions are necessary other than baptism (28:19), which plays a role in one's entrance to the community.

As we have seen, Matthew places a priority on family life. But in one way the family unit is transcended. He gives qualifications for belonging to Jesus' family (i.e., his community) in 12:46–50 (a triple tradition: Mark 3:31–35; Luke 8:19–21). There Jesus points to his disciples (only in Matthew) and announces that they are his family. These disciples do the will of the Father. "Father" is Matthean (Mark has "God"; Luke omits it). Matthew has also modified the patriarchal social manifestation somewhat in that he has elevated the role of women. For instance, he has included three women in his genealogy (two of whom were non-Jewish) and made men equally responsible for the integrity and breakdown of marriage, as reflected in the divorce texts.

d. Matthew and Paul. This social picture of Matthew's community allows us to contrast it to that of the Pauline communities reflected in the Pastoral Epistles. The concept of the household (*oikos*) in the larger Hellenistic society provides the model of "church" there. The head of the household oversees the church. Thus the Pauline communities are oriented more toward the idea of a "house church" as opposed to Matthew's "community." Paul's communities have more of the strong "fatherly" leader than Matthew's modified patriarchal kinship society.

III. Conclusion. Matthew's Gospel offers a new model for the contemporary church. This model calls for charismatic activity such as miracles and prophecy but, at the same time, places restrictions and guidelines on charismatic manifestation. Jesus is the center of all prophecy and for all interpretation of Scripture, and the Spirit is given to these ends. The community discerns all manifestations in light of the Jesus tradition. Belonging to this community calls for a different lifestyle; the relationships are intimate and personal. The quality of life of the community must be maintained by forgiving one another and seeking those who have wandered away. And it is not a closed community to outsiders. Its mission is to all people, especially those of its own kind.

See also JESUS CHRIST.

Bibliography: B. C. Aker, "New Directions in Lucan Theology: Reflections on Luke 3:21–22 and Some Implications," in P. Elbert, ed., *Faces of Renewal* (1988); G. Bornkamm, G. Barth, and H. J. Held, *Tradition and Interpretation in Matthew*, trans. P. Scott (1963); R. E. Brown, *The Birth of the Messiah: A Commentary on the Infancy Narratives in Matthew and Luke* (1977); D. A. Carson, "Matthew," *EBC*, vol. 8 (1984); E. Cothenet, "*Les prophetes chrétiens dans l'Evangile selon Matthieu,*" in *L'Evangile selon Matthieu*, ed. M. Didies (1978), 282–308; J. E. Davison, "*Anomia* and the Question of an Antinomian Polemic in Matthew," *JBL* 104 (1985): 617–35; J. A. Fitzmyer, *Essays on the Semitic Background of the New Testament* (1974); idem, "The Matthean Divorce Texts and Some New Palestinian Evidence," *To Advance the Gospel* (1981), 79–111 (originally in *TS* 37 [1976]: 197–226); L. Goppelt,

Theology of the New Testament, 2 vols. (1982); R. A. Guelich, The Sermon on the Mount: A Foundation for Understanding (1982); R. H. Gundry, Matthew: A Commentary on His Literary and Theological Art (1981); idem, The Use of the Old Testament in St. Matthew's Gospel With Special Reference to the Messianic Hope (1975); J. P. Heil, "Some Significant Aspects of Healing Miracles in Matthew," CBQ 41 (1979): 274–87; D. Hill, "False Prophets and Charismatics: Structure and Interpretation in Matthew 7:15–23," Bib 57 (1976): 327–48; J. Jeremias, Jesus' Promise to the Nations (1958); S. E. Johnson, "The Gospel According to St. Matthew," vol. 7, IB (1951); H. Kee, Christian Origins in Sociological Perspective (1980); J. Kingsbury, "The Figure of Peter in Matthew's Gospel as a Theological Problem," JBL 98 (1979): 67–83; idem, Matthew (1977); idem, Matthew: Structure, Christology, Kingdom (1975); idem, The Parables of Jesus in Matthew 13: A Study in Redaction-Criticism (1969); J. P. Meier, Law and History in Matthew's Gospel: A Redactional Study of Mt. 5:17–48, AB (1976), 71; B. M. Metzger, "The Formulas Introducing Quotations in Scripture in the New Testament and the Mishnah," JBL 70 (1951): 306–7; C. F. D. Moule, "Fulfillment Words in the NT: Use and Abuse," NTS 4 (1967–68): 293–320; M. Pamment, "The Kingdom of Heaven According to the First Gospel," NTS (1980–81): 211–32; G. Strecker, Der Weg der Gerechtigkeit (1962); W. Trilling, Das wahre Israel: Studien zur theologie des Matthaus–Evangeliums (1964); H. C. Waetjen, "The Genealogy as the Key to the Gospel According to Matthew," JBL 95 (1976): 205–30.   B. C. Aker

Joseph Mattsson-Boze came to America in 1933 from Sweden to pastor a Chicago church. He edited the Herald of Faith and was a leader in the New Order of the Latter Rain.

MATTSSON-BOZE, JOSEPH D. (1905–). Swedish-American missionary and evangelist. Joseph Boze was born in Marstrand, Bohuslan, Sweden. As a young man, Boze converted from the Mission Covenant Church to Pentecostalism and soon became a copastor of one of Sweden's leading Pentecostal churches, the Smyrna Assem-

bly of Gothenburg. He came to the U.S. after receiving an invitation to pastor Chicago's leading Scandinavian Pentecostal church, the Filadelfia-Forsamlinger, in 1933. From 1943 to 1970 Boze was the editor of the prominent Scandinavian-American Pentecostal periodical, the Herald of Faith. In the late 1940s he became a well-known proponent of the New Order of the Latter Rain revival. He resigned his pastorate in Chicago in 1958 and for the next twenty years traveled as an evangelist, holding crusades in such countries as Honduras, India, Kenya, Singapore, Spain, Thailand, and Yugoslavia. Though living in the U.S., Boze has been a dominant figure in Sweden's Pentecostal movement. He was responsible for bringing such notable evangelists to Sweden as William Branham, William Freeman, and Kathryn Kuhlman.

Bibliography: Personal papers of Joseph Mattsson-Boze, David J. du Plessis Archives, Fuller Theological Seminary Library, Pasadena, California; Trons Harold 5 (3, March 1936): 11–12.   J. Colletti

MEAD, SAMUEL J. AND ARDELLA (KNAPP) (1849–1936) (1843–1934). Missionaries to Africa. Having been farmers in Vermont, the Meads and their niece Bertha traveled as pioneer Methodist Episcopal missionaries (as members of the original "Pioneer Forty") to Angola in 1885 under the direction of Bishop William Taylor. After arriving they opened a mission station at Malange. Samuel's responsibilities included evangelizing the lost, teaching school, and supervising a large farm to support the work. Having no children, the couple adopted several African children. Bishop Taylor wrote of the Meads in his book, The Flaming Torch in Darkest Africa (1898): "If there were a thousand such trainers such as Samuel Mead and his wife, Ardella, there would in a few years be twenty thousand native evangelists and pastors in Africa under the leadership of our all-conquering King."

Feeling a lack of spiritual power, the Meads returned to the U.S. in 1904 and were seeking for a deeper work of God in their lives. Claiming to have been led by God to settle in Los Angeles, they began attending the revival services at the Azusa Street Mission and received the baptism in the Holy Spirit in 1906. The Apostolic Faith, a newspaper published by the leaders of the mission, reported that the Meads identified several African dialects being spoken by some who were experiencing glossolalia in the services. The Meads returned to Africa along with other early Pentecostal missionaries from Los Angeles in late 1906. In 1909 they retired from the Methodist Board of Foreign Missions and settled in California.

Bibliography: W. C. Barclay, Widening Horizons, 1845–1895. History of Methodist Missions (1957); A. A. Boddy, "Some Los Angeles Friends," Confidence (November 1912), 246–47; A. K. Mead, "Sister Mead's Baptism," AF (November 1906), 3; S. J. Mead, "From a Missionary to Africa," AF (September 1906), 3.
                    G. B. McGee

MEARES, JOHN L. (1920–). Pentecostal leader with inner-city ministry. Born in Largo, Florida, of Pentecostal parents, Meares graduated from Lee College, Cleveland, Tennessee, in 1944 and then married Mary Lee Bell. After pastoring a Church of God in Memphis, Tennessee, Meares heard a call to Washington, D.C., in 1955, beginning his ministry in a tent meeting in a black area of the city. He immediately established a worship center for his new congregation, first in leased premises and from 1957 in a purchased theater on Georgia Avenue renamed the Washington Revival Center. In 1967 Meares sensed a call to deepen his ministry beyond a revival-healing work to an emphasis on teaching and worship, from more random evangelism to the formation of a church to minister unto the Lord. In 1975 the present Evangel Temple was opened on Rhode Island Avenue, N.E.

In the 1970s Meares developed a practical interest in the church and church formation, which led to closer relationships with John McTernan (Rome, Italy), Robert McAlister (Rio de Janeiro, Brazil), and Earl Paulk (Decatur, Georgia). Out of this came the legal corporation The International Evangelical Church, the spiritual fellowship of The International Communion of Charismatic Churches, and Meares's own consecration as bishop (1982).

Possibly Meares's greatest contribution has been in interracial reconciliation between black and white Christians. In Washington, D.C., the city council proclaimed the week of Evangel Temple's thirtieth anniversary in 1985 as Evangel Temple/Bishop John L. Meares Week in recognition of this ministry. This reconciling emphasis has been spread nationally through the Inner City Pastors' Conferences begun in 1984, and since 1987 by Evangel Temple's new magazine *Bridge-Builder*. Meares, long a close friend of David du Plessis, was a core committee member in the Roman Catholic–Pentecostal dialogue (1972–82).

Bibliography: *Evangel Temple's 30th Anniversary Historical Journal* (1985).   P. D. Hocken

MEDJUGORJE Site of Marian apparitions in Yugoslavia since 1981. The phenomenon of Medjugorje has had from its inception an undoubted affinity and association with Catholic Charismatic Renewal (CCR). At an International Leaders' meeting in Rome in May 1981, a Yugoslav charismatic, Fr. Tomislav Vlasic, asked other leaders to pray with him for the healing of the church. Sr. B. McKenna had a mental picture of Vlasic seated and surrounded by a great crowd, while streams of water flowed from the seat. Fr. E. Tardif gave a prophecy, "Do not fear. I am sending you my mother." The following month, on June 24 the apparitions began in Medjugorje, a village in southern Herzegovina, to six young people: five then ages fifteen to sixteen (four girls and one boy) and a ten-year-old boy. Vlasic soon became assistant pastor in Medjugorje and spiritual adviser to the visionaries.

Medjugorje has from an early date drawn large crowds of pilgrims, increasingly from many nations. While the Roman Catholic church is slow to approve such phenomena, apparitions even eventually recognized as authentic may have only a relatively local significance. Medjugorje, how-ever, shows signs of becoming internationally significant on the scale of Lourdes and Fatima. Medjugorje is distinctive in that the apparitions have continued, virtually on a daily basis, over many years, which is without obvious historical precedent.

The Medjugorje visionaries report seeing the figure of the Virgin Mary and holding conversations with her, of which neither side can be heard by others present. The messages have consistently emphasized faith in Jesus as the only Savior, his atoning death on the cross, repentance for sin, prayer, and fasting. The messages have insisted that the world is hovering on the brink of catastrophe, which can be mitigated or averted only by prayer and fasting. Peace through reconciliation with God and one another is a constant theme. Medjugorje's situation underlines the importance of reconciliation, where Christians live in a Marxist state and where conflicts have long troubled Catholic Croats and Serbian Orthodox; Christians and Moslems; and among Catholics, diocesan clergy and Franciscan friars.

Over the years, the visionaries have been entrusted with a number of secrets; for those who have received the full ten secrets, the daily apparitions have ceased. As the apparitions have continued, some other young people in Medjugorje have received "interior visions."

The links between Medjugorje and CCR have been numerous. In Medjugorje numerous prayer groups have been formed in which the spiritual gifts are exercised. Theologians and pastoral leaders active in CCR have sensed an affinity between the messages of Mary at Medjugorje and what they were hearing from the Lord in the renewal. The French scholar, R. Laurentin, has become the main chronicler of the apparitions and their repercussions, writing to date eight books on the topic. A movie on the apparitions has been made by Bobbie Cavnar of Dallas and J. Bertolucci. While the apparitions have received extensive publicity since 1985 (the BBC made a documentary of quality in 1987), the first news reached many Catholics from Catholic charismatic journals. Moreover, the most ardent Catholic opponents of Medjugorje have generally been among the strongest critics of CCR.

The messages given to the visionaries at Medjugorje are more evidently evangelical in tone and content than those of previous Marian apparitions, with an emphasis on personal love of Jesus, the role of the Holy Spirit, an emphasis on the Scriptures, and a commendation of prayer meetings. One reported message stated, "The important thing is to beg the Holy Spirit that he may come down. When you have the Spirit, you have everything. People are deceiving themselves when they only turn to the saints to ask for anything."

It is too soon to pronounce on the effects of the Medjugorje events on the Roman Catholic church and on CCR. Much will clearly depend on the results of the official church investigations currently proceeding. The church response may have been delayed both by the open hostility of the local bishop of Mostar and by the continuation of the apparitions. However, it is likely that the Medjugorje events will strengthen in CCR the centrality of repentance for sin and give the movement a greater sense of its historic significance at a critical moment in world history.

See also CATHOLIC CHARISMATIC RENEWAL; MARY AND THE HOLY SPIRIT.

Bibliography: D. du Plessis, *Simple and Profound* (1986); R. Faricy and L. Rooney, *Mary, Queen of Peace: Is the Mother of God Appearing in Yugoslavia?* (1984); idem, *Medjugorje Unfolds* (1985); R. Laurentin, *Learning from Medjugorje* (1987); idem, *Is the Virgin Mary Appearing at Medjugorje?* (1984); idem, *Medjugorje: Récit et Message des Apparitions* (1986).

P. D. Hocken

MELODYLAND CHRISTIAN CENTER A large Christian center in Anaheim, California, pastored by Ralph A. Wilkerson. In 1961 Wilkerson began a ministry with some 28 people in the growing Orange County area, and by 1964 a 750-seat church had been built. However, even with three morning services the facilities became overcrowded. Youth rallies on a monthly basis, frequent charismatic conferences, and varied interdenominational activities began to call for still larger accommodations. In 1969 the Melodyland Theater complex near Disneyland became available for purchase, and Wilkerson's congregation purchased the 3,600-seat theater at a bankruptcy sale and converted it into Melodyland Christian Center. Before long, the number of people attending the multiple Sunday services at Melodyland was between 10,000 and 15,000. As an extension of Melodyland in 1972 a delinquency prevention center (Melodyland Hotline) with twenty-four-hour coverage for troubled youth, dope addicts, suicidals, etc., was incorporated and began to serve an ever-increasing number of people. In 1973, in conjunction with Melodyland Christian Center, the Melodyland School of Theology was founded, and within a few years it was training hundreds of students from across the U.S. and from many foreign countries to serve in various kinds of Christian ministry. In 1976 Melodyland High School and later Melodyland Christian College were instituted to serve the growing needs for education within a genuinely Christian context. Melodyland Christian Center has continued to expand its facilities by adding buildings to serve educational and other purposes.

In the history of the modern charismatic movement, Melodyland Christian Center will probably be best remembered for annual charismatic clinics. Melodyland became known as an international crossroads of the movement, attracting speakers of many denominations. People came from around the world to participate in the clinics. The charismatic movement remains indebted to Ralph Wilkerson for his vision and energy in making possible these memorable occasions.

In recent years Melodyland Christian Center has suffered a number of crises, including serious financial difficulties, reported misconduct charges, and contested departure of several of the church-sponsored ministers. It has experienced a drop in Sunday attendance to fewer than 3,000; however, a recent report from Pastor Wilkerson speaks of a fresh vision and new programs for the years ahead.

Bibliography: "Coast Clinic Held by Charismatics," *New York Times* (August 26, 1973), 30; "Melodyland Makes a Comeback," *Charisma* (August 1987), 58, 61; J. N. Vaughn, *The World's Twenty Largest Churches* (1984).   J. R. Williams

Cal Kaufman is the executive secretary of Mennonite Renewal Services with offices in Goshen, Indiana. He was baptized in the Spirit in 1972.

MENNONITE CHARISMATICS When, as a young Mennonite minister, Gerald Derstine and some of his parishioners experienced a renewal in the Holy Spirit (1955), he was told by his bishop that he would be separated from the Mennonite church: "What you have permitted and practiced in your church and home is contrary to our church theology and doctrine and we must ask you to refrain from talking about it or teaching it" (Derstine, 1980, 170).

Not until 1972, when a consultation on the Holy Spirit was held at Eastern Mennonite College, Harrisonburg, Virginia, did the Mennonite church change that stance and give official recognition to the reality of the movement of God's Spirit within its ranks.

Mennonite Renewal Services (MRS), with headquarters in Goshen, Indiana, was formed in 1977. Until recently MRS has been an advocate and source of apologetic for Holy Spirit renewal, particularly at the personal level, exploring and interpreting the movement of the Spirit among Mennonite people and providing organization for those seeking to bring renewal within the church.

"Renewal in the Spirit" in Mennonite circles denotes much more than "speaking in tongues." That may well be a sign of one's being renewed or "baptized in the Spirit," but it is not essential. Indeed, no single event is requisite. Instead, Dan

Two charismatic Mennonite women dance during a worship service at Morton, Illinois, in 1985.

Yutzy, professor at Taylor University, Upland, Indiana, writes:

> Difficulty, severe testing or spiritual challenge may be a more typical consequence of the baptism. A fresh and vivid sense of the presence of Jesus, a hunger for the Word, a joy and enthusiasm, and a warm love and affection towards others, especially believers, are also typical. . . . Each one has a unique and personal set of experiences with the baptism (1983, 4).

For those in the renewal, MRS has organized churchwide and regional renewal conferences that give opportunity for persons to gather for fellowship, worship, encouragement, and instruction. M. Miller, president of MRS and pastor of Trinity Mennonite Church, Morton, Illinois, notes that approximately twelve regional renewal conferences were planned for 1987 (Miller, 1987, 9). Currently MRS is undergoing change in structure and direction. Calvin Kaufman, executive secretary of MRS, reported its merger with the Church of the Brethren Renewal Committee (1987, 14; see also idem, 1987b, 14). Subject to the approval of MRS members in annual meeting, April 1988, the united group shall be called Believers Church Renewal Ministries (BCRM). Its focus is toward corporate and intercongregational renewal. To that end a Network of Congregations in Renewal is being formed, appealing for membership to congregations that already participate in MRS and those that are without Mennonite conference or even denominational affiliation.

According to Virgil Vogt, pastor of Reba Place Church, Evanston, Illinois, the MRS−BCRM is renewing or rediscovering significant forms of leadership, especially in "trans-local relationships" (1988, 8−9). The ministry gifts of pastor, teacher, and evangelist have long been recognized, affirmed, and active among Mennonites. Now, however, apostolic and prophetic ministries are appearing and being cultivated. "Prophets are those who frequently and reliably hear the Word of the Lord" (ibid., 8). "Apostles are people with a unique gift for extending or expanding the witness of the Kingdom—going to regions beyond" (ibid., 9). M. Miller observes that the ministry of the prophet has been restored in the Mennonite community since 1980 but that the apostle is only now emerging (Miller, 1987, 9). To facilitate the actualization of these two ministry gifts, a national-level Apostolic and Prophetic Council has been formed. Members include Allen Yoder, Keith Yoder, Alvin Frey, Virgil Vogt, Harold Gingerich, Harold E. Bauman, Doug Fike, and Art Good.

Mennonite renewal is an international movement. The periodical *Empowered* frequently includes reports of the Mennonite church's efforts in evangelization and/or renewal among other nations, e.g., Tanzania, Israel, Argentina, Ethiopia, Honduras, Germany, and the Philippines.

The recurring theme in the Mennonite Renewal is a focus upon unity in Jesus. John Toews, a Mennonite Brethren (Fresno, California) and Hugo Zorilla, a Mennonite Brethren missionary to Spain from Columbia, South America—in a joint address to the Mennonite World Conference on Renewal (1984)—stated:

> God is building a new Mennonite house. The new house is Jesus centered. . . . It is not Conrad Grebel or Menno Simons, or Swiss, or Dutch, or Russian-centered. Ethnocentrism of all forms and varieties is sin. The new Mennonite reality calls for a Mennonite identity that is profoundly Jesus-centered and genuinely universal (*Empowered* 2 [7, 1984]: 6).

See also CHARISMATIC MOVEMENT.

Bibliography: G. Derstine, *Following the Fire* (1980); C. Kaufman, "MRS Expands Its Ministry," *Empowered* 5 (4, 1987) 14; idem, "MRS Projects Future Course," *Empowered* 5 (3, 1987b); R. S. Koch and M. Koch, *My Personal Pentecost* (1977); M. Miller, "A Fellowship of Congregations in Renewal," *Empowered* 5 (2, 1987): 9; V. Vogt, "New Dimensions of Renewal," *Empowered* 6 (1, 1958): 8–9. D. Yutzy, "The Baptism with the Spirit," *Empowered* 1 (1, 1983): 4.   J. A. Hewett

MENNONITE RENEWAL SERVICES See MENNONITE CHARISMATICS.

MENZIES, WILLIAM WATSON (1931–). Assemblies of God pastor, educator, and author. Menzies was born to Sophie B. and William E. Menzies. He married Doris L. Dresselhaus in 1955, and they had two sons, Glen Wesley (1956) and Robert Paul (1958). After completing a B.A. at Central Bible College, Springfield, Missouri (1952), he earned both a second B.A. and an M.A. at Wheaton (Ill.) College. He earned a Ph.D. in American church history at the University of Iowa in 1968. Ordained in 1956, he founded or pastored churches in Michigan and Iowa (1954–58, 1963–64). As an educator he taught at all three schools of the Assemblies of God (AG) in Springfield, Missouri: Central Bible College (1958–70), Evangel College (1970–80 and 1987–), and the Assemblies of God Theological Seminary (1980–84).

At the AG headquarters in the same city he also served on numerous denominational committees—often in theologically advisory roles—and edited the denominational youth magazine. He wrote the commissioned denominational history of the AG, *Anointed to Serve* (1971)—an adaptation of his doctoral thesis. In 1970 Menzies cofounded (with Vinson Synan and Horace

Assemblies of God educator William W. Menzies is the author of *Anointed to Serve*, a history of the Assemblies of God.

Ward) the Society for Pentecostal Studies. He was its first president and the first editor of its journal, *Pneuma*, from 1979 to 1983.

Long interested in missions education, Menzies lectured and traveled extensively in the U.S., Europe, South America, Scandinavia, and countries within and upon the Pacific rim. Since at least 1972 he has had a formative influence on the Far East Advanced School of Theology, Baguio, Philippines and served as that school's president in 1984–85 and from 1988 onward. From 1985 to 1987 he was vice-president for academic affairs at the California Theological Seminary, Fresno. As a respected interpreter of the Pentecostal theology, he participated in the Lausanne Consultation (1984) and serves on its subsequent committees. In 1986 he was named a consulting editor for *Christianity Today*. His other writings, besides several dozen articles and reviews, include *Understanding the Times of Christ* (1971), *Understanding Our Doctrine* (1970), and *Philippians: The Joyful Life* (1981).   R. P. Spittler

MESSIANIC JUDAISM

I. History. Jewish believers in Jesus have reflected their Jewish roots as part of their new covenant faith in limited ways throughout history. However, it was not until the nineteenth century that their efforts produced significant institutions. The Hebrew Christian Alliance of Great Britain formed in the 1860s, an American Alliance in 1915, and an International Alliance in 1925. These organizations provided membership and fellowship for individual Jewish believers.

Various perspectives were held among Alliance members concerning Jewish lifestyle. In general the majority did not live a significantly Jewish life, either by the calendar of Judaism or by other Jewish observances. However, a significant minority argued for a Hebrew Christianity that would be both congregationally based and Hebraic in worship and liturgy. Most noteworthy in this regard was Mark John Levy, the general secretary of the Hebrew Christian Alliance of America (HCAA), who even convinced the Episcopal denomination of his position. Ironically the HCAA rejected his position!

Other significant leaders and trends should also be noted. Theodore Lukey edited *The Messianic Jew* in Eastern Europe at the turn of the century. Jacob Rabinowitz planted a famous Messianic synagogue in Kiev in the late nineteenth century. Before his adoption of dispensational theology, A. C. Gaebelein, a noted American theologian, forcefully argued for Messianic Judaism. His journal, *Our Hope*, edited with Ernest Stroeker, put forth this case (Rausch, 1979, 94–99, 212–62).

In 1921 a converted tailor, David Bronstein, founded the Peniel Community Center in Chicago. Bronstein completed Moody Bible Institute and McCormick Theological Seminary and was ordained as a Presbyterian minister. He was to have a marked effect on Jewish outreach. In 1934 Bronstein founded the First Hebrew Christian Church in Chicago (Presbyterian). Bronstein was also able to win many of his family members to his faith. His brother-in-law, Jacob Peltz, became general secretary of the American Alliance. Morris Kaminskey, another brother-in-law, started a similar congregation in Toronto under Anglican auspices. The Presbyterian church also established congregations in Los Angeles, Baltimore, and Philadelphia (Bronstein, Jr., 1947).

Jewish missions in America and Europe also achieved significant growth during this period. Some mission work both then and to this day eventuated in congregations. Mission policies on congregations have varied.

The late 1960s and early 1970s produced new beginnings toward a Messianic Jewish congregational direction. Manny Brotman, in the mid 1960s, came in contact with many of the old Alliance leaders and with the Chicago work of David Bronstein, Sr. (Bronstein was succeeded by Morris Kaminskey and Kaminskey by Larry Rich, later the HCAA general secretary.) While in Chicago Brotman founded the Young Hebrew Christian Alliance (YHCA). He greatly influenced young Jewish believers toward a Messianic Jewish direction. Joel Chernoff was part of the new YHCA. He, with Rick Coghill, became a significant influence for Messianic music, forming the noted musical team called Lamb. The influence of the youth eventually persuaded the late Martin Chernoff, saved under the ministry of Morris Kaminskey in Toronto, to move his congregation in Cincinnati toward a Messianic Jewish direction (1971) (Rausch, 1981, 102–11).

The Jews for Jesus outreach under Moishe Rosen also raised Jewish consciousness among Jewish followers of Jesus. Literature and Jewish gospel music exemplified by the Liberated Wailing Wall proclaimed that one could be a Jew for Jesus.

Others during the early seventies also began to move in a Messianic Jewish direction. This included Daniel Juster, under whose leadership the Chicago congregation (Bronstein's) became Adat ha Tikvah (1974); and Beth Messiah Congregation in Rockville, Maryland, founded by Paul Liberman, Sid Roth, and Sandra Sheskin and first pastored by Manny Brotman (1973–75) and later by Juster (1978–86). Herb Links also took his Presbyterian related group in a Messianic Jewish direction. It became Beth Messiah, Philadelphia (1973). During this period, John Fischer and Mike Becker founded B'nai Macabim in the North Chicago suburbs. Dr. James Hutchin, Wheaton College chaplain, wrote a significant doctoral dissertation, *The Case for Messianic Judaism,* as part of the requirement for the Ph.D. at Fuller Theological Seminary. He also became involved in the planting of Messianic Jewish congregations.

Members of these congregations swelled the ranks of the HCAA. In 1975 their numbers provided the votes to change the name of the organization to the Messianic Jewish Alliance of America (MJAA). This was a clear affirmation of new Messianic Jewish directions.

A significant move toward Messianic Judaism was also taking place in Assemblies of God-related works. Ray Gannon and Phil Goble founded Beth Immanuel in the Los Angeles area (1971). Gan-

non went on to establish Beth Immanuel on Long Island, and Goble, congregations in Miami, Fort Lauderdale, and northern New Jersey. These men were influenced by the indigenous concepts of Fuller Seminary's School of World Mission (Goble and Gannon, 1975).

In the late 1970s attempts were made by several leaders to form a union—the Union of Messianic Jewish Congregations (UMJC). This union included nineteen congregations at its inception (1979) and includes almost sixty as of this writing. Conferences, leadership training, congregational planting, and materials development have been important services of this fellowship.

II. Philosophy. Those who identify primarily as Messianic Jews vary in philosophy. The author's description of common elements reflects predominant viewpoints. Messianic Jews affirm classical evangelical doctrines but express these doctrines in more Judaic terms. Messianic Jews also believe in the value of planting Messianic Jewish congregations as a home for Jews and Gentiles who desire a Jewishly rooted expression of their faith. These congregations reflect a corporate Jewish lifestyle greatly furthering the goal of fostering a New Covenant people movement in the Jewish community. By maintaining connections to their people, Messianic Jews have natural opportunities to share their faith. Furthermore, Messianic Jews believe they are called by God to maintain a biblically rooted Jewish life (Juster, 1986, 157–90; Rausch, 1981, 117–42).

Varieties of opinion may be found on the place of the Law in this lifestyle. The basic consensus is that the Law has continued value in its universal moral principles (2 Tim. 3:16–17). Also the Law is seen as a focus for defining Jewish lifestyle since it provides the roots of Jewish life in the memory maintained by feasts and other observances. Yet all must be celebrated with regard to Yeshua's (Jesus') fulfillment in a new covenant context (UMJC, "The Place of the Law," 1983).

Messianic Jews are predominantly charismatic in orientation. The gifts of the Spirit are seen as important for accomplishing God's work. This emphasis is connected to the conviction that convincing Jewish people of the claims of Jesus will require a supernatural demonstration of God's kingdom.

Messianic Jews are usually Zionist. Some believe that Jewish people have a right to their land under standards of justice and mercy. Others see the present regathering to the land as the fulfillment of the biblical promise to Israel. Some see the present regathering as a stage of God's working to eventually bring the promised fulfillment after Israel's repentance with regard to accepting Jesus as the Messiah. All hope for Israel's ultimate salvation and reingrafting (Rom. 11).

The Messianic Jewish movement continues to grow, with more than eighty-five identifiable groups in North America. Several visible groups exist in Israel as well, notably: Ramat ha Sharon, under Ari and Shira (Lindsey) Sor-koram; Nativya, under Joe Shulam in Jerusalem; and Bet Immanuel in Jaffe. New congregations are being planted in Israel. Others exist in England, France, and Australia.

Recently a full-time Bible and graduate school program to train Messianic leaders was established in Rockville, Maryland, called Messiah Yeshiva.

See also UNION OF MESSIANIC JEWISH CONGREGATIONS.

Bibliography: D. Bronstein, Jr., *Peniel Portrait* (1947); P. Goble and R. Gannon, *Everything You Need to Grow a Messianic Synagogue* (1975); D. C. Juster, *Jewish Roots* (1986); P. Liberman, *The Fig Tree Blossoms* (1976); D. Rausch, *Messianic Judaism, Its History, Theology, and Policy* (1981); idem, *Zionism in Early American Fundamentalism* (1979).   D. C. Juster

METHODIST CHARISMATICS See UNITED METHODIST CHARISMATICS.

Audrey Mieir is a musician, well-known for her many compositions and Mieir Choir Clinics.

MIEIR, AUDREY (1916–). Musician, composer, and humanitarian. Raised in a Christian home, Audrey received the Holy Spirit at age ten, about the time she started piano lessons. Church pianist at thirteen, she taught piano while attending L.I.F.E Bible College. She was married to Charles Mieir in 1936 by Aimee Semple McPherson, who later ordained them.

Mieir ministered in music for many churches. The Phil Kerr Monday night musicals in the Pasadena Civic Auditorium, with her 150-voice Harmony Chorus, were a revolution in religious music as she popularized the Hollywood sound in spite of conservative resistance. Her Mieir Choir Clinics spread her compositions and style worldwide.

The Mieirs founded Mieir Ministries, Inc., supporting and relocating Amerasian orphans of the Korean and Vietnam Wars.

Bibliography: A. Mieir, *The Audrey Mieir Song Book: A Biography in Words and Music* (1977); idem, *The Laughter and the Tears* (1976).   D. J. Wilson

MILLENNIALISM See ESCHATOLOGY, PENTECOSTAL PERSPECTIVES ON.

MILLS, WATSON EARLY (1939–). NT scholar, author, and educator best known for his contribution to the academic study of the Pentecostal and charismatic movements. Mills (Th.D., Southern Baptist Seminary, 1968; Ph.D., Baylor University, 1973) has authored more than thirteen books, eight of which deal directly with Pentecostal or charismatic issues. Some of his more significant contributions include *Charismatic Religion in Modern Research* (1984), *A Theological/Exegetical Approach to Glossolalia* (1985), and *A Bibliography on the Holy Spirit* (1988). The Society for Pentecostal Studies published his *Speaking in Tongues: A Classified Bibliography* (1974).

Currently Mills is professor of Christianity and vice-president for research and publication at Mercer University (Southern Baptist). He also serves as editor for *Perspectives in Religious Studies* and is involved in numerous professional societies.

While not himself a participant in the charismatic movement, Mills can be characterized as supportive and understanding. He acknowledges that the presence of the Pentecostal and charismatic movements "serves to underscore a real problem within Christendom today, namely there exist less than adequate categories for dealing with the experience of the Spirit" (1984, preface). Moreover, Mills's work has contributed significantly toward providing scholars with some of the tools necessary for filling that void.

Bibliography: W. E. Mills, *Charismatic Religion in Modern Research: A Bibliography* (1984); curriculum vitae (1986).   P. H. Alexander

MINOR PROPHETS, BOOKS OF THE
Minor prophets are only "minor" in the sense that their books are shorter. They all were inspired by the Holy Spirit, though some do not specifically mention him. Most Pentecostals accept a conservative classification into four groups: Early— Obadiah (about 845 B.C.), Joel (about 830 B.C.), Jonah (about 760 B.C.); Assyrian times—Amos (about 755 B.C.), Hosea (about 725 B.C.), Micah (about 710 B.C.); Babylonian times—Zephaniah (about 621 B.C.), Nahum (about 615 B.C.), Habakkuk (about 607 B.C.); and restoration times—Haggai (520 B.C.), Zechariah (520–500 B.C.), Malachi (about 430 B.C.).

I. Hosea. Hosea is the prophet of God's love. From his own experience with an unfaithful, idolatrous wife, he learned how God reaches out in love to restore a backslidden people. Sin, judgment, and love are the great themes he stresses. Hosea, though himself wholly dedicated to God and sensitive to the Spirit, says nothing about his own experience with the Spirit. At one point he does speak of the common attitudes of the people of his day: "Because your sins are so many and your hostility so great, the prophet is considered a fool, the inspired man a maniac" (9:7). But this reflected the corruption of the people (9:9).

II. Joel. Joel, the prophet of Pentecost, ministered at a time when the people were going through the forms of temple worship without real love or faith toward God. The first half of his book is a call to repentance and fits well with the early part of the reign of Joash while Jehoiada the priest was in control.

The second half of the book is the Lord's reply and indicates that the people did repent. Then God promised them not only physical restoration of the land but also "a teacher for righteousness" (2:23). Some versions do translate this phrase of the former (autumn) rains, but the Hebrew word *moreh* used here clearly means teacher (as in Job 36:22; Prov. 5:13; Isa. 30:20), and was so understood by the copyists of the Dead Sea Scrolls.

Thus we see that the outpouring of the Spirit in Joel 2:28 comes after God sends the Teacher of righteousness, in other words, after the work of Christ in his first coming. There was, of course, the sending of literal rain in Joel's day. But this gave assurance also that God would fulfill the rest of his promise and send the Teacher for righteousness and for the outpouring of the Holy Spirit. In the light of this, it seems significant that the most common title of Jesus in the Greek NT is *didaskalos*, literally, "Teacher" (often translated "Master" in the KJV).

Peter, under the inspiration of the Holy Spirit, further identified *afterward* (LXX, *meta tauta*; Heb. *hayah 'ahºy-kēn*) to mean "in the last days" (Acts 2:17)—that is, in the last age before the coming kingdom age. Thus he saw "last days" as the entire church age.

Joel also noted that the outpouring of the Spirit would bypass all the usual barriers in society. It would be abundant for all people ("all flesh"; meaning all humankind, as in Gen. 6:12–13; Deut. 5:26; Job 12:10; 34:14–15; Pss. 65:2; 145:21; Isa. 40:6; Jer. 25:31; Zech. 2:13). It would come upon both men and women, both young and old, both free people and slaves. Moreover, the Hebrew *eshpok*, "I will pour out," normally indicates progressive or repeated action, making this experience available to all from the time of the initial outpouring on the Day of Pentecost until the end of the age.

III. Micah. Micah, a country prophet who was a contemporary of Isaiah, specifically states what he experienced as the result of God's call. He says, "But as for me, I am filled with power, with the Spirit of the LORD,/and with justice [including right decisions] and might [courageous strength], to declare to Jacob his transgression [rebellion, guilt], to Israel his sin" (3:8). In the midst of a society that was calling evil good and good evil God filled him with the Holy Spirit so that he could make right judgments and come to grips with sin.

Micah also points out that the false prophets were telling him not to prophesy, for they supposed that the very speaking of the words of judgment would have a magic effect and bring the judgment (2:6). Thus they believed that if Micah would cease prophesying judgment, then the disgrace of such judgment would not overtake the people. In response Micah asked, "Is the Spirit of the LORD angry [Heb. *qatsar*, "shortened"—that is, impatient, discontented]?" The Hebrew con-

struction here calls for a negative answer. God had not changed. He is still a good God. But the people had changed. They had risen against God "as an enemy" (2:8).

The people were showing their rebellion by the way they were listening to the false prophets and rejecting the true prophets like Micah. They preferred prophets who were liars and deceivers but who prophesied for them easy living and prosperity (2:11). In other words, the people wanted teachers who would tell them what they wanted to hear. They rejected the truth that God's Spirit is indeed holy. The Spirit's purpose was to turn people away from lust and the degrading practices of sin in order to bring them into the joy and blessings of the Lord.

IV. Habakkuk. Habakkuk shows us that a Spirit-filled prophet could have doubts and serious theological problems. But he had the wisdom to take his questions to the Lord, and the Lord strengthened his faith.

V. Haggai. Haggai's chief purpose was to encourage the people to rebuild the temple after their return from Babylonian exile. But he does make an important statement about the Spirit. He told both leaders and people that God wanted them to be strong and to work. God's word to them was "I am with you." The Lord further declared, "This is what I covenanted with you when you came out of Egypt. And my Spirit remains [is still taking his stand] among you. Do not fear [stop being afraid]" (2:4–5). What a wonderful declaration of the Spirit's divine, unchanging, eternal nature, character, and purpose!

VI. Zechariah. God raised up Zechariah, as he did Haggai, to encourage the people to rebuild the temple. He did this through a series of eight visions that let them know that what they were doing was part of the plan of God, a greater plan than they knew, a plan that extended into the times of the Messiah and the redemption and restoration he would bring.

The fourth vision shows the high priest Joshua, as a representative of the people, cleansed and restored even though Satan accused him. This restoration is identified as the work of the "Branch," the new branch from the line of David (cf. Isa. 11:1; 53:2; Jer. 23:5). This prophecy of the Messiah's work is then significantly followed by a vision of a golden lampstand that pictures the Spirit of God as the Giver of power (cf. Acts 1:8). In 4:2 the Hebrew indicates that there were seven spouts on each of the seven lamps, each with a wick, thus making forty-nine lights to give a fullness of light. Then (v. 6) God's word was that his work must be done, not by human might and power, but by his Spirit. Most Pentecostals take this to symbolize the Spirit's work through the church today (cf. Matt. 5:14; Luke 12:35; Rev. 1:20).

Bibliography: G. L. Archer, Jr., *A Survey of Old Testament Introduction* (rev. ed., 1974); J. Calvin, *Commentaries on the Twelve Minor Prophets* (reprint, 1950); H. L. Ellison, *Men Spake From God*, 2d ed. (1958); S. M. Horton, *What the Bible Says About the Holy Spirit* (1976); C. F. Keil, *The Twelve Minor Prophets* (reprint, 1954); T. Laetsch, *The Minor Prophets* (1965); H. C. Leupold, *Exposition of Zechariah* (1965);

H. G. Mitchell, *A Critical and Exegetical Commentary on Haggai and Zechariah* (1912); T. V. Moore, *A Commentary of Zechariah* (1856, reprint 1961); E. B. Pusey, *The Minor Prophets* (1885); M. F. Unger, *Zechariah* (1965).
S. M. Horton

MIRACLE LIFE FELLOWSHIP A ministerial fellowship founded by A. A. Allen in 1956 that later became a part of the Don Stewart Association. Originally called Miracle Revival Fellowship, it was formed the year Allen left the Assemblies of God (AG). Allen advertised it as a fellowship that would give ministers "freedom from denominational bondage."

The international office was at Allen's Miracle Valley in Arizona, which later became the home of Southern Arizona Bible College (AG). Stewart's office is now in Phoenix.

Miracle Life Fellowship in 1987 had 1,635 affiliated churches in the U.S., England, Ghana, Honduras, Jamaica, Liberia, the Philippines, Mexico, and Nigeria. More than two thousand credentialed ministers are associated with the organization.

The Don Stewart Association also operates eleven kindergartens, sixteen day schools, one residential deaf school, three Bible schools, and fifteen medical clinics. In addition, the association claims to feed 50,000 children in 150 feeding centers in Third World countries.

Bibliography: D. E. Harrell, Jr., *All Things Are Possible* (1975); C. Jones, *Guide to the Pentecostal Movement* (1983); W. Wagner, *Born to Lose, Bound to Win* (1970). W. E. Warner

MIRACLE REVIVAL FELLOWSHIP See MIRACLE LIFE FELLOWSHIP.

MIRACLES, GIFT OF The term "operations/workings of powerful deeds" *(energemata dynameon)* occurs fifth in a list of "manifestations" of the Holy Spirit in 1 Co 12:7-10. A shorter form of the same expression ("powerful deeds," *dynameis)*is found in Paul's resume of the list in 1 Co 12:28,29. The plural form is used most probably to evoke the notion of variety and abundance as is the case with the corresponding terminology concerning healing: "gifts of healings" *(charismata iamaton;* 1 Co 12:9,28,30).

The root *dyn* connotes "ability, capacity, power" (see Grundmann, 1964). It is sometimes used in the Septuagint as a translation of the Hebrew root *gbr* when this refers to the power of God to effect his will: 1 Ch 29:11; Job 12:13; Ps 54:1; 145:12. The frequency with which the term *dyanmis* is employed to denote a powerful deed or "miracle" in the NT probably reflects intertestamental usage. As witness to this, we may point to the frequency with which the Hebrew word *gbrh* in the Qumran literature (1QH 1:35; 4:28-29; 11:3, etc.) refers to the wonderful and powerful works of God. In a saying of Jesus belonging to what Mussner (1970, 19) terms "the oldest tradition of the gospels," we find this prophetic condemnation of Korazin, Bethsaida and Capernaum: "had the powerful deeds *(dynameis)* been done in Tyre and Sidon/Sodom that were done in your midst. . ." (Mt 11:21,23/Luke 10:13). The notion that God's powerful works were being performed to lead people to repent and under-

stand his intentions is found rather frequently in the NT: Mt 7:22; 13:54,58/Mk 6:2,5; Lk 19:37; Ac 2:22; 8:13; 10:38; 19:11; 2 Co 12:12; Gal 3:5; Heb 2:4; 6:5.

The fact that, in the Corinthian lists, "powerful deeds" are distinguished from "healings" is probably due to the special ability of healing miracles to symbolize and communicate the saving power of God. (See article on Healing, Gift of.) On other occasions, *dynamis* is a generic term which includes acts of healing. In Mk 6:2, we encounter the reaction to Jesus on the part of his fellow townsmen: "What is the wisdom given to him so that even such powerful deeds are done at his hands?" Mark then goes on to report, "he was not able to perform any deed of power *(dynamin)*, except, putting his hands on a few sick, *he cured them.*" (Mk 6:5/Mt 13:54,58.)

The fact that Paul himself lists "powerful deeds" alongside the common OT expression "signs and wonders" in 2 Co 12:12 (see also Ac 2:22; Heb 2:4), entitles us to think that *dynameis* may be a generic term to him as well. Certainly the multiplication of food, the power over weather and other cosmic forces, some forms of exorcism, and the like should be classified as "powerful deeds," but such realities do not exhaust the possibilities. We have seen that healing itself can be considered a demomstration of power. There are other indications as well which point to a broader understanding of what Paul may mean by such expressions as we find in Gal 3:5: "the one who grants you the Spirit and effects powerful deeds *(energon dynameis:* note resemblence to 1 Co 12:10) in your midst: [is this] from works of the Law or the obedience of faith?"

Powerful deeds may refer to any aspect of the divine activity by which people are "cut to the heart" (Ac 2:37), a lifetime of habit patterns of sin are erased, spiritual blindness is overcome in an instant, physical and moral healing takes place as the Gospel is preached, and enemies are both touched and brought to the Lord. This is what Paul refers to when he says that he preached in such a way that the Corinthians, faith "might not rest on men's wisdom but on God's power" (1 Co 1:5 NIV), or when he refers to his assurance concerning God's choice of the Thessalonians because "our Gospel came to you not simply with words, but also with power, with the Holy Spirit and deep conviction." (1 Th 1:5 NIV)

The charasmatic gift designated in 1 Co 12 refers to a particular spiritual endowment by which a person is able to demonstrate God's justifying and saving power, and to manifest the Lordship of Jesus Christ over the whole universe by bringing about physical and moral effects that clearly transcend the power of merely human resources. Though many of these effects may be imitated and indeed co-opted by satan, the criteria for discerning God's activity are clearly given in the NT. (See article on Discernment). One of the surest signs that God is the source of the event is thawt "workings of powerful deeds" proceed from and lead to faith. The Christian community in every age has need of this precious gift in order that faith grow both in extension and depth.

Bibliography: W. Grundmann, Article, *"dynamai/dynamis"* in TDNT 2 (1964); H. Van Der Loos, *The Miracles of Jesus* (Supplements to Novum Testamentum, 9) (1965); F. Mussner, *The Miracles of Jesus* (1970); A. Bittlinger, *Gifts and Graces. A Commentary on 1 Corinthians 12-14* (1973); R. Laurentin, *Miracles in El Paso?* (tr. J. Otto) (1982).   R. F. Martin

MISSIOLOGY

I. Introduction. A review of Pentecostal missiology must include an evaluation of at least three important factors: (1) What are the central theological beliefs that have propelled the Pentecostal-charismatic movements into a worldwide evangelistic force? (What do they believe about mission?); (2) Who are the persons and what are the methods employed to missionize? (How do they do mission?); (3) What is on the future agenda for Pentecostal missiology? (Where are they headed in mission?).

II. What Do They Believe About Mission? Pentecostal mission theology has tended to be a "theology on the move," its character often having been more experiential than cognitive, more activist than reflective. Early Pentecostals were characterized by an "urgent missiology" that caused them to seek immediate world evangelization in light of their conviction of the imminent return of Christ. Systematic theologizing, research, and writing on the world mission of the church were therefore postponed in the early years of the movement (McClung, 1986a). In more recent years "Pentecostal missiologists" have emerged and have begun to develop a more formalized "Pentecostal missions theology" (Hodges, 1972 and 1977; McClung, 1986b; McGee, 1986a and 1986b; Pomerville, 1986; Smeeton, 1986).

It may not be possible to isolate *the* Pentecostal statement on mission. The theology of the Pentecostal movement, like its history, personalities, and polities is far from being monolithic, typical, or generic. The river of Pentecostalism flows from many streams and tributaries (Nichol, 1966, 55). This should not erase the fact, however, that from its inception, the movement has had underlying theological assumptions that have formed the impulse for its missionary expansion. In scanning the field of Pentecostal literature, there are at least five major theological themes that relate to missions.

A. A Literal Biblicism. Pentecostals have been marked by their exactness in following a literal interpretation of Scripture—so much so that they have been characterized as "people of The Book." For Pentecostals, the issue of biblical authority is nonnegotiable and is *the* beginning point for missions theology and strategy. If the Bible says, "Go into all the world . . ." and records the actions of the early church obeying this commission, then Pentecostals have believed that this is a command and a model to be taken literally for this generation. Every major Pentecostal group has strong statements regarding the authority of Scripture and the missionary obligation of the church.

B. An Experiential Christianity. Pentecostal pioneer David J. du Plessis called it "truth on fire" (1977, 181–82). In spite of accusations of shallow hermeneutics and subjectivity, Pentecostals have remained insistent that God is to be personally experienced through the Holy Spirit. For Pentecostals, there need not be any polarization between doctrine and experience. If the Holy Spirit is the originator and impetus for world mission and if Christians are to experience the Holy Spirit personally, then (as Pentecostals believe), the natural outflow of this personal experience is involvement in the world mission of the Holy Spirit.

C. The Personality and Power of the Holy Spirit. For Pentecostals, the Holy Spirit is personally active, living in and directing his servants in world evangelization (Acts 8, 13). Missiologically speaking, the Holy Spirit is not just a force or influence but is also personally and powerfully potent on the frontiers of mission. Prudencio Damboriena observed in Latin American Pentecostalism that Pentecostal beliefs and practices cannot be understood until people grasp

> the centrality of the Third Person of the Trinity in their theology and in their lives. To them Pentecost is not a mere historical event that took place almost two thousand years ago, but an always renewed presence of the Spirit in the world. The Holy Spirit is now, as then, the "creator" and the "vivifier" of men (1969, 87).

Pentecostals understand the experience of the baptism of the Holy Spirit as an indispensable enduement of power for world evangelization (Luke 24:49; Acts 1:8) and insist that it is normative and imperative for each believer to seek for a "personal Pentecost." In fact, the ministry of the Holy Spirit is directly mentioned or inferred in every one of the Great Commission passages in the Gospels and the Book of Acts.

D. A Strong Christology. Since the baptism of the Holy Spirit and the accompanying evidence of speaking in tongues has been central to Pentecostal experience, the movement has been criticized for too much emphasis on one person of the Godhead, namely, the Holy Spirit. In fact, however, early Pentecostal writings reveal the opposite—the literature is replete with a strong christology. Jesus Christ is personally present as the Lord of the world harvest in the experience of empowerment for this harvest. He is seen as the Baptizer in the Holy Spirit (Matt. 3:11; Mark 1:8; Luke 3:16; John 1:33; McClung, 1986b, 50–51).

E. An Urgent Missiology. Eschatological urgency is at the heart of understanding the missionary fervor of early Pentecostalism. "Eschatology," says Damboriena, "belongs to the essence of Pentecostalism" (1969, 82). It is difficult to rightly understand Pentecostal missiology apart from its roots found in premillennialism, dispensationalism, and the belief in the imminent return of Jesus Christ (McClung, 1986b, 8–10; 51–52).

III. How Do Pentecostals Do Mission? Pentecostals have been known as "doers." Missiologists from many theological and ecclesiastical directions have not majored so much on Pentecostal origins and theology as they have on the growth dynamics of the worldwide movement. A large part of the answer to this inquiry can be found in the personnel and the methodology of Pentecostal missiology.

A. The Personnel of Pentecostal Missiology. Sociological and historical studies have reflected on the humble social origins of the Pentecostals and the development of preachers from among the common people of the poorer class. Since they have not had a long history of formal theological training for the professional clergy (as a class set apart), the Pentecostals have emphasized that all in the body of Christ are ministers and everyone a preacher. C. Peter Wagner's study of Latin American Pentecostalism found aggressive lay ministry as a key factor in Pentecostal growth (1986, 43). By and large, this is yet true in non-Western settings. On the North American and European scene, however, Wagner and others warn of signs of institutionalism and clear distinctions between a "professional clergy" and lay ministry (Wagner, 1982, 9).

A large part of the dynamic worldwide growth of the Pentecostal movement is due to its ability since its inception to mobilize and effectively deploy women into missionary service. A 1985 study from Fuller Theological Seminary showed a higher percentage of women ministers and missionaries in Pentecostal groups (per capita) than in their evangelical counterparts ("Women in Ministry," 1985, 6). Interestingly, seven of the twelve members of the Azusa Street "Credential Committee" were women. This committee selected and approved candidates for licensing and deployed them into missionary service (Corum, 1981, 6). Paul Yonggi Cho has espoused the leadership and involvement of women as a key ingredient in the successful growth of the Yoido Full Gospel Church in Seoul, Korea—the world's largest local church (Cho, 1981; 1984).

Pentecostal missiological tradition has placed high value on being sent by the Holy Spirit (characterized by du Plessis's book title, *The Spirit Bade Me Go*, 1972). McGee, for example, discusses the precedence of the "leading of the Spirit" over administrative structures and scientific church growth formulas and some of the tensions felt on this issue in the Assemblies of God (AG) (1986b, 166–70). High value has been placed on supernatural recruitment through dreams, visions, prophecy, tongues and interpretations, words/inner impressions, and even the audible voice of God (McClung, 1986b, 11–15).

B. The Methodology of Pentecostal Missiology. As with theological motivations, there are numerous issues, elements, and practices associated with Pentecostal methodology and strategy (McClung, 1985, 19). Among the variety of strategies employed, five practices should be noted:

1. *Indigenous Churches.* Pentecostal missions have sought from the outset to develop indigenous churches. In many overseas situations the national Pentecostal churches have expanded rapidly. One of the Pentecostal missiologists most responsible for this emphasis in the last forty years is Melvin L. Hodges, whose book *The Indigenous Church* (1953) has become the standard work on

the subject in evangelical circles. A sequel, *The Indigenous Church and the Missionary*, was published in 1978.

2. *Church Planting.* William R. Read found in his research on Brazilian Pentecostalism that the Pentecostals were not only expanding rapidly, but almost wholly through church planting (Read, 1965, 12). Pentecostals stress the importance of planting responsible, reproducing congregations as the abiding fruit of world evangelization and measure their progress by the number of new congregations set in order and new buildings constructed.

3. *Urban Strategies.* In the non-Western world Pentecostal growth and urbanization have developed side by side. Read's conclusion was that in Latin America the Pentecostal strength was in the city (Read, 1965, 219–21). McGavran also discovered that Pentecostals have taken advantage of the migration from villages to cities and noted that they were "buying up urban opportunities" (McGavran, 1979, 247).

4. *Literature Distribution/Publishing.* Among some fifteen "Causes For the Initial Success of Pentecostalism," Nichol has given strong emphasis to tabloid-sized newspapers and other early publications that became the "means of disseminating the message of Pentecostalism to the far-flung corners of the globe" (Nichol, 1966, 60–61). Though analytical and systematized theologies did not emerge until later in Pentecostalism, the Pentecostal message has been distributed widely to the common man through massive literature campaigns.

Today publishing ministries remain high in priority in all major Pentecostal groups. Denominations publish a variety of papers and journals in many languages, and an International Pentecostal Press Association has been formed. Interdenominational Pentecostal journals such as *Pneuma* (the journal of the Society for Pentecostal Studies), *EPTA Bulletin* (the journal of the European Pentecostal Theological Association), and *World Pentecost* (the journal of the Pentecostal World Conference) carry occasional articles on Pentecostal missions. Departments of world mission in Pentecostal denominations publish specialized world missions papers, and by 1987 there was a call for an international journal of Pentecostal missiology/church growth (McClung, 1987, 11).

5. *Missions Stewardship.* Pentecostals have given generously to the cause of world missions since the earliest days of the movement. In the pioneering years whole families sold their possessions and either started for the field or supported others who went. In the classical Pentecostal denominations of North America, missions budgets continue to receive the largest share of donations. Missions stewardship has received number-one priority.

IV. Where Are Pentecostals Headed in Mission? Out of the backdrop of a history of worldwide expansion, there is evidence from all sources in the Pentecostal world that there is optimism for the future of Pentecostal missions. A special issue of the *Pentecostal Minister* journal on the subject of world evangelization highlights the projections toward the year 2000 among leading

Pentecostal denominations and charismatic networks (Buxton, 1987).

This optimism is seen in the commitment to the perpetuation of the movement worldwide through leadership training in Bible schools and seminaries, indigenous church leadership, and continued church planting (McClung, 1986b, 39).

In addition, Pentecostals have responded to the challenge of unreached people. By the early 1980s terms such as "unreached people," "hidden people," and "people groups" were making their way into regular Pentecostal missions publications (McClung, 1986a, 144; Buxton, 1987, 33). There has been much discussion of the urban challenge, Third World missions, and the formation of new missions structures in traditional Pentecostal churches and in the charismatic movement (McClung, 1986b, 145–48; Buxton, 1987, 21, 42).

By the late 1980s the concepts of *countdown* and *closure* were entering the discussions of Pentecostal missions leaders. Pentecostals joined with the widespread evangelical trend toward taking aim on the year 2000 with specific goals for increasing world evangelization efforts during the decade of the 1990s. A survey of mainline Pentecostal organizations and missions departments revealed ambitious faith projections with such programs as "Target 2000" (Pentecostal Holiness Church) and "Project 2000" (Church of God, Cleveland, Tenn.).

In July 1987 the North American Congress on World Evangelization and the Holy Spirit met in the New Orleans Superdome for a massive statement on Pentecostal-charismatic unity toward world evangelization. The clearly stated primary goal of the convocation was to bring the majority of the human race to Jesus Christ by the end of the century (Synan, 1987). The plan from New Orleans was to hold a *world* follow-up congress for Pentecostal-charismatic leaders in the early 1990s to usher in a decade of evangelization leading up to the end of the twentieth century. By the end of 1987 many nonaffiliated charismatic churches and organizations had begun to affiliate with a network known as AIMS, the Association of International Missions Services.

A review of the historical dynamics in the spread of early Pentecostalism around the world reveals a clear-cut, if not systematic, theology of missions. Pentecostal missions methods have employed the laity, including the leadership of women in missions. International expansion has resulted from indigenous church planting with a focus on urban mission, literature distribution, and missions stewardship. Prior to the last decade of the twentieth century, a science of Pentecostal missiology has emerged with optimistic projections toward world evangelization by the year 2000.

See also CHURCH GROWTH; MISSIONS, OVERSEAS.

Bibliography: C. Buxton, ed., *The Pentecostal Minister* (Winter 1987); P. Y. Cho, *More Than Numbers* (1984); idem, *Successful Home Cell Groups* (1981); F. T. Corum, comp., *Like As of Fire: A Reprint of the Old Azusa Street Papers* (1981); P. Damboriena, *Tongues As of Fire: Pentecostalism in Contemporary Christianity* (1969); D. J. du Plessis, *A Man Called Mr. Pentecost* (1977); M. L. Hodges, *A Theology of The Church and Its Mission: A Pentecostal Perspective* (1977); L. G. McClung, Jr., ed., *Azusa Street and Beyond: Pentecostal Missions and Church Growth in the Twentieth Century* (1986b); idem, "Explosion, Motivation, and Consolidation: The Historical Anatomy of the Pentecostal Missionary Movement" *Missiology* (April 1986a), 159–72; idem, "Spontaneous Strategy of the Spirit: Pentecostal Missionary Practices," *World Pentecost* (March 1985), 19–22; idem, "Theology and Strategy of Pentecostal Missions," *International Bulletin of Missionary Research* (January 1988), 2–6; idem, "Why I am Optimistic About the Future of Pentecostal Missions," *The Pentecostal Minister* (Winter 1987), 6–11; G. B. McGee, "Assemblies of God Mission Theology: A Historical Perspective," *International Bulletin of Missionary Research* (October 1986b), 166, 168–70; idem, *This Gospel Shall Be Preached* (1986a); J. T. Nichol, *Pentecostalism* (1966); P. A. Pomerville, *The Third Force in Missions* (1986); W. R. Read, *New Patterns of Church Growth in Brazil* (1965); D. D. Smeeton, ed., "Toward a Pentecostal Missiology," *EPTA Bulletin* 5 (4, 1986): 128–36; V. Synan, "A Vision for the Year 2000," *Charisma* (August 1987): 42–44, 46; C. P. Wagner, *Spiritual Power and Church Growth* (1986); "Women in Ministry," *Theology, News and Notes* (October 1985).
L. G. McClung, Jr.

MISSIONARY CHURCH OF CHRIST One of several Puerto Rican Pentecostal denominations. The group began as the Iglesia de Cristo en las Antillas (Church of Christ in the Antilles) as a result of Francisco Olazábal's campaign in Puerto Rico in 1934. Within a few months twelve churches in the northeastern part of the island organized a general council. In March 1938 the group changed its name to the Iglesia de Cristo Misionera (Missionary Church of Christ) in order to be more inclusive. The dominant personality during the early years was Florentino Figueroa Rosa, who held the position of general supervisor for more than twenty-five years, beginning in 1940. The group reported 125 congregations in Puerto Rico with seven thousand members. A remnant that retained the name Iglesia de Cristo en las Antillas after 1938 has also grown substantially.

See also IGLESIA DE CRISTO EN LAS ANTILLAS.

Bibliography: D. Barratt, *World Christian Encyclopedia* (1982); E. Carver, "Showcase for God. A Study of Evangelical Church Growth in Puerto Rico," unpublished M.A. thesis, Fuller Theological Seminary, 1972; D. Moore, *Puerto Rico Para Cristo* (1969). E. A. Wilson

MISSIONARY CONFERENCE, THE A nondenominational conference of missionaries called by the General Council of the Assemblies of God (AG) "to include every person in Pentecost who was interested in missions, regardless of their affiliation, to discuss better cooperation, in the home and foreign fields, better facilities for carrying on missionary work, and above all, to raise the standard of missions to the place it should rightfully hold in the heart and mind of every Christian" ("First Conference of Pentecostal Missionaries," 1917, 13). As a matter of convenience, the first conference followed the general council meeting at St. Louis in September 1917. John W. Welch, chairman of the AG, assured the conference that it was independent and not

subject to general council legislation; nevertheless, the latter would welcome suggestions that
would advance the cause of missions. Thirty
missionaries attended, including Christian
Schoonmaker, Fannie Simpson, Nettie D. Nichols, Ivan Kauffman, C. W. Doney, Blanche Appleby, H. C. Ball, Charles C. Personeus, and
Florence Murcutt. The conference chose S. A.
Jamieson to be the chairman and Anna C. Reiff as
the secretary. Various issues were addressed,
notably the use of native workers, the need for
missionary rest homes in the U.S., and additional
financial support. Ten resolutions were passed,
with the last one declaring the Missionary Conference to be a permanent organization.

The conference normally continued to follow
the meetings of the general council, while retaining its independent status. Later officers included
Daniel W. Kerr as chairman, and Zella Reynolds,
sister of Alice Reynolds Flower, as secretary.

The significance of the organization centered
on the need to provide guidelines for the burgeoning missionary enterprise. Conferences provided opportunities for missionaries to receive
inspiration, express their needs to pastors and
general council officers, and pass helpful resolutions. In addition, laypersons received information about conditions abroad and the challenge to
be faithful in giving. The close association of the
general council to an undenominational organization also reflects the state of early Pentecostal
ecumenicity.

Due to the positive relationships developed at
the gatherings many independent missionaries
joined the AG. Consequently, the Missionary
Conference eventually outlived its usefulness, and
the last meeting was held in 1921.

See also MISSIONS, OVERSEAS.

Bibliography: G. B. McGee, *This Gospel Shall Be Preached* (1986); A. C. Reiff, "First Conference of Pentecostal Missionaries," *LRE* (October 1917), 13–17.
                                              G. B. McGee

MISSIONS, OVERSEAS (NORTH AMERI-CAN)

I. The Azusa Street Revival and the Pente-
   costal Missions Movement
   A. Historical Context of Pentecostal
      Missions
   B. Pentecostal Missions Begin
      1. The Topeka Revival (1901)
      2. The Azusa Street Revival (1906–
         09)
   C. Early Missionaries
      1. Three Groups
      2. Women Missionaries
   D. Effectiveness
   E. Early Attempts at Organization
II. The Emergence of Pentecostal Missions
   Agencies After 1910
   A. The Need for Organization
   B. North American Agencies
      1. Pentecostal Mission in South and
         Central Africa
      2. General Council of the Assemblies
         of God
      3. Pentecostal Assemblies of Canada
      4. Pentecostal Holiness Church
      5. Church of God (Cleveland, Tenn.)
      6. Russian and Eastern European
         Mission
      7. Other Agencies
   C. Oneness Agencies
   D. Cooperation and Ecumenicity
III. Growth and Expansion Since 1945
   A. Increased Cooperation
   B. Major Agencies:
      1. Church of God (Cleveland, Tenn.)
      2. Pentecostal Assemblies of Canada
      3. General Council of the Assemblies
         of God
      4. United Pentecostal Church Inter-
         national
      5. 1987 Statistics
IV. Historical Development of Pentecostal
   Missiology
   A. Early Missiological Perspectives
   B. The Influence of A. B. Simpson and
      the CMA
   C. The Emerging Influence of Roland
      Allen
   D. The Achievement of Melvin L.
      Hodges
   E. Recent Publications and Statements
   F. Historical Perspectives
V. Missions Education
VI. Independent Ministries
VII. Missions and the Charismatic Movement
   A. North American Congresses on the
      Holy Spirit and World Evangeliza-
      tion
   B. Association of International Mission
      Services (AIMS)

**I. The Azusa Street Revival and the Pente-
costal Missions Movement.**

*A. Historical Context of Pentecostal Mis-
sions.* The origins of the Protestant missionary
movement can be traced to the spiritual awakenings of the seventeenth and eighteenth centuries,
which produced Pietism, Moravianism, the Great
Awakening, and the Wesleyan revival in England.
Kenneth Scott Latourette noted that this evangelical strain within Protestantism "made much of
the transformation of the individual through the
Christian gospel and it also gave rise to many
efforts for the elimination of social ills and for the
collective betterment of mankind" (1941, 4:65).

In the nineteenth century, the Western colonial
powers raced to build overseas empires, often
undergirded by presuppositions of their own
cultural and racial superiority and propelled by
new means of transportation. At the same time,
many devout Christians followed the summons of
the Great Commission (Matt. 28:19–20) and
traveled abroad as missionaries. This evangelical
trend in missions was reinforced by the revival
campaigns of Dwight L. Moody (1837–99),
among others, and the organization of the Student Volunteer Movement for Foreign Missions
(1888). As a result, the widest expansion of
Christianity since the time of the ancient Christian
church began to occur in the late nineteenth
century.

Millennial expectations figured heavily into the
missionary movement. The postmillennial vision
of an emerging kingdom of God on earth through

the propagation of the gospel and the establishment of human institutions (schools, orphanages, hospitals, etc.) held the loyalty of Christian denominations and missionaries during most of the century. However, a decided shift occurred in the last decades when premillennial teaching (both the dispensational and nondispensational forms) rapidly gained widespread popularity. This perspective, reflecting a pessimistic appraisal of human progress, anticipated an imminent return of Christ prior to the establishment of his millennial kingdom on earth.

The growing acceptance of premillennialism extended into the Holiness movement, among Wesleyans (George D. Watson, W. B. Godbey, et al.) as well as "higher life" teachers with Reformed-Keswick sympathies. Reflecting the higher-life perspective, A. J. Gordon (1836–95), A. B. Simpson (1843–1919), and others became well known for their premillennial teachings and missionary endeavors. In their view, Christians were living in "the last days" (Joel 2:28–32) and the evangelization of the heathen required a mighty outpouring of the Holy Spirit to accomplish that objective. Simpson expressed this concern to the membership of the Christian and Missionary Alliance (CMA) by saying, "We believe God wants us to deeply realize our special calling as a distinct spiritual and missionary agency in these last days. . . . May the Holy Spirit help us to behold the vision, to receive anew the great commission, and then go forth in the power of a new baptism of the Holy Ghost to make it real" (Simpson, 1900, 32). Many shared this concern as the end of the century approached. The preaching, publications, schools, and sometimes missions agencies that Gordon, Simpson, and others founded or supported, exercised a profound influence on the later Pentecostal missionary movement.

B. Pentecostal Missions Begin.

1. The Topeka Revival (1901). The Pentecostal movement began with a revival on January 1, 1901, at Charles F. Parham's Bethel Bible School in Topeka, Kansas. Parham believed that the glossolalia (i.e., speaking in tongues) that he and many of his students experienced was specifically xenolalia (actual foreign languages). Thus the Spirit's linguistic provision with dynamic power would afford an unparalleled missionary advance before Christ's return. Parham's linkage of the baptism in the Holy Spirit to glossolalia also laid the foundation for classical Pentecostalism's belief in "initial evidence."

Surprisingly, the Topeka revival produced no foreign missionaries. Perhaps the hopes for sending missionaries waned amid the persecution and discouragement that followed. Notwithstanding, spiritual awakenings and missionary zeal have long been associated on the American religious scene, and Topeka ultimately proved to be no exception. Its actual impact on world missions can be found in the results of the later revivals that it spawned, notably the Azusa Street revival in Los Angeles, California.

2. The Azusa Street Revival (1906–09). Sparked by the ministry of William J. Seymour, a black Holiness preacher and former student of Parham's at his Bible school in Houston, Texas, the Azusa Street revival generated one of the greatest spiritual awakenings of the twentieth century. Its long-range impact has been that millions at home and overseas have entered the ranks of the Christian church, representing an almost unprecedented expansion of the Christian faith. To understand its importance, three aspects of the revival must be considered. First, the participants at Azusa Street (Seymour, Florence L. Crawford, A. G. Garr, et al.), considered their new-found languages to be the languages of the world, reflecting Parham's xenolalic perspective. *The Apostolic Faith,* a newspaper published occasionally from 1906 to 1908 by the revival's leadership, reported: "God is solving the missionary problem, sending out new-tongued missionaries . . . without purse or scrib [*sic*], and the Lord is going before them preparing the way (*Apostolic Faith* [November 1906], 2). While this view was widely shared by other contemporary Pentecostals (including W. F. Carothers and Levi R. Lupton), it soon became apparent that glossolalia did not equip people to preach in other languages, although Parham himself never flinched in his belief to the contrary.

Second, those who attended the revival services believed that the apostolic "signs and wonders" that had characterized the advance of the early Christians in the Book of Acts had been restored. This pneumatological emphasis, while rejected by many, underscored a reliance on the leading of the Holy Spirit to the point of representing a unique posture toward the Christian world mission. Indeed, their wholesale return to the apostolic pattern of first-century Christianity was without parallel on the missionary landscape.

Third, the enthusiasm for world evangelization prompted a dispersion of new missionaries. Although the leaders of the revival constituted a credentials committee and issued licenses for missionaries and evangelists, they did not organize a missions agency. This conceivably reflects their concerns about the urgency of the hour, reluctance to rely on the support of a human agency (reflecting the "faith" principle held by the British Christian philanthropist George Müller and the missiology of William Taylor, famed Methodist missionary bishop), naïvete about conditions overseas, and the desire to be directed completely by the Spirit. Thus, most of the early missionaries traveled abroad on "faith" (without pledged support) and with their perceived new language for overseas preaching. The records also indicate that all Christians—whether men or women, clergy or laity, blacks or whites, could be called to foreign missions.

Alfred G. ("A. G.") Garr, pastor of the Burning Bush Mission in Los Angeles, and his wife, Lillian, both of whom had received the Pentecostal baptism at the Azusa Street Mission in June 1906, sailed for India (and eventually Hong Kong) several months later. They were among the first and best-known Pentecostals to leave for "the regions beyond." Others included Louise Condit and Lucy M. Leatherman (Jerusalem), Lucy Farrow (Africa), Lizzie Fraser (India), Samuel J. and Ardella K. Mead (veteran Methodist mission-

The first Pentecostal missionaries from the Northwest to the Orient in 1907. The leader is M. L. Ryan, seated in the center of the second row.

aries who returned to Africa), Henry M. Turney (South Africa), and Ansel and Etta Post (Egypt). Generally speaking, the early missionaries traveled to the traditional sites of Protestant endeavor: Africa, the Middle East, India, and China. While some returned home disillusioned, as early as late 1906, this dispersion represents the concern among the Azusa Street participants for world evangelization, as well as the leveling effect of the revival.

The publication and widespread distribution across North America of the newspaper, the *Apostolic Faith,* carried the teachings and news of the revival, testimonials from around the country, and reports from missionaries. Numerous Pentecostal publications assisted in the dissemination of this information as well.

Other revivals generated by Parham and the Azusa Street revival also significantly influenced the missionary effort. Among other places, revivals occurred in Indianapolis, Indiana; Alliance, Akron, and Cleveland, Ohio; Rochester and Nyack, New York; Dunn, North Carolina; Portland, Oregon; Houston, Texas; and Toronto and Winnipeg, Canada. Parham's revival in Zion City, Illinois, resulted in the journey of John G. Lake and Thomas Hezmalhalch (who had attended Azusa Street) to South Africa in 1908, after which they contributed to the founding of the Apostolic Faith Mission. A revival in Spokane, Washington, triggered by news of the happenings at the Azusa Mission, produced several parties of missionaries who left the Pacific Northwest in 1907 for Japan, China, India, Africa, and Scandinavia; these included H. L. and Emma Lawler, Will Colyar, Rosa Pittman Downing, Cora Fritsch Falkner, the Reverend Edward Reilly, E. May Law, and Bertha Milligan.

Influential personalities touched by the Azusa Street revival included Thomas B. Barratt, who received the baptism in the Holy Spirit while visiting New York City. He returned to Norway with the new message and eventually carried it to England, Sweden, and other European countries; Pentecostal missionaries from these countries soon traveled overseas. Others who developed international ministries include Cecil Polhill, founder of the Pentecostal Missionary Union in Great Britain (1909), the first successful Pentecostal missions agency to be established; Minnie T. Draper, one of the founders of the Pentecostal Mission in South and Central Africa (1910); William F. P. Burton and James Salter, founders of the Congo Evangelistic Mission (later the Zaire Evangelistic Mission) (1915); Luigi Francescon, Daniel Berg, and Gunnar Vingren, missionaries to Brazil (1910); and G. R. Polman, organizer of the Pentecostal Mission Alliance in the Netherlands (1920). Historian Vinson Synan proposes that "directly or indirectly, practically all the Pentecostal groups in existence can trace their lineage to the Azusa Mission" (Synan, 1971, 114). Nevertheless, there is limited evidence to suggest that some contemporary indigenous Pentecostal revivals did occur overseas without its tutelage.

From North America alone, over 185 Pentecostal missionaries had traveled overseas by 1910. Their travels, needs, and triumphs were heralded to the members of the burgeoning movement by means of early Pentecostal periodicals such as the *Apostolic Faith* (Los Angeles, 1906), *Bridegroom's Messenger* (1907), *Word and Witness* (1907), *Latter-Rain Evangel* (1908), *New Acts* (1904), *Pentecost* (1908), *Evening Light and Church of God Evangel* (1910), *Christian Evangel* (1913),

Pentecostal Holiness Advocate (1917), and *Word and Work* (1879). In addition, the editors received funds from readers and distributed them to the designated missionaries.

C. Early Missionaries.

1. Three Groups. At least three different groups of missionaries went overseas. The first were those who felt called, but because of their eschatology, belief in xenolalia, and adherence to the faith principle, ventured abroad without adequate financial resources or an understanding of the history, culture, or language of the people to whom they wished to minister. They shared their testimonies, often attempting to proselytize other Protestant missionaries to the new-found Pentecostal blessing. Their attempts to convert the non-Christians were limited by lack of preparation.

The second group was composed of veteran missionaries who received the baptism in the Holy Spirit and joined the Pentecostal movement. These individuals brought maturity and respectability to the movement, though they often faced hardships after leaving their parent agencies. Numbered among them were Minnie F. Abrams (Methodist), H. A. Baker (Christian Church), Susan Easton (American Women's Board of Missions in India), J. C. Lehman (independent Holiness), William W. Simpson (CMA), Christian Schoonmaker (CMA), Samuel J. Mead (Methodist), and Alice C. Wood (Friends and CMA).

The graduates of Bible institutes formed the third group of missionaries. Undoubtedly the most influential school on Pentecostal missions before 1920 (among the small minority of missionaries who had received such training) was A. B. Simpson's Missionary Training Institute at Nyack. Before long, however, distinctively Pentecostal Bible institutes appeared (either founded as Pentecostal or having become so later) such as the Altamont Bible and Missionary Institute (later Holmes College of the Bible), Paris Mountain, South Carolina (1898); Rochester Bible Training School, Rochester, New York (1906); Beulah Heights Bible and Missionary Training School, North Bergen, New Jersey (1912); Bethel Bible Training School, Newark, New Jersey (1916); Bible Training School (later Lee College), Cleveland, Tennessee (1918); Glad Tidings Bible Institute (later Bethany Bible College), San Francisco, California (1919); Southern California Bible School (later Southern California College), Los Angeles, California (1920); Central Bible Institute (later Central Bible College), Springfield, Missouri (1922); and the Evangelistic and Missionary Training Institute (later Lighthouse of International Foursquare Evangelism, now L.I.F.E. Bible College), Los Angeles, California (1923). The training these schools provided in Bible instruction and spirituality, though lacking in missiological studies, prepared a committed force of Pentecostal missionaries who eventually brought stability to the overseas endeavors of the movement.

2. Women Missionaries. The extensive role of women in Pentecostal missions reflects that of the Protestant missions movement in general. Single Pentecostal women maintained that the Lord had

called them to serve overseas, having been assured by Peter's statement on the Day of Pentecost "Even on my servants, both men and women, I [God] will pour out my Spirit in those days, and they will prophesy" (Acts 2:18). While sometimes denied full ministerial opportunities at home, they found considerable liberty to pastor, teach, evangelize, and administer charitable institutions abroad.

Throughout most, if not all, of the history of Pentecostal missions, married and single women missionaries have constituted a majority. The achievements of married women have been substantial (e.g., Maria W. Atkinson [CG], Louise Jeter Walker [AG], and Jean Firth [ICFG]). The number of single women serving as missionaries, however, has steadily declined, at least in the denominational agencies. Nevertheless, their impact on the development of national churches and charitable institutions is without dispute. Single women like Lillian Trasher (CG, and later AG), Nellie Hendrickson (PAOC), Lucille Jenkins (Mitchell) (OBSC), and Marie Stephany (AG) made notable contributions. Other prominent women, including Elizabeth V. Baker, Marie Burgess Brown, Florence L. Crawford, Minnie T. Draper, Christine Gibson, Aimee Semple McPherson, Carrie Judd Montgomery, Virginia E. Moss, and Avis Swiger, while not serving as missionaries (with the exception of McPherson), impacted Pentecostal missions through the institutions that they founded (schools, missions agencies, denominations) or served.

D. Effectiveness.

The general impact of the earliest missionaries (1906–08) appears to have been short-lived and disappointing. Disillusionment quickly crept in because of the harsh realities they faced, their inability to communicate with the people, financial instability, and lack of preparation.

Observers within the movement began to notice the deficiencies as early as 1906. An outsider, A. B. Simpson, referred in 1908 to these early missionaries as "unhappy victims of some honest but mistaken impression" (Simpson, 1908, 11–12). Although Simpson accurately described the failures of some (and there was a high turnover rate before 1920), there were those who persevered: among others, the A. G. Garrs, Henry M. Turney, and E. May Law. A later observer, Bishop Joseph H. King of the Pentecostal Holiness Church, made a world tour (1909–12) to "visit all the Pentecostal centers in foreign lands. These centers needed special help in order to be established in the doctrine of the Pentecostal baptism, as well as in those truths closely related to it" (King, 1949, 142). Significantly, King portrayed the mission enterprise in a positive light and made no reference to xenolalia.

Despite later pronouncements that described this seminal period (1906–20) as a "golden era" of Pentecostal missions, such was not the case. The death toll in some fields was staggering. In some cases missionaries refused vaccination for epidemics due to their steadfast belief in faith healing. While many took inspiration from the sacrifice and dedication of these individuals, there were unscrupulous persons who caused embarrassment. Others such as T. J. McIntosh traveled around the world (twice between 1907 and 1909) without settling down to do permanent mission work. Despite the problems, however, the number of Pentecostals volunteering for foreign service continued to increase each year; permanent works were gradually established and converts gained.

E. Early Attempts at Organization. Perceptive observers recognized that the lack of accountability, financial stability, legal recognition, and long-range strategy produced problems that needed to be addressed. The earliest attempt on the part of American Pentecostals to organize a missions agency may have been in Alliance, Ohio, at the close of the Pentecostal Camp Meeting in 1907—a meeting organized by Levi R. Lupton, Ivey Campbell, and Claude A. McKinney. The proposed Apostolic Evangelization Association, however, failed to materialize.

At the next annual camp meeting the participants issued a "Pentecostal Manifesto," which laid the groundwork for an agency. Nevertheless, this did not transpire until 1909, when the Pentecostal Missionary Union (PMU) in the U.S. became a reality, with Lupton as its president. The manifesto and the later organization of the PMU called for missionary preparation in the form of Bible training and practical ministerial experience, reflecting a mature level of thinking. Concerns that the missionary have a definite call, adequate legal recognition, and the confidence of a local church point to major problems that Lupton and his associates wanted to address. In a short time, the PMU endorsed and partially supported seventy-five missionaries. It is notable that the structural authority of the agency was minimal. Early Pentecostal missionaries tended to be staunchly independent, often "living by faith" and receiving financial assistance from many sources. Unfortunately, the PMU collapsed in December 1910 with Lupton's public confession of moral failure and the questionable sincerity of his repentance. In addition, the agency had become the target of anti-organizational sentiments. A parallel attempt in 1909 to establish a PMU in Canada also failed.

Providing the model and inspiration for these efforts was the successful Pentecostal Missionary Union founded in Great Britain in January 1909 by Cecil Polhill, one of the original "Cambridge Seven" of athletic and missionary fame. Having been a missionary on the Tibetan border with the China Inland Mission (CIM), Polhill received the Pentecostal baptism in Los Angeles in 1908. With the establishment of the PMU, modeled after the CIM, he served as its president for many years. In 1924 the PMU was integrated into the newly formed Assemblies of God in Great Britain and Ireland.

II. The Emergence of Pentecostal Missions Agencies After 1910.

A. The Need for Organization. The failure of the American PMU did not erase the need for addressing the problems of the enterprise. The inability to purchase property in certain countries because of lack of legal recognition, the occasional practice of acquiring property under the name of a recognized Protestant missions board, the inadequate and often inequitable funding of missionaries, and the unfortunate turnover in personnel continued to cause alarm. By 1913 Anna C. Reiff, the successor to William H. Piper as editor of the *Latter-Rain Evangel,* began to address "the missionary problem." Specifically she questioned whether every believer received the "George Müller call" to faith living and argued that missionaries need regular assistance from the saints at home. The costs of their basic needs left no available funds to open new works in their mission areas. For the welfare of the missionaries Reiff appealed to Pentecostals to reach the middle ground between the organizational restrictions of missions boards and total independence.

B. North American Agencies.

1. Pentecostal Mission in South and Central Africa (PMSCA). The first major Pentecostal missions agency in America to be established following the debacle of the PMU was the Pentecostal Mission in South and Central Africa (1919) founded by the Executive Council of the Bethel Pentecostal Assembly, Newark, New Jersey, "to maintain and conduct a general evangelistic work in the State of New Jersey, in all other States of the United States and any and all foreign countries" (Beach and Fahs, eds., 1925, 24). Begun by members of the Ossining, New York, Gospel Assembly, notably Minnie T. Draper (1857–1921), and the Bethel Pentecostal Assembly in Newark, the "Bethel Board" sponsored works in Liberia, the Union of South Africa (later the Republic of South Africa), Swaziland, and Portuguese East Africa (later Mozambique), and Venezuela. For a short time, it included William F. P. Burton's Congo Evangelistic Mission under its wing. Draper directed the affairs of the agency until her death in 1921, at which time she was succeeded by Christian J. Lucas.

This agency, funded by wealthy Pentecostals who were members of the board and by generous offerings from supporting churches, invested its monies in a trust fund to gain additional revenue. By 1925 the Pentecostal Mission had an income of $30,150, making it second only in size and financial underpinnings to the Assemblies of God (AG). With the collapse of the stock market in 1929, the trust fund suffered a serious blow and the agency's activities declined. Many of its missionaries—including Fred Burke, Anna Richards Scoble, and the Edgar Pettengers—transferred to the AG. The PMSCA churches in South Africa eventually became known as the Full Gospel Church. A merger in 1951 with the Church of God (Cleveland, Tenn.) resulted in a change of name to Full Gospel Church of God.

2. General Council of the Assemblies of God. The next major agency to appear came with the organization of the AG at Hot Springs, Arkansas, in 1914. The following statement was among the reasons for calling this conference:

We come together . . . that we may get a better understanding of the needs of each foreign field, and may know how to place our money in such a way that one mission or missionary shall not suffer, while another not any more worthy, lives in luxuries. Also that we may discourage wasting money on those who are running here and there accomplishing nothing, and may concentrate our support on those who mean business for our King (*Word and Witness,* December 20, 1913, 1). The formation of an executive presbytery at Hot Springs accorded them the responsibility to function also as a "missionary presbytery." In the following months approximately twenty-seven missionaries became affiliated with the AG. Thus from the beginning, the new organization concentrated on the goal of world evangelization as one of its primary objectives; by 1920 giving had reached $90,812.40 (representing a 43 percent increase over the previous year).

With the growing responsibilities of the executive presbytery, the missionary department was established in 1919 with J. Roswell Flower appointed secretary-treasurer. At this time, the department served largely as a distribution center for funds designated for specific missionaries; undesignated monies were allocated equally. It exercised little authority over the missionary personnel and did not provide strategic planning for the global effort.

AG missions turned an important corner in 1927 with the permanent appointment of Noel Perkin as missionary secretary to superintend the responsibilities of the department and the overseas personnel. His past missionary experience in Argentina, rapport with pastors, bookkeeping skills, and gentle manner insured the future maturity of AG missions. In 1931 the first *Missionary Manual* was published, containing policies and missiological perspectives. Promotions became an important priority as did the need for establishing a solid financial base to cover administrative expenses; the latter has been a continuing problem over the years. By 1939 the AG had 380 missionaries (a 1,400 percent increase since 1914), mission works in 48 countries, 1,131 churches and preaching points overseas, 44 missionary institutions (Bible institutes, orphanages, elementary schools, etc.), and 1,231 national ministers. Church members also contributed $811,766 to foreign missions between 1937 and 1939.

Noteworthy missionaries included Blanche R. Appleby (China), the Alfred A. Blakeneys (India), the Henry B. Garlocks (Africa), the Carl F. Juergensens (Japan), the Maynard L. Ketchams (India), Juan L. Lugo (Puerto Rico), Nettie D. Nichols (China), the Nicholas Nikoloffs (Eastern Europe), the Victor G. Plymires (China), Lillian Trasher (Egypt), the Ralph D. Williamses (Central America), the Arthur E. Wilsons (Burkina Faso), and Anna Ziese (China).

3. *Pentecostal Assemblies of Canada* (PAOC). Canada felt the impact of the Azusa Street revival through the ministry of Robert E. McAlister, who received the baptism in the Holy Spirit in Los Angeles in 1906. An important revival also occurred in Winnipeg, through the ministry of A. H. Argue, who received the Pentecostal baptism at the North Avenue Mission in Chicago. Without external influence, however, Mrs. Ellen

Hebden received the same experience in November 1906. In Toronto she and her husband directed the Hebden Mission, which became the Canadian "Azusa." These revivals played key roles in sending missionaries. Early personnel included the Charles W. Chawners (South Africa), the Thomas Hindles (Mongolia), the Arthur Atters (China), the Otto Kellers (East Africa), the Alex Lindsays (India), and Robert and Aimee Semple (Hong Kong).

Since many of the Canadian Pentecostal churches were initially linked to the American AG, practical considerations (including problems distinct to Canadian missionary efforts) finally led to the friendly separation and incorporation of the Pentecostal Assemblies of Canada in 1922.

4. *Pentecostal Holiness Church* (PHC). Among Holiness bodies that entered the Pentecostal movement, the PHC was the first to establish a "missionary board" at its Fayetteville, North Carolina, convention in 1904. Two years later, T. J. McIntosh became the first missionary to receive support but did not travel overseas under the auspices of the church. Within a short time the Fire-Baptized Holiness Church and the Tabernacle Pentecostal Church, both of which later amalgamated with the PHC (1911, 1915), sent out missionaries as well. Bishop Joseph H. King's world tour of Pentecostal missions (1909–12) helped to enlist independent missionaries into the church.

While the PHC experienced rapid turnover in missionary personnel during the early years, the denomination nevertheless witnessed continued growth abroad. Notable missionaries included Kenneth and Geraldine Spooner (Africa), Lucy Jones (China), and the W. H. Turners (China).

5. *Church of God* (Cleveland, Tenn., CG). The CG traces the beginning of its missions effort to the trip of R. M. and Ida Evans to the Bahamas in 1910. Evans, an elderly former Methodist minister, achieved some success, but after great personal sacrifice he and his wife had to return to the U.S. because of lack of financial support.

CG missions grew slowly during this period because of the disruptions of the war, no plan of regular support (reflecting the socio-economic conditions of the church members), and the inner turmoil that the church experienced in 1923. Notwithstanding, some missionaries did travel abroad without assurance of consistent financial provision. These included Sam C. Perry (Cuba), the Peter N. Johnsons (China), and the P. F. Branewalls and J. F. Carscaddens (French West Africa).

A missions board was appointed in 1926, but stability and steady growth did not begin until the 1930s. During these years, J. H. Ingram, the missions overseer of California and Arizona, became a powerful force for missions in the denomination through his world-wide travels. Ingram contacted many independent Pentecostal missionaries and encouraged them to unite with the CG. Thus important mission works founded by pioneer missionaries quickly expanded the scope of the church's mission and responsibilities; these included the efforts of Mary W. Atkinson (Mexico), Robert F. Cook (India), and Herman

Lauster (Germany), among others. By 1941 the CG had a missions budget of $83,101.89 and an overseas constituency of 18,362 people.

6. *Russian and Eastern European Mission* (REEM). The Russian and Eastern European Mission was organized in Chicago in 1927. It had roots in the Eastern European ministries of missionaries Nicholas Nikoloff, Gustave H. Schmidt, and Paul B. Peterson. In the following year the agency established in Danzig (Gdansk), Poland, both a field office to supervise the work in Europe and a Bible institute for the training of ministers. The Bible institute paid large dividends by preparing young men for the ministry (Poles, Hungarians, Yugoslavs, Bulgarians, Russians, et al.) Through the evangelistic work of its missionaries and the graduates of the school in Danzig, REEM reported eighty thousand converts in Eastern Europe and Russia by the time of World War II. Its activities were published in the *Gospel Call,* the official voice of the agency.

From 1927 to 1940, REEM maintained close ties with the AG by sharing personnel and mutual support. Its refusal, however, to amalgamate with the AG, as well as differences over financial policies and its gradual departure from a distinctively Pentecostal theology, led the AG to sever the relationship in 1940. Eventually REEM changed its name to Eastern European Mission and more recently to Eurovision.

7. *Other Agencies.* The number of missions agencies and denominations increased as Pentecostals recognized that the goal of world evangelization required coordination, regular financial support, and promotion. Such organizations included the Apostolic Faith movement (Portland, Ore.), begun by Florence L. Crawford in 1907 (first missionary sent in 1911); National and International Pentecostal Missionary Union, founded by Philip Wittich in 1914 (later it became part of the International Pentecostal Church of Christ); Pentecostal Church of God (1919); the Evangelization Society (TES) of the Pittsburgh Bible Institute, founded by Charles Hamilton Pridgeon in 1920; Fellowship of Christian Assemblies (1922); Church of God of Prophecy (CGP, 1923); Pentecostal Assemblies of Newfoundland, pioneered by Alice Belle Garrigus and organized in 1925; Church of God in Christ (CGIC), founded by Charles H. Mason and C. P. Jones in 1897 (first Home and Foreign Missions Board in 1925); International Church of the Foursquare Gospel (ICFG), established by Aimee Semple McPherson in 1927; Christian Church of North America (CCNA, its missions agency was founded in 1929); Elim Fellowship (1933, originally Elim Ministerial Fellowship, later Elim Missionary Assemblies); and Open Bible Standard Churches (OBSC), formed from the merger of the Open Bible Evangelistic Association and the Bible Standard Churches in 1935.

C. *Oneness Agencies.* The entry of the "New Issue" (the Oneness view of the Trinity) into the Pentecostal movement in 1913 created new divisions and ultimately led to a split within the AG in 1916. While a considerable number of ministers left the AG, the impact on the missionary personnel appears to have been minimal, although the controversy did arise on some foreign fields.

As a result, several Oneness organizations came into existence. Like other Pentecostals, they shared the same concerns for world evangelization. Two months after the schism within the AG, a large group of Oneness believers gathered in Eureka Springs, Arkansas, and formed the General Assembly of the Apostolic Assemblies (GAAA). The *Blessed Truth,* edited by D. C. O. Opperman, the newly elected chairman, was designated the official voice of the organization. The membership voted that missionary funds should be sent to Opperman, who would then distribute them to the missionaries. Seven missionaries were named on the ministerial list.

The GAAA was short-lived, however, and merged in c. 1918 with the Pentecostal Assemblies of the World (PAW), which had been formed earlier in Portland, Oregon (1914). Andrew D. Urshan, a former missionary to Persia (later Iran), received an appointment as foreign missionary secretary in 1923.

Dissatisfaction with the PAW led to a division along racial lines, and three new white organizations came into existence. One gathering of ministers founded the Pentecostal Ministerial Alliance (PMA) in 1925 and expressed the usual concerns about missions. To administer the foreign missions department, Edgar C. Steinberg, a former missionary to China, was chosen to serve as the first missionary secretary-treasurer in 1927. The seventeen missionaries listed on the roster, receiving some or all of their support from this agency, included O. W. Coote (Japan), the C. M. Hensleys (China), the A. J. Holmeses (Liberia), and Dorothy McCarty (India).

A second group of ministers organized the Emmanuel's Church in Jesus Christ in 1925. Urshan was selected as its foreign missions secretary and every church was requested to send regular monthly support. Ten missionaries received assistance, some of whom also received monies from PMA. A third constituency from PAW began the Apostolic Church of Jesus Christ (ACJC) in 1925.

The continuing disunity among Oneness believers distressed many people and resulted in the merger of ACJC and part of the remaining white constituency of PAW in 1932 to form the Pentecostal Assemblies of Jesus Christ. The new denomination supported twenty missionaries and adopted a nine-point missions policy.

A further development came in 1932 when the PMA changed its name to the Pentecostal Church, Inc. (PC). During that decade missions giving increased dramatically, and twenty-six missionaries received support. In 1944 the PC adopted a comprehensive missions policy.

While many had left PAW to form new Oneness organizations, the blacks and some whites remained separate and retained the original name. After years of instability, PAW appointed a foreign missions board, and the work achieved some progress under the direction of Bishop Earl Parchia.

D. *Cooperation and Ecumenicity.* An early ecumenical endeavor on the homefront emerged from the AG in 1917 when it called for a nondenominational conference of missionaries to address the needs of the Pentecostal missions enterprise. Known as the Missionary Conference, its first meeting took place following the AG general council meeting at St. Louis in the same year. Although independent of the AG, officers of the latter attended its sessions and welcomed suggestions. The conferences continued to follow meetings of the general council until the last meeting in 1921, when it was perceived that the body had outlived its usefulness. Many of the missionaries who participated eventually affiliated with the AG.

Ecumenical cooperation abroad often characterized the early (Trinitarian) Pentecostal missionaries for several reasons. First, many shared the ideal of unity among Spirit-baptized believers. Second, the relatively small numbers of Pentecostal missionaries in any given country fostered fellowship among those of like faith. Third, with the belief in Christ's imminent return, coupled with the relative youth and limitations of Pentecostal missions agencies, many missionaries did not perceive of themselves as overseas representatives of particular church organizations. Thus for spiritual and practical reasons they were willing in some instances to form fellowships to provide some direction to their efforts. The Pentecostal Interior Mission in Liberia, representing all the missionaries there, was a notable example of such cooperation. A similar attempt occurred in India but collapsed with the untimely death of Christian Schoonmaker. The Truth Bible Institute in Beijing, China, represented another ecumenical venture. In the same spirit of cooperation and mutual concern, the AG organized the Scandinavian Missionary Relief Fund during World War II to assist over one hundred Norwegian and Swedish Pentecostal missionaries in China, Argentina, and Brazil who had been cut off from their regular sources of income.

With the growing size of missions agencies, the missionaries became more closely linked to others who had been sent out by the same organization; consequently, they became less familiar with other Pentecostal missionaries. In reference to training, more and more missionaries received Bible institute training and hence grew in denominational loyalty. The ever-increasing demands for more financial assistance also required them to broaden their base of support beyond a few congregations, thus gradually requiring extensive itineration when they were home on furlough. With these changes, missionaries forged stronger ties to their sending agencies.

In the U.S., denominationalism continued to splinter the Pentecostal movement, setting the stage for increased isolation among the leaders. Generally there was little contact between Pentecostal missions boards in the U.S. until after World War II. However, the fraternal relationships between the AG and the PAOC, and between the AG and REEM, were notable exceptions in ecumenical endeavors.

Although Pentecostals experienced considerable isolation from Fundamentalists and Evangelicals before World War II, the AG did belong to the Foreign Missions Conference of North America. While AG leaders detested the growing theological liberalism within the conference, they nevertheless profited from the practical assistance that came with membership.

III. Growth and Expansion Since 1945.

A. Increased Cooperation. A major turn of events came with the founding of the National Association of Evangelicals (NAE) in 1942 and the willingness of its leadership to include Pentecostal denominations. Consequently Pentecostal executives came into contact with one another and their interest in fellowship played an important role in the formation of the Pentecostal World Conference (PWC, 1947) and the Pentecostal Fellowship of North America (PFNA, 1948). The PFNA adopted seven criteria for cooperation in missions and promised to promote spiritual fellowship and coordination of overseas efforts. However, since neither the PWC nor the PFNA has any legislative powers but serve only to promote consultation and good-will, their actual impact on missions policies has been minimal. After the establishment of the NAE, its missions arm, the Evangelical Foreign Missions Association (EFMA), commenced operation in 1945. The AG, CG, OBSC, and PHC became charter members (the CCNA and ICFG joined later). With this affiliation the Pentecostals gained broader exposure to each other's missions programs and those of other evangelical agencies. Notwithstanding, a formal caucus of Pentecostal missions agencies has never developed.

The relationship with EFMA proved to be difficult during its early years. Citing the resentment expressed by some members against Pentecostal representation, the unproved benefits of association, and the cost of contributions, the AG withdrew in 1950. Three years later, at the urging of Clyde W. Taylor, the executive secretary, they rejoined. Since then the connection has been cordial and positive. Noel Perkin, director of AG foreign missions (1927–59), became the first Pentecostal to serve as EFMA president in 1959–60. His successor over AG missions, J. Philip Hogan, has served three terms as president.

B. Major Agencies.

1. Church of God (Cleveland, Tenn.). CG churches continued to increase their giving to missions during World War II, and a growing number of youth volunteered for missionary service. M. P. Cross received an appointment as the first full-time executive missions secretary in 1941. Before long, field superintendents were appointed to oversee the administration of large geographical sectors of ministry. In 1951 the CG amalgamated with the Full Gospel Church of South Africa, significantly adding to its overseas constituency. Other notable mergers occurred with the Bethel Full Gospel Church in Indonesia (1967), the Evangelical Church of Christ in Yugoslavia (1968), and the Apostolic Church of God in Romania (1980).

By 1964 world missions giving in the CG had exceeded one million dollars annually. Strong auxiliary agencies (e.g., Youth World Evangelism Action, YWEA) have also made important contributions. A significant milestone was passed in

1966 when the overseas membership exceeded that of the U.S. and Canada. To spearhead a thrust on church growth and the internationalization of the organization, the CG conducted its first international meeting outside of the U.S.—in Mexico City in 1973, the International Evangelism Congress. Another was held in Puerto Rico in 1977, and the theme appealed to the church to "Double in a Decade."

In 1980 the general assembly of the CG restructured the world missions department to allow for the election of the director of world missions (formerly the appointed position of executive secretary). Jim O. McClain, Sr., became the first to fill the new position. From 1984 to 1988 J. Herbert Walker served as director of world missions. Walker was a former missionary to Haiti, academic dean of Lee College, superintendent for Europe, and coordinator of mission schools.

In keeping with the central organizational philosophy of the CG, the decision-making process of the missions program has been closely linked to the denomination's world missions board, though the amalgamated churches overseas have retained autonomy. Missionaries have been appointed by the board to be national overseers or top administrators. Their responsibilities involve administration and the training of national leaders and workers. In turn the national ministers serve as pastors, evangelists, and, increasingly, as national overseers.

The CG has remained committed to a centralized form of government that superintends its global constituency. The objectives of CG missions are:

to help (1) unchurched or nominal Christians to become committed disciples of Christ, and (2) non-Christian people to become Christians. For this reason we send missionaries to preach the gospel of Christ, to train national leaders, to proclaim the gospel to their own people and to other nations, to help relieve people who are suffering, and to develop mature disciples for the kingdom of God (*World Missions Policy Manual* 1984, 8).

While commitment to world evangelization is firmly stated, its philosophy of sponsoring indigenous churches abroad is less clear, due no doubt to the structure of the organization. Nevertheless, many national ministers now serve as overseers in their own countries, reflecting the high level of indigenization that has actually occurred on most of its mission fields.

To promote world missions among its constituency, the CG began to publish *Save Our World* (*SOW*) magazine in 1962.

2. Pentecostal Assemblies of Canada. The PAOC established a distinct missions department in 1944, the first to be formed in the denomination. G. R. Upton became the first missionary secretary.

Missions policy has emphasized evangelism, Bible institute instruction, and the building of strong indigenous national church organizations (e.g., Pentecostal Assemblies of the West Indies,

Pentecostal Assemblies of God in Kenya). PAOC printing presses in Africa supply the largest amount of Christian literature on the continent. The Emergency Relief and Development Overseas (ERDO) division was established in 1983 to assist in famine relief, ministry to refugees, adult literacy, vocational and industrial training, water supply, and health clinics.

Among other publications the overseas missions department publishes *ACTION* magazine to inform the denomination of its activities. The current executive director of the department is W. C. Cornelius.

3. General Council of the Assemblies of God. The rapid growth of fraternal AG constituencies overseas after 1960 can be traced to several important factors: the (1) planning for the post–World War II period in 1943; (2) increasing enrollments in the denomination's Bible colleges; (3) mounting numbers of young ministers applying for missionary service; (4) appointment of field directors beginning in 1943; (5) improved coordination through appointment of district missionary secretaries; (6) establishment of a promotions office in 1949 and the already demonstrated effectiveness of promotional literature; (7) growing articulation of a Pentecostal missions strategy with a strong commitment to fostering self-reliant national church organizations abroad, aided by the publication of Melvin L. Hodges' *The Indigenous Church* (1953); (8) the founding of the School of Missions in 1959 to provide specialized instruction to new and furloughed missionaries; (9) the rapid multiplication of overseas Bible institutes to train national pastors, evangelists, and other Christian workers; (10) effective implementation of auxiliary ministries to support the effort (e.g., Speed-the-Light, Boys and Girls Missionary Crusade [BGMC], Light for the Lost, Mobilization and Placement Service [MAPS], Ambassadors in Mission [AIM], Women's Ministries Department, etc.); and (11) the continuing commitment to the belief that only the power and demonstration of the Holy Spirit can bring about world evangelization before the return of Christ.

Since the retirement of Noel Perkin in 1959 as director of AG missions, the Division of Foreign Missions has been led by J. Philip Hogan, a former missionary to China and Taiwan and director of promotions. Under Hogan's leadership, the plans, promotions, and support of the agency's efforts have continued to expand. The agency has sponsored significant international ministries, including International Correspondence Institute and International Media Ministries. Advanced schools of theology as well as creative ventures (e.g., Brazilian Extension School of Theology, Christian Training Network in Latin America) have enhanced the achievement of the agency's goals.

The objectives reflect a careful balancing of priorities: (1) evangelism, (2) the building of indigenous churches after the NT pattern, (3) the training of national believers for preaching the gospel, and (4) acts of compassion. Along with other promotional literature, the AG division of foreign missions publishes *Mountain Movers* magazine.

5. 1987 Statistics

	Regular Missionaries	Countries	Overseas Constituents	Overseas Churches	Missions Budget
AG	1464	118	14,241,714	110,608	$76,679,376
CCNA	20	35	165,000	1,800	$1,000,000
CG	397	113	1,129,343	10,627	$8,000,000
CGP	66	87	172,153	3,048	*
CGIC	8	46	330,207	2,000	$500,000
ICFG	89	62	1,755,732	17,657	$4,755,732
OBSC	30	30	*	*	$900,000
PAOC	168	30	950,000	6,882	$7,500,000
PHC	126	40	111,840	1,396	$4,000,000
UPCI	308	74	681,845	8,550	$11,227,696

Statistics supplied by above agencies. *Not available.

The emphasis on building strong national churches abroad has resulted in fraternal relationships between the American AG and its sister denominations abroad. While no formal worldwide AG organization has ever developed, the mutual concern for world evangelization before the year A.D. 2000 has led this fellowship of churches to promote a "Decade of Harvest." In preparation for this strategic thrust in missions, leaders from AG and other Pentecostal constituencies around the world met in Springfield, Missouri, in the summer of 1988 to "link arms in intercessory prayer for God's direction and anointing. Leaders have also begun to confer to formulate a united strategy for world evangelization" (AG Division of Foreign Missions, "Decade of Harvest" [n.d.]).

4. *United Pentecostal Church International* (UPCI). In 1945 two of the major Oneness organizations—the Pentecostal Church, Inc., and the Pentecostal Assemblies of Jesus Christ—merged to form the United Pentecostal Church International. Since both agencies had sponsored some of the same missionaries, amalgamation of the missions programs was easy. By 1954 there were seventy-one missionaries under appointment serving in sixteen fields. The missions efforts of the UPCI grew rapidly after the merger. The first foreign missionary secretary of the new organization was Wynn T. Stairs; in 1956 the title was changed to director of foreign missions. A promotions department was formed in 1968.

The foreign missions division of the UPCI is supervised by a foreign missions board consisting of the director, secretary, coordinator of overseas ministries, and nine other members. The Foreign Missions Administrative Committee is a resident committee that oversees the daily operation of the agency, chaired by Harry E. Schism, director of foreign missions. The objectives include the sending forth of missionaries, training of national ministers, building indigenous national church organizations abroad, establishing an international fellowship of the UPCI, and creating a love for truth and holiness in every member. To advertise the news of its missions program, the UPCI publishes *Global Witness* magazine.

IV. Historical Development of Pentecostal Missiology.

A. Early Missiological Perspectives. Early Pentecostals often referred to three Scripture passages that articulated their mission to the world: Matthew 24:14; Mark 16:15–18; and Acts 1:8. The Great Commission of Jesus, the promise of apostolic power to accompany proclamation, and the imminent return of Christ provided the motivation for the growing dispersion of missionaries. Hence, the Pentecostals aimed to convert the heathen to Christianity ("plucking brands from the burning") with no thought of universalism.

Not all Pentecostals accepted Parham's xenolalic interpretation of glossolalia. In *The Baptism of the Holy Ghost and Fire,* an important early treatise by Minnie F. Abrams, the author noted that when one receives Spirit baptism, "the fire of God's love will so burn within you that you will desire the salvation of souls . . . and realize that He to whom all power is given has imparted some of that power to you, sufficient to do all that He has called you to do" (1906, 44). To Abrams, the baptism in the Holy Spirit brought a deeper relationship with Christ and filled the believer with love for the lost. Consequently, "when those anointed to preach the gospel are bold enough to accept and exercise the gifts of the Spirit, and to do the signs and miracles authorized in the word of God, in three years time the gospel will spread more rapidly and bring more under its power, than it has in the past 300 years" (ibid., 72–73). In a similar vein, J. Roswell Flower, later a founding father and missionary secretary of the AG, wrote in 1908: "The baptism of the Holy Ghost does not consist in simply speaking in tongues. . . . It fills our souls with the love of God for lost humanity, and makes us much more willing to leave home, friends, and all to work in His vineyard, even if it be far away among the heathen" (McGee, 1986, 45). As Pentecostals found the xenolalic interpretation of tongues to be inaccurate, they increasingly turned to the perspective of Abrams, Flower, and others, which focused on the value of glossolalia for empowerment, prayer, praise, and love for the unsaved.

Through the years, therefore, Pentecostal publications have contained thousands of accounts of healings, exorcisms, and deliverances from chemical addictions; many of these miraculous testimonies were in foreign lands and were a result of gospel proclamation. Missionaries have attested their willingness to confront evil powers due to the spiritual dynamic of the baptism in the Holy Spirit.

B. The Influence of A. B. Simpson and the CMA. Since a large contingent of early pastors and missionaries received training at Simpson's Missionary Training Institute at Nyack, New York, the first Bible institute in America, the CMA had a marked influence on the development of Pentecostal missions, especially that of the AG (the largest Pentecostal missions agency). At least three areas of influence are detectable. First, the Bible institute program at Nyack, which focused attention more on spiritual than on academic training, became the pattern for the Bethel Bible Training Institute at Newark, New Jersey (1916) and Central Bible Institute, Springfield, Missouri (1922), both begun by former members of the CMA. The various emphases on missions at Nyack were repeated at Bethel and Central, and probably elsewhere. Both trained many students who became missionaries.

Since the early missionaries rarely had college or university training (there were notable exceptions), the Pentecostals readily adopted the Bible institute approach for theological training. Short-

Roland Allen, an Anglican missionary to China, unwittingly exerted a profound influence on Pentecostal missions through his writings, particularly *Missionary Methods: St. Paul's or Ours?*

er than the traditional program of ministerial preparation, it offered students an intensely biblical education, a dynamic spiritual atmosphere through daily chapel services and prayer meetings, and a speedier entry into the ministry. A former CMA pastor, David Wesley Myland, who joined the ranks of the Pentecostal movement, echoed Simpson's concerns by stating that he "would rather see one person baptized in the Holy Ghost and fire, dead in love with God's Word, reading it day and night and praying the heathen through to salvation than to see a score of missionaries go out with only intellectual equipment" (1911, 71).

The emphasis on the Christian life of faith represents a second influence of Simpson; its roots, however, extend beyond him to George Müller and leaders in the late-nineteenth-century faith-healing movement. Müller's philanthropic enterprises in England exemplified the benefits of the faith life and God's miraculous provision. Without publicly mentioning his needs, finances and material assistance were always forthcoming. Simpson urged CMA missionaries to trust God for their needs, since they traveled abroad without fixed salaries; he did, however, encourage the membership to contribute regularly.

Similarly, Simpson believed that the benefits of Christ's atonement extend beyond the spiritual to the physical nature of humankind. Missionaries, therefore, should exercise faith for their own healing and pray for the sick on the foreign field. The healing of diseases and other manifestations of divine power would then propel the success of Christian missions. Simpson's missionaries usually shunned medicines and vaccines. The early Pentecostal missionaries, some directly influenced by him, usually held the same view. They easily linked prayer for the sick with the work of the Spirit. As was true of the CMA, the Pentecostals suffered the loss of some missionaries (e.g., Christian Schoonmaker, an AG missionary to India [formerly with the CMA], died from smallpox in 1919, having refused inoculation).

The missiological perspectives taught at Nyack represent the third influence on Pentecostals. Rooted in the writings of Rufus Anderson and Henry Venn, the strategy of building strong national churches overseas through application of indigenous church principles received new attention at the turn of the century. These principles, expressed succinctly in the "three selfs" (self-propagating, self-supporting, self-governing), were popularized through the publication of *The Planting and Development of Missionary Churches* (1886) by John L. Nevius, a Presbyterian missionary to China. It is important to note that students at Nyack studied the teachings of Nevius. The AG, in the second year of its existence, resolved "to promote the evangelization of heathen lands according to New Testament methods" (General Council Minutes [Combined Minutes], 1914–17, 9). This limited statement may well indicate the foundation for indigenous principles (in part transmitted through the CMA), on which the longer AG declaration on missions was based in 1921.

C. The Emerging Influence of Roland Allen. For decades of the Pentecostal missions enterprise, many missionaries followed the paternalistic practices of the established Protestant denominations. When the Lord did not return as quickly as expected, they naturally followed the lead of others. Missionaries often lived on "mission compounds," operating charitable institutions such as orphanages and schools and retaining tight control over local pastors and evangelists by paying them with funds raised in America. Although the missionaries cherished their freedom to be directed personally by the Holy Spirit, their paternalism in some instances actually stifled the building of strong national churches. As time passed, many, but not all, Pentecostals moved away from paternalism to plan and work for the development of indigenous church organizations.

The high Anglican missionary to North China, Roland Allen, reflecting the missiological perspectives of Anderson, Venn, and Nevius, proved to be the most powerful influence in the development of Pentecostal missiology. With the publication of his books *Missionary Methods: St. Paul's or Ours?* (1912) and *The Spontaneous Expansion of the Church and the Causes Which Hinder It* (1927), Allen unwittingly shaped the future course of Pentecostal missions. Through these books several key individuals were able to mold a new generation of missionaries. Allen's emphasis on the Pauline methods of church planting, as seen in the Book of Acts, naturally appealed to the Pentecostals who believed that the dynamic power ("signs and wonders") of the NT church had been restored.

Alice E. Luce, a former missionary to India with the Church Missionary Society and later to Hispanics in America, may have been the first Pentecostal exponent of Allen's teachings. His first book made a deep impression on her while she was still in India. Later, as an AG missionary, she wrote a series of articles for the *Pentecostal Evangel* in 1921; these articles helped set the stage for the denomination's strong endorsement of indigenous church principles at its general council gathering later that year. Through these articles, Luce advocated Allen's perspectives on church planting. Foreign leadership may be necessary for a time, but it cannot be based on attitudes of racial or cultural superiority. Such guidance must be founded on greater experience and spiritual maturity. Missionary leadership should model humility and obedience to the Holy Spirit if younger national ministers are to be properly trained to take their places.

While Luce approved Allen's methods, her Pentecostal theology led her to believe that apostolic methods of evangelism and church planting would be followed by the power and demonstration of the Holy Spirit. She challenged her readers by asking, "When we go forth to preach the Full Gospel [salvation, baptism in the Holy Spirit, divine healing, second coming of Christ], are we going to expect an experience like that of the denominational missionaries, or shall we look for the signs to follow?" (*Pentecostal Evangel* [January 22, 1921], 6). Luce had a particularly strong influence on Ralph D. Williams and Henry C. Ball, both indigenous-church pioneers among Latin Americans.

Another and more influential voice supporting these methods within AG missions was that of Noel Perkin. Perkin had served as a missionary to Argentina with Harry L. Turner, a later president of the CMA. As director, Perkin urged missionary candidates to familiarize themselves with Allen's books before going overseas.

D. The Achievement of Melvin L. Hodges. One missionary who followed Perkin's advice was Melvin L. Hodges (1909–88), an AG missionary to Central America and later field director for Latin America and the West Indies. Upon arriving in Central America in 1936, he began working with Ralph D. Williams to put indigenous principles into effect.

In 1953 the Gospel Publishing House published *The Indigenous Church* written by Hodges. A series of lectures at the 1950 Missionary Conference in Springfield, Missouri, provided the basis for the book. A year later, when Moody Press gained permission to reprint the book, it gained wider publicity. The book proved to be the most significant work on missions strategy and theology that the Pentecostal movement had produced. In eleven chapters, Hodges discussed the nature of a NT church and its implementation. Relying on his experiences in working with national church organizations, he also discussed how to change an existing paternalistic structure to an indigenous one. To a considerable extent, Hodges repeated the methods advocated by Anderson, Venn, Nevius, and particularly Allen. The book's uniqueness consisted in its practical nature and fusion of indigenous principles with Pentecostal theology. He asserted that "the faith which Pentecostal people have in the ability of the Holy Spirit to give spiritual gifts and supernatural abilities to the common people . . . has raised up a host of lay preachers and leaders of unusual spiritual ability—not unlike the rugged fishermen who first followed the Lord" (Hodges, 1953, 132). The application of Hodges' teachings have played a major role in the spectacular spread of Pentecostalism overseas, particularly in Latin America.

The timing of this publication coincided with the AG's growing concern to further articulate its mission and provide more specialized training for missionary candidates. Hodges' exposition assisted the agency at a critical time in its history when forces (e.g., T. L. Osborn's Association for Native Evangelism) were at work to undermine the commitment to indigenous principles.

E. Recent Publications and Statements. The need for missions education in the home churches prompted the AG to publish *Our World Witness* (1963) by Noel Perkin and John Garlock, and the CG to publish *The Church and World Missions* (1970) by Vessie D. Hargrave. The prolific Melvin L. Hodges continued to contribute books on missiology and church growth including *Build My Church* (1957), *Growth in Your Christian Ministry* (1960), *A Guide to Church Planting* (1973), *A Theology of the Church and Its Mission* (1977), and *The Indigenous Church and the Missionary* (1978). When *The Indigenous Church* was published by Moody Press and later articles were published in edited works and journals (e.g.,

"A Pentecostal's View of Mission Strategy," *International Review of Missions* 57 [July 1968]: 304–10), Hodges became the first Pentecostal to publish on missiology outside of denominational publications.

A significant strategy of Pentecostal missions appeared with *Breaking the Stained-Glass Barrier* (1973) by David A. Womack, a former AG missionary to Latin America. The publication of this book by Harper and Row contributed to its widespread popularity. A CG perspective on the missionary enterprise appeared in the same year with *Unto the Uttermost* (1973) by Wade H. Horton. Successful church planter David E. Godwin (AG) published *Church Planting Methods* (1984). AG missionaries Delmer R. and Eleanor R. Guynes contributed *The Apostolic Nature of the Church* (1986), a theology of missions. Practical advice on indigenous church relationships (national church organizations with sending agencies) can be found in *Partnership in Mission* (1979, 1986) by Morris O. Williams, a former AG missionary and field director for Africa.

The most significant Pentecostal missiology to appear in recent years is *The Third Force in Missions* (1985) by Paul A. Pomerville, formerly an AG missionary. Pomerville notes that the lack of emphasis in evangelical missions on the work of the Holy Spirit can be traced to the rationalistic impact of Protestant scholasticism through its overidentification of the Spirit with the written Word and an abhorrence of personal "experience" as a factor in spiritual authority. Accordingly, he states that "as a renewal movement, emphasizing a neglected dimension of the Holy Spirit's ministry, Pentecostalism sets the subtle influence of post-Reformation scholasticism in bold relief. It is at this point that Pentecostalism functions as a 'corrective' in contemporary missions" (Pomerville, 1985, 79).

Pomerville also maintains that the NT theology of the kingdom of God lays the groundwork for properly understanding the outpouring of the Spirit both then and now. The proclamation of the gospel, coupled with the dynamic work of the Spirit should characterize the extension of God's kingdom before the return of Christ. This should form the heart of Pentecostal missiology. Although he praises George Eldon Ladd (*The Presence of the Future*, 1974) for his insights on the kingdom of God, he faults him for not adequately addressing the work of the Spirit that must accompany it.

This emphasis on nondispensational premillennialism also reflects a trend in Pentecostal theology away from the specially adapted dispensationalism that has been popular in Pentecostalism since its beginning (e.g., Finis Jennings Dake, *Dake's Annotated Reference Bible* [1963]; cf. Gerald T. Sheppard, "Pentecostalism and the Hermeneutics of Dispensationalism: Anatomy of an Uneasy Relationship," *Pneuma* 6 [Fall 1984]: 5–33). Pomerville's formulation of a Pentecostal missiology is an important achievement in this vital area but is not the final word.

A valuable resource for the study of Pentecostal missions and church growth is *Azusa Street and Beyond* (1986) edited by L. Grant McClung, Jr., a former CG missionary to Europe. Articles come under the topics of historical perspectives, theological motivations, strategic/practical issues, the Church Growth movement, and future cautions and challenges.

Two major Pentecostal denominations have reviewed their mission to the world within the last two decades and have issued statements explaining their commitments. The AG Council on Evangelism, meeting in St. Louis, Missouri, in 1968, issued the "Declaration at St. Louis." The papers for this gathering are found in Richard Champion, Edward S. Caldwell, and Gary Leggett, eds., *Our Mission in Today's World* (1968). In 1983 the CG conducted an International Congress on World Evangelism that convened in Cleveland, Tennessee, and adopted "A Covenant on World Evangelization" (McClung, 1986, 171–72).

F. Historical Perspectives. Early Pentecostal literature reflects a strong triumphalism, no doubt caused by its restorationist impulse. Surprisingly, the same statement on the place of Pentecostal missions in the history of the church appears in two early missions documents: the AG *Missionary Manual* (1931) and Horace McCracken's *History of Church of God Missions* (1943). The original author of the statement (possibly Noel Perkin, but this is uncertain), stated that the Lord's Pentecostal missionary movement began on the Day of Pentecost. Led and energized by the Holy Spirit, it spawned a remarkable expansion of the Christian faith until the close of the first century. At that time people rejected the Spirit's leadership, and the movement halted; the Dark Ages followed. Although the Reformation brought partial restoration, it failed to complete its task. In the twentieth century, "the professing church is largely in apostasy, neither cold nor hot, and is ready to be spued out" (McCracken, 1943, 8). With the "outpouring of the Spirit" in 1901 "the Lord's Pentecostal missionary movement was resumed" (*Missionary Manual*, 1931, 7). As a result of its resumption, hundreds of missionaries have traveled overseas and hundreds of thousands of converts have been made.

This restorationist interpretation of history actually says more about the contemporary feelings of isolation and rejection by other Christians that the Pentecostals experienced than it does about the course of church history. With the growing alignment of denominational (Trinitarian) Pentecostals with Evangelicals (NAE, etc.) in the 1940s, later histories and manuals made little or no reference to it. Valuable surveys of the Pentecostal movement addressing its history and missions expansion include Stanley H. Frodsham, *With Signs Following* (rev. ed., 1946); Donald Gee, *To the Uttermost Part* (c. 1932) and *The Pentecostal Movement* (rev. ed., 1949); Gordon F. Atter, *The Third Force* (1962); and Karl Roebling, *Pentecost Around the World* (1978).

Many Pentecostal missionaries realized from the earliest years that they had to maintain contact with publications such as *Apostolic Faith, New Acts, Latter Rain Evangel*, et al. to publicize their ministries and inform the readers of their needs. Hence, letters from missionaries, frequently containing accounts of healings and deliverances, abound in these periodicals. However, historical treatments of the enterprise from the earliest period are rare; a notable exception is E. May Law's *Pentecostal Mission Work in South China* (c. 1916). As the missions agencies (independent and denominational) grew in size and sophistication, they increasingly produced their own magazines to highlight their activities, sometimes including references to the role of Pentecostal missions in the history of the church. Independent missions agencies sponsored such publications as *The Gospel Call* (REEM), *The Record of Faith* (TES), and *Full Gospel Missionary Herald* (PMSCA). Denominational publications such as the *Church of God Evangel* (CG, formerly *Evening Light and Church of God Evangel*), *Pentecostal Evangel* (AG), and the *Bridal Call Foursquare* (ICFG) included sections devoted to missions. Later they produced magazines to focus entirely on missions (e.g., the AG *Missionary Challenge* [1944]). In addition, the AG department of foreign missions developed a series of booklets in the 1930s and 1940s describing the work of its missionaries on various fields (e.g., Jacob J. Mueller, *With Our Missionaries in North India* [1937], Arthur E. Wilson, *A Visit to Mosi Land, French West Africa* [c. 1932], and H. C. Ball and A. E. Luce, *Glimpses of Our Latin American Work in the United States and Mexico* [1940]). These contain valuable historical accounts for tracing the development of the work.

Missionary biographies and autobiographies began to appear, especially in the 1930s. These accounts served to promote the cause of missions and provide more information and personal details about the work of individuals overseas (e.g., Marion Keller, *Twenty Years in Africa: 1913–1933* [n.d.]; Stanley H. Frodsham, *Wholly for God* [1934], and Helen I. Gustavson, *Tsinan, China: The Opening of an Effectual Door* [1941]).

Broader and more scholarly historical treatments of Pentecostal missions appeared later in denominational histories (e.g., Joseph E. Campbell, *The Pentecostal Holiness Church: 1898–1948* [1951]) or in studies of the entire movement (e.g., Nils Bloch-Hoell, *The Pentecostal Movement* [1964]; John T. Nichol, *Pentecostalism* [1966]; Prudencio Damboriena, S. J., *Tongues As of Fire* [1969]; and Walter J. Hollenweger, *The Pentecostals* [1972]). These proved to be especially helpful because historians of Christian missions have until recently given only scant attention to the Pentecostal movement. Helpful studies of Pentecostal church growth overseas by outside observers have also been helpful in interpreting its progress and importance (e.g., William R. Read, Victor M. Monterroso, and Harmon A. Johnson, *Latin American Church Growth* [1969]; Steven D. Glazier, *Perspectives on Pentecostalism* (1980); and the popular treatment by C. Peter Wagner, *Look Out! The Pentecostals Are Coming* [1973]).

The first history devoted entirely to an agency's program appeared with Horace McCracken's *History of Church of God Missions* (1943); this was surpassed in scope and detail by Charles W. Conn's *Where the Saints Have Trod* (1959). Historical treatments of AG missions have included Serena M. Hodges, ed., *Look on the Fields* (1956); B. P. Wilson, *Early Pentecostal and Assemblies of God Missionaries of the Northwest District* (n.d.); and Joyce Wells Booze, *Into All the World* (1980). Major histories of AG missions began to appear with the publication of *Making Many Rich* (1955) by Elizabeth A. Galley Wilson; *The Silent Pentecostals* (1979) by Victor De Leon; and the recent *This Gospel Shall Be Preached* (1986) by Gary B. McGee. Important articles on AG missions history also have appeared in the denomination's archival quarterly, *Assemblies of God Heritage*.

V. Missions Education. Curricular offerings in missiology were slim in the early Pentecostal Bible institutes. When Central Bible Institute (CBI), Springfield, Missouri, opened in 1922, it offered one course in missions: "Missions and Missionaries." The course covered the history of Christian missions, the present efforts of Pentecostal missionaries, and "Home Missionary" work as well (McGee, 1986, 88). The recognition that specialized training would enhance the success of missionaries developed in the 1940s. The AG offered an advanced course of study at CBI beginning in 1944. With the founding of the American Association of Bible Colleges in 1947, Pentecostal schools began to offer four-year baccalaureate programs, and majors in missions studies soon appeared.

In 1959 the AG instituted the School of Missions, which offered specialized training to missionaries and continuing education for those home on furloughs. The school has continued to meet annually in the summers for several weeks. An additional instructional period for new recruits has been provided and is currently called Pre-Field Orientation (formerly Extended Session, 1982–1984).

Graduate and seminary training in missions began to appear in the 1970s. These institutions, some offering advanced degrees in missiology, include Oral Roberts University (1965), Assemblies of God Theological Seminary (1973), Church of God School of Theology (1975), CBN University (1977), California Theological Seminary (1983), and Southern California College Graduate School (1983).

VI. Independent Ministries. Since the beginning of Pentecostal missions, there has been a strong current of independency. The anti-organizational sentiments of many missionaries reflected the painful rejection by former denominations over their newfound theology, as well as their intense desire to live by faith and be led totally by the Spirit in their ministries. Thus, relying on individuals and supporting congregations, independent Pentecostal missionaries have continued in ministry for many years, some with considerable success. Their number, the scope of their ministries, and the success they have achieved is nevertheless difficult to ascertain.

While the fears of many were allayed by the benefits of joining with Pentecostal agencies (e.g., the personnel in the Missionary Conference who joined the AG), the tension between independency and structure has continued to the present. Although the denominational agencies place high value on team work and have believed that the Spirit can work through committees and boards as well as individuals, the desire to be directed personally by the Spirit lies at the core of Pentecostal concerns. (For a study of the utilization of the gifts of the Spirit in church-planting, see Paul B. Watney, "Ministry Gifts: God's Provision for Effective Mission," D. Miss. diss., Fuller Theological Seminary, 1979).

Over the years various individual and group initiatives have surfaced to promote effective overseas evangelism without the strictures of denominational boards. These include the efforts of the faith-healing evangelists in overseas crusades in the 1950s and 1960s (e.g., M. A. Daoud, Tommy Hicks, and Morris Cerullo). T. L. Osborn, another evangelist, began the Association for Native Evangelism in 1953. Gordon Lindsay's foreign missions efforts were advertised through the pages of his *Voice of Healing* magazine, known later as *Christ for the Nations.* Jimmy Swaggart began Jimmy Swaggart Ministries as a parachurch agency (to the AG) to promote world evangelization through his television ministry and to subsidize the building of Bible institutes, churches, schools, and child-care ministries. Other important ministries include Youth With a Mission (YWAM), founded by Loren Cunningham; Asian Outreach, directed by Paul E. Kauffman; Christian Fellowship Union, led by Steven P. Johnson; and Christ for India, Inc., directed by P. J. Titus.

In some instances, independent missionaries have been supported by networks of churches such as the Fellowship of Christian Assemblies, which reflect the congregational influence of Swedish Pentecostalism. Their approach to missiology can be found in many countries (e.g., Brazil) where Swedish missionaries and others holding to congregational church polity have ministered. At times, tensions have emerged on fields between agencies that promote national church organizations and Bible institutes for training clergy and advocates of the local congregation as the primary base for missions and education.

VII. Missions and the Charismatic Movement. Unlike the Pentecostals who had to start their own agencies, the charismatics who remained in their churches had the benefits of established missions boards. As the denominational renewals gathered strength and gained internal approval, the number of charismatic missionaries serving on these boards increased, although their numbers are difficult to obtain, perhaps because of denominational sensitivities in some cases. On the other hand, independent charismatics have begun their own missions agencies, and only limited information on them is available.

Criticisms by some Pentecostals have been leveled at charismatics (both denominational and independent) for their seeming failure to take a more active involvement in world evangelization. Since revivalism and missions have been associated on the American scene, the lack of missions involvement appears to challenge the legitimacy of the charismatic movement as a genuine revival movement.

This perspective appears to be short-sighted, however, since it is important to consider the differences in development between the Pentecostal and charismatic movements. Those charismatics who remained within their denominations to work for renewal were challenged to revitalize existing churches with their new-found spiritual insights. The need to address theological and ecclesiastical issues and gain denominational acceptance necessarily consumed considerable energy. Nevertheless, there are strong indicators that the various branches of the charismatic movement are increasingly focusing their efforts on world evangelism.

A. North American Congresses on the Holy Spirit and World Evangelization. Of great importance were the recent North American Congresses on the Holy Spirit and World Evangelization in New Orleans (1986, 1987), sponsored by the North American Renewal Service Committee, attracting thousands of charismatics. Chaired by Pentecostal historian Vinson Synan, the gatherings included participants from a wide range of churches (Roman Catholic, Presbyterian and Reformed, Lutheran, Baptist, Episcopal, Wesleyan Holiness, Mennonite, Covenant, Methodist, and classical Pentecostal). As many as 35,000 to 40,000 attended the sessions of the second congress (July 22–26, 1987). The announced goal called for the registrants to make the 1990s a decade of evangelization in order to win at least half of the world's population to Christ by the year 2000. Synan observed that "this conference brought evangelization into the thinking of the charismatic renewal. . . . Where evangelization has never before'been a big part of the charismatic experience, now it will become the major thrust of the renewal" (Lawson, 1987, 58).

B. Association of International Mission Services (AIMS). The growing charismatic interest in foreign missions is also illustrated by the recent formation of the Association of International Mission Services. The idea for such an organization originated in a 1985 meeting at Christ for the Nations Institute in Dallas, Texas. The agency commenced operation in the following year "to challenge and mobilize the church for World missions and to expand its capabilities and opportunities to fulfill the Great Commission. AIMS will provide a framework for unity and fellowship among churches, mission agencies, and training institutions in cooperative efforts for world evangelization" (Association of International Mission Services 1986, 3). AIMS also serves as a clearinghouse to accredit charismatic agencies following a self-study and screening process.

There are four categories of members: agencies, organizations, institutes, and churches. Agencies and organizations include African Intercontinental Missions, Bibles for India, China Ministries International, David Livingstone Missionary Foundation, Evangel Bible Translators, and Tentmakers International. Member institutes include California Theological Seminary, CBN University, Christ for the Nations Institute, and Oral Roberts University. The membership also contains ninety-two churches. Currently the organization has 185 members.

The leaders of AIMS hope to eventually influence all branches of the charismatic movement. Howard Foltz, a former missionary to Europe and currently professor at CBN University, serves as president. *The AIMS Report* publicizes the activities of the organization. See also MISSIOLOGY; CHURCH GROWTH; STATISTICS, GLOBAL.

Bibliography: M. F. Abrams, *The Baptism of the Holy Ghost and Fire*, 2d ed. (1906); Assemblies of God Division of Foreign Missions, "Decade of Harvest" (n.d.); idem, *1987 Annual Report* (1987); Association of International Mission Services, *The AIMS Report* 1 (Summer 1986): 3; idem, "Background Paper" (1987); H. P. Beach and C. H. Fahs, eds., *World Missionary Atlas* (1925); D. L. Burk, ed., *The Foreign Missions Story 1988* (1988); Church of God World Missions, *World Missions Policy Manual* (1984); A. W. Clanton, *United We Stand* (1970); G. D. Clementson, *Charles Hamilton Pridgeon* (1963); W. T. Coggins, "Evangelical Foreign Missions Association: A Brief History" (1984); C. W. Conn, *Like a Mighty Army* (rev. ed., 1977); idem, *Our First 100 Years* (1986); L. De Caro, *Our Heritage* (1977); General Council Minutes [Combined Minutes] 1914–17; D. E. Harrell, Jr., *All Things Are Possible* (1975); P. Hawkes, "Pentecostalism in Canada," in *The Holy Spirit in the Scriptures and the Church*, ed. R. Stronstad and L. M. Van Kleek (1987), 63–76; M. L. Hodges, *The Indigenous Church* (1953); P. Humphrey [Scarborough], *J. H. Ingram: Missionary Dean* (1966); J. H. King, *Yet Speaketh* (1949); G. G. Kulbeck, *What God Hath Wrought* (1958); K. S. Latourette, *A History of the Expansion of Christianity*, 4 (1941); S. Lawson, "The Big Charismatic Get-Together," *Charisma* (September 1987), 56–58; A. E. Luce, "Paul's Missionary Methods" (part 3), *PE* (February 5, 1921), 6–7; I. Lundgren, "Lewi Petrus and the Swedish Pentecostal Movement," in *Essays on Apostolic Themes*, ed. P. Elbert (1985), 158–72; G. McClung, "From BRIDGES (McGavran, 1955) to WAVES (Wagner, 1983): Pentecostals and the Church Growth Movement," *Pneuma* 7 (Spring 1985): 5–18; L. G. McClung, Jr., ed., *Azusa Street and Beyond* (1986); G. B. McGee, "Assemblies of God Mission Theology: A Historical Perspective," *International Bulletin of Missionary Research* 10 (October 1986): 166, 168–70; idem, "The Azusa Street Revival and Twentieth-Century Missions," *International Bulletin of Missionary Research* 12 (April 1988): 58–61; idem, "Levi R. Lupton and the Ill-Fated Pentecostal Missionary Union in America," paper presented at the 16th meeting of the Society for Pentecostal Studies, Costa Mesa, California, November 14, 1986; idem, *This Gospel Shall Be Preached* (1986); W. W. Menzies, *Anointed to Serve* (1971); T. W. Miller, "The Canadian 'Azusa': The Hebden Mission in Toronto," *Pneuma* 8 (Spring 1986): 5–29; R. B. Mitchell, *Heritage and Horizons* (1982); C. C. Moree, ed., *Into All the World* (1984); D. W. Myland, *The Latter Rain Covenant and Pentecostal Power* (2d ed., 1911); D. Shibley, "Charismatics Aim for Missions," *Charisma* (December 1987), 65; A. B. Simpson, *Annual Report of the Superintendent and Board of Managers*, May 4, 1900; idem, *The Eleventh Annual Report of the Christian and Missionary Alliance*, May 27, 1908; V. Synan, *The Holiness-Pentecostal Movement in the United States* (1971); idem, "A Vision for the Year 2000," *Charisma* (August 1987), 42–44, 46; J. H. Walker, Jr., "Reaping the Harvest," in *The Promise and the Power*, ed. D. N. Bowdle (1980), 53–83.

G. B. McGee

MITCHELL, ROBERT BRYANT (1905–). Administrator, educator, and missionary leader for Open Bible Standard Churches (OBSC). He is the eldest of the six A. E. Mitchell children, all of whom followed their parents into the ministry. He graduated from the Bible Institute of Los Angeles (Biola, 1924) and attended UCLA to prepare for a medical career but transferred to L.I.F.E. Bible College and prepared for the ministry. Following ordination with the International Church of the Foursquare Gospel (ICFG) in 1929, he founded three churches in the Midwest and taught at two ICFG schools. Along with thirty-two other ministers, he withdrew in 1932 to form the Open Bible Evangelistic Association (later OBSC). He served as dean of Open Bible College (1935–53), general chairman of OBSC (1953–67), missionary director of OBSC (1967–73), and part-time instructor at Eugene Bible College (1975–79). He also served as chairman of the Pentecostal Fellowship of North America (1967–68) and on committees of the National Association of Evangelicals. He wrote the official history of OBSC, *Heritage and Horizons* (1982).

A charter member of the Open Bible Standard Churches, R. Bryant Mitchell served as general superintendent, director of missions, and educator.

Bibliography: R. Mitchell, *Heritage and Horizons* (1982).

W. E. Warner

MJORUD, HERBERT (1910–). Pioneer exponent of charismatic renewal among Lutherans. In 1962 Mjorud received the gift of tongues during a visit to the Episcopal parish of Dennis Bennett, in Seattle, Washington. He was serving as an evangelist for the American Lutheran Church (ALC) at the time. He had earlier experienced miraculous healings while serving a congregation in Anchorage, Alaska.

Mjorud began to include a charismatic message in his evangelistic meetings, which led to controversy. When his six-year term as an evangelist with the ALC expired, his call was not renewed. He formed his own evangelistic association and continued to hold meetings throughout the U.S.

In 1968 he began a series of around-the-world evangelistic tours, with particular concentration of work in Sri Lanka, where he was instrumental in starting two Bible schools. Key elements of his personal experience, pastoral concern, and theological perspective are summed up in the books and articles that he authored.

Mjorud was healed of cancer in 1981 after he had been sent home to die.

Bibliography: L. Christenson, ed., *Welcome, Holy Spirit* (1987); H. Mjorud, *Dare to Believe* (1975); idem, *Fighting Cancer with Christ* (1983); idem, *What's Baptism All About?* (1979).   L. Christenson

Mary Gill Moise operated a "faith home" in St. Louis and also helped train future ministers. Mary Barnes worked with her in her home of mercy.

MOISE, MARY GILL (1850–1930). A pioneer in Pentecostal social ministry in St. Louis. "Mother" Moise began her mission work under Episcopal bishop Daniel S. Tuttle. About 1907 she united with Pentecostals and operated her home of mercy. Her home was also called a "faith home" and practiced an open-door policy for wayward girls, drunks, prostitutes, and other social outcasts. The home was also used as a Bible training center for future preachers. Early Pentecostals traveling through St. Louis always found a welcome. Her work with homeless girls won for her a first prize in the 1904 World's Fair.

Moise accepted rebaptism in the name of Jesus, which placed her and the work in the Oneness branch of Pentecostalism. She also accepted the belief that Christians need never die. At her death a St. Louis newspaper called her "one of the most widely known mission workers in the country."

Bibliography: W. Warner, "Mother Mary Moise of St. Louis," *AG Heritage* (Spring 1986), 6–7, 13–14.
                    W. E. Warner

MONTAGUE, GEORGE T. (1929–). Catholic charismatic leader and biblical scholar. Montague joined the Marianist order as a young man, was ordained as a priest in 1958, and completed his doctoral dissertation on Paul in 1960. Baptized in the Spirit in 1970, he soon became a popular speaker at charismatic conferences. His personal testimony is given in *Riding the Wind* (1974), and his charismatic experience is joined with biblical scholarship in *The Spirit and His Gifts* (1974) and *The Holy Spirit: Growth of a Biblical Tradition* (1976). Montague served on the National Service Committee for Catholic Charismatic Renewal (1978–82).

Montague has held responsible positions in academic and ecclesiastical circles, being closely associated with the Catholic Biblical Quarterly (general editor [1973–75]) and serving as seminary rector and university professor in St. Louis, Missouri, and Toronto, Ontario. Other books include *Maturing in Christ* (1964), *Building Christ's Body* (1975), and *Mark: Good News for Hard Times* (1981). Since 1982 Montague was director of novices for the Marianists in Katmandu, Nepal. He returned to the U.S. in 1988.
                    P. D. Hocken

MONTGOMERY, CARRIE JUDD (1858–1946). A minister-teacher, writer, editor, director of faith homes, and social worker whose ministry spanned more than sixty-five years. Worldwide, Carrie Judd Montgomery was best known for her *Triumphs of Faith;* the subtitle described the magazine as "A Monthly Journal Devoted to Faith Healing and to the Promotion of Christian Holiness." Her religious associations included the Episcopal Church, the Holiness healing movement, the Christian and Missionary Alliance (CMA), the Salvation Army, and the Pentecostal movement. Always interested in building bridges between diverse groups, she operated several transdenominational ministries.

I. The Early Years and Her Healing. Reared in an Episcopal home in Buffalo, New York, where piety was practiced daily, Carrie Judd was one of eight children. At the age of eleven she made a spiritual commitment and was later confirmed at the Episcopal Church. Two of the Judd children died of tuberculosis, and Carrie was not well. While attending the Buffalo Normal School, she suffered a fall that forced her to drop out of school. She became an invalid and was not expected to live. Through the ministry of a black woman, Mrs. Edward Mix, Carrie was healed, and her story was told in the *Buffalo Commercial Advertiser* on October 20, 1880.

Judd later wrote a book, *The Prayer of Faith* (1880), which gave her testimony and encouraged others to believe for healing. A. B. Simpson read the book and later developed a lifelong friendship with her. Her miraculous healing also brought her into the leadership circle of the growing faith movement. In addition to Simpson,

Montgomery shared the faith healing platform with Charles Cullis, W. E. Boardman, Maria B. Woodworth-Etter, and Mrs. Michael Baxter of Bethshan, London.

II. Publications. Judd's first literary effort was published when she was fifteen. A Buffalo newspaper published a poem she had written and then published others. Also as a teen she began working in the office of a health magazine, an experience that would help prepare her for the publishing phase of her life. In addition to her book *The Prayer of Faith,* she wrote her autobiography, *Under His Wings* (c. 1936), and other books, including *Secrets of Victory* (1921), *Heart Melody* (c. 1922), and *The Life of Praise.* Her biggest literary output, however, was *Triumphs of Faith,* a magazine she founded in 1881 and edited for sixty-five years. The magazine bridged the Holiness and Pentecostal movements, and its pages provided a nonsectarian forum for a variety of denominations to express concern and teachings on common themes that greatly influenced the healing movement, social work, and worldwide missions.

III. Early Ministry. Although it was unusual to hear women speak in public during the 1880s, the timid Carrie Judd began to give her testimony of healing. She received a good response among holiness believers, and she began to speak at conventions that A. B. Simpson sponsored. In 1885 William E. Boardman invited Judd to speak at his healing convention in London, but she was unable to accept the invitation. When the CMA was organized in 1885, Judd was named recording secretary of the board. Even though she later was associated with the Salvation Army and the Pentecostal movement, she maintained strong ties with the CMA.

The room in which Montgomery was confined during her illness became a faith sanctuary, a place where people could pray. Then a weekly meeting began in her home. Soon Faith Rest Cottage was established in Buffalo, where the sick could receive comfort, encouragement, prayer, and teaching. The home was one of several established across the country in the late nineteenth century by people who believed in divine healing.

IV. Ministry in the West. After ministering in the East during the 1880s, Judd moved to Oakland, California, in 1890. That spring she married a wealthy businessman, George S. Montgomery, who owned property in an area near Oakland called Beulah (later Beulah Heights). Here the Montgomerys established the Home of Peace in 1893 in a big three-story Victorian house, which is still being used by the organization. The Home of Peace was destined to have a far greater outreach than the Buffalo home. Various ministries were established as the Montgomerys saw the need. An orphanage was operated from 1895 to 1908. An average of fifty to a hundred children were in the home. The Salvation Army took over its operation in 1908. Shalom Training School was established in 1894 to train missionary candidates.

Foreign mission work was always a priority with the Montgomerys. They made missionary trips and welcomed missionaries to stay at the

George and Carrie Judd Montgomery were a team for four decades, she as the minister and editor and he a supporting husband and businessman. This portrait was made in about 1907.

Home of Peace while they were on furlough. Support for the missionaries was channeled through Home of Peace, and freight was shipped from the facilities. Missionaries from a hundred societies have used the home and its services.

Montgomery organized a CMA church the first year she lived in Oakland. Since the early CMA was a loosely organized fellowship of believers rather than a strict denomination, the Montgomerys also joined the Salvation Army and were active for several years. They also organized the People's Mission in San Francisco but turned it over to the Salvation Army following the death of the director. Land at Beulah Heights was donated to the Salvation Army for a rescue home for girls.

Another parachurch project was the campground called "Elim Groves" at Cazadera. Notable Pentecostal and non-Pentecostal leaders ministered there.

V. Involvement in the Pentecostal Movement. Always interested in a deeper spiritual experience, Montgomery became aware of the Pentecostal revival and began to pray for the baptism in the Holy Spirit. She received the experience at the home of a friend in Chicago in 1908. Due in part to her conservative Pentecostal image, Montgomery maintained relationships with non-Pentecostals, including A. B. Simpson and other Alliance leaders. Following a missionary trip around the world in 1909, she ministered in two of Simpson's services and spoke at four other CMA conventions. Several CMA ministers were influenced to seek a Pentecostal experience, including D. W. Kerr and John Salmon.

After her baptism in the Spirit, Montgomery began publishing articles about the Pentecostal outpouring around the world. Her emphasis on holiness in *Triumphs of Faith* shifted to that of power, but she never neglected holiness and divine healing themes.

One of the points that helped Montgomery maintain credibility with her non-Pentecostal friends was her position on speaking in tongues. She highly valued her own experience but believed some people in the Pentecostal movement had given tongues too prominent a place in the church. Her emphasis was on unity and love. She was a charter member of the General Council of the Assemblies of God.

After Montgomery's death in 1946, the organization continued publishing *Triumphs of Faith* as a ministry to missionaries into the 1970s. The Montgomery's one child, Faith Berry, who was born in 1891, lives in an apartment at the Home of Peace.

Bibliography: D. Albrecht, "The Life and Ministry of Carrie Judd Montgomery," graduate research paper, Western Evangelical Seminary, 1984; C. Judd, *The Prayer of Faith* (1880); C. Montgomery, *Under His Wings* (1936); R. Niklaus, J. Sawin, and S. Stoesz, *All For Jesus* (1986). "With Christ," obituary, *PE* (July 26, 1946). W. E. Warner

A leader in the Pentecostal Holiness Church, G. H. Montgomery became prominent as editor of the denomination's *Advocate* magazine. He was later the editor-in-chief for Oral Roberts.

MONTGOMERY, GRANVILLE HARRISON (1903–66). Pentecostal Holiness Church (PHC) pastor, superintendent, evangelist, and editor. Best known as editor of Oral Roberts' publications (1952–61). Born into poverty in the coal mining community of Merrimac, Virginia, Montgomery left school at age twelve to work in the mines to help the family's income following his father's death. He was converted in 1918 after two women founded a PHC nearby. He was issued a PHC license when he was sixteen and later graduated from Holmes Bible and Missionary Institute (later Holmes Bible College). He also taught for a year at this school.

During the 1920s and 1930s Montgomery pastored in the South and East. In 1937 he began devoting his time to writing and evangelism, becoming the editor of the Pentecostal Holiness *Advocate* (1937–49). During part of this period he also served as editor for all PHC publications, managed the PHC publishing house, and was superintendent of evangelism.

Oral Roberts, who was himself a member of the denomination at the time, hired Montgomery to edit his publications in 1952. During the nearly ten years with Roberts, Montgomery wrote most of Roberts' many books. He also left the PHC during this time and joined the Open Bible Standard Churches.

After leaving Roberts in 1961, Montgomery edited *The Christian Challenge*, published by Jack Coe's widow, Juanita. A series of critical articles he wrote on some of the practices in the salvation-healing movement and published in the *Challenge* created friction with some of his Pentecostal friends.

In 1963 Montgomery joined the staff of Defenders of the Christian Faith (founded by Gerald B. Winrod) and became editor and president, which he remained until his death. Defenders published his biography, *This Man Montgomery,* edited by M. L. Flowers, in 1964.

Three of Montgomery's seven children were born deaf. One of these, Paula, ministered to the deaf in Jamaica. His son William is an Assemblies of God (AG) minister, and his daughter Bonnie is married to an AG minister.

In addition to ghost-written books, Montgomery wrote *Practical Holiness* (n.d.), *After Armageddon — What?* (n.d.), *The History of Defenders of the Christian Faith, Gerald Burton Winrod* (1965), and several others. He also founded *The Christian Challenge* magazine in the late 1940s (this name was later used on the Coe publication).

Bibliography: M. Flowers, *This Man Montgomery* (1964). W. E. Warner

MOORE, JACK (1905–). Pastor and co-founder of *Voice of Healing* magazine. Jack Moore was converted at age twelve in a small Pentecostal church in his hometown of Shreveport, Louisiana. He became a successful building contractor in Shreveport before building and copastoring the Life Tabernacle Church (1940). Members of this United Pentecostal congregation attended the meetings of William Branham being held in Arkansas and invited Branham to come to Shreveport. Branham came to Life Tabernacle and held a meeting with much success. This led to Moore's writing a letter to his friend Gordon Lindsay, an Assemblies of God evangelist and pastor, in the hopes of gaining a wider acceptance of Branham's ministry. Lindsay and Moore soon joined together to publish the *Voice of Healing* to promote Branham's work. After Branham briefly withdrew because of illness, the *Voice of Healing* was broadened to report on other ministries, and this broader view continued after Branham returned to active ministry.

Bibliography: D. E. Harrell, Jr., *All Things Are Possible* (1975); A. J. Price, "The Jack Moore Story I &

II," *Voice of Healing* (October–November 1955).
                                        J. R. Zeigler

MOORE, JENNIE EVANS (1883–1936).
Evangelist and pastor. A gifted, cheerful black
woman of high intellect, Jennie E. Moore worked
as a maid and resided at 217 North Bonnie Brae
Street in Los Angeles. She attended the Seymour-
led cottage prayer meetings across the street
during the spring of 1906. On Monday, April 9,
1906, she became the first woman in Los Angeles
to speak in tongues. She also played the piano, an
instrument for which she claimed to have no prior
training, and sang in tongues under the inspiration of the Spirit on that occasion. The following
Sunday morning (Easter), she worshiped with her
regular congregation, the First New Testament
Church. After the sermon by Pastor Joseph
Smale, she shared her testimony and spoke in
tongues. Reaction was quick and mixed, but
many of those present accompanied her that week
to the newly opened mission on Azusa Street.

From the beginning, Jennie was active at the
Azusa Street Mission, where she continued to
share her testimony, exhort, and lead in singing.
A capable evangelist in her own right, she
itinerated with two other women between Los
Angeles and Chicago, in 1907–08, visiting William Durham's mission. While there, she wrote
letters home in glowing terms of what a "blessed
place" it was.

On May 13, 1908, she married William J.
Seymour in a simple ceremony in Los Angeles.
The couple are reported to have adopted a
daughter. Together they resided on the second
floor of the Azusa Street Mission, where they
continued to minister. In 1915 she was listed as
one of the trustees of the mission. Following
Seymour's death in 1922, Jennie stayed on as
pastor. By 1935 her health had deteriorated to the
extent that she was hospitalized. She died on July
2, 1936.

Bibliography: *AF* 1 (8, 1907): 3; 1 (12, 1908):1;
Confidence 5 (10, 1912): 232–34; 5 (11, 1912): 244–
45; D. J. Nelson, "For Such a Time As This," unpublished Ph.D. diss., University of Birmingham, 1981; C.
W. Shumway, "Study of 'The Gift of Tongues,'"
unpublished A.B. thesis, University of Southern California, 1914.   C. M. Robeck, Jr.

MORGAN, ARTHUR THEODORE (1901–
67). General superintendent of the United Pentecostal Church (UPC) from 1951 to 1967.
Although born in Texas, Morgan grew to adulthood in Louisiana. In 1929 he was ordained in
the Pentecostal Assemblies of the World but later
joined the Pentecostal Ministerial Alliance. He
pastored in Louisiana and Texas. In 1944–45 he
served as the superintendent of the South Central
District of the Pentecostal Church, Incorporated.
Morgan also served as secretary-treasurer of the
Texas District of the UPC from 1945 to 1951,
when he was elected as general superintendent, a
position he held until his death.

Bibliography: A. L. Clanton, *United We Stand*
(1970).   J. L. Hall

MORMONS Mormonism, or the Church of
Jesus Christ of the Latter Day Saints (Salt Lake
City, Utah), gave form to Joseph Smith's version

of the restorationist hope. Smith (1805–44), a
native of Vermont, moved with his family in
1816 to Palmyra, New York, the so-called
burned-over district, where intense revivals yielded various new forms of religious expression.
Smith claimed a heavenly visitation that informed him of his call to a special task. He maintained
that he had been led by the angel Moroni to
discover long-lost golden plates that told of the
early history of the American continent and
revealed that Christ had visited America after his
resurrection. Smith discovered seer stones that
enabled him to decipher the hieroglyphics. He
published his translation of the Book of Mormon
in 1830.

Smith's scripture offered a resolution to the
quandary of many denominations. It asserted that
the true church had been removed and that in
1830 it had been divinely restored. The writing
offered answers to all the religious questions that
surfaced in the wake of revivals in upstate New
York. A series of revelations followed the first,
people proved willing to accept the new prophet's
authority, and the restored church began to grow.

It is hardly surprising that in this restorationist
setting, with its millenarian thrust, some adherents began to assert the place of apostolic gifts in
the church. Smith claimed to believe in all the
apostolic gifts, but he was not the first to
experience them all. Tongues speech broke out
early in Mormon history, and during their so-
journ in Kirkland, Ohio, in the 1830s, Brigham
Young claimed the experience. Smith understood
it to be "pure Adamic language" and soon
engaged in tongues speech himself. Prayer for the
sick, with the laying on of hands, was also
practiced. Such ecstatic experiences did not survive, however. Prophecy came to be the primary
form of inspired utterance among this restorationist consistency, whose leader is known as a
prophet.

Bibliography: T. O'Dea, *The Mormons* (1957);
G. H. Williams and Edith L. Waldvogel (Blumhofer),
"Speaking in Tongues and Related Gifts," in *The
Charismatic Movement*, ed. M. Hamilton (1975), 87–
88.   E. L. Blumhofer

MOSS, VIRGINIA E. (1875–1919). Pastor
and educator. With a great-grandmother who had
been a country preacher and a mother active in
Woman's Christian Temperance Union crusades
in the mid 1870s, the idea of feminine involvement in preaching and social work was not new to
Virginia E. Moss.

Born in Susquehanna, Pennsylvania, Moss suffered from frail health and various ailments for
her entire life. With her husband, she moved in
1899 to the Newark, New Jersey, area, where
most of her ministry activities eventually occurred, particularly in North Bergen.

A fall on ice when Moss was thirteen years old
left her with permanent spinal damage. By 1904
paralysis had spread from her waist to her feet. In
that year she received a complete healing from
this condition. With the healing came a consecration to Christian service. Her testimony was
warmly received by many, but not by the pastor
and members of the local Methodist church to

which she belonged. Home prayer meetings with other believers led to the opening of the Door of Hope Mission on February 7, 1906. Although emphasizing evangelism and faith healing, the mission also cared for wayward women.

Upon reading in a West Coast publication, *The Triumphs of Faith*, published by Carrie Judd Montgomery, that the "latter rain" was falling, she began to seek a deeper work of the Holy Spirit. Moss and several others traveled to Nyack in the summer of 1907 because "there a meeting was being held for the purpose of seeking God, and the baptism of the Holy Ghost and fire, and speaking in tongues." One member of their party received the baptism in the Spirit and spoke in tongues at the meeting. After this, others at the Door of Hope Mission sought for the Pentecostal baptism and consequently spoke in tongues, which Moss also received after the Nyack visit. Nightly services were held through 1908 to assist other seekers; outstanding healings were also recorded.

Moss felt led to open a "rest home" (faith home) in 1909. This ministry, as well as her mission, enlarged in 1910 when property was purchased in North Bergen. There the work proceeded as the Beulah Heights Assembly.

A view of the world in need of the gospel was never far from Moss's thoughts. Her mother had been called to go to India but never went. Remorse over this failure haunted the mother, but the daughter determined to aid the cause of world evangelization. She recounted that the Lord spoke to her and said, "I want witnesses of my Word and Spirit to go forth from a Missionary Training School at Beulah." Aware that many Pentecostals viewed formal theological education with suspicion since the baptism in the Spirit supposedly made this unnecessary, she nevertheless heeded Paul's admonition to Timothy: "Study to shew thyself approved unto God . . ." (2 Tim. 2:15 KJV) and opened the Beulah Heights Bible and Missionary Training School in 1912.

Many early graduates of this school distinguished themselves in Assemblies of God (AG) foreign missions. Two later field directors, Henry B. Garlock (Africa) and Maynard L. Ketcham (India and the Far East) attended this school. Other notable graduates included Edgar Barrick (India), Frank Finkenbinder (Latin America), John Juergensen (Japan), Lillian Merian Riggs (Africa), Marie Stephany (North China), and Fred Burke (South Africa).

Virginia E. "Mother" Moss died in 1919 after directing the school for seven years and the church for thirteen. The church and school eventually became closely linked to the AG for several years. Later the school was renamed the Metropolitan Bible Institute and was operated by the New York–New Jersey district of the AG for several years.

Bibliography: G. B. McGee, "Three Notable Women in Pentecostal Ministry," *AG Heritage* 1 (1986): 3–5, 12, 16; V. E. Moss, *Following the Shepherd* (1919).
                                                    G. B. McGee

MOTHER ANGELICA   See ANGELICA, MOTHER.

MOTHER BARNES   See BARNES, LEANORE O. ("MOTHER MARY.")

MOTHER COTTON   See COTTON, EMMA L.

MOTHER MOISE   See MOISE, MARY GILL.

MOTHER OF GOD (GAITHERSBURG, MD.)   See CHARISMATIC COMMUNITIES.

MOUNT SINAI HOLY CHURCH OF AMERICA   Founded in 1924 by Ida Robinson, pastor in the United Holy Church, as a Pentecostal denomination giving full rights to women as bishops and elders. The predominantly black connection has grown from its beginnings in Philadelphia to more than 120 churches in sixteen states and the District of Columbia, foreign missions in Cuba and Guyana, a nursing home, and a farm/retreat center. Central to the life of Mount Sinai are (1) the convocation—the annual meeting of bishops, ministers, and delegates who oversee organization, doctrine, and appointments; (2) doctrine, based on the Apostles' Creed, with special emphasis on the life of Christ (his virgin birth, miracles, crucifixion, resurrection, and second coming), the baptism of the Holy Spirit as a gift of God upon a sanctified life, and the Tribulation and Great White Throne Judgment; (3) the ordinances of baptism, Communion, footwashing, blessing of children, and tithing, along with emphasis on marriage with strict prohibitions against divorce and remarriage; and (4) the standard, a set of rules governing principles of holy conduct, including prohibitions against alcohol, tobacco, artificial adornings, secret societies, and arms-bearing in military service.

Bibliography: A. Fauset, *Black Gods of the Metropolis* (1944); M. M. Fisher, "Organized Religion and the Cults," *Crisis* 44 (January 1937): 8–10; C. Gilkes, "The Roles of Church and Community Mothers," *Journal of Feminist Studies in Religion* 2 (1, 1986): 41–59; *The Manual of the Mount Sinai Holy Church* (1984); J. Ratliffe, "The Enabling of a Local Pentecostal Congregation to Rethink the Role of Women in the Church," D.Min. thesis, Interdenominational Theological Center, Atlanta, Georgia, 1976; H. Trulear, "The Lord Will Make a Way Somehow," *Journal of the Interdenominational Theological Center* 13 (1985): 87–104.
                                                    H. D. Trulear

MÜHLEN, HERIBERT (1927–). One of the most prominent Catholic theologians to be renewed in the Spirit. Ordained in 1955, Mühlen became professor of dogmatics at Paderborn in 1964. Author of two major works on the Holy Spirit: *Una Mystica Persona* (1964) and *Der Heilige Geist als Person* (1969), Mühlen's first contact with the Spirit-baptized was at the Catholic-Pentecostal dialogue in 1973, after which he himself received. Subsequently Mühlen has become the foremost leader of *Charismatische Gemeinde Erneuerung* (charismatic parish renewal) in West Germany and coeditor of *Erneuerung in Kirche und Gesellschaft*. He advocates a form of renewal fully integrated into church pastoral structures and differentiates this from the worldwide charismatic renewal. One of the Catholic members of the dialogue team with Pentecostals in the third quinquennium, he has written extensively on renewal in the Spirit. Only *A Charismatic Theology* (1978) and a few articles (e.g., in *One in Christ,* and *Theological Renewal*) are available in English.   P. D. Hocken

MÜLHEIM ASSOCIATION (MA). The oldest segment of German Pentecostalism. The Mülheim Association, the *Christliche Gemeinschaftsverband GmbH Mülheim/Ruhr,* was formed when the Pentecostal issue, especially the gift of tongues, split the *Gemeinschaftsbewegung,* the network of Holiness groupings within the state churches. Though MA was formed in 1913, Mülheim had been the site of annual Pentecostal conferences since 1907 and was the home base of MA's first president, E. Humburg. From the start, MA was an interdenominational movement, rather like the Christian and Missionary Alliance, with member fellowships from the state churches (Lutheran and Reformed), such as those of E. Edel and C. O. Voget, and from free assemblies, thus including both pedobaptists and practitioners of believer's baptism. Its most respected teacher was J. Paul.

MA never defined itself against other traditions, and so, unusual for a Pentecostal group, some congregations upheld the historic creeds as well as the Lutheran Augsburg Confession. Despite this ecumenicity, MA was even more firmly rejected by German Evangelicals in the Berlin Declaration than the Pentecostal movement elsewhere. MA affirms all the spiritual gifts without requiring glossolalia as initial evidence for baptism in the Spirit. Holiness of life is a major emphasis, continuing a Keswick-type emphasis on victory over sin. MA published *Pfingstgresse* monthly from 1909, renamed *Grusse aus dem Heiligtum* in 1919, now known as *Heilszeugnisse.* MA, which has increasingly become a form of independent free church, has been open to some ecumenical contacts since 1967. Membership has suffered from the division of Germany and now totals some four thousand committed members.

See also EUROPEAN PENTECOSTALISM.

Bibliography: W. J. Hollenweger, *The Pentecostals* (1972); idem, "'Touching' and 'Thinking' the Spirit: Some Aspects of European Charismatics," *Perspectives on the New Pentecostalism,* ed. R. P. Spittler (1976); C. Krust, *50 Jahre Deutsche Pfingstbewegung* (1976); idem, *Was wir glauben, lehren und bekennen* (1963).
                                                                                    P. D. Hocken

MUMFORD, BERNARD C., JR. ("BOB") (1930–). Pastor, Bible teacher, and author. Mumford was born in Steubenville, Ohio, and was spiritually renewed at age twenty-four at an Assemblies of God church in Atlantic City while in the Navy. He graduated from Valley Forge Christian College and studied at Bethesda Missionary Medical School, Toronto, Canada. In 1964 he earned an M.Div. from Reformed Episcopal Seminary, Philadelphia, Pennsylvania.

Mumford served as senior pastor at interdenominational churches in Kane, Pennsylvania, and Wilmington, Delaware. He served as dean and professor of NT and missions at Elim Bible Institute, and while there was inspired by David du Plessis to take the message of charismatic renewal to denominational churches. He traveled both nationally and internationally in a transdenominational ministry to churches, renewal seminars, and pastoral leadership training sessions.

Bob Mumford was one of the founders of Christian Growth Ministries and later founded Lifechangers, Inc.

Mumford was involved in conferences on the Holy Spirit in Fort Lauderdale, Florida. These were so successful that the sponsoring committee of forty pastors and laymen formed the Holy Spirit Teaching Mission, which assumed publication of *New Wine* magazine in 1969. A covenant relationship developed among four men—Mumford, Derek Prince, Don Basham, and Charles Simpson. They shared their teachings with each other for confirmation. Their teachings resulted in some controversy in the area of submission, discipleship, and shepherding. In 1972 the men changed their organization's name to Christian Growth Ministries.

In 1986 *New Wine* ceased publication and Mumford moved to San Rafael, California, where he established his ministry, Lifechangers, Inc. He continues his Bible teaching ministry in conferences and leadership seminars and by means of television, audio and video cassettes, bimonthly periodicals, and books. He has authored twelve books.

Bibliography: J. Buckingham, "New Wine Ceases Publication," *Ministries Today* (November–December 1986), 24; S. Strang, "Discipleship Controversy Three Years Later," *Charisma* (September 1978), 14–24.
                                                                                    S. Strang

MURRAY, GEORGE A. AND ANNIE (c. 1860–1909) (d. 1912). Pentecostal pioneers in Toronto, Ontario. Natives of Dundee, Scotland, and married in 1889, the Murrays both suffered from lifelong handicaps, George being lame in both feet and Annie blind in both eyes. Hearing God's call, they went as missionaries to Palestine in 1890, initially unsponsored but later associated with the Christian and Missionary Alliance. Moving to Toronto in 1904, the Murrays were baptized in the Spirit soon after "Pentecost" arrived in the city, and they opened a Pentecostal mission at Concord and Hepbourne. Teachers of Keswick-type Holiness doctrine, they were committed to Pentecostal unity, and George became secretary of the United Pentecostal Missions of Toronto, a voluntary association that organized the city-wide convention in October 1908. After George's death in August 1909, Annie responded to a call to India, where she served in Bombay from December 1910 until her death in December 1912. P. D. Hocken

MUSIC See PENTECOSTAL AND CHARISMATIC MUSIC.

MYERSCOUGH, THOMAS (1858–1932). British estate agent, Bible School leader, and missionary secretary. Converted in 1874 Myerscough was leader of a group of Bible students associated with the Brethren in Preston, Lancashire. First introduced to Pentecostal teaching at nearby Lytham, he was baptized in the Spirit at the Sunderland Convention in 1909. His gifts as a Bible teacher were recognized and his Bible class work developed into the Pentecostal Missionary Union (PMU) Bible School (1911–14). Among its students were W. F. P. Burton, E. J. Phillips (1893–1973), James Salter, R. E. Darragh (1886–1959), and George Jeffreys. These were formative years, and his sound teaching had a lasting impact on his students. He took an active part in the PMU and served on its council. He was a founding member of the Assemblies of God of Great Britain and Ireland and was a member of its executive council from 1924. He was the first secretary-treasurer of the Congo Evangelistic Mission until his death in March 1932, when his son succeeded him. He was pastor of the Preston Assembly and a great promoter of missionary work.

Bibliography: *Confidence* 58 (January 1913): 5–6; D. Gee, *These Men I Knew* (1980); idem, *Showers of Blessing*, vol. 4 (1910). D. W. Cartwright

MYLAND, DAVID WESLEY (1858–1943). Evangelist, pastor, author, and Bible school teacher. Myland, Canadian born, grew up in a log cabin close to Cleveland, Ohio. He received four years of training to be a Methodist preacher. During his life, Myland was miraculously healed seven times when close to death. As a result, he preached healing in addition to the Holiness doctrine of crisis sanctification. Since the Methodists did not approve the teaching of healing, he became associated with the Christian and Missionary Alliance (CMA) in 1890.

While with the CMA Myland wrote hymns, coauthored a hymnal with James M. Kirk, and

was part of the Ohio Quartet. He also held three positions with the Ohio District of the CMA: secretary (1894), superintendent (1898–1904), and evangelist (1910). During one of his evangelistic meetings, he appeared with D. L. Moody. Additionally, Myland operated El Shaddai, a home for rest and healing, in Cleveland for three years; and he pastored a CMA church in Columbus, Ohio (1904–12). He also published the *Christian Messenger*, a paper devoted to the fourfold gospel: salvation, sanctification, healing, and Second Coming.

David Wesley Myland, pictured with his wife, was an early and prominent leader in the Christian and Missionary Alliance but later identified with the Pentecostal movement.

Myland's theology changed following his seeking and receiving the baptism in the Spirit and his seventh healing in November 1906, having heard about the outpouring of the Spirit at Azusa Street seven months earlier. Immediately Myland began preaching the Pentecostal message until 1912, when the CMA officially broke with Pentecostalism over the issue of tongues. This resulted in Myland and twenty-four other pastors leaving the organization.

During 1906–19 Myland had a major writing ministry. He wrote the first Pentecostal hymn, "The Latter Rain," (1906); three Pentecostal hymnals (1907, 1911, 1919); and the first definitive Pentecostal theology that was widely distributed, the *Latter Rain Covenant* (1910). When Myland wrote this book, he utilized two hermeneutical principles: translating Scripture from the original language and interpreting Scripture by Scripture under the illumination of the Holy Spirit. This led him to view Scripture passages as having three possible interpretations: historical, spiritual, and dispensational; or in other words: literal, typological, and prophetical. Thus he interpreted the early and latter rains referred to in Deuteronomy 11:13–15 as literally meaning the spring and autumn rains; typologically meaning justification of the believer and baptism in the Spirit; and prophetically meaning baptism in the Spirit and the second coming of Christ. His meaning of the last dispensation differed from the standard dispensational interpretation. Myland justified the use of the gifts of the Spirit before the second coming of Christ, while the dispensationalists used it to deny the use of the gifts of the Spirit during the church age.

Myland was also concerned about Christians being overcomers so that they might be raptured during the first resurrection. His theology of the Rapture was pretribulational and premillennial (cf. Myland, *The Revelation of Jesus Christ* [1911]).

Upon leaving the CMA, Myland became a leader in the Pentecostal movement. His ministerial experience and prior writing gave him the credentials he needed to found and teach at the Gibeah Bible School in Plainfield, Indiana, among former CMA people (1912–14). While at Gibeah he taught (1912–13) and ordained (1913) J. Roswell Flower and Alice Reynolds Flower, who were involved in establishing the Assemblies of God (AG). Myland was also a weekly contributor to the *Christian Evangel*, which was edited by J. Roswell Flower and later became the *Pentecostal Evangel*, the official organ of the AG. While in Plainfield, Myland formed the Association of Christian Assemblies and became its general superintendent (1913–14). The organization disbanded in 1914.

Myland did not accompany Flower to the organizational meeting in Hot Springs, Arkansas, in April 1914 of the General Council of the AG, nor did he affiliate with it. Apparently, he was not ready to commit himself to a Pentecostal organization and wanted to maintain contact with the CMA. Since Myland was held in such high esteem by the early leaders of the AG, he undoubtedly would have been one of the major leaders if he had affiliated.

After leaving Plainfield, Myland continued to teach. He founded and taught at Ebenezer Bible Institute in Chicago (1915–18). Gibeah and Ebenezer, however, closed their doors for various reasons when Myland left them. Next he taught at Beulah Heights Bible Institute in Atlanta (1918–20) and became the first chairman of the board of

trustees for the institute. It is known today as Beulah Heights Bible College.

Myland continued his administrative ministry as the first chairman (1919–20) of the general council for the Apostolic Christian Association, which incorporated on October 29, 1919, in Atlanta, Georgia. This association later merged with what is now the International Pentecostal Church of Christ. While in Atlanta Myland associated with Paul and Elizabeth Barth, who continued the work when he left. The Barth family was instrumental in publishing the *Bridegroom's Messenger*.

After leaving Atlanta Myland pastored churches until he was eighty-three years old in Philadelphia, Pennsylvania; Jackson, Redford, and Detroit, Michigan; and Toledo, Van Wert, and Columbus, Ohio. At least one of these congregations was black.

In Van Wert, Myland opened another El Shaddai, a school and a home for healing (1932–33). He continued to write hymns, manuscripts, and letters. One of these letters refutes the doctrine of eternal security (1933). The last ten years of his life were spent in Columbus pioneering a new church and preaching in established churches. Interestingly enough, he maintained his credentials with the Methodist church through all of these changes in his religious career.

Bibliography: "Annual Report of Alliance: 1905–1906," unpublished document (1906); "Apostolic Christian Association," *Bridegroom's Messenger* 13 (November–December 1919) 2; J. K. Butcher, "The Holiness and Pentecostal Labors of David Wesley Myland, 1890–1918," unpublished Th.M. thesis, Dallas Theological Seminary, 1982; "CMA Board of Managers Minutes: April, 1898," unpublished document, 1898; "CMA Board of Managers Minutes: June 4, 1910," unpublished document, 1910; R. B. Eckvall, H. M. Schuman, and A. C. Smead, *After Fifty Years* (1939); D. W. Faupel, "The Function of 'Models' in the Interpretation of Pentecostal Thought," *Pneuma* 2 (1980): 51–71; A. R. Flower, *Grace for Grace* (1961); C. E. Jones, *A Guide to the Study of the Pentecostal Movement*, (1983); W. W. Menzies, *Anointed to Serve* (1971); "Minutes of the General Council of the Assemblies of God, Hot Springs, Arkansas: April 2–12, 1914," unpublished 1914; S. Murray, "Minutes of Board of Trustees of Beulah Heights Bible Institute," unpublished, 1918; D. W. Myland, *The Latter Rain Covenant* (1910); idem, "Philadelphia Assembly," church advertisement (c. 1920); idem, *The Revelation of Jesus Christ* (1911); idem, "Special Services at the Glory Barn," announcement (1930). Letters: Myland to Beloved in Christ Jesus (December 18, 1932), Myland to Elder in Christ Jesus (September 16, 1930), Myland to Gordon (May 5, 1933; April 18, 1938; May 31, 1941; June 30, 1941), Myland to Palmer (December 23, 1927), Myland to Sister in Christ (January 24, 1933).   E. B. Robinson

N

NAME IT, CLAIM IT DOCTRINE See POSITIVE CONFESSION THEOLOGY.

NATIONAL ASSOCIATION OF EVANGELICALS (NAE). An association of evangelical, Holiness, and Pentecostal individuals, local churches, and denominations formed in 1942 to provide visibility and advocacy for the concerns of conservative Christians in the U.S. Its membership in 1987 was about 5 million. The ten largest groups in 1987 were the Assemblies of God (2,082,878), Church of God (Cleveland, Tenn.) (550,000), Church of the Nazarene (522,082), Christian and Missionary Alliance (227,846), Presbyterian Church in America (177,917), International Church of the Foursquare Gospel (177,787), Baptist General Conference (132,546), International Pentecostal Holiness Church (113,000), Wesleyan Church (109,541), and the Conservative Congregational Christian Churches (108,115).

From its inception this group has been distinguishable from the smaller, highly vocal and often strident organization of Fundamentalists organized in 1940 by Carl McIntire, the American Council of Christian Churches (ACCC: 1987 membership 1.5 million). The NAE is fundamental in its doctrinal commitment yet more inclusive and less sectarian than the ACCC. For many it also provided a conservative alternative to the Federal Council of Churches of Christ in America (FCCCA), succeeded by the now 40-million-member National Council of Churches of Christ in the USA—whose theological and political agenda seemed to represent exclusively the concerns of more liberal Protestants. The NAE was unique in that it did not wish to condemn these other ecumenical agencies but rather to occupy territory between them.

To describe the NAE in ecumenical terms may, at first glance, seem odd. Most of its members view genuine Christian unity as spiritual unity and champion the doctrine of an invisible church. They tend to shy away from any contact with the formal "ecumenical movement." Yet the NAE provides cross-denominational fellowship, shares common doctrinal and social agendas, and it raises a visible voice that is demonstrative of the Christian character and commitments of those involved. These factors are indicative of its basic ecumenical nature. The most significant difference between what is normally identified as the ecumenical movement and the NAE is the list of candidates that are welcomed into membership.

In many ways the NAE could be termed the brainchild of J. Elwin Wright. In 1929 he had launched the New England Fellowship to bring a modicum of cohesiveness to isolated conservative Christians who felt lonely in the seemingly theologically hostile and dominantly Roman Catholic world of New England. The New England Fellowship was highly successful from its inception, recruiting cooperation from a broad spectrum of fundamentalist and evangelical groups, among them Pentecostals. Wright was pro-active in his recruitment of Pentecostals in this venture, a fact that was not always appreciated in many fundamentalist circles.

The New England Fellowship organized a range of activities and events for its constituency, including camps, seminars, Bible studies, and a series of radio programs. From 1937 to 1939 Wright traveled the U.S., taking the pulse of American "Evangelicalism." By 1939 he began to share with people like Harold John Ockenga, pastor of the famed Park Street Church in Boston, and other church and denominational leaders around the country, his dream of a similar organization to be formed on the national scale. Wright visited many leaders personally during those years and continued to include Pentecostals as he had done in the New England Fellowship.

A "National Conference for United Action Among Evangelicals" was convened in St. Louis, Missouri, April 7–9, 1942. Its purpose was to discuss the necessity of founding a "front" to represent the concerns of evangelical organizations before various governmental agencies, the need for a kind of "clearing house" for items of common interest and concern, and a concern to provide a visible means to demonstrate before an otherwise unbelieving world the determination of many to stand against the forces of unbelief and apostasy. Several Pentecostal groups showed immediate interest in this proposal, including the Pentecostal Holiness Church (PHC), Open Bible Standard Churches (OBSC), the Church of God (Cleveland, Tenn.) (CG), and the Assemblies of God (AG). Of the 150 delegates present at this meeting, about 10 percent were Pentecostals.

In spite of early Pentecostal interest in the NAE, full participation did not come easily. Pentecostals were chary of the positive response they were given by these "Calvinists," and, as J. R. Flower noted, some Pentecostals kept their "fingers crossed" lest they lose this "good fortune." Harold Ockenga did much to alleviate Pentecostal fears, arguing repeatedly that Pentecostals and Holiness groups such as the Free Methodists and the Nazarenes should have an equal voice with others who called themselves evangelical.

For many the issue of Pentecostal participation peaked in April 1944 when Carl McIntire published several articles in his paper, the *Christian Beacon*, repudiating Pentecostals. "Tongues," his paper claimed, "is one of the great signs of the apostasy." The real gift of tongues had long since ceased to exist. McIntire announced his willingness to merge the ACCC into the NAE if the NAE would, among other things, " . . . get rid of the . . . tongues groups."

Flower wondered aloud whether the NAE had hurt its chances of representing evangelical Christians in the U.S. by including Pentecostals in their numbers. But Ockenga reassured him that the course was set and that Pentecostals would participate. As late as 1947 Ockenga was still defending that decision. By then Pentecostals were committed to stay. Flower, with E. S. Williams' encouragement, had led the AG into the organization. G. H. Montgomery had urged participation in the NAE by the Pentecostal Holiness Church. Frank Smith, Gerald Crooks, R. Bryant Mitchell, and Roy E. Southard led the OBSC into the NAE, and the CG took its cue from J. H. Walker, Earl P. Paulk, E. L. Simmons, M. P. Cross, and E. C. Clark. Since its founding meeting, these groups have been joined by the Christian Church of North America, Church of God of the Mountain Assembly, Elim Fellowship, Full Gospel Pentecostal Association, International Church of the Foursquare Gospel (ICFG), International Pentecostal Church of Christ (IPCC), Pentecostal Church of God (PCG), and the Pentecostal Evangelical Church (PEC) as Pentecostal member churches in the NAE.

While Pentecostals were in the minority of NAE membership in the 1940s and 50s, their rapid growth since then has moved them into a majority position. According to 1987 figures on the roughly 5 million members in these NAE denominations, nearly 3.1 million are Pentecostal. Of the forty-four member denominations, twelve are Pentecostal. The AG contributes 66 percent of all the Pentecostal membership, the NAE could be said to represent Pentecostal thinking. Still, of the twenty-four presidents who have led the NAE, only three have been Pentecostals. Thomas F. Zimmerman served two terms as president in 1960 and 1961 while holding the position of general superintendent of the AG. Bishop J. Floyd Williams, General Superintendent of the PHC, was elected to a two-year term in 1980–81. More recently Ray H. Hughes, first assistant general overseer of the CG, served as president in 1986–87. Pentecostal participation on the various commissions of the NAE, including the commissions on the chaplaincy, churchmen, stewardship, and women has been much more evident. Similarly, Pentecostals have served as convention coordinators in recent years.

Although other Pentecostal groups have joined the NAE, as of 1987 the NAE has had no black or Hispanic Pentecostal denominations as members, indicating that the NAE has not been pro-active in an attempt to include these ethnic groups, but it may also point to some racial bias. Some black Pentecostals, however, have participated in the National Black Evangelical Association (NBEA) founded in Los Angeles, California, in 1963. Nor does the NAE grant admission to "Jesus Name" or Oneness Pentecostals. These groups are precluded from joining on the basis of the NAE's Trinitarian statement of faith.

The NAE publishes *United Evangelical Action*

six times annually; in it articles on a variety of socially relevant issues are addressed. Among recent topics have been medical ethics, nuclear war, liberation theology, the sanctuary movement, Evangelicals in the mainline, racism, and pornography. Occasionally it also publishes articles that highlight Pentecostal works or articles by Pentecostal authors. *Washington Insight,* a regular newsletter, has done much to inform NAE members of "evangelical concerns and the federal government," thereby encouraging active participation by Evangelicals and Pentecostals in political concerns.

The Pentecostal groups that have joined the NAE have benefited in several ways. First, they have gained visibility and respectability among their evangelical peers. Formerly viewed as sectarians, they are now often addressed as *bona fide* Christian denominations.

Second, Pentecostal concerns that were shared by other Christians now have a greater bearing in the church, and through cooperation with the NAE membership, Pentecostals have a larger voice in the public arena. Third, Pentecostals inevitably came to the place where they recognized the need for dialogue with one another. Out of this recognition, NAE member Pentecostals formed the Pentecostal Fellowship of North America (PFNA) in 1948. Fourth, membership in the NAE has contributed to the broadening, or "evangelicalization," of those Pentecostal groups who have participated.

While Pentecostals have gained through participation in the NAE, they have also lost some things. The "evangelicalization" of Pentecostals has brought them into dialogue with evangelical Christians, but this interaction has been at the risk of certain distinctives. First, most Pentecostals were pacifists prior to World War II. Evangelism on military bases was allowed, but Pentecostal military chaplains were nonexistent, and Pentecostals were discouraged from serving in the military, especially in combatant roles. The NAE first gave Pentecostals entrée to the military through its Chaplain's Commission. By the Vietnam era the AG, as one representative group, had rewritten its position on military service. It no longer declared that as a fellowship it could not "participate in war and armed resistance which involves the actual destruction of human life" in accordance with Scripture, but left the decision to the individual. This allowed the fellowship to identify more clearly with the NAE members whose traditions, for the most part, had not shared a pacifist past. More often than not, they identify with the political right and have been hard on those with whom they have disagreed. Second, less overt is the movement away from support for women in ministry. Some Pentecostals have never ordained women, others have. At the very least, women have traditionally played a more significant role in ministry within the Pentecostal tradition than they have in the larger evangelical tradition. But as evangelical values have been adopted by Pentecostals, the role of women in ministry has suffered. Third, the doctrinal concerns of Evangelicals have become the doctrinal concerns of Pentecostals. Some

Pentecostal groups have rewritten their statements of faith, and others have imported such "evangelical" issues as "inerrancy" into their theological arenas for the first time. Fourth, to take membership in the NAE has meant that Pentecostals have stood in solidarity with the NAE in its suspicion of the ecumenical movement as embodied in the World and National Councils of Churches. Thus Pentecostals have effectively been cut off from meaningful interaction with the conciliar sector of the church, in part to maintain a position acceptable to other NAE member denominations, but at the expense of forfeited witness.

On balance, the NAE has aided many Pentecostal concerns. Pentecostal missions have been represented in the Evangelical Foreign Missions Association (EFMA), a group formed from within the missions committee of the NAE in 1945. The AG, CG, OBSC, and PHC were all charter members. Likewise, the National Religious Broadcasters (NRB) was formed in 1944 from NAE concerns "to safeguard free and complete access to the broadcast media." Pentecostals have also benefited significantly from the work of the NRB as Pentecostal evangelists have pioneered the field of televangelism. The headquarters of the NAE are located at 450 Gunderson Dr., P.O. Box 28, Wheaton, IL, 60189.

Bibliography: J. Carpenter, "From Fundamentalism to the New Evangelical Coalition," in G. Marsden, ed. *Evangelicalism and Modern America* (1984); idem, "The Fundamental Leaven and the Rise of an Evangelical United Front" in L. Sweet, ed., *The Evangelical Tradition in America* (1984); E. C. Clark, "Chicago Conventional Evangelicals," *Church of God Evangel* (May 29, 1943); C. W. Conn, *Like a Mighty Army: Moves the Church of God* (1955); Constitution and By-Laws of The General Council of the Assemblies of God 1939, 1987; C. H. Jacquet, ed. *Yearbook of American and Canadian Churches* (1987); G. Marsden, *Reforming Fundamentalism* (1987); W. H. Menzies, *Anointed to Serve* (1971); R. B. Mitchell, *Heritage and Horizons: The History of Open Bible Standard Churches* (1982); V. Synan, *The Old Time Power: A History of the Pentecostal Holiness Church* (1973); G. H. Montgomery, "Does United Evangelical Action Include Pentecostal Holiness?" *Pentecostal Holiness Advocate* 27 (4, May 27, 1943): 2–3; J. D. Murch, *Cooperation Without Compromise: A History of the National Association of Evangelicals* (1956); idem, *Evangelical Action! A Report of the Organization of the National Association of Evangelicals for United Action* (1942); R. Robins, "A Chronology of Peace: Attitudes Toward War and Peace in the Assemblies of God: 1914–1918," *Pneuma* 6 (1984); B. L. Shelley, *Evangelicalism in America* (1967); "Foursquare Gospel Church Joins NAE," *United Evangelical Action* 11 (May 1, 1952): 6; Correspondence located in the Assemblies of God Archives in Springfield, Missouri, including J. R. Flower to H. J. Ockenga, June 1, 1943; July 5, 1943; May 4, 1944; H. J. Ockenga to J. R. Flower, May 28, 1943; May 22, 1944; "Ockenga Disavows Barnhouse's Speech at NAE Convention"; "Confusion"; "Tongues"; and W. O. J. Garman, "Analysis of National Association Convention and Constituency" in *Christian Beacon* 9 (2, April 27, 1944); H. J. Ockenga, "The 'Pentecostal' Bogey," *United Evangelical Action* 6 (1, 1947).

C. M. Robeck, Jr.

NATIONAL DAVID SPIRITUAL TEMPLE OF CHRIST UNION See UNIVERSAL CHRIS-

TIAN SPIRITUAL FAITH AND CHURCHES FOR ALL NATIONS.

NATIONAL LEADERSHIP CONFERENCE See CHARISMATIC MOVEMENT.

NATIONAL SERVICE COMMITTEE (GREAT BRITAIN) See CHARISMATIC MOVEMENT.

NATIONAL SERVICE COMMITTEE (U.S.) See CATHOLIC CHARISMATIC RENEWAL.

NAZARENE CHARISMATICS See WESLEYAN CHARISMATICS.

An immigrant from Denmark, P. C. Nelson became a minister, first as a Baptist and then as a Pentecostal. He founded Southwestern Bible School in Enid, Oklahoma (now Southwestern Assemblies of God College, Waxahachie, Texas).

NELSON, PETER CHRISTOPHER (1868– 1942). Evangelist and educator. Born in Denmark, Nelson immigrated with his family to the U.S. in 1872. He felt called to the ministry at a youthful age and later enrolled at Denison University in 1890 to begin preparation. He married Myrtle Garmong in 1893 and completed his bachelor's degree in 1897. In 1899 he entered Rochester Theological Seminary, where he studied under Augustus H. Strong. After completing his studies, Nelson entered the Baptist ministry, engaging in evangelism and pastoring; he also worked with the YMCA during World War I. Following the war he was called to pastor the Conley Memorial Baptist Church in Detroit.

Nelson embraced Pentecostalism in 1920. Because his congregation refused to accept his new doctrines on faith healing and the baptism in the Holy Spirit, he resigned and spent seven years in evangelistic ministry. Settling in Enid, Oklahoma, in 1927, he founded a church and opened

Southwestern Bible School. These initiatives prompted him to affiliate with the Assemblies of God. Traveling widely in the promotion of the school, Nelson became well-known for his pulpit ministry. His contribution to Pentecostal education was expanded by the publication of his writings: *The Young Minister's Guide* (1932), *Bible Doctrines* (1934), *Life of Paul* (1939), *Does Christ Heal Today?* (1941), *Word Studies* (1941), *The Baptism in the Holy Spirit* (1942), and *The Letters of Paul* (1945). He translated Eric Lund's *Hermeneutics* from Spanish into English in 1934.

In 1941 Nelson negotiated for the merger of Southwestern Bible School and South Central Bible Institute in Fort Worth, Texas, to form Southwestern Bible Institute (now Southwestern Assemblies of God College). Two years later it moved to Waxahachie, Texas, to occupy the former campus of Trinity University. He died shortly before the move.

Bibliography: K. Kendrick, "A Pioneer Pentecostal Educator," *AG Heritage* 2 (Spring 1982): 2, 4; P. C. Nelson, "Autobiography of P. C. Nelson," Enid, Oklahoma (1928, typewritten). G. B. McGee

NEO-PENTECOSTALISM See CHARISMATIC MOVEMENT.

NEW ISSUE See ONENESS PENTECOSTALISM; UNITED PENTECOSTAL CHURCH INTERNATIONAL; PENTECOSTAL ASSEMBLIES OF THE WORLD.

NEW ORDER OF THE LATTER RAIN See LATTER RAIN MOVEMENT.

NICHOL, JOHN THOMAS (1928–). Historian and educator. Born in Dorchester, Massachusetts, Nichol (originally Nykiel) is the son of John and Felixa Nykiel. He married Dorothy Marie Jashinsky on August 30, 1952. Nichol received his A.B. from Gordon College (1949) and his A.M. (1953) and Ph.D. (1965) degrees from Boston University. He also earned S.T.B. (1953) and S.T.M. (1954) degrees from Harvard University. Nichol has served on the faculties of Gordon College, New England College of Pharmacy, and Bentley College. In 1971 he was appointed vice-president for academic affairs and dean of faculties at Bentley College, Waltham, Massachusetts.

Nichol's book *Pentecostalism* was published in 1966. This sympathetic treatment chronicled the movement's proliferation and problems in America at a time when the emerging charismatic movement made its message timely. This book, published by a major publisher (Harper and Row), marked the beginning of a new scholarly interest in American Pentecostalism.

Nichol has also written on business and religion as well as on Christianity in his parents' native Poland. E. L. Blumhofer

NICKEL, THOMAS ROY (1900–). The founder and editor for ten years of *Full Gospel Business Men's Voice*. Born and raised in Missouri, Nickel graduated from Southwest Missouri State College (now University) and had a long and varied career in journalism before moving to California during World War II. Early in 1953 he felt impressed to attend a Los Angeles meeting of the fledgling Full Gospel Business Men's Fellowship International, where he offered his press and services to Demos Shakarian, the organization's founder and president. Nickel was immediately appointed to edit and publish a magazine. The *Voice's* initial circulation of 5,000 grew to 250,000 by 1962 and proved a significant factor in the growth of the organization and the charismatic movement. On leaving the magazine in 1962, Nickel founded another called *Testimony*. He has written three books and hundreds of articles.

Bibliography: *Full Gospel Business Men's Voice* (February 1953), 2; J. Sherrill, *The Happiest People on Earth* (1975). L. F. Wilson

NIKOLOFF, NICHOLAS (1900–1964). Pastor, educator, and missionary to Eastern Europe. Nicholas Nikoloff was born to Greek Orthodox parents in Bulgaria. His mother had been educated at an American college, and through her influence he attended a Protestant church in Bourgas. He was converted in 1914 while reading a Bible that he had purchased. Five years later he began to study law at the University of Sofia. When Ivan Varonaev passed through Bulgaria on his way to evangelize in Russia, Nikoloff learned of the baptism in the Holy Spirit.

Immigrating to the U.S. in 1920, Nikoloff attended college in New York City and received the baptism in the Holy Spirit under the ministry of Robert and Marie Brown at Glad Tidings Tabernacle. He pastored several churches in New York and New Jersey and at the same time attended Bethel Bible Training School in Newark, New Jersey, graduating in 1924. He then taught at the school until 1926.

Feeling called of God to return to Bulgaria, Nikoloff and his American-born wife, Martha, spent five years (1926–31) evangelizing and pastoring in Bourgas. He also served as the first superintendent of the Evangelical Pentecostal churches in Bulgaria. From 1935 to 1938 he worked as principal of the Biblical Institute in the Free City of Danzig (now Gdansk, Poland). While there he assisted in the training of young people who went back to various Eastern European countries to preach the gospel. He returned to Bulgaria in 1939 to evangelize and teach.

With the coming of World War II, Nikoloff returned to the U.S. and served as president of Metropolitan Bible Institute, North Bergen, New Jersey (1941–50), and New England Bible Institute, Framingham, Massachusetts (1950–52). In 1952 he joined the faculty of Central Bible Institute of Springfield, Missouri, where he served (chairman of the Department of Religious Education in 1954; the Bible department beginning in 1956) until his retirement in 1961 due to ill health.

During his years in the U.S., Nikoloff earned the B.R.E. and M.R.E. degrees from the Biblical Seminary in New York (now New York Theological Seminary). In 1956 he completed the Ph.D. from New York University; his dissertation was entitled: "Bogomilism, A Study of the Bulgarian Heresy as an Expression of the Principle of Puritanism." In recognition of his scholastic record, he received the University's Founders Day Certificate of Achievement.

Nikoloff's publications included two Bulgarian church magazines, several books and tracts, and a songbook in that language. He also worked for five years (1954–59) as the editor of the Sunday school quarterly *Youth Teacher* at the Gospel Publishing House. The Nikoloffs had three children: a daughter born in Danzig who died at an early age; another daughter, Natalie (Eliott); and a son, Dr. Paul H. Nichols.

Nicholas Nikoloff made important contributions to the development of the Pentecostal churches in Bulgaria, the advance of Pentecostalism in Eastern Europe and the Soviet Union, and the training of AG ministers and missionaries.

Bibliography: "Martha Nikoloff, a Life Committed to Ministry," *Onward* (May 1988), 2; N. Nikoloff, *Report on Europe* (1943); idem, "The Signs Follow in Bulgaria," *PE* (June 25, 1932), 1; "Nicholas Nikoloff With the Lord," *PE* (December 13, 1964), 15; T. Salzer, *"The Danzig Gdanska Instytut Biblijny: Its History and Impact"* (unpublished, 1988).   G. B. McGee

NONDENOMINATIONAL PENTECOSTAL AND CHARISMATIC CHURCHES

It is nearly impossible to tabulate the number of nondenominational charismatic churches in the U.S. According to a 1980 *Christianity Today* Gallup poll, 19 percent of all adult Americans (over 29 million) consider themselves to be Pentecostal or charismatic Christians. Many of these people attend independent charismatic churches.

When asked for the explanation of the amazing growth of independent charismatic congregations over the past decade or two, leaders of the movement noted the effects of twenty-five years of Oral Roberts, Full Gospel Business Men's Fellowship, the television ministries of CBN and PTL, and the evangelistic fervor of these churches. Also the charismatic movement can be seen as the attempt to fill an emotional, experiential vacuum left in American Christendom that had become more liberal and rationalistic.

Many of today's charismatics were once Catholics or members of mainline Protestant churches. They recall their former churches as formal, cold, or dead, while they perceive their charismatic churches as free, warm, and alive. Typically, the worship of a charismatic congregation has no liturgical trappings. Nor is a charismatic church identical with classical Pentecostal churches, especially in any preoccupation with avoidance of "worldly dress," which once was the hallmark of women in Pentecostal congregations. Both men and women in charismatic congregations wear attire typical of their communities. Women feel free to attend services in slacks or jeans, men in casual clothing. Such matters as women's hairstyles, makeup, and the wearing of jewelry are not considered significant to spiritual stature. Many of these cultural changes have been adopted recently by Pentecostal congregations, especially the larger ones.

While not as legalistic as yesterday's Pentecostals, today's charismatics consider it inappropriate to indulge in the use of tobacco, alcoholic beverages, or drugs. In some quarters the use of wine in moderation is not condemned; in others total abstinence from any form of alcohol is advocated.

The matter of divorce, which tends to put some Pentecostals into a "second-class" status, is less of a problem in most charismatic churches, since hard and fast rules were not adopted years ago when divorce was not such a common circumstance. Generally speaking, converts are accepted in whatever marital state they find themselves at the time of their conversion. Divorce for a converted person is frowned upon as a sin, but a convert who happens to be a divorced person is welcomed into the body without reservation. Some churches offer support groups or classes for divorced persons, and others provide counsel for those considering remarriage.

Generally there is no outright condemnation for members attending motion pictures, theater, plays, sporting events, musical concerts, and the like. However, most charismatics find themselves so taken up with a wide variety of church activities that they have little time for secular entertainment.

The one trait that marks the charismatics is their exuberance in worship: they raise their hands and sometimes clap or wave in time to the music as they sing choruses. The lyrics for their choruses are usually displayed by overhead projection on a wall or screen or are sung from memory, and they sing heartily. They seldom rely on hymnals for an entire song service. Many of the choruses are based on biblical passages, often from the Psalms.

Some churches have spontaneous praise as well as dancing in time to music, but this dancing could not be compared to what takes place on a dance floor. Other churches have praise-dance groups who have learned Hebrew dance patterns and who "dance before the Lord" while the congregation watches and worships with them.

Most charismatic churches have choirs and employ musical instruments—from a few guitars and a drummer to full orchestras. Vocal soloists, ensembles, and choirs often sing with commercially produced musical accompaniment tapes.

In vocal worship some churches make a distinction between praise and "high praise"—the former being expressed aloud in the common language, the latter being uttered in unknown tongues, sometimes called "singing in the Spirit." While classical Pentecostals practice praying aloud (sometimes called praying in concert), charismatics emphasize praising aloud, often accompanied with hand clapping.

To many the charismatic congregation's contributions to the church are a new awareness of the gifts of the Holy Spirit as a ministry to the life of the church, new devotional techniques for public and private worship (not just tongues), exercise of "body life," and an emphasis on discipleship.

When Pentecostal believers were forced out of mainline denominations in the early twentieth century, they formed independent churches that tended to hold denominations suspect. Many remained as independent entities, but some nevertheless formed "fellowships" and avoided using the term "denomination." This was the case with the General Council of the Assemblies of God (AG). In some respects this parallels what has occurred in the charismatic renewal in recent years. The Church of God (CG, Cleveland Tenn.), founded prior to the turn of the century as a Holiness denomination, simply accepted the baptism of the Holy Spirit as an authentic biblical experience. Something similar to this took place in the 1960s in several denominations after respected clergy and laity testified to speaking in tongues. In several instances denominations appointed committees to study the biblical validity of the phenomenon, and favorable reports were adopted along with guidelines about charismatic manifestations.

When the Neo-Pentecostal or charismatic movement began in the 1950s and became full-blown in the 1960s, at first many Neo-Pentecostals stayed in their churches. David du Plessis was one leader who encouraged them to do this. "There is no doubt the Holy Spirit is hard at work at bringing unity," he said. "Dialogue is becoming more and more acceptable."

Some congregations, such as Everett ("Terry") Fullam's St. Paul's Episcopal Church in Darien, Connecticut, and Morris Vaagenes's North Heights Lutheran Church in Roseville, Minnesota, became known as "charismatic parishes."

Yet other charismatics, such as Jamie Buckingham and Ken Sumrall, both Southern Baptists from Florida, were forced to withdraw from their denominations because of their new-found charismatic experiences.

Most of these ministers and their congregations preferred to remain independent rather than to affiliate with the classical Pentecostal denominations. And most also wanted to avoid starting new denominations because of the stigma they identified with denominations.

Yet the charismatics typically were not loners. Most emphasized the unity of believers, and they sought out other charismatics for fellowship. To fan the flames of renewal, charismatic conferences and meetings were sponsored with names such as Camps Farthest Out and National Leadership Conference.

Slowly, new groups began to form, often based on personal relationships between ministers. Among the first to emerge in the early 1970s were groups affiliated with Derek Prince, Bernard "Bob" Mumford, Charles Simpson, Don Basham, and later W. J. "Ern" Baxter. In 1975 these men called a "Shepherds' conference" in Kansas City. Some saw this as the forming of a new charismatic denomination, and the matter was hotly debated that year. Those men maintained that they were not starting a denomination, and they held to this so firmly that their group of churches never really became a strong force within the charismatic renewal and finally disintegrated in late 1986.

After a few years there were so many nondenominational charismatics that when the historic 1977 Conference on Charismatic Renewal in the Christian Churches was held in Kansas City, the nondenominationals were allowed to hold their own meetings while the denominational charismatics (Roman Catholics, Lutherans, Episcopalians, etc.) were holding theirs. In fact, there were two nondenominational meetings—one was for the Prince-Mumford-Simpson-Basham group (which went under a number of different names over the years), and the other for the other nondenominationals who did not want to be affiliated with those men. (The discipleship controversy was raging at this time.)

When the nondenominational ministers formed their own congregations, they found they had to take on some of the trappings of a denomination in order to qualify for nonprofit status by the Internal Revenue Service (IRS). They had to form nonprofit corporations. (The IRS expects churches to have: a distinct legal existence, a recognized creed and form of worship, a definite and distinctive ecclesiastical government, a formal code of doctrine and discipline, a distinct religious history, a membership not associated with any other church denomination, a complete organization of ordained ministers ministering to their congregations, ordained ministers selected after completing a prescribed course of study, a literature of its own, established places of worship, regular congregations, regular religious services, Sunday schools for religious instruction of the young, and schools for the preparation of its ministers.)

Few, if any, churches could satisfy all of these criteria, but organizations meeting a preponderance of these items clearly could be recognized by the IRS as a church. In their efforts to satisfy IRS scrutiny, attempts to form single independent local churches sometimes grew into mini-denominations. At times, IRS audits or the fear of audits caused independent charismatic churches to add ministries, such as Bible schools, that were not their original intent.

Some charismatic churches—especially the larger ones—were so totally dominated by a strong pastor who, in some instances, had almost unlimited control over the finances, that several of these churches came under scrutiny by the IRS. So in the 1970s some "fellowships" were formed that served as umbrella organizations to some of these nondenominational groups that wished to be affiliated and to add legitimacy before the eyes of the IRS. The International Convention of Faith Ministries, Tulsa, Oklahoma, with approximately 1,000 ministers, and Liberty Fellowship, Birmingham, Alabama, which currently lists thirty-two churches and 242 pastors, were formed in this era.

At the same time, younger men were beginning their own ministries. Some of these set about to recapture certain aspects of church life and mission that others deemphasized. These young ministers formed what they called "New Testament" churches according to what they considered to be the biblical blueprint. Some of these churches are informally linked to each other. Pastors establishing new churches look to existing churches for oversight, although there is an absence of legal or formal ties such as exist in a denomination.

An example of these younger leaders is Larry Tomczak, a minister in the Washington, D.C., area. Tomczak, thirty-seven, a former Roman Catholic, emerged as a leader around the time of the Jesus movement in the early 1970s. For several years he along with C. J. Mahaney and others held Tuesday night "Take and Give" (T.A.G.) charismatic services in rented facilities. After a few years it was obvious that a committed group of believers who needed pastoral oversight had developed, and most of them did not relate closely with any other group. So they began holding Sunday services in a high school gymnasium. They named their first church Covenant Life Church and since then have planted other churches throughout the country.

Some of the more successful independent charismatic pastors are, like Tomczak, under forty: Bob Weiner, thirty-nine, started Maranatha Campus Ministries in 1972 in Kentucky. With its headquarters now in Gainesville, Florida, Maranatha has established churches on a hundred college campuses. Larry Lea, thirty-six, founded Church on the Rock in Rockwall, Texas, in 1979. Today the church has 12,000 in attendance. Ron Tucker, thirty-five, founded Grace World Outreach Center in Maryland Heights, a suburb of St. Louis, Missouri, in 1978. Average Sunday attendance is 3,500. Billy Joe Daugherty, thirty-five, founded Victory Christian Center in Tulsa, Oklahoma. The church offices, Victory Christian School (K–12, eight hundred students), Victory Bible Institute, and Victory World Mission Training Center are located in a former public school building. The congregation meets each Sunday at Mabee Center on the campus of Oral Roberts University, with attendance averaging around 6,000. The Living Word Church in Middleton, Ohio, is building a sanctuary that will seat 14,000, making it the largest auditorium of any charismatic church in this country.

Black Pentecostals also have many large, independent charismatic churches. They provide theological conservatism and political-social radicalism that will both challenge and contribute to the development of evangelism. One of the largest charismatic churches pastored by a black minister is Crenshaw Christian Center, which occupies the old Pepperdine University Campus in Los Angeles, California. Its pastor, Frederick K. C. Price, also conducts a nationwide television ministry.

Other charismatics have developed "Christian Centers" on a congregationalist community-church model that, at least in the beginning stages, seeks to do without buildings and sometimes has a very informal sacramental practice. Typical of these structures are the Neo-Pentecostal missions of the Jews, which tend to form charismatic Messianic synagogues with a loose relationship to one another.

In the early 1980s hundreds of new churches were started by eager young pastors who had been trained at the new charismatic institutions such as Rhema Bible Training Center in Tulsa, Oklahoma; Christ for the Nations Institute in Dallas, Texas; Liberty Bible College in Pensacola, Florida; or a host of smaller Bible schools affiliated with churches. Often these churches had names such as Word of Faith or Faith Fellowship.

By 1984 there were so many of these nondenominational congregations that the Pentagon recognized them so they could send chaplains to the military. Founded by James Ammerman of Dallas, a former chaplain, the Chaplaincy of Full Gospel Churches estimates that approximately 40,000 independent charismatic churches have been started since 1960. Ammerman now represents about 1.5 million members. In his listings are twenty-four "fellowships," some of which have the trappings of a denomination and some of which are merely umbrella organizations. Ammerman estimates that there are at least three million believers in independent churches that are not affiliated with his group. By 1987 Ammerman had placed ten chaplains in the Army, four in the Navy, one in the Air Force, eighteen in the National Guard reserves, two in prisons, and one in a hospital.

Even though many fellowships had formed, few if any used the word "charismatic" in their titles, and almost all were unknown other than by the pastors or churches with whom they were affiliated. Then in 1986 Oral Roberts founded the Charismatic Bible Ministries (CBM) as a fellowship. Roberts invited seventy-seven men and women as trustees who represented a virtual "who's who" of the nondenominational charismatic segment of the Pentecostal–charismatic movement. Within a year more than two thousand had joined.

The trustees adopted a statement of purpose:

> The purpose of this fellowship is to provide a broad range of spiritual, educational and professional benefits to ministers who choose to participate. The foremost benefit is mutual fellowship—spiritual enrichment during conferences, sharing of methods, revelations, prophecies, and teachings in the fullness of the Holy Spirit; and personal encouragement from one minister to another.

While advancing specific goals, CBM is not a denomination. It is neither opposed to church denominations, nor does it discourage its members from involvement in their respective or independent group.

The Network of Christian Ministries formed in 1984. Its purpose is to link together fellowships, independent churches, and ministries. Charles Green serves as chairman and Everett Strong as administrator.

But much more than networks or fellowships or denominations, the dynamic of these Pentecostal/charismatic churches is the element of the supernatural—the gifts of the Holy Spirit and miracles being available to everyone. It is not the fact that a church is independent or part of a denomination that is emphasized; it is the fact that the people who worship at that church experience a consciousness of God's presence. In that presence they worship him, not in a distant formal manner, but with an awareness that he is actually present.

See also CHARISMATIC MOVEMENT.

Bibliography: J. Guinn, "Church Audits Under the Tax Reform Act," *Ministries Today* (September–October 1986), 16–18; L. Howard, "Humble Young Men, Enormous New Churches," *Charisma* (September 1984), 78–83; K. S. Kantzer, "Charismatics: Who We Are and What We Believe," *Charisma* (April 1980), 43–

49; D. Roberts, "They Called Him Mr. Pentecost," *Charisma* (November–December 1978), 19–25; S. Strang, "The Ever-Increasing Faith of Fred Price," *Charisma* (September 1986), 52.   S. Strang

NORTH AMERICAN CONGRESSES ON THE HOLY SPIRIT AND WORLD EVANGELIZATION

The first North American Congress on the Holy Spirit and World Evangelization was held in New Orleans on October 8–11, 1986. More than 7,000 leaders from a total of 40 denominations and church groups attended the conference. The theme of this leadership conference was a challenge to work together for the evangelization of the world. One of the main speakers was John Wimber, who also led three workshops on "Signs and Wonders." Roman Catholic leader Tom Forrest urged the group to unite in the belief that "Jesus Christ is Lord." Honored at this meeting for their contributions were Oral Roberts, Demos Shakarian, David du Plessis, and Mennonite renewal leader Nelson Litwiller. Two denominational renewal groups were formed at this meeting, one of Southern Baptists and the other a mix of the Churches of Christ, the Christian Church, and the Disciples of Christ.

The second congress, with up to 35,000 registrants and perhaps as many as 40,000 in attendance, was a general conference open to the public and held in New Orleans on July 22–26, 1987. The theme of this conference seemed to be a call to personal holiness and commitment to evangelization. Participants had their choice of 110 different workshops such as "God's Call to the Single Adult," "Messianic Worship in the Local Congregation," "Discovering Your Ministry in the Body of Christ," and "Spiritual Warfare." Workshop leaders included James Robison, Ken Sumrall, Michael Scanlan, Anne Gimenez, Shirley Boone, Charles and Francis Hunter, Dennis Bennett, Marilyn Hickey, Charles Simpson, and John Meares.

Chairman Vinson Synan reported that 3,500 to 5,000 persons went to the prayer room each night in response to the altar call. Many of these were first time converts. Responding to a call to change New Orleans, over 10,000 participants gathered for a parade in the port area on the Mississippi River. Except for Mardi Gras it was the largest parade in New Orleans' history.

One of the most remarkable moments occurred when German evangelist Reinhard Bonnke gave an altar call for salvation and one-third of those present stood to their feet. He repeated the call and more stood! David Sklrenko, Sr., a Roman Catholic, suggested that Bonnke's call could have been understood by Roman Catholics as a "renewing of Christian vows" rather than as a first-time commitment. Many remarkable healings were reported under Bonnke's ministry as well.

Chairman Synan remarked, "This Conference brought evangelization into the thinking of the charismatic renewal. Where evangelization has never before been a big part of the charismatic experience, now it will become the major thrust of the renewal."

A world congress is to be held some time in 1990.

Bibliography: S. Lawson, "The Big Charismatic Get-Together," *Charisma* (Sept. 1987), 56–58; idem, "Focus on Miracles and Evangelism," *Charisma* (June 1987), 65; idem, "Leaders Unite in New Orleans," *Charisma* (Dec. 1986), 58–59.   J. R. Zeigler

NORTH AMERICAN RENEWAL SERVICE COMMITTEE

(NARSC). Steering committee for the North American Congresses on the Holy Spirit and World Evangelization.

After the meeting on the Holy Spirit held in Kansas City in 1977 there was talk of another national meeting. On May 6–7, 1985, thirty-two Christian leaders met in St. Louis, Missouri, to discuss plans for a national conference. Vinson Synan, assistant general superintendent of the Pentecostal Holiness Church, served as chairman of the group. The decision was made to hold a national leadership conference in New Orleans in October of 1986, a general North American conference in July 1987, and a world conference sometime in 1990. Kevin Ranaghan, chairman of the Kansas City meeting and serving on the steering committee of the NARSC, said one of the goals of the NARSC was to emphasize the role of the Holy Spirit in world evangelization and added, "[We want to show] that we are people who are depending on the power of the Holy Spirit in Christian life and the power of the Holy Spirit in spiritual gifts."

Bibliography: S. Haggerty, "Kansas City 2," *Charisma* (July 1985), 84–85.   J. R. Zeigler

NORTON, ALBERT

(d. 1923). Missionary in India. A university-trained minister from Chicago, Norton was an early proponent of faith missions: he exhibited tenacity and self-sacrifice in reaching the Kurkus of central India. He collaborated with Pandita Ramabai in famine relief in 1899 and was on hand to witness the outpouring that occurred at her nearby Mukti Mission in 1905. A similar revival with Pentecostal phenomena was experienced at his home for boys.

Bibliography: F. J. Ewart, *The Phenomenon of Pentecost* (1947); S. Frodsham, *With Signs Following* (1941); B. F. Lawrence, "Apostolic Faith Restored," published serially in *Weekly Evangel* (April 1, 1916), 4; C. Montgomery, *Under His Wings* (1936); J. E. Norton, "In Memorium of Albert Norton," *LRE* (April 1924), 13.   E. A. Wilson

NORWEGIAN CHARISMATICS
See CHARISMATIC MOVEMENT.

NORWEGIAN PENTECOSTALS
See EUROPEAN PENTECOSTALISM.

NOTRE DAME CONFERENCES
See CATHOLIC CHARISMATIC RENEWAL.

NUNN, DAVID OLIVER

(1921–). Healing evangelist. Having been reared in poverty and hunger, David Nunn has never forgotten his origins. He formed a ministry, Bible Revival Evangelistic Association (1962), that is today dedicated to foreign missions, especially feeding the hungry. Through his "Free Food Kitchens" in Africa, India, China, Mexico, and the Philippines, 500,000 per month are fed. Two orphanages operate in India, as well as a hospital that his agency supports (Mission of Mercy, Calcutta). Three Bible schools and a college serve converts in India and the Philippines. Bibles and other Christian literature are distributed worldwide, including Nepal and western China.

Nunn was born and reared in a Pentecostal family, served with the Army Air Force during World War II, and was an alcoholic by age twenty-two (Nunn, 1960, 4). After his conversion in November 1946, he began a preaching ministry in the Assemblies of God in June 1949. By January of the new year he had heard God's call to "get up from this city and go into every city I shall show thee and heal the sick therein" (ibid).

During the 1950s Nunn worked intensively with Gordon Lindsay and the *Voice of Healing*. His articles were often one of the magazine's primary features. He reports in one article that "as many as twenty-five totally blind received their sight in one single service. . . . In one single campaign I counted thirty-three people who were healed of paralysis or of a crippled condition." From 1959 until 1961 Nunn was active in the radio ministry of Lindsay's Voice of Healing organization, serving as a principal evangelist.

Bibliography: D. Nunn, *The Life and Ministry of David Nunn* (n.d.); D. Nunn, ed., *The Healing Messengers* (March 1963–current); idem, "How God Led Me into a Miracle Ministry" *Voice of Healing* 13 (4, 1960): 9; idem, personal letter to the author (1988).

J. A. Hewett

O

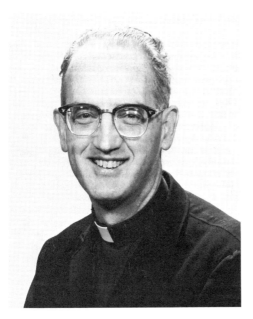

Edward D. O'Connor was one of the first Catholic priests to receive the baptism in the Spirit in 1967. He has taught at the University of Notre Dame since 1952.

O'CONNOR, EDWARD DENNIS

(1922–). Prominent priest-theologian in the early stages of the Catholic Charismatic Renewal. O'Connor entered the Holy Cross Congregation in 1939 and was ordained priest in 1948. He taught theology at the University of Notre Dame from 1952, becoming an associate professor of theology. O'Connor was one of the first priests to receive the baptism in the Spirit in 1967. His book *The Pentecostal Movement in the Catholic Church* (1971) describes the origins at Notre Dame, interpreting them in a Catholic framework. In the first years of the movement O'Connor wrote several pamphlets on charismatic topics and theological articles, mostly concerning ecclesiology and the spiritual life. He served on the National Service Committee from 1970 to 1973, resigning over his unease with its attitude toward church authority. O'Connor, who still participates in charismatic prayer meetings, has edited *Perspectives on Charismatic Renewal* (1975) and authored *Pope Paul and the Spirit* (1978).

P. D. Hocken

OLAZÁBAL, FRANCISCO (1886–1937).
Hispanic evangelist. Considered to have been the most effective Hispanic preacher of the early

Pentecostal movement, the Mexican-born Olazábal was converted in San Francisco under the influence of George and Carrie Judd Montgomery about 1900. He completed studies at the Methodist seminary in San Luis Potosí, Mexico, and had brief pastorates before returning to the U.S. to enter Moody Bible Institute, where he met R. A. Torrey. His ministry with the Methodist Church reached its height during World War I when he pastored a congregation in Los Angeles and was given oversight of churches in northern California. His reacquaintance with the Montgomerys— who in the meantime had become Pentecostal— led to his own baptism and his affiliation with the Assemblies of God in 1917.

Known affectionately as "El Azteca," Francisco Olazábal was considered the most effective Hispanic preacher in the early years of the Pentecostal movement.

In 1923, having grown restive within the predominantly Anglo organization, he led a group of disaffected pastors in forming the Latin American Council of Christian Churches (LACCC). In the following fourteen years he conducted numerous well-attended crusades in California, Texas, the Midwest, and Puerto Rico, and on the East Coast. Known affectionately as "El Azteca," the well-educated, physically imposing, and unusually effective evangelist dominated his devoted following. By 1937, when he met an untimely death in an auto accident, the LACCC numbered an estimated 150 churches with 50,000 adherents in Puerto Rico, New York, Chicago, Texas, and California.

Bibliography: H. C. Ball, "De los Primeros Cincuenta Años de las Asambleas de Dios Latinas," *La Luz Apostólica* 50 (9, 1966): 3, 11; V. De Leon, *The Silent Pentecostals* (1979); R. Domínguez, *Pioneros de Pentecostés* (1971); C. L. Holland, *The Religious Dimensions in Hispanic Los Angeles* (1974).   E. A. Wilson

ONENESS PENTECOSTALISM
   I. Origins
   II. Birth
   III. Organizational Development
   IV. Theology
       A. A Jewish Christian Theology of the Name
       B. The Name and the Nature of God
       C. The Name and Christology
       D. The Name and the Christian

Oneness Pentecostalism (OP) is a religious movement that emerged in 1914 within the Assemblies of God (AG) branch of the early American Pentecostal movement, challenging the traditional Trinitarian doctrine and baptismal practice with a modalistic view of God, a revelational theory of the name of Jesus, and an insistence on rebaptism in the name of the Lord Jesus Christ. It took on organizational form in 1917 as a result of the expulsion of its adherents from the AG. Originally called the "New Issue" or "Jesus Only" movement, by 1930 the self-designation was "Jesus' Name," "Apostolic," or "Oneness" Pentecostalism (OP).

I. Origins. In its distinctive teachings as well as in the doctrines that it continues to share with its AG counterpart, OP is an inheritor of nineteenth-century revivalism and in particular of the form of evangelical pietism found in the Keswick Holiness movement and the works of A. B. Simpson (founder of the Christian and Missionary Alliance) at the turn of the century.

As a form of evangelical experiential religion, the movement emphasized the importance of divine power in the individual Christian life, centering primarily on the experience of the "baptism of the Holy Spirit." A shift had been occurring toward an increased use of the name "Jesus" in piety, hymnody, and teaching. This focus soon extended to the name of Jesus as an object of devotion and source of spiritual power.

For their developing theology of the centrality and name of Jesus, the first Oneness leaders drew heavily from the writings of Arno C. Gaebelein, J. Monro Gibson, A. J. Gordon, William Phillips Hall, Essex W. Kenyon, and A. B. Simpson. They were less dependent in their "oneness" view of God and their advocacy of baptism in the name of the Lord Jesus Christ.

II. Birth. The Oneness movement received its first direct impulse in April 1913 at an international Pentecostal camp meeting in Arroyo Seco, outside Los Angeles. In an environment of expectancy, a baptismal sermon preached by Canadian evangelist R. E. McAlister noted that the apostles baptized in the name of the Lord Jesus Christ (see Acts 2:38), not in the triune formula of Matthew 28:19.

An otherwise unknown figure, John G. Scheppe, meditated on McAlister's observation throughout the night. In the early hours of the morning he ran through the camp shouting that the Lord had revealed to him the truth on baptism in the name of the Lord Jesus Christ.

The initial observation of the two baptismal formulas in Matthew 28:19 and Acts 2:38, and the attempt to harmonize them, made little impact except in the mind of another witness to McAlister's sermon, Frank J. Ewart. Australian by birth and a former Baptist minister, Ewart had been converted to Pentecostalism while pastoring in Canada. He moved to Los Angeles and became associated at Seventh Street Mission with William H. Durham, the first Pentecostal leader to convert from the Holiness to the baptistic "finished work of Calvary" teaching. This association eventually placed the Oneness movement within the organizational fellowship of the AG.

Following the 1913 camp meeting, Ewart continued to minister in the Los Angeles area while privately studying the baptismal question raised by McAlister. One year later he was ready to act on his growing convictions. He erected a tent in the town of Belvedere outside Los Angeles and preached his first public sermon on Acts 2:38 on April 15, 1914. He was joined by Glenn A. Cook, another prominent evangelist, and together they baptized each other in a baptismal tank set up in the tent. While other early Pentecostals had been baptized in the name of Jesus, notably Howard A. Goss and Andrew Urshan, this was the first public baptism using the apostolic formula to receive its rationale from a more comprehensive theology of the nature and name of God. This action credits Ewart as the first to chart a new direction within the early Pentecostal movement. It was he who formulated a theology of the name of Jesus to validate the new baptismal practice.

The new doctrine spread rapidly through evangelistic tours and a periodical edited by Ewart, *Meat In Due Season.* Since its circulation extended to the mission field, many converts were made there. The message was effectively planted in the Midwest through an evangelistic tour by Cook in the early months of 1915. The result was a number of baptisms at Mother Mary Barnes's Faith Home in St. Louis. It was there that J. Roswell Flower, an early convert of Cook and leader of the newly formed AG, first heard but strongly resisted the doctrine.

Cook traveled to Indianapolis, where he was successful in winning another leader, L. V. Roberts, and his entire congregation. More significant was the acceptance by the prominent black preacher, Garfield T. Haywood, who was baptized with 465 members of his thriving congregation. Haywood's conversion was strategic, for he was a popular preacher throughout the country and a singular black leader within the non-Wesleyan Pentecostal fellowship. Although he did not officially hold credentials with the AG, his ministry was with those who eventually made up that constituency. As a result, large numbers of black Pentecostals followed Haywood into the Oneness movement.

This painting of a night baptismal scene by Ransom Rambo, titled "Never Too Late," hangs in the United Pentecostal Church Archives, Hazelwood, Missouri.

By the spring of 1915 the new movement was spreading rapidly. Louisiana lost all twelve of its AG ministers. Advances were being made across Canada through the efforts of R. E. McAlister, Franklin Small (a Pentecostal leader from Winnipeg), and numerous American evangelists.

As the "new issue" spread, controversy intensified. A leading figure in the debate was E. N. Bell, member of the executive presbytery of the AG and editor of its two magazines, *Weekly Evangel* and *Word and Witness*. His assistant editor was Flower, already an opponent and soon to be an archenemy of the new movement. During the spring of 1915 Bell published articles and editorials denouncing the movement. He supported the validity of baptism in the name of the Lord Jesus Christ but opposed the requirement of rebaptism. Throughout his writings he remained cordial and conciliatory.

The summer brought a change in Bell. At an AG camp meeting in Jackson, Tennessee, under the strain of conscience and perhaps fatigue, he requested to be rebaptized by Roberts. The apparent defection caused confusion throughout the AG. In the fall Bell absented himself from the headquarters for the remainder of the year. Flower became responsible for the editorial work.

In articles that Bell published (which were edited by Flower), his religious enthusiasm centered on the centrality of Jesus Christ and the importance of the name "Lord." In a deleted portion he defended his personal conviction of the propriety of baptizing in the name of the Lord Jesus Christ without insisting that others be required to do so. But Bell never denied his Trinitarian beliefs. He refused to align himself with the new movement. He denounced contention and factionalism, recommended freedom in the use of baptismal formulae, discouraged rebaptism, and admonished visiting preachers to refrain

from promoting their baptismal preference without expressed permission from the pastor.

The rapid and aggressive spread of the Oneness movement, Bell's rebaptism, and the growing confusion within the AG ranks thrust Flower into the center of the controversy as defender of the Trinitarian cause. Seeing a need to reverse the current confusion, he obtained permission to call the Third General Council for October 1–10, 1915, in St. Louis. The purpose was to address the new issue in debate and discussion. At the assembly attention was given primarily to an examination of the baptismal formula. Although no consensus was reached, the council called for neutrality, liberality, and respect for the rights of conscience of both the ministers and the local congregations. It denounced aspects of the Oneness teaching on God and Christ that it regarded to be at variance with the Scriptures.

The coming months were a trial period, but they failed to achieve the goal of the Third Council. The Oneness proponents were still aggressively evangelizing within the fellowship. The Trinitarian faction was clarifying the theological issues and becoming increasingly irritated with the divisiveness.

As the hostility mounted, the agenda for the Fourth General Council in the fall of 1916 was set to settle the doctrinal issue of the Oneness movement. The Trinitarians entered the meeting in control of the key positions and committees. The committee to draft a "statement of fundamental truths" (*Council Minutes, 1916*, 10) was solidly Trinitarian, including Bell, who by then was back in full favor with the council leadership.

Although the council at its inception in 1914 disavowed any intention of creating an organization "that legislates or forms laws and articles of faith" (*Council Minutes, 1914*, 4), the Fourth Council was faced with the pressure to establish doctrinal limits. The result was a seventeen-point

"Statement of Fundamental Truths" that included a strongly worded section affirming the traditional doctrine of the Trinity. With the adoption of the Statement, 156 of the 585 ministers were barred from membership and with them many congregations.

III. Organizational Development. Amid rumors of its demise, the disenfranchised company of dissidents reappeared within months to ensure itself a future. Leaders such as Goss, H. G. Rodgers, and D. C. O. Opperman, who less than three years earlier had been instrumental in the formation of the AG, called for an organizational meeting on December 28, 1916, in Eureka Springs, Arkansas. Six days later the General Assembly of Apostolic Assemblies (GAAA) was formed, with a membership of 154 ministers, missionaries, elders, deacons, and evangelists.

The life of the GAAA, however, was short. Most ministers needed an organization that could issue credentials. But with the pending American involvement in World War I, it was discovered that the GAAA was formed too late to recognize ministers of military age.

Through the intervention of Haywood, a small organization was found that had embraced the Oneness message, the Pentecostal Assemblies of the World (PAW). It had been formed in 1906 as a loose fellowship in the Los Angeles area. Haywood himself had held credentials since 1911. Undoubtedly it was his influence as well as his contacts with the GAAA members that led to a merger of the two groups. In January 1918 they met in St. Louis, Missouri, where they negotiated the merger under the charter of the PAW.

By the following year three publications already in existence were officially recognized—Ewart's *Meat in Due Season*, Haywood's *Voice in the Wilderness*, and Opperman's *The Blessed Truth*.

Prominent early Oneness leaders varied in their relationship to the PAW. Ewart, the architect of the new doctrine, was listed in the membership of the GAAA and the PAW. But he held no official position, and his name disappeared completely from the rolls by 1920. He continued his ministry in the Los Angeles area and maintained fellowship with others in the movement but showed little interest in organizational matters.

Franklin Small, a former Baptist minister from Winnipeg, held credentials with the apostles for the purpose of fellowship. But in 1921 he formed a Canadian organization, the Apostolic Church of Pentecost (ACOP), to promote the movement in western Canada. The ACOP continues to be unique among the theologically Arminian Pentecostals with its Calvinistic doctrine of the eternal security of the believer.

Andrew Urshan, a Persian immigrant and convert to Pentecostalism, was a prominent evangelist with the AG until the early part of 1919. He had practiced baptism in the name of the Lord Jesus Christ since 1911, but after 1916 he came under increasing suspicion for holding views sympathetic to the Oneness cause. After joining the PAW in 1919, Urshan promoted the new doctrine through evangelism and the publication of a periodical, *The Witness of God*.

Haywood was wide-ranging in his influence as a preacher, teacher, hymnwriter, organizational leader, and periodical publisher. He was an outspoken advocate of racial integration within the PAW. His doctrinal teaching and leadership continued to inspire the black Oneness movement long after his death in 1931.

The vision for a racially integrated body gradually eroded between 1920 and 1924. With the moving of the PAW headquarters to Indianapolis and the influence of Haywood, the blacks were increasing in numbers until they were a majority in the North. Because of segregation policies in the South, conventions were held in the North. Financial limitations prevented large numbers of the white southern majority to attend. In 1921 the southern constituency held a Bible conference in Little Rock, Arkansas, that resulted in both unifying the white members and deepening the rift between them and the blacks.

The whites argued pragmatically that an integrated organization was a barrier to the spread of the movement in the South. However, their racist attitudes were exposed in complaints that a black official was signing ministerial credentials for the white ministers; namely, Haywood, who was general secretary at the time. A compromise resolution in 1923 to allow T. C. Davis, a black, and Goss, a white, to sign certificates for those demanding it, failed to stem the tide of disunity.

The whites entered the 1924 general conference with a proposal for two racially separate administrations under one organizational structure. With its failure to meet the approval of the blacks, the majority of the whites withdrew from the PAW, cutting its rolls by over 50 percent. The schism left a legacy of hostility on both sides. It was regarded as a special affront to the black members who had struggled to maintain the racial unity of the fragile movement.

The years 1924–31 were slow and troublesome for both segments. The names and number of members in the PAW remained virtually unchanged. While the whites grew faster, dissension within their ranks increased. They divided organizationally into two groups, based in part on regional concentration.

One group began as Emmanuel's Church in Jesus Christ (ECJC), representing the tri-state region of Oklahoma, Texas, and Louisiana. It merged in 1927 with a small group that had been formed in St. Louis, changing its name to the Apostolic Church of Jesus Christ (ACJC). Theologically many of its members embraced the "new birth" teaching that equated the new birth and salvation with water baptism in the name of the Lord Jesus Christ and the Pentecostal experience of the baptism of the Holy Spirit accompanied by speaking in tongues.

Another group formed in Tennessee in 1925 as the Pentecostal Ministerial Alliance (PMA). Its baptistic influences were evident organizationally in its preference for a less centralized government and theologically in its definition of the new birth as a conversion experience distinct from water baptism and the baptism of the Holy Spirit. In 1932 it changed its name to Pentecostal Church, Incorporated (PCI).

This time period was one of fragmentation,

failed attempts to reunify, and slight numerical growth. Finally, a large Unity Conference of all Oneness groups was held in September 1931 in Columbus, Ohio, to explore the possibility of reunification. From that meeting came a flurry of negotiations, with both white organizations approaching the PAW. The PMA's proposal, which included a separate administration system, failed in the negotiation stage.

The offer by the ACJC of a racially balanced, integrated structure quickly won the support of many PAW leaders. A swift merger was achieved by November 1931 under a new name, the Pentecostal Assemblies of Jesus Christ (PAJC). The speed with which the leaders negotiated the merger, however, soon became a source of suspicion on the part of some black leaders in the PAW. They feared that insincerity and opportunism were the motives prompting the white negotiators.

The charges, the compromise to change the name of the organization, and the abandonment of the episcopal form of government practiced since 1925 were sufficient reasons for ministers like Samuel Grimes, E. F. Akers, and A. W. Lewis to take action. The original PAW charter was salvaged from obscurity shortly before its expiration date. A meeting to reorganize was called in Dayton, Ohio, and the old organization re-emerged under the leadership of Grimes.

The continuing PAJC was soon fraught with racial tension. Due to the selection of the southern city of Tulsa, Oklahoma, as the site of the 1937 general convention, black ministers were confronted with segregated accommodations. With this affront, most of the ministers who had supported the new experiment returned to the PAW. With it also came sufficient disillusionment to thwart any future serious attempts at merger.

A persistent drive for unity continued between the two white organizations, the PAJC and PCI. One unsuccessful attempt was made in 1936. In 1941 a significant schism occurred when L. R. Ooton from Indiana led nearly a thousand ministers from the tri-state region of Indiana, Ohio, and West Virginia out of the PAJC to form the Apostolic Ministerial Alliance.

In 1945 the two organizations finally negotiated a merger to form the largest Oneness organization, the United Pentecostal Church (UPC). Creating a ministerial strength of nearly 1,800 ministers and more than 900 congregations, the union was built on a delicate compromise over the theological interpretation of the new birth. All agreed on the practice of baptism in the name of the Lord Jesus Christ and the Pentecostal experience of the baptism of the Holy Spirit according to the pattern of Acts 2:38, but they could not agree that this pattern signifies the new birth. The compromise called upon each member to refrain from promoting one position at the expense of the unity of the fellowship. The compromise succeeded in maintaining the structural unity of the organization, with the exception of two minor disaffections in later years. But eventually the segment that equates Acts 2:38 with the new birth increased more rapidly in numerical growth

and finally gained control of most of the positions of leadership.

The UPC claims approximately one-half of the numerical strength of the Oneness movement. It maintains an aggressive evangelistic program, publishes its own Sunday school curriculum, and supports nine Bible schools in the U.S. and Canada.

Although much of its doctrine and organizational structure are similar to the AG, there are differences. Due in part to the Holiness roots of some of the early leaders prior to 1945, the UPC maintains a more centralized form of church government. It expects a higher degree of conformity to its code of conduct and allegiance to the organizational fellowship. There are ministerial restrictions on the public fellowshiping of any minister or group that has been formerly disfellowshiped by the UPC for doctrinal or moral reasons. Theologically it teaches the baptistic doctrine of progressive sanctification it inherited from the AG. In practice, however, it reflects Holiness tendencies to specify certain religious customs as a standard by which to express one's piety. For instance, there is a strong injunction against women cutting their hair (see 1 Cor. 11). Ministers are not permitted to own a television, and the faithful are strongly admonished against it.

The PAW has continued to be a predominantly black organization since 1931. Although whites are a small minority, a conscientious policy in integration is maintained. White representation is encouraged at all levels, including that of the episcopate. The PAW continues a high degree of commitment to an episcopal form of government.

Most of the black Oneness groups have their origin directly or indirectly in the PAW. There has been little variance from the Oneness doctrinal teachings of Haywood. Most disputes and schisms have occurred over conflict in leadership, the stand on divorce and remarriage, and the use of wine in Communion.

The growing institutionalization of the movement and a desire for a larger Oneness identity among the smaller organizations led in 1971 to the formation of the Apostolic World Christian Fellowship (AWCF). Unrepresented for doctrinal reasons in the Pentecostal World Conference and the Pentecostal Fellowship of North America, the AWCF provides a means to express the worldwide unity of Oneness Pentecostals, to assess their strength, and to coordinate evangelistic efforts.

The momentum for the founding of the AWCF was provided largely by Worthy Rowe, a pastor from South Bend, Indiana. The initial meeting attracted representatives from eight organizations. As a result, the international fellowship was established as an affiliation of organizations, respecting the sovereignty of each. Voting rights were granted only to official organizational representatives, although independent clergy were encouraged to attend.

The conspicuous absence of the UPC from the outset was due to Rowe's association with a doctrinal deviation taught by his father, G. B. Rowe. The latter had held official positions in the early PAW, PAJC, and UPC. With his refusal to abandon the teaching of a form of adoptionistic christology, he was disfellowshiped from the UPC in the early fifties. His son, having never recanted the father's teaching, has continued under the ban. The UPC, therefore, has extended the ban to the AWCF, since it has continued under his chairmanship. The AWCF, however, has gained the respect and support of more than fifty Oneness organizations worldwide.

Like the Pentecostal movement in general, a small segment of Oneness believers can be found on the fringe. There are numerous independent churches that have affiliation with no organization and are frequently founded and pastored by a single leader. In addition, Oneness beliefs can be found among approximately two dozen small Sabbatarian groups. Some are Yahwist groups devoted to the sacred name of Yahweh, water baptism in the name of Jesus or Yahshua, and the monarchy of God. Finally, some of the snake-handling sects in West Virginia, Tennessee, and Kentucky hold to some form of Oneness belief.

IV. Theology.

A. A Jewish-Christian Theology of the Name.

Historically OP is part of the modern Pentecostal movement within the American revivalist tradition. Many of its beliefs and practices can be traced to these roots. Within the larger theological horizon, it is a modern sectarian expression of a Jewish-Christian theology of the Name.

From the NT texts emerges the perennial possibility of modes of thinking and motifs borrowed from Judaism. These may be concepts or practices pushed aside by advancing Gentile Christianity. Richard Longenecker observes this tendency in the early christological disputes:

> In reaction to the direction that the crystalization [sic] of thought in mainstream Christianity was taking, some undoubtedly latched onto earlier titles which they felt were being ignored and certain perspectives which they considered illegitimately relegated to an inferior position in the structure of Christian thought (1970, 153).

In its distinctive doctrines of God, Christ, and Christian initiation, OP is a modern sectarian expression of this desire to restore some aspect of primitive Christianity. It focuses on a distinctly Jewish theme or idea that becomes its point of identity. Part of its sectarian pattern is to place all other doctrines at the service of this one and by it to define the group's relationship to all other Christian bodies.

The specifically Jewish characteristics of the Oneness doctrine of God are the belief that the name of God reveals his true nature, that in his being he is radically one, and that he "dwells" in tabernacle, temple, and in particular his name.

From this view of God dwelling in his name, Oneness christology develops the belief that the name "Jesus" is a major christological designation connoting his deity. The Jewish concept of divine presence as "dwelling" supports the Nestorian tendency in OP to keep the two natures in Christ separate.

The Jewish-Christian theology of the Name takes on significance for the believer when that person invokes the name of Jesus in water baptism. By so doing, the initiate is linked with the risen Lord. Subsequent to baptism the name of Jesus becomes an instrument of power in the life of the one who bears that name, manifesting the signs of the kingdom.

B. The Name and the Nature of God.

The core of Oneness theology is the belief that God has revealed himself through his name, beginning in the OT. The Name is more than a human designation for divine reality. It is God's method of revealing his presence and character and the means by which one encounters him (Exod. 33:18–19). Although the OT records various names for God that designate divine characteristics, the name of Yahweh defines God in his self-revelation in the Old Covenant. The singularity of this Name corroborates the radical oneness of God's nature. In the words of Frank Ewart, "The unity of God is sustained by the absolute unity or oneness of His name" (n.d., 21). Treating Yahweh as a proper name prepares the way for a theology of the name of Jesus as the NT name given by God as a means of self-revelation and salvation.

The radical unity of God is demonstrated in the *Shema* (Deut. 6:4) and in other passages that affirm God's oneness, leading Oneness writers such as David Bernard to claim for OP the designation "Christian Monotheism" (1983, 13).

Oneness theology builds its alternative to the traditional Trinitarian doctrine of the nature of God on three theological principles. First, the nature of God is a simple dialectic of transcendence and immanence. The only distinction within the Godhead is otherness and expressibility. In the NT it is expressed as Spirit and Word, or more personally as Father and Son. The monarchy of God is preserved in his transcendence; his threeness in revelation. Therefore, unlike Trinitarian theology, the divine threefold reality exists only on the side of God's immanence.

Second, the "personhood" of God is reserved for his immanent and incarnate presence in Jesus, while "Spirit" designates God in his transcendence. Unaware of the complexity of traditional Trinitarian terminology, "person" is given the modern definition of a corporal human being. This makes comprehensible the Oneness accusation of crypto-tritheism in Trinitarian thought. To describe the transcendent pole of God's nature as "Spirit" does not imply that God is an impersonal force. The character of personality is preserved in the theology of the Name that reveals and embodies it. This "Spirit-person" dialectic is the principle by which Oneness theology explains the Incarnation. It is not the Second Person of the Trinity but the Spirit, the full undifferentiated Deity, who becomes incarnate in the human person, Jesus. In Oneness language, the Father indwells the Son.

Third, the threefold divine reality is defined as "three manifestations" of the one Spirit in the person of Jesus. Taken from the christological hymn in 1 Timothy 3:16, the term "manifestation" bars the threeness from God's nature and restricts it to his self-revelation. As a form of modalism, it preserves the radical monarchy of

God and affirms the triune revelation. Believing, mistakenly, that Trinitarianism teaches that God exists as three *separate* and distinct persons, it is concerned to show that the whole essential Godhead is present in Jesus, not just one divine Person (see Col. 2:9).

The functional term "offices" is preferred by some writers instead of "manifestations." But its lack of biblical reference and impersonal tone make it less appealing to most Oneness representatives.

The Oneness interpretation of the traditional "us" passages in the OT (e.g., Gen. 1:26; 3:22), which some Trinitarians interpret as conversation among the members of the Trinity, varies with the authors. Gordon Magee argues that God is speaking to angels (n.d.). John Paterson, who holds a variant position that the Word had a distinct status before the Incarnation, believes that God was conversing with the Word, "the embodiment of the invisible God" (n.d.). Embodiment here refers to a divine hypostatic distinction. The plural name, "Elohim," is generally interpreted as a plurality of attributes or majesty, not persons.

Analogies are used by Oneness writers to illustrate their view of the Three-in-One, such as the triune nature of humanity as body, soul, and spirit; a man as son, husband, and father; a tree with roots, branches, and sap; a light ray giving illumination, warmth, and power; and fire, which also gives light, heat, and power. The Oneness choice of analogies, however, is poor; because of their Trinitarian implications, the Oneness point is lost. Some analogies would legitimately place the Oneness view within the acceptable range of Western Trinitarian thought.

The three manifestations of Father, Son, and Holy Spirit function in much the same way as persons do in Trinitarian theology. Personality is attributable to all three. The difference is that there is but one divine being whose essence is revealed as Father *in* the Son and as Spirit *through* the Son. The attention is christocentric in that as a human being Jesus *is* the Son, and as Spirit (i.e., in his deity) he reveals—indeed *is* the Father—and sends—indeed *is* the Holy Spirit as the Spirit of Christ who indwells the believer. Because the nature of God is one, the Father, Son, and Holy Spirit are all present in the manifestation of each.

Oneness Pentecostalism is a form of simultaneous modalism that, unlike Sabellianism, regards all three manifestations as present at the same time, not in successive revelatory periods. Occasional statements that parallel views of economic Trinitarianism are not developed sufficiently to warrant identification with it. There is also a corrective element to the general criticism that modalism does not adequately support an incarnational bond between the being of God and his revelation. One is a radical Jesus-centrism whereby God is not blocked from incarnating himself but is drawn out of eternity in his fullness in Jesus. Additionally, the theology of the Name bonds the revelation to the nature of God by identifying the name "Jesus" as the proper name of God for the New Covenant age.

C. The Name and Christology. The most distinctive aspect of Oneness christology, and

fundamental to it, is its theology of the name of Jesus. Since "Jesus" etymologically embodies the name of Yahweh and the latter theologically anticipates the revealing of a future new name, the name of Jesus is regarded as the proper name of God for this age. It reveals the identity of Jesus and describes his function as Savior of the world (see Matt. 1:21; see also John 5:43; Acts 4:12; Phil. 2:9–11; Heb. 1:4).

In the compound name "Lord Jesus Christ," the name of Jesus is seen with few exceptions as the revealed name, with "Lord" and "Christ" functioning as descriptive titles to set him apart from all others by that name. Departing from the traditional interpretation of the name of Jesus as a designation for his humanity, the name uniquely bears the stamp of divinity.

The Jewish-Christian characteristics are evident in the Oneness description of the person of Christ. To the Hebrew *Shema* (Deut. 6:4), which is a favorite passage for defending the monarchy of God, is added a supporting NT text, Colossians 2:9, "In him dwelleth all the fulness of the Godhead bodily" (KJV). The incipient tritheism of Trinitarianism is seen to minimize the full revelation of God in Christ. If only one person in the Godhead becomes incarnate, then Jesus is neither the full revelation of deity nor the revelation of the full deity. Furthermore, it leads to an unwarranted subordination of the Son in his deity. The mission is to elevate the Son to his rightful place in the Godhead and in revelation.

Two images coming from Jewish-Christian roots that shape Oneness christology are "dwelling" and "glory." The more prominent one is dwelling, taken primarily from Colossians 2:9. Recalling the Jewish experience of God's dwelling temporarily in localized places, God now dwells permanently in the human tabernacle of Jesus. This is consistent with the fundamental principle of one undifferentiated Spirit and one human person. In Father-Son terms, the Father is the divine Spirit who indwells the human Son. In his deity Jesus is Father; in his humanity, Son. Yet the Father continues in transcendence after the Incarnation in the same manner as does the divine Logos in Trinitarian theology.

Integral to the dwelling image is that of glory. Like the glory tradition in pre-NT Hellenistic Judaism, Oneness theology gives special attention to NT words such as "manifestation" (1 Tim. 3:16), "image" (Heb. 1:3), "form" (Phil. 2:7), and "face" (2 Cor. 4:10). They are all used to express the divine-human reality in terms of the Spirit-person principle. In Christ the hidden God becomes manifest. He who is without form takes on the form of a servant. The Invisible One reveals himself as in a mirror, Christ being the true and perfect image. The OT theophanies are regarded as temporary manifestations that anticipate the future permanent attachment of God to the human body of Jesus.

The preexistence of Christ is developed in three stages. To protect the monarchy of God, the first stage is God's utter transcendent, undifferentiated being, which has existed from eternity. Prior to the creation of the world, God had a plan. It is only as the thought of God, as his eternal purposeful plan, that Christ preexisted.

From solitary thought emerges the second stage of expression. The creative and redemptive activity of God reveals him as Logos. "Spirit" defines God in his eternal being; "Word" is God-in-relation or God-in-time. Unwilling to find a hypostatic distinction within God, the Word is both a coming forth from God and God himself. He is everything that can be implied by personification without creating a second personality.

The third stage is the divine self-disclosure in the Incarnation. God as Spirit is without differentiation or form. When he assumes a form, he is present in his full essential being. As the form of God, Jesus is the preexistent Word. But in his full deity, he is indwelled by the full Godhead. In his final expression the deity of Christ is the one Spirit (Father) who proceeds from eternity, through the Word, into the human form of Jesus (Son).

The sonship of Jesus begins with his birth. In his humanity the Son is subordinate to the Father. In his deity there can be no subordination or inferiority of position. While both natures are affirmed, the relationship follows the Jewish-Christian pattern that maintains a clear distinction between the two.

Although there is a serious desire to keep the integrity and unity of the two natures in Christ, the Nestorian bias gives a tentativeness to the union. The distinctive theology of the Name holds some potential for strengthening the bond in that the giving of the name of Jesus at the Annunciation to Mary is suggestive of the permanent union that exists between the divine name and the person.

It is in the ministry of Jesus that the inherent weakness of the union appears. Various human acts are attributed to either his deity or his humanity, thus depicting him as functioning with two parallel systems, switching from one to the other as the occasion demands, but never as an integrated person.

While Oneness teaching is not uniform on this issue, there is not a developed theology of the two natures. This is evident in the Oneness doctrine of the Atonement. In Jesus' cry of dereliction from the cross, "My God, my God, why hast thou forsaken me?" (Matt. 27:46 KJV), many teach that a withdrawal of God from the body occurs. Following a theology inherited from a strand of early Fundamentalism, Jesus as sin-bearer takes on the sins of the world at his moment of death. Because a holy God cannot encounter sin directly, he prepares in Jesus a sinless body as a sacrifice. In the moment of death, while the sin of the world is vicariously laid upon Jesus, the Spirit of God departs. The union is broken, and the Spirit remains separated from the body until the Resurrection.

The provisional nature of the union is confirmed in the eschatological vision of Christ. Some teach that the sonship will cease at the end of history. With the mediatorial work of Christ completed, he may return to the form in which he existed prior to the Creation or simply be known as the Almighty God.

With the concern that pervades all Oneness literature to restore the centrality and exclusiveness of Christ, the humanity and sonship ultimately become dispensable in order that he may ultimately be known as the Lord of glory. Whereas the Trinitarian doctrine holds to an eternal relationship between the Father and Son, the Oneness view sees sonship as primarily functional and in some cases temporary. Consequently, termination or substantial change is consistent with a monarchian view of God.

D. The Name and the Christian. The theology of the Name is carried consistently into the status and life of the Christian. As the name of Jesus is central to a knowledge of God, so it is equally essential for salvation. The point of convergence of the Name and salvation is the rite of water baptism in the name of the Lord Jesus Christ. Instead of the familiar evangelistic text of John 3:16, the essentials of Christian initiation are summed up in Peter's instructions on the Day of Pentecost: "Repent, and be baptized every one of you in the name of Jesus Christ for the remission of sins, and ye shall receive the gift of the Holy Ghost" (Acts 2:38 KJV). From this text OP blends a conversionist theology and a Pentecostal doctrine of Spirit baptism with its own theology of the Name to form a unique three-stage soteriology.

Repentance, the first step, is defined as faith acting in obedience. Repentance and obedience are the active elements in faith, without which salvation cannot be appropriated. Rejecting the conversionist axiom that the disposition of a heart turned toward God is sufficient for salvation, OP anticipates in the obedient act of repentance a willingness to take the ultimate step of obedience—baptism in the name of Jesus Christ.

A test of true obedience, the second stage of baptism is the point of binding the name of Jesus to the new believer. Although consistent with its theology of the Name, the practice of rebaptism remains a major point of contention and division with other Christian bodies.

The third stage, the giving of the Holy Spirit, conforms to the traditional Pentecostal experience of the baptism in the Spirit accompanied by speaking in tongues.

Oneness soteriology from the earliest years has been divided into two main schools of thought. One follows the baptistic tradition of the AG in which the new birth is experienced in conversion. Baptism in the name of Jesus conforms the believer to the NT pattern of Christian initiation. Spirit baptism is a second work of grace that gives the Christian power for ministry (see K. Reeves, *The Great Commission Re-Examined* and F. Small, *Living Waters—A Sure Guide for Your Faith* [n.d.]). This interpretation consciously and theologically places OP within the larger evangelical-Pentecostal tradition.

The other position, expressed in sacramental terms, identifies all three elements in Acts 2:38 as constitutent of the new birth. To be born of water and Spirit (John 3:5) means to be baptized in the name of Jesus and to receive the Pentecostal experience of Spirit baptism. Adapting the traditional interpretation of Colossians 2:11–13, which equates baptism with New Covenant circumcision, the identification with Christ and cleansing from sin occur through baptism. The insistence that baptism is "for the remission of sins" (Acts 2:38) draws the charge of baptismal regeneration. It is countered, however, with the qualification that to be efficacious the water must be accompanied by an active faith and invocation of the name of Jesus. In the words of Haywood, "To be saved by water baptism, it must be administered in the name of Jesus" (n.d., 24).

In both traditions the invocation of the name of Jesus according to Acts 2:38 is harmonized with the Trinitarian baptismal formula in Matthew 28:19 by means of differentiating between "name" and "titles." Whereas "Jesus" is the one revelatory and proper name of God, "Father, Son, and Holy Spirit" are descriptive titles. The singular use of "name" in Matthew 28:19 points forward to Jesus as the one name of the Father, Son, and Holy Spirit. Rejecting the traditional interpretation that "Father, Son, and Holy Spirit" is a compound name, Matthew 28:19 is regarded as the command to baptize in the one name of the Father, Son, and Holy Spirit, and Acts 2:38 provides the formula.

By incorporating the third stage of Spirit baptism into the new birth, the sacramental group transfers the initial entry of the Spirit from the traditional conversion experience to the Pentecostal one. Taking "born" to be synonymous with "baptize," a highly exclusive theology of salvation is erected in which one is neither truly born again nor indwelled by the Spirit until the three stages of Acts 2:38 are completed. The roots of this teaching are traced to Haywood (*The Birth of the Spirit and the Mystery of the Godhead* [n.d.]) and Andrew Urshan (*The Doctrine of the New Birth or The Perfect Way to Eternal Life* [1921]).

The baptistic stream theologically recognizes as born again those who share in a conversion experience, while only Oneness believers enjoy the "full gospel." The sacramentalists have more difficulty in that by definition Trinitarian Christians are not born again. Haywood and Urshan attempt to circumvent the problem by likening the difference to that which exists between the conception and birth of a child. In eschatological terms, Oneness believers represent the church that will enter the eternal kingdom in a secret resurrection called the "Rapture." Trinitarians, OT saints, and the righteous people of other faiths will be saved according to their faithfulness to obey God to the limits of their knowledge of him and to their perseverance in enduring persecution. A total break with the wider church is avoided by introducing a stage in Christian initiation whereby one can be validly reconciled to God prior to being born again. Not unlike many Evangelicals, the born-again theology functions to identify those Christians who are deemed to have appropriated the gospel in its fullness.

The two-tier classification of Christians, however, tends to inhibit relations with other Christian groups. The separation is most apparent in white organizations such as the UPC. More acknowledgment of and cooperation with other

Christians is exhibited by the blacks and some indigenous groups in Third World countries.

OP represents a unique expression of Christianity on the fringe of the evangelical-Pentecostal movement. While sharing a common religious heritage and inheriting much of its theology, OP stands outside the accepted canons of orthodoxy by its rejection of the doctrine of the Trinity and Trinitarian baptism. Unlike the cults that claim exclusive rights to salvation, OP is obligated to acknowledge a common religious experience in its Trinitarian counterparts. Many Oneness representatives actively engage in wider Christian fellowship and cooperation.

A more inclusive theology in OP will weaken the trend toward isolationism and strengthen its ties with the wider evangelical-Pentecostal tradition. Conversely, the Christian church is confronted in OP with the challenge to identify and understand those groups that have not gone the way of the cult but speak a different language than orthodoxy.

See also JESUS CHRIST; PENTECOSTAL ASSEMBLIES OF THE WORLD; UNITED PENTECOSTAL CHURCH, INTERNATIONAL.

Bibliography: D. Bernard, *The Oneness of God* (1983); idem, *The New Birth* (1984); A. Clanton, *United We Stand—A History of Oneness Organizations* (1970); F. Ewart, *The Revelation of Jesus Christ* (n.d.); M. Golder, *History of the Pentecostal Assemblies of the World* (1973); G. T. Haywood, *The Birth of the Spirit and the Mystery of the Godhead* (n.d.); R. N. Longenecker, *The Christology of Early Jewish Christianity* (1970); G. Magee, *Is Jesus in the Godhead or Is the Godhead in Jesus?* (n.d.); J. Paterson, *God in Christ Jesus* (n.d.); D. Reed, "Origins and Development of the Theology of Oneness Pentecostalism in the United States," Ph.D. diss., Boston University, 1978; F. Small, *Living Waters—A Sure Guide for Your Faith* (n.d.); V. Synan, ed., *Aspects of Pentecostal-Charismatic Origins* (1975); A. D. Urshan, *The Doctrine of the New Birth or The Perfect Way to Eternal Life* (1921). D. A. Reed

OPEN BIBLE EVANGELISTIC ASSOCIATION See OPEN BIBLE STANDARD CHURCHES, INC.

OPEN BIBLE STANDARD CHURCHES, INC. A Pentecostal denomination that traces its lineage to the Azusa Street revival by way of the Apostolic Faith (AF) (Portland) and the Pentecostal revivals in the Midwest. Headquarters for the Trinitarian "finished work" group is in Des Moines, Iowa.

In 1986 there were 281 affiliated churches in the U.S., with a constituency of 46,020; there are 350 congregations in twenty-five other countries. Official statistics also list 29 churches in the U.S. that are pastored by Open Bible Standard Church ministers and that add another 5,863 to the constituency. There are 1,300 ministers worldwide.

I. Northwest Element—Bible Standard Conference (BSC) (1919–35). An AF (Portland) minister, Fred Hornshuh, was a successful church planter along the Pacific Coast, especially in the Northwest. But he and a few other ministers became disenchanted with certain AF policies: (1) the exclusiveness of the group, which forbade fellowship with other Pentecostal groups;

(2) the unkind treatment of those with whom they differed; (3) the requirement that divorced and remarried people should renounce their present marriage and return to their first mate; (4) the centralized form of government, which among other things, required ministers to attend the three-month camp meeting; and (5) feminine domination (i.e., Florence Crawford). A break in 1919 brought about a new organization that was first called the Bible Standard Mission (later Conference).

Three former general chairmen of the Open Bible Standard Churches get together in a 1970 meeting. Left to right are Everett Fulton, John Richey, and R. Bryant Mitchell.

Hornshuh had started a dynamic church in Eugene, Oregon (later called Lighthouse Temple), in 1913, which was the first Pentecostal church in the area. Following the break with the AF, Hornshuh began publishing the *Bible Standard* magazine. What is now Eugene Bible College was founded in 1925 as Bible Standard Theological School. Hornshuh and his small band of ministers and laymen took the Pentecostal message to many cities and communities in the Northwest.

II. Open Bible Evangelistic Association (OBEA) (1932–35). Like the Bible Standard, its counterpart in the Northwest, OBEA was a split from another Pentecostal group—also formed by a woman—Aimee Semple McPherson's International Church of the Foursquare Gospel (ICFG).

In 1927 a small Des Moines Pentecostal group headed by John Goben invited Mrs. McPherson to the city for widely promoted meetings. She returned the next year, and many conversions and healings were reported. As a result, three congregations were organized and united with the ICFG.

When Goben took a position with Mrs. McPherson's work in California, he arranged for Willard H. Pope to take his place in Des Moines. John R. Richey later succeeded Pope, and other young Foursquare couples followed Richey to pioneer churches in the Midwest.

In 1930 the Midwest group began to question the wisdom of ICFG's episcopal plan of holding church property. There was no change, however. Then in 1931 Mrs. McPherson, who was divorced, married David L. Hutton. The next year the ministers in the Midwest voted to withdraw from ICFG and subsequently formed OBEA.

Both groups—Hornshuh's BSC and OBEA—were formed in reaction to policies that their parent organizations legislated.

III. Amalgamation. Recognizing their similar doctrinal beliefs and visions, the BSC and the OBEA united their forces in 1935. The new name—a combination of the two—was adopted: Open Bible Standard Evangelistic Association. A total of 210 ministers made up the new association. The name was changed to the present OBSC in 1940.

IV. Doctrine and Polity. Despite the fact that the BSC in its beginning had started in the Holiness wing of the Pentecostal movement and the OBEA had accepted the "finished work" position, this was not an issue by 1935. BSC had also practiced footwashing, but it too was not an issue in the amalgamation.

The doctrinal statement adopted was similar to that of the General Council of the Assemblies of God (AG), ICFG, and other Trinitarian "finished work" Pentecostal groups. These beliefs include salvation by faith, healing in the Atonement, the pretribulation rapture of the church, and speaking in tongues as the initial physical evidence of the baptism in the Holy Spirit.

V. Administration. The local church is ruled by the congregation, calling its own pastor, electing its own officials, and having a voice in the divisional and national conferences. There are five U.S. divisions: Pacific, Midwest, Central, Eastern, and Southeastern. The denomination meets biennially in a general conference. An elected general board of directors conducts the business of the organization.

VI. Schools. Because of economic pressures and declining enrollments, in the fall of 1986 the denomination merged Open Bible College (Des Moines) and Dayton Bible Institute (Dayton, Ohio) with the oldest and apparently the most prosperous, Eugene Bible College. Plans are for the school to increase its correspondence courses to give the constituency additional opportunities to receive Bible training.

VII. Publications. *Message of the Open Bible* is the official monthly magazine. *The Overcomer* is published quarterly for youth. In the past the denomination published a Sunday school curriculum; but in recent years it has been relying on other publishers to fill this need.

VIII. Affiliation. The OBSC is a member of the National Association of Evangelicals, the

Pentecostal Fellowship of North America, and the Pentecostal World Conference.

IX. Overture for Amalgamation. The AG in the late 1950s made a formal invitation for the OBSC to unite with them. However, the OBSC chose to remain a separate organization.

X. Official History. A charter member of the Midwest group and former superintendent, R. Bryant Mitchell, is the author of the 414-page official history, *Heritage and Horizons* (1982), published by the denomination. Despite the fact that the denomination has had little numerical growth in the past thirty years and that the schools saw it necessary to combine, there is optimism that OBSC has a bright future. The immediate future, it seems, does not include an amalgamation with the AG or with any other Pentecostal group.

Bibliography: R. Mitchell, *Heritage and Horizons* (1982); "Policies and Principles of OBSC" (1985).
                                    W. E. Warner

Daniel Opperman is best remembered in the Pentecostal movement for his efforts in education. He was one of the organizers of the Assemblies of God but later helped form a Oneness organization.

OPPERMAN, DANIEL CHARLES OWEN (1872–1926). Evangelist and educator. Daniel Charles Owen Opperman was born on July 13, 1872, in Clinton Township, Elkhart County, Indiana. The family moved to Nevada, Missouri, in 1881, and settled in Florida in 1884. In 1884 Opperman had a conversion experience. He was a member of the German Baptist Brethren. After his father's death in 1887, the mother and four children returned to Indiana, settling in Goshen. Opperman did farm work and studied. In 1893 he enrolled in a Brethren college in Mt. Morris, Illinois. He later studied for one year at Manchester College in North Manchester, Indiana. From

May 23 until July 6, 1899, Opperman was enrolled at Moody Bible Institute.

While a Moody student, Opperman began attending John Alexander Dowie's Zion. He joined Dowie's Christian Catholic Church and eventually directed Zion City's education program. On March 10, 1900, Opperman married Ella Syler. Their son, Daniel Paul, was born on January 22, 1901. Ella died a week later. A bout with tuberculosis resulted in Opperman's move to Texas, where he met Charles Parham in 1906. Opperman became a Pentecostal evangelist before experiencing Spirit baptism (which he did on January 13, 1908, in Belton, Tex.). He married Hattie Ruth Allen near Rogers, Texas, on July 22, 1907. A son, Joseph, was born to this union.

Opperman's prior teaching experience prompted his recognition as an educator, and he conducted numerous short-term Bible institutes that served early Pentecostal needs. A founding member of the Assemblies of God and an executive presbyter (Nov. 1914–15), Opperman withdrew in 1916 to become chairman of a fledgling Oneness association, the General Assembly of Apostolic Assemblies, with headquarters in Eureka Springs, Arkansas. During his years in Oneness Pentecostal leadership, Opperman edited *The Blessed Truth* and became a pastor in Lodi, California. He died in a car/train accident in Baldwin Park, California, on September 15, 1926.

Bibliography: G. P. Gardiner, "Out of Zion . . . Into All the World," *Bread of Life* (February 1983), 7–9, 14; D. C. O. Opperman, "Journal," unpublished manuscript, Assemblies of God Archives.   E. L. Blumhofer

ORAL ROBERTS EVANGELISTIC ASSOCIATION See ROBERTS, GRANVILLE ORAL.

ORDINANCES, PENTECOSTAL This article focuses on what traditional Pentecostalism has labeled "ordinances." Since Protestant charismatics and Roman Catholic charismatics have generally accepted the sacramental traditions of their respective heritage, these traditions will not be covered. Independent Protestant charismatics are excluded, although many of these groups have not inherited their understanding of ordinances from a parent group. Classical Pentecostals have essentially been uniform in fundamentals; however, in particularities they have shown considerable diversity.

I. The Words "Sacrament" and "Ordinance." The two terms "ordinance" and "sacrament" can have the same basic meaning, yet some Pentecostals have deliberately spurned the word "sacrament" because it seemed to imply a self-contained efficacy, independent of the participant's faith. That is an unnecessary conclusion; using "sacrament" will be important, because it functions to identify only water baptism and the Lord's Supper as sacraments, and "footwashing" as something less. In this context a sacrament refers to those external rites directed by Scripture and observed by the gathered people of God.

"Sacrament" will be used here in a cognitive/symbolic way, rather than in the casual way that might suggest that salvation is conveyed *ex opera operato.* On the one hand, if there is no faith by the recipient, there is no sacrament. On the other hand, the administration of the sacraments should not be the sole prerogative of the ordained ministry. The practice of denominationally licensed ministers administering the sacraments seems biblically allowable but not mandatory.

II. Water Baptism. The biblical imagery for baptism probably extends into the OT religious and ceremonial lustrations in which water was the medium for cleansing from the defilement of sin. It would seem axiomatic to say that North American Pentecostals consider water the appropriate element for the ceremony, yet it does not seem theologically inappropriate to suggest that another liquid would be appropriate, especially under certain conditions that limit the availability of water.

All major Pentecostal denominations in the U.S. practice water baptism by immersion (some even break ice in rivers to immerse the candidate), yet under the influence of J. H. King, the Pentecostal Holiness Church officially sanctions sprinkling. Pentecostals have been so emphatic about water baptism being a response to faith that they not only reject paedobaptism (although not "infant salvation") and sometimes lack urgency in performing the rite, but some have insisted on rebaptism if a person was baptized as an infant or sprinkled as an adult. Furthermore, some groups counsel rebaptism if a person "backslides" then is "saved again." Oneness Pentecostalism reflects a departure from the Trinitarian formulas used by other Pentecostal groups. While traditional Trinitarian formulas are to be preferred, the approach of Oneness Pentecostals is not to be considered sub-Christian.

The early Pentecostal preference in the U.S. for immersion may lie as much in the continuity of the demonstrative nature of regular worship services as in their finding scriptural support for the practice. There was a general dearth of serious inquiry into the subject, and an overall consensus on the subject was lacking. The NT term translated "to baptize" (*baptizō*) and specific texts like Acts 8:39, seem to endorse immersion. But Scripture taken in its entirety does not preclude the appropriateness of sprinkling or pouring.

The crucial concern in the sacrament of baptism is the subject. To those committed to the cognitive view of the sacraments, no proxy faith is sufficient. Fortunately, most advocates of causal sacramentalism, specifically proponents of baptismal regeneration, expect to move recipients past the ceremony to a full and complete allegiance to the gospel. The NT does not envision such a thing as an unbaptized Christian, and a sense of urgency should undergird this sacrament.

III. The Eucharist. The Synoptic accounts and the Pauline elaborations describe Jesus as instituting this sacrament. The elements used in the original Last Supper probably included unleavened bread and fermented wine. Pentecostals in the U.S. have often not been willing to locate unleavened bread, thus many substitutes, like crackers, have been used. Most Pentecostals, however, have been quite adamant in their refusal to partake of fermented wine. A primary concern here is that to use fermented wine would not only

contravene a doctrine of total abstinence of such things, but it would provide a working premise for alcoholism. Emerging Pentecostal scholarship and international Pentecostal practice have challenged this point of view.

In the socioeconomic stratum and cultural climate of early Pentecostalism it was easier to deny any possible connection to the dreaded practice of drinking. At the same time, the historical reality of the first Eucharist need not be denied nor pressed too far. It seems that the early church's use of unleavened bread and fermented wine was something of a historical accident. That is, these elements are not intrinsic to the ceremony, but were incorporated because of the historical situation. The process of distilling intoxicating drinks has changed since the first century, but the biblical mandate prohibiting drunkenness has not. Again, it is not theologically necessary to insist on the fruit of the vine, but it is encouraged by apostolic precedent.

Other things are not as value laden for Pentecostals, such as the posture of the body, the manner of the breaking of the bread, the use of a table, or an incorporated liturgy. In years past it often seemed that enthusiastic worship was the supremely important catalyst. They have insisted on all endorsed candidates (ruling out infants and adult unbelievers) partaking of both elements while recalling the death of Jesus and experiencing his presence.

IV. Footwashing. The Johannine account of the Lord's Supper includes a scene not found in the Synoptics. Because the story (John 13:1ff.) recounts Jesus' washing the disciples' feet at the same occasion as the "first Eucharist" (cf. 1 Tim. 5:10), some have viewed footwashing as an ordinance and have insisted that it should always follow the observance of the Lord's Supper. Some Pentecostal groups have practiced footwashing as an ordinance (among others, e.g., Church of God of Prophecy; Church of God, Cleveland, Tenn.). Such an insistence wrongly infers a moral necessity in Jesus' actions known only to water baptism and the Eucharist.

This object lesson in humility, as portrayed by Christ, is not an extraneous rite. It can be engaged in with full confidence that the participating Christian community has taken a positive step toward realizing koinonia. The ceremony can draw attention to Christian servitude, while at the same time demonstrating publicly that Christian commitment transcends societal barriers of race, nationality, gender, and social class.

See also CHURCH, THEOLOGY OF THE; SACRAMENTS.

Bibliography: G. Duffield and N. M. Van Cleave, *Foundations of Pentecostal Theology* (1984); P. K. Jewett, "Systematic Theology" (n.d.); R. Pruitt, *Fundamentals of the Faith* (1981).   H. D. Hunter

ORTHODOX RENEWAL MOVEMENT
See STEPHANOU, EUSEBIUS A.; HOLY SPIRIT, DOCTRINE OF: THE MEDIEVAL CHURCH.

ORTIZ, JUAN CARLOS (1934–).
Argentine evangelist and conference speaker. Ortiz's unique ministry emphasizing Christian unity and biblical truth rather than conventionality began with the

Beginning in the early 1950s, T. L. and Daisy Osborn have ministered in overseas mass evangelism crusades.

Assemblies of God. He was secretary of the Tommy Hicks meetings in Buenos Aires in 1954 and gained prominence as pastor of the city's Hidalgo church. Increasingly well known in Latin America, he extended his ministry to the U.S. through association with various leaders of the charismatic renewal. As Ortiz's provocative messages brought him recognition, his sometimes iconoclastic style and fellowship with Catholics and mainline Protestants alienated him from his denominational colleagues. He has spoken in settings as diverse as Lutheran churches, a Trappist monastery, and the Latin American Mission Church in San Jose, Costa Rica. He was a vocal figure in the Lausanne Congress on World Evangelization in 1974 and has subsequently worked with Evangelicals promoting interagency coordination. His most widely read book, *Disciple,* appeared in 1975. Increasingly identified with prominent Evangelicals, in the 1980s he became a minister-at-large with a California Presbyterian church and now resides in Buenos Aires.

Bibliography: J. E. Orr, *Evangelical Awakenings in Latin America* (1978); J. C. Ortiz, *Disciple* (1975); idem, "Just Getting 'Fatter' Isn't Growth," *Eternity* 26 (15, 1975): 15–16ff.; idem, "When Is Jesus With You?" *Christian Life* 44 (7, 1982): 38–44; C. Peter Wagner, *Look Out! The Pentecostals Are Coming* (1973).
                                                                E. A. Wilson

OSBORN, TOMMY LEE (1923–). Missionary, healing evangelist, pastor, and author. Born on an Oklahoma farm, T. L. Osborn was converted to Christ at age twelve and was called to preach at age fourteen. The following year he assisted E. M. Dillard with revivals in Arkansas, Oklahoma, and California, where he met Daisy Washburn (1924–) in 1940 and married her the following year.

In 1941 the Osborns went into the Kiamichi

Mountains of Oklahoma as evangelists. They soon returned to California, where they itinerated for two years before pioneering a new work, Montaville Tabernacle, in Portland, Oregon.

They went to India in 1945 as missionaries. While there T. L. contracted typhoid fever and their infant son struggled with cholera and amoebic dysentery. The following year they returned to the U.S. to pastor the Full Gospel church of McMinnville, Oregon.

After Charles S. Price died in 1947, Osborn wept. "I thought of Wigglesworth, of Gipsy Smith, of Kenyon, of Price, of Dowie, and of others, not one of whom I had ever met or heard preach, but they were gone forever from the world's scene of action" (Osborn, September 1949, 11). He then heard Hattie Hammond at a camp meeting in Brooks, Oregon, preaching on "Seeing Jesus." The next morning he was awakened with a vision of Jesus Christ that changed his life.

In September of 1947 the Osborns returned to the pastorate of Montaville Tabernacle. Soon afterward, William Branham conducted a healing campaign in Portland's Civic Auditorium, where Osborn observed a young girl's deliverance when Branham prayed, "Thou deaf and dumb spirit, I adjure thee in Jesus' name, leave the child." When Branham snapped his fingers, she heard and spoke perfectly. Osborn said, "When I witnessed this, there seemed to be a thousand voices speaking to me at once, all in one accord saying over and over, 'You can do that'" (October 1949, 9).

After many days of prayer and fasting, Osborn and his wife began a ministry as healing evangelists in the spring of 1948. Early the following year they reported from Jamaica, "The people are so hungry . . . they eat the Word like starving birds" (Osborn, February 1949, 14). Scores of healings were reported, with hundreds of conversions. The Osborns returned to the U.S. for highly successful campaigns in Flint, Michigan, with William Branham and F. F. Bosworth; in Detroit with Bosworth and Benham; and in Pennsylvania, Tennessee, and Texas with Gordon Lindsay.

The following year Osborn reported over 18,000 conversions within twelve days in Puerto Rico, and in January of 1951, 50,000 in Camaguey, Cuba. In 1952 thousands more came to Christ in Punto Fijo, Venezuela, before police arrested Osborn for "witchcraft" after many reports of healings had been received by physicians and Roman Catholic priests. In Guatemala City, during a political upheaval in February and March of 1953, another 50,000 people were brought to Christ.

In 1953 Osborn formed the Association for Native Evangelism to facilitate the spreading of the gospel by trained nationals. This program, financed by many different denominations, has produced about four hundred new self-supporting indigenous churches every year since it began. By 1964 the Osborns had ministered in over forty countries, with startling successes in Kenya, Indonesia, Formosa, Japan, Java, Holland, Chile, Switzerland, and elsewhere.

Osborn's ministry is characterized by flexibility. In an effort to reach youth in the late 1960s, he grew a beard and modified his wardrobe and vocabulary. Recently, they have emphasized that Daisy has functioned as a minister in her own right, serving as president of the Osborn Foundation, international editor of *Faith Digest* magazine, and director of Overseas Evangelism.

The Osborn Foundation maintains headquarters in Tulsa, with international branches in major cities throughout the world, and has produced tapes, films, and printed literature in more than eighty languages, reaching multiplied millions worldwide.

Bibliography: D. Graham, "DMO: Directing the Action of National Evangelism Worldwide," *Faith Digest* 24 (July 1979): 2–5, 10–11; D. E. Harrell, Jr., *All Things Are Possible* (1975); T. L. Osborn, "From the Island of Jamaica," *Elim Pentecostal Herald* (February 1949), 14; idem, "My Life Story and Call to the Healing Ministry," *Voice of Healing* (September 1949), 11; ibid., (October 1949), 9, 13; idem, *Young In Faith* (1964).
											R. M. Riss

OSTEEN, JOHN HILLERY (1921–). Charismatic pastor and broadcaster. Born in Paris, Texas, Osteen received his B.A. from John Brown University and an M.R.E. from Northern Baptist Theological Seminary. He was ordained as a Southern Baptist minister in 1942 and served as assistant pastor of a church in San Diego, California, and as pastor of churches in Hamlin, Baytown, and Houston, Texas. In 1958, while pastor at Hibbard Memorial Baptist Church in Houston, Osteen was baptized in the Holy Spirit. About that time, his daughter, who was born with cerebral palsy, was healed. This ushered Osteen into a healing ministry.

Osteen established Lakewood Baptist Church, Houston, Texas, with about 150 members. Now known as Lakewood Church (charismatic), with a membership of 20,000, the church places strong emphasis on world missions, having touched 111 nations. They have national and international television ministries carried on various local networks and on the CBN satellite network. Osteen is the editor/publisher of *Manna* magazine and author of thirty books.

John Osteen, a former Baptist minister, founded the charismatic Lakewood Church, Houston, Texas.

Bibliography: "Runners Up," *Charisma* (August 1985), 132–33.
											S. Strang

OTTOLINI, PETER (1870–1962). Italian-American evangelist. Ottolini was born in Pescaglia, a city in the province of Lucca, Italy. At age twenty-one Ottolini immigrated to the U.S., arriving in Chicago on September 11, 1891. In 1900 he converted from Catholicism, becoming a member of Chicago's First Italian Presbyterian Church. In 1907 he became a Pentecostal after receiving the baptism in the Holy Spirit with the evidence of speaking in tongues during a meeting conducted by William H. Durham at the North Avenue Mission. During the next few years, Ottolini served as an elder in the Assemblea Cristiana. He traveled to New York in 1908 and helped to establish Pentecostal churches among the Italian communities in Buffalo, Holley, and New York City. Beginning in 1910, Ottolini made several trips to northern and southern Italy and helped establish the first Pentecostal churches in those regions. In 1917 he moved his family to St. Louis and established the Italian Evangelical Church. He spent the rest of his life supporting the churches he helped establish and resided in St. Louis until his death.

Bibliography: "Biography of Peter Ottolini," personal papers of Anthony DeGregorio, Du Plessis Center Archives, Fuller Theological Seminary Library, Pasadena, California; R. Bracco, *Risveglio Pentecostale in Itallia* (n.d.); L. DeCaro, *Our Heritage: The Christian*

Agnes N. Ozman was the first to speak in tongues at Charles F. Parham's Bethel Bible College in Topeka, Kans., in 1901. This picture was taken in 1937, the year of her death.

Church of North America (1977); P. Ottolini, *Storia dell'Opera Italiana* (1945); idem, *The Life and Mission of Peter Ottolini* (n.d.).   J. Colletti

OZMAN, AGNES N. (1870–1937). Evangelist. Agnes Ozman was assured a place in Pentecostal history when she became the first to speak in tongues at Charles Parham's Bethel Bible College in Topeka, Kansas. Despite conflicting accounts about her expectations and the sequence of events, her experience is usually credited with establishing the validity of Parham's assertion that tongues speech evidenced Spirit baptism.

Ozman was born in Albany, Wisconsin, on September 15, 1870. She grew up in rural Nebraska, where she attended a Methodist Episcopal church. A participant in various nondenominational settings as well, she eventually espoused both premillennialism and healing. In 1892 she enrolled for the winter term at T. C. Horton's Bible school in St. Paul, Minnesota. In 1894 she moved to New York to continue her training at A. B. Simpson's training institute. Unsettled and driven by the need to pursue spiritual reality, she served briefly as a city missionary in Kansas City. From there she went, in the fall of 1900, to Parham's school in Topeka, Kansas.

After her tongues experience in 1901, Ozman returned to city missionary work. In Lincoln in 1906 she heard about Pentecostalism, related her earlier experience, and identified with the emerging movement. In 1911 she married Pentecostal preacher Philemon LaBerge. The two traveled about the country, holding meetings wherever possible. In 1917 LaBerge affiliated with the Assemblies of God, receiving credentials as an evangelist. She died in Los Angeles on November 29, 1937.

Bibliography: E. L. Blumhofer, *The Assemblies of God* (1988); A. O. LaBerge, *What God Hath Wrought* (n.d.).   E. L. Blumhofer

P

PACIFISM The literature of the early Pentecostals indicates that they were generally but not universally pacifist. Pentecostal history is characterized over the years by a declining pacifism that basically corresponded to the trends in public opinion in the population at large.

There was little attempt at theorizing about pacifism in any systematic way. The limited pacifist tendencies reflected the prevailing premillennialist eschatology. Because most Pentecostals believed that the end times would feature wars and rumors of wars, there was no active pacifism that tried to prevent war but only a passive type that prevented the individual Christian from participating in war or, at least, killing if conscripted. The moderating influence undermining the initial pacifism has usually been the belief that the established government power was divinely ordained and that, therefore, the Christian was to support the government's decision to go to war. There was little discussion of the traditional differentiation of just and unjust wars.

I. Pre–World War I. The pacifist elements in Pentecostalism may be accounted for in the roots of the movement—particularly in the Holiness churches, but also in the evangelical and pietist traditions. Significant pacifist strains may be found in the Church of the Nazarene, the Free Methodists, and the Wesleyan Methodists. The Evangelicals were influenced by such dominant personalities as leader Alexander Campbell of the Disciples of Christ, who was an absolute pacifist, and revivalist Dwight L. Moody, who identified himself with Quaker concepts and was a conscientious objector in the Civil War. John Alexander Dowie, the founder of Zion City, Illinois, did not allow soldiers into membership. Two thousand of his American followers would become Pentecostals, as well as some in Holland, Switzerland, and the Republic of South Africa.

Early Pentecostal leaders expressed their pacifism even prior to the crisis situation engendered by the outbreak of World War I. Charles Fox Parham had married a Quaker and claimed that for twenty years prior to the war he had taught that true Christians should not go to war. He believed at the same time, however, that peace conferences were hopeless. In 1912 to 1914 Frank Bartleman taught in Europe in opposition to the developing war spirit there. Shortly after World War I he published a tract, "Christian Citizenship," which forbade Christians' going to war. In response to the Boer War, the British Pentecostal preacher, Arthur Sydney Booth-Clibborn, wrote a pacifist book, *Blood Against Blood,* which was touted in 1915 by the *Weekly Evangel* of the Assemblies of God (AG).

II. World War I. The outbreak of World War I created a crisis for the fledgling Pentecostal movement on both sides of the Atlantic. Independent congregations and recently formed denominations had difficulty establishing themselves in government eyes as organized religions that could qualify their members as (1) exempt from military service because their organization was opposed to war or (2) at least exempt from combatant service because their church opposed killing.

Donald Gee, who later was to become chairman of the British AG, was a conscientious objector and was exempted to do farm labor. He continued to promote pacifism longer than any other major Pentecostal leader. Some British Pentecostals were sent to prison for their pacifist stands. Howard Carter was imprisoned, whereas John Carter was exempted.

Prior to U.S. entry into the war in 1917, it appeared that most American Pentecostals were adamantly opposed to war. Frank Bartleman, writing in the *Weekly Evangel,* opposed the U.S. support of Britain's involvement. Upon entry of the U.S. into the war, the passage of the Espionage and Sedition Acts made it a crime to obstruct recruiting or to cause someone to refuse duty in the military services. This generally produced the development of a more moderate position, advocating noncombatant service rather than conscientious objection to war altogether. The AG in 1917 officially declared its opposition to participation in war that involved the destruction of human life, basing its position on scriptural precepts, "Follow peace," "Love your enemies," and "Thou shalt not kill." Although this was defined as a historical Quaker position, the organization claimed that it did not discourage enlistment of people whose conscientious principles were not involved. In the same year, the Church of God (CG, Cleveland, Tenn.) took a position against its members going to war. The Church of God in Christ (CGIC) also reflected a pacifist position, and its founder, Bishop Charles H. Mason, was jailed and accused of being a German sympathizer. Similar positions were indicated in Pentecostal churches in Russia, Germany, Switzerland, and Canada.

It is impossible to know to what extent the pacifist leadership influenced the rank and file members. There is indication of opposition to the prevailing pacifist tendency. S. A. Jamieson, one of the founding fathers of the AG, opposed the pacifist point of view, and Bartleman complained that "one dare not pray publicly in a meeting for God's saints in prison [conscientious objectors] without being assailed by a torrent of abuse."

In the total American population, 20,873 men claimed noncombatant status, but only 3,989 persisted in their position after induction. Of these, 450 were sent to prison, 17 of them

Pentecostals. Out of one group of 1,000 of these inductees in camps, 13 were listed as Pentecostal, another 20 were probably members of the CGIC, and some others from smaller sects also may have been Pentecostal.

III. Interwar Period. Between the world wars the pacifist position continued to erode among Pentecostals. Some did continue to preach absolute pacifism. Frank Bartleman published a tract, "War and the Christian," boldly asserting, "A 'War Church' is a Harlot Church." But the Russian Pentecostals who had held a pacifist line during the 1917 revolution modified that stance in 1927, advising members to serve in the armed forces. This transition did, however, produce objections within the AG that threatened to withdraw support. The AG at this time was under the influence of Stanley H. Frodsham, editor of the *Pentecostal Evangel* (1921–48), whose pacifism was derived from a general withdrawal from the affairs of this world. The trend, though, lay with the thinking of Eudorus N. Bell, chairman of the general council in 1914 and again from 1920 to 1923, who hinted at a *just war* philosophy by insisting that a soldier who killed in battle was not a murderer but a vehicle of justice. Thus the way of the combatant was justified. In 1928 the CG moderated its 1917 attitude "against members going to war" to "against members going to war in combatant service."

In a 1930 article in the *Pentecostal Evangel* the British leader Donald Gee lamented the lack of teaching on war and continued to reassert the view that conscientious objection was the only option open to the Christian. But his moderation was reflected in a call for tolerance of those who believed otherwise. Britain's Elim Pentecostal churches continued an antiwar attitude in the 1930s; but as war came, James McWhirter of that denomination declared pacifism itself to be the unbiblical position.

IV. World War II. The beginning of World War II in 1939 again brought the issues to the forefront. AG General Superintendent Ernest S. Williams encouraged Christians to request noncombatant status and recommended the statement developed by New York's Broadway Tabernacle: "I cannot reconcile the way of Christ with the way of war." Williams did not approve, however, of the belief that a person who killed in battle was a murderer. The beginning of conscription brought an immediate response in the *Pentecostal Evangel*, reasserting the pacifist position adopted in 1917 and restated in the 1927 AG constitution. This statement was far afield from the value system of the denomination as a whole; the AG would claim 50,000 men in the armed services, including wholesale enlistments. The CG also maintained a pacifist position; but, likewise, few of its young men complied.

Although the Pentecostal Holiness Church (PHC) apparently had never adopted a pacifist statement, at the beginning of the war it favored isolation; but when war came, the church gave total support to the war effort, sending thousands of men to fight. Chief Bishop Dan T. Muse condemned all protest to the war and said that those who refused to register for the draft were dishonoring God.

With so many men under arms, the Pentecostals appropriated their due proportion of chaplain positions in the armed services. The beginning of the Pentecostal chaplaincy may be seen as the tacit admission of the transition from pacifism to nonpacifism within the movement. The AG had thirty-four appointments by 1944, and the PHC received a total of twelve. This chaplain's lobby within the AG would become a major force after the war to change the denomination's official position so as to conform to practice.

The Selective Service records show a total of 11,950 conscientious objectors in World War II. Of these only 131 are listed as Pentecostals of various hue.

V. Post-World War II. At the end of World War II the CG altered its official pacifist position to allow liberty of conscience of its members to be combatants, noncombatants, or conscientious objectors. This has generally become the position of most American Pentecostals. In the Korean War and Vietnam War Pentecostals rarely sought noncombatant or conscientious objector status.

Amazingly, in 1947 a committee reported to the General Council of the AG that after due consideration no change was necessary in the statement of the denomination. But in 1957 the scriptural reference of "Thou shalt not kill" was dropped without comment from the supporting statements on military service. In 1961 the executive presbytery of the AG blocked publication in the *Pentecostal Evangel* of an article advocating conscientious objection to war. As the popular romanticism of the general population leaned in the direction of antinuclear views and opposition to the Vietnam War, the conservatism of the AG toughened, finally culminating in the 1967 statement allowing each member to choose combatant, noncombatant, or conscientious objector status.

This development may be contrasted, however, with a growing anti-militarism in the postwar German and British Pentecostal churches, the British leadership strongly supporting the banning of atomic weapons. But the general American trend may be further illustrated by the defeat of a resolution by the AG in 1981 that would have supported the establishment of a World Peace Tax Fund. The fund would have allowed those opposed to military spending to allocate their taxes to peaceful resources.

Thus while some Pentecostals retained residues of the general pacifism of an earlier era, others had even gone beyond nonpacifism and had hardened into an antipacifist position, continuing to merely reflect, rather than to instruct, public opinion.

See also QUAKERS.

Bibliography: R. M. Anderson, *Vision of the Disinherited* (1979); J. Beaman, "Pentecostal Pacifism: The Origin, Development, and Rejection of Pacific Belief Among Pentecostals," M.Div. thesis, North American Baptist Seminary, 1982; W. J. Hollenweger, *The Pentecostals* (1972); W. W. Menzies, *Anointed to Serve: The Story of the Assemblies of God* (1971); R. Robins, "A Chronology of Peace: Attitudes Toward War and Peace in the Assemblies of God: 1914–1918," *Pneuma* 6 (1, 1984): 3–25.   D. J. Wilson

PARHAM, CHARLES FOX (1873–1929). American Pentecostal pioneer and author. Parham formulated classical Pentecostal theology in Topeka, Kansas, in 1901 and thus deserves recognition as founder of the Pentecostal movement. Born amidst a panorama of religious ideas and persuasions, he connected the basic tenets that later defined the movement: evangelical-style conversion, sanctification, divine healing, premillennialism, and the eschatological return of Holy Spirit power evidenced by glossolalia. Parham's efforts gave Pentecostalism a definable theological corpus and instilled within the movement a fervent missionary emphasis. Believing that glossolalia was actually xenolalia (known foreign language), he surmised that the gift of Holy Spirit power foreshadowed a period of unequaled missions activity. This end-time revival would mark the conclusion of the present church age and herald the return of a triumphant Christ. With his student-disciples, Parham launched the first sustained period of Pentecostal growth; through his influence, others later made his ideas a global phenomenon.

Born in Muscatine, Iowa, on June 4, 1873, Parham fought an early struggle for survival. As an infant he suffered a virus (probably encephalitis) that weakened his childhood constitution and permanently stunted his growth. After moving with his parents to Cheney, Kansas, in 1878, he endured an even greater physical malady. At the age of nine, Parham was stricken with rheumatic fever—a condition that plagued him throughout his life despite long periods of remission. With the first bout of rheumatic fever, he felt a call to the ministry and began imitating revival preachers he had seen. Because of his weakened physical condition, he spent much of his childhood performing light farm chores in the presence of his deeply religious mother. When she died in 1885, Parham vowed to meet her in heaven. He was converted shortly thereafter and became active in the local Congregational church.

In 1890 Parham entered Southwest Kansas College and for three years struggled with his studies and his call to preach. Survival after a particularly severe attack of rheumatic fever in 1891 convinced him to reaffirm his ministerial call and also left him with a firm belief in the doctrine of divine healing. In 1893 he quit school to assume a supply pastorate of a Methodist church. Enamored with the theology of the Holiness movement and spurred by his college experience with divine healing, Parham left the Methodist Church in 1895 to assume an independent ministry. The following year, he married Sarah Thistlethwaite, and together in 1898 they founded the Beth-el Healing Home in Topeka. The home offered lodging and faith training for individuals seeking a divine cure. Parham's ministry in Topeka also included publication of a bimonthly Holiness journal, the *Apostolic Faith,* and some interest in rescue missions for the city's homeless.

In the summer of 1900 Parham embarked on a tour of Holiness religious centers. The focus of his twelve-week journey was Frank W. Sandford's Holiness commune at Shiloh, Maine. Impressed with the emphasis throughout the Holiness movement on a "latter rain" outpouring of the Holy Spirit, Parham sought for himself a greater personal manifestation of this power. Through Sandford, he heard isolated reports of xenolalic tongues among missionaries. Privately he drew great significance from the discovery. Convinced that Christ's premillennial return would occur on the heels of a worldwide revival, Parham viewed xenolalic tongues as proof of Spirit baptism, since it made all recipients instant missionaries. The emergence of large numbers of divinely trained mission workers and the example of apostolic power restored in the last days would prompt the start of the expected global revival.

Charles F. Parham, who had at one time pastored a Methodist church in Kansas, founded a Bible school in Topeka where the Pentecostal movement began in 1901.

Parham returned to Topeka in September 1900 and optimistically secured quarters for a Bible school to prepare prospective missionaries for the outpouring of Holy Spirit power. In an elaborate old mansion on the edge of town, he taught his students the essentials of Holiness doctrine and challenged them to search for the true evidence of Holy Spirit reception. He strategically directed them to the account of Acts 2 where xenolalic tongues sparked the initial phase of Christian growth, and on January 1, 1901, one of Parham's students (Agnes Ozman) experienced the expected blessing and sign. During the next few days, Parham and about half of his student body of thirty-four were likewise baptized. Parham followed the Topeka revival with an ambitious effort to spread what he now believed was the true "apostolic faith." By April, however, his plan was dashed. Negative publicity and marginal numbers quelled the initial enthusiasm, and Parham spent the next few years in relative obscurity. He continued to proclaim Pentecostal doctrine, however, and kept a small core of followers.

Parham's Apostolic Faith movement (AF) received a renewed thrust with the outbreak of revival in Galena, Kansas, in late 1903. There the message of the Pentecostal baptism fused with divine healing to create a mass outpouring of support in the boom towns of the lead and zinc mining district. Newspaper coverage generated widespread interest, and Parham quickly garnered several thousand converts. On the strength of this success he invaded Texas early in 1905 and established a string of AF churches centered in the growing suburbs of Houston. In December 1905 Parham launched another Bible school effort to train missionary evangelists. The Houston Bible school prompted further growth as Parham's disciples fanned out into the rural sections of Texas. Most significant in this ten-week training session was the attendance for several weeks of William J. Seymour, a black Holiness evangelist. Seymour subsequently carried the new message to Los Angeles, where through the Azusa Street revival he succeeded in winning increased numbers of Pentecostal converts.

By mid 1906 Parham was at the height of his popularity and enjoyed between eight and ten thousand followers. The previous year he had resumed publication of the *Apostolic Faith*—now decisively Pentecostal in theology. He also launched a program of organization to link his scattered flock and to monitor the success of the impending missionary revival. Naming himself "Projector," he formulated a loosely constructed federation of assemblies to promote increased evangelical activity. Unfortunately for Parham, events of the next year would prevent him from successfully establishing this organizational agenda. Late in 1906 he turned his attentions to the opportunity of securing faction-riddled Zion City, Illinois, as a Pentecostal capital. Despite an amazing growth rate and good press coverage, Parham's forces failed to win control of Zion from John Alexander Dowie's heir apparent, Wilbur Glenn Voliva. The strategic shift toward Zion also prevented him from visiting Seymour's revival in Los Angeles until late in October, by which time the revival had begun to assume its own separate identity. Parham's belated attempt to harness the religious enthusiasm and establish his own authority created a backlash, and he was forced to establish a rival mission. Meanwhile, Voliva's forces in Zion consolidated to effectively stifle his influence there. By the end of 1906 Parham's position as leader of the movement was left seriously in doubt.

The final blow to Parham's prominence came in the summer of 1907 when he was arrested in San Antonio, Texas, on a charge of sodomy. The details of the case are extremely sketchy and filled with innuendo and rumor. It is clear, however, that questions about Parham's reputation surfaced late in 1906—precisely the period in which his collapse as Pentecostal leader began. All charges were dropped by Texan authorities without explanation, and most of the damaging press came

from the religious press of Parham's opponent, Wilbur Voliva. Parham himself refused extensive comment on the charges, expecting his followers to simply accept that the whole affair had been an elaborate frame. In the end the debacle ruined any impact that he might have retained over the growing Pentecostal movement. Marred by scandal, he spent the final two decades of his life alienated from the bulk of the movement he had begun. From a base in Baxter Springs, Kansas, he retained a core of only several thousand followers, although his nationwide revival efforts touched many more. At the time of his death in 1929, he was almost unknown among the developing second generation of the Pentecostal denominations. Yet to no one individual did the movement owe a greater debt.

Parham's contributions to Pentecostalism included the crucial definition of tongues as initial evidence and the particularly acute level of "latter rain" millenarianism. Tongues as evidence provided Pentecostals with an identity significantly different from that of the Holiness movement by making Holy Spirit baptism a demonstrable experience. The missionary emphasis engendered by the perceived millenarian function of xenolalic tongues, despite the fading of that dream after 1908, played a crucial role in the growth of Pentecostalism around the world. In addition, Parham contributed as one of the movements most prolific authors. He edited the *Apostolic Faith* with varying regularity throughout his ministry (Topeka, Kans.: 1889–90; Melrose, Kans., and Houston, Tex.: 1905–06; Baxter Springs, Kans.: 1910–17, 1925–29) and published two books: *Kol Kare Bomidbar: A Voice Crying in the Wilderness* (1902) and *The Everlasting Gospel* (c. 1919).

See also APOSTOLIC FAITH MOVEMENT, ORIGINS; APOSTOLIC FAITH (BAXTER SPRINGS, KANS.); AZUSA STREET REVIVAL; CLASSICAL PENTECOSTALISM.

Bibliography: R. Anderson, *Vision of the Disinherited* (1979); J. Goff, *Fields White Unto Harvest* (1988); D. Nelson, "For Such a Time as This," Ph.D. diss., University of Birmingham, 1981; S. Parham, *Life of Charles F. Parham* (1930).   J. R. Goff, Jr.

PARISH RENEWAL COUNCIL An interchurch organization formed by denominational renewal fellowships for the promotion of congregational renewal in the Holy Spirit. In informal discussions at a meeting of the Charismatic Concerns Committee at Glencoe, Missouri, several denominational leaders from mainline Protestant churches expressed their concern that congregational renewal, where they saw the movement's future, was being neglected. One reason was that the focus of its largest segments, the Roman Catholic and the nondenominational, was elsewhere. So in September 1980, ten leaders from four renewal fellowships met at Aurora, Illinois, seeking how to cooperate so as "to open the local churches to the ministry of the Holy Spirit." As a result, some sixty leaders came together at Tulsa, Oklahoma, in January 1981 to form the Parish Renewal Council (PRC).

The aims of PRC were "to centralize some of

the charismatic renewal activities for parish pastors, priests, lay leaders and to cooperate with church denominational leaders." The five groups initially forming PRC were the Presbyterian Charismatic Communion, Lutheran Charismatic Renewal Services, Episcopal Renewal Ministries, United Methodist Renewal Services Fellowship, and the Fellowship of Charismatic Christians in the United Church of Christ. The American Baptist Charismatic Fellowship joined PRC in 1983 and Mennonite Renewal Services in 1985. PRC has an executive committee with two representatives from each member fellowship.

In fact, many of the functions originally envisaged for PRC did not materialize, e.g., the sponsoring of regional and national parish renewal conferences and the publication of theological-biblical position papers and treatises. An evaluation of its role was undertaken by the PRC executive committee in 1984, and one of its goals was specified as identifying and highlighting those congregations that could be labeled as "lighthouse renewal groups." In fact, the PRC concept remained more attractive than it was immediately practical, and the meetings ended in 1985 without any formal dissolution.   P. D. Hocken

PARR, JOHN NELSON (1886–1976). British Assemblies of God leader. Converted in 1904, Parr's early association was with the Methodist Church and Star Hall Holiness, Manchester. Introduced to Pentecostal teaching when a friend visited Sunderland, he was baptized in the Spirit in 1910. In 1917, while holding a senior position in a large factory, he became part-time pastor of a small Pentecostal church. At the end of the war he continued to pastor the assembly. He took a leading part in the formation of the Assemblies of God of Great Britain and Ireland in 1924. He was chairman–general secretary (1924–32) and first editor of *Redemption Tidings* from 1924. False accusations were made against him (later withdrawn), and he resigned and joined Fred Squire (1904–62) in the Full Gospel Testimony, serving as general superintendent.

Parr's ministry was continued in Manchester, and a crusade by Stephen Jeffreys in 1927 brought in hundreds of new converts. Parr resigned his position at the factory and built up a large assembly. He opened Bethshan Tabernacle in 1928 and later enlarged it. He continued there until his retirement in 1964 at the age of seventy-eight. Energetic and pugnacious, he took up radio work at age sixty-nine. He was active to the last as a soul winner.

Bibliography: J. N. Parr, *Incredible* (1972).
                                                    D. W. Cartwright

PASTOR, ROLE OF The word "pastor" (Gk. *poimēn*) derives from the same word as "shepherd" and carries with it all the meaning inherent in the biblical culture and economy. The major OT reference to the pastoral ministry is in the Book of Jeremiah where the Lord promises "and I will give you pastors according to my own heart, which shall feed you with knowledge and understanding" (3:15). The same prophet pronounced judgment on pastors who failed to feed and visit the sheep, thereby scattering them (23:1–2).

Indeed, Psalm 23 depicts the Lord himself as the Good Shepherd who feeds and leads his sheep to green pastures and still waters. Thus the model of the shepherd and the sheep is integral to the OT understanding of spiritual leadership among the people of God.

I. The Pastor in the New Testament. In the NT, pastoral leadership was initially charismatic and itinerant. The apostles served as prophets and evangelists, carrying the gospel to the known nations of their world. The offices of bishop (overseer or supervisor), elder (presbyter), and deacon (server), were established in the NT churches but are not mentioned in Ephesians 4:11. Evidently the former related to the charismatic functions of leadership while the latter referred to their offices.

In the Ephesians list only the pastor-teacher (they refer to one office) were local ministers, while the first three (apostle, prophet, and evangelist) were itinerant. Thus the first ministers to live with the people and exercise a continuing local ministry were the pastor-teachers.

In reference to the roles of the bishops and elders, it is clear from the NT that they were used interchangeably and at first seemed to refer to the same office. In time, however, the bishops became the supreme pastors of the local churches with the elders (presbyters and priests), serving as their assistants. As the functions of each became more specialized, the bishops were permitted to exercise the exclusive rights of ordination, confirmation, and appointment of pastors, while the presbyters (priests) were permitted to celebrate the Eucharist and to baptize with water.

The diaconate served as a first step into the ministry and was based on the functions of the first deacons elected in Acts 6:1–6. In addition to these offices of the local church, there were added over the centuries the "minor orders," which consisted variously of exorcists, ministering widows, and acolytes.

II. The Pastor in the Patristic Age. By the third century the essentially charismatic ministries were largely forgotten as the hierarchic ministries developed. Thus prophets, speakers in tongues, interpreters, healers, discerners of spirits, and exorcists practically ceased to exist as regular pastoral ministries in the churches.

The first bishops were considered to be the pastors of a local church of a major city and its surrounding environs, with the priests serving as pastors of subdivided units called parishes. The local church was called a diocese or the "see" (seat) of the bishop. A later development was the creation of "metropolitans" or "archbishops" who exercised authority over an entire province or region. The ultimate development of the episcopate was the gradual recognition of the bishop of Rome as the "first among equals" among the bishops of the church, and in time in the West, with the pope claiming supreme pastoral authority over all Christendom.

As the pastoral system developed in the West, authority flowed from the top down through a pastoral "hierarchy" that included all the pastors of the church from the pope down to the minor orders.

III. The Protestant Heritage. The Protestant Reformation saw the development of new forms of pastoral authority. The episcopal system had been the common form of government in both the Eastern and Western branches of the church for a thousand years. In this system, pastors were ordained and assigned to parishes by the bishop with no elections coming from either the presbyters or the congregations.

An early Reformation change was the Presbyterian form of government where pastors were ordained and assigned by the eldership, or "presbytery" of the pastors. In other words, the pastors ordained and assigned each other to the churches. In this system pastoral power was transferred from the bishops to the pastors themselves. The Presbyterian churches, as the name implies, instituted and used this system.

The radical Reformation introduced the congregational system of government in which pastors were elected and ordained by the local churches, thus bypassing both bishops and presbyteries. In pure congregational government, pastoral authority lies with the local church, with the pastor serving as "first among equals." The Anabaptists and Mennonite churches were the first to use this system.

Advocates of all three systems claim to find authority and precedents for each in the NT. The latest scholarship now concedes that all three were indeed present to some degree in the NT and may all claim some biblical validity.

IV. The Role of the Pastor. Whatever the system used, there are clear directions for the role and character of the pastor in the Pauline Epistles. In 1 Timothy 3:1–7 Paul requires that a pastor (bishop) be blameless, the husband of one wife, vigilant, sober, of good behavior, hospitable, apt to teach, not given to much wine, not greedy, patient, nonviolent, not a novice, one who rules his own house well, and one with a good reputation outside of the church.

The major role of the pastor was the care and feeding of the sheep. This Jesus said three times to Simon Peter, who represented the first pastors of the church. The preaching and teaching ministry was the principal way that the sheep were to be fed and cared for. This could not be done regularly by an itinerant apostle, prophet, or evangelist. It was a duty that naturally inhered in one who lived with the sheep as a local shepherd.

The pastor was also to protect the sheep from the wolves who might attempt to seduce them with new and heretical doctrines. Thus developed the teaching function of the magisterium (the entire clergy of the church), which was to defend the sheep from errors promulgated by false teachers. This is stressed in Paul's last letter to Timothy, which has been used from time immemorial in the ordination charge. The newly ordained pastor is to "preach the word, be instant in season and out of season." He is to "reprove, rebuke, and exhort with all longsuffering and doctrine." This instruction was given in light of the time "when they shall not endure sound doctrine" but follow false teachers (2 Tim. 4:1–5).

V. The Personal Life of the Pastor. Paul instructed Timothy in both letters about the personal life and character of the bishop (pastor). The requirements in 1 Timothy 3 deal with the personal qualities of the pastor, calling for integrity and self-control in all aspects of his life, at home, in the church, and in the community.

VI. The Modern Role of the Pastor. Whatever the church or tradition represented, the role of the modern pastor is much the same as in biblical times. He is the primary preacher and teacher to his flock. He is the chief administrator of the congregation, overseeing all of the ministries for which he is responsible. He also is the chief evangelist ("do the work of an evangelist," 2 Tim. 4:5) to the congregation, who either evangelizes in the normal ministry of the church or invites itinerant evangelists to minister in local revival crusades.

A major duty is that of counselor to those in distress, many of whom are not members of the church family. For this responsibility, most seminaries now offer courses in psychology and counseling.

The role of pastors in large, or "super," churches involves the leading and equipping of a large staff of pastoral and professional assistants who carry out most of the counseling and administrative workload. The most recent model for this type of pastoral ministry is that of a "rancher" who supervises many undershepherds as assistants who lead "cell groups" and other smaller subcongregations that make up the larger body.

See also CHURCH LEADERSHIP; PREACHING, A PENTECOSTAL PERSPECTIVE.

Bibliography: J. Adams, *Shepherding God's Flock* (1979); C. Gore, *The Church and the Ministry* (1902; C. P. Wagner, *A Theology of Church Leadership* (1984).
                                        H. V. Synan

PASTORAL COUNSELING   See PASTOR, ROLE OF.

PATHWAY PRESS The trade division, particularly for book publication, of the Church of God (CG) Publishing House (Cleveland, Tenn.). Other divisions of the firm are Tennessee Music and Printing Company and local Pathway Bookstores, which are located in a half-dozen cities of the southeastern U.S.

The CG began its publishing ministry in 1910 with a weekly journal, *Church of God Evangel.* (It has been published continuously ever since, although it is now a biweekly journal.) In 1917 the CG established its own printing plant for production of its Sunday school literature. In 1929 a youth magazine, *The Lighted Pathway*, was begun. Other materials and publications featuring every aspect of Christian ministry have been added to the literary output. In 1986 Pathway Press, valued at $7,284,773, was one of the largest and most modern Christian publishing establishments in the U.S. (See photo on page 664.)

Bibliography: C. W. Conn, *The Evangel Reader* (1958).   C. W. Conn

PATTERSON, JAMES OGLETHORPE (1912–). Church executive. In November 1968

The Church of God Publishing House in Cleveland, Tenn., houses Pathway Press and Tennessee Music.

J. O. Patterson is the presiding bishop of the Church of God in Christ, the largest black Pentecostal organization in the U.S.

J. O. Patterson succeeded C. H. Mason (1866–1961) as presiding bishop of the Church of God in Christ (CGIC). This action, taken as a result of the denomination's first constitutional convention in February that year, ended a seven-year crisis during which, as senior bishop, O. T. Jones (1890–1972) had served as head. Under Patterson the Memphis-based body outgrew all other North American Pentecostal churches, both black and white. The 1982 membership of 3,709,661 was ten times as large as at Bishop Mason's death. A native of Derma, Mississippi, Patterson is married to the former Deborah Mason, daughter of the founder. He also serves as pastor of Pentecostal Temple in Memphis, the headquarters church.

Bibliography: F. B. Kelley, *Here I Am, Send Me* (1970); J. O. Patterson, *History and Formative Years of the Church of God in Christ* (1969); J. S. Tinney, "Black Pentecostals: Setting Up the Kingdom," *Christianity Today* 20 (December 5, 1975): 42–43.   C. E. Jones

PAUL, JONATHAN ANTON ALEXANDER

(1853–1931). German Pentecostal leader and author. After graduating from the Studium der Theologie in Griefswald, Paul pastored in Pommeren from 1880. He was active in the Gnadauer Verband (a revivalist group within the state church), in youth work and social action concerns, including industrial missions and ministry to railway workers. He wrote and preached extensively about "full salvation," drawing upon the Pietist and Anglo-Saxon revivalist traditions; and in 1907, after a visit to Oslo, he became a Pentecostal believer. Attacked by the Gnadauer Verband, the infamous Berlin Declaration, Paul became a founder of the Mülheim Pentecostal movement. A prolific writer, he edited several periodicals, including *Heiligung, Lied des Lammes, Pfingstgrusse,* and *Heilszeugnisse.* A skillful poet, many of his works are included in the Mülheim hymnal, *Pfingstjubel.* He (with five others) provided the first modern German language translation of the NT, *Das Neue Testament in der Sprache der Gegenwart* (1914).

See also EUROPEAN PENTECOSTALISM.

Bibliography: Selected Works: J. A. A. Paul, *Ihr werdet die Kraft des Heiligen Geistes empfangen, ein Zeugnis von der Taufe mit dem Heiligen Geist und Feuer* (1896), Swedish trans. *Andeopet* (1906); idem, *Siegreiches Leben durch das Blut Jesu* (n.d.); idem, *Unsere Botschaft an die Kranken* (n.d.); idem, *Was ist die Pfingstbewegung* (n.d.); idem, *Wie ich in die Pfingstbewegung kam* (n.d.); idem, *Zur Daimonenfrage, Ein Wort zur Verstandigung* (n.d.). **Selected Secondary Literature:** P. Fleisch, *Die Geschichte der deutschen Gemeinschaftsbewegung bis zum Auftreten des Zungenredens (1875–1907)* (1912, reprint 1985); idem, *Die Pfingstebewegung in Deutschland* (1957): idem, "Paul, Jonathan," *RGG,* 2, 4:1015–16; E. Geise, *Jonathan Paul, Ein Knecht Jesu Christi* 2. Aufl. (1965); E. Geldbach, "Paul Jonathan," *Evangelisches Gemeindelexikon* (1978), 398–99; C. H. Krust, *50 Jahre, Deutsche Pfingstbewegung, Mulheimer Richtung* (1958); D. Lange, *Eine Bewegung bricht zich Bahn* (1979).   D. D. Bundy

Two prominent German Pentecostal leaders: Emil Humburg (L), first president of the Mühlheim Association, and Jonathan Paul (R), a founder of the association and a prolific writer. In the center, H. Schober.

PAULINE LITERATURE Along with Luke-Acts, the letters of Paul present the most significant material on the ministry of the Holy Spirit in the NT. Whereas Luke presents the work of the Spirit in terms of promise and fulfillment in the form of historical narrative, Paul speaks of the Spirit, in both reflective and non-reflective ways, as the absolutely crucial element for Christian life, both individual and corporate.

    I. Presuppositions About the Literature
       A. Authenticity/Integrity
       B. Chronology
   II. The Data
       A. Spirit Language in Paul
          1. Holy Spirit and Human Spirit
          2. "A Spirit/The Spirit of . . ."
          3. The Adjective "Spiritual"
          4. Other Difficulties
       B. The Spirit and Power
  III. Finding the Center in Pauline Theology
  IV. The Spirit and the Godhead
       A. Personal Attributes
       B. Relationship to the Godhead
          1. The Spirit and God
          2. The Spirit and Christ
       C. Trinitarian Implications
   V. The Spirit and Eschatology
       A. The NT Framework
       B. The Role of the Spirit
          1. The Fulfilled Promise
             a. The Spirit and the New Covenant
             b. The Spirit–Flesh Contrast
          2. The Guarantee of the Future
             a. The Spirit as Seal and Down Payment

      b. The Spirit as Firstfruits
    C. The Charismata and Eschatology
VI. The Spirit and the Christian Life
    A. Preliminary Observations
    B. The Hearing of the Gospel
        1. Paul's Own Preaching
        2. The Spirit and Ministry
        3. The Place of Revelation
    C. The Spirit and Conversion
        1. The Crucial Role of the Spirit
        2. The Pauline Images
            a. Adoption
            b. Birth and Washing
            c. Life-giving
            d. Sanctification
        3. The Spirit and Water Baptism
        4. Conversion and Spirit Baptism
    D. Life in the Spirit
        1. The Spirit and Ethical Life
            a. Walking in the Spirit
            b. The Spirit as "Holy"
            c. The Spirit–Flesh Tension
            d. The Spirit and the Body
        2. The Fruit of the Spirit
        3. Other Spirit Activity
VII. The Spirit and the Community
    A. The Formation of the Community
    B. The Pauline Images
        1. Family
        2. Temple
        3. Body
    C. The Spirit and Worship
        1. Prayer
        2. Song
        3. Worship and the Charismata
    D. The Charismata and the Spirit
        1. The Linguistic Data
        2. Their Number and Variety
            a. Service
            b. Miracles
            c. Inspired Utterance
                i. Glossolalia
                ii. Prophecy
        3. Their Extent in the Pauline
            Churches

I. Presuppositions About the Literature.

A. Authenticity/Integrity. Since we are dealing with the Pauline literature, all thirteen letters of Paul are included here. The authenticity of the ten major letters is assumed (including those most often suspected: 2 Thessalonians, Colossians, Ephesians), as is the basic Pauline perspective of the Pastoral Epistles, which are considered ultimately to have come from him, despite the acknowledged difficulties of language and style (cf. Fee, 1984, xxxiv–xxxvii). The point is that even if these letters are not directly from Paul, they clearly reflect Pauline ideas throughout; this is especially true in their use of Spirit language, despite frequent assertions to the contrary (e.g., Dunn, 1975, 347–50).

The unity of all the letters is also assumed, except for 2 Corinthians, as it seems highly probable that chapters 10–13 are from yet another letter of Paul to this community; but in contrast to the opinion of many, that letter most likely follows chapters 1–9, not the other way

around (cf. Barrett, 1973, 11–17; Furnish, 1984, 30–41).

B. Chronology. Concerning the chronological order of the letters, the consensus of a former day seems to have the better of it: Galatians was most likely written shortly before Romans and is therefore not the earliest of the extant letters. Their assumed order—and the normal order of discussion—is: 1 Thessalonians, 2 Thessalonians, 1 Corinthians, 2 Corinthians, Galatians, Romans, Colossians, Philemon, Ephesians, Philippians, 1 Timothy, Titus, 2 Timothy.

II. The Data.

A. Spirit Language in Paul. Although the broad outlines of Paul's understanding of the Spirit and his ministry are easily discernible, just enough flexibility in language exists to make precision difficult to achieve. The word "spirit" (*pneuma*) occurs 145 times in the thirteen letters, the vast majority of which unambiguously refer to the Holy Spirit, although the full name occurs but 17 times (he also uses the term "the Spirit of God"/"his Spirit" 16 times; and "Spirit of Christ" 3 times). The word refers to Satan once (Eph. 2:2) and in the plural to demons at least once (1 Tim. 4:2; on "the discerning of spirits" in 1 Corinthians 12:10 see sections A.2 and VII.D below). Paul uses *pneuma* to refer to the basic interior component of the human personality in 14 unambiguous instances. The difficulties in usage occur in four areas.

1. Holy Spirit or Human Spirit. There are several instances of an unqualified use of *pneuma* in Paul's letters where one cannot be certain whether he intends to refer to the Holy Spirit or the human spirit, or perhaps to some genuine interplay between the two. Thus English translations vary between "spirit" and "Spirit" in 1 Corinthians 6:17; 14:2, 15, 16; 2 Corinthians 6:6; 11:4; Romans 1:4; 12:11; and Ephesians 2:18. The solution to these exegetical problems is to be found in two areas: Pauline grammar (usage) and the fact that in some cases there is genuine fluidity in language.

Some of these problems occur in the dative in the formula *pneumati* or *en pneumati* ("in spirit" or "in/by Spirit"). Here Paul's own usage seems determinative: When he intends the human spirit in this formula, he always includes the Greek article (1 Cor. 5:3; 14:15, 16; 2 Cor. 2:13; Rom. 1:9; 8:16; Col. 2:5; Eph. 4:23), but when he intends the Holy Spirit, he usually does not (1 Cor. 12:3; Gal. 3:3; 5:16, 18, 25 [2x]; Rom. 2:29; 8:9, 13, 14). On the basis of this usage, as well as other exegetical factors, one can be quite sure that Paul is referring to the Holy Spirit in 1 Corinthians 14:2, 16; 2 Corinthians 6:6; and Ephesians 2:18; whereas in Romans 12:11 the primary reference is to the human spirit.

Other instances are to be resolved in terms of Paul's apparent conviction that the believer's spirit is the place where, by means of God's own Spirit, the human and the divine interface in the individual believer's life. The key to this usage is to be found in some difficult plurals in 1 Corinthians 12–14: "the discerning of spirits" (12:10), "since you are zealots for spirits" (14:12), and "the spirits of the prophets are subject to the prophets"

(14:32). In light of the context of 14:32, these almost certainly refer to "the prophetic Spirit" by which each of them speaks through his or her own spirit (see Fee, 1987, 696); thus the prophetic utterance, inspired by the Divine Spirit, is subject to the speaker and must be "discerned" by others in the community. This usage is also the clue to 1 Corinthians 14:15 ("my spirit/Spirit prays/sings") and 1 Corinthians 6:17 ("the person who is joined to the Lord becomes one spirit/Spirit with him"). In both cases *pneuma* might best be translated "S/spirit," since something like this is almost certainly what Paul's somewhat flexible language intends. To these one might also add 1 Corinthians 5:3–5, where Paul speaks of being present in their gatherings "in S/spirit." Perhaps this is how one should also understand Romans 12:11 ("be fervent in S/spirit") and Philippians 1:27 ("stand fast in one S/spirit").

2. *"A spirit/the Spirit of . . . ."* This kind of genitive qualifier of *pneuma* occurs ten times in the Pauline corpus. As above, one cannot be sure in some instances whether Paul intends the human or divine Spirit (e.g., Rom. 1:4: "a spirit of holiness" or "the Spirit of holiness" = "the Holy Spirit," with emphasis on holiness), and in other instances whether Paul intends a human attitude or an attitude brought forth by the Holy Spirit (e.g., 1 Cor. 4:21, "a spirit of gentleness" [= "a gentle spirit"] or "the Spirit of gentleness" [= "gentleness that the Spirit brings"]). In three cases this usage is set up by Paul's standard "not–but" contrast (1 Cor. 2:12; Rom. 8:15; 2 Tim. 1:7). In each of these cases English translations tend to render the negative part "a spirit of" but are ambiguous with the positive part (sometimes "but the Spirit"; sometimes "but a spirit"). Here Paul's usage is certain. In each case he is referring to the reception of the Holy Spirit, who did not come from the "world" or bring "slavery" or "cowardice"; rather the Spirit comes from God (1 Cor. 2:12) and brings "adoption" (Rom. 8:15) or "power" and "sound-mindedness" (2 Tim. 1:7).

The other instances can be resolved only contextually. Paul certainly means the Holy Spirit when he refers to "the Spirit of life" (= the Spirit who brings life) in Romans 8:2; so also Romans 1:4 (the Spirit characterized by holiness); 2 Corinthians 4:13 (the same Spirit who brings faith); and Ephesians 1:17 (the Spirit who brings wisdom and revelation). The usage in Galatians 6:1, which as above probably means "in the S/spirit of gentleness," may be the clue to the identical phrase in 1 Corinthians 4:21, although in the latter the emphasis is more likely on Paul's own attitude.

3. *The Adjective "Spiritual."* In many ways the adjective *pneumatikos,* "spiritual") is the most difficult of all. In several instances it seems clearly to refer to the Holy Spirit. This is especially true of several instances in 1 Corinthians (2:13–3:4; 12:1; 14:1, 37), where the whole context requires an understanding in terms of the Spirit. Thus the context of 2:13 argues for a meaning something like "we speak words taught by the Spirit," which means "we explain the things of the Spirit by means of words taught by the Spirit." Likewise

the "spiritual person" in 2:14 means "the person who has the Spirit" in contrast to an unbeliever ("the natural person"), who does not; and the meaning of the plural in 12:1 is most likely "the things of the Spirit," which would thus include both the "gifts" of the Spirit and "spiritual [Spirit] people." Even in some cases where the word is used to contrast more earthly concerns (e.g., 1 Cor. 9:10–11, where material support is "physical" in contrast to the benefits of the gospel, which are "spiritual"), it is arguable that the ultimate referent is the Spirit. Perhaps the most ambiguous usage is in Ephesians 1:3—"God has blessed you with all spiritual blessings in heavenly places in Christ Jesus." Because of the occurrence of the phrase "heavenly places," some argue that this means "heavenly blessings," in contrast to those of earth. More likely, however, especially in light of Paul's usage in the rest of this letter and of verses 13–14, with which this benediction concludes, Paul is here referring to the benefits that the Spirit bestows, benefits that result from the work of Christ—a fact that is elaborated in verses 4–12. So also the "spiritual songs" in Colossians 3:16 and Ephesians 5:19 refer to songs that are inspired of the Spirit for individuals to sing to the gathered community.

4. *Other Difficulties.* Because of their especially ad hoc character, Paul's letters also frequently display flexibility as to how something is said. Thus, e.g., there has been considerable debate over the meaning of Galatians 4:5–7, where Paul explicitly says that "the Spirit [not the believer] cries" and that because we "are children God sent the Spirit of his Son into our hearts," implying that the Spirit is received after one becomes a child of God. However, the parallel in Romans 8:15–16 (we cry; the Spirit brings about our adoption as children) leads us to see that our understanding of Paul's way of expressing himself in Galatians needs to be modified in light of the broader picture. So also with the various references to Timothy's experience of Spirit in 1 Timothy 1:18; 4:14; and 2 Timothy 1:6–7 (see below, VI.B.2).

Besides these difficulties, there is the matter of Spirit phenomena that appear in Paul's letters, where one can be sure that from Paul's perspective one is dealing with the activity of the Spirit, but where Spirit language as such does not occur. This is true, e.g., of such passages as Romans 12:1–2 ("be transformed by the renewing of your mind"); Galatians 2:2 ("I went up in response to a revelation"); and 2 Corinthians 12:1–7 ("a man caught up to the third heaven").

B. The Spirit and Power. In contrast to the common perspective of the contemporary church, the first-century believers understood—and assumed—the Spirit to be manifested in power. So much is this so that "Spirit" and "power" at times are used interchangeably. Thus Luke, for example, interchanges the two words in the balanced lines of Semitic poetry in Luke 1:35; and since Jesus' whole public ministry is to be understood in terms of the Spirit's activity (3:22; 4:1, 14), there can be little question that in 5:17 Luke meant that the "power of the Spirit" was present with Jesus to heal.

So also with Paul. Not only does he specifically use such terminology as "the power of the Spirit" (Rom. 15:13, 19), but he also regularly joins the two terms together in such a way that the presence of the Spirit means the presence of power (1 Thess. 1:5; 1 Cor. 2:4; Gal. 3:5; Rom. 1:4; Eph. 3:16; 2 Tim. 1:7). Several of these references are in the context of Paul's own ministry (1 Thess. 1:5; 1 Cor. 2:4; Rom. 15:19), but others clearly refer to the powerful working of the Spirit in the lives of believers. One may thus assume not only that Paul's other references to the Spirit always imply the presence of power, but also that many of his references to power imply the presence of the Spirit (e.g., 2 Thess. 1:11; 1 Cor. 4:20; 5:4; 2 Cor. 4:7; 6:7; 12:9, 12; 13:4; Col. 1:11, 29; Eph. 1:19, 21; 3:7, 20; 2 Tim. 1:8).

One cannot always be sure what "power" might have meant for Paul. Most often it refers to clearly visible manifestations that evidence the Spirit's presence (e.g., 1 Cor. 2:4–5; Gal. 3:5; Rom. 15:19). The evidence from 1 Thessalonians 5:19–22; 1 Corinthians 12–14; Galatians 3:2–5; and Romans 12:6 makes it certain that the Pauline churches were "charismatic" in the sense that a dynamic presence of the Spirit was manifested in their gatherings (cf. Dunn, 1975, 260–65). And even where power means that believers apprehend and live out the love of Christ in a greater way (Eph. 3:16–20), Paul recognizes here a miraculous work of the Spirit that will be evidenced by the way renewed people behave toward one another. Probably more than anything else, this dynamic, evidential dimension of life in the Spirit is what tends to separate believers in later church history from those in the Pauline churches. Whatever else, the Spirit was experienced in the Pauline churches; he was not simply a matter of creedal assent.

III. Finding the Center in Pauline Theology. There has been a long debate in scholarship as to what constitutes the "heart" of Pauline theology. The traditional view, fostered by the Reformers and perpetuated by generations of Protestants, is that "justification by faith" is the key to Paul's theology. This view puts the emphasis on Christ's historical act of redemption and its appropriation by the believer through faith. The inadequacy of such a view should be apparent from a thorough reading of Paul's letters. Not only does such an approach focus on one metaphor of salvation to the exclusion of others, but it also fails to throw the net broadly enough so as to capture all of Paul's theological concerns.

In response to this, others have sought this center in Paul's "mystical experience of being *in Christ*" (see esp. Schweitzer, 1931). This view shifts the focus from Christ's historical work and its appropriation by the believer to the believer's (especially Paul's) ongoing experience of Christ. While in some ways this serves as a corrective to the traditional view, most contemporary Pauline scholars have recognized the inadequacy of both of these somewhat limiting approaches.

The best approach to Paul is to see eschatology as the essential framework of all his theological reflection and salvation in Christ as the essential

concern within that framework. Salvation is "eschatological" in the sense that final salvation, which still awaits the believer, is already a present reality through Christ and the Spirit (see section V below). It is "in Christ" in the sense that what originated in God was effected historically by the death and resurrection of Christ, to be appropriated experientially through the Holy Spirit, who also empowers Christian living until the final consummation at Christ's parousia. Any understanding that does not see the crucial role of the Spirit in Pauline theology quite misses Paul's own concerns and emphases.

IV. The Spirit and the Godhead.
A. Personal Attributes. Paul's interest in the Spirit is basically limited to the Spirit's *activity*. He does not, therefore, speak directly to the question of his *person*; and his letters are both too early and too ad hoc for him to be involved in Trinitarian discussion or speculation. Nonetheless, several converging pieces of evidence make it certain that Paul understood the Spirit in personal terms, intimately associated with both the Father and the Son, yet distinct from them.

That Paul understood the Spirit as personal is evidenced in two ways. First, although most often the Spirit is the agent of God's activity (e.g., 2 Thess. 2:13; Titus 3:5), he is also the subject of a large number of personal actions. The Spirit knows (1 Cor. 2:11), teaches (1 Cor. 2:13), works (1 Cor. 12:11), gives life (2 Cor. 3:6), cries (Gal. 4:6), leads (Gal. 5:18; Rom. 8:14), bears witness (Rom. 8:16), helps us in our weakness (Rom. 8:26), intercedes (Rom. 8:26–27), and may be grieved (Eph. 4:30).

Second, the Spirit is sometimes the subject of a verb or implied activity, which elsewhere is attributed to either the Father or the Son. Thus in 1 Corinthians 12:6 Paul says of God (the Father is implied) that he "produces" (*energei*) all of these activities in all people, whereas in a similar sentence in verse 11 the Spirit is the subject of the identical verb (cf. "gives life" in Rom. 8:11 [of the Father] and in 2 Cor. 3:6 [the Spirit]; and "intercedes," of Christ in Rom. 8:34 and of the Spirit in 8:26–27).

B. Relationship to the Godhead. Given the reality of the Spirit's personal attributes, the greater questions have to do with his relationship to the Father and the Son and whether there is in fact a latent Trinitarianism in Paul's letters. These issues are made especially complex by the fluidity of Paul's language, Romans 8:9–11 being the classic example, where in successive sentences Paul speaks of believers as being indwelt by "the Spirit of God," "the Spirit of Christ," and "Christ" himself.

1. The Spirit and God. Despite some suggestions to the contrary, Paul thinks of the Spirit primarily in terms of his relationship to God (the Father, though he never uses this imagery of this relationship). Not only does he more often speak of the "Spirit of God" than of the "Spirit of Christ" (16 to 3), but God is invariably the subject of the verb when Paul speaks of human reception of the Spirit. Thus God "sent forth the Spirit of his Son into our hearts" (Gal. 4:6), "gives" us his Spirit (1 Thess. 4:8; 2 Cor. 1:22;

5:5; Gal. 3:5; Rom. 5:5; Eph. 1:17), and pours out his Spirit on us (Titus 3:6). This relationship is in Paul's case almost certainly determined by his OT roots, where God "fills with" (Exod. 31:3) or "pours out" his Spirit (Joel 2:28), and the "Spirit of God" comes on people for all sorts of extraordinary ("charismatic") activities (e.g., Num. 24:2; Judg. 3:10).

Two passages in particular give insight into Paul's own understanding of this relationship. In 1 Corinthians 2:10–12 he uses the analogy of human interior consciousness (only one's "spirit" knows one's mind), to insist that the Spirit alone knows the mind of God. Paul's own concern in this analogy is with the Spirit as the source of our understanding the cross as God's wisdom; nonetheless the analogy itself draws the closest kind of relationship between God and his Spirit. The Spirit alone "searches all things," even "the depths of God" (an idea that reflects Paul's background in the OT and Jewish apocalyptic [cf. Dan 2:22–23]); and because of this singular relationship with God, the Spirit alone knows and reveals God's otherwise hidden wisdom (1 Cor. 2:7).

In Romans 8:26–27 this same idea is now expressed obversely. Among other matters, Paul is here concerned to show how the Spirit, in the presence of our own weaknesses and inability to speak for ourselves, is able to intercede adequately on our behalf. The effectiveness of the Spirit's intercession lies precisely in the fact that God, who searches our hearts, likewise "knows the mind of the Spirit," who is making intercession for us.

Some mystery is involved here, because finally we are dealing with divine mysteries. There can be little question that Paul sees the Spirit as distinct from God; yet at the same time he is both the interior expression of the unseen God's own personality and the visible manifestation of God's activity in the world. The Spirit is truly God in action; yet he is neither simply an outworking of God's own personality, nor is he all there is to say about God.

2. The Spirit and Christ. In Christian theology in general and Pauline theology in particular, the coming of Christ has forever marked our understanding of God. The transcendent God of the universe is henceforth known as "the father of our Lord Jesus Christ" (2 Cor. 1:3; Eph. 1:3; 1 Peter 1:3), who "sent his Son" into the world to redeem (Gal. 4:4–5). Likewise the coming of Christ has forever marked our understanding of the Spirit. The Spirit of God is also the Spirit of Christ (Gal. 4:6; Rom. 8:9; Phil. 1:19), who carries on the work of Christ following Christ's resurrection and subsequent assumption of the place of authority at God's right hand. To have received the Spirit of God (1 Cor. 2:12) is to have the mind of Christ (v. 16). For Paul, therefore, Christ gives definition to the Spirit: Spirit people are God's children, fellow heirs with God's Son (Rom. 8:14–17), who simultaneously know both the power of Christ's resurrection and the fellowship of his sufferings (Phil. 3:3, 10); at the same time Christ is the absolute criterion for what is truly Spirit activity (e.g., 1 Cor. 12:3). Thus it is fair to say with some that Paul's

doctrine of the Spirit is Christocentric, in the sense that Christ and his work give definition to the Spirit and his work in the Christian life.

In fact in some passages (e.g., 1 Cor. 6:17; 15:45; 2 Cor. 3:17–18) Paul speaks of the risen Lord in such a way that some scholars have argued that Paul, in part at least, identifies the Spirit with the risen Lord. But such an identification is negated by a contextual understanding of these texts. The language of 1 Corinthians 6:17 and 15:45 has been dictated by their contexts, where certain contrasts set up by the argument itself call forth this usage. Neither of these passages offers a theology of the Spirit, nor do they suggest an identification of the Spirit with the risen Lord (see Fee, 1987, 257–60; 788–95).

So also in 2 Corinthians 3:17–18. Even though Paul explicitly says that "the Lord is the Spirit," he scarcely intends an ontological identification of Christ with the Spirit. The words "the Lord" in verse 17 are anaphoric; i.e., "the Lord" just mentioned in verse 16 (alluding to Exod. 34:34) to whom people now turn is the Spirit—the Spirit of the new covenant, who brings freedom and transforms God's people into "the glory of the Lord."

Although Paul does not make this identification, he does assume the same kind of close relationship between the Spirit and Christ as between the Spirit and God the Father. They are clearly distinct from each other, as a passage like Galatians 4:4–6 makes certain, yet at times Paul moves easily from the mention of the one to the other, especially when using the language of "indwelling" (e.g., Rom. 8:10–11, from "have the Spirit of Christ" to "Christ is in you"; cf. Eph. 3:16–17). Thus when Paul in Galatians 2:20 speaks of Christ as living in him, he almost certainly means "Christ lives in me by his Spirit," referring to the ongoing work of Christ in his life that is being carried out by the indwelling Spirit.

This fluid use of language most likely results from the fact that Paul's concern with both Christ and the Spirit is not ontological (i.e., the nature of their being God), but soteriological (i.e., their role in salvation) and experiential. Paul thus often speaks of salvation in terms of the activities of the three divine Persons. For example, in Galatians 4:4–6, God the Father initiated salvation by sending forth his Son, who effected redemption within history, which in turn was made effectual in the life of the believer by the Spirit of the Son, whom God also sent forth. So also in Titus 3:5–7 "God saved us" through the regenerating work of the Spirit, predicated on the prior justifying work of Christ (cf. 1 Cor. 6:11; Rom. 1:3–4; 5:1–5; 8:3–4; 15:18; Eph. 1:4–14; 2:17–18; 2:22). In this threefold activity—God the Father as ultimate cause and initiator, God the Son as working it out in our human history, and God the Spirit as effecting it in our lives and in the church—one has the clue both to Pauline theology as a whole (section III above) and to the beginnings of Trinitarian theology itself.

C. Trinitarian Implications. Paul never specifically calls the Spirit "God" (whether he so refers to Christ is a moot point, depending on how one understands some crucial issues in two very difficult passages [Rom. 9:5; Titus 2:13]). Nonetheless, an implicit Trinitarianism in Paul's understanding of God seems certain. Besides the several texts noted above, three in particular (1 Cor. 12:4–6; 2 Cor. 13:13; Eph. 4:4–6) offer the kind of Trinitarian language that provides the basis for the later formulations of the early church.

In 1 Corinthians 12 Paul urges that the Corinthians broaden their perspective to recognize the rich diversity of the Spirit's manifestations among them (over against their apparently singular interest in glossolalia). He begins in verses 4–6 by noting that such diversity reflects the character of God himself and is therefore the true evidence of the work of the one God in their midst. The Trinitarian implications of these three sentences are undeniable.

The threefold benediction in 2 Corinthians 13:13 moves in the same direction. As elsewhere, the three phrases reflect Paul's interest in God's threefold soteriological activity (God's love initiates; Christ's grace effects historically; the Spirit creates an ongoing fellowship). However, this is not a piece of prose, but a benediction; and benediction involves one in speaking about God himself. That God is herewith understood as Father, Son, and Spirit is implied in the strongest possible way.

In Ephesians 4:4–6 one finds this same combination: a creedal formulation expressed in terms of the distinguishable activities of the Triune God. The basis for Christian unity is God himself. The one body is the work of the one Spirit (cf. 1 Cor. 12:13); we live our present eschatological existence in one hope, effected for us by the one Lord, in whom all believe (we have "one faith"), and to this faith all have given witness through their "one baptism." The source of all these realities is the one God himself, "who is over all and through all and in all."

If the last phrase in this passage reemphasizes the unity of the one God, who is ultimately responsible for all things—past, present, and future—and subsumes the work of the Spirit and the Son under that of God, the whole passage at the same time puts into creedal form the affirmation that God is experienced as a threefold reality. Precisely on the basis of such experience and language the later church maintained its biblical integrity by expressing all of this in explicitly Trinitarian language. And Paul's formulations, which include the work of the Spirit, form a part of this basis.

V. The Spirit and Eschatology.

A. The New Testament Framework.
The essential framework for NT theology, both for its central personages and for all of its documents, is eschatology. The early church, taking its clue from Jesus' own proclamation of the kingdom as a present reality in his own ministry, understood itself to be an eschatological community. The resurrection of Christ and the gift of the promised (eschatological) Spirit, completely altered their perspective, both of the mission and message of Jesus and of their own self-understanding. In place of the totally future eschatology of their Jewish roots, with its hope of the coming Messiah and its culmination in the resurrection of the dead, the early church recognized that the future had already been set in motion. The resurrection of Christ marked the beginning of the End, the turning of the ages. However, the End had only begun; they still awaited the final event, the parousia of their Messiah Jesus, at which time they too would experience the resurrection of the body. They lived "between the times"; already the future had begun, it had not yet been consummated. In the NT the whole of Christian existence—and theology—has this eschatological tension as its basic framework.

This framework is the absolute key to understanding Paul's theology as well. With Christ's death and resurrection the old (former age) has gone, the new has begun (2 Cor. 5:14–17). We are those on whom the ends of the ages have come (1 Cor. 10:11), yet we await the final glory and inheritance (Rom. 8:17–26). Salvation is both "already" (Eph. 2:8) and "not yet" (Rom. 5:9), as is the gift of righteousness (Rom. 5:1; Gal. 5:5). Redeemed already (Eph. 1:7), we yet await the day of redemption (Eph. 4:30); already adopted as children (Rom. 8:15), we wait eagerly for our adoption as children (v. 23). Believers thus constitute an eschatological community, marked by resurrection and Spirit, among whom God has begun a good work that he will complete on the day of the Lord (Phil. 1:6). But Paul is no triumphalist. Because we are "already," we know the power of Christ's resurrection; but because we are "not yet" we also presently share in the fellowship of his sufferings (Phil. 3:10). Such an eschatological view of existence totally determines one's present relationships and values (1 Cor. 6:2–4; 7:29–31). The certain future, already begun with Christ's resurrection, completely radicalizes God's new people. They live as aliens on earth; their true citizenship is in heaven (Phil. 3:20).

B. The Role of the Spirit.
Along with the resurrection of Jesus, the present gift of the Spirit has especially determined this theological perspective in Paul. From his Jewish heritage he well understood that the Spirit was part of the promise for the future; therefore the gift of the outpoured Spirit meant that the messianic age had already arrived. For Paul the Spirit is both the certain evidence that the future had dawned and the guarantee of its final consummation.

1. The Fulfilled Promise. It has been suggested (correctly, I think) that the theme of the Spirit's ministry making already present for the believer the glory that is to be "is in fact the most distinctive feature in Paul's doctrine of the Spirit" (Bruce, 1982, 232). This theme is found in a variety of passages and metaphors. For example, the certain evidence that the time of the law is passed and that Gentiles have at last inherited the promise made to Abraham (Gen. 12:3) is that they have received the substance of the promise, the Holy Spirit himself (Gal. 3:14). Likewise in Ephesians 1:13–14, again addressing Gentiles, Paul says that they have been marked with a seal, the Holy Spirit of promise (i.e., "the promised Holy Spirit").

Similarly, in 1 Corinthians 2:6–16 Paul argues that God's secret wisdom, which he destined for our glory before time began, but which until now has been hidden in God himself, has at last been revealed by his Spirit—although it is still hidden to those without the Spirit.

a. The Spirit and the New Covenant. This same theme is picked up in a slightly different way in those passages where Paul contrasts the past and present in terms of the old and new covenants (2 Cor. 3:1–4:6; Rom. 2:29; 7:6). The old covenant of law, even though it came with glory, was written on stone tablets. For Paul this imaged its "deadness," its basic inability to set people free. It had become a covenant of "letter" (i.e., a merely written code) leading to death; and a veil like that which covered Moses' face to hide the fading glory now covers the hearts of all who hear it read.

In contrast, the new covenant, by means of the Spirit, is written on "tablets of human hearts" (2 Cor. 3:3); its rite of "circumcision" is that "of the heart" (Rom. 2:29). The gospel and its ministry is accompanied by a much greater and more enduring glory, the ministry of the Spirit himself. The new covenant is life-giving, precisely because its content, Christ, is administered by the Spirit, through whom also we behold—and are transformed into—the glory of the Lord (2 Cor. 3:4–18). Thus the promised new covenant has replaced the old, the gift of the Spirit being the certain evidence.

b. The Spirit–Flesh Contrast. Paul's well-known contrast between living *kata sarka* ("according to the flesh") and *kata pneuma* ("according to the Spirit") is also primarily to be understood within this eschatological framework (Gal. 5:13–6:10 [cf. the analogy in 4:29]; Rom. 8:3–17; Phil. 3:3). These phrases do not refer to "physical" and "spiritual" existence, but to living under the influence of two radically opposite "powers." The one, the sinful nature, has been decisively crippled by the death and resurrection of Christ. As with the "old age" to which it belongs, the "flesh" is on its way out; it has been rendered ineffective through death (Rom. 7:4–6). Those who have so died with Christ must now live "according to the Spirit"; they are to walk by the Spirit (Gal. 5:16), be led of the Spirit (v. 18), bear the fruit of the Spirit (v. 22), behave according to the Spirit (v. 25), and sow to the Spirit (6:8). The coming of the Spirit marks the beginning of the end of life "according to the flesh."

Thus believers live "between the times." As Romans 8:9–11 makes clear, they are in the flesh (body) but not of the flesh (sinful nature). The body is still subject to decay, awaiting its final transformation into a "spiritual body" (i.e., a body adapted to the final life of the Spirit). We live in that hope precisely because we are already Spirit people. The already-crippled flesh (sinful nature) will be finally brought to ruin at the Parousia. The Spirit, already our present possession, will be fully realized at the same parousia.

2. *The Guarantee of the Future.* The present reality of the Spirit, however, is not triumphalism. Paul is a completely eschatological man; the future has thoroughly conditioned life in the present. But he is also a realist. Indwelt by the Spirit, one must by that same Spirit walk in newness of life. There are no guarantees of sinlessness or perfection in the "already"; there are only guarantees of the Spirit's effective working in and through our present weaknesses and of the final glory, of which the Spirit is the present installment. Thus the Spirit is not only the evidence that the new has come and the old is on its way out, but he is at the same time the sure guarantee of the final glory itself. This is made especially clear by three Pauline metaphors for the Spirit: seal (2 Cor. 1:21–22; Eph. 1:13; 4:30), earnest (*arrabōn*, first installment; 2 Cor. 1:21–22; 5:5; Eph. 1:14), and firstfruits (Rom. 8:23).

a. The Spirit as Seal and Down Payment. These two metaphors occur together in 2 Corinthians 1:21–22. In a paragraph (vv. 18–22) that is something of an aside as he recounts some changes to his itinerary and the reasons for it, Paul appeals to the faithfulness of God as guaranteeing his own trustworthiness as an apostle. As a conclusion to this aside, he affirms that their very existence in Christ, brought about by God himself, is the guarantee. The God whose promises have all been confirmed in Christ (v. 20) is the same God who confirms us (present tense) as well, which has been certified by the gift of the Spirit, with whom God has "anointed" us and who functions for us as both "seal" and "down payment."

Except for the verb "anointed," this entire sentence is expressed in a business metaphor ("confirmation" is here a metaphor from the selling of property). The "seal," usually a stamped imprint in wax, denotes ownership, and carries with it the protection of the owner (see BAGD, 796; MM, 617–18). As Ephesians 1:13 and 4:30 make certain, the "seal" is the Spirit himself, by whom God has marked believers and claimed them for his own. The eschatological guarantee in the metaphor is expressly stated in Ephesians 4:30 ("with whom you were sealed for the day of redemption").

The word *arrabōn* is amply attested in the Greek commercial papyri as a technical term for the first installment (hence "down payment") of a total amount due (see MM, 79). As such, it functions both to establish the contractual obligation and to guarantee its fulfillment. As Ephesians 1:14 makes certain, the genitival phrase "of the Spirit" in 2 Corinthians 1:22 and 5:5 is to be understood as in apposition to "down payment." Thus the Spirit is the down payment, God's down payment in our lives that guarantees our certain future. Not only so, this metaphor, as well as the next one (firstfruits), suggests that what is given is part of the whole. For Paul the gift of the Spirit is the first part of the redemption of the whole person, the beginning of the process that will end when believers assume their spiritual bodies (that is, when they enter into a mode of existence determined solely by the Spirit; cf. Dunn, 1975, 311).

b. The Spirit as Firstfruits. This metaphor reflects both the tension of our present existence as already–not yet and the guarantee of our certain future. The larger context of Romans

8:12–27 is especially noteworthy. In verses 15–17, with the Spirit playing the leading role, Paul has struck the dual themes of our present position as children, who are thus joint-heirs with Christ of the Father's glory, and our present existence as one of weakness and suffering, as we await that glory. These are the two themes taken up in verses 18–27. By the Spirit we have already received our "adoption" as God's children, but what is "already" is also "not yet"; therefore, by the same Spirit, who functions for us as firstfruits, we await our final "adoption as children, the redemption of our bodies." The first sheaf is God's pledge to us of the final harvest.

With the body in particular this motif is played out to the full in Paul. Our mortal bodies, mere jars of clay (2 Cor. 4:7), presently carry about in them the death of Jesus (v. 10). Because they bear the likeness of the man of earth (1 Cor. 15:47), they are subject to weakness, decay, and finally death (15:42–44). Nonetheless, by the Spirit they will be made alive (Rom. 8:11), transformed into the likeness of the heavenly person (1 Cor. 14:47), and thus become "spiritual" (both "supernatural" and adapted to final life in the Spirit) like that of him who by his resurrection is already a life-giving spirit (14:44–45). Therefore, in the present we abound in hope by the power of the Spirit (Rom. 15:13).

C. The Charismata and Eschatology. In 1 Corinthians 13:8–13 Paul also places the *charismata* into an eschatological framework. In this case he is arguing against an "overspiritualized" eschatology on the part of the Corinthians. Apparently they had placed emphasis on the "already" in such a way as to negate rather thoroughly the "not yet." Already they were rich and full and had begun to reign (4:8). Glossolalia apparently served for them as the "sign" (cf. 14:20–22) of their "arrival." Speaking the language of angels (13:1) meant they were already partakers of the ultimate state of spiritual existence, leading them to deny a future bodily resurrection (15:12).

As part of his argument against this wrong emphasis on tongues, Paul insists in 13:8–13 that the gifts do not belong to the future, but only to the present. On this matter they were deluded. The irony is that the gifts, the evidence of future existence, will pass away (v. 8a); they are "partial" (v. 9); they are as childhood in comparison with adulthood (v. 11); they are like looking into a mirror in comparison with seeing someone face to face (v. 12).

But this is not a devaluation of the gifts themselves; it is making them relative. We are in fact still in the present, so in chapter 14 Paul goes on not only to correct abuse, but to urge proper use. In the present we should pursue love (14:1), because that alone is both for now and forever (13:13); but that also means that in the already we should eagerly desire manifestations of the Spirit so as to build up the community. The final glory (completeness) still awaits.

VI. The Spirit and the Christian Life.

A. Preliminary Observations. Two preliminary observations need to be made. First, Paul's concerns about the Christian life are primarily with its corporate, not its individual, expression. The command in Ephesians 5:18 to keep filled with the Spirit, for example, is not addressed to individuals with regard to Christian life in general; rather Paul is addressing a community setting, in which believers teach one another with various kinds of songs.

On the other hand, such a text by its very nature applies first to individual believers, who must respond to the exhortation if the community is to be filled with the Spirit. So it is with the majority of texts here under discussion. Therefore, even though Paul's own emphasis tends to be in reverse order, it is nonetheless more convenient in attempting to systematize what he says about the Spirit to deal with the individual believer first.

Second, all of Paul's statements about the role of the Spirit in the Christian life are ad hoc and do not easily yield to a precise scheme as to the *ordo salutis* (order of salvation). What one finds in fact are several components that make up the complex of Christian conversion (hearing the gospel, faith, various metaphors for conversion, the gift of the Spirit, baptism in water), and there is indeed a certain logic as to how they are mentioned; but beyond that, everything is more speculative. What is crucial to note is the central role that the Spirit plays in most of the process, except for baptism.

B. The Hearing of the Gospel. Christian life begins with the hearing of the gospel, which both precedes faith (Rom. 10:14) and is accompanied by faith (1 Thess. 2:13; 2 Thess. 2:13–14; Eph. 1:13). According to Paul the effectual hearing of the gospel is a work of the Holy Spirit. Two things are involved here: the gospel itself as God's very Word (1 Thess. 2:13) and therefore the truth that must be believed (2 Thess. 2:13; 1 Tim. 2:4), revealed as such by the Spirit, and the dual act of preaching and responding, which are also the work of the Spirit.

1. Paul's Own Preaching. Paul frequently refers to his own effective ministry as a direct result of the work of the Spirit (see 1 Thess. 2:5–6; 1 Cor. 2:1–5; cf. 2 Cor. 6:6–7; Rom. 15:18–19; Eph. 3:7).

In 1 Thessalonians 1:5–6 he begins his encouragement of this new—and persecuted—Christian community by reminding them of two experienced realities: his ministry among them and the nature of their own conversion. They became converts (v. 5), not because of Paul's words alone, words that carried the content of the gospel, but because those words were accompanied by the power of the Spirit, including a deep conviction (probably in them as to the truthfulness of the gospel). Their own reception of the gospel was itself accompanied by much affliction and with the joy of the Holy Spirit (v. 6), that untrammeled joy the Spirit brings to those who have come to know the living and true God (v. 9).

So also 1 Corinthians 2:1–5. In defending his ministry among them against his detractors (cf. 4:1–21; 9:1–27), Paul here takes up the matter of his own preaching when he had first come to Corinth. Both the content (1:18–25) and the form of his preaching were without persuasive wisdom or rhetoric; indeed, it was far more effective than these human characteristics could have made it. It was accompanied by a demonstration of the Spirit's power, evidenced by the conversion of the Corinthians themselves (cf. 2 Cor. 3:3).

Thus Paul's service in the gospel was in keeping with God's effective power (Eph. 3:7)—i.e., through the working of the Spirit, as 3:16 makes clear.

2. *The Spirit and Ministry*. Although the evidence is more scanty, what was true of Paul's ministry is probably how he understood the effective preaching of the gospel in general. This at least is implied by the plural "we" in 1 Thessalonians 1:5–6, which included both Silas and Timothy. Similarly, in 1 Corinthians 15:11 Paul includes the preaching of the other "apostles" as also bringing about faith.

Paul's understanding of the relationship of the Spirit to ministry is best found in three passages addressed to Timothy (1 Tim. 1:18; 4:14; 2 Tim. 1:6–7; cf. v. 14). Each of these recalls Timothy's own experience of "call" to ministry; because of context, each emphasizes a different aspect of that experience. Several things may be deduced from the passages together: (1) Timothy's gift (charisma) refers first to the Spirit (2 Tim. 1:6–7) but is also broadened to refer to the gift of ministry that came by the Spirit (1 Tim. 4:14). The experience therefore is first of all something that happened to (or within) Timothy. (2) The experience took place in a community setting, since it also came by way of prophetic utterances spoken over/about/to him (1 Tim. 1:18; 4:14). (3) The community of elders responded to the prior work of the Spirit by the laying on of hands (4:14; 2 Tim. 1:6; cf. a similar sequence in Acts 13:1–3). The Spirit as an experienced reality is the obvious key to these appeals.

3. *The place of Revelation*. Part of Paul's conviction that his message would be, and was, accompanied by the Spirit's power, was his corresponding conviction that it came to him by revelation, again as the work of the Spirit. Although Paul does not mention the Spirit in his defense in Galatians 1:12, both 1 Corinthians 2:10–13, 16 and Ephesians 3:5–7 affirm that his own insight into the gospel came by the Spirit's revelation.

This revelation involved a twofold unveiling of God's mystery. First, 1 Corinthians 2:6–16 states that the Spirit has revealed what was formerly hidden, and is still hidden to those without the Spirit, namely that God in his own wisdom has chosen to redeem his fallen race by means of the ultimate foolishness (from a merely human point of view)—by means of a crucified Messiah. Thus Paul's preaching of the cross came with "words taught by the Spirit" (v. 13), which included "explaining spiritual things by spiritual means" (i.e., the things taught by the Spirit with language appropriate to the Spirit). To have the Spirit in this way means not to be subject to merely human judgments; rather, it means to have the mind of Christ (vv. 15–16; cf. 1 Cor. 7:25, 40).

Crucial to Paul's argument here is that this revelation should be the common experience of all who have received the Spirit. Paul's problem with the Corinthians was that they considered themselves to be people of the Spirit but were abandoning the Cross for merely human wisdom and rhetoric. Hence the crucial role of the Spirit, who has revealed to those who love God what was formerly hidden (vv. 9–10), namely what God in Christ has freely given us (v. 12).

Second, in Ephesians 3:2–13 this mystery—God's hidden wisdom now revealed by the Spirit—includes the fact that "Gentiles are heirs together with Israel, members together of one body, and sharers together in the promise in Christ Jesus" (v. 6). Therefore for Paul both the revelation of it and the actual inclusion of Jews and Gentiles together in Christ (1:13–14; 2:18, 22) is the work of the Spirit.

A further aspect of revelation connected with the hearing of the gospel occurs in 1 Corinthians 14:24–25. Here it comes by means of prophetic utterances within the believing community when unbelievers are present. What is revealed in this case are the secrets of the unbelievers' own hearts, leading to repentance and conversion. This serves for believers as the sure sign of God's favor and presence among them (v. 22). All of this is the work of the Spirit. Moreover, in Ephesians 6:17 part of the believer's armor is described as the "sword of the Spirit," which is defined as the "word of God." "Word" (*rhema*) in this case less likely refers to Scripture as to the message of the gospel itself that they proclaim by the Spirit's power.

Thus for Paul both the understanding of the gospel and the event of preaching itself, including the hearing of faith, are the powerful work of the Spirit. In this sense one may legitimately argue that faith itself therefore is also a prior work of the Spirit in the life of the one who becomes a believer (cf. 2 Cor. 4:13, "the same S/spirit of faith").

C. The Spirit and Conversion. The crucial role of the Spirit in Christian conversion is recognized by all; however, there is less than full agreement as to the precise nature of that role. This is due in part to some ambiguity in Paul's own statements; but mostly it is due to our reading the texts from the vantage point of later experience or ecclesiology—not to mention vested interests. Our difficulty stems from the fact that people experienced the Spirit in the Pauline churches, so explanations as to the *ordo salutis* are simply not given. Total precision is therefore not possible.

1. *The Crucial Role of the Spirit.* Christian conversion has both an objective and a subjective dimension to it. On the one hand, Christ's death and resurrection have secured eternal salvation for those who believe. This objective historical reality is expressed with a variety of metaphors, each of which emphasizes a significant aspect of the believer's new relationship with God (redemption, reconciliation, washing, propitiation, justification, adoption, birth). At the point of conversion, this objective historical reality becomes for the believer an objective positional reality as well, in terms of one's individual relationship to God

through Christ. But for Paul there is also a clearly subjective, experiential appropriation of this reality, producing some radical changes in the believer; and the Spirit is the absolutely crucial element for this dimension of conversion. This can be illustrated in several ways.

First, quite in passing Paul frequently refers to his readers' conversion(s) and does so in terms of the Spirit. God gave them his Spirit (1 Thess. 4:8; Rom. 5:5), anointed them with the Spirit (2 Cor. 1:21), poured out his Spirit generously on them (Titus 3:6), and sealed them with the Spirit (Eph. 1:13; 4:30). Obversely, believers have received the Spirit (1 Cor. 2:12; 2 Cor. 11:4), have been saved through the sanctifying work of the Spirit (2 Thess. 2:13), have been circumcised in their hearts by the Spirit (Rom. 2:29), and have been joined to Christ so as to become one S/spirit with him (1 Cor. 6:17). In the analogy of Ishmael and Isaac in Galatians 4:29, the former was "born of the flesh" (NIV "in the ordinary way"), while the latter (the Galatian believers) was born of the Spirit.

Second, in several "conversion" texts, the Spirit plays the leading role in describing what has happened to the believer (Gal. 3:2–5; 1 Cor. 6:11; 12:13; Eph. 1:13–14; Titus 3:5–7). Most significant of these is Galatians 3:2–5, made so by the nature of Paul's appeal. To counteract the influence of the Judaizers, he begins by appealing to the Galatians' own conversion(s), precisely because it was experienced and visible. So he does not ask, "Were you saved? or justified? etc.," but, "Did you receive the Spirit by observing the law, or by believing what you heard? Are you so foolish? After beginning with the Spirit, are you now trying to attain your goal by human effort?" (NIV). For Paul the Spirit is the crucial element to all of Christian life; therefore his argument stands or falls on their recalling their own experience of conversion at the beginning, in terms of the Spirit. Later, in 4:6 (cf. the parallel in Rom. 8:15) he refers to this experience again, this time with the metaphor of adoption as children; and again the Spirit, who has made them children and enables them to cry out to God as *Abba,* is clearly the crucial element.

Ephesians 1:13–14 and Titus 3:4–7 are significant in yet another way, since Paul here describes conversion in language that has a more creedal ring to it. Again, in both cases, the Spirit is the central element in terms of what happens to the believer.

Third, in three texts Paul distinguishes believers from nonbelievers in terms of the former having the Spirit, the latter not (1 Cor. 2:6–16; 12:3; Rom. 8:9). Most significant of these is 1 Corinthians 2:6–16, where Paul sets out the basic contrasts between the "natural" and the "spiritual" person. The "natural person" is one who does not have the Spirit and is therefore quite incapable of understanding what God is doing in the world; whereas the opposite prevails for the believer. Likewise no one can make the basic Christian confession that Jesus is Lord, except by the Holy Spirit (1 Cor. 12:3); and if one does not have the Spirit, that person simply does not belong to Christ (Rom. 8:9).

2. *The Pauline Images.* How Paul perceived this converting work of the Spirit is best seen by looking at the various metaphors he uses. On the one hand, the more common metaphors, because they refer to Christ's saving work in our behalf, are seldom used in conjunction with the Spirit (e.g., propitiation, reconciliation, redemption). Justification is connected with the Spirit in 1 Corinthians 6:11 (perhaps Rom. 14:17), most likely in terms of the believer's appropriation.

On the other hand, metaphors that emphasize the believer's own experience of salvation are usually expressed in Spirit language. Many of these texts, however, are full of ambiguities, on which scholarly opinion is considerably divided.

a. Adoption. This metaphor appears first in Galatians 4:4–6, where Paul is contrasting living under law with the life of faith, life in the Spirit. Living under law is like being a son before he has obtained maturity; he may technically own the whole estate, but he is still no better off than a slave. So with believers, who are no longer under slavery (which for the sake of Paul's Gentile readers is seen as slavery to the "powers," the so-called "elements of the world"); rather, they are "sons" with full rights, the evidence of which is their experience of the Spirit, especially the Spirit in them crying out, *"Abba"* (i.e., Father) to God (*Abba* is the word Jesus taught his disciples to use when praying).

The difficulties in this text come with verse 6, where Paul, in making his new point (after vv. 4–5), starts the sentence by saying that because they are "sons," God has sent the Spirit of his Son into their hearts. That sounds as if the one thing (objective sonship) preceded the other (the gift of the Spirit). This awkwardness has been variously handled by scholars, including some Pentecostals who hereby argue for two works of grace (conversion followed by Spirit baptism). That Paul has little concern for such "ordering" of things can be seen both from 3:2–5, where the Spirit alone is the key to their conversion, and from the parallel in Romans 8:15–17, where the Spirit is understood to be responsible for their adoption. Hence Paul's point in both texts is to remind believers that their very reception of the Spirit is what makes them children, as is evidenced by the cry "Abba."

b. Birth and Washing. These two metaphors occur together in a very difficult phrase in Titus 3:5. As the central feature of salvation Paul says (literally), "God saved us . . . through washing of rebirth and renewal of the Holy Spirit." Does this refer to two experiences (the washing of rebirth and the renewal of the Spirit = baptism and confirmation, or conversion and Spirit-baptism) or to one (a washing that involves rebirth and renewal, both of which are effected by the Spirit)? Although one cannot be certain here, the latter option is favored by Greek grammar (one would expect a repeated preposition [through] if Paul intended the former), by language (the words "rebirth" and "renewal" are synonyms), and by Pauline usage elsewhere (see Fee, 1984, 157–58).

But opinion is also divided among those who take this position. Does "washing" refer to water baptism or more simply to the "washing away of sin," and what relationship does the Spirit have to this "washing"? Conclusions tend to follow ecclesiological lines. That it probably alludes to "baptism" one need not doubt; but that Paul uses a metaphor and not the word "baptism" itself implies that his own emphasis is on the metaphor as such, not on the event of baptism. In any case, the final genitival phrase, "of the Spirit," is the key to the whole. Salvation is not appropriated through baptism—that is quite foreign to Paul—but through the work of the Spirit, which in this case is imaged as a "new birth" (cf. John 3:3) or a "renewal" in the new believer's life.

The metaphor "washing" as a work of the Spirit also occurs earlier in 1 Corinthians 6:11. Here again many see a reference to baptism, especially in this case because it is followed by the phrase "in the name of the Lord Jesus Christ," which is argued to be a baptismal formula. But that runs aground on Paul's usage elsewhere (he always uses eis, not en, with that formula) and the structure of the sentence, where both prepositions modify all three verbs. As above, that it might allude to baptism need not be doubted, but in context the emphasis falls on the metaphor of "washing away of sin"—especially those just mentioned in verses 9–10 (see Fee, 1987, 246–48).

c. *Life Giving.* Related to the metaphor of rebirth, but less a metaphor and more an essential reality is the Spirit as the one who gives life. Although not frequent in Paul, this way of expressing Christian conversion appears especially where Paul is contrasting living under law with living by grace. To live under law results ultimately in death (1 Cor. 15:56; 2 Cor. 3:6; cf. Rom. 7:9–10; 8:2). In contrast, believers live "by the Spirit" (i.e., according to the experience of and under the direction of the Spirit; Gal. 5:25). In contrast to "the law of sin and death" (i.e., the OT law that arouses sin and leads to death), there is another "law," that of the Spirit, who gives life to those who believe (Rom. 8:2). Likewise in 2 Corinthians 3:6, "the letter kills, but the Spirit gives life."

d. *Sanctification.* Paul's primary use of the term "sanctification" is also as a metaphor for conversion, not a reference to a work of grace following conversion. This can be seen most clearly in 2 Thessalonians 2:13, where Paul refers to the Thessalonians' experience of salvation as being effected "by sanctification of the Spirit and belief in the truth." The metaphor is drawn from Jewish religious practices, where the sacred rites and utensils have become so by their being "sanctified" unto God, i.e., set apart solely for his holy purposes. A more full use of the metaphor, referring to Gentile conversions under Paul's ministry, is found in Romans 15:16, and again is claimed as the work of the Spirit (see also 1 Cor. 6:11; cf. 1:2, 30).

When one adds to these the metaphors "anointing," "seal," "down payment," and "firstfruits" discussed above (under V. "The Spirit and Eschatology"), certain conclusions can be drawn: (1) The wide variety of metaphors in itself indicates that no single one will do. The work of the Spirit in Christian conversion is simply too multifaceted to allow of a single metaphor. (2) The metaphors tend to be used in keeping with the emphasis of the moment, thus the point in context is what is at issue, not the precise timing or relationships in conversion. (3) There is no such thing as Christian conversion that does not have the coming of the Spirit into the believer's life as the crucial ingredient. However variously expressed, the presence of the Spirit is the one constant. (4) It is highly doubtful whether Paul saw the Spirit as connected directly to water baptism or whether his language implies yet a second experience of the Spirit after conversion. To these latter two issues we must turn in further detail.

3. *The Spirit and Water Baptism.* In the early church, water baptism was the believer's immediate response to God's saving action by the Spirit. Since some of the texts discussed above seem to suggest a close connection between the two, those in the more liturgical Christian traditions argue that the Spirit actually comes to the believer through the event of baptism itself—much as the dove descended on Jesus in the waters of baptism, which is viewed as a paradigm for later Christians (a paradigm, interestingly, that Pentecostals have seen as expressing Spirit baptism as subsequent to his birth by the Spirit). The key texts here are 1 Corinthians 6:11; 12:13; and Titus 3:5, although some would add Galatians 3:28–4:6; the imagery of the "seal" in 2 Corinthians 1:21–22; and Ephesians 1:13–14; 4:30.

In the preceding section it was pointed out that this will scarcely work for 1 Corinthians 6:11 and is doubtful in Titus 3:5. The more significant passage is 1 Corinthians 12:13, where Paul specifically says that they were "all baptized in [en] one Spirit into [eis] one body, . . . and all were made to drink to the full of the one Spirit." As elsewhere every kind of experience has been argued for (baptism and confirmation, conversion and Spirit-baptism, baptism and the Lord's Supper [!], one experience [conversion] expressed in two ways). In this case the contextual and grammatical evidence decisively favors the latter option.

First, Paul is not trying to explain how people become believers, but how believers from such diverse backgrounds (Jew, Greek, slave, free) all form the one body of Christ. To make this point, Paul, with a fine piece of Semitic parallelism, uses two metaphors (immersion into and drinking to one's fill of) to express their common, lavish experience of the Spirit (the repeated "all" indicates that he is referring to their conversion).

Second, Paul's usage elsewhere strongly suggests that the prepositions en and eis should be translated respectively as locative (the Spirit is the "element" into which they were submerged) and telic (i.e., so as to form one body).

The point is that Paul is not referring to water baptism at all—although again an allusion to it might be recognized. That is simply outside his frame of reference in this context. It is not baptism that makes them one body; it is Spirit— as they themselves would agree; this is why Paul uses such a metaphor in the first place. In the context his ultimate interest is to argue for the need for diversity in the one body. To get to that point he must appeal to the fact that they are indeed one body, and, as they should well appreciate, the Spirit alone makes them so.

This is not to downplay baptism, any more than Paul himself intends to downplay it in 1 Corinthians 1:13–17. Rather, it is to see it in its proper Pauline perspective—as the believer's proper response to the hearing of faith and the gift of the Spirit that brought about conversion.

4. Conversion and Spirit Baptism. The urgent question for Pentecostals is whether Paul also envisaged a work of grace beyond conversion to which the language "the baptism of the Spirit" might correctly apply. They have sometimes interpreted such texts as 1 Corinthians 12:13 or Galatians 4:4–6 in this way (Horton, 1976, 173, 215–17), but the full contextual data make this doubtful. On the other hand, whether Paul knew of such an experience is a moot point, argued against primarily on the basis of silence. Two further points need to be made.

First, as was pointed out in the discussion of "Spirit language" (II.B), Paul makes a clear connection between the Spirit and the experience of power. What becomes additionally clear from the preceding discussion is that the Spirit was not only experienced in conversion, but was experienced in a dynamic, undoubtedly visible way. This is precisely why Paul appeals to the Spirit, the lavish experience of Spirit, to make his points in both Galatians 3:2–3 and 1 Corinthians 12:13. This is made the more certain by Galatians 3:5, where, as further evidence of their having no relationship to law, Paul specifically appeals to their ongoing experience of the Spirit as dynamically present among them with miraculous deeds (one can scarcely interpret the two present tenses otherwise ["God gives the Spirit and works miracles among you"]). By reemphasizing this dimension of Christian life in their experience of "baptism," Pentecostals see themselves as having recaptured what is at the heart of Paul's understanding of the Spirit and Christian life, even if they have (less convincingly) also made a virtue out of their timing of this dimension as well (see Fee, 1985).

Second, as is pointed out in the succeeding section, Paul does not see life in the Spirit as the result of a single experience of the Spirit at conversion. The Spirit is the key to all of Christian life, and frequently Paul speaks in such a way as to imply further, ongoing appropriations of the Spirit's power. This is certainly intended in Galatians 3:5; it is the further implication of such present-tense verbs as one finds in 1 Thessalonians 4:8 and Ephesians 5:18. In 1 Thessalonians 4:8 Paul's first referent is surely to the conversion of the Thessalonians; but the argument in context and the present tense ("God gives you his Holy Spirit") suggest that what happened at conversion needs renewed appropriation in light of their pagan past. All of this suggests that perhaps too much is made on both sides of single experiences. For Paul life in the Spirit begins at conversion; at the same time that experience was both dynamic and renewable.

D. Life in the Spirit. For Paul Christian life not only begins by means of the Spirit; the whole of Christian life is a matter of Spirit. In the kingdom of God not only righteousness (i.e., right standing with God), but also peace and joy are effected by the Spirit (Rom. 14:17). The Spirit is also the key to Christian growth. On the one hand, he illumines believers so that they may better understand God and his ways (Eph. 1:17–19); such illumination will also include more wisdom and understanding as to God's will in their individual and corporate lives (Col. 1:9; cf. Rom. 12:1–2).

On the other hand, the Spirit also empowers them to grow and be built up in Christ. In Ephesians 3:14–21, at the conclusion of his presentation of God's mystery (the inclusion of Jew and Gentile together in Christ; 2:1–22) and of his own role in making that mystery known (3:1–13). Paul offered prayer for these Gentile believers whom he did not know personally (cf. 1:15; 3:2). The urgency of the prayer is for their growth in the love of Christ—that they may better comprehend Christ's love for them and have the same love for one another (cf. 4:2–3, 14–16). The key to such life is the empowering of the Spirit in the inner person, as Christ by the Spirit dwells in believers' hearts by faith. The benediction in verses 20–21 reassures them that God will do this very thing by his power (i.e., by his Spirit) at work in them. In Galatians 3:3, Paul had asked rhetorically (about their conversion): "Having made a beginning by means of the Spirit, are you now hoping to be made complete in the flesh?" The intended reply is "Of course not!" One must finish in the same way as one began, through the empowering and appropriating work of the Spirit. Thus the Spirit is as crucial to Paul's understanding of ethical life as for conversion itself. Here again Paul's emphasis focuses primarily on the community. Nonetheless, several dimensions of this life are individual before they are corporate.

1. The Spirit and Ethical Life. In Pauline ethics Christ is the pattern (1 Cor. 4:16–17; 11:1; Eph. 4:20), love is the principle (Gal. 5:13–14; 1 Cor. 13; Rom. 13:8–10; Eph. 5:2, et al.), and the Spirit is the power. Thus the role of the Spirit is crucial. Since he is the Spirit of Christ, and since the first-mentioned fruit of the Spirit is love, the Spirit not only empowers the believer for ethical behavior, but by indwelling also reproduces the pattern and the principle.

a. Walking in the Spirit. The central role of the Spirit is most clearly spelled out in Galatians 5:13–6:10, where with a series of verbs modified by the word *pneumati* ("in [or by] the Spirit"), Paul urges them to "make a completion" (3:3) by means of the same Spirit by whom they had been converted. They are commanded to "walk in the Spirit" (v. 16); they are "led by the Spirit" and thus are not under law (v. 18), which should evidence itself by "the fruit of the Spirit" (vv. 22–23). Since they "live by the Spirit" (i.e., have been brought to life by the life-giving Spirit), they must also "behave in accordance with the Spirit" (v. 25). Finally, only those who "sow to the Spirit" in this way "will reap the eternal life" that is also from the Spirit (6:8).

Two things are clear from this passage: that the Spirit is the key to ethical life and that Paul expected Spirit people to exhibit changed behavior. The first imperative, "walk in the Spirit," is the basic imperative in Pauline ethics. This verb was common in Judaism to refer to one's whole way of life. It was taken over by Paul as his most common metaphor for ethical conduct (seventeen occurrences in all). All other imperatives proceed from this one.

But ethics for Paul are not simply some ideal, to be actualized only by those who are truly "spiritual," as over against some who are still "carnal." Precisely because the Spirit empowers this new life, Paul has little patience for the point of view that allows people to be "justified sinners" without appropriate changes in attitudes and conduct (cf. 1 Cor. as a whole, Gal. 5–6, Rom. 6 and 12, Col. 3, and Phil. 2–4).

b. *The Spirit as "Holy."* Although Paul uses the term "sanctification" primarily to refer to Christian conversion (see above, VI.C.2.c), the metaphor tends to appear precisely where his concern is with his converts' improper (sinful) behavior. For example, in 1 Thessalonians 4:3–8 he takes up the issue of sexual immorality with a group of former pagans for whom such activity was not considered a moral issue. The argument begins, "This is God's will for you, even your sanctification" (v. 3) and concludes by saying that the person who rejects Paul's instruction on this matter does not reject what a mere man has to say, "but rejects the very God who gives [present tense] . . . his Holy Spirit." This further explains the use of this metaphor in reminding them of their conversion in 2 Thessalonians 2:13, as well as the repeated emphasis on this metaphor in 1 Corinthians (see 1:2, 30; 6:11).

Here one sees at least in part the significance of the early church's referring to the Spirit as the Holy Spirit, a name that seldom occurs in the OT. The early believers understood themselves to be dedicated to God but not in a ritual way, as in the OT use of the term "sanctified." Rather, they were set apart for God, to be his "holy" people in the world. Hence the emphasis in 1 Thessalonians 4:3–8.

For Paul "holiness," i.e., walking by means of the Holy Spirit, was two-dimensional. On the one hand, it meant abstaining from certain sins. Precisely because in Christ they had died to both sin (the flesh) and the law, believers are to serve God "in the newness of the Spirit" (Rom. 7:6). They must put to death the former way of life (Rom. 6:1–18; Col. 3:5–11), portrayed in Galatians 5:19–21 as "the works of the flesh." Paul understands such "putting aside" as the work of the Spirit.

On the other hand, "holiness" also (especially) means the Holy Spirit living in believers, reproducing the very life of Christ within/among them, especially in their communal relationships. To do otherwise is to "grieve the Holy Spirit of God" (Eph. 4:30), who by his presence has given them both unity and mutual growth.

c. *The Spirit-Flesh Tension.* One of the most disputed areas of Pauline ethics is the tension between Spirit and "flesh," noted earlier (under "the Spirit and eschatology" V.B.1.b). Does Paul in fact see believers as living in a constant struggle between their inherent sinful natures (the "flesh") and the now resident Spirit? The difficulty stems from comparing the language of Galatians 5:17 and Romans 7:13–15—language that seems to imply a continual struggle—with the contexts, which seem to imply otherwise. The answer to whether there is a continuing conflict is something of yes and no, but mostly no.

Paul nowhere in fact actually says that a great conflict goes on within the believer between the "flesh" and the Spirit. Rather, he says that these two "principles," representing the two ages, are themselves in conflict with each other (Gal. 5:17, "the two are in opposition to each other"). The final clause in this passage, therefore, most likely means something like, "so that the person who lives by the 'flesh' is unable to do as he or she wishes." Thus one finds a subtle change of nuance in the use of the word "flesh." In 3:3 to finish "in the flesh" meant "to continue the Christian life under the demands of the law," thus reverting to living in the former age that is now passing away. But those who belong to the new age of "Spirit" are not under law (v. 18), and neither shall they live any longer under the domination of the "flesh" (v. 16), understood now as "the sinful nature" whose "works" are manifest in sinful behavior (vv. 19–21), as well as by circumcision and the keeping of days (4:10, 21; 5:2). Indeed Spirit people, "who belong to Christ Jesus, have crucified the sinful nature with its passions and desires" (v. 24). Thus they cannot "finish in the flesh" under either sense of the term.

So also in Romans 7. In context the believer has been freed in Christ from both the law and the "flesh" (7:4–6), which was an unrecognized presence until the coming of the law. Beginning with verse 7, Paul then bursts into a vivid description of what life is like under law. Law caused the resident sin to spring to life, resulting in a "living death" (v. 25), so much so that one is helpless in sin's clutches. The law was a good thing—indeed "spiritual" (v. 12); but it was simply helpless in the presence of resident sin (vv. 15–25; 8:3–4). But this describes life prior to the coming of the Spirit. The expressions of personal helplessness in chapter 7 and the inability of the law to help in 8:3 are, in light of chapters 6 and 8, the certain indicators that Paul is not speaking about an ongoing struggle within the heart of the believer over indwelling sin. That one must continually walk in the Spirit, so as not to yield to the ever-present "desires" of the "flesh," is a thoroughly Pauline idea; that one is engaged in a helpless struggle before these "desires" simply contradicts the clear point of both Galatians 5 and Romans 6 and 8. The Spirit, who gives birth and life, is ever present to produce within one the life of Christ himself, expressed in Galatians 5:22–23 as the fruit of the Spirit.

d. *The Spirit and the Body.* But if the "flesh" is to be considered dead, the same is not true of the body. In its present form it is in fact subject to decay and death, but it is neither evil nor the source of evil. Rather, the body is a part of the purchase of redemption (1 Cor. 6:20), a dwelling (temple) of the Spirit and destined for resurrection. This goes in two directions for Paul.

On the one hand, because of its "glorious" destiny (cf. Phil. 3:21), one may not sin against the body by indulging in sexual immorality (1 Cor. 6:18). It is the "bodily" nature of this sin that makes it singularly a sin against the body. One who has previously been joined "in S/spirit" to Christ cannot join physically with a prostitute, because the believer's body is also destined for a resurrection like Christ's.

On the other hand, because it is subject to decay, the body is the point of tension for present eschatological life in the Spirit (see esp. Rom. 8:18–25; cf. 1 Cor. 15:35–58; Phil 3:10–11, 21). Even though we are now Spirit people, who through the Spirit have received the adoption of "sons," we have received only the firstfruits (Rom. 8:23). As long as we are in the present body, we are still subject to weakness and join with the whole created order in awaiting our final "adoption." Precisely this weakness, represented for Paul especially by the body (cf. 2 Cor. 12:1–10), kept him from triumphalism—i.e., a view of life in the Spirit in which there is no sin or sickness. Moreover, he sees such weakness, and all expressions of affliction and suffering, as our present form of bearing the likeness of the pre-risen Lord, as we will eventually bear his likeness in resurrection.

2. The Fruit of the Spirit. In Galatians 5:22–23 Christian ethical life is specified as the fruit of the Spirit, in contrast to the works of the "flesh." But this is not to be understood as passivity on the part of the believer. Indeed, the imperatival nature of Pauline ethics found elsewhere leaves exactly the opposite impression. Believers are called to active obedience. What one must not disregard is the element of the miraculous. Just as in conversion, where there is a "hearing of faith" and a receiving of the Spirit, so in Pauline ethics there is a walking in the Spirit—that is, being led by the Spirit. The Spirit produces the fruit as the believer continually walks with the Spirit's help.

The essential nature of the "fruit" is the reproduction of the life of Christ in the believer. This is confirmed by several pieces of evidence: (1) that the Spirit is in fact the Spirit of Christ, a point made especially strongly in Romans 8:9–11; (2) that many of the words listed here to describe that fruit are used elsewhere of Christ; and (3) that Paul elsewhere understands ethical conduct in terms of "learning Christ" (Eph. 4:20).

Two observations are needed about the "fruit" listed in Galatians 5:22–23. First, they are not intended to be exhaustive, but representative, just as is the preceding list of vices in verses 19–21. Paul concludes both lists by referring to "such things" (*toi outon*), meaning all other vices and virtues similar to these. All such lists, including the descriptions of love in 1 Corinthians 13 and of *charismata* in chapter 12, are quite ad hoc and thus tailored to their contexts. This means that a full discussion of the fruit of the Spirit would need to spread a wide net so as to include, for example, the further items mentioned in Colossians 3:12–13 (compassion, humility, forbear-

ance, forgiveness) as well as the specific applications such as one finds in Romans 12:9–21.

Second, this "fruit" covers a broad range, including all manner of attitudes, virtues, and behavior. Christian life across the broadest possible spectrum is the work of the Spirit. Such fruit includes the experience of joy and peace and attitudes such as love and patience, as well as all kinds of behavior consonant with such experience and attitudes.

What they do not cover is any attempt to "regulate" Christian behavior by rules of religious conduct. For truly Christian ethics, precisely because they are the product of walking and living in the Spirit, there can be no law (Gal. 5:23), especially of the kind that regulates food, clothing, the observance of days, entertainment, recreation, or religious practices as such. These may have an appearance of wisdom, but finally they are of no value at all, since they are but the "commandments of men" (Col. 2:20–23).

3. Other Spirit Activity. Finally, it should be noted that not all of ongoing Christian life comes under the rubric of ethics. All sorts of other activities are also seen to be the work of the Spirit in the believer's life.

For example, by the Spirit we live out our present lives in hope of the certain future (Gal. 5:5; Rom. 15:13). In Romans 9:1 Paul implies that his clear conscience about what he will say as to his own yearning for his fellow-countrymen is the work of the Spirit in his life. If Romans 12:11 refers to the Spirit at work in the believer's spirit (see above, II.A.1), then the Spirit is also the source of zeal for service. And however one finally understands Philippians 1:19, Paul expects the combination of the Philippians' praying and the "support of the Spirit" to make it possible for him to experience either deliverance or death without shaming the gospel, and to the glory of Christ.

All of these texts together demonstrate further what has already been said—that Paul's view of life in Christ is so thoroughly dominated by the Spirit that he is the one absolutely essential ingredient for that life. Moreover, both the community imperative in Ephesians 5:18 ("be filled with the Spirit") and the individual imperative to Timothy in 2 Timothy 1:6–7 ("fan the gift into flame") imply the need for ongoing appropriation. The Spirit's presence is the crucial matter, but that presence does not automatically ensure a quickened, fervent spiritual life. Both individuals and the church as a whole are exhorted to keep the gift aflame.

VII. The Spirit and the Community. As noted above, most of Paul's words about the Spirit, including almost all of his ethical imperatives, assume the presence of the believing community. They are to love one another, encourage and build up one another, forgive one another, bear with one another, pursue what is good for one another, consider one another better than themselves, and be kind to one another. Even when an individual needs correction, the stronger words are directed toward the community that is tolerating the sin (1 Cor. 5:1–13; 6:1–11).

In these matters Paul's thinking is still dominated by his OT heritage. God is not simply saving individuals and preparing them for heaven; rather, he is creating a people for his name, among whom he can dwell and who in their life together will reproduce his life and character. Such a view of salvation is thoroughgoing in Paul; it is evidenced nowhere more clearly than in his words about the Spirit.

A. The Formation of the Community. What was noted about the individual Christian life, that it both began and was sustained by the Spirit, is equally true of the believing community. Life together as a body begins through the common experience of the Spirit (1 Cor. 12:13); inscribed by the Spirit, they become an epistle of Christ (2 Cor. 3:1–3).

Created and formed by the Spirit, the early communities thus became a fellowship of the Spirit (2 Cor. 13:13; Phil. 2:1). The concept of "fellowship" is a broad one in Paul. It begins as fellowship with God through Christ (1 Cor. 1:9), which in turn brings believers into fellowship with one another. In the Trinitarian benediction of 2 Corinthians 13:13 Paul thus selects "fellowship" as the word that characterizes the ministry of the Spirit. Although this could mean "a participation in the Spirit himself," most likely it refers to the fellowship created and sustained by the Spirit. So also in Philippians 2:1–4, part of the basis of his appeal to unity and harmony in verse 1 is their common fellowship (both his and theirs together) in the Spirit (cf. 1:27, "Stand firm in one S/spirit"). And common love brought about by the Spirit serves as the basis of an appeal to the Roman believers to support him with their prayers (Rom. 15:30; cf. Col. 1:8).

For Paul the inclusion of Jews and Gentiles together is the most remarkable aspect of this newly formed fellowship; God had triumphed over the former prejudices on both sides (Eph. 2:14–18). Paul's sense of wonder at this shines through the whole of Ephesians. Thus 1:13–14 is not about individual conversions. Rather, Paul is rejoicing because Gentiles ("you also") have been included in Christ along with Jews as God's inheritance, certified by the singular reality that they were given the promised Holy Spirit as a "seal" and "down payment" of that inheritance. This is also the point of 2:18 ("through him both have access to the Father by one Spirit"; cf. v. 22).

B. The Pauline Images. That the Spirit is crucial to Paul's view of the believing community emerges especially in his three major images for the church (family, temple, body).

1. Family. This image, which occurs only twice (Eph. 2:19; 1 Tim. 3:15), flows naturally out of Paul's reference to God as Father, believers as brothers and sisters, and the apostle as a household manager. The imagery itself receives no elaboration. What is significant is the role of the Spirit, as both responsible for and evidence of believers' becoming members of God's family (Gal. 4:6; Rom. 8:14–17).

2. Temple. This image occurs four times referring to the church (1 Cor. 3:16–17; 2 Cor. 6:16; Eph. 2:19–22; 1 Tim. 3:15–16). It is particularly well-suited to the Spirit, since it derives from the sanctuary (*naos*) in Jerusalem,

the earthly "dwelling" of the living God. The Spirit among them means that God has taken up his dwelling in the gathered community.

Paul's use of the imagery in 1 Corinthians 3 begins with verse 9 ("You [the church in Corinth] are God's building"). Their foundation (Christ crucified) had been laid by the apostle, but currently the superstructure was being erected with materials incompatible to that foundation (wood, hay, etc.—here referring to their current fascination with wisdom and rhetoric). They had to build with enduring materials (gold, silver, etc.—the gospel of the crucified One), imagery taken from the building of Solomon's temple (1 Chron. 29:2; 2 Chron. 3:6). Then in verse 16 Paul asks rhetorically, "Do you not know what kind of building you are? God's temple in Corinth!" As a gathered community, they formed the one temple of the living God—God's alternative to Corinth; and what made them his alternative was the presence of the Spirit in their midst.

But the Corinthians were in the process of dismantling God's temple—because their strife and fascination with wisdom meant the banishing of the Spirit from their midst. Hence this strongest of warnings, that the people responsible for the destruction would themselves be destroyed by God.

3. Body. With this imagery, which occurs several times (1 Cor. 10:16–17; 12:12–26; Rom. 12:4–5; Col. 1:18; 3:15; Eph. 1:23; 2:16; 4:1–16; 5:23), Paul essentially makes two points: the need for unity and diversity in the believing community, both of which are the work of "the one and the same Spirit" (1 Cor. 12:11).

First, the imagery both presupposes and contends for unity. That is the clear point of Ephesians 4. The church, composed of both Jew and Gentile, forms one body (2:16). The urgency of the appeal that begins with 4:1 and carries through to the end is that the Ephesian Christians "keep the unity that the Spirit has given them" (4:3). The basis for the appeal is the unity of the Triune God (vv. 4–6), which begins by noting that the one body is the product of the one Spirit.

Furthermore, all of the sins listed in verses 25–31 are sins of discord. By giving in to such sin, they thereby grieve the Holy Spirit (v. 30), who has formed them into a body and whose continuing presence is intended to bring the body to full maturity. Hence the need to "keep filled with the Spirit" (5:18), so as to ensure proper worship (vv. 19–20) and proper relationships (5:21–6:9).

So also in 1 Corinthians 12:12–26. Here the greater concern is diversity; but the earlier use of the imagery in 10:16–17, with reference to the bread of the Table, had focused on their need for unity. When the imagery is picked up in 12:12, both unity and diversity are stressed. The role of the much-debated verse 13 fits in right at this point. With two sentences (vv. 13 and 14) that begin with the identical applicational signal ("for indeed"), Paul argues first that the many of them (Jew, Gentile, slave, free) are one body because of their common lavish experience of the Spirit (v. 13). After verse 14 and its application (vv. 15–20) that stress diversity, the second application (vv. 21–25) picks up the theme of unity once more. Whatever else, the Spirit creates and preserves unity and harmony in the body of Christ, in terms both of relationships within the body and of their corporate gatherings.

Second, the Spirit is also responsible for maintaining a necessary and healthy diversity in the church. This is the point of the whole argument in 1 Corinthians 12. Their singular and imbalanced emphasis on tongues as the evidence of a fully developed spirituality requires some theological correctives (chs. 12 and 13) before the specific abuse itself is corrected (ch. 14). Thus every paragraph (except for vv. 21–25) has this singular theme—the need for diversity in order for the community to be built up. God himself as three Persons illustrates—and thus serves as the basis for—this diversity-in-unity (vv. 4–6); and the Spirit in particular is responsible for its being evidenced among them, especially in the many manifestations of his presence "given to each one for the common good" (vv. 7–11). A body cannot be only one thing (v. 14); that is a monstrosity (vv. 15–20).

Significantly, the body imagery in Ephesians, with its concern for unity, focused primarily on relationships within the church. In 1 Corinthians 12, however, the focus primarily is on the church as a community gathered for worship, which is true also of the temple imagery in 3:16–17. This is due to the respective errors that were taking place within the gathered community. The early believers did not have buildings called "churches"; they did not "go to church." They were the church, and at appointed times assembled as the church (1 Cor. 11:18). As God's temple, inhabited by his Spirit, they formed a powerful fellowship, evidenced by manifestations of the Spirit (1 Cor. 12:7), including miracles (Gal. 3:5) and prophetic utterances (1 Thess. 5:19–20; 1 Cor. 14:24–25; outsiders exclaim, "Surely God is among you"). Here by the same Spirit they lived out the Christian ethic so that no one was in need (1 Cor. 12:25–26). This emphasis on the gathered community serves as the essential background to Paul's understanding of charismata, especially in 1 Corinthians 12–14.

C. The Spirit and Worship. Because of the ad hoc nature of Paul's letters, they contain nothing close to a systematic presentation of the worship of the early church. What we learn is only in response to problems and is therefore fragmentary. Nonetheless, for Paul the gathered church was primarily a worshiping community; and the key to their worship was the presence of the Holy Spirit. Thus, in Philippians 3:3, in his strong attack against the "mutilators of the flesh" (through circumcision), he begins by asserting that "we are the circumcision, who worship by the Spirit of God." Their worship is a matter of a religious rite performed in the flesh; ours is a matter of Spirit.

Not only is the Spirit seen as responsible for worship (see esp. 1 Cor. 14:6, 24, 26), but when the church was assembled in this way Paul understood himself to be present in S/spirit (probably in the reading of the letter as his prophetic voice among them), along with the "power of the Lord Jesus" (1 Cor. 5:3–5; see

Fee, 1987, 203–8). Thus, even though he makes no direct allusion to the presence of the Spirit at the Lord's Table (1 Cor. 10:16–17; 11:17–34), we may assume his understanding of the bread as representing Christ's body the church (10:16–17; 11:29), made so by the Spirit, to be leading in that direction. In fact, one would not be far wrong to see the Spirit's presence at the Table as Paul's way of understanding "the real presence." In any case, the Spirit is specifically noted as responsible for all other expressions of Christian worship.

1. Prayer. Prayer in particular has been radically transformed by the coming of the Spirit. Whether set prayers were ever said in the Pauline churches cannot be known; in any case, spontaneous prayer by the Spirit is the norm. The beginning of Christian life is marked by the indwelling Spirit crying out *"Abba"* to God (Gal. 4:6; Rom. 8:15). "On all occasions," Paul urges elsewhere, "pray in [or by] the Spirit," which is to include every form of prayer (Eph. 6:18). Here in particular the Spirit helps us in our "already–not yet" existence. Because in our present weakness we do not know how (or for what) to pray, the Spirit himself makes intercession for us with "sighs too deep for words" (Rom. 8:26–27 RSV). Some have seen this as referring to glossolalia, and in light of 1 Corinthians 14:2 it may indeed include such prayer; but in context it pictures the believer at the end of himself, as it were, with the Spirit stepping in to intercede where the believer cannot find words.

Prayer (and praise) also seems the best way to view Paul's understanding of glossolalia. At no point in 1 Corinthians 14 does Paul suggest that tongues is speech directed toward people; three times he indicates that it is speech directed toward God (14:2, 14–16, 28). In verses 14–16 he specifically refers to tongues as "praying with [his] S/spirit"; and in verse 2 such prayer is described as "speaking mysteries to God," which is why the mind of the speaker is left unfruitful, and also why such prayer without interpretation is not to be part of the corporate setting.

2. Song. As with prayer, song has also become the special province of the Spirit (1 Cor. 14:14–15, 26; Col. 3:16; Eph. 5:19). The evidence from Colossians and Ephesians suggests that some of the singing was corporate; the language of these passages further indicates that besides being addressed as praise to God, such hymns served as vehicles of instruction in the gathered assembly. Furthermore, both passages, as well as 1 Corinthians 14:15, indicate that some of the singing might best be called "a kind of charismatic hymnody" (Dunn, 1975, 238), in which spontaneous hymns of praise were offered to God in the congregation, although some may have been known beforehand. Both 1 Corinthians 14:15 and 26 suggest that some of this singing at least was "solo."

3. Worship and the Charismata. Several of the "gifts" discussed in the next section are also to be understood as belonging to the context of corporate worship. This is especially true of those that involve speech directed toward the community, as Paul's correctives in 1 Corinthians 14 make clear.

These would include prophecy, teaching, knowledge, and revelation (v. 6), however we are finally to define some of these in relationship to each other.

What is most noteworthy in all the passages is the free, spontaneous nature of worship in the Pauline churches, apparently orchestrated by the Spirit himself. Worship is expressed in a variety of ways, and with the (potential) participation of everyone (1 Cor. 14:26). There is no hint of a worship leader, although that cannot be ruled out. But neither is chaos permitted. The God whom they worship is a God of peace (v. 33), whose character is to be reflected in both the manner and the content of their worship. Therefore, disorder is out. Although all may participate (vv. 23, 24, 26, 31), there are some guidelines. Speakers of inspired utterances must be limited to two or three at a time, and they must be followed by interpretation and evaluation. And they must have respect for one another. Speakers must make way for others, since the "S/spirit of the prophet is subject to the prophet" (v. 32). Thus, spontaneity does not mean lack of order; it means "peace" and "decency and orderliness"—also the work of the Spirit.

D. The Charismata and the Spirit. As already noted, community worship included several extraordinary phenomena Paul variously calls *charismata, pneumatika,* or "manifestations of the Spirit." Such phenomena are especially the activity of the Spirit in the community. This is an area, however, where there is also great diversity in understanding, both among scholars and within ecclesiastical contexts. The primary reason for this is the basic assumption by most that Paul is intending to give instruction in the various places where he mentions charismata; what we have in fact is ad hoc correction, that is neither systematic nor exhaustive.

1. The Linguistic Data. Part of the difficulty lies with Paul's use of language, especially the words *charismata* and *pneumatika.* Both words tend to put emphasis on their root ideas of grace (*charis*) and Spirit (*pneuma*). That is, these phenomena are both gracious bestowments for the sake of the church and the evidence (or result) of Spirit activity in their midst. As a description of these phenomena, the word *pneumatika* occurs only in 1 Corinthians 12:1 (probably) and 14:1 (certainly); and in this case Paul is almost certainly picking up a favorite Corinthian word. Because they thought of glossolalia as being the language of angels, they apparently considered it the evidence of their having arrived at an advanced state of "spirituality" (i.e., being *pneumatikoi*). Thus Paul uses their word in the neuter to refer to the Spirit phenomena they believed made them so.

The word *charismata,* on the other hand, is especially difficult to pin down. It is a distinctively Pauline word (found elsewhere in the NT only in 1 Peter 4:10 and otherwise rarely in Greek literature at all), used to cover a broad range of ideas, not all of which are specifically tied to the Spirit, and certainly not always intended to be understood as "spiritual gifts" (e.g., salvation in Rom. 6:23; celibacy and marriage in 1 Cor. 7:7;

deliverance from deadly peril in 2 Cor. 1:11). In fact Paul uses the adjective *pneumatikon* with the word *charisma* in Romans 1:11 in order to make the latter specifically mean "spiritual gift."

On the other hand, since *charismata* is used in 1 Corinthians 12:4 and 31 to refer to the basically extraordinary phenomena that in the same context are also called *pneumatika* (14:1) and "manifestations of the Spirit" (12:7), it seems legitimate in that context at least to translate something like "gracious gifts" ("of the Spirit," being implied). That seems easy enough until one notes the usage in Romans 12:6, where the body imagery also expresses concern for diversity-in-unity. In this case the focus is very little on the church as a worshiping community; therefore, of the items listed, only prophesying and teaching carry over from 1 Corinthians 12–14, and there is no mention of the Spirit whatsoever. Although one may assume the latter always to be in Paul's mind, there is no guarantee that the community in Rome would have picked that up.

2. Their Number and Variety. Several things need to be said about the various lists in 1 Corinthians 12–14. First, none of them is intended to be exhaustive, as though Paul were setting forth everything that might legitimately be called a "gift of the Spirit." This is evidenced in part by the very fact that no two lists are identical—not even the rhetorical repetition in 12:30 of verses 28–29. It simply goes beyond the evidence—and Paul's own concerns—to speak of "the nine spiritual gifts."

Second, the items in 12:8–10 are in fact called "manifestations of the Spirit," which in context almost certainly means, "diverse ways the Spirit manifests himself when the community is gathered together." Paul's point here is their need for diversity. The list seems especially tailored to the situation in Corinth. Paul's own structural signals (the omission of the connective particle *de* along with a different word for "another" for the third and eighth items) suggest a listing in three parts. The first two pick up words that held high court in Corinth ("wisdom" and "knowledge") and seem to be an attempt by Paul to recapture them for the Spirit and the gospel. The next five have in common that they are, like glossolalia itself, extraordinary phenomena. It would scarcely do for Paul to try to broaden their perspective with regard to tongues by listing less visible phenomena. Finally, after diversity is well heard, he includes the problem child, glossolalia, along with its necessary companion—at least in the community—the interpretation of glossolalia.

Third, attempts to categorize the items in the various lists are tentative at best; when those in Romans 12:6–8 and Ephesians 4:11 are included as well, one encounters a wide variety of nomenclature (e.g., "motivational," "ministerial," etc.) that the apostle would scarcely recognize and that at best are exegetically suspect. The broad spectrum of phenomena are best grouped under the three natural headings hinted at in 1 Corinthians 12:4–6: service, miracles, and inspired utterance. (Paul himself does not refer to visionary experiences such as one finds in 2 Corinthians 12:1–6 as *charismata*—although they belong legitimately to a discussion of Spirit phenomena. Nor are people [apostles, pastors, etc.] *charismata*; to be sure, they are "gifts" to the church, as Ephesians 4:11 makes clear, but only their ministries, not the people themselves, are legitimately termed *charismata*.)

a. Service. Items listed here include "serving," "giving," and "caring for" (in the sense of leadership) from Romans 12:7–8 and "helpful deeds" and "acts of guidance" from 1 Corinthians 12:28. These are the least visibly "charismatic" of the "gifts" and the least obvious as expressions of corporate worship. In fact they belong to Paul's ever-present interest in relationships within the church.

b. Miracles. Included here are three items from 1 Corinthians 12:9–10: "faith" (i.e., the supernatural gift of faith that can "move mountains"; cf. 13:2), "gifts [*charismata*] of healings" (of the physical body; also vv. 28, 30), and "workings of miracles" (i.e., all other such phenomena not included in healing). The use of the plurals, "gifts" and "workings," for the latter two probably means that these "gifts" are not permanent, but each occurrence is a "gift" in its own right. That such phenomena were a regular part of the apostle's own ministry is evidenced by 2 Corinthians 12:12 and Romans 15:18–19. That they were also the regular expectation of the Pauline churches is evidenced by Galatians 3:5.

c. Inspired Utterance. Included here are "the message of wisdom," "the message of knowledge," "prophecy," "the discernments of S/spirits," "tongues," and "the interpretation of tongues" from 1 Corinthians 12:10; "teaching" and "revelation" from 14:6; and (perhaps) "exhortation" from Romans 12:8—it might also include "singing" from Ephesians 5:19 (cf. 1 Cor. 14:26). Attempts to distinguish some of these items from one another are generally futile, as is any distinction between their charismatic or noncharismatic expression (e.g., teaching or singing).

The "message of wisdom" and "knowledge," for example, is language created by the situation in Corinth. For Paul the "message of wisdom" is the preaching of the cross (see 1 Cor. 1:18–2:16; the terminology occurs nowhere else). "Knowledge," on the other hand, is closely related to "mysteries" in 13:2 and elsewhere stands close to the concept of "revelation" (13:8–9, 12; 14:6). Similarly, prophecy itself is closely connected to "revelation" in 14:6, and especially 14:25, 26, 30. Are these to be understood as distinctively different gifts? Or, as seems more likely, do they suggest different emphases for the expression of the prophetic gift, since that, too, seems to fluctuate between "revealing mysteries" and more straightforward words of edification, comfort, and exhortation (or encouragement)? In any case, the use of uninterpreted tongues in the assembly is what brought forth the whole argument, and Paul uses prophecy as representative of all other intelligible inspired utterances that are to be preferred to tongues in that setting.

i. Glossolalia. Paul's actual term is "different kinds of tongues." Enough is said in 1 Corinthians 13–14 to give us a fairly good idea as to how

Paul understood it. (1) It is Spirit-inspired utterance; that is made plain by 12:7 and 11 and 14:2. (2) The regulations for its community use in 14:27–28 make it clear that the speaker is not in "ecstasy" or "out of control." Quite the opposite: the speakers must speak in turn, and they must remain silent if there is no one to interpret. (3) It is speech essentially unintelligible both to the speaker (14:14) and to other hearers (14:16), and this is why it must be interpreted in the assembly. (4) It is speech directed basically toward God (14:2, 14–15, 28); one may assume, therefore, that what is interpreted is not speech directed toward others, but the "mysteries" spoken to God. (5) As a gift for use in private prayer, Paul held it in the highest regard (14:5, 15, 17–18).

Whether Paul also understood it to be an actual earthly language is a moot point, but the overall evidence suggests not. He certainly does not envisage the likelihood of someone's being present who might understand without interpretation; and the analogy of earthly language in 14:10–12 implies that it is not an earthly language (a thing is not usually identical with that to which it is analogous).

ii. Prophecy. In all the *charismata*, prophecy is the one mentioned most often in the Pauline letters (1 Thess. 5:20; 1 Cor. 11:4–5; 12–14; Rom. 12:6; Eph. 2:20; 3:5; 4:11; 1 Tim. 1:18; 4:14; and probably "through the Spirit" in 2 Thess. 2:2), implying the widest range of occurrence in the Pauline churches. Although it was also a widespread phenomenon in the Greek world, Paul's understanding was thoroughly conditioned by his own history in Judaism. The prophet was a person who spoke to God's people under the inspiration of the Spirit. In Paul such "speech" consisted of spontaneous, intelligible messages, orally delivered in the gathered assembly, intended for the edification or encouragement of the people. Those who prophesied were clearly understood to be "in control" (see 14:29–33). Although some people are called "prophets," the implication of 1 Corinthians 14:24–25 and 30–31 is that the gift is available—at least potentially—to all.

But it is also clear that it does not have independent authority. The combined evidence of 1 Thessalonians 5:21–22 and 1 Corinthians 12:10 and 14:29 is that all such prophesying must be "discerned" by the charismatic community. That is almost certainly the first intent of the gift of the "discernments of S/spirits" in 1 Corinthians 12:10, since the cognate verb of the noun "discernments" appears in 14:29 as the needed response to prophetic utterances, as interpretation is needed with tongues.

3. Their Extent in the Pauline Churches. The very fact that Paul can list all these items in such a matter-of-fact way, especially in 1 Corinthians 12:7–11, indicates that the worship of the church in the first century was far more charismatic than has been true for most of its subsequent history. Some indeed have tried to make a virtue of this lack, arguing that the more extraordinary phenomena were relatively limited in the early church—they belonged to more "immature" believers like the Corinthians—and that they were no longer needed once the NT was canonized. But that quite misses the evidence in Paul, as well as his point in 1 Corinthians 13:8–13 (see Fee, 1987, 641–52). One may as well argue that the other Pauline churches did not celebrate the Lord's Supper, since it is mentioned only in 1 Corinthians.

In fact the evidence is considerable that a visible, charismatic dimension of life in the Spirit was the normal experience of the Pauline churches. That Paul should speak of it in a direct way only twice (1 Thess. 5:19–22; 1 Cor. 12–14) is the "accident" of history—only here were there problems of abuse. Indeed, the problem in Thessalonica is especially telling, since apparently there was a tendency to "play down" the prophetic Spirit in their gatherings; but Paul will have none of that.

Even more telling are the off-handed, matter-of-fact ways these phenomena are mentioned elsewhere. For example, in 2 Thessalonians 2:2 Paul knows that someone has falsely informed them as to "the day of the Lord." What he does not know is the source of this false information; one possibility that automatically comes to mind is "through the Spirit" (most likely a "nondiscerned" prophetic utterance). Likewise in 1 Corinthians 11:2–16 in the matter of head-coverings, Paul refers to worship as "praying and prophesying," the two primary ways of addressing God and people in the assembly. In Galatians 3:5 a major point of his argument rests on their ongoing experience of "miracles." And in the case of Timothy's ministry (1 Tim. 1:18; 4:14), his own gifting is related to prophetic utterances in the community. In none of these instances is Paul arguing for something; rather, the visible, "charismatic" expression of their common life in the Spirit is the presupposition from which he argues for something else.

We may conclude, therefore, that all the evidence points in one direction: For Paul and the churches he founded, not only is the Spirit the absolute key to their understanding of Christian life—from beginning to end—but also, above all else, he was experienced, and experienced in ways that were essentially powerful and visible.

Bibliography: D. E. Aune, *Prophecy in Early Christianity and the Ancient Mediterranean World* (1983); C. K. Barrett, *Commentary on First Corinthians* (1971); idem, *Commentary on Second Corinthians* (1973); A. Bittlinger, *Gifts and Graces* (1967); F. F. Bruce, *Commentary on Galatians* (1982); D. A. Carson, *Showing the Spirit* (1987); J. D. G. Dunn, *Baptism in the Holy Spirit* (1970); idem, *Jesus and the Spirit* (1975); H. M. Ervin, *Conversion-Initiation and the Baptism in the Holy Spirit* (1984); idem, *Spirit Baptism* (1987); D. Ewert, *The Holy Spirit in the New Testament* (1983); G. Fee, *1 and 2 Timothy, Titus* (1984); idem, "Baptism in the Holy Spirit: The Issue of Separability and Subsequence," *Pneuma* 7 (1985): 87–99; idem, *The First Epistle to the Corinthians* (1987); V. P. Furnish, *II Corinthians* (1984); D. Gee, *Concerning Spiritual Gifts* (1947); M. Green, *I Believe in the Holy Spirit* (2d ed., 1985); W. Grudem, *The Gift of Prophecy in 1 Corinthians* (1982); N. Q. Hamilton, *The Holy Spirit and Eschatology in Paul* (1957); D. Hill, *New Testament Prophecy* (1979); S. Horton, *What the Bible Says About the Holy Spirit* (1976); R. B. Hoyle, *The Holy Spirit in Paul* (1928); H. Hunter, *Spirit-Baptism: A Pentecostal Alternative* (1983); J. Koenig, *Charismata: God's Gifts for God's People* (1978); G. E. Ladd, *A Theology of the New Testament* (1974); G. W. H. Lampe, *The Seal of the Spirit* (1967); C. F. D. Moule, *The Holy Spirit* (1978); H. Ridderbos, *Paul: An Outline of His Theology* (1975); S. Schatzmann, *A Pauline Theology of Charismata* (1986); A. Schweitzer, *The Mysticism of Paul the Apostle* (1931); E. Schweizer, *The Holy Spirit* (1978); E. F. Scott, *The Spirit in the New Testament* (1923); H. B. Swete, *The Holy Spirit in the New Testament* (1910); A. W. Wainwright, *The Trinity in the New Testament* (1962).   G. D. Fee

Pastor of the Chapel Hill Harvester Church in Atlanta, Earl P. Paulk, Jr., also conducts a weekly television ministry and the Earl Paulk College.

PAULK, EARL PEARLY, JR. (1927–). Televangelist, pastor, and bishop. Bishop Earl P. Paulk, Jr., grew up in a classical Pentecostal family as the son of Earl P. Paulk, Sr., a former assistant general overseer of the Church of God (CG, Cleveland, Tenn.). His grandfather, Elisha Paulk, was a Freewill Baptist preacher.

Paulk was called to the ministry and began preaching at age seventeen in Greenville, South Carolina. Two years later he became the state Sunday school and youth director for South Carolina (CG); later he pastored the Hemphill Church of God in Atlanta, Georgia (now known as Mount Paran Church of God). Paulk earned a B.A. at Furman University in 1947 and completed an M.Div. at the Candler School of Theology of Emory University in 1952.

In 1960 Paulk and his brother Don founded the Gospel Harvester Church in Atlanta's inner-city. The church moved to the suburbs in 1973 and became known as Chapel Hill Harvester Church. By 1988 the church had grown to more than 10,000 with twenty-one full-time pastors and a "Harvester Television Network" (a weekly national telecast). The church also developed ministries for unwed mothers, homosexuals, prisoners, and those with chemical addictions. In September 1986 the church opened Earl Paulk College, a liberal arts institution with three initial areas of study: biblical studies; business enterprise; music, art, and drama.

Paulk has become well-known for his "kingdom message" through his preaching, the monthly publication of *Thy Kingdom Come,* and his many books. The latter include: *The Divine Runner* (1978), *Satan Unmasked* (1984), *The Wounded Body of Christ* (1985), *Sex Is God's Idea* (1985), *Held in the Heavens Until . . .* (1985), *To Whom Is God Betrothed?* (1985), *Thrust in the Sickle and Reap* (1986), and *Ultimate Kingdom* (1987). His autobiography is entitled *The Provoker* (1986, ed. Tricia Weeks).

In 1982 Paulk was named to the office of bishop in the International Communion of Charismatic Churches. L. G. McClung, Jr.

PAYNE, LEANNE (1932–). Teacher and minister of inner healing. Like Agnes Sanford, Payne was led into the healing ministry through a personal healing, and she experienced a filling with the Holy Spirit and other spiritual gifts some time before receiving the gift of tongues. Her first contact with charismatic renewal was in 1963 with R. Winkler of Wheaton, Illinois. Payne, who is an Episcopalian, emphasizes the indwelling presence of Christ, and perhaps more than other ministers of divine healing she has realized the importance of rooting this ministry in a framework of a strong Trinitarian theology. This concern led to her first book, *Real Presence: The Holy Spirit in the Works of C. S. Lewis* (1979). Her ministry, through Pastoral Care Ministries founded in Milwaukee, Wisconsin, in 1982, sees gender identity as vital for human wholeness. This conviction is clearly expressed in *The Broken Image: Restoring Personal Wholeness Through Healing Prayer* (1981), *The Healing of the Homosexual* (1984), and *Crisis in Masculinity* (1985). P. D. Hocken

PEARLMAN, MYER (1898–1943). Educator and author. Born in Edinburgh, Scotland, Myer Pearlman, a Jew, immigrated to New York City in 1915 and later moved to San Francisco. While passing by Glad Tidings Mission in San Francisco, he felt drawn inside, where the people were singing "Honey in the Rock," composed by F. A. Graves. After several months of attending meetings at the church, he was converted to Christianity and received the baptism of the Holy Spirit. He graduated from Central Bible Institute, Springfield, Missouri, in 1925 and was asked to join the faculty. In 1927 he married one of his pupils, Irene Graves, daughter of F. A. Graves.

For many years Pearlman prepared the *Adult Teacher's Quarterly,* as well as the *Adult Student's Quarterly* for the Gospel Publishing House. He also edited *Reveille,* a devotional publication geared to American servicemen. He is best remembered for his monumental outline of theology called *Knowing the Doctrines of the Bible* (1937). Overwork caused his health to break at a comparatively early age.

Bibliography: I. P. Pearlman, *Myer Pearlman and His Friends* (1953). G. W. Gohr

PECOS BENEDICTINES IN NEW MEXICO See CHARISMATIC COMMUNITIES.

PEDERSON, W. DENNIS (1938–). A leader in the Lutheran charismatic movement who combines gifts of teaching and administration with a broad missionary vision. Pederson graduated from Augsburg Theological Seminary, Minneapolis, in 1963, and received the D.Min. from the Jesuit School of Theology in Berkeley in 1978. He served as a principal staff assistant to the governor of Minnesota from 1971 to 1975. Having experienced a personal spiritual renewal during Holy Week 1972, Pederson began relating to other Lutheran charismatics the following August at the first International Lutheran Conference on the Holy Spirit, in Minneapolis.

Pederson returned to the active ordained ministry in 1975 as minister of evangelism and education in a Lutheran congregation in California. In 1978 he was called as an associate pastor and administrator to North Heights Lutheran Church, St. Paul, Minnesota, one of the leading Lutheran charismatic churches in the country.

Together with senior pastor Morris Vaagenes, he cofounded the International Lutheran Center for Church Renewal as a ministry of North Heights Lutheran Church (1980), which merged with Lutheran Charismatic Renewal Services in 1983 to form the International Lutheran Renewal Center (ILRC). Pederson became coordinator of ILRC's international ministries. He traveled extensively abroad, helping develop a worldwide network of relationships among Lutheran charismatic leaders.

Bibliography: L. Christenson, ed., *Welcome, Holy Spirit* (1987). L. Christenson

PENDLETON, WILLIAM H. (b. 1847). Early Pentecostal pastor. Pendleton was born in Arkansas. In 1866 he was married, and he and his wife, Sarah, had thirteen children. A white Civil War veteran, Pendleton embraced "second work" teaching while a Baptist deacon in 1879. In an 1893 Downey, California, camp meeting of the Holiness churches, he experienced "full sanctification." Recognized as a Holiness church minister from 1895 onward, he became pastor of the Los Angeles Holiness Church. A frequent and popular camp meeting speaker, Pendleton was elected to the denominational board of elders (1898). During the summer of 1906 he attended Azusa Street, after which he became the focus of controversy in the Holiness church because he experienced and taught baptism in the Spirit evidenced by tongues as subsequent to sanctification. Defrocked (August 27, 1906), he and twenty-eight members moved to the Eighth and Maple mission, where he succeeded Bartleman as pastor through 1910. As late as 1913 he was listed as pastor at a Pentecostal assembly at 1162 East 43rd, residing at 2010 Hunter in Los Angeles.

Bibliography: F. Bartleman, *How Pentecost Came to Los Angeles* (1925); J. M. Washburn, *History and Reminiscences of the Holiness Church Work in Southern California and Arizona* (1912). C. M. Robeck, Jr.

PENTATEUCH

I. Introduction
II. The Term *Rûaḥ*
III. The Wind of God
IV. The Spirit Upon Prophets and Leaders
V. Spirit of Wisdom
VI. Affecting Volition; Source of Life
VII. Conclusions

I. Introduction. "Pentateuch" is the designation given to the first five books of the Bible, from the Greek term meaning "five-volume book." The name given to this section in the Hebrew canon is the Torah, which is best translated "The Instruction" although "The Law" is the traditional rendering.. The books are anonymous, but conservative Christianity and Judaism have commonly attributed authorship to Moses.

In the middle of the eighteenth century, biblical scholarship in general started to shift away from the view that Moses wrote the entire five-volume work in the final form as we now possess it. The views that have resulted can be described as developmental—i.e., the material of the Pentateuch evolved in several parallel strands over a period of hundreds of years, strands that were woven together at different points in time into a literary tapestry that was completed at the latest by the time of Ezra, roughly 450 B.C.

Many Pentecostal biblical scholars have rejected any hint of development in the Pentateuchal materials. Others hold that one can allow for a certain amount of development and editing without jettisoning the theories of revelation and inspiration that have tended to mark Pentecostals as biblical conservatives, though these theories must therefore increase in complexity. Pentecostal scholars, standing in a biblically conservative tradition, will generally give serious attention to claims that much of the material, especially the legal, derives in one way or another from Moses as the human originator.

Questions of authorship and dating do not greatly impact this study. The primary relevance of decisions in these areas would be to allow the Pentateuch to shed light on the diachronic aspects of Israel's view of the Spirit of God, especially in such areas as symbols used for the Spirit and their significance and the Spirit's relation to prophecy, including Moses as prophet par excellence.

II. The Term *Rûaḥ*. The term "spirit," *rûaḥ* in Hebrew, often refers to such things as wind, breath, life or principle of life, heart in the sense of the core of personality, and anger. It can also refer to the Spirit of God. In view of the range of meanings, it is best to consider *rûaḥ* as pointing directly to the Spirit of God only when one or more of the following factors suggest it: (1) phraseology, e.g., "*rûaḥ* of God," "his [God's] *rûaḥ*"; (2) statements within the context that move the thought away from a physical meaning (wind, breath) toward "Spirit"; or (3) a clear reference to God's Spirit in the context.

III. The Wind of God. The reader first encounters the Spirit of God in the second verse of the Bible, the familiar line (KJV) reading "and the Spirit of God moved upon the face of the waters." Many scholars, however, argue that *rûaḥ* here means wind, and "of God" (*elohim*) denotes

a superlative degree of intensity. As an example, von Rad (1972, 49–50) argues that the verb in the clause means to stir or agitate. He prefers to translate the expression *rûaḥ elohim* as a "terrible storm," which is part of the initial chaos; the rest of the narrative then relates God imposing order upon that chaos. Von Rad notes that the Spirit of God is not seen elsewhere in the opening narrative of Genesis and states that the Spirit never has such a cosmological significance elsewhere in the OT. He concludes that this *rûaḥ* is not part of the creative activity nor preparation for it.

In support of the interpretation of wind in Genesis 1:2, it could be significant that wind also plays a part in the Akkadian *Creation Epic*. Although the existence of any parallel is hotly contested, attention is often drawn to the similarity in the biblical creation narrative's *tehom*, "deep," over which the *rûaḥ* swept, and Tiamat in the *Epic*. In this epic, the gods make Marduk their king and commission him to eliminate Tiamat, their vicious ancestress. In the ensuing battle, Marduk waits until Tiamat opens her mouth to devour him, then he forces the wind into her to keep her mouth open. She becomes distended, and he kills her with an arrow. After capturing her forces, Marduk splits her in two and makes half into the earth, and the other half into the vault of heaven (*The Creation Epic*, Tablet IV, 96–105, 128–40, in *ANET*, 66–67). Even if the comparison is valid, however, the narrative in Genesis does not make use of the mythological, nor does it make use of the battle motif.

Rather than interpreting *rûaḥ* in Genesis 1:2 as wind, Pentecostals generally take it to refer to the Holy Spirit and have seen the activity as preparatory to the events of creation related in chapters 1–2. Horton, for example, pointing to Psalm 104:30 and Isaiah 40:12–13, states that the Spirit of God is seen in the OT as active in God's creating and continued care for the world. Here in Genesis 1:2, then, the Spirit of God participates in creation (cf. the activity of the Son of God in texts such as John 1:3), even though the text does not reveal him as a distinct personality. The OT talks about God making the world by his wisdom and power, either in those abstract terms or using such anthropomorphic terms as God's hands or fingers. Most OT scholars agree that the "Spirit of God" is one way of talking about God's power and presence in action in the world. It should not be surprising to see the Spirit, thought of in terms of God's power and presence, as active in creation. The verb used should be translated "hovering" (not "brooding"), and probably refers to some preparatory work for the acts of creation that follow, though the text is not specific. Dark it may have been, but there was no chaos, for God was there (see Horton, 1976, 17–20).

Which interpretation is better? First, a good definition of chaos is in order. Chaos in the biblical sense is not helter-skelter activity; rather, it is to be pictured as a lack of defining attributes, characteristics, and differentiation—darkness, desolation, or shapelessness. In these terms chaos may be seen in Genesis 1:2, and much of the Creation narrative involves imposing form, differentiation, and order on that chaos, turning it into cosmos, an ordered world. Second, it is quite probable that there is an OT motif of God's victory over chaos in such creation texts as Job 38:8–11 and Psalm 74:13–17, where dividing the sea in verse 13a could refer to the Exodus under the influence of verse 12 but, in view of verses 13b–14 and 16–17, may well refer to the separation of the primordial sea described in Genesis 1:6–7. Leviathan and the dragons in Psalm 74:13b–14 are the mythological monsters representing chaos, as is Leviathan in Job 3:8, where Job wants to return the day of his birth to darkness, i.e., to the original unordered chaos; the chaos monster is designated by the names *yām*, "sea[-god]" and *rāhab* in Job 9:8, 13. Third, as we shall see below, the Pentateuchal description of the *rûaḥ* of God sometimes is borderline between the senses of "Spirit of God" and a mighty wind at God's command. Fourth, the use of *elohim* in the Creation narrative as a mere superlative seems emaciated. Given these factors, it is best not to choose between the alternatives but to allow that both contribute to the picture intended. We do not have a clear-cut reference to the Holy Spirit, but, in view of the parallels with Genesis 8:1, we should read the use here in Genesis 1:2 as "wind" but with the overtones of God at work beginning to impose order on the as yet chaotic creation. These overtones, of course, will suggest to the Christian interpreter the One whom systematic theologians later call "the Holy Spirit."

In Genesis 8:1 God caused a *rûaḥ* to blow over the earth, and the floodwater subsided. A fast reading of the text might suggest evaporation, but this conclusion is not required by the text, which only states that the waters went down. The *rûaḥ* also seems to be behind the closing of the windows of the heavens and the fountains of the deep. The latter especially indicates something more than a wind, since these fountains are pictured as being in the depths of the oceans. In referring to this text, von Rad (1972, 128) notes that the Flood narrative involves some of the same elements as the Creation narrative in Genesis 1, viz., the waters above the heavens and the waters below the earth. Thus, the catastrophe is one of cosmological proportions. With this dimension in focus, the *rûaḥ* sweeping across the waters is noteworthy. The earth has again been reduced to chaos as the two halves of the primeval sea reunite and cover all distinguishing characteristics, but God sends *rûaḥ*, and the process of restoring order out of chaos begins. (This text may thus give *rûaḥ* cosmological significance, contra the view of von Rad mentioned above.)

There are several other places in the Pentateuch where *rûaḥ* means "wind" yet where the picture is still one of God at work in the world. The sequence is (1) God caused the wind, and (2) the wind performed God's work. These texts are Exodus 10:13, 19; 14:21; 15:8–10; and Numbers 11:31.

The clearest pair of these texts is Exodus 14:21; 15:8–10. In 14:21 the Lord drove back the sea all night by a strong east wind, leaving dry ground so that the Israelites could cross. Later, in his song of celebration, Moses called the wind "the blast (*rûaḥ*) of his [God's] nostrils" (15:8),

and, more importantly for this study, we read, "You blew them with your *rûaḥ*" (15:10). It is true that in context the referent of *rûaḥ* is wind, but that context and the phrasing in verses 8 and 10 connect the personal activity of God very closely with the working of the wind. Indeed, no completely physical wind could hold the waters at bay and still allow the Israelites to cross. While the sea in this text is not as overtly connected with chaos, it does represent an otherwise insurmountable obstacle to continued life for the Israelites, and hence death; it does prove to be death to the army of Egypt. The separation of the waters on either side of the Israelites could be read as a horizontal echo of the vertical separation of the primeval sea in Genesis 1:6–8; the reuniting of the Red Sea is reminiscent of the reuniting of the two halves of the primeval sea in the Flood account, and the covering of all the Egyptians reminds the reader of the definition of chaos and its resurgence in the Flood story. One significant difference in thematic development is the direct involvement of the *rûaḥ* in the reuniting of the two halves of the Red Sea (Exod. 15:10), and, of course, the Red Sea is not redivided. On the other hand, as in the Flood account, God's favored do make it through, and the unfavored fall victim to the waters.

Another instance where *rûaḥ* means "wind" is found in Exodus 10:13, 19, where the Lord brought an east wind over the land all day and all night; by morning the east wind had brought a plague of locusts. Following Moses' encounter with Pharaoh, the Lord sent a very strong west wind that picked up the locusts and drove them into the sea. Here the *rûaḥ* involved is clearly wind, because it is given a directional designation, yet it is *rûaḥ* that accomplishes God's purpose. A similar use is found in Numbers 11:31, in which there goes forth a *rûaḥ* from the Lord, and the *rûaḥ* brought quail from the sea (seacoast) to provide meat for the Israelites. One might simply pass this off as mere wind except that there is a reference close in context to the Lord's Spirit in 11:29. Although the text in Exodus involves judgment (perhaps this and the other plague texts could be described as a partial and controlled unleashing of the forces of chaos upon Egypt; cf. the treatment above of Exod. 14–15) and the text in Numbers involves provision, both have connections with the sea, the one as the place of disposal of locusts (perhaps viewing the sea as the repository of chaos) and the other as the source of quail.

To be sure, the explanation for some of these texts could lie in a text like Psalm 104:4, which says that God "makes winds his messengers," i.e., God simply uses wind to accomplish his purposes. On the other hand, the preceding discussion would suggest that, in the Pentateuch at least, there is not only an etymological link among the meanings of *rûaḥ*—"breath," "wind," and "spirit"—but a conceptual or symbolic one as well. The wind, the *rûaḥ*, sometimes designated as the "breath of God," is used as a tangible symbol of God at work and is actually found where God is at work, even though wind as such cannot account for the results. This use shades off into the more "spiritual" meaning that points more directly to the person of God. (This usage may well lie behind the symbolic meaning of the sound of wind in Acts 2:2.)

IV. The Spirit Upon Prophets and Leaders. In Numbers 11, as part of the incident with the quail, God put some of the *rûaḥ* that was on Moses upon seventy elders of Israel so that they could help Moses bear the burden of the people. There are four references to *rûaḥ* in this section of the story. The key reference is verse 29, where Moses identifies this *rûaḥ* as the Spirit of the Lord, clarifying the references in verses 17, 25, and 26. When the Lord did put the Spirit upon the elders, the result was that they prophesied, but only for this once and only for a time. The activity denoted by "prophesying" must have been clearly recognizable and unusual, for the two men who stayed in the camp and did not join the others were noted to be prophesying. It may be that prostration was one characteristic aspect, if the description in Numbers 24:4c, 16 is significant: "falling down" (cf. 1 Sam. 19:20).

Numbers 11 implies that since the Spirit was the one who rested upon Moses and that some of the Spirit's power was shared with the elders, the elders received a lesser portion, distributed among seventy of them. The unique status of Moses as the prime spokesman for God is thereby safeguarded; that status is again preserved in the following chapter, when it was threatened by two other prophets, viz., Miriam and Aaron. Further, verse 29 makes the equation that the one upon whom the Spirit of the Lord rests is a prophet.

Stronstad argues that this passage is part of a larger OT theme that involves the transference of the Spirit as an integral aspect of appointment to God's service, including a sign that leadership has been transferred and that one has been enabled for that leadership role (1984, 20–24). We must note that in Numbers 11 leadership is not actually transferred from Moses to the seventy elders; rather, they were now to assist Moses. Since his role was prophetic, theirs must be prophetic, at least to a limited extent. Joshua was one of these seventy elders (v. 28), and later God does transfer leadership of Israel to him (27:16–23), at which time God describes him to Moses as "a man in whom is the spirit" (27:18).

Balaam is another figure in Numbers upon whom the Spirit comes; a prophetic oracle is once more the result (24:2). The phrase "the Spirit of God came upon him" is, in addition to the repeated phrase "he uttered his oracle," the only major variation in the introductions to his oracles. The oracle where it occurs also includes a description of Balaam's prophetic function: "the oracle of one who hears the words of God . . . who sees a vision from the Almighty, who falls prostrate, and whose eyes are opened" (cf. vv. 15–16). Both the visionary and auditory strands of the prophetic are represented in these lines. This description is interesting when read in the light of the statements of the Lord to Aaron and Miriam in Numbers 12. There the Lord says that he communicates with all of the Israelite prophets except for Moses in dreams and visions, while he speaks with Moses directly, clearly, and while Moses is in his normal state of consciousness.

V. Spirit of Wisdom. In Genesis 41:38 Pharaoh describes Joseph as having the Spirit of God in him, then connects this description with receiving revelation from God, being wise, and therefore having the ability to govern Egypt. The Spirit of God thus gives wisdom in a sense that is familiar to modern readers. Further, the intertwining of the wisdom with the reference to the interpretation of dreams suggests the prophetic in God's speech to Moses, Aaron, and Miriam in Numbers 12.

Another reference to being full of the Spirit of Wisdom is in the closing passage of the Pentateuch, Deuteronomy 34:9. The verse is a clear reference to Numbers 27:16–23. Joshua was full of the Spirit of Wisdom and thus was able to lead Israel. These two texts are strongly similar in thought to the leadership texts discussed above.

The term "wisdom" has a more practical meaning, too: ability as a craftsman. The Spirit endows with this kind of wisdom those who will prepare the cultic (ceremonial worship) materials. In Exodus 31:3–5 God states that he has filled Bezalel with the Spirit of God, i.e., with skill (*ḥokmah*, "wisdom"), ability, and knowledge in all kinds of crafts (for a similar list, cf. Isa. 11:2 and the possible allusion to it in Rev. 3:1). A less clear reference is Exodus 28:3, where God tells Moses that he has given ability to all who have it, i.e., he has given them a spirit of wisdom (NIV "wisdom," RSV "able mind"). The two texts are linked by Exodus 31:6–10, which serves to clarify Exodus 28:3 as indeed a reference to the Spirit of God. Both of these passages are recapitulated in Exodus 35:30–36:1. These texts allow the reader to conclude that the Spirit of God can be called the Spirit of Wisdom.

VI. Affecting Volition; Source of Life. There may be one or two texts that describe God's Spirit as affecting volition, but in both cases this meaning is not probable. In Exodus 35:21 the text describes the offerings made for the tabernacle as brought by [rendered with wooden literalness] "every man whom his heart drove him, and every [man] whom his spirit moved him." If the "his" with "spirit" referred to God, then this text would refer to God's Spirit dealing with people's hearts to make them respond favorably to his will. The tight parallel within the sentence, however, and the parallel expressions of verses 22, 25, and 29 (note that vv. 25, 29 bring in the women as well), suggest that it is the human spirit as a close synonym for "heart" that is in view in verse 21.

The meaning of the other text, Genesis 6:3, is in doubt due to the difficulty in determining the meaning of the verb involved, which normally would mean to act as judge, govern, or the like (BDB, s.v. *dîn*, cf. also 1122). The traditional English translation of the KJV is "My spirit shall not always strive with man" (NIV "contend"), but this meaning elsewhere occurs only in Ecclesiastes 6:10, where the preposition "with" is *'im*; here the preposition is *b*. While *b* can be translated "with" in certain senses, it does not fit with this kind of meaning.

Different meanings proposed for the verb are "abide" (RSV), "remain" (NIV), or "rule," "be mighty" (von Rad, 1972, 114) if the verb form is derived from a similarly spelled verb, *dûn*. The resulting idea is that the Spirit of God is in humanity, most probably in the sense of giving life. These alternatives fit well with the preposition *b* and also can account for the reason that God's Spirit will not continue to give life: humanity is flesh, and thus weak and frail and therefore cannot live forever (or must not; cf. Gen. 3:22–24). God thus decides that he will not allow humanity to continue on its present course; a limit has been set, even if it is a rather conventionally stylized round number. This limit may be a limit to individual life spans, or it may be a period of time that God will delay his judgment. The latter fits best with the singular *'ādām* ("man" or "humanity") in verse 3 and with the context, specifically verses 5–7, 12–13. The Spirit not abiding in and thus being withdrawn from humanity is then equivalent to God destroying humanity in verses 7 and 13. The Spirit is seen as the source of life for flesh; this idea is also behind the expressions in Genesis 6:17; 7:15; and especially the MT of 7:22, "the breath of the spirit of life" (cf. Gen. 2:7; Num. 16:22; 27:16; and the non-Pentateuchal texts Job 34:14; Ps. 104:29–30; and Eccl. 12:7).

VII. Conclusions The major picture of the Spirit of the Lord that is developed in the Pentateuch is that of wind. Wind is used by the Lord to perform his will. In some texts the wind and the power of God at work are so closely identified that the wind is viewed as an extension of Yahweh himself. It is but a short step from these texts to those in which there is no chance of seeing any physical reference in the term *rûah*. To be sure, no text in the Pentateuch describes the Spirit as a distinct person, though from a NT perspective the reader often perceives the Holy Spirit in the text.

In terms of activity, the Pentateuch several times in some way connects the spirit-wind with the sea, at least twice being an agent of imposing order upon it. In some of these cases the sea is the repository, representative, or is even the agent of chaos. The *rûah*, on the other hand, is the agent of God and assists in the imposition of order on chaos. Withdrawal of *rûah* is connected with the eruption of chaos and death; God may use these eruptions in a controlled way to bring judgment. In a complementary sense, the *rûah* of God is the source of life for all flesh.

God also places his Spirit upon individuals. One possible result is that the person will prophesy; another is that the person receives wisdom or ability for a specific task, including manufacture of cultic materials or leadership of a nation. The prophetic result is connected to the gift of wisdom both in the persons of Moses, Joshua, the seventy elders, and to some extent, Joseph. The "Spirit of Wisdom," with "wisdom" being broadly defined, can be another term for the Spirit of God.

Bibliography: *ANET*, 3d ed. with supplement (1969); BDB, corrected ed., 1953; S. Horton, *What the Bible Says About the Holy Spirit* (1976); R. Stronstad,

The Charismatic Theology of St. Luke (1984); G. von Rad, *Genesis: A Commentary* (1972).   D. A. Johns

PENTECOST, FEAST OF   The Feast of Pentecost, commemorated in the church as the day on which the Holy Spirit descended (Acts 2) in fulfillment of the promise of Jesus (John 16:7, 13; Acts 1:4, 14), is traditionally recognized as the birth of the church as an institution.

"Pentecost," meaning "fifty," is the Greek name for the OT Feast of Weeks, since this festival occurred on the fiftieth day (seven weeks) after Passover. Along with the feasts of Passover and Tabernacles, Pentecost was one of the three annual pilgrimage feasts among the Jews. A harvest festival, it marked the beginning of the time when the people brought their offerings of firstfruits. Leviticus 23:15–21 provides the most detailed account of the ritual observed during the feast. The observance is also known as the Feast of Ingathering (Exod. 23:16) and Day of Firstfruits (Num. 28:26).

In Judith 6:17–21 (c. 100 B.C.), Pentecost is the feast of covenant renewal, an understanding also reflected within the Qumran community. After the destruction of the Jerusalem temple in A.D. 70, Jews celebrated Pentecost to commemorate the giving of the law at Sinai.

The coming of the Holy Spirit on the Day of Pentecost (Acts 2) implies the passing of the old system of worship, as well as the climax and fulfillment of the promises that system foreshadowed. For the church, Pentecost has become a time to celebrate God's bestowal of the gift of the Spirit. Modern Christians who believe in the possibility of receiving the same experience of the Holy Spirit as the apostles on the Day of Pentecost (Acts 1:1–4) are called "Pentecostals."

Bibliography: R. de Vaux, *Ancient Israel*, 2 vols. (1961); J. D. G. Dunn, "Pentecost, Feast of," *NIDNTT* (1976), 2:783–88; C. Feinberg, "Pentecost," *ZPEB* (1976), 4:692–94; S. Gilmour, "Easter and Pentecost," *JBL* 81 (1962): 62–66; E. Lohse, "*Pentēkostē*," *TDNT* (1968), 6:44–53; H. Schauss, *The Jewish Festivals* (1938).   T. Powell

PENTECOST OVER EUROPE CONFERENCE   See CHARISMATIC MOVEMENT.

PENTECOSTAL AND CHARISMATIC MUSIC   The Pentecostal movement has long been distinguished for the important role it gives to music in all aspects of the lives of its adherents. Fervent, spiritual singing is and has been typical of the Pentecostal-charismatic tradition of worship. The value of music for the worship, evangelism, education, and nurture of the church has emerged as a major emphasis of the movement. Music occupies a vital place in the religious experience of typical Pentecostal-charismatic believers, expressing a wide range of economic, political, and social values; styles of worship; and musical tastes.

Music can be a powerful influence when it is performed by devout believers and anointed by the presence of the Holy Spirit. This spiritual approach, encompassing a variety of music types and styles, is an identifying characteristic of music associated with the Pentecostal-charismatic tradition and has its basis in both the Bible and historical church traditions.

The subject is here treated as follows:

I. Roots of Pentecostal-Charismatic Music
 A. Biblical Influences
  1. Old Testament Practices
  2. New Testament Practices
 B. Historical-Musical Influences
  1. Reform and Revival
  2. Early American Music
  3. The Gospel Hymn
II. The Tradition Develops
 A. The New Hymnals
 B. Choral Music and Chorus Singing
 C. Music Education
III. Expansion and New Directions
 A. Contemporary Christian Music
 B. The Charismatic Renewal
IV. Coming of Age
 A. Organization of Music Ministry
 B. Music Education
 C. Music and Media
 D. Toward the Future

I. Roots of Pentecostal-Charismatic Music.
The roots of music representing the Pentecostal-charismatic tradition run deep and strong. They are firmly embedded in scriptural practices, yet influenced by the historical traditions of Christian church music. From the beginning of the twentieth century, music of the Pentecostal tradition has emphasized a heartfelt, sincere, and enthusiastic approach to singing and instrumental performance. Early revival meetings typically saw worshipers caught up in the exuberant and spirited singing of gospel hymns. Their singing was joyful in spirit and consisted primarily of congregational expressions of praise and testimony. Early accounts tell of singing, praising, hand clapping, shouting, and even dancing unto the Lord.

Following what they believed to be the NT model, early Pentecostal believers placed little emphasis on ritual and ceremony in worship. Adherents of such bodies as the Assemblies of God (AG), Church of God (CG), Pentecostal Holiness Church (PHC), Church of God of Prophesy (CGP), International Church of the Foursquare Gospel (ICFG), Church of God in Christ (CGIC), Pentecostal Assemblies of Canada (PAOC), and more recently, charismatic groups developing within the traditional denominations, believe worship to be primarily a matter of the heart and personally oriented. They have developed an attitude of freedom in worship that they perceive to have existed in the early church.

The movement has emphasized congregational participation through singing and performing a variety of types and styles of music. Most important, perhaps, this tradition recognizes the work of the Holy Spirit in guiding and influencing the experience of the individual in both corporate and private worship. The importance of singing and performing with the aid and direction of the Holy Spirit is a central aspect of Pentecostal-charismatic music.

This attitude quite naturally leads to musical expression and ministry that tends to be less liturgical and formal in its organization and practice than many Christian church traditions.

Music comes to be more subjective in its expression, and it is demonstrably emotional in its style of performance. Consequently, Pentecostal-charismatic music has some characteristic qualities in both sound and concept that distinguish it from other eras and practices of both liturgical and evangelical traditions.

A. Biblical Influences. The importance of music in the life of believers can be seen throughout Scripture. Music is an integral part of the universe, born in the heart of God (Job 38:7; Isa. 14:7; 44:23). Scripture reveals that God created music, both sacred and secular, and established it as part of the total lifestyle of his people (Exod. 15:1–21; Josh. 6:4–5).

In addition, God provided for the use of music in the worship and in the training programs of the temple and tabernacle (2 Chron. 5:11–14; Pss. 100:1–2; 150).

Finally, God designed and established music as a specialized ministry within the church, to be well organized and spiritually administered (1 Chron. 16:1–10; 2 Chron. 29:25–28). An analysis of musical interests and practices within the Pentecostal-charismatic movement reveals a significant influence of these biblical models on the organization of programs, manner of performance in worship, and acceptance of diversity of style.

1. Old Testament Practices. The role of music in ministry and praise and worship, both vocal and instrumental, is modeled in the OT. Music was intended not only for religious functions but also for secular purposes, such as call to battle, celebration, work activities, and social life.

The music and worship of the tabernacle and temple provide organizational models for music ministry, including emphasis on congregational singing, prominent use of choirs and special singers, and love and appreciation of instrumental music (1 Chron. 16:37–42; 25:1–6; 2 Chron. 5:11–14).

Perhaps the most significant OT influence is the importance placed on singing psalms and other Scriptures. This practice has enjoyed immense popularity, especially in Pentecostal-charismatic music from 1970 to the present. Yet the earliest Pentecostals used the various psalters that were popular during the late nineteenth century along with traditional hymnals. In addition, they made liberal use of various kinds of musical instruments. The rise of singing psalms and Scripture songs, as well as the rebirth of dance in worship, in the charismatic movement is directly attributed to OT examples. And this resurgence of singing choruses and Scripture songs, along with spontaneous, exuberant worship has spread widely in non-Pentecostal settings, in large part because of the influence of the Pentecostal-charismatic movement.

2. New Testament Practices. In the earliest years of Pentecostalism, music was a vital and expected part of church life and ministry, home, street meetings, jail services, and even work activity (Conn, 1977, 109, 158, 180, 196). The heavy dependence of the Pentecostal-charismatic tradition on the NT for doctrine and lifestyle also helped to shape its beliefs and ideas concerning the use of music.

Variety in music forms and tastes is a strong characteristic of the Pentecostal-charismatic tradition that derives from the NT. The gospel hymn, traditional hymn, chorus, gospel song, and Scripture song are all part of the repertory enjoyed by congregations and individuals. The acceptance of diversity can be most attributed perhaps to Paul's writings to the Colossians and Ephesians, in which he suggests at least three different song types or texts. In Colossians 3:16 (KJV) the apostle writes, "Let the word of Christ dwell in you richly in all wisdom; teaching and admonishing one another in psalms and hymns and spiritual songs, singing with grace in your hearts to the Lord." Music historians have corroborated the early Christian practice of using song types other than OT psalms (Reese, 1940). There is evidence that even the earliest music services of the AG, CG, and PHC churches used a variety of song types. Gospel hymns, psalms, and later on, gospel songs and choruses all gained common use and popularity.

This appreciation and tolerance of different music styles also applied to performance. Using guitars, rhythm instruments, and keyboards together with various combinations of traditional band and orchestral instruments has become the norm. The AG music program had been particularly distinctive in its use of musical instruments in the church. Instrumental music combined with solo, group, and eventually choral singing all came to be accepted components to supplement the fervent, enthusiastic congregational singing so typical of the movement. This inclusiveness continues today as a prominent feature of Pentecostal-charismatic music.

The psalm represents inspired text given by God to humanity to express various themes and emotions. The hymn embodies the believer's expression of praise, thanksgiving, and prayer to God. The gospel song offers to the believer and nonbeliever alike a vehicle for testimony and prophecy. These comprise the basic elements for developing a rich and satisfying music ministry in the Pentecostal-charismatic tradition. Chorus singing, Scripture songs, praise, and dance are elements that evolved later out of this background.

The manner of singing—spirited, enthusiastic, jubilant, with purpose—so typical of Pentecostal music during the entire history of the movement is also perceived to be based on biblical example. In 1 Corinthians 14:15 (KJV), Paul encourages edification of the church through singing: "I will sing with the spirit, and I will sing with the understanding also." These two concepts—spiritual or spirited singing, and communicative or impactive singing—can be described as a double-stranded thread that weaves through the entire fabric of Pentecostal-charismatic music.

Music and singing that call for the performer's involvement emotionally and physically, while making provision for the prompting, directing, and moving of the Holy Spirit, are thought to be both necessary and good. Yet it is also deemed necessary that music effectively communicate the text, its message, and its meaning in their intellectual dimension.

B. Historical-Musical Influences. Numerous musical styles, approaches, and practices of the past have influenced Pentecostal-charismatic music, but it is music most directly associated with evangelical reform that has had the greatest impact. Church music from A.D. 300 to 1500 is important primarily in relation to the significance it had for music born out of the Protestant Reformation.

1. Reform and Revival. Out of the Reformation came an understanding of the importance of the effective use of hymns for worship and for individual and corporate expression of doctrine and faith. Martin Luther's contribution through his chorales is fundamental to the development of hymn singing in the evangelical movement. Even so, the psalter long remained the basic song book of the reform movement, while the hymn achieved popularity and widespread use more slowly.

Hymn singing became the most popular form of musical expression by the mid-eighteenth century. But the emerging Pentecostals in the early twentieth century used gospel hymns and psalters along with the traditional hymnals. Describing CG meetings of the early 1900s, C. W. Conn writes that "the meetings were begun with singing, without musical accompaniment unless some person with a guitar happened to bring his instrument along. Such hymns as 'Amazing Grace,' 'Blessed Assurance,' 'At the Cross,' and 'What a Friend We Have in Jesus' were invariably sung, for what is now properly called 'gospel singing' was unknown" (1977, 19). This description applies not just to meetings held in the South but also to practices on the West Coast and in middle America. During this time some use was also made of folk music, spirituals, and simple choruses.

The influence of Luther's thought can be seen not only in the popularity of hymn singing but in the importance placed on music training. This emphasis was reflected in a fondness for presenting week-long singing schools to develop music-reading skills and to teach new songs. This practice is in vogue today, particularly in rural areas in the southern U.S. Such schools are also enjoyed by non-Pentecostals of various denominations.

The works of Isaac Watts, noted English hymnist of the eighteenth century, have exerted tremendous influence on the music of Evangelicals of the late eighteenth and nineteenth centuries and, subsequently, the Pentecostal movement of the twentieth century. Several of Watts' hymns are favorites in Pentecostal-charismatic churches today. "When I Survey the Wondrous Cross," "At the Cross," "O God, Our Help in Ages Past," and "Joy to the World" continue to be sung with conviction and frequency.

The hymns of John and Charles Wesley and the widespread influence of the Wesleyan revival also hold great significance for the Holiness and Pentecostal traditions. Typical hymns from Charles Wesley's prolific pen that are still sung today include "Hark the Herald Angels Sing,"

"Love Divine All Loves Excelling," and "O for a Thousand Tongues to Sing." Charles' hymns were more personal and intimate than those of Watts. John was concerned that singing be at the same time spiritual and of good musical quality. His instructions to the congregation included admonishments to "Sing All, Sing Lustily, Sing Modestly, Sing in Time and above all, Sing Spiritually" (Reynolds, 1963, 55–56).

2. *Early American Music.* The psalms and hymns brought to America by the colonists exerted a direct influence on Pentecostal-charismatic music, as did the development of singing schools, which were a popular part of American music in the late seventeenth and early eighteenth centuries (Alford, 1967, 43–46). Music associated with the great revival movements of the eighteenth and nineteenth centuries, especially the popularity of the folk-oriented hymn (which came to be known as the camp meeting or revival spiritual) also had far-reaching effects on Pentecostal-charismatic music.

Black music and Negro spirituals were a major part of these revivals and camp meetings, creating a repertory and tradition that not only influenced white Pentecostals from traditional denominations but also provided the basis for much of the rich music expressions of American black Pentecostals today. Churches like the CGIC are renowned for their great choirs, soloists, impressive congregational singing, and upbeat instrumental music, all of which have become a major part of the music scene in the twentieth century.

The writing of Lowell Mason, Thomas Hastings, George Root, William Bradbury, and Isaac Woodbury continued to expand the popularity and importance of hymns while developing a new form known as the Sunday school song, which is still popular in Pentecostal-charismatic churches.

Then there was the shape-note system of music notation, a purely American tradition of music notation and an approach to singing that has strong historical significance. It became the primary vehicle in development of a new form of music composition and style of singing that has flourished in the Pentecostal movement since the early twentieth century. The work of Andrew Law in the *Music Primer* and Smith and Little in *The Easy Instructor* effectively launched the shape-note tradition in this country.

"The basis of the system was the providing of a simple method of visually identifying the pitch of the note by a particular note shape. These shapes then represented certain pitches, and the singer could find the pitch through the visual shape rather than actually reading the music" (Alford, 1967, 46). The system began with a four-way— fa, so, la, mi—approach that gave way to a new seven-shape system. Each shape represents one note of the diatonic scale. This system of notation and publishing became extremely popular and influential; it provided an opportunity for development and dissemination of the gospel or "convention song."

3. *The Gospel Hymn.* Clearly the gospel hymn occupies a place of great importance in any description of Pentecostal-charismatic music. Its value and appropriateness are described by Rob-

ert M. Stevenson: "Gospel hymnody has the distinction of being America's most typical contribution to Christian song. . . . Its very obviousness has been its strength. . . . In an age when religion must win mass approval in order to survive, in an age when religion must at least win a majority vote, . . . gospel hymnody is inevitable" (1953, 162).

The gospel hymn (song of testimony) exists in several forms. E. S. Lorenz perhaps best defines the gospel hymn as "a sacred folk song, free in form, emotional in character, devout in attitude, evangelistic in purpose and spirit" (1923, 342). This is an apt description of a form that was to have lasting influence on music of the Pentecostal movement.

Along with traditional publishers, several Pentecostal denominations joined the early rush to publish these newly popular gospel or convention songs in collections. By the third decade of the twentieth century these collections, or "convention" song books, were in wide use in churches, revival meetings, camp meetings, and conventions. Local church choirs made much use of them, and their popularity eventually led to a period of dominance of this form in the Pentecostal-charismatic movement. The gospel hymn also encouraged singing by special choirs and groups rather than just by a congregation.

Publishers in the AG (Gospel Publishing House; Melody Music), PHC (Advocate Press), and the CG (Tennessee Music and Printing; Pathway Press) joined with other prominent gospel hymn publishers such as Stamps-Baxter Music, Vaughan Music, and Hartford Music in producing hundreds of collections that spread this type of song and approach to singing throughout the movement. Tennessee Music and Printing Company of the CG has emerged as the single largest producer of gospel hymn collections.

Popular Pentecostal writers of gospel hymns during the first four decades of the twentieth century included Otis L. McCoy, "I'm on the Battlefield"; Vep Ellis, "Have Faith in God"; Cleavant Derricks, "When God Dips His Love in My Heart"; and Herbert Buffum, "Lift Me Up Above the Shadows" and "He Abides." These were preceded in the genre before the Pentecostal era by prominent writers and composers of the late nineteenth century, e.g., Ira D. Sankey, "I Am Praying for You"; Fanny Crosby, "Blessed Assurance" and "Near the Cross"; William Bradbury, "He Leadeth Me"; James Rowe, "Love Lifted Me"; W. J. Kirkpatrick, "The Comforter Has Come"; and Charles Gabriel, "Send the Light."

Twentieth-century writers whose works are familiar to the Pentecostal-charismatic movement have included Norman J. Clayton, John W. Peterson, Thomas A. Dorsey, Charles Weigle, George Schuler, Charles Bartlett, Charles Wycuff, Bill and Gloria Gaither, Albert Brumley, Joe Parks, Ralph Carmichael, Lanny Wolfe, and Jack Hayford.

While the gospel hymn has not had a significant role in the charismatic movement, it has an essential place in the development of music in the Pentecostal tradition. Its popularity and influence among a broad spectrum of Pentecostal believers are immeasurable.

Denton Alford concludes that "Pentecostal musicians, ministers and believers attach great importance to the use and value of the gospel song in the religious lives of twentieth century Christians. While Pentecostal church music has always encompassed . . . hymns and psalms . . . the very nature of the Pentecostal outreach and ministry has lent itself to an emphasis on the gospel hymn or gospel song" (1967, 49).

II. The Tradition Develops. The prominence of music in the Pentecostal-charismatic movement can be gauged by the time devoted to singing and instrumental music in worship. It is not unusual for up to two-thirds of worship services to be given over to music performance. Moreover, music is used in the sanctuary and in the home with equal fervor.

By the 1930s a new style of music called the gospel song had gained prominence. Songs tended to tell the story of redemption—"Oh, Happy Day," "A New Name in Glory"—or announce the second coming of Christ and the joys of an eternity spent in heaven—"When I Take My Vacation in Heaven," "When I Make My Last Move," and "I'll Fly Away." Many songs related experiences of the perceived joys or hardships of the Christian life—"We'll Soon Be Done With Troubles and Trials," "I've Got That Old Time Religion in My Heart," and "Victory In Jesus." Texts were often more experientially oriented than praise or worship related.

The emergence of gospel music and the increasing emphasis placed on training also produced teachers of great renown like Homer Rodeheaver, Virgil Stamps, Adgar Pace, and Otis McCoy. The popularity of the all-male gospel quartet began in the early 1930s and lasted well into the fifties. There seemed to be a particular liking for the timbre of the male voice in the genre of gospel music. These quartets sang in churches, schools, singing conventions, and revivals and later on radio and television. Their singing style and their music gained immediate acceptance among Pentecostals in America, particularly the AG, CG, CGP, PHC, and PAOC. Many of the featured soloists were Pentecostals and included such people as James Blackwood, Connor B. Hall, and J. D. Sumner. Eva LeFevre was one of the few female soloists featured with these quartets. Later the quartets developed recording and concert careers, moving out of the churches and onto the stage. Hundreds of groups formed during that era, some of the most prominent being the Blackwood Brothers, the Homeland Harmony Quartet, the Statesmen, and the Singing LeFevres.

For a time, gospel music became primary in the Pentecostal-charismatic movement, almost to the exclusion of other forms. This emphasis lasted until the 1950s, when a return to a more middle-of-the-road flavor became the trend.

A. The New Hymnals. In an effort to become more balanced and retain the best of past traditions while exploring the fresh and new, mainstream Pentecostal denominations returned to using hymns, gospel hymns, and other musical forms during the 1950s. Several denominational publishers exerted leadership by compiling, editing, and publishing hymnals for their constituencies.

While these efforts did not produce hymnals of the traditional variety, they did culminate in some noteworthy collections that contain traditional hymns, gospel songs, and music for special occasions and choirs. A popular publication of this type was *Church Hymnal*, published in 1951 by Tennessee Music and Printing Company of the CG. This hymnal is heavily weighted toward gospel songs, and it has remained popular since its inception with more than four million copies in print. It is used not only by Pentecostals, but also by churches of many other denominations. The *Foursquare Hymnal*, published in 1957 by the ICFG, and *The Gospel Hymnal*, published in 1973 by Advocate Press of the PHC, are other examples of this type.

Hymns of Glorious Praise, published in 1969 by Gospel Publishing House of the AG, and *Hymns of the Spirit*, published in 1969 by Pathway Press of the CG, are examples of more traditional hymnals.

The broadening musical tastes and interests in the Pentecostal-charismatic movement affected repertory, style, and content. Hymn singing witnessed a new prominence, and congregational participation in worship through singing was emphasized once again.

B. Choral Music and Chorus Singing. During most of the first half of the twentieth century, Pentecostal groups were known as a singing church. Congregational singing and participation in worship was an identifying characteristic until the 1940s. By this time, due to influences already mentioned, congregational music diminished in favor of performances by soloists and special groups. This trend lasted until the 1960s, when there developed greater equality between congregational singing and choral singing.

The sixties ushered in a time of effective use of church choirs, encouraged by the enhancement of choirs and music departments in denominational colleges and Bible training schools. Choral singing fueled the development of local church sanctuary choirs, youth choirs, and children's choirs and other specialized groups (e.g., camp meeting choirs and minister's choirs). In addition, denominational publishers and music departments began publishing choral octavos and collections, prominently featuring the compositions and arrangements of Pentecostal musicians like Cyril McClellan, Hope Collins, and Ralph Carmichael of the AG and Delton Alford of the CG.

Another development was the rise of chorus singing. Fresh, new melodies and texts combined with a simple compositional form to provide an ideal vehicle for corporate and personal praise and worship through music. This development was to blossom a decade or more later and be expressed in the exuberant Scripture and praise songs of the charismatic movement.

C. Music Education. Of great significance to the music explosion occurring in the Pentecostal-charismatic movement during the 1960s and 1970s was the contribution of colleges and Bible schools of the traditional Pentecostal denominations. While the singing school, church music school, and Bible school had always exerted influence in music training, these two decades witnessed an intensified impact of education on music, particularly in institutions of higher learning. These schools were now training not only singers and instrumentalists, but also ministers of music, choral and band directors, and arrangers and composers. Evangel College, Central Bible College, and Southern California College (AG), Lee College (CG), Emmanuel College (PHC), and L.I.F.E. Bible College (ICFG) increased efforts to educate Christian men and women for greater effectiveness through music ministry.

This trend has since grown and enlarged in scope, and today's Pentecostal music and musicians still reflect this influence.

III. Expansion and New Directions. Beginning in the mid-1960s there has been rapid growth and development of music as the Pentecostal-charismatic revival has grown to worldwide proportions. The U.S. has also witnessed, with the appearance of large mega-churches, huge and sophisticated music programs and the opportunity for unprecedented acceptance by the non-Pentecostal Christian community. Pentecostal churches are no longer only on "the other side of the tracks," and their influence is mounting. The dynamic growth and tension produced by the historical Pentecostal-charismatic continuum has exerted considerable influence on Pentecostal-charismatic music.

A. Contemporary Christian Music. Pentecostal musicians have always considered themselves to be contemporary—that is, worshiping through music styles created in their own particular era. In each decade of this century, the music was certainly reflective of contemporary styles: gospel singing, piano styles reminiscent of jazz, popular singing of the quartets, and so on. However, from the mid-fifties to the late sixties, young people in particular became increasingly restless because what they were hearing in church had little in common with the music they were listening to elsewhere.

Ralph Carmichael, one of the first to notice and respond to this point of alienation between youth and the church, was a popular and talented composer-arranger with roots in the AG. Through his music he attempted to build a bridge between the generations and introduced new styles of music together with "new" instruments like drum sets, electric guitars, electric keyboards, and sophisticated electronic sound systems. Herein lies the birth of what is called today contemporary christian music (CCM). CCM has had far-reaching effects on the entire Christian church, not without stirring controversy and arousing resistance.

The late sixties ushered in a time (much like the early Pentecostal revival) where music was taken out of the church and shared with the world beyond through street services, outdoor concerts, coffee house performances, and the like. There was an attempt to take the message of Jesus anywhere people would listen. Christian bands, vocal groups, soloists, and recording artists came into prominence; many of the writers, arrangers,

and star performers were Pentecostal-charismatic in background.

Traditions, beliefs, musical tastes, and demographics have all led to the highly pluralistic music ministry found in the Pentecostal-charismatic movement today, so much so that an acceptance of "new" and innovative approaches has virtually become the norm.

A few of the major CCM influences important to an understanding of the state of music in the Pentecostal-charismatic movement of the 1980s include: (1) youth musicals and religious folk music, early 1960s; (2) music of the "Jesus Movement," late '60s, early '70s; (3) folk, gospel, and popular artists of the '50s–'70s; (4) crossover music and middle-of-the-road, easy-listening music, late '70s and '80s; (5) emergence of Christian "rock music," late '70s and '80s; and (6) popularity of singing choruses and Scripture songs, '60s–'80s.

Prominent songwriters, some of whom are Pentecostal, making noteworthy contributions during this time include Bill and Gloria Gaither, Andrae Crouch (CGC), Lanny Wolfe (UPC), David Binion (CG), and Jack Hayford (ICFG). Artists and groups, many of whom come from the Pentecostal-charismatic tradition, who are making or have made impact on CCM include George Beverly Shea, the Cathedrals, Evie Tornquist, Sandi Patti, Amy Grant, the Bill Gaither Trio, Phil Driscoll, Mylon LeFevre, Petra, Steve Taylor, Walter Hawkins, and the Imperials.

B. The Charismatic Renewal. The charismatic renewal of the mid-twentieth century—that outpouring of the Holy Spirit on believers in traditional denominational and independent churches—has brought about a revival of emphasis on praise and worship in American religious life. Freedom in worship, joyful singing, both vocal and physical expressions of praise, instrumental accompaniment of singing, and acceptance of a wide variety of music styles are all characteristic of this renewal.

As in the early days of the Pentecostal revival, it is not unusual to find charismatic worshipers singing, shouting, clapping hands, leaping, and even dancing before the Lord as they offer him sincere praise and thanksgiving. Yet among some classical Pentecostals there is discomfort with the freshness and exuberance found in the music of the charismatics. Concern is expressed about dancing, marching, chanting, and frequent clapping of hands; however, there are those who remember when it was usual and expected to find traditional Pentecostal believers also dancing before the Lord, happily participating in "Jericho marches" and "singing in the Spirit."

Music contributions of note relating to the charismatic renewal include: (1) the importance of singing psalms and Scripture songs; (2) heavy use of music for praise and worship, not only in the sanctuary but also in conferences, festivals, small groups, home churches, and in private; (3) use of musical instruments, both formally and informally; (4) a return to emphasis on spirited congregational singing featuring praise leaders rather than choirs; (5) use of spontaneous and choreographed dance and pageantry; (6) use of drama, mime, and hand-signing; and (7) emphasis on the prophetic role of the musician.

IV. Coming of Age. The first century of music in the Pentecostal-charismatic movement has culminated in the development of a strong biblically based, experientially oriented ministry that draws from many traditions and styles. Pentecostal-charismatic music can be said to have come of age through the development of music traditions by classical Pentecostals, the charismatic infusion of new perspectives, and the response to the popularity and acceptance of contemporary Christian music. It is not only thriving and surviving but also exerting influence on music ministry ideals of other traditions. This maturity can be seen in several particular areas of influence.

A. Organization of Music Ministry. Churches and denominations within the Pentecostal-charismatic movement have begun to develop and organize music ministries of substance with programs that effectively use music in worship, evangelism, education, and Christian growth. The liturgy of the Pentecostal-charismatic worship service itself has developed more meaningfully. Larger churches have begun to develop impressive, sophisticated music ministries with graded choral programs, instrumental and orchestral programs, music schools and academies of the arts, production of musicals, cantatas, and pageants featuring music.

Some denominations have also begun to sponsor general programs and departments of music (e.g., CG, AG, CGP) to meet effectively the growing needs of music ministry.

B. Music Education. Church music schools, conferences, seminars, and festivals are constantly being developed in all corners of the Pentecostal-charismatic movement to provide avenues for effective training. Denominational institutions of higher learning have been joined by independent schools within the tradition in producing music degree programs for the development of performers, composer-arrangers, music ministers, and professionals who are competent musically yet sensitive to Pentecostal-charismatic distinctives. Institutions of notable achievement include Evangel College and Central Bible College (AG), Lee College (CG), Emmanuel College (PHC), and Oral Roberts University (independent).

Denominational and independent publishers have contributed to the impact of education by providing music resources. Music publishers of influence include Pathway Music (CG), Melody Music (AG), Hosanna-Integrity Music (independent) and Lexicon-Light Music (independent).

C. Music and Media. Opportunities for music outreach through media ministries are abundant. Pentecostal-charismatic churches have used music as a part of their media ministries. Formats have changed and expanded in relation to the technology of the time.

Radio broadcasting has long been a popular endeavor for Pentecostal-charismatic ministers and churches. The format and quality of the broadcast often depends on the type of church or ministry it represents. Practically all Pentecostal denominations have been or are involved in radio broadcasting. The list of individual or church-related radio broadcasts is virtually endless, and coverages vary from local stations to powerful regional stations, to world-wide efforts via networks and satellites.

When television replaced radio as the most influential medium of communication during the mid-twentieth century, Evangelicals and later Pentecostal-charismatics seized the opportunity to speak directly to the public. By the 1970s, Pentecostal-charismatic preaching and music were reaching across America and around the world. The decades of the 1960s–1980s have prominently featured independent television ministries, including prominent figures in the Pentecostal-charismatic movement, e.g., Oral Roberts, Jim Bakker (PTL), Pat Robertson (700 Club), Jimmy Swaggart, and Kenneth Copeland.

While the denominations as such have not enjoyed equal success in their television efforts, there is a growing trend for individual congregations to produce television outreach locally and regionally. The advent of nationwide cable systems featuring religious programming almost exclusively, together with satellite broadcasting and link-up capabilities for international outreach, have rendered the possibility of global impact through television broadcasting. Music is a vital ingredient in all these efforts.

D. Toward the Future. While the past produced challenge, success, adversity, and triumph, and the present signals maturity and stability of impressive dimensions, the future holds the greatest possibilities for music ministry.

The time has come for development of a total music ministry that will serve the spiritual, emotional, aesthetic, and educational needs of the Pentecostal-charismatic movement. Such a ministry concept will recognize contributions of the past while encouraging acceptance of new ideas and efforts. It will emphasize education and training in music both in preparation and performance and provide organized programs denominationally and locally. Finally, it will always recognize and promote excellent and proficient performance of religious music without lessening the importance of the spiritual dimension that must accompany music offered in praise and service to God.

Bibliography: D. L. Alford, *Music in the Pentecostal Church* (1967); R. Allen and G. Borror, *Worship: Rediscovering the Missing Jewel* (1982); A. E. Bailey, *The Gospel in Hymns* (1950); L. S. Blackwell, *Wings of the Dove: The Story of Gospel Music in America* (1978); C. Brumback, *What Meaneth This?* (1947); J. Burt and D. Allen, *History of Gospel Music* (1971); G. Chase, *America's Music* (1955); C. W. Conn, *Like a Mighty Army* (1977); D. P. Ellsworth, *Christian Music in Contemporary Witness* (1979); C. L. Etheringston, *Protestant Worship Music* (1962); D. J. Grout, *A History of Western Music* (1960); W. J. Hollenweger, *The Pentecostals* (1972); L. Hooper, *Church Music in Transition* (1963); A. Z. Idelsohn, *Jewish Music* (1967); G. P. Jackson, *The Story of the Sacred Harp* (1944); P. Kerr, *Music in Evangelism* (1952); C. B. Knight, ed., *Pentecostal Worship* (1974); E. S. Lorenz, *Church Music: What a Minister Should Know About It* (1923); A. C. Lovelace and W. C. Rice, *Music and Worship in the Church* (rev. ed., 1976); J. T. Nichol, *Pentecostalism* (1966); K. W. Osbeck, *The Ministry of Music* (1961);

Headquarters of the Pentecostal Assemblies of Canada, Toronto.

G. Reese, *Music in the Middle Ages* (1940); W. J. Reynolds, *A Survey of Christian Hymnody* (1963); P. Scholes, ed., *Oxford Companion to Music* (1950); R. M. Stevenson, *Patterns of Protestant Church Music* (1953); E. L. Thomas, *Music in Christian Education* (1953); P. L. Walker, *The Ministry of Church and Pastor* (1965); F. L. Whittlesey, *A Comprehensive Program of Church Music* (1957).   D. L. Alford

PENTECOSTAL ASSEMBLIES OF CAN-ADA (PAOC). Part of the fastest-growing religious grouping in the country. The Pentecostal Assemblies of Canada's history has been characterized both by vision leading to aggressive evangelistic outreach and by stability. This becomes obvious as one traces the denomination through three periods.

I. Beginnings (1906–25). Within months of the outpouring of the Spirit at Azusa Street in Los Angeles, Pentecostalism had taken root in Canada. By 1910 it had spread to both coasts, with comparatively large concentrations in Toronto and Winnipeg. When comparisons are made to respective populations, in the early decades of the century the Prairie provinces had the largest proportions of Pentecostals. Not coincidentally these provinces also had the largest proportions of American immigrants. It has often been observed that throughout the history of the country Canadian sectarianism has been fundamentally American in nature, and in no case has this been more true than for PAOC. Alongside American brethren, Canadian Pentecostals had dynamic Christian experiences focusing simultaneously on Christ and the Holy Spirit.

The first attempt to create an organization among Canadian Pentecostals occurred in the East in 1909. It collapsed in the face of intense opposition. Nine years later it was decided to form the PAOC and then to join the Pentecostal Assemblies of the World (PAOW), an American body. The PAOC received its charter on May 17, 1919, but the PAOW was never contacted.

In 1919 Pentecostals in Saskatchewan and Alberta, as yet unattached officially to the PAOC, joined the Assemblies of God (AG) (U.S.). J. W. Welch, general superintendent of the AG, was present at the conference at which this decision was made, and another American, Hugh Cadwalder, was elected district superintendent.

One year later the PAOC itself decided to join the AG. This was particularly significant, for the PAOC had been "Jesus Only" when it received its charter. By this decision it repudiated that stance. This act brought most Canadian Pentecostals into membership with the AG (some even held ministerial credentials with both the American and the Canadian group, the PAOC continuing to exist as a separate entity). It also united most Canadian Pentecostals, because as a part of the action, those from the West had joined the PAOC. It also precipitated the first major split in Canadian Pentecostalism.

One of the group's charter members, Frank Small from Winnipeg, regarded the move away from the Jesus Only position as an unwarranted compromise. After having been dropped from the ranks of the PAOC, Small founded the Apostolic Church of Pentecost in 1921. Again, numbering among its charter members were prominent American Oneness Pentecostals.

The organizational relationship between the AG and the PAOC persisted until 1925, when the PAOC asked to be released from the AG, primarily because of differences over missionary policy. The request was granted, leading to an amiable parting.

These organizational discussions were closed to all except leaders. While they were going on, the PAOC was continuing to experience growth. In 1920 it established a national paper, *The Pentecostal Testimony*, and it articulated a centralized missionary policy to facilitate the overseas evangelism that had already been carried on by Canadian Pentecostals for twelve years. During this period the PAOC had been able to find strong leadership. Some, like G. A. Chambers, A. G. Ward, R. L. Dutaud, J. C. Ball, and F. M. Bellsmith, came from other denominations, while others, for example, A. H. Argue and C. E. Baker, left business to assume prominent positions. The contribution made by these people cannot be overestimated. First and foremost, it was their religious experiences, their understanding of Scripture, and their life experience that defined the nature of the emerging movement. They gave it their priorities and formulated its doctrine. They also exemplified its view of spirituality. In

The historic Calvary Temple, Winnipeg, Manitoba, is a member of the PAOC.

these areas, there has been little change since 1920. In short, they established the ideological framework in which the PAOC and its members would grow and develop.

In spite of strong American roots, the PAOC achieved an autonomous Canadian identity. It also made significant strides in defining itself doctrinally. By 1925 it had clearly made a place for itself among Canadian religious groups.

II. Consolidation (1926–51). The year 1925 was an important date for the PAOC. The next twenty-five years saw it consolidate and enlarge its position. Leadership at the beginning of the period was provided by the same men who had been involved in the creation of the group. However, in 1925 several men who had active ministries within other denominations came into the PAOC. Three were Presbyterians, one a Methodist, and one an Anglican. All were in the West, one in Saskatchewan and the others in Manitoba. They contributed significantly to the shape the PAOC acquired.

The concern that had dominated Canadian Pentecostalism from its beginning—the evangelization of the lost—continued to preoccupy it. *The Pentecostal Testimony* carried articles stressing the importance of evangelism. By December 1951 it had also carried more than 150 reports of evangelistic meetings. These reports were careful to give statistics regarding the number of people who had been converted, healed, or baptized in the Holy Spirit. This was vital information, serving both as an encouragement and as a stimulus. Large evangelistic campaigns carried on by prominent personalities were also a feature. Aimee Semple McPherson, Charles Price, Harvey McAlister, and Lorne Fox were active across the country. The same burden for the lost motivated international missionary service. By 1927 Canadian Pentecostals were supporting missionaries on five fields. The fundamental concerns of the PAOC remained intact, but around them changes were occurring.

The denomination was growing numerically, and hand in hand with that went economical growth. Pentecostals were acquiring the financial resources vital to carrying out its ministry. This is made apparent in a somewhat crude comparison of denominational receipts. In a twelve-month period in 1927 to 1928, it received $71,000, but from January to September 1952, it took in $530,000. Through its national periodical the PAOC began to offer advice to its members with regard to financial planning. Examples of this were the annuity bonds and wills that were mentioned for the first time in 1928.

More money also meant better and larger facilities. In 1927 the church in Kitchener, Ontario, erected a building that seated 800, and one year later Calvary Temple in Winnipeg bought

An early convention of the PAOC in Kitchener, Ontario.

the First Baptist Church, which accommodated 1,500 people. Increasing growth was obvious.

During this same period the PAOC also became active in theological education. The motivation throughout was to prepare people, both men and women, for ministry. The first efforts were concentrated on short-term schools. In 1925 it opened Canadian Pentecostal Bible College in Winnipeg, placing the leadership in the hands of J. Eustace Purdie, an Anglican minister who had recently been baptized in the Holy Spirit. Purdie held this post until his retirement in 1950. Through the school he trained a generation of leaders for the denomination.

The development of an organization also increased. This, too, came about in the pursuit of basic objectives. In 1935 General Secretary A. G. Ward wrote:

I feel we must not fail to recognize that as a movement grows numerically and new departments are opened up, of necessity it must be carried on in the most efficient business-like way. We have certainly outgrown some of our former policies and methods of conducting affairs, and now we must either make the necessary changes and improvements or be forced into retrogression.

In this spirit Pentecostals turned their hands to creating a structure. In the 1920s district conferences and attending organizations began to appear, and in the 1930s and 1940s national departments were added. Along with many others, the prominent figure involved in this process was D. N. Buntain. Basic priorities—evangelism and the ministry of the Holy Spirit—were retained. However, important and far-reaching changes were taking place in the PAOC, and not everyone was comfortable with what he or she saw.

In the 1940s *The Pentecostal Testimony* began to carry articles with titles like "The Love of Many Waxen Cold," "Is Pentecost Doomed to Defeat?" and "Is Pentecost Passing?" G. A. Chambers, the denomination's first general superintendent, said, "We have not only turned aside, but have stepped down to the level of other religious bodies who long ago lost the anointing. . . ." The PAOC was experiencing something of a crisis of identity. In the light of this it is not surprising that the PAOC was wracked by another major split that occurred in 1947–48. One of its leaders, George Hawtin, said:

The Great Pentecostal revival of the twentieth century was no sooner under way than we like all our predecessors, began to divide ourselves up into denominational groups. We like all others before us set up our fences, and made our statement as to what we believed, making it impossible to go on to the next glory and the next revelation of truth.

This new movement began in Saskatchewan and was known as "The Latter Rain" or "The

James MacKnight, general superintendent of the Pentecostal Assemblies of Canada, conducting business at the 36th Biennial General Conference, August 1984.

Sharon Movement." It placed particular emphasis on the gifts of the Spirit and on fasting, and it developed its own missionary arm called Global Outreach. Faced with this challenge, up to 50 percent of the PAOC churches in Saskatchewan and smaller proportions elsewhere in western Canada left the denomination and "went Latter Rain."

From 1925 to 1951 the PAOC experienced significant growth and developed a strong infrastructure. It also experienced a tension within itself that led to the defection of a significant number of people and churches primarily in the West. In spite of this, it emerged from the period with a high level of vigor and a clear sense of itself and its mission.

III. Growth (1952–87). Having passed through a particularly turbulent period, the PAOC moved into three decades of strong growth. The most important concern in the collective mind of the denomination continued to be evangelism, but at the same time the PAOC took its place among the other Canadian denominations. Several features make this obvious.

Economically, the PAOC continued to experience significant gains. In the 1950s this led to some attempt to rationalize and to understand the implications. In that decade *The Pentecostal Testimony* carried articles that promoted private enterprise and investment and that showed how money could be used to further denominational objectives. Two decades later a national stewardship department was created in order to provide investment counsel and estate planning.

The stronger financial base also provided the resources necessary for aggressive building programs. Mentioning only three, Central Tabernacle in Edmonton was built in 1972 with a seating capacity of 2,000; Winnipeg's Calvary Temple, capable of accommodating 2,500, was completed in 1974; and Queensway Cathedral in Toronto, seating 4,500, was dedicated in 1985. The last

cost $4.5 million to build. The rash of building programs in the last decade precipitated a mild centralizing tendency. High mortgage interest rates in 1981 and 1982 helped create national guidelines that are designed to preclude congregations from undertaking building projects that would jeopardize them financially.

A second feature marking increasing maturity within the PAOC is a developing social awareness. Some members of the denomination have held public office. One, Sam Jenkins, served as president of the Marine Workers and Boilermakers Union of the Canadian Coalition of Laborers. Another, Everett Wood, held a seat for the socialist New Democratic Party in the legislative assembly of the province of Saskatchewan for sixteen years. For most of that time he was a member of the cabinet. Others have represented right of center political parties.

Philanthropy has also been a prominent part of PAOC ministry. This has been expressed through a home for girls, a major regional hospital, and numerous senior citizens' residences. The first of these residences appeared in 1942, but as the denomination ages, they are becoming common in connection with major churches. A number of PAOC churches was also active in the late 1970s in the relocation of Vietnamese refugees. Local committees found accommodations; provided food, clothing, and furniture; and arranged language training and employment for the refugees.

The denomination has also become acutely aware of moral and ethical issues in Canada. In 1982 it funded an ethics and social concerns committee. This committee has been very active, creating an interchurch committee to deal with pornography; articulating positions on prayer in schools and abortion; and attempting to mobilize denominational members to express opinions locally, provincially, and nationally.

Educationally, the PAOC has undergone significant changes. With the rest of the population of Canada, general educational levels have risen steadily within the denomination. There are an increasing number of university graduates and professionals within its membership. Theological colleges (the PAOC operates six, four in English and two in French) have been part of the same trend. One is affiliated with a major university and holds an association with a Lutheran seminary through which it offers a master of divinity degree. Another is accredited with the American Association of Bible Colleges, and yet another has candidate status. All four English colleges grant bachelor degrees.

In the midst of economic, social, and educational developments, the PAOC has retained its intense interest in evangelism. During the 1950s it began to experience some difficulties with large campaigns that led to a refocusing of energy. A number of programs were created among youth. Ambassadors in Missions and Team Canada have both conducted direct evangelism on streets and in parks in connection with major events such as the 1976 Olympics in Montreal and Expo '86 in Vancouver. Meanwhile the denomination developed national programs such as Canada for Christ, which organized crusades for widely recognized evangelists, and Pentecostal Assemblies Church Expansion, which attempted to teach church growth principles. In 1976 these and other programs were amalgamated and are now known as the Department of National Spiritual Life and Evangelism.

There is currently great emphasis being placed on church planting. At the 1984 general conference, General Superintendent James MacKnight set before the denomination a goal of 75 new churches in two years. By the 1986 conference 102 churches had been established. MacKnight's ten-year goal for 1994 is 400 new assemblies.

Again under MacKnight's leadership, the PAOC held a major policy and planning conference in 1987—the Congress on Pentecostal Leadership. The theme was "On Track" and the goal was to move toward the twenty-first century with a well-coordinated thrust.

The constant feature of the PAOC's experience, especially since 1952, has been change. Conditions in its sociohistorical context and forces within itself have prompted growth and development. While immersed in this, leaders and people alike have continued to hold to well-established priorities.

No religious group is static, but the PAOC has evidenced a particularly high energy level. This has meant that the denomination has had a bumpy history. It has been characterized by pragmatism and "entrepreneurial" innovation as it has striven to fulfill its mandate. It may settle into a homogeneous denominational form, but at this point its ideals of openness to the Spirit and evangelism are propelling it into the future.

Bibliography: G. F. Atter, *The Third Force* (1970); G. G. Kulbeck, *What God Hath Wrought* (1958); E. A. Peters, *The Contribution to Education by the Pentecostal Assemblies of Canada* (1970).   R. A. N. Kydd

PENTECOSTAL ASSEMBLIES OF JESUS CHRIST   Formed in 1931 as an attempt to

return to the original interracial fellowship that marked Oneness Pentecostalism. At the initial stages of Pentecostal organization all Oneness Pentecostals were affiliated with the multiracial Pentecostal Assemblies of the World (PAW). In 1924 many white constituents, citing increased effectiveness in world evangelism, withdrew to form the Pentecostal Church, Incorporated.

The remaining membership of the PAW then affiliated with the Apostolic Church of Jesus Christ in 1931, forming the Pentecostal Assemblies of Jesus Christ (PAJC) in an ill-fated attempt to restore interracial harmony. Within weeks, black followers of Bishop Samuel Grimes met in Dayton, Ohio, to decide to continue the PAW under the old charter. Following a decision to hold the 1937 conference in Tulsa, Oklahoma (a city with segregated facilities), most of the blacks who had remained in the Pentecostal Assemblies of Jesus Christ returned to the PAW. In 1945, since there was virtually no doctrinal difference and great congruity in constituency, the PAJC merged with the Pentecostal Church, Incorporated, to form the United Pentecostal church, which is the largest of the Oneness Pentecostal bodies.

See also ONENESS PENTECOSTALISM; UNITED PENTECOSTAL CHURCH, INTERNATIONAL.

Bibliography: J. Gordon Melton, ed., *The Encyclopedia of American Religions*, vol. 1 (1978); J. T. Nichol, *Pentecostalism* (1966).   B. M. Stout

PENTECOSTAL ASSEMBLIES OF NEWFOUNDLAND   (PAN). The expansion of Pentecostalism to Newfoundland and Labrador is traced to the ministry of Alice Belle Garrigus, a Pentecostal evangelist from Boston, Massachusetts. She opened the Bethesda Mission (later Bethesda Pentecostal Church) in St. John's, Newfoundland, on Easter Sunday, 1911. As the Pentecostal revival spread, more converts were gained and churches were established. By 1925 the numbers had increased sufficiently to gain legal recognition from the provincial government. For the next five years it was known as the Bethesda Pentecostal Assemblies, becoming the Pentecostal Assemblies of Newfoundland in 1930. Using a coastal vessel, *The Gospel Messenger*, PAN began its ministry outreach to Labrador two years later.

Since Newfoundland and Labrador constituted a separate dominion from Canada in the British Commonwealth until 1949, PAN developed independently of the Pentecostal Assemblies of Canada. Nevertheless, they share a common statement of faith and work closely in overseas missions and in the governance of Eastern Pentecostal Bible College in Peterborough, Ontario. A unique distinctive of PAN is the large school system which it sponsors, maintaining both elementary and high schools. Roy D. King currently serves as the general superintendent.

The national census (1981) reported 162 churches in PAN and 37,450 members.

Bibliography: B. K. Janes, *The Lady Who Came* (1982); idem, *The Lady Who Stayed* (1982); C. E. Jones, *A Guide to the Study of the Pentecostal Movement* (1983);

The ministerial certificate of R. B. Chisolm, given by the Pentecostal Assemblies of the World in 1922, and signed by G. T. Haywood. Chisolm founded a Christian school in Mississippi.

R. D. King, ed., *Good Tidings* (1935–); A. C. Piepkorn, *Profiles in Belief*, 3 vols. (1979).　　J. A. Hewett

PENTECOSTAL ASSEMBLIES OF THE WORLD One of the oldest interracial Oneness Pentecostal organizations. A product of the Azusa Street revival, it held its first recorded meeting in 1907 in Los Angeles. J. J. Frazee from Portland, Oregon, the first secretary, was general secretary from 1912 to 1916. G. T. Haywood, prominent black Oneness leader from Indianapolis, held credentials since 1911. In 1918 he assisted in a merger with the one-year-old General Assembly of Apostolic Assemblies, a group formed by the original dissidents ousted by the AG in 1916 and who were seeking an organization that could provide protection from military duty.

Following incorporation in 1919, the number of blacks increased dramatically in the North with Haywood's influence. Although the PAW was fully integrated, racial tension with the southern white members finally led to a schism in 1924. The Pentecostal Assemblies of the World (PAW) reorganized with episcopal government, electing Haywood as first presiding bishop, a position he held until his death in 1931.

The whites splintered into two groups. An unstable merger between the PAW and one group, the Apostolic Church of Jesus Christ, was accomplished in 1931, creating the Pentecostal Church of Jesus Christ. Due to the church's changing its name and abandoning the episcopal form of government, A. W. Lewis, a white, led a move to reconstitute the PAW. Within months it reemerged under the leadership of a black leader,

Samuel Grimes. The interracial experiment of the Pentecostal Assemblies of Jesus Christ collapsed in 1937, and most black members returned to the PAW.

Predominantly black, the organization is conscientiously integrated at every level. It has suffered only one schism since 1931. This occurred under the leadership of one of its bishops, S. N. Hancock, in 1957, the result of a power struggle.

The PAW adheres strictly to the Oneness "new birth" teaching of Haywood, practices footwashing and advocates the use of wine in Communion, and permits divorce and remarriage in the case of adultery or separation by an unsaved partner. Headquarters are in Indianapolis. In 1987 its Annual Convention reported a worldwide membership of 500,000 in 1,400 U.S. and 1,400 foreign churches. It is represented in every state, Africa, Asia, Europe, and West Indies.

See also ONENESS PENTECOSTALISM; UNITED PENTECOSTAL CHURCH, INTERNATIONAL.

Bibliography: M. Golder, *History of the Pentecostal Assemblies of the World* (1973); D. Reed, "Origins and Development of the Theology of Oneness Pentecostalism in the United States," Ph.D. diss., Boston University, 1978.   D. A. Reed

PENTECOSTAL CHURCH, INCORPORATED

The all-white Pentecostal Ministerial Alliance was organized at St. Louis, Missouri, November 3, 1925, in the wake of the breakup of the biracial Pentecostal Assemblies of the World. Race, not doctrine, was the issue. The 1926–27 roll contained 222 names. Although membership was restricted to clergy, fellowship soon developed among churches served by members. In 1932 adoption of a new name: The Pentecostal Church, Incorporated, and of a plan for district and local church government, established a milestone on the road to denominational order. That destination was reached at St. Louis thirteen years later when the Pentecostal Church, Incorporated, claimed 175 congregations and 810 ministers.

See also UNITED PENTECOSTAL CHURCH, INTERNATIONAL.

Bibliography: A. L. Clanton, *United We Stand* (1970).   C. E. Jones

PENTECOSTAL CHURCH OF CHRIST

See INTERNATIONAL PENTECOSTAL CHURCH OF CHRIST.

PENTECOSTAL CHURCH OF GOD

(PCG). A baptistic Pentecostal organization with headquarters in Joplin, Missouri, that probably owes its existence to the fact that the General Council of the Assemblies of God (AG) adopted a statement of faith in 1916. A group of Pentecostals who shared beliefs similar to those of the AG but were fearful of any type of rigid statement met in December 1919 under the leadership of former AG executive presbyter, John C. Sinclair, and formed the Pentecostal Assemblies of the U.S.A.

Other ministers who were at one time associated with the AG included A. D. and Violet McClure, Eugene N. Hastie, C. A. McKinney, Cyrus B. Fockler, Will C. Trotter, and later, Frank Lindblad. Another minister, William E. Kirschke, served as national youth leader with the Pentecostal Young People's Association from 1937 to 1939 and later was a prominent Sunday school leader in the AG.

Sinclair came to the U.S. from Scotland when he was a youth. He was associated with the Holiness movement before receiving the baptism in the Holy Spirit while pastoring a church in Chicago. Elmer Moon, in *The Pentecostal Church* (p. 138), states that it was reported that Sinclair was the first to receive the Pentecostal experience in Chicago.

A layman, George C. Brinkman, became the first secretary of the PCG and donated his paper, *The Pentecostal Herald,* to the new organization.

A name change, from the Pentecostal Assemblies of the U.S.A. to the Pentecostal Church of God, was effected in 1922 when the church went through a financial and leadership struggle. A second name change came in 1934 when the group added "of America" to distinguish it from a local church in Kansas City. The PCG offices and publishing interests were in Chicago until 1927 when they were moved to Ottumwa, Iowa. From Iowa the group moved to Kansas City in 1934 and then to the present headquarters in Joplin, Missouri, in 1951.

The PCG doctrinal statement, an instrument that the founding fathers were careful not to include in 1919, was deemed essential by 1933. It is similar to the AG statement and other Pentecostal Baptistic statements.

The PCG's greatest period of growth came during the 1940s when the number of churches and ministers doubled. During the late 1940s, however, the Northwest District was decimated by the New Order of the Latter Rain. Most of the churches and the district superintendent joined the new movement. By 1955 that district gained new churches and members to offset the loss to the Latter Rain.

Although work among the American Indian tribes has been strong for many years, foreign mission efforts had been somewhat neglected until recent years. This can be seen by the fact that it was not until 1949 that the church saw the need for a full-time foreign missions administrator and a board of directors—even though the world missions department was established in 1932. By 1986 PCG missions had established nine hundred churches and ten Bible schools in more than twenty countries.

Local churches, which practice the congregational form of government, are located in forty-two states. The U.S. is divided into thirty-three districts. The 1984 annual report showed a total of 1,138 U.S. churches, 3,008 ministers, and a constituency of 93,338.

The PCG owns and operates the Messenger Publishing House in Joplin, which publishes the *Pentecostal Messenger,* the official periodical since 1927. Other departments are Christian Education, Pentecostal Young Peoples Association (PYPA), Pentecostal Ladies Auxiliary, King's Men Fellowship, and Senior Christian Fellowship. In 1986 the PCG had seven military chaplains on active duty.

The PCG's first Bible school was Pentecostal Bible Institute, founded in 1946, in Gilroy,

This new international headquarters building for the Pentecostal Church of God in Joplin, Missouri, was occupied in 1987. The denomination was formed in 1919.

California. It is now Evangelical Christian College and is located in Fresno. Southern Bible College was opened in 1958 in Houston; it was moved to Joplin, Missouri, in 1987 and renamed Messenger College. A third school, the School of Bible Theology and Christian Dynamics, was founded in San Jacinto, California, in 1978.

The general superintendent to serve the longest (1953–75) was R. Dennis Heard. He was born in Arkansas but moved with his family to California, where he became involved with the PCG. He was a pastor, district official, and active in PYPA leadership. Heard led the PCG into the National Association of Evangelicals, the Pentecostal Fellowship of North America, and the Pentecostal World Congress. Roy M. Chappell followed Heard as superintendent.

Bibliography: "Facts of Interest about the PCG" (1985); C. Jones, *Guide to the Pentecostal Movement* (1983); K. Kendrick, *The Promise Fulfilled* (1961); E. Moon, *The Pentecostal Church* (1966); "PCG General Constitution and Bylaws" (1984); "Presenting the PCG World Ministries" (n.d.). **W. E. Warner**

PENTECOSTAL CHURCH OF GOD IN PUERTO RICO See IGLESIA DE DIOS PENTECOSTAL DE PUERTO RICO.

PENTECOSTAL CHURCHES OF THE APOSTOLIC FAITH ASSOCIATION A predominantly black Oneness group of churches and ministers organized in 1957 by Bishop S. N. Hancock and others following a split with the Pentecostal Assemblies of the World. In 1987 the group reported 400 ministers, 125 churches, and approximately 50,000 adherents. Headquarters are in Louisville, Kentucky.

Bibliography: D. R. Bell, *The Pentecostal Churches of the Apostolic Faith* (1982); J. Collins, Jr., *With Water and Spirit* (1980). **W. E. Warner**

PENTECOSTAL COALITION FOR HUMAN RIGHTS (PCHR). An advocacy and support organization for racial and sexual minorities within Pentecostal churches, with a strong emphasis on homosexual rights.

Formed in 1981 by Dr. James S. Tinney, a minister in the Church of God in Christ (CGIC), its founding signaled a growing social consciousness among a younger generation of Pentecostals. From the beginning, PCHR had a largely black following; its novelty was its devotion to liberation movements of all types, especially homosexual rights.

PCHR sought to secure these rights not only in the civil arena but also by pressing Pentecostal churches to acknowledge confessed homosexuals as full participants in the body of Christ. This latter crusade caused PCHR to be identified almost exclusively with the gay rights issue and the political activism of its founder, James S. Tinney, a Howard University professor and historian of black Pentecostalism.

Chapters were organized in Washington, D.C.; Portland, Oregon; and Los Angeles; with regional representatives in four other cities.

Although gay caucuses existed in all major denominations, Pentecostal leaders saw PCHR as a foreboding development. A national magazine (*Logos Journal* [May–June 1981], 4) urged Tinney's excommunication, and CGIC dutifully responded. Seventeen PCHR protesters bearing signs and banners picketed Sunday services in front of Temple Church of God in Christ, the judiciary headquarters for Bishop Samuel Kelsey, who had expelled Tinney.

During its confrontational years, PCHR became the first group to picket a Pentecostal church, to stage demonstrations at Pentecostal conferences, to secure homosexual-oriented advertising on a gospel radio station (WYCB-AM), and to successfully challenge licensing and programming of radio and TV stations carrying anti-gay Pentecostal preaching.

In 1982 PCHR conducted the first "City-wide Lesbian and Gay Revival." Eventually the founding chapter developed into the organization of Faith Temple, an independent Pentecostal church in Washington, D.C., comprised mostly of black homosexuals.

More recently, PCHR has become less strident, functioning more in terms of counseling and education. More than fifty publications seek to reinterpret Scriptures thought to condemn homosexuality. PCHR also conducts dialogues with clergy groups around concerns such as pastoral counseling for homosexuals and ministry to persons with AIDS.

Racial integration of many Pentecostal churches and abandonment of radical political rhetoric by PCHR have narrowed its focus to homosexual issues. A national hotline is main-

In this 1964 picture former chairmen of the PFNA were presented with engraved gavels. They are, left to right and the years they served, James A. Cross (1962-63), Walter E. McAlister (1959-60), Gayle F. Lewis (1956-58), E. J. Fulton (1954-55), H. D. Mitzner standing in for Howard P. Courtney (1952-53), J. A. Synan (1950-51, 1964-65), and J. C. Jernigan (1948-49). The organization was founded in 1948.

tained for Pentecostals "experiencing a faith crisis over their homosexuality."

Bibliography: "Coalition to Press for Human Rights Among Pentecostals," Religious News Service (March 5, 1981); H. Hostetler, "Dealing With Immorality Among the Saints," *Logos Journal* (May–June 1981), 4; G. Sheppard, "James Tinney's PCHR Versus Jerry Falwell's Moral Majority," *Agora* 4 (1981): 18–20; D. Willingham, "Pentecostal Gay Rights?" *Church of God Evangel* (August 10, 1981), 4.   J. S. Tinney

PENTECOSTAL EUROPEAN CONFERENCES   See EUROPEAN PENTECOSTALISM.

PENTECOSTAL EVANGELICAL CHURCH   An association of churches and a ministerial fellowship. Organized by G. F. C. Fons in 1936 in Fort Smith, Arkansas, the fellowship in 1987 numbered approximately one hundred churches and 250 ministers. Prior to organizing the association, Fons had served as moderator of the Pentecostal Church of God (1934–35). The church's fifteen missionaries are in the Philippines, India, and Central America. Jack Hill serves as the general bishop. Headquarters for the association are in Bremerton, Washington, where *Gospel Tidings*, the official magazine, is published. The Pentecostal Evangelical Church is a member of the National Association of Evangelicals.

Bibliography: General By-laws of the Pentecostal Evangelical Church (1966).   W. E. Warner

PENTECOSTAL FELLOWSHIP OF NORTH AMERICA   (PFNA). A fellowship of

twenty-four Pentecostal groups that meets annually to promote fellowship and to demonstrate unity among Pentecostals.

I. History.   Ironically, it took the formation of the National Association of Evangelicals (NAE) in 1942 to bring Pentecostals together. Some Pentecostals had proposed unity meetings in the 1920s, but nothing of substance resulted. When Pentecostals got acquainted in NAE meetings, they began to think seriously about a fellowship among themselves. Then when the Pentecostal World Fellowship (PWC) was created in 1947 at Zurich, Switzerland, a challenge was thrown out to North American Pentecostals to work toward a cooperative fellowship.

The first visible sign of Pentecostal cooperation came on May 7, 1948, in Chicago, following the annual NAE meeting. Twenty-four leaders of eight Pentecostal groups met in an exploratory conference concerning unity. Nobody was interested in amalgamation of denominations, but it was determined that the groups would benefit in numerous foreign and domestic areas from a fellowship of Pentecostal organizations.

A second exploratory meeting in Chicago later that year attracted twenty-seven leaders from twelve denominations. Noel Perkin, secretary for the foreign missions department of the Assemblies of God (AG), told the group that the denominations represented did not have to create fellowship but had to recognize that it already existed. He also suggested the name Pentecostal Fellowship of North America.

An important part of the second meeting was the appointment of a committee to draw up articles of the fellowship. The four selected for the committee were J. Roswell Flower (AG), E. J. Fulton (Open Bible Standard Churches), Herman D. Mitzner (International Church of the Foursquare Gospel), and H. L. Chesser (Church of God, Cleveland, Tenn.). Their job was not particularly difficult, because they simply modified the NAE statement of faith with a Pentecostal paragraph and brought it back to the body.

The PFNA was organized at Des Moines, Iowa, October 26–28, 1948. One of the speakers was an evangelist who was then beginning to gain national attention, Oral Roberts.

II. Objectives. With the exceptions of an expansion of the first paragraph and the insertion of "endeavoring" in paragraph 4, the objectives of the PFNA adopted in 1948 have remained unchanged:

1. To provide a vehicle of expression and coordination of efforts in matters common to all member bodies, including missionary and evangelistic effort throughout the world.

2. To demonstrate to the world the essential unity of Spirit-baptized believers, fulfilling the prayer of the Lord Jesus "that they all may be one" (John 17:21).

3. To provide services to its constituents which will enable them to accomplish more quickly and efficiently their responsibility for the speedy evangelization of the world.

4. To encourage the principles of comity for the nurture of the body of Christ, endeavoring to keep the unity of the Spirit until we all come to the unity of the faith.

Although the PFNA is not a legislative body, it has through its history issued resolutions involving political, religious, or social actions. In 1951 a resolution was prepared protesting the Universal Military Training Program. Other resolutions included showing support for the charismatic movement (1965) and encouraging Pentecostal youth to consider public school teaching as a career (1964).

III. Structure. The PFNA operates with a board of administration with representation of member bodies. The board meets in the spring to plan fall meetings and to conduct other business relating to the fellowship and the PWC. Beginning with the organizational meeting in 1948, the annual meeting has been hosted by a number of American and Canadian cities.

For several years the PFNA encouraged local churches to establish chapters in key cities, but by 1966 only thirty-seven chapters were operating. One former official stated that a great deal of enthusiasm was shown in the early years as local chapters united churches for the purpose of sponsoring evangelistic meetings and other special events. But apparently local churches eventually preferred to remain independent of united efforts, much to the consternation of the denominational leaders. Eventually the local chapter idea died from a lack of interest.

Other committees that have functioned included those on youth, foreign missions, radio, and women's ministries. A quarterly, *PFNA News*, is printed for the organization by the AG.

IV. Doctrinal Statement and Membership. A Oneness leader, Howard A. Goss, represented the United Pentecostal Church at the second exploratory meeting in Chicago in 1948. His group, however, became ineligible for membership as soon as the doctrinal statement—with its Trinitarian paragraph—was adopted. The brief statement permits any Pentecostal group to belong as long as they are Trinitarian and otherwise orthodox.

On the eve of its fortieth anniversary the PFNA had not attracted a single black Pentecostal denomination. Groups such as the Church of God in Christ have been invited to join the PFNA, but they have chosen to remain outside.

V. The Future. The format of the 1986 annual meeting held in Oklahoma City was a departure from meetings of the past. Dwindling interest and attendance in recent years prompted PFNA participants to change the meetings from rally to leadership type and was open by invitation.

VI. PFNA Records. Having never established a permanent office or salaried employees, the PFNA records remained with whomever was secretary at the time. In 1982 the records were deposited in the AG Archives for safekeeping and to be made available to PFNA members and researchers.

See also PENTECOSTAL WORLD CONFERENCE.

Bibliography: Minutes, PFNA Board of Administration and Annual Meetings (1948–); W. Menzies, *Anointed to Serve* (1971); *PFNA News* (1960–).

          W. E. Warner

PENTECOSTAL FIRE-BAPTIZED HOLINESS CHURCH Formed in 1918 as a schism from the Pentecostal Holiness church, this is one of the smallest Pentecostal denominations in North America. Originally formed by those who wanted stricter standards, this denomination enforces the following standards: Women's dresses are to be at least mid-calf in length, and women are not allowed to cut their hair or wear jewelry. Men are not allowed to wear neckties. Swimming pools, theaters, and fairs are on the list of forbidden activities.

Doctrinally, the church stresses sanctification as a second definite work of grace, subsequent to regeneration. The baptism of the Holy Spirit, with the evidence of speaking in other tongues, is then after sanctification.

The church has a general convention that meets biennially. A campground and printing press are part of a headquarters complex located at Toccoa Falls, Georgia. With missions work in Mexico, the church has less than one thousand members in the U.S.

Bibliography: D. Wood and W. H. Preskitt, Jr., *Baptized with Fire: A History of the Pentecostal Fire-Baptized Church* (1983).   B. M. Stout

PENTECOSTAL FREE WILL BAPTIST CHURCH A large segment of the Free-Will Baptist Church that became Pentecostal in experience and doctrine. In 1855 a group of seven congregations in North Carolina who believed in freedom of the will and instantaneous sanctification formed the Camp Fear Conference of the Free Will Baptist Church. Later, in 1907, the Camp Fear Conference adopted Pentecostal views of the baptism of the Holy Spirit. So the Pentecostal Free-Will Baptist Church (PFWBC) was an existing conference that embraced Pentecostal doctrine and experience. As the work spread, additional conferences were formed: Wilmington in 1908, New River in 1911, and a South Carolina conference in 1912. These four united into a general conference in 1943.

The general conference organized under the name PFWBC in 1959. There were seven thousand members, 135 churches, and 180 ministers. Herbert Carter was elected general overseer. (The South Carolina Conference declined to organize with the North Carolina conferences and became the Free-Will Baptist Church of the Pentecostal Faith). In 1960 the organization established headquarters in Dunn, North Carolina, and initiated an official journal, *The Messenger*.

The PFWBC has now expanded into Virginia, Georgia, and Florida, and has missions in India, the Philippines, Mexico, Nicaragua, Venezuela, and Puerto Rico. In 1971 it established Heritage Bible College in Dunn. At the 1986 general conference the PFWBC reported 11,104 members and 228 ministers.

Bibliography: H. Carter, *History of the Pentecostal Free-Will Baptist Church* (1978); *Faith and Practices of the Pentecostal Free-Will Baptist Church* (1977).

C. W. Conn

PENTECOSTAL HOLINESS CHURCH

See INTERNATIONAL PENTECOSTAL HOLINESS CHURCH.

PENTECOSTAL HOLINESS CHURCH OF CANADA

The Pentecostal Holiness Church (PHC) was one of the first Pentecostal denominations to minister in the dominion of Canada. First organized as the Fire-Baptized Holiness Association by B. H. Irwin, the church had conventions in Ontario and Manitoba when the denomination was formed in Anderson, South Carolina, in 1898. Canadian "ruling elders" included Oliver Fluke of Ontario, and Albert E. Robinson in Manitoba.

Early congregations included the Evangelistic Centre in Toronto, founded by George Fisher in 1906, and the Apostolic Faith Mission congregation in Vancouver, British Columbia, begun by George S. Paul in 1907.

In 1926 the Ontario Conference of the PHC was organized in Toronto by E. D. Reeves. The high water mark for the denomination was reached in the 1930s when the Evangelistic Centre Church of Toronto, pastored by O. E. Sproull, was, for a time, the largest attended Pentecostal congregation in the nation.

The western portion of the church was begun in 1938 as the Pacific Coast Missionary Society, a group of churches with roots in the Apostolic Faith Mission of Portland, Oregon. In 1942 these churches merged with the Pentecostal Holiness Church.

For many years the PHC of Canada was listed as part of the American denomination. This was changed in 1971 when the PHC was legally chartered as a Canadian church. The first Canadian general superintendent was Bishop Harry Nunn. Today the Canadian PHC consists of thirty-six congregations in three conferences located in Ontario, Quebec, British Columbia, and Nova Scotia. The 1985 membership was three thousand.

Bibliography: V. Synan, *The Old-Time Power* (1973).

H. V. Synan

PENTECOSTAL MINISTERIAL ALLIANCE

See PENTECOSTAL CHURCH, INC.

PENTECOSTAL MISSION IN SOUTH AND CENTRAL AFRICA

(PMSCA). An early Pentecostal missions agency founded in 1910 by the executive council of the Bethel Pentecostal Assembly of Newark, New Jersey (often referred to as the "Bethel Board") "to maintain and conduct a general evangelistic work in the State of New Jersey, and in all other States of the United States and any and all foreign countries" (Beach and Fahs, 1925, 24). By 1925 PMSCA had a budget of $30,150 and supported missionaries in Liberia, the Republic of South Africa, Swaziland, Mozambique, Mexico, and Venezuela. A separate field council directed the activities in South Africa. The organization promoted its work by publishing the *South and Central African Pentecostal Herald* (1917); the publication was later renamed the *Full Gospel Missionary Herald* (1921). The executive council also directed the affairs of the Bethel Pentecostal Assembly and sponsored the Bethel Bible Training School (1916–29).

Members of the council included Minnie T. Draper, president and, for many years, an associate of A. B. Simpson in the Christian and Missionary Alliance; Joseph R. Potter; Mr. and Mrs. Lewis B. Heath; Mary S. Stone; (Mrs.) Eleanor B. Schoenborn; and Christian J. Lucas. Several members were wealthy and invested their contributions in a trust fund that helped to support the foreign endeavors. The Bethel Bible Training School served as a recruiting ground for its overseas endeavors. Missionaries to Africa with the agency included George and Eleanor Bowie, Fred Burke, Ernest Hooper, Edgar and Mabel Pettenger, Ralph and Lillian Riggs, and Anna Richards Scoble.

With the stock market crash in 1929, the trust fund suffered a serious setback, and much of the missionary work was curtailed. A proposed amalgamation with the Assemblies of God (AG) in the same year never occurred. Many of the missionaries eventually affiliated with the AG and made significant contributions. Among American Pentecostal missions agencies before 1929, it was second only to the AG for the size and financial underpinnings of its operation.

The churches founded by the PMSCA missionaries merged with the Churches of God in South Africa (a group of breakaway congregations from the PMSCA that organized in 1917 at Pretoria) at the Kroonstad Conference in 1920 to become "one body, the Church cemented together through the love and sacrifice of Jesus Christ" and took the name Full Gospel Church (FGC). The first constitution for the new body was ratified at Bloemfontein on April 19, 1922. The relationship granting joint jurisdiction of the FGC to the executive council of the Bethel Pentecostal Assembly ended in 1933. In 1951 the FGC amalgamated with the Church of God (Cleveland, Tenn.) and changed its name to Full Gospel Church of God. In 1985 the church reported 1,219 churches, 1,717 ministers, ten missions, three Bible schools, and 169,849 members.

Bibliography: R. S. Armstrong, "The Get Acquainted Page," *LRE* (July 1936), 14–15; H. P. Beach and C. H. Fahs, eds., *World Missionary Atlas* (1925), 24; C. W. Conn, *Like a Mighty Army*, 2d ed. (1977); G. B. McGee, *This Gospel Shall Be Preached* (1986); D. W. Slocumb, comp., *Leaders in World Evangelism* (1985); A. Thompson, "The Full Gospel Church of God—South Africa," *World Pentecost* (3, 1972), 14–15; "Editorials," *Full Gospel Missionary Herald* (January 1921), 8–9; E. L. Schoenborn, "Reports from Other Lands," *Full Gospel Missionary Herald* (January 1921), 16.   G. B. McGee

PENTECOSTAL MISSIONARY UNION

The first Pentecostal missionary agency, the Pentecostal Missionary Union was formed in Great Britain under the leadership of C. Polhill. The Pentecostal Missionary Union of Great Britain and Ireland (PMU), formed in January 1909, reflected Polhill's passion for the world mission, the strong missionary thrust among early Pentecostals, and the availability of missionaries expelled from other societies for the Pentecostal witness.

I. PMU Council. The PMU was administered by a council of between four and ten members. Throughout the PMU's sixteen-year history, the role of President C. Polhill was dominant because of his missionary experience, his administrative expertise, his social standing, and, not least, his money. Membership over the years included many well-known pioneers in the movement in Britain, including A. A. Boddy, E. W. Moser, T. Myerscough, S. Wigglesworth, and a Mrs. Crisp, first principal of the PMU training home for women. The handwritten PMU minute books at Nottingham are the most important resource, giving a full picture of the human problems not mentioned in the encouraging reports regularly published in *Confidence* and *Flames of Fire*.

II. Doctrine. The PMU required that all candidates had received the baptism of the Holy Spirit and were sincere in professing the fundamentals of evangelical faith. The "Principles" specify those truths, adding that candidates "be able to have fellowship with all believers holding these fundamental truths, even if widely differing in their judgment as to points of church government," a point later applied to the practice of water baptism. At least three council members were asked to resign for holding extreme views.

III. Training Homes. The PMU opened two training homes in London, one for young men, the other for young women. The superintendency of the men's home presented a constant problem, as few of Polhill's nominees lived up to expectations and were acceptable to the Pentecostal grassroots. The interlude when the council asked

T. Myerscough in Preston to train the male students (among whom were W. F. P. Burton, G. Jeffreys, and E. J. Phillips) was perhaps its peak-period, at least until the final years under H. Carter.

IV. Missionaries. The first PMU missionaries went to India (1909) and China (1910). China was the preferred mission field, due to Polhill's commitment and connections. Thus almost all the candidates from the London training homes went to China, while most in India were formerly with non-Pentecostal societies. From 1911 the Chinese work was based on Yunnan-fu in the southwest, with a hope of eventually penetrating Tibet. By 1915 there were eighteen PMU missionaries in China, six in India, and one new arrival in Africa in the Belgian Congo. Later a field was opened in Brazil.

The PMU minutes reveal the constant problem posed by the missionaries. Many were seen as instances of independence and lack of discipline, e.g., the incurring of expenses without reference to the council, impulsive journeys, disregard of the council's rules about engagement and marriage (a two-year period was required on the field before engagement), and reliance on undiscerned prophetic messages. Other difficulties arose from death and ill health caused by the rigors of an alien climate.

Polhill made strenuous efforts to provide oversight both in India and in China. In 1911 a question was added to the application form: "Are you willing to work in harmony with those who may be placed over you in the Lord?" At one stage there was talk of the Irish barrister John Leech going to India as superintendent, but no appointment was ever made, despite a decision in 1915 not to send any more members to India until a superintendent had been found. In China attempts were made through Polhill's contacts with other missionary societies, especially the China Inland Mission and the Christian and Missionary Alliance, to have their leader oversee newly arrived PMU missionaries, though this did not generally work well in practice. Only in 1921 was a superintendent appointed for China, William Boyd, who had gone out in 1915. A greater stability appeared at that time, with much heroic groundwork being done, as for example, by A. Lewer, who tragically drowned on the Burma-China border in 1924.

V. Support. The official principles of the PMU stated: "The Mission is supported entirely by the free will offerings of the Lord's people." These donations were listed at the end of each issue of *Confidence*. However, Polhill's personal generosity was always important. His numerous donations were always for specific projects (e.g., the lease of the women's training home, some travel costs to the mission field, students' vacation expenses). In the PMU's last years, however, there was a worsening shortage of funds, caused by an increasing number of missionaries and a growing lack of confidence in the PMU by the Pentecostal assemblies in Britain. This reflected a widening gap between the educated Anglican patriots, Polhill and Boddy, and the rank and file working-class Pentecostals, who included many conscientious objectors to military service.

VI. Its End. The formation of the Assemblies of God of Great Britain and Ireland (AGGBI) in 1925 came at a natural time for Polhill's retirement and for the PMU to become their missionary arm. During 1925 the PMU council included five nominees from AGGI, and from 1926 it was replaced by the Assemblies' Home Missionary Reference Council, on which E. Moser and T. H. Mundell remained.

Bibliography: D. Gee, *Wind and Flame* (1967).
P. D. Hocken

PENTECOSTAL MISSIONS See MISSIONS, OVERSEAS; MISSIOLOGY.

PENTECOSTAL PREACHING See PREACHING, A PENTECOSTAL PERSPECTIVE.

PENTECOSTAL WORLD CONFERENCE (PWC). A triennial, international, ecumenical gathering of Pentecostals first convened in 1947.

Known through 1958 as the World Pentecostal Conference, it has been incorrectly identified in the literature under the names World Conference of International Pentecostal Churches, World Federation of Pentecostal Churches, and World Pentecostal Fellowship. In the 1961 meeting it was identified for the first time as the Pentecostal World Conference. Its purposes include the promotion of *spiritual* fellowship among Pentecostals regardless of denominational affiliation or the lack of it, demonstration to the world of the "essential unity of Spirit-baptized believers" in fulfillment of John 17:21, promotion of courtesy, mutual understanding, and "scriptural purity among the various pentecostal groups," maintenance of those Pentecostal truths "most surely believed among us," and cooperation on items of mutual concern in fulfilling the Great Commission.

The beginnings of the Pentecostal movement in the twentieth century found a widespread hope among its adherents that the Pentecostal renewal would sweep over the churches, producing a new and visible unity among all Christians in answer to Jesus' prayer (John 17:21). Hopes were soon turned to frustration when divisions emerged over issues of polity, doctrine, mores, and personalities. In spite of the divisions, there was a growing concern that some differences could be ignored for the sake of common witness in worship. Hence, the earliest days of Pentecostalism in the U.S. saw camp meetings emerge with national and international invitations for Pentecostals of all stripes to attend.

As the Pentecostal movement matured, groups like the General Council of the Assemblies of God (1914) emerged, seeking to coordinate efforts on such issues as missions, publications, and education. In Europe as early as 1908 Alexander A. Boddy, rector at All Saints Church in Sunderland, England, began the Sunderland Conference, which the next year was renamed International Conferences. The Hamburg Conference, held in Germany in 1908, also brought many international Pentecostal leaders together. These conferences were soon joined by others in Mülheim and Zurich.

In 1911, Thomas B. Barratt issued "An Urgent Call for Charity and Unity," in which he proposed an international Pentecostal union or alliance. While his proposal was not accepted initially, it did not fall on deaf ears. In June 1912 a Consultative International Pentecostal Council emerged from the Sunderland Convention, and by December a full-fledged Consultative Council was held in Amsterdam to provide advisory counsel to the Pentecostal movement. Additional meetings of the International Advisory Council were held in Sunderland in May of 1913 and 1914. The beginning of World War I brought an end to such councils.

In 1920 invitations to an International Pentecostal Convention to be held in January 1921 in Amsterdam were sent out by Mr. and Mrs. G. R. Polham. Pentecostals from Britain, Scandinavia, Germany, and Switzerland attended. A tendency toward a preaching of the Cross (*theologia cruxes*) by the Germans and a triumphalistic critique by the Scandinavians led to some division, but, Donald Gee reported, participants generally were able to rise above their differences.

In the U.S. the vision for unity among Pentecostals fell to two provocative Pentecostal leaders. Frank Bartleman repeatedly rebuked Pentecostals in his writings for their divisiveness, and he consistently exhorted them to greater unity. After all, he wrote, "the Spirit is laboring for the unity of believers today, for the 'one body,' that the prayer of Jesus may be answered, 'that they all may be one that the world may believe.'"

Warren F. Carothers, originally affiliated with Charles F. Parham and the Apostolic Faith Movement, joined the Assemblies of God (AG) in 1914 and in 1921 was instrumental in the passage of the resolution by the general council on "World-Wide Cooperation." He was appointed to a committee whose purpose was to encourage an "ecumenical union of Pentecostal believers." That committee moved too slowly for Carothers, and shortly thereafter he withdrew from the AG, establishing a committee of his own. He convened unity conferences in St. Louis, Missouri (October 1922), Chicago, Illinois (November 1923), and Owensboro, Kentucky (July 1924). The committee published a periodical, *The Herald of the Church,* to spread its message. Carothers' vision survived for more than a decade. But by 1934 it had foundered.

In 1937 the General Council of the Assemblies of God (U.S.) invited Pentecostal leaders from around the world to attend its general council. These leaders decided to call a World Conference in London during 1940. May 1939 saw a Pentecostal Unity Conference in London among several British Pentecostal groups, while a second one was convened in January 1940. The most significant conference of that period was held June 5–12, 1939, in Stockholm. It came at the suggestion of Donald Gee and was given form by Lewi Pethrus. Delegates from nearly twenty countries were present, and as many as eight thousand people attended some meetings. Its primary value lay in personal fellowship, encouragement, and the opportunity to share a variety of

The 14th Pentecostal World Conference advisory committee meeting in 1983, Springfield, Missouri. Front row, J. Floyd Williams, Jakob Zopfi, T. F. Zimmerman, Ray H. Hughes, and Reinhold Ulonska. 2nd row, Cornelio Castelo, A. M. Cakau, M. L. Badenhorst, Carlis L. Moody, Sr., and James Worsfold. 3rd row, James MacKnight, John Thannickal, Karl-Erik Heinerborg, Richard Ondeng'.

viewpoints without formally adopting them as policy.

World War II put an end to the hope of a PWC in 1940 but did little to dampen Pentecostal interests in greater cooperation with each other. In the U.S. Pentecostals found unanticipated acceptance in the National Association of Evangelicals (NAE). Four Pentecostal denominations joined the NAE in 1942. Others soon joined with them, although certain independent Pentecostals criticized these groups for entering into a formal organization. Emerging from the Pentecostal membership of the NAE was the Pentecostal Fellowship of North America (PFNA) in October 1948.

On the European side, interest in a worldwide conference was the logical outgrowth of the highly successful 1939 European Pentecostal Conference in Stockholm. Following a preliminary meeting in September 1946 in Paris, it was decided that such a World Pentecostal Conference would be convened in Zurich, Switzerland, May 4–9, 1947, with Leonard Steiner acting as the organizing secretary. This was the first of what later became a regular triennial event. Subsequent meetings have been held in Paris (1949), London (1952), Stockholm (1955), Toronto (1958), Jerusalem (1961), Helsinki (1964), Rio de Janeiro (1967), Dallas (1970), Seoul (1973), London (1976), Vancouver, B.C. (1979), Nairobi (1982), and Zurich (1985). After a four-year

hiatus, the 1989 meeting is scheduled for Singapore.

Organizers for the first PWC hoped that it might become a fellowship of Pentecostal groups that could provide a worldwide perspective on what God was doing in the Pentecostal revival, implement relief efforts in a postwar Europe, and coordinate missionary and evangelistic efforts throughout the world. While some of these agenda items were enacted (e.g., the establishment of an office in Basel to coordinate relief efforts), it soon became apparent that it would not be possible to organize a world Pentecostal fellowship on anything like denominational lines. Issues of polity, especially among Scandinavian and American independent Pentecostals proved too rigid for such an organization. Thus the 1947 meeting has at times been termed a failure. Yet, this conference did provide an item of singular importance to the Pentecostal revival. It was agreed that there should be a world-wide Pentecostal missionary magazine edited by Donald Gee on behalf of this and any future PWC.

Donald Gee's assignment gave him free rein to speak to the issues he believed were crucial to the Pentecostal movement. To guarantee objectivity and freedom, he was "to be answerable to God alone." He kept at the task until his death on July 20, 1966, having edited and published seventy-seven issues of *Pentecost*. In nearly all of these issues Gee penned an editorial in which he reflected on the state of the Pentecostal movement and its role in the church. His insight and wisdom, his breadth of knowledge, and his humility were carefully blended in these editorials as he assessed the critical issues facing Pentecostalism. Indeed, so successful was he in this regard that his biographer, Brian Ross, described the inside back cover where Gee's editorials normally appeared as ". . . the most openly honest and perceptive pages in all Pentecostal literature."

Donald Gee, on the left, stepped down as the chairman of the Advisory Committee of the Pentecostal World Conference at the Helsinki meeting in 1964. He was succeeded by Thomas F. Zimmerman, on the right.

Following the death of Donald Gee, the PWC sought a new editor. In 1970 Percy S. Brewster (Elim Pentecostal Church) became the editor of the newly titled *World Pentecost*. He was succeeded in December 1978 by Eric C. Dando (AG in Great Britain and Ireland). With the death of Dando in April 1983, the task was passed to Jakob Zopfi (Swiss Pentecostal Mission). In 1987 *World Pentecost* went to a bilingual (English-German) format. With the addition of French in the March 1988 issue, it became trilingual. The magazine continues to provide news items on Pentecostals around the world, as well as historical articles, sermons by leading Pentecostal figures, and news concerning the PWC. Yet its editorials generally lack the significance that Donald Gee's had.

The meetings of the PWC are planned and coordinated by an elected secretary and advisory committee. In addition, a five-person presidium is also elected at each gathering. The advisory committee, a group of approximately twenty-five and the most diverse and truly representative group in the conference, is responsible for site, theme, and speaker selection. Members of the presidium are expected to chair the various sessions of the conference. Since their inception,

the positions of secretary and chair of the conferences have been dominated by American, British, Swiss, and Swedish members. In 1967 A. P. Vasconcelos, general superintendent of the AG in Brazil, served a term as secretary, coordinating the meeting in Rio de Janeiro, and in 1958 Canadian W. E. McAlister, general superintendent of the Pentecostal Assemblies of Canada (PAOC), chaired the meeting in Toronto.

During the first two decades of its existence the chair of the advisory committee was shared by L. Steiner (Switzerland), D. Gee (England), L. Pethrus (Sweden), W. E. McAlister (Canada) H. P. Courtney (U.S.), and T. F. Zimmerman (U.S.). Zimmerman, former general superintendent of the AG (U.S.), has chaired the PWC since 1967 with the exception of 1970 when Percy S. Brewster (England) held that position. Since 1973 the editor of *World Pentecost* has also served as secretary to the conference.

Through the years, the PWC has functioned remarkably well in providing an international ecumenical witness in worship. Its themes have been edifying or challenging to the Pentecostal movement as a whole, and only rarely, such as in 1961, have some speakers attempted to politicize them, using their speeches as a forum to bring what they perceived to be dissident or maverick Pentecostals into line. The diversity of the conference leadership in its early years was capable of including a broad agenda from the top down. Undoubtedly, the fact that T. F. Zimmerman has chaired the conference almost without interruption since 1967 and the fact that the editor of *World Pentecost* has served as secretary since 1973, have added a measure of stability to the PWC.

Dangers inherent in this change are equally obvious. First, it centralizes power in a single individual or a small number of individuals. Second, it detracts from the fact that the conference is truly representative of *world* Pentecostalism. Third, it runs the risk of hampering younger Pentecostal leaders, especially from non-Western nations, from obtaining a world-wide forum in the Pentecostal movement. Fourth, until leadership is more representative of the Pentecostal movement as a whole, the PWC runs the risk of being perceived as "inbred," determined to maintain the *status quo*.

Early leaders such as Donald Gee and David du Plessis had hoped to see the PWC embrace, or at least take seriously, the charismatic renewal among the historic churches. By 1988 it has not done so and as a result has lost opportunity for wider global impact. Competition from regional or national conferences may also ultimately prove to be a strong factor that reduces the impact of the PWC to a shadow of its former hope.

Bibliography: J. M. Boze, "Human Organization or Divine Administration," *Herald of Faith* 14 (2, February 1949); "Can There be Real Unity in the Pentecostal Movement in the United States? Some Suggestions," *Herald of Faith* 14 (5, May 1949); W. F. Carothers, *The Herald of the Church* 1 (1925): 3; D. J. du Plessis, *A Brief History of the World Pentecostal Fellowship* (c. 1951); H A. Fischer, *Progress of Pentecostal Fellowship* (1952); D. Gee, ed. *Pentecost: A Review of World-Wide Pentecos-*

tal Missionary and Revival News (1947–66); idem, *Wind and Flame* (1941, 1947, rev. 1967); W. J. Hollenweger, *The Pentecostals* (1972); K. Kendrick, *The Promise Fulfilled* (1961); W. W. Menzies, *Anointed to Serve* (1971); L. Pethrus, "No Pentecostal World Organization," *Herald of Faith* 12 (July 1947): 7; B. R. Ross, "Donald Gee: Sectarian in Search of a Church," *Evangelical Quarterly* 50 (1978); L. F. Sumrall, "International Pentecostal Conference in Switzerland," *Pentecostal Evangel* (May 31 and June 7, 1947); C. van der Laan, "The Proceedings of the Leaders' Meetings (1908–1911) and of the International Pentecostal Council (1912–1914)," *EPTA Bulletin* 6 (3, 1987) and *Pneuma* 10 (1, 1988); E. S. Williams, "Fellowship in the Will of God: Pentecostal Bodies Consolidate?" in *Herald of Faith* 13 (10, October 1948).   C. M. Robeck, Jr.

PENTECOSTALISM See BLACK HOLINESS–PENTECOSTALISM; CLASSICAL PENTECOSTALISM; PENTECOSTAL AND CHARISMATIC MOVEMENTS (INTRODUCTORY ESSAY); HISPANIC PENTECOSTALISM; ONENESS PENTECOSTALISM.

PEOPLE OF DESTINY, INTERNATIONAL See CHARISMATIC MOVEMENT.

PEOPLE OF PRAISE (SOUTH BEND, IND.) See CATHOLIC CHARISMATIC RENEWAL; CHARISMATIC COMMUNITIES.

PERFECTION See CHRISTIAN PERFECTION.

When Noel Perkin (seated) completed his more than 30 years as director of the AG Division of Foreign Missions in 1959, one of his assistants, J. Philip Hogan was elected to succeed him.

PERKIN, NOEL (1893–1979). Missions executive. Born in England, Perkin grew up in the Wesleyan Methodist Church. Perkin's initial in-

terest in dentistry changed to banking, and he accepted a position with the Bank of Montreal in Canada, eventually working at the branch office in Toronto. While there he came into contact with the Christian and Missionary Alliance (CMA), whose teaching strongly influenced him. He later identified with Christian Schoonmaker and others who left the CMA because of their Pentecostal theology. Ordained in 1918, he left for Argentina and served there for three years with Harry L. Turner, a later president of the CMA.

In 1921 Perkin returned to Canada and subsequently entered the U.S. While visiting the Rochester Bible Training School in Rochester, New York, he met and married Ora Blanchard. They had five children. Perkin served two pastorates in western New York (1922–26) before he joined the Assemblies of God (AG) headquarters staff in Springfield, Missouri. Given permanent appointment as missionary secretary in 1927, he served until his retirement in 1959.

Perkin exerted a profound influence on the development of AG foreign missions. During his long tenure, the first *Missionary Manual* (1931) was produced; the administrative structure grew; promotional activities expanded; and the number of missionary personnel, overseas converts, and foreign Bible institutes dramatically increased. He was instrumental in changing the missions department from an agency that largely distributed funds to one that provided leadership and planning to the entire missions enterprise. At the same time, his fervor and gentle demeanor assured the supporting constituency that the spiritual objectives of the effort remained at the forefront.

Perkin's impact also can be detected in the orientation toward establishing indigenous churches abroad. Perkin was strongly influenced by the writings of Roland Allen. In turn he encouraged the missionaries, notably Melvin L. Hodges, to study them as well. His missiological perspectives are best found in *Our World Witness* (1963), coauthored with John Garlock.

By the time of Perkin's retirement in 1959, the AG had become a leader in the Christian world mission. In the same year he was elected to a one-year term as president of the Evangelical Foreign Missions Association, the first Pentecostal to hold the office.

Bibliography: G. B. McGee, *This Gospel Shall Be Preached* (1986); I. Spence, *Mr. Missions* (n.d.).
G. B. McGee

PERRY, TROY DEROY (1940–). Founder of Universal Fellowship of Metropolitan Community Churches (UFMCC), a mostly homosexual denomination. He began preaching at thirteen, attended Moody Bible Institute, briefly served as assistant state overseer of Florida for the Emmanuel Holiness Church, and pastored the Santa Ana, California, Church of God of Prophecy until 1963, when he was ousted for homosexuality.

Arrested numerous times, he led a sit-in at the 1972 Democratic National Convention and a public fast on federal property in Los Angeles for sixteen days to draw attention to movement goals. In 1968 he founded the first UFMCC church in Los Angeles, where its headquarters are located.

He holds an honorary D.Min. from Samaritan College.

As UFMCC moderator, he oversees 267 churches in twelve countries. Membership is 35,000. Some local congregations are charismatic, but the denomination is broadly ecumenical. A 1987 decision by the U.S. attorney general gave Perry's group rights to minister in all federal prisons.

Bibliography: R. Enroth and G. Jamison, *The Gay Church* (1974); T. Perry, *The Lord is My Shepherd and He Know's I'm Gay* (1972); S. Warren, "Never Ask Permission," *New York Native* (June 15, 1987), 21–23.
                                                                    J. S. Tinney

PETERSON, PAUL BERNHARD (1895–1978). Cofounder of the Russian and Eastern European Mission. Born in Chicago on February 11, 1895, Paul Peterson was the oldest child of G. Edward and Bengta (Svenson) Peterson. As a young man he heard continuous reports about the mass conversions taking place in Russia. Gripped by the reports, Peterson decided to become one of the organizers and eventually a trustee of the Russian Missionary Society when it decided to move its headquarters from Philadelphia to Chicago in 1920. While working for the society, he decided to devote his life to the evangelization of Russia and the Eastern European countries. Under the society's auspices Peterson and his wife, Signe E. Anderson, whom he married in 1922, left Chicago in 1924 to serve as missionaries in Poland and Latvia. Upon his return to America, he cofounded the Russian and Eastern European Mission with G. Herbert Schmidt and a Chicago businessperson in Chicago in 1927. He was immediately appointed the organization's general secretary and later elected its president in 1931. He served in that capacity until his death. Peterson spent the rest of his life traveling across the world for the purpose of acquainting people with the needs and opportunities for evangelism in Russia and Eastern Europe. He made several trips throughout the U.S., Asia, and Europe. At times he also visited Russia and Eastern Europe. During the war years he appealed to people throughout the world to send parcels of food and clothing to Russia and Eastern Europe. In 1952 Peterson moved to Pasadena, California, after the decision was made to relocate the headquarters of the Eastern European Mission to Pasadena (earlier the name Russian was dropped from its title). While in Pasadena, Peterson directed the mission's evangelistic efforts into Western Europe as well. Germany, Greece, and the Netherlands were three countries in which workers were supported. He also helped develop Bible correspondence courses, the publication of Christian literature, and radio broadcasts as means of evangelization. Peterson lived in Pasadena until his death on December 8, 1978.

Bibliography: "He Served His Generation by the Will of God," *Gospel Call* (January–February 1979); G. B. McGee, *This Gospel Shall Be Preached* (1986); P. B. Peterson, *History of the First Fifty Years (1927–1977) of the Eastern European Mission* (n.d.).   J. Colletti

PETHRUS, PETRUS LEWI (1884–1974). Swedish pastor and international Pentecostal leader. The son of a factory worker, Pethrus grew up in the Baptist Church. He was baptized at age fifteen. After several years as a factory worker himself, Pethrus became an evangelist (1902–04) and attended Bethel Seminary in Stockholm (1905–06). He was elected pastor of the Baptist Church in Lidkoping (1906–11) and of Filadelfia Church, Stockholm (1911).

Pethrus, attracted by reports of the Sunderland and Oslo revivals, journeyed to Oslo, where in 1907 under the guidance of T. B. Barratt, he became a Pentecostal. His congregation also accepted the Pentecostal message, as did numerous other churches in Sweden. In 1913 the Swedish Baptist Convention expelled Pethrus and his entire congregation from the convention ostensibly because they practiced open Communion, but in reality, because of their Pentecostal theology and liturgy. Despite the schism, Pethrus continued to be influenced by his Baptist heritage and would, for example, insist upon Baptist ecclesiology as the pattern for Swedish Pentecostal polity.

The structure of the Swedish Pentecostal movement was officially egalitarian, but Pethrus was, in actuality, its leader. He determined the priorities of the movement, represented it to the international movement, and determined the careers of individuals within the church. He could tolerate no competition to his leadership and forced talented individuals such as Sven Lidman (journalist) and A. P. Franklin (missiologist) to work outside the movement. He also caused Allan Tornburg, pastor and theologian, to lose the race for a seat in Parliament by declaring, on the eve of the election, that Pentecostals should not be in politics.

On the other hand, Pethrus encouraged a number of daring enterprises. He founded the Filadelfia Church Rescue Mission (1911); the Filadelfia Publishing House (1912); the Filadelfia Bible School (1915); the periodical *Evangelii Harold* (1916–); the Kaggeholms Folkhogskola (a secondary school) (1942); a national daily newspaper, *Dagen* (1945–); a savings bank, Allmanna Spar-och Kreditkassen (1952); and a worldwide radio network, I.B.R.A. Radio (1955).

Pethrus was also a prolific author. His first book, *Jesus Kommer* (1912) was also the first publication of the Forlaget Filadelfia (Filadelfia Publishing House). His collected writings comprise ten volumes, not counting his five-volume memoirs and a number of books written after 1956. He also contributed widely to periodical publications. His books and essays have been translated into many languages.

As pastor, Pethrus led his own congregation to become the largest in the Pentecostal world (until c. 1975) and the Pentecostal movement in Sweden to become the largest Free Church in Sweden, primarily by his ability to relate the church to all aspects of life. His holistic vision for the Christian life and the moderation, dignity, and realism of his expectations of spiritual development won him a hearing throughout Europe, North America, and the Third World. He demonstrated to the Pentecostal world that the movement did not have to be alienated from the national culture of which it is a part.

A former Baptist pastor in Sweden, Lewi Pethrus became the leader of Pentecostalism in Sweden. He founded the Filadelfia Church in Stockholm which became the largest in the Pentecostal movement worldwide.

Pethrus, after initial reservations about international cooperation, hosted the 1939 World Pentecostal Conference with twenty nations represented and would thereafter be active in Pentecostal ecumenism. He remained pastor at Filadelfia, Stockholm, until his retirement in 1958 and active in the movement until his death in 1974.

See also EUROPEAN PENTECOSTALISM.

Bibliography: Works: L. Pethrus, *Memoarer,* (5 vols. 1953–56); idem, *Samlade Skrifter,* 10 vols. (1958–59); **Selected Secondary Literature:** B. Andstrom, *Lewi Pethrus* (1966); N. Bloch-Hoell, *Pinsebevegelsen, en undersøkelse av pinsebevegelsens tilblivelse . . .* (1956, partial English trans., *The Pentecostal Movement* [1964]); B. Carlsson, *Organizations and Decision Procedures Within the Swedish Pentecostal Movements* (1978); W. J. Hollenweger, *Handbuch der Pfingstbewegung,* diss., Zurich, 1966; A. Holmberg, *Lewi Pethrus, ratt man paå ratt plats ratt tid* (1976); J. Kallmark, ed. *Saå minns vi Lewi Pethrus* (1984); S. Lidman, *Vildaasnor och paadrivare; en arbetsbok* (1968); R. Struble, *Den Samfundsfria Församlingen och de karismatiska gaå vorna och tjänsterna. Den Svenska Pingströckelsen Församlingssyn 1907–1947* (1982); A. Sundsted, *Pingstväckelsen,* 5 vols. (1969–73).   D. D. Bundy

PETRINE LITERATURE The NT writings called 1 and 2 Peter, although many scholars do not think the documents were written by the same author, and many are reluctant to affix the name Peter to either. The uncertainty over the question of authorship, the unquestionable literary relationship between Jude and 2 Peter, and the differences in literary style and theology have resulted in 1 and 2 Peter being separated. Second Peter is normally examined in conjunction with Jude, whereas 1 Peter is investigated in its own right. Almost no one, whether holding to Petrine authorship of both or not, seriously analyzes the books in light of one another.

I. 1 Peter. First Peter 1:1 asserts that "Peter, apostle of Christ Jesus" is writing to "God's

chosen ones, exiles of the Diaspora." There is substantial endorsement of Petrine authorship from the early church (e.g., Irenaeus, *Against Heresies* 4.9.2; cf. 2 Peter 3:1, which some regard as a reference to 1 Peter), but scholarship remains divided over the issue. Those who reject Petrine authorship usually do so on the basis of the Greek, which they regard as too sophisticated for a Galilean fisherman, and on the assumption that 1 Peter presupposes Pauline theology. The problem of dating and identifying the persecution depicted in the document also determines how some view the author (e.g., Kümmel, 1973, 433; Beare, 1958, 24–31). Defenders of Petrine authorship are almost constrained to resort to a theory that depends on a "secretary" who wrote down Peter's words (Selwyn [1946] 1981, 7), although some have insisted that it is not mandatory (Guthrie, 1965, 778–81). Others are reluctant to call the document pseudonymous but admit that that possibility "certainly cannot be excluded" (Kelly, 1969, 32).

The "genre" of 1 Peter might best be described as a "diaspora letter" (e.g., 2 Macc. 1:1–10a; 1:10b–2:18; 2 Bar. 78–87; Acts 15:23; James [see JAMES, BOOK OF]). As such, it originally circulated among the primarily Gentile Christian communities in Asia Minor (Michaels, 1988, intro.). Dating the letter usually depends on how one stands on authorship. Those advocating Peter as author posit a date prior to Peter's traditional date of martyrdom under Nero; hence, prior to A.D. 64–65. Those who see the circumstances in 1 Peter reflecting a post-65 situation (e.g., under Trajan [A.D. 98–117]), have argued for non-Petrine authorship. This practice has been challenged, however. Evidence also suggests that Peter may not have been martyred at the traditional date of A.D. 62–65. Thus the date for 1 Peter cannot be too tightly linked to the question of authorship (Michaels, 1988, intro.).

It is not clear whether all the recipient communities are undergoing persecution or not (1 Peter 1:6; cf. 4:12). Nonetheless, encouragement to endure suffering and to live holy lives in the face of adversity characterizes the entire letter. Beare, among others, contends that the central concern of 1 Peter is the "nature of Christian life." He, following others, also discerns in 1 Peter portions of a baptismal homily (1:3–4:11). This appears untenable, however, for it requires 1 Peter to be a composite structure and demands the presence of an elaborate baptismal liturgy in which the rite has become sacrament. It also suffers from a lack of explicit reference in 1 Peter to baptism except in 1 Peter 3:21.

II. The Spirit in 1 Peter. There are only four unmistakable references to the Spirit in 1 Peter (1:2, 11, 12; 4:14 [cf. below on the variant reading there]). First Peter 3:18 and 4:6 may be two other references to the Spirit (cf., ad loc., the NIV's translations), and even 1 Peter 3:4 could possibly refer to the Holy Spirit within the individual. In 1:2 it is the "sanctifying" Spirit who has chosen God's elect. This should not be read in terms of the Spirit's giving power to live a "sanctified" life but in terms of the Spirit's ability to make what was formerly unholy holy through the sacrifice of Christ.

Through the "Spirit of Christ" *in them* (*en autois*) the prophets spoke of the sufferings of Christ that made possible the preaching of the gospel (1:10). The "prophets" spoken of here obviously include the OT prophets; however, Christian prophets also "searched the Scriptures" to explicate the Christ event (e.g., Selwyn, 1981, 134; and despite the NIV's "predicted").

The mention of the Holy Spirit in 1 Peter 1:12 implies that the Spirit is equally the force behind Christian evangelization. That the Spirit is "sent from heaven" need not be interpreted as an allusion to Pentecost, but it does remind one of a coming of the Spirit from the realm of the divine (heaven) into the realm of this world. The textual problems surrounding *en* in 1:12 make it awkward to insist on an instrumental reading of "by." Thus it should not be demanded that it is "by" the Holy Spirit that the gospel was preached.

First Peter 4:14 speaks of the "Spirit of the glory of God which rests upon" those insulted because of the name of Christ. (A variant reading attested in PΨ Maj r t z vg^{ww} accepted by some modern commentators [e.g., Michaels] says that the Spirit is blasphemed by those who reproach believers; believers, on the other hand, glorify the Spirit in them.) The reading of most modern versions parallels the earlier statement that if one suffers because of righteousness, that one is blessed (3:14; cf. Luke 6:22). Now, though, the resting of the Spirit of glory upon the individual implies that the individual shares in eschatological blessing "to be revealed" (cf. 1:5, 7, 13; 3:9; 4:13; 5:1, 4, 6, 10). There may be some implicit sense in which the Spirit empowers the believer to endure suffering and persecution, for in 1:5 God's power "shields" those who have had to suffer. This recalls Gospel texts like Luke 12:11–12 and 21:12–14.

The adjective *pneumatikos* occurs twice in 1 Peter 2:5. Elliot has called into question any reading of *oikos pneumatikos* ["spiritual house"] that reads *pneumatikos* as "spiritual" in any abstract, metaphorical, or immaterial sense. Instead he recommends that it is the "house [i.e. community] in which the [divine] Spirit resides" (Elliot, 1981, 169; 1966, 154–56).

Beare insists that the author does not associate the word *charismata* ("gifts of grace") with the activity of the Spirit. While it is true that one should not impose a Pauline understanding of that term (actually Paul speaks more of "manifestations" in 1 Corinthians anyway), it is nonetheless clearly a divine gift of service (grace) given by God for the sake of others in a community. Moreover, if *pneuma* should be interpreted "Spirit" (if not in a full-orbed Trinitarian sense, at least in the sense of "divine") in 1 Peter 4:6 rather than "spirit" (NIV, RSV, KJV), then "living according to God" (4:6) involves exercising one's gifts (of the Spirit?) on behalf of others (4:8–11). This also puts the phrase "if anyone speaks" (*ei tis lalei*) he should speak "as [speaking] words of God" (*hos logia theou*) in an entirely new light. The context is the exercise of one's gifts within the community. One need not read ecstatic speech here;

however, it is probably divinely "inspirited," whereby the community is edified and in turn gives glory to God (cf. 1 Cor. 12–14).

Whereas the Spirit may not have as prominent a place in 1 Peter as he does in the writings of Paul, the Spirit nonetheless works within the community to distinguish God's people from the world. The Spirit is active in gospel proclamation; and in the life of the community the *charismata* of God bind the members in service to one another. The Spirit enables the Christian to live a godly life in spite of persecution and suffering.

III. 2 Peter. Second Peter has been surrounded by a sea of controversy. Eusebius grouped it among the "disputed" writings (*Ecclesiastical History* 3.25.3), and the Peshitta Syriac version (4th–5th cent.), in fact, does not even contain 2 Peter (or 2 and 3 John and Revelation). Second Peter exhibits the form of an ancient letter (opening, salutation, body, doxology [cf. 3:1]), but many have regarded this as artificial (e.g., Becker, but cf. Bauckham). Second Peter also resembles testamentary literature, i.e., a "farewell speech" (Bauckham, 1983, 132).

Most who regard 2 Peter as dependent on Jude contend that it is impossible for the document to have been written by the apostle Peter (e.g., Kümmel, 1973, 430; but cf. Bauckham). Main arguments against Petrine authorship include: language, the presence of ideas that seem to reflect a later period in church history (e.g., 3:4, 16), and the distinctly Hellenistic influence (e.g., the attitude toward "virtue," "faith," "knowledge" [1:2, 3, 6, 8; 2:20; 3:18]).

The recipients of 2 Peter are usually regarded as several Gentile Christian communities throughout the Mediterranean world. Whether one takes 2 Peter to be Petrine or not, almost all would agree that the threat of false teachers has prompted the document. With regard to precisely who these false teachers were (gnostics, libertines, pseudoprophets?), what they taught, or when they existed (A.D. 62–180?), there is little agreement.

IV. The Spirit in 2 Peter. The expression "Holy Spirit" occurs only once in 2 Peter, in 1:21. There the author asserts that "prophecy never had its origin in the human will, but people spoke from God as they were carried along by the Holy Spirit." One need not restrict prophecy here to prophecies in the OT Scriptures. Nonwriting prophets and early Christian prophets are also in view, as are the prophets and pseudoprophets (false teachers, 2:1) addressed in the letter. In fact, the remainder of false prophets of the past is an allusion to the false teachers whose teachings (i.e., interpretations of Scripture; 1:16; 2:3; 3:16) originate from their own greed and sinful nature (1:4; 2:3, 10, 12, 14, 18; 3:3) rather than from the Holy Spirit.

To counter the false teachings of these errorists, the faithful have the certainty of the word of the true prophets, who are energized by the Holy Spirit rather than their sinful nature (1:19; 3:2). Their foundation is the eyewitness testimony of those with Jesus (1:16). The false teachers have received the same "sacred command" (2:21) given through the holy prophets and apostles (3:2), but they have turned away to their own desires.

Although it is plain that 2 Peter does not have any developed pneumatology, it is equally clear that the author regards the activity of the Spirit in prophecy as a crucial check against false teaching. The "authentic" teaching is characterized by holy living (1:5–8; 3:11, 14) and by faithfulness to what has been handed down by the apostles (1:12–21; 2:21; 3:1–2). Remaining faithful to apostolic teaching will ensure the believer's security (1:10–11, 12–15; 2:9; 3:14, 17).

Bibliography: R. J. Bauckham, *Jude, 2 Peter, WBC* (1983); F. W. Beare, *The First Epistle of Peter* (1958); J. C. Becker, "Peter, Second Letter of," *IDB* (1962), 3:767–71; H. C. C. Cavallin, "The False Teachers of 2 Pt as Pseudo-Prophets," *NovT* 3 (21, 1977): 263–70; J. H. Elliot, *The Elect and the Holy* (1966); idem, *A Home for the Homeless* (1981); E. E. Ellis, *Prophecy and Hermeneutic in Early Christianity* (1978); T. Fornberg, *An Early Church in a Pluralistic Society* (1977); D. Guthrie, *New Testament Introduction* (1970); D. Hill, *New Testament Prophecy* (1979); E. Käsemann, *Essays on New Testament Themes* (1964); J. N. D. Kelly, *A Commentary on the Epistles of Peter and Jude, HNTC* (1969); W. G. Kümmel, *Introduction to the New Testament* (1973); J. R. Michaels, *1 Peter, WBC* (1988); E. G. Selwyn, *The First Epistle of St. Peter* (1946; reprint 1981).   P. H. Alexander

PFOTENHAUER, C. DONALD (1930–). One of the first exponents of charismatic renewal in the Lutheran Church–Missouri Synod (LCMS). Pfotenhauer graduated from Concordia Seminary, St. Louis, Missouri, in 1955 and then served a parish in Canada for six years. In 1961 he was called to a LCMS congregation in Blaine, Minnesota, a suburb of Minneapolis.

While serving in that congregation, he experienced the baptism with the Holy Spirit and testified to it in his congregation. He was suspended from the ministry in 1964 and was expelled from the LCMS in 1970 after a prolonged trial.

Pfotenhauer continued to serve as a leader in the Lutheran charismatic movement. In 1980 he was released by his congregation from many responsibilities in order to minister to a number of nondenominational pastors and congregations in the north-central U.S., as well as to groups overseas, particularly Lutherans in East Germany.

Bibliography: L. Christenson, ed., *Welcome, Holy Spirit* (1987).   L. Christenson

PHAIR, ROBERT (1837–1931). Canadian clergyman and archdeacon. Born in County Tyrone, Ireland, Phair experienced an evangelical conversion in 1859 in his homeland. This launched him into a life of deep devotion to Christ. Two years later he enrolled at the Church Missionary Society (CMS) college at Islington in England in preparation for Canada, where he began what would be a forty-eight-year ministry among the native people.

Ordained first to the diaconate in 1864, then to the priesthood in 1866, Phair began his ministry with an appointment to the area that would be the scene of most of his life's work, northwestern Ontario, part of the extremely rugged Canadian Shield. His diary for 1887 reveals the privations

that his ministry sometimes entailed. It tells of him tramping through heavy snow in subzero temperatures and sleeping in an overcrowded tepee in order to pray with a dying chief.

In 1888 Phair was appointed archdeacon of Islington and superintendent and secretary of the CMS in the diocese of Rupert's Land—a position that he filled until his retirement in 1912. Following this, he traveled extensively in the Far East, Britain, and North America, holding Bible conferences and preaching, often through interpreters.

Phair was baptized in the Spirit shortly after 1907 in Winnipeg, Manitoba. Without compromising his position in the Anglican church, he frequently appeared among Pentecostal leaders. In 1912 he attended meetings in Dallas, and in 1915 he was at a convention in London, England.

Given the fact that there were no official positions in Canadian Pentecostalism until 1919, when Phair was eighty-two, he never held office or credentials. His prime contribution was probably made through lending counsel. Documentation does not permit greater precision. It is likely that he also added credibility. When Pentecostals spoke of him, they always did so with great respect, being careful to use his title.

Bibliography: T. C. B. Boon, *The Anglican Church From the Bay to the Rockies: A History of the Ecclesiastical Province of Rupert's Land and Its Dioceses From 1820 to 1950* (1962).   R. A. N. Kydd

PHILLIPS, EVERETT L. (1905–88). Pioneer missionary to Nigeria. Phillips, born in Kentucky, was influenced by missionaries as a youth. After attending Central Bible Institute he married Dorothy Prohaska in 1932. They had one son, Don (d. 1985), who also became a missionary.

The Phillipses traveled as pioneer ministers to Nigeria in response to a call by a group of Spirit-filled Nigerians in 1940. They soon opened a Bible school that became the Assemblies of God (AG) Divinity School and is the largest AG school there today. They also started printing notes and lessons and began a women's program in the churches. In 1943 the Phillipses were prevented from returning to Nigeria following a furlough, because Everett had developed a heart problem. Before returning to Nigeria in 1951 Phillips served as pastor and vice-president of the Great Lakes Bible Institute and as assistant superintendent of the Illinois District. Upon returning to Nigeria he served as superintendent of the Nigerian AG and assisted in founding 120 churches.

In 1954 Phillips was appointed field director for Africa. He retired from that position in 1971 and pastored a church in Venice, Florida, later settling in Springfield, Missouri.

Bibliography: AG Office of Information, media release (February 1988); "Everett L. Phillips with Christ," *PE* (March 6, 1988), 7; "God Had A Man," *PE* (February 28, 1971), 16–17; W. E. Warner, "The Ministry of Everett and Dorothy Phillips in Nigeria, Africa," taped interview (October 3, 1980). S. Shemeth

PIETISM See EUROPEAN PIETISTIC ROOTS OF PENTECOSTALISM.

PIKE, JOHN MARTIN (1840–1932). Pastor, author, editor, and publisher. A native of Newfoundland, J. M. Pike came to the U.S., where he became an important figure in the Holiness movement. Settling in Columbia, South Carolina, he was associated with the Methodist Episcopal Church, South, but was broadly supportive of a variety of Holiness ventures. The Christian and Missionary Alliance credits Pike with making it possible for them to enter South Carolina through his Oliver Gospel Mission. For several years he provided space for Nickles J. Holmes's Bible institute. In addition, Pike wrote for a variety of Holiness periodicals, including Carrie Judd Montgomery's *Triumphs of Faith,* and he contributed to works such as Abbie Clemans Morrow Brown's *Jesus Only: A Full Salvation Year Book* published by God's Revivalist Office in Cincinnati.

Pike's prominence in Pentecostalism is derived largely from his publishing work. Beginning in 1890 and extending through 1931, he published *The Way of Faith,* a weekly periodical of devotional articles, news items, and testimonies designed to provide advocacy for biblical holiness, divine healing, and the second "personal" coming of Christ. When the Pentecostal revival broke out in Los Angeles in April 1906, one of Pike's frequent contributors, Frank Bartleman, kept Pike's subscribers informed of its progress with a series of firsthand reports. Pike was greatly impressed with the movement, and he, too, wrote articles that were supportive of it.

The publishing interests of J. M. Pike went beyond his periodical. He was also instrumental in publishing a number of devotional paperback books, such as Holiness author Mary Mabette Anderson's, *Lights and Shadows of the Life in Canaan* (1906). With the emergence of the Pentecostal revival Pike published Frank Bartleman's first autobiography, *My Story: "The Latter Rain"* (1908), and collected correspondence between Dr. Lilian B. Yeomans and her mother, Dr. Amelia Yeomans, in *Pentecostal Papers* (n.d.). This latter work provided careful reflection on the meaning of Pentecostal experience for these women.

J. M. Pike remained in Columbia, South Carolina, most of his life, dying there May 16, 1932.

Bibliography: C. E. Jones, *Guide to the Study of the Pentecostal Movement* (1983); *The Ninth Annual Report of the Christian and Missionary Alliance* (1906); J. M. Pike, "The Bride of the Lamb," *TF* 21 (7, 1901): 154–56; idem, "Needed: Much Waiting Upon God," *TF* 28 (8, 1908): 189–90; idem, "One Taken—the Other Left," *TF* 34 (10, 1914): 225–26; idem, "Pentecostal Movement" *TF* 30 (11, 1910): 250–51; idem, "Rivers of Living Water," *TF* 30 (12, 1910): 282–83; V. Synan, *The Holiness-Pentecostal Movement in the United States* (1971).   C. M. Robeck, Jr.

PINSON, MACK M. (1873–1953). Early Pentecostal evangelist and pastor. Pinson's important contribution to the Pentecostal movement was in the South prior to 1920. Reared on cotton farms in Georgia, Pinson was one of seven children. His parents were not practicing Christians, and his father deserted the family. The death of his sister while giving birth had a lasting effect on Mack—or M. M., as he is better known—when she asked each family member to meet her in heaven. He was converted in 1893, when he was twenty, in a Missionary Baptist church revival. He met some Holiness people but disputed their teaching; later, however, he had a deep spiritual experience, which he was told was the baptism in the Spirit. He felt a call to preach and soon began holding meetings.

An executive presbyter elected at the organizational meeting of the Assemblies of God, M. M. Pinson had a Holiness background. He founded the Pentecostal periodical *Word and Witness.*

Pinson met J. O. McClurkan, president of a holiness school in Nashville, the Pentecostal Mission Bible and Literary Institute. He began attending the school in 1902, was ordained in 1903, and remained with the organization until shortly after he was baptized in the Holy Spirit in 1907. (This school is now Trevecca College, a Nazarene school.) During his years with the mission, Pinson held very successful meetings throughout the South. Later, after being baptized in the Spirit, he went back to some of the same towns and cities to preach the Pentecostal message.

His contact with Pentecostals came in 1907 when he went to Birmingham to hear G. B. Cashwell, who was spreading the Pentecostal teaching following his Azusa Street Mission experience. Pinson, however, had trouble accepting the new message. When Cashwell went to Memphis, Pinson went along. While seeking for the baptism in the Spirit in Memphis, he attended C. H. Mason's Church of God in Christ. Mason too had just returned from the Azusa Street Mission and had turned his Holiness church into a Pentecostal fellowship. After seeking for some time, Pinson was baptized in the Spirit while praying in bed. His friend, H. G. Rodgers, was kneeling at the bed, and he too received the experience. The two later organized several Pentecostal churches in the South.

After Pinson's Memphis experience, he returned to Birmingham, where he ministered with Cashwell and others. He became a "corresponding editor" for the *Bridegroom's Messenger*, a paper Cashwell had founded in Atlanta.

Through the influence of William Durham and others, Pinson accepted the Baptistic view of sanctification in 1910, or the "finished work," as it was called. When the editor of the *Bridegroom's Messenger*, Mrs. E. A. Sexton, wanted to change Pinson's "finished work" articles that he was submitting, he founded his own paper, the *Word and Witness*, in Nashville. He later consolidated this paper with E. N. Bell's *Apostolic Faith*, retaining the name *Word and Witness*. Bell, who was a pastor in Malvern, Arkansas, became editor; Pinson, because of his itinerant ministry, became a "field correspondent." Many of his insightful reports and often sharp articles can be found in the paper.

Few people of the early years of the Pentecostal movement had doubts where Pinson stood on social and doctrinal issues. Although reared in the South, he was sympathetic to blacks, even trying to integrate a meeting in the South. He signed the "call" for the General Council of the Assemblies of God (AG) organizational meeting and was selected as the keynote speaker and as an executive presbyter. When the Oneness issue surfaced, Pinson played an important role for the AG in slowing down the rebaptizing of believers.

Pinson studied Spanish and ministered along the Mexican border and pastored churches. After 1920 his influence waned in the AG. When he became inactive in his later years, he returned his credentials to the AG, the organization he helped to found.

Bibliography: C. Brumback, *Suddenly . . . From Heaven* (1961); correspondence between M. Pinson and J. Flower (1949–51, in AG Archives); R. Leverett, "M. M. Pinson and the Pentecostal Mission, 1902–07," *AG Heritage* (Fall 1984), 5, 10–11; W. Menzies, *Anointed to Serve* (1971); M. Pinson, "Sketch of the Life and Ministry of Mack M. Pinson" (1949); R. Spence, *The First Fifty Years, The Story of the Assemblies of God in Alabama* (1965, excerpts reprinted in *AG Heritage* [Fall 1984]).
                                                        W. E. Warner

PIPER, WILLIAM HAMNER (1868–1911). Influential early Pentecostal pastor and editor. Born in Lydia, Maryland, on June 8, 1868, Piper was ordained in the Brethren Church at Philadelphia in 1893. On December 29, 1912, he married Lydia Markley. The next year, he identified with John Alexander Dowie's newly formed Christian Catholic Church. Two years before, he had experienced healing, and he fully embraced Dowie's radical stance on faith. His wife, too, had been healed under Dowie's ministries, of paralysis in one leg, which had also been shorter than the other. Dowie had publicized her story in his *Leaves of Healing,* and she had frequently given public testimony to her healing. Lydia Piper was one of the better-known members of Zion. One of the first group of six elders Dowie ordained as

his assistants, Piper served Dowie's movement as an overseer. When Dowie opened his community, Zion City, Illinois, for settlement in 1901, Piper became one of its most influential and prominent citizens.

After serving as an associate of John Alexander Dowie, William H. Piper founded Chicago's Stone Church in 1906.

In 1906, disillusioned with events in Zion, Piper forsook the movement and moved to Chicago. On December 9, 1906, he opened the Stone Church, where he preached a message similar to Dowie's, though shorn of apostolic pretensions. Most of his congregation were Chicago area people who had formerly associated with Zion. Prejudiced against the Pentecostalism that had further divided Zion City's citizens in the fall of 1906, Piper purposely excluded Pentecostal teaching from his church.

By the spring of 1907, with attendance down significantly, Piper decided that his opposition to Pentecostalism was adversely affecting his ministry. He invited three former Dowie followers who had accepted Pentecostal teaching to present their message in his pulpit late in June 1907. The congregation responded positively and readily identified with Pentecostal worship patterns. Attendance increased dramatically, and the church became a prominent center, noted for its Pentecostal conventions, missionary focus, and ongoing revival emphasis. Piper fully endorsed the Pentecostal view of Spirit baptism as enduement with power for service; he refused, however, to be dogmatic about evidential tongues. Lydia Piper was among the first in the Stone Church to receive Spirit baptism (July 1907); her husband received the experience in February 1908.

In October 1908 the church began publishing *The Latter Rain Evangel,* a monthly magazine that circulated Pentecostal teaching and news to a broad, far-flung constituency. Edited first by Piper then by his former assistant, Anna Reiff, the *Evangel* greatly extended the Stone Church's visibility and stature throughout the movement. The church also published other tracts, pamphlets, and books that offered teaching about the movement's emphases. Probably the most influential of these was D. Wesley Myland's *The Latter Rain Covenant* (1910).

On December 29, 1911 (his fifteenth wedding anniversary), the forty-three-year-old Piper died unexpectedly after a brief illness. His wife served as pastor of the Stone Church until 1914, when she moved the family to California for two years. After ten more years in Chicago, she returned to the West Coast, where she taught briefly at the Bible school that later became Southern California College. She died on January 15, 1949. The Pipers had six children: Ruth, William, Theodore, Irene, Dorothy, and Esther.

Under new leadership, the Stone Church affiliated with the General Council of the Assemblies of God. Its commodious facilities accommodated the second and seventh General Councils.

Bibliography: Gordon P. Gardiner, "Out of Zion . . . Into All the World," *Bread of Life* (April 1982), 7–8, 11; (May 1982), 7–10, 13; *LRE* (October 1908); (January 1912).   E. L. Blumhofer

PISGAH HOME MOVEMENT   Founded about 1895 by Finis Ewing Yoakum, M.D. The Pisgah Home Movement reached its peak between 1911 and 1914. Yoakum, originally from Texas, had attended half a dozen colleges and had been a member of at least one medical school faculty. After receiving a miraculous healing in his own body following a near fatal accident, he began to seek ways to bring health and healing to those who were unable to afford it.

Headquartered in Highland Park, California, Yoakum established a variety of outreach ministries in the greater Los Angeles basin that were financed totally through faith. Theses efforts he named "Pisgah" after the mountain where Moses stood to view the Promised Land (Num. 21:20; 23:14; Deut. 3:27; 4:49; 34:1). Among them was Pisgah Home, 6044 Echo Street in Highland Park. In 1911 it provided regular housing for 175 workers and stable indigents and made provision for an average of 9,000 clean beds and 18,000 meals monthly to the urban homeless, the poor, and the social outcasts, including alcoholics, drug addicts, and prostitutes. Each week Yoakum sent his workers into the city distributing nickels (the price of trolley fare to Pisgah) so that these people could come to Pisgah Home and Tabernacle. There they received two free meals and spent the day in evangelistic and healing services where Dr. Yoakum preached. They sang from *Pisgah Home Songs,* a book of hymns selected and published by Stanley H. Frodsham. At the end of the day those who wished were allowed to continue at the home, while the others were given another nickel to return to Los Angeles.

Dr. Yoakum established a "free" Pisgah store at the corner of Avenue 58 and Benner Street. It was a two-story concrete block structure a short distance from Pisgah Home. Staffed entirely by volunteers, it served as a distribution center for used and donated clothing and food goods along with those made or grown by residents of the various Pisgah projects.

Near the store, on a hill called Mount Ararat (symbolic of a new beginning) at 140 Hayes Avenue, Yoakum constructed Pisgah Ark, a wooden frame structure, as a haven for recovering prostitutes, drug addicts, and alcoholic women. Housing about two dozen, including the staff of matrons, it provided serene accommodations and a rigorous schedule of work and disciplined Bible study.

Seventeen miles from the Highland Park campus, Yoakum purchased a 24-acre plot near Lankershim Boulevard in North Hollywood. Known as Pisgah Gardens, it was designed to provide rehabilitative exercise and fresh air to those with tuberculosis and other diseases for whom it was thought some exercise would be useful. This acreage was dotted with small dwellings and tents, and it housed a small orphanage between 1913 and 1914. Three-fourths of this property was under cultivation, and the vegetables and fruit raised and dried there were distributed through the Pisgah free store, cooked for the "inmates" of the various Pisgah endeavors in the form of vegetarian stews, or distributed freely to the poor.

On March 14, 1914, Yoakum exchanged the Pisgah Ark and Garden properties for a 3,225-acre parcel of land about forty miles north of Los Angeles, near Chatsworth. Known as Pisgah Grande, it was the establishment of a Utopian-like community that would house a number of Pisgah enterprises, including the ones uprooted in the purchase. Cattle were raised, fruit trees were planted, some gardening was undertaken, and tents were set up or small red brick cottages were constructed to house the workers. By 1916 there were about 130 workers who called it home. A longer-term Pisgah Bible School was established there under the direction of William C. Stevens; this drew a number of younger people to the community. Plans were made to establish a home for the feeble-minded and insane, a cancer treatment center, and a home for illegitimate children. The death of Dr. Yoakum in 1920 brought the development scheme to a halt.

C. M. White, a close friend of Yoakum, incorporated Pisgah at that time, enabling it to continue operation. During the 1930s property was obtained in the San Bernardino Mountains, but in 1943 it was sold because it was not easily managed year round. Property was purchased at a lower altitude, ten miles from San Bernardino. In 1947, a 500-acre farm parcel near Pikesville, Tennessee, was donated to the Pisgah Home Movement. Today the tabernacle in Highland Park is called Christ Faith Mission. It continues to minister to the alcoholic and addicted, although the city has recently put restrictions upon those it can serve. Pisgah maintains a Mountain Home at 7220 Sierra Highway in the Antelope Valley near Pisgah Grande, operating it as a camp meeting center. A small community also flourishes on the Tennessee site.

Bibliography: *Confidence* 5 (11, November 1912): 248–51, 255–58; 7 (5, May 1914): 92; J. Creek, *Footprints of a Human Life* (1949); *Dictionary of American Biography* (1936), 20:611–12; *Pisgah Journal* 48 (1, March 1962); *Word and Work* 33 (1911).
                                                                      C. M. Robeck, Jr.

PLYMIRE, VICTOR GUY (1881–1956). Missionary to Tibet and China. Plymire was born to Christian parents in Loganville, Pennsylvania. In 1887, at age sixteen, he consecrated his life to God at a street meeting and began attending the Christian and Missionary Alliance (CMA) church. At first he found work with an electrical construction company, but God began to call him into full-time Christian service. Plymire attended the Missionary Training Institute at Nyack, New York, and was ordained by the CMA. He pioneered several churches in the U.S. before he felt impressed to apply for missionary service.

In 1908 Plymire was accepted as a missionary and was sent to northwest China on the border of Tibet. He married missionary Grace Harkless in 1919. There were many struggles and hardships in Tibet, but Plymire was determined to serve the Lord at any cost. It was sixteen years before he had the joy of baptizing his first convert.

After returning home on furlough in 1920, Plymire received the baptism of the Spirit at Lancaster, Pennsylvania. He was immediately ordained by the Assemblies of God (AG) and was appointed to serve again in Tibet. In 1927 his wife and baby son died of smallpox. The following year, Plymire married Ruth Weidman, also a missionary to China. The Plymires continued to minister in Tibet and China until 1949, when China was closed to missions. They returned to the U.S., serving churches in Ohio and Missouri. Ruth Plymire served as a missionary to Taiwan from 1959 until she retired in 1970.

Bibliography: D. Plymire, *High Adventure in Tibet* (1959).   G. W. Gohr

POLHILL, CECIL H. (1860–1938). First major promoter of Pentecostal missions. Polhill was one of the "Cambridge Seven" who went out as missionaries with the China Inland Mission (CIM) in 1885. After years on the Tibetan border, Polhill returned home on doctors' orders in 1900 and was soon invited to join the CIM council. He inherited the family estate near Bedford in 1903 and was widowed in 1904. Returning from a trip to China, he was baptized in the Spirit in Los Angeles early in 1908. Soon making common cause with fellow Anglican A. A. Boddy, Polhill used his social position and finances to promote the nascent Pentecostal movement, through prayer meetings in several London locations and through regular conferences. His consuming interest was the salvation of the lost through missionary work, especially in China. After urging this cause at the Hamburg conference in December 1908, Polhill and Boddy took immediate steps to form the Pentecostal Missionary Union for Great Britain and Ireland (PMU), of which Polhill soon became the president. He was instrumental in the establishment of missionary training homes for both men and women and from his experience emphasized the practical over the theoretical.

Polhill, a disciplined man, inspired respect rather than love and undoubtedly endured ridicule by the upper class for his Pentecostal witness and contacts. Although continuing to preside at the annual London conferences each Pentecost, as the years passed Polhill devoted himself more exclusively to the missionary task. He paid several visits to PMU missionaries in the Far East, the last in 1924. When PMU was integrated into the newly formed Assemblies of God in Great Britain and Ireland in 1925, Polhill went into retirement. His publication *Fragments of Flame* became *Flames of Fire* in 1911 and ended with the demise of PMU.

Bibliography: D. Gee, *Wind and Flame* (1967); P. Hocken, 'Cecil Polhill—Pentecostal Layman," *Pneuma* 2 (1988, forthcoming).   P. D. Hocken

POLISH CHARISMATICS See CHARISMATIC MOVEMENT.

POLISH PENTECOSTALS See EUROPEAN PENTECOSTALISM.

POLMAN, GERRIT ROELOF (1868–1932). Founder of the Dutch Pentecostal movement. Polman began ministry in the Salvation Army under the direction of Arthur S. Booth-Clibborn, through whom he made contact with the Dowie movement in Zion City, Illinois, which he visited in about 1904. He returned to found a Dowie Zionist center in Amsterdam. Influenced by the Welsh revival and reports of the Azusa Street revival, the group became Pentecostal in 1907. Polman published the periodical, *Spade Regen* (April 1908–31) and hosted the International Pentecostal Conference, January, 9–16, 1921.

Bibliography: H. Bakker, *Stroomingen en Sekten van onzen tijd* (1924), 161–68; D. Bundy, "Pentecostalism in Belgium," *Pneuma* 8 (1986): 41–56; W. J. Hollenweger, "Handbuch der Pfingstbewegung," diss., Zurich, 1966, 05.20.004; C. van der Laan and P. N. van der Laan, *Pinksteren in beweging* (1982); *Vijfenzeventig Jaar Pinkstergemeente Immanuel* (n.d.); G. A. Wumkes, *De Pinksterbeweging voornamelijk in Nederland* (1916).
                                                                      D. D. Bundy

PORTUGUESE CHARISMATICS See CHARISMATIC MOVEMENT.

PORTUGUESE PENTECOSTALS See EUROPEAN PENTECOSTALISM.

POSITIVE CONFESSION THEOLOGY An alternative title for faith-formula theology or the prosperity doctrine promulgated by several contemporary televangelists under the leadership and inspiration of Essek William Kenyon (1867–1948). The phrase "positive confession" may be legitimately interpreted in several ways. Most significantly of all, the phrase "positive confession" refers quite literally to bringing into existence what we state with our mouth, since faith is a confession. This perspective, embraced by Kenyon and his disciples in their relatively new biblical-theological emphasis, regarded the value of the power of the tongue as a key to the confession theory. Since Kenyon's demise in

1948, several "word ministries," including such personalities as Kenneth Hagin, Kenneth Copeland, Charles Capps, Frederick K. C. Price, and others have mined the teachings of their revered teacher.

Conceptually, the views espoused by E. W. Kenyon can be traced to his exposure to metaphysical ideas derived from attendance at Emerson College of Oratory in Boston, a spawning ground for New Thought philosophical ideas. The major tenets of the New Thought movement are health or healing, abundance or prosperity, wealth and happiness.

New Thought philosophy can be traced to Phineas P. Quimby (1802–66), whose ideas gained prominence toward the close of the last century. Not only regarded as the founder of the New Thought philosophy, Quimby studied spiritism, occultism, hypnosis, and other aspects of parapsychology. It was Quimby who was said to have healed Mary Baker Patterson Eddy, the founder of Christian Science, in 1862. He attempted to make witchcraft credible by the use of scientific language. It appears that Eddy borrowed the term Christian Science from Quimby along with his theoretical formulations, and these became the basis for the Mind Science cult she founded. Quimby labeled his formulation the science of Christ. From Quimby, William Branham, E. W. Kenyon, and John G. Lake, a view of God emerged that is currently espoused by Hagin, Copeland, Capps, and Price.

John G. Lake asserted, "Man is not a separate creation detached from God, he is part of God Himself. . . . God intends us to be gods. The inner man is the real governor, the true man that Jesus said was a god." Bishop Earl Paulk of Atlanta recently wrote, "Just as dogs have puppies and cats have kittens, so God has little gods. Until we comprehend that we are little gods and we begin to act like little gods, we cannot manifest the Kingdom of God." Kenneth Copeland further asserted, "You impart humanity into a child that's born of you. Because you are a human, you have imparted the nature of humanity into that born child. That child wasn't born a whale. It was born a human. Well, now, you don't have a God in you. You are one." The origin of this view is derived from the words of the serpent in Genesis 3:4. This recent emphasis in the Positive Confession movement poses the greatest danger. It raises humankind to God's level and thereby creates a false pride that generates the belief that humans can save themselves from disaster by claiming their "divine right." The logical conclusion is that we can purge the earth of sickness, sin, and even the "demon of poverty." Robert Tilton, pastor of the Word of Faith World Outreach Center in Dallas, Texas, espouses such a view: "He's given us power to create wealth and we're already seeing this thing happen, and I believe that in those last days the believer is not going to be at the back of the bus taking a back seat any longer! We're the righteousness of God." This theological claim, while based on faulty presuppositions, has a universal appeal because of its promise of humanistic plans to change history. This form of godism appears to be the basis of faith for Positive

Confession adherents who attempt to use their "divine right" to manipulate the Divine. "Now you live in the present tense." "He is what He says He is, and you are what He says you are!" "His Word cannot lie, and you hold fast to that Word in your confession." E. W. Kenyon went beyond the scientific shamanism of the New Thought movement when he first taught "the positive confession of the Word of God." But he did not go so far as to espouse that "faith is a confession," therefore "what I confess, I possess," or to assert that we can indeed "create reality with the words of our mouths." Such confession creates "now faith."

The disciples of Kenyon speak of prosperity as a "divine right" and have formulated laws of prosperity to be rehearsed daily by persons seeking health and wealth. Positive Confessionism is rooted in an easy believism with no grounding or fundamental point of reference. Its doctrinal formulations are rooted in a strained biblicism without an object of faith, often placing an undue stress upon gifts rather than on the fruit of a believer.

The Rhema doctrine is the primary key to Positive Confession theology. Romans 10:8 is the primary passage or archtext of the Rhema doctrine. In its classical Greek usage, the word *rhēma* has to do with stating something specifically. The major premise of Rhema doctrine is that whatever is spoken by faith becomes immediately inspired and therefore dynamic in the particular situation or event to which it is addressed. Kenyon held that there are two kinds of knowledge, revelation or faith knowledge and sense knowledge. Revelation knowledge is "the knowledge that deals with things that the senses cannot discover or know without assistance from revelation knowledge." Revelation knowledge, for Kenyon and Positive Confession adherents, is the realm above sense knowledge. Kenyon's use of the category of revelation knowledge appears to be apologetic and calls the uninitiated into a true and higher knowledge of God.

Faith formula theology for Charles Farah has gnostic tendencies, and its revelation doctrine is informed by its presuppositions. This revelation or "higher knowledge" becomes the hermeneutical principle by which adherents either discount or destroy traditional biblical themes of suffering, cross-bearing, self-sacrifice, poverty, and martyrdom.

Proverbs 6:2; Romans 10:8; Romans 4:17; and 3 John 2 are the basic Scriptures used by Positive Confession adherents to give credence to the Rhema doctrine that they embrace. To be "ensnared by the words of your mouth" in Proverbs 6:2 has reference to a financial transaction that involves a security deposit within a contractual relationship. Romans 4:17 and 10:8 are usually taken out of context and strained to mean that anyone can "call those things which be not as though they were." By the blessings of Abraham, adherents "nullify the curse of Adam and enter in almost all of the kingdom benefits before the kingdom has fully come." However, Romans 4:17 is a description of Abraham's faith, specifically, not ours. Romans 10:8 apart from verses 9–11 loses its true meaning. The passages cited refer primarily to the truth that comprises the message of salvation as proclaimed in the apostolic tradition. Such truths must be believed and relied on and confessed if salvation is to be realized as verse 13 indicates. The context is about special faith given to us. It is obtained as a divine gift and not attained as an acquired skill. It is like grace, an offer in the righteousness of God. Such "faith comes by hearing the Word of God" (v. 17). Third John 2 is a formal greeting and not a promise; neither can it be evoked as God's will for all believers to be "healthy and prosperous."

The problem with exponents of the Rhema interpretation is their biased selection of biblical passages, often without due regard to their context. The self-defined phrase "confessing the Word of God" takes precedence over hermeneutical principles and rules for biblical interpretation. This approach not only does violence to the text but forces the NT linguistic data into artificial categories that the biblical authors themselves could not affirm. The Rhema doctrinal premise (that whatever is spoken by faith becomes immediately inspired in the situation addressed) has a tendency to confuse *want* and *need*.

The easy believism of the Positive Confession movement appears to be grounded in *fides qua* (i.e., how Jesus believed) rather than *fides quae* (i.e., Jesus as the object of faith). Authentic biblical faith reveals the former but is always grounded in the latter, Jesus as the object of faith. Indeed, to grasp biblical faith, one must move beyond a mere *mind* over *matter* wish or belief and examine the Hebraic meaning of faith, which stresses firmness, reliability, or steadfastness. The power or efficacy of faith for right relationship with God is never to be found or sought in the act itself but rather in that to which one holds firm by believing. God must be the object of our faith and never of our ego wishes or selfish wants.

As Christians we are urged in Luke 12:22 to take no thought about our basic needs, that they are already included in the divine providential plan. Those who are preoccupied with life's basic necessities are said to be persons of little faith, for it is "after such things that the Gentiles seek," says Jesus. Christians of all walks are urged to grasp more fully the notion that faith does not always secure from God everything we desire, but it does get from God everything *he wants us to have*, and there is a fundamental difference. In the NT, faith is active; it is a "response term" that presumes the initiative of the grace of God. Within the Christian faith the biblical meaning of the noun and the associated verb "to believe" denotes the criterion of right relationship with God. (1) In the NT it appears that love is given primacy over faith, especially in the Pauline literature. Positive Confessionists reverse this emphasis. The true evidence of the arrival and sign of the kingdom is indeed based on the presence and evidence of love (John 13:34–35). "By this shall all men know that you are my disciples, if you have love one to another." Faith is never presented as a tool to manipulate God for our selfish ends and nowhere in the teachings of Jesus receives primacy. (2) Paul, in the hymn of love in 1 Corinthians 13,

assigns primacy to love as the greatest of faith, hope, and love. Love was indeed the balancing ideal between ecstasy and order for the gifted and the nongifted. (3) At the very core of our being is the need to be loved by the One who created us for his glory, and who alone as perfect love can totally satisfy our deepest needs. It is God's liberating love that breaks the shackles forged by the demonic powers of oppression, thus releasing us to become all we were meant to be in God.

Bibliography: C. S. Braden, *Spirits in Rebellion: The Rise and Development of New Thought* (1966); C. Capps, *How to Have Faith in Your Faith* (1986); idem, *Seedtime and Harvest* (1986); idem, *The Tongue—A Creative Force* (1976); P. Y. Cho, *The Fourth Dimension* (1979); G. Copeland, *God's Will Is Prosperity* (1978); K. Copeland, *The Force of Faith* (1981); idem, *The Power of The Tongue* (1980); idem, "Questions and Answers" in *Believer's Voice of Victory* (June 1986); C. Farah, Jr., "A Critical Analysis: The Roots and Fruits of Faith-Formula Theology," *Society of Pentecostal Studies* (Fall 1980); G. D. Fee, "The Gospel of Prosperity—An Alien Gospel," *Reformation Today* (November–December, 1984), 39; K. Hagin, Sr., *Having Faith in Your Faith* (1980); idem, *How to Write Your Own Ticket With God* (1979); idem, *New Thresholds of Faith* (1985); idem, *Plead Your Case* (1985); idem, *Right and Wrong Thinking* (1966); idem, *The Word of Faith* (1984); idem, *Words* (1979); idem, *You Can Have What You Say* (1980); D. Hunt, *Beyond Seduction* (1987); D. Hunt and J. A. McMahon, *The Seduction of Christianity* (1985); E. W. Kenyon, *Jesus the Healer* (1943); idem, *The Two Kinds of Faith: Faith's Secrets Revealed* (1942); idem, *What Happened From the Cross to the Throne?* (1945); E. W. Kenyon and D. Gossett, *The Positive Confession of the Word of God* (1981); G. Lindsay, *Spiritual Hunger, The God-men and Other Sermons by Dr. John G. Lake* (1976); D. R. McConnell, *A Different Gospel* (1988); E. Paulk, *Satan Unmasked* (1984); F. Price, *Faith, Foolishness or Presumption?* (1979); idem, *How Faith Works* (1976); R. Tilton, *God's Laws of Success* (1983).   L. Lovett

POST, ANSEL HOWARD (d. 1931). Early Pentecostal missionary. After thirty years as a Baptist minister, Post came into contact with the Azusa Street revival while he was living in Los Angeles, California. He received the baptism in the Holy Spirit in 1906 and then propagated the new Pentecostal message with other believers in nearby Pasadena; they were known as the "Household of God." In 1907 he began traveling abroad to spread the news about the revival. His travels took him to South Africa, England, Wales, and Ceylon.

In 1910 Post and his wife Etta began ministry in Egypt as independent Pentecostal missionaries. They affiliated with the Assemblies of God in December 1916. His ministry there focused on church planting and the promotion of Pentecostal revivals until his death.

Bibliography: "Head of Sect Is Disturber," *Pasadena Daily News* (July 13, 1906), 12; "Household Is on Move Again," *Pasadena Daily News* (July 18, 1906), 12; "In Memoriam," *PE* (August 15, 1931), 8; A. H. Post, "Testimony of a Minister," *AF* (January 1907), 4.   G. B. McGee

PRANGE, ERWIN (1917–). Lutheran charismatic leader with a widely recognized ministry of deliverance and counseling. Prange graduated from Concordia Seminary, St. Louis, Missouri, in

1954. He served ghetto parishes of the Lutheran Church–Missouri Synod (LCMS) in New York and Baltimore for most of the next eighteen years.

Prange pursued extensive graduate and post-graduate studies in psychology and counseling in the 1960s. While serving in his second LCMS parish he experienced the infilling of the Holy Spirit and spoke in tongues (1963). In 1976 he moved to St. Paul, Minnesota, and became an associate pastor at North Heights Lutheran Church, one of the leading charismatic churches in the American Lutheran Church (ALC). Prange developed the most extensive and well-known

Built in 1967, the prayer tower on the Oral Roberts University campus, Tulsa, Oklahoma, is 200 feet tall. Paid prayer counselors of the Abundant Life Prayer group answer telephones around the clock.

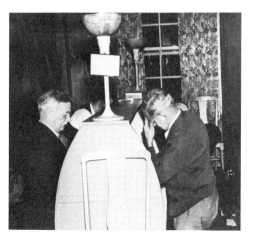

Men at prayer in Angelus Temple prayer tower.

ministry of deliverance and counseling in the Lutheran charismatic movement. Key elements of his personal experience, pastoral concern, and theological perspective are included in a substantial authorship of books and articles.

Bibliography: L. Christenson, ed., *Welcome, Holy Spirit* (1987); E. Prange, *The Gift Is Already Yours* (1973); idem, *How to Pray for Your Children* (1979); idem, *A Time for Intercession* (1979); idem, *A Time to Grow* (1976). L. Christenson

PRAYER See SPIRITUALITY, PENTECOSTAL AND CHARISMATIC; FASTING.

PRAYER TOWERS A place set aside for prayer either for oneself or for specific needs of others. Numerous organizations, individuals, Bible schools, and local churches have designated rooms or buildings for prayer. Often these places are built on a second floor or higher.

Symbolically, the prayer tower idea probably comes from at least two scriptural accounts of people who prayed in places that were higher than the ground floor. When Elijah stayed with the widow and her son (1 Kings 17), he stayed in an upper room. There Elijah prayed life back into the dead son. A second upper room, of course, was the one referred to in Acts 2 in which the 120 prayed and waited for the Day of Pentecost. Another symbolic idea is a watch tower on a city wall. People in prayer can think of themselves as "watchmen."

Through the centuries believers have set aside places of prayer, sometimes in upper rooms or towers and other places of solitude. Since Pentecostals and charismatics believe in waiting on God for the baptism in the Spirit and for healing, prayer towers and other places set aside for prayer seem natural.

Carrie Judd Montgomery set aside a prayer room in an unused parlor in her parents' home in the 1880s after she read an article on the subject in a Christian magazine. Sanford's work at Shiloh, Maine, featured a prayer tower, as did other nineteenth-century ministries. Charles F. Parham followed the examples of others after he moved his Bible school into Stone's Folly, an unfinished mansion in Topeka, Kansas. One of the domes of the mansion was converted into a prayer tower. An early Pentecostal mission in Los Angeles was called the Upper Room Mission. Later Aimee Semple McPherson had an upper room built in her Angelus Temple. Believers could seek for the Pentecostal experience or pray for other needs around the clock.

The best-known prayer tower of recent years has been the ultramodern 200-foot structure on the Oral Roberts University campus. Built in 1967, this tower is manned twenty-four hours a day by employees of the Abundant Life Prayer Group. The employees answer several thousand calls each month from people asking for prayer. The Upper Room at PTL has been designed for visitors to pray and receive prayer. Callers can call the Upper Room staff for prayer.

Bibliography: K. Kendrick, *The Promise Fulfilled* (1961); promotional materials from the International Church of the Foursquare Gospel, Oral Roberts University, and PTL. W. E. Warner

PENTECOSTAL PREACHING See PREACH-ING, A PENTECOSTAL PERSPECTIVE.

PREACHING, A PENTECOSTAL PERSPECTIVE

I. Introduction. One must not attempt, through definition, to separate totally, Pentecostal preaching from the normal understanding of what it means "to preach" or "to proclaim" the good news of Jesus Christ.

As commonly understood, Pentecostal preaching means a type of message and a style of delivery characteristic of Pentecostal worship. Pentecostal preaching is the best of one's study and meditation, warmed by the Spirit of God, and made to glow in the heart by the anointing of the same Holy Spirit.

The word "Pentecostal" brings to the subject of preaching a unique emphasis. It presents a clear track for interpreting events and actions of the NT church as recorded in the Book of Acts, and it provides a vehicle for emphasizing some positives often overlooked or ignored by more convention-al definitions of preaching.

II. The Basics of Pentecostal Preaching. What is today referred to as the Pentecostal-charismatic revival has its roots in large part in the mid- and late-nineteenth-century Holiness movement. It is important therefore to remember that there are some fundamental truths relating to preaching that influenced attitudes. Let us look at three such basics on which Pentecostals agree.

A. True Pentecostal Preaching Must Center on the Word of God. Pentecostals have been so identified by an emphasis on the work of the Holy Spirit in every believer's life that some overlook the fact that a cardinal principle of Pentecostalism has always been strict adherence first and foremost to the Bible. For one properly to understand the role of Pentecostal preaching as herein interpret-ed, this basic first principle—the centrality of the Word of God—will have to be kept in mind.

An overview of the Book of Acts reveals that the early church was Christ-centered, Spirit-domi-nated, and Word-based. All the members were continually spreading the Word of God, honoring the Word, and explaining the Word. The Word of God constituted the message and became the authority for all claims of the church. The Word was the source of all preaching, the standard for all doctrine, the medium by which to judge all experience (Acts 2:41; 4:4, 29; 6:7; 8:4, 14; 10:44; 12:24; 13:49).

For Pentecostals today the Word is central to all life-practice as well as to all doctrine. It is both the manual by which to operate and the standard by which to judge. To think otherwise, or to try and understand Pentecostalism from any other perspective, is erroneous.

B. Pentecostal Preaching Must Always Exalt Jesus Christ. Preaching that is anthropocentric, that glorifies the human either physically or in terms of works, or that extols anything other than grace manifested in the person and work of Jesus Christ is not Pentecostal preaching no matter how it is labeled.

Jesus set forth this principle when he first told his disciples that he would send them another Counselor: "When the Counselor comes, whom I will send to you from the Father, the Spirit of truth who goes out from the Father, he will testify about me" (John 15:26).

It has been suggested by some that Pentecostals exalt the Holy Spirit to the exclusion of Jesus Christ, and it may be that there have been times when this emphasis has appeared to be true, but such is a false conclusion, denied by true Pente-costals. Those who are led of the Spirit of God proclaim, exalt, and extol the lordship of Jesus Christ.

"But when he, the Spirit of truth, comes, he will guide you into all truth. He will speak on his own; he will speak only what he hears, and he will tell you what is yet to come. He will bring glory to me by taking from what is mine and making it known to you. All that belongs to the Father is mine. That is why I said the Spirit will take from what is mine and make it known to you" (John 16:13–15).

C. Pentecostal Preaching Should Always Be Directed and Empowered by the Holy Spirit. People are capable of structuring speeches. They are able to do research, to study, and are also quite capable, in terms of human talent, of entertaining, of presenting interesting lectures, and of persuading others. But, for the Pentecos-tal, all these things do not constitute preaching in the real sense. Pentecostal preaching takes place only in terms of the dynamic of the Holy Spirit.

It is the Holy Spirit who directs and guides the minister of the Word (John 16:13). The Spirit teaches the minister all things and brings all things to his or her remembrance (John 14:26). The Spirit also anoints the minister for the performance of his or her task, as clearly wit-nessed in the words of our Lord, "The Spirit of the Lord *is* upon me" (Luke 4:18 KJV), and in other references (Acts 1:8; 10:38; 2 Cor. 1:22; 1 John 2:20, 27).

This is not to say that the same Holy Spirit does not function in the lives of other preachers of the gospel—he certainly does—but it is to point out that a proper understanding of the Holy Spirit's role in preaching lets the person of God be more sensitive and open to the Spirit's leading. This sensitivity to the Spirit constitutes an impor-tant element in what is commonly known as the anointing of the Spirit.

The word "anointing" is used in a rather broad and twofold sense. The anointing of the Holy Spirit should be present in the individual's study, in the prayer closet, in daily devotions, in personal witnessing and ministering to others, as well as in pulpit activity.

The word "anointing" is also used to set forth the divine element of preaching, that which pricks the human heart and conscience, that which burns the Word first into the minister's heart and then into the consciousness of the listener, and without which the mere human words become powerless and ineffective.

III. The Dimensions of Pentecostal Preach-ing. There are many facets to Pentecostal preach-ing; the following should be considered:

A. Pentecostal Preaching Should Be Precise, Exact in Meaning, Relevant, Always Being Carried Out in a Certain Degree of Refinement. The word "precise" is used here in opposition to that preaching which is pointless, without specific and concrete objectives.

The Holy Spirit breathes fresh inspiration on those willing to listen, and the Bible illumines Scripture truths for the minister willing to study, to discover, and to share. Every minister must study. Meditation in the Word, searching the Scriptures, examination and self-application of the Word to one's own life—these too are spiritual activities wherein the Holy Spirit anoints the person of God.

Routine operation and pseudoprofessionalism have no place in Pentecostal preaching. God's servants do not have the time for dealing in unfelt truths. Rather, they must give heed to Paul's admonition to "live a life worthy of the calling you have received" (Eph. 4:1). Study furnishes a person with materials, and prayer sanctifies those ideas and concepts, but God gives the message through the Holy Spirit.

Preaching with precision—truly great preaching—includes knowing and understanding the audience. It means the establishing of preaching goals, long-range and immediate, and it aims to convert sinners, to inspire saints, to comfort, to teach, to correct, to motivate, to make aware, to call to commitment, to challenge, to instruct, to reprove, to lead in the giving of thanks, and to guide in worship.

B. Pentecostal Preaching Should Be Prophetic. The prophet Joel gave Israel a message of hope in a dark hour (Joel 2:23–29). Above and beyond the temporal blessings mentioned, there was to be an outpouring of the Spirit that would be accompanied by the prophetic gift in a most unusual manner. Sons and daughters of the family, as well as servants of the household, were to become partakers of the Spirit who made Elijah and Elisha stand head and shoulders above others of their day.

Joel prophesied of an age of blessing when the prophetic unction was to be shared by many. The essential facts of his prediction were these: first, a great age of salvation was to be opened; second, this coming era would be distinguished by the gift of the Holy Spirit; third, the presence of the Holy Spirit was to be marked by an extraordinary manifestation of prophetic power.

Prophecy was thus promised to be a distinctive gift of Pentecost. No one can doubt that the 120 on the Day of Pentecost were endowed with divine energy and speech such as was not known before. According to the message of the apostle Peter, Joel's prophecy was specifically fulfilled (Acts 2:17–18).

Modern usage of the word "prophecy" is understood to mean almost exclusively the predicting of future events. The predictive element is certainly not absent from NT prophecy, but a more common definition is "forthtelling." In the scriptural sense, the NT prophet is one empowered by authority of the Holy Spirit to declare the mind of God. He or she therefore proclaims truth put in his or her heart by the Holy Spirit.

This brings us to the full definition of what it means "to prophesy," which makes the minister one who speaks for another: the prophet speaks for God. Not only does he or she receive authority to speak through the Spirit but the message comes through the Holy Spirit as well. Prophets are moved by the Spirit to speak. Their minds are illumined by the Spirit to deliver the message that God sends. The Holy Spirit quickens their mental powers, guides their thoughts, and moves them to deal in certain topics of need. This is preaching prophetically, Pentecostal preaching at its best.

C. Pentecostal Preaching Is Uniquely Effective. Pentecostal preaching has the same power and authority it evidenced on the Day of Pentecost nearly two thousand years ago. Pentecostal preaching today will produce the same miraculous results it produced during the early days of the NT church. It is the same uniting of human instrument and divine power, the same blending of human commitment and phenomenal results as set forth in the Book of Acts.

"Signs," "wonders," "powers," and "works" were terms applied to the ministry of Jesus Christ. These were the evidences by which Jesus verified his claim to messiahship. These were also the evidences found in the NT church as recorded in the Book of Acts. These evidences *should* and *will* follow true believers in the twentieth century.

Let us look now, briefly, at some of the unique results that ought always to follow Pentecostal preaching.

1. Convicts of Sin. Pentecostal preaching builds on the Word, according to the leading of the Holy Spirit, and it depends on that same Spirit to convict and bring men and women to Christ. It is not the persuasiveness of men nor the rational arguments of the theologian, but it is the Holy Spirit who moves people and has sparked this present-day revival impacting Christianity around the world.

2. Produces Faith. Christian faith, saving faith, is of divine origin. It does not originate with individuals. Not only is this truth set forth explicitly in the Scriptures—"For it is by grace you have been saved, through faith, and this not from yourselves, it is the gift of God" (Eph. 2:8)—but it is likewise verified through human experience.

3. Sparks Our Faith. We may not have been converted during the preaching of a sermon or even in a church building, but it was the Word—what Paul referred to as "the power of God for the salvation of everyone" (Rom. 1:16)—that planted the seed of faith; and the Holy Spirit brought forth a new creation in Christ Jesus.

4. Confronts Demonic Powers. This world is in rebellion against God. There can be no compromise between righteousness and wickedness. While one sees evidence of this conflict on many levels, none is more clearly exposed than when the anointed preacher speaks as God's voice. Such preaching may stir up opposition, it may upset economic and social orders, it may conflict with established patterns and habits. Nevertheless, God's people must continue to proclaim the

Word, for herein will come victory of a miraculous nature (Acts 7:54, 57–58; 19:23–41).

5. *Produces Godly Reverence (Acts 5:1–10).* Effectiveness in preaching is not in words alone but rather in the listener's understanding of what God is saying and doing at the moment. When the Word is preached uncompromisingly, when the Word goes forth with power and under the anointing of the Holy Spirit, people will develop an awesome respect for spiritual things. This is the soil from which come miracles and transformed lives.

6. *Confirmed by Operation of Spiritual Gifts.* Paul instructed believers at Corinth to "eagerly desire the greater gifts" (1 Cor. 12:31). When one places this statement alongside what follows in chapter 13—Paul's "more excellent way"— and when these two passages are viewed within the context of the first part of chapter 12 and with chapter 14, balance is achieved. Paul did not wish the church to ignore or forget spiritual gifts, as some tend to do today, nor did he wish spiritual gifts to become an end in themselves. In fact, Paul clearly profiles the error of the latter choice. Instead, Paul wished the church to realize that the operation of spiritual gifts goes hand in hand with the preaching and teaching of God's Word.

As noted earlier, a key ingredient in Pentecostal preaching is prophecy. Under the anointing of the Holy Spirit, God's servants prophesy—they "speak forth"—the things of God. Prophecy is a key operation of the Holy Spirit (1 Cor. 12:8–10). Prophecy is a gift that may be further confirmed by the operation of other gifts.

IV. Conclusion. The objective of preaching has not changed in today's world, for God has not changed. The person of God who is called and anointed of the Holy Spirit and who will faithfully yield to the leading of the Spirit, has the same commission and enablement as was given to the disciples of old. Such is the grand objective and overall purpose of Pentecostal preaching as seen and understood by Pentecostals in today's world.

Bibliography: W. R. Bowie, *Preaching* (1954); J. Dawson, ed., *John Wesley on Preaching* (1904); G. Duffield, *Pentecostal Preaching* (1957); G. Holmes, *Toward an Effective Pulpit Ministry* (1971); R. H. Hughes, *Pentecostal Preaching* (1981); C. E. Macartney, *Preaching Without Notes* (1946); I. Macpherson, *Burden of the Lord* (1955); G. C. Morgan, *Preaching* (1955); W. E. Sangster, *The Craft of the Sermon* (1954); J. S. Stewart, *Heralds of God* (1946).   R. H. Hughes

PRESBYTERIAN AND REFORMED CHARISMATICS

Despite a natural tension between a theology believed and a faith experienced, those Christians in the Presbyterian and Reformed tradition have often been pioneers in movements of the Holy Spirit within the body of Christ.

John Calvin, who is referred to as the father of Reformed theology, has been called by many the theologian of the Holy Spirit in the Protestant Reformation. He had much to say about the person and work of the Holy Spirit in his classic *Institutes of the Christian Religion.* In his theology he sought a balance between the written Word and the Holy Spirit and emphasized the Christian's absolute need for the power of the Holy Spirit in order to live a life of righteousness in Christ to which the heavenly Father has called all Christians.

It is true that Calvin intimated that the "extraordinary" gifts of the Holy Spirit had ceased. He attributed this to the facts that God did not want them further abused on the one hand and that Christians lacked the faith to appropriate them on the other. Unfortunately, Professor Benjamin B. Warfield of Princeton Theological Seminary in the late nineteenth century went a step further by stating that the "extraordinary" gifts had ceased with the apostles. This view quenched the Holy Spirit in the lives of numerous clergy who in turn influenced their church members.

History does record that periodically the Holy Spirit has used Presbyterians as pioneers in renewal and revival movements, enabling them to move from the theological to the experiential. Occasionally this has led to an upheaval or division within congregations and to resistance or caution by presbyteries. It may even lead to the formation of a new denomination.

A case in point occurred when the Holy Spirit moved mightily among Presbyterians living in the Cumberland Mountains of Tennessee. Ninety years ahead of the Pentecostal movement, these Presbyterians were experiencing "the New Testament baptism of the Holy Spirit" as church historian B. W. McDonald described it in his book *History of the Cumberland Presbyterian Church.* The preachers of the emerging Cumberland Presbyterian Church in the early 1800s were convinced that it was essential for the clergy to seek an enduement of Holy Spirit power before embarking upon their ministry.

When the Neo-Pentecostal or charismatic movement began in the mainline churches in the U.S. after World War II, the Presbyterians were again in the forefront of renewal. The first well-known Presbyterian pastor to experience speaking in tongues and healing to remain in his church was James Brown, pastor of the Upper Octorara United Presbyterian Church near Parkesburg, just outside of Philadelphia, Pennsylvania. About 1957 Brown was baptized with the Holy Spirit. Perplexed as to what course of action he should follow, Brown asked David du Plessis for advice. "Stay in your church and renew it" was the word from the famous Pentecostal and charismatic leader. This Brown determined to do.

Brown's decision was to conduct traditional Presbyterian worship in the regular Sunday services but to have Neo-Pentecostal worship in informal Saturday evening sessions in the sanctuary. This strategy worked for more than twenty years with a minimum of friction. In time the Saturday services attracted hundreds of enthusiastic worshipers each week, with the little country church jammed with as many as six hundred people. Thousands of clergy and laity were baptized in the Holy Spirit in these services.

These events were taking place in the late 1950s before the more famous events in Van Nuys, California, surrounding the ministry of Dennis Bennett. For several years prior to 1960, Brown had the largest charismatic prayer meeting in the

U.S. In 1977 he retired after thirty-seven years in the same pastorate, an early success story of the renewal movement.

In May 1966 Brown and five other Presbyterian charismatic ministers took an important step. They organized the Charismatic Communion of Presbyterian Ministers, which later took the name Presbyterian Charismatic Communion (PCC) in order to include the laity. This was the first charismatic organization to be formed in a mainline denomination. George C. "Brick" Bradford was chosen from among the six as the general secretary, a position he holds today. In one year the new group had 125 Presbyterian ministers on its rolls, and in a short time hundreds of pastors and laypersons joined forces in this well-organized ministry.

Not long after this move Bradford and the PCC were confronted with a landmark case that tested the place of the gifts of the Spirit in the Presbyterian system. This case arose because of a dispute concerning the ministry of Robert C. Whitaker, pastor of the First Presbyterian Church, Chandler, Arizona, near Phoenix.

In 1962 Whitaker had been baptized in the Holy Spirit and had seen the Holy Spirit slowly but surely revolutionize his ministry and the ministry of the Chandler church. By 1967 a number of his members had experienced the power of the Holy Spirit in their lives. Also, like James Brown, no tongues or laying on of hands were practiced in the regular services of the church. However, in home prayer meetings revival broke out.

In 1967 a small group of dissenting elders was able to persuade the presbytery of Phoenix to appoint an administrative commission to investigate Whitaker's ministry and the use of the gifts of the Holy Spirit within the life of the congregation. When Whitaker refused to take a vow to stop speaking in tongues, praying for the sick, and casting out demons, the presbytery removed him as pastor of First Presbyterian Church in Chandler. Rather than accepting this decision, he decided to appeal to the Synod of Arizona on grounds that the verdict was contrary to Scripture and violated his conscience according to a provision within the Book of Order of the United Presbyterian Church.

In February 1968, when the appeal failed, Whitaker was faced with accepting the decision or appealing it further. Giving a strong counsel and aid to Whitaker was a leading figure in world Presbyterianism, the late John A. Mackay, president emeritus of Princeton Theological Seminary. Both Mackay and Bradford strongly encouraged Whitaker to continue the fight. As providence would have it, Brick Bradford had been a lawyer before entering the ministry and offered his services as counsel for the plaintiff.

Bradford added a third reason for appealing to the Permanent Judicial Commission of the general assembly, the highest court of the United Presbyterian Church. He argued that no lower judicatory (presbytery or synod) could add vows to the ordination vows set forth in the church constitution. In May 1968 *The Reverend Robert C.*

Two leaders of the Presbyterian & Reformed Renewal Ministries, Brick Bradford (left) and James H. Brown, visit at a 1974 conference.

Whitaker vs. The Synod of Arizona was decided in favor of Whitaker.

It was a great moral victory for all charismatics in the mainline churches. But the victory did not end with the successful appeal. As a result of the Whitaker case, every Presbyterian minister was protected from arbitrary removal by a presbytery from his/her pastorate on grounds of involvement in the charismatic renewal. Because the case did not rule on the theological implications, the 180th General Assembly (1968) ordered a theological study to be made on the question of tongues, healing, exorcism, and the Neo-Pentecostal movement in general.

The study commissioned by the general assembly was the first and possibly the most thorough one ever done by a major denomination. The members of the commission were made up of persons versed in theology, psychology, psychiatry, pastoral ministry, and ecclesiology. The report was so groundbreaking and comprehensive that it served as a model for many other denominational reports in the following years. Again the Presbyterians were pioneers in renewal.

The exegetical sections of the report, while rejecting a separate experience of Holy Spirit baptism, did allow for the exercise of spiritual gifts in the contemporary church as long as they did not lead to disorder and division.

A set of guidelines was offered for both Presbyterians who were considered Neo-Pentecostal and those who were not, with a view toward keeping peace in the churches. Overall the report was positive in its exegetical, psychological, and pastoral sections. The report's guidelines were adopted overwhelmingly, and the *Report on the Work of the Holy Spirit* as a whole was received by the 182nd General Assembly of the United Presbyterian Church in 1970. It has been the official policy of the church since that time.

Throughout the 1970s the renewal moved ahead with ever-increasing force. In Hollywood's First Presbyterian Church, one of the largest in the world, more than six hundred members were said to be speaking in tongues. Such prominent

Presbyterian leaders as Senior Pastor Louis Evans of the National Presbyterian Church in Washington, D.C., and his wife, Colleen Townsend Evans, and the late Catherine Marshall and her husband, Leonard LeSourd, have been openly active in the movement. Robert L. Wise, Reformed Church in America pastor, is another well-known figure in the renewal.

An important addition to the movement came in 1965 when J. Rodman Williams was baptized in the Holy Spirit while serving as professor of systematic theology at the Austin Presbyterian Theological Seminary in Texas. Already an able and well-known theologian among Presbyterians, Williams added serious theological depth to the charismatic movement as a whole. In later years he made significant contributions through his books and teaching positions at Melodyland School of Theology and the Graduate School of Theology at CBN University. Presbyterian Charles Farah served the renewal in a similar fashion from his teaching position at Oral Roberts University as professor of theology.

In 1984 the name was changed to Presbyterian and Reformed Renewal Ministries International (PRRM). By 1986 PRRM had close to 1,000 clergy members out of the 3,000 to 3,500 who had been baptized in the Holy Spirit. The total membership of the group is about 3,500 contributing members. This relatively small group is representative of some 250,000 charismatics in the Presbyterian and Reformed churches in the U.S. PRRM has members in twenty-six Presbyterian and Reformed denominations scattered throughout forty-two nations.

See also CHARISMATIC MOVEMENT. (Major portions reprinted with permission from *Charisma* [April 1986], 37–39. Copyright 1986, Strang Communications Company.)

Bibliography: H. Berkhof, *The Doctrine of the Holy Spirit* (1964); B. Bradford, *Releasing the Power of the Holy Spirit* (1983); idem, *Report on the Work of the Holy Spirit* (1970); J. R. Williams, *The Era of the Spirit* (1971).   H. V. Synan

PRESBYTERIAN AND REFORMED RENEWAL MINISTRIES, INTERNATIONAL
See PRESBYTERIAN AND REFORMED CHARISMATICS

PRICE, CHARLES SYDNEY (1880?–1947).
Pentecostal evangelist, pastor, and teacher. He commanded deep respect as one of the greatest teachers of the early Pentecostal movement. Originally from Britain, he was trained in law at Wesley College, Oxford, and immigrated to Canada. He later had a conversion experience at a Free Methodist mission in Spokane, Washington, and attracted the attention of Dr. Henry I. Rasmus, who convinced him to enter the ministry. When Price was invited to a Pentecostal prayer meeting shortly after the outpouring of the Spirit at Azusa Street, another minister dissuaded him and successfully convinced him to study the works of Modernism instead. Although he gradually gained prestige within the Columbia River Conference of the Methodist church, he became disenchanted with the Methodist episcopal sys-

Charles S. Price was pastoring a Congregational Church in Lodi, California, when he was baptized in the Spirit at an Aimee Semple McPherson meeting. He then launched his own evangelistic ministry, gaining widespread popularity for his prayers for the sick.

tem, becoming pastor of a Congregational church in Valdez, Alaska.

During World War I, he attained popularity as a public speaker at theaters in San Francisco selling war bonds. He later became pastor of the First Congregational Church in Lodi, California. In early 1920 some members of his church began attending Aimee Semple McPherson's meetings in San Jose. They convinced him to go, but he intended to discredit them, until "a masterful message came from the lips of the evangelist and my modernistic theology was punctured until it looked like a sieve" (Price, 1944, 34–35). On the third night he answered the altar call. He was later baptized in the Spirit at tarrying meetings held at a Baptist church in San Jose pastored by Dr. William Keeny Towner, who had sponsored McPherson's meetings. Price returned to his church at Lodi, where "the power of God commenced to fall" (Price, 1944, 45). When denominational officials began to interfere, he started an independent church, Lodi Bethel Temple.

In 1922 Price began itinerating as an evangelist, holding meetings in Oregon and British Columbia. There were several miraculous healings in Victoria that became well publicized. During the following year, meetings in Vancouver attracted 250,000 people over the course of three weeks. Price later held meetings in Calgary and Edmonton, where people smashed windows to gain admittance after the 12,000 seats at the ice arena were taken. At the amphitheater in Winnipeg, Manitoba, Price had to climb through a kitchen window to get into the building. Later meetings were held in Toronto, Minneapolis, Duluth, St. Louis, and Belleville, Illinois. One thousand conversions per day were reported during the last ten days of the Belleville campaign.

In 1926 Price began publishing his periodical, *Golden Grain*. Continuing his itinerant ministry in the Pacific Northwest, he began to find it necessary to construct tabernacles in which to hold his meetings.

By 1944 Price had preached in Sweden, Norway, England, Egypt, Palestine, Turkey, Syria, Lebanon, Italy, and other parts of Europe, as well as in many additional places throughout the U.S. and Canada.

Bibliography: C. S. Price, *The Real Faith,* new ed. (1972); idem, *The Story of My Life,* 3d ed. (1944).   R. M. Riss

PRICE, FREDERICK K. C. (1932–). Pastor and television evangelist. Price was born in Santa Monica, California, and was reared in a Jehovah's Witness environment. Converted at a tent crusade in 1953, Price entered the Christian ministry in 1955. During his first seventeen years of ministry he belonged to four denominations: Baptist, African Methodist Episcopal, Presbyterian, and Christian and Missionary Alliance. He received the baptism of the Holy Spirit in 1970 and soon began to develop a "faith" ministry.

In 1973 Price founded an independent church called Crenshaw Christian Center. The multiracial congregation now exceeds 15,000 people and is headquartered on thirty-two acres that formerly housed Pepperdine University. Price began a nationally broadcast television ministry in 1978 called "Ever Increasing Faith," which is featured on nearly a hundred stations in the U.S. and abroad. In 1982 he bean teaching his faith message in crusades across the U.S.

Price is the author of several books, including *Is Healing for All?* (1976); *How Faith Works* (1976); *How to Obtain Strong Faith* (1977); *The Holy Spirit—the Missing Ingredient: My Personal Testimony* (1978); and *Faith, Foolishness or Presumption?* (1979).

Bibliography: V. B. Lowe, "Frederick Price: The Making of a Ministry," *Religious Broadcasting* (February 1987), 26–28.   G. W. Gohr

PRIDGEON, CHARLES HAMILTON (1863–1932). Pastor, educator, and missions executive. Born in Baltimore, Maryland, and educated at Lafayette College (B.A., 1886; M.A., 1889) and Princeton Theological Seminary (graduated 1889). Further studies took him to Free Church College and United Presbyterian College, Edinburgh, Scotland; University of Leipzig; and Worcester University.

Pridgeon was ordained to the Presbyterian ministry and pastored at Canonsburg, Pennsylvania (1890–1901). In 1892 he sought for the fullness of the Holy Spirit; this proved to be a turning point in his ministry. Later contact with A. B. Simpson led to his invitation to address the Christian and Missionary Alliance (CMA) convention at Old Orchard campground in Maine. While there he met Louise Shepard (d. 1928), whom he married in 1901; they had one daughter. Conflict over Pridgeon's preaching on faith healing led to his withdrawal from the Presbyterian church in the same year.

Moving to Pittsburgh, Pridgeon founded the Wylie Avenue Church in December 1901. Following this he established the Pittsburgh Bible Institute (c. 1902); the doctrines taught at the school strongly reflected those of the CMA. In 1908–09 he traveled overseas to investigate possible sites for ministry. This trip resulted in the dispatching of missionaries to China. Later Pridgeon founded the Evangelization Society of the Pittsburgh Bible Institute (1920), which placed missionaries in India and Africa as well. His other efforts included an orphanage, open air evangelism, a hospital ministry, a printing plant, and the publication of the *Record of Faith*.

In the winter of 1920 Pridgeon went to Dayton, Ohio, to attend a revival conducted by Aimee Semple McPherson. Stirred by what he saw, he returned home and urged the students to pray for the baptism in the Holy Spirit. A remarkable revival began the following April with more than 1,500 persons receiving the Pentecostal baptism in the following two to three years.

Beginning in 1918 Pridgeon generated controversy over his teaching that hell is not eternal. He explained his views in *Is Hell Eternal; or Will God's Plan Fail?* To him it was a place of limited duration required by the sins of humankind. After purification humanity could discover the love of God. The terms used to describe this form of universalism included the "restitution" or "reconciliation" of all things, and "Pridgeonism." The "Pridgeon doctrine" was condemned as heretical by the General Council of the Assemblies of God in 1925.

Bibliography: G. D. Clementson, *Charles Hamilton Pridgeon* (1963); idem, *Louise Shepard Pridgeon* (1955); *Combined Minutes of the General Council of the Assemblies of God,* 1914–25; W. W. Menzies, *Anointed to Serve* (1971); idem, "The Non-Wesleyan Origins of the Pentecostal Movement," in *Aspects of Pentecostal-Charismatic Origins,* ed. V. Synan (1975); C. H. Pridgeon, *Is Hell Eternal; or Will God's Plan Fail?* 3d ed. (1931); "Pridgeon, Charles Hamilton," *Who Was Who in America,* vol. I: 1897–1942; "Pridgeonism," *The Pentecostal Testimony* (November 1923), 7–8.   G. B. McGee

PRINCE, PETER DEREK V. (1915–). Author and teacher. Prince was born in Bangalore, India, into a British military family. He was educated at Eton College and Cambridge University (B.A. and M.A.) in England and at Hebrew University, Israel. As a student he was a philosopher and self-proclaimed atheist.

While in the British Medical Corps (1940–41), Prince began to study the Bible. Converted through a powerful encounter with Christ, he was baptized in the Holy Spirit a few days later. He was discharged from the army in Jerusalem in

1946, and he married Lydia Christensen, founder of a Danish children's home in Jerusalem. After her death he married Ruth Baker in 1978.

In 1949 Prince founded a Pentecostal church in London and served as pastor until 1956. He then served as principal of the African Teacher Training College in Kenya (1957–61).

Prince came to Canada in 1962, where he spent a year traveling in behalf of missions for the Pentecostal Assemblies of Canada. He and his family moved to the U.S. in 1964 and pastored a church in Seattle, Washington. During this time he became involved in a deliverance ministry.

Prince was attacked by many for his stand on demonology. Some said he taught that a Christian could be demon-possessed. What Prince said was that a Christian could be demonized (bothered by demons).

Prince moved to Ft. Lauderdale, Florida, in 1968, and in 1974 he established the Good News Church, along with Don Basham and Bernard "Bob" Mumford. A quasi-denomination, based on disciplining or "shepherding" concepts, formed around the men and resulted in considerable debate and controversy.

Prince renounced the basic principles of the "shepherding" movement in 1984 and separated from the team, although he did maintain a personal relationship with the other men.

Prince conducts an internationally recognized radio ministry, established in 1979, called "Today with Derek Prince." In addition to airing in many U.S. cities, the program is translated into several languages and transmitted to many countries. He has also written more than twenty books, of which the best known are the *Foundation Series* books (1965–66).

Bibliography: J. Buckingham, "New Wine Ceases Publication," *Ministries Today* (November–December 1986), 24; S. Strang, "Discipleship Controversy Three Years Later," *Charisma* (September 1978), 14–24.

S. Strang

PROPHECY, GIFT OF
I. Prophetic Speech in the Ancient World
  A. Near Eastern Prophecy Outside Israel
  B. Greek and Roman Prophetic Activity
  C. Prophecy in Israel
II. Prophecy in the New Testament
  A. A Pauline Perspective
  B. A Lukan Perspective
  C. Prophecy and the Gospel Writers
III. The Gift of Prophecy in Church History
  A. The Early Church
  B. The Middle Ages
  C. Reformation and Post Reformation Understandings
IV. Prophecy in Contemporary Understanding
  A. True and False Prophecy
  B. Limits of Prophetic Authority

One of several charisms or "gifts" (*charismata*) of the Holy Spirit mentioned by Paul in 1 Corinthians 12:10 and elsewhere. Prophecy (Gk. *prophētia*) has been alternatively identified as (1) an oracle, spontaneously inspired by the Holy Spirit and spoken in a specific situation; (2) a form of expositional preaching from the biblical text; or (3) a public pronouncement of a moral or ethical nature that confronts society. The commonly held understanding of prophecy as a predictive word of future events, and therefore as foreknowledge, has ancient precedence but it does not provide an adequate basis for understanding this gift. Prophecy more commonly includes a component of "forthtelling," or the conveyance of a message with or without the predictive element. Pentecostal and charismatic Christians tend to emphasize the nature of prophecy as spontaneous, though many allow for prophetic gifts to function in "anointed" preaching and in some "inspired" social commentary.

The history of prophetic claims is an ancient and diverse one, limited neither to the church nor to the people of Israel. Prophetic claims are common in ancient Near Eastern (G. A. Guillaume; R. Wilson) and Far Eastern religions (H. H. Rowley), in Greek and Roman religious life (J. Fontenrose; H. W. Parke; D. E. W. Wormell), and in contemporary non-Christian religions such as Islam (F. Rahman), as well as in the Christian context. Even within the larger "Christian" context, spontaneous prophetic claims arise from groups as diverse as Roman Catholics, Seventh-day Adventists, Mormons, and Pentecostals. Thus the biblical discussions of prophets, prophecy, and prophetic activity should be viewed within this larger historical, religious, and cultural context. Although non-Jewish and non-Christian claims to prophetic activity do not fit the Pauline criteria for *genuine* manifestations of the gift of prophecy, a look at these claims to spirit possession, their content, and their methodology provides many parallels to Jewish and Christian claims, and may nonetheless help us understand the nature of genuine prophetic activity.

I. Prophetic Speech in the Ancient World.
A. Near Eastern Prophecy Outside Israel. Prophetic activity in ancient Near Eastern society has been observed as early as the nineteenth century B.C. It took various forms but was often associated with the use of omens, and it more clearly followed the pattern of divination. In Mesopotamian society, events were observed in such a way that though they might not be seen as having a causal relationship to one another, yet they were understood to have some relationship due at least to a shared proximity of moment. The recurrence of one such event was then thought to have some relationship to the repetition of the other. If an owl flew overhead and someone's home burned down, the next time an owl was seen to fly overhead, it might be predicted that some destructive event would soon transpire.

Mesopotamian prophetic specialists or diviners banded together into schools or guilds. Entrance into such a guild was both competitive and selective. Following initiatory rites the diviner (*bārû*) was then taught such things as the use of dice, divination of oil as it was spread upon water, interpretation of dreams, the examination of the entrails of sacrificial animals, and other "arts" commonly used in the trade. While it is clear that many similar methods were used in Israel, such as the casting of lots (1 Sam. 14:41–42) or the interpretation of dreams (Gen. 40:5–8; 41:1–8; Dan. 2:1–11), some of these "arts" were clearly understood to be forms of divination, which was expressly forbidden (Deut. 18:10–11). It is not at all clear whether Israel's own prophetic guilds borrowed any of these methods directly from their Mesopotamian neighbors, but rather, it appears that these methods developed independently.

In Mesopotamia, the preferred method of divination and of predicting the future was that of examination of an animal's liver. By the Babylonian period there was a sophisticated system for interpreting the meaning of various liver configurations. Ezekiel told his hearers that the Babylonian king would engage in the casting of lots, the consulting of idols, and the examination of livers (Ezek. 21:21–23) in order to determine the future of Jerusalem. Still, those who had sworn allegiance to him would interpret it as a false omen.

The Mari Letters give further evidence of "prophetic" activity in that region of the Near East. The "answerers" or *āpilus* served a variety of localized cultic deities. Their utterances were quite rational but not particularly profound. Often they involved personal requests on behalf of the deity, requests that, if fulfilled, would improve the personal situation of the *āpilu*. Alongside the *āpilu* was the *muhhû*, one who entered into a sometimes violent form of trance or ecstasy and gave an oracle, sometimes while in the trance and sometimes later. In the cases of both the *āpilu* and the *muhhû*, their oracles were often submitted to testing and scrutiny by still other forms of divination.

The Assyrians provided a parallel to the Israelite "seer" in the person of the *sabrû*. The messages from the *sabrû* were derived from visions or dreams, sometimes providing reassurance in times of peril. One example from the reign of Assurbanipal involved a prayer to the goddess Ishtar or Arbela just prior to an attack. It was recorded that she appeared to the *sabrû* with words of encouragement for the king.

On the whole, divination and prophetic, even apocalyptic, activity were present throughout the Near East and running both prior to and concurrent with Israel's own prophetic activity. Israel's prophetic activity, however, claimed to be unique, for it was derived solely from Yahweh, Israel's God.

B. Greek and Roman Prophetic Activity. As early as the eighth century B.C., Homer mentioned the existence of prophetic activity in Pythea or Delphi, as well as at Dodona. Prophetic activity in the Greek world was generally associated with Zeus (at Dodona), and with Apollo (at Delphi). As was the case of Abram's God, who was at one point associated with the oak tree at Moreh (Gen. 12:6), so Zeus was associated with an oak at Dodona, and Apollo with a laurelwood at Delphi. The Greek deity Zeus, who controlled storms and was thought to be the supreme god in a pantheon of gods, and the god Apollo, who was largely a pastoral and agricultural deity, were most commonly addressed and invoked at Dodona and Delphi.

Plutarch (*Obsolescence of Oracles* 414B) observed that of the two cities noted for their prophetic activity, Delphi was not only the more ancient, it was also the more famous. For a time it was closely associated with the activity of a serpent who was, according to Greek mythology, originally the guardian of the Oracles of Delphi but was killed by Apollo.

Herodotus, a Greek historian writing in the fifth century, B.C., gives an idea of how widespread prophetic activity was in this region when he mentions oracles in Delphi, Abae in Phocia, Dodona, Amphriaraus, Trophonius, Branchidae in the Milesian country, and Ammon in Libya (Herodotus, *Histories* 1.46). It is also known that oracles were delivered at such ancient sites as Olympia, Patara, Argos, and Agamemnon. Herodotus wrote during the apex of Delphic activity, while Plutarch (c. A.D. 50–120), a biographer and philosopher, wrote of Delphi during its decline.

At the height of Delphic activity, multitudes kept two prophetesses fully employed, with a third one in reserve to accommodate any overflow business (Plutarch, *Obsolescence of Oracles* 414B). Those who prophesied at Delphi were young virgins who, Plutarch maintained, were of ordinary birth and experience. They had no prior training, no technical skill, and no previously demonstrated talents that enabled them to prophesy (*Oracles at Delphi* 405C). These young women, however, were alternatively described as servants to their god (*tō theō synestin*), as prophetesses (*prophētisin*), and as mantics (*mantia*).

The method by which these women performed their religious function involved their willingness to act as intermediaries between the god and a paying customer who sought information. Strabo (*Geography* 9.3.5) reports that they entered a cave from which gases were emitted. There they sat upon a tripod, received these gases into their bodies and began to "prophesy." Plutarch says that at such times it was actually the god who entered their bodies and prompted "their utterances, employing their mouths, and voices as instruments" (*Obsolescence of Oracles* 414E). Plutarch, who idealized this activity as involving divine possession, was concerned that the populace, however, was more interested in the winds, vapors, exhalations, and the external wonders than they were in the god who spoke.

In the early days of professional prophetism at Delphi, it was claimed that these virgins prophesied in metered verse. (See, for example, Herodotus, *Histories* 1.47, which contains an oracle given in hexameter verse.) By Plutarch's day, metered verse was extremely rare. Simple statements needing interpretation were the norm. Thus at times the young girl, who acted as the intermediary, was described as having a mantic power by which she foretold the future, but it was also necessary to have an oracular interpreter called a "prophet" (*prophētēs*), who stood by her to help those who had made inquiry understand the meaning of her response. This relationship between the inspired speaker and the interpreter may provide a helpful parallel to the relationship between the gift of tongues and the interpretation of tongues as it was described by Paul in 1 Corinthians 12 and 14. This is even more probable in the cases where the virgin spoke unintelligible speech while possessed.

Plutarch argued that the inspiration of the young girls came from gods (*theia*) and demigods (*daimonios*) and that each intermediary or girl responded to her possession by them in different ways. In one highly publicized case, a girl went unwillingly to do the job. When she was possessed by Apollo, Plutarch said, she was as one who had a change of voice. She acted like a "labouring ship." She became hysterical, screamed, and threw herself to the ground, and within a few days she was dead (*Obsolescence of Oracles* 438A). This more or less uncontrollable behavior, however, was not typical of Delphic prophetic activity.

As one might imagine, the inquiries made to these prophetesses were relatively uncomplicated questions on matters of daily life. Questions of whether or when to embark on a trip, how to invest money, and whether or whom one ought to marry were very common. Examples of such inquiry have been found inscribed on lead strips at the sites of the caves where the inquiry was made. The community of the Coragraeans, for instance, inquired during the late fifth century, "to what god or hero by making sacrifice and prayer [may we] dwell in the fairest and best way both now and in time to come?" Others, such as one Callicrates, were concerned with things closer to their own personal well-being. Callicrates requested that the prophetess ask "the god whether I will have offspring from Mike whom I have by remaining with her and praying to which of the gods." Questions concerning illness and healing were addressed to the god in this way as well, as in the case of Leontios, who consulted the oracle "concerning his son Leon whether there will be recovery from the disease on his breast which seizes him" (Parke).

On occasion, consultations were made to two prophetesses to determine whether the answers were true to the facts and consistent with one another. Herodotus records that Croesus, king of Lydia, made simultaneous inquiry of both Greek and Libyan oracles to determine whether he should engage in battle with the Persians. The test of *consistency* was applied to these oracles. A second test that was commonly applied was the test of *fulfillment*. If the word of the prophetess came true, it was judged to have been divinely sent. A third test was also used by Croesus. Through a messenger he asked each oracle what he had done at a specific hour. At that time he had cut up a tortoise and a lamb, then boiled them in a covered bronze caldron. Only by *revelation*, he argued, could they respond rightly, and by this means he acknowledged that genuine divination had been made only at Delphi (Herodotus, *Histories* 1.46–48).

The NT suggests that such activity was widespread at the time of Jesus and his disciples. Paul and Silas were harassed in Philippi by a slave girl who "earned a great deal of money for her owners, by fortune-telling" (*manteuomenē*, Acts 16:16). Paul recognized that this was accomplished by means of a spirit of divination, literally, a pythian spirit (*pneuma pythōna*), and he exorcised it.

The fathers of the church were unanimous in their condemnation of these prophetic activities in Greek and Roman religion. Justin Martyr (*Apology* 1.18, 44, 56) saw the source of their inspiration as demonic. Origen reached the same conclusion in his work *Against Celsus* 7.7.3–4 because, he noted, the divine spirit does not put a person into such "a state of ecstasy and madness that she loses control of herself," nor would the divine spirit fill her mind and cloud her judgment with darkness. Tertullian concluded that Croesus' question of what he was cooking had been answered by means of revelation, but it was by means of demonic revelation (*Apology* 1.22), not divine revelation. In spite of this condemnation, many patterns exist in Greek and Roman prophetic activity, and these patterns help to shed light on similar ones that may be observed in the gift of prophecy as it is described in Scripture and employed in the church.

C. Prophecy in Israel. Usually when we think of prophecy, we think of a predictive word about something that will take place in the future. When we think of prophets, our minds typically picture the literary prophets of Israel who gave us so many of the OT books. While both of these images are helpful in describing prophecy, the basic concept of prophecy as it is found in the canonical writings of Israel is quite simple. The experience of Moses and Aaron described in Exodus 4:10–16 (cf. 7:1–2) provides an early and paradigmatic understanding of prophecy. This passage indicates that *the prophet is essentially a person who speaks on behalf of another*.

God asked Moses to speak to Pharaoh about the release of the people of Israel. Moses declined God's request, on grounds that he had a speech impediment. God then directed Moses to enlist the help of Aaron to convey the message. Thus before Pharaoh, Moses would appear as God ('*elohim*), while Aaron would act as the "mouth" or the "prophet" (*nabi* '). Moses would give Aaron the message that Aaron would deliver to Pharaoh.

From such a description several observations can be made. First, the person who prophesies is not the inventor of the words to be spoken. That person is merely the conveyor of the message. Aaron spoke what Moses told him to speak, and no more. The message was Moses' message, though the precise words used to convey it were Aaron's words. Second, in this paradigm there is no confusion between the person who speaks the message and the person whose message is spoken. There is a discrete prophetic consciousness that can be clearly articulated. God gives the word. The prophet speaks. Moses gave Aaron the message and was likened by Pharaoh to God. Aaron delivered the message and was likened to the prophet. Third, the person who acts as the "prophet" does so only when conveying the message that has been given to him or her. Every word spoken by Aaron during his lifetime was clearly not to be considered as having equal importance with the specific thoughts or words that Moses gave him to speak to Pharaoh. Only the message that God gave to Moses and which Moses gave to Aaron from God were prophetically important.

In 1 Samuel, two texts provide additional information that helps further to define this gift. First Samuel 9:6–9 describes Saul's entrance into the land of Zeph when he was searching for his father's lost asses. He was told that Samuel, a man devoted to the service of Yahweh, was there. Saul sought him out to ascertain where the herd could be found. The editor of this passage provides an interesting side note for the reader. Those who were currently called "prophets" (nabi'), he wrote, had formerly been called "seers" (ro'eh). This emphasis on the prophet as a "seer" suggests a connection between prophecy, dreams, and visions.

Visions continued to play a significant role in the oracles of the literary prophets (cf. Isa. 6:1ff.; Ezek. 1:1ff.; 8:1ff.; Amos 7:1–9). Dreams were sometimes also used (cf. Jer. 23:25). At other times prophets heard the voice of Yahweh while pondering the significance of current events (such as the locust invasion, drought, and brush fires, which Joel [1:1–2:11] saw as harbingers of the Day of the Lord) or while studying simple everyday acts, such as Jeremiah's encounter with the potter who formed the clay (18:1ff.). Yet it appears that the earliest claims to prophetic activity involved some ability to interpret dreams or visions.

In the second text, 1 Samuel 10:6, Samuel anointed Saul on behalf of Yahweh to be a prince over Israel. Samuel told Saul that when Saul came to Gibeathelohim, he would meet a band of prophets prophesying with musical accompaniment and that when he did so, the Spirit of the Lord would fall upon Saul, he would prophesy, and "be turned into another man."

At other times also prophecy was given to the accompaniment of music. It should come as no surprise when we note the relationship of singing to prophesying (1 Chron. 25:1, 3, 6) or the prophetic forms of some of Israel's hymns, psalms (cf. Pss 50; 60; 89:19–37). The Pauline encouragement for Christians to sing "spiritual songs" (Eph. 5:18–19; Col. 3:16) may also have a prophetic component to it.

In the OT there were those who banded together into prophetic schools. Amos denied that he was either a prophet or the "son of a prophet" (7:14), that is, he was not a member of any professional prophetic guild or school.

A connection to some form of "ecstatic" experience might also be derived from the statement that Saul would "be turned into another man." Samuel's own prophecy of this was fulfilled in verses 9–12 to such an extent that the origin of the proverb "Is Saul also among the prophets?" was understood to have arisen here. The ecstatic elements of a trancelike state, Saul's lying prostrate on the ground while prophesying and his seeming obliviousness to his own "nakedness," might be described as extreme in the light of later Pauline reflection on the subject of prophecy, but, nonetheless, they may be observed in this text. Such "ecstatic" activity ultimately led to the

description of a prophet as a "man of the Spirit" or an inspired "maniac" (Hos. 9:7) and may also lie behind the imagery suggested by the prophet as one on whom Yahweh's hand has been placed (Ezek. 3:14–16; 8:1–4).

Prophecy in the OT, then, shows great diversity. At times it comes almost silently in thoughts, visions, or dreams. On other occasions it comes quite forcefully, in a moment of significant emotion, reminiscent of drunkenness. In Moses' day it came to a limited group of elders, two of whom caused such a stir by their behavior that even Joshua attempted to have them silenced (Num. 11:24–29). The prophets of Baal also created a commotion on Mount Carmel when they shouted and engaged in self-flagellation (1 Kings 19:28–29).

Prophecy was taken seriously, whether it was announced on someone's inquiry (1 Kings 22:5–6), or at God's initiative, such as in the case of Moses and Aaron's confrontation with Pharaoh. It was treated with great care whether it was given to an individual (1 Sam. 12:1–15) or was proclaimed to a crowd gathered in a sacred place (Amos 7:10–13), though at times the message being announced cut to the hearts of those who listened.

Prophetic words were also tested. Sometimes they were predictive (cf. Jer. 31:27ff.) and therefore subject to tests of fulfillment, while on other occasions they were prescriptive (Hag. 1:1–12) and thus were tested on the basis of existing revelation or other grounds. In cases where these oracles proved to be false, the prophet's credibility was to be doubted, and the so-called prophet was to be ignored (Deut. 18:15–22) or even put to death (Deut. 13:1–5). The bottom line, however, was that genuine prophecy was given by Yahweh to certain individuals, to be spoken as an inspired word on behalf of Yahweh. Moses wished that all of God's people could prophesy (Num. 11:29), and Joel promised that it would finally happen when the Spirit was poured out upon all flesh (Joel 2:28–29).

In the OT and certain intertestamental literature, both apocryphal and pseudepigraphic, there are several passages that appear to suggest that the prophetic Spirit ceased to function for a period of time. In Psalm 74:9, for instance, there appears a lament that "we are given no miraculous signs; no prophets are left, and none of us knows how long this will be." Similarly, when the Maccabees recaptured the temple from the Greeks, they dismantled the altar that had been profaned, and they set the stones aside "until there should come a prophet to tell them what to do with them" (1 Macc. 4:46). At first glance these passages seem to affirm the silence of the prophetic voice, but Aune has demonstrated the complexity of the times, noting that there were others who prophesied simultaneously with these claims. Furthermore, Psalm 74:9 probably refers to the fact that the temple prophets at the close of the Solomic temple period (586 B.C.) had lost credibility in the eyes of the psalmist. Similarly, the Maccabees were probably looking for a specific type of cultic prophet to provide inspired leadership.

The intertestamental period did, however,

make a substantial contribution to prophetism in the form of apocalyptic. While it is not precisely the same as prophecy, it is very clearly related to it. The term *apocalypse* is derived from the Greek term *apokalypsis* meaning "revelation" or "disclosure." Thus the NT Book of Revelation is often called the Apocalypse of John. The term *apocalyptic eschatology* is often used to describe a system of religious beliefs related to a specific type of millenarianism that was present during that period of time. There was even a social movement known as "apocalypticism," which was motivated by these phenomena.

Most clearly related to the gift of prophecy, though, is the appearance of a genre of literature known as apocalyptic literature. The single OT book of this type and the earliest of the apocalypses is Daniel. There are many noncanonical works that emerged during this time, however—many of them pseudonymous (e.g., 1 and 2 Enoch, Apocalypse of Abraham). Their writers and readers took their revelations seriously. Commonly these apocalyptic works were based on "visions" that the writer claims to have experienced. These visions were often, though not always, interpreted by an angel or some other heavenly being, and the author of the apocalypse dutifully recorded the vision and its interpretation in the apocalyptic work. Often these visions were recorded as transcendent realities within a theoretical framework of history, using a high degree of symbolism (e.g., numerology).

II. Prophecy in the New Testament.

A. A Pauline Perspective.
Paul speaks of prophecy on several occasions, and it is he who first labeled it among the *charismata*, the gifts of the Holy Spirit. As a manifestation of God's grace (*charis*), it is to be uttered in faith (Rom. 12:6). While the prophet is mentioned as one of God's gifts to the church (Eph. 4:11), it is in the long exposition of 1 Corinthians 12–14 that we get the clearest understanding of Paul's thought on the subject.

Like Moses, Paul had a wish that all might prophesy, and repeatedly he exhorted his readers to desire or seek this gift (1 Cor. 14:1, 5, 39). Yet he always viewed prophetic activity as but one manifestation of God's varied grace within the body of Christ, which contained a rich diversity of such manifestations. While it might be the potential for *all* to prophesy, since each Christian possessed the Spirit (Rom. 8:9) and the Spirit was the bestower of this gift (1 Cor. 12:8–11), Paul's metaphor of the body of Christ suggests that he anticipated that only *some* people would be given this gift for use within that body. His rhetorical question in 1 Corinthians 12:29, "Are all prophets?" which clearly anticipates a negative response, serves further to underscore this observation. It may also be noted that there are no gender restrictions placed on this gift (1 Cor. 11:5). In each Pauline passage in which prophecy is mentioned (1 Cor. 12–14; Rom. 12; and Eph. 4), it is simply listed in relation to the metaphor of the body of Christ.

Paul was clearly concerned that the exercise of this gift be of benefit to the church. Prophecy had its limitations, of course. It was described as both imperfect and, ultimately, temporary (1 Cor. 13:8). It would disappear when "the perfect" had come. But in the meantime, its purposes were clearly articulated in 1 Corinthians 14:3. There were three clearly identifiable purposes: edification, exhortation, and comfort. To put it another way, prophecy was to build up, encourage, and/or console the people of God. While its primary functions aided the believer (1 Cor. 14:22), this gift could also hold an evangelistic and/or an ethical edge. Paul noted that an unbeliever who happened to come into the assembly where this gift was manifest, might recognize the presence of God and be convicted of the reality of his or her own sinfulness. The result would be that this person, too, might come to worship God (1 Cor. 14:24–25). Jesus' own prophetic character was recognized in much this same way by the woman at the well (John 4:9) as she moved from distrust to faith.

Paul argued that in order to provide the body of Christ with clear benefit, prophecy needs to be used according to general guidelines whose aim is to guarantee a properly functioning body. First and foremost among these guidelines was a recognition that the proper use of this gift was to serve as a reflection of the Giver. Since God is a God of peace and order, the use of this gift should be consistent with that fact. If it seeks to call attention to itself or to the person who claims to possess it, it denies the character of God (1 Cor. 14:26–33).

Second, it is a gift that is sovereignly bestowed by the Spirit of God (1 Cor. 12:11). As such, and consistent with the OT pattern, some people would be given this gift while others would not. Paul's contention was, however, that such diversity contributes to the body's smooth functioning, which includes the orderly proclamation of prophetic oracles. How was this to be done?

Whenever the congregation gathered, Paul argued, prophetic leadership was to be shared. Each person with a prophetic word was to be given a turn. But he was not to control the floor; rather, preference was to be given to others through whom God might choose to speak (1 Cor. 14:29–31). As Paul described the use of this gift, he did so in a very matter-of-fact way. It was simply a means for the Holy Spirit to convey a message from God to his people through an inspired intermediary. It came in the language of those who heard it, enabling the gift to provide edification to the congregation (1 Cor. 14:6).

The orderliness with which this gift was to be used is equally significant. Paul clearly did not define prophecy as some form of wild-eyed ecstatic phenomenon. The speaker had final control over how the prophetic word was proclaimed. The spirits of the prophets, he wrote, are subject to the prophets (1 Cor. 14:32). Those who prophesy are not out of control, driven into some ecstatic frenzy, nor are they so "Spirit-possessed" that their personality is lost in the "divine." The speaker is human and totally in control of his or her ability to speak. Prophets may begin to speak or cease from speaking at their own initiative (1 Cor. 14:30). There can be no legitimate claim that the Spirit has "overcome" them, forcing them to act.

Paul also recommended that the congregation even recognize a limited role for prophetic utterances that would be allowed in a given service. He suggested that two or three persons be allowed to speak (1 Cor. 14:29) before testing. It is clear that this gift of prophecy, while very significant for the life of the congregation, should be only one component of the Christian meeting, not the whole meeting. Room should be left for a variety of other Spirit-inspired contributions; a hymn, a word of instruction, a revelation, even a tongue and its interpretation (1 Cor. 14:26). Prophecy was not to dominate, nor was it to have an independent authority.

To guarantee that the prophetic offerings were indeed the mind of the Holy Spirit, Paul noted that an assessment needed to be made. It was an assessment of *what was spoken* (content) more than it was an assessment of the person *who spoke* (medium). In his instructions written to the Thessalonian Christians, Paul had already exhorted the church not to quench the Spirit or to despise prophesying. Instead, he had offered the advice to *test* it (*dokimazete*), accepting what was good in it while avoiding what was not (1 Thess. 5:19–22). In that context, his words were addressed to the entire congregation, not merely to a specific group of prophets within it.

In 1 Corinthians 14:29, he stated that the weighing or testing (*diakrinetōsan*) of the prophetic oracles was to be undertaken by the "others." It is possible to argue that "the others" to whom Paul refers here, are other specially equipped "prophets" within the congregation. Indeed, this is a very popular interpretation of this passage. But if this injunction in 14:29 is read in the light of Paul's words to the Thessalonian Christians, the pool of "testers" is broadened to include members from throughout the congregation. The "others," may well be the rest of the congregation, including the other "prophets." This interpretation is also possible from the text, provides more consistency with Paul's overall argument, and allows for a wider dimension of the Spirit's activity in the whole congregation.

For Paul the gift of the discerning of spirits (*diakriseis pneumatōn*) is repeatedly understood to have a complementary relationship to the gift of prophecy (1 Cor. 12:10; 1 Thess. 5:20–21) in much the same way that the gift of tongues is complemented by the gift of the interpretation of tongues. Yet the metaphor of the body of Christ governs Paul's observation that the sovereign work of the Spirit is to grant the ability to test to whomever God may choose to give it, not merely to certain "prophets."

Paul is convinced that the community is best protected and edified by testing prophetic claims. So strongly does he hold to this belief, that he describes his guidelines for the proper use of the gift of prophecy as being a "command of the Lord" (1 Cor. 14:37). In Paul's teaching, then, the Spirit inspires the prophetic utterance, demands that it be tested, and provides through the community of faith the means to determine its trustworthiness. Those who wish to speak but who refuse to allow for such testing may, like those in the OT, safely be ignored (1 Cor. 14:38) by the Christian community.

B. A Lukan Perspective. In the second volume that Luke addressed to Theophilus (cf. Luke 1:1–4; Acts 1:1–5), Luke provides examples of genuine Christian prophecy and mentions pagan "prophetic" practice. In Acts 16:16–18 he records an incident with some parallels to the prophetic phenomena prevalent in the Apollo or Pythian cult at Delphi (cf. above, Greek and Roman Prophetic Activity). In Philippi, there was a slave girl who worked by divining or telling fortunes. She followed Paul and Silas, crying, "These men are servants of the Most High God, who are telling you the way to be saved" (Acts 16:17). After repeated encounters with her, Paul became annoyed. What she proclaimed was true, but Paul apparently recognized the demonic origin of her words, and he spoke to the spirit within her, saying, "In the name of Jesus Christ I command you to come out of her!" Implicitly, at least, Luke is obviously in agreement with Paul. Prophecy needs to be tested, since some oracles, even those with what appears to be acceptable or truthful content can be demonically inspired.

Luke also recorded two striking incidents of genuine Christian prophecy. In each case, the prophet was Agabus, though the incidents were separated by some twelve intervening years. The first took place in Antioch. There Agabus stood up and signified, or foretold (*esēmanen*), by the Spirit that a famine was coming over all the earth (Acts 11:27–30). His prophecy was accepted by Luke as genuine on the grounds that it was fulfilled when Claudius was Caesar (11:28). The question can be raised, however, "How did the Christians at Antioch know that it was genuine?" Luke does not provide the answer to that question, *but* for them not to act until after the famine would have been not to take advantage of the warning. Thus it appears that at times prophecy has value within specific limits of time and space. It has context specificity, and the ability to test the prophetic gift adequately also lies within that context. The Christian community in Antioch had to act when it discerned that God was actually speaking through Agabus. It is probable that Agabus' word was accepted simply because there were those in Antioch who exercised the ability to discern spirits.

It is equally clear that Agabus' warning, while a part of what the church has come to recognize as Scripture, has no similar hold on the action of the contemporary church. The famine had come and gone. But the Christians whom Agabus addressed in the first century apparently believed the prediction to be genuine, for they acted according to their ability to provide a relief offering for those who would feel the results of the famine the most, their brothers and sisters in Judea. For today's church, Agabus' prophecy must be understood against a different hermeneutical construct; it merely provides instruction and example for such truths as how God provides for the needs of people, how generous the congregation at Antioch was, or how the gift of prophecy functioned in a specific situation.

The second illustration from the prophetic ministry of Agabus took place in Caesarea (Acts 21:10–14). According to Acts 20:22–23, Paul believed that the Holy Spirit was directing him to go to Jerusalem. A problem arose in that as he proceeded along his journey the Holy Spirit also told him (presumably by a word of prophecy) that he would undergo imprisonment and suffering. After sailing from Asia Minor, he landed in the coastal town of Tyre where, Luke notes, certain Christians told Paul "through the Spirit" (*dia tou pneumatos*) that he was *not* to go to Jerusalem (21:4). Paul had to make a decision. Would he continue the trip or stop it altogether? He chose to continue. When he traveled to Caesarea, the hometown of Philip the evangelist and his four virgin daughters who had the ability to prophesy, Paul and his companions were met by Agabus, who had come from Jerusalem.

In this instance, the actions of Agabus are reminiscent of those of the OT prophets. He not only *spoke* a prophetic word, he also *illustrated* the word by means of a "symbolic action," a graphic picture that, when acted out, made the same point as the spoken oracle (cf. Jer. 13:1–11; 27:1–28:17; Isa. 20:2–6). In this case, Agabus took Paul's belt and bound his own hands and feet with it. Then he proclaimed: "The Holy Spirit says, 'In this way the Jews of Jerusalem will bind the owner of this belt and will hand him over to the Gentiles'" (Acts 21:11). It is clear that this particular oracle was given in a *form* that is similar to many found in the OT. Among the OT prophets, a frequently cited introduction, or "messenger formula," included the words "Thus saith the Lord." Agabus used the same basic form, but it was the Lord the Spirit who spoke. Thus the "messenger formula" was transformed from "Thus saith the Lord" to "Thus says the Holy Spirit" or "The Holy Spirit says."

What is even more clear from this passage is that here a genuine oracle from God is subject to interpretation and is therefore in need of testing *and* application. The Christians at Caesarea clearly understood this to be a prophetic warning that Paul should *stop* his journey. On the other hand, Paul was still determined to follow his initial direction, that he was to go to Jerusalem even if it meant his death. The people understood it to mean, "Paul, don't go!" Paul apparently understood it to mean, "Go, but be prepared for suffering." After extensive discussion as to its meaning, Luke records that those who had confronted and challenged Paul, finally, perhaps even reluctantly, gave in and prayed that the Lord's will would be done (Acts 21:14).

By using concrete examples from everyday life, Luke has provided a series of pictures that reveal much about the gift of prophecy. While false prophecy or divination comes from other spirits, genuine prophecy comes from the Holy Spirit. It *may* have a predictive element at times, such as in the prophecies of Agabus, though this is not always the case. Prophecy needs assessment and demands application. It is possible for the whole Christian community to misunderstand a genuine prophetic word. It is important, then, to seek clarity on God's will on each occasion when the gift of prophecy is manifest.

One final passage in Acts shows that Peter and Luke understood the breadth that is possible in prophetic speech. In short, they shared the perspective on prophecy that has been noted in Exodus 4. In Acts 2:16–18 Peter declared that when the 120 spoke in tongues on the Day of Pentecost, a clear indication that the Holy Spirit had come, the prophecy of Joel (2:28–29) had been fulfilled. In Joel 2, however, there is no reference to speaking in tongues. What there is, is a reference to the ability to prophesy. Evidently, then, the ability to speak in tongues, the ecstatic activity that led some in the multitude to charge the 120 with public drunkenness, was understood first by Peter, then by many in the multitude, to be a form of "prophetic" speech. This allowed Peter to appeal to Joel in the way he did. It is clear that in one sense Luke, like Paul, distinguished the ability to speak in tongues from the ability to prophesy. Yet in another sense, Luke, in particular, agreed with Peter and the long-standing picture of the OT that prophecy at its most basic level is nothing less than inspired speech given by God through an individual.

C. Prophecy and the Gospel Writers. Two people who serve in transitional roles between Israel and the church are John the Baptist and Jesus. Each of them is understood to have a prophetic role, John a more focused one, and Jesus, a more paradigmatic one. It is clear that the Gospel writers wish to establish John the Baptist as a prophet in continuity with the church. Repeatedly they refer to him as a prophet (e.g., Luke 1:76; 7:26 = Matt. 11:9; John 1:21, 25), and the people around John are said to have understood that he was a prophet (e.g., Mark 11:32 = Matt. 21:26 = Luke 20:6; Matt. 14:5).

A look at John's life finds him "filled with the Holy Spirit even from birth" (Luke 1:15). The angel Gabriel who appeared to Zechariah before John's birth predicted that John's task would be one of bringing people back to God, and in the power of Elijah before him he would prepare the way for the Lord (Luke 1:16–17). Thus John preached near the Jordan, addressing multitudes as a "brood of vipers." His message was one of repentance and forgiveness (Matt. 3:7–10 = Luke 3:7–9; Mark 1:4–5). Furthermore, he pointed the way to the one who would follow him, the one who would both purge and baptize with the Holy Spirit and fire (Matt. 3:11–12 = Luke 3:16–17; Mark 1:7–8). While the *form* of John's message as recorded in the Gospels is not identical to the prophetic forms in the OT, there are a number of parallels, especially with Amos' admonition (Amos 5:4–5) and Jeremiah's "summons to flee" (Jer. 4:4–5; 6:1; 50:8–10). More significantly, John the Baptist stands firmly within the prophetic-apocalyptic stream, preaching an imminent divine intervention into history ("the ax is already at the root of the tree" [Matt. 3:10 = Luke 3:9]) with an eschatological judgment in response to Israel's wickedness.

R. B. Y. Scott has helped to differentiate between prophecy as it occurred in the OT and preaching as it was carried on in the NT. If the ministry of John the Baptist is studied, the initial reaction might be that he was preaching, not prophesying. But in the NT, preaching (*kērussō*) always includes the announcement of Good News. Prophecy, on the other hand, merely declares the urgency of belief in and obedience to the declaration of God's will and purpose. With this as a working definition, we can clearly understand that John the Baptist served in a prophetic role.

If some understood John the Baptist to be Elijah *redivivus,* or the eschatological prophet (John 1:21), people see Jesus in much the same light (Mark 8:27–28 = Matt. 16:13–14 = Luke 9:18–19; Luke 7:16). Luke in particular develops the prophetic role of Jesus, pointing toward the inevitable fate of prophets who from the first are not acceptable in their home towns (Luke 4:24) and ultimately are persecuted (Matt. 5:11–12 = Luke 6:22–23) or even put to death (Matt. 23:37–39 = Luke 13:34–35). But John also repeatedly depicts Jesus as a prophet (e.g., John 4:19; 6:14–15; 7:40; 9:17).

What John the Baptist, as well as Jesus, suggests for those who exercise the gift of prophecy is that they have a somewhat angular fit within church and society. They are not always warmly regarded, nor are their words readily received. Indeed, many who know them may ultimately reject them, precisely because they are prophets. On the other hand, simply because someone claims to be a prophet is no reason to accept everything he or she says. Jesus warned his own disciples on several occasions that false prophets would arise, parading as part of the church. They might appear to be harmless, but in reality they are bent on destruction of the flock (Matt. 7:15; 24:11, 24).

Jesus' concern was apparent in that he noted that such individuals would ultimately be rejected from entering the kingdom of heaven because (1) they were not known by him and (2) they were evildoers. Indeed, he warned his disciples beforehand (Matt. 24:24), he told them to be on guard for those who would lead them astray (v. 4), and he taught them that the false prophet ultimately produces evil fruit (Matt. 7:16–20). Jesus, then, taught that his followers should assess the fruit of those who claim prophetic authority to be sure that it is good. For the church, the norm for "good fruit" lies in Jesus, who is described for us in the apostolic writings, Scripture.

John is the only Gospel writer to have written on the role of the Spirit as "Paraclete." He incorporated the teachings of Jesus on the Spirit in a series of what have become known as "Paraclete Sayings" (John 14:16–17, 26; 15:26–7; 16:7–15). These sayings make clear the ongoing role of the Spirit among the followers of Christ. The term "paraclete" is related to the term "exhortation" (*paraklēsis*), whose verbal form means literally "to stand beside," or "to act as an advocate." When Paul wrote on the gift of prophecy, he used this term to describe one purpose of the gift (1 Cor. 14:3). According to Jesus, the Paraclete brings things to the remembrance of his followers (John 14:26), bears witness to Christ (15:26), and guides his follow-

ers into all truth (16:13). Indeed, the Paraclete, or Holy Spirit, conveys the mind of Christ to the church.

John also understood himself as functioning within the prophetic tradition of the church. He was well aware that there were many false prophets in the world (1 John 4:1), so he argued that all prophetic words should be tested. Yet he was confident of the genuineness of his own prophetic experience as when "on the Lord's Day [he] was in the Spirit [*en pneumati*]" (Rev. 1:10). What he experienced while "in the Spirit" he proclaimed as a "prophecy," but he also used the terms "revelation" and "apocalypse" (Rev. 1:10) to describe it, thereby demonstrating his own continuity in the prophetic-apocalyptic tradition.

III. The Gift of Prophecy in Church History.

A. The Early Church. Within the first several centuries A.D. the church was no stranger to continuing prophetic activity. Room was made within the church structure for prophets to function on both itinerant and local levels. Indeed, the writer to the Ephesians understood them to be foundational to the church (Eph. 2:20), for they received the mystery of Christ that the Gentiles were, through Christ, made "heirs together with Israel, members together of one body" (Eph. 3:6).

One important first-century writing, the *Didache* (c. A.D. 90), was concerned with both types of prophetic activity, although it appears that the predominant prophetic activity within the communities that accepted the tradition of the *Didache* was an itinerant ministry (*Did.* 10.7; 11:1–12; but see 13:1–7). Following Jesus' admonition to assess the fruit of the "prophet," the writer of the *Didache* instructed his readers to disregard anyone who benefited financially from his or her own prophetic activity. This was particularly true of itinerants. Those who settled down in a particular Christian community, however, were to be supported for their contribution to the spiritual welfare of the community.

The early second century reveals the claims that Ignatius, bishop of Antioch, made regarding his own experience with this gift (Ign. 7:1–2). While preaching to the congregation at Philadelphia on one occasion, he claimed that the Holy Spirit spoke through him, revealing a problem of disunity within that congregation. Ignatius maintained that until that point in his sermon he had been unaware of the problem, and its exposure in his sermon led to its ultimate resolution.

The Shepherd of Hermas, a devotional work most probably originating in Rome in the first third of the second century included a series of visions and provided guidelines for distinguishing between true and false prophetic claims (*Herm. Man.* 11). The esteem with which this work was held in the life of the church varied. Irenaeus (*Against Heresies* 4:20.2) called it *hē graphē* or *scriptura,* a term usually reserved for the canonical writings, although there is some ambiguity attached to Irenaeus' meaning when he used this term. Clement of Alexandria cited the work repeatedly in his *Stromata* (cf. 1.1.1; 1.85.4; 2.3.4; 4.74.4; et al.). Similarly there is a marked resemblance between portions of Hermas and the visions found in the *Passion of Perpetua and Felicitas* (cf. *Passion* 4.6–7 and *Herm. Vis.* 4.1.4–8). Tertullian, on the other hand, found it offensive because he believed it was lenient on those who had lapsed from the faith during times of persecution (*On Modesty* 10.12). Still, it was believed to provide good devotional food for thought by much of the church, including those who framed the Muratorian canon.

Hermas was particularly concerned for the impact that so-called prophets had on the newly committed Christian, the young, and the spiritually immature. Like the writer of the *Didache* and Jesus before him, he advocated the test of "good fruit." Those who function as false prophets, he argued, are bold and shameless. Some are motivated by power, others by money. He notably singled out those who prophesy on the fringe of a congregation, unnoticed or disregarded by the larger body. He argued against the usefulness of privately given "personal" prophecies. Typically they were nothing more than "empty words" that often left the immature at the mercy of the false prophet (*Herm. Man.* 11).

Competition between at least three different groups for recognition and acceptance of their prophetic claims was intense during this early period. On the one side were those who embraced one or another brand of *Gnosticism*. Gnostics highlighted exclusive revelation claims as authoritative. Typically they judged the traditions of the apostles to be imperfect (Irenaeus, *Against Heresies* 1.13.6; 1.25.2; 3.12.12; Tertullian, *Prescription Against Heretics* 23.1). They held up their own visions and prophecies as being not only indicative of a legitimate and vibrant spirituality, but an authoritative one as well (Hippolytus, *Refutation of All Heresies* 6.37; 7.26; 10.26).

The Montanists, too, believed in the continuation of prophetic phenomena. Originating in Asia Minor in the last half of the second century, they held considerable strength in Phrygia and later in North Africa. Problematic though they were, recent scholarship suggests that these believers were essentially orthodox in theology (Hippolytus, *Refutation of All Heresies* 8.12; Epiphanius, *Panarion* 48.1; Jerome, *Epistle* 41.3). Their tendencies toward asceticism and apocalypticism, however, often brought them into conflict with church leaders.

Tertullian (*On Monogamy* 4.1; 2.2) found in the Paraclete saying of John 16:12–13 ample justification for even the ascetic claims of this prophetic movement. From this passage he argued that through continuing prophetic activity, the Holy Spirit reveals to the church the mind of Christ little by little. The disciples had been unable to accept and process adequately everything that Jesus had intended for them to hear. Thus, by means of a form of progressive apostolic tradition found in Scripture and the *regula fidei* or "rule of faith" (Tertullian, *On Monogamy* 2.2–3), the church had opportunity to accept or reject what the Spirit had revealed to the church in the form of visions and prophecies.

To be sure, there were excesses in some Montanist prophecies. It appears that some pre-

dicted the imminent return of Christ, perhaps with setting dates for that event (Epiphanius, *Heresies* 48.2), while others pointed to Pepuza, a city in Asia Minor, as the New Jerusalem (Eusebius, *Ecclesiastical History* 5.18.1). Most, however, were understood as providing guidance in specific situations (Tertullian, *On Flight in Persecution* 9.4) or as providing supplementary support for certain teachings thought already to be evident in Scripture (cf. Tertullian, *On Modesty* 21.7; *On Chastity* 10.5; *On the Resurrection of the Flesh* 11.2). The most substantial problem associated with Montanist prophecy was the question of authority. How far did it legitimately extend and what relationship did it have to the official church authorities of the day?

The third group that claimed the activity of prophetic gifts were the orthodox themselves. The *Didache* clearly fell within this context, as did the *Shepherd of Hermas*. Irenaeus (*Against Heresies* 5.6.1) noted the existence of genuine prophecies in his day, and spoke against those who rejected the gift (*Demonstrations of the Apostolic Preaching* 99). In the East, Origen, who lived in Alexandria (203–231), then moved to Caesarea (232–253), had little time for either Pythian or Montanist claims. He rejected all forms of ecstasy (*ekstasia*), frenzy (*maniken*), or trance as signs of genuine prophetic activity. Yet he did believe in the genuineness of some prophetic claims. As Origen taught it, prophecy came at a moment of revelation in which the prophet saw things clearly and was then able to communicate the profound truths of Christian doctrine revealed by the Holy Spirit, truths that had been received in that moment (*Against Celsus* 7.3). It helped to provide biblical understanding and spiritual growth to the Christian community. Thus Origen appears to have been the first Christian writer to identify the gift with a form of exposition on the biblical text. The revealed understanding of the text was a prophetic word.

Prophecy, dreams, and visions found a unique place in the life of many early martyrs, as well as within the life of the much-persecuted North African church. Indeed, because of the presence of the martyr Perpetua; the advocate of Montanism, Tertullian; and the charismatic bishop Cyprian, the North African church seems to have been more actively involved in such activities than any other church of the third century.

At least four categories of prophetic revelations may be found in writings that originated from the church at Carthage at that time. First among these is the fact that many individuals received ecclesiastical appointment or confirmation of an appointment by this means (Cyprian, *Epistles* 39.1, 4; 40; 48.4; 63.1; 66.5, 10). That this practice was widespread may be observed from the fact that more than thirty other people joined Cyprian in one appointment made by this means (Cyprian, *Epistle* 70).

Second, were the many visions/prophecies that were given to provide comfort to the Confessors, those who had already been tried for their faith and were either awaiting sentencing, serving a sentence, or awaiting their execution (Cyprian, *Epistles* 10.4; 58.1; 78.1–2, 6.1–3). Indeed, the persecuted church understood the ability of an individual to make a confession before the magistrates to be a fulfillment of Jesus' promise that at such a time as they were persecuted, the Holy Spirit would provide them with a prophetic response (Matt. 10:19–20; Mark 13:9–13; Luke 12:11–12; 21:11–19). Thus there appears to have been a close relationship between prophecy and martyrdom.

Third, there were those times when visions and prophecies provided personal guidance or direction. Cyprian claimed to have been directed into hiding by the Lord (Cyprian, *Epistle* 16.4; and 7) at the time of a severe persecution about A.D. 252. During a later persecution, in A.D. 257, Cyprian received another revelation that allegedly foretold of his martyrdom (*Life and Passion of Cyprian* 7), thereby enabling him to set his house in order.

At times, appeals to such revelations were also used to provide direction to a congregation. Such a usage of revelatory claims does raise questions of discernment and the possibility of improper manipulation of the gullible (cf. von Harnack), but the claim still remains. On at least four occasions Cyprian provided leadership and exhortation to the congregations over which he presided as bishop by appealing to prophetic claims (*Epistle* 11.1–4) that exhorted the churches to unity in a time of deep conflict.

In spite of the widespread character of the gift of prophecy, it did lose some of its spontaneity as time progressed. Adolf von Harnack saw that fact as in some way related to the formation of the biblical canon. David Hill and David Aune have suggested that prophetic phenomena came into disrepute by their association with such sects as the Montanists and the rise of a class of more "rational" theologians and teachers. James Ash has argued that the decline in the prophetic gifts was due to the identification of these gifts with those in church leadership and especially with the bishop. Undoubtedly there are elements of truth in each of these explanations. Indeed, only by a movement from the spontaneous to an emphasis on the formalized did it become possible for Chrysostom (*Homily* 29 on 1 Cor. 12:1–2) to plead ignorance of what Paul meant when he wrote about spiritual gifts because they "no longer take place." Still, prophetic gifts were present even in the more routine aspects and offices of a maturing church. It is also possible to identify them outside the church's formal structure.

B. The Middle Ages. In the church of the Middle Ages, much of divine activity was viewed as operating within the bounds of official ecclesiastical structure. Prophetic activity was not limited to the formal structure by any means, for there were numerous outbursts of a more spontaneous nature among many, especially those who had embraced monastic life. This was true even more in the East than in the West. There were also many others to whom charismatic abilities were attributed and who were ultimately canonized by official church action as "saints," in part because of these abilities. On the whole, however, there is clear evidence that the regular church understood the *charismata* as being present in a

more or less routine way with the order of Christian leadership. As early as Basil of Caesarea (A.D. 330–379), those called to Christian leadership were assumed to stand in the prophetic tradition.

Thomas Aquinas, a leading scholastic theologian of the medieval church (A.D. 1225–1274), did much not only to systematize Catholic thinking in his day, but he has been a primary factor within Roman Catholic thinking ever since. Among his works were *De Veritate* and his multifaceted *Summa Theologica,* in which he addressed himself to the nature and working of the gift of prophecy at some length (2a 2ae. 171–75).

Arguing from an Aristotelian philosophical base, Thomas attempted to show the usefulness of this gift for the church. He understood it to be a charism or gratuitous gift (*gratias gratis datae*) given by God. It was, he argued, but one of several gifts including the words of knowledge and of wisdom, faith, and the discernment of spirits that could be subsumed under the broader category of "prophecy," because each of these shared a form of "prophetic revelation." Prophetic revelation not only involves prediction of future human events but also discloses contemporary divine realities (*res divinas;* 2a 2ae. 171, *Prol.*). Thus for Thomas, the prophet becomes a mediator of divine revelation, who through this gift instructs people in "whatever is necessary for salvation" (*De Veritate,* p. 12, a.2c).

The person who receives such a gift is divinely chosen, since it is a charism of grace (2a 2ae. 172, a3a). It is given to those whom God determines are best suited to receive it. Thus it is sometimes given to those who, humanly speaking, appear to be immature. The granting of this gift comes independently of sanctification or spiritual maturity. The best and deepest use of this gift, however, may be enhanced by sanctification since this gift requires the maximum elevation of the mind (*maxima meatis elevatio*) to things contemplative and spiritual. This "elevation" of the mind to see things that God chooses to uncover or disclose is hampered when things of the flesh such as passions (*passionum*) or a preoccupation with externalities (*exteriorum*) enter into the picture (2a 2ae. 172,a5d).

As for the method by which prophetic revelation occurs, Aquinas believed it is principally through the mind. The prophet's mind (*mens*) is moved (*movetus*) by the Holy Spirit in the same way a defective instrument is moved by its first cause. Thus the Holy Spirit moves the prophet's mind in such a way as to perceive or apprehend, speak, or act. At times, all three of these outcomes could result from the Spirit's movement. And while it is possible that the prophet might understand all that transpires in this way, it is not necessarily the case that this will be so, for there is a possibility that the prophet's own knowledge will be defective.

Thomas also held that there were both true and false prophecies and that demons were capable of inspiring false prophecy. While a true prophet inspired by the Spirit of truth (*Spiritu veritatis*) could prophesy without a trace of falsehood, the false prophet, instructed by the spirit of falsehood, would intermingle truth with falsehood. Thus ultimately the prophecy given by the false prophet was false prophecy.

C. Reformation and Post-Reformation Understandings. The issue of prophecy was an important factor during the Reformation. About 1529, Martin Luther penned his famous hymn "A Mighty Fortress Is Our God" in which he affirmed that "the Spirit and the gifts are ours." He believed in the priesthood of believers and the presence of *charismata* in his day. Yet he was troubled both by Roman abuses and what he perceived to be the subjective excesses of the so-called heavenly prophets. In Luther's thinking, "when Paul or the other apostles interpreted the Old Testament, their interpretation *was* prophecy" (*On Joel* 2:28). Furthermore, he seemed to place all "who can expound the Scriptures and ably interpret and teach the difficult books" as prophesying (*On Zechariah* [preface]).

Martin Luther, however, disagreed violently with the claims of the Zwickau prophets led by Thomas Münzer. He believed that their expositions and their signs were "worthless" (*On Joel* 2:28). Similarly, Luther's former colleague Andreas Karlstadt became known as a "heavenly prophet" after he defected from Luther. In 1525 Luther wrote of Karlstadt's interpretations of Scripture as "false prophecies," and he warned the churches against them. As a means of responding to these false "prophecies," Luther urged the readers of his work *Against the Heavenly Prophets* to pray for a "right understanding" of God's Word, and he exhorted them to stand guard against false prophetic claims.

John Calvin held a position on the gift of prophecy that was similar to that of Martin Luther. He noted that all the ancient prophecies and divine oracles were concluded in Christ and the gospel. Thus the canon appears to have entered into Calvin's understanding as the ultimate or final word spoken to the church. Further prophetic activity was limited to. a clearer understanding of this final word. In his *Commentary on Romans* (12:5) he said: "Prophecy . . . is simply the right understanding of Scripture and the particular gift of expounding it." Clearly, though, emphasis was placed on the prophetic as something that did not occur spontaneously but, like Origen's position, was more akin to the concept of illumination. It did not seem to be fresh revelation but primarily correct understanding and application of existing revelation.

If the Protestant Reformation and its leaders brought about renewal in the church, they also made it possible for a resurgence of more or less independent prophetic claims. During the late seventeenth and early eighteenth centuries, Christians in Cévennes raised a considerable stir by making prophetic claims. "Prophetic" manifestations were particularly common among younger people, male and female, who upon entering into trances, recited extended passages of Scripture, preached sermons, and indicted those who listened, sometimes addressing specific individuals. Other prophetic phenomena can be traced in groups that were largely marginal to mainstream Christianity. The Quakers preserved a more or less radical notion of the Spirit through experiences of the Inner Light. Others who made prophetic claims included the Ranters, an English extremist group, and the Shakers. In both cases they adopted unorthodox, even heretical, positions. Perhaps the most significant movement to claim spontaneous prophetic inspiration during the early nineteenth century was that associated with Church of Scotland minister Edward Irving. Unfortunately his adoption of an aberrant Christology led to his being deposed from Church of Scotland ranks. He later became associated with the Holy Catholic Apostolic Church where a variety of *charismata* were welcome. For the most part, however, the gift of prophecy since the Reformation has been closely identified with preaching. It is only as the Holiness movement drew toward the end of the nineteenth century that the issues of spontaneous inspiration began to reemerge.

IV. Prophecy in Contemporary Understanding. Within the Pentecostal-charismatic movements, the gift of prophecy has held a significant place. It was present in the earliest Pentecostal and charismatic meetings, and it continues to play an important role in the contemporary experience of these renewal movements. Discussion most frequently revolves around two basic issues. They are the question of (1) how to distinguish genuine oracles from false ones and (2) what authority contemporary oracles have in light of a closed canon of Scripture.

A. True and False Prophecy. It is clear from Scripture that prophecy is meant to be understood as a gift that is inspired by God through the Holy Spirit; granted to individuals for purposes of edification, exhortation, and comfort; and intended to communicate the mind of God. But for someone to claim that he or she is speaking on behalf of God makes the issue of discerning between true and false claims a critical one. The early Christian community was undoubtedly faced with this problem when it attempted to determine the limits of apostolic and prophetic claims, especially as questions of *regulae fidei* (rules of faith) and canon emerged. Modern discussions on the nature of canon and how it functioned in the earliest Christian community, then, may be informative here.

Questions were raised then, as they should be now, as to what relationship contemporary prophetic claims had to accepted apostolic tradition. Today, the major link with the apostles and their teachings is the NT, just as the writings of the OT played an authoritative role in the apostles' lives and provided a link for them with the people of God who had preceded them. Thus Scripture becomes the key by which contemporary "prophets" and prophecies may be assessed. Questions of how well prophetic claims contribute to the stability of the Christian community or challenge it within the limits of the apostolic faith and tradition and how widely adaptable such utterances are for the whole Christian community are equally significant. Mere personal claims to ecstatic experience and self-reported tales of visionary activity prove fruitless as sources of authentication for prophetic authority.

With Scripture as the norm, at least three basic criteria emerge that may aid the community in the assessment of prophetic claims. There may be more, but these three are found repeatedly in Scripture and in the workings of the church. They include an assessment of the person who prophesies, reflection on the process by which the prophecy is transmitted, and an evaluation of its content.

Guidelines on who may prophesy in a Christian meeting vary. Within those churches that view it solely as Christian preaching, the answer lies in the preacher or exhorter. Within a large congregation testing is sometimes accomplished in advance by having the would-be "prophet" pass the word before authorized elders or "prophets" or, within a Roman Catholic setting, before the priest. On other occasions, people may be allowed to speak from the floor and the whole group is given opportunity to weigh the words. Yet in each case, it is usually understood that those who speak are part of the community of faith, and thus they come under the authority of the community and its canon, Scripture, or else the person has been referred by another community whose judgment is trusted. Hence, the problems raised by prophetic claims made by strangers or by non-Christians are greatly reduced.

The test of methodology is equally helpful. Paul argued that God is a God of peace and order, and as such the use of charismata should reflect God's nature (1 Cor. 14:32–39). In addition, Scripture repeatedly recommends and invites testing to occur (Deut. 13:1–3; Matt. 7:15–23; 1 Thess. 5:19–22). Indeed, Paul noted that the Holy Spirit provides a testing charism, the discerning of spirits, for just such a purpose. Hence, those who are disruptive; who refuse to submit to community orders or its canon, Scripture; who refuse to be tested; or who place themselves in a position of authority beyond the ability of the community to provide testing, are to be ignored (1 Cor. 14:29–33a, 37–38).

Often the most helpful test may focus on what is actually said. If Scripture is normative within the Christian community, then one does not anticipate that a contemporary prophetic statement will contradict it. In the postapostolic age many prophetic claims were rejected simply because they were inconsistent with the apostolic tradition as it was found in the apostolic or NT writings and various regulae fidei. Perhaps the most notable of these were the many Gnostic claims that sought a legitimate place in the Christian community by claiming new revelations or personal visitations from one apostle who attempted to undermine the authority of other apostles (e.g., Apocalypse of James [C.G. 1.1.2]) or to generate the new teachings said to supersede the prior teachings of those in the biblical tradition (e.g., Apocalypse of John [C.G. 2.1.13]; Irenaeus Against Heresies [1.10.1–2]).

In recent years, prophetic claims have had more to do with personal guidance than with predictions of the future and more to say to local congregations than to the larger church. There are exceptions to this, such as the numerous "prophecies" that have been recorded and widely circulated within the numerous magazines and newsletters in charismatic renewal circles. David Wilkerson's book The Vision is one that is clearly meant to convey a predictive word to the larger church. Although Wilkerson has denied prophetic status, the reader of his Vision is hard pressed to reach the same conclusion. Care must be exercised in accepting a word of prediction in that a test of fulfillment must ultimately be invoked, and great damage and disillusionment may occur if it is ultimately found to be false. Likewise, the circulation of written prophecies can be confusing since some will ultimately treat them with some form of an ongoing canonical status. Joseph Smith's alleged revelation that produced the Book of Mormon and the esteem with which certain writings of Ellen G. White are held provide significant examples.

B. Limits of Prophetic Authority. The second issue is related to the first one. Given that the Christian community recognizes the need to test prophetic claims, and given that there exist within the body of Christ the necessary gifts and people to make possible an assessment of these claims, how far does prophetic authority extend? Many within the Reformed and dispensational camps suggest that the issue is easily resolved. Appeal is made to Hebrews 1:1–2 to demonstrate that all genuine prophetic authority has ceased, since God has given the ultimate Word to humankind in the person of Jesus Christ. This passage is then used as a key to 1 Corinthians 13:10 to argue that "the perfect" has come in Jesus Christ and that therefore prophecies have ceased. Prophetic activity is understood to have reached its apex in Jesus and in those through whom he revealed his will, the NT apostles and prophets. Thus the NT writings are understood to be the final prophetic words given through human beings, with the gifts of prophecy generally understood to have ceased around the end of the second century (cf. Warfield) or at the time in which the NT canon was formally recognized.

This position provides the church with protection from Mormon or Pentecostal claims today, but it seems necessarily to avoid a great deal of historical data. Similarly it tends to move 1 Corinthians 13:10 outside the immediate context of 1 Corinthians 13 for interpretation. The immediate context seems to suggest that "the perfect" (to teleion) to which Paul makes reference is the Parousia. The parallels that exist between this critical passage and the obviously eschatological reference found in 1 John 3:2 are significant.

The majority of the church, however, has never argued that prophecy ceased upon the deaths of the apostles or with the completion of the NT canon. A review of historical data appears to demonstrate that prophecy became more or less routine, was captured by the episcopacy, and was used in a way that further established the authority of the episcopacy. This position has found its ultimate form in the Roman Catholic doctrine of papal infallibility, where ex cathedra statements are made. Still, this act has been infrequently invoked, and all such pronouncements following the teaching of Paul are subject to scrutiny by the Roman magisterium before acceptance.

In spite of apparent attempts to limit the prophetic spirit—by the adoption of a theological system that in essence rules all later utterances as illegitimate prophetic claims, by anticipating that all legitimate claims originate within the episcopacy, or by removing the potentially spontaneous character of this gift by defining it as did Luther and Calvin as a form of expository preaching or teaching—the spontaneous character of this gift has been demonstrated frequently in the church in a variety of sects and cults. But this fact brings the discussion back to the beginning. What is the limit of prophetic authority? Within the Christian tradition it must be limited by the teachings of Scripture as understood by the members of the community of faith as they seek to submit themselves one to another and to live under the guidance of Scripture as the ultimate written authority in all matters of faith and practice.

The renewal of interest in the gift of prophecy speaks well for the church at the end of the twentieth century. While some are occupied with debates on whether early Christian prophets later "created" prophetic statements attributed to Jesus, others argue that the prophetic vocation holds great importance for the ecumenical vision of the church for the future. Insofar as Christians listen for the voice of God, discern what is that voice, and act upon it, this *charisma* will be of profit to the whole church as it faces the challenge of a new millennium. See also GIFTS OF THE SPIRIT; PAULINE LITERATURE.

Bibliography: A. Aubert, ed. *Prophets in the Church* (1968); D. E. Aune, *Prophecy in Early Christianity and the Ancient Mediterranean World* (1983); J. Blenkinsopp, *A History of Prophecy in Israel* (1983); E. M. Boring, *Sayings of the Risen Christ: Christian Prophecy in the Synoptic Tradition* (1982); S. M. Burgess, *The Spirit and the Church: Antiquity* (1984); R. P. Carroll, *When Prophecy Failed* (1979); A. H. Chroust, "Inspiration in Ancient Greece," in E. D. O'Connor, ed., *Perspective on Charismatic Renewal* (1975); R. E. Clements, *Prophecy and Covenant* (1965); R. Coggins, A. Phillips, and M. Knibb, eds., *Israel's Prophetic Tradition* (1982); T. M. Crone, *Early Christian Prophecy: A Study of Its Origin and Function* (1973); G. Dautzenberg, *Urchristliche Prophetie* (1975); A. B. Davidson, *Old Testament Prophecy* (1904); E. Ellis, *Prophecy and Hermeneutic in Early Christianity* (1978); J. Fontenrose, *The Delphic Oracle: Its Responses and Operations* (1978); C. Garrett, *Spirit Possession and Popular Religion: From the Camisards to the Shakers* (1987); D. Gee, *Concerning Spiritual Gifts* (rev. 1980); W. A. Grudem, *The Gift of Prophecy in 1 Corinthians* (1982); A. Guillaume, *Prophecy and Divination* (1938); H. A. Guy, *New Testament Prophecy: Its Origin and Significance* (1947); A. J. Heschel, *The Prophets*, 2 vols. (1962); D. Hill, *New Testament Prophecy* (1979); H. Horton, *The Gifts of the Spirit* (1971); E. C. Huber, *Women and the Authority of Inspiration* (1985); A. R. Johnson, *The Cultic Prophet in Ancient Israel* (1944, 1962); C. Klein, *The Psychological Pattern of Old Testament Prophecy* (1956); K. Koch, *The Prophets*, 2 vols. (1983, 1984); T. A. Kselman, *Miracles and Prophecies in Nineteenth-Century France* (1983); R. A. N. Kydd, *Charismatic Gifts in the Early Church* (1984); G. W. H. Lampe, "Martyrdom and Inspiration," in W. Horbury, *Suffering and Martyrdom in the New Testament,* (1981); R. E. Lerner, *The Powers of Prophecy* (1983); J. Lindblom, *Prophecy in Ancient Israel* (1973); U. B. Müller, *Prophetie und Predigt im Neuen Testament* (1975); N. I. Nidiokwere, *Prophecy and Revolution: The Role of Prophets in the Independent African Churches and in Biblical Tradition* (1981); J. Panagopoulos, *He'Ekklēsia tōn prophētikōn: To prophētikon charisma en tē 'Ekklēsia tōn duo prōtōn aiōnōn* (1979); idem, *Prophetic Vocation in the New Testament Today* (1977); H. W. Parke, *The Oracles of Zeus* (167); H. W. Parke and D. E. W. Wormell, *The Delphic Oracle,* 2 vols. (1956); D. L. Peterson, *The Roles of Israel's Prophets* (1981); J. R. Pridie, *The Spiritual Gifts* (1921); F. Rahman, *Prophecy in Islam: Philosophy and Orthodoxy* (1958, reprint 1979); K. Rahner, *Visions and Prophecies* (1983); J. Reiling, *Hermas and Christian Prophecy* (1973); C. M. Robeck, Jr., "Canon, *Regulae Fidei,* and Continuing Revelation in the Early Church," in J. E. Bradley and R. A. Muller, eds., *Church, Word and Spirit* (1987), 65–91; idem, "The Gift of Prophecy in Acts and Paul, Parts I & II," in *Studia Biblica et Theologica* (1975); idem, "The Role and Function of Prophetic Gifts for the Church at Carthage: A.D. 202–58," Ph.D. diss. (1985); idem, "Written Prophecies: A Question of Authority," *Pneuma* 2 (2, 1980): 26–45; H. W. Robinson, *Inspiration and Revelation in the Old Testament* (1946, reprint 1967); T. H. Robinson, *Prophecy and the Prophets in Ancient Israel* (1923, 1953, reprint 1967); F. Rousseau, *L'Apocalypse et le Milieu Prophétique du Nouveau Testament* (1971); C. Rowland, *The Open Heaven: A Study of Apocalyptic in Judaism and Early Christianity;* H. H. Rowley, "The Nature of Old Testament Prophecy in the Light of Recent Study," in H. H. Rowley, *The Servant of the Lord* (1952, 1965), 97–134; D. S. Russell, *The Method and Message of Jewish Apocalyptic* (1964); R. B. Y. Scott, *The Relevance of the Prophets* (1944); R. R. Wilson, *Prophecy and Society in Ancient Israel* (1980); H. W. Wolff, *Confrontations with Prophets* (1983); B. Yocum, *Prophecy: Exercising the Prophetic Gifts of the Spirit in the Church Today* (1976); E. J. Young, *My Servants the Prophets* (1952).

C. M. Robeck, Jr.

PSALMS, THE Because this book ends in a great climax of "Praise the Lord" (Heb. *hallelu YAH*), its original title was *Tehillim,* "Praises." When it was translated into Greek, the Septuagint version gave it the title, *Psalmoi,* "Songs to the accompaniment of a stringed instrument." Actually, some psalms are designated in the superscriptions by the Hebrew *mizmor* which has the same meaning as the Greek *psalmoi.* Others are called prayers or are given technical Hebrew designations.

These superscriptions (which were probably added to each psalm when it was placed in the temple collection) indicate that David wrote seventy-three. Of these, five are among the fifteen songs of degrees that some believe were added to the collection to celebrate the fifteen added years the Lord promised to Hezekiah (Isa. 38:5). They may have been added by the same men of Hezekiah who copied out proverbs of Solomon from the extant literature and added them to the Book of Proverbs (Prov. 25:1). The remainder of the psalms come from the time of Moses down to the period of the Exile. Though some literary critics of the nineteenth century claimed that all of the psalms were written after the Babylonian exile, there is no real evidence that any were written after 500 B.C.

The psalms express a great variety of feeling and most include the response of the psalmist to their situation and to the love, mercy, and grace of God. It was the hymn book of the Jews and of the early church. It still is one of the most popular parts of the Bible. Many believers read from it every day as a part of their private or personal devotions. No matter how a person feels, the Psalms help to give expression to the cry of the heart, and at the same time they bring encouragement to our faith in God. Portions of the psalms have been incorporated in many of the worship choruses that are so popular among Pentecostals and charismatics today.

I. David's Experience. After David was anointed by Samuel (1 Sam. 16:13), the Spirit of the Lord came into David with a rush of mighty power (Heb. *titslah*) and continued to indwell him from that day on, literally, "upward" (Heb. *maalah*). His was a rising, growing experience. Again and again songs poured forth from his Spirit-filled inner being to the accompaniment of his harp. They expressed his joy and his sorrow; his trust and his questions; and above all, his praise to God and his confidence in him. Then at the end of his life he was still able to say, "The Spirit of the LORD spoke through me, his word was on my tongue" (2 Sam. 23:2). The psalms he wrote and sang were thus the product of the inspiration of the Holy Spirit.

II. Five Books. David instituted the Levitical choir and orchestra and made music an important part of the worship of the Lord. He began the sacred collection we call the Psalms. The superscriptions sometimes include the words: *lamenatstseah*, "for the music director [of the Levitical choir and orchestra]," which seems to mean that these psalms were written with the intention that they would be included in the sacred collection.

In later times the Jews arranged the collection into five books, apparently to make the Book of Psalms have the same number of divisions as the Book of Moses (which we call the Pentateuch). Each of these divisions of the Psalms ends with a doxology, which is a further reason for the Hebrew title *Tehillim*, "Praises" (see Pss. 41:13; 72:19; 89:52; 106:48; 150:6). Otherwise, the five divisions seem to have little significance for the interpretation of the psalms. Occasionally there seems to be a brief sequence, as in the case of Psalms 22, 23, and 24. But the fact that the book is a collection means that each psalm is a unit in itself and has its own outline, so that each psalm must be studied individually for its own message and for its own emotional impact.

III. The Holy Spirit in the Psalms. The Spirit of God is mentioned in five psalms (51, 104, 106, 139, and 143). David used the term "Holy Spirit" only once, however. In Psalm 51 he expressed his genuine repentance for his great sins of adultery and murder. Verse 11 gives us his earnest petition, "Do not cast me from your presence or take your Holy Spirit from me." This was preceded by a cry for forgiveness which recognized that though God had been very patient with him, God's patience did not indicate approval of his sin. Thus, though he may not have understood the distinct personality of the Holy Spirit as we see it in the NT, he recognized that the Spirit of God is indeed holy. He also knew by experience that the Spirit was personally active, convicting

him of sin and then restoring the joy of God's salvation.

In this connection, verse 10 tells us that David wanted God to create in him (or, for him) a pure (unalloyed) heart and to renew (restore) a steadfast (firm, faithful, reliable) spirit within him (within his inner being). The Hebrew *bara*, "create," is used in the Bible only of God's unique, unprecedented, divine actions or activity. David, by his own efforts or thought processes, could not manufacture a pure heart for himself. Only God could do that. Neither could David renew or restore the steadfast, faithful spirit that desired above all things to do God's will. Sin had robbed his human spirit of that purpose and desire which before had made him always willing and ready to move when God moved.

Notice too, in spite of David's sin, that God did not take his Holy Spirit from him, nor had God removed his presence. In fact, God's presence here is parallel to God's Spirit, and it is evident that the Holy Spirit was making David aware of God's presence. Furthermore, the work of the Holy Spirit in convicting David of his sin made him aware that God had not yet cast him out on the slag heap as totally rejected or as totally beyond hope of restoration. The joy of his salvation had been lacking in that year during which he tried to cover up his sin, but now he had hope that God would not only forgive him but would also restore the joy.

Psalm 51:12 goes on to say, "Grant me a willing spirit to sustain me." However, "grant me" (Heb. *tismekeni*) is better translated "assist me," "support me," or "give me aid." This aid is given, not by his own spirit, but by God's willing, generous (Heb. *nedivah*) Spirit. David felt that he needed the support and aid of the Spirit, not only to keep him from falling again but also to open the mouth that sin had closed and to enable him to teach others the ways of God (v. 13). Later events show that God did answer David's prayer. The Spirit of God continued to be on his tongue.

Psalm 104 glorifies God as the Creator and Sustainer of the earth and its creatures. Verse 24 says, "How many are your works, O LORD! In wisdom you made them all; the earth is full of your creatures." Verse 30 goes on to say, "When you send your Spirit, they are created, and you renew the face of the earth." This is parallel to Genesis 1:2 as well as to Job 33:4. The psalmist thus sees a connection also between God's creative work and his providence and care for his creation, all carried out through the work of his Spirit, whom he sends. The fact that God sends his Spirit is significant also. Even though his Spirit is parallel with his presence, there is both a distinction and an identity implied. This is part of the mystery of the Trinity.

Psalm 106 speaks on the failures of the Israelites who rebelled in spite of the marvelous way God delivered them out of Egypt. Verses 32 and 33 put the blame on them for what happened to Moses: "By the waters of Meribah they angered the LORD, and trouble came to Moses because of them; for they rebelled against the Spirit of God, and rash words came from Moses' lips." Here the Hebrew simply says *ruho*, "his spirit" (the Heb.

does not distinguish between capital and lower case letters), which might mean either Moses' spirit or God's Spirit. But here it is clear from the parallelism between verses 32 and 33 that verse 33 is talking about God's Spirit and Moses' lips.

In Psalm 139 David recognizes God's knowledge of him and God's guidance. In verse 7 he cries out, "Where can I go from your Spirit? Where can I flee from your presence?" Then he answers, "If I go up to the heavens, you are there; if I make my bed in the depths (Heb. *sheol*), you are there. If I rise on the wings of the dawn, if I settle on the far side of the sea, even there your hand will guide me, your right hand will hold me fast." The question of verse 7 is rhetorical. As David's answer shows, he had no desire to get away from God's Spirit or to flee from his presence. Instead, he was declaring his faith and confidence that God's Spirit, power, and presence are everywhere in all the universe.

In Psalm 143:10, as David is crying out for mercy, relief, and deliverance from his enemies, he says, "Teach me to do your will, for you are my God; may your good Spirit lead me on level ground." He wanted God to help him really learn to do his will. He wanted God to let his good Spirit guide him into level country where nothing would cause him to stumble or fall, where he could live in righteousness, and where he could make the spiritual progress he so wanted to make.

The Bible makes it clear from beginning to end that God is indeed a good God, that his purposes for us are good, and that the Holy Spirit he sends to help us is also good. Nehemiah, near the end of God's OT dealings with Israel, also reminded the people of how God sent his good Spirit (Neh. 9:20).

Many other passages in the Psalms show us how the Holy Spirit must have inspired the worship of ancient Israel. He made them feel that God is indeed worthy of praise. The hallelujahs of the psalmists were not expressions of mere form and ceremony. They rolled out of the depths of their inner beings and out of the reality of their experience with God. It is no wonder that the Book of Psalms is still the greatest hymn book in the world!

Bibliography: J. A. Alexander, *The Psalms Translated and Explained,* 2 vols. (1873); G. L. Archer, Jr., *A Survey of Old Testament Introduction* (1974); D. S. Brisco, *A Heart for God* (n.d.); M. J. Dahood, *Psalms II* (1968); D. Guthrie, ed., *New Bible Commentary* (1970); S. M. Horton, *What the Bible Says About the Holy Spirit* (1976); A. Maclaren, *The Psalms* (1908); G. C. Morgan, *Notes on the Psalms* (1947); A. B. Simpson, *The Holy Spirit* (1895); C. H. Spurgeon, *The Treasury of David* (nineteenth century); J. W. Thirtle, *Old Testament Problems* (1916). S. M. Horton

PTL TELEVISION NETWORK See BAKKER, JAMES ORSEN "JIM" AND TAMMY FAYE.

PUBLIC WORSHIP See WORSHIP.

PUBLICATIONS The Pentecostal and charismatic movements, like other religious organizations, have looked at the printed page as perhaps the most effective medium to reach not only their own constituencies but also prospective converts. Numerous accounts are documented in these movements' literature of people who have been either converted and/or inspired through periodicals, tracts, books, or other printed matter. This was especially true during the first half of the twentieth century, when there was no television and only limited use of radio.

I. Introduction: Focus of Publications
  A. Evangelism
  B. Indoctrination
  C. Introduction of Distinctives
  D. Inspirational Literature
  E. Promotion
  F. Leadership Helps
II. Publications of the Pentecostal Movement
  A. Early Publications
  B. Recent Publications
III. Publications of the Salvation-Healing Movement
  A. The Rise of the Movement
  B. A Flood of Publications
IV. Publications of the Charismatic Movement
  A. The Origin of the Movement
  B. Segments Within the Charismatic Movement
  C. New Periodicals
V. Books Published on the Pentecostal-Charismatic Movement
  A. *Logos* Leads the Way
  B. Most Important Literature (1961–87)
VI Summary

I. Introduction: Focus of Publications. The focus of the print media can be divided into six broad categories with additional specialized use as needed.

A. Evangelism. This has been an emphasis in Pentecostal publications from the very beginning of the movement. It can be seen in the later charismatic movement's publications as well. The strong mission programs of early Pentecostals are one indication that their main objective was to convert the non-Christian, not just to convert believers to Pentecostalism.

B. Indoctrination. Most early leaders in the Pentecostal and charismatic movement came from denominations that relied on the printed page to indoctrinate their church members. Such a heritage influenced them later to incorporate similar publishing strategies within their own budding ministries. Both movements have utilized indoctrinational tactics in Sunday school literature, curriculum design, and other publications.

C. Introduction of Distinctives. In addition to publishing materials dealing with evangelical-fundamental doctrines, Pentecostals and charismatics use the printed medium to introduce their distinctive doctrines and practices: physical healing, sanctification, baptism in the Spirit, gifts of the Spirit, feet washing, and other doctrines and practices.

D. Inspirational Literature. Personal testimonies and other inspirational accounts have long been a means to attract others or encourage the faithful. Often these accounts are given at a local church during a "testimony" service, but the more important use of inspirational stories has been through the printed page.

E. Promotion. Missionary work, especially among the classical Pentecostal, has been promoted in periodicals almost from the beginning of the movement. The accounts not only served to attract additional missionaries to the "regions beyond" but also to raise support. Periodicals are used to promote various meetings and programs.

F. Leadership Helps. Early Pentecostals, for the most part, were not well educated. Therefore, leaders who did benefit from a good education saw the need for ongoing leadership training programs. This has included published leadership training courses, and in more recent times, audio and video training courses. Some denominations select a book—or assign a writer to produce a book on a certain subject—and then add an instructor's manual so that the material can be taught to Sunday school teachers and other church leaders.

Many of the publications produced by the Pentecostal-charismatic movement are being preserved in denominational and college archives, independent ministries' collections, and even some state libraries and historical societies. The Oral Roberts University collection is probably the most extensive available on the charismatic and salvation-healing movements. Two other important independent sources are the Billy Graham Center Archives at Wheaton College and David J. du Plessis Center for Christian Spirituality at Fuller Theological Seminary. Serious researchers should also consult the extensive bibliographical works by Charles Edwin Jones.

Researchers and collectors, however, are aware that many publications produced by Pentecostals are rare if available at all. Many of the publications were not kept, thus leaving gaps in the documentation of some early Pentecostal groups. The charismatic movement is young in comparison, which makes it easier to find its publications. The focus of this article will be on the older Pentecostal movement (and its salvation-healing offshoot) and the charismatic movement, and will examine the various publications and how they were used.

II. Publications of the Pentecostal Movement.

A. Early Publications. The modern Pentecostal movement's origins are generally traced to Charles F. Parham's Bethel Bible College in Topeka, Kansas, in 1901. Numerous stories were told of people around the world who read about the outpouring of the Spirit and later outpourings in other cities and communities. The first publicity on the Pentecostal gatherings came from the secular press—although these reports were usually derogatory. It was not long, however, before various individuals and ministries that had accepted the Pentecostal message began to publish their own periodicals and other literature.

Some of the periodicals that appeared on the scene during the first ten years of the revival predated the Pentecostal outpourings—they simply made room for their new Pentecostal doctrines. When the editors became Pentecostal, so did the periodicals. Four examples are Parham's *Apostolic Faith* (1899), J. M. Pike's *The Way of*

Faith (1890), Samuel G. Otis's *Word and Work* (1879), and Carrie Judd Montgomery's *The Triumphs of Faith* (1881).

By the end of 1908, J. Roswell Flower listed twenty-one Pentecostal papers in an "Apostolic Faith Directory" published in his monthly *The Pentecost* (1908). Of the twenty-one, fourteen were published in the U.S. Also included in the directory were missionaries, missions (local churches), missionary societies, and three song book publishers.

The Pentecost (1908), Indianapolis, Indiana. J. Roswell Flower.
The New Acts (1904), Alliance, Ohio. Levi R. Lupton.
Household of God (1908), Dayton, Ohio.
Good Tidings (1908), Dayton, Ohio.
The Bridegroom's Messenger (1907), Atlanta, Georgia. G. B. Cashwell and E. A. Sexton.
The Apostolic Witness (1908), Dallas, Oregon.
Trust (1902), Rochester, New York.
The Apostolic Faith (1899), Houston, Texas. C. F. Parham.
The Apostolic Faith (1906), Portland, Oregon. Florence Crawford.
The Pentecostal Record and Outlook (1908), Spokane, Washington. H. R. Bursell.
God's Latter Rain, Johannesburg, South Africa.
The Apostolic Standard, Doxey, Oklahoma.
The Christian Assembly, Cincinnati, Ohio.
The Midnight Cry (1908), Seattle, Washington.
The Latter Rain, Watertown, New York. J. E. Sanders.
The Spirit of Truth, Hants, England. W. L. Lake.
Confidence (1908), Sunderland, England. A. A. Boddy.
The Cloud of Witnesses, Bombay, India. Max Wood Moorehead.
Pentecostal Truths (Chinese), Hong Kong. Mok Lai Chi.
The Apostolic Light (c. 1904), Yokohama, Japan. M. L. Ryan.
Spade Regen, Amsterdam, Holland. G. R. Polman.

Some of the publications were free while others carried a nominal subscription fee (usually fifty cents a week). Some publishers who charged a subscription fee reasoned that it was the only way they could continue the publications. Other publishers, who offered their papers free, with an occasional low-key request for financial support, believed that the gospel and the Pentecostal message should be offered without charge, citing biblical reasons for their positions. Flower's own *The Pentecost* was offered at a subscription fee; but when he turned it over to A. S. Copley in 1910, Copley changed the name to *Grace and Glory* and offered it free. Seventy-seven years later it was still being published as a free publication.

It is obvious that publishers of early Pentecostal papers did not use their publications to make money. Many of them apologized for the nominal charge, and some of the free publications failed because of a lack of financial support. The publishers honestly believed their papers were divinely ordained; and when they failed, it was not the publisher's fault, the readers simply "missed God" by failing to support the endeavor.

When early Pentecostal organizations were formed, they either created their own periodicals or accepted existing ones. *The Christian Evangel* (1913) and the *Word and Witness* (c. 1911), which were given to the Assemblies of God in 1914, are examples of the latter. Another example of a group picking up an existing periodical is Florence Crawford's *Apostolic Faith* in Portland, Oregon. She moved to Portland in 1906 and by 1908 had taken over the *Apostolic Faith* paper, which was started by William J. Seymour and the Azusa Street Mission in Los Angeles. (Some have pointed at evidence that indicates the takeover was against Seymour's knowledge.) The paper was renamed *The Light of Hope* in 1965.

One of the early papers to be founded as a Pentecostal periodical was G. B. Cashwell's *The Bridegroom's Messenger* in 1907; it is still being published by the International Pentecostal Church of Christ. Two others are *The Evening Light and Church of God Evangel* (now called *Church of God Evangel* and published in Cleveland, Tenn.), founded in 1910, and the *Pentecostal Holiness Advocate,* which was founded in 1917 and continues to be published by the Pentecostal Holiness Church.

Many of the periodicals had limited circulation while others claimed unusually wide coverage for such young enterprises. Seymour claimed by the end of 1907 that his *Apostolic Faith* boasted a 40,000 press run. A year later, after Florence Crawford became the publisher and the paper moved to Portland, the circulation jumped to 80,000. It seems reasonable to assume, however, that the high circulation of the *Apostolic Faith* was an exception to the rule for early Pentecostal periodicals.

Many periodicals began in local churches, but most of them either were discontinued or combined with other periodicals. The *Latter Rain Evangel,* which was started by William H. Piper and his Stone Church in Chicago (1908), surprisingly continued as a local church publication for more than thirty years. Piper, who had at one time been an assistant to John Alexander Dowie, picked up ideas for a quality publication from Dowie's *Leaves of Healing.* Probably the most astute move Piper made was to hire Dowie's former secretary, Anna C. Reiff, as the editor of the *Latter Rain Evangel.* This monthly magazine carried news of missionaries, revival meetings, sermons, and articles. The magazine merged with the *Gospel Call* in 1939.

Aimee Semple McPherson very early saw the value of the printed page. She began her *Bridal Call* magazine in 1917, and it became one of the most attractive religious magazines of its day. After her death, the *Bridal Call* and the *Crusader* were combined and became the *Foursquare Magazine.*

Since the early Pentecostal publications were mailed to subscribers around the world, and not just for local readership, their purposes are of concern. In the beginning the primary purpose was to spread the news about the Latter Rain, or the baptism in the Holy Spirit. Pentecostals could

As a young woman, Carrie Judd Montgomery was healed of a serious illness. For the rest of her life she ministered to people in need. She edited *Triumphs of Faith* for more than 60 years.

not expect favorable treatment in secular and non-Pentecostal periodicals, so out of necessity, to promote and preserve the revival, they started their own.

As the revival continued, different views and misunderstandings arose, creating a need for defining some of the doctrinal points. Just because, at the turn of the century, two preachers spoke in tongues was no assurance that they agreed on the finer points of doctrines and practices.

Therefore, numerous articles were published on various views within the movement. The first major difference came over the doctrine of sanctification. Parham and Seymour, with their Holiness background, believed that nobody received the baptism in the Spirit until they had been converted and sanctified. William H. Durham began teaching a progressive sanctification, which was known as the "finished work," rather than an instantaneous experience. The end result was the same: believers were baptized in the Spirit and spoke in tongues, but the route to that experience was on two different roads.

Parham and Seymour (and later Florence Crawford in Portland) used their papers, both of which were called *Apostolic Faith,* to promote their particular ideas on sanctification and the baptism in the Holy Spirit. Durham countered with the "finished work" teaching in his *The Pentecostal Testimony* (1907).

Later, other major differences argued in Pentecostal papers, tracts, and books included the correct mode of water baptism (which led to the great Trinitarian–Oneness debate) and the initial evidence controversy (whether or not speaking in tongues was the exclusive evidence of the baptism in the Holy Spirit). Small differences, though perhaps not small in the eyes of the proponents, included outward holiness practices, washing of the saints' feet, use of the gifts of the Spirit, separation from the world, snake handling, eating pork, pacifism, church organizations, local church polity, women's rights in the gospel, and countless other "essentials."

The arguments presented in the early periodicals were hardly friendly, charitable debates. A good example of intolerance is Parham's reaction to Durham's finished work teaching. Parham wrote in the July 1912 issue of *Apostolic Faith* that either Durham or he himself was wrong about the issue. Parham prayed that God would smite the one who was in error. Durham's death six months later seemed to satisfy Parham and perhaps other Wesleyan Pentecostals that God had indeed spoken.

Another major issue, the Trinitarian and Oneness controversy, erupted in 1915. Three papers used to promote the Oneness side of the issue were G. T. Haywood's *Voice Crying in the Wilderness* (1910), Frank Ewart's *Meat in Due Season* (1914), and David Lee Floyd's (later D. C. Opperman's) *Blessed Truth* (1915). The *Christian Evangel* and the *Word and Witness* stood by the Trinitarian view during the controversy.

With all of the different doctrines that were being taught (many of which came by "revelation" according to the proponents), it is no wonder that publications became the most effective means to present "correct" interpretations.

The *Christian Evangel* was also a pacesetter in the publishing of Sunday school lesson materials. J. Roswell and Alice R. Flower presented a Pentecostal slant to the International Sunday School Lessons for their readers. Started in 1913, the *Evangel* later became known as the *Weekly Evangel* when the Assemblies of God (AG) moved to St. Louis and discovered another *Christian Evangel* being published there. The name was changed back to the *Christian Evangel* when the denomination moved to Springfield, Missouri. In 1919 the magazine became known as the *Pentecostal Evangel*.

In comparison to an editor today who operates with the latest state-of-the-art word processing equipment and who never sees the press unless he or she wants to, early editors often wore many hats. They often wrote the articles, set type, ran the press, mailed the finished product, and even repaired the press when it broke down. Ironically, with all of the primitive production methods used in the first half of the twentieth century, editors had a shorter lead time than editors of modern times. What took two to three weeks in the early years might take six weeks today.

Most libraries early in the twentieth century looked at the Pentecostal publications as "fly-by-night" operations and as unimportant for their collections. Consequently, there are few extant full collections of Pentecostal publications. One paper, Seymour's *Apostolic Faith* (1906–08), was reprinted as *Like as of Fire*. Many of the lesser known periodicals are cited in books and other publications but are difficult to find today.

The list is long of people who were influenced by the early publications. Seymour's *Apostolic Faith* became the most prominent paper in the early months of the Azusa Street outpouring. Numerous people were brought into the Pentecostal movement by first reading the *Apostolic Faith*, including Thomas H. Ball, A. H. Argue, C. A. McKinney, and J. H. King, just to name a few.

B. Recent Publications. In recent years the classical Pentecostal groups have maintained an "official organ" and have added specialized periodicals designed to promote various church departments and interests: publications for women, men, youth, history buffs, ministers, Sunday school teachers, home and foreign missionaries, and others.

Most of the groups have also published books, tracts, Sunday school curricula, and other material. Some are producing curricula for the growing Christian school movement. The smaller Pentecostal groups find that purchasing curricula and other material from large publishers is more practical than publishing their own. One large publisher who serves many smaller groups and independent churches, Gospel Publishing House, avoids certain controversial subjects so that more groups will be able to use the materials.

Agora, an independent journal published largely by AG ministers and teachers survived for five years (1977–82). This publication gave authors opportunity to write articles that would never be published in the church-sponsored publications due to their controversial character or critical views. Lack of finances and writers (the publisher claimed denominational officials threatened writers with loss of ministerial credentials if they contributed) ended this journal's short and controversial life.

III. Publications of the Salvation-Healing Movement.
A. The Rise of the Movement. The salvation-healing movement, popularly associated with an evangelist and a huge tent and beginning in the late 1940s and running for about the next twenty years, brought to the American scene a phenomenon that created either uncritical acclaim or total repudiation. It all depends on whether one reads the evangelists' periodicals or the local newspaper. And in the Pentecostal movement it would be argued by some that the movement was responsible for church growth; others, however, claimed that the excitement and big crowds created little lasting results.

This is the movement that gave America such healing luminaries as Oral Roberts, William Branham, A. A. Allen, Jack Coe, and dozens of others of less notoriety. Each of them, to survive, needed publications, often gaudy and filled with claims of healing and deliverance from demons, financial curses, and other calamities. By 1960, however, only a handful of salvation-healing evangelists were able to attract the crowds of the heyday years. Some of them had taken pastorates, some had gone into other ministries, at least two (Allen and Roberts) had founded a college and a university, and still others had dropped out of the ministry.

Although the salvation-healing movement peaked during the 1950s, several key evangelists are credited with breaking ground for the success of this period. These include John Alexander Dowie, John G. Lake, Maria B. Woodworth-Etter, Aimee Semple McPherson, Raymond T. Richey, F. F. Bosworth, Smith Wigglesworth, and Charles S. Price. Like their successors, these pioneers used periodicals, tracts, and books to report healings, to promote their meetings, to keep in touch with their supporters, and to build faith.

Historian David Edwin Harrell, Jr., considers Charles S. Price as the most influential for later salvation-healing evangelists. A former Congregational minister who became a Pentecostal under the ministry of Aimee Semple McPherson, Price left a pastorate in Lodi, California, for the nomadic life of an evangelist in 1922. He was considered an anomaly among Pentecostals in that he was well educated and was a professional master of ceremonies and speaker on chautauqua circuits. And unlike his successors with their big staffs, in later years Price would often lead his own song service before preaching. An associate said Price felt more comfortable if he had full control over the meetings.

Golden Grain, a monthly periodical that Price started in 1925, carried his sermons, news of his meetings, and healing testimonies. Considered an extremely modest man by the standards set by some of the later flamboyant evangelists, Price seldom published his own photograph with Golden Grain. Although Price remained independent during his years with the salvation-healing movement, he conducted many campaigns in AG churches and camp meetings. (Price family members donated issues of Golden Grain, healing cards used in meetings, copies of his books, and a newspaper clipping scrapbook to the Assemblies of God Archives.)

The story of Joseph Conlee, a minister-turned-atheist, who returned to Christ during the gold rush in Alaska, was told many times in sermons by Price and published in tract and magazine form as "The Cabin on the 40 Mile." Price also wrote several books, including The Story of My Life (1935).

His death in 1947 did not end the Golden Grain. Lorne Fox, who was healed in a Price meeting in 1923, was associate editor for several years. The same year Price died also saw the rise of two men who would become the giants of the salvation-healing movement—William Branham and Oral Roberts. Their appearance signaled the beginning of other large ministries. Healing tents were soon common in every major city in America, and little-known evangelists began preaching to thousands and praying for the sick. It was the beginning of a new era.

B. A Flood of Publications. With the great number of tent evangelists moving from city to city, the need for printed materials became evident, and some kind of coordination was needed. The man to fill the need was Gordon Lindsay, an AG pastor who traced his spiritual heritage to the likes of John Alexander Dowie, John G. Lake, and Charles F. Parham. He used his writing and organizational skills to publicize the dozens of campaigns taking place simultaneously across the country. Lindsay formed the Voice of Healing and began publishing a magazine with the same name. Many of the evangelists united with Lindsay and were pleased to see reports of their meetings published in the Voice of Healing (1948). Others, like Oral Roberts, remained independent and published their own periodicals and other literature.

One of the reasons Lindsay's Voice of Healing and other periodicals came on the scene is that denominational editors, operating on official policy, gave very little publicity to the evangelists. Denominational officials generally shunned the high-flying tent evangelists because of the often wild and undocumented healing claims and questionable practices.

Secular newspapers and magazines often covered the tent meetings, but reporters, who knew little about Pentecostal worship and practices, saw an Elmer Gantry in every evangelist. Their stories reflected that suspicion. At times, however, the critical reporting only increased interest, drawing thousands to the meetings.

Pentecost (1947), the official publication of the Pentecostal World Conference, was more sympathetic to the healing evangelists than were many of the denominational publications. One reason is that Donald Gee, the English Pentecostal teacher and writer, was the editor. His lifelong plea for unity among believers kept him open to any who were orthodox and moral. After Gee's death in 1966, Pentecost was replaced by World Pentecost (1971).

The most important book written on the salvation-healing movement is David Edwin Harrell's All Things Are Possible (1975). His bibliographical essay documents the movement's major periodicals and other literature. Monumental bibliographical works by Charles Edwin Jones give serious scholars handy reference tools not only for the salvation-healing movement but also for the Holiness, Pentecostal, and charismatic movements. Probably the best sources for periodicals from the salvation-healing movement are in the Oral Roberts University collection.

In addition to periodicals published by the evangelists, scores of books and tracts were published. It was an unusual evangelist who did not publish his own story. Other books dealt with exercising faith for everything from physical healings to raising the dead. Demonology and financial prosperity were two other popular topics. Since few established publishers would accept book manuscripts from the evangelists, the individual ministries became book publishers. They would hire a printer to produce the books, and then they would sell them in the meetings. The books would also be offered on the radio and television or in publications as a premium for an offering.

Publications produced by the salvation-healing ministries served their purposes in encouraging faith and promoting the ministries. Without this important medium, much of the movement's momentum would have been lost.

IV. Publications of the Charismatic Movement.

A. The Origin of the Movement. The charismatic movement received its early thrust in the 1960s after Episcopalian Dennis Bennett was baptized in the Holy Spirit. Since that experience in a Van Nuys, California, church, the movement has expanded throughout the world. Not the least of the reasons given for this phenomenon are the periodicals, books, and other literature of the charismatics. And just as the *Apostolic Faith* and similar publications created a hunger in the lives of believers around the world at the turn of the century, so a new batch of publications whetted the spiritual appetites of a new generation.

Whereas Pentecostal denominational publications primarily focus on people and events within their own fellowships, or at least on those who have a doctrinal and lifestyle affinity with their own, the new independent charismatic publications reached to believers of all charismatic groups. Along with this freedom and openness came risks and vulnerability—publishing articles or literature by or about people whose accounts were not fully documented or who lacked spiritual maturity. The freedom of the independent publications and the restrictions imposed on the denominational publications in the 1960s and 1970s gave readers the impression that the latter were ingrown and lacked a vision for any spiritual happenings outside their own denominational barriers.

The way Pentecostals after 1960 began to look at the charismatic renewal was similar to the cautious attitude mainline denominational publications took early in this century regarding the Pentecostal renewal. However, the Pentecostals of the 1960s were more sympathetic than the mainline denominations were sixty years before. Countless stories were recounted of how the early Pentecostals were kicked out of the mainline denominations whenever they embraced the doctrines of speaking in tongues, spiritual gifts, and physical healing. Articles published in the denominational publications of that period were usually very critical. Even the venerable Reuben A. Torrey, in referring to charges against Charles F. Parham, wrote that the movement was founded by a sodomite.

The charismatics, beginning in the early 1960s, had their critics, and many of them were asked to leave their churches. But others were permitted to stay, and in many cases the churches became Pentecostal, or as they preferred to be called, charismatic or Neo-Pentecostal.

Denominational publications even published favorable, or at least objective, articles about the renewal. Unofficial denominational periodicals and other literature began to appear, giving the movement respectability, something early Pentecostals found difficult to obtain.

The Pentecostal movement publicly acknowledged the charismatic renewal as a genuine spiritual happening but grew increasingly wary of some of the charismatic claims and activities. Along with the cautious approval by the Pentecostals came a division in their ranks: some advised the charismatics to leave their old-line denominations and join the existing Pentecostal congregations, while others urged them to stay in their own groups and thus influence noncharismatics toward spiritual renewal.

One influential voice among the Pentecostals that urged charismatics to leave their noncharismatic churches was Evangelist Jimmy Swaggart. He focused especially on Roman Catholic charismatics, urging them to leave their church and join Protestant congregations, preferably classical Pentecostal congregations.

B. Segments Within the Charismatic Movement. Before looking at the periodicals and other literature of the charismatic movement, it is important to examine the various segments within the movement. The first group includes denominational congregations that became charismatic, following the lead of their minister, and were permitted to remain in the organization. Dennis Bennett's St. Luke's Episcopal Church in Seattle is one such example. A second group of charismatics represent independent churches that were formed by leaders who had been baptized in the Holy Spirit but who were no longer allowed to remain in their denomination. A third group, alluded to above, is made up of Catholic charismatics, those who basically want to add the charismatic teachings and experiences to their traditions. Still a fourth element among charismatics, which developed in the 1970s, is the "Word" or "Faith" groups. These groups have been spearheaded by such strong leaders as Kenneth Hagin, Derek Prince, Kenneth Copeland, Fred Price, and others. Leadership of the later has come from both classical and Neo-Pentecostal traditions.

There are in addition many divisions within the above four charismatic groups, created by certain worship styles and practices (worship dancing, particular uses of the gifts of the Spirit, and other distinctives) and by doctrinal points (including shepherding, financial prosperity, demon exorcism, healing, etc.). Another division is created when charismatic scholars emphasize a scholarly treatment of the renewal rather than an emotional experience.

One fellowship that has tried to bridge the entire Pentecostal-charismatic renewal, with considerable success, has been the Full Gospel Business Men's Fellowship International (FGBMFI). This organization, with its roots in classical Pentecostal traditions, recognized its ability to draw various groups together and has had an important impact on these believers. The same can be said of Women's Aglow, a counterpart to the FGBMFI. Both groups can be described as experience oriented. Since the 1970s the Society for Pentecostal Studies (SPS) has been successful in attracting scholars from various wings of the Pentecostal and charismatic traditions. The association publishes *Pneuma: Journal of the Society for Pentecostal Studies,* as a semiannual journal. Beginning primarily as a classical Pentecostal fellowship, the group elected a Catholic charismatic as president in 1985.

C. New Periodicals. Just as in the early years of the Pentecostal movement, the charismatic groups

Early Pentecostal periodicals flourished in all shapes and sizes, each carrying the message of the outpouring of the Holy Spirit.

soon began to publish their own periodicals and literature. Being a nebulous form with little to hold themselves together except their new experiences, charismatic groups began to publish various small periodicals. Many of these periodicals reported testimonials of people who had been baptized in the Spirit. Some of the more serious began to define the theology.

It was not until 1971 that any one magazine was able to speak for and to the majority of charismatic groups that were springing up worldwide. That magazine was the *Logos Journal*, established in 1971 by Daniel Malachuk. He had been reared in a classical Pentecostal church, the famous Glad Tidings Tabernacle (AG) in New York. The *Journal*, edited in the beginning by Alden West, filled the need for a magazine that ministered to charismatics and as an evangelism tool for the noncharismatic. It also became an important promotional medium for Malachuk's new charismatic book publishing venture. Almost overnight, from a small operation in Malachuk's kitchen, Logos Fellowship International (LFI) became the leading publisher of charismatic books, far surpassing the output of classical Pentecostal book publishers. LFI was soon publishing as many as fifty books a year.

Logos's meteoric rise to fame among charismatics ended dramatically in 1981 when the company filed for Chapter XI in the U.S. Bankruptcy Court of New Jersey. It was the painful end of an important publishing venture of the charismatic movement. Others would pick up the spoils and carry on the exciting publishing idea that the risk-taking Malachuk created with his first book published in 1968.

The *Logos Journal* actually had its beginning with a previous magazine consolidation. Joseph Mattsson-Boze's *Herald of Faith* and charismatic Mennonite Gerald Derstine's *Harvest Time* had merged in 1970 as *Herald of Faith, Harvest Time*. Malachuk reached an agreement with the publishers to take over the periodical in 1971, renaming it the *Logos Journal*. Given a new burst of energy and a broader base, the *Journal* soon reached many parts of the world and all segments of the Pentecostal-charismatic movement. Within three years the *Journal* had nearly 50,000 subscribers.

With an aggressive publisher, a professional editorial staff, and some of the biggest charismatic names contributing articles, the *Journal* became the most important periodical of the renewal. Readers could expect a balance of personal testimonies, news from charismatic circles, and the treatment of important doctrinal subjects. The effort was somewhat successful in helping to stabilize an often fluctuating renewal movement.

Ironically, the medium that gave LFI and the charismatic movement such wide exposure also became its downfall. In 1975 Malachuk announced that God had led him into starting the *National Courier*, a biweekly newspaper. The *Courier* folded in 1977, leaving the company deep in debt, an indebtedness that caused it to collapse four years later.

In 1981 the *Journal's* circulation dropped to 20,000. Like other aspects of the LFI venture, the *Journal's* life ended with the September/October 1981 issue.

Benefiting most from the *Journal's* failure was *Charisma*, a magazine started by Stephen Strang and sponsored by Calvary Assembly of God in Winter Park, Florida. Begun in 1975 as a competitor to the *Journal, Charisma* took over the *Journal's* subscription list when it closed.

Strang, who later became the sole owner of *Charisma*, started a church leader's magazine, *Ministries Today*. He later bought *Christian Life* magazine, which also included the *Christian Bookseller* trade magazine and the Creation House book publishing division. (*Christian Life* merged with *Charisma* in 1987 to become *Charisma and Christian Life*.) By 1987 Strang Communications Company, now in Altamonte Springs, Florida, was considered one of the most influential and important publishing companies in the charismatic movement. Strang's editorial latitude embraces the entire Pentecostal-charismatic segment of the Christian church, giving him a strong base of operation.

Although it was not strictly a charismatic publication, *Christian Life*, with charismatic founder-editor Bob Walker, became an important medium in reporting activities in the movement beginning in the 1960s. Articles telling of spiritual renewal in various denominational churches established this interdenominational magazine as a voice in the renewal. Readers learned of the charismatic experiences of such leaders as Dennis Bennett, James Brown, Howard Ervin, Don Basham, Jean Stone, John Osteen, and others. Because of its sympathy toward the renewal, *Christian Life* suffered losses in subscriptions among noncharismatics but gained new subscribers among believers who were interested in the movement.

The Full Gospel Business Men's *Voice*, begun in 1953, despite its masculine laity focus, was an important publication in the renewal. Dedicated men in local FGBMFI chapters spread the word through the magazine by distributing it in doctors' offices, bus stations, churches, and wherever else reading material would be picked up. Published testimonies of men in various walks of life helped spread the news of the renewal to church and nonchurch men alike.

Thomas R. Nickel, who was the founding editor of the FGBMFI *Voice*, left the organization in 1962 and founded the Great Commission International. He also established *Testimony* (1962), a magazine similar in appearance to *Voice*.

Christian Growth Ministries, Fort Lauderdale, Florida (later called Integrity Communications, Mobile, Ala.), published *New Wine* magazine (1969–86). Four ministers from varied backgrounds sponsored the publication: Derek Prince, Bernard "Bob" Mumford, Don Basham, and Charles Simpson. Controversy surrounded this organization, primarily because of the shepherding movement and teachings on demon possession of believers. Integrity Communications was dissolved at the end of 1986, and the ministers involved began their own independent ministries. Charles Simpson remained in Mobile and formed a new organization but retained the name of Integrity Communications. He publishes a bimonthly magazine, *Christian Conquest* (1987).

Another ministry that bridges the Pentecostal-charismatic movement is the work of Oral Roberts. Originally from the Pentecostal Holiness Church, Roberts later joined the Methodist Church. Although his tent meetings in the salvation-healing era were sponsored primarily by classical Pentecostals, he later moved into charismatic circles with no apparent loss of following. His *Abundant Life* magazine (called *Healing Waters* [1947–53]; *America's Healing Magazine* [1953–55]; *Healing* [1956]; and *Abundant Life* [1956–]) appeals to most segments of the renewal besides his old following in the Pentecostal movement. *Abundant Life* and his *Daily Blessing* devotional magazine are used to promote Oral Roberts University, the City of Faith, and other Roberts ministries, with a heavy emphasis on "seed faith" giving.

Among the magazines established to appeal to specific denominations within the renewal were *Trinity* and *New Covenant*. Founded in 1961 and surviving for only a short time, *Trinity* was published by Episcopalians. *New Covenant*, which began in 1969, is a magazine published for Roman Catholic charismatics. Other denominations are represented in the renewal with magazine and book publishing interests.

V. Books Published on the Pentecostal-Charismatic Movement.

A. Logos *Leads the Way*. As mentioned earlier in this article, Logos Fellowship International became the leading publisher of charismatic books as well as of the *Logos Journal*, the most important charismatic periodical during the early 1970s. Publishing nearly a book a week, LFI was propelled into a select book publishing crowd, matching or surpassing many Christian publishers who had been in the business for decades. The first big seller for Logos was Nicky Cruz's *Run Baby Run*, which sold well over eight million copies. Other best-selling books included books by Merlin Carothers (*Prison to Praise* et al.), Dennis Bennett, Jamie Buckingham, David du Plessis, and many others. Most non-Pentecostal publishers avoided writers in the charismatic renewal. An exception is Fleming H. Revell Co., which profited on a paperback edition of David Wilkerson's *The Cross and the Switchblade*.

B. *Most Important Literature* (1961–87). Cecil M. Robeck, Jr., examines what he terms as the most important literature produced in the renewal in his "The Decade (1973–82) in Pentecostal-Charismatic Literature: A Bibliographic Essay" (Fuller Theological Seminary, *Theology, News, and Notes* [March 1983], 24–29, 34).

Robeck correctly points out that the roots of the charismatic renewal are in classical Pentecostalism and that much of the theology and practice has been greatly influenced by the older movement. He cites several books published between 1973 and 1982 that trace the history of classical Pentecostalism and help to explain the relationship between the two groups. These include Frank Bartleman, *Azusa Street* (1980), a reprint of *How "Pentecost" Came to Los Angeles* (1925); A. C. Valdez, *Fire on Azusa Street* (1980); Robert Mapes Anderson, *Vision of the Disinherited: The Making of American Pentecostalism* (1979); David Edwin Harrell, Jr., *All Things Are Possible* (1975); Walter J. Hollenweger, *The Pentecostals: The Charismatic Movement in the Churches*

This collection of foreign language periodicals in 1953 demonstrates the wide coverage of the Pentecostal message.

(1972); Stephen D. Glazier, *Perspectives on Pentecostalism* (1980); Victor de Leon, *The Silent Pentecostals* (1979); Melvin D. Williams, *Community in a Black Pentecostal Church* (1974); Arthur E. Paris, *Black Pentecostalism: Southern Religion in an Urban Setting* (1982); David Bradfield, *Neo-Pentecostalism: A Sociological Assessment* (1979); Vinson Synan, ed., *Aspects of Pentecostal-Charismatic Origins* (1975); and Russell P. Spittler, ed., *Perspectives on the New Pentecostalism* (1976).

To this list can be added *The Old-Time Power: A History of the Pentecostal Holiness Church* (1973) by Vinson Synan. Other important books published before 1973 that deal with classical Pentecostal origins include Klaude Kendrick, *The Promise Fulfilled: A History of the Modern Pentecostal Movement* (1961); Vinson Synan, *The Holiness-Pentecostal Movement in the United States* (1971); Elmer Louis Moon, *The Pentecostal Church* (PCG) (1966); Carl Brumback, *Suddenly . . . From Heaven* (AG) (1961); William W. Menzies, *Anointed to Serve* (AG) (1971); Charles W. Conn, *Like a Mighty Army* (CG) (1955, 1977); *A Historical Account of the Apostolic Faith* (Portland) (1965); and John L. Sherrill, *They Speak With Other Tongues* (1964). Another denominational history, *Heritage & Horizons* (Open Bible Standard Churches), by Robert Bryant Mitchell, was published in 1982.

Denominational studies of the charismatic movement include Kilian McDonnell, *Charismatic Renewal and the Churches* (Catholic) (1976); Dow Kirkpatrick, ed., *The Holy Spirit* (Methodist) (1974); Paul D. Opsahl, ed., *The Holy Spirit in the Life of the Church* (Lutheran) (1978); Larry Christenson, *Welcome, Holy Spirit* (Lutheran) (1987); and Edward D. O'Connor, *Perspectives on Charismatic Renewal* (Catholic) (1975). Two other books that are broader in their scope are Michael P. Hamilton, ed., *The Charismatic Movement* (1975); and J. Elmo Agrimson, ed., *Gifts of the Spirit and the Body of Christ: Perspectives on the Charismatic Movement* (Lutheran) (1974).

A great number of books have been written, pro and con, regarding Pentecostal-charismatic doctrines. Many of these deal with the Holy Spirit, the baptism of the Holy Spirit, prosperity, and healing.

Kilian McDonnell collected all of the major formal statements on the subject of charismatic renewal within various traditions around the world. These were published in the three-volume work *Presence, Power, Praise* (1981).

VI. Summary. The movements cited in this article—Pentecostal, salvation-healing, and charismatic—are interwoven in theology and in many practices. Much of the theology of healing, deliverance, speaking in tongues, gifts of the Spirit, etc., used in the salvation-healing and charismatic movements has been borrowed from classical Pentecostalism.

It is no wonder then that publications from each of the traditions reflect similar concerns. Each of them looks at the printed page as an important tool to evangelize, indoctrinate, introduce distinctives, inspire, promote their ministries, and offer leadership helps. Both movements owe much of their success to periodicals and to other publications.

See also BIBLIOGRAPHY AND HISTORIOGRAPHY OF PENTECOSTALISM (U.S.).

Bibliography: R. Anderson, *Vision of the Disinherited* (1979); D. Harrell, Jr., *All Things Are Possible* (1975); C. Jones, *Black Holiness: A Guide to the Study of Black Participation in the Wesleyan Perfectionist and Glossolalic Pentecostal Movement* (1987); idem, *The Charismatic Movement: A Guide to the Study of Neo-Pentecostalism With Emphasis on Anglo-American Sources* (1988); idem, *Guide to the Study of the Pentecostal Movement* (1983); K. Kendrick, *The Promise Fulfilled* (1961); K. McDonnell, *Catholic Pentecostalism* (1970); J. Nichols, *Pentecostalism* (1966); C. M. Robeck, Jr., "The Decade (1973– 1982) in Pentecostal-Charismatic Literature: A Bibliographic Essay," Fuller Theological Seminary, *Theology, News, and Notes* (March 1983); V. Synan, *The Holiness-Pentecostal Movement in the United States* (1971).
W. E. Warner

PULKINGHAM, WILLIAM GRAHAM

(1926–). Episcopal priest. Ordained in 1958, William G. Pulkingham became rector of the Church of the Redeemer in Houston, Texas, in 1963. The poverty of the slum district and the futility of ministry there drove him to seek the power of the Holy Spirit. Under his leadership committed families moved into the neighborhood, eventually rejuvenating worship and parish life. Their common life soon became an inspiration for others seeking such relationships in their own church settings.

In 1972 Pulkingham moved to England and later founded Community of Celebration, which was based on Cumbrae Island. Its extension ministry, the Fisherfolk, traveled worldwide teaching folk arts in worship. Hymns and liturgical settings developed by the Fisherfolk and Pulkingham's gifted wife, Betty, have contributed significantly to modern Christian community worship. In 1985 the Community of Celebration moved to Aliquippa, Pennsylvania.

Bibliography: M. Durran, *The Wind at the Door* (1986); W. Pulkingham, *Gathered for Power* (1972); idem, *They Left Their Nets* (1973).
C. M. Irish

PURDIE, JAMES EUSTACE (1880–1977).

Canadian churchman and educator. Having graduated in 1907 from Wycliffe College, an Anglican seminary in Toronto, Purdie immediately launched into a successful ministry in the Anglican church in Canada, serving parishes in Manitoba, New Brunswick, and Saskatchewan from 1907 to 1922. He was baptized in the Holy Spirit in 1919 in the midst of his tenure in one of these. After a brief ministry in Philadelphia in a Reformed Episcopal church in 1925 he was invited to become the founding principal of Canadian Pentecostal Bible College to be situated in Winni-

peg, Manitoba, the first full-time Bible school to be operated by the Pentecostal Assemblies of Canada (PAOC). Purdie held this position until his retirement in 1950. Following retirement, he continued to minister widely within the PAOC, but he also maintained ties with the Anglican Church. He preached and assisted at Communion in a parish in Winnipeg until as late as 1975.

Purdie's outstanding contribution was theological. He modeled his college's curriculum after that of Wycliffe College, insisting on a thorough understanding of doctrine and emphasizing church history along with biblical studies. "Pastoralia" was also important, with stress being placed on preaching and conducting worship services. His work is widely credited with providing the foundation for the theological stability enjoyed by the PAOC.

The other major theme of Purdie's ministry was evangelism. As a young Anglican, he held outdoor services and saw rapid growth in his parishes. He also organized evangelistic missions and Bible conferences.

Bibliography: K. R. Davis, "Purdie, James Eustace," *NIDCC* (1974), 814; R. A. N. Kydd, "The Contribution of Denominationally Trained Clergymen to the Emerging Pentecostal Movement in Canada," *Pneuma* 5 (1983): 17–33; idem, "Pentecostals, Charismatics, and the Canadian Denominations," *Église et Théologie* 13 (1982): 224–25; B. R. Ross, "The Emergence of Theological Education Within the Pentecostal Assemblies of Canada," M.Th. Thesis, University of Toronto, 1971; idem, "James Eustace Purdie: The Story of Pentecostal Theological Education," *Journal of the Canadian Church Historical Society* 17 (1975): 94–103.
R. A. N. Kydd

PYTCHES, DAVID (1931–). International

Anglican renewal teacher. Ordained as a priest in 1956, Pytches volunteered for service with the South American Missionary Society and went out with his wife Mary to Chile in 1959. In 1969 his wife was baptized in the Spirit on the boat returning to Chile; this led Pytches to seek the same experience, which followed some months later. In 1970 he became suffragan bishop, being appointed bishop of Chile, Bolivia, and Peru in 1972. Some of Pytches's experiences of renewal as bishop are described in "The Spirit and Evangelism" in *Bishops' Move* (1978), edited by Michael Harper.

Pytches resigned as bishop in Latin America in 1976, and in 1977 he followed John Perry as vicar of St. Andrew's, Chorleywood, Herts, England. The Pytcheses' experience of the miraculous in Latin America had prepared them for the "signs and wonders" teaching of John Wimber. Pytches' book *Spiritual Gifts in the Local Church* (*Come, Holy Spirit* in the British edition), published in 1985, has almost acquired textbook status among Anglican charismatics. Mary Pytches' book on inner healing, *Set My People Free* (1987), complements her husband's earlier work. Pytches, chairman of the Sharing of Ministries Abroad (SOMA) executive committee, became in 1983 one of SOMA's international directors.
P. D. Hocken

Q

QUAKERS (SOCIETY OF FRIENDS) The Society of Friends was founded by George Fox (1624–90) in the context of radical English Puritanism during the turbulent Interregnum period (1649–60). In his early adulthood, Fox began a search for spiritual reality. He went from minister to minister to find answers to the spiritual longing in his heart. In every case, the advice offered did not satisfy him. After four years as a "seeker," Fox heard a voice speak to him, telling him that God alone could communicate to him in his condition.

In 1647 Fox began preaching. He was followed by a group of enthusiasts, numbering in the thousands by the mid 1650s. Brought to trial for his attacks on the ordained clergy, he told the judge that the latter should tremble at the Word of God, and the justice then called Fox "a Quaker"—a name that has remained. Persecution continued but only served to strengthen the movement.

The Quakers believed that every true Christian minister, whether ordained or lay, was endowed by the Holy Spirit. Christ is revealed by the "inner word" of God, or "inner voice," which is given directly to human hearts by the Spirit of God. Hereby the Christian's relationship to God, the nature of Christian doctrine, and the correct interpretation of Scripture are revealed. The "outer word," or Scripture, apart from the revelation of the Holy Spirit, has no necessary relation to spiritual enlightenment.

The Quaker distinction between the "inner" and the "outer" words was a reaction against the biblicism to which most Puritans had fallen prey by Fox's time. In his view, the Puritans left out the fundamental element in spiritual enlightenment, the experience of the Holy Spirit. For Fox, experiential knowledge of the Holy Spirit was the only basis for true Christianity. In turn, the Puritans denied the Quaker doctrine of the Spirit with assertions of the priority of Scripture, which they equated with the Word of God.

Fox argued that a true revelation from God could not contradict Scripture. According to his own experience, the Holy Spirit speaks according to Scripture. Revelation leads to an understanding of Scripture. Scripture corroborates and interprets one's prior spiritual experience.

Because of their dependence on the Holy Spirit for direct inspiration, Quakers developed a unique form of corporate worship. Sitting in silence, they waited for God to speak through one or more of them. Because any or all present could be moved upon by the Spirit of God, there was no need for clergy.

Early Quaker literature records visions, healings, prophecies, and a power from God that they likened to first-century Pentecost. There is even evidence of tongues-speech among them. Fox eventually discouraged such ecstatic utterances, and glossolalia died out among the Quakers.

The Quakers speak to modern Pentecostals and charismatics in a variety of ways. They certainly provided antecedents for the current concepts of "life in the Spirit." They faced the issue of the relationship between the divine Spirit and the Scripture in opposition to Puritanism, just as twentieth-century Pentecostals have been forced to deal with the same issue raised by biblicists in Evangelical and Fundamentalist camps. Quakers even provided arguments for early Pentecostals who tended to be strongly pacifistic.

See also EUROPEAN PIETISTIC ROOTS OF PENTE-COSTALISM; PACIFISM.

Bibliography: J. L. Ash, Jr., "Oh No, It Is Not the Scriptures!" *Quaker History* 63 (August 1974): 94–107; H. Barbour and A. O. Roberts, *Early Quaker Writings 1650–1700* (1973); B. L. Bresson, *Studies in Ecstasy* (1966); R. M. Jones, *Spiritual Reformers in the Sixteenth and Seventeenth Centuries* (1914); R. A. Knox, *Enthusiasm* (1950).   S. M. Burgess

QUEBEDEAUX, RICHARD ANTHONY (1944–). Author of numerous books about Evangelicals. Quebedeaux was born in Los Angeles, California. After obtaining his B.A. and M.A. degrees from University of California at Los Angeles, he received an S.T.B. from Harvard Divinity School in 1968 and a Ph.D. from Oxford University in 1975. A member of the United Church of Christ, Quebedeaux served as a consultant on church renewal for the United Church Board for Homeland Ministries before accepting appointment as a consultant at the Unification Theological Seminary in Barrytown, New York. He became a senior consultant at the New Ecumenical Research Association in Barrytown in 1980.

Much of Quebedeaux's published work examines, from a sociological perspective, subjects related to Pentecostalism. While his books *The Young Evangelicals* (1974) and *The Worldly Evangelicals* (1978) deal with trends in the broader evangelical culture, his studies of the charismatic movement, *The New Charismatics* (1976) and *The New Charismatics II* (1983), account in cultural terms for the emergence and evolution of a broad renewal movement.   E. L. Blumhofer

R

Bennie S. Triplet, speaker for the Church of God *Forward in Faith* radio program, in a "live" service. The radio choir is in the background.

RADIO BROADCASTING See Radio.

RADIO Pentecostals recognized the evangelism and teaching potential of radio shortly after commercial stations began to be licensed in 1920. Despite the growing popularity of Christian television, radio continues to be an effective medium for proclaiming the gospel worldwide. By 1987 *The Directory of Religious Broadcasting* listed 1,370 radio stations in the U.S. that carried at least a part-time Christian schedule. This figure was up 236 from the year before. The directory also lists 596 organizations producing religious programs for U.S. release.

Classical Pentecostals, "Word" or "Faith" groups, and the salvation-healing evangelists of the 1950s have used radio regionally and nationally; few charismatics, however, have been known to develop radio ministries. Several ministries that use television primarily as their means of preaching the gospel began with radio. Three examples are Oral Roberts, the Christian Broadcasting Network (Pat Robertson), and Jimmy Swaggart.

I. History. After radio was made available for preaching the gospel, ministers soon learned that effective communication with people by radio outside their sanctuaries required a different style.

With a "live" audience the preacher uses gestures, facial expressions, and other movements. On radio he or she is limited to content and voice quality. Consequently, some preachers never successfully made the transition. Producing the program and obtaining air time is not so difficult, but communicating with listeners is critical. A pioneer in radio, RCA's president Robert W. Sarnoff, probably said it best: "To communicate anything you must first have an audience; and second, you must have its attention." Gaining an audience and getting its attention has been the goal of gospel broadcasters ever since Calvary Episcopal Church, Pittsburgh, aired what is thought to have been the first broadcast church service on January 2, 1921.

It is no surprise that the flamboyant Aimee Semple McPherson is said to have been one of the first women to preach on radio in 1922. This well-known Pentecostal also built one of the first commercial stations, KFSG, at Angelus Temple in Los Angeles in 1924. Apparently the first gospel station was licensed to the National Presbyterian Church, Washington, D.C., in 1922. Some of the first well-known evangelical radio preachers included John Zoller, Paul Rader, R. R. Brown, Charles E. Fuller, Donald Grey Barnhouse, Wal-

Tommy Emmett, right, pastor of the Gospel Tabernacle, Aberdeen, South Dakota, and church musicians prepare for a radio broadcast in 1941.

ter A. Maier, Paul Myers, J. Harold Smith, and John Roach Straton.

In addition to McPherson, other Pentecostals went on the air in the beginning years of commercial radio. F. F. Bosworth developed a radio ministry that supplemented his city-wide salvation-healing meetings. Pastors across the country were broadcasting over local radio stations during the 1920s. These included Richard and Adele Carmichael, parents of musician Ralph Carmichael.

Robert Craig, founder of Glad Tidings Temple (Assemblies of God), San Francisco, and what is now Bethany Bible College, established KGTT in 1925. In neighboring San Jose, First Baptist Church—which had experienced a great Pentecostal revival under McPherson's ministry in 1921—bought the existing KQW in 1925.

Not all Pentecostals during the early years of radio accepted the medium as a viable method for preaching the gospel. Some looked at the "air" as the devil's territory and not to be used. Broadcasting the gospel on radio, which was also being used for worldly entertainment, was also thought by some to compromise the gospel—a criticism later leveled against television ministries.

During the salvation-healing movement era beginning in the late 1940s, several evangelists used radio. Oral Roberts gained a faithful following on his "Healing Waters" program. One of the longest running programs was A. A. Allen's fifteen-minute daily broadcast. Allen's protégé, R. W. Schambach, has used radio as well. The Voice of Healing, which was directed by Gordon Lindsay, sponsored a radio broadcast, as did Kathryn Kuhlman. With a few exceptions, listeners to the salvation-healing programs usually heard on-location taped broadcasts rather than studio-produced programs. What the programs lacked in quality, they made up in drama, excitement, and expectancy.

II. Objectives of the Broadcasters. Evangelicals began to use radio in the 1920s as an evangelism-teaching tool. But they soon recognized other important purposes. A morning worship service on radio reached believers who were unable to attend because of sickness or other reasons. Gospel music programs became popular, and later talk shows and news programs were developed to communicate the gospel and to inform listeners on important issues.

Pentecostals added another reason for broadcasting. They began praying for the sick on the air and mailing prayer cloths to persons who requested them. Oral Roberts urged listeners to touch their radios as a "point of contact" and then to "release [their] faith."

Some preachers began to use what they termed the word of knowledge on the air to declare that a person in the audience was receiving healing for a particular need. Other speakers spoke in tongues on their broadcasts. These practices have had both critics and supporters. Criticism has also been leveled at broadcasters who use radio time for raising money rather than for preaching the gospel.

Radio—and later television—has been a medium to promote the local church. Countless people have been attracted to a local church by radio, and many of them have been converted and become members.

III. Radio's Vast Coverage. Almost anywhere in America one can turn on a radio and hear a gospel program coming from one of the 1,370 stations broadcasting religious programs. Several producers release their programs on hundreds of outlets daily. For example, Kenneth Hagin's "Faith Seminar of the Air" is aired on approximately two hundred stations. On some stations he might be followed by Kenneth Copeland's "Believer's Voice of Victory" or another of the scores of daily programs being produced today. Three weekly programs sponsored by Pentecostal denominations also have wide coverage: The Church of God, (Cleveland, Tennessee), sponsors "Forward in Faith"; the United Pentecostal Church produces "Harvestime"; and the Assemblies of God has produced "Revivaltime" since 1950. The latter is heard on nearly six hundred stations worldwide and for twenty-five years featured the familiar voice of C. M. Ward.

Missionary radio has been used for more than fifty years. Clarence Jones and Reuben Larson established HCJB in Quito, Ecuador, in 1931. After World War II, Paul Freed built Trans World Radio at Monte Carlo. Three Pentecostals—Robert Bowman, John C. Broger, and William J. Roberts—built a network of powerful stations in the Far East which they called the Far East Broadcasting Company. These missionary stations produce their own programs with the help of missionaries and nationals. They also sell time to selected U.S. producers.

Many of the Pentecostal broadcasters belong to the National Religious Broadcasters (NRB), a 1,250-member association that was formed in 1944. The association publishes *Religious Broadcasting* and an annual directory of radio and television stations, programs, producers, and others involved in gospel broadcasting. NRB has established principles and guidelines for fundraising, accounting, and financial reporting. NRB offices are in Morristown, New Jersey.

IV. Gospel Radio's Future. As indicated by the growing number of radio stations that broadcast the gospel and an increasing number of radio receivers, the future looks extremely bright. In 1952 Americans owned 105 million radios. By 1986 that figure had jumped to nearly 500 million.

It has been estimated that 90 percent of the world listens to radio or watches television every day. Gospel radio producers know that quality programs targeted for a specific market—whether over U.S. stations or powerful missionary stations abroad—will have an audience. Gospel radio is an important outreach of the kingdom, reaching into hospital rooms, behind prison walls, into homes and vehicles, behind the Bamboo and Iron Curtains, and into portable receivers everywhere.

See also EVANGELISM.

Bibliography: B. Armstrong, ed., *Directory of Religious Broadcasting* (annual); *Religious Broadcasting* magazine; S. Siedell, *Gospel Radio, A 20th Century Tool for a 20th Century Challenge* (1971).   W. E. Warner

RAINBOW REVIVAL CHURCH In 1957 Eldridge and Ruth Plunkett incorporated the Rainbow Revival Church. At that time the pastors were veterans of fifteen years in the evangelistic field. The organization has two ministry strategies. These consist of regular Sunday services in its Los Angeles center and "written church services" and pastoral counseling by mail. Items sent to constituents include mimeographed testimonials of healings and other blessings; prayer handkerchiefs; and questionnaires, the latter to be completed and returned with a record of such things as the person's amount of time spent in personal prayer and Bible reading, prayer requests, answers to prayer, and offerings being sent to the ministry. In the mid 1970s the active mailing list contained an average of six thousand to seven thousand names.

Bibliography: A. C. Piepkorn, *Profiles in Belief*, vol. 3 (1979).   C. E. Jones

RAMABAI, SARASVATI (PANDITA) (c. 1858–1922). Indian educator, writer, and missionary. Born of high-caste Hindu parents, Pandita Ramabai was fortunate in that her father defied his culture by teaching her to read and write Sanskrit. As a young woman Ramabai became convinced that Christianity was the true religion. Her wide reading in Hindu literature, however, uncovered the fact that all Indian men agreed that "women of high and low caste, as a class, were bad, very bad, worse than demons, as unholy as untruth . . ." (Dyer, n.d., 26).

In 1883 Ramabai left India for England to prepare for what she considered her "life's work"—that of ministering to India's women. Before returning to India, she spent six years in the U.S., where she formed the Ramabai Association, a group that sponsored her first mission for ten years.

In order to establish an educational institution for women in Bombay, Ramabai appealed to the Reformed Hindus, suggesting that she could educate their daughters. She also took in high-caste widows who were often blamed for their husbands' deaths and badly mistreated by their husbands' families. These two groups were kept separate from each other but were treated equally well by Ramabai. She did not insist that the students observe her Christian ways but quietly asserted her faith while they continued to observe her changed life. Gradually students began to be won over to Christianity. After several years, Ramabai moved her school to Poona, where living costs were lower, eventually naming it Mukti Mission. At a camp meeting at Lanouli in 1896 several young women became Christians, and Ramabai became more bold in her Christian witness. In 1897 she began religious instruction for all the pupils enrolled in her school. As well, she embarked on a number of faith missions by going to cities that were suffering from famine

Two of the key leaders in the Catholic charismatic movement is this husband-wife team, Kevin and Dorothy Ranaghan.

and gathering up poor women whom she then brought back to Mukti Mission to be cared for and educated. By 1898 she had helped five hundred widows, received $91,500 in support from the Ramabai Association, and owned property valued at $60,000 (Dyer, 65).

Ramabai's missionary zeal led her to establish orphanages in a number of villages for girls who would otherwise be forced to live on the streets. Realizing that she would not be able to take in prostitutes at Mukti Mission, she opened a home for them where they, too, were given shelter and educated and taught Christian doctrine. During famines Ramabai courageously opened the doors of Mukti Mission to starving women, often stretching her resources to the limit in order to minister to them.

In January 1905 Ramabai encouraged the girls at Mukti to prayerfully seek for a revival. Many responded, and a Pentecostal revival began on June 29 when one girl was baptized in the Holy Spirit. Some were "slain in the Spirit" under the conviction of sin, and others experienced a burning sensation said to result from their baptism "in fire" (Matt. 3:11). The participants also experienced glossolalia. The revival soon spread, and a number of missionaries received Spirit-baptism (e.g., Albert Norton). A Chicago reporter, William Ellis, reports that in 1907 he witnessed evidence of revival going on among the women at the mission. Ramabai told him that meetings were held two times a day and led by "girls who have been baptized with the Holy Spirit and with fire" (Ellis, 1982–83, 5).

Ramabai ran Mukti Mission with consummate organizational skill. In the school the women were taught to read and write and to be teachers. Outside the school women were trained in weaving, needlework, farming, and printing. Ramabai

appointed department heads over the various areas of the mission, but she personally supervised the building program and print shop where she taught her women assistants to set type and print books and articles in many Indian dialects. Ramabai herself wrote *The High-Caste Hindu Woman* (c. 1885), translated the Bible into Marathi, wrote a Marathi concordance based on Greek and Hebrew etymology, and wrote many tracts that were then distributed all over India. In 1918 she wrote and printed 23,000 copies of a *Life of Christ* in Marathi and distributed them free of charge (Dyer, 129). Her managerial method was to move her office from place to place on the mission grounds to keep in contact with all that was happening. In 1919 the Kaiser-i-Hind medal was given to Ramabai for her outstanding contribution to Indian society (ibid., 145). A visitor to the mission said of her, "She represents . . . the most remarkable combination of executive, intellectual, and religious powers that I know of in recent times in either man or woman" (ibid.).

Bibliography: J. Chappell, *Pandita Ramabai: A Great Life in Indian Missions* (n.d.); H. Dyer, *Pandita Ramabai: Her Vision, Her Mission and Triumph of Faith* (n.d.); T. Ellis, "Pentecostal Revival Touches India," *AG Heritage* (Winter 1982–83), 1, 5 (first published in *Chicago Daily News*, January 14, 1908); S. H. Frodsham, *With Signs Following* (1946).   F. Bixler

RANAGHAN, KEVIN MATHERS (1940–) **AND DOROTHY** (1942–). Leaders in the Catholic Charismatic Renewal (CCR) since its inception early in 1967. The Ranaghans soon became widely known through their book *Catholic Pentecostals* (1969), which has served as a standard introduction to the renewal and has recently been updated under the title *Catholic Pentecostals Today*.

Kevin Ranaghan has been a key figure in the

organization and planning of many national and international conferences in the CCR. He served on the National Service Committee (NSC) from 1970 to 1985 as executive director and as North American delegate to the International Catholic Charismatic Renewal Office (ICCRO) from 1978–84. He also served as chairperson of the 1977 Kansas City conference. Dorothy Ranaghan has also served on the NSC (1978–84) and since 1983 has been editor of the NSC's *Newsletter*.

Both of the Ranaghans have degrees in theology—Dorothy an M.A. (Notre Dame, 1966) and Kevin an M.A. (1964) and Ph.D. (1974), with a dissertation on "Rites of Initiation in Representative Pentecostal Churches in the United States, 1901–1972." As teachers, writers, and conference speakers, both have become prominent public figures in the CCR. Other writings include K. and D. Ranaghan (eds.), *As the Spirit Leads Us* (1971); K. Ranaghan, *The Lord, the Spirit and the Church* (1973) and *Renew the Face of the Earth* (1982); D. Ranaghan, *A Day in Thy Courts* (1986).

The Ranaghans, who have six children, have been members of the People of Praise, an ecumenical covenant community in South Bend, Indiana, since its beginning in 1971. Kevin works full time as a coordinator for the community.

See also CATHOLIC CHARISMATIC RENEWAL.

Bibliography: F. Lilly, "Kevin Ranaghan and Renewal," *Charisma* (April 1980), 29–33; E. D. O'Connor, *The Pentecostal Movement in the Catholic Church* (1971). P. D. Hocken

RAPTURE OF THE CHURCH See ESCHATOLOGY, PENTECOSTAL PERSPECTIVES ON.

RASMUSSEN, ANDREW W. (1905–). American evangelist. Andrew Rasmussen was born in Pennock, Minnesota. At the age of thirteen Rasmussen had a conversion experience during a revival meeting conducted by evangelist A. B. Ost. In 1929 he became a Pentecostal after receiving the baptism in the Holy Spirit during a prayer meeting in Michigan. He served as an ordained pastor of the Independent Assemblies of God at the Bethel Pentecostal Assembly in Tacoma, Washington, from 1933 to 1936; the Salem Gospel Tabernacle in Brooklyn, New York, from 1936 to 1940; and the Philadelphia Church in Chicago, Illinois, from 1941 to 1944 and 1950 to 1954. Rasmussen became a supporter of the New Order of the Latter Rain revival while in Edmonton in 1947. He continued to support the revival after returning to Chicago. When the Independent Assemblies of God split over the New Order controversy, Rasmussen organized the pro-New Order group of ministers into another fellowship under the name Independent Assemblies of God International, which is presently under his administration.

Bibliography: J. R. Colletti, "Lewi Pethrus: His Influence Upon Scandinavian–American Pentecostalism," *Pneuma* 5 (2, 1983): 18–29; A. W. Rasmussen, *The Last Chapter* (1973). J. Colletti

REBA PLACE FELLOWSHIP See CHARISMATIC COMMUNITIES.

REED, WILLIAM STANDISH (1922–). Charismatic surgeon. A physician since 1945 and a surgeon since 1955, William Reed has encouraged Christians to accept the concept of medicine for the whole person. Through *Surgery of the Soul* (1969, 1975) and *A Doctor's Thoughts on Healing* (audiotape, n.d.). Reed has continued to develop his ideas based on 1 Thessalonians 5:23. An active member of the Episcopal Church, the Order of St. Luke, Camps Farthest Out, former director of Full Gospel Business Men's Fellowship (1961–71), and founder of the Christian Medical Foundation (1959), Reed has contributed greatly to integrating medical science and Christian faith.

Bibliography: D. Bennett, *Nine O'Clock in the Morning* (1970); J. L. Sherrill, *They Speak With Other Tongues* (1964). F. Bixler

RELIGIOUS EDUCATION See CHRISTIAN DAY SCHOOLS; SUNDAY SCHOOLS.

REVELATION. See APOCALYPSE, BOOK OF THE.

John and Louise Richey, early leaders of the Open Bible Standard Churches.

RICHEY, JOHN R. AND LOUISE H. (1899–1984) (1894–1986). Founders of the Open Bible Evangelistic Association (OBEA) (1932). Beginning their ministry with Aimee Semple McPherson and the International Church of the Foursquare Gospel (ICFG) in Southern California, John and Louise Richey were transferred to Des Moines in 1928, where John became the ICFG leader for the Midwest. He pastored two thriving churches in Des Moines simultaneously and started a Bible school. His vigorous leadership and evangelistic preaching helped establish Pentecostal churches in the area.

When thirty-two ministers withdrew from ICFG in 1932 and formed OBEA, Richey became their chairman and later was elected first chairman of Open Bible Standard Churches

(1935–38). He was related to E. N. and Raymond T. Richey of the Assemblies of God.

Louise H. Richey was healed of a goiter in 1918 under the ministry of Maria B. Woodworth-Etter and later attended L.I.F.E. Bible College, where she met her husband. They were copastors and coevangelists for nearly sixty years.

Bibliography: R. Mitchell, *Heritage and Horizons* (1982).   W. E. Warner

Raymond T. Richey conducted city-wide salvation-healing meetings beginning in 1920.

RICHEY, RAYMOND THEODORE

(1893–1968). World-famous healing evangelist. Born into a devout family in Illinois, Richey led a life of dissipation during his adolescence, until his eyesight began to fail due to a serious boyhood injury. In 1911 he surrendered his life to Christ after his eyes were healed at meetings held by Arch P. Collins in Fort Worth, Texas. A few years later his father, E. N. Richey, was called to a pastorate in Houston, and Raymond became assistant pastor.

During World War I, Raymond established the United Prayer and Workers' League for the distribution of literature. He erected a tabernacle in Houston near an army camp where hundreds were converted to Christ. While ministering to the dying during the influenza epidemic, Richey contracted tuberculosis. He went to southern California, where he received a miraculous healing in September 1919.

A year later he intended to assist Warren Collins of Fort Worth, Texas, with meetings in Hattiesburg, Mississippi. After all of the arrangements had been made, Collins canceled, and Richey held meetings on his own, praying for the sick. This marked the beginning of his ministry as a healing evangelist, which took him to huge city

auditoriums in all parts of the U.S. In the spring of 1923, at Tulsa, Oklahoma, there were 11,000 reported conversions. Those who were healed paraded through the streets, with "a truck piled high with discarded crutches" (Richey, 1925, 107).

During World War II, Richey traveled with a large tent of red, white, and blue stripes, holding meetings for members of the armed forces, thousands of whom professed conversion. After his father's death in 1945, Richey returned to Houston to pastor Evangelistic Temple. In the 1950s he continued his traveling ministry, going to Central and South America in 1951, and Germany, Switzerland, Japan, and Korea in 1957–58.

Bibliography: T. R. Nickel, "Evang. Raymond T. Richey Now Is With His Lord," *Testimony* 23 (Second Quarter 1968): 9; "Raymond T. Richey Back From Europe," *Voice of Healing* (December 1957), 7, 22; E. M. Richey, *What God Hath Wrought* (1925).
                                                        R. M. Riss

A former missionary and pastor, Ralph M. Riggs was general superintendent of the Assemblies of God from 1953 to 1959.

RIGGS, RALPH MEREDITH (1895–1971).

Pastor, missionary, educator, author, and administrator. Ralph Riggs was born in Coal Creek, Tennessee, to a physician father and devout mother who moved the family to Hattiesburg, Mississippi, to enable her children to attend a Holiness academy. At the age of ten he was converted, and four years later he was baptized in the Holy Spirit. While still in his teens, he came into contact with many of the early Pentecostal leaders, including three future general superintendents of the Assemblies of God. Consequently he attended that denomination's formational meeting at Hot Springs, Arkansas, in 1914, and remained with the Assemblies for the rest of his life.

Riggs had planned to study architecture, but believing that he was called to the ministry, he enrolled in the Rochester Bible Training School in Rochester, New York. On completion of the two-year course in 1916, he was ordained and became pastor of a Syracuse church. Three years later, under the auspices of the Pentecostal Mission, he went to South Africa, where he met and married another missionary, Lillian Merian. After three years of ministry in the cities, the Riggses moved into the northern Transvaal, often traveling by donkey cart. The difficult living conditions, exacerbated by the failure of promised support, took their toll, forcing the family, which now included two daughters, Merian and Venda, to return home in 1925.

Riggs returned to his former pastorate at Syracuse for a year, followed by pastorates at Ossining, New York, and Newark, New Jersey. While in Newark he also taught at Bethel Bible Training School and in 1929 moved with it to Springfield, Missouri. For the next thirty years Springfield was to be his home, but after only two years he left the classroom to serve as pastor of Central Assembly, which was regarded as the denominational headquarters church. It flourished during his eight years of ministry, and several daughter churches were founded. In recognition of his leadership, Riggs was made district superintendent of the Southern Missouri District. Four years later he was elected to national office as an assistant general superintendent and, after eight years, as general superintendent.

During Riggs's six-year tenure as the leader of the Assemblies of God, much was accomplished, including major construction projects at the administrative headquarters and at Central Bible Institute. Though he had various responsibilities, Riggs was best known for his service to education. He served on the first board of the American Association of Bible Colleges and worked to strengthen each of his denomination's nine colleges. Under his leadership, Evangel College, a denominational liberal arts school, was created and located in Springfield. In recognition of his contribution to higher education, he was awarded an honorary doctorate.

On leaving office Riggs moved to Santa Cruz, California, where he returned to the classroom for nine years before retiring as professor emeritus at Bethany Bible College. Five of his books have been published, including *The Spirit Himself* (1949) and *A Successful Pastor* (c. 1931).

Bibliography: C. Brumback, *Suddenly . . . From Heaven* (1971); *Glad Tidings* (March 1971), 8–14; "With Christ," *PE* (February 21, 1971), 3–4.

L. F. Wilson

ROBERSON, LIZZIE (1860–1945). First national supervisor of women in the Church of God in Christ. While serving as matron of women at Dermott Arkansas College, Roberson was exposed to the message of Charles H. Mason,

who was conducting revivals in that city. Upon recommendation of Lillian Brooks Coffey, Lizzie Roberson was invited by Elder Mason to assist in organizing the women's department of the denomination. Not only did Roberson lay the foundation for the women's department for the denomination, she also organized several auxiliaries, such as the Bible Band, sewing circle, and the Home and Foreign Mission. She was distinguished by her gifted teaching ministry. Her daughter, Ida Baker, eventually became the secretary of the Home and Foreign Mission department. Lizzie Roberson's brilliance as an organizer was foundational to the work of women in the denomination and set the pace for years to come.

L. Lovett

ROBERTS, GRANVILLE ORAL (1918–). America's premier healing evangelist. Born in Pontotoc County, Oklahoma, Roberts was reared in abject poverty, the son of a Pentecostal Holiness preacher. At age seventeen he was diagnosed as having tuberculosis and was bedridden for more than five months. In July 1935, under the ministry of evangelist George W. Moncey, he was healed of both tuberculosis and stuttering. The following two years he served an apprenticeship under his father in evangelistic ministry. Ordained by the Pentecostal Holiness church in 1936, he quickly became one of the outstanding young ministers in the denomination. Between 1941 and 1947 he served four pastorates.

In 1947 Roberts launched a healing ministry with his first city-wide campaign in Enid, Oklahoma. The same year he published his first book on healing, *If You Need Healing—Do These Things!*; took the message of healing to the radio airwaves; started his own monthly magazine, *Healing Waters*; and established his ministry headquarters in Tulsa, Oklahoma. The following year he began crisscrossing America with the largest portable tent ever used to promote the gospel. Eventually his "tent cathedral" would seat crowds of over 12,500.

Roberts' success in healing evangelism thrust him to the leadership of a generation of dynamic revivalists who took the message of divine healing around the world after 1947. His ecumenical crusades were instrumental in the revitalization of Pentecostalism in the post-World War II era. He was also influential in the formation of the Full Gospel Business Men's Fellowship International in 1951 as well as a leading figure in laying the foundation for the modern charismatic movement. Roberts' most significant impact upon American Christianity came in 1955 when he initiated a national weekly television program that took his healing crusades inside the homes of millions who had never been exposed to the healing message. Through this program the healing message was literally lifted from the Pentecostal subculture of American Christianity to its widest audience in history. By 1980 a Gallup Poll revealed that Roberts' name was recognized by a phenomenal 84 percent of the American public, and historian Vinson Synan observed that Roberts was considered the most prominent Pentecostal in the world.

Oral Roberts, the best-known salvation-healing evangelist during the 1950s and 1960s, prays for a small girl in his prayer line during a 1965 tent meeting.

Between 1947 and 1968 Roberts conducted more than three hundred major crusades, personally praying for millions of people. By the mid-1950s his healing message was broadcast on more than five hundred radio stations, and for almost thirty years his Sunday morning television program was the number one syndicated religious program in the nation. His monthly magazine, renamed *Abundant Life* in 1956, reached a circulation of over a million, while his devotional magazine, *Daily Blessing,* exceeded a quarter million subscribers and a monthly column was written for 674 newspapers. By the 1980s there were more than 15 million copies of his eighty-eight books in circulation, and his yearly mail from supporters exceeded five million letters.

Indicative of his growing acceptance by mainline denominations, Roberts was invited in 1966 to be a participant in Billy Graham's Berlin Congress on World Evangelism, transferred his religious affiliation to the United Methodist church in 1968, and began an ambitious television outreach in 1969 with prime-time religious variety shows. The success of the prime-time programming was remarkable, reaching as many as 64 million viewers. This led Edward Fiske, religious editor of the *New York Times,* to declare that Roberts commanded more personal loyalty in the 1970s than any minister in America.

In 1965 Roberts opened a coeducational liberal arts college in Tulsa. Receiving regional accreditation in a record six years, Oral Roberts University became a major institution when seven graduate colleges were added between 1975 and 1978: Medicine, Nursing, Dentistry, Law, Business, Education, and Theology. The $250 million university, with its ultramodern architecture and facilities, has an average enrollment of 4,600 students. Dedicated in 1967 by Billy Graham, it is considered the premier charismatic university in America. Adjacent to the university Roberts

established a 450-resident retirement center in 1966.

The apex of Roberts' ministry came with the opening in 1981 of the $250 million City of Faith Medical and Research Center. The complex consists of a thirty-story hospital, sixty-story medical center, and twenty-story research facility. The philosophy of the center is to merge prayer and medicine, the supernatural and natural, in the treatment of the whole person. In conjunction with the medical school, doctors are being prepared to serve as medical missionaries around the world.

Theologically Roberts is basically a classical Pentecostal, who maintains that speaking in tongues is normative for every believer. His trademark, however, has been essentially an upbeat message of hope. The whole thesis of his ministry has been that God is a good God and that he wills to heal and prosper his people (3 John 2).

See also HEALING MOVEMENTS.

Bibliography: D. Harrell, Jr., *All Things Are Possible* (1975); idem, *Oral Roberts: An American Life* (1985); E. Roberts, *His Darling Wife, Evelyn Roberts* (1976); E. M. Roberts, *Our Ministry and Our Son Oral* (1960); O. Roberts, *The Call* (1972); idem, *Oral Roberts's Life Story* (1952); idem, *My Story* (1961); W. Robinson, *Oral* (1976). (The reader may also wish to consult R. Frame, "Did Oral Roberts Go Too Far?" *Christianity Today* [Feb. 20, 1987], 43–45; and O. Roberts, "The Media Have Had Their Say. Now the Truth . . . ," *Abundant Life* [September–October 1987], 2–11.— EDS.)   P. G. Chappell

ROBERTS, RICHARD (1948–). Faith healer and televangelist. Richard Roberts is the third child of Oral and Evelyn Roberts, and although he accepted Christ as a child during one of his father's crusades, he did not turn his life over to God until after he enrolled at Oral Roberts University. Married at age nineteen to a fellow singer in his father's ministry, Richard gave up his ambitions to be a night-club singer. His first marriage ended in divorce in 1978. Richard married Lindsay Salem in 1980, and together they began to seek God for a healing ministry. Richard began to see results in his prayers for the sick as he began to call out healings given to him through the "word of knowledge." In September 1984 the daily television program "Richard Roberts Live" began with a Christian talk show format, and many healings have been reported on that program. Roberts also serves as president of the Oral Roberts Evangelistic Association.

Bibliography: R. Roberts, *He's the God of a Second Chance* (1985). (The reader may wish to consult P. Roberts and S. Andrews, *Ashes to Gold* [1987] — EDS.)   J. R. Zeigler

ROBERTS, THOMAS (1902–83). Much-loved Welsh evangelist in France. Brought up in the Welsh revival, Thomas Roberts was sent to France by the Apostolic Church in 1926. Uncomfortable with Apostolic exclusivism but retaining his Pentecostal convictions, he became pastor of an independent Reformed church in Paris in 1936. His friendship with L. Dallière and his involvement in the Union de Prière shaped the direction of his life's work. Roberts, a man of deep prayer, increasingly longed for revival, the integration of Israel, and the reconciliation of divided Christians. Thrilled by news of the charismatic renewal from America, Roberts entered the most important part of his ministry as a minister of reconciliation and as an ecumenical evangelist. He became a key figure in the annual Porte Ouverte Conventions near Chalon from 1971.

His vision of a European convocation in the spring took flesh in "Pentecost over Europe" at Strasbourg in 1982.

Bibliography: Supplement to *Tychique*, no. 59, "Thomas Roberts."   P. D. Hocken

ROBERTSON, MARION GORDON ("PAT") (1930–). Television evangelist, politician, and the founder of the Christian Broadcasting Network (CBN). Born March 22, 1930, in Lexington, Virginia. Pat Robertson is the son of the late U.S. senator A. Willis Robertson and the late Gladys Churchill Robertson. He is a graduate of Washington and Lee University (B.A., 1950), Yale University Law School (J.D., 1955), and New York Theological Seminary (M.Div., 1959). He served as a first lieutenant in the U.S. Marine Corps (1950–52). Robertson married Adelia ("Dede") Elmer in 1954. They have four children: Timothy, Elizabeth, Gordon, and Ann. He was an ordained Southern Baptist clergyman (1961–87).

The turning point in Robertson's life, according to his own testimony, was a day in New York (the year 1956) when he accepted Jesus Christ as his Savior ("I passed from death into life"). Later, while in seminary, Robertson was baptized in the Holy Spirit and for a time served as associate to Harald Bredesen, charismatic pastor of the Reformed Church in Mount Vernon, New York.

Robertson moved from New York to Ports-

Thomas Roberts worked for revival and Christian reconciliation as a Pentecostal in France.

Founder of CBN and CBN University, Pat Robertson left the Virginia Beach complex in 1987 to become a presidential candidate.

mouth, Virginia, in 1959, and with initial capital of seventy dollars bought a defunct UHF television station. Since that time Robertson has built the worldwide Christian Broadcasting Network (CBN). His flagship weekday television program, "The 700 Club," is beamed live into more than 7 million homes and 15,000 cities throughout America, and the CBN cable network has more than 30 million subscribers in fifty states. In a year, viewers of "The 700 Club" log some 4 million prayer calls to 4,500 volunteers in sixty counseling centers. Since 1982 CBN's Middle East television station in southern Lebanon has provided daily outreach to Israel and surrounding countries. It is estimated that more than sixty countries around the world are being touched regularly by CBN. CBN is now a sprawling complex of Williamsburg-style buildings on 680 acres in Virginia Beach and has an annual operating budget of more than $200 million and more than 4,000 employees worldwide.

In 1977 Pat Robertson founded CBN University on the CBN complex. Beginning with a graduate School of Communications, the university now also includes the graduate Schools of Education, Business Administration, Biblical Studies, Public Policy, Law, and an Institute of Journalism. CBNU has been given full accreditation by the Southern Association of Colleges and Schools. The stated mission of the university is to bring biblical truth to bear on every discipline in every area of life.

Another outreach of CBN is Operation Blessing, which, beginning in 1978, has become one of America's largest private organizations helping the poor. In 1985 Operation Heads Up began teaching reading to functionally illiterate persons across America. This program has been especially effective in urban ghettos.

Books by Pat Robertson include *Shout It from the Housetop* (with Jamie Buckingham, 1972), *My Prayer for You* (1977), *The Secret Kingdom* (number one religious book in America, 1983), *Beyond Reason* (1984), *Answers to 200 of Life's Most Probing Questions* (1985), and *America's Dates with Destiny* (1986).

In September 1986 Robertson announced his intention to run for the presidency of the U.S. if three million registered voters signed petitions by September 1987 to support his candidacy financially and with prayer. That intent was realized in 1988 when Robertson unsuccessfully sought the Republican nomination.

Bibliography: John W. Mashek, "A Scrambled Deck for '88," *U.S. News & World Report* (July 14, 1986), 20–25; Richard N. Ostling, "Power, Glory—and Politics," *Time* (February 17, 1986), 62–69; "Pat Robertson and Politics," *Christian Life* (August 1986), 44–46; M. D. SerVaas, Cory and Stoddard, and Maynard Good, "CBN's Pat Robertson: White House Next?" *Saturday Evening Post* (March 1985), 50–57, 106–9; Beth Spring, "Pat Robertson for President?" *Christianity Today* (November 8, 1985), 48–51; Steven Strand and Bert Ghezzi, "Pat Robertson—What Would He Do If He Were President?" *Charisma* (May 1986), 31–35; David H. Van Biema, "Heaven Only Knows," *People Magazine* (August 11, 1986), 27–31. J. R. Williams

ROBINSON, ALBERT ERNEST (1877–1950). As a layman Albert Robinson was a charter member of the Pentecostal Holiness Church (PHC) and was that organization's first general secretary (1911–25). He was a member of the general board of administration during his latter years.

A Canadian by birth, Robinson became acquainted with members of the Fire-Baptized Holiness Church following his conversion while serving as a printer in their literature ministry. Later he began a long friendship with Joseph H. King, who would become the bishop of the PHC. His publishing work included the printing of *Live Coals of Fire, Apostolic Evangel, The Pentecostal Holiness Advocate,* and PHC Sunday school literature. He also wrote and published a magazine, *The Apologist*. His book, *A Layman and the Book* (1936), was required reading for PHC ministers.

Bibliography: C. Bradshaw, *Profiles of Faith* (1984); A. Robinson, *A Layman and the Book* (1936). W. E. Warner

ROBINSON, IDA (1891–1946). Black female evangelist. Born in Georgia, Ida Robinson came to Philadelphia in 1917, assuming the pastorate of a small mission. In 1924, while fasting and praying, she received a vision from God to "Come out on Mt. Sinai and loose the women." She subsequently organized the Mt. Sinai Holy Church of America, a connection that gave full clerical and episcopal rights to women. As first bishop of Mt. Sinai, she conducted revivals from New York to Florida and established a network of churches where men and women had equal access to leadership. Bishop Robinson based her claim for full clerical rights for women on four biblical premises: (1) God created male and female in his own image and gave them both dominion before forming them as distinctly sexual beings; (2) the role of women in announcing the resurrection of Jesus; (3) the relationship of the Virgin Mary to Jesus ("If Mary could carry the Word of God in her womb, then I can carry the Word of God on my lips"); and (4) the equality of male and female in the body of Christ.

Bibliography: A. Fauset, *Black Gods of the Metropolis* (1944); P. Jones, "A Minority Report: Black Pentecostal Women," *Spirit* 1 (2, 1977): 31–44; *The Manual of the Mount Sinai Holy Church* (1984); R. Ruether, ed., *Women in American Religion,* vol. 3 (1986); H. Trulear, "There's a Bright Side Somewhere," *Journal of the Afro-American Historical and Genealogical Society* 2 (8, 1987): 51–56. H. D. Trulear

ROBISON, JAMES (1945–). Televangelist. Born out of wedlock to Myra Wattinger and Joe Robison, an alcoholic, James Robison spent much of formative years living with foster parents, Herbert and Katie Hale. Hale was pastor of Memorial Baptist Church in Pasadena, Texas, where Robison was saved at age 13.

Called to preach in 1961, he attended East Texas Baptist College at Marshall, Texas, and married Betty Freeman in February 1963. During three years of Bible college he preached in several large Baptist churches in the South, including W.A. Criswell's First Baptist Church in Dallas. Billy Graham encouraged Robison to broadcast a message on television, and soon he became known as a televangelist, developing the James Robison Evangelistic Association in Fort Worth, Texas. In his early ministry he endorsed issues central to Fundamentalism, taking firm stands against the feminist movement, homosexuality, evolution, and secular humanism.

In 1981, after a prayer session with a friend, Milton Green, Robison reported personal deliverance from demons which had plagued him for close to fifteen years. He was healed of a number of bodily ailments and received a new zeal to serve God. Soon afterwards his wife and three children each received physical healing. Since 1982 Robison has emphasized love and Christian unity, along with teachings on healing of the sick, deliverance from demons, and the gifts of the Holy Spirit. As a Southern Baptist, his recent ministry has become controversial, but he neither accepts nor denies the label "charismatic." Both his daily television program and his weekly show, "Restoration with James Robison," can be seen on major Christian networks.

Bibliography: J. Robison, *Thank God, I'm Free: The James Robison Story* (1988).   G.W. Gohr

ROMAN CATHOLIC CHURCH   See CATHOLIC CHARISMATIC RENEWAL; DIALOGUE, ROMAN CATHOLIC AND CLASSICAL PENTECOSTAL; VATICAN II.

ROMANIAN PENTECOSTALS   See EUROPEAN PENTECOSTALISM.

ROSSIN, DELBERT   (1932–). Pastor in the Lutheran Church–Missouri Synod (LCMS) who became the most widely recognized spokesman and leader of the charismatic movement in that denomination. He graduated from Concordia Seminary, St. Louis, Missouri, in 1963. In 1966 he experienced the baptism with the Holy Spirit and shared with his congregation (Faith Lutheran, Geneva, Ill.) what had happened to him. The congregation prospered as it incorporated the charismatic message into its life and structure. After building a strong charismatic congregation in Geneva, Rossin began to spend time traveling to counsel with other pastors and congregations who wanted to move into charismatic renewal. He and his congregation became articulate exponents of charismatic renewal among Lutherans.

Rossin's strong emphasis on worship and his program for training elders attracted particular notice. He was widely sought as a counselor, teacher, and worship leader. He was one of the founding members of the International Lutheran Conference on the Holy Spirit (1972). In 1985 his congregation released him to serve more than half time as coordinator of pastoral and parish renewal with the International Lutheran Renewal Center in St. Paul, Minnesota.

Bibliography: L. Christenson, ed., *Welcome, Holy Spirit* (1987).   L. Christenson

RUIBAL, JULIO CESAR   See CHARISMATIC MOVEMENT.

RUSSIAN AND EASTERN EUROPEAN MISSION   A missionary society first organized (1927) under the name Russian and Eastern European Mission (later changed to Eastern European Mission [EEM]). Its founder, Paul Bernhard Peterson felt personally challenged to evangelize Russia after hearing reports of mass conversions of Russians to Protestantism after the country's revolution in 1917. While in Chicago, Peterson came into contact with E. W. Olson, a Russian missionary who was supported by the Swedish Baptist General Conference, and William Fetler, director of the Russian Missionary Society (RMS). The dedication of these persons to the evangelization of Russia motivated Peterson to do the same. He first became involved by becoming a trustee of RMS after it decided to move its headquarters from Philadelphia to Chicago in 1920. Two years later the society decided to support Peterson as a full-time missionary, and he left for Eastern Europe in 1924 and remained there until 1926.

As a result of his missionary work, Peterson decided to organize a new missionary society shortly after he returned to the U.S. After gaining additional support, the Russian and Eastern European Mission was founded in the spring of 1927. G. Herbert Schmidt, who previously served as a missionary in Poland, was chosen to establish a headquarters in Eastern Europe, and Peterson worked as general secretary of the Chicago office, which was designated as the mission's international headquarters.

In the summer of 1928 Schmidt was able to establish field headquarters for the mission in Danzig (now Gdansk), Poland. In 1930 the agency supported N. J. Poysti as a missionary in Manchuria and eastern Siberia. As a result of the Japanese occupation of Manchuria, Poysti returned to the U.S. in 1935. Shortly afterward, he established a local headquarters in New York City, where he began publishing a periodical in the Russian language known as *The Way of Faith* and began broadcasting a weekly radio program in Russian. Under the direction of these persons EEM began to serve as an interdenominational society that supported foreign and national missionaries in the Soviet Union and Eastern Europe. Prior to World War II EEM struggled to establish itself in the Soviet Union. Up until 1928 there was considerable freedom to evangelize in Soviet Russia. Under the antireligious law of 1929, however, religious conditions radically changed. By 1930 all of EEM's missionaries in the Soviet Union were arrested and either imprisoned or exiled. It was not until after World War II that the agency was able to evangelize again in the Soviet Union.

During the 1930s the organization met with better success in Poland. It began a Bible school in Danzig and conducted short-term Bible courses in neighboring areas for students from surrounding countries such as Romania, Lithuania, Bulgaria, Yugoslavia, Hungary, and Latvia. The Bible school remained open until shortly before World War II.

For many years EEM had worked closely with the Department of Foreign Missions of the Assemblies of God (AG), sharing personnel and providing mutual support for the work in Europe and Russia. This relationship ended in 1940,

A graduating class of the Danzig Bible Institute before World War II. Pictured in the second row are Gustav H. Schmidt (third from left), Donald Gee, Nicholas Nikoloff, and Gustav Kinderman. Martha Nikoloff is second from the right in the second row.

however, over AG dissatisfaction with Russian and Eastern European Mission financial policies, its move away from a distinctly Pentecostal posture theologically, and related problems.

The outbreak of the war greatly affected the entire operation in Eastern Europe. All of its foreign missionaries were forced to return to America, and the organization lost contact with its national workers as well. Forced out of Europe, EEM decided to focus its ministry on Russians and Eastern Europeans living in western Canada and the southern half of South America. It undertook the support of missionaries and evangelists who helped to establish churches in these areas. During this time Poysti conducted a weekly radio broadcast in Russian to the Slavic people in Ecuador and its surrounding countries.

Beginning in 1945 the agency began its refugee ministry by sending food and clothing to various camps that were established to help displaced persons uprooted from their homes as a result of the war. As its relief work expanded EEM began to support many evangelists who ministered in the camps. In 1953 it established a center in West Berlin to provide material and spiritual aid to those persons who fled East Berlin to seek resettlement in the West. The center remained open until the wall was erected in 1961.

Since the 1950s EEM has extended its ministries in Western Europe. The organization has also established offices near Amsterdam, Athens, Munich, and Vienna. From its center near Amsterdam EEM has helped to evangelize the Netherlands through Bible correspondence courses, radio broadcasting, and the establishment of coffee houses. Near Munich other coffee houses were established. In Athens EEM has published Sunday school materials for children and adults. It has also founded a conference center and a retirement home for the elderly. Near Vienna EEM directs several of its evangelistic programs to Eastern Europe. It has continued to supply Christian literature and relief supplies to churches and organizations in Bulgaria, Poland, Romania and Yugoslavia. In Poland EEM conducts weekly radio broadcasts known as "The Voice of the Gospel from Warsaw." It conducts six weekly programs from other countries that are broadcasted to the Soviet Union; it has also continued to supply the Soviet people with Bibles. Since 1985 EEM has conducted short-term outreach opportunities to Eastern Europe and the Soviet Union for persons interested in relief and Christian literature distribution. Since 1987 the international headquarters for Eurovision (formerly EEM), which had moved from Chicago to Pasadena, California, in 1952, is located in Claremont, California.

See also EUROPEAN PENTECOSTALISM; MISSIONS, OVERSEAS.

Bibliography: G. B. McGee, *This Gospel Shall Be Preached* (1986); P. B. Peterson, *History of the First Fifty Years (1927–1977) of the Eastern European Mission* (n.d.).   J. Colletti

RUSSIAN PENTECOSTALS See EUROPEAN PENTECOSTALISM; RUSSIAN AND EASTERN EUROPEAN MISSION.

S

SACRAMENTS Since there are no common answers to questions concerning the nature, number, or efficacy of the sacraments, it is necessary that this article offer the answers of a particular Christian confession. The understanding of sacraments that will be proposed here is that of the Roman Catholic church.

The word "sacrament" is the English equivalent of the Latin *sacramentum,* which, in early Christian Latin, was the common translation of the Greek *mystērion,* "mystery." The NT writers, especially Paul, identified the "mystery" as God's hidden plan of salvation for all, finally and definitively revealed in Christ. Indeed, Jesus Christ was himself identified as the sacrament, or visible manifestation, of the Father's mysterious will with regard to humanity.

The Latin Fathers used the term *sacramentum* to refer to various things that in one sense or another were manifestations or symbols of saving grace. Thus the religious rites were seen as symbols of the mysteries of Christ's life, death, and resurrection. In the course of time, in Western theology, the term came to be used more exclusively of those acts of Christian worship that were understood to be not only symbolic but in some way efficacious of the grace that they signified. It was only at the Council of Trent that the Catholic church definitively declared the number of such sacraments to be seven, identifying them as baptism, confirmation, Eucharist, penance, holy orders, matrimony, and the anointing of the sick.

Catholics believe that in each of these liturgical actions, the church, as Christ's body, is in a special way united to its Head as the High Priest who eternally offers himself to the Father on our behalf. Each of the sacraments is seen as a uniquely efficacious sign of Christ's power, as the Risen Lord, to confer the fruits of his sacrifice on those who believe in him. Christ himself is understood to have instituted the seven sacraments and to be the principal agent of the effects that they bring about.

While in each case there is a human minister, and in most of the sacraments the minister is required to have been duly ordained in order to represent both Christ and the church in this liturgical act, the effectiveness of the sacraments does not depend on the faith or holiness of the minister, since in these acts of the church it is Christ himself who confers grace through the agency of his Spirit. However, it is required that the minister intend to do what the church does in celebrating the sacraments.

On the other hand, the effectiveness of the sacraments to confer the gift of the Spirit does depend on the faith of the recipients and on their being properly disposed to receive such grace.

Lack of faith or refusal to renounce grave sin would prevent a sacrament from having its intended effects. However, in the case of the baptism of infants, Catholics, relying on an ancient Christian tradition, hold that the faith of the church and the intention of the parents to bring up the child as a Christian justify the belief that the infant receives the saving grace of Christ at baptism without being able to make an act of personal faith at that time. Of course he or she must make such an act of faith when capable of it, and the special occasions for this confession of faith will be at the reception of confirmation and the Eucharist, which complete that person's Christian initiation. By these sacraments, which symbolize Christ's death and resurrection and the outpouring of the Spirit at Pentecost, new Christians are brought into a saving encounter with Christ in his mysteries and begin to enjoy the life of grace that is their fruit. Their incorporation into Christ is also their incorporation into his body, the church, initiating them into the priesthood of the faithful and enabling them to live the Christian life and to take an active part in the public worship of the church.

The principal actions in which the faithful exercise their baptismal priesthood are the celebrations of the other sacraments. Chief among these is the celebration of the Eucharist, in which Christ's sacrifice of himself for the world's salvation is symbolized by the offering of bread and wine, which are transformed by the power of the Holy Spirit into the body and blood of Christ. Catholics believe that Christ becomes truly present in the Eucharist as the High Priest who offers himself to the Father and joins the church to himself in the sacramental offering of this same unique, eternal sacrifice. By receiving the Eucharist in Holy Communion, the faithful become more deeply one body with Christ and with one another.

While the sacraments of initiation confer the grace to live up to the demands of Christian life, human failure to correspond with grace results in sin, which involves the need of reconciliation with the Lord and with the church. Such reconciliation calls for repentance on the part of the sinner, and also an action on the part of the church, since Christ entrusted to his disciples the power to forgive sin in his name (cf. John 20:23). Catholics understand the exercise of this power to be a sacrament, symbolizing and effecting the pardon that Christ himself offers to the repentant sinner.

Liturgical initiation into two states of life that are especially vital to the life of the church and also involve a particular need of grace—marriage and ministry—is also understood to have sacramental efficacy. In holy matrimony the partners themselves are the ministers of the sacrament, which consists in the marriage covenant by which they bind themselves to one another in Christ. Ordination to the diaconate, the priesthood, or the episcopate is also a sacrament, of which the bishop is the only valid minister. This sacrament, like baptism and confirmation, is believed to have a permanent effect distinct from sanctifying grace and is traditionally spoken of as a "character." The most common interpretation of this is the one given by St. Thomas Aquinas, who saw it as a participation in the priesthood of Christ, which is shared, in different ways, by the baptized, the confirmed, and the ordained.

The seventh sacrament is the anointing of the sick, which for a long time was seen as a preparation for death but has recently been again recognized in its true nature as symbolic of Christ's ministry of healing of both spiritual and physical ills.

See also ORDINANCES, PENTECOSTAL; CHURCH, THEOLOGY OF THE.

Bibliography: P. F. Fransen, *Faith and the Sacraments* (1958); B. Leeming, *Principles of Sacramental Theology* (1960); A. G. Martimort, *The Signs of the New Covenant* (1963); K. Rahner, *The Church and the Sacraments* (1963); E. Schillebeeckx, *Christ: The Sacrament of the Encounter With God* (1963).   F. A. Sullivan

SAINT SAMUEL See SAMUEL, SAINT.

SALMON, JOHN (1831–1918). Born in Glasgow, Scotland, John Salmon spent ten years of his youth at sea, during which (1854) he was converted to faith in Jesus Christ. Serving in Canada first as a Methodist and later as a Congregationalist minister, he became interested in divine healing in the 1880s, being healed in 1885 of a kidney disease at an A. B. Simpson convention. Salmon was present in 1887 at the formation of the Christian Alliance, becoming a vice-president. He was the founding father of the Christian and Missionary Alliance in Canada and founding pastor of Bethany Church in Toronto. At an Alliance convention in Ohio in 1907, Salmon received the gift of tongues, and he became for some years a proponent of the Pentecostal baptism. He retired to California in 1911, where he experienced some disillusionment with Pentecostal developments.

Bibliography: L. Reynolds, *Footprints* (1982).
P. D. Hocken

SALTER, JAMES (1890–1972). British pioneer missionary and cofounder with W. F. P. Burton of the Congo Evangelistic Mission. Born in Preston, he was associated with Thomas Myerscough's Bible School and the Pentecostal Missionary Union. He sailed for Africa in May 1915 to join his friend William F. P. Burton. They arrived together in the Belgian Congo in September. One of their party died en route, and Salter survived attacks of malaria and blackwater fever. In 1919 he returned to Britain and visited a number of Pentecostal churches and met many of their leaders. They formed the Congo Evangelistic Mission after the Whitsun Convention at Kingsway Hall, London. Headquarters were established at Preston, with Myerscough as secretary-treasurer. "Jimmy" Salter became home di-

rector. He returned to the Congo in 1920, accompanied by several recruits, including Alice Wigglesworth, daughter of Smith Wigglesworth. Salter married her, and she stayed in the Congo only two years. The Salters spent much of their time traveling with Wigglesworth. Salter served on the executive council of the Assemblies of God of Great Britain and Ireland and was chairman of their conference. He returned to the Congo regularly, sometimes for long periods. Loving, gracious and wise, cautious and brave, he was given the Congolese nickname, "Inabanza," which means "wise counselor."

Bibliography: C. C. Whittaker, *Seven Pentecostal Pioneers* (1983).   D. W. Cartwright

SALVATION ARMY CHARISMATICS See WESLEYAN CHARISMATICS.

SAMUEL, SAINT (c. 1885–1934). Evangelist and convocation worship leader (Church of God in Christ). Samuel was converted under the ministry of Bishop Charles H. Mason in a revival conducted at Norfolk, Virginia, in 1907. While some details of his life are sketchy, he was married and held pastorates in Memphis, Tennessee; Rockingham, North Carolina; and Norfolk, Virginia. Through him God wrought special miracles, and he also distinguished himself as a worship leader at the national convocations in Memphis. Many believers were blessed as they watched Samuel literally "wrestle the Devil." He would stamp his feet and make a weird noise as though he were chasing an animal and then begin to rebuke Satan. His rebukes were, "Get out of here, you fool"; "On your way to hell"; "God rebuke you"; "God is your boss"; or "I'll get the Boss on you." After his death, many saints reported that they heard him singing in the Spirit his favorite, "My Soul Loves Jesus," and saw him entering the funeral service.   L. Lovett

SANCTIFICATION See CHRISTIAN PERFECTION; HOLINESS MOVEMENT; KESWICK HIGHER LIFE MOVEMENT.

SANDFORD, FRANK (1862–1948). Author, publisher, pastor, evangelist, Bible school founder, and utopian visionary who played a pivotal role in the training of many Holiness people who would later become Pentecostals, among them C. F. Parham and A. J. Tomlinson. Born in Bowdomham, Maine, Sandford received his primary education at Nichols Latin School in Lewiston. He was converted on February 29, 1880.

Upon graduation from Bates College (1886), Sandford entered Cobb Divinity School. The following year he dropped out of seminary claiming that it did not satisfy his "intense spiritual hunger," and he became pastor of the Free Baptist church in Topsham. That first summer he was influenced heavily by Hannah Whitall Smith's *The Christian's Secret of a Happy Life*, which seemed to satisfy the "craving" of his soul. His congregation grew rapidly.

In 1890 he moved to a second pastorate in Grand Falls (Somersworth), New Hampshire. While there, he attended Methodist meetings on the campgrounds of Old Orchard, Maine, and accepted the Holiness teaching on sanctification. Contact with the Christian Alliance led him to a belief in divine healing as well. He attended summer schools led by D. L. Moody in Northfield, Maine, and as a result, he entered the Student Volunteer Movement. With T. H. Stacey, a pastor from Auburn, Maine, and a denominational executive, Sandford traveled the globe and became convinced that current missionary efforts were so fruitless that he could no longer be bound by a single denomination and that the final work of God on earth would include the separation of humanity into two groups: Christ's and Antichrist's, through the use of "signs, wonders, and mighty deeds."

Toward the end of his second pastorate Sandford married Helen C. Kinney, who had served as a Christian Alliance missionary in Japan, following in her parents' footsteps. They left Great Falls, and traveled to Texas, New York, and New Jersey, finally settling in Lancaster, Maine.

Sandford recounted the years 1893–99 as his "journey back to apostolic life and power," and he wrote of them in *Seven Years with God* (1900, reprint 1957). During this time he founded the Holy Ghost and Us Bible School, held evangelistic crusades, studied divine healing, and edited and published a periodical initially called *Tongues of Fire* (1894). His concern for the unreached led him to claim divine direction when, in a project financed by faith and built in large part with student labor, he constructed a large, white, Victorian structure named Shiloh, complete with turrets, towers, and flags, on a hilltop near Durham, Maine. From here, the gospel would go throughout the world as students, steeped in faith, evangelism, and divine healing went forth. In the meantime this project attracted a large following, many of whom moved to the area. By 1904 some six hundred residents who had donated all they owned to Shiloh, were living together in community. Still, all was not well at Shiloh, for rumors flew concerning Sandford's authoritarian rule and abusive discipline.

Sandford's missionary concern led in 1905 to the purchase of a schooner, the *Coronet,* and a barkentine, the *Kingdom,* for use in worldwide evangelization. It was this enterprise that brought about Sandford's downfall. In June 1911, while on a missionary trip, the *Kingdom* was wrecked off the African coast. All personnel were placed on board the *Coronet.* Sandford was on board, providing leadership and waiting on God for direction. A series of bad decisions compounded the predicament of those on board, and by the time they reached Portland, Maine, on October 21, 1911, several had died from lack of food and water, and others were nearly dead. By November 1 a total of nine had died.

Sandford was soon plagued by renewed reports of his iron rule and disciplinary measures. He was arrested and charged with manslaughter. His trial began on December 1, 1911, and ultimately he was convicted and sentenced to a ten-year term in the federal penitentiary at Atlanta, Georgia. Sandford constantly maintained that God had directed him in all that he did, but he never fully recovered from this blow. Bartleman, for instance, classed

him with J. A. Dowie as a spiritual charlatan who "severely abused and fleeced the flock of God" and came "to a most disreputable and execrable end." Released early from prison, Sandford lived in semiretirement until 1948 when at age eighty-five he died.

The Shiloh movement continues to the present, with headquarters in Dublin, New Hampshire. It has kept many of Sandford's works in print through its own Kingdom Press.

Bibliography: F. Bartleman, "All Things in Common," *Confidence* 6 (4, 1918): 79; H. F. Day, "The Saints of Shiloh," *Leslie's Monthly Magazine* (April 1905), 682–91; W. C. Hiss, "Shiloh: Frank W. Sandford and the Kingdom: 1893–1948," Ph.D. diss., Tufts University, 1978; F. S. Murray, *The Sublimity of Faith, The Life and Work of Frank W. Sandford* (1981); F. W. Sandford, *The Art of War for the Christian Soldier* (1904, reprint 1966); A. L. White, "The Tragic Voyage of the Shiloh Schooner 'Coronet,'" *Down East* (May 1974), 54–57, 72–76; E. P. Woodward, "Sandfordism: An Exposure," *The Safeguard and Armory* 6 (January 3, 1902): 105.   C. M. Robeck, Jr.

SANFORD, AGNES MARY (1897–1982).

Pioneer in healing ministry. The child of Presbyterian missionaries, Agnes White spent her youth in China, except for her college years, which she spent in the U.S. She married an Episcopal priest, Edgar Sanford, in 1923, and they returned to the U.S. in 1925.

Mrs. Sanford's interest in healing developed after she was healed of long-standing depression. Studying the Scriptures, she discovered that she had a gift of healing. Her wider ministry began when her first book, *The Healing Light,* was published in 1947 and became a best seller. Around 1953–54, Sanford experienced a definite empowering of the Holy Spirit, and then received the gift of tongues after contact with some Pentecostals. In 1955 the Sanfords launched School of Pastoral Care—residential conferences for clergy, their wives, and medical personnel on the ministry of healing. These continued after her husband's death in 1960.

Though Sanford never spoke in public of the Pentecostal experience, she frequently did so in private, urging discretion on the recipients, many of them clergy. Through contacts in the School of Pastoral Care, Camps Farthest Out, and the Order of St. Luke, Sanford was one of the foremost promoters of renewal in the Holy Spirit within the historic churches in the English-speaking world. Her teaching had a sacramental dimension that gave a greater place to natural processes than evangelical and Pentecostal healing ministries, presenting God's healing work as following the laws of nature and positive thinking. Sanford was the major pioneer in ministry for the healing of memories, which for her was all one with the forgiveness of sin. Her other major books include *Behold Your God* (1958); *The Healing Gifts of the Spirit* (1966); *The Healing Power of the Bible* (1969); and her autobiography, *Sealed Orders* (1972).

Bibliography: J. T. Connelly, "Neo-Pentecostalism: the Charismatic Revival in the Mainline Protestant and Roman Catholic Churches of the United States, 1960–1971," Ph.D. diss., University of Chicago, 1977.   P. D. Hocken

SCANDINAVIAN INDEPENDENT AS-SEMBLIES OF GOD See FELLOWSHIP OF CHRISTIAN ASSEMBLIES.

Michael Scanlan has been prominent in the Catholic charismatic movement since 1969. He is president of the Franciscan University of Steubenville.

SCANLAN, MICHAEL (1931–). Prominent figure in Catholic Charismatic Renewal (CCR). A qualified lawyer, admitted to the bar of New York State in 1956, Scanlan entered the T.O.R. Franciscans in 1957. Ordained priest in 1964, he immediately became dean at the College of Steubenville, Ohio. Appointed rector of St. Francis' Seminary, Loretto, Pennsylvania, in 1969, he was baptized in the Spirit there that fall, following a talk by two visiting Catholic leaders.

Scanlan's main contribution to charismatic renewal among Catholics has been: (1) as president at Steubenville; (2) as a prominent preacher-teacher; (3) as promoter-organizer of Steubenville conferences; and (4) as a member of renewal committees. Of these, the first is probably the most significant. Returning to Steubenville in 1974, Scanlan transformed a small Catholic college into a thriving university (achieving university status in 1980) with a reputation for Christian orthodoxy and a strong, Spirit-filled campus life. As a regular speaker at renewal conferences in the U.S. and elsewhere, Scanlan was already a recognized preacher when, in 1983, he joined Ralph Martin, John Bertolucci, and Ann Shields in "F.I.R.E.," which held rallies in major cities (preaching faith, intercession, repentance, and evangelism). Scanlan has pioneered annual residential conferences at Steubenville for priests and deacons (from 1975), for youth (from 1982), and for prayer group leaders (from 1983). He was for some years a member of the national service committee for CCR, being chairman from 1976

to 1978. He is a member of the Servants of Christ the King community in Steubenville, which is part of the Sword of the Spirit (see CHARISMATIC COMMUNITIES), of which Scanlan is a leader. Among Scanlan's published books are: *The Power in Penance* (1972); *Inner Healing* (1974); *And Their Eyes Were Opened* (with A. Shields, 1976); *Deliverance From Evil Spirits* (with R. Cirner, 1980); and *Let the Fire Fall* (1986), an autobiography.   P. D. Hocken

SCHAEPE, JOHN G. (1870–1939). The person credited with receiving the initial revelation concerning the Oneness doctrine and baptism in Jesus' name. John Schaepe was reared in a German Lutheran home, one of at least three children. At age fourteen he left home, taking a job aboard a ship. He spent the next five years sailing to South American ports. Deserting ship in Argentina when he was eighteen, John worked his way to the Pampas, where he learned to ride horses, herd cattle, and qualify as a "cowboy" and "bronco-buster." After a time in Argentina he came to the U.S. and worked on the ranges of Wyoming and Montana. While in these states he became a fugitive from justice because of his constant brawling and fled to Hawaii.

In 1903, shortly after arriving in Hawaii, Schaepe was unable to find work. Instead, he found his way toward the Honolulu waterfront, where he intended to mug a passing sea captain with the aid of his 38 caliber pistol. What he found was a Salvation Army Mission into which he was drawn by the music. There he heard testimonies that made him desire "a better way of living." He returned to his hotel room where he was converted and then quickly joined the Salvation Army.

Schaepe stated in his testimony that God "baptized me with the Holy Spirit" on February 23, 1906, and that he spoke in Chinese, Japanese, and Korean. This would place his experience prior to the Azusa Street revival. It is probable, however, that it was actually in 1907 when he received his "baptism," since he was apparently working in Southern California, breaking horses, at the time the revival broke in Los Angeles.

The occasion for Schaepe's now famous revelation was a sermon delivered by Robert E. McAlister in April 1913 at the Apostolic Faith World-Wide Camp Meeting held in the Arroyo Seco of Los Angeles. McAlister observed that in the Book of Acts, the apostles always baptized the newly converted "in the name of Jesus Christ." He emphasized that the Matthew 28:19 trinitarian formula was not used. John Schaepe was sufficiently inspired by the message that he spent the entire night in prayer. Toward morning, this "would-be preacher" raced through the camp shouting out his revelation on the power of the name of Jesus. Many of the campers began to study the issue. Some, including Frank J. Ewart, came to accept it, were rebaptized, and began to share their beliefs from the pulpit. Out of these beginnings came the Oneness Pentecostal churches.

In 1917 Schaepe was living just blocks from the Arroyo Seco campground at 6340 Arroyo Seco

After working with A. A. Allen for several years, R. W. Schambach struck out on his own in the salvation-healing movement. Here he leads a tent crowd in praise.

Avenue. He remained in that general area, moving a short distance to 3810 Eagle Rock Boulevard, where he remained until his death. He is buried in Vahalla Cemetery in Burbank, California.

Bibliography: A. Clanton, *United We Stand* (1970), 15–16; F. Foster, *Think It Not Strange* (1965), 52; W. Menzies, *Anointed to Serve* (1971), 111–12; Obituary, *Los Angeles Times* (February 23, 1939); J. Schaepe, "A Remarkable Testimony," *Meat in Due Season* 1 (August 21, 1917): 4; V. Synan, *The Holiness-Pentecostal Movement in the United States* (1971), 154; W. Warner, "The 1913 Worldwide Camp Meeting," *AG Heritage* 3 (1, 1983): 4.   C. M. Robeck, Jr.

SCHAMBACH, ROBERT W. (1926–). Healing evangelist. R. W. Schambach was licensed with the Assemblies of God (AG) in 1951 and became an important part of A. A. Allen's ministry in 1953. Schambach dropped his credentials with the AG when the denomination disciplined Allen. Leaving Allen's ministry on good terms in 1959, he launched his own ministry known as Schambach Miracle Revivals.

Schambach's financial base was rooted in four churches that he had founded and that were pastored by his full-time assistants. Commitment to old fashioned revivalism, including the use of a tent, has been a high priority to Schambach. His central message focused on deliverance from sickness, and the services included spontaneous audience participation. His ministry distinctively aims at bringing a positive message to the lower

classes with the goal of moving them out of despair.

In 1970 Schambach started the periodical *Power*, edited by Lexie Allen, and by 1974 it had a circulation near 100,000. In 1974 his radio program was on fifty stations.

Bibliography: D. E. Harrell, Jr., *All Things Are Possible* (1975).   S. Shemeth

SCHEPPE, JOHN G. See SCHAEPE, JOHN G.

SCHLINK, BASILEA (1904–). Cofoundress of the Evangelical Sisterhood of Mary and prolific author. Born Klara Schlink and brought up in Brunswick, Germany, she had a conversion experience in 1922 and thereafter saw her life in terms of Christian service. Increasingly led to work with her friend Erika Madauss, Schlink experienced the twenty years following her graduation as a divine preparation for her later call. In 1945, in the ruins of Darmstadt, Schlink and Madauss witnessed a revival including manifestation of the spiritual gifts among the girls in their Bible study, in which repentance was a key factor. From this revival grew the Sisterhood of Mary, an evangelical Protestant community consecrated to a faith-life of simplicity and celibacy for love of Jesus. Together Schlink and Madauss (now known as Mothers Basilea and Martyria) led the Mary Sisters in a life characterized by faith in God's call, promise, and provision. Schlink played a leading role in responding to a call to purchase a twenty-two-acre site near Darmstadt in 1955, which was renamed Canaan. With funds and materials trusted for in faith without solicitation, the basic plan for Canaan was completed in 1963, with chapels, a home for the aged and infirm, and a retreat house. Schlink has also helped to found a total of twenty-four branches of the Sisterhood in twenty-one different countries, including one in Phoenix, Arizona. She has written approximately a hundred books and booklets, concentrating on the themes of God's call to repentance, the dire spiritual need of the modern world, the divine judgment and mercy, the bridal love of Jesus, and the role of Israel. Schlink's own life is told in *I Found the Key to the Heart of God* (1975), and the experiences of the Sisterhood in *Realities of Faith* (1966). Other important books include *Israel— My Chosen People* (1963, rev. 1987), *Repentance—The Joy Filled Life* (1968), *Ruled by the Spirit* (1970), *My All for Him* (1972), *The Unseen World of Angels and Demons* (1986), *Patmos— When the Heavens Opened* (1976), and *Mary, the Mother of Jesus* (1986). Schlink's books have been translated into more than sixty languages, and she has also written many songs.   P. D. Hocken

SCHMIDT, GUSTAV HERBERT (1891– 1958).

Missionary to Eastern Europe. Born in Annapol, Wolynia, Russia, to Jacob and Wilhelmine Schmidt. The younger Schmidt attended a public school in Russia from 1898 to 1905. He was converted to Christ in 1908 and received the baptism in the Holy Spirit two or three years later. He continued his education by attending business college in Berlin, Germany, and then immigrated to the U.S., where he attended the Rochester Bible Training School in Rochester, New York (1915–18).

In 1919 Schmidt received appointment as an Assemblies of God (AG) missionary to Poland and arrived there in 1920. He immediately engaged in relief work and evangelism. Success followed quickly with Schmidt baptizing a hundred converts within four months. After several years of ministry there, he recognized the need to establish a Bible institute for the training of ministers. Returning to the U.S. in 1925, he asked the AG for permission to start such a school; they declined due to heavy financial pressures for other missions projects.

In the following year, he met C. W. Swanson, a California businessman, who financed the publication of *The Gospel Call of Russia* to publicize the ministry and needs of Eastern Europe. In 1927 he met Paul B. Peterson, a former missionary to Russia, and together they organized the Russian and Eastern European Mission (REEM) to extend their ministry in this region of Europe; it worked in close collaboration with the AG until 1940. Schmidt's publication became the official voice of REEM, later with a shortened title, *The Gospel Call.*

Schmidt returned to Poland in 1929 and on March 2, 1930, the Danzig Instytut Biblijny opened in the Free City of Danzig, the first Pentecostal Bible institute in Eastern Europe. He served as dean until he was followed in this capacity by Nicholas Nikoloff in 1935. With the increase of Nazi sympathies in Danzig and the

approach of the war, the Bible school was closed in 1938. After the war broke out, Schmidt was imprisoned for six months by the Nazis for his Pentecostal beliefs but escaped incarceration in a concentration camp in 1941 because of his American citizenship. He smuggled on board a Swedish ship leaving Danzig to escape from the Gestapo, leaving his family behind. After the war, the family was reunited and returned to America, where Schmidt continued in ministry. While on a preaching tour of Germany, he died in 1958. His escape from Danzig is recorded in his book, *Songs in the Night* (1945); he also authored *The Journey Home* (1945).

Bibliography: "Application for Endorsement as Missionary" (1919); "G. H. Schmidt Dies in Germany," *PE* (July 13, 1958), 27; T. Salzer, "The Danzig Gdanska Instytut Biblijny: Its History and Impact" (unpublished, 1988).   G. B. McGee

Christian Schoonmaker was a pioneer missionary to India for the Christian and Missionary Alliance. After he received the baptism in the Holy Spirit, he led other Alliance missionaries into this experience.

SCHOONMAKER, CHRISTIAN H. (1881–1919).

Missionary to India. Schoonmaker, who was born in New York, was one of the first American Assemblies of God (AG) missionaries to India and the first chairman of the Indian AG developed in 1918 at Saharanpur, India. As chairman he intended for the Indian AG to include all the Pentecostal groups; but it was disbanded shortly after he died in 1919.

Schoonmaker's religious heritage included having a Methodist mother; working for the Salvation Army; being trained in the Christian and Missionary Alliance (CMA) school in Nyack, New York; and attending a convention where people received the baptism in the Spirit. When he became a missionary to India in 1907 he preached that people should wait for the baptism in the Spirit, which he received in 1908. Schoonmaker had a vision of Christ, facilitated others receiving the baptism in the Spirit, discerned spirits, was sensitive to the Spirit's leading, and had a healing ministry. He was ordained by the American AG and returned to India in 1917 despite the diseases his family had experienced in India. He died of smallpox, having refused the vaccination due to his faith. Following his death, his wife, Violet, continued working as a missionary; five of their six children became missionaries to India.

Bibliography: C. H. Schoonmaker, "God's Estimate of a Heathen Soul. What Is Yours?" *LRE* 10 (1917): 13–17; V. Schoonmaker, *A Man Who Loved the Will of God* (c. 1959).   E. B. Robinson

SCOFIELD REFERENCE BIBLE   Highly influential, dispensationally oriented edition of the Bible named after its editor, Cyrus Ingerson Scofield (1843–1921). Initially begun in 1900, *The Scofield Reference Bible* was first published by Oxford University Press in 1909. Scofield was aided by an eight-member group of editorial consultants on both the 1909 first edition and the 1917 "New and Improved Edition." Copyrights were reissued in 1937 and again in 1945.

At the invitation of Oxford University Press, in 1954 a committee of nine men under the editorial guidance of E. Schuyler English, Litt.D., began revising *The Scofield Reference Bible,* and in 1967 an edition entitled *The New Scofield Reference Bible* was released. *The New Scofield Reference Bible* reflected among other things some

important word changes in the text to help the reader; . . . revision of many of the introductions to the books of the Bible . . . ; more subheadings; clarification of some footnotes, deletion of others, and the addition of many new notes; more marginal references; an entirely new chronology [Ussher's chronology was omitted]; a new index; . . . a concordance.

Despite new editorial leadership, the dispensational character of its predecessor remained substantially intact.

Scofield's own spiritual roots began with his conversion in 1879. Within three years (1882) he had accepted a Congregational pastorate in Dallas, Texas. Soon afterward, under the tutelage of Presbyterian minister J. H. Brookes, Scofield was exposed to and highly taken with the writings of John Nelson Darby (1800–1882) and other Plymouth Brethren. Although lacking any formal theological training, Scofield began his writing career with a book called *Rightly Dividing the Word of Truth* (1885) and *The Comprehensive Bible Correspondence Course* (1896). These laid the groundwork for his most significant work, *The Scofield Reference Bible.* Scofield also penned a collection of essays entitled *Addresses on Prophecy* (1900) and a little-known volume on the doctrine of the Holy Spirit (1906), which was reissued in 1973 by Baker Book House under the title *A Mighty Wind: Plain Papers on the Doctrine of the Holy Spirit.*

The impact of *The Scofield Reference Bible* on the Pentecostal and charismatic movements in this country can scarcely be understated, despite attempts to show that Pentecostals were not originally dispensational (Sheppard, 1984). Many of the over two million copies that were sold or given away fell into the eager hands of members of both movements. Pentecostals were affected early and directly. Some charismatics, however, as often was the case with theological issues, accepted dispensationalism by default as part of the theological package accompanying the baptism in the Holy Spirit. Other, more progressive, charismatic groups, chose another route. (E.g., The Vineyard Christian Fellowship tacitly rejects dispensationalism and opts for an eschatology based more upon G. E. Ladd's "already–not yet" perspective.)

Although dispensationalism denies that spiritual gifts are valid under the present dispensation (e.g., see Scofield's notes on 1 Cor. 14: "Tongues and the sign gifts are to cease"; cf. Walvoord, *The Holy Spirit* [1954]), that did not stop Pentecostal pioneers from using its framework. Among Pentecostal denominations, Scofield's premillennial, pretribulational brand of dispensationalism rode the coattails of nineteenth-century Fundamentalism and soon nearly became "dogma."

Pentecostal publications like Frank M. Boyd's *Ages and Dispensations* (1955) found it "an easy exercise to adapt the teaching and literature of Scofieldian dispensationalism to the Pentecostal emphasis. . . . the dispensational motif, given a proper Pentecostal baptism, [was seen] as a helpful aid in underscoring the importance of the doctrine of the second coming of Christ" (Menzies, 1971, 328–29). P. C. Nelson, in *Bible Doctrines* (1916, 1948, 1961, 1969, 1971), a series of studies on the Statement of Fundamental Truths adopted by the Assemblies of God (AG), encouraging that readers who "wish to go deeper into the subject [of Israel's return to Palestine] will do well to read Blackstone's *Jesus is Coming,*" which was virtually a dispensationalist's primer. The more recent trend, however, is away from dispensational categories (Menzies, 1971, 328–29; but cf. Menzies in Synan, 1975, 85), although as recently as the 1970s dispensationalist John G. Hall (*God's Dispensational and Prophetic Plan,* 1972) was invited to speak at Central Bible College, flagship Bible college of the AG. *The Book of Doctrine* (Church of God [CG, Cleveland, Tenn.]), published in 1922, is another clear reflection of Scofield's influence in Pentecostal circles (see p. 144; cf. the more recent *This We Believe* [1963], by CG author J. L. Slay).

See also DISPENSATIONALISM.

Bibliography: *Book of Doctrines* (1922); F. M. Boyd, *Ages and Dispensation* (1955); W. E. Cox, *An Examination of Dispensationalism* (1979); W. N. Kerr, "Scofield, Cyrus Ingerson," EDT, 988–89; G. N. Kraus, *Dispensationalism in America* (1958); D. MacPherson, *The Great Rapture Hoax* (1983); F. C. Masserano, "A Study of Worship Forms in the Assemblies of God Denomination," Master's thesis, Princeton, 1966; W. C. Meloon, *We've Been Robbed* (1971); W. Menzies, *Anointed to Serve, The Story of the Assemblies of God* (1971); P. C. Nelson, *Bible Doctrines* (1971); C. I. Scofield, ed., *The Scofield Reference Bible* (1909, 1917, 1937, 1945); idem,

A Mighty Wind, Plain Papers on the Doctrine of the Holy Spirit (1906, reprint 1973); idem, *The New Scofield Reference Bible* (1967); G. Sheppard, "Pentecostals and the Hermeneutics of Dispensationalism. The Anatomy of an Uneasy Relationship," *Pneuma* 6 (2, 1984): 5–33; J. L. Slay, *This We Believe* (1963); V. Synan, ed., *Aspects of Pentecostal-Charismatic Origins* (1975).

P. H. Alexander

SCOTT, DOUGLAS R. (1900–1967). Pioneer Pentecostal apostle in France. Born in Ilford, Essex, Scott was brought up in a religious family, and from his adolescence attended a Congregational church. Talented at sports and music, Scott had been troubled in soul for some years. He finally was converted in 1925 when he heard a Polish Pentecostal student, A. Bergholc, preach on the Cross. Some months later he was baptized in the Spirit following the laying on of hands by George Jeffreys and being healed of a speech impediment. Convinced that the Lord had empowered him to bring the word of salvation to others, he soon shared the Elim emphasis on healing signs and wonders to demonstrate the truth of the gospel to the unconverted. Scott threw himself into evangelistic work with complete dedication, gaining experience in street meetings and door-to-door evangelism.

Hearing the call of the Lord to missionary work, Scott arranged to visit Le Havre, France, to learn the language before traveling to Africa. In Le Havre, at the Ruban Bleu mission of Hélène Biolley in 1927, Scott began preaching in his limited French, and some remarkable healings occurred. Urged to return, Scott sought the Lord and received confirmation through prophecy. In 1929 he married Clarice Weston, gave up his job, and in January, 1930, the Scotts arrived in Le Havre. From this point, Scott became God's instrument for establishing the Pentecostal movement in France. Through missions and campaigns, initially in Normandy, and then in southern Belgium (through contact with H. de Worm) and in western Switzerland and southeast France, Scott initiated revival with numerous conversions. He decisively influenced the men who became key figures in the French AG, including P. Nicolle, and was the catalyst in the 1932 Ardèche revival, bringing the Pentecostal experience to L. Dallière and other Reformed pastors. Besides spending the war years in the Congo, the Scotts were also called to French North Africa, where they evangelized in 1952–56. Between 1946 and 1952, Scott labored particularly in Perpignan and Carcassonne in southwest France.

Scott's enormous impact on French Pentecostalism cannot be explained alone by his undoubted dedication, which showed most clearly in his last years with a deteriorating heart condition. He was recognized as a man of the Spirit who always sought the Lord's guidance before he acted. He was noted for the directness of his preaching, for his ability to make the Scriptures live, for his humor, and his compassion for people's burdens. He mirrored an apostle's care for the churches he had founded. If one phrase catches Scott's personality, it might be *"Une église qui ne missione pas démissionne."* (A church that does not evangelize hands in its resignation).

See also EUROPEAN PENTECOSTALISM.

Bibliography: G. R. Stotts, *Le Pentecôtisme au pays de Voltaire* (1981). P. D. Hocken

SCOTT, EUGENE W. (1929–). Pastor and television personality. Eugene Scott, born in Buell, Idaho, into the family of a rural Assemblies of God (AG) minister, was raised in an atmosphere of camp meetings and fundamental Bible teaching. The close bond to his parents has never diminished, his mother acting as his closest adviser. Scott married Betty Ann Frazer in the early 1950s. Receiving his Ph.D. in philosophy of education from Stanford University in 1957, he attempted to apply philosophy to Christian teachings (he has no degree in religion or theology). A study of the Resurrection brought Scott out of three years of agnosticism, after which he traveled about as a preacher and teacher.

Scott worked with Oral Roberts when Oral Roberts University was being formed. He later joined the faculty of Evangel College (1964–65). In 1966 he assisted with the reorganization of the AG as research director of the Committee on Advance; however, he dropped out of the denomination in 1970.

When Faith Center Church of Glendale, California, and its Faith Broadcasting Network hit difficult times in 1976, the church elected Scott as pastor and president. Scott settled for a one dollar a year salary and an unlimited expense account. His approach to ministry has not been orthodox. His life has been shadowed by accusations of mishandling of funds and irregularities in broadcasting fund-raising techniques. After twenty-three years of marriage, his wife left him, saying she no longer wanted to be associated with him. Despite the controversies surrounding his ministry, his ministry has been popularized through the daily television broadcast "Festival of Faith."

Bibliography: "Dr. W. Eugene Scott and Faith Center Church," AG Archives (c. 1977); "Life and Times of an Electronic Pastor," *Los Angeles Times: View* (August 10, 1980), 1–8. S. Shemeth

SECOND DEFINITE WORK OF GRACE See CHRISTIAN PERFECTION; HOLINESS MOVEMENT.

SEMINARIES AND GRADUATE SCHOOLS The last third of the twentieth century will be noted for a maturing of the Pentecostal movement on the subject of education in general and of theological education in particular. During that period the movement has begun to offer a variety of graduate programs. By the fall of 1987, about 1,300 students were enrolled in eight graduate schools or programs offered within the Pentecostal and charismatic movements.

Much of early Pentecostalism treated education with ambivalence. Theological education was often treated with outright contempt, most probably because of two related factors. First, the Pentecostal renewal did not begin among the highly educated nor within the theological seminaries of the day. It began at the grassroots in small local churches and prayer meetings. Second, those who became Pentecostals in the early days of the movement believed that the general tenor

Students engaged in research at Cordas C. Burnett Library, Assemblies of God Theological Seminary, Springfield, Missouri.

of things in most historic churches and especially in their seminaries was such that they undercut the working of God and deprived the people of God's truth. Seminaries were viewed as preoccupied with the intellectual and as having little regard for experience. As such, those with theological degrees such as the doctor of divinity (D.D.) were sometimes nicknamed "Dumb Dogs," and theological seminaries became theological "cemeteries."

Yet Pentecostals did appreciate and recognize the need for some formal training. Sometimes that took the form of younger people attaching themselves to a local pastor or evangelist in a mentoring relationship. This ultimately led to a series of short-term Bible schools. In a few cases, the "instructor" waited upon God for direction and inspiration and "taught" the class by means of "prophecies" or "interpretations" to utterances in tongues. More frequently, the *Scofield Reference Bible* was adopted as the sole or primary text to which students were given a more or less verse-by-verse exposition.

Initially these schools lasted for six to eight weeks and were run by such men as D. C. O. Opperman or C. F. Parham. These short-term schools, which tended to move from place to place, were soon replaced by longer-term schools, Bible institutes such as those of N. J. Holmes (Greenville, S.C.) or T. K. Leonard (Findlay, Ohio) which charged little tuition and were run almost entirely on a "faith" basis. Teachers were drawn from the ranks of successful evangelists and

pastors who brought a topical, systematic, or expositional approach to the text.

As the movement entered its second generation, some of the early matriarchs and patriarchs had begun to die. That meant finding ways to collect and share their stories and experiences for the edification of the next generation of Pentecostals. At the same time, Pentecostals attempted to relate to the Bible institute movement in Fundamentalism. As a result Pentecostals also established two-year Bible institutes.

In March 1923 Aimee Semple McPherson founded the Lighthouse of International Foursquare Evangelism, better known as L.I.F.E. Bible College, which eventually offered a three-year course of study leading to the bachelor of theology (Th.B.) degree. By 1936 she had clearly moved ahead of her peers by offering a doctor of theology (Th.D.) degree program. It required a high school diploma and a four-year course of study, one more than the Th.B., including four years of Greek and a 20,000-word thesis. In later years the Greek requirement was reduced to three years and a one-year Hebrew requirement was added. The Th.D. was last advertised in 1948, but by 1955 it had produced forty graduates. While the degree ultimately did not measure up to the rigor of accredited Th.D. programs elsewhere, it nonetheless pointed the way toward higher academic standards for Pentecostals.

During the 1940s and 1950s most other Pentecostal Bible institutes followed the leading of their fundamentalist and evangelical peers adopting three- and four-year programs and expanded their schools to become Bible colleges. Many received accreditation from the conservative American Association of Bible Colleges (AABC). A few of the more "progressive" sought regional accreditation. A few shed the name "Bible" and attempted to become fully functional "liberal arts" colleges whose purpose it was to prepare Pentecostal young people for ministry in the arts and science professions without having to face the full force of a "secular" education.

In the Assemblies of God (AG), movement toward a fifth-year B.Th. degree was made at the 1947 general council. The 1945 general council had authorized Central Bible Institute (CBI) to "provide a Full Theological Seminary Course" in addition to the Bible Institute course "as progress and growth" demanded. By 1947 the demand had been identified, and CBI was authorized to offer a fifth-year course beginning in 1949. A 155-semester-hour B.Th. was advertised in the 1948–49 catalog, and the school became known as Central Bible Institute and Seminary (Central Bible College after 1965). By 1957 it had dropped the name "seminary" and established a graduate school of religion. It offered a master of arts in Religion degree, designed to provide "advanced but terminal training" for the "mature student" following the normal Bible college course. Northwest Bible College (now Northwest College of the AG) followed suit in 1958 with the establishment of a graduate division offering a Master of Arts in Theology degree.

When the AABC registered concern that the M.A. was a degree that fell under the jurisdiction

Students from diverse cultures and denominations study at California Theological Seminary, Fresno, California.

of the American Association of Theological Schools (AATS, now the ATS), the standard accreditation agency for seminaries, Northwest College withdrew its offer of the M.A. and replaced it the following year with a five-year bachelor of theology (Th.B.) degree. Central Bible College, however, continued to offer the M.A. in Religion through 1966 when it seemed that the AG would, indeed, establish a seminary.

In 1963, Pentecostal healing evangelist Oral Roberts opened a university in Tulsa, Oklahoma, under his own name and financed by his ministry. It was the first Pentecostal university, and it caught the attention of Donald Gee in *Pentecost* magazine. He wrote that early Pentecostal leaders had justifiably feared an "arid intellectualism" which had damaged many churches out of which these leaders had come. But, he noted, fear "drove them too far." He exhorted his readers to ever higher academic standards on the condition that the "Holy Spirit is honored" and prescribed that those who wished to place academic degrees after their names should earn them by "hard work in a reputable place of learning."

Two years later Oral Roberts added to his university a short-lived Graduate School of Theology. Announced first in 1963, it opened its doors with 29 students on September 7, 1965. Under the leadership of Roberts' long-time friend, R. O. Corvin of the Pentecostal Holiness Church, this program provided an opportunity to study theology at the graduate level within the Pentecostal tradition, but theoretically, at least, not under the auspices of any single Pentecostal denomination. A series of governance, administration, and personality problems quickly developed, however, and this attempt failed in 1969.

It was the largely black Church of God in Christ (CGIC) that actually launched the first successful and fully accredited theological seminary in American Pentecostal history. Intentionally ecumenical from its inception in September

1970, the Charles H. Mason Theological Seminary, under the leadership of founding President-Dean Leonard Lovett, brought Pentecostal students into the mainstream of theological education. The CGIC established its seminary with the larger six-school consortium of black seminaries in Atlanta, Georgia, known as the Interdenominational Theological Center (ITC). The 1986 enrollment for this consortium was 304 students. It is accredited by the ATS and the regional Southern Association of Colleges and Schools (SACS). Students at Mason Seminary may pursue a variety of masters and doctoral (D.Min. and S.T.D.) degrees, sharing a common theological curriculum, classrooms, and faculty with the other member schools of the ITC. They receive from Mason a variety of student services as well as specific course offerings that are distinctive to the history, theology, and polity of the CGIC. Since its opening, the seminary has graduated more than 100 students.

The charismatic renewal was running at full steam when in the autumn of 1973 Melodyland Christian Center in Anaheim, California, under the leadership of Pastor Ralph Wilkerson, established the Melodyland School of Theology. With Presbyterian J. Rodman Williams as its president, a board of regents, and a faculty that drew heavily from the range of charismatic and Pentecostal leadership, the school held great promise of becoming a key training institution for mainline and Pentecostal students who identified with the renewal. It received candidate status with the regional accreditation body in 1977, the Western Association of Schools and College (WASC). It also received associate membership with the ATS. Melodyland offered the M.A. and master of divinity (M.Div.) degrees and by 1979 boasted a student body of 218 drawn from thirty-eight states and twenty-one denominations. It also enrolled more than 70 students from independent charismatic churches.

The academic year 1978–79 brought a series of reversals to this institution that ultimately led to its demise. Questions of its financial integrity and soundness, problems in the governance of the institution in relation to Melodyland Christian Center, and questions of theological orthodoxy were all raised. The latter, raised by Wilkerson, Dr. Walter Martin, and Dr. John W. Montgomery, ultimately proved to be the school's undoing. When the faculty was asked to sign a statement of faith designed by these men and including an "inerrancy of Scripture" clause, many of its members resigned in protest. Most of the school's better students transferred to other seminaries in an attempt to salvage their academic investment. By 1981 the school had ceased to function in any viable way as a graduate school and had changed its name to the American Christian Theological Seminary. By the mid-eighties it ceased to exist.

In 1961 the General Council of the Assemblies of God authorized the executive presbytery and the board of education to establish a graduate school of theology, "as soon as it was deemed feasible." Significant in the discussion was whether to call it a "graduate school of theology" or a "seminary." Because of concern for the

The Church of God School of Theology was founded in 1975 and adjoins Lee College campus in Cleveland, Tennessee.

feelings of many older Pentecostals, it became known as the Assemblies of God Graduate School (AGGS) and opened September 4, 1973, in Springfield, Missouri.

Housed in the administrative headquarters complex of the AG, this theological venture was allowed to expand under the watchful eye of denominational leadership. Offering the M.A. and M.Div. degrees in Biblical Studies, Christian Education, and Missions, the school moved quickly to receive regional accreditation from the North Central Association of Colleges and Schools (NCACS) and received associate status with the ATS. With its 1984 accreditation review came a recommendation that AGGS change its name to reflect more accurately its mission. As a result, in August 1984 it became the Assemblies of God Theological Seminary (AGTS). In 1987 H. Glynn Hall was appointed its first full-time president. Current enrollment is approximately three hundred students.

On September 1, 1975, the Church of God (CG, Cleveland, Tenn.) became the third classical Pentecostal denomination to open its own School of Theology. Housed initially in rented facilities, in 1980 it occupied a newly designed and built facility in Cleveland, Tennessee, adjacent to properties of the CG headquarters building. The School of Theology shares library facilities with the denomination's Lee College, which also acts as a recruitment base for the school. In 1984 the School of Theology received accreditation from the SACS, and in 1987 ATS granted candidate status to the school. The student body is in excess of 250.

After a six-year hiatus a new attempt was made to establish a graduate school of theology at Oral Roberts University in 1975. With United Methodist James Buskirk at the helm as dean, the faculty was more broadly mainline than in the previous attempt. The school sought to be broadly inclusive, choosing the terms "catholic, evangelical, reformed, and charismatic" to describe its philosophy of education, but clearly attempting to integrate elements of a classical theological education into the theological grid of Oral Roberts,

with an interest in the whole person, "body, mind, and spirit."

This second attempt by Oral Roberts has proved to be more successful than the first. The school currently offers the M.A. and M.Div. degrees as well as the doctor of ministry (D.Min.) degree. Yet it has met substantial problems in recent years. Questions of governance, financial stability, and identity as well as morale problems among faculty and staff, with a high turnover rate, have all contributed to the concerns. They are further compounded by the ever-present scrutiny of the president, Oral Roberts. Thus, within the past two years the School of Theology has undergone two name changes and has now received a new dean, Larry Lea, who is attempting to turn it into a School of Theology and Missions with an emphasis on practical ministry in signs and wonders.

In 1977 televangelist Pat Robertson unveiled his vision for graduate charismatic education in the form of CBN University located in Virginia Beach, Virginia. The project received accreditation from SACS in 1984 and currently offers to its nine hundred students master's degrees in five areas of specialization. The College of Theology and Ministry is divided into two schools featuring the same faculty. The School of Biblical Studies is intent upon developing Bible knowledge and hermeneutical skills. It offers the M.A. degree in biblical studies and encourages its students to pursue further academic work. The School of Ministry, on the other hand, attempts to bring an integrative structure that equips for ministry. It is this latter school where the M.Div. and an assortment of M.A. degrees may be undertaken.

CBN seeks to be both interdisciplinary and contemporary, interacting with and transforming contemporary culture. It is housed in an open area on a well-planned campus featuring finely furnished facilities with high-tech, state-of-the-art equipment available only at a well-financed institution.

Southern California College in Costa Mesa, California, a highly successful liberal arts college of the AG, entered the graduate market in 1983 with the establishment of a well-designed graduate studies program. Offering a WASC accredited M.A. degree in religion, the program offers concentrations in biblical studies and in church leadership, providing a background to pastoral ministry or to further study.

The California Theological Seminary was formed in 1984 in Fresno, California. An educational experiment of the People's Church in Fresno, the seminary has hopes of bringing together scholars from a variety of Pentecostal denominations. By 1988 the faculty included members from the AG and the CG. Under the leadership of Del Tarr, the seminary is attempting to provide a multidenominational, charismatic approach to academic training for ministry which is anthropologically and culturally sensitive to the needs of the Third World. Its strength lies in its global vision. In 1987 it formed a relationship with the Asia Theological Centre for Evangelism and Missions (ATCEM) in Singapore. The isolated location of CTS is a factor against the school, which to date has been troubled by low enrollment, financial difficulties, and potential governance issues.

The latest attempt to establish a Pentecostal seminary has been undertaken by a third televangelist, Jimmy Swaggart. Called the Jimmy Swaggart Theological Seminary (JSTS), it is located in Baton Rouge, Louisiana, in proximity to Swaggart's World Ministry Center. Unabashedly conservative, its outlook lies in contrast to that of CBN, as one which stands over *against* contemporary culture. It is considered to be the "advanced academic training division" of Swaggart's multifaceted ministry and is being advertised as lying on the "cutting edge" of world evangelization by incorporating and perpetuating Swaggart's principles of "inerrancy, Pentecostal distinctives, and worldwide evangelism."

JSTS opened in the autumn of 1988 offering the M.A. and M.Div. degrees. Its programs are focused upon practical "hands-on" experience, but their academic components are somewhat restricted by such tone-setting requirements as a course in "Dispensational Theology." An emphasis is planned to provide a variety of team-taught interdisciplinary courses.

There are currently eight overtly Pentecostal-charismatic alternatives available in graduate education in the U.S. today. Because there are several evangelical seminaries such as Gordon-Conwell Theological Seminary (South Hamilton, Mass.) with its Pentecostal president, Robert E. Cooley, and Fuller Theological Seminary in Pasadena, California, with its several Pentecostal and charismatic faculty members and the presence of the David J. du Plessis Center for Christian Spirituality which houses the personal papers of du Plessis and other Pentecostal leaders, Pentecostal or charismatic students are faced with a variety of options that represent quite different emphases, foci, and commitments to academic excellence and freedom of inquiry. See also BIBLE INSTITUTES, COLLEGES, UNIVERSITIES.

Bibliography: D. Gee, "Bible Schools Become Bible 'Colleges'," *Pentecost* 74 (December 1965–February 1966): 18; D. E. Harrell, Jr., *Oral Roberts: An American*

Life (1985); *Oral Roberts University: Graduate and Professional Schools*, 1984–85 and 1985–86; *ORU Academic Programs Catalog*, 1986–88; *CBN University, Graduate Catalog*, 1987–88; *Assemblies of God Graduate School Catalog*, 1978–80; *AGTS 1986–88 Catalog*, vol. 11:2; *Southern California College 1984–86 Graduate Studies Bulletin; Church of God School of Theology Catalog*, 1985–87 and 1987–88; K. Yurica, "Dissonance Jars the Melodyland Harmony," *CT* 23 (5, 1978): 46–47; "Melodyland Lingers: Is the Song Ended?" *CT* 23 (6, 1978), 42; *Melodyland School of Theology Catalog*, 1980–1982; *Jimmy Swaggart Theological Seminary Academic Catalog*, 1988–89; "Jimmy Swaggart Theological Seminary Mission. Philosophy, Objectives, and Distinctives," *The Evangelist* 19 (December 12, 1987), 22–23.

C. M. Robeck, Jr.

An evangelist and missionary, Robert J. Semple served in China only a few months before contracting malaria where he died in 1910. His wife Aimee Semple (McPherson) later became an evangelist and founded the International Church of the Foursquare Gospel.

SEMPLE, ROBERT JAMES (1881–1910). Evangelist and missionary. Semple was born to Scotch-Irish parents who ran the general store near Magherafelt, thirty miles from Belfast, North Ireland. One of five children, including two brothers (Samuel and William) and two sisters (Marion and Maggie), Robert was reared in a Presbyterian family. At age seventeen he immigrated to the U.S., landing first in New York, where he was employed in a variety of menial jobs—dishwasher, street and hallway sweep, then as clothes salesman. In a short time he moved to Chicago, where he was employed at Marshall Fields Department Store. While there, Semple entered the fledgling Pentecostal movement through a small storefront mission, most probably that of William H. Durham. By late 1907 Semple, a six-foot-six-inch, handsome and eloquent speaker, had launched into an evangelistic ministry, first in Toronto, then in Ingersoll near Salford, where he met Aimee Elizabeth Kennedy. From there he went to Stratford. Returning to Ingersoll, where he had held meetings through the winter of 1908, Robert Semple married Aimee on August 12, 1908, in a ceremony conducted by Lt.-Col. John D. Sharp of the Salvation Army. Following their honeymoon they returned to Stratford, where Robert worked as a boilermaker in a locomotive factory during the day and preached in the evening. Next they moved to London, Ontario, where they pioneered a church, then on to Chicago, where on January 2, 1909, Robert Semple was ordained by William H. Durham.

The Semples remained with Durham at the North Avenue Mission for several months of teaching and service. They accompanied him on evangelistic tours in Findlay, Ohio, and in several Canadian towns. The couple had anticipated a full-time ministry of faith as missionaries in China, and the Italians at Durham's mission provided their initial financial backing. Leaving Chicago in 1910 they again ministered in Canada, then sailed the *Empress of Ireland* from St. John's, New Brunswick, to Liverpool, England. They went north to Belfast, where Robert Semple held a three-week evangelistic crusade. Aimee reported forty converts to Pentecostalism there, and the mayor of Belfast met Semple, giving him the key to the city. From Ireland, the Semples journeyed to London for a one-week stay with Cecil Polhill.

The Semples sailed from London to Hong Kong by way of the Suez Canal, stopping at a number of ports on the way, where they kept abreast of the many Pentecostal news reports. Arriving in Hong Kong, they were plunged into a foreign culture and climate that soon took its toll. Robert engaged in literature distribution and preached through an interpreter. The couple also immersed themselves in Cantonese language study. On a trip to Macao, Robert contracted malaria. He was returned to Hong Kong by steamer and transferred to an English sanitarium, where he died on August 19, 1910, shortly after their second wedding anniversary. Robert Semple was buried in the Happy Valley Cemetery in Hong Kong. Aimee gave birth to their daughter, Roberta Star Semple, just six weeks later, on September 17, 1910.

Bibliography: G. G. Kulbeck, *What God Hath Wrought* (1958); N. B. Mavity, *Sister Aimee* (1931); A. S. McPherson, *This is That* (1919); idem, *The Story of My Life* (1951); idem, *In the Service of the King* (1927).
C. M. Robeck, Jr.

SERPENT HANDLING The practice of endangering one's health by committing dangerous feats is not new to church history. Predecessors paralleling classical Pentecostals who were so engaged included the following: Madame Guyon (seventeenth century), the Camisards (early eighteenth century), and the Convulsionaries (eighteenth century). The origin of serpent handling among classical Pentecostals centers around the person of George Went Hensley. His 1910 Spirit baptism was accomplished in a Church of God (CG, Cleveland, Tenn.) congregation. He became

quite interested in Mark 16:18, and while praying on White Oak Mountain he told the Lord to let him find a serpent if it was God's will to handle it. Soon he noticed a timber rattler, which he handled without difficulty then and at the next church service. Hensley eventually brought this practice to the local Church of God in Cleveland, Tennessee, with the approval of A. J. Tomlinson. Hensley joined the CG in 1912, and the resultant problems led A. J. Tomlinson, in his 1917 annual address, to say that handling serpents and fire were acceptable "under the proper conditions" but that such experiences were not "a test of salvation." In the meantime, a sister denomination which was losing members to the CG, the Pentecostal Holiness Church, denounced all such behavior as "fanaticisms." By 1922 Hensley was no longer a member of the CG.

Handling serpents can range from wrapping these poisonous creatures around necks, stuffing them into shirts, rubbing them over faces, or walking on them with barefeet, and then throwing them to a fellow worshiper.

Practitioners of serpent handling also engage in other potentially life-threatening stunts, such as drinking poison or handling fire. The strychnine or other poison that is drunk usually is diluted but is still lethal. The fire can come from self-made fire bombs and is applied directly to any exposed portion of the body. The majority of those who actually do these things are men. The practice became so widespread that by the late 1930s some states — Kentucky, Georgia, Virginia, Tennessee, North Carolina, and Alabama — started passing legislation prohibiting such activity. By the 1940s the practitioners received national attention through the coverage of magazines like *Newsweek* and *Time* along with the *New York Times*. Outside observers were surprised to learn that very few people had died from snake bites despite the fact that some communicants had been bitten several times. Steven Kane counts sixty-one deaths from snake bites between 1934 and 1978 and five from the drinking of strychnine. The use of fire resulted in some physical harm, but apparently no deaths were recorded during this time. Typically, most incidents of these practices leave the person without bite or without hairs singed and free from pain or harm. In the earliest years it was the scoffers who brought snakes to the meetings, but most recently the practitioners of serpent handling hunt for snakes between April and September. Reportedly no deaths have resulted from these annual hunts. Once captured, the snakes are fed and bathed regularly.

The devotees of serpent handling, fire contact, and strychnine drinking are adamant that these things are commanded in Scripture. Passages like Exodus 4:2–4; Job 26:13; Luke 10:19; and Acts 28:3–5 are used along with the suggestion that John 20:30 implies that Jesus himself handled venomous serpents. The principle text is Mark 16:18, and none of these people know, or would believe, that this is not part of the original text of the Gospel of Mark. Their doctrine of the "anointing" means that they refuse to do any of these things without this perceived direct intervention from God. Usually the "anointing" is

A church member tests his faith by handling a venomous snake during a revival meeting at the Holiness Church of God In Jesus' Name, Kingston, Georgia. These people believe that they are commanded to handle snakes according to Mark 16:8: "They shall take up serpents . . . it shall not hurt them."

thought to be present in the midst of a demonstrative worship service that includes loud music, tongues speech, and physical agitations. When someone is bitten and dies, one of the following explanations may be offered: (1) The anointing was not present. This is a primary concern about photographers and their distraction and about insincere practitioners. (2) Such deaths prove to outsiders that the snakes have not been defanged—some have handled deadly Indian cobras. (3) God wills their death. It could be a punishment, and others add that their refusal to use medicine that could have saved them brings glory to God. Sometimes snakes are handled at the funeral of the one who died from a snakebite.

Despite the ridicule of fellow Christians and the laws passed against these practices, they continue to this day. The number of adherents is not large, and they are from the lower spectrum of the socioeconomic ladder and are geographically centered in the Appalachians. These practices are not sanctioned by any international Pentecostal denomination.

Bibliography: K. W. Carden and R. W. Pelton, *The Persecuted Prophets* (1976); "Holy Ghost People" (n.d.); *Appalachian Journal* 1 (Spring 1974): 255–62; S. M. Kane, "Snake Handlers of Southern Appalachia" (1979).   H. D. Hunter

SERVANT PUBLICATIONS   See CHARISMATIC COMMUNITIES.

SEVENTH DAY PENTECOSTAL CHURCH OF THE LIVING GOD Founded in Washington, D.C., in the 1940s by Charles Gamble, this church has remained in that area and nearby states. Theologically it confesses the "oneness" of the Godhead, immersion baptism exclusively in the name of Jesus Christ, speaking in other tongues as the initial sign of Holy Spirit baptism, physical healing available in the Atonement, and the bodily physical return of the Lord Jesus Christ prior to the establishment of a millennial kingdom.

The Scriptures of the Bible are interpreted in a literal fashion. Believers observe a sabbatarian week. Though there is no affiliation per se with other Pentecostal and sabbatarian groups, limited fellowship with like-minded believers is practiced.

An active membership of about one thousand was reported in 1979.

Bibliography: A. C. Piepkorn, *Profiles in Belief*, vol. 3 (1979).   J. A. Hewett

SEYMOUR, WILLIAM JOSEPH (1870–1922). Prominent early Pentecostal leader and pastor of the Azusa Street Mission. William Joseph Seymour, the leading figure in the Azusa Street Pentecostal revival in Los Angeles in 1906–09, was born in Centerville, Louisiana, on May 2, 1870, to former slaves Simon and Phillis Seymour. Raised as a Baptist, Seymour was given to dreams and visions as a young man. Although little is recorded about his early life, it is known

One of the most influential and respected early Pentecostal leaders, William J. Seymour played a key role in the Azusa Street revival and the development of the Pentecostal movement. Seymour had moved to California after sitting under the teaching of Charles F. Parham in Houston.

William J. Seymour was only 52 when he died in 1922. He is buried in Evergreen Cemetery, Los Angeles; nearby are buried Charles Price Jones, the hymn writer, and Ivey G. Campbell, an early Pentecostal evangelist.

that he migrated to Indianapolis, Indiana, in 1895, where he took a job as a waiter in a fashionable restaurant. While in Indianapolis, he joined a local black congregation of the Methodist Episcopal Church.

From 1900 to 1902, Seymour lived in Cincinnati, Ohio, where he came in contact with the Holiness movement under the influence of the "God's Revivalist" movement founded by Martin Wells Knapp (1853–1901). Accepting the Holiness emphasis on entire sanctification, Seymour joined the Church of God Reformation movement, also known as the "Evening Light Saints." Founded in 1880 by Daniel S. Warner (1853–1895), the church was headquartered in Anderson, Indiana, and stressed the probability of a great outpouring of the Holy Spirit before the rapture of the church.

While Seymour was in Indianapolis, he contracted smallpox, which left him without the use of his left eye. While reflecting on his illness, he accepted a call to preach and in a short time was licensed and ordained as a minister of the "Evening Light Saints" movement.

In 1903 Seymour moved to Houston, Texas, in search of his family. Here he began to attend a Holiness church pastored by Lucy Farrow. When Pastor Farrow went to Kansas in 1905 to work as a governess in the home of Charles Fox Parham (1873–1929), a Holiness preacher who had been leading a Pentecostal movement in the Midwest since 1901, Seymour was asked to become pastor of the church. In October 1905 Farrow returned to Houston with a new experience of speaking in tongues, which she had accepted under Parham's influence. By December 1905 Parham moved his

Bible School to Houston, where he taught that the "initial evidence" of receiving the baptism in the Holy Spirit was speaking in tongues.

Ever hungry for biblical training, Seymour enrolled in Parham's school, despite the prevailing system of racial segregation in the South. To satisfy southern law and mores, Seymour was permitted to sit in a hall where he could hear the classes through the doorway. Under Parham's teaching Seymour accepted the premise that glossolalia was a present-day sign of the baptism in the Holy Spirit, although he himself did not receive the experience at the time.

While in the Houston church, Seymour was visited by Neely Terry, a young woman from a Holiness church in Los Angeles. She invited him to visit her California congregation with the possibility of becoming pastor. The church, which was connected with the Southern California Holiness Association, was founded and pastored by Julia W. Hutchins. On his way to Los Angeles, Seymour stayed in the Pillar of Fire headquarters in Denver led by Alma White. In his first sermon in Los Angeles, Seymour preached on Acts 2:4, and to the dismay of Pastor Hutchins, he announced the necessity of speaking in other tongues as evidence of the Pentecostal experience. Because of opposition from the Holiness Association, Hutchins was forced to find refuge in the home of Richard Asberry on Bonnie Brae Avenue.

After several weeks of prayer meetings in the Asberry home, Seymour and others received the sought-for tongues experience, an event that sparked an intense revival. For a time, services were held on the front porch, where Seymour preached to crowds gathered in the streets. As the numbers increased, larger quarters were obviously needed if the services were to continue. A search of the downtown area of Los Angeles turned up an old building at 312 Azusa Street that had formerly been an African Methodist Episcopal church but had been more recently used as a stable and warehouse.

On April 14, 1906, Seymour held his first service on Azusa Street. On April 18, the day of the San Francisco earthquake, the first report in the Los Angeles Times spoke of "a weird babble of tongues" amid "wild scenes" in the mission. By May more than a thousand persons were trying to enter the small 40-by-60-foot mission to witness the scenes that rivaled those of Cane Ridge a century earlier.

The central feature at Azusa Street, however, was glossolalia, which electrified the services and attracted many to the altars to receive "the baptism." An observer at these early meetings was Frank Bartleman (1871–1935), whose diary indicated links between the Los Angeles Pentecost and the Welsh revival.

Since Seymour recognized Parham as his "spiritual father," and the "projector of the movement," he invited the Kansas evangelist to hold a "union revival" in October 1906. When Parham arrived he was repelled by the noisy demonstrations and the perceived influence of spiritualists in the meetings. His attempts at correction only alienated Seymour and his followers. The two suffered an irreparable break when Parham was rejected by the Azusa Street elders.

Despite this rupture, the revival continued with increasing force. By the end of 1906 Seymour officially incorporated his ministry as the Pacific Apostolic Faith Movement and began publication of a periodical titled the *Apostolic Faith,* which soon mushroomed to 50,000 subscribers, many of whom lived outside the U.S.

Soon visitors from around the nation and from foreign lands journeyed to Los Angeles to receive their own Pentecostal experience. Azusa Street pilgrims included William H. Durham and John C. Sinclair, who brought the Pentecostal message to Chicago; G. B. Cashwell, who spread the message in the Holiness churches of the Southeast; and C. H. Mason, who brought the Pentecostal movement to the Church of God in Christ, a mostly black church based in Memphis, Tennessee. Other important American pilgrims included Rachel Sizelove, Glenn Cook, D. W. Kerr, and Marie Burgess.

Those entering the ranks of the Pentecostals outside the U.S. influenced by the Azusa Street meetings included Thomas Ball Barratt of Norway, Canon Harford Battersby and Cecil Polhill of England, Pandita Ramabai of India, and A. H. Argue and R. E. McAlister of Canada.

For three years the Azusa Street meetings continued with increasing force and influence. Meetings were held three times a day, seven days a week. In the pages of the *Apostolic Faith* Seymour wrestled with the theological implications of the tongues-attested Pentecostal experience. Here he demonstrated a grasp of theology that marked him as a pioneer formulator of the new Holiness-Pentecostal theology that characterized the movement in its beginnings.

Seymour's influence mushroomed as the Pentecostal movement quickly spread around the world. Missionaries sent from Azusa Street included A. G. Garr (1874–1944), who went to India in 1907 expecting to preach to the natives in unknown tongues, as taught by Parham and Seymour. After failing in this attempt, Garr went on to Hong Kong, where he experienced success using more traditional linguistic methods. Despite this failure, outstanding Pentecostal revivals were reported from such far-off places as Jerusalem, India, China, Europe, South America, and the islands of the sea.

The unity of Seymour's Azusa Street revival was remarkable in that people of practically every nationality, race, and culture attended the services. This unique mixing of blacks and whites under Seymour's leadership caused Bartleman to exult, "The color line has been washed away by the blood." Women's ministries were also encouraged. Helping Seymour were several white women who aided him in publishing the magazine. These included Clara Lum and Florence Crawford (1872–1936).

Seymour's style of leadership was one of meekness. He encouraged freedom in the Spirit and often sat with his head covered behind the rough shoe boxes used as a makeshift pulpit. His speaking ministry was not in the tradition of black pulpit oratory but was more that of a teacher.

By 1908 Seymour's leadership of the movement was crippled when Lum and Crawford took the mailing list for the *Apostolic Faith* with them to their Portland, Oregon, headquarters. This was done in part because of Seymour's marriage to Jenny Moore on May 13, 1908, which Lum and Crawford opposed because of the shortness of time before the rapture of the church. Without the mailing list Seymour could not communicate with the thousands of persons who looked to him and Azusa Street for leadership.

A further erosion in Seymour's leadership came in 1911 when Durham returned to the mission to promote his new "finished work" teaching, which directly attacked Seymour's position that sanctification was a "second work of grace" necessary before one could speak in tongues. When it seemed that Durham was about to usurp his leadership, Seymour returned from an eastern preaching tour and padlocked the mission against Durham and his followers. Those who followed Durham's teaching eventually organized the Assemblies of God denomination in 1914.

The struggles with Parham, Crawford, and Durham effectively ended Seymour's major role of leadership in the Pentecostal movement. This also ended Seymour's dream of an interracial Pentecostal movement that would serve as a positive witness to a racially segregated America.

By 1914, with the outbreak of World War I, Azusa Street had become a local black church with an occasional white visitor. For several years after the war Seymour and a retinue of about twenty followers held revival campaigns across America. In 1915 he revised the Doctrines and Discipline and the Constitution of the church to recognize him as "bishop" of the Pacific Apostolic Faith movement, including a provision that his successors would always be "a man of color."

When Seymour died on September 28, 1922, in Los Angeles, his wife continued as pastor of the Azusa Mission. For years afterward the Azusa Street property was tied up in court battles over nonpayment of taxes. After Mrs. Seymour's death in 1936, the mission was sold for tax liens and ultimately torn down to make a parking lot in the Little Tokyo section of Los Angeles.

For decades after his death Seymour's role in the origins of the Pentecostal movement was largely ignored as the movement gained ground among whites and in many Third World nations. But in recent years Seymour's place as the catalyst of the worldwide Pentecostal movement has been assured. Practically every early Pentecostal movement in the world can trace its origins directly or indirectly to Seymour's Azusa Street Mission.

See also AZUSA STREET REVIVAL; BLACK HOLINESS–PENTECOSTALISM.

Bibliography: D. Nelson, "For Such a Time as This: The Story of Bishop William J. Seymour and the Azusa Street Revival" (1981); V. Synan, *Holiness-Pentecostal Movement in the United States* (1971); J. Tinney, "William J. Seymour: Father of Modern-Day Pentecostalism," in R. Burkett and R. Newman, eds., *Black Apostles* (1978).   H. V. Synan

SHAKARIAN, DEMOS (1913–). Dairy farmer and founder of the Full Gospel Business Men's Fellowship International (FGBMFI).

Demos Shakarian is of Armenian descent. His family escaped the Armenian holocaust due to a warning from a Pentecostal prophet whom God had raised up to warn the Armenian people of disaster that would come upon them. The Shakarian family heeded the words of the prophet and fled to America. Shakarian grew up in the Armenian Pentecostal Church and gave his heart to God as a young man. When he experienced the baptism of the Holy Spirit in 1926 at age thirteen, he also received a healing for his impaired hearing.

A successful California dairyman, Demos Shakarian had been reared in a Pentecostal home. With encouragement from Oral Roberts, Shakarian founded the Full Gospel Business Men's Fellowship International.

In 1933 Shakarian married Rose Gabrielian in a traditionally arranged Armenian wedding. Since their wedding, Rose and Demos have devoted their lives to serving God in any way they could and felt led to sponsor revival meetings to bring the message of Jesus to their community. During this time Shakarian became friends with Dr. Charles S. Price through the remarkable healing of Shakarian's sister who had been severely injured in an automobile accident and was not expected to live. (Dr. Price laid hands on Shakarian's sister and as her body shook for twenty minutes under the power of God her shattered pelvis was healed. The next morning new X-rays revealed a completely restored pelvis in place of the crushed and dislocated one of the day before.)

As God prospered the Shakarians through their dairy farm (one of the largest private dairies in the world) Shakarian continued to support and work in revival meetings. In 1951 after helping set up Oral Roberts' Los Angeles crusade, he told Roberts of his feeling that God was leading him to start a group called the Full Gospel Business Men's Fellowship International. Roberts agreed to attend the first meeting of the group, held at Clifton's cafeteria, and prayed an anointed prayer that called for this group to be a mighty force for the spread of the gospel. However, Shakarian experienced a year of frustration until, in a night of prayer, God gave him a vision of the work God would do in the world through this group. As he led meetings, God would direct him to the individuals he should call upon to give testimony. As businessmen told the story of how God was working in their lives and businesses, many of their friends were converted and the goal of sharing Christ in an organization of businessmen was realized. The FGBMFI has spread the message of the fullness of the Spirit and the truth of divine healing as well as the message of salvation. The FGBMFI has grown to have chapters in 87 countries with over three hundred thousand members. In 1984 Demos suffered a stroke that left him with some impairment but he continues in an advisory capacity.

See also FULL GOSPEL BUSINESS MEN'S FELLOWSHIP INTERNATIONAL.

Bibliography: B. Bird, "The Legacy of Demos Shakarian," *Charisma* (June 1986), 20–25; D. Shakarian, *The Happiest People on Earth* (1975); J. R. Zeigler

SHAKERS The followers of Ann Lee (1736–81), who immigrated from England to Watervliet, New York, with eight sympathizers in 1774, the Shakers introduced a version of millenarian perfectionism within a communal setting. The wife of a blacksmith in Manchester, Lee was the mother of four children, all of whom died in infancy. Her subsequent emotional distress found relief in religious enthusiasm. She was deeply influenced by radical Quakers and French Camisard prophets, and she concluded that she was the second appearing of Christ. A concomitant interest in an end times restoration of spiritual gifts to the church resulted in her espousal of healing and tongues.

In 1787 Lee organized her followers as the United Society of Believers in Christ's Second Appearing. Given her own unhappy marriage, it is hardly surprising that she taught them that the source of evil was the sex act and that Christians who coveted perfection should eliminate greed, pride, and sex. By regulating every minute detail of daily existence, substituting communal property for private possessions, and enjoining celibacy, Shaker communities responded to these issues.

The Shakers generally gained adherents during periods of local revival, when they challenged converts with their call to perfection. After 1787 the spontaneity and enthusiasm that marked religious gatherings under Ann Lee yielded to systematized doctrine and elaborate regulation under the supervision of Lee's successor, Joseph Meacham. As awakenings spread across the northern states after the Revolutionary War, the Shakers experienced rapid growth. They moved westward to reap a harvest from the revivals that focused in Cane Ridge, Kentucky. By 1825 there were Shaker communities in Ohio, Indiana, and

This old engraving shows the Shakers at their dance of worship, from which their name was derived. In their dances they "shook off sin" and "trampled evil underfoot" to rid themselves of sexual desire.

Kentucky as well as in New England and New York. Membership surged to approximately six thousand. For several years after 1837 spiritualism flourished in Shaker settings. The waning of revival fervor combined with internal tensions to discourage further growth. The prosperous Shaker communities merged until only one active but dying community remains.

During Lee's lifetime, Shaker services resembled early Quaker gatherings. Visitors reported that spiritual gifts operated and that these gifts validated the message of Christ's second appearing. Reports of signs, visions, prophecies, and gifts attracted the curious and convinced some; others considered Lee's personal dealings compellingly persuasive.

Lee's message was essentially restorationist: the primitive church had lost the gifts, but an end-time restoration had been promised. It was being realized in the 1780s. After Lee's death, religious enthusiasm was channeled into ritualistic dance, and tongues speech was confined to "quick meetings" held during the Christmas holiday season.

Bibliography: E. D. Andrews, *The People Called Shakers* (1953); G. H. Williams and E. L. Waldvogel (Blumhofer), "Speaking in Tongues and Related Gifts," *The Charismatic Movement,* ed. M. Hamilton (1975), 81–84.   E. L. Blumhofer

SHARING OF MINISTRIES ABROAD (SOMA) SOMA began in 1978 at the first Anglican Conference on Spiritual Renewal held in Canterbury, U.K. Leaders gathered from twenty-five countries believed that the Lord was directing them to share the blessings and power of the Holy Spirit with the body of Christ worldwide. The Reverend Canon Michael Harper left his ministry at the Fountain Trust to accept leadership of SOMA as its executive director. SOMA's international council included Bill Burnett, Everett L. Fullam, and Charles M. Irish.

The leaders' vision for SOMA was a fresh approach to overseas mission. They envisioned one part of the body of Christ sharing with another so as to empower the local church to do God's work among its own people. As a first step, a series of international conferences were organized; they were held in Singapore in 1981; Limuru, Kenya, in 1983; and Suva, Fiji, in 1984. A second step was the sending out of clergy and lay teams, at its own expense, to minister in various countries in the context of short-term missions. SOMA then developed affiliated organizations in the U.S., Canada, and Far East.

C. M. Irish

SHEPHERDING MOVEMENT (Discipleship Controversy). When the Protestant charismatic movement burgeoned in the 1960s, the majority of adherents maintained denominational affiliation. It was not long before many charismatics were changing churches. They went to Protestant churches that accommodated charismatics or to Pentecostal churches, like the Assemblies of God (AG), that readily received charismatics. There had been a few independent charismatic churches prior to 1960, but by the 1970s these churches became a faction with which to reckon. Several organizations feigning nondenominationalism rose up to deal with this increased fragmentation. By the middle of the decade, one such group would be the center of one of the most violent controversies in Protestant charismatic history.

The central organization of those committed to a form of "shepherding" was the Christian Growth Ministries (CGM) headquartered in Fort Lauderdale, Florida. This came out of the 1969 Holy Spirit Teaching Mission that originally published *New Wine*. There were six men—Derek Prince, Bob Mumford, Charles Simpson, Don Basham, Ern Baxter, and John Poole—who were propagating a government of delegated authority and covenant loyalty. The key players were Mumford, Simpson, Basham, and Prince. Mumford, converted through the ministries of the AG, had attended Reformed Episcopal Seminary and pastored while teaching at Elim Bible Institute. Simpson, formerly a Southern Baptist minister, after receiving his B.D. degree, experienced Spirit baptism in 1964 through the ministry of Ken Sumrall. An ordained Disciples of Christ minister, Basham earned a B.D. from Phillips University Graduate Seminary and later pastored. Prince received a master's degree in philosophy from King's College, Cambridge University, worked with Pentecostal churches in the 1950s, and after engendering considerable controversy over his demonology, quickly moved to the Full Gospel Business Men's Fellowship International (FGBMFI) circuit. The notoriety and influence of these men, in addition to the circulation of *New Wine*, along with books like Mumford's *The Problem of Doing Your Own Thing* (1973), made their discipleship doctrines a national phenomenon.

Because they were concerned about the increasing numbers of nomadic charismatics who were free from any system of accountability, they taught a covenant love that evidenced devotion to God by submission to some man. They had a national network of followers who formed pyramids of sheep and shepherds. Down through the pyramid went the orders, it was alleged, while up the same pyramid went the tithes. The use of masculine language here is deliberate, as Basham made clear when he spoke of conforming women to the "sheltered, protected role God has reserved for them." These roles include: the ministry of spiritual gifts when under proper covering of authority as they minister, ministry in the company of their husbands to whom they are properly subject, and the teaching of younger women by older women.

The year 1975 was a time of national turmoil for the Protestant charismatic movement. Pat Robertson banned the CGM leaders and erased all tapes that included them. Robertson used CBN to pronounce the shepherding teaching "witchcraft" and said the only difference between the discipleship group and Jonestown was "Kool-Aid." Kathryn Kuhlman refused to appear together with Bob Mumford at the 1975 Conference on the Holy Spirit in Jerusalem. Demos Shakarian and the director of FGBMFI declared the CGM leaders persona non grata. The number of voices swelled as criticism came from Dennis Bennett, Ken Sumrall, Thomas F. Zimmerman, and David du Plessis.

The heat of the controversy can be captured by reading an open letter, dated June 27, 1975, from Pat Robertson to Bob Mumford. Robertson said that in a recent visit to Louisville, Kentucky, he found cultish language like "submission" rather than churches, "shepherds" not pastors, and "relationships" but not Jesus. Robertson traveled to ORU and found a twenty-year-old "shepherd" who drew tithes from fellow students as part of their submission. Robertson, drawing from Juan Carlos Ortiz's *Call to Discipleship*, charged the leaders with placing personal revelations (*rhēma*) on par with Scripture. He quoted a devotee as saying, "If God Almighty spoke to me, and I knew for a certainty that it was God speaking, and if my shepherd told me to do the opposite, I would obey my shepherd." Robertson claimed that communicants had complete latitude in choosing from a broad spectrum of possible shepherds but once engaged had to reveal intimate details of their lives.

An important meeting of concerned charismatic leaders convened December 16–17, 1975, in Ann Arbor, Michigan. Things did not improve, and on March 18, 1976, several gathered again in Oklahoma City, with the shepherding movement as their primary focus. Michael Harper would later comment that the CGM leaders held their fire when others were shooting recklessly at them. CGM had been seeking reconciliation, clarification, and correction, and so Prince read a letter that summarized some of what they had been saying. As Kilian McDonnell noted, it made 1976 the watershed year.

CGM accepted responsibility for the excesses of those influenced by them, and they printed their side of well-traveled horror stories. One example was a young convert whom CGM stopped from handing out tracts on the beach. CGM explained that the young man in question was a recent convert from the Jesus movement who spent all of his time on the beach handing out tracts while failing to provide adequate support for his wife and young child. The young man was advised to get a job, support his family, and pass out tracts as best possible. In 1976 Prince released the small book *Discipleship, Shepherding, Commitment* that enumerated four safeguards: Scripture is the final authority, anyone seeking leadership positions should be properly tested, a leader must submit to a group of his peers, and Christ will promote or remove. Mumford contributed to moderation by articulating seven principles for balance, such as pointing to the struggle between mindless collectivism and rugged individualism.

By the end of the decade Fort Lauderdale was abandoned by CGM, and the stronghold became Charles Simpson's eight-hundred-member Gulf Coast Covenant Church in Mobile, Alabama. Prince was the first openly to break with the group. Against their original advice, he married a Jewess and built a house in Jerusalem but later returned to Florida. In 1986 the remnant of CGM announced that they were no longer tied together organizationally—Basham in Ohio, Baxter and Mumford in different parts of California—and that *New Wine* would be discontinued. Nevertheless, in 1977 the leaders pulled together to bring one of the largest segments to the Pentecostal-charismatic conference in Kansas City (a total of 50,000 people attended). They have done the same for the 1986 and 1987 Congresses on the Holy Spirit and World Evangelization held in New Orleans. There remain numerous affiliated Covenant churches making the whole a protodenomination.

See also HOLY SPIRIT TEACHING MISSION; INTEGRITY COMMUNICATIONS.

Bibliography: J. Buckingham, "Changing Attitudes Among Discipleship Leaders," *Buckingham Report* 1 (6, March 20, 1985): 1ff.; K. McDonnell, ed., *Presence, Power, Praise: Documents on the Charismatic Renewal* 2 (1980); S. Strang, "The Discipleship Controversy Three Years Later," *Charisma* (September 1978), 14ff.

H. D. Hunter

SHERRILL, JOHN LEWIS (1923–) **AND ELIZABETH** (1928–). Authors and ghost writers for several charismatic best sellers. The Sherrills were married in 1947 and worked as freelance writers for some years. John was senior editor for *Guideposts* from 1951 to 1969. Around 1961 he contacted H. Bredesen for a possible article but realized the resurgence of glossolalia in the twentieth century required a book. During its writing, Sherrill, an Episcopalian, was himself baptized in the Spirit. The resulting book, *They Speak With Other Tongues* (1964), with its autobiographical element, became a best seller. Possibly even more influential in the charismatic movement was *The Cross and the Switchblade* (1963), on which the Sherrills worked with David Wilkerson. They also collaborated on Brother Andrew's *God's Smuggler* (1967) and Corrie ten Boom's *The Hiding Place* (1975). Elizabeth has also acted as editor for other well-known authors, such as Catherine Marshall and Charles Colson.

Bibliography: "John and Elizabeth Sherrill Tell Their Own Story," *Charisma* (September 1985), 64–70.

P. D. Hocken

SHIELDS, ANN ELIZABETH (1939–). Popular teacher in Catholic Charismatic Renewal. Professed as a Sister of Mercy in 1960, Sr. Ann was baptized in the Spirit in January 1971. Frequent speaker at national and international conferences, she has a gift for simple and challenging presentation. She was a member of the National Service Committee (1978–84) and has coauthored (with M. Scanlan) *And Their Eyes Were Opened—Encountering Jesus in the Sacraments* (1976). From its inception in 1983, Shields has been a member of the F.I.R.E. team and edits

the F.I.R.E. magazine. She resigned from the Mercy Sisters in 1984, following disagreement with the changing direction of the order, and now heads the Servants of God's Love, an ecumenical group of consecrated women in the Word of God community, Ann Arbor, Michigan.   P. D. Hocken

SHLEMON, BARBARA LEAHY (1936–). Catholic charismatic and editor. Born in Canton, Ohio, Barbara Leahy obtained a diploma in nursing in 1957, marrying Ben Shlemon the same year. Mother of five children, she was one of the first Catholics to receive the baptism in the Spirit, which happened at Trinity Episcopal Church, Wheaton, Illinois, in March 1965. Schlemon developed a healing ministry, working with F. MacNutt and later the Linn brothers. A founding member of the Association of Christian Therapists in 1976, she became editor of the *Journal of Christian Healing* (1977–80). In 1980 Shlemon was cofounder of a House of Prayer in Clearwater, Florida. She is the author of *Healing Prayer* (with D. and M. Linn, 1976); *To Heal As Jesus Healed* (1978); *Healing the Hidden Self* (1982); and *Living Each Day by the Power of Faith* (1986).   P. D. Hocken

SIBERIAN SEVEN A Pentecostal *cause célèbre* of five years' duration ended happily on June 28, 1983, when sixteen members of the Vashchenko family (five of whom had spent all of the preceding five years in the U.S. embassy in Moscow) were reunited in Israel. Still in the Soviet Union, but soon to be granted exit visas also, were Maria Chmykhalov and her son, Timofei. The so-called Siberian Seven, these members of two peasant families of Chernogorsk in Siberia had been for many years at the forefront of a struggle with Soviet bureaucrats for religious freedom. In 1963 Augustina Vashchenko (her husband then in the third year of confinement in a labor camp) joined thirty-one other Pentecostals in requesting exit visas from the U.S. embassy in Moscow. Powerless to comply, embassy officials persuaded the petitioners to return home. Fifteen years of persecution (labor camp, prison, job discrimination, and forced relocation) followed. Not knowing that to emigrate a Soviet citizen must have a formal invitation from a close relative abroad, they tried again on June 27, 1978. Denied, the seven fled into the U.S. embassy and refused to leave. (One Vashchenko son was arrested in the process and imprisoned.) Notoriety gained for them by news coverage and interested groups in the West resulted in standing invitations to the U.S., Canada, the U.K., and Sweden. Numerous appeals to the American government to place pressure on the Soviet authorities proved fruitless, as did hearings in 1981 and 1982 by the U.S. Senate and House of Representatives. The breaking of the deadlock came from the seven themselves. On December 25, 1982, Mrs. Vashchenko and her daughter, Lidiya, went on a hunger strike. Hospitalized, Lidiya agreed to return to Chernogorsk, where she successfully applied for an exit visa. Once she was in Israel, the others decided to follow a similar course.

Bibliography: T. Chmykhalov, *The Last Christian: The Release of the Siberian Seven* (1986); idem, *Release!* (1984); J. Pollock, *The Siberian Seven* (1979); U.S. Congress. House Judiciary Committee. *Siberian Seven; Hearing, December 16, 1982* (1983); U.S. Congress. Senate Judiciary Committee. *Relief of Seven Soviet Pentecostals; Hearing, November 19, 1981* (1982); L. Vashchenko, *Cry Freedom* (1987).   C. E. Jones

SIGNS AND WONDERS See GIFTS OF THE SPIRIT; LUKE–ACTS; PAULINE LITERATURE; CHURCH GROWTH; THIRD WAVE.

SIMPSON, ALBERT BENJAMIN (1843–1919). Founder of the Christian and Missionary Alliance (1897). Born in 1843 at Bayview, Prince Edward Island. Following his graduation in 1865 from Knox College in Toronto, Ontario, Simpson was ordained into the Presbyterian ministry and served churches in Hamilton, Ontario (1865–73); Louisville, Kentucky (1874–79); and New York City (1879–81). He resigned as pastor of Thirteenth Street Presbyterian Church in New York City in 1881 to establish an independent church, later named the Gospel Tabernacle, for the purpose of evangelizing the unchurched masses of New York City.

Simpson's spiritual journey and beliefs were crystallized in the phrase "Fourfold Gospel," which he coined to exalt Christ as Savior, Sanctifier, Healer, and Coming King. He was simultaneously a revivalist preacher, a Holiness prophet of the "deeper" or "higher Christian life," a promoter of world missions, an eschatological speculator, and a theological synthesizer. Not surprisingly, his theology, spirituality, ministry, and polity became an inspiration to many in the Pentecostal movement who had in the late-nineteenth century sat by and drunk from some of the same streams of spiritual awakening in which Simpson himself had been refreshed.

The ideological continuity between Simpson's doctrines and those espoused by early Pentecostals can be established at several points. His restorationist interpretation of the evolution of church history since the Protestant Reformation underscored a conviction that the present age would conclude with the days of the "latter rain," which had already begun to "sprinkle" in Simpson's own time. This anticipated outpouring of the Holy Spirit would be accompanied by supernatural manifestations of the Spirit, such as tongues, miracles, and prophecy, reminiscent of the "early rain" at Pentecost (Acts 2). He exhorted believers to pray for those special evidences of divine power typical of past revivals.

Simpson adamantly opposed any dispensational notion that the gifts of the Holy Spirit had necessarily ceased with the close of the apostolic age. On the basis of Joel 2 and 1 Corinthians 12, he contended that the gifts of the Holy Spirit were to continue in the church until the Second Advent. Prior to the outbreak of the Azusa Street revival in 1906, Simpson acknowledged the value of the gift of tongues in the church as "an expression of lofty spiritual feeling and intense moving of the heart," noting also that it was mentioned last in Paul's list of charismata and seemed most prone to abuse. He described the nature of tongues as both known and unknown languages, but he rejected the prevalent popular misconception that the gift could be expected by missionaries for the purpose of preaching the gospel to the heathen.

For Simpson, the Book of Acts depicted church life as God intended it to be throughout all ages of church history. Like Pentecostals who followed him, he was fully prepared to use the standard of spiritual life portrayed in Acts as the existential norm by which to measure the shortcomings of the church in his own time. He asserted that an openness to the supernatural quality of Christian life as exhibited by the early apostolic church was the only prevention against a deterioration into "conventional formalism."

In his writings, Simpson foreshadowed the Pentecostal hermeneutical practice of deriving doctrinal truth from the narrative accounts of Acts. Though he rejected as unbiblical the "initial evidence doctrine," Simpson nevertheless made full use of the classical prooftexts of Pentecostalism (Acts 2, 8, 19) to substantiate his claim that regeneration and the baptism of the Holy Spirit were two distinct events in the life of the believer. The Samaritans and the Ephesian disciples provided support for his two-step model of Christian initiation.

The entire Simpson corpus testifies uniformly to his conception of Spirit baptism as occurring subsequently to regeneration. Spurred on by the reading of W. E. Boardman's *The Higher Christian Life* (1858), Simpson received the baptism of the Spirit in 1874 during his second pastorate in Louisville, Kentucky. He variously termed Spirit baptism a "second blessing," "crisis sanctification," "the anointing," "the sealing," "receiving the Holy Spirit," "the fullness of the Spirit," and "the indwelling of Christ."

Simpson made several criticisms of the Pentecostal movement in "Special Revival Movements," a report he delivered to the Alliance general council in 1908. He charged that the "initial evidence doctrine" spawned a preoccupation with spiritual manifestations rather than cultivating a devotion to God and tended to reduce evangelistic zeal. Moreover, those professing the Pentecostal baptism had allegedly divided Alliance branches, thereby reducing missionary contributions. He observed that on the foreign field, some inexperienced missionaries naively assumed that they would receive tongues as a substitute for language study. Lastly, in his address Simpson noted a style of "prophetic authority" within the movement that resembled "the Romish confessional" or "spiritualism." Despite the drawbacks of Pentecostalism, Simpson remained open to the movement that had produced impressive spiritual fruit where stable leadership had emerged.

A diary kept by Simpson from 1907 to 1916 discloses that the Pentecostal movement prompted him to make "a new claim for a Mighty Baptism of the Holy Spirit in His complete fullness embracing all the gifts and graces of the Spirit." He could not, however, testify to having received tongues or similar gifts as had several of his friends. As both a forerunner of Pentecostalism and a seeker of the Pentecostal baptism with tongues, he remained a critic of the "initial evidence doctrine" to the end of his life.

See also CHRISTIAN AND MISSIONARY ALLIANCE; HEALING MOVEMENTS; KESWICK HIGHER LIFE MOVEMENT.

Bibliography: D. Hartzfeld and C. Nienkirchen, eds., *The Birth of a Vision* (1986); A. B. Simpson, "The Baptism of the Holy Spirit, A Crisis or an Evolution," *Living Truths* 5 (1905): 705–15; idem, "The Ministry of the Spirit," *Living Truths* 7 (1907): 438–46; idem, "A Story of Providence," *Living Truths* 7 (1907): 150–65.   C. Nienkirchen

SIMPSON, CHARLES VERNON (1937–).

Pastor, teacher, and publisher. Son of Baptist missionaries in Louisiana, Charles Simpson was born in New Orleans and educated at William Carey College (B.A.) and New Orleans Baptist Theological Seminary. He was asked to serve a Southern Baptist church in Mobile, Alabama, in the summer of 1957, and was ordained in December of that year. He remained as pastor until 1971.

Simpson received the baptism of the Holy Spirit in 1964 through the ministry of Ken Sumrall of Pensacola, Florida, and became active in the charismatic renewal. In 1970 Simpson, with Don Basham, Bob Mumford, and Derek Prince, began to work together and formed Christian Growth Ministries. They assumed publication of *New Wine* magazine with offices in Fort Lauderdale, Florida. The magazine became, along with audio teaching tapes, the primary vehicle for what became known as the shepherding or discipleship movement. A quasi-denomination, based on discipleship, or "shepherding," concepts, formed around the four men, plus Ern Baxter. Simpson gave pastoral leadership to the others. He was the first among the five to encourage the tight relationships that came to characterize discipleship ministry.

Simpson established the Gulf Coast Fellowship in 1973, and in 1978 *New Wine* magazine moved to Mobile. That year Simpson became chairman of Integrity Communications, which published it. In December 1986 *New Wine* ceased publication, and he began *Christian Conquest* magazine.

Gulf Coast Fellowship changed its name in 1987 to Covenant Church of Mobile. Simpson continues to serve as senior pastor and as leader of the Fellowship of Covenant Ministers and Churches. Simpson has a radio program that is released on eight stations. He has written three books, including *The Challenge to Care* (1986).

Bibliography: J. Buckingham, "New Wine Ceases Publication," *Ministries Today* (November–December 1986), 24; C. Simpson, *The Challenge to Care* (1986); S. Strang, "The Discipleship Controversy Three Years Later," *Charisma* (September 1978), 14–24.   S. Strang

SIMPSON, WILLIAM WALLACE (1869–1961).

Pioneer missionary to China. Born in White County, Tennessee, Simpson (no relation to A. B. Simpson) attended an academy of the Congregational church. He surrendered his life to Christ in 1881 and ministered in a rural area of the state. Preparing on one occasion to preach on Mark 16:15, he was personally confronted with

the challenge of overseas evangelism and decided to pursue that objective. Attending A. B. Simpson's New York Missionary Training College (later Nyack College) in 1891, the following year he headed for the Far East with other missionaries of the Christian and Missionary Alliance (CMA). Receiving instructions and encouragement from J. Hudson Taylor, Simpson and his colleagues headed for Tibet—considered by many at that time to be the "uttermost" part of the world.

In December 1895 Simpson married Otilia Ekvall, an appointed CMA missionary to China. From this union came two daughters and a son, William Ekvall Simpson (1901–32), who later was killed while serving as a missionary on the China–Tibetan border.

Attending a convention of missionaries in Taochow, China, in 1912, Simpson received the baptism in the Holy Spirit and spoke in tongues. Due to his uncompromising belief that the evidence for this was glossolalia, tension mounted between him and the other missionaries, as well as with the officials of the CMA, particularly Robert H. Glover. Simpson returned to the U.S. in 1915 due to his wife's poor health and his stance on the Pentecostal baptism. In the same year, he was forced to resign from the CMA and subsequently joined the Assemblies of God (AG). Prevented from returning to China because of his wife's deteriorating health, he accepted the post of principal at the recently established Bethel Bible Training School at Newark, New Jersey, in 1916. Following the death of his wife, he resigned his post and returned to China. In 1925 he married Martha Merrill, also a missionary, and they had six children.

Over the years, Simpson evangelized in all of the provinces of China with the exception of the seven in the southern part; he also ministered in Tibet, Mongolia, and Manchuria. He preferred to travel on foot for much of his ministry. An advocate of indigenous church principles, he assisted in the training of national clergy by teaching in Bible institutes, including the Truth Bible Institute in Beijing, China. Simpson took great interest in forming eschatological interpretations of contemporary events, often approaching the bizarre in speculation.

After World War II, Simpson returned to China, but he retired to the U.S. following the Communist takeover in 1949. He continued to promote foreign missions until his death.

During his lifetime, Simpson became one of the best-known missionaries of the Pentecostal movement. His legacy included the converts from his front-line evangelism, the Chinese clergy he trained, and his courageous example of endurance in the face of discouraging circumstances.

Bibliography: G. F. Atter, *The Third Force*, 2d ed. (1965); N. Blan, *Rugged Mountains* (n.d.); W. W. Simpson, *Evangelizing in West China* (n.d.).
G. B. McGee

SIN AGAINST THE HOLY SPIRIT See BLASPHEMY AGAINST THE HOLY SPIRIT.

SINCLAIR, JOHN CHALMERS (1863–1936).

Early Pentecostal pastor. The career of John C. Sinclair of Chicago illustrates the priority many early Pentecostals gave to ecclesiastical independence. Born in Lydster, Scotland, Sinclair immigrated as a youth to the U.S., settling in Wisconsin. There he met and married a fellow Presbyterian, Mary E. Bie. Before the turn of the century, the Sinclairs moved to Chicago, where he was employed by the U.S. Steel Corporation. There he accepted the Wesleyan Holiness teaching and was called and ordained to the ministry. In 1907 as pastor of an independent church at 328 West 63rd Street, Sinclair was reported to be the first person in Chicago to claim the Pentecostal experience. Destined to spend most of his life as an independent, he was a participant in two early attempts at organizational unity. In 1914 he was one of three members added to the original executive presbytery of the Assemblies of God following the first general council meeting in Hot Springs, Arkansas; however, he soon withdrew. Five years later as pastor of the Christian Apostolic Assembly of Chicago, he served as first general chairman of the Pentecostal Assemblies of the U.S. (parent to the Pentecostal Church of God), but again withdrew. In both cases fear of latent denominationalism appears to have been the cause. With Chicago as home base, Sinclair traveled widely in his last years. He died at La Porte, Indiana, in 1936 and is buried in Chicago. His daughter, Dorothy, was wife of the prominent evangelist, John H. Bostrom (1899–1974).

Bibliography: C. Brumback, *Suddenly . . . From Heaven* (1961); E. L. Moon, *The Pentecostal Church* (1966);.   C. E. Jones

SINGING IN TONGUES

In 1 Corinthians 14:15 Paul writes, "I will sing with my spirit, but I will also sing with my mind." The larger section in which this text occurs, verses 13–19, gives detail to the principle set forth in verse 12, viz., "strive for the edification of the church, that is, not self-edification" (Conzelmann, 1975, 237).

"Singing with my spirit" is set in tight parallel with "praying with my spirit." Neither statement in verse 15 contains the pronoun "my," but the NIV correctly interprets the definite article (*the* spirit) as either anaphoric or possessive following Paul's explicit "my spirit" in verse 14. Singing and praying "with my spirit" are contrasted with praying and singing "with my mind." Framed by verses 13–14 and 18–19, it is clear that singing and praying with the/my spirit refers to singing or praying in tongues. In the light of verses 16–17, it is further probable that Paul views these songs as songs of praise (Fee, 1987, 671; Barrett, 1968, 320).

Fee (1987, 670) interprets "my spirit prays" as "my S/spirit prays," i.e., Paul's own spirit prays "as the Holy Spirit gives the utterance" (using an admittedly Lucan phrase). Thus, singing with the spirit would have the same characteristic of inspiration by the Spirit.

Paul establishes the validity of glossolalic singing and praying when he says that he will do both (v. 15) and that the one who gives thanks in a tongue does so well enough (v. 17). On the other hand, he establishes that singing and praying in the vernacular are preferable in the assembly because the assembly can be edified only if the words are understood. Further, singing with the spirit would come under Paul's rule in verse 27: any utterances in tongues must be done one at a time, each must be interpreted, and there is a limit of three glossolalic utterances in any gathering.

Some have tried to see another reference to singing in the Spirit in the "spiritual songs" of Ephesians 5:18–19: "be filled with the Spirit. Speak to one another with psalms, hymns, and spiritual songs." "Speak" is grammatically subordinate to "be filled with the Spirit," so a leap is made to the interpretation "singing in the spirit" in the sense of 1 Corinthians 14:15. However, the Spirit can, and in a group would rather, inspire speech in the vernacular. This interpretation founders on the phrase "speak to one another." Glossolalic singing could hardly be addressed to anyone who did not understand the language spoken.

Bibliography: C. K. Barrett, *A Commentary on the First Epistle to the Corinthians* (1968); H. Conzelmann, *1 Corinthians* (1975); G. D. Fee, *First Epistle to the Corinthians* (1987).   D. A. Johns

SISSON, ELIZABETH

(1843–1934). Missionary, writer, evangelist, and church planter. Elizabeth Sisson was born the second of three sisters to New England whaling captain William Sisson and Elizabeth (Hempstead) Sisson. She was converted in 1863 in New London, Connecticut, where she joined the Second Congregational Church. Her interest in ministry came early, and in an autobiographical account she describes sitting in an Episcopal ordination service wishing she were a man so that she could be ordained. Later, while meditating on that service, she had a vision of Christ, whom she described as the Great Bishop, who said, "I have ordained you." Her response from that time onward was that "all human ordination shrivelled into utter insignificance."

Under the influence of W. S. Boardman, Sisson received sanctification. In 1871 she left the U.S. to serve in India as a missionary for the American Board of Commissioners for Foreign Missions, where she ministered largely among the Hindu population with occasional incursions among Moslems as well.

Stricken with severe illness, Sisson was forced to leave India for a period of recuperation in a healing home in London. In 1887 she returned to the U.S. and took up a teaching and writing ministry. During this period she was associated with Carrie Judd Montgomery and became the associate editor of *Triumphs of Faith*. The two women went to San Francisco in the fall of 1889, where Carrie became engaged to George H. Montgomery. During this time Sisson attended the tent meetings held by Maria B. Woodworth-Etter in Oakland. At one meeting a prophecy was given that predicted the destruction of San Francisco and Oakland by a tidal wave. Sisson, along with many others, believed and propagated the prophecy, which proved to be false, and because of this "error in judgment" her reputation was heavily damaged. She resigned her post with the *Triumphs of Faith* and for a time "sank into obscurity."

Sisson returned to New England, where she received her Pentecostal baptism at Old Orchard, Maine. In the early days of the Pentecostal outpouring, Sisson, who never married, traveled across Canada and throughout the U.S., often accompanied by her sister Charlotte W. Sisson. She made an evangelistic tour to the British Isles in 1908, spent four months ministering with F. F. Bosworth in Dallas (1915), and ministered in Detroit for a period during that same year. She became affiliated with the fledgling Assemblies of God, from which she received credentials in December 1917 at age seventy-four.

A prolific writer and conference speaker, Sisson used her home at 17 Jay Street in New London, Connecticut, as her headquarters. Elizabeth's articles were published regularly in *Word and Work* (Framingham, Mass.), *Confidence* (Sunderland, England), *The Latter Rain Evangel* (Chicago), *The Weekly Evangel* (St. Louis), *The Pentecostal Evangel* (Springfield, Mo.), and *Triumphs of Faith* (Oakland, Calif.). Many of these were simultaneously published in tract form.

Bibliography: "At Rest," *TF* 54 (10, 1934): 235; "The Envelope," *Confidence* 10 (8, 1915): 183–86; idem, *Foregleams of Glory* (1912); idem, "Four Years' Continuous Revival," *Confidence* 8 (4, 1915): 68, 70–72; idem, "God's Prayer House," *TF* 28 (10, 1908): 230–34; idem, "Kept by the Power of God" (August 1915); *Confidence* 8 (9, 1915): 176–77; idem, "The Lord's Healing," *LRE* 1 (7, 1909): 2–6; idem, "Miss Sisson's Miraculous Healing" *Confidence* 3 (2, 1909): 55–58; idem, "Miss Sisson's Restoration," *Confidence* 2 (1, 1909): 23; idem, "The Holy Ghost and Fire," *LRE* 1 (8, 1909): 6–10.   C. M. Robeck, Jr.

SIZELOVE, RACHEL ARTAMISSIE (1864–1941). Evangelist. A former Free Methodist evangelist, Rachel A. Sizelove introduced the Pentecostal teaching in Springfield, Missouri, and foresaw that place as a Pentecostal center. In May 1907, after receiving the baptism of the Holy Spirit the preceding July at the Azusa Mission in Los Angeles, she returned to Springfield, where her sister and her mother then lived. Commissioned by the Azusa workers, she and Lucy Farrow, a black en route to Liberia as a missionary, traveled as far as Dallas together. The first convert of her cottage meetings in Missouri was her sister, Lillie Corum, mother of the future Pentecostal editor, Fred Tice Corum (1900–1982). When Sizelove returned six years later, the nucleus gathered in 1907 had become a thriving congregation. She recorded, "One afternoon" during the second visit, "there appeared before me a beautiful, bubbling, sparkling fountain in the heart of the city of Springfield. It sprang up gradually, but irresistibly, and began to flow toward the East and toward the West, toward the North and toward the South, until the whole land was deluged with living water." Although the General Council of the Assemblies of God was not to be formed for yet another year and was not to establish offices there for yet another five years, she and many others regarded the selection of Springfield as the headquarters site as the fulfillment of prophecy. A native of Marengo, Indiana, Rachel Sizelove lived most of her adult life in southern California. She died in Long Beach in 1941.

Bibliography: C. Brumback, *Suddenly . . . From Heaven* (1961); F. T. Corum, *Like as of Fire* (1981); R. A. Sizelove, *A Sparkling Fountain for the Whole Earth* (n.d.).   C. E. Jones

SLAIN IN THE SPIRIT A relatively modern expression denoting a religious phenomenon in which an individual falls down; the cause of this is attributed to the Holy Spirit. The phenomenon is known within modern Pentecostalism and charismatic renewal under various names, including "falling under the power," "overcome by the Spirit," and "resting in the Spirit." Within the discipline of the sociology of religion "slain in the Spirit" might fall under the general rubric of "possession trance"; however, sociologists have paid little specific attention to what is recognized in Pentecostal and charismatic circles as a distinct, identifiable experience (see, e.g., Bourguignon, 1973, 1976). It is generally acknowledged that in addition to God, the source of the experience can be a purely human response to autosuggestion, group "peer pressure," or simply a desire to experience the phenomenon. Furthermore, although the nomenclature may not have been in place for very long, it is generally recognized that the phenomenon (or something closely akin to it) has occurred throughout the history of the church; indeed, sociologists would insist that it is common to many religions (i.e., the possession trance).

Defenders of the legitimacy of the experience as distinctly Christian point to similar examples of the phenomenon prior to the modern Pentecostal and charismatic movements. For example, one could point to similarities between being "slain in the Spirit" and the experience of Perpetua at her martyrdom, who "being roused from what seemed like sleep, so completely had she been in the Spirit and in ecstasy . . ." (*The Passion of Perpetua and Felicitas*, 20). Or, one might, as MacNutt does, see in an account of a fourteenth-century Dominican monk an allusion to being slain in the Spirit (MacNutt, 1978, 194–95).

It is perhaps more popular to see the phenomenon of being slain in the Spirit as an accompaniment to great Protestant revivals. John Wesley's *Journal* tells of people who during his preaching "were struck to the ground and lay there groaning" (Knox, 1950, 472, citing Wesley's *Journal*, p. 118). The Methodist circuit-rider Peter Cartwright's preaching was also accompanied by listeners falling under the power. Similar results accompanied George Whitefield's preaching and are attested in the writings of Jonathan Edwards as well (ibid., 526, 529, 530). Charles G. Finney's *Autobiography* recounts episodes in which people could not move or speak, in one instance for sixteen hours (Wessel, 1977, reprint, 58).

The one person most associated with the phenomenon in early Pentecostalism is Maria B. Woodworth-Etter. However, it is noteworthy that people were experiencing being slain in the Spirit in her evangelistic meetings several years *prior* to her participation in the Pentecostal movement. Thus an 1890 copy of the *St. Louis*

Post-Dispatch contains an artist's rendering of people "under the power" at her meeting (Warner, 1986, 144). Indeed, perhaps more than anything else, this phenomenon characterized her meetings. One account in the September 25, 1885, issue of the Muncie, Indiana, *Daily News* tells of "Dozens lying around pale and unconscious, rigid, and lifeless as though in death" (ibid., 55). In her own account of Muncie she says that many of the infidels and scoffers "were the first to fall under the slaying power of God" (Woodworth-Etter, 1984 ed., 69). She also speaks of large audiences in which "hundreds of people were struck down by the power" (Warner, 1986, 229). It seems as if the Pentecostal-charismatic association of slain in the Spirit with particular personalities stems from Woodworth-Etter more than any other person.

The modern Pentecostal and charismatic movements particularly associate being slain in the Spirit with the ministries of Kathryn Kuhlman, Kenneth Hagin, Sr., and Charles and Frances Hunter. Kuhlman was perhaps the one most responsible for the entrance of the "practice" of slaying in the Spirit, principally because her meetings were so characterized by the phenomenon (Buckingham, 1976, 40, 41, 224–29).

Characteristics of the "blessing" of being "slain in the Spirit" include a loss of feeling or control; sometimes those who fall under the power reportedly feel no pain, even if they bump their heads on the way down should "catchers" fail to do their job. On many occasions the experience is accompanied by tongues speech; at other times laughing, weeping, or praising of God are manifest.

Whereas during earlier revivals the experience "struck down" (and converted) many of the "convicted," the "scoffers," and the "mockers," in modern Pentecostalism and charismatic circles the experience is a spiritual experience to be sought. Almost all see the experience as deeply spiritual in nature, and afterward a general euphoria is present.

The length of time people are "under" varies. Usually the experience lasts from a few seconds to several minutes, though on some occasions it is reported to last for hours. One undocumented story about Maria Woodworth-Etter asserts that she "stood like a statue for three days and three nights" (Hagin, 1980, 5).

Almost all would see the experience in a positive way—at least initially. Some aberrant, negative examples of being slain in the Spirit do exist, however. Kenneth Hagin relates that his wife and a coworker, both of whom had questioned his authority, were unable to approach him without falling down under the power. Hagin interpreted this as a kind of "touch not the Lord's anointed" lesson (McConnell, 1988). Such a judgmental, personal "use" of "slaying in the Spirit" is unprecedented.

An entire battalion of Scripture proof texts is enlisted to support the legitimacy of the phenomenon, although Scripture plainly offers no support for the phenomenon as something to be expected in the normal Christian's life. Passages appealed to from the OT include the following. In Genesis 15:12–21 Abram is said to have been overcome

by a "deep sleep," at which time God spoke to him about the future of his descendants. Numbers 24:4 tells of one who "falls prostrate, and whose eyes are opened" (the text is clear that this is a visionary experience). Another passage appealed to is 1 Samuel 19:20, where Saul's men are sent to capture David. They come upon "a group of prophets prophesying, with Samuel standing there as their leader." That Samuel is "standing" is seen to imply that the prophets were "slain in the Spirit"; the text goes on to say that the Spirit came upon Saul's men. Likewise, the visionary experiences of Ezekiel the prophet are viewed as times when he was slain in the Spirit (cf. Ezek. 1:28, Ezekiel "fell facedown"; Ezek. 2:1 says "Son of man, *stand up on your feet*" [italics mine]).

But the NT receives the most attention. Two passages in Matthew 17:1–6 and 28:1–4, are said to justify the phenomenon. In Matthew 17:6 the disciples "fell facedown" at the voice of God, and in Matthew 28:1–4 the tomb guards "shook and became like dead men" at the appearance of the angel of the Lord. Both the Matthean texts refer to instances of fear. One is clearly a normal response of awe-struck worship (Matt. 17:6 [*epi prosopon auton*]) while the other is probably simply a figurative way of saying the guards were "petrified." Even if the guards were "slain," their experience is entirely secondary to the story and did not have any redemptive value as far as the text is concerned.

Perhaps foremost in support of the phenomenon is John 18:1–6. In that passage Jesus replies to the officers from the chief priests and Pharisees who come to seize him, and at his word "they drew back and fell to the ground." There is no mention of the Spirit here, and John portrays no relationship between Spirit, power, and Jesus. The text remains enigmatic, especially since John offers neither explanation for, nor effect of, their fall. Obviously they were not converted, because they proceeded to arrest Jesus.

Of course Acts 9:4 and 26:14, the accounts of Paul's conversion, are thought to be Paul's experience of being slain in the Spirit. The text offers no phenomenological explanation for the event, and none should be expected. In terms of resembling the modern experience one finds close parallels; however, Luke in no way intimates that this is normal. In fact, it is the uniqueness of the event that prompts Luke to recount it three times. It is certainly legitimate to discern here a genuine spiritual experience similar to the modern phenomenon in description but distinct in purpose.

Paul's remembrance (if indeed 2 Cor. 12:2 is autobiographical) tells of "a man in Christ who . . . was caught up to the third heaven." While this is appealed to as evidence that Paul experienced being slain in the Spirit, there is simply not enough data to justify the conclusion that the "third heaven" and the state of being slain in the Spirit are identical.

The evidence for the phenomenon of being "slain in the Spirit" is thus inconclusive. From an experiential standpoint it is unquestionable that through the centuries Christians have experienced a psychophysical phenomenon in which people fall down; moreover, they have attributed the experience to God. It is equally unquestionable that there is no biblical evidence for the experience as normative in Christian life.

Bibliography: E. Bourguignon, *Possession* (1976); idem, *Religion, Altered States of Consciousness, and Social Change* (1973); J. Buckingham, *Daughter of Destiny* (1976); K. Hagin, *Why Do People Fall Under the Power?* (1980); R. Knox, *Enthusiasm* (1950); D. McConnell, *A Different Gospel* (1988); F. MacNutt, *Healing* (1974); idem, *The Power to Heal* (1977); W. Warner, *The Woman Evangelist* (1986); H. Wessel, ed., *Autobiography of Charles G. Finney* (1908, reprint 1984); M. Woodworth-Etter, *Miracles, Signs and Wonders* (1916; abridged and reprinted 1977).

P. H. Alexander

SMAIL, THOMAS A. (1928–). Teacher and theologian. Smail studied under Karl Barth for a year and was ordained in the Church of Scotland in 1953. Baptized in the Spirit through the ministry of Dennis Bennett (1965), he served as a pastor in Northern Ireland (1968–72). Smail then became general secretary of the Fountain Trust, taking over editorship of *Renewal* in 1975. A gifted expositor with a rigorous theological mind, Smail edited all twenty-five issues of *Theological Renewal* (1975–83). Ordained an Anglican priest in 1979, he left Fountain Trust to become vice-principal at St. John's College, Nottingham, in 1980. Smail has been critical of mindless enthusiasm, emphasizing especially in his editorials in *Theological Renewal* the Trinitarian character of all Christian life and demanding a solid theological basis for spiritual renewal within the church. Smail became rector of Sanderstead, Surrey, in 1985. He has authored *Reflected Glory* (1975) and *The Forgotten Father* (1980).

P. D. Hocken

SMALE, JOSEPH (1867–1926). Los Angeles, California, pastor. Son of John and Ann (Stephens) Smale, Joseph Smale was born in England and received his theological education at Spurgeon's College in London. At the age of twenty-one he entered the Baptist ministry, in which he remained for most of his life. His earliest ministry experience was obtained in street meetings in London and in a three-year pastorate at Ryde, on the Isle of Wight. He was married to Esther Isabelle (b. November 23, 1879).

At the age of twenty-four Smale immigrated to the U.S., taking a Baptist pastorate in Prescott, Arizona. About 1895 he moved to the Los Angeles area, where he became the pastor of First Baptist Church located at 725 South Flower.

When news came to Los Angeles about the Welsh revival, Smale was interested enough to travel to Wales to visit Evans Roberts and observe the revival firsthand. Upon his return to Los Angeles, he began home prayer meetings and nineteen weeks of protracted meetings in anticipation of a similar outpouring of the Holy Spirit. Many "spiritual workers" from a variety of denominational backgrounds were attracted to Smale's church, but the spontaneity of worship sought by Smale was not accepted by the church leaders. Smale withdrew to establish First New Testament Church in Burbank Hall at 542 South Main Street, Los Angeles, in early 1906.

On Easter Sunday 1906, First New Testament Church experienced its first incident of speaking in tongues. The speaker was Jennie Moore, the future wife of William J. Seymour. At first Smale was reticent to accept tongues. A dozen or more of his followers moved to Azusa Street, but by June 22 Smale had invited his people back with a promise to allow full freedom in the Spirit. Some returned, and for a time this congregation prospered. Those who did not return joined one of four other Pentecostal missions existing in Los Angeles by October 1906.

Smale and his congregation were the subject of two articles in the *Los Angeles Daily Times* during July 1906. The congregation was described as racially mixed, including the poor and the prosperous. Dr. Henry Sheridan Keyes, president of the Emergency and General Hospital in Los Angeles, featured in one of these articles, was but one of Smale's regular parishioners. Services were well attended, and people stood along the walls and in the entry rather than leaving. Manifestations such as speaking in tongues, jumping, "slayings in the Spirit," and shouting were common. Meetings often ran all night. It was at First New Testament Church where Elmer K. Fisher received his Pentecostal experience. Soon after, he founded the Upper Room Mission.

Smale is said to have written an eighteen-page apology for the Pentecostal movement titled *A Tract for the Times* (Shumway). He resided at 1249 South Bonnie Brae (1905), an address later taken by Keyes (1908), and continued to serve First New Testament Church for several years. Although he was a Baptist, he was active in Holiness circles, too, appearing with Carrie Judd Montgomery and several others on the docket of speakers who addressed a four-day convention of the Christian Alliance held at Trinity Methodist Church South on Grand Avenue in December 1906 or January 1907.

While Smale allowed others to manifest the gift of tongues in his services and to seek for the fullness of the Spirit in his presence, he never "received the 'baptism' with the 'speaking in tongues.' " This fact led Frank Bartleman to describe him as God's "Moses" for Pentecostalism, an obvious reference to Moses' inability to cross into the Promised Land. This may also have led to Smale's disillusionment with the Pentecostal movement against whose abuses he wrote in January 1907. He continued to serve as the pastor of First New Testament Church for several years but ultimately founded Grace Baptist Church, of which he was pastor at the time of his death.

Following a lengthy illness, Smale died on September 16, 1926, at his South Pasadena home, leaving a daughter, Esther Grace, and his wife. At the time of his death a brother, Ebenezer Smale, lived in Long Beach, while a sister, Mrs. J. G. Van Houten, lived in Los Angeles. Joseph and Esther (d. August 3, 1958) are buried in Mountain View Cemetery in Pasadena, California.

Bibliography: F. Bartleman, *How Pentecost Came to Los Angeles* (1925); B. F. Lawrence, *The Apostolic Faith Restored* (1916); C. W. Shumway, "Queer Gift Given Many," *Los Angeles Daily Times* (July 22, 1906), 8; idem, "Rolling on Floor in Smale's Church," *Los Angeles*

Daily Times (July 14, 1906), 1; idem, "A Study of 'the Gift of Tongues,' " unpublished A.B. thesis, University of Southern California, 1914; A. S. Worrell, "Christian Alliance Convention," *Triumphs of Faith* 27 (1, 1907): 11; idem, "The Gift of Tongues," *Living Truths* 7 (1, 1907): 32–43; idem, "The Movements in Los Angeles, California," *Triumphs of Faith* 26 (12, 1906): 257; idem, "Rites for Churchman Tomorrow," *Los Angeles Daily Times* (September 18, 1926), 2:1.   C. M. Robeck, Jr.

SMALL, FRANKLIN (1873–1961). Canadian pastor and administrator. Born at Revenna near Collingwood, Ontario, he was one of the first in Winnipeg to receive the baptism of the Holy Spirit in 1907. He soon became assistant pastor to A. H. Argue and was ordained by the American Assemblies of God in 1914. He then became one of the seven charter members of the Pentecostal Assemblies of Canada (PAOC) in 1917.

In 1921 Small severed his connections with the PAOC due to doctrinal differences on water baptism. He promoted the "Jesus Only" view and led in the formation of the Apostolic Church of Pentecost of Canada, Incorporated (ACPC). In 1953 the Evangelical Churches of Pentecost, which included many believers in the triunity of the Godhead, merged with the ACPC, resulting in tolerance of both views of the Godhead.

Small pastored Zion Apostolic Church in Winnipeg for the last twenty-nine years of his life.

Bibliography: G. F. Atter, *The Third Force*, 3d ed. (1970).   G. W. Gohr

SMITH, CAMPBELL BANNERMAN (1900–1961). Canadian pastor and administrator. Born at Eganville, near Pembroke, Ontario, Smith came into contact with the Pentecostal movement during the winter of 1924 and was soon converted and filled with the Holy Spirit. Having previously been a bank manager, he left that career to follow a call to the ministry. He entered the Pentecostal Bible College in Winnipeg in the fall of 1926 and also became secretary and bookkeeper of the college. He was ordained in 1928. In July 1928 he married Beulah Argue, daughter of A. H. Argue.

Smith served pastorates in Saskatchewan, Ontario, and British Columbia and was twice president of Eastern Pentecostal Bible College (1940–44, 1958–61). He was also superintendent of the Eastern Ontario District of the PAOC before serving as general superintendent (1944–52).

Smith was killed in an automobile accident near Napanee, Ontario.

Bibliography: "Rev. C. B. Smith," *Pentecostal Testimony* (March 1962), 11, 33–34.   G. W. Gohr

SMITH, CHARLES ("CHUCK") (1927–). Pastor and youth leader. Charles Smith was reared in Pentecostal churches by Christian parents. He and his wife, Kay, have four children. Following high school he attended junior college in Santa Ana, California, and then studied at L.I.F.E. Bible College in Los Angeles. Upon his graduation from L.I.F.E., Smith was ordained with the International Church of the Foursquare Gospel (ICFG). He held pastorates in Prescott and Tucson, Arizona, then in several locations in Southern California. In the early 1960s he opened

Chuck Smith came into prominence during the late 1960s and early 1970s as a leader of what became known as the Jesus Movement. He is pastor of Calvary Chapel, Costa Mesa, California, and leader of a church organization spawned by the Costa Mesa church.

his home to small Bible study groups. His simple, clear, and practical messages met the needs of those who attended, and he soon led a half-dozen such burgeoning groups. He was asked in 1965 to serve as associate pastor of a struggling congregation in Costa Mesa, California, called Calvary Chapel. Three years later the congregation moved to a Lutheran church in Newport Beach and later purchased eleven acres in Costa Mesa where it remains today.

Under the leadership of Chuck Smith, Calvary Chapel became famous for its biblical teaching, balanced use of charismata, evangelistic fervor, social concern for "hippies" and drug users, and willingness to accept the misunderstood and unloved of society. Smith became the center of national attention in the early 1970s with his mass beach baptisms in Corona del Mar and has been acknowledged as a prominent leader in the Jesus People movement of those years. Today he continues to serve as pastor of Calvary Chapel, ministering to as many as 25,000 people each week.

Bibliography: R. Enroth et al., *The Jesus People* (1972), esp. ch. 4; C. Smith, *Charisma vs. Charismania* (1983); C. Smith with H. Steven, *The Reproducers: New Life for Thousands* (1972).   C. M. Robeck, Jr.

SMITH, FRANK W. (1909–). A charter member of the Open Bible Standard Churches (OBSC), long-time pastor, and denominational leader. Getting his Pentecostal start in the First Baptist Church, San Jose, California, Frank Smith went to L.I.F.E. Bible College and then pastored his first church, a Foursquare Gospel congregation in West Hollywood. Moving to Des Moines, he pastored in the city for the next forty-two years, retiring in 1976.

In addition to Smith's pastorates in Iowa, he served in several administrative capacities, including president of Open Bible College and divisional and general superintendent of OBSC; he taught at the college for twenty years. Active in the National Association of Evangelicals, he was the Midwest section president for three years and a member of the general board and executive committee for thirty years. He also served as president of the Pentecostal Fellowship of North America. He is the author of *Pentecostal Positives* (1967).

Bibliography: R. Mitchell, *Heritage and Horizons* (1982).   W. E. Warner

Ray Smith, general superintendent of the Open Bible Standard Churches, 1967-1976, 1979-.

SMITH, RAYMOND EVERETT (1932–). General superintendent of the Open Bible Standard Churches (1967–76; 1979–). Following graduation in 1953 from Open Bible College, Raymond Smith established a church in Billings, Montana, where he remained until 1959. His second pastorate was in Rapid City, South Dakota (1959–67). During his Midwest pastorates he also served in executive positions with his denomination. He was elected to his church's highest office while pastoring at Rapid City. Except for a three-year pastorate in Eugene, Oregon (1976–79), he has been general superintendent since that time.

As superintendent Smith has been involved in various interdenominational efforts, including Iowa state chairman, Key '73; member of the board of administration, National Association of Evangelicals; and member of the board of directors, Pentecostal Fellowship of North America.

He is also involved in several citizens groups. He has a brother and two sisters who have served in foreign missions.

Bibliography: R. Mitchell, *Heritage and Horizons* (1982).   W. E. Warner

SNAKE HANDLING   See SERPENT HANDLING.

SOCIETY FOR PENTECOSTAL STUDIES (SPS). Following World War II the American Pentecostal movement clearly established itself among Evangelicals—perhaps largely due to the statesmanship of Thomas F. Zimmerman as the chief executive officer of the Assemblies of God (AG) for over a quarter century. By the 1950s, teachers in classical Pentecostal schools were often trained at evangelical institutions such as Wheaton College, Gordon-Conwell Theological Seminary (South Hamilton, Mass.), and Fuller Theological Seminary (Pasadena, Calif.). With the precedent of the Evangelical Theological Society, established in 1949, it was natural to expect a similar organization among emerging Pentecostal scholars. Discussions through the 1960s, when Pentecostal teachers increasingly undertook university doctorates, are known to have occurred among such persons as J. Robert Ashcroft, R. O. Corvin, Klaude Kendrick, John T. Nichol, and others. But the founding of the SPS occurred under the leadership of William W. Menzies, Vinson Synan, and Horace Ward at a dinner held on November 6, 1970, in conjunction with the ninth Pentecostal World Conference meeting in Dallas, Texas. Of the 139 persons who attended, 108 signed on as charter members. Menzies was elected the first president, and Synan became the initial secretary. An occasional newsletter has appeared at least once each year since 1971. By 1978 the need for a journal was felt. Twice yearly since the spring of 1979 *Pneuma—the Journal of the Society for Pentecostal Studies* has been published. One of the few learned periodicals to arise within the Pentecostal movement, *Pneuma*, by the end of 1987 was received at ninety-eight libraries on six continents. At the same time the membership of SPS numbered 524 additional—mainly Pentecostal and charismatic—scholars, teachers, pastors, writers, denominational executives, and students. In its early years, the SPS sought to maintain close connection with the Pentecostal World Conference and with the Pentecostal Fellowship of North America (PFNA). But the varying purposes of these organizations did not lead to a fruitful relationship. Besides, interest in the society had arisen among charismatic scholars who did not subscribe to the precise theological views of the American Pentecostal establishment. At its 1982 meeting the SPS took action that had the effect of opening leadership positions to persons other than members of a classical Pentecostal denomination. Within a few years a striking series of "firsts" occurred in the presidency of the organization, an office held for a year: the first charismatic (J. Rodman Williams, a Presbyterian theologian, 1985), the first Roman Catholic (Fr. Peter Hocken, 1986), the first woman (Edith Waldvogel Blumhofer, 1987), the first non-American (Ronald Kydd, of Canada, 1988), the first non-Pentecostal (Donald Dayton, a Wesleyan, 1989), and the first representative from the Jesus-Name sector of classical Pentecostalism (Manuel Gaxiola-Gaxiola, of Mexico, 1990). Regularly, the SPS has held an annual meeting featuring invited papers and, at times, planned discussions. Mostly such papers have related to historical and theological themes of interest to emerging theologians in the Pentecostal and charismatic movements. The more neutral and exploratory character of an academic society, where members function as individuals and not as representatives of their denomination, has on occasion permitted unprecedented advance in intra-Pentecostal fellowship. Notable in this regard was the participation of Oneness Pentecostals in the third annual meeting held in 1973 at Cleveland, Tennessee, which focused on the distinctives of that sector of the movement. Not since the Oneness (or "Jesus-Only") issue had resulted in the withdrawal of a fourth of the ministers from the AG in 1916 had such an encounter between establishment Pentecostals and their shunned siblings occurred. In 1987 the SPS voted to affiliate with the Council of Societies for the Study of Religion—an umbrella organization of academic societies in the U.S. About to conclude its second decade, the SPS faces a delicate balance between its growing acceptance among scholarly and ecumenical circles and its mixed reception on the part of the classical Pentecostal establishment.

Bibliography: C. M. Robeck, Jr., "The Society for Pentecostal Studies," *Ecumenical Trends* (February 14, 1985), 28–30. Among scholarly outcomes of the SPS are two bibliographies: D. W. Faupel, *The American Pentecostal Movement* (1972), and W. Mills, *Speaking in Tongues—A Classified Bibliography* (1974); and three edited collections of papers read at annual meetings: C. M. Robeck, Jr., ed., *Charismatic Experiences in History* (1985); R. Spittler, ed., *Perspectives on the New Pentecostalism* (1976); V. Synan, ed., *Aspects of Pentecostal-Charismatic Origins* (1975). R. P. Spittler

SOCIETY OF FRIENDS See QUAKERS.

SOCIOLOGY OF PENTECOSTALISM

I. Pentecostalism: A Sociological Perspective. In broad terms, the sociology of Pentecostalism is a category within the sociology of religion, since the dynamics of the Pentecostal experience are usually expressed within a religious context. The sociology of religion, according to Roberts (1984, 3),

> focuses on religious groups and institutions (their formation, maintenance, and demise), on the behavior of individuals within those groups (social processes which effect conversion, ritual behavior), and on conflicts between religious groups (Catholic versus Protestant, Christian versus Moslem, mainline denomination versus cult).

While there has been considerable interest in the systematic study of religion since the early development of sociology, interest in the sociology of Pentecostalism is fairly recent.

The sociological study of religion has been influenced by at least three broad social and intellectual trends. First, during the latter decades of the nineteenth century and continuing into the first two decades of the twentieth century, an interest in evolutionary theories was the primary intellectual means of explaining changes occurring in natural and social phenomena. Second, a positivist reaction against evolutionary theories emerged during the early decades of the twentieth century. This reaction took two related but distinct directions. One direction is the psychological study of religion. The other is the sociological study of religion. Both approaches developed along historical and empirical lines. Third, a more recent trend is an interest in the values, symbols, and ideological structures of religion that has led to a study of the characteristics of the movement in which religious experience is expressed.

This article will view Pentecostalism as a specific religious movement engaged in by persons attempting to make sense of, and thus bring cognitive order to, what is seen as a complex and, at times, alien world structure. It is defined as a social movement rather than as a social group, because during the early days of its development, the majority of Pentecostals were an amorphous collection of individuals outside the mainstream Christian denominations, and today the category encompasses many entire groups as well as parts of others and includes people who are not members of any definable group. The Pentecostals who remain in their home churches rather than joining the Pentecostal groups are called charismatics or Neo-Pentecostals, while those who are members of no formal organization are usually referred to as Jesus People (Hamilton, 1975; Quebedeaux, 1976, 1974). The sociology of Pentecostalism is an attempt to use systematic means to understand the social processes whereby Pentecostals, as a specific religious movement, have been able to delimit the definitions of the world situation to one that is best understood from a Pentecostal perspective. (For additional information see CHURCH GROWTH; STATISTICS, GLOBAL.)

II. Background to the Sociological Approach to Religion. Auguste Comte, who gave sociology its name, saw history as a series of evolutionary social stages, moving from theological explanations through metaphysical explanations to positive, or empirical, explanations. Borrowing from Comte as well as from Charles Darwin, Herbert Spencer, who had an influential impact on American notions of social Darwinism, saw religious development as moving from less rational to more rational interpretations, until the time when humans no longer need to interpret social and/or natural phenomena by referring to religion. Rather, a scientific explanation would be sufficient for the modern person.

These early attempts at sociological explanations of religious phenomena were articulated within the intellectual framework of evolutionary theories, and by the first decades of the twentieth century, popular and scholarly reactions against social Darwinism were crystallizing. The criticism from scholars centered on the notion that evolutionary theories rely on analytic or synthetic assumptions, while science, including social science, could progress only by experimentation and empirical testing.

The division between evolutionary science and positive science is not neatly drawn. Most of the evolutionary theorists believed in the inevitable victory of the positivist approach, although for the most part they were not positivists themselves. Also, many of the early positivists held to an evolutionary theory of progress. The difference in emphasis can be seen as the difference between the types of questions the two approaches might ask. An evolutionary theorist might ask, "Why did religion emerge in the first place?" while a positivist would turn the question around: "What part does religion play in the total structure of society?" The latter question would be more concerned with "Why does religion persist?" rather than "Why did religion emerge?"

The works of Sigmund Freud and Emile Durkheim illustrate the movement from evolutionary to positivist theories. In his study *Totem and Taboo* (1959 [1913]), Freud hypothesized that religious beliefs and practices reflect neurotic tendencies in the society, which are then reflected in the neurotic behavior of the individual. A modern society that retains religious beliefs and practices represents an evolutionary lag in which not every part of the society evolves at the same rate. This hypothesis stemmed from Freud's argument that a healthy personality depends on one's ability to make a realistic resolution of the conflict between the superego and the id. However, when an individual in a modern society adheres to a system of religious beliefs, then that individual is neurotic and unable or unwilling to adequately resolve the conflict between the super-ego and the id. If the religion is particularly expressive, with tendencies toward emotional outbursts, then the id is dominant over the superego. If the religion is repressive or if its members engage in philosophical discourses on abstract points of theology or if it has a substantial liturgy, then the superego dominates the id. Both cases represent neurosis. Freud stated, however, that even if religious belief is neurotic, it is often necessary to protect the individual during times of real or perceived helplessness.

Following a somewhat different line of reasoning, Emile Durkheim (1965 [1915]) merged Darwin's analytical evolutionary reasoning with his hypothesis that societies move from sacred explanations, where everything in the culture can be explained by its relation to deity or other sacred phenomena, to profane explanations, where little or nothing in the culture has sacred meaning but rather has practical, utilitarian meaning. Durkheim argued that one function of religion is to reflect the structure of society. What happens, however, when the structure of society is fragmented? Of the several possibilities, one likely occurrence is an increase in conflict as different groups attempt to make their own image of society the prevailing image through education or politics (Wuthnow, 1976).

While Durkheim's interest was the relation between the structure of society and individual response, Max Weber's (1963 [1922]) concern focused on ever-increasing complexities of rationalization, progressing through three states, which are: charismatic authority, where people's ideas of right and wrong are based on an outstanding and revered leader's perception of right and wrong; traditional authority, where ideas of right and wrong are based on what has been done in the past; and rational-legal authority, where people follow an ever-increasing complex set of rules or laws that provide the basis for right and wrong. Weber hypothesized that the loosely focused religious interests of "primitive" peoples gradually develop, or evolve, into highly structured bureaucratic organizations, ruled by laws rather than by either people or traditions. At the same time, he recognized that rationalization by itself is not sufficient to motivate people to do right. Nonrational elements are important in human motivation, and Weber identified two: the manner in which a society defines the meaning of life and its attendant problems and the charisma of an individual in relation to a group's ability to create a definition of meaning and to forge action toward achieving group goals. He tested this hypothesis in *The Protestant Ethic and the Spirit of Capitalism* (1958 [1904–05]), where he argued that the Protestant Reformation, with its emphases on Greek rationality and intellectual thought, provided the social framework for the rise of capitalism, industrialization, and modernization; but the Calvinist doctrine of divine selection, or predestination, provided the nonrational element necessary to keep people working, even when immediate payoffs were meager.

A further example of the linkage between the evolutionary and positivist approach to religion can be seen in the work of Ernst Troeltsch (1960 [1931]), who defined modern religions according to their type of organizational structure: churches, denominations, sects, or cults. A church is a religious organization linked to the dominant society. The leading members of a church are likely to be influential in the larger society. While a church tends to be synonymous with the dominant structure of society, a denomination competes with other denominations and with the larger society for loyalty from its members. At the same time, a denomination usually defines its best interests as similar to the best interests of society (Niebuhr, 1929). A sect both rejects the larger society and is rejected by it. To join a sect, an adherent must "convert" to the belief structure of the group. A cult is an extreme form of sect that calls for the total separation of its adherents from the world. Cults usually form around a dominant leader or personality and tend to glorify the leader rather than a system of beliefs.

Following Troeltsch, E. T. Clark (1949) classified the smaller sects that have emerged in American religion as: (1) pessimistic sects (e.g., Seventh-Day Adventists), (2) perfectionist sects (e.g., early Methodists and Holiness groups), (3) communistic sects (e.g., Shakers, Amanas, House of David), (4) legalistic sects (e.g., Mennonites, Primitive Baptists), (5) egocentric sects (e.g., Christian Science, Unity School), and (6) esoteric sects (e.g., Theosophists, Spiritualists).

The Pentecostal movement has its roots in the perfectionist sects (e.g., Kendrick, 1961; Synan,

1971, 1975; but cf. Mills, 1985), with a few outbreaks of tongues speaking found in the pessimistic and legalistic sects. Almost no Pentecostal phenomena occurred among communistic, egocentric, or esoteric sects, except for individuals who left these sects and joined one more conducive to the Pentecostal message. However, Clark notes that the types should be seen as being theoretical models, with the boundaries between the types obscured. For example, many Pentecostal groups are pessimistic in that they believe in the catastrophic end of the world. Many of these same groups are legalistic in that they believe in the literal authority of the Bible. They are perfectionist in that they believe that regeneration or the baptism in the Holy Spirit removes the consequences of sin from the believer's life.

Bryan Wilson (1959b, 1970), building on Clark's typology, has distinguished four general categories of sects: (1) adventist sects (e.g., Jehovah's Witnesses), (2) introversionist sects (e.g., Quakers and some Holiness sects), (3) conversionist sects (e.g., Pentecostals and the Salvation Army), and (4) gnostic sects (e.g., Christian Science, New Thought, and New Age). Wilson presents the hypothesis that those sects that argue for drastic changes in the structure of society, e.g., Adventist and Introversionist sects, are not likely to become churches or denominations, in Troeltsch's use of the concept. Rather, they will remain sects because they refuse to compromise with the dominant social structure; however, conversionist and gnostic sects are more likely to become denominations, because they are more willing to compromise with the dominant value structure. He points to the larger Pentecostal denominations as examples of conversionist sects that have become integrated into the dominant society.

III. Pentecostalism As a Value-oriented Society Movement.

Neil J. Smelser (1962) has advanced a useful theory of behavior that helps organize the growing material on the Pentecostal movement. Smelser has proposed six predeterminants of social movements, each of which is added to the others to create a cumulative effect. These are: (1) structural conduciveness, where social inequality is present; (2) structural strain, where people become aware of the social inequality; (3) growth and spread of a generalized belief system that offers an alternative explanation as to why the inequality exists; (4) factors that may precipitate people acting on the belief system; (5) mobilization of the participants to action; and (6) a weakening of general and social control.

An example contrasting two types of social movements, Pentecostalism and the Social Gospel movement, may help clarify how different social movements can emerge from similar social conditions yet maintain distinctiveness and alternative action choices. Evangelicals in general and Pentecostals in particular have been criticized for their emphasis on individual salvation as a solution to what have been described as intolerable social conditions rather than join with and support the Social Gospel movement (Moberg, 1965; Christensen, 1974, 1976). But when seen in perspective, the issue is less striking than when first proposed. Liston Pope (1942), for example, found in the mill towns of Gaston County, North Carolina, that preachers, regardless of denomination, preached sermons along lines of individual morality but ignored broader social issues, such as low pay, child labor, and shift work for women. The mill towns studied by Pope included people from the same social classes as those that spawned the Pentecostal movement. But one should not be surprised that the early Pentecostals did not address social problems.

People tend to respond to adverse social conditions in ways they perceive as appropriate. Those who are outside the political structure of society are not likely to define their situation as one appropriate or amenable to a political solution. If people define their situations as ones in which only God can intervene, then so far as they are concerned, a religious response is the only appropriate behavior. Smelser calls this component "situational facilities," by which he means that the nature of the situation is likely to facilitate, in this case, a religious response. Smelser distinguishes between value-oriented responses and norm-oriented responses and suggests that the Pentecostal movement is a type of value-oriented response. This is more than a semantic distinction. A value-oriented movement is "a collective attempt to restore, protect, modify, or create values in the name of a generalized belief" (1962, 313).

The Pentecostal movement as a value-oriented movement is broader and more inclusive than the Social Gospel movement, which was a norm-oriented, or reform, movement (e.g., Rauschenbusch, 1945, 1964). As a value-oriented movement, the Pentecostals attempted to reconstitute values, redefine norms along value lines, reorganize the motivation of individuals, and redefine situational facilities. The Social Gospel movement, as a norm-oriented, or reform, movement, attempted to change the behavior of individuals and groups by changing the laws (i.e., norms) that govern behavior. This was attempted in two ways. First, there were appeals to the logic and good graces of the parties involved. Second, there was an effort to induce government agencies to enact changes that would help alleviate social problems.

A value-oriented movement is more radical than a norm-oriented movement (Smelser, 1962), since an emphasis on values is an emphasis on restructuring the basis of social organization. A norm-oriented movement is a social reform movement, emphasizing the legitimacy of the existing social order, with responsibility of the privileged classes to orchestrate gradual social change and help alleviate problems generated by the same social processes that produced the privileges enjoyed by the upper classes in the first place. The success or failure of the Social Gospel movement lay in its ability to change norms without changing structure. The fact that American society, in the first decades of the twentieth century, was in the throes of rapid structural change rather than normative change, while not a guarantee of the success of a value-oriented movement, does with a fair degree of certainty, guarantee opposition to a norm-oriented movement. The ideas of the Social

Gospel movement still have an impact, and, in fact, many of the specific points made by Bushnell, Gladden, Rauschenbusch, and their followers have been included in the agendas of many of the groups that originally were in opposition to the Social Gospel movement (White and Hopkins, 1976).

Seen from this perspective, the content of the argument is only one aspect of the distinctiveness between the Pentecostal movement and the Social Gospel movement. There are at least two major social distinctions between the two. First, the Pentecostal movement received its largest support from rural residents: southern and midwestern tenant farmers, farm laborers, and small-town residents. In the larger cities, where Pentecostal churches had any success, their adherents were drawn chiefly from the recent migrants from the rural areas, both black and white (Kendrick, 1961; Synan, 1971, 1975; Schwartz, 1970). In addition, many of the early Pentecostal preachers were black, including pastors and evangelists in predominantly white congregations; and the early Pentecostal movement, while marked by instances of individual bigotry, had no official or structural color barriers. Many independent white Pentecostal ministers, in order to obtain railroad discounts given to ministers and to perform weddings, were ordained by the Church of God in Christ, a black Pentecostal organization. By contrast, the Social Gospel movement's greatest success and support was among the churches that either ministered to the recent European immigrants who worked in the urban factories and sweatshops or those upper-middle-class churches supported by the owners and managers of the factories (White and Hopkins, 1976).

A second distinction between the two movements was in the sources of leaders who emerged. The Pentecostal leaders tended to come from the same social sources as the adherents, while the leaders of the Social Gospel movement tended to be seminary- or university-trained members of the middle classes (Kendrick, 1961; Synan, 1971; White and Hopkins, 1976). Many of these were the descendants of recent European immigrants or were Anglo-Saxon ministers or members of mainline denominations who were influenced by the then relatively young field of sociology and who had genuine compassion and concern for the plight of the urban working classes. In addition, many had access to people in positions of power and thus felt they could exert some influence to get social conditions changed.

Thus, important to the success of the Pentecostal movement has been its ability to differentiate between values and norms. Value-oriented movements arise when alternative means of expressing grievances are inadequate (or perceived as such). Norm-oriented movements demand political solutions to problems. The participants in the early Pentecostal movement perceived political solutions as unattainable for at least two reasons. First, as poor rural residents, they experienced the uncomfortable reality that they were outsiders in the political process and thus had no faith in a political solution to their problems. Second, lacking the accoutrements of power, and having little or no organizational expertise, they did not possess the means to effect changes in the political systems even if they so desired.

A further factor affecting the success of the value-oriented movement was its ability to isolate itself from the influences of the dominant social structure (Gerlach, 1970; Gerlach and Hine, 1968). Thus, appeals by Pentecostal preachers to "come out from the world and be separate" had a practical impact. It allowed the ministers to control the interpretation of world events. The reluctance to participate in political or legal attempts to redress grievances forced ministers to emphasize appeals to God as a solution to problems. Higher education was suspect because it was a representative of a worldly value system, so Bible institutes and colleges were established to train not only ministers but lay members as well. The relative social isolation of adherents allowed the leaders to control communication at a time when other means of communication were relatively ineffective.

In addition, the leaders of the early Pentecostal movement offered alternative explanations of social conditions primarily because of their own isolation from dominant intellectual explanations. Many of the explanations were intended to dismiss commonly understood wisdom and at the same time, make sense of the relative deprivation of adherents to the Pentecostal movement while nonadherents seemed to experience relative prosperity.

Further social strains existed as industrialization expanded its dominance in the economic spheres and agriculture lost its prominence (Bellah, 1975; Wuthnow, 1976; Marty, 1984). These changes brought many different ethnic and cultural groups together. They saw the emergence of blacks as a competing economic group with poor, southern whites, and increasingly, after World War I, with poor northern urban whites. Add to these changes the intellectual unfashionableness of social Darwinism; the emergence of higher criticism as a methodological tool of biblical analysis, which was rejected by Evangelicals in general and Pentecostals in particular as a trend toward modernism; and a renewed spiritual awakening as evidenced by a number of worldwide revival movements that occurred around the turn of the century.

As strain increases, explanations of social phenomena tend to focus on the nature of good and evil (Flora, 1973; Dynes, 1955; Gerlach and Hine, 1968). This generalized belief system is necessary because the strains in society make old explanations untenable and thus increase the need for new elaborations or explanations. The leaders of the Pentecostal movement had a somewhat limited social and professional experience and thus had to formulate alternative interpretations. It was easy, then, to formulate strictly religious interpretations of social events and even to develop a singular religious experience, i.e., the Pentecostal or charismatic experience, as an exclusive interpretation of a general value-oriented movement. It provided something other groups did not have. Defined as a unique religious experience given by God to those he deemed worthy, it gave the Pentecostals a reason to feel that they had a greater degree of spirituality than other religious groups. This generalized belief system allowed the Pentecostals to define themselves as special, having an aspect of true spirituality rejected by other groups. Some Pentecostals called themselves "Full Gospel," after the Holiness groups, implying that others who were not Pentecostal had less than a Full Gospel. Thus the isolation with its resulting strain and the Pentecostal message being used as an explanation to help relieve the pressure generated by the strain, increased the probabilities of survival for the Pentecostals.

When the members of value-oriented movements perceive themselves to be the preservers and upholders of the good and right, while others are perceived as either ignoring the good and right or actively pursuing the path of evil, then any confrontation can be interpreted as a precipitating event. Revival meetings are evidences of success in the encounters, and it makes little difference, at least initially, whether the revival meetings produce an absolute increase in the numbers of adherents. The revival meeting is its own success. When people receive salvation, speak in tongues, or are healed, a lack of increase in numbers in the worship services on Sunday morning could be dismissed as unimportant. Many preachers could say with conviction, "Numbers aren't important. The move of the Spirit is." Some could justify small numbers in regular worship services as "God separating the wheat from the chaff."

Linked closely to the success of the revival meetings is the personality of the evangelist. This person is the focus of attention of the local congregation. In a revival-centered movement, the evangelist is the closest to a superstar most people get. Well traveled, well dressed, sometimes well connected, at least with other like-minded religious leaders, the evangelist is the link connecting isolated people. This tendency has continued, with evangelists serving the same function for Pentecostals as movie and television stars serve for general audiences.

In addition to the impact that revival meetings had on the success of the Pentecostal movement was the growth of the Sunday School movement. The Sunday School movement was an evangelistic outreach that not only educated children but recruited adults as well (Hudson, 1981). The Sunday school movement was primarily an urban phenomena and can be seen as one type of organizational structure that helped the newly arrived urbanites cope with what to them was an alien society.

Another factor evident in the Pentecostal movement that helped increase the structural strain was the initial opposition of mainline denominations to the Pentecostal experience. Many of the lower-class and disinherited members were forced to leave their home denominations as they became interested in the Pentecostal experience. Some felt they were already excluded because of their lower-class status. They then affiliated with the fledgling Pentecostal movement, and the struggles of the members and the struggles of the movement

became united. Later, when the leaders of the mainline denominations began to worry that this tactic was causing too many people to leave, the tactics were changed, and the denominations attempted to include and encourage the Pentecostals, or charismatics, as those who remained in the mainline churches became known (Kelly, 1972). The charismatics who have remained have experienced another cycle of strain and conflict.

Part of the impetus to the rise of the Pentecostal movement has to do with the search for religious identity going on in America during the early days of the twentieth century. Martin E. Marty, in *Pilgrims in Their Own Land* (1984), notes that not only have Americans been on a religious quest, their religion has been changing as well, so that no permanent establishment can be expected to last much past the generation of those who created the establishment, sometimes not even that long. Yet, as Marty has pointed out, this restlessness has become an essential part of the definition of American religion. Glenn (1987), however, writes that poll data indicate that American religion is not just becoming more restless. Americans are becoming less religious, or more secular, a process linked closely to modernization. Religious groups are responding to the modernization of society by becoming more alike, a point made more than three decades ago by Herberg (1955).

The trend toward secularization has several explanations. First, as Durkheim noted several years ago, as specialization and division of labor increases in society, so too will religious groups, so that persons with different religious needs can find groups that specialize in that need. Thus the new religious consciousness, including the Neo-Pentecostal and Jesus movements, are specialized responses to specialized needs that other groups either were not meeting or could not meet. This point is given empirical support by Finke and Stark (1988), who, in an analysis of the 1906 U.S. Census of Religious Bodies, argue that in the early days of the twentieth century, as urbanization and the numbers of religious groups increased, so did the percentage of the population who were church adherents. They conclude that the trend toward urbanization is conducive to the growth of church attendance, because the urban centers provide many more choices for participation than do rural areas.

Second, the new religious consciousness, like the earlier Pentecostal movement, is seen as a reaction to the strain produced by the changes incurred by modernization. Bellah (1967), for example, argues that as the dominant social institutions lose their traditional authority (reminiscent of Weber), people search for alternative sources of certainty and absoluteness. This idea also has been advanced by Kelley (1972), in explaining the growth of conservative churches and the increase in Protestant Neo-Pentecostals, and by O'Connor (1975) and Ranaghan and Ranaghan (1969) in discussing the growth of Catholic Neo-Pentecostals.

Third, the new religious consciousness is explained by Campbell (1978) as an adjustment to modern society by people who are unhappy about traditional religion's resistance to modernity. Thus the new religiousness is seen as an attempt to integrate science, individualism, personal growth, and other aspects of modern culture, such as the arts, music, and literature. It is an embracing of the modern, an argument also advanced by Bellah et al. in their *Habits of the Heart* (1985).

This article has used Smelser's elements of collective behavior as illustrative of the social conditions connected with the growth of the Pentecostal movement. The kind of response depends on the ways in which the elements combine.

One cannot take Smelser's model carte blanche, as several problems can be identified. First, the lines between the different elements are blurred when analyzing actual events so that it is difficult to ascertain the distinctions between, e.g., structural conduciveness and structural strain. Second, not all of the elements are identifiable in some cases so that the logical possibilities for combinations are limited. Third, the identification of the important precipitating event is difficult, especially when, in most movements, there are a number of events occurring simultaneously. Fourth, the utility of the model depends on the accuracy and completeness of the records of the movement. Thus, while it provides a general model for orientation, it is less useful for generating testable hypotheses.

Part of the problem facing sociologists of religion is that, at the present time, no adequate theory of the interaction of religion and society exists. Specific recommendations would likely be foolhardy given our present state of knowledge, although some general parameters can be sketched. For example, the saliency of the interchanges between language and religion, following Burke (1961), have only been touched upon. Also, while Darrand (1983) has conducted a very good analysis of the Pentecostal experience as a mechanism of social control, there are ramifications still not clearly understood. In addition, we still have only a limited understanding of the sources and styles of Pentecostal leaders, as well as the similarities and differences between beliefs and lifestyles of leaders and adherents. And the impact of the electronic church on the development of belief structures, not to mention personal identities, still demands additional research. Further, the assumption that Pentecostals are likely to be politically conservative has left another segment of the population—namely politically liberal or radical Pentecostals whose concern is with social justice and with liberation theology—underresearched. Finally, there are not enough social scientists studying the processes of modernization in relation to the growth or decline of social and religious movements, especially in non-Western societies.

Bibliography: R. M. Anderson, *Vision of the Disinherited* (1979); R. Bellah, *The Broken Covenant: American Civil Religion in Time of Trial* (1975); idem, "Civil Religion in America," *Daedalus* 96 (1967): 1–20; R. Bellah, R. Madsen, W. M. Sullivan, A. Swidler, and S. M. Tipton, *Habits of the Heart: Individualism and Commitment in American Life* (1985); K. Burke, *The Rhetoric of Religion* (1961, 1970); E. Clarke, *The Small Sects in America* (1949); L. Christenson, *A Charismatic Approach to Social Action* (1974); idem, *Social Action Jesus Style* (1976); T. C. Darrand, *Metaphors of Social Control in a Pentecostal Sect* (1983); E. Durkheim, *The Elementary Forms of the Religious Life* (1965 [1915]); R. Dynes, "Church-Sect Typology and Socio-Economic Status," *American Sociological Review* 20 (1955): 555–60; R. Finke and R. Stark, "Religious Economies and Sacred Canopies: Religious Mobilization in American Cities, 1906," *American Sociological Review* 53 (1988): 41–49; C. B. Flora, "Social Dislocation and Pentecostalism: A Multivariate Analysis," *Sociological Analysis* 34 (1973): 296–304; S. Freud, *Totem and Taboo* (1959 [1913]); L. Gerlach, "Pentecostalism: Revolution or Counter-Revolution?" in I. I. Zaretsky and M. P. Lerne, eds., *Religious Movements in Contemporary America* (1974); idem, *People, Power, Change: Movements of Social Transformation* (1970); L. Gerlach and V. Hine, "Five Factors Crucial to the Growth and Spread of a Modern Religious Movement," *Journal for the Scientific Study of Religion* (Spring 1968), 23–40; N. D. Glenn, "Social Trends in the United States: Evidence From Sample Surveys," *Public Opinion Quarterly* 51 (1987): 109–26; A. Greeley, *The Denominational Society* (1972); M. P. Hamilton, ed., *The Charismatic Movement* (1975); W. Herberg, *Protestant–Catholic–Jew* (1955); W. J. Hollenweger, *The Pentecostals* (1972); W. S. Hudson, *Religion in America* (1981); C. E. Jones, *A Guide to the Study of the Pentecostal Movement* (1983); D. M. Kelley, *Why Conservative Churches Are Growing: A Study in the Sociology of Religion* (1972); K. Kendrick, *The Promise Fulfilled: A History of the Modern Pentecostal Movement* (1961); M. E. Marty, *Pilgrims in Their Own Land* (1984); W. E. Mills, *Charismatic Religion in Modern Research: A Bibliography* (1985); D. O. Moberg, *Inasmuch: Christian Social Responsibility in the Twentieth Century* (1965); H. R. Niebuhr, *The Social Sources of Denominationalism* (1929); E. D. O'Connor, ed., *Perspectives on Charismatic Renewal* (1975); M. M. Poloma, *The Charismatic Movement: Is There a New Pentecost?* (1982); idem, "Toward a Christian Sociological Perspective: Religious Values, Theory, and Methodology," *Sociological Analysis* 43 (1982): 95–108; L. Pope, *Millhands and Preachers* (1942); R. Quebedeaux, *The New Charismatics: The Origins, Development, and Significance of Neo-Pentecostalism* (1976); idem, *The Young Evangelicals: Revolution in Orthodoxy* (1974); K. and D. Ranaghan, *Catholic Pentecostals* (1969); W. Rauschenbusch, *Christianity and the Social Crisis* (1964); idem, *A Theology for the Social Gospel* (1945); K. Roberts, *Religion in Sociological Perspective* (1984); G. Schwartz, *Sect Ideologies and Social Status* (1970); N. J. Smelser, *Theory of Collective Behavior* (1962); L. J. Suenens and C. D. Helder, *Charismatic Renewal and Social Action: A Dialogue* (1980); V. Synan, *Aspects of Pentecostal-Charismatic Origins* (1975); idem, *The Holiness-Pentecostal Movement* (1971); E. Troeltsch, *The Social Teaching of the Christian Churches* (1960 [1931]); J. Wach, *Sociology of Religion* (1944); M. Weber, *The Protestant Ethic and the Spirit of Capitalism* (1958 [1904–5]); idem, *The Sociology of Religion* (1964 [1922]); R. C. White, Jr., and C. H. Hopkins, *The Social Gospel: Religion and Reform in Changing America* (1976); B. R. Wilson, "An Analysis of Sect Development," *American Sociological Review* 24 (1959): 3–15; idem, "The Pentecostalist Minister: Role Conflicts and Status Contradictions," *American Journal of Sociology* 64 (1959): 494–504; idem, *Religious Sects: A Sociological Study* (1970); idem, *Sects and Society: A Sociological Study of the Elim Tabernacle, Christian Science, and Christadelphians* (1961); R. Wuthnow, *The Consciousness Reformation* (1976).   J. W. Shepperd

SOMA   See SHARING OF MINISTRIES ABROAD.

SPANISH CHARISMATICS   See CHARIS-
MATIC MOVEMENT.

SPANISH PENTECOSTALS   See EUROPEAN
PENTECOSTALISM.

SPEAKING IN TONGUES.   See BAPTISM IN
THE HOLY SPIRIT; GLOSSOLALIA; INITIAL EVI-
DENCE, A BIBLICAL PERSPECTIVE; INITIAL EVI-
DENCE, A HISTORICAL PERSPECTIVE; INTER-
PRETATION, GIFT OF.

SPENCER, IVAN CARLTON   (1914–).
Educator, church executive. Son of Ivan Quay
Spencer (1888–1970), Carlton Spencer succeeded his father as head both of the school and
church he had founded. A native of West Burling-
ton (Bradford County), Pennsylvania, he graduated from the Elim Bible Institute, then moved to
Hornell, New York, in 1933 and was ordained to
the ministry by the Elim Ministerial Fellowship
(now Elim Fellowship) two years later. He served
the school as instructor from 1938 to 1949, as
president from 1949 to 1982, and as chairman of
the board of trustees from 1982 to date. He was
general chairman of the fellowship, based in
Lima, New York, from 1954 to 1984; and was a
member of the administrative board of the National Association of Evangelicals from 1948 to
1984 and of the Pentecostal Fellowship of North
America from 1961 to 1984. Upon retirement as
head of the Elim Fellowship, Carlton Spencer
became first president of a new sister organization: Elim Fellowship of Evangelical Churches
and Ministers, also based in Lima. Under his
leadership, the Elim Bible Institute and Elim
Fellowship spearheaded acceptance of the Latter
Rain, charismatic, and discipling movements
among older Pentecostals. In 1977 Spencer
served on the planning committee for the first
Conference on the Charismatic Renewal in the
Christian Churches in Kansas City.
   Bibliography: C. E. Jones, *Guide to the Study of the
Pentecostal Movement* (1983); D. Manuel, *Like a Mighty
River* (1977).   C. E. Jones

SPENCER, IVAN QUAY   (1888–1970). President of Elim Bible Institute and founder of Elim
Fellowship. Reared on a farm in the Allegheny
foothills of northern Pennsylvania, Ivan Spencer
grew up in the Methodist Church. From early
childhood he had an interest in spiritual things.
Converted at age twenty-one, he immediately felt
the call to preach. For a short time he attended
Wyoming Seminary near Scranton, Pennsylvania,
but left school when he was stricken with typhoid
fever. While returning home on the train, he was
instantly healed.
   Spencer soon found work with a farmer in
Macedon, New York, who encouraged him to
visit the nearby Elim Tabernacle in Rochester,
sponsored by the Duncan Sisters. After visiting
the church, he enrolled in the Rochester Bible
Training School, which it sponsored in the fall of
1911. The next year Spencer received the baptism
of the Holy Spirit. In 1913 he graduated from the
school and was married to fellow student Minnie
Back.
   For the first years of their marriage, Spencer
farmed and did evangelistic work. He held a

Methodist pastorate in upstate New York for a
short time. In 1920 Spencer joined the Assemblies of God and pioneered a church at Hornell,
New York.

Ivan Q. Spencer founded Elim Bible Institute in
1924. The school is now in Lima, New York.

   During the summer of 1924 Spencer opened
Elim Bible Institute at Endwell, New York, to
train Pentecostal ministers. Intending for this new
school to carry the mantle of the Rochester Bible
Training School which had closed, the Duncan
sisters then invited Spencer to move his school to
Rochester in 1927. Disagreement arose, however,
over the school's affiliations, and Elim Bible
Institute moved to Red Creek, New York, in
1928. Here Spencer began editing the *Elim
Pentecostal Herald* in January 1931. By 1932 the
school moved into larger facilities at Hornell,
New York. In the following year, the Elim
Ministerial Fellowship was founded as an agency
to grant ministerial credentials. During the 1940s
Ivan Spencer and Elim Bible Institute were closely
associated with the New Order of the Latter
Rain. The school moved again in 1951 to Lima,
New York, where it now occupies the campus of
the old Genessee Wesleyan Seminary. The Elim
Ministerial Fellowship was expanded and became
the Elim Missionary Assemblies in 1947 and since
1972 has been called Elim Fellowship.
   Spencer was a founding delegate of the National Evangelical Association in May 1943. He
also served on the board of administration for
Pentecostal Fellowship of North America at its
inception in 1948. In 1960 Spencer's son Carlton
took over as fellowship chairman and as president
of the school.
   Bibliography: M. Meloon, *Ivan Spencer: Willow in
the Wind* (1974).   G. W. Gohr

SPIRIT BAPTISM See Baptism in the Holy Spirit; Glossolalia; Initial Evidence, a Biblical Perspective; Initial Evidence, a Historical Perspective.

SPIRIT IN SCRIPTURE The term "spirit" when used in the OT is almost always a translation of the Hebrew word *rûaḥ,* though in a very few cases "spirit" renders the Hebrew *nᵉšamah.* In the NT "spirit" translates the Greek *pneuma.* We shall survey the various ways in which the Hebrew and Greek terms are used, concentrating on expressions designating the divine Spirit. The intention here is not a full conceptual or theological study of the divine Spirit in the Bible (see bibliography), but the more modest aim of describing the relevant linguistic data.

I. Rûaḥ in the Hebrew Old Testament.

A. General. The word *rûaḥ* occurs approximately 380 times in the Hebrew OT and in the great majority of cases is taken to mean "spirit" with various connotations. The next most common meanings of the term are "wind" or "breath." To take the KJV translation as an example, Young's concordance shows *rûaḥ* translated as "spirit" 240 times, the next most frequent translations being "wind" (92 times) and "breath" (28 times). In the Septuagint *rûaḥ* is translated as *pneuma* 264 times (usually meaning "spirit"), the next most frequent translation being *anemos* ("wind," 49 times).

Thus, the precise meaning of *rûaḥ* depends on the context. But in some cases it is difficult to be sure exactly what connotation is to be given to *rûaḥ.* For example, it has been debated whether in Genesis 1:2 the *rûaḥ ʾelôhîm* that "was moving upon the face of the waters" of the primordial world is to be taken as "the spirit of God," the more common view (so, e.g., the NIV), or "the wind of God," as in Job 26:13, where God's *rûaḥ* (here usually taken as "breath" [NIV] or "wind" [RSV]) is referred to in a poetic passage alluding to the creation of the world. Other passages where *rûaḥ* means "wind" include, e.g., Genesis 8:1; Numbers 11:31; and 1 Kings 18:45. In Isaiah 40:7, the *rûaḥ yahweh* is frequently translated as "the breath of the LORD," but in 40:13 the same expression is usually translated "the Spirit of the LORD."

Likewise, in Ezekiel 37:1–14 translations show some uncertainty as to how the various occurrences of *rûaḥ* are to be taken. The *rûaḥ yahweh* of 37:1, which takes Ezekiel to the valley of bones, is usually translated "the Spirit of the LORD." However, in 37:5–6, is the *rûaḥ* which God promises "breath" (so, e.g., NIV, RSV) or (divine?) "spirit" (NIV and RSV mg.)? In 37:9–10 Ezekiel is told to "prophesy to the breath [ha rûaḥ]," which enters the dead and they come to life. This "breath" comes from "the four winds [rûḥôt, pl. of rûaḥ]," but in 37:14 the *rûaḥ* God promises to put within the Israelites is usually taken as God's "Spirit."

In Ezekiel 37:1–14, in fact, it is likely that the author plays with possible connotations of *rûaḥ,* making the "breath" or "wind" of the vision in 37:4–10 a dramatic representation of God's "Spirit" promised to the exiled Israelites. That is,

the *rûaḥ* of 37:4–10 may be taken as *both* "breath" and the divine "Spirit."

Numerous passages use *rûaḥ* in the simple sense of "breath," almost indistinguishably from *nᵉšamah.* For example, "breath of life" translates *rûaḥ ḥayyim* in Genesis 6:17 and *nišmat ḥayyim* in Genesis 2:7 (cf. Gen. 7:15, 22). In Job 33:4 and 34:14, *rûaḥ* and *nᵉšamah* appear in parallel parts of poetic passages. In several poetic passages, we read of God's "breath" (*rûaḥ*) as a powerful force (e.g., Exod. 15:10; 2 Sam. 22:16; Job 4:9; 15:30; Pss. 18:15; 33:6). Other passages refer to the *rûaḥ,* "breath" (and, by extension, the life) of humans (e.g., Job 9:18; 12:10; Eccl. 3:19). When God takes away the *rûaḥ* of his creatures they die (Ps. 104:29; cf. 146:4), and when he sends his *rûaḥ* ("Spirit"? "breath"?) "they are created" (104:30).

The term is also used to mean a person's temper or disposition (e.g., Gen. 41:8, "mind"—NIV; Ps. 32:2), strength, or vivacity (e.g., Gen. 45:27; Judg. 15:19; 1 Kings 10:5, lit. "there was no more spirit in her," "she was overwhelmed"— NIV). It is also used in a variety of related senses for which English translations supply an assortment of renderings.

Isaiah 31:3 declares that "the Egyptians are men and not God; their horses are flesh [*bāśar*] and not spirit [*rûaḥ*]." The point is that the Egyptians and their horses are mortal, vulnerable to the forces God will bring against them. "Spirit" here represents a mode of existence not subject to mortality.

B. The Divine Spirit. Of most importance here, however, are the many cases (approx. 90) where the Hebrew OT references to God's *rûaḥ* have to do with God's "Spirit." The most frequent construction is "the Spirit of the LORD" (*rûaḥ yahweh,* 23 times). This expression appears mainly in the books of Judges, 1 and 2 Samuel, 1 and 2 Kings, and in a few other places (2 Chron. 20:14; Isa. 11:2; 40:7, 13; 63:14; Ezek. 11:15; 37:1; Mic. 2:7; 3:8). Other constructions include "the Spirit of God" (*rûaḥ ʾelôhîm,* 11 times, e.g., Exod. 31:3; 1 Sam. 10:10), "the Spirit" (*ha rûaḥ,* 11 times, nearly all in Ezekiel, e.g., 2:2; 3:12), and "my Spirit" (*rûḥi,* 10 times, mainly in the Prophets, e.g., Isa. 42:1).

Most scholars are persuaded that the ancient Israelite conception of God's "Spirit" underwent development. From earlier portrayals as an almost impersonal force, the Spirit came to be seen more and more as having personal characteristics. Certainly in a number of OT references, the divine "Spirit" is basically a powerful force.

For example, in the stories of the Israelite "judges" the Spirit "came upon" (*hāya ʾāl*) the human individuals and they were emboldened for war (Judg. 3:10; 11:29). The literal sense of the Hebrew in 6:34 is that the Spirit "clothed itself" with Gideon (*lābšāh,* "took possession"—RSV; cf. the same verb in 1 Chron. 12:18; 2 Chron. 24:20). The Spirit of the Lord "came mightily upon" (*sālaḥ ʾāl*) Samson, giving him extraordinary strength (Judg. 14:6, 19; 15:14).

In the stories of Saul, the Spirit operates like an overwhelming force from God. When Saul meets a band of prophets, the Spirit comes upon him and he is moved to prophesy (1 Sam. 10:5–11; cf. 11:6). In 1 Samuel 19:18–24 the Spirit comes upon Saul and his servants, deflecting them from their hostile purposes and throwing them into a kind of prophetic frenzy.

In other passages, "the Spirit of God" conveys to the human agent special understanding and craft, as in the equipping of Bezalel as artisan in the construction of the tabernacle (Exod. 31:1–5; 35:30–35). The notion of the Spirit as equipping one for service/office is shown by the Spirit leaving Saul after his disobedience to God and transferring to David, God's newly approved choice to be king (1 Sam. 16:13–14). In the latter passage especially, the "Spirit" also seems to represent the agency by which divine approval for office is tended. In Numbers 11:24–30 God distributes his "Spirit" to the Israelite elders at their installation as assistants to Moses, and they too "prophesy."

This understanding of God's "Spirit" as the means through which God equips people for special tasks is reflected in the prophecies of a future Davidic king on whom "the Spirit of the LORD will rest" (Isa. 11:1–5), giving him great insight and good judgment. Likewise, the "servant" of Isaiah 42:1–4 bears the divine Spirit and is thus enabled for his task.

As indicated already, in the OT the divine Spirit is the power generating prophecy. The Gentile Balaam utters prophetic oracles whose content he cannot control when "the Spirit of God [comes] upon him" (Num. 24:2–25). In 2 Samuel 23:1–2 David is the vehicle through whom "the Spirit of the LORD" spoke oracles and songs. In 1 Kings 22:24 (cf. 2 Chron. 18:23), two prophets argue over which one is the true spokesman for the divine Spirit, reflecting the common prophetic claim. Micah declares himself to be "filled with power [kōaḥ], with the Spirit of the LORD [rûaḥ yahweh]," and thus is able "to declare to Jacob his transgression and to Israel his sin" (3:8).

This close connection of the Spirit with prophecy becomes a somewhat standardized conception in postexilic Israelite thought as is indicated in Nehemiah 9:20, 30, where the prophets are pictured as the vehicles through whom God's Spirit frequently admonished Israel. A similar idea is reflected in Acts 7:51–53, where Israel's rejection of prophets sent from God is called resisting the Holy Spirit.

The divine Spirit and prophecy are frequently associated in the Book of Ezekiel in colorful ways. We encounter a number of references to "the Spirit" without further qualifiers, suggesting that the concept of the divine Spirit was already sufficiently developed and familiar as to require no modifiers (but cf. 11:5; 37:1 ["the Spirit of the LORD"]; and 11:24 ["the Spirit of God"]). After the vision in chapter 1, which leaves Ezekiel prostrate and weak, we are told that "the Spirit came into me and raised me to my feet" (2:2; cf. 3:12–15, 24). Several times, "the Spirit" induces in Ezekiel experiences that involve being transported in visions (8:3; 11:1, 24; 43:5). In other passages (e.g., 40:1–3) it is "the hand of the LORD," apparently synonymous with "the Spirit."

Often in prophetic oracles we encounter the expression "my Spirit" (rûḥi), in promises of divine restoration of his people. In Isaiah 44:3, God promises, "I will pour out my Spirit" on Israel, and this is parallel with the promise to bestow "my blessings on your descendants." The most famous example of this expression, however, is Joel 2:28–32, where again the Spirit is pictured as "poured out" upon Israel, producing prophecies, dreams, and visions as part of a great redemption.

In these passages, the verbs evoke an image of the "Spirit" as a fluid, but the language should not be taken woodenly. It is the nature of poetic oracles to use colorful and striking imagery for rhetorical effect. Note the different imagery in Ezekiel 36:27, where God promises, "I will put my Spirit in you and move you to follow my decrees and be careful to keep my laws" (but cf. 39:29). This imparting of God's "Spirit" produces thoroughly changed behavior and is apparently synonymous with the "new heart [lēb ḥādāš]" and "new spirit [rûaḥ ḥᵉdāšāh]" that will characterize the redeemed Israel (18:31; 36:26). Clearly behind the varying imagery is a strong connotation of the "Spirit" as a divine force effecting profound moral change.

In Psalm 139:7 God's rûaḥ and "presence" (pāneh) are linked, and both seem to function as verbal representations of God's inescapable power and sovereignty. In Psalm 143:10, however, God's rûaḥ is sought as a guide in doing the divine will. The psalmist in 51:10–11 asks for a divinely wrought moral renewal and implores God not to cast him from the divine "presence" (pāneh) or to take away "[his] Holy Spirit [rûaḥ qādšᵉkā]." In this last passage "Holy Spirit" seems to represent a mode of fellowship with God and also (in view of the modifier "Holy") the agency of divine moral purpose and power. The personal moral renewal prayed for here is a "steadfast spirit [rûaḥ nākôn]" and "a willing spirit [rûaḥ nᵉdibāh]" that reflects the intents of the divine "Spirit." Also relevant here is Isaiah 63:7–14, where there are two more instances of the construction "Holy Spirit." God "set his Holy Spirit" among ancient Israel (v. 11), and their rebellion against God "grieved his Holy Spirit" (v. 10). Here again, "Holy Spirit" seems to be a way of referring to the special presence of God among his people, and the adjective emphasizes the sacredness and sanctity of the divine Spirit. The fact that the term rûaḥ was a way of speaking of God's direct action and presence probably contributed to the tendency more evident in later Israelite texts to think of the divine "Spirit" as possessing personal characteristics.

II. Pneuma in the New Testament.

A. General. Like rûaḥ, the NT term pneuma can mean "wind" (e.g., Heb. 1:7), or "breath" (e.g., 2 Thess. 2:8). But we also find references to "unclean spirits" (pneuma akatharton, e.g., Mark 1:23–27), meaning demonic powers (cf. 1 John 4:1–6). First Peter 3:19 mentions "the spirits in prison" (disobedient angels? cf. Jude 6) to whom Christ preached. Hebrews 12:23 refers to "the spirits of righteous men made perfect," reflecting the idea that the dead (or righteous dead) have some continuing existence as "spirits" (e.g., 1 Cor. 5:5; or "souls" [*psychē*], e.g., Rev. 6:9). And Hebrews 1:14 describes angels as "ministering spirits [*leitourgika pneumata*] sent to serve those who will inherit salvation."

Pneuma is also used to describe the inward aspect of the human person associated with emotions and thought. For example, Paul says he serves God with his "spirit" (Rom. 1:9, "whole heart"NIV), and refers to the Spirit of God testifying "with our spirit that we are God's children" (Rom. 8:16). In 1 Corinthians 2:11 Paul states that only a "man's spirit within him" (*to pneuma tou anthrōpou*) can know his thoughts. But in 14:14 he defines prayer in tongues by saying "my spirit [*pneuma*] prays, but my mind [*nous*] is unfruitful," and he does not elaborate on the distinction (cf. Eph. 4:23, "the spirit of your mind"). Elsewhere, Paul refers to the "refreshing" of the spirits of various people through the kindness of others (e.g., 1 Cor. 16:18; 2 Cor. 7:13). The *pneuma* can also be the life-force within a person, as in James 2:26. At death the individual "gives up" the spirit, i.e., yields life back to God (e.g., Matt. 27:50; cf. Acts 7:59).

The statement "God is spirit [*pneuma ho theos*]," in the context of John 4:24, probably means that as "spirit" God transcends all human shrines and all attempts to restrict access to him to particular places and customs of worship. Worship "in spirit" probably does not mean "within the human spirit." Instead, it is likely worship prompted by the divine Spirit by whom all must be born anew (John 3:5–8; cf. Phil. 3:3).

B. God's Spirit. Of the 379 occurrences of *pneuma* in the NT more than 250 refer to God's Spirit. We shall survey this usage and highlight the distinctive features of NT expressions.

The construction "Holy Spirit" (*pneuma hagion*) appears much more often than in the OT (e.g., Matt. 28:19; Luke 11:13; Acts 1:8), but we also frequently find "Spirit of God" (*pneuma theou*, e.g., Matt. 3:16; Rom. 8:14; 15:19). Apart from the OT quote in Luke 4:18, the expression "the Spirit of the Lord" ([*to*] *pneuma kyriou*) appears only a few times, and always with some degree of textual variation in the manuscript tradition: Acts 5:9; 8:39; 2 Corinthians 3:17 (and the variant at Acts 16:7). In many cases, however, there is the simple construction, "the Spirit," indicating the familiarity of early Christians with the concept (e.g., John 1:32; 7:39; Acts 2:4; Gal. 3:3–5).

Distinctively Christian expressions referring to the Spirit include "the Spirit of his Son" (*to pneuma tou hyiou autou*, Gal. 4:6), "the Spirit of Christ" (*pneuma christou*, Rom. 8:9; 1 Peter 1:11), and "the Spirit of Jesus" (*to pneuma Iēsou*, Acts 16:7). These constructions reflect the conviction that the divine Spirit is the agency by which the glorified Christ manifests his power and will among believers. Linking the divine Spirit so closely with Christ also contributed to the Christian emphasis on the Spirit as possessing full characteristics of "personhood." Especially interesting is the statement in 2 Corinthians 3:17, "the Lord is the Spirit." This "Lord" is likely the exalted Christ (v. 18), and we have here the

strongest verbal connection between Christ and the divine Spirit in the NT. In 1 Corinthians 15:45 Paul contrasts Adam, "a living being" (*psychēn zōsan*) with Christ, who was made "a life-giving spirit" (*pneuma zōopoioun*).

This link of the divine Spirit and Christ finds expression also in 1 Peter 1:11, where the OT prophets are said to have been inspired by "the Spirit of Christ" (cf. 2 Peter 1:21). In Revelation 19:10 the reference to "the spirit of prophecy" (*to pneuma tēs prophēteias*) as "the testimony of Jesus" likewise shows a strong Christian redefinition of the nature and role of the Spirit.

Another important NT innovation is in John 14–16, where the Spirit is termed the "Counselor" (*paraklētos*). He is also "the Spirit of truth" (14:17; 15:26; 16:13) and is described as possessing strong personal characteristics. Given and sent by God "the Father" (14:16, 26) and by Christ (15:26; 16:7), the Spirit will "teach" (14:26), "testify" (15:26), "convict" (16:8), "guide" (16:13), "glorify" Christ (16:14), and make known the things concerning Christ (16:14–15). Also relevant is the consistent use of the masculine pronoun (*ekeinos;* "he" or "that one") throughout John 14–16 to refer to the Spirit (*pneuma* is a neuter noun in Greek), further suggesting a strong conception of the Spirit in "personal" categories. Research has demonstrated that the reference to the Spirit as *paraklētos* here probably represents a transference to the Spirit of certain roles and characteristics associated with chief angels in some pre-Christian Jewish circles (e.g., Brown, 1970, 2:1135–44; cf. 1 John 2:1, where Christ is *paraklētos* for Christians before God).

The NT claims that God's OT promise to "pour out" his Spirit has now been fulfilled (e.g., Acts 2:14–21, 32–33). Jesus, who was "anointed" with the Spirit (John 1:32–34; Acts 10:38), bestows the Spirit to his followers (John 20:21–23; note the play on the meaning of *pneuma* as "breath"); though more frequently it is God who gives his Spirit (e.g., Rom. 5:5; 1 Thess. 4:8). Thus, in the NT the bestowal and activity of the Spirit is evidence that the eschatological hopes for final redemption from God have begun to be fulfilled. The expression "firstfruits of the Spirit" (Rom. 8:23) reflects this eschatological viewpoint, as does the reference to the Spirit as a "deposit [*arrabōn*], guaranteeing what is to come" (2 Cor. 1:22; 5:5; cf. Eph. 1:14). Also related to this is Hebrews 6:4–6, where Christian believers, who "share" in the Holy Spirit, are said to have "tasted . . . the powers of the coming age."

Very important for the later development of the classical Christian doctrine of the Trinity are NT passages that link the Spirit with God and Christ in formulaic triads (Matt. 28:20; 2 Cor. 13:14). These formulas seem to indicate an emergent notion of the Spirit later expressed in more sophisticated terms of the "persons" (Latin *persona*) of the Godhead.

The NT is replete with expressions concerning the experience of the Spirit, both individually and collectively in Christian circles. People are said to be "filled" or "full" of the Spirit (e.g., Acts 2:4;

4:8, 31; 6:5), and so have unusual enthusiasm, eloquence, and even miraculous power. The Spirit directs via such phenomena as visions (e.g., Acts 11:12) and prophetic oracles (e.g., Acts 11:28; 21:4, 10–11). Paul refers to various phenomena of early Christian experience as "gifts" (*charismata*) of the Spirit (1 Cor. 12:4), including such things as prophecy, tongues speaking, healings, etc. (12:4–11). Paul's description of the tongues speaker as uttering *mystēria* ("mysteries") *pneumati* may mean "with his [own] spirit" (NIV) or "in the Spirit" (RSV). In Revelation the expression "in the Spirit" (*en pneumati,* 1:10; 4:2; 17:3; 21:10) describes a state in which John the prophet receives visions from God.

Indeed, Christian existence can be called "walking" or living "according to" (Rom. 8:4) or "in" the Spirit (8:9; Gal. 5:25). Christians are "letters of Christ" (*epistolē christou*) written "with [or by] the Spirit [*pneumati*] of the living God" (2 Cor. 3:3). The Christian church is a "temple" (*naos*) in which God's Spirit dwells (1 Cor. 3:16–17), as are the bodies of individual Christians (6:18–20). In colorful imagery, Paul refers to Christian initiation as baptism "by [or in] one Spirit [*heni pneumati*] into one body" of believers and as being given "the one Spirit to drink" (1 Cor. 12:13). In 1 Thessalonians 5:19, he warns, "Do not quench the Spirit," meaning that the Spirit-inspired phenomena such as prophecies are not to be suppressed. Also worth noting is the image of being "sealed" (*en hō esphragisthēte*) by or with the Spirit (marked and set apart until the day of redemption; Eph. 1:13; 4:30), and the exhortation not to "grieve [*mē lupeite*] the Holy Spirit of God" by improper behavior.

In light of this, it should be recognized that NT usage of the term "spiritual" (*pneumatikos*) characteristically refers to the Spirit of God, does not usually mean simply "nonphysical," and does not carry overtones of asceticism found in later Christian usage. Thus, e.g., "spiritual songs" (*ōdais pneumatikais*, Eph. 5:19) are lyrical expressions inspired by God's Spirit, and "the spiritual man" (*ho pneumatikos*) of 1 Corinthians 2:15 is a person in whom the Holy Spirit is active.

The frequency and variety of expressions referring to the Spirit are linguistic evidence of the importance of the concept of the Holy Spirit and the pervasiveness of religious experiences attributed to the work of the Spirit in the early church.

Bibliography: R. E. Brown, *The Gospel According to John,* 2 vols. (1970); J. Dunn, *Baptism in the Holy Spirit* (1970); idem, *Jesus and the Spirit* (1975); H. Gunkel, *The Influence of the Holy Spirit* (1979); E. Kamlah, J. D. G. Dunn, and C. Brown, "Spirit, Holy Spirit," *NIDNTT,* 3:689–709; H. Kleinknecht, F. Baumgärtel, W. Bieder, E. Sjöberg, and E. Schweizer, "*pneuma,* etc.," *TDNT,* 6:332–455; G. T. Montague, *The Holy Spirit: Growth of a Biblical Tradition* (1976).   L. W. Hurtado

SPIRITUALITY, PENTECOSTAL AND CHARISMATIC

Spirituality refers to a cluster of acts and sentiments that are informed by the beliefs and values that characterize a specific religious community. *Liturgy* describes what all members of a community do together when assembled for worship. *Theology* defines systematized, ordinarily written, reflections on religious

experience. *Spirituality,* by contrast, focuses on the pietistic habits of ordinary individuals. The vagueness and elasticity of the word *spirituality* rise in large part from the wide variety in which worshipers express themselves, even in a single religious communion.

Spirituality as the *gestalt* of piety is, however, not native to the Pentecostal tradition. Pentecostals more easily use the adjective *spiritual* than they do the abstract noun. They more easily speak of persons than of deeds or manners, as spiritual (or unspiritual). In the far less frequent times when "spirituality" *is* used in ordinary Pentecostal conversation, it applies not to what people do but to how religious they are. Statements like the following are typical: "Of course she can teach the class, she's a very spiritual person." "I'm greatly impressed by the new pastor's spirituality: he's deep in the Lord, a real man of God." In Pentecostal usage, spirituality admits of degrees. "Consecrated" and "consecration" are close synonyms (no doubt acquired from the Pentateuchal vocabulary of ritual sacrifice in the KJV, with antecedents in the Holiness movement), but these terms are now archaic in the Pentecostal tradition and seem not to have been picked up at all in the charismatic movement.

This article describes facets of Pentecostal and charismatic spirituality, chiefly as expressed in the North American context, and with an effort to observe nuances in practice between Pentecostals and charismatics where that can be done. There is a geography of spirituality: this analysis needs adjustment for other cultures.

Five *implicit values* govern Pentecostal spirituality:

1. By far the most pervasive is the worth accorded to individual *experience.* Included are not only religious feeling, and emotions of joy, or sorrow, but Pentecostals consider personal experience the arena of true religion. The point is well made by Lesslie Newbigin in *Household of God* (1954), where he describes three broad approaches to Christian realities. (1) Protestants view religion as belief, orthodoxy, doctrinal assent—a matter of the intellect. (2) The Catholic churches (he includes highly liturgical Protestant groups, not merely the Roman Catholic church) think rather in terms of obedience, participation, and religious acts. (3) Members of the Pentecostal churches—not at all limited to the classical Pentecostal churches, about which he knew little when he wrote—achieve religious satisfaction through personal experience, and this always brings an emphasis on the Holy Spirit. Classical Pentecostals are of the third variety, and charismatics in the mainstream churches add a significant experiential component to the traditional intellectual or volitional character of their various Christian traditions.

The bent toward emotional experience among Pentecostals may account in part for occasional moral failure among them, since religious and sexual experience are among the deepest of human experiences. But there is little concrete evidence to suggest that moral failure among Pentecostals exceeds that in any other Christian tradition—

except in visibility, given the prominence of Pentecostal ministers among the televangelists.

Ministerial ineptitude, doctrinal deviation, divergent mores—these and more can long be tolerated or even forgiven if profound personal experience prevails, known usually from shared personal testimony. A quoted aphorism often heard in Pentecostal circles runs this way: "The person with an experience is never at the mercy of another person with a doctrine." Of course such an emphasis lays Pentecostal piety open to charges of individualism, narcissism, or elitism. But most are only barely conscious of these charges and would hardly consider them faults if they were aware of them. Pentecostals and charismatics say, "You have to experience it for yourself." "God has no grandchildren," Pentecostal leader David du Plessis tirelessly insisted—meaning you cannot hand on to another your own experience of God. Seekers must always themselves find God in their own experience.

2. *Orality* as a fundamental quality of Pentecostal piety has been emphasized especially by Walter Hollenweger (1983, 1986). No one can rightly appreciate Pentecostal spirituality merely by reading what Pentecostals have written. Now approaching their fourth generation, Pentecostals have not yet produced any substantial theological literature. They write tracts and simple studies for purposes of evangelism. Their first scholars have been historians tempted by triumphant apologetic. Expected behaviors like avoidance of gambling or alcoholic beverages might go entirely unwritten. Nonetheless, by a lively oral tradition a newcomer soon learns.

As classical Pentecostalism moves from a sect to a church, the subculture will of course become more literary. It is likely that the astonishing success of Pentecostals in Third World evangelization, as well as its success in nonliterate cultures, can in large part be attributed to a shared reliance on the spoken word.

3. *Spontaneity* is prized in Pentecostal piety. The Holy Spirit guides worship and leads each believer, and he moves unpredictably (John 3:8). All the members expect anyone of the local assembly to follow the Spirit's leading and to do so at once. Hence, printed orders of service for public worship are not provided—though something of the sort can now be found in large metropolitan Pentecostal churches, but only in the hands of the organist, the pianist, and the supervising minister. In small-group prayer meetings, the leaders and the Spirit are in charge. Usually such gatherings give much time for "waiting on God," and no one is offended—indeed the leader may be cheered by perceived progress—if someone leads out in a prayer, a Scripture reading, or a musical chorus that everyone knows by heart. Long pauses, as in the Quaker tradition, are uncommon in Pentecostal spirituality, for Pentecostals do not consider silence a virtue (Baer, 1976; Malz, 1985).

The mix of spontaneity with the unpredictable, sometimes uncontrolled urges of the Spirit call for the best resources of pastoral guidance. From time to time, if leadership in worship sags,

Pauline fears of perceived madness (1 Cor. 14:23) are warranted.

4. *Otherworldliness* is a fading value among North American Pentecostals, given the upward slope of their economic progress and the surrounding cultural affluence. Mainline charismatics, mostly from upper-middle class circles, less clearly reflect otherworldliness though they share with Pentecostals the sort of simple dualism otherworldliness implies. "This world is not my home" is heard less frequently now among Pentecostals, and it would be unimaginable among most charismatics. The social and economic deprivation of the earlier Pentecostals no doubt accented the contrast between their own straits and the pearly gates and golden streets of heaven.

Yet Pentecostal otherworldliness reflects an authentic biblical motif, one more Johannine (1 John 2:15–17, 19; 4:4–6) than Pauline (1 Cor. 5:9–10). Such an outlook controls Pentecostal cosmology: the *real* world is the eternal one, "up there" in heaven. It informs their eschatology: Christ will at any moment return to set at right what is wrong. It accounts for the unripened social conscience of Pentecostals linked with their worldly pessimism: "The world passes away" (1 John 2:17). Among them, social justice is a part of eschatological hope. Cultural pessimism makes the correction of social ills inappropriate as a feature of any contemporary ecclesiastical agenda and accounts for earlier Pentecostal mores: their women were not to use cosmetics, since it is the business of the church to "come out from them and be separate" (2 Cor. 6:14–7:1; cf. Isa. 52:11). They were not to engage in worldly activities—mixed swimming, theater attendance, card playing. Most available photos of William J. Seymour, the Azusa Street pastor, show him without a tie, which by many early Pentecostals was thought "worldly." Otherworldliness linked with experiential individualism makes it nearly impossible for Pentecostals to comprehend the notion of structural or systemic evil—except to say that the Devil controls unredeemed human society.

5. Finally, a commitment to *biblical authority* characterizes both the Pentecostal and the charismatic sectors of the church. It is important to distinguish biblical *authority* from biblical *inspiration*. Pentecostal discussions about biblical inerrancy provide a case study in theology as learned behavior. It is the authoritative role of Scripture that more naturally characterizes Pentecostalism than intricate arguments about the inerrant quality of the biblical text. Yet when the question was raised by evangelical neighbors, Pentecostals readily joined the more conservative inerrantist party—a logical deduction from the divinely originated written Word of God. This important nuance finds illustration in the doctrinal formulation of the American Assemblies of God. When this formulation was first produced in 1916, its opening statement concerning Scripture read this way: "The Bible is the inspired Word of God, a revelation from God to man, the infallible rule of faith and conduct, and is superior to conscience and reason, but not contrary to reason (2 Tim. 3:15, 16; 1 Pet. 2:2)." In 1961, the Assemblies of

God sealed its postwar acceptance among Evangelicals by retrofitting the statement on Scripture so as to read: "The Scriptures, both the Old and New Testaments, are verbally inspired of God and are the revelation of God to man, the infallible authoritative rule of faith and conduct (2 Tim. 3:15–17; 1 Thess. 2:13; 2 Pet. 1:21)." Noteworthy is the insertion of the word "verbally" ("verbal inspiration" was an evangelical catchword at the time) and the unexplained deletion of the marvelous phrase ". . . superior to conscience and reason, but not contrary to reason." A clear mark of a classical Pentecostal is the ubiquitous presence of a Bible in hand, well marked.

The lofty regard for biblical authority, coupled with an inclination to take the words of Scripture at face value, illuminates both beliefs and practices that occur within Pentecostalism. The emergence of the doctrinal curio present in the "Jesus Name" or "Jesus Only" species of (Oneness) Pentecostalism, a neglected sister to establishment Pentecostalism, which shuns the group, presents a case in point. Denial of the Trinity, assertion that "Jesus" is God's true name and is himself the one God, and rebaptism "in the name of Jesus only"—all these emerge from the plain fact that in every place where water baptism is mentioned in the Book of Acts the biblical text specifies that the baptism was "in the name of Jesus." Similarly, if speaking in tongues is described in Scripture as an acknowledged and approved part of Christianity, Pentecostals can see no good reason to eliminate it from contemporary spirituality. Indeed they think it their providential role in history to restore to the church that long neglected "experience."

Many of the marginal eccentricities of Pentecostalism, both what the Pentecostals believe and what they experience, can be understood as contemporized forms of biblical precedents. These include out-of-the-body experiences (2 Cor. 12:2–3), visits by angels (Gen. 6:7–12; Acts 5:17–20), hearing an audible voice (1 Sam. 3:2–9; Acts 9:4), visionary tours of heaven or hell (Rev. 1:11; 4:1—all remarkably similar to a species of apocalyptic literature common in sectarian Judaism during NT times), and even miraculous Spirit transport (Acts 8:39–40; cf. Gen. 5:24) can readily be found in the literature of Pentecostal testimony or on the Pentecostal and charismatic television talk shows—where orality and experience easily converge.

Beliefs such as the prosperity teaching (Christians should be wealthy because God is) or positive confession (the believer participates in God's creative authority: say it, aloud and with faith, and you'll have it) draw from the same biblical sources, though invariably with a highly selective hermeneutic.

These five implicit values—experience, orality, spontaneity, otherworldliness, and biblical authority—combine variously to yield a constellation of *characteristic practices* found in Pentecostal and/or charismatic spirituality quite apart from the central features of speaking in tongues, the baptism in the Holy Spirit, and prayer for divine healing (see BAPTISM IN THE HOLY SPIRIT; DIVINE HEALING; GLOSSOLALIA; JESUS). The style of *prayer and praise* is instructive. Quite

usual is collective oral prayer, all praying at once, mostly vernacular or mostly glossolalic or some mix of the two. This pattern expresses the personal experience of each. Such collective group prayer is usually cued by a leader, but it can emerge spontaneously—in which cases glossolalia often predominates. On the whole, collective prayer in Pentecostal services is louder and more emotionally expressive than in charismatic circles. *Fasting* often accompanies prayer, but it is rarely mandated for congregations.

The *raising of hands* in joint or individual prayer reflects literal response to biblical precedents (Exod. 17:11–12) and commands (1 Tim. 2:8). One or two hands may be used. Pentecostals are more likely to extend the arms fully upward, palms forward. Charismatics, again more restrained, often extend arms from the waist, with bent elbows, palms upward.

Proxy prayer appears in charismatic small groups. It hardly ever occurred in earlier classical Pentecostalism, but it appears increasingly in contemporary Pentecostalism as a learned technique acquired from charismatics. There is no biblical precedent for the action, nor any injunction against it. An interested third party sits on a chair in the midst of the gathered Christians. The *laying on of hands* might be done by all present in groups of up to six to ten members or by a spontaneously assembled representative delegation of two or three persons. The idea is that prayer here is offered on behalf of an identified person not present and, quite possibly not interested in the prayers offered. In some instances, more often in charismatic than in Pentecostal groups, hands will not be laid fully on the persons who are objects of prayer but intentionally held five or six inches above the shoulders: the reason for this, if not social discretion, is unclear.

In both Pentecostal and charismatic circles, leading ministers may ask gathered congregation members to extend their arms toward a person or a group during prayer. This serves as a sort of collective, symbolic laying on of hands. Finally, some Pentecostal televangelists ask viewers to *touch* the television set as a "point of contact." *Touch* is an important, though largely unrecognized, feature of Pentecostal and charismatic spirituality. "He touched me," they gratefully sing, or in hope: "Reach out and touch the Lord as he goes by" (cf. Mark 5:25–34). Laying on of hands frequently accompanies prayer for the Pentecostal baptism in the Holy Spirit. But there is no universal requirement for this practice among Pentecostals and charismatics, probably because of the clear precedent at Acts 10:44–45, when the Holy Spirit fell on those gathered at the household of Cornelius while Peter was still speaking—with no laying on of hands.

Expressive personal experience occurs when an individual Pentecostal believer engages in *dancing in the Spirit*. Always individually done, never in couples, always unplanned and never scheduled, at almost any point in the service—during hymns or during the sermon, a believer so moved will leave the seat and move up and down the aisles of the church, eyes often closed, arms usually uplifted—lost in abandon to the worship of God. This practice more often appears among black Pentecostals, where usually purer forms of Pentecostal worship survive. Some charismatics have intentionally inserted liturgical dance into planned services, but "scheduled" and "liturgical" dance would be twice embarrassing to classical Pentecostals—on grounds both of their preference for spontaneity and their Johannine avoidance of "dance" as worldly entertainment. Only "dancing in the Spirit" has legitimacy among Pentecostals: was it not David himself who "danced before the LORD with all his might" as the Scriptures say (2 Sam. 6:14)?

Like dancing in the Spirit, which would be unlikely (but not impossible) if alone in prayer, some features of Pentecostal spirituality appear only in corporate settings. The most colorful and lively of these is a *Jericho March,* so named from the march of the children of Israel seven times around the city of Jericho till the walls fell down (Joshua 6:1–27). In an atmosphere of high enthusiasm, a congregant may rise and make for the aisles, possibly inviting others to join. Around the perimeter of the place of assembly they go, gathering more worshipers till a full column is formed. Quite possibly most of the congregation who are able and willing join in as do the platform ministers. During the march, there is much singing, maybe some shouting (as happened also in the Bible, and at the bidding of the leader: Joshua 6:10, 16, 20). The whole affair might last as long as an hour or two, and it might even displace the preaching. Afterwards, the marchers return to their seats and the service goes on. At times, a Jericho March begins with one person dancing in the Spirit, who is joined by another, then another, till the whole group is caught up. The corporate jubilation and joy of the Jericho March—which is always spontaneous and unrehearsed—affords stunning contrast to routine liturgies denounced regularly by the Pentecostals—who never thought it wrong for worship to be fun. Anything like a Jericho March among upper-class charismatics would suggest classical Pentecostal influence.

The most likely scene for a Jericho March is the *camp meeting.* Begun by Kentucky Presbyterians in the early 1800s and used widely among the nineteenth-century Holiness churches, this venerable remnant of the frontier still widely appears among North American classical Pentecostals. (But not among charismatics, who have moved to metropolitan four-star hotel ballrooms.) "Camp meetings," with a bit of forgiveable metaphor, have occurred into the 1980s at velvet-seated, multimillion-dollar Pentecostal megachurches. As recently as the 1950s, tents were used. Later, simple cabins were constructed. But these are now being upgraded to year-round cottages. A large wooden "tabernacle" seating up to two or three thousand would be the center of activity. Bareground floors covered with straw or with sweetsmelling wood chips from a nearby sawmill have been replaced increasingly by poured concrete. There might be a morning Bible teacher and an evening evangelist. The camp might run one or two weeks, sometimes longer, with a succession of ministers and campers. Red checkerboard

tablecloths are draped over long tables where, when the bell rings—a bell rescued from some decaying rural church—all queue up for tasty meals in common, prepared by the industrious laywomen of the camp. Afternoons allowed peaceful walks through the surrounding country woods setting.

These camp meetings were also frequent settings for the Pentecostal "wave offering" (after Lev. 23:9–10, 20–21 and similar references, with a permitted hermeneutical wink.) At the direction of the leading minister, men and women would retrieve from purse or pocket a fresh handkerchief and, to the accompaniment of great singing "present a wave offering to the Lord." Battlefield imagery prevailed, and the crowd waved, not in surrender, but to welcome symbolically the coming King until whose impending arrival they would sing with triumphant resolve:

"Hold the fort, for I am coming!"
　　Jesus signals still:
Wave the answer back to heaven
　　"By Thy grace we will!"

For many Pentecostals the summer camp meetings were the occasions when they were baptized in the Spirit, perhaps also being baptized in water at a nearby creek. *Altar services* at the camps could go on through the night, yielding fresh testimonies of deepened personal experience with the Lord that might be given in the services the next day. Pentecostal services often end, unnervingly to the unaccustomed, with people going in two directions: some toward the altar for prayer, others out the rear door.

Public Pentecostal services, whether at a camp meeting or a local church, form the occasions for other practices common to Pentecostal spirituality. One of those that occurred from the beginning was *"falling under the power,"* being "slain in the Spirit"—a virtual faint, almost always supine, sometimes accompanied by soft glossolalic prayer, sometimes conspicuously silent, sometimes with arms fully raised from the lying position accompanied with loud prayer. In this posture many early Pentecostals received the baptism in the Holy Spirit and, for the first time, spoke in tongues. In later Pentecostalism, "falling under the power" came to be associated with certain ministers credited with having a gift that led to the phenomenon. (It flourished under Kathryn Kuhlman as early as the mid- and late-1940s, for example.) This practice occurs also among charismatics, who have renamed it "resting in the Spirit" to escape the militaristic imagery.

Expressiveness among Pentecostals and, to a lesser degree, among charismatics makes a playful appearance in the use of what may be called *sacred expletives*—happy exclamations like "Glory to God!" "Hallelujah!" "Thank you, Jesus!" often sprinkled through Pentecostal rhetoric. These are at points comparable to the "boos" and "yeas" that are heard in ball games. They may resemble profanity, but have their origin in experiential piety.

A *word of knowledge* may occur in the public gatherings of either Pentecostals or charismatics.

Going beyond the strict exegetical demands of the listed spiritual gift of that name (1 Cor. 12:8, but compare 14:26; John 1:48–50), these Christians allow that a minister (a word of knowledge "could happen to any believer," but certain ministers regularly use the gift) may be told by God certain information about one or more people present at a meeting. Several variant settings have emerged. A minister so gifted may describe a medical disorder or a specific ailment and say that if that sufferer will identify himself or herself, God will heal the condition. In certain charismatic Roman Catholic circles, a different sociology has been observed. A lay congregant will rise, describe a hazy vision including the gender and approximate age of a person, then describe a condition of need not limited to physical ills, and then be seated. The clustered group leaders (plural leadership is characteristic of Roman Catholic prayer group leadership) may ask for self-identification and suggest a group nearby gather for immediate prayer.

In one regrettable case in the late 1980s an eager evangelist fraudulently "aided" the Spirit through use of a tiny radio receiver in his ear tuned to a concealed transmitter operated by his wife, who interviewed unknowing attendees and fed the information to her husband. Such a ruse cannot account for the surprising accuracy of these "words of knowledge." But misuse or abuse of the gift is an occupational hazard in Pentecostal spirituality.

The authority of biblical precedent (Acts 19:12) also lies behind the long use in Pentecostalism (not observed among charismatics) of *anointed prayer cloths*. In a local church a concerned family member might present a handkerchief after describing someone in particular need. Following congregational prayer, as part of a regular service (or, perhaps, private prayer with the pastor, and maybe with the elders also) the sponsor carries the cloth to the needy one in hopeful imitation of the biblical precedent. Pentecostal evangelists, in a few unfortunate instances, have huckstered anointed prayer cloths available through the mails "for a gift of a minimum of [so many] dollars to the ministry."

Biblical precedent and command (Acts 28:3–6; Mark 16:18) lie behind the bizarre practice among certain isolated Pentecostal congregations in the Appalachians where *snake handling* is practiced (La Barre, 1962). Deaths still occur. The practice is often accompanied by intentional *drinking of poison*—strychnine, usually—again "because the Bible says we should do it" (Mark 16:18, a passage regarded by a large majority of biblical scholars as a second-century addition to the original Gospel but present in the KJV most familiar to classical Pentecostals). Organized Pentecostalism deplores these practices, and the charismatics only read about them.

Of course, Pentecostals and charismatics *speak in tongues*, both in corporate gatherings and in private prayer. Charismatics as a whole are less emotional in their use of glossolalia. The noise level and the appearance of possession vary widely with the broad cultural differences among Pentecostals. Even the deaf speak in tongues, though

that is rarely observed and has gone virtually unnoticed in research.

Holy laughter occurred in early Pentecostalism. A believer, ordinarily praying at the altar, may fall into spasms of laughter, lasting minutes or upwards of an hour. This is understood as an expression of joy in the Lord. There is no social pressure to generate or repeat the experience, and it is rare today.

Prayer for *divine healing* regularly marks Pentecostal and charismatic services. Charismatic mainstreamers, given their backgrounds, more realistically regard suffering. Wise Pentecostal pastors deal regularly with failed healings, the consequence of an imbalanced call, often via the one-way electronic church, for "faith": "overbelief" is a constant threat in Pentecostal spirituality (Parker, 1980).

Leg-lengthening, the act of bringing a person's shorter leg to the length of the other, when both are extended, gives the appearance of an instant miracle. The practice seems to have originated after World War II and perhaps most instances of it occur among independent charismatics. But it also appears in some "Third Wave" Pentecostalized evangelical prayer groups.

Exorcisms are not frequent anywhere, but they are serious and demanding when they occur. They most often take place among those independent Pentecostals and charismatics who foster a sort of *pandemonism*—a belief that not only sins but faults and even bad habits are caused by demons, which must be expelled. Such environments on the distant margins of organized Pentecostalism at times generate bizarre practices: in a central California valley in the early 1970s attendees at independent Pentecostal meetings, where much was made of demons as the cause of life's ills, were asked to bring small brown paper bags to the services. At the right moment, the evangelist directed them to cough and spit into the bag—producing an exorcism by expectoration.

Dreams and, especially, *visions* give another example of the power of biblical example (Acts 9:10–18). One sector of the charismatic movement, a sector that could be called the "The Jungian school" (Agnes Sanford popularized the approach) takes dreams very seriously and finds in the intricate psychological writings of Carl Jung a theoretic basis (Kelsey, 1964, 1968). *Inner healing* was an understandable development that emerged out of this school. Classical Pentecostals, on the other hand are suspicious of psychology and with it such "inner healing." They neither need nor want any theory for a practice that is already found in the Bible (Acts 16:9–10), and among them visions outnumber dreams, neither of which are frequent, however. Some report visionary trips to heaven (or hell) and back, and itinerant ministries are born of such experiences.

All these may seem a curious conglomeration of practices cited as features of spirituality. But each springs from the values listed earlier. Pentecostals and charismatics are Christians who value the Bible highly, take their commitment with utmost seriousness, prizing the spontaneity of life in the Spirit and conveying all of this through oral testimonies and "sharing." They are members of a

Christian subculture whose burgeoning numbers already exceed the total membership of Protestantism and who, by the year A.D. 2000, are expected to predominate in the new church of the southern hemisphere.

See also DANCING IN THE SPIRIT; SINGING IN THE SPIRIT; SLAIN IN THE SPIRIT.

Bibliography: R. A. Baer, Jr., "Quaker Silence, Catholic Liturgy, and Pentecostal Science—Some Functional Similarities," in R. P. Spittler, ed., *Perspectives on the New Pentecostalism* (1976); W. Benn and M. Burkill, "A Theological and Pastoral Critique of the Teachings of John Wimber," *Churchman* 101 (1987):101–13; E. Coppin, *Slain in the Spirit: Fact or Fiction* (1976); R. Cummings, *Gethsemane* (1944); C. Farah, *From the Pinnacle of the Temple* (n.d., charismatic critique of the "positive confession" movement); J. W. Follette, *Broken Bread* (1957); S. Frodsham, *Spirit-Filled, -Led, and -Taught* (n.d.); D. Gee, *After Pentecost* (1945); idem, *Concerning Spiritual Gifts* (1937); idem, *The Fruit of the Spirit* (1928); idem, *Keeping in Touch* (1951); idem, *The Ministry Gifts of Christ* (1930); idem, *Pentecost* (1932); idem, *Trophimus I Left Sick: Our Problems of Divine Healing* (1952); J. Gunstone, *The Charismatic Prayer Group: A Handbook* (1976); W. J. Hollenweger, "Pentecostal Research: Problems and Promises," in Charles E. Jones, *A Guide to the Study of the Pentecostal Movement* vol. 1 (1983), vii–ix; idem, "Pentecostals and the Charismatic Movement," in C. Jones et al., eds., *The Study of Spirituality* (1986); D. Hunt and T. A. McMahon, *Seduction of Christianity* (1985); C. A. Johnston, *The Frontier Camp Meeting* (1955); M. Kelsey, *Dreams: the Dark Speech of the Spirit* (1968); idem, *Tongue Speaking* (1964); W. LaBarre, *They Shall Take up Serpents: Psychology of the Southern Snake Handling Cult* (1962); D. N. Malz, "Joyful Noise and Reverent Silence: The Significance of Noise in Pentecostal Worship," in D. Tannen and M. Saville-Truike, eds., *Perspectives on Silence* (1985); D. McConnell, *A Different Gospel* (1988); F. McNutt, *Healing* (1974); L. Newbigin, *The Household of God* (1954); L. Parker as told to D. Tanner, *We Let Our Son Die* (1980); M. Pearlman, *The Heavenly Gift* (1935); C. M. Robeck, Jr., "Growing Up Pentecostal," *Theology News and Notes* (Pasadena, California) 35 (March 1988): 4–7, 26; A. Sanford, *The Healing Gifts of the Spirit* (1966); R. P. Spittler, "Scripture and the Theological Enterprise: View From a Big Canoe," in R. K. Johnston, ed., *The Use of the Bible in Theology: Evangelical Options* (1985); D. Wilkerson, with J. and E. Sherrill, *The Cross and the Switchblade* (1963); R. Wise, ed., *The Church Divided: The Holy Spirit and a Spirit of Seduction* (1986).   R. P. Spittler

SPITTLER, RUSSELL PAUL (1931–). NT scholar and theologian. Reared in the Assemblies of God (AG) in Pittsburgh, Pennsylvania, Russell Spittler began his ministerial education at Southeastern College (Lakeland, Fla.), continuing at Florida Southern College (A.B.), Wheaton College Graduate School (M.A.), Gordon-Conwell Theological Seminary (B.D.), and Harvard University (Ph.D.). His dissertation on the *Testament of Job* gave rise to his translation and notes now standard on the subject. Following faculty assignments at Central Bible College (1958–62) and Southern California College (1967–76), where he also served as academic dean (1973–76), he moved to Fuller Theological Seminary, where from 1976 to 1986 he served as associate dean for academic systems in the School of Theology. In 1986 he became founding director of the David J. du Plessis Center for Christian Spirituality at

Fuller, where he also holds the post of professor of NT.

New Testament scholar Russell P. Spittler directs the David J. du Plessis Center for Christian Spirituality at Fuller Theological Seminary.

In 1955 Spittler married Bobbie Watson. Ordained by the AG (1961), he has served as U.S. Naval Reserve Chaplain (now captain) since 1963, was a member of the Board of Regents of Melodyland School of Theology (1974–81), and president of the Society for Pentecostal Studies (1973). He is author of several books and many articles.

Selected publications include *Cults and Isms* (1962); *God the Father* (1976); *Perspectives on the New Pentecostalism* (ed.) (1976); *The Corinthian Correspondence* (1976); *The Church* (1977); and "The Testament of Job" in J. H. Charlesworth, ed., *The Old Testament Pseudepigrapha*, 2 vols. (1983).   C. M. Robeck, Jr.

SQUIRE, FREDERICK HENRY (1904–62). British pastor, evangelist, and educator. While serving as an Assemblies of God (Assemblies of God in Great Britain and Ireland [AGGBI]) pastor in East Kirkby, Nottinghamshire, England, Squire felt called to enter itinerant evangelism in 1932. A successful revival campaign in Northampton prompted him to conduct, with his Full Gospel Testimony Revival Party, campaigns throughout the South Midlands and elsewhere. These contributed to the development of Pentecostalism in Britain. Squire emphasized faith healing, and the reported healings drew attention to his meetings.

Squire left the AGGBI to organize his converts into congregations, forming the Full Gospel Testimony with headquarters first in Southend-on-Sea and later at Leamington Spa. The *Full Gospel Testimony* (1935–52) publicized the activities of the organization, which eventually disbanded in the early 1950s. The International Bible Training Institute, which Squire founded at Leamington Spa in 1947, has endured as a nondenominational institution.

Bibliography: C. E. Jones, *A Guide to the Study of the Pentecostal Movement* (1983).   G. B. McGee

A minister, singer, and composer, Ira Stanphill is best known for his gospel songs such as "Mansion Over the Hilltop," "Suppertime," and "Room at the Cross."

STANPHILL, IRA (1914–). Assemblies of God minister, singer, and gospel songwriter. His contribution to gospel music, both in style and writing, is immense. He has written more than five hundred songs, including "Mansion Over the Hilltop," "Suppertime," "Follow Me," "He Washed My Eyes With Tears," "Room at the Cross," "We'll Talk It Over," "You Can Have a Song in the Night," and "I Know Who Holds Tomorrow." Many of his songs were written as a result of deep personal trials, including divorce in his first marriage and later the death of his first wife.

"Suppertime" was popularized by former Louisiana Governor Jimmie Davis; "Room at the Cross" has been heard for many years as a theme for the weekly "Revivaltime" broadcast. Stanphill was inducted into the Gospel Music Hall of Fame in 1981. His candid autobiography, *This Side of Heaven* (1983), gives the stories behind the writing of many of his more popular songs.

Bibliography: I. Stanphill, *This Side of Heaven* (1983).   W. E. Warner

STAPLETON, RUTH CARTER (1930–83). American evangelist. Though a Baptist, Ruth Stapleton actively engaged in a public faith healing ministry and a private commitment to speaking in tongues. She emphasized emotional, spiritual, and physical healing through the work of the Holy Spirit and the commitment of a person's imaginative powers to wholeness (*The Gift of Inner Healing* [1976]; *The Experience of Inner Healing* [1977]). Her faith in God's healing power resulted in her refusal to accept medical treatment for cancer. Though she did not survive her bout with cancer, her faith encouraged many.

Bibliography: "Healer of Memories," *Time* (April 16, 1976): 42, 107; "Jimmy Carter's Sister: How Faith Can Heal," *McCall's* (April 1977), 32, 104; "Walking People Out of Their Past: An Interview with Ruth Carter Stapleton," *Christianity Today* (November 4, 1977), 10–14.   F. Bixler

STARK, EDMOND F. (1913–39). First Church of God (CG, Cleveland, Tenn.) missionary to Angola. Stark, a native of Oklahoma, married Pearl Pickel, a former missionary to China and Liberia, who accompanied him to Angola in 1938. In Angola they went to Quanza Sol, a district where there were no Christians, no Bibles, and no schools. In March 1939 Stark was stricken with malaria and died. The nearest missionary was two days away, and death came so suddenly that help never reached him. His death, however, had a dramatic effect on the missionary impulse of the CG. Eventually his work was salvaged and continued by others who were inspired by his sacrifice.

Bibliography: C. W. Conn, *Where the Saints Have Trod* (1959).   C. W. Conn

STATISTICS, GLOBAL This is a survey of what is best described as, and best termed, the Twentieth-Century Pentecostal-Charismatic Renewal in the Holy Spirit, with its goal of world evangelization.

I. Three Waves of Renewal. The tables that follow trace the expansion of this Renewal across ten decades and two centuries, and also across eight continents and the entire world. Historically, the Renewal can be seen to have arrived in three massive surges or waves whose origins are traced in Global Table 1 to the years 1741, 1907, and 1970. The first wave is known today as Pentecostalism (line 3), the second wave as the Charismatic Movement (line 25), followed by a third wave of non-Pentecostal, noncharismatic, mainstream church renewal (line 39). (References are to numbered lines in the table plus their related numbered footnotes). The Pentecostals, charismatics, and third-wavers who make up this Renewal today number 21 percent of organized global Christianity. They are here classified under thirty-eight different categories (twenty-one relating to Pentecostals, thirteen to charismatics, and four to third-wavers).

Even with these three waves and thirty-eight categories, an underlying unity pervades the movement. This survey views the Renewal in the Holy Spirit as one single cohesive movement into which a vast proliferation of all kinds of individuals and communities have been drawn in a whole range of different circumstances. This explains the massive babel of diversity evident today.

These members are found in 11,000 Pentecostal denominations and in 3,000 independent charismatic denominations. Charismatics are now also found across the entire spectrum of Christianity. They are found within all 150 traditional non-Pentecostal ecclesiastical confessions, families, and traditions. Pentecostals/charismatics (the generic term preferred here) are found in 8,000 ethnolinguistic cultures, speaking 7,000 languages, covering 95 percent of the world's total population.

The sheer magnitude and diversity of the numbers involved beggar the imagination. Global Table 1 and its footnotes document a 1988 total of 332 million affiliated church members (line 44). Of these, 176 million are Pentecostals, 123 million are charismatics, and 28 million are third-wavers. Some 29 percent of all members worldwide are white, 71 percent nonwhite. Members are more urban than rural, more female than male, more children (under eighteen) than adults, more Third World (66 percent) than Western world (32 percent), more living in poverty (87 percent) than affluent (13 percent), more family-related than individualist.

Members are more harassed, persecuted, suffering, and martyred than perhaps any other Christian tradition in recent history. Their incredible variety and diversity can be seen from the fact that to do justice to this diversity we have had to create a whole variety of neologisms and new statistical categories. Those described in the table include: pre-Pentecostals, quasi-Pentecostals, indigenous Pentecostals, isolated radio Pentecostals, post-Pentecostals, postcharismatics, crypto-charismatics, radio/TV charismatics, and independent charismatics.

Of these nine categories only the last two have been recognized up to now as genuine Pentecostals/charismatics. In this survey we are taking the position that all of these categories need to be recognized and enumerated as part of the Renewal.

II. The Tide Surges In. All three waves are still continuing to surge in. Massive expansion and growth continue at a current rate of 19 million new members a year or over 54,000 a day (columns 19–20). One-third of this is purely demographic (births minus deaths in the Pentecostal/charismatic community); two-thirds are converts and other new members. In the early days of all three waves annual rates of growth were enormous (columns 11–12); now they have declined gradually to 5 percent per year for Pentecostals, 7 percent for charismatics, and 6 percent per year for the Renewal as a whole (column 15). These overall figures hide a number of situations of saturation, some spheres of decline, and many situations of explosive, uncontrollable growth.

Charismatics outnumber Pentecostals in numbers of annual converts worldwide (column 21). They do, however, have a growing dilemma in that charismatics in the non-Pentecostal mainline Protestant and Catholic churches experience an average involvement of only two or three years—

after this period as active weekly attenders at prayer meetings, they become irregular or nonattending, justifying our term postcharismatics (line 34). This "revolving door syndrome" results in an enormous annual turnover, a serious problem that has not yet begun to be adequately recognized or investigated.

III. Permeation of Global Christianity. Global Table 2 shows the geographical spread of the Renewal today. Large numbers exist on every continent and in 230 countries. This table solves the eighty-year-old puzzle as to why Europe has always had the lowest response to Pentecostalism of any continent. Europe has always remained less than 1 percent Pentecostal. The reason Europeans rejected the first wave is because they were not prepared to leave the great state churches to become Pentecostals; since 1970, however, they have responded enormously as charismatics *within* those churches. With 24 million charismatics and third-wavers, Europe now has the highest ratio (4.5) of charismatics to Pentecostals of all continents across the world (column 24).

At the other end of the spectrum from rejection to acceptance is East Asia, whose Christians have become massively Pentecostalized (column 23). This is due mainly to the phenomenal spread of the Renewal in Korea and in mainland China.

All state churches and national denominations, with their myriads of agencies and institutions, are now rapidly becoming permeated with charismatics (see footnote to line 72). In addition, roughly 14 percent of charismatics in these mainline churches have seceded or become independent each year since 1970, forming some 100,000 white-led independent charismatic churches across the world, loosely organized into forty or so major networks (line 38).

The enormous force of the Renewal can be observed in many ways. One is that a majority of the fifty or so megachurches—the world's largest single congregations, each with over 50,000 members—are Pentecostal/charismatic (line 50, footnote).

Another indication of the Renewal's dynamic is the disproportionately high Pentecostal/charismatic penetration of the media (lines 71–2). Charismatics in particular have seized the global initiative in radio, television, movies, audio, video, publishing, literature, magazines, citywide evangelistic campaigns (eight hundred each year), and so on. Virtually all varieties of ministries engaged in by institutionalized Christianity worldwide has now been penetrated by stalwarts of the Renewal.

Finance, stewardship, and giving also have risen well above the global Christian average (lines 62–69). Personal annual income of church members in the Renewal has grown this year to $880 billion (line 63). Of this, $34 billion is donated to Christian causes (line 64). This means that the rank and file of the Renewal do not need to be further exhorted regarding stewardship. Its lay members are doing all they should, and more. There is, however, an almost universal failure by leaders of the Renewal to garner and organize these vast sums coherently for mission and ministry at the world level. In consequence, giving to

A SURVEY OF THE 20TH-CENTURY PENTECOSTAL/CHARISMATIC RENEWAL IN THE HOLY SPIRIT, WITH ITS GOAL OF WORLD EVANGELIZATION
David B. Barrett

Global Table 1. The Global Expansion of the Renewal Across the 20th Century, AD 1900–2000

Column		Year	1900	1970	1975	1980	1985
1	2		3	4	5	6	7
1. AFFILIATED CHURCH MEMBERS							
2.	Prepentecostals (individual quasipentecostals) (1738)		2,500,000	3,824,000	4,084,000	4,438,000	4,813,000
3. FIRST WAVE: PENTECOSTALISM			**1,216,300**	**64,334,970**	**78,690,730**	**104,545,600**	**149,656,990**
4.	Denominational Pentecostals/pentecostals		1,216,300	61,254,240	75,036,370	100,186,050	144,392,240
5.	Non-White indigenous quasipentecostals (1741)		1,161,000	22,368,200	28,420,600	35,724,120	43,758,670
6.	Black/Non-White indigenous pentecostals (1783, 1886, 1906)		30,300	20,146,880	24,278,520	29,257,410	34,236,290
7.	Indigenous revivalist pentecostals (1783)		30,000	9,375,850	11,346,140	13,710,750	16,045,350
8.	Indigenous holiness-pentecostals (1886)		300	2,830,050	3,077,260	3,364,160	3,651,060
9.	Indigenous baptistic-pentecostals (1906)		0	4,533,450	5,565,880	6,831,100	8,096,330
10.	Indigenous oneness-pentecostals (1916)		0	1,693,820	2,075,430	2,485,110	2,894,790
11.	Indigenous pentecostal-apostolics (1917)		0	1,701,710	2,189,120	2,808,370	3,427,610
12.	Indigenous radical-pentecostals (c1960)		0	12,000	24,690	57,920	121,150
13.	Catholic Apostolics (1830, 1863)		20,000	1,610,100	1,749,000	1,887,300	2,030,800
14.	Classical Pentecostals (1895, 1901, 1904)		5,000	16,329,060	18,688,250	26,317,220	35,366,480
15.	Holiness-Pentecostals (1895)		5,000	2,553,920	2,816,620	3,123,230	3,429,850
16.	Pentecostal Apostolics (1904)		0	700,500	795,490	911,510	1,027,520
17.	Oneness-Pentecostals (1913)		0	988,430	1,081,720	1,196,180	1,310,640
18.	Baptistic-Pentecostals (1914)		0	11,820,390	13,720,580	20,802,300	29,304,300
19.	Radical-Pentecostals (c1940)		0	265,820	273,840	284,000	294,170
20.	Chinese house-church pentecostals (1906, 1955)		0	800,000	1,900,000	7,000,000	29,000,000
21.	Isolated radio pentecostals (1924, 1931)		0	2,080,730	2,454,360	2,859,550	3,264,750
22.	White pentecostal radio believers (1924)		0	806,000	893,000	971,000	1,049,000
23.	Non-White indigenous radio believers (1931)		0	1,274,730	1,561,360	1,888,550	2,215,750
24.	Postpentecostals (1930)		0	1,000,000	1,200,000	1,500,000	2,000,000
25. SECOND WAVE: CHARISMATIC MOVEMENT			**0**	**3,788,700**	**16,861,080**	**45,535,390**	**97,498,700**
26.	Mainline charismatics (active)		0	1,588,700	5,261,080	11,035,390	16,998,700
27.	Anglican charismatics (1907, 1914, 1918, 1925, 1956, 1962)		0	109,900	519,650	1,090,200	1,660,750
28.	Protestant charismatics (1910, 1918, 1950, 1956, 1966)		0	824,100	2,112,700	4,286,800	6,460,900
29.	Orthodox charismatics (1944, 1968)		0	15,200	73,000	157,000	400,000
30.	Catholic charismatics (1962, 1966)		0	238,500	1,995,730	4,771,390	7,547,050
31.	Old Catholic charismatics		0	1,000	10,000	30,000	80,000
32.	Black charismatics (1975)		0	400,000	550,000	700,000	850,000
33.	Radio/television charismatics (1953)		0	199,000	990,000	1,960,000	2,910,000
34.	Mainline postcharismatics (1960, 1970)		0	900,000	8,000,000	26,000,000	64,000,000
35.	Protestant postcharismatics (1960)		0	400,000	3,000,000	11,000,000	21,000,000
36.	Catholic postcharismatics (1970)		0	500,000	5,000,000	15,000,000	43,000,000
37.	Messianic Jewish charismatics (1965)		0	1,000	10,000	40,000	90,000
38.	White independent charismatics (1965)		0	1,100,000	2,600,000	6,500,000	13,500,000
39. THIRD WAVE: MAINSTREAM CHURCH RENEWAL			**0**	**50,000**	**1,000,000**	**4,000,000**	**20,700,000**
40.	Mainstream third-wavers		0	0	0	1,000,000	15,700,000
41.	Third-Wave White Evangelicals (1980)		0	0	0	1,000,000	8,500,000
42.	Third-Wave Black/Non-White Evangelicals (1982)		0	0	0	0	7,200,000
43.	Crypto-charismatics (1970)		0	50,000	1,000,000	3,000,000	5,000,000
44. Total all pentecostal/charismatic church members			**3,716,300**	**71,997,670**	**100,635,810**	**158,518,990**	**272,668,690**
45. Total as % of world's church-member Christians			0.70	6.40	8.20	12.00	19.10
46. PROFESSING PENTECOSTALS/CHARISMATICS							
47. Pentecostals/charismatics unaffiliated to churches or groups			0	3,362,000	5,800,000	10,700,000	20,550,000
48. Total all professing pentecostals/charismatics			**3,716,300**	**75,359,670**	**106,435,810**	**169,218,990**	**293,218,690**
49. Total as % of whole world's Christians			0.70	6.20	8.10	11.80	18.90

	1988	1990	2000	Annual rate of change, %								1988 increase		
				1970	1975	1980	1985	1988	1990	2000	Demo	Annual	Daily	Converts
1	8	9	10	11	12	13	14	15	16	17	18	19	20	21
1.														
2.	5,165,200	5,400,000	7,300,000	1.36	1.50	1.64	2.00	2.27	3.07	2.60	1.60	117,250	321	34,610
3.	176,070,330	193,679,230	268,149,500	4.46	5.11	6.79	5.96	5.00	4.08	2.78	1.57	8,803,516	24,119	6,041,700
4.	169,971,940	187,025,070	258,192,800	4.50	5.19	6.92	6.01	5.02	4.06	2.76	1.59	8,532,591	23,377	5,832,430
5.	47,765,450	50,436,630	65,461,900	5.41	4.70	4.29	3.36	2.80	2.87	2.30	1.8	1,337,432	3,664	477,650
6.	36972700	38796970	48715100	4.10	3.75	3.40	2.79	2.47	2.49	2.04	1.60	913,225	2,502	319,870
7.	17,257,820	18,032,800	22,218,400	4.20	3.82	3.43	2.69	2.30	2.28	1.88	1.5	438,191	1,200	138,060
8.	3,811,300	3,918,120	4,482,000	1.75	1.74	1.71	1.52	1.40	1.41	1.26	1.00	53,358	146	15,250
9.	8,785,630	9,245,160	11,717,400	4.55	4.13	3.70	2.98	2.62	2.61	2.11	1.90	230,183	630	63,260
10.	3,132,180	3,290,440	4,102,300	4.51	3.81	3.30	2.78	2.53	2.45	1.98	1.10	79,244	217	44,790
11.	3,759,610	3,980,940	5,356,500	5.73	5.06	4.41	3.42	2.94	3.23	2.57	2.3	110,532	302	24,060
12.	226,170	329,510	838,500	21.15	18.60	16.65	22.42	18.43	14.51	6.07	3.2	41,672	114	34,450
13.	2,113,960	2,169,400	2,500,000	1.73	1.58	1.49	1.39	1.31	1.44	1.32	1.00	27,692	75	6,550
14.	41,519,830	45,622,070	71,515,800	2.89	5.34	6.34	5.46	4.94	5.28	3.62	1.75	2,051,079	5,619	1,325,960
15.	3,600,640	3,714,500	4,316,800	2.06	2.02	1.96	1.72	1.58	1.59	1.40	0.90	56,890	155	24,480
16.	1,090,830	1,133,030	1,359,800	2.71	2.65	2.55	2.16	1.93	1.96	1.67	0.40	21,052	57	16,690
17.	1,372,970	1,414,520	1,638,100	1.89	0.15	1.91	1.67	1.51	1.54	1.36	0.90	20,731	56	8,370
18.	35,251,200	39,215,800	63,878,000	3.22	6.55	6.28	6.28	5.62	5.88	3.86	2.00	1,981,117	5,427	1,276,090
19.	299,620	303,260	323,100	0.60	0.17	0.65	0.65	0.64	0.61	0.61	0.50	1,827	5	330
20.	41,600,000	50,000,000	70,000,000	27.50	32.63	38.71	14.83	10.10	5.47	2.86	1.20	4,201,600	11,511	3,702,400
21.	3,498,400	3,654,160	4,456,700	3.59	3.17	2.83	2.43	2.23	2.17	1.80	1.22	78,014	213	35,330
22.	1,098,500	1,131,500	1,289,800	2.16	1.85	1.61	1.53	1.50	1.42	1.23	0.60	16,477	45	9,890
23.	2,399,900	2,522,660	3,166,900	4.50	3.93	3.47	2.86	2.56	2.51	2.03	1.50	61,437	168	25,440
24.	2,600,000	3,000,000	5,500,000	4.00	4.17	5.33	7.50	7.69	7.78	4.55	1.00	199,940	547	173,940
25.	123,342,710	140,572,050	222,076,500	69.01	24.76	17.71	9.75	6.98	5.91	3.67	1.76	8,609,321	23,587	6,439,400
26.	21,032,710	23,722,050	41,301,500	46.23	17.96	10.64	7.46	6.39	6.83	4.26	1.65	1,343,990	3,682	996,920
27.	1,954,840	2,150,900	2,662,200	74.57	18.86	10.47	6.39	5.01	3.10	1.92	1.60	97,937	268	66,660
28.	7,499,710	8,192,250	10,818,000	31.27	16.39	10.14	6.04	4.62	3.55	2.43	1.70	346,486	949	218,990
29.	442,540	470,900	3,000,000	76.05	19.42	20.83	7.85	3.20	36.81	8.43	1.00	14,161	38	9,740
30	10,106,920	11,813,500	23,101,300	147.36	22.71	11.63	9.33	8.44	8.78	4.89	1.70	853,024	2,337	681,210
31.	88,700	94,500	120,000	180.00	29.00	23.33	8.06	3.27	2.82	2.12	0.40	2,900	7	2,550
32.	940,000	1,000,000	1,600,000	7.50	5.45	4.29	3.53	3.19	5.00	3.75	1.30	29,986	82	17,770
33.	4,060,000	4,830,000	9,550,000	79.50	17.79	9.80	9.86	9.46	9.16	4.94	0.90	399,840	1,095	347,540
34.	80,710,000	91,850,000	140,775,000	157.78	31.37	21.54	10.29	6.90	5.57	3.48	2.02	5,568,990	15,257	3,937,440
35.	27,360,000	31,600,000	53,900,000	130.00	35.33	16.36	9.81	7.75	6.94	4.14	1.10	2,120,400	5,809	1,819,440
36.	53,350,000	60,250,000	86,875,000	180.00	29.00	25.33	10.52	6.47	4.85	3.06	2.50	3,451,745	9,456	2,118,000
37.	140,000	170,000	450,000	180.00	39.00	20.00	11.11	11.43	14.12	6.22	1.20	16,002	44	14,320
38.	17,400,000	20,000,000	30,000,000	27.27	20.77	16.77	10.00	7.47	5.50	3.33	0.90	1,299,780	3,561	1,143,180
39.	28,080,000	33,000,000	65,000,000	380.00	39.50	49.25	14.01	8.76	8.95	4.92	1.43	2,459,808	6,739	2,059,320
40.	21,880,000	26,000,000	55,000,000	0.00	0.00	157.00	15.92	9.41	10.08	5.27	1.37	2,058,908	5,640	1,758,620
41.	12,400,000	15,000,000	25,000,000	0.00	0.00	85.00	16.47	10.48	7.33	4.00	0.90	1,299,520	3,560	1,187,920
42.	9,480,000	11,000,000	30,000,000	0.00	0.00	0.00	15.28	8.02	13.82	6.33	2.00	760,296	2,083	570,700
43.	6,200,000	7,000,000	10,000,000	380.00	29.50	13.33	8.00	6.45	4.76	3.00	1.60	399,900	1,095	300,700
44.	332,658,240	372,651,280	562,526,000	7.96	8.60	10.85	7.85	6.01	5.19	3.38	1.63	19,992,760	54,774	14,575,030
45.	21.4	23.2	28.6	5.62	6.83	9.08	5.86	3.83	2.73	1.89	—	—	—	—
46.														
47.	27,960,000	32,900,000	56,800,000	14.50	12.65	13.79	10.80	8.83	7.35	4.21	1.00	2,468,868	6,764	2,189,270
48.	360,618,240	405,551,280	619,326,000	8.25	8.82	11.04	8.06	6.23	5.36	3.45	1.58	22,466,516	61,552	16,764,300
49.	21.4	23.3	29.1	6.13	6.91	9.15	6.08	4.11	2.92	1.99	—	—	—	—

A SURVEY OF THE 20TH-CENTURY PENTECOSTAL/CHARISMATIC RENEWAL IN THE HOLY SPIRIT, WITH ITS GOAL OF WORLD EVANGELIZATION (cont'd)

David B. Barrett

Global Table 1. The Global Expansion of the Renewal Across the 20th Century, AD 1900–2000

Column		Year	1900	1970	1975	1980	1985
1	2		3	4	5	6	7
50. CHURCHES, CONGREGATIONS AND HOUSE GROUPS							
51.	Denominational pentecostal churches		15,010	253,170	321,500	518,200	734,000
52.	Non-White indigenous quasipentecostal churches		10,000	65,500	80,000	100,000	120,000
53.	Black/Non-White indigenous pentecostal churches		3,000	66,310	82,000	150,000	205,000
54.	Catholic Apostolic churches		2,000	7,160	7,500	8,200	9,000
55.	Classical Pentecostal churches		10	94,200	120,000	180,000	260,000
56.	Chinese pentecostal house churches		0	10,000	12,000	30,000	50,000
57.	Isolated radio pentecostal house groups		0	54,140	60,000	66,000	75,000
58.	Mainline charismatic house groups		0	35,000	50,000	130,000	300,000
59.	White independent charismatic churches		0	10,000	20,000	50,000	90,000
60.	Mainstream third-wave house groups		0	2,000	10,000	50,000	100,000
61. Total all pentecostal/charismatic churches/groups			**15,010**	**352,310**	**441,500**	**764,200**	**1,209,000**
62. PENTECOSTAL/CHARISMATIC FINANCE AND GIVING							
63.	Personal income of church members, per year		$250 million	157 billion	240 billion	395 billion	693 billion
64.	Giving to all Christian causes, per year		$3 million	8 billion	12 billion	18 billion	29 billion
65.	Giving to all Christian causes per member per week		$0.02	$2.14	$2.29	$2.18	$2.05
66.	Giving to pentecostal/charismatic causes, per year		$2 million	200 million	1 billion	2 billion	3 billion
67.	Giving to pentecostal/charismatic causes per member per week		$0.01	$0.05	$0.19	$0.24	$0.21
68.	Giving to global foreign missions, per year		$50,000	530 million	900 million	1 billion	2 billion
69.	Giving to global foreign missions per member per week		$0.00	$0.14	$0.17	$0.12	$0.14
70. PENTECOSTAL/CHARISMATIC AGENCIES							
AND INSTITUTIONS							
71.	Service agencies		20	600	1,000	1,500	2,100
72.	Institutions		100	1,300	3,000	5,000	7,500
73. Total all parachurch/service agencies and institutions			**120**	**1,900**	**4,000**	**6,500**	**9,600**
74. PENTECOSTAL/CHARISMATIC WORKERS							
75.	Nationals (pastors, evangelists, et alii)		2,000	237,270	308,060	420,400	740,830
76.	Aliens: foreign missionaries		100	3,790	8,940	34,600	59,170
77.	Aliens: short-termers		0	1,000	3,000	15,000	50,000
78. Total all pentecostal/charismatic full-time workers			**2,000**	**240,000**	**320,000**	**470,000**	**850,000**
79. WORLD CHRISTIANITY							
80.	Christians (all varieties)		558,056,300	1,216,579,400	1,316,780,900	1,432,686,500	1,548,592,200
81.	Affiliated church members		521,563,200	1,131,809,600	1,220,852,100	1,323,389,700	1,425,927,300
82. WORLD EVANGELIZATION							
83.	Unevangelized populations		788,159,000	1,391,956,000	1,393,054,000	1,380,576,000	1,335,212,000
84.	Unevangelized as % of world		48.70	38.60	35.10	31.60	27.90
85.	Unreached peoples with no churches at all		3,500	1,300	1,000	700	580
86.	Unevangelized non-Christian or anti-Christian megacities		5	65	78	95	121
87.	Unevangelized persons to each pentecostal/charismatic		212	18.47	13.09	8.16	4.55
88.	World evangelization global plans since AD 30		246	496	546	602	673

	1988	1990	2000	Annual rate of change, %								1988 increase		
				1970	1975	1980	1985	1988	1990	2000	Demo	Annual	Daily	Converts
1	8	9	10	11	12	13	14	15	16	17	18	19	20	21
50.														
51.	839,480	909,800	1,111,000	5.40	8.24	7.96	5.34	4.19	2.76	1.81	—	35,174	96	—
52.	150,000	170,000	220,000	4.43	4.31	4.00	5.83	6.67	3.92	2.27	—	10,005	27	—
53.	220,000	230,000	260,000	4.73	10.21	8.20	3.90	2.27	1.59	1.15	—	4,994	13	—
54.	9,480	9,800	11,000	0.95	1.39	1.83	1.78	1.69	1.36	1.09	—	160	0	—
55.	296,000	320,000	400,000	5.48	7.15	7.78	5.38	4.05	2.92	2.00	—	11,988	32	—
56.	65,000	75,000	100,000	4.00	16.67	12.67	9.00	7.69	4.44	2.50	—	4,998	13	—
57.	81,000	85,000	100,000	2.16	1.98	2.27	2.53	2.47	1.96	1.50	—	2,000	5	—
58.	330,000	350,000	550,000	8.57	19.00	19.23	7.33	3.03	4.76	3.64	—	9,999	27	—
59.	99,000	105,000	120,000	20.00	20.00	14.00	6.11	3.03	1.90	1.25	—	2,999	8	—
60.	118,000	130,000	180,000	80.00	48.00	18.00	8.00	5.08	4.10	2.78	—	5,994	16	—
61.	**1,368,480**	**1,474,800**	**1,941,000**	**5.06**	**9.33**	**10.04**	**5.88**	**3.88**	**3.31**	**2.40**	—	**53,097**	**145**	—
62.														
63.	880 billion	1,005 billion	1,550 billion	6.91	9.91	11.47	8.80	7.09	5.68	3.52	—	—	—	—
64.	34 billion	37 billion	54 billion	6.67	8.33	9.45	6.55	4.71	4.51	3.15	—	—	—	—
65.	$1.97	$1.91	$1.85	1.40	0.17	-1.10	-1.32	-1.42	-0.70	-0.32	—	—	—	—
66.	3.6 billion	4 billion	5 billion	16.00	18.00	10.00	6.67	5.56	3.33		—	—	—	—
67.	$0.21	$0.21	$0.17	56.00	10.00	0.83	0.00	0.00	-1.27	-2.35	—	—	—	—
68.	2.6 billion	3 billion	4 billion	8.22	5.22	11.00	10.00	7.69	4.44	2.50	—	—	—	—
69.	$0.15	$0.15	$0.14	4.29	-1.18	-2.50	-2.14	1.33	0.00	-0.71	—	—	—	—
70.														
71.	2,500	2,800	4,000	13.33	9.00	7.33	6.19	5.60	4.52	3.00	—	140	—	—
72.	9,000	11,000	14,000	26.15	12.33	9.00	8.00	7.78	3.94	2.14	—	700	2	—
73.	**11,500**	**13,800**	**18,000**	**22.11**	**11.50**	**4.46**	**10.58**	**12.00**	**5.36**	**2.33**	—	**1,380**	**4**	—
74.														
75.	857,030	934,500	1,133,000	5.97	5.94	10.29	6.94	4.52	2.80	1.75	—	38,737	106	—
76.	74,970	85,500	167,000	27.18	34.46	14.52	8.60	7.02	8.41	4.88	—	5,262	14	—
77.	68,000	80,000	300,000	40.00	46.67	31.33	13.00	8.82	20.83	7.33	—	5,997	16	—
78.	**1,000,000**	**1,100,000**	**1,600,000**	**6.67**	**7.19**	**11.28**	**7.41**	**5.00**	**4.55**	**3.12**	—	**50,000**	**137**	—
79.														
80.	1,684,533,500	1,742,000,000	2,130,000,000	1.65	1.64	1.62	2.00	2.30	2.23	1.82	1.3	38,744,300	106,150	16,845,335
81.	1,555,199,600	1,608,700,000	1,967,000,000	1.57	1.57	1.55	2.00	2.35	2.24	1.82	1.3	36,547,200	100,130	16,329,595
82.														
83.	1,295,304,700	1,265,000,000	1,038,819,000	0.02	-0.08	-0.42	-0.64	-0.61	-1.53	-2.47	1.7	-7,906,400	-21,650	29,921,540
84.	25.38	24.11	16.6	-1.81	-1.99	-2.28	-2.68	-2.98	-3.12	-4.52		—	—	—
85.	490	430	200	-4.62	-6.00	-6.00	-4.66	-6.12	-5.89	-11.50	—	—	—	—
86.	140	152	202	4.62	3.85	4.53	4.71	4.43	3.55	2.48	—	—	—	—
87.	3.64	3.19	1.68	-5.58	-7.88	-10.47	-10.92	-7.47	-6.00	-8.99	—	—	—	—
88.	770	900	1,500	—	—	—	—	—	—	—	—	—	—	—

Global Table 2. The Geographical Spread of the Renewal Across the World's 8 Continental Areas, 1988.

			Church members in Renewal by 8 continental areas			
Column		World	Africa	East Asia	Europe	Latin America
1	2	8	22	23	24	25
1. AFFILIATED CHURCH MEMBERS						
2.	Prepentecostals (individual quasipentecostals) (1738)	5,165,200	774,780	304,750	315,080	108,470
3. FIRST WAVE: PENTECOSTALISM		**176,070,330**	**42,128,880**	**47,590,900**	**4,415,820**	**37,410,010**
4.	Denominational Pentecostals/pentecostals	169,971,940	41,450,490	46,936,920	4,144,830	37,096,010
5.	Non-White indigenous quasipentecostals (1741)	47,765,450	14,663,990	3,964,530	100,310	7,546,940
6.	Black/Non-White indigenous pentecostals (1783, 1886, 1906)	36,972,700	18,471,130	498,060	84,260	10,467,230
7.	Indigenous revivalist pentecostals (1783)	17,257,820	13,029,650	69,030	18,980	3,313,500
8.	Indigenous holiness-pentecostals (1886)	3,811,300	678,410	72,420	30,490	41,920
9.	Indigenous baptistic-pentecostals (1906)	8,785,630	904,920	96,640	8,790	6,448,650
10.	Indigenous oneness-pentecostals (1916)	3,132,180	21,610	259,970	22,240	519,940
11.	Indigenous pentecostal-apostolics (1917)	3,759,610	3,748,330	0	3,760	7,520
12.	Indigenous radical-pentecostals (c1960)	226,170	88,210	0	0	135,700
13.	Catholic Apostolics (1830, 1863)	2,113,960	697,610	2,110	885,750	179,690
14.	Classical Pentecostals (1895, 1901, 1904)	41,519,830	7,617,760	872,220	3,074,510	18,902,150
15.	Holiness-Pentecostals (1895)	3,600,640	579,700	39,610	50,410	720,130
16.	Pentecostal Apostolics (1904)	1,090,830	942,480	0	101,450	5,450
17.	Oneness-Pentecostals (1913)	1,372,970	146,910	20,600	12,360	127,690
18.	Baptistic-Pentecostals (1914)	35,251,200	5,886,950	810,780	2,820,100	18,048,610
19.	Radical-Pentecostals (c1940)	299,620	61,720	1,230	90,190	270
20.	Chinese house-church pentecostals (1906, 1955)	41,600,000	0	41,600,000	0	0
21.	Isolated radio pentecostals (1924, 1931)	3,498,400	158,390	419,980	10,990	38,400
22.	White pentecostal radio believers (1924)	1,098,500	0	0	10,990	0
23.	Non-White indigenous radio believers (1931)	2,399,900	158,390	419,980	0	38,400
24.	Postpentecostals (1930)	2,600,000	520,000	234,000	260,000	275,600
25. SECOND WAVE: CHARISMATIC MOVEMENT		**123,342,710**	**2,833,810**	**10,798,400**	**21,930,160**	**37,986,630**
26.	Mainline charismatics (active)	21,032,710	869,810	3,120,910	2,998,660	6,276,880
27.	Anglican charismatics (1907, 1914, 1918, 1925, 1956, 1962)	1,954,840	326,460	1,960	1,043,890	9,770
28.	Protestant charismatics (1910, 1918, 1950, 1956, 1966)	7,499,710	194,990	2,309,910	787,470	1,649,940
29.	Orthodox charismatics (1944, 1968)	442,540	44,210	490	97,360	13,280
30.	Catholic charismatics (1962, 1966)	10,106,920	303,210	808,550	1,010,690	4,548,110
31.	Old Catholic charismatics	88,700	0	0	31,050	8,780
32.	Black charismatics (1975)	940,000	940	0	28,200	47,000
33.	Radio/television charismatics (1953)	4,060,000	40,600	36,540	162,400	243,600
34.	Mainline postcharismatics (1960, 1970)	80,710,000	1,751,000	7,606,000	16,128,300	31,398,890
35.	Protestant postcharismatics (1960)	27,360,000	684,000	5,472,000	4,924,800	9,685,440
36.	Catholic postcharismatics (1970)	53,350,000	1,067,000	2,134,000	11,203,500	21,713,450
37.	Messianic Jewish charismatics (1965)	140,000	140	150	30,800	16,800
38.	White independent charismatics (1965)	17,400,000	172,260	34,800	2,610,000	50,460
39. THIRD WAVE: MAINSTREAM CHURCH RENEWAL		**28,080,000**	**2,528,400**	**2,134,640**	**2,490,720**	**2,899,800**
40.	Mainstream third-wavers	21,880,000	1,908,400	2,004,440	630,720	2,868,800
41.	Third-Wave White Evangelicals (1980)	12,400,000	12,400	13,640	621,240	24,800
42.	Third-Wave Black/Non-White Evangelicals (1982)	9,480,000	1,896,000	1,990,800	9,480	2,844,000
43.	Crypto-charismatics (1970)	6,200,000	620,000	130,200	1,860,000	31,000
44. Total all pentecostal/charismatic church members		**332,658,240**	**48,265,870**	**60,828,690**	**29,151,780**	**78,404,910**
45. Total as % of world's church-member Christians		21.40	22.72	80.30	7.15	18.95

	(as defined by United Nations)				Church member in Renewal by 8 continental areas, as % world total							
	Northern America	Oceania	South Asia	USSR	Africa	East Asia	Europe	Latin America	Northern America	Oceania	South Asia	USSR
1	26	27	28	29	30	31	32	33	34	35	36	37
1.												
2.	3,099,120	98,140	464,870	0	15.00	5.90	6.10	2.10	60.00	1.90	9.00	0.00
3.	**22,551,620**	**584,210**	**19,544,230**	**1,977,610**	**23.93**	**27.03**	**2.51**	**21.25**	**12.81**	**0.33**	**11.10**	**1.12**
4.	21,563,620	555,610	17,490,700	866,690	20.00	27.61	2.44	21.82	12.69	0.33	10.29	0.51
5.	11,177,120	90,750	10,221,810	0	30.70	8.30	0.21	15.80	23.40	0.19	21.40	0.00
6.	3,388,700	19,340	4,043,960	0	49.96	1.35	0.23	28.31	9.17	0.05	10.94	0.00
7.	51,770	15,530	759,340	0	75.50	0.40	0.11	19.20	0.30	0.09	4.40	0.00
8.	2,827,990	3,810	156,260	0	17.80	1.90	0.80	1.10	74.20	0.10	4.10	0.00
9.	158,140	0	1,168,490	0	10.30	1.10	0.10	73.40	1.80	0.00	13.30	0.00
10.	350,800	0	1,957,610	0	0.69	8.30	0.71	16.60	11.20	0.00	62.50	0.00
11.	0	0	0	0	99.70	0.00	0.10	0.20	0.00	0.00	0.00	0.00
12.	0	0	2,260	0	39.00	0.00	0.00	60.00	0.00	0.00	1.00	0.00
13.	287,500	8,460	52,850	0	33.00	0.10	41.90	8.50	13.60	0.40	2.50	0.00
14.	6,710,300	437,050	3,172,080	866,690	18.35	2.10	7.40	45.53	16.16	1.05	7.64	2.09
15.	1,357,440	3,600	846,150	7,200	16.10	1.10	1.40	20.00	37.70	0.10	23.50	0.20
16.	2,180	34,910	3,270	0	86.40	0.00	9.30	0.50	0.20	3.20	0.30	0.00
17.	630,190	9,610	418,760	6,870	10.70	1.50	0.90	9.30	45.90	0.70	30.50	0.50
18.	4,582,660	387,760	1,903,570	846,030	16.70	2.30	8.00	51.20	13.00	1.10	5.40	2.40
19.	137,830	1,170	330	6,590	20.60	0.41	30.10	0.09	46.00	0.39	0.11	2.20
20.	0	0	0	0	0.00	100.00	0.00	0.00	0.00	0.00	0.00	0.00
21.	0	0	1,783,130	1,087,520	4.53	12.00	0.31	1.10	0.00	0.00	50.97	31.09
22.	0	0	0	1,087,520	0.00	0.00	1.00	0.00	0.00	0.00	0.00	99.00
23.	0	0	1,783,130	0	6.60	17.50	0.00	1.60	0.00	0.00	74.30	0.00
24.	988,000	28,600	270,400	23,400	20.00	9.00	10.00	10.60	38.00	1.10	10.40	0.90
25.	**43,212,450**	**1,758,440**	**5,133,540**	**752,250**	**2.30**	**8.75**	**17.78**	**30.80**	**35.03**	**1.43**	**4.16**	**0.61**
26.	6,027,330	397,500	1,047,800	293,850	4.14	14.84	14.26	29.84	28.66	1.89	4.98	1.40
27.	361,650	199,390	11,730	0	16.70	0.10	53.40	0.50	18.50	10.20	0.60	0.00
28.	2,159,920	82,500	239,990	75,000	2.60	30.80	10.50	22.00	28.80	1.10	3.20	1.00
29.	66,380	4,430	88,510	127,890	9.99	0.11	22.00	3.00	15.00	1.00	20.00	28.90
30	2,526,730	111,180	707,480	90,960	3.00	8.00	10.00	45.00	25.00	1.10	7.00	0.90
31.	48,790	0	90	0	0.00	0.00	35.00	9.90	55.00	0.00	0.10	0.00
32.	863,860	0	0	0	0.10	0.00	3.00	5.00	91.90	0.00	0.00	0.00
33.	3,532,200	0	40,600	0	1.10	0.90	4.00	6.00	87.00	0.00	1.00	0.00
34.	19,602,900	837,200	4,021,800	430,910	2.17	9.42	19.98	38.90	24.29	1.04	4.98	0.53
35.	5,198,400	410,400	820,800	164,160	2.50	20.00	18.00	35.40	19.00	1.50	3.00	0.60
36.	14,404,500	426,800	3,201,000	266,750	2.00	4.00	21.00	40.70	25.00	0.80	6.00	0.50
37.	86,520	0	4,200	1,390	0.10	0.11	22.00	12.00	61.80	0.00	3.00	0.99
38.	13,963,500	523,740	19,140	26,100	0.99	0.20	15.00	0.29	80.25	3.01	0.11	0.15
39.	**11,672,010**	**76,110**	**5,044,520**	**1,233,800**	**9.00**	**7.60**	**8.87**	**10.33**	**41.57**	**0.27**	**17.96**	**4.39**
40.	11,666,430	69,290	2,731,920	0	8.72	9.16	2.88	13.11	53.32	0.32	12.49	0.00
41.	11,656,000	60,760	11,160	0	0.10	0.11	5.01	0.20	94.00	0.49	0.09	0.00
42.	10,430	8,530	2,720,760	0	20.00	21.00	0.10	30.00	0.11	0.09	28.7	0.00
43.	5,580	6,820	2,312,600	1,233,800	10.00	2.10	30.00	0.50	0.09	0.11	37.3	19.90
44.	**80,535,200**	**2,516,900**	**30,187,160**	**3,963,660**	**14.51**	**18.29**	**8.76**	**23.57**	**24.21**	**0.76**	**9.07**	**1.19**
45.	43.04	14.34	22.41	3.76	14.51	18.29	8.76	23.57	24.21	0.76	9.07	1.19

Methodological Notes. This pair of tables presents a descriptive survey of the phenomenon usually known as the Pentecostal/Charismatic Renewal, or, by participants, as the Renewal in the Holy Spirit. It takes in the somewhat expanded boundaries of the movement that most leaders now understand it as inhabiting. At the same time, the Renewal recognizes the existence and reality of large numbers of other branches or segments of global Christianity, to which it is related in varying degrees of closeness. This means that these tables do not claim to be describing a tradition of Christianity distinct and separate from all other traditions, but a contemporary movement which overlaps with the rest of the Christian world to a large degree (47% in 1988, rising to 53% by AD 2000). By 1987, in fact, the Renewal had penetrated, and had secured committed representation in, every one of the Christian world's 156 distinct ecclesiastical confessions, traditions, and families. The tables enumerate the progress of all branches of the Renewal across the 20th century, with projections to the years 1990 and AD 2000 based on current long-term trends.

Definitions and Additional Data (referring to numbered lines). Each line in the Global Tables 1 and 2 above refers to the global (total, worldwide) situation (in Global Table 2 divided into continental totals), in which pentecostals/charismatics are found in 90% of the world's total of 254 countries (in which 99% of the world's population is found). A number of subjects are shown above on the left broken down into divisions and subdivisions or components listed below them, indented. All indented titles in the tables therefore form part of, and are included in, unindented or less-indented categories above them. Lines Nos. 2–43 are listed in approximate chronological order of their emergence (shown by dates in parentheses) and similarly with divisions, subdivisions, and components. Definitions of major categories are as given and explained in *World Christian Encyclopedia* (1982), which contains details of all the denominations involved; additional data and explanations are given below. Totals of denominations listed below (e.g. under Nos. 5–12) refer to large or significant bodies only. Sources include in-process world surveys by author, including the monograph *Cosmos, Chaos, and Gospel: A Chronology of World Evangelization From Creation to New Creation* (1987). Basic data and bibliographies on the Pentecostal/Charismatic Renewal may be found in C.E. Jones, *A Guide to the Study of Pentecostalism* (1983, 2 volumes, 9,883 entries), also Jones, *Black Holiness: A Guide to the Study of Black Participation in Wesleyan Perfectionist and Glossolalic Pentecostal Movements* (1987), and W.J. Hollenweger (ed), *Pentecostal Research in Europe: Problems, Promises and People* (1986).

Columns (1–21 in Global Table 1, and 22–37 in Global Table 2).
1. Reference number of line.
2. Usual current terminology for all major components of the Renewal.
3–8. Statistics for the years 1900–1988.
9–10. Projections for 1990 and 2000 based on current trends, conservatively estimated.
11–17. Rate of change (% per year) at the year indicated. This rate is computed for a particular column in table (e.g. 1980) as the next column (1985) minus the previous column (1975), divided by number of years' difference (in this case, 10), divided by current figure (for 1980), multiplied by 100: result = annual growth rate, % per year (for 1980). In line with United Nations' and most countries' statistical reporting, this section (columns 11–17) presents annual growth rates, rather than the sometimes-quoted decadal growth rates or 5-year growth rates, because the latter 2 mask shorter-term fluctuations important to the understanding of rapidly-growing movements such as the present Renewal.
18. Annual growth rate in 1988 due to purely demographic factors (births minus deaths in the churches).
19. 1988 increase (column 15) expressed as an annual figure. (Computed as column 15, divided by 100, multiplied by column 8).
20. 1988 increase (column 15) expressed as an average daily figure.
21. Annual converts (persons not previously in this category but who have joined in the last 12 months) in 1988, measured as total annual increase minus demographic increase. (Computed as column 15 minus column 18, divided by 100, multiplied by column 8).
22–29. Church members in Renewal by 8 continental areas of the world as standardized by the United Nations, 1988 (actual numbers, equal to columns 30–37 times column 8 divided by 100).
30–37. Church members in Renewal by the 8 continental areas of the world as standardized by the United Nations, given as percent in 1988 of total church members on each row (column 8).

The Renewal as a Single Movement. The above tables view the 20th-century Renewal in the Holy Spirit as one single cohesive movement into which a vast proliferation of all kinds of individuals and communities have been drawn in a whole range of different circumstances over a period of 250 years. Whether termed pentecostals, charismatics, or third-wavers, they share a single basic experience. Their contribution to Christianity is a new awareness of spiritual gifts as a ministry to the life of the church. The case for this thesis could be made by listing historical, missiological, theological, sociological and other data. It could also be made by drawing attention to the fact that in the 1900–1904–1906 revivals, news of these travelled throughout the globe (by rail, by ship, by telegraph) in a few days and weeks; while today, news of such happenings—conversions, blessings, healings, movements—travels worldwide within a few seconds by telephone, radio, television, electronic mail, etc. Such rapid communication across time, space, and all varieties of the Renewal, implies an underlying unity.

The case for the statistical presentation of the Renewal as a single interconnected movement can however best be made by considering how the movement starts off and spreads in any area, from the days of the earliest pentecostals to those of current charismatics and third-wavers.

The start of the movement anywhere has always been an unexpected or unpredictable happening rather than any result of human planning or organization. First individuals (at random across the existing churches), then groups, then large numbers in organized movements, become filled with the Spirit and embark on the common charismatic experience. All of them, originally, can collectively and correctly be termed charismatics. All these charismatics find themselves living initially within existing mainline nonpentecostal churches and denominations. There, over the last 200 years they have been termed or labelled as charismatics, revivalists, enthusiasts, spirituals, or pentecostals; and often have been dismissed as cranks, fanatics, sectarians, heretics, schismatics or worse. However, all of them initially attempt to stay within, and work within, those churches. But before long evictions begin, and ejections, withdrawals, and secessions occur in varying degrees. First various individuals, then groups, then whole movements are forced into schism or opt for it and so begin separate ecclesiastical structures and new denominations.

From its beginnings in this way, the Renewal has subsequently expanded in 3 massive surges or waves. We can further divide these waves into a typology of 9 stages, explained and described as follows.

A Typology of the Evolution of Charismatics Within Churches

Notes on the 9 columns below:
1 = stage in evolution of new charismatic developments
2 = first year of new stage
3 = main or majority race involved in stage, either Whites or Non-Whites
4 = fate of charismatics in their existing parent churches
5 = percent of charismatics evicted from parent churches
6 = percent of charismatics who voluntarily secede from parent churches
7 = percent of charismatics lost to parent churches (= cols 5 + 6)
8 = percent remaining in parent churches (= 100 - col 7)
9 = new organizations or developments resulting

Stage	Start	Race	History of charismatics	Fate, %				Resulting organizations
1	2	3	4	5	6	7	8	9

FIRST WAVE: Rejection, eviction, secession, new denominations; = PENTECOSTALISM

1.	1741	Non-Whites	Immediate eviction	100	0	100	0	Black/Non-White denominations
2.	1901	Whites	Eventual secession	95	5	100	0	White Classical Pentecostal denominations

SECOND WAVE: Friction, toleration, new mainline networks; = CHARISMATIC MOVEMENT

3.	1918	Non-Whites	Majority eviction	80	10	90	10	Isolated mainline prayer groups
4.	1930	Whites	Minority eviction	40	30	70	30	Isolated healing ministries
5.	1960	Whites	Partial eviction	10	15	25	75	Large-scale mainline networks
6.	1970	Whites	Few evictions	4	10	14	86	Denominational charismatic agencies

THIRD WAVE: Power evangelism, renewed structures, renewed churches; = MAINSTREAM CHURCH RENEWAL

7.	1980	Whites	Occasional evictions	2	8	10	90	Renewed parishes and structures
8.	1990	Non-Whites	Rare evictions	1	1	2	98	Renewed denominations
9.	2000	Non-Whites	No evictions	0	0	0	100	Renewed global Christianity

These 9 stages and categories are approximate and descriptive, not watertight or exclusive. For instance, as a result of the global influenza pandemic of 1918, large numbers of Blacks in Anglican churches in Africa (Nigeria, Kenya, Uganda, South Africa) became charismatics and formed charismatic prayer groups within Anglican parishes. The majority however were soon evicted (and so are enumerated here in Global Tables 1 and 2 under line No. 6, and 7–12, becoming what we now refer to as Black pentecostals); only a minority (10%) remained within Anglicanism as charismatics in what later became known as the Anglican Charismatic Movement.

Having described how the Renewal can be seen as a single movement, we will next describe its component elements.

Three Waves of Twentieth-Century Renewal. The tables classify the various movements and types under the following 3 consecutive waves of the Renewal in the Holy Spirit, defining its 3 key terms as follows.

Pentecostals. These are defined as Christians who are members of explicitly-pentecostal denominations in Pentecostalism or the Pentecostal Movement whose major characteristic is a rediscovery of, and a new experience of, the supernatural with a powerful and energizing ministry of the Holy Spirit in the realm of the miraculous that most other Christians have considered to be highly unusual. This is interpreted as a rediscovery of the spiritual gifts of New Testament times, and their restoration to ordinary Christian life and ministry. Pentecostalism is usually held to have begun in the USA in 1901 (although the present survey shows the year of origin as 1741). For a brief period it was a charismatic revival expecting to remain an interdenominational movement within the existing churches without beginning a new denomination; but from 1909 onwards its members were increasingly ejected from all mainline bodies and so forced to begin new organized denominations.

Pentecostal denominations hold the distinctive teaching that all Christians should seek a post-conversion religious experience called baptism in the Holy Spirit, and that a Spirit-baptized believer may receive one or more of the supernatural gifts known in the Early Church: instantaneous sanctification, the ability to prophesy, to practise divine healing through prayer, to speak in tongues (glossolalia), or to interpret tongues; singing in tongues, singing in the Spirit; praying with upraised hands; dreams, visions, discernment of spirits, words of wisdom, words of knowledge; emphasis on miracles, power encounters, exorcisms (casting out demons), resuscitations, deliverances, signs and wonders. From 1906 onwards, the hallmark of explicitly Pentecostal denominations, by comparison with Holiness/Perfectionist denominations, has been the single addition of speaking with other tongues as the "initial evidence" of one's having received the baptism of the Holy Ghost (or Holy Spirit), whether or not one subsequently experiences regularly the gift of tongues. Most Pentecostal denominations teach that tongues-speaking is mandatory for all members, but in practice today only 35% of all members have practiced this gift either initially or as an ongoing experience. Pentecostal denominations proclaim a "full" or "four-fold" gospel of Christ as Savior, Baptizer with the Holy Spirit, Healer, and Coming King. Collectively, all these denominations are sometimes referred to as the "First Wave" of this whole 20th-century movement of Holy-Spirit-centered renewal. In the USA, Pentecostals usually name the entire body of these denominations by the blanket term "Classical Pentecostals" to distinguish them from the subsequent "Neopentecostals" or "Charismatics" in the nonpentecostal denominations.

Charismatics. These are defined as Christians with the above experiences in the Charismatic Movement whose roots go back to 1907 and 1918 but whose rapid expansion has been mainly since 1950 (later called the Charismatic Renewal), usually describing themselves as having been renewed in the Spirit and experiencing the Spirit's supernatural and miraculous and energizing power, who remain within, and form organized renewal groups within, their older mainline nonpentecostal denominations (instead of leaving to join pentecostal denominations), who demonstrate any or all of the *charismata pneumatika* (Greek New Testament: gifts of the Spirit) including signs and wonders (but with glossolalia regarded as optional); joined increasingly since 1965 by thousands of schismatic or other independent charismatic churches coming out of the Charismatic Movement; these independents have from 1970 to the present day averaged 14% of the whole Charismatic Movement. The whole Movement is sometimes termed the "Second Wave" of the 20th-century Renewal. Concerning the key word, note that "In the technical Pauline sense charismata (AV, gifts) denote extraordinary powers, distinguishing certain Christians and enabling them to serve the church of Christ, the reception of which is due to the power of divine grace operating in their souls by the Holy Spirit" (*Thayer's Greek-English Lexicon of the New Testament*, 1886, 1977:667).

Third-wavers. These are Evangelicals and other Christians who, unrelated to Pentecostalism or the Charismatic Movement, have recently become filled with the Spirit, or empowered or energized by the Spirit and experiencing the Spirit's supernatural and miraculous ministry (though usually without recognizing a baptism in the Spirit separate from conversion), who exercise gifts of the Spirit (with much less emphasis on tongues, as optional or even absent or unnecessary), and emphasize signs and wonders, supernatural miracles and power encounters, but who remain within their mainline nonpentecostal denominations and who do not identify themselves as either pentecostals or charismatics. In a number of countries they exhibit pentecostal and charismatic phenomena but combine this with rejection of pentecostal terminology. There is less emphasis also on organizing distinct and separate renewal groups. These believers are increasingly being identified by their leadership as a "Third Wave" of the whole 20th-century renewal (the terms Third Wave and third-wavers having been coined by a participant, C. Peter Wagner, in 1983—see his articles "A Third Wave?" in *Pastoral Renewal*, 8, 1(July–August, 1983), 1–5, and "The Third Wave" in *Christian Life* (September, 1984),90, and his 1988 book *The Third Wave of the Holy Spirit: Encountering the Power of Signs and Wonders Today*). Because they constitute a major new revitalizing force, in this table we also term the movement "Mainstream church renewal" (after definition in Webster's: mainstream = "the middle of a stream, where the current is strongest; a major or prevailing trend").

Layout of lines below. The explanatory notes below have numbers referring to the numbered lines in Global Tables 1 and 2. They are set out with each line's title in column 2 being given below in boldface type.

1. **AFFILIATED CHURCH MEMBERS.** (Lines Nos. 2–45, with key years of origin or watersheds added in parentheses). Total Christian community affiliated to (on the rolls of) denominations, churches or groups, including baptized members, their children and infants, catechumens, enquirers, attenders, but excluding interested non-Christian attenders, casual attenders, visitors, et alii. Many Pentecostal denominations enumerate their children and infants, and a number are pedobaptist (infant-baptizing). Most however ignore their children's statistics, which has led to serious underenumeration of the spread of the Renewal. Whenever statistics of church members are compared to total population figures (which almost always include children and infants), such membership figures must also include its children and infants. Like must always be compared with like.

2. **Prepentecostals.** Scattered individual quasipentecostals in mainline nonpentecostal denominations ("quasi" means apparent, seemingly, largely, to a great extent, to some extent). There have always been sizeable numbers of such individuals who have experienced or demonstrated pentecostal phenomena in their own lives or ministries. Those in the last 200 years, and which may reasonably be regarded as antecedents of the 20th century Renewal, fall into 4 main categories. (1) Several thousands of individual monks, priests, brothers, sisters, in Catholic, Orthodox, Anglican and other monastic and religious orders, who have been allowed unhindered to exercise personal gifts of the Spirit including glossolalia, faith healing, et alia. Many of these were indirectly responsible for the Encyclical letter "On the Holy Spirit" issued in 1897 by pope Leo XIII, directing attention to the 7-fold gifts of the Spirit (Isaiah 11) and promoting a universal novena (9-day cycle of prayer) to the Holy Spirit before Pentecost Sunday each year, which influenced millions of Roman Catholics. (2) Numerous Mormons (Latter-day Saints) including founder Joseph Smith and organizer Brigham Young have practiced glossolalia (though not included here in the statistics of prepentecostals). (3) Charismatic groupings in new movements of the 19th century which have now become denominations which define themselves as part of the Renewal; thus Salvation Army headquarters (London) states: "The history of the Salvation Army (beginning in 1865) is only intelligible as a work of the Holy Spirit. For this reason, the Salvation Army could itself be called a charismatic movement and its early meetings resembled charismatic meetings of today" (A. Bittlinger, ed, *The Church Is Charismatic*, 1981:42). (4) Sanctified/perfectionist Anglicans and Protestants in holiness movements within the churches. Especially in the years 1855–1900 which saw the rise in the USA of the doctrine of baptism in the Holy Spirit, the term prepentecostals describes individuals with a perfectionist or "second-blessing" experience plus related pentecostal phenomena but belonging as members to antipentecostal, nonpentecostal or prepentecostal denominations, particularly Holiness/Perfectionist bodies, popular American revivalism, and other denominations opposed to pentecostal phenomena (especially glossolalia), which claim instead that conversion and sanctification (often termed "infilling with the Spirit") are the only 2 necessary and complete experiences promised to believers. On the eve of the year 1900, this category included (a) in the USA alone, several thousand scattered glossolalists, 100,000 "come-outers" (adults in Holiness splitoffs and higher-life movements), and over 1,000,000 White (with some Black) "loyalists" with the sanctification/infilling experience, belonging to Holiness, Wesleyan and Methodist denominations; and (b) similar numbers abroad in Holiness/Wesleyan/Methodist denominations and movements and missions in Europe, South Africa, India, Chile, et alia. (For a detailed treatment of the relation between the Holiness and Pentecostal movements, see H.V. Synan, *The Holiness-Pentecostal Movement in the United States*, 1971). Historically, the prototype prepentecostal has been regarded as the Anglican revivalist priest John Wesley (1703–1791). For this reason, the first 2 words of Synan's study were deliberately chosen as "John Wesley" (Synan 1971:13—"John Wesley, the indomitable founder of Methodism, was also the spiritual and intellectual father of the modern holiness and pentecostal movements which have issued from Methodism within the last century"). The best-known prepentecostal preacher before 1900 was the evangelist Dwight L. Moody, whose preaching from 1875 onwards sometimes resulted in glossolalia (Synan 1971:99; the term "pre-pentecostal" appears to have originated in this

passage). Before 1900 there were many such cases: thus, tongues were a significant feature, according to some scholars, of the Camp Creek holiness revival in North Carolina in 1896; other scholars produce contrary evidence.

For the years 1970–2000 on line No. 2, the statistics refer mainly to similar "sanctified Methodists" and other phenomenological pentecostals and quasipentecostals in these nonpentecostal denominations at present (especially in: Church of the Nazarene, Wesleyan Church, Free Methodist Church, Salvation Army), most of which differ from pentecostalism only in the absence of tongues-speaking or in the absence of a doctrine that tongues-speaking is the essential evidence of baptism in the Holy Spirit. Most of these prepentecostals are unrelated to, and are uninvolved with, either Pentecostalism, or the Charismatic Movement, or the Third Wave of the 1980s; they do not identify themselves by the terms pentecostals, charismatics, or third-wavers. However, a new complication by 1985 is that a number of these denominations' largest congregations in the Third World have independently become Third-Wave; these are not enumerated on line No. 2 but later in the tables, on line No. 42 (Third-Wave Black/Non-White Evangelicals). Since by 1987 the total of members of Pentecostal denominations (the First Wave of the Renewal) who have never spoken in tongues had risen to 65%, and since members of the Charismatic Movement from 1950 onwards (the Second Wave) also regard tongues as a gift some (but not all) may receive, it is logical to include prepentecostals in the present enumeration, and the above tables therefore do so. In 1985 these prepentecostals are enumerated here as including 20% of the world's 6,092,000 members of 350 major Holiness denominations plus 10% of the world's 31,717,000 members of 210 major Methodist denominations, plus 10% of the world's 4,227,000 Salvationists.

3. **FIRST WAVE: PENTECOSTALISM.** Pentecostals are defined here as all associated with explicitly-pentecostal denominations which identify themselves in explicitly-pentecostal terms (see definition of "Pentecostals" near the beginning of these footnotes), or with other denominations which as a whole are phenomenologically pentecostal in teaching and practice. Current practice in the USA is to analyse the phenomenon as basically an American one, and as one distinct from Neopentecostalism (the Charismatic Movement), and so to label the whole of denominational Pentecostalism worldwide by the parallel or synonymous term "Classical Pentecostalism". In the present table however we are concerned more to see the entire phenomenon as a global one requiring a different set of descriptive terms. We therefore divide the movement into 2 major streams as shown by 2 different spellings: (1) the term "Pentecostal" with a capital P denotes what we are terming Classical Pentecostalism (which is mainly White-originated), whereas (2) the term "pentecostal" with a lowercase p refers to the huge phenomenon of Black/Non-White/Third-World indigenous pentecostalism unrelated to Western Classical Pentecostalism (see notes below on lines Nos. 6–12). To avoid excessive repetition of the comprehensive adjective "Pentecostal/pentecostal" the adjective "pentecostal" is often used below to denote the whole. Historically, the First Wave developed out of Black slavery in the USA, the Evangelical (Wesleyan) Revival from 1738 in Britain, and the Holiness (Perfectionist) movement in Britain, the USA, and its worldwide missions in the 19th century. Although many Pentecostal/pentecostal denominations had antecedents going back to the 18th century, the year 1901 is usually quoted as the year of origin of Pentecostalism because that is when the movement took off on a massive universal scale with widespread tongues and other pentecostal phenomena. Other scholars cite 1906 (Azusa Street), for the same reasons. (This line's statistics are computed as the sum of lines Nos. 4,21 and 24).

4. **Denominational Pentecostals/pentecostals.** In over 3,000 major recognized, clear-cut, wholly-pentecostal or wholly-charismatic denominations of pentecostal theology or practice or stance, committed as denominations to Pentecostal distinctives; there are also thousands of minor or very small denominations, which bring the grand total of all such denominations to around 11,000, in 230 different countries. (This line is computed as the sum of the 5 lines Nos. 5,6,13,14, and 20). Note that the Non-White-originated segment of this total (lines Nos. 5,6 and 20) preceded the USA-White-originated segment historically (line No. 14) and is today 3 times as numerous.

5. **Non-White indigenous quasipentecostals.** Apparent/seemingly/largely pentecostal or semi-pentecostal members of this 250-year-old movement of churches indigenous to, and begun without reference to Western Christianity by, Christians in Non-White races across the world; estimated in 1970 as 60% (rising by 1985 to 75%) of all members of the over 1,000 Non-White/Third-World indigenous denominations which, though not explicitly pentecostal, nevertheless have the main phenomenological hallmarks of pentecostalism (charismatic spirituality, oral liturgy, narrative witness/theology, dreams and visions, emphasis on filling with the Holy Spirit, healing by prayer, atmospheric communication (simultaneous audible prayer), emotive fellowship, et alia). These denominations are found today in 170 different countries. The case for enumerating adherents of these movements as pentecostals has been fully made by W.J. Hollenweger in his writings, most recently in "After Twenty Years' Research on Pentecostalism," International Review of Mission (April, 1986). Note that the term "indigenous" as used

here refers to the auto-origination of these movements, begun among Non-White races without Western or White missionary support.

6. **Black/Non-White indigenous pentecostals.** Black, Non-White or Third-World Christians in over 800 explicitly-pentecostal denominations, indigenous to Non-White races in that they were begun without outside Western or White missionary assistance or support. There are 4 varieties: (a) USA Black denominations including the largest, the Church of God in Christ (begun 1895), and (b) over 750 Third-World denominations unrelated to foreign missions from Western denominations (often being schisms out of them), in 140 different countries; being joined more recently by (c) networks of Non-White independent charismatic churches (as in Brazil, Argentina, Colombia, Nigeria, India, et alia), and (d) since 1980, rapidly-increasing numbers of independent youth churches, video churches, et alia, meeting in hotels, theatres, secular halls, warehouses, shops, or in the open air. (Sum of lines Nos. 7–12). Most Pentecostal spokesmen in the USA define variety (a) above as an integral part of Classical Pentecostalism, although in this table we give this term a more restricted definition (see line No. 14). Our reasoning is that, seen in the total global perspective, variety (a) above is far more accurately located as the archetype of global Non-White pentecostalism. Furthermore, many Black pentecostals regard the terms "Pentecostal" and "charismatic" as largely White in origin, and have traditionally preferred the term "sanctified".

7. **Indigenous revivalist pentecostals.** Begun in 1783 in Jamaica (Native Baptists, Revival Zionists, Shouters, Shakers, et alii), in 1860 in Trinidad & Tobago (West Indies Spiritual Baptist Churches, National Evangelical Spiritual Baptist Church, National Spiritual Baptist Council of Churches), now in 400 denominations in 80 countries across the world; this earliest variety of denomination remains a general one without the refinements of theology and practice later developed in the next 5 lines Nos. 8–12).

8. **Indigenous holiness-pentecostals.** In some 60 denominations, teaching 3-crisis experience (conversion, sanctification, baptism in the Spirit); in 35 different countries.

9. **Indigenous baptistic-pentecostals.** In 70 denominations, teaching 2-crisis experience (conversion, baptism in the Spirit); in 45 different countries.

10. **Indigenous oneness-pentecostals.** In 60 denominations practising baptism in name of Jesus only; the major such body with missions worldwide is the True Jesus Church (begun in China, 1917). The first such new denomination, a schism from the (mainly White) Assemblies of God (USA), was the Pentecostal Assemblies of the World (1916). These bodies are found in 38 countries today.

11. **Indigenous pentecostal-apostolics.** In over 60 denominations in 18 countries; stress on complex hierarchy of living apostles, prophets and other charismatic officials.

12. **Indigenous radical-pentecostals.** In over 100 deliverance-pentecostal denominations (similar to, and defined as in, line No.19), in at least 40 countries and expanding rapidly. Most of the mushrooming new youth churches, hotel churches, theatre churches, cinema churches, store churches, and open-air churches are in this category.

13. **Catholic Apostolics.** 1832 schism (Irvingites) in London ex Church of Scotland (Presbyterian) stressing Catholic features, hierarchy of living apostles, glossolalia, and that all the New Testament charismata have now been restored; Old Apostolics; 1863 formation of Universal Catholic Church (Germany), later renamed New Apostolic Church, emphasizing the gifts of the Holy Spirit including prophecy, tongues, interpretation of tongues, miraculous healing, sacraments, hierarchy of 48 living Apostles (1980: 1,600,000 members worldwide). Total countries involved: 48.

14. **Classical Pentecostals.** As explained above, in this global classification we define this as a blanket term for those in 690 traditional Western-related denominations which identify themselves as explicitly Pentecostal; almost all of White origin in USA, but now worldwide with adherents in all races, found in 200 countries. (Sum of lines Nos. 15–19). USA Pentecostal spokesmen use a somewhat wider definition which identifies "Classical Pentecostals" (a term which dates from 1970) with all denominational Pentecostals in contrast to Neopentecostals (Charismatics); they therefore include under this term the major early Black pentecostal denominations in the USA, notably the Church of God in Christ with its 3 million members today (which however we here classify under lines Nos. 6 and 8). In essence, our procedure is saying that the whole phenomenon of denominational Pentecostalism/pentecostalism is best understood when classified into the 2 subdivisions, (a) Black-originated pentecostalism and (b) White-originated Pentecostalism. As the better-organized and better-articulated form, category (b) then better merits the appellation "Classical" Pentecostalism.

There has been a certain amount of blurred boundaries and movement between Pentecostalism and the Charismatic Movement. Thus in 1948 the Latter Rain Revival (New Order of the Latter Rain) erupted among classical Pentecostals in Saskatchewan, Canada, and spread rapidly to Europe, USA, and across the world. It emphasised laying on of hands with prophecy, and government by an order of living apostles; it began Global Missions Broadcast (over radio); but from 1965, it merged into the Charismatic Movement.

15. **Holiness Pentecostals.** Also known as Wesleyan Pentecostals, or Methodistic Pentecostals, this was the universal Pentecostal position until the 1910 Northern USA change (see note 18 below), and still remains the major Southern USA position. It is found today in 170 denominations worldwide, teaching a 3-crisis experience (conversion, sanctification, baptism in the Spirit). First claimed glossolalia manifestations: 1897 Fire-Baptized Holiness Church, 1896 Church of God (Cleveland), 1906 Pentecostal Holiness Church. Total countries involved: 95.

16. **Pentecostal Apostolics.** The 1904 Welsh Revival under Evan Roberts, which is often regarded by European writers as the origin of the worldwide Pentecostal movement, prepared the way for British Pentecostalism, especially Apostolic-type teaching resulting in 1908 in the Apostolic Faith Church (Bournemouth), from which a schism in 1916 formed the Apostolic Church (HQ in Wales). Apostolics are now found worldwide in 55 denominations, stressing complex hierarchy of living apostles, prophets and other charismatic officials. Total countries involved: 35.

17. **Oneness-Pentecostals.** In 90 denominations in 57 countries; termed by outsiders Unitarian Pentecostals or Jesus-Only Pentecostals, but calling themselves Oneness-Pentecostals or Jesus Name Pentecostals; baptism in name of Jesus only; widely accepted ecclesiastically as Evangelicals but theologically as modal monarchians; since 1920 they have included 25% of all Pentecostals in the USA. The major denomination is the United Pentecostal Church, a 1945 union of the Pentecostal Assemblies of Jesus Christ (1913) and the Pentecostal Church (1916). In contrast to this emphasis within denominational Pentecostalism, the Charismatic Movement has remained explicitly trinitarian throughout.

18. **Baptistic-Pentecostals.** Mainline Classical Pentecostals teaching "finished work" or 2-crisis experience (conversion, baptism in the Spirit); in over 350 denominations in 180 countries. This category also includes quasidenominational networks such as Full Gospel Fellowship of Churches & Ministers International (begun 1962; 425 churches). Scores of Pentecostal denominations trace their origin to the 1906–09 Azusa Street Revival in Los Angeles, USA, under bishop W.J. Seymour et alios, at which thousands first spoke in tongues; but the "finished work" teaching (combining conversion with sanctification or "second blessing") of W.H. Durham in 1910 shifted many Northern USA Pentecostals out of the Wesleyan 3-crisis teaching into the 2-crisis position now known as Baptistic Pentecostalism. The first new denomination to hold this position was the Assemblies of God, founded in 1914, which with its foreign mission work now in 118 countries is by far the largest Pentecostal worldwide denomination. Its meticulously-kept annual statistics for each country form Pentecostalism's most solid body of statistical data and hence the main documentation for the Renewal's phenomenal growth. This denomination's growth can be briefly summarized as follows: AG (USA) home and overseas adherents (adult baptized persons usually over 18 years whom the AG enumerates under 2 heads: (a) "Baptized members", which refers only to adults who have taken the further step after baptism of formally joining a local church and signing to its rules and conditions; and (b) "Other believers", which refers to other baptized adults who have not yet taken this step, or do not intend to): these adherents have risen from 1,499,241 (1960) to 3,800,965 (1970), to 5,833,977 (1975), 10,562,541 (1980), 15,258,629 (1985), and to 16,376,818 (1986). Adding children and teenagers, the total AG world community in 1985 was 43.7% larger at 21,930,500, increasing annually by 6.2% (1,360,000), to 23,290,000 in 1986.

19. **Radical-Pentecostals.** Perfectionist-Pentecostals, Free Pentecostals, Deliverance-Pentecostals, Revivalist-Pentecostals, teaching 4-crisis experience including deliverance/ecstatic-confession/ascension/perfectionism/prophecy; in over 40 denominations, in over 30 countries and rapidly expanding.

20. **Chinese house-church pentecostals.** A strong tradition beginning in 1906, widespread by 1955, expanding rapidly throughout mainland China by 1982; by 1985, almost 25% of all Protestants were tongues-speakers; estimates of the proportion of all Chinese Christians who are phenomenologically pentecostals/charismatics range from 50% to 85%, in large numbers and networks of de facto independent pentecostal or charismatic churches.

21. **Isolated radio pentecostals.** Those in isolated regions with no denominations or churches, whose ongoing corporate Christian life derives only from foreign radio broadcasts. (Sum of lines Nos. 22–23).

22. **White pentecostal radio believers.** Converts through Christian radio in 10 Communist countries.

23. **Non-White indigenous radio believers.** Converts through Christian radio in 65 countries closed to foreign missions or overt evangelism.

24. **Postpentecostals.** Former members of Pentecostal denominations who have left to join nonpentecostal denominations (due to marriage, family moves, job transfers, upward mobility, new interests in liturgy and theology, et alia), but who have not renounced their pentecostal experience, and who still identify themselves as pentecostal. Example: postpentecostals formerly members of the International Pentecostal Holiness Church are nowadays estimated at 450,000 in the USA which is 3 times IPHC's present membership of 150,000.

25. **SECOND WAVE: CHARISMATIC MOVEMENT.** Charismatics (or, until recently, Neopentecostals) are usually defined as those baptized or renewed in the Spirit within the mainline nonpentecostal denominations, from its first mass stirrings in 1918 in Africa on to the large-scale rise from 1950 of the Charismatic Movement (initially also termed Neopentecostalism to distinguish it from Classical Pentecostalism), who remain within their mainline nonpentecostal denominations; but the term also includes recent schismatic or secessionist bodies and other independent churches which since 1950 have clearly arisen in the context of the Charismatic Movement (later called the Charismatic Renewal). The exact definition used here is given above near the beginning of these footnotes. Note that many individuals and groups in the mainline churches had already received baptism in the Spirit without publicity for many years before the usually-quoted beginning dates of 1950, 1959, 1962, 1967, etc. (This line's statistics are computed as the sum of lines Nos. 26,33,34,37, and 38).

26. **Mainline charismatics (active).** Active members regularly (weekly, or once a month or more) involved in prayer groups within the Charismatic Movement in the older mainline denominations. (Sum of lines Nos. 27–32). During the period 1906–1950, many thousands of mainline clergy and hundreds of thousands of laity received the pentecostal experience and spoke in tongues, but many were ejected and later joined the Pentecostal denominations. By 1987 the Renewal had penetrated every one of the Christian world's 156 distinct ecclesiastical confessions, traditions and families, with charismatics within every tradition.

27. **Anglican charismatics.** Anglican pentecostals, begun 1907 with clergyman A.A. Boddy (Sunderland, England); then from 1918, due to the global influenza pandemic, numerous prayer and healing groups in the Anglican church of Nigeria, inter alia; then from 1925 the Spirit Movement (Aladura), which was then expelled and seceded as today's African indigenous churches (with total membership of 32 million, here enumerated in lines Nos. 5 and 6); subsequently, numerous isolated clergy and groups in several countries up to US Episcopalian Agnes Sanford's healing ministry from 1953, priests R. Winkler in 1956 and D. Bennett in 1959, Blessed Trinity Society (1961), and Church of England clergyman M.C. Harper in 1962 (who then founded Fountain Trust in 1964); in 18 countries by 1978, expanding to 95 countries by 1987 (with 850,000 active adherents in UK, served by Anglican Renewal Ministries (ARM); 520,000 (18% of all Episcopalians) in USA served by Episcopal Renewal Ministries; with branches of ARM in other countries also). Much of this expansion is due to a unique structured international charismatic ministry body, SOMA (Sharing of Ministries Abroad), begun 1979, which now covers 17 of the 31 Anglican Provinces worldwide and partially covers 9 more, working by 1987 in 50 countries.

28. **Protestant charismatics.** 1909 Lutheran prayer groups in state churches (Germany), 1918 charismatics in African countries secede to form AICs (African indigenous churches), 1931 Reformed groups related to 1946 Union de Pri/ere (south of France), 1932 charismatic revival in Methodist Church (Southern Rhodesia) leading to massive AACJM schism, 1945 Darmstadt Sisters of Mary (Germany), 1950 Dutch Reformed Church (Netherlands); 1950 origins of Protestant neopentecostals in USA; 1958 large-scale neopentecostal movements in Brazil's Protestant churches (Renovação); in 38 countries by 1978, and in 130 by 1987. Some representative figures: (East Germany) 500,000 participants (7% of all members) in state Lutheran church.

29. **Orthodox charismatics.** Contemporary successors of scores of charismatic movements within Russian Orthodox Church dating from Spiritual Christians (AD 1650); also charismatics in Greek Orthodox Church in Greece, and Eastern and Oriental Orthodox churches in USA (1967, fr A. Emmert, who by 1987 had become a Melkite Catholic convert), Canada, Australia, Lebanon, Uganda, Kenya, Tanzania, Egypt, and some 30 other countries. Agency: Service Committee for Orthodox Spiritual Renewal (SCOSR). A recent significant development is the rapid spread of the Brotherhood of Lovers of the Church, a charismatic renewal within the Armenian Apostolic Church in the USSR. Despite these stirrings, Orthodox authorities have generally harassed charismatics relentlessly, this hostility being due to the Orthodox assertion that they never lost the Spirit nor the charismata.

30. **Catholic charismatics.** Catholic pentecostals, in Roman Catholic Charismatic Renewal, begun with early stirrings in Third World countries (Africa, Latin America), then definitively in 1966 in USA; in 1987, 60,000 prayer groups in 140 countries worldwide (in USA 10,500 English, Vietnamese, Korean, Filipino, Haitian, Hispanic and several other language groups). Since 1978 there have been National Service Committees in over 80 countries uniting Catholic charismatics, as well as 2 streams of different emphasis in the USA and several other countries: (a) that centered on Word of God Community (Servant Ministries, University Christian Outreach, New Covenant magazine, in Ann Arbor, MI, with overseas communities and work in Belgium, Honduras, Hong Kong, India, Indonesia, Lebanon, Nicaragua, Northern Ireland, Philippines, South Africa, Sri Lanka) with cohesive, authoritarian leadership, which originated ICCRO in Brussels, Belgium; and (b) that centered on People of Praise Community (South Bend, IN), ICCRO after its relocation in Vatican City in 1985, and a wide international network of covenant communities, with a less authoritarian structure and leadership style. Priests. Since 1974 some

5% of USA priests have been active in the Renewal, with a further 5% now as postcharismatics. Priests are less involved than bishops; foreign missionaries are more involved than home clergy.

A 5-fold statistical typology. With a mushrooming movement such as this it is essential to understand the exact definition of each and every statistic that is generated, published or quoted. As the Charismatic Movement's best-documented membership data, Catholic statistics each refer to one of the following 5 types or categories, (a) to (e). The first category is the basic grassroots head count, which is of adults only; the following 4 categories are then derived from it. The first 3 categories refer to adults only (over 18 years old); the last 2 categories are demographic totals including children and infants. These last 2 are just as important because the whole Renewal is not a movement of isolated adults but is largely a family movement in which children cannot be ignored.

(a) *Weekly-attending Catholic charismatics.* These are defined as those adults actually attending (involved in/enrolled in/participating in) the Movement's officially-recognized prayer meetings regularly every week. These have been called the "shock troops" of the movement. Official membership was enumerated by ICCRO in 1986 at 4 million weekly-participating adults worldwide (Latin America 2 million in 21 countries; North America and Caribbean 1.2 million; Middle East, Asia and Oceania 400,000 in 26 countries; Europe 300,000 in 22 countries; Africa 100,000 in 29 countries). (b) Active Catholic charismatics. These are defined as adults attending the Movement's prayer meetings once a month or more, enumerated at 7 million worldwide in 1986 (including the 4 million in category (a) above). (c) Total involved Catholic charismatics. During its 20 years of existence, the renewal is known to have influenced the lives of over 30 million adult Catholics who have become baptized in the Spirit (figures from ICCRO et alia). This category clearly includes those enumerated under categories (a) and (b) above.

To all these statistics of adults must now be added their children and infants, to get demographic figures or family figures which can be directly and legitimately compared with secular population figures, and also with standard Catholic statistics of baptized Catholics, which always include children and infants. Two more categories result, as follows. (d) Active Catholic charismatic total community. This is defined as monthly-attending adults plus their children and infants, enumerated in this table (in the statistics on line No. 30) at 10.1 million in 1988. Lastly, (e) Total Catholic charismatic demographic community. This is defined as consisting of 2 distinct figures: (i) the 10.1 million active community of category (d) above (line No. 30), plus (ii) 53.4 million Catholic postcharismatics (those irregular, or less active, or annually active, or formerly active, or inactive, or elsewhere active, defined and enumerated here in line No. 36). Together these 2 constitute the total Catholic charismatic demographic community, amounting to 50 million in 1985, increasing to 63.5 million by 1988.

31. **Old Catholic charismatics.** Mainly within Old Catholic Churches in Netherlands, USA, and 10 other countries. At its origin in the Netherlands in the 1723 Schism of Utrecht, the Jansenist Church (later Old Catholic Church) specifically embraced "signs and wonders" (miracles, healings, supernatural signs, spiritual gifts).

32. **Black charismatics.** Black neopentecostals within USA Black Baptist and Methodist denominations in around 20 countries, who identify themselves with the Charismatic Movement.

33. **Radio/television charismatics.** Those whose worship life is centered only on radio/TV Pentecostal or charismatic preachers and is unrelated to the numerous local churches and charismatic fellowships nearby.

34. **Mainline postcharismatics.** Self-identified charismatics within mainline nonpentecostal denominations who are no longer regularly active in the Charismatic Movement but have moved into other spheres of witness and service in their churches. (Sum of lines Nos. 35–36). A detailed explanation of this phenomenon is given above in line No. 30.

35. **Protestant postcharismatics.** Charismatics formerly active in Renewal, now inactive but in wider ministries; these inactive persons are much fewer than inactive Catholics because of the more developed teaching, pastoral care, and ministry opportunities offered by the 20 or so organized denominational renewal fellowships in the USA and their counterparts in Europe. An indication of the rapid turnover in membership is the fact that 25% of the 12,000 attenders at the Lutheran ILCOHS annual charismatic conferences in Minneapolis (USA) are first-timers, which implies an average 4-year turnover.

36. **Catholic postcharismatics.** Charismatics formerly active in Renewal (for average turnover period of 2 to 3 years of active involvement in officially-recognized Catholic charismatic prayer groups), now in wider ministries; inaccurately called "graduates" or "alumni" of Renewal; in the USA, these consist of 9 million inactive in addition to the 700,000 active adults or 1 million weekly-active or 2 million monthly-active Catholic charismatic community including children. Added to active persons (line No. 30) this means that in 1985 Catholic charismatics worldwide numbered 50 million (5.8% of the entire Roman Catholic Church, rising to over 9% by AD 2000). A detailed explanation is given in line No. 30. A number of Catholic theologians hold that Spirit baptism is as irreversible as water baptism.

37. **Messianic Jewish charismatics.** Some 2% of all Jews (350,000) are believers in Jesus Christ (Yeshua the Mashiach/Messiah), also known as Jewish Christians, Christian Jews, Hebrew Christians, or Messianic Jews (the latter being those who emphasize Jewish roots and rituals). Of the 150,000 Messianic Jews, 75% (110,000) identify themselves as charismatic, particularly in the 53 churches of the Union of Messianic Jewish Congregations (USA); other charismatics are found in Britain (London Messianic Fellowship), France (Paris), Italy, USSR (aided by Finnish Lutheran Jewish missions broadcasts), Argentina, Israel (3,000, including Beth Emmanuel, Tel Aviv). A smaller number of other Jewish charismatics are found in Pentecostal denominations (Assemblies of God with 37 centers in USA, International Church of the Foursquare Gospel, et alia), or in Anglican/Catholic/Protestant charismatic groupings, so are classified here under lines Nos. 14,27,28,30, et alia.

38. **White independent charismatics.** Independent charismatic churches which either have separated from the charismatic renewal in parent mainline denominations (thus 50% of all Presbyterian charismatics in USA are known to have left to join these new churches), or have recently been founded independently (though from out of the same milieux), all being either independent congregations or in loose networks, and all being mainly or predominantly of White membership (Europeans, North Americans): especially in house church movements in England (Restoration, and 5 other major groupings), Scotland, Norway, Sweden (many, including Rhema Fellowship), Denmark, Hungary, Poland, France (several communities), Switzerland, Spain (Witnessing), Netherlands (many), New Zealand, South Africa (many, including International Fellowship of Charismatic Churches, with 300 churches, Hatfield Christian Centre (162 churches), etc), Soviet Union/USSR (in Central Russia, Northern Russia, Ukraine, Baltic, Georgia, et alia), USA (60,000 recently-formed churches in several major groupings or networks (with some overlap): International Fellowship of Faith Ministries (2,000 churches), International Convention of Faith Churches & Ministries (495 churches; in Tulsa), Faith Christian Fellowship International (1,000 ordained ministers), Melodyland Christian Center, People of Destiny, International Communion of Charismatic Churches (former classical Pentecostals, very large, fastest growing network in 1988), Network of Christian Ministries (Latter Rain emphasis), Fellowship of Christian Assemblies (101 churches), Maranatha Christian Churches (57 churches), Fellowship of Covenant Ministers & Churches (250 churches), Association of Vineyard Churches (200 churches, founder John Wimber; note that he and the churches regard themselves as third-wavers rather than charismatics, though most observers hold the reverse is truer), National Leadership Conference, Charismatic Bible Ministries (1,500 ministers), Word Churches (Word of Faith Movement), Calvary Ministries International (200 churches), Local Covenant Churches (Shepherding), Rhema Ministerial Association (525 churches), International Ministers Forum (500 churches), Full Gospel Chaplaincy (1.5 million independent charismatics), Christ for the Nations (600 churches), Abundant Life Community Churches (25 churches), et alia). There are similar movements, related and unrelated, in over 40 other countries also.

39. **THIRD WAVE: MAINSTREAM CHURCH RENEWAL.** These terms describe a completely new wave of the 20th-century Renewal in the Holy Spirit gathering momentum in the 1980s with no direct affiliation to either Pentecostalism or the Charismatic Movement. Participants belong to mainline nonpentecostal denominations (Evangelical and others); see exact definition near beginning of these footnotes (mainstream = "the middle of a stream, where the current is strongest"). (This line's statistics are computed as the sum of lines Nos. 40 and 43; which is the sum of lines Nos. 41,42 and 43). Note that large numbers of phenomenological charismatics (in Korea, East Germany, Poland, et alia) do not identify themselves as either pentecostal or charismatic, and instead exhibit a marked rejection of pentecostal terminology.

40. **Mainstream third-wavers.** Persons in mainline nonpentecostal denominations, recently filled with or empowered with the Spirit but usually non-glossolalic, who do not identify themselves with the terms pentecostal or charismatic. Because they demonstrate the charismata and the phenomena of pentecostalism, they are also being termed (by outside observers) quasicharismatics or neocharismatics. (Sum of lines Nos. 41–42).

41. **Third-Wave White Evangelicals.** As No. 40; mainline Evangelicals (USA, UK) who have recently begun to demonstrate gifts of the Spirit (with tongues in many instances) but who do not join the First Wave (pentecostals) or Second Wave (charismatics), nor identify with them, and instead describe their movement as the Third Wave; many unorganized individuals, but also increasingly organized intradenominational bodies with their own periodicals such as Fulness movement (2,000 Southern Baptist pastors). This movement is strongest in the USA because Evangelicals there opposed the earlier Charismatic Movement in reaction against its emphasis on the miraculous, whereas a number of influential Evangelicals in Britain and Europe publicly endorsed and supported charismatics as early as 1965.

42. **Third-Wave Black/Non-White Evangelicals.** As Nos. 40–41, but rapidly spreading by 1987 among African, Asian and Latin American Evangelicals; this category includes many large, widely known or outstanding Third-World churches and congregations belonging to nonpentecostal denominations founded by nonpentecostal or even antipentecostal mission boards from

Europe and North America. Among the most prominent of such congregations are 4 from Korea: Sung Rak Baptist Church, Seoul (at 25,000 members the largest Southern Baptist-related congregation in the world until its secession in September 1987); Central Evangelical Holiness Church, Seoul (at 6,000 members the largest Holiness congregation in the world); and the world's 2 largest Methodist congregations, in Inchon and Seoul (25,000 members each). All of these congregations exhibit charismatic and pentecostal phenomena.

43. **Crypto-charismatics.** Persons in other mainline confessions recently filled with the Spirit but not joining either pentecostal denominations or the mainline Charismatic Movement, nor linking up with Third-Wave Evangelicals; including those who for reasons of family security in closed countries do not reveal their charismatic experience.

44. **Total all pentecostal/charismatic church members.** Sum of lines Nos. 3,25 and 39 (the Three Waves of Renewal), plus No. 2; i.e. the sum of lines Nos. 2,4,21,24,26,33,34,37,38,40 and 43.

45. **Total as % of world's church-member Christians.** Computed as line No. 44 divided by line No. 81, times 100. For columns 22–29, the figures are percentages of continent-wide church-member Christians. The high figure for East Asia is due mainly to China and Korea.

46. **PROFESSING PENTECOSTALS/CHARISMATICS.** All Christians who identify themselves or regard themselves as, or profess to be, pentecostals or charismatics or quasipentecostals or neocharismatics or crypto-charismatics or third-wavers.

47. **Pentecostals/charismatics unaffiliated to churches or groups.** Professing pentecostals/charismatics who do not, or do not yet, belong to pentecostal or charismatic or third-wave organized churches or groups or communities or denominations. Large numbers become pentecostals/charismatics in personal experience several weeks, months or even years before they find a church or group and get enrolled and therefore enumerated. They can be estimated, as here, by careful comparison of those professing with those affiliated (enrolled).

48. **Total all professing pentecostals/charismatics.** Sum of lines Nos. 44 and 47.

49. **Total as % of whole world's Christians.** Computed as line No. 48 divided by line No. 80, times 100.

50. **Churches, Congregations and House Groups.** All distinct organized local congregations, worship centers, parishes, fellowships or groupings of all kinds, which are explicitly identified with or attached to the Renewal. Megachurches. A majority of the 50 or so largest megachurches (the world's largest single congregations, each with over 50,000 members) are pentecostal/charismatic. The largest Protestant church is Full Gospel Central Church, Seoul, Korea, with 600,000 members by 1988.

55. **Classical Pentecostal churches.** Largest grouping, Assemblies of God (USA and overseas): churches excluding outstations (1985) 77,976, (1986) 92,355 (15.6% per year increase).

61. **Total all pentecostal/charismatic churches/groups.** Totals of the 10 distinct categories shown in the table as the sum of lines Nos. 52–60.

62. **PENTECOSTAL/CHARISMATIC FINANCE AND GIVING (in US$, per year).** Defined as in article "Silver and Gold Have I None," in *International Bulletin of Missionary Research* (October, 1983), page 150.

70. **PENTECOSTAL/CHARISMATIC AGENCIES AND INSTITUTIONS.** Defined as in WCE (1982) pages 93–95, 830, 844.

71. **Service agencies.** National, countrywide, regional or international bodies, parachurch organizations and agencies which assist or serve the churches but are not themselves denominations or church-planting mission bodies. (Defined in WCE page 95, with listing of 61 categories in Part 13). Among the most significant categories are (a) Pentecostal agencies (missions, evangelism, publishing, etc), (b) denominational charismatic agencies: Anglican Renewal Ministries (UK), Episcopal Renewal Ministries (USA), International Catholic Charismatic Renewal Office (Vatican City), National Service Committees for the Catholic Charismatic Renewals (in over 80 countries), and 100 more such bodies, (c) global mission agencies: SOMA, Advance, AIMS (with 75 member mission agencies) and other missionary bodies serving the Charismatic Movement, and (d) Third-World mission agencies: over 300 locally-organized and -supported charismatic sending bodies. One of the fastest growing varieties of renewal agency is: TV production organizations, numbering over 500 by 1987.

72. **Institutions.** Major pentecostal/charismatic church-operated or -related institutions of all kinds, i.e. fixed centers with premises, plant and permanent staff, excluding church buildings, worship centers, church headquarters or offices; including high schools, colleges, universities, medical centers, hospitals, clinics, presses, bookshops, libraries, radio/TV stations and studios, conference centers, study centers, research centers, seminaries, religious communities (monasteries, abbeys, convents, houses), etc. (Defined in WCE pages 93–94). Many of these have been originated by Pentecostal bodies, and a growing number by mainline charismatics. But in countries where new initiatives are prohibited or repressed (e.g. East Germany, Poland), thousands of traditionally-Christian institutions have been infiltrated and virtually taken over by charismatics. Charismatic covenant communities. Since 1958 (Community of Jesus, Cape Cod, Massachusetts, now with 900 members) and 1965 (Episcopal Church of the Redeemer, Houston, Texas), residential communities committed to intentional corporate charismatic life,

service and mission, mainly ecumenical or interdenominational, with married couples and families as well as celibates, have arisen in 50 countries across the world (see list of Catholic-originated communities, in note under line No. 30). Size varies from under 20 persons each to 4,000 (Emmanuel Community, Paris, France, begun 1972). Total communities in 1987: some 2,000, with over quarter of a million members. A very detailed survey is given by P. Hocken, "The Significance of Charismatic Communities", in P. Elbert, ed, *Charismatic Renewal in the Churches* (forthcoming).

73. **Total all parachurch/service agencies and institutions.** Sum of lines Nos. 71 and 72.
74. **PENTECOSTAL/CHARISMATIC WORKERS.** Full-time church workers, pastors, clergy, ministers, evangelists, missionaries, executives, administrators, bishops, moderators, church leaders, et alii. (Defined as in WCE pages 94–95).
75. **Nationals (pastors, clergy, evangelists, et alii).** Some representative statistics: (1) Pentecostalism. Assemblies of God (USA and overseas) credentialed ministers 111,788 (1985), 121,425 (1986), annual increase 8% per year. (2) Charismatic Movement. Percentage of charismatics among clergy (some representative figures): (East Germany) Bund der Evangelische Kirchen in der DDR (state Lutheran church): 500 pastors (10% of all clergy) are charismatics. (UK) Church of England: 25% of all 17,000 clergy. (USA) Episcopal Church in the USA: 21% of 14,111 clergy are involved, and 64% receive ERM periodicals. Lutheran Church Missouri Synod: 400 out of 6,000 clergy are charismatic; several clergy have been unfrocked since 1970. Many ecumenical and evangelical parachurch agencies have 20–60% charismatics on staff. In the 2,000 or so Pentecostal agencies, virtually all staff are Pentecostal.
76. **Aliens: foreign missionaries.** These include Pentecostals, and the following varieties of charismatics (renewed in the Spirit): (1985) 25% of all Anglican foreign missionaries, 20% of all RCs, 40% of all Protestants (60% of WEC, 42% of ABCIM, etc); by AD 2000, these figures are likely to have increased at least to 50% of Anglicans, 25% of RCs, 50% of Protestants, and 90% of Third-World missionaries. (See definitions of foreign missionaries in WCE pages 92–93).
77. **Aliens: short-termers.** Defined as full-time workers, missionaries, volunteers, or others who go abroad for less than a 2-year period (usually one year or thereabouts).
78. **Total all pentecostal/charismatic full-time workers.** Sum of lines Nos. 75,76, and 77.
79. **WORLD CHRISTIANITY.** The following 2 lines supply the context of the world total of all Christians.
80. **Christians (all varieties).** Total all Christians, i.e. professing Christians plus crypto-Christians (or affiliated Christians plus nominal Christians). See Global Table 4 in *World Christian Encyclopedia* (1982), page 6, updated in Barrett, "Status of Global Mission, 1988", *International Bulletin of Missionary Research* (January, 1988), page 17, line 9.
81. **Affiliated church members.** Persons (adults and children) on the rolls of the churches and so of organized Christianity, as defined in "Status of Global Mission, 1988", page 17, line 21.
82. **WORLD EVANGELIZATION.** This last section is added because it has always been the focus and goal of the movement as a whole.
83. **Unevangelized populations.** Total persons in the world who have never heard the name of Jesus Christ and remain unaware of Christianity, Christ, and the gospel.
84. **Unevangelized as % of world.** Line No. 83 divided by world population, times 100.
85. **Unreached peoples with no churches at all.** Ethnolinguistic peoples among whom no churches of any kind have yet been organized or begun.
86. **Unevangelized non-Christian or anti-Christian megacities.** Cities of over 1 million population which are predominantly Muslim, Hindu, Buddhist, Marxist, or of other non-Christian persuasion. Anti-Christian cities are those which are actively hostile to Christianity, evangelism, mission and missionaries.
87. **Unevangelized persons to each pentecostal/charismatic.** Computed as line No. 83 divided by No. 48.
88. **World evangelization global plans since AD 30.** Grand total of all distinct plans and proposals for accomplishing world evangelization made by Christians since AD 30. Most of these are each described in D.B. Barrett, *Cosmos, Chaos, and Gospel: A Chronology of World Evangelization from Creation to New Creation* (Birmingham, AL: New Hope, 1987). All 720 are listed, enumerated, described, analyzed and interpreted in T. Wang, P.E. McKaughan, J.W. Reapsome, and D.B. Barrett, *Seven Hundred Plans to Evangelize the World: The Rise of a Global Evangelization Movement* (New Hope, 1988).

global foreign missions per member per week is stuck at the paltry figure of fifteen U.S. cents (line 69).

A further illustration of the permeation of global Christianity lies in the huge numbers of ordained pastors, priests, ministers, bishops, and other church leaders involved (lines 74–78). One quarter of the world's full-time Christian workers are Pentecostals/charismatics.

IV. Penetration of the World. Throughout the history of the Renewal, leaders have summoned members to the task of world evangelization. A favorite theme has been the saying of Jesus: "The fields are white unto harvest" (John 4:35). The unharvested or unreached harvest field today consists of 1.3 billion unevangelized persons who have never heard of Jesus Christ (line 83), in 3,000 unevangelized population segments (cities, peoples, countries). It includes 2,000 unreached ethnolinguistic peoples, 175 unreached megapeoples (of over one million population each), 140 unevangelized megacities, 300 unevangelized Islamic metropolises. The harvest force, or harvesters committed to harvesting, consists of 4 million full-time Christian workers: of these, one million are Pentecostals/charismatics (line 78).

Another indicator concerns global plans to evangelize the world (line 88). Of the world's 720 such plans since A.D. 30, some 12 percent have been definitely Pentecostal/charismatic. Probably 20 percent altogether—150 plans—have had significant charismatic participation. In the last twenty years, this percentage has risen markedly. Of the world's 20 current megaplans launched since 1968, 13, or 65 percent, are Pentecostal-charismatic. So are 8 (73 percent) of the 11 current gigaplans (global plans to evangelize the world spending over one billion U.S. dollars) launched since 1968.

In 1988 a loose affiliation of national and confessional charismatic service agencies, Charismatics United for World Evangelization, began planning major congresses and processes to implement the goal of all persons on earth hearing the gospel by the year 2000.

New bodies are continually emerging. Over one hundred new charismatic mission agencies have recently been formed in the Western world, and over three hundred more in the Third World. Many are taking on the challenge of unevangelized population segments in restricted-access countries by appointing nonresidential missionaries.

With Pentecostals/charismatics now active in 80 percent of the world's 3,300 large metropolises, all in process of actively implementing networking and cooperation with Great Commission Christians of all confessions, a new era in world mission is clearly underway.

See also CHURCH GROWTH.   D. B. Barrett

STEELBERG, WESLEY ROWLAND

(1902–52). A boy preacher who grew up to become the general superintendent of the General Council of the Assemblies of God (AG) (1949–52). Wesley Steelberg's parents had emigrated from Sweden. At the age of six he suffered from

spinal meningitis and was given up to die but was healed.

Steelberg was converted in a small Pentecostal church in Denver and later received the baptism in the Holy Spirit. After the family moved to Los Angeles, he began preaching at age sixteen and was ordained the next year. He married Ruth Fisher, daughter of Elmer Fisher, pastor of the Upper Room Mission in Los Angeles.

While pastoring in California, Steelberg helped organize what later became Christ's Ambassadors, the youth organization of the AG. He was the speaker for "Sermons in Song" and "Revivaltime" radio programs while he was general superintendent. He died after suffering a heart attack while ministering in Wales. Mrs. Steelberg later married Howard Carter, former general superintendent of the Assemblies of God in Great Britain and Ireland.

Bibliography: "Brother Steelberg Is With the Lord" and "All for Jesus," *PE* (July 27, 1952), 5; (August 10, 1952), 3; L. Sumrall, *All for Jesus, The Life of Wesley R. Steelberg* (1955).   W. E. Warner

STEIDEL, FLORENCE

(1897–1962). Missionary to Liberia, nurse, and founder of a leper colony. Steidel was born in Illinois and raised in the Ozark Mountains of Arkansas and Missouri. During a vision and a dream one day in 1924, she was called to help the sick and dying in Africa and was shown the home in Liberia in which she would later live. She prepared for this call by obtaining nurses' training at Missouri Baptist Hospital (1924–28) and attending Southern Baptist Theological Seminary (1929–31). While staying at Mizpah Missionary Home (Assemblies of God [AG]) in New York, Steidel became acquainted with AG missionaries and received the baptism in the Spirit in 1934. She obtained a missionary appointment with the AG in 1935 and later studied at Central Bible College (CBC) when home on furlough in 1944. Upon arriving in 1935 at her first missionary assignment, a girls' school in Palipo, Liberia, Steidel immediately recognized the home in her 1924 dream. She knew she was where God called her. She worked in this girls' school, which had been moved to Newaka, Liberia, for twelve years before she started the leper colony.

Steidel is remembered for her work at New Hope Town, a leper colony she founded in 1947 with a hundred dollars and the labor of lepers. Over the next fifteen years she oversaw the construction of seventy permanent buildings and the planting of 2,500 rubber trees to help the colony become self-sufficient. In addition, she was responsible in 1956 for the building of an eighteen-mile road connecting the colony to the nearest government road. New Hope Town housed and medically treated more than eight hundred lepers. It also had separate housing and educational facilities for the children of the lepers who had not contracted leprosy. Usually it took four years for the people to be cured of their leprosy. Each year one hundred people were given "symptom free certificates" indicating that they had been symptom free for a year.

The daily schedule began with a service in the

thousand-seat chapel. Before people left New Hope Town, 90 percent had been saved and many had received the baptism in the Spirit. Steidel built a Bible school in 1961; by 1962 seventy-one students were preparing for ministry. The development of New Hope Town was complicated by 380 inches of rain per year, its inaccessibility, and fifty tribal languages being spoken in the colony. Steidel received two honors for her work: Knight Official of the Humane Order of African Redemption, awarded by William V. S. Tubman, president of the Republic of Liberia, in 1957; and CBC Alumna of the Year in 1960.

Bibliography: R. F. Brock, "Florence Steidel, A Devoted Worker Who Gave Lepers New Hope," *PE* (May 27, 1962), 8; C. Carmichael, *New Hope Leprosy Mission* (c. 1959); I. Spence, *These Are My People: Florence Steidel* (1961); I. Winehouse, *The Assemblies of God: A Popular Survey* (1959).   E. B. Robinson

STEINER, LEONHARD (1903–). Major figure in Swiss Pentecostalism. Converted as a young man, Steiner heard a call to the ministry in 1923 and was baptized in the Spirit. Steiner was a preacher in the Swiss Pentecostal Mission from 1927, becoming in 1945 editor of *Verheissung des Vaters* (*Promise of the Father*) and missions secretary, as well as pastor of the Basel assembly. He was led to convene the first Pentecostal World Conference in Zurich in 1947 and was unanimously elected its chairman.

Since 1939 Steiner has rejected the two-stage view of new birth and Spirit baptism and the sign of tongues. One of the most ecumenical among European Pentecostal leaders, he was chairman of a 1966 consultation between representatives of the World Council of Churches and of some European Pentecostals. Steiner is the author of *Mit Folgenden Zeichen* (*With Signs Following*), a study of Pentecostal history and doctrine published in 1954 but not reprinted due to his changed attitude toward the healing evangelists.
                                                          P. D. Hocken

STENHOUSE, EVERETT RAY (1931–). Pastor, missionary, and denominational executive. Born in Minco, Oklahoma, Stenhouse was reared in California, where he later attended the University of California. He engaged in evangelistic ministry from 1951 to 1954. In 1955 he became pastor of Wayside Chapel in Bakersfield, California, and was ordained by the Southern California District of the Assemblies of God (AG) in the same year. During the years 1960–63, 1968–69, and 1974–79 Stenhouse served as pastor or associate pastor in three other Southern California District churches. From 1963 to 1967 he was the district's youth president, and he served for one term (1969–73) as a missionary to Greece.

In 1979 Stenhouse became superintendent of the Southern California District. Two years later he was elected to serve as the nonresident executive presbyter for the Southwest region of the U.S. During his tenure as superintendent, the California Graduate School of Theology conferred on him an honorary doctor of divinity degree. When the General Council of the AG met in 1985, he was elected to serve as the denomina-

tion's assistant general superintendent and took office on January 1, 1986. Stenhouse and his wife, Alice (married 1948), have four children: Brenda (Jones), Judy (Lundberg), Steve, and Andrew.

Bibliography: AG Office of Information, media release.   G. B. McGee

STEPHANOU, EUSEBIUS A. (1924–). Charismatic priest of the Greek Orthodox Church. Stephanou was born in Fond du Lac, Wisconsin, in 1924, the son and grandson of priests. He graduated from high school in Detroit, Michigan, in 1942; received the B.A. degree from the University of Michigan; the B.D. from Holy Cross Greek Orthodox Seminary in Brookline, Massachusetts; the S.T.M. from Nashotah House Seminary, Nashotah, Wisconsin; and the Th.D. from the General Theological Seminary, New York City. Postdoctoral studies were taken at the University of Athens, Greece.

Ordained a priest in Greece in 1953, Stephanou pastored Greek Orthodox churches in Ann Arbor, Michigan; Woburn, Massachusetts; Canton, Ohio; Chicago, Illinois; and Fort Wayne, Indiana. From 1955 to 1962 he served on the faculty of Holy Cross Greek Orthodox Seminary as professor of theology. He later taught in the department of theology at Notre Dame University as visiting professor (1967–68).

In 1968 Stephanou founded the Logos Ministry for Orthodox Renewal and began publication of the *Logos* monthly periodical. At that time he embarked on an itinerant ministry of evangelism among Orthodox Christians in the U.S. and abroad, including such countries as Greece, Australia, Cyprus, and Kenya. Increasingly aware of the dichotomy between orthodoxy in doctrine and orthodoxy in actual practice, he sensed a calling from God for reevangelization of Orthodox Christians.

In 1972 Stephanou received the baptism in the Holy Spirit, having been introduced to the charismatic renewal by fellow Orthodox priest, Athanasius Emmert. Thereafter he has been actively involved in the Holy Spirit renewal. He soon was recognized inside and outside his church as a leader in the Orthodox charismatic renewal. Not only did he continue to publish the *Logos* magazine but also sponsored the first five annual Orthodox charismatic conferences between 1972 and 1978 and then again in 1986 and 1987. His communications center was located in Fort Wayne, Indiana, until 1988 when he relocated in Destin, Florida.

Stephanou's ministry of evangelism has stressed an end-time message of salvation, healing, and deliverance. He has attempted to demonstrate to the worldwide Orthodox community that the charismatic renewal can find a natural home in the Orthodox church because it is the church par excellence that has been intrinsically charismatic for almost two millennia.

Stephanou's evangelical and prophetic outreach has met with misunderstanding and even the open opposition of the official Orthodox Church. He has been placed under suspension off and on since 1968. In 1986 he was notified that proceedings were in progress for the purpose of his defrock-

ing. However, the petition of the Greek Orthodox Archdiocese of North and South America was
turned down by the Ecumenical Patriarchate of
Constantinople. While numerous Orthodox
priests have recanted their charismatic theology
and practice, Eusebius Stephanou has courageously and vigorously continued his attempts to
bring the renewal of the Holy Spirit to the
Orthodox church.

Stephanou has authored the following books:
Belief and Practice in the Orthodox Church (1965),
Charismatic Renewal in the Orthodox Church
(1976), *The Worldwide Outpouring of the Holy
Spirit* (in Greek) (1976), *Charisma and Gnosis in
Orthodox Thought* (n.d.), *Desolation and Restora-
tion in the Orthodox Church* (1977), *Pathway to
Orthodox Renewal* (1978), *World Orthodoxy in
Crisis* (1980), and *Renewal Pains in the Orthodox
Church* (1982). He is also the author of numerous
articles on the charismatic movement and histori-
cal pneumatology.

Bibliography: "Archdiocese Seeks to Defrock Priest,"
*The Greek Star: The Voice of Chicago's Hellenic Commu-
nity* (May 15, 1986), n.p.; " 'Charismatic' Priest May Be
Defrocked," *The Illuminator: The Newspaper of the Greek
Orthodox Diocese of Pittsburgh* 7 (56, 1986): n.p.;
curriculum vitae supplied by Eusebius Stephanou; letter
from E. A. Stephanou to Rt. Rev. Philotheos, Titular
Bishop of Meloa, Greek Orthodox Archdiocese, March
27, 1987.   S. M. Burgess

STEWART, DONALD LEE (1939–). Healing evangelist. Don Stewart was born in Arizona
and began preaching at age twenty-one. He was
ordained by Miracle Valley Fellowship (A. A.
Allen's organization) in 1961. In 1960 he married
Kathleen Rogers. They have two children.

Don Stewart, a graduate of A. A. Allen's
Miracle Valley School and one of Allen's associate
evangelists after 1958, took over the ministry at
Allen's death in 1970. The scandal surrounding
Allen's death and the internal struggle for control
made the transition no easy task, but Stewart
believed that Allen's mantle had fallen on him.
After a two-year legal battle (which caused heavy
losses to the ministry) and after a successful New
York revival, Stewart emerged the leader of what
remained, changing the name to the Don Stewart
Evangelistic Association. It has become a multi-
million dollar per year operation.

Stewart is a simple but powerful preacher.
Healing remains central to his ministry. He
encourages the audience to expect from God.
Prosperity for Christians is another emphasis. He
is the author of *Fakes, Frauds, and Fools* (1972)
and *The Man From Miracle Valley* (1971).

Bibliography: D. E. Harrell, Jr., *All Things Are
Possible* (1975); R. Jones, *The Faith Healers* (1987);
"Who Is Don Stewart? What Is He Trying To Do?"
(n.d.).   S. Shemeth

STEWART, LEON OTTO (1929–). Pastor,
editor, and denominational official. Born in Pine-
ville, Florida, to John Wesley and Susie Ann
(Allen) Stewart. Reared in Florida and Alabama,
Stewart attended Holmes Bible College (now
called Holmes College of the Bible), Greenville,
South Carolina. He graduated from there with a
Th.B. degree in 1952 and was ordained in the
same year. Although his eyesight failed early in his

ministry, he successfully pastored Pentecostal
Holiness churches in Greenville, Alabama;
Kreole, Mississippi; and Roanoke, Virginia.
From 1960 to 1969 he served as conference
superintendent for the Alabama Conference of
the International Pentecostal Holiness Church
(PHC).

Bishop Leon O. Stewart is the general superintendent of the International Pentecostal Holiness
Church.

In 1969 he was elected assistant general superintendent of the denomination and held this
position until 1981; he also filled the post of vice-
chairman from 1977 to 1981. During these years
as a national officer of PHC, Stewart worked
variously as general director of the following
departments: Superannuation, Loan Fund, Publications, World Intercessory Network (WIN),
Armed Forces, Archives, Men's Fellowship,
Video, and Evangelism.

Stewart's editorial responsibilities have included *Prep*, a Sunday school teaching magazine
for youth (1961–74); *Witness*, a publication of
the Department of Evangelism (1974–81); and
Advocate, the official voice of PHC (1981–). He
also authored *Too Late* (1958), a religious novel.

Since 1981 Stewart has served as general
superintendent of the denomination, carrying the
honorary title of "bishop." His administration has
brought tranquility and renewed confidence in
the national leadership of the PHC, following a
short period of turmoil. He also currently represents the PHC on the board of administration and
executive committee of the National Association
of Evangelicals. In recognition of his leadership
Stewart has received honorary doctor of divinity
degrees from the following institutions: Holmes
College of the Bible, Greenville, South Carolina;
Heritage Bible College, Dunn, North Carolina;
Pacific Coast Bible College, Sacramento, Califor-

nia; and Southwestern College of Christian Ministries, Oklahoma City, Oklahoma.

In 1952 he married Donna Dooley. They have two daughters: Dianne Marie and Karen Denise.

Bibliography: *Who's Who in Religion*, 3d ed. (1985).
G. B. McGee

STONE, JEAN See WILLANS, JEAN STONE.

STRADER, KARL DAVID (1929–). Assemblies of God (AG) pastor. Reared a Methodist in western Oklahoma, Karl Strader became interested in Pentecostalism after attending an Oral Roberts' tent meeting. Educated at Bob Jones University, he married Joyce Wead of a prominent AG family and joined that denomination. Since 1966 he has pastored First Assembly of God in Lakeland, Florida, which had grown to five thousand members in 1987. In 1985 he built a 10,000-seat sanctuary—the largest in the nation at the time—and named the building the Carpenter's Home Church. He is known as a powerful preacher who quotes long passages of Scripture from memory in his sermons. Considered somewhat of a maverick within his denomination, he has served as a bridge builder with other charismatics by initiating in 1980 annual "Idea Exchanges" that brought together leaders from the charismatic renewal to discuss and sometimes debate problematic issues.

Bibliography: S. Andrew, "The Pastor Who Built a 10,000-Seat Church in a City of 58,000," *Charisma* (January 1985), 20–28.
S. Strang

Stephen Strang is the founding editor of *Charisma* magazine. He is president of Strang Communications Company, which in addition to publishing *Charisma*, publishes *Ministries* magazine and books under the name Creation House.

STRANG, STEPHEN EDWARD (1951–). Magazine editor and publisher. Stephen Strang was born to A. Edward and Amy Alice Strang in Springfield, Missouri. The family later moved to Florida where the younger Strang attended the University of Florida College of Journalism. Prior to his graduation with a B.S. degree in 1973, he won the writing championship award sponsored by the William Randolph Hearst Foundation, reputed to be the highest journalism honor given to a college student in America. In 1972 he married Joy Ferrell; they have two sons. From 1973 to 1976 he worked as a reporter for *The Orlando Sentinel* (then called *Sentinel Star*).

Although reared in a Christian home, Strang became rebellious as a teenager. During the height of the Jesus movement, as a college sophomore, Strang rediscovered the gospel and had a life-changing experience with the Lord. While employed as a newspaper reporter, he envisioned a Christian magazine as a forum for sharing his faith with people outside the church. In 1975, while a member of Calvary Assembly of God in Winter Park, Florida, he proposed to the church leadership that the congregation sponsor a magazine entitled *Charisma* by underwriting the first six issues with $15,000. Beginning as a church magazine with only 420 subscribers, it gained a national audience of approximately 50,000 subscribers during the next five years. Initially Strang edited the magazine on a part-time basis; a year later in 1976, he quit his post with the local newspaper to work full time for *Charisma*. The relationship with Calvary Assembly of God ended on June 1, 1981, when the church's leadership allowed him to form a corporation to purchase the magazine.

With incorporation came other publishing enterprises by the newly formed Strang Communications Company. *Ministries Today,* a quarterly for ministers, began in 1983 and has a current subscription list of 20,000. Three years later, Strang Communications, now located in Altamonte Springs, Florida, accepted the offer of Robert Walker, president of Christian Life Missions, to purchase *Christian Life, Christian Bookseller,* and Creation House books. As a result, *Christian Bookseller* became *Christian Retailing* in December 1986 and adopted a trade-tabloid format. In addition, *Christian Life* was merged with *Charisma* in the spring of 1987; this resulted in a combined circulation of 220,000, making it one of the most widely read Christian magazines in America with a paid circulation.

Since the founding of *Charisma* magazine, it has become one of the most influential publications among charismatic Christians. Strang's ecumenical stance toward cooperation among Pentecostals and charismatics is reflected in the editorial direction of *Charisma* and in his 1985 call to the leadership of the Pentecostal World Conference

to meet with leaders in the renewal movements in the historic churches, as well as with leaders of independent Charismatic or Pentecostal groups. We believe that such meetings would, at the least, result in a better understanding on both sides. Such meetings could also result in denominational Pentecostals cooperating more with their independent and Charismatic counterparts. And at best, such meetings could contribute to building the kingdom of God, the avowed goal of all believers" (Strang, 1985, 8).

Bibliography: S. Strang, "A Call for Cooperation," *Charisma* (September 1985), 8; idem, "One Small Step," *Charisma* (June 1981), 8; S. Strang to G. B. McGee, February 18, 1988.   G. B. McGee

STRATON, WARREN BADENOCH

(1907–66). Artist, sculptor, architect, violin-maker, and minister. The son of John R. Straton, pastor of Calvary Baptist Church in New York City, Warren Straton began to draw seriously before the age of six. By age eleven he was selling paintings in New York galleries, and at eighteen he sold statuary at Tiffany's. He studied at the Art Students League, the Beaux Arts Institute of Design, Cooper Union in New York, the University of Rochester, and in Italy.

His architectural achievements include designing the Nelson Tower and the Chrysler Building in New York City. He worked on the Pennsylvania state capitol building and the Department of Justice Building in Washington, D.C. He sculpted the eagles for Arlington Memorial Bridge in Washington, D.C., and the eagles for the American embassy in Paris, France. Among his many outstanding murals are the hands of God reaching out to humankind and encircling the universe (for Oral Roberts), and Christ of the Apocalypse riding a white horse (Assemblies of God [AG] Headquarters Building).

Straton also was known as a violin-maker and restorer, following the patterns of Stradivari and Guarnieri. He developed a varnish that he believed to be an exact reproduction of that used by Stradivari. In addition, he restored numerous valuable sixteenth- and seventeenth-century paintings to their original beauty.

He was ordained by the AG and pastored in Rochester, New York, for twenty-three years. For nine years he was head of the art department at Evangel College, Springfield, Missouri. He also served on the Oral Roberts University faculty and on the faculty of the American Academy in Rome. He died in an automobile accident on April 18, 1966.

Bibliography: J. Fairfield, *Known Violinmakers* (1942); "Rev. Straton Dies in Crash," *Springfield* [Missouri] *Daily News* (April 19, 1966).   S. M. Burgess

STUDD, GEORGE B.

(1859–1945). The second of the three cricket-playing Studd brothers. Though George Studd had become a Christian while at Eton, he made a full commitment during an extended visit with his brother C. T. in China ten years later. He helped build Peniel Hall, a Holiness church in Los Angeles, and by 1907 accepted the Pentecostal message. He taught a Bible class at the Azusa Street Mission, and in 1913 he helped organize the Worldwide Camp Meeting at Arroyo Seco. He later accepted the Oneness doctrine and worked with its early leaders although he continued to fellowship with Trinitarian Pentecostals. His great passion was missions, and he supported and corresponded with many missionaries. He gradually gave away his inherited fortune and lived very modestly.

Bibliography: F. Ewart, *The Phenomenon of Pentecost* (1975); N. Grubb, *C. T. Studd, Cricketeer and Pioneer* (1933).   L. F. Wilson

Léon-Joseph Cardinal Suenens is a prelate, theologian, and author in Belgium who was influential at Vatican Council II.

SUENENS, LÉON-JOSEPH

(1904–). Roman Catholic cardinal, theologian, and author. Suenens studied at the Pontifical Gregorian University (Rome) and was ordained in Malines, Belgium (1927), where he taught philosophy until 1939. During the Nazi occupation, 1940–45, he was vice-rector of the University of Louvain and from 1945–61 auxiliary bishop of Malines. In 1961 he was appointed archbishop of Malines-Brussels (until 1979). He was made cardinal in 1962 by Pope John XXIII.

An astute and persuasive politician and member of the commission that prepared the agenda for the council, Suenens became an initiator and leader of the reform movement that dominated the Vatican II Council. He urged developing lay charismata and ecumenical cooperation in issues of social and humanitarian concern. He also urged that the church adapt, without compromising essential doctrines, to modern culture.

In 1972 and 1973 Suenens first came into contact with the Catholic Charismatic Renewal (CCR) in the U.S. and visited Notre Dame. He hosted a conference at Malines that attempted to evaluate the CCR and provided *Theological and Pastoral Guidelines on the Catholic Charismatic Renewal* (1974). He invited two American CCR leaders, Ralph Martin and Stephen Clark, to develop a CCR International Information Office in Brussels (later moved to Rome). Suenens became concerned about trends of the CCR, especially its tendency to act independently of the church. Thus, concerned about the parachurch qualities, he decreed (c. 1976) that (in Belgium) only priests could lead prayer groups, and he developed his ideas concerning the importance of complete integration of the CCR into the ecclesial structure of the church.

Selected English translations of Suenens's works include: *The Gospel to Every Creature* (1957), *Mary, the Mother of God* (1959), *Christian Life Day by Day* (1964), *Theology of the Apostolate* (1954), *The Right View of Moral Rearmament* (1954), *Love and Control* (1962), *The Church in Dialogue* (1965), *Coresponsibility in the Church* (1968), *The Future of the Christian Church* (1970), *A New Pentecost?* (1975), *Come, Holy Spirit* (1976), *Ways of the Spirit* (1976), *Essays on Renewal* (1977), *Your God?* (1977), *Ecumenism and Charismatic Renewal* (1978), *Charismatic Renewal and Social Action* (1979), *Open the Frontiers* (1980), *Renewal and the Powers of Darkness* (1983).

Bibliography: R. J. Bord and J. E. Faulkner, *The Catholic Charismatics* (1983); D. Bundy, "Charismatic Renewal in Belgium: A Bibliographical Essay," *EPTA Bulletin* 5 (1986): 76–90; *Contemporary Authors* 61–64 (1976): 542; *Current Biography Yearbook, 1965,* 420–22; E. Hamilton, *Suenens, A Portrait* (1975); *International Who's Who 1986–1987*; P. Lesourd and J. Ramiz, *Leon Josef Cardinal Suenens* (1964); J. L. Sandidge, "Origin and Development of the Catholic Charismatic Movement in Belgium," unpublished M.R.S.C. thesis, University of Leuven, 1976.

D. D. Bundy

Founder of Lester Sumrall Evangelistic Assn. (LESEA), Lester Sumrall owns Christian television and radio stations, is an author, and operates World Harvest Bible College in South Bend, Indiana.

SUMRALL, LESTER FRANK (1913–). Missionary, pastor, and broadcaster. Sumrall was born in New Orleans, Louisiana. He began preaching at age seventeen, just three weeks after being miraculously cured of tuberculosis. At age nineteen he founded a church in Green Forest, Arkansas, and was ordained by the Assemblies of God (AG). In 1934 he began to travel abroad, preaching in Tahiti, New Zealand, and Australia, where he established a church in Brisbane. He traveled with Howard Carter through Indonesia, French Indo-China, Tibet, China, Mongolia, Korea, Siberia, Russia, Poland, Germany, France, and Scandinavia.

On a trip to South America he met Louise Layman, a Canadian missionary to Argentina. A year later they were married in London, Ontario. On their honeymoon they evangelized in Nova Scotia, other parts of Canada, the Caribbean Islands, and South America.

The Sumralls spent several years in the Philippines. After a successful evangelistic effort with crowds that newspapers estimated at 50,000 and thousands of conversions, Sumrall founded in Manila what became the largest church in the Philippines during the 1950s.

In 1963 the Sumralls moved to South Bend, Indiana, where Lester has since served as a pastor. The church, now called Christian Center Cathedral of Praise, has expanded three times. It has a domed sanctuary with a seating capacity of 3,500.

Separating from the AG, Sumrall founded Lester Sumrall Evangelistic Association (LeSea), World Harvest Bible College, World Harvest Homes for orphans, and *World Harvest Magazine*.

Sumrall ventured into broadcasting with a vision to bring millions to salvation in Christ. He established WHME, an FM radio station in 1968. LeSea also bought television stations in Indianapolis (1972) and South Bend (1977). In 1986 LeSea purchased three other stations, one each in Honolulu, Tulsa, and Kenosha, Wisconsin. Since December 1985 World Harvest Radio International transmits shortwave to Latin America, Canada, Europe, Russia, and North Africa.

Sumrall is the author of more than a hundred books, including *Gifts & Ministries of the Holy Spirit* (1982), *Faith to Change the World* (1983), *Dominion Is Yours* (n.d.), and *My Story to His Glory* (n.d.).

Bibliography: F. Lily, "Lester Sumrall: Cathedral of Praise," *Charisma* (November 1985), 48–52. S. Strang

SUNDAY SCHOOLS Although evangelism was foremost in the hearts of the founders of the Pentecostal denominations, there was a widespread practice of including Sunday school as part of the church program. At the first general assembly of the Church of God (CG, Cleveland, Tenn.) in 1906 there was a call for each congregation to establish a Sunday school for training children. Almost from its beginning the leaders and laypersons of the Assemblies of God (AG) promoted Sunday schools as a means of conserving and instructing its children and youth. Sunday schools were operated in the International Pentecostal Holiness Church (IPHC) from its founding.

The Pentecostal Sunday schools took a similar philosophy of the early twentieth-century Protestant Sunday schools: reaching persons for Christ and establishing them in the faith. This was in contrast to the purpose of the founder of the modern Sunday school movement in 1780. Robert Raikes in Gloucester, England, hired teachers to instruct poor children in the basics of reading, writing, arithmetic, and religious instruction in the Bible. Since the children worked six days a week from dawn to dusk, Sunday was their only day for school. Initial opposition was overcome as John Wesley and George Fox encouraged the establishment of Sunday schools as a primary method of religious instruction. Within a few years the Sunday school became well known and spread to the U.S. The Sunday school movement probably has had its greatest success in America as it became the primary church program of Bible study for all ages, while in England and many parts of the world Sunday school was for children only. It still retains its unique role as primarily a lay movement. This is particularly true since a majority of Pentecostal churches have not been large enough to hire professional religious educators to administer and supervise Christian education programs.

The most popular time for Sunday school has always been the hour before the worship service whether morning or afternoon. It was not uncommon for a new Pentecostal church to hold afternoon Sunday school and worship services because it lacked its own building. A few churches have chosen to conduct Sunday school on Sunday evening.

Most churches provide classes for preschoolers, elementary age children, young adults, and adults. A general superintendent and one or two other officers usually oversee these. As the Sunday school increases in attendance, most schools begin to departmentalize and add other officers at the department and general level. A medium-size school will function with three departments—children, youth, and adult. Larger schools provide a department for each of the age group classifications: baby nursery, teaching nursery, kindergarten (or preprimary), primary, junior, junior high (or young teen), senior high (or high school), youth, young adult, adult, and senior adult. Extension and cradle roll departments that minister to shut-ins and babies who do not attend Sunday school have been important in reaching new persons and building relationships with the elderly and others who cannot attend church regularly. Most Sunday schools provide from thirty to sixty minutes for Bible study. Team teaching is commonly practiced in many children's classes and in some youth classes.

The larger Pentecostal denominations publish their own curriculum or work with one of the large independent religious publishers in adapting or adopting their literature. David C. Cook, Scripture Press, and Gospel Light service many denominations and independent churches and offer various types of adaptation and imprinting of curriculum materials.

The Bible is the center and foundation of the Sunday school curriculum. Before the formation of the National Association of Evangelicals (NAE) in 1942, most curricula followed the outlines prepared by the International Sunday School Lessons. After the founding of the National Sunday School Association (NSSA), an affiliate of the NAE, in 1945, a new series of

Uniform Bible Lessons were prepared, beginning in 1946. These lesson outlines were considered to be more evangelical and biblically based. Currently the AG, CG, IPHC, and Pentecostal Church of God cooperate in preparing uniform outlines titled *Evangelical Sunday School Lessons*. Excluding the AG, the other denominations use an annual *Evangelical Sunday School Commentary*. Pathway Press of the CG publishes about 60,000 of these annual commentaries. The AG publishes its own annual Sunday school teacher's manual.

There has been very little cooperation among the major Pentecostal churches in preparing and printing curriculum materials. Each denomination began publishing picture cards and Sunday school lesson comments during the founding periods of organization. Mrs. J. R. Flower (AG) began preparing lesson comments for *The Pentecostal Evangel* in 1914. In the 1927 bylaws prepared by the AG, the executive presbytery was authorized to publish Sunday school literature. However, the AG had been printing their materials for several years. The IPHC did not begin publishing its material until 1929. Prior to that they purchased materials published by one of their ministers, G. F. Taylor. Curriculum preparation and publishing has been one of the primary functions of the Pentecostal publishing houses.

Current curriculum materials are attractive, group graded, well written, and often published in full color. It retains its emphasis on the Bible as the center and heart of the lessons, but pupil-centered methodology and current social application of the gospel are integral to doctrinal content. Only the adult lessons follow the uniform outlines.

Recognition of the need for trained Sunday school teachers gradually swept across the denominations. In the beginning, many felt that the Holy Spirit baptism and a burning testimony were the primary requirements for teachers. The first worker's training book published by the Pentecostals was *A Successful Sunday School*, written by Ralph M. Riggs in 1933. At the time he was pastoring Central Assembly in Springfield, Missouri. This book set the pattern for AG Sunday schools for many years. Additional training books were added quickly and continued to be published. The CG published its first text in its church training course program in 1955, although it had adopted other materials earlier for training workers. The CG also continues to publish one or more new books annually. It has also adopted training books from other publishers, notably from the International Center for Learning (Gospel Light). The IPHC adopted the texts published by the Evangelical Teaching Training Association, Wheaton, Illinois, as its training program.

In the 1940s the NSSA began conducting annual Sunday school conventions. Pentecostals who were members of the NAE cooperated and were actively involved in these great conventions of 10,000 to 20,000 attendants. The AG and CG began their own convention programs that gradually eclipsed the NSSA conventions. The denominational conventions declined also, possibly because of cost, problems in staffing, and the increasing diversity of other church programs. The emphasis moved toward regional, territorial, or state Christian education conventions that sought to include all church educational programs such as boys' and girls' clubs, youth ministries, evangelism, counseling, etc.

The IPHC was the first denomination to establish a national Sunday school department (1945). Gospel Publishing House set up a promotions office for Sunday school in 1935, but the AG national Sunday school department was officially opened in 1953. The CG appointed a national youth office in 1946, only two years later adding Sunday school to it. The AG and CG publish national Sunday school promotional magazines, although the CG includes more than Sunday school, as its title reflects: *Youth and Christian Education Leadership*.

In 1984 the AG had forty churches that averaged more than one thousand in Sunday school. In spite of this, there has not been the increase in Sunday school attendance to correspond with increases in attendance at Sunday worship and praise services. After World War II there was a tremendous surge in Sunday school attendance in most evangelical denominations. This contrasted with heavy losses in the mainline denominations. However, from the mid-1970s many evangelical denominations held their own or had slight decreases. The CG has continued to have increases while the AG has suffered some decline, particularly as compared to their large increases in Sunday worship service attendance. At the AG National Sunday School Conference in Springfield, Missouri, in February 1986, research findings indicated that the decline was caused by declining adult attendance. Negative consequences to local churches were that adults were lacking in basic Bible knowledge, were not committed to the church, did not cherish many of the beliefs of Pentecostal Christianity, or did not volunteer to work in the church. In addition, youth dropped out of church at a much earlier age when adults did not attend Sunday school. The AG has begun an aggressive program to involve more adults in regular Bible study in Sunday school. The small Sunday school class is important to spiritual development and maturity because it is a caring fellowship where class members build a powerful community of faith as lay persons study the Word of God, pray together, and build relationships. So far in history, no Christian education program reaches more persons for consistent, regular, weekly Bible study than the Sunday school.

Many charismatic churches have not discovered the benefits of Sunday school. In their emphasis on praise and worship they have generally neglected the nurturing role of small Bible study classes or have weekday Bible classes that usually do not involve as many persons as a traditional Sunday school does. There seems to be a growing awareness that there needs to be opportunities for both small and large group activities in the church. The small group (as a Sunday school class) is needed for identity, fellowship, and life-changing learning while the large group is needed for celebration and praise.

Pentecostals are attempting to reach persons cross-culturally as they begin Sunday schools and churches for new immigrants. Gospel Publishing House (AG) recently began publishing Spanish Sunday school literature for the larger Hispanic community. The CG and Church of God of Prophecy have published foreign literature for many years.

Some large churches have developed Saturday Bible schools where an aggressive program of evangelism and outreach is combined with Bible study. Such innovation reflects the desire of Pentecostals and charismatics to reach out to the lost with the message of salvation and Bible study for spiritual nurture.

Bibliography: J. E. Campbell, *The Pentecostal Holiness Church* (1951); C. W. Conn, *Like a Mighty Army* (1955); M. G. Hoover, "Origin and Structural Development of the Assemblies of God," M.A. thesis, Southwest Missouri State University, 1968; H. Jansen, *The Making of a Sunday School* (1972); W. W. Menzies, *Anointed to Serve: The Story of the Assemblies of God* (1971); V. Synan, *The Old-Time Power* (1973). Periodicals: *Advance; Church of God Evangel; Foursquare World Advance; Pentecostal Evangel; International Pentecostal Holiness Advocate; Pentecostal Holiness Advocate; The Pentecostal Minister; PFNA News; Pentecostal Testimony; Sunday School Counselor.*   J. M. Baldree

SWAGGART, JIMMY LEE (1935–). Evangelist, televangelist. Born during the Depression a few miles outside of Ferriday, Louisiana, Swaggart began attending an Assemblies of God (AG) church at the age of six. He was converted and baptized in the Holy Spirit at age eight. He began preaching on a street corner in Mangham, Louisiana, shortly after his marriage at age seventeen to Francis Anderson. The chosen topic of his first sermon was judgment on America, setting the tone for his following ministry.

Swaggart began itinerant preaching at the age of twenty-two. Attendance at his meetings was boosted when he let it be known that he was the cousin of Jerry Lee Lewis, a rock and roll singer who was then at the zenith of his popularity. This relationship helped to lift Swaggart from the ranks of evangelistic mediocrity and to swell his audience in churches across the South. The relationship was a double-edged sword, however, for because of it and his unique country music style, Swaggart was denied ordination with the AG at his first application.

A year later Swaggart was accepted for ordination and pastored a church for a short time with his father. His lack of contentment in the pastorate led to his resignation and propelled him to redouble his efforts in itinerant evangelism. In 1964, after six successful years on the evangelistic circuit, he began preaching camp meetings and holding meetings four to six weeks long in AG churches. In 1969 Swaggart began broadcasting his fiery brand of preaching and singing on the radio. He reinvested the royalties from his albums in expanding his radio outreach. As radio exposure grew, album sales increased, setting in motion a cyclical process of funding and furthering radio exposure.

In 1972 Swaggart virtually ceased holding meetings in churches and started holding weekend crusades in city auditoriums. These crusades were openly patterned on the model of the Graham crusades, with local pastors heading steering committees in advertising, recruitment, and transportation.

Before confessing to a moral failure in 1988, Jimmy Swaggart was one of the most watched televangelists in the world.

In 1973 Swaggart began production of a weekly, half-hour television program that focused on his music. Even though he was preaching on 550 radio stations, in 1981 he went exclusively to television, allowing him to channel all of his money and energy to one medium. This, along with a change of emphasis to his preaching ministry, resulted in increased popularity for Swaggart's ministry.

Swaggart's burgeoning constituency consisted of those holding to fundamentalistic Christian values. His dualistic morality and oversimplification of social issues found a growing audience in the U.S. and many foreign countries. While the core supporters were Pentecostal, Swaggart also had a wide following among other conservative Protestant and Roman Catholic constituencies.

As Swaggart's audience grew, he instituted a local church (Family Worship Center) and a college (Jimmy Swaggart Bible College), planned for a seminary, published a monthly magazine (*The Evangelist*), supported many missionary ventures, and held several media properties through his organization based in Baton Rouge, Louisiana.

While Swaggart's ministry was dramatic and emotional, it was also tinged with hostility. Observers of Swaggart's ministry noticed a concentric trend in the focal points of his attack. He began by attacking the "world," i.e., the value system of the larger culture outside of Christian-

ity. He narrowed the attack by searing the Roman Catholic church and liberal Protestant churches. He then criticized Pentecostal denominations, most notably his own denominational leadership. Last of all, he grievously damaged his own ministry.

Swaggart was on the verge of starting his own Pentecostal fellowship centered around Family Worship Center when allegations surfaced that connected him with voyeuristic activities involving a prostitute. This led to a loss of credibility and to cash flow problems for Swaggart's organization. Although Swaggart confessed that the charges were true and claimed repentance, he refused to accept rehabilitative discipline from his denomination. He was subsequently defrocked by the Assemblies of God in April 1988.

Bibliography: C. Moritz, ed., *Current Biography Yearbook* (1987); J. Swaggart with R. P. Lamb, *To Cross a River* (1977). B. M. Stout

SWEDISH CHARISMATICS See CHARISMATIC MOVEMENT.

SWEDISH PENTECOSTALS See EUROPEAN PENTECOSTALISM.

SWEET, HENRY CHARLES (1866–1960). Canadian pastor and educator. Having begun ministry in 1887 in southern Manitoba among Baptists and the Salvation Army, Sweet went on to have a remarkably diverse career. He pastored Baptist and Presbyterian churches across western Canada, and at the conclusion of his ministry he was serving a black African Methodist Episcopal church in Winnipeg. For brief periods, he was principal of a Presbyterian residential school for native children in Saskatchewan and headed up a nondenominational, evangelical Bible school in Winnipeg.

Sweet is further distinguished by his education. Having completed a nondegree program at Crozer Theological Seminary in 1897, he then graduated with a B.A. from the University of Manitoba in 1906. He returned to Crozer, where he earned a B.D. in 1925, and then, at sixty years of age, went to Evangelical Theological College in Dallas (later, Dallas Theological Seminary), from which he graduated with the Th.D. degree in 1928.

While Sweet never officially held ministerial credentials with any Pentecostal body, he was on the faculty of Western Pentecostal Bible College, under the auspices of the Pentecostal Assemblies of Canada (PAOC) from 1931 to 1950, with a gap of several years from the late 1930s until 1943. While there, he taught Bible and homiletics.

The most interesting period of Sweet's association with the Pentecostals followed immediately upon his first becoming involved with the movement in 1916. During these years, he was prominent in Pentecostal missions in Winnipeg. While there he made contact with Franklin Small, the founder of the "Oneness" Apostolic Church of Pentecost of Canada. When that group applied for a federal charter in 1921, Sweet was among the signatories. Coming from an unusually strong academic background and from a ministry that

Some of the many expressions of Evangelist Jimmy Swaggart as caught by a photographer during a sermon.

spanned racial and denominational lines, Sweet helped shape Pentecostalism in western Canada.

Bibliography: *First Baptist Church, Moose Jaw: Souvenir of the Fiftieth Anniversary* (1933); E. Hildebrandt, *A History of Winnipeg Bible Institute and College from 1925–1960* (1965); R. A. N. Kydd, "H. C. Sweet: Canadian Churchman," *Journal of the Canadian Church Historical Society* 20 (1978): 19–30; " 'Sweet' Memories," *The Portal* (1949), 4.   R. A. N. Kydd

SWISS PENTECOSTALS See EUROPEAN PENTECOSTALISM.

SWORD OF THE SPIRIT, THE See CHARISMATIC COMMUNITIES.

SYNAN, HAROLD VINSON (1934–). American Pentecostal church executive and author. He was born the twin of Vernon, sons of Joseph A. and Minnis E. Synan—the father having served a quarter century as bishop of the Pentecostal Holiness Church (PHC). In 1960 Vinson married Carol Lee Fuqua. They have four children: Mary C. (1961); Virginia L. (1963); Harold Vinson, Jr. (1966); and Joseph A. III (1968). Following a B.A. at the University of Richmond (1958), he completed an M.A. (1964) and a Ph.D. (1967) in American social and intellectual history at the University of Georgia.

Ordained in 1954 by the PHC, Synan pastored churches in Virginia (1956–62) and Georgia (1967–74)—the latter while teaching at Emmanuel College, Franklin Springs, Georgia. During this time he was a cofounder (with William W. Menzies and Horace Ward in 1970) of the Society for Pentecostal Studies, and he also wrote his most substantial work, *The Holiness-Pentecos-*

tal Movement in the United States (1971), as well as histories of his college (*Emmanuel College,* 1968) and his denomination (*The Old-Time Power,* 1973).

A Pentecostal scholar who is also a leader in the charismatic movement, Vinson Synan is author of several books, including *The Holiness-Pentecostal Movement in the United States.*

Synan was general secretary of the PHC from 1973 to 1977, assistant general superintendent from 1977 to 1981, and director of evangelism from 1981 to 1986—a dozen years in classical Pentecostal denominational leadership. Participation in the International Roman Catholic-Pentecostal Dialogue in 1973 (core member, 1976–81) foreshadowed his later ecumenical and charismatic leadership. Since 1986 he has chaired the New Orleans Congresses on the Holy Spirit and World Evangelization—which have attracted up to 40,000 charismatics and have deepened cooperation and understanding between Pentecostals and charismatics.

Ordained as a Pentecostal Holiness Church minister in 1926, Joseph A. Synan served his denomination as general superintendent for 24 years.

His later writings, though more popular in style, reflect a fine historical sense coupled with a readable style. These include: *Charismatic Bridges* (1974), *Aspects of Pentecostal Origins* (1975), *Azusa Street* (1980), *In the Latter Days* (1984), and *The Twentieth-Century Pentecostal Explosion* (1987). R. P. Spittler

SYNAN, JOSEPH ALEXANDER (1905–84). Church planter and bishop of the Pentecostal Holiness Church (PHC). Synan was born in Tazewell County, Virginia, the second of thirteen children born to Thomas and Maude Synan. His marriage to Minnis Evelyn Perdue in 1926 produced seven children. Called to preach as a youth, he joined a local Methodist church that promised to send him to college to study for the ministry. His plans changed in 1921 when he was converted in a tent revival near Fredericksburg, Virginia, and joined a nearby Pentecostal Holiness congregation.

After being ordained in the Baltimore Conference of the PHC in 1926, Synan planted several churches in the Tidewater area of Virginia. In 1934 he was elected superintendent of the Eastern Virginia Conference. In 1945 he was elected to the position of general superintendent, a position he held for twenty-four years. From 1950 to 1969, he served as the presiding chairman and bishop of the PHC.

A leader in ecumenical relations, J. A. Synan was one of the founding fathers of the National Association of Evangelicals (NAE) in 1943, and of the Pentecostal Fellowship of North America (PFNA) in 1948. In 1967, he negotiated an affiliation between the PHC and the Pentecostal Methodist Church of Chili.

During Synan's chairmanship, the PHC grew from 30,000 to 67,000 members in the U.S. Two of his sons became ministers in the church, including Pentecostal historian, Vinson Synan.

Bibliography: V. Synan, *The Old-Time Power* (1973). H. V. Synan

T

TABERNACLE PENTECOSTAL CHURCH
See International Pentecostal Holiness
Church.

**TABERNACLE PRESBYTERIAN
CHURCH** See International Pentecostal
Holiness Church.

TAITINGER, ROBERT W. (1927–). General superintendent (1969–82) of the Pentecostal Assemblies of Canada (PAOC). Taitinger pastored the Central Pentecostal Tabernacle, Edmonton, Alberta, for thirteen years (1955–68) before his election to the leadership of the PAOC at the age of forty-one. Converted at age twelve, he took up ministry upon completing high school and succeeded D. N. Buntain in his Edmonton pastorate at the age of twenty-eight. He served on the faculty of the Canadian Northwest Bible Institute and was chairman of the Pentecostal Fellowship of North America (1972–74). An enthusiastic supporter of foreign missions, his congregation led PAOC missions giving for fifteen years.

Bibliography: "General Officers Leave Executive Posts," *Pentecostal Testimony* 63 (12, 1982): 2; R. W. Taitinger, "Sixty Years in the Marketplace," *Pentecostal Testimony* 59 (11, 1978): 16–18.   E. A. Wilson

Robert W. Taitinger served the PAOC as general superintendent for 13 years (1969-82) and more recently as president of Eastern Pentecostal Bible College, Peterborough, Ontario.

TAPE MINISTRIES Pentecostals and charismatics have in their ranks effective preachers who minister under "the anointing." Many of these ministers do not produce written matter and so tape record their messages. Sometimes popular teaching series are put into "tape books" for distribution.

It could be said that the charismatic renewal in the 1960s was spread by tapes. Large charismatic conferences were often taped, and thousands of tapes were sold and shared. Some parachurch ministries developed "tape ministries" that made tapes available for donation or sold them for modest amounts.

Since high-speed duplicators have become affordable, it has become customary for many charismatic churches to record all services and to have tapes available as the congregation leaves the service. Today video tapes are popular, but they have not yet become as well used as audio cassettes.

Bibliography: "Marilyn Hickey Tapes Available for Cell Groups," *Ministries* (Winter 1983), 26.   S. Strang

TARDIF, EMILIEN (1928–). Catholic charismatic healing evangelist. Born in Quebec, Tardif joined the Sacred Heart Fathers and went as a missionary to the Dominican Republic in 1956, becoming in the mid 1960s head of his order there. Sent back to Canada with acute tuberculosis in 1973, Tardif was healed when prayed over by members of a charismatic prayer group. Returning to the Dominican Republic, he bore witness to his healing, and many extraordinary healings took place. Since 1975 Tardif has preached and ministered in every continent, especially in French and Spanish-speaking countries. His ministry has often been attended with enormous crowds and regularly accompanied by sensational cures. He has also given many retreats for fellow Catholic priests. His witness is given in *Jesus a fait de moi un témoin* (1984), which is also available in both Portuguese and Spanish.
                                          P. D. Hocken

TARI, MELCHIOR ("MEL") (1946–). Evangelist. Tari was born near Soe, Timor Island, Indonesia, to a Christian elementary school principal. He graduated in 1964 from a Reformed Church academy and was offered a university scholarship in Moscow. But, accepting Christ at home in August 1965, he declined the scholarship. Accompanied by the sound of rushing wind, revival broke out in his Soe Reformed Church on September 26, 1965. Lay evangelistic teams were organized immediately. Four days later a communist coup of Indonesia failed. Many miracles occurred in the next years, including water repeatedly turned to wine. Tari evangelized on a team for five years in Timor.

In September 1970 Tari began touring America telling about the revival. His *Like a Mighty Wind* (1971) was translated into ten other languages. He married an American in 1972, and they returned to Indonesia. They coauthored *The Gentle Breeze of Jesus* (1974). Tari now resides in California and preaches worldwide in evangelistic meetings.											J. Rea

TAYLOR, GEORGE FLOYD (1881–1934). Church leader, educator, and author. One of the early leaders of the Pentecostal Holiness Church (PHC), George Floyd Taylor was born in Duplin County, North Carolina, near the town of Magnolia. Afflicted from birth with a palsy-like condition, Taylor accomplished much in spite of his physical handicap.

A member of the Methodist Episcopal Church, South, Taylor was swept into the Holiness movement in 1903 under the ministry of A. B. Crumpler. In that same year he was licensed to preach in the Holiness Church of North Carolina, (the Pentecostal Holiness Church after 1908). His interest in education led him to found the Bethel Holiness School in Rose Hill, North Carolina, in 1903. Four years later he founded the Falcon Holiness School near Dunn, North Carolina, which he headed from 1907 to 1916. While in Falcon, he began in 1913 the publication of a line of Pentecostal Sunday school literature that was later bought by the PHC.

When the Pentecostal movement swept the South under the ministry of G. B. Cashwell (1862–1916), Taylor was one of the first ministers to speak in tongues in the Dunn meeting of 1907. His defense of the new Pentecostal experience, *The Spirit and the Bride*, appeared in September of 1907 in ringing support of the new Pentecostal experience. This was possibly the first book-length defense of Pentecostalism ever published. In the debates over speaking in tongues that shook the PHC in 1908, Taylor's staunch stand for the "initial evidence" theory helped swing the PHC into the growing Pentecostal movement.

In 1913 Taylor was elected general superintendent of the PHC, a position he held for two years. In 1917 he became the founding editor of the official voice of the church, the *Pentecostal Holiness Advocate*. A talented writer, Taylor continued to write and edit the Sunday school literature while editing the *Advocate*. In 1919 he was called on to serve as the founding president of the Franklin Springs Institute (FSI) located in Franklin County, Georgia. At first a high school and Bible college, the school became Emmanuel College in 1933.

In 1928 Taylor resigned as president of FSI and moved back to North Carolina, where he earned an M.A. degree in history at the University of North Carolina at Chapel Hill. After a trip to the Holy Land in 1929, he published a book titled *A Tour of Bible Lands*. His last years were spent as a faculty member at Emmanuel College.

Bibliography: V. Synan, *Emmanuel College, The First Fifty Years* (1968).											H. V. Synan

TEEN CHALLENGE An evangelistic program started by David Wilkerson, a young preacher from Philipsburg, Pennsylvania, who went to New York City with a burning desire to share Christ with youth in trouble. What started as an evangelistic ministry to New York City gang members in 1958 has grown to a worldwide ministry aimed at reaching teenagers and young adults caught up in drugs, alcohol, and other life-controlling problems.

From its first days, the Teen Challenge ministry was supported by offerings received from churches where Wilkerson's story was told. The late Reginald Yake, pastor of the Assembly of God in Irvington, New Jersey, a suburb of New York City, told Wilkerson that it was the responsibility of the local churches to raise the needed money to carry on his work. Subsequently, two hundred ministers in the New York City area were invited to meet at Glad Tidings Tabernacle, Manhattan, New York (R. Stanley Berg, pastor), to determine how the new youth ministry could be supported. Twenty ministers responded to the invitation. When asked what it would take to keep him on the street full time, Wilkerson stated that he needed a hundred dollars per week. Each minister pledged that his church would contribute five dollars weekly.

From the twenty ministers present for that initial December 1958 meeting, a central committee of nine men was selected to form the first board of directors of Teen Age Evangelism, as the organization was originally known. R. Stanley Berg was made committee chairman; Frank M. Reynolds, secretary; and Paul DiLena, treasurer.

In those early days Teen Age Evangelism aimed to inspire and organize Christian youth to do street evangelism. Converts were directed to local churches to be discipled in the Word of God and in Christian living. Focus at the end of the first decade of ministry continued to be on New York City street gangs. Nicky Cruz's dramatic conversion inspired and expanded the Teen Challenge ministry. *The Cross and the Switchblade* (1963) by David Wilkerson sets forth the dramatic way the Holy Spirit directed the early years of this ministry.

As workers shared their faith on the streets they came in frequent contact with drug addicts, regarded by everyone as hopeless cases. Following one of the New York City street meetings, Ralph, a young man who had been a heroin addict for three years, approached the intrepid youth minister and asked if "he could have that too," with reference to the salvation about which he just had heard, so evident in the lives of the workers. Not recognizing that Ralph was a drug addict, Wilkerson assured Ralph that he could experience new life in Christ. He then prayed for Ralph that he might receive Christ as Savior. The next day Ralph was back with the testimony that he had not had any heroin for twenty-four hours and was not having any withdrawal pains. Ralph became an instant evangelist to other drug addicts, telling the youth that he had found the answer to their drug problems.

Drug addicts began flocking to Wilkerson's services and were led to Christ. Many of these addicts suffered no withdrawal pains. Ministry to drug addicts brought excitement to the Teen

Challenge organization—at last there was an answer to the epidemic drug problem. News of what was transpiring in New York City spread across the country. Invitations for Wilkerson to speak in meetings came from many churches and groups.

Between 1960 and 1962 Teen Challenge ministries branched out from New York City to other cities facing the same gang and drug problems—Chicago, Los Angeles, San Francisco, Boston, and Philadelphia. Teen Challenge workers were recruited from Bible institutes and colleges and from churches to help with new centers. Christian workers planned, sacrificed, and prayed, looking for an immediate sweep of the Holy Spirit to revolutionize their cities.

The success of the evangelistic outreach in the urban areas was clearly evident in those first years. A serious problem was also evident—many drug addicts and gang members, after receiving deliverance, were returning after a few weeks to their old ways. That truth brought soul searching, much prayer, and a complete reevaluation of the evangelism methods used by Teen Challenge. Why were the new Christians not succeeding? It was found, first of all, that few churches to which the converts were directed were willing and able to work with these people. It further became apparent that new converts did not have basic skills to handle all the adjustments they needed to make—housing, jobs, pressures of old relationships, legal entanglements, and other changes. When asked what would help them most, converts requested help in getting away from their environment temporarily, where they could learn how to be Christians.

In August 1961 a committee was appointed to develop an adequate program and to find a suitable place for meeting the obvious need. On the committee were David Wilkerson, Frank M. Reynolds, and Reginald Yake. They recommended the development of a five-to-eight month program in a rural setting. They further recommended that a productive farm be purchased. Buildings would be constructed to meet the needs. Land in Rehrersburg, Pennsylvania, was purchased in June 1962 from Arthur Graybill, on which the Teen Challenge Training Center was to be constructed and developed. Reynolds became superintendent of the center in August of that year. He was charged with overseeing the construction of the first buildings and of developing the Christian growth training program.

This was the beginning of what has been considered one of the most successful drug rehabilitation programs. The primary goal of the program was to teach new converts how to live disciplined Christian lives. Four key truths have provided the foundation for Teen Challenge ministry to drug addicts and other troubled youths: (1) there is hope; (2) sin is the problem; (3) Jesus Christ can change your life; (4) the power of the Holy Spirit is essential for consistent Christian living. The first students at the Rehrersburg Training Center came from New York, Chicago, Boston, Los Angeles, San Francisco, and Philadelphia. Originally these new Christians stayed three weeks at the Teen Challenge center in one of these cities before going to the Training Center at Rehrersburg.

Rapid expansion of the ministry came as Teen Challenge centers opened across the nation. Since Wilkerson did not desire to be responsible for the administration and funding of all those ministries, each center became an autonomous unit, operating with its respective board of directors. In 1963 it was decided that Teen Challenge should come under the general supervision of the national Division of Home Missions of the General Council of the Assemblies of God, with specific supervision given to district councils. Teen Challenge has worked interdenominationally and intradenominationally; people of various denominations have served on local boards and staff. The one source of unity is the belief that students should seek the baptism of the Holy Spirit, with the evidence of speaking in other tongues.

Many Teen Challenge centers have developed ministry programs to inner-city children, including drug prevention seminars for schools. Teen Challenge has also helped start twenty-eight churches, most in inner-city areas.

In 1969 Howard Foltz, Teen Challenge director in Dallas–Fort Worth, felt called to develop a Teen Challenge program in Europe. The same basic principles were followed. In 1972 teams of Teen Challenge staff members and graduates were sent to Vietnam under contract with the U.S. Department of Defense. They were effective in assisting military personnel with drug abuse problems.

By 1987 more than 100 Teen Challenge ministries had been established in the U.S. and more than 150 ministries overseas. Today the primary motivation for the development of a Teen Challenge ministry is to reach the lost where they are with the message of salvation through Jesus Christ. After receiving Christ as Savior, sound discipling of the convert follows, either in a Teen Challenge center or in a local church.

Bibliography: F. M. Reynolds, "Teen Challenge at the Quarter-Century Mark," *PE* (June 19, 1983); additional information comes from the minutes of Teen Challenge board meetings and from personal records of the author, F. M. Reynolds; D. Wilkerson, *The Cross and the Switchblade* (1963).   F. M. Reynolds

THEOLOGICAL SEMINARIES   See SEMINARIES AND GRADUATE SCHOOLS.

THEOPHANIE (MONTPELLIER, FRANCE)   See CHARISMATIC COMMUNITIES.

THIRD DEFINITE WORK OF GRACE   See HOLINESS MOVEMENT; IRWIN, BENJAMIN HARDIN.

THIRD WAVE   The term "third wave" is used to designate a movement that is similar to the Pentecostal movement (first wave) and charismatic movement (second wave), but which perceives itself to have some fairly important differences. It is composed largely of evangelical Christians who, while applauding and supporting the work of the Holy Spirit in the first two waves, have chosen not to be identified with either. The desire of those in the third wave is to experience the power of the Holy Spirit in healing the sick, casting out demons, receiving prophecies, and participating in other charismatic-type manifestations without disturbing the current philosophy of ministry governing their congregations.

While the shape of the third wave is in its formation stage at this writing, some distinctives may include:

1. Belief that the baptism of the Holy Spirit occurs at conversion (1 Cor. 12:13) rather than as a second work of grace subsequent to the new birth.

2. Expectation of multiple fillings of the Holy Spirit subsequent to the new birth, some of which may closely resemble what others call "baptism in the Holy Spirit."

3. A low-key acceptance of tongues as one of many NT spiritual gifts that God gives to some and not to others. Speaking in tongues is not considered the initial physical validation of a certain spiritual experience but rather a gift used by some for ministry or prayer language.

4. Ministry under the power and anointing of the Holy Spirit as the portal of entrance into the third wave rather than a spiritual experience as is typical of the first two waves. The context of ministry is most commonly a body of believers rather than individual activities such as those of a faith healer.

5. Avoidance of divisiveness at almost any cost. Compromise in areas such as raising of hands in worship, public tongues, methods of prayer for the sick, and others is cordially accepted in order to maintain harmony with those not in the third wave. Semantics become important, with terms such as "charismatic" and "Spirit-filled" being rejected because of their alleged implication that those who are so labeled form a sort of spiritual elite of first-class as over against second-class Christians.

The third wave became prominent around 1980, with the term itself being coined in 1983 by Peter Wagner. David Barrett estimates that worldwide there are some 20 million believers who could be counted as fitting into the third wave pattern.

See also CHURCH GROWTH; STATISTICS, GLOBAL.

Bibliography: V. Synan, *In the Latter Days* (1984), 136–39; C. P. Wagner, "A Third Wave?" *Pastoral Renewal* (July–August 1983), 1–5; idem, "The Third Wave," *Christian Life* (September 1984), 90.
C. P. Wagner

THISTLETHWAITE, LILIAN T. (1873–1939). American Pentecostal pioneer. Under the direction of her brother-in-law, Charles F. Parham, Lilian Thistlethwaite pioneered many of the earliest Pentecostal churches in the American Midwest following the Topeka revival of January 1901. In March 1906 Parham named her the first "general secretary of the Apostolic Faith Movement." Thistlethwaite also contributed one of the most detailed accounts of the Topeka revival in "The Wonderful History of the Latter Rain" (in S. Parham, 1930, 57–68).

Bibliography: J. Goff, *Fields White Unto Harvest* (1988); S. Parham, *Life of Charles F. Parham* (1930).
J. R. Goff, Jr.

THOMAS, E. C. (1920–). General overseer of the Church of God (CG, Cleveland, Tenn.) from 1982 to 1986. A native of Florida, he served brief pastorates in Florida and North Carolina.

Thomas' business acumen and preparation equipped him for financial service and stewardship responsibilities in the church. For fifteen years (1955–70) he was publisher of CG publications. Thomas also served during those years as president of the National Sunday School Association.

Additional years as state superintendent (1970–78) and general secretary-treasurer (1978–82) brought Thomas to the general overseership of the CG. In this post his business ability guided the denomination in stringent years. He was deeply involved in the events of the denomination's centennial year, 1986.

Bibliography: Archives of the Church of God (Cleveland, Tenn.).
C. W. Conn

THOMPSON, FRANK CHARLES (1858–1940). Compiler of the *Thompson Chain Reference Bible*. Thompson was born in Elmira, New York. He attended classes at Boston University School of Theology as a "special student" (1884–86), without ever enrolling in a regular program of study. Rutherford College in North Carolina later conferred an honorary D.D. degree on him. Thompson and his wife Laura were the parents of two daughters.

Thompson became a licensed Methodist preacher in 1879 and joined the Genesee (N.Y.) Conference. After serving numerous parishes he served as associate pastor of Asbury Methodist Church in Rochester, New York (1911–23).

The origin of the reference Bible dates back to his pastoral work in Genesee County, New York, when he recognized the need for a quality reference Bible. After church members expressed admiration for the quality of his marginal references in his Oxford Wide Margin Bible (KJV), several offered to underwrite its publication. This resulted in the formation of the Chain Reference Bible Publishing Company. The first edition appeared in 1908 but proved to be slow in gaining market exposure. In 1914 B. B. Kirkbride, a student at Cotner College and a Bible salesman during the summer, became familiar with it while working for a Nebraska firm. Impressed with the volume, he offered to sell a minimum of three thousand per year for Thompson. The offer was accepted, and the sales surpassed the goal.

Originally Thompson's Bible contained only the text and marginal references; other items, such as the concordance, the outline of the books, and the maps of Paul's journeys (prepared by Laura Thompson) came later as a result of suggestions from customers. The B. B. Kirkbride Bible Company, with headquarters in Indianapolis, Indiana, emerged in 1915 from the agreement with Thompson and has offered the reference Bible as its sole product. Since that time approximately 3 million copies have been sold. It has also proved to be a favorite among Pentecostal believers. During Thompson's lifetime the volume went through two revisions (1929, 1934).

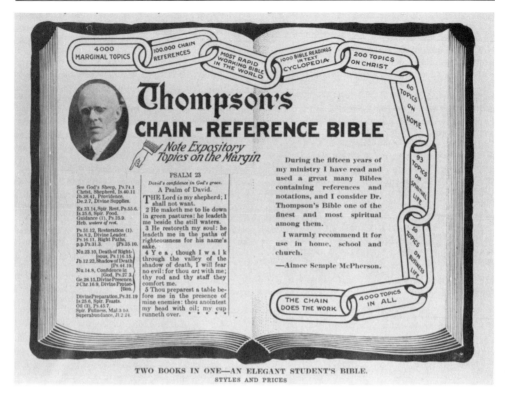

This advertisement for the Thompson Chain Reference Bible appeared in Aimee Semple McPherson's *Bridal Call* in 1924. Thompson was a faculty member of L.I.F.E. Bible College, the Foursquare school in Los Angeles.

While living in Rochester, Thompson warmly supported Aimee Semple McPherson's divine-healing crusade there in 1921. Following his retirement from the Rochester church, Thompson and his wife moved to California. Although Thompson was an "old-fashioned Methodist" and never became a Pentecostal, Aimee Semple McPherson admired his reference Bible and endorsed it in *The Bridal Call Foursquare*. Consequently, she invited him to teach at L.I.F.E. Bible College (c. 1924–c. 1931), where he also held the title of honorary dean.

Thompson's other publications included *Barriers to Eden* (c. 1939) and *Bob's Hike to the Holy City* (n.d.).

Bibliography: "A Brief History of the 'Thompson Chain-Reference Bible' and the Publisher, the B. B. Kirkbride Bible Company, Inc." (n.d.); A. Alhand to G. B. McGee (December 17, 1987); S. Baker to G. B. McGee (December 21, 1987); R. B. Mitchell to G. B. McGee (November 14, 1987); A. Sorenson, "People in Progress: B. B. Kirkbride Bible Co., Inc.," *Bookstore Journal* (November 1984), 73–74; "Dr. Thompson Passes at 82 in California," *Rochester Democrat and Chronicle* (May 5, 1940); F. C. Thompson, "A Great Revival Campaign," *The Bridal Call* (Dec. 1921), 23–25.   G. B. McGee

TILTON, ROBERT GIBSON (1946–). Pastor and television personality. Born in McKinney, Texas, he was educated at Cook County Junior College and Texas Technological University. Til-

ton was converted as a result of young people coming to his home with a Christian witness when his marriage was in difficulty and he was using drugs.

Tilton is founder and pastor of Word of Faith Outreach Center, an eight-thousand-member congregation with a four-thousand-seat auditorium in Dallas. His closed-circuit satellite network carries monthly seminars to approximately two thousand churches. His televised Bible school reaches four thousand students via six hundred locations. He has written several books.

Tilton teaches that Christians are "the righteousness of Christ" and that they can be all God intends. He insists that Christ has redeemed us from the curse of the law, which includes sickness, poverty, and death. Some have accused Tilton of preaching a "gospel of success" that leaves out aspects of the gospel dealing with suffering.

Bibliography: S. Strang, "Facts About Word of Faith," *Charisma* (July 1985), 31; idem, "Robert Tilton Wants You to Be a Success in Life," *Charisma* (July 1985), 24–28.   S. Strang

TINNEY, JAMES STEVEN (1942–88). Editor and historian. A native of Kansas City, Missouri, James S. Tinney focused his efforts as a historian of Pentecostalism on two themes: blackness and homosexuality. He was ordained to the ministry at age eighteen but worked mostly as a teacher and journalist. From 1974 to 1975, he served as editor of the *Washington Afro-American* and from 1977 to 1979 as editor of *Spirit: a Journal of Issues Incident to Black Pentecostalism.* The final issue of the latter consisted of a bibliography on the black movement. In these years Tinney emerged as a leading contender for the black origins of the Pentecostal movement, holding the black William J. Seymour (1870–1922), not the white Charles F. Parham (1873–1929), to be the real founder. Sympathetic articles on Pentecostal homosexuals elicited sharp reactions from others in the movement. In 1980, he organized the Pentecostal Coalition for Human Rights, a support group for racial and sexual minorities which includes lesbians and gays. In 1982 he founded Faith Temple, a predominantly black gay church in Washington, D.C. He also served on the journalism faculty at Howard University. His untimely death occurred on June 12, 1988.

Bibliography: *Spirit* (Washington), 1–3, (2, 1977–79).   C. E. Jones

TITHE GIVING   Pentecostal leaders today emphasize Christian stewardship of time, talents, and money. Yet tithe giving has always been emphasized and plays an important part in the teaching and preaching of the local churches. There is hardly a pastor who has not preached a sermon based on Malachi 3:8–10, with special emphasis on verse 10: "Bring the whole tithe into the storehouse. . . and see if I will not throw open the floodgates of heaven and pour out so much blessing that you will not have room enough for it"—interpreting the "storehouse" to mean the local church in our time.

Actually, the Bible shows that the tithe was given before the law of Moses. Both Abraham and Jacob tithed (Gen. 14:20; 28:22). Furthermore, the primary emphasis of tithing in the Bible always relates to blessing, even under the Law.

Malachi 3:10, however, was dealing with exceptional circumstances. The people were robbing God by failing to bring their tithes. They had lost the blessing. By tithing the blessing would be restored. But the normal order in the Bible is "you are blessed, therefore tithe."

By NT times many Pharisees turned tithing into a burden by demanding much more than the Law required. Jesus condemned that, but he recognized that tithing was something they should do nevertheless (Luke 11:42). This was enough for the early church. (See Milo Kauffman, *Stewards of God,* 1975, 189–90). The cheerful giver that the Lord loves will be a steward of all God gives, but systematic tithing is the least we can do. Experience shows that those who are faithful in tithing are usually faithful in all their service to the Lord.   S. M. Horton

TOMLINSON, AMBROSE JESSUP (1865–1943). Ambrose Jessup Tomlinson was born on September 22, 1865, near Westfield, Indiana, to Milton and Delilah Tomlinson. He was anemic at birth but exhibited unusual stamina throughout his life. His Quaker grandparents actively opposed slavery. His paternal grandfather, Robert Tomlinson, also denounced war and capital punishment. In other respects, his earliest years

typified the life of a farm boy from Westfield, Indiana. Through these years none in his immediate family were much involved with church services or related activities. He described a spiritual experience at age twelve (he heard his name called three times), but when he attended Westfield Academy he concentrated on athletics and drama. During these high school days a number of his classmates professed Christian commitment as a result of a revival, but he refused to follow their example. He then became consumed with politics, and it was only after almost being hit by lightning that, as a new groom, he turned to the Scriptures and, at age twenty-four, made allegiance to the gospel. He soon applied to his life the doctrine of divine healing that he learned first from a Carrie Judd Montgomery tract.

Elected as the first general overseer of the Church of God (Cleveland, Tenn.), A. J. Tomlinson held the position until removed from office by the denomination in 1923. His work and the congregations that remained loyal to him were then labeled the Tomlinson Church of God (now known as the Church of God of Prophecy).

Ambrose became busily engaged in Sunday school work and contributed to the growth of a nearby Quaker congregation. Before long he became acquainted with J. B. Mitchell. Mitchell had been converted under the ministry of Charles G. Finney and had attended Oberlin College. Through this contact and travel with Mitchell, Ambrose learned firsthand about the Oberlin views on sanctification, missions, and the distribution of clothes and Bibles to the poor. Within a few years, his travels introduced him to the ministries of Moody, Morrison, Robinson, Simpson, Watson, Knapp, Reese, Merritt, Taylor, and others. When Ambrose attended God's Bible School, Mount of Blessing, Cincinnati, Ohio, fellow students placed the sign "The Prevailer" over his door.

Thereafter, Tomlinson committed himself to colportage work for the American Bible Society and the American Tract Society. Starting in 1899, he centered his activities in Culbertson, North Carolina, where he organized, on April 9, 1900, an orphanage and published a religious (eight-page) monthly paper called *Samson's Foxes*. The paper, published from 1901 to 1902, featured articles and news from the Holiness movement (Tomlinson had earlier claimed the Holiness type of sanctification), the healing movement, and appeals to assist the needy. Tomlinson's approach produced considerable hostilities from the upper class in North Carolina, and in 1901 he made his way to Frank W. Sandford's Shiloh in Maine. He had been water baptized in 1897 by Gleason in Maine and reportedly in 1901 by Stephen Merritt in New York. However, as a result of his time at the Bible school, he was baptized again by Sandford. On October 1, 1901, Tomlinson joined the fledgling group who identified themselves as "The Church of the Living God for the Evangelization of the World, Gathering of Israel, New Order of Things at the Close of the Gentile Age."

Tomlinson's most far-reaching commitment came out of a relationship with some Holiness adherents in western North Carolina. Richard Spurling, Jr., and W. F. Bryant were Holiness leaders who in May 1902 organized a small band as the Holiness Church at Camp Creek. A. J. Tomlinson had at least four or five years of contact with Holiness people in the area. After a time of intense prayer near the Bryant home on the morning of June 13, 1903, he joined the group with the proclamation that this was the Church of God of the Bible. His leadership ability is shown in that he was then elected pastor of the church, while Spurling and Bryant turned to evangelism. By 1904 Tomlinson was pastor of three out of the four affiliated congregations and edited, with M. S. Lemons, a periodical titled *The Way*. This publication lasted at least one year, used original biblical languages, and centered on Holiness thought. Tomlinson himself was an avid reader of magazines like *Evangelical Visitor, Tongues of Fire, The Mountain Missionary, The Way of Faith, God's Revivalist,* and *The Bible Advocate*, and he was familiar with the writings of George Foxe, George Müller, David Brainerd, the ante-Nicene Fathers, and the church history of Eusebius. He was himself a prolific writer as evidenced in the journal started in 1899, the daily church book record, the pocket memorandum, the 1913 book entitled *Last Great Conflict,* and his numerous articles in the official church publication.

By the end of 1904, the A. J. Tomlinson family was living in Cleveland, Tennessee (population just under five thousand). The local church was set in order in Cleveland by late 1906 after a revival held by M. S. Lemons, Sister McCanless, and A. J. Tomlinson (who had conducted meetings there prior to this). For some time, A. J. Tomlinson served this church as pastor and Sunday school superintendent, although he also traveled extensively.

When the affiliated churches convened during January 1906, for what was considered the first general assembly, A. J. Tomlinson served as moderator and clerk (he was one of the few of the twenty-one there who could read and write). He penned these words as an addendum to the minutes: "We hope and trust that no person or body of people will ever use these minutes, or any part of them, as articles of faith upon which to establish a sect or denomination." The name Church of God was adopted the next year even though the name was in use elsewhere. At the fourth annual meeting, A. J. Tomlinson not only served again as the conference moderator and clerk but was elected as the primary leader. The original title of general moderator was changed to general overseer at the next annual meeting. After the general overseer's annual address, the testimony of the prominent leaders, and various interpreted tongues messages, the general assembly of 1914 unanimously made Tomlinson's selection as general overseer permanent.

In January 1907 A. J. Tomlinson became "more fully awakened" about the fledgling Pentecostal movement. The result was that he preached the emerging doctrine of Spirit baptism with tongues speech as the initial evidence during the assembly that year. Several received this experience, but as he preached this throughout the year, he joined the seekers at the altar for the very thing he had just prescribed. In June 1907 A. J. Tomlinson and M. S. Lemons went to Birmingham, Alabama, in an attempt to meet with G. B. Cashwell. They met, instead, with M. M. Pinson. In 1908 Cashwell came to Cleveland and preached a sermon at the conclusion of the Church of God general assembly. During Cashwell's Sunday morning service, January 12, 1908, A. J. Tomlinson uttered what he judged to be ten different languages. From August 11 to October 14 of that year, Tomlinson preached a revival in Cleveland that resulted in 258 recorded spiritual "experiences" and 106 new church members. The next year, Tomlinson's Spirit baptism doctrine was challenged by his assistant pastor, John B. Goins, and a few members, all of whom would depart because of their opposition to his view on initial evidence.

For the next fourteen years, Tomlinson not only traveled widely holding revivals and camp meetings and organizing new churches, he also either initiated or at least was a key player in the development of the principal ministries of the Church of God. Dated March 1, 1910, the first issue of *The Evening Light and Church of God Evangel* rolled off the presses, with A. J. Tomlinson as editor (he later added the *Faithful Standard*). The first publishing house was built in 1913 with Tomlinson's prodding. His first international campaign began in February 1911 in the Bahamas, where he had been preceded one year by Church of God minister R. M. Evans. In the various general assemblies Tomlinson was always a prime mover in doctrinal considerations (including the foundational twenty-nine teachings). At many assemblies he stood and responded to

In one of the strangest religious demonstrations in the 20th century Homer Tomlinson announced himself as "King of the World." Here, in his robes and crown, he stands in Rome's ancient Colosseum.

various questions and, starting in 1911, initiated annual addresses, which served as a platform to engage the body theologically. Probably the only Church of God leader in Bible school experiences, he used his 1917 annual address to bring attention to the need for an institution to train workers. Thus a Bible Training School opened in Cleveland on January 1, 1918, with Tomlinson as superintendent. In Tomlinson's 1919 annual address, he brought to the general assembly the need for sponsoring an orphanage. The first home opened on December 17, 1920, in Cleveland.

Tomlinson's leadership was also marked by an intense interest in treating all races equally. He met Charles H. Mason on more than one occasion and shared with him the concern to break racial barriers. Tomlinson tried to incorporate all races into the Church of God; nevertheless, there was a major exodus of blacks in 1921. After that Tomlinson's work moved his church toward racial egalitarianism. He was like-minded on the ministry of women, although he did not support women as participants in business meetings or sharing the full rights of ordination. However, he constantly wrote in support of female ministers and utilized them in strategic church positions.

A full account cannot be given of the 1922–23 controversy between A. J. Tomlinson and the council of elders. Tomlinson was central in 1916–17 in forming this group of twelve. However, the result of the various complications was that Tomlinson, age fifty-nine, started over with between 2,000 and 3,000 adherents. The courts exonerated Tomlinson of financial wrongdoing

and decreed his organization should be called the Tomlinson Church of God in nonreligious matters. The group never used this name but preferred "Church of God, over which A. J. Tomlinson is General Overseer." At the time of his death on October 2, 1943, the Church of God of Prophecy (CGP; as it would be designated by the courts in 1952) had a membership of just less than 32,000. Three of his four children survived him in death. Milton Ambrose succeeded his father as the duly chosen general overseer of the CGP. Homer Aubrey left the church and formed his own denomination.

Bibliography: L. Duggar, *A. J. Tomlinson* (1964); D. D. Preston, *The Era of A. J. Tomlinson* (1984); idem, *God's Twentieth Century Pioneer* (1962); A. J. Tomlinson, "Diary" (1899–1943), the original is in the Library of Congress; idem, *Historical Notes* (1970), originally published in 1943 under the title *A. J. Tomlinson: God's Anointed—Prophet of Wisdom*; idem, *Last Great Conflict* (1913); H. A. Tomlinson, *Diary of A. J. Tomlinson*, 3 vols. (1949–55). H. D. Hunter

TOMLINSON, HOMER AUBREY (1892–1968). General overseer, Church of God (Queens, N.Y.) The oldest son of A. J. Tomlinson, Homer Aubrey Tomlinson was born in Westfield, Indiana. Homer grew up with the Church of God (CG, Cleveland, Tenn.), and was influenced in various ways by his father's ministry of leadership. Knowing the hardships endemic to a minister's life and seeing Pentecostals experience persecution, Homer was not interested in joining the ministry. In 1913, after two years at the University of Tennessee and a year of teaching school, he went to Indianapolis, entering a career in advertising. By 1916 he was in New York, where he opened a small advertising agency. During a 1919 Aimee Semple McPherson tent service, he met Marie Wunch, and they were married two months later. He served in the military during World War I. Homer also accepted considerable publishing responsibilities on behalf of his father, including the *Evangel* and the *Faithful Standard*. Later he composed religious dramas and gospel songs. In 1923 Homer entered the ministry to aid his father (see TOMLINSON, AMBROSE JESSUP), who was starting over (see CHURCH OF GOD OF PROPHECY). He expected to succeed his father as head of the Church of God of Prophecy, but when that did not materialize in 1943, he struck out on his own still using the name Church of God (Queens, N.Y.).

Homer is best remembered for his activities between 1954 and 1966. He repeated a coronation service in the capitals of 101 nations (including Russia and Israel). Typically, after his arrival in a capital city he notified the press, went to some public area wearing a scarlet academic robe, displayed his inflatable plastic globe, crowned himself, suspended the flag from his neck, and took his seat on the portable "throne." He then removed the flag and addressed the audience, always promising some form of peace or prosperity. By his reckoning, his visit to Ghana ended a year-long drought there, while his presence in the Congo halted an uprising and massacre. Revolutions in Guatemala, Costa Rica, and Haiti were said to have stopped abruptly with his arrival. He reportedly headed off a war between the Arabs and the Israelis and flew over Korea in December 1952 to lay the ground work for the end of that war. Only two capitals refused his ceremony: that of the U.S. and Vietnam. This, he said, explained the tragedy of the prolonged Vietnam War. He further claimed ownership to the land of Druze, while also accepting credit for President Roosevelt's welfare programs and the 1940s European Famine Relief Effort. In 1952, 1960, 1964, and 1968, he ran as a Theocratic Party candidate for president of the U.S. His running platform proposed uniting church and state; abolishing taxes and substituting tithing; stopping all divorce, gambling, and use of liquor, narcotics, and tobacco; and promoting racial equality. He desired to create two new cabinet posts: secretary of righteousness and secretary of the Holy Bible. He selected prominent Catholics, Protestants from various denominations, and Jews as his cabinet officers for his projected presidency. Also, he lectured in many prominent universities in the U.S.

In all of this, Homer remained good humored and aware that only a small band of followers gave him credit for these and other things (note his use of Josh. 1:3). The wide media coverage of his sensationalizing and long list of his publications drew regular attention to his point of view, but such was usually treated with derision, if not outright opposition. His response was that his claim to power could come from humility and not pride. Yet his surrealistic *Shout of the King* moves well beyond reality when he claims to have been

with the Wright brothers when they invented the airplane and to have become personal friends with the likes of Eisenhower and Roosevelt. At home, however, Tomlinson sustained a quality relationship with his immediate family.

Tomlinson's wife disbelieved many of his exaggerations, and their two sons and some of the grandchildren have held positions in the established community (both sons are retired railroad executives, and one grandson is an M.D.). Homer A. Tomlinson died on December 4, 1968, in his home, and his position of general overseer was assumed by his designated successor, Voy M. Bullen. Bullen centers the activities of the group out of his home in Huntsville, Alabama.

See also CHURCH OF GOD (HUNTSVILLE, ALABAMA).

Bibliography: R. H. Huff, "The Preacher Who Wanted to Be President," *Liberty* (6, 1978); H. A. Tomlinson, *Diary of A. J. Tomlinson*, 3 vols. (1949–55); idem, *The Shout of a King* (1968); W. Whitworth, "Profiles: Bishop Homer A. Tomlinson," *The New Yorker* (September 24, 1966). H. D. Hunter

Milton A. Tomlinson succeeded his father, A. J. Tomlinson, in 1943 as general overseer of the Tomlinson Church of God (now Church of God of Prophecy).

TOMLINSON, MILTON AMBROSE

(1906–). General overseer, Church of God of Prophecy. Milton Ambrose Tomlinson was born October 19, 1906, in Cleveland, Tennessee, the last child of A. J. and Mary Jane Tomlinson. His early years featured mostly the effects of various facets of his father's ministry. Teenage "Tony" exhibited some mischievousness, and he did not give up old friends after the events of 1923 (see TOMLINSON, AMBROSE JESSUP). He worked at the Herald Publishing Company, a print shop, after he completed high school. It was 1927 when his conversion, sanctification, and Spirit baptism were recorded and he joined the Church of God of Prophecy (the 1952 name). The next year he married Ina Mae Turner. For ten years he served the local church as youth leader and treasurer/clerk, and he was a member of the Tabernacle Brass Band. On October 17, 1932, he was ordained as a deacon. Following the general assembly of 1942 he began serving as pastor in Henderson, Kentucky.

After the death of Tomlinson's father the thirty-nine state and national overseers who could travel to Cleveland met to select an interim general overseer. Some candidates were discussed, but the choice was unanimous after a tongues message ("Bring forth the younger son . . .") was interpreted to refer to Milton Tomlinson. By acclamation, on September 15, 1944, the next general assembly enthusiastically endorsed him as the new general overseer. There seemed to be several reasons why many people (including Milton Tomlinson and his wife) had not envisioned Tomlinson as a general overseer. Part of this must have been the contrast between father and son: the father a dynamic preacher, gifted organizer, and prolific writer; the son self-effacing and deliberate in speech. Although Milton's call into the ministry was recent, and he had no experience in the work of the world headquarters. He began as general overseer on October 7, 1943, and was ordained a bishop on October 13, 1943. His ordination included the laying on of hands by a field secretary and a state overseer and his own signature on the bishop's license. Later sermons by numerous church leaders turned typology into allegory by paralleling Milton to Joshua and predicting his death and/or completion of the church's work by 1983.

Most of Tomlinson's views have been molded by his father's last decade. His irenic spirit is displayed in that while some around him used an exclusive ecclesiology to proselytize, such has not been his practice. In recent years he has demonstrated some willingness to encourage dialogue between different Christian traditions (Pentecostals with non-Pentecostals, charismatics, and Roman Catholics). Until his late seventies Tomlinson kept up a local church assignment in addition to transporting people to church and helping various ones in need. He and his wife have two children, Wanda and Joy, both of whom are married to ministers. He is now in his forty-fifth year (1987–88) as general overseer.

Bibliography: M. A. Tomlinson, *Basic Bible Briefs* (1961); idem, *The Glorious Church of God* (1968); various interviews with M. A. Tomlinson, 1976–87.
H. D. Hunter

TONGUES, GIFT OF See BAPTISM IN THE HOLY SPIRIT; GLOSSOLALIA; INITIAL EVIDENCE, A BIBLICAL PERSPECTIVE; INITIAL EVIDENCE, A HISTORICAL PERSPECTIVE; INTERPRETATION, GIFT OF.

TONGUES-SPEECH. See BAPTISM IN THE HOLY SPIRIT; GLOSSOLALIA; INITIAL EVIDENCE, A BIBLICAL PERSPECTIVE; INITIAL EVIDENCE, A HISTORICAL PERSPECTIVE; INTERPRETATION, GIFT OF.

TOPEKA REVIVAL The Topeka revival in Topeka, Kansas, in early 1901 marked the birth of the Pentecostal movement. The manifestation of glossolalia on a dozen and a half students at the Bethel Bible School solidified the unique theological tenet of Pentecostalism that tongues speech provided the initial evidence of the baptism of the Holy Spirit. The reception also implanted a fervent millenarian belief that Pentecostal gifts marked the imminent return of Christ and promised worldwide revival during the last years before the dawn of the eschaton.

The Topeka outbreak was a product of the ministry of Charles F. Parham. By 1900 Parham accepted a variety of theological speculations promulgated by Holiness evangelists. Nothing impressed him more than the concept of apostolic power as a sign of history's final generation. Drawing from several isolated reports of xenolalia, Parham decided that this phenomenon gave full evidence of an end-time baptism of the Holy Spirit because it promised the utilitarian method for a global revival. Spirit-filled believers could fan out and preach the gospel message without the painstaking process of learning a new language.

On this premise, Parham established the Bethel Bible School in October 1900 in the Stone mansion, a rented—though elaborately designed—structure on the outskirts of Topeka. He organized the school as a missionary training center but kept quiet about his conclusions on missionary xenolalia. Rather, Parham instructed his thirty-four students in Holiness theology and then, in late December, challenged them to search for the true evidence of the end-time spiritual outpouring. Strategically, he pointed them to Acts 2 where tongues speech clearly accompanied the dawn of apostolic power in the early church.

Much of the story of the initial outbreak of Pentecost at Topeka is obscured by the incongruity of two conflicting accounts. Parham recalled that, to his amazement, all his students agreed independently that tongues were the only "indisputable proof" of the end-time Holy Spirit baptism. At the students' New Year's Eve service in 1900, Agnes Ozman requested that Parham lay hands on her and pray specifically that she receive this baptism with the "biblical sign." Parham reported that after a brief prayer "a halo seemed to surround her head and face, and she began speaking in the Chinese language, and was unable to speak English for three days" (Parham, 1930, 52–53). Ozman, however, dated the experience to the evening of January 1, 1901, and recalled nothing about the student consensus. She recalled, "I did not know that I would talk with tongues when I received the Baptism," and claimed to find biblical support for the phenomenon only *after* the experience (Ozman, 1921, 28–29). Both agreed that at a service several days later Parham and about half the students were likewise empowered.

An unfinished mansion in Topeka, Kansas, which was dubbed "Stone's Folly," became the home of Charles F. Parham's Bible school in 1900. It was here that the first reported tongues speaking happened in the 20th century, marking the beginning of the Pentecostal movement.

This 50th anniversary symbol of the Pentecostal outpouring at Topeka, Kansas, was used in the *Pentecostal Evangel* in 1951.

The two accounts cannot be totally reconciled, but a couple of things are clear. In his earliest recounting Parham dated the initial outbreak to New Year's Day, thus confirming Ozman's timetable (Parham, 1902, 34). On the more important question of ideological origins, Parham's xenolalic theory provided the foundation for the belief in tongues as initial evidence. He led his students to an expectation of their unique roll in an end-time global revival. Ozman was, like the other students, deeply interested in foreign missions and duly impressed when her tongues speech was "confirmed" by a local Bohemian who claimed to understand her words perfectly.

Publicity of the revival emerged a week after the initial outbreak when reporters were alerted by Stanley Riggins, a student who defected in opposition to the new doctrine. News reports centering on the strange tongues generated attention as far away as St. Louis. Late in January, Parham and a handful of Spirit-filled students set out for Kansas City intent on establishing a string of missionary posts in major cities across the Northeast. After only marginal results and amidst an acute shortage of funds, Parham postponed further campaigns in mid February. Undaunted by the setback, he planned and publicized a summer camp meeting for Holiness evangelists nationwide, expecting "thousands" to visit the Bible School and adopt his new Pentecostal plank. However, tragedy struck in March and ended the optimism that poor turnouts and belittling news reports had failed to dampen. Parham's one-year-old son suddenly became ill and died. Shortly thereafter the Bible school was lost when Stone mansion was sold to a new owner, and Parham and his students were forced off the premises. New quarters in the city were secured briefly, but

Lillian Trasher founded the Assiout Orphanage in Egypt in 1911 and took homeless children and widows. Here she is with some of her orphans during the early part of her ministry.

by the end of the summer the school closed and the initial wave of Pentecostal optimism ended.

Parham moved his family to Kansas City and spent the next two years in evangelistic work. Though he kept a small band of followers in Topeka and Kansas City, it was not until late in 1903 that he achieved a level of sustained growth. Nevertheless, the theological concept of tongues as evidence and xenolalia as an end-time missions tool remained a solid part of his ministerial efforts after Topeka. From those optimistic, yet humble, beginnings would rise the Pentecostal movement of the twentieth century.

See also APOSTOLIC FAITH MOVEMENT, ORIGINS.

Bibliography: J. Goff, *Fields White Unto Harvest* (1988); A. LaBerge, *What God Hath Wrought* (1921); C. Parham, *Voice Crying in the Wilderness* (1902); S. Parham, *Life of Charles F. Parham* (1930).   J.R. Goff, Jr.

TOPPI, FRANCESCO (1928–). Italian pastor, evangelist, educator, and church official.

Born in Rome, Italy, Toppi worked as a public accountant and later attended the International Bible Training Institute in Burgess Hill, England, directed by Frederick Squire. In 1959 he married Anna Maria Ferretti.

Toppi began his ministry in 1949 with the Italian Assemblies of God (ADI, Assembles di Dio d'Italia) and received ordination in the same year. He engaged in evangelistic work in Southern Italy (1950–1953) and in evangelistic and pastoral work in Turin (1953–1959). He became a member of the executive presbyters council of the denomination in 1954. With the founding of the Italian Bible Institute in Rome in 1953, Toppi was appointed secretary-treasurer for the school and also taught.

In recent years Toppi has served as pastor of the Evangelistic Center in Rome and as the general superintendent of the ADI, which now claims over nine hundred churches and owns fifty radio stations, one orphanage, and three senior citizens'

homes. During his administration, the ADI, the largest Protestant church body in Italy, with over 100,000 members and adherents, has gained legal recognition from the government equal to that afforded the Roman Catholic church, and the Italian Bible Institute has received full accreditation.

Bibliography: Personal vita; "Pentecostals in Italy Given Government Approval to Evangelize After 80 Years of Limited Freedom," *PE* (April 19, 1987), 24.
G. B. McGee

TRASHER, LILLIAN HUNT (1887–1961). Missionary to Egypt. Lillian Trasher was born in Florida to a successful businessman and an educated mother. When young, she committed her life to Roman Catholicism. In her late teens, after reading the Bible and attending Bible studies at a newly converted friend's house, she knelt and prayed with all her heart and knew she had met God.

At age eighteen Trasher left for God's Bible School in Cincinnati, Ohio, for one term and subsequently went to work at an orphanage in North Carolina. After a few months, she left for Altamont Bible School in South Carolina, where she was baptized in the Holy Spirit and began a successful pastorate of a Pentecostal church. Despite the success, she left the church to accompany an evangelist, and then returned to the orphanage.

During the evangelistic tour, she became engaged to Tom Jordan. Because of her call to Africa as a missionary and her fiancé's lack of interest in missions, she broke the engagement ten days before the wedding date. That same year, 1910, she left for Africa in the face of her family's strong disapproval. Her sister went with her to take care of her and later proved to be an invaluable asset amidst severe persecution. The Lord gave Lillian a verse (Acts 7:34) as she prayed in her cabin before setting sail, which verified her calling to Egypt.

As Trasher cared for a starving baby after watching its mother die, she realized that her earlier training at the orphanage was all part of God's plan. She rented a house and started an orphanage in Assiout, Egypt (230 miles south of Cairo). Within one year, and with the help of Egyptian and American friends, eight children were supported in the home. She capitalized on the Egyptian belief that giving to the poor brings healing more quickly. The Egyptian government also helped her. She realized the effectiveness of prayer and that God was her source.

Trasher was ordained with the Church of God (Cleveland, Tenn.) in 1912. In 1916, after five years, she had fifty children. On a trip to America, she was impressed by the giving and prayers of the Assembly of God (AG) constituency and as a result became a part of that organization in 1919.

Over the years, many of the children who have been reared at the orphanage have been sought after as wives and workers. Some return to the orphanage if they become pregnant or if they lose their jobs. Trasher delivered hundreds of babies; most of the girls were promptly named "Lillian." She loved to be called "Mamma." Her dedication kept her working from 1929 until 1954 without a furlough. In 1955 her family numbered 1,200. She became known worldwide.

"Mamma Lillian" was buried at the site of her orphanage, which today is made up of thirteen main buildings on twelve acres, housing about 650 children, widows, and blind women. Today it is known as the Lillian Trasher Memorial Orphanage.

"I believe that when she dies, in spite of the fact she is a woman and a Christian, God will take her directly to paradise." This statement, representative of her reputation in Egypt, is the highest of compliments—especially when coming from a Moslem official (Crouch, 1984–85, 7).

Bibliography: J. Beatty, "Nile Mother," *AG Heritage* 4 (Winter 1984–85): 1, 3–6, 8; J. Booze, *Into All the World* (1980); P. Crouch, "Why They Called Her the Greatest Woman in Egypt," *AG Heritage* 4 (Winter 1984–85): 7–8; B. P. Howell, *Lady on a Donkey* (1960); N. Perkin, ed., *Light Along the Nile* (1942); *Letters From Lillian* (1983).   S. Shemeth

TRIBULATION PERIOD See Eschatology, Pentecostal Perspectives on.

TRINITY BROADCASTING NETWORK See Crouch, Paul Franklin.

TRIPLETT, LOREN OTIS, JR. (1926–). Missionary and field director for the Assemblies of God (AG). Born in San Jose, California, Triplett grew up in California, Michigan, and Oregon. After graduating from Glad Tidings Bible Institute, he began his ministry as an assistant pastor at Red Bluff, California, in 1946. He married Mildred Johnson of Newburg, Oregon, in 1949 and was ordained by the AG in 1950.

Triplett pastored churches in Oregon and Nebraska before serving as a missionary to Nicaragua from 1954 to 1966. He became assistant superintendent of the AG in Nicaragua and director of the Nicaraguan Bible Institute.

From 1966 to 1973 Triplett was manager of Life Publishers in Miami, Florida. While in this capacity, he edited *Poder*, a monthly magazine serving the churches in Latin America. Since 1973 he has served as field director for Latin America and the West Indies for the AG Division of Foreign Missions.

Bibliography: Personal data sheet, AG Office of Information (1980).   G. W. Gohr

TROUT, EDGAR J. (1912–68). Prominent figure in the initial stages of the charismatic movement in Britain. A local politician and Methodist lay preacher, Edgar Trout became leader of Bath Street Mission in Plymouth (1956); he was baptized in the Spirit in 1958. Leaving Bath Street at the end of 1961, he formed the All for Christ Fellowship, developing a more national ministry. His conferences (especially in Devon from 1962) did much to spread Pentecostal blessing. In his later years he received a vision for national revival. Trout was much sought out by those fighting the occult, and his ministry was noted for manifestations of supernatural power, many people receiving significant words of knowledge for their future. Regarded as a key figure among British charismatics in the mid-1960s, Trout's early death was a great shock, and not being an author, his contribution is largely unknown to later charismatics.

Bibliography: P. Hocken, *Streams of Renewal* (1986).   P. D. Hocken

During the Congo uprising in 1964, AG missionary J. W. Tucker became a martyr for the cause of Christ.

TUCKER, J. W. (1915–64). Missionary martyr. J. W. Tucker served as a missionary in the Belgian Congo (now known as Zaire) for more than twenty-five years. During the latter part of his service there, rebel forces were attempting to overthrow the then New Republic of Congo. Tucker, a white American, was considered a threat to the rebel cause and was imprisoned and eventually beaten to death. At the time, Tucker's wife, Angeline, and their three children were also in great danger, but the rebels spared their lives. J. W. Tucker remains one of the outstanding missionary martyrs of the Assemblies of God.

Bibliography: A. Tucker, *He Is in Heaven* (1965).
F. Bixler

TUGWELL, SIMON (1943–). English Catholic authority on traditional, especially Dominican, spirituality. Brought up as an Anglican, Tugwell became a Catholic at Oxford University. He entered the Dominican order in 1965. In the late 1960s he had some experience of spiritual gifts, following contact with British Pentecostals. Before the Catholic Charismatic Renewal developed in Britain, Tugwell helped many Catholics to benefit from the experience of Pentecostal churches. His book, *Did You Receive the Spirit?* (1972, rev. 1979), illustrated the life of the Spirit from the riches of patristic and medieval sources; widely acclaimed, it became for many their first introduction to things Pentecostal. Tugwell never identified himself with organized charismatic renewal and, after some further writings on glossolalia, e.g., in *Prayer* (1974) and *New Heaven? New Earth?* (1976), he has not pursued such topics since. He teaches theology in Oxford and Rome and has published works on the history of spirituality.   P. D. Hocken

TURNEY, HENRY MICHAEL (1850–1920). Early Pentecostal missionary. Turney was born to Irish Catholic parents in Louisville, Kentucky. He later became an alcoholic, but his life changed when he was converted to Christ. In 1897 he received an experience of sanctification. While doing evangelistic work in Alaska in 1906, he heard about the Azusa Street revival in Los Angeles. Leaving for California, he arrived at the Azusa Street Mission on October 5, 1906, and received the baptism in the Holy Spirit on the following night.

Shortly after his experience at Azusa Street, Turney established an Apostolic Faith mission in San Jose, California. In February 1907 he married Anna E. Arian (d. 1954), and they departed for ministry in Hawaii. Returning to the U.S., he preached in Pentecostal churches across the country before sailing to England in 1908. After several months, the Turneys sailed for South Africa and arrived in 1909. During the following year, the Turneys and Hanna James opened a mission in Doornkop in eastern Transvaal. They later became closely linked to the American Assemblies of God (AG), registering a number of South African Pentecostal churches under that name in 1917. At approximately the same time they affiliated with the American AG.

Bibliography: H. M. Turney, "Alaska Brother Proves Acts 1:8," *The Apostolic Faith* (December 1906), 3; idem, "Article VIII.—Letter from H. M. Turney of South Africa," *The Weekly Evangel* 17 (June 1916): 4.
G. B. McGee

Baptized in the Spirit in 1966, Judith Tydings became involved in the Catholic charismatic movement.

TYDINGS, JUDITH C. (1935–). One of the women leaders in the early years of the Catholic Charismatic Renewal (CCR). A teacher and wife with four young children, Tydings was baptized in the Spirit in about 1966, soon meeting up with Edith Difato. Together in 1968 they began the first Catholic charismatic prayer group on the East Coast in Potomac, Maryland, that evolved into the predominantly Catholic and ecumenical community known as Mother of God. Tydings served on the advisory committee to the national service committee for the CCR (1973–80). With a history degree and previous involvement in the Franciscan Third Order, Tydings has specialized in the study of Catholic saints. From this background she has seen charismatic renewal as an outpouring of God's Spirit calling all Christians to holiness of life and mutual commitment in community, as illustrated in her book *Gathering a People: Catholic Saints in Charismatic Perspective* (1976).   P. D. Hocken

TYSON, TOMMY (1922–). Pastor and evangelist. Tommy Tyson was born in Farmville, North Carolina, and was educated at Duke University (B.A.) and Duke Divinity School (M.Div.).

Tyson had a profound new-birth experience in 1947 and responded to a call to preach in 1948. After serving six years as a pastor in the North Carolina annual conference of the United Methodist Church (UMC), he received appointment as an approved evangelist through that body and continues to serve in that capacity. It was largely through the witness and life of Professor J. Rufus Moseley that Tyson was led into the experience of the baptism in the Holy Spirit in 1952 while serving as a UMC pastor. From 1965 to 1968 he served as director of spiritual life at the newly founded Oral Roberts University, an appointment approved by the bishop of the North Carolina Conference.

Most of Tyson's ministry as an evangelist has been in the work of church renewal at denominational, interdenominational, and ecumenical levels. He and his wife, Frances, live in Chapel Hill, North Carolina, at the Aqueduct, a Christian growth conference center.

S. Strang

U

UNFORGIVABLE SIN See BLASPHEMY AGAINST THE HOLY SPIRIT.

UNION DE PRIÈRE (UP). An association formed in 1946 under the leadership of Louis Dallière among those touched by the Ardèche revival in the Reformed church in France in the 1930s. Though not using the term, the Union de Prière was the pioneer "charismatic" body, with baptism in the Spirit and the spiritual gifts being received and exercised with a firm commitment to a historic church tradition. UP's charter specifies four intercessory concerns: the revival of the churches through the conversion of souls, the salvation of the Jewish people, the visible unity of the body of Christ, and the return of Jesus Christ and the resurrection of the dead. An official accord was reached between UP and the French Reformed Church in 1972.

Bibliography: W. J. Hollenweger, "'Touching' and 'Thinking' the Spirit: Some Aspects of European Charismatics," in *Perspectives on the New Pentecostalism,* ed. R. P. Spittler (1976); J. Thoorens, L'union de prière de Charmes-sur-Rhone, unpublished diss., Institut Catholique de Paris.   P. D. Hocken

UNION OF MESSIANIC JEWISH CONGREGATIONS

(UMJC). The UMJC is a transdenominational fellowship of almost sixty Messianic Jewish congregations. The fellowship consists of seven Assemblies of God (AG) related congregations, two Presbyterian related congregations and nearly fifty nonaffiliated congregations.

The UMJC was formed to serve the needs of the increasing number of Messianic Jewish congregations. These congregations are homes for Jews and Gentiles who appreciate a Jewish rooted expression of their new covenant faith.

The roots of this movement can be traced to the establishment of Hebrew Christian churches in the past decades, the Messianic Jewish orientation of Manny Brotman in the mid 1960s and the establishment of several Messianic congregations in the early 1970s. Some Hebrew Christian congregations reoriented themselves to the new Jewish directions (Adat ha Tikvah, formerly the First Hebrew Christian Church, under Daniel Juster [1974]; Beth Messiah, Philadelphia, under Herb Links [1971]; and Beth Messiah, Cincinnati, under Martin Chernoff [1971]). New congregations included Beth Messiah, Washington, D.C., founded by Paul Liberman, Sid Roth, and Sandra Sheskin, and first pastored by Manny Brotman (1973); Beth Immanuel in Encino, California, under Ray Gannon and Phil Goble (1971) (Goble, 1975); and B'nai Macabium, in Highland Park, Illinois (Rausch, 1981, 99–108), under John Fischer (1975).

The desire began to grow among several congregations for a mutual affiliation. In 1976 James Hutchins of B'nai Macabium and Daniel Juster of Adat ha Tikveh asked the Messianic Jewish Alliance of America (MJAA), an organization for individuals of Jewish birth, to consider affiliation for congregations. The MJAA board noted the need for such an affiliation but stated that it should be formed separately from the Alliance (Minutes of March 1976 MJAA board meeting).

In 1976 Manny Brotman and Jim Hutchins sought to form a union of congregations. This effort received little response and was halted. In 1978 invitations were sent by the two Chicago area congregations to all known Messianic Jewish congregations to discuss the possible formation of a union. This meeting was followed up by a spring 1979 meeting in which there was almost unanimous agreement to form a union. A brief incorporation meeting took place in July 1979 in Mechanicsburg, Pennsylvania. Nineteen of the twenty-two known congregations joined (Juster, 1986, 148–55).

Since that time the UMJC has fostered many services, including a planters program for establishing new congregations, educational materials development and publication, leadership training courses and seminars, national and regional conferences, pastoral fellowships, and a program for ordination for those without other adequate sources of credentials. The UMJC maintains doctrinal and moral standards as agreed upon by its constituents.

The UMJC is charismatic in orientation reflecting the perspective of the great majority of Messianic Jewish congregations.

The government of the UMJC is by delegate representation with most congregations sending their head pastor and another leader. These delegates elect a four-member executive board. The board appoints committee chairmen and regional coordinators subject to delegate approval. A general secretary, who is an appointed member of the executive board, oversees the daily operations of the organization.

Bibliography: P. Goble and R. Gannon, *Everything You Need to Grow a Messianic Synagogue* (1975); D. Juster, *Jewish Roots* (1986); P. Liberman, *The Fig Tree Blossoms* (1976); D. Rausch, *Messianic Judaism, Its History, Theology, and Policy* (1981).   D. C. Juster

UNITED APOSTOLIC FAITH CHURCH

Originally formed in 1907 as the Apostolic Faith Church under the leadership of W. O. Hutchinson, the denomination is now headquartered in London, England. The movement publishes the *Pentecostal Times* and *Kingdom Evangel* even though the number of congregations in England is fewer than twenty.

In addition to emphasizing the gift of prophecy in making group decisions, the denomination has embraced the British Israel teaching. There are missionaries for the church in Zimbabwe, Canada, and South Africa. There are approximately six congregations in America with a combined membership of about five hundred people.

Bibliography: J. G. Melton, ed., *Encyclopedia of American Religions*, vol. 1 (1978); J. T. Nichol, *Pentecostalism* (1966).   B. M. Stout

UNITED CHURCH OF CHRIST, FELLOWSHIP OF CHARISMATIC CHRISTIANS IN THE

(FCC/UCC). The FCC/UCC began as seventy-three members of the United Church of Christ (UCC) attending the 1977 Conference on Charismatic Renewal in the Christian Churches (Kansas City, Mo.) decided to address the need for "a denominational nationwide fellowship for those who were interested in the charismatic renewal" (FCC/UCC pamphlet, n.d.). With every intention of remaining in the church, the FCC/UCC organized in the winter of 1977–78 to strengthen and encourage those who had a "charismatic experience" within the UCC religious tradition.

Programs of the FCC/UCC include: Acts Alive, a three weekend lay witness event designed to be experienced over a two- or three-year period within the local congregation; Ekklesia, a followup program to Acts Alive, wherein selected "pilot" churches provide further teaching, research, and development for renewal; *Focus* newspaper (containing articles, book reviews, announcements, and other renewal information); mailings of reprint and resource materials; correspondence with pastors and laity who are seeking information concerning the renewal; and liaison relationships with the Office of Church Life and Leadership in the UCC.

FCC/UCC is expanding its ministry, beginning with a proposed new name—"Focus Renewal Ministries in the United Church of Christ" (*Newsletter* [Christmas 1987]). Vernon Stoop, Jr., is the director of services for FCC/UCC.

Other visionary agenda are being pursued, including: exploring "varieties of future growth opportunities such as developing renewal seminars, establishing Christian Healing Centers, developing apostolic ministries, exploring ways to assist in the placement of pastors, developing a book treatise on renewal and encouraging the formation of FCC/UCC . . . regional representatives" (*Focus* 12 [9, 1987]: 2).

See also CHARISMATIC MOVEMENT.

Bibliography: "Fellowship of Charismatic Christians in the United Christian Church," pamphlet, n.d.
J. A. Hewett

UNITED CHURCH OF CHRIST, FOCUS RENEWAL MINISTRIES IN THE

See UNITED CHURCH OF CHRIST, FELLOWSHIP OF CHARISMATIC CHRISTIANS IN THE.

UNITED CHURCH OF JESUS CHRIST

Distinctive practices of the United Church of Jesus Christ (UCJC) include invocation of the name of Jesus while persons being baptized are under water and use of wine mixed with water in the Lord's Supper. Ministers are addressed as "Reverend." Former members of the Church of Jesus Christ, then based in Cleveland, Tennessee, established the UCJC in 1948. There were twenty-five congregations, one hundred ministers, and 1,250 members in the early 1970s. At that time, W. C. Gibson of Sweetwater, Tennessee, was chairperson.

Bibliography: A. C. Piepkorn, *Profiles in Belief*, vol. 3 (1979).   C. E. Jones

UNITED EVANGELICAL CHURCHES

Organized in 1960 as a response to the charismatic renewal in the mainline churches, the denomination is headquartered in Monrovia, California. It was founded by ministers who were made to feel that their experience with the baptism in the Holy Spirit was incompatible with the stance of their various denominations.

The church is governed by an executive council and convenes in conference every two years. In addition to churches in most states, the denomination has a missions outreach in at least fifteen countries.

The tenets of faith include various orthodox statements such as belief in the Bible as the Word of God, the Virgin Birth, the resurrection of Christ, salvation in Christ, regeneration by the Holy Spirit, the inability of humankind to save itself, and the judgment of Christ. Pentecostal distinctives include belief that the present ministry of the Holy Spirit enables the believer through gifts and ministries. The church continues to identify with the charismatic tradition.

Bibliography: J. G. Melton, ed., *The Encyclopedia of American Religions*, vol. 1 (1978).   B. M. Stout

UNITED HOLY CHURCH OF AMERICA

During the late nineteenth century, the Holiness movement spread among blacks in the South. In 1886 one group met in Method, North Carolina, and from that meeting arose the United Holy Church of America. Referring to themselves as the "Holy People," the movement spread throughout the state. In 1894 many gathered in Durham for the first convocation of Holy People in North Carolina. Then in 1900 this and several other Holiness associations met together to form the "Holy People of North Carolina and Virginia," with Elder L. M. Mason of Goldsboro, North Carolina, as president. Expansion dictated the adoption of the name United Holy Church of America in 1916. Although Mason was the first president, and other church fathers such as H. L. Fisher, G. J. Branch, and J. D. Diggs gave great form and direction to the movement, church doctrine claims "no earthly founder," pointing rather to the initiative of Jesus Christ by the Holy Spirit. The church is organized around a Holy Convocation structure, meeting in convocation by districts as well as holding an annual convocation for the whole church. Church doctrine includes strong emphasis on sanctification as a second work of grace and the baptism of the Holy Ghost as empowerment for service. The church teaches that speaking in tongues is one of the spiritual gifts that comes with Spirit baptism but is not necessarily the initial evidence. Over the years, three schisms have taken place, resulting in new denominations that maintain basically the same structures and beliefs as the mother church. The first schism resulted in the formation of the Mt. Sinai Holy Church in Philadelphia in 1924. The second yielded the Mt. Calvary Holy Church in Boston in 1929. The third group, the Original United Holy Church, International, was formed in 1977 and maintains headquarters at its United Christian College at Goldsboro. Interestingly, relations between the groups have remained amicable even amidst the schisms. Membership in the United Holy Church is estimated to be between 30,000 and 40,000, primarily along the East Coast. The church maintains ministries in England, the West Indies, Liberia, and the Philippines.

Bibliography: H. L. Fisher, *The History of the United Holy Church of America, Inc.* (1945), reprinted in *The Holiness Union* (1979); J. A. Forbes, "A Ministry of Hope From a Double Minority," *Theological Education 9* (4, 1973): 305–16; C. W. Gregory, *The History of the United Holy Church of America, Inc., 1886–1986* (1986); A. W. Lawson, *The Doctrine of the United Holy Church of America, Inc.* (1980); L. Lovett, "Black Holiness Pentecostalism: Implications for Social Transformation," Ph.D. diss., Emory University, 1979; A. Paris, *Black Pentecostalism: Southern Religion in an Urban World* (1982); J. Shopshire, "A Socio-Historical Characterization of the Black Pentecostal Movement in America," Ph.D. diss., Northwestern University, 1975; J. Tinney, "New Missions Thrust for the United Holy Church," *Washington Afro-American* (September 22, 1973), 14; idem, "Prospects of Black Pentecostalism: An Emerging Third World Religion," in D. J. Jones and W. H. Matthews, *The Black Church: A Community Resource* (1977), 134–56; W. C. Turner, "The United Holy Church of America: A Study in Black Holiness-Pentecostalism," Ph.D. diss., Duke University, 1984.
H. D. Trulear

UNITED HOUSE OF PRAYER FOR ALL PEOPLE, CHURCH ON THE ROCK OF THE APOSTOLIC CHURCH   The first House of Prayer was founded by Charles Emmanuel "Sweet Daddy" Grace (1881–1961) in West Wareham, Massachusetts, in 1919. A native of the Cape Verde Islands, he worked in a variety of jobs at the same time he was evangelizing. Grace incorporated the organization in 1927 and focused his energies on reaching the poor in urban areas. Centers were established in leading cities, including New York, Philadelphia, Atlanta, Baltimore, and Washington, D.C. Low-cost housing as well as employment in church-related businesses is provided to church members.

Worship in the centers of the United House of Prayer for All People allows for unrestrained emotionalism. Services are also characterized by dancing, falling in trances, and glossolalia. Criticisms have been leveled at the organization for its excessive veneration of the founder. With Grace's death in 1961, his office was eventually filled by Walter McCullough (1915–), known to the members as "Sweet Daddy Grace" McCullough. With his ascendancy, a split occurred within the ranks leading to the organization of the True Grace Memorial House of Prayer. At the time of the split, 137 churches, with an approximate membership of 27,500 remained with McCullough.

Bibliography: C. E. Jones, *A Guide to the Study of the Pentecostal Movement* (1983).   G. B. McGee

UNITED METHODIST CHARISMATICS
I. Methodists in the Early Pentecostal Movement. Methodists and Wesleyan-Holiness proponents were heavily involved in the early Pentecostal movement. Charles Fox Parham was a Methodist minister, as were T. B. Barratt of Norway, Johannes Van Kesteren of Belgium and Harold Horton of England. Entire denominations and/or congregations became Pentecostal during the early decades of the Pentecostal movement in Chile, Germany, Great Britain, India, Norway, Sweden, and the U.S. Many features of Pentecostal theology and spirituality were borrowed or adapted from the heritage of Methodism and its derivative movements, the Wesleyan–Holiness and Keswick–Higher Life traditions.

II. Development of the Charismatic Movement in the United Methodist Church, U.S. After the institutionalization of the Pentecostal movement, there is no published record of Methodist charismatics until Tommy Tyson's 1952 experience of "baptism of the Holy Spirit." Tyson, pastor of Bethany Methodist Church in Durham, North Carolina, was encouraged by Bishop Paul Garber to remain within the church. Tyson was appointed conference evangelist in 1954 and became a national leader of the charismatic renewal, both within Methodism and in other denominations. He later became friends with Oral Roberts and served as director of Religious Life at Oral Roberts University.

Many Methodist charismatics of the 1950s and 1960s became involved in Full Gospel Business Men's Fellowship International (FGBMFI) activities. That organization published a volume of testimonies of pastors, laymen, and a district superintendent (Jolly Harper, Shreveport, La.), *The Methodists and the Baptism of the Holy Spirit* (1963). *Voice,* the FGBMFI magazine, was influential. Another important instrument of communication was the periodical *"He is Able"* (1961–78). This "journal dedicated to aid the revival of the Ministry of Healing in the Methodist Church," was edited by James and Virginia Johnson in Chattanooga, Tennessee.

Oral Roberts, long-time Pentecostal Holiness evangelist, became a United Methodist in 1968, first as a member of Boston Avenue United Methodist Church (Tulsa) and, by transfer, as an ordained elder in the Oklahoma Conference. He recruited Methodist faculty for the university, including James Buskirk, dean of the Graduate School of Theology (1976–84), Methodist bishop Mack Stokes, Bob Stamps, and Robert Tuttle. Oral Roberts University achieved recognition as a seminary for training United Methodist clergy. Through Roberts' involvement, the charismatic movement in the United Methodist Church achieved recognition and an element of respectability. During 1984 to 1986, however, most Methodists were fired from the School of Theology and the school lost (1986) the recognition of the United Methodist University Senate.

Because of the increased numbers of charismatic Methodist clergy and the controversies over

Headquarters for the United Pentecost Church, International is located in Hazelwood (St. Louis area), Missouri.

God (AG) in 1914 (Anderson, 1979, 167). In 1910 he and others worked out an arrangement with C. H. Mason to obtain ministerial licenses with his organization, the Church of God in Christ, for legal recognition (Brumback, 1961, 154). In 1912 he became acquainted with H. G. Rodgers and his group in Alabama and solicited their support. In late 1913 he persuaded E. N. Bell, D. C. O. Opperman, and others to issue the call for ministers to attend a conference to form an organization for Pentecostals. This conference, held in Hot Springs, Arkansas, where Goss was the host pastor, organized the AG. Goss, Bell, and Opperman were chosen along with others to be officials in the new organization, and from this beginning the AG has grown to be a large and respected organization.

III. Doctrinal Issues. The first doctrinal division in the Pentecostal movement came when William H. Durham preached what came to be known as the Finished Work doctrine. Although Durham had earlier embraced the "second work" view, he came to believe that the act of sanctification is accomplished at the time of conversion and that it continues toward perfection throughout a person's life. By 1912 most of the independent Pentecostal ministers had accepted Durham's teaching (Ewart, 1975, 200). The AG and later the UPC were formed by ministers who believed the Finished Work message.

The second doctrinal issue to divide the Pentecostal movement had its beginning in 1913 at the Arroyo Seco World Wide Camp Meeting near Los Angeles. Ministering at a baptismal service, R. E. McAlister noted that the church in the Book of Acts always baptized in the name of Jesus Christ and not in the traditional formula, "in the name of the Father, and of the Son, and of the Holy Ghost." His observation immediately stirred the interest of many Pentecostal ministers, including Frank J. Ewart (Ewart, 1975, 105–6).

During the next several months Ewart searched

the Bible for the answer to the apparent conflict between the command Jesus gave in Matthew 28:19 and the formula used by the church in the Book of Acts. He noted that without exception the baptismal formula administered in Acts was "in the name of Jesus Christ" or "in the name of the Lord Jesus" (Acts 2:38; 8:16; 10:48; 19:5; 22:16). Moreover, the baptismal references in the epistles supported the apostolic formula and not the traditional formula.

By the spring of 1914, Ewart reached the conclusion that the singular "name" in Matthew 28:19 was Jesus Christ. He came to believe that the one true God who had revealed himself as Father, in the Son, and as the Holy Spirit was none other than Jesus Christ. To support this view, he pointed to Colossians 2:9, which states that in Jesus dwells all the fullness of the Godhead bodily.

Ewart explained his discovery to other Pentecostal ministers, some of whom rejected his teaching, but others enthusiastically embraced it. On April 15, 1914, Ewart rebaptized Glenn A. Cook, his assistant and a veteran evangelist of the Azusa Street Mission, in the name of Jesus Christ, and Cook rebaptized Ewart. This one act set in motion an issue that would divide the Pentecostal movement between the Trinitarians and the Jesus Name, or Oneness, believers.

Although Parham had apparently used the Jesus Name formula as early as 1903 (Foster, 1981, 98), and A. D. Urshan began baptizing converts in the name of Jesus in 1910 (Urshan, 1967, 169), no issue was raised about the practice until Ewart began rebaptizing Pentecostals in the name of Jesus Christ.

After Ewart and Cook were rebaptized, they rebaptized thousands of Pentecostals with the shorter formula. Pentecostals from the West Coast flocked to Ewart's church in Belvedere, California, to be baptized in the name of Jesus Christ. Cook, who had brought the Pentecostal message to the Midwest in 1907, returned to Oklahoma, Missouri, and Indiana in January 1915 preaching water baptism in the name of Jesus Christ. He rebaptized hundreds of Pentecostals in the name of Jesus Christ, including Mother Barnes and her staff in St. Louis, and Garfield Thomas Haywood and about five hundred members of the large Pentecostal church he pastored in Indianapolis.

With Cook's successful tour in the Midwest, the leaders of the newly formed AG, including E. N. Bell, J. R. Flower, and Howard Goss, readily denounced the "new issue" (Menzies, 1971, 114). Writing in the July 17, 1915, issue of *Word and Witness*, Flower expressed his opinion that the matter was only a fad and would soon fade away on its own. Bell had earlier expressed the same view in the June 12 issue (Brumback, 1961, 195). But their expectations were shattered by the middle of 1915. Indeed, by the time the general council was held in St. Louis in October 1915, it appeared that the entire AG organization might embrace baptism in the name of Jesus Christ.

A frightening event for the leaders was Bell's rebaptism during a camp meeting in Jackson, Tennessee, in August 1915. Joining him were many other ministers, including H. G. Rodgers, and hundreds of saints. Later that summer Bell rebaptized Goss in a meeting in Arkansas. When the general council convened in October, the list of prominent Pentecostal leaders that had been rebaptized had grown to include not only Bell, Goss, Ewart, Cook, Haywood, and Rodgers, but also R. E. McAlister, D. C. O. Opperman, George B. Studd, Harvey Shearer, L. C. Hall, B. F. Lawrence, Harry Van Loon, L. V. Roberts, and Frank Small (Menzies, 1971, 115).

Many Trinitarian ministers feared that the "Jesus Only" message, a name derived from the shorter baptismal formula, would become the doctrinal position of the AG. The overwhelming majority of the ministers still believed in the traditional formula, but the matter had to be handled with tact since so many of the leaders had embraced the Jesus Name formula. The "new issue" was debated at the general council in 1915. E. N. Bell and G. T. Haywood were chosen to argue on the side for water baptism in the name of Jesus Christ, and A. P. Collins and Jacob Miller were chosen to present the view for using the traditional formula, "in the name of the Father, and of the Son, and of the Holy Ghost" (Brumback, 1961, 201).

The general council in 1915 took no official action on the matter of water baptism, and it was the general feeling that time for prayer and study should be given to the matter. It is significant, however, that all Oneness leaders were replaced with confirmed Trinitarians on the executive presbytery (Anderson, 1979, 179). While the Trinitarians wanted time to strengthen their position, they attempted to impose a period of silence on the Jesus Name ministers (Anderson, 1979, 179). During the year before the next general council the leadership of J. W. Welch, J. R. Flower, and M. M. Pinson successfully regained some of the ministers who had accepted the Jesus Name formula. Their most important victory was the winning back of Bell to the Trinitarian position.

By the time the general council convened in St. Louis in October 1916, the majority had effectively organized to force the Oneness ministers to accept the Trinitarian formula or to leave the organization. The leaders appointed a committee of staunch Trinitarians to draw up a "Statement of Fundamental Truths." This statement embraced the traditional formula and made the doctrine of the Trinity a basis for membership.

In spite of the protests by the Oneness ministers that passing the Statement of Fundamental Truths was a violation of the organizational charter that rejected the formulation of a creed or any statement of faith other than the Bible itself, each item of the statement was passed by a majority vote. The council also charged the chairman and secretary with the responsibility of annually renewing ministerial credentials to ensure conformity to the new Statement of Fundamental Truths.

The passing of the Statement effectively forced the withdrawal of about one-fourth of the ministers from the AG. Some of the ministers withdrew not because of the doctrinal issue but because they compared the harsh actions against the Oneness faction with the way they were treated by the Holiness organizations a few years earlier. After the council the list of ordained ministers in the AG fell from 585 to 429.

IV. The Oneness Ministers Organize. In January 1917 a group of Oneness ministers meeting in St. Louis formed the General Assembly of the Apostolic Assemblies. The officers chosen were D. C. O. Opperman, general chairman; Lee Floyd, secretary; Howard A. Goss, credential committee; and H. G. Rodgers, member of credential committee. This organization lasted only a year, however, since the government would not grant military exemption or railroad discount fares to the ministers in the young organization.

In January 1918 the General Assembly of the Apostolic Assemblies merged with the Pentecostal Assemblies of the World, a Pentecostal organization that began in Los Angeles in 1906 (Golder, 1973, 31). The merger effected a reorganization of the Pentecostal Assemblies of the World with new officers: J. J. Frazee, general chairman; D. C. O. Opperman, secretary; and Howard A. Goss, treasurer. By its next conference in October 1918 Edward W. Doak had become general chairman, and W. E. Booth-Clibborn had become the secretary. In January 1919 the headquarters of the Pentecostal Assemblies of the World was moved from Portland, Oregon, to Indianapolis, Indiana, and the organization was incorporated in the state of Indiana. E. W. Doak remained as general overseer, and G. T. Haywood became general secretary.

For the first few years this racially integrated organization functioned smoothly, but by 1921 racial tension became evident. Southern white ministers complained about the conferences always being held in the North to accommodate the blacks due to the social prejudices in the South.

Since travel was not easy, the black ministers were usually in a majority at the conferences. Some abuse by both races added to the tension.

V. Division and Mergers. In spite of efforts by ministers of both races, misunderstandings continued to grow until in the fall of 1924 a division came on racial lines. Most of the white ministers withdrew to form a white organization, but by the end of 1925 they had formed three organizations.

In February 1925 a group of white ministers met in Jackson, Tennessee, to form the Pentecostal Ministerial Alliance. They chose L. C. Hall as general chairman and Goss as secretary-treasurer. Later, in 1932, the name of this organization was changed to Pentecostal Church, Incorporated (PCI).

Many ministers who felt that the Pentecostal Ministerial Alliance was only a ministerial organization and that it did not properly recognize the status of churches met in Houston, Texas, in October 1925 to organize the Emmanuel's Church in Jesus Christ, with W. T. Lyons as chairman and G. C. Stroud as secretary. O. F. Fauss was the third member of the board.

Between February and November 1925 a third group organized under the name of Apostolic Church of Jesus Christ, with headquarters in St. Louis. Under the leadership of W. H. Whittington, this group held its first conference in April 1926 to draw up a statement of doctrine.

Most ministers were not satisfied with the division among Oneness believers. From the outset they sought for a way to unite again all groups into one organization. Many of their attempts failed, but there were successes. The first merger occurred in 1928 between the Emmanuel's Church of Jesus Christ and the Apostolic Church of Jesus Christ, using the latter's name except changing "Church" to "Churches." O. F. Fauss was chosen as chairman, W. H. Whittington as secretary, and E. D. Browning as treasurer.

The next merger took place in 1932. The Apostolic Churches of Jesus Christ merged with the Pentecostal Assemblies of the World, once again creating a racially integrated organization. The new organization was named the Pentecostal Assemblies of Jesus Christ (PAJC). This merger was not accepted by all the black ministers, however, and they continued under the charter of the Pentecostal Assemblies of the World.

VI. The United Pentecostal Church. The UPC was formed in 1945 by the merger of the PAJC and the PCI. Many Oneness believers felt that this union fulfilled a dream of many years.

In the spring of 1945 a committee composed of members from both organizations met twice in St. Louis to work toward an agreement on the proposed merger. The leaders carefully explored various potential problems and found acceptable solutions. The most difficult question had to do with the new birth. While most Oneness ministers identified the new birth with Acts 2:38, others did not take such a firm view.

The solution came when W. T. Witherspoon, chairman of the PAJC, retired to a private room and wrote the Fundamental Doctrine Statement, which was readily accepted by all. The statement reads:

> The basic and fundamental doctrine of this organization shall be the Bible standard of full salvation, which is repentance, baptism in water by immersion in the name of the Lord Jesus Christ, and the baptism of the Holy Ghost with the initial sign of speaking with other tongues as the Spirit gives utterance. We shall endeavor to keep the unity of the Spirit until we all come into the unity of the faith, at the same time admonishing all brethren that they should not contend for their different views to the disunity of the body.

This statement, later amended to include the phrase "for the remission of sins" after the clause on water baptism, remains the basic doctrine of the UPC.

At the merger conference, the ministers elected officers from both former organizations: Howard A. Goss, general superintendent; W. T. Witherspoon, assistant general superintendent; Stanley W. Chambers, secretary-treasurer; T. R. Dungan, assistant general secretary-treasurer; and Wynn T. Stairs as foreign mission secretary. M. J. Wolff became the editor of the *Pentecostal Herald*, the official voice of the organization. The united organization had about 1,800 ministers and more than seven hundred churches.

A. Organizational Ministries. The UPC has experienced rapid growth since 1945. Its first headquarters building in St. Louis was enlarged immediately after the merger. A larger building was purchased in 1952, and it was enlarged in 1954. In 1970 a two-story headquarters building was constructed at 8855 Dunn Road, in Hazelwood, Missouri. In 1983 a third floor was added to this building to provide additional office space.

The UPC sponsors missionaries and national workers in more than one hundred nations and on every continent. Its annual foreign missionary budget was approximately 12 million dollars in 1987, serving 428 missionaries (annual reports to general conference, 1987).

The organization has operated a publishing house since 1945, and it publishes tracts, books, church supplies, and since 1970 a complete curriculum of Sunday school materials for all ages and grade levels. By 1987 it had more than ninety books in print under the label of Word Aflame Press. The organization also publishes seven national periodicals, including the *Pentecostal Herald*.

Among the endorsed institutions of the UPC are nine Bible colleges, an orphanage, a rehabilitation center for boys, and a ministry to those addicted to alcohol and other drugs. The organization maintains a heritage center in its headquarters building, operates a chaplaincy ministry to penal institutions, and provides endorsement of chaplains to the military. It also assists ministries for evangelizing ethnic groups in the U.S. and Canada.

B. Doctrines and Beliefs. Since the UPC emerged from the Holiness movement of the nineteenth century and the Pentecostal revival that began during the early years of this century, its doctrinal views reflect many of the beliefs of the Holiness-Pentecostal movement, with the exception of the "second work of grace," the historic doctrine of the Trinity, and the traditional Trinitarian formula in water baptism. It embraces the Pentecostal view that speaking in tongues is the initial sign of receiving the Holy Spirit. It shares the hope of the second coming of Jesus Christ, the rapture of the church, the resurrection of the dead, the judgment and eternal punishment of the wicked, the Millennium, and the eternal bliss of the redeemed.

The UPC also holds a fundamental view of the Bible: "The Bible is the only God-given authority which man possesses; therefore all doctrine, faith, hope, and all instructions for the church must be based upon and harmonize with the Bible" (*Manual of the United Pentecostal Church,* 19). It rejects all extrabiblical revelations and writings and accepts church creeds and articles of faith only as the thinking of men.

The distinctive beliefs of the UPC center on a non-Trinitarian view of God and on the practice of water baptism in the name of Jesus Christ. It holds that the Trinitarian concept is not an adequate explanation of God's revelation of himself as the Father, in the Son, and as the Holy Spirit, and that an emphasis upon separate eternal persons in the Godhead tends toward tritheism.

In distinction to the doctrine of the Trinity, the UPC holds to a Oneness view of God. The one God who revealed himself in the OT as Jehovah also revealed himself in his Son, Jesus Christ. Thus Jesus Christ was and is absolute deity; he was the one true God manifested in flesh, and in him dwells all the fullness of the Godhead bodily. Moreover, the Holy Spirit is God with us and in us. Thus God is manifested as Father in creation and as the Father of the Son, in the Son for our redemption, and as the Holy Spirit in our regeneration.

At the same time, Oneness believers hold to the full humanity of Jesus Christ. He was God of very God, but he was also man. God was manifest in flesh; he took upon himself human nature. As the Son of God, Jesus died for our sins, was raised by God, and was exalted to a position of power—as Lord and Christ (Acts 2:36). The man Christ Jesus is our Mediator and Advocate. His humanity did not detract from his deity, nor did his deity detract from his humanity. He was both God and man.

Since Jesus Christ is the redemptive name of God revealed in the NT economy of salvation, it is through this name that salvation and blessings are appropriated and bestowed upon believers (Matt. 1:21; Luke 24:47; John 1:12; 20:31; Acts 2:38; 3:16; 4:12). As the name of God in redemption, Jesus is the singular name of God manifested as Father, in the Son, and as the Holy Spirit. For this reason, the apostles and early Christians baptized in the singular name of Jesus Christ or Lord Jesus and not in the titles of Father, Son, and Holy Spirit (Acts 2:38; 8:16; 10:48; 19:5; 22:16; Rom. 6:3–4; 1 Cor. 1:13–15; Gal. 3:27; Col. 2:12).

The UPC holds that water baptism by immer-

sion in the name of Jesus Christ is a command, not an option, and that it has to do with the remission of sins. It does not believe, however, in baptismal regeneration.

Salvation is held to be by grace through faith in Jesus Christ, not by works. It is by faith in Jesus Christ that sinners are justified. At the same time, the sinner must believe the gospel; he is commanded to repent of his sins and to be baptized in water; and he is promised the gift of the Holy Spirit. The UPC believes that these various aspects of faith and obedience work together in God's grace to reconcile us to God.

The members of the UPC observe the Communion service and practice the ordinance of footwashing.

Although the matter is left to the conscience of each member, the official position of the UPC in regard to military service is conscientious objection to killing. They accept, however, noncombatant military service.

The members of the UPC hold to a standard of conduct and dress similar to that held by Pentecostals during the early years of this century. They shun movies, worldly sports and amusements, dancing, public swimming, immodest dress, and wearing make-up and jewelry. Women are taught not to cut their hair, and men are taught to wear short hair. The organization stresses and supports the family as God's primary institution and teaches that the church is God's redemptive fellowship for all believers.

C. Church Government. The basic governmental structure is congregational, with each local church autonomous in the conduct of its business. The organization embraces a modified presbyterian structure in that ministers meet in sectional, district, and general conferences or assemblies to elect officials and to conduct business. Only ministers are allowed to vote and to participate in business at these conferences.

Much of the business of the organization is conducted by officials, boards, and committees. A general superintendent, two assistant general superintendents, a secretary-treasurer, divisional directors, district superintendents, and executive presbyters are members of the general board of presbyters, the highest authority under the general conference. An executive board, consisting of members from the general board, conducts necessary business between meetings of the general board.

In 1945 Howard A. Goss was elected as the first general superintendent. In 1951 Arthur T. Morgan was elected general superintendent and served until his sudden death in 1967. Oliver F. Fauss was chosen to fill the unexpired term, until January 1968. Stanley W. Chambers was elected as general superintendent and served until 1977, when Nathaniel A. Urshan, the present general superintendent, was elected.

The headquarters building, located at 8855 Dunn Road, Hazelwood, Missouri, houses offices for its general officials and the Pentecostal Publishing House. In addition to church administration, the work is organized into divisions: foreign missions, home missions, Sunday school, editorial, education, youth, ladies auxiliary, Harvestime (radio), and publishing.

The basic structure of the UPC has changed little during its history. As the organization has grown, more districts have been organized and divisional operations expanded. In the years since the merger, the home missions, youth, ladies auxiliary, education, and Harvestime divisions have been formed.

In 1987 the UPC reported 3,496 churches, 7,064 ministers, and a membership exceeding 350,000 in the U.S. and Canada. It reports a foreign membership of more than 680,000.

See also ONENESS PENTECOSTALISM.

Bibliography: R. M. Anderson, *Vision of the Disinherited* (1979); C. Brumback, *Suddenly . . . From Heaven* (1961); A. L. Clanton, *United We Stand* (1970); F. T. Corum, *Like As of Fire* (1981); F. J. Ewart, *The Phenomenon of Pentecost* (1975); F. J. Foster, *Their Story: 20th Century Pentecostals* (1981); M. E. Golder, *History of the Pentecostal Assemblies of the World* (1973); E. E. Goss, *Winds of God* (1958); W. W. Menzies, *Anointed to Serve* (1971); C. F. Parham, *Voice Crying in the Wilderness* (1902); S. E. Parham, *The Life of Charles F. Parham* (1930); A. D. Urshan, *Life of Andrew Bar David Urshan* (1967).　　　　　　　　　J. L. Hall

UNIVERSAL CHRISTIAN SPIRITUAL FAITH AND CHURCHES FOR ALL NATIONS

In 1952 the National David Spiritual Temple of Christ Union (Inc.), U.S.A.; the St. Paul's Spiritual Church Convocation; and the King David's Spiritual Temple of Truth Association united to form the Universal Christian Spiritual Faith and Churches for All Nations. Heading the new body was David William Short, a former Missionary Baptist who twenty years before had founded the National David Spiritual Temple of Christ Union in Kansas City, Missouri ("David" in the church name refers to him). It claims the Day of Pentecost as its date of origin and teaches that although some who indeed have the Spirit of Christ do not speak in tongues, those with "a full and complete baptism of the Holy Ghost as poured out on the Day of Pentecost" always experience the gift of tongues or some other powerful sign. In the mid-1960s the group (using the name National David Spiritual Temple) claimed sixty-six churches, 40,816 members, and 275 clergy. Since that time headquarters have been moved from Kansas City to Los Angeles.

Bibliography: E. T. Clark, *Small Sects in America* (1965); C. E. Jones, *Black Holiness* (1987), 105–6; J. G. Melton, *Encyclopedia of American Religions* (1987).　　　　　　　　　　　　　　C. E. Jones

UNIVERSAL FELLOWSHIP OF METROPOLITAN COMMUNITY CHURCHES

See PERRY, TROY DEROY.

UNIVERSITIES

See BIBLE INSTITUTES, COLLEGES, UNIVERSITIES; SEMINARIES AND GRADUATE SCHOOLS.

UNPARDONABLE SIN

See BLASPHEMY AGAINST THE HOLY SPIRIT.

UPPER ROOM MISSION

Founded in the fall of 1906, this Pentecostal mission located at 327½ South Spring Street in Los Angeles, California, became for several years the "strongest" mission in town. Established by the former pastor of the First Baptist Church in Glendale, Elmer Kirk Fisher, the mission was formed with the help of several families from Glendale as well as many of the white people who were originally at the Azusa Street Mission. In February 1911 when William Durham came to Los Angeles from Chicago seeking to preach, he went first to the Upper Room Mission. Fisher did not allow him to do so, however, because of his views on sanctification. Durham then went to the Azusa Street Mission.

The Upper Room was located on the second floor of an office building. Poorly ventilated, it consisted of a three-hundred-seat auditorium, three small apartments, and several tiny rooms that served as offices. The motto adopted by the congregation was "Exalt Jesus Christ; Honor the Holy Ghost."

Worship services were held three times each Sunday (11:00 A.M., 3:00 P.M., and 7:30 P.M.). Each Monday evening a group of German-speaking Pentecostals, who were considered part of the congregation but who had a service of their own, held services in the facility. Bible studies, generally surveys of such books as Acts, Romans, Daniel, and Hebrews were conducted from 11:00 A.M.– 1:00 P.M. each Tuesday through Friday. On each of those days, there also were evening meetings beginning at 7:30. The last week of the month was set aside to conduct baptismal services (Wednesday) and to celebrate the Lord's Supper (Thursday). Baptismal services were generally held near Terminal Island in the Los Angeles harbor and were attended by hundreds.

In addition to the meetings held at the main facility on Spring Street, people from the mission gathered together each evening and conducted two or three street meetings in Los Angeles, often targeting bars and the red-light district. At times the youth group led such meetings in neighboring Glendale.

The impact of the Upper Room may be assessed partially in the number of missionaries and missionary projects it helped to support. This was documented in a more or less monthly publication of the mission begun in June 1909 and jointly edited by Elmer K. Fisher and George B. Studd. Studd, however, did most of the editorial work. Like many of the early Pentecostal periodicals, *The Upper Room*, as it was called, printed articles that had already appeared in other Pentecostal publications, letters from missionaries, responses to the paper, personal testimonies, and articles by the staff. The periodical ran at least through May 1911.

The issue of tongues as the "Bible evidence" of baptism in the Spirit was very important to this mission. Azusa appears to have been more fluid on the subject and in 1915 rejected the idea completely, coming to view tongues as a sign or gift that might follow the baptism. Fisher, however, repeatedly kept the issue before his readers.

Bibliography: C. Brumback, *Suddenly . . . From Heaven* (1961); W. Frodsham, "A Pentecostal Journey in Canada, British Columbia, and the Western States," *Confidence* 4 (6, 1911): 139; *The Upper Room* 1 (1, 1909); *The Upper Room* 2 (5, 1911).　　C. M. Robeck, Jr.

URQUHART, COLIN

URQUHART, COLIN (1940–). Founder of the Bethany Fellowship in Sussex, England, and a prominent teacher and minister within the charismatic movement in Europe. Ordained in 1964, Colin Urquhart was baptized in the Spirit early in his ministry at St. Hugh's Church, Lewsey, Luton (1970–76), where he was instrumental in building up one of the leading charismatic Anglican parishes in Britain. Since 1976 he has concentrated on an international teaching and healing ministry centered from 1978 on the interdenominational Bethany Fellowship, consisting in 1986 of some 150 members. This ministry, focusing on "kingdom faith," has increasingly crossed church boundaries. Urquhart's story is told in *When the Spirit Comes* (1974) and *Faith for the Future* (1982). His other books include *Anything You Ask* (1978), *The Positive Kingdom* (1985), and *Receive Your Healing* (1986). His wife, Caroline, has authored *His God, My God* (1983).

P. D. Hocken

costal Assemblies of the World in 1923. In 1925 he became a founding member of the Emmanuel's Church of Jesus Christ, serving as its first foreign missions secretary. Beginning in 1917, Urshan published the periodical *The Witness of God*. He is the author of several books, including *The Life of Andrew D. Urshan* (n.d.), *The Almighty God in the Lord Jesus Christ* (1919), *My Study of Modern Pentecostals* (n.d.), *Apostolic Faith Doctrine of the New Birth* (n.d), *Timely Messages of Comfort* (1918), *The Supreme Need of the Hour* (1923), *Timely Messages of Warning* (1917), and *The Doctrine of Redemption of the Body* (1925). He was known as the Persian evangelist.

Bibliography: A. L. Clanton, *United We Stand* (1970).

J. L. Hall

A native of Persia, Andrew D. Urshan returned to his native land as a Pentecostal during the early years of the movement. He later embraced the Oneness teaching.

URSHAN, ANDREW DAVID

URSHAN, ANDREW DAVID (1884–1967). Pentecostal preacher, missionary, and author. The oldest son of a Presbyterian pastor in Iran, Urshan immigrated to the U.S. in 1901. While living in Chicago, he received the Holy Spirit in 1908 and established a Persian mission. He was ordained by William Durham in 1910. In 1914 Urshan returned to Iran as a missionary. During World War I he became a refugee in Russia for several months during 1915 and 1916, establishing Pentecostal churches in Tiflis, Armaear, and Leningrad. It was at Leningrad that he was baptized in the name of Jesus Christ. Urshan served as foreign missions secretary in the Pente-

Nathaniel A. Urshan is the general superintendent of the United Pentecostal Church, International, and speaker for the *Harvestime* radio program.

URSHAN, NATHANIEL ANDREW

URSHAN, NATHANIEL ANDREW (1920–). General superintendent of the United Pentecostal Church, International (UPC; 1978–). The son of Andrew D. Urshan, he was born in Minnesota but spent his early years in several other states. Urshan began evangelizing in 1941 and later pastored in New York City before he accepted the pastorate of Calvary Tabernacle in Indianapolis, Indiana. He continued to pastor this large and influential church until 1979. In 1961 Urshan became the speaker on "Harvestime," the radio program of the UPC, and he remains a speaker on this program. He served as assistant general superintendent of the UPC from 1972 to 1977. In 1978 he was elected to the office of general superintendent.

J. L. Hall

UTTERBACH, CLINTON AND SARAH
(1931–) (1937–). Pastors of the Redeeming
Love Christian Center, one of the largest (2,600)
predominantly black independent charismatic
congregations on the East Coast. "Clint," an
accomplished musician and composer and former
director of the Utterbach Concert Ensemble,
along with wife, Sarah, a former corporate executive, came under the teaching of Kenneth Copeland. Through his assistance, they attended Rhema Bible Training Center. While at Rhema, they
also traveled with Kenneth Hagin as part of his
crusade team. In 1980 they founded Redeeming
Love Christian Center in their home. The congregation moved to Teanech, New Jersey, in 1982
before settling in its present location in 1985 in
Nanuet, New York. The Utterbachs also operate a
national broadcast, a preschool learning center,
and a music ministry. Their central message is
"the authority of the believer" based on a covenant relationship with God through the new
birth. The Utterbach's ministry features an emphasis on biblical teaching, total prosperity (spiritual, mental, physical, financial, and social),
ordinances of baptism and the Lord's Supper, the
acceptance of women in ministry, and a witness
for strong family life modeled on their own
marriage.

Bibliography: K. Dow, "Nanuet Church Gets
Message Across in Style," *Rockland County Journal-News*
(June 2, 1987), 1ff.; C. Utterbach, "Heirs to the
Promise," *Horizons Unlimited* 1 (1987): 4ff; S. Utter-
bach, "Heirs Can Afford to Wait," *Horizons Unlimited* 1
(1987): 8–10.   H. D. Trulear

V

A. C. Valdez, Sr., became a Pentecostal as a result of his contact with the Azusa Street Mission. He held successful meetings in Australia in the 1920s.

VAAGENES, MORRIS G. C., JR. (1929–). Senior pastor of North Heights Lutheran Church (American Lutheran Church), St. Paul, Minnesota, a congregation prominently identified with the Lutheran charismatic movement. Vaagenes graduated from Augsburg Theological Seminary, Minneapolis, in 1954. He received the D.Min. from Luther-Northwestern Seminary, St. Paul, in 1979.

Vaagenes and his wife served as missionaries in Madagascar until a health problem with one of their children forced them to return to the U.S. In 1961 he was called to North Heights, a congregation with a few hundred members. He and his wife experienced the baptism with the Holy Spirit in 1962. His weekly Bible study became a gathering place for the nascent charismatic renewal in the Minneapolis–St. Paul area.

The congregation grew dramatically in a major expression of charismatic renewal among Lutherans in that area as well as internationally, with the annual International Institute on Church Renewal and the two-year program of the International Lay Ministry Training Center.

By the mid 1980s the congregation had grown to more than four thousand members.

Bibliography: L. Christenson, ed., *Welcome, Holy Spirit* (1987). L. Christenson

VALDEZ, A. C., SR. (1896–1988). Evangelist and missionary. A. C. Valdez, Sr., attended the historic Azusa Street meetings as a boy from 1906–09. The Valdez family was Roman Catholic, having been influenced by a Franciscan-style of Catholicism that believed in the gifts of the Spirit, including speaking in tongues (Valdez, 1980, 22). The Valdez family embraced the outpouring of the Spirit at Azusa Street and became part of the revival that resulted from those meetings. Ordained by a mission in Long Beach, California, in 1916, Valdez moved quickly from part-time ministry into a long fruitful life of preaching the gospel around the world. Together with his son, A. C. Valdez, Jr., he held campaigns in South America, Australia, New Zealand, India, China, Japan, the South Sea Islands, and Hawaii. After the death of his first wife he continued his evangelistic ministry and frequently preached for his son at his successful church, Milwaukee Evangelistic Temple. After the death of his son, Valdez continued his ministry and appeared on the "700 Club" and the "PTL Club," telling of his early experiences in the founding of the Pentecostal Movement.

Bibliography: A. C. Valdez, Sr., *Fire on Azusa Street* (1980). J. R. Zeigler

VAN CLEAVE, NATHANIEL MOORE (1907–). Foursquare pastor, educator, and executive. He was born to Herbert Roland and Elsie Chase Van Cleave in Fort Smith, Arkansas. He studied at L.I.F.E. Bible College (Th.D., 1943), Los Angeles Baptist Theological Seminary, and the extension division of the University of California. Van Cleave was ordained in the International Church of the Foursquare Gospel (ICFG) in 1929 and married Lois Standlee the following year; they have two children. Pastoral ministry began in 1930 in Lamar, Colorado, and continued later in Van Nuys, California; Decatur, Illinois; Pasadena and Long Beach, California; and Portland, Oregon. From 1943 to 1949 he served as a missionary to the West Indies. At different times he also served on the faculty of L.I.F.E. Bible College, including a year as president of the school (1976–77). He received the status of professor emeritus in 1985.

Van Cleave's executive responsibilities in the ICFG included that of district supervisor (1954–60, 1968–76), interim general supervisor (1981, 1986), and membership on the board of directors (1976–80) and missionary cabinet (1954–88). He also served on the board of regents of L.I.F.E. Bible College (1976–87). For his service to the denomination, the latter conferred an honorary D.D. on him in 1970.

Van Cleave's publications include *Handbook of Preaching* (1943) and (with Guy P. Duffield) *Foundations of Pentecostal Theology* (1983).

Bibliography: Resume supplied to this writer; *Who's Who in Religion,* 3d ed. (1985).   G. B. McGee

VAN DUSEN, HENRY PITNEY (1897–1975). Theologian and seminary president. The appearance in the June 9, 1958, issue of *Life* magazine of "The Third Force in Christendom," by Henry P. Van Dusen, sent waves of self-affirmation into the Pentecostal world. In it the president of the liberal Union Theological Seminary (N.Y.) described in highly complimentary terms mission successes of Pentecostal, Holiness, Adventist, and Church of Christ groups. Unused to such praise from outsiders, Pentecostals eagerly adopted "Third Force" as being particularly applicable to them. In 1962 the Canadian Pentecostal Gordon F. Atter (b. 1905) even used the phrase as the title of his general history of the world movement. Secular historians such as William McLoughlin (b. 1922) were less sure of its applicability, however. A Presbyterian, Van Dusen devoted his entire career to theological education.

Bibliography: G. F. Atter, *The Third Force* (1962); W. G. McLoughlin, "Is There a Third Force in Christendom?" *Daedalus* 96 (Winter 1967): 43–68; H. P. Van Dusen, "The Third Force in Christendom," *Life* 44 (June 9, 1958): 113–22, 124.   C. E. Jones

VASSAR, THEODORE ROOSEVELT (1909–75). Minister and missionary. Ted Vassar was born in Tryon, Oklahoma, the son to Dr. John Alexander and Lenora Isabelle (Scott) Vassar. He graduated in 1930 from Southwestern Bible School (later Southwestern AG College) in Enid, Oklahoma, where he had studied under P. C. Nelson. Two years later, Vassar married Freddie Estelle Barnett (1912–1980), a flamboyant lady evangelist with a "call to India."

After pastoring AG churches in Texas and Oklahoma, the Vassars became missionaries to Maharashtra State, India, in 1937. Following their first term of service in Pune, they were placed in charge of the Boys' Orphanage, a farming project, and an elementary school in Junnar. Vassar also served as superintendent of the South India District Council of the AG, although he labored to make the Indian church self-supporting and self-governing. It was his vision that those under his care be encouraged into full-time ministry. He was not disappointed, as dozens of orphans followed him into Christian service, among them Benjamin Shinde (late professor at Southern Asia Bible College, Bangalore) and Solomon Wasker (missionary to the province of Assam, and pastor in Bombay).

The Vassars returned to the United States in 1952, pastoring several churches in Texas. Ted Vassar had a ministry to youth and a ministry of teaching, balancing evangelism with social action. He was known as a "thinking Pentecostal," emphasizing the importance of exercising creative and cognitive gifts in Christian service.

Five children were born to the Vassars: Bobby Joe (1935–1937), Ruth Lenora [Burgess] (1939–), Theodore Roosevelt, Jr. (1943–), Helen Elizabeth [Sullivan] (1945–), and Rose Marie (1948). Two children, Bobby Joe and Rose Marie, died on the mission field from disease.

Bibliography: Ruth V. Burgess, "Obeying the Great Commission: The Acts of Obedience of Ted and Estelle Vassar," unpublished, 1983; interviews with Ruth Vassar Burgess and Helen Elizabeth Sullivan, March–April 1988.   S. M. Burgess

VATICAN II

I. Description. The Second Vatican Council is the twenty-first of the councils that the Catholic church reckons as "ecumenical"—that is, as councils of the universal church. Of these twenty-one councils, eight took place in the first millennium, before the split between Eastern and Western Christianity; ten were councils of the pre-Reformation Western church, and three of the post-Reformation Roman Catholic church.

Vatican II was by far the most global of these councils, for it brought together about 2,400 Catholic bishops from every continent and from practically every country in the world. Every Catholic bishop, whether of the Latin rite or of one of the Eastern rites, whether actually in charge of a diocese or not, was invited to take part with full voting rights. Along with the bishops, about a hundred general superiors of the religious orders of men (such as the Benedictines, Franciscans, and Jesuits) also participated with full voting rights.

The new approach to the ecumenical movement that Pope John XXIII intended the council to take was already shown prior to the opening of the council in his establishment of the Vatican Secretariat for Promoting Christian Unity and in the invitation extended to the other Christian churches and church federations to send their delegates as official observers to the council. The number of such delegated observers increased from forty-nine, representing seventeen churches or federations during the first period of the council, to ninety-nine, representing twenty-eight churches or federations in the final period. These observers were invited to attend all the sessions of the council, were given all the documents distributed to the bishops, and had many opportunities to meet the bishops and discuss the matter before the council with them in various formal and informal meetings.

II. Chronology. The surprise announcement of his intention to summon an ecumenical council was made by Pope John XXIII on January 25, 1959. Within the following year the various preparatory commissions were established, and all the Catholic bishops, heads of religious orders, and faculties of theology were requested to submit their proposals regarding possible agenda for the council. In July 1962 invitations went out to the other Christian churches to send delegates as official observers.

The solemn opening of the council took place on October 11, 1962. The first period ended on December 8 without the promulgation of any completed document. Perhaps the most significant feature of that first period was the manifestation of the fact that a large majority of the bishops were dissatisfied with the work that had been done by the preparatory commissions. It became evident that a new, more progressive approach to many questions would be taken by the new commissions that had been established by the council, along with the help of the theologians whom the bishops had brought to Rome as their advisors. These commissions worked not only during the periods when the council was in session but during the intervals as well.

Pope John XXIII lived to see only the first period of the council that he had summoned. His death on June 3, 1963, had the effect of automatically suspending the council. However, the first official act of his successor, Pope Paul VI, was to announce that the work of the council should go forward.

The second period lasted from September 29 to December 4, 1963, and concluded with the promulgation of the Constitution on the Sacred Liturgy and the Decree on the Instruments of Social Communication. This period was very largely taken up with the discussion of the draft of the document on the church: the one generally considered the most basic document of the council and certainly the one that was most keenly debated. Consensus was reached through the process of taking a distinct vote on every crucial paragraph of the text.

The third period, from September 14 to November 21, 1964, closed with the promulgation of three important documents, all having to do with Catholic doctrine about the church: the Dogmatic Constitution on the Church, the Decree on Ecumenism, and the Decree on the Eastern Catholic Churches.

During the course of the fourth and final period, from September 14 to December 8, 1965, the remaining eleven documents were promulgated: on October 28 the Decree on the Bishop's Pastoral Office, the Decree on the Renewal of Religious Life, the Decree on Priestly Formation, the Declaration on Christian Education, and the Declaration on the Relationship of the Church to the Non-Christian Religions. On November 18 the Dogmatic Constitution on Divine Revelation and the Decree on the Apostolate of the Laity were promulgated, followed on December 7 by the Declaration on Religious Freedom, the Decree on the Ministry and Life of Priests, and the Pastoral Constitution on the Church in the Modern World.

A few days before the solemn close of the council, a "Prayer Service for Promoting Christian Unity" was held, with the participation of the observers from the other Christian communities, along with Pope Paul VI and the whole assembly of the council.

III. Doctrine. As it would be impossible, within the limits of this article, to give even a brief summary of the contents of the sixteen documents produced by Vatican II, I shall only indicate some of the highlights of the documents that would be of most interest to the readers of this dictionary.

A. The Dogmatic Constitution on the Church. While two documents of Vatican II are entitled "Dogmatic Constitutions," in neither of them did the council define any doctrine as a "dogma of faith"—an action that would have had the effect of condemning the contrary doctrine as heretical. Following the direction that Pope John XXIII gave to the council in his opening address, where he called for a council whose exercise of its teaching authority would be "predominantly pastoral in character," the council sought to express Catholic doctrine positively, in language that would be better adapted to a modern mentality, rather than to condemn contrary points of view.

In contrast to what had been the typical Catholic description of the church as a hierarchically structured society, Vatican II began by presenting the church as a mystery of faith, having its origin in the mystery of the Trinity. Various aspects of this mystery were then illustrated by the multiple images that are found in Scripture, in recognition of the impossibility of adequately expressing the nature of the church in any one description of it. A highly significant change was made in the text, when the previous assertion of identity between the Church of Christ and the Roman Catholic church was dropped in favor of saying that the Church of Christ subsists in the Catholic church, while many elements of sanctification and truth are found outside its visible structure. This decision led the way to a more explicit recognition of the ecclesiastical reality of the other Christian communities, in the Decree on Ecumenism.

While previous Catholic ecclesiology had stressed the notion of the church as "mystical body of Christ," Vatican II preferred the equally biblical concept of the church as "people of God," thus putting a stronger accent on the historical reality of the church as a body of people who had to struggle with weakness and sin on their pilgrim way to the Kingdom of God. It is also significant that the chapter on the church as people of God comes before the chapter on the hierarchical structure of the church. The main achievement of this chapter was to clarify the role of bishops: determining that they receive their offices of ruling and teaching not from the pope, but by their sacramental ordination to the episcopate, and that they constitute a body or "college" which shares with the pope the pastoral care of the universal church. The "Synod of Bishops" that now meets every three years to discuss matters of concern to the whole church is one fruit of Vatican II's doctrine of episcopal collegiality.

B. The Dogmatic Constitution on Divine Revelation. After an introductory chapter on the nature of revelation and the response of faith, the major portion of this document is devoted to the question of the ways in which this revelation is handed on in the church. Here the first question that needed to be clarified was whether tradition is rightly seen as a source of revelation, distinct from Holy Scripture. The answer of Vatican II, which in fact is also the answer of the Council of Trent, is that there is but one source of revelation: the gospel itself, which was handed on by the apostles both in writing and by their preaching and example. "Now what was handed on by the apostles includes everything which contributes to the holiness of life, and the increase in faith of the People of God; and so the church, in her teaching, life and worship, perpetuates and hands on to all generations all that she herself is, all that she believes." Hence, while sacred Scripture is the Word of God, inasmuch as this Word was put in writing under divine inspiration, the Word of God is also handed on in the faith and life of the church, where there can also be authentic growth in the understanding of what God has revealed.

The greater part of this document (four of its six chapters) can be described as an instruction addressed to the Catholic faithful as to how they should esteem, read, and understand the Bible. While insisting that the Bible must be interpreted in the light of the church's faith, it also recognizes the important contributions that modern biblical scholarship can make to our grasp of the authentic meaning of the sacred text.

C. The Decree on Ecumenism. The Decree on Ecumenism is the official declaration of the Catholic church's decision to participate fully in the modern ecumenical movement. It begins with the recognition that this movement, which began among the "separated brethren," was "fostered by the grace of the Holy Spirit." It goes on to admit that men of both sides were to blame for the developments that have led to the disunity of the Christian people and that all are called to repentance as the first step toward reunion. Going beyond the admission of the presence of "elements of sanctification and truth" outside the limits of the Catholic church, the decree recognizes that the "sacred actions of the Christian religion" that are carried out in other churches can truly engender a life of holiness and lead to salvation. From this the conclusion is drawn that these separated churches and communities as such are being used by the Holy Spirit as means of grace and salvation for their adherents. This positive assessment of the salvific role of the other churches is balanced by the assertion that it is only the Catholic church that is believed to possess the fullness of the means of grace and that it is in the Catholic church that the unity that Christ gave to the church has been preserved, as an endowment that the church can never lose.

D. The Declaration on Religious Liberty. The Declaration on Religious Liberty is the only document of the council that has a subtitle spelling out the limits of the question that it is going to treat. This subtitle reads, "On the rights of the person and communities to social and civil liberty in religious matters." The essential teaching of this document is that the dignity of the human person requires that every person be free from coercion on the part of any human power whatever, in such wise that no one is to be forced to act in a manner contrary to his religious beliefs, or to be restrained from acting in accordance with his beliefs, provided that the just requirements of public order are observed. Since this declaration is addressed to the whole world, its primary argument is one that ought to appeal to all people, whatever their religious beliefs. However, in the second part of the document, it is shown how consonant this teaching is with the fundamental tenet of Christian faith that the act of faith must be a free response of man to God.

There can be no doubt that this declaration is the fruit of a development of Catholic thinking with regard to the rightful exercise of religious liberty to non-Catholics in countries where Catholicism enjoys special legal recognition as the religion of the great majority of the people. The position of Vatican II is clearly stated in the following sentence: "If, in view of peculiar circumstances obtaining among certain peoples, special legal recognition is given in the constitutional order of society to one religious body, it is at the same time imperative that the right of all citizens and religious bodies to religious freedom should be recognized and made effective in practice." Later on a frank admission of past failure to observe this principle is made: "In the life of the People of God as it has made its pilgrim way through the vicissitudes of human history, there have at times appeared ways of acting which were less in accord with the spirit of the gospel and even opposed to it." Here we see a practical fruit of a fundamental choice made earlier by the council, to view the church not as a "perfect society," but as a "pilgrim people of God."

See also CATHOLIC CHARISMATIC RENEWAL; CHARISMATIC MOVEMENT; DIALOGUE, ROMAN CATHOLIC AND CLASSICAL PENTECOSTAL.

Bibliography: W. M. Abbott, ed., *The Documents of Vatican II* (1966); A. Flannery, ed., *Vatican Council II. The Conciliar and Post Conciliar Documents* (1975); H. Vorgrimler, ed., *Commentary on the Documents of Vatican II* 5 (1967–69). F. A. Sullivan

VERHOEF, W. W. (1928–). Pioneer leader in the charismatic movement in Holland. While a theological student in the Dutch Reformed church in 1951, Verhoef was baptized in the Spirit as he was prayed over by a faith healer. Associating briefly with a movement known as *Stromen van Kracht* (Streams of Power), Verhoef began his own charismatic monthly, *Vuur* (Fire), in March 1957, when his former colleagues started to rebaptize. As editor, he sought to promote charismatic renewal within the historic churches on an ecumenical basis and soon had wide representation on the editorial board, including a Catholic priest as early as 1964. In 1972 *Vuur* with Verhoef became one of the main component elements in the *Charismatische Werkgemeenschap Nederland* (Dutch Charismatic Working Fellowship). Verhoef's contribution in Holland has been important through his leadership of national conventions; his sponsoring of days of theological reflection; and his writings, none of which are available in English.

Bibliography: C. and P. van der Laan, *Pinksteren in Beweging*. P. D. Hocken

VINEYARD CHRISTIAN FELLOWSHIP

Vineyard Christian Fellowship refers to a group of more than 250 churches led by John Wimber, founding pastor of the central church of the organization, Vineyard Christian Fellowship of Anaheim, California. The church, which reported membership of five thousand in 1987, was started by Wimber's wife, Carol, in a home fellowship meeting in October 1976. The first public service was held in May 1977 with John Wimber as pastor under the name of Calvary Chapel of Yorba Linda, California. It remained associated with Chuck Smith's Calvary Chapel fellowship until 1983, when Wimber decided to join a group of six churches called "Vineyards," led by Kenn Gulliksen.

The churches are affiliated organizationally under the Association of Vineyard Churches, established in 1985 and administered by Wimber's associate, Sam Thompson. Six regional pastoral coordinators report to Thompson.

The Vineyard Ministries International is an umbrella organization that supervises and coordinates the ministries of John Wimber and his colleagues nationally and internationally through seminars, books, tapes, and other resources.

Bibliography: K. N. Springer, "Applying the Gifts to Everyday Life," *Charisma* (September 1985), 26–34; T. Stafford, "Testing the Wine from John Wimber's Vineyard," *Christianity Today* (August 8, 1986), 17–22; C. P. Wagner, ed., *Signs and Wonders Today* (1987); C. Wimber, "A Hunger for God," *Riding the Third Wave*, J. Wimber and K. Springer, eds. (1987); *The Winepress* (1987).   C. P. Wagner

VINGREN, ADOLF GUNNAR (1879–1933). Swedish Pentecostal missionary. Vingren was born in Ostra Husby Parish, Ostergötland, Sweden. In 1897 Vingren became a member of the Swedish Baptist movement after he was baptized in a church in Wraka, Smaland. He came to the U.S. in 1903, and while living with his uncle in Kansas, he worked as a laborer until he decided in 1905 to attend the Swedish Department of the University of Chicago Divinity School. Upon graduation in 1909 he became the pastor of a Swedish Baptist church in Menominee, Michigan.

Shortly afterward, while visiting Sweden, Vingren came into contact with the country's Pentecostal movement. Upon his return to Chicago, he attended a Pentecostal conference sponsored by the First Swedish Baptist church and converted to Pentecostalism. Vingren traveled back to Michigan, resigned from his pastorate, and returned to Chicago. While in Chicago, Vingren attended several Pentecostal churches, including William H. Durham's North Avenue Mission and the Svenska Pingst Forsamlingen, Chicago's first Scandinavian Pentecostal church.

During the summer of 1910 Vingren accepted the pastorate of a Swedish Baptist church in South Bend, Indiana. During a Saturday evening prayer meeting, Adolf Uldine, a member of the church, prophesied to Vingren that he should go to Para and preach about Jesus. Shortly afterward, Uldine gave the same prophecy to Daniel Berg, whom Vingren had met a year earlier in Chicago. After finding out that Para was in Brazil, Vingren and Berg returned to Chicago and were dedicated as missionaries by Durham at the North Avenue Mission. They also visited the Svenska Pingst Forsamlingen and received nearly four hundred dollars from the church to help finance their trip to Brazil.

Together, Vingren and Berg left the U.S. on November 4 and arrived in Brazil two weeks later. After finding a Baptist church, they were invited to attend the church and live in the pastor's home. They were soon asked to leave the church, however, because of their Pentecostal preaching. Vingren and Berg, who were now living on their own, conducted evening services for the eighteen church members who had also left the Baptist Church. Less than a year later these persons decided to organize a church called the Apostolic Faith Mission in the home of Henrique Albuquerque at Rua Siqueira Mendes in the neighborhood of Cidade Velha. They elected Vingren as their pastor. When church members began to meet in the new home of Albuquerque at 224 Sao Jeronimo Avenue, they officially registered themselves as a church called the Assembly of God. From this small congregation grew the Assemblies of God, presently the largest Protestant denomination in Brazil.

During the next eighteen years, Vingren often went to Sweden and the U.S. to enlist support for his ministry in Brazil. He also traveled along the East Coast of Brazil to support the growing number of Pentecostal churches that had developed within this region's cities. In 1930 Vingren became very weak as a result of stomach cancer. He returned to Sweden in the fall of 1932 and died the following spring.

Bibliography: W. J. Hollenweger, *The Pentecostals* (1972); I. Vingren, *Pionjarens dagbok* (1968).

J. Colletti

VINYARD, RICHARD (1913–). Faith healer and Voice of Healing evangelist. Richard Vinyard was an Assemblies of God pastor during the first great William Branham crusade (1948) in Kansas City. Branham's ministry caused such a stir that Vinyard overheard two young men in Sunday school speculating as to why Pastor Vinyard was not used of God in the same way as Branham. This stirred the heart of Vinyard to speak to the boys, and in response to their question as to why he didn't do the same things as "Brother Branham," he had to confess, "I was not where I should be with God." Vinyard set himself to seek God, and after a period of several months he was awakened by God at 4:00 one morning and told that from that day on he would have a ministry of healing. Vinyard told the story to his church the next Sunday, and several were healed. This was the beginning of many years of fruitful ministry not only in the U.S. but in many foreign lands as well. Vinyard also served on the staff of *Voice of Healing* for several years during its early days.

Bibliography: G. Lindsay, "The Story of the Great Restoration Revival—Part IV," *World-wide Revival* (June 1958).   J. R. Zeigler

VOICE OF HEALING From April 1948 until May 1967, when the magazine *Voice of Healing* changed its name to *Christ for the Nations* (vol. 20, no. 2), Gordon Lindsay labored as its founder, editor, and director.

Voice of Healing began as a promotional tool for the William Branham revival meetings. No sooner had the first issue appeared, however, than Branham announced his retirement from active campaigning, leaving Lindsay with many subscriptions for a magazine that had unexpectedly lost its chief reason for being.

About the same time, other evangelists who were engaged in deliverance ministries began requesting coverage in *Voice of Healing*, which

These ministers who were associated with the Voice of Healing attended the second VOH convention in Kansas City, Dec. 19-21, 1950. Gordon Lindsay, founder of VOH is standing on the left.

Lindsay chose to grant. During the next ten years *Voice of Healing* became the primary voice of the worldwide salvation healing revivals, featuring the crusades and schedules of numerous evangelists and publishing photographs and documented accounts of miracles that occurred in these services (healings of the blind, deaf, crippled, and those with other ailments).

Though Lindsay was himself an Assemblies of God (AG) minister before entering the publishing field, his magazine was not intended as a promotion of that, or any other, denomination. Neither did the subscribers of *Voice of Healing* represent an organized denomination. Instead, "The avowed purpose of *Voice of Healing* from the beginning [was] not to become a denomination but to serve all groups. We ordained no ministers but encouraged them to remain in their own organizations and be a blessing there, but at the same time, ministering to, and recognizing the whole body of Christ" (*Voice of Healing* 10 [1, 1957]: 2). This explicit affirmation of an ecumenical spirit permeated *Voice of Healing* through the 1950s and well into the 1960s.

Rather than a denomination, *Voice of Healing* was, first, a magazine and second, a loosely knit fellowship of evangelists who shared the following characteristics: they had a mature healing ministry, accepted and subscribed to the articles of *Voice of Healing*'s constitution, had personal character that was above reproach, practiced the ideals of *Voice of Healing*'s fellowship, labored for unity among God's people, were willing and helpful in cultivating the circulation of *Voice of Healing*'s magazine, and they were evangelists— not pastors (*Voice of Healing* 5 [3, 1952]: 2).

Though *Voice of Healing* began as a fellowship

of American evangelists ministering in the U.S., a growing awareness of and commitment to foreign mission needs came to dominate the magazine in the late 1950s. By February 1958 Lindsay announced that *Voice of Healing* was changing its name with the next issue to *World-Wide Revival*, a move intended to reflect more fully the scope of the organization's world-wide activities. Though that name lasted only through July 1958, the foreign mission emphasis took over the magazine, while that of the American evangelists on the local campaign trail gradually disappeared.

During the late 1950s and early 1960s Tommy Hicks, R. W. Culpepper, David Nunn, Morris Cerullo, and others associated with *Voice of Healing* circled the world with their message of salvation in Jesus with attendant miracles of healing and deliverance. Reports concerning their crusades provided the bulk of many of those issues.

On the same page of that February 1958 issue of *Voice of Healing* Lindsay reported that he and other evangelists were "joining forces in an all out move for world-evangelization." Lindsay's own contributions to that effort came through several programs. He reviewed them in "The Story of the Winning the Nations Crusade" (*Voice of Healing* 19 [6, 1966]: 2–4, 14).

The Winning the Nations Crusade, as his work of world evangelism was known, had as its centerpiece an effort to raise monies that would establish funds to sponsor indigenous revival centers and churches (cf. *Voice of Healing* 10 [1, 1957]: 7). *Voice of Healing* contributed monies to a fund that in turn loaned these monies to a developing congregation for church building. The latter repaid the money interest free, which funds were again circulated. This effort, coupled with the Native Church Crusade (see *Voice of Healing* 17 [6, 1964]: 3, 15) had, by 1966, established or supported some 1,200 native churches. *Voice of Healing* reported the commissioning of some 1,500 native evangelists since 1953.

The Holy Land Crusade was the second important ministry of *Voice of Healing*. Since 1959 gospel teams had traversed Israel distributing messianic literature (some 170,000 books in 1965 alone).

Lindsay early recognized the importance of the written word for evangelization. Between 1954 and 1966, through the "Native Literature Crusade" and his world literature program, *Voice of Healing* distributed millions of pieces of gospel literature, including more than one hundred of Lindsay's own titles (some having circulations of 50,000–100,000 copies). In 1965 alone about 1 million books printed in a dozen languages and concerning a host of evangelical topics were distributed.

Finally, *Voice of Healing* sponsored international evangelistic radio programs. A more notable work was that in Central America, begun in 1957, with Paul Finkenbinder. *Christ for the Nations* reported that his ministry was being carried over several hundred radio stations in Central America, with 10,000 program releases per month.

The first issue of *Christ for the Nations* (20 [2, 1967]: 2) carried an editorial in which Lindsay wrote: "Divine healing is the means, and *Christ for the Nations* is the objective—and has been our objective from the beginning. Truly our call is to put the Gospel before all nations."

See also CHRIST FOR THE NATIONS INSTITUTE; HEALING MOVEMENTS.

Bibliography: G. Lindsay, ed., *The Voice of Healing*, vols. 1–20 (1948–67).   J. A. Hewett

VORONAEV, IVAN EFIMOVICH (b. 1886). Russian Pentecostal missionary. Voronaev was born in the province of Orenburg in central Russia. As a young man Voronaev served as a Cossack under the Tsar before his conversion in 1908. Shortly afterward, he served as a Baptist pastor in the Siberian cities of Irkutsk and Krasnoyarsk. During a period of severe persecution of Protestants by the state church, Voronaev left Russia for the U.S. He first settled in San Francisco and became a pastor of the Russian Baptist Church. Three years later he accepted an invitation to pastor the Russian Baptist Church in New York City. While in New York, he converted to Pentecostalism. As a result, Voronaev resigned from his pastorate and founded the first Russian Pentecostal church in New York City. He soon felt a deep conviction for his homeland and decided to return to Russia in 1920. There he helped establish several Pentecostal churches. Under the antireligious law of 1929, Voronaev was arrested and spent nearly the rest of his life in prison.

Bibliography: S. Durasoff, *Bright Wind of the Spirit: Pentecostalism Today* (1972); W. J. Hollenweger, *The Pentecostals* (1977); P. Voronaeff, *My Life in Soviet Russia* (1969).   J. Colletti

VOUGA, OSCAR (1903–1978). Pentecostal preacher and leader. Born in Missouri in a Presbyterian home, Vouga moved to California in 1921 and was converted to the Pentecostal movement in 1924. He held pastorates in Idaho, Alabama, Texas, Tennessee, Georgia, and Canada. Later responsibilities included being the general secretary of the Pentecostal Church, Incorporated (1944–45), and editor of *The Apostolic Herald* (1943–45), the official organ of the same organization. In 1945 Vouga served as the secretary for the joint committee, general board, and general conference that formed the United Pentecostal Church (UPC). He was the assistant general superintendent (1949–62) and the foreign missions director (1963–69) of the UPC. He is the author of *Our Gospel Message* (1967).

Bibliography: A. L. Clanton, *United We Stand* (1970).   J. L. Hall

W

WAGNER, CHARLES PETER (1930–). Missionary, educator, author, and church growth authority. C. Peter Wagner was born in New York City to C. Graham and Mary Wagner. In 1950 he married Doris Mueller; they have three children. Wagner earned degrees at the following institutions: Rutgers University (B.S., summa cum laude, 1952; Phi Beta Kappa), Fuller Theological Seminary (M.Div., 1955), Princeton Theological Seminary (Th.M., 1962), Fuller Theological Seminary School of World Mission (M.A. in Missiology, 1968), University of Southern California (Ph.D. in Social Ethics, 1977).

Ordained to the ministry in 1955 by the Conservative Congregational Christian Conference, Wagner and his wife traveled to Bolivia for missionary service under the South America Mission and Andes Evangelical Mission (now SIM International). During those years he served as a professor at George Allan Theological Seminary, Cochabamba (1962–71), and as associate general director of the Andes Evangelical Mission (1964–71).

Having studied under church growth specialist Donald A. McGavran, Wagner joined the faculty of Fuller Theological Seminary School of World Mission in 1971 as his understudy. He has served at Fuller in several capacities: vice-president, Charles E. Fuller Institute for Evangelism and Church Growth (1971–79), and professor in the School of World Mission (1971–). In 1984 he was appointed as the first Donald A. McGavran Professor of Church Growth. He also designed and taught, with John Wimber, the controversial course MC510, "Signs and Wonders."

With the formation of the Lausanne Committee for World Evangelization in 1974, Wagner became a charter member. For six years he served on its executive committee. He was the first chairperson of the Lausanne Strategy Working Group, which focused on reaching unreached peoples. With Edward R. Dayton he initiated and coedited the first three *Unreached Peoples* annuals.

In 1985 Wagner became the founding president of the North American Society for Church Growth. Wagner also coined the phrase "third wave" to describe noncharismatic Evangelicals who believe that signs and wonders of the Holy Spirit will accompany the proclamation of the gospel. Wagner's status as an authority on worldwide church growth, which has often highlighted the growth of Pentecostals and charismatics, can be traced to his own work in Latin America, research, frequent traveling, and extensive publications. A prolific writer, he has contributed many magazine and journal articles. His books include *Latin American Theology: Radical or Evangelical?* (1970), *The Protestant Movement in Bolivia* (1970), *Frontiers in Missionary Strategy* (1972),

Church/Mission Tensions Today (ed., 1972), *Look Out! The Pentecostals Are Coming* (1973; later, *What Are We Missing?*), *Your Church Can Grow: Seven Vital Signs of a Healthy Church* (1976), *Your Spiritual Gifts Can Help Your Church Grow* (1979), *Your Church Can Be Healthy* (1979), *Our Kind of People: The Ethical Dimensions of Church Growth in America* (1979), *Church Growth and the Whole Gospel* (1981), *Effective Body Building: Biblical Steps to Spiritual Growth* (1982), *Helping Your Church Grow* (1982), *On the Crest of the Wave: Becoming a World Christian* (1983), *Leading Your Church to Growth: The Secret of Pastor/People Partnership in Dynamic Church Growth* (1984), *Church Growth: State of the Art* (ed., 1986), *Strategies for Church Growth: Tools for Planning Evangelism and Missions* (1987), and *Signs and Wonders Today* (ed., rev. ed., 1987).

C. Peter Wagner is considered one of the leading church growth authorities in the world.

Bibliography: Resume supplied to this writer; "Testing the Wine from John Wimber's Vineyard," *Christianity Today* (August 8, 1986), 17–22; *Who's Who in Religion*, 3d ed. (1985).   G. B. McGee

WALDVOGEL, HANS R. (1893–1969). Pastor and founder of *The Bread of Life*. A native of Switzerland, Waldvogel was the son of Adam and Anna Waldvogel. Adam was a German Baptist minister who immigrated with his family of two sons and four daughters to Chicago in 1908. The children followed their father into

A leader among German Pentecostals in the U.S., Hans R. Waldvogel pastored the Ridgewood Pentecostal Church and founded the *Bread of Life* magazine.

ministry: both sons became Pentecostal pastors; two daughters married German Baptist pastors, and one served as a full-time Pentecostal church staff member.

Waldvogel came into contact with the Zion Faith Homes in 1919. He attended services there and was deeply influenced by two of the leaders of that independent Pentecostal center, Eugene Brooks and Martha Wing Robinson. The Zion Faith Homes did not accept evidential tongues. The leaders also looked askance at the ongoing "denominationalizing" of Pentecostalism. They stressed instead a Christocentric experiential piety similar to that espoused by A. B. Simpson, adding the practice of spiritual gifts and replacing premillennialism with an amillennial stress on the presence of God's kingdom within believers. They preserved a strong emphasis on divine healing, rooted in their participation with Zion's founder, John Alexander Dowie.

After training for the ministry by working under a pastor in Kenosha, Wisconsin, Waldvogel accepted a call to a small German Pentecostal mission in Brooklyn, New York, in 1925. In time, he transformed it into a thriving center of German Pentecostal outreaches known as the Ridgewood Pentecostal Church. Located in a predominantly German neighborhood in Brooklyn, the congregation soon added English services and supported aggressive evangelism, which resulted in the opening of other congregations around the city. From 1947 Waldvogel increasingly left pastoral responsibilities to his brother, Gottfried (a gradu-

ate of the Christian and Missionary Alliance's Nyack College in its institute days), and his nephew, Edwin Waldvogel. He traveled as an evangelist in Germany, Switzerland, and Austria, where he conducted large tent campaigns that both helped establish new congregations and nurtured war-devastated older groups.

In the U.S. Waldvogel not only gave leadership to a network of independent Pentecostal congregations but also preached weekly on a half-hour German radio program; founded a monthly periodical, *The Bread of Life*, which extended the Pentecostal emphases of the early Zion Faith Home leaders to others interested in the "deeper" life; established a camp in upstate New York; and conducted a faith home in Woodhaven, New York.   E. L. Blumhofer

WALKEM, CHARLES WILLIAM (d. 1982). Musician, pastor, teacher, and author. During the 1930s and 1940s Walkem collaborated with Aimee Semple McPherson by arranging much of her music, "setting down the strains at her dictation." Walkem's musical career spanned three decades, beginning in the 1920s and continuing long after the death of McPherson in 1944. A number of his arrangements may be found in the *Foursquare Hymnal* (1937). He was particularly used to help write and arrange songs for L.I.F.E. Bible College, such as "Long Live LIFE" (1945) and "L.I.F.E., I Love You" (1946), and to edit and arrange many of the tunes in McPherson's sacred operas, such as "Bells of Bethlehem."

In 1931 Walkem accompanied Aimee Semple McPherson and her entourage in a trip around the world as she recouperated from a breakdown brought on by overwork. During this period they worked together on her sacred operas. Upon their arrival in New York he acted as the family spokesperson, indicating to members of the press that she was still too ill to handle the fatigue of a press interview.

Ordained by the International Church of the Foursquare Gospel, Walkem was used widely as a speaker and teacher. A "self-made scholar," he was the author of a number of smaller pamphlets on theological subjects. He held an honorary D.D. from L.I.F.E. Bible College (1943) and served on the faculty from 1930 to 1978.

Bibliography: S. F. Middlebrook, *Preaching from a Pentecostal Perspective* (1970); "Poet of the Piano," *Foursquare World Advance* (January–February 1983), 14; L. Thomas, *Storming Heaven* (1970).
C. M. Robeck, Jr.

WALKER, DAVID DAVILLO ("LITTLE DAVID") (1934–). Evangelist. As a child of traveling evangelists, Walker's early home was typically a "converted bus, house truck, [or a] tent" (Walker, n.d., 3). Born in Phoenix, Arizona, he was in Dallas by age six; Cudahy, Wisconsin, as a seven year old; and Long Beach, California, at age nine.

Both Walker and his parents had been healed by God in his early years: his father of burns, his mother of cancer in advanced stages, and he himself of poisonous snake bites and an eye infection that had led to blindness. After a three-day fast and prayer time, he was healed of his

At the age of 9, David Walker was called to preach. To thousands in North America and in foreign countries he became known as "Little David Walker," the boy evangelist.

blindness and baptized in the Holy Spirit (Walker, n.d., 7–10).

Walker preached his first sermon at age nine in Colton, California, where he reported he was changed from a little boy to a "minister and soul winner for the Kingdom" (Walker, n.d., 13). He began a deliverance and healing ministry that ranged up the Pacific Coast, into Mexico, and Jamaica. When he was fourteen he preached in the Royal Albert Hall, London, for two weeks, as well as Birmingham, England, and Paris, France.

At age seventeen Walker began a church in Lansing, Michigan. After a five-year pastorate, in March 1958 he joined R. W. Culpepper's round-the-world evangelistic, healing campaign.

Walker faded from the revival-healing scene after appearing at the Second World Convention of Deliverance Evangelists (summer 1963). In 1976 he was ordained with the Assemblies of God. He continues to evangelize in North America and in overseas campaigns.

Bibliography: D. D. Walker, *Little David's Life Story: He Began Preaching at the Age of Nine* (n.d.); "Little David's Life Story" *Voice of Healing* 12 (10, 1960): 8–9, 14–15.   J. A. Hewett

WALKER, JOHN HERBERT, JR. (1928–). Missionary and educator of the Church of God (CG, Cleveland, Tenn.). The son of J. H. Walker, a veteran Pentecostal leader, J. Herbert Walker, Jr., grew up in the Pentecostal movement. He earned academic degrees at Vanderbilt University (B.A., 1947), George Peabody College (M.A., 1953), Vanderbilt School of Religion (M.Div., 1955), and the University of Tennessee (Ph.D., 1967).

Walker and his wife, Lucille, were missionaries to Haiti from 1947 to 1952. He then was an administrator for Latin America (1955–57), Europe, the Middle East (1970–76), and Church of God World Missions (1980–84). He served as executive director (1984–88). In the area of education Walker was academic dean and professor of sociology at Lee College (1957–70) and coordinator of education for missions (1976–80). His literary works include *Haiti* (1950) and *God's Living Room* (1971).

Bibliography: Archives of the Church of God (Cleveland, Tenn.); C. W. Conn, *Where the Saints Have Trod* (1959).   C. W. Conn

WALKER, J. HERBERT, SR. (1900–1976). Fourth general overseer of the Church of God (CG, Cleveland, Tenn.) and a Pentecostal minister and leader for more than fifty years. A native of Louisiana, Herbert Walker began his ministry in the CG in 1922. After serving as president of Lee College (1930–35), Walker was elected general overseer at the age of thirty-five, the youngest man ever chosen, serving for nine years (1935–44). His other executive positions were editor-in-chief of CG publications (1946–48) and director of CG world missions (1948–52).

Walker was a member of the constitution committee of the National Association of Evangelicals in 1942 and the Pentecostal World Conference in 1949. He was a strong voice in bringing the Pentecostal movement to its present role of leadership and cooperation in the evangelical world.

Bibliography: Archives of the Church of God (Cleveland, Tenn.); C. W. Conn, *Like a Mighty Army* (rev. 1977).   C. W. Conn

WALKER, PAUL HAVEN (1901–1975). A Pentecostal pioneer from North Dakota, whose ministry in the Church of God (CG, Cleveland, Tenn.) and the Pentecostal world spanned fifty-six years. In 1919 Walker began a new field ministry that established churches in Maryland, North Dakota, South Dakota, and Minnesota. His later ministry as state overseer and executive missions secretary of the CG (1952–58) was largely administrative. He led in establishing churches in ten mission fields in Latin America, Europe, and Asia.

Active in worldwide Pentecostal ministry, Walker was a member of the Pentecostal World Conference advisory board (1955–58) and the Evangelical Foreign Missions Association. He produced two books: *The Baptism With the Holy Ghost and the Evidence* (c. 1935) and his autobiography, *Paths of a Pioneer* (1971).

Bibliography: C. W. Conn, *Our First 100 Years* (1986); P. H. Walker, *Paths of a Pioneer* (1971).   C. W. Conn

WALKER, PAUL LAVERNE (1932–). Senior pastor of the Mt. Paran Church of God in Atlanta, Georgia. Born in Minot, North Dakota, the son of Pentecostal pioneer Paul H. Walker, he holds degrees from Lee College, Presbyterian College (B.A., 1953), Emory University (B.D., 1964), and Georgia State University (M.Ed., 1970; Ph.D., 1972).

During the 1950s Walker pastored churches in South Carolina and Florida and in 1960 became pastor of the 565-member Mt. Paran congregation. In 1987 the church had 6,432 members in multiple sanctuaries.

Walker is a staff member of the Atlanta Counseling Center and a prominent speaker at interdenominational conferences. Among his published books are *The Ministry of Church and Pastor* (1965), *Counseling Youth* (1967), *Knowing the Future* (1976), *Understanding the Bible and Sci-*

ence (1976), *Courage for Crisis Living* (1978), and *How to Keep Your Joy* (1987).

Bibliography: Files of the Mt. Paran Church of God (Atlanta).   C. W. Conn

WALKER, ROBERT ALANDER (1912–). Magazine editor, author, and publisher. Born in Syracuse, New York, he married Jean Browning Clements in 1937. After earning a B.S. (1936) and M.S. (1941) from Northwestern University, Walker became the founder and editor of *HIS Magazine*, published by Inter-Varsity Christian Fellowship (1941–43), and served as director and sales manager for Scripture Press Ministries in Chicago (1945–56).

From 1943 to 1986, Walker served as editor of *Christian Life*, a monthly magazine with a strong emphasis on spiritual renewal aimed at the evangelical Christian community. In addition to testimonies of Evangelicals, the magazine began carrying news of the charismatic renewal around the world in the 1960s. Walker also served as chief executive officer of Christian Life Missions, Inc., in Wheaton, Illinois (1956–86), which was the publisher of *Christian Life, Christian Bookseller*, and Creation House books. In December 1986 Christian Life Missions sold out to Strang Communications Company. Subsequently, *Christian Life* magazine merged with *Charisma* in the spring of 1987, and *Christian Bookseller* became *Christian Retailing*. Walker is now editor emeritus for *Charisma*.

Walker has authored several books, including *A New Song* (with Pat Boone, 1970); *Finger Licking Good* (with Col. Harland Sanders, 1975); *The Successful Writer and Editor* (1979); and *Leads and Story Openings* (1984).

Bibliography: *Who's Who in America,* 44th ed. (1986–87).   G. W. Gohr

WALLIS, ARTHUR R. (1923–1988). Major figure in the House Church movement in Great Britain. From a Plymouth Brethren background, Wallis began to pray and fast for revival in the early 1950s, soon experiencing the Spirit's power. Influenced by G. H. Lang and D. Lillie, he developed a vision for the restoration of the NT church. Wallis served as a convener with Lillie, of the Devon conferences (1958, 1961, 1962). With growing interest in spiritual gifts, Wallis received tongues in 1962, leading to exclusion from Brethren assemblies during his New Zealand tour (1963–64). Between 1965 and 1972 Wallis worked both with the Fountain Trust and with leaders who believed that renewal must lead to reformation and restoration of the church. Covenanting with a group of these men in 1972, Wallis became a major teacher and father figure in the "restorationist" movement, centered on Bradford. His major books are *In the Day of Thy Power* (1956, reprinted as *Rain From Heaven: God's Chosen Fast* [1968]), *Pray in the Spirit* (1970), and *The Radical Christian* (1981).

Bibliography: P. Hocken, *Streams of Renewal* (1986); A. Walker, *Restoring the Kingdom* (1985).
                                        P. D. Hocken

WANNENMACHER, JOSEPH P. (1895–) **AND HELEN (INNES)** (1890–1985). Pioneer Assemblies of God (AG) pastors. Helen Innes was born in Cincinnati, Ohio, and moved with her family to John Alexander Dowie's Zion City, Illinois, in 1901. Receiving a scholarship to Chicago University, she graduated with a teaching degree in 1914. While on a visit to Zion City in 1915 she attended a service at the Faith Home and received salvation. Soon afterward, she received the baptism of the Holy Spirit and later decided to move to the Faith Home to train for Christian work. While there, she met her husband, Joseph, who was preparing for the ministry.

Joseph Wannenmacher was born to a German Catholic family in Hungary. His family immigrated to Milwaukee, Wisconsin, in 1909, and he found work as a foreman of a tool shop. When he became afflicted with tuberculosis, he was forced to change professions. He then took up music for a livelihood. For a time, Wannenmacher turned to Christian Science for a possible cure for his condition. Then in 1917 he attended a Pentecostal mission in Milwaukee pastored by Hugo Ulrich. There he received salvation, healing, and the baptism of the Holy Spirit. Afterward he began playing the violin and giving his testimony everywhere he went.

Immediately after their marriage in 1921, Joseph and Helen pioneered a Hungarian mission that became known as the Full Gospel Church (now Calvary Assembly of God) of Milwaukee, Wisconsin. They were both ordained by the Assemblies of God in 1923. The Wannenmachers published Hungarian literature and began conducting Hungarian and English services in the same building. After World War II Joseph ministered and helped with relief work in Austria and Germany. Since 1963 Joseph Wannenmacher has served as pastor emeritus of Calvary Assembly of God in Milwaukee. Three children were born to the Wannenmachers: John, Philip, and Lois (Graber); all have been involved in AG ministries.

Bibliography: *Bread of Life* (November 1985), 5–7; "When God's Love Came In," *PE* (October 29, 1949), 2–3, 11–13.   G. W. Gohr

WARD, ALFRED GEORGE (1881–1960). Assemblies of God (AG) educator, evangelist, and administrator. Best known as the father of "Revivaltime" speaker C. M. Ward, A. G. Ward served as a minister in the Christian and Missionary Alliance until his ordination with the AG in 1919.

After several years as an itinerant evangelist, he became pastor of Central Assembly of God in Springfield, Missouri, from 1926 to 1928. He then served as an instructor at Central Bible Institute in 1928 and 1929. The following year he became field secretary for the Pentecostal Assemblies of Canada. He was secretary-treasurer of the Canadian fellowship from 1932 to 1938. He also served on the faculty of North Central Bible College before his retirement in 1950. His most notable booklet was *The Minister and His Work,* (1945) published by Gospel Publishing House.

Bibliography: C. M. Ward, *Elder A. G. Ward: Intimate Glimpses of My Father's Life* (1955); "A G. Ward Ends His Earthly Pilgrimage," *PE* (January 22, 1961), 20–21.   B. M. Stout

C. Morse Ward's voice was one of the most familiar to radio listeners between 1953-78. During that 25-year period, Ward was speaker for the Assemblies of God radio program *Revivaltime*.

WARD, CHARLES MORSE (1909–). Evangelist. For twenty-five years the speaker on "Revivaltime," the radio outreach of the Assemblies of God (AG), Ward also served as president of Bethany Bible College.

In 1929 Ward graduated from Central Bible Institute in Springfield, Missouri. His father, A. G. Ward, had served as general secretary of the Pentecostal Assemblies of Canada and as pastor of Central Assembly in Springfield, Missouri.

After graduation C. M. Ward served as a pastor, editor, and evangelist in Canada. For several years he taught at North Central Bible College in Minneapolis, Minnesota, and served in missionary promotional work.

In 1945 Ward began a nine-year term as pastor of the Full Gospel Tabernacle in Bakersfield, California. His successful ministry there was the basis for his appointment as speaker for Revivaltime on the ABC radio network.

Over the next twenty-five years Ward preached 1,306 radio sermons, which were published in annual volumes. He also wrote hundreds of booklets, articles, and tracts to complement the ministry of "Revivaltime."

While still serving as the speaker for "Revivaltime," Ward was elected as president of Bethany Bible College in 1973. He still serves as chancellor for the institution.

Always controversial, Ward stirred feelings with the publication of his autobiography in 1976. In it he criticized leaders of the denomination for their lack of freshness and employed some rather vigorous language in describing impolite events in his life.

Bibliography: *Revivaltime Pulpit*, published by Revivaltime; C. M. Ward with Doug Wead, *The C. M. Ward Story* (1976).   B. M. Stout

WARE, R. KENNETH (1917–). Pentecostal missionary in France. In his youth Ware had a speech impediment, which was healed during a campaign of Smith Wigglesworth, who told him "This tongue will preach the gospel." Ordained in 1935 in Switzerland, his mother's homeland, he ministered in Toulon, France, until 1943. With his wife, Suzy, a Pentecostal of Jewish background, whom he married in 1942, Ware ministered to Jewish refugees. The Wares escaped to Switzerland from the German occupation in 1943, returning to Paris in 1948. Receiving Assemblies of God (AG) (U.S.) ministerial approval in 1953, Ware specialized in producing written materials and for a time had printing equipment in his home. He initiated a Sunday school program in 1960 and served on the committee that produced the Colombe Bible (1978). In 1981 he took over direction of the Centre de Formation Biblique of the French AG at Bievres, near Paris, a position he was forced through illness to relinquish in 1985.

P. D. Hocken

WATER BAPTISM See ORDINANCES, PENTECOSTAL; SACRAMENTS.

Known widely for his ecumenical ministry in England, David C. K. Watson was one of the first Anglican ministers to be baptized in the Spirit in the 1960s.

WATSON, DAVID C. K. (1933–84). Possibly the spiritual leader who in life and death has made the greatest impact on contemporary Christian life in Britain. The archbishop of Canterbury visited David Watson on his death-bed to thank him for his contribution to the Church of England. His first appointment at St. Mark's, Gillingham (1959–62), and under John Collins was an important preparation for receiving the baptism in the Spirit while serving in Cambridge (1962–65). Taking over St. Cuthbert's, York, which was destined for closure, in 1965, Watson developed team ministry and strong teaching programs, necessitating a move to a larger church, St. Michael-le-Belfrey alongside York Minster by 1973. Watson was a gifted evangelist, and some of his deepest impact was in student milieu through the many university missions he led. In York he encouraged the creative arts in worship and used gifted Christian artists in his evangelistic teams. From an evangelical churchmanship, Watson became strongly committed to the Spirit's ecumenical work across all the churches, doing much to open doors between Protestants and Catholics

He married his wife, Anne, in 1964. His autobiography, *You are My God* (1983), reveals the importance of his marriage for his ministry and yet is unusually open about the trials they together experienced. Watson moved to London in 1982 to concentrate on a wider teaching ministry but was soon diagnosed as having cancer. His account of the struggle with cancer, *Fear No Evil*, published just after his death, was an instant best seller. Other books include *My God is Real* (1970); *One in the Spirit* (1973); *Anyone There?* (1979); *Discipleship* (1981); and two volumes in an evangelical series, *I Believe in Evangelism* (1976) and *I Believe in the Church* (1978).

Bibliography: E. England, *The Spirit of Renewal*; E. England, ed., *David Watson: A Portrait by His Friends.*   P. D. Hocken

WATT, JAMES GAIUS (1938–). U.S. Secretary of the Interior (1981–83). He earned B.S. and J.D. degrees at the University of Wyoming before moving to Washington as an aide to Senator Milward Simpson in 1962. Two years later he was born again and in time affiliated with the Assemblies of God. He became known as a natural resource specialist and for eleven years moved through key positions in the Department of the Interior before his appointment to President Ronald Reagan's cabinet. An outspoken man, his tenure as Secretary of the Interior was marked by controversy, and many of his positions were bitterly opposed by conservationists. His casual remarks were seized on and interpreted as racist and sexist, eventually leading to his resignation and return to private life.

Bibliography: R. Arnold, *At the Eye of the Storm* (1982); J. Watt, *The Courage of a Conservative* (1984).
L. F. Wilson

WAY INTERNATIONAL (WI). A cult-like movement with Pentecostal tendencies. In 1957 Victor Paul Wierwille (1916–85) left the Evangelical and Reformed Church, the denomination in which he had served as a pastor for sixteen years, to devote his full energies to the Way, an educational ministry he had chartered two years earlier. The outgrowth of a Lima, Ohio, radio broadcast (successively called "Vesper Chimes," "The Chimes Hour," and "The Chimes Hour

Youth Caravan") dating from the early years of his ministry, the Way (renamed the Way International [WI] in 1975) centers in the twelve-session *Power for Abundant Living* course. Instituted in 1953, this sequence of lectures and readings summarizes the founder's teachings. At the end students are taught to speak in tongues. (Wierwille had come to his experience of glossolalia under the tutelage of the maverick Pentecostal evangelist J. E. Stiles.) This and other unusual teachings are placed in a dispensational schema that regards Jesus as the Son of God but rejects him as God the Son. Participants pay for instruction and materials.

The WI organization is patterned after a tree. It has roots (headquarters) as well as trunk (national), limb (state and provincial), branch (city and town), and twig (small group) fellowships. Individual members are described as leaves. The Wierwille family gave its farm near New Knoxville, Ohio, as the headquarters. Here are located the American Christian Press and annual (since 1971) Rock of Ages Festival. In addition to New Knoxville, root locations in the U.S. include Emporia, Kansas (site of the Way College of Emporia); Rome City, Indiana (site of the Way College of Biblical Research); Tinnie, New Mexico; and Gunnison, Colorado. In 1983 the WI reported approximately 30,000 participants in 2,657 twigs, and more than 2,000 Word Over the World Ambassadors on one-year appointments. Some critics regard the organization as a cult. Upon Wierwille's death, L. Craig Martindale became president, and Donald E. Wierwille, the founder's son, became vice-president.

Bibliography: J. P. Juedes, *From Vesper Chimes to The Way International* (1982); J. G. Melton, *Encyclopedia of American Religions* (1987); E. S. Whiteside, *The Way: Living in Love* (1972); V. P. Wierwille, *Jesus Christ Is Not God* (1975); idem, *Power for Abundant Living* (1971); idem, *Witnessing and Undershepherding* (1974).
C. E. Jones

WEAD, ROY H. (1916–87). An Assemblies of God (AG) pastor, denominational official, and school administrator who had strong ties with the charismatic and salvation-healing movements. His first important association with the salvation-healing movement came in his native North Dakota when he was healed in a meeting conducted by Charles S. Price. He left North Dakota in 1933 for schooling at Central Bible Institute. While pastoring and serving as superintendent of the Indiana District of the AG, he became acquainted with healing evangelist William Branham. Wead assisted Branham in some of his early meetings. While pastoring in South Bend he became involved in the initial outpouring of the Holy Spirit in the Roman Catholic Church. In 1968 he returned to North Dakota, where he served as president of Trinity Bible College for fourteen years. He also served as an executive presbyter of the AG from 1957 to 1983.

Bibliography: W. Menzies, *Anointed to Serve* (1971); R. D. Wead, *The Great Multi-million Dollar Miracle* (1975).   W. E. Warner

WEINER, ROBERT THOMAS (1948–). Church planter, editor, and evangelist. Born in

Chicago, Illinois, Weiner later attended Trinity College. After leaving his studies there, he joined the U.S. Air Force and served as a chaplain's assistant.

Weiner received the baptism in the Holy Spirit in the home of baseball player Albie Pearson after hearing him preach the previous night. After his discharge from the Air Force, he became the youth pastor in a growing Assemblies of God (AG) church in southern California.

In 1972 Weiner and his wife, Rose, founded Maranatha Campus Ministries in Paducah, Kentucky, following a successful evangelistic effort among high school students. Later in the same year Weiner established Maranatha's first church at Murray State University in Murray, Kentucky.

Now, with headquarters in Gainesville, Florida, Maranatha Campus Ministries, International, has established churches on more than 150 college campuses in the U.S. and in sixteen foreign countries. Weiner directs the organization and publishes *The Forerunner on Campus,* an evangelistic newspaper with a current circulation of 75,000, and he also edits *The Forerunner,* a newspaper designed for inspiring Christian leaders across the nation.

In 1986 Weiner founded World Ambassadors, an international student ministry reaching foreign students in American colleges and universities. He also hosts the nationally televised "Forerunner" as well as the Maranatha Satellites Prayer Network.

Bibliography: S. Andrews, "Maranatha Ministries," *Charisma* (May 1982), 20–27.   S. Strang

WELCH, JOHN WILLIAM (1858–1939). Pastor, church executive, and educator. J. W. Welch gave maturity and dignity to the General Council of the Assemblies of God (AG) in its early years. An original executive presbyter and general chairman (1915–20 and 1923–25), the staunchly Trinitarian Welch proved himself during the "New Issue" crisis. Both times he succeeded E. N. Bell (1866–1923) as presiding officer. Born in Seneca, New York, he spent many years as an organizer for the American Sunday School Union and as an evangelist for the Christian and Missionary Alliance (CMA). He was ordained by the latter at age forty-one. Assignment by the CMA in 1910 as superintendent in Oklahoma brought him into contact with A. B. Cox, pioneer Pentecostal evangelist, at Muskogee. Similarities of the AG and the CMA may be attributed in part to Welch's leadership in the formative years. Pentecostal ministry included pastorates at Galena, Kansas; Essex, Missouri; and Modesto, California. In 1915 he served a brief stint as editor of the *Christian Evangel* in St. Louis. Following a year as teacher in the Glad Tidings Bible Institute in San Francisco, he became president of Central Bible Institute in 1931. He died in Springfield, Missouri, on July 14, 1939, at age eighty.

Bibliography: C. Brumback, *Suddenly . . . From Heaven* (1961), *PE* (July 29, 1939).   C. E. Jones

WELSH REVIVAL The *cause célèbre* of turn-of-the century Anglo-American Evangelicalism was the awakening that erupted in November

The Welsh revival of 1905 was led by this man, Evan Roberts. Although it was not considered a Pentecostal revival, the Welsh Revival had a great impact on the Pentecostal movement.

1903 in a church served by Joseph Jenkins at New Quay on Cardigan Bay. Lasting scarcely more than a year, the Welsh revival of 1904 was destined to make distinctive marks on key actors and characteristic practices of the Pentecostal movement soon to be born. Among the very first converts was Evan Roberts (1878–1947), a miner-blacksmith turned evangelist, who so influenced the course of the revival as to make his name synonymous with it. Peculiarities of the revival outburst included hour-long singing, deemphasis on preaching, praying in concert, interruptions by worshipers, stress on the baptism of the Spirit and on Spirit guidance, and the *Hwyl*, a spontaneous half-sung, half-spoken hymn of thanks or penitence. Lay preachers such as Roberts at center-stage were assisted at times by regular clergy such as Alexander A. Boddy (1854–1930) (Anglican), and Seth Joshua (Calvinistic Methodist). Roberts and Joshua (under whom the influential Donald Gee [1891–1966] was converted), never embraced Pentecostalism. Boddy, on the other hand, experienced the Pentecostal baptism three years later in Christiana (Oslo) under Thomas B. Barratt (1862–1940), another Roberts admirer, and returned to his parish (All Saints, Sunderland) to become leader of the movement in the Church of England.

Americans were likewise drawn to the happening in Wales. Some visited the scene; others read the accounts of W. T. Stead (1849–1912), S. B. Shaw (b. 1854), and G. Campbell Morgan (1863–1945). Among those in Los Angeles before and during the Azusa Street meeting with firsthand knowledge of the Welsh revival were F. B. Meyer (1847–1929), Joseph Smale, and Alexander A. Boddy. Smale, one-time pastor of the First Baptist Church of Los Angeles, who toyed with Pentecostalism, then rejected it, was an early evangelistic colleague of Frank Bartleman (1871–1935), participant and historian of Azusa Street and of the events that followed. The three main Pentecostal bodies in the U.K.—the Elim Pentecostal Church, the Assemblies of God in Great Britain and Ireland, and the Apostolic Church—credit the Welsh revival for early leaders and patterns of worship and organization. Elim founders George Jeffreys (1889–1962) and his brother Stephen Jeffreys (1876–1943) were products of the revival, as was the Assemblies of God mainstay, Donald Gee. The Apostolic Church, whose first apostle was W. J. Williams, a Welsh miner, is centered in Penygroes, South Wales. It depends heavily on Spirit guidance and prophecy in decision making.

Bibliography: R. M. Anderson, *Vision of the Disinherited* (1979); W. J. Hollenweger, *The Pentecostals* (1972).   C. E. Jones

WESLEY, JOHN   See EUROPEAN PIETIST ROOTS OF PENTECOSTALISM.

WESLEYAN CHARISMATICS   Persons within the Charismatic Renewal whose ecclesiastical parentage is traced to John Wesley (but are typically not United Methodists) have formed the Wesleyan Holiness Charismatic Fellowship (WHCF), also known as Fellowship of Charismatic Nazarenes. Wilbur Jackson is chairman, and Stan Puliam is secretary. Membership is largely from the Nazarene, Wesleyan, Free Methodist, Church of God (Anderson, Ind.), and Salvation Army churches.

A review of the list of participants in recent WHCF activities shows that members are frequently "former Nazarene," or "former Free Methodist," etc. This observation helps the reader understand the stated purpose of the fellowship: to be "an information and communications link, a hand of fellowship and support to those who have been 'disfellowshiped' from former ties or who feel alone in their new walk" ("Newsletter," 1987, 1). WHCF additionally seeks to foster understanding and dialogue between Wesleyan charismatics and denominational leadership in the light of differences of experiences.

The particular spiritual experience to which the leadership within the various Wesleyan family of churches has been closed or resistant is the ability to speak and worship God in tongues as the Spirit gives utterance.

See also CHARISMATIC MOVEMENT.

Bibliography: W. Jackson, "The Wesleyans and the Charismatic Movement," lecture at the 1986 New Orleans Leaders Congress, the WHCF sessions, cassette; H. A. Snyder, *The Divided Flame: Wesleyans and the Charismatic Renewal* (1986); idem, "Wesleyans and Charismatics—Tensions vs. Cooperation," lecture at the 1986 New Orleans Leaders Congress, the WHCF sessions, cassette; WHCF "Newsletter" (Spring 1987).   J. A. Hewett

WESLEYAN CHURCH CHARISMATICS   See WESLEYAN CHARISMATICS.

WESLEYAN HOLINESS CHARISMATIC FELLOWSHIP   See WESLEYAN CHARISMATICS.

WHEATON, ELIZABETH RYDER (1844–1923). Social reformer and evangelist. Elizabeth Ryder was born to John and Mary Van Nest Ryder in Wayne County, Ohio. Her parents, both Christians, died by the time she was five years of age. At the death of her mother, Elizabeth was separated from her siblings and was reunited only with her brothers, J. M. and Emanuel, and her sister, Lida Ryder Hoffman, in 1902.

At first Elizabeth was placed in a foster home where she remained until the family moved away. Subsequently she was reared by her grandparents. As a child, she worshiped among the Methodists. Later she would describe her commitment to Christianity at this time as "normal."

At age eighteen Elizabeth married J. A. Wheaton. They had one son, but within two years of their marriage, both her husband and their infant son had died. Elizabeth's self-acknowledged conversion came in the wake of their deaths. In the years that followed, she heard of "holiness" and "the baptism of the Holy Spirit for service." She began to attend a Holiness church some distance from her home. It was there that she received her "sanctification." On November 11, 1883, she claimed to have received a vision of Jesus in which she was asked to follow him. Thus she began her prison ministry.

Mother Wheaton, as she was frequently called, was known primarily as a prison evangelist, although she was also engaged in rescue work. She was not attached to any single denomination but ministered frequently in street meetings, especially in front of bars and houses of prostitution, on railroad cars, in Peniel Missions, and in various Crittenden rescue centers. From 1895 onward, she made the Missionary Training Home in Tabor, Iowa, under the supervision of Elder Weavers, her home address.

For a period of time Wheaton was accompanied and assisted by a Mrs. Hattie Worcester Kelly. In later years Mother Wheaton continued her independent faith venture alone, ministering to those in state and federal prisons in nearly every state and territory of the U.S. and in Canada and Mexico. She carried numerous letters of reference, signed by governors and wardens alike. Her reputation was widely known, and she is said to have become such a well-known figure on the railroads that she was frequently allowed to travel at no charge.

Mother Wheaton was a featured speaker at the semiannual camp meeting of the Holiness Church in Southern California in April 1905, where she told of her work in the slums and prisons and engaged in altar work among the seekers present.

In the spring of 1906 Wheaton was a guest in the Frank Bartleman home, accompanying him to meetings at the cottage on Bonnie Brae Street and an all night prayer meeting at Joseph Smale's First New Testament Church. She also went with Frank Bartleman on his first visit to the Apostolic Faith Mission on Azusa Street. It was later reported in *The Apostolic Faith* that she had come "tarrying for her Pentecost." By January 1907, at age sixty-two, it was reported by Henry McLain that she had gone to a meeting in Clearwater, California, where she "was baptized with the Holy Spirit and spoke in two languages."

Always one who was interested in foreign missions, Mother Wheaton made two trips to Europe. She was jailed in Edinburgh, Scotland, for holding a street meeting. Touched by reports from famine-ravaged India, Mrs. Wheaton donated twenty dollars annually to support a young Indian boy at the Frontier Faith Mission superintended by Robert and Laura E. Jarvis in Lahore, India. He was named John Ryder Wheaton in honor of Mother Wheaton's brother.

In her declining years, Mother Wheaton was unable to continue her heavy travel schedule. She suffered both physical and emotional trauma and was ultimately confined to her home in Tabor, Iowa. A letter she wrote just six weeks before her death indicates that she was lonely and living in anticipation of her imminent death. She died on July 28, 1923, at the Faith Home in Tabor, Iowa.

Bibliography: F. Bartleman, How Pentecost Came to Los Angeles (1925, reprint 1985); "A Nationally Known Prison Worker Died Here Saturday," Beacon-Enterprise (Tabor, Iowa) 42 (31, 1923): 1, 4; J. M. Washburn, History and Reminiscences of the Holiness Church Work in Southern California and Arizona (1912, reprint 1985), 352–53; E. R. Wheaton, Prisons and Prayer or A Labor of Love (1906).   C. M. Robeck, Jr.

WHETSTONE, ROSS (1919–). Pastor, educator, and Methodist charismatic leader. Ross Whetstone was a leader in organizing, in 1977, the United Methodist Renewal Service Fellowship (UMRSF). At that time he held the Ruth Jones Cadwallader Chair of Evangelism at Scarritt College in Nashville (Manna, December 1977, 1). This is "a group of United Methodist Christians [who are] seeking to glorify Christ and serve his Body, the church, in all ministries which relate to renewal by the power of His Spirit" (Manna, 10 [2, 3, 4, December 1987]: 3). He now serves as executive director of UMRSF and editor of Manna, the agency's newsletter.

After his baptism in the Holy Spirit (1937), Whetstone became active in the Salvation Army. He joined in 1938 and was commissioned an officer in 1939. In 1950 he transferred his ordination to the Central New York Conference of the Methodist Church. During the early 1950s he completed theological studies, first attending Pennsylvania State College at Mansfield and then Colgate-Rochester Divinity School. After several local pastorates in Pennsylvania and New York, he joined the national board of evangelism of the United Methodist Church (UMC) (1957) as leader for the Contact Teleministry movement. He then became assistant general secretary for the evangelism section in the UMC.

Bibliography: P. Guinn, "Ross Whetstone: Forty Years of Miracles," Manna 4 (4, October 1980): 5; R. Whetstone, ed., Manna 10 (2, 3, 4, 1987): 3.
                                                          J. A. Hewett

WHITE, KENT (1860–1940). Minister, evangelist, teacher, editor, and author. Born in Beverly, Randolf County, Virginia (later West Virginia) to Francis Marion and Elizabeth (Buckley) White. Reared on a farm, Kent was educated in local schools. From 1882 onward he attended courses at the University of Denver. On a trip through Montana in March 1883 White preached to a Methodist congregation normally served by another pastor. There he met Mollie Alma Bridwell, whom he married in Denver, Colorado, on December 21, 1887. Ordained a deacon (1889) and later an elder (1891) in the Colorado Methodist conference, White pioneered several churches and served as pastor in Lamar and Morrison. His connection with the Methodists was severed in 1902 when he identified with the fruit of his wife's evangelistic labor, known pejoratively as the "Holy Jumpers." This group organized in 1902 under the name Pillar of Fire.

The paths of the Whites repeatedly crossed those of Pentecostals prior to 1909. During this period, White accepted the Pentecostal teaching and embraced its experience. It was this doctrinal difference between Alma and Kent that became the excuse for their separation in 1909. Kent identified with the Apostolic Faith, then in 1922 he moved to England, where he served as an Apostolic Faith pastor and teacher until 1939. Returning to Denver in 1939, he died there the following year. White was the author of The Word of God Coming Again (1919) and The Hostel of the Good Shepherd (1938), as well as numerous articles.

Bibliography: A. White Demons and Tongues (1910); idem, My Heart and My Husband (1923); idem, National Cyclopedia of American Biography (194) 35:152; idem, The Story of My Life (1921).
                                                          C. M. Robeck, Jr.

WIERWILLE, VICTOR PAUL (1916–85). Organization executive. Founder of The Way International, Victor Paul Wierwille is significant to the history of Pentecostalism because of his routinization of glossolalia. From 1941 to 1957 he served as a pastor in the Evangelical and Reformed Church, a body later merged into the United Church of Christ. Early in his ministry, Wierwille began a radio Bible study successively called the "Vesper Chimes," "The Chimes Hour," and "The Chimes Hour Youth Caravan," which provided the foundation later for the Power for Abundant Living course and for The Way International. In 1951 he experienced tongues through the ministry of Pentecostal evangelist J. E. Stiles, who claimed to have developed a technique for inducing the gift. Two years later Wierwille inaugurated his twelve-session course, which culminated in students being taught to speak in tongues. In 1957 he established the headquarters of The Way, a cultlike organization for nurturing converts, on the farm near New Knoxville, Ohio, where he had been born. He died there in 1985 at age sixty-eight. At that time The Way International claimed more than 30,000 adherents.

Bibliography: W. J. Cummins, The Living Word Speaks (1981); J. A. MacCollam, The Way of Victor Paul Wierwille (1978); R. L. Sumner, Jesus Christ is God (1983).   C. E. Jones

WIGGLESWORTH, SMITH (1859–1947). An English evangelist known throughout many parts of the world for his strong faith and legendary answers to prayer. An indication of Wigglesworth's continued popularity is the fact that no fewer than six books by or about him are in print—three of which were first published in the 1980s. What makes his life more unusual than most of the healing evangelists of the twentieth century is that he was hardly known outside of his hometown until he was forty-eight. That was in 1907 when he received the Pentecostal experience at Sunderland under the ministry of Vicar and Mrs. Boddy. Until that happened he was operating a plumbing business in Bradford and assisting his wife Polly in a mission. He had been an aggressive personal evangelist but did little preaching.

Born to a very poor family, Wigglesworth was deprived of an education because he had to help support his family from the time he was six. As a consequence, he never learned to read well until he was an adult. Later he claimed he never read anything but the Bible. He would not take credit for two books, *Ever Increasing Faith* (c. 1924) and *Faith That Prevails* (1938), explaining that others had taken his sermons in shorthand and published them.

Wigglesworth's healing ministry began before he was baptized in the Spirit. He received healing from a ruptured appendix and wrote later that God gave him great faith for people suffering with appendicitis. He would usually conclude a sermon by praying for the sick, regardless of what text he had taken.

Wigglesworth's wife, Polly, died about the time his ministry began to broaden. He was soon preaching in other countries, becoming one of the better-known evangelists in the Pentecostal movement. His daughter, Alice Salter, who was a missionary to Africa, frequently accompanied him on his international trips.

Wigglesworth was often accused of being rough on the people who came for prayer. It was claimed that he would strike a sick person with his fist; a person suffering from stomach problems might receive prayer along with a sharp hit to the afflicted area. Others who were crippled were ordered to run across the platform after he prayed for them. Criticism came from such leaders as E. S. Williams, former general superintendent of the General Council of the Assemblies of God. Close associates, however, told of Wigglesworth's compassion for suffering people, often praying and weeping over requests he had received.

Wigglesworth's ministry centered on salvation for the unconverted, healing for the sick, and a call to believers to be baptized in the Holy Spirit. Donald Gee, in reporting Wigglesworth's death in 1947, wrote that a "unique ministry, a gift of Christ to His church, has been taken from the worldwide Pentecostal Movement. He died in the harness—nearly 88 years of age."

Bibliography: "Awaiting the Resurrection," *PE* (April 5, 1947), 3, 11; S. Frodsham, *Smith Wigglesworth: Apostle of Faith* (1948); W. Warner, taped interview with E. S. Williams, Assemblies of God Archives (1979).   W. E. Warner

WILKERSON, DAVID RAY   (1931–). Founder of Teen Challenge and evangelist. David Wilkerson was born and reared in a Pentecostal home under the influence of Pentecostal preaching by both his parents, Kenneth and Ann Wilkerson, and his grandfather, Jay Wilkerson. He attended Central Bible Institute (now College) from 1951 to 1952. He and his wife Gwen have four children.

Wilkerson started his ministry in a traditional way by pastoring a small church in Philipsburg, Pennsylvania. Yet he was innovative in that he produced a television program from the Assemblies of God (AG) church in Philipsburg at a time when many Pentecostal and Holiness people were questioning whether or not it was worldly for Spirit-filled Christians to own or watch a television.

The dramatic story of Wilkerson's launch into a worldwide ministry is well told in the book *The Cross and the Switchblade* (1963). His faith in the Bible as the Word of God has been the balance wheel that has guided him in some unusual areas of ministry. His prayer life has been the place where God has been able to get his attention, when no one else could persuade him.

During a prayer vigil in 1958 Wilkerson's attention was drawn to an article in *Life* magazine. The story graphically depicted the murder trial of seven young men who had killed a crippled boy, Michael Farmer. As he looked at the artist's drawing of these seven young men sitting in the court room, he did not see seven ruthless murderers but scared young men. He asked himself if they had ever heard the story of Jesus.

Smith Wigglesworth was a plumber with a limited formal education; after being baptized in the Spirit in 1907, he became a noted Pentecostal evangelist.

When David Wilkerson took an interest in New York gang members being tried for murder, it was the beginning of an effort which formed Teen Challenge. In this 1983 photo he is seen preaching to an outdoor crowd.

Led by the Holy Spirit, Wilkerson went to New York City to try to talk to the seven young men. He was told he would have to get permission from the trial judge. Unable to contact the judge, he again was told to attend court and ask to speak to the judge in his chambers. This led to his being ejected from the court room and getting his picture on the front page of the *New York Daily News* (March 1, 1958). Although Wilkerson was unable to talk with these young men personally, the experience was used by God to begin his ministry to the gangs on the streets of New York. The picture in the newspaper became a passport to the gangs. The gangs welcomed him as "the guy the cops don't like," and Wilkerson seized the opportunity to witness to them. The success of his street evangelism led to the founding of the Teen Challenge ministry with close ties to the AG. Wilkerson was appointed executive director of this New York City ministry in 1958 and continues to the present to hold this position. Many of the new converts were drug addicts and alcoholics, so Wilkerson established a home in Brooklyn where these young men and women could receive intensive discipleship training.

Many graduates of Teen Challenge chose to enter full-time Christian ministry. They often faced difficulty being accepted into established Bible colleges, so in 1966 Wilkerson established Teen Challenge Bible Institute, Rhinebeck, New York, to provide Bible school education for those completing the Teen Challenge program.

The growth of the Teen Challenge ministry and its spread across the U.S. and overseas brought about an ever-increasing public exposure in all media to Wilkerson and his message. The bold stance he took on the "born again" experience and being filled with the Holy Spirit with the evidence of "speaking in tongues" caused a stir in the church world. The beginning of the charismatic movement in many circles, both Roman Catholic and Protestant, was sparked by *The Cross and the Switchblade*.

Students and teachers at Duquesne University read about "speaking in tongues" in *The Cross and the Switchblade*. A hunger was created for this experience that could transform their lives. As a result, the modern "outpouring" of the Holy Spirit among Roman Catholics traces back to Duquesne University. By 1969 forty-two ministers in the United Methodist Church in the Western Conference in Pennsylvania had testified to the experience of "speaking in tongues." They described *The Cross and the Switchblade* as the key in creating a hunger for a personal encounter with the Holy Spirit.

The widespread popularity of Wilkerson's book resulted in many invitations for him to preach to a wide spectrum of inter- and intra-denominational circles. His ministry soon expanded to preaching at city-wide crusades across America and Canada. In 1972 Wilkerson established World Challenge to coordinate his ministry outside of New York City. Through World Challenge he expanded his city-wide crusades, summer street evangelism, and missionary outreach. He has assisted in starting numerous Teen Challenge centers in countries around the world. Wilkerson has been a prolific writer in calling the church to the work of evangelism and in spreading the prophetic message of repentance and holiness (nineteen books by 1985). World Challenge also produced several movies on evangelism and prophetic themes. In 1987 David Wilkerson; his brother, Don Wilkerson; and Robert Philips founded Times Square Church in New York City. He resigned from the AG in the same year.

The influence of Wilkerson through preaching, writing, and example has been felt not only in the free world but has opened up doors to the gospel in Iron Curtain countries as well.

Wilkerson's books have included: *The Cross and the Switchblade* (1963); *Twelve Angels From Hell* (1966); *The Little People* (1966); *Get Your Hands Off My Throat* (1966); *I'm Not Mad at God* (1967); *Parents on Trial* (1967); *Hey, Preach . . . You're Coming Through!* (1968); *Man, Have I Got Problems* (1968); *Purple Violet Squish* (1969); *Rebel's Bible* (1970); *The Untapped Generation* (1971); *Life on the Edge of Time* (1972); *David Wilkerson Speaks Out* (1973); *The Vision* (1974); *Racing Toward Judgement* (1976); *Beyond the Cross and the Switchblade* (1976); *Suicide* (1978); *Sipping Saints* (1978); *Have You Felt Like Giving Up Lately?* (1980); *Set the Trumpet to Thy Mouth* (1985).

See also TEEN CHALLENGE.

Bibliography: D. Wilkerson, *The Cross and the Switchblade* (1963).   F. M. Reynolds

WILKERSON, RALPH A. (1927–). The founder and pastor of Melodyland Christian Center. Born in 1927 to Benjamin and Lela Wilkerson in Ponca, Oklahoma, Wilkerson graduated from Tulsa University and was ordained by the Assemblies of God in 1948. He married Allene Work, and they have two daughters, Angela and Debi. Wilkerson is the author of several books: *Loneliness: The World's Number One Killer* (1978); *The Redwoods* (1977); *Success from Stress* (1978); *Satellites of the Spirit* (1978); *ESP or HSP?* (1978); and *Beyond and Back* (1977). For the last of these, *Beyond and Back*, Wilkerson was the recipient in 1977 of a Religion in Media (RIM) award. In the same year he received an honorary doctorate from Oral Roberts University.

Ralph Wilkerson expanded the outreach of Melodyland Christian Center to include a delinquency prevention center (hotline), a school of theology, and a Christian high school and college. For many years he sponsored the annual Melodyland Charismatic Clinics that featured speakers from many denominations and attracted people from around the world.

See also MELODYLAND CHRISTIAN CENTER.

J. R. Williams

WILLANS, JEAN STONE (1924–). Important figure in the origins of the charismatic movement. In 1959 Jean Stone was a high church Episcopalian, belonging to St. Mark's Church, Van Nuys, California. That fall, being baptized in the Spirit, she joined a group of parishioners likewise touched by God, including the rector, Dennis Bennett. After Bennett announced his experience and then resigned (April 1960), Stone was responsible for the national publicity in *Newsweek* and *Time*. In 1960 she founded the Blessed Trinity Society, which published numerous leaflets and pamphlets and, from 1961, a quarterly magazine, *Trinity*, the first non-Pentecostal journal in America devoted to this new move of the Spirit. With others in the society, Stone organized conferences called "Christian Advances" in the Pacific Coast states. With Harald Bredesen she was responsible for the term "charismatic renewal" being used to designate the new movement.

Between 1960 and 1965 Stone was an indefatigable promoter of charismatic renewal in the historic churches. Vigorous and determined, with a directness of approach, she traveled frequently, including a brief visit to Britain in 1964. Stone's influence in America declined in 1966 with the cessation of *Trinity* magazine, which was linked to financial troubles outside Stone's control and to her divorce and subsequent marriage to Richard Willans.

The Willanses then moved to the Far East, settling in Hong Kong in 1968. They founded the Society of Stephen, led an ecumenical prayer group, and assisted with the beginning of Catholic charismatic renewal in Hong Kong. In particular they ministered to drug addicts and had close association with the work of Jackie Pullinger. The Willanses returned to Altadena, California, in 1983. Jean Stone Willans' account of her charismatic experience was published in *The Acts of the Green Apples* (1973).

See also BLESSED TRINITY SOCIETY.

Bibliography: J. T. Connelly, "Neo-Pentecostalism," Ph.D diss., University of Chicago (1977); R. Quebedeaux, *The New Charismatics II* (1983).   P. D. Hocken

WILLIAMS, ERNEST SWING (1885–1981). Pastor, dean, author, and denominational executive. Born in 1885 in San Bernardino, California, E. S. Williams entered the home of Christian parents who were charter members of the First Holiness Church in that city. That his parents were strongly tied to this group may be seen from the fact that his middle name was derived from James R. Swing, the president of the Southern California and Arizona Holiness Association at the time of his birth. His father was a carpenter, but he supplemented the family income through odd jobs. Because of the poor economic situation, his education was at first limited to grammar school. Later, when the family moved to Santa Ana (1899), he attended business school for a time.

Ernest S. Williams, who was baptized in the Spirit at the Azusa Street Mission, served the Assemblies of God as general superintendent from 1929 to 1949.

In 1904, through the continued urging of his mother and a strong sense of personal anxiety in a Free Methodist service, Williams made a commitment to Christ. Shortly thereafter, he and a friend decided to enroll in a "holiness school in Chicago." They got as far as Denver, where he worked on a ranch. His mother wrote weekly, and it was she who told him of the Azusa Street revival. In the fall of 1906 Williams traveled by train to the Los Angeles depot, then walked to the mission on Azusa Street, arriving after the sermon but in time for the altar call. A few days later, on October 2, 1906, he received his Pentecostal experience.

Almost immediately Williams was drawn toward ministry. He continued to attend the Azusa Street Mission, telling Pastor William J. Seymour that he wanted to enter the ministry. In his timidity, he interpreted Seymour's silence as not affirming his call. For a time he was "defeated," but during the first camp meeting of Azusa, in August 1907, Williams was asked to accept the leadership of an Apostolic Faith mission in San Francisco. He was soon ordained and remained in San Francisco for two years. Following a short pastorate in Colorado Springs, he returned to the West Coast, where he engaged from 1909 to 1911 in evangelistic work. In 1911 he married Laura O. Jacobson, from Portland, Oregon.

Following their marriage, the Williamses moved eastward, conducting meetings in Kentucky and Indiana, then in 1912 accepting a two-year pastorate in Conneaut, Ohio. The couple then went to Bradford, a town located in the mountains of Pennsylvania. While there, Williams read of the founding meeting of the Assemblies of God (AG) in Hot Springs, Arkansas (April 1914). He wrote, asking to be enrolled in this new general council. Late that same year he was recognized as an ordained minister with the AG.

Williams's early years of ministry may be described as difficult ones, filled with hardships and self-denial. He was invited in 1917 to serve as pastor of Bethel Pentecostal Assembly in Newark, New Jersey, a significant Pentecostal church in the region.

In 1920 Williams became pastor of Highway Mission Tabernacle in Philadelphia. The congregation was small at first, but it grew rapidly, purchased an old Presbyterian church building, and expanded it with a large balcony. The year 1920 also brought him into the position of executive presbyter for the Eastern District of the AG. For a decade Williams and his wife remained as pastors of Highway Tabernacle, but his exposure as an executive presbyter in the East and as general presbyter for the new movement, as well as his election to the executive presbytery of the denomination in 1927, led to nationwide exposure.

The 1929 General Council of the AG saw Williams elected to the office of general superintendent for the denomination, and the following October he left Philadelphia and moved to Springfield, Missouri, where he served until 1949. Membership in the AG tripled under his leadership as did the number of churches and ordained ministers. Missionary giving expanded, and new mission fields were opened.

Williams's term as general superintendent was marked by the Great Depression of the 1930s. He provided a strong sense of stability for the denomination during those years. It was he who led the AG, cautiously at first, into association with American Evangelicals by bringing the AG into the National Association of Evangelicals in 1943. He helped pioneer the Radio Department, establishing "Sermons in Song," a fifteen-minute weekly radio broadcast for which he began preaching January 6, 1946. He guided the AG into dialogue with other world and American Pentecostals, participating in the initial meetings

of the Pentecostal World Conference and giving the keynote address at the first convention of the Pentecostal Fellowship of North America (1949).

Upon his retirement from the office of general superintendent, Williams taught at Central Bible Institute for seven years and served as its academic dean for a year. He continued to speak and to write.

Throughout his ministry, Williams had submitted short synopses of his sermons for publication to the denomination's weekly publication, the *Pentecostal Evangel*. Later his writing included several books, including the first systematic theology by a Pentecostal. Williams also had a weekly question-and-answer column in the *Evangel*. Many of these questions and answers, like those of the first general superintendent, E. N. Bell, were collected and published in book form by Gospel Publishing House.

Laura Williams died on February 26, 1980, and Ernest S. Williams spent his remaining months in Maranatha Village, an AG retirement center in Springfield, Missouri. He has often been described as a quiet, humble, wise, and godly man. His prayers were powerful, his demeanor gentle.

Bibliography: "Long-Time General Council Leader with Christ," *PE* (December 13, 1981), 7–8; "Memories of Azusa Street Mission," *PE* (April 4, 1966), 7; W. Menzies, *Anointed to Serve* (1971); D. D. Merrifield, ed., "The Life Story of Reverend Ernest S. Williams" (unpublished ms., 1980); "Pentecostal Origins: James S. Tinney Interviews E. S. Williams," *Agora* (Winter 1979), 4–6; E. S. Williams, *Encouragement to Faith* (1946); idem, *A Faithful Minister* (1941); idem, *Not I But Christ* (1939); idem, *Questions and Answers on Faith and Practice* (1963); idem, *Systematic Theology*, 3 vols. (1935); idem, *Temptation and Triumph* (n.d.); idem, *Your Questions Answered* (1968).   C. M. Robeck, Jr.

WILLIAMS, JOHN RODMAN (1918–). Presbyterian charismatic theologian and educator. Born August 21, 1918, to John Rodman and Odessa Lee (Medford) Williams in Clyde, North Carolina. John Williams received the A.B. from Davidson College (N.C.) in 1939, graduating Phi Beta Kappa. Earning his B.D. (1943) and Th.M. (1944) at Union Theological Seminary (Va.), he was ordained in the Presbyterian Church of the U.S. (1943) and served as a U.S. marine chaplain 1944–46. He later earned the Ph.D. in philosophy of religion at Columbia University and Union Theological Seminary (N.Y.) (1954).

In 1949 Williams married Johanna Servaas and was appointed associate professor of philosophy at Beloit College (Wis.), where he served until 1952. Thereafter he was pastor of First Presbyterian Church, Rockford, Illinois (1952–59), then professor of systematic theology at Austin Presbyterian Seminary (1959–72). As an early participant in charismatic renewal, he played an active role, becoming president of the International Presbyterian Charismatic Communion, then in 1972 becoming the founding president and professor of theology at Melodyland School of Theology in Anaheim, California. During that time he participated in the International Roman Catholic–Pentecostal Dialogue. Currently he serves as professor of theology at CBN University School of Biblical Studies in Virginia Beach,

A Presbyterian pastor and seminary educator, J. Rodman Williams was an early participant in the charismatic renewal.

Virginia. In 1985 he served as president of the Society for Pentecostal Studies. Among his publications are *The Era of the Spirit* (1971), *The Pentecostal Reality* (1972), *The Gift of the Holy Spirit Today* (1980), and *Renewal Theology: God, the World, and Redemption* (1988).

C. M. Robeck, Jr.

WILLIAMS, MORRIS OLIVER (1920–). Missionary and author. Williams was born in Kansas and reared in Egeland, North Dakota. While attending North Central Bible College, he married Alice Mae ("Macey") Lundquist. He later served in pastoral ministry at Sioux City (1941–42) and Moville, Iowa (1942–44). He also served as youth director for the West Central District of the Assemblies of God (AG) (1944–46).

Feeling the call of the Great Commission, the couple applied to the AG Division of Foreign Missions in 1945 and arrived in Malawi in March 1946. Ministry there and in the Republic of South Africa prompted Williams to work toward improving relationships with national church organizations. Beginning in 1971, he served as AG field director for Africa. He retired from the post in December 1985. In 1976 North Central Bible College conferred an honorary D.D. on him for services rendered to the cause of foreign missions. He currently serves as associate professor of missions at the Assemblies of God Theological Seminary.

A prolific writer, Williams has also written Sunday school curricula for African churches. His

perspectives on missiology are best found in *Partnership in Mission* (2d ed., 1986).

Bibliography: "A Tribute to Morris Williams," *Mountain Movers* (December 1985), 12–13.

G. B. McGee

WILLIAMS, RALPH DARBY (1902–1982). Pioneer missionary to Latin America. Williams was born in Sudbrook, Monmouthshire, England. He was converted and baptized in the Holy Spirit during a Pentecostal revival in 1919. Later he and his brother Richard (d. 1931; see L. J. Walker, *Peruvian Gold*, 1985, 56) traveled to the U.S. and graduated from Glad Tidings Bible Institute (later Bethany Bible College) in 1924, where he studied the missiology of Roland Allen. A year later he was ordained by the Assemblies of God (AG) and married fellow student Jewyl Stoddard (d. 1976); they had four children.

Before leaving England, Alice E. Luce, an indigenous church pioneer among Mexican-Americans, had visited Ralph and Richard Williams and encouraged them to consider becoming missionaries to Latin America. Later Ralph and his brother received appointments (1926) as AG missionaries and assisted Luce in her church and in the Berean Bible Institute in San Diego, California (later Latin American Bible Institute). Ralph served as associate pastor and instructor in the school.

The Williamses arrived in El Salvador in 1929 as the first AG missionaries to that country and contributed to the organization and guidance of the Pentecostals there. A constitution was approved in 1930 that placed the churches on an indigenous footing. Ralph Williams also established a Bible institute in 1931 and introduced, with Francisco R. Arbizu, the "Reglamento" ("Standard for Doctrine and Conduct") for church members and pastors.

After a furlough to the U.S., Williams returned to El Salvador in 1936 with Melvin L. Hodges and his wife Lois, newly appointed missionaries to Central America. In the following year Williams built Bethel Church and Bethel Bible Institute in Santa Ana, El Salvador. Election as field superintendent for Central America followed in 1940 and considerably increased the scope of his work. During his ministry the number of churches grew from twelve to more than four hundred in the region. Later activities took Williams to Nicaragua, Costa Rica, Honduras, Guatemala, Mexico, Venezuela, Colombia, Panama, Cuba, Puerto Rico, and the Spanish Eastern District of the AG. He married Lois Alma Stewart in 1976 and returned to the U.S. to work at the office of Program of Applied Christian Education (PACE), an AG educational agency that provides advanced training for ministers in Latin America.

Williams's contribution to foreign missions lay in his application of indigenous church principles for the building of strong national churches and in pioneering quality educational training for national pastors and leaders. His Bible institute program in El Salvador became a model for other such institutions throughout Latin America.

Bibliography: R. D. Williams, unpublished "Memoirs" (1981); G. B. McGee, *This Gospel Shall Be Preached* (1986); idem, "Missionaries With Christ," *PE* (July 25, 1982), 29.   G. B. McGee

John Wimber is the founding pastor of the Vineyard Christian Fellowship of Anaheim, California, and president of Vineyard Ministries International.

WIMBER, JOHN (1934–). Founding pastor of the Vineyard Christian Fellowship of Anaheim, California, and president of Vineyard Ministries International. Born and raised in a non-Christian home, he developed a successful career in the music industry. A dramatic conversion experience in 1963 drew him into a commitment to full-time Christian service. After graduation from Azusa Pacific University, Wimber was recorded (ordained) in 1970 by the California Yearly Meeting of Friends and served as copastor of the Yorba Linda Friends Church for five years.

In 1975 Wimber joined C. Peter Wagner of the Fuller Evangelistic Association in pioneering what is now the Charles E. Fuller Institute of Evangelism and Church Growth. In his role as church growth consultant, he worked with hundreds of churches across the denominational spectrum.

Wimber left Fuller to establish the Anaheim Vineyard in 1977. Soon afterward he and his congregation began praying for the sick and, after an agonizing period of ineffectiveness, began seeing dramatic results. This launched Wimber, a gifted leader and public speaker, into a renowned national and international "signs and wonders" ministry that has had a profound effect on tens of thousands of charismatics and noncharismatics alike. Meanwhile his church grew to five thousand, and he has sparked an aggressive church-

planting effort that now includes more than 250 churches affiliated with the Association of Vineyard churches.

Wimber has lectured with Wagner in the Fuller Theological Seminary Doctor of Ministry program since 1975. He first introduced a lecture, "Signs, Wonders and Church Growth," in 1981. Then from 1982 to 1985 he taught a full course in the Fuller School of World Mission, "The Miraculous and Church Growth," which became not only the most popular course in the seminary's history but also the most controversial. Currently Wimber participates in a restructured course under Wagner and Charles H. Kraft.

Bibliography: E. Gibbs, "My Friend John Wimber," *Signs and Wonders Today*, C. Peter Wagner, ed. (1987); K. N. Springer, "Applying the Gift to Everyday Life," *Charisma* (September 1985), 26–34; T. Stafford, "Testing the Wine from John Wimber's Vineyard," *Christianity Today* (August 8, 1986), 17–22; J. Wimber, *Power Healing* (1987); J. Wimber with K. Springer, Power Evangelism (1986).   C. P. Wagner

WINKLER, RICHARD EDWARD (1916–). Episcopal priest. Trained as an engineer, he was ordained in 1953. He served at Trinity Episcopal Church in Wheaton, Illinois, as curate and then rector until 1967.

Under Winkler's leadership a prayer group was begun in the mid 1950s that was significantly blessed by the Holy Spirit. Tongues were spoken and miraculous healings took place. He pioneered many practices that are now standard features of a renewal ministry. These included prayer and praise meetings with prophecy, tongues and interpretation, lengthy evening prayer sessions, and healing services.

Because Trinity was one of the first mainline Protestant churches to experience speaking in tongues, some controversy resulted. The Episcopal Diocese of Chicago issued a report on tongues urging that the phenomenon not be allowed to divide the parish.

In 1967 Winkler became rector of Good Shepherd Episcopal Church in Wailuku, Hawaii. From 1967 to 1973 he was archdeacon of Maui and Molokai. In 1976 he retired for health reasons.   C. M. Irish

WINSETT, ROGER EMMET (1876–1952). A popular songwriter and song book publisher in the early years of the Pentecostal movement. Winsett's own compositions included "In the Great Triumphant Morning," "The Message of His Coming," and others, but he is best known for the many song books he published during the first half of the twentieth century. He obtained rights to hundreds of songs, including "In the City Where the Lamb Is the Light," "Look to the Lamb of God," "Joy Unspeakable," "Victory," "Victory Ahead," and "Living by Faith."

The R. E. Winsett Music Company is now owned by Sacred Music Company.   W. E. Warner

WISDOM LITERATURE The wisdom literature (WL) of the OT consists of Job, Proverbs, Ecclesiastes, and according to some interpreters, the Song of Songs. In the WL the term "spirit," *rûah*, is not often used to refer to the One whom we now call the Holy Spirit (it does not appear at all in the Song of Songs). The term more often refers to other things, such as wind, breath, life or principle of life, heart in the sense of the core of personality, and anger.

Because of the ambiguity of meaning, it is best to consider *rûaḥ* as referring to the Spirit of God only when one or more of the following factors suggest it: (1) phraseology, e.g., "*rûaḥ* of God," "his [God's] *rûaḥ*"; (2) parallels within the poetry that move the thought away from a physical meaning (wind, breath) toward "Spirit"; (3) a clear reference to God's Spirit in the near context. Under these criteria, only in Job does the term *rûaḥ* point directly to God's Spirit, but there it does so at least five times (out of eleven occurrences; four of these five are in the speeches of Elihu [32:8, 18; 33:4; 34:14]; the other relatively certain use is 27:3). Three more instances possibly refer to the Spirit of God (4:9, 15; 26:13), and three more may have a metaphoric reference based on an interplay between the meanings of wind and spirit (15:30; and less likely, 21:18; 30:22).

In the five clear references in Job, the role of the Spirit of God is fourfold. Giving life is the most frequently seen aspect; the Spirit in a sense creates and gives life to the individual (Job 33:4) and thus forms the basis for all human life (Job 27:3; in 34:14–15 perhaps even the basis of all animate life).

The second role, that of giving wisdom, is rather surprising in the WL where observation and reflection would be the more normal source of wisdom. The Book of Job, however, deals more in that branch of wisdom that concerns the ultimate questions of life. Though humanity is not privy to the answers to these questions, God is. For humanity to understand in these areas, God must speak (Job 28:12–28), and in Job 32:8 Elihu states that this communication comes via the Spirit, the breath of God. Similar thoughts are voiced by the writer of the introduction to the Book of Proverbs in 1:7 and 9:10. There wisdom must operate within the framework of the fear of Yahweh. He created wisdom (Prov. 8:22–31, cf. Job 28:25–27), which then addresses people and invites them to receive instruction (Prov. 1–8, passim).

The third role of the Spirit of God in Job is that of moving to action. In Job 32:18 Elihu says that the Spirit within him forces him to speak to Job and the three friends. Depending on one's view of the function of Elihu in the book, it could be argued that the *rûaḥ* in him here is anger or even wind, but the parallel with 32:8 shows that Elihu believes himself to be pressured by the Spirit of God into speaking up.

The combination of the second and third roles in relation to Elihu suggests a rather prophetic tone to his character that I have argued is confirmed by other facets of his speeches (Johns, 1983, 163–69). Von Rad argues that in both Elihu and Eliphaz (Job 4:12–17) there is a nearness to the prophetic. In these texts a decisive gain in knowledge must have its origin in God; thus a wise man may be to some extent inspired in a way similar to a prophet (1972, 54–57).

The fourth role of the Spirit in Job involves

judgment. Since the Spirit forms the basis for life, his retraction by God would be the equivalent of the sentence of death (Job 34:14; cf. the [non-judgmental] return of the *rûaḥ* at death "to God, who gave it" in Eccl. 12:7). Job 4:9 is a clearer reference to judgment if perhaps a less clear reference to the Spirit.

A fifth role may be detected in 26:12–13 unless the translation "wind" is preferred. Here God's *rûaḥ* is paralleled with his power, and both are at work in his creation.

In the WL the Spirit is not seen as distinct from God; rather, the Spirit of God is God at work within the world and especially at work with humanity, giving life and wisdom and calling into account in judgment. Yet in the light of later biblical texts, i.e., NT texts, the reader may sometimes glimpse the NT "Holy Spirit" at work here as well.

Bibliography: J. L. Crenshaw, *Old Testament Wisdom: An Introduction* (1981); D. Johns, "Literary and Theological Functions of the Elihu Speeches in the Book of Job," Ph.D. diss., St. Louis University, 1983; J. W. McKay, "Elihu—A Proto-Charismatic?" *ExpT* 90 (1979): 167–71; R. B. Y. Scott, *The Way of Wisdom in the Old Testament* (1971); G. von Rad, *Wisdom in Israel* (1972).   D. A. Johns

WISDOM, WORD OF (Gk. *logos sophia*). One of several charismata; mentioned by Paul only in 1 Corinthians 12:8. The fact that Paul does not elaborate on the use of this charism or provide further definition of its character has left it open to a variety of interpretations. In Pentecostal circles it has been commonly understood to be a word of revelation given by the Holy Spirit to provide wisdom to the Christian community at a particular time of need, often applying scriptural wisdom to the situation. It may best be understood by looking at the larger wisdom tradition of Israel in general, then by studying the concept of wisdom as it appears within the context of 1 Corinthians.

In the tradition of Israel, wisdom played an important role. This may be observed by studying the various forms that it took in the literature of the nation. It was present in the preaching of Qoheleth and in the extended poetry of Job. It appeared often in the pithy one- and two-line Proverbs, and it was both personified and highly praised in Proverbs 8. Wisdom made its appearance in other OT writings as well. The Spirit or *rûaḥ* of God was believed to have provided wisdom, literally, to have made "wise-hearted" (*el kol ḥōkmê lēḇ*) those who made clothes for members of the Aaronic priesthood (Exod. 28:3). Joshua was said to have received the spirit of wisdom through the laying on of hands (Deut. 34:9), and it was anticipated that the messianic figure would also receive the spirit of wisdom (Isa. 11:2).

In addition there are several references that connect the subject of wisdom (Heb. *ḥōkma*) to that of the *rûaḥ* of God. One example occurs in Genesis 41 where we are told that Pharaoh dreamed a dream in which seven gaunt cows had devoured seven healthy ones, and seven thin stalks of grain had swallowed up seven healthy ones. His own court magicians and wisemen were unable to interpret it for him. Joseph was summoned. He told Pharaoh that God would give him the answer. He went on to interpret the dream as meaning that seven abundant years of crop production would be followed by seven lean years and to recommend that Pharaoh appoint a discerning and wise person to oversee Egypt's agricultural production during the good years to ensure survival in the lean ones.

Pharaoh acknowledged the wisdom of the plan. He asked his own court officials, "Can we find anyone like this man, one in whom is the Spirit of God [*rûah 'elohîm*]?" Turning back to Joseph, Pharaoh continued, "Since God has made all this known to you, there is no one so discerning and wise [*wᵉhakam*] as you" (Gen. 41:38–39). Thus the *rûah* was recognized as being with Joseph. Wisdom was identified within a specific situation, given to a particular end. The interpretation of the dream, with its application to Egypt's need, provided also the revelation of wisdom made known by God. The result was not only that Egypt was saved through the systematic storage of grain but that ultimately it proved to be God's means for preserving the Abrahamic line.

The prophet Daniel was also skilled in wisdom, endowed with knowledge, and capable of understanding visions and dreams (Dan. 1:4, 17). God was the source of Daniel's wisdom, for he acknowledged that God

> gives wisdom to the wise
> and knowledge to the discerning.
> He reveals deep and hidden things;
> He knows what lies in darkness.

In Nebuchadnezzar's second year as regent over Babylon, the king had a dream that none of his wisemen could discern or interpret. Daniel, concerned that the king had overreacted by sending forth an order to destroy all his men, rallied three of his friends to pray that God would reveal the dream and its meaning to him. The answer came in the form of a vision, and the "mystery" was revealed. Daniel informed Nebuchadnezzar that God had given him the key. He advised, "This mystery has been revealed to me, not because I have greater wisdom (*hokmâ*) than other living men, but so that you, O king, may know the interpretation and that you may understand what went through your mind" (Dan. 2:30). After Daniel told him the dream and its interpretation, the king declared, "Surely, your God is God of gods and Lord of kings, and a revealer of mysteries, for you were able to reveal this mystery" (2:47).

Later Nebuchadnezzar issued a decree in which he spelled out that his own wisemen (Dan. 4:6 [MT 4:3]) had been unable to reveal either the dream or its meaning but that Daniel, in whom the king identified what he called the "Spirit of the gods" (*rûah 'elohîm*, Dan. 4:8–9 [MT 4:5–6]), was able to do both. Once again, the idea of wisdom, the presence of the *rûah* or Spirit, and the fact of revelation are all present. The word itself is specific and interpretive in nature, and it ultimately led to Nebuchadnezzar's recognition that Daniel's God is indeed God.

The term "wisdom" (Gk. *sophia*) is an important one for the apostle Paul; and it is with him that we meet the charism. It appears in the Pauline corpus twenty-eight times, of which seventeen are found in 1 Corinthians, the majority of which occur in 1:18–4:21. Paul stood squarely within the tradition of the Hebrews and was well versed in both Jewish and Greek views of wisdom. In the Corinthian situation, however, it is almost certain that he takes on the terms "knowledge" and "wisdom" from a group of the Corinthians themselves. This leads him, in his first letter to Corinth, to distinguish between two types of wisdom: human wisdom, or the wisdom of the "wise," and the wisdom of God.

The wisdom of the "wise" is a form of wisdom that is an intellectual accomplishment pursued especially by the Gentiles (1 Cor. 1:22). The acquisition of this worldly wisdom was considered to be a status symbol (1:26–27). Before God, however, it appears as a foolish quest (1:20; 3:19), a human attainment that falls below even the "foolishness" of God (1:25). Humanity has sought to know God. They have pursued salvation through the attainment of wisdom, but through the divine plan people have been unable to know God in this way (1:21). Their "wisdom" has been of a speculative nature. Ultimately, God will destroy the wisdom of the "wise" (1:19). It seems clear that Paul was not disparaging the intellectual attainment of wisdom, per se, but the acquisition of wisdom, which was thought to be inherently salvific. Such humanly derived wisdom was ultimately doomed to failure and would not transcend the ages (2:6).

In contrast to human wisdom, the wisdom of God was described as a secret and hidden wisdom (2:7) that goes uncomprehended by the natural human being (2:13–16) as well as by demonic powers (2:8). This wisdom is revealed (*apekalypsen* [cf. Eph. 3:3–6]) by the Spirit (2:10). It is related to the plan of salvation (2:7, 9), and it has its origin in the mind of God (2:11) from eternity past (2:7). Its purpose is the glorification of God's people (2:7), and it involves the impartation or interpretation (*synkrinontes*)—perhaps more literally, "making a judgment by means of comparison" of spiritual truth, to those who possess the Spirit (2:12–13). Thus the utterance or word of wisdom comes through the Spirit in such a way as to proclaim Christ, the wisdom of God, crucified.

Isaiah wrote that the Spirit of wisdom (*rûah hokmâ*) would come upon the shoot of the stump of Jesse (Isa. 11:2). Hence, both testaments perceive the source of God's wisdom to be the Spirit. In Isaiah's prophecy this bestowal of wisdom would, among other things, enable the messianic figure to rule with righteousness (11:4–5). He would also assemble the outcasts of Israel (v. 12), recover a remnant (v. 11), and destroy their enemies (vv. 14–16). In short, the concepts that Paul mentions as being present in Jesus (1 Cor. 1:30), including wisdom, righteousness, sanctification, and redemption, may have their background in this Isaiah 11 prophecy. It appears that the wisdom of God is provided so that God's people may have direction within the ongoing plan of God. It is a form of spiritual guidance. Thus the suggestion of James (1:5) that those who lack wisdom should ask God for it may apply to the general category of wisdom as a way of life so prevalent among the people of Israel and the wisdom of tradition, but it may also take on a special significance in relationship to utterances of wisdom that may be requested to fill a specific need.

In 1 Corinthians 12:8 Paul calls this charism a "word" (*logos*), "message," or "utterance" of wisdom. The connection between wisdom and *logos* in the form of "wise words," or "wisdom characterized by word (rhetoric)" may be all that Paul means by this construction as some have suggested. Yet the fact that *logos* appears in the same way with knowledge raises the distinct possibility that Paul has in mind a *specific type* of utterance. It is a word, revealed by God, providing direction from the wisdom of God, which may interpret a situation and enable a congregation to move in accordance with the will of God in light of the plan of salvation. Not all Christians are given this gift, since it is sovereignly distributed by the Holy Spirit (12:11) for the community welfare (12:7–8).

In the postapostolic era, the word of wisdom continued to be accepted as a legitimate charism. Justin Martyr (*Dialog with Trypho* 87) relied on Isaiah 11:2 to explain the continuing spirit of wisdom in the church. Origen worked with the Pauline catalogue of gifts in 1 Corinthians 12 to argue that the charismata there were listed in descending order of value to the life of the church. The word of wisdom, which Origen described as possessing an intuitive or transrational (*thĕŏrēma*) character (*On Prayer* 25:2), was singled out as God's greatest gift (*Comm. on Matt.* 3). Through it, prophets spoke (*Exhort. to Mart.* 8), and the more intelligent Christian came to understand the "spiritual significance" of Scripture (*On First Prin.*, Pref. 8). This enabled them to be Bible teachers (*Ag. Celsus* 1:44; *Comm. on Matt.* 15:37; 16:13).

Origen's observations that Paul gave a hierarchy of charisms in 1 Corinthians 12:8–10, as well as his connection of the word of wisdom with the prophet and with the teacher are common in the church today. The weakness in the theory of hierarchy in this particular catalogue of gifts, however, is that it fails to take seriously all other Pauline catalogues of gifts (Rom. 12:6–8; Eph. 4:11; 1 Cor. 12:28–30) as being either legitimate catalogues or as listing legitimate charisms.

The connection of words of wisdom with prophecy or the view that words of wisdom are a form of prophetic speech is a common one. Jesus told his disciples that when they were brought before those who would persecute them, he would give them words (lit. "a mouth" [*stoma*]) *and* wisdom (*sophia*) to respond (Luke 21:15; Matt. 10:19–20). Early Christians viewed these words alternately as prophetic words and words of wisdom (e.g., Cyprian, *Ep.* 10.4; 57.4; 58.5; 76.5; 81.1). Such manifestations and more particularly those utterances that revealed the mind of God in specific ways are often denied as having validity since the completion of the canon (Unger, Baxter) or are tolerated with ambivalence,

leaning toward condemnation (Bridge and Phypers).

Fears motivating such arguments are real, since the understanding of this charism as a form of prophetic speech must include the claims of the Mormon "prophet" Joseph Smith, who allegedly received a "word of wisdom" in 1833 on the evils of tobacco, wine, and hot drinks such as coffee (*Doc. & Cov.* 89). Questions are raised relating to the infallibility of such utterances and their relationship to Scripture as well as to the role that a completed Christian canon might play in testing. Within the mainstream of Pentecostalism, Harold Horton comes closest to Smith by arguing that the word of wisdom is a word of revelation concerning God's purpose for people, things, or events in the future. This definition is broad enough to include even Smith's utterances, and in the opinion of this author, provides inadequate safeguards.

The connection of this gift with teaching is a more mediating one. In this regard Griffiths has rendered *logos* as "teaching" so that what results is a "teaching of wisdom" derived from Scripture. Close to this but clearly more spontaneous in its orientation is Donald Gee's contention that a "word of wisdom" is a revelation that occurs when one preaches or teaches Christ and the cross and the hearts of the hearers "burn" within them. It approaches the Calvinist concept of an inner testimony of the Spirit, the Wesleyan concept of illumination, and the Barthian concept in which Scripture becomes the Word of God to those who hear God speak as it is proclaimed.

See also GIFTS OF THE SPIRIT; PAULINE LITERATURE.

Bibliography: R. E. Baxter, *Gifts of the Spirit* (1983); A. Bittlinger, *Gifts and Graces* (1967, reprint 1972); D. Bridge and D. Phypers, *Spiritual Gifts and the Church* (1973); G. D. Fee, *The First Epistle to the Corinthians* (1987); D. Gee, *Concerning Spiritual Gifts* (rev. 1980); M. Griffiths, *Grace Gifts* (1978); H. Horton, *The Gifts of the Spirit* (1934, reprint 1971); K. C. Kinghorn, *Gifts of the Spirit* (1976); M. F. Unger, *The Baptism and Gifts of the Holy Spirit* (1978). C. M. Robeck, Jr.

WITHERSPOON, WILLIAM THOMAS

(1880–1947). Pentecostal preacher and leader. Born in Pennsylvania in a home that was not religious, Witherspoon joined a Methodist church after his marriage. Later he worshiped with the Christian and Missionary Alliance, but when he received the baptism of the Holy Spirit in 1912 his fellowship with this group ended. He founded Apostolic Gospel Church in Columbus, Ohio, in 1914 and served as the pastor of this church until his death. In 1932 Witherspoon became the first foreign missionary chairman of the Pentecostal Assemblies of Jesus Christ (PAJC). He was elected general chairman of the PAJC in 1938 and served until the merger that formed the United Pentecostal Church (UPC) in 1945. He was the first assistant general superintendent of the UPC, serving from 1945 until his death.

Bibliography: A. L. Clanton, *United We Stand* (1970). J. L. Hall

WOMEN MINISTERS See WOMEN, ROLE OF.

WOMEN MISSIONARIES   See Missions, Overseas; Women, Role of.

WOMEN, ROLE OF   Women have had extremely important leadership roles in the Pentecostal and charismatic movements, as has been the case in most awakenings and movements of spiritual vitality throughout Christian history.

Many pioneers of Pentecostalism were women, including Florence L. Crawford, founder of the Apostolic Faith movement in the Pacific Northwest; Marie Burgess Brown, who founded Glad Tidings Tabernacle in New York City; and Aimee Semple McPherson, founder of the International Church of the Foursquare Gospel. Some, such as Maria B. Woodworth-Etter and Carrie Judd Montgomery, had already established ministries during the nineteenth-century Holiness movement.

I. Nineteenth Century Precursors to Pentecostalism.

A. The Holiness Movement. There had been a strong tradition of women in leadership in the Holiness movement. Phoebe Palmer had been pivotal in its development with her "Tuesday Meetings for the Promotion of Holiness" held in New York City from 1835 until 1874, and with the wide circulation of her books and tracts, including *The Way of Holiness*, which had appeared in fifty-two editions by 1867. In constant demand as a public speaker, she brought countless people into a full consecration to God.

Hannah Whitall Smith, author of *The Christian's Secret of a Happy Life* (1875), catalyzed the development of the Holiness movement in Britain and throughout Europe. Her activities in England led to the founding of the Keswick Convention in 1874. Later the great Christian author Jessie Penn-Lewis also became an important Keswick leader.

B. The Healing Movement. Women had also been instrumental in the leadership of the healing movement of the same era, beginning with the ministry of Lucy Drake, whose powerful testimony of healing so impressed William E. Boardman that in 1870 he persuaded her to accompany him in his itinerant ministry. As Lucy Drake Osborn, she later founded a faith home in Brooklyn, N.Y., for terminally ill patients.

Another important early figure in the healing movement was Mrs. Elizabeth Mix of Wolcottville, Connecticut, a black woman who regularly ministered at the faith healing conventions of Charles Cullis in Old Orchard, Maine. Among those who received healing through her ministry was Carrie F. Judd (Montgomery), who herself became a great healing evangelist.

II. Early Pentecostalism.

A. Women Associated With Charles F. Parham. Within the context of the twentieth-century Pentecostal movement, the first person to receive the baptism of the Holy Spirit with the gift of tongues was Agnes N. Ozman. As a student at Charles F. Parham's Bethel Bible College in Topeka, Kansas, on January 1, 1901, she asked that hands be laid on her for the baptism of the Holy Spirit, and she began to speak in tongues and "had great joy and was filled with glory"

(LaBerge, n.d., 29). With this, the modern Pentecostal movement was born. Some of the most important early accounts of these events were written by women, such as Parham's wife, Sarah Parham, and her sister, Lillian Thistlethwaite (Parham, 1930, 65–68).

From 1901 onward there were many local revivals taking place in Kansas, Missouri, Texas, and Zion City, Illinois, where many women functioned as important leaders. One of them was a Wesleyan minister who, in the spring of 1903, invited Parham to speak at the mission she pastored in Nevada, Missouri (Menzies, 1971, 42–43; Kendrick, 1961, 57). This meeting was a turning point in Parham's ministry, and from this time onward his message became more widely accepted.

Another important woman, Mrs. Mary A. Arthur, was healed of several very serious physical disabilities in El Dorado Springs, Missouri, on August 17, 1903, while Parham was ministering. After she returned to her home in Galena, Kansas, she and her husband started meetings on a lot adjoining their home. These became so well attended that they found it necessary to secure the Grand Leader building on Main Street in Galena. They invited Parham to preach, and there were literally hundreds of reports of healings, attracting the attention of the Cincinnati *Enquirer* and other local newspapers. Soon afterward a mission was opened on Third Street in Galena by Mary Arthur and Francene Dobson, which was later served by such people as J. W. Welch and E. N. Bell (Brumback, 1961, 29; Goss, 1977, 59).

In 1904 the message of Pentecost was taken to Zion City, Illinois, as a result of the ministry of Mrs. Waldron, who had received the baptism in the Spirit in Lawrence, Kansas, before moving to Illinois. A Mrs. Hall had also moved there from Lawrence and received the baptism of the Spirit at a prayer meeting in Mrs. Waldron's home in Zion City. Both of them carried on a fruitful ministry, leading many others to this experience (Brumback, 1961, 72; Blumhofer, 1985, 136). This prepared the way for Parham's successes at Zion City during September and October 1906.

Anna Hall, one of Parham's workers, was another important leader during this time. At the bidding of Mr. and Mrs. Walter Oyler, she went to Orchard, Texas, to touch off a revival beginning on March 21, 1905. News of this revival traveled rapidly. Mrs. John C. Calhoun of Houston wrote that a report had reached her that "the Latter Rain was falling," and she traveled forty-five miles to Orchard, where "a matronly lady, whom she afterwards learned was Mrs. Anna Hall, gave a soul-stirring message" (Frodsham, 1946, 27). She returned to Houston, testifying of these things to Pastor W. Fay Carothers, a leader of the Holiness church in Brunner, a suburb of Houston, where he and his congregation received the Pentecostal message. His church soon became the headquarters of the Apostolic Faith movement in Texas.

Anna Hall and Mr. and Mrs. Oyler were later selected by Parham to go to Azusa Street in answer to William J. Seymour's requests for help (Parham, 1930, 148). While associated with the

The best-known woman preacher of the 20th century was the flamboyant Aimee Semple McPherson, shown in this photo taken in about 1920.

mission at Azusa Street, Anna Hall preached among Armenians and Russians in Los Angeles, who reportedly understood her in their own languages (Anderson, 1971, 70; Ewart, 1975, 83).

As the Pentecostal movement in the southwestern U.S. gained momentum, many women surfaced in leadership as evangelists and pastors. Among the evangelists were Rosa Cadwalder, Millicent McClendon, Sarah Bradbury, Cora Lane, Nora Byrd, Mabel Wise, Hattie Allen, Mabel Smith-Hall, and "Sister" Coffee. Ethel Goss (1977, 137) wrote of Millicent McClendon that "God mightily used her as an evangelist . . . . Our workers called her 'Little David' because of her remarkable preaching ability." At meetings in Austin "God used her mightily, . . . as she did most of the night preaching"; and in Arlington, Texas, this "freckled-faced, red-headed, girl evangelist mightily preached under the power of the Spirit" (Goss, 1977, 137, 145). Some of the pastors included Fannie Dobson, Ethel Wright, and an unnamed "lady minister" of a church in Texas (Goss, 1977, 179).

Some women had powerful ministries as intercessors. In Malvern, Arkansas, one woman "spent the greater part of every day for five years travailing in intercessory prayer, pleading for the souls of her neighbors, acquaintances, and the surrounding countryside," after which "there was

a mighty outpouring" of the Holy Spirit in the city" (Goss, 1977, 117).

B. Women Associated With William J. Seymour. Lucy Farrow became a key figure in the outpouring of the Holy Spirit at Azusa Street. The leader of a black Holiness mission in Houston, she had received the baptism of the Holy Spirit under Parham's ministry. When Parham's Bible school opened in Houston in December 1905, she and William J. Seymour both attended. That winter, after a visitor from Los Angeles, Neely Terry, returned home, she recommended that Seymour be engaged as pastor of her church. He was invited, and he arrived in March. Although he had not yet spoken in tongues, Seymour was convinced of Parham's view that the gift of unknown tongues was the evidence of the baptism in the Holy Spirit. Because of this, he was locked out of the church after his first sermon, but he and some of the members began meeting at the home of Richard and Ruth Asberry on North Bonnie Brae Street to seek the baptism of the Spirit.

Seymour then requested help from Parham, who sent Lucy Farrow and J. A. Warren in his place. Lucy Farrow had already been quite successful in leading other people into the baptism with the laying on of her hands (Anderson, 1979, 65–66). Within a few days of her arrival "the power fell" on April 9. According to Frank J. Ewart (1975, 75–76), Seymour had laid his hands on Edward Lee, who fell under the power of God but did not speak in tongues. After Lucy Farrow arrived at Lee's home, "Brother Lee asked her to lay hands on him that he might receive the baptism of the Holy Ghost. She did as he requested, and once again Brother Lee dropped to the floor. This time, however, he began to speak in other tongues." Lee, Seymour, and Farrow then went to the meeting already in progress at the Asberry home. As they entered, Lee "threw up his arms and once again spoke in tongues. As he did, the power of God fell on six people who were on their knees praying and they instantly began to speak with other tongues as the Spirit gave utterance" (Ewart, 1975, 65).

The following August, Farrow returned to Houston to preach at a camp meeting. Ethel Goss (1977, 98) observed that after she preached, as she laid hands on people and prayed, "everyone for whom she prayed was speaking in tongues." Farrow later established a work in Portsmouth, Virginia, and went on to Africa as a missionary, where she spent the rest of her life.

Also important to the early Pentecostal movement was another black woman, Jennie Evans Moore, who eventually married W. J. Seymour. She was one of the seven people who first received the gift of tongues at the Asberry home on April 9. On Easter Sunday, April 15, she took Mr. and Mrs. Asberry to her church, pastored by Joseph Smale. After the sermon, when Smale invited testimonies, Moore rose to her feet and testified to the outpouring of the Holy Spirit at the Asberry home. It may have been as a result of this publicity that so many people began visiting the Asberry home that the floor collapsed. Meetings were then moved to 312 Azusa Street. As this building was being renovated, one of the women cleaning it "had one of the workmen down on his knees and soundly converted even before the place was opened" (Cartwright, 1985, 7).

Of the twelve elders at the Apostolic Faith Mission at Azusa Street who were "selected to examine candidates for licenses as missionaries and evangelists" (Coram, 1981, 19), at least six were women: Jennie Evans Moore, "Sister" Prince, Mrs. G. W. Evans, Clara Lum, Phoebe Sargent, and Florence L. Crawford. Sister Prince was described as "a mother in Israel," while Clara Lum was a "stenographer and wonderful helper in editing the paper, and spreading the good news all over the world" (Cook, n.d., 1). There were many other women associated with the work at Azusa Street whose faithful labors were essential to the operation of the mission. Mrs. I. May Throop, for example, handled much of the heavy load of correspondence and other paperwork associated with the mission and its periodical, *The Apostolic Faith*.

C. Emissaries From Azusa Street. In the summer of 1906, Florence L. Crawford left the Apostolic Faith Mission to hold meetings in many California cities, including San Francisco and Oakland, where there were many dramatic conversions to Christ. After her return to Los Angeles, she felt she received a definite call from God to go out and preach. Her son wrote, "One day, as she sat meditating on her call, it seemed that a door opened right before her, revealing the radiant light of Heaven. God spoke to her, saying: 'I have set before thee an open door, and no man can shut it'" (Apostolic Faith Mission, 1965, 63). She responded in obedience, and setting out with her young daughter and with Mr. and Mrs. G. W. Evans, she went to preach at a series of meetings in Salem, Oregon. While there, she received an invitation to hold services at a mission hall in Portland, where she arrived to preach on Christmas Day, 1906. There were many conversions under her preaching, and soon the pastor turned his work over to her. A "real revival broke out" within a short while. "Every chair was filled, the aisles packed, the doorway jammed. Crowds stood out into the streets" (Apostolic Faith Mission, 1965, 64). Crawford's fruitful ministry soon brought her to prominence as leader of the Apostolic Faith movement in the Pacific Northwest.

Another emissary from Azusa Street was Miss Mabel Smith, who brought with her a team of workers to Chicago in the fall of 1906. She "preached nightly to overflowing crowds and wonderful scenes were witnessed," and she "seldom failed to bring pungent conviction to the hearts of the hearers" (Frodsham, 1946, 43). She may have been the evangelist from Texas who, as Mabel Smith-Hall, continued in Galveston, her hometown, where many visiting sailors from foreign nations often reported hearing her preach in their own languages (Goss, 1977, 93–94).

Miss Ivey Campbell, after receiving the baptism in the Spirit at the Azusa Mission, returned to her home city, East Liverpool, Ohio, and then traveled to Akron, Ohio, where she spoke in December 1906 at the Union Gospel Mission pastored by C. A. McKinney. The pastor and many in the congregation received the baptism, and this church soon became a center of Pentecostal activity (Frodsham, 1946, 71). Campbell then went to a Christian and Missionary Alliance church in Cleveland where another powerful revival resulted from her preaching (Niklaus, 1986, 34).

In May 1907 Rachel A. Sizelove left for Springfield, Missouri, after the believers at Azusa Street had laid hands upon her and issued her a minister's license. On the afternoon of her arrival she arranged a prayer meeting that lasted all night. "From that time on, the power began to fall and has been falling ever since" (Brumback, 1961, 68).

D. Other Pentecostal Pioneers.

1. United States. Other pioneers of the Pentecostal movement in the U.S. included the wife of an Iowa state supreme court justice, Mrs. Scott Ladd, who opened a Pentecostal mission in Des Moines in 1907 (Menzies, 1971, 67); the Duncan sisters, who had opened the Rochester Bible Training School at Elim Faith Home where there was a tremendous Pentecostal visitation in June 1907; and "Mother" Barnes of St. Louis, Missouri, who held tent meetings with her son-in-law, B. F. Lawrence, in southern Illinois in the spring of 1908 (Brumback, 1961, 116). According to J. H. Duke, Mother Barnes was involved in the resurrection of Joe French from the dead at the Railroad Hotel in Thayer, Missouri, in June of the same year (Ewart, 1975, 176).

One of the most effective pioneers of the early Pentecostal movement was Marie Burgess, who was won to Pentecostalism in Zion City, Illinois, on October 18, 1906, under the ministry of Charles F. Parham. She preached in Chicago, Toledo, and Detroit and went in January 1907 to New York City to conduct meetings at a Holiness mission. The leader of this mission did not like the Pentecostal message and terminated her meetings after four weeks. Burgess then conducted services in private homes before opening Glad Tidings Hall on New York's 42nd Street in May. Her church soon became an important center for the spread of the Pentecostal revival, igniting it in other parts of New York State and in New Jersey. In October 1909 she married Robert Brown, a Methodist pastor from Ireland who had been baptized in the Holy Spirit at Glad Tidings, which was later moved to 33rd Street. It soon became a focal point for missions to China, India, Africa, and many other places throughout the world. She remained pastor of the church throughout her long life, surviving her husband by many years.

Another early Pentecostal pioneer in New York was Miss Maud Williams (Haycroft), who had been baptized in the Holy Spirit in Canada. On November 15, 1906, T. B. Barratt of Norway first spoke in tongues during her meetings on 14th Street when Lucy Leatherman and a man from Norway laid hands on him. Barratt soon afterward became the father of the Pentecostal movement in Norway, Finland, and many other parts of Europe.

2. *Canada.* On November 17, 1906, Ellen Hebden of Toronto also received the Pentecostal baptism, and her East End Mission soon became important to the development of worldwide Pentecostalism, sending out more than a dozen missionaries in its first few years. Its influence was quickly felt throughout Canada and many parts of the world, and it became a focal point for Canadian Pentecostalism. Mrs. Hebden and her husband remained preeminent in the Pentecostal movement in Toronto for almost a decade. Some of the Pentecostal leaders who came into the movement through her ministry included C. W. Chawner, Arthur Atter, and Robert Semple.

Some of the other significant leaders of the Pentecostal movement in Canada included Ella M. Goff of Winnipeg, Manitoba; Alice B. Garrigus of Boston, Massachusetts, who pioneered the Pentecostal work in Newfoundland; and the Davis sisters, who brought the message of Pentecost to the Maritime provinces shortly after World War I. While ministering in Saint John, New Brunswick, they experienced great revival and established a church of several hundred members. From there, other assemblies were opened throughout New Brunswick, as well as in Nova Scotia and Prince Edward Island.

Mrs. C. E. Baker, who had been healed of cancer in May 1911 at R. E. McAlister's mission in Ottawa, later opened a work in Montreal with her husband. Stanley H. Frodsham (1946, 54) wrote of it that "God has graciously visited Montreal and many hundreds have been saved in that mission and filled with the Spirit." In 1920 they invited Aimee Simple McPherson to Montreal for meetings that "have been described as the greatest revival in the history of Quebec" (Miller, Spring 1986, 14). In the same year, Mr. and Mrs. Baker invited A. H. Argue and his daughter, Zelma, to hold meetings, and there was continued revival, launching Zelma Argue into an important evangelistic ministry with her father in Canada and throughout the U.S. (Miller, Fall 1986, 138–45), and the South Pacific (Atter, 1970, 272–73).

III. Some Major Figures in the Pentecostal Movement.

A. North America.

1. *Carrie Judd Montgomery.* Carrie Judd Montgomery had been healed miraculously in 1879 when she received a letter from Mrs. Elizabeth Mix exhorting her to rise from her deathbed and walk by faith, which she did, to the astonishment of her nurse, her family, and the local Buffalo newspapers, which published articles on her healing. She became a healing evangelist of considerable prominence, and her book *The Prayer of Faith* (1880) soon gained widespread circulation. She published a periodical, *The Triumphs of Faith*, and established Faith Rest Cottage in 1882, a center for divine healing in Buffalo, New York. She became a founding member of A. B. Simpson's Christian and Missionary Alliance in 1887.

After her marriage to George H. Montgomery in 1890, she began a multifaceted ministry in San Francisco, which included a mission, a girl's rescue home, a faith home (Home of Peace), and

a "town" for orphanages (Beulah Heights), which soon became a center for various missionary activities. A training school for missionaries (Shalom Training School) was established, and a church (Beulah Chapel) was built.

In June 1908 Mrs. Montgomery was baptized in the Holy Spirit while in Chicago. She continued with all of the ministries she had established, adding to them a heavy speaking schedule. She eventually decentralized the children's homes and donated them to other individuals and organizations, and she became ordained as a minister by the Assemblies of God in 1917, continuing her multifaceted ministry until her death in 1946.

2. *Maria B. Woodworth-Etter.* Maria B. Woodworth-Etter was also involved in the Holiness movement before she rose to prominence as an early Pentecostal leader. She committed her life to God during meetings in Damascus, Ohio, in 1879, and began ministering in various places near her home in Columbiana County, Ohio, for the next three or four years, venturing into Indiana in 1883 and 1884. At this time she was granted a license to preach by the Churches of God general conference, founded by John Winebrenner in 1825.

In the beginning of 1885 Woodworth-Etter's meetings already began to receive national press coverage, and within a few months she began preaching about divine healing. During the period 1885–89 she widened the geographical scope of her ministry and "was responsible for starting about a dozen churches, adding 1,000 members, erecting six churches, [and] starting several Sunday schools. In addition, 12 preachers were licensed as a result of her ministry" (Warner, 1986, 32). The revivals she held during this time were attended with unusual manifestations of God's power, many healings, and mass conversions. In 1890 she was thought to have incorrectly predicted an earthquake in San Francisco, and her ministry went into relative obscurity until April 18, 1906, when San Francisco received one of the worst earthquakes in recorded history just a few days after the initial outpouring of the Holy Spirit in Los Angeles. During these sixteen years there had been continued manifestations of unusual power at her meetings (Woodworth-Etter, 1916, 108–50).

During the early Pentecostal movement Woodworth-Etter was in continual demand, becoming a featured speaker at the Worldwide Pentecostal Camp Meeting at Arroyo Seco, California, in April 1913. She founded the Woodworth-Etter Tabernacle in western Indianapolis in 1918, which she pastored until her death in 1924.

3. *Aimee Semple McPherson.* Aimee Semple McPherson was converted and baptized in the Spirit in late 1907 and early 1908 at meetings held by Robert Semple in Ingersoll, Ontario. She later married him, and in the winter of 1909–10 they began holding meetings in London, Ontario, at the home of a local resident. They soon went to Hong Kong as missionaries, where Robert Semple died. With a baby daughter, Aimee went to New York City to visit her mother in 1911 until her marriage to Harold McPherson of Providence, Rhode Island, the following year. In 1914 she began preaching at Wednesday night prayer meetings and Sunday night services in small Pentecostal churches near Providence. While there, she became acquainted with Christine Gibson, who, with her husband, later started a small Pentecostal mission, the Church of the Firstborn, a forerunner of Zion Bible Institute.

In 1915 Aimee began preaching at meetings in Ontario, Canada. From 1916 onward she began preaching along the U.S. Eastern Seaboard, taking an evangelistic tour across the country in 1918. She established a home base in Los Angeles in 1919, where Angelus Temple was dedicated in 1923. She continued as senior pastor there, carrying on a radio ministry and accepting speaking engagements worldwide. Despite the "kidnapping scandal" of 1926, when she was accused of carrying on an adulterous liaison during an absence of several weeks in May and June of that year, she incorporated the International Church of the Foursquare Gospel in 1927, which soon became a major Pentecostal denomination. In the late 1930s a tremendous revival swept Angelus Temple, which she continued to serve as pastor until her death in 1944.

4. Kathryn Kuhlman. Kathryn Kuhlman's ministry began in the summer of 1923, two years after her conversion in Concordia, Missouri, at the age of fourteen. Her sister Myrtle brought her to Oregon to join her and her husband, Everett Parrot, in their ministry as itinerant evangelists. Also on their team was a pianist, Helen Gulliford, who began working with Kathryn Kuhlman independently in 1928. Kuhlman was ordained by the Evangelical Church Alliance in Joliet, Illinois, during the early 1930s, and she established the Denver Revival Tabernacle in 1935, where she remained as pastor until her marriage in 1938 to Burroughs A. Waltrip, who had divorced his wife to marry her. Her ministry was rendered ineffective by this union, which she renounced in 1944. She began preaching in Pennsylvania, Ohio, Illinois, Indiana, West Virginia, and Georgia. In each case, she preached with considerable success, although in many cases her meetings were cut short when details of her marriage were discovered. In 1946 she returned to Franklin, Pennsylvania, where she began to thrive as a preacher and radio evangelist. Many people were healed at her meetings beginning in 1947, and she began to gain a reputation as one of the world's outstanding healing evangelists, carrying on as a leading figure during the charismatic movement until her death in 1976.

B. Women in Foreign Countries. Some of the women who were pioneers of the Pentecostal movement outside of North America, either as indigenous pastors or evangelists or as missionaries, included Ethel Abercrombie, Grace Agar, Blanch Appleby, Maria Atkinson, Ethel Bingeman, Hélène Biolley, Anna Larssen Bjorner, Susan Easton, Margaret Felch, Marguerite Flint, Maria Fraser, Lizzie Frazer, Mrs. A. G. Garr, Mrs. George Hansen, Phoebe Holmes, Lillian Keys, Lucy Leatherman, Bernice Lee, Anna Lewini, Ingrid Lokken, Alice E. Luce (to Hispanics in America), Nettie Moomau, Dr. Florence Murcutt, Johanna Nxumalo, Nukwase Nxumalo, Olga

Olsson, Catharine S. Price, Pandita Ramabai, Violet Schoonmaker, Fanny Simpson, Sarah A. Smith, Lillian Trasher, Kathryn B. Vogler, Lettie Ward, and Alice C. Wood.

C. Women in the Charismatic Movement. A few of the women working as Pentecostal pastors during the charismatic movement of the 1960s and 1970s included Charlotte Baker, Myrtle D. Beall, Helen Beard, Aimee Cortese, Sue Curran, B. Maureen Gaglardi, Anne Giminez, Ione Glaeser, Hattie Hammond, Alpha O. Henson, Marilyn Hickey, Violet Kitely, Janet Kreis, Freda Lindsay, Fuchsia T. Pickett, Iverna Thompkins, and Rachel Titus. A sampling of a few of the other women who were vital during the time of the charismatic movement as speakers, authors, or evangelists, would include Eleanor and Roberta Armstrong, Rita Bennett, Edith Blumhofer, Hazel Bonawitz, Roxanne Brant, Mary Ann Brown, Shirley Carpenter, Jean Darnall, Josephine Massyngberde Ford, Katie Fortune, Shirlee Green, Nina Harris, Sue Malachuk, Daisy Osborn, Dorothy Ranaghan, Agnes Sanford, Gwen Shaw, Bernice Smith, Ruth Carter Stapleton, Jean Stone, Joni Eareckson Tada, and Corrie Ten Boom.

IV. Analysis. Although women had great freedom to preach at the beginning of the Pentecostal movement, the proportion of women in leadership dropped dramatically after 1920 (Barfoot and Sheppard, 1980, 2) until the time of the charismatic renewal, when this trend was reversed (Garlock, 1981, 44).

A. Why Women Originally Had Freedom to Preach. At the beginning of the twentieth century there were a number of factors favorable for the leadership of women among Pentecostals:

1. Historical Circumstances. During the nineteenth century, the process of industrialization and the rise of the urban family freed many women from the traditional household duties that had made any significant activities outside of the context of the home nearly impossible. With smaller families (Hassey, 1986, 7) and labor-saving devices, women had more time to devote to social and religious causes.

During the abolition movement beginning in the 1830s people began thinking of freedom and equality not only for slaves but also for women. Many of the most outspoken abolitionists were women such as Sara Grimké, who spoke publicly against slavery when there were serious social taboos against a woman addressing a mixed public assembly (Dayton, 1976, 47).

The resulting movement for women's rights was another factor that paved the way for greater acceptance of the possibility of women's leadership in the church. Such women as Frances Willard had had the Holiness experience of entire sanctification and believed themselves called of God to become active in the women's suffrage movement (Hardesty, Dayton, and Dayton, 1979, 234–35). Organizations such as the Woman's Christian Temperance Union (WCTU), the Young Women's Christian Association (YWCA), and many women's missionary societies began to afford women opportunities for leadership roles. By the turn of the century, women had a far greater status among Evangelicals than ever before or afterward (Hassey, 1986, 9). There had been an "egalitarian thrust" in the revivalism of the nineteenth century (Dayton, 1976, 48), emphasizing Galatians 3:28, according to which in Christ there is neither Jew nor Greek, slave nor free, male nor female.

2. Early Pentecostalism Was a Revival Movement. During times of revival, women have often had greater freedom. There is usually a tremendous emphasis on evangelism and/or missions, coupled with a sense of extreme urgency. During a revival, the time is considered short, and all available personnel are mobilized immediately, whether men or women, laity or clergy, formally educated or not.

During reawakenings of Christian faith, authority is usually grounded more on experience than on educational or ecclesiastical qualifications. As a basis for the authority to preach, formal ordination begins to pale in significance compared to evidence of the anointing of the Holy Spirit on an individual (Blumhofer, 1985, 137). Great stress is laid on the experience of a divine call (Barfoot and Sheppard, 1980, 4). During the Holiness and Pentecostal revivals, many women did not find it easy to resist the call of God on their lives to preach (Barfoot and Sheppard, 1980, 8; Scanzoni and Setta, 1986, 226, 237; Hardesty, Dayton, and Dayton, 1979, 243).

3. The Influence of the Holiness Movement. The Pentecostal revival arose from the Holiness movement of the nineteenth century, which had had a long tradition of openness toward women in ministry. In fact, many women joined the Pentecostal movement after recognized ministry in various Holiness denominations. There had been an emphasis on social reform in the Holiness movement, and the idea of equal rights for women was a part of this thrust (Dayton, 1976, 53). Many people in the Holiness movement had written books and tracts advocating the right of women to preach (Dayton, 1985; Scanzoni and Setta, 1986, 224–25).

Under the ministry of Charles G. Finney, women had been encouraged to speak in mixed assemblies as early as the 1830s, despite social strictures against this practice. This freedom for women was strengthened during the Holiness movement as both men and women were encouraged to make immediate public confession of entire sanctification. Women were also able to participate in "Bible readings," where a speaker would read a passage from the Bible and comment on it as appropriate. This practice enabled women and laymen to preach without giving a formal sermon (Hardesty, Dayton, and Dayton, 1979, 247). As Holiness denominations came into existence, many of them, such as the Church of the Nazarene and the Church of God (Anderson, Indiana), ordained women as pastors (Scanzoni and Setta, 1986, 225–26).

Because the Holiness movement stressed the doctrine of sanctification and the restoration, to a degree, of the prefallen state of humankind by God's transforming grace, it was felt that any elements of the curse laid on women as a result of the Fall need not apply to the church, the company of the redeemed and restored (Dayton,

1976, 54). The perfectionistic theology of both the Holiness and Pentecostal movements saw the subordination of women as part of the sinful state out of which redemption was needed. In both movements there was an expectation of the dawning of a new era in which such evils as the subordination of women would be overcome. There was an emphasis on the outpouring of the Holy Spirit as recorded in Acts 2, according to which both men and women were baptized in the Spirit. The fact that the Spirit was being poured out on all flesh and that both men and women were prophesying indicated that the latter rain of God's Spirit was falling, signifying that the end of the age was very near.

B. Why the Role of Women Later Became More Restricted. There were several reasons for the decline in the leadership of women among Pentecostals after 1920.

1. Historical Circumstances. The abolition movement had ended in victory with the Emancipation Proclamation, which had taken effect at the beginning of 1863. Moreover, the Nineteenth Amendment was ratified in 1920, extending to women the right to vote. This major victory put an end to much of the activity of the movement for women's rights. Pentecostalism was not as concerned about women's rights as the Holiness movement had been, and it did not produce a body of literature on the right of women to preach comparable to that of the Holiness movement. Among Pentecostals, the equality of women was often affirmed with qualifications and reservations (Barfoot and Sheppard, 1980, 4, 7, 14; Scanzoni and Setta, 1986, 229).

2. The Fear of Apostasy. The Fundamentalist-Modernist controversy engendered a fear of apostasy among many believers. Culturally specific applications of the Scriptures increasingly came to be viewed with alarm and suspicion (Scanzoni and Setta, 1986, 233). People began to worry that changes in the traditional role of women might bring about the collapse of the home and the destruction of society (Scanzoni and Setta, 1986, 231). As a result, the Fundamentalist movement began to drift away from the ordination of women, contrary to its earlier practices in many quarters (Hassey, 1986, xiii–xiv). The *Scofield Reference Bible* (1909), which gained wide circulation and did not treat women favorably, had a powerful influence on evangelical opinions with respect to biblical teachings on women (Scanzoni and Setta, 1986, 233).

3. The Decline of Revival. A decline in spiritual vitality usually brings with it fewer opportunities for women and laymen to preach. Sociologist Max Weber has observed that it is only in rare cases that the practice of allotting equality to women extends beyond the first stage of the formation of a religious community (Barfoot and Sheppard, 1980, 2). As the sense of urgency decreases, so does the utilization of all available personnel. There is usually a concern for increased social respectability, resulting in a greater accommodation to the culture. After the initial phase of the Pentecostal movement, bureaucratization and institutionalization resulted in a growing professionalism of the ministry and fewer opportunities for leadership for women in a society that considered the woman's place to be in the home (Barfoot and Sheppard, 1980, 14, 16; Scanzoni and Setta, 1986, 233).

Bibliography: D. E. Albrecht, "Carrie Judd Montgomery; Pioneering Contributor to Three Religious Movements," *Pneuma* 8 (Fall 1986): 101–19; Apostolic Faith Mission, *A Historical Account of the Apostolic Faith* (1965); R. Bahr, *Least of All Saints* (1979); C. H. Barfoot and G. T. Sheppard, "Prophetic Vs. Priestly Religion: The Changing Role of Women Clergy in Classical Pentecostal Churches," *Review of Religious Research* 22 (September 1980): 2–17; F. Bartleman, *How Pentecost Came to Los Angeles* (1925); D. Basham, "Women in Ministry," *New Wine* 6 (October 1974): 18–22; H. Beard, *Women in Ministry Today* (1980); E. Blumhofer, "The Christian Catholic Apostolic Church and the Apostolic Faith: A Study in the 1906 Pentecostal Revival," in C. M. Robeck, Jr., ed., *Charismatic Experiences in History* (1985), 126–46; idem, "The Role of Women in the Assemblies of God," *AG Heritage* 7 (Winter 1987–88): 13–17; idem, "The Role of Women in Pentecostal Ministry," *AG Heritage* 6 (Spring 1986): 11, 14; C. Booth, *Female Ministry; or, Woman's Right to Preach the Gospel* (1859); J. Buckingham, *Daughter of Destiny* (1976); K. Bushnell, *God's Word to Women* (1912); D. W. Cartwright, "Your Daughters Shall Prophesy: The Contribution of Women in Early Pentecostalism," in *Papers of the Fifteenth Annual Meeting of the Society for Pentecostal Studies* (1985); P. J. Cole, Introduction to A. J. Gordon's "The Ministry of Women," Gordon-Conwell Theological Seminary Monograph #61; F. T. Coram, *Like As of Fire* (1981); D. W. Dayton, "Evangelical Roots of Feminism," *The Covenant Quarterly* 34 (November 1976): 41–56; D. W. Dayton, ed., *Holiness Tracts Defending the Ministry of Women* (1985); F. Franson, *Prophesying Daughters* (1896); R. Garlock, "Women: Pentecost and the Release of Women in Ministry," *Logos Journal* 11 (March–April, 1981): 42–45; W. B. Godbey, *Woman Preacher* (1891); A. J. Gordon, "The Ministry of Women," *MRW* 7 (n.s., December 1894): 910–21; S. Grimké, *Letters on the Equality of the Sexes and the Condition of Woman* (1838); G. P. Hayes, *May Women Speak?* (1889); N. Hardesty, *Women Called to Witness: Evangelical Feminism in the Nineteenth Century* (1984); N. Hardesty, L. Dayton, and D. W. Dayton, "Women in the Holiness Movement: Feminism in the Evangelical Tradition," in R. Ruether and E. McLaughlin, eds., *Women of Spirit* (1979), 226–54; J. Hassey, *No Time For Silence* (1986); F. M. Hunter, *Women Preachers* (1905); J. W. James, *Women in American Religion* (1980); P. King, "Aglow," *Logos Journal* 4 (May–June 1974): 34–35; A. N. O. LaBerge, *What God Hath Wrought* (n.d.); L. Lee, *Woman's Right to Preach the Gospel* (1853); F. Lindsay, *Freda* (1984); J. O. McClurkan, *Chosen Vessels* (1901); G. B. McGee, "Three Notable Women in Pentecostal Ministry," *AG Heritage* 6 (Spring 1986): 3–5, 12; A. S. McPherson, *This Is That* (1919); T. W. Miller, "The Canadian 'Azusa': The Hebden Mission in Toronto," *Pneuma* 8 (Spring 1986): 5–29; R. L. Niklaus, J. S. Sawin, and S. J. Stoesz, *All For Jesus* (1986); P. Palmer, *The Promise of the Father; or a Neglected Specialty of the Last Days* (1859); S. E. Parham, *The Life of Charles F. Parham* (1930); J. Penn-Lewis, *The Magna Charta of Women* (1919); D. Prince, "A Stormy Christmas in the Holy Land," *New Wine* 8 (December 1976): 4–8; D. Prince, "Single, Married— and Single Again," *New Wine* 9 (February 1977): 4–9; S. C. Rees, *The Ideal Pentecostal Church* (1897); R. M. Riss, *A Survey of Twentieth Century Revival Movements in North America* (1988); idem, *Latter Rain* (1987); B. T. Roberts, *Ordaining Women* (1891); R. R. Ruether and R. S. Keller, eds., *Women & Religion in America*, 3 vols. (1981–1986); L. D. Scanzoni and S. Setta, "Women in Evangelical, Holiness, and Pentecostal Traditions," in R. R. Ruether and R. S. Keller, eds., *Women and Religion in America* 8 (1986): 223–65; W. A. Sellew, *Why Not?* (1894); L. A. Starr, *Bible Status of Women* (1926); C. Trombley, *Who Said Women Can't Teach?* (1985); M. H. Wallace, *Pioneer Pentecostal Women*, 2 vols. (1981); W. E. Warner, *The Woman Evangelist: The Life and Times of Charismatic Evangelist Maria B. Woodworth-Etter* (1986); idem, *Touched by the Fire* (1978); M. B. Woodworth-Etter, *Signs and Wonders* (1916).   R. M. Riss

Women praying for each other during the 1984 conference of the Women's Aglow Fellowship.

WOMEN'S AGLOW FELLOWSHIP

(WAF). Interdenominational evangelistic outreach. The Women's Aglow Fellowship originated in 1967 in Seattle, Washington, with a group of women coming together for lunch, prayer, and fellowship. The organization has grown from its small beginnings to a worldwide community of more than 1,300 fellowships (*Aglow*). Under a program called World Literature Thrust, WAF has distributed 44,000 Bible study books in Africa, 28,500 in India (WAF Memo, 3). Other literature has been distributed all over the world. WAF also publishes a national magazine: *Aglow*. The fellowship's central goals are to share worship, witness for Christ, work for unity among believers, foster fellowship, and encourage women to participate fully in the local church.

Bibliography: "Women's Aglow Fellowship Executive Board Memo" (March 16, 1987), 3; Women's Aglow Fellowship, *What Is Aglow?* (n.d.).   F. Bixler

WOODWORTH-ETTER, MARIA BEU-LAH (1844–1924). One of the best-known and most successful itinerant evangelists at the turn of the century. Although often controversial because of her emphasis on the power of the Holy Spirit and faith healing, Maria B. Woodworth-Etter ministered with the Winebrennerian Churches of God (CG) for twenty years (1884–1904). Later, among Pentecostals, even though she was in her sixties and seventies, she was still one of the most popular evangelists on the sawdust trail.

Much of Woodworth-Etter's popularity and notoriety—which carried over into the Pentecostal movement—can be traced to the practice of faith healing and other charismatic gifts she began to employ in meetings in about 1885. Those features attracted an estimated 25,000 people to a camp meeting near Alexandria, Indiana, in 1885. Newspapers gave varied reports of her exploits, usually calling attention to the trances (or being "slain in the Spirit") and general pandemonium but not failing to notice the many conversions usually registered in every meeting. (See *The Woman Evangelist* for numerous newspaper quotes from coast to coast.) In most cities where she conducted her nineteenth-century meetings—some as long as five months—newspaper editors were caught up by the huge crowds, the excitement, and a woman in the pulpit, and they regarded her meetings as the biggest news story at the time. Generous front-page coverage, which was often critical and satirical, was common. Woodworth-Etter, however, took it all in stride, even after the editorial broadsides, and after being arrested and charged with obtaining money under false pretenses in one city and practicing medicine without a license in another.

Woodworth-Etter never lost sight of her "call" to preach, which she said God gave to her when she was a child. Her preaching netted conversions (as many as five hundred a week in 1885), planted churches, and spread Holiness teaching in the nineteenth century and Pentecostalism in the twentieth. She became probably the best-known Holiness preacher to embrace Pentecostalism. Her contribution to women's rights in the ministry would be difficult to measure, but it must be immense. Ironically, historians outside of the Pentecostal movement have largely ignored Woodworth-Etter's contribution to revival movements in America.

I. Early Life and Preaching. Born Maria Beulah Underwood near Lisbon, Ohio, in 1844, she was one of eight children. Their father died when Maria was twelve, so she dropped out of school to help her mother. A Dr. Belding (possibly Warren A.) conducted a revival meeting at the Lisbon Christian Church when Maria was thirteen. She was converted and baptized and felt a call to the ministry even though she knew her church did not have women preachers.

Woodworth-Etter's disastrous marriage to P. H. Woodworth and the rearing of her six children made a preaching career highly unlikely. In a series of deep sorrows, the Woodworths lost five of their six children to illnesses. When Maria was thirty-five, in 1879, she attended a Friends revival meeting and renewed her spiritual com-

Probably the best known 19th-century Holiness minister to embrace Pentecostalism was Maria B. Woodworth-Etter. She became a popular Pentecostal evangelist in 1912.

mitment. Soon she began having success in preaching local revivals, and those successes launched her into a lifelong itinerant ministry. Apparently her first church association was with the United Brethren, but then she joined the Churches of God (Winebrenner) in 1884. Her attitude throughout her career was ecumenical, however, even accepting an invitation from Mormons to preach in Nebraska in 1920.

II. Nineteenth-Century Mass Evangelism. Woodworth-Etter's meetings took on gigantic proportions beginning in 1885, after she had been preaching about five years. When she opened a campaign in Hartford City, Indiana, in January, the crowds poured in from miles around, and soon no building in town could hold them. As many as twenty reporters attended and filed stories. Even the *New York Times* took notice and published stories. Conversions and trances became popular. Lawyers and doctors joined the common people at the once despised "mourner's bench." Hartford City was only the beginning of exciting meetings—somewhat of a Woodworth-Etter prototype—which made her a household name throughout the Midwest and beyond. Some amazing accounts of healings and conversions were frequently reported in newspaper stories and later repeated in Woodworth-Etter's journal-type books.

During the nineteenth century, Woodworth-Etter preached a subsequent spiritual experience that she called "the power." This was often accompanied by a trance and a vision that could go on for hours. She regarded the phenomenon as the same type that the apostle Peter experienced at Joppa (Acts 10). She often went into trances herself during a service, standing like a statue for an hour or more with her hands raised while the service continued. As would be expected, the trances drew much criticism in and out of the church. She was soon dubbed the "trance evangelist." Later she was called the "priestess of divine healing" and the "voodoo priestess." A frequent charge was that she hypnotized the people. Two doctors in St. Louis tried to have her committed as insane during a meeting she conducted there in 1890.

Woodworth-Etter undoubtedly picked up bits and pieces of her theology from Finney, Mahan, Simpson, Boardman, and other nineteenth-century ministers and theologians. She did not originate the teachings and practices but certainly popularized them through her mass meetings and many books.

The gift of prophecy operated in her meetings from the beginning, Woodworth-Etter claimed. Possibly the best-known prophecy, and one she never reported in her books, was that the San Francisco Bay area would be destroyed by an earthquake and tidal wave in 1890. Newspapers said that about a thousand people fled to the hills because of the prophecy.

In 1891 Woodworth-Etter divorced P. H. Woodworth, charging him with adultery. He died the next year. She married Samuel Etter in 1902 and so hyphenated her two last names.

III. The Pentecostal Movement. Woodworth-Etter's involvement with the Pentecostal movement on a major scale began in 1912, at age sixty-eight, in Dallas, where F. F. Bosworth had founded a church. He invited her to conduct a meeting, which ran from July until December. The meeting was momentous for both Woodworth-Etter and the Pentecostal movement (not to speak of the boost it gave to Bosworth's local church). It gave Woodworth-Etter a national platform as a Pentecostal heavyweight, inasmuch as many important leaders in the movement were attracted to the meeting from all over the country. Pentecostalism and Woodworth-Etter received favorable publicity through published reports in the movement's periodicals as far away as England. The next spring Woodworth-Etter was the main speaker at the Worldwide Camp Meeting in Los Angeles.

With the exception of Charles F. Parham, Frank J. Ewart, and a few others, it appears that most early Pentecostals looked at Woodworth-Etter as a godsend to the movement and accepted her uncritically. They knew about her legendary nineteenth-century ministry and were certain that she would have success in the Pentecostal movement. From eyewitnesses and published reports, it appears that the movement was not disappointed with her ministry.

Although Woodworth-Etter claimed that people spoke in tongues in her meetings from the beginning, this claim never was documented. In looking back on her own ministry after the Pentecostal movement began, she equated her subsequent experience of the 1880s as the baptism in the Holy Spirit, but she does not claim to have spoken in tongues in the early years. Her particular brand of holiness, however, put her in a vanguard that helped usher in the Pentecostal movement.

In 1918 Woodworth-Etter established a local church in Indianapolis. She was the pastor but continued to conduct meetings in the Midwest during the last six years of her life. That church is now the large Lakeview Christian Center.

In examining Woodworth-Etter's forty-plus years as a Holiness-Pentecostal preacher, primarily as an evangelist, one is amazed at what she was able to accomplish as a woman between 1880 and 1924. She was organizing and preaching huge campaigns with little or no local church backing thirty to forty years before women could vote in national elections. She took salvation, faith healing, and a subsequent spiritual experience of power to the masses. Amazingly, her eight-thousand-seat tent, which she began to use in 1889, was often too small to hold the seekers, the faithful, the curious, and the usual troublemakers. And her holiness star kept rising, right into the fledgling Pentecostal movement.

Maria B. Woodworth-Etter was no theologian, but in the words of D. William Faupel, she was "a monumental figure in terms of spreading the pentecostal message" (*The Woman Evangelist*, 175).

Bibliography: W. Warner, "Indiana's Forgotten Women on the Sawdust Trail," *Indianapolis Star* (September 16, 1984); idem, "Maria B. Woodworth-Etter and the Early Pentecostal Movement," *AG Heritage* (Winter 1986–87), 11; idem, *The Woman Evangelist* (1986); M. Woodworth-Etter, *Signs and Wonders* (1916, reprinted 1980).　　　W. E. Warner

WORD OF FAITH MOVEMENT See POSITIVE CONFESSION THEOLOGY.

WORD OF FAITH See FAITH, GIFT OF.

WORD OF GOD (ANN ARBOR, MICH.) See CATHOLIC CHARISMATIC RENEWAL; CHARISMATIC COMMUNITIES.

WORD OF KNOWLEDGE See KNOWLEDGE, WORD OF.

WORD OF WISDOM See WISDOM, WORD OF.

WORLD COUNCIL OF CHURCHES (WCC). Officially formed in August 1948 in Amsterdam, the WCC was designed to be "composed of churches which acknowledge Jesus Christ as God and Savior." It is not the intention that the WCC be a church above the churches. Origins of the WCC began in the nineteenth century. However, the World Missionary Conference held in Edinburgh, Scotland, in 1910 played a very significant role, and the modern "ecumenical movement" is usually dated from this meeting. The original impetus was to bring unity of witness among Western churches working on the mission frontiers of the world. A few years later the first *Life and Work* world conference was held in Stockholm, Sweden (1925), followed by the first *Faith and Order* world conference in Lausanne, Switzerland (1927). *Life and Work* and *Faith and Order* combined to form the WCC in

1948. The International Missionary Conference (IMC), formed in 1921, joined forces with the WCC at its third assembly, held in New Delhi (1961).

Fundamentalist Christian groups refused to cooperate in the WCC and in its sister organization in the U.S., the National Council of Churches of Christ (NCCC) (est. 1950). A "rival ecumenical machine" was established, known as the American Council of Christian Churches (1941), followed by the International Council of Christian Churches (ICCC, 1948). These groups, heatedly opposed to the WCC, refused membership of Pentecostals to their organizations. A more moderate group, also opposed to the WCC but in less outspoken measures, was the National Association of Evangelicals (NAE, 1942), in which classical Pentecostal denominations were allowed membership. Several Pentecostal denominations are charter members of the NAE.

Pentecostals have generally been skeptical of the WCC, fearing a compromise of faith on fundamental doctrines. There were, however, signs of a new openness to the ecumenical movement by two pioneers of ecumenism within the Pentecostal movement. David J. du Plessis (1905–87) and Donald Gee (1891–1966) were Pentecostal leaders who urged their brethren to become involved in the WCC. In 1960 they attended a meeting of Faith and Order in St. Andrews, Scotland. Keith Bridston recorded his impression of the Pentecostal presence:

The words of Dr. David du Plessis, former general secretary of the World Conference of Pentecostal Churches [PWC], were heard with special interest when he said he was "privileged to share in two Pentecostal revivals; one still outside the World Council of Churches [classical Pentecostalism], and the other, more recent one, inside the Historic Churches [charismatic renewal] within the Ecumenical Movement" (1960, 4).

Du Plessis also attended the Third Assembly of the WCC in New Delhi and was listed in the program as an "observer . . . personally invited." But the overriding opinion of Pentecostals has been that "contact produces compromise." A watered-down theology, liberalism, and the social gospel are major objections against associating with the WCC or its member churches.

In 1965 the Assemblies of God (AG) passed a resolution at their general council opposing the "Ecumenical Movement." This statement has become Article VIII, Section 11 of the bylaws and reads in part: "The General Council of the Assemblies of God disapproves of ministers or churches participating in any of the modern ecumenical organizations on a local, national, or international level in such a manner as to promote the Ecumenical Movement. . ." *Minutes . . . The Forty-Second General Council, August 6–11, 1987,* 133. Although the statement does not mention the WCC, it is directed toward the WCC as well as the NCCC. Of the major Pentecostal denominations in the U.S., only the AG has incorporated such a statement into their constitu-

tion and bylaws, although the other Pentecostal groups (in the U.S.) are no more sympathetic toward the WCC than the AG.

Besides the positive efforts of du Plessis and Gee, not all Pentecostals took a negative view of the WCC. At the third assembly in New Delhi there were two small Pentecostal denominations that joined the WCC—the first Pentecostal groups to do so: the *Iglesia Pentecostal de Chile* (Pentecostal Church of Chile) and *Misión Iglesia Pentecostal* (Pentecostal Mission Church). These two Chilean Pentecostal groups reported the reason that they did not join the WCC sooner was because they had been misinformed about the organization. Lesslie Newbigin, on his first visit to Latin America, saw the division between Evangelicals (including the Pentecostals) and the historic churches. He soon realized that "evangelical Christianity in this vast continent had been founded on a negation. Not the beauty of the Gospel but the horror of Rome seemed to be the deepest motive." Of his visit Newbigin said, "When one begins by exalting a negative it is very difficult to get out of that posture" (1985, 184). Augusto E. Fernandez Arlt, a Lutheran, says that the reason for the Pentecostals from Chile joining the WCC was more in the field of service than in dimensions of theological discussions. The earthquake of 1960 in Chile brought Pentecostals and relief workers from the WCC together to assist in the moral and financial rebuilding of the country.

These two groups are Chilean in their origin, their leadership, and their financial structure. They do not depend on any North American or European mission board. Arlt reports that the significance of these groups joining the WCC shows the openness of the World Council and the opportunity for other Latin American Pentecostal churches to consider membership. It was possible for these two groups to associate with the council without losing any of their authenticity as Pentecostals.

Since the two small Chilean groups joined the WCC, there have been others desiring membership. Other Pentecostal denominations to join the WCC since 1961 include: the Igreja Evangélica Pentecostal "O Brasil para Christo" (The Evangelical Pentecostal Church "Brazil for Christ"); the International Evangelical Church (U.S.); the Eglise du Christ sur la Terre par le Prophète Simon Kimbangu (Church of Christ on Earth by the Prophet Simon Kimbangu) in Zaïre (some Pentecostals may question if this group should be considered a Pentecostal church, although W. J. Hollenweger would so classify it); and the Union of Evangelical Christian Baptists of U.S.S.R., of which the Pentecostals are a part. In Argentina, La Iglesia de Dios (The Church of God) recently became associate members of the WCC.

Barry Till, in *The Churches Search for Unity* (1972) says of Pentecostals and the WCC: "As far as Pentecostal membership is concerned the absence of the great majority of the Pentecostalist churches is a serious matter, a weakness second only to the official absence of Rome" (284–85). The possibility of a better relationship between Pentecostals and the WCC came about through the birth of the charismatic movement within the historic Protestant churches and the Roman Catholic church, although it took some years for the WCC to take a serious look at the charismatic renewal.

In August 1980 the Central Committee of the WCC adopted a four-point recommendation made to it by the subunit on Renewal and Congregational Life concerning the charismatic renewal. These recommendations came as a result of an important task force meeting in West Germany (1978) and theological consultation in Bossey, Switzerland (1980), to investigate the charismatic renewal and its implications for all the churches. The result has been an ongoing interest in the worldwide charismatic renewal by the WCC leadership. Two books dealing with the charismatic movement have been published in Geneva, as well as many articles in *The Ecumenical Review* and *International Review of Mission*.

Currently there is a more evangelical orientation within the WCC, as was apparent at the sixth assembly in Vancouver (1983). This is also reflected in its rather conservative president, Emilio Castro, with his openness to Pentecostals, and the renewed concern for world evangelization. It is possible that a new era of possibility can exist between the WCC and classical Pentecostals. The contribution of millions of charismatic Christians in the historic churches has allowed the doors of fellowship and contact to remain open. David Barrett's, *World Christian Encyclopedia* (1983, 838), lists more than 100 million Pentecostal-charismatic Christians worldwide, but more recent figures estimate there are 332 million. With Pentecostalism (and charismatics) on the increase in virtually every part of the world and positive signs of openness to dialogue being demonstrated in the conciliar churches, there just may be an exciting period of acceptance and cooperation on the horizon.

Bibliography: Ecumenism: R. Rouse and S. Neill, eds., *A History of the Ecumenical Movement 1517–1948* (1954); B. Till, *The Churches Search for Unity* (1972). **Pentecostals:** A. E. F. Arlt, "The Significance of the Chilean Pentecostals' Admission to the World Council of Churches," *International Review of Missions* 51 (204, October 1962): 480–82; C. L. d'Epinay, *Haven of the Masses. A Study of the Pentecostal Movement in Chile* (1969); **WCC:** A. J. van der Bent, *What in the World is the World Council of Churches?* (1978, 1981); *Handbook Member Churches. World Council of Churches* (1982); K. Bridston, "Faith and Order: 1960," *Lutheran World* 8 (3, 1960): 1–6; D. P. Gaines, *The World Council of Churches* (1966); H. Martin, *Beginning at Edinburgh* (1960); L. Newbigin, *Unfinished Agenda* (1985); J. C. Smith, *From Colonialism to World Community* (1982); W. A. Visser 't Hooft, *The Genesis and Formation of the World Council of Churches* (1982); idem, *Has the Ecumenical Movement a Future?* (1974). **WCC and Charismatics:** A Bittlinger, ed., *The Church Is Charismatic* (1981); R. David, *Locusts and Wild Honey* (1978); D. Gee, "Amsterdam and Pentecost" *Pentecost* 6 (December 1948); idem, "Contact Is Not Compromise," *Pentecost* 53 (September–November 1960); idem, "Missions and 'Prophets,'" *Pentecost* 10 (December 1949); idem, "Pentecost and Evanston," *Pentecost* 30 (December 1954); idem, "Pentecostals at New Delhi," *Pentecost* 59 (March–May 1962); P. Hocken, *Streams of Renewal* (1986); W. J. Hollenweger, "Towards an Intercultural History of Christianity," *International Review of Missions* 76 (October 1987): 235–37; M. de Mello, "Participation Is Everything," *International Review of Mission*, 60 (238, April 1971): 245–48; C. M. Robeck, Jr., "Pentecostal Perspectives on the Ecumenical Challenge," unpublished paper delivered at the American Academy of Religion, Chicago (December 1984); M. Robinson, "To the Ends of the Earth—The Pilgrimage of an Ecumenical Pentecostal, David J. du Plessis (1905–1987)," Ph.D. diss., University of Birmingham, Birmingham, England, 1987.   J. L. Sandidge

WORLD PENTECOSTAL CONFERENCE
See PENTECOSTAL WORLD CONFERENCE.

WORRELL, ADOLPHUS SPALDING
(1831–1908). A well-known Baptist scholar, teacher, editor, evangelist, and—in later life—a seeker for the baptism in the Spirit at the Azusa Street Mission. At Worrell's death in 1908 the *Louisville Courier-Journal* ran a full-column obituary, "Divine Healer to the Last," which described him as something of an eccentric but godly man who refused any kind of medical help for the stomach cancer that took his life.

Educated at Mercer University, Worrell was regarded as a Greek scholar in the nineteenth century, and he devoted much of his early career to teaching. He was also president of Mt. Pleasant College in Missouri. During the Civil War he was a captain for the Confederate forces and then became a Baptist evangelist. In the 1890s he was an editor for the *Western Recorder*, the Kentucky Baptist paper. He later published his own periodical, *The Gospel Witness*. In 1903 he completed a translation, *Worrell New Testament*, which is still being published by Gospel Publishing House.

Worrell had been in the ministry for nearly forty years by 1891, when he told of a spiritual experience in which Christ was revealed to him and "enthroned in his heart as permanent Ruler thereof" (*Didactic and Devotional Poems*). After personally investigating the Pentecostal movement, he wrote "An Open Letter to the Opposers of This Pentecostal Movement," in which he—while not accepting everything that was going on under the name of Pentecostal—attempted to reason with people who had formed negative opinions of the movement.

Bibliography: "Divine Healer to the Last," *Louisville Courier-Journal* (August 1, 1908); *The Western Recorder* (1890s); A. Worrell, *Didactic and Devotional Poems* (1906); idem, "An Open Letter to the Opposers of This Pentecostal Movement," *Triumphs of Faith* (November 1907).   W. E. Warner

WORSHIP
Worship, in the general sense, refers to piety or spirituality. In the more specific, or narrow, sense, it refers to the *form or style of expression* of piety or spirituality and is a public witness to the union of God and humanity. An early Pentecostal educator and minister, M. E. Collins (n.d., 7) defines worship as "the act of expressing profound love, appreciation, reverence, and devotion to a thing, person or God." Defined in this way, worship is a social, or human, choice to help remind the believer of God's presence and provision. In this article, worship will be viewed in the narrow sense by which Collins defined it, that is, as an *expression* of piety and spirituality. Focus will be chiefly on the contributions of the Lutheran, Reformed,

Free Church, Anglican, Quaker, and Methodist worship traditions as background to Pentecostal worship.

Two phrases can sum the Protestant tradition: justification by faith and the priesthood of all believers (Bartlett, 1925). The appropriate social response to these notions is thanksgiving. As a result, two ordinances, or observances, are common as praise, celebration, or thanksgiving to most Protestant groups. Baptism and initiation is carried over from the Roman Catholic practice of baptism and confirmation. The observance of the Lord's Supper replaced the Mass as a distinctive ordinance of worship. The Lord's Supper is generally seen as a memorial of thanksgiving to the saving work in Christ. To a Protestant, the elements are a reminder of the death and resurrection of Christ and are not assumed by most to be a sacrifice. In the observance of both baptism and the Lord's Supper, the believer offers her or his life as a sacrifice to Christ. The vows of initiation, whether they are taken in baptism or in sharing the Lord's Supper are renewed on a regular basis in some Protestant denominations. In addition, wedding and funeral services can be included within the category of worship.

I. Lutheran. Lutheran worship is strongly conservative and formal (White, 1976). Martin Luther initially wanted to reform the Catholic church rather than establish an alternative worship experience. At the same time, many of his innovations were drastic for the times and provided the model for a significant portion of Protestant liturgical worship. For example, Luther emphasized the sacraments but was the first prominent leader to point out that the sacraments were not sacrificial.

The Lord's Supper for Luther contained the physical and spiritual presence of Christ in the worship service, but he also believed that preaching should be the center of the service. In addition, music and the visual arts have been emphasized in Lutheran worship. Many of the well-known hymns sung by the different denominations were written by Lutheran hymnwriters, and composers have provided the Western world with standards of excellence.

II. Reformed. John Calvin is largely responsible for the pattern of the Reformed worship service and has had considerable impact on other Protestant churches, most notably in the simplicity of style and in the lack of liturgy (Bartlett, 1925; tenZythoff, 1986). Through the influence of Luther and Calvin, the preaching of the Word on each Lord's Day gradually became the central focus of Protestant worship. Calvin thought the Catholic worship style was too passive and allowed the worshiper to entertain stray thoughts. In order for worship to have the desired effect, i.e., to produce a change in the lives of believers, Calvin argued that believers had to play an active part in the worship experience by meditation, reflection, and self-examination. This was possible only if the Scriptures were available in the believers' languages and if preaching was done under the anointing of the Holy Spirit so as to engage the minds of believers. As the saving work of grace came to be understood as the work of the Holy Spirit, preaching was seen to be the expression of the uttered word of God as revealed through the words of Scripture. As each believer is a priest, each has access to God through the Word, as revealed by the Holy Spirit, rather than through the sacraments. Calvin thought that the Lord's Supper should be observed no oftener than once a month lest it lose its symbolic significance, which, for Calvin, was its chief significance.

Calvin encouraged singing because singing also required active engagement by the worshiper. Calvin saw music as being both a symbolic aid to help focus the believer's mind on Christ and thus an aid in worship, and as an expression of worship in its own right. Public prayer, for Calvin, was also an aid to worship and should be spontaneous rather than written, and patterned after the NT prayers.

III. Free Church. The Free Church tradition contributed two specific expressions to Protestant worship (Mead, 1963). First, the autonomy of the local congregation meant that no form of expression became standard. Second, an emphasis on the authority of the Word of God as the model for worship precluded prayerbooks and liturgy.

There are three general categories of Free Church tradition: the Anabaptist, the Puritan, and the Disciples of Christ (White, 1976; Hughes, 1986). The Anabaptist movement began as a resistance to official churches. As a result, the form of worship was simple, with a great deal of local variation. Some stressed singing; others stressed the Lord's Supper. All limited baptism to believers.

The Puritans believed that worship should include only what Scripture allowed. No liturgy or ceremony was included, and some opposed the recitation of the Lord's Prayer. In opposition to the Anabaptists, however, they practiced infant baptism.

The Disciples of Christ are a product of the American frontier revivals, and, in contrast to the Puritans, they attempt to avoid all that Scripture avoided. Systematic theology and formal creeds receive less emphasis, while preaching receives greater emphasis as a result. Disciples of Christ reject infant baptism as unscriptural but give the Lord's Supper central place in the worship experience.

IV. Anglican. The Anglican tradition of worship revolves around the 1549 edition of the *Book of Common Prayer* by Thomas Cranmer and its later revisions. The congregation participates in worship by reciting Scriptures, prayers, and readings. Initially, hymns and the Lord's Supper were excluded but were added later, though some conservatives among Anglicans are still opposed to both.

V. Quaker. The Quaker contribution to worship has been the removal of sermons, public prayers, and hymns from the service (Flew, 1934). Even Scripture is considered less important than the voice of the Holy Spirit, who provides an inner light within each worshiper. Emphasis is placed on corporate worship, or meeting, where each person waits patiently and quietly for the Holy Spirit to speak to him or her, who then tells the others what the Spirit revealed.

While the Quakers stress the work of the Holy Spirit in revealing inner light, they do not believe in the outward manifestation of the baptism of the Holy Spirit, such as glossolalia, which most modern Quakers view as disruptive.

In addition, Quakers stress the equality of all believers, with no categorization by gender, racial, or income differences.

VI. Methodist. The Methodist worship style is a pragmatic blend of several traditions (Hughes, 1986). Under the influence of John and Charles Wesley, Methodism began as a renewal movement within the Anglican church and included elements from Moravian worship, Puritan evangelicalism, and Reformed preaching. The worship experience included hymns set to popular music, informal preaching, and spontaneous prayer.

In the U.S., because of the influence of Bishop Francis Asbury, the formal, liturgical contribution of the Anglican tradition was dropped, while preaching, hymn singing, and spontaneous prayer were underscored. For ceremonies such as baptisms, weddings, funerals, and some other special observances, aspects of the *Book of Common Prayer* have been retained (White, 1976).

The Methodists were instrumental in the revival movements of the nineteenth century and represented a distinctively American religious movement. The Methodists emphasized hymns in the revival meetings and involved the worshipers as active, joyous participants rather than as mere observers.

VII. Pentecostals. Pentecostal worship is an eclectic amalgamation of a variety of traditions, reflecting, to some extent, the denominational origins of its adherents, with some congregations maintaining a significant form of liturgical worship, while others appear, at least to the outsider, to have no coherent pattern or order. All, however, are characterized by an attitude of allowing the Holy Spirit to lead, an attitude that means Pentecostal worship tends to be less structured than that of other groups, even those with which it shares similarities. Historically, Pentecostal worship style is linked to the frontier revivals conducted primarily by Methodists, Disciples of Christ, and Baptists in nineteenth-century America (Mead, 1963).

The Pentecostal churches that were organized during the first decades of the twentieth century place emphasis on the work of the Holy Spirit in worship. The central focus of the service is not the sermon or the music, but the moving of the Holy Spirit. There is the expectation that God will minister in love to the worshiper through the agency of the Holy Spirit (Collins, n.d.). Normally, the service will stop for the moving of the Holy Spirit, usually expressed through glossolalia, or speaking in tongues.

Some of the larger Pentecostal and charismatic churches have developed specialized worship leaders, such as song leaders, who not only select songs, but actively participate in the worship experience, being sensitive to the needs of those who are present. A holdover from the frontier revival meetings, the altar service has become an institutionalized part of the service in some churches. Many churches have specific persons

designated as altar workers. The practice can vary from having mature Christians in the congregation pray and counsel those who come forward, to having a volunteer staff of lay "prayer counselors," led either by another volunteer or by a staff member of the church (Collins, 1986).

Since the early '60s there has been dramatic increase in the numbers of charismatics in the historical or mainline denominations, including the Catholic church. Usually designated charismatics or Neo-Pentecostals, these enthusiasts are developing a new style of worship that combines both glossolalia and the traditional worship style of the denomination in which they are centered. This certainly is one of the more interesting trends in modern expressions of worship (Randall, 1986).

While most Pentecostal worship services have only recently begun to be racially integrated, blacks have shared leadership from the beginning of the modern Pentecostal movement, taking an active part in the historical Pentecostal revivals. As a result, black influence can be seen in preaching style and in music, both of which play significant roles in Pentecostal worship (Patterson et al., 1969; Synan, 1971).

As a result of the many possible combinations of worship styles, people with different worship needs are able to find the style most appropriate to them. People from different traditions now are being brought together in meaningful worship experiences. The isolation of traditional Pentecostals is being penetrated, and the number of Pentecostals around the world is increasing. In short, Pentecostals and Neo-Pentecostals are discovering that God can be worshiped in a variety of ways; Christians thereby may live a life energized by the Holy Spirit (Synan, 1987).

See also PENTECOSTAL AND CHARISMATIC MUSIC; SPIRITUALITY, PENTECOSTAL AND CHARISMATIC.

Bibliography: J. V. Bartlett "Worship (Christian)" in J. Hastings, ed., *Encyclopedia of Religion and Ethics* (1925), 12:762–76; G. Collins, *Innovative Approaches to Counseling*, 1986; M. E. Collins, *Worship* (n.d.); R. N. Flew, *The Ideas of Perfection in Christian Theology* (1934); J. W. Fowler, *Faith Development and Pastoral Care* (1987); R. T. Hughes, "Christian Primitivism as Perfectionism: From Anabaptists to Pentecostals," in S. M. Burgess, ed., *Reaching Beyond: Chapters in the History of Perfectionism* (1986); S. Mead, *The Lively Experiment* (1963); J. O. Patterson, *History and Formative Years of the Church of God in Christ with Excerpts from the Life and Writings of C. H. Mason* (1969); C. Randall "The Importance of the Pentecostal and Holiness Churches in the Ecumenical Movement," *Pneuma*, 50–60 (Spring 1987); V. Synan, "Pentecostalism: Varieties and Contributions," *Pneuma* (Spring 1987), 31–49; idem, *The Holiness-Pentecostal Movement* (1971); G. J. tenZythoff, "The Non-Perfectionism of John Calvin," in S. M. Burgess, ed., *Reaching Beyond: Chapters in the History of Perfectionism* (1986); J. F. White *Christian Worship in Transition* (1976).

J. W. Shepperd

WRIGHT, JAMES ELWIN (1890–1973). Minister, real estate developer, religious executive, and author. He was born in Corinth, Vermont, to Joel Adams and Mary Melissa (Goodwin) Wright, and was married to Florence

Daisy Dunkling in 1911. They had one daughter, Muriel Virginia (Evans). For a time Wright entered the ministry, having received a theological education at the Missionary Training Institute (Christian and Missionary Alliance) at Nyack, New York, in 1921. His strengths, however, lay in organizational skills and ability to work one on one.

Laboring as a real estate developer in New England, Wright attached himself to Park Street Church in Boston. During the 1920s he sought to establish an organization that would provide a unified identity and voice to conservative Christians in New England. His New England Fellowship, formed in 1929, quickly gained a broad following, inclusive of Pentecostals; it gathered together over a thousand churches in its first five years of existence.

Wright began a nationwide trip in 1937 to test the waters on the feasibility of a similar organization on the national level. By 1939 he was openly promoting the idea, and in April 1942 he called a National Conference for United Action Among Evangelicals to be convened in St. Louis, Missouri. This meeting gave birth to the National Association of Evangelicals (NAE).

From its inception Wright helped to include Pentecostals in the NAE, often at considerable personal expense. He remained with the NAE as executive secretary of the commission on international relations (1948–57). In 1951 he became cosecretary to the World Evangelical Fellowship. He authored *The Old Fashioned Revival Hour* (1940, rev. 1942), *Evangelical Action!* (1942), and *Manna in the Morning* (1943). In his later years he made his home in Rumney Depot, New Hampshire, while maintaining an office in Boston.

Bibliography: J. Carpenter, "The Fundamentalist Leaven and the Rise of an Evangelical United Front," in L. I. Sweet, *The Evangelical Tradition in America* (1984); G. M. Marsden, *Reforming Fundamentalism* (1987); J. D. Murch, *Co-Operation Without Compromise* (1956); *Who's Who in America, 1958–59.*   C. M. Robeck, Jr.

WYATT, THOMAS (d. 1964). Evangelist and radio speaker. Reared in hardship and deprivation in Jasper County, Iowa, Wyatt left school at age eleven when his father became a semi-invalid.

After his conversion in the Methodist church at Ira, Iowa, he had a near-death experience. While in an eighteen-hour coma he heard the words, "I am the Lord that healeth thee." Subsequent to his recovery, he began a Midwestern healing ministry that even attracted the attention of *Look* magazine (November 23, 1937).

In that same year Wyatt moved to Portland, Oregon, where he established a ministry that continued for twenty-two years. "Wings of Healing," his pioneer radio healing ministry, was first heard on Mother's Day, 1942. By June 21, 1953, his broadcasts were carried on both the ABC network and 552 Mutual Broadcasting Company stations. In July 1957 he began "Global Frontiers Telecast," an expansion of an intensely patriotic, anticommunist campaign begun in 1954 (*The March of Faith* 9 [7, 1954]: 14–15; 9 [8, 1954]: 14–15). Round-the-world short-wave radio broadcasts began in 1959.

A 1953 evangelistic and healing crusade in West Africa prompted the establishment in Portland of Bethesda World Training Center (Bethesda Bible Institute had been established in 1947). From this school Wyatt sent forth "Gospel invasion teams" on an international level as an evangelistic effort and patriotic American resistance to the spread of communism.

The ministry established new headquarters in the Embassy Building, Los Angeles, in October 1959.

During 1962–63 Wyatt conducted numerous evangelistic tours of America. A massive heart attack felled him on December 9, 1962. After recovering, he reestablished his fast pace. He continued his preaching tours, speaking against threats from world communism, militant atheism, and apathy and indifference in the church (see "Report on 'World Crisis Conference,'" *March of Faith* 18 [10, 1963]: 2–4).

Struck down again in November 1963, he still continued his radio ministry. He died peacefully in his sleep on April 19, 1964.

Bibliography: *A Memorial Tribute to Thomas Wyatt—A Man of Vision* (1964); B. Miller, *Grappling With Destiny* (1962); T. Wyatt, *Give Me This Mountain* (n.d.); T. Wyatt, ed., *The March of Faith* (1946–) (continued after his death by his wife, Evelyn).
                                                                J. A. Hewett

X Y Z

XENOLALIA   See GLOSSOLALIA.

YAHVAH TEMPLE   Founded in 1947 as the Church of Jesus, shortened to the Jesus Church in 1953, the present name was adopted in 1982. Yahvah Temple is a group with a loose affiliation that has operated in Cleveland, Tennessee. Its founder and bishop is Samuel E. Officer. A periodical, *Light of the World*, has been discontinued. The group is a Oneness body that worships on Saturday. Although admitting that his interpretations of Scripture had not been widely accepted by 1987, Officer believes God will raise up a successor who will be successful in spreading the Yahvah Temple message. Followers believe that Jesus is the Yahweh of the OT.

Bibliography: C. Jones, *Guide to the Pentecostal Movement* (1983); E. Moore, "Handbook of Pentecostal Denominations in the United States," M.A. thesis, 1954; *Light of the World* (1947–); various tracts by Samuel E. Officer.   W. E. Warner

YEOMANS, LILIAN BARBARA (1861–1942). Faith healer. Born in Calgary, Alberta, Canada, the eldest of three daughters, to medical doctor parents. Lilian Yeomans was reared in a Christian home, attending Sunday school and church regularly. During the Civil War her family moved to the U.S., where her father served as a surgeon for the U.S. Army. This led to Lilian's interest in a medical career. Ultimately she was graduated with the M.D. degree from the University of Michigan (Ann Arbor) and returned to Canada, where she went into practice in a partnership with her mother Amelia Le Sueur Yeomans, as a physician and surgeon.

To manage her stress from her heavy practice she began to rely on drugs, among them morphine and chloral hydrate. She soon became addicted to morphine. When she showed signs of advanced addiction, she attempted all known medical cures, including a detoxification program at the Keeley Gold Cure Institute. That proved to be ineffective, and she was placed in a sanitorium for nervous diseases. She journeyed from Winnipeg to New York City, where she also attempted a cure through Christian Science practitioners. That, too, proved to be ineffective, and she began to read her Bible. Her healing came on January 12, 1898, under the ministry of John Alexander Dowie of Chicago, Illinois.

In true Holiness fashion, Lilian sought for a crisis experience of sanctification; she claimed to have received it in September 1907. That same night she also spoke in tongues. Over the next several months she wrote a variety of letters to her mother and other acquaintances, which were subsequently published in the *Way of Faith,* and separately under the title of *Pentecostal Letters,* which was compiled by her mother. These letters outline her understanding of speaking in tongues and her feelings about the value of the Pentecostal experience. She encouraged her mother, who had been the vice-president of the Canadian Woman's Christian Temperance Union and president of that country's Suffrage Club, to ask God for the experience; she subsequently received it in January 1908. Lilian Yeomans later held evangelistic meetings throughout the U.S. and Canada. She attempted to pioneer Pentecostal works especially in Alberta.

In her later years Yeomans settled in Manhattan Beach, California. She served on the faculty of L.I.F.E. Bible College under Aimee Semple McPherson, where she taught courses on divine healing and church history. She authored several devotional books and works on healing, all of which were published between her sixty-fifth and eighty-first years. In 1940, at the age of eighty, she was still conducting evangelistic meetings. In 1941, at the encouragement of her friend Carrie Judd Montgomery, she published a short book of her sister's works titled *Gold of Ophir: Spiritual Songs Given Through Amy Yeomans.* Yeomans died on December 9, 1942, and is buried in Forest Lawn Cemetery, Glendale, California.

Bibliography: Lilian B. Yeomans, *Balm of Gilead* (1935); idem, *Divine Healing Diamonds* (1933); idem, *Healing From Heaven* (1926); idem, *The Hiding Place* (1940); idem, *Resurrection Rays* (1930); idem, *The Royal Road to Health-ville* (1938); idem, *The Upper Room* 1 (1910): 3.   C. M. Robeck, Jr.

YOAKUM, FINIS EWING (1851–1920). Faith healer and social reformer. A medical doctor in Texas, Colorado, and California, Finis Yoakum gave up his lucrative career (he reportedly earned $18,000 per month) following a personal healing to found the Pisgah Home Movement. His parents were Franklin and Narcissa (Teague) Yoakum; his father was a country physician in Texas, who later became a minister with the Cumberland Presbyterian Church and served as the president of their college in Larrisan. A younger brother, Benjamin Franklin Yoakum, was an important figure in American commerce, serving as president of the San Antonio and Arkansas Pass Railway and chairman of the board for the St. Louis and San Francisco Railroad ("Frisco") as well as several other major railroads and business enterprises.

In 1873 Finis took a wife, Mary. They had three sons, Modrall G., Charles O., and Finis E. Yoakum, Jr. Their twin daughters, Ruth and Ruby married Harold E. Wing and William N. Whitney, respectively.

Yoakum studied at Larissa College as well as at another in the Dallas–Fort Worth area. Ultimately, he graduated from the Hospital College of Medicine, in Louisville, Kentucky, with the M.D.

degree on June 16, 1885. Following medical school he specialized in neurological disorders and finally occupied the Chair of Mental Diseases on the faculty of the Gross Medical College in Denver, Colorado.

On the evening of July 18, 1894, while on his way to organize a Class Leader's Association for the Methodist Church, he was struck by a buggy driven by a drunken man. A piece of metal pierced his back, broke several ribs, and caused internal hemorrhaging. A medical assessment of his injuries predicted them to be fatal. Plagued by infection for several months, he moved to Los Angeles hoping to gain relief. There, on February 5, 1895, he was prayed for by W. C. Stevens of the Christian Alliance (107½ North Main) at which time he began a remarkable recovery, nearly doubling his weight within three months. On July 2, 1895, he was awarded a license to practice medicine in California.

That year, Dr. Yoakum received a vision directing him toward a mission to the needy. While Yoakum continued to hold his medical certification until his death, he closed his official medical practice, moved out of his house into a tent, and adopted the habit of wearing second-hand clothes. He built a tabernacle that doubled as a dormitory in Arroyo Seco between Los Angeles and Pasadena, vowing to spend the remainder of his life serving the chronically ill, poor, destitute, and social outcasts.

While in the Los Angeles area, he associated with the Holiness churches, frequently speaking on divine healing at their camp meetings and annual gatherings between 1901 and 1904. When the Azusa Street revival broke in 1906 Yoakum visited the mission. He spoke in tongues as early as 1902, and he wrote of this continuing experience in 1911. He maintained a cordial, even supportive, relationship with the fledgling Pentecostal movement but never identified himself closely with it. This lack of close identification led to criticism of him by E. N. Bell, who warned his readers that Yoakum was not really "Pentecostal."

Yoakum held regular healing services for several years at 1 P.M. on Mondays at the Spring Street Mission and at 1 P.M. on Thursdays at the assembly on Eighth and Maple. He held Sunday services at his tabernacle and conducted other services on his properties in what would later become North Hollywood. When he was not on his Pisgah properties he could be found most days in an office suite between 10 A.M. and 1 P.M. in the Bradley Building (1896) and in later years in an upper floor of the San Fernando Building on Main Street near 4th in downtown Los Angeles. There he laid hands on and prayed for the sick and needy who sought him out. He distributed handkerchiefs or prayer cloths.

From 1907 onward Yoakum began a wider public ministry that reached its peak between 1911 and 1914. In addition to his own periodical, *Pisgah*, his work was widely publicized by Carrie Judd Montgomery in *Triumphs of Faith*, by Alexander A. Boddy in *Confidence*, by William Hamner Piper in the *Latter Rain Evangel*, and by Samuel Otis in *Word and Work*. During these years he engaged in a public speaking ministry throughout the U.S., Canada, and Great Britain.

Yoakum was a controversial figure throughout the latter part of his life. He was the object of a love-hate relationship with the city of Los Angeles, because his ministry attracted indigents to the city from other areas of the country, yet the city was happy to send many of their own to him for care. He encountered criticism, too, because he refused to make his financial books available for public scrutiny. His comment was that those who did not trust him should not give and those who gave should trust him. Finally, he alienated some because he received ordination as a "bishop" from a self-appointed bishop in the East.

Yoakum was compared by some to John Alexander Dowie, for in 1914 he purchased a 3,225-acre parcel in Lime Valley, northeast of Los Angeles, where he intended to establish a utopian center under the name of Pisgah Grande. His death from a heart attack in 1920 left that work unfinished.

Bibliography: A. A. Boddy, "Dr. Yoakum's Work at Los Angeles, *Confidence* 5 (11, 1912): 248–51, 255–58; "Founder of Pisgah Dies," *Los Angeles Daily Times* 2 (August 19, 1920): 7; "Some Information," *Work and Witness* (December 20, 1913), 1; P. D. Smith, *He Is Just the Same Today* (1931), 119–21.   C. M. Robeck, Jr.

Loren Cunningham founded Youth With a Mission (YWAM).

YOUTH WITH A MISSION (YWAM). A nondenominational parachurch organization whose purpose is to provide Christian service and to evangelize the world with youth. It had its

origin in a vision given to a young Assemblies of God (AG) Bible college student, Loren Cunningham, in 1956. The vision consisted of waves of youth going ashore on every continent in the world to evangelize. Cunningham began YWAM in his parents' California home in December 1960. He incorporated YWAM in the summer of 1961 and became its director. His first two missionaries went to a Liberian leper colony as vocational volunteers (1961–62).

Cunningham sought the acceptance of YWAM as part of the foreign missions effort of the AG (1961), and the AG responded by offering him a position in the AG international headquarters. However, in 1964, after 146 young YWAM volunteers had spent eight weeks in the Bahama Islands winning 6,000 souls, AG officials and Cunningham were unable to agree on the structure for YWAM. Cunningham never responded to the job offer, gave up his AG ministerial credentials, and developed YWAM as an interdenominational evangelistic ministry including street meetings, door-to-door evangelism, music, drama, urban evangelism, Olympic evangelism, and mercy service.

The structure established by Cunningham consists of one region containing two ships and three international regions that are divided and subdivided into areas, nations, and districts. Each region has its own council; however, the authority is decentralized and located in three hundred-plus autonomous centers around the world. Each center has its own separate funding, constitution, bylaws, board, incorporation, and IRS clearance. The operation of YWAM is unified by an international council consisting of a board of seven men and an annual strategy conference attended by the four regional councils. There are two international offices: one is in Kailua-Kona, Hawaii, where the Pacific and Asia Christian University (PACU) and Cunningham, the president, are located; and the second one is in Amsterdam, Netherlands, where Floyd McClung, director of international operations, is located. Currently YWAM sends 50,000 short-term (two to three months) volunteers out each summer to do evangelistic work; has 6,000 full-time workers; has more than one hundred Discipleship Training Schools with a five-month curriculum; offers a two-year degree at the School of Urban Missions in Amsterdam; operates PACU, which focuses on preparing people for missionary work in Asia; and owns two mercy ships, the *Good Samaritan* and *Anastasis*, which provide medical and engineering services, deliver relief and emergency supplies, and do discipleship training and evangelism. There are no salaried employees in this structure; instead, each person must raise his or her own funding; YWAM has no definite ties with any specific denomination. Thus far, YWAM has ministered in 218 of the 223 countries on earth.

Bibliography: M. A. Berry, ed., *The Great Commission Handbook*, 1988 ed. (1987); L. Cunningham, "Chronology of Steps of YWAM's Relationship with Springfield," director's report (c. September 1962); L. Cunningham and J. Rogers, *Is That Really You, God? Hearing the Voice of God* (1984); Evangel Press, "Abused Teen Who Killed Dad Sentenced to YWAM Work,"

Charisma 9 (1984): 62; R. Grant, "Olympic Challenge," *Charisma* 9 (1984): 58–61; B. Joffe, "Man With a Mission," *Charisma* 11 (1985): 21–26; R. M. Wilson, *God's Guerrillas: Youth With a Mission* (1971).

E. B. Robinson

YUGOSLAVIAN PENTECOSTALS   See EUROPEAN PENTECOSTALISM.

YWAM   See YOUTH WITH A MISSION.

ZAIRE EVANGELISTIC MISSION   Originally founded as the Congo Evangelistic Mission by William F. P. Burton and James Salter. Burton was a student at the Pentecostal Missionary Union (PMU) Bible School, Preston, Lancashire. Due to sail for Africa with James McNeill, he was in disagreement with leaders of the PMU and sailed alone in March 1914. Joined later by his friend "Jimmy" Salter, they journeyed together with two others to the Belgian Congo, arriving there in September 1915. Taking the name Pentecostal Mission, for a time they were part of the Pentecostal Mission in South and Central Africa. Burton become their legal representative.

One of their party died en route, and the others were seriously ill. With the continuation of the war in Europe, the only help came from the U.S. Burton went to South Africa in 1918 and returned with four helpers, including Hettie Trollip, whom he married. Salter returned to Britain for Easter 1919. Traveling extensively, he made a great impact and gathered several new workers, including Cyril Taylor, a final year medical student from Cambridge; Smith Wigglesworth's daughter, Alice, whom Salter married; and Edmund Hodgson from Preston.

Following the Kingsway Convention in Whitsun 1919, at which many of the leaders were present, the Congo Evangelistic Mission was established, with offices in Preston. A. E. Saxby (1873–1960) was chosen president and Thomas Myerscough, secretary–treasurer. Burton became field director and Salter became home director. Support and personnel came from the Elim Pentecostal churches, and from independent churches and the Assemblies of God.

F. D. Johnstone, a former Preston student and worker in the Congo since 1914, and his wife joined the group. Fevers and dysentery struck many times, and some fourteen workers died, with more being compelled to return incapacitated. In spite of the difficulties, the work expanded. In total, some 189 missionaries served on the field. In addition there were many national workers from a total of 25 in 1925 to 578 in 1960. In 1960 there was a staff of 80 on thirteen stations; 65 were Europeans. There were 40,000 registered believers in 950 assemblies.

Independence from Belgian rule in June 1960 saw a period of civil unrest when many believers were killed. The missionaries were withdrawn for a time, but in the following unsettled conditions New Zealander Elton Knauf and E. Hodgson were killed in November 1960.

The Pentecostal Church of Zaire is now indigenous with all its office holders Zairian. Since independence the work has more than doubled, with nearly 3,000 assemblies and 190,000 believers.

Bibliography: W. Burton, *God Working With Them* (1933); Max W. Moorhead, *Missionary Pioneering in the Congo Forests* (1922); H. Womersley, *Congo Miracle* (1974).   D. W. Cartwright

An international Pentecostal leader, T. F. Zimmerman was general superintendent of the Assemblies of God (U.S.A.) from 1959 to 1985.

ZIMMERMAN, THOMAS FLETCHER

(1912–). Assemblies of God (AG) minister and administrator. Thomas F. Zimmerman was born in Indianapolis, Indiana, the son of Thomas Fletcher and Carrie D. (Kenagy) Zimmerman. He was converted at the age of seven, at approximately the time that his mother was healed of tuberculosis; he experienced the Pentecostal baptism of the Holy Spirit four years later. While still in high school, Zimmerman felt called into full-time gospel ministry, initially intending to go as a missionary to China.

After a year at Indiana University, which he left because of family financial pressures, Zimmerman worked for a printing business. In 1928 he became assistant pastor to John Price of Indianapolis, whose daughter he married five years later. He was ordained by the AG in 1936. In turn, he pastored AG churches in Kokomo, Indiana (1933); Harrodsburg, Indiana (1934); South Bend, Indiana (1935–39); Granite City, Illinois (1939–42); Springfield, Missouri (1943–47); and Cleveland, Ohio (1951–52). From 1941 to 1943 he served as assistant superintendent, Illinois District of the AG; from 1943 to 1947 as assistant superintendent, Southern Missouri District of the AG; and from 1949 to 1951 as

secretary-treasurer, Southern Missouri District of the AG.

The radio department of the AG was born in 1945, and Zimmerman was chosen as its director. From 1946 to 1949 he was narrator of a fifteen-minute weekly program, "Sermons in Song." Because of his interest in radio evangelism, he also was among the founders of the National Religious Broadcasters, an organization he served both as vice-president and president.

In 1953 Zimmerman became an assistant general superintendent of the AG; and at the general council meeting at San Antonio in 1959, he assumed the chief leadership role, a position he retained until 1985. During his twenty-six years as general superintendent, the AG experienced phenomenal growth, doubling in numbers of members, adherents, and ministers. By 1985 the AG had eleven accredited colleges (he served on the boards of directors of Central Bible College and Evangel College, Springfield, Mo.), and the AG Theological Seminary (originally the AG Graduate School) had been founded, with Zimmerman serving as president from 1973 to 1985. Maranatha Village Retirement Complex also originated under his leadership, and he was chairman of the board of directors from 1976 to 1985.

Zimmerman's strong influence has been felt outside the AG as well. He was the first Pentecostal to be elected as president of the National Association of Evangelicals, which the AG joined in 1942. He also served as a member of the executive committee, Lausanne Committee for World Evangelization; as president, Lausanne Committee for World Evangelization—U.S.A.; as chairman of the Pentecostal Fellowship of North America; and as a member of the board of managers, American Bible Society, since 1967. He also has served with the International Advisory Committee of the Pentecostal World Conference as chairman for the past six conferences: 1970 in Dallas; 1973 in Seoul, Korea; 1976 in London; 1979 in Vancouver, British Columbia; 1982 in Nairobi, Kenya; and 1985 in Geneva, Switzerland.

Zimmerman has been active in civic affairs as a Rotarian; a member of the board of directors, Lester E. Cox Medical Centers in Springfield, Missouri; a director of KOZK Public TV Station in Springfield; and a member of the board of directors of the United Way of Springfield. In 1974 he was honored as Springfieldian of the Year by the Springfield Area Chamber of Commerce.

He has been awarded honorary degrees from Northwest College, Kirkland, Washington (D.D.), and Central Bible College, Springfield, Missouri (LL.D.)

Thomas Zimmerman has become known for his personal charisma and drive, his exceptionally strong leadership style (although this occasionally has been controversial), and his prominent level of participation in the life of his church and community.

Bibliography: C. Brumback, *Suddenly . . . From Heaven* (1961); W. W. Menzies, *Anointed to Serve* (1971); *Minutes of the General Council of the Assemblies of God* (especially 1959ff.); "No Regrets for AG's

Shepherd," *The Springfield News-Leader* (September 8, 1985), E1, E6; *Who's Who in America* (1975ff.); *Who's Who in Religion* (1976).   S. M. Burgess

ZION EVANGELISTIC FELLOWSHIP Established in 1935, the Zion Evangelistic Fellowship brought together independent churches in at least a half-dozen northeastern states. Christine A. Gibson (1879–1955), the founder, designed it as an agency for life service of graduates of Zion Bible Institute, East Providence, Rhode Island, which she headed, and as means of enlisting financial and prayer support for the school and foreign missions. In 1953 the ninety-six congregations in the fellowship had a combined membership of 10,000. Most of the twenty-two missionaries it then endorsed were working in Africa. Teachings were similar to those of the General Council of the Assemblies of God. In 1956, a year after Gibson's death, the Zion Evangelistic Fellowship was dissolved. Shortly thereafter former members in New Hampshire and Maine formed the Apostolic Challenge, a ministerial fellowship similar to the original organization.

Bibliography: R. Crayne, *Pentecostal Handbook* (1986); R. L. Moore, "Handbook of Pentecostal Denominations in the United States," M.A. thesis, Pasadena College, 1954.   C. E. Jones

ZOPFI, JAKOB (1932–). Swiss Pentecostal pastor and evangelist. Born in Switzerland, Zopfi was educated at Elim Bible College in London, England. He began his ministry as pastor of the Swiss Pentecostal Mission in Basel (1961–65) and was ordained in 1964. Leaving the pastorate, he engaged in evangelistic ministry for five years. In 1970 he became secretary and later chairman of the Swiss Pentecostal Mission. He has also served as chairman of the Pentecostal European Fellowship.

Zopfi's editorial responsibilities have included *Wort + Geist, Schwarmgeist,* and more recently *World Pentecost,* the official publication of the Pentecostal World Conference, of which he currently holds the post of secretary of the advisory committee.

Bibliography: Assemblies of God Office of Information, personal data sheet.   G. B. McGee

Picture Sources

l = left column; r = right column; t = top; b = bottom

Apostolic Faith Mission (Portland) 18

Archives of the Hal Bernard Dixon, Jr., Pentecostal Research Center 21b, 198, 199, 201, 451, 538, 664t, 753, 846

Assemblies of God Archives 8, 17t+b, 21t, 23l, 28, 33, 35, 49, 51, 53, 62, 91l, 94, 97, 99r, 101r, 104, 108, 220, 222, 225, 229l+r, 248, 249, 256, 269, 270, 290, 312, 313, 328, 329, 330, 331, 342, 343, 349r, 366, 369, 448, 531, 542, 543, 620, 626, 636, 643r, 660, 700, 703, 712, 715, 716, 726, 744, 748, 750, 754, 758l+r, 770, 780, 851t+b, 853, 873, 886, 894, 900

Assemblies of God, Division of Home Missions 24, 26, 39b, 885

Assemblies of God, Office of Information 162, 708, 709, 838, 910

Assemblies of God Theological Seminary 404, 446r, 773

Assemblies of God, Division of Foreign Missions 90, 102, 274, 275, 310, 405, 464

Baker, James and Marjorie 38

Berean College 23r

Bethesda Missionary Temple, Detroit 52

Bohlin, Kathryn (Fullness Magazine) 392

CBN 60, 519, 761r

California Theological Seminary 774

Calvary Chapel, Santa Ana, California 792

Campbell, Faith Frodsham 317

Cartwright, Desmond 32, 50, 91r, 92, 346, 409, 479l+r, 779, 881, 884

Chapel Hill Harvester Church 683

Chariscenter 115, 118, 121, 566, 584, 756l+r, 768, 834, 854

Christ for the Nations 361, 540l+r

Christian Retreat 239

Christian and Missionary Alliance 164

Church of God (Cleveland, Tenn.) 224, 775

Church of God in Christ 586, 664b

Church of God of Prophecy 207, 307t, 849

Church on the Way, The 349l

Crouch Music Corporation 230l

Dake Bible Sales 235

Doug Grandstaff Photography 363, 529

Duin, Julia 536

Eastern Pentecostal Bible College, Peterborough, Ontario 841

Episcopal Renewal Ministries 262, 324, 348, 470

Full Gospel Business Men's Voice 322, 390r, 782, 868

Fullness Magazine 48

Gibson, Naomi D. 657

Gospel Publishing House 27, 59, 98, 165, 612, 632, 710, 852

Harper, Canon Michael (SOMA) 147, 154

Harvest Temple, Largo, Florida 261

Herrstrom, Beth 627

Hocken, Peter (Mother of God Community) 113, 123, 761l

Hoover, Mario 445

International Church of the Foursquare Gospel 10, 569, 571, 721b, 776

International Lutheran Renewal Center 163, 513, 563

International Pentecostal Holiness Church 832

John Osteen Ministries 656

Kenneth Hagin Ministries 345

Kenyon's Gospel Publishing Society 517

Kuzmic, Peter 271

Latter Rain Evangel 7

Lester Sumrall Evangelistic Association 835

Marilyn Hickey Ministries 389r

Mattson-Boze, Winston 272, 598

McGee, Gary B. 764

Mennonite Renewal Services 541, 600, 601

Mitchell, R.B. 652

Montgomery, William 628

Mumford, Bob 461

New Covenant Magazine 138, 143

Nicky Cruz Outreach 232

Nikoloff, Martha 273

Open Bible Standard Churches, Inc. 793

Oral Roberts Evangelistic Association 218, 286, 359, 721t, 760

Pentecostal Assemblies of Canada 695, 696, 697, 698

Pentecostal Church of God 702

Pentecostal Evangel 127, 233

Presbyterian and Reformed Renewal Ministries 99l, 725, 888

R.W. Schambach Revivals 354, 769

Religious News Service Photo/Wide World 39t+b, 492, 778, 783, 839t, 848

Revivaltime 572l, 879l

Rock Church, Virginia Beach, Va. 335

Rogers, Truitt 48

Sandidge, Jerry L. 242

Schoch, Paul C. 389l

Spencer, Carlton 800

St. Luke's Episcopal Church, Seattle 133

Strang Communications Co. 1011, 833

Terry, Huegha (Church of God in Christ) 204, 205

Trinity Broadcasting Network 230r

United Pentecostal Church International 5, 861

University of Notre Dame, South Bend, Ind. 6431

University of Stuebenville, Ohio 55

Vineyard Ministries International 889

Voice of God Recordings 96, 356

Warner, Wayne 371, 625, 757

Watson, Anne 879r

Williams, Jan 446l

Women's Aglow 899

Youth With a Mission 908

The Dictionary of Pentecostal and Charismatic Movements
was typeset by
the Photocomposition Department
of Zondervan Publishing House,
Grand Rapids, Michigan
Compositor: Nancy Wilson
Equipment: Mergenthaler Linotron 202/N
Text type: Galliard Roman and Palatino Italic
Copy Editors: Laura Dodge Weller and Claire M. Hughes
Picture Layout: Rachel Hostetter
Printer: R. R. Donnelly & Sons, Harrisonburg, Virginia